Psychology, Thirteenth Edition in Modules

David G. Myers
Hope College
Holland, Michigan

C. Nathan DeWall
University of Kentucky
Lexington, Kentucky

worth publishers
Macmillan Learning
New York

SENIOR VICE PRESIDENT, CONTENT STRATEGY: **Charles Linsmeier**
PROGRAM DIRECTOR, SOCIAL SCIENCES: **Shani Fisher**
SENIOR EXECUTIVE PROGRAM MANAGER: **Carlise Stembridge**
DEVELOPMENT MANAGER, SOCIAL SCIENCES: **Christine Brune**
DEVELOPMENT EDITORS: **Nancy Fleming, Trish Morgan, Danielle Slevens**
ASSISTANT EDITOR: **Anna Munroe**
EXECUTIVE MARKETING MANAGER: **Katherine Nurre**
MARKETING ASSISTANT: **Steven Huang**
DIRECTOR OF MEDIA EDITORIAL & ASSESSMENT, SOCIAL SCIENCES: **Noel Hohnstine**
EXECUTIVE MEDIA EDITOR, PSYCHOLOGY: **Laura Burden**
ASSISTANT MEDIA EDITOR: **Conner White**
SUPPLEMENTS EDITOR: **Betty Probert**
DIRECTOR, CONTENT MANAGEMENT ENHANCEMENT: **Tracey Kuehn**
SENIOR MANAGING EDITOR: **Lisa Kinne**
SENIOR CONTENT PROJECT MANAGER: **Won McIntosh**
DIRECTOR OF DIGITAL PRODUCTION: **Keri deManigold**
SENIOR MEDIA PROJECT MANAGER: **Chris Efstratiou**
MEDIA PROJECT MANAGER: **Eve Conte**
SENIOR WORKFLOW SUPERVISORS: **Susan Wein, Paul W. Rohloff**
PRODUCTION SUPERVISOR: **Lawrence Guerra**
EXECUTIVE PERMISSIONS EDITOR: **Robin Fadool**
PHOTO RESEARCHER AND LUMINA PROJECT MANAGER: **Donna Ranieri**
DIRECTOR OF DESIGN, CONTENT MANAGEMENT: **Diana Blume**
DESIGN SERVICES MANAGER: **Natasha Wolfe**
DESIGN MANAGER, COVER: **John Callahan**
INTERIOR DESIGN: **Maureen McCutcheon**
LAYOUT DESIGN: **Lee Ann McKevitt**
COVER DESIGN: **John Callahan**
ART MANAGER: **Matthew McAdams**
INTERIOR ILLUSTRATIONS: **Shawn Barber, Keith Kasnot, Matthew McAdams, Evelyn Pence, and Don Stewart**
COMPOSITION: **Lumina Datamatics, Inc.**
PRINTING AND BINDING: **LSC Communications**
COVER PHOTO: **Eva-Katalin/Getty Images**

To John Sargent, with gratitude for his enduring friendship and support, and his example of progressive corporate leadership.

DM

•

To Barb Gillilan: A loving aunt, skilled nurse, and inspiration to many.

ND

Library of Congress Control Number: 2020910398

ISBN-13: 978-1-319-13209-5
ISBN-10: 1-319-13209-X

© 2021, 2018, 2015, 2013 by Worth Publishers

Printed in the United States of America

1 2 3 4 5 6   25 24 23 22 21 20

David Myers' royalties from the sale of this book are assigned to the David and Carol Myers Foundation, which exists to receive and distribute funds to other charitable organizations.

Worth Publishers
One New York Plaza
Suite 4600
New York, NY 10004-1562
www.macmillanlearning.com

About the Authors

Photographer Steven Herppich, courtesy of Hope College Public Affairs and Marketing

David Myers received his B.A. in chemistry from Whitworth University, and his psychology Ph.D. from the University of Iowa. He has spent his career at Michigan's Hope College, where he has taught dozens of introductory psychology sections. Hope College students have invited him to be their commencement speaker and voted him "outstanding professor." His research and writings have been recognized by the Gordon Allport Intergroup Relations Prize, an Honored Scientist award from the Federation of Associations in Behavioral & Brain Sciences, an Award for Distinguished Service on Behalf of Social-Personality Psychology, a Presidential Citation from APA Division 2, election as an American Association for the Advancement of Science Fellow, and three honorary doctorates.

With support from National Science Foundation grants, Myers' scientific articles have appeared in three dozen scientific periodicals, including *Science, American Scientist, Psychological Science,* and *American Psychologist.* In addition to his scholarly and textbook writing, he digests psychological science for the general public. His writings have appeared in four dozen magazines, from *Today's Education* to *Scientific American.* He has authored five general audience books, including *The Pursuit of Happiness* and *Intuition: Its Powers and Perils.* And he blogs about psychology and life at TalkPsych.com.

David Myers has chaired his city's Human Relations Commission, helped found a thriving assistance center for families in poverty, and spoken to hundreds of college, community, and professional groups worldwide.

Drawing on his experience, he also has written articles and a book (*A Quiet World*) about hearing loss, and he is advocating a transformation in American assistive listening technology (see HearingLoop .org). For his leadership, he has received awards from the American Academy of Audiology, the hearing industry, and the Hearing Loss Association of America.

David and Carol Myers met and married while undergraduates, and have raised sons Peter and Andrew, and a daughter, Laura. They have one grandchild, Allie (see p. 177).

J.A. Laub Photography, LLC

Nathan DeWall is professor of psychology at the University of Kentucky. He received his bachelor's degree from St. Olaf College, a master's degree in social science from the University of Chicago, and a master's degree and Ph.D. in social psychology from Florida State University. DeWall received the College of Arts and Sciences Outstanding Teaching Award, which recognizes excellence in undergraduate and graduate teaching. The Association for Psychological Science identified DeWall as a "Rising Star" early in his career for "making significant contributions to the field of psychological science." He is in the top 1 percent of all cited scientists in psychology and psychiatry on the Institute for Scientific Information list, according to the Web of Science.

DeWall conducts research on close relationships, self-control, and aggression. With funding from the National Institutes of Health, the National Science Foundation, and the John Templeton Foundation, he has published over 200 scientific articles and chapters. DeWall's research awards include the SAGE Young Scholars Award from the Foundation for Personality and Social Psychology, the Young Investigator Award from the International Society for Research on Aggression, and the Early Career Award from the International Society for Self and Identity. His research has been covered by numerous media outlets, including *Good Morning America, The Wall Street Journal, Newsweek, The Atlantic Monthly, The New York Times, The Los Angeles Times, Harvard Business Review, USA Today,* National Public Radio, the BBC, and *The Guardian.* He has lectured nationally and internationally, including in Hong Kong, China, the Netherlands, England, Greece, Hungary, Sweden, Australia, and France.

Nathan is happily married to Alice DeWall and is the proud father of Beverly "Bevy" and Ellis. He enjoys playing with his two golden retrievers, Finnegan and Atticus. As an ultramarathon runner, he completed numerous races, including the Badwater 135 in 2017 (dubbed "the World's toughest foot race"). In his spare time now, he writes novels, watches sports, and plays guitar and sings in a rock band called *Roar Shock.*

Brief Contents

Contents

Instructor Preface

From its first edition, this text has focused on teaching *critical thinking,* and helping students understand the *research* underlying psychological discoveries. We've expanded that focus in this new edition. (See p. xii to learn more about the Myers/DeWall research and critical thinking story.) This new edition offers 2100 research citations dated 2015–2020, making these *the most up-to-date introductory psychology course resources available.* With so many exciting new findings, and every module updated with current new examples and ideas, students will see the importance and value of psychological research, and how psychology can help them make sense of the world around them. For example, we discuss new research on how the COVID-19 pandemic may affect: our need to belong (Module 34), the social responsibility norm and prejudice (Module 43), and suicidal behavior (Module 47). The abundant, high quality teaching and learning resources in *LaunchPad* and in *Achieve Read & Practice,* carefully matched to the text content, help students succeed, and help make life easier and more enjoyable for instructors. Our integrated resources help bring students to class better prepared, and offer instructors more ways to engage them.

- ➡ **APA Introductory Psychology Initiative, and Learning Goals and Outcomes for the Psychology Major**
- ➡ **Myers/DeWall Research and Critical Thinking Story**
- ➡ **What's New in the Thirteenth Edition?**
- ➡ **Why Should I Use *Psychology, Thirteenth Edition in Modules* Resources?**
- ➡ **LaunchPad and Achieve Read & Practice Resources**
- ➡ **Myers and DeWall's Eight Guiding Principles**
- ➡ **In Appreciation**

APA Introductory Psychology Initiative, and Learning Goals and Outcomes for the Psychology Major

As of our press date, the American Psychological Association (APA) was scheduled to release the results of its **Introductory Psychology Initiative (IPI)** in August, 2020 in hopes of improving "the quality of the introductory psychology experience" (APA.org /Ed/Precollege/Undergrad/Introductory-Psychology-Initiative). The APA IPI, with its five "Integrative Themes" and six "Student Learning Outcomes," encourages instructors to integrate these themes throughout the course, with regular opportunities for practicing, thinking, and communicating about them, and regular assessment of student understanding.

In summary, the APA IPI encourages instructors to use the *five Integrative Themes* to help students (1) adapt their thinking in response to empirical evidence; (2) recognize general principles but individual differences; (3) acknowledge biological, psychological, and social-cultural influences; (4) be aware of perceptual and thinking errors; and (5) apply psychology's principles to improve their own lives.

The *six Learning Outcomes* charge students to (1) fully understand the five themes; (2) apply psychology in their daily lives; (3) use empirical evidence in judgments and decision making; (4) evaluate claims using psychological science; (5) design, carry out, and evaluate research studies; and (6) know ethical principles for research and therapy.

Psychology, Thirteenth Edition in Modules and its resources offer a perfect match for those interested in following these new guidelines, with full text coverage of relevant content, and abundant student and classroom activities and assessment opportunities (see **TABLE 1** and **TABLE 2**).

TABLE 1 APA 2020 Introductory Psychology Initiative's *Expected Integrative Themes*

APA's Five "Integrative Themes"	APA's "Sample Concepts or Ideas"
a. Psychological science relies on empirical evidence, and adapts as new data develop.	• Experimental methods • Statistics • Memory models • Subliminal perception • Therapy interventions
b. Psychology explains general principles that govern behavior, while recognizing individual differences.	• Intelligence • Resilience • Personality testing • Supertasters • Synesthesia
c. Psychological, biological, social, and cultural factors influence mental processes and behavior.	• Psychological disorders • Aging • Health and wellness • Attachment • Personality theories
d. Our perceptions filter experience of the world through an imperfect personal lens.	• Perceptual illusions • Schemas • Cognitive errors • Self-serving bias • Ingroup bias
e. Applying psychological principles can change our lives in positive ways.	• Psychotherapy • Study skills • Coping • Conflict resolution • Behavioral change

*NOTE that these are the *expected* integrative themes—from the July 2019 APA Summit on Introductory Psychology. As of our press date, final recommendations were scheduled to be released in August, 2020. *For final Integrative Themes, please see APA.org/Ed /Precollege/Undergrad/Introductory-Psychology-Initiative.*

TABLE 2 *Psychology, Thirteenth Edition in Modules* Corresponds to APA 2020 Introductory Psychology Initiative's *Expected Student Learning Outcomes*

APA's Six Student Learning Outcomes	*Psychology, Thirteenth Edition in Modules* Coverage
1. Identify basic concepts and research findings, and give examples of psychology's integrative themes.	This first outcome is content-based, challenging students to demonstrate the five "Integrative Themes" outlined in Table 1. *Psychology, Thirteenth Edition in Modules* offers a compelling and complete survey of the field, including all of the "Sample Concepts or Ideas" outlined in Table 1.
1a. Psychological science relies on empirical evidence and adapts as new data develop.	• The **empirical approach** is introduced as a key term on p. 2, and the reality that psychology is a science and that research matters is emphasized throughout the text. See Preface section **"Myers/DeWall Research and Critical Thinking Story"** (p. xii). • In addition, David Myers regularly blogs at **TalkPsych,** where he shares the most exciting new psychological science discoveries, how the field is adapting in response, and how psychology helps explain the rapidly changing world around us.
1b. Psychology explains general principles that govern behavior, while recognizing individual differences.	• Since the first edition of this text, one of Myers and DeWall's "Eight Guiding Principles" has been **"to convey respect for human unity and diversity."** Readers will learn about human kinship in our shared biology and need for affiliation; our shared mechanisms for learning and remembering, emotional expression, and the stress response; and our shared vulnerability to perceptual and thinking errors. Yet they will learn much about our individual diversity—in development and aptitudes, temperament and characteristics, sexual orientation and gender identity, attitudes and motivations, disorder and health— and about cultural and other group variations.
1c. Psychological, biological, social, and cultural factors influence mental processes and behavior.	• The **biopsychosocial approach** is introduced in Module 1 and carried through the rest of the book, with regular narrative reflections on the biological, psychological, and social/cultural factors influencing our understanding of behavior and mental processes. The text includes flow charts outlining the biopsychosocial influences on key topics, including development, aging, disordered drug use, learning, sexual motivation, aggressive behavior, personality, and psychological disorder.
1d. Our perceptions filter our experiences of the world through an imperfect personal lens.	• The Module 17 discussion of *"Processing Sensations and Perceptions"* outlines the impressive strengths and numerous weaknesses in our ability to detect and interpret incoming stimuli. Other coverage of our "imperfect personal lens" includes: cognitive errors (Module 26), ingroup bias (Module 42), and self-serving bias (Module 46).
1e. Applying psychological principles can change our lives in positive ways.	• This edition has a new student preface—**Student Success: How to Apply Psychology to Live Your Best Life.** This preface offers brief discussions of "Thinking Critically and Scientifically," "Self-Control and Self-Improvement," "Time Management and Study Tips," "Social Life," and "Finding Meaning and Pursuing Goals." • New **"Ask Yourself"** questions appear throughout each module to help students apply what they are learning to improve their own lives. This helps make the material more meaningful and memorable. • **Self-applications** are built into the narrative throughout the text, including "Use Psychology to Become a Stronger Person—and a Better Student" in Module 1, tips for getting a "Better Night's Sleep" in Module 8, goal-setting to "Change Your Own Behavior" in Module 21, "Goal-Setting" strategies in Module 34, "Improving Memory" in Module 25, ways to "boost the creative process" in Module 26, building a "Growth Mindset" in Module 30, "Tips for Weight Management" in Module 32, "Connecting and Social Networking" in Module 34, "Evidence-Based Suggestions for a Happier Life" in Module 37, guidance for coping with stress in Module 39, "How to Be Persuasive" in Module 40, "Cognitive Therapy Techniques" in Module 53, "When should a person seek therapy and what should people look for when selecting a therapist?" in Module 54, "Therapeutic Lifestyle Change" in Module 55, and tips for finding "flow" in Appendix C. • In the **"Assess Your Strengths" activities** in LaunchPad, students apply what they are learning from the text to their own lives and experiences by considering key "strengths." Students assess themselves on the strength (critical thinking, quality of sleep, self-control, relationship strength, and more), then get guidance for nurturing that strength in their own lives. • The value of **community psychology** and preventive mental health work is discussed in Module 1, Module 55, and Appendix B. Related discussions include: the social toxicity of extreme income inequality (Module 37), the importance of community communication (Module 43), and the relationship of poverty and empowering communities to mental disorders (Module 47).
2. Apply psychological principles to everyday life.	• Since the first edition of the text, one of the "eight guiding principles" has been "to provide applications of principles." The authors strive throughout to make psychology meaningful and memorable to students by showing how it relates to their lives. (See above examples.)
3. Draw appropriate, logical, and objective conclusions about behavior and mental processes from empirical evidence.	• There are **"Thinking Critically About…" infographics,** with associated activities in LaunchPad, for every group of modules to guide students to consider available empirical evidence before drawing conclusions. Topics include parenting styles, gender bias, sexual aggression, effects of violence-viewing, lie detection, and introversion. • Module 26 outlines the obstacles to effective decision making, judgment, and problem solving, including confirmation bias, fixation, mental set, representativeness and availability heuristics, overconfidence, belief perseverance, and framing.

4. Evaluate misconceptions or erroneous behavioral claims based on evidence from psychological science.	• "To teach critical thinking" has been the first of the "Eight Guiding Principles" that have guided Myers and DeWall's work on this text since the first edition. • Table 4 in the Preface (p. xiv) outlines coverage of "Critical Examinations of Pop Psychology," "Thinking Critically With Psychological Science," and "Scientific Detective Stories." • Module 2 offers a new section on "Psychological Science in a Post-Truth World," which is accompanied by Myers' new tutorial animation "Thinking Critically in Our Post-Truth World" in LaunchPad, and also at tinyurl.com/PostTruthMyers. • There is coverage integrated throughout of misconceptions related to diversity, including prejudice toward various "outgroups," and the value in embracing diverse perspectives (see p. xii).
5. Design, conduct, or evaluate basic psychological research.	• "How Would You Know?" **research activities** for each group of modules in LaunchPad allow students to play the role of researcher as they design and interpret studies. Students consider possible confounding factors and other issues that affect interpretation of results. Students learn about how key decision points can alter the meaning and value of a psychological study, and they develop scientific literacy skills in the process. Topics include "How Would You Know If a Cup of Coffee Can Warm Up Relationships?," "How Would You Know If People Can Learn to Reduce Anxiety?", and "How Would You Know If Schizophrenia Is Inherited?" • **New research-oriented iClicker questions,** based on research presented in the text, are available for each group of modules, helping build student understanding of research design and interpretation.
6. Describe ethical principles that guide psychologists in research and therapy.	• Module 2, Research Strategies: How Psychologists Ask and Answer Questions, includes discussion of "Psychology's Research Ethics," with a **new section on "Ensuring Scientific Integrity"** as well as coverage of "Studying and Protecting Animals," "Studying and Protecting Humans," and "Values in Psychology." • Module 54 has new coverage of **Ethical Principles in Psychotherapy** and the **Ethics of Research on Mental Illness.**

*NOTE that these are the *expected* Student Learning Outcomes—from the July 2019 APA Summit on Introductory Psychology. As of our press date, final recommendations were scheduled to be released in August, 2020. **For final Student Learning Outcomes, please see APA.org/Ed/Precollege/Undergrad/Introductory-Psychology-Initiative.**

In addition, **APA's 2013 Learning Goals and Outcomes,** from their *Guidelines for the Undergraduate Psychology Major,* Version 2.0, were designed to gauge progress in students graduating with psychology majors. (See apa.org/ed/precollege/about/psymajor-guidelines.pdf.) Many psychology departments use these goals and outcomes to help establish their own benchmarks for departmental assessment purposes. **TABLE 3** outlines the way *Psychology, Thirteenth Edition in Modules* can help you and your department to address the APA's Learning Goals and Outcomes. There is a detailed APA Correlation Guide in LaunchPad's Instructor Resources for this thirteenth edition. In addition, *all of the Test Bank items for this text are coded for the APA Outcomes.*

TABLE 3 *Psychology, Thirteenth Edition in Modules,* **Corresponds to APA Learning Goals**

Relevant Feature from *Psychology, Thirteenth Edition in Modules*	APA Learning Goals				
	Knowledge Base in Psychology	Scientific Inquiry and Critical Thinking	Ethical and Social Responsibility in a Diverse World	Communication	Professional Development
Text content	•	•	•	•	•
Myers/DeWall research and critical thinking story	•	•	•		
"Thinking Critically About…" infographics and their new LaunchPad activities	•	•	•		
"Learning Objective Questions" previewing main sections	•	•			
"Retrieval Practice" self-tests throughout	•	•	•		
New "Ask Yourself" questions integrated throughout	•	•	•	•	•
"Try this" style activities integrated throughout the text and LaunchPad resources	•	•		•	•
"Mastering the Material" self-tests	•	•		•	
"Psychology at Work" appendix	•	•	•		•
"The Story of Psychology" timeline (Appendix A)	•		•		•

"Career Fields in Psychology" appendix, with "Pursuing a Psychology Career" online appendix	•	•			•
LearningCurve adaptive quizzing	•	•	•	•	•
"Assess Your Strengths" activities in LaunchPad	•	•	•		•
"How Would You Know?" research activities in LaunchPad	•	•	•	•	•
New research-oriented iClicker questions	•	•	•		

Myers/DeWall Research and Critical Thinking Story

2100 References Dated 2015–2020

The most important task for us as your authors is to report the current state of psychology, including each sub-discipline's latest research insights. Thus, you will find 2100 references in this edition dated 2015–2020. A lot has changed since 2014: Barack Obama is no longer the U.S. president, #MeToo and the COVID-19 pandemic have happened, a little-known app called Instagram now has over a billion users, and efforts to improve replicability in psychological science have ramped up dramatically.

The end-of-book *References* section highlights these 2100 recent citations in blue. The work of writing this text is mostly reading: With thousands of studies published each year, it takes a daily effort to keep up with all that is happening in our exciting field. In winnowing new research findings, we consider:

- *Reliability*: Does either replication or the inherent scale of the finding make it trustworthy?

- *Importance*: Is this, for psychology, a significant new finding? And is this something an educated person needs to know?

- *Clarity*: Is this something our readers could understand and remember?

The new findings met these high standards for inclusion. Each confirms key concepts or informs the way we present them. The remaining thousands of reference citations include important classic studies that have formed the structure of our discipline.

We all want students to walk away with the most accurate, current understandings of psychology to apply in their own lives and work. Having the latest research engages students so much more effectively. Here are two examples of new research areas—from just the last couple of years—that are important for students' understanding of psychological science and its application in their lives.

1. *People often spurn those with differing worldviews, yet the recent scientific evidence we share in this new edition demonstrates value in embracing diverse perspectives:*

   - Diverse scientific teams make more scientific breakthroughs (AlShebli et al., 2018; see Module 42, Antisocial Relations).

   - Children raised with competent, secure, and nurturing care can flourish regardless of parents' gender and sexual orientation (Calzo et al., 2019; see Module 14, Infancy and Childhood).

   - People who identify as transgender have a more positive therapeutic experience when therapists affirm them (Bettergarcia & Israel, 2018; see Module 54, Evaluating Psychotherapies).

   - Politically conservative and liberal people are similarly biased against those who hold differing political views (Ditto et al., 2019a,b; see Module 2, Research Strategies: How Psychologists Ask and Answer Questions).

- Social media communication often occurs in an ideological vacuum, in which we surround ourselves with mostly like-minded individuals (Hills, 2019; see Module 41, Social Influence).

2. *Social media use has soared, and the new research we present in Module 2 and 34 explores correlational, longitudinal, and experimental studies of its possible effects, such as on depression and suicidal thoughts in teen girls.*

Other new, student-relevant research explores

- navigating our "post-truth" world,
- understanding how gene–environment interactions affect us,
- distinguishing substance use from abuse,
- weighing parent/peer influences on our development,
- appreciating our unique sensory and perceptual windows on the world,
- figuring out how to learn and remember most effectively,
- successfully connecting socially with others to build our health and well-being,
- understanding gender identity and sexual orientation,
- learning about our hunger and sexual motivations,
- coping with stress and determining how to thrive,
- recognizing inborn personality variations,
- dealing with the challenges of mental illness,
- appreciating *neurodiversity* (including those on the autism spectrum, and those challenged by ADHD, a learning disorder, or brain injury),
- finding hope in psychological and biomedical therapies, and
- seeking "flow" in our daily lives and work.

Expanded Focus on Critical Thinking and Research

Throughout the text, we help students *think critically*. By examining sources and evidence, students can apply psychology's concepts to their own lives and to their studies—using evidence-based principles to boost their relationships, academic success, stress-management, and so much more (see **TABLE 4**). "To teach critical thinking" has been the first of the "Eight Guiding Principles" that have guided our work on this text since the first edition. (See p. xxvii.) The first subsection in Module 1 is headed *"Psychology Is a Science,"* and Modules 2 and 3 take a critical-thinking approach to introducing students to psychology's research methods. "Critical thinking" is a key term on p. 3 and is encouraged throughout the text and its resources. *New resources include:*

- a new *Student Preface,* "Student Success: How to Apply Psychology to Live Your Best Life," which includes discussion of "Thinking Critically and Scientifically."
- a new Module 2 section on *"Psychological Science in a Post-Truth World"* (accompanied by my [DM's] new tutorial animation, "Thinking Critically in Our Post-Truth World" in LaunchPad, and also at tinyurl.com/PostTruthMyers),
- new Module 2 coverage of *"Ensuring Scientific Integrity,"*
- new Module 54 coverage of *Ethical Principles in Psychotherapy* and the *Ethics of Research on Mental Illness,*
- new *research-oriented iClicker questions* for each module, contributed by Jennifer Zwolinski (University of San Diego), and
- new *"Thinking Critically About…" infographic activities* (along with our popular "How Would You Know" research design activities) for every group of modules in LaunchPad.

TABLE 4 Critical Thinking and Scientific Inquiry

Critical thinking coverage and in-depth stories of psychology's process of *scientific inquiry* can be found on the following pages:

Thinking Critically About . . . infographics:
The Scientific Attitude, p. 4
Correlation and Causation, p. 34
Do We Use Only 10 Percent of Our Brain?, p. 80
Tolerance and Addiction, p. 111
Gender Bias in the Workplace, p. 153
Sexual Aggression, p. 159
Parenting Styles—Too Hard, Too Soft, Too Uncaring, and Just Right?, p. 187
Subliminal Sensation and Subliminal Persuasion, p. 215
The Effects of Viewing Media Violence, p. 289
Can Memories of Childhood Sexual Abuse Be Repressed and Then Recovered?, p. 320
The Fear Factor, p. 331
Cross-Sectional and Longitudinal Studies, p. 367
The Challenges of Obesity and Weight Control, p. 392
Lie Detection, p. 424
Stress and Health, p. 451
How To Be Persuasive, p. 474
The Internet as Social Amplifier, p. 486
The Stigma of Introversion, p. 534
ADHD—Normal High Energy or Disordered Behavior?, p. 595
Therapeutic Lifestyle Change, p. 621

Critical Examinations of Pop Psychology:
The need for psychological science, pp. 22–24
Perceiving order in random events, pp. 23–24
Do we use only 10 percent of our brain?, p. 80
Near-death experiences, p. 118
Critiquing the evolutionary perspective, pp. 139–140

How much credit or blame do parents deserve?, pp. 143–144
Sensory restriction, pp. 235–236
Can hypnosis be therapeutic? Alleviate pain?, pp. 246–247
Is there extrasensory perception?, pp. 253–255
Do other species have language?, pp. 346–348
Do violent video games teach social scripts for violence?, pp. 499–500
Is Freud credible?, pp. 523–526
Is repression a myth?, p. 524
How valid is the Rorschach test?, pp. 526–527
Is psychotherapy effective?, pp. 612–615
Evaluating alternative therapies, p. 616

Thinking Critically With Psychological Science:
"Critical thinking" introduced as a key term, p. 3
Psychological science in a post-truth world, pp. 13–14
The limits of intuition and common sense, p. 22
The scientific method, pp. 25–39
Exploring cause and effect, pp. 31–37
Regression toward the mean, p. 33
Correlation and causation, p. 34
Random assignment, p. 35
Independent and dependent variables, pp. 36–37
Choosing the right research design, p. 38
Statistical reasoning, pp. 44–48
Describing data, pp. 44–46
Making inferences, pp. 47–48
The evolutionary perspective on human sexuality, pp. 138–140

Scientific Detective Stories:
Superforecasters avoid overconfidence, p. 23
Big data enables naturalistic observation, p. 28
Girls' social media use and risk of depression and self-harm, pp. 35–36

Natural endorphins discovery, p. 59
Our divided brain, pp. 82–85
What affects our sleep patterns, and why do we sleep?, pp. 99–101
Why we dream, pp. 106–109
Twin and adoption studies, pp. 128–130
How a child's mind develops, pp. 174–175
How do we see in color?, pp. 225–226
Parallel processing, p. 228
How can hypnosis provide pain relief?, pp. 246–247
How are memories constructed?, pp. 294–301
How do we store memories in our brain?, pp. 302–307
Do other species exhibit language?, pp. 346–348
Aging and intelligence, pp. 368–369
Why do we feel hunger?, pp. 387–389
What determines sexual orientation?, pp. 401–404
The pursuit of happiness: Who is happy, and why?, pp. 434–440
How does stress contribute to heart disease?, p. 450
How is social support linked with health?, pp. 457–459
Why do people fail to help in emergencies?, pp. 508–510
Self-esteem versus self-serving bias, pp. 547–549
What causes depressive disorders and bipolar disorders?, pp. 574–578
Do prenatal viral infections increase the risk of schizophrenia?, p. 582
Is psychotherapy effective?, pp. 612–615

What's New in the Thirteenth Edition?

In addition to our thorough, line-by-line updating of every module, and our ongoing efforts to make no assumptions about student readers' gender identity, sexual orientation, culture, relationship or family status, age, economic background, or physical ability, we offer much that is new in this thirteenth edition:

1. **Over 2100 research citations dated 2015–2020**. Our ongoing scrutiny of dozens of scientific periodicals and science news sources, enhanced by commissioned reviews and countless emails from instructors and students, enables integrating our field's most important, thought-provoking, and student-relevant new discoveries. Part of the pleasure that sustains this work is learning something new every day! *See MacmillanLearning.com for a list of significant Content Changes.*

2. **More support for teaching that *psychology is a science*, and that *critical thinking* and research matter!** (See "Expanded Focus on Critical Thinking and Research," p. xiii.)

3. NEW Student Preface—*Student Success: How to Apply Psychology to Live Your Best Life*. When we ask our teaching colleagues to share the most important lessons they wish to impart to students, they often tell us they want to teach students to *think critically*, and to *apply psychology to their own lives* so that they can live better and be more successful. This brief new Student Success preface, which previews relevant resources in the text and in LaunchPad, helps get students on the right path with sections on

- Thinking Critically and Scientifically,
- Self-Control and Self-Improvement,
- Time Management and Study Tips,
- Social Life, and
- Finding Meaning and Pursuing Goals.

4. **Improved, updated coverage of gender identity and sexual orientation.** A lot has changed in the field of psychology since the last edition was written, especially in the fast-moving subfields of human sexuality and gender psychology. We sought extra reviews from experts and instructors and made extensive updates to this coverage. In Modules 11, 12, 33, and elsewhere, we've worked to be appropriately inclusive and fully up-to-date in our presentation—representing the abundance of current research in this area, but also encompassing the lived experiences of many people, which may not yet be well represented in the literature.

5. **Ask Yourself Questions.** New "Ask Yourself" questions appear periodically throughout each module to help students apply what they are learning to their own lives. This helps make the material more meaningful, and more memorable. These questions are repeated in the Lecture Guides, for use as classroom discussion starters. We continue to offer "Assess Your Strengths" personal self-assessments in LaunchPad, allowing students to actively apply key principles to their own experiences and develop their strengths.

ASK YOURSELF

Are you the same person you were as a preschooler? As an 8-year-old? As a 12-year-old? How are you different? How are you the same?

ASK YOURSELF

Imagine a situation in which you would like to change the way you feel. How could you do so by altering your facial expressions or the way you carry yourself? In what other settings could you apply your knowledge of these feedback effects?

Sample "Ask Yourself" questions Here are two samples, taken from the Developing Through the Life Span and Emotions, Stress, and Health modules.

6. **"Thinking Critically About . . ." Infographic Activities.** All of these infographics in the text have been revised and updated for the new edition, with two entirely new pieces on "Sexual Aggression" (Module 12) and "How to Be Persuasive" (Module 40; see **FIGURE 1**). They are also now accompanied by *new corresponding activities in LaunchPad.*

7. **Active Learning.** Our Instructor's Resources have long been considered the "gold standard" in the field, and they nicely support students' active learning in class. There are additional NEW Classroom Exercises, Student Projects, Demonstrations, and Lecture/Discussion Topics that work well for think-pair-share, small-group, and large-group activities. These new activities for each group of modules cover diversity in psychology and were created by Salena Brody (University of Texas, Dallas).

8. **New research and research design-oriented iClicker questions.** We have new iClicker questions for each group of modules, written by Jennifer Zwolinski (University of San Diego), that help engage students on research topics, such as designing an effective study, understanding the component parts of key research that's presented in the text, and weighing the implications of research results.

Thinking Critically About:

How to Be Persuasive

LOQ 40-4   How can we share our views more effectively?

Would you like to be persuasive with those whose views differ from yours?

Do not:

Loudly argue your position before listening. Yelling backfires.

Humiliate people, or imply that they are ignorant. Insults breed defensiveness.

^%*&#!!   idiot   Stupid   *#*&#!!

Bore people with complex and forgettable information.

Therefore, with that said, direct your attention to this very dull and wonky and boring statistic that you will never remember. Now, however, on the other hand, here are yet more data points that are even more dry and overly complicated than the last... Let us continue...

Do:

Identify your shared values or goals, such as, "We all want to graduate, yes? Find a better job? Let's study for the test before we take time off to hang out."

Appeal to others' admirable motives.
Relate your aims to their yearnings.[1] For example:

"I would like us to **recover the good old days**, when people owned hunting rifles and pistols, but not assault rifles."

"I would prefer to **make a change**, so that in the future people may own hunting rifles and pistols, but no one will have assault rifles."

Political conservatives tend to respond to nostalgia. Those promoting gun safety legislation to this group should frame their message as an affirmation of yesteryear.

Political liberals respond better to future-focused messages.

Make your message vivid. People remember dramatic visual examples well. Pictures of unvaccinated children suffering from preventable diseases, or hungry children starving speak to the heart as well as the head.

Repeat your message. People often come to believe repeated falsehoods, but they also tend to believe oft-repeated truths.

Science Evidence-based Science Evidence-based Science Evidence-based Consider alternatives Science

Engage your audience in restating your message or, better yet, acting on it. Engage them in actively owning it—not just passively listening.

1. Lammers & Baldwin, 2018.

⬆ FIGURE 1
Sample "Thinking Critically About" infographic

Why Should I Use *Psychology, Thirteenth Edition in Modules* and Its Resources?

There are several reasons we think you should consider using this text and its resources for your classes:

1. **These resources are *top quality*.** Our resources offer *up-to-date, carefully checked content and assessment you can rely on,* with a study system that follows best practices from learning and memory research. This new thirteenth edition includes *2100 citations* dated 2015–2020, representing the field's most important, thought-provoking, and student-relevant new discoveries. We have worked with dozens of helpful reviewers, and with our editors we have run the text manuscript through *eight* drafts. Our dedicated Media and Test Bank authors and editors have focused similar intensity on their work. (For example, our 10,000 Test Bank questions go through four stages of checking to ensure there is appropriate, useful coverage for each new edition, and that different levels and kinds of questions have been included.)

2. **This text and its resources *make life easier for instructors*.** We've imagined the worst-case scenario of being asked to teach a course on a Friday and being ready to teach on a Monday. Step 1: Assign a book students tell us they love! Step 2: You have what you need with *LaunchPad's full course solution* (e-book, LearningCurve adaptive quizzing and other assessments, iClicker questions, classroom activities and other Instructor Resources, abundant videos, and numerous engaging student tutorials and activities for each module—all reporting to an easy-to-use gradebook). Or you may opt for the simplified (and extra-affordable) *Achieve Read & Practice* (e-book and LearningCurve adaptive quizzing, reporting to a gradebook with analytics on student performance). These engaging, integrated, top-notch options are both ready to use as is, with default courses set up, or you can readily tweak them to suit your needs. Our popular LearningCurve adaptive quizzing system has been shown to bring students to class better prepared, and help them do better in class. We've included callouts from the text pages to especially pertinent, helpful online resources. (See **FIGURE 2** for a sample.)

3. **Macmillan Learning offers students *affordable options*.** The digital-only, rental, or looseleaf options compete with Open Educational Resources (OER) printouts on price, and far surpass OER on success in the course for students, and ease of use and success for instructors.

4. **We wrote this text to be *inclusive of diverse student readers*.** From the first edition, we have endeavored to make no assumptions in terms of students' gender identity, sexual orientation, culture, relationship or family status, age, economic background, or physical ability. The text includes abundant, integrated coverage of psychology's diversity, and plenty of everyday life applications to draw all students into the content. Since this text's first edition, one of its Eight Guiding Principles has been "To convey respect for human unity and diversity." This edition offers an even more thoroughly **cross-cultural perspective** on psychology, with a world-based presentation for our worldwide student readers. We have included important new research and fresh examples from around the world in our efforts to help students understand *human* behavior in a broad sense, and to expose students to the world beyond their own culture. Salena Brody (University of Texas, Dallas) created new classroom activities for each group of modules covering diversity in psychology topics, and she revised our newly illustrated Timeline (Appendix A) to reflect the many contributions from women and people of color to the history of psychology. (See **TABLE 5**, The Psychology of Gender, Gender Identity, and Sexuality, and **TABLE 6**, The Psychology of Cultural Diversity and Inclusion.)

> For an animated tutorial on correlations, engage online with *Concept Practice: Positive and Negative Correlations.* See also the *Video: Correlational Studies* for another helpful tutorial animation.

FIGURE 2
Sample LaunchPad callout from Module 2

TABLE 5 The Psychology of Gender, Gender Identity, and Sexuality

Coverage of the *psychology of gender, gender identity, and sexuality* can be found on the following pages:

TABLE 6 The Psychology of Cultural Diversity and Inclusion

Coverage of the *psychology of cultural diversity and inclusion* can be found on the following pages:

(Continued)

same-sex orientation and, p. 443
social support and, p. 457
transgender people and, p. 443
Substance use
cultural expectations, p. 110
rates of, pp. 112, 114, 115–116, 122
Suicide and nonsuicidal self-injury,
pp. 557–559

Taste preferences, p. 390
Teen sexuality, pp. 398–399
Terrorism
fear/aggression and, p. 493
group polarization and,
p. 485
vivid cases and, p. 495
Testing bias, pp. 378–379
Therapy, p. 618

Trait stability, p. 536
adaptation and, p. 536
Trauma, pp. 106, 134, 184–185, 443,
524, 565
Universal emotions, pp. 428–429
Universal expressions, pp. 11,
428–429
Video-game playing, compulsive,
p. 111

Violence, media models for,
pp. 498–499
Weight, p. 392
WEIRD cultures, pp. 11, 68
Well-being, pp. 438–439
See also Modules 10, 11, 12, 40, 41,
42, and 43.

5. **These resources teach** *critical thinking.* See p. xiii and Table 4 for details and a deeper list of coverage.

6. **This text offers excellent** *neuroscience* **coverage, maps almost exactly to the MCAT Behavioral Sciences Section, and is perfect for nursing and premed students.** We have continued to improve our strong neuroscience, behavior genetics, and evolutionary psychology coverage in this new edition, reflecting the dynamic nature of these subfields. See **TABLE 7** and **TABLE 8** for a list of topics covered. *Psychology, Thirteenth Edition in Modules* also maps well onto the MCAT's behavioral sciences section. Since 2015, the MCAT has devoted 25 percent of its questions to the "Psychological, Social, and Biological Foundations of Behavior." The new section's topics match up almost exactly with the topics in this text. See **TABLE 9** for a sample. For a complete pairing of the MCAT behavioral science topics with this book's contents, see the MCAT Correlation Guide provided in LaunchPad's Instructor Resources. In addition, the Test Bank questions for *Psychology, Thirteenth Edition in Modules* are keyed to the MCAT behavioral science section's topics.

TABLE 7 Neuroscience

In addition to the coverage found in Modules 4, 5, and 6, *neuroscience* can be found on the following pages:

Aggression, pp. 496–497
Aging: physical exercise and the brain, p. 202
Animal cognition, pp. 337–338
Animal language, pp. 346–347
Antisocial personality disorder, pp. 588–589
Arousal, pp. 397–398
Attention-deficit hyperactivity disorder (ADHD) and the brain, p. 595
Autism spectrum disorder (ASD), pp. 592–594
Biofeedback, p. 461
Biological psychology, p. 52
Biopsychosocial approach, pp. 12–13
to aggression, pp. 495–500
to aging, pp. 207–209
to Alzheimer's, pp. 100, 202, 204–205, 307, 459
to development, pp. 161–162
to disordered drug use, pp. 120–123
to dreams, pp. 106–109
to emotion, pp. 304–305, 422–424
to learning, pp. 278–281
to pain, pp. 343–345

to personality, pp. 541–542
to psychological disorders, pp. 553–554
to sexual motivation, pp. 397–398
to sleep, pp. 95–97
to therapeutic lifestyle change, pp. 620–622
Brain development
in adolescence, pp. 190–191
experience and, pp. 142–143
in infancy and childhood, pp. 173–174
pruning and, pp. 100, 142, 173, 190, 253
sexual differentiation in utero, p. 155
Brain imaging techniques, pp. 66–69, 73
Cognitive neuroscience, pp. 9, 68, 89–90
Drug use, pp. 120–121
adolescent brain development and, p. 113
Dual processing, pp. 92–93, 193, 228, 247
Electroconvulsive therapy, pp. 625–626
Emotion and cognition, pp. 418–422
Fear-learning, pp. 264, 568–569

Fetal alcohol syndrome and brain abnormalities, pp. 170–171
Frequent head trauma, risks of, pp. 73–74
Functional connectivity, p. 81
Hallucinations, p. 97
hallucinogens and, pp. 79, 117–119
near-death experiences and, p. 188
psychological disorders and, p. 560
schizophrenia and, pp. 36, 578–581, 622
sleep and, pp. 97, 107
Hormones, pp. 63–64
abuse and, p. 185
appetite and, pp. 388–389
in autism spectrum disorder, treatment of, p. 594
development and, pp. 154–157, 173, 190
in adolescents, pp. 155–156, 190
of sexual characteristics, pp. 155–156, 190
emotion and, pp. 419–420, 422–423
gender and, pp. 154–157
memory and, pp. 305, 524
sex and, pp. 154–157, 190
sexual behavior and, pp. 394–395, 397, 405

sleep and, pp. 99, 101, 102
stress and, pp. 170, 181, 185, 304, 315, 422–423, 446–447, 449, 451, 453–454, 566
weight control and, pp. 392
Hunger, pp. 387–389
Insight, pp. 85, 327, 333–334, 462
Intelligence, pp. 354–357
creativity, pp. 334–336
twins, pp. 370–371
Language, pp. 345–346, 375
deafness and, p. 345
thinking in images and, pp. 350–351
Meditation, pp. 88–89, 246, 439, 461–464
mindfulness and mindfulness meditation, pp. 463–464
Memory
emotional memories, pp. 304–305
explicit and implicit memories, pp. 296–298
physical storage of, pp. 302–306
sleep and, p. 100
synaptic changes and, pp. 305–306
Mirror neurons, pp. 284–286
Neurocognitive disorders and Alzheimer's disease, pp. 204, 292, 250, 306

TABLE 8 Behavior Genetics and Evolutionary Psychology

In addition to the coverage found in Module 10, *behavior genetics* is covered on the following pages:

In addition to the coverage found in Module 11, the *evolutionary perspective* is covered on the following pages:

TABLE 9 Sample MCAT Correlation With *Psychology, Thirteenth Edition in Modules*

MCAT 2015 Content Category 6C: Responding to the world	*Psychology, Thirteenth Edition in Modules* Correlations	Page Numbers
Emotion	Emotion: Introduction to emotion; Expressing emotion; Experiencing emotion	417–440
Three components of emotion (i.e., cognitive, physiological, behavioral)	Emotion: Arousal, behavior, and cognition	417–422
Universal emotions (e.g., fear, anger, happiness, surprise, joy, disgust, and sadness)	Culture and emotional expression—including the universal emotions	428–430
	Experiencing emotion—including the basic emotions	432–440
Adaptive role of emotion	Emotion as the body's adaptive response	418, 422–423, 433–434, 445–446
	Emotions and the autonomic nervous system	422–423
Theories of emotion		
James-Lange theory	James-Lange theory: Arousal comes before emotion	418–419
Cannon-Bard theory	Cannon-Bard theory: Arousal and emotion occur simultaneously	419
Schachter-Singer theory	Schachter and Singer two-factor theory: Arousal + label = emotion	419–420
Zajonc; LeDoux; Lazarus	Zajonc, LeDoux, and Lazarus: Does cognition always precede emotion?	420–422
The role of biological processes in perceiving emotion	Emotions and the autonomic nervous system	422–423
Brain regions involved in the generation and experience of emotions	The physiology of emotions—including the brain's pathways for emotions	420–422, 423
	Zajonc, LeDoux, and Lazarus: Does cognition always precede emotion?	420–422
The role of the limbic system in emotion	Emotions and the autonomic nervous system	422–423
	The limbic system	71–72
	Physiological differences among specific emotions	423–424
Emotion and the autonomic nervous system	Emotions and the autonomic nervous system	422–423
Physiological markers of emotion (signatures of emotion)	The physiology of emotions	420–422
Stress	Stress and illness	441–452
The nature of stress	Stress: Some basic concepts	441–446
Appraisal	Stress appraisal	441
Different types of stressors (i.e., cataclysmic events, personal)	Stressors—things that push our buttons	442–445
Effects of stress on psychological functions	The stress response system	445–446
Stress outcomes/response to stressors	The stress response system	445–446
Physiological	The stress response system	445–446
	Stress and vulnerability to disease	446–452
	Thinking critically about: Stress and health	451
Emotional	Stress and heart disease: The effects of personality, pessimism, and depression	449–451
	Coping with stress	453–459
	Posttraumatic stress disorder	565–566
Behavioral	The stress response system	445–446
	Coping with stress	453–459
Managing stress (e.g., exercise, relaxation techniques, spirituality)	Reducing Stress: aerobic exercise; relaxation and meditation; faith communities	459–466

Make Things Memorable!

How to study and LEARN more effectively.
With David G. Myers, author

FIGURE 3
How to learn and remember For my [DM's] 5-minute animated guide to more effective studying, visit tinyurl.com/HowToRemember.

FIGURE 4 →
Sample Retrieval Practice feature

Scattered throughout this book, students will find interesting and informative review notes and quotes from researchers and others that will encourage them to be active learners and to apply their new knowledge to everyday life.

→ **key terms** Look for complete definitions of each important term near the term's introduction in the narrative.

7. **The study system follows best practices from learning and memory research.** This text's learning system harnesses the *testing effect,* which documents the benefits of actively retrieving information through regular testing (**FIGURE 3**). Thus, our popular LearningCurve adaptive quizzing provides a personalized study plan. In the text, each module offers **Retrieval Practice** questions interspersed throughout (**FIGURE 4**). Creating these *desirable difficulties* for students along the way optimizes the testing effect, as does *immediate feedback* via answers that are available for checking. In addition, each main section of text begins with a numbered question that establishes a **learning objective** and directs student reading. The **Review** sections repeat these questions as a further self-testing opportunity (with answers available to check). The Review sections also offer a self-test on the **Terms and Concepts to Remember,** and **Master the Material** questions to promote optimal retention.

RETRIEVAL PRACTICE

RP-2 What does a good theory do?

RP-3 Why is replication important?

ANSWERS IN APPENDIX E

---

8. **You won't find better service and support anywhere.** The Macmillan representatives who market and sell these resources, help set up instructors' courses, and in many other ways service instructor and student course needs are the best in the business. Many of these folks have become personal friends. We've been grateful to be working with a family-owned publisher that has been so supportive of our teaching mission and has encouraged us to create the best teaching and learning materials.

LaunchPad and Achieve Read & Practice Resources

LaunchPad

It has been a joy for me [ND] to teach the course with **LaunchPad** (LaunchPadWorks .com), which my students love. LaunchPad makes it easy to engage students effectively starting on Day 1 of the class when I make a LaunchPad assignment. With immediate engagement, and active learning throughout the course, most students have fun with the material and stay in my class.

LaunchPad facilitates active learning as it solves key challenges in the course (**FIGURE 5**). In combination with the meticulously created text, these online resources give students everything they need to succeed, while giving you, the instructor, everything *you* need to quickly set up a course, shape the content to your syllabus, craft presentations, assign and assess homework, and guide the progress of individual students and the class as a whole:

- Our **e-book** can go with any student, anywhere. It is fully mobile-compatible and meets accessibility standards.

- **LearningCurve game-like quizzing** motivates students and adapts to their needs based on their performance. Additional reporting tools and metrics will help you assess the progress of individual students and the class as a whole.

- **iClicker offers active learning simplified, and now includes the REEF mobile app** (iClicker.com). iClicker's simple, flexible tools in LaunchPad help you give students a voice, facilitate active learning and engage remote learners. Students can use iClicker remotes, or the REEF mobile app on their phone, tablet, or laptop to participate more meaningfully. LaunchPad includes a robust collection of iClicker questions for each

i>clicker.

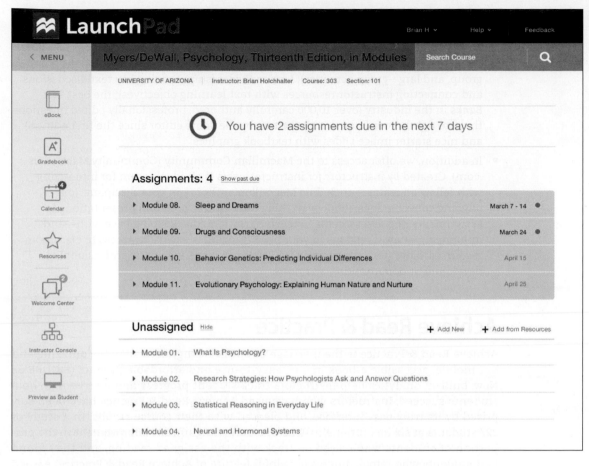

group of modules, including new questions for each group of modules designed to help students understand the value and importance of research.

- The **Concept Practice collection** offers 120 dynamic, interactive 5-minute tutorials that teach and reinforce the course's foundational ideas.

- The **Topic Tutorials: PsychSim6,** Thomas Ludwig's (Hope College) award-winning interactive psychology simulations, place students in the role of scientist or participant in activities that highlight important concepts, processes, and experimental approaches.

- In the **Assess Your Strengths** activities, students apply what they are learning from the text to their own lives and experiences by considering key "strengths." Each activity starts with a personalized video introduction from us [DM and ND], and students assessing themselves on the strength (critical thinking, quality of sleep, self-control, relationship strength, belonging, hope, and more) using scales developed by researchers. Next, students get tips for nurturing that strength in their own lives, and take a quiz to help solidify their learning.

- NEW **"Thinking Critically About . . ." infographic activities** teach and reinforce critical-thinking skills.

- **LMS integration** into your school's system is readily available. Check with your local sales representative for details.

- **The Video Assignment Tool** makes it easy to assign and assess video-based activities and projects, and provides a convenient way for students to submit video coursework.

- **The Gradebook** gives a clear window on performance for the whole class, for individual students, and for individual assignments.

- A **streamlined interface** helps students manage their schedule of assignments, while *social commenting tools* let them connect with classmates and learn from one another. 24/7 help is a click away, accessible from a link in the upper right corner.

- LaunchPad offers curated **optional pre-built units,** which can be used as is or customized. Or choose not to use them and build your course from scratch.

- Our **Instructor Resources** include suggestions for lectures, classroom exercises and demonstrations, and student projects (which work well for think-pair-share, small-group, and large-group activities); *Lecture Guides* (summarizing key text discussions and connecting instructor resources with text learning objectives); the best *Test Banks* in the industry (over 10,000 carefully authored, professionally edited questions that are tightly coordinated with the text by the same editor since the first edition); and nice starter image slides with textbook graphics.

- In addition, we offer access to the **Macmillan Community** (Community.Macmillan .com). Created *by* instructors *for* instructors, this is an ideal forum for interacting with fellow educators—including Macmillan authors—in your discipline. Join ongoing conversations about everything from course prep and presentations to assignments and assessments to teaching with media, keeping pace with—and influencing—new directions in your field. It includes exclusive access to classroom resources, blogs (including my [DM's] TalkPsych.com), webinars, professional development opportunities, and more.

Achieve Read & Practice

Achieve Read & Practice is the marriage of our LearningCurve adaptive quizzing and our mobile, accessible e-book in one, easy-to-use and affordable product (**FIGURE 6**). New, built-in analytics help instructors track student progress and intervene to help students succeed. Instructors who have used Achieve Read & Practice have been surprised by its truly easy interface, and pleased with their course results. In a study of 227 students at six institutions, instructors found a significant improvement in the proportion of students who stayed on track with the assigned reading, and they found that students who retook quizzes (a helpful feature of Achieve Read & Practice) earned higher grades in the course. (Access the full report at MacmillanLearning.com/Catalog/Page/LearningScience.)

FIGURE 6
Sample from Achieve Read & Practice

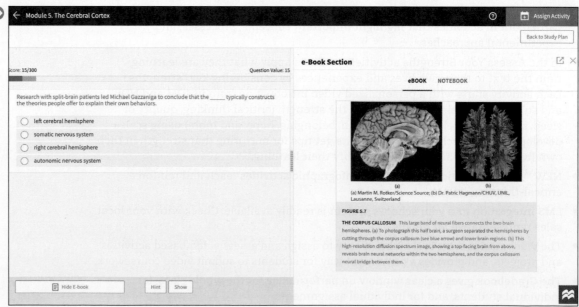

Myers' and DeWall's Eight Guiding Principles

We have retained the goals—the guiding principles—that have animated this text since its first edition.

Facilitating the Learning Experience

1. To teach critical thinking By presenting research as intellectual detective work, we model a scientific mindset. Students will discover how critical thinking can help them evaluate competing ideas and popular claims—from ESP and memory construction to group differences in intelligence and alternative therapies. Our "Thinking Critically About" infographic features help engage students in this learning. (See p. xii, and Table 4, for more about critical thinking in this text.)

2. To provide applications of principles Throughout the narrative, illustrations, and online resources we relate psychology's findings to real-world applications. We make psychology meaningful to students by showing how it relates to their lives—their life-span development, their search for relationships and happiness, their understanding of negative forces, such as prejudice, and so much more. The "Ask Yourself" questions throughout each module, and our "Assess Your Strengths" activities in LaunchPad invite students to apply important concepts to their own lives, and to learn ways to develop key personal strengths. (See **TABLE 10**, Positive Psychology, for more about how we encourage understanding of happiness and human strengths, and see the new Student Preface—Student Success: How To Apply Psychology to Live Your Best Life on p. xxxi.)

3. To reinforce learning at every step Everyday examples and thought-provoking questions encourage students to process the material actively. Self-testing opportunities throughout the text and online resources help students learn and retain important concepts and terminology.

Demonstrating the Science of Psychology

4. To show the process of inquiry We try to show students not just the outcome of research, but how the research process works, often by putting them in the role of experimenter or participant in classic studies. We introduce research stories as mysteries that unravel as one clue after another falls into place. Our "How Would You Know?" activities in LaunchPad allow students to play the role of researcher in thinking about research questions and how they may be studied effectively.

5. To be as up-to-date as possible While retaining psychology's classic studies and concepts, we also present the most important recent developments. In this edition, 2100 references are dated 2015–2020. Likewise, new photos and new everyday examples are drawn from today's world.

6. To put facts in the service of concepts Our intention is not to overwhelm students with facts, but to reveal psychology's major concepts—to teach students how to think, and to offer psychological ideas worth thinking about. Learning Objective Questions and Retrieval Practice questions throughout each module help students focus on the most important concepts. Concept Practice and Topic Tutorial activities in LaunchPad help ensure student understanding of key points.

Promoting Big Ideas and Broadened Horizons

7. To enhance comprehension by providing continuity We often present concepts with a significant issue or theme that links subtopics, forming a thread that ties ideas together. The Learning modules convey the idea that bold thinkers can serve as intellectual

TABLE 10 Positive Psychology	
Coverage of *positive psychology* topics can be found in the following modules:	
Topic	**Module**
Altruism/compassion	2, 10, 22, 37, 39, 40, 43, 45
Coping	14, 34, 39, 47, 49, 55
Courage	37, 41, 43, 45, 51, Appendix C
Creativity	2, 26, 28, 34, 37, 39, Appendix C
Emotional intelligence	28
Empathy	12, 19, 22, 36, 41, 43, 45, 53, 54
Flow	37, Appendix C
Gratitude	37, 53
Happiness/life satisfaction	1, 2, 16, 34, 36, 37, 38, 39, 43, Appendix C
Humility	1, 12, 46, Appendix C
Humor	37, 39, 48
Integrity	13, 15, 16, 37
Justice	15, 54
Leadership	34, 37, 38, 39, 45, 46, Appendix C
Love	10, 14, 16, 17, 25, 31, 34, 37, 39, 42, 43, 45
Morality	6, 11, 12, 15, 22, 26, 40, 43
Optimism	14, 16, 37, 39, 45, 53
Personal control	12, 20, 30, 32, 34, 37, 38, 39, 41, 47, 55
Resilience	12, 14, 16, 30, 37, 38, 47, 48, 55
Self-awareness	19, 28, 45, 53
Self-control	16, 20, 32, 34, 35, 36, 37, 39, 40, 46, 53
Self-discipline	15, 30, 32, 34, 39
Self-efficacy	46, 54
Self-esteem	9, 14, 16, 31, 34, 37, 45, 46, 47, Appendix C
Spirituality	9, 31, 37, 38, 39, 55
Toughness (grit)	28, 30, 34
Wisdom	1, 14, 26, 29, 37, 45, Appendix C

pioneers. The Thinking and Language modules raise the issue of human rationality and irrationality. The Psychological Disorders modules convey empathy for, and understanding of, troubled lives. Other threads, such as cognitive neuroscience, dual processing, and individual and group diversity, weave throughout the whole book, and students hear a consistent voice.

8. **To convey respect for human unity and diversity** Throughout the book, readers will see evidence of human kinship in our shared biology—our common mechanisms of seeing and learning, hungering and feeling, loving and hating. They will also better understand our diversity—our individual diversity in development and aptitudes, temperament and personality, and disorder and health; and our cultural diversity in attitudes and expressive styles, child-raising and care for the elderly, and life priorities and experiences.

In Appreciation

Aided by input from thousands of instructors and students over the years, this has become a better, more effective, more accurate book than two authors alone (these authors at least) could write. Our indebtedness continues to the innumerable researchers who have been so willing to share their time and talent to help us accurately report their research, and to the hundreds of instructors who have taken the time to offer feedback.

Our gratitude extends to the colleagues who contributed criticism, corrections, and creative ideas related to the content, pedagogy, and format of this new edition and its resources. For their expertise and encouragement, and the gift of their time to the teaching of psychology, we thank the reviewers and consultants listed here:

Michelle Butler
United States Air Force Academy

Gary Creasey
Old Dominion University

Brian Day
Clemson University

Joseph Eastwood
University of Ontario Institute of Technology

Perry Fuchs
The University of Texas at Arlington

Antonia Henderson
Langara College

Carrie Kobelsky
University of Victoria

Erin Lea
Langara College

Valerie L. Lloyd
Langara College

Beth Morling
University of Delaware

Robin Musselman
Lehigh Carbon Community College

Levente Orban
Kwantlen Polytechnic University

John M. O'Brien
University of Maine at Augusta

Elaine M. O'Reilly
University of North Carolina at Charlotte

L. Alison Phillips
Iowa State University

Alan Roberts
Indiana University

Jon Sigurjonsson
Caldwell University

Kamara Taylor
Michigan Technological University

Elizabeth Veinott
Michigan Technological University

Jeanne Viviani
LaGuardia Community College

Kimberly Wood
Samford University

We'd like to offer special thanks to the reviewers and consultants who helped us update and improve the gender and human sexuality discussions, and who helped us shape the new "Thinking Critically About: Sexual Aggression" infographic feature in Module 12:

Michael Bailey
Northwestern University

Andrea Brown
College of Southern Nevada

Christia Brown
University of Kentucky

Ann Coker
University of Kentucky

Jane Dickie
Hope College

Sara Dorer
Hope College

Angela B. Dortch
Ivy Tech Community College

Heather V. Ganginis Del Pino
Montgomery College

Jerry Green
Tarrant County College

Ruth Hallongren
Triton College

Regina M. Hughes
Collin College

Kellie McCants-Price
Anne Arundel Community College

Michelle Merwin
The University of Tennessee at Martin

Hayley Kleitz Nelson
Delaware County Community College

Thelisa E. Nutt
Tarrant County College District—Southeast Campus

Claire Renzetti
University of Kentucky

David L. Roby
Texas Southmost College

We'd also like to offer our thanks to the instructors who shared their input and expertise to help us shape the content of our new Student Preface—Student Success: How to Apply Psychology to Live Your Best Life:

Andrea Brown
College of Southern Nevada

Douglas Dinero
Onondaga Community College

Angela B. Dortch
Ivy Tech Community College

Timothy Flemming
Georgia State University

Dann Hazel
Polk State College

David L. Roby
Texas Southmost College

Edie Sample
Metropolitan Community College

Melissa S. Terlecki
Cabrini University

Carol Wilkinson
Whatcom Community College

We also appreciate Salena Brody's (University of Texas, Dallas) careful review of our Psychology Timeline (Appendix A), including her added entries relating to the contributions of women and people of color, and the new classroom exercises, lecture/discussion topics, and think-pair-share activities she created for the Instructor's Resources on diversity in psychology.

At Macmillan Learning, a host of people played key roles in creating this thirteenth edition.

Senior Executive Program Manager Carlise Stembridge has been a valued team leader, thanks to her dedication, creativity, and sensitivity. Carlise oversees, encourages, and guides our author-editor team, and she serves as an important liaison with our colleagues in the field.

Noel Hohnstine and Laura Burden expertly coordinated creation of the media resources. Betty Probert efficiently edited and produced the Test Bank questions (working with Chrysalis Wright, University of Central Florida), Instructor's Resources, and Lecture Guides and, in the process, also helped fine-tune the whole book. Anna Munroe provided invaluable support in commissioning and organizing the multitude of reviews, coordinating our development and production schedules, and providing editorial guidance. Lee McKevitt did a splendid job of laying out each page of the printed text. Robin Fadool and Donna Ranieri worked together to create the lovely photo program.

Won McIntosh, Susan Wein, and Paul Rohloff masterfully kept the book to its tight schedule, and Natasha Wolfe skillfully directed creation of the beautiful new design.

Christine Brune, chief editor for the last three decades, is a wonder worker. She offers just the right mix of encouragement, gentle admonition, attention to detail, and passion for excellence. Her authors could not ask for more. Development Editors Trish Morgan and Danielle Slevens also amazed us with their meticulous focus, impressive knowledge, and helpful editing—and with kindred spirits to our own. And Deborah Heimann did an excellent job with the copyediting.

To achieve our goal of supporting the teaching of psychology, these resources not only must be authored, reviewed, edited, and produced, but also made available to teachers of psychology, with effective guidance and professional and friendly servicing close at hand. For their exceptional success in doing all this, our author team is grateful to Macmillan Learning's professional sales and marketing team. We are especially grateful to Executive Marketing Manager Kate Nurre, and Learning Solutions Specialists Robyn Burnett and Elizabeth Chaffin Woosley for tirelessly working to inform our teaching colleagues of our efforts to assist their teaching, and for the joy of working with them.

At Hope College, Kathryn Brownson researched countless bits of information and edited and proofed hundreds of pages. Kathryn is a knowledgeable and sensitive adviser on many matters. At the University of Kentucky, Lorie Hailey showcased a variety of indispensable qualities, including a sharp eye and a strong work ethic.

Again, I [DM] gratefully acknowledge the editing assistance and mentoring of my writing coach, poet Jack Ridl, whose influence resides in the voice you will be hearing in the pages that follow. He, more than anyone, cultivated my delight in dancing with the language, and taught me to approach writing as a craft that shades into art. Likewise, I [ND] am grateful to my intellectual hero and mentor, Roy Baumeister, who taught me how to hone my writing and embrace the writing life. I'm also indebted to John Tierney, who has offered unending support and served as a role model of how to communicate to a general audience.

And we have enjoyed our ongoing work with each other on this our eighth co-authored book. Nathan's fresh insights and contributions continue to enrich this book as we work together on each module. With support from our wonderful editors, this is a team project. In addition to our work together on the textbook, Nathan and I contribute to the monthly "Teaching Current Directions in Psychological Science" column in the *APS Observer* (tinyurl.com/MyersDeWall). I [DM] also blog at TalkPsych.com, where I share exciting new findings, everyday applications, and observations on all things psychology (with special thanks to my talented, longtime editor, Nancy Fleming).

Finally, our gratitude extends to the many students and instructors who have written to offer suggestions, or just an encouraging word. It is for them, and those about to begin their study of psychology, that we have done our best to introduce the field we love.

• • •

The day this book went to press was the day we started gathering information and ideas for the next edition. Your input will influence how this book continues to evolve. So, please, do share your thoughts.

Hope College
Holland, Michigan 49422-9000 USA
DavidMyers.org
@DavidGMyers

University of Kentucky
Lexington, Kentucky 40506-0044 USA
NathanDeWall.com
@cndewall

Student Success: How to Apply Psychology to Live Your Best Life

As you will see in the modules to come, some things—including our temperament, body type, sexual orientation, and personality traits—can be restrained with willpower, yet are mostly beyond our power to change. In such ways it's better to accept than to fight who we are.

In other ways, we *can* change and become the person we aspire to be. Consider five ways we can use psychology to live our best life (more on each in the modules to come):

- thinking critically when forming judgments and making decisions,
- attending to self-control and self-improvement,
- managing our time and study,
- enjoying a satisfying social life, and
- finding meaning while pursuing goals.

➔ **Thinking Critically and Scientifically**

➔ **Self-Control and Self-Improvement**

➔ **Time Management and Study Tips**

➔ **Social Life**

➔ **Finding Meaning and Pursuing Goals**

Thinking Critically and Scientifically

To live your best life, you will need to learn to think critically—guidance for which you will find in every module of this book. You will need to base your hopes, your fears, and your decisions on a foundation of truth, and to understand the importance of scientific thinking and the careful research that underlies all of what we will be presenting.

Alas, misinformation spreads readily. Many people fear terrorism, mass shootings, and air travel more than the vastly greater threats they face from in-home guns and car travel. In the United States, 2 in 3 people have, year after year, perceived crime as rising—even while it has been dramatically falling (McCarthy, 2019). And "how many of the world's 1-year old children have been vaccinated against some disease"—20, 50, or 80 percent? In most countries, more than 4 in 5 people guess 20 or 50 percent, when the truth is 88 percent (Rosling, 2018).

Not only does it help us individually to know the truth about what threatens and benefits us, it also helps us collectively. Democracy presumes our wisdom. When we voters grasp truth—when facts prevail over false news—we can support sensible policies and elect benevolent leaders.

Misinformation comes from various sources:

- Some people or organizations aim to deceive us, in order to sell a product or to undermine a political opponent.
- Sensationalized news can be misleading—vivid images of horrific shootings or plane crashes may lead us to disproportionately fear some dangers too much, and others too little.
- If we interact only with people, websites, and news sources that reflect our way of thinking, we will confirm rather than challenge our presumptions.
- We have a natural "truth bias," an inclination to believe what others say, especially when repeated.

Fortunately, ignorance of our ignorance can be remedied by education. And that brings you to this book and its resources, which offer psychology's contribution to critical thinking. To learn how we can protect ourselves against errors and biases that may hack our brain, and to better understand the importance of current, scientific research and the careful procedures it follows, read on. You will also want to explore the "How Would You Know?" research activities in LaunchPad, which give you a hands-on opportunity to experience the value of research from the inside out. And check out my [DM's] new tutorial animation, "Thinking Critically in Our Post-Truth World" in LaunchPad, and also at tinyurl.com/PostTruthMyers.

With a mix of open-minded curiosity and evidence-seeking questioning we can better sift falsehood from fact. And we can live smarter and more flourishing lives.

Self-Control and Self-Improvement

We can apply our smart thinking to all aspects of living our best life, including appropriate self-care. Family, work, and school commitments can make it difficult to find time to achieve our goals, sustain our health, and have fun. But to care for others, we first need to care for ourselves.

Self-Control

Success starts with **self-control**—the ability to restrain impulses and delay short-term gratification for greater long-term rewards. What's your level of self-control? On a scale from 1 *(not at all like me)* to 5 *(very much like me)*, indicate how much each of the following statements reflects how you typically are (Tangney et al., 2004):

1. ___ I am good at resisting temptation.
2. ___ I have a hard time breaking bad habits.
3. ___ I am lazy.
4. ___ I say inappropriate things.
5. ___ I do certain things that are bad for me, if they are fun.
6. ___ I refuse things that are bad for me.
7. ___ I wish I had more self-discipline.
8. ___ People would say that I have iron self-discipline.
9. ___ Pleasure and fun sometimes keep me from getting work done.
10. ___ I have trouble concentrating.
11. ___ I am able to work effectively toward long-term goals.
12. ___ Sometimes I can't stop myself from doing something, even if I know it is wrong.
13. ___ I often act without thinking through all the alternatives.

To tally your total score:

- *Reverse* your rating for items 2, 3, 4, 5, 7, 9, 10, 12, and 13 (1=5, 2=4, 3=3, 4=2, 5=1).
- Now *add* your ratings to establish your **total score**.
- Total scores range from 13 to 65, with higher scores indicating more self-control. The average score was 39 in two studies of college students (Tangney et al., 2004).

To improve your self-control, watch my [ND's] video, "Self-Control—Our Greatest Inner Strength," available in LaunchPad or at tinyurl.com/DeWallSelf-Control.

> 📖 **LaunchPad** Alternatively, you can have your score automatically calculated in the LaunchPad activity *Assess Your Strengths: How Much Self-Control Do You Have, and Why Is This Worth Working to Increase?*

Self-Improvement

Here are some tips for improving your self-care:

- **Set and announce your goals.** Specific and realistic goals—such as "draft that paper by next Friday"—direct attention, promote effort, and motivate persistence. To make yourself accountable, announce your goal to friends or family.

- **Develop an action plan.** Specify *how* you will progress toward your goal. People who flesh out goals with detailed plans become more focused, and are more likely to finish on time. Fantasizing your ultimate success (a great paper turned in on time, a good course grade, a sports victory) helps. But imagining the step-by-step details helps more.

- **Form beneficial habits.** Is there some behavior, such as exercising, that you would like to make automatic? Make yourself do it every day for two months and you will have transformed a hard-to-do behavior into a must-do habit.

- **Plan for a full night's sleep.** Work commitments, family stresses, and other challenges can interfere with sleep. Screen time and social time can also intrude. The first step in changing your sleep routine starts with a question, "Do I want to increase my happiness, energy, focus, and health?" If so, try to find a way to give your body more of the sleep it craves. (See Module 8 for tips on getting better sleep.)

- **Create a supportive environment.** It's easier to eat healthy when you don't have junk food around. At meals, control portion size by using smaller plates and bowls. To focus on a project, remove distractions. At night, stash your phone so you can sleep undisturbed. Engage with friends who bring out the best rather than the worst in you.

- **Control substance use.** Many psychoactive drugs, such as nicotine, are highly addictive and can readily hijack our daily lives, long-term goals, and good health. Although some drugs, such as caffeine, may be safely consumed in moderation, many others will seriously disrupt our best life unless avoided entirely. (More on this in Module 9.)

- **Make time for exercise.** Frequent aerobic exercise is a great time investment. Even in small amounts, aerobic exercise boosts health, increases energy, lifts mood, improves memory, and calms anxiety.

- **Incorporate mindfulness meditation.** Practicing mindfulness can help you manage your stress and regulate your emotions more healthfully.

- **Build coping skills and a healthy lifestyle.** Strengthening our *resilience* and managing our emotions helps us cope with stress. We can also boost our mental health with lifestyle changes—daily practices that mark flourishing lives. For more information, see Module 39, and also "Thinking Critically About: Therapeutic Lifestyle Change" in Module 55.

> **LaunchPad** Consider ways to build your resilience by engaging with the LaunchPad activity *Assess Your Strengths: How Resilient Are You, and Why Should You Build More Resilience?*

Time Management and Study Tips

Some students fail. Some survive. And some thrive. So, what choices can you make to thrive?

You can start by making a plan for how you will manage your time and maximize your learning. As legendary basketball coach John Wooden (1977) said, "When you fail to prepare, you're preparing to fail."

It may seem as if there are not enough hours in the week to get everything done. It may be that you are not using your time as efficiently as you could. To assess your current time management and study skills, complete the survey below by answering YES or NO:[1]

1. _____Have you estimated how many hours you will need to study each week?

2. _____Do you tend to complete your assignments on time?

3. _____Have you estimated how long it takes to complete each of your assignments?

4. _____Do you begin to work on long-term assignments at the beginning of the term?

5. _____Do you make lists of things to do in your head rather than on paper or in a digital scheduling program?

6. _____Do you participate in social activities even when you know you should be studying?

7. _____Do you schedule time to study for exams?

8. _____Do you have a job that requires more than 20 hours a week?

---

[1]Source: Van Blerkom, D. L. (2012). *Orientation to learning* (7th ed.). Wadsworth.

9. _____ Do you know exactly what tasks you are going to do when you sit down to study?

10. _____ Do you attempt the assignments from your most difficult class first?

Give yourself one point for each *NO* answer to questions 5, 6, and 8, and one point for each *YES* answer to all the other questions. How many total points did you earn? People who score higher than 7 tend already to have good time management and study skills; people who score below 5 benefit most from learning how to improve. We can all use a reminder of best practices. Here are a few tips.

Manage Your Time

Your time is your most precious resource. Managing your time requires intentionally planning *when* you will progress toward your goals. Start by carefully tracking your time use for a week—including all personal, school, and work time—and watching for patterns and opportunities. (We [DM and ND] have each done this and were surprised by how much time we were wasting!) Next, create a "time budget" that allows you to enjoy life, be energized, and complete your study, work, and family tasks. Plan time for recreation and friends; social media; sleep, eating, and personal care; class time and study; and any employment or home obligations. Determine precisely when you will do each, by *creating weekly and daily schedules that make guilt-free space for each activity.* To become the person you wish to be, live intentionally, day by day.

Manage Your Mental Energy

Some tasks are mentally demanding. Plan your day to make space for such tasks when you have the most energy. Allow time to rest and recover before engaging the next demanding task. By tracking your mental energy, you will know when to spend it and when to save it.

Play Offense

Car troubles, family problems, and work challenges happen. Sometimes we have to play "defense" against life's demands and problems, leaving us stressed and short of our goals. The solution: When possible, play "offense" against your environment. Rather than just letting the day happen to you, start each day with a plan. Control how you spend your time. Establishing routines and making decisions in advance conserves energy by reducing daily decision making. If you know you are going to study two hours in the morning before class, you won't waste time weighing what to do.

Time for success Making a realistic, day-to-day schedule will allow you time for what you *need* to do as well as time for what you *want* to do.

stock_colors/Getty Images

Study Smart

To remember what you read, use the SQ3R (Survey, Question, Read, Retrieve, Review) system: Survey the module organization. Identify Questions your reading should answer. Read actively, seeking answers. Retrieve and rehearse key ideas. Finally, Review the module's organization and concepts.

Those last two "R's" are especially important: You will retain information best through repeated self-testing and rehearsal of previously studied material. Getting *immediate feedback* makes this *testing effect* even stronger. That's the idea behind our effective online adaptive quizzing system, LearningCurve, and the frequent self-testing opportunities throughout this text.

Distributing your study time, rather than cramming, will also help. Establishing a schedule, and sticking to it, will spread the load out across the term. For more information, see "Use Psychology to Become a Stronger Person—and a Better Student" at the end of Module 1 and "Improving Memory" in Module 25, and view my [DM's] 5-minute animation at tinyurl.com/HowToRemember.

Social Life

Living your best life requires social support. Here are some tips for forming and maintaining healthy, supportive relationships:

- **Prioritize people.** We humans are social animals. We need to belong. We are happier and healthier when supported by, and giving support to, our friends. So, make the effort to make friends, such as by joining a club, sports team, or fellowship group. Get to know your instructors. And do not take your friends and loved ones for granted. Attend to them. Affirm them. Share your daily experiences and feelings with them.

- **Enjoy social media and your phone without letting them control you.** Use social media and your phone to stay connected with friends and family, but without hijacking your time and other priorities. And when posting on social media, remember that someday a potential employer may be Googling your name.

- **Embrace a speak-up culture rather than a call-out culture.** To disagree is to be human. You will disagree with others, and others will disagree with you. Indeed, we often learn by exploring these other perspectives. (This is why it is so important for psychological scientists to practice humility.) When you disagree, avoid *calling out* others (publicly shaming them). Instead, *speak up*: Approach the person and explain

Social success Nurturing relationships is an important part of a successful life. Make time and energy for important others, and you will have better physical and psychological health.

LaunchPad To assess and nurture your feelings of belonging and your relationship strength, engage online with these two LaunchPad activities (1) *Assess Your Strengths: How Strong Is Your Need to Belong, and How Can you Strengthen Your Feelings of Belonging?* and (2) *Assess Your Strengths: How Strong Is Your Relationship, and How Might You Increase Its Strength?*

your disagreement without blaming them. We have a natural tendency to explain others' behaviors based on their personality traits ("He's a selfish jerk") rather than their situation ("He's sleep-deprived and stressed"). To resist this tendency, take the other person's perspective.

- **It's time to be the adult in the room.** As we grow up, we pass through different stages of development. Most adolescents seek social acceptance while still depending on family. The transition from adolescence to adulthood requires becoming more independent. As adults, we need to own our goals, attitudes, values, and beliefs, and to make our own decisions and solve our own problems.

Finding Meaning and Pursuing Goals

To have meaning is to have a life filled with purpose, coherence, and significance. Most people want a meaningful life, but they report feeling unfulfilled in some area of their life. They may not be fully engaged in their work. Or they may feel stuck in a daily routine that brings money without meaning. To live your best life, take the following steps to promote meaning and pursue goals:

- **Imagine your possible self.** Who is the person you wish to be? Who is the "possible self" you dream of becoming? *Define who you hope to be and what you aim to achieve.* With that vision in mind, you can then lay out specific goals and strategies that will take you where you want to go.

- **Live your dream daily.** Here's a good rule for success: Whatever you hope to achieve, *do something toward that every day.* Do you want to be kinder, more educated, more assertive? Then, every day, do a kind act, learn something new, or practice asserting yourself. Although many days you may accomplish less than you'd hoped, even small daily steps toward a goal can, over time, take you to your destination— transforming your possible self into your actual self.

- **Adopt a "growth mindset."** It's surprisingly powerful to believe that our abilities are changeable through energy and effort. Some things we should accept, but many things we have the power to change. If you see your math or writing or speaking ability as like a muscle—something that gets stronger with training and practice—you will, in fact, develop more skill. Your mindset matters. (More on this in Module 30.)

LaunchPad To further develop your goal-setting ability, engage with the LaunchPad activity *Assess Your Strengths: How Might Your Willingness to Think of the Future Affect Your Ability to Achieve Long-Term Goals?*

- **Find your calling.** No need to rush it. Most students change their vocational plans along the way, and you likely will, too. But notice what sorts of activities absorb you and make time fly. Is it being with people? Working with your hands? Solving problems with your mind? Watch for work and activities that will enable you to do what you love and to love what you do, and pursue those paths.

* * *

Throughout this book you will encounter additional pointers to a flourishing life— counting your blessings, expressing gratitude, finding *flow,* acting happy, training your willpower, becoming mindful, opting for optimism, and more. In such ways, you can not only survive, you can thrive. Don't be too hard on yourself if you experience setbacks. If you try to do a little better each day, you can, over time, accomplish goals that might seem impossible at the outset. As Reinhold Niebuhr suggested, seek the serenity to accept things you cannot change, but also feel empowered to change the things you can.

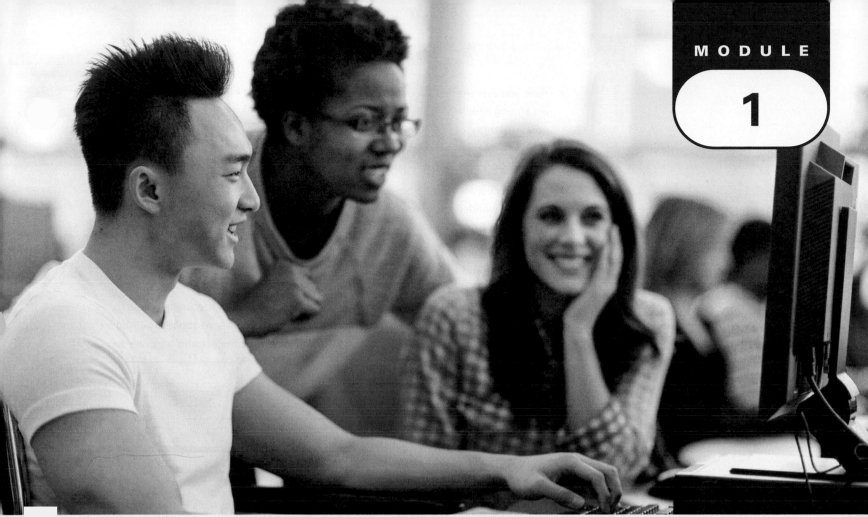

The Story of Psychology

Astronomer Owen Gingerich has described the human brain as "by far the most complex physical object known to us in the entire cosmos" (2006, p. 29). On the scale of outer space, we are less than a single grain of sand on all the oceans' beaches, and our lifetime lasts but a relative nanosecond. Yet there is nothing more awe inspiring than our own inner space. Our consciousness—our mind somehow arising from matter—remains a profound mystery. Our thinking, emotions, and actions (and their interplay with others' thinking, emotions, and actions) fascinate us. Outer space staggers us with its enormity. But inner space enthralls us. Enter psychological science.

From news and media portrayals, you might think that psychologists offer counseling, analyze personality, dispense child-raising advice, examine crime scenes, and testify in court. Do they? *Yes*—and much more. Consider some of psychology's questions that you may wonder about:

- Have you ever found yourself reacting to something as one of your biological parents would—perhaps in a way you vowed you *never* would—and then wondered how much of your personality you inherited? *To what extent do genes predispose our individual differences in personality? How do home and community environments shape us?*

- Have you ever worried about how to act among people of a different culture, gender identity, or sexual orientation? *How are we alike as members of the human family? How do we differ?*

- Have you ever awakened from a night-mare and wondered why you had such a crazy dream? *Why do we dream?*

- Have you ever played peekaboo with a 6-month-old and wondered why the baby finds your disappearing/reappearing act so delightful? *What do babies actually perceive and think?*

- Have you ever wondered what fosters school and work success? *Does inborn intelligence explain why some people get richer, think more creatively, or relate more sensitively? Or does gritty effort, and a belief in the power of persistence, matter more?*

- Have you ever become depressed or anxious and wondered whether you'll ever feel "normal"? *What triggers our bad moods—and our good ones? What's the line between a routine mood swing and a psychological disorder?*

Psychology is a science that seeks to answer such questions about us all—how and why we think, feel, and act as we do.

① What Is Psychology?

Once upon a time, on a planet in our neighborhood of the universe, there came to be people. Soon thereafter, these creatures became intensely interested in themselves and in one another: "Who are we? What produces our thoughts? Our feelings? Our actions? And how are we to understand and manage those around us?"

Psychology Is a Science

LEARNING OBJECTIVE QUESTION **LOQ** **1-1** How is psychology a science?

To assist your learning, numbered Learning Objective Questions appear at the beginning of major sections. You can test your understanding by trying to answer the question before, and then again after, you read the section.

Underlying all science is, first, a passion to explore and understand without misleading or being misled. Some questions (*Is there life after death?*) are beyond science. Answering them requires a leap of faith. With many other ideas (*Can some people demonstrate extrasensory perception?*), the proof is in the pudding. We can let the facts speak for themselves.

Magician James Randi has used this **empirical approach** when testing those claiming to see glowing auras around people's bodies:

> *Randi:* Do you see an aura around my head?
>
> *Aura seer:* Yes, indeed.
>
> *Randi:* Can you still see the aura if I put this magazine in front of my face?
>
> *Aura seer:* Of course.
>
> *Randi:* Then if I were to step behind a wall barely taller than I am, you could determine my location from the aura visible above my head, right?

Throughout the text, the most important concepts are **boldfaced**. As you study, you can find these terms defined nearby and in the Glossary at the end of the book. (In the e-book, definitions are always a click away.)

Randi once told me [DM] that no aura seer had agreed to take this simple test.

No matter how sensible-seeming or how wild an idea, the smart thinker asks: *Does it work?* When put to the test, do the data support its predictions? Subjected to such scrutiny, crazy-sounding ideas sometimes find support. During the 1700s, scientists scoffed at the notion that meteorites had extraterrestrial origins. When two Yale scientists challenged the conventional opinion, Thomas Jefferson reportedly scoffed, "Gentlemen, I would rather believe that those two Yankee professors would lie than to believe that stones fell from Heaven." Sometimes scientific inquiry turns jeers into cheers.

 empirical approach an evidence-based method that draws on observation and experimentation.

More often, science becomes society's garbage collector, sending crazy-sounding ideas to the waste heap atop previous claims of perpetual motion machines, miracle cancer cures, and out-of-body travels into centuries past. To sift reality from fantasy and fact from fiction therefore requires a *scientific attitude:* being skeptical but not cynical, open-minded but not gullible. When ideas compete, careful testing can reveal which ones best fit the facts. Do some people have a psychic power to predict an unexpected catastrophe? Is *electroconvulsive therapy* (delivering an electric shock to the brain) an effective treatment for severe depression? As we will see, putting such claims to the test has led psychological scientists to answer *No* to the first question and *Yes* to the second.

Putting a scientific attitude into practice requires not only curiosity and skepticism but also *humility*—an awareness of our own vulnerability to error and an openness to new perspectives (Leary et al., 2017). What matters is not my opinion or yours, but the truths revealed by our questioning and testing. If people or other animals don't behave as our ideas predict, then so much the worse for our ideas. This humble attitude was expressed in one of psychology's early mottos: "The rat is always right." (See Thinking Critically About: The Scientific Attitude.)

Humility predicts helpfulness and realistic academic confidence (Erlandsson et al., 2018). One nine-country study asked 40,000 teens which of 16 math concepts they were familiar with, including three fake terms: "proper number," "subjective scaling," and "declarative fraction." Those who arrogantly claimed to know the nonexistent concepts were often men from advantaged backgrounds (Jerrim et al., 2019). *The point to remember:* Knowing what we *don't* know enables generosity and intellectual humility.

> **ASK YOURSELF**
>
> Were you surprised to learn that psychology is a science? How would you explain that now if someone asked you about it?

Critical Thinking

LOQ 1-3 How does critical thinking feed a scientific attitude, and smarter thinking for everyday life?

The scientific attitude—curiosity + skepticism + humility—prepares us to think smarter. This smart thinking, called **critical thinking,** examines assumptions, appraises the source, discerns hidden biases, evaluates evidence, and assesses conclusions. When reading a research report, an online opinion, or a news story, critical thinkers ask questions: *How do they know that? What is this person's agenda? Is the conclusion based on anecdote, or on evidence? Does the evidence justify a cause-effect conclusion? What alternative explanations are possible?*

Critical thinkers wince when people make factual claims based on their gut: "I *feel like* climate change is [or isn't] happening." "I *feel like* self-driving cars are more [or less] dangerous." "I *feel like* my candidate is more honest." Such beliefs (commonly mislabeled as feelings) may or may not be true. Critical thinkers are open to the possibility that they might be wrong. Sometimes the best evidence confirms what we believe. Other times it challenges and beckons us to a different way of thinking. Cynics often seem smart, but most demonstrate less cognitive ability and academic competence than average (Stavrova & Ehlebracht, 2018). To believe everything—or to reject everything—is to be a fool. Critical thinking, informed by science, helps clear the colored lenses of our biases. Consider: Does climate change threaten our future, and, if so, is it human-caused? In 2016, some climate-action advocates interpreted record Louisiana flooding as proof of climate change. In 2015, climate-change skeptics perceived North American bitter winter cold as discounting global warming. Rather than having their understanding of climate change swayed by such local examples of today's weather, critical thinkers say, "Show me the evidence." Over time, is the Earth actually warming? Are the polar ice caps melting? Are vegetation patterns changing? Are extreme weather events becoming more frequent? And is human activity emitting atmospheric CO_2 that would lead us to expect such changes?

Throughout the book, information sources are cited in parentheses, with researchers' names and the date the research was published. Every citation can be found in the end-of-book References section, with complete documentation that follows American Psychological Association (APA) style.

From a tongue-in-cheek Twitter feed: "The problem with quotes on the internet is that you never know if they're true."
— Abraham Lincoln

critical thinking thinking that does not automatically accept arguments and conclusions. Rather, it examines assumptions, appraises the source, discerns hidden biases, evaluates evidence, and assesses conclusions.

Thinking Critically About:
The Scientific Attitude

LOQ **1-2** What are the three key elements of the scientific attitude, and how do they support scientific inquiry?

Three basic attitudes helped make modern science possible.

1 CURIOSITY:

Does it work?

When put to the test, can its predictions be confirmed?

Can some people read minds? ●

Are stress levels related to health and well-being? ○

● No one has yet been able to demonstrate extrasensory mind-reading.

○ Many studies have found that higher stress relates to poorer health.

2 SKEPTICISM:

What do you mean?

How do you know?

Sifting reality from fantasy requires a healthy skepticism—an attitude that is not cynical (doubting everything), but also not gullible (believing everything).

Do our facial expressions and body postures affect how we actually feel? ○

Do parental behaviors determine children's sexual orientation? ○

○ Our facial expressions and body postures can affect how we feel.

○ Module 34 explains that there is not a relationship between parental behaviors and children's sexual orientation.

3 HUMILITY:

That was unexpected! Let's explore further.

Researchers must be willing to be surprised and follow new ideas. People and other animals don't always behave as our ideas and beliefs would predict.

The rat is always right.

When contemplating such issues, critical thinkers will also consider the credibility of sources. They will look at the evidence (*Do the facts support them, or are they just makin' stuff up?*). They will recognize multiple perspectives. And they will expose themselves to news sources that challenge their preconceived ideas.

Some religious people may view critical thinking and scientific inquiry, including psychology's, as a threat. Yet many leaders of the scientific revolution, including Copernicus and Newton, were deeply religious people acting on the idea that "in order to love and honor God, it is necessary to fully appreciate the wonders of his handiwork" (Stark, 2003a,b).

Critical inquiry can lead us to surprising findings. Other modules illustrate some examples from psychological science: Massive losses of brain tissue early in life may have minimal long-term effects. Within days, newborns can recognize their mother by her odor. After brain damage, a person may be able to learn new skills yet be unaware of such learning. Diverse groups—all genders, old and young, wealthy and not wealthy, with varying physical abilities—report roughly comparable levels of personal happiness.

Critical inquiry sometimes debunks popular presumptions, as we may also see in other modules. Sleepwalkers are *not* acting out their dreams. Our past experiences are *not* all recorded verbatim in our brains; with brain stimulation or hypnosis, one *cannot* simply replay and relive long-buried or repressed memories. Most people do *not* suffer from unrealistically low self-esteem, and high self-esteem is *not* all good. Opposites tend *not* to attract. In these instances and many more, what psychological scientists have learned is not what is widely believed.

Psychology's critical inquiry can also identify effective policies. To deter crime, should we invest money in lengthening prison sentences, or should we increase the likelihood of arrest? To help people recover from a trauma, should counselors help them relive it, or not? To increase voting, should we tell people about the low turnout problem, or emphasize that their peers are voting? What matters is not what we "feel" is true, but what is true. When put to critical thinking's test—and contrary to common practice—the second option in each of this paragraph's examples wins (Shafir, 2013). Thinking critically can—and sometimes does—change the world.

Critical thinking can also change us, by helping us assess popular applications of psychology. Looking at a self-help book, we can consider the author's expertise and goals. We can ask: Are the suggestions based on evidence or anecdote? And how might the author's personal values and agenda affect the advice? If you defer to guidance about how to live—how to raise children, how to achieve self-fulfillment, how to respond to sexual feelings, how to get ahead at work—you are accepting value-laden advice. A science of behavior and mental processes can help us reach our goals. But it cannot decide which goals are worth pursuing. Psychological scientists teach, but they do not preach.

> "My deeply held belief is that if a god anything like the traditional sort exists, our curiosity and intelligence are provided by such a god. We would be unappreciative of those gifts . . . if we suppressed our passion to explore the universe and ourselves."
> — Carl Sagan, *Broca's Brain*, 1979

RETRIEVAL PRACTICE

RP-1 Describe what's involved in critical thinking.

ANSWERS IN APPENDIX E

Study Tip: Memory research reveals a *testing effect:* We retain information much better if we actively retrieve it by self-testing and rehearsing. (More on this at the end of this module.) To bolster your learning and memory, take advantage of the Retrieval Practice opportunities you'll find throughout this text—with answers for checking in Appendix E, or a click away in the e-book.

Psychological Science Is Born

LOQ 1-4 What were some important milestones in psychology's early history?

To be human is to be curious about ourselves and the world around us. Before 300 B.C.E., the Greek naturalist and philosopher Aristotle theorized about learning and memory, motivation and emotion, perception and personality. Today we chuckle at some of his guesses, like his suggestion that a meal makes us sleepy by causing gas and heat to collect around what he believed was the source of our personality, the heart. But credit Aristotle with asking the right questions.

Psychology's First Laboratory

Philosophers' thinking about thinking continued until the birth of psychology as we know it. That happened on a December day in 1879, in a small, third-floor room at Germany's University of Leipzig. There, two young men were helping an austere,

Wilhelm Wundt (1832–1920)
Wundt established the first psychology laboratory at the University of Leipzig, Germany.

middle-aged professor, Wilhelm Wundt, create an experimental apparatus. Their machine measured how long it took for people to press a telegraph key after hearing a ball hit a platform (Hunt, 1993). Curiously, people responded in about one-tenth of a second when asked to press the key as soon as the sound occurred—and in about two-tenths of a second when asked to press the key as soon as they were consciously aware of perceiving the sound. (To be aware of one's awareness takes a little longer.) Wundt was seeking to measure "atoms of the mind"—the fastest and simplest mental processes. So began the first psychological laboratory, staffed by Wundt and psychology's first graduate students.

Psychology's First Schools of Thought

Before long, this new science of psychology became organized into different branches, or schools of thought, each promoted by pioneering thinkers. Two early schools were **structuralism** and **functionalism.**

STRUCTURALISM Much as chemists developed the periodic table to classify chemical elements, so psychologist Edward Bradford Titchener aimed to classify and understand elements of the mind's structure. He engaged people in self-reflective *introspection* (looking inward), training them to report elements of their experience as they looked at a rose, listened to a metronome, smelled a scent, or tasted a substance. What were their immediate sensations, their images, their feelings? And how did these relate to one another? Alas, structuralism's technique of introspection proved somewhat unreliable. It required smart, verbal people, and its results varied from person to person and experience to experience. As introspection waned, so did structuralism. Hoping to assemble the mind's structure from simple elements was rather like trying to understand a car by examining its disconnected parts.

Edward Bradford Titchener (1867–1927)
Titchener used introspection to search for the mind's structural elements.

FUNCTIONALISM Philosopher-psychologist William James sought to go beyond labeling our inward thoughts and feelings by considering their evolved *functions*. Smelling is what the nose does; thinking is what the brain does. But *why* do the nose and brain do these things? Under the influence of evolutionary theorist Charles Darwin, James assumed that thinking, like smelling, developed because it was *adaptive*—it helped our ancestors survive and reproduce. Consciousness serves a function. It enables us to consider our past, adjust to our present, and plan our future. To explore the mind's adaptive functions, James studied down-to-earth emotions, memories, willpower, habits, and moment-to-moment streams of consciousness.

James' writings moved the publisher Henry Holt to offer James a contract for a textbook on the new science of psychology. James agreed and began work in 1878, with an apology for requesting two years to finish his writing. The text proved an unexpected chore and actually took him 12 years. (Why are we not surprised?) More than a century later, people still read the resulting *Principles of Psychology* (1890) and marvel at the brilliance and elegance with which James introduced psychology to the educated public.

Psychology's First Women

James' legacy stems from his Harvard mentoring as well as from his writing. In 1890—thirty years before American women had the right to vote—he admitted Mary Whiton Calkins into his graduate seminar over the objections of Harvard's president (Scarborough & Furumoto, 1987). When Calkins joined, the other students (all men) dropped out. So James tutored her alone. Later, she finished all of Harvard's Ph.D. requirements, outscoring all the male students on the qualifying exams. Alas, Harvard denied her the degree she had earned, offering her instead a doctorate from Radcliffe College, its undergraduate "sister" school for women. Calkins resisted the unequal treatment and refused the degree. She nevertheless went on to become a distinguished memory researcher and, in 1905, the first female president of the American Psychological Association (APA).

structuralism an early school of thought promoted by Wundt and Titchener; used introspection to reveal the structure of the human mind.

functionalism an early school of thought promoted by James and influenced by Darwin; explored how mental and behavioral processes function—how they enable the organism to adapt, survive, and flourish.

William James (1842–1910) and Mary Whiton Calkins (1863–1930)
James was a legendary teacher-writer who authored an important 1890 psychology text. He mentored Calkins, who became a pioneering memory researcher and the first female president of the American Psychological Association.

Margaret Floy Washburn (1871–1939)
The first woman to receive a psychology Ph.D., Washburn synthesized animal behavior research in *The Animal Mind* (1908).

The honor of being the first official female psychology Ph.D. later fell to Margaret Floy Washburn, who also wrote an influential book, *The Animal Mind,* and became the second female APA president in 1921. But Washburn's gender barred doors for her, too. Although her thesis was the first foreign study Wundt published in his psychology journal, she could not join the all-male organization of experimental psychologists founded by Titchener, her own graduate adviser (Johnson, 1997). What a different world from the recent past: Between 1997 and 2019, more than half of the elected presidents of the science-focused Association for Psychological Science (APS) were women. In the United States, Canada, and Europe, women now earn most psychology doctorates.

(a)

(b)

Psychology increasing diversity At this 1964 meeting of the Society of Experimental Psychologists (a), Eleanor Gibson was easy to spot among the many male members, all in a sea of White faces. By contrast, women now are 62 percent of Association for Psychological Science members and 75 percent of its psychology student affiliates, as is clear in this current photo of APS graduate students (b). People of color have made enormous contributions to the field (see, for example, coverage of Kenneth Clark and Mamie Phipps Clark in Module 2), and psychology's diversity continues to grow. For more on the history of these changes, see Appendix A, the Story of Psychology: A Timeline.

behaviorism the view that psychology (1) should be an objective science that (2) studies behavior without reference to mental processes. Most psychologists today agree with (1) but not with (2).

ASK YOURSELF

How do you think psychology might change in the future as more women, and others from historically excluded groups, contribute their ideas to the field?

RETRIEVAL PRACTICE

RP-2 What event defined the start of scientific psychology?

RP-3 Why did introspection fail as a method for understanding how the mind works?

RP-4 The school of _____ used introspection to define the mind's makeup; _____ focused on how mental processes enable us to adapt, survive, and flourish.

ANSWERS IN APPENDIX E

Psychological Science Matures

LOQ 1-5 How did behaviorism, Freudian psychology, and humanistic psychology further the development of psychological science?

In psychology's early days, many psychologists shared with the English essayist C. S. Lewis the view that "there is one thing, and only one in the whole universe which we know more about than we could learn from external observation." That one thing, Lewis said, is ourselves. "We have, so to speak, inside information" (1960, pp. 18–19). Wundt and Titchener focused on inner sensations, images, and feelings. James also engaged in introspective examination of the stream of consciousness and of emotion, hoping to understand how they help humans survive and thrive. For these and other early pioneers, *psychology* was defined as "the science of mental life."

Behaviorism

That definition endured until the 1920s, when the first of two provocative American psychologists challenged it. John B. Watson and, later, B. F. Skinner dismissed introspection and redefined *psychology* as "the scientific study of observable behavior." After all, they said, science is rooted in observation: What you cannot observe and measure, you cannot scientifically study. You cannot observe a sensation, a feeling, or a thought, but you *can* observe and record people's *behavior* as they are *conditioned*—as they respond to and learn in different situations. Many agreed, and **behaviorism** was one of two major forces in psychology well into the 1960s.

John B. Watson (1878–1958) and Rosalie Rayner (1898–1935)
Working with Rayner, Watson championed psychology as the scientific study of behavior. In a controversial study on a baby who became famous as "Little Albert," he and Rayner showed that fear could be learned.

B. F. Skinner (1904–1990) This leading behaviorist rejected introspection and studied how consequences shape behavior.

Freudian (Psychoanalytic) Psychology

The other major force was Sigmund Freud's *psychoanalytic psychology*, which emphasized the ways our unconscious mind and childhood experiences affect our behavior. (In other modules, we'll look more closely at Freud's teachings, including his theory of personality, and his views on unconscious sexual conflicts and the mind's defenses against its own wishes and impulses.)

Humanistic Psychology

As the behaviorists had rejected the early twentieth-century definition of *psychology*, other groups rejected the behaviorist definition. In the 1960s, **humanistic psychologists,** led by Carl Rogers and Abraham Maslow, found both behaviorism and Freudian psychology too limiting. Rather than focusing on conditioned responses or childhood memories, the humanistic psychologists focused on our growth potential, our needs for love and acceptance, and the environments that nurture or limit personal growth.

Sigmund Freud (1856–1939)
The controversial ideas of this famed personality theorist and therapist have influenced humanity's self-understanding.

> **RETRIEVAL PRACTICE**
>
> **RP-5** From the 1920s through the 1960s, the two major forces in psychology were
> _____ and _____ psychology.
>
> *ANSWERS IN APPENDIX E*

Contemporary Psychology

LOQ 1-6 How has contemporary psychology focused on cognition, on biology and experience, on culture and gender, and on human flourishing?

Simultaneous with humanistic psychology's emergence, psychologists in the 1960s pioneered a *cognitive revolution.* This led the field back to its early interest in how our mind processes and retains information. **Cognitive psychology** today continues its scientific exploration of how we perceive, process, and remember information, and of how thinking and emotion interact in anxiety, depression, and other disorders. The marriage of cognitive psychology (the science of mind) and neuroscience (the science of brain) gave birth to **cognitive neuroscience.** This specialty, with researchers in many disciplines, studies the brain activity underlying mental activity.

Today's psychology builds on the work of many earlier scientists and schools of thought. To encompass psychology's concern with observable behavior *and* with inner thoughts and feelings, we now define **psychology** as the *science of behavior and mental processes.* Let's unpack this definition. *Behavior* is anything an organism *does*—any action we can observe and record. Yelling, smiling, blinking, sweating, talking, tweeting, and questionnaire marking are all observable behaviors. *Mental processes* are our internal, subjective experiences—our sensations, perceptions, dreams, thoughts, beliefs, and feelings.

The key word in today's definition of psychology is *science.* Psychology is less a set of findings than a way of asking and answering questions. Our aim, then, is not merely to report results but also to show you how psychologists play their game. You will see how researchers evaluate conflicting opinions and ideas. And you will learn how all of us, whether scientists or simply curious people, can think harder and smarter when experiencing and explaining the events of our lives.

Psychology—the science of behavior and mental processes—has roots in many disciplines and countries. The young science of psychology developed from the more established fields of philosophy and biology. Wundt was both a philosopher and a physiologist. James was an American philosopher. Freud was an Austrian physician. Ivan Pavlov, who pioneered the study of learning, was a Russian physiologist. Jean Piaget, the last century's most influential observer of children, was a Swiss biologist. These "Magellans of the mind," as psychology historian Morton Hunt (1993) called them, illustrate the diversity of psychology's origins.

humanistic psychology a historically significant perspective that emphasized human growth potential.

cognitive psychology the study of mental processes, such as occur when we perceive, learn, remember, think, communicate, and solve problems.

cognitive neuroscience the interdisciplinary study of the brain activity linked with cognition (including perception, thinking, memory, and language).

psychology the science of behavior and mental processes.

nature–nurture issue the longstanding controversy over the relative contributions that genes and experience make to the development of psychological traits and behaviors. Today's science sees traits and behaviors arising from the interaction of nature and nurture.

natural selection the principle that the inherited traits enabling an organism to survive and reproduce in a particular environment will (in competition with other trait variations) most likely be passed on to succeeding generations.

evolutionary psychology the study of the evolution of behavior and the mind, using principles of natural selection.

behavior genetics the study of the relative power and limits of genetic and environmental influences on behavior.

Like those pioneers, today's estimated 1+ million psychologists are citizens of many lands (Zoma & Gielen, 2015). The International Union of Psychological Science has 82 member nations, from Albania to Zimbabwe. In China, the first university psychology department was established in 1978; by 2016 there were 270 (Zhang, 2016). Psychology is both *growing* and *globalizing*. The story of psychology is being written in many places, with interests ranging from the study of nerve cell activity to the study of international conflicts. Contemporary psychology, shaped by many forces, is particularly influenced by our understanding of biology and experience, culture and gender, and human flourishing.

ASK YOURSELF

How would you have defined psychology before taking this class?

Evolutionary Psychology and Behavior Genetics

Are our human traits inherited, or do they develop through experience? This has been psychology's biggest and most persistent issue. But the debate over the **nature–nurture issue** is ancient. The Greek philosopher Plato (428–348 B.C.E.) assumed that we inherit character and intelligence and that certain ideas are inborn. Aristotle (384–322 B.C.E.) countered that there is nothing in the mind that does not first come in from the external world through the senses.

In the 1600s, European philosophers rekindled the debate. John Locke argued that the mind is a blank slate on which experience writes. René Descartes disagreed, believing that some ideas are innate. Descartes' views gained support from a curious naturalist two centuries later. In 1831, an indifferent student but ardent collector of beetles, mollusks, and shells set sail on a historic round-the-world journey. The 22-year-old voyager, Charles Darwin, pondered the incredible species variation he encountered, including tortoises on one island that differed from those on nearby islands. Darwin's *On the Origin of Species* (1859) explained this diversity by proposing the evolutionary process of **natural selection:** From among chance variations, nature selects traits that best enable an organism to survive and reproduce in a particular environment. Darwin's principle of natural selection—what philosopher Daniel Dennett (1996) has called "the single best idea anyone has ever had"—is still with us 160+ years later as biology's organizing principle. Evolution also has become an important principle for twenty-first-century psychology. This would surely have pleased Darwin, who believed his theory explained not only animal structures (such as a polar bear's white coat) but also animal behaviors (such as the emotional expressions associated with human lust and rage).

The nature–nurture issue recurs throughout this text as today's psychologists explore the relative contributions of biology and experience. They ask, for example: How are we humans *alike* because of our common biology and evolutionary history? That's the focus of **evolutionary psychology.** And how do we individually *differ* because of our differing genes and environments? That's the focus of **behavior genetics.**

We can, for example, ask: Are gender differences biologically predisposed or socially constructed? Is children's grammar mostly innate or formed by experience? How are intelligence and personality differences influenced by heredity and by environment?

Charles Darwin (1809–1882)
Darwin argued that natural selection shapes behaviors as well as bodies.

Macmillan Learning

A nature-made nature–nurture experiment Identical twins have the same genes. This makes them ideal participants in studies designed to shed light on hereditary and environmental influences on personality, intelligence, and other traits. Fraternal twins have different genes but often share a similar environment. Twin studies provide a wealth of findings—described in other modules—showing the importance of both nature and nurture.

Are sexual behaviors more "pushed" by inner biology or "pulled" by external incentives? Should we treat psychological disorders—depression, for example—as disorders of the brain, disorders of thought, or both?

Such debates continue. Yet over and over again we will see that in contemporary science the nature–nurture tension dissolves: *Nurture works on what nature provides.* In other modules, you'll also learn about *epigenetics*—how experience can influence genetic expression. And you will see that our species has been graced with the great biological gift of brain *plasticity*: an enormous capacity to learn and adapt. Moreover, every psychological event (every thought, every emotion) is simultaneously a biological event. Thus, depression can be both a brain disorder *and* a thought disorder.

> **culture** the enduring behaviors, ideas, attitudes, values, and traditions shared by a group of people and transmitted from one generation to the next.

ASK YOURSELF

Think of one of your own traits. (For example, are you a planner or a procrastinator—do you usually complete assignments on time, or late? Are you more an extravert or introvert—do you become energized by social interactions, or recharge by spending time alone?) How do you think that trait was influenced by nature and nurture?

RETRIEVAL PRACTICE

RP-6 How did the cognitive revolution affect the field of psychology?

RP-7 What is natural selection?

RP-8 What is contemporary psychology's position on the nature–nurture issue?

ANSWERS IN APPENDIX E

Cross-Cultural and Gender Psychology

What can we learn about people in general from psychological studies done in one time and place—often with participants from what psychologists have called the WEIRD cultures (Western, Educated, Industrialized, Rich, and Democratic [Henrich et al., 2010; Hruschka et al., 2018])? As we will see time and again, **culture**—shared ideas and behaviors that one generation passes on to the next—matters. Our culture shapes our standards of promptness and frankness, our attitudes toward premarital sex and varying body shapes, our tendency to be casual or formal, our willingness to make eye contact, our conversational distance, and much, much more. Being aware of such differences, we can restrain our assumptions that others will think and act as we do.

It is also true, however, that our shared biological heritage unites us as a universal human family. Some aspects of our humanity—how we see and hear, how our bodies respond to stress, how our smiles communicate feeling—we share with all humans (Stroebe et al., 2018). The same underlying processes guide people everywhere. Some examples:

- People diagnosed with *specific learning disorder* (formerly called dyslexia) exhibit the same brain malfunction whether they are Italian, French, or British (Paulesu et al., 2001).

- Variation in languages may impede communication across cultures. Yet all languages share deep principles of grammar.

- People in different cultures vary in feelings of loneliness (Lykes & Kemmelmeier, 2014). But across cultures, loneliness is magnified by shyness, low self-esteem, and being unmarried (Jones et al., 1985; Rokach et al., 2002).

We are each in certain respects like all others, like some others, and like no other. Studying people from all cultures helps us discern our similarities and our differences, our human kinship and our diversity.

You will see throughout this book that our *gender identity*—our sense of being male, female, neither, or some combination of male and female—also matters, as does our biologically influenced *sex*.

> "All people are the same; only their habits differ." — Confucius, 551–479 B.C.E.

A smile is a smile the world around This book tells the story of psychology as a global science, one that studies and celebrates cultural and gender similarities and differences. For example, cultural norms vary in when and how often people should smile, but a naturally happy smile *means* the same thing anywhere in the world.

Roy Toft/National Geographic Creative

Antonia Brune

Culture and kissing Kissing crosses cultures. Yet how we do it varies. Imagine yourself kissing someone on the lips. Do you tilt your head right or left? In Western cultures, in which people read from left to right, about two-thirds of couples kiss right, as in Prince Harry and Duchess Meghan's wedding kiss and Auguste Rodin's sculpture, *The Kiss*. In one study, 77 percent of Hebrew- and Arabic-language right-to-left readers kissed tilting left (Shaki, 2013).

Today's researchers report gender differences in what we dream, in how we express and detect emotions, and in our risk for alcohol use disorder, depression, and eating disorders. Gender differences fascinate us, and studying them is potentially beneficial. For example, many researchers have observed that women carry on conversations more readily to build relationships, while men talk more to give information and advice (Tannen, 2001). Understanding these differences can help us prevent conflicts and misunderstandings in everyday interactions.

But again, psychologically as well as biologically, humans are overwhelmingly similar. Regardless of gender, we learn to walk at about the same age. We experience the same sensations of light and sound. We remember vivid emotional events and forget mundane details. We feel the same pangs of hunger, desire, and fear. We exhibit similar overall intelligence and well-being.

The point to remember: Even when specific attitudes and behaviors vary by gender or across cultures, as they often do, the underlying processes are much the same.

ASK YOURSELF

How have your cultural experiences influenced your development?

Positive Psychology

Psychology's first hundred years often focused on understanding and treating troubles, such as abuse and anxiety, depression and disease, prejudice and poverty. Much of today's psychology continues the exploration of such challenges. Without slighting the need to repair damage and cure disease, Martin Seligman and others (2002, 2011, 2016) have called for more research on *human flourishing*—on understanding and developing the emotions and traits that help us to thrive. These psychologists call their approach **positive psychology.** They believe that happiness is a by-product of a pleasant, engaged, and meaningful life. Thus, positive psychology uses scientific methods to explore the building of a "good life" that engages our skills, and a "meaningful life" that points beyond ourselves.

Psychology's Three Main Levels of Analysis

LOQ **1-7** How do psychologists use the biopsychosocial approach, and how can it help us understand our diverse world?

We all share a biologically rooted human nature. Yet many psychological and social-cultural influences fine-tune our assumptions, values, and behaviors. We differ individually by gender identity, physical ability, and sexual orientation. And each of us is a complex system that is part of a larger social system—a family, ethnic group, culture, and *socioeconomic* status (combines education, income, and occupation). The **biopsychosocial approach** integrates these three **levels of analysis**—the biological, psychological, and social-cultural.

Consider horrific school shootings. Do they occur because the shooters have brain disorders or genetic tendencies that cause them to be violent? Because they observe brutality in the media or play violent video games? Because they live in a gun-toting society? The biopsychosocial approach enables psychologists to move beyond labels ("school shooter") and to consider the interconnected factors that may lead to violent acts (Pryor, 2019) (**FIGURE 1.1**). Clinical psychologists use this approach to help people with mental disorders (Teachman et al., 2019).

Each level of analysis offers a perspective for looking at a behavior or mental process, yet each by itself is incomplete. Each perspective described in **TABLE 1.1** asks different questions and has its limits, but together they complement one another. Consider, for example, how they shed light on anger:

* Someone working from a *neuroscience perspective* might study brain circuits that cause us to be red in the face and "hot under the collar."
* Someone working from an *evolutionary perspective* might analyze how anger facilitated the survival of our ancestors' genes.

⮿ Our online learning tools will help you excel in this course. Take advantage of the adaptive quizzing that adjusts to your individual needs, *Assess Your Strengths* personal self-assessments, interactive simulations, and *How Would You Know?* research activities.

⮿ For an excellent tour of psychology's roots, view the 9.5-minute *Video: The History of Psychology.*

---

positive psychology the scientific study of human flourishing, with the goals of discovering and promoting strengths and virtues that help individuals and communities to thrive.

biopsychosocial approach an integrated approach that incorporates biological, psychological, and social-cultural levels of analysis.

levels of analysis the differing complementary views, from biological to psychological to social-cultural, for analyzing any given phenomenon.

Jane Barlow/Getty Images

Hemis/Alamy

Biological influences:
- genetic *predispositions* (genetically influenced traits)
- genetic *mutations* (random errors in gene replication)
- natural selection of adaptive traits and behaviors passed down through generations
- genes responding to the environment

Psychological influences:
- learned fears and other learned expectations
- emotional responses
- cognitive processing and perceptual interpretations

Behavior or mental process

Social-cultural influences:
- presence of others
- cultural, societal, and family expectations
- peer and other group influences
- compelling models (such as in the media)

FIGURE 1.1
Biopsychosocial approach This integrated viewpoint incorporates various levels of analysis and offers a more complete picture of any given behavior or mental process.

- Someone working from a *behavior genetics perspective* might study how heredity and experience influence our individual differences in temperament.
- Someone working from a *psychodynamic perspective* might view an outburst as an outlet for unconscious hostility.
- Someone working from a *behavioral perspective* might attempt to determine what triggers aggressive acts.
- Someone working from a *cognitive perspective* might study how our interpretation of a situation affects our anger and how our anger affects our thinking.
- Someone working from a *social-cultural perspective* might explore how expressions of anger vary across cultural contexts.

TABLE 1.1 Psychology's Theoretical Perspectives

Perspective	Focus	Sample Questions	Examples of Subfields Using This Perspective
Neuroscience	How the body and brain enable emotions, memories, and sensory experiences	How do pain messages travel from the hand to the brain? How is blood chemistry linked with moods and motives?	Biological; cognitive; clinical
Evolutionary	How the natural selection of traits has promoted the survival of genes	How does evolution influence behavior tendencies?	Biological; developmental; social
Behavior genetics	How our genes and our environment influence our individual differences	To what extent are psychological traits such as intelligence, personality, sexual orientation, and vulnerability to depression products of our genes? Of our environment?	Personality; developmental; legal/forensic
Psychodynamic	How behavior springs from unconscious drives and conflicts	How can someone's personality traits and disorders be explained by unfulfilled wishes and childhood traumas?	Clinical; counseling; personality
Behavioral	How we learn observable responses	How do we learn to fear particular objects or situations? What is the most effective way to alter our behavior, say, to lose weight or stop smoking?	Clinical; counseling; industrial-organizational
Cognitive	How we encode, process, store, and retrieve information	How do we use information in remembering? Reasoning? Solving problems?	Cognitive neuroscience; clinical; counseling; industrial-organizational
Social-cultural	How behavior and thinking vary across situations and cultures	How are we affected by the people around us, and by our surrounding culture?	Developmental; social; clinical; counseling

The point to remember: Like two-dimensional views of a three-dimensional object, each of psychology's perspectives is helpful. But each by itself fails to reveal the whole picture.

ASK YOURSELF

Which of psychology's theoretical perspectives do you find most interesting? Why?

RETRIEVAL PRACTICE

RP-9 What advantage do we gain by using the biopsychosocial approach in studying psychological events?

RP-10 The _____-_____ perspective in psychology focuses on how behavior and thought differ from situation to situation and from culture to culture, while the _____ perspective emphasizes observation of how we respond to and learn in different situations.

ANSWERS IN APPENDIX E

Psychology's Subfields

LOQ 1-8 What are psychology's main subfields?

Picturing a chemist at work, you may envision a laboratory scientist surrounded by test tubes and high-tech equipment. Picture a psychologist at work, and you would be right to envision

- a white-coated scientist probing a rat's brain.
- an intelligence researcher measuring how quickly an infant shows boredom by looking away from a familiar picture.
- an executive evaluating a new "healthy lifestyles" training program for employees.
- a researcher at a computer analyzing "big data" from social media status updates or Google searches.
- a therapist actively listening to a depressed client's thoughts.
- a traveling academic visiting another culture and collecting data on variations in human values and behaviors.
- a teacher or writer sharing the joy of psychology with others.

The cluster of subfields we call psychology is a meeting ground for different disciplines. Thus, it's a perfect home for those with wide-ranging interests. In its diverse activities, from biological experimentation to cultural comparisons, the tribe of psychology is united by a common quest: *describing and explaining behavior and the mind underlying it.*

Some psychologists conduct **basic research** that builds psychology's knowledge base. We will meet a wide variety of such researchers, including *biological psychologists* exploring the links between body and mind; *developmental psychologists* studying our changing abilities from womb to tomb; *cognitive psychologists* experimenting with how we perceive, think, and solve problems; *personality psychologists* investigating our persistent traits; and *social psychologists* exploring how we view and affect one another.

These and other psychologists also may conduct **applied research,** tackling practical problems. *Industrial-organizational psychologists,* for example, use psychology's concepts and methods in the workplace to help organizations and companies select and train employees, boost morale and productivity, design products, and implement systems.

Psychology is a science, but it is also a profession that helps people have healthier relationships, overcome feelings of anxiety or depression, and raise thriving children. *Counseling psychology* and *clinical psychology* grew out of different historical traditions. Early counseling psychologists offered job skills guidance, whereas clinical psychologists worked alongside psychiatrists to assess and provide psychotherapy to people in the first psychology clinics. Today's counseling psychologists and clinical psychologists have a lot in common. **Counseling psychologists** help people to cope with challenges and crises (including academic,

"I'm a social scientist, Michael. That means I can't explain electricity or anything like that, but if you ever want to know about people I'm your man."

basic research pure science that aims to increase the scientific knowledge base.

applied research scientific study that aims to solve practical problems.

counseling psychology a branch of psychology that assists people with problems in living (often related to school, work, or relationships) and in achieving greater well-being.

clinical psychology a branch of psychology that studies, assesses, and treats people with psychological disorders.

psychiatry a branch of medicine dealing with psychological disorders; practiced by physicians who sometimes provide medical (for example, drug) treatments as well as psychological therapy.

community psychology a branch of psychology that studies how people interact with their social environments and how social institutions (such as schools and neighborhoods) affect individuals and groups.

vocational, and relationship issues) and assist those with psychological disorders to improve their personal and social functioning. **Clinical psychologists** focus on assessing and treating people with mental, emotional, and behavior disorders. Both counseling and clinical psychologists administer and interpret tests, provide counseling and therapy to people with all levels of psychological difficulties, and undergo the same licensing exams. They sometimes also conduct basic and applied research. By contrast, **psychiatrists,** who also may provide psychotherapy, are medical doctors licensed to prescribe drugs and otherwise treat physical causes of psychological disorders.

Rather than seeking to change people to fit their environment, **community psychologists** work to create social and physical environments that are healthy for all (Bradshaw et al., 2009; Trickett, 2009). To prevent bullying, they might consider ways to improve the culture of the school and neighborhood, and how to increase bystander intervention (Polanin et al., 2012).

With perspectives ranging from the biological to the social, and with settings ranging from the laboratory to the clinic to the office, psychology relates to many fields. Psychologists teach in medical schools, business schools, law schools, and theological seminaries, and they work in hospitals, factories, and corporate offices. They engage in interdisciplinary studies, such as psychobiography (the study of the lives and personalities of public figures), psycholinguistics (the study of language and thinking), and psychoceramics (the study of crackpots).[1]

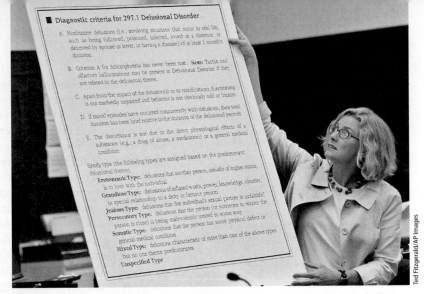

Psychology in court *Forensic psychologists* apply psychology's principles and methods in the criminal justice system. They may assess witness credibility or testify in court about a defendant's state of mind and future risk.

ASK YOURSELF

When you signed up for this course, what did you know about different psychology specialties?

Want to learn more? See Appendix B, Career Fields in Psychology, at the end of this book, and go to our online *Pursuing a Psychology Career* resource to learn about the many interesting options available to those with bachelor's, master's, and doctoral degrees in psychology. To review and test your understanding of psychology's perspectives and subfields, engage online with *Concept Practice: Psychology's Current Perspectives* and *Concept Practice: Psychology's Subfields.*

Psychology: A science and a profession Psychologists experiment with, observe, test, and help modify behavior. Here we see psychologists testing a child, measuring emotion-related physiology, and doing face-to-face therapy.

[1]Confession: I [DM] wrote the last part of this sentence on April Fool's Day.

"The mind, once stretched by a new idea, never returns to its original dimensions."
— Ralph Waldo Emerson, 1803–1882

"I have uttered what I did not understand, things too wonderful for me." — Job 42:3

Psychology also influences culture. Knowledge transforms us. Learning about the solar system and the germ theory of disease alters the way people think and act. Learning about psychology's findings also changes people: They less often judge psychological disorders as moral failings, treatable by punishment and ostracism. They less often regard and treat women as men's mental inferiors. They less often view and raise children as ignorant, willful beasts in need of taming. "In each case," noted Morton Hunt (1990, p. 206), "knowledge has modified attitudes, and, through them, behavior." Once aware of psychology's well-researched ideas—about how body and mind connect, how a child's mind grows, how we construct our perceptions, how we learn and remember, how people across the world are alike (and different)—your mind may never again be the same.

But bear in mind psychology's limits. Don't expect it to answer the ultimate questions, such as those posed by Russian novelist Leo Tolstoy (1904): "Why should I live? Why should I do anything? Is there in life any purpose which the inevitable death that awaits me does not undo and destroy?"

Although many of life's significant questions are beyond psychology, some very important ones are illuminated by even a first psychology course. Through painstaking research, psychologists have gained insights into brain and mind, dreams and memories, depression and joy. Even the unanswered questions can renew our sense of mystery about things we do not yet understand. Moreover, your study of psychology can help teach you how to ask and answer important questions—how to think critically as you evaluate competing ideas and claims.

Psychology deepens our appreciation for how we humans perceive, think, feel, and act. By so doing, it can enrich our lives and enlarge our vision. Through this book we hope to help guide you toward that end. As educator Charles Eliot said a century ago: "Books are the quietest and most constant of friends, and the most patient of teachers."

RETRIEVAL PRACTICE

RP-11 Match the specialty (i through iii) with the description (a through c).

i.	Clinical psychology	**a.**	works to create social and physical environments that are healthy for all
ii.	Psychiatry	**b.**	studies, assesses, and treats people with psychological disorders but usually does not provide medical therapy
iii.	Community psychology	**c.**	is a branch of medicine dealing with psychological disorders

ANSWERS IN APPENDIX E

Use Psychology to Become a Stronger Person—and a Better Student

LOQ 1-9 How can psychological principles help you learn, remember, and thrive?

Psychology is not just about understanding others; it is also about understanding ourselves. It is only through such learning that we can be—and show to the world—our best selves. Throughout this text, we will offer evidence-based suggestions that you can use to live a happy, effective, flourishing life, including the following:

- *Manage your time to get a full night's sleep.* Unlike sleep-deprived people, who live with fatigue and gloomy moods, well-rested people live with greater energy, happiness, and productivity.

- *Make space for exercise.* Aerobic activity not only increases health and energy; it also is an effective remedy for mild to moderate depression and anxiety.

- *Set long-term goals, with daily aims.* Successful people take time each day to work toward their goals, such as exercising or sleeping more, or eating more healthfully. Over time, they often find that their daily practice becomes a habit.

- *Have a growth mindset.* Rather than seeing their abilities as fixed, successful people view their abilities as like a muscle—something that grows stronger with effortful use.

- *Prioritize relationships.* We humans are social animals. We flourish when connected in close relationships. We are both happier and healthier when supported by (and when supporting) caring friends.

Psychology's research also shows how we can learn and retain information. Many students assume that the way to cement new learning is to reread. What helps more—and what this book therefore encourages—is *repeated self-testing and rehearsal* of previously studied material. Memory researchers Henry Roediger and Jeffrey Karpicke (2006) call this phenomenon the **testing effect.** (It is also sometimes called the *retrieval practice effect* or *test-enhanced learning.*) They note that "testing is a powerful means of improving learning, not just assessing it." In one study, English-speaking students who had been tested repeatedly recalled the meaning of 20 previously learned Lithuanian words better than those who had spent the same time restudying the words (Ariel & Karpicke, 2018). Repetitive testing's rewards also make it reinforcing: Students who used repetitive testing once found it helped, and more often used it later when learning new material.

Many other studies, including in college classrooms, confirm that *frequent quizzing and self-testing boosts students' retention* (Cho et al., 2017; Foss & Pirozzolo, 2017; Trumbo et al., 2016).

As you will see in the Memory modules, to master information you must *actively process it.* In one digest of 225 studies, students engaged in active learning showed the highest examination performance in science, technology, engineering, and mathematics (the STEM fields) (Freeman et al., 2014). Likewise, when learning a new language, those who practice speaking it learn better than those who passively listen to it (Hopman & MacDonald, 2018). Better to talk than listen. So don't treat your mind like your stomach, something to be filled passively. Treat it more like a muscle that grows stronger with exercise. Countless experiments reveal that people learn and remember best when they put material in their own words, rehearse it, and then retrieve and review it again.

The SQ3R study method incorporates these principles (McDaniel et al., 2009; Robinson, 1970). **SQ3R** is an acronym for its five steps: Survey, Question, Read, Retrieve,[2] Review.

To study a module, first *survey,* taking a bird's-eye view. Scan each module's headings, and notice how the module is organized.

Before you read each main section, try to answer its numbered Learning Objective *Question* (for this section: "How can psychological principles help you learn, remember, and thrive?"). Researchers Roediger and Bridgid Finn (2010) have found that "trying and failing to retrieve the answer is actually helpful to learning." Those who test their understanding *before* reading, and discover what they don't yet know, will learn and remember better.

Then *read,* actively searching for the answer to the Learning Objective Question (LOQ).

At each sitting, read only as much of the module (usually a single main section) as you can absorb without tiring. Read actively and critically. Ask questions. Take notes. Make the ideas your own: How does what you've read relate to your own life? Does it support or challenge your assumptions? How convincing is the evidence? (Our new *Ask Yourself* questions and *Apply Psychological Science* features throughout each module will help you engage personally with the material.) Write out what you know. "Writing is often a tool for learning," say researchers (Arnold et al., 2017).

Having read a section, *retrieve* its main ideas: "Active retrieval promotes meaningful learning," says Karpicke (2012). So *test yourself.* This will not only help you figure out what you know; the testing itself will help you learn and retain the information more effectively. Even better, test yourself repeatedly. To facilitate this, we offer periodic *Retrieval Practice* questions throughout each module (for example, the questions at the end of this section). After answering these questions for yourself, you can check the answers in Appendix E and reread the material as needed.

testing effect enhanced memory after retrieving, rather than simply rereading, information. Also referred to as a *retrieval practice effect* or *test-enhanced learning.*

SQ3R a study method incorporating five steps: *Survey, Question, Read, Retrieve, Review.*

"If you read a piece of text through twenty times, you will not learn it by heart so easily as if you read it ten times while attempting to recite it from time to time and consulting the text when your memory fails." — Francis Bacon, *Novum Organum,* 1620

"It pays better to wait and recollect by an effort from within, than to look at the book again." — William James, *Principles of Psychology,* 1890

[2]Also sometimes called "Recite."

Finally, *review*: Read over any notes you have taken, again with an eye on the module's organization, and quickly review the whole module. Write or say what a concept is before rereading to check your understanding.

Survey, question, read, retrieve, review. We have organized this book to facilitate your use of the SQ3R study system. Each group of modules begins with an outline that aids your *survey*. Headings and Learning Objective *Questions* suggest issues and concepts you should consider as you *read*. The material is organized into sections of readable length. The Retrieval Practice questions will challenge you to *retrieve* what you have learned, and thus *retain* it better. The end-of-section *Review* is set up as a self-test, with the collected Learning Objective Questions and key terms listed, along with Master the Material questions in a variety of formats. In the e-book, answer-checking is a click away. In the printed text, answers may be found in Appendix C and Appendix D. Survey, question, read . . .

Four additional study tips may further boost your learning:

Distribute your study time. One of psychology's oldest findings is that *spaced practice* promotes better retention than *massed practice*. You'll remember material better if you space your time over several study periods—perhaps one hour a day, six days a week—rather than cram it into one week-long or all-night study blitz. For example, rather than trying to read an entire module in a single sitting, read just one main section and then turn to something else. *Interleaving* your study of psychology with your study of other subjects boosts long-term retention and protects against overconfidence (Kornell & Bjork, 2008; Taylor & Rohrer, 2010).

Spacing your study sessions requires a disciplined approach to managing your time. For more tips on time management, see the new Student Preface—Student Success: How to Apply Psychology to Live Your Best Life at the beginning of this text.

Learn to think critically. Both inside and outside of this course, critical thinking—smart thinking—is a key to wisdom. Whether you are reading or conversing, note people's assumptions and values. What perspective or bias underlies an argument? Evaluate evidence. Is it anecdotal? Or is it based on informative experiments? Assess conclusions. Are there alternative explanations?

Process class information actively. Listen for the main ideas and sub-ideas of a lecture. *Write them down.* Ask questions during and after class. In class, as in your private study, process the information actively and you will understand and retain it better. As psychologist William James urged a century ago, "*No reception without reaction, no impression without . . . expression.*" Make the information your own. Engage with the Ask Yourself questions and the Apply Psychological Science features found periodically throughout each module to relate what you read to your own life. Tell someone else about it. (As any teacher will confirm, to teach is to remember.)

Also, take notes *by hand*. Handwritten notes, in your own words, typically engage more active processing, with better retention, than does verbatim note taking on laptops (Mueller & Oppenheimer, 2014).

Overlearn. Psychology tells us that overlearning improves retention. We are prone to overestimating how much we know. You may understand a module as you read it, but that feeling of familiarity can be deceptively comforting. By using the Retrieval Practice and Master the Material questions as well as our online learning opportunities, you can test your knowledge and *overlearn* in the process.

Memory experts Elizabeth Bjork and Robert Bjork (2011, p. 63) offer simple, scientifically supported advice for how to improve your retention and your grades:

> Spend less time on the input side and more time on the output side, such as summarizing what you have read from memory or getting together with friends and asking each other questions. Any activities that involve testing yourself—that is, activities that require you to retrieve or generate information, rather than just representing information to yourself—will make your learning both more durable and flexible.

More learning tips To learn more about the testing effect and the SQ3R method, view the 5-minute animation, "Make Things Memorable," at tinyurl.com/HowToRemember.

ASK YOURSELF

Of all of these helpful principles, which ones seem most relevant and important for improving your own life and studies? How will you add them to your usual routines?

ANSWERS IN APPENDIX E

RETRIEVAL PRACTICE

RP-12 The _____ _____ describes the enhanced memory that results from repeated retrieval (as in self-testing) rather than from simple rereading of new information.

RP-13 What does SQ3R stand for?

MODULE

1 REVIEW The Story of Psychology

LEARNING OBJECTIVES

Test yourself Answer these repeated Learning Objective Questions on your own (before checking the answers in Appendix D) to improve your retention of the concepts (McDaniel et al., 2009, 2015).

LOQ 1-1 How is psychology a science?

LOQ 1-2 What are the three key elements of the scientific attitude, and how do they support scientific inquiry?

LOQ 1-3 How does critical thinking feed a scientific attitude, and smarter thinking for everyday life?

LOQ 1-4 What were some important milestones in psychology's early history?

LOQ 1-5 How did behaviorism, Freudian psychology, and humanistic psychology further the development of psychological science?

LOQ 1-6 How has contemporary psychology focused on cognition, on biology and experience, on culture and gender, and on human flourishing?

LOQ 1-7 How do psychologists use the biopsychosocial approach, and how can it help us understand our diverse world?

LOQ 1-8 What are psychology's main subfields?

LOQ 1-9 How can psychological principles help you learn, remember, and thrive?

TERMS AND CONCEPTS TO REMEMBER

Test yourself Write down the definition in your own words, then check your answer.

empirical approach, p. 2
critical thinking, p. 3
structuralism, p. 6
functionalism, p. 6
behaviorism, p. 8
humanistic psychology, p. 9
cognitive psychology, p. 9

cognitive neuroscience, p. 9
psychology, p. 9
nature–nurture issue, p. 10
natural selection, p. 10
evolutionary psychology, p. 10
behavior genetics, p. 10
culture, p. 11

positive psychology, p. 12
biopsychosocial approach, p. 12
levels of analysis, p. 12
basic research, p. 14
applied research, p. 14

counseling psychology, p. 14
clinical psychology, p. 14
psychiatry, p. 14
community psychology, p. 14
testing effect, p. 17
SQ3R, p. 17

MASTER THE MATERIAL

Test yourself Answer the following questions on your own first, then check your answers in Appendix E.

1. How can critical thinking help you evaluate claims in the media, even if you're not a scientific expert on the issue?

2. In 1879, in psychology's first experiment, _____ _____ and his students measured the time lag between hearing a ball hit a platform and pressing a key.

3. William James would be considered a(n) _____. Wilhelm Wundt and Edward Titchener would be considered _____.
   a. functionalist; structuralists
   b. structuralist; functionalists
   c. evolutionary theorist; structuralists
   d. functionalist; evolutionary theorists

4. In the early twentieth century, _____ redefined psychology as "the science of observable behavior."
   a. John B. Watson
   b. Abraham Maslow
   c. William James
   d. Sigmund Freud

5. Nature is to nurture as
   a. personality is to intelligence.
   b. biology is to experience.
   c. intelligence is to biology.
   d. psychological traits are to behaviors.

6. "Nurture works on what nature provides." Describe what this means, using your own words.

7. Which of the following is true regarding gender differences and similarities?

    a. Differences among the genders outweigh any similarities.

    b. Despite some gender differences, the underlying processes of human behavior are the same.

    c. Both similarities and differences among the genders depend more on biology than on environment.

    d. Gender differences are so numerous that it is difficult to make meaningful comparisons.

8. Martin Seligman and other researchers who explore various aspects of human flourishing refer to their field of study as _____ _____.

9. A psychologist treating emotionally troubled adolescents at a local mental health agency is most likely to be a(n)

    a. research psychologist.

    b. psychiatrist.

    c. industrial-organizational psychologist.

    d. clinical psychologist.

10. A mental health professional with a medical degree who can prescribe medication is a _____.

11. A psychologist conducting basic research to expand psychology's knowledge base may

    a. design a computer screen with limited glare and assess the effect on computer operators' eyes after a day's work.

    b. treat older people who are overcome by depression.

    c. observe 3- and 6-year-olds solving puzzles and analyze differences in their abilities.

    d. interview children with behavioral problems and suggest treatments.

Continue testing yourself with 📖 **LearningCurve** or 📖 **Achieve Read & Practice** to learn and remember most effectively.

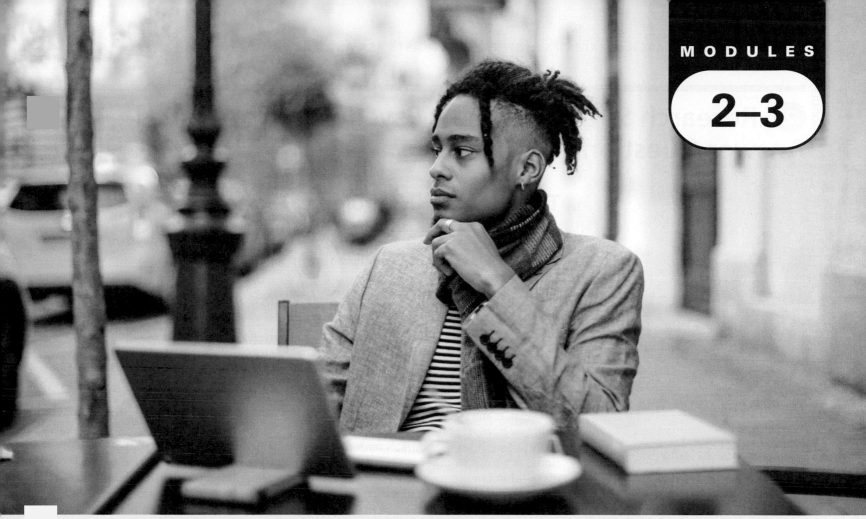

Eva-Katalin/Getty Images

Thinking Critically With Psychological Science

Hoping to satisfy their curiosity about people and to relieve their own woes, millions turn to "psychology." They read advice columns aimed at helping people cope with their problems, overcome their addictions, and save their marriages. They watch "celebrity psychics" demonstrate their supposed powers. They attend stop-smoking hypnosis seminars. They play online games, hoping to strengthen their brain. They immerse themselves in self-help books, websites, and lectures that promise to teach the path to love, the road to personal happiness, and the "hacks," or shortcuts, to success.

Others, intrigued by claims of psychological truth, wonder: How—and how much—does parenting shape children's personalities and abilities? Are first-born children more driven to achieve? Do dreams have deep meaning? Do we sometimes remember events that never happened? Does psychotherapy heal?

In working with such questions, the science of psychology does more than speculate. To separate uninformed opinions from examined conclusions, psychologists use the *scientific method* to conduct research. Let's consider how psychology's researchers do their science.

Research Strategies: How Psychologists Ask and Answer Questions

The Need for Psychological Science

LEARNING OBJECTIVE QUESTION **LOQ** **2-1** How does our everyday thinking sometimes lead us to a wrong conclusion?

Some people think that psychology merely proves what we already know and then dresses it in jargon: "You get paid for using fancy methods to tell me what my grandmother knew?"

Indeed, Grandma's common sense is often right. As the baseball great Yogi Berra (1925–2015) once said, "You can observe a lot by watching." (We also have Berra to thank for other gems, such as "Nobody goes there anymore—it's too crowded," and "If the people don't want to come out to the ballpark, nobody's gonna stop 'em.") Because we're all behavior watchers, it would be surprising if many of psychology's findings had *not* been foreseen. Many people believe that love breeds happiness, for example, and they are right (we have what researchers call a deep "need to belong").

But sometimes Grandma's common sense, informed by countless casual observations, is wrong. In other modules, we will see how research has overturned popular ideas—that familiarity breeds contempt, that dreams predict the future, and that most of us use only 10 percent of our brain. We will also see how research has surprised us with discoveries about how the brain's chemical messengers control our moods and memories, about other animals' abilities, and about the effects of stress on our capacity to fight disease.

Other things seem like commonsense truth only because we so often hear them repeated. Mere repetition of statements—whether true or false—makes them easier to process and remember, and thus more true-seeming (Dechêne et al., 2010; Fazio et al., 2015). Easy-to-remember misconceptions ("Vitamin C prevents the common cold") can therefore overwhelm hard truths. This power of familiar, hard-to-erase falsehoods is a lesson well known to political manipulators, and kept in mind by critical thinkers.

Three common flaws in commonsense thinking—*hindsight bias, overconfidence,* and *perceiving order in random events*—illustrate how, as novelist Madeleine L'Engle (1973) observed, "The naked intellect is an extraordinarily inaccurate instrument."

Did We Know It All Along? Hindsight Bias

Consider how easy it is to draw the bull's-eye *after* the arrow strikes. After the stock market drops, people say it was "due for a correction." After the athletic match, we credit the coach if a "gutsy play" wins and criticize the same "stupid play" if it doesn't. After a war or an election, its outcome usually seems obvious. Although history may therefore seem like a series of inevitable events, the actual future is seldom foreseen. No one's diary recorded, "Today the Hundred Years War began."

This **hindsight bias** is easy to demonstrate by giving half the members of a group some purported psychological finding and giving the other half an opposite result. Tell the first group, for example: "Psychologists have found that separation weakens romantic attraction. As the saying goes, 'Out of sight, out of mind.'" Ask them to imagine why this might be true. Most people can, and after hearing an explanation, nearly all will then view this true finding as unsurprising.

Tell the second group the opposite: "Psychologists have found that separation strengthens romantic attraction. As the saying goes, 'Absence makes the heart grow fonder.'" People given this untrue result can also easily imagine it, and most will also see it as unsurprising. When opposite findings both seem like common sense, there is a problem.

"All effective propaganda must be limited to a very few points and must harp on these in slogans." — Adolf Hitler, *Mein Kampf*, 1926

"Those who trust in their own wits are fools." — Proverbs 28:26

"Life is lived forwards, but understood backwards." — Philosopher Søren Kierkegaard, 1813–1855

"Anything seems commonplace, once explained." — Dr. Watson to Sherlock Holmes

Such errors in people's recollections and explanations show why we need psychological research. It's not that common sense is usually wrong. Rather, common sense describes, after the fact, what *has* happened better than it predicts what *will* happen.

More than 800 scholarly papers have shown hindsight bias in people young and old from around the world (Roese & Vohs, 2012). As physicist Niels Bohr reportedly jested, "Prediction is very difficult, especially about the future."

Overconfidence

We humans tend to think we know more than we do. Asked how sure we are of our answers to factual questions *(Is Boston north or south of Paris?)*, we tend to be more confident than correct.[1] Consider these three anagrams, shown beside their solutions (from Goranson, 1978):

WREAT ⟶ WATER

ETRYN ⟶ ENTRY

GRABE ⟶ BARGE

About how many seconds do you think it would have taken you to unscramble each of these? Did hindsight influence you? Knowing the answers tends to make us overconfident. (Surely the solution would take only 10 seconds or so?) In reality, the average problem solver spends 3 minutes, as you also might, given a similar anagram without the solution: OCHSA.[2]

Are we any better at predicting social behavior? Psychologist Philip Tetlock (1998, 2005) collected more than 27,000 expert predictions of world events, such as the future of South Africa or whether Quebec would separate from Canada. His repeated finding: These predictions, which experts made with 80 percent confidence on average, were right less than 40 percent of the time. It turns out that only about 2 percent of people do an excellent job predicting social behavior. Tetlock (with Gardner, 2016) calls them "superforecasters." Superforecasters avoid overconfidence. Faced with a difficult prediction, a superforecaster "gathers facts, balances clashing arguments, and settles on an answer."

ASK YOURSELF

Do you have a hard time believing you may be overconfident? Could overconfidence be at work in that self-assessment? How might reading this section about overconfidence help reduce your tendency to be overconfident?

RETRIEVAL PRACTICE

RP-1 Why, after friends start dating, do we often feel that we *knew* they were meant to be together?

ANSWERS IN APPENDIX E

Perceiving Order in Random Events

We're born with an eagerness to make sense of our world. People see a face on the Moon, hear Satanic messages in music played backward, or perceive the Virgin Mary's image on a grilled cheese sandwich. Even in random data, we often find patterns, because—here's a curious fact of life—*random sequences often don't look random* (Falk et al., 2009; Nickerson, 2002, 2005). Flip a coin 50 times and you may be surprised at the streaks of heads or tails—much like supposed "hot" and "cold" streaks in basketball shooting and baseball hitting. In actual random sequences, patterns and streaks (such as repeating digits) occur more often than people expect (Oskarsson et al., 2009). That also makes it hard for people to generate random-like sequences. When embezzlers try to simulate random digits when specifying how much to steal, their nonrandom patterns can alert fraud experts (Poundstone, 2014).

---

[1]Boston is south of Paris.
[2]The anagram solution: CHAOS.

Everett Collection/Newscom

Hindsight bias When drilling its Deepwater Horizon oil well in 2010, BP employees took shortcuts and ignored warning signs, without intending to harm people, the environment, or their company's reputation. *After* an explosion killed 11 employees and caused the largest ever marine oil spill, the foolishness of those judgments became (in hindsight) obvious.

Fun anagram solutions from Wordsmith (wordsmith.org):
Snooze alarms = Alas! No more z's
Dormitory = dirty room
Slot machines = cash lost in 'em

Overconfidence in history:
"We don't like their sound. Groups of guitars are on their way out." — Decca Records, in turning down a recording contract with the Beatles in 1962

"Computers in the future may weigh no more than 1.5 tons." — *Popular Mechanics*, 1949

"They couldn't hit an elephant at this distance." — General John Sedgwick just before being killed during a U.S. Civil War battle, 1864

"No woman in my time will be prime minister." — Margaret Thatcher, 1969 (British Prime Minister, 1979–1990)

hindsight bias the tendency to believe, after learning an outcome, that one would have foreseen it. (Also known as the *I-knew-it-all-along phenomenon.*)

Why are people prone to pattern-seeking? For most people, a random, unpredictable world is unsettling (Tullett et al., 2015). Making sense of our world relieves stress and helps us get on with daily living (Ma et al., 2017).

"The really unusual day would be one where nothing unusual happens."
— Statistician Persi Diaconis (2002)

Some happenings, such as winning a lottery twice, seem so extraordinary that we find it difficult to conceive an ordinary, chance-related explanation. "But with a large enough sample," said statisticians Persi Diaconis and Frederick Mosteller (1989), "any outrageous thing is likely to happen." An event that happens to but 1 in 1 billion people every day occurs about 7 times a day, more than 2500 times a year.

The point to remember: Our commonsense thinking is flawed due to three powerful tendencies—hindsight bias, overconfidence, and our tendency to perceive patterns in random events. But scientific inquiry can help us sift reality from illusion.

> Play the role of a researcher using scientific inquiry to think smarter about random hot streaks in sports. Engage online with the activity *How Would You Know If There Is a "Hot Hand" in Basketball?*

Psychological Science in a Post-Truth World

LOQ 2-2 Why are we so vulnerable to believing untruths?

In 2017, the Oxford English Dictionary's word of the year was *post-truth*—describing a modern culture where people's emotions and personal beliefs often override their acceptance of objective facts.

Consider two U.S. examples of such "truth decay"—of widely shared misinformation:

Belief: *The crime rate is rising.* Every recent year, 7 in 10 adults told Gallup that there is more crime "than there was a year ago" (Swift, 2016).

Fact: For several decades, both violent and property crime rates have been *falling*. In 2015, the violent crime rate was less than half the 1990 rate (BJS, 2017; Statista, 2017).

Belief: *Many immigrants are criminals* (McCarthy, 2017). Memorable incidents feed this narrative. Stories of an immigrant murdering, burglarizing, or lying spread through social networks and news outlets. Such fears are commonplace not only in North America but also in Europe and Australia (Nunziata, 2015).

Fact: Most immigrants are *not* criminals. Compared with native-born Americans, immigrants are 44 percent *less* likely to be imprisoned (CATO, 2017; Flagg, 2018, 2019). The same has been true in Italy, the United Kingdom, and elsewhere (Di Carlo et al., 2018).

Political party bias has distorted Americans' thinking. Psychologist Peter Ditto and his colleagues (2019a,b) reported that researchers have found "partisan bias in both liberals and conservatives, and at virtually identical levels." In the United States, a majority of Republicans believed unemployment had increased under Democratic President Barack Obama (it decreased), while a majority of strong Democrats believed inflation had worsened under Republican President Ronald Reagan (it improved) (Gelman, 2009; PPP, 2016). One study found that both U.S. Democrats and Republicans discriminate against the other-party candidates for college scholarships (Iyengar & Westwood, 2015). So, let none of us smugly think "Yes, but bias doesn't apply to *me*." Bias goes both ways.

U.S. Democrats and Republicans share concern about failures to separate fact from fiction. In his farewell address, President Barack Obama (2017) warned that without a "common baseline of facts," democracy is threatened: "We become so secure in our bubbles that we start accepting only information, whether it's true or not, that fits our opinions, instead of basing our opinions on the evidence that is out there." The late Republican Senator John McCain (2017) similarly expressed alarm about "the growing inability, and even unwillingness, to separate truth from lies."

So why do post-truth era people so often, in the words of psychologist Tom Gilovich (1991), "know what isn't so?"

False news Some misinformation gets fed to us intentionally. It's "lies in the guise of news" (Kristof, 2017). In the 2016 U.S. election cycle, 6 percent of all Twitter-enabled news consumption was fake news (Grinberg et al., 2019). And made-up news persists. In one analysis of 126,000 stories tweeted by 3 million people, falsehoods—especially false political news—"diffused significantly farther, faster, deeper, and more broadly than the truth" (Vosoughi et al., 2018). The good news is that most people can often tell the difference between high- and low-quality information sources (Pennycook & Rand, 2019).

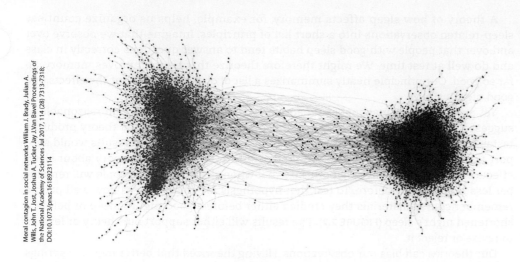

Moral contagion in social networks William J. Brady, Julian A. Wills, John T. Jost, Joshua A. Tucker, Jay J.Van Bavel Proceedings of the National Academy of Sciences Jul 2017, 114 (28) 7313-7318; DOI:10.1073/pnas.1618923114

FIGURE 2.1
The meeting of like minds On social media, most people discuss contentious issues, such as gun control, same-sex marriage, and climate change, only with likeminded others. In this graph of politically charged Twitter activity, each node represents a user who sent a message; each line represents a user who retweeted another user. As we can see, users overwhelmingly sent messages to, and retweeted messages from, those who shared their liberal (blue) or conservative (red) ideology (Brady et al., 2017).

Repetition In experiments, statements become more believable when they are repeated (De keersmaecker et al., 2019). What we hear over and over—perhaps a made-up smear of a political opponent—gets remembered and comes to seem true (Fazio et al., 2015).

Availability of powerful examples In the media, "if it bleeds it leads." Gruesome violence—a horrific murder, a mass killing, a plane crash—gets reported, with vivid images that color our judgments. No wonder Americans grossly overestimate their risk of being victimized by crime, terror, and plane crashes.

Group identity and the echo chamber of the like-minded Our social identities matter. Feeling good about our groups helps us feel good about ourselves. On social media we tend to friend people who think as we do (see **FIGURE 2.1**). We often read news sources that affirm our views and demonize news sources that do not.

The good news is that we can build a real-truth world by embracing a scientific mindset. With a mix of curiosity, skepticism, and humility, we can adopt the spirit of critical thinking: To accept everything is to be gullible; to deny everything is to be a cynic.

> To experience my [DM's] recap of some important, scientific thinking strategies, view the 3.5-minute animated video: *Thinking Critically in Our "Post-Truth" World* (also at tinyurl.com/PostTruthMyers).

"We have . . . become sloppier than ever: Tweet first, research later. Post first, rescind later. Guess first, confirm later." — Luvvie Ajayi, *I'm Judging You: The Do-Better Manual*, 2016

The Scientific Method

The foundation of all science is a scientific attitude that combines *curiosity, skepticism,* and *humility.* Psychologists arm their scientific attitude with the *scientific method*—a self-correcting process for evaluating ideas with observation and analysis. Psychological science welcomes hunches and plausible-sounding theories. And it puts them to the test. If a theory works—if the data support its predictions—so much the better for that theory. If the predictions fail, the theory gets revised or rejected. When researchers submit their work to a scientific journal, *peer reviewers*—other scientists who are experts in that field— provide anonymous evaluations of a study's theory, originality, and accuracy. With this feedback in hand, the journal editor decides whether the research deserves publication.

"I'm sorry, Jeannie, your answer was correct, but Kevin shouted his incorrect answer over yours, so he gets the points."

Constructing Theories

LOQ **2-3** How do theories advance psychological science?

In everyday conversation, we often use *theory* to mean "mere hunch." Someone might, for example, discount evolution as "only a theory"—as if it were mere speculation. In science, a **theory** explains behaviors or events by offering ideas that organize observations. By using deeper principles to organize isolated facts, a theory summarizes and simplifies. As we connect the observed dots, a coherent picture emerges.

theory an explanation using an integrated set of principles that organizes observations and predicts behaviors or events.

hypothesis a testable prediction, often implied by a theory.

operational definition a carefully worded statement of the exact procedures (operations) used in a research study. For example, *human intelligence* may be operationally defined as what an intelligence test measures. (Also known as *operationalization*.)

replication repeating the essence of a research study, usually with different participants in different situations, to see whether the basic finding can be reproduced.

A theory of how sleep affects memory, for example, helps us organize countless sleep-related observations into a short list of principles. Imagine that we observe over and over that people with good sleep habits tend to answer questions correctly in class and do well at test time. We might therefore theorize that sleep improves memory. So far so good: Our principle neatly summarizes a list of observations about the effects of a good night's sleep.

Yet no matter how reasonable a theory may sound—and it does seem reasonable to suggest that sleep boosts memory—we must put it to the test. A good theory produces testable *predictions*, called **hypotheses.** Such predictions specify what results would support the theory and what results would disconfirm it. To test our theory about sleep effects on memory, we might hypothesize that when sleep deprived, people will remember less from the day before. To test that hypothesis, we might assess how well people remember course materials they studied either before a good night's sleep or before a shortened night's sleep (**FIGURE 2.2**). The results will either support our theory or lead us to revise or reject it.

Our theories can bias our observations. Having theorized that better memory springs from more sleep, we may see what we expect: We may perceive sleepy people's comments as less accurate. The urge to see what we expect is strong, both inside and outside the laboratory, as when people's views of climate change influence their interpretation of local weather events.

As a check on their own biases, psychologists report their research with precise, measurable **operational definitions** of research procedures and concepts. *Sleep deprived,* for example, may be defined as "at least 2 hours less" than the person's natural sleep. (Likewise, a study of "aggression" may observe how many pins you stab into a doll that represents a lab partner, or a study of "helping" may record dollars donated.) Using these carefully worded statements, others can **replicate** (repeat) the original observations with different participants, materials, and circumstances. If they get similar results, confidence in the finding's reliability grows. The first study of hindsight bias, for example, aroused psychologists' curiosity. Now, after many successful replications with differing people and questions, we feel sure of the phenomenon's power. Replication is confirmation.

Replication is an essential part of good science. Psychology experienced a "replication crisis" when recent multi-lab efforts to replicate as many as 100 studies produced mixed results—ranging from 36 percent to 85 percent of studies replicating (Camerer et al., 2018a; Klein et al., 2014, 2018; Open Science Collaboration, 2015). (None of these nonreproducible findings appear in this text.) Replication failures often result when samples are small, so

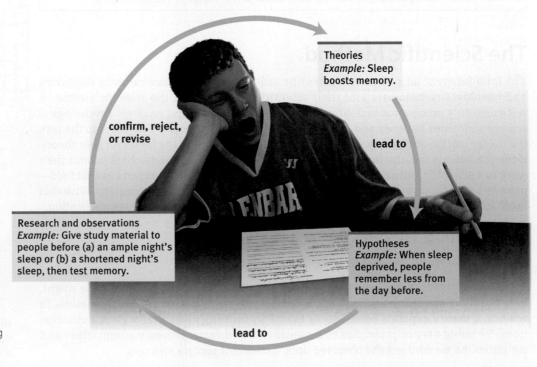

Theories
Example: Sleep boosts memory.

confirm, reject, or revise

lead to

Research and observations
Example: Give study material to people before (a) an ample night's sleep or (b) a shortened night's sleep, then test memory.

Hypotheses
Example: When sleep deprived, people remember less from the day before.

lead to

FIGURE 2.2
The scientific method A self-correcting process for asking questions and observing nature's answers.

psychologists increasingly study large samples of people (Camerer et al., 2018b; Sassenberg & Ditrich, 2019; Stanley et al., 2018). Bigger sample = a bigger chance of replication.

Today's psychological research is benefitting from more replications, more rigorous research methods, and more sharing of research data (Dougherty et al., 2018; Smaldino & McElreath, 2016; Zwaan et al., 2018). More and more psychologists use **preregistration** to publicly communicate their planned study design, hypotheses, data collection, and analyses (Nosek et al., 2018). (This openness and transparency also prevents later modifications, such as changing the hypotheses to fit the data.) There is still a place for *exploratory research:* Investigators gather data and seek patterns that inspire theories, which can then be tested with *confirmatory research* (with preregistered hypotheses and preplanned analyses).

Explorations, replications, preregistrations, and the open sharing of raw data are enabling "Psychology's Renaissance" of improved scientific practices (Motyl et al., 2017; Nelson et al., 2018).

Psychological and medical science also harness the power of **meta-analysis.** Meta-analysis is a procedure for statistically synthesizing a body of scientific evidence. By combining the results of many studies, researchers avoid the problem of small samples and arrive at a bottom-line result.

In the end, our theory will be useful if it (1) *organizes* observations and (2) implies *predictions* that anyone can use to check the theory or to derive practical applications. (Does people's sleep predict their retention?) Eventually, our research may (3) stimulate further research that leads to a revised theory that better organizes and predicts.

As we will see next, we can test our hypotheses and refine our theories using *descriptive* methods (which describe behaviors, often through case studies, surveys, or naturalistic observations), *correlational* methods (which associate different factors), and *experimental* methods (which manipulate factors to discover their effects). To think critically about popular psychology claims, we need to understand these methods and know what conclusions they allow.

> "Failure to replicate is not a bug; it is a feature. It is what leads us along the path—the wonderfully twisty path—of scientific discovery." — Lisa Feldman Barrett, "Psychology Is Not in Crisis," 2015

RETRIEVAL PRACTICE

RP-2 What does a good theory do?

RP-3 Why is replication important?

ANSWERS IN APPENDIX E

Description

LOQ 2-4 How do psychologists use case studies, naturalistic observations, and surveys to observe and describe behavior, and why is random sampling important?

The starting point of any science is description. In everyday life, we all observe and describe people, often drawing conclusions about why they think, feel, and act as they do. Psychologists do much the same, though more objectively and systematically, through

- *case studies* (in-depth analyses of individuals or groups).
- *naturalistic observations* (recording the natural behavior of many individuals).
- *surveys* and interviews (asking people questions).

THE CASE STUDY Among the oldest research methods, the **case study** examines one individual or group in depth in the hope of revealing things true of us all. Some examples:

- *Brain damage.* Much of our early knowledge about the brain came from case studies of individuals who suffered particular impairments after damage to a certain brain region.
- *Children's minds.* Jean Piaget taught us about children's thinking after carefully observing and questioning only a few children.
- *Animal intelligence.* Studies of various animals, including a few chimpanzees, have revealed their capacity for understanding and language.

preregistration publicly communicating planned study design, hypotheses, data collection, and analyses.

meta-analysis a statistical procedure for analyzing the results of multiple studies to reach an overall conclusion.

case study a descriptive technique in which one individual or group is studied in depth in the hope of revealing universal principles.

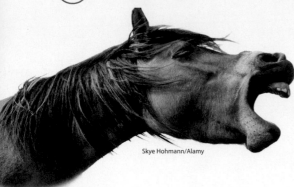

Skye Hohmann/Alamy

Freud and Little Hans Sigmund Freud's case study of 5-year-old Hans' extreme fear of horses led Freud to his theory of childhood sexuality. He conjectured that Hans felt unconscious desire for his mother, feared castration by his rival father, and then transferred this fear into his phobia about being bitten by a horse. Today's psychological science discounts Freud's theory of childhood sexuality but does agree that much of the human mind operates outside our conscious awareness.

See the *Video: Case Studies* for an animated tutorial.

Intensive case studies are sometimes very revealing, and they often suggest directions for further study.

But atypical individual cases may mislead us. Both in our everyday lives and in science, unrepresentative information can lead to mistaken judgments and false conclusions. Indeed, anytime a researcher mentions a finding (*Smokers die younger: 95 percent of men over 85 are nonsmokers*) someone is sure to offer a contradictory anecdote (*Well, I have an uncle who smoked two packs a day and lived to be 89!*).

Dramatic stories and personal experiences (even psychological case examples) command our attention and are easily remembered. Journalists understand that and often begin their articles with compelling stories. Stories move us. But stories can mislead. Which of the following do you find more memorable? (1) "In one study of 1300 dream reports concerning a kidnapped child, only 5 percent correctly envisioned the child as dead" (Murray & Wheeler, 1937). (2) "I know a man who dreamed his sister was in a car accident, and two days later she died in a head-on collision!" Numbers can be numbing, but *the plural of anecdote is not evidence*. A single story of someone who supposedly changed from gay to straight is not evidence that sexual orientation is a choice. As psychologist Gordon Allport (1954, p. 9) said, "Given a thimbleful of [dramatic] facts we rush to make generalizations as large as a tub."

The point to remember: Individual cases can suggest fruitful ideas. What's true of all of us can be glimpsed in any one of us. But to find those general truths, we must employ other research methods.

RETRIEVAL PRACTICE

RP-4 We cannot assume that case studies always reveal general principles that apply to all of us. Why not?

ANSWERS IN APPENDIX E

NATURALISTIC OBSERVATION A second descriptive method records responses in natural environments. These **naturalistic observations** range from watching chimpanzee societies in the jungle, to videotaping and analyzing parent-child interactions in different cultures, to recording racial differences in students' self-seating patterns in a school lunchroom. In the digital age, naturalistic observations have increased—thanks to "big data" harvested from phone apps, social media, Google searches, and more.

Until recently, naturalistic observation was mostly "small science"—possible to do with pen and paper rather than fancy equipment and a big budget (Provine, 2012). But today's digital technologies have transformed naturalistic observations into big science. Want to keep track of how often people go to the gym, a café, or the library? All you need is access to their phone's global positioning system (GPS) (Harari et al., 2016). And new technologies—wearable cameras and fitness sensors, and internet-connected smart-home sensors—offer increasing possibilities for people to allow accurate recording of their activity, relationships, sleep, and stress (Nelson & Allen, 2018; Yokum et al., 2019).

The billions of people entering personal information online have also enabled big-data observations (without disclosing anyone's identity). One research team studied the ups and downs of human moods by counting positive and negative words in 504 million Twitter messages from 84 countries (Golder & Macy, 2011). As **FIGURE 2.3** shows, people seemed happier on weekends, shortly after waking, and in the evenings. (Are late Saturday evenings often a happy time for you, too?) Another study found that negative emotion (especially anger-related) words in 148 million tweets from 1347 U.S. counties predicted the counties' heart disease rates *better* than smoking and obesity rates (Eichstaedt et al., 2015). Google enables us to learn about the world, and people's Google use enables us to learn about them. For example, the words people search and the questions they ask can pinpoint a geographical area's level of racism and depression. But Google searches also reveal our universal human likeness—as illustrated by the word "pregnant" being searched in conjunction with the same food cravings across varied countries (Stephens-Davidowitz, 2017). Across the globe, we are kin beneath the skin.

Like the case study, naturalistic observation does not *explain* behavior. It *describes* it. Nevertheless, descriptions can be revealing. We once thought, for example, that only humans use tools. Then naturalistic observation revealed that chimpanzees sometimes insert a stick in a termite mound and withdraw it, eating the stick's load of termites.

naturalistic observation a descriptive technique of observing and recording behavior in naturally occurring situations without trying to manipulate and control the situation.

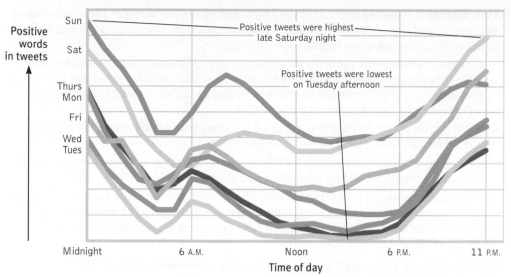

FIGURE 2.3
Twitter message moods, by time and by day This graph illustrates how, without knowing anyone's identity, researchers can use big data to study human behavior on a massive scale. It now is also possible to associate people's moods with, for example, their locations or with the weather, and to study the spread of ideas through social networks. (Data from Golder & Macy, 2011.)

Such unobtrusive naturalistic observations paved the way for later studies of animal thinking, language, and emotion, which further expanded our understanding of our fellow animals. Thanks to researchers' observations, we know that chimpanzees and baboons use deception: Psychologists repeatedly saw one young baboon pretending to have been attacked by another as a tactic to get its mother to drive the other baboon away from its food (Whiten & Byrne, 1988).

Naturalistic observations also illuminate human behavior. Here are two findings you might enjoy:

- *A funny finding.* We humans laugh 30 times more often in social situations than in solitary situations (Provine, 2001). (Have you noticed how seldom you laugh when alone?)

- *Culture and the pace of life.* Naturalistic observation also enabled Robert Levine and Ara Norenzayan (1999) to compare the pace of life—walking speed, accuracy of public clocks, and so forth—in 31 countries. Their conclusion: Life is fastest paced in Japan and Western Europe, and slower paced in economically less-developed countries.

Naturalistic observation offers interesting snapshots of everyday life, but it does so without controlling for all the factors that may influence behavior. It's one thing to observe the pace of life in various places, but another to understand what makes some people walk faster than others. Nevertheless, descriptions can be revealing: The starting point of any science is description.

A natural observer "Observations, made in the natural habitat," noted chimpanzee observer Jane Goodall (1998), "helped to show that the societies and behavior of animals are far more complex than previously supposed."

MICHAEL NICHOLS/National Geographic Creative

RETRIEVAL PRACTICE

RP-5 What are the advantages and disadvantages of naturalistic observation?

ANSWERS IN APPENDIX E

📺 See the *Video: Naturalistic Observation* for a helpful tutorial animation.

survey a descriptive technique for obtaining the self-reported attitudes or behaviors of a particular group, usually by questioning a representative, *random sample* of the group.

random sample a sample that fairly represents a population because each member has an equal chance of inclusion.

population all those in a group being studied, from which random samples may be drawn. (*Note:* Except for national studies, this does *not* refer to a country's whole population.)

correlation a measure of the extent to which two factors vary together, and thus of how well either factor predicts the other.

correlation coefficient a statistical index of the relationship between two things (from −1.00 to +1.00).

variable anything that can vary and is feasible and ethical to measure.

scatterplot a graphed cluster of dots, each of which represents the values of two variables. The slope of the points suggests the direction of the relationship between the two variables. The amount of scatter suggests the strength of the correlation (little scatter indicates high correlation).

THE SURVEY A **survey** looks at many cases, asking people to report their behavior or opinions. Questions about everything from sexual practices to political opinions are put to the public. Here are some recent survey findings:

- Compared at the same age with those born in the 1960s and 1970s, twice as many Millennials born in the 1990s reported having no sexual partners since age 18 (Twenge et al., 2017). Today's less attached young adults are experiencing what one writer termed a "sex recession" (Julian, 2018).
- 1 in 2 people across 24 countries reported believing in the "existence of intelligent alien civilizations in the universe" (Lampert, 2017).
- 68 percent of all humans—some 5.2 billion people—say that religion is important in their daily lives (from Gallup World Poll data analyzed by Diener et al., 2011).

But asking questions is tricky. People may shade their answers in a socially desirable direction, such as by underreporting their cigarette consumption or overreporting their voting. And the answers often depend on how questions are worded and how respondents are chosen.

Wording Effects Even small changes in the order or wording of questions can make a big difference (**TABLE 2.1**). When U.S. White evangelical Christians were asked whether (1) "Humans have evolved over time" or (2) "Humans have existed in their present form since the beginning of time," only 32 percent expressed a belief in evolution (Funk, 2019). But when asked whether (1) "Humans have evolved over time due to processes such as natural selection; God or a higher power had no part in this process"; (2) "Humans have evolved over time due to processes that were guided or allowed by God or a higher power"; or (3) "Humans have existed in their present form since the beginning of time," more than twice as many—68 percent—expressed a belief in evolution. Because wording is such a delicate matter, critical thinkers will reflect on how the phrasing of a question might affect people's expressed opinions.

Random Sampling In everyday thinking, we tend to generalize from samples we observe, especially vivid cases. An administrator who reads (a) a statistical summary of a professor's student evaluations and (b) the vivid comments of two irate students may be influenced as much by the biased sample of two unhappy students as by the many favorable evaluations in the statistical summary. The temptation to succumb to the *sampling bias*—to generalize from a few vivid but unrepresentative cases—is nearly irresistible.

So how do you obtain a *representative sample?* Say you want to learn how students at your college or university feel about a proposed tuition increase. It's often not possible to survey the whole group. How then could you choose a group that would represent the total student body? Typically, you would seek a **random sample,** in which every person in the entire **population** has an equal chance of being included in the sample group. You might number the names in the general student listing and use a random-number generator to pick your survey participants. (Sending each student a questionnaire wouldn't work because the conscientious people who returned it would not be a random sample.) Large representative samples are better than small ones, but a smaller representative sample of 100 is better than a larger unrepresentative sample of 500. You cannot compensate for an unrepresentative sample by simply adding more people.

Political pollsters sample voters in national election surveys just this way. Without random sampling, large samples—such as from website polls—often give misleading results. But by using some 1500 randomly sampled people, drawn from all areas of

TABLE 2.1 Survey Wording Effects	
Garners More Approval	**Garners Less Approval**
"aid to the needy"	"welfare"
"affirmative action"	"preferential treatment"
"undocumented workers"	"illegal aliens"
"gun safety laws"	"gun control laws"
"revenue enhancers"	"taxes"
"enhanced interrogation"	"torture"

a country, they can provide a remarkably accurate snapshot of the nation's opinions. Moreover, pollsters can assess the accuracy of their sampling by asking unrelated questions—such as whether the respondents live alone or are married—for which government statistics are available as benchmarks (Bialik, 2018). If the survey sample closely matches the national breakdown of people, so much the better.

Given polling's margin of error and last-minute voter swings, political polls are good but imperfect estimates of likely outcomes. Immediately before the 2016 U.S. presidential election, popular polling analysis website FiveThirtyEight.com gave candidate Hillary Clinton an estimated 71 percent chance of winning. When Donald Trump was then elected, many regarded the prediction as a failure. But consider: When a prediction model estimates a 71 percent chance for one candidate, that candidate should *lose* nearly one third of the time. (Imagine a weather forecast that predicts a 70 percent chance of rain. If it then *always* rained, that would be a flawed forecast.) One analysis of 30,000 general election political predictions in 45 countries between 1942 and 2017 summed it up: Contrary to popular belief, polls are pretty accurate (Jennings & Wlezien, 2018).

The point to remember: Before accepting survey findings, think critically. Consider the sample. The best basis for generalizing is from a representative, random sample.

RP-6 What is an unrepresentative sample, and how do researchers avoid it?

ANSWERS IN APPENDIX E

With very large samples, estimates become quite reliable. The letter *E* is estimated to represent 12.7 percent of the letters in written English. *E*, in fact, is 12.3 percent of the 925,141 letters in Melville's *Moby-Dick*, 12.4 percent of the 586,747 letters in Dickens' *A Tale of Two Cities*, and 12.1 percent of the 3,901,021 letters in 12 of Mark Twain's works (*Chance News,* 1997).

Correlation

LOQ 2-5 What does it mean when we say two things are correlated, and what are positive and negative correlations?

Describing behavior is a first step toward predicting it. Naturalistic observations and surveys often show us that one trait or behavior tends to coincide with another. In such cases, we say the two **correlate.** A statistical measure (the **correlation coefficient**) helps us figure out how closely two things vary together, and thus how well either one *predicts* the other. Knowing how much aptitude test scores *correlate* with school success tells us how well the scores *predict* school success.

Throughout this book, we often ask how strongly two **variables** are related: For example, how closely related are the personality test scores of identical twins? How well do intelligence test scores predict career achievement? How much do people's depressive symptoms predict their anxiety? In such cases, **scatterplots** can be very revealing.

Each dot in a scatterplot represents the values of two variables. The three scatterplots in **FIGURE 2.4** illustrate the range of possible correlations from a perfect positive to a perfect negative. (Perfect correlations rarely occur in the real world.) A correlation is positive if two sets of scores, such as for height and weight, tend to rise or fall together.

Saying that a correlation is "negative" says nothing about its strength. A correlation is negative if two sets of scores relate inversely, one set going up as the other goes down. The correlation between people's height and the distance from their head to the ceiling is strongly (perfectly, in fact) negative.

FIGURE 2.4
Scatterplots, showing patterns of correlation Correlations—abbreviated *r*—can range from +1.00 (scores for one variable increase in direct proportion to scores for another), to 0.00 (no relationship), to −1.00 (scores for one variable decrease precisely as scores for the other rise).

Perfect positive correlation (*r* = +1.00)   No relationship (*r* = 0.00)

Perfect negative correlation (*r* = −1.00)

TABLE 2.2 People's Fear and Disgust Responses to Various Animals

Animal	Average Fear	Average Disgust
Ant	2.12	2.26
Bat	2.11	2.01
Bull	3.84	1.62
Cat	1.24	1.17
Cockroach	3.10	4.16
Dog	2.25	1.20
Fish	1.15	1.38
Frog	1.84	2.48
Grass snake	3.32	2.47
Horse	1.82	1.11
Lizard	1.46	1.46
Louse	3.58	4.83
Maggot	2.90	4.49
Mouse	1.62	1.78
Panda	1.57	1.17
Pigeon	1.48	2.01
Rat	2.11	2.25
Rooster	1.78	1.34
Roundworm	3.49	4.79
Snail	1.15	1.69
Spider	4.39	4.47
Tapeworm	3.60	4.83
Viper	4.34	2.83
Wasp	3.42	2.84

Statistics can help us understand what we might miss with casual observation. To demonstrate, consider the responses of 2291 Czech and Slovakian volunteers who were asked by Jakub Polák and his colleagues (2019) to rate, on a 1 to 7 scale, their *fear* and *disgust* related to each of 24 animals. With all the relevant data right in front of you (**TABLE 2.2**), can you tell whether the correlation between participants' fear and their disgust is positive, negative, or close to zero?

When comparing the columns in Table 1.2, most people don't detect a relationship between fear and disgust. In fact, the correlation in this imaginary example is positive ($r = +.72$), as we can see if we display the data as a scatterplot (**FIGURE 2.5**).

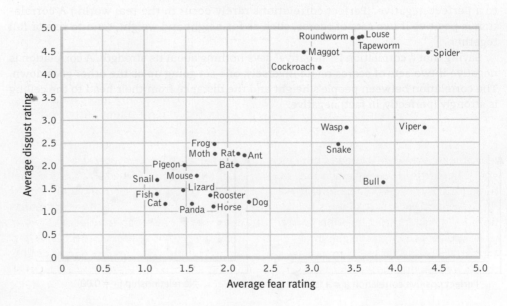

→ **FIGURE 2.5**
Scatterplot for fear and disgust felt toward 24 animals This display of average self-reported fear and disgust (each represented by a data point) reveals an upward slope, indicating a positive correlation. The considerable scatter of the data indicates the correlation is much lower than +1.00.

If we don't easily recognize a strong relationship when data are presented systematically, as in Table 2.2, how much less likely are we to notice them in everyday life? To see what is right in front of us, we sometimes need statistical illumination. We can easily see evidence of gender discrimination when given statistically summarized information about job level, seniority, performance, gender, and salary. But we often see no discrimination when the same information dribbles in, case by case (Twiss et al., 1989). Thinking like a psychological scientist helps us value everyone equally—not just those who catch our attention.

The point to remember: A correlation coefficient helps us see the world more clearly by revealing the extent to which two things relate.

> **RETRIEVAL PRACTICE** ────────────────────

RP-7 Indicate whether each association is a positive correlation or a negative correlation.

1. The more husbands viewed internet pornography, the worse their marital relationships (Muusses et al., 2015). _____

2. The more time teen girls spend absorbed with online social media, the more at risk they are for depression and suicidal thoughts (Kelly et al., 2018; Twenge & Campbell, 2019). _____

3. The longer children were breast-fed, the greater their later academic achievement (Horwood & Fergusson, 1998). _____

4. The more leafy vegetables older adults eat, the less their mental decline over the ensuing 5 years (Morris et al., 2018). _____

ANSWERS IN APPENDIX E

ILLUSORY CORRELATIONS AND REGRESSION TOWARD THE MEAN

LOQ **2-6** What are *illusory correlations,* and what is *regression toward the mean?*

Correlations not only make clear the relationships we might otherwise miss; they also keep us from falsely observing nonexistent relationships. When we believe there is a relationship between two things, we are likely to notice and recall instances that confirm our belief. If we believe that dreams forecast actual events, we may notice and recall confirming instances more than disconfirming instances. The result is an **illusory correlation.**

Illusory correlations can feed an illusion of control—that chance events are subject to our personal control. Gamblers, remembering their lucky rolls, may come to believe they can influence the roll of the dice by again throwing gently for low numbers and hard for high numbers. The illusion that uncontrollable events correlate with our actions is also fed by a statistical phenomenon called **regression toward the mean.** Average results are more typical than extreme results. Thus, after an unusual event, things tend to return toward their average level; extraordinary happenings tend to be followed by more ordinary ones. Students who score much lower or higher on an exam than they usually do are likely, when retested, to return to their average. Extrasensory perception (ESP) test subjects who defy chance when first tested nearly always lose their "psychic powers" when retested.

Failure to recognize regression is the source of many superstitions and of some ineffective practices—in sports coaching and in the workplace, for example. After berating an employee (or athlete) for poorer-than-usual performance, a manager may—when the employee regresses to normal—feel rewarded by the "improvement." After lavishing praise for an exceptionally fine performance, the manager may be disappointed when the employee's behavior again migrates back toward his or her average. Ironically, then, regression toward the average can mislead us into feeling rewarded after criticizing others ("That criticism really made him work harder!") and feeling punished after praising them ("All those compliments made her slack off!") (Tversky & Kahneman, 1974).

The point to remember: When a fluctuating behavior returns to normal, fancy explanations for why it does so are often wrong. Regression toward the mean is probably at work.

Moreover, although correlational research helpfully reveals relationships, it does not explain them. If teen social media use correlates with (predicts) teen risk of depression, that may—or may not—indicate that social media use affects depression risk. Other explanations are possible (see Thinking Critically About: Correlation and Causation).

illusory correlation perceiving a relationship where none exists, or perceiving a stronger-than-actual relationship.

regression toward the mean the tendency for extreme or unusual scores or events to fall back (regress) toward the average.

▣ For an animated tutorial on correlations, engage online with *Concept Practice: Positive and Negative Correlations.* See also the *Video: Correlational Studies* for another helpful tutorial animation.

"Once you become sensitized to it, you see regression everywhere." —Psychologist Daniel Kahneman (1985)

Thinking Critically About:
Correlation and Causation

LOQ 2-7 Why do correlations enable prediction but not cause-effect explanation?

Mental illness *correlates* with smoking—meaning that those who experience mental illness are also more likely to be smokers.[1] Does this tell us anything about what *causes* mental illness or smoking? **NO.**

There may be something about smoking that leads to mental illness.

Those with mental illness may be more likely to smoke.

OR

There may be some *third variable*, such as a stressful home life, for example, that triggers *both* smoking and mental illness.

So, then, how would you interpret these recent findings?
a) Sexual hook-ups correlate with college women's experiencing depression.
b) *Delaying* sexual intimacy correlates with positive outcomes such as greater relationship satisfaction and stability.[2]

Possible explanations:

1. Sexual restraint	→ Better mental health and stronger relationships
2. Depression	→ People being more likely to hook up
3. Some third factor, such as lower impulsivity	→ Sexual restraint, psychological well-being, and better relationships

Correlations do help us predict. Consider: Self-esteem correlates negatively with (and therefore predicts) depression. The lower people's self-esteem, the greater their risk for depression.

Possible interpretations:

1. Low self-esteem	→ Depression
2. Depression	→ Low self-esteem
3. Some third factor, such as distressing events or biological predisposition	→ Both low self-esteem and depression

You try it!
A survey of over 12,000 adolescents found that the more teens feel loved by their parents, the less likely they are to behave in unhealthy ways—having early sex, smoking, abusing alcohol and drugs, exhibiting violence.[3] What are three possible ways we could interpret that finding?[4]

The point to remember: **Correlation does not prove causation.**
Correlation suggests a possible cause-effect relationship but does not prove it. Remember this principle and you will be wiser as you read and hear news of scientific studies.

1. Belluck, 2013. 2. Fielder et al., 2013; Willoughby et al., 2014. 3. Resnick et al., 1997. 4. *ANSWERS*: A. Parental love may produce healthy teens. B. Well-behaved teens may feel more parental love and approval. C. Some third factor, such as income or neighborhood, may influence both parental love AND teen behaviors.

RP-8 You hear the school basketball coach telling her friend that she rescued her team's winning streak by yelling at the players after an unusually bad first half. What is another explanation of why the team's performance improved?

RP-9 Length of marriage positively correlates with hair loss in men. Does this mean that marriage causes men to lose their hair (or that balding men make better husbands)?

Nancy Brown/Getty Images

ANSWERS IN APPENDIX E

experiment a research method in which an investigator manipulates one or more factors (independent variables) to observe the effect on some behavior or mental process (the dependent variable). By *random assignment* of participants, the experimenter aims to control other relevant factors.

experimental group in an experiment, the group exposed to the treatment, that is, to one version of the independent variable.

control group in an experiment, the group *not* exposed to the treatment; contrasts with the experimental group and serves as a comparison for evaluating the effect of the treatment.

random assignment assigning participants to experimental and control groups by chance, thus minimizing preexisting differences between the different groups.

Experimentation

LOQ 2-8 What are the characteristics of experimentation that make it possible to isolate cause and effect?

Happy are they, remarked the Roman poet Virgil, "who have been able to perceive the causes of things." How might psychologists sleuth out the causes in correlational studies, such as the small correlation between teen girls' social media use and their risk of depression and self-harm?

EXPERIMENTAL MANIPULATION Our sleuthing starts with two plain facts:

1. Beginning in 2010, worldwide smart phone and social media use mushroomed.

2. Simultaneously, Canadian, American, and British teen girls' rates of depression, anxiety, self-harm, and suicide also mushroomed (Mercado et al., 2017; Morgan, 2017; Statistics Canada, 2016).

What do such findings mean? Is there a cause-effect connection? If so, should parents limit their middle schoolers' time on Instagram or Snapchat? Even big correlational data from a million teens couldn't tell us. The answers are being debated and the data are mixed. Moving beyond the simple correlation, one research summary noted that, in six of eight *longitudinal* (over time) studies, teens' current social media use predicted future mental health issues (Haidt, 2019). Even so, to identify cause and effect, researchers must **experiment.** Experiments enable researchers to isolate the effects of one or more factors by (1) *manipulating the factors of interest* and (2) *holding constant ("controlling") other factors*. To do so, they often create an **experimental group** in which people receive the treatment (such as reduced screen time), and a contrasting **control group** in which they do not.

To minimize any preexisting differences between the two groups, experimenters **randomly assign** people to each condition. Random assignment—whether with a random numbers table or flip of the coin—effectively equalizes the two groups. If one-third of the volunteers for an experiment can wiggle their ears, then about one-third of the people in each group will be ear wigglers. So, too, with age, attitudes, and other characteristics, which will be similar in the experimental and control groups. Thus, if the groups differ at the experiment's end, we can surmise that the treatment had an effect. (Note the difference between random *sampling*—which creates a representative survey sample—and random *assignment,* which equalizes the experimental and control groups.)

So, what do *experiments* reveal about the relationship between girls' social media use and their risk of depression and self-harm? While there have been few actual experiments that vary social media use, one identified nearly 1700 people who agreed to deactivate their Facebook account for four weeks (Allcott et al., 2019). Compared with people in the control group, those randomly assigned to the deactivation group spent more time watching TV and socializing with friends and family—and they reported lower depression, and greater happiness and satisfaction with their lives (and less post-experiment Facebook use). Less Facebook time meant a happier life.

The debate over the effects of prolonged social media use is ongoing. For now, most researchers agree that unlimited teen social media use poses a modest mental health risk. With more large-scale correlational and longitudinal studies, and further experimentation, researchers will refine this tentative conclusion.

The point to remember: Correlational studies, which uncover naturally occurring relationships, are complemented by experiments, which manipulate a factor to determine its effect.

PROCEDURES AND THE PLACEBO EFFECT Consider, then, how we might assess therapeutic interventions. Our tendency to seek new remedies when we are ill or emotionally down can produce misleading testimonies. If three days into a cold we start taking zinc tablets and find our cold symptoms lessening, we may credit the pills rather than the cold naturally subsiding. In the 1700s, bloodletting *seemed* effective. People sometimes improved after the treatment; when they didn't, the practitioner inferred the disease was too advanced to be reversed. So, whether or not a remedy is truly effective, enthusiastic users will probably endorse it. To determine its effect, we must control for other factors.

And that is precisely how new drugs and new methods of psychological therapy are evaluated. Investigators randomly assign participants in these studies to research groups. One group receives a pseudotreatment—an inert *placebo* (perhaps a pill with no drug in it). The other group receives a treatment, such as an antidepressant medication. (You can think of the placebo versus the actual drug as "trick or treatment.") The participants are often *blind* (uninformed) about what treatment, if any, they are receiving. If the study is using a **double-blind procedure,** neither the participants nor those who administer the drug and collect the data will know which group is receiving the treatment.

In double-blind studies, researchers check a treatment's actual effects apart from the participants' and the staff's belief in its healing powers. Just *thinking* you are getting a treatment can boost your spirits, relax your body, and relieve your symptoms. This **placebo effect** is well documented in reducing pain, depression, anxiety, and auditory hallucinations in schizophrenia (Dollfus et al., 2016; Kirsch, 2010). Athletes have run faster when given a supposed performance-enhancing drug (McClung & Collins, 2007). Decaf-coffee drinkers have reported increased vigor and alertness when they thought their brew had caffeine in it (Dawkins et al., 2011). People have felt better after receiving a phony mood-enhancing drug (Michael et al., 2012). And the more expensive the placebo, the more "real" it seems to us—a fake pill that costs $2.50 worked better than one costing 10 cents (Waber et al., 2008). To know how effective a therapy really is, researchers must control for a possible placebo effect.

RETRIEVAL PRACTICE

RP-10 What measures do researchers use to prevent the *placebo effect* from confusing their results?

ANSWERS IN APPENDIX E

INDEPENDENT AND DEPENDENT VARIABLES Here is an even more potent example: The drug Viagra was approved for use after 21 clinical trials. One trial was an experiment in which researchers randomly assigned 329 men with erectile disorder to either an experimental group (Viagra takers) or a control group (placebo takers given an identical-looking pill). The procedure was double-blind—neither the men taking the pills nor the person giving them knew what participants were receiving. The result: At peak doses, 69 percent of Viagra-assisted attempts at intercourse were successful, compared with 22 percent for men receiving the placebo (Goldstein et al., 1998). Viagra performed.

This simple experiment manipulated just one factor: the drug (Viagra versus no Viagra). We call this experimental factor the **independent variable** because we can vary it *independently* of other factors, such as the men's age, weight, and personality. Other factors that can potentially influence a study's results are called **confounding variables.** Random assignment controls for possible confounding variables.

Experiments examine the effect of one or more independent variables on some measurable behavior, called the **dependent variable** because it can vary *depending* on what takes place during the experiment. Both variables are given precise *operational definitions,* which specify the procedures that manipulate the independent variable (the exact drug dosage and timing in this study) or measure the dependent variable (the men's

---

See the *Video: Random Assignment* for a tutorial animation.

"If I don't think it's going to work, will it still work?"

double-blind procedure an experimental procedure in which both the research participants and the research staff are ignorant (blind) about whether the research participants have received the treatment or a placebo. Commonly used in drug-evaluation studies.

placebo [pluh-SEE-bo; Latin for "I shall please"] **effect** experimental results caused by expectations alone; any effect on behavior caused by the administration of an inert substance or condition, which the recipient assumes is an active agent.

independent variable in an experiment, the factor that is manipulated; the variable whose effect is being studied.

confounding variable in an experiment, a factor other than the factor being studied that might influence a study's results.

dependent variable in an experiment, the outcome that is measured; the variable that may change when the independent variable is manipulated.

Random assignment (controlling for other confounding variables, such as temperament and environment)

Group	Independent variable	Dependent variable
Experimental	Deactivated Facebook account	Depression test score 4 weeks later
Control	Did not deactivate Facebook account	Depression test score 4 weeks later

Lucy Lambriex/Getty Images

FIGURE 2.6

Experimentation To discern causation, psychologists control for confounding variables by randomly assigning some participants to an experimental group, others to a control group. Measuring the dependent variable (depression test score) will determine the effect of the independent variable (social media exposure).

responses to questions about their sexual performance). These definitions offer a level of precision that enables others to replicate the study. (See **FIGURE 2.6** for the Facebook experiment design.)

Let's pause to check your understanding using a simple psychology experiment: To test the effect of perceived ethnicity on the availability of rental housing, Adrian Carpusor and William Loges (2006) sent identically worded email inquiries to 1115 Los Angeles–area landlords. The researchers varied the ethnic connotation of the sender's name and tracked the percentage of positive replies (invitations to view the apartment in person). "Patrick McDougall," "Said Al-Rahman," and "Tyrell Jackson" received, respectively, 89 percent, 66 percent, and 56 percent invitations. In this experiment, what was the independent variable? The dependent variable?[3]

Experiments can also help us evaluate social programs. Do early childhood education programs boost impoverished children's chances for success? What are the effects of different antismoking campaigns? Do school sex-education programs reduce teen pregnancies? To answer such questions, we can experiment: If an intervention is welcomed but resources are scarce, we could use a lottery to randomly assign some people (or regions) to experience the new program and others to a control condition. If later the two groups differ, the intervention's effect will be supported (Passell, 1993).

Let's recap. A *variable* is anything that can vary (infant nutrition, intelligence, social media exposure—anything within the bounds of what is feasible and ethical to measure). Experiments aim to *manipulate* an *independent* variable, *measure* a *dependent* variable, and *control confounding* variables. An experiment has at least two different conditions: an *experimental condition* and a *comparison* or *control condition*. *Random assignment* works to minimize preexisting differences between the groups before any treatment effects occur. In this way, an experiment tests the effect of at least one independent variable (what we manipulate) on at least one dependent variable (the outcome we measure).

A similar experiment on a drug approved to increase women's sexual arousal produced a result described as, um, anticlimactic—an additional "half of one satisfying sexual encounter a month" (Ness, 2016; Tavernise, 2016).

"[We must guard] against not just racial slurs, but . . . against the subtle impulse to call Johnny back for a job interview, but not Jamal." — U.S. President Barack Obama, eulogy for state senator and church-shooting victim Clementa Pinckney, June 26, 2015

See the *Videos: Experiments* and *Confounding Variables* for helpful tutorial animations.

RETRIEVAL PRACTICE

RP-11 By using *random assignment,* researchers are able to control for _____ _____, which are other factors besides the independent variable(s) that may influence research results.

RP-12 Match the term on the left (i through iii) with the description on the right (a through c).

i.   Double-blind procedure

ii. Random sampling

iii. Random assignment

a. helps researchers generalize from a small set of survey responses to a larger population

b. helps minimize preexisting differences between experimental and control groups

c. controls for the placebo effect; neither researchers nor participants know who receives the real treatment

RP-13 Why, when testing a new drug to control blood pressure, would we learn more about its effectiveness from giving it to half the participants in a group of 1000 than to all 1000 participants?

ANSWERS IN APPENDIX E

[3]The independent variable, which the researchers manipulated, was the implied ethnicity of the applicants' names. The dependent variable, which researchers measured, was the rate of positive responses from the landlords.

Research Design

LOQ 2-9 How would you know which research design to use?

Throughout this book, you will read about amazing psychological science discoveries. But how do psychological scientists choose research methods and design their studies in ways that provide meaningful results? Understanding how research is done—how testable questions are developed and studied—is key to appreciating all of psychology. **TABLE 2.3** compares the features of psychology's main research methods. Other modules explain additional research designs, including *twin studies* and *cross-sectional* and *longitudinal research*.

In psychological research, no questions are off limits, except untestable (or unethical) ones: Does free will exist? Are people born evil? Is there an afterlife? Psychologists can't test those questions. But they *can* test whether free will beliefs, aggressive personalities, and a belief in life after death influence how people think, feel, and act (Dechesne et al., 2003; Shariff et al., 2014; Webster et al., 2014).

Having chosen their question, psychologists then select the most appropriate research design—*experimental, correlational, case study, naturalistic observation, twin study, longitudinal,* or *cross-sectional*—and determine how to set it up most effectively. They consider how much money and time are available, ethical issues, and other limitations. For example, it wouldn't be ethical for a researcher studying child development to use the experimental method and randomly assign children to loving versus punishing homes.

Next, psychological scientists decide how to measure the behavior or mental process being studied. For example, researchers studying aggressive behavior could measure participants' willingness to blast a stranger with supposed intense noise.

Researchers want to have confidence in their findings, so they carefully consider confounding variables—factors other than those being studied that may affect their interpretation of results.

Psychological research is a creative adventure. Researchers *design* each study, *measure* target behaviors, *interpret* results, and learn more about the fascinating world of behavior and mental processes along the way.

> ### ASK YOURSELF
> If you could conduct a study on any psychological question, which question would you choose? How would you design the study?

To help you build your understanding, your critical thinking, and your *scientific literacy skills,* we created online research activities. In these *How Would You Know?* activities, you get to play the role of researcher, making choices about the best ways to test interesting questions. Some examples: How Would You Know If Having Children Relates to Being Happier?, How Would You Know If a Cup of Coffee Can Warm Up Relationships?, and How Would You Know If People Can Learn to Reduce Anxiety?

To review and test your understanding of research methods, engage online with *Concept Practice: Psychology's Research Methods* and *The Language of Experiments,* and the interactive *Topic Tutorial: PsychSim6, Understanding Psychological Research.* For a 9.5-minute video synopsis of psychology's scientific research strategies, see the *Video: Research Methods.*

TABLE 2.3 Comparing Research Methods

Research Method	Basic Purpose	How Conducted	What Is Manipulated	Weaknesses
Descriptive	To observe and record behavior	Do case studies, naturalistic observations, or surveys	Nothing	No control of variables; single cases may be misleading
Correlational	To detect naturally occurring relationships; to assess how well one variable predicts another	Collect data on two or more variables; no manipulation	Nothing	Cannot specify cause and effect
Experimental	To explore cause and effect	Manipulate one or more factors; use random assignment	The independent variable(s)	Sometimes not feasible; results may not generalize to other contexts; not ethical to manipulate certain variables

Predicting Everyday Behavior

LOQ 2-10 How can simplified laboratory conditions illuminate everyday life?

When you see or hear about psychological research, do you ever wonder whether people's behavior in the lab will predict their behavior in everyday life? Does detecting the blink of a faint red light in a dark room say anything useful about flying an airplane at night? After viewing a violent, sexually explicit film, does a man's increased willingness to push buttons that he thinks will deliver a noise blast to a woman really say anything about whether viewing violent pornography makes a man more likely to abuse a woman?

Before you answer, consider: The experimenter *intends* the laboratory environment to be a simplified reality—one that simulates and controls important features of everyday life. Just as a wind tunnel lets airplane designers re-create airflow forces under controlled conditions, a laboratory experiment lets psychologists re-create psychological forces under controlled conditions.

An experiment's purpose is not to re-create the exact behaviors of everyday life, but to test *theoretical principles* (Mook, 1983). In aggression studies, deciding whether to push a button that delivers a noise blast may not be the same as slapping someone in the face, but the principle is the same. *It is the resulting principles—not the specific findings— that help explain everyday behaviors.*

When psychologists apply laboratory research on aggression to actual violence, they are applying theoretical principles of aggressive behavior, principles they have refined through many experiments. Similarly, it is the principles of the visual system, developed from experiments in artificial settings (such as looking at red lights in the dark), that researchers apply to more complex behaviors such as night flying. And many investigations show that principles derived in the laboratory do typically generalize to the everyday world (Mitchell, 2012).

The point to remember: Psychological science focuses less on specific behaviors than on revealing general principles that help explain many behaviors.

Psychology's Research Ethics

LOQ 2-11 Why do psychologists study animals, and what ethical research guidelines safeguard human and animal welfare? How do psychologists' values influence what they study and how they apply their results?

We have reflected on how a scientific approach can restrain biases. We have seen how case studies, naturalistic observations, and surveys help us describe behavior. We have also noted that correlational studies assess the association between two factors, showing how well one predicts another. We have examined the logic that underlies experiments, which use control conditions and random assignment of participants to isolate the causal effects of an independent variable on a dependent variable.

Yet, even knowing this much, you may still be approaching psychology with a mixture of curiosity and apprehension. So before we plunge in, let's entertain some common questions about psychology's ethics and values.

> See the *Video: Research Ethics* for a helpful tutorial animation.

Studying and Protecting Animals

Many psychologists study nonhuman animals because they find them fascinating. They want to understand how different species learn, think, and behave. Psychologists also study animals to learn about people. We humans are not *like* animals; we *are* animals, sharing a common biology. Animal experiments have therefore led to treatments for human diseases—insulin for diabetes, vaccines to prevent polio and rabies, transplants to replace defective organs.

Humans are complex. But some of the same processes by which we learn are present in other animals, even sea slugs and honeybees. The simplicity of the sea slug's nervous system is precisely what makes it so revealing of the neural mechanisms of learning. Ditto for the honeybee, which resembles us humans in how it learns to cope with stress (Dinges et al., 2017).

"Rats are very similar to humans except that they are not stupid enough to purchase lottery tickets." — Dave Barry, July 2, 2002

"Please do not forget those of us who suffer from incurable diseases or disabilities who hope for a cure through research that requires the use of animals." — Psychologist Dennis Feeney (1987)

"The greatness of a nation can be judged by the way its animals are treated." — Mahatma Gandhi, 1869–1948

Animal research benefiting animals
Psychologists have helped zoos enrich animal environments—for example, by giving animals more choices to reduce the *learned helplessness* of captivity (Kurtycz, 2015; Weir, 2013). Thanks partly to research on the benefits of novelty, control, and stimulation, these gorillas are enjoying an improved quality of life in New York's Bronx Zoo.

MARY ALTAFFER/AP Images

Sharing such similarities, should we not respect our animal relatives? The animal protection movement protests the use of animals in psychological, biological, and medical research. "We cannot defend our scientific work with animals on the basis of the similarities between them and ourselves and then defend it morally on the basis of differences," noted Roger Ulrich (1991). In U.S. national surveys, half of adults oppose and half favor "the use of animals in scientific research"—with support greater among those most informed about science (Strauss, 2018).

Out of this heated debate, two issues emerge. The basic one is whether it is right to place the well-being of humans above that of other animals. In experiments on stress and cancer, is it right that mice get tumors in the hope that people might not? Should some monkeys be exposed to an HIV-like virus in the search for an AIDS vaccine? Humans raise and slaughter 56 billion animals a year (Thornton, 2019). Is our use and consumption of other animals as natural as the behavior of carnivorous hawks, cats, and whales?

For those who give human life top priority, a second question emerges: What safeguards should protect the well-being of animals in research? One survey of animal researchers gave an answer. Some 98 percent supported government regulations protecting primates, dogs, and cats, and 74 percent also supported regulations providing for the humane care of rats and mice (Plous & Herzog, 2000). Many professional associations and funding agencies already have such guidelines. British Psychological Society (BPS) guidelines call for housing animals under reasonably natural living conditions, with companions for social animals (Lea, 2000). American Psychological Association (APA) guidelines state that researchers must provide "humane care and healthful conditions" and that testing should "minimize discomfort" (APA, 2012). The European Parliament also mandates standards for animal care and housing (Vogel, 2010). Most universities screen research proposals, often through an animal care ethics committee, and laboratories are regulated and inspected.

Animals have themselves benefited from animal research. One Ohio team of research psychologists measured stress hormone levels in samples of millions of dogs brought each year to animal shelters. They devised handling and stroking methods to reduce stress and ease the dogs' transition to adoptive homes (Tuber et al., 1999). Other studies have helped improve care and management in animals' natural habitats. By revealing our behavioral kinship with animals and the remarkable intelligence of chimpanzees, gorillas, and other animals, experiments have also led to increased empathy and protection for them. At its best, a psychology concerned for humans and sensitive to animals serves the welfare of both.

Studying and Protecting Humans

What about human participants? Does the image of white-coated scientists seeming to deliver electric shocks trouble you? Actually, most psychological studies are free of such stress. Blinking lights, flashing words, and pleasant social interactions are more common.

Occasionally, researchers do temporarily stress or deceive people, but only when they believe it is essential to a justifiable end, such as understanding and controlling violent behavior or studying mood swings. Some experiments won't work if participants know everything beforehand. (Wanting to be helpful, the participants might try to confirm the researcher's predictions.)

The ethics codes of the APA and Britain's BPS urge researchers to (1) obtain potential participants' **informed consent** to take part, (2) protect participants from greater-than-usual harm and discomfort, (3) keep information about individual participants confidential, and (4) fully **debrief** people (explain the research afterward, including any temporary deception). To enforce these ethical standards, universities and research organizations have *Institutional Review Boards* that screen research proposals and safeguard "the rights, welfare and well-being of human research participants" (NIEHS, 2019).

Ensuring Scientific Integrity

In science, as in everyday life, mistakes happen. When data get accidentally miscomputed or misreported, that's forgivable and correctable. What's not acceptable—and will get a scientist banished from the profession—is fraud. Indeed, leading scientists cite honesty as the most important scientific value, followed by curiosity and perseverance (*Nature*, 2016). To seek career advancement by plagiarizing another's words or ideas, or to make up data, is to risk finding one's career ended. Such was the rare case when a Dutch psychologist fabricated data that made it into 58 research articles—fakery that was sniffed out by alert colleagues (Retraction Watch, 2015).

Fake science also has the potential to cause great harm. This happened in 1998 when a now-disbarred British physician, Andrew Wakefield, published an article in the prestigious *Lancet,* reporting a dozen cases in which British children given the measles, mumps, and rubella (MMR) vaccine supposedly developed autism afterward. Other studies failed to reproduce the finding (replication matters!) (Hviid et al., 2019). An investigation revealed a fraud—with falsified data—and the journal retracted the report (Godlee, 2011). Alas, by then the widely publicized finding—"the most damaging medical hoax of the last 100 years" (Flaherty, 2011)—had produced an "anti-vax" movement and declining vaccination rates. Instead of following the typical path toward disease elimination, U.S. measles rates in 2019 rose to their highest levels in 25 years (CDC, 2019; Graham et al., 2019). Unvaccinated children may suffer long-term harm or even death, as well as placing at risk those children too young to be fully vaccinated. Though the science self-corrected, the damage lingers on. Nevertheless, the good news is that scientific scrutiny, complete with replication, can inform and protect us.

Values in Psychology

Values affect what we study, how we study it, and how we interpret results. Researchers' values influence choice of research topics. Should we study worker productivity or worker morale? Sex discrimination or gender differences? Conformity or independence? Values can also color "the facts"—our observations and interpretations. Sometimes we see what we want or expect to see (**FIGURE 2.7**).

Even the words we use to describe traits and tendencies can reflect our values. In psychology and in everyday speech, labels describe and labels evaluate: One person's *rigidity* is another's *consistency*. One person's *faith* is another's *fanaticism*. One person's *adultery* is another person's *open marriage*. Our labeling someone as *firm* or *stubborn*, *careful* or *picky*, *discreet* or *secretive* reveals our own attitudes.

So, values inform psychological science—and psychological science has the power to persuade. This may lead some to feel distrustful: Is psychology dangerously powerful?

The New Yorker Collection, Paul Noth, from cartoonbank.com. All Rights Reserved.

"There can be no peace until they renounce their Rabbit God and accept our Duck God."

(a)

Rubberball/Mike Kemp/Getty Images

(b)

FIGURE 2.7
What do you see? Our expectations influence what we perceive in (a). Did you see a duck or a rabbit? Show some friends this image with the rabbit photo (b) covered up and see if they are more likely to perceive a duck. (Inspired by Shepard, 1990.)

Psychology speaks In making its historic 1954 school desegregation decision, the U.S. Supreme Court cited the expert testimony and research of psychologists Kenneth Clark and Mamie Phipps Clark (1947). The Clarks reported that, when given a choice between Black and White dolls, most African-American children chose the White doll, which indicated that they had likely absorbed and internalized anti-Black prejudice.

Might it be used to manipulate people? Knowledge, like all power, can be used for good or evil. Nuclear power has been used to light up cities—and to demolish them. Persuasive power has been used to educate people—and to deceive them. Although psychology does have the power to deceive, its purpose is to enlighten. Every day, psychologists explore ways to enhance learning, creativity, and compassion. Psychology speaks to many of our world's great problems—war, overpopulation, inequality, climate change, prejudice, family crises, crime—all of which involve attitudes and behaviors. Psychology also speaks to our deepest longings—for nourishment, for love, for happiness. Psychology cannot address all of life's great questions, but it speaks to some mighty important ones.

ASK YOURSELF

What other questions or concerns do you have about psychology?

RETRIEVAL PRACTICE

RP-14 How are animal and human research participants protected?

ANSWERS IN APPENDIX E

MODULE

2 REVIEW Research Strategies: How Psychologists Ask and Answer Questions

LEARNING OBJECTIVES

Test Yourself Answer these repeated Learning Objective Questions on your own (before checking the answers in Appendix D) to improve your retention of the concepts (McDaniel et al., 2009, 2015).

LOQ 2-1 How does our everyday thinking sometimes lead us to a wrong conclusion?

LOQ 2-2 Why are we so vulnerable to believing untruths?

LOQ 2-3 How do theories advance psychological science?

LOQ 2-4 How do psychologists use case studies, naturalistic observations, and surveys to observe and describe behavior, and why is random sampling important?

LOQ 2-5 What does it mean when we say two things are correlated, and what are positive and negative correlations?

LOQ 2-6 What are *illusory correlations,* and what is *regression toward the mean?*

LOQ 2-7 Why do correlations enable prediction but not cause-effect explanation?

LOQ 2-8 What are the characteristics of experimentation that make it possible to isolate cause and effect?

LOQ 2-9 How would you know which research design to use?

LOQ 2-10 How can simplified laboratory conditions illuminate everyday life?

LOQ 2-11 Why do psychologists study animals, and what ethical research guidelines safeguard human and animal welfare? How do psychologists' values influence what they study and how they apply their results?

TERMS AND CONCEPTS TO REMEMBER

Test Yourself Write down the definition in your own words, then check your answer.

hindsight bias, p. 23

theory, p. 25

hypothesis, p. 26

operational definition, p. 26

replication, p. 26

preregistration, p. 27

meta-analysis, p. 27

case study, p. 27

naturalistic observation, p. 28

survey, p. 30

random sample, p. 30

population, p. 30

correlation, p. 30

correlation coefficient, p. 30

variable, p. 30

scatterplot, p. 30

illusory correlation, p. 33

regression toward the mean, p. 33

experiment, p. 35

experimental group, p. 35

control group, p. 35

random assignment, p. 35

double-blind procedure, p. 36

placebo [pluh-SEE-bo] effect, p. 36

independent variable, p. 36

confounding variable, p. 36

dependent variable, p. 36

informed consent, p. 41

debriefing, p. 41

MASTER THE MATERIAL

Test Yourself Answer the following questions on your own first, then check your answers in Appendix E.

1. _____ _____ refers to our tendency to perceive events as obvious or inevitable after the fact.

2. As scientists, psychologists
   a. keep their methods private so others will not repeat their research.
   b. assume the truth of articles published in leading scientific journals.
   c. reject evidence that competes with traditional findings.
   d. are willing to ask questions and to reject claims that cannot be verified by research.

3. A theory-based prediction is called a(n) _____.

4. Which of the following is NOT one of the *descriptive* methods psychologists use to observe and describe behavior?
   a. A case study
   b. Naturalistic observation
   c. Correlational research
   d. A phone survey

5. For your survey, you need to establish a group of people who represent your country's entire adult population. To do this, you will need to question a _____ sample of the population.

6. A study finds that the more childbirth training classes women attend, the less pain medication they require during childbirth. This finding can be stated as a _____ (positive/negative) correlation.

7. A _____ provides a visual representation of the direction and the strength of a relationship between two variables.

8. In a _____ correlation, the scores rise and fall together; in a(n) _____ correlation, one score falls as the other rises.
   a. positive; negative
   b. positive; illusory
   c. negative; weak
   d. strong; weak

9. How can regression toward the mean influence our interpretation of events?

10. Knowing that two events are correlated provides
    a. a basis for prediction.
    b. an explanation of why the events are related.
    c. proof that as one increases, the other also increases.
    d. an indication that an underlying third factor is at work.

11. Here are some recently reported correlations, with interpretations drawn by journalists. Knowing just these correlations, can you come up with other possible explanations for each of these?
    a. Alcohol use is associated with violence. (One interpretation: Drinking triggers or unleashes aggressive behavior.)
    b. Educated people live longer, on average, than less-educated people. (One interpretation: Education lengthens life and enhances health.)
    c. Teens engaged in team sports are less likely to use drugs, smoke, have sex, carry weapons, and eat junk food than are teens who do not engage in team sports. (One interpretation: Team sports encourage healthy living.)
    d. Adolescents who frequently see smoking in movies are more likely to smoke. (One interpretation: Movie stars' behavior influences impressionable teens.)

12. To explain behaviors and clarify cause and effect, psychologists use _____.

13. To test the effect of a new drug on depression, we randomly assign people to control and experimental groups. Those in the control group take a pill that contains no medication. This pill is a _____.

14. In a double-blind procedure,
    a. only the participants know whether they are in the control group or the experimental group.
    b. experimental and control group members will be carefully matched for age, sex, income, and education level.
    c. neither the participants nor the researchers know who is in the experimental group or control group.
    d. someone separate from the researcher will ask people to volunteer for the experimental group or the control group.

15. A researcher wants to determine whether noise level affects workers' blood pressure. In one group, she varies the level of noise in the environment and records participants' blood pressure. In this experiment, the level of noise is the _____.

16. The laboratory environment is designed to
    a. exactly re-create the events of everyday life.
    b. re-create psychological forces under *controlled* conditions.
    c. re-create psychological forces under *random* conditions.
    d. minimize the use of animals and humans in psychological research.

17. In defending their experimental research with animals, psychologists have noted that
    a. animals' physiology and behavior can tell us much about our own.
    b. animal experimentation sometimes helps animals as well as humans.
    c. animals are fascinating creatures and worthy of study.
    d. all of these statements are correct.

Continue testing yourself with 📙 **LearningCurve** or 📘 **Achieve Read & Practice** to learn and remember most effectively.

MODULE

3 Statistical Reasoning in Everyday Life

In descriptive, correlational, and experimental research, statistics are tools that help us see and interpret what the unaided eye might miss. But accurate statistical understanding benefits everyone. To be an educated person today is to be able to apply simple statistical principles to everyday reasoning. One needn't memorize complicated formulas to think more clearly and critically about data.

Off-the-top-of-the-head estimates often misread reality and mislead the public. Someone throws out a big, round number. Others echo it, and before long the big, round number becomes public misinformation. Three examples:

- *Ten percent of people are gay*. Or is it 2 to 4 percent, as suggested by various national surveys?

- *We ordinarily use only 10 percent of our brain*. Or is it closer to 100 percent?

- *To be healthy, walk 10,000 steps a day*. Or will 8,500 or 13,000 steps do the trick, or swimming or jogging (Mull, 2019)?

When setting goals, we love big, round numbers. We're far more likely to want to lose 20 pounds than 19 or 21 pounds (or an even 10 kilograms rather than 9.07 kilograms). And batters try to improve their batting average shortly before the season's end, making them nearly four times more likely to finish with a .300 average than with a .299 average (Pope & Simonsohn, 2011).

If you see an attention-grabbing headline presented without evidence—that nationally there are one million teen pregnancies, two million homeless seniors, or three million alcohol-related car accidents—you can be pretty sure that someone is guessing. If they want to emphasize the problem, they will be motivated to guess big. If they want to minimize the problem, they will guess small. *The point to remember*: Use critical thinking when presented with big, round, undocumented numbers.

Statistical illiteracy also feeds needless health scares (Gigerenzer, 2010). In the 1990s, the British press reported a study showing that women taking a particular contraceptive pill had a 100 percent increased risk of blood clots that could produce strokes. The story went viral, causing thousands of women to stop taking the pill. What resulted? A wave of unwanted pregnancies and an estimated 13,000 additional abortions (which also are associated with increased blood-clot risk). Distracted by big, round numbers, few people focused on the study's actual findings: A 100 percent increased risk, indeed—but only from 1 in 7000 to 2 in 7000. Such false alarms underscore the need to think critically, to teach statistical reasoning, and to present statistical information more transparently.

Describing Data

LOQ 3-1   How do we describe data using three measures of central tendency, and what is the relative usefulness of the two measures of variation?

Once researchers have gathered their data, they may organize that data using *descriptive statistics*. One way to do this is to convert the data into a simple *bar graph*, as in **FIGURE 3.1**, which displays a distribution of different brands of trucks still on the road after a decade. When reading statistical graphs such as this one, take care. It's easy to design a graph to make a difference look big (Figure 3.1a) or small (Figure 3.1b). The secret lies in how you label the vertical scale (the *y-axis*).

The point to remember: Think smart. When interpreting graphs, consider the scale labels and note their *range*.

mode   the most frequently occurring score(s) in a distribution.

mean   the arithmetic average of a distribution, obtained by adding the scores and then dividing by the number of scores.

median   the middle score in a distribution; half the scores are above it and half are below it.

ASK YOURSELF

Think of a time when you used statistics to make a point—maybe in class, in a paper, or in a discussion with a friend or family member. Looking back, were the data you cited credible and accurate? How do you know?

RP-1 A truck manufacturer offered Figure 3.1's graph (a)—with actual brand names included—to suggest the much greater durability of its trucks. What does graph (b) make clear about the varying durability, and how is this accomplished?

⬇ **FIGURE 3.1**
Read the scale labels

Percentage still functioning after 10 years

(a)

(b)

Brand of truck

Transtock/SuperStock

ANSWERS IN APPENDIX E

Measures of Central Tendency

The next step is to summarize the data using a *measure of central tendency*, a single score that represents a whole set of scores. The simplest measure is the **mode,** the most frequently occurring score or scores. The most familiar is the **mean,** or arithmetic average—the total sum of all the scores divided by the number of scores. The midpoint—the 50th percentile—is the **median.** On a divided highway, the median is the middle. So, too, with data: If you arrange all the scores in order from the highest to the lowest, half will be above the median and half will be below it.

Measures of central tendency neatly summarize data. But consider what happens to the mean when a distribution is lopsided—when it's *skewed* by a few way-out scores. With income data, for example, the mode, median, and mean often tell very different stories (**FIGURE 3.2**). This happens because the mean is biased by a few extreme incomes. When Amazon founder Jeff Bezos sits down in a small café, its average (mean) customer instantly becomes a billionaire. But median customer wealth remains unchanged.

⬇ **FIGURE 3.2**
A skewed distribution This graphic representation of the distribution of a village's incomes illustrates the three measures of central tendency—mode, median, and mean. Note how just a few high incomes make the mean—the fulcrum point that balances the incomes above and below—deceptively high.

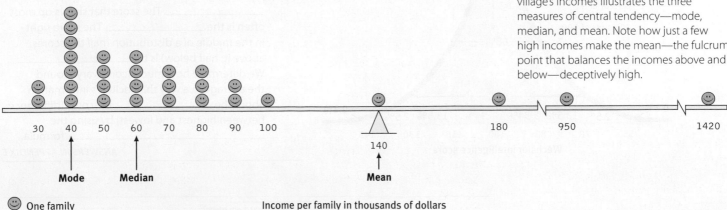

Mode   Median   Mean

😊 One family   Income per family in thousands of dollars

The average person has one ovary and one testicle.

Understanding this, you can see why, according to the 2010 U.S. Census, nearly 65 percent of U.S. households have "below average" income. The bottom half of earners receive much less than half of the total national income. So, most Americans make less than average (the mean). Mean and median tell different true stories.

The point to remember: Always note which measure of central tendency is reported. If it is a mean, consider whether a few atypical scores could be distorting it.

Measures of Variation

Knowing the value of an appropriate measure of central tendency can tell us a great deal. But the single number omits other information. It helps to know something about the amount of *variation* in the data—how similar or diverse the scores are. Averages derived from scores with low variability are more reliable than averages based on scores with high variability. Consider a basketball player who scored between 13 and 17 points in each of the season's first 10 games. Knowing this, we would be more confident that she would score near 15 points in her next game than if her scores had varied from 5 to 25 points.

The **range** of scores—the gap between the lowest and highest—provides only a crude estimate of variation. A couple of extreme scores in an otherwise similar group, such as the $950,000 and $1,420,000 incomes in Figure 3.2, will create a deceptively large range.

The more useful standard for measuring how much scores deviate (differ) from one another is the **standard deviation.** It better gauges whether scores are packed together or dispersed, because it uses information from each score. The computation[4] assembles information about how much individual scores differ from the mean, which can be very telling. Let's say test scores from Class A and Class B both have the same mean (75 percent correct), but very different standard deviations (5.0 for Class A and 15.0 for Class B). Have you ever had test experiences like that—where two-thirds of your classmates in one course score in the 70 to 80 percent range, with scores in another course more spread out (two-thirds between 60 and 90 percent)? The standard deviation, as well as the mean score, tell us about how each class is faring.

You can grasp the meaning of the standard deviation if you consider how scores naturally tend to be distributed. Large numbers of data—heights, intelligence scores, life expectancy (though not incomes)—often form a symmetrical, *bell-shaped* distribution. Most cases fall near the mean, and fewer cases fall near either extreme. This bell-shaped distribution is so typical that we call the curve it forms the **normal curve.**

As **FIGURE 3.3** shows, a useful property of the normal curve is that roughly 68 percent of the cases fall within one standard deviation on either side of the mean. About 95 percent of cases fall within two standard deviations. Thus, about 68 percent of people taking an intelligence test will score within ±15 points of 100. About 95 percent will score within ±30 points.

 For an interactive review of these statistical concepts, visit *Topic Tutorial: PsychSim6, Descriptive Statistics.*

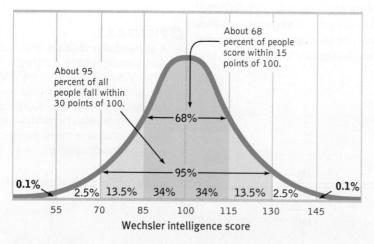

FIGURE 3.3
The normal curve Scores on aptitude tests tend to form a normal, or bell-shaped, curve. The most commonly used intelligence test, the Wechsler Adult Intelligence Scale, calls the average score 100.

Number of scores

About 95 percent of all people fall within 30 points of 100.

About 68 percent of people score within 15 points of 100.

68%

95%

0.1%   2.5%   13.5%   34%   34%   13.5%   2.5%   0.1%

55   70   85   100   115   130   145

Wechsler intelligence score

RETRIEVAL PRACTICE

RP-2 The average of a distribution of scores is the _____. The score that shows up most often is the _____. The score right in the middle of a distribution (half the scores above it; half below) is the _____. We determine how much scores vary around the average in a way that includes information about the _____ of scores (difference between highest and lowest) by using the _____ _____ formula.

ANSWERS IN APPENDIX E

[4]The actual standard deviation formula is: $\sqrt{\dfrac{\text{Sum of (deviations from mean)}^2}{\text{Number of scores} - 1}}$

Significant Differences

LOQ 3-2 How do we know whether an observed difference can be generalized to other populations?

Data are "noisy." The average score in one group (those who deactivated their Facebook account, in one experiment) could conceivably differ from the average score in another group (those who didn't) not because of any real difference, but merely because of chance fluctuations in the people sampled. How confidently, then, can we *infer* that an observed difference is not just a fluke—a chance result from the research sample? For guidance, we can ask how reliable and statistically significant the differences are. These *inferential statistics* help us determine if results can be generalized to a larger population (all those in a group being studied).

When Is an Observed Difference Reliable?

In deciding when it is safe to generalize from a sample, we should keep three principles in mind:

1. *Representative samples are better than biased (unrepresentative) samples.* The best basis for generalizing is not from the exceptional and memorable cases one finds at the extremes but from a representative sample of cases. Research never randomly samples the whole human population. Thus, it pays to keep in mind what population a study has sampled.

2. *Less-variable observations are more reliable than those that are more variable.* As we noted earlier in the example of the basketball player whose game-to-game points were consistent, an average is more reliable when it comes from scores with low variability.

3. *More cases are better than fewer.* An eager prospective student visits two universities, each for a day. At the first, the student randomly attends two classes and finds both instructors to be witty and engaging. At the second, the two sampled instructors seem dull and uninspiring. Returning home, the student (discounting the small sample size of only two teachers at each institution) tells friends about the "great teachers" at the first school and the "bores" at the second. Again, we know it but we ignore it: *Averages based on many cases are more reliable* (less variable) than averages based on only a few cases. After noticing that small schools were overrepresented among the most successful schools, several foundations invested in splitting larger schools into smaller ones—without realizing that small schools were also overrepresented among the *least* successful, because schools with fewer students have more variable outcomes (Nisbett, 2015). Again, more cases make for a more reliable average and a more replicable study.

The point to remember: Smart thinkers are not overly impressed by a few anecdotes. Generalizations based on a few unrepresentative cases are unreliable.

When Is an Observed Difference Significant?

Let's say you compared men's and women's scores on a laboratory test of aggression. You found that men behaved more aggressively than women. But individuals differ. How likely is it that your observed gender difference was just a fluke?

Researchers use statistical steps to answer this question. Statistical tests begin with the assumption that no differences exist between groups, an assumption called the *null hypothesis.* Using statistics we may conclude that the gender difference we observed is so large that it's unlikely to fit the null hypothesis. That's when we reject the null hypothesis of no differences, and we say that the result is **statistically significant.** Such a large difference would support an *alternative hypothesis*—that a difference (in aggression, for our example) does exist between the groups being studied (men and women).

How does the size of the difference between them—the *effect size*—determine statistical significance? First, when averages from two samples are each reliable measures of their respective populations (as when each is based on many observations that have

"The poor are getting poorer, but with the rich getting richer it all averages out in the long run."

range the difference between the highest and lowest scores in a distribution.

standard deviation a computed measure of how much scores vary around the mean score.

normal curve a symmetrical, bell-shaped curve that describes the distribution of many types of data; most scores fall near the mean (about 68 percent fall within one standard deviation of it) and fewer and fewer near the extremes. (Also called a *normal distribution.*)

statistical significance a statement of how likely it is that a result (such as a difference between samples) occurred by chance, assuming there is no difference between the populations being studied.

low variability), then any difference between the two samples is more likely to be statistically significant. (For our example: The less the variability in women's and in men's aggression scores, the more confidence we would have that our observed gender difference is real.) When the difference between the sample averages is *large* (as long as the samples are based on many observations), we also have more confidence that the difference between them reflects a real difference in their populations.

In short, when samples are large, and when the difference between them is relatively large, we say the difference has statistical significance. This means that the observed difference is probably more than just chance variation between the samples, and we can reject the null hypothesis of no existing differences.

In judging statistical significance, psychologists are conservative. They are like juries that must presume innocence until guilt is proven. Many psychological tests provide *p*-values, which indicate the probability of the null hypothesis given the sample data. For most psychologists, proof beyond a reasonable doubt means not making much of a finding unless the probability (*p*-value) of the null hypothesis is less than 5 percent ($p < .05$). Some researchers argue that statistical significance is overemphasized, noting that a "nonsignificant" result does *not* mean—as people often assume—a complete lack of difference between the groups (Amrhein et al., 2019). It only indicates greater uncertainty. For now, many psychologists continue to use $p < .05$, but stay tuned.

When learning about research, you should remember that, given large enough or homogeneous enough samples, a difference between them may be "statistically significant" yet have little *practical* significance. They might be statistically significant but have a small effect size. Comparisons of intelligence test scores among hundreds of thousands of first-born and later-born individuals indicate a highly significant tendency for first-born individuals to have higher average scores than their later-born siblings (Rohrer et al., 2015; Zajonc & Markus, 1975). But because the scores differ only slightly, the "significant" difference has a small effect size and little practical importance.

The point to remember: Statistical significance indicates the *likelihood* that a result would happen by chance if the null hypothesis (of no difference) were true. But this does not say anything about the *importance* of the result.

PEANUTS

Reprinted by permission of Andres McMeel Syndicate, Inc.

ASK YOURSELF

Can you think of a situation where you were fooled by a writer or speaker's attempts to persuade you with statistics? What have you learned in this module that will be most helpful in the future to avoid being misled?

RETRIEVAL PRACTICE

RP-3 Can you solve this puzzle?

The registrar's office at the University of Michigan has found that about 100 students in Arts and Sciences usually have perfect marks at the end of their first term. However, only about 10 to 15 students graduate with perfect marks. What do you think is the most likely explanation for the fact that there are more perfect marks after one term than at graduation (Jepson et al., 1983)?

RP-4 _____ statistics summarize data, while _____ statistics determine if data can be generalized to other populations.

ANSWERS IN APPENDIX E

📖 For a review, engage online with *Concept Practice: Statistical Significance.*

3 REVIEW Statistical Reasoning in Everyday Life

LEARNING OBJECTIVES

Test Yourself Answer these repeated Learning Objective Questions on your own (before checking the answers in Appendix D) to improve your retention of the concepts (McDaniel et al., 2009, 2015).

LOQ 3-1 How do we describe data using three measures of central tendency, and what is the relative usefulness of the two measures of variation?

LOQ 3-2 How do we know whether an observed difference can be generalized to other populations?

TERMS AND CONCEPTS TO REMEMBER

Test Yourself Write down the definition in your own words, then check your answer.

mode, p. 44

mean, p. 44

median, p. 44

range, p. 47

standard deviation, p. 47

normal curve, p. 47

statistical significance, p. 47

MASTER THE MATERIAL

Test Yourself Answer the following questions on your own first, then check your answers in Appendix E.

1. Which of the three measures of central tendency is most easily distorted by a few very high or very low scores?

   a. The mode

   b. The mean

   c. The median

   d. They are all equally vulnerable to distortion from atypical scores.

2. The standard deviation is the most useful measure of variation in a set of data because it tells us

   a. the difference between the highest and lowest scores in the set.

   b. the extent to which the sample being used deviates from the bigger population it represents.

   c. how much individual scores differ from the mode.

   d. how much individual scores differ from the mean.

3. Another name for a bell-shaped distribution, in which most scores fall near the middle and fewer scores fall at each extreme, is a _____ _____.

4. When sample averages are _____ and the difference between them is _____, we can say the difference is more likely to be statistically significant.

   a. reliable; large

   b. reliable; small

   c. due to chance; large

   d. due to chance; small

Continue testing yourself with 📖 **LearningCurve** or 📖 **Achieve Read & Practice** to learn and remember most effectively.

The Biology of Mind

Two transplant surgeons, Italy's Sergio Canavero and China's Xiaoping Ren, have built an international team for an audacious medical venture—a head transplant (Kean, 2016; Ren & Canavero, 2017; Ren et al., 2019). Wang Huanming, who is paralyzed from the neck down, volunteered to have his fully functioning head transferred to a brain-dead person's still-functioning body.

Ignore for the moment the ethical issues of such an experiment, which some have called "reckless and ghastly" and part of the scientists' "ghoulish fantasies" (Illes & McDonald, 2017; Wolpe, 2018). Ignore the procedure's cost, estimated at up to $100 million (Hjelmgaard, 2019). And ignore the seeming impossibility of precisely connecting the head-to-spinal-cord nerves. Imagine, just imagine, that the procedure could work. With the same brain and a new body, would Wang still be Wang? To whose home should he return? If the old Wang was a skilled musician, would the new Wang conceivably retain that skill—or would that depend on the muscle memories stored in the new body? And if he (assuming the new body was male) later had a child, whom should the birth certificate list as the father?

Most of us twenty-first-century people (you, too?) presume that, even with a new body, Wang would still be Wang. We presume that our brain, designed by our genes and sculpted by our experiences, provides our identity and enables our mind. No brain, no mind.

We are, indeed, living brains, but more. We are bodies alive. No principle is more central to today's psychology, or to this book, than this: *Everything psychological is simultaneously biological.* Your every idea, every mood, every urge is a biological happening. You love, laugh, and cry with your body. To think, feel, or act without a body would be like running without legs. Without your body—your genes, your nervous system, your hormones, your appearance—you truly would be nobody. Moreover, your body and your brain influence and are influenced by your experiences. Throughout this book, you will find many examples of the interplay between biology and psychology.

As you will also see throughout this book, we humans share the same basic biological design. Yet thanks to our individual genes, experiences, and cultural traditions and teachings, we differ from one another. Our traits and behaviors arise from the interaction of nature and nurture. Our thoughts, feelings, and actions influence our blood pressure, hormones, health—and our brain. As we wend our way from cradle to grave, our biology changes in response to our behaviors and environments.

In Modules 4 through 6, we explore the mind's biology. We start small and build from the bottom up—from nerve cells up to the brain. But we'll also discuss how our behavior and environment can influence our biology from the top down. Life changes us. You've heard it before and you'll hear it again: *Nurture works on what nature provides.*

4 Neural and Hormonal Systems

> **biological psychology** the scientific study of the links between biological (genetic, neural, hormonal) and psychological processes. Some biological psychologists call themselves *behavioral neuroscientists, neuropsychologists, behavior geneticists, physiological psychologists,* or *biopsychologists.*
>
> **neuroplasticity** the brain's ability to change, especially during childhood, by reorganizing after damage or by building new pathways based on experience.

Biology, Behavior, and Mind

LEARNING OBJECTIVE QUESTION **LOQ** **4-1** Why are psychologists concerned with human biology?

Our understanding of how the brain gives birth to the mind has come a long way. The ancient Greek physician, Hippocrates, correctly located the mind in the brain. His contemporary, the philosopher Aristotle, believed the mind was in the heart, which pumps warmth and vitality to the body. The heart remains our symbol for love, but science has long since overtaken philosophy on this issue: It's your brain, not your heart, that falls in love.

In the early 1800s, German physician Franz Gall proposed that *phrenology*, studying bumps on the skull, could reveal a person's mental abilities and character traits (**FIGURE 4.1**). At one point, Britain had 29 phrenological societies, and phrenologists traveled North America giving skull readings (Dean, 2012; Hunt, 1993). Using a false name, humorist Mark Twain put one famous phrenologist to the test. "He found a cavity [and] startled me by saying that that cavity represented the total absence of the sense of humor!" Three months later, Twain sat for a second reading, this time identifying himself. Now "the cavity was gone, and in its place was . . . the loftiest bump of humor he had ever encountered in his life-long experience!" (Lopez, 2002). The "science" of phrenology remains known today as a reminder of our need for critical thinking and scientific analysis. Phrenology did at least succeed in focusing attention on the *localization of function*—the idea that various brain regions have particular functions.

Today, we are living in a time Gall could only dream about. **Biological psychologists** use advanced technologies to study the links between biological (genetic, neural, hormonal) processes and psychological processes. They and other researchers working from a biological perspective are announcing discoveries about the interplay of our biology and our behavior and mind at an exhilarating pace. Within little more than the past century, researchers seeking to understand the biology of the mind have discovered that

- our adaptive brain is wired by our experiences.
- among the body's cells are nerve cells that conduct electricity and "talk" to one another by sending chemical messages across a tiny gap that separates them.
- specific brain systems serve specific functions (though not the functions Gall supposed).
- we integrate information processed in these different brain systems to construct our experience of sights and sounds, meanings and memories, pain and passion.

"You're certainly a lot less fun since the operation."

Gahan Wilson/Cartoon Stock

(a)   (b)

⊙ FIGURE 4.1

A wrongheaded theory (a) Despite initial acceptance of Franz Gall's speculations, bumps on the skull tell us nothing about the brain's underlying functions. Nevertheless, some of his assumptions have held true. Though they are not the functions Gall proposed, different parts of the brain do control different aspects of behavior, as suggested in (b) (from *The Human Brain Book*).

We have also realized that we are each a system composed of subsystems that are in turn composed of even smaller subsystems. Tiny cells organize to form body organs. These organs form larger systems for digestion, circulation, and information processing. And those systems are part of an even larger system—the individual, who in turn is a part of a family, community, and culture. Thus, we are *biopsychosocial* systems. To understand our behavior, we need to study how these biological, psychological, and social-cultural systems work and interact. Let's begin with the brain's ability to rewire itself as it adapts to experience.

RETRIEVAL PRACTICE

RP-1 What do phrenology and biological psychology have in common?

ANSWERS IN APPENDIX E

The Power of Plasticity

LOQ 4-2 How do biology and experience together enable neuroplasticity?

Your brain is sculpted not only by your genes but also by your life. Under the surface of your awareness, your brain is constantly changing, building new pathways as it adjusts to new experiences. This neural change is called **neuroplasticity.** Although neuroplasticity is greatest in childhood, it continues throughout life (Gutchess, 2014).

To see neuroplasticity at work, consider London's taxi driver trainees. They spend years learning and remembering the city's 25,000 street locations and connections. For the half who pass the difficult final test, big rewards are in store: not only a better income but also an enlarged hippocampus, one of the brain's memory centers that processes spatial memories. London's bus drivers, who navigate a smaller set of roads, gain no similar neural rewards (Maguire et al., 2000, 2006; Woollett & Maguire, 2012).

We also see neuroplasticity in well-practiced pianists, who have a larger-than-usual auditory cortex area, a sound-processing region (Bavelier et al., 2000; Pantev et al., 1998). Practice likewise sculpts the brains of ballerinas, jugglers, and unicyclists (Draganski et al., 2004; Hänggi et al., 2010; Weber et al., 2019).

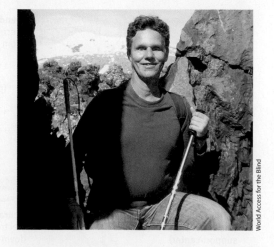

The mind's eye Daniel Kish, who is completely blind, enjoys going for walks in the woods. To stay safe, he uses echolocation—the same navigation method used by bats and dolphins. Blind echolocation experts such as Kish engage the brain's visual centers to navigate their surroundings (Thaler et al., 2011, 2014). Although Kish is blind, his flexible brain helps him "see."

Marian Diamond (1926–2017) This ground-breaking neuroscientist's research fundamentally changed how we understand the brain. She pioneered the exploration of how experience changes the brain. Diamond also analyzed Albert Einstein's brain after his death, which helped unlock the neural mechanics of his mind.

Your brain is a work in progress. The brain you were born with is not the brain you will die with. Even limited practice times may produce neural benefits. If you spend six weeks training your sense of smell, as did participants in one study, you may grow your smell-related brain areas (Al Aïn et al., 2019). Just an hour of learning produces subtle brain changes (Brodt et al., 2018). Remember that the next time you attend class!

Neuroplasticity is part of what makes the human brain exceptional (Gómez-Robles et al., 2015). Think of how much the world has changed over the past 50 years, and how much more it will change in the next 50. More than for any other species, our neuroplasticity enables us to adapt to our rapidly changing world (Roberts & Stewart, 2018).

RETRIEVAL PRACTICE

RP-2 How does learning a new skill affect the structure of our brain?

ANSWERS IN APPENDIX E

Neural Communication

For scientists, it is a happy fact of nature that the information systems of humans and other animals operate similarly—so much so that you could not distinguish between small samples of brain tissue from a human and a monkey. This similarity allows researchers to study much simpler animals, such as squids and sea slugs, to discover how our neural systems operate. It allows them to study other mammals' brains to understand the organization of our own. Cars differ, but all have accelerators, steering wheels, and brakes. A space alien could study any one of them and grasp the operating principles. Likewise, animals differ, yet their nervous systems operate similarly.

Neurons

LOQ **4-3** What are *neurons,* and how do they transmit information?

Our body's neural information system is complexity built from simplicity. Its building blocks are **neurons,** or nerve cells. Throughout life, new neurons are born and unused neurons wither away (O'Leary et al., 2014; Shors, 2014). To fathom our thoughts and actions, our memories and moods, we must first understand how neurons work and communicate.

Neurons differ, but all are variations on the same theme (**FIGURE 4.2**). Each consists of a **cell body** and its branching fibers. The often bushy **dendrite** fibers receive and integrate information, conducting it toward the cell body (Stuart & Spruston, 2015). From there, the cell's single lengthy **axon** fiber passes the message through its terminal branches to other neurons or to muscles or glands (**FIGURE 4.3**). Dendrites listen. Axons speak.

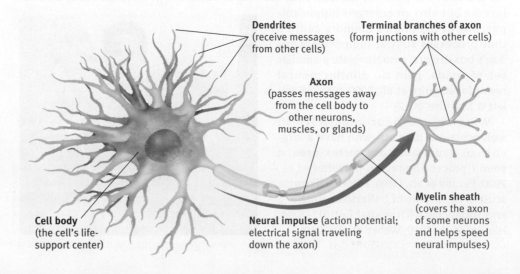

Dendrites (receive messages from other cells)

Terminal branches of axon (form junctions with other cells)

Axon (passes messages away from the cell body to other neurons, muscles, or glands)

Cell body (the cell's life-support center)

Neural impulse (action potential; electrical signal traveling down the axon)

Myelin sheath (covers the axon of some neurons and helps speed neural impulses)

→ **FIGURE 4.2**
A motor neuron

David Scharf/Science Source

⊘ FIGURE 4.3
Neurons communicating Our billions of neurons exist in a vast and densely interconnected web. One neuron's terminal branches send messages to neighboring dendrites. Read on to learn more about this complex and fascinating electrochemical communication process.

John Shearer/Getty Images

Managing multiple sclerosis Actor Selma Blair's multiple sclerosis results from a loss of the myelin sheath that insulates her motor axons and speeds their neural impulses. She has openly discussed her challenges, including difficulty speaking and walking. In 2018, Blair attended a Hollywood event walking with a cane.

Unlike the short dendrites, axons may be very long, projecting several feet through the body. A human neuron carrying orders to a leg muscle, for example, has a cell body and axon roughly on the scale of a basketball attached to a rope that's 4 miles (6.4 kilometers) long. Much as home electrical wire is insulated, some axons are encased in a **myelin sheath,** a layer of fatty tissue that insulates them and speeds their impulses. As myelin is laid down up to about age 25, neural efficiency, judgment, and self-control grow (Fields, 2008; Nakamura et al., 2018; Van Munster et al., 2015). If the myelin sheath degenerates, *multiple sclerosis* results: Communication to muscles and brain regions slows, with diminished muscle control and sometimes impaired cognition.

Supporting these billions of nerve cells are spidery **glial cells** ("glue cells"). Neurons are like queen bees; on their own they cannot feed or sheathe themselves. Glial cells are worker bees. They provide nutrients and insulating myelin, guide neural connections, and mop up *ions* and *neurotransmitters*. Glia also play a role in learning, thinking, and memory. By "chatting" with neurons, they participate in information transmission and memory (Fields, 2011, 2013; Martín et al., 2015).

In more complex animal brains, the proportion of glia to neurons increases. A postmortem analysis of Albert Einstein's brain did not find more or larger-than-usual neurons, but it did reveal a much greater concentration of glial cells than found in an average person's head (Fields, 2004). Einstein's glial cells kept his brain abuzz with activity.

The Neural Impulse

Neurons transmit messages when stimulated by our senses or by neighboring neurons. A neuron sends a message by firing an impulse, called the **action potential**—a brief electrical charge that travels down its axon.

Depending on the type of fiber, a neural impulse travels at speeds ranging from a sluggish 2 miles (3 kilometers) per hour to more than 200 miles (320 kilometers) per hour. But even its top speed is 3 million times slower than that of electricity through a wire. We measure brain activity in milliseconds (thousandths of a second) and computer activity in nanoseconds (billionths of a second). Thus, unlike the nearly instantaneous reactions of a computer, your reaction to a sudden event, such as a child darting in front of your car, may take a quarter-second or more. Your brain is vastly more complex than a computer, but slower at executing simple responses. And if you were an elephant—whose round-trip message travel time from a yank on the tail to the brain and back to the tail is 100 times longer than that of a tiny shrew—your reflexes would be slower yet (More et al., 2010).

Like batteries, neurons generate electricity from chemical events. In the neuron's chemistry-to-electricity process, *ions* (electrically charged atoms) are exchanged. The fluid outside an axon's membrane has mostly positively charged sodium ions. A resting axon's fluid interior (which includes both large, negatively charged protein ions and smaller, positively charged potassium ions) has a mostly negative charge. Like a tightly guarded facility, the axon's surface is selective about what it allows through its gates. We say the axon's surface is *selectively permeable*. This positive-outside/negative-inside state is called the *resting potential*.

When a neuron fires, however, the security parameters change: The first section of the axon opens its gates, rather like a storm sewer cover flipping open, and positively charged sodium ions (attracted to the negative interior) flood in through the now-open channels (**FIGURE 4.4**). The loss of the inside/outside charge difference, called

"I sing the body electric." — Walt Whitman, "Children of Adam," 1855

neuron a nerve cell; the basic building block of the nervous system.

cell body the part of a neuron that contains the nucleus; the cell's life-support center.

dendrites a neuron's often bushy, branching extensions that receive and integrate messages, conducting impulses toward the cell body.

axon the segmented neuron extension that passes messages through its branches to other neurons or to muscles or glands.

myelin [MY-uh-lin] **sheath** a fatty tissue layer segmentally encasing the axons of some neurons; enables vastly greater transmission speed as neural impulses hop from one node to the next.

glial cells (glia) cells in the nervous system that support, nourish, and protect neurons; they also play a role in learning, thinking, and memory.

action potential a neural impulse; a brief electrical charge that travels down an axon.

2. This initial depolarization influences the electrical charge of the next portion of the axon. Gates in this neighboring area now open, allowing positively charged sodium ions to flow in and depolarize that area. Meanwhile, other gates open in the first part of the axon, allowing potassium ions to flow out, repolarizing this section.

Sodium ions (Na+)

1. Neuron stimulation causes a brief change in electrical charge. If strong enough, this opens gates to allow positively charged sodium ions to flood in, producing a momentary depolarization called the action potential.

Potassium (K+)

Na+

3. As the action potential moves speedily down the axon, sodium/potassium pumps in the cell membrane finish restoring the first section of the axon to its resting potential.

K+ Na+

Direction of action potential: toward axon terminals

⑦ FIGURE 4.4

Action potential Bodily sensations and actions—detecting a hug or kicking a soccer ball—happen when our neurons are stimulated enough that their membrane's electrical charge reaches a threshold (–55 mV in this example—see graph). This prompts each of those neurons to "fire" an impulse—an action potential—which travels down its axon (see numbered drawings) and transmits a message to other neurons, muscles, or glands.

depolarization, causes the next section of axon channels to open, and then the next, like falling dominos. This temporary inflow of positive ions is the neural impulse—the action potential. Each neuron is itself a miniature decision-making device performing complex calculations as it receives signals from hundreds, even thousands, of other neurons. The mind boggles when imagining this electrochemical process repeating up to 100 or even 1000 times a second. But this is just the first of many astonishments.

Most neural signals are *excitatory*, somewhat like pushing a neuron's accelerator. Some are *inhibitory*, more like pushing its brake. If excitatory signals exceed the inhibitory signals by a minimum intensity, or **threshold** (see Figure 4.4), the combined signals trigger an action potential. (Think of it this way: If the excitatory party animals outvote the inhibitory party poopers, the party's on.) The action potential then travels down the axon, which branches into junctions with hundreds or thousands of other neurons or with the body's muscles and glands.

Neurons need short breaks (a tiny fraction of an eyeblink). During a resting pause called the **refractory period,** subsequent action potentials cannot occur until the axon returns to its resting state. Then the neuron can fire again.

Increasing the level of stimulation above the threshold will not increase the neural impulse's intensity. The neuron's reaction is an **all-or-none response:** Like guns, neurons either fire or they don't. How, then, do we detect the intensity of a stimulus? How do we distinguish a gentle touch from a big hug? A strong stimulus can trigger *more* neurons to fire, and to fire more often. But it does not affect the action potential's strength or speed. Squeezing a trigger harder won't make a bullet go faster.

"What one neuron tells another neuron is simply how much it is excited." — *Francis Crick, The Astonishing Hypothesis,* 1994

ASK YOURSELF

Does it surprise you to learn that despite your brain's complexity, your reaction time is slower than a computer's? Does this suggest which tasks might be more readily performed by computers than by humans?

RP-3 When a neuron fires an action potential, the information travels through the axon, the dendrites, and the cell body, but not in that order. Place these three structures in the correct order.

RP-4 How does our nervous system allow us to experience the difference between a slap and a tap on the back?

ANSWERS IN APPENDIX E

> For an interactive, animated explanation of this process, engage online with *Concept Practice: Action Potentials.*

How Neurons Communicate

LOQ **4-4** How do nerve cells communicate with other nerve cells?

Neurons interweave so intricately that even with a microscope, you would struggle to see where one neuron ends and another begins. Scientists once believed that the axon of one cell fused with the dendrites of another in an uninterrupted fabric. Then British physiologist Sir Charles Sherrington (1857–1952) noticed that neural impulses were taking an unexpectedly long time to travel a neural pathway. Inferring that there must be a brief interruption in the transmission, Sherrington called the meeting point between neurons a **synapse.**

We now know that the axon terminal of one neuron is in fact separated from the receiving neuron by a tiny—less than a millionth of an inch wide—*synaptic gap* (or *synaptic cleft*). Spanish anatomist Santiago Ramón y Cajal (1852–1934) marveled at these near-unions of neurons, calling them "protoplasmic kisses." "Like elegant ladies air-kissing so as not to muss their makeup, dendrites and axons don't quite touch," noted poet Diane Ackerman (2004, p. 37). How do the neurons execute this protoplasmic kiss, sending information across the synaptic gap? The answer is one of the important scientific discoveries of our age.

When an action potential reaches the button-like terminals at an axon's end, it triggers the release of chemical messengers, called **neurotransmitters** (FIGURE 4.5).

threshold the level of stimulation required to trigger a neural impulse.

refractory period in neural processing, a brief resting pause that occurs after a neuron has fired; subsequent action potentials cannot occur until the axon returns to its resting state.

all-or-none response a neuron's reaction of either firing (with a full-strength response) or not firing.

synapse [SIN-aps] the junction between the axon tip of the sending neuron and the dendrite or cell body of the receiving neuron. The tiny gap at this junction is called the *synaptic gap* (or *synaptic cleft*).

neurotransmitters chemical messengers that cross the synaptic gap between neurons. When released by the sending neuron, neurotransmitters travel across the synapse and bind to receptor sites on the receiving neuron, thereby influencing whether that neuron will generate a neural impulse.

> "All information processing in the brain involves neurons 'talking to' each other at synapses." —Neuroscientist Solomon H. Snyder (1984)

**FIGURE 4.5
How neurons communicate**

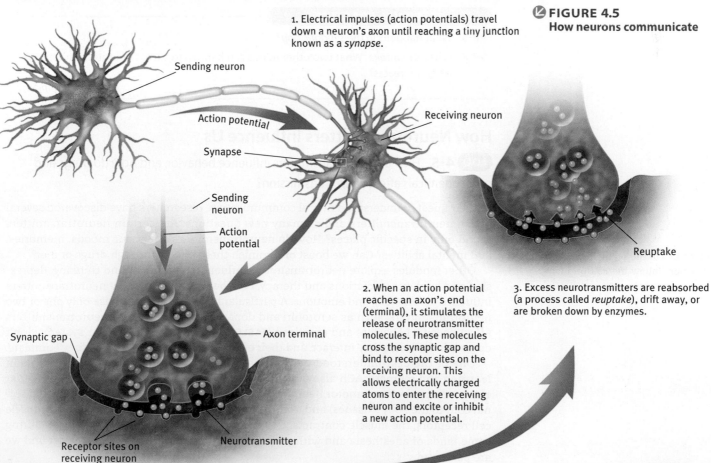

1. Electrical impulses (action potentials) travel down a neuron's axon until reaching a tiny junction known as a *synapse*.

Sending neuron

Action potential

Receiving neuron

Synapse

Sending neuron

Action potential

Axon terminal

Reuptake

Synaptic gap

Receptor sites on receiving neuron

Neurotransmitter

2. When an action potential reaches an axon's end (terminal), it stimulates the release of neurotransmitter molecules. These molecules cross the synaptic gap and bind to receptor sites on the receiving neuron. This allows electrically charged atoms to enter the receiving neuron and excite or inhibit a new action potential.

3. Excess neurotransmitters are reabsorbed (a process called *reuptake*), drift away, or are broken down by enzymes.

Message is sent across synaptic gap.

Message is received; excess serotonin molecules are reabsorbed by sending neuron.

Prozac partially blocks normal reuptake of the neurotransmitter serotonin; excess serotonin in synapse enhances its mood-lifting effect.

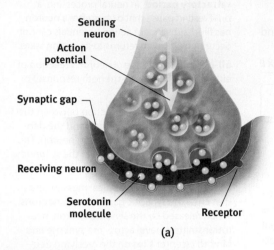

Sending neuron
Action potential
Synaptic gap
Receiving neuron
Serotonin molecule
Receptor

(a)

Reuptake

(b)

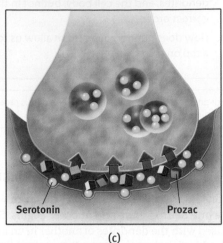

Reuptake
Serotonin
Prozac

(c)

⑦ FIGURE 4.6
Biology of antidepressants Selective serotonin reuptake inhibitors (SSRIs) are popularly prescribed antidepressants. They are designed to relieve depression by partially blocking the reuptake of the neurotransmitter serotonin. Shown here is the action of the SSRI Prozac.

Within 1/10,000th of a second, the neurotransmitter molecules cross the synaptic gap and bind to receptor sites on the receiving neuron—as precisely as a key fits a lock. For an instant, the neurotransmitter unlocks tiny channels at the receiving site, and electrically charged atoms flow in, exciting or inhibiting the receiving neuron's readiness to fire. The excess neurotransmitters finally drift away, are broken down by enzymes, or are reabsorbed by the sending neuron—a process called **reuptake.** Some antidepressant medications partially block the reuptake of mood-enhancing neurotransmitters (**FIGURE 4.6**).

> **ASK YOURSELF**
>
> Why was the discovery of neurons' communication mechanism so important?

> **RETRIEVAL PRACTICE**
>
> **RP-5** What happens in the *synaptic gap*?
>
> **RP-6** What is *reuptake*? What two other things can happen to excess neurotransmitters after a neuron reacts?

ANSWERS IN APPENDIX E

How Neurotransmitters Influence Us

LOQ 4-5 How do neurotransmitters influence behavior, and how do drugs and other chemicals affect neurotransmission?

In their quest to understand neural communication, researchers have discovered several dozen neurotransmitters and as many new questions: Are certain neurotransmitters found only in specific places? How do neurotransmitters affect our moods, memories, and mental abilities? Can we boost or diminish these effects through drugs or diet?

Other modules explore neurotransmitter influences on hunger and thinking, depression and euphoria, addictions and therapy. For now, let's glimpse how neurotransmitters influence our motions and emotions. A particular brain pathway may use only one or two neurotransmitters, such as serotonin and dopamine, and particular neurotransmitters affect specific behaviors and emotions (**TABLE 4.1**). But neurotransmitter systems don't operate in isolation; they interact, and their effects vary with the receptors they stimulate.

One of the best-understood neurotransmitters, *acetylcholine* (ACh), plays a role in learning and memory. ACh also enables muscle action, by acting as the messenger at every junction between motor neurons (which carry information from the brain and spinal cord to the body's tissues) and skeletal muscles. When ACh is released to our muscle cell receptors, the muscle contracts. If ACh transmission is blocked, as happens during some kinds of anesthesia and with some poisons, the muscles cannot contract and we are paralyzed.

"When it comes to the brain, if you want to see the action, follow the neurotransmitters." — Neuroscientist Floyd Bloom (1993)

TABLE 4.1 Commonly Studied Neurotransmitters and Their Functions

Neurotransmitter	Function	Examples of Malfunctions
Acetylcholine (ACh)	Enables muscle action, learning, and memory	With Alzheimer's disease, ACh-producing neurons deteriorate.
Dopamine	Influences movement, learning, attention, and emotion	Oversupply linked to schizophrenia. Undersupply linked to tremors and decreased mobility in Parkinson's disease.
Serotonin	Affects mood, hunger, sleep, and arousal	Undersupply linked to depression. Some drugs that raise serotonin levels are used to treat depression.
Norepinephrine	Helps control alertness and arousal	Undersupply can depress mood.
GABA (gamma-aminobutyric acid)	A major inhibitory neurotransmitter	Undersupply linked to seizures, tremors, and insomnia.
Glutamate	A major excitatory neurotransmitter; involved in memory	Oversupply can overstimulate the brain, producing migraines or seizures.
Endorphins	Neurotransmitters that influence the perception of pain or pleasure	Oversupply with opiate drugs can suppress the body's natural endorphin supply.

Noam Galai/Getty Images

ASSOCIATED PRESS

Dependent upon dopamine The neurotransmitter dopamine helps us move, think, and feel. Too little dopamine may produce the tremors and loss of motor control of Parkinson's disease (NIA, 2019; Weinstein et al., 2018). More than 10 million people worldwide have Parkinson's disease, including actor Michael J. Fox and the late boxing legend Muhammad Ali (Parkinson's Foundation, 2018).

Candace Pert and Solomon Snyder (1973) made an exciting discovery about neurotransmitters when they attached a harmless radioactive tracer to morphine, an opiate drug that elevates mood and eases pain. As the researchers tracked the morphine in an animal's brain, they noticed it was binding to receptors in areas linked with mood and pain sensations. But why would the brain have these "opiate receptors"? Why would it have a chemical lock, unless it also had a key—a natural painkiller—to open it?

Researchers soon confirmed that the brain does indeed produce its own naturally occurring opiates. Our body releases several types of neurotransmitter molecules similar to morphine in response to pain and vigorous exercise. These **endorphins** (short for *endo*genous [produced within] m*orphine*) help explain good feelings such as the "runner's high," the painkilling effects of acupuncture, and the indifference to pain in some severely injured people (Boecker et al., 2008; Fuss et al., 2015). But once again, new knowledge led to new questions.

Physician Lewis Thomas, on the endorphins: "There it is, a biologically universal act of mercy. I cannot explain it, except to say that I would have put it in had I been around at the very beginning, sitting as a member of a planning committee." — *The Youngest Science*, 1983

ASK YOURSELF

Can you recall a time, perhaps after a workout, when you felt the effects of endorphins? How would you describe those feelings?

RETRIEVAL PRACTICE

RP-7 Serotonin, dopamine, and endorphins are all chemical messengers called _____.

ANSWERS IN APPENDIX E

HOW DRUGS AND OTHER CHEMICALS ALTER NEUROTRANSMISSION If natural endorphins lessen pain and boost mood, why not increase this effect by flooding the brain with artificial opiates, thereby intensifying the brain's own "feel-good" chemistry? Because it would disrupt the brain's chemical balancing act. When flooded with opiate drugs such as heroin, morphine, and fentanyl (a powerful synthetic opioid), the brain—to maintain its chemical balance—may stop producing its own natural opiates. When the drug is withdrawn, the brain may then be deprived of *any* form of opiate, causing intense discomfort. For suppressing the body's own neurotransmitter production, nature charges a price.

Drugs and other chemicals affect brain chemistry, often by either exciting or inhibiting neurons' firing. **Agonist** molecules *increase* a neurotransmitter's action. Some agonists may increase the production or release of neurotransmitters, or block reuptake in the synapse. Other agonists may be similar enough to a neurotransmitter to bind to its receptor

reuptake a neurotransmitter's reabsorption by the sending neuron.

endorphins [en-DOR-fins] "morphine within"—natural, opiate-like neurotransmitters linked to pain control and to pleasure.

agonist a molecule that increases a neurotransmitter's action.

and mimic its excitatory or inhibitory effects. Some opiate drugs, then, are agonists and produce a temporary "high" by amplifying normal sensations of arousal or pleasure.

Antagonists *decrease* a neurotransmitter's action by blocking production or release. Botulin, a poison that can form in improperly canned food, causes paralysis by blocking ACh release. (Small injections of botulin—Botox—smooth wrinkles by paralyzing the underlying facial muscles.) These antagonists are enough like the natural neurotransmitter to occupy its receptor site and block its effect, but are not similar enough to stimulate the receptor (rather like foreign coins that fit into, but won't operate, a vending machine). Curare, a poison some South American Indigenous people have applied to hunting-dart tips, occupies and blocks ACh receptor sites on muscles, producing paralysis in their prey.

⊠ For an illustrated review of neural communication, visit *Topic Tutorial: PsychSim6, Neural Messages.*

RETRIEVAL PRACTICE

RP-8 Curare poisoning paralyzes animals by blocking ACh receptors involved in muscle movement. Morphine mimics endorphin actions. Which is an agonist, and which is an antagonist?

ANSWERS IN APPENDIX E

The Nervous System

LOQ 4-6 What are the functions of the nervous system's main divisions, and what are the three main types of neurons?

Neurons communicating via neurotransmitters make up our body's **nervous system,** a communication network that takes in information from the world and the body's tissues, makes decisions, and sends back information and orders to the body's tissues (**FIGURE 4.7**).

A quick overview: The brain and spinal cord form the **central nervous system (CNS),** the body's decision maker. The **peripheral nervous system (PNS)** is responsible for gathering information and for transmitting CNS decisions to other body parts. **Nerves,** electrical cables formed from bundles of axons, link the CNS with the body's sensory receptors, muscles, and glands. The optic nerve, for example, bundles a million axons into a single cable carrying the messages from the eye to the brain (Mason & Kandel, 1991).

Information travels in the nervous system through three types of neurons. **Sensory neurons** carry messages from the body's tissues and sensory receptors inward (thus, they are *afferent*) to the brain and spinal cord for processing. **Motor neurons** (which are *efferent*) carry

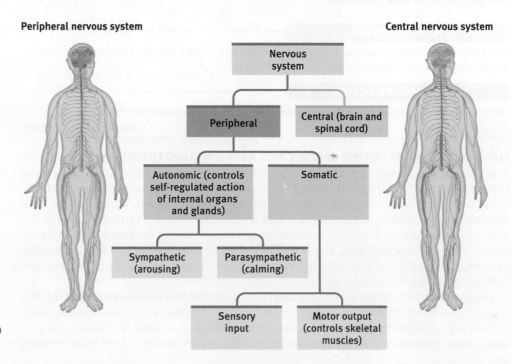

Peripheral nervous system   **Central nervous system**

Nervous system

Peripheral — Central (brain and spinal cord)

Autonomic (controls self-regulated action of internal organs and glands) — Somatic

Sympathetic (arousing) — Parasympathetic (calming)

Sensory input — Motor output (controls skeletal muscles)

⊜ **FIGURE 4.7**
The functional divisions of the human nervous system

instructions from the central nervous system outward to the body's muscles and glands. Between the sensory input and motor output, information is processed via **interneurons.** Our complexity resides mostly in these interneurons. Our nervous system has a few million sensory neurons, a few million motor neurons, and billions and billions of interneurons.

The Peripheral Nervous System

Our peripheral nervous system has two components—somatic and autonomic. Our **somatic nervous system** enables voluntary control of our skeletal muscles. As your friend taps your shoulder, your somatic nervous system reports to your brain the current state of your skeletal muscles and carries instructions back, triggering your head to turn toward her.

Our **autonomic nervous system (ANS)** controls our glands and our internal organ muscles. The ANS influences functions such as glandular activity, heartbeat, and digestion. (*Autonomic* means "self-regulating.") Like a self-driving car, this system may be consciously overridden, but usually operates on its own (autonomously).

The autonomic nervous system's subdivisions serve two important functions (**FIGURE 4.8**). The **sympathetic nervous system** arouses and expends energy. If something alarms or challenges you, such as a longed-for job interview, your sympathetic nervous system will accelerate your heartbeat, raise your blood pressure, slow your digestion, raise your blood sugar, and cool you with perspiration, making you alert and ready for action. When the stress subsides once the interview is over, your **parasympathetic nervous system** will produce the opposite effects, conserving energy as it calms you. The sympathetic and parasympathetic nervous systems work together, as accelerator and brake, to keep us in a steady internal state called *homeostasis*.

antagonist a molecule that inhibits or blocks a neurotransmitter's action.

nervous system the body's speedy, electrochemical communication network, consisting of all the nerve cells of the peripheral and central nervous systems.

central nervous system (CNS) the brain and spinal cord.

peripheral nervous system (PNS) the sensory and motor neurons that connect the central nervous system (CNS) to the rest of the body.

nerves bundled axons that form neural cables connecting the central nervous system with muscles, glands, and sensory organs.

sensory (afferent) neurons neurons that carry incoming information from the body's tissues and sensory receptors to the brain and spinal cord.

motor (efferent) neurons neurons that carry outgoing information from the brain and spinal cord to the muscles and glands.

interneurons neurons within the brain and spinal cord; they communicate internally and process information between the sensory inputs and motor outputs.

somatic nervous system the division of the peripheral nervous system that controls the body's skeletal muscles. Also called the *skeletal nervous system*.

autonomic [aw-tuh-NAHM-ik] **nervous system (ANS)** the part of the peripheral nervous system that controls the glands and the muscles of the internal organs (such as the heart). Its *sympathetic* division arouses; its *parasympathetic* division calms.

sympathetic nervous system the division of the autonomic nervous system that arouses the body, mobilizing its energy.

parasympathetic nervous system the division of the autonomic nervous system that calms the body, conserving its energy.

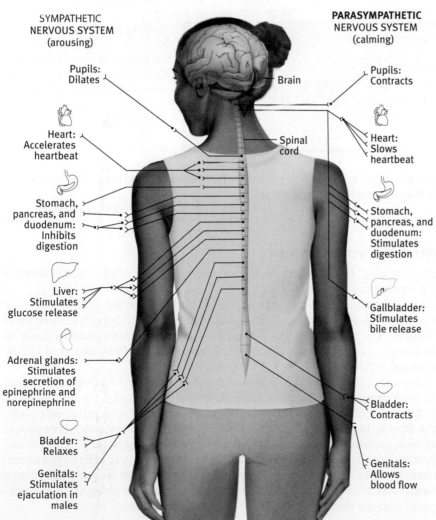

SYMPATHETIC
NERVOUS SYSTEM
(arousing)

PARASYMPATHETIC
NERVOUS SYSTEM
(calming)

Pupils:
Dilates

Brain

Pupils:
Contracts

Heart:
Accelerates
heartbeat

Spinal
cord

Heart:
Slows
heartbeat

Stomach,
pancreas, and
duodenum:
Inhibits
digestion

Stomach,
pancreas, and
duodenum:
Stimulates
digestion

Liver:
Stimulates
glucose release

Gallbladder:
Stimulates
bile release

Adrenal glands:
Stimulates
secretion of
epinephrine and
norepinephrine

Bladder:
Contracts

Bladder:
Relaxes

Genitals:
Stimulates
ejaculation in
males

Genitals:
Allows
blood flow

FIGURE 4.8
The dual functions of the autonomic nervous system The autonomic nervous system controls the more autonomous (or self-regulating) internal functions. Its sympathetic division arouses the body and expends energy. Its parasympathetic division calms the body and conserves energy, allowing routine maintenance activity. For example, sympathetic stimulation accelerates heartbeat, whereas parasympathetic stimulation slows it.

I [DM] recently experienced my ANS in action. Before sending me into an MRI machine for a shoulder scan, the technician asked if I had issues with claustrophobia. "No, I'm fine," I assured her, with perhaps a hint of macho swagger. Moments later, as I found myself on my back, stuck deep inside a coffin-sized box and unable to move, my sympathetic nervous system had a different idea. Claustrophobia overtook me. My heart began pounding, and I felt a desperate urge to escape. Just as I was about to cry out for release, I felt my calming parasympathetic nervous system kick in. My heart rate slowed and my body relaxed, though my arousal surged again before the 20-minute confinement ended. "You did well!" the technician said, unaware of my ANS roller-coaster ride.

ASK YOURSELF

Think back to a stressful moment when you felt your sympathetic nervous system kick in. What was your body preparing you for? Were you able to sense your parasympathetic nervous system's response when the challenge had passed?

RETRIEVAL PRACTICE

RP-9 Match the type of neuron (i–iii) to its description (a–c).

Type	Description
i. Motor neurons	**a.** Carry incoming messages from sensory receptors to the CNS.
ii. Sensory neurons	**b.** Communicate within the CNS and process information between incoming and outgoing messages.
iii. Interneurons	**c.** Carry outgoing messages from the CNS to muscles and glands.

Ballistic stress In 2018, Hawaiians received this terrifying alert, amid concerns about North Korean nuclear warheads. "We fully felt we were about to die," reported one panicked mother (Nagourney et al., 2018). Thirty-eight minutes later, the alert was declared a false alarm.

RP-10 How was the ANS involved in Hawaiians' terrified responses, and in calming their bodies once they realized it was a false alarm?

ANSWERS IN APPENDIX E

The Central Nervous System

From neurons "talking" to other neurons arises the complexity of the central nervous system's brain and spinal cord.

It is the brain that enables our humanity—our thinking, feeling, and acting. Tens of billions of neurons, each communicating with thousands of other neurons, yield an ever-changing wiring web. By one estimate—projecting from neuron counts in small brain samples—our brain has some 86 billion neurons (Azevedo et al., 2009; Herculano-Houzel, 2012).

Just as individual pixels combine to form a picture, the brain's individual neurons cluster into work groups called *neural networks*. To understand why, Stephen Kosslyn and Olivier Koenig (1992, p. 12) have invited us to "think about why cities exist; why don't people distribute themselves more evenly across the countryside?" Like people networking with people, neurons network with nearby neurons with which they can have short, fast connections; each layer's cells connect with various cells in the neural network's next layer. Learning—to play the violin, speak a foreign language, or solve a math problem—occurs as experience strengthens connections. To paraphrase one neuropsychologist, neurons that fire together wire together (Hebb, 1949).

"The body is made up of millions and millions of crumbs."

© Tom Swick/Cartoonstock.com

1. In this simple hand-withdrawal reflex, information is carried from skin receptors along a sensory neuron (shown by the large red arrow) to the spinal cord. From there it is passed via interneurons to motor neurons (blue arrow) that lead to the muscles in the hand and arm.

Sensory neuron
(incoming information)

Brain

◀ FIGURE 4.9
A simple reflex

Interneuron

Muscle

Spinal cord

Skin receptors

Motor neuron
(outgoing information)

2. Because this reflex involves only the spinal cord, the hand jerks away from the candle flame even before information about the event has reached the brain, where pain is experienced.

The other part of the CNS, the *spinal cord*, is a two-way information highway connecting the peripheral nervous system and the brain. Ascending neural fibers send up sensory information, and descending fibers send back motor-control information. The neural pathways governing our **reflexes,** our automatic responses to stimuli, illustrate the spinal cord's work. A simple spinal reflex pathway is composed of a single sensory neuron and a single motor neuron. These often communicate through an interneuron. The knee-jerk reflex, for example, involves one such simple pathway. A headless warm body could do it.

Another neural circuit enables the pain reflex (**FIGURE 4.9**). When your finger touches a flame, neural activity (excited by the heat) travels via sensory neurons to interneurons in your spinal cord. These interneurons respond by activating motor neurons leading to the muscles in your arm. Because the simple pain-reflex pathway runs through the spinal cord and right back out, your hand jerks away from the candle's flame *before* your brain receives and responds to the information that causes you to feel pain. That's why it feels as if your hand jerks away not by your choice, but on its own.

Information travels to and from the brain by way of the spinal cord. Were the top of your spinal cord severed, you would not feel pain from your paralyzed body below. Nor would you feel pleasure. With your brain literally out of touch with your body, you would lose all sensation and voluntary movement in body regions with sensory and motor connections to the spinal cord below its point of injury. You would exhibit the knee-jerk reflex without feeling the tap. Men paralyzed below the waist may be capable of an erection (a simple reflex) if their genitals are stimulated (Gomes et al., 2017; Hess & Hough, 2012). Women who are similarly paralyzed may respond with vaginal lubrication. But, depending on where and how completely their spinal cord is severed, they may be genitally unresponsive to erotic images and have no genital feelings (Kennedy & Over, 1990; Sipski et al., 1999). To produce bodily pain or pleasure, the sensory information must reach the brain.

"If the nervous system be cut off between the brain and other parts, the experiences of those other parts are nonexistent for the mind. The eye is blind, the ear deaf, the hand insensible and motionless." — William James, *Principles of Psychology,* 1890

The Endocrine System

LOQ 4-7 How does the endocrine system transmit information and interact with the nervous system?

So far, we have focused on the body's speedy electrochemical information system. Interconnected with your nervous system is a second communication system, the **endocrine system** (FIGURE 4.10). The endocrine system contains glands and fat tissue that secrete another form of chemical messenger, **hormones.** Hormones travel through the bloodstream and affect other tissues, including the brain. When hormones act on the brain, they influence our interest in sex, food, and aggression.

reflex a simple, automatic response to a sensory stimulus, such as the knee-jerk reflex.

endocrine [EN-duh-krin] **system** the body's "slow" chemical communication system; glands and fat tissue that secrete hormones into the bloodstream.

hormones chemical messengers that are manufactured by the endocrine glands, travel through the bloodstream, and affect other tissues.

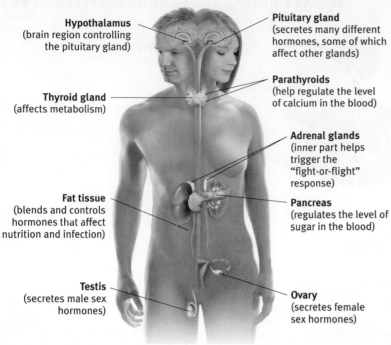

Hypothalamus
(brain region controlling
the pituitary gland)

Pituitary gland
(secretes many different
hormones, some of which
affect other glands)

Thyroid gland
(affects metabolism)

Parathyroids
(help regulate the level
of calcium in the blood)

Adrenal glands
(inner part helps
trigger the
"fight-or-flight"
response)

Fat tissue
(blends and controls
hormones that affect
nutrition and infection)

Pancreas
(regulates the level of
sugar in the blood)

Testis
(secretes male sex
hormones)

Ovary
(secretes female
sex hormones)

🔾 **FIGURE 4.10**
The endocrine system

fizkes/Getty Images

Prejudice causes stress An experience
of prejudice may trigger release of the stress
hormone cortisol (Deer et al., 2018).

Some hormones are chemically identical to neurotransmitters (the chemical messengers that diffuse
across a synapse and excite or inhibit an adjacent neuron). The endocrine system and nervous system are
therefore close relatives: Both produce molecules that
act on receptors elsewhere. Like many relatives, they also
differ. The speedier nervous system zips messages from
eyes to brain to hand in a fraction of a second. Endocrine
messages trudge along in the bloodstream, taking several
seconds or more to travel from the gland to the target
tissue. If the nervous system transmits information with
text-message speed, the endocrine system delivers an
old-fashioned letter.

But slow and steady sometimes wins the race. Endocrine messages tend to outlast the effects of neural messages. Have you ever felt angry long after the cause of your
angry feelings was resolved (say, your friend apologized for
her rudeness)? You may have experienced an "endocrine
hangover" from lingering emotion-related hormones. The
persistence of emotions—even without conscious aware-
ness of what caused them—was dramatically evident in one ingenious experiment.
Brain-damaged patients unable to form new conscious memories watched a sad film
and later a happy film. After each viewing, they did not consciously recall the films, but
the sad or happy emotion persisted (Feinstein et al., 2010).

In a moment of danger, the ANS orders the **adrenal glands** on top of the kidneys to
release *epinephrine* and *norepinephrine* (also called *adrenaline* and *noradrenaline*). These hormones increase heart rate, blood pressure, and blood sugar, providing a surge of energy.
When the emergency passes, the hormones—and the feelings—linger a while.

The most influential endocrine gland is the **pituitary gland,** a pea-sized structure
located in the core of the brain, where it is controlled by an adjacent brain area, the
hypothalamus (more on that shortly). Among the hormones released by the pituitary is
a growth hormone that stimulates physical development. Another is *oxytocin*, which
enables labor contractions, milk flow while nursing, and orgasm. Oxytocin can also promote social bonding (Bartz et al., 2019; Kreuder et al., 2018; Tan et al., 2019). It strengthens our close relationships and alerts us to threats to our group (Nitschke et al., 2019;
Sunahara et al., 2019; Zhang et al., 2019).

Pituitary secretions also direct other endocrine glands to release their hormones. The
pituitary, then, is a *master gland* (whose own master is the hypothalamus). For example,
under the brain's influence, the pituitary triggers your sex glands to release sex hormones. These in turn influence your brain and behavior (Goetz et al., 2014). So, too, with
stress. A stressful event triggers your hypothalamus to instruct your pituitary to release
a hormone that causes your adrenal glands to flood your body with *cortisol*, a stress hormone that increases blood sugar.

This feedback system (brain → pituitary → other glands → hormones → body and
brain) reveals the intimate connection of the nervous and endocrine systems. The nervous system directs endocrine secretions, which then affect the nervous system. Conducting and coordinating this whole electrochemical orchestra is that flexible maestro
we call the brain.

⊖ **adrenal** [ah-DREEN-el] **glands** a pair of
endocrine glands that sits just above the
kidneys and secretes hormones (epinephrine
and norepinephrine) that help arouse the
body in times of stress.

pituitary gland the endocrine system's
most influential gland. Under the influence
of the hypothalamus, the pituitary regulates
growth and controls other endocrine glands.

ASK YOURSELF

Do you remember feeling the lingering effects of a hormonal response, such as anger, after
some particularly aggravating event? How did it feel? How long did it last?

RETRIEVAL PRACTICE

RP-11 Why is the pituitary gland called the *master gland*?

RP-12 How are the nervous and endocrine systems alike, and how do they differ?

ANSWERS IN APPENDIX E

4 REVIEW Neural and Hormonal Systems

LEARNING OBJECTIVES

Test Yourself Answer these repeated Learning Objective Questions on your own (before checking the answers in Appendix D) to improve your retention of the concepts (McDaniel et al., 2009, 2015).

LOQ 4-1 Why are psychologists concerned with human biology?

LOQ 4-2 How do biology and experience together enable neuroplasticity?

LOQ 4-3 What are *neurons*, and how do they transmit information?

LOQ 4-4 How do nerve cells communicate with other nerve cells?

LOQ 4-5 How do neurotransmitters influence behavior, and how do drugs and other chemicals affect neurotransmission?

LOQ 4-6 What are the functions of the nervous system's main divisions, and what are the three main types of neurons?

LOQ 4-7 How does the endocrine system transmit information and interact with the nervous system?

TERMS AND CONCEPTS TO REMEMBER

Test Yourself Write down the definition in your own words, then check your answer.

biological psychology, p. 52

neuroplasticity, p. 52

neuron, p. 55

cell body, p. 55

dendrites, p. 55

axon, p. 55

myelin [MY-uh-lin] sheath, p. 55

glial cells (glia), p. 55

action potential, p. 55

threshold, p. 57

refractory period, p. 57

all-or-none response, p. 57

synapse [SIN-aps], p. 57

neurotransmitters, p. 57

reuptake, p. 59

endorphins [en-DOR-fins], p. 59

agonist, p. 59

antagonist, p. 61

nervous system, p. 61

central nervous system (CNS), p. 61

peripheral nervous system (PNS), p. 61

nerves, p. 61

sensory (afferent) neurons, p. 61

motor (efferent) neurons, p. 61

interneurons, p. 61

somatic nervous system, p. 61

autonomic [aw-tuh-NAHM-ik] nervous system (ANS), p. 61

sympathetic nervous system, p. 61

parasympathetic nervous system, p. 61

reflex, p. 63

endocrine [EN-duh-krin] system, p. 63

hormones, p. 63

adrenal [ah-DREEN-el] glands, p. 64

pituitary gland, p. 64

MASTER THE MATERIAL

Test Yourself Answer the following questions on your own first, then check your answers in Appendix E.

1. What do psychologists mean when they say the brain is "plastic"?

2. The neuron fiber that passes messages through its branches to other neurons or to muscles and glands is the _____.

3. The tiny space between the axon of one neuron and the dendrite or cell body of another is called the

   a. axon terminal.   c. synaptic gap.

   b. branching fiber.   d. threshold.

4. Regarding a neuron's response to stimulation, the intensity of the stimulus determines

   a. whether or not an impulse is generated.

   b. how fast an impulse is transmitted.

   c. how intense an impulse will be.

   d. whether reuptake will occur.

5. In a sending neuron, when an action potential reaches an axon terminal, the impulse triggers the release of chemical messengers called _____.

6. Endorphins are released in the brain in response to

   a. morphine or heroin.   c. the all-or-none response.

   b. pain or vigorous exercise.   d. all of the above.

7. The autonomic nervous system controls internal functions, such as heart rate and glandular activity. The word *autonomic* means

   a. calming.   c. self-regulating.

   b. voluntary.   d. arousing.

8. The sympathetic nervous system arouses us for action and the parasympathetic nervous system calms us down. Together, the two systems make up the _____ nervous system.

9. The neurons of the spinal cord are part of the _____ nervous system.

10. The most influential endocrine gland, known as the *master gland*, is the _____

    a. pituitary.   c. thyroid.

    b. hypothalamus.   d. pancreas.

11. The _____ _____ secrete(s) epinephrine and norepinephrine, helping to arouse the body during times of stress.

Continue testing yourself with 📖 **LearningCurve** or 📖 **Achieve Read & Practice** to learn and remember most effectively.

⑤ Tools of Discovery, Older Brain Structures, and the Limbic System

"I am a brain, Watson. The rest of me is a mere appendix." — Sherlock Holmes, in Arthur Conan Doyle's "The Adventure of the Mazarin Stone," 1921

We are convinced that we live "somewhere north of the neck" (Fodor, 1999). And for good reason: The brain enables the mind—seeing, hearing, smelling, feeling, remembering, thinking, speaking, dreaming. An acquaintance of mine [DM's] received a new heart from a woman who, in a rare operation, had received a matched heart-lung transplant. When the two chanced to meet in their hospital ward, she introduced herself: "I think you have my heart." But only her heart. Her self, she assumed, still resided inside her skull. It is the brain that self-reflectively analyzes the brain. When you think *about* your brain, you're thinking *with* your brain—by releasing billions of neurotransmitter molecules across trillions of synapses. The effect of hormones on experiences such as love reminds us that we would not be of the same mind if we were a bodiless brain. Nevertheless, brain, behavior, and cognition are an integrated whole. But precisely where and how are the mind's functions tied to the brain? Let's first see how scientists explore such questions.

The Tools of Discovery: Having Our Head Examined

LOQ 5-1 How do neuroscientists study the brain's connections to behavior and mind?

For most of human history, scientists had no tools high-powered yet gentle enough to reveal a living brain's activity. Early case studies helped localize some brain functions. Damage to one side of the brain often caused numbness or paralysis on the body's opposite side, suggesting that the body's right side is wired to the brain's left side, and vice versa. Damage to the back of the brain disrupted vision, and to the left-front part of the brain produced speech difficulties. Gradually, these early explorers were mapping the brain.

Now the human brain has invented new ways to study itself. A new generation of neural mapmakers is charting the known universe's most amazing organ. Scientists can selectively **lesion** (destroy) tiny clusters of normal or defective brain cells, observing any effect on brain function. In the laboratory, such studies have revealed, for example, that damage to one area of the hypothalamus in a rat's brain reduces eating, to the point of starvation, whereas damage in another area produces overeating.

Today's neuroscientists can *stimulate* various brain parts—electrically, chemically, or magnetically—and note the effect. Depending on the stimulated brain part, people may—to name a few examples—giggle, hear voices, turn their head, feel themselves falling, or have an out-of-body experience (Selimbeyoglu & Parvizi, 2010).

Scientists can even snoop on the messages of individual neurons. With tips small enough to detect the electrical pulse in a single neuron, modern microelectrodes can, for example, now detect exactly where the information goes in a cat's brain when someone tickles its belly (Ishiyama & Brecht, 2017). Promising new tools include *optogenetics*, a technique that allows neuroscientists to control the activity of individual neurons (Boyden, 2014). By programming neurons to become receptive to light, researchers can examine the biological basis of sensations, fear, depression, and substance use disorders (Dygalo & Shishkina, 2019; Firsov, 2019; Juarez et al., 2019; Nikitin et al., 2019).

Researchers can also eavesdrop on the chatter of billions of neurons. Right now, your mental activity is emitting telltale electrical, metabolic, and magnetic signals that would enable neuroscientists to observe your brain at work. Electrical activity in your brain's billions of neurons sweeps in regular waves across its surface. An **EEG (electroencephalogram)** is an amplified readout of such waves. Researchers record the brain waves through a shower-cap-like hat that is filled with electrodes covered with a conductive gel. Studying an EEG of the brain's activity is like studying a blender's motor by listening to its hum. With no direct access to the brain, researchers present a stimulus repeatedly and have a computer filter out brain activity unrelated to the stimulus. What remains is the electrical wave evoked by the stimulus.

A living human brain exposed Today's neuroscience tools enable us to "look under the hood" and glimpse the brain at work, enabling the mind.

← FIGURE 5.1

The PET scan To obtain a PET scan, researchers inject volunteers with a low and harmless dose of a short-lived radioactive sugar. Detectors around the person's head pick up the release of gamma rays from the sugar, which has concentrated in active brain areas. A computer then processes and translates these signals into a map of the brain at work.

A related technique is **MEG (magnetoencephalography).** To isolate the brain's magnetic fields, researchers create special rooms that cancel out other magnetic signals, such as the Earth's magnetic field. Participants sit underneath a head coil that resembles a hair salon hairdryer. While participants complete activities, tens of thousands of neurons create electrical pulses, which in turn create magnetic fields. The speed and strength of the magnetic fields enable researchers to understand how certain tasks influence brain activity (Eldar et al., 2018; Ruzich et al., 2019; Uhlhaas et al., 2018).

"You must look into people, as well as at them," advised Lord Chesterfield in a 1746 letter to his son. Newer neuroimaging techniques give us super hero-like ability to see inside the living brain. One such tool, the **PET (positron emission tomography)** scan (**FIGURE 5.1**), depicts brain activity by showing each brain area's consumption of its chemical fuel, the sugar glucose. Active neurons gobble glucose. Our brain, though only about 2 percent of our body weight, consumes 20 percent of our calorie intake. After a person receives temporarily radioactive glucose, the PET scan can track the gamma rays released by this "food for thought" as a task is performed. Rather like weather radar showing rain activity, PET-scan "hot spots" show the most active brain areas as the person does mathematical calculations, looks at images of faces, or daydreams.

In **MRI (magnetic resonance imaging)** brain scans, the person's head is put in a strong magnetic field, which aligns the spinning atoms of brain molecules. Then, a radio-wave pulse momentarily disorients the atoms. When the atoms return to their normal spin, they emit signals that provide a detailed picture of soft tissues, including the brain. MRI scans have revealed a larger-than-average neural area in the left hemisphere of musicians who display perfect pitch (Schlaug et al., 1995). They have also revealed enlarged *ventricles*—fluid-filled brain areas (marked by the red arrows in **FIGURE 5.2**)—in some patients who have schizophrenia.

A special application of MRI—**fMRI (functional MRI)**—can reveal the brain's functioning as well as its structure. Where the brain is especially active, blood goes. By comparing successive MRI scans, researchers can watch as specific brain areas activate, showing increased oxygen-laden blood flow. As a person looks at a scene, for example, the fMRI machine detects blood rushing to the back of the brain, which processes visual information. Another tool, *functional near-infrared spectroscopy (fNIRS)*, uses infrared light that shines

lesion [LEE-zhuhn] tissue destruction. A brain lesion is a naturally or experimentally caused destruction of brain tissue.

EEG (electroencephalogram) an amplified recording of the waves of electrical activity sweeping across the brain's surface. These waves are measured by electrodes placed on the scalp.

MEG (magnetoencephalography) a brain-imaging technique that measures magnetic fields from the brain's natural electrical activity.

PET (positron emission tomography) a technique for detecting brain activity that displays where a radioactive form of glucose goes while the brain performs a given task.

MRI (magnetic resonance imaging) a technique that uses magnetic fields and radio waves to produce computer-generated images of soft tissue. MRI scans show brain anatomy.

fMRI (functional MRI) a technique for revealing blood flow and, therefore, brain activity by comparing successive MRI scans. fMRI scans show brain function as well as structure.

(a) (b)

← FIGURE 5.2

MRI scan of a healthy individual (a) and a person with schizophrenia (b) Note the enlarged ventricle—the fluid-filled brain region at the tip of the arrow in the image—in the brain of the person with schizophrenia (b).

Mark Straccia/UCLA Social Cognitive Neuroscience Laboratory

Understanding the non-WEIRD brain Most neuroscience research studies people from Western, educated, industrial, rich, and democratic (WEIRD) populations (Falk et al., 2013). Using functional near-infrared spectroscopy (fNIRS), the researchers shown here were able to identify brain areas involved in persuasion among a Jordanian sample (Burns et al., 2019).

 To check your understanding of brain scans and their functions, engage online with *Concept Practice: Scanning the Brain.*

onto blood molecules to identify brain activity. The fNIRS equipment can fit in a large backpack, enabling researchers to study the biology of mind in difficult-to-reach populations (Burns et al., 2019; Perdue et al., 2019).

See **TABLE 5.1** for a comparison of some of these imaging techniques.

Such snapshots of the brain's changing activity provide new insights into how the brain divides its labor and reacts to changing needs. A mountain of recent fMRI studies tells us which brain areas are most active when people feel pain or rejection, listen to angry voices, think about scary things, feel happy, or become sexually aroused. fMRI can even reveal what happens if we deliberately suppress our own personality, as actors do. (Brown et al., 2019).

Can brain imaging enable mind reading? fMRI technology has enabled a crude eavesdropping on the mind. One neuroscience team scanned 129 people's brains as they did eight different mental tasks (such as reading, gambling, or rhyming). Later, they were able, with 80 percent accuracy, to identify which of these mental activities their participants had been doing (Poldrack, 2018). Other research has used the brain's activity to predict public health campaign effectiveness and future behavior, such as school performance, drug use, and who we choose as friends (Chung et al., 2017; Cooper et al., 2019; Kranzler et al., 2019; Zerubavel et al., 2018).

You've seen the pictures—of colorful brains with accompanying headlines, such as "your brain on music." Although brain areas don't actually "light up," vivid brain-scan images seem impressive. People rate scientific explanations as more believable and interesting when they contain neuroscience (Fernandez-Duque et al., 2015; Im et al., 2017). But "neuroskeptics" caution against overblown claims about any ability to predict customer preferences, to detect lies, and to foretell crime (Rose & Rose, 2016; Satel & Lilienfeld, 2013; Schwartz et al., 2016). Neuromarketing, neuroleadership, neurolaw, and neuropolitics are often neurohype. Imaging techniques illuminate brain structure and activity, and sometimes help us test different theories of behavior (Mather et al., 2013). But given that all human experience is brain-based, it's no surprise that different brain areas become active when one listens to a lecture or lusts for a lover.

* * *

Today's techniques for peering into the thinking, feeling brain are doing for psychology what the microscope did for biology and the telescope did for astronomy. From them we have learned more about the brain in the last 100 years than in the previous 10,000. And the next decade will reveal much more, as each year massive funding goes into brain research. To advance brain science, Europe's Human Brain Project has budgeted $1 billion between 2013 and 2023 (Salles et al., 2019). The $40 million Human Connectome

TABLE 5.1 Common Types of Neural Measures		
Name	**How Does It Work?**	**Sample Finding**
EEG (Electroencephalogram)	Electrodes placed on the scalp measure electrical activity in neurons.	Symptoms of depression and anxiety correlate with increased activity in the right frontal lobe, a brain area associated with behavioral withdrawal and negative emotion (Thibodeau et al., 2006).
MEG (Magnetoencephalography)	A head coil records magnetic fields from the brain's natural electrical currents.	Soldiers with posttraumatic stress disorder (PTSD), compared with soldiers who do not have PTSD, show stronger magnetic fields in the visual cortex when they view trauma-related images (Todd et al., 2015).
Positron emission tomography (PET)	Tracks where in the brain a temporarily radioactive form of glucose goes while the person given it performs a task.	Monkeys with an anxious temperament have brains that use more glucose in regions related to fear, memory, and expectations of reward and punishment (Fox et al., 2015).
Magnetic resonance imaging (MRI)	People sit or lie down in a chamber that uses magnetic fields and radio waves to provide a map of brain structure.	People with a history of violence tend to have smaller frontal lobes, especially in regions that aid moral judgment and self-control (Glenn & Raine, 2014).
Functional magnetic resonance imaging (fMRI)	Measures blood flow to brain regions by comparing continuous MRI scans.	Years after surviving a near plane crash, passengers who viewed material related to their trauma showed greater activation in the brain's fear, memory, and visual centers than when they watched footage related to the 9/11 terrorist attacks (Palombo et al., 2015).

Project seeks to map the brain's long-distance connections by harnessing the power of *diffusion spectrum imaging,* a type of MRI technology (Glasser et al., 2016; Wang & Olson, 2018) (**FIGURE 5.3**). Such efforts have produced a new brain map with 100 neural centers not previously described (Glasser et al., 2016). Building on this work, a new project seeks to understand typical brain aging from age 36 to 100+ (Bookheimer et al., 2019). Stay tuned for future fascinating findings.

To learn about the neurosciences now is like studying world geography when Magellan explored the seas. This truly is the golden age of brain science.

Tom Barrick, Chris Clark, SGHMS/Science Source

◉ FIGURE 5.3
Beautiful brain connections The Human Connectome Project is using cutting-edge methods to map the brain's interconnected network of neurons. Scientists created this multicolored "symphony" of neural fibers transporting water through different brain regions.

"As heady as our progress has been . . . we have only discovered a tiny fraction of what there is to know about the human brain. But [it] makes for a story more exciting than any Sherlock Holmes novel."
— V. S. Ramachandran, *The Tell-Tale Brain*, 2011

ASK YOURSELF

Were you surprised to learn that there are so many technological tools to study the brain's structures and functions? Which techniques do you find most interesting? Why?

RETRIEVAL PRACTICE

RP-1 Match the scanning technique (i–iii) with the correct description (a–c).

Technique	**Description**
i. fMRI scan	**a.** Tracks radioactive glucose to reveal brain *activity*.
ii. PET scan	**b.** Tracks successive images of brain tissue to show brain *function*.
iii. MRI scan	**c.** Uses magnetic fields and radio waves to show brain *anatomy*.

ANSWERS IN APPENDIX E

🎬 For an introductory 12.5-minute overview of the brain, see the *Video: The Central Nervous System— Spotlight on the Brain.*

Older Brain Structures

LOQ 5-2 What structures make up the brainstem, and what are the functions of the brainstem, thalamus, reticular formation, and cerebellum?

An animal's capacities come from its brain structures. In primitive animals, such as sharks, a not-so-complex brain primarily regulates basic survival functions: breathing, resting, and feeding. In lower mammals, such as rodents, a more complex brain enables emotion and greater memory. In advanced mammals, such as humans, a brain that processes more information enables increased foresight as well.

The brain's increasing complexity arises from new systems built on top of the old, much as Earth's landscape covers the old with the new. Digging down, one discovers the fossil remnants of the past—brainstem components performing for us much as they did for our distant ancestors. Let's start with the brain's base and work up to the newer systems.

The Brainstem

The **brainstem** is the brain's oldest and innermost region. Its base is the **medulla,** the slight swelling in the spinal cord just after it enters the skull (**FIGURE 5.4**). Here lie the controls for your heartbeat and breathing. As some brain-damaged patients in a vegetative state illustrate, we need no higher brain or conscious mind to orchestrate our heart's pumping and lungs' breathing. The brainstem handles those tasks. Just above the medulla sits the *pons,* which helps coordinate movements and control sleep.

brainstem the oldest part and central core of the brain, beginning where the spinal cord swells as it enters the skull; the brainstem is responsible for automatic survival functions.

medulla [muh-DUL-uh] the base of the brainstem; controls heartbeat and breathing.

➔ FIGURE 5.4
The brainstem and thalamus
The brainstem, including the pons and medulla, is an extension of the spinal cord. The thalamus is attached to the top of the brainstem. The reticular formation passes through both structures.

Thalamus

Reticular formation

Pons

Brainstem

Medulla

Andrew Swift

⬆ FIGURE 5.5
The body's wiring

RP-2 The _____ is a crossover point where nerves from the left side of the brain are mostly linked to the right side of the body, and vice versa.

ANSWERS IN APPENDIX E

If a cat's brainstem is severed from the rest of the brain above it, the animal will still breathe and live—and even run, climb, and groom (Klemm, 1990). But cut off from the brain's higher regions, it won't *purposefully* run or climb to get food.

The brainstem is a crossover point, where most nerves to and from each side of the brain connect with the body's opposite side (**FIGURE 5.5**). This peculiar cross-wiring is but one of the brain's many surprises.

The Thalamus

Sitting atop the brainstem is the **thalamus,** a pair of egg-shaped structures that acts as the brain's sensory control center (see Figure 5.4). The thalamus receives information from all the senses except smell, and routes that information to the higher brain regions that deal with seeing, hearing, tasting, and touching. The thalamus also receives some of the higher brain's replies, which it then directs to the medulla and to the *cerebellum*. For sensory information, your thalamus is something like what Seoul is to South Korea's trains, a hub through which traffic passes on its way to various destinations.

The Reticular Formation

Inside the brainstem, between your ears, lies the **reticular** ("netlike") **formation,** a nerve network extending from the spinal cord right up through the thalamus. As the spinal cord's sensory input flows up to the thalamus, some of it travels through the reticular formation, which filters incoming stimuli and relays important information to other brain areas. Have you multitasked today? You can thank your reticular formation (Wimmer et al., 2015).

The reticular formation also controls arousal, as Giuseppe Moruzzi and Horace Magoun discovered in 1949. Electrically stimulating a sleeping cat's reticular formation almost instantly produced an awake, alert animal. When Magoun *severed* a cat's reticular formation without damaging nearby sensory pathways, the effect was equally dramatic: The cat lapsed into a coma from which it never awakened.

The Cerebellum

Extending from the rear of the brainstem is the baseball-sized **cerebellum,** meaning "little brain," which is what its two wrinkled halves resemble (**FIGURE 5.6**). The cerebellum (along with the *basal ganglia*, deep brain structures involved in motor movement) enables nonverbal learning and skill memory. It plays an important role in a lot that happens just outside your awareness. Quickly answer these questions. How long have you been reading this text? Do your clothes feel soft or rough against your skin? How's your mood today? You probably answered easily, thanks to your cerebellum. This little brain, which actually has more than half your brain's neurons, helps you judge time,

Cerebellum

Spinal cord

◀ **FIGURE 5.6**
The brain's organ of agility Hanging at the back of the brain, the cerebellum coordinates our voluntary movements, as when soccer player Mallory Pugh controls the ball.

discriminate textures and sounds, and control your emotions and social behaviors (Bower & Parsons, 2003; Carta et al., 2019). It aids your vocabulary, reading, and ability to store information (Moore et al., 2017). With assistance from the pons, it also coordinates voluntary movement. When a soccer player masterfully controls the ball, give her cerebellum some credit. Under alcohol's influence, coordination suffers. And if you injured your cerebellum, you would have difficulty walking, keeping your balance, or shaking hands. Your movements would be jerky and exaggerated. Gone would be any dreams of being a dancer or guitarist.

* * *

Note: These older brain functions all occur without any conscious effort. This illustrates another of our recurring themes: *Our brain processes most information outside of our awareness.* We are aware of the *results* of our brain's labor—say, our current visual experience—but not *how* we construct the visual image. Likewise, whether we are asleep or awake, our brainstem manages its life-sustaining functions, freeing our newer brain regions to think, talk, dream, or savor a memory.

RETRIEVAL PRACTICE

RP-3 In what brain region would damage be most likely to (a) disrupt your ability to jump rope? (b) disrupt your ability to hear? (c) leave you in a coma? (d) cut off the very breath and heartbeat of life?

ANSWERS IN APPENDIX E

thalamus [THAL-uh-muss] the brain's sensory control center, located on top of the brainstem; it directs messages to the sensory receiving areas in the cortex and transmits replies to the cerebellum and medulla.

reticular formation a nerve network that travels through the brainstem into the thalamus; filters information and plays an important role in controlling arousal.

cerebellum [sehr-uh-BELL-um] the "little brain" at the rear of the brainstem; functions include processing sensory input, coordinating movement output and balance, and enabling nonverbal learning and memory.

limbic system neural system (including the *amygdala, hypothalamus,* and *hippocampus*) located below the cerebral hemispheres; associated with emotions and drives.

amygdala [uh-MIG-duh-la] two lima-bean-sized neural clusters in the limbic system; linked to emotion.

The Limbic System

LOQ 5-3   What are the limbic system's structures and functions?

We've considered the brain's oldest parts, but we've not yet reached its newest and highest regions, the *cerebral hemispheres* (the two halves of the brain). Between the oldest and newest brain areas lies the **limbic system** (*limbus* means "border"). This system, which is associated with emotions and drives, contains the *amygdala,* the *hypothalamus,* and the *hippocampus* (**FIGURE 5.7**).

The Amygdala

The **amygdala**—two lima-bean-sized neural clusters—enables aggression and fear. In 1939, psychologist Heinrich Klüver and neurosurgeon Paul Bucy surgically removed a rhesus monkey's amygdala, turning the normally ill-tempered animal into the most mellow of creatures. In studies with other wild animals, including the lynx, wolverine, and wild rat, researchers noted the same effect. So, too, with humans. One woman with an amygdala lesion, patient S. M., has been called "the woman with no fear," even if being threatened with a gun (Feinstein et al., 2013). Even healthy people who have a smaller-than-average amygdala display reduced arousal to threatening stimuli (Foell et al., 2019). Little amygdala, little fear.

Hypothalamus

Pituitary gland

Amygdala   Hippocampus

◀ **FIGURE 5.7**
The limbic system This neural system sits between the brain's older parts and its cerebral hemispheres. The limbic system's hypothalamus controls the nearby pituitary gland.

hypothalamus [hi-po-THAL-uh-muss] a neural structure in the limbic system lying below (*hypo*) the thalamus; it directs several maintenance activities (eating, drinking, body temperature), helps govern the endocrine system via the pituitary gland, and is linked to emotion and reward.

What then might happen if we electrically stimulated the amygdala of a normally placid domestic animal, such as a cat? Do so in one spot and the cat prepares to attack, hissing with its back arched, its pupils dilated, its hair on end. Move the electrode only slightly within the amygdala, cage the cat with a small mouse, and now it cowers in terror.

These and other experiments have confirmed the amygdala's role in fear and rage. Monkeys and humans with amygdala damage become less fearful of strangers (Harrison et al., 2015). Other studies link criminal behavior with amygdala dysfunction (da Cunha-Bang et al., 2017; Dotterer et al., 2017; Ermer et al., 2012). When people view angry and happy faces, only the angry ones increase activity in the amygdala (Mende-Siedlecki et al., 2013). And when negative events energize the amygdala, they become more memorable (Admon et al., 2018).

But we must be careful. The brain is not neatly organized into structures that correspond to our behavior categories. The amygdala is engaged with other mental phenomena as well. And when we feel afraid or act aggressively, there is neural activity in many areas of our brain—not just the amygdala. If you destroy a car's battery, the car won't run. But the battery is merely one link in an integrated system.

RETRIEVAL PRACTICE

GK Hart/Vikki Hart/Getty Images

RP-4 Electrical stimulation of a cat's amygdala provokes angry reactions. Which *autonomic nervous system* division is activated by such stimulation?

ANSWERS IN APPENDIX E

The Hypothalamus

Just below (*hypo*) the thalamus is the **hypothalamus** (**FIGURE 5.8**), an important link in the command chain governing bodily maintenance. Some neural clusters in the hypothalamus influence hunger; others regulate thirst, body temperature, and sexual behavior. Together, they help maintain a steady (*homeostatic*) internal state.

To monitor your body state, the hypothalamus tunes in to your blood chemistry and any incoming orders from other brain parts. For example, picking up signals from your brain's cerebral cortex that you are thinking about sex, your hypothalamus will secrete hormones. These hormones will in turn trigger the adjacent "master gland" of the endocrine system, your pituitary (see Figure 5.7), to influence your sex glands to release *their* hormones. These hormones will intensify the thoughts of sex in your cerebral cortex. (Note the interplay between the nervous and endocrine systems: The brain influences the endocrine system, which in turn influences the brain.)

A remarkable discovery about the hypothalamus illustrates how progress in science often occurs—when curious, open-minded investigators make an unexpected observation. Two young McGill University neuropsychologists, James Olds and Peter Milner (1954), were trying to implant an electrode in a rat's reticular formation when they made a magnificent mistake: They placed the electrode incorrectly (Olds, 1975). Curiously, as if seeking more stimulation, the rat kept returning to the location where it had been stimulated by this misplaced electrode. On discovering that they had actually placed the device in a region of the hypothalamus, Olds and Milner realized they had stumbled upon a brain center that provides pleasurable rewards.

Later experiments located other "pleasure centers" (Olds, 1958). (What the rats actually experience only they know, and they aren't telling. Rather than attribute human feelings to rats, today's scientists refer to *reward centers*.) Just how rewarding are these

ISM/Medical Images USA

⑦ FIGURE 5.8

The hypothalamus This small but important structure, colored yellow/orange in this MRI scan, helps keep the body's internal environment in a steady state.

reward centers? Enough to cause rats to self-stimulate these brain regions more than 1000 times per hour.

In other species, including dolphins and monkeys, researchers later discovered other limbic system reward centers, such as the *nucleus accumbens* in front of the hypothalamus (Hamid et al., 2016). Animal research has also revealed both a general dopamine-related reward system and specific centers associated with the pleasures of eating, drinking, and sex. Animals, it seems, come equipped with built-in systems that reward activities essential to survival.

Researchers have experimented with ways of using brain stimulation to control non-human animals' actions in search-and-rescue operations. By rewarding rats for turning left or right, one research team trained previously caged rats to navigate natural environments (Talwar et al., 2002). By pressing buttons on a laptop, the researchers were then able to direct the rat—which carried a receiver, power source, and video camera all in a tiny backpack—to turn on cue, climb trees, scurry along branches, and return.

Do humans have limbic centers for pleasure? Some evidence indicates we do. When we meet likable people, our brain bursts with reward center activity (Zerubavel et al., 2018). Ditto when we read kind messages from friends and family members, such as, "You light up my entire world" (Inagaki et al., 2019). Stimulating reward centers can also help control the cruelest individuals. But as one neurosurgeon found by implanting electrodes in violent patients' limbic system areas, the patients reported only mild pleasure. Unlike Olds and Milner's rats, the patients were not driven to a frenzy (Deutsch, 1972; Hooper & Teresi, 1986). Moreover, newer research reveals that stimulating the brain's "hedonic hotspots" (its reward circuits) produces more *desire* than pure enjoyment (Kringelbach & Berridge, 2012).

Experiments have also revealed the effects of a dopamine-related reward system in people. For example, experimentally boosting dopamine levels increases the pleasurable "chills" response to a favorite piece of music, whereas reducing dopamine levels decreases musical pleasure (Ferreri et al., 2019). Some researchers believe that many disordered behaviors may stem from malfunctions in natural brain systems for pleasure and well-being. People genetically predisposed to this *reward deficiency syndrome* may crave whatever provides that missing pleasure or relieves negative feelings, such as aggression, fattening food, or drugs and alcohol (Blum et al., 1996, 2014; Chester et al., 2016).

The Hippocampus

The **hippocampus**—a seahorse-shaped brain structure—processes conscious, explicit memories. Variations in hippocampal development predict academic achievement (Wilkey et al., 2018). Humans who lose their hippocampus to surgery or injury lose their ability to form new memories of facts and events (Clark & Maguire, 2016). Those who survive a hippocampal brain tumor in childhood struggle to remember new information in adulthood (Jayakar et al., 2015). National Football League players who experience one or more loss-of-consciousness concussions may later have a shrunken hippocampus and poor memory (Strain et al., 2015; Tharmaratnam et al., 2018). Hippocampus size and function

> **hippocampus** a neural center located in the limbic system; helps process explicit (conscious) memories—of facts and events—for storage.

> "If you were designing a robot vehicle to walk into the future and survive, . . . you'd wire it up so that behavior that ensured the survival of the self or the species—like sex and eating—would be naturally reinforcing." — Neuroscientist Candace Pert (1986)

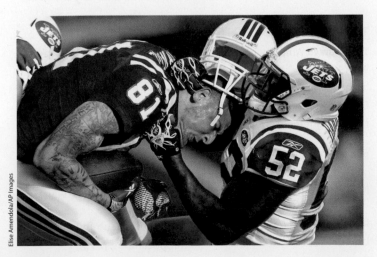

Elise Amendola/AP Images

Are football players' brains protected?
When researchers analyzed the brains of 111 deceased National Football League players, 99 percent showed signs of degeneration related to frequent head trauma (Mez et al., 2017). In 2017, NFL player Aaron Hernandez (#81) died by suicide while imprisoned for murder. An autopsy revealed that his brain, at age 27, was already showing advanced degeneration (Kilgore, 2017). One small study showed that those who played even a single college football season, with or without experiencing a concussion, were more likely than not to exhibit brain damage (Hirad et al., 2019). In hopes of protecting players, today's teams and scientists use more protective gear and portable brain-imaging tools (Canadian Press, 2018).

Left hemisphere

Right hemisphere

Corpus callosum: axon fibers connecting the two cerebral hemispheres

Thalamus: relays messages between lower brain centers and cerebral cortex

Hypothalamus: controls maintenance functions such as eating; helps govern endocrine system; linked to emotion and reward

Pituitary: master endocrine gland

Reticular formation: helps control arousal

Pons: helps coordinate movement and control sleep

Medulla: controls heartbeat and breathing

Spinal cord: pathway for neural fibers traveling to and from brain; controls simple reflexes

Cerebellum: coordinates voluntary movement and balance and supports learning and memories of such

Cerebral cortex: ultimate control and information-processing center

Amygdala: linked to emotion

Hippocampus: linked to conscious memory

■ Cerebral cortex   ■ Limbic system   ■ Brainstem

⑦ **FIGURE 5.9**
Brain structures and their functions

decrease as we grow older, which furthers cognitive decline (O'Callaghan et al., 2019). The Memory modules explain how our two-track mind uses the hippocampus to process our memories.

* * *

FIGURE 5.9 locates the brain areas we've discussed, as well as the *cerebral cortex*—the body's ultimate control and information-processing center.

📖 To review and assess your understanding, engage online with *Concept Practice: The Limbic System.*

RETRIEVAL PRACTICE

RP-5   What are the three key structures of the limbic system, and what functions do they serve?

ANSWERS IN APPENDIX E

---

5   **REVIEW** Tools of Discovery, Older Brain Structures, and the Limbic System

LEARNING OBJECTIVES

Test Yourself Answer these repeated Learning Objective Questions on your own (before checking the answers in Appendix D to improve your retention of the concepts (McDaniel et al., 2009, 2015).

LOQ 5-1   How do neuroscientists study the brain's connections to behavior and mind?

LOQ 5-2   What structures make up the brainstem, and what are the functions of the brainstem, thalamus, reticular formation, and cerebellum?

LOQ 5-3   What are the limbic system's structures and functions?

TERMS AND CONCEPTS TO REMEMBER

Test Yourself Write down the definition in your own words, then check your answer.

lesion [LEE-zhuhn], p. 67

EEG (electroencephalogram), p. 67

MEG (magnetoencephalography), p. 67

PET (positron emission tomography), p. 67

MRI (magnetic resonance imaging), p. 67

fMRI (functional MRI), p. 67

brainstem, p. 69

medulla [muh-DUL-uh], p. 69

thalamus [THAL-uh-muss], p. 71

reticular formation, p. 71

cerebellum [sehr-uh-BELL-um], p. 71

limbic system, p. 71

amygdala [uh-MIG-duh-la], p. 71

hypothalamus [hi-po-THAL-uh-muss], p. 72

hippocampus, p. 73

MASTER THE MATERIAL

Test Yourself Answer the following questions on your own first, then check your answers in Appendix E.

1. The part of the brainstem that controls heartbeat and breathing is the
   a. cerebellum.
   b. medulla.
   c. cortex.
   d. thalamus.

2. The thalamus functions as a
   a. memory bank.
   b. balance center.
   c. breathing regulator.
   d. sensory control center.

3. The lower brain structure that governs arousal is the
   a. spinal cord.
   b. cerebellum.
   c. reticular formation.
   d. medulla.

4. The part of the brain that coordinates voluntary movement and enables nonverbal learning and memory is the
   _____.

5. Two parts of the limbic system are the amygdala and the
   a. cerebral hemispheres.
   b. hippocampus.
   c. thalamus.
   d. pituitary.

6. A cat's ferocious response to electrical brain stimulation would lead you to suppose the electrode had touched the
   _____.

7. The neural structure that most directly regulates eating, drinking, and body temperature is the
   a. endocrine system.
   b. hypothalamus.
   c. hippocampus.
   d. amygdala.

8. The initial reward center discovered by Olds and Milner was located in the _____.

Continue testing yourself with 📚 **LearningCurve** or 📚 **Achieve Read & Practice** to learn and remember most effectively.

MODULE

6 The Cerebral Cortex

LOQ 6-1 What four lobes make up the cerebral cortex, and what are the functions of the motor cortex, somatosensory cortex, and association areas?

Older brain networks sustain basic life functions and enable memory, emotions, and basic drives. Newer neural networks within the *cerebrum*—the two cerebral hemispheres contributing 85 percent of the brain's weight—form specialized work teams that enable our perceiving, thinking, and speaking. Like other structures above the brainstem (the oldest part of the brain)—including the thalamus, hippocampus, and amygdala—the cerebral hemispheres come as a pair. Covering those hemispheres, like bark on a tree, is the **cerebral cortex,** a thin surface layer of interconnected neural cells. In our brain's evolutionary history, the cerebral cortex—our brain's thinking crown—is a relative newcomer.

As we move up the ladder of animal life, the cerebral cortex expands, tight genetic controls relax, and the organism's adaptability increases. Frogs and other small-cortex amphibians operate extensively on preprogrammed genetic instructions. The larger cortex of mammals offers increased capacity for learning and thinking, enabling them to adapt to ever-changing environments. What makes us distinctively human is the size and interconnectivity of our cerebral cortex (Donahue et al., 2018). Let's take a look at its structure and function.

The people who first dissected and labeled the brain used the language of scholars—Latin and Greek. Their words are actually attempts at graphic description: For example, *cortex* means "bark," *cerebellum* is "little brain," and *thalamus* is "inner chamber."

RETRIEVAL PRACTICE

RP-1 Which area of the human brain is most similar to that of less complex animals? Which part of the human brain distinguishes us most from less complex animals?

ANSWERS IN APPENDIX E

cerebral [seh-REE-bruhl] **cortex** the intricate fabric of interconnected neural cells covering the cerebral hemispheres; the body's ultimate control and information-processing center.

frontal lobes the portion of the cerebral cortex lying just behind the forehead; involved in speaking and muscle movements and in making plans and judgments.

parietal [puh-RYE-uh-tuhl] **lobes** the portion of the cerebral cortex lying at the top of the head and toward the rear; receives sensory input for touch and body position.

occipital [ahk-SIP-uh-tuhl] **lobes** the portion of the cerebral cortex lying at the back of the head; includes areas that receive information from the visual fields.

temporal lobes the portion of the cerebral cortex lying roughly above the ears; includes the auditory areas, each receiving information primarily from the opposite ear.

motor cortex a cerebral cortex area at the rear of the frontal lobes that controls voluntary movements.

Structure of the Cortex

If you opened a human skull, exposing the brain, you would see a wrinkled organ, shaped somewhat like the meat of an oversized walnut. Without these wrinkles, a flattened cerebral cortex would require triple the area—roughly that of a large pizza. The brain's left and right hemispheres are filled mainly with axons connecting the cortex to the brain's other regions. The cerebral cortex—that thin surface layer—contains some 20 to 23 billion of the brain's nerve cells and 300 trillion synaptic connections (de Courten-Myers, 2005). Being human takes a lot of nerve.

Each hemisphere's cortex is subdivided into four *lobes*, separated by prominent *fissures*, or folds (**FIGURE 6.1**). Starting at the front of your brain and moving over the top, there are the **frontal lobes** (behind your forehead), the **parietal lobes** (at the top and to the rear), and the **occipital lobes** (at the back of your head). Reversing direction and moving forward, just above your ears, you find the **temporal lobes.** Each of the four lobes carries out many functions, and many functions require the interplay of several lobes.

Functions of the Cortex

More than a century ago, surgeons found damaged cortical areas during autopsies of people who had been partially paralyzed or speechless. This rather crude evidence did not prove that specific parts of the cortex control complex functions like movement or speech. A laptop with a broken power cord might go dead, but we would be fooling ourselves if we thought we had "localized" the internet in the cord.

Motor Functions

Scientists had better luck in localizing simpler brain functions. For example, in 1870, German physicians Gustav Fritsch and Eduard Hitzig made an important discovery: Mild electrical stimulation to parts of an animal's cortex made parts of its body move. The effects were selective: Stimulation caused movement only when applied to an arch-shaped region at the back of the frontal lobe, running roughly ear to ear across the top of the brain. Moreover, stimulating parts of this region in the left or right hemisphere caused movements of specific body parts on the *opposite* side of the body. Fritsch and Hitzig had discovered what is now called the **motor cortex.**

MAPPING THE MOTOR CORTEX Lucky for brain surgeons and their patients, the brain has no sensory receptors. Knowing this, in the 1930s, Otfrid Foerster and Wilder Penfield were able to map the motor cortex in hundreds of wide-awake patients by stimulating different cortical areas and observing responses. They discovered that body areas requiring precise control, such as the fingers and mouth, occupy the greatest amount of cortical space (**FIGURE 6.2**). In one of his many demonstrations of motor behavior

The brain has left and right hemispheres

Frontal lobe
Parietal lobe
Temporal lobe
Occipital lobe

FIGURE 6.1
The cortex and its basic subdivisions

Output: Motor cortex
(Right hemisphere section
controls the body's left side)

Input: Somatosensory cortex
(Left hemisphere section receives
input from the body's right side)

Macmillan Learning

⬆ **FIGURE 6.2**
**Motor cortex and somatosensory
cortex tissue devoted to each body
part** As you can see from this classic though
inexact representation, the amount of cortex
devoted to a body part in the motor cortex
(in the frontal lobes) or in the somatosensory
cortex (in the parietal lobes) is not
proportional to that body part's size. Rather,
the brain devotes more tissue to sensitive
areas and to areas requiring precise control.
So, your fingers have a greater representation
in the cortex than does your upper arm.

mechanics, Spanish neuroscientist José Delgado stimulated a spot on a patient's left
motor cortex, triggering the right hand to make a fist. Asked to keep the fingers open
during the next stimulation, the patient, whose fingers closed despite his best efforts,
remarked, "I guess, Doctor, that your electricity is stronger than my will" (Delgado,
1969, p. 114).

Scientists can predict a monkey's arm motion *just before* it moves—by repeatedly measuring motor cortex activity preceding specific arm movements (Livi et al., 2019). Scientists have also observed monkeys' motor cortex neurons responding differently when
executing a social act (putting an object in an experimenter's hand) rather than a nonsocial act (putting something in a container or in their own mouth) (Coudé et al., 2019). Such
findings have opened the door to research on brain-controlled computer technology.

RETRIEVAL PRACTICE

RP-2 If you are able, try moving your right hand in a circular motion, as if cleaning a table.
Then start your right foot doing the same motion, synchronized with your hand. Now
reverse the right foot's motion, but not the hand's. Finally, try moving the *left* foot
opposite to the right hand.

a. Why is reversing the right foot's motion so hard?

b. Why is it easier to move the left foot opposite to the right hand?

ANSWERS IN APPENDIX E

BRAIN-MACHINE INTERFACES Researchers wondered: By eavesdropping on
the brain, could we enable a paralyzed person to move a robotic limb? Could a brain-
machine interface help people learn to command a cursor to write email or work online?
To find out, they implanted 100 tiny recording electrodes in the motor cortexes of three
monkeys (Nicolelis, 2011; Serruya et al., 2002). As the monkeys gained rewards by using
a joystick to follow a moving red target, the researchers matched the brain signals with
the arm movements. Then they programmed a computer to monitor the signals and
operate the joystick. When a monkey merely thought about a move, the mind-reading
computer moved the cursor with nearly the same proficiency as had the reward-seeking
monkey. Monkey think, computer do.

⊙ **FIGURE 6.3**

Brain-machine interaction Electrodes planted in the hand area of the motor cortex, and in the hand, elbow, and shoulder muscles helped a man with paralysis in all four limbs use his paralyzed arm to take a drink of coffee (Ajiboye et al., 2017). Such research advances are paving the way for restored movement in daily life, outside the controlled laboratory environment (Andersen, 2019; Andersen et al., 2010).

In another demonstration of machine learning, researchers scanned the brains of physics students when they thought about 30 physics-relevant concepts, such as gravity and momentum (Mason & Just, 2016). A computer program learned to accurately identify the links between specific brain region activations and the concepts.

Clinical trials of such *cognitive neural prosthetics* have since been under way with people who have severe paralysis or have lost a limb (Andersen et al., 2010; Nurmikko et al., 2010; Rajangam et al., 2016; Velliste et al., 2008). The first patient, a 25-year-old man with paralysis, was able to mentally control a TV, draw shapes on a computer screen, and play video games—all thanks to an aspirin-sized chip with 100 microelectrodes recording activity in his motor cortex (Hochberg et al., 2006). Others with paralysis who have received implants have learned to direct robotic arms with their thoughts (Clausen et al., 2017).

And then there is Ian Burkhart, who lost the use of his arms and legs at age 19. Ohio State University brain researchers implanted recording electrodes in his motor cortex (Schwemmer et al., 2018). Using computer *machine learning*, they instruct Burkhart to stare at a screen that shows a moving hand. Next, Burkhart imagines moving his own hand. Brain signals from his motor cortex begin feeding into the computer, which gets the message that he wants to move his arm and thus stimulates those muscles. The result? Burkhart, with his very own paralyzed arm, grasps a bottle, dumps out its contents, and picks up a stick. He can even play the video game *Guitar Hero*. By learning Burkhart's unique brain response patterns, the computer can predict his brain activity to help him make these movements. "It's really restored a lot the hope I have for the future to know that a device like this will be possible to use in everyday life," Burkhart says, "for me and for many other people" (Wood, 2018). (See tinyurl.com/ControlMotorCortex.)

If everything psychological is also biological—if, for example, every thought is also a neural event—microelectrodes could someday detect complex thoughts well enough to enable many people to control their environment with ever-greater precision (see **FIGURE 6.3**). Scientists have even created a prosthetic voice. The virtual voice creates (mostly) understandable speech by reading the brain's motor commands that direct vocal movement (Anumanchipalli et al., 2019).

Sensory Functions

If the motor cortex sends messages out to the body, where does the cortex receive incoming messages? Wilder Penfield identified a cortical area—at the front of the parietal lobes, parallel to and just behind the motor cortex—that specializes in receiving information from the skin senses, such as touch and temperature, and from the movement of body parts. We now call this area the **somatosensory cortex.** Stimulate a point on the top of this band of tissue and a person may report being touched on the shoulder; stimulate some point on the side and the person may feel something on the face.

The more sensitive the body region, the larger the somatosensory cortex area devoted to it (see Figure 6.2). Your supersensitive lips project to a larger brain area than do your toes, which is one reason we kiss rather than touch toes. Rats have a large area of the brain devoted to their whisker sensations, and owls to their hearing sensations.

 somatosensory cortex a cerebral cortex area at the front of the parietal lobes that registers and processes body touch and movement sensations.

Imperial College London

(a)   (b)

◀ **FIGURE 6.4**
Seeing without eyes The psychoactive drug LSD often produces vivid *hallucinations*. Why? Because it dramatically increases communication between the visual cortex (in the occipital lobe) and other brain regions. These fMRI (functional MRI) scans show (a) a research participant with closed eyes who has been given a placebo and (b) the same person under the influence of LSD. Color represents increased blood flow (Carhart-Harris et al., 2016). Other researchers have confirmed that LSD increases communication between brain regions (Preller et al., 2019; Timmerman et al., 2018).

Scientists have identified additional areas where the cortex receives input from senses other than touch. Any visual information you are receiving now is going to the visual cortex in your occipital lobes, at the back of your brain (**FIGURES 6.4** and **6.5**). If you have normal vision, you might see flashes of light or dashes of color if stimulated in your occipital lobes. (In a sense, we *do* have eyes in the back of our head!) Having lost much of his right occipital lobe to a tumor removal, a friend of mine [DM's] was blind to the left half of his field of vision. Visual information travels from the occipital lobes to other areas that specialize in tasks such as identifying words, detecting emotions, and recognizing faces.

Any sound you now hear is processed by your auditory cortex in your temporal lobes (just above your ears; see Figure 6.5). Most of this auditory information travels a circuitous route from one ear to the auditory receiving area above your opposite ear. If stimulated in your auditory cortex, you might hear a sound. MRI scans of people with schizophrenia have revealed active auditory areas in the temporal lobes during the false sensory experience of auditory *hallucinations* (Lennox et al., 1999). Even the phantom ringing sound experienced by people with hearing loss (tinnitus) is—if heard in one ear—associated with activity in the temporal lobe on the brain's opposite side (Muhlnickel, 1998).

Auditory cortex

Visual cortex

🅐 **FIGURE 6.5**
The visual cortex and auditory cortex The visual cortex in the occipital lobes at the rear of your brain receives input from your eyes. The auditory cortex in your temporal lobes—above your ears—receives information from your ears.

RETRIEVAL PRACTICE

RP-3 Our brain's _____ cortex registers and processes body touch and movement sensations. The _____ cortex controls our voluntary movements.

ANSWERS IN APPENDIX E

Association Areas

So far, we have pointed out small cortical areas that either receive sensory input or direct muscular output. Together, these occupy about one-fourth of the human brain's thin, wrinkled cover. What, then, goes on in the remaining vast regions of the cortex? In these **association areas,** neurons are busy with higher mental functions—many of the tasks that make us human. Electrically probing an association area won't trigger any observable response. So, unlike the somatosensory and motor areas, association area functions cannot be neatly mapped. Does this mean we don't use them—or that, as some 4 in 10 people agreed in two surveys, "We use only 10 percent of our brains" (Furnham, 2018; Macdonald et al., 2017)? (See Thinking Critically About: Do We Use Only 10 Percent of Our Brain?)

Association areas are found in all four lobes. The *prefrontal cortex* in the forward part of the frontal lobes enables judgment, planning, social interactions, and processing of new memories (de la Vega et al., 2016; Silwa & Frehwald, 2017; Yin & Weber, 2019). People with damage to this area may have high intelligence test scores and great cake-baking skills. Yet they would not be able to plan ahead to *begin* baking a cake for a birthday party (Huey et al., 2006). If they did begin to bake, they might forget the recipe (MacPherson et al., 2016). And despite being responsible for the absence of birthday cake at the party, they may fail to feel regret (Bault et al., 2019).

association areas areas of the cerebral cortex that are not involved in primary motor or sensory functions; rather, they are involved in higher mental functions such as learning, remembering, thinking, and speaking.

Thinking Critically About:
Do We Use Only 10 Percent of Our Brain?

LOQ 6-2 Is it true that 90 percent of our brain isn't really used?

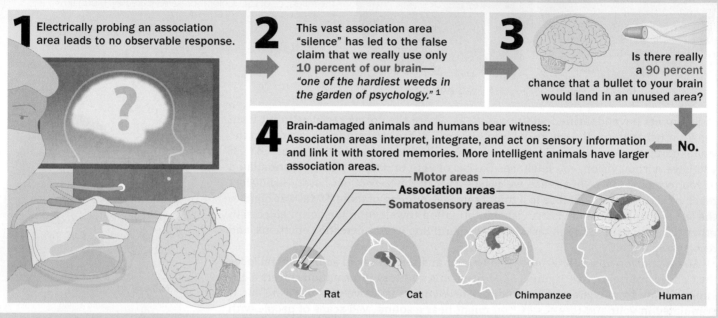

1 Electrically probing an association area leads to no observable response.

2 This vast association area "silence" has led to the false claim that we really use only 10 percent of our brain—*"one of the hardiest weeds in the garden of psychology."* [1]

3 Is there really a 90 percent chance that a bullet to your brain would land in an unused area?

No.

4 Brain-damaged animals and humans bear witness: Association areas interpret, integrate, and act on sensory information and link it with stored memories. More intelligent animals have larger association areas.

Motor areas
Association areas
Somatosensory areas

Rat   Cat   Chimpanzee   Human

1. McBurney, 1996, p. 44

FIGURE 6.6

A blast from the past (a) Phineas Gage's skull was kept as a medical record. Using measurements and modern neuroimaging techniques, researchers have reconstructed the probable path of the rod through Gage's brain (Van Horn et al., 2012). (b) This photo shows Gage after his accident. (The image has been reversed to show the features correctly. Early photos, including this one, were actually mirror images.)

Warren Anatomical Museum in the Francis A. Countway Library of Medicine. Gift of Jack and Beverly Wilgus

(a)   (b)

Frontal lobe damage also can alter personality and remove a person's inhibitions. Consider the classic case of railroad worker Phineas Gage. One afternoon in 1848, Gage, then 25 years old, was using a tamping iron to pack gunpowder into a rock. A spark ignited the gunpowder, shooting the rod up through his left cheek and out the top of his skull, leaving his frontal lobes damaged (**FIGURE 6.6**). To everyone's amazement, Gage was immediately able to sit up and speak, and after the wound healed, he returned to work. But the blast damaged connections between his frontal lobes and brain regions that enable emotion control and decision making (Thiebaut de Schotten et al., 2015; Van Horn et al., 2012). How did this damage affect Gage's personality? The normally friendly, soft-spoken man was now irritable, profane, and dishonest. Gage, said his friends, was "no longer Gage." Gage later lost his railroad job, but over time he adapted to his disability and found work as a stagecoach driver (Macmillan & Lena, 2010).

Studies of others with damaged frontal lobes have revealed similar impairments. Not only do they become less inhibited (without the frontal lobe brakes on their impulses), but their moral judgments also seem unrestrained. Cecil Clayton lost 20 percent of his left frontal lobe in a 1972 sawmill accident. Thereafter, his intelligence test score dropped to an elementary school level and he displayed increased impulsivity. In 1996, he fatally shot a deputy sheriff. In 2015, when he was 74, the State of Missouri executed him (Williams, 2015).

Would you advocate pushing one person in front of a runaway trolley to save five others? Most people would not, because of strong social norms against murder. But people with damage to the prefrontal cortex are often untroubled by such ethical dilemmas (Koenigs et al., 2007). The frontal lobes help steer us toward kindness and away from violence (Lieberman et al., 2019;

Molenberghs et al., 2015; Yang & Raine, 2009). With their frontal lobes ruptured, people's moral compass seems separated from their actions. They know right from wrong but often don't care.

Association areas also perform other mental functions. The parietal lobes, parts of which were large and unusually shaped in Einstein's normal-weight brain, enable mathematical and spatial reasoning (Amalric & Dehaene, 2019; Wilkey et al., 2018). Stimulation of one parietal lobe area in brain-surgery patients produced a feeling of wanting to move an upper limb, the lips, or the tongue without any actual movement. With increased stimulation, patients falsely believed they *had* moved. Curiously, when surgeons stimulated a different association area near the motor cortex in the frontal lobes, the patients did move but had no awareness of doing so (Desmurget et al., 2009). These head-scratching findings suggest that our perception of moving flows not from the movement itself, but rather from our intention and the results we expected.

On the underside of the right temporal lobe, another association area enables us to recognize faces. If a stroke or head injury destroyed this area of your brain, you would still be able to describe facial features and to recognize someone's gender and approximate age, yet be strangely unable to identify the person as, say, Ariana Grande, or even your grandmother.

Nevertheless, to reemphasize, we should be wary of using pictures of brain "hot spots" to create a new phrenology that locates complex functions in precise brain areas (Beck, 2010; Shimamura, 2010; Uttal, 2001). During a complex task, a brain scan shows many islands of brain activity working together—some running automatically in the background, and others under conscious control (Chein & Schneider, 2012). Your memory, language, attention, and social skills result from *functional connectivity*—communication among distinct brain areas and neural networks (Bassett et al., 2018; Knight, 2007; Silston et al., 2018). What happens when brain areas struggle to communicate with each other? People are at increased risk for a variety of mental disorders (Baker et al., 2019; Zhang et al., 2019). *The point to remember:* Our mental experiences—and our psychological health—rely on coordinated brain activity.

RETRIEVAL PRACTICE

RP-4 Why are association areas important?

ANSWERS IN APPENDIX E

Cecil Clayton's brain scan, included with request for stay of execution filed with the Supreme Court, showing a missing portion of his frontal lobe.

Missing frontal lobe brakes With part of his left frontal lobe (in this downward facing brain scan) lost to injury, Cecil Clayton became more impulsive and killed a deputy sheriff. Nineteen years later, his state executed him for this crime.

"We held Einstein's brain in our hands and realized that this is the organ that was responsible for changing our perceptions of the universe . . . we were in awe."
— Neuroscientist Sandra Witelson (2011)

 Check your understanding of the parts of the brain by engaging online with *Concept Practice: Brain Areas Within the Head.* And to learn more about case studies, such as the study of Phineas Gage, see the *Video: Case Studies* for a helpful tutorial animation.

Responses to Damage

LOQ 6-3 To what extent can a damaged brain reorganize itself, and what is *neurogenesis?*

Our brain displays an extraordinary **neuroplasticity**—an ability to change in response to experiences, both good and bad. Here we will explore the brain's ability to modify itself after damage.

Most brain-damage effects can be traced to two hard facts: (1) Severed brain and spinal cord neurons, unlike cut skin, usually do not regenerate. (If your spinal cord were severed, you would probably be permanently paralyzed.) And (2) some brain functions seem preassigned to specific areas. One newborn who suffered damage to temporal lobe facial recognition areas was never able to recognize faces (Farah et al., 2000). But there is good news: Some neural tissue can *reorganize* in response to damage.

Neuroplasticity may also occur after serious damage, especially in young children (Kolb, 1989; see also **FIGURE 6.7**). *Constraint-induced therapy* aims to rewire brains and improve the dexterity of a brain-damaged child or even an adult stroke victim (Taub, 2004). By restraining a fully functioning limb, therapists force patients to use the "bad" hand or leg, gradually reprogramming the brain. One stroke victim, a surgeon in his fifties, was put to work cleaning tables, with his good arm and hand restrained. Slowly, the bad arm recovered its skills. As damaged-brain functions migrated to other brain regions, he gradually learned to write again and even to play tennis (Doidge, 2007).

The brain's plasticity is good news for those blind or deaf. Blindness or deafness makes unused brain areas available for other uses, such as sound and smell (Amedi et al., 2005;

neuroplasticity the brain's ability to change, especially during childhood, by reorganizing after damage or by building new pathways based on experience.

Courtesy of Dr. Danielle Bassett

Physics of the mind MacArthur Genius Award winner Danielle Bassett's work crosses disciplines. She applies concepts from physics and mathematics to explain the brain's neural network connections.

Joe McNally/Hulton Archive/Getty Images

Living Art Enterprises, LLC/Science Source

⑦ **FIGURE 6.7**

Brain work is child's play This 6-year-old had surgery to end her life-threatening seizures. Although most of an entire hemisphere was removed (see MRI of hemispherectomy), her remaining hemisphere compensated by putting other areas to work. One Johns Hopkins medical team reflected on the child hemispherectomies they had performed. Although use of the opposite arm was compromised, the team reported being "awed" by how well the children had retained their memory, personality, and humor (Vining et al., 1997). The younger the child, the greater the chance that the remaining hemisphere can take over the functions of the one that was surgically removed (Choi, 2008; Danelli et al., 2013).

📺 For more on how our brain responds to damage, see the *Video—Brain Plasticity: Rewiring the Visual Cortex.*

neurogenesis the formation of new neurons.

corpus callosum [KOR-pus kah-LOW-sum] the large band of neural fibers connecting the two brain hemispheres and carrying messages between them.

split brain a condition resulting from surgery that separates the brain's two hemispheres by cutting the fibers (mainly those of the corpus callosum) connecting them.

Bauer et al., 2017). If a blind person uses one finger to read Braille, the brain area dedicated to that finger expands as the sense of touch invades the visual cortex that normally helps people see (Barinaga, 1992; Sadato et al., 1996). Neuroplasticity also helps explain why deaf people who learned sign language before another language may have enhanced peripheral and motion-detection vision (Bosworth & Dobkins, 1999; Shiell et al., 2014). In deaf people whose native language is sign, the temporal lobe area normally dedicated to hearing waits in vain for stimulation. Finally, it looks for other signals to process, such as those from the visual system used to see and interpret signs.

Similar reassignment may occur when disease or damage frees up other brain areas normally dedicated to specific functions. If a slow-growing left hemisphere tumor disrupts language (which resides mostly in the left hemisphere), the right hemisphere may compensate (Thiel et al., 2006). When people who are born without hands use their feet to perform everyday tasks, their somatosensory cortex for the hand area becomes active—even though they have never had hands (Striem-Amit et al., 2018). So what do you suppose was the sexual intercourse experience of one patient whose lower leg had been amputated? "I actually experience my orgasm in my [phantom] foot. [Note that in Figure 6.2, the toes region is adjacent to the genitals.] And there it's much bigger than it used to be because it's no longer just confined to my genitals" (Ramachandran & Blakeslee, 1998, p. 36).

Although the brain often attempts self-repair by reorganizing existing tissue, researchers are debating whether it can also mend itself through **neurogenesis**—producing new neurons (Boldrini et al., 2018; Kempermann et al., 2018; Sorrells et al., 2018). Researchers have found baby neurons deep in the brain of adult mice, birds, monkeys, and humans (He & Jin, 2016; Jessberger et al., 2008). These neurons may then form connections with neighboring neurons (Gould, 2007; Luna et al., 2019). Neurogenesis varies among individuals, offering another example of how we experience a common process in our own unique way (Kempermann, 2019).

Master *stem cells,* which can develop into any type of brain cell, have also been discovered in the human embryo. If mass-produced in a lab and injected into a damaged brain, might neural stem cells turn themselves into replacements for lost brain cells? Researchers at universities and biotech companies continue to break new ground on how to produce stem cells that resemble functioning human neurons (Lu et al., 2016; Paşca et al., 2015). Such stem cell research not only helps treat the diseased or damaged brain, but also aids understanding of brain development, memory, and other basic psychological processes (Mariani et al., 2012; Sun et al, 2015; Zhang et al., 2016). Might surgeons someday be able to rebuild damaged brains, much as we reseed damaged sports fields? Stay tuned. In the meantime, we can all benefit from natural promoters of neurogenesis, such as exercise, sleep, and nonstressful but stimulating environments (Liu & Nusslock, 2018; Monteiro et al., 2014; Nollet et al., 2019).

The Divided Brain

LOQ 6-4 What do split brains reveal about the functions of our two brain hemispheres?

Our brain's look-alike left and right hemispheres serve differing functions. This *lateralization* is apparent after brain damage. Research spanning more than a century has shown that left hemisphere accidents, strokes, and tumors can impair reading, writing, speaking, arithmetic reasoning, and understanding. Similar right hemisphere damage has less visibly dramatic effects. Does this mean that the right hemisphere is just along for the ride? Many believed this was the case until the 1960s, when a fascinating chapter in psychology's history began to unfold: Researchers found that the "minor" right hemisphere was not so limited after all.

(a)   (b)

Martin M. Rotker/Science Source

Dr. Patric Hagmann/CHUV, UNIL, Lausanne, Switzerland

←FIGURE 6.8
The corpus callosum This large band of neural fibers connects the two brain hemispheres. (a) To photograph this half brain, a surgeon separated the hemispheres by cutting through the corpus callosum (see blue arrow) and lower brain regions. (b) This high-resolution diffusion spectrum image, showing a top-facing brain from above, reveals brain neural networks within the two hemispheres, and the corpus callosum neural bridge between them.

Splitting the Brain

In the early 1960s, two neurosurgeons speculated that major epileptic seizures were caused by an amplification of abnormal brain activity bouncing back and forth between the two cerebral hemispheres, which work together as a whole system (Bogen & Vogel, 1962). If so, they wondered, could they end this biological tennis match by severing the **corpus callosum,** the wide band of axon fibers connecting the two hemispheres and carrying messages between them (see **FIGURE 6.8**)? The neurosurgeons knew that psychologists Roger Sperry, Ronald Myers, and Michael Gazzaniga had divided cats' and monkeys' brains in this manner, with no serious ill effects.

So the surgeons operated. The result? The seizures all but disappeared. The patients with these **split brains** were surprisingly normal, their personality and intellect hardly affected. Waking from surgery, one even joked that he had a "splitting headache" (Gazzaniga, 1967). By sharing their experiences, these patients have greatly expanded our understanding of interactions between the intact brain's two hemispheres.

To appreciate these findings, we need to focus for a minute on the peculiar nature of our visual wiring, illustrated in **FIGURE 6.9**. Note that each eye receives sensory information from the entire visual field. But in each eye, information from the left half of your field of vision goes to your right hemisphere, and information from the right half of your visual field goes to your left hemisphere, which usually controls speech. Information received by either hemisphere is quickly transmitted to the other across the corpus callosum. In a person with a severed corpus callosum, this information-sharing does not take place.

Knowing these facts, Sperry and Gazzaniga could send information to a patient's left or right hemisphere. As the person stared at a spot, they flashed a stimulus to its right or left. They could do this with you, too, but in your intact brain, the hemisphere receiving the information would instantly pass the news to the other side. Because the split-brain surgery had cut the communication lines between the hemispheres, the researchers could, with these patients, quiz each hemisphere separately.

In an early experiment, Gazzaniga (1967) asked split-brain patients to stare at a dot as he flashed HE·ART on a screen (**FIGURE 6.10**). Thus, HE appeared in their left visual field (which transmits to the right hemisphere) and ART in the right field (which transmits to the left hemisphere). When he then asked them to *say* what they had seen, the patients reported that they had seen ART. But when asked to *point* to what they had seen, they were startled when their left hand (controlled by the right hemisphere) pointed to HE. Given an opportunity to express itself, each hemisphere indicated what it had seen. The right hemisphere (controlling the left hand) intuitively knew what it could not verbally report.

When a picture of a spoon was flashed to their right hemisphere, the patients could not *say* what they had viewed. But when asked to *identify* what they had viewed by feeling an assortment of hidden objects with their left hand, they readily selected the spoon. If the experimenter said, "Correct!" the patient might reply, "What? Correct? How could I possibly pick out the correct object when I don't know what I saw?" It is, of course, the left hemisphere doing the talking here, bewildered by what the nonverbal right hemisphere knows.

A few people who have had split-brain surgery have been for a time bothered by the unruly independence of their left hand. It seemed the left hand truly didn't know what the right hand was doing. The left hand might unbutton a shirt while the right hand buttoned it, or put grocery store items back on the shelf after the right hand put them in the cart. It was as if each hemisphere was thinking, "I've half a mind to wear my green (blue) shirt today." Indeed, said Sperry (1964), split-brain surgery leaves people "with two

↓FIGURE 6.9
The information highway from eye to brain

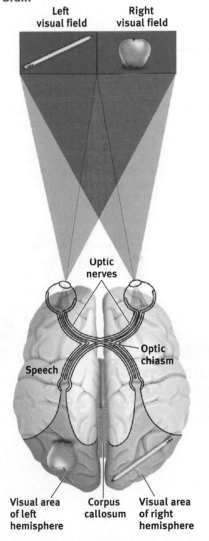

Left visual field

Right visual field

Optic nerves

Optic chiasm

Speech

Visual area of left hemisphere

Corpus callosum

Visual area of right hemisphere

"Do not let your left hand know what your right hand is doing." — Matthew 6:3

FIGURE 6.10
One skull, two minds When an experimenter flashes HE•ART across the visual field, a woman with a split brain verbally reports seeing the word transmitted to her left hemisphere. However, if asked to indicate with her left hand what she saw, she points to the word transmitted to her right hemisphere (Gazzaniga, 1983).

"Look at the dot."

(a)

Two words separated by a dot are momentarily projected.

(b)

"What word did you see?"   or   "Point with your left hand to the word you saw."

(c)

FIGURE 6.11
Try this! People who have had split-brain surgery can simultaneously draw two different shapes.

separate minds." With a split brain, both hemispheres can comprehend and follow an instruction to copy—*simultaneously*—different figures with the left and right hands (Franz et al., 2000; see also **FIGURE 6.11**). Today's researchers believe that a split-brain patient's mind resembles a river that has branched into separate streams, each unaware of the other (Pinto et al., 2017). (Reading these reports, can you imagine a patient enjoying a solitary game of "rock, paper, scissors"—left versus right hand?)

When the "two minds" are at odds, the left hemisphere does mental gymnastics to rationalize reactions it does not understand. If a patient follows an order ("Walk") sent to the right hemisphere, a strange thing happens. The left hemisphere, unaware of the order, doesn't know why the patient begins walking. But if asked, the patient doesn't reply, "I don't know." Instead, the left hemisphere improvises—"I'm going into the house to get a Coke." Gazzaniga (1988), who described these patients as "the most fascinating people on earth," realized that the conscious left hemisphere resembles an interpreter that instantly constructs explanations. The brain, he concluded, often runs on autopilot; it acts first and then explains itself.

RETRIEVAL PRACTICE

RP-5 (a) If we flash a red light to the right hemisphere of a person with a split brain, and flash a green light to the left hemisphere, will each observe its own color? (b) Will the person be aware that the colors differ? (c) What will the person verbally report seeing?

ANSWERS IN APPENDIX E

Have you ever been asked if you are "left-brained" or "right-brained"? Consider this popular misconception—supported by 64 percent of the public in one survey (Macdonald et al., 2017)—by engaging online with the activity *How Would You Know If People Can Be "Left-Brained" or "Right-Brained"?*

Right-Left Differences in the Intact Brain

So, what about the 99.99+ percent of us with undivided brains? Does each of *our* hemispheres also perform distinct functions? The short answer is *Yes*. When a person performs a *perceptual* task, a brain scan often reveals increased activity (brain waves, blood flow, and glucose consumption) in the *right* hemisphere. When the person speaks or does a math calculation, activity usually increases in the *left* hemisphere.

A dramatic demonstration of hemispheric specialization happens before some types of brain surgery. To locate the patient's language centers, the surgeon injects a sedative into the neck artery feeding blood to the left hemisphere, which usually controls speech. Before the injection, the patient is lying down, arms in the air, chatting with the doctor. Can you predict what happens when the drug puts the left hemisphere to sleep? Within seconds, the person's right arm falls limp. If the left hemisphere is controlling language, the patient will be speechless until the drug wears off. If the drug is injected into the artery to the right hemisphere, the left arm will fall limp, but the person will still be able to speak.

To the brain, language is language, whether spoken or signed. Just as hearing people usually use the left hemisphere to process spoken language, deaf people use the left hemisphere to process sign language (Corina et al., 1992; Hickok et al., 2001). Thus, a left hemisphere stroke disrupts a deaf person's signing, much as it would disrupt a hearing person's speaking (Corina, 1998).

Although the left hemisphere is skilled at making quick, literal interpretations of language, the right hemisphere

- *excels in making inferences* (Beeman & Chiarello, 1998; Bowden & Beeman, 1998; Mason & Just, 2004). Primed with the flashed word *foot*, the left hemisphere will be especially quick to recognize the closely associated word *heel*. But if given an insight-like problem—"What word goes with *boot, summer,* and *ground?*"—the right hemisphere more quickly comes to a reasoned conclusion and recognizes the solution: *camp*. As one patient explained after a right hemisphere stroke, "I understand words, but I'm missing the subtleties." The right side of the brain is also better than the left at copying drawings, recognizing faces, noticing differences, perceiving emotion, and expressing emotion through the more expressive left side of the face. Right hemisphere damage can greatly disrupt these abilities.

- *helps us modulate our speech* to make meaning clear—as when we say, "Let's eat, Grandpa!" instead of "Let's eat Grandpa!" (Heller, 1990).

- *helps orchestrate our self-awareness*. People who suffer partial paralysis will sometimes stubbornly deny their impairment—constantly claiming they can move a paralyzed limb—if the damage is to the right hemisphere (Berti et al., 2005).

Simply looking at the two hemispheres, so alike to the naked eye, who would suppose they each contribute uniquely to the harmony of the whole? Yet a variety of observations—of people with split brains, of people with normal brains, and even of other species' brains—converge beautifully, leaving little doubt that we have unified brains with specialized parts (Hopkins & Cantalupo, 2008; MacNeilage et al., 2009).

Brain scans show that, like humans, dogs usually process words with their left hemisphere and intonation with a right hemisphere region. One study demonstrated that giving praise was ineffective if what the dogs heard didn't match *how* it was spoken (Andics et al., 2016).

ASK YOURSELF

Why do you think our brain evolved into so many interconnected structures with varying functions?

For a helpful animated review of this research, see *Topic Tutorial: PsychSim6, Hemispheric Specialization*.

* * *

We have glimpsed an overriding principle: Everything psychological is simultaneously biological. We have focused on how our thoughts, feelings, and actions arise from our specialized yet integrated and wondrously adaptable brain. Elsewhere in this text, we will further explore the significance of the biological revolution in psychology.

From nineteenth-century phrenology to today's neuroscience, we have come a long way. Knowing neuroscience helps us to understand ourselves and our fellow humans. As noted by one of the founders of modern neuroscience, Marian Diamond (2016), "Take away the brain, you take away the person." Yet psychological scientists need to practice intellectual humility: What is unknown still dwarfs what is known. We can describe the brain. We can learn the functions of its parts. We can study how the parts communicate. But how do we get mind out of meat? How does the electrochemical whir in a hunk of tissue the size of a small cabbage give rise to elation, a creative idea, or that memory of Grandmother?

Much as gas and air can give rise to something different—fire—so also does the complex human brain give rise to something different: *consciousness*. The mind, Roger Sperry argued, emerges from the brain's dance of ions, yet is not reducible to it. As neuroscientist Donald MacKay (1978) observed, "[My brain activity] reflects what I am thinking, as [computer] activity reflects the equation it is solving." Mind and brain activities are yoked, he noted, but are complementary and conceptually distinct.

Cells cannot be fully explained by the actions of atoms, nor minds by the activity of cells. Psychology is rooted in biology, which is rooted in chemistry, which is rooted in physics. Yet psychology is more than applied physics. As Jerome Kagan (1998) reminded us, the meaning of the Gettysburg Address is not reducible to neural activity. Sexual love is more than blood flooding to the genitals. Morality and responsibility become possible when we understand the mind as a "holistic system," said Sperry (1992). We are not mere jabbering robots. Brains make thoughts. And thoughts change brains.

The mind seeking to understand the brain—that is indeed among the ultimate scientific challenges. And so it will always be. To paraphrase cosmologist John Barrow, a brain simple enough to be fully understood is too simple to produce a mind able to understand it.

"All psychological phenomena are caused by the brain, but many are better understood at the level of the mind." — Tweet from psychologist Steven Pinker, 2013

MODULE 6 REVIEW The Cerebral Cortex

LEARNING OBJECTIVES

Test Yourself Answer these repeated Learning Objective Questions on your own (before checking the answers in Appendix D) to improve your retention of the concepts (McDaniel et al., 2009, 2015).

LOQ 6-1 What four lobes make up the cerebral cortex, and what are the functions of the motor cortex, somatosensory cortex, and association areas?

LOQ 6-2 Is it true that 90 percent of our brain isn't really used?

LOQ 6-3 To what extent can a damaged brain reorganize itself, and what is *neurogenesis*?

LOQ 6-4 What do split brains reveal about the functions of our two brain hemispheres?

TERMS AND CONCEPTS TO REMEMBER

Test Yourself Write down the definition in your own words, then check your answer.

cerebral [seh-REE-bruhl] cortex, p. 75

frontal lobes, p. 76

parietal [puh-RYE-uh-tuhl] lobes, p. 76

occipital [ahk-SIP-uh-tuhl] lobes, p. 76

temporal lobes, p. 76

motor cortex, p. 76

somatosensory cortex, p. 78

association areas, p. 79

neuroplasticity, p. 81

neurogenesis, p. 82

corpus callosum [KOR-pus kah-LOW-sum], p. 82

split brain, p. 82

MASTER THE MATERIAL

Test Yourself Answer the following questions on your own first, then check your answers in Appendix E.

1. If a neurosurgeon stimulated your right motor cortex, you would most likely
   a. see light.
   b. hear a sound.
   c. feel a touch on the right arm.
   d. move your left leg.

2. How do different neural networks communicate with one another to let you respond when a friend greets you at a party?

3. Which of the following body regions has the greatest representation in the somatosensory cortex?
   a. Upper arm
   b. Toes
   c. Lips
   d. All regions are equally represented.

4. Judging and planning are enabled by the _____ lobes.

5. The "uncommitted" areas that make up about three-fourths of the cerebral cortex are called _____.

6. The flexible brain's ability to respond to damage is especially evident in the brains of
   a. split-brain patients.
   b. young adults.
   c. young children.
   d. right-handed people.

7. An experimenter flashes the word HERON across the visual field of a man whose corpus callosum has been severed. HER is transmitted to his right hemisphere and ON to his left hemisphere. When asked to indicate what he saw, the man says he saw _____ but his left hand points to _____.

8. Studies of people with split brains and brain scans of those with undivided brains indicate that the left hemisphere excels in
   a. processing language.
   b. visual perceptions.
   c. making inferences.
   d. neurogenesis.

9. Damage to the brain's right hemisphere is most likely to reduce a person's ability to
   a. recite the alphabet rapidly.
   b. make inferences.
   c. understand verbal instructions.
   d. solve arithmetic problems.

We Are/Getty Images

Consciousness and the Two-Track Mind

Consciousness can be a funny thing. It offers us weird experiences, as when entering sleep or leaving a dream. And sometimes it leaves us wondering who is really in control. After zoning me [DM] out with nitrous oxide, my dentist tells me to turn my head to the left. My conscious mind resists: *"No way,"* I silently say. *"You can't boss me around!"* Whereupon my robotic head, ignoring my conscious mind, turns obligingly under the dentist's control.

Playing basketball, I have sometimes been mildly irritated as my body passes the ball while my conscious mind says, *"No, stop! Sarah is going to intercept!"* Alas, my body completes the pass. Other times, as psychologist Daniel Wegner (2002) noted in

The Illusion of Conscious Will, people believe their conscious mind is controlling their actions when it isn't. In one experiment, two people jointly controlled a computer mouse. Even when their partner (who was actually the experimenter's accomplice) caused the mouse to stop on a predetermined square, the participants perceived that *they* had caused it to stop there.

Then there are those times when consciousness seems to split. Sometimes, my [ND's] mind wanders while singing portions of the *Moana* soundtrack daily with my young daughter. When reading *Green Eggs and Ham* to one of my [DM's] preschoolers for the umpteenth time, my obliging mouth could say the words while my mind flitted in and out of the story. And if a friend interrupts you mid-text to ask what you're doing for lunch, it's not a problem. Your thumbs complete their keyboard dance as you suggest getting tacos.

What do such experiences tell us? Does the mind's wandering while singing, reading, or texting reveal a split in consciousness, and what exactly is *consciousness* (Module 7)? How do our states of consciousness play out in our sleep and dreams (Module 8)? And was that drug-induced dental episode akin to people's experiences with other mood- and perception-altering *psychoactive drugs* (Module 9)?

MODULE 7 Basic Consciousness Concepts

Roz Chast The New Yorker Collection/The Cartoon Bank

Every science has concepts so fundamental they are nearly impossible to define. Biologists agree on what is alive but not on precisely what *life* is. In physics, *matter* and *energy* elude simple definition. To psychologists, *consciousness* is similarly a fundamental yet slippery concept.

Defining Consciousness

LEARNING OBJECTIVE QUESTION **LOQ** 7-1

What is the place of consciousness in psychology's history?

At its beginning, *psychology* was "the description and explanation of states of consciousness" (Ladd, 1887). But during the first half of the twentieth century, the difficulty of scientifically studying consciousness led many psychologists—including those in the emerging school of *behaviorism*—to turn to direct observations of behavior. By the 1960s, psychology had nearly lost consciousness and was defining itself as "the science of behavior." Consciousness was likened to a car's speedometer: "It doesn't make the car go, it just reflects what's happening" (Seligman, 1991, p. 24).

After 1960, mental concepts reemerged. Neuroscience advances linked brain activity to sleeping, dreaming, and other mental states. Researchers began studying consciousness altered by drugs, hypnosis, and meditation. (More on meditation in Module 40.) Psychologists of all persuasions were affirming the importance of *cognition*, or mental processes. Psychology was regaining consciousness.

Today, consciousness is a thriving area of study (Michel et al., 2019). By **consciousness,** most psychologists mean our subjective awareness of ourselves and our environment (Feinberg & Mallatt, 2016):

- Conscious awareness helps us make sense of our life, including our sensations, emotions, and choices (Weisman et al., 2017).

- Conscious awareness allows us to set and achieve goals as we reflect on our past, adapt to our present, and plan for our future.

- When learning a behavior, conscious awareness focuses our attention (Logan, 2018; Rand et al., 2017; Servant et al., 2018). Over time, the automatic system takes over and your mind tends to run on autopilot (Logan, 2018; Rand et al., 2017). When learning to drive, we focus intensely on the car and the traffic. With practice, the mechanics of driving become semiautomatic. We may find our mind wandering on a long stretch of highway—only to have our attention jolted back to the car and the traffic when someone cuts in front of us and we need to react.

- Over time, we flit between different *states of consciousness*, including normal waking awareness and various altered states (**FIGURE 7.1**).

"Psychology must discard all reference to consciousness." — Behaviorist John B. Watson (1913)

consciousness our subjective awareness of ourselves and our environment.

hypnosis a social interaction in which one person (the hypnotist) suggests to another (the subject) that certain perceptions, feelings, thoughts, or behaviors will spontaneously occur.

cognitive neuroscience the interdisciplinary study of the brain activity linked with cognition (including perception, thinking, memory, and language).

Some states occur spontaneously	Daydreaming	Drowsiness	Dreaming
Some are physio-logically induced	Hallucinations	Orgasm	Food or oxygen starvation
Some are psycho-logically induced	Sensory deprivation	Hypnosis	Meditation

⊖ FIGURE 7.1
Altered states of consciousness In addition to normal, waking awareness, consciousness comes to us in altered states, including daydreaming, sleeping, drug-induced hallucinating, and meditating.

INSADCO Photography/Alamy

Hypnosis

Through **hypnosis,** we may experience an altered state of consciousness involving changes in perceptions, feelings, thoughts, or behaviors. Researchers and health care providers have for many years used hypnosis to lessen pain related to medical procedures, headaches, burn injuries, heart disease, and dental issues (Milling et al., 2002; Montgomery et al., 2000; Patterson & Jensen, 2003). Hypnosis can also reduce emotional distress, unpleasant thinking, and the pain of social rejection (Rainville et al., 1997; Raz & Fan, 2005; Schnur et al., 2008). For people who are obese, hypnosis can aid weight loss, especially when used with *psychotherapy* (Milling et al., 2018). (More on hypnosis in Module 19.)

* * *

So, consciousness helps us adapt and survive. But that leaves us with what researchers call the "hard problem": How do brain cells jabbering to one another create our awareness of the taste of toast, the idea of infinity, the feeling of fright? The question of how consciousness arises from the material brain is one of life's deepest mysteries.

Cognitive Neuroscience

Scientists assume, in the words of neuroscientist Marvin Minsky (1986, p. 287), that "the mind is what the brain does." We just don't know *how* it does it. Even with all the world's technology, we still don't have a clue *how* to make a conscious robot. Yet today's **cognitive neuroscience**—the interdisciplinary study of the brain activity linked with our mental processes—is relating specific brain states to conscious experiences.

If you just *think* about kicking a soccer ball, an fMRI scan could detect increased blood flow to the brain region that plans such action. In one study, researchers asked soccer players to imagine they were making either creative moves (bicycle kick) or ordinary moves (kicking the ball from one foot to the other). Scans showed that thinking of creative moves produced the most coordinated brain activity across different brain regions (Fink et al., 2019).

If brain activity can reveal conscious thinking, could brain scans allow us to discern mental activity in unresponsive patients? *Yes.* A stunning demonstration of consciousness appeared in brain scans of a noncommunicative patient—a 23-year-old woman who had been in a car accident and showed no outward signs of conscious awareness (Owen, 2017a; Owen et al., 2006). When researchers asked her to *imagine* playing tennis, fMRI scans revealed activity in a brain area that normally controls arm and leg movements (**FIGURE 7.2**). Even in a motionless, noncommunicative body, researchers concluded, the brain—and the mind—may still be active. Follow-up studies of brain activity in dozens of unresponsive patients suggest that 25 to 30 percent may be experiencing meaningful conscious awareness (Owen, 2017b; Stender et al., 2014).

Many cognitive neuroscientists are exploring and mapping the conscious functions of the cortex. Based on your cortical activation patterns, they can now, in limited ways, read your mind (Bor, 2010). They could, for example, tell which of 10 similar objects (hammer, drill, and so forth) you were viewing (Shinkareva et al., 2008).

Courtesy of Adrian M. Owen, the Brain and Mind Institute, Western University

⬆ FIGURE 7.2
Evidence of awareness? When a noncommunicative patient was asked to imagine playing tennis or navigating her home, her brain (top) exhibited activity similar to a healthy person's brain (bottom). Researchers wonder if such fMRI scans might enable a "conversation" with some unresponsive patients, by instructing them, for example, to answer *yes* to a question by imagining playing tennis (top and bottom left), and *no* by imagining walking around their home (top and bottom right).

→ **selective attention** focusing conscious awareness on a particular stimulus.

inattentional blindness failing to see visible objects when our attention is directed elsewhere.

Conscious experience, including retrieved memories, arises from synchronized activity across the brain (Chennu et al., 2014; Mashour, 2018; Vaz et al., 2019). If a stimulus activates enough cortex-wide coordinated neural activity—as strong signals in one brain area trigger activity elsewhere—it crosses a threshold for consciousness. A weaker stimulus—perhaps a word flashed too briefly to be consciously perceived—may trigger only visual cortex activity that quickly fades. A stronger stimulus will engage other brain areas, such as those involved with language, attention, and memory. Such reverberating activity (detected by brain scans) is a telltale sign of conscious awareness (Boly et al., 2011; Silverstein et al., 2015). Coordinated activity across brain areas can therefore provide another indication of awareness in unresponsive patients (Demertzi et al., 2019). How the synchronized activity produces awareness—how matter makes mind—remains a mystery.

RETRIEVAL PRACTICE

RP-1 Those working in the interdisciplinary field called _____ _____ study the brain activity associated with the mental processes of perception, thinking, memory, and language.

ANSWERS IN APPENDIX E

Selective Attention

LOQ **7-2** How does selective attention direct our perceptions?

Through **selective attention,** our awareness focuses, like a flashlight beam, on a minute aspect of all that we experience. We may think we can fully attend to a conversation or a class lecture while checking and returning text messages. Actually, our consciousness focuses on but one thing at a time.

By one estimate, our five senses take in 11,000,000 bits of information per second, of which we consciously process about 40 (Wilson, 2002). Yet our mind's unconscious track intuitively makes great use of the other 10,999,960 bits.

What captures our limited attention? Things we deem important. A classic example of selective attention is the *cocktail party effect*—your ability to attend to only one voice within a sea of many as you chat with a party guest. But what happens when another voice speaks your name? Your cognitive radar, operating on your mind's other track, instantly brings that unattended voice into consciousness. Even cats selectively respond to their own names (Saito et al., 2019). This effect might have prevented an embarrassing and dangerous situation in 2009, when two Northwest Airlines pilots "lost track of time." Focused on their laptops and in conversation, they ignored alarmed air traffic controllers' attempts to reach them and overflew their Minneapolis destination by 150 miles. If only the controllers had known and spoken the pilots' names.

Selective Attention and Accidents

Have you, like 60 percent of American drivers, read or sent a text message or viewed a phone map while driving in the last month (Gliklich et al., 2016)? If so, you likely thought—wrongly—that you could simultaneously attend to the road. Such digital distraction can have tragic consequences, as our selective attention shifts more than we realize (Stavrinos et al., 2017). One study left people in a room for 28 minutes with both internet and television access. On average, they guessed their attention switched 15 times. But they were not even close. Eye-tracking revealed eight times that many attentional switches—120 on average (Brasel & Gips, 2011).

Rapid toggling between activities is today's great enemy of sustained, focused attention. The more we mindlessly check our phone, the more we're distracted from our everyday tasks (Marty-Dugas et al., 2018). When we switch attentional gears, and especially when we shift to complex tasks, such as noticing and avoiding cars around us, we pay a toll—a slight and sometimes fatal delay in coping (Rubenstein et al., 2001). When a driver attends to a conversation, activity in brain areas vital to driving decreases an average of 37 percent (Just et al., 2008).

Reprinted with permission of Bill Whitehead

Just how dangerous is distracted driving? Each day, distracted driving kills about 9 Americans (CDC, 2018b). One video cam study of teen drivers found that driver distraction from passengers or phones occurred right before 58 percent of their crashes (AAA, 2015). Talking with passengers makes the risk of an accident 1.6 times higher than normal. Using a cell phone (even hands-free) makes the risk 4 times higher than normal—equal to the risk of drunk driving (McEvoy et al., 2005, 2007). And while talking is distracting, texting wins the danger game. One 18-month video cam study tracked the driving habits of long-haul truckers. When they were texting, their risk of a collision increased 23 times (Olson et al., 2009)! Many European countries, most Canadian provinces, and 48 of 50 U.S. states now ban texting while driving (CBC News, 2014; Rosenthal, 2009). So the next time you're behind the wheel, put the brakes on your texts. Your passengers and fellow drivers will thank you.

> Watch the thought-provoking *Video: Automatic Skills—Disrupting a Pilot's Performance.*

Inattentional Blindness

At the level of conscious awareness, we are "blind" to all but a tiny sliver of visual stimuli. Ulric Neisser (1979) and Robert Becklen and Daniel Cervone (1983) demonstrated this **inattentional blindness** dramatically by showing people a 1-minute video of basketball players, three in black shirts and three in white shirts, tossing a ball. Researchers told viewers to press a key every time they saw a black-shirted player pass the ball. Most were so intent on their task that they failed to notice a young woman carrying an umbrella saunter across the screen midway through the video (**FIGURE 7.3**). Watching a replay, viewers were astonished to see her (Mack & Rock, 2000). This inattentional blindness is a by-product of what we are really good at: focusing attention on some part of our environment.

⌃ FIGURE 7.3
Inattentional blindness Viewers who were attending to basketball tosses among the black-shirted players usually failed to notice the umbrella-toting woman sauntering across the screen (Neisser, 1979).

In a repeat of the experiment, smart-aleck researchers sent a gorilla-suited assistant through the swirl of players (Simons & Chabris, 1999). During its 5- to 9-second cameo appearance, the gorilla paused and thumped its chest. But the gorilla did not steal the show: Half the conscientious pass-counting viewers failed to see it. Psychologists like to have fun, and have continued to do so with "invisible" gorillas. When 24 radiologists were looking for cancer nodules in lung scans, 20 of them missed a tiny gorilla superimposed on the image—though, to their credit, their focus enabled them to spot the much tinier cancer tissue (Drew et al., 2013). The point of these purposeful pranks: Attention is powerfully selective. Your conscious mind is in one place at a time.

This phenomenon extends to *inattentional numbness*. Pickpockets have long understood that bumping into people makes them unlikely to notice a hand slipping into their pocket. British researchers experimented with this tactile inattention: Sure enough, when distracted, participants failed to perceive an otherwise easily-noticed vibration to their hand (Murphy & Dalton, 2016, 2018). Inattentional numbness can lead us to ignore information right beneath our noses. When people focused on a distracting task, they failed to notice a coffee scent in the room (Forster & Spence, 2018). Our attention is a wonderful gift, given to one thing at a time.

Given that most people miss someone in a gorilla suit while their attention is riveted elsewhere, imagine the fun that magicians can have by manipulating our selective attention. "Every time you perform a magic trick, you're engaging in experimental psychology," says magician Teller, a master of mind-messing methods (2009). Clever thieves know this, too. One Swedish psychologist was surprised in Stockholm by a woman suddenly exposing herself; only later did he realize that he had been pickpocketed, outwitted by thieves who understood the limits of our selective attention (Gallace, 2012).

"Has a generation of texters, surfers, and twitterers evolved the enviable ability to process multiple streams of novel information in parallel? Most cognitive psychologists doubt it." — Steven Pinker, "Not at All," 2010

⊙ **FIGURE 7.4**

Change blindness While a man (in red) provides directions to another (a), two experimenters rudely pass between them carrying a door (b). During this interruption, the original direction seeker switches places with another person wearing different-colored clothing (c). Most people, focused on their direction giving, do not notice the switch (Simons & Levin, 1998).

(a)   (b)   (c)

🖾 For more on the limits of our attention, engage online with *Concept Practice: Selective Attention and Multitasking*. And for more on change blindness, watch the 3-minute *Video: Visual Attention*.

In other experiments, people exhibited a form of inattentional blindness called **change blindness**. Viewers failed to notice that, after a brief visual interruption, a big Coke bottle had disappeared, a railing had risen, clothing had changed color—and someone they'd been talking to had been replaced by a different person (**FIGURE 7.4**) (Chabris & Simons, 2010; Resnick et al., 1997). Out of sight, out of mind.

ASK YOURSELF

Can you recall a recent time when, as your attention focused on one thing, you were oblivious to something else—perhaps to pain, to someone's approach, or to music lyrics? (If you're reading this while listening to exciting music, you may have struggled to understand the question 😊 [Vasilev et al., 2018]).

RETRIEVAL PRACTICE

RP-2   Explain two attentional principles that magicians may use to fool us.

ANSWERS IN APPENDIX E

Dual Processing: The Two-Track Mind

LOQ **7-3**   What is the *dual processing* being revealed by today's cognitive neuroscience?

Discovering which brain regions become active with a particular conscious experience strikes many people as interesting, but not mind-blowing. If everything psychological is simultaneously biological, then our ideas, emotions, and spirituality must all, somehow, be embodied. What is mind-blowing to many of us is evidence that we have, so to speak, two minds, each supported by its own neural equipment.

At any moment, we are aware of little more than what's on the screen of our consciousness. But beneath the surface, unconscious information processing occurs simultaneously on many parallel tracks. When we look at a bird flying, we are consciously aware of the result of our cognitive processing ("It's a hummingbird!") but not of our subprocessing of the bird's color, form, movement, and distance. One of the grand ideas of recent cognitive neuroscience is that much of our brain work occurs off stage, out of sight. Perception, memory, thinking, language, and attitudes all operate on two independent levels—a conscious, deliberate "high road" and an unconscious, automatic "low road" (Wang et al., 2017). The high road is reflective, the low road intuitive (Kahneman, 2011; Pennycook et al., 2018). Today's researchers call this **dual processing.** We know more than we know we know.

If you are a driver, consider how you move into the right lane. Drivers know this unconsciously but cannot accurately explain it (Eagleman, 2011). Most say they would bank to the right, then straighten out—a procedure that would actually steer them off the road. In reality, an experienced driver, after moving right, automatically reverses the steering wheel just as far to the left of center, and only then returns to the center position. The lesson: The human brain is a device for converting conscious into unconscious knowledge.

⊙ **change blindness** failing to notice changes in the environment; a form of *inattentional blindness*.

dual processing the principle that information is often simultaneously processed on separate conscious and unconscious tracks.

Or consider this story, which illustrates how science can be stranger than science fiction. During my sojourns at Scotland's University of St Andrews, I [DM] came to know cognitive neuroscientists David Milner and Melvyn Goodale (2008). They studied a local woman, D. F., who suffered brain damage when overcome by carbon monoxide, leaving her unable to recognize and discriminate objects visually. Consciously, D. F. could see nothing. Yet she exhibited **blindsight**—she acted as though she could see. Asked to slip a postcard into a vertical or horizontal mail slot, she could do so without error. Asked the width of a block in front of her, she was at a loss, but she could grasp it with just the right finger–thumb distance. Likewise, if your right and left eyes view different scenes, you will only be consciously aware of one at a time. Yet you will display some blindsight awareness of the other (Baker & Cass, 2013).

How could this be? Don't we have one visual system? Goodale and Milner knew from animal research that the eye sends information simultaneously to different brain areas, which support different tasks (Weiskrantz, 2009, 2010). Sure enough, a scan of D. F.'s brain activity revealed normal activity in the area concerned with reaching for, grasping, and navigating objects, but damage in the area concerned with consciously recognizing objects.[1] (See another example in **FIGURE 7.5**.)

How strangely intricate is this thing we call vision, conclude Goodale and Milner in their aptly titled book, *Sight Unseen*. We may think of our vision as a single system that controls our visually guided actions. Actually, it is a dual-processing system (Foley et al., 2015). A *visual perception track* enables us "to think about the world"—to recognize things and to plan future actions. A *visual action track* guides our moment-to-moment movements.

The dual-track mind also appeared in a patient who lost all of his left visual cortex, leaving him blind to objects and faces presented on the right side of his field of vision. He nevertheless could sense the emotion expressed in faces that he did not consciously perceive (de Gelder, 2010). The same is true of normally sighted people whose visual cortex has been disabled with magnetic stimulation. Such findings suggest that brain areas below the cortex process emotion-related information.

Much of our everyday thinking, feeling, and acting operates outside our conscious awareness (Bargh & Chartrand, 1999). Some "80 to 90 percent of what we do is unconscious," says Nobel laureate and memory expert Eric Kandel (2008). Sometimes we're motivated to avoid thinking, especially when careful thought ("How many calories are in that dessert?") conflicts with our goals ("I want to eat that piece of cake!") (Woolley & Risen, 2018). Yet most people, most of the time mistakenly believe that their intentions and deliberate choices rule their lives. They don't.

Consciousness, though enabling us to exert voluntary control and to communicate our mental states to others, is but the tip of the information-processing iceberg. Just ask the volunteers who chose a card after watching a magician shuffle through the deck (Olson et al., 2015). In nearly every case, the magician swayed participants' decisions by subtly allowing one card to show for longer—but 91 percent of the participants believed they had made the choice on their own. Being intensely focused on an activity (such as reading this module, we hope) increases your total brain activity no more than 5 percent above its baseline rate. Even when you rest, activity whirls inside your head (Raichle, 2010).

Unconscious parallel processing is faster than conscious sequential processing, but both are essential. **Parallel processing** enables your mind to take care of routine business (more on this in Module 17). **Sequential processing** is best for solving new problems, which requires our focused attention on one thing at a time. Try this if you are able: If you are right-handed, move your right foot in a smooth counterclockwise circle and write the number 3 repeatedly with your right hand—at the same time. Or try something equally difficult: Tap a steady beat three times with your left hand while tapping four times with your right hand. Both tasks require conscious attention, which can be in only one place at a time. If time is nature's way of keeping everything from happening at once, then consciousness is nature's way of keeping us from thinking and doing everything at once.

FIGURE 7.5

When the blind can "see" In this compelling demonstration of blindsight and the two-track mind, researcher Lawrence Weiskrantz trailed a blindsight patient down a cluttered hallway. Although told the hallway was empty, the patient meandered around all the obstacles without any awareness of them.

blindsight a condition in which a person can respond to a visual stimulus without consciously experiencing it.

parallel processing processing many aspects of a stimulus or problem simultaneously.

sequential processing processing one aspect of a stimulus or problem at a time; generally used to process new information or to solve difficult problems.

---

[1]So, would the reverse damage lead to the opposite symptoms? Indeed, there are a few such patients—who can see and recognize objects but have difficulty pointing toward or grasping them.

To think further about conscious awareness and decision making, engage online with *Topic Tutorial: PsychSim6, Who's in Charge?*

RETRIEVAL PRACTICE

RP-3 What are the mind's two tracks, and what is *dual processing*?

ANSWERS IN APPENDIX E

7 REVIEW Basic Consciousness Concepts

LEARNING OBJECTIVES

Test Yourself Answer these repeated Learning Objective Questions on your own (before checking the answers in Appendix D) to improve your retention of the concepts (McDaniel et al., 2009, 2015).

LOQ 7-1 What is the place of consciousness in psychology's history?

LOQ 7-2 How does selective attention direct our perceptions?

LOQ 7-3 What is the *dual processing* being revealed by today's cognitive neuroscience?

TERMS AND CONCEPTS TO REMEMBER

Test Yourself Write down the definition in your own words, then check your answer.

consciousness, p. 88

hypnosis, p. 88

cognitive neuroscience, p. 88

selective attention, p. 90

inattentional blindness, p. 90

change blindness, p. 92

dual processing, p. 92

blindsight, p. 93

parallel processing, p. 93

sequential processing, p. 93

MASTER THE MATERIAL

Test Yourself Answer the following questions on your own first, then check your answers in Appendix E.

1. Failure to see visible objects because our attention is occupied elsewhere is called _____ _____.

2. We register and react to stimuli outside of our awareness by means of _____ processing. When we devote deliberate attention to stimuli, we use _____ processing.

3. Inattentional blindness is a product of our _____ attention.

Continue testing yourself with **LearningCurve** or **Achieve Read & Practice** to learn and remember most effectively.

8 Sleep and Dreams

LOQ 8-1 What is *sleep*?

We humans have about a 16-hour battery life before we lay down on our comfy wireless charging pad and slip into **sleep.** Sleep—the irresistible tempter to whom we inevitably succumb. Sleep—the equalizer of presidents and peasants. Sleep—sweet, renewing, mysterious sleep. While sleeping, we may feel "dead to the world," but we are not. Although the roar of my [ND's] neighborhood garbage truck leaves me undisturbed, my baby's cry will shatter my sleep. Even when you are deeply asleep, your perceptual window is open a crack. You move around on your bed, but you manage not to fall out. The sound of your name can also cause your unconscious body to perk up. EEG recordings confirm that the brain's auditory cortex responds to sound stimuli even during sleep (Kutas, 1990). And when you sleep, as when awake, you process most information outside your conscious awareness.

By recording the brain waves and muscle movements of sleeping participants, and by observing and occasionally waking them, researchers are solving some of sleep's deepest mysteries. Perhaps you can anticipate some of their discoveries. Are the following statements true or false?

"I love to sleep. Do you? Isn't it great? It really is the best of both worlds. You get to be alive and unconscious." — Comedian Rita Rudner, 1993

1. When people dream of performing some activity, their limbs often move in concert with the dream.

2. Older adults sleep more than young adults.

3. Sleepwalkers are acting out their dreams.

4. Sleep experts recommend treating insomnia with an occasional sleeping pill.

5. Some people dream every night; others seldom dream.

All these statements (adapted from Palladino & Carducci, 1983) are *false*. To see why, read on.

Biological Rhythms and Sleep

Like the ocean, life has its rhythmic tides. Over varying time periods, our bodies fluctuate, and with them, our minds. Let's look more closely at two of those biological rhythms—our 24-hour biological clock and our 90-minute sleep cycle.

Circadian Rhythm

LOQ 8-2 How do our biological rhythms influence our daily functioning?

The rhythm of the day parallels the rhythm of life—from our waking at a new day's birth to our nightly return to what Shakespeare called "death's counterfeit." Our bodies roughly synchronize with the 24-hour cycle of day and night thanks to an internal biological clock called the **circadian rhythm** (from the Latin *circa*, "about," and *diem*, "day"). As morning nears, body temperature rises; it then peaks during the day, dips for a time in early afternoon (when many people take siestas or drink a caffeinated beverage), and begins to drop again in the evening. Thinking and memory improve as we approach our daily peak in circadian arousal. Have you ever pulled an all-nighter? You might remember feeling groggiest in the middle of the night, but gaining a sense of new alertness with the arrival of your normal wake-up time.

Age and experience can alter our circadian rhythm. Most 20-year-olds are evening-energized "owls," with performance improving across the day (May & Hasher, 1998). The older you get, the more you look forward to bedtime. Most older adults experience more fragile sleep and are morning-loving "larks." For our ancestors (and for today's hunter-gatherers), a grandparent who awakened easily and early helped protect the family from predators (Samson et al., 2017). By mid-evening, when the night has hardly begun for many young adults, retirement homes are typically quiet. After about age 20 (slightly earlier for women), we begin to shift from being owls to being larks (Roenneberg et al., 2004). Age is one influence, but in general, night owls tend to be smart, creative, and hard-working (Giampietro & Cavallera, 2007; Schmidt et al., 2009). Morning types tend to do better in school, take more initiative, be more punctual, and be less vulnerable to depression (Preckel et al., 2013; Randler, 2008, 2009; Werner et al., 2015).

ASK YOURSELF

Would you consider yourself a night owl or a morning lark? When do you usually feel most energetic? What time of day works best for you to study?

Sleep Stages

LOQ 8-3 What is the biological rhythm of our sleeping and dreaming stages?

Seeking sleep, we crawl into bed and fake it until we make it. Eventually, sleep overtakes us, and consciousness fades as different parts of our brain's cortex stop communicating (Massimini et al., 2005). Sleep may feel like time traveling a few hours into the future. Yet the sleeping brain remains active and has its own biological rhythm.

About every 90 minutes, we cycle through distinct sleep stages. This fact came to light when 8-year-old Armond Aserinsky went to bed one night in 1952. His father, Eugene, a

sleep a periodic, natural loss of consciousness—as distinct from unconsciousness resulting from a coma, general anesthesia, or hibernation. (Adapted from Dement, 1999.)

circadian [ser-KAY-dee-an] **rhythm** our biological clock; regular bodily rhythms (for example, of temperature and wakefulness) that occur on a 24-hour cycle.

Eric Isselee/Shutterstock

In one famous case, a man stayed up all night to see where the Sun went. (Then it dawned on him.)

Peter Chadwick/Science Source

⊖ **FIGURE 8.1**
Measuring sleep activity Sleep researchers measure brain-wave activity, eye movements, and muscle tension with electrodes that pick up weak electrical signals from the brain, eyes, and facial muscles (Dement, 1978).

Left eye movements

Right eye movements

EMG (muscle tension)

EEG (brain waves)

Hank Morgan/Science Source

⊖ **FIGURE 8.2**
Brain waves and sleep stages The beta waves of an alert, waking state and the regular alpha waves of an awake, relaxed state differ from the slower, larger delta waves of deep N3 sleep. Although the rapid REM sleep waves resemble the near-waking N1 sleep waves, the body is more internally aroused during REM sleep than during NREM sleep (the N1, N2, and N3 stages).

Dolphins, porpoises, and whales sleep with one side of their brain at a time (Miller et al., 2008).

Waking beta waves

Waking alpha waves

100 nV

N1

N2

N3 (delta waves)

REM

Rebecca Spencer, University of Massachusetts, assisted with this illustration.

6 sec

University of Chicago graduate student, needed to test an electroencephalograph he had repaired that day (Aserinsky, 1988; Seligman & Yellen, 1987). So, like many good scientists, he involved his family in his research! Placing electrodes near Armond's eyes to record the rolling eye movements then believed to occur during sleep, Aserinsky watched the machine go wild, tracing deep zigzags on the graph paper. Could the machine still be broken? As the night proceeded and the activity recurred, Aserinsky realized that the periods of fast, jerky eye movements were accompanied by energetic brain activity. Awakened during one such episode, Armond reported having a dream. Aserinsky had discovered what we now know as **REM sleep** (rapid *eye movement* sleep; sometimes called *R sleep*).

Similar procedures used with thousands of volunteers showed the cycles were a normal part of sleep (Kleitman, 1960). To appreciate these studies, imagine yourself as a participant. As the hour grows late, you feel sleepy and yawn in response to reduced brain metabolism. (Yawning, which is also socially contagious, stretches your neck muscles and increases your heart rate, which increases your alertness [Moorcroft, 2003].) When you are ready for bed, a researcher comes in and tapes electrodes to your scalp (to detect your brain waves), on your chin (to detect muscle tension), and just outside the corners of your eyes (to detect eye movement; **FIGURE 8.1**). Other devices may record your heart rate, respiration rate, and genital arousal.

When you are in bed with your eyes closed, the researcher in the next room sees on the EEG the relatively slow **alpha waves** of your awake but relaxed state (**FIGURE 8.2**). Your eyes may be closed, but you can still attend to what the researcher says through the intercom (Legendre et al., 2019). As time wears on, you adapt to all this equipment, grow tired, and, in an unremembered moment, slip into sleep (**FIGURE 8.3**). This transition is marked by the slowed breathing and irregular brain waves of what the American Academy of Sleep Medicine classifies as N1 sleep—the first stage of non-REM (NREM) sleep (Silber et al., 2007).

In one of his 15,000 research participants, William Dement (1999) observed the moment the brain's perceptual window to the outside world slammed shut. Dement asked a sleep-deprived young man with eyelids taped open to press a button every time a strobe light flashed in his eyes (about every 6 seconds).

◀ **FIGURE 8.3**
The moment of sleep We seem unaware of the moment we fall into sleep, but someone watching our brain waves could tell (Dement, 1999).

After a few minutes, the young man missed one. Asked why, he said, "Because there was no flash." But there was a flash. He missed it because (as his brain activity revealed) he had fallen asleep for 2 seconds, missing not only the flash 6 inches from his nose but also the awareness of the abrupt moment of entry into sleep.

During this brief N1 sleep you may experience fantastic images resembling **hallucinations**—sensory experiences that occur without a sensory stimulus. You may have a sensation of falling (when your body may suddenly jerk) or of floating weight-lessly. These *hypnagogic* (also called *hypnic*) sensations may later be incorporated into your memories. People who claim they were abducted by aliens—often shortly after getting into bed—commonly recall being floated off of or pinned down on their beds (Clancy, 2005; McNally, 2012).

You then relax more deeply and begin about 20 minutes of N2 sleep, with its periodic *sleep spindles*—bursts of rapid, rhythmic brain-wave activity that aid memory processing (Studte et al., 2017). Although you could still be awakened without too much difficulty, you are now clearly asleep.

Then you transition to the deep sleep of N3. During this slow-wave sleep, which lasts for about 30 minutes, your brain emits large, slow **delta waves** and you are hard to awaken. Have you ever said, "That thunder was so loud last night!" only to have a friend respond, "What thunder?" Those who missed the storm may have been in delta sleep. (It is at the end of this stage that children may wet the bed.)

> 📺 To better understand EEG readings and their relationship to consciousness, sleep, and dreams, experience the tutorial and simulation in *Topic Tutorial: PsychSim6, EEG and Sleep Stages.*

REM Sleep

About an hour after you first fall asleep, a strange thing happens. Rather than continuing in deep slumber, you ascend from your initial sleep dive. Returning through N2 (where you'll ultimately spend about half your night), you enter the most intriguing sleep phase—REM sleep (**FIGURE 8.4**). For about 10 minutes, your brain waves become rapid and saw-toothed, more like those of the nearly awake N1 sleep. But unlike N1, during REM sleep your heart rate rises, your breathing becomes rapid and irregular, and every half-minute or so your closed eyes dart around in momentary bursts of activity. These eye movements announce the beginning of a dream—often emotional, usually story-like, and richly hallucinatory. Dreams aren't real, but REM sleep tricks your brain into responding as if they were (Andrillon et al., 2015). Because anyone watching a sleeper's eyes can notice these REM bursts, it is amazing that science was ignorant of REM sleep until 1952.

Except during very scary dreams, your genitals become aroused during REM sleep. You may have an erection or increased vaginal lubrication and clitoral engorgement, regardless of whether the dream's content is sexual (Karacan et al., 1966). Men's common "morning erection" stems from the night's last REM period, often just before waking. Many men troubled by occasional erectile difficulties still get sleep-related erections, suggesting the problem is not between their legs.

During REM sleep, your brain's motor cortex is active, but your brainstem blocks its messages. This leaves your muscles relaxed, so much so that, except for an occasional finger, toe, or facial twitch, you are essentially paralyzed. Moreover, you cannot easily be awakened. (This immobility may occasionally linger as you awaken from REM sleep, producing a disturbing experience of *sleep paralysis* [Santomauro & French, 2009].) REM sleep is thus sometimes called *paradoxical sleep:* The body is internally aroused, with waking-like brain activity, yet asleep and externally calm. We spend about 600 hours a year experiencing some 1500 dreams, or more than 100,000 dreams over a typical lifetime—dreams swallowed by the night but not acted out, thanks to REM's protective paralysis.

To catch your own hypnagogic experiences, you might use your alarm's snooze function.

"*My problem has always been an overabundance of alpha waves.*"

REM sleep rapid eye movement sleep; a recurring sleep stage during which vivid dreams commonly occur. Also known as *paradoxical sleep,* because the muscles are relaxed (except for minor twitches) but other body systems are active. (Sometimes called *R sleep.*)

alpha waves the relatively slow brain waves of a relaxed, awake state.

hallucinations false sensory experiences, such as seeing something in the absence of an external visual stimulus.

delta waves the large, slow brain waves associated with deep sleep.

→ **FIGURE 8.4**

The stages in a typical night's sleep People pass through a multistage sleep cycle several times each night. As the night goes on, periods of deep sleep diminish and, for younger adults, REM sleep increases. As people age, sleep becomes more fragile, with awakenings common among older adults (Kamel & Gammack, 2006; Neubauer, 1999).

The sleep cycle repeats itself about every 90 minutes for younger adults (with shorter, more frequent cycles for older adults). As the night goes on, deep N3 sleep grows shorter and disappears, and REM and N2 sleep periods get longer (see Figure 8.4). By morning, we have spent 20 to 25 percent of an average night's sleep—some 100 minutes—in REM sleep. In sleep lab studies, 37 percent of participants have reported rarely or never having dreams that they "can remember the next morning" (Moore, 2004). Yet even they, more than 80 percent of the time, could recall a dream after being awakened during REM sleep. Neuroscientists have also identified brain regions that are active during dreaming, which enables them to detect when dreaming occurs (Sicarli et al., 2017).

Horses, which spend 92 percent of each day standing and can sleep standing, must lie down for REM sleep (Morrison, 2003).

RETRIEVAL PRACTICE

RP-1 Why would communal sleeping provide added protection for those whose safety depends on vigilance, such as these refugees in Paris?

RP-2 What are the sleep stages, and in what order do we normally travel through those stages?

RP-3 Match the sleep stage (i–iii) with the cognitive experience (a–c).

Sleep stage:
i. N1
ii. N3
iii. REM

Cognitive experience:
a. story-like dream
b. fleeting images
c. minimal awareness

ANSWERS IN APPENDIX E

What Affects Our Sleep Patterns?

LOQ 8-4 How do biology and environment interact in our sleep patterns?

True or false? "Everyone needs 8 hours of sleep." *False.* Newborns often sleep two-thirds of their day, most adults no more than one-third (with some thriving on fewer than 6 hours nightly, others racking up 9 or more). But there is more to our sleep differences than age. Some are awake between nightly sleep periods—sometimes called "first sleep" and "second sleep" (Randall, 2012). And some find that a 15-minute midday nap is as effective as another hour of nighttime sleep (Horne, 2011).

Sleep patterns are genetically influenced. Researchers are tracking the sleep-regulating genes in humans and other animals (Hayashi et al., 2015; Mackenzie et al., 2015). One analysis of 1.3 million people identified 956 genes related to sleep patterns such as *insomnia* (Jansen et al., 2019). Another such analysis identified genes associated with being a morning person (Jones et al., 2019).

Sleep patterns are also culturally, socially, and economically influenced. In Britain, Canada, Germany, Japan, and the United States, adults average 7 hours of sleep a night on workdays and 7 to 8 hours on other days (NSF, 2013). The weeknight sleep of many students and workers falls short of this average, however (NSF, 2008). Earlier school start times, more extracurricular activities, and fewer parent-set bedtimes lead American adolescents to get less sleep than their Australian counterparts (Short et al., 2013). Those who struggle to pay their bills also struggle to get enough sleep (Johnson et al., 2018; Mai et al., 2019; Vancampfort et al., 2018). With sleep, as with waking behavior, biology and environment interact.

Whether for work or play, bright light tweaks the circadian clock by activating light-sensitive retinal proteins. These proteins control the circadian clock by triggering signals to the brain's **suprachiasmatic nucleus (SCN)**—a pair of grain-of-rice-sized, 10,000-cell clusters in the hypothalamus (**FIGURE 8.5**). The SCN does its job partly by causing the brain's pineal gland to decrease its production of the sleep-inducing hormone *melatonin* in the morning and to increase it in the evening (Chang et al., 2015; Gandhi et al., 2015). (A 2017 Nobel Prize was awarded for research on the molecular biology that runs our biological clock.)

Being bathed in (or deprived of) light disrupts our 24-hour biological clock (Czeisler et al., 1999; Dement, 1999). One study simulated a space mission to Mars, in which astronauts-in-training spent 520 days deprived of natural sunlight (Basner et al., 2013). As a result, they experienced *desynchronization.* This condition, which night-shift workers also tend to experience, may lead to fatigue, stomach problems, heart disease, and, for women, breast cancer (Knutsson & Bøggild, 2010; Lin et al., 2015; Puttonen et al., 2009). Our ancestors' body clocks were attuned to the rising and setting sun of the 24-hour day, leading them to get more sleep during the dark winter months and less during the sunny summer months (van Egmond et al., 2019).

Today's young adults adopt something closer to a 25-hour day, by staying up too late to get 8 hours of sleep. For this, we can thank (or blame) Thomas Edison, inventor

suprachiasmatic nucleus (SCN) a pair of cell clusters in the hypothalamus that controls circadian rhythm. In response to light, the SCN causes the pineal gland to adjust melatonin production, thus modifying our feelings of sleepiness.

People rarely snore during dreams. When REM starts, snoring stops.

▼ **FIGURE 8.5**
The biological clock (a) Light striking the retina signals the suprachiasmatic nucleus (SCN) to suppress the pineal gland's production of the sleep hormone melatonin. (b) At night, the SCN quiets down, allowing the pineal gland to release melatonin into the bloodstream.

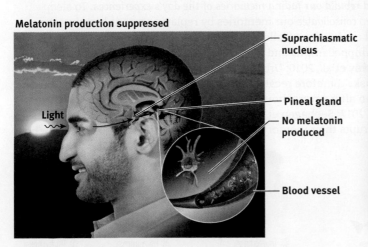

Melatonin production suppressed

- Suprachiasmatic nucleus
- Light
- Pineal gland
- No melatonin produced
- Blood vessel

(a)

Melatonin produced

- Suprachiasmatic nucleus
- Pineal gland
- Melatonin produced
- Blood vessel

(b)

I WOKE UP IN THE MIDDLE OF THE NIGHT AND QUICKLY CHECKED INSTAGRAM, TWITTER, FACEBOOK, GMAIL, MY WEATHER APP, AND MY TEXTS, AND NOW I'M A TAD TOO STIMULATED TO CLOSE MY EYES AGAIN.

Phil McAndrew/The Cartoonbank/The New Yorker

A circadian disadvantage: One study of more than 24,000 Major League Baseball games found that teams that had crossed three time zones before playing a series had a nearly 60 percent chance of losing their first game (Winter et al., 2009). A follow-up study replicated this effect in the National Basketball Association and National Hockey League (Roy & Forest, 2018).

of the light bulb. Approximately 90 percent of Americans report using a light-emitting electronic device one hour before going to sleep (Chang et al., 2015). Such artificial light delays sleep and affects sleep quality. For first-year college students, staying up late watching television interfered with the onset, quality, and duration of their sleep (Exelmans & Van den Bulck, 2018). Streaming disrupts dreaming.

Sleep often eludes those who stay up late and sleep in on weekends, and then go to bed earlier on Sunday evening in preparation for the new workweek (Oren & Terman, 1998). Like New Yorkers readjusting after a trip to California, they experience "social jet lag." For North Americans who fly to Europe and need to be up when their circadian rhythm cries "SLEEP," bright light (spending the next day outdoors) helps reset the biological clock (Czeisler et al., 1986, 1989; Eastman et al., 1995).

RETRIEVAL PRACTICE

RP-4 The _____ nucleus helps monitor the brain's release of melatonin, which affects our _____ rhythm.

ANSWERS IN APPENDIX E

Why Do We Sleep?

LOQ 8-5 What are sleep's functions?

So, our sleep patterns differ from person to person and from culture to culture. But why do we have this need for sleep? Psychologists offer five possible reasons:

1. *Sleep protects.* When darkness shut down the day's hunting, gathering, and travel, our distant ancestors were better off asleep in a cave, out of harm's way. Those who didn't wander around dark cliffs were more likely to leave descendants. This fits a broader principle: A species' sleep pattern tends to suit its ecological niche (Siegel, 2009). Animals with the greatest need to graze and the least ability to hide tend to sleep less. Animals also sleep less, with no ill effects, during times of mating and migration (Siegel, 2012). (For a sampling of animal sleep times, see **FIGURE 8.6**.)

2. *Sleep helps us recuperate.* Sleep gives our body and brain the chance to repair, rewire, and reorganize. It helps the body heal from infection and restores the immune system (Dimitrov et al., 2019). Sleep gives resting neurons time to repair themselves, while pruning or weakening unused connections (Ascády & Harris, 2017; Ding et al., 2016; Li et al., 2017). Bats and other animals with high waking metabolism burn a lot of calories, producing *free radicals,* molecules that are toxic to neurons. Sleep sweeps away this toxic waste, along with protein fragments that for humans can cause Alzheimer's disease (Beil, 2018; Xie et al., 2013). Think of it this way: When consciousness leaves our house, workers come in to clean, saying "Good night. Sleep tidy."

3. *Sleep helps restore and rebuild our fading memories of the day's experiences.* To sleep is to strengthen. Sleep *consolidates* our memories by replaying recent learning and strengthening neural connections (Paller & Oudiette, 2018). It reactivates recent experiences stored in the hippocampus and shifts them for permanent storage elsewhere in the cortex (Racsmány et al., 2010; Urbain et al., 2016). Adults, children, and infants trained to perform tasks therefore recall them better after a night's sleep, or even after a short nap, than after several hours awake (Friedrich et al., 2015; Horváth et al., 2017; Sandoval et al., 2017; Seehagen et al., 2015). Older adults' more frequently disrupted sleep also disrupts their memory consolidation (Boyce et al., 2016; Pace-Schott & Spencer, 2011).

◥ FIGURE 8.6

Animal sleep time Would you rather be a brown bat and sleep 20 hours a day or a giraffe and sleep 2 hours a day? (Data from NIH, 2010.)

20 hours
Kruglov_Orda/Shutterstock

16 hours
Andrew D. Myers

12 hours
Utekhina Anna/Shutterstock

10 hours
Steffen Foerster/Shutterstock

8 hours
RubberBall Productions/Getty Images

4 hours
Eric Isselee/Shutterstock

2 hours
pandapaw/Shutterstock

4. *Sleep feeds creative thinking.* Dreams can inspire noteworthy artistic and scientific achievements, such as the dreams that clued chemist August Kekulé to the structure of benzene (Ross, 2006) and inspired medical researcher Carl Alving (2011) to invent the vaccine patch. More commonplace is the boost that a complete night's sleep gives to our thinking and learning. After working on a task, then sleeping on it, people solve difficult problems more insightfully than do those who stay awake (Barrett, 2011; Sio et al., 2013). They also are better at spotting connections among novel pieces of information (Ellenbogen et al., 2007; Whitehurst et al., 2016). To think smart and see connections, it often pays to ponder a problem just before bed and then sleep on it.

5. *Sleep supports growth.* During slow-wave sleep, which occurs mostly in the first half of a night's sleep, the pituitary gland releases human growth hormone, which is necessary for muscle development.

A regular full night's sleep can "*dramatically* improve your athletic ability," report James Maas and Rebecca Robbins (2010). REM sleep and N2 sleep—which occur mostly in the final hours of a long night's sleep—help strengthen the neural connections that build enduring memories, including the "muscle memories" learned while practicing tennis or shooting baskets. Sleep scientist Cheri Mah and her colleagues (2011) advise athletes on how to build sleep into their training. She helped transform professional basketball player Andre Igoudala from an afternoon-napping, late-night videogamer into someone with healthy sleep habits (Gonzalez, 2018). The result? Igoudala played more minutes, shot more effectively, and received the 2015 National Basketball Association Finals Most Valuable Player award. Given all the benefits of sleep, it's no wonder that sleep loss hits us so hard.

Ample sleep supports skill learning and high performance Figure skater Sarah Hughes was advised to cut her early-morning practices as part of a recommended sleep regimen. This led to improved performances, better scores, and finally a 2002 Olympic gold medal.

TIMOTHY A. CLARY/AFP/Getty Images

"Sleep faster, we need the pillows." — Yiddish proverb

"Corduroy pillows make headlines." — Anonymous

> **RETRIEVAL PRACTICE**
>
> **RP-5** What are five proposed reasons for our need for sleep?
>
> *ANSWERS IN APPENDIX E*

Sleep Deprivation and Sleep Disorders

LOQ 8-6 How does sleep loss affect us, and what are the major sleep disorders?

When our body yearns for sleep but does not get it, we begin to feel terrible. Trying to stay awake, we will eventually lose. In the tiredness battle, sleep always wins.

Effects of Sleep Loss

Modern sleep patterns—the "Great Sleep Recession"—leave us not only sleepy but drained of energy and our sense of well-being (Keyes et al., 2015; Thorarinsdottir et al., 2019). After several 5-hour nights, we accumulate a sleep debt that cannot be satisfied by one long sleep. "The brain keeps an accurate count of sleep debt for at least two weeks," reported sleep researcher William Dement (1999, p. 64).

Obviously, then, we need sleep. Sleep commands roughly one-third of our lives—some 25 years, on average. Allowed to sleep unhindered, most adults—who are paying off a sleep debt—will sleep at least 9 hours a night (Coren, 1996). One experiment demonstrated the benefits of unrestricted sleep by having volunteers spend 14 hours daily in bed for at least a week. For the first few days, the volunteers averaged 12 hours of sleep or more per day, apparently paying off a sleep debt that averaged 25 to 30 hours. That accomplished, they settled back to 7.5 to 9 hours nightly and felt energized and happier (Dement, 1999).

College and university students are especially sleep deprived; 69 percent in one U.S. survey reported "feeling tired" or "having little energy" on at least several days during the two previous weeks (AP, 2009). One in four Chinese university students has serious sleep problems (Li et al., 2018). U.S. surveys reveal that 75 percent of high school students report getting fewer than 8 hours of nightly sleep, and that 28 percent of them acknowledged falling asleep in class at least once a week (CDC, 2019; NSF, 2006). The going needn't get boring before students start snoring.

In 1989, Michael Doucette was named America's Safest Driving Teen. In 1990, while driving home from college, he fell asleep at the wheel and collided with an oncoming car, killing both himself and the other driver. Michael's driving instructor later acknowledged never having mentioned sleep deprivation and drowsy driving (Dement, 1999).

Sleep loss also affects our mood. Tiredness triggers testiness: Less sleep predicts more anger and relationship conflicts (Keller et al., 2019; Krizan & Hisler, 2019; Madrid-Valero et al., 2019). And sleep loss is a strong predictor of depressive disorders (Palagini et al., 2019). Researchers who studied thousands of adolescents across two studies found that those who slept 5 or fewer hours a night had a 70 and 80 percent higher risk of depression and suicidal thinking than their peers who slept 8 hours or more (Gangwisch et al., 2010; Whitmore et al., 2018). Among a half million 30- to 79-year-olds from China, those who slept 5 or fewer hours a night had a more than doubled rate of depression (Sun et al., 2018). This link does not appear to reflect an effect of depression on sleep. When children and youth are followed through time, sleep loss predicts depression rather than vice versa (Gregory et al., 2009). For people at risk for suicide, a night of poor sleep increases their next-day suicidal thinking (Littlewood et al., 2019).

But there is hope: REM sleep's processing of emotional experiences helps protect against depression (Walker & van der Helm, 2009). This may help to explain why parentally enforced bedtimes predict less depression. It also helps explain why later secondary school start times consistently produce more sleep, better and more on-time attendance, improved alertness, and fewer car accidents among students (Bowers & Moyer, 2017; Foss et al., 2019; Morgenthaler et al., 2016). When the Seattle School District moved secondary school start times 55 minutes later, the results were clear: more sleep and better grades (Dunster et al., 2018). Thus, European high schools rarely start before 9 A.M. (Fischetti, 2014). The American Academy of Pediatrics (2014) advocates delaying adolescents' school start times to "allow students the opportunity to achieve optimal levels of sleep (8.5–9.5 hours)." As psychologist Roxanne Prichard notes, "Nothing gets worse with better sleep, and a lot of things get better" (Brody, 2018).

When one psychology professor challenged students to sleep at least 8 hours each night during final exams week, those who completed the challenge earned the highest final exam grades (Scullin, 2019). *The bottom line:* Sleep better to perform better.

Lack of sleep can also make you gain weight. Sleep deprivation messes with our hormones, our metabolism, and our brain's responses to food by

- increasing *ghrelin,* a hunger-arousing hormone, and decreasing its hunger-suppressing partner, *leptin* (Shilsky et al., 2012).

- increasing *cortisol,* a stress hormone that stimulates the body to make fat.

- decreasing metabolic (energy use) rate (Schmid et al., 2015; Potter et al., 2017).

- disrupting gene expression, which increases risk for heart disease and other negative health outcomes (Möller-Levet et al., 2013; Mure et al., 2018).

- enhancing limbic brain responses to the mere sight of food and decreasing cortical responses that help us resist temptation (Benedict et al., 2012; Greer et al., 2013; St-Onge et al., 2012).

Thus, children and adults who sleep less are heavier than average, and in recent decades people have been sleeping less and weighing more (Hall et al., 2018; Miller et al., 2018). Moreover, experimental sleep deprivation increases appetite and junk food eating; our tired brain finds fatty foods more enticing (Fang et al., 2015; Hanlon et al., 2015; Rihm, 2019). So, sleep loss helps explain the weight gain common among sleep-deprived students (Hull et al., 2007).

Sleep also affects our physical health. When infections do set in, we typically sleep more, boosting our immune cells. Sleep deprivation can suppress immune cells that battle viral infections and cancer (Möller-Levet et al., 2013; Motivala & Irwin, 2007; Opp & Krueger, 2015). One experiment exposed volunteers to a cold virus. Those who averaged less than 5 hours' sleep a night were 4.5 times more likely to develop a cold than those who slept more than 7 hours a night (Prather et al., 2015). Sleep's protective effect may help explain why people who sleep 7 to 8 hours a night tend to outlive those who are chronically sleep deprived (Dew et al., 2003; Parthasarathy et al., 2015; Scullin & Bliwise, 2015).

Sleep deprivation slows reactions and increases errors on visual attention tasks similar to those involved in screening airport baggage, performing surgery, and reading X-rays (Caldwell, 2012; Lim & Dinges, 2010). When especially drowsy, we may unknowingly

"Remember to sleep because you have to sleep to remember." — James B. Maas and Rebecca S. Robbins, *Sleep for Success,* 2010

Sleep stealers "You wake up in the middle of the night and grab your smartphone to check the time—it's 3 A.M.—and see an alert. Before you know it, you fall down a rabbit hole of email and Twitter. Sleep? Forget it." — Nick Bilton, "Disruptions: For a Restful Night, Make Your Smartphone Sleep on the Couch," 2014

FIGURE 8.7
Less sleep = more accidents (a) On the Monday after the spring time change, when people lose one hour of sleep, accidents increased, as compared with the Monday before. (b) In the fall, traffic accidents normally increase because of more snow, ice, and darkness, but they diminished after the time change. (Data from Coren, 1996.)

experience a 1- to 6-second "microsleep" (Koch, 2016). Slow responses and microsleeps can spell disaster for those operating equipment, piloting, or driving. Drowsy driving has contributed to an estimated 1 in 6 American traffic accidents (AAA, 2010) and to some 30 percent of Australian highway deaths (Maas, 1999). Consider the engineers of two New York-area commuter trains, whose fatigue from *sleep apnea* caused them to crash, injuring 100 people and killing one bystander (McGeehan, 2018). When sleepy frontal lobes confront an unexpected situation, misfortune often results.

Stanley Coren capitalized on what is, for many North Americans, a semi-annual sleep-manipulation experiment—the "spring forward" to daylight saving time and "fall back" to standard time. Searching millions of Canadian and American records, Coren found that accidents increased immediately after the spring-forward time change, which shortens sleep (**FIGURE 8.7**).

FIGURE 8.8 summarizes the effects of sleep deprivation. But there is good news! Psychologists have discovered a treatment that strengthens memory, increases

"So shut your eyes
Kiss me goodbye
And sleep
Just sleep." — My Chemical Romance, "Sleep"

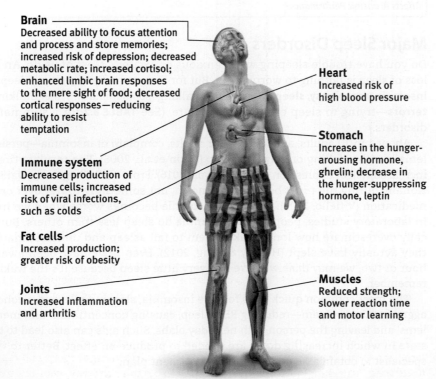

Brain
Decreased ability to focus attention and process and store memories; increased risk of depression; decreased metabolic rate; increased cortisol; enhanced limbic brain responses to the mere sight of food; decreased cortical responses—reducing ability to resist temptation

Immune system
Decreased production of immune cells; increased risk of viral infections, such as colds

Fat cells
Increased production; greater risk of obesity

Joints
Increased inflammation and arthritis

Heart
Increased risk of high blood pressure

Stomach
Increase in the hunger-arousing hormone, ghrelin; decrease in the hunger-suppressing hormone, leptin

Muscles
Reduced strength; slower reaction time and motor learning

FIGURE 8.8
How sleep deprivation affects us

TABLE 8.1 Get a Better Night's Sleep: Natural Sleep Aids

- Exercise regularly but not in the late evening (Lowe et al., 2019). (Late afternoon is best.)

- Avoid caffeine after early afternoon, and avoid food and drink near bedtime. The exception would be a glass of milk, which provides raw materials for the manufacture of serotonin, a neurotransmitter that facilitates sleep.

- Relax before bedtime, using dimmer light.

- Sleep on a consistent schedule (rise at the same time, even after a restless night) and avoid long naps (Jansson-Fröjmark et al., 2019).

- Hide time displays so you aren't tempted to check repeatedly.

- Reassure yourself that temporary sleep loss happens, and it's normal to struggle to sleep sometimes. Just try to do your best each day.

- Focus your mind on nonarousing, engaging thoughts, such as song lyrics or vacation travel (Gellis et al., 2013). (Thinking about falling asleep may keep you awake.)

- Manage stress. Realize that for any stressed organism, being vigilant is natural and adaptive. Less stress = better sleep.

concentration, boosts mood, moderates hunger, reduces obesity, fortifies the immune system, improves school performance, and lessens the risk of fatal accidents. Even better news: The treatment feels good, it can be self-administered, and it's free! If you are a typical college or university student, often going to bed late, you might feel trapped in a cycle of sleeplessness. Your stressful living situation might make sleep seem more of a luxury than a necessity. One night this week, try to add 15 minutes to your sleep. If you feel more rested and less like a zombie, try adding more sleep as often as you can. For some additional tips on getting better quality sleep, see **TABLE 8.1**.

ASK YOURSELF

What have you learned about sleep that you could apply to yourself?

To see whether you are one of the many sleep-deprived students, engage online with the self-assessment activity *Assess Your Strengths: Are You Sleep Deprived? How Can You Improve Your Sleep?* And consider how researchers have addressed these issues by engaging online with *How Would You Know If Sleep Deprivation Affects Academic Performance?*

Major Sleep Disorders

Do you have trouble sleeping when anxious or excited? Most of us do. An occasional loss of sleep is nothing to worry about. But for those who have a major sleep disorder—**insomnia, narcolepsy, sleep apnea,** sleepwalking (*somnambulism*), sleeptalking, or **night terrors**—trying to sleep can be a nightmare. (See **TABLE 8.2** for a summary of these disorders.)

About 1 in 10 adults, and 1 in 4 older adults, complain of insomnia—persistent problems in either falling or staying asleep (Irwin et al., 2006). The result is tiredness and increased risk of depression (Baglioni et al., 2016). From middle age on, awakening occasionally during the night becomes the norm, not something to fret over or treat with medication (Vitiello, 2009). Ironically, insomnia becomes worse when we fret about it. In laboratory studies, people with insomnia do sleep less than others. But they typically overestimate how long it takes them to fall asleep and underestimate how long they actually have slept (Harvey & Tang, 2012). Even if we have been awake only an hour or two, we may *think* we have had very little sleep because it's the waking part we remember.

The most common quick fixes for true insomnia, sleeping pills and alcohol, typically aggravate the problem—reducing REM sleep, causing concentration and memory problems, and leaving the person with next-day blahs. Such aids can also lead to *tolerance*—a state in which increasing doses are needed to produce an effect. Better to visit a sleep specialist to obtain a healthy long-term treatment plan.

"Sleep is like love or happiness. If you pursue it too ardently it will elude you."
— Wilse Webb, *Sleep: The Gentle Tyrant*, 1992

"There is a gulf fixed between those who can sleep and those who cannot. It is one of the great divisions of the human race."
— Iris Murdoch, *Nuns and Soldiers*, 1980

TABLE 8.2 Sleep Disorders

Disorder	Rate	Description	Effects
Insomnia	1 in 4 adults (based on past year's symptoms)	Ongoing difficulty falling or staying asleep.	Chronic tiredness, increased risk of depression, obesity, hypertension, and arthritic and fibromyalgia pain (Olfson et al., 2018). Reliance on sleeping pills and alcohol, which reduce REM sleep and lead to tolerance—a state in which increasing doses are needed to produce an effect.
Narcolepsy	1 in 2000 adults	Sudden attacks of overwhelming sleepiness.	Risk of falling asleep at a dangerous moment. Narcolepsy attacks usually last less than 5 minutes, but they can happen at the worst and most emotional times. Everyday activities, such as driving, require extra caution.
Sleep apnea	1 in 20 adults	Stopping breathing repeatedly while sleeping.	Fatigue and depression (as a result of slow-wave sleep deprivation). Associated with obesity (especially among men).
Sleepwalking and sleeptalking	1–15 in 100 in the general population for sleepwalking (NSF, 2016); about half of young children for sleeptalking (Reimão & Lefévre, 1980)	Doing normal waking activities (sitting up, walking, speaking) while asleep. Sleeptalking can occur during any sleep stage. Sleepwalking happens in N3 sleep.	Few serious concerns. Sleepwalkers return to their beds on their own or with the help of a family member, rarely remembering their trip the next morning.
Night terrors	1 in 100 adults; 1 in 30 children	Appearing terrified, talking nonsense, sitting up, or walking around during N3 sleep; different from nightmares.	Doubling of a child's heart and breathing rates during the attack. Luckily, children remember little or nothing of the fearful event the next day. As people age, night terrors become increasingly rare.

RETRIEVAL PRACTICE

RP-6 A well-rested person would be more likely to have _____ (trouble concentrating/quick reaction times) and a sleep-deprived person would be more likely to _____ (gain weight/fight off a cold).

ANSWERS IN APPENDIX E

Dreams

LOQ 8-7 What do we dream, and what functions have theorists proposed for dreams?

Now playing at an inner theater near you: the premiere of a sleeping person's vivid dream. This never-before-seen mental movie features captivating characters wrapped in a plot so original and unlikely, yet so intricate and so seemingly real, that the viewer later marvels at its creation.

REM **dreams** are vivid, emotional, and often bizarre (Loftus & Ketcham, 1994). Waking from one, we may wonder how our brain can so creatively, colorfully, and completely construct this alternative world. In the shadowland between our dreaming and waking consciousness, we may even wonder for a moment which is real. Awakening from a nightmare, a 4-year-old may be sure there is a bear in the house.

insomnia recurring problems in falling or staying asleep.

narcolepsy a sleep disorder characterized by uncontrollable sleep attacks. The sufferer may lapse directly into REM sleep, often at inopportune times.

sleep apnea a sleep disorder characterized by temporary cessations of breathing during sleep and repeated momentary awakenings.

night terrors a sleep disorder characterized by high arousal and an appearance of being terrified; unlike nightmares, night terrors occur during N3 sleep, within 2 or 3 hours of falling asleep, and are seldom remembered.

dream a sequence of images, emotions, and thoughts passing through a sleeping person's mind.

Discovering the link between REM sleep and dreaming began a new era in dream research. Instead of relying on someone's hazy recall hours later, researchers could catch dreams as they happened, awakening people during or within 3 minutes of a REM sleep period to hear a vivid account.

What We Dream

We spend 6 years of our life in dreams, many of which are anything but sweet. For women and men, 8 in 10 dreams are marked by at least one negative event or emotion (Domhoff, 2007). Common themes include repeatedly failing in an attempt to do something; being attacked, pursued, or rejected; or experiencing misfortune (Hall et al., 1982). Dreams with sexual imagery occur less often than you might think (though more often after consuming sexual media [Van den Bulck et al., 2016]). In one study, only 1 in 10 dreams among young men and 1 in 30 among young women had sexual content (Domhoff, 1996).

More commonly, a dream's story line incorporates traces of previous days' nonsexual experiences and preoccupations (Nikles et al., 2017):

- *Trauma and dreams* After suffering a trauma, people commonly report nightmares, which help extinguish daytime fears (Levin & Nielsen, 2007, 2009). Auschwitz concentration camp inmates, Palestinian children living amid conflict, and Americans after the 9/11 terrorist attacks all have experienced frequent trauma-related dreams (Owczarski, 2018; Propper et al., 2007; Punamäki & Joustie, 1998).

- *Musicians' dreams* Compared with nonmusicians, musicians report twice as many dreams of music (Uga et al., 2006).

- *Blind people's dreams* Studies in four countries have found blind people mostly dreaming of using their nonvisual senses (Buquet, 1988; Taha, 1972; Vekassy, 1977). But even natively blind people sometimes "see" in their dreams (Bértolo, 2005). Likewise, people born paralyzed below the waist sometimes dream of walking, standing, running, or cycling (Saurat et al., 2011; Voss et al., 2011).

- *Media experiences and dreams* In a study of 1287 Turkish people, "participants who consumed violent media tended to have violent dreams, and participants who consumed sexual media tended to have sexual dreams" (Van den Bulck et al., 2016).

Our two-track mind continues to monitor our environment while we sleep. Sensory stimuli—a particular odor or a phone's ringing—may be instantly and ingeniously woven into the dream story. In a classic experiment, researchers lightly sprayed cold water on dreamers' faces (Dement & Wolpert, 1958). Compared with sleepers who did not get the cold-water treatment, these people were more likely to dream about a waterfall, a leaky roof, or even about being sprayed by someone.

So, could we learn a foreign language by hearing it played while we sleep? If only. While sleeping we can learn to associate a sound with a mild electric shock (and to react to the sound accordingly). We can also learn to associate a particular sound with a pleasant or unpleasant odor (Arzi et al., 2012). But we do not remember recorded information played while we are soundly asleep (Eich, 1990; Wyatt & Bootzin, 1994). In fact, anything that happens during the 5 minutes just before we fall asleep is typically lost from memory (Roth et al., 1988). This explains why sleep apnea patients, who repeatedly awaken with a gasp and then immediately fall back to sleep, do not recall the episodes. Ditto someone who awakens momentarily, sends a text message, and the next day can't remember doing so. It also explains why dreams that momentarily awaken us are mostly forgotten by morning. To remember a dream, get up and stay awake for a few minutes.

Why We Dream

Dream theorists have proposed several explanations of why we dream, including these:

To satisfy our own wishes. In 1900, in his landmark book *The Interpretation of Dreams*, Sigmund Freud offered what he thought was "the most valuable of all the discoveries it has been my good fortune to make." He proposed that dreams provide a psychic safety valve that discharges otherwise unacceptable feelings. He viewed a dream's **manifest content** (the apparent and remembered story line) as a censored, symbolic version of its **latent content,** the unconscious drives and wishes (often erotic) that would be threatening if expressed directly. Thus, a gun might be a disguised representation of a penis.

A popular sleep myth: If you dream you are falling and hit the ground (or if you dream of dying), you die. Unfortunately, those who could confirm these ideas are not around to do so. Many people, however, have had such dreams and are alive to report them.

"Follow your dreams, except for that one where you're naked at work." — Attributed to comedian Henny Youngman

manifest content according to Freud, the symbolic, remembered story line of a dream (as distinct from its latent, or hidden, content).

latent content according to Freud, the underlying meaning of a dream (as distinct from its manifest content).

Freud considered dreams the key to understanding our inner conflicts. However, his critics say it is time to wake up from Freud's dream theory, which they regard as a scientific nightmare. Legend has it that even Freud, who loved to smoke cigars, acknowledged that "sometimes, a cigar is just a cigar." Seth Stephens-Davidowitz (2017) analyzed whether phallic foods "sneak into our dreams with unexpected frequency." His answer: They do not. Cucumbers, for example, are the seventh most dreamed-of vegetable and the seventh most common vegetable. "There is no reason to believe any of Freud's specific claims about dreams and their purposes," observed dream researcher William Domhoff (2003). Sometimes, a cucumber is just a cucumber.

Some contend that even if dreams are symbolic, they could be interpreted any way one wished. Others maintain that dreams hide nothing. Freud's wish-fulfillment theory of dreams has in large part given way to other theories.

To file away memories. The *information-processing* perspective proposes that dreams may help sift, sort, and fix the day's experiences in our memory. Some studies support this view. When tested the day after learning a task, those who had been deprived of both slow-wave and REM sleep did not do as well as those who had slept undisturbed (Stickgold, 2012). Other studies showed similar memory lapses for new material among people who were awakened every time they began REM sleep (Empson & Clarke, 1970; Karni & Sagi, 1994).

Brain scans confirm the link between REM sleep and memory. The brain regions that were active as rats learned to navigate a maze, or as people learned to perform a visual-discrimination task, became active again later during REM sleep (Louie & Wilson, 2001; Maquet, 2001). So precise were these activity patterns that scientists could tell where in the maze the rat would be if awake. To sleep, perchance to remember.

This is important news for students, many of whom, observed researcher Robert Stickgold (2000), suffer from a kind of sleep bulimia—sleep deprived on weekdays and binge sleeping on the weekend. "If you don't get good sleep and enough sleep after you learn new stuff, you won't integrate it effectively into your memories," he warned. That helps explain why high school students with high grades slept about 25 minutes longer each night than their lower-achieving classmates (Wolfson & Carskadon, 1998; see **FIGURE 8.9**). Sacrificing sleep time to study actually *worsens* academic performance, by making it harder the next day to understand class material or do well on a test (Gillen-O'Neel et al., 2013).

To develop and preserve neural pathways. Perhaps dreams, or the brain activity associated with REM sleep, serve a *physiological* function, providing the sleeping brain with periodic stimulation. This theory makes developmental sense. Stimulating experiences preserve and expand the brain's neural pathways. Infants, whose neural networks are fast developing, spend much of their abundant sleep time in REM sleep (**FIGURE 8.10**).

To make sense of neural static. Other theories propose that dreams erupt from neural activation spreading upward from the brainstem (Antrobus, 1991; Hobson, 2003, 2004, 2009). According to the *activation-synthesis theory*, dreams are the brain's attempt to synthesize random neural activity. Much as a neurosurgeon can produce hallucinations by stimulating different parts of a patient's cortex, so can stimulation originating within the brain.

"When people interpret [a dream] as if it were meaningful and then sell those interpretations, it's quackery." — Sleep researcher J. Allan Hobson (1995)

Rapid eye movements also stir the liquid behind the cornea; this delivers fresh oxygen to corneal cells, preventing their suffocation.

⬇ FIGURE 8.9
A sleeping brain is a working brain

(a) Learning.

(b) Sleep consolidates our learning into long-term memory.

(c) Learning is retained.

swissmacky/Shutterstock

⑦ FIGURE 8.10

Sleep across the life span As we age, our sleep patterns change. During our first few months, we spend progressively less time in REM sleep. During our first 20 years, we spend progressively less time asleep. (Data from Snyder & Scott, 1972.)

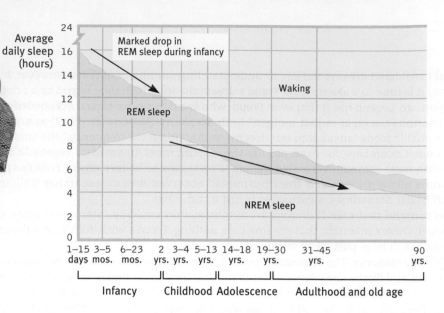

Question: Does eating spicy foods cause us to dream more?

Answer: No, but a spicy food that causes you to awaken more increases your chance of *recalling* a dream (Moorcroft, 2003).

As Freud might have expected, PET scans of sleeping people also reveal increased activity in the emotion-related limbic system (in the amygdala) during emotional dreams (Schwartz, 2012). In contrast, frontal lobe regions responsible for inhibition and logical thinking seem to idle, which may explain why we are less inhibited in our dreams than we are when awake (Maquet et al., 1996). Add the limbic system's emotional tone to the brain's visual bursts and—Voila!—we dream. Damage either the limbic system or the visual centers active during dreaming, and dreaming itself may be impaired (Domhoff, 2003).

To reflect cognitive development. Some dream researchers prefer to see dreams as part of brain maturation and cognitive development (Domhoff, 2010, 2011; Foulkes, 1999). For example, prior to age 9, children's dreams seem more like a slide show and less like an active story in which the dreamer is an actor. Dreams overlap with waking cognition and feature coherent speech. They *simulate reality* by drawing on our concepts and knowledge. They engage brain networks that also are active during daydreaming—and so may be viewed as intensified mind-wandering, enhanced by visual imagery (Fox et al., 2013). Unlike the idea that dreams arise from bottom-up brain activation, the cognitive perspective emphasizes our mind's top-down control of our dream content (Nir & Tononi, 2010). Dreams, says G. William Domhoff (2014), "dramatize our wishes, fears, concerns, and interests in striking scenarios that we experience as real events."

TABLE 8.3 compares these major dream theories. Although today's sleep researchers debate dreams' function—and some are skeptical that dreams serve any function—there is one thing they agree on: We need REM sleep. Deprived of it by repeated awakenings, people return more and more quickly to the REM stage after falling back to sleep. When finally allowed to sleep undisturbed, they literally sleep like babies—with increased REM sleep, a phenomenon called **REM rebound.** Most other mammals also experience REM rebound, suggesting that the causes and functions of REM sleep are deeply biological.

TABLE 8.3 Dream Theories

Theory	Explanation	Critical Considerations
Freud's wish-fulfillment	Dreams provide a "psychic safety valve"—expressing otherwise unacceptable feelings; dreams contain manifest (remembered) content and a deeper layer of latent content (a hidden meaning).	Lacks any scientific support; dreams may be interpreted in many different ways.
Information processing	Dreams help us sort out the day's events and consolidate our memories.	But why do we sometimes dream about things we have not experienced and about past events?
Physiological function	Regular brain stimulation from REM sleep may help develop and preserve neural pathways.	This does not explain why we experience *meaningful* dreams.
Activation synthesis	REM sleep triggers neural activity that evokes random visual memories, which our sleeping brain weaves into stories.	The individual's brain is weaving the stories, which still tells us something about the dreamer.
Cognitive development	Dream content reflects dreamers' level of cognitive development—their knowledge and understanding. Dreams simulate our lives, including worst-case scenarios.	Does not propose an adaptive function of dreams.

(That REM sleep occurs in mammals—and not in animals such as fish, whose behavior is less influenced by learning—fits the information-processing theory of dreams.)

So does this mean that because dreams serve physiological functions and extend normal cognition, they are psychologically meaningless? Not necessarily. Every psychologically meaningful experience involves an active brain. We are once again reminded of a basic principle: *Biological and psychological explanations of behavior are partners, not competitors.*

Dreams are a fascinating altered state of consciousness. But they are not the only altered state. As we will see next, drugs also alter conscious awareness.

> **REM rebound** the tendency for REM sleep to increase following REM sleep deprivation.

ASK YOURSELF

Which explanation for why we dream makes the most sense to you? How well does it explain your own dreams?

RETRIEVAL PRACTICE

RP-7 What five theories propose explanations for why we dream?

ANSWERS IN APPENDIX E

---

8 REVIEW Sleep and Dreams

LEARNING OBJECTIVES

Test Yourself Answer these repeated Learning Objective Questions on your own (before checking the answers in Appendix D) to improve your retention of the concepts (McDaniel et al., 2009, 2015).

LOQ 8-1 What is *sleep*?

LOQ 8-2 How do our biological rhythms influence our daily functioning?

LOQ 8-3 What is the biological rhythm of our sleeping and dreaming stages?

LOQ 8-4 How do biology and environment interact in our sleep patterns?

LOQ 8-5 What are sleep's functions?

LOQ 8-6 How does sleep loss affect us, and what are the major sleep disorders?

LOQ 8-7 What do we dream, and what functions have theorists proposed for dreams?

TERMS AND CONCEPTS TO REMEMBER

Test Yourself Write down the definition in your own words, then check your answer.

sleep, p. 95

circadian [ser-KAY-dee-an] rhythm, p. 95

REM sleep, p. 97

alpha waves, p. 97

hallucinations, p. 97

delta waves, p. 97

suprachiasmatic nucleus (SCN), p. 99

insomnia, p. 105

narcolepsy, p. 105

sleep apnea, p. 105

night terrors, p. 105

dream, p. 105

manifest content, p. 106

latent content, p. 106

REM rebound, p. 109

MASTER THE MATERIAL

Test Yourself Answer the following questions on your own first, then check your answers in Appendix E.

1. Our body temperature tends to rise and fall in sync with a biological clock, which is referred to as the
   _____ _____.

2. During the N1 sleep stage, a person is most likely to experience
   a. sleep spindles.   c. night terrors or nightmares.
   b. hallucinations.   d. rapid eye movements.

3. The brain emits large, slow delta waves during
   _____ sleep.

4. As the night progresses, what happens to the REM stage of sleep?

5. Which of the following is NOT one of the reasons that have been proposed to explain why we need sleep?
   a. Sleep has survival value.
   b. Sleep helps us recuperate.
   c. Sleep rests the eyes.
   d. Sleep plays a role in the growth process.

6. What is the difference between narcolepsy and sleep apnea?

7. In interpreting dreams, Freud was most interested in their
   a. information-processing function.
   b. physiological function.
   c. manifest content, or story line.
   d. latent content, or hidden meaning.

8. How has *activation-synthesis* been used to explain why we dream?

9. "For what one has dwelt on by day, these things are seen in visions of the night" (Menander of Athens [342–292 B.C.E.], *Fragments*). How might we use the information-processing perspective on dreaming to interpret this ancient Greek quote?

10. The tendency for REM sleep to increase following REM sleep deprivation is referred to as _____ _____.

Continue testing yourself with **LearningCurve** or **Achieve Read & Practice** to learn and remember most effectively.

9 **Drugs and Consciousness**

→ **psychoactive drug** a chemical substance that alters perceptions and moods.

substance use disorder a disorder characterized by continued substance craving and use despite significant life disruption and/or physical risk.

tolerance the diminishing effect with regular use of the same dose of a drug, requiring the user to take larger and larger doses before experiencing the drug's effect.

addiction an everyday term for compulsive substance use (and sometimes for dysfunctional behavior patterns, such as out-of-control gambling) that continues despite harmful consequences. (See also *substance use disorder*.)

withdrawal the discomfort and distress that follow discontinuing an addictive drug or behavior.

Tolerance and Addiction in Substance Use Disorders

LOQ 9-1 What are *substance use disorders?*

Let's imagine a day in the life of a make-believe drug-using student. It begins with a few cups of coffee to feel alert and Adderall to help focus on a morning lecture. At midday, an energy drink helps offset post-lunch drowsiness. A little vaping with friends calms frazzled nerves before a class presentation. An after-dinner study session means another Adderall, followed by smoking marijuana with friends before heading to a local bar. It used to take only a drink or two to feel relaxed, but now three or four are needed to produce the desired effect. Back home, two Advil PMs help reduce the night's stimulating effects. The alarm clock beeps a few hours later, and after a night of poor sleep, the daily cycle of drug use resumes. Over time, our imagined student— and many actual students—may struggle to keep up with school, work, and family responsibilities; experience strained relationships; and have difficulty limiting their substance use. How do we know when substance use becomes a problem?

The substances our imaginary student uses are **psychoactive drugs,** chemicals that change perceptions and moods. Most of us manage to use some psychoactive drugs in moderation and without disrupting our lives. But sometimes, drug use crosses the line between moderation and **substance use disorder** (TABLE 9.1).

Today's psychiatric diagnostic system also includes *substance/ medication-induced disorders* (APA, 2018). A substance/medication-induced disorder occurs when people misuse drugs and alcohol, causing changes that resemble various psychological disorders. These include sexual dysfunctions, obsessive-compulsive disorder (OCD), depression, psychosis, and sleep and neurocognitive disorders.

A drug's overall effect depends not only on its biological effects but also on the user's expectations, which vary with social and cultural contexts (Gu et al., 2015; Ward, 1994). If one culture assumes that a particular drug produces euphoria (or aggression or sexual arousal) and another does not, each culture may find its expectations fulfilled. We'll take a closer look at these interacting forces in the use and potential abuse of particular psychoactive drugs. But first, to consider what contributes to the disordered use of various substances, see Thinking Critically About: Tolerance and Addiction.

TABLE 9.1 When Is Drug Use a Disorder?

According to the American Psychiatric Association, a person may be diagnosed with *substance use disorder* when drug use continues despite significant life disruption. Resulting brain changes may persist after quitting use of the substance (thus leading to strong cravings when exposed to people and situations that trigger memories of drug use). The severity of substance use disorder varies from *mild* (two to three of the indicators listed below) to *moderate* (four to five indicators) to *severe* (six or more indicators). (*Source:* American Psychiatric Association, 2013.) If you are concerned about your substance use or that of a loved one, contact your school counseling center, health clinic, or physician.

Diminished Control

1. Uses more substance, or for longer, than intended.
2. Tries unsuccessfully to regulate use of substance.
3. Spends much time acquiring, using, or recovering from effects of substance.
4. Craves the substance.

Diminished Social Functioning

5. Use disrupts commitments at work, school, or home.
6. Continues use despite social problems.
7. Causes reduced social, recreational, and work activities.

Hazardous Use

8. Continues use despite hazards.
9. Continues use despite worsening physical or psychological problems.

Drug Action

10. Experiences tolerance (needing more substance for the desired effect).
11. Experiences withdrawal when attempting to end use.

Tolerance and Addiction

LOQ 9-2 What roles do tolerance and addiction play in substance use disorders, and how has the concept of *addiction* changed?

Tolerance

With continued use of alcohol and some other drugs (but not marijuana), users develop **tolerance** as their brain chemistry adapts to offset the drug effect (*neuroadaptation*). To experience the same effect, users require larger and larger doses, which increase the risk of becoming **addicted** and developing a *substance use disorder*.

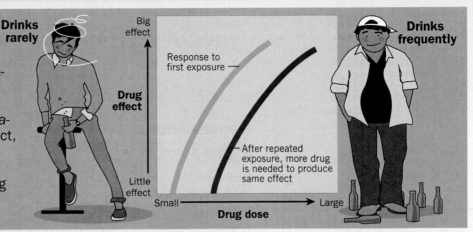

Drinks rarely

Drinks frequently

Big effect

Drug effect

Response to first exposure

Little effect

After repeated exposure, more drug is needed to produce same effect

Small — **Drug dose** — Large

Addiction

Caused by ever-increasing doses of most psychoactive drugs (including prescription painkillers). Prompts user to crave the drug, to continue use despite adverse consequences, and to struggle when attempting to **withdraw** from it. These behaviors suggest a substance use disorder. Once in the grip of addiction, people *want* the drug more than they *like* the drug.[1]

4% of the world's people have an alcohol use disorder.[2]

4%

The lifetime odds of getting hooked after using various drugs:

9%	Marijuana
21%	Cocaine
23%	Alcohol
68%	Tobacco

Source: National Epidemiologic Survey on Alcohol and Related Conditions [3]

Therapy or group support, such as from Alcoholics Anonymous, may help. It also helps to believe that addictions are controllable and that people can change. Many people do voluntarily stop using addictive drugs without any treatment. Most ex-smokers have kicked the habit on their own.[4]

Behavior Addictions

Psychologists try to avoid using "addiction" to label driven, excessive behaviors such as eating, work, sex, and accumulating wealth.

I'm ADDICTED to cheeseburgers!

Yet some behaviors can become compulsive and dysfunctional—similar to problematic alcohol and drug use.[5] Behavior addictions include *gambling disorder. Internet gaming disorder* is also now a diagnosable condition.[6] Such gamers display a consistent inability to resist logging on and staying on, even when this excessive use impairs their work and relationships. One international study of 19,000 gamers found that 1 in 3 had at least one symptom of the disorder. But fewer than 1 percent met criteria for a diagnosis.[7]

Psychological and drug therapies may be "highly effective" for problematic internet use.[8]

1. Berridge et al., 2009; Robinson & Berridge, 2003. 2. WHO, 2014b. 3. Lopez-Quintero et al., 2011. 4. Newport, 2013b. 5. Gentile, 2009; Griffiths, 2001; Hoeft et al., 2008. 6. WHO, 2018b. 7. Przybylski et al., 2017. 8. Winkler et al., 2013.

RETRIEVAL PRACTICE

RP-1 What is the process that generally leads to drug tolerance?

RP-2 Can someone become "addicted" to shopping?

ANSWERS IN APPENDIX E

Types of Psychoactive Drugs

The three major categories of psychoactive drugs are *depressants, stimulants,* and *hallucinogens.* All do their work at the brain's synapses, stimulating, inhibiting, or mimicking the activity of the brain's own chemical messengers, the neurotransmitters.

Depressants

LOQ 9-3 What are *depressants,* and what are their effects?

Depressants are drugs such as alcohol, barbiturates (tranquilizers), and opiates that calm neural activity and slow body functions.

ALCOHOL True or false? Alcohol is a depressant in large amounts but is a stimulant in small amounts. *False.* In any amount, alcohol is a depressant. Low doses of alcohol may, indeed, enliven a drinker, but they do so by acting as a *disinhibitor*—they slow brain activity that controls judgment and inhibitions, causing 3 million yearly deaths worldwide (WHO, 2018a).

Alcohol is an equal-opportunity drug: It increases (disinhibits) helpful tendencies—as when tipsy restaurant patrons leave extravagant tips and social drinkers bond in groups (Fairbairn & Sayette, 2014; Lynn, 1988). And it increases harmful tendencies, as when sexually aroused men become more disposed to sexual aggression. One University of Illinois campus survey showed that before sexual assaults, 80 percent of the male assailants and 70 percent of the female victims had been drinking (Camper, 1990). Another survey of 89,874 American collegians found alcohol or other drugs involved in 79 percent of unwanted sexual intercourse experiences (Presley et al., 1997). Drinking increases men's and women's desire for casual sex and perception of others' attractiveness (Bowdring & Sayette, 2018; Johnson & Chen, 2015). Yet women, especially, often regret their alcohol-related sexual behavior (Peterson et al., 2019). *The bottom line:* The urges you would feel if sober are the ones you will more likely act upon when intoxicated.

The prolonged and excessive drinking that characterizes **alcohol use disorder** can shrink the brain and contribute to premature death (Kendler et al., 2016; Mackey et al., 2019). Girls and young women (who have less of a stomach enzyme that digests alcohol) can become addicted to alcohol more quickly than boys and young men do, and they are at risk for lung, brain, and liver damage at lower consumption levels (CASA, 2003). With increased heavy drinking among women, these gender differences have grown, with life-or-death consequences: Canadian women's risk for alcohol-related death between 2001 and 2017 increased at five times the rate of men's (Tam, 2018) (**FIGURE 9.1**). Canadian and Australian researchers are now using computer-based *machine learning* to identify other risk factors and to predict problem alcohol use (Afzali et al., 2019).

Slowed Neural Processing Alcohol slows sympathetic nervous system activity. Larger doses cause reactions to slow, speech to slur, and skilled performance to deteriorate. Alcohol is a potent sedative, especially when paired with sleep deprivation. Add these physical effects to lowered inhibitions, and the result can be deadly. As blood-alcohol levels rise and judgment falters, people's qualms about drinking and driving lessen. When drunk, people aren't aware of how drunk they are (Moore et al., 2016). In experiments, virtually all drinkers who had insisted when sober that they would not drive under the influence later decided to drive home from a bar, even if given a Breathalyzer test and told they were intoxicated (Denton & Krebs, 1990; MacDonald et al., 1995). Alcohol can be life threatening when heavy drinking follows an earlier period of moderate drinking, which depresses the vomiting response. People may poison themselves with an overdose that their bodies would normally throw up.

Scan of woman with alcohol use disorder **(a)**

Scan of woman without alcohol use disorder **(b)**

Daniel Hommer, NIAAA, NIH, HHS

FIGURE 9.1
Disordered drinking shrinks the brain MRI scans show brain shrinkage in women with alcohol use disorder (a) compared with women in a control group (b).

depressants drugs (such as alcohol, barbiturates, and opiates) that reduce neural activity and slow body functions.

alcohol use disorder (popularly known as *alcoholism*) alcohol use marked by tolerance, withdrawal, and a drive to continue problematic use.

Drinking disaster demo Firefighters reenacted the trauma of an alcohol-related car accident, providing a memorable demonstration for these high school students. Alcohol consumption leads to feelings of invincibility, which become especially dangerous behind the wheel of a car.

Lon Clark Diehl

Memory Disruption Alcohol can disrupt memory formation, and heavy drinking can also have long-term effects on the brain and cognition. In rats, at a developmental period corresponding to human adolescence, binge drinking contributes to nerve cell death and reduces the birth of new nerve cells. It also impairs the growth of synaptic connections (Crews et al., 2006, 2007). In humans, heavy drinking may lead to blackouts, in which drinkers are unable to recall people they met the night before or what they said or did while intoxicated. These blackouts result partly from the way alcohol suppresses REM sleep, which helps fix the day's experiences into permanent memories.

Reduced Self-Awareness In one experiment, those who consumed alcohol (rather than a placebo beverage) were doubly likely to be caught mind-wandering during a reading task, yet were *less* likely to notice that they zoned out (Sayette et al., 2009). Sometimes we mind-wander to give our brains a break, but unintentional zoning out—while driving, for example—can cause later regret (Seli et al., 2016). Alcohol also produces a sort of "myopia" by focusing attention on an arousing situation (say, provocation) and distracting it from normal inhibitions and future consequences (Giancola et al., 2010; Hull & Bond, 1986; Steele & Josephs, 1990).

Reduced self-awareness may help explain why people who want to suppress their awareness of failures or shortcomings are more likely to drink than are those who feel good about themselves. Losing a business deal, a game, or a romantic partner sometimes elicits a drinking binge.

Expectancy Effects Expectations influence behavior. Expectations help explain why adolescents—presuming that alcohol will lift their spirits—sometimes drink when they're upset and alone (Bresin et al., 2018). Solitary drinking actually does not boost mood, but it does increase the likelihood of developing a substance use disorder (Creswell et al., 2014; Fairbairn & Sayette, 2014).

Simply *believing* we're consuming alcohol can cause us to act out alcohol's presumed influence (Christiansen et al., 2016; Moss & Albery, 2009). In a now-classic experiment, researchers gave Rutgers University men (who had volunteered for a study on "alcohol and sexual stimulation") either an alcoholic or a nonalcoholic drink (Abrams & Wilson, 1983). (Both had strong tastes that masked any alcohol.) After watching an erotic movie clip, the men who *thought* they had consumed alcohol were more likely to report having strong sexual fantasies and feeling guilt-free. Being able to *attribute* their sexual responses to alcohol released their inhibitions—whether or not they had actually consumed any alcohol. Fourteen "intervention studies" have educated college drinkers about that very point (Scott-Sheldon et al., 2014). Most participants have come away with lower positive expectations of alcohol and reduced their drinking the ensuing month. *The point to remember*: Alcohol's effect lies partly in that powerful sex organ, the mind.

Lives lost to opioids Prince and Tom Petty are among the tens of thousands who have died of tragic, accidental opioid overdoses in recent years. Both musicians had been prescribed narcotic painkillers for chronic pain conditions.

barbiturates drugs that depress central nervous system activity, reducing anxiety but impairing memory and judgment.

opiates opium and its derivatives, such as morphine and heroin; depress neural activity, temporarily lessening pain and anxiety.

stimulants drugs (such as caffeine, nicotine, and the more powerful cocaine, amphetamines, methamphetamine, and Ecstasy) that excite neural activity and speed up body functions.

amphetamines drugs (such as *methamphetamine*) that stimulate neural activity, causing accelerated body functions and associated energy and mood changes.

nicotine a stimulating and highly addictive psychoactive drug in tobacco products.

BARBITURATES Like alcohol, the **barbiturate** drugs, which are *tranquilizers*, depress nervous system activity. Barbiturates such as Nembutal, Seconal, and Amytal are sometimes prescribed to induce sleep or reduce anxiety. In larger doses, they can impair memory and judgment. If combined with alcohol—as sometimes happens when people take a sleeping pill after an evening of heavy drinking—the total depressive effect on body functions can be lethal.

OPIATES The **opiates**—opium and its derivatives—also depress neural functioning. Opiates include *heroin* and its medically prescribed substitute, *methadone*. They also include pain-relief *narcotics* such as codeine, OxyContin, Vicodin, and morphine (and morphine's much more powerful synthetic counterpart, fentanyl). As blissful pleasure replaces pain and anxiety, the user's pupils constrict, breathing slows, and lethargy sets in. Those who become addicted to this short-term pleasure may pay a long-term price: a gnawing craving for another fix, a need for progressively larger doses (as tolerance soon develops), and the extreme discomfort of withdrawal. When repeatedly flooded with an artificial opiate, the brain eventually stops producing *endorphins,* its own opiates. If the artificial opiate is then withdrawn, the brain will lack the normal level of these painkilling neurotransmitters.

An alarming number of Americans have been unable or unwilling to tolerate this state and have paid an ultimate price—death by overdose. Between 2013 and 2017, the U.S. rate of opioid overdose deaths increased almost *ten times* to 43,036 (NIDA, 2018; NSC, 2019). "For the first time in U.S. history, a person is more likely to die from an accidental opioid overdose than from a motor vehicle crash," reported the National Safety Council in 2019.

What started the opioid crisis? Drug companies played a large part by aggressively promoting opioid drugs while downplaying the dangers, and by sending millions of pills to pharmacies known to sell the drugs illegally (Rashbaum, 2019). As a result, pharmaceutical companies have been fined billions of dollars, including one company in 2019 for "false, misleading, and dangerous marketing" of opioids (Hoffman, 2019). Some doctors have overprescribed pills, making their patients more likely to become addicted (Tompkins et al., 2017). Social influence also matters. People with parents and friends who use opioids are more likely to use opioids (Griesler et al., 2019; Keyes et al., 2014).

RETRIEVAL PRACTICE

RP-3 Alcohol, barbiturates, and opiates are all in a class of drugs called _____.

ANSWERS IN APPENDIX E

Stimulants

LOQ 9-4 What are *stimulants,* and what are their effects?

A **stimulant** excites neural activity and speeds up body functions. Pupils dilate, heart and breathing rates increase, and blood sugar levels rise, reducing appetite. Energy and self-confidence also rise.

Stimulants include caffeine, nicotine, and the more powerful cocaine, **amphetamines,** methamphetamine (also known as *speed*), and Ecstasy. People use stimulants to feel alert, lose weight, or boost mood or athletic performance. Simply showing students in Western cultures pictures of coffee made them feel more alert (Chan & Maglio, 2019). Some students resort to stronger stimulant drugs in hopes of boosting their grades, despite the fact that they offer little or no benefit (Ilieva et al., 2015; Teter et al., 2018). Stimulants can be addictive, as many know from the fatigue, headaches, irritability, and depression that result from missing their usual caffeine dose (Silverman et al., 1992). A mild dose typically lasts three or four hours, which—if taken in the evening—may impair sleep.

NICOTINE Tobacco products deliver highly addictive **nicotine.** Imagine that cigarettes were harmless—except, once in every 25,000 packs, an occasional innocent-looking one was filled with dynamite instead of tobacco. Not such a bad risk of having your head blown off. But with 250 million packs a day consumed worldwide, we could expect more than 10,000 gruesome daily deaths (more than three times the 9/11 terrorist fatalities each and every day)—surely enough to have cigarettes banned everywhere.[2]

The lost lives from these dynamite-loaded cigarettes approximate those from today's actual cigarettes. A teen-to-the-grave smoker has a 50 percent chance of dying from the habit, and each year, tobacco kills nearly 5.4 million of its 1.3 billion customers world-wide. (Imagine the outrage if 25 loaded jumbo jets crashed today, let alone tomorrow and every day thereafter.) By 2030, annual tobacco deaths are expected to increase to 8 million. That means that 1 *billion* twenty-first-century people may be killed by tobacco (WHO, 2012). Most tobacco deaths will occur in low- and middle-income countries, where 80 percent of the world's smokers live (Akanbi et al., 2019).

Tobacco products include cigarettes, cigars, chewing tobacco, pipe tobacco, snuff, and—most recently—e-cigarettes. Inhaling e-cigarette vapor ("vaping") gives users a jolt of nicotine without cancer-causing tar. Thanks to vaping's rapid increase—the fastest drug use increase on record—U.S. high school students in 2019 used e-cigarettes at five times the rate of traditional cigarettes (Miech et al., 2019). In one survey of regular e-cigarette users from the United States, England, Canada, and Australia, 85 percent reported they vaped because they believed it would help them cut down on smoking traditional cigarettes (Yong et al., 2019). Unfortunately, e-cigarettes are addictive nicotine dispensers. They deliver toxic chemicals. And they increase one's chances of using conventional cigarettes (Prochaska, 2019). In a British study, nonsmoking teens who started vaping became four times more likely to move on to cigarette smoking (Miech et al., 2017).

Teen use has prompted legal restrictions as well as investigations, including one by the U.S. Food and Drug Administration to determine whether e-cigarette companies target teenage users (Richtel & Kaplan, 2018). Lacing e-cigarettes with fruity flavors, for example, increases teen use (Buckell & Sindelar, 2019; O'Connor et al., 2019). These troubling trends prompted U.S. Surgeon General Jerome Adams to "officially declar[e] e-cigarette use among youth an epidemic" (Stein, 2018).

Smoke a cigarette and nature will charge you 12 minutes—ironically, just about the length of time you spend smoking it (*Discover*, 1996). (Researchers don't yet know how e-cigarette smoking affects life expectancy.) Compared with nonsmokers, smokers' life expectancy is "at least 10 years shorter" (CDC, 2013b). Eliminating smoking would increase life expectancy more than any other preventive measure. Why, then, do so many people smoke?

Tobacco products are powerfully and quickly addictive. Attempts to quit tobacco use even within the first weeks often fail (DiFranza, 2008). And, as with other addictions, users develop *tolerance*. Those who attempt to quit will experience nicotine-withdrawal symptoms—craving, insomnia, anxiety, irritability, and distractibility. When trying to focus on a task, their mind wanders at three times the normal rate (Sayette et al., 2010). When not craving a cigarette, they tend to underestimate the power of such cravings (Sayette et al., 2008).

All it takes to relieve the aversive state of craving is a single inhale. With that inhale, a rush of nicotine will signal the central nervous system to release a flood of neurotransmitters (**FIGURE 9.2**). Epinephrine and norepinephrine will diminish appetite and boost alertness and mental efficiency. Dopamine and opioids will temporarily calm anxiety and reduce sensitivity to pain (Ditre et al., 2011; Gavin, 2004). No wonder some ex-users, under stress, resume their habit—as did some 1 million Americans after the 9/11 terrorist attacks (Pesko, 2014). Ditto for people experiencing major depressive disorder, who are more likely than others to see their efforts to quit go up in smoke (Zvolensky et al., 2015).

Cigarette smoking is the leading cause of preventable death in the United States, killing 480,000 people each year (CDC, 2018c). Although 3 in 4 smokers wish they could stop, each year fewer than 1 in 7 will be successful (Newport, 2013b). Even those who know they are committing slow-motion suicide may be unable to stop (Saad, 2002).

"No adult who has never used nicotine should ever use our product." — Ashley Gould, Chief Administrative Officer of e-cigarette company Juul Labs, 2018

"Smoking cures weight problems . . . eventually." — Comedian-writer Steven Wright

"To cease smoking is the easiest thing I ever did; I ought to know because I've done it a thousand times." — Mark Twain (1835–1910)

---

[2] This analogy, adapted here with world-based numbers, was suggested by mathematician Sam Saunders, as reported by K. C. Cole (1998).

⊜ **FIGURE 9.2**
Physiological effects of
nicotine Nicotine reaches the brain within
7 seconds, twice as fast as intravenous
heroin. Within minutes, the amount in the
blood soars.

1. Arouses the brain to a state of increased alertness

2. Increases heart rate and blood pressure

3. At high levels, relaxes muscles and triggers the release of neurotransmitters that may reduce stress

4. Reduces circulation to extremities

5. Suppresses appetite for carbohydrates

Humorist Dave Barry (1995) recalling why he smoked his first cigarette the summer he turned 15: "Arguments against smoking: 'It's a repulsive addiction that slowly but surely turns you into a gasping, gray-skinned, tumor-ridden invalid, hacking up brownish gobs of toxic waste from your one remaining lung.' Arguments for smoking: 'Other teenagers are doing it.' Case closed! Let's light up!"

 cocaine a powerful and addictive stimulant derived from the coca plant; produces temporarily increased alertness and euphoria.

methamphetamine a powerfully addictive drug that stimulates the central nervous system, with accelerated body functions and associated energy and mood changes; over time, reduces baseline dopamine levels.

Ecstasy (MDMA) a synthetic stimulant and mild hallucinogen. Produces euphoria and social intimacy, but with short-term health risks and longer-term harm to serotonin-producing neurons and to mood and cognition.

Nevertheless, repeated attempts seem to pay off. The worldwide smoking rate—25 percent among men and 5 percent among women—is down about 30 percent since 1990 (GBD, 2017). Half of all Americans who have ever smoked have quit, sometimes aided by a nicotine replacement drug and with encouragement from a counselor or support group. Some researchers argue that it is best to quit abruptly—to go "cold tur-key" (Lindson-Hawley et al., 2016). Others suggest that success is equally likely whether smokers quit abruptly or gradually (Fiore et al., 2008; Lichtenstein et al., 2010). For those who endure, the acute craving and withdrawal symptoms gradually dissipate over the ensuing 6 months (Ward et al., 1997). After a year's abstinence, only 10 percent will relapse in the next year (Hughes, 2010). These nonsmokers may live not only healthier but also happier lives. Smoking correlates with higher rates of depression, chronic disabilities, and divorce (Doherty & Doherty, 1998; Edwards & Kendler, 2012; Vita et al., 1998). Healthy living seems to add both years to life and life to years. Awareness of non-smokers' better health and happiness has contributed to U.S. twelfth graders' 88 percent disapproval of smoking a pack or more a day, and also to a plunge in their daily smoking rate, from 22 percent in 1998 to 2 percent in 2018 (Miech et al., 2019).

ASK YOURSELF

Think of a friend or family member who is addicted to nicotine. What do you think would be most effective to say to that person to convince them to try to quit?

RETRIEVAL PRACTICE

RP-4 What withdrawal symptoms should your friend expect when quitting smoking?

ANSWERS IN APPENDIX E

COCAINE **Cocaine** is a powerfully addictive stimulant derived from the coca plant. The recipe for Coca-Cola originally included coca extract, creating a cocaine tonic intended for tired elderly people. Between 1896 and 1905, Coke was indeed "the real thing." Today, cocaine is snorted, injected, or smoked (sometimes as *crack cocaine*, a faster-working

Sending neuron

Action potential

Synaptic gap

Receiving neuron

Neurotransmitter molecule

Receptor sites

(a)

Neurotransmitters carry a message from a sending neuron across a synapse to receptor sites on a receiving neuron.

Reuptake

(b)

The sending neuron normally reabsorbs excess neurotransmitter molecules, a process called *reuptake*.

Cocaine

(c)

By binding to the sites that normally reabsorb neurotransmitter molecules, cocaine blocks reuptake of dopamine, norepinephrine, and serotonin (Ray & Ksir, 1990). The extra neurotransmitter molecules therefore remain in the synapse, intensifying their normal mood-altering effects and producing a euphoric rush. When the cocaine level drops, the absence of these neurotransmitters produces a crash.

FIGURE 9.3
Cocaine euphoria and crash

crystallized form that produces a briefer but more intense high, followed by a more intense crash). Cocaine enters the bloodstream quickly, producing a rush of euphoria that depletes the brain's supply of the neurotransmitters dopamine, serotonin, and norepinephrine (**FIGURE 9.3**). Within the hour, a crash of agitated depression follows as the drug's effect wears off. After several hours, the craving for more wanes, only to return several days later (Gawin, 1991).

In situations that trigger aggression, ingesting cocaine may heighten reactions. Caged rats fight when given foot shocks, and they fight even more when given cocaine *and* foot shocks. Likewise, humans who voluntarily ingest high doses of cocaine in laboratory experiments impose higher shock levels on a presumed opponent than do those receiving a placebo (Licata et al., 1993). Cocaine use may also lead to emotional disturbances, suspiciousness, convulsions, cardiac arrest, or respiratory failure.

Cocaine powerfully stimulates brain reward pathways (Keramati et al., 2017; Walker et al., 2018). Alcohol or nicotine use, which often precedes cocaine use, amplifies the brain's response to cocaine (Griffin et al., 2017). Cocaine's psychological effects vary with the dosage and form consumed, but the situation and the user's expectations and personality also play a role. Given a placebo, cocaine users who *thought* they were taking cocaine often had a cocaine-like experience (Van Dyke & Byck, 1982).

In national surveys, 2 percent of American twelfth graders and 6 percent of British 18- to 24-year-olds reported having tried cocaine during the past year (ACMD, 2009; Miech et al., 2019). Of those, nearly half had smoked crack.

METHAMPHETAMINE Amphetamines stimulate neural activity. As body functions speed up, the user's energy rises and mood soars. Amphetamines are the parent drug for the highly addictive **methamphetamine,** which is chemically similar but has greater effects (NIDA, 2002, 2005). Methamphetamine triggers the release of the neurotransmitter dopamine, which stimulates brain cells that enhance energy and mood, leading to 8 hours or so of heightened energy and euphoria. Its aftereffects may include irritability, insomnia, hypertension, seizures, social isolation, depression, and occasional violent outbursts (Homer et al., 2008). Over time, methamphetamine may reduce baseline dopamine levels, leaving the user with continuing depressed functioning.

ECSTASY **Ecstasy,** a street name for **MDMA** (methylenedioxymethamphetamine, also known in its powder form as *Molly*), is both a stimulant and a mild hallucinogen. As an amphetamine derivative, Ecstasy triggers dopamine release, but its major effect is releasing stored serotonin and blocking its reuptake, thus prolonging serotonin's feel-good flood (Braun, 2001). Users feel the effect about a half-hour after taking an Ecstasy pill. For 3 or 4 hours, they experience high

"Cocaine makes you a new man. And the first thing that new man wants is more cocaine." — Comedian George Carlin (1937–2008)

Dramatic drug-induced decline In the 18 months between these two mug shots, this woman's methamphetamine addiction led to obvious physical changes.

1.5 Years Later

Multnomah County Sheriff's Office

energy, emotional elevation, and (given a social context) connectedness with those around them ("I love everyone!"). Octopuses became similarly sociable when researchers gave them MDMA (Edsinger et al., 2018). Whether you have two or eight arms, MDMA will make you want to reach out.

Ecstasy's popularity first soared in the late 1990s as a "club drug" taken at nightclubs and all-night dance parties (Landry, 2002). The drug's popularity crosses national borders, with an estimated 60 million tablets consumed annually in Britain (ACMD, 2009). There are, however, reasons not to be ecstatic about Ecstasy. One is its dehydrating effect, which—when combined with prolonged dancing—can lead to severe overheating, increased blood pressure, and death. Another is that long-term, repeated leaching of brain serotonin can damage serotonin-producing neurons, leading to decreased output and increased risk of permanently depressed mood (Croft et al., 2001; McCann et al., 2001; Roiser et al., 2005). Ecstasy also suppresses the immune system, impairs memory, slows thought, and disrupts sleep by interfering with serotonin's control of the circadian clock (Laws & Kokkalis, 2007; Schilt et al., 2007; Wagner et al., 2012). Ecstasy delights for the night but dispirits the morrow.

The hug drug MDMA, known as Ecstasy and often taken at clubs, produces a euphoric high and feelings of intimacy. But repeated use can destroy serotonin-producing neurons, impair memory, and permanently deflate mood.

Hallucinogens

LOQ 9-5 What are *hallucinogens,* and what are their effects?

Hallucinogens distort perceptions and evoke sensory images in the absence of sensory input (which is why these drugs are also called *psychedelics,* meaning "mind-manifesting"). Some, such as LSD and MDMA (Ecstasy), are synthetic. Others, including psilocybin mushrooms, ayahuasca brew, and the mild hallucinogen marijuana, are natural substances. Experiments are exploring psilocybin and ayahuasca as possible treatments for persistent depression.

Whether provoked to hallucinate by drugs, loss of oxygen, or extreme sensory deprivation, the brain hallucinates in basically the same way (Siegel, 1982). The experience typically begins with simple geometric forms, such as a spiral. Then come more meaningful images, which may be superimposed on a tunnel; others may be replays of past emotional experiences. Brain scans of people on an LSD trip reveal that their visual cortex becomes hypersensitive and strongly connected to their brain's emotion centers (Carhart-Harris et al., 2016). As the hallucination peaks, people frequently feel separated from their body and experience dreamlike scenes. Their sense of self dissolves, as does the border between themselves and the external world (Lebedev et al., 2015).

These sensations are strikingly similar to the **near-death experience,** an altered state of consciousness reported by about 10 to 15 percent of those revived from cardiac arrest (Agrillo, 2011; Greyson, 2010; Parnia et al., 2014). Many describe visions of tunnels (**FIGURE 9.4**), bright lights, a replay of old memories, and out-of-body sensations (Siegel, 1980). These experiences can later enhance spirituality and promote feelings of personal growth (Khanna & Greyson, 2014, 2015). Given that oxygen deprivation and other insults to the brain are known to produce hallucinations, it is difficult to resist wondering whether a brain under stress manufactures the near-death experience. During epileptic seizures and migraines, people may experience similar hallucinations of geometric patterns (Billock & Tsou, 2012). So have solitary sailors and polar explorers while enduring monotony, isolation, and cold (Suedfeld & Mocellin, 1987). The philosopher-neuroscientist Patricia Churchland has called such experiences "neural funny business" (Churchland, 2013, p. 70).

LSD Chemist Albert Hofmann created—and on one Friday afternoon in April 1943 accidentally ingested—**LSD (lysergic acid diethylamide).** The result—"an uninterrupted stream of fantastic pictures, extraordinary shapes with intense, kaleidoscopic play of colors"—reminded him of a childhood mystical experience that had left him longing for another glimpse of "a miraculous, powerful, unfathomable reality" (Siegel, 1984; Smith, 2006).

The emotions of an LSD (or *acid*) trip vary from euphoria to detachment to panic. Users' mood and expectations (their "high hopes") color the emotional experience, but the perceptual distortions and hallucinations have some commonalities.

⊽ FIGURE 9.4

Near-death vision or hallucination?
Psychologist Ronald Siegel (1977) reported that people under the influence of hallucinogenic drugs often see "a bright light in the center of the field of vision.... The location of this point of light create[s] a tunnel-like perspective." This is very similar to others' near-death experiences.

MARIJUANA The straight dope on marijuana: Marijuana leaves and flowers contain **THC** (delta-9-tetrahydrocannabinol). Whether smoked (getting to the brain in about 7 seconds) or eaten (traveling at a slower, unpredictable rate), THC produces a mix of effects.

Marijuana is usually classified as a mild hallucinogen because it amplifies sensitivity to colors, sounds, tastes, and smells. But like the depressant alcohol, it relaxes, disinhibits, and may produce a euphoric high. As with alcohol, people sometimes consume marijuana to help them sleep or improve their mood (Buckner et al., 2019; Wong et al., 2019). Both alcohol and marijuana impair the motor coordination, perceptual skills, and reaction time necessary for safely operating an automobile or other machine. "THC causes animals to misjudge events," reported Ronald Siegel (1990, p. 163). "Pigeons wait too long to respond to buzzers or lights that tell them food is available for brief periods; and rats turn the wrong way in mazes."

Marijuana and alcohol also differ. The body eliminates alcohol within hours, while THC and its by-products linger in the body for more than a week. Regular users may experience a less abrupt withdrawal, and achieve a high with smaller-than-usual amounts. This is the opposite of typical tolerance, in which repeat users need larger doses for the same effect.

After considering more than 10,000 scientific reports, the U.S. National Academies of Sciences, Engineering, and Medicine (2017) concluded that marijuana use

- alleviates chronic pain and chemotherapy-related nausea;
- is not associated with tobacco-related diseases such as lung cancer;
- predicts increased risk of traffic accidents, chronic bronchitis, psychosis, social anxiety disorder, and suicidal thoughts; and
- likely contributes to impaired attention, learning, and memory, and possibly to academic underachievement.

The more often the person uses marijuana, especially during adolescence, the greater the risk of anxiety, depression, psychosis, and suicidal behavior (Gage, 2019; Gobbi et al., 2019; Huckins, 2017). One study of nearly 4000 Canadian seventh-graders concluded that marijuana use at that early age was "neurotoxic": It predicted long-term cognitive impairment (Harvey, 2019). Marijuana can also function as a "gateway drug" for future alcohol and opioid use (Gunn et al., 2018; Olfson et al., 2017). "Nearly 1 in 5 people who begin marijuana use during adolescence become addicted," warned U.S. Surgeon General Jerome Adams (Aubrey, 2019).

Over the last half-century, attitudes toward marijuana use have changed remarkably—from 12 percent support for legalizing marijuana in 1969 to 66 percent in 2019 (De Pinto, 2019; McCarthy, 2018). Some countries and U.S. states have passed laws legalizing marijuana possession. Greater legal acceptance helps explain why rates of Americans who have tried marijuana rose dramatically between 1969 and 2017, from 4 to 45 percent (Gallup, 2019).

* * *

Despite their differences, the psychoactive drugs summarized in **TABLE 9.2** (with the exception of marijuana) share a common feature: They trigger negative aftereffects that offset their immediate positive effects and grow stronger with repetition. This helps explain both tolerance and withdrawal.

hallucinogens psychedelic ("mind-manifesting") drugs, such as LSD, that distort perceptions and evoke sensory images in the absence of sensory input.

near-death experience an altered state of consciousness reported after a close brush with death (such as cardiac arrest); often similar to drug-induced hallucinations.

LSD (lysergic acid diethylamide) a powerful hallucinogenic drug; also known as *acid*.

THC the major active ingredient in marijuana; triggers a variety of effects, including mild hallucinations.

Synthetic marijuana (*K2*, also called *Spice*) mimics THC. Its harmful side effects can include agitation and hallucinations (Fattore, 2016; Sherif et al., 2016).

TABLE 9.2 A Guide to Selected Psychoactive Drugs

Drug	Type	Pleasurable Effects	Negative Aftereffects
Alcohol	Depressant	Initial high followed by relaxation and disinhibition	Depression, memory loss, organ damage, impaired reactions
Heroin	Depressant	Rush of euphoria, relief from pain	Depressed physiology, agonizing withdrawal
Caffeine	Stimulant	Increased alertness and wakefulness	Anxiety, restlessness, and insomnia in high doses; uncomfortable withdrawal
Nicotine	Stimulant	Arousal and relaxation, sense of well-being	Heart disease, cancer
Cocaine	Stimulant	Rush of euphoria, confidence, energy	Cardiovascular stress, suspiciousness, depressive crash
Methamphetamine	Stimulant	Euphoria, alertness, energy	Irritability, insomnia, hypertension, seizures
Ecstasy (MDMA)	Stimulant; mild hallucinogen	Emotional elevation, disinhibition	Dehydration, overheating, depressed mood, impaired cognitive and immune functioning
LSD	Hallucinogen	Visual "trip"	Risk of panic
Marijuana (THC)	Mild hallucinogen	Enhanced sensation, relief of pain, distortion of time, relaxation	Impaired learning and memory, increased risk of psychological disorders

To review the basic psychoactive drugs and their actions, and to play the role of experimenter as you administer drugs and observe their effects, visit *Topic Tutorial: PsychSim6, Your Mind on Drugs.*

"How curiously [pleasure] is related to what is thought to be its opposite, pain! . . . Wherever the one is found, the other follows up behind." (Plato, *Phaedo*, fourth century B.C.E.)

RP-5 How does this pleasure-pain description apply to the repeated use of psychoactive drugs?

ANSWERS IN APPENDIX E

Influences on Drug Use

LOQ 9-6 Why do some people become regular users of consciousness-altering drugs?

Drug use by North American youth increased during the 1970s. Then, with increased drug education and a more realistic and deglamorized media depiction of taking drugs, drug use declined sharply (except for a small rise in the mid-1980s). After the early 1990s, the cultural antidrug voice softened, and some drugs for a time were again glamorized in music and films. Consider these historical trends in the use of marijuana:

- In the University of Michigan's annual survey of 15,000 U.S. twelfth graders, the proportion who said there is "great risk" in regular marijuana use rose from 35 percent in 1978 to 79 percent in 1991, then retreated to 30 percent in 2018 (Miech et al., 2019).

- After peaking in 1978, marijuana use by U.S. twelfth graders declined through 1992, then rose and held steady until beginning to trend back up in 2017 (see **FIGURE 9.5**). Canadian use among 15- to 24-year-olds has been similarly trending upward since 2012, and by late 2018 was 15 percent among all Canadians age 15 and older (CCSA, 2017; Statistics Canada, 2019). European teen drug use has been lower, but with trends mirroring those in North America: rising marijuana and declining cigarette use (Wadley & Lee, 2016).

For some adolescents, occasional drug use represents thrill seeking. Yet why do some teens, but not others, become regular drug users? In search of answers, researchers have engaged biological, psychological, and social-cultural levels of analysis.

→ FIGURE 9.5

Trends in drug use The percentage of U.S. twelfth graders who said they had used alcohol or marijuana during the past 30 days largely declined from the late 1970s to the 1990s, when it partially rebounded for a few years. Reported cocaine use has declined since the mid-1980s, and opioids peaked in 2009. (Data from Miech et al., 2016, 2019.) Outside the United States, teens' drug use has also declined. In Europe, 15-year-olds' weekly alcohol use has plummeted—dropping from 26 to 13 percent between 2002 and 2014; in Britain it dropped from 46 percent to 10 percent (WHO, 2018b).

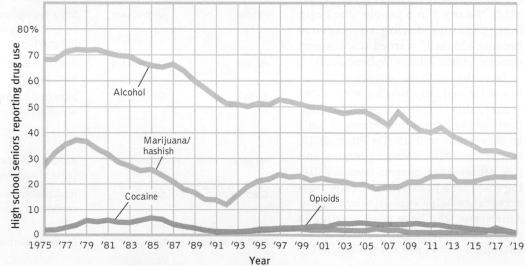

Biological Influences

Some people may be biologically vulnerable to particular drugs. For example, evidence accumulates that heredity influences some aspects of substance use problems, especially those appearing by early adulthood (Crabbe, 2002):

- *Genetics.* Researchers have identified genes associated with alcohol use disorder, and they are seeking genes that contribute to tobacco addiction (Stacey et al., 2012).

These culprit genes seemingly produce deficiencies in the brain's natural dopamine reward system: While triggering temporary dopamine-produced pleasure, the addictive drugs disrupt normal dopamine balance. Studies of how drugs reprogram the brain's reward systems raise hopes for anti-addiction drugs that might block or blunt the effects of alcohol and other drugs (Volkow & Boyle, 2018).

- *Twin studies.* If an identical rather than fraternal twin is diagnosed with alcohol use disorder, the other twin is at increased risk for alcohol problems (Kendler et al., 2002). In marijuana use, too, identical twins more closely resemble each other than do fraternal twins.

- *Adoption studies.* One study tracked 18,115 Swedish adoptees. Those with drug-abusing biological parents were at doubled risk of drug abuse, indicating a genetic influence—a finding confirmed in another Swedish study of 14,000+ twins and 1.3 million other siblings. But then those with drug-abusing adoptive siblings also had a doubled risk of drug abuse, indicating an environmental influence (Kendler et al., 2012; Maes et al., 2016). So, what might those environmental influences be?

> See the *Video: Twin Studies* for a helpful tutorial animation about this type of research design.

Psychological and Social-Cultural Influences

Throughout this text, you will see that biological, psychological, and social-cultural factors interact to produce behavior. So, too, with problematic drug use (**FIGURE 9.6**). Those without close, secure attachments with family and friends are more likely to turn to substance use (Fairbairn et al., 2018). One psychological factor that has appeared in studies of youth and young adults is the feeling that life is meaningless and direction-less (Newcomb & Harlow, 1986). This feeling is common among school dropouts who subsist without job skills, without privilege, and with little hope.

Sometimes the psychological influence is obvious. Many heavy users of alcohol, marijuana, and cocaine have experienced significant stress or failure and are depressed. Girls with a history of depression, eating disorders, or sexual or physical abuse are at increased risk for problematic substance use. So are youth undergoing school or neighborhood transitions (CASA, 2003; Logan et al., 2002). Undergraduates who have not yet achieved a clear identity are also at greater risk (Bishop et al., 2005). By temporarily dulling the pain of self-awareness, psychoactive drugs may offer a way to avoid coping with depression, anger, anxiety, or insomnia. (As the Learning modules explain, behavior is often controlled more by its immediate consequences than by its later ones.)

Warning signs of alcohol use disorder:
- Drinking binges (five drinks for men and four for women over two hours)
- Craving alcohol
- Use results in unfulfilled work, school, or home tasks
- Failing to honor a resolve to drink less
- Continued use despite health risk
- Avoiding family or friends when drinking

Biological influences:
- genetic predispositions
- variations in neurotransmitter systems

Psychological influences:
- lacking sense of purpose
- significant stress
- psychological disorders, such as depression

Disordered drug use

Social-cultural influences:
- difficult environment
- cultural acceptance of drug use
- negative peer influences

← **FIGURE 9.6**
Levels of analysis for disordered drug use The biopsychosocial approach enables researchers to investigate disordered drug use from complementary perspectives.

Nic-A-Teen Few people start smoking or vaping past the vulnerable teen and early-adult years. Eager to hook customers whose addiction will give them business for years to come, tobacco product companies focus on a young target market. Seeing celebrities smoking or vaping, such as singer Lily Allen, may tempt young people to imitate. In 2017, more than a third of youth-rated (G, PG, PG-13) American movies showed smoking (CDC, 2018b).

VYPE/MEGA/Newscom

Smoking and vaping usually begin during early adolescence. (If you are in college or university, and the cigarette manufacturers haven't yet made you their devoted customer, they almost surely never will.) Adolescents, self-conscious and often thinking the world is watching their every move, are especially vulnerable. They may first light up to imitate glamorous celebrities, to project a mature image, to handle stress, or to get the social reward of acceptance by other users (Cin et al., 2007; DeWall & Pond, 2011; Tickle et al., 2006). Mindful of these tendencies, tobacco product companies have effectively modeled smoking with themes that appeal to youths: attractiveness, independence, adventurousness, social approval (Surgeon General, 2012).

Rates of drug use also vary across cultural and ethnic groups. One survey of European teens found that lifetime marijuana use ranged from 5 percent in Norway to more than eight times that in the Czech Republic (Romelsjö et al., 2014). Alcohol and other drug addiction rates have also been low among actively religious people, with extremely low rates among Orthodox Jews, Mormons, Mennonites, and the Amish (DeWall et al., 2014; Salas-Wright et al., 2012).

Typically, teens who start smoking also have friends who smoke, who suggest its pleasures and offer them cigarettes (Rose et al., 1999). Among teens whose parents and best friends are nonsmokers, the smoking rate is close to zero (Moss et al., 1992; also see **FIGURE 9.7**). Similarly, if teens' friends use drugs, the odds are double that they will, too (Liu et al., 2017). Peers throw the parties and provide (or don't provide) the drugs. Teens who come from happy families, who do not begin drinking before age 15, and who do well in school tend not to use drugs, largely because they rarely associate with those who do (Bachman et al., 2007; Hingson et al., 2006; Odgers et al., 2008).

Adolescents' expectations—what they *believe* friends are doing and favoring—also influence their behavior (Vitória et al., 2009). One study surveyed sixth graders in 22 U.S. states. How many believed their friends had smoked marijuana? About 14 percent. How many of those friends acknowledged doing so? Only 4 percent (Wren, 1999). University students are not immune to such misperceptions: Drinking dominates social occasions partly because students overestimate their peers' enthusiasm for alcohol and underestimate their views of its risks (Prentice & Miller, 1993; Self, 1994) (**TABLE 9.3**). When students' overestimates of peer drinking are corrected, alcohol use often subsides (Moreira et al., 2009).

People whose beginning use of drugs was influenced by their peers are more likely to stop using when friends stop or their social network changes (Chassin & MacKinnon, 2015). One study that followed 12,000 adults over 32 years found that smokers tend to quit in clusters (Christakis & Fowler, 2008). Within a social network, the odds of a person quitting increased when a spouse, friend, or co-worker stopped smoking. Similarly, most U.S. soldiers who engaged in problematic drug use while in Vietnam ceased after returning home (Robins et al., 1974).

⮕ **FIGURE 9.7**

Peer influence Kids don't smoke if their friends don't (Philip Morris, 2003). A correlation-causation question: Does the close link between teen smoking and friends' smoking reflect peer influence? Teens seeking similar friends? Or both?

Percentage of 11- to 17-year-olds who smoked a cigarette at least once in the past 30 days

45%

30

15

0

All/Most of my friends smoke | Some of my friends smoke | None of my friends smoke

TABLE 9.3 Facts About "Higher" Education

- College and university students drink more alcohol than their nonstudent peers and exhibit 2.5 times the general population's rate of substance abuse. After college, most adults "mature out" of problem alcohol use (Lee et al., 2018).
- Fraternity and sorority members report nearly twice the binge-drinking rate of nonmembers.
- Since 1993, campus smoking rates have declined, alcohol use has been steady, and abuse of prescription opioids, stimulants, tranquilizers, and sedatives has increased, as has marijuana use.

Source: NCASA, 2007.

As always with correlations, the traffic between friends' drug use and our own may be two-way: Our friends influence us. Social networks matter. But we also select as friends those who share our likes and dislikes.

What do the findings on drug use suggest for drug prevention and treatment programs? Three channels of influence seem possible:

- Educate young people about the long-term costs of a drug's temporary pleasures.
- Help young people find other ways to boost their self-esteem and discover their purpose in life.
- Attempt to modify peer associations or to "inoculate" youth against peer pressures by training them in refusal skills.

People rarely abuse drugs if they understand the physical and psychological costs, feel good about themselves and the direction their lives are taking, and are in a peer group that disapproves of using drugs. These educational, psychological, and social-cultural factors may help explain why 26 percent of U.S. high school dropouts, but only 6 percent of those with a postgraduate education, report smoking (CDC, 2011).

SNAPSHOTS at jasonlove.com

Once upon a time, peer pressure caused Bob to start smoking.

Twenty years later, it forces him to quit.

(c) Love A141

Jason Love

"Substance use disorders don't discriminate; they affect the rich and the poor; they affect all ethnic groups. This is a public health crisis, but we do have solutions."
— U.S. Surgeon General Vivek Murthy, 2016

RETRIEVAL PRACTICE

RP-6 Why do tobacco companies try so hard to get customers hooked as teens?

RP-7 Studies have found that people who begin drinking in their early teens are much more likely to develop alcohol use disorder than are those who begin at age 21 or after. What possible explanations might there be for this correlation?

ANSWERS IN APPENDIX E

9 REVIEW Drugs and Consciousness

LEARNING OBJECTIVES

Test Yourself Answer these repeated Learning Objective Questions on your own (before checking the answers in Appendix D) to improve your retention of the concepts (McDaniel et al., 2009, 2015).

LOQ 9-1 What are *substance use disorders?*

LOQ 9-2 What roles do tolerance and addiction play in substance use disorders, and how has the concept of *addiction* changed?

LOQ 9-3 What are *depressants*, and what are their effects?

LOQ 9-4 What are *stimulants*, and what are their effects?

LOQ 9-5 What are *hallucinogens*, and what are their effects?

LOQ 9-6 Why do some people become regular users of consciousness-altering drugs?

TERMS AND CONCEPTS TO REMEMBER

Test Yourself Write down the definition in your own words, then check your answer.

psychoactive drug, p. 110

substance use disorder, p. 110

tolerance, p. 110

addiction, p. 110

withdrawal, p. 110

depressants, p. 112

alcohol use disorder, p. 112

barbiturates, p. 114

opiates, p. 114

stimulants, p. 114

amphetamines, p. 114

nicotine, p. 114

cocaine, p. 116

methamphetamine, p. 116

Ecstasy (MDMA), p. 116

hallucinogens, p. 119

near-death experience, p. 119

LSD, p. 119

THC, p. 119

MASTER THE MATERIAL

Test Yourself Answer the following questions on your own first, then check your answers in Appendix E.

1. After continued use of a psychoactive drug, the drug user needs to take larger doses to get the desired effect. This is referred to as _____.

2. The depressants include alcohol, barbiturates,
   a. and opiates.
   b. cocaine, and morphine.
   c. caffeine, nicotine, and marijuana.
   d. and amphetamines.

3. Why might alcohol make a person more helpful *or* more aggressive?

4. Long-term use of Ecstasy can
   a. depress sympathetic nervous system activity.
   b. deplete the brain's supply of epinephrine.
   c. deplete the brain's supply of dopamine.
   d. damage serotonin-producing neurons.

5. Near-death experiences are strikingly similar to the experiences evoked by _____ drugs.

6. Use of marijuana
   a. impairs motor coordination, perception, reaction time, and memory.
   b. inhibits people's emotions.
   c. leads to dehydration and overheating.
   d. stimulates brain cell development.

7. An important psychological contributor to drug use is
   a. inflated self-esteem.
   b. the feeling that life is meaningless and directionless.
   c. genetic predispositions.
   d. overprotective parents.

Continue testing yourself with 🅜 **LearningCurve** or 🅜 **Achieve Read & Practice** to learn and remember most effectively.

Sisoje/Getty Images

Nature, Nurture, and Human Diversity

What makes you you? In important ways, we are each unique. We are each a one-of-a-kind package of looks, language, personality, interests, abilities, and cultural background.

Yet we are also the leaves of one tree. Our human family shares not only a common biological heritage—cut us and we bleed—but also common behavioral tendencies. Our shared brain architecture disposes us to sense the world, develop language, and feel hunger through identical mechanisms. Whether we live by the Arctic Ocean or the Atacama Desert, we prefer sweet tastes to sour. We divide the color spectrum into similar colors. And we feel drawn to behaviors that produce and protect offspring.

Our kinship also appears in our social behaviors. Whether named Gonzales, Nkomo, Ahmadi, Smith, or Wong, we start fearing strangers at about 8 months, and as adults we prefer the company of those with attitudes and attributes similar to our own. Coming from different parts of the globe, we know how to read one another's smiles and frowns. As members of one species, we affiliate, conform, return favors, punish offenses, organize hierarchies of status, and anguish over a child's death. A visitor from outer space could drop in anywhere and find humans dancing and feasting, singing and worshiping, playing sports and games, laughing and crying, living in families and forming groups. Taken together, such universal behaviors define our human nature.

What causes our striking diversity, and also our shared human nature? How much are our individual differences shaped by our differing genes? And how much by our environment—by every external influence, from maternal nutrition while in the womb to social support while nearing the tomb? To what extent are we formed by our upbringing? By our culture? By our gender? By our current circumstances? By people's reactions to our genetic dispositions? By our own choices and efforts? Modules 10, 11, and 12 tell the scientific story of how our genes (nature) and environments (nurture) together knit us.

MODULE ⑩ Behavior Genetics: Predicting Individual Differences

LEARNING OBJECTIVE QUESTION **LOQ** **10-1** What are *chromosomes, DNA, genes,* and the human *genome*? How do behavior geneticists explain our individual differences?

So, if Beyoncé and JAY-Z's eldest daughter, Blue Ivy, grows up to be a popular recording artist, should we attribute her musical talent to her "superstar genes"? To her growing up in a musically rich environment? To high expectations? Such questions intrigue **behavior geneticists,** who study our differences and weigh the effects and the interplay of **heredity** and **environment.**

Genes: Our Codes for Life

Behind the story of our body and its brain—surely the most awesome thing on our little planet—is the heredity that interacts with our experience to create both our universal nature and our individual and social diversity. On the eve of the twentieth century, few would have guessed that every cell nucleus in your body contains the genetic master code for your entire body. It's as if every room in Dubai Creek Tower (the world's tallest structure) contained a book detailing the architect's plans for the entire structure. The plans for your own book of life run to 46 chapters—23 donated by your mother's egg and 23 by your father's sperm. Each of these 46 chapters, called a **chromosome,** is composed of a coiled chain of the molecule **DNA (deoxyribonucleic acid). Genes,** small segments of the giant DNA molecules, form the words of those chapters (**FIGURE 10.1**). Altogether, you have some 20,000 genes, which are either active (*expressed*) or inactive. Environmental events "turn on" genes. When turned on, genes provide the code for creating *protein molecules,* our body's building blocks.

Genetically speaking, every other human is nearly our identical twin. Human **genome** researchers have discovered a common sequence within human DNA. This shared genetic profile is what makes us humans, rather than tulips, bananas, or chimpanzees.

Yet we aren't all that different from our chimpanzee cousins. At a genetic level, humans and chimpanzees are 96 percent identical (Mikkelsen et al., 2005). At "functionally important" DNA sites, this number reaches 99.4 percent (Wildman et al., 2003)! Yet that wee 0.6 percent difference matters. It took a human, Shakespeare, to do what a chimpanzee cannot—intricately weave 17,677 words into literary masterpieces.

Small differences matter among other species, too. Common chimpanzees and bonobos resemble each other in many ways. They should—their genomes differ by much less than 1 percent. But they display markedly differing behaviors. Chimpanzees are aggressive and male dominated. Bonobos are peaceable and female led.

The occasional variations found at particular gene sites in human DNA fascinate geneticists and psychologists. Slight person-to-person variations from the common pattern give clues to our uniqueness—why one person has a disability that another does not, why one person is tall and another short, why one is anxious and another calm. Should people use newly available gene-editing technologies to reduce their unborn children's risk of disease? Only 26 percent of Americans approve (Scheufele et al., 2017).

The nurture of nature Parents everywhere wonder: Will my baby grow up to be agreeable or aggressive? Successful or struggling at every step? What comes built in, and what is nurtured—and how? Research reveals that nature and nurture together shape our development—every step of the way.

"Thanks for almost everything, Dad."

"We share half our genes with the banana."
— Evolutionary biologist Robert May, president of Britain's Royal Society, 2001

"Your DNA and mine are 99.9 percent the same. . . . At the DNA level, we are clearly all part of one big worldwide family."
— Francis Collins, Human Genome Project director, 2007

DNA

Chromosome

Gene

Cell

Nucleus

◀ **FIGURE 10.1**
The life code The nucleus of every human cell contains chromosomes, each of which is made up of two strands of DNA connected in a double helix. Genes are DNA segments that, when expressed (turned on), direct the development of proteins that influence a person's individual development.

behavior genetics the study of the relative power and limits of genetic and environmental influences on behavior.

heredity the genetic transfer of characteristics from parents to offspring.

environment every nongenetic influence, from prenatal nutrition to the people and things around us.

chromosomes threadlike structures made of DNA molecules that contain the genes.

DNA (deoxyribonucleic acid) a complex molecule containing the genetic information that makes up the chromosomes.

genes the biochemical units of heredity that make up the chromosomes; small segments of DNA capable of synthesizing proteins.

genome the complete instructions for making an organism, consisting of all the genetic material in that organism's chromosomes.

Most of our traits have complex genetic roots. How tall you are, for example, reflects the size of your face, vertebrae, leg bones, and so forth—each of which may be influenced by different genes interacting with your specific environment. Traits such as intelligence, happiness, and aggressiveness are each similarly influenced by a whole orchestra of genes (Holden, 2008). Indeed, one of the big take-home findings of today's behavior genetics is that there is no single gene that predicts your smarts, sexual orientation, or personality. And gene analyses of more than 800,000 people have identified 269 genes associated with depression (Howard et al., 2019). Another study of 1.1 million people identified 1271 gene variations that together predicted about 12 percent of the differences in people's years of schooling (Lee et al., 2018). *The bottom line:* Our differing traits are *polygenetic*—they are influenced by "many genes of small effect" (Lee et al., 2018; Matoba et al., 2019; Plomin, 2018).

So, our many genes help explain both our shared human nature and our human diversity. But—another take-home finding—knowing our heredity tells only part of our story. To form us, environmental influences interact with our genetic predispositions.

Charles Sykes/AP Images

Nature or nurture or both?
When talent runs in families, as with Wynton Marsalis, Branford Marsalis, and Delfeayo Marsalis, how do heredity and environment together do their work?

RETRIEVAL PRACTICE

RP-1 Put the following cell structures in order from smallest to largest: nucleus, gene, chromosome.

ANSWERS IN APPENDIX E

Twin and Adoption Studies

LOQ **10-2** How do twin and adoption studies help us understand the effects and interactions of nature and nurture?

To scientifically tease apart the influences of heredity and environment, behavior geneticists could wish for two types of experiments. The first would control heredity while varying the home environment. The second would control the home environment while varying heredity. Such experiments with human infants would be unethical, but nature has done this work for us.

Identical Versus Fraternal Twins

Identical (monozygotic) twins develop from a single fertilized egg that splits. Thus they are *genetically* identical—nature's own human clones (**FIGURE 10.2**). Indeed, they are clones who share not only the same genes but the same conception and uterus, and usually the same birth date and cultural history. Two slight qualifications:

* Although identical twins have the same genes, they don't always have the same *number of copies* of those genes repeated within their genome, and they sometimes differ in their brain's tiny wiring structures. These variations help explain why one twin may have a greater risk for certain illnesses and disorders, including schizophrenia (Lee et al., 2019; Maiti et al., 2011).

* During prenatal development, most identical twins share a *placenta* (transfers nutrients and oxygen from mother to embryo), but one of every three sets has separate placentas. One twin's placenta may provide slightly better nourishment, which may contribute to a few identical twin differences (Marceau et al., 2016; van Beijsterveldt et al., 2016).

Fraternal (dizygotic) twins develop from two separate fertilized eggs. Although they share a prenatal environment, they are genetically no more similar than ordinary siblings.

Shared genes can translate into shared experiences. A person whose identical twin has *autism spectrum disorder,* for example, has about a 3 in 4 risk of being similarly diagnosed. If the affected twin is fraternal, the co-twin has about a 1 in 3 risk (Tick et al., 2016). To study the effects of genes and environments, several thousand medical and psychological researchers have studied nearly 15 million identical and fraternal twin pairs (Polderman et al., 2015).

Are genetically identical twins also *behaviorally* more similar than fraternal twins? Studies in 12 countries have found that, compared with fraternal twins, identical twins are much more alike in *openness, conscientiousness, agreeableness, extraversion,* and *neuroticism* (Vukasović & Bratko, 2015). As identical twins grow older, their behaviors remain similar (McGue & Christensen, 2013). Genes also influence many specific behaviors. For example, among marijuana users, identical twins begin at a more similar age than do fraternal twins (Minică et al., 2018).

Identical twins, more than fraternal twins, look alike—so much so that most have difficulty distinguishing a flashed photo of their face from their co-twin's face (Martini et al., 2015). So, do people's responses to their looks account for their similarities? *No.* In a clever approach, researcher (and fraternal twin) Nancy Segal (2013; Segal et al., 2013) compared personality similarity between identical twins and unrelated lookalike pairs. Only the identical twins reported similar personalities. Other studies have shown that identical twins whose parents treated them alike (for example, dressing them identically) were not psychologically more alike than other identical twins (Kendler et al., 1994; Loehlin & Nichols, 1976). In explaining individual differences, genes matter.

 See the *Video: Twin Studies* for a helpful tutorial animation.

FIGURE 10.2
Same fertilized egg, same genes; different eggs, different genes Identical twins develop from a single fertilized egg, fraternal twins from two.

Identical twins	Fraternal twins
Same sex only	Same or different sex

Do look-alikes act alike? Genetically unrelated look-alikes, called doppelgangers, tend not to have notably similar personalities (Segal, 2013). Amazingly, these two bearded, red-haired minor league baseball pitchers also share the same unusual name—Brady Feigl—but are unrelated and grew up unaware of each other.

Separated Twins

Imagine the following science fiction experiment: A mad scientist, given two pairs of identical twins, swaps one in each pair. The resulting pairs are then raised in separate environments as if they were fraternal twins. Better yet, consider a *true* story (Dominus, 2015; Segal & Montoya, 2018):

In 2015, William Velasco was working as a butcher in Bogotá, Colombia. One day, customer Laura Vega Garzón mistook him for a colleague, Jorge, who looked the same—matching high cheek bones, same smile, same walking style. Was it Jorge, pretending to be someone else? Confused, she returned to the butcher shop to show William a picture of his look-alike, Jorge. William laughed and didn't take it seriously, but Laura later showed Jorge a photograph of William. "That's me!" Jorge exclaimed. Scrolling through William's social media photos, Jorge continued to see mirror images of himself. He saw something else that surprised him—his look-alike, William, sitting next to Jorge's fraternal twin brother (at least that's who it looked like to Jorge).

Until then, William and Jorge had lived utterly separate lives. William grew up in a rural village, whereas Jorge was city-raised. William and Jorge both—thanks to a colossal hospital mistake—believed they had fraternal twin brothers, Wilber and Carlos, respectively. In reality, Wilber and Carlos, like William and Jorge, were identical twins born in 1988. The hospital had sent William home with Wilber, and Carlos home with Jorge.

Although they were raised apart, William and Jorge both were jokesters, physically strong, and supportive. Wilber and Carlos were moody and serious, always organized, and prone to crying, and they had the same speech impediment. Each of them had wondered why he felt so different from his supposed fraternal twin. Meeting their identical twin revealed the power of genetics.

Genes matter, but so does environment. Urban-dwellers Jorge and Carlos had better nutrition, and were taller than rural-raised William and Wilber. Wilber didn't have access to the speech therapy that Carlos did, which meant that only Wilber struggled with speaking as an adult.

The remarkable story of the "Bogotá brothers" (see tinyurl.com/BogotaBrothers for more) resembles that of many separated twin pairs tested by psychologists Thomas Bouchard and Nancy Segal. These studies find similarities not only of tastes and physical attributes but also of personality, abilities, attitudes, interests, and fears.

Stories of startling twin similarities have not impressed critics, who remind us that "the plural of *anecdote* is not *data*." They note that if any two strangers were to spend hours comparing their behaviors and life histories, they would probably discover many coincidental similarities. If researchers created a control group of biologically unrelated pairs of the same age, sex, and ethnicity, who had not grown up together but who were as similar to one another in economic and cultural background as are many of the separated twin pairs, wouldn't these pairs also exhibit striking similarities (Joseph, 2001)?

identical (monozygotic) twins individuals who developed from a single fertilized egg that split in two, creating two genetically identical organisms.

fraternal (dizygotic) twins individuals who developed from separate fertilized eggs. They are genetically no closer than ordinary siblings, but shared a prenatal environment.

Separated Jims

In 1979, Jim Lewis awoke next to his second wife, for whom he often left love notes around the house. As he lay in bed, he thought about others he loved, including his son, James Alan, and his dog, Toy. Jim enjoyed building furniture in his basement woodworking shop, including a white bench circling a tree in his front yard, and he also liked driving his Chevy, watching stock-car racing, and drinking Miller Lite beer.

Shockingly, there existed another Jim for whom all these things were also true![1] Thirty-seven days after their birth, Jim Lewis and Jim Springer, genetically identical twins, were separated, adopted, and raised with no contact or knowledge of each other until the day Jim Lewis received a call from his genetic clone (who, having been told he had a twin, set out to find him).

These 39-year-old brothers became the first of 74 separated twin pairs tested by psychologist Thomas Bouchard and his colleagues (2009; Miller, 2012c). The brothers' voice intonations and inflections were so similar that, hearing an earlier interview, Jim Springer guessed, "That's me." Wrong—it was Jim Lewis. Tests measuring their personality, intelligence, heart rate, and brain waves were virtually as alike as the same person tested twice.

Siblings so different: Hermann Goering was outgoing, loved crowds, and became Hitler's right-hand man and founder of the Nazi Gestapo. His younger brother Albert Goering was quiet and reclusive, and worked to save the Jews that brother Hermann's regime was killing (Brennan, 2010).

Twin researchers have replied that separated fraternal twins do not exhibit similarities comparable to those of separated identical twins.

Even the impressive data from personality assessments are clouded by the reunion of many of the separated twins some years before they were tested. When adoption agencies are involved, separated twins tend to be placed in similar homes. Despite these criticisms, the striking twin-study results helped shift scientific thinking toward a greater appreciation of genetic influences.

Biological Versus Adoptive Relatives

For behavior geneticists, nature's second real-life experiment—adoption—creates two groups: *genetic relatives* (biological parents and siblings) and *environmental relatives* (adoptive parents and siblings). For personality or any other given trait, we can therefore ask whether adopted children are more like their biological parents, who contributed their genes, or their adoptive parents, who contribute a home environment. And while sharing that home environment, do adopted siblings come to share traits?

The stunning finding from studies of hundreds of adoptive families is that, apart from identical twins, people who grow up together—whether biologically related or not—do not much resemble one another in personality (McGue & Bouchard, 1998; Plomin, 2011; Rowe, 1990). In personality traits such as extraversion and agreeableness, for example, people who have been adopted are more similar to their *biological* parents than their caregiving adoptive parents.

The finding is important enough to bear repeating: The normal range of environments shared by a family's children has little discernible impact on their personalities. Two adopted children raised in the same home are no more likely to share personality traits with each other than with the child down the block.

Heredity shapes other primates' personalities, too. Macaque monkeys raised by foster mothers exhibit social behaviors that resemble their biological, rather than foster, mothers (Maestripieri, 2003).

Why are children in the same family so different? Why does shared family environment have so little effect on children's personalities? Is it because each sibling experiences unique peer influences and life events? Because sibling relationships ricochet off each other, amplifying their differences? Because siblings—despite sharing half their genes—have very different combinations of genes and may evoke very different kinds of parenting? Such questions fuel behavior geneticists' curiosity.

The genetic leash may limit the family environment's influence on personality, but it does not mean that adoptive parenting is a fruitless venture. One study followed more than 4000 Swedish children of parents who had criminal convictions or had substance use problems. Compared with their not-adopted siblings, those raised by an adoptive family were 44 percent less likely to be convicted of a crime (Kendler et al., 2016). As an adoptive parent, I [ND] find it heartening to know that parents do influence their children's attitudes, values, manners, politics, education, and faith (Gould et al., 2019; Kandler & Riemann, 2013). This was dramatically illustrated during World War II by separated identical twins Jack Yufe, a Jew, and Oskar Stöhr, a member of Germany's Hitler Youth. After later reuniting, Oskar mused to Jack: "If we had been switched, I would have been the Jew, and you would have been the Nazi" (Segal, 2005, p. 70). Parenting—and the cultural environments in which parents place children—matters!

Moreover, child neglect and abuse and even parental divorce are rare in adoptive homes. (Adoptive parents are carefully screened; biological parents are not.) One study looked at the parenting of siblings being raised apart—some with their biological mother, some with an adoptive mother (Natsuaki et al., 2019). Compared with the biological mothers, the adoptive mothers used gentler parenting, gave more guidance, and experienced less depression. So it is not surprising that, despite a somewhat greater risk of psychological disorder, most adopted children thrive, especially when adopted

---

[1]Actually, this description of the two Jims errs in one respect: Jim Lewis named his son James Alan. Jim Springer named his James Allan.

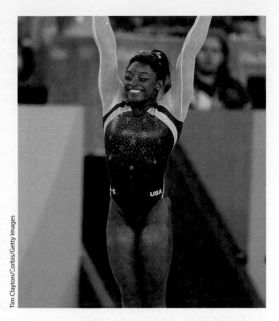

Adoption matters Country music singer Faith Hill and Olympic gold medal gymnast Simone Biles both benefited from one of the biggest gifts of love: adoption.

as infants (Loehlin et al., 2007; van IJzendoorn & Juffer, 2006; Wierzbicki, 1993). Seven in eight adopted children have reported feeling strongly attached to one or both adoptive parents. As children of self-giving parents, they have grown up to be more self-giving and altruistic than average (Sharma et al., 1998). Many scored higher than their biological parents and raised-apart biological siblings on intelligence tests, and most grew into happier and more stable adults (Kendler et al., 2015b; van IJzendoorn et al., 2005). In one Swedish study, children adopted as infants grew up with fewer problems than were experienced by children whose biological mothers initially registered them for adoption but then decided to raise the children themselves (Bohman & Sigvardsson, 1990). *The bottom line:* Most adopted children benefit from adoption.

ASK YOURSELF

Do you know biological siblings who, despite having been raised together, have very different personalities? (Are *you* one of these siblings perhaps?) Knowing what you do of their lives and upbringing, what do you think contributed to these differences?

RETRIEVAL PRACTICE

RP-2 How do researchers use twin and adoption studies to learn about psychological principles?

ANSWERS IN APPENDIX E

Temperament and Heredity

LOQ 10-3 What have psychologists learned about temperament?

As most parents with multiple children report, babies differ right out of the womb (Willoughby et al., 2019). One aspect of personality—**temperament** (emotional reactivity and intensity)—is quickly apparent, and it is genetically influenced (Kandler et al., 2013; Raby et al., 2012). Identical twins, more than fraternal twins, often have similar temperaments (Fraley & Tancredy, 2012; Kandler et al., 2013). Temperament differences typically persist. The most emotionally reactive newborns tend also to be the most reactive 9-month-olds (Wilson & Matheny, 1986; Worobey & Blajda, 1989). Emotionally intense preschoolers tend to become relatively intense young adults (Larsen & Diener, 1987). One study of 1037 New Zealanders found that a 45-minute assessment of 3-year-olds'

temperament a person's characteristic emotional reactivity and intensity.

frustration tolerance, impulsivity, and intelligence could predict "with considerable accuracy" which of them would, by age 38, consume the most welfare benefits, parent then abandon the most children, and commit the most crime (Caspi et al., 2016).

The genetic effect appears in physiological differences. Anxious, inhibited infants have high and variable heart rates and a reactive nervous system. When facing new or strange situations, they become more physiologically aroused (Kagan & Snidman, 2004; Roque et al., 2012).

Heritability

LOQ 10-4 What is *heritability,* and how does it relate to individuals and groups?

So, our biology helps form our personality. Yet asking whether our personality is more a product of our genes or our environment is like asking whether a basketball court's size is more the result of its length or its width. We could, however, ask whether different court sizes are more the result of *differences* in their length or differences in their width. Similarly, we can ask whether person-to-person personality differences are influenced more by nature or by nurture.

Using twin and adoption studies, behavior geneticists can mathematically estimate the **heritability** of a trait—the extent to which variation among individuals in a group can be attributed to their differing genes. For many personality traits, heritability is about 40 percent; for major depressive disorder, heritability is about 30 percent (Haworth et al., 2010; Pettersson et al., 2019). Everyday estimates for the heritability of intelligence range from 50–80 percent (Madison et al., 2016; Plomin et al., 2016; Plomin & von Stumm, 2018). This does *not* mean that *your* intelligence is 50–80 percent genetic. Rather, it means that genetic influence explains between 50–80 percent of the observed *variation among people*. We can never say what percentage of an *individual's* personality or intelligence is inherited. It makes no sense to say that your personality is due *x* percent to your heredity and *y* percent to your environment. This point is so often misunderstood that we repeat: Heritability refers to how much *differences among people* are due to genes.

The heritability of traits such as intelligence varies from study to study. Consider humorist Mark Twain's (1835–1910) fictional idea of raising boys in barrels to age 12, feeding them through a hole. If we were to follow his suggestion, the boys would all emerge with lower-than-normal intelligence scores at age 12. Yet given their equal environments, their test score differences could be explained only by their heredity. With the same environment, heritability—differences due to genes—would be near 100 percent.

As environments become more similar, heredity becomes the primary source of differences. If all schools were of uniform quality, all families equally loving, and all neighborhoods equally healthy, then heritability would *increase* (because differences due to environment would *decrease*). But consider the other extreme: If all people had similar heredities but were raised in drastically different environments (some in barrels, some in luxury homes), heritability would be much lower. So, heritability is not a single fixed score; it varies with changing environments.

If genetic influences help explain variations in traits among individuals in a group, can the same be said of trait differences *between* groups? Not necessarily. Height is 90 percent heritable, yet nutrition (an environmental factor) rather than genes explains why, as a group, today's adults are taller (Floud et al., 2011). In 1896, the global average height for men was 5 feet 3 inches (162 centimeters) and for women was 4 feet 10 inches (151 centimeters) (Our World in Data, 2019). In the 1990s, their male and female counterparts stood 3.5 inches (9 centimeters) taller. The two groups differ, but not because human genes have changed in this eyeblink of time. South Korean men and women, with their better diets, now average 6 inches (15 centimeters) taller than genetically similar North Koreans (Johnson et al., 2009). Genes matter, but so does environment.

As with height, so with personality and intelligence scores: Heritable individual differences need not imply heritable group differences. And, if some *individuals* are genetically disposed to be more aggressive than others, that needn't explain why some *groups* are more aggressive than others. Putting people in a new social context can change their aggressiveness. Today's peaceful Scandinavians carry many genes inherited from their Viking warrior ancestors.

Play the role of a researcher studying temperament and personality by engaging online with the activity *How Would You Know If Personality Runs in Our Genes?*

"The title of my science project is 'My Little Brother: Nature or Nurture.'"

RETRIEVAL PRACTICE

RP-3 Those studying the *heritability* of a trait try to determine how much of the person-to-person variation in that trait among members of a specific group is due to their differing _____.

ANSWERS IN APPENDIX E

For a 7-minute explanation of genes and environment, watch the *Video: Behavior Genetics.*

Gene–Environment Interaction

Among our similarities, the most important—the behavioral hallmark of our species—is our enormous adaptive capacity. Some human traits develop the same way in virtually every environment. But other traits are expressed only in particular environments. Go barefoot for a summer and you will develop toughened, callused feet—a biological adaptation to friction. Meanwhile, your shod neighbor will remain a tenderfoot. The difference between the two of you is an effect of environment. But it is the product of a biological mechanism—*adaptation*. Our shared biology enables our developed diversity (Buss, 1991). Thus, to say that genes and experience are *both* important is true. But more precisely, they **interact.** Just *how* our genes and our experiences interact to form us as unique individuals is one of the hottest topics in psychology today. Gene–environment interaction studies are revealing, for example, who is most at risk of permanent harm from stress or abuse and who is most likely to benefit from interventions (Byrd et al., 2019; Manuck & McCaffery, 2014). The National Institutes of Health *All of Us* research program is now studying 1 million people to pinpoint precisely how their genes and environment together predict physical and mental health (NIH, 2019).

Molecular Behavior Genetics

LOQ 10-5 How is molecular genetics research changing our understanding of the effects of nature and nurture?

Behavior geneticists have progressed well beyond asking "Do genes influence behavior?" The newest frontier of behavior-genetic research draws on "bottom-up" **molecular genetics,** which studies the molecular structure and function of genes.

SEARCHING FOR SPECIFIC GENES INFLUENCING BEHAVIOR As we've seen, genes typically are not solo players. For example, twin and adoption studies have revealed no single "obesity gene." Some genes influence how quickly the stomach tells the brain, "I'm full" (Adetunji, 2014). Others might dictate how much fuel the muscles need, how many calories are burned off by fidgeting, and how efficiently the body converts extra calories into fat. So, one goal of **molecular behavior genetics** is to find some of the many genes that together orchestrate complex traits such as body weight, sexual orientation, and impulsivity.

EPIGENETICS: TRIGGERS THAT SWITCH GENES ON AND OFF Genes can be either active (expressed, as hot water activates a tea bag) or inactive. **Epigenetics** (meaning "in addition to" or "above and beyond" genetics) studies the molecular mechanisms by which environments can trigger or block genetic expression. Genes are *self-regulating*. Rather than acting as blueprints that lead to the same result no matter the context, genes react. An African butterfly that is green in summer turns brown in fall, thanks to a temperature-controlled genetic switch. The same genes that produce green in one situation produce brown in another.

Our experiences also create *epigenetic marks,* which are often organic methyl molecules attached to part of a DNA strand (**FIGURE 10.3**). If a mark instructs the cell to ignore any gene present in that DNA segment, those genes will be "turned off"—they will prevent the DNA from producing the proteins normally coded by that gene. As one geneticist explained, "Things written in pen you can't change. That's DNA. Things written in pencil you can. That's epigenetics" (Reed, 2012).

Environmental factors such as diet, drugs, and stress can affect the epigenetic molecules that regulate gene expression. Mother rats normally lick their infants. In

Genetic space exploration In 2015, Scott Kelly (left) spent 340 days orbiting the planet in the International Space Station. His identical twin, Mark Kelly (right), remained on Earth. Both twins underwent the same physical and psychological testing (Garrett-Bakelman et al., 2019). Compared with his Earth-bound brother, Scott Kelly's immune system temporarily went into overdrive, possibly due to the stresses of living in space and exposure to greater-than-average levels of radiation. The study results are helping scientists understand how genes and environment—in outer space and on Earth—interact.

heritability the proportion of variation among individuals in a group that we can attribute to genes. The heritability of a trait may vary, depending on the range of populations and environments studied.

interaction the interplay that occurs when the effect of one factor (such as environment) depends on another factor (such as heredity).

molecular genetics the subfield of biology that studies the molecular structure and function of genes.

molecular behavior genetics the study of how the structure and function of genes interact with our environment to influence behavior.

epigenetics "above" or "in addition to" *(epi)* genetics; the study of the molecular mechanisms by which environments can influence gene expression (without a DNA change).

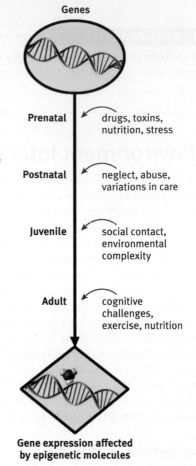

Genes

Prenatal	drugs, toxins, nutrition, stress
Postnatal	neglect, abuse, variations in care
Juvenile	social contact, environmental complexity
Adult	cognitive challenges, exercise, nutrition

Gene expression affected by epigenetic molecules

⊘ **FIGURE 10.3**

Epigenetic expression Beginning in the womb, life experiences lay down *epigenetic marks*—often organic methyl molecules—that can influence the expression of any gene in the DNA segment they affect. (Research from Champagne, 2010.)

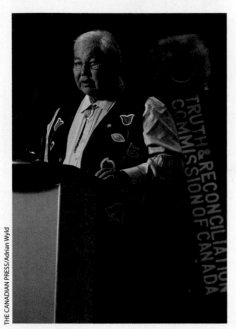

THE CANADIAN PRESS/Adrian Wyld

Lasting effects Canadian Senator Murray Sinclair received a humanitarian award from the Canadian Psychological Association for an in-depth report on the devastating effects of Canada's long running residential school program that removed Indigenous children from their families. Psychologist Susan Pinker (2015) observed that the epigenetic effects of forced family separation "can play out, not only in the survivors of residential schools but in subsequent generations."

experiments, infant rats deprived of this licking had more epigenetic molecules blocking access to their brain's "on" switch for developing stress hormone receptors. When stressed, those animals had above-average levels of free-floating stress hormones and were more stressed (Champagne et al., 2003; Champagne & Mashoodh, 2009).

Epigenetics provides a possible mechanism by which the effects of childhood trauma, poverty, or malnutrition may last a lifetime (Nugent et al., 2016; Peter et al., 2016; Swartz et al., 2016). Such experiences may leave their fingerprints in a person's genome. Some epigenetic changes may even get passed down to future generations. Studies of Holocaust trauma survivors and former U.S. Civil War prisoners of war showed shared epigenetic alterations with their offspring (Costa et al., 2018; Yehuda et al., 2016). Some critics question these findings' reliability (Horsthemke, 2018; Yasmin, 2017). Stay tuned: This scientific story is still being written.

Epigenetics research may solve some scientific mysteries, such as why only one member of an identical twin pair may develop a genetically influenced mental disorder (Spector, 2012). Epigenetics can also help explain why identical twins may look slightly different. Researchers studying mice have found that in utero exposure to certain chemicals can cause genetically identical twins to have different-colored fur (Dolinoy et al., 2007).

RETRIEVAL PRACTICE

RP-4 Match the following terms (i–iii) to the correct explanation (a–c).

i. Epigenetics

ii. Molecular behavior genetics

iii. Behavior genetics

a. Study of the relative effects of our genes and our environment on our behavior.

b. Study of how the structure and function of specific genes interact with our environment to influence behavior.

c. Study of environmental factors that affect how our genes are *expressed*.

ANSWERS IN APPENDIX E

❿ REVIEW Behavior Genetics: Predicting Individual Differences

LEARNING OBJECTIVES

Test Yourself Answer these repeated Learning Objective Questions on your own (before checking the answers in Appendix D) to improve your retention of the concepts (McDaniel et al., 2009, 2015).

LOQ 10-1 What are *chromosomes, DNA, genes,* and the human *genome?* How do behavior geneticists explain our individual differences?

LOQ 10-2 How do twin and adoption studies help us understand the effects and interactions of nature and nurture?

LOQ 10-3 What have psychologists learned about temperament?

LOQ 10-4 What is *heritability,* and how does it relate to individuals and groups?

LOQ 10-5 How is molecular genetics research changing our understanding of the effects of nature and nurture?

TERMS AND CONCEPTS TO REMEMBER

Test Yourself Write down the definition in your own words, then check your answer.

behavior genetics, p. 127

heredity, p. 127

environment, p. 127

chromosomes, p. 127

DNA (deoxyribonucleic acid), p. 127

genes, p. 127

genome, p. 127

identical (monozygotic) twins, p. 129

fraternal (dizygotic) twins, p. 129

temperament, p. 131

heritability, p. 133

interaction, p. 133

molecular genetics, p. 133

molecular behavior genetics, p. 133

epigenetics, p. 133

MASTER THE MATERIAL

Test Yourself Answer the following questions on your own first, then check your answers in Appendix E.

1. The threadlike structures made largely of DNA molecules are called _____.

2. A small segment of DNA that codes for particular proteins is referred to as a _____.

3. When the mother's egg and the father's sperm unite, each contributes
   a. one chromosome pair.
   b. 23 chromosomes.
   c. 23 chromosome pairs.
   d. 25,000 chromosomes.

4. Fraternal twins result when
   a. a single egg is fertilized by a single sperm and then splits.
   b. a single egg is fertilized by two sperm and then splits.
   c. two eggs are fertilized by two sperm.
   d. two eggs are fertilized by a single sperm.

5. _____ twins share the same DNA.

6. Adoption studies seek to understand genetic influences on personality. They do this mainly by
   a. comparing adopted children with nonadopted children.
   b. evaluating whether adopted children's personalities more closely resemble those of their adoptive parents or their biological parents.
   c. studying the effect of prior neglect on adopted children.
   d. studying the effect of children's age at adoption.

7. From the very first weeks of life, infants differ in their characteristic emotional reactions, with some infants being intense and anxious, while others are easygoing and relaxed. These differences are usually explained as differences in _____.

8. _____ is the proportion of variation among individuals in groups that we can attribute to genes.

9. Epigenetics is the study of the molecular mechanisms by which _____ trigger or block genetic expression.

 Continue testing yourself with 🎧 **LearningCurve** or 🎵 **Achieve Read & Practice** to learn and remember most effectively.

⓫ Evolutionary Psychology: Explaining Human Nature and Nurture

LOQ 11-1 How do evolutionary psychologists use natural selection to explain behavior tendencies?

Behavior geneticists explore the genetic and environmental roots of human differences. **Evolutionary psychologists** instead focus mostly on what makes us so much alike as humans. They use Charles Darwin's principle of **natural selection**—"arguably

evolutionary psychology the study of the evolution of behavior and the mind, using principles of natural selection.

natural selection the principle that inherited traits that better enable an organism to survive and reproduce in a particular environment will (in competition with other trait variations) most likely be passed on to succeeding generations.

the most momentous idea ever to occur to a human mind," said Richard Dawkins (2007)—to understand the roots of behavior and mental processes. The idea, simplified, is this:

- Organisms' varied offspring compete for survival.
- Certain biological and behavioral variations increase organisms' reproductive and survival chances in their particular environment.
- Offspring that survive are more likely to pass their genes to ensuing generations.
- Thus, over time, population characteristics may change.

To see these principles at work, let's consider a straightforward example in foxes.

Natural Selection and Adaptation

A fox is a wild and wary animal. If you capture a fox and try to befriend it, be careful: If the timid fox cannot flee, it may snack on your fingers. In the early 1950s, Russian scientist Dmitry Belyaev wondered how our human ancestors had domesticated dogs from their equally wild wolf forebears. Might he, within a comparatively short stretch of time, accomplish a similar feat by transforming the fearful fox into a friendly fox?

To find out, Belyaev set to work with 100 female and 30 male foxes selected from fox farms (where some domestication would have occurred through routine feeding and confinement [Gorman, 2019]). From their offspring he selected and mated the tamest 20 percent of females and 5 percent of males. (He measured tameness by the foxes' responses to attempts to feed, handle, and stroke them.) Over 57 generations of foxes, Belyaev and his successor, Lyudmila Trut, have repeated that simple procedure (Dugatkin & Trut, 2017). After forty years and 45,000 foxes, they had a new breed of foxes that, in Trut's (1999) words, were "docile, eager to please, and unmistakably domesticated. . . . Before our eyes, 'the Beast' has turned into 'beauty,' as the aggressive behavior of our herd's wild [ancestors] entirely disappeared." A transformation had occurred. So friendly and eager for human contact were these animals, so inclined to whimper to attract attention and to lick people like affectionate dogs, that the cash-strapped institute seized on a way to raise funds—marketing its friendly foxes as house pets.

Does the same process work with naturally occurring selection? Does natural selection explain our human tendencies? Nature has indeed selected advantageous variations from the new gene combinations produced at each human conception plus the **mutations** (random errors in gene replication) that sometimes result. But the tight genetic leash that predisposes a dog's retrieving, a cat's pouncing, or a bird's nesting is looser on humans. The genes selected during our ancestral history provide more than a long leash; they give us a great capacity to learn and therefore to *adapt* to life in varied environments, from the tundra to the jungle. Genes and experience together wire the brain. Our adaptive flexibility in responding to different environments contributes to our *fitness*—our ability to survive and reproduce.

Courtesy Institute of Cytology and Genetics, SB RAS

How to tame a fox Over six decades, Lyudmila Trut has genetically bred silver foxes into friendly human companions.

RETRIEVAL PRACTICE

RP-1 How are Belyaev and Trut's breeding practices similar to, and how do they differ from, the way natural selection normally occurs?

ANSWERS IN APPENDIX E

Evolutionary Success Helps Explain Similarities

Human differences grab our attention. Guinness World Records entertain us with the tallest, oldest, longest-haired, and most-tattooed humans. But our deep similarities also demand explanation. At the Amsterdam Airport's international arrivals area, one sees the same delighted joy on the faces of Indonesian grandmothers, Chinese children, and homecoming Dutch. "Even at a time when everything seems to be changing," notes physician-sociologist Nicholas Christakis (2019), "fundamental ways that humans live together remain constant."

mutation a random error in gene replication that leads to a change.

Our Genetic Legacy

Our similarities arise from our shared human *genome*, our common genetic profile. No more than 5 percent of the genetic differences among humans arise from population group differences. Some 95 percent of genetic variation exists *within* populations (Rosenberg et al., 2002). The typical genetic difference between two South Africans or between two Singaporeans is much greater than the *average* difference between the two groups. Thus, if after a worldwide catastrophe only South Africans or Singaporeans survived, the human species would suffer only "a trivial reduction" in its genetic diversity (Lewontin, 1982).

And how did we develop this shared human genome? At the dawn of human history, our ancestors faced certain questions: Who is my ally, who is my foe? With whom should I mate? What food should I eat? Some individuals answered those questions more successfully than others. For example, women who experienced nausea in the critical first three months of pregnancy were genetically predisposed to avoid certain bitter, strongly flavored, and novel foods. Avoiding such foods had survival value, since they are the very foods most often toxic to prenatal development (Profet, 1992; Schmitt & Pilcher, 2004). Early humans disposed to eat nourishing rather than poisonous foods survived to contribute their genes to later generations. Those who deemed leopards "nice to pet" often did not.

Similarly successful were those whose mating helped them produce and nurture offspring. Over generations, the genes of individuals not disposed to mate or nurture tended to be lost from the human gene pool. As success-enhancing genes continued to be selected, behavioral tendencies and learning capacities emerged that prepared our Stone Age ancestors to survive, reproduce, and send their genes into the future—and into you.

Across our cultural differences, we even share a "universal moral grammar" (Mikhail, 2007). Men and women, young and old, liberal and conservative, living in Sydney or Seoul, all respond negatively when asked, "If a lethal gas is leaking into a vent and is headed toward a room with seven people, is it okay to push someone into the vent—saving the seven but killing the one?" And they all respond more approvingly when asked if it's okay to *allow* someone to fall into the vent, again sacrificing one life but saving seven. Our shared moral instincts survive from a distant past where we lived in small groups in which direct harm-doing was punished. For all such universal human tendencies, from our intense need to give parental care to our shared fears and lusts, evolutionary theory proposes a one-stop-shopping explanation (Schloss, 2009).

As heirs to this prehistoric legacy, we are genetically predisposed to think and act in ways that promoted our biological ancestors' surviving and reproducing. On campus, we easily remember survival-related information ("In case of fire, use the stairs") and pay close attention to those we find romantically desirable (Nairne et al., 2019; Nakamura et al., 2017). But in some ways, we are biologically prepared for a world that no longer exists. We love the taste of sweets and fats, nutrients that prepared our physically active ancestors to survive food shortages. Few of us now gather and hunt for our food; instead, we too readily find sweets and fats in fast-food outlets and vending machines. Our deeply rooted natural dispositions are mismatched with today's junk-food and often inactive lifestyle.

Evolutionary Psychology Today

Darwin's theory of evolution has become one of biology's fundamental organizing principles and lives on in the *second Darwinian revolution*: the application of evolutionary principles to psychology. In concluding *On the Origin of Species*, Darwin (1859, p. 346) anticipated this, foreseeing "open fields for far more important researches. Psychology will be based on a new foundation."

Elsewhere in this text, we address questions that intrigue evolutionary psychologists: Why do infants start to fear strangers about the time they become mobile? Why do more people develop a *specific phobia* in response to spiders, snakes, and heights than to modern threats such as guns? And why do we fear air travel more than driving (which is riskier)?

To see how evolutionary psychologists think and reason, let's pause to explore their answers to two questions: How are males and females alike? How and why does their sexuality differ?

Consider yourself fortunate: Despite high infant mortality and rampant disease in past millennia, not one of your countless ancestors died childless.

Those who are troubled by an apparent conflict between scientific and religious accounts of human origins may find it helpful to consider that different perspectives on life can be complementary. For example, the scientific account attempts to tell us *when* and *how;* religious creation stories usually aim to tell about an ultimate *who* and *why.* As Galileo explained to the Grand Duchess Christina, "The Bible teaches how to go to heaven, not how the heavens go."

An Evolutionary Explanation of Human Sexuality

LOQ 11-2 How might an evolutionary psychologist explain male-female differences in sexuality and mating preferences?

Having faced many similar challenges throughout history, all genders have adapted in similar ways: We eat the same foods, avoid the same dangers, and perceive, learn, and remember similarly. When looking for a mate, we all prize many of the same traits—kindness, honesty, and intelligence—and we all avoid our close genetic relatives (Dandine-Roulland et al., 2019). It is only in those domains where we have faced differing adaptive challenges—most obviously in behaviors related to reproduction—that we differ, say evolutionary psychologists.

Male-Female Differences in Sexuality

And differ we do. Consider sex drives. Men and women are sexually motivated, some women more so than many men. Yet on average, who thinks more about sex? Hooks up more often? Masturbates more often? Views more pornography? The answers worldwide: *men, men, men,* and *men* (Baumeister et al., 2001; Hall et al., 2017; Lippa, 2009; Petersen & Hyde, 2010). Even among 65- to 80-year-old Americans, 12 percent of women and 50 percent of men reported being "very" or "extremely" interested in sex (Malani et al., 2018).

Unattached heterosexual men are alert for women's interest, and often misperceive a woman's friendliness as a sexual come-on (Abbey, 1987). This *sexual overperception bias* was evident in speed-dating men, who believed their dating partners expressed more sexual interest than the partners reported actually expressing (Perilloux et al., 2012). (This may be partially explained by unattached heterosexual women underreporting their own sexual interests [Engeler & Raghubir, 2018]). Long-term couples do better at gauging their partners' sexual interest (Dobson et al., 2018).

Many gender similarities and differences transcend sexual orientation. Compared with gay women, gay men (like straight men) report more responsiveness to visual sexual stimuli, and more concern with their partner's physical attractiveness (Bailey et al., 1994; Doyle, 2005; Schmitt, 2007; Sprecher et al., 2013). Gay male couples also report having sex more often than do gay female couples (Peplau & Fingerhut, 2007). And (also like straight men) gay men report more interest in uncommitted sex (Schmitt, 2003).

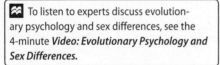 To listen to experts discuss evolutionary psychology and sex differences, see the 4-minute *Video: Evolutionary Psychology and Sex Differences.*

Natural Selection and Mating Preferences

Natural selection is nature selecting traits and appetites that contribute to survival and reproduction. Over time, traits that give an individual or a species a reproductive advantage are selected and will prevail. Evolutionary psychologists use the principle of *sex selection* to explain how females and males tend to differ in mating-related domains, whether they're chimpanzees or elephants, rural peasants or corporate presidents (Buss & Schmitt, 2019; Geary, 2010). Our natural yearnings, they say, are our genes' way of reproducing themselves.

Why do women tend to be choosier than men when selecting sexual partners? Women have more at stake. To send her genes into the future, a woman must—at a minimum—conceive and protect a fetus growing inside her body for up to 9 months, and may nurse for months following birth. No surprise then, that heterosexual women prefer partners who will offer their joint offspring support and protection—stick-around dads over likely cads (Meeussen et al., 2019). Straight women are attracted to tall men with slim waists and broad shoulders—all signs of reproductive success (Mautz et al., 2013). And straight American, Chinese, and European women overwhelmingly prefer men who seem affluent (Wang et al., 2018).

"Is that all you can think about?"

One study of hundreds of Welsh pedestrians asked people to rate a driver pictured at the wheel of a humble Ford Fiesta or a swanky Bentley. Men said a female driver was equally attractive in both cars. Women, however, found a male driver more attractive if he was in the luxury car (Dunn & Searle, 2010). Similarly, when people viewed pictures of others in luxury or standard apartments, women found men more attractive when they appeared in the luxury apartment, but men's perceptions were not affected by the backdrop (Dunn & Hill, 2014).

The data are in, say evolutionists: Men pair widely; women pair wisely. And what traits do straight men find desirable? Some, such as smooth skin and a youthful shape, cross place and time, and they convey health and fertility (Buss & Von Hippel, 2018). Mating with such women might increase a man's chances of sending his genes into the future. And sure enough, men feel most attracted to women whose waist is roughly a third narrower than their hips—a likely sign she has not yet had children (Lassek & Gaulin, 2018, 2019; Lewis et al., 2015). Even blind men show this preference for women with a low waist-to-hip ratio (Karremans et al., 2010). Men are most attracted to women whose ages in the ancestral past (when ovulation began later than today) would be associated with peak fertility (Kenrick et al., 2009). Thus, teen boys are most excited by women several years older than themselves, mid-twenties men prefer women around their own age, and older men prefer younger women. This pattern consistently appears across European singles ads, Indian marital ads, and marriage records from North and South America, Africa, and the Philippines (Singh, 1993; Singh & Randall, 2007).

Nature selects behaviors that increase genetic success. As mobile gene machines, say evolutionary psychologists, we are designed to prefer whatever worked for our ancestors in their environments. Had they not been genetically predisposed to act in ways that would produce children, we wouldn't be here. As carriers of their genetic legacy, we are similarly predisposed.

MGP/Photodisc/Getty Images

Critiquing the Evolutionary Perspective

LOQ 11-3 What are the key criticisms of evolutionary explanations of human sexuality, and how do evolutionary psychologists respond?

Most psychologists agree that natural selection prepares us for survival and reproduction. But critics say there is a weakness in evolutionary psychology's explanation of our mating preferences. Let's consider how an evolutionary psychologist might explain the findings in a startling, classic study of heterosexual women and men (Clark & Hatfield, 1989), and how a critic might object.

In this experiment, a woman or man posing as a stranger approached men or women and remarked, "I have been noticing you around campus. I find you to be very attractive." The "stranger" then asked a question, which was sometimes "Would you go to bed with me tonight?" What percentage of women and men do you think agreed? An evolutionary explanation of sexuality would predict that women would be choosier than men in selecting their sexual partners. Indeed, *not a single woman agreed*—but 70 percent of the men did. A French replication of this study produced a similar result (Guéguen, 2011).

Did the research support evolutionary psychology? Critics note that evolutionary psychologists start with an effect—in this case, the survey result showing that men were more likely to accept casual sex offers—and work backward to explain what happened. What if research showed the opposite effect? If men refused an offer for casual sex, might we not reason that men who partner with one woman for life make better fathers, whose children more often survive?

Other critics ask why we should try to explain today's behavior based on decisions our distant ancestors made thousands of years ago. Don't cultural expectations also bend the genders? Alice Eagly and Wendy Wood (1999, 2013) point to the smaller behavioral differences between women and men in cultures with greater gender equality. Such critics believe that *social learning theory* offers a better, more immediate explanation. We all learn **social scripts**—our culture's guide to how people should act in certain situations. By watching and imitating others in their culture, women may learn that sexual encounters with strange men can be dangerous, that casual sex may not offer much sexual pleasure, and that women (more than men) who engage in casual sex face reputational harm (Conley, 2011; Muggleton et al., 2019). This alternative explanation suggests that women are reacting to sexual encounters in socially scripted ways. And men's reactions may reflect *their* learned social scripts: "Real men" take advantage of every opportunity to have sex.

A third criticism focuses on evolutionary psychology's possible social effects. Are straight men truly hardwired to have sex with any woman who approaches them? If so, does it mean that men have no moral responsibility to remain faithful to their partners? Does this explanation excuse inappropriate sexual behavior as men's evolutionary legacy? Might evolutionary psychology weaken social movements aimed at reducing *sexual aggression*, such as #MeToo?

Evolutionary psychologists agree that much of who we are is *not* hardwired. "Evolution forcefully rejects a genetic determinism," insisted one research team (Confer et al., 2010). Genes are not destiny. And evolutionary psychology research confirms that men and women, having faced similar adaptive problems, are far more alike than different. Natural selection has prepared us to be flexible. We humans have a great capacity for learning and social progress. We adjust and respond to varied environments. We adapt and survive, whether we live in the arctic or the desert.

Evolutionary psychologists also agree with their critics that some traits and behaviors, such as suicide, are hard to explain in terms of natural selection (Barash, 2012; Confer et al., 2010). But they ask us to remember evolutionary psychology's scientific goal: to explain behaviors and mental traits by offering testable predictions using principles of natural selection (Lewis et al., 2017). We may, for example, predict that people are more likely to perform favors for those who share their genes or can later return those favors. Is this true? (The answer is *Yes*.) And evolutionary psychologists remind us that studying how we *came to be* need not dictate how we *ought to be*. Understanding our tendencies can help us overcome them.

"It is dangerous to show a man too clearly how much he resembles the beast, without at the same time showing him his greatness. It is also dangerous to allow him too clear a vision of his greatness without his baseness. It is even more dangerous to leave him in ignorance of both." — Blaise Pascal, *Pensées*, 1659

> ### ASK YOURSELF
> Based on what you've learned so far, how would you say that genes and environment work together to influence sexual behavior?

> ### RETRIEVAL PRACTICE
>
> **RP-2** How do evolutionary psychologists explain male-female differences in sexuality?
>
> **RP-3** What are the three main criticisms of the evolutionary explanation of human sexuality?
>
> *ANSWERS IN APPENDIX E*

To observe an experiment showing men's and women's attitudes toward casual sex, see the *Video: Openness to Casual Sex—A Study of Men Versus Women.* And for an interactive demonstration of evolutionary psychology and mating preferences, visit *Topic Tutorial: PsychSim6, Dating and Mating.*

social script a culturally modeled guide for how to act in various situations.

11 REVIEW Evolutionary Psychology: Explaining Human Nature and Nurture

LEARNING OBJECTIVES

Test Yourself Answer these repeated Learning Objective Questions on your own (before checking the answers in Appendix D) to improve your retention of the concepts (McDaniel et al., 2009, 2015).

LOQ 11-1 How do evolutionary psychologists use natural selection to explain behavior tendencies?

LOQ 11-2 How might an evolutionary psychologist explain male-female differences in sexuality and mating preferences?

LOQ 11-3 What are the key criticisms of evolutionary explanations of human sexuality, and how do evolutionary psychologists respond?

TERMS AND CONCEPTS TO REMEMBER

Test Yourself Write down the definition in your own words, then check your answer.

evolutionary psychology, p. 135

natural selection, p. 135

mutation, p. 136

social script, p. 140

MASTER THE MATERIAL

Test Yourself Answer the following questions on your own first, then check your answers in Appendix E.

1. Behavior geneticists are most interested in exploring _____ (commonalities/differences) in our behaviors. Evolutionary psychologists are most interested in exploring _____ (commonalities/differences).

2. Evolutionary psychologists are most likely to focus on
   a. how individuals differ from one another.
   b. the social consequences of learned behaviors.
   c. the natural selection of traits that helped our ancestors survive and reproduce.
   d. social scripts.

3. How do evolutionary psychologists use the principle of *natural selection* to explain differences in mating preferences in women and men?

Continue testing yourself with 📚 **LearningCurve** or 📖 **Achieve Read & Practice** to learn and remember most effectively.

---

12 Cultural and Gender Diversity: Understanding Nature and Nurture

From conception onward, we are the product of a cascade of *interactions* between our genetic predispositions and our surrounding environments (McGue, 2010). Our genes affect how people react to and influence us. And they affect our family environment (Barlow, 2019; Kong et al., 2018). Forget nature *versus* nurture; think nature *via* nurture.

Imagine two babies, one genetically predisposed to be attractive, sociable, and easygoing, the other less so. Assume further that the first baby attracts more affectionate and stimulating care and so develops into a warmer and more outgoing person. As the two children grow older, the more naturally outgoing child may seek more activities and friends that encourage further social confidence.

What has caused their resulting personality differences? Neither heredity nor experience acts alone. Environments trigger gene activity. And our genetically influenced traits *evoke* significant responses in others. Thus, a child's impulsivity and aggression may evoke an angry response from a parent or teacher, who reacts warmly to well-behaved children in the family or classroom. In such cases, the child's nature and the parents' nurture interact. Gene and scene dance together.

Identical twins not only share the same genetic predispositions, they also seek and create similar experiences that express their shared genes (Kandler et al., 2012). This helps explain why identical twins raised in different families have recalled their parents' warmth as remarkably similar—almost as similar as if they had been raised by the same parents (Plomin et al., 1988, 1991, 1994). Fraternal twins have more differing recollections of their early family life—even if raised in the same family. "Children experience us as different parents, depending on their own qualities," noted Sandra Scarr (1990).

How Does Experience Influence Development?

Our genes, when expressed in specific environments, influence our developmental differences. We are like coloring books, with certain lines predisposed and experience filling in the full picture. We are formed by nature and nurture, but what are the most influential components of our nurture? How do our early experiences, our family and peer relationships, and all our other experiences guide our development and contribute to our diversity?

The formative nurture that conspires with nature begins at conception, with the prenatal environment in the womb, where embryos receive differing nutrition and varying levels of exposure to toxic agents. Nurture then continues outside the womb, where our early experiences foster brain development.

Experience and Brain Development

LOQ 12-1 How do early experiences modify the brain?

Developing neural connections prepare our brain for thought, language, and other later experiences. So how do early experiences leave their fingerprints in the brain? Mark Rosenzweig, David Krech, and their colleagues (1962) opened a window on that process when they raised some young rats in solitary confinement and others in a communal playground. When they later analyzed the rats' brains, those who died with the most toys had won. The rats living in the enriched environment, which simulated a natural environment, usually developed a heavier and thicker brain cortex (**FIGURE 12.1**).

Rosenzweig was so surprised that he repeated the experiment several times before publishing his findings (Renner & Rosenzweig, 1987; Rosenzweig, 1984). So great are the effects that, shown brief video clips of the rats, you could tell from their activity and curiosity whether their environment had been impoverished or enriched (Renner & Renner, 1993). After 60 days in the enriched environment, the rats' brain weights increased 7 to 10 percent and the number of brain *synapse* connections mushroomed by about 20 percent (Kolb & Whishaw, 1998). The enriched environment literally increased brain power. In humans, too, lack of stimulation can slow brain and cognitive development (Farah, 2017).

Such results have motivated improvements in environments for laboratory, farm, and zoo animals—and for children in institutions. Stimulation by touch or massage also benefits infant rats and premature babies (Field et al., 2007; Sarro et al., 2014). "Handled" infants of both species develop faster neurologically and gain weight more rapidly. Preemies who have had skin-to-skin contact with their parents sleep better, experience less stress, and show better cognitive development 10 years later (Britto et al., 2017; Feldman et al., 2014).

Nature and nurture interact to sculpt our synapses. Brain maturation provides us with an abundance of neural connections. Experience—sights and smells, touches and tastes, music and movement—activates and strengthens some neural pathways while others weaken from disuse. Similar to paths through a forest, less-traveled neural pathways gradually disappear and popular ones are broadened (Dahl et al., 2018; Gopnik et al., 2015). By puberty, this *pruning process* results in a massive loss of unemployed connections.

FIGURE 12.1
Experience affects brain development Researchers raised rats either alone in an environment without playthings, or with other rats in an environment enriched with playthings that changed daily (Rosenzweig et al., 1962). In 14 of 16 repetitions of this basic experiment, rats in the enriched environment developed significantly more cerebral cortex (relative to the rest of the brain's tissue) than did those in the impoverished environment.

Impoverished environment **Impoverished rat brain cell** **Enriched environment** **Enriched rat brain cell**

Here at the juncture of nurture and nature is the biological reality of early childhood learning. During early childhood—while excess connections are still on call—youngsters can most easily master such skills as the grammar and accent of another language. Lacking any exposure to language before adolescence, a person will never master any language. Likewise, lacking visual experience during the early years, a person whose vision is later restored by cataract removal will never achieve normal perceptions (Gregory, 1978; Wiesel, 1982). Without that early visual stimulation, the brain cells normally assigned to vision will die or be diverted to other uses. The maturing brain's rule: Use it or lose it.

Courtesy of C. Brune

Stringing the circuits young String musicians who started playing before age 12 have larger and more complex neural circuits controlling the note-making left-hand fingers than do string musicians whose training started later (Elbert et al., 1995).

Although normal stimulation during the early years is critical, brain development does not end with childhood. Thanks to the brain's amazing *neuroplasticity*, our neural tissue is ever changing and reorganizing in response to new experiences. New neurons are also born. If a monkey pushes a lever with the same finger many times a day, brain tissue controlling that finger will change to reflect the experience (Karni et al., 1998). Human brains work similarly. Whether learning to keyboard, skateboard, or navigate London's streets, we perform with increasing skill as our brain incorporates the learning (Ambrose, 2010; Maguire et al., 2000).

Genes and experiences are just two ways of doing the same thing—wiring synapses."

— Joseph LeDoux, *The Synaptic Self*, 2002

ASK YOURSELF

What skills did you practice the most as a child—sports, music, cooking, video gaming? How do you think this affected your brain development? How will you continue to develop your brain with new learning and new skills?

How Much Credit or Blame Do Parents Deserve?

LOQ 12-2 In what ways do parents and peers shape children's development?

Biological parents shuffle their gene decks and deal a life-forming hand to their child-to-be, who is then subjected to countless influences beyond their control. But all parents—whether biological or adoptive—feel enormous satisfaction in their children's successes or guilt and shame over their failures. They beam over the child who wins trophies and titles. They wonder where they went wrong with the child who is repeatedly in trouble.

Freudian psychiatry and psychology encouraged such ideas, blaming problems from asthma to schizophrenia on "bad mothering." Believing that parents shape their offspring as a potter molds clay, many people praise parents for their children's virtues and blame them for their children's vices, and for the psychological harm that toxic parents presumably inflict on their fragile children. No wonder having and raising children can seem so risky.

But do parents really produce wounded future adults by being (take your pick from the toxic-parenting lists) overbearing—or uninvolved? Pushy—or indecisive? Overprotective—or distant? Should we then blame our parents for our failings, and ourselves for our children's failings? Or does talk of wounding fragile children through normal parental mistakes trivialize the brutality of real abuse? To paraphrase developmental psychologist Alison Gopnik (2016), are parents less like potters and more like gardeners who provide the soil for their children's natural growth?

Parents do matter. But parenting wields its largest effects at the extremes: the abused children who become abusive, the deeply loved but firmly handled who become self-confident and socially competent. The power of the family environment also appears in the remarkable academic and vocational successes of many children of people who leave their home countries, such as those of refugees who fled war-torn Vietnam and Cambodia—successes attributed to close-knit, supportive, even demanding families (Caplan et al., 1992). Asian Americans and European Americans often differ in their parenting expectations. An Asian-American mother may push her children to do well, but usually not in a way that strains their relationship (Fu & Markus, 2014). Having a supportive "Tiger Mother"—one who

"To be frank, officer, my parents never set boundaries."

"So I blame you for everything—whose fault is that?"

Mom in charge Amy Chua, law professor and author of *Battle Hymn of the Tiger Mother* (2011), sparked controversy by comparing strict "Chinese" and more permissive "Western" parenting styles. In raising her two daughters, Chua came to appreciate the benefits and the costs of the more externally controlled traditional Chinese parenting.

pushes her children and works alongside them—tends to motivate such children (whose culture prepares them to expect such pushing) to work harder. European Americans, however, might see this as going overboard and undermining children's motivation (Deal, 2011).

Yet in personality measures, shared environmental influences from the womb onward typically account for less than 10 percent of children's differences. Referring to our traits rather than our values, behavior geneticist Robert Plomin (2018b) noted, "We would essentially be the same person if we had been adopted at birth and raised in a different family."

This research has stunning implications. To developmental psychologist Sandra Scarr (1993), it implies that "parents should be given less credit for kids who turn out great and blamed less for kids who don't." So, knowing that children's personalities are not easily sculpted by parental nurture, perhaps parents can relax and love their children for who they are.

Peer Influence

As children mature, what other experiences do the work of nurturing? At all ages, but especially during childhood and adolescence, we seek to fit in with our groups (Blakemore, 2018; Harris, 1998, 2000):

- Preschoolers who disdain a certain food often will eat that food if put at a table with a group of children who like it.

- Children who hear English spoken with one accent at home and another in the neighborhood and at school will invariably adopt the accent of their peers, not their parents. Accents (and slang) reflect culture, "and children get their culture from their peers," as Judith Rich Harris (2007) has noted.

- Teens who start smoking typically have friends who model smoking, suggest its pleasures, and offer cigarettes (Liu et al., 2017). Part of this peer similarity may result from a *selection effect*, as adolescents seek out peers with similar attitudes, interests, and traits (Domingue et al., 2018). Those who smoke (or don't) may select as friends those who also smoke (or don't).

Peer power As we develop, we play, mate, and partner with peers. No wonder children and youths are so sensitive and responsive to peer influences.

The power to select a child's neighborhood and schools gives some parents the ability to influence the culture that shapes the child's peer group. And because neighborhood influences matter, parents may want to become involved in intervention programs that aim at a whole school or neighborhood. If the vapors of a toxic climate are seeping into a child's life, that climate—not just the child—needs reforming. Even so, peers are but one medium of cultural influence. As an African proverb declares, "It takes a village to raise a child."

RP-1 What is the *selection effect*, and how might it affect a teen's decision to join sports teams at school?

ANSWERS IN APPENDIX E

RETRIEVAL PRACTICE

---

culture the enduring behaviors, ideas, attitudes, values, and traditions shared by a group of people and transmitted from one generation to the next.

norm an understood rule for accepted and expected behavior. Norms prescribe "proper" behavior.

Cultural Influences

LOQ 12-3 How does culture affect our behavior?

Compared with the narrow path taken by flies, fish, and foxes, the road along which environment drives humans is wider. The mark of our species—nature's great gift to us—is our ability to learn and adapt. We come equipped with a huge cerebral mobile device, ready to receive cultural apps.

Culture is the behaviors, ideas, attitudes, values, and traditions shared by a group of people and transmitted from one generation to the next (Brislin, 1988; Cohen, 2009). Human nature, noted Roy Baumeister (2005), seems designed for culture. We are social animals, but more. Wolves are social animals; they live and hunt in packs. Ants are incessantly social, never alone. But "culture is a better way of being social," observed Baumeister. Wolves function pretty much as they did 10,000 years ago. We enjoy electricity, indoor plumbing, antibiotics, and the internet—things unknown to most of our ancestors. Culture works.

Other animals exhibit smaller kernels of culture. Chimpanzees sometimes invent customs—using leaves to clean their bodies, slapping branches to get attention, and doing a "rain dance" by slowly displaying themselves at the start of rain—and pass them on to their peers and offspring (Whiten et al., 1999). Culture supports survival and reproduction by transmitting learned behaviors that give a group an edge. But human culture does more.

Thanks to our culture's mastery of language, we humans enjoy the *preservation of innovation*. Within the span of this day, we have used Google, our phones, digital hearing technology [DM], and a digital guitar tuner [ND]. On a grander scale, we have culture's accumulated knowledge to thank for the last century's 30-year extension of the average human life expectancy (in most countries where this book is being read). Moreover, culture enables an efficient *division of labor*. Although two lucky people get their name on this book (which transmits accumulated cultural wisdom), it actually results from the coordination and commitment of a team of gifted people, no one of whom could produce it alone.

Across cultures, we differ in our language, money, sports, religion, and customs. But beneath differences is our great similarity—our capacity for culture. Culture transmits the customs and beliefs that enable us to communicate, to exchange money for things, to play, to eat, and to drive with agreed-upon rules and without crashing into one another.

Variation Across Cultures

We see our adaptability in cultural variations among our beliefs and our values, in how we nurture our children and bury our dead, and in what we wear (or whether we wear anything at all). We are ever mindful that the worldwide readers of this book are culturally diverse. You and your ancestors reach from Australia to Algeria and from Singapore to Sweden.

Riding along with a unified culture is like biking with the wind: As it carries us along, we hardly notice it is there. When we try biking *against* the wind, we feel its force. Face-to-face with a different culture, we become aware of the cultural winds. Visiting Europe, most North Americans notice the smaller cars, the left-handed use of the fork, the uninhibited swimwear. Stationed in Iraq, Afghanistan, and Kuwait, American and European soldiers alike realized how comparatively liberal their home cultures were. Arriving in North America, visitors from Japan and India struggle to understand why so many people wear their dirty street shoes in the house.

But humans in varied cultures nevertheless share some basic moral ideas. Even before they can walk, babies prefer helpful people over naughty ones (Hamlin et al., 2011). Worldwide, people prize honesty, fairness, and kindness (McGrath, 2015). Yet each cultural group also evolves its own **norms**—rules for accepted and expected behavior.

Gender equity: Among the Aka people of Central Africa, men and women interchangeably perform roles such as hunting and child care. As a result, fathers form an especially close bond with their infants, even suckling the babies with their own nipples when hunger makes the child impatient for Mother's return. Fathers in this culture are holding or within reach of their babies 47 percent of the time (Hewlett, 1991).

The British have a norm for orderly waiting in line. Many in South Asia, Africa, and the Middle East use only the right hand for eating. Sometimes social expectations seem oppressive: "Why should it matter how I dress?" Yet, norms—how to greet, how to eat—grease the social machinery.

When cultures collide, their differing norms often befuddle. Should we greet people by shaking hands, bowing, or kissing each cheek? Knowing what sorts of gestures and compliments are culturally appropriate, we can relax and enjoy one another without fear of embarrassment or insult.

When we don't understand what's expected or accepted, we may experience *culture shock*. People from Mediterranean cultures have perceived northern Europeans as efficient but cold, and preoccupied with punctuality (Triandis, 1981). People from time-conscious Japan—where pedestrians walk briskly and postal clerks fill requests speedily—have found themselves growing impatient when visiting Indonesia, where the pace of life is more leisurely (Levine & Norenzayan, 1999). Someone from the European community, which requires 20 paid vacation days each year, may also experience culture shock when working in the United States, which does not guarantee workers any paid vacation (Ray et al., 2013).

Variation Over Time

Like biological creatures, cultures vary and compete for resources, and thus evolve over time (Mesoudi, 2009). Consider how rapidly cultures may change. English poet Geoffrey Chaucer (1342–1400) is separated from a modern Briton by only 25 generations, but the two would have great difficulty communicating. At the beginning of the last century, your ancestors lived in a world without cars, radio broadcasting, or electric lighting. And in the thin slice of history since 1960, most Western cultures have changed with astonishing speed. Middle-class people enjoy the convenience of air-conditioned housing, online shopping, anywhere-anytime electronic communication, and—enriched by doubled per-person real income—they eat out more than twice as often as did their grandparents. People now enjoy expanded human rights. And with greater economic independence, today's women more often marry for love and less often endure abusive relationships.

But some changes seem not so wonderfully positive. Had you fallen asleep in the United States in 1960 and awakened today, you would open your eyes to a culture with more depression and more economic inequality. You would also find North Americans—like their counterparts in Britain, Australia, and New Zealand—spending more hours at work, fewer hours with friends and family, and fewer hours asleep (BLS, 2011; Twenge, 2017).

Whether we love or loathe these changes, we cannot fail to be impressed by their breathtaking speed. And we cannot explain them by changes in the human gene pool, which evolves far too slowly to account for high-speed cultural transformations. Cultures vary. Cultures change. And cultures shape our lives.

Culture and the Self

LOQ **12-4** How do individualist and collectivist cultures differ in their values and goals?

Imagine that someone ripped away your social connections, making you a solitary refugee in a foreign land. How much of your identity would remain intact?

If you are an **individualist,** a great deal. You would have an independent sense of "me," and an awareness of your unique personal convictions and values. Individualists prioritize personal goals. They define their identity mostly in terms of personal traits. They strive for personal control and individual achievement.

The human need to belong is universal, so individualists do seek out and join groups. But they are less focused on group harmony and doing their duty to the group (Brewer & Chen, 2007). As children, they value a sense of free will (Chernyak et al., 2019). Being more self-contained, individualists move in and out of social groups more easily. They feel relatively free to switch places of worship, change jobs, or even leave their extended families and migrate to a new place. Marriage is often for as long as they both shall love.

individualism giving priority to one's own goals over group goals and defining one's identity in terms of personal attributes rather than group identifications.

collectivism giving priority to the goals of one's group (often one's extended family or work group) and defining one's identity accordingly.

If set adrift in a foreign land as a **collectivist,** you might experience a greater loss of identity. Cut off from family, groups, and loyal friends, you would lose the connections that have defined who you are. *Group identifications* provide a sense of belonging, a set of values, and an assurance of security. Collectivists have deep attachments to their groups—their family, clan, company, or country. Elders receive respect. For example, Chinese law states that parents aged 60 or above can sue their sons and daughters if they fail to provide "for the elderly, taking care of them and comforting them, and cater[ing] to their special needs."

Collectivists are like athletes who take more pleasure in their team's victory than in their own performance. They find satisfaction in advancing their groups' interests, even at the expense of personal needs. They preserve group spirit by avoiding direct confrontation, blunt honesty, and uncomfortable topics. They value humility, not self-importance (Bond et al., 2012). They view forgiveness as a way to strengthen group harmony (Joo et al., 2019). Instead of dominating conversations, collectivists hold back and display shyness when meeting strangers (Cheek & Melchior, 1990). Given the priority on "we," not "me," that satisfying, super-customized North American latte might seem selfishly demanding in Seoul (Kim & Markus, 1999).

> "One needs to cultivate the spirit of sacrificing the *little me* to achieve the benefits of the *big me.*" — Chinese saying

"I'D LIKE a DeCAFFACiNNO FRAPPA CHAPPA DAPPA DiNGO ICE BLeNDED LAST OF THe MOCCAHiCANS VANiLLA ICe ICe BeTTeR LATTe' THAN NeVeR SMOOTHie WiTH a SHOT OF SeLF-eXPRESSO."

The tolerance of a Starbucks barista is severely tested.

Cartoon by Buddy Hickerson

A question: What do you think of people who willingly change their behavior to suit different people and situations? People in individualist countries (for example, the United States and Brazil) typically describe such people as "dishonest," "untrustworthy," and "insincere" (Levine, 2016). In traditionally collectivist countries (China, India, and Nepal, for example), people more often describe them as "mature," "honest," "trustworthy," and "sincere."

To be sure, there is also diversity *within* cultures. Many countries also have distinct subcultures related to religion, economic status, and region (Cohen, 2009). Southern Chinese farmers typically grow rice, a crop that requires group cooperation and builds collectivist values. Northern Chinese farmers often grow wheat, a crop that involves individual effort and leads to more individualist values. These differences lead people from Southern and Northern China to adopt different ways of thinking, feeling, and acting (Dong et al., 2019; Obschonka et al., 2018; Talhelm et al., 2014). In one clever study, researchers moved chairs together in Starbucks coffeehouses across China to block the aisle. They observed who acted like a typical individualist—controlling the environment by moving one of the chairs out of the way—and who acted like a typical collectivist—adapting to the environment by squeezing through the chairs (Talhelm et al., 2018). Compared with the more collectivist Southern Chinese, the Northern Chinese were more likely to move the chair.

In collectivist Japan, a spirit of individualism marks the "northern frontier" island of Hokkaido (Kitayama et al., 2006). And even in the most individualist countries, people have some collectivist values. But in general, people (especially men) in competitive, individualist cultures have more personal freedom, are less geographically bound to their families, enjoy more privacy, and take more pride in personal achievements (**TABLE 12.1**).

TABLE 12.1 Value Contrasts Between Individualism and Collectivism		
Concept	Individualism	Collectivism
Self	Independent (identity from individual traits)	Interdependent (identity from belonging to groups)
Life task	Discover and express one's uniqueness	Maintain connections, fit in, perform role
What matters	Me—personal achievement and fulfillment; rights and liberties; self-esteem	Us—group goals and solidarity; social responsibilities and relationships; family duty
Coping method	Change reality	Accommodate to reality
Morality	Defined by the individual (self-based)	Defined by social networks (duty-based)
Relationships	Many, often temporary or casual; confrontation acceptable	Few, close, and enduring; harmony is valued
Attributing behavior	Behavior reflects the individual's personality and attitudes	Behavior reflects social norms and roles

Information from Thomas Schoeneman (1994) and Harry Triandis (1994).

→ **FIGURE 12.2**
A child like no other
Americans' individualist tendencies are reflected in their choice of names for their babies. In recent years, the percentage of American babies receiving one of that year's 10 most common names has plunged. (Data from Twenge et al., 2010a, 2016a.)

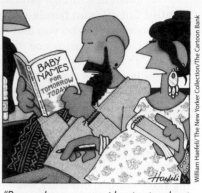

"Remember—we want her to stand out and fit in."

Individualists even prefer unusual names, as psychologist Jean Twenge noticed while seeking a name for her first child. When she and her colleagues (2010a, 2016a) analyzed the first names of 358 million American babies born between 1880 and 2015, they discovered that the most common baby names had become less common. As **FIGURE 12.2** illustrates, the percentage of boys and girls given one of the 10 most common names for their birth year has plunged. Collectivist Japan provides a contrast: Half of Japanese baby names are among the country's 10 most common names (Ogihara et al., 2015).

The individualist-collectivist divide appears in reactions to Olympic medals received. U.S. gold medal winners and the U.S. media covering them have attributed the achievements mostly to the athletes themselves (Markus et al., 2006). "I think I just stayed focused," explained swimming gold medalist Misty Hyman. "It was time to show the world what I could do." Japan's gold medalist in the women's marathon, Naoko Takahashi, had a different explanation: "Here is the best coach in the world, the best manager in the world, and all of the people who support me—all of these things . . . became a gold medal."

Individualists frequently demand romance and personal fulfillment in marriage (Dion & Dion, 1993). In contrast, collectivist love songs have often expressed enduring commitment and friendship, as in this one from China: "We will be together from now on. . . . I will never change from now to forever" (Rothbaum & Tsang, 1998).

What predicts change in one culture over time, or differences between cultures? Social history matters. Individualism and independence have been fostered by voluntary emigration, a capitalist economy, and a sparsely populated, challenging environment (Kitayama et al., 2009, 2010; Varnum et al., 2010). In Western cultures over the last century and now in all but the poorest countries, individualism has increased, following closely on the heels of increasing affluence (Grossmann & Varnum, 2015; Santos et al., 2017). Might biology also play a role? One study comparing collectivists' and individualists' brain activity suggested that collectivists experienced greater emotional pain when they viewed others in distress (Cheon et al., 2013). As we have seen, we are biopsychosocial creatures.

Collectivist culture
Although the United States is largely individualist, many cultural subgroups remain collectivist. This is true for many Alaska Natives, who demonstrate respect for tribal elders, and whose identity springs largely from their group affiliations.

To explore your individualist versus collectivist self, engage online with *Assess Your Strengths—What Is Your Self-Concept?*

Culture and Child Raising

Variations in child-raising values reflect individual and cultural diversity, as well as changes over time. Do you prefer children who are independent, or children who comply with what others think? Compared with families in Asian cultures, families in Western cultures more often prefer independence: "You are responsible for yourself." "Follow your conscience. Be true to yourself. Discover your gifts." Some Western parents have recently gone further, telling their children, "You are more special than other children" (Brummelman et al., 2015). Many with Western cultural values no longer prioritize obedience, respect, and sensitivity to others (Alwin, 1990; Remley, 1988). In the 1950s, Western parents were more likely to teach their children, "Be true to your traditions." "Be loyal to your heritage and country." "Show respect toward your parents and other superiors." Cultures vary. And cultures change.

Children across place and time have thrived under various child-raising systems. Upper-class British parents traditionally handed off routine caregiving to nannies, then sent their 10-year-olds away to boarding school.

Those from Asian and African cultures more often value emotional closeness. Infants and toddlers may spend their days close to a family member (Morelli et al., 1992; Whiting & Edwards, 1988). Many of these cultures encourage a strong sense of *family self*—which may mean that what shames the child shames the family, and what brings honor to the family brings honor to the self.

In traditional Gusii society, in western Kenya, babies nursed freely but spent most of the day on their mother's or a sibling's back—with lots of body contact but little face-to-face and language interaction. What might appear as a lack of interaction to many Westerners might to these Gusii parents seem far preferable to the lesser body contact experienced by babies pushed in strollers, carried in car seats, and left in playpens

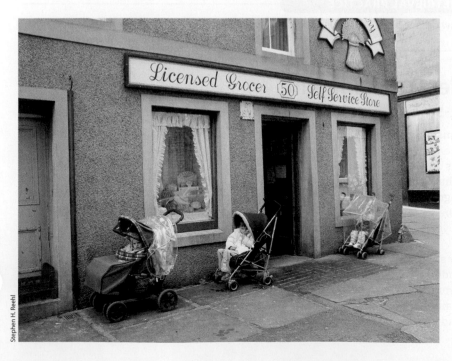

Cultures vary Parents everywhere care about their children, but raise and protect them differently depending on the surrounding culture. In big cities, parents keep children close. In smaller, close-knit communities, such as Scotland's Orkney Islands' town of Stromness, social trust has enabled parents to park their toddlers outside shops.

Stephen H. Reehl

(Small, 1997). In some rural villages in Senegal, cultural traditions discourage caregivers' talking with young children. Programs encouraging verbal interaction improved the children's language development one year later (Weber et al., 2017). But were the programs worth the cultural disruption? Diversity in child raising cautions us against presuming that any one culture's way is the only way to raise children successfully.

Developmental Similarities Across Groups

Mindful of how others differ from us, we often fail to notice the similarities predisposed by our shared biology. One 49-country study revealed smaller than expected nation-to-nation differences in personality traits, such as conscientiousness and extraversion (Terracciano et al., 2006). National stereotypes exaggerate differences that, although real, are modest: Australians see themselves as outgoing. German-speaking Swiss see themselves as conscientious. And Canadians see themselves as agreeable. Actually, compared with the person-to-person differences within groups, between-group differences are small. Regardless of our culture, we humans are more alike than different. We share the same life cycle. We speak to our infants in similar ways and respond similarly to their coos and cries (Bornstein et al., 1992a,b).

Even differences *within* a culture, such as those sometimes attributed to race, are often easily explained by an interaction between our biology and our culture. Consider this illustration (Rowe et al., 1994, 1995): Black men tend to have higher blood pressure than White men. Suppose that (1) in both groups, salt consumption correlates with blood pressure, and (2) salt consumption is higher among Black men than among White men. The blood pressure "race difference" might then actually, at least partly, reflect nothing about race—and more about a difference in diet.

And that parallels psychological findings. Ethnic groups sometimes differ, such as in average school achievement. But such differences are, as the researchers noted, "no more than skin deep." To the extent that family structure and economics, peer influences, and parental education predict behavior in one of these ethnic groups, they do so for the others as well.

So as members of different ethnic and cultural groups, we may differ in surface ways. But as members of one species we are subject to the same psychological forces. Our outward reactions vary, yet our basic emotions are universal. Our tastes vary, yet they reflect common principles of hunger. Our social behaviors vary, yet they reflect pervasive principles of human influence. Cross-cultural research helps us appreciate both our cultural diversity *and* our human similarity.

RETRIEVAL PRACTICE

RP-2 How do people in individualist and collectivist cultures differ?

ANSWERS IN APPENDIX E

Gender Development

LOQ 12-5 How does the meaning of *gender* differ from the meaning of *sex?*

We humans share an irresistible urge to organize our worlds into simple categories. Among the ways we classify people—as tall or short, dull or smart, cheerful or churlish—one stands out. It's what everyone first wanted to know about you: "Boy or girl?" Your parents may have tried to offer clues with pink or blue clothing; their answer described your birth-assigned **sex.** For most people, those biological traits help define their assigned **gender,** their culture's expectations about what it means to be a man or a woman. In recent years, cultural and scientific understandings of gender development have grown.

Simply said, your body defines your sex; your mind defines your gender. But your mind's understanding of gender arises from the complex interplay between your biology and your experiences (Eagly & Wood, 2013). Before we consider that interplay in more detail, let's take a closer look at some ways that males and females are both similar and different.

Cultural norms vary and change. "The generally accepted rule is pink for the boy and blue for the girl," declared the *Earnshaw's Infants' Department* in 1918 (Frassanito & Pettorini, 2008). "Pink being a more decided and stronger color is more suitable for the boy, while blue, which is more delicate and dainty, is prettier for the girls."

Similarities and Differences

LOQ 12-6 What are some of the ways in which males and females tend to be alike and to differ?

Whether male, female, or **intersex,** most of us receive 23 chromosomes from our mother and 23 from our father. Of those 46 chromosomes, 45 are *unisex*—the same for everyone. Our similar biology helped our evolutionary ancestors face similar adaptive challenges. For example, survival for men and women involved traveling long distances (migration, running down prey, running away from threats), which today is reflected biologically in men's and women's similar finishing times for ultralong-distance races. Everyone needed to survive, reproduce, and avoid predators, and so we are in most ways alike. Do you identify yourself as male, female, neither, or some combination of the two (Hyde et al., 2019)? No matter your answer, you gave no clues to your vocabulary, happiness, or ability to see, learn, and remember. Whatever our gender, we are, on average, comparably creative and intelligent and feel the same emotions and longings (Hyde, 2014; Lauer et al., 2019; Reilly et al., 2019).

But in some areas, female and male traits do differ, and differences command attention. Some oft-noted differences (such as the difference in self-esteem) are actually quite modest (Zell et al., 2015). And the average female and male intelligence test scores are near-identical (Lynn & Kanazawa, 2011; Tran et al., 2014). Other differences are more striking. The average female enters puberty about two years earlier than the average male, and her life expectancy is 4 years longer. She expresses emotions more freely, smiling and crying more, and, in Facebook updates, more often expresses "love" and being "sooo excited!!!" (Fischer & LaFrance, 2015; Schwartz et al., 2013). She is better at spelling and reading (Reilly et al., 2019). She can detect fainter odors and can become sexually re-aroused sooner after orgasm. She also has twice the risk of developing depression and anxiety, and 10 times the risk of developing an eating disorder. Yet the average male is 4 times more likely to die by suicide, to abuse tobacco, and to develop an alcohol use disorder. His "more likely to have" list includes greater size and strength, but also autism spectrum disorder, color-deficient vision, and attention-deficit/hyperactivity disorder (ADHD). And as an adult, he is more at risk for antisocial personality disorder. Male and female each have their own heightened risks.

Gender similarities and differences appear throughout this book, but here let's take a closer look at three gender differences. Although individuals vary widely, the *average* male and female differ in aggression, social power, and social connectedness.

AGGRESSION To a psychologist, **aggression** is any physical or verbal behavior intended to hurt someone physically or emotionally (Bushman & Huesmann, 2010). Think of examples of aggressive people. Are most of them men? Likely yes. Men generally admit to more aggression, especially extreme physical violence (Yount et al., 2017). Nearly half of 14- to 19-year-old U.S. boys feel pressure to be "willing to punch someone if provoked" (PLAN USA, 2018). In romantic relationships between women and men, minor acts of physical aggression, such as slaps, are roughly equal, but the most violent acts are mostly committed by men (Archer, 2000; Tremblay et al., 2018).

Laboratory experiments confirm a gender difference in aggression. Men have been more willing to blast people with what they believed was intense and prolonged noise (Bushman et al., 2007). And outside the laboratory, men—worldwide—commit more violent crime (Antonaccio et al., 2011; Caddick & Porter, 2012; Frisell et al., 2012). Worldwide, 95 percent of people convicted of murder are men (HEUNI, 2015). Men also take the lead in hunting, fighting, warring, and supporting war (Liddle et al., 2012; Wood & Eagly, 2002, 2007).

Here's another question: Think of examples of people harming others by passing along hurtful gossip, or by shutting someone out of a social group or situation. Were most of those people men? Perhaps not. Those behaviors are acts of **relational aggression,** and women are slightly more likely than men to commit them (Archer, 2004, 2007, 2009).

In 2019, the American Psychological Association (APA) released guidelines to help therapists work with men and boys. (Similar guidelines for working with women and girls were released in 2007.)

sex in psychology, the biologically influenced characteristics by which people define *male, female,* and *intersex.*

gender in psychology, the behavioral characteristics that people associate with *boy, girl, man,* and *woman.* (See also *gender identity.*)

intersex possessing male and female biological sexual characteristics at birth.

aggression any physical or verbal behavior intended to harm someone physically or emotionally.

relational aggression an act of aggression (physical or verbal) intended to harm a person's relationship or social standing.

Cadet Hallie H. Pound/U.S. Army

Making history In 2019, West Point's 34 Black female cadets were part of its most diverse graduating class in history.

"I hate to say there are female and male ways of dealing with power, because I think each of us has a male and a female part. But based on my own experience, women will tend to be inclusive, to reach out more, to care a little more." — Christine Lagarde, president of the European Central Bank, 2011

Mansplaining:

Emily Bernstein/The New Yorker Collection/The Cartoon Bank

"Oh, you've read it? I'll just describe it to you as if you hadn't."

SOCIAL POWER Imagine you've walked into a job interview and are taking your first look at the two interviewers. The unsmiling person on the left oozes self-confidence and independence, maintaining steady eye contact. The person on the right gives you a warm, welcoming smile, but makes less eye contact and seems to expect the other interviewer to take the lead.

Which interviewer is male?

If you said the person on the left, you're not alone. Around the world, from Nigeria to New Zealand, people have perceived gender differences in power (Williams & Best, 1990). (For more on this topic, see Thinking Critically About: Gender Bias in the Workplace.)

Now imagine a heterosexual couple negotiating a car purchase price. "If you won't change your price, we're leaving," says one of them, prompting the salesperson to counteroffer.

Which member of the couple—male or female—is the negotiator?

If you said the male, you're again in good company. People tend to associate negotiation with males, which helps explain why men often have an advantage in negotiation outcomes (Mazei et al., 2015)

SOCIAL CONNECTEDNESS Whatever our gender, we all have a need to belong, though we may satisfy this need in different ways (Baumeister, 2010). Males tend to be *independent*. Even as children, males typically form large play groups that brim with activity and competition, with little intimate discussion (Rose & Rudolph, 2006). As adults, men usually enjoy side-by-side activities, and their conversations often focus on problem solving (Baumeister, 2010; Tannen, 1990). When asked a difficult question to which they don't know the answer—"Do you have any idea why the sky is blue?"—men are more likely than women to hazard answers than to admit they don't know, a phenomenon researchers have called the *male answer syndrome* (Giuliano et al., 1998).

Brain scans show no striking sex differences (Ritchie et al., 2018; Wierenga et al., 2019). "Human brains cannot be categorized into two distinct classes—male brain/female brain," report neuroscientist Daphna Joel and her colleagues (2015). Brain scans do, however, reveal that a sex difference in brain network connections occurs prenatally, before culture's influence (Wheelock et al., 2019). And scans have suggested that a woman's brain, more than a man's, is usually wired in a way that enables social relationships (Ingalhalikar et al., 2013). This helps explain why females tend to be more *interdependent*. In childhood, girls usually play in small groups, often with one friend. They compete less and imitate social relationships more (Maccoby, 1990; Roberts, 1991). Teen girls spend more time with friends and less time alone (Wong & Csikszentmihalyi, 1991). In late adolescence, they spend more time on social networking sites, and average more text messages per day than boys (Pew, 2015; Yang et al., 2018). Girls' and women's friendships are more intimate, with more conversation that explores relationships (Maccoby, 2002). In one analysis of 10 million posts to Facebook (which more women use), women's status updates were as assertive as men's, but used warmer words; men more often swore or expressed anger (Gramlich, 2018; Park et al., 2016). An analysis of over 700 million Facebook words found women also used more family-related words, whereas men used more work-related words (Schwartz et al., 2013).

Thinking Critically About:
Gender Bias in the Workplace

LOQ 12-7 What factors contribute to gender bias in the workplace?

Differences in PERCEPTION

She's so aggressive!

He's so take-charge!

Among politicians who seem power-hungry, women are less successful than men.[1]

Most political leaders are men:

men

Men held 76% of seats in the world's governing parliaments in 2019.[2]

Political leaders

People around the world tend to see men as more powerful.[3]

women

When groups form, whether as juries or companies, leadership tends to go to males.[4]

Differences in COMPENSATION

Women in traditionally male occupations have received less than their male colleagues.[5]

Medicine U.S. salary disparity between male and female physicians:[6]

$171,880 women

$243,072 men

Academia Female research grant applicants have received lower quality of researcher ratings and have been less likely to be funded.[7] (But as we will see, gender attitudes and roles are changing.)

Differences in FAMILY-CARE RESPONSIBILITY

U.S. mothers still do nearly **twice** as much child care as **fathers**.[8] In the workplace, women are less often driven by money and status, compromise more, and more often opt for reduced work hours.[9]

What else contributes to WORKPLACE GENDER BIAS?

Social norms

In most societies, men place more importance on power and achievement, and are socially dominant.[10]

Leadership styles

Men are more *directive*, telling people what to do and how to do it.

Women are more *democratic*, welcoming others' input in decision making.[11]

Interaction styles

Women are more likely to express support.[12]

Men are more likely to offer opinions.[12]

Everyday behavior

Women smile and apologize more than men.[13]

Men are more likely to talk assertively, interrupt, initiate touches, and stare.[13]

Yet GENDER ROLES VARY WIDELY across place and time.

Women are increasingly represented in leadership (now 50% of Canada's cabinet ministers) and in the workforce. In 1963, the Harvard Business School admitted its first women students. Among its Class of 2020, 41% were women.[14] In 1960, women were 6% of U.S. medical students. Today they are slightly more than half.[15]

1. Okimoto & Brescoll, 2010. 2. IPU, 2019. 3. Williams & Best, 1990. 4. Colarelli et al., 2006. 5. Willett et al., 2015. 6. Census Bureau, 2018. 7. Witteman et al., 2019. 8. CEA, 2014; Parker & Wang, 2013; Pew, 2015. 9. Nikolova & Lamberton, 2016; Pinker, 2008. 10. Gino et al., 2015; Schwartz & Rubel-Lifschitz, 2009. 11. Eagly & Carli, 2007; van Engen & Willemsen, 2004. 12. Aries, 1987; Wood, 1987. 13. Leaper & Ayres, 2007; Major et al., 1990; Schumann & Ross, 2010. 14. Harvard Business School, 2019. 15. AAMC, 2018.

Every man for himself, or tend and befriend? Gender differences in the way we interact with others begin to appear at a very young age.

When searching for understanding from someone who will share their worries and hurts, people usually turn to women. Women and men have reported that their friendships with women are more intimate, enjoyable, and nurturing (Kuttler et al., 1999; Rubin, 1985; Sapadin, 1988). Bonds and feelings of support are stronger among women than among men (Rossi & Rossi, 1993). Women's ties—as mothers, daughters, sisters, aunts, and grandmothers—bind families together. As friends, women talk more often and more openly (Berndt, 1992; Dindia & Allen, 1992). "Perhaps because of [women's] greater desire for intimacy," reported Joyce Benenson and colleagues (2009), first-year college and university women are twice as likely as men to change roommates. When stressed, women are also more likely than men to turn to others for support. They are said to *tend and befriend* (Tamres et al., 2002; Taylor, 2002).

Gender differences in both social connectedness and power are greatest in adolescence and early adulthood—the prime years for dating and mating (Hoff et al., 2018). By their teen years, girls appear less assertive and more insecure, and boys seem more dominant and less expressive (Chaplin, 2015). In adulthood, after the birth of a first child, attitude and behavior differences often peak. Mothers especially may express more traditionally female attitudes and behaviors (Ferriman et al., 2009; Katz-Wise et al., 2010). By age 50, most gender differences subside, especially among parents. Men become less domineering and more empathic, and women—especially those with paid employment—become more assertive and self-confident (Kasen et al., 2006; Maccoby, 1998). Worldwide, fewer women than men work for pay. But, like men, women tend to be more satisfied with their lives when gainfully employed (Ryan, 2016).

So, although women and men are more alike than different, there are some behavior differences between the average woman and man, some of which also occur in non-human primates (Lonsdorf, 2017). Are such differences dictated by their biology? Shaped by their cultures and other experiences? Do we vary in how gender-conforming or non-conforming we are? Read on.

"In the long years liker must they grow;
  The man be more of woman, she of man."
— Alfred Lord Tennyson, *The Princess*, 1847

RETRIEVAL PRACTICE

RP-3 _____ (Men/Women) are more likely to commit relational aggression, and _____ (men/women) are more likely to commit physical aggression.

ANSWERS IN APPENDIX E

The Nature of Gender

LOQ 12-8 How do sex hormones influence prenatal and adolescent sexual development?

In most physical ways—regulating heat with sweat, preferring energy-rich foods, growing calluses where the skin meets friction—we are all similar. Although biology does not *dictate* gender, it can influence our gender psychology in two ways:

- *Genetically*—We have differing *sex chromosomes*.
- *Physiologically*—We have differing concentrations of *sex hormones*, which trigger other anatomical differences.

These two influences began to form you long before you were born.

PRENATAL SEXUAL DEVELOPMENT Six weeks after you were conceived, you looked much the same as any other tiny embryo. Then, as your genes kicked in, your biological sexual characteristics—determined by your twenty-third pair of chromosomes (the two sex chromosomes)—became more apparent. If you are male or female, your mother's contribution to that chromosome pair was an **X chromosome.** From your father, you received the 1 chromosome out of the usual 46 that is not unisex—either another X chromosome, making you female, or a **Y chromosome,** making you male. There are other sexual development variations, as we will see shortly.

About 7 weeks after conception, a single gene on the Y chromosome throws a master switch, which triggers the testes to develop and to produce **testosterone,** the main *androgen* (male hormone) that promotes male sex organ development. Females also have testosterone, but less of it; the main female sex hormones are the **estrogens,** such as estradiol.

Later, during the fourth and fifth prenatal months, sex hormones bathe the fetal brain and influence its wiring. Different patterns for males and females develop under the influence of the male's greater testosterone and the female's estrogens (Hines, 2004; Udry, 2000). If, however, females are prenatally exposed to unusually high levels of male hormones, they tend to grow up with more male-typical interests (Endendijk et al., 2016).

ADOLESCENT SEXUAL DEVELOPMENT A flood of hormones triggers another period of dramatic physical change, when we enter **puberty.** In this 2-year period of rapid sexual maturation, pronounced female-male differences emerge. A variety of changes begin at about age 10 in girls and at about age 12 in boys, though the subtle beginnings of puberty, such as budding breasts or enlarging testes, appear earlier (Biro et al., 2012; Herman-Giddens et al., 2012). A year or two before visible physical changes, we often feel the first stirrings of sexual attraction (McClintock & Herdt, 1996).

Girls' slightly earlier entry into puberty can at first propel them to greater height than boys of the same age (**FIGURE 12.3**). But boys catch up when they begin puberty, and by age 14, they are usually taller than girls. During these growth spurts, the **primary sex characteristics**—the reproductive organs and external genitalia—develop dramatically. So do the nonreproductive **secondary sex characteristics.** Girls develop breasts and larger hips. Boys' facial hair begins growing and their voices deepen. Pubic and underarm hair emerges in girls and boys (**FIGURE 12.4**).

For boys, puberty's landmark is the first ejaculation, which often occurs first during sleep (as a "wet dream"). This event, called **spermarche,** usually happens by about age 14.

In girls, the landmark is the first menstrual period, **menarche,** usually within a year of age 12½ (Anderson et al., 2003). Scientists have identified nearly 250 genes that predict

X chromosome the sex chromosome found in males and females. Females typically have two X chromosomes; males typically have one. An X chromosome from each parent produces a female child.

Y chromosome the sex chromosome typically found only in males. When paired with an X chromosome from the mother, it produces a male child.

testosterone the most important male sex hormone. Males and females have it, but the additional testosterone in males stimulates the growth of the male sex organs during the fetal period, and the development of the male sex characteristics during puberty.

estrogens sex hormones, such as estradiol, that contribute to female sex characteristics and are secreted in greater amounts by females than by males.

puberty the period of sexual maturation, when a person becomes capable of reproducing.

primary sex characteristics the body structures (ovaries, testes, and external genitalia) that make sexual reproduction possible.

secondary sex characteristics nonreproductive sexual traits, such as female breasts and hips, male voice quality, and body hair.

spermarche [sper-MAR-key] the first ejaculation.

menarche [meh-NAR-key] the first menstrual period.

Pubertal boys may not at first like their sparse beard. (But then it grows on them.)

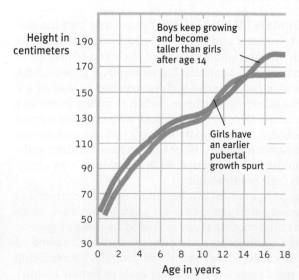

Height in centimeters

Boys keep growing and become taller than girls after age 14

Girls have an earlier pubertal growth spurt

Age in years

■ Boys ■ Girls

George Doyle/Getty Images

ⓝ FIGURE 12.3
Height differences (Data from Tanner, 1978.)

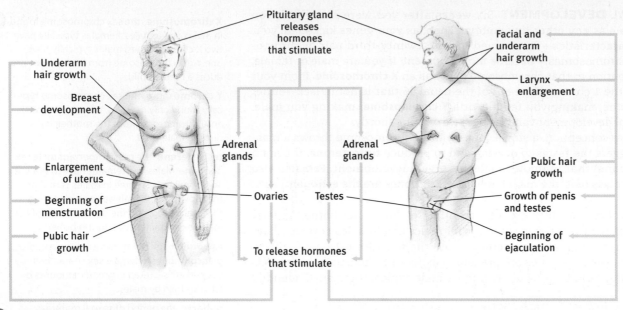

⊘ FIGURE 12.4
Body changes at puberty At about age 10 in girls and age 12 in boys, a surge of hormones triggers a variety of visible physical changes.

age at menarche (Day et al., 2017). But environment matters, too. Early menarche is more likely following stresses related to father absence, sexual abuse, insecure attachments, or a history of a mother's smoking during pregnancy (Richardson et al., 2018; Shrestha et al., 2011; Sung et al., 2016). Girls in various countries are developing breasts and reaching puberty earlier today than in the past. Suspected triggers include increased body fat, increased hormone-mimicking chemicals in the diet, and increased stress related to family disruption (Biro et al., 2010, 2012; Ellis et al., 2012; Herman-Giddens, 2013). But the good news is that a secure child-mother attachment can provide a buffer against childhood stresses, including those related to early puberty (Sung et al., 2016). Remember: *Nature and nurture interact.*

RETRIEVAL PRACTICE

RP-4 Prenatal sexual development begins about _____ weeks after conception. Adolescence is marked by the onset of _____ .

ANSWERS IN APPENDIX E

For a 7-minute discussion of gender development, see the *Video: Gender Development.*

"I am who I am." Dramatic improvements in South African track star Caster Semenya's race times prompted the International Association of Athletics Federations (IAAF) to undertake sex testing beginning in 2009. Semenya was reported to have physical characteristics not typically male or female. In 2016, she won an Olympic gold medal. The IAAF prevented her from competing in 2019 unless she took testosterone suppressants, which Semenya refused to do. As she fights for her right to race, Semenya said she would "continue to inspire young women and athletes in South Africa and around the world" (Reuters, 2019).

Michael Dalder/SEMENYA Reuters/Newscom

SEXUAL DEVELOPMENT VARIATIONS Nature may blur the biological line between males and females. People who are intersex may be born with unusual combinations of male and female chromosomes, hormones, and anatomy. For example, a genetic male may be born with two or more X chromosomes as well as a Y chromosome (*Klinefelter syndrome*), often resulting in sterility and small testes. Genetic females born with only one normal X chromosome (*Turner syndrome*) may not have menstrual periods, develop breasts, or be able to have children without reproductive assistance. Such individuals may struggle with their *gender identity.*

In the past, medical professionals often recommended *sex-reassignment surgery* to create an unambiguous sex identity for such children. One study reviewed 14 cases of genetic boys who had undergone early surgery and been raised as girls. Of those cases, 6 later identified as male, 5 were living as females, and 3 reported an unclear male or female identity (Reiner & Gearhart, 2004).

In one famous case, a little boy lost his penis during a botched circumcision. His parents followed a psychiatrist's advice to raise him as a girl rather than as a boy. So, with male chromosomes and hormones and a female upbringing, did nature or nurture form this child's gender identity? "Brenda" Reimer was not like most other girls. "She" didn't like dolls. She tore her dresses with rough-and-tumble play. At puberty she wanted no part of kissing boys. Finally, Brenda's parents explained what had happened, which led Brenda immediately to reject the assigned female identity. He underwent surgery to remove the breasts he'd developed from hormone therapy. He cut his hair and chose a male name, David. He eventually married a woman and became a stepfather. Sadly, he later died by suicide—as had his depressed identical twin brother (Colapinto, 2000). Today, most experts recommend postponing surgery until a child's naturally developing physical appearance and gender identity become clear.

The Nurture of Gender

For many people, birth-assigned sex and gender coexist in harmony. Biology draws the outline, and culture paints the details. The physical traits that define a newborn as male, female, or intersex are the same worldwide. But the gender traits that define how men (or boys) and women (or girls) should act, interact, or feel about themselves differ across time and place (Zentner & Eagly, 2015).

GENDER ROLES

LOQ 12-9   What are some cultural influences on gender roles?

Cultures shape our behaviors by defining how we ought to behave in a particular social position, or **role.** We can see this shaping power in **gender roles**—the social expectations that guide people's behavior as men or as women.

In just a thin slice of history, gender roles worldwide have undergone an extreme makeover. At the beginning of the twentieth century, only one country in the world—New Zealand—granted women the right to vote (Briscoe, 1997). By 2015, all countries granted that right. A century ago, American women could not vote in national elections, serve in the military, or divorce a husband without cause. If a woman worked for pay, she would more likely have been a cook than a college professor. When asked to draw a scientist in the 1960s and 1970s, less than 1 percent of U.S. children drew a woman. In more recent studies, 28 percent did so (Miller et al., 2018). Now, women are more than 40 percent of many countries' workforce (BLS, 2019; Fetterolf, 2017).

Globally, women are often underrepresented in the STEM fields (science, technology, engineering, and mathematics) (UNESCO, 2017). Men around the world tend to hold most faculty positions, receive greater financial research support, and have more articles accepted in the most prestigious journals (Odic & Wojcik, 2020; Oliveira et al., 2019; Shen et al., 2018). In many countries, women still experience sexism, subtle or otherwise, that discourages a STEM-related career (Kuchynka et al., 2018; Leaper & Starr, 2019). But signs point to increases in supply and demand for STEM women. In high school, U.S. women outperform men on reading and writing (Reilly et al., 2019). At the college level, U.S. women, compared with men, earn more college degrees and higher college grades, and show equal competence in science and math (Stoet & Geary, 2018; Terrell et al., 2017). When researchers invited U.S. professors to recommend candidates for STEM positions, most said they preferred hiring the highly qualified women over the equally qualified men (Williams & Ceci, 2015). This is good news for budding female scientists and engineers,

> **role** a set of expectations (norms) about a social position, defining how those in the position ought to behave.
>
> **gender role** a set of expected behaviors, attitudes, and traits for men and for women.

> "#MeToo, Time's Up, the Women's March, these movements tell us that we need to have a critical discussion on women's rights, equality, and the power dynamics of gender. . . . Sexual harassment, for example—in business and in government—is a systemic problem and it is unacceptable. As leaders, we need to act to show that truly, time is up." — Canadian Prime Minister Justin Trudeau, 2018

MARWAN NAAMANI/Getty Images

Driving change Thanks to the advocacy of Manal al-Sharif and others, driving a car became a universal right for women in 2018, when Saudi Arabia lifted its ban. She said, "The fight for women's rights anywhere contributes to the fight for women's rights everywhere" (2019).

The gendered tsunami In Sri Lanka, Indonesia, and India, the gendered division of labor helps explain the excess of female deaths from the 2004 tsunami. In some villages, 80 percent of those killed were women, who were mostly at home while the men were more likely to be at sea fishing or doing tasks elsewhere. Many women also died trying to save children and elderly relatives (Oxfam, 2005).

> "You cannot put women and men on an equal footing. It is against nature." — Turkish President Recep Tayyip Erdoğan, 2014

> "We need to keep changing the attitude that raises our girls to be demure and our boys to be assertive, that criticizes our daughters for speaking out and our sons for shedding a tear." — Former U.S. President Barack Obama, 2016

sexual aggression any physical or verbal behavior of a sexual nature that is unwanted or intended to harm someone physically or emotionally. Can be expressed as either *sexual harassment* or *sexual assault*.

gender identity our sense of being male, female, neither, or some combination of male and female.

social learning theory the theory that we learn social behavior by observing and imitating and by being rewarded or punished.

gender typing the acquisition of a traditional masculine or feminine role.

androgyny displaying both traditionally masculine and traditionally feminine psychological characteristics.

who benefit from having capable and motivated female mentors and role models (Dennehy & Dasgupta, 2017; Moss-Racusin et al., 2018).

Gender roles also vary from one place to another. Nomadic societies of food-gathering people have had little division of labor by sex. Boys and girls receive much the same upbringing. In agricultural societies, where women typically work in the nearby fields and men roam while herding livestock, cultures have shaped children to assume more distinct gender roles (Segall et al., 1990; Van Leeuwen, 1978).

Take a minute to check your own gender expectations. Would you agree that "When jobs are scarce, men should have more rights to a job"? In Sweden and Spain, barely more than 10 percent of adults agree. In Egypt and Jordan, about 90 percent of adults agree (UNFPA, 2016). We're all human, but my, how our views differ.

Expectations about gender roles also factor into cultural attitudes about **sexual aggression.** In the aftermath of credible accusations of sexual aggression by famous and powerful men, many countries are making efforts to reduce sexual harassment and assault. (See Thinking Critically About: Sexual Aggression.)

> **RETRIEVAL PRACTICE**
>
> **RP-5** What are gender roles, and what do their variations tell us about our human capacity for learning and adaptation?
>
> *ANSWERS IN APPENDIX E*

GENDER IDENTITY

LOQ 12-11 How do we form our gender identity?

A *gender role* describes how others expect us to think, feel, and act. Our **gender identity,** when *binary* (involving only two options), is our personal sense of being male or female. Those with a *nonbinary* gender identity may not feel male or female, or they may identify as some combination of male *and* female. How do we develop our gender identity?

Social learning theory assumes that we acquire our identity in childhood, by observing and imitating others' gender-linked behaviors and by being rewarded or punished for acting in certain ways. ("Tatiana, you're such a good mommy to your dolls"; "Big boys don't cry, Armand.") But critics note that there's more to gender identity than imitation and reward. They point out that **gender typing**—taking on a traditional female or male role—varies from child to child (Tobin et al., 2010).

Parents do help to transmit their culture's views on gender. In one analysis of 43 studies, parents with traditional gender views were more likely to have gender-typed children who shared their expectations about how males and females should act (Tenenbaum & Leaper, 2002). When fathers share equally in housework, their daughters develop higher aspirations for work outside the home (Croft et al., 2014).

But no matter how much parents encourage or discourage traditional gender behavior, children may drift toward what feels right to them. Some organize themselves into "boy worlds" and "girl worlds," each guided by their understanding of the rules. Others conform to these rules more flexibly. Still others prefer **androgyny:** A blend of male and female roles feels right to them. Androgyny has benefits. As adults, androgynous people are more adaptable. They are more flexible in their actions and in their career choices (Bem, 1993). From childhood onward, they tend to be more resilient and self-accepting, and they experience less depression (Lam & McBride-Chang, 2007; Mosher & Danoff-Burg, 2008; Pauletti et al., 2017).

Thinking Critically About:

Sexual Aggression

LOQ **12-10** What are the effects of sexual aggression? How have cultural views changed, and how can we reduce sexual aggression?

Definition of Sexual Aggression

Sexual harassment involves making unwanted sexual advances, obscene remarks, or requests for sexual favors.[1]

Sexual assault is "any type of sexual contact or behavior that occurs without the explicit consent of the recipient," such as unwanted touching, molestation, and attempted or completed rape.[2]

Cultural Effects on Our Views

By Place: Some cultures view victims of sexual aggression as guilty of disgracing their families. In India and Pakistan, male family members kill an unknown number of women—one source estimates 1000 annually in each country[9]— for dishonoring their families.

Over Time: Changes in global norms have made it less acceptable to blame victims of sexual aggression.

1970

1990

2020

1970s
The first significant studies of rape victim blaming

1991
Landmark U.S. Supreme Court nominee Clarence Thomas sexual harassment case

2017
Tipping point:
Many people from different professions (journalism, politics, academia, sports, entertainment) lost their jobs because of alleged sexual aggression.

2019
#MeToo movement active in more than 85 nations[10]

Blaming the victim becomes less acceptable.

Victims

In the U.S., **81%** of women and **43%** of men report having experienced sexual aggression in their lifetime.[3]

Sexual aggression affects people of *all ethnic groups*.[4]

Nearly **70%** of rape victims are between the ages of 11 and 24.4.[4]

In a National School Climate survey, **8** out of **10** gay or lesbian adolescents reported experiencing sex-related harassment in the prior year.[5]

How to Reduce Sexual Aggression

Therapy to treat sexual aggressors has not been very effective.[11] However, other, broader-based strategies do work:

Encourage victims to report their experiences to authority figures (parents, supervisors, law enforcement officials) and to share their experiences publicly.

Empower victims to take control of their situation and refuse to let their perpetrators dominate or manipulate them. Adjust social norms so that victims feel safe reporting their experiences.

Educate people about preventive bystander intervention strategies, such as "Green Dot," which has reduced sexual aggression in communities by as much as 20%.[12]

Effects on Well-Being

Thanks to human resilience, victims of sexual aggression often recover and lead healthy and meaningful lives. Yet many also suffer serious setbacks, including:

- Disrupted sleep[6]
- Poor physical health[7]
- Difficulty trusting new relationship partners[8]

1. McDonald, 2012; U.S.E.E.O.C., 2018. 2. U.S.D.O.J., 2018. 3. Stop Street Harassment, 2018. 4. Black et al., 2011. 5. GLSEN, 2012; Krahé & Berger, 2017; Snipes et al., 2017; Zanarini et al., 1997. 6. Krakow et al., 2001, 2002. 7. Schuyler et al., 2017; Zinzow et al., 2011. 8. Muldoon et al., 2016; Starzynski et al., 2017. 9. HBVA, 2018. 10. Stone & Vogelstein, 2019. 11. Grønnerød et al., 2015. 12. Coker et al., 2017. 13. Jesse, 2019.

transgender an umbrella term describing people whose gender identity or expression differs from that associated with their birth-assigned sex.

Feelings matter, but so does how we think. Early in life, we all form *schemas,* or concepts that help us make sense of our world. Our *gender schemas* organize our experiences of male-female characteristics and help us think about our gender identity, about who we are as unique individuals (Bem, 1987, 1993; Martin et al., 2002).

As young children, we were "gender detectives" (Martin & Ruble, 2004). Before our first birthday, we knew the difference between a typically male and female voice or face (Martin et al., 2002). After we turned 2, language forced us to label the world in terms of gender. The English language has classified people as *he* and *she.* Other languages classify objects as masculine ("*le* train") or feminine ("*la* table").

Children tend to learn that two sorts of people exist—that they are "supposed" to be one of these two sorts—and they begin to search for clues about gender. In every culture, people communicate their gender in many ways. Their *gender expression* drops hints not only in their language but also in their clothing, interests, and possessions. Having picked up such clues, 3-year-olds may divide the human world in half. "Girls," they may decide, are the ones who love *Frozen* and have longer hair. "Boys" think *Captain Underpants* is hilarious and don't wear dresses. Armed with their newly collected "proof," they then adjust their behaviors to fit their concept of gender. These stereotypes are most rigid at about age 5 or 6. If the new neighbor is a girl, a 6-year-old boy may assume he cannot share her interests.

So for young children, gender looms large. What they learn has, however, slowly been broadening from the "two sorts of people" found in the animated classics and separate toy aisles for dolls and action heroes. In 2019, the popular children's cartoon *Arthur* showed Arthur's teacher marrying another male character. "Art reflects life," said creator Marc Brown, "and kids need to see what's happening in the world" (Wong, 2019).

For people who identify as *cisgender,* gender corresponds with birth sex. For those who identify as **transgender,** gender identity differs from what's typical for that person's birth-assigned sex (APA, 2010; Bockting, 2014). From childhood onward, a person may, for example, feel like a male in a female body, or a female in a male body (Olson et al., 2015). One study of three hundred 3- to 12-year-old transgender children found these "early transitioning" children to be as strongly gender-typed and gender identified as their cisgender siblings and those in a cisgender control group (Gülgöz et al., 2019). Brain scans are revealing: Those who seek medical sex-reassignment (about 75 percent men) have some neural tracts that differ from those whose gender identity matches their birth-assigned sex (Kranz et al., 2014; Van Kesteren et al., 1997). And brain scans have also revealed differences between transgender and cisgender people, suggesting a biological influence on gender identity (Williams, 2018). Biologist Robert Sapolsky (2015) explains: "It's not that [these] individuals think they are a different gender than they actually are. It's that they [are] stuck with bodies that are a different gender from who they actually are."

In most countries, it's not easy being transgender. In a national survey of lesbian, gay, bisexual, and transgender Americans, 71 percent saw "some" or "a lot" of social acceptance for gay men, and 85 percent said the same for gay women. But only 18 percent saw similar acceptance for transgender people (Sandstrom, 2015). In another survey—of 27,175 transgender Americans—46 percent reported being verbally harassed in the last year (James et al., 2016). Transgender people in Europe and Asia also experience frequent insults, prejudice, and discrimination (Amnesty International, 2018). Some transgender people experience profound distress, increasing their risk for a diagnosis of *gender dysphoria* (McNeil et al., 2017; Mueller et al., 2017). To receive a gender dysphoria diagnosis, you must experience *clinical levels of distress* associated with your gender identity. Simply identifying as transgender does not indicate you have a psychological disorder. Perhaps due to experiencing prejudice within the U.S. military, transgender veterans have twice the risk of dying by suicide as cisgender military veterans (Tucker, 2019). And in one study of 27,000 transgender adults, those who received "conversion therapy" had double the risk of dying by suicide (Turban et al., 2020).

Transgender people may attempt to align their outward appearance and everyday lives with their gender identity. In 2019, the U.S. Supreme Court upheld a ruling that transgender people have the right to use the restroom that matches their gender identity (Wolf, 2019). Such validation of gender identity can help transgender people avoid depression and low self-esteem (Glynn et al., 2017). Indeed, gender-affirming medical procedures (hormone use, surgery) appear to reduce transgender people's depression, anxiety, and posttraumatic stress (Tomita et al., 2018).

"Being trans should be a personal or social identity, not a psychiatric one." — Anthropologist Roy Richard Grinker (2018)

"My father . . . is . . . a woman." So said Mark Morris (2015) of his famous parent, the transgender Welsh writer Jan Morris. After sex-reassignment surgery in 1973, Jan Morris was forced by law to divorce Mark's mother. "They continued to live together in a remarkably strong marital bond," until remarrying when same-sex marriages became legal in Britain.

Colin McPherson/Getty Images

Note that *gender identity* is distinct from *sexual orientation* (the direction of one's sexual attraction). Transgender people may be sexually attracted to people of the other gender, the same gender, all genders, or to no one at all. Your sexual orientation is who you fantasize going to bed *with*; your gender identity is who you go to bed *as*.

Worldwide, an estimated 25 million people identify as transgender (WHO, 2016). In the United States, about 1 million people identify as transgender (Meerwijk & Sevelius, 2017). Roughly 30 percent in that group have broader nonbinary gender identities—feeling a combination of male and female, or feeling neither male nor female (Barr et al., 2016; James et al., 2016; Mikalson et al., 2012). In North America and Europe, the number is rising, especially among adolescents who were designated female at birth. Some wonder whether the increase is partly a social phenomenon, or simply today's teens feeling freer to own their private identities (Wadman, 2018). But many who transition already preferred gender-nonconforming clothes, toys, and hair as younger children (Rae et al., 2019).

Beloved son Chaz Bono, writer, musician, advocate, and actor, is the transgender son of singer and actor Cher, and the late musician and politician Sonny Bono.

ASK YOURSELF

How gender-typed are you? What has influenced your feelings of being male, female, neither, or some combination of male and female?

> For a 6.5-minute exploration of one pioneering transgender person's journey, see the *Video: Renée Richards—A Long Journey.*

Reflections on Nature, Nurture, and Their Interaction

LOQ 12-12 How do nature, nurture, and our own choices influence gender roles and other aspects of our lives?

"There are trivial truths and great truths," reflected the physicist Niels Bohr on the paradoxes of science. "The opposite of a trivial truth is plainly false. The opposite of a great truth is also true." Our ancestral history helped form us as a species. Where there is variation, natural selection, and heredity, there will be evolution. The unique gene combination created when our mother's egg engulfed our father's sperm predisposed both our shared humanity and our individual differences. Our genes form us. This is a great truth about human nature.

But our experiences also shape us. Our families and peer relationships teach us how to think and act. Differences initiated by our nature may be amplified by our nurture. If their genes and hormones predispose males to be more physically aggressive than females, culture can amplify this gender difference through norms that reward macho men and gentle women. If men are encouraged toward roles that demand physical power, and women toward more nurturing roles, each may act accordingly. Roles remake their players. Lawyers in time become more lawyerly, professors more professorial. Gender roles similarly shape us.

In many modern cultures, gender roles are merging. Brute strength has become less important for power and status (think "philanthrocapitalists" Priscilla Chan and Mark Zuckerberg). From 1965 to 2019, women soared from 9 percent to 52 percent of U.S. medical students (AAMC, 2014, 2018). In 1965, U.S. married women devoted eight times as many hours to housework as did their husbands; by 2012, this gap had shrunk to less than twice as many (Parker & Wang, 2013; Sayer, 2016). A survey of 30 countries showed a similar shrinking gender gap in housework and other unpaid work, such as child care (OECD, 2018). Such swift changes signal that biology does not fix gender roles.

If nature and nurture jointly form us, are we "nothing but" the product of nature and nurture? Are we rigidly determined?

We *are* the product of nature and nurture, but we are also an open system (**FIGURE 12.5**). Genes are all-pervasive but not all-powerful. People may reject their evolutionary role as transmitters of genes and choose not to reproduce. Culture, too, is all-pervasive but not all-powerful. People may defy peer pressures and resist social expectations.

Culture matters As this exhibit at a San Diego museum illustrates, children learn their culture. A baby's foot can step into any culture.

FIGURE 12.5
The biopsychosocial approach to development

Biological influences:
• Shared human genome
• Individual genetic variations
• Prenatal environment
• Sex-related genes, hormones, and physiology

Psychological influences:
• Gene–environment interaction
• Neurological effect of early experiences
• Responses evoked by our own temperament, gender, etc.
• Beliefs, feelings, and expectations

Individual development

Social-cultural influences:
• Parental influences
• Peer influences
• Cultural individualism or collectivism
• Cultural gender norms

Moreover, we cannot excuse our failings by blaming them solely on bad genes or bad influences. In reality, we are both creatures and creators of our worlds. So many things about us—including our gender roles—are the products of our genes and environments. Yet the stream that runs into the future flows through our present choices. Our decisions today design our environments tomorrow. We are the architects. Our hopes, goals, and expectations influence our destiny. And that is what enables cultures to vary and to change. Mind matters.

> **RETRIEVAL PRACTICE**

RP-6 How does the biopsychosocial approach explain our individual development?

ANSWERS IN APPENDIX E

* * *

We know from our correspondence and from surveys that some readers are troubled by the naturalism and evolutionism of contemporary science. (A note to readers from other nations: In the United States there can be a wide gulf between scientific and lay thinking about evolution.) "The idea that human minds are the product of evolution is . . . unassailable fact," declared a 2007 editorial in *Nature*, a leading science journal. In *The Language of God*, Human Genome Project director Francis Collins (2006, pp. 141, 146), a self-described evangelical Christian, compiled the "utterly compelling" evidence that led him to conclude that Darwin's big idea is "unquestionably correct." Yet Gallup pollsters have reported that 38 percent of U.S. adults believe that humans were created "pretty much in their present form" within the last 10,000 years (Swift, 2017). Many people who dispute the scientific story worry that a science of behavior (and evolutionary science in particular) will destroy our sense of the beauty, mystery, and spiritual significance of the human creature. For those concerned, we offer some reassuring thoughts.

When Isaac Newton explained the rainbow in terms of light of differing wavelengths, the British poet John Keats feared that Newton had destroyed the rainbow's mysterious beauty. Yet, as evolutionary biologist Richard Dawkins (1998) noted in *Unweaving the Rainbow*, Newton's analysis led to an even deeper mystery—Einstein's theory of special relativity. Nothing about Newton's optics need diminish our appreciation for the dramatic elegance of a rainbow arching across a brightening sky.

When Galileo assembled evidence that the Earth revolved around the Sun, not vice versa, he did not offer irrefutable proof for his theory. Rather, he offered a coherent explanation for a variety of observations, such as the changing shadows cast by the Moon's mountains. His explanation eventually won the day because it described and explained things in a way that made sense, that hung together. Darwin's theory of evolution likewise is a coherent view of natural history. It offers an organizing principle that unifies various observations.

"Let's hope that it's not true; but if it is true, let's hope that it doesn't become widely known." — Lady Ashley, commenting on Darwin's theory

"Is it not stirring to understand how the world actually works—that white light is made of colors, that color measures light waves, that transparent air reflects light . . . ? It does no harm to the romance of the sunset to know a little about it." — Carl Sagan, *Skies of Other Worlds*, 1988

Many people of faith find the scientific idea of human origins congenial with their spirituality. In the fifth century, St. Augustine (quoted by Wilford, 1999) wrote, "The universe was brought into being in a less than fully formed state, but was gifted with the capacity to transform itself from unformed matter into a truly marvelous array of structures and life forms." In the fourteenth century, Muslim historian Ibn Khaldun (1377) wrote, "One should then look at the world of creation. It started out from the minerals and progressed, in an ingenious, gradual manner to plants and animals." Some 800 years later, Pope Francis in 2015 welcomed a science-religion dialogue, saying, "Evolution in nature is not inconsistent with the notion of creation, because evolution requires the creation of beings that evolve."

heromen30/Shutterstock

Meanwhile, many people of science are awestruck at the emerging understanding of the universe and the human creature. It boggles the mind—the entire universe popping out of a point some 14 billion years ago, and instantly inflating to cosmological size. Had the energy of this Big Bang been the tiniest bit less, the universe would have collapsed back on itself. Had it been the tiniest bit more, the result would have been a soup too thin to support life. Astronomer Sir Martin Rees has described *Just Six Numbers* (1999), any one of which, if changed ever so slightly, would produce a cosmos in which life could not exist. Had gravity been a tad stronger or weaker, or had the weight of a carbon proton been a wee bit different, our universe just wouldn't have worked.

What caused this almost-too-good-to-be-true, finely tuned universe? Why is there something rather than nothing? How did it come to be, in the words of Harvard-Smithsonian astrophysicist Owen Gingerich (1999), "so extraordinarily right, that it seemed the universe had been expressly designed to produce intelligent, sentient beings"? On such matters, a humble, awed, scientific silence is appropriate, suggested philosopher Ludwig Wittgenstein: "Whereof one cannot speak, thereof one must be silent" (1922, p. 189).

Rather than fearing science, we can welcome its enlarging our understanding and awakening our sense of awe. In *The Fragile Species*, Lewis Thomas (1992) described his utter amazement that the Earth in time gave rise to bacteria and eventually to Bach's Mass in B Minor. In a short 4 billion years, life on Earth has come from nothing to structures as complex as a 6-billion-unit strand of DNA and the incomprehensible intricacy of the human brain. Atoms no different from those in a rock somehow formed dynamic entities that produced extraordinary, self-replicating, information-processing systems—us (Davies, 2007). Although we appear to have been created from dust, over eons of time, the end result is a priceless creature, one rich with potential beyond our imagining.

"The possession of knowledge does not kill the sense of wonder and mystery. There is always more mystery." — Anaïs Nin, *The Diary of Anaïs Nin*, 1934

⑫ REVIEW Cultural and Gender Diversity: Understanding Nature and Nurture

LEARNING OBJECTIVES

Test Yourself Answer these repeated Learning Objective Questions on your own (before checking the answers in Appendix D) to improve your retention of the concepts (McDaniel et al., 2009, 2015).

LOQ 12-1 How do early experiences modify the brain?

LOQ 12-2 In what ways do parents and peers shape children's development?

LOQ 12-3 How does culture affect our behavior?

LOQ 12-4 How do individualist and collectivist cultures differ in their values and goals?

LOQ 12-5 How does the meaning of *gender* differ from the meaning of *sex*?

LOQ 12-6 What are some of the ways in which males and females tend to be alike and to differ?

LOQ 12-7 What factors contribute to gender bias in the workplace?

LOQ 12-8 How do sex hormones influence prenatal and adolescent sexual development?

LOQ 12-9 What are some cultural influences on gender roles?

LOQ 12-10 What are the effects of sexual aggression? How have cultural views changed, and how can we reduce sexual aggression?

LOQ 12-11 How do we form our gender identity?

LOQ 12-12 How do nature, nurture, and our own choices influence gender roles and other aspects of our lives?

TERMS AND CONCEPTS TO REMEMBER

Test Yourself Write down the definition in your own words, then check your answer.

culture, p. 145

norm, p. 145

individualism, p. 146

collectivism, p. 146

sex, p. 151

gender, p. 151

intersex, p. 151

aggression, p. 151

relational aggression, p. 151

X chromosome, p. 155

Y chromosome, p. 155

testosterone, p. 155

estrogens, p. 155

puberty, p. 155

primary sex characteristics, p. 155

secondary sex characteristics, p. 155

spermarche [sper-MAR-key], p. 155

menarche [meh-NAR-key], p. 155

role, p. 157

gender role, p. 157

sexual aggression, p. 158

gender identity, p. 158

social learning theory, p. 158

gender typing, p. 158

androgyny, p. 158

transgender, p. 160

MASTER THE MATERIAL

Test Yourself Answer the following questions on your own first, then check your answers in Appendix E.

1. Individualist cultures tend to value _____; collectivist cultures tend to value _____.

   a. interdependence; independence

   b. independence; interdependence

   c. solidarity; uniqueness

   d. duty; fulfillment

2. In psychology, _____ is the biologically influenced characteristics by which people define male, female, and intersex. The behavioral characteristics that people associate with *boy, girl, man,* and *woman* is _____.

3. Females and males are very similar, but one way they differ is that

   a. females interrupt more often than males.

   b. males are more democratic than females in their leadership roles.

   c. as children, females tend to play in small groups, while males tend to play in large groups.

   d. females are more likely to die by suicide.

4. A fertilized egg will develop into a male if it receives a/n _____ chromosome from its father.

5. Primary sex characteristics relate to _____; secondary sex characteristics refer to _____.

   a. spermarche; menarche

   b. breasts and facial hair; ovaries and testes

   c. emotional maturity; hormone surges

   d. reproductive organs; nonreproductive traits

6. On average, girls begin puberty at about the age of _____, boys at about the age of _____.

7. A person born with a combination of male and female biological sexual characteristics is _____.

8. *Gender role* refers to our

   a. sense of being male, female, neither, or some combination of male and female.

   b. culture's expectations about the "right" way for men and women to behave.

   c. assigned birth sex—our chromosomes and anatomy.

   d. unisex characteristics.

9. Our sense of being male, female, neither, or some combination of male and female is known as our _____.

Continue testing yourself with ⓩ **LearningCurve** or ⓜ **Achieve Read & Practice** to learn and remember most effectively.

Tanya Constantine/Getty Images

Developing Through the Life Span

Life is a journey, from womb to tomb. So it is for me [DM], and so it will be for you. My story, and yours, began when a man and a woman together contributed 20,000+ genes to an egg that became a unique person. Those genes coded the protein building blocks that, with astonishing precision, form our body and predispose our traits. My grandmother bequeathed to my mother a rare hearing loss pattern, which she, in turn, gave to me (the least of her gifts). My father was an amiable extravert, and sometimes I forget to stop talking (although as a child, my talking was impeded by embarrassing stuttering, for which Seattle Public Schools provided speech therapy).

Along with my parents' nature, I also received their nurture. Like you, I was born into a particular family and culture, with its own way of viewing the world. My values have been shaped by a family culture filled with talking and laughter, by a religious culture that speaks of love and justice, and by an academic culture that encourages critical thinking (asking, *What do you mean? How do you know?*).

We are formed by our genes and by our contexts, so our stories all differ. But in many ways we are each like nearly everyone else on Earth. Being human, you and I have a need to belong. My mental video library, which began after age 4, is filled with scenes of social attachment. Over time, my attachments to parents loosened as peer friendships grew. After lacking confidence to date in high school, I fell in love with a college classmate and married at age 20. Natural selection predisposes

165

us to survive and perpetuate our genes. Sure enough, two years later a child entered our lives, and I experienced a new form of love that surprised me with its intensity.

But life is marked by change. That child and his brother now live 2000 miles away, and their sister has found her calling in South Africa. The tight rubber bands linking parent and child have loosened, as yours likely have as well.

Change also marks most vocational lives, which for me transitioned from a teen working in the family insurance agency, to a premed chemistry major and hospital aide, to (after discarding my half-completed medical school applications) a psychology professor and author. I predict that in 10 years you, too, will be doing things you do not currently anticipate.

Stability also marks our development: Our life situations change, but we experience a continuous self. When I look in the mirror, I do not see the person I once was, but I feel like the person I have always been. I am the same person who, as a late teen, played basketball and discovered love. Sixty years later, I still enjoy basketball and still love (with less passion but more security) the life partner with whom I have shared life's griefs and joys.

Continuity morphs through stages—for me, growing up, raising children, enjoying a career, and, eventually, life's final stage, which will demand my presence. As I wend my way through this cycle of life and death, I am mindful that life is a journey, a continuing process of development, seeded by nature and shaped by nurture, animated by love and focused by work, begun with wide-eyed curiosity and completed, for those blessed to live to a good old age, with peace and never-ending hope.

Across the life span, we grow from newborn to toddler, from toddler to teenager, and from teenager to mature adult. At each stage of life there are physical, cognitive, and social milestones. We begin with prenatal development and the newborn (Module 13). Then we'll turn our attention to infancy and childhood (Module 14), adolescence (Module 15), and adulthood (Module 16).

MODULE

⑬ Developmental Issues, Prenatal Development, and the Newborn

developmental psychology a branch of psychology that studies physical, cognitive, and social development throughout the life span.

cross-sectional study research that compares people of different ages at the same point in time.

longitudinal study research that follows and retests the same people over time.

"Nature is all that a man brings with him into the world; nurture is every influence that affects him after his birth." — Francis Galton, *English Men of Science*, 1874

Developmental Psychology's Major Issues

(LEARNING OBJECTIVE QUESTION) (LOQ) **13-1** What three issues have engaged developmental psychologists?

Researchers find human development interesting for the same reasons most of us do— they want to understand more about how we've become our current selves, and how we may change in the years ahead. **Developmental psychology** examines our physical, cognitive, and social development across the life span. Developmental psychologists often do **cross-sectional studies** (comparing people of different ages) and **longitudinal studies** (following people across time) to explore three major issues:

1. *Nature and nurture:* How does our genetic inheritance (our nature) interact with our experiences (our nurture) to influence our development? (This is our focus in Modules 10–12.)

2. *Continuity and stages:* What parts of development are gradual and continuous, like riding an escalator? What parts change abruptly in separate stages, like climbing rungs on a ladder?

3. *Stability and change:* Which of our traits persist through life? How do we change as we age?

📹 See the *Video: Longitudinal and Cross-Sectional Studies* for a helpful tutorial animation.

Continuity and Stages

Do adults differ from infants as a giant redwood differs from its seedling—a difference created by gradual, cumulative growth? Or do they differ as a butterfly differs from a caterpillar—a difference of distinct stages?

Researchers who emphasize experience and learning typically see development as a slow, continuous shaping process. Those who emphasize biological maturation tend to see development as a sequence of genetically predisposed stages or steps: Although progress through the various stages may be quick or slow, everyone passes through the stages in the same order.

Are there clear-cut stages of psychological development, as there are physical stages such as walking before running? The *stage theories* we will consider—of Jean Piaget on cognitive development, Lawrence Kohlberg on moral development, and Erik Erikson on psychosocial development—propose developmental stages (summarized in **FIGURE 13.1**). But as we will also see, some research casts doubt on the idea that life proceeds through neatly defined age-linked stages.

Although many modern developmental psychologists do not identify as stage theorists, the stage concept remains useful. The human brain does experience growth spurts during childhood and puberty that correspond roughly to Piaget's stages (Thatcher et al., 1987). And stage theories contribute a developmental perspective on the whole life span, by suggesting how people of one age think and act differently when they arrive at a later age.

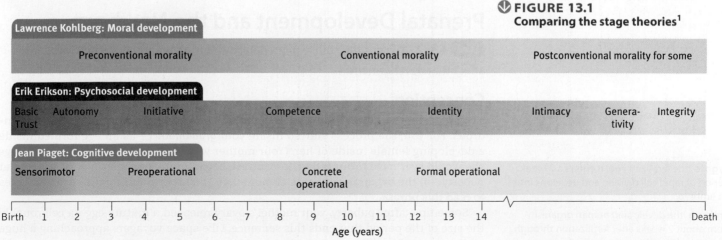

TOO MUCH COFFEE MAN BY SHANNON WHEELER

LIFE:

PLAY, SCHOOL, PLAY, SCHOOL, PLAY, SCHOOL, PLAY, SCHOOL, FIRST LOVE, BRIEF HAPPINESS, BREAK UP, REGRET, SCHOOL, SCHOOL, SCHOOL, SCHOOL, SCHOOL, SCHOOL, SCHOOL, SCHOOL, SCHOOL, SCHOOL, SCHOOL, SCHOOL, SCHOOL, SCHOOL, PLAY, WORK, PLAY, WORK, PLAY, WORK, PLAY, WORK, IDEALISM, EFFORT, REJECTION, FAILURE, WORK, EFFORT, FAILURE, COMPROMISE, WORK, WORK, WORK, WORK, WORK, WORK, PLAY, COMMITMENT, WORK, WORK, WORK, WORK, WORK, WORK, PLAY, WORK, WORK, WORK, WORK, WORK, WORK, WORK, WORK, PLAY, WORK, WORK, WORK, WORK, WORK, WORK, WORK, WORK, PLAY, WORK, WORK, WORK, WORK, WORK, WORK, WORK, WORK, PLAY, WORK, WORK, WORK, WORK, WORK, WORK, WORK, WORK, PLAY, WORK, WORK, WORK, WORK, WORK, WORK, WORK, WORK, PLAY, WORK, WORK, WORK, WORK, WORK, WORK, WORK, WORK, PLAY, WORK, WORK, WORK, WORK, WORK, WORK, WORK, WORK, PLAY, WORK, WORK, WORK, WORK, WORK, WORK, WORK, WORK, PLAY, WORK, WORK, WORK, WORK, WORK, WORK, WORK, WORK, PLAY, WORK, WORK, WORK, WORK, WORK, WORK, WORK, WORK, PLAY, WORK, WORK, WORK, WORK, WORK, WORK, WORK, WORK, PLAY, WORK, WORK, WORK, WORK, WORK, WORK, WORK, WORK, PLAY, WORK, WORK, WORK, WORK, WORK, WORK, WORK, WORK, PLAY, WORK, WORK, WORK, WORK, WORK, WORK, WORK, WORK, PLAY, RETIRE, PLAY, DIE.

Stages of the life cycle

Stability and Change

As we follow lives through time, do we find more evidence for stability or change? If reunited with a long-lost childhood friend, do we instantly realize that "it's the same old Andy"? Or do long-ago friends now seem like strangers? (At least one acquaintance of mine [DM's] would choose the second option. At his 40-year college reunion, he failed to recognize a former classmate. The understandably appalled classmate was his first wife!)

We experience both stability and change. Some of our characteristics, such as *temperament,* are very stable. Studying thousands of people in New Zealand and the United States over several decades, research teams have been struck by the consistency of temperament and emotionality across time (Kassing et al., 2019; Moffitt et al., 2013; Slutske et al., 2012). Researchers also confirmed stability of moods when they followed 174 Scots across 63 years—from age 14 to 77 (Harris et al., 2016). Out-of-control young children were later the most likely to engage in teen smoking, adult criminal behavior, or out-of-control gambling. Inattentive Canadian kindergarteners become less likely to earn high salaries in their adult careers (Vergunst et al., 2019). Moreover, children observed being repeatedly cruel to animals often became violent adults (Hensley et al., 2018). But on a happier note, the widest smilers in childhood and college photos are the ones most likely to enjoy enduring marriages (Hertenstein et al., 2009).

"When I look at myself in the first grade and I look at myself now, I'm basically the same. The temperament is not that different." — Donald Trump to his biographer in *Never Enough,* 2015

"As at 7, so at 70." — Jewish proverb

FIGURE 13.1
Comparing the stage theories[1]

Lawrence Kohlberg: Moral development		
Preconventional morality	Conventional morality	Postconventional morality for some

Erik Erikson: Psychosocial development
Basic Trust · Autonomy · Initiative · Competence · Identity · Intimacy · Generativity · Integrity

Jean Piaget: Cognitive development
Sensorimotor · Preoperational · Concrete operational · Formal operational

Birth 1 2 3 4 5 6 7 8 9 10 11 12 13 14 Death
Age (years)

[1]With thanks to Dr. Sandra Gibbs, Muskegon Community College, for inspiring this illustration.

Smiles predict marital stability In one study of 306 U.S. college graduates, 1 in 4 with yearbook expressions like the one in photo (a) later divorced, as did only 1 in 20 with smiles like the one in photo (b) (Hertenstein et al., 2009).

(a)

(b)

We cannot, however, predict all aspects of our future selves based on our early life. Our social attitudes, for example, are much less stable than our temperament, especially during the impressionable late adolescent years (Krosnick & Alwin, 1989; Rekker et al., 2015). Older children and adolescents learn new ways of coping. Although delinquent children have elevated rates of later problems, many confused and troubled children blossom into mature, successful adults (Moffitt et al., 2002; Roberts et al., 2013; Thomas & Chess, 1986). Life is a process of becoming. Our present struggles may lay the foundation for a happier tomorrow.

In some ways, we *all* change with age. Most shy, fearful toddlers begin opening up by age 4, and after adolescence most people gradually become more conscientious, stable, agreeable, and self-confident (Lucas & Donnellan, 2009; Shaw et al., 2010; Van den Akker et al., 2014). Risk-prone adolescents tend, as adults, to become more cautious (Mata et al., 2016). Indeed, many irresponsible 18-year-olds have matured into 40-year-old business or cultural leaders. (If you are the former, you aren't done yet.) Yet when asked how they have changed in the last decade and will change in the next decade, people—both young and old—exhibit an *end of history illusion*. They recognize that they have changed, but presume they will change little in the future (Quoidbach et al., 2013).

Life requires *both* stability and change. Stability provides our identity. Change gives us our hope for a brighter future, allowing us to adapt and grow from experience.

As adults grow older, there is continuity of self.

> ### ASK YOURSELF
> Are you the same person you were as a preschooler? As an 8-year-old? As a 12-year-old? How are you different? How are you the same?

> ### RETRIEVAL PRACTICE
> **RP-1** Developmental researchers who emphasize learning and experience are supporting _____; those who emphasize biological maturation are supporting _____.
>
> **RP-2** What findings in psychology support (1) the stage theory of development and (2) the idea of stability in personality across the life span?

ANSWERS IN APPENDIX E

Prenatal Development and the Newborn

LOQ 13-2 What is the course of prenatal development, and how do teratogens affect that development?

Conception

Nothing is more natural than a species reproducing itself. And nothing is more wondrous. For you, the process started inside your *grandmother*—as an egg formed inside a developing female inside of her. (Your mother was born with all the immature eggs she would ever have.) Your father, in contrast, began producing sperm cells nonstop at puberty—in the beginning at a rate of more than 1000 sperm during the second it takes to read this phrase.

Some time after puberty, your mother's ovary released a mature egg—a cell roughly the size of the period that ends this sentence. Like space voyagers approaching a huge planet, some 250 million deposited sperm began their frantic race upstream, approaching a cell 85,000 times their own size. The small number reaching the egg released digestive enzymes that ate away the egg's protective coating (**FIGURE 13.2a**). As soon as the one

zygote the fertilized egg; it enters a 2-week period of rapid cell division and develops into an embryo.

embryo the developing human organism from about 2 weeks after fertilization through the second month.

fetus the developing human organism from 9 weeks after conception to birth.

Eye of Science/Science Source

David M. Phillips/Science Source

(a)   (b)

⊲ **FIGURE 13.2**
Life is sexually transmitted (a) Sperm cells surround an egg. (b) One sperm penetrates the egg's jellylike outer coating, triggering a series of chemical events that will cause sperm and egg to fuse into a single cell. If all goes well, that cell will subdivide again and again to emerge 9 months later as a 37-trillion-cell human being (Bianconi et al., 2013).

winning sperm penetrated that coating and was welcomed in (Figure 13.2b), the egg's surface blocked out the others. Before half a day elapsed, the egg nucleus and the sperm nucleus fused: The two became one.

Consider it your most fortunate of moments. Among 250 million sperm, the one needed to make you, in combination with that one particular egg, won the race. And so it was for innumerable generations before us. If any one of our ancestors had been conceived with a different sperm or egg, or died before conceiving, or not chanced to meet their partner, or. . . . The mind boggles at the improbable, unbroken chain of events that produced us.

Prenatal Development

How many fertilized eggs, called **zygotes,** survive beyond the first 2 weeks? Fewer than half (Grobstein, 1979; Hall, 2004). But for us, good fortune prevailed. One cell became 2, then 4—each just like the first—until this cell division had produced some 100 identical cells within the first week. Then the cells began to differentiate—to specialize in structure and function ("I'll become a brain, you become intestines!").

About 10 days after conception, the zygote attaches to the mother's uterine wall, beginning approximately 37 weeks of the closest human relationship. Near the beginning of this maternal bodybuilding feat, the tiny clump of cells forms two parts. The inner cells become the **embryo** (**FIGURE 13.3a**). Many of the outer cells become the *placenta,* the life-link that transfers nutrients and oxygen from mother to embryo. Over the next 6 weeks, the embryo's organs begin to form and function. The heart begins to beat.

By 9 weeks after conception, an embryo looks unmistakably human (Figure 13.3b). It is now a **fetus** (Latin for "offspring" or "young one"). During the sixth month, organs such as the stomach develop enough to give the fetus a good chance of surviving and thriving if born prematurely.

At each prenatal stage, genetic and environmental factors affect our development. By the sixth month, the fetus is responsive to sound. Microphone readings taken inside

⊽ **FIGURE 13.3**
Prenatal development (a) The embryo grows and develops rapidly. At 40 days, the spine is visible and the arms and legs are beginning to grow. (b) By the start of the ninth week, when the fetal period begins, facial features, hands, and feet have formed. (c) As the fetus enters the sixteenth week, its 3 ounces could fit in the palm of your hand.

(a)   (b)   (c)

Review prenatal development

Zygote: Conception to 2 weeks

Embryo: 2 weeks through 8 weeks

Fetus: 9 weeks to birth

"You shall conceive and bear a son. So then drink no wine or strong drink." — Judges 13:7

the uterus reveal that the fetus is exposed to the sound of its mother's muffled voice (Ecklund-Flores, 1992; Hepper, 2005). Immediately after emerging from their underwater world, newborns prefer their mother's voice to another woman's, or to their father's (DeCasper et al., 1986, 1994; Lee & Kisilevsky, 2014).

They also prefer hearing their mother's language. In one study, day-old American and Swedish newborns paused more in their pacifier sucking when listening to familiar vowels from their mother's language (Moon et al., 2013). After repeatedly hearing a fake word (*tatata*) in the womb, Finnish newborns' brain waves displayed recognition when hearing the word after birth (Partanen et al., 2013). If their mother spoke two languages during pregnancy, newborns displayed interest in both (Byers-Heinlein et al., 2010). And just after birth, the melodic ups and downs of newborns' cries bear the tuneful signature of their mother's native tongue (Mampe et al., 2009). Babies born to French-speaking mothers tended to cry with the rising intonation of French; babies born to German-speaking mothers cried with the falling tones of German (Mampe et al., 2009). Would you have guessed? The learning of language begins in the womb.

In the 2 months before birth, fetuses demonstrate learning in other ways, as when they adapt to a vibrating, honking device placed on their mother's abdomen (Dirix et al., 2009). Like people who adapt to the sound of trains in their neighborhood, fetuses get used to the honking. Moreover, 4 weeks later, they recall the sound (as evidenced by their blasé response, compared with the reactions of those fetuses not previously exposed).

Sounds are not the only environmental factors that impact fetal development. In addition to transferring nutrients and oxygen from mother to fetus, the placenta screens out many harmful substances. But some slip by. **Teratogens,** agents such as viruses and drugs, can damage an embryo or fetus. This is one reason pregnant women are advised not to drink alcoholic beverages or use nicotine or marijuana (Kuehn, 2019; Saint Louis, 2017). A pregnant woman never smokes, vapes, or drinks alone. When alcohol enters her bloodstream, and that of her fetus, it reduces activity in both their central nervous systems. Alcohol use during pregnancy may prime the woman's offspring to like alcohol and put them at risk for heavy drinking and alcohol use disorder during their teen years. In experiments, when pregnant rats drank alcohol, their young offspring later displayed a liking for alcohol's taste and odor (Youngentob & Glendinning, 2009; Youngentob et al., 2007).

Worldwide, 1 in 10 women report consuming alcohol while pregnant (Popova et al., 2019). Even light drinking, occasional binge drinking, or marijuana smoking can affect the fetal brain (CDC, 2018; Ghazi Sherbaf et al., 2019; Marjonen et al., 2015). Persistent heavy drinking puts the fetus at risk for birth defects, future behavior problems, and lower intelligence. For 1 in about 130 children worldwide and 1 in 30 in the United States, the effects are visible as *fetal alcohol spectrum disorder* (Lange et al., 2017; May et al., 2018). Its most serious form is **fetal alcohol syndrome (FAS),** which is marked by lifelong physical and mental abnormalities. The fetal damage may occur because alcohol has an *epigenetic effect:* It leaves chemical marks on DNA that switch genes abnormally on or off (Liu et al., 2009). Smoking cigarettes or marijuana during pregnancy also leaves epigenetic scars that may increase vulnerability to stress or addiction (Stroud et al., 2014; Szutorisz & Hurd, 2016).

If a pregnant woman experiences extreme stress, the stress hormones flooding her body may indicate a survival threat to the fetus and produce an earlier delivery. And famine or malnourishment puts a child at increased risk for health problems such as hypertension, heart disease, obesity, and psychiatric disorders (Glynn & Sandman, 2011; Santavirta et al., 2018).

For an interactive review of prenatal development, see *Topic Tutorial: PsychSim6, Conception to Birth.* See also the 8-minute *Video: Prenatal Development.*

> **RETRIEVAL PRACTICE**
>
> **RP-3** The first two weeks of prenatal development is the period of the _____.
> The period of the _____ lasts from 9 weeks after conception until birth. The time between those two prenatal periods is considered the period of the
> _____.
>
> *ANSWERS IN APPENDIX E*

The Competent Newborn

LOQ 13-3 What are some newborn abilities, and how do researchers explore infants' mental abilities?

Babies come with apps preloaded. Having survived prenatal hazards, we as newborns came equipped with automatic reflex responses ideally suited for our survival. We withdrew our limbs to escape pain. If a cloth over our face interfered with our breathing, we turned our head from side to side and swiped at it.

New parents are often in awe of the coordinated sequence of reflexes by which their baby gets food. When something touches their cheek, babies turn toward that touch, open their mouth, and vigorously *root* for a nipple. Finding one, they automatically close on it and begin *sucking*. (Failing to find satisfaction, the hungry baby may cry—a sound that parents find highly unpleasant, and very rewarding to relieve.) Other adaptive reflexes include the *startle* reflex (when arms and legs spring out, quickly followed by fist clenching and loud crying) and the surprisingly strong *grasping* reflex, both of which may have helped infants stay close to their caregivers.

The pioneering American psychologist William James presumed that the newborn experiences a "blooming, buzzing confusion," an assumption few people challenged until the 1960s. But then scientists discovered that babies can tell you a lot—if you know how to ask. To ask, you must capitalize on what babies can do—gaze, suck, and turn their heads. So, equipped with eye-tracking machines and pacifiers wired to electronic gear, researchers set out to answer parents' age-old questions: What can my baby see, hear, smell, and think?

Consider how researchers exploit **habituation**—a decrease in responding with repeated stimulation. We saw this earlier when fetuses adapted to a vibrating, honking device placed on their mother's abdomen. The novel stimulus gets attention when first presented. With repetition, the response weakens. This seeming boredom with familiar stimuli gives us a way to ask infants what they see and remember.

As newborns, we prefer sights and sounds that facilitate social responsiveness. We turn our head in the direction of human voices. We gaze longer at a drawing of a face-like image (**FIGURE 13.4**). Even late-stage fetuses look more at face-like patterns in red lights shined into the womb (Reid et al., 2017). As young infants, we also prefer to look at objects 8 to 12 inches away, which—wonder of wonders—just happens to be about the distance between a nursing infant's eyes and its mother's (Maurer & Maurer, 1988). Our brain's default settings help us connect socially.

Within days after birth, our brain's neural networks were stamped with the smell of our mother's body. Week-old nursing babies, placed between a gauze pad from their mother's bra and one from another nursing mother, have usually turned toward the smell of their own mother's pad (MacFarlane, 1978). What's more, that smell preference lasts. One experiment capitalized on the fact that some nursing mothers in a French maternity ward used a chamomile-scented balm to prevent nipple soreness (Delaunay-El Allam et al., 2010). Twenty-one months later, their toddlers preferred playing with chamomile-scented toys! Their peers who had not sniffed the scent while breast-feeding showed no such preference. (This makes us wonder: Will these children grow up to become devoted chamomile tea drinkers?) Such studies reveal the remarkable abilities with which we enter our world.

FIGURE 13.4
Newborns' preference for faces When shown these two images with the same three elements, Italian newborns spent nearly twice as many seconds looking at the face-like image (Valenza et al., 1996). Newborns—average age 53 minutes in one Canadian study—have an apparently inborn preference for looking toward faces (Mondloch et al., 1999).

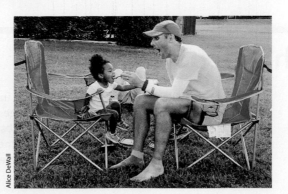

Prepared to feed and eat Like birds and other animals, we are predisposed to respond to our offspring's cries for food—even if we are in the middle of a 314-mile ultramarathon, as I [ND] was when my 18-month-old, Bevy, decided that only Daddy could feed her.

RP-4 Infants' _____ to repeated stimulation helps developmental psychologists study what infants can learn and remember.

ANSWERS IN APPENDIX E

MODULE 13

13 **REVIEW** **Developmental Issues, Prenatal Development, and the Newborn**

LEARNING OBJECTIVES

Test Yourself Answer these repeated Learning Objective Questions on your own (before checking the answers in Appendix D) to improve your retention of the concepts (McDaniel et al., 2009, 2015).

LOQ **13-1** What three issues have engaged developmental psychologists?

LOQ **13-2** What is the course of prenatal development, and how do teratogens affect that development?

LOQ **13-3** What are some newborn abilities, and how do researchers explore infants' mental abilities?

TERMS AND CONCEPTS TO REMEMBER

Test Yourself Write down the definition in your own words, then check your answer.

developmental psychology, p. 166

cross-sectional study, p. 166

longitudinal study, p. 166

zygote, p. 168

embryo, p. 168

fetus, p. 168

teratogens, p. 171

fetal alcohol syndrome (FAS), p. 171

habituation, p. 171

MASTER THE MATERIAL

Test Yourself Answer the following questions on your own first, then check your answers in Appendix E.

1. How do cross-sectional and longitudinal studies differ?

2. The three major issues that interest developmental psychologists are nature/nurture, stability/change, and _____ / _____.

3. Although development is lifelong, there is stability of personality over time. For example,

   a. most personality traits emerge in infancy and persist throughout life.

   b. temperament tends to remain stable throughout life.

   c. few people change significantly after adolescence.

   d. people tend to undergo greater personality changes as they age.

4. Body organs first begin to form and function during the period of the _____; within 6 months, during the period of the _____, the organs are sufficiently functional to provide a good chance of surviving and thriving.

   a. zygote; embryo

   b. zygote; fetus

   c. embryo; fetus

   d. placenta; fetus

5. Chemicals that the placenta isn't able to screen out that can harm an embryo or fetus are called _____.

Continue testing yourself with 📘 **LearningCurve** or 📗 **Achieve Read & Practice** to learn and remember most effectively.

MODULE 14

14 **Infancy and Childhood**

➤ **maturation** biological growth processes that enable orderly changes in behavior, relatively uninfluenced by experience.

As a flower unfolds in accord with its genetic instructions, so do we. **Maturation**—the orderly sequence of biological growth—decrees many of our commonalities. Babies stand, then walk. Toddlers use nouns, then verbs. Severe deprivation or abuse can slow development, but genetic growth patterns come "factory-installed"—they are inborn. Maturation (nature) sets the basic course of development; experience (nurture) adjusts it. Genes and scenes interact.

Physical Development

LOQ **14-1** During infancy and childhood, how do the brain and motor skills develop?

Brain Development

In your mother's womb, your developing brain formed nerve cells at the explosive rate of nearly one-quarter million per minute. The developing brain cortex actually overproduces neurons, with the number peaking at 28 weeks (Rabinowicz et al., 1996, 1999).

From infancy on, brain and mind—neural hardware and cognitive software—develop together. On the day you were born, you had most of the brain cells you would ever have. However, your nervous system was immature: After birth, the branching neural networks that eventually enabled all your abilities had a wild growth spurt (**FIGURE 14.1**). This rapid development helps explain why infant brain size increases rapidly in the early days after birth (Holland et al., 2014). From ages 3 to 6, the most rapid growth was in your frontal lobes, which enable rational planning. During those years, your brain required vast amounts of energy (Kuzawa et al., 2014). This energy-intensive process caused rapid progress in your ability to control your attention and behavior (Garon et al., 2008; Thompson-Schill et al., 2009).

The brain's association areas—those linked with thinking, memory, and language—were the last cortical areas to develop. As they did, your mental abilities surged (Chugani & Phelps, 1986; Thatcher et al., 1987). Fiber pathways supporting agility, language, and self-control proliferated into puberty. Under the influence of adrenal hormones, tens of billions of synapses formed and organized, while a use-it-or-lose-it *synaptic pruning* process shut down unused links (Paus et al., 1999; Thompson et al., 2000).

Motor Development

The developing brain enables physical coordination. Skills emerge as infants exercise their maturing muscles and nervous system. With occasional exceptions, the motor development sequence is universal. Babies roll over before they sit unsupported, and they usually crawl before they walk. These behaviors reflect not imitation but a maturing nervous system; blind children, too, crawl before they walk.

Genes guide motor development. In the United States, 25 percent of all babies walk by age 11 months, 50 percent within a week after their first birthday, and 90 percent by age 15 months (Frankenburg et al., 1992). Identical twins typically begin walking on nearly the same day (Wilson, 1979). Maturation—including the rapid development of the cerebellum at the back of the brain—creates our readiness to learn walking at about age 1. The same is true for other physical skills, including bowel and bladder control. Before necessary muscular and neural maturation, neither pleading nor punishment will produce successful toilet training. You can't rush a child's first flush.

Still, nurture may amend what nature intends. In some regions of Africa, the Caribbean, and India, caregivers often massage and exercise babies, which can accelerate the process of learning to walk (Karasik et al., 2010). The recommended infant *back to sleep position* (putting babies to sleep on their backs to reduce crib-death risk) has been associated with somewhat later crawling but not with later walking (Davis et al., 1998; Lipsitt, 2003).

| Newborn | 3 months | 15 months |

⬆ **FIGURE 14.1**

Infant brain development In humans, the brain is immature at birth. As the child matures, the neural networks grow increasingly complex.

PA Archive/The Image Works

Baby brains This electrode cap allows researchers to detect changes in brain activity triggered by different stimuli.

Physical development Sit, crawl, walk, run—the sequence of these motor development milestones is the same around the world, though babies reach them at varying ages.

Juice Images/JupiterImages/Getty Images

In the 8 years following the 1994 launch of a U.S. Back to Sleep educational campaign, the number of infants sleeping on their stomach dropped from 70 to 11 percent—and sudden unexpected infant deaths fell significantly (Braiker, 2005).

RETRIEVAL PRACTICE

RP-1 The biological growth process called _____ explains why most children begin walking by about 12 to 15 months.

ANSWERS IN APPENDIX E

"Someday we'll look back at this time in our lives and be unable to remember it."

Brain Maturation and Infant Memory

Can you recall your third birthday? Most of us *consciously* recall little from before age 4. Mice and monkeys also forget their early life, as rapid neuron growth disrupts the circuits that stored old memories (Akers et al., 2014). But as children mature, this *infantile amnesia* wanes, and they become increasingly capable of remembering experiences, even for a year or more (Bauer & Larkina, 2014; Morris et al., 2010). The brain areas underlying memory, such as the hippocampus and frontal lobes, continue to mature during and after adolescence (Luby et al., 2016; Murty et al., 2016).

Despite consciously recalling little from our early years, our brain was processing and storing information. While finishing her doctoral work in psychology, Carolyn Rovee-Collier observed nonverbal infant memory in action. Her 2-month-old, Benjamin, could be calmed by a moving crib mobile. Hoping to keep the baby entertained while she worked, she strung a cloth ribbon connecting the mobile to Benjamin's foot. Soon, he was kicking his foot to move the mobile. Thinking about her unintended home experiment, Rovee-Collier realized that, contrary to popular opinion in the 1960s, babies can learn and remember. To know for sure that her son wasn't just a whiz kid, she repeated the experiment with other infants (Rovee-Collier, 1989, 1999). Sure enough, they, too, soon kicked more when hitched to a mobile, both on the day of the experiment and the day after. If, however, she hitched them to a different mobile the next day, the infants showed no learning, indicating that they remembered the original mobile and recognized the difference. Moreover, when tethered to the familiar mobile a month later, they remembered the association and again began kicking.

Traces of forgotten childhood languages may also persist. One study tested English-speaking British adults who had no conscious memory of the Hindi or Zulu they had spoken as children. Yet, up to age 40, they could relearn subtle sound contrasts in these languages that other English speakers could *not* learn (Bowers et al., 2009). Chinese adoptees living in Canada since age 1 process Chinese sounds as do fluent Chinese speakers, even if they have no conscious recollection of Chinese words (Pierce et al., 2014). We see our two-track mind at work here: What the conscious mind does not know and cannot express in words, the nervous system and unconscious mind somehow remember.

ASK YOURSELF

What do you regard as your earliest memory? Now that you know about infantile amnesia, has your opinion changed about the accuracy of that memory?

Cognitive Development

LOQ **14-2** How did Piaget broaden our understanding of the way a child's mind develops, and how have today's researchers built on his work?

Somewhere on your precarious journey "from egghood to personhood" (Broks, 2007), you became conscious. When was that? In search of the conscious thoughts of an infant—or, rather, a neural signal that marks early conscious awareness—one French research team flashed faces on a screen. At first, the faces appeared so briefly that even a typical adult could not consciously perceive them. Gradually, the presentation slowed until an adult brain-wave response signaled conscious awareness, about 300 milliseconds after an image appeared. With enough time to process the faces, 5-month-old infants displayed the same brain signature of visual awareness (Dehaene, 2014; Kouider et al., 2013).

Once conscious, how did your mind grow? Developmental psychologist Jean Piaget [pee-ah-ZHAY] spent his life searching for the answer. He studied children's developing **cognition**—all the mental activities associated with thinking, knowing, remembering, and communicating. His interest in children's cognitive development began in 1920, when he was in Paris developing questions for children's intelligence tests. While administering the tests, Piaget became intrigued by children's wrong answers, which were often strikingly similar among same-age children. Where others saw childish mistakes, Piaget saw developing intelligence at work. Such accidental discoveries are among the fruits of psychological science.

Jean Piaget (1896–1980) "If we examine the intellectual development of the individual or of the whole of humanity, we shall find that the human spirit goes through a certain number of stages, each different from the other" (1930).

FIGURE 14.2
A changing marriage schema Most people once had a *marriage* schema as a union between a man and a woman. Today, more than two dozen countries have legalized same-sex marriage.

A half-century spent with children convinced Piaget that a child's mind is not a miniature model of an adult's. Thanks partly to his careful observations, we now understand that children reason differently than adults, in "wildly illogical ways" (Brainerd, 1996).

Piaget's studies led him to believe that a child's mind develops through a series of stages, in an upward march from the newborn's simple reflexes to the adult's abstract reasoning power. Thus, an 8-year-old can comprehend things a toddler cannot, such as the analogy that "getting an idea is like having a light turn on in your head."

Piaget's core idea was that our intellectual progression reflects an unceasing struggle to make sense of our experiences. To this end, the maturing brain builds **schemas**—concepts or mental molds into which we pour our experiences (**FIGURE 14.2**).

To explain how we use and adjust our schemas, Piaget proposed two more concepts. First, we **assimilate** new experiences—we interpret them in terms of our current schemas (understandings). Having a simple schema for *dog,* for example, a toddler may call all four-legged animals *dogs.* But as we interact with the world, we also adjust, or **accommodate,** our schemas to incorporate information provided by new experiences. Thus, the child soon learns that the original *dog* schema is too broad and accommodates by refining the category.

ASK YOURSELF

Can you recall a time when you misheard some song lyrics because you assimilated them into your own schema? (For hundreds of examples of this, visit KissThisGuy.com.)

Piaget's Theory and Current Thinking

Piaget believed that children construct their understanding of the world while interacting with it. Their mind experiences spurts of change, followed by greater stability as they move from one cognitive plateau to the next, each with distinctive characteristics that permit specific kinds of thinking. In Piaget's view, cognitive development consisted of four major stages—*sensorimotor, preoperational, concrete operational,* and *formal operational.*

SENSORIMOTOR STAGE In the **sensorimotor stage,** from birth to nearly age 2, babies take in the world through their senses and actions—through looking, hearing, touching, mouthing, and grasping. As their hands and limbs begin to move, they learn to make things happen.

Very young babies seem to live in the present: Out of sight is out of mind. In one test, Piaget showed an infant an appealing toy and then flopped his beret over it. Before the age of 6 months, the infant acted as if the toy ceased to exist. Young infants lack **object permanence**—the awareness that objects continue to exist even when not perceived. By 8 months, infants begin exhibiting memory for things no longer seen. If you hide a toy, the infant will momentarily look for it (**FIGURE 14.3**). Within another month or two, the infant will look for it even after being restrained for several seconds.

So does object permanence in fact blossom suddenly at 8 months, much as tulips blossom in spring? Today's researchers believe object permanence unfolds gradually, and they see development as more continuous than Piaget did. Even young infants will at least momentarily look for a toy where they saw it hidden a second before (Wang et al., 2004).

cognition all the mental activities associated with thinking, knowing, remembering, and communicating.

schema a concept or framework that organizes and interprets information.

assimilation interpreting our new experiences in terms of our existing schemas.

accommodation adapting our current understandings (schemas) to incorporate new information.

sensorimotor stage in Piaget's theory, the stage (from birth to nearly 2 years of age) at which infants know the world mostly in terms of their sensory impressions and motor activities.

object permanence the awareness that things continue to exist even when not perceived.

FIGURE 14.3

Object permanence Infants younger than 6 months seldom understand that things continue to exist when they are out of sight. But for this older infant, out of sight is definitely not out of mind.

Researchers also believe Piaget and his followers underestimated young children's competence. Young children think like little scientists. They test ideas, make causal inferences, and learn from statistical patterns (Gopnik et al., 2015). Consider these simple experiments:

- *Baby physics:* Like adults staring in disbelief at a magic trick (the *"Whoa!"* look), infants look longer at and explore impossible scenes—a car seeming to pass through a solid object, a ball stopping in midair, or an object violating object permanence by magically disappearing (Shuwairi & Johnson, 2013; Stahl & Feigenson, 2015). Why do infants show this visual bias? Because impossible events violate infants' expectations (Baillargeon et al., 2016).

- *Baby math:* Karen Wynn (1992, 2000, 2008) showed 5-month-olds one or two objects (**FIGURE 14.4a**). Then she hid the objects behind a screen, and visibly removed or added one (Figure 14.4d). When she lifted the screen, the infants sometimes did a double take, staring longer when shown a wrong number of objects (Figure 14.4f). But were they just responding to a greater or smaller *mass* of objects, rather than a change in *number* (Feigenson et al., 2002)? Later experiments showed that babies' number sense extends to larger numbers, to ratios, and to such things as drumbeats and motions (Libertus & Brannon, 2009; McCrink & Wynn, 2004; Spelke et al., 2013). If accustomed to a Daffy Duck puppet jumping three times on stage, they showed surprise if it jumped only twice.

"It is a rare privilege to watch the birth, growth, and first feeble struggles of a living human mind." — Annie Sullivan, in Helen Keller's *The Story of My Life*, 1903

PREOPERATIONAL STAGE Piaget believed that until about age 6 or 7, children are in a **preoperational stage**—able to represent things with words and images but too young to perform *mental operations* (such as imagining an action and mentally reversing it).

FIGURE 14.4

Baby math Shown a numerically impossible outcome, 5-month-old infants stare longer (Wynn, 1992). Clearly, infants are smarter than Piaget appreciated. Even as babies, we had a lot on our minds.

(a) Objects placed in case   (b) Screen comes up   (c) Empty hand enters   (d) One object removed

Then either: possible outcome
(e) Screen drops revealing 1 object

or: impossible outcome
(f) Screen drops revealing 2 objects

For a 5-year-old, the milk that seems "too much" in a tall, narrow glass may become just right if poured into a short, wide glass. Focusing only on the height dimension, this child cannot perform the operation of mentally pouring the milk back. Before about age 6, said Piaget, children lack the concept of **conservation**—the principle that quantity remains the same despite changes in shape (**FIGURE 14.5**).

Pretend Play Symbolic thinking and *pretend play* appear at an earlier age than Piaget supposed. Judy DeLoache (1987) discovered this when she showed children a model of a room and hid a miniature stuffed dog behind its miniature couch. The 2½-year-olds easily remembered where to find the miniature toy, but they could not use the model to locate an actual stuffed dog behind a couch in a real room. Three-year-olds—only 6 months older—usually went right to the actual stuffed animal in the real room, showing they *could* think of the model as a symbol for the room. Although Piaget did not view the stage transitions as abrupt, he probably would have been surprised to see symbolic thinking at such an early age.

Egocentrism Piaget taught us that preschool children are **egocentric:** They have difficulty perceiving things from another's point of view. They are like the person who, when asked by someone across a river, "How do I get to the other side?" answered, "You're *on* the other side." Asked to "show Mommy your picture," 2-year-old Gabriella holds the picture up facing her own eyes. Three-year-old Gray makes himself "invisible" by putting his hands over his eyes, assuming that if he can't see his grandparents, they can't see him. Asked what he would do if he saw a bear, 3-year-old Grant replies, "We cover our eyes so the bears can't see us."

Children's conversations also reveal their egocentrism, as one young boy demonstrated (Phillips, 1969, p. 61):

"Do you have a brother?"

"Yes."

"What's his name?"

"Jim."

"Does Jim have a brother?"

"No."

Like Gabriella, TV-watching preschoolers who block your view of the TV assume that you see what they see. They simply have not yet developed the ability to take another's viewpoint. Even adolescents egocentrically overestimate how much others are noticing them (Lin, 2016). And adults may overestimate the extent to which others share their opinions, knowledge, and perspectives. We assume that something will be clear to others if it is clear to us, or that email recipients will "hear" our "just kidding" intent (Epley et al., 2004; Kruger et al., 2005). Perhaps you can recall asking someone to guess a simple tune such as "Happy Birthday" as you clapped or tapped it out. With the tune in your head, it seemed so obvious! But you suffered the egocentric *curse of knowledge*, assuming that what was in your head was also in someone else's.

FIGURE 14.5
Piaget's test of conservation This visually focused preoperational child does not yet understand the principle of conservation. When the milk is poured into a tall, narrow glass, it suddenly seems like "more" than when it was in the shorter, wider glass. In another year or so, she will understand that the amount stays the same.

Egocentrism in action "Look, Granddaddy, a match!" So said my [DM's] granddaughter, Allie, at age 4, when showing me two memory game cards with matching pictures—that faced her.

"It's too late, Roger—they've seen us."
Roger has not outgrown his early childhood egocentrism.

preoperational stage in Piaget's theory, the stage (from about 2 to 6 or 7 years of age) at which a child learns to use language but does not yet comprehend the mental operations of concrete logic.

conservation the principle (which Piaget believed to be a part of concrete operational reasoning) that properties such as mass, volume, and number remain the same despite changes in the forms of objects.

egocentrism in Piaget's theory, the preoperational child's difficulty taking another's point of view.

CONCRETE OPERATIONAL STAGE By about age 7, said Piaget, children enter the **concrete operational stage.** Given concrete (physical) materials, they begin to grasp operations such as conservation. Understanding that change in form does not mean change in quantity, they can mentally pour milk back and forth between glasses of different shapes. They also enjoy jokes that use this new understanding:

> Mr. Jones went into a restaurant and ordered a whole pizza for his dinner. When the waiter asked if he wanted it cut into 6 or 8 pieces, Mr. Jones said, "Oh, you'd better make it 6, I could never eat 8 pieces!" (McGhee, 1976)

Piaget believed that during the concrete operational stage, children become able to comprehend mathematical transformations and conservation. When my [DM's] daughter, Laura, was 6, I was astonished at her inability to reverse simple arithmetic. Asked, "What is 8 plus 4?" she required 5 seconds to compute "12," and another 5 seconds to then compute 12 minus 4. By age 8, she could answer a reversed question instantly.

FORMAL OPERATIONAL STAGE By age 12, our reasoning expands from the purely concrete (involving actual experience) to encompass abstract thinking (involving imagined realities and symbols). As children approach adolescence, said Piaget, they can ponder hypothetical propositions and deduce consequences: *If* this, *then* that. Systematic reasoning, what Piaget called **formal operational** thinking, is now within their grasp.

Although full-blown logic and reasoning await adolescence, the rudiments of formal operational thinking begin earlier than Piaget realized. Consider this simple problem:

> If John is in school, then Mary is in school. John is in school. What can you say about Mary?

Formal operational thinkers have no trouble answering correctly. But neither do most 7-year-olds (Suppes, 1982). **TABLE 14.1** summarizes the four stages in Piaget's theory.

TABLE 14.1 Piaget's Stages of Cognitive Development

Typical Age Range	Stage and Description	Key Milestones	
Birth to nearly 2 years	*Sensorimotor* Experiencing the world through senses and actions (looking, hearing, touching, mouthing, and grasping)	• Object permanence • Stranger anxiety	
About 2 to 6 or 7 years	*Preoperational* Representing things with words and images; using intuitive rather than logical reasoning	• Pretend play • Egocentrism	
About 7 to 11 years	*Concrete operational* Thinking logically about concrete events; grasping concrete analogies and performing arithmetical operations	• Conservation • Mathematical transformations	
About 12 through adulthood	*Formal operational* Reasoning abstractly	• Abstract logic • Potential for mature moral reasoning	**Pretend play** Liz Banfield/Getty Images

RETRIEVAL PRACTICE

RP-2 Object permanence, pretend play, conservation, and abstract logic are developmental milestones for which of Piaget's stages, respectively?

RP-3 Label each of the following developmental phenomena (i–vi) with the correct cognitive developmental stage: (a) sensorimotor, (b) preoperational, (c) concrete operational, or (d) formal operational.

  i.   Thinking about abstract concepts, such as "freedom."

  ii. Enjoying imaginary play (such as dress-up).

  iii. Understanding that physical properties stay the same even when objects change form.

  iv. Having the ability to reverse math operations.

  v.   Understanding that something is not gone for good when it disappears from sight, as when Mom "disappears" behind the shower curtain.

  vi. Having difficulty taking another's point of view (as when blocking someone's view of the TV).

ANSWERS IN APPENDIX E

Reflecting on Piaget's Theory

What remains of Piaget's ideas about the child's mind? Plenty—enough to merit his being singled out by *Time* magazine as one of the twentieth century's 20 most influential scientists and thinkers, and his being rated in a survey of British psychologists as the last century's greatest psychologist (*Psychologist*, 2003). Piaget identified significant cognitive milestones and stimulated worldwide interest in how the mind develops. His emphasis was less on the ages at which children typically reach specific milestones than on their sequence. Studies around the globe, from Australia to Algeria to North America, have confirmed that human cognition unfolds basically in the sequence Piaget described (Lourenco & Machado, 1996; Segall et al., 1990).

However, today's researchers see development as more continuous than did Piaget. By detecting the beginnings of each type of thinking at earlier ages, they have revealed conceptual abilities Piaget missed. Moreover, they see formal logic as a smaller part of cognition than he did. Today, as part of our own cognitive development, we are adapting Piaget's ideas to accommodate new findings.

IMPLICATIONS FOR PARENTS AND TEACHERS Future parents and teachers, remember: Young children are incapable of adult logic. Preschoolers who block one's view of the TV simply have not learned to take another's viewpoint. What seems simple and obvious to us—getting off a seesaw will cause a friend on the other end to crash—may be incomprehensible to a 3-year-old. And it's important for all of us to remember that children are not passive receptacles waiting to be filled with knowledge. Better to build on what they already know, engaging them in concrete demonstrations and stimulating them to think for themselves. Finally, accept children's cognitive immaturity as adaptive. It is nature's strategy for keeping children close to protective adults and providing time for learning and socialization (Bjorklund & Green, 1992).

An Alternative Viewpoint: Lev Vygotsky and the Social Child

LOQ 14-3 How did Vygotsky view children's cognitive development?

As Piaget was forming his theory of cognitive development, Russian psychologist Lev Vygotsky was also studying how children think and learn. Where Piaget emphasized how the child's mind grows through interaction with the physical environment, Vygotsky emphasized how the child's mind grows through interaction with the *social* environment. If Piaget's child was a young scientist, Vygotsky's was a young apprentice. By giving children new words and mentoring them, parents, teachers, and other children provide what we now call a temporary **scaffold** from which children can step to higher levels of thinking (Renninger & Granott, 2005; Wood et al., 1976). Children learn best when their social environment presents them with something in the sweet spot between too easy and too difficult.

Language, an important ingredient of social mentoring, provides the building blocks for thinking, noted Vygotsky (who was born the same year as Piaget, but died prematurely of tuberculosis). By age 7, children increasingly think in words and use words to solve problems. They do this, Vygotsky said, by internalizing their culture's language and relying on inner speech (Fernyhough, 2008). Parents who say, "No, no, Bevy!" when pulling their child's hand away from a cup of hot coffee are giving their child a self-control tool. When Bevy later needs to resist temptation, she may likewise think, "*No, no, Bevy!*" Second graders who muttered to themselves while doing math problems grasped third-grade math better the following year (Berk, 1994). Whether out loud or inaudibly, talking to themselves helps children control their behavior and emotions and master new skills. (It helps adults, too. Adults who motivate themselves using self-talk—"You can do it!"—experience better performance [Kross et al., 2014].)

Theory of Mind

LOQ 14-4 What does it mean to develop a *theory of mind*, and how is this impaired in those with autism spectrum disorder?

When Little Red Riding Hood realized her "grandmother" was really a wolf, she swiftly revised her ideas about the creature's intentions and raced away. Preschoolers, although still egocentric, develop this ability to infer others' mental states when they begin forming a **theory of mind** (Premack & Woodruff, 1978).

"Assessing the impact of Piaget on developmental psychology is like assessing the impact of Shakespeare on English literature."
— Developmental psychologist Harry Beilin (1992)

"Childhood has its own way of seeing, thinking, and feeling, and there is nothing more foolish than the attempt to put ours in its place." — Philosopher Jean-Jacques Rousseau, 1798

For a 7-minute synopsis of Piaget's concepts, see the *Video: Cognitive Development.*

concrete operational stage in Piaget's theory, the stage of cognitive development (from about 7 to 11 years of age) at which children gain the mental operations that enable them to think logically about concrete events.

formal operational stage in Piaget's theory, the stage of cognitive development (normally beginning about age 12) at which people begin to think logically about abstract concepts.

scaffold in Vygotsky's theory, a framework that offers children temporary support as they develop higher levels of thinking.

theory of mind people's ideas about their own and others' mental states—about their feelings, perceptions, and thoughts, and the behaviors these might predict.

This is Sally. *This is Anne.*

Sally puts her ball in the red cupboard.

Sally goes away.

Anne moves the ball to the blue cupboard.

Where will Sally look for her ball?

⊘ FIGURE 14.6
Testing children's theory of mind This simple problem illustrates how researchers explore children's presumptions about others' mental states. (Inspired by Baron-Cohen et al., 1985.)

Infants as young as 7 months show some knowledge of others' beliefs (Kovács et al., 2010). With time, the ability to take another's perspective develops. They come to understand what made a playmate angry, when a sibling will share, and what might make a parent buy a toy. They begin to tease, empathize, and persuade. And when making decisions, they use their understanding of how their actions will make others feel (Repacholi et al., 2016). Preschoolers and young children who have an advanced ability to understand others' minds tend to be well-liked (McElwain et al., 2019; Slaughter et al., 2015).

Between about ages 3 and 4½, children come to realize that others may hold false beliefs (Callaghan et al., 2005; Rubio-Fernández & Geurts, 2013; Sabbagh et al., 2006). Jennifer Jenkins and Janet Astington (1996) showed Canadian children a Band-Aid box and asked them what was inside. Expecting Band-Aids, the children were surprised to discover that the box actually contained pencils. Asked what a child who had never seen the box would think was inside, 3-year-olds typically answered "pencils." By age 4 to 5, the children's theory of mind had leapt forward, and they anticipated their friends' false belief that the box would hold Band-Aids.

In a follow-up experiment, children viewed a doll named Sally leaving her ball in a red cupboard (**FIGURE 14.6**). Another doll, Anne, then moved the ball to a blue cupboard. Researchers then posed a question: When Sally returns, where will she look for the ball? Children with *autism spectrum disorder* had difficulty understanding that Sally's state of mind differed from their own— that Sally, not knowing the ball had been moved, would return to the red cupboard. They also have difficulty reflecting on their own mental states. They are, for example, less likely to use the personal pronouns I and me. Deaf children with hearing parents and minimal communication opportunities have had similar difficulty inferring others' states of mind (Peterson & Siegal, 1999).

RETRIEVAL PRACTICE

RP-4 What does *theory of mind* have to do with autism spectrum disorder?

ANSWERS IN APPENDIX E

Social Development

LOQ 14-5 How do caregiver-infant attachment bonds form?

From birth, most babies are social creatures, developing an intense attachment to their caregivers. Infants come to prefer familiar faces and voices, then to coo and gurgle when given a caregiver's attention. By 4.5 months, infants can tell apart familiar and unfamiliar languages (Fecher & Johnson, 2019). After about 8 months, soon after object permanence emerges and children become mobile, a curious thing happens: They develop **stranger anxiety.** They may greet strangers by crying and reaching for familiar caregivers: "No! Don't leave me!" Children this age have schemas for familiar faces; when they cannot assimilate the new face into these remembered schemas, they become distressed (Kagan, 1984). Once again, we see an important principle: *The brain, mind, and social-emotional behavior develop together.*

Origins of Attachment

One-year-olds typically cling tightly to a caregiver when they are frightened or expect separation. Reunited after being apart, they often shower that special someone with smiles and hugs. This striking caregiver-infant **attachment** bond is a powerful survival impulse that keeps infants close to their caregivers. Infants normally become attached to those—typically their parents—who are comfortable and familiar. For many years, psychologists reasoned that infants became attached to those who satisfied their need for nourishment. But an accidental finding overturned this explanation.

BODY CONTACT During the 1950s, University of Wisconsin psychologists Harry Harlow and Margaret Harlow bred monkeys for their learning studies. To equalize experiences and to isolate any disease, they separated the infant monkeys from their mothers

stranger anxiety the fear of strangers that infants commonly display, beginning by about 8 months of age.

attachment an emotional tie with others; shown in young children by their seeking closeness to caregivers and showing distress on separation.

critical period an optimal period early in the life of an organism when exposure to certain stimuli or experiences produces normal development.

imprinting the process by which certain animals form strong attachments during early life.

shortly after birth and raised them in individual cages, each including a cheesecloth baby blanket (Harlow et al., 1971). Then came a surprise: When their soft blankets were taken to be washed, the monkeys became distressed.

The Harlows recognized that this intense attachment to the blanket contradicted the idea that attachment derives from an association with nourishment. But how could they show this more convincingly? To pit the drawing power of a food source against the comfort of the blanket, they created two artificial mothers. One was a bare wire cylinder with a wooden head and an attached feeding bottle, the other a cylinder wrapped with terry cloth.

When raised with both, the monkeys overwhelmingly preferred the comfy cloth mother (**FIGURE 14.7**). Like other infants clinging to their live mothers, anxious monkey babies would cling to their cloth mothers, soothed by this *contact comfort*. When exploring their environment, they used her as a *secure base,* as if attached to her by an invisible elastic band that stretched only so far before pulling them back. Researchers soon learned that other qualities—rocking, warmth, and feeding—made the cloth mother even more appealing.

Human infants, too, become attached to parents who are soft and warm and who rock, feed, and pat. Much parent-infant emotional communication occurs via touch, which can be either soothing (snuggles) or arousing (tickles) (Hertenstein et al., 2006). People across the globe agreed that the ideal mother "shows affection by touching" (Mesman et al., 2015). Such parental affection not only feels good, it boosts brain development and later cognitive ability (Davis et al., 2017).

Human attachment also consists of one person providing another with a secure base from which to explore and a safe haven when distressed. As we mature, our secure base shifts—from parents to peers and partners (Cassidy & Shaver, 1999; Schmidt et al., 2019). But at all ages we are social creatures. We gain strength when someone offers, by words and actions, a safe haven: "I will be here. I am interested in you. Come what may, I will support you" (Crowell & Waters, 1994).

FAMILIARITY Contact is one key to attachment. Another is familiarity. In many animals, attachments based on familiarity form during a **critical period**—an optimal period when certain events must take place to facilitate proper development (Bornstein, 1989). For goslings, ducklings, or chicks, that period falls in the hours shortly after hatching, when the first moving object they see is normally their mother. From then on, the young fowl follow her, and her alone.

Konrad Lorenz (1937) explored this rigid attachment process, called **imprinting.** He wondered: What would ducklings do if he was the first moving creature they observed? What they did was follow him around: Everywhere that Konrad went, the ducks were sure to go. Although baby birds imprint best to their own species, they also will imprint to a variety of moving objects—an animal of another species, a box on wheels, or a bouncing ball (Colombo, 1982; Johnson, 1992). Once formed, this attachment is difficult to reverse.

Children—unlike ducklings—do not imprint. However, they do become attached to what they've known. *Mere exposure* to people and things fosters fondness. Children like to reread the same books, rewatch the same movies, reenact family traditions. They prefer to eat familiar foods, live in the same familiar neighborhood, attend school with the same old friends. Familiarity is a safety signal. Familiarity breeds content.

PR INK/Science Source

⑦ FIGURE 14.7

The Harlows' monkey mothers
Psychologists Harry Harlow and Margaret Harlow raised monkeys with two artificial mothers—one a bare wire cylinder with a wooden head and an attached feeding bottle, the other a cylinder with no bottle but covered with foam rubber and wrapped with terry cloth. The Harlows' discovery surprised many psychologists: The infants much preferred contact with the comfortable cloth mother, even while feeding from the nourishing wire mother.

For some people, a perceived relationship with God functions as do other attachments, by providing a secure base for exploration and a safe haven when threatened (Granqvist et al., 2010; Kirkpatrick, 1999).

Nina Leen/Getty Images

Daddy duck? Konrad Lorenz demonstrated that ducks will imprint on the first moving thing they see, which in this case was him!

basic trust according to Erik Erikson, a sense that the world is predictable and trustworthy; said to be formed during infancy by appropriate experiences with responsive caregivers.

RP-5   What distinguishes imprinting from attachment?

ANSWERS IN APPENDIX E

Attachment Differences

LOQ **14-6**   How have psychologists studied attachment differences, and what have they learned?

What accounts for children's attachment differences? To answer this question, Mary Ainsworth (1979) designed the *strange situation* experiment. She observed mother-infant pairs at home during their first six months. Later she observed the 1-year-old infants in a strange situation (usually a laboratory playroom) with and without their mothers. Such research has shown that about 60 percent of infants and young children display *secure attachment* (Moulin et al., 2014). In their mother's presence they play comfortably, happily exploring their new environment. When she leaves, they become distressed; when she returns, they seek contact with her.

Other infants show *insecure attachment,* marked either by anxiety or avoidance of trusting relationships. These infants are less likely to explore their surroundings; they may even cling to their mother. When she leaves, they either cry loudly and remain upset or seem indifferent to her departure and return (Ainsworth, 1973, 1989; Kagan, 1995; van IJzendoorn & Kroonenberg, 1988).

Ainsworth and others found that sensitive, responsive mothers—those who noticed what their babies were doing and responded appropriately—had infants who exhibited secure attachment (De Wolff & van IJzendoorn, 1997). Insensitive, unresponsive mothers—mothers who attended to their babies when they felt like doing so but ignored them at other times—often had infants who were insecurely attached. The Harlows' monkey studies, with unresponsive artificial mothers, produced even more striking effects. When put in strange situations without their artificial mothers, the deprived infants were terrified (**FIGURE 14.8**).

Many remember Harry Harlow as the researcher who tortured helpless monkeys, and today's climate of greater respect for animal welfare would likely prevent such primate studies. But Harlow defended his methods: "Remember, for every mistreated monkey there exist a million mistreated children," he said, expressing the hope that his research would sensitize people to child abuse and neglect. "No one who knows Harry's work could ever argue that babies do fine without companionship, that a caring mother doesn't matter," noted Harlow biographer Deborah Blum (2011, pp. 292, 307). "And since we . . . didn't fully believe that before Harry Harlow came along, then perhaps we needed—just once—to be smacked really hard with that truth so that we could never again doubt."

So, caring parents (and other caregivers) matter. But is attachment style the result of parenting? Or is attachment style the result of genetically influenced *temperament?* Studies reveal that heredity affects temperament, and that temperament affects attachment style (Picardi et al., 2011; Raby et al., 2012). Shortly after birth, some babies are noticeably *difficult*—irritable, intense, and unpredictable. Others are *easy*—cheerful, relaxed, and with predictable feeding and sleeping schedules (Chess & Thomas, 1987). By neglecting such inborn differences, the parenting studies, noted Judith Harris (1998), are like "comparing foxhounds reared in kennels with poodles reared in apartments." So, to separate nature and nurture, we would need to vary parenting while controlling temperament. (Pause and think: If you were the researcher, how might you do this?)

Dutch researcher Dymphna van den Boom's (1994) solution was to randomly assign 100 temperamentally difficult 6- to 9-month-olds to either an experimental group, in which mothers received personal training in sensitive responding, or to a control group, in which they did not. At 12 months of age, 68 percent of the infants in the experimental group were securely attached, as were only

FIGURE 14.8
Social deprivation and fear In the Harlows' experiments, monkeys raised with artificial mothers were overwhelmed when placed in strange situations without those mothers.

Science Source

TABLE 14.2 Dual Parenting Positives

- *Active dads are caregiving more.* Today's co-parenting fathers are more engaged, with a doubling in the weekly hours spent with their children, compared with fathers in 1965 (Livingston & Parker, 2011).

- *Couples that share housework and child care are happier in their relationships and less divorce prone* (Wilcox & Marquardt, 2011).

- *Dual parenting supports children.* After controlling for other factors, children average better life outcomes "if raised by both parents" (Taylor, 2014).

- *Parents' gender and sexual orientation do not affect children's well-being.* The American Academy of Pediatrics (2013) reports that what matters is competent, secure, nurturing parents. The American Sociological Association (2013) concurs: Parental stability and resources matter, but "whether a child is raised by same-sex or opposite-sex parents has no bearing on a child's well-being." One analysis of 21,000 American children aged 4 to 17 found that, compared to those with straight parents, children with gay or lesbian parents experienced similar levels of well-being (Calzo et al., 2019).

Lorie Hailey

28 percent of the control-group infants. Other studies confirm that intervention programs can increase parental sensitivity and, to a lesser extent, infant attachment security (Bakermans-Kranenburg et al., 2003; Van Zeijl et al., 2006). Such "positive parenting" interventions seem to be especially beneficial for children with difficult temperaments (Slagt et al., 2016).

As these examples indicate, researchers have more often studied mother care than father care. Infants who lack a caring mother are said to suffer "maternal deprivation"; those lacking a father's care merely experience "father absence." This reflects a wider attitude in which "fathering a child" has meant impregnating, and "mothering" has meant nurturing. But fathers are more than just mobile sperm banks. Across nearly 100 studies worldwide, a father's love and acceptance have been comparable with a mother's love in predicting their offspring's health and well-being (Rohner & Veneziano, 2001; see also **TABLE 14.2**). Fathers matter.

In one large British study following 7259 children from birth to adulthood, those whose fathers were most involved in parenting (through outings, reading to them, and taking an interest in their education) tended to achieve more in school, even after controlling for other factors such as parental education and family wealth (Flouri & Buchanan, 2004). Girls with supportive fathers expect that other men will treat them with care and respect, and they are less prone to risky sexual behavior (DelPriore et al., 2017, 2019). Increasing nonmarital births and the greater instability of cohabiting versus married partnerships has, however, meant more father-absent families (Hymowitz et al., 2013). In Europe and the United States, for example, children born to married parents (compared to cohabiting parents) are about half as likely to experience their parents' separation, which often entails diminished father care (Brown et al., 2016; Wilcox & DeRose, 2017). Even after controlling for parents' income, education, and race, children co-parented by two married parents experience a lower rate of school problems (Zill & Wilcox, 2017).

Children's anxiety over separation from parents peaks at around 13 months, then gradually declines (**FIGURE 14.9**). This happens whether they live with one parent or two, are cared for at home or in day care, live in North America, Guatemala, or the Kalahari Desert. Does this mean our need for and love of others also fades away? Hardly. Our capacity for love grows, and our pleasure in touching and holding those we love never ceases.

ATTACHMENT STYLES AND LATER RELATIONSHIPS Developmental psychologist Erik Erikson (1902–1994), working with his wife, Joan Erikson (1902–1997), believed that securely attached children approach life with a sense of **basic trust**—a sense that the world is predictable and reliable. He attributed basic trust not to environment or inborn temperament, but to early parenting. He theorized that infants blessed with sensitive, loving caregivers form a lifelong attitude of trust rather than fear.

Jouke van Keulen/Shutterstock

⊘ **FIGURE 14.9**

Infants' distress over separation from parents In an experiment, infants were left by their mothers in an unfamiliar room. Regardless of whether the infant had experienced day care, the percentage who cried when the mother left peaked at about 13 months of age (Kagan, 1976).

Percentage of infants who cried when their mothers left

Day care

Home

Age (months)

Many researchers now believe that our early attachments form part of the foundation for our adult relationships and our comfort with affection and intimacy (Birnbaum et al., 2006; Fraley et al., 2013). People who report secure relationships with their parents tend to enjoy secure friendships (Gorrese & Ruggieri, 2012). Students leaving home to attend college or university—another kind of "strange situation"—tend to adjust well if closely attached to parents (Mattanah et al., 2011). Children with sensitive, responsive mothers tend to flourish socially and academically (Raby et al., 2014).

Feeling insecurely attached to others may take either of two main forms (Fraley et al., 2011). One is *anxious attachment,* in which people constantly crave acceptance but remain vigilant to signs of possible rejection. (Being sensitive to threat, anxiously attached people also tend to be skilled lie detectors and poker players [Ein-Dor & Perry, 2012, 2013].) The other is *avoidant attachment,* in which people experience discomfort getting close to others and use avoidant strategies to maintain distance from others. In romantic relationships, an anxious attachment style creates constant concern over rejection, leading people to cling to their partners. An avoidant style decreases commitment and increases conflict (DeWall et al., 2011; Overall et al., 2015).

Adult attachment styles can also affect relationships with one's own children. But say this for those (nearly half of all people) who exhibit wary, insecure attachments: Anxious or avoidant tendencies have helped our groups detect or escape dangers (Ein-Dor et al., 2010).

> **ASK YOURSELF**
>
> How has your upbringing affected your attachment style?

Deprivation of Attachment

LOQ 14-7 How does childhood neglect or abuse affect children's attachments?

If secure attachment nurtures social competence, what happens when circumstances prevent a child's forming any attachments? In all of psychology, there is no sadder research literature. Babies locked away at home under conditions of abuse or extreme neglect are often withdrawn, frightened, even speechless. The same is true of those raised in institutions without the stimulation and attention of a regular caregiver, as was tragically illustrated during the 1970s and 1980s in Romania. Having decided that economic growth for his impoverished country required more human capital, Nicolae Ceaușescu, Romania's Communist dictator, outlawed contraception, forbade abortion, and taxed families with fewer than five children. The birthrate skyrocketed. But unable to afford the children they had been coerced into having, many families had to leave them at government-run orphanages with untrained and overworked staff. Child-to-caregiver ratios often were 15 to 1, so the children were deprived of healthy attachments with at least one adult.

When tested after Ceaușescu's 1989 execution, and compared with children assigned to quality foster care, these socially deprived children had lower intelligence scores, reduced brain development, abnormal stress responses, and quadruple the rate of attention-deficit/hyperactivity disorder (ADHD) (Bick et al., 2015; Kennedy et al., 2016; McLaughlin et al., 2015; Nelson et al., 2014). Dozens of other studies across 19 countries have shown that orphaned children generally fare better on later intelligence tests when raised in family homes from an early age (van IJzendoorn et al., 2008, 2017).

Most children growing up under adversity (as did the surviving children of the Holocaust) are *resilient;* they withstand the trauma and become well-adjusted adults (Helmreich, 1992; Masten, 2001). So do most victims of childhood sexual abuse, noted researcher Susan Clancy (2010). And hardship short of trauma often boosts mental toughness (Seery, 2011). Children who have coped with some adversity become hardier when facing future stresses (Ellis et al., 2017). Moreover, although enduring the hardship of growing up poor puts children at risk for some social pathologies, growing up rich puts them at risk for others. Affluent children are at elevated risk for substance abuse,

"Out of the conflict between trust and mistrust, the infant develops hope, which is the earliest form of what gradually becomes faith in adults." — Erik Erikson (1983)

To consider how your own attachment style may be affecting your current relationships, engage online with the activity *Assess Your Strengths: What Is Your Attachment Style?*

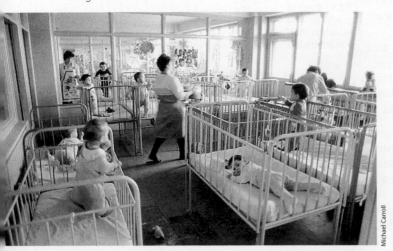

The deprivation of attachment In this 1980s Romanian orphanage, children between ages one and five outnumbered caregivers 15 to 1.

Michael Carroll

eating disorders, anxiety, and depression (Lund & Dearing, 2012; Luthar et al., 2013). So when you recall some adversity you have faced, consider the silver lining. Your coping may have strengthened your resilience—your tendency to bounce back and go on to lead a better life.

But many who experience enduring abuse don't bounce back so readily. The Harlows' monkeys raised in total isolation, without even an artificial mother, bore lifelong scars. As adults, when placed with other monkeys their age, they either cowered in fright or lashed out in aggression. When they reached sexual maturity, most were incapable of mating. If artificially impregnated, females often were neglectful, abusive, even murderous toward their first-born. Another primate experiment confirmed the abuse-breeds-abuse phenomenon: 9 of 16 female monkeys who had been abused by their mothers became abusive parents, as did *none* of the females raised by a nonabusive mother (Maestripieri, 2005).

In humans, too, the unloved may become the unloving. Most abusive parents—and many condemned murderers—have reported being neglected or battered as children (Kempe & Kempe, 1978; Lewis et al., 1988). Some 30 percent of people who have been abused later abuse their children—four times the U.S. national rate of child abuse (Dumont et al., 2007; Kaufman & Zigler, 1987). And parents tend to abuse their own children in the ways they were abused as children, such as through neglect, emotional abuse, physical abuse, or sexual abuse (Madigan et al., 2019).

Although most abused children do *not* later become violent criminals or abusive parents, extreme early trauma may nevertheless leave footprints on the brain (Teicher & Samson, 2016). Like battle-stressed soldiers, abused children's brains respond to angry faces with heightened activity in threat-detecting areas (McCrory et al., 2011). In conflict-plagued homes, even sleeping infants' brains show heightened reactivity to hearing angry speech (Graham et al., 2013). As adults, these children struggle to regulate their negative emotions, exhibit stronger startle responses, and are more than twice as likely to attempt suicide (Angelakis et al., 2019; Jovanovic et al., 2009; Lavi et al., 2019).

If repeatedly threatened and attacked while young, normally placid golden hamsters grow up to be cowards when caged with same-sized hamsters, or bullies when caged with weaker ones (Ferris, 1996). Such animals show changes in the brain chemical serotonin, which calms aggressive impulses. A similarly sluggish serotonin response has been found in abused children who become aggressive teens and adults. By sensitizing the stress response system, early stress can permanently heighten reactions to later stress and increase stress-related disease (Fagundes & Way, 2014; van Zuiden et al., 2012; Wei et al., 2012). Child abuse can also leave *epigenetic* marks—chemical tags—that can alter normal gene expression (Lutz et al., 2017; McKinney, 2017).

Such findings help explain why young children who have survived severe or prolonged physical abuse, sexual abuse, bullying, or wartime atrocities are at increased risk for health problems, psychological disorders, substance abuse, criminality, and, for women, earlier death (Chen et al., 2016; Jakubowski et al., 2018; Schaefer et al., 2018). An analysis of 135,000 adolescents in 48 countries showed that those bullied had triple the normal rate of attempted suicide (Koyanagi et al., 2019). In one national study of 43,093 adults, 8 percent reported experiencing physical abuse at least fairly often before age 18 (Sugaya et al., 2012). Among these, 84 percent had experienced at least one psychiatric disorder. Moreover, the greater the abuse, the greater the odds of anxiety, depression, substance use disorder, and attempted suicide. Childhood abuse victims also experience more troubled adult romantic relationships (Labella et al., 2018).

Abuse victims are at especially heightened risk for depression if they carry a gene variation that spurs stress-hormone production (Bradley et al., 2008). As we will see again and again, behavior and emotion arise from a particular environment interacting with particular genes.

We adults also suffer when our attachment bonds are severed. Whether through death or separation, a break produces a predictable sequence. Agitated preoccupation with the lost partner is followed by deep sadness and, eventually, the beginnings of emotional detachment and a return to normal living (Hazan & Shaver, 1994). Newly separated couples who have long ago ceased feeling affection are sometimes surprised at their desire to be near the former partner. Detaching is a process, not an event.

self-concept all our thoughts and feelings about ourselves, in answer to the question, "Who am I?"

Self-awareness Mirror images fascinate infants from the age of about 6 months. Only at about 18 months, however, does the child recognize that the image in the mirror is "me."

Kate Nurre

Robert Weber/The New Yorker Collection/The Cartoon Bank

"Thank you, Adrian. Parenting is a learning process, and your criticisms help."

"Before I got married I had six theories about bringing up children; now I have six children and no theories." — attributed to John Wilmot, 2nd Earl of Rochester (1647–1680)

Developing a Self-Concept

LOQ **14-8** How do children's self-concepts develop?

Infancy's major social achievement is attachment. *Childhood's* major social achievement is a positive sense of self. By the end of childhood, at about age 12, most children have developed a **self-concept**—an understanding and assessment of who they are. Parents often wonder when and how this sense of self develops. "Is my baby aware of herself— does she know she is a person distinct from everyone else?"

Of course we cannot ask the baby directly, but we can again capitalize on what she can do—letting her *behavior* provide clues to the beginnings of her self-awareness. In 1877, biologist Charles Darwin offered one idea: Self-awareness begins when we recognize ourselves in a mirror. To see whether a child recognizes that the girl in the mirror is indeed herself, researchers sneakily dabbed color on her nose. At about 6 months, children reach out to touch their mirror image as if it were another child (Courage & Howe, 2002; Damon & Hart, 1982, 1988, 1992). By 15 to 18 months, they begin to touch their own noses when they see the colored spot in the mirror (Butterworth, 1992; Gallup & Suarez, 1986). Apparently, 18-month-olds have a schema of how their face should look, and they wonder, "What is that spot doing on *my* face?"

By school age, children's self-concept has blossomed. It now includes their gender identity, group memberships, psychological traits, and similarities and differences compared with other children (Newman & Ruble, 1988; Stipek, 1992). They come to see themselves as good and skillful in some ways but not others. They form a concept of which traits, ideally, they would like to have. By age 8 or 10, their self-image is quite stable.

Children's views of themselves affect their actions. Children who form a positive self-concept are more confident, independent, optimistic, assertive, and sociable (Maccoby, 1980). So how can parents encourage a positive yet realistic self-concept?

Parenting Styles

LOQ **14-9** What are the four main parenting styles?

Some parents spank; others reason. Some are strict; others are lax. Some show little affection; others liberally hug and kiss. How do parenting-style differences affect children?

The most heavily researched aspect of parenting has been how, and to what extent, parents seek to control their children. Parenting styles can be described as a combination of two traits: how *responsive* and how *demanding* parents are (Kakinami et al., 2015). Investigators have identified four parenting styles (Baumrind, 1966, 1989, 1991; Maccoby & Martin, 1983; Steinberg et al., 1994):

1. *Authoritarian* parents are *coercive*. They impose rules and expect obedience: "Don't interrupt." "Keep your room clean." "Don't stay out late or you'll be grounded." "Why? Because I said so."

2. *Permissive* parents are *unrestraining*. They make few demands, set few limits, and use little punishment.

3. *Neglectful* parents are *uninvolved*. They are neither demanding nor responsive. They are careless, inattentive, and do not seek a close relationship with their children.

4. *Authoritative* parents are *confrontive*. They are both demanding and responsive. They exert control by setting rules, but, especially with older children, they encourage open discussion and allow exceptions.

For more on parenting styles and their associated outcomes, see Thinking Critically About: Parenting Styles.

Parents who struggle with conflicting advice should remember that *all advice reflects the advice-giver's values.* For parents who prize unquestioning obedience, or whose children live in dangerous environments, an authoritarian style may have the desired effect. For those who value children's sociability and self-reliance, there is wisdom in authoritative firm-but-open parenting.

Thinking Critically About:

Parenting Styles—Too Hard, Too Soft, Too Uncaring, and Just Right?

LOQ 14-10 What outcomes are associated with each parenting style?

Researchers have identified four parenting styles,[1] which have been associated with varying outcomes.

1 Authoritarian parents

↗↙

Children with less social skill and self-esteem, and a brain that overreacts when they make mistakes[2]

2 Permissive parents

↗↙

Children who are more aggressive and immature[3]

HOWEVER, Correlation ≠ Causation!

What other factors might explain this parenting-competence link?

• Children's traits may influence parenting. Parental warmth and control vary somewhat from child to child, even in the same family.[6] Maybe socially mature, agreeable, easygoing children get greater trust and warmth from their parents? Twin studies have supported this possibility.[7]

• Some underlying third factor may be at work. Perhaps, for example, competent parents and their competent children share genes that make social competence more likely. Twin studies have also supported this possibility.[8]

3 Neglectful parents

↗↙

Children with poor academic and social outcomes[4]

4 Authoritative parents

↗↙

Children with the highest self-esteem, self-reliance, self-regulation, and social competence[5]

1. Kakinami et al., 2015. 2. Meyer et al., 2019. 3. Luyckx et al., 2011. 4. Pinquart, 2016; Steinberg et al., 1994. 5. Baumrind, 1996, 2013; Buri et al.,1988; Coopersmith, 1967; Sulik et al., 2015. 6. Holden & Miller, 1999; Klahr & Burt, 2014. 7. Kendler, 1996. 8. South et al., 2008.

"You are the bows from which your children as living arrows are sent forth." — Kahlil Gibran, *The Prophet*, 1923

The investment in raising a child buys many years of joy and love, but also of worry and irritation. Yet for most people who become parents, a child is one's legacy—one's personal investment in the human future. To paraphrase psychiatrist Carl Jung, we reach backward into our parents and forward into our children, and through their children into a future we will never see, but about which we must therefore care.

ASK YOURSELF

What mistakes do you think parents of the past most often made? What mistakes do you think today's parents might be making, and that as a parent you would want to (or already try to) avoid?

RETRIEVAL PRACTICE

RP-6 For those who value children's self-reliance, the four parenting styles may be described as "too hard, too soft, too uncaring, and just right." Which parenting style goes with each of these descriptions, and how do children benefit from the "just right" style?

ANSWERS IN APPENDIX E

See the *Video: Correlational Studies* for a helpful tutorial animation about correlational research design.

MODULE 14 REVIEW Infancy and Childhood

LEARNING OBJECTIVES

Test Yourself Answer these repeated Learning Objective Questions on your own (before checking the answers in Appendix D) to improve your retention of the concepts (McDaniel et al., 2009, 2015).

LOQ 14-1 During infancy and childhood, how do the brain and motor skills develop?

LOQ 14-2 How did Piaget broaden our understanding of the way a child's mind develops, and how have today's researchers built on his work?

LOQ 14-3 How did Vygotsky view children's cognitive development?

LOQ 14-4 What does it mean to develop a *theory of mind*, and how is this impaired in those with autism spectrum disorder?

LOQ 14-5 How do caregiver-infant attachment bonds form?

LOQ 14-6 How have psychologists studied attachment differences, and what have they learned?

LOQ 14-7 How does childhood neglect or abuse affect children's attachments?

LOQ 14-8 How do children's self-concepts develop?

LOQ 14-9 What are the four main parenting styles?

LOQ 14-10 What outcomes are associated with each parenting style?

TERMS AND CONCEPTS TO REMEMBER

Test Yourself Write down the definition in your own words, then check your answer.

maturation, p. 172

cognition, p. 175

schema, p. 175

assimilation, p. 175

accommodation, p. 175

sensorimotor stage, p. 175

object permanence, p. 175

preoperational stage, p. 177

conservation, p. 177

egocentrism, p. 177

concrete operational stage, p. 179

formal operational stage, p. 179

scaffold, p. 179

theory of mind, p. 179

stranger anxiety, p. 180

attachment, p. 180

critical period, p. 180

imprinting, p. 180

basic trust, p. 182

self-concept, p. 186

MASTER THE MATERIAL

Test Yourself Answer the following questions on your own first, then check your answers in Appendix E.

1. Stroke a newborn's cheek and the infant will root for a nipple. This illustrates
   a. a reflex.
   b. nurture.
   c. a preference.
   d. continuity.

2. Between ages 3 and 6, the human brain experiences the greatest growth in the _____ lobes, which enable reasoning and planning.

3. Which of the following is true of motor-skill development?

a. It is determined solely by genetic factors.

b. The sequence, but not the timing, is universal.

c. The timing, but not the sequence, is universal.

d. It is determined solely by environmental factors.

4. Why can't we consciously recall learning to walk?

5. Use Piaget's first three stages of cognitive development to explain why young children are not just miniature adults in the way they think.

6. Although Piaget's stage theory continues to inform our understanding of children's thinking, many researchers believe that

a. Piaget's stages begin earlier and development is more continuous than he realized.

b. children do not progress as rapidly as Piaget predicted.

c. few children progress to the concrete operational stage.

d. there is no way of testing much of Piaget's theoretical work.

7. An 8-month-old infant who reacts to a new babysitter by crying and clinging to his father's shoulder is showing _____ _____.

8. In a series of experiments, the Harlows found that monkeys raised with artificial mothers tended, when afraid, to cling to their cloth mother rather than to a wire mother holding the feeding bottle. Why was this finding important?

Continue testing yourself with 🅰 **LearningCurve** or 🅼 **Achieve Read & Practice** to learn and remember most effectively.

MODULE

⑮ Adolescence

LOQ 15-1 How is *adolescence* defined, and how do physical changes affect developing teens?

Many psychologists once believed that childhood sets our traits. Today's developmental psychologists see development as lifelong. As this *life-span perspective* emerged, psychologists began to look at how maturation and experience shape us not only in infancy and childhood, but also—after we are no longer handed the children's menu—in adolescence and beyond. **Adolescence**—the years spent morphing from child to adult—starts with the physical beginnings of sexual maturity and ends with the social achievement of independent adult status. Thus, in cultures where teens are self-supporting, adolescence hardly exists. And in Western cultures, where sexual maturation is occurring earlier and independence later, adolescence is lengthening (Sawyer et al., 2018; Worthman & Trang, 2018).

In industrialized countries, what are the teen years like? In Leo Tolstoy's *Anna Karenina*, the teen years were "that blissful time when childhood is just coming to an end, and out of that vast circle, happy and gay, a path takes shape." But another teenager, Anne Frank, writing in her diary while hiding from the Nazis, described tumultuous teen emotions:

> My treatment varies so much. One day Anne is so sensible and is allowed to know everything; and the next day I hear that Anne is just a silly little goat who doesn't know anything at all and imagines that she's learned a wonderful lot from books. . . . Oh, so many things bubble up inside me as I lie in bed, having to put up with people I'm fed up with, who always misinterpret my intentions.

G. Stanley Hall (1904), one of the first psychologists to describe adolescence, believed that this tension between biological maturity and social dependence creates a period of "storm and stress." It's a time of diminishing parental control (Lionetti et al., 2019). It's also a time when teens crave social acceptance, but often feel socially disconnected. Three in four U.S. friendships started in seventh grade dissolve by the end of eighth grade (Hartl et al., 2015). Such social disconnection hits adolescents hard—increasing their risk for substance abuse and depressive symptoms (Hussong et al., 2019). Indeed, after age

adolescence the transition period from childhood to adulthood, extending from puberty to independence.

puberty the period of sexual maturation, during which a person usually becomes capable of reproducing.

30, many who grow up in independence-fostering Western cultures look back on their teenage years as a time they would not want to relive—a time when their peers' social approval was imperative, their sense of direction in life was in flux, and their feeling of alienation from their parents was deepest (Arnett, 1999; Macfarlane, 1964). But for others, adolescence is a time of vitality without the cares of adulthood—a time of rewarding friendships, heightened idealism, and a growing sense of life's exciting possibilities.

ASK YOURSELF

How will you look back on your life 10 years from now? What could you change so that someday you will recall your choices with satisfaction?

Physical Development

Adolescence begins with **puberty,** the time when we mature sexually. Puberty follows a surge of hormones, which may intensify moods and which trigger the bodily changes discussed in Module 12, Culture, Gender, and Other Environmental Influences.

The Timing of Puberty

Just as in the earlier life stages, the *sequence* of physical changes in puberty (for example, breast buds and visible pubic hair before *menarche*—the first menstrual period) is far more predictable than their *timing*. Some girls start their growth spurt at 9, some boys as late as age 16.

Early maturation can be a challenge. "Early maturing adolescents may be more likely to experience mental health problems attributable to [puberty-related] stress and difficulties," report Josie Ullsperger and Molly Nikolas (2017). This vulnerability is greatest for teen girls and boys with emotionally reactive temperaments. Also, if a girl's physical development outpaces her emotional maturity and her friends' development, she may associate with older adolescents, suffer teasing or sexual harassment, and become anxious or depressed (Alloy et al., 2016; Ge & Natsuaki, 2009; Weingarden & Renshaw, 2012).

The Teenage Brain

The adolescent brain is a work in progress. Until puberty, brain cells increase their connections, like trees growing more roots and branches. Then during adolescence comes a selective *pruning* of unused neurons and connections (Blakemore, 2008). What we don't use, we lose.

As teens mature, their frontal lobes also continue to develop. The continuing growth of *myelin*, the fatty tissue that forms around axons and speeds neurotransmission, enables better communication with other brain regions (Whitaker et al., 2016). These developments bring improved judgment, impulse control, and long-term planning. A landmark study of 11,000 participants from late childhood to early adulthood is examining the factors that influence teens' brain development, such as drugs, screen time, and sleep (NIMH, 2019; Wadman, 2018).

Frontal lobe maturation nevertheless lags behind that of the emotional limbic system. Puberty's hormonal surge and limbic system development help explain teens' occasional impulsiveness, risky behaviors, and emotional storms—slamming doors and turning up the music (Casey & Caudle, 2013; Fuhrmann et al., 2015; Smith, 2018). No wonder younger teens (whose unfinished frontal lobes aren't yet fully equipped for making long-term plans and curbing impulses) may succumb to the lure of smoking or vaping. Teens actually don't underestimate the risks of smoking—or fast driving or unprotected sex. Teens' brains are just biased toward immediate rewards—which helps explain why teens worldwide struggle with self-control (Hansen et al., 2019; Steinberg et al., 2018). The teenage brain is like a car with a forceful accelerator and underdeveloped brakes (**FIGURE 15.1**).

⬇️ **FIGURE 15.1**
Impulse control lags reward seeking Surveys of more than 7000 American 12- to 24-year-olds reveal that sensation seeking peaks in the mid-teens, with impulse control developing more slowly as frontal lobes mature. (National Longitudinal Study of Youth and Children and Young Adults survey data presented by Steinberg, 2013.)

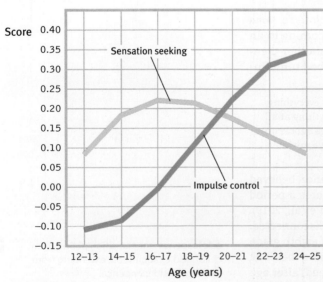

So, when Junior drives recklessly and academically self-destructs, should his parents reassure themselves that "he can't help it; his frontal cortex isn't yet fully grown"? They can at least take hope: Brain changes underlie teens' new self-consciousness about what others are thinking as well as their valuing of risky rewards (Barkley-Levenson & Galván, 2014; Somerville et al., 2013). And the brain with which Junior begins his teens differs from the brain with which he will end his teens. Unless he slows his brain development with heavy drinking—leaving him prone to impulsivity and addiction—his frontal lobes will continue maturing until about age 25 (Crews et al., 2007; Giedd, 2015). They will also become better connected with the limbic system, enabling better emotion regulation (Cohen et al., 2016; Steinberg, 2012).

In 2004, the American Psychological Association (APA) joined seven other medical and mental health associations in filing U.S. Supreme Court briefs, arguing against the death penalty for 16- and 17-year-olds. The briefs documented the teen brain's immaturity "in areas that bear upon adolescent decision making." Brain scans of young teens reveal that frontal lobe immaturity is most evident among juvenile offenders and drug users (Shannon et al., 2011; Whelan et al., 2012). Thus, teens are "less guilty by reason of adolescence," suggested psychologist Laurence Steinberg and law professor Elizabeth Scott (2003; Steinberg et al., 2009). In 2005, by a 5-to-4 margin, the Court concurred, declaring juvenile death penalties unconstitutional. In 2012, the APA offered similar arguments against sentencing juveniles to life without parole (Banville, 2012; Steinberg, 2013). Once again, the Court, by a narrow 5-to-4 vote, concurred.

"Young man, go to your room and stay there until your cerebral cortex matures."

Cognitive Development

LOQ 15-2 How did Piaget, Kohlberg, and later researchers describe adolescent cognitive and moral development?

During the early teen years, *egocentrism* endures, and reasoning is often self-focused. Capable of thinking about their own and others' thinking, teens also begin imagining what others are thinking about *them* and develop an intense awareness of this *imaginary audience*. (They might worry less if they understood their peers' similar self-focus.) Teens also have a tendency to develop a *personal fable*—believing that they are unique and special and what happens to "most people" would never happen to them. "My vaping is just for fun; I would never end up an addicted smoker like my uncle."

Developing Reasoning Power

When adolescents achieve the intellectual summit that Jean Piaget called *formal operations,* they apply their new abstract reasoning tools to the world around them. They may think about what is ideally possible and compare that with the imperfect reality of their society, their parents, and themselves. They may debate human nature, good and evil, truth and justice. Their sense of what's fair changes from simple equality to equity—to what's proportional to merit (Almås et al., 2010). Having left behind the concrete images of early childhood, they may search for spirituality and a deeper meaning of life (Boyatzis, 2012; Elkind, 1970). Reasoning hypothetically and deducing consequences also enables adolescents to detect inconsistencies and spot hypocrisy in others' reasoning. This can lead to heated family debates and silent vows never to lose sight of their own ideals (Peterson et al., 1986).

"When the pilot told us to brace and grab our ankles, the first thing that went through my mind was that we must all look pretty stupid." — Jeremiah Rawlings, age 12, after surviving a 1989 plane crash in Sioux City, Iowa

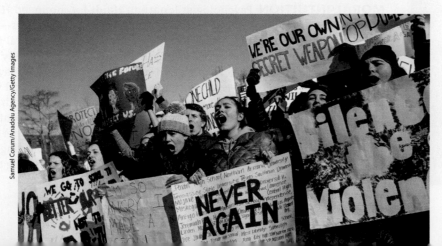

Fed up with firearms After a 2018 mass shooting at a high school in Parkland, Florida, student survivors started the #NeverAgain movement to demand U.S. gun law reform. Hundreds of thousands of teens have since participated in school walkouts and marches, demonstrating their ability to think logically about abstract topics and to voice their ideals. According to Piaget, these teens are in the final cognitive stage, formal operations.

TABLE 15.1 Kohlberg's Levels of Moral Thinking

Kohlberg posed moral dilemmas, such as: "Is it okay to steal medicine to save a loved one?"

Level (approximate age)	Focus	Example of Moral Reasoning
Preconventional morality (before age 9)	Self-interest; obey rules to avoid punishment or gain concrete rewards.	"If you steal the medicine, you will go to jail."
Conventional morality (early adolescence)	Uphold laws and rules to gain social approval or maintain social order.	"We are supposed to take care of our loved ones, so you should steal the drug."
Postconventional morality (adolescence and beyond)	Actions reflect belief in basic rights and self-defined ethical principles.	"People have a right to live."

"I helped a so-called friend commit armed robbery and murder. . . . I was just 17 years old. . . . Been in prison for over 20 years . . . longer than I was ever free. . . . I am among the 300 plus "Juvenile Lifers" in Michigan prisons. I learned and matured a lot since my time incarcerated. I experience great remorse and regret over the tragedy that I ashamedly participated in. But I salvage this experience by learning and growing from it." — M. H., Michigan prison inmate, personal correspondence, 2015

Moral reasoning Bahamians faced a moral dilemma in 2019 when Hurricane Dorian devastated their northern islands. Should they take in family and friends who now had no home? Their reasoning likely reflected different levels of moral thinking, even if they behaved similarly.

Ramon Espinosa/AP Images

Developing Morality

Two crucial tasks of childhood and adolescence are discerning right from wrong and developing character—the psychological muscles for controlling impulses. Children learn to empathize with others, an ability that continues to develop in adolescence. To be a moral person is to *think* morally and *act* accordingly. Jean Piaget and Lawrence Kohlberg proposed that moral reasoning guides moral actions. A newer view builds on psychology's game-changing recognition that much of our functioning occurs not on the "high road" of deliberate, conscious thinking but on the "low road," unconscious and automatic.

MORAL REASONING Piaget (1932) believed that children's moral judgments build on their cognitive development. Agreeing with Piaget, Lawrence Kohlberg (1981, 1984) sought to describe the development of *moral reasoning,* the thinking that occurs as we consider right and wrong. Kohlberg posed moral dilemmas (for example, whether a person should steal medicine to save a loved one's life) and asked children, adolescents, and adults whether the action was right or wrong. His analysis of their answers led him to propose three basic levels of moral thinking: *preconventional, conventional,* and *postconventional* (**TABLE 15.1**). Kohlberg claimed these levels form a moral ladder. As with all stage theories, the sequence is unvarying. We begin on the bottom rung and rise to varying heights; at the postconventional level, we may place others' comfort above our own (Crockett et al., 2014). Infants recognize right and wrong, preferring moral over immoral action (Cowell & Decety, 2015). Preschoolers, typically identifying with their cultural group, conform to and enforce its moral norms (Tomasello, 2019; Yudkin et al., 2019). When those norms reward kind actions, preschoolers help others (Carragan & Dweck, 2014). From a young age, we seem hard-wired to dislike unfairness (Elenbaas, 2019).

Kohlberg's critics have noted that his postconventional stage is culturally limited. It appears mostly among people from large *individualist* societies that give priority to personal goals, rather than from *collectivist* societies that place more value on group goals (Barrett et al., 2016; Eckensberger, 1994). In more collectivist India, morality is less a matter of personal choice and more a role-related duty (Miller et al., 2017). Kohlberg's theory can also be viewed as male-focused, given women's tendency to emphasize care for others in need over what is "fair" (Gilligan, 1982, 2015).

MORAL INTUITION Psychologist Jonathan Haidt [pronounced HITE] (2002, 2012) believes that much of our morality is rooted in *moral intuitions*—"quick gut feelings." According to this intuitionist view, the mind makes moral judgments in much the same way that it makes aesthetic judgments—quickly and automatically. Feelings of disgust or of elation trigger moral reasoning, says Haidt.

One woman recalled traveling through her snowy neighborhood with three young men as they passed "an elderly woman with a shovel in her driveway. . . . [O]ne of the guys . . . asked the driver to let him off there. . . . [M]y mouth dropped in shock as I realized that he was offering to shovel her walk for her." Witnessing this unexpected goodness triggered elevation: "I felt like jumping out of the car and hugging this guy. I felt like singing and running, or skipping and laughing. I felt like saying nice things about people" (Haidt, 2000).

"Could human morality really be run by the moral emotions," Haidt wonders, "while moral reasoning struts about pretending to be in control?" Consider the desire to punish. Laboratory games reveal that the desire to punish wrongdoing is mostly driven not by reason (such as an objective calculation that punishment deters crime) but rather by emotional reactions, such as moral outrage and the pleasure of revenge (Chester & DeWall, 2016; Darley, 2009). After the emotional fact, moral reasoning—our mind's press secretary—aims to convince us and others of the logic of what we have intuitively felt.

This intuitionist perspective on morality finds support in a study of moral paradoxes. Imagine seeing a runaway trolley headed for five people. All will certainly be killed unless you throw a switch that diverts the trolley onto another track, where it will kill one person. Should you throw the switch? Most say *Yes*. Kill one, save five.

Now imagine the same dilemma, with one change. This time, you must save the five by pushing a large stranger onto the tracks, where he will die as his body stops the trolley. In both versions of this famous "trolley problem," the logic is the same— kill one, save five—but most now say *No*. One brain-imaging study showed that only the body-pushing type of moral dilemma activated emotion-area neural responses (Greene et al., 2001). Thus, our moral judgments provide another example of the two-track mind—of dual processing (Feinberg et al., 2012). Moral reasoning, centered in one brain area, says throw the switch. Our intuitive moral emotions, rooted in other brain areas, override reason when saying *don't* push the man. We may liken our moral cognition to our phone's camera settings. Usually, we rely on the default settings. Yet sometimes we use reason to manually override those settings or to adjust the resulting image (Greene, 2010).

THE LITTLE ENGINE THAT FACED A TOUGH MORAL DILEMMA

Trevor Spaulding/The New Yorker Collection/The Cartoon Bank

MORAL ACTION Our moral thinking and feeling surely affect our moral talk. But sometimes talk is cheap and emotions are fleeting. Morality involves *doing* the right thing, and what we do also depends on social influences. As political theorist Hannah Arendt (1963) observed, many Nazi concentration camp guards during World War II were ordinary "moral" people corrupted by a powerfully evil situation.

Today's character education programs tend to focus on the whole moral package— thinking, feeling, and *doing* the right thing. In service-learning programs, teens have tutored, cleaned up their neighborhoods, and assisted older adults. The result? The teens' sense of competence and desire to serve has increased, school absenteeism and dropout rates have fallen, and violent behavior has diminished (Andersen, 1998; Heller, 2014; Piliavin, 2003). *Moral action* feeds moral attitudes.

These programs also teach the self-discipline needed to restrain one's own impulses. Those who have learned to *delay gratification*—to live with one eye on the future—have become more socially responsible, academically successful, and productive (Daly et al., 2015; Funder & Block, 1989; Sawyer et al., 2015). A preference for large-later rather than small-now rewards also minimizes one's risk of problem gambling, smoking, and delinquency (Callan et al., 2011; Ert et al., 2013; Lee et al., 2017).

In one of psychology's best-known experiments, Walter Mischel (2014) gave 4-year-olds a choice between one marshmallow now, or two marshmallows when he returned a few minutes later. The children who delayed gratification went on to have higher college completion rates and incomes, and less often suffered addiction problems. A replication of this famous study found a more modest effect (Watts et al., 2018). But the big idea remains: Maturity and life success grow from the ability to spurn small pleasures now in favor of greater pleasures later (Watts et al., 2018). Delaying gratification fosters flourishing.

"It is a delightful harmony when doing and saying go together." — Michel Eyquem de Montaigne (1533–1592)

"The best time to plant a tree was 20 years ago. The second best time is now." — Chinese proverb

identity our sense of self; according to Erikson, the adolescent's task is to solidify a sense of self by testing and integrating various roles.

social identity the "we" aspect of our self-concept; the part of our answer to "Who am I?" that comes from our group memberships.

ASK YOURSELF

Think about a difficult decision you had to make in early adolescence and later regretted. What did you do? How would you do things differently now?

RETRIEVAL PRACTICE

RP-1 According to Kohlberg, _____ morality focuses on self-interest, _____ morality focuses on self-defined ethical principles, and _____ morality focuses on upholding laws and social rules.

RP-2 How has Kohlberg's theory of moral reasoning been criticized?

ANSWERS IN APPENDIX E

Social Development

LOQ 15-3 What are the social tasks and challenges of adolescence?

Theorist Erik Erikson (1963) contended that each stage of life has its own *psychosocial* task, a crisis that needs resolution. Young children wrestle with issues of *trust,* then *autonomy* (independence), then *initiative.* School-age children strive for *competence,* feeling able and productive. The adolescent's task is to synthesize past, present, and future possibilities into a clearer sense of self (**TABLE 15.2**). Adolescents wonder, "Who am I as an individual? What do I want to do with my life? What values should I live by? What do I believe in?" Erikson called this quest the adolescent's *search for identity.*

As sometimes happens in psychology, Erikson's interests were bred by his own life experience. As the son of a Jewish mother and a Danish Gentile father, Erikson was "doubly an outsider," reported Morton Hunt (1993, p. 391). He was "scorned as a Jew in school but mocked as a Gentile in the synagogue because of his blond hair and blue eyes." Such episodes fueled his interest in the adolescent struggle for identity.

"Somewhere between the ages of 10 and 13 (depending on how hormone-enhanced their beef was), children entered adolescence, a.k.a. 'the de-cutening.'" — Jon Stewart et al., *Earth (The Book)*, 2010

TABLE 15.2 Erikson's Stages of Psychosocial Development

Stage (approximate age)	Issue	Description of Task
Infancy (to 1 year)	Trust vs. mistrust	If needs are dependably met, infants develop a sense of basic trust.
Toddlerhood (1 to 3 years)	Autonomy vs. shame and doubt	Toddlers learn to exercise their will and do things for themselves, or they doubt their abilities.
Preschool (3 to 6 years)	Initiative vs. guilt	Preschoolers learn to initiate tasks and carry out plans, or they feel guilty about their efforts to be independent.
Elementary school (6 years to puberty)	Competence vs. inferiority	Children learn the pleasure of applying themselves to tasks, or they feel inferior.
Adolescence (teen years into 20s)	Identity vs. role confusion	Teenagers work at refining a sense of self by testing roles and then integrating them to form a single identity, or they become confused about who they are.
Young adulthood (20s to early 40s)	Intimacy vs. isolation	Young adults struggle to form close relationships and to gain the capacity for intimate love, or they feel socially isolated.
Middle adulthood (40s to 60s)	Generativity vs. stagnation	Middle-aged people discover a sense of contributing to the world, usually through family and work, or they may feel a lack of purpose.
Late adulthood (late 60s and up)	Integrity vs. despair	Reflecting on their lives, older adults may feel a sense of satisfaction or failure.

chee gin tan/Getty Images

Competence vs. inferiority

Forming an Identity

To refine their sense of identity, adolescents in individualist cultures usually try out different "selves" in different situations. They may act out one self at home, another with friends, another online, and still another at school. If two situations overlap—as when a teenager brings new friends home—the discomfort can be considerable (Klimstra et al., 2015). The teen often wonders, "Which self should I be? Which is the real me?" The eventual resolution is a self-definition that unifies the various selves into a consistent and comfortable sense of who one is—an **identity.**

For both adolescents and adults, group identities are often formed by how we differ from those around us—in gender and sexual orientation, in age and relative wealth, in abilities and beliefs. When living in Britain, I [DM] become conscious of my Americanness. When spending time in Hong Kong, I [ND] become conscious of my White race. For international students, for those of a minority ethnic or religious group, for gay and transgender people, or for people with a disability, a **social identity** often forms around their distinctiveness. (You can find more on social identity and prejudice in the Social Psychology modules.)

Erikson noticed that some adolescents forge their identity early, simply by adopting their parents' values and expectations. Other adolescents may adopt the identity of a particular peer group—jocks, preps, geeks, band kids, debaters. Traditional, collectivist cultures teach adolescents who they are, rather than encouraging them to decide on their own. Bicultural adolescents form complex identities as they integrate group memberships and their feelings about them (Marks et al., 2011).

Most young people develop a sense of contentment with their lives. Which statement best describes you: "I would choose my life the way it is right now" or "I wish I were somebody else"? When American teens answered, 81 percent picked the first, and 19 percent the second (Lyons, 2004). Reflecting on their existence, 75 percent of American college and university students say they "discuss religion/spirituality" with friends, "pray," and agree that "we are all spiritual beings" and "search for meaning/purpose in life" (Astin et al., 2004; Bryant & Astin, 2008). This would not surprise researchers who have contended that a key task of adolescence is to achieve a purpose—a desire to accomplish something personally meaningful that makes a difference to the world beyond oneself (Damon et al., 2003; Sumner et al., 2018).

Interventions that aim to boost adolescents' health and well-being work best when appealing to their desires for self-esteem, status, and respect (Yeager et al., 2018). Rather than saying "Eating well is important for your health," a more effective message would be "Buying junk food gives money to rich adults who disrespect you by thinking you don't know better."

During the early to mid-teen years, self-esteem typically falls and, for girls, depression scores often increase (Salk et al., 2017). But self-image rebounds during the late teens and twenties, and self-esteem gender differences shrink (Zuckerman et al., 2016). Agreeableness and emotional stability scores also increase in late adolescence (Klimstra et al., 2009).

> "Self-consciousness, the recognition of a creature by itself as a 'self,' [cannot] exist except in contrast with an 'other,' a something which is not the self." — C. S. Lewis, *The Problem of Pain*, 1940

> "I don't think any of us like to be reduced to just one label." — Actor Riz Ahmed, 2016

Teen depression and suicide rates have increased since the spread of social media and the peer comparisons they enable. (There is more on this in Module 35.) If your life feels dull compared with all the fun experiences your online friends are posting, be consoled: Most of your friends feel the same way (Deri et al., 2017).

Ian Cook/Image Source

Who shall I be today? By varying the way they look, adolescents try out different "selves." Although we eventually form a consistent and stable sense of identity, the self we present may change with the situation.

intimacy in Erikson's theory, the ability to form close, loving relationships; a primary developmental task in young adulthood.

emerging adulthood a period from about age 18 to the mid-twenties, when many in Western cultures are no longer adolescents but have not yet achieved full independence as adults.

These are the years when many people in industrialized countries begin exploring new opportunities by attending college or working full time. Many college and university seniors have achieved a clearer identity and a more positive self-concept than they had as first-year students (Waterman, 1988). Those who have achieved a clear sense of identity are less prone to alcohol misuse (Bishop et al., 2005).

Erikson contended that adolescent identity formation (which continues into adulthood) is followed in young adulthood by a developing capacity for **intimacy,** the ability to form emotionally close relationships. When Mihaly Csikszentmihalyi [chick-SENT-me-hi] and Jeremy Hunter (2003) used a beeper to sample the daily experiences of American teens, they found them unhappiest when alone and happiest when with friends. Romantic relationships, which tend to be emotionally intense, are reported by some two in three North American 17-year-olds, but by fewer in collectivist countries such as China (Collins et al., 2009; Li et al., 2010). Those who enjoy high-quality (intimate, supportive) relationships with family and friends tend also to enjoy similarly high-quality romantic relationships in adolescence, which set the stage for healthy adult relationships. Such relationships are, for most of us, a source of great pleasure. As Aristotle long ago recognized, we humans are "the social animal." We have a deep need to belong. Relationships matter.

> For an interactive self-assessment of your own identity, see *Topic Tutorial: PsychSim6, Who Am I?*

FIGURE 15.2
The changing parent-child relationship In a large national study of Canadian families, the typically close, warm relationships between children and their parents loosened as they became teens (Pepler & Craig, 2012).

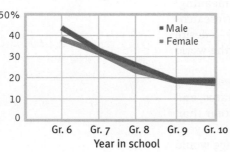

"I love u guys." — Emily Keyes' final text message to her parents before dying in a Colorado school shooting, 2006

"She says she's someone from your past who gave birth to you, and raised you, and sacrificed everything so you could have whatever you wanted."

Parent and Peer Relationships

LOQ 15-4 How do parents and peers influence adolescents?

Adolescence is typically a time of diminishing parental influence and growing peer influence (Blakemore, 2018). The preschooler who can't be close enough to her mother, who loves to touch and cling to her, becomes the 14-year-old who wouldn't be caught dead holding hands with Mom. The transition occurs gradually (**FIGURE 15.2**). As children, we more readily recognize adult faces than other children's faces; by adolescence, we display superior recognition for our peers' faces (Picci & Scherf, 2016). Puberty alters attachments and primes perceptions.

By adolescence, parent-child arguments occur more often, usually over mundane things—household chores, bedtime, homework (Tesser et al., 1989). Conflict during the transition to adolescence tends to be greater with first-born than with second-born children, and greater with mothers than with fathers (Burk et al., 2009; Shanahan et al., 2007).

For a minority of parents and their adolescents, differences lead to real splits and great stress (Steinberg & Morris, 2001). But most disagreements are at the level of harmless bickering. With sons, the issues often are behavior problems, such as acting out or hygiene; for daughters, the issues commonly involve relationships, such as dating and friendships (Schlomer et al., 2011). In a survey of nearly 6000 adolescents in 10 countries—from Australia to Bangladesh to Turkey—most said they like their parents (Offer et al., 1988). "We usually get along but . . . ," adolescents often reported (Galambos, 1992; Steinberg, 1987).

Positive parent-teen relations and positive peer relations often go hand in hand. High school girls who had the most affectionate relationships with their mothers tended also to enjoy the most intimate friendships with girlfriends (Gold & Yanof, 1985). And teens who felt close to their parents have tended to be healthy and happy and to do well in school (Resnick et al., 1997). Of course, we can state this correlation the other way: Misbehaving teens are more likely to have tense relationships with parents and other adults.

Although heredity does much of the heavy lifting in forming individual temperament and personality differences, parents and peers influence teens' behavior and attitudes. When with peers, teens discount the future and focus more on immediate rewards (O'Brien et al., 2011). Most teens are herd animals. They talk, dress, and act more like their peers than their parents. What their friends are, they often become, and what "everybody's doing," they often do. Teens' social media use illustrates the power of peer influence. Compared to photos with few likes, teens prefer photos with many other likes. Moreover, when viewing many-liked photos, teens' brains become more active in areas associated with reward processing and imitation (Sherman et al., 2016). Liking and doing what everybody else likes and does feels good.

"First, I did things for my parents' approval, then I did things for my parents' disapproval, and now I don't know why I do things."

Both online and face-to-face, for those who feel excluded and bullied by their peers, the pain is acute. Most excluded "students suffer in silence. . . . A small number act out in violent ways against their classmates" (Aronson, 2001). The pain of exclusion also persists. In one large study, those who were bullied as children showed poorer physical health and greater psychological distress 40 years later (Takizawa et al., 2014).

ASK YOURSELF

What are the most positive and the most negative things you remember about your own adolescence? Who do you credit or blame more—your parents or your peers?

Emerging Adulthood

LOQ 15-5 What is *emerging adulthood*?

In the Western world, adolescence now roughly corresponds to the teen years. At earlier times, and in other parts of the world today, this slice of life has been much smaller (Baumeister & Tice, 1986). Shortly after sexual maturity, young people would assume adult responsibilities and status. The event might be celebrated with an elaborate initiation—a public rite of passage. The new adult would then work, marry, and have children.

When schooling became compulsory in many Western countries, independence was put on hold until after graduation. Adolescents are now taking more time to establish themselves as adults. Today's adolescents are less likely to work for pay, drive, or have romantic attachments (Twenge & Park, 2019). In the United States, the average age at first marriage has increased more than 5 years since 1960, to 29 for men, and 27 for women. In 1960, three in four women and two in three men had, by age 30, finished school, left home, become financially independent, married, and had a child. In the early twenty-first century, fewer than half of 30-year-old women and one-third of men were meeting these five milestones (Henig, 2010). In 2016, 15 percent of 25- to 35-year-old Americans—double the 1981 proportion—were living in their parents' home (Fry, 2017).

As we noted, later independence and earlier sexual maturity have widened the once-brief interlude between biological maturity and social independence (**FIGURE 15.3**). In prosperous communities, the time from 18 to the mid-twenties is an increasingly not-yet-settled phase of life, now often called **emerging adulthood** (Arnett, 2006, 2007; Reitzle, 2006). No longer adolescents, these emerging adults—having not yet assumed full adult responsibilities and independence—feel "in between."

▼ **FIGURE 15.3**
The transition to adulthood is being stretched from both ends In the 1890s, the average interval between a woman's first menstrual period and marriage, which typically marked a transition to adulthood, was about 7 years. By 2006, in industrialized countries, that gap had widened in well-off communities to about 14 years (Finer & Philbin, 2014; Guttmacher Institute, 1994). Although many adults are unmarried, later marriage combines with prolonged education and earlier menarche to help stretch out the transition to adulthood.

Barbara Smaller/Cartoon Stock

"I just don't know what to do with myself in that long stretch after college but before social security."

Those furthering their education or working may be managing their own time and priorities. Yet they may be doing so from their parents' home, unable to afford their own place and perhaps still emotionally dependent as well (Fry, 2017). Recognizing today's more gradually emerging adulthood, the U.S. government now allows dependent children up to age 26 to remain on their parents' health insurance (Cohen, 2010).

ASK YOURSELF

What do you think makes a person an adult? Do you feel like an adult? Why or why not?

RETRIEVAL PRACTICE

RP-3 Match the psychosocial development stage below (i–viii) with the issue that Erikson believed we wrestle with at that stage (a–h).

i.	Infancy	a.	Generativity vs. stagnation
ii.	Toddlerhood	b.	Integrity vs. despair
iii.	Preschool	c.	Initiative vs. guilt
iv.	Elementary school	d.	Intimacy vs. isolation
v.	Adolescence	e.	Identity vs. role confusion
vi.	Young adulthood	f.	Competence vs. inferiority
vii.	Middle adulthood	g.	Trust vs. mistrust
viii.	Late adulthood	h.	Autonomy vs. shame and doubt

ANSWERS IN APPENDIX E

---

15 REVIEW Adolescence

LEARNING OBJECTIVES

Test Yourself Answer these repeated Learning Objective Questions on your own (before checking the answers in Appendix D) to improve your retention of the concepts (McDaniel et al., 2009, 2015).

LOQ 15-1 How is *adolescence* defined, and how do physical changes affect developing teens?

LOQ 15-2 How did Piaget, Kohlberg, and later researchers describe adolescent cognitive and moral development?

LOQ 15-3 What are the social tasks and challenges of adolescence?

LOQ 15-4 How do parents and peers influence adolescents?

LOQ 15-5 What is *emerging adulthood*?

TERMS AND CONCEPTS TO REMEMBER

Test Yourself Write down the definition in your own words, then check your answer.

adolescence, p. 189

puberty, p. 190

identity, p. 194

social identity, p. 194

intimacy, p. 196

emerging adulthood, p. 196

MASTER THE MATERIAL

Test Yourself Answer the following questions on your own first, then check your answers in Appendix E.

1. Adolescence is marked by the onset of
   a. an identity crisis.
   b. puberty.
   c. moral reasoning.
   d. parent-child conflict.

2. According to Piaget, a person who can think logically about abstractions is in the _____ _____ stage.

3. In Erikson's stages, the primary task during adolescence is
   a. attaining formal operations.
   b. forging an identity.
   c. developing a sense of intimacy with another person.
   d. living independent of parents.

4. Some developmental psychologists refer to the period that occurs in some Western cultures from age 18 to the mid-twenties as _____ _____.

Continue testing yourself with 🅐 **LearningCurve** or 🅰 **Achieve Read & Practice** to learn and remember most effectively.

MODULE 16 Adulthood

The unfolding of our lives continues across the life span. It is, however, more difficult to generalize about adulthood stages than about life's early years. If you know that James is a 1-year-old and Jamal is a 10-year-old, you could say a great deal about each child. Not so with adults who differ by a similar number of years. The boss may be 30 or 60; the marathon runner may be 20 or 50; the 19-year-old may be a parent who supports a child or a child who receives an allowance. Yet our life courses are in some ways similar. Physically, cognitively, and especially socially, we differ at age 50 from our 25-year-old selves. In the discussion that follows, we recognize these differences and use three terms: *early adulthood* (roughly twenties and thirties), *middle adulthood* (to age 65), and *late adulthood* (the years after 65). Within each of these stages, people vary in physical, psychological, and social development.

ASK YOURSELF

Imagining the future, how do you think you might change? How might you stay the same? In what ways do you most want to grow as a person?

How old does a person have to be before you think of him or her as old? Depends on who you ask. For 18- to 29-year-olds, 67 was old. For those 60 and over, old was 76 (Yankelovich Partners, 1995).

Physical Development

LOQ 16-1 What physical changes occur during middle and late adulthood?

Like the declining daylight after the summer solstice, our physical abilities—muscular strength, reaction time, sensory keenness, and cardiac output—all begin an almost imperceptible decline in our mid-twenties. Athletes are often the first to notice. Baseball players peak at about age 27—with 60 percent of Most Valuable Player awardees since 1985 coming within 2 years of that age (Silver, 2012). But most of us—especially those of us whose daily lives do not require top physical performance—hardly perceive the early signs of decline.

Rick Doyle/Getty Images

Adult abilities vary widely George Blair was, at age 92, the world's oldest barefoot water skier. He is shown here in 2002 when he first set the record, at age 87. (He died at age 98.)

Physical Changes in Middle Adulthood

Athletes over 40 know all too well that physical decline gradually accelerates. As a lifelong basketball player, I [DM] am playing less often and no longer racing for that loose ball. But even diminished vigor is sufficient for normal activities. Moreover, during early and middle adulthood, physical vigor has less to do with age than with a person's health and exercise habits. Many physically fit 50-year-olds run 4 miles with ease, while sedentary 25-year-olds find themselves huffing and puffing up two flights of stairs.

Aging also brings a gradual decline in fertility, especially for women. For a 35- to 39-year-old woman, the chance of getting pregnant after a single act of intercourse is half that of a woman 19 to 26 (Dunson et al., 2002). Men experience a gradual decline in sperm count, testosterone level, and speed of erection and ejaculation. Women experience **menopause** as menstrual cycles end, usually within a few years of age 50. Some may experience distress, as do some men who experience declining virility and physical capacities. But most people age without such problems.

Sexual activity remains satisfying, though less frequent, after middle age. This was true of 70 percent of Canadians surveyed (ages 40 to 64) and 75 percent of Finns (ages 65 to 74) (Kontula & Haavio-Mannila, 2009; Wright, 2006). In one survey, 75 percent of respondents reported being sexually active into their eighties (Schick et al., 2010).

The New Yorker Collection, 1999 Tom Cheney from cartoonbank.com

"Happy fortieth. I'll take the muscle tone in your upper arms, the girlish timbre of your voice, your amazing tolerance for caffeine, and your ability to digest french fries. The rest of you can stay."

menopause the time of natural cessation of menstruation; also refers to the biological changes a woman experiences as her ability to reproduce declines.

"The things that stop you having sex with age are exactly the same as those that stop you riding a bicycle (bad health, thinking it looks silly, no bicycle)." — Alex Comfort, *The Joy of Sex*, 2002

"I intend to live forever—so far, so good."
— Comedian Steven Wright

And in an American Association of Retired Persons sexuality survey, it was not until age 75 or older that most women and nearly half of men reported little sexual desire (DeLamater, 2012; DeLamater & Sill, 2005). Most older people sustain sexual satisfaction even as sexual frequency subsides (Forbes et al., 2017; Schick et al., 2010). Given good health and a willing partner, desire, though simmered down, lives on.

Physical Changes in Late Adulthood

Is old age "more to be feared than death" (Juvenal, *The Satires*)? Or is life "most delightful when it is on the downward slope" (Seneca, *Epistulae ad Lucilium*)? What is it like to grow old?

LIFE EXPECTANCY From 1950 to 2015, worldwide life expectancy at birth increased from 50 to 73 years (Dicker et al., 2018). (See **FIGURE 16.1**.) What a gift—two decades more of life! In China, the United States, the United Kingdom, Canada, and Australia (to name some countries where students read this book), life expectancy has risen to 76, 79, 81, 82, and 82, respectively (World Bank, 2019). This increasing life expectancy (humanity's greatest achievement, say some) combines with decreasing birthrates: Older adults are a growing population segment, creating an increasing demand for hearing aids, retirement villages, and nursing homes. Today, 13 percent of people worldwide are 60 or older. The United Nations (2017) projects that proportion will more than double by 2100.

Throughout the life span, males are more prone to dying. Although 126 male embryos begin life for every 100 females, the sex ratio is down to 105 males for every 100 females at birth (Strickland, 1992). During the first year, male infants' death rates exceed females' by one-fourth. Worldwide, women outlive men by 4.7 years (WHO, 2016b). (Rather than marrying a man older than themselves, 20-year-old women who want a husband who shares their life expectancy should wait for the 16-year-old boys to mature.) By age 100, women outnumber men 5 to 1.

But few of us live to 100. Disease strikes. The body ages. Its cells stop reproducing. It becomes frail and vulnerable to tiny insults—hot weather, a fall, a mild infection—that at age 20 would have been trivial. Tips of chromosomes, called *telomeres*, wear down, much as the tip of a shoelace frays. This wear is accelerated by smoking, obesity, or stress. Breast-fed children have longer telomeres, while those who suffer frequent abuse or bullying exhibit the biological scars of shortened telomeres (Shalev et al., 2013). As telomeres shorten, aging cells may die without being replaced with perfect genetic replicas (Epel, 2009).

World record for longevity? French woman Jeanne Calment, the oldest human in history with authenticated age, died in 1998 at age 122 (Robine & Allard, 1999). At age 100, she was still riding a bike.

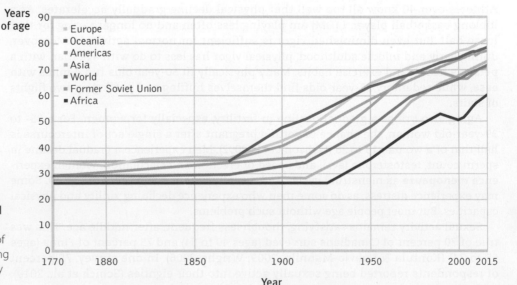

➔ FIGURE 16.1
Life expectancy since 1770, by world regions With improved sanitation, modern medicine, and the introduction of antibiotics, infant mortality declined during the twentieth century and life expectancy increased (Roser, 2019).

Chronic anger and depression increase our risk of premature death. But low stress and good health habits enable longevity, as does a positive spirit. Researchers have even observed an intriguing *death-deferral* phenomenon (Shimizu & Pelham, 2008). Across one 15-year period, 2000 to 3000 more Americans died on the 2 days after Christmas than on Christmas and the 2 days before. The death rate also increases when people reach their birthdays, and when they survive until after other milestones, like the first day of the new millennium.

SENSORY ABILITIES, STRENGTH, AND STAMINA Although physical decline begins in early adulthood, we are not usually acutely aware of it until later in life, when the stairs get steeper, the print gets smaller, and other people seem to mumble more. Visual sharpness diminishes, as does distance perception and adaptation to light-level changes. Muscle strength, reaction time, and stamina also diminish, as do smell, hearing, and touch. In Wales, teens' loitering around a convenience store has been discouraged by a device that emits an aversive high-pitched sound that almost no one over 30 can hear (Lyall, 2005).

With age, the eye's pupil shrinks and its lens becomes less transparent, reducing the amount of light reaching the retina. A 65-year-old retina receives only about one-third as much light as its 20-year-old counterpart (Kline & Schieber, 1985). Thus, to see as well as a 20-year-old when reading or driving, a 65-year-old needs three times as much light—a reason for buying cars with untinted windshields. This also explains why older people sometimes ask younger people, "Don't you need better light for reading?"

HEALTH As people age, they care less about what their bodies look like and more about how their bodies function. For those growing older, there is both bad and good news about health. The bad news: The body's disease-fighting immune system weakens, making older adults more susceptible to life-threatening ailments such as cancer and pneumonia. The good news: Thanks partly to a lifetime's accumulation of antibodies, people over 65 suffer fewer short-term ailments, such as common flu and cold viruses. One study found they were half as likely as 20-year-olds and one-fifth as likely as preschoolers to suffer upper respiratory flu each year (National Center for Health Statistics, 1990).

THE AGING BRAIN Up to the teen years, we process information with greater and greater speed (Fry & Hale, 1996; Kail, 1991). But compared with teens and young adults, older people take a bit more time to react, to solve perceptual puzzles, even to remember names (Bashore et al., 1997; Verhaeghen & Salthouse, 1997). At video games, most 70-year-olds are no match for a 20-year-old. This processing lag can also have deadly consequences (Aichele et al., 2016). As **FIGURE 16.2** indicates, fatal accident rates per mile driven increase sharply after age 75. By age 85, they exceed the 16-year-old level. Older drivers appear to focus well on the road ahead, but attend less to other vehicles approaching from the side (Pollatsek et al., 2012).

Brain regions important to memory begin to atrophy during aging (Fraser et al., 2015; Ritchie et al., 2015). The blood-brain barrier also breaks down beginning in the hippocampus,

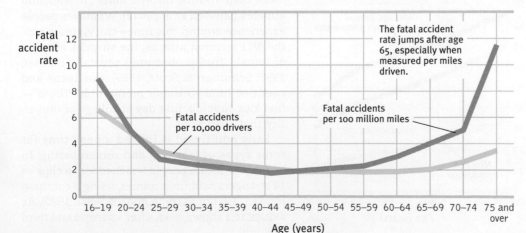

Fatal accident rate

The fatal accident rate jumps after age 65, especially when measured per miles driven.

Fatal accidents per 10,000 drivers

Fatal accidents per 100 million miles

Age (years): 16–19 20–24 25–29 30–34 35–39 40–44 45–49 50–54 55–59 60–64 65–69 70–74 75 and over

Suiting up for old age A long life is a gift. To reach old age, it takes good genes, a nurturing environment, and a little luck. New technology allows you to put yourself in your elders' shoes. In these special suits, younger people can hear, see, and move like a typical 85-year-old.

"For some reason, possibly to save ink, the restaurants had started printing their menus in letters the height of bacteria."
— Dave Barry, *Dave Barry Turns Fifty*, 1998

Most stairway falls taken by older people occur on the top step, precisely where the person typically descends from a window-lit hallway into the darker stairwell (Fozard & Popkin, 1978). Our knowledge of aging could be used to design environments that would reduce such accidents.

FIGURE 16.2
Age and driver fatalities Slowing reactions contribute to increased accident risk among those 75 and older, and older adults' greater fragility increases their risk of death when accidents happen (NHTSA, 2000). Would you favor driver exams based on performance, not age, to screen out those whose slow reactions or sensory impairments indicate accident risk?

which furthers cognitive decline (Montagne et al., 2015). No wonder older adults feel even older after taking a memory test: It's like "aging 5 years in 5 minutes," joked one research team (Hughes et al., 2013). In early adulthood, a small, gradual net loss of brain cells begins, contributing by age 80 to a brain-weight reduction of 5 percent or so. We know that our frontal lobes help us override undesirable urges—their slow development (not fully mature until about age 25) helps account for teen impulsivity. Late in life, some of that impulsiveness often returns as those same frontal lobes begin to atrophy, seemingly explaining older people's occasional blunt questions ("Have you put on weight?") or inappropriate comments (von Hippel, 2007, 2015). But good news: There is still some *plasticity* in the aging brain, which partly compensates for what it loses by recruiting and reorganizing neural networks (Park & McDonough, 2013). During memory tasks, for example, the left frontal lobes are especially active in young adult brains, while older adult brains use both left and right frontal lobes.

EXERCISE AND AGING   And more good news: Exercise slows aging, as shown in studies of identical twin pairs in which only one twin exercised (Iso-Markku et al., 2016; Rottensteiner et al., 2015). Midlife and older adults who do more exercising and less sitting around tend to be mentally quick older adults (Kramer & Colcombe, 2018; Won et al., 2019). Physical exercise not only enhances muscles, bones, and energy and helps prevent obesity and heart disease; it maintains the telomeres that protect the chromosome ends and even appears to slow the progression of Alzheimer's disease (Kivipelto & Håkansson, 2017; Loprinzi et al., 2015; Smith et al., 2014).

Exercise also appears to stimulate *neurogenesis*—the development of new brain cells—and neural connections, thanks perhaps to increased oxygen and nutrient flow (Erickson et al., 2010; Pereira et al., 2007). Sedentary older adults randomly assigned to aerobic exercise programs exhibited enhanced memory, sharpened judgment, and reduced risk of severe cognitive decline (Northey et al., 2018; Raji et al., 2016; Smith, 2016). In the aging brain, exercise reduces brain shrinkage (Gow et al., 2012). And it increases the cellular mitochondria that help power both muscles and brain cells (Steiner et al., 2011). We are more likely to rust from disuse than to wear out from overuse. Fit bodies support fit minds.

Cognitive Development
Aging and Memory

LOQ 16-2   How does memory change with age?

Among the most intriguing developmental psychology questions is whether adult cognitive abilities, such as memory, intelligence, and creativity, parallel the gradually accelerating decline of physical abilities.

As we age, we remember some things well. Looking back in later life, adults asked to recall the one or two most important events over the last half-century tend to name events from their teens or twenties (Conway et al., 2005; Rubin et al., 1998). They also display this "reminiscence bump" when asked to name their all-time favorite music, movies, and athletes (Janssen et al., 2012). Whatever people experience around this time—the Vietnam war, the 9/11 terrorist attacks, the surprise election of Donald Trump—becomes pivotal (Pillemer, 1998; Schuman & Scott, 1989). Our teens and twenties hold so many memorable "firsts"—first kiss, first job, first day at college or university, first apartment.

Early adulthood is indeed a peak time for some types of learning and remembering. In one test of recall, people watched video clips as 14 strangers said their names, using a common format: "Hi, I'm Larry" (Crook & West, 1990). As **FIGURE 16.3** shows, even after a second and third

The New Yorker Collection Kaamran Hafeez from cartoonbank.com

"I've been working out for six months, but all my gains have been in cognitive function."

If you are within five years of 20, what experiences from the past year will you likely never forget? (This is the time of your life you may best remember when you are 50.)

➔ FIGURE 16.3

Tests of recall   Recalling new names introduced once, twice, or three times is easier for younger adults than for older ones. (Data from Crook & West, 1990.)

replay of the introductions with more personal information, younger adults consistently remembered more names than older adults. How well older people remember depends in part on the task. In another experiment, when asked to *recognize* 24 words they had earlier tried to memorize, older adults showed no memory decline. When asked to *recall* that information without clues, however, the decline was greater (**FIGURE 16.4**).

Teens and young adults surpass both young children and 70-year-olds at *prospective memory* ("Remember to . . .") (Zimmermann & Meier, 2006). But older people's prospective memory remains strong when events help trigger a memory (as when walking by a convenience store triggers "Pick up milk!"). Time-based tasks ("Client meeting at 3:00 P.M.") and especially habitual tasks ("Take medications at 9:00 A.M., 2:00 P.M., and 6:00 P.M.") can be challenging (Einstein & McDaniel, 1990; Einstein et al., 1995, 1998). To minimize such problems, older adults rely more on time management and reminder cues, such as notes to themselves (Henry et al., 2004). This might have helped John Basinger, who, at age 76, memorized all 12 volumes of John Milton's epic poem *Paradise Lost* and became the subject of a psychology journal article (Seamon et al., 2010; Weir, 2010). A local paper scheduled an interview with Basinger, which he forgot to attend. Calling the reporter to apologize, he noted the irony of forgetting his interview about memory!

In our capacity to learn and remember, as in other areas of development, we show individual differences. Younger adults vary in their abilities to learn and remember, but 70-year-olds vary much more. "Differences between the most and least able 70-year-olds become much greater than between the most and least able 50-year-olds," reported Oxford researcher Patrick Rabbitt (2006). Some 70-year-olds perform below nearly all 20-year-olds; other 70-year-olds match or outdo the average 20-year-old.

No matter how quick or slow we are, remembering seems also to depend on the type of information we are trying to retrieve. If the information is meaningless—nonsense syllables or unimportant events or experiences—then the older we are, the more errors we are likely to make. If the information is *meaningful,* as was *Paradise Lost* for John Basinger, older people's rich web of existing knowledge will help them to hold it. But they may take longer than younger adults to *produce* the words and things they know. Older adults also more often experience tip-of-the-tongue forgetting (Ossher et al., 2012). Quick-thinking game show winners have usually been young or middle-aged adults (Burke & Shafto, 2004).

Maintaining Mental Abilities

Psychologists who study the aging mind debate whether "brain fitness" computer-based training programs can build mental muscles and stave off cognitive decline. Our brain remains plastic throughout life (Gutchess, 2014). So, can exercising our brains on a "cognitive treadmill"—with memory, visual tracking, and problem-solving exercises—avert losing our minds? "At every point in life, the brain's natural plasticity gives us the ability to improve . . . function," said one neuroscientist-entrepreneur (Merzenich, 2007). One analysis of cognitive training programs showed that they consistently improved scores on tests related to their training (Simons et al., 2016). Video game playing may also enhance people's attention (Bediou et al., 2018).

Based on such findings, some computer game makers have been marketing daily brain-exercise programs for older adults. But researchers, after reviewing all the available studies, advise skepticism (Melby-Lervåg et al., 2016; Redick et al., 2017; Sala et al., 2018). One team of experts reported "extensive evidence that brain-training interventions improve performance on the trained tasks, less evidence that such interventions improve performance on closely related tasks, and little evidence that training enhances performance on distantly related tasks or that training improves everyday cognitive performance" (Simons et al., 2016, p. 103). As researcher Zach Hambrick (2014) explains, "Play a video game and you'll get better at that video game, and maybe at very similar video games"—but not at driving a car or filling out your tax return. One experiment found that, compared with mere online video game playing, a prominent brain-training program by Lumosity did not improve mental performance (Kable et al., 2017).

Modules 28–31 explore another dimension of cognitive development: intelligence. As we will see, *cross-sectional studies* and *longitudinal studies* have identified mental abilities that

"I am still learning." — Michelangelo, 1560, at age 85

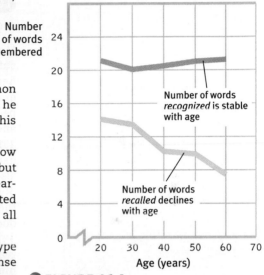

⑦ FIGURE 16.4

Recall and recognition in adulthood In this experiment, the ability to *recall* new information declined during early and middle adulthood, but the ability to *recognize* new information did not. (Data from Schonfield & Robertson, 1966.)

"The sudden knowledge of the fragility of his life narrowed his focus and altered his desires. . . . It made him visit with his grandchildren more often, put in an extra trip to see his family in India, and tamp down new ventures." — Atul Gawande, *Being Mortal: Medicine and What Matters in the End,* 2014, describing his father's terminal condition

do and do not change as people age. Age is less a predictor of memory and intelligence than is proximity to a natural death, which does give a clue to someone's mental ability. In the last three or four years of life, and especially as death approaches, cognitive decline typically accelerates (Vogel et al., 2013; Wilson et al., 2007b). Researchers call this near-death drop *terminal decline* (Backman & MacDonald, 2006). Our goals also shift: We're driven less to learn and more to connect socially (Carstensen, 2011).

Neurocognitive Disorders and Alzheimer's Disease

LOQ **16-3** How do neurocognitive disorders and Alzheimer's disease affect cognitive ability?

Most people who live into their nineties do so with clear minds. Some, unfortunately, suffer substantial psychological decline that is *not* normal aging. Among older adults, hearing loss, and its associated social isolation, predicts risk of depression and accelerated mental decline (Lin et al., 2011a,b, 2013; Loughrey et al., 2018). Compared with people with good hearing, those with hearing loss show declines in memory, attention, and learning about three years earlier—but less if they get hearing aids (Maharani et al., 2018). A series of small strokes, a brain tumor, or alcohol use disorder can progressively damage the brain, causing that mental erosion we call a **neurocognitive disorder** (**NCD,** also called *dementia*). Heavy midlife smoking more than doubles later risk of the disorder (Rusanen et al., 2011). The feared brain ailment **Alzheimer's disease** strikes 3 percent of the world's population by age 75. Up to age 95, the incidence of mental disintegration doubles roughly every 5 years.

Alzheimer's destroys even the brightest of minds. First memory deteriorates, then reasoning. (Occasionally forgetting where you laid the car keys—the sort of "episodic memory" that subsides with normal aging—is no cause for alarm. Forgetting how to get home may suggest Alzheimer's.) Robert Sayre (1979) recalled his father shouting at his afflicted mother to "think harder," while his mother, confused, embarrassed, on the verge of tears, randomly searched the house for lost objects. As the disease runs its course, after 5 to 20 years, the person becomes emotionally flat, then disoriented and disinhibited, then incontinent, and finally mentally vacant—a sort of living death, a mere body stripped of its humanity.

Underlying the symptoms of Alzheimer's are a loss of brain cells and a deterioration of neurons that produce the neurotransmitter acetylcholine, which is vital to memory and thinking. An autopsy reveals two telltale abnormalities in these acetylcholine-producing neurons: shriveled protein filaments in the cell body, and clumps of a free-floating protein fragment that accumulate as plaque at neuron tips where synaptic communication normally occurs. Long before symptoms appear, new technologies can now test for the Alzheimer's susceptibility gene or check spinal fluid for the culprit protein fragments (De Meyer et al., 2010; Luciano et al., 2009). Such discoveries have stimulated a race to invent and test drugs that may forestall the disease, such as by reducing the activity of a memory-inhibiting neurotransmitter called GABA (Chen et al., 2014). The discovery of 21 associated genes may help (Lambert et al., 2013).

A diminishing sense of smell and slowed or wobbly walking may foretell Alzheimer's (Belluck, 2012; Wilson et al., 2007a). In people at risk for Alzheimer's, brain scans (**FIGURE 16.5**) have also revealed—before symptoms appear—the degeneration of critical brain cells and diminished activity in Alzheimer's-related brain areas (Apostolova et al., 2006; Johnson et al., 2006; Wu & Small, 2006). When people memorized words, scans also showed diffuse brain activity, as if more exertion was required to achieve the same performance (Bookheimer et al., 2000).

Alzheimer's is somewhat less common among those who sleep well and who keep their minds and bodies active, through activities like reading, attending educational lectures, and running or lifting weights (Agrigoroaei & Lachman, 2011; Noble &

🔻 FIGURE 16.5

Predicting Alzheimer's disease During a memory test, MRI scans of the brains of people at risk for Alzheimer's (a) revealed more intense activity (yellow, followed by orange and red) when compared with normal brains (b). As brain scans and genetic tests make it possible to identify those likely to suffer Alzheimer's, would you want to be tested? At what age?

(a)

(b)

Spires-Jones, 2019; Reynolds, 2019). In one four-decade-long study that followed nearly 1500 middle-aged Swedish women, a high fitness level delayed the onset of dementia by 9.5 years (Hörder et al., 2018). As with muscles, so with the brain: Those who use it less often lose it.

Social Development

LOQ 16-4 What themes and influences mark our social journey from early adulthood to death?

Try completing this statement five times: "I am _____."

In response, teens mostly describe their individual traits. Young adults more often define themselves in terms of their social roles, such as their occupation or being a parent (Hards et al., 2019). Many differences between teens, younger adults, and older adults are created by significant life events. A new job means new relationships, new expectations, and new demands. Marriage brings the joy of intimacy and the stress of merging two lives. The 3 years surrounding the birth of a child bring increased life satisfaction for most couples (Dyrdal & Lucas, 2011). The death of a loved one creates an irreplaceable loss. Do these adult life events shape a sequence of life changes?

Adulthood's Ages and Stages

As people enter their forties, they undergo a transition to middle adulthood, a time when they realize that life will soon be mostly behind instead of ahead of them. Some psychologists have argued that for many the *midlife transition* is a crisis, a time of great struggle, regret, or even feeling struck down by life. The popular image of the midlife crisis—an early-forties man who forsakes his family for a younger romantic partner and a hot sports car—is more a myth than reality. Unhappiness, job dissatisfaction, marital dissatisfaction, divorce, anxiety, and suicide do *not* surge during the early forties (Hunter & Sundel, 1989; Mroczek & Kolarz, 1998). Divorce, for example, is most common among those in their twenties, suicide among those in their seventies and eighties. One study of emotional instability in nearly 10,000 men and women found "not the slightest evidence" that distress peaks anywhere in the midlife age range (McCrae & Costa, 1990).

For the 1 in 4 middle-aged adults who report experiencing a life crisis, the trigger is not age, but a major event, such as illness, divorce, or job loss (Lachman, 2004). Some middle-aged adults describe themselves as a "sandwich generation," simultaneously supporting their aging parents and their emerging adult children or grandchildren (Riley & Bowen, 2005).

Life events trigger transitions to new life stages at varying ages. The **social clock**—the definition of "the right time" to leave home, get a job, marry, have children, and retire—varies from era to era and culture to culture. The once-rigid sequence has loosened; the social clock still ticks, but people feel freer to keep their own time.

Even *chance events* can have lasting significance, by deflecting us down one road rather than another. Albert Bandura (1982, 2005) recalls the ironic true story of a book editor who came to one of Bandura's lectures on the "Psychology of Chance Encounters and Life Paths"—and ended up marrying the woman who happened to sit next to him. The sequence that led to my [DM's] authoring this book (which was not my idea) began with my being seated near, and getting to know, a distinguished colleague at an international conference. The road to my [ND's] co-authoring this book began in a similarly unplanned manner: After stumbling on an article about my professional life, DM invited me to visit his college. There, we began a conversation that resulted in our collaboration. Chance events can change our lives.

Adulthood's Commitments

Two basic aspects of our lives dominate adulthood. Erik Erikson called them *intimacy* (forming close relationships) and *generativity* (being productive and supporting future generations). Sigmund Freud (1935/1960) put this more simply: The healthy adult, he said, is one who can *love* and *work*.

neurocognitive disorders (NCDs) acquired (not lifelong) disorders marked by cognitive deficits; often related to Alzheimer's disease, brain injury or disease, or substance abuse. Also called *dementia* in older adults.

Alzheimer's disease a neurocognitive disorder marked by neural plaques, often with onset after age 80, and entailing a progressive decline in memory and other cognitive abilities.

social clock the culturally preferred timing of social events such as marriage, parenthood, and retirement.

"I am very curious. . . . I wouldn't still be working if I didn't find it exciting."
— 99-year-old neuropsychologist Brenda Milner, 2017

"The important events of a person's life are the products of chains of highly improbable occurrences." — Joseph Traub, "Traub's Law," 2003

Andersen Ross/Blend Images/Alamy

Love Intimacy, attachment, commitment—love by whatever name—is central to healthy and happy adulthood.

What do you think? Does marriage correlate with happiness because marital support and intimacy breed happiness, because happy people more often marry and stay married, or both?

LOVE Although more and more people live single lives, most eventually pair up romantically. People typically flirt, fall in love, and commit—one person at a time. "Pair-bonding is a trademark of the human animal," observed anthropologist Helen Fisher (1993). From an evolutionary perspective, relatively monogamous pairing makes sense: Parents who cooperated to nurture their children to maturity were more likely to have their genes passed along to posterity than were parents who didn't.

Adult bonds of love are most satisfying and enduring when marked by a similarity of interests and values, a sharing of emotional and material support, and intimate self-disclosure. And for better or for worse, our standards have risen over the years: We now hope not only for an enduring bond, but also for a mate who is a wage earner, caregiver, intimate friend, and warm and responsive lover (Finkel, 2017). There also appears to be "vow power." Straight and gay relationships sealed with commitment more often endure (Balsam et al., 2008; Rosenfeld, 2014). Such bonds are especially likely to last when couples marry after age 20 and are well educated. Compared with their counterparts of 30 years ago, people in Western countries *are* better educated and marrying later (Wolfinger, 2015). These trends may help explain why the American divorce rate, which surged from 1960 to 1980, has since declined. Canadian divorce rates since the 1980s have followed a similar pattern (Statistics Canada, 2011).

Might test-driving life together minimize divorce risk? In Europe, Canada, and the United States, those who live together before marriage (and especially before engagement) have had *higher* rates of divorce and marital dysfunction than those who did not (Goodwin et al., 2010; Jose et al., 2010; Manning & Cohen, 2012; Stanley et al., 2010). In 11 developed countries studied, cohabiting partners were more likely than spouses to agree that in the past year, they have had serious doubts their relationship will last (Wang & Wilcox, 2019). Three factors contribute. First, those who live together tend to be initially less committed to the ideal of enduring marriage. Second, they may become even less marriage-supporting while living together. Third, it's more awkward to break up with a cohabiting partner than with a dating partner, leading some cohabiters to marry someone "they otherwise would have left behind" (Stanley & Rhoades, 2016a,b).

Although there is more variety in relationships today, the institution of marriage endures. More than 9 in 10 American adults either have married during their lifetime or want to (Newport & Wilke, 2013). In Western countries, what counts as a "very important" reason to marry? Among Americans, 31 percent say financial stability, and 93 percent say love (Cohn, 2013). And marriage is a predictor of happiness, sexual satisfaction, income, and physical and mental health (Scott et al., 2010; Wilcox & Wolfinger, 2017). Between 1972 and 2018, surveys of more than 60,000 Americans revealed that 40 percent of married adults were "very happy," compared with 23 percent of those never married (NORC, 2019). Lesbian couples, too, have reported greater well-being than those who are single (Peplau & Fingerhut, 2007; Wayment & Peplau, 1995). Moreover, neighborhoods with high marriage rates typically have low rates of social pathologies such as crime, delinquency, and emotional disorders among children (Myers & Scanzoni, 2005; Wilcox et al., 2018).

Relationships that last are not always devoid of conflict. Some couples fight but also shower each other with affection. Other couples never raise their voices yet also seldom praise each other or nuzzle. Both styles can last. After observing the interactions of 2000 couples, John Gottman and Julie Gottman (2018) report one indicator of marital success: at least *a five-to-one ratio of positive to negative interactions*. Stable marriages provide five times more instances of smiling, touching, complimenting, and laughing than of sarcasm, criticism, and insults. So, if you want to predict which couples will stay together, don't pay attention to how passionately they are in love. The pairs who make it are more often those who refrain from putting down their partners. To prevent a cancerous negativity, successful couples learn to fight fair (to state feelings without insulting) and to steer conflict away from chaos with comments like "I know it's not your fault" or "I'll just be quiet for a moment and listen."

Often, love bears children. For most people, this most enduring of life changes is a happy event—one that adds meaning, joy, and occasional stress (Nelson-Coffey et al., 2019; Witters, 2014). "I feel an overwhelming love for my children unlike anything I feel for anyone else," said 93 percent of American mothers in a national survey (Erickson & Aird, 2005). Many fathers feel the same. A few weeks after the birth of my first child I [DM] was suddenly struck by a realization: "So *this* is how my parents felt about me!"

When children begin to absorb time, money, and emotional energy, parents' satisfaction with their own relationship may decline (Doss et al., 2009). This is especially likely among employed women who, more than they expected, may also carry the burden of doing more chores at home. Putting effort into creating an equitable relationship can thus pay double dividends: greater satisfaction, which breeds better parent-child relations (Erel & Burman, 1995).

Eventually, children leave home. This departure is a significant and sometimes difficult event. But for most people, an empty nest is a happy place (Adelmann et al., 1989; Gorchoff et al., 2008). Many parents experience a "postlaunch honeymoon," especially if they maintain close relationships with their children (White & Edwards, 1990). As Daniel Gilbert (2006) said, "The only known symptom of 'empty nest syndrome' is increased smiling."

> Play the role of a researcher exploring the connection between parenting and happiness by engaging online with the activity *How Would You Know If Having Children Relates to Being Happier?*

WORK For many adults, the answer to "Who are you?" depends a great deal on the answer to "What do you do?" For women and men, choosing a career path is difficult, especially during uncertain economic times. Even in the best of times, few students in their first 2 years of college or university can predict their later careers.

In the end, happiness is about having work that fits your interests and provides you with a sense of competence and accomplishment. It is giving generously of your time and resources (Mogilner & Norton, 2016; Whillans et al., 2016). It is having a close, supportive companion, or family and friends, who notice and cheer your accomplishments (Campos et al., 2015). And for some, it includes having children who love you and whom you love and feel proud of.

> **RETRIEVAL PRACTICE**
>
> **RP-1** Freud defined the healthy adult as one who is able to _____ and to
> _____.
>
> *ANSWERS IN APPENDIX E*

Well-Being Across the Life Span

LOQ 16-5 How does our well-being change across the life span?

To live is to grow older. This moment marks the oldest you have ever been and the youngest you will henceforth be. That means we all can look back with satisfaction or regret, and forward with hope or dread. When asked what they would have done differently if they could relive their lives, people's most common answer has been "taken my education more seriously and worked harder at it" (Kinnier & Metha, 1989; Roese & Summerville, 2005). Other regrets—"I should have told my father I loved him," "I regret that I never went to Europe"—have also focused less on mistakes made than on the things one *failed* to do (Gilovich & Medvec, 1995).

But until the very end, the over-65 years are not notably unhappy. Self-esteem, for example, remains stable (Wagner et al., 2013). Gallup asked 658,038 people worldwide

"To understand your parents' love, bear your own children." — Chinese proverb

"Our love for children is so unlike any other human emotion. I fell in love with my babies so quickly and profoundly, almost completely independently of their particular qualities. And yet 20 years later I was (more or less) happy to see them go—I had to be happy to see them go. We are totally devoted to them when they are little and yet the most we can expect in return when they grow up is that they regard us with bemused and tolerant affection." — Developmental psychologist Alison Gopnik, "The Supreme Infant," 2010

Job satisfaction and life satisfaction Work can provide us with a sense of identity and competence, and opportunities for accomplishment. Perhaps this is why challenging and interesting occupations enhance people's happiness. For more on work, including discovering your own strengths, see Appendix C, Psychology at Work.

FIGURE 16.6

Humans are social creatures Both younger and older adults report greater happiness when spending time with others. (Note this correlation could also reflect happier people being more social.) (Gallup survey data reported by Crabtree, 2011.)

Percentage of Americans reporting a lot of stress-free enjoyment and happiness the previous day

Ages 65+

Ages 18–29

Hours spent with others the previous day

"When you were born, you cried and the world rejoiced. Live your life in a manner so that when you die the world cries and you rejoice." — Native American proverb

"Still married after all these years?
No mystery.
We are each other's habit,
And each other's history."
— Judith Viorst, "The Secret of Staying Married," 2007

to rate their lives on a ladder from 0 ("the worst possible life") to 10 ("the best possible life"). Age—from 15 to over 90 years—gave no clue to life satisfaction (Morrison et al., 2014). Positive feelings, supported by enhanced emotional control, tend to grow after midlife, and negative feelings subside (Stone et al., 2010; Urry & Gross, 2010). Compared with younger Chinese and American adults, for example, older adults are *more* attentive to positive news (Isaacowitz, 2012; Wang et al., 2015a).

Like people of all ages, older adults are happiest when not alone (**FIGURE 16.6**). Compared with teens and young adults, older adults do tend to have a smaller social network, with fewer friendships and greater loneliness (Luhmann & Hawkley, 2016; Wagner et al., 2016). However, older adults experience fewer problems in their relationships—less attachment anxiety, stress, and anger (Chopik et al., 2013; Fingerman & Charles, 2010). With age, we become more stable and trusting (Bailey & Leon, 2019; Shallcross et al., 2013).

The aging brain may help nurture these positive feelings. Brain scans of older adults show that the amygdala, a neural processing center for emotions, responds less actively to negative events (but still responds to positive events) (Mather et al., 2004). Brain-wave reactions to negative images also diminish with age (Kisley et al., 2007). As we reach the later chapters of our lives, our brain enables a contented culmination (Mather, 2016).

Moreover, unlike younger people, older adults remember the good more than the bad events of their lives (Addis et al., 2010). This happy phenomenon leaves most older people with the comforting feeling that life, on balance, has been mostly good. Thanks to biological, psychological, and social-cultural influences, more and more people flourish into later life (**FIGURE 16.7**).

Biological influences:
• no genetic predisposition to early cognitive or physical decline
• appropriate nutrition

Psychological influences:
• optimistic outlook
• physically and mentally active lifestyle

Successful aging

Social-cultural influences:
• support from family and friends
• cultural respect for aging
• safe living conditions

FIGURE 16.7

Biopsychosocial influences on successful aging

The resilience of well-being across the life span obscures some interesting age-related emotional differences. When researchers mapped people's emotional terrain by periodically signaling them with electronic beepers to report their current activities and feelings, they found that teenagers typically come down from elation or up from gloom in less than an hour, but that adult moods are less extreme and more enduring (Csikszentmihalyi & Larson, 1984). As the years go by, feelings mellow (Brose et al., 2015). Highs become less high, lows less low. Compliments provoke less elation and criticisms less despair, as both become merely additional feedback atop a mountain of accumulated praise and blame. As we age, life therefore becomes less of an emotional roller coaster.

> "At 70, I would say the advantage is that you take life more calmly. You know that 'this, too, shall pass'!" — Eleanor Roosevelt, 1954

RETRIEVAL PRACTICE

RP-2 What are some of the most significant challenges and rewards of growing old?

ANSWERS IN APPENDIX E

Death and Dying

LOQ 16-6 What range of reactions does a loved one's death trigger?

Warning: If you begin reading the next paragraph, you will die.

But of course, if you hadn't read this, you would still die in due time. "Time is a great teacher," noted the nineteenth-century composer Hector Berlioz, "but unfortunately it kills all its pupils." Death is our inevitable end. Good health, as has been said, is simply the slowest way to die.

Most of us will also cope with the deaths of relatives and friends. Typically, the most difficult separation a person experiences is the death of a partner—a loss suffered by four times more women than men. Maintaining everyday engagements and relationships increases resilience in the face of such a loss (Infurna & Luthar, 2016). But for some, grief is severe, especially when a loved one's death comes suddenly and before its expected time on the social clock. I [ND] experienced this firsthand when a tragic accident claimed the life of my 60-year-old mother. Such tragedies may trigger a year or more of memory-laden mourning (Lehman et al., 1987).

> "The best thing about being 100 is *no peer pressure.*" — Lewis W. Kuester, 2005, on turning 100

For some, the loss is unbearable. One Danish long-term study of more than 1 million people found that about 17,000 of them had suffered the death of a child under 18. In the 5 years following that death, 3 percent of them had a first psychiatric hospitalization—a 67 percent higher rate than among other parents (Li et al., 2005).

Reactions to a loved one's death range more widely than most suppose. Some cultures encourage public weeping and wailing; others hide grief. Within any culture, individuals differ. Given similar losses, some people grieve hard and long, others less so (Ott et al., 2007). Some popular misconceptions persist, however:

- *Are there stages of grieving?* Terminally ill and bereaved people do not go through identical predictable stages, such as denial before anger (Friedman & James, 2008; Nolen-Hoeksema & Larson, 1999).

- *Should we purge our grief?* Those who express the strongest grief immediately do not purge their grief more quickly (Bonanno & Kaltman, 1999; Wortman & Silver, 1989). But grieving parents who try to protect their partner by "staying strong" and not discussing their child's death may actually prolong the grieving (Stroebe et al., 2013).

- *Is therapy needed?* Bereavement therapy and self-help groups offer support, but there is similar healing power in the passing of time, the support of friends, and the act of giving support and help to others (Baddeley & Singer, 2009; Brown et al., 2008; Neimeyer & Currier, 2009). Grieving spouses who talk often with others or receive grief counseling adjust about as well as those who grieve more privately (Bonanno, 2004; Stroebe et al., 2005).

- *Is impending death terrifying?* Compared to what people *imagine* they would feel when facing death, those actually facing imminent death due to terminal illness are more positive and less sad and despairing. After studying terminally ill patients' blog posts and death row inmates' last words, Amelia Goranson and her colleagues (2017) concluded that "Meeting the grim reaper may not be as grim as it seems."

Facing death with dignity and openness helps people complete the life cycle with a sense of life's meaningfulness and unity—the sense that their existence has been good and that life and death are parts of an ongoing cycle. Although death may be unwelcome, life itself can be affirmed even at death. This is especially so for people who review their lives not with despair but with what Erik Erikson called a sense of *integrity*—a feeling that one's life has been meaningful and worthwhile.

16 REVIEW Adulthood

LEARNING OBJECTIVES

Test Yourself Answer these repeated Learning Objective Questions on your own (before checking the answers in Appendix D) to improve your retention of the concepts (McDaniel et al., 2009, 2015).

LOQ 16-1 What physical changes occur during middle and late adulthood?

LOQ 16-2 How does memory change with age?

LOQ 16-3 How do neurocognitive disorders and Alzheimer's disease affect cognitive ability?

LOQ 16-4 What themes and influences mark our social journey from early adulthood to death?

LOQ 16-5 How does our well-being change across the life span?

LOQ 16-6 What range of reactions does a loved one's death trigger?

TERMS AND CONCEPTS TO REMEMBER

Test Yourself Write down the definition in your own words, then check your answer.

menopause, p. 199

neurocognitive disorders (NCDs), p. 205

Alzheimer's disease, p. 205

social clock, p. 205

MASTER THE MATERIAL

Test Yourself Answer the following questions on your own first, then check your answers in Appendix E.

1. By age 65, a person would be most likely to experience a cognitive decline in the ability to
   a. recall and list all the important terms and concepts in a module.
   b. select the correct definition in a multiple-choice question.
   c. recall their own birth date.
   d. practice a well-learned skill, such as knitting.

2. Freud defined the healthy adult as one who is able to love and work. Erikson agreed, observing that the adult struggles to attain intimacy and _____.

3. Contrary to what many people assume,
   a. older people are significantly less happy than adolescents are.
   b. people become less happy as they move from their teen years into midlife.
   c. positive feelings tend to grow after midlife.
   d. those whose children have recently left home—the empty nesters—have the lowest level of happiness of all groups.

Continue testing yourself with 🔲 **LearningCurve** or 🔲 **Achieve Read & Practice** to learn and remember most effectively.

Artem Varnitsin/EyeEm/Getty Images

Sensation and Perception

"I have perfect vision," explains writer and teacher Heather Sellers. Her vision may be perfect, but her perception is not. In her 2010 memoir, *You Don't Look Like Anyone I Know*, she tells of awkward moments resulting from her lifelong *prosopagnosia*—face blindness:

> In college, on a date at the Spaghetti Station, I returned from the bathroom and plunked myself down in the wrong booth, facing the wrong man. I remained unaware he was not my date even as my date (a stranger to me) accosted Wrong Booth Guy, and then stormed out. . . . I do not recognize myself in photos or videos. I can't recognize my stepsons in the soccer pick-up line; I [have] failed to determine which husband was mine at a party, in the mall, at the market.

To avoid being perceived as snobby or aloof, Sellers sometimes fakes recognition. She often smiles at people she passes, in case she knows them. Or she pretends to know the person with whom she is talking. But, Sellers points out, there is an upside: When encountering someone who previously irritated her, she typically feels no ill will—she doesn't recognize the person.

Unlike Sellers, most of us have a functioning area on the underside of our brain's right hemisphere that helps us recognize a familiar human face as soon as we detect it—in only one-seventh of a second (Jacques & Rossion, 2006). Our remarkable ability illustrates a broader principle: *Nature's sensory gifts enable each animal to obtain essential information*. Other examples:

- Human ears are most sensitive to sound frequencies that include human voices, especially a baby's cry.

- Frogs, which feed on flying insects, have cells in their eyes that fire only in response to small, dark, moving objects. A frog could starve to death knee-deep in motionless flies. But let one zoom by and the frog's "bug detector" cells snap awake. (As Kermit the Frog said, "Time's fun when you're having flies.")

- Male silkworm moths' odor receptors can detect one-billionth of an ounce of chemical sex attractant per second, released by a female one mile away (Sagan, 1977). That is why there continue to be silkworms.

In these modules, we'll look at what psychologists have learned about how we sense and perceive our world. We begin by considering some basic principles of sensation and perception that apply to all our senses (Module 17), followed by a focus on visual processes (Module 18), and then the non-visual senses (Module 19).

17 Basic Concepts of Sensation and Perception

How do we create meaning from the blizzard of sensory stimuli that bombards our bodies 24 hours a day? In its silent, cushioned, inner world, our brain floats in utter darkness. By itself, it sees nothing. It hears nothing. It feels nothing. *So, how does the world out there get in?* To phrase the question scientifically: How do we construct our representations of the external world? How do a campfire's flicker, crackle, heat, and smoky scent activate neural connections? And how, from this living neurochemistry, do we create our conscious experience of the fire's motion and temperature, its aroma and beauty?

Processing Sensations and Perceptions

LEARNING OBJECTIVE QUESTION LOQ 17-1 What are *sensation* and *perception*? What do we mean by *bottom-up processing* and *top-down processing*?

Heather Sellers' curious mix of "perfect vision" and face blindness illustrates the distinction between *sensation* and *perception*. When she looks at a friend, her **sensation** is normal. Her **sensory receptors** detect the same information any sighted person's would, and her nervous system transmits that information to her brain. Her **perception**—the processes by which her brain organizes and interprets sensory input—is *almost* normal. Thus, she may recognize people from their hair, gait, voice, or particular physique, just not from their face. Her experience is much like the struggle any human would have trying to recognize a specific penguin.

Under normal circumstances, sensation and perception blend into one continuous process.

- **Bottom-up processing** starts at your sensory receptors and works up to higher levels of processing.

- **Top-down processing** constructs perceptions from this sensory input by drawing on your experience and expectations.

As your brain absorbs the information in **FIGURE 17.1**, bottom-up processing enables your sensory systems to detect the lines, angles, and colors that form the images. Using top-down processing, you interpret what your senses detect.

Transduction

LOQ 17-2 What three steps are basic to all of our sensory systems?

Your sensory systems perform an amazing feat: They convert one form of energy into another. Vision processes light energy. Hearing processes sound waves. All our senses

FIGURE 17.1

What's going on here? Our sensory and perceptual processes work together to help us sort out complex images, including the hidden donkey rider in Sandro Del-Prete's drawing, *Homage to Leonardo da Vinci.*

Sandro Del-Prete

- *receive* sensory stimulation, often using specialized receptor cells.
- *transform* that stimulation into neural impulses.
- *deliver* the neural information to our brain.

The process of converting one form of energy into another that our brain can use is called **transduction.** Transduction is rather like translation—of a physical energy such as light waves into the brain's electrochemical language. **Psychophysics** studies the relationships between the physical energy we can detect and its effects on our psychological experiences.

In Modules 18 and 19, we'll focus on individual sensory systems. How do we see? Hear? Feel pain? Taste? Smell? Keep our balance? In each case, one of our sensory systems receives, transforms, and delivers the information to our brain. And our senses work together.

Let's explore some strengths and weaknesses in our ability to detect and interpret stimuli in the sea of energy around us.

RETRIEVAL PRACTICE

RP-1 What is the rough distinction between sensation and perception?

ANSWERS IN APPENDIX E

Thresholds

LOQ **17-3** How do *absolute thresholds* and *difference thresholds* differ?

At this moment, we are being struck by X-rays and radio waves, ultraviolet and infrared light, and sound waves of very high and very low frequencies. To all of these we are blind and deaf. Other animals with differing needs detect a world that lies beyond our experience. Migrating birds stay on course aided by an internal magnetic compass. Bats and dolphins locate prey using sonar, bouncing echoing sound off objects. Bees navigate on cloudy days by detecting invisible (to us) polarized light.

Our senses open the shades just a crack, allowing us a restricted awareness of this vast sea of energy. But for our needs, this is enough.

Absolute Thresholds

To some stimuli we are exquisitely sensitive. Standing atop a mountain on an utterly dark, perfectly clear night, most of us could see a candle flame atop another mountain 30 miles (nearly 50 kilometers) away. We could feel the wing of a bee falling on our cheek. We could smell a single drop of perfume in a three-room apartment (Galanter, 1962).

German scientist and philosopher Gustav Fechner (1801–1887) studied the edge of our awareness of these faint stimuli, which he called an **absolute threshold.** To test your absolute threshold for sounds, a hearing specialist would send tones, at varying levels, into each of your ears and record whether you could hear each tone (**FIGURE 17.2**). The test results would show the point where, for any sound frequency, half the time you could detect the sound and half the time you could not. That 50-50 point would define your absolute threshold.

Detecting a weak stimulus, or signal (such as a hearing-test tone), depends not only on its strength but also on our psychological state—our experience, expectations, motivation, and alertness. **Signal detection theory** predicts when we will detect weak signals (measured as our ratio of "hits" to "false alarms"). Signal detection theorists seek to understand why people respond differently to the same stimuli, and why the same person's reactions vary as circumstances change.

Percentage of correct detections

100%

75

50

25

0

Subliminal stimuli

Low — **Absolute threshold** — Medium

Intensity of stimulus ⟶

Sidebar definitions

sensation the process by which our sensory receptors and nervous system receive and represent stimulus energies from our environment.

sensory receptors sensory nerve endings that respond to stimuli.

perception the process by which our brain organizes and interprets sensory information, enabling us to recognize objects and events as meaningful.

bottom-up processing information processing that begins with the sensory receptors and works up to the brain's integration of sensory information.

top-down processing information processing guided by higher-level mental processes, as when we construct perceptions drawing on our experience and expectations.

transduction conversion of one form of energy into another. In sensation, the transforming of stimulus energies, such as sights, sounds, and smells, into neural impulses our brain can interpret.

psychophysics the study of relationships between the physical characteristics of stimuli, such as their intensity, and our psychological experience of them.

absolute threshold the minimum stimulus energy needed to detect a particular stimulus 50 percent of the time.

signal detection theory a theory predicting how and when we detect the presence of a faint stimulus *(signal)* amid background stimulation *(noise)*. Assumes there is no single absolute threshold and that detection depends partly on a person's experience, expectations, motivation, and alertness.

FIGURE 17.2
Absolute threshold Can I detect this sound? An *absolute threshold* is the intensity at which a person can detect a stimulus half the time. Hearing tests locate these thresholds for various sound frequencies.

Dan Dunkley/Science Source

Signal detection When reading mammograms, health professionals seek to detect the presence of a faint cancer stimulus *(signal)* amid background stimulation *(noise)*, and without raising false alarms. New 3-D ultrasound breast-imaging technologies aim to clarify the signal and reduce the rate of false alarms.

Stimuli you cannot consciously detect 50 percent of the time are **subliminal**—below your absolute threshold (Figure 17.2). One experiment using subliminal stimuli illustrated the deep reality of sexual orientation. As people gazed at the center of a screen, a photo of a nude person was flashed on one side and a scrambled version of the photo on the other side (Jiang et al., 2006). Because the nude images were immediately masked by a colored checkerboard, viewers consciously perceived nothing but flashes of color and so were unable to state on which side the nude had appeared. To test whether this unseen image unconsciously attracted their attention, the experimenters then flashed a geometric figure on one side or the other. This, too, was quickly followed by a masking stimulus. When asked to give the figure's angle, straight men guessed more accurately when it appeared where a nude *woman* had been a moment earlier. Gay men and straight women guessed more accurately when the geometric figure replaced a nude *man*. Thus, though not consciously perceived, the more appealing sexual image had drawn their attention.

This experiment indicates that sexual orientation is something deeper than a conscious moral choice. And it illustrates how the unconscious mind is like the wind: We don't see it, but we see its effects. So, can we be *controlled* by subliminal messages? (See Thinking Critically About: Subliminal Sensation and Subliminal Persuasion.)

> For a helpful tutorial animation about the experimental research method, see the *Video: Experiments.*

→ **subliminal** below one's absolute threshold for conscious awareness.

difference threshold the minimum difference between two stimuli required for detection 50 percent of the time. We experience the difference threshold as a *just noticeable difference* (or *jnd*).

Weber's law the principle that, to be perceived as different, two stimuli must differ by a constant minimum percentage (rather than a constant amount).

priming the activation, often unconsciously, of certain associations, thus predisposing one's perception, memory, or response.

Difference Thresholds

To function effectively, we need absolute thresholds low enough to allow us to detect important sights, sounds, textures, tastes, and smells. We also need to detect small differences among stimuli. A musician must detect minute discrepancies when tuning an instrument. Parents must detect the sound of their own child's voice amid other children's voices. Even after 2 years in Scotland, all lamb *baas* sounded alike to my [DM's] ears. But not to lamb mothers. After shearing, I observed, each ewe would streak directly to the *baa* of *her* lamb amid the chorus of other distressed lambs.

The **difference threshold** (or the *just noticeable difference [jnd]*) is the minimum stimulus difference a person can detect half the time. That detectable difference increases with the size of the stimulus. If we listen to our music at 40 decibels, we might barely detect an added 5 decibels (the jnd). But if we increase the volume to 110 decibels, we probably won't detect an additional 5-decibel change.

Eric Isselee/Shutterstock

In the late 1800s, German physician Ernst Weber described this with a principle so simple and so widely applicable that we still refer to it as **Weber's law:** For an average person to perceive a difference, two stimuli must differ by a constant minimum *percentage* (not a constant *amount*). The exact percentage varies, depending on the stimulus. Two lights, for example, must differ in intensity by 8 percent. Two objects must differ in weight by 2 percent. And two tones must differ in frequency by only .3 percent (Teghtsoonian, 1971).

The difference threshold In this copy of the Twenty-third Psalm, each line of the typeface increases in size slightly. How many lines are required for you to experience a just noticeable difference?

The LORD is my shepherd;
    I shall not want.
He maketh me to lie down
        in green pastures:
    he leadeth me
        beside the still waters.
He restoreth my soul:
    he leadeth me
        in the paths of righteousness
        for his name's sake.
Yea, though I walk through the valley
        of the shadow of death,
    I will fear no evil:
    for thou art with me;
        thy rod and thy staff
        they comfort me.
Thou preparest a table before me
        in the presence of mine enemies:
    thou anointest my head with oil,
        my cup runneth over.
Surely goodness and mercy
        shall follow me
        all the days of my life:
    and I will dwell
        in the house of the LORD
        for ever.

RETRIEVAL PRACTICE

RP-2 Using sound as your example, explain how these concepts differ: *absolute threshold, subliminal stimulation,* and *difference threshold.*

ANSWERS IN APPENDIX E

We can be affected by *subliminal* sensations—stimuli so weak that we don't consciously notice them.

Researchers use **priming** to activate unconscious associations.

Participant views slides of people and offers either favorable or unfavorable ratings of each person.

BUT
an instant before each slide appears, the trickster researcher subliminally flashes another image—either pleasant (for example, kittens), or unpleasant (for example, a werewolf).

or

Participants consciously perceive these images only as flashes of light.

Will participants' ratings of the faces be affected?

Yes![1]

More **favorable** ratings of people

More **unfavorable** ratings of people

Our two-track mind: Priming happens even though the viewer's brain does not have time to consciously perceive the flashed images. We may evaluate a stimulus even when we are not consciously aware of it.[2]

So, we can be *primed*, but can we be *persuaded* by subliminal stimuli, for example to lose weight, stop smoking, or improve our memory?

Quiz 100%

Audio and video messages subliminally (without recipients' conscious awareness) announce:

"I am thin,"
"Cigarette smoke tastes bad,"
and
"I do well on tests. I have total recall of information."

Results from 16 experiments[3] showed no powerful, enduring influence on behavior. Not one of the recordings helped more than a placebo, which works only because we believe it will.

1. Krosnick et al., 1992.   2. Ferguson & Zayas, 2009.   3. Greenwald et al., 1991, 1992.

FIGURE 17.3
The jumpy eye Our gaze jumps from one spot to another every third of a second or so, as eye-tracking equipment illustrated as a person looked at this photograph of Edinburgh's Princes Street Gardens (Henderson, 2007). The circles represent visual fixations, and the numbers indicate the time of fixation in milliseconds (300 milliseconds = 3/10ths of a second).

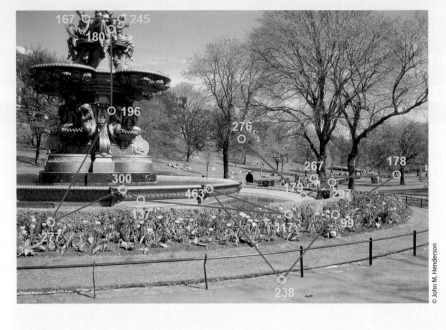

"We need above all to know about changes; no one wants or needs to be reminded 16 hours a day that his shoes are on."
— Neuroscientist David Hubel (1979)

Sensory Adaptation

LOQ **17-5** What is the function of sensory adaptation?

It's one of life's little curiosities: You may not notice a fan's noise until it's turned on or off. The same is true for odors. Sitting down on the bus, you are struck by your seatmate's heavy perfume. You wonder how she endures it, but within minutes you no longer notice. **Sensory adaptation** has come to your rescue. When constantly exposed to an unchanging stimulus, we become less aware of it because our nerve cells fire less frequently. (To experience sensory adaptation, roll up your sleeve. You will feel it—but only for a few moments.)

Why, then, if we stare at an object without flinching, does it *not* vanish from sight? Because, unnoticed by us, our eyes are always moving. This continual flitting from one spot to another ensures that stimulation on the eyes' receptors continually changes (**FIGURE 17.3**).

What if we actually could stop our eyes from moving? Would sights seem to vanish, as odors do? To find out, psychologists have devised ingenious instruments that maintain a constant image on the eye's inner surface. Imagine that we have fitted a volunteer, Mary, with such an instrument—a miniature projector mounted on a contact lens. When Mary's eye moves, the image from the projector moves as well. So everywhere that Mary looks, the scene is sure to go. Can you guess the weird result? (See **FIGURE 17.4**.)

Although sensory adaptation reduces our sensitivity, it offers an important benefit: freedom to focus on informative changes in our environment. Technology companies understand the attention-grabbing power of changing stimulation: Our phone's new tweets, likes, messages, breaking news stories, and other chatter are hard to ignore. As one of Instagram's founding engineers said, "There's always another hashtag to click on" (Alter, 2017). If we're performing other tasks, these intrusions can harm our performance (Stothart et al., 2015).

FIGURE 17.4
Sensory adaptation: Now you see it, now you don't! (a) A projector mounted on a contact lens makes the projected image move with the eye. (b) Initially, the person sees the stabilized image. But thanks to sensory adaptation, her eye soon becomes accustomed to the unchanging stimulus. Rather than the full image, she begins to see fragments fading and reappearing.

(a)

(b)

The point to remember: Our sensory system is alert to novelty; bore it with repetition and it frees our attention for more important things. *We perceive the world not exactly as it is, but as it is useful for us to perceive it.*

sensory adaptation diminished sensitivity as a consequence of constant stimulation.

perceptual set a mental predisposition to perceive one thing and not another.

ASK YOURSELF

What types of sensory adaptation have you experienced in the last 24 hours?

RETRIEVAL PRACTICE

RP-3 Why is it that after wearing shoes for a while, you cease to notice them (until questions like this draw your attention back to them)?

ANSWERS IN APPENDIX E

Perceptual Set

LOQ 17-6 How do our expectations, contexts, motivation, and emotions influence our perceptions?

To see is to believe. As we less fully appreciate, to believe is to see. Through experience, we come to expect certain results. Those expectations may give us a **perceptual set,** a set of mental tendencies and assumptions that affects, top-down, what we hear, taste, feel, and see.

Consider **FIGURE 17.5**: Is image (b) an old or young woman? What we see in such a drawing can be influenced by first looking at either image (a) or image (c), which are both unambiguous versions (Boring, 1930).

Do you perceive a number or a letter in the middle? If you read from left to right, you likely perceive a letter. But if you read from top to bottom, you may perceive the same center image as a number.

W.E. Hill 1915

(a)   (b)   (c)

FIGURE 17.5

Perceptual set Show a friend *either* image (a) or image (c). Then show image (b) and ask, "What do you see?" Whether your friend reports seeing an old woman's face or young woman's profile may depend on which of the other two drawings was viewed first. In images (a) and (c), the meaning is clear, and it will establish perceptual expectations.

Everyday examples abound of perceptual set—of "mind over mind." In 1972, a British newspaper published unretouched photographs of a "monster" in Scotland's Loch Ness, proclaiming them "the most amazing pictures ever taken." If this information creates in you the same expectations it did in most of the paper's readers, you, too, will see the monster in a similar photo in **FIGURE 17.6**. But when a skeptical researcher approached the original photos with different expectations, he saw a curved tree limb—as had others the day that photo was shot (Campbell, 1986). What a difference a new perceptual set makes.

Perceptual set also affects what we hear—"stuffy nose" or "stuff he knows"? Consider the kindly airline pilot who, on a takeoff run, looked over at his sad co-pilot and said, "Cheer up." Expecting to hear the usual "Gear up," the co-pilot promptly raised the wheels—before they left the ground (Reason & Mycielska, 1982). Or ask the little boy who loved the prelude to Major League Baseball games when people rose to sing to him: "José, can you see?" Or tell people about a couple who suffered from their experience with some "bad sects" and (depending on what's on their mind) they may hear something quite different ("bad sex").

Now consider this odd question: If you said one thing but heard yourself saying another, what would you think you said? To find out, a clever Swedish research team

There
Are Two
Errors in The
The Title Of
This Book
— Title of a book by Robert M. Martin, 2002

Did you perceive what you expected in this title—and miss the errors? If you are still puzzled, see the explanation below.[1]

"We hear and apprehend only what we already half know." — Henry David Thoreau, *Journal,* 1860

[1] The title's first error is its repeated "The." Its ironic second error is its misstatement that there are two errors, when there is only one.

FIGURE 17.6
Believing is seeing What do you perceive? Is this Nessie, the Loch Ness monster, or a log?

FIGURE 17.7
Culture and context effects What is above the woman's head? In one classic study, most rural East Africans questioned said the woman was balancing a metal box or can on her head (a typical way to carry water at that time). They also perceived the family as sitting under a tree. Westerners, used to tap water and box-like houses and apartments with corners, were more likely to perceive the family as being indoors, with the woman sitting under a window (Gregory & Gombrich, 1973).

Hearing hype Why do people pay millions of dollars for old Italian violins? Many people believe the sound quality is unmatched. Unfortunately, a recent study showed that, under blind conditions, expert violin soloists generally preferred the sound of less expensive, modern violins over expensive, old Italian violins (Fritz et al., 2017).

invited people to name a font color, such as saying "gray" when the word *green* appeared in a gray font (Lind et al., 2014). While participants heard themselves speaking over a noise-canceling headset, the wily experimenters occasionally substituted the participant's own previously recorded voice, such as saying "green" instead of "gray." Surprisingly, people usually missed the switch—and experienced the inserted word as self-produced. Again, hearing was believing.

Our expectations can influence our taste perceptions, too. In one experiment, preschool children, by a 6-to-1 margin, thought french fries tasted better when served in a McDonald's bag rather than a plain white bag (Robinson et al., 2007). Another experiment invited campus bar patrons at the Massachusetts Institute of Technology to sample free beer (Lee et al., 2006). When researchers added a few drops of vinegar to a brand-name beer and called it "MIT brew," the tasters preferred it—unless they had been told they were drinking vinegar-laced beer. In that case, they expected, and usually experienced, a worse taste.

What determines our perceptual set? Through experience we form concepts, or *schemas,* that organize and interpret unfamiliar information. Our preexisting schemas for monsters and tree trunks influence how we apply top-down processing to interpret ambiguous sensations.

In everyday life, stereotypes—about culture, ethnicity, gender identity, sexual orientation, income, age, disabilities, and more—can color perception. People (especially children) have, for example, perceived new baby "David" as bigger and stronger than when the same infant was called "Diana" (Stern & Karraker, 1989). Some differences, it seems, exist merely in the eyes of their beholders.

Context, Motivation, and Emotion

Perceptual set influences how we interpret stimuli. But our immediate context, and the motivation and emotion we bring to a situation, also affect our interpretations.

CONTEXT Social psychologist Lee Ross invites us to recall our own perceptions in different contexts: "Ever notice that when you're driving you hate . . . the way [pedestrians] saunter through the crosswalk, almost daring you to hit them, but when you're walking you hate drivers?" (Jaffe, 2004). People's expectations influence their perceptions constantly, whether about an angry man (*Is he reaching for his keys or a weapon?*) or a person coming too close (*Is this a threat or a come-on?*).

Some other examples of the power of context:

• Black men, compared with White men, are perceived as being taller, heavier, and more muscular (Wilson et al., 2017). This biased size perception leads people to more often perceive Black men as threatening and to justify using force against Black criminal suspects. Such perception biases may contribute to police officers' tendency to mistakenly shoot unarmed Black individuals (Johnson et al., 2018; Plant & Peruche, 2005).

• Imagine hearing a noise interrupted by the words "eel is on the wagon." Likely, you would actually perceive the first word as *wheel*. Given "eel is on the orange," you would more likely hear *peel*. In each case, the context creates an expectation that, top-down, influences our perception of a previously heard phrase (Grossberg, 1995).

- Cultural context helps inform our perceptions, so it's not surprising that people's varying cultures may cause them to view things differently, as in **FIGURE 17.7**. Perception is influenced by culture.

- And how is the woman in **FIGURE 17.8** feeling? The context provided in **FIGURE 17.9** will leave no doubt.

Craig Klomparens/Hope College

ASK YOURSELF

Can you think of a time when your expectations caused you to misperceive the intentions of a person or a group? How might you use awareness of *context effects* to modify your expectations?

RETRIEVAL PRACTICE

RP-4 Does *perceptual set* involve bottom-up or top-down processing? Why?

ANSWERS IN APPENDIX E

⟲ FIGURE 17.8
What emotion is this? (See Figure 17.9)

MOTIVATION Motives give us energy as we work toward a goal. Like context, they can bias our interpretations of neutral stimuli:

- Desirable objects, such as a water bottle viewed by a thirsty person, seem closer than they really are (Balcetis & Dunning, 2010). And closeness can increase desire itself. Straight men, for example, find women who are physically closer more desirable (Shin et al., 2019).

- A to-be-climbed hill can seem steeper when we are carrying a heavy backpack, and a walking destination further away when we are feeling tired (Burrow et al., 2016; Philbeck & Witt, 2015; Proffitt, 2006a,b). When heavy people lose weight, hills and stairs no longer seem so steep (Taylor-Covill & Eves, 2016).

- A softball appears bigger when you're hitting well, as researchers observed after asking players to choose a circle the size of the ball they had just hit well or poorly. There's also a reciprocal phenomenon: Seeing a target as bigger—as happens when athletes focus directly on a target—improves performance (Witt et al., 2012).

"When you're hitting the ball, it comes at you looking like a grapefruit. When you're not, it looks like a black-eyed pea." — Former Major League Baseball player George Scott

EMOTION Other clever experiments have demonstrated that emotions can shove our perceptions in one direction or another:

- Hearing sad music can predispose people to perceive a sad meaning in spoken homophonic words—*mourning* rather than *morning, die* rather than *dye, pain* rather than *pane* (Halberstadt et al., 1995).

- Hearing major-key (bright, cheery-sounding) music speeds up identification of happy emotion words (Tay & Ng, 2019). Thus, Beyoncé's "Single Ladies"—a major-key song—may make happy things in your environment easier to spot.

- When angry, people more often perceive neutral objects as guns (Baumann & DeSteno, 2010). When made to feel mildly upset by subliminal exposure to a scowling face, people perceive a neutral face as less attractive and less likable (Anderson et al., 2012).

Emotions and motives color our *social* perceptions, too. People more often perceive solitary confinement, sleep deprivation, and cold temperatures as "torture" when experiencing a small dose of such themselves (Nordgren et al., 2011). Spouses who feel loved and appreciated perceive less threat in stressful marital events—"He's just having a bad day" (Murray et al., 2003).

The point to remember: Much of what we perceive comes not just from what's "out there," but also from what's behind our eyes and between our ears. Through top-down processing, our experiences, assumptions, expectations—and even our context, motivation, and emotions—can shape and color our views of reality.

FIGURE 17.9
Context makes clearer The Hope College volleyball team celebrates its national championship winning moment.

Craig Klomparens/Hope College

MODULE

17 **REVIEW** Basic Concepts of Sensation and Perception

LEARNING OBJECTIVES

Test Yourself Answer these repeated Learning Objective Questions on your own (before checking the answers in Appendix D) to improve your retention of the concepts (McDaniel et al., 2009, 2015).

LOQ **17-1** What are *sensation* and *perception?* What do we mean by *bottom-up processing* and *top-down processing?*

LOQ **17-2** What three steps are basic to all our sensory systems?

LOQ **17-3** How do *absolute thresholds* and *difference thresholds* differ?

LOQ **17-4** How are we affected by subliminal stimuli?

LOQ **17-5** What is the function of sensory adaptation?

LOQ **17-6** How do our expectations, contexts, motivation, and emotions influence our perceptions?

TERMS AND CONCEPTS TO REMEMBER

Test Yourself Write down the definition in your own words, then check your answer.

sensation, p. 213

sensory receptors, p. 213

perception, p. 213

bottom-up processing, p. 213

top-down processing, p. 213

transduction, p. 213

psychophysics, p. 213

absolute threshold, p. 213

signal detection theory, p. 213

subliminal, p. 214

difference threshold, p. 214

Weber's law, p. 214

priming, p. 214

sensory adaptation, p. 217

perceptual set, p. 217

MASTER THE MATERIAL

Test Yourself Answer the following questions on your own first, then check your answers in Appendix E.

1. Sensation is to _____ as perception is to _____.

   a. absolute threshold; difference threshold

   b. bottom-up processing; top-down processing

   c. interpretation; detection

   d. grouping; priming

2. The process by which we organize and interpret sensory information is called _____.

3. Subliminal stimuli are

   a. too weak to be processed by the brain.

   b. consciously perceived more than 50 percent of the time.

   c. strong enough to affect our behavior at least 75 percent of the time.

   d. below our absolute threshold for conscious awareness.

4. Another term for *difference threshold* is the _____ _____ _____.

5. Weber's law states that for a difference to be perceived, two stimuli must differ by

   a. a fixed or constant energy amount.

   b. a constant minimum percentage.

   c. a constantly changing amount.

   d. more than 7 percent.

6. Sensory adaptation helps us focus on

   a. visual stimuli.

   b. auditory stimuli.

   c. constant features of the environment.

   d. important changes in the environment.

7. Our perceptual set influences what we perceive. This mental tendency reflects our

   a. experiences, assumptions, and expectations.

   b. sensory adaptation.

   c. priming ability.

   d. difference thresholds.

Continue testing yourself with 📚 **LearningCurve** or 📖 **Achieve Read & Practice** to learn and remember most effectively.

18 Vision: Sensory and Perceptual Processing

Light Energy and Eye Structures

LOQ 18-1 What are the characteristics of the energy that we see as visible light? What structures in the eye help focus that energy?

Our eyes receive light energy and *transduce* (transform) it into neural messages. Our brain—in one of life's greatest wonders—then creates what we consciously see. How does such a taken-for-granted yet extraordinary thing happen?

The Stimulus Input: Light Energy

When you look at a bright red tulip, the stimuli striking your eyes are not particles of the color red, but pulses of electromagnetic energy that your visual system *perceives* as red. What we see as visible light is but a thin slice of the wide spectrum of electromagnetic energy, ranging from imperceptibly short gamma waves to the very long waves of radio transmission (**FIGURE 18.1**). Other portions are visible to other animals. Bees, for instance, cannot see what we perceive as red but can see ultraviolet light.

Light travels in waves, and the shape of those waves influences what we see. Light's **wavelength** is the distance from one wave peak to the next (**FIGURE 18.2a**). Wavelength determines **hue,** the color we experience, such as the tulip's red petals or green leaves. A light wave's *amplitude,* or height, determines its **intensity**—the amount of energy the wave contains. Intensity influences *brightness* (Figure 18.2b).

To understand *how* we transform physical energy into color and meaning, we need to know more about vision's window—the eye.

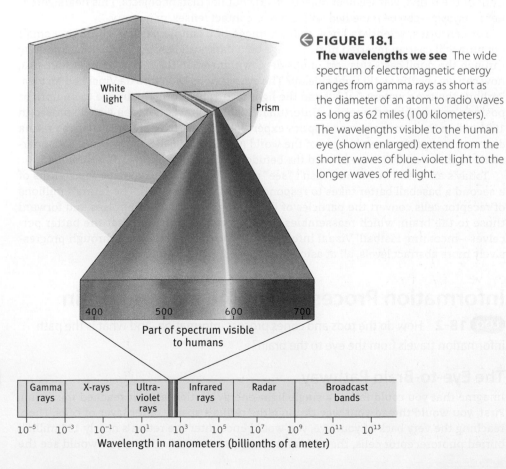

FIGURE 18.1

The wavelengths we see The wide spectrum of electromagnetic energy ranges from gamma rays as short as the diameter of an atom to radio waves as long as 62 miles (100 kilometers). The wavelengths visible to the human eye (shown enlarged) extend from the shorter waves of blue-violet light to the longer waves of red light.

White light

Prism

400 500 600 700

Part of spectrum visible to humans

| Gamma rays | X-rays | Ultra-violet rays | | Infrared rays | Radar | | Broadcast bands |

10^{-5} 10^{-3} 10^{-1} 10^{1} 10^{3} 10^{5} 10^{7} 10^{9} 10^{11} 10^{13}

Wavelength in nanometers (billionths of a meter)

wavelength the distance from the peak of one light or sound wave to the peak of the next. Electromagnetic wavelengths vary from the short blips of gamma rays to the long pulses of radio transmission.

hue the dimension of color that is determined by the wavelength of light; what we know as the color names *blue, green,* and so forth.

intensity the amount of energy in a light wave or sound wave, which influences what we perceive as brightness or loudness. Intensity is determined by the wave's amplitude (height).

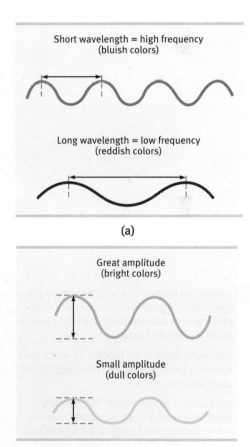

Short wavelength = high frequency (bluish colors)

Long wavelength = low frequency (reddish colors)

(a)

Great amplitude (bright colors)

Small amplitude (dull colors)

(b)

FIGURE 18.2

The physical properties of waves
(a) Waves vary in *wavelength* (the distance between successive peaks). *Frequency,* the number of complete wavelengths that can pass a point in a given time, depends on the wavelength. The shorter the wavelength, the higher the frequency. Wavelength determines the perceived *color* of light. (b) Waves also vary in *amplitude* (the height from peak to trough). Wave amplitude influences the perceived *brightness* of colors.

FIGURE 18.3

The eye Light rays reflected from a candle pass through the cornea, pupil, and lens. The curvature and thickness of the lens change to bring nearby or distant objects into focus on the retina. Rays from the top of the candle strike the bottom of the retina, and those from the left side of the candle strike the right side of the retina. The candle's image on the retina thus appears upside down and reversed.

Pascal Goetgheluck/Science Source

The Eye

Light enters the eye through the *cornea*, which bends light to help provide focus. The light then passes through the *pupil*, a small adjustable opening. Surrounding the pupil and controlling its size is the *iris*, a colored muscle that dilates or constricts in response to light intensity. Each iris is so distinctive that iris-scanning technology can often confirm your identity.

The iris responds to your cognitive and emotional states. If you have full vision, imagine a sunny sky—your iris will constrict; imagine a dark room and it will dilate (Laeng & Sulutvedt, 2014). The iris also constricts when you are about to answer *No* to a question, or when you feel disgust (de Gee et al., 2014; Goldinger & Papesh, 2012). And when you're feeling amorous or trusting, your telltale dilated pupils subtly signal your feelings (Attard-Johnson et al., 2016, 2017; Kret & De Dreu, 2017; Prochanzkova et al., 2018).

After passing through your pupil, light hits the transparent *lens* in your eye. The lens then focuses the light rays into an image on your **retina,** the multilayered tissue on the eyeball's sensitive inner surface. To focus the rays, the lens changes its curvature and thickness in a process called **accommodation.** If the lens focuses the image on a point in front of the retina, you see near objects clearly but not distant objects. This nearsightedness—*myopia*—can be remedied with glasses, contact lenses, or surgery.

For centuries, scientists knew that an image of a candle passing through a small opening will cast an inverted mirror image on a dark wall behind. If the image passing through the pupil casts this sort of upside-down image on the retina, as in **FIGURE 18.3,** how can we see the world right side up? The ever-curious Leonardo da Vinci had an idea: Perhaps the eye's watery fluids bend the light rays, reinverting the image to an upright position as it reaches the retina. Unfortunately for da Vinci, that idea was disproved in 1604, when the astronomer and optics expert Johannes Kepler showed that the retina *does* receive upside-down images of the world (Crombie, 1964). So how could we understand such a world? "I leave it," said the befuddled Kepler, "to natural philosophers."

Today's answer: The retina doesn't "see" a whole image. Consider the four-tenths of a second a baseball batter takes to respond to a pitcher's fastball. The retina's millions of receptor cells convert the particles of light energy into neural impulses and forward those to the brain, which reassembles them, right side up, into what the batter perceives—incoming fastball! Visual information processing percolates through progressively more abstract levels, all at astonishing speed.

Information Processing in the Eye and Brain

LOQ 18-2 How do the rods and cones process information, and what is the path information travels from the eye to the brain?

The Eye-to-Brain Pathway

Imagine that you could follow a single light-energy particle after it reached the retina. First, you would thread your way through the retina's sparse outer layer of cells. Then, reaching the very back of your eye, you would encounter the retina's nearly 130 million buried photoreceptor cells, the **rods** and **cones** (FIGURE 18.4). There, you would see the

retina the light-sensitive inner surface of the eye, containing the receptor rods and cones plus layers of neurons that begin the processing of visual information.

accommodation the process by which the eye's lens changes shape to focus near or far objects on the retina.

rods retinal receptors that detect black, white, and gray, and are sensitive to movement. Rods are necessary for peripheral and twilight vision, when cones don't respond.

cones retinal receptors that are concentrated near the center of the retina and that function in daylight or in well-lit conditions. Cones detect fine detail and give rise to color sensations.

optic nerve the nerve that carries neural impulses from the eye to the brain.

blind spot the point at which the optic nerve leaves the eye, creating a "blind" spot because no receptor cells are located there.

fovea the central focal point in the retina, around which the eye's cones cluster.

1. Light entering eye triggers chemical reaction in rods and cones at back of retina.

2. Chemical reaction in turn activates bipolar cells.

Light

Ganglion cell

Bipolar cell

Cone

Rod

Neural impulse

Cross section of retina

Optic nerve

To the brain's visual cortex via the thalamus

3. Bipolar cells then activate the ganglion cells, whose combined axons form the optic nerve. This nerve transmits information (via the thalamus) to the brain's visual cortex.

◀ **FIGURE 18.4**
The retina's reaction to light

light energy trigger chemical changes. That chemical reaction would spark neural signals in nearby *bipolar cells.* You could then watch the bipolar cells activate neighboring *ganglion cells,* whose axons twine together like the strands of a rope to form the **optic nerve.** After a momentary stopover at the thalamus, the information would fly on to the final destination, your visual cortex, in the occipital lobe at the back of your brain.

The optic nerve is an information highway from the eye to the brain. This nerve can send nearly 1 million messages at once through its nearly 1 million ganglion fibers. (The auditory nerve, which enables hearing, carries much less information through its mere 30,000 fibers.) We pay a price for this high-speed connection. Your eye has a **blind spot,** with no receptor cells, where the optic nerve leaves the eye (**FIGURE 18.5**). Close one eye. Do you see a black hole? *No,* because, without seeking your approval, your brain fills in the hole.

RETRIEVAL PRACTICE

RP-1 There are no receptor cells where the optic nerve leaves the eye. This creates a blind spot in your vision. To demonstrate, close your left eye, look at the black dot, and move your face away until one of the cars disappears. (Which one do you predict it will be?) Repeat with your right eye closed—and note that now the other car disappears. Can you explain why?

◀ **FIGURE 18.5**
The blind spot

ANSWERS IN APPENDIX E

Rods and cones differ in where they're found and in what they do (**TABLE 18.1**). *Cones* cluster in and around the **fovea,** the retina's area of central focus (Figure 18.3). Many cones have their own hotline to the brain: One cone transmits its message to a single bipolar cell, which relays the message to the visual cortex (where a large area receives input from the fovea). These direct connections preserve the cones' precise information, making them better able to detect fine detail. Cones can detect white and enable you to perceive color—but not at night (Sabesan et al., 2016).

Rods, which (unlike cones) are located around the retina's outer regions, remain sensitive in dim light, and they enable black-and-white vision. Rods have no hotline to the brain. If cones are soloists, rods perform as a chorus. Several rods pool their faint energy output and funnel it onto a single bipolar cell, which sends the combined message to your brain.

TABLE 18.1 Receptors in the Human Eye: Rod-Shaped Rods and Cone-Shaped Cones

	Cones	Rods
Number	6 million	120 million
Location in retina	Center	Periphery
Sensitivity in dim light	Low	High
Color sensitivity	High	Low
Detail sensitivity	High	Low

Omikron/Science Source

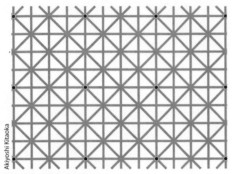

Akiyoshi Kitaoka

FIGURE 18.6
How many disappearing dots can you see at once? Look at or near any of the 12 and you can see them, but not in your peripheral vision.

Cones and rods each provide a special sensitivity—cones to detail and color, and rods to faint light and peripheral motion. Stop for a minute and experience this rod–cone difference. Pick a word in this sentence and stare directly at it, focusing its image on the cones in your fovea. Notice that words distant from it appear blurred? They lack detail because their image is striking your retina's outer regions, where rods predominate. Thus, when you drive or bike, rods help you detect a car in your peripheral vision well before you perceive its details. And in **FIGURE 18.6**, which has 12 black dots, you can see barely two at a time, with your brain filling in the less distinct peripheral input (Kitaoka, 2016, adapting Ninio & Stevens, 2000).

When you enter a darkened theater or turn off the light at night, your pupils dilate to allow more light to reach your retina. Your eyes adapt, but fully adapting typically takes 20 minutes or more. This period of dark adaptation matches the average natural twilight transition between the Sun's setting and darkness. How wonderfully made we are.

At the entry level, the retina's neural layers don't just pass along electrical impulses; they also help to encode and analyze sensory information. (The third neural layer in a frog's eye, for example, contains those "bug detector" cells that fire only in response to moving fly-like stimuli.) In human eyes, any given retinal area relays its information to a corresponding location in your visual cortex, in the occipital lobe. The brain's peculiar wiring means that half of each eye's sensory information arrives in the opposite side of the brain, by crossing the X-shaped *optic chiasm* (**FIGURE 18.7**).

The same sensitivity that enables retinal cells to fire messages can lead them to misfire, as you can demonstrate. Turn your eyes to the left, close them, and then gently rub the right side of your right eyelid with your fingertip. Note the patch of light to the left, moving as your finger moves.

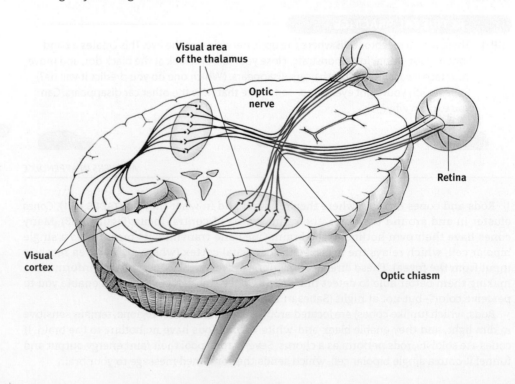

FIGURE 18.7
Pathway from the eyes to the visual cortex The retina's ganglion axons form the optic nerve. It runs to the thalamus, where the axons synapse with neurons that run to the visual cortex.

Why do you see light? Why at the left? This happens because your retinal cells are so responsive that even pressure triggers them. But your brain interprets their firing as light. Moreover, it interprets the light as coming from the left—the normal direction of light that activates the right side of the retina.

ASK YOURSELF

Consider your activities in the last day. Which of them relied on your rods? Which relied on your cones? How would these activities be different—or impossible—without these cells' different abilities?

RETRIEVAL PRACTICE

RP-2 Some nocturnal animals, such as toads, mice, rats, and bats, have impressive night vision thanks to having many more _____ (rods/cones) than _____ (rods/cones) in their retinas. These creatures probably have very poor _____ (color/black-and-white) vision.

Kruglov_Orda/Shutterstock

RP-3 Cats are able to open their _____ much wider than we can, which allows more light into their eyes so they can see better at night.

ANSWERS IN APPENDIX E

Color Processing

LOQ 18-3   How do we perceive color in the world around us?

We talk as though objects possess color: "A tomato is red." Recall the old question, "If a tree falls in the forest and no one hears it, does it make a sound?" We can ask the same of color: If no one sees the tomato, is it red?

The answer is *No*. First, the tomato is everything *but* red, because it *rejects* (reflects) the long wavelengths of red. Second, the tomato's color is our mental construction. As Sir Isaac Newton (1704) noted, "The [light] rays are not colored." Like all aspects of vision, our perception of color resides not in the object itself but in the theater of our brain; even while dreaming, we usually perceive things in color.

One of vision's most basic and intriguing mysteries is how we see the world in color. How, from the light energy striking the retina, does our brain construct our experience of such a multitude of colors?

Modern detective work on the mystery of color vision began in the nineteenth century, when German scientist Hermann von Helmholtz built on the insights of an English physicist, Thomas Young. They knew that any color can be created by combining the light waves of three primary colors—red, green, and blue. So Young and von Helmholtz's research led to a hypothesis: The eye must therefore have three corresponding types of color receptors.

Researchers later confirmed the **Young-Helmholtz trichromatic (three-color) theory,** by measuring the response of various cones to different color stimuli. The retina does indeed have three types of color receptors, each especially sensitive to the wavelengths of red, green, or blue. When light stimulates combinations of these cones, we see other colors. For example, the retina has no separate receptors especially sensitive to yellow. But when red and green wavelengths stimulate both red-sensitive and green-sensitive cones, we see yellow. Said differently, when your eyes see red and green without blue, your brain says *yellow*.

By one estimate, most of us can see differences among more than 1 million color variations (Neitz et al., 2001). Some lucky people, mostly female, can see up to 100 million colors thanks to a genetic condition known as *tetrachromatic color vision* (Jordan et al., 2010). Asked to look at a leaf, a woman with tetrachromatic color vision said, "You might see dark green but I'll see violet, turquoise, blue. It's like a mosaic of color" (Ossola, 2014). Others less fortunate, mostly male, have the genetically sex-linked condition of *color-deficient vision*. Worldwide, about 1 in 12 males and 1 in 200 females are "color blind." Most are not actually blind to all colors: They simply lack functioning red- or green-sensitive cones, or sometimes both. Their vision—perhaps unknown to them, because their lifelong vision *seems* normal—is monochromatic (one-color) or dichromatic (two-color) instead of trichromatic, making it impossible to distinguish the red and green in **FIGURE 18.8** (Boynton, 1979). Dogs, too, lack receptors for the wavelengths of red, giving them only limited, dichromatic color vision (Neitz et al., 1989).

"It is in the brain that the poppy is red, that the apple is odorous, that the skylark sings." — Oscar Wilde, love letter to Alfred Douglas, 1896

In Singapore, yellow taxis—which are strikingly visible—have had 9 percent fewer accidents than blue taxis (Ho et al., 2017).

Young-Helmholtz trichromatic (three-color) theory the theory that the retina contains three different types of color receptors—one most sensitive to red, one to green, one to blue—which, when stimulated in combination, can produce the perception of any color.

FIGURE 18.8

Color-deficient vision The photo in image (a) shows how people with red-green deficiency perceived a 2015 Buffalo Bills versus New York Jets football game. "For the 8 percent of Americans like me that are red-green colorblind, this game is a nightmare to watch," tweeted one fan. "Everyone looks like they're on the same team," said another. The photo in image (b) shows how the game looked for those with normal color vision.

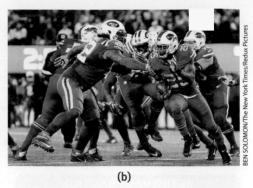

(a)   (b)

BEN SOLOMON/The New York Times/Redux Pictures

But why do people blind to red and green often still see yellow? And why does yellow appear to be a pure color and not a mixture of red and green, the way purple is of red and blue? As physiologist Ewald Hering—a contemporary of von Helmholtz—noted, trichromatic theory leaves some parts of the color vision mystery unsolved.

Hering found a clue in *afterimages*. If you stare at a green square for a while and then look at a white sheet of paper, you will see red, green's *opponent color*. Stare at a yellow square and its opponent color, blue, will appear on the white paper. (To experience this, try the flag demonstration in **FIGURE 18.9**.) Hering formed another hypothesis: Color vision must involve two *additional* color processes, one responsible for red-versus-green perception, and one for blue-versus-yellow perception.

Indeed, a century later, researchers also confirmed Hering's hypothesis, now called the **opponent-process theory.** This concept is tricky, but here is the gist: Color vision depends on three sets of opposing retinal processes—*red-green, blue-yellow,* and *white-black*. As impulses travel to the visual cortex, some neurons in both the retina and the thalamus are turned "on" by red but turned "off" by green. Others are turned on by green but off by red (DeValois & DeValois, 1975). Like red and green marbles sent down a narrow tube, "red" and "green" messages cannot both travel at once. Red and green are thus opponents, so we see either red or green, not a reddish-green mixture. But red and blue travel in separate channels, so we *can* see a reddish-blue magenta.

So how does opponent-process theory help us understand negative afterimages, as in the flag demonstration? Here's the answer (for the green changing to red): First, you stared at green bars, which tired your green response. Then you stared at a white area. White contains all colors, including red. Because you had tired your green response, only the red part of the green-red pairing fired normally.

The present solution to the mystery of color vision is therefore roughly this: *Color processing occurs in two stages.*

1. The retina's red-, green-, and blue-sensitive cones respond in varying degrees to different color stimuli, as the Young-Helmholtz trichromatic theory suggested.

2. The cones' responses are then processed by opponent-process cells, as Hering's opponent-process theory proposed.

ASK YOURSELF

Does it surprise you to learn that colors don't "live" in the objects we perceive—that in fact, these objects are everything but the color we experience? If someone had asked you, "Is grass green?" before you read this section, how would you have responded?

FIGURE 18.9

Afterimage effect Stare at the center of the flag for a minute and then shift your eyes to the dot in the white space beside it. What do you see? (After tiring your neural response to black, green, and yellow, you should see their opponent colors.) Stare at a white wall and note how the size of the flag grows with the projection distance.

RP-4 What are two key theories of color vision? Are they contradictory or complementary? Explain.

ANSWERS IN APPENDIX E

📶 For an interactive review of these color vision principles, visit *Topic Tutorial: PsychSim6, Colorful World.*

Feature Detection

LOQ 18-4 Where are feature detectors located, and what do they do?

Scientists once likened the brain to a movie screen on which the eye projected images. Then along came David Hubel and Torsten Wiesel (1979), who showed that our visual processing deconstructs visual images and then reassembles them. Hubel and Wiesel received a Nobel Prize for their work on **feature detectors,** nerve cells in the occipital lobe's visual cortex that respond to a scene's specific features—to particular edges, lines, angles, and movements.

Using microelectrodes, they had discovered that some neurons fired actively when cats were shown lines at one angle, while other neurons responded to lines at a different angle. They surmised that these specialized neurons, now known as feature detectors, receive information from individual ganglion cells in the retina. Feature detectors pass this specific information to other cortical areas, where teams of cells *(supercell clusters)* respond to more complex patterns.

For biologically important objects and events, monkey brains (and surely ours as well) have a "vast visual encyclopedia" distributed as specialized cells (Perrett et al., 1990, 1992, 1994). These cells respond to one type of stimulus, such as a specific gaze, head angle, posture, or body movement. Other supercell clusters integrate this information and fire only when the cues collectively indicate the direction of someone's attention and approach. This instant analysis, which aided our ancestors' survival, also helps a hockey player anticipate where to shoot the puck, and a driver to anticipate a pedestrian's next movement.

One temporal lobe area by your right ear (**FIGURE 18.10**) enables you to perceive faces and, thanks to a specialized neural network, to recognize them from varied viewpoints (Connor, 2010). This *fusiform face area* helps us identify faces from friends and strangers, from people who look different from us and from those of similar ethnic background (Hughes et al., 2019; Wiese et al., 2019). If your fusiform face area were stimulated, you might spontaneously see faces. One participant reported to an experimenter, "You just turned into someone else. Your face metamorphosed" (Koch, 2015). Damage the fusiform face area and you might recognize other forms and objects, but not familiar faces.

When researchers temporarily disrupt the brain's face-processing areas with magnetic pulses, people are unable to recognize faces. But they can still recognize other objects, such as houses, because the brain's face perception occurs separately from its object perception (McKone et al., 2007; Pitcher et al., 2007). Thus, functional MRI (fMRI) scans have shown different brain areas activating when people viewed varied objects (Downing et al., 2001). Brain activity is so specific that, with the help of brain scans, researchers can tell whether people are "looking at a shoe, a chair, or a face, based on the pattern of their brain activity" (Haxby, 2001).

opponent-process theory the theory that opposing retinal processes (red-green, blue-yellow, white-black) enable color vision. For example, some cells are stimulated by green and inhibited by red; others are stimulated by red and inhibited by green.

feature detectors nerve cells in the brain's visual cortex that respond to specific features of the stimulus, such as shape, angle, or movement.

Face recognition area
(fusiform face area)

⊘ **FIGURE 18.10**

How your brain processes faces In social animals such as humans, a large right temporal lobe area (shown here in a right-facing brain) is dedicated to the crucial task of face recognition. Viewing famous people's faces, compared with famous buildings, increases activation in this fusiform face area (Gorno-Tempini & Price, 2001).

Supercells score In this 2017 National Hockey League game, Alex Ovechkin (in red) instantly processed visual information about the positions and movements of three opponents. By using his pattern-detecting supercells, Ovechkin somehow managed to get the puck into the net.

parallel processing processing many aspects of a stimulus or problem simultaneously.

gestalt an organized whole. Gestalt psychologists emphasized our tendency to integrate pieces of information into meaningful wholes.

figure-ground the organization of the visual field into objects (the *figures*) that stand out from their surroundings (the *ground*).

grouping the perceptual tendency to organize stimuli into coherent groups.

Parallel Processing

LOQ 18-5 How does the brain use parallel processing to construct visual perceptions?

Our brain achieves these and other remarkable feats by **parallel processing:** doing many things at once. To analyze a visual scene, the brain processes its subdimensions—motion, form, depth, color—simultaneously.

To recognize a face, your brain integrates information projected by your retinas to several visual cortex areas and compares it with stored information, thus enabling your fusiform face area to recognize the face: *Grandmother!* Scientists have debated whether this stored information is contained in a single cell or, as now seems more likely, distributed over a network of cells that build a facial image bit by bit (Tsao, 2019). But some supercells—actually nicknamed *"grandmother cells"*—do appear to respond very selectively to 1 or 2 faces in 100 (Bowers, 2009; Quiroga et al., 2013). The whole face-recognition process requires tremendous brain power, involving connections between visual, memory, social, and auditory networks (Ramot et al., 2019). Supercells require super-sized brain power.

Destroy or disable the neural workstation for a visual subtask, and something peculiar results, as happened to "Mrs. M." (Hoffman, 1998). After a stroke damaged areas near the rear of both sides of her brain, she could not perceive motion. People in a room seemed "suddenly here or there but I [had] not seen them moving." Pouring tea into a cup was a challenge because the fluid appeared frozen—she could not perceive it rising in the cup.

After stroke or surgery has damaged the brain's visual cortex, others have experienced *blindsight*. Shown a series of sticks, they report seeing nothing. Yet when asked to guess whether the sticks are vertical or horizontal, their visual intuition typically offers the correct response. When told, "You got them all right," they are astounded. There is, it seems, a second "mind"—a parallel processing system—operating unseen. These separate visual systems for perceiving and for acting illustrate once again the astonishing dual processing of our two-track mind.

* * *

Think about the wonders of visual processing. As you read these words, the letters reflect light rays onto your retina, which triggers a process that sends formless nerve impulses to several areas of your brain, which integrate the information and decode its meaning. The amazing result: We have transferred information across time and space, from our minds to yours (**FIGURE 18.11**). That all of this happens instantly, effortlessly, and continuously is indeed awesome. As Roger Sperry (1985) observed, the "insights of science give added, not lessened, reasons for awe, respect, and reverence."

"I am . . . wonderfully made." — King David, Psalm 139:14

RETRIEVAL PRACTICE

RP-5 What is the rapid sequence of events that occurs when you see and recognize a friend?

ANSWERS IN APPENDIX E

For a 4-minute depiction of a blindsight patient, see the *Video—Blindsight: Seeing Without Awareness.*

FIGURE 18.11
A simplified summary of visual information processing

Tom Walker/Getty Images

| Scene | → | **Retinal processing:** Receptor rods and cones → bipolar cells → ganglion cells | → | **Feature detection:** Brain's detector cells respond to specific features—edges, lines, and angles | → | **Parallel processing:** Brain cell teams process combined information about color, movement, form, and depth | → | **Recognition:** Brain interprets the constructed image based on information from stored images—it's a tiger! |

Perceptual Organization

LOQ 18-6 How did the Gestalt psychologists understand perceptual organization, and how do figure-ground and grouping principles contribute to our perceptions?

Our understanding of how we organize and interpret sights into *meaningful* perceptions—a rose in bloom, a familiar face, a sunset—was advanced early in the twentieth century by a group of German psychologists. They noticed that people given a cluster of sensations tend to organize them into a **gestalt,** a German word meaning a "form" or a "whole." As we look straight ahead with both eyes open, we cannot separate the perceived scene into our left and right fields of view (each as seen with one eye closed). Our conscious perception is, at every moment, a seamless scene—an integrated whole.

Consider **FIGURE 18.12**: The individual elements of this figure, called a *Necker cube,* are really nothing but eight hexagons, each containing three converging white lines. What happens when we view these elements together? The resulting Necker cube nicely illustrates a favorite saying of Gestalt psychologists: *In perception, the whole may exceed the sum of its parts.*

Over the years, the Gestalt psychologists demonstrated many principles we use to organize our sensations into perceptions (Wagemans et al., 2012a,b). Underlying all of them is a fundamental truth: *Our brain does more than register information about the world.* Perception is not a picture printing itself on the brain. We filter incoming information and *construct* perceptions. Mind matters.

Form Perception

Imagine designing one of today's video-computer systems that, like your eye-brain system, recognizes faces at a glance. What abilities would it need?

FIGURE AND GROUND To start with, the system needs to perceive **figure-ground**—to separate faces from their backgrounds. In our eye-brain system, this is our first perceptual task—perceiving any object (the *figure*) as distinct from its surroundings (the *ground*). As you read, the words are the figure; the white space is the ground. This perception applies to our hearing, too. As you hear voices at a party, the one you attend to becomes the figure; all others are part of the ground. Sometimes the same stimulus can trigger more than one perception. In **FIGURE 18.13**, the figure-ground relationship continually reverses. First we see the vase (or the faces), then the faces (or the vase), but we always organize the stimulus into a figure seen against a ground.

GROUPING Having discriminated figure from ground, we (and our video-computer system) must also organize the figure into a *meaningful* form. Some basic features of a scene—such as color, movement, and light-dark contrast—we process instantly and automatically (Treisman, 1987). Our mind brings order and form to other stimuli by following certain rules for **grouping,** also identified by the Gestalt psychologists. These rules, which we apply even as infants and even in our touch perceptions, illustrate how the perceived whole differs from the sum of its parts, rather as water differs from its hydrogen and oxygen parts (Gallace & Spence, 2011; Quinn et al., 2002; Rock & Palmer, 1990). See **FIGURE 18.14** for three examples.

◄ FIGURE 18.12
A Necker cube What do you see: hexagons with white lines, or a cube? If you stare at the cube, you may notice that it reverses location, moving the tiny X from the front edge to the back. At times, the cube may seem to float forward, with hexagons behind it. At other times, the hexagons may become holes through which the cube appears, as though it were floating behind them. There is far more to perception than meets the eye. (From Bradley et al., 1976.)

◄ FIGURE 18.13
Reversible figure and ground

◄ FIGURE 18.14
Three principles of grouping (a) Thanks to *proximity*, we group nearby figures together. We see not six separate lines, but three sets of two lines. (b) Through *continuity*, we perceive smooth, continuous patterns rather than discontinuous ones. This pattern could be a series of alternating semicircles, but we perceive it as two continuous lines—one wavy, one straight. (c) Using *closure*, we fill in gaps to create a complete, whole object. Thus, we assume that the circles on the left are complete but partially blocked by the (illusory) triangle. Add nothing more than little line segments to close off the circles and your brain may stop constructing a triangle.

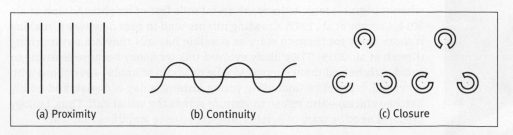

| (a) Proximity | (b) Continuity | (c) Closure |

➔ **depth perception** the ability to see objects in three dimensions, although the images that strike the retina are two-dimensional; allows us to judge distance.

visual cliff a laboratory device for testing depth perception in infants and young animals.

➔ **FIGURE 18.15**
Great Gestalt! What's the secret to this impossible doghouse? You probably perceive this doghouse as a gestalt—a whole (though impossible) structure. Actually, your brain imposes this sense of wholeness on the picture. As **FIGURE 18.19** shows, Gestalt grouping principles such as closure and continuity are at work here.

Such principles usually help us construct reality. Sometimes, however, they lead us astray, as when we look at the doghouse in **FIGURE 18.15**.

RETRIEVAL PRACTICE

RP-6 In terms of perception, a band's lead singer would be considered _____ (figure/ground), and the other musicians would be considered _____ (figure/ground).

RP-7 What do we mean when we say that, in perception, "the whole may exceed the sum of its parts"?

ANSWERS IN APPENDIX E

Depth Perception

LOQ 18-7 How do we use binocular and monocular cues to see in three dimensions, and how do we perceive motion?

Our eye-brain system performs many remarkable feats, among which is **depth perception.** From the two-dimensional images falling on our retinas, we somehow organize three-dimensional perceptions that, for example, let us estimate the distance of an oncoming car. How do we acquire this ability? Are we born with it? Did we learn it?

As psychologist Eleanor Gibson picnicked on the rim of the Grand Canyon, her scientific curiosity kicked in. She wondered: *Would a toddler peering over the rim perceive the dangerous drop-off and draw back?* To answer that question and others, Gibson and Richard Walk (1960) designed a series of experiments in their Cornell University laboratory using a **visual cliff**—a model of a cliff with a "drop-off" area that was actually covered by sturdy glass. They placed 6- to 14-month-old infants on the edge of the "cliff" and had one of the parents coax the infants to lean over the glass or crawl out onto it (**FIGURE 18.16**). Most infants refused to do so, indicating that they could perceive depth.

Creating three-dimensional perceptions from two-dimensions Several of the world's cities slow traffic with illusory 3-D crosswalk paintings, thanks to artists Saumya Pandya Thakkar and Shakuntala Pandyaand, who created the first of these in India.

Had they *learned* to perceive depth? Learning appears also to be part of the human story. Years after Gibson and Walk's classic visual cliff studies, psychologist Karen Adolph continued to study infant motor development (Adolph & Hoch, 2019). Adolph and others showed that crawling, no matter when it begins, seems to increase an infant's fear of heights (Adolph et al., 2014; Campos et al., 1992). Crawling infants tend to gaze downward, making it more likely for them to stare at possible hazards they are approaching (Kretch et al., 2014). They likely evolved this tendency because learning to avoid cliffs helped them survive. Mobile newborn animals—even those with no visual experience (including young kittens, a day-old goat, and newly hatched chicks)—also refuse to venture across the visual cliff. Thus, biology prepares us to be wary of heights, and experience amplifies that fear.

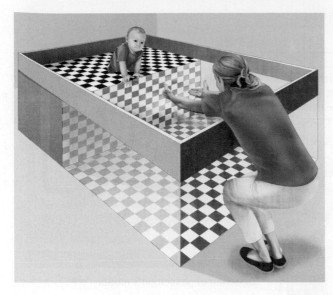

FIGURE 18.16
Visual cliff Eleanor Gibson and Richard Walk devised this glass-covered miniature cliff to determine whether crawling infants and newborn animals can perceive depth.

If we were to build the ability to perceive depth into our video-computer system, what rules might enable it to convert two-dimensional images into a single three-dimensional perception? A good place to start would be the depth cues our brain receives from information supplied by one or both eyes.

BINOCULAR CUES People who see with two eyes perceive depth thanks partly to **binocular cues.** Here's a demonstration you might try: With both eyes open, hold two pens or pencils in front of you and touch their tips together. Now do so with one eye closed. A more difficult task, yes?

We use binocular cues to judge the distance of nearby objects. One such cue is *convergence,* the inward angle of the eyes focusing on a near object. Another is **retinal disparity.** Because there is space between your eyes, each retina receives a slightly different image of the world. By comparing these two images, your brain can judge how close an object is to you. The greater the disparity (difference) between the two retinal images, the closer the object. Try it. Hold your two index fingers, with the tips just barely not touching, in front of your nose, and your retinas will receive quite different views. If you close one eye and then the other, you can see the difference. (With your fingers close to your face you will create a finger sausage, as in **FIGURE 18.17**.) At a greater distance—say, when you hold your fingers at arm's length—the disparity is smaller.

We could easily include retinal disparity in our video-computer system. Moviemakers sometimes film a scene through two lenses placed a bit apart. Viewers then watch the film through glasses that allow the left eye to see only the image from the left camera, and the right eye to see only the image from the right camera. The resulting effect, as 3-D movie fans know, mimics or exaggerates normal retinal disparity, giving the perception of depth.

FIGURE 18.17
The floating finger sausage Hold your two index fingers about 5 inches (12 centimeters) in front of your eyes, with their tips half an inch (1 centimeter) apart. Now look beyond them and note the weird result. Move your fingers out farther and the retinal disparity—and the finger sausage—will shrink.

binocular cue a depth cue, such as retinal disparity, that depends on the use of two eyes.

retinal disparity a binocular cue for perceiving depth. By comparing retinal images from the two eyes, the brain computes distance—the greater the disparity (difference) between the two images, the closer the object.

Relative height We perceive objects higher in our field of vision as farther away. Because we assume the lower part of a figure-ground illustration is closer, we perceive it as figure (Vecera et al., 2002). Invert this illustration and the black will become ground, like a night sky.

Image courtesy of Shaun P. Vecera, Ph.D., adapted from stimuli that appeared in Vecera et al., 2002.

Relative size If we assume two objects are similar in size, *most* people perceive the one that casts the smaller retinal image as farther away.

BIZARRO © 2014 Dan Piraro, Dist. By King Features

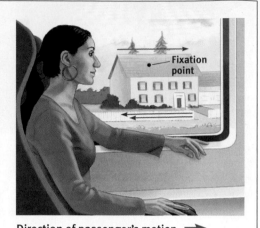

Direction of passenger's motion →

Relative motion As we move, stable objects may also appear to move. If while riding on a bus you fix your gaze on some point—say, a house—the objects beyond the fixation point will appear to move with you. Objects in front of the point will appear to move backward. The farther an object is from the fixation point, the faster it will seem to move.

Rhymes with Oranges © 2010 Hilary B. Price. Distributed by King Features Syndicate, Inc.

Linear perspective Parallel lines appear to meet in the distance. The sharper the angle of convergence, the greater the perceived distance.

Philip Mugridge/Alamy

Interposition If one object partially blocks our view of another, we perceive it as closer.

⬆ **FIGURE 18.18**
Monocular depth cues

Unlike carnivores, whose eyes enable forward focus on prey and offer binocular vision-enhanced depth perception, grazing herbivores typically have eyes on either side of their skull. Although lacking superior depth perception, herbivores have sweeping peripheral vision, all the better to detect predators.

MONOCULAR CUES How do we judge whether a person is 10 or 100 meters away? Retinal disparity won't help us here, because there won't be much difference between the images cast on our right and left retinas. At such distances, we depend on **monocular cues** (depth cues available to each eye separately). See **FIGURE 18.18** for some examples.

RETRIEVAL PRACTICE

RP-8 How do we normally perceive depth?

ANSWERS IN APPENDIX E

🔖 Check your understanding of these cues by engaging online with *Concept Practice: Depth Cues.*

monocular cue a depth cue, such as interposition or linear perspective, available to either eye alone.

phi phenomenon an illusion of movement created when two or more adjacent lights blink on and off in quick succession.

perceptual constancy perceiving objects as unchanging (having consistent color, brightness, shape, and size) even as illumination and retinal images change.

Motion Perception

Imagine that, like Mrs. M. described earlier, you could perceive the world as having color, form, and depth but that you could not see motion. Not only would you be unable to bike or drive, you would have trouble writing, eating, and walking.

Normally your brain computes motion based partly on its assumption that shrinking objects are retreating (not getting smaller) and enlarging objects are approaching. In young children, this ability to correctly perceive approaching (and enlarging) vehicles is not yet fully developed, which puts them at risk for pedestrian accidents (Wann et al., 2011). But it's not just children who have occasional difficulties with motion perception.

Our adult brain is sometimes tricked into believing what it is not seeing. When large and small objects move at the same speed, the large objects appear to move more slowly. Thus, trains seem to move slower than cars, and jumbo jets seem to land more slowly than little jets.

Have you noticed how often you interrupt your vision with a .1 second blink—about 15 times per minute or 15,000 times per day? Probably not. Our brain perceives a rapid series of slightly varying images as continuous movement (a phenomenon called *stroboscopic movement*). As film animators know well, a superfast slide show of 24 still pictures a second will create an illusion of movement. We construct that motion in our heads, just as we construct movement in blinking marquees and holiday lights. We perceive two adjacent stationary lights blinking on and off in quick succession as one single light moving back and forth. Lighted signs exploit this **phi phenomenon** with a succession of lights that creates the impression of, say, a moving arrow.

Perceptual Constancy

LOQ 18-8 How do perceptual constancies help us construct meaningful perceptions?

So far, we have noted that our video-computer system must perceive objects as we do—as having a distinct form, location, and motion. Its next task is to recognize objects without being deceived by changes in their color, brightness, shape, or size—a *top-down* process called **perceptual constancy.** Regardless of the viewing angle, distance, and illumination, we can identify people and things in less time than it takes to draw a breath. This feat is a huge challenge for a video computer system.

COLOR AND BRIGHTNESS CONSTANCIES James Gibson (1979) argued for an *ecological approach* to perception, in which our perceptions depend on an object's context. Consider how you experience the color of a tomato—and how it would change if you viewed it through a paper tube over the course of a day. As the light—and thus the tomato's reflected wavelengths—changed, the tomato's color would also seem to change. But if you discarded the paper tube and viewed the tomato as one item in a salad bowl, its perceived color would remain essentially constant, a consistent perception we call *color constancy*.

Though we take color constancy for granted, this ability is truly remarkable. A blue poker chip under indoor lighting reflects wavelengths that match those reflected by a sunlit gold chip (Jameson, 1985). Yet bring a goldfinch indoors and it won't look like a bluebird. The color is not in the bird's feathers. We see color thanks to our brain's computations of the light reflected by an object *relative to the objects surrounding it*. **FIGURE 18.20** dramatically illustrates the ability of a blue object to appear very different in three different contexts. Yet we have no trouble seeing these disks as blue. Nor does knowing the

⤵ **FIGURE 18.19**

The solution Another view of the impossible doghouse in Figure 18.15 reveals the secrets of this illusion. From the photo angle, the grouping principles of closure and continuity lead us to perceive the boards as continuous.

"From there to here, from here to there, funny things are everywhere." — Dr. Seuss, *One Fish, Two Fish, Red Fish, Blue Fish*, 1960

R. Beau Lotto/Lottolab

(a)   (b)

⤺ **FIGURE 18.20**

Color depends on context (a) Believe it or not, these three blue disks are identical in color. (b) Remove the surrounding context and see what results.

Seeing color?
Surprise! This is actually a black and white photo. Did the colorful, overlaid grid lines trick your eyes, too?

⊘ FIGURE 18.21
Relative luminance
Because of its surrounding context, we perceive Square A as lighter than Square B. But believe it or not, they are identical. To channel comedian Richard Pryor, "Who you gonna believe: me, or your lying eyes?" If you believe your lying eyes—actually, your lying brain—you can photocopy (or screen-capture and print) the illustration, then cut out the squares and compare them. (Information from Edward Adelson.) Such human mistakes are so reliable that one computer system uses them to identify human website users—knowing that computer spam robots answer *correctly*.

"Sometimes I wonder: Why is that Frisbee getting bigger? And then it hits me." — Anonymous

truth—that these disks are identically colored—diminish our perception that they are quite different. Because we construct our perceptions, we can simultaneously accept alternative objective and subjective realities.

Brightness constancy (also called *lightness constancy*) similarly depends on context. We perceive an object as having a constant brightness even as its illumination varies. This perception of constancy depends on *relative luminance*—the amount of light an object reflects *relative to its surroundings* (**FIGURE 18.21**). White paper reflects 90 percent of the light falling on it; black paper, only 10 percent. Although a black paper viewed in sunlight may reflect 100 times more light than does a white paper viewed indoors, it will still look black (McBurney & Collings, 1984). But try viewing sunlit black paper through a narrow tube so nothing else is visible and it may look gray, because in bright sunshine it reflects a fair amount of light. View it without the tube and it is again black, because it reflects much less light than the objects around it.

This principle—that we perceive objects not in isolation but in their environmental context—matters to artists, interior decorators, and clothing designers. Our perception of the color and brightness of a wall or of a streak of paint on a canvas is determined not just by the paint itself but by the surrounding colors. The take-home lesson: *Context governs our perceptions.*

SHAPE AND SIZE CONSTANCIES Thanks to *shape constancy*, we perceive the form of familiar objects, such as the door in **FIGURE 18.22**, as constant even while our retinas receive changing images of them. Our brain manages this feat because visual cortex neurons rapidly learn to associate different views of an object (Li & DiCarlo, 2008).

Thanks to *size constancy*, we perceive an object as having an unchanging size, even while our distance from it varies. We assume a bus is large enough to carry people, even when we see its tiny image from two blocks away. This assumption also illustrates the close connection between perceived *distance* and perceived *size*. Perceiving an object's distance gives us cues to its size. Likewise, knowing its general size—that the object is a bus—provides us with cues to its distance.

Even in size-distance judgments, however, we consider an object's context. This interplay between perceived size and perceived distance helps explain several well-known illusions, including the *Moon illusion*: The Moon looks up to 50 percent larger when near the horizon than when high in the sky. Can you imagine why?

For at least 22 centuries, scholars have wondered (Hershenson, 1989). One reason is that monocular cues to an object's distance make the horizon Moon seem farther away. If it's farther away, our brain assumes, it must be larger than the Moon high in the night sky (Kaufman & Kaufman, 2000). But again, if you use a paper tube to take away the distance cue, the horizon Moon will immediately seem smaller.

⊘ FIGURE 18.22
Shape constancy A door casts an increasingly trapezoidal image on our retinas as it opens. Yet we still perceive it as rectangular.

Perceptual illusions reinforce a fundamental lesson: Perception is not merely a projection of the world onto our brain. Rather, our sensations are disassembled into information bits that our brain then reassembles into its own functional model of the external world. During this reassembly process, our assumptions—such as the usual relationship between distance and size—can lead us astray. *Our brain constructs our perceptions.*

* * *

Form perception, depth perception, motion perception, and perceptual constancies illuminate how we organize our visual experiences. Perceptual organization applies to our other senses, too. Listening to an unfamiliar language, we have trouble hearing where one word stops and the next one begins. Listening to our own language, we automatically hear distinct words. This, too, reflects perceptual organization. But it is more, for we even organize a string of letters—THEDOGATEMEAT—into words that make an intelligible phrase; it's more likely "The dog ate meat" than "The do gate me at" (McBurney & Collings, 1984). This process involves not only the organization we've been discussing, but also interpretation—discerning meaning in what we perceive.

> To experience more visual illusions, and to understand what they reveal about how you perceive the world, visit *Topic Tutorial: PsychSim6, Visual Illusions.*

Perceptual Interpretation

Philosophers have debated whether our perceptual abilities should be credited to our nature or our nurture. To what extent do we *learn* to perceive? German philosopher Immanuel Kant (1724–1804) maintained that knowledge comes from our *inborn* ways of organizing sensory experiences. Indeed, we come equipped to process sensory information. But British philosopher John Locke (1632–1704) argued that through our experiences we also *learn* to perceive the world. Indeed, we learn to link an object's distance with its size. So, just how important is experience? How radically does it shape our perceptual interpretations?

Experience and Visual Perception

LOQ 18-9 What does research on restored vision, sensory restriction, and perceptual adaptation reveal about the effects of experience on perception?

RESTORED VISION AND SENSORY RESTRICTION Writing to John Locke, William Molyneux wondered whether "a man *born* blind, and now adult, taught by his *touch* to distinguish between a cube and a sphere" could, if made to see, visually distinguish the two. Locke's answer was *No,* because the man would never have *learned* to see the difference.

Molyneux's hypothetical case has since been put to the test with people who, though blind from birth, later gained sight (Gandhi et al., 2017; Gregory, 1978; von Senden, 1932). Most were born with cataracts—clouded lenses that allowed them to see only diffused light, rather as a sighted person might see a foggy image through a table-tennis ball sliced in half. After cataract surgery, the patients could distinguish figure from ground, differentiate colors, and distinguish faces from nonfaces—suggesting that these aspects of perception are innate. But much as Locke supposed, they often remained unable to visually recognize objects that were familiar by touch.

Seeking to gain more control than is provided by clinical cases, researchers have restricted the vision of infant kittens (Hubel & Wiesel, 1963). After infancy, when their vision was restored, the kittens behaved much like the humans born with cataracts. They could distinguish color and brightness, but not the form of a circle from that of a square. Their eyes had not

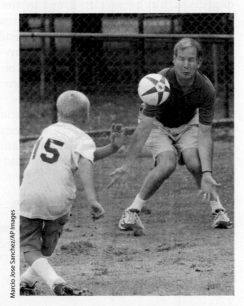

Marcio Jose Sanchez/AP Images

"Let us then suppose the mind to be, as we say, white paper void of all characters, without any ideas: How comes it to be furnished? . . . To this I answer, in one word, from EXPERIENCE." — John Locke, *An Essay Concerning Human Understanding,* 1690

Learning to see At age 3, Mike May lost his vision in an explosion. Decades later, after a new cornea restored vision to his right eye, he got his first look at his wife and children. Alas, although signals were now reaching his visual cortex, it lacked the experience to interpret them. May could not recognize expressions or faces, apart from features such as hair. Yet he can see an object in motion and has learned to navigate his world and to marvel at such things as dust floating in sunlight (Abrams, 2002; Gorlick, 2010; Huber et al., 2015).

> **perceptual adaptation** the ability to adjust to changed sensory input, including an artificially displaced or even inverted visual field.

degenerated; their retinas still relayed signals to their visual cortex. But lacking early stimulation, their brain's cortical cells had not developed normal connections. Thus, the animals remained functionally blind to shape.

Surgery on children in India reveals that those who are blind from birth can benefit from removal of cataracts, and the younger they are, the more they benefit. But their visual acuity (sharpness) may never be normal (Chatterjee, 2015; Gandhi et al., 2014). For normal sensory and perceptual development, there is a *critical period*—an optimal period when exposure to certain stimuli or experiences is required.

Once this critical period has passed, sensory restrictions later in life do no permanent harm. When researchers cover an adult animal's eye for several months, its vision will be unaffected after the eye patch is removed. When surgeons remove cataracts that developed during late adulthood, most people are thrilled at the return to normal vision.

Perceptual adaptation
"*Oops, missed,*" thought researcher Hubert Dolezal as he attempted a handshake while viewing the world through inverting goggles. Yet, believe it or not, kittens, monkeys, and humans can adapt to an inverted world.

PERCEPTUAL ADAPTATION Given a new pair of glasses, we may feel slightly disoriented, even dizzy. Within a day or two, we adjust. Our **perceptual adaptation** to changed visual input makes the world seem normal again. But imagine a far more dramatic new pair of glasses—one that shifts the apparent location of objects 40 degrees to the left. When you first toss a ball to a friend, it sails off to the left. Walking forward to shake hands with someone, you veer to the left.

Could you adapt to this distorted world? Not if you were a baby chicken. When fitted with such lenses, baby chicks continue to peck where food grains *seem* to be (Hess, 1956; Rossi, 1968). But we humans adapt to distorting lenses quickly. Within a few minutes your throws would again be accurate, your stride on target. Remove the lenses and you would experience an aftereffect: At first your throws would err in the *opposite* direction, sailing off to the right; but again, within minutes you would readapt.

Indeed, given an even more radical pair of glasses—one that literally turns the world upside down—you could still adapt. Psychologist George Stratton (1896) experienced this. He invented, and for 8 days wore, optical headgear that flipped left to right *and* up to down, making him the first person to experience a right-side-up retinal image while standing upright. The ground was up, the sky was down.

At first, when Stratton wanted to walk, he found himself searching for his feet, which were now "up." Eating was nearly impossible. He became nauseated and depressed. But he persisted, and by the eighth day he could comfortably reach for an object and, if his hands were in view, could walk without bumping into things. When Stratton finally removed the headgear, he readapted quickly. So did research participants who later wore such gear—while riding a motorcycle, skiing the Alps, or flying an airplane (Dolezal, 1982; Kohler, 1962). By actively moving about in their topsy-turvy world, they adapted to their new context and learned to coordinate their movements.

So, do we learn to perceive the world? In part we do, as we constantly adjust to changed sensory input. Research on critical periods teaches us that early nurture sculpts what nature has provided. In less dramatic ways, nurture continues to do so throughout our lives. Experience guides, sustains, and maintains the brain pathways that enable our perceptions.

ASK YOURSELF

Consider someone you know (could be yourself) who has a visual disability of some kind. What sort of disruption in the visual process might cause that disability?

18 REVIEW Vision: Sensory and Perceptual Processing

LEARNING OBJECTIVES

Test Yourself Answer these repeated Learning Objective Questions on your own (before checking the answers in Appendix D) to improve your retention of the concepts (McDaniel et al., 2009, 2015).

LOQ 18-1 What are the characteristics of the energy that we see as visible light? What structures in the eye help focus that energy?

LOQ 18-2 How do the rods and cones process information, and what is the path information travels from the eye to the brain?

LOQ 18-3 How do we perceive color in the world around us?

LOQ 18-4 Where are feature detectors located, and what do they do?

LOQ 18-5 How does the brain use parallel processing to construct visual perceptions?

LOQ 18-6 How did the Gestalt psychologists understand perceptual organization, and how do figure-ground and grouping principles contribute to our perceptions?

LOQ 18-7 How do we use binocular and monocular cues to see in three dimensions, and how do we perceive motion?

LOQ 18-8 How do perceptual constancies help us construct meaningful perceptions?

LOQ 18-9 What does research on restored vision, sensory restriction, and perceptual adaptation reveal about the effects of experience on perception?

TERMS AND CONCEPTS TO REMEMBER

Test Yourself Write down the definition in your own words, then check your answer.

wavelength, p. 221
hue, p. 221
intensity, p. 221
retina, p. 222
accommodation, p. 222
rods, p. 222
cones, p. 222
optic nerve, p. 222
blind spot, p. 222
fovea, p. 222
Young-Helmholtz trichromatic (three-color) theory, p. 225
opponent-process theory, p. 227

feature detectors, p. 227
parallel processing, p. 228
gestalt, p. 228
figure-ground, p. 228
grouping, p. 228
depth perception, p. 230
visual cliff, p. 230
binocular cue, p. 231
retinal disparity, p. 231
monocular cue, p. 232
phi phenomenon, p. 232
perceptual constancy, p. 232
perceptual adaptation, p. 236

MASTER THE MATERIAL

Test Yourself Answer the following questions on your own first, then check your answers in Appendix E.

1. The characteristic of light that determines the color we experience, such as blue or green, is _____.

2. The amplitude of a light wave determines our perception of
   a. brightness.
   b. color.
   c. meaning.
   d. distance.

3. The blind spot in your retina is located where
   a. there are rods but no cones.
   b. there are cones but no rods.
   c. the optic nerve leaves the eye.
   d. the bipolar cells meet the ganglion cells.

4. Cones are the eye's receptor cells that are especially sensitive to _____ light and are responsible for our _____ vision.
   a. bright; black-and-white
   b. dim; color
   c. bright; color
   d. dim; black-and-white

5. Two theories together account for color vision. The Young-Helmholtz trichromatic theory shows that the eye contains _____, and Hering's theory accounts for the nervous system's having _____.
   a. opposing retinal processes; three pairs of color receptors
   b. opponent-process cells; three types of color receptors
   c. three pairs of color receptors; opposing retinal processes
   d. three types of color receptors; opponent-process cells

6. What mental processes allow you to perceive a lemon as yellow?

7. The cells in the visual cortex that respond to certain lines, edges, and angles are called _____.

8. The brain's ability to process many aspects of an object or a problem simultaneously is called _____.

9. In listening to a concert, you attend to the solo instrument and perceive the orchestra as accompaniment. This illustrates the organizing principle of
   a. figure-ground.
   b. shape constancy.
   c. grouping.
   d. depth perception.

10. Our tendencies to fill in the gaps and to perceive a pattern as continuous are two different examples of the organizing principle called
    a. interposition.
    b. depth perception.
    c. shape constancy.
    d. grouping.

11. The visual cliff experiments suggest that
    a. infants have not yet developed depth perception.
    b. crawling human infants and very young animals perceive depth.
    c. we have no way of knowing whether infants can perceive depth.
    d. unlike other species, humans are able to perceive depth in infancy.

12. Depth perception underlies our ability to
    a. group similar items in a gestalt.
    b. perceive objects as having a constant shape or form.
    c. judge distances.
    d. fill in the gaps in a figure.

13. Two examples of _____ depth cues are interposition and linear perspective.

14. Perceiving a tomato as consistently red, despite lighting shifts, is an example of
    a. shape constancy.
    b. perceptual constancy.
    c. a binocular cue.
    d. continuity.

15. After surgery to restore vision, adults who had been blind from birth had difficulty
    a. recognizing objects by touch.
    b. recognizing objects by sight.
    c. distinguishing figure from ground.
    d. distinguishing between bright and dim light.

16. In experiments, people have worn glasses that turned their visual fields upside down. After a period of adjustment, they learned to function quite well. This ability is called _____ _____.

Continue testing yourself with 📚 **LearningCurve** or 📖 **Achieve Read & Practice** to learn and remember most effectively.

19 The Nonvisual Senses

Hearing

Like our other senses, our hearing—**audition**—helps us adapt and survive. Hearing provides information and enables relationships. Hearing humanizes: People seem more thoughtful, competent, and likable when we hear, not just read, their words (Schroeder & Epley, 2015, 2016). And hearing is pretty spectacular. It lets us communicate invisibly—we shoot unseen air waves across space and receive the same from others. Hearing loss is therefore the great invisible disability. To not catch someone's name, to not grasp what someone is asking, and to miss the hilarious joke is to be deprived of what others know, and sometimes to feel excluded. As a person with inherited hearing loss, I [DM] know the feeling, and can understand why adults with significant hearing loss experience increased risk of depression and anxiety (Blazer & Tucci, 2019; Scinicariello et al., 2019).

Most of us, however, can hear a wide range of sounds, and the ones we hear best are those in the range of the human voice. With normal hearing, we are remarkably sensitive to faint sounds, such as a child's whimper. (If our ears were only slightly more sensitive, we would hear a constant hiss from the movement of air molecules.) Our distant ancestors' survival depended on this keen hearing when hunting or being hunted.

The sounds of music A violin's short, fast waves create a high pitch. The longer, slower waves of Chi-chi Nwanoku OBE's double bass create a lower pitch. Differences in the waves' height, or amplitude, also create differing degrees of loudness.

Vereshchagin Dmitry/Shutterstock

Courtesy of Eric Richmond/The Chineke! Foundation

We are also remarkably attuned to sound variations. Among thousands of possible voices, we easily recognize an unseen friend's. Moreover, hearing is fast. "It might take you a full second to notice something out of the corner of your eye, turn your head toward it, recognize it, and respond to it," notes auditory neuroscientist Seth Horowitz (2012). "The same reaction to a new or sudden sound happens at least 10 times as fast." A fraction of a second after such events stimulate your ear's receptors, millions of neurons have simultaneously coordinated in extracting the essential features, comparing them with past experience, and identifying the stimulus (Freeman, 1991). For hearing, as for our other senses, we wonder: How do we do it?

The Stimulus Input: Sound Waves

LOQ 19-1 What are the characteristics of the air pressure waves that we hear as sound?

Draw a bow across a violin, and you will unleash the energy of sound waves. Air molecules, each bumping into the next, create waves of compressed and expanded air, like the ripples on a pond circling out from a tossed stone. As we swim in our ocean of moving air molecules, our ears detect these brief air pressure changes.

Like light waves, sound waves vary in shape (**FIGURE 19.1**). The height, or *amplitude*, of sound waves determines their perceived *loudness*. Their **frequency** (measured in *hertz*) determines the **pitch** (the high or low tone) we experience. Long waves have low frequency—and low pitch. Short waves have high frequency—and high pitch. Sound waves produced by a soprano are much shorter and faster than those produced by a baritone singer.

We measure sound intensity in *decibels*, with zero decibels representing the absolute threshold for hearing. Every 10 decibels corresponds to a tenfold increase in sound intensity. Thus, normal conversation (60 decibels) is 10,000 times more intense than a 20-decibel whisper. And a temporarily tolerable 100-decibel passing subway train is 10 billion times more intense than the faintest detectable sound. If prolonged, exposure to sounds above 85 decibels can produce hearing loss. Tell that to basketball fans at the University of Kentucky who, in 2017, broke the Guinness World Record for the noisiest indoor stadium at 126 decibels (WKYT, 2017). Hear today, gone tomorrow.

(a)   (b)

The Ear

LOQ 19-2 How does the ear transform sound energy into neural messages?

How does vibrating air trigger nerve impulses that your brain can decode as sounds? The process begins when sound waves strike your *eardrum*, causing this tight membrane to vibrate (**FIGURE 19.2**).

In your **middle ear,** a piston made of three tiny bones—the *hammer* (malleus), *anvil* (incus), and *stirrup* (stapes)—picks up the vibrations and transmits them to the **cochlea,** a snail-shaped tube in your **inner ear.**

The incoming vibrations then cause the cochlea's membrane-covered opening (the *oval window*) to vibrate, jostling the fluid inside the cochlea. This motion causes ripples in the *basilar membrane*, bending the *hair cells* lining its surface, rather like grass blades bending in the wind.

audition the sense or act of hearing.

frequency the number of complete wavelengths that pass a point in a given time (for example, per second).

pitch a tone's experienced highness or lowness; depends on frequency.

middle ear the chamber between the eardrum and cochlea containing three tiny bones—hammer (malleus), anvil (incus), and stirrup (stapes)—that concentrate the vibrations of the eardrum on the cochlea's oval window.

cochlea [KOHK-lee-uh] a coiled, bony, fluid-filled tube in the inner ear; sound waves traveling through the cochlear fluid trigger nerve impulses.

inner ear the innermost part of the ear, containing the cochlea, semicircular canals, and vestibular sacs.

FIGURE 19.1
The physical properties of waves
(a) Waves vary in *wavelength* (the distance between successive peaks). *Frequency,* the number of complete wavelengths that can pass a point in a given time, depends on the wavelength. The shorter the wavelength, the higher the frequency. Wavelength determines the *pitch* of sound. (b) Waves also vary in *amplitude* (the height from peak to trough). Wave amplitude influences sound *intensity*.

(a)

OUTER EAR | MIDDLE EAR | INNER EAR

Sound waves

Auditory canal

Bones of the middle ear

Semicircular canals

Bone

Auditory nerve

Cochlea

Eardrum

Oval window (where stirrup attaches)

Auditory cortex of temporal lobe

(b)

Enlargement of middle ear and inner ear, showing cochlea partially uncoiled for clarity

Hammer (malleus)

Anvil (incus)

Cochlea, partially uncoiled

Sound waves

Eardrum

Stirrup (stapes)

Oval window

Auditory nerve

Nerve fibers to auditory nerve

Protruding hair cells

Basilar membrane

Motion of fluid in the cochlea

⬆ **FIGURE 19.2**

Hear here: How we transform sound waves into nerve impulses that our brain interprets (a) The outer ear funnels sound waves to the eardrum. The bones of the middle ear (malleus, incus, and stapes) amplify and relay the eardrum's vibrations through the oval window into the fluid-filled cochlea. (b) As shown in this detail of the middle ear and inner ear, the resulting pressure changes in the cochlear fluid cause the basilar membrane to ripple, bending the hair cells on its surface. Hair cell movements trigger impulses at the base of the nerve cells, whose fibers converge to form the auditory nerve. That nerve sends neural messages to the thalamus and on to the auditory cortex.

What do you hear at www.tinyurl.com /YannyLaurel? With a unique, top-down hearing system, each of us may process the same sound differently. Some people hear *Yanny* and some hear *Laurel*—two rather different names.

sensorineural hearing loss the most common form of hearing loss, caused by damage to the cochlea's receptor cells or to the auditory nerve; also called *nerve deafness.*

conduction hearing loss a less common form of hearing loss, caused by damage to the mechanical system that conducts sound waves to the cochlea.

cochlear implant a device for converting sounds into electrical signals and stimulating the auditory nerve through electrodes threaded into the cochlea.

The hair cell movements in turn trigger impulses in adjacent nerve cells, whose axons converge to form the *auditory nerve.* The auditory nerve carries the neural messages to your thalamus and then on to the *auditory cortex* in your brain's temporal lobe. From vibrating air, to tiny moving bones, to fluid waves, to electrical impulses to the brain: Voila! You hear!

Perhaps the most intriguing part of the hearing process is the hair cells—"quivering bundles that let us hear" thanks to their "extreme sensitivity and extreme speed" (Goldberg, 2007). A cochlea has 16,000 of them, which sounds like a lot until we compare that with an eye's 130 million or so photoreceptors. But consider a hair cell's responsiveness. Deflect the tiny bundles of *cilia* on its tip by only the width of an atom, and the alert hair cell, thanks to a special protein, will trigger a neural response (Corey et al., 2004).

Damage to the cochlea's hair cell receptors or the auditory nerve can cause **sensorineural hearing loss** (or nerve deafness). With auditory nerve damage, people may hear sound but have trouble discerning what someone is saying (Liberman, 2015).

Occasionally, disease damages hair cell receptors, but more often the culprit is biological changes linked with heredity and aging. I [DM] understand—as one who lives with severe hearing loss passed down from my grandmother and mother, thanks to a single mutation in one gene (WFS1). Toxic noise, such as prolonged exposure to ear-splitting music, is another culprit. Sensorineural hearing loss is more common than **conduction hearing loss,** which is caused by damage to the mechanical system—the eardrum and middle ear bones—that conducts sound waves to the cochlea.

The cochlea's hair cells have been likened to carpet fibers. Walk around on them and they will spring back. But leave a heavy piece of furniture on them and they may never rebound. As a general rule, any noise we cannot talk over (loud machinery, fans screaming at a concert or sports event, our daily music mix blasting at maximum volume) may be harmful, especially if prolonged and repeated (Roesser, 1998) (**FIGURE 19.3**). And if our ears ring after such experiences, we have been bad to our unhappy hair cells. As pain alerts us to possible bodily harm, ringing of the ears alerts us to possible hearing damage. It is hearing's equivalent of bleeding.

Worldwide, 1.23 billion people are challenged by hearing loss and about half a billion have a disabling hearing loss (Global Burden of Disease, 2015; Wilson et al., 2017). Since the early 1990s, teen hearing loss has risen by a third and affects 1 in 6 teens (Shargorodsky et al., 2010; Weichbold et al., 2012). Exposure to loud music, both live and through headphones, is a culprit: After three hours of a rock concert averaging 99 decibels, 54 percent of teens reported temporarily not hearing as well, and 1 in 4 had ringing in their ears (Derebery et al., 2012). Teen boys more than teen girls or adults blast themselves with loud volumes for long periods (Widén et al., 2017; Zogby, 2006). Greater noise exposure may help explain why men's hearing tends to be less acute than women's. Anyone who spends many hours in a loud nightclub, behind a power mower, or above a jackhammer should wear earplugs, or risk needing a hearing aid later. "Condoms," say sex educators. "Earplugs," say hearing educators.

Decibels	
140	Rock band (amplified) at close range
130	
120	Loud thunder
110	Jet plane at 500 feet
100	Subway train at 20 feet
90	
80	Busy street corner
70	
60	Normal conversation
50	
40	
30	
20	Whisper
10	
0	Threshold of hearing

Prolonged exposure above 85 decibels produces hearing loss.

sebra/Shutterstock

FIGURE 19.3
The intensity of some common sounds One study found 3 million professional musicians with almost four times the normal rate of noise-induced hearing loss (Schink et al., 2014). Noise-blocking earpieces and headphones reduce the need to blast the music at dangerous volumes.

Nerve deafness cannot, as yet, be reversed. One way to restore hearing is a sort of bionic ear—a **cochlear implant.** Some 50,000 people, including some 30,000 children, receive these electronic devices each year (Hochmair, 2013). The implants translate sounds into electrical signals that, wired into the cochlea's nerves, convey information about sound to the brain (**FIGURE 19.4**). When given to deaf kittens and human infants, cochlear implants have seemed to trigger an "awakening" of the pertinent brain area (Klinke et al., 1999; Sireteanu, 1999). These devices can help children become proficient in oral communication (especially if they receive them as preschoolers or ideally before age 1) (Dettman et al., 2007; Schorr et al., 2005). Hearing, like vision, has a *critical period.* Cochlear implants can help restore hearing for most adults, but only if their brain learned to process sound during childhood. The restored hearing can also reduce social isolation and the risk of depression (Mosnier et al., 2015).

RETRIEVAL PRACTICE

RP-1 What are the basic steps in transforming sound waves into perceived sound?

RP-2 The amplitude of a sound wave determines our perception of _____ (loudness/pitch).

RP-3 The longer the sound waves, the _____ (lower/higher) their frequency and the _____ (higher/lower) their pitch.

ANSWERS IN APPENDIX E

Perceiving Loudness, Pitch, and Location

LOQ 19-3 How do we detect loudness, discriminate pitch, and locate sounds?

RESPONDING TO LOUD AND SOFT SOUNDS How do we detect loudness? If you guessed that it's related to the *intensity* of a hair cell's response, you'd be wrong. Rather, a soft, pure tone activates only the few hair cells attuned to its frequency. Given louder sounds, neighboring hair cells also respond. Thus, your brain interprets loudness from the *number* of activated hair cells.

If a hair cell loses sensitivity to soft sounds, it may still respond to loud sounds. This helps explain another surprise: Really loud sounds may seem loud to people with or without normal hearing. Given my hearing loss, I [DM] used to wonder what really loud music must sound like to people with normal hearing. Now I realize it sounds much the same; where we differ is in our perception of soft sounds (and our ability to isolate one sound amid noise). This is why we hard-of-hearing people do not want *all* sounds (loud and soft) amplified. We like sound *compressed,* which means harder-to-hear sounds are amplified more than loud sounds (a feature of today's digital hearing aids).

FIGURE 19.4
Hardware for hearing Cochlear implants work by translating sounds into electrical signals that are transmitted to the cochlea and, via the auditory nerve, relayed to the brain.

Transmitter

Receiver/Stimulator

Electrode

Speech processor

place theory in hearing, the theory that links the pitch we hear with the place where the cochlea's membrane is stimulated. (Also called *place coding*.)

frequency theory in hearing, the theory that the rate of nerve impulses traveling up the auditory nerve matches the frequency of a tone, thus enabling us to sense its pitch. (Also called *temporal coding*.)

HEARING DIFFERENT PITCHES How do we know whether a sound is the high-frequency, high-pitched chirp of a bird or the low-frequency, low-pitched roar of a truck? Current thinking on how we discriminate pitch combines two theories.

- **Place theory** (also called *place coding*) presumes that we hear different pitches because different sound waves trigger activity at different places along the cochlea's basilar membrane. Thus, the brain determines a sound's pitch by recognizing the specific place (on the membrane) that is generating the neural signal. When Nobel laureate-to-be Georg von Békésy (1957) cut holes in the cochleas of guinea pigs and human cadavers and looked inside with a microscope, he discovered that the cochlea vibrated, rather like a shaken bedsheet, in response to sound. High frequencies produced large vibrations near the beginning of the cochlea's membrane. Low frequencies vibrated more of the membrane and were not so easily localized. So, there is a problem: Place theory can explain how we hear high-pitched sounds but not low-pitched sounds.

- **Frequency theory** (also called *temporal coding*) suggests another explanation: The brain reads pitch by monitoring the frequency of neural impulses traveling up the auditory nerve. The whole basilar membrane vibrates with the incoming sound wave, triggering neural impulses to the brain at the same rate as the sound wave. If the sound wave has a frequency of 100 waves per second, then 100 pulses per second travel up the auditory nerve. But frequency theory also has a problem: An individual neuron cannot fire faster than 1000 times per second. How, then, can we sense sounds with frequencies above 1000 waves per second (roughly the upper third of a piano keyboard)? Enter the *volley principle*: Like soldiers who alternate firing so that some can shoot while others reload, neural cells can alternate firing. By firing in rapid succession, they can achieve a *combined frequency* above 1000 waves per second.

So, place theory and frequency theory work together to enable our perception of pitch. Place theory best explains how we sense *high pitches*. Frequency theory, extended by the volley principle, explains how we sense *low pitches*. Finally, some combination of place and frequency theories likely explains how we sense *pitches in the intermediate range*.

RETRIEVAL PRACTICE

RP-4 Which theory of pitch perception would best explain a symphony audience's enjoyment of a high-pitched piccolo? How about a low-pitched cello?

ANSWERS IN APPENDIX E

LOCATING SOUNDS Why don't we have one big ear—perhaps above our one nose? "All the better to hear you with," as the wolf said to Little Red Riding Hood. Thanks to the placement of our two ears, we enjoy stereophonic ("three-dimensional") hearing. Two ears are better than one for at least two reasons (**FIGURE 19.5**). If a car to your right honks, your right ear will receive a more *intense* sound, and it will receive the sound slightly *sooner* than your left ear.

Because sound travels fast and human ears are not very far apart, the intensity difference and the time lag are extremely small. A just noticeable difference in the direction of two sound sources corresponds to a time difference of just 0.000027 second! Lucky for us, our supersensitive auditory system can detect such minute differences and locate the sound (Brown & Deffenbacher, 1979; Middlebrooks & Green, 1991).

For an interactive review of how we perceive sound, visit *Topic Tutorial: PsychSim6, The Auditory System.* For an animated test of your knowledge, engage online with *Concept Practice: The Auditory Pathway.*

Air

Sound shadow

FIGURE 19.5
How we locate sounds Sound waves strike one ear sooner and more intensely than the other. From this information, our nimble brain can compute the sound's location. As you might therefore expect, people who lose all hearing in one ear often have difficulty locating sounds.

The Other Senses

Sharks and dogs rely on their outstanding sense of smell, aided by large smell-related brain areas. Our human brain allocates more real estate to seeing and hearing. But extraordinary happenings also occur within our other senses. Without our senses of touch, taste, smell, and body position and movement, we humans would be seriously hampered, and our capacities for enjoying the world would be greatly diminished.

Touch

LOQ **19-4** What are the four basic touch sensations, and how do we sense touch?

Touch, our tactile sense, is vital. From infancy to adulthood, affectionate touches promote our well-being (Jakubiak & Feeney, 2017). Right from the start, touch aids our development. Infant rats deprived of their mother's grooming produce less growth hormone and have a lower metabolic rate—a good way to keep alive until the mother returns, but a reaction that stunts growth if prolonged. Infant monkeys that are allowed to see, hear, and smell—but not touch—their mother become desperately unhappy (Suomi et al., 1976). Premature human babies gain weight faster and go home sooner if they are stimulated by hand massage (Field et al., 2006). Sensing a disaster or grieving a death, we find comfort in a hug. As adults, we still yearn to touch—to kiss, to stroke, to snuggle.

Humorist Dave Barry (1985, p. 2) was perhaps right to jest that your skin "keeps people from seeing the inside of your body, which is repulsive, and it prevents your organs from falling onto the ground." But skin does much more. Touching various spots on the skin with a soft hair, a warm or cool wire, and the point of a pin reveals that some spots are especially sensitive to *pressure*, others to *warmth*, others to *cold*, still others to *pain*. Our "sense of touch" is actually a mix of these four basic and distinct skin senses, and our other skin sensations are variations of pressure, warmth, cold, and pain. For example, stroking adjacent pressure spots creates a tickle. Repeated gentle stroking of a pain spot creates an itching sensation. Touching adjacent cold and pressure spots triggers a sense of wetness (which you can experience by touching dry, cold metal).

Touch sensations involve more than tactile stimulation, however. A self-administered tickle produces less somatosensory cortex activation than does the same tickle from something or someone else (Blakemore et al., 1998). Likewise, a sensual leg caress evokes a different somatosensory cortex response when a heterosexual man believes it comes from an attractive woman rather than a man (Gazzola et al., 2012). Such responses reveal how quickly cognition influences our brain's sensory response.

The precious sense of touch As William James wrote in his *Principles of Psychology* (1890), "Touch is both the alpha and omega of affection."

Pain

LOQ **19-5** What biological, psychological, and social-cultural influences affect our experience of pain? How do placebos, distraction, and hypnosis help control pain?

Be thankful for occasional pain. Pain is your body's way of telling you something has gone wrong. Drawing your attention to a burn, a break, or a sprain, pain orders you to change your behavior—"Stay off that ankle!" Pain also serves a psychological purpose, enhancing our self-awareness, arousing others' empathy, and promoting social connections (Bastian et al., 2014).

The rare people born without the ability to feel pain may experience pain-free childbirth, but also are at risk of severe injury or even early death (Habib et al., 2019). Without the discomfort that makes us shift position, their joints can fail from excess strain. Without the warnings of pain, infections can run wild and injuries can accumulate (Neese, 1991).

More numerous are those who live with chronic pain, which is rather like an alarm that won't shut off. Persistent backaches, arthritis, headaches, and cancer-related pain prompt two questions: What is pain? How might we control it?

UNDERSTANDING PAIN Our experience of pain reflects both *bottom-up* sensations and *top-down* cognition. Pain is a biopsychosocial event (Hadjistavropoulos et al., 2011). As such, pain experiences vary widely, from group to group and from person to person. Viewing pain from the biological, psychological, and social-cultural perspectives can help us better understand it, and also help us cope with it and treat it (**FIGURE 19.6**).

"Pain is a gift." So said a doctor studying Ashlyn Blocker, who has a rare genetic mutation that prevents her from feeling pain. At birth, she didn't cry. As a child, she ran around for two days on a broken ankle. She has put her hands on a hot machine and burned the flesh off. And she has reached into boiling water to retrieve a dropped spoon. "Everyone in my class asks me about it, and I say, 'I can feel pressure, but I can't feel pain.' *Pain!* I cannot feel it!" (Heckert, 2012).

FIGURE 19.6
Biopsychosocial approach to pain Our experience of pain is much more than the neural messages sent to our brain.

Biological influences:
• activity in spinal cord's large and small fibers
• genetic differences in endorphin production
• the brain's interpretation of CNS activity

Psychological influences:
• attention to pain
• learning based on experience
• expectations

Social-cultural influences:
• presence of others
• empathy for others' pain
• cultural expectations

Personal experience of pain

Biological Influences Pain is a physical event produced by your senses. But pain differs from some of your other sensations. No one type of stimulus triggers pain the way light triggers vision. And no specialized receptors process pain signals the way your retina receptors react to light rays. Instead, sensory receptors called *nociceptors*—mostly in your skin, but also in your muscles and organs—detect hurtful temperatures, pressure, or chemicals (**FIGURE 19.7**).

Your experience of pain depends in part on the genes you inherited and on your physical characteristics (Gatchel et al., 2007; Reimann et al., 2010). Women are more sensitive to pain than men are (their senses of hearing and smell also tend to be more sensitive) (Ruau et al., 2012; Wickelgren, 2009).

FIGURE 19.7
The pain circuit Sensory receptors *(nociceptors)* respond to potentially damaging stimuli by sending an impulse to the spinal cord, which passes the message to the brain, which interprets the signal as pain.

Projection to brain

Pain impulse

Cross section of the spinal cord

Cell body of nociceptor

Nerve cell

Tissue injury

No pain theory can explain all available findings. One useful model, **gate-control theory,** suggests that the spinal cord contains a neurological "gate" that controls the transmission of pain messages to the brain (Melzack & Katz, 2013; Melzack & Wall, 1965, 1983).

Small spinal cord nerve fibers conduct most pain signals, so an injury activates the small fibers and opens the gate. The pain signals can then travel to your brain, and you feel pain. But large-fiber activity (stimulated by massage, electrical stimulation, or acupuncture) can close the pain gate by blocking pain signals. Brain-to-spinal-cord messages can also close the gate. Thus, chronic pain can be treated both by "gate-closing" stimulation, such as massage, and by mental activity, such as distraction (Wall, 2000).

We also benefit from our own natural pain-killers, *endorphins,* which are released in response to severe pain or vigorous exercise. People who carry a gene that boosts the availability of endorphins are less bothered by pain, and their brain is less responsive to pain (Zubieta et al., 2003). Others, who carry a mutated gene that disrupts pain circuit neurotransmission, may be unable to experience pain (Cox et al., 2006). Such discoveries point the way toward future pain medications that mimic these genetic effects.

Pain is not merely a physical phenomenon of injured nerves sending impulses to a definable brain or spinal cord area—like pulling on a rope to ring a bell. The brain can also create pain, as it does in *phantom limb sensations*. Without normal sensory input from a missing limb, the brain may misinterpret and amplify spontaneous but irrelevant central nervous system activity. As the dreamer may see with eyes closed, so 7 in 10 such people feel pain or movement in nonexistent limbs (Melzack, 1992, 2005). Some may even try to lift a cup with a phantom hand, or step off a bed onto a phantom leg. Even those born without a limb sometimes perceive sensations from the absent arm or leg; the brain may come prepared to anticipate "that it will be getting information from a body that has limbs" (Melzack, 1998).

Phantoms may haunt other senses, too. People with hearing loss often experience the sound of silence: *tinnitus,* the phantom sound of ringing in the ears that's accompanied by auditory brain activity (Sedley et al., 2015). Those who lose vision to glaucoma, cataracts, diabetes, or macular degeneration may experience phantom sights—nonthreatening hallucinations (Painter et al., 2018). Others with nerve damage in the systems for tasting and smelling have experienced phantom tastes or smells, such as ice water that seems sickeningly sweet or fresh air that reeks of rotten food (Goode, 1999). *The point to remember:* We feel, see, hear, taste, and smell with our brain.

Psychological Influences One powerful influence on our perception of pain is the attention we focus on it. Athletes, focused on winning, may perceive pain differently and play through it.

We also seem to edit our *memories* of pain, which often differ from the pain we actually experienced. In experiments, and after painful medical procedures or childbirth, people overlook a pain's duration. Their memory snapshots instead record two factors: their pain's *peak* moment (which can lead them to recall variable pain, with peaks, as worse [Chajut et al., 2014; Stone et al., 2005]), and how much pain they felt at the *end.* In one experiment, people immersed one hand in painfully cold water for 60 seconds, and then the other hand in the same painfully cold water for 60 seconds followed by a slightly less painful 30 seconds more (Kahneman et al., 1993). Which experience would you expect they recalled as most painful?

Curiously, when asked which trial they would prefer to repeat, most preferred the 90-second trial, with more net pain—but less pain at the end. Physicians have used this principle with patients undergoing colon exams—lengthening the discomfort by a minute, but lessening its intensity at the end (Kahneman, 1999). Imagine undergoing a painful procedure and having the doctor ask if you'd rather go home now or bear a few more minutes of milder discomfort. There's a case to be made for prolonging a tapered hurt.

The end of an experience can color our memory of pleasures, too. In one simple experiment, some people, on receiving a fifth and last piece of chocolate, were told it was their "next" one. Others, told it was their "last" piece, liked it better and also rated the whole experiment as being more enjoyable (O'Brien & Ellsworth, 2012). Endings matter.

Social-Cultural Influences Pain is a product of our attention, our expectations, and also our culture (Gatchel et al., 2007; Reimann et al., 2010). Not surprisingly, then, our perception of pain varies with our social situation and our cultural traditions. We tend to perceive more pain when others also seem to be experiencing pain (Symbaluk et al., 1997). This may help explain the apparent social aspects of pain, as when groups of Australian keyboard operators during the mid-1980s suffered outbreaks of severe pain while typing or performing other repetitive work—without any discernible physical abnormalities (Gawande, 1998). Sometimes the pain in sprain is mainly in the brain— literally. When people feel empathy for another's pain, their own brain activity partly mirrors the activity of the actual brain in pain (Singer et al., 2004).

gate-control theory the theory that the spinal cord contains a neurological "gate" that blocks pain signals or allows them to pass on to the brain. The "gate" is opened by the activity of pain signals traveling up small nerve fibers and is closed by activity in larger fibers or by information coming from the brain.

"I'd know my tinnitus anywhere and this isn't it."

"Pain is increased by attending to it."
— Charles Darwin, *The Expression of the Emotions in Man and Animals,* 1872

Distracted from the pain After a tackle in the first half of a competitive game, Mohammed Ali Khan (here playing for BK Häcken in white) said he "had a bit of pain" but thought it was "just a bruise." With his attention focused on the game, he played on. In the second half he was surprised to learn from an attending doctor that his leg was broken.

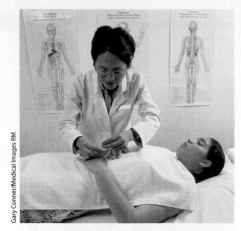

Acupuncture: A jab well done This acupuncturist is attempting to help this woman gain relief from back pain by using needles on points of the patient's hand.

"It's like I'm actually walking."

CONTROLLING PAIN If pain is where body meets mind—if it is both a physical and a psychological phenomenon—then it should be treatable both physically and psychologically. Depending on the symptoms, pain control therapies may include drugs, surgery, acupuncture, electrical stimulation, massage, exercise, hypnosis, relaxation training, meditation, and thought distraction.

Placebos Even *placebos* can help, by dampening the central nervous system's attention and responses to painful experiences—mimicking painkilling drugs (Eippert et al., 2009; Wager & Atlas, 2013). After being injected in the jaw with a stinging saltwater solution, men in one experiment received a placebo they had been told would relieve the pain. It did—they immediately felt better. "Nothing" worked. The men's belief in the fake painkiller triggered their brain to respond by dispensing endorphins, as revealed by activity in an area that releases natural painkilling opiates (Scott et al., 2007; Zubieta et al., 2005).

Another experiment pitted two placebos—fake pills and pretend acupuncture—against each other (Kaptchuk et al., 2006). People with persistent arm pain received either sham acupuncture (with trick needles that retracted without puncturing the skin) or blue cornstarch pills that looked like a medication often prescribed for strain injury. After two months, both groups were reporting less pain, with the fake acupuncture group reporting the greater pain drop. A quarter of those receiving the nonexistent needle pricks and 31 percent of those receiving the fake pills even complained of side effects, such as painful skin or dry mouth and fatigue.

Distraction Have you ever had a health care professional suggest that you focus on a pleasant image ("Think of a warm, comfortable environment") or perform some task ("Count backward by 3s")? Drawing attention away from the painful stimulation is an effective way to activate brain pathways that inhibit pain and increase pain tolerance (Edwards et al., 2009). For burn victims receiving excruciating wound care, an even more effective distraction is escaping into virtual reality. Functional MRI (fMRI) scans have revealed that playing in the computer-generated 3-D world reduces the brain's pain-related activity (Hoffman, 2004). Because pain is in the brain, diverting the brain's attention may bring relief. Being "fully immersed in a virtual environment [is] like a 'brain hack,'" said one doctor who uses virtual reality to treat pain. "You can't be engaged in anything else" (Brody, 2019).

Hypnosis Better yet, research suggests, try maximizing pain relief by combining a placebo with distraction (Buhle et al., 2012) and amplifying their effects with **hypnosis.** Imagine you are about to be hypnotized. The hypnotist invites you to sit back, fix your gaze on a spot high on the wall, and relax. You hear a quiet, low voice suggest, "Your eyes are growing tired. . . . Your eyelids are becoming heavy . . . now heavier and heavier. . . . They are beginning to close. . . . You are becoming more deeply relaxed. . . . Your breathing is now deep and regular. . . . Your muscles are becoming more and more relaxed. Your whole body is beginning to feel like lead." After a few minutes of this *hypnotic induction*, you may experience hypnosis. Words can temporarily change your brain activity.

Hypnotists have no magical mind-control power; they merely focus people's attention on certain images or behaviors. To some extent, we are all open to suggestion. But highly hypnotizable people—such as the 20 percent who can carry out a suggestion not to react to an open bottle of smelly ammonia—are especially suggestible and imaginative (Barnier & McConkey, 2004; Silva & Kirsch, 1992). Their brain also displays altered activity when under hypnosis (Jiang et al., 2016).

Can hypnosis relieve pain? *Yes.* When unhypnotized people put their arm in an ice bath, they felt intense pain within 25 seconds (Elkins et al., 2012; Jensen, 2008). When hypnotized people did the same after being given suggestions to feel no pain, they indeed reported feeling little pain. Hypnosis can also reduce some forms of chronic and disability-related pain (Adachi et al., 2014; Bowker & Dorstyn, 2016).

In surgical experiments, hypnotized patients have required less medication, recovered sooner, and left the hospital earlier than unhypnotized control patients (Askay & Patterson, 2007; Hammond, 2008; Spiegel, 2007). Nearly 10 percent of us can become so deeply hypnotized that even major surgery can be performed without anesthesia. Half of us can gain at least some pain relief from hypnosis. The surgical use of hypnosis has flourished in Europe, where one Belgian medical team has performed more than 5000 surgeries with a combination of hypnosis, local anesthesia, and a mild sedative (Facco, 2016; Song, 2006).

Psychologists have proposed two explanations for how hypnosis works:

- *Social influence theory* contends that hypnosis is a by-product of normal social and mental processes (Lynn et al., 1990, 2015; Spanos & Coe, 1992). In this view, hypnotized people, like actors caught up in a role, begin to feel and behave in ways appropriate for "good hypnotic subjects." They may allow the hypnotist to direct their attention away from pain.

- *Dissociation theory* proposes that hypnosis is a special dual-processing state of **dissociation**—a split between different levels of consciousness. Dissociation theory seeks to explain why, when no one is watching, previously hypnotized people may later carry out **posthypnotic suggestions** (Perugini et al., 1998). It also offers an explanation for why people hypnotized for pain relief may show brain activity in areas that receive sensory information, but not in areas that normally process pain-related information (Rainville et al., 1997).

Selective attention may also play a role in hypnotic pain relief. Brain scans show that hypnosis increases activity in frontal lobe attention systems (Oakley & Halligan, 2013). So, while hypnosis does not block sensory input itself, it may block our attention to those stimuli. This helps explain why injured soldiers, caught up in battle, may feel little or no pain until they reach safety.

Courtesy of Elizabeth Jecker

Dissociation or social influence? This hypnotized woman being tested by researcher Ernest Hilgard showed no pain when her arm was placed in an ice bath. The water felt cold, but not painful. But asked to press a key if some part of her felt the pain, she did so. To Hilgard (1986, 1992), this was evidence of divided consciousness, or "dissociation" of the cold from the pain. The social influence perspective, however, maintains that people responding this way are caught up in playing the role of "good subject."

ASK YOURSELF

What methods of pain control do you usually turn to when you need it? Has learning about these ways to control pain given you some new ideas about other effective strategies to try?

RETRIEVAL PRACTICE

RP-5 Which of the following options has NOT been proven to reduce pain?

    a. Distraction b. Hypnosis c. Phantom limb sensations d. Endorphins

ANSWERS IN APPENDIX E

Taste

LOQ **19-6** In what ways are our senses of taste and smell similar, and how do they differ?

Like touch, **gustation**—our sense of taste—involves several basic sensations. Taste's sensations were once thought to be *sweet, sour, salty,* and *bitter,* with all others stemming from mixtures of these four (McBurney & Gent, 1979). Then, as investigators searched for specialized nerve fibers for the four taste sensations, they encountered a receptor for what we now know is a fifth—the savory, meaty taste of *umami,* best experienced as the flavor enhancer monosodium glutamate (MSG).

Tastes exist for more than our pleasure (see **TABLE 19.1**). Pleasureful tastes attracted our ancestors to energy- or protein-rich foods that enabled their survival. Aversive tastes deterred them from new foods that might be toxic. We see the inheritance of this biological wisdom in today's 2- to 6-year-olds, who are typically fussy eaters, especially when offered new meats or bitter-tasting vegetables, such as spinach and brussels sprouts (Cooke et al., 2003). Meat and plant toxins were both potentially dangerous sources of food poisoning for our ancestors, especially children. Given repeated small tastes of disliked new foods, however, most children begin to accept them (Wardle et al., 2003). We come to like what we eat. Compared with breast-fed babies, German babies bottle-fed vanilla-flavored milk grew up to be adults with a striking preference for vanilla flavoring (Haller et al., 1999). The taste-exposure phenomenon even extends to the womb. In one experiment, babies whose mothers drank carrot juice during the end of pregnancy and the early weeks of nursing developed a liking for carrot-flavored cereal (Mennella et al., 2001).

hypnosis a social interaction in which one person (the hypnotist) suggests to another (the subject) that certain perceptions, feelings, thoughts, or behaviors will spontaneously occur.

dissociation a split in consciousness, which allows some thoughts and behaviors to occur simultaneously with others.

posthypnotic suggestion a suggestion, made during a hypnosis session, to be carried out after the subject is no longer hypnotized; used by some clinicians to help control undesired symptoms and behaviors.

gustation our sense of taste.

TABLE 19.1 The Survival Functions of Basic Tastes	
Taste	**Indicates**
Sweet	Energy source
Salty	Sodium essential to physiological processes
Sour	Potentially toxic acid
Bitter	Potential poisons
Umami	Proteins to grow and repair tissue

Lauren Burke/Getty Images

Macmillan Learning

Linda Bartoshuk (born 1938) As a student in the late 1950s era of gender discrimination, Bartoshuk (2010) abandoned her interest in astronomy when she learned that "women weren't allowed to use the big telescopes." This led her to *psychophysics*— the study of how physical stimuli, such as substances on the tongue, create our subjective experience. While studying taste experiences, she discovered *supertasters*.

Taste is a chemical sense. Inside each little bump on the top and sides of your tongue are 200 or more taste buds, each containing a pore that catches food chemicals and releases neurotransmitters (Roper & Chaudhari, 2017). In each taste bud pore, 50 to 100 taste receptor cells project antenna-like hairs that sense food molecules. Some receptors respond mostly to sweet-tasting molecules, others to salty-, sour-, umami-, or bitter-tasting ones. Each receptor transmits its message to a matching partner cell in your brain's temporal lobe (Barretto et al., 2015). Some people have more taste buds than others, enabling them to experience more intense tastes. Psychologist Linda Bartoshuk (2000) has researched these *supertasters* and how they can taste some things that the rest of us cannot.

For most people, it doesn't take much to trigger a taste response. If a stream of water is pumped across your tongue, the addition of a concentrated salty or sweet taste for but one-tenth of a second will get your attention (Kelling & Halpern, 1983). When a friend asks for "just a taste" from your smoothie, you can squeeze off the straw after a mere instant.

Taste receptors reproduce themselves every week or two, so if you burn your tongue it hardly matters. However, as you grow older, the number of taste buds decreases, as does taste sensitivity (Cowart, 1981). (No wonder adults enjoy strong-tasting foods that children resist.) Smoking and alcohol use accelerate these declines. Those who have lost their sense of taste have reported that food tastes like "straw" and is hard to swallow (Cowart, 2005).

There's more to taste than meets the tongue. Wear a blindfold when eating a meal and you will attend more to (and savor) its taste (O'Brien & Smith, 2019). Expectations also influence taste. When told a sausage roll was "vegetarian," nonvegetarian people judged it decidedly inferior to its identical partner labeled "meat" (Allen et al., 2008). In another experiment, hearing that a wine cost $90 rather than its real $10 price made it taste better and triggered more activity in a brain area that responds to pleasant experiences (Plassmann et al., 2008). Contrary to Shakespeare's presumption (in *Romeo and Juliet*) that "A rose by any other name would smell as sweet," labels matter. And speaking of smell . . .

Smell

Inhale, exhale. Between birth's first inhale and death's last exhale, an average 500 million breaths of life-sustaining air bathe human nostrils in a stream of scent-laden molecules. The resulting experience of smell—**olfaction**—is strikingly intimate. With every breath, you inhale something of whatever or whoever it is you smell.

Smell, like taste, is a chemical sense. We smell something when molecules of a substance carried in the air reach a tiny cluster of receptor cells at the top of each nasal cavity (**FIGURE 19.8**). These 20 million olfactory receptors, waving like sea anemones on a reef, respond selectively—to the aroma of a cake baking, to a wisp of smoke, to a friend's fragrance. Instantly, they alert the brain through their axon fibers.

Being part of an old, primitive sense, olfactory neurons bypass the brain's sensory control center, the thalamus. Eons before our cerebral cortex had fully evolved, our mammalian ancestors sniffed for food—and for predators. They also smelled molecules called *pheromones*, especially those secreted by other members of their species. Some pheromones serve as sexual attractants. When straight men smelled ovulating women's T-shirts, the men became more sexually interested and experienced increased testosterone (Miller & Maner, 2010, 2011).

Impress your friends with your new word for the day: People unable to see are said to experience blindness. People unable to hear experience deafness. People unable to smell experience *anosmia*. The 1 in 7500 people born with anosmia not only have trouble cooking and eating, but also are somewhat more prone to depression, accidents, and relationship insecurity (Croy et al., 2012, 2013).

 olfaction our sense of smell.

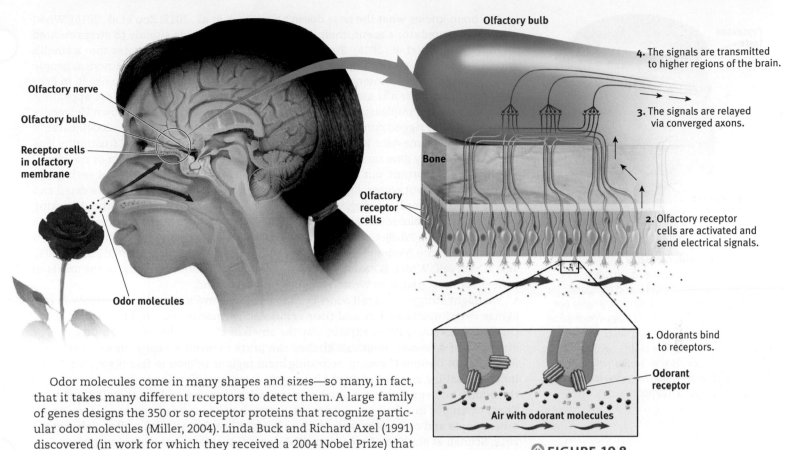

Olfactory bulb

Olfactory nerve

Olfactory bulb

Receptor cells in olfactory membrane

Odor molecules

Bone

Olfactory receptor cells

4. The signals are transmitted to higher regions of the brain.

3. The signals are relayed via converged axons.

2. Olfactory receptor cells are activated and send electrical signals.

1. Odorants bind to receptors.

Odorant receptor

Air with odorant molecules

Odor molecules come in many shapes and sizes—so many, in fact, that it takes many different receptors to detect them. A large family of genes designs the 350 or so receptor proteins that recognize particular odor molecules (Miller, 2004). Linda Buck and Richard Axel (1991) discovered (in work for which they received a 2004 Nobel Prize) that these receptor proteins are embedded on the surface of nasal cavity neurons. As a key slips into a lock, so odor molecules slip into these receptors. Yet we don't seem to have a distinct receptor for each detectable odor. Odors trigger combinations of receptors, in patterns that are interpreted by the olfactory cortex. As the English alphabet's 26 letters can combine to form many words, so odor molecules bind to different receptor arrays, producing at least 1 trillion odors that we could potentially discriminate (Bushdid et al., 2014). Neuroscientists have identified complex combinations of olfactory receptors that trigger different neural networks, allowing us to distinguish between delightful and disagreeable odors (Zou et al., 2016).

Animals that have many times more olfactory receptors than we do also use their sense of smell to survive, to communicate, and to navigate. Elephants can smell the difference between small and large amounts of food—letting them know whether they have enough to feed themselves or their herd (Plotnik et al., 2019). And long before a shark can see its prey, or a moth its mate, olfactory cues direct their way, as they also do for migrating salmon returning to their home stream. After being exposed in a hatchery to one of two odorant chemicals, returning salmon will later seek whichever stream was spiked with the familiar smell (Barinaga, 1999).

Aided by smell, a mother fur seal returning to a beach crowded with pups will find her own. Human mothers and nursing infants also quickly learn to recognize each other's scents (McCarthy, 1986). When people in relationships catch a whiff of their romantic partner's scent, their stress levels drop (Granqvist et al., 2019; Hofer et al., 2018). As any dog or cat with a good nose could tell us, we each have our own identifiable chemical signature. (One noteworthy exception: A dog will follow the tracks of one identical twin as though they had been made by the other person [Thomas, 1974].)

⬆ **FIGURE 19.8**
The sense of smell To smell a flower, airborne molecules of its fragrance must reach receptors at the top of your nose. By sniffing, you swirl air up to those receptors, enhancing the aroma. The receptor cells send messages to the brain's olfactory bulb, and then onward to the temporal lobe's primary smell cortex and to the parts of the limbic system involved in memory and emotion.

LAYNE BAILEY/AP Images

The nose knows Humans have some 20 million olfactory receptors. A bloodhound has 220 million (Herz, 2007).

Processes taste

Processes smell (near memory area)

⑦ FIGURE 19.9

Taste, smell, and memory Information from the taste buds travels to an area between the brain's frontal and temporal lobes (yellow area). It registers in an area not far from where the brain receives information from our sense of smell (red area), which interacts with taste. The brain's circuitry for smell also connects with areas involved in memory storage, which helps explain why a smell can trigger a memory.

"You have to see and smell and feel the circumstances of people to really understand them." — U.S. Senator Kamala Harris, 2019

→ kinesthesia [kin-ehs-THEE-zhuh] our movement sense—our system for sensing the position and movement of individual body parts.

vestibular sense our balance sense—our sense of body movement and position that enables our sense of balance.

The brain knows what the nose doesn't like (Cook et al., 2017; Zou et al., 2016). When mice sniff a predator's scent, their brain instinctively sends signals to stress-related neurons (Kondoh et al., 2016). But smell expert Rachel Herz (2001) notes that a smell's appeal—or lack of it—also depends on cultural experiences. In North America, people associate the smell of wintergreen with candy and gum, and they tend to like it. In Britain, wintergreen often is associated with medicine, and people find it less appealing. Odors also evoked unpleasant emotions when researchers frustrated Brown University students with a rigged computer game in a scented room (Herz et al., 2004). Later, if exposed to the same odor while working on a verbal task, the students' frustration was rekindled and they gave up sooner than others exposed to a different odor or no odor.

Although important, our sense of smell is less acute than our senses of seeing and hearing. Looking out across a garden, we see its forms and colors in exquisite detail and hear a variety of birds singing, yet we miss some of a garden's scents without sticking our nose into the blossoms. We can learn to identify subtle smell differences, but it isn't easy (Al Aïn et al., 2019). Compared with how we experience and remember sights and sounds, smells are harder to describe and recall (Richardson & Zucco, 1989; Zucco, 2003). Test it yourself: Which is easier, describing the *sound* of coffee brewing, or the *aroma* of coffee? For most people in Western cultures, it's the sound.

We might struggle to recall odors by name, but we have a remarkable capacity to recognize long-forgotten odors and their associated memories (Engen, 1987; Schab, 1991). Our brain's circuitry helps explain why the smell of the sea, the scent of a perfume, or an aroma of a favorite relative's kitchen can bring to mind a happy time. Other odors remind us of traumatic events, activating brain regions related to fear (Kadohisa, 2013). Indeed, a hotline runs between the brain area receiving information from the nose and the brain's ancient limbic centers associated with memory and emotion (**FIGURE 19.9**). Thus, when put in a foul-smelling room, people have expressed harsher judgments of other people and of immoral acts (such as lying or keeping a found wallet) (Inbar et al., 2012; Schnall et al., 2008). Exposed to a fishy smell, people became more suspicious (Lee et al., 2015; Lee & Schwarz, 2012). And when riding on a train car with the citrus scent of a cleaning product, people have left behind less trash (de Lange et al., 2012).

Gender and age influence our ability to identify scents. Women and young adults tend to have the best sense of smell (Wysocki & Gilbert, 1989). Physical condition also matters. Smokers and people with Alzheimer's disease, Parkinson's disease, or alcohol use disorder typically have a diminished sense of smell (Doty, 2001). Moreover, the smells we detect and the ways we experience them differ, thanks to our individual genes (Trimmer et al., 2019). The scent of a flower may be different for you than for a friend. For all of us, however, the sense of smell tends to peak in early adulthood and gradually declines thereafter.

RETRIEVAL PRACTICE

RP-6 How does our system for sensing smell differ from our systems for touch and taste?

ANSWERS IN APPENDIX E

☒ Test your understanding of how we smell by engaging online with *Concept Practice: Sense of Smell.*

Body Position and Movement

LOQ 19-7 How do we sense our body's position and movement?

Without sensing your body's position and movement, you could not put food in your mouth, stand up, or reach out and touch someone. Nor could you perform the "simple" act of taking one step forward. That act requires feedback from, and instructions to, some 200 muscles, and it engages brain power that exceeds the mental activity involved in reasoning. Millions of position and motion sensors in muscles, tendons, and joints all over your body, called *proprioceptors,* provide constant feedback to your brain, enabling your sense of **kinesthesia,** which keeps you aware of your body parts' position and movement. Twist your wrist one degree and your brain receives an immediate update.

If you have full vision and hearing, you can momentarily imagine being blind and deaf by closing your eyes and plugging your ears to experience the dark silence. But what would it be like to live without touch or kinesthesia—without being able to sense the positions of your limbs when you wake during the night? Ian Waterman of Hampshire, England, knows. At age 19, Waterman contracted a rare viral infection that destroyed the nerves enabling his sense of light touch *and* of body position and movement. People with this condition report feeling disembodied, as though their body is dead, not real, not theirs (Sacks, 1985). With prolonged practice, Waterman learned to walk and eat—by visually focusing on his limbs and directing them accordingly. But if the lights went out, he would crumple to the floor (Azar, 1998).

Vision interacts with kinesthesia for you, too. If you are able, stand with your right heel in front of your left toes. Easy. Now close your eyes and try again. Did you wobble?

A companion **vestibular sense** monitors your head's (and thus your body's) position and movement. The biological gyroscopes for this sense of equilibrium are two structures in your inner ear. The first, your fluid-filled *semicircular canals*, look like a three-dimensional pretzel (see Figure 19.2a). The second structure is the pair of calcium-crystal–filled *vestibular sacs*. When your head rotates or tilts, the movement of these organs stimulates hair-like receptors, which send nerve signals to your cerebellum at the back of your brain, enabling you to sense your body position and maintain your balance.

If you twirl around and then come to an abrupt halt, neither the fluid in your semicircular canals nor your kinesthetic receptors will immediately return to their neutral state. The dizzy aftereffect fools your brain with the sensation that you're still spinning. This research illustrates a principle that underlies perceptual illusions: *Mechanisms that normally give us an accurate experience of the world can, under special conditions, fool us. Understanding how we get fooled provides clues to how our perceptual system works.*

Your vestibular sense is super speedy. If you slip, your vestibular sensors automatically and instantly order your skeletal response, well before you have consciously decided how to right yourself. You might try this: Hold one of your thumbs in front of your face, then move it rapidly right to left and back. Notice how your thumb blurs (your vision isn't fast enough to track it). Now hold your thumb still and swivel your *head* from left to right—just as fast. Voila! Your thumb stays clear—because your vestibular system, which is monitoring your head position, speedily moves the eyes. Head moves right, eyes move left. Vision is fast, but the vestibular sense is faster.

* * *

For a summary of our sensory systems, see **TABLE 19.2.**

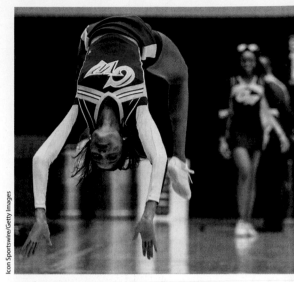

Body in space This college cheerleader shows that by using information from the inner ears, the brain expertly monitors body position.

TABLE 19.2 Summarizing the Senses

Sensory System	Source	Receptors	Key Brain Areas
Vision	Light waves striking the eye	Rods and cones in the retina	Occipital lobes
Hearing	Sound waves striking the outer ear	Cochlear hair cells (*cilia*) in the inner ear	Temporal lobes
Touch	Pressure, warmth, cold, harmful chemicals	Receptors (including pain-sensitive *nociceptors*), mostly in the skin, which detect pressure, warmth, cold, and pain	Somatosensory cortex
Taste	Chemical molecules in the mouth	Basic taste receptors for sweet, sour, salty, bitter, and umami	Frontal/temporal lobe border
Smell	Chemical molecules breathed in through the nose	Millions of receptors at top of nasal cavities	Olfactory bulb
Kinesthesia— position and movement	Any change in position of a body part, interacting with vision	Kinesthetic sensors in joints, tendons, and muscles (*proprioceptors*)	Cerebellum
Vestibular sense— balance and movement	Movement of fluids in the inner ear caused by head/body movement	Hair-like receptors (*cilia*) in the ears' semicircular canals and vestibular sacs	Cerebellum

Touch
Taste
Hearing
Smell
Vision

sensory interaction the principle that one sense can influence another, as when the smell of food influences its taste.

embodied cognition the influence of bodily sensations, gestures, and other states on cognitive preferences and judgments.

extrasensory perception (ESP) the controversial claim that perception can occur apart from sensory input; includes telepathy, clairvoyance, and precognition.

RETRIEVAL PRACTICE

RP-7 Where are the kinesthetic receptors and the vestibular sense receptors located?

ANSWERS IN APPENDIX E

Sensory Interaction

LOQ 19-8 How does sensory interaction influence our perceptions, and what is *embodied cognition?*

We have seen that vision and kinesthesia interact. Actually, none of our senses act alone. All our senses—seeing, hearing, tasting, smelling, touching—eavesdrop on one another, and our brain blends their inputs to interpret the world (Rosenblum, 2013). This is **sensory interaction** at work. One sense can influence another.

Consider how smell sticks its nose into the business of taste. Hold your nose, close your eyes, and have someone feed you various foods. A slice of apple may be indistinguishable from a chunk of raw potato. A cracker may taste like cardboard. Without their smells, a cup of cold coffee may be hard to distinguish from a glass of red wine. A big part of taste is right under your nose.

We normally inhale the aroma through our nose. Like smoke rising in a chimney, food molecules rise into our nasal cavity. This is why food tastes bland when you have a bad cold. Smell can also change our perception of taste: A drink's strawberry odor enhances our perception of its sweetness. Even touch can influence our taste. Depending on its texture, a potato chip "tastes" fresh or stale (Smith, 2011). Smell + texture + taste = flavor. Yet perhaps you have noticed: Flavor *feels* located in the mouth (Stevenson, 2014).

Vision and hearing may similarly interact. Baseball umpires' vision informs their hearing of when the ball hits a player's glove, influencing their judgments of whether baserunners are safe or out (Krynen & McBeath, 2019). Likewise, a weak flicker of light becomes more visible when accompanied by a short burst of sound (Kayser, 2007). The reverse is also true: Soft sounds are more easily heard when paired with a visual cue. If I [DM], as a person with hearing loss, watch a video with on-screen captions, I have no trouble hearing the words I am seeing. But if I then decide I don't need the captions and turn them off, I quickly realize I do need them. The eyes guide the ears (**FIGURE 19.10**).

So our senses do not function in isolation; they interact. But what happens if they disagree? What if our eyes *see* a speaker form one sound but our ears *hear* another sound? Surprise: Our brain may perceive a third sound that blends both inputs. Seeing mouth movements for *ga* while hearing *ba*, we may perceive *da*. This phenomenon is known as the *McGurk effect,* after Scottish psychologist Harry McGurk, who, with his assistant John MacDonald, discovered the effect (1976). For most of us, lip reading is part of hearing.

We have seen that our perceptions have two main ingredients: Our bottom-up sensations and our top-down cognitions (such as expectations, attitudes, thoughts, and memories). In everyday life, sensation and perception are two points on a continuum. It's not surprising, then, that the brain circuits processing our physical sensations sometimes interact with brain circuits responsible for cognition. The result is **embodied cognition.** We think from within a body. Three examples from playful experiments:

- *Judgments may mimic body sensations.* Sitting at a wobbly desk and chair may make relationships seem less stable (Forest et al., 2015; Kille et al., 2013).
- *Physical warmth may promote social warmth.* On days when people feel physically warm, they feel socially warm and friendly (Fetterman et al., 2018). Want to perceive others and yourself as socially warmer? Try wearing a sweater rather than a T-shirt.

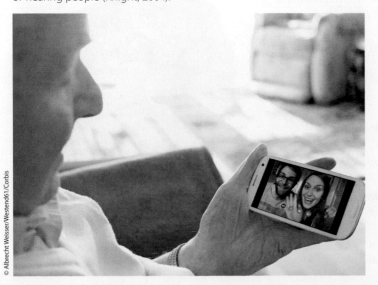

FIGURE 19.10

Sensory interaction Seeing the speaker forming the words in video chats makes those words easier to understand for hard-of-hearing people (Knight, 2004).

© Albrecht Weisser/Westend61/Corbis

- *Hard objects may make you hard on crime.* People who sat in a hard chair, compared with a soft chair, gave harsher punishments to criminals, and to college students who cheated on a final paper (Schaefer et al., 2018). Hard chair, hard on crime.

As we attempt to decipher our world, our brain blends inputs from multiple channels. But in a few select individuals, the brain circuits for two or more senses become joined in a phenomenon called *synesthesia,* where the stimulation of one sense (hearing a number or musical note) triggers an experience of another (sensing a specific color, taste, or smell) (**FIGURE 19.11**). Early in life, "exuberant neural connectivity" produces some arbitrary associations among the senses, which later are normally—but not always—pruned (Wagner & Dobkins, 2011). Equipped with a brain that blends sensations, hearing music may activate color-sensitive cortex regions and trigger a sensation of color (Brang et al., 2008; Hubbard et al., 2005). Seeing a number may evoke a taste or color sensation (Newell & Mitchell, 2016; Ranzini & Girelli, 2019). People with synesthesia experience such sensory shifts.

ASK YOURSELF

When have you experienced a feeling that you think could be explained by embodied cognition?

Think of even numbers

Person without synesthesia

Person with synesthesia

⬆ **FIGURE 19.11**
Synesthesia's symphony A person with synesthesia experiences blended sensations. For example, hearing numbers may evoke an experience of specific colors or smells or musical notes.

ESP—Perception Without Sensation?

LOQ 19-9 What are the claims of ESP, and what have most research psychologists concluded after putting these claims to the test?

The river of perception is fed by sensation, cognition, and emotion. If perception is the product of these three sources, what can we say about **extrasensory perception (ESP),** which claims that perception can occur without sensory input? Are there indeed people—any people—who can read minds, see through walls, or foretell the future? Nearly half of all Americans surveyed believe we are capable of extrasensory perception and 41 percent believe in psychics (Gecewicz, 2018; Kim et al., 2015).

If ESP is real, we would need to overturn the scientific understanding that we are creatures whose minds are tied to our physical brains and whose perceptual experiences of the world are built of sensations. The most testable and, for this discussion, most relevant ESP claims are

- *telepathy:* mind-to-mind communication.
- *clairvoyance:* perceiving remote events, such as a house on fire across the country.
- *precognition:* perceiving future events, such as an unexpected death in the next month.

Closely linked to these ESP claims is *psychokinesis,* or "mind moving matter," such as levitating a table or controlling the roll of a die. (The claim, also called *telekinesis,* is illustrated by the wry request, "Will all those who believe in psychokinesis please raise my hand?") In Britain, psychologists created a "mind machine" to see if festival visitors could influence or predict a coin toss (Wiseman & Greening, 2002). Participants were given four attempts to call heads or tails, playing against a computer. By the time the experiment ended, nearly 28,000 people had predicted 110,959 tosses—with 49.8 percent correct.

PSYCHIC DIVING COMPETITION.

Jon Carter/Cartoonstock

Most psychological scientists are skeptical that paranormal phenomena exist. But in several reputable universities, **parapsychology** researchers search for possible ESP phenomena by performing scientific experiments (Cardeña, 2018; Storm et al., 2010a,b; Turpin, 2005). Before seeing how they conduct their research, let's consider some popular beliefs.

Premonitions or Pretensions?

Can psychics see into the future? No greedy—or charitable—psychic has been able to make billions on the stock market. Where were the psychics the day before the 9/11 terrorist attacks? Why could no psychics help locate Osama bin Laden afterward? And why, when the Chilean government consulted four psychics after a mine collapse trapped 33 miners in 2010, did those psychics sorrowfully decide "they're all dead" (Kraul, 2010)? Imagine their surprise when all 33 miners were rescued 69 days later.

Psychic visions offered to police departments have been no more accurate than guesses made by others (Nickell, 2005; Palmer, 2013; Radford, 2010). But their sheer volume increases the odds of an occasional correct guess, which psychics can then report to the media. Such visions can sound amazingly correct when later retrofitted to match events. Nostradamus, a sixteenth-century French psychic, explained in an unguarded moment that his ambiguous prophecies "could not possibly be understood till they were interpreted after the event and by it."

Are everyday people's "visions" any more accurate than psychic predictions? Do our dreams foretell the future, as people from both Eastern and Western cultures tend to believe (Morewedge & Norton, 2009)? Or do they only seem to do so when we recall or reconstruct them in light of what has already happened? Are our remembered visions merely revisions? After famed aviator Charles Lindbergh's baby son was kidnapped and murdered in 1932, but before the body was discovered, two Harvard psychologists invited people to report their dreams about the child (Murray & Wheeler, 1937). How many visionaries replied? 1300. How many accurately envisioned the child dead? Five percent. How many also correctly anticipated the body's location—buried among trees? Only 4. Although this number was surely no better than chance, to those 4 dreamers, the accuracy of their apparent precognitions must have seemed uncanny.

Given countless daily events, and given enough days, some stunning coincidences are bound to occur. By one careful estimate, chance alone would predict that more than a thousand times per day, someone on Earth will think of another person and then, within the next 5 minutes, learn of that person's death (Charpak & Broch, 2004). Thus, when explaining an astonishing event, we should "give chance a chance" (Lilienfeld, 2009). With enough time and people, the improbable becomes inevitable.

Putting ESP to Experimental Test

When faced with claims of mind reading or out-of-body travel or communication with the dead, how can we separate fiction from strange-but-true fact? Psychological science offers a simple answer: *Test claims to see if they work.* If they do, so much the better for the ideas. If they don't, so much the better for our skepticism.

Both believers and skeptics agree that what parapsychology needs is a reproducible phenomenon and a theory to explain it. Parapsychologist Rhea White (1998) spoke for many in saying that "the image of parapsychology that comes to my mind, based on nearly 44 years in the field, is that of a small airplane [that] has been perpetually taxiing down the runway of the Empirical Science Airport since 1882 . . . its movement punctuated occasionally by lifting a few feet off the ground only to bump back down on the tarmac once again. It has never taken off for any sustained flight."

How might we test ESP claims in a controlled, reproducible experiment? An experiment differs from a staged demonstration. In the laboratory, the experimenter controls what the "psychic" sees and hears. On stage, the psychic controls what the audience sees and hears.

Daryl Bem, a respected social psychologist, once quipped that "a psychic is an actor playing the role of a psychic" (1984). Yet this one-time skeptic reignited hopes for replicable evidence of ESP with nine experiments that seemed to show people anticipating

A headline you've never seen: "Psychic wins lottery."

"A person who talks a lot is sometimes right." — Spanish proverb

parapsychology the study of paranormal phenomena, including ESP and psychokinesis (also called *telekinesis*).

future events (Bem, 2011). In one, when an erotic scene was about to appear on a screen in one of two randomly selected positions, Cornell University participants guessed the right placement 53.1 percent of the time (beating chance by a small but statistically significant margin). Bem wondered if his "anomalous" findings reflected an evolutionary advantage to those who can precognitively anticipate future dangers.

Despite Bem's research surviving critical reviews by a top-tier journal, critics found the methods and statistical analyses "badly flawed" and "biased" (Alcock, 2011; Wagenmakers et al., 2011). Others predicted the results would fail to replicate (Helfand, 2011). Anticipating such skepticism, Bem made his research materials available to anyone who wished to replicate his studies. Multiple attempts have met with minimal success and continuing controversy (Bem et al., 2015; Ritchie et al., 2012; Wagenmakers, 2014). Regardless, science is doing its work:

- It has been open to a finding that challenges its own assumptions.
- Through follow-up research, it has assessed the reliability and validity of that finding.

And that is how science sifts crazy-sounding ideas, leaving most on the historical waste heap while occasionally surprising us.

For 19 years, skeptic and magician James Randi offered $1 million "to anyone who proves a genuine psychic power under proper observing conditions" (Randi, 1999; Thompson, 2010). French, Australian, and Indian groups have made similar offers of up to 200,000 euros (CFI, 2003). Large as these sums are, the scientific seal of approval would be worth far more. To refute those who say there is no ESP, one need only produce a single person who can demonstrate a single, reproducible ESP event. (To refute those who say pigs can't talk would take but one talking pig.) So far, no such person has emerged.

> "At the heart of science is an essential tension between two seemingly contradictory attitudes—an openness to new ideas, no matter how bizarre or counterintuitive they may be, and the most ruthless skeptical scrutiny of all ideas, old and new." — Carl Sagan (1987)

RETRIEVAL PRACTICE

RP-8 If an ESP event did occur under controlled conditions, what would be the next step to confirm that ESP really exists?

ANSWERS IN APPENDIX E

Have you ever tried to see if you have ESP? Test your skills by engaging online with the activity *Assess Your Strengths—ESP and Critical Thinking.*

* * *

To feel awe, mystery, and a deep reverence for life, we need look no further than our own perceptual system and its capacity for organizing formless nerve impulses into colorful sights, vivid sounds, and evocative smells. As Shakespeare's Hamlet recognized, "There are more things in Heaven and Earth, Horatio, than are dreamt of in your philosophy." Within our ordinary sensory and perceptual experiences lies much that is truly extraordinary—surely much more than has so far been dreamt of in our psychology.

19 REVIEW The Nonvisual Senses

LEARNING OBJECTIVES

Test Yourself Answer these repeated Learning Objective Questions on your own (before checking the answers in Appendix D) to improve your retention of the concepts (McDaniel et al., 2009, 2015).

LOQ **19-1** What are the characteristics of the air pressure waves that we hear as sound?

LOQ **19-2** How does the ear transform sound energy into neural messages?

LOQ **19-3** How do we detect loudness, discriminate pitch, and locate sounds?

LOQ **19-4** What are the four basic touch sensations, and how do we sense touch?

LOQ **19-5** What biological, psychological, and social-cultural influences affect our experience of pain? How do placebos, distraction, and hypnosis help control pain?

LOQ **19-6** In what ways are our senses of taste and smell similar, and how do they differ?

LOQ **19-7** How do we sense our body's position and movement?

LOQ **19-8** How does sensory interaction influence our perceptions, and what is *embodied cognition?*

LOQ **19-9** What are the claims of ESP, and what have most research psychologists concluded after putting these claims to the test?

TERMS AND CONCEPTS TO REMEMBER

Test Yourself Write down the definition in your own words, then check your answer.

audition, p. 239

frequency, p. 239

pitch, p. 239

middle ear, p. 239

cochlea [KOHK-lee-uh], p. 239

inner ear, p. 239

sensorineural hearing loss, p. 240

conduction hearing loss, p. 240

cochlear implant, p. 240

place theory, p. 242

frequency theory, p. 242

gate-control theory, p. 245

hypnosis, p. 247

dissociation, p. 247

posthypnotic suggestion, p. 247

gustation, p. 247

olfaction, p. 248

kinesthesia [kin-ehs-THEE-zhuh], p. 250

vestibular sense, p. 250

sensory interaction, p. 252

embodied cognition, p. 252

extrasensory perception (ESP), p. 252

parapsychology, p. 254

MASTER THE MATERIAL

Test Yourself Answer the following questions on your own first, then check your answers in Appendix E.

1. The snail-shaped tube in the inner ear, where sound waves are converted into neural activity, is called the
_____.

2. What are the basic steps in transforming sound waves into perceived sound?

3. _____ theory explains how we hear high-pitched sounds, and _____ theory explains how we hear low-pitched sounds.

4. The sensory receptors that are found mostly in the skin and that detect painful temperatures, pressure, or chemicals are called
_____.

5. The gate-control theory of pain proposes that
   a. special pain receptors send signals directly to the brain.
   b. the pain gate is controlled by the thalamus.
   c. small spinal cord nerve fibers conduct most pain signals, but large-fiber activity can close access to those pain signals.
   d. pain can often be controlled and managed effectively through the use of relaxation techniques.

6. How does the biopsychosocial approach explain our experience of pain? Provide examples.

7. We have specialized nerve receptors for detecting which five tastes? How did this ability aid our ancestors?

8. _____ is your sense of body position and movement. Your _____
_____ specifically monitors your head's movement, with sensors in the inner ear.

9. Why do you feel a little dizzy immediately after a roller-coaster ride?

10. A food's aroma can greatly enhance its taste. This is an example of
    a. olfaction.
    b. synesthesia.
    c. kinesthesia.
    d. sensory interaction.

11. Which of the following ESP phenomena is supported by solid, replicable scientific evidence?
    a. Telepathy
    b. Clairvoyance
    c. Precognition
    d. None of these answers

Continue testing yourself with **LearningCurve** or **Achieve Read & Practice** to learn and remember most effectively.

Learning

In the early 1940s, University of Minnesota graduate students Marian Breland and Keller Breland witnessed the power of a new learning technique. Their mentor, B. F. Skinner, would become famous for *shaping* rat and pigeon behaviors by delivering well-timed rewards as the animals inched closer and closer to a desired behavior. Impressed by Skinner's results, the Brelands began shaping the behavior of cats, chickens, parakeets, turkeys, pigs, ducks, and hamsters (Bailey & Gillaspy, 2005). The company they formed spent the next half-century training more than 15,000 animals from 140 species. Their efforts helped pave the way for training animals to help police officers and people with vision loss.

Like other animals, humans learn from experience. Indeed, nature's most important gift may be our *adaptability*—our capacity to learn new behaviors that help us cope with our changing world. We can learn how to build grass huts or snow shelters, submarines or space stations, and thereby adapt to almost any environment.

Oprah Winfrey is a living example of adaptability. Growing up in poverty with her grandmother, Winfrey wore dresses made of potato sacks. She experienced constant racism, and she was molested by a cousin, an uncle, and a family friend, beginning at age 9. Winfrey ran away from home at age 13 and became pregnant at age 14, but her son died shortly after birth.

To overcome such tremendous adversity, Winfrey learned how to adapt to new situations. She joined her high school speech team and used this talent to win a college scholarship. After graduating, she moved to Chicago and took over as the host of a struggling show, transforming it into the most popular daytime talk show in America. Winfrey continues to influence the world as a media executive, philanthropist, and political activist. "Education," said Winfrey, "is the key to unlocking the world, a passport to freedom."

Learning breeds hope. What is learnable we may be able to teach—a fact that encourages animal trainers, and also parents, educators, and coaches. What has been learned we may be able to change by new learning—an assumption underlying stress management and counseling programs. No matter how unhappy or unsuccessful or unloving we are, that need not be the end of our story.

No topic is closer to the heart of psychology than *learning*. Psychologists study infants' learning, and the learning of visual perceptions, of a drug's expected effect, and of gender roles. They also consider how learning shapes our thoughts and language, our motivations and emotions, our personalities and attitudes. Here in Modules 20–22 we examine the heart of learning: classical conditioning, operant conditioning, the effects of biology and cognition on learning, and learning by observation.

20 Basic Learning Concepts and Classical Conditioning

How Do We Learn?

LEARNING OBJECTIVE QUESTION **LOQ** **20-1** How do we define *learning,* and what are some basic forms of learning?

By **learning,** we humans adapt to our environments. We learn to expect and prepare for significant events such as the arrival of food or pain *(classical conditioning)*. We learn to repeat acts that bring rewards and avoid acts that bring unwanted results *(operant conditioning)*. We learn new behaviors by observing events and people, and through language, we learn things we have neither experienced nor observed *(cognitive learning)*. But *how* do we learn?

One way we learn is by *association*. Our mind naturally connects events that occur in sequence, and we find such learned connections rewarding (Kobayashi & Hsu, 2019; Rodríguez & Hall, 2019). We evolved to like learning (Clark & Gilchrist, 2018). Suppose you see and smell freshly baked bread, eat some, and find it satisfying. The next time you see and smell fresh bread, you will expect that eating it will again be satisfying. So, too, with sounds. If you associate a sound with a frightening consequence, hearing the sound alone may trigger your fear. As one 4-year-old exclaimed after watching a TV character get mugged, "If I had heard that music, I wouldn't have gone around the corner!" (Wells, 1981).

Learned associations also feed our habitual behaviors (Urcelay & Jonkman, 2019; Wood et al., 2017). Habits can form when we repeat behaviors in a given context—sleeping in a certain posture in bed, biting our nails in class, eating popcorn in a movie theater. As behavior becomes linked with the context, our next experience of that context will evoke our habitual response. Especially when our willpower is depleted, as when we're mentally fatigued, we tend to fall back on our habits (Neal et al., 2013). That's true of both good habits (eating fruit) and bad (overindulging in alcohol) (Graybiel & Smith, 2014). To increase our self-control, and to connect our resolutions with positive outcomes, the key is forming "beneficial habits" (Galla & Duckworth, 2015).

How long does it take to form a beneficial habit? To find out, one British research team asked 96 university students to choose some healthy behavior (such as running before dinner or eating fruit with lunch), to do it daily for 84 days, and to record whether the behavior felt automatic (something they did without thinking and would find it hard not to do). On average, behaviors became habitual after about 66 days (Lally et al., 2010).

learning the process of acquiring through experience new and relatively enduring information or behaviors.

associative learning learning that certain events occur together. The events may be two stimuli (as in classical conditioning) or a response and its consequence (as in operant conditioning).

stimulus any event or situation that evokes a response.

respondent behavior behavior that occurs as an automatic response to some stimulus.

operant behavior behavior that operates on the environment, producing a consequence.

Two related events:

Stimulus 1:
Lightning

+

Stimulus 2:
Thunder

BOOM!

⟹

Response:
Startled
reaction;
wincing

Result after repetition:

Stimulus:
Lightning

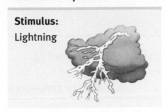

⟹

Response:
Anticipation
of booming
thunder;
wincing

⬅ FIGURE 20.1
Classical conditioning

Is there something you'd like to make a routine or essential part of your life? Just do it every day for two months, or a bit longer for exercise, and you likely will find yourself with a new habit. This happened for both of us—with a midday workout [DM] or a late afternoon guitar practice session [ND] having long ago become an automatic daily routine.

Other animals also learn by association. Disturbed by a squirt of water, the sea slug *Aplysia* protectively withdraws its gill. If the squirts continue, as happens naturally in choppy water, the withdrawal response diminishes. But if the sea slug repeatedly receives an electric shock just after being squirted, its protective response to the squirt instead grows stronger. The animal has associated the squirt with the impending shock.

Complex animals can learn to associate their own behavior with its outcomes. An aquarium seal will repeat behaviors, such as slapping and barking, that prompt people to toss it a herring.

By linking two events that occur close together, both sea slugs and seals are exhibiting **associative learning.** The sea slug associates the squirt with an impending shock; the seal associates slapping and barking with a herring treat. Each animal has learned something important to its survival: anticipating the immediate future.

This process of learning associations is *conditioning*. It takes two main forms:

- In *classical conditioning* (**FIGURE 20.1**), we learn to associate two stimuli and thus to anticipate events. (A **stimulus** is any event or situation that evokes a response.) We learn that a flash of lightning signals an impending crack of thunder; when lightning flashes nearby, we start to brace ourselves. We associate stimuli that we do not control, and we respond automatically (exhibiting **respondent behavior**).

- In *operant conditioning,* we learn to associate a response (our behavior) and its consequence. Thus, we (and other animals) learn to repeat acts followed by good results (**FIGURE 20.2**) and avoid acts followed by bad results. These associations produce **operant behaviors** (which operate on the environment to produce consequences).

To simplify, we will explore these two types of associative learning separately. Often, though, they occur together, as on one Japanese cattle ranch, where the clever rancher outfitted his herd with electronic pagers, which he called from his cell phone. After a week of training, the animals learned to associate two stimuli—the beep of their pager and the arrival of food (classical conditioning). But they also learned to associate their hustling to the food trough with the pleasure of eating (operant conditioning), which simplified the rancher's work. Classical conditioning + operant conditioning did the trick.

"Watch your thoughts, they become words; watch your words, they become actions; watch your actions, they become habits; watch your habits, they become character; watch your character, for it becomes your destiny." — Attributed to nineteenth-century fugitive Frank Outlaw, 1977

Most of us would be unable to name the order of the songs on our favorite album or playlist. Yet, hearing the end of one piece cues (by association) an anticipation of the next. Likewise, when singing your national anthem, you associate the end of each line with the beginning of the next. (Pick a line out of the middle and notice how much harder it is to recall the *previous* line.)

⬇ FIGURE 20.2
Operant conditioning

(a) Behavior: Being polite   (b) Consequence: Getting a treat   (c) Behavior strengthened

Conditioning is not the only form of learning. Through **cognitive learning** we acquire mental information that guides our behavior. *Observational learning,* one form of cognitive learning, lets us learn from others' experiences. Chimpanzees, for example, sometimes learn behaviors merely by watching other chimpanzees perform them. If one animal sees another solve a puzzle and gain a food reward, the observer may perform the trick more quickly. So, too, in humans: We look and we learn.

Let's look more closely now at classical conditioning.

RETRIEVAL PRACTICE

RP-1   Why are habits, such as having something sweet with that cup of coffee, so hard to break?

ANSWERS IN APPENDIX E

Classical Conditioning

LOQ   20-2   What is behaviorism's view of learning?

For many people, the name Ivan Pavlov (1849–1936) rings a bell. His early twentieth-century experiments—now psychology's most famous research—are classics, and the phenomenon he explored we justly call **classical conditioning.**

Pavlov's work laid the foundation for many of psychologist John B. Watson's ideas. In searching for laws underlying learning, Watson (1913) urged his colleagues to discard reference to inner thoughts, feelings, and motives. The science of psychology should instead study how organisms respond to stimuli in their environments, said Watson: "Its theoretical goal is the prediction and control of behavior. Introspection forms no essential part of its methods." Simply said, psychology should be an objective science based on observable behavior.

This view, which Watson called **behaviorism,** influenced North American psychology, especially during the first half of the twentieth century. Pavlov and Watson came to share both a disdain for "mentalistic" concepts (such as consciousness) and a belief that the basic laws of learning were the same for all animals—whether sea slugs or dogs or humans. Few researchers today agree that psychology should ignore mental processes, but most do agree that classical conditioning is a basic form of learning by which all organisms adapt to their environments.

Pavlov's Experiments

LOQ   20-3   Who was Pavlov, and what are the basic components of classical conditioning?

Pavlov was driven by a lifelong passion for research. After setting aside his initial plan to follow his father into the Russian Orthodox priesthood, Pavlov earned a medical degree at age 33 and spent the next two decades studying dogs' digestive system. This work earned him Russia's first Nobel Prize. But Pavlov's novel experiments on learning, which consumed the last three decades of his life, earned this feisty, intense scientist his place in history (Todes, 2014).

Pavlov's new direction came when his creative mind seized on an incidental observation. Without fail, putting food in a dog's mouth caused the animal to salivate. Moreover, the dog began salivating not only to the taste of the food, but also to the mere sight of the food, or the food dish, or the person delivering the food, or even the sound of that person's approaching footsteps. At first, Pavlov considered these "psychic secretions" an annoyance—until he realized they pointed to a simple but fundamental form of learning.

Pavlov and his team of researchers—over half of whom were women (Hill, 2019)—tried to imagine what the dog was thinking and feeling as it drooled in anticipation of the food. This only led them into fruitless debates. So, to explore the phenomenon more

Ivan Pavlov "Experimental investigation . . . should lay a solid foundation for a future true science of psychology" (1927).

John B. Watson Watson (1924) admitted to "going beyond my facts" when offering his famous boast: "Give me a dozen healthy infants, well-formed, and my own specified world to bring them up in and I'll guarantee to take any one at random and train him to become any type of specialist I might select—doctor, lawyer, artist, merchant-chief, and, yes, even beggar-man and thief, regardless of his talents, penchants, tendencies, abilities, vocations, and race of his ancestors."

➡ FIGURE 20.3
Pavlov's device for recording salivation A tube in the dog's cheek collects saliva, which is measured in a cylinder outside the chamber.

objectively, they experimented. To eliminate other possible influences, they isolated the dog in a small room, secured it in a harness, and attached a device to divert its saliva to a measuring instrument (**FIGURE 20.3**). From the next room, they presented food—first by sliding in a food bowl, later by blowing meat powder into the dog's mouth at a precise moment. They then paired various **neutral stimuli (NS)**—events the dog could see or hear but didn't associate with food—with food in the dog's mouth. If a sight or sound regularly signaled the arrival of food, would the dog learn the link? If so, would it begin salivating in anticipation of the food?

The answers proved to be *Yes* and *Yes*. Just before placing food in the dog's mouth to produce salivation, Pavlov sounded a tone. After several pairings of tone and food, the dog, now anticipating the meat powder, began salivating to the tone alone. In later experiments, a buzzer,[1] a light, a touch on the leg, even the sight of a circle set off the drooling. (This procedure works with people, too. When hungry young Londoners viewed abstract figures before smelling peanut butter or vanilla, their brain soon responded in anticipation to the abstract images alone [Gottfried et al., 2003].)

A dog does not learn to salivate in response to food in its mouth. Rather, food in the mouth automatically, *unconditionally*, triggers a dog's salivary reflex (**FIGURE 20.4**). Thus, Pavlov called this drooling an **unconditioned response (UR).** And he called the food an **unconditioned stimulus (US).**

cognitive learning the acquisition of mental information, whether by observing events, by watching others, or through language.

classical conditioning a type of learning in which we link two or more stimuli; as a result, to illustrate with Pavlov's classic experiment, the first stimulus (a tone) comes to elicit behavior (drooling) in anticipation of the second stimulus (food).

behaviorism the view that psychology (1) should be an objective science that (2) studies behavior without reference to mental processes. Most research psychologists today agree with (1) but not with (2).

neutral stimulus (NS) in classical conditioning, a stimulus that elicits no response before conditioning.

unconditioned response (UR) in classical conditioning, an unlearned, naturally occurring response (such as salivation) to an unconditioned stimulus (US) (such as food in the mouth).

unconditioned stimulus (US) in classical conditioning, a stimulus that unconditionally—naturally and automatically—triggers an unconditioned response (UR).

⬇ FIGURE 20.4
Pavlov's classic experiment
Pavlov presented a neutral stimulus (a tone) just before an unconditioned stimulus (food in mouth). The neutral stimulus then became a conditioned stimulus, producing a conditioned response.

BEFORE CONDITIONING

US (food in mouth) → UR (salivation)

An unconditioned stimulus (US) produces an unconditioned response (UR).

NS (tone) → No salivation

A neutral stimulus (NS) produces no salivation response.

DURING CONDITIONING

NS (tone) + US (food in mouth) → UR (salivation)

The US is repeatedly presented just after the NS.
The US continues to produce a UR.

AFTER CONDITIONING

CS (tone) → CR (salivation)

The previously neutral stimulus alone now produces a conditioned response (CR), thereby becoming a conditioned stimulus (CS).

---

[1]The "buzzer" (English translation) was perhaps the bell people commonly associate with Pavlov (Tully, 2003). Pavlov used various stimuli, but some have questioned whether he used a bell.

PEANUTS

Peanuts reprinted with permission of United Features Syndicate

Salivation in response to a tone, however, is learned. It is *conditional* upon the dog's associating the tone with the food. Thus, we call this response the **conditioned response (CR).** The stimulus that used to be neutral (in this case, a previously meaningless tone that now triggers salivation) is the **conditioned stimulus (CS).** Distinguishing these two kinds of stimuli and responses is easy: Conditioned = learned; *unconditioned* = *unlearned.*

If Pavlov's demonstration of associative learning was so simple, what did he do for the next three decades? What discoveries did his research factory publish in his 532 papers on salivary conditioning (Windholz, 1997)? He and his associates explored five major conditioning processes: *acquisition, extinction, spontaneous recovery, generalization,* and *discrimination.*

RETRIEVAL PRACTICE

RP-2 An experimenter sounds a tone just before delivering an air puff that causes your eye to blink. After several repetitions, you blink to the tone alone. What is the NS? The US? The UR? The CS? The CR?

ANSWERS IN APPENDIX E

ACQUISITION

LOQ **20-4** In classical conditioning, what are the processes of *acquisition, extinction, spontaneous recovery, generalization,* and *discrimination?*

To understand the **acquisition,** or initial learning, of the stimulus-response relationship, Pavlov and his associates wondered: How much time should elapse between presenting the NS (the tone, the light, the touch) and the US (the food)? In most cases, not much—half a second usually works well.

What do you suppose would happen if the food (US) appeared before the tone (NS) rather than after? Would conditioning occur? Not likely. Conditioning usually won't occur when the NS follows the US. Remember: *Classical conditioning is biologically adaptive because it helps humans and other animals prepare for good or bad events.* To Pavlov's dogs, the originally neutral tone became a CS after signaling an important biological event—the arrival of food (US). To deer in the forest, the snapping of a twig (CS) may signal a predator's approach (US).

Research on male Japanese quail shows how a CS can signal another important biological event (Domjan, 1992, 1994, 2005). Just before presenting a sexually approachable female quail, the researchers turned on a red light. Over time, as the red light continued to herald the female's arrival, the light alone caused the male quail to become excited. They developed a preference for their cage's red-light district, and when a female appeared, they mated with her more quickly and released more semen and sperm (Matthews et al., 2007). This capacity for classical conditioning supports reproduction.

In humans, too, objects, smells, sounds, and sights associated with sexual pleasure—even a geometric figure, in one experiment—can become conditioned stimuli for sexual arousal (Byrne, 1982; Hoffman, 2012, 2017). Onion breath does not usually produce sexual arousal. But when repeatedly paired with a passionate kiss, it can become a CS and do just that (**FIGURE 20.5**).

The larger lesson: *Conditioning helps an animal survive and reproduce—by responding to cues that help it gain food, avoid dangers, locate mates, and produce offspring* (Hollis, 1997). Learning makes for yearning.

---

conditioned response (CR) in classical conditioning, a learned response to a previously neutral (but now conditioned) stimulus (CS).

conditioned stimulus (CS) in classical conditioning, an originally neutral stimulus that, after association with an unconditioned stimulus (US), comes to trigger a conditioned response (CR).

acquisition in classical conditioning, the initial stage—when one links a neutral stimulus and an unconditioned stimulus so that the neutral stimulus begins triggering the conditioned response. (In operant conditioning, the strengthening of a reinforced response.)

higher-order conditioning a procedure in which the conditioned stimulus in one conditioning experience is paired with a new neutral stimulus, creating a second (often weaker) conditioned stimulus. For example, an animal that has learned that a tone predicts food might then learn that a light predicts the tone and begin responding to the light alone. (Also called *second-order conditioning.*)

extinction the diminishing of a conditioned response; occurs in classical conditioning when an unconditioned stimulus (US) does not follow a conditioned stimulus (CS); occurs in operant conditioning when a response is no longer reinforced.

spontaneous recovery the reappearance, after a pause, of an extinguished conditioned response.

◀ **FIGURE 20.5**

An unexpected CS Psychologist Michael Tirrell (1990) recalled: "My first girlfriend loved onions, so I came to associate onion breath with kissing. Before long, onion breath sent tingles up and down my spine. Oh what a feeling!"

Through **higher-order conditioning,** a new NS can become a new CS without the presence of a US. All that's required is for it to become associated with a previously conditioned stimulus. If a tone regularly signals food and produces salivation, then a light that becomes associated with the tone (light → tone → food) may also begin to trigger salivation. Although this higher-order conditioning (also called *second-order conditioning*) tends to be weaker than first-order conditioning, it influences our everyday lives. If a dog bites you, just the sound of a barking dog may later make you feel afraid.

Remember:
NS = Neutral Stimulus
US = Unconditioned Stimulus
UR = Unconditioned Response
CS = Conditioned Stimulus
CR = Conditioned Response

ASK YOURSELF

Psychologist Michael Tirrell recalled coming to associate his girlfriend's onion breath with arousal. Can you remember ever experiencing something that would normally be neutral (or even unpleasant), but came to mean something special to you?

EXTINCTION AND SPONTANEOUS RECOVERY What would happen, Pavlov wondered, if, after conditioning, the CS occurred repeatedly without the US? If the tone sounded again and again, but no food appeared, would the tone still trigger salivation? The answer was mixed. The dogs salivated less and less, a reaction known as **extinction.** Extinction is the diminished response that occurs when the CS (tone) no longer signals an impending US (food). But if, after several hours' delay, Pavlov sounded the tone again, the dogs drooled in response (**FIGURE 20.6**). This **spontaneous recovery**—the reappearance of a (weakened) CR after a pause—suggested to Pavlov that extinction was suppressing the CR rather than eliminating it.

RETRIEVAL PRACTICE

RP-3 If the aroma of a baking cake sets your mouth to watering, what is the US? The CS? The CR?

RP-4 The first step of classical conditioning, when an NS becomes a CS, is called _____. When a US no longer follows the CS, and the CR becomes weakened, this is called _____.

ANSWERS IN APPENDIX E

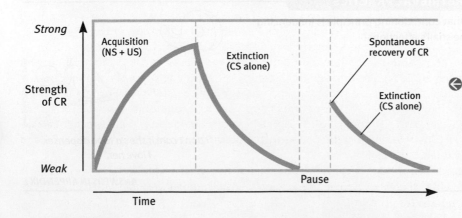

◀ **FIGURE 20.6**

Idealized curve of acquisition, extinction, and spontaneous recovery The rising curve shows the CR rapidly growing stronger as the NS becomes a CS due to repeated pairing with the US *(acquisition)*. The CR then weakens rapidly as the CS is presented alone *(extinction)*. After a pause, the (weakened) CR reappears *(spontaneous recovery)*.

FIGURE 20.7
Generalization Pavlov demonstrated generalization by attaching miniature vibrating devices to various parts of a dog's body. After conditioning salivation to stimulation of the thigh, he stimulated other areas. The closer a stimulated spot was to the dog's thigh, the stronger the conditioned response. (Data from Pavlov, 1927.)

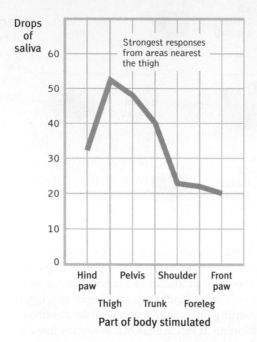

Strongest responses from areas nearest the thigh

Drops of saliva / Part of body stimulated

Hind paw — Thigh — Pelvis — Trunk — Shoulder — Foreleg — Front paw

FIGURE 20.8
Child abuse leaves tracks in the brain Abused children's sensitized brains react more strongly to angry faces (Pollak et al., 1998). This generalized anxiety response may help explain their greater risk of psychological disorder.

generalization (also called *stimulus generalization*) in classical conditioning, the tendency, once a response has been conditioned, for stimuli similar to the conditioned stimulus to elicit similar responses. (In operant conditioning, generalization occurs when responses learned in one situation occur in other, similar situations.)

discrimination in classical conditioning, the learned ability to distinguish between a conditioned stimulus and similar stimuli that do not signal an unconditioned stimulus. (In operant conditioning, the ability to distinguish responses that are reinforced from similar responses that are not reinforced.)

GENERALIZATION Pavlov and his students noticed that a dog conditioned to the sound of one tone also responded somewhat to the sound of a new and different tone. Likewise, a dog conditioned to salivate when rubbed would also drool a bit when scratched (Windholz, 1989) or when touched on a different body part (**FIGURE 20.7**). This tendency to respond to stimuli similar to the CS is called **generalization** (or *stimulus generalization*).

Generalization can be adaptive, as when toddlers who learn to fear moving cars also become afraid of moving trucks and motorcycles. And generalized fears can linger, sticking in memory (Simon-Kutscher et al., 2019; Stout et al., 2018). For two months after being in a car collision, sensitized young drivers are less vulnerable to repeat collisions (O'Brien et al., 2017). Years after being tortured, one Argentine writer reported still flinching with fear at the sight of black shoes—his first glimpse of his torturers as they approached his cell (Timerman, 1980). Generalized anxiety reactions have been demonstrated in laboratory studies comparing abused with nonabused children (**FIGURE 20.8**).

Stimuli related to naturally disgusting or morally objectionable objects will, by association, also evoke some physical or moral disgust. Would most people eat otherwise desirable fudge shaped to resemble dog feces? Or hold an English dictionary apparently owned and used by Adolf Hitler? Or wrap themselves in a blanket thought to be previously owned by members of the al-Qaeda terrorist group? No, No, and No. These situations cause people to feel repulsed (Fedotova & Rozin, 2018; Rozin et al., 1986, 2015). These examples show how people's emotional reactions to one stimulus can generalize to other, related stimuli.

DISCRIMINATION Pavlov's dogs also learned to respond to the sound of a particular tone and *not* to other tones. One stimulus (tone) predicted the US, and the others did not. This learned ability to *distinguish* between a conditioned stimulus (which predicts the US) and other, irrelevant stimuli is called **discrimination.** Being able to recognize differences is adaptive. Slightly different stimuli can be followed by vastly different consequences. After eating a poisonous butterfly, birds will generalize—they will avoid preying on similar butterflies. But they will also discriminate such butterflies from other butterfly species that are edible (Sims, 2018). Kenyan elephants flee the scent of Maasai hunters, whom they have learned to fear, but not the scent of nonthreatening Kamba men (Rhodes, 2017). Facing a guard dog, your heart may race; facing a guide dog, it probably will not.

RETRIEVAL PRACTICE

RP-5 What conditioning principle is influencing the snail's affections?

"I don't care if she's a tape dispenser. I love her."

ANSWERS IN APPENDIX E

Pavlov's Legacy

LOQ 20-5 Why does Pavlov's work remain so important?

What remains today of Pavlov's ideas? A great deal. Most psychologists now agree that classical conditioning is a basic form of learning. Modern neuroscience has also supported Pavlov's ideas—by identifying neural circuits that link a conditioned stimulus (warning signal) with an impending unconditioned stimulus (threat) (Harnett et al., 2016; Yau & McNally, 2018). Judged with today's knowledge of the interplay of our biology, psychology, and social-cultural environment, some of Pavlov's ideas were incomplete. But if we see further than Pavlov did, it is because we stand on his shoulders.

Why does Pavlov's work remain so important? If he had merely taught us that old dogs can learn new tricks, his experiments would long ago have been forgotten. Why should we care that dogs can be conditioned to salivate to the sound of a tone? The importance lies, first, in the finding that *many other responses to many other stimuli can be classically conditioned in many other organisms*—in fact, in every species tested, from microscopic creatures to earthworms to fish to dogs to monkeys to people (Schwartz, 1984; Zhou et al., 2019). Thus, classical conditioning is one way that virtually all organisms learn to adapt to their environment.

Second, *Pavlov showed us how a process such as learning can be studied objectively.* He was proud that his methods involved virtually no subjective judgments or guesses about what went on in a dog's mind. The salivary response is a behavior measurable in cubic centimeters of saliva. Pavlov's success therefore suggested a scientific model for how the young discipline of psychology might proceed—by isolating the basic building blocks of complex behaviors and studying them with objective laboratory procedures.

Psych nerd joke:
"Why was Pavlov's hair so soft?"
"Because he conditioned it."

RETRIEVAL PRACTICE

RP-6 Companies often pay to make their products visible in popular movies—such as when admired actors drink certain beverages. Based on classical conditioning principles, what might be an effect of this pairing?

ANSWERS IN APPENDIX E

Play the role of an experimenter in classical conditioning research by engaging *Topic Tutorial: PsychSim6, Classical Conditioning.* And review Pavlov's classic work by watching a 3-minute re-creation of Pavlov's lab in the *Video: Pavlov's Discovery of Classical Conditioning.*

APPLICATIONS OF CLASSICAL CONDITIONING

LOQ 20-6 What have been some applications of Pavlov's work to human health and well-being? How did Watson apply Pavlov's principles to learned fears?

In many areas of psychology, including consciousness, motivation, emotion, health, psychological disorders, and therapy, Pavlov's principles are used to influence human health and well-being. Three examples:

- *Drug cravings:* Classical conditioning may inform treatments for *substance use disorder.* Former drug users often feel a craving when they are again in the drug-using context, because their brain has become conditioned to associate that context with a drug's reward (Wang et al., 2018; Wilar et al., 2018). Breaking this association can reduce cravings (Ananth et al., 2019; Martínez-Rivera et al., 2019). Many drug counselors advise clients to steer clear of the people and settings associated with previous highs (NIDA, 2017; Siegel, 2005).

- *Food cravings:* Classical conditioning makes dieting difficult. Sugary substances evoke sweet sensations. Researchers have conditioned healthy volunteers to experience cravings after only one instance of eating a sweet food (Blechert et al., 2016). So, the next time you think "I can definitely eat just one cookie," think twice. People who struggle with their weight often have strongly conditioned responses to eat the very foods that will keep them in poor health (Hill, 2007).

- *Immune responses:* Classical conditioning even works on the body's disease-fighting immune system. When a particular taste accompanies a drug that influences immune responses, the taste by itself may come to produce an immune response (Ader & Cohen, 1985).

Pavlov's work also provided a basis for Watson's (1913) idea that human emotions and behaviors, though biologically influenced, are mainly a bundle of conditioned responses. Working with an 11-month-old, Watson and his graduate student Rosalie Rayner (1920; Harris, 1979) showed how specific fears might be conditioned. Like most infants, "Little Albert" feared loud noises but not white rats. Watson and Rayner presented a white rat and, as Little Albert reached to touch it, struck a hammer against a steel bar just behind his head. After seven repeats of seeing the rat and hearing the frightening noise, Albert burst into tears at the mere sight of the rat. Five days later, he reportedly generalized this startled fear reaction to the sight of a rabbit, a dog, and even a furry coat. A modern reanalysis questioned Watson's evidence for Albert's conditioning, but the case remains legendary (Powell & Schmaltz, 2017).

For years, people wondered what became of Little Albert. Sleuthing by Russell Powell and his colleagues (2014) found a well-matched child of one of the hospital's wet nurses. The child, William Albert Barger, went by Albert B.—precisely the name used by Watson and Rayner. This Albert was an easygoing person, though, perhaps coincidentally, he had an aversion to dogs. He died in 2007 without ever knowing of his role in psychology's history.

People also wondered what became of Watson. After losing his Johns Hopkins professorship over an affair with Rayner (whom he later married), he joined an advertising agency as the company's resident psychologist. There, he used his knowledge of associative learning to conceive many successful advertising campaigns, including one for Maxwell House that helped make the "coffee break" an American custom (Hunt, 1993).

Some psychologists had difficulty repeating Watson and Rayner's findings with other children. (These experiments would be unethical by today's standards.) Nevertheless, Little Albert's learned fears led many psychologists to wonder whether each of us might be a walking warehouse of conditioned emotions. If so, might extinction procedures or new conditioning help us change our unwanted responses to emotion-arousing stimuli?

One patient, who for 30 years had feared entering an elevator alone, did just that. Following his therapist's advice, he forced himself to enter 20 elevators a day. Within 10 days, his fear had nearly vanished (Ellis & Becker, 1982). Comedian-writer Mark Malkoff extinguished his fear of flying by taking 135 flights in 30 days, spending 14 hours a day in the air (NPR, 2009). After a week and a half, his fears had faded, and he began playing games with fellow passengers. His favorite was the "toilet paper experiment": Put one end of a roll in the toilet, unroll the rest down the aisle, and flush, sucking down the whole roll in three seconds! In the Therapy modules, we will see more examples of how psychologists use behavioral techniques such as *counterconditioning* to treat psychological disorders and promote personal growth.

RETRIEVAL PRACTICE

RP-7 In Watson and Rayner's experiments, "Little Albert" learned to fear a white rat after repeatedly experiencing a loud noise as the rat was presented. In these experiments, what was the US? The UR? The NS? The CS? The CR?

Archives of the History of American Psychology, The Center for the History of Psychology, The University of Akron

ANSWERS IN APPENDIX E

📷 See the *Video: Research Ethics* for a helpful tutorial animation.

20 REVIEW Basic Learning Concepts and Classical Conditioning

LEARNING OBJECTIVES

Test Yourself Answer these repeated Learning Objective Questions on your own (before checking the answers in Appendix D) to improve your retention of the concepts (McDaniel et al., 2009, 2015).

LOQ 20-1 How do we define *learning,* and what are some basic forms of learning?

LOQ 20-2 What is behaviorism's view of learning?

LOQ 20-3 Who was Pavlov, and what are the basic components of classical conditioning?

LOQ 20-4 In classical conditioning, what are the processes of *acquisition, extinction, spontaneous recovery, generalization,* and *discrimination?*

LOQ 20-5 Why does Pavlov's work remain so important?

LOQ 20-6 What have been some applications of Pavlov's work to human health and well-being? How did Watson apply Pavlov's principles to learned fears?

TERMS AND CONCEPTS TO REMEMBER

Test Yourself Write down the definition in your own words, then check your answer.

learning, p. 258

associative learning, p. 258

stimulus, p. 258

respondent behavior, p. 258

operant behavior, p. 258

cognitive learning, p. 261

classical conditioning, p. 261

behaviorism, p. 261

neutral stimulus (NS), p. 261

unconditioned response (UR), p. 261

unconditioned stimulus (US), p. 261

conditioned response (CR), p. 262

conditioned stimulus (CS), p. 262

acquisition, p. 262

higher-order conditioning, p. 262

extinction, p. 262

spontaneous recovery, p. 262

generalization, p. 264

discrimination, p. 264

MASTER THE MATERIAL

Test Yourself Answer the following questions on your own first, then check your answers in Appendix E.

1. Learning is defined as "the process of acquiring through experience new and relatively enduring _____ or _____."

2. Two forms of associative learning are classical conditioning, in which the organism associates _____, and operant conditioning, in which the organism associates _____.

   a. two or more responses; a response and its consequence

   b. two or more stimuli; two or more responses

   c. two or more stimuli; a response and its consequence

   d. two or more responses; two or more stimuli

3. In Pavlov's experiments, the tone started as a neutral stimulus, and then became a(n) _____ stimulus.

4. Dogs have been taught to salivate to a circle but not to a square. This process is an example of _____.

5. After Watson and Rayner classically conditioned Little Albert to fear a white rat, the child later showed fear in response to a rabbit, a dog, and a furry coat. This illustrates

   a. extinction.

   b. generalization.

   c. spontaneous recovery.

   d. discrimination between two stimuli.

6. "Sex sells!" is a common saying in advertising. Using classical conditioning terms, explain how sexual images in advertisements can condition your response to a product.

Continue testing yourself with 📚 **LearningCurve** or 📚 **Achieve Read & Practice** to learn and remember most effectively.

21 Operant Conditioning

LOQ 21-1 What is *operant conditioning?*

It's one thing to classically condition a dog to salivate to the sound of a tone, or a child to fear moving cars. But to teach an elephant to **learn** to walk on its hind legs or a child to say *please,* we turn to operant conditioning.

Classical conditioning and operant conditioning are both forms of **associative learning,** yet their differences are straightforward:

- *Classical conditioning* forms associations between **stimuli** (a CS and the US it signals). It also involves **respondent behavior**—automatic responses to a stimulus (such as salivating in response to meat powder and later in response to a tone).

learning the process of acquiring through experience new and relatively enduring information or behaviors.

associative learning learning that certain events occur together. The events may be two stimuli (as in classical conditioning) or a response and its consequence (as in operant conditioning).

stimulus any event or situation that evokes a response.

respondent behavior behavior that occurs as an automatic response to some stimulus.

operant conditioning a type of learning in which a behavior becomes more likely to recur if followed by a reinforcer or less likely to recur if followed by a punisher.

operant behavior behavior that operates on the environment, producing a consequence.

law of effect Thorndike's principle that behaviors followed by favorable consequences become more likely, and that behaviors followed by unfavorable consequences become less likely.

operant chamber in operant conditioning research, a chamber (also known as a *Skinner box*) containing a bar or key that an animal can manipulate to obtain a food or water reinforcer; attached devices record the animal's rate of bar pressing or key pecking.

reinforcement in operant conditioning, any event that *strengthens* the behavior it follows.

shaping an operant conditioning procedure in which reinforcers guide behavior toward closer and closer approximations of the desired behavior.

positive reinforcement increasing behaviors by presenting a pleasurable stimulus. A positive reinforcer is any stimulus that, when *presented* after a response, strengthens the response.

• In **operant conditioning,** organisms associate their own actions with consequences. Actions followed by reinforcers increase; those followed by punishments often decrease. Behavior that *operates* on the environment to produce rewarding or punishing stimuli is called **operant behavior.**

RETRIEVAL PRACTICE

RP-1 With classical conditioning, we learn associations between events we _____ (do/do not) control. With operant conditioning, we learn associations between our behavior and _____ (resulting/random) events.

ANSWERS IN APPENDIX E

Skinner's Experiments

LOQ **21-2** Who was Skinner, and how is operant behavior reinforced and shaped?

B. F. Skinner (1904–1990) was a college English major and aspiring writer who, seeking a new direction, enrolled as a graduate student in psychology. He went on to become modern behaviorism's most influential and controversial figure. Skinner's work elaborated on what psychologist Edward L. Thorndike (1874–1949) called the **law of effect:** Rewarded behavior tends to recur (**FIGURE 21.1**), and punished behavior is less likely to recur. Using Thorndike's law of effect as a starting point, Skinner developed a behavioral technology that revealed principles of *behavior control.* Working from a rooftop office in a Minneapolis flour mill in 1943, Skinner and his students Keller Breland and Norman Guttman looked at the flocks of pigeons sitting on the windowsills and jokingly wondered, "Could we teach a pigeon how to bowl?" (Goddard, 2018; Skinner, 1960). By shaping pigeons' natural walking and pecking behaviors, Skinner and his students did just that (Peterson, 2004). Skinner later used his new learning principles to teach pigeons other unpigeon-like behaviors, including how to walk in a figure 8, play Ping-Pong, and keep a missile on course by pecking at a screen target.

For his pioneering studies, Skinner designed an **operant chamber,** popularly known as a *Skinner box* (**FIGURE 21.2**). The box has a bar (a lever) that an animal presses—or a key (a disc) the animal pecks—to release a reward of food or water. It also has a device that records these responses. This creates a stage on which rats and other animals act out Skinner's concept of **reinforcement:** any event that strengthens (increases the frequency of) a preceding response. What is reinforcing depends on the animal and the conditions. For some people, it may be praise, attention, or a paycheck. For others, it may be drugs that reduce distress or produce euphoria (Bechara et al., 2019). For hungry and thirsty rats, food and water work well. Skinner's experiments have done far more than teach us how to pull habits out of a rat. They have explored the precise conditions that foster efficient and enduring learning.

Shaping Behavior

Imagine that you wanted to condition a hungry rat to press a bar. Like Skinner, you could tease out this action with **shaping,** gradually guiding the rat's actions toward the desired behavior. First, you would watch how the animal naturally behaves, so that you could

⚫ **FIGURE 21.1**
Cat in a puzzle box Thorndike used a fish reward to entice cats to find their way out of a puzzle box through a series of maneuvers. The cats' performance tended to improve with successive trials, illustrating Thorndike's *law of effect.* (Data from Thorndike, 1898.)

Time required to escape (seconds)

Successive trials in the puzzle box

build on its existing behaviors. You might give the rat a bit of food each time it approaches the bar. Once the rat is approaching regularly, you would give the food only when it moves close to the bar, then closer still. Finally, you would require it to touch the bar to get food. By rewarding *successive approximations*, you reinforce responses that are ever closer to the final desired behavior, and you ignore all other responses. By making rewards contingent on desired behaviors, researchers and animal trainers gradually shape complex behaviors.

We can also shape our own behavior. Let's say you want to train for your first 5K race. You set up a daily plan with a mixture of walking and running. At each stage, you give yourself a nice reward—perhaps first for a 15-minute walk, then for walking and running a mile, then for running a mile, then for running every additional half mile—rewarding successive approximations of your target behavior.

Shaping can also help us understand what nonverbal organisms can perceive. Can a dog distinguish red and green? Can a baby hear the difference between lower- and higher-pitched tones? If we can shape them to respond to one stimulus and not to another, then we know they can perceive the difference. Such experiments have even shown that some nonhuman animals can form concepts. When experimenters reinforced pigeons for pecking after seeing a human face, but not after seeing other images, the pigeons' behavior showed that they could recognize human faces (Herrnstein & Loveland, 1964). In this experiment, the human face was a *discriminative stimulus*. Like a green traffic light, discriminative stimuli signal that a response will be reinforced. After being trained to discriminate among classes of events or objects—flowers, people, cars, chairs—pigeons can usually identify the category in which a new pictured object belongs (Bhatt et al., 1988; Wasserman, 1993). They have even been trained to discriminate between the music of Bach and Stravinsky (Porter & Neuringer, 1984).

Skinner noted that we continually reinforce and shape others' everyday behaviors, though we may not mean to do so. Erlinda's nagging annoys her mom, for example, but consider how Mom typically responds:

ERLINDA: *Could you take me to the mall?*

MOM: *(Continues checking her phone.)*

ERLINDA: *Mom, I need to go to the mall.*

MOM: *Uh, yeah, in a few minutes.*

ERLINDA: *MOM! The mall!*

MOM: *Show some manners! Okay, where are my keys . . .*

Erlinda's nagging is reinforced, because she gets something desirable—a trip to the mall. Mom's response is reinforced, because it gets rid of something aversive—Erlinda's nagging.

Or consider a teacher who sticks gold stars on a wall chart beside the names of children scoring 100 percent on spelling tests. As everyone can then see, some children consistently do perfect work. The others, who may have worked harder than the academic all-stars, get no rewards. The teacher would be better advised to apply the principles of operant conditioning—to reinforce all spellers for gradual improvements (successive approximations toward perfect spelling of words they find challenging).

ASK YOURSELF

Can you recall a time when a teacher, coach, family member, or employer helped you learn something by shaping your behavior in little steps until you achieved your goal?

Types of Reinforcers

LOQ 21-3 How do positive and negative reinforcement differ, and what are the basic types of reinforcers?

Until now, we've mainly been discussing **positive reinforcement,** which strengthens responding by *presenting* a typically *pleasurable* stimulus immediately after a response. But, as the nagging Erlinda story illustrates, there are two basic kinds of reinforcement

FIGURE 21.2

A Skinner box Inside the box, the rat presses a bar for a food reward. Outside, measuring devices (not shown here) record the animal's accumulated responses.

Reinforcers vary with circumstances What is reinforcing (a heat lamp) to one animal (a cold meerkat) may not be to another (an overheated bear). What is reinforcing in one situation (a cold snap at the Taronga Zoo in Sydney) may not be in another (a sweltering summer day). Reinforcers also vary among humans. A chocolate treat that is reinforcing to Clarice might not be to Clarence, who prefers vanilla.

Bird brains spot tumors After being rewarded with food when correctly spotting breast tumors, pigeons became as skilled as humans at discriminating cancerous from healthy tissue (Levenson et al., 2015). Other animals have been shaped to sniff out land mines or locate people amid rubble (La Londe et al., 2015).

TABLE 21.1 Ways to Increase Behavior

Operant Conditioning Term	Description	Examples
Positive reinforcement	Add a desirable stimulus	Pet a dog that comes when you call it; pay someone for work done.
Negative reinforcement	Remove an aversive stimulus	Take painkillers to end pain; fasten seatbelt to end loud beeping.

(TABLE 21.1). **Negative reinforcement** strengthens a response by *reducing or removing* something *negative*. Erlinda's nagging was *positively* reinforced, because Erlinda got something desirable—a trip to the mall. Her mom's response (doing what Erlinda wanted) was *negatively* reinforced, because it ended an aversive event—Erlinda's nagging. Similarly, taking aspirin may relieve your headache, and hitting *snooze* will silence your irritating alarm. These welcome results provide negative reinforcement and increase the odds that you will repeat these behaviors. For those with a drug addiction, the negative reinforcement of ending withdrawal pangs can be a compelling reason to resume using (Baker et al., 2004). Note that *negative reinforcement is not punishment*. (Some friendly advice: Repeat those italicized words in your mind.) Rather, negative reinforcement—psychology's most misunderstood concept—*removes* a punishing (aversive) event. Think of negative reinforcement as something that provides relief—from that nagging person, bad headache, or annoying alarm clock.

Sometimes negative and positive reinforcement coincide. Imagine a worried student who, after goofing off and getting a bad exam grade, studies harder for the next exam. This increased effort may be *negatively* reinforced by reduced anxiety, and *positively* reinforced by a better grade. We reap the rewards of escaping the aversive stimulus, which increases the chances that we will repeat our behavior. *The point to remember:* Whether it works by reducing something aversive, or by providing something desirable, *reinforcement is any consequence that strengthens behavior.*

RETRIEVAL PRACTICE

RP-2 How is operant conditioning at work in this cartoon?

ANSWERS IN APPENDIX E

PRIMARY AND CONDITIONED REINFORCERS Getting food when hungry or having a painful headache go away is innately satisfying. These **primary reinforcers** are unlearned. **Conditioned reinforcers,** also called *secondary reinforcers*, get their power through learned association with primary reinforcers. If a rat in a Skinner box learns that a light reliably signals a food delivery, the rat will work to turn on the light (see Figure 21.2). The light has become a conditioned reinforcer. Our lives are filled with conditioned reinforcers—money, good grades, a pleasant tone of voice—each of which has been linked with more basic rewards.

IMMEDIATE AND DELAYED REINFORCERS Let's return to the imaginary shaping experiment in which you were conditioning a rat to press a bar. In addition to performing this "wanted" behavior, the hungry rat will engage in other, "unwanted" behaviors—scratching, sniffing, and moving around. If you present food immediately after any one

---

negative reinforcement increasing behaviors by stopping or reducing an aversive stimulus. A negative reinforcer is any stimulus that, when *removed* after a response, strengthens the response. (*Note:* Negative reinforcement is not punishment.)

primary reinforcer an innately reinforcing stimulus, such as one that satisfies a biological need.

conditioned reinforcer a stimulus that gains its reinforcing power through its association with a primary reinforcer. (Also known as a *secondary reinforcer.*)

reinforcement schedule a pattern that defines how often a desired response will be reinforced.

continuous reinforcement schedule reinforcing the desired response every time it occurs.

partial (intermittent) reinforcement schedule reinforcing a response only part of the time; results in slower acquisition of a response but much greater resistance to extinction than does continuous reinforcement.

fixed-ratio schedule in operant conditioning, a reinforcement schedule that reinforces a response only after a specified number of responses.

of these behaviors, the rat will likely repeat that rewarded behavior. But what if the rat presses the bar while you are distracted, and you delay giving the reinforcer? If the delay lasts longer than about 30 seconds, the rat will not learn to press the bar (Austen & Sanderson, 2019; Cunningham & Shahan, 2019). Delays also decrease human learning. Students learn class material better when they complete frequent quizzes that provide them with immediate feedback (Healy et al., 2017). Immediate feedback produces immediate learning.

But unlike rats, humans *can* respond to delayed reinforcers: the paycheck at the end of the week, the good grade at the end of the term, the trophy at the end of the sports season. Indeed, to function effectively we must learn how to master the difficult task of delaying gratification. In one of psychology's most famous studies, some 4-year-olds showed this ability. In choosing a piece of candy or a marshmallow, these impulse-controlled children preferred having a big one tomorrow to munching on a small one right away. Children who delay gratification have tended to become socially competent and high-achieving adults (Mischel, 2014). A recent study showed a similar (though weaker) relationship between delay of gratification and achievement later (Watts et al., 2018). Learning to control our impulses in order to achieve more valued rewards can even protect us from later committing an impulsive crime (Åkerlund et al., 2016; Logue, 1998a,b). *The bottom line:* It pays to delay.

To our detriment, small but immediate pleasures (the enjoyment of watching late-night TV, for example) are sometimes more alluring than big but delayed rewards (feeling rested for a big exam tomorrow). For many teens, the immediate gratification of risky, unprotected sex in passionate moments prevails over the delayed gratifications of safe sex or saved sex. And for many people, the immediate rewards of today's gas-guzzling vehicles, air travel, and air conditioning prevail over the bigger future consequences of global climate change, rising seas, and extreme weather.

Reinforcement Schedules

(LOQ) 21-4 How do different reinforcement schedules affect behavior?

In most of our examples, the desired response has been reinforced every time it occurs. But **reinforcement schedules** vary. With **continuous reinforcement,** learning occurs rapidly, which makes it the best choice for mastering a behavior. But extinction also occurs rapidly. When reinforcement stops—when we stop delivering food after the rat presses the bar—the behavior soon stops (is *extinguished*). If a normally dependable candy machine fails to deliver a chocolate bar twice in a row, we stop putting money into it (although a week later we may exhibit *spontaneous recovery* by trying again).

Real life rarely provides continuous reinforcement. Salespeople do not make a sale with every pitch. But they persist because their efforts are occasionally rewarded. This persistence is typical with **partial (intermittent) reinforcement schedules,** in which responses are sometimes reinforced, sometimes not. Learning is slower to appear, but *resistance to extinction* is greater than with continuous reinforcement. Imagine a pigeon that has learned to peck a key to obtain food. If you gradually phase out the food delivery until it occurs only rarely, in no predictable pattern, the pigeon may peck 150,000 times without a reward (Skinner, 1953). Slot machines reward gamblers in much the same way—occasionally and unpredictably. And like pigeons, slot players keep trying, time and time again. With intermittent reinforcement, hope springs eternal.

Lesson for parents: Partial reinforcement also works with children. *Occasionally* giving in to children's tantrums for the sake of peace and quiet intermittently reinforces the tantrums. This is the very best procedure for making a behavior persist.

Skinner (1961) and his collaborators compared four schedules of partial reinforcement and their effects on behavior.

Fixed-ratio schedules reinforce behavior after a set number of responses. Coffee shops may reward us with a free drink after every 10 purchased. Once conditioned, rats may be reinforced on a fixed ratio of, say, one food pellet for every 30 responses. Once conditioned, animals will pause only briefly after a reinforcer before returning to a high rate of responding.

"Oh, not bad. The light comes on, I press the bar, they write me a check. How about you?"

TABLE 21.2 Schedules of Partial Reinforcement		
	Fixed	**Variable**
Ratio	*Every so many:* reinforcement after every *nth* behavior, such as buy 10 coffees, get 1 free, or pay workers per product unit produced	*After an unpredictable number:* reinforcement after a random number of behaviors, as when playing slot machines or fly fishing
Interval	*Every so often:* reinforcement for behavior after a fixed time, such as Tuesday discount prices	*Unpredictably often:* reinforcement for behavior after a random amount of time, as when checking our phone for a message

"The charm of fishing is that it is the pursuit of what is elusive but attainable, a perpetual series of occasions for hope." — Scottish author John Buchan (1875–1940)

Variable-ratio schedules provide reinforcers after a seemingly unpredictable number of responses. This unpredictable reinforcement is what slot-machine players and fly fishers experience, and it's what makes gambling and fly fishing so hard to extinguish even when they don't produce the desired results. Because reinforcers increase as the number of responses increases, variable-ratio schedules produce high rates of responding.

Fixed-interval schedules reinforce the first response after a fixed time period. Animals on this type of schedule tend to respond more frequently as the anticipated time for reward draws near. People check more frequently for the mail as the delivery time approaches. Pigeons peck keys more rapidly as the time for reinforcement draws closer. This produces a choppy stop-start pattern rather than a steady rate of response (**FIGURE 21.3**).

Variable-interval schedules reinforce the first response after *varying* time intervals. At unpredictable times, a food pellet rewarded Skinner's pigeons for persistence in pecking a key. Like the longed-for message that finally rewards persistence in checking our phone, variable-interval schedules tend to produce slow, steady responding. This makes sense, because there is no knowing when the waiting will be over (**TABLE 21.2**).

In general, response rates are higher when reinforcement is linked to the number of responses (a ratio schedule) rather than to time (an interval schedule). But responding is more consistent when reinforcement is unpredictable (a variable schedule) than when it is predictable (a fixed schedule). (See Figure 21.3.) Animal behaviors differ, yet Skinner (1956) contended that the reinforcement principles of operant conditioning are universal. It matters little, he said, what response, what reinforcer, or what species you use. The effect of a given reinforcement schedule is pretty much the same: "Pigeon, rat, monkey, which is which? It doesn't matter . . . . Behavior shows astonishingly similar properties."

● FIGURE 21.3
Intermittent reinforcement schedules Skinner's (1961) laboratory pigeons produced these response patterns to each of four reinforcement schedules. (Reinforcers are indicated by diagonal marks.) For people, as for pigeons, reinforcement linked to number of responses (a *ratio* schedule) produces a higher response rate than reinforcement linked to amount of time elapsed (an *interval* schedule). But the predictability of the reward also matters. An unpredictable *(variable)* schedule produces more consistent responding than does a predictable *(fixed)* schedule. (Data from Skinner, 1961.)

Vitaly Titov/Shutterstock

RETRIEVAL PRACTICE

RP-3 People who send spam email are reinforced by which schedule? Home bakers checking the oven to see if the cookies are done are reinforced on which schedule? Sandwich shops that offer a free sandwich after every 10 purchased are using which reinforcement schedule?

ANSWERS IN APPENDIX E

Punishment

LOQ **21-5** How does punishment differ from negative reinforcement, and how does punishment affect behavior?

Reinforcement increases a behavior; **punishment** does the opposite. So, while negative reinforcement *increases* the frequency of a preceding behavior (by withdrawing something negative), a *punisher* is any consequence that *decreases* the frequency of a preceding behavior (**TABLE 21.3**). Swift and sure punishers can powerfully restrain unwanted behavior. The rat that is shocked after touching a forbidden object and the child who is burned by touching a hot stove will learn not to repeat those behaviors.

Criminal behavior, much of it impulsive, is also influenced more by swift and sure punishers than by the threat of severe sentences (Darley & Alter, 2013). Thus, when Arizona introduced an exceptionally harsh sentence for first-time drunk drivers, the drunk-driving rate changed very little. But when Kansas City police started patrolling a high crime area to increase the swiftness and sureness of punishment, that city's crime rate dropped dramatically.

What do punishment studies imply for parenting? One analysis of over 160,000 children found that physical punishment rarely corrects unwanted behavior (Gershoff & Grogan-Kaylor, 2016). With support from an American Psychological Association resolution on the ineffectiveness and potential harm of physical punishment, psychologists have noted five major drawbacks (APA, 2019; Finkenauer et al., 2015; Gershoff et al., 2018; Marshall, 2002):

1. *Punished behavior is suppressed, not forgotten. This temporary state may (negatively) reinforce parents' punishing behavior.* The child swears, the parent swats, the child stops swearing when the parent is nearby, so the parent believes the punishment successfully stopped the behavior. No wonder spanking is a hit with so many parents—with 60 percent of children around the world spanked or otherwise physically punished (UNICEF, 2014).

2. *Physical punishment does not replace the unwanted behavior.* Physical punishment may reduce or even eliminate unwanted behavior, but it does not provide direction for appropriate behavior. A child who is spanked for screaming in the car may stop yelling but continue to throw her food or steal her brother's toys.

3. *Punishment teaches discrimination among situations.* In operant conditioning, *discrimination* occurs when an organism learns that certain responses, but not others, will be reinforced. Did the punishment effectively end the child's swearing? Or did the child simply learn that while it's not okay to swear around the house, it's okay elsewhere?

4. *Punishment can teach fear.* In operant conditioning, *generalization* occurs when an organism's response to similar stimuli is also reinforced. A punished child may associate fear not only with the undesirable behavior but also with the person who delivered the punishment or where it occurred. Thus, children may learn to fear a punishing teacher and try to avoid school, or may become anxious (Gershoff et al., 2010). For such reasons, most European countries and 31 U.S. states now ban hitting children in public schools (EndCorporalPunishment.org). As of 2019, 156 countries had outlawed hitting in the home. A large survey in Finland, the second country to pass such a law, revealed that children born after the law passed were, indeed, less often slapped and beaten (Österman et al., 2014).

5. *Physical punishment may increase aggression by modeling violence as a way to cope with problems.* Studies find that spanked children are at increased risk for aggression (MacKenzie et al., 2013). We know, for example, that many aggressive delinquents and abusive parents come from abusive families (Straus & Gelles, 1980; Straus et al., 1997).

variable-ratio schedule in operant conditioning, a reinforcement schedule that reinforces a response after an unpredictable number of responses.

fixed-interval schedule in operant conditioning, a reinforcement schedule that reinforces a response only after a specified time has elapsed.

variable-interval schedule in operant conditioning, a reinforcement schedule that reinforces a response at unpredictable time intervals.

punishment an event that tends to *decrease* the behavior that it follows.

TABLE 21.3 Ways to Decrease Behavior

Type of Punisher	Description	Examples
Positive punishment	Administer an aversive stimulus.	Spray water on a barking dog; give a traffic ticket for speeding.
Negative punishment	Withdraw a rewarding stimulus.	Take away a misbehaving teen's driving privileges; block a rude commenter on social media.

Some researchers question this logic. Physically punished children may be more aggressive, they say, for the same reason that people who have undergone psychotherapy are more likely to suffer depression—because they had preexisting problems that triggered the treatments (Ferguson, 2013a; Larzelere, 2000; Larzelere et al., 2019). So, does spanking cause misbehavior, or does misbehavior trigger spanking? Correlations don't hand us an answer.

So, how should parents discipline their children? Many psychologists encourage *time-out from positive reinforcement*: removing a misbehaving child from access to desired stimuli such as siblings' and parents' attention (Dadds & Tully, 2019). Effective time-outs come with clear expectations for replacing problem behavior (hitting siblings) with alternative positive behaviors (telling siblings they have hurt your feelings) (O'Leary et al., 1967; Patterson et al., 1968). Children learn that time-out helps the family enjoy positive and caring interactions.

Parents of delinquent youths are often unaware of how to achieve desirable behaviors without screaming, hitting, or threatening their children with punishment (Patterson et al., 1982). Training programs can help transform dire threats ("You clean up your room this minute or no dinner!") into positive incentives ("You're welcome at the dinner table after you get your room cleaned up"). Stop and think about it. Aren't many threats of punishment just as forceful, and perhaps more effective, when rephrased positively? Thus, "If you don't get your homework done, there'll be no car" could be phrased more positively as . . . .

In classrooms, too, teachers can give feedback by saying, "No, but try this . . ." and "Yes, that's it!" Such responses reduce unwanted behavior while reinforcing more desirable alternatives. Remember: *Punishment tells you what not to do; reinforcement tells you what to do.* Thus, punishment trains a particular sort of morality—one focused on prohibition (what *not* to do) rather than positive obligations (Sheikh & Janoff-Bulman, 2013).

What punishment often teaches, said Skinner, is how to avoid it. Most psychologists now favor an emphasis on reinforcement: Notice people doing something right and affirm them for it.

> **"A pat on the back, though only a few vertebrae removed from a kick in the pants, is miles ahead in results."** — Attributed to publisher Bennett Cerf (1898–1971)

RETRIEVAL PRACTICE

RP-4 Fill in the blanks with one of the following terms: positive reinforcement (PR), negative reinforcement (NR), positive punishment (PP), or negative punishment (NP). We have provided the first answer (PR) for you.

Type of Stimulus	Give It	Take It Away
Desired (for example, a teen's use of the car)	1. PR	2.
Undesired/aversive (for example, an insult)	3.	4.

ANSWERS IN APPENDIX E

> See the *Video: Correlational Studies* for a helpful tutorial animation. And simulate operant conditioning and shaping by engaging *Topic Tutorial: PsychSim6, Operant Conditioning* and also *Topic Tutorial: PsychSim6, Shaping.*

Skinner's Legacy

LOQ 21-6 Why did Skinner's ideas provoke controversy, and how might his operant conditioning principles be applied?

B. F. Skinner stirred a hornet's nest with his outspoken beliefs. He repeatedly insisted that external influences, not internal thoughts and feelings, shape behavior. He argued that brain science isn't needed for psychological science, saying that "a science of behavior is independent of neurology" (Skinner, 1938/1966, pp. 423–424). And he urged people to use operant conditioning principles to influence others' behavior at school, work, and home. Knowing that behavior is shaped by its results, he argued that we should use rewards to evoke more desirable behavior.

Skinner's critics objected, saying that he dehumanized people by neglecting their personal freedom and by seeking to control their actions. Skinner's reply: External consequences already haphazardly control people's behavior. Why not administer those consequences toward human betterment? Wouldn't reinforcers be more humane than the punishments used in homes, schools, and prisons? And if it is humbling to think that our history has shaped us, doesn't this very idea give us hope that we can apply operant conditioning to shape our future?

B. F. Skinner "I am sometimes asked, 'Do you think of yourself as you think of the organisms you study?' The answer is yes. So far as I know, my behavior at any given moment has been nothing more than the product of my genetic endowment, my personal history, and the current setting" (1983).

Applications of Operant Conditioning

Psychologists apply operant conditioning principles to help people with a variety of challenges, from moderating high blood pressure to gaining social skills. Reinforcement techniques are also at work in schools, sports, computer programs, workplaces, and homes, and these principles can support our self-improvement as well (Flora, 2004).

AT SCHOOL More than 50 years ago, Skinner and others worked toward a day when "machines and textbooks" would shape learning in small steps, by immediately reinforcing correct responses. Such machines and textbooks, they said, would revolutionize education and free teachers to focus on each student's special needs. "Good instruction demands two things," said Skinner (1989). "Students must be told immediately whether what they do is right or wrong and, when right, they must be directed to the step to be taken next."

Skinner might be pleased to know that many of his ideals for education are now possible. Teachers used to find it difficult to pace material to each student's rate of learning, and to provide prompt feedback. Online adaptive quizzing, such as the LearningCurve and Achieve Read & Practice systems available with this text, do both. Students move through quizzes at their own pace, according to their own level of understanding. And they get immediate feedback on their efforts, including personalized study plans.

Immediate reinforcement Muffet McGraw, the coach of Notre Dame's 2018 national championship women's basketball team, focuses on catching her players doing things right and applauds them for it on the spot.

> Operant conditioning principles may help us achieve our goals. What else affects our goal achievement? To find out, engage online with *Assess Your Strengths: How Might Your Willingness to Think of the Future Affect Your Ability to Achieve Long-Term Goals?*

IN SPORTS The key to shaping behavior in athletic performance, as elsewhere, is first reinforcing small successes and then gradually increasing the challenge. Golf students can learn putting by starting with very short putts, and then, as they build mastery, stepping back farther and farther. Novice batters can begin with half swings at an oversized ball pitched from 10 feet away, giving them the immediate pleasure of smacking the ball. As the hitters' confidence builds with their success and they achieve mastery at each level, the pitcher gradually moves back and eventually introduces a standard baseball. Compared with children taught by conventional methods, those trained by this behavioral method have shown faster skill improvement (Simek & O'Brien, 1981, 1988).

IN COMPUTER PROGRAMS Using reinforcement principles, developers have created computer programs that mimic human learning. Such *artificial intelligence* (AI) programs perform actions—playing chess, poker, or the multi-player videogame *Quake III*—faster than humans do, enabling the programs to quickly learn to repeat reinforced actions and avoid punished responses (Botvinick et al., 2019; Jaderberg et al., 2019). AI programs are teaching humans about the limits of human learning.

AT WORK How might managers successfully motivate their employees, and coaches motivate their players? It helps to make the reinforcement *immediate,* and reward specific, achievable behaviors, not vaguely defined "merit." People, unlike pigeons, also

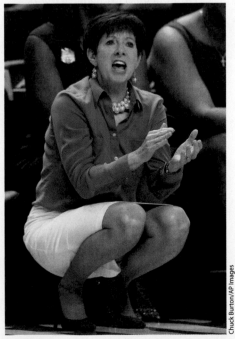

respond to delayed positive and negative reinforcers. General Motors CEO Mary Barra understood this. In 2015, she observed workers' high performance and awarded record bonuses (Vlasic, 2015). But rewards don't have to be monetary. An effective manager may simply walk the floor and sincerely praise people for good work.

IN PARENTING As we have seen, parents can learn from operant conditioning practices. Parent-training researchers remind us that by saying, "Get ready for bed" and then caving in to protests or defiance, parents reinforce such whining and arguing (Wierson & Forehand, 1994). Exasperated, they may then yell or gesture menacingly. When the child, now frightened, obeys, that reinforces the parents' angry behavior. Over time, a destructive parent-child relationship develops.

To disrupt this cycle, parents should remember the basic rule of shaping: *Notice people doing something right and affirm them for it*. Give children attention and other reinforcers when they are behaving *well*. If you want your teen to drive safely, reward her for safe driving (Hinnant et al., 2019). Target a specific behavior, reward it, and watch it increase. When children misbehave, don't yell at them or hit them. Simply explain the misbehavior and take away the iPad, remove a misused toy, or give a brief time-out.

TO CHANGE YOUR OWN BEHAVIOR Finally, we can use operant conditioning in our own lives. To reinforce your own desired behaviors (perhaps to improve your study habits) and extinguish the undesired ones (to stop smoking, for example), psychologists suggest taking these steps:

1. *State a realistic goal in measurable terms and announce it.* You might, for example, aim to boost your study time by an hour a day. To increase your commitment and odds of success, share that goal with friends.

2. *Decide how, when, and where you will work toward your goal.* Take time to plan. From North American undergraduates to Swedish entrepreneurs, those who specify how they will implement goals become more focused on those goals and more often fulfill them (Gollwitzer & Oettingen, 2012; van Gelderen et al., 2018).

3. *Monitor how often you engage in your desired behavior.* You might log your current study time, noting under what conditions you do and don't study. (When we began writing textbooks, we each logged our time and were amazed to discover how much time we were wasting.)

4. *Reinforce the desired behavior.* People's persistence toward long-term goals is powered mostly by immediate rewards (Woolley & Fishbach, 2017). So to increase your study time, give yourself a reward (a snack or some activity you enjoy) only after you finish your extra hour of study. Agree to join your friends for weekend activities only if you have met your realistic weekly studying goal.

5. *Reduce the rewards gradually.* As your new behaviors become more habitual, give yourself a mental pat on the back instead of a cookie.

"I wrote another five hundred words. Can I have another cookie?"

Mick Stevens/Cartoon Stock

ASK YOURSELF

Think of a bad habit of yours. How could you use operant conditioning to break it?

RETRIEVAL PRACTICE

RP-5 Joslyn constantly misbehaves at preschool even though her teacher scolds her repeatedly. Why does Joslyn's misbehavior continue, and what can her teacher do to stop it?

ANSWERS IN APPENDIX E

Conditioning principles may also be applied in clinical settings. Play the role of a researcher exploring these applications by engaging online with the activity *How Would You Know If People Can Learn to Reduce Anxiety?*

Contrasting Classical and Operant Conditioning

LOQ 21-7 How does operant conditioning differ from classical conditioning?

Both classical and operant conditioning are forms of *associative learning*. Both involve *acquisition, extinction, spontaneous recovery, generalization,* and *discrimination*. But these two forms of learning also differ. Through classical (Pavlovian) conditioning, we associate different stimuli we do not control, and we respond automatically (*respondent behaviors*) (**TABLE 21.4**). Through operant conditioning, we associate our own behaviors—which act on our environment to produce rewarding or punishing stimuli (*operant behaviors*)—with their consequences.

As we shall see next, our biology and cognitive processes influence both classical and operant conditioning.

TABLE 21.4 Comparison of Classical and Operant Conditioning

	Classical Conditioning	Operant Conditioning
Basic idea	Learning associations between events we do not control.	Learning associations between our behavior and its consequences.
Response	Involuntary, automatic.	Voluntary, operates on environment.
Acquisition	Associating events; NS is paired with US and becomes CS.	Associating a response with a consequence (reinforcer or punisher).
Extinction	CR decreases when CS is repeatedly presented alone.	Responding decreases when reinforcement stops.
Spontaneous recovery	The reappearance, after a rest period, of an extinguished CR.	The reappearance, after a rest period, of an extinguished response.
Generalization	The tendency to respond to stimuli similar to the CS.	Responses learned in one situation occurring in other, similar situations.
Discrimination	Learning to distinguish between a CS and other stimuli that do not signal a US.	Learning that some responses, but not others, will be reinforced.

"O! This learning, what a thing it is."
— William Shakespeare, *The Taming of the Shrew*, 1597

RETRIEVAL PRACTICE

RP-6 Salivating in response to a tone paired with food is a(n) _____ behavior; pressing a bar to obtain food is a(n) _____ behavior.

ANSWERS IN APPENDIX E

MODULE 21 REVIEW Operant Conditioning

LEARNING OBJECTIVES

Test Yourself Answer these repeated Learning Objective Questions on your own (before checking the answers in Appendix D) to improve your retention of the concepts (McDaniel et al., 2009, 2015).

LOQ 21-1 What is *operant conditioning*?

LOQ 21-2 Who was Skinner, and how is operant behavior reinforced and shaped?

LOQ 21-3 How do positive and negative reinforcement differ, and what are the basic types of reinforcers?

LOQ 21-4 How do different reinforcement schedules affect behavior?

LOQ 21-5 How does punishment differ from negative reinforcement, and how does punishment affect behavior?

LOQ 21-6 Why did Skinner's ideas provoke controversy, and how might his operant conditioning principles be applied?

LOQ 21-7 How does operant conditioning differ from classical conditioning?

TERMS AND CONCEPTS TO REMEMBER

Test Yourself Write down the definition in your own words, then check your answer.

learning, p. 267
associative learning, p. 267
stimulus, p. 267
respondent behavior, p. 267
operant conditioning, p. 268
operant behavior, p. 268
law of effect, p. 268
operant chamber, p. 268
reinforcement, p. 268
shaping, p. 268
positive reinforcement, p. 268
negative reinforcement, p. 270

primary reinforcer, p. 270
conditioned reinforcer, p. 270
reinforcement schedule, p. 270
continuous reinforcement schedule, p. 270
partial (intermittent) reinforcement schedule, p. 270
fixed-ratio schedule, p. 270
variable-ratio schedule, p. 273
fixed-interval schedule, p. 273
variable-interval schedule, p. 273
punishment, p. 273

MASTER THE MATERIAL

Test Yourself Answer the following questions on your own first, then check your answers in Appendix E.

1. Thorndike's law of effect was the basis for _____'s work on operant conditioning and behavior control.

2. One way to change behavior is to reward natural behaviors in small steps, as the organism gets closer and closer to a desired behavior. This process is called _____.

3. Your dog is barking so loudly that it's making your ears ring. You clap your hands, the dog stops barking, your ears stop ringing, and you think to yourself, "I'll have to do that when he barks again." The end of the barking was for you a

   a. positive reinforcer.

   b. negative reinforcer.

   c. positive punishment.

   d. negative punishment.

4. How could your psychology instructor use negative reinforcement to encourage your attentive behavior during class?

5. Reinforcing a desired response only some of the times it occurs is called _____ reinforcement.

6. A restaurant is running a special deal. After you buy four meals at full price, you will get a free appetizer. This is an example of a _____-_____ schedule of reinforcement.

   a. fixed-ratio

   b. variable-ratio

   c. fixed-interval

   d. variable-interval

7. The partial reinforcement schedule that reinforces a response after unpredictable time periods is a _____-_____ schedule.

8. A medieval proverb notes that "a burnt child dreads the fire." In operant conditioning, the burning would be an example of a

   a. primary reinforcer.

   b. negative reinforcer.

   c. punisher.

   d. positive reinforcer.

Continue testing yourself with ⚞ **LearningCurve** or ⚞ **Achieve Read & Practice** to learn and remember most effectively.

MODULE

22 Biology, Cognition, and Learning

From drooling dogs, running rats, and pecking pigeons we have learned much about the basic processes of **learning.** But conditioning principles don't tell us the whole story. Today's learning theorists recognize that learning is the product of the interaction of biological, psychological, and social-cultural influences (**FIGURE 22.1**).

Biological Constraints on Conditioning

LOQ 22-1 How do biological constraints affect classical and operant conditioning?

Ever since Charles Darwin, scientists have assumed that all animals share a common evolutionary history and thus share commonalities in their makeup and functioning. Pavlov and Watson, for example, believed the basic laws of learning were essentially similar in all animals. So, it should make little difference whether one studied pigeons or people. Moreover, it seemed that any natural response could be conditioned to any neutral stimulus.

Biological influences:
- genetic predispositions
- unconditioned responses
- adaptive responses
- neural mirroring

Psychological influences:
- previous experiences
- predictability of associations
- generalization
- discrimination
- expectations

Learning

Social-cultural influences:
- culturally learned preferences
- motivation, affected by presence of others
- modeling

→ **FIGURE 22.1**
Biopsychosocial influences on learning Our learning results not only from environmental experiences, but also from cognitive and biological influences.

learning the process of acquiring through experience new and relatively enduring information or behaviors.

preparedness a biological predisposition to learn associations, such as between taste and nausea, that have survival value.

Biological Limits on Classical Conditioning

In 1956, learning researcher Gregory Kimble proclaimed, "Just about any activity of which the organism is capable can be conditioned and . . . these responses can be conditioned to any stimulus that the organism can perceive" (p. 195). Twenty-five years later, he humbly acknowledged that "half a thousand" scientific reports had proven him wrong (Kimble, 1981). More than the early behaviorists realized, an animal's capacity for conditioning is limited by biological constraints. For example, each species' predispositions *prepare* it to learn the associations that enhance its survival—a phenomenon called **preparedness.** Environments are not the whole story. Biology matters.

John Garcia (1917–2012) was among those who challenged the prevailing idea that all associations can be learned equally well. While researching the effects of radiation on laboratory animals, Garcia and Robert Koelling (1966) noticed that rats began to avoid drinking water from the plastic bottles in radiation chambers. Could classical conditioning be the culprit? Might the rats have linked the plastic-tasting water (a CS) to the sickness (UR) triggered by the radiation (US)?

To test their hunch, Garcia and Koelling exposed the rats to a particular taste, sight, or sound (CS) and later also to radiation or drugs (US) that led to nausea and vomiting (UR). Two startling findings emerged: First, even if sickened as late as several hours after tasting a particular novel flavor, the rats thereafter avoided that flavor. This appeared to violate the notion that for conditioning to occur, the US must immediately follow the CS.

Second, the sickened rats developed aversions to tastes but not to sights or sounds. This contradicted the behaviorists' idea that any perceivable stimulus could serve as a CS. But it made adaptive sense. For rats, the easiest way to identify tainted food is to taste it; if sickened after sampling a new food, they thereafter avoid it. This response, called *taste aversion*, makes it difficult to eradicate a population of "bait-shy" rats by poisoning.

Humans, too, seem biologically prepared to learn some associations rather than others. If you become violently ill four hours after eating contaminated oysters, you will probably develop an aversion to the *taste* of oysters more readily than to the sight of the associated restaurant, its plates, the people you were with, or the music you heard there. (In contrast, birds, which hunt by sight, appear biologically primed to develop aversions to the *sight* of tainted food [Nicolaus et al., 1983].)

Garcia's early findings on taste aversion were met with an onslaught of criticism. As the German philosopher Arthur Schopenhauer (1788–1860) once said, important ideas are first ridiculed, then attacked, and finally taken for granted. Leading journals refused to publish Garcia's work: The findings are impossible, said some critics. But, as sometimes happens in science, Garcia and Koelling's taste-aversion research replicated often, from the simple snail to the complex human (Aonuma et al., 2018). Conditioned taste aversion is now basic textbook material.

It is also a good example of experiments that begin with the discomfort of some laboratory animals and end by enhancing the welfare of many others. In one conditioned taste-aversion study, coyotes and wolves were tempted into eating sheep carcasses laced with a sickening poison. Thereafter, they developed an aversion to sheep meat; two wolves later penned with a live sheep seemed actually to fear it (Gustavson et al.,

Macmillan Learning

John Garcia As the laboring son of California farmworkers, Garcia attended school only in the off-season during his early childhood years. After entering junior college in his late twenties, and earning his Ph.D. in his late forties, he received the American Psychological Association's Distinguished Scientific Contribution Award "for his highly original, pioneering research in conditioning and learning." He was also elected to the National Academy of Sciences.

Classical Conditioning Review:
NS = Neutral Stimulus
US = Unconditioned Stimulus
UR = Unconditioned Response
CS = Conditioned Stimulus
CR = Conditioned Response

Jose Oto/BSIP SA/Alamy

Taste aversion If you became violently ill after eating oysters, you would probably have a hard time eating them again. Their smell and taste would have become a CS for nausea. This learning occurs readily because our biology prepares us to learn taste aversions to toxic foods.

Animal taste aversion As an alternative to killing wolves and coyotes that preyed on sheep, some ranchers have sickened the animals with lamb laced with a drug to create a taste aversion.

blickwinkel/Alamy

1974, 1976). These studies not only saved the sheep from their predators, but also saved the sheep-shunning coyotes and wolves from angry ranchers and farmers who had wanted to destroy them. Similar applications have prevented baboons from raiding African gardens, raccoons from attacking chickens, and ravens and crows from feeding on crane eggs. In all these cases, research helped preserve both the prey and their predators, all of which occupy an important ecological niche (Dingfelder, 2010; Garcia & Gustavson, 1997).

Such research supports Darwin's principle that natural selection favors traits that aid survival. Our ancestors learned to avoid foods and situations that made them sick, which helped them survive and leave descendants (Bernal-Gamboa et al., 2018). Nausea, like anxiety, pain, and other bad feelings, serves a good purpose. Like a car's low-fuel warning light, each alerts the body to a threat (Davidson & Riley, 2015; Neese, 1991).

Our preparedness to associate a CS with a US that follows predictably and immediately is adaptive. Causes often do immediately precede effects. But as we saw in the taste-aversion findings, our predisposition to associate an effect with a preceding event can trick us. When chemotherapy triggers nausea and vomiting more than an hour following treatment, cancer patients may, over time, develop classically conditioned nausea (and sometimes anxiety) to the sights, sounds, and smells associated with the clinic (Hall, 1997) (**FIGURE 22.2**). Merely returning to the clinic's waiting room or seeing the nurses can provoke these conditioned feelings (Burish & Carey, 1986; Davey, 1992). Under normal circumstances, such revulsion to sickening stimuli would be adaptive.

> "All animals are on a voyage through time, navigating toward futures that promote their survival and away from futures that threaten it. Pleasure and pain are the stars by which they steer." — Psychologists Daniel T. Gilbert and Timothy D. Wilson, "Prospection: Experiencing the Future," 2007

> "Once bitten, twice shy." — G. F. Northall, *Folk-Phrases,* 1894

⬇ **FIGURE 22.2**
Nausea conditioning in cancer patients

| Before conditioning | US (drug) | → | UR (nausea) |

| Conditioning | NS (waiting room) | ➕ | US (drug) | → | UR (nausea) |

| After conditioning | CS (waiting room) | → | CR (nausea) |

RETRIEVAL PRACTICE

RP-1 How did Garcia and Koelling's taste-aversion studies help disprove Gregory Kimble's early claim that "just about any activity of which the organism is capable can be conditioned . . . to any stimulus that the organism can perceive"?

ANSWERS IN APPENDIX E

Biological Limits on Operant Conditioning

Nature also constrains each species' capacity for operant conditioning. Science fiction writer Robert Heinlein (1907–1988) said it well: "Never try to teach a pig to sing; it wastes your time and annoys the pig."

We most easily learn and retain behaviors that reflect our biological and psychological predispositions (Iliescu et al., 2018). Thus, using food as a reinforcer, you could easily condition a hamster to dig or to rear up, because these are among the animal's natural food-searching behaviors. But you won't be so successful if you use food as a reinforcer to shape face washing and other hamster behaviors that aren't normally associated with food or hunger (Shettleworth, 1973). Similarly, you could easily teach pigeons to flap their wings to avoid being shocked, and to peck to obtain food: Fleeing with their wings and eating with their beaks are natural pigeon behaviors. However, pigeons would have a hard time learning to peck to avoid a shock, or to flap their wings to obtain food (Foree & LoLordo, 1973). The principle: *Biological constraints predispose organisms to learn associations that are naturally adaptive.*

In the early years of their work, animal trainers Marian Breland and Keller Breland presumed that operant principles would work on almost any response an animal could make. But along the way, they too learned about biological constraints. In one act, pigs trained to pick up large wooden "dollars" and deposit them in a piggy bank began to drift back to their natural ways. They dropped the coin, pushed it with their snouts as pigs are prone to do, picked it up again, and then repeated the sequence—delaying their food reinforcer. This **instinctive drift** occurred as the animals reverted to their biologically predisposed patterns.

Natural athletes Animals can most easily learn and retain behaviors that draw on their biological predispositions, such as horses' inborn ability to move around obstacles with speed and agility.

For more information on animal behavior, see books by (we are not making this up) Robin Fox and Lionel Tiger.

> 📖 To learn more about biology's Influence on learning, engage online with *Concept Practice: Biologically Adaptive Associations.*

Cognition's Influence on Conditioning

LOQ **22-2** How do cognitive processes affect classical and operant conditioning?

Cognition and Classical Conditioning

In their dismissal of "mentalistic" concepts such as consciousness, Pavlov and Watson underestimated the importance of not only biological constraints such as preparedness and instinctive drift, but also the effects of cognitive processes (thoughts, perceptions, expectations). The early behaviorists believed that rats' and dogs' learned behaviors could be reduced to mindless mechanisms, so there was no need to consider cognition. But Robert Rescorla and Allan Wagner (1972) showed that an animal can learn the *predictability* of an event. If a shock always is preceded by a tone, and then may also be preceded by a light that accompanies the tone, a rat will react with fear to the tone but not to the light. Although the light is always followed by the shock, it adds no new information; the tone is a better predictor. The more predictable the association, the stronger the conditioned response. It's as if the animal learns an *expectancy*, an awareness of how likely it is that the US will occur.

Classical conditioning treatments that ignore cognition often have limited success. For example, people receiving therapy for alcohol use disorder may be given alcohol spiked with a nauseating drug. Will they then associate alcohol with sickness? If classical conditioning were merely a matter of "stamping in" stimulus associations, we might hope so, and to some extent this does occur. However, one's awareness that the nausea is induced by the drug, not the alcohol, often weakens the association between drinking alcohol and feeling sick, reducing the treatment's effectiveness. So, even in classical conditioning, it is—especially with humans—not simply the CS-US association, but also the thought that counts.

"All brains are, in essence, anticipation machines." — Daniel C. Dennett, *Consciousness Explained,* 1991

Cognition and Operant Conditioning

B. F. Skinner acknowledged the biological underpinnings of behavior and the existence of private thought processes. Nevertheless, many psychologists criticized him for discounting cognition's importance.

instinctive drift the tendency of learned behavior to gradually revert to biologically predisposed patterns.

A mere 8 days before dying of leukemia in 1990, Skinner stood before the American Psychological Association convention. In this final address, he still resisted the growing belief that cognitive processes (thoughts, perceptions, expectations) have a necessary place in the science of psychology and even in our understanding of conditioning. He viewed "cognitive science" as a throwback to early twentieth-century introspectionism. For Skinner, thoughts and emotions were behaviors that follow the same laws as other behaviors.

Nevertheless, the evidence of cognitive processes cannot be ignored. For example, animals on a *fixed-interval reinforcement schedule* respond more and more frequently as the time approaches when a response will produce a reinforcer. Although a strict behaviorist would object to talk of "expectations," the animals behave as if they expected that repeating the response would soon produce the reward.

Evidence of cognitive processes has also come from studying rats in mazes. Rats exploring a maze, given no obvious rewards, seem to develop a **cognitive map,** a mental representation of the maze. When an experimenter then places food in the maze's

The New Yorker Collection, 2000, Pat Byrnes, from cartoonbank.com. All Rights Reserved.

"Bathroom? Sure, it's just down the hall to the left, jog right, left, another left, straight past two more lefts, then right, and it's at the end of the third corridor on your right."

goal box, these rats run the maze as quickly as other rats that were previously reinforced with food for this result. Like people sightseeing in a new town, the exploring rats seemingly experienced **latent learning** during their earlier tours (Tolman & Honzik, 1930). That learning became apparent only when there was some incentive to demonstrate it. Children, too, may learn from watching a parent but demonstrate the learning only much later, as needed

The point to remember: There is more to learning than associating a response with a consequence; there is also cognition.

In the Thinking and Language modules, we encounter more striking evidence of animals' cognitive abilities in solving problems and in using aspects of language. And in Module 35, we see how, due to cognition, excessive rewards can make us *less* motivated to perform a desired behavior.

TABLE 22.1 compares the biological and cognitive influences on classical and operant conditioning.

TABLE 22.1 Biological and Cognitive Influences on Conditioning		
	Classical Conditioning	**Operant Conditioning**
Biological influences	Natural predispositions constrain what stimuli and responses can easily be associated.	Organisms most easily learn behaviors similar to their natural behaviors; unnatural behaviors instinctively drift back toward natural ones.
Cognitive influences	Organisms develop an expectation that a CS signals the arrival of a US.	Organisms develop an expectation that a response will be reinforced or punished; they also exhibit latent learning, without reinforcement.

cognitive map a mental representation of the layout of one's environment. For example, after exploring a maze, rats act as if they have learned a cognitive map of it.

latent learning learning that occurs but is not apparent until there is an incentive to demonstrate it.

observational learning learning by observing others.

modeling the process of observing and imitating a specific behavior.

ASK YOURSELF

Can you remember examples from your childhood of learning through *classical conditioning* (salivating at the sound or smell of some delicious food cooking in the kitchen?), *operant conditioning* (deciding not to repeat a behavior because you disliked its consequence?), and *cognitive learning* (repeating or avoiding what you watched someone else do)?

RETRIEVAL PRACTICE

RP-2 Instinctive drift and latent learning are examples of what important idea?

ANSWERS IN APPENDIX E

Learning by Observation

LOQ **22-3** What is *observational learning?*

Cognition supports **observational learning** (also called *social learning*), in which higher animals, especially humans, learn without direct experience, by watching and imitating others. A child who sees his sister burn her fingers on a hot stove learns not to touch it. We learn our native languages and various other specific behaviors by observing and imitating others, a process called **modeling.**

Picture this scene from an experiment by Albert Bandura, the pioneering researcher of observational learning (Bandura et al., 1961): A preschool child works on a drawing. An adult in another part of the room builds with Tinkertoys. As the child watches, the adult gets up and for nearly 10 minutes pounds, kicks, and throws around the room a large inflated Bobo doll, yelling, "Sock him in the nose. . . . Hit him down. . . . Kick him."

The child is then taken to another room filled with appealing toys. Soon the experimenter returns and tells the child she has decided to save these good toys "for the other children." She takes the now-frustrated child to a third room containing a few toys, including a Bobo doll. Left alone, what does the child do?

Unlike children not exposed to the adult model (none of whom imitated the model), those who viewed the model's actions often lashed out at the doll (Bandura, 2017). Observing the aggressive outburst apparently lowered their inhibitions. But *something more* was also at work, for the children imitated the very acts they had observed and used the very words they had heard (**FIGURE 22.3**).

That "something more," Bandura suggests, was this: By watching models, we experience *vicarious reinforcement* or *vicarious punishment,* and we learn to anticipate a behavior's consequences in situations like those we are observing. We are especially likely to learn from people we perceive as successful, admirable, or similar to ourselves. fMRI scans show that when people observe someone winning a reward (and especially when it's someone likable and similar to themselves), their own brain reward systems activate, much as if they themselves had won the reward (Mobbs et al., 2009). When we identify with someone, we experience their outcomes vicariously. Even our learned fears may extinguish as we observe another safely navigating the feared situation (Golkar et al., 2013). Lord Chesterfield (1694–1773) had the idea: "We are, in truth, more than half what we are by imitation."

Polaris/Newscom

Albert Bandura "The Bobo doll follows me wherever I go. The photographs are published in every introductory psychology text and virtually every undergraduate takes introductory psychology. I recently checked into a Washington hotel. The clerk at the desk asked, 'Aren't you the psychologist who did the Bobo doll experiment?' I answered, 'I am afraid that will be my legacy.' He replied, 'That deserves an upgrade. I will put you in a suite in the quiet part of the hotel'" (2005). A recent analysis of citations, awards, and textbook coverage identified Bandura—shown here receiving a 2016 U.S. National Medal of Science from President Obama—as the world's most eminent psychologist (Diener et al., 2014).

© Albert Bandura, Dept. of Psychology, Stanford University

← FIGURE 22.3 The famous Bobo doll experiment Notice how the children's actions directly imitate the adult's.

mirror neurons frontal lobe neurons that some scientists believe fire when we perform certain actions or observe another doing so. The brain's mirroring of another's action may enable imitation and empathy.

Bandura's work provides an example of how basic research "pursued for its own sake" can have a broader purpose. "The Bobo Doll studies," he reflected (2016, 2017), "provided the principles for unforeseen global applications 25 years later." Insights derived from his research have been used not only to restrain televised violence, but also to offer social models in African, Asian, and Latin American television and radio series that have helped reduce unplanned childbearing, protect against AIDS, and promote environmental conservation.

> 📺 For 3 minutes of classic footage, see the **Video: Bandura's Bobo Doll Experiment.**

Mirrors and Imitation in the Brain

LOQ 22-4 How may observational learning be enabled by neural mirroring?

In 1991, on a hot summer day in Parma, Italy, a lab monkey awaited its researchers' return from lunch. The researchers had implanted wires next to its motor cortex, in a frontal lobe brain region that enabled the monkey to plan and enact movements. The monitoring device would alert the researchers to activity in that region of the monkey's brain. When the monkey moved a peanut into its mouth, for example, the device would buzz. That day, as one of the researchers reentered the lab, ice cream cone in hand, the monkey stared at him. As the researcher raised the cone to lick it, the monkey's monitor buzzed—as if the motionless monkey had itself moved (Blakeslee, 2006; Iacoboni, 2008, 2009).

The same buzzing had been heard earlier, when the monkey watched humans or other monkeys move peanuts to their mouths. The flabbergasted researchers, led by Giacomo Rizzolatti (2002, 2006), had, they believed, stumbled onto a previously unknown type of neuron. These presumed **mirror neurons,** they argued, provide a neural basis for everyday imitation and observational learning. When one monkey sees, its neurons mirror what another monkey does. (For a debate regarding the importance of mirror neurons, which have been overblown in the popular press, see Gallese et al., 2011; Hickok, 2014.)

"Your back is killing me!"
Mirror neurons at work?

Imitation is widespread in other species. Primates observe and imitate all sorts of novel tool use behaviors, such as how to crack nuts using stone hammers (Fragaszy et al., 2017). These types of behaviors are then transmitted from generation to generation within their local culture (Hopper et al., 2008; Whiten et al., 2007). In one 27-year analysis of 73,790 humpback whale observations, a single whale in 1980 whacked the water to drive prey fish into a clump. In the years since, this "lobtail" technique spread among other whales (Allen et al., 2013).

Animal social learning (a) Whacking the water to boost feeding has spread among humpback whales through social learning (Allen et al., 2013). (b) Likewise, monkeys learn to prefer whatever color corn they observe other monkeys eating.

(a)

(b)

Meltzoff, A. N., Kuhl, P. K., Movellan, J. & Sejnowski, T. J. (2009). Foundations for a new science of learning. *Science, 325*, 284–288.

⬆ **FIGURE 22.4**

Imitation This 12-month-old infant sees an adult look left, and immediately follows her gaze (Meltzoff et al., 2009).

So, too, with monkeys. Erica van de Waal and her co-researchers (2013) trained groups of vervet monkeys to prefer either blue or pink corn by soaking one color in a disgusting-tasting solution. Four to six months later, after a new generation of monkeys was born, the adults stuck with whatever color they had learned to prefer—and, on observing them, so did all but one of 27 infant monkeys. Moreover, when blue- (or pink-) preferring males migrated to the other group, they switched preferences and began eating as the other group did. Monkey see, monkey do.

In humans, imitation is pervasive. Our catchphrases, fashions, ceremonies, foods, traditions, morals, and fads all spread by one person copying another. Children, and even infants, are natural imitators (Marshall & Meltzoff, 2014). From 8 to 16 months, infants come to imitate various novel gestures (Jones, 2007, 2017). By 12 months (**FIGURE 22.4**), they look where an adult is looking (Meltzoff et al., 2009). And by 14 months, children imitate acts modeled on TV (Meltzoff, 1988; Meltzoff & Moore, 1989, 1997). Even as 2½-year-olds, when many of their mental abilities are near those of adult chimpanzees, young humans surpass chimps at social tasks such as imitating another's solution to a problem (Herrmann et al., 2007). Children see, children do.

So strong is the human predisposition to learn from watching adults that 2- to 5-year-old children *overimitate*. Whether living in urban Australia or rural Africa, they copy even irrelevant adult actions. Before reaching for a toy in a plastic jar, they will first stroke the jar with a feather if that's what they have observed (Lyons et al., 2007). Or, imitating an adult, they will wave a stick over a box and then use the stick to push on a knob that opens the box—when all they needed to do to open the box was to push on the knob (Nielsen & Tomaselli, 2010).

Humans, like monkeys, have brains that support empathy and imitation. Researchers cannot insert experimental electrodes in human brains, but they can use fMRI scans to see brain activity associated with performing and with observing actions. So, is the human capacity to simulate another's action and to share in another's experience due to specialized mirror neurons? Or is it due to distributed brain networks? That issue is under debate (Fox et al., 2016; Gallese et al. 2011; Hickok, 2014; Iacoboni, 2009). Regardless, children's brains do enable their empathy and their ability to infer another's mental state, an ability known as *theory of mind*.

Our brain's response to observing others makes emotions contagious. Our brain simulates and vicariously experiences what we observe. So real are these mental instant replays that we may misremember an action we have observed as one we have performed (Lindner et al., 2010). Watching someone experience electric shocks, we become more fearful in our own choices—as if we had experienced the shocks ourselves (Lindström et al., 2019). But through these reenactments, we grasp others' states of mind. Observing others' postures, faces, voices, and writing styles, we unconsciously synchronize our own to theirs—which helps us feel what they are feeling (Bernieri et al., 1994; Ireland & Pennebaker, 2010). Imitation helps us gain friends, leading us to mimic those we like, who then like us more in return (Chartrand & Lakin, 2013; Salazar Kämpf, 2018). We find ourselves yawning when they yawn, smiling when they smile, laughing when they laugh.

Seeing a loved one's pain, our faces mirror the other's emotion. But as **FIGURE 22.5** shows, so do our brains. Observing others' pain also releases our body's natural painkillers, thus calming our distress and enabling our helping (Haaker et al., 2017). Even fiction

"This instinct to humiliate, when it's modeled by someone in the public platform, by someone powerful, it filters down into everybody's life, because it . . . gives permission for other people to do the same thing." — Meryl Streep, U.S. Golden Globe Award speech, 2017

"Children need models more than they need critics." — Joseph Joubert, *Pensées,* 1842

(a) Pain   (b) Empathy

⊖ **FIGURE 22.5**
Experienced and imagined pain in the brain In these fMRI scans, brain activity related to actual pain (a) is mirrored in the brain of an observing loved one (b) (Singer et al., 2004). Empathy in the brain shows up in areas that process emotions, but not in the somatosensory cortex, which receives the physical pain input.

reading may trigger such activity, as we mentally simulate (and vicariously experience) the experiences described (Mar & Oatley, 2008; Speer et al., 2009). In a series of experiments, reading about Harry Potter and his acceptance of people such as the "Mudbloods" reduced prejudice against immigrants, refugees, and gay people (Vezzali et al., 2015).

Applications of Observational Learning

LOQ 22-5 What is the impact of prosocial modeling and of antisocial modeling?

The big news from Bandura's studies and mirror-neuron research is that we look, we mentally imitate, and we learn. Models—in our family, our neighborhood, or the media we consume—may have effects, good and bad.

PROSOCIAL EFFECTS The good news is that people's modeling of **prosocial** (positive, helpful) **behaviors** can have prosocial effects. Many business organizations effectively use *behavior modeling* to help new employees learn communications, sales, and customer service skills (Taylor et al., 2005). Trainees gain these skills faster when they are able to observe the skills being modeled effectively by experienced workers (or actors simulating them).

People who exemplify nonviolent, helpful behavior can also prompt similar behavior in others. After observing someone helping (assisting a woman with dropped books), people became more helpful, such as by assisting someone who dropped a dollar (Burger et al., 2015). India's Mahatma Gandhi and America's Martin Luther King, Jr., both drew on the power of modeling, making nonviolent action a powerful force for social change in both countries (Matsumoto et al., 2015). The media offer models. Across many countries and dozens of studies, viewing prosocial TV, movies, and video games boosted later helping behavior (Coyne et al., 2018; Prot et al., 2014).

Parents are also powerful models. European Christians who risked their lives to rescue Jews from the Nazis usually had a close relationship with at least one parent who modeled a strong moral or humanitarian concern; this was also true for U.S. civil rights activists in the 1960s (London, 1970; Oliner & Oliner, 1988). The observational learning of morality begins early. Socially responsive toddlers, who readily imitate their parents, tend to become preschoolers with a strong internalized conscience (Forman et al., 2004).

Models are most effective when their actions and words are consistent. To encourage children to read, read to them and surround them with books and people who read. To increase the odds that your children will practice your religion, worship and attend religious activities with them (Lanman & Buhrmester, 2017). To teach your children persistence, let them see

A model caregiver This girl is learning orphan-nursing skills, as well as compassion, by observing her mentor in this Humane Society program. As the sixteenth-century proverb states, "Example is better than precept."

Zumapress/Newscom

persistence in you (Butler, 2017). Sometimes, however, models say one thing and do another. Many parents seem to operate according to the principle "Do as I *say*, not as I *do*." Experiments suggest that children learn to do both (Rice & Grusec, 1975; Rushton, 1975). Exposed to a hypocrite, they tend to imitate the hypocrisy—by doing what the model did and saying what the model said.

> **prosocial behavior** positive, constructive, helpful behavior. The opposite of antisocial behavior.

RP-3 Emily's parents and older friends all drive over the speed limit, but they advise her not to. Hannah's parents and friends drive within the speed limit, but they say nothing to deter her from speeding. Will Emily or Hannah be more likely to speed?

ANSWERS IN APPENDIX E

ANTISOCIAL EFFECTS The bad news is that observational learning may also have *antisocial effects*. This helps us understand why abusive parents might have aggressive children, why children who are lied to become more likely to cheat and lie, and why many men who beat their wives had wife-battering fathers (Hays & Carver, 2014; Jung et al., 2019; Stith et al., 2000). Critics note that such aggressiveness could be genetic. But with monkeys, we know it can be environmental. In study after study, young monkeys separated from their mothers and subjected to high levels of aggression grew up to be aggressive themselves (Chamove, 1980). The lessons we learn as children are not easily replaced as adults, and they are sometimes visited on future generations.

David Strickler/The Image Works

Children see, children do? Children who often experience physical punishment tend to display more aggression.

Observational learning influences adults, too. Those repeatedly exposed to hate speech become desensitized to hateful words. And they become more prejudiced toward its targets (Soral et al., 2018). As social psychologists Chris Crandall and Mark White (2016) remind us, political leaders have the power to influence norms, and norms matter: "People express the prejudices that are socially acceptable and they hide the ones that are not."

TV shows, movies, and videos are sources of observational learning. While watching, children may learn that bullying is an effective way to control others, that free and easy sex brings pleasure without later misery or disease, or that men should be tough and women gentle. Some films glorify high-speed and risky driving. Do these films "teach" viewers that such driving is acceptable? An analysis of nearly 200,000 speeding tickets showed increased average speed among drivers who received tickets on the weekends following the release of *The Fast and the Furious* films (Jena et al., 2018).

And children have ample time to learn such lessons. During their first 18 years, most children in developed countries spend more time watching TV than they spend in school. The average teen watches more than 4 hours a day; the average adult, 3 hours (Robinson & Martin, 2009; Strasburger et al., 2010).

Viewers are learning about life from a peculiar storyteller, one that reflects the culture's mythology rather than its reality. Between 1998 and 2006, prime-time violence on TV reportedly increased 75 percent (PTC, 2007). An analysis of more than 3000 network and cable programs aired during one closely studied year revealed that nearly 6 in 10 featured violence, that 74 percent of the violence went unpunished, that 58 percent did not show the victims' pain, that nearly half the incidents involved "justified" violence, and that nearly half involved an attractive

Paul Noth/The New Yorker Collection/The Cartoon Bank

"Screen time . . . screen time . . ."

Screen time's greatest effect may stem from what it displaces. Children and adults who spend several hours a day in front of a screen spend that many fewer hours in other pursuits—talking, studying, playing, reading, or socializing face-to-face with friends. What would you have done with your extra time if you had spent even half as many hours in front of a screen? How might you be different as a result?

perpetrator. These conditions define the recipe for the *violence-viewing effect* described in many studies around the world and recognized by most media researchers (Anderson et al., 2017; Bushman, 2018; Martins & Weaver, 2019; Teng et al., 2019). (See Thinking Critically About: The Effects of Viewing Media Violence.)

* * *

Bandura's work—like that of Ivan Pavlov, John Watson, B. F. Skinner, and thousands of others who advanced our knowledge of learning principles—illustrates the impact that can result from single-minded devotion to a few well-defined problems and ideas. These researchers defined the issues and impressed on us the importance of learning. As their legacy demonstrates, intellectual history is often made by people who risk going to extremes in pushing ideas to their limits (Simonton, 2000).

ASK YOURSELF

Who has been a significant role model for you? What did you learn from observing this person? For whom are you a role model? How might you become a better role model for others?

RETRIEVAL PRACTICE

RP-4 Match the examples (i–v) to the appropriate underlying learning principle (a–e):

i.	Knowing the way from your bed to the bathroom in the dark	a.	Classical conditioning
ii.	Your little brother getting in a fight after watching a violent action movie	b.	Operant conditioning
iii.	Salivating when you smell brownies in the oven	c.	Latent learning
		d.	Observational learning
iv.	Disliking the taste of chili after becoming violently sick a few hours after eating chili	e.	Biological predispositions
v.	Your dog racing to greet you on your arrival home		

ANSWERS IN APPENDIX E

Introduction of TV, 1957–1974 ↔ Doubling of homicide rate in U.S. and Canada[1] ↔ Introduction of TV for White South Africans in 1975 ↔ Near-doubling of homicide rate in South Africa[1] ↔ Heavy exposure to media violence for U.S. 9–11-year-olds ↔ Increased fighting, and more violent behavior later as teens[2]

BUT, CORRELATION ≠ CAUSATION!

Experimental studies have also found that media violence viewing can cause aggression:

Viewing violence (compared to entertaining nonviolence) ➔ participants react more cruelly when provoked. (Effect is strongest if the violent person is attractive, the violence seems justified and realistic, the act goes unpunished, and the viewer does not see pain or harm caused.)

What prompts the *violence-viewing effect*?

1 IMITATION:

Watching violent cartoons ➔ Sevenfold increase in violent play[3]

Limited exposure to violent programs ➔ Reduced aggressive behavior[4]

2 DESENSITIZATION:

Prolonged exposure to violence ➔ Viewers are later indifferent (desensitized) to violence on TV or in real life.[5]

meh.

Adult males spent 3 evenings watching sexually violent movies. ➔ Viewers became progressively less bothered by the violence shown. Compared to a control group, they expressed less sympathy for domestic violence victims and rated victims' injuries as less severe.[6]

Violent moviegoers ➔ less likely to help

Nonviolent moviegoers ➔ more likely to help[7]

• **APA Task Force on Violent Media (2015)** found that the "research demonstrates a consistent relation between violent video game use and increases in aggressive behavior, aggressive cognitions, and aggressive affect, and decreases in prosocial behavior, empathy, and sensitivity to aggression."

• **American Academy of Pediatrics (2009)** has advised pediatricians that "media violence can contribute to aggressive behavior, desensitization to violence, nightmares, and fear of being harmed."

Critics suggest that these statements may ignore some weakness in media violence research, such as reliability and the size of the effect. They also note that some places, such as Japan, have similarly violent media but much less violent behavior.[8]

1. Centerwall, 1989.   2. Boxer et al., 2009; Gentile et al., 2011; Gentile & Bushman, 2012.   3. Boyatzis et al., 1995.   4. Christakis et al., 2013.
5. Fanti et al., 2009; Jin et al., 2018; Rule & Ferguson, 1986.   6. Mullin & Linz, 1995.   7. Bushman & Anderson, 2009.   8. Elson et al., 2019.

22 REVIEW Biology, Cognition, and Learning

LEARNING OBJECTIVES

Test Yourself Answer these repeated Learning Objective Questions on your own (before checking the answers in Appendix D) to improve your retention of the concepts (McDaniel et al., 2009, 2015).

LOQ 22-1 How do biological constraints affect classical and operant conditioning?

LOQ 22-2 How do cognitive processes affect classical and operant conditioning?

LOQ 22-3 What is *observational learning*?

LOQ 22-4 How may observational learning be enabled by neural mirroring?

LOQ 22-5 What is the impact of prosocial modeling and of antisocial modeling?

LOQ 22-6 What is the violence-viewing effect?

TERMS AND CONCEPTS TO REMEMBER

Test Yourself Write down the definition in your own words, then check your answer.

learning, p. 278

preparedness, p. 278

instinctive drift, p. 281

cognitive map, p. 282

latent learning, p. 282

observational learning, p. 282

modeling, p. 282

mirror neurons, p. 284

prosocial behavior, p. 287

MASTER THE MATERIAL

Test Yourself Answer the following questions on your own first, then check your answers in Appendix E.

1. Garcia and Koelling's _____-_____ studies showed that conditioning can occur even when the unconditioned stimulus (US) does not immediately follow the neutral stimulus (NS).

2. Taste-aversion research has shown that some animals develop aversions to certain tastes but not to sights or sounds. Which of Darwin's principles does this support?

3. Evidence that cognitive processes play an important role in learning comes in part from studies in which rats running a maze develop a _____ _____ of the maze.

4. Rats that explored a maze without any reward were later able to run the maze as well as other rats that had received food rewards for running the maze. The rats that had learned without reinforcement demonstrated _____ _____.

5. Children learn many social behaviors by imitating parents and other models. This type of learning is called _____ _____.

6. According to Bandura, we learn by watching models because we experience _____ reinforcement or _____ punishment.

7. Parents are most effective in getting their children to imitate them if
   a. their words and actions are consistent.
   b. they have outgoing personalities.
   c. one parent works and the other stays home to care for the children.
   d. they carefully explain why a behavior is acceptable in adults but not in children.

8. Some scientists believe that the brain has _____ neurons that enable empathy and imitation.

9. Most experts agree that repeated viewing of media violence
   a. makes all viewers significantly more aggressive.
   b. has little effect on viewers.
   c. is a risk factor for viewers' increased aggression.
   d. makes viewers angry and frustrated.

Continue testing yourself with **📘 LearningCurve** or **📖 Achieve Read & Practice** to learn and remember most effectively.

Memory

Be thankful for memory. We take it for granted, except when it malfunctions. But it is our memory that accounts for time and defines our life. It is our memory that enables us to recognize family, speak our language, and find our way home. It is our memory that enables us to enjoy an experience and then mentally replay it to enjoy again. It is our memory that enables us to build histories with those we love. And it is our shared memories that bind us together as Irish or Iranian, Somalian or Samoan—and that occasionally pit us against others whose offenses we cannot forget.

In large part, we are what we remember. Without memory—our archive of accumulated learning—there would be no savoring of past joys, no guilt or anger over painful recollections. We would instead live in an enduring present, each moment fresh. Each person would be a stranger, every language foreign, every task—dressing, cooking, biking—a new challenge. You would even be a stranger to yourself, lacking that continuous sense of self that extends from your distant past to your momentary present.

Researchers study memory from many perspectives. Module 23 introduces the measuring, modeling, and encoding of memories. Module 24 examines how memories are stored and retrieved. Module 25 explores what happens when our memories fail us, and looks at ways to improve memory.

23 Studying and Encoding Memories

Studying Memory

(LEARNING OBJECTIVE QUESTION) **LOQ** **23-1** What is *memory,* and how is it measured?

Memory is learning that persists over time; it is information that has been acquired and stored and can be retrieved. Research on memory's extremes has helped us understand how memory works. At age 92, my [DM's] father suffered a small stroke that had but one peculiar effect. His genial personality was intact. He knew us and enjoyed poring over family photo albums and reminiscing about his past. But he had lost most of his ability to form new memories of conversations and everyday episodes. He could not tell me what day of the week it was, or what he'd had for lunch. Told repeatedly of his brother-in-law's recent death, he was surprised and saddened each time he heard the news.

Some disorders slowly strip away memory. *Alzheimer's disease* begins as difficulty remembering new information, progressing to an inability to do everyday tasks. Complex speech becomes simple sentences; family members and close friends become strangers; the brain's memory centers, once strong, become weak and wither away (Desikan et al., 2009). Over several years, those with Alzheimer's may become unknowing and unknowable. Their sense of self weakens, leaving them wondering, "Who am I?" (Ben Malek et al., 2019). Lost memory strikes at the core of their humanity, robbing them of their joy, meaning, and companionship.

At the other extreme are people who win gold medals in memory competitions. When two-time World Memory champion Feng Wang was a 21-year-old college student, he didn't need help from his phone to remember his friends' numbers. The average person could parrot back a string of about 7—maybe even 9—digits. Feng could reliably repeat up to 200, if they were read about 1 second apart in an otherwise silent room (Ericsson et al., 2017). At one competition, he even memorized 300 digits!

Amazing? Yes, but consider your own impressive memory. You remember countless faces, places, and happenings; tastes, smells, and textures; voices, sounds, and songs. In one study, students listened to snippets—a mere four-tenths of a second—from popular songs. How often did they recognize the artist and song? More than 25 percent of the time (Krumhansl, 2010). We often recognize songs as quickly as we recognize a familiar voice.

So, too, with faces and places. Imagine viewing more than 2500 slides of faces and places for 10 seconds each. Later, you see 280 of these slides, paired with others you've never seen. Actual participants recognized 90 percent of the slides they had viewed in the first round (Haber, 1970). In a follow-up experiment, people exposed to 2800 images for only 3 seconds each spotted the repeats with 82 percent accuracy (Konkle et al., 2010). Look for a target face in a sea of faces and you later will recognize other faces from the scene as well (Kaunitz et al., 2016).

The average person permanently stores and recognizes about 5000 faces (Jenkins et al., 2018). But some super-recognizers display an extraordinary ability to recognize faces. Using closed-circuit television street footage, British, Asian, and German police have used super-recognizers to solve difficult cases (Keefe, 2016; NPR, 2018). Eighteen months after viewing a video of an armed robbery, one police officer spotted and arrested the robber walking on a busy street (Davis et al., 2013). And it's not just humans who have shown remarkable memory for faces. Sheep remember faces, too **(FIGURE 23.1)**. And so has at least one fish species—as demonstrated by their spitting at familiar faces to trigger a food reward (Newport et al., 2016).

How do we humans accomplish such memory feats? How does our brain pluck information out of the world around us and tuck it away for later use? How can we remember things we have not thought about for years, yet forget the name of someone we just met? How are memories stored in our brain? Why will you be likely, later in this module, to misrecall this sentence: *"The angry rioter threw the rock at the window"*?

National Institute on Aging, National Institutes of Health

Healthy brain / **Severe Alzheimer's disease**

Extreme forgetting Alzheimer's disease severely damages the brain, and in the process strips away memory.

Want to test your memory? Try to memorize the first 10 digits of pi (π): 3.141592653. In 2015, Rajveer Meena of India broke the world record by reciting 70,000 digits of pi (*Guinness World Records,* 2019).

FIGURE 23.1
Other animals also display face smarts After food rewards are repeatedly associated with some sheep and human faces, but not with others, sheep remember food-associated faces for two years (Kendrick & Feng, 2011; Knolle et al., 2017).

A. Jennifer Morton/University of Cambridge

ASK YOURSELF

Imagine having an injury that significantly impairs your ability to form new memories. Now, imagine having a record-setting ability to remember, like Feng Wang. How would each condition affect your daily routine?

Measuring Retention

To a psychologist, evidence that learning persists includes these three *retention measures*:

- **recall**—*retrieving* information that is not currently in your conscious awareness but that was learned at an earlier time. A fill-in-the-blank question tests your recall.

- **recognition**—*identifying* items previously learned. A multiple-choice question tests your recognition.

- **relearning**—*learning something more quickly* when you learn it a second or later time. When you review the first weeks of course work to prepare for your final exam, or engage a language used in early childhood, it will be easier to relearn the material than when you first learned it.

Psychologists can measure these different forms of memory separately. The Wechsler Memory Scale, first developed by David Wechsler in 1945 and now in its fourth edition (WMS-IV), includes a global assessment of memory functioning. Long after you cannot recall most of the people in your high school graduating class, you may still be able to recognize their yearbook pictures and spot their names in a list of names. In one experiment, people who had graduated 25 years earlier could not recall many of their old classmates. But they could *recognize* 90 percent of their pictures and names (Bahrick et al., 1975). If you are like most students, you, too, could probably recognize more names of Snow White's seven dwarfs than you could recall (Miserandino, 1991).

Our recognition memory is impressively quick and vast. "Is your friend wearing a new or old outfit?" *Old.* "Have you read this textbook material before?" *No.* "Have you ever seen this person before—this minor variation on the same old human features (two eyes, one nose, and so on)?" *No.* Before the mouth can form our answer to any of millions of such questions, the mind knows, and knows that it knows.

Our response speed when recalling or recognizing information indicates memory strength, as does our speed at *relearning*. Pioneering memory researcher Hermann Ebbinghaus (1850–1909) showed this in the nineteenth century, using nonsense syllables. He randomly selected a sample of syllables, practiced them, and tested himself. To get a feel for his experiments, rapidly read aloud, eight times over, the following list of syllables (from Baddeley, 1982), then look away and try to recall the items:

JIH, BAZ, FUB, YOX, SUJ, XIR, DAX, LEQ, VUM, PID, KEL, WAV, TUV, ZOF, GEK, HIW.

The day after learning such a list, Ebbinghaus could recall few of the syllables. But they weren't entirely forgotten. As **FIGURE 23.2** portrays, the more frequently he repeated the

Time in minutes taken to relearn list on Day 2

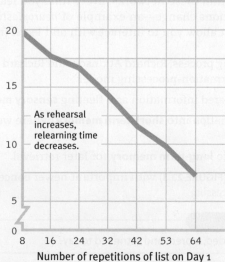
As rehearsal increases, relearning time decreases.

Number of repetitions of list on Day 1

⊖ **FIGURE 23.2**
Ebbinghaus' retention curve
Ebbinghaus found that the more times he practiced a list of nonsense syllables on Day 1, the less time he required to relearn it on Day 2. Speed of relearning is one measure of memory retention. (From Baddeley, 1982.)

memory the persistence of learning over time through the encoding, storage, and retrieval of information.

recall a measure of memory in which the person must retrieve information learned earlier, as on a fill-in-the-blank test.

recognition a measure of memory in which the person identifies items previously learned, as on a multiple-choice test.

relearning a measure of memory that assesses the amount of time saved when learning material again.

Famous faces Even if Taylor Swift and Barack Obama had not become famous, their high school classmates would most likely still recognize them in these photos.

list aloud on Day 1, the less time he required to relearn the list on Day 2. Additional rehearsal (overlearning) of verbal information increases retention, especially when practice is distributed over time. For students, this means that it helps to rehearse course material over time, even after you know it. Better to rehearse and overlearn than relax and remember too little.

The point to remember: Tests of recognition and of time spent relearning demonstrate that we remember more than we can recall.

RETRIEVAL PRACTICE

RP-1 Multiple-choice questions test our _____. Fill-in-the-blank questions test our _____.

RP-2 If you want to be sure to remember what you're learning for an upcoming test, would it be better to use *recall* or *recognition* to check your memory? Why?

ANSWERS IN APPENDIX E

Memory Models

LOQ **23-2** How do memory models help us study memory, and how has later research updated the three-stage information-processing model?

Architects create virtual models to help clients imagine their future homes. Similarly, psychologists create memory models. Such models aren't perfect, but they help us think about how our brain forms and retrieves memories. History has offered varied memory models: a wax tablet (Aristotle); a "mystic writing pad" (Freud); a house, a library, a telephone switchboard, a videotape (Roediger, 1980). Today's *information-processing model* likens human memory to computer operations. Thus, to remember we must

- **encode**—get information into our brain.
- **store**—retain that information.
- **retrieve**—later get the information back out.

Like all analogies, computer models have their limits. Our memories are less literal and more fragile than a computer's. Most computers also process information *sequentially*, even while alternating between tasks. Our agile brain processes many things *simultaneously* (some of them unconsciously) by means of **parallel processing**. To focus on this multitrack processing, one information-processing model, *connectionism*, views memories as products of interconnected neural networks. Specific memories arise from particular activation patterns within these networks. Every time you learn something new, your brain's neural connections change—an example of *neuroplasticity*—forming and strengthening pathways that allow you to interact with and learn from your constantly changing environment.

To explain our memory-forming process, Richard Atkinson and Richard Shiffrin (1968, 2016) proposed a three-stage information-processing model:

1. We first record to-be-remembered information as a fleeting **sensory memory.**

2. From there, we process information into **short-term memory,** where we encode it through *rehearsal*.

3. Finally, information moves into **long-term memory** for later retrieval.

This model has been updated (**FIGURE 23.3**) with important newer concepts, including *working memory* and *automatic processing*.

ASK YOURSELF

What has your memory system encoded, stored, and retrieved today?

---

encoding the process of getting information into the memory system—for example, by extracting meaning.

storage the process of retaining encoded information over time.

retrieval the process of getting information out of memory storage.

parallel processing processing many aspects of a stimulus or problem simultaneously.

sensory memory the immediate, very brief recording of sensory information in the memory system.

short-term memory briefly activated memory of a few items (such as digits of a phone number while calling) that is later stored or forgotten.

long-term memory the relatively permanent and limitless archive of the memory system. Includes knowledge, skills, and experiences.

WORKING MEMORY Atkinson and Shiffrin saw short-term memory merely as a space for briefly storing recent thoughts and experiences. Alan Baddeley and others (Baddeley, 2002; Barrouillet et al., 2011; Engle, 2002) extended our understanding. They began calling this stage **working memory** because it resembled an active "scratch pad" where our brain makes sense of new experiences and links them with our long-term memories. This "system for holding information in mind and working on it" (Oberauer et al., 2018) also functions in the opposite direction, by retrieving and processing previously stored information.

Working memory is influenced by nature and nurture. Some people possess consistently better working memory than others do (Balaban et al., 2019). Heredity is thought to explain about half the person-to-person variation in working memory (Blokland et al., 2011; Knowles et al., 2014). Compared with fraternal twins, identical twins have more similar working memory capacity (Kremen et al. 2007). Moreover, experiments find that people don't expand their overall working memory capacity with training. Practicing on computerized working memory tasks improves performance only on those and closely related tasks (Redick, 2019). But our environment does matter. Children exposed to stressful situations tend to have poorer working memory as adults (Goodman et al., 2019). Even momentary mental fatigue can reduce our working memory capacity (Garrison et al., 2019).

As you integrate new information with your existing long-term memory, your attention is focused. In Baddeley's (2002) model, a *central executive* coordinates this focused processing. Without focused attention, information typically fades. If you think you can look something up later, you attend to it less and forget it more quickly. In one experiment, people read and typed new bits of trivia they would later need, such as "an ostrich's eye is bigger than its brain." If they knew the information would be available online, they invested less energy and remembered it less well (Wegner & Ward, 2013). Online, out of mind.

Right now, your working memory is actively linking what you're reading with what you already knew (Cowan, 2010, 2016; deBettencourt et al., 2019). If you hear "eye-scream," you may encode it as *ice cream* or *I scream,* depending on both your experiences and the context (snack shop or horror film).

For most of you, reading enters sensory memory and then working memory through vision. You might also use auditory rehearsal. Some groups, such as the Inuit in northern Canada, use repeated oral histories to help younger group members remember important information. In one dramatic case, repeated information passed down through many generations was crucial to the archeological discovery of the doomed ships of the 1845 Franklin Expedition—ships that sunk near where local Inuit lived (Neatby & Mercer, 2018). Whether we soak up information using our eyes or our ears, working memory helps us integrate our previous experiences to make smart decisions.

FIGURE 23.3

A modified three-stage information-processing model of memory Atkinson and Shiffrin's classic three-step model helps us to think about how memories are processed, but researchers now recognize other ways that long-term memories form. For example, some information slips into long-term memory via a "back door," without our consciously attending to it *(automatic processing).* And so much active processing occurs in the short-term memory stage that we now call it *working memory.*

RETRIEVAL PRACTICE

RP-3 How does the *working memory* concept update the classic Atkinson-Shiffrin three-stage information-processing model?

RP-4 What are two basic functions of working memory?

ANSWERS IN APPENDIX E

📹 For a 14-minute explanation and demonstration of our memory systems, see the *Video: Models of Memory.*

working memory a newer understanding of short-term memory; conscious, active processing of both incoming sensory information, and information retrieved from long-term memory.

Encoding Memories

Dual-Track Memory: Effortful Versus Automatic Processing

LOQ 23-3 How do explicit and implicit memories differ?

Atkinson and Shiffrin's model focuses on how we process our **explicit** (*declarative*) **memories**—the facts and experiences that we can consciously know and "declare." We encode many explicit memories through conscious **effortful processing.** But our mind has a second, unconscious track. Behind the scenes, other information skips the conscious encoding track and barges directly into storage. This **automatic processing,** which happens without our awareness, produces some things we can know without actively thinking about them (the shape of the cafeteria tray in our hands), and also produces our **implicit** (*nondeclarative*) **memories.**

Our two-track mind, then, helps us encode, retain, and retrieve information through both effortful and automatic tracks. Let's begin by seeing how automatic processing assists the formation of implicit memories.

Automatic Processing and Implicit Memories

LOQ 23-4 What information do we process automatically?

Our implicit memories include *procedural* memory for automatic skills (such as how to ride a bike) and classically conditioned *associations* among stimuli. If once attacked by a dog, years later you may, without recalling the conditioned association, automatically tense up as a dog approaches.

Without conscious effort you also automatically process information about

- *space.* While studying, you often encode the place where certain material appears; later, when you want to retrieve the information, you may visualize its location.

- *time.* While going about your day, you unintentionally note the sequence of its events. Later, realizing you've left your phone somewhere, the event sequence your brain automatically encoded will enable you to retrace your steps.

- *frequency.* You effortlessly keep track of how many times things happen, as when you realize, "This is the third time I've run into her today!"

Our two-track mind engages in impressively efficient information processing. As one track automatically tucks away routine details, the other track is free to focus on conscious, effortful processing. Mental feats such as vision, thinking, and memory may seem to be single abilities, but they are not. Rather, we split information into different components for separate and simultaneous processing.

Effortful Processing and Explicit Memories

Automatic processing happens effortlessly. When you see familiar words on the side of a delivery truck, you can't help but read them and register their meaning. *Learning* to read wasn't automatic. You may recall working hard to pick out letters and connect them to certain sounds. But with experience and practice, your reading became automatic. Imagine now learning to read sentences in reverse:

.citamotua emoceb nac gnissecorp luftroffE

At first, this requires effort, but after enough practice, you would also perform this task much more automatically. We develop many skills in this way: driving, texting, and speaking a new language.

ASK YOURSELF

Does it surprise you to learn how much of your memory processing is automatic? What might life be like if *all* memory processing were effortful?

---

explicit memory retention of facts and experiences that we can consciously know and "declare." (Also called *declarative memory.*)

effortful processing encoding that requires attention and conscious effort.

automatic processing unconscious encoding of incidental information, such as space, time, and frequency, and of familiar or well-learned information, such as sounds, smells, and word meanings.

implicit memory retention of learned skills or classically conditioned associations independent of conscious recollection. (Also called *nondeclarative memory.*)

iconic memory a momentary sensory memory of visual stimuli; a photographic or picture-image memory lasting no more than a few tenths of a second.

echoic memory a momentary sensory memory of auditory stimuli; if attention is elsewhere, sounds and words can still be recalled within 3 or 4 seconds.

SENSORY MEMORY

LOQ 23-5 How does sensory memory work?

Sensory memory (recall Figure 23.3) feeds our active working memory, recording momentary images, sounds, and strong scents. But sensory memory, like a lightning flash, is fleeting. How fleeting? In one experiment, people viewed three rows of three letters each, for only one-twentieth of a second (**FIGURE 23.4**). After the nine letters disappeared, they could recall only about half of them.

Was it because they had insufficient time to glimpse them? No. People actually *could* see and recall all the letters, but only momentarily. We know this because rather than ask them to recall all nine letters at once, researcher George Sperling sounded a high, medium, or low tone immediately *after* flashing the nine letters. The pitch of the tone directed participants to report only the letters of the top, middle, or bottom row, respectively. Now they rarely missed a letter, showing that all nine letters were momentarily available for recall.

Sperling's experiment demonstrated **iconic memory,** a fleeting sensory memory of visual stimuli. For a few tenths of a second, our eyes register a picture-image memory of a scene, and we can recall any part of it in amazing detail. But delaying the tone signal by more than half a second caused the image to fade and memory to suffer. We also have an impeccable, though fleeting, memory for auditory stimuli, called **echoic memory** (Cowan, 1988; Lu et al., 1992). Picture yourself in class being distracted by a text message. If your mildly irked instructor tests you by asking, "What did I just say?" you can recover the last few words from your mind's echo chamber. Auditory echoes tend to linger for 3 or 4 seconds.

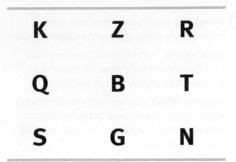

FIGURE 23.4
Total recall—briefly

SHORT-TERM MEMORY CAPACITY

LOQ 23-6 What is our short-term memory capacity?

Recall that short-term memory—and working memory, its actively processing manager—refers to what we can briefly retain. What are the limits of what we can hold in this middle, short-term stage?

George Miller (1956) proposed that we can store about seven pieces of information (give or take two) in short-term memory. Miller's magical number seven is psychology's contribution to the list of magical sevens—the seven wonders of the world, the seven seas, the seven deadly sins, the seven colors of the rainbow, the seven-note musical scale, the seven days of the week—seven magical sevens.

Other research confirms that we can, if nothing distracts us, recall about seven bits of information. But the number varies by task; we tend to remember about six letters and only about five words (Baddeley et al., 1975; Cowan, 2015). And how quickly do our short-term memories disappear? To find out, Lloyd Peterson and Margaret Peterson (1959) asked people to remember three-consonant groups, such as *CHJ*. To prevent rehearsal, the researchers distracted participants (asking them, for example, to start at 100 and begin counting aloud backward by threes). After 3 seconds, people recalled the letters only about half the time; after 12 seconds, they seldom recalled them at all (**FIGURE 23.5**). Without the active processing that we now understand to be a part of our working memory, short-term memories have a limited life.

Working memory capacity varies, depending on age and other factors. Young adults tend to have greater working memory capacity—the ability to juggle multiple items while processing information—than do children and older adults (Bopp & Verhaeghen, 2020; Jaroslawska & Rhodes, 2019). This helps young adults to better retain information and to solve problems creatively (De Dreu et al., 2012; Fenn & Hambrick, 2012; Wiley & Jarosz, 2012). But because task-switching reduces working memory, everyone does better and more efficient work when focused, without

After Miller's 2012 death, his daughter recalled his best moment of golf: "He made the one and only hole-in-one of his life at the age of 77, on the seventh green . . . with a seven iron. He loved that" (quoted by Vitello, 2012).

FIGURE 23.5
Short-term memory decay (Data from Peterson & Peterson, 1959; see also Brown, 1958.)

chunking organizing items into familiar, manageable units; often occurs automatically.

mnemonics [nih-MON-iks] memory aids, especially those techniques that use vivid imagery and organizational devices.

spacing effect the tendency for distributed study or practice to yield better long-term retention than is achieved through massed study or practice.

testing effect enhanced memory after retrieving, rather than simply rereading, information. Also sometimes referred to as a *retrieval practice effect* or *test-enhanced learning*.

distractions, on one task at a time (Steyvers et al., 2019). *The bottom line:* It's probably a bad idea to try to watch a live stream, text your friends, and write a psychology paper simultaneously, with your attention switching among them (Willingham, 2010)!

Working memory capacity appears to reflect intelligence level (Cowan, 2008; Shelton et al., 2010). Imagine seeing a letter of the alphabet, then a simple question, then another letter, followed by another question, and so on. In such experiments, those who could juggle the most mental balls—who could remember the most letters despite the interruptions—tended in everyday life to exhibit high intelligence and an ability to maintain their focus (Kane et al., 2007; Unsworth & Engle, 2007). When beeped to report in at various times, they were less likely than others to report that their mind was wandering.

RETRIEVAL PRACTICE

RP-5 What is the difference between *automatic* and *effortful* processing, and what are some examples of each?

RP-6 At which of Atkinson-Shiffrin's three memory stages would *iconic* and *echoic* memory occur?

ANSWERS IN APPENDIX E

For a review of memory stages and a test of your own short-term memory capacity, visit *Topic Tutorial: PsychSim6, Short-Term Memory.*

EFFORTFUL PROCESSING STRATEGIES

LOQ **23-7** What are some effortful processing strategies that can help us remember new information?

Several effortful processing strategies boost our ability to form new memories. Later, when we try to retrieve a memory, these strategies can make the difference between success and failure.

Chunking Glance for a few seconds at the first set of letters (row 1) in **FIGURE 23.6,** then look away and try to reproduce what you saw. Impossible, yes? But you can easily reproduce set 2, which is no less complex. Similarly, you will probably remember sets 4 and 6 more easily than the same elements in sets 3 and 5. As this demonstrates, **chunking** information—organizing items into familiar, manageable units—enables us to recall it more easily (Thalmann et al., 2018). Try remembering 43 individual numbers and letters. It would be impossible, unless chunked into, say, seven meaningful chunks, such as "Try remembering 43 individual numbers and letters." 😊

Chunking usually occurs so naturally that we take it for granted. Native English speakers can reproduce perfectly the 150 or so line segments that make up the words in the three phrases of set 6 in Figure 23.6. It would astonish someone unfamiliar with the language. Similarly amazing is a Chinese reader's ability to glance at **FIGURE 23.7** and then reproduce all the strokes, or a varsity basketball player's recall of all the players' positions after a 4-second peek at a picture of a basketball play (Allard & Burnett, 1985). We all remember information best when we can organize it into personally meaningful arrangements.

1. M ᗡ ∀ ⋝ ᴚ W ⊥

2. W G V S R M T

3. VRESLI UEGBN GSORNW CDOUL LWLE NTOD WTO

4. SILVER BEGUN WRONGS CLOUD WELL DONT TWO

5. SILVER BEGUN WRONGS CLOUD DONT TWO HALF MAKE WELL HAS A EVERY IS RIGHT A DONE LINING

6. WELL BEGUN IS HALF DONE EVERY CLOUD HAS A SILVER LINING TWO WRONGS DONT MAKE A RIGHT

FIGURE 23.6

Chunking effects Organizing information into meaningful units, such as letters, words, and phrases, helps us recall it more easily (Hintzman, 1978).

Mnemonics To help encode lengthy passages and speeches, ancient Greek scholars and orators developed **mnemonics.** Many of these memory aids use vivid imagery, because we are particularly good at remembering mental pictures. We more easily remember concrete, visualizable words than we do abstract words (Akpinar & Berger, 2015). (When we quiz you later, which three of these words—*bicycle, void, cigarette, inherent, fire, process*—will you most likely recall?) If you still recall the rock-throwing rioter sentence, it is probably not only because of the meaning you encoded but also because the sentence painted a mental image.

Memory whizzes understand the power of such systems. Star performers in the World Memory Championships do not usually have exceptional intelligence, but rather are superior at using mnemonic strategies (Maguire et al., 2003b). Frustrated by his ordinary memory, science writer Joshua Foer wanted to see how much he could improve it. After a year of intense practice, he won the U.S. Memory Championship, memorizing a pack of 52 playing cards in under two minutes. How did Foer do it? He added vivid new details to memories of a familiar place—his childhood home. Each card, presented in any order, could then match up with the clear picture in his head. As the test subject of his own wild memory experiment, he learned the power of painting pretty pictures in his mind (Foer, 2011).

When combined, chunking and mnemonic techniques can be great memory aids for unfamiliar material. Want to remember the planets in order of distance from the Sun? Think of the mnemonic My Very Educated Mother Just Served Us Noodles (Mercury, Venus, Earth, Mars, Jupiter, Saturn, Uranus, Neptune). Need to recall the names of North America's five Great Lakes? Just remember HOMES (Huron, Ontario, Michigan, Erie, and Superior). In such cases, we chunk information into a more familiar form by creating a sentence from the first letters of the to-be-remembered items.

Hierarchies When people develop expertise in an area, they often process information in *hierarchies* composed of a few broad concepts divided and subdivided into narrower concepts and facts. Organizing knowledge in hierarchies helps us retrieve information efficiently, as Gordon Bower and his colleagues (1969) demonstrated by presenting words either randomly or grouped into categories. When the words were grouped, recall was two to three times better. Such results show the benefits of organizing what you study—of giving special attention to module headings, and, in this text, to numbered Learning Objective Questions. Taking lecture and text notes in outline format—a type of hierarchical organization—may also prove helpful.

ASK YOURSELF

How have you used hierarchies to organize material that you are trying to remember? How would you do so for a section of this module?

DISTRIBUTED PRACTICE

LOQ 23-8 How do distributed practice, deep processing, and making new material personally meaningful aid memory?

We retain information better when our encoding is distributed over time. Experiments have consistently revealed the benefits of this **spacing effect** (Cepeda et al., 2006; Soderstrom et al., 2016). *Massed practice* (cramming) can produce speedy short-term learning and an inflated feeling of confidence. But to paraphrase early memory researcher Hermann Ebbinghaus (1885), those who learn quickly also forget quickly. *Distributed practice* produces better long-term recall. After you've studied long enough to master the material, further study at that time becomes inefficient. Better to spend that extra reviewing time later—a day later if you need to remember something 10 days hence, or a month later if you need to remember something 6 months hence (Cepeda et al., 2008). The spacing effect is one of psychology's most reliable findings, and it extends to motor skills and online game performance, too (Stafford & Dewar, 2014). Memory researcher Henry Roediger (2013) sums it up: "Hundreds of studies have shown that distributed practice leads to more durable learning."

One effective way to distribute practice is *repeated* self-testing, a phenomenon that researchers Roediger and Jeffrey Karpicke (2006, 2018) have called the **testing effect.** Testing does more than assess learning and memory: It improves them (Pan & Rickard, 2018). In this book, the Retrieval Practice questions and Review sections, including the Master the Material questions, offer opportunities to improve learning and memory. Better to practice retrieval (as any exam will demand) than to merely reread material (which may lull you into a false sense of mastery). Roediger (2013) explains, "Two techniques that students frequently report using for studying—highlighting (or underlining) text and rereading text—[have been found] ineffective." Happily, "retrieval practice (or testing) is a powerful and general strategy for learning." As another memory expert

FIGURE 23.7 An example of chunking—for those who read Chinese After looking at these characters, can you reproduce them exactly? If so, you can read Chinese.

春夏秋冬

The acronym of *The Only Day After Yesterday:* TODAY.

"The mind is slow in unlearning what it has been long in learning." — Roman philosopher Seneca (4 B.C.E.–65 C.E.)

For suggestions on how to apply the *testing effect* to your own learning, watch my [DM's] 5-minute *Video: Make Things Memorable* or at tinyurl.com /HowToRemember.

explained, "What we recall becomes more recallable" (Bjork, 2011). No wonder daily quizzing improves introductory psychology students' course performance (Batsell et al., 2017; Pennebaker et al., 2013).

The point to remember: Spaced study and self-assessment beat cramming and rereading. Practice may not make perfect, but smart practice—occasional rehearsal with self-testing—makes for lasting memories.

LEVELS OF PROCESSING Memory researchers have discovered that we process verbal information at different levels, and that depth of processing affects our long-term retention. **Shallow processing** encodes on an elementary level, such as a word's letters or, at a more intermediate level, a word's sound. Thus, we may type *there* when we mean *their,* *write* when we mean *right,* and *two* when we mean *too.* **Deep processing** encodes *semantically,* based on the meaning of the words. The deeper (more meaningful) the processing, the better our retention.

In one classic experiment, researchers Fergus Craik and Endel Tulving (1975) flashed words at viewers. Then they asked them questions that would elicit different levels of processing. To experience the task yourself, rapidly answer the questions in **TABLE 23.1**.

TABLE 23.1			
Sample Questions to Elicit Different Levels of Processing	**Word Flashed**	**Yes**	**No**
Most shallow: Is the word in capital letters?	CHAIR	_____	_____
Shallow: Does the word rhyme with train?	brain	_____	_____
Deep: Would the word fit in this sentence? The girl put the _____ on the table.	puzzle	_____	_____

Which type of processing would best prepare you to recognize the words at a later time? In Craik and Tulving's experiment, the deeper, semantic processing triggered by the third question yielded a much better memory than did the shallower processing elicited by the second question or the very shallow processing elicited by the first question (which was especially ineffective).

MAKING MATERIAL PERSONALLY MEANINGFUL If new information is neither meaningful nor related to our experience, we have trouble processing it. Imagine being asked to remember the following recorded passage:

> The procedure is actually quite simple. First you arrange things into different groups. Of course, one pile may be sufficient depending on how much there is to do. . . . After the procedure is completed, one arranges the materials into different groups again. Then they can be put into their appropriate places. Eventually they will be used once more and the whole cycle will then have to be repeated. However, that is part of life.

When some students heard the paragraph you have just read, without a meaningful context, they remembered little of it (Bransford & Johnson, 1972). When others were told the paragraph described washing clothes (something meaningful), they remembered much more of it—as you probably could now after rereading it.

Can you repeat the sentence about the angry rioter that we gave you at this module's beginning? Perhaps, like those in an experiment by William Brewer (1977), you recalled the sentence by the meaning you encoded when you read it (for example, "The angry rioter threw the rock *through* the window") and not as it was written ("The angry rioter threw the rock *at* the window"). Referring to such mental mismatches, some researchers have likened our minds to theater directors who, given a raw script, imagine the finished stage production (Bower & Morrow, 1990). Asked later what we heard or read, we recall not the literal text but *what we encoded.* Thus, studying for an exam, you may remember your lecture notes rather than the lecture itself.

In the discussion of mnemonics, we gave you six words and told you we would quiz you about them later. How many of these words can you now recall? Of these, how many are high-imagery words? How many are low-imagery?[1]

---

[1]bicycle, void, cigarette, inherent, fire, process.

We can avoid significant mismatches by rephrasing what we see and hear into meaningful terms. From his experiments on himself, Ebbinghaus estimated that, compared with learning nonsense syllables, learning meaningful material required one-tenth the effort. As memory researcher Wayne Wickelgren (1977, p. 346) noted, "The time you spend thinking about material you are reading and relating it to previously stored material is about the most useful thing you can do in learning any new subject matter."

Psychologist-actor team Helga Noice and Tony Noice (2006) have described how actors inject meaning into the daunting task of learning "all those lines." They do it by first coming to understand the flow of meaning: "One actor divided a half-page of dialogue into three [intentions]: 'to flatter,' 'to draw him out,' and 'to allay his fears.'" With this meaningful sequence in mind, the actor more easily remembered the lines.

Most people excel at remembering personally relevant information. Asked how well certain adjectives describe a stranger, we often forget them; asked how well the adjectives describe us, we often remember them. To remember their passwords, people often use self-relevant information (Taylor & Garry, 2019). The tendency to remember self-relevant information, called the *self-reference effect,* is especially strong in individualist Western cultures (Jiang et al., 2019; Symons & Johnson, 1997). In contrast, people from collectivist Eastern cultures tend to remember self-relevant and family-relevant information equally well (Sparks et al., 2016). Knowing this, you can understand why some people best retain information deemed "relevant to me," while others are also skilled at remembering information relevant to "my family."

The point to remember: You can profit from taking time to find personal meaning in what you are studying.

> **shallow processing** encoding on a basic level, based on the structure or appearance of words.
>
> **deep processing** encoding semantically, based on the meaning of the words; tends to yield the best retention.

RETRIEVAL PRACTICE

RP-7 Which strategies are better for long-term retention: cramming and rereading material, or spreading out learning over time and repeatedly testing yourself?

RP-8 If you try to make the material you are learning personally meaningful, are you processing at a shallow or a deep level? Which level leads to greater retention?

ANSWERS IN APPENDIX E

MODULE

23 REVIEW Studying and Encoding Memories

LEARNING OBJECTIVES

Test Yourself Answer these repeated Learning Objective Questions on your own (before checking the answers in Appendix D) to improve your retention of the concepts (McDaniel et al., 2009, 2015).

LOQ 23-1 What is *memory,* and how is it measured?

LOQ 23-2 How do memory models help us study memory, and how has later research updated the three-stage information-processing model?

LOQ 23-3 How do explicit and implicit memories differ?

LOQ 23-4 What information do we process automatically?

LOQ 23-5 How does sensory memory work?

LOQ 23-6 What is our short-term memory capacity?

LOQ 23-7 What are some effortful processing strategies that can help us remember new information?

LOQ 23-8 How do distributed practice, deep processing, and making new material personally meaningful aid memory?

TERMS AND CONCEPTS TO REMEMBER

Test Yourself Write down the definition in your own words, then check your answer.

memory, p. 293
recall, p. 293
recognition, p. 293
relearning, p. 293
encoding, p. 294
storage, p. 294
retrieval, p. 294
parallel processing, p. 294
sensory memory, p. 294
short-term memory, p. 294
long-term memory, p. 294
working memory, 295
explicit memory, p. 296

effortful processing, p. 296
automatic processing, p. 296
implicit memory, p. 296
iconic memory, p. 296
echoic memory, p. 296
chunking, p. 298
mnemonics [nih-MON-iks], p. 298
spacing effect, p. 298
testing effect, p. 298
shallow processing, p. 301
deep processing, p. 301

MASTER THE MATERIAL

Test Yourself Answer the following questions on your own first, then check your answers in Appendix E.

1. A psychologist who asks you to write down as many objects as you can remember having seen a few minutes earlier is testing your _____.

2. The psychological terms for taking in information, retaining it, and later getting it back out are _____, _____, and _____.

3. The concept of working memory

   a. clarifies the idea of short-term memory by focusing on the active processing that occurs in this stage.

   b. splits short-term memory into two substages—sensory memory and iconic memory.

   c. splits short-term memory into two types: implicit and explicit memory.

   d. clarifies the idea of short-term memory by focusing on space, time, and frequency.

4. Sensory memory may be visual (_____ memory) or auditory (_____ memory).

5. Our short-term memory for new information is limited to about _____ bits of information.

6. Memory aids that use visual imagery or other organizational devices are called _____.

Continue testing yourself with 🎓 **LearningCurve** or 🎓 **Achieve Read & Practice** to learn and remember most effectively.

MODULE

(24) Storing and Retrieving Memories

Memory Storage

LOQ **24-1** What is the capacity of long-term memory? Are our long-term memories processed and stored in specific locations?

In Arthur Conan Doyle's *A Study in Scarlet,* Sherlock Holmes offers a popular theory of memory capacity:

> [A] brain originally is like a little empty attic, and you have to stock it with such furniture as you choose. . . . It is a mistake to think that that little room has elastic walls and can distend to any extent. Depend upon it, there comes a time when for every addition of knowledge you forget something that you knew before.

Contrary to Holmes' "memory model," our brain is *not* like an attic, which once filled can store more items only if we discard old ones. Our capacity for storing long-term memories is essentially limitless. One research team, after studying the brain's neural connections, estimated its storage capacity as "in the same ballpark as the World Wide Web" (Sejnowski, 2016).

Retaining Information in the Brain

I [DM] marveled at my aging mother-in-law, a retired pianist and organist. At age 88, her blind eyes could no longer read music. But let her sit at a keyboard and she would flawlessly play any of hundreds of hymns, including ones she had not thought of for 20 years. Where did her brain store those thousands of sequenced notes?

For a time, some surgeons and memory researchers marveled at patients' apparently vivid memories triggered by brain stimulation during surgery. Did this prove that our whole past, not just well-practiced music, is "in there," in complete detail, just waiting to be relived? On closer analysis, the seeming flashbacks appeared to have been invented, not a vivid reliving of long-forgotten experiences (Loftus & Loftus, 1980). In a further demonstration that memories do not reside in single, specific spots, psychologist Karl Lashley (1950) trained rats to find their way out of a maze, then surgically removed pieces of their brain's cortex and retested their memory. No matter which small brain section he removed, the rats retained at least a partial memory of how to navigate the maze. Memories *are* brain-based, but the brain distributes the components of a memory across a network of locations. These specific locations include some of the neural circuitry involved in the original experience: Some brain cells that fire when we experience something fire again when we recall it (Miller, 2012a; Miller et al., 2013).

 semantic memory explicit memory of facts and general knowledge; one of our two conscious memory systems (the other is *episodic memory*).

episodic memory explicit memory of personally experienced events; one of our two conscious memory systems (the other is *semantic memory*).

hippocampus a neural center located in the limbic system; helps process explicit (conscious) memories—of facts and events—for storage.

memory consolidation the neural storage of a long-term memory.

The point to remember: Despite the brain's vast storage capacity, we do not store information as libraries store their books, in single, precise locations. Instead, brain networks encode, store, and retrieve the information that forms our complex memories.

EXPLICIT MEMORY SYSTEM: THE FRONTAL LOBES AND HIPPOCAMPUS

LOQ 24-2 What roles do the frontal lobes and hippocampus play in memory processing?

Explicit, conscious memories are either **semantic** (facts and general knowledge) or **episodic** (experienced events). The network that processes and stores new explicit memories for facts and episodes includes your frontal lobes and hippocampus. When you summon up a mental encore of a past experience, many brain regions send input to your prefrontal cortex (the front part of your frontal lobes) for working memory processing (de Chastelaine et al., 2016; Michalka et al., 2015). The left and right frontal lobes process different types of memories. Recalling a password and holding it in working memory, for example, would activate the left frontal lobe. Calling up a visual party scene would more likely activate the right frontal lobe. And women, whose episodic memory surpasses men's, are most likely to accurately remember what happened at the party (Asperholm et al., 2019).

Cognitive neuroscientists have found that the **hippocampus,** a temporal lobe neural structure located in the limbic system, can be likened to a "save" button for explicit memories (**FIGURE 24.1**). As children mature, their hippocampus grows, enabling them to construct detailed memories (Keresztes et al., 2017). Brain scans reveal activity in the hippocampus and nearby brain networks as people form explicit memories of names, images, and events (Norman et al., 2019; Terada et al., 2017).

Damage to this structure therefore disrupts the formation and recall of explicit memories. If their hippocampus is severed, chickadees and other birds will continue to cache food in hundreds of places, but later be unable to find them (Kamil & Cheng, 2001; Sherry & Vaccarino, 1989). With left-hippocampus damage, people have trouble remembering verbal information, but they have no trouble recalling visual designs and locations. With right-hippocampus damage, the problem is reversed (Schacter, 1996).

So, the hippocampus is complex, with subregions that serve different functions. One part is active as people and mice learn social information (Okuyama et al., 2016; Zeineh et al., 2003). Another part is active as memory champions engage in spatial mnemonics (Maguire et al., 2003a). The rear area, which processes spatial memory, grows bigger as London cabbies navigate the city's complicated maze of streets (Woolett & Maguire, 2011).

Memories are not permanently stored in the hippocampus. Instead, the hippocampus acts as a loading dock where the brain registers and temporarily holds the elements of a to-be-remembered episode—its smell, feel, sound, and location. Then, like older files shifted to be archived, memories migrate to the cortex for storage. This storage process is called **memory consolidation.**

Sleep supports memory consolidation. In one experiment, students who learned material in a study/sleep/restudy condition remembered material better, both a week and six months later, than did students who studied in both the morning and evening without intervening sleep (Mazza et al., 2016). During deep sleep, the hippocampus processes memories for later retrieval. After a training experience, the greater one's hippocampus activity during sleep, the better the next day's memory will be (Peigneux et al., 2004; Whitehurst et al., 2016). Researchers have watched the hippocampus and brain cortex displaying simultaneous activity rhythms during sleep, as if they were having a dialogue (Euston et al., 2007; Khodagholy et al., 2017). The brain seems to replay the day's experiences as it transfers them to the cortex for long-term storage (Squire & Zola-Morgan, 1991). When our learning is distributed over days rather than crammed into a single day, we experience more sleep-induced memory consolidation. And that helps explain the spacing effect.

> "Our memories are flexible and superimposable, a panoramic blackboard with an endless supply of chalk and erasers."
> — Elizabeth Loftus and Katherine Ketcham, *The Myth of Repressed Memory,* 1994

Roger Harris/Science Source

⊙ **FIGURE 24.1**
The hippocampus Explicit memories for facts and episodes are processed in the hippocampus (orange structures) and fed to other brain regions for storage.

Tim Zurowski/All Canada Photos

Hippocampus hero One contender for champion memorist is a mere birdbrain—the Clark's Nutcracker—which can locate up to 6000 caches of pine seed it had previously buried (Gould et al., 2013; Shettleworth, 1993).

Mark Parisi/offthemark.com

flashbulb memory a clear memory of an emotionally significant moment or event.

long-term potentiation (LTP) an increase in a nerve cell's firing potential after brief, rapid stimulation; a neural basis for learning and memory.

IMPLICIT MEMORY SYSTEM: THE CEREBELLUM AND BASAL GANGLIA

LOQ 24-3 What roles do the cerebellum and basal ganglia play in memory processing?

Your hippocampus and frontal lobes are processing sites for your *explicit* memories. But you could lose those newer areas of the brain and still, thanks to automatic processing, lay down *implicit* memories for skills and newly conditioned associations. Joseph LeDoux (1996) recounted the story of a patient with brain damage whose amnesia left her unable to recognize her physician as, each day, he shook her hand and introduced himself. One day, she yanked her hand back, for the physician had pricked her with a tack in his palm. The next time he returned to introduce himself she refused to shake his hand but couldn't explain why. Having been classically conditioned, she just wouldn't do it. Implicitly, she felt what she could not explain.

The *cerebellum* plays a key role in forming and storing the implicit memories created by classical conditioning. With a damaged cerebellum, people cannot develop certain conditioned reflexes, such as associating a tone with an impending puff of air—and thus do not blink in anticipation of the puff (Daum & Schugens, 1996; Green & Woodruff-Pak, 2000). Implicit memory formation needs the cerebellum.

The *basal ganglia,* deep brain structures involved in motor movement, facilitate formation of our procedural memories for skills (Mishkin, 1982; Mishkin et al., 1997). The basal ganglia receive input from the cortex, but do not return the favor by sending information back to the cortex for conscious awareness of procedural learning. If you have learned how to ride a bike, thank your basal ganglia.

Our implicit memory system, enabled by these more ancient brain areas, helps explain why the reactions and skills we learned during infancy reach far into our future. Yet as adults, our *conscious* memory of our first four years is largely blank—due to *infantile amnesia.* As an adult, my [ND's] daughter, Bevy, will not consciously remember her happy visit to Hong Kong Disneyland at age 2. Two influences contribute to infantile amnesia: First, we index much of our explicit memory with a command of language that young children do not possess. Second, the hippocampus is one of the last brain structures to mature, and as it does, more gets retained (Akers et al., 2014).

RETRIEVAL PRACTICE

RP-1 Which parts of the brain are important for *implicit* memory processing, and which parts play a key role in *explicit* memory processing?

RP-2 Your friend has experienced brain damage in an accident. He can remember how to tie his shoes but has a hard time remembering anything you tell him during a conversation. How can implicit versus explicit information processing explain what's going on here?

ANSWERS IN APPENDIX E

THE AMYGDALA, EMOTIONS, AND MEMORY

LOQ 24-4 How do emotions affect our memory processing?

Our emotions trigger stress hormones that influence memory formation. When we are excited or stressed, these hormones make more glucose energy available to fuel brain activity, signaling the brain that something important is happening. Moreover, stress hormones focus memory. Stress provokes the *amygdala* (two limbic system, emotion-processing clusters) to initiate a *memory trace*—a lasting physical change as the memory forms—that boosts activity in the brain's memory-forming areas (Buchanan, 2007; Kensinger, 2007) (**FIGURE 24.2**). It's as if the amygdala says, "Brain, encode this moment for future reference!" The result? Emotional arousal can sear certain events into the brain, while disrupting memory for irrelevant events (Brewin et al., 2007; McGaugh, 2015).

Significantly stressful events can form almost unforgettable memories. After a traumatic experience—a school shooting, a house fire, a rape—vivid recollections of the horrific event may intrude again and again. It is as if they were burned in: "Stronger emotional experiences make for stronger, more reliable memories," noted James McGaugh (1994, 2003). Such experiences even strengthen recall for relevant, immediately

FIGURE 24.2
Review key memory structures in the brain
Frontal lobes and *hippocampus:* explicit memory formation
Cerebellum and *basal ganglia:* implicit memory formation
Amygdala: emotion-related memory formation

preceding events (Dunsmoor et al., 2015: Jobson & Cheraghi, 2016). This makes adaptive sense: By waving warning flags, memory protects us from future dangers (Leding, 2019).

But emotional events produce tunnel vision memory. They focus our attention and recall on high priority information, and reduce our recall of irrelevant details (Mather & Sutherland, 2012). Whatever captures our attention gets well recalled, at the expense of the surrounding context.

Emotion-triggered hormonal changes help explain why we long remember exciting or shocking events, such as our first kiss or our whereabouts when learning of a loved one's death. Where were you, for example, when you learned that Donald Trump was elected U.S. president in 2016? In a 2006 Pew survey, 95 percent of American adults said they could recall exactly where they were or what they were doing when they first heard the news of the 9/11 terrorist attacks. This perceived clarity of memories of surprising, significant events leads some psychologists to call them **flashbulb memories.**

Our flashbulb memories are noteworthy for their vividness and our confidence in them. But as we relive, rehearse, and discuss them, even these memories may come to err. With time, some errors crept into people's 9/11 recollections (compared with their earlier reports taken right afterward). Mostly, however, people's memories of 9/11 remained consistent over the next ten years (Hirst et al., 2015).

Dramatic experiences remain clear in our memory in part because we rehearse them (Hirst & Phelps, 2016). We think about them and describe them to others. Memories of personally important experiences also endure (Storm & Jobe, 2012; Talarico & Moore, 2012). Compared with non-Catholics, devout Catholics recalled better the resignation of Pope Benedict XVI (Curci et al., 2015). A similar memory boost occurred following Japan's 2011 Fukishima nuclear disaster (Talarico et al., 2019). In Germany, repeated political discussions about the dangers of nuclear energy led to longer-lasting memories of the disaster than in the Netherlands, where fewer political discussions occurred.

Synaptic Changes

LOQ **24-5** How do changes at the synapse level affect our memory processing?

As you now think and learn about memory processes, your flexible brain is changing. Given increased activity in particular pathways, neural interconnections are forming and strengthening.

The quest to understand the physical basis of memory—how information becomes embedded in brain matter—has sparked study of the synaptic meeting places where neurons communicate with one another via their neurotransmitter messengers. Eric Kandel and James Schwartz (1982) recruited a seemingly unlikely candidate for memory research by observing synaptic changes during learning in the neurons of the California sea slug, *Aplysia*. A sea slug is a simple animal, with a mere 20,000 or so unusually large and accessible nerve cells. It can be classically conditioned (with mild electric shock) to reflexively withdraw its gills when squirted with water, much as a soldier traumatized by combat might jump at the sound of a firecracker. When learning occurs, Kandel and Schwartz discovered, the slug releases more of the neurotransmitter *serotonin* into certain neurons. These cells' synapses then become more efficient at transmitting signals. Experience and learning can increase—even double—the number of synapses, even in slugs (Kandel, 2012).

In experiments with people, rapidly stimulating certain memory-circuit connections has increased their sensitivity for hours or even weeks to come. The sending neuron now needs less prompting to release its neurotransmitter, and more connections exist between neurons. This increased efficiency of potential neural firing, called **long-term potentiation (LTP),** provides a neural basis for learning and remembering associations (Lynch, 2002; Whitlock et al., 2006) (**FIGURE 24.3**). Several lines of evidence confirm that LTP is a physical basis for memory. For example, drugs that block LTP interfere with learning (Lynch & Staubli, 1991). Drugs that mimic what happens during learning increase LTP (Harward et al., 2016). And rats given a drug that enhanced LTP learned a maze with half the usual number of mistakes (Service, 1994).

After LTP has occurred, passing an electric current through the brain won't disrupt old memories. But the current will wipe out very recent memories. Such is the

Which is more important—your experiences or your memories of them?

📺 For an 8-minute examination of emotion's effect on memory, see the *Video: The Role of Emotion.*

Aplysia The California sea slug, which neuroscientist Eric Kandel studied for 45 years, has increased our understanding of the neural basis of learning and memory.

Renata Rodrigues Pereira/Shutterstock

(a)

(b)

From N. Toni et al, *Nature, 402,* Nov. 25, 1999, Dominique Muller

FIGURE 24.3

Doubled receptor sites An electron microscope image (a) shows just one receptor site (gray) reaching toward a sending neuron before long-term potentiation. Image (b) shows that, after LTP, the receptor sites have doubled. This means the receiving neuron has increased sensitivity for detecting the presence of the neurotransmitter molecules that may be released by the sending neuron. (From Toni et al., 1999.)

experience both of laboratory animals and of severely depressed people given *electroconvulsive therapy (ECT).* A blow to the head can do the same. Football players and boxers momentarily knocked unconscious typically have no memory of events just before the knockout (Yarnell & Lynch, 1970). Their working memory had no time to consolidate the information into long-term memory before the lights went out. I [ND] can confirm this from having been knocked unconscious while playing high school football (in what turned out to be my final game).

Recently, I [DM] did a little test of memory consolidation. While on an operating table for a basketball-related tendon repair, I was given a face mask and soon could smell the anesthesia gas. "So how much longer will I be with you?" I asked the anesthesiologist (knowing that our last seconds before falling asleep go unremembered). My last moment of memory was her answer: "About 10 seconds." My brain spent that 10 seconds consolidating a memory for her 2-second answer, but could not tuck any further memory away before I was out cold.

Some memory-biology explorers have helped found companies that are competing to develop memory-altering drugs. The target market for memory-boosting drugs is massive: people with Alzheimer's disease or the *mild cognitive impairment* that often becomes Alzheimer's, people with more typical age-related memory decline, and anyone who simply wants a better memory. Meanwhile, students can already strive to boost one safe and free memory enhancer: effective study techniques followed by adequate *sleep!*

One approach to improving memory focuses on drugs that boost the LTP-enhancing neurotransmitter *glutamate* (Lynch et al., 2011). Another approach involves developing drugs that boost production of CREB, a protein that also enhances the LTP process (Fields, 2005). Boosting CREB production might trigger increased production of other proteins that help reshape synapses and transfer short-term memories into long-term memories.

Some of us may wish for memory-*blocking* drugs that, when taken after a traumatic experience, might blunt intrusive memories (Adler, 2012; Kearns et al., 2012). In experiments, victims of traumatic events such as car accidents and rapes received, on 6 to 10 occasions following their horrific event, either one such drug, propranolol, or a placebo. Later testing for signs of stress revealed a greater reduction in the drug-treated group (Brunet et al., 2018; Pitman et al., 2002).

FIGURE 24.4 summarizes the brain's two-track memory processing and storage system for implicit (automatic) and explicit (effortful) memories. *The bottom line:* Learn something and you change your brain a little.

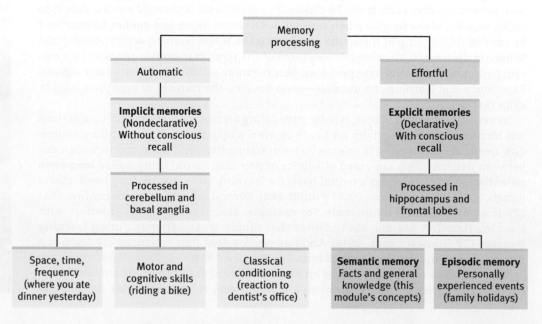

FIGURE 24.4

Our two memory systems

RP-3 Which brain area responds to stress hormones by helping to create stronger memories?

RP-4 Increased efficiency at the synapses is evidence of the neural basis of learning and memory. This is called _____-_____ _____.

ANSWERS IN APPENDIX E

priming the activation, often unconsciously, of particular associations in memory.

Memory Retrieval

After the magic of brain encoding and storage, we still have the daunting task of retrieving the information. What triggers retrieval?

Retrieval Cues

LOQ **24-6** How do external cues, internal emotions, and order of appearance influence memory retrieval?

Imagine a spider suspended in the middle of her web, held up by the many strands extending outward from her in all directions to different points. If you were to trace a pathway to the spider, you would first need to locate an anchor point and then follow the strand into the web.

The process of retrieving a memory follows a similar principle, because memories are held in storage by a web of associations, each piece of information interconnected with others. When you encode into memory a target piece of information, such as the name of the person sitting next to you in class, you associate with it other bits of information about your surroundings, mood, seating position, and so on. These bits can serve as *retrieval cues* that you can later use to access the information. The more retrieval cues you have, the better your chances of finding a route to the suspended memory. Thus, meeting someone and being told either his occupation (baker) or name (Baker), we would—though the words are the same—better remember his occupation, with its richer network of associations (Cohen, 1990).

We need to retrieve memories for both our past (called *retrospective memory*) and our intended future actions *(prospective memory)*. To remember to do something (say, to text someone after class), one effective strategy is to mentally associate the act with a cue (perhaps putting your phone on the desk) (Rogers & Milkman, 2016). It pays to plan ahead, which helps explain why people spend more time thinking about their future than their past (Anderson & McDaniel, 2019).

The best retrieval cues come from associations we form at the time we encode a memory—smells, tastes, and sights that can evoke our memory of the associated person or event (Tamminen & Mebude, 2019). To call up visual cues when trying to recall something, we may mentally place ourselves in the original context. After losing his sight, British scholar John Hull (1990, p. 174) described his difficulty recalling such details:

> I knew I had been somewhere, and had done particular things with certain people, but where? I could not put the conversations . . . into a context. There was no background, no features against which to identify the place. Normally, the memories of people you have spoken to during the day are stored in frames which include the background.

To help people recall older memories, *reminiscence therapy* uses the power of retrieval cues (İnel Manav & Simsek, 2019; Park et al., 2019). One study had older people with Alzheimer's disease spend time in a room styled as a 1950s museum, filled with sights, sounds, and smells that triggered their youthful memories (Kirk et al., 2019). Compared with people who received standard assistive care, those who experienced the immersive reminiscence therapy performed better on memory tests. Retrieval cues helped them regain memories.

PRIMING Often our associations are activated without our awareness. Philosopher-psychologist William James referred to this process, which we call **priming,** as the "wakening of associations." After seeing or hearing the word *rabbit*, we are later more likely to spell the spoken word *hair/hare* as *h-a-r-e*, even if we don't recall seeing or hearing *rabbit* (Bower, 1986) **(FIGURE 24.5)**.

"Memory is not like a container that gradually fills up; it is more like a tree growing hooks onto which memories are hung."
— Peter Russell, *The Brain Book,* 1979

For an 8-minute synopsis of how we access what's stored in our brain, see the *Video: Memory Retrieval.*

⊕ **FIGURE 24.5**
Priming associations unconsciously activates related associations

Seeing or hearing the word *rabbit*

Activates concept

Primes spelling the spoken word *hair/hare* as *h-a-r-e*

Ask a friend three rapid-fire questions:
1. What color is snow?
2. What color are clouds?
3. What do cows drink?
If your friend answers "milk" to the third question, you have demonstrated priming.

Priming is often "memoryless memory"—an implicit, invisible memory, without your conscious awareness. If you see a poster of a missing child, you will then unconsciously be primed to interpret an ambiguous adult-child interaction as a possible kidnapping (James, 1986). Although you no longer have the poster in mind, it predisposes your interpretation. Priming can also influence behaviors (Weingarten et al., 2016). Adults and children primed with money-related words and materials change their behavior in various ways, such as by reducing helpfulness (Gasiorowska et al., 2016; Lodder et al., 2019). Money may prime our materialism and self-interest.

CONTEXT-DEPENDENT MEMORY Have you noticed? Putting yourself back in the context where you earlier experienced something can prime your memory retrieval. Remembering, in many ways, depends on our environment (Palmer, 1989). When you visit your childhood home or neighborhood, old memories surface. When scuba divers listened to a word list in two different settings (either 10 feet underwater or sitting on the beach), they recalled more words when later tested where they first heard the list (Godden & Baddeley, 1975).

By contrast, experiencing something outside the usual setting can be confusing. Have you ever run into a former teacher in an unusual place, such as at a store or park? Perhaps you felt a glimmer of recognition, but struggled to realize who it was and how you were acquainted. The **encoding specificity principle** helps us understand how *specific* cues will most effectively trigger that memory. In new settings, you may be missing the memory cues needed for speedy face recognition. Our memories are *context-dependent*, and are affected by the cues we have associated with that context.

In several experiments, Carolyn Rovee-Collier (1993) found that a familiar context could activate memories even in 3-month-olds. After infants learned that kicking would make a crib mobile move (via a connecting ribbon from the ankle), the infants kicked more when tested again in the same crib than when in a different context.

STATE-DEPENDENT MEMORY Closely related to context-dependent memory is *state-dependent memory*. What we learn in one state—be it drunk or sober—may be more easily recalled when we are again in that state. What people learn when drunk they don't recall well in *any* state (alcohol disrupts memory storage). But they recall it slightly better when again drunk. Someone who hides money when drunk may forget the location until drunk again.

Moods also provide an example of memory's state dependence. Emotions that accompany good or bad events become retrieval cues (Gaddy & Ingram, 2014). Thus, our memories are somewhat **mood congruent.** If you've had a bad day—your social media feed showed your friends having fun last night without you, your work boss refuses to give you time off, and your midterms are next week—your gloomy mood may facilitate recalling other bad times. Being depressed sours memories by priming negative associations, which we then use to explain our current mood. In many experiments, people put in a buoyant mood—whether under hypnosis or just by the day's events (a World Cup soccer victory for German participants in one study)—recall the world through rose-colored glasses (DeSteno et al., 2000; Forgas et al., 1984; Schwarz et al., 1987). They recall their behaviors as competent and effective, other people benevolent, happy events more frequent.

"I can't remember what we're arguing about, either. Let's keep yelling, and maybe it will come back to us."

Have you ever noticed that your current mood influences your perceptions of family members? In one study, adolescents' ratings of parental warmth in one week gave little clue to how they would rate their parents 6 weeks later (Bornstein et al., 1991). When teens were down, their parents seemed cruel; as their mood brightened, their parents morphed from devils into angels. We may nod our heads knowingly. Yet, in a good or bad mood, we persist in attributing to reality our own changing judgments, memories, and interpretations. In a bad mood, we may read someone's look as a glare and feel even worse. In a good mood, we may encode the same look as interest and feel even better. Moods magnify.

Mood effects on retrieval help explain why our moods persist. When happy, we recall pleasant events and therefore see the world as a wonderful place, which helps prolong our good mood. When depressed, we recall sad events, which darkens our interpretations of current events. For those of us predisposed to depression, this process can help maintain a vicious, dark cycle.

encoding specificity principle the idea that cues and contexts specific to a particular memory will be most effective in helping us recall it.

mood-congruent memory the tendency to recall experiences that are consistent with one's current good or bad mood.

serial position effect our tendency to recall best the last *(recency effect)* and first *(primacy effect)* items in a list.

ASK YOURSELF

What sort of mood have you been in lately? How has your mood colored your memories, perceptions, and expectations?

SERIAL POSITION EFFECT Another memory-retrieval quirk, the **serial position effect,** explains why we may have large holes in our memory of a list of recent events. Imagine it's your first day in a new job, and your manager is introducing co-workers. As she leads you to meet each person, you silently repeat everyone's name, starting from the beginning. As the last person smiles and turns away, you feel confident you'll be able to greet your new co-workers by name the next day.

Don't count on it. Because you have spent more time rehearsing the earlier names than the later ones, those are the names you'll probably recall more easily the next day. In experiments, when people viewed a list of items (words, names, dates) or experienced a series of odors or tastes, and then immediately tried to recall them in any order, they fell prey to the serial position effect (Daniel & Katz, 2018; Dimsdale-Zucker et al., 2019). They briefly recalled the last items especially quickly and well (a *recency effect*), perhaps because those last items were still in working memory. But after a delay, when their attention was elsewhere, their recall was best for the first items (a *primacy effect;* see **FIGURE 24.6**).

RETRIEVAL PRACTICE

RP-5 What is *priming?*

RP-6 When tested immediately after viewing a list of words, we tend to recall the first and last items best, which is known as the _____ _____ effect.

ANSWERS IN APPENDIX E

For a simulated experiment showing the probability of recalling a specific item from a list, engage online with *Concept Practice: The Serial Position Effect.*

Percentage of words recalled

Immediate recall: last items best (recency effect)

Later recall: only first items recalled well (primacy effect)

Position of word in list

Kevork Djansezian/Getty Images

FIGURE 24.6
The serial position effect Immediately after actor Mahershala Ali made his way down the red carpet at the 2019 Academy Awards, he would probably have best recalled the last few people he greeted *(recency effect).* But later he may have been able to recall the first few people best *(primacy effect).*

24 REVIEW Storing and Retrieving Memories

LEARNING OBJECTIVES

Test Yourself Answer these repeated Learning Objective Questions on your own (before checking the answers in Appendix D) to improve your retention of the concepts (McDaniel et al., 2009, 2015).

LOQ 24-1 What is the capacity of long-term memory? Are our long-term memories processed and stored in specific locations?

LOQ 24-2 What roles do the frontal lobes and hippocampus play in memory processing?

LOQ 24-3 What roles do the cerebellum and basal ganglia play in memory processing?

LOQ 24-4 How do emotions affect our memory processing?

LOQ 24-5 How do changes at the synapse level affect our memory processing?

LOQ 24-6 How do external cues, internal emotions, and order of appearance influence memory retrieval?

TERMS AND CONCEPTS TO REMEMBER

Test Yourself Write down the definition in your own words, then check your answer.

semantic memory, p. 302

episodic memory, p. 302

hippocampus, p. 302

memory consolidation, p. 302

flashbulb memory, p. 304

long-term potentiation (LTP), p. 304

priming, p. 307

encoding specificity principle, p. 309

mood-congruent memory, p. 309

serial position effect, p. 309

MASTER THE MATERIAL

Test Yourself Answer the following questions on your own first, then check your answers in Appendix E.

1. The hippocampus seems to function as a
   a. temporary processing site for explicit memories.
   b. temporary processing site for implicit memories.
   c. permanent storage area for emotion-based memories.
   d. permanent storage area for iconic and echoic memories.

2. Hippocampus damage typically leaves people unable to learn new facts or recall recent events. However, they may be able to learn new skills, such as riding a bicycle, which is an _____ (explicit/implicit) memory.

3. Long-term potentiation (LTP) refers to
   a. emotion-triggered hormonal changes.
   b. the role of the hippocampus in processing explicit memories.
   c. an increase in a cell's firing potential.
   d. aging people's potential for learning.

4. Specific odors, visual images, emotions, or other associations that help us access a memory are examples of _____ _____.

5. When you feel sad, why might it help to look at pictures that reawaken some of your best memories?

6. When tested immediately after viewing a list of words, people tend to recall the first and last items more readily than those in the middle. When retested after a delay, they are most likely to recall
   a. the first items on the list.
   b. the first and last items on the list.
   c. a few items at random.
   d. the last items on the list.

Continue testing yourself with 📚 **LearningCurve** or 📚 **Achieve Read & Practice** to learn and remember most effectively.

25 Forgetting, Memory Construction, and Improving Memory

Forgetting

LOQ 25-1 Why do we forget?

Amid all the applause for memory—all the efforts to understand it, all the books on how to improve it—have any voices been heard in praise of forgetting? William James (1890, p. 680) was such a voice: "If we remembered everything, we should on most occasions be as ill off as if we remembered nothing." Psychologists Robert Bjork and Elizabeth Bjork (2019) agree, calling forgetting "the friend of learning." To discard the clutter of useless information—where we parked yesterday, our old phone number, restaurant orders already cooked and served—is surely a blessing (Nørby, 2015). In the 1920s, Russian journalist and memory whiz Solomon Shereshevsky had merely to listen while other reporters scribbled notes. Although his memory was not perfect, he could—performing in front of a crowd—memorize streams of nonsensical information, such as cantos from Dante's *Inferno* in a language he didn't know (Johnson, 2017). But his junk heap of memories dominated his conscious mind (Luria, 1968). He had difficulty thinking abstractly—generalizing, organizing, evaluating. After reading a story, he could recite it but would struggle to summarize its gist.

Jill Price's incredibly accurate memory of her life's events since age 14 has been closely studied by a University of California at Irvine research team. She reports that her super-memory, called *highly superior autobiographical memory*, interferes with her life, with one memory cuing another (McGaugh & LePort, 2014; Parker et al., 2006): "It's like a running movie that never stops. . . . It is nonstop, uncontrollable, and totally exhausting." Although their memories are not perfect, people like Price are prone to having their mind fill up with information that, once in memory storage, never leaves (Frithsen et al., 2019; Patihis, 2016). In such rare individuals—sixty of whom have been identified worldwide—researchers have identified enlarged brain areas and increased brain activity in memory centers (Dutton, 2018; Mazzoni et al., 2019; Santangelo et al., 2018). A good memory is helpful, but so is the ability to forget. If a memory-enhancing pill ever becomes available, it had better not be *too* effective.

More often, however, our unpredictable memory dismays and frustrates us. Memories are quirky. My [DM's] own memory can easily call up such episodes as that wonderful first kiss with the woman I love, or trivial facts like the air mileage from London to Detroit. Then it abandons me when I discover I have failed to encode, store, or retrieve a student's name or where I left my keys. See how you do with remembering this sentence when we ask you about it later: *The fish attacked the swimmer.*

As we process information, we sift, change, or lose most of it (**FIGURE 25.1**).

Forgetting and the Two-Track Mind

For some, memory loss is severe and permanent. Consider Henry Molaison (or H. M., as he was known until his 2008 death). Surgeons removed much of his hippocampus in order to stop severe seizures. This resulted "in severe disconnection of the remaining hippocampus" from the rest of the brain (Annese et al., 2014). For his remaining 55 years, he was unable to form new conscious memories. Molaison suffered from **anterograde amnesia**—he could remember his past, but he could not form new memories. (Those who cannot remember their past—the old information stored in long-term memory—suffer from **retrograde amnesia**.) He was, as before his surgery, intelligent and did daily crossword puzzles. Yet, reported neuroscientist Suzanne Corkin (2005, 2013), "I've known H. M. since 1962, and he still doesn't know who I am." For about half a minute he could keep something in mind, enough to carry on a conversation. When distracted, he would lose what was just said or what had just occurred. Without the neural tissue for turning new information into long-term memories, he never could name the current U.S. president (Ogden, 2012).

Neurologist Oliver Sacks (1985, pp. 26–27) described another patient, Jimmie, who had anterograde amnesia resulting from brain damage. Jimmie had no memories—thus, no sense of elapsed time—beyond his injury in 1945.

When Jimmie gave his age as 19, Sacks set a mirror before him: "Look in the mirror and tell me what you see. Is that a 19-year-old looking out from the mirror?"

Jimmie turned ashen, gripped the chair, cursed, then became frantic: "What's going on? What's happened to me? Is this a nightmare? Am I crazy? Is this a joke?" When his attention was diverted to some children playing baseball, his panic ended, the dreadful mirror forgotten.

Sacks showed Jimmie a photo from *National Geographic*. "What is this?" he asked.

"It's the Moon," Jimmie replied.

"No, it's not," Sacks answered. "It's a picture of the Earth taken from the Moon."

"Doc, you're kidding! Someone would've had to get a camera up there!"

"Naturally."

"Hell! You're joking—how the hell would you do that?" Jimmie's wonder was that of a bright young man from the 1940s, amazed by his travel back to the future.

"Amnesia seeps into the crevices of our brains, and amnesia heals." — Joyce Carol Oates, "Words Fail, Memory Blurs, Life Wins," 2001

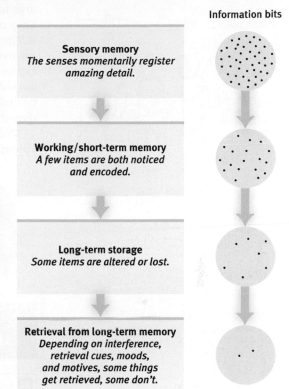

Information bits

Sensory memory
The senses momentarily register amazing detail.

Working/short-term memory
A few items are both noticed and encoded.

Long-term storage
Some items are altered or lost.

Retrieval from long-term memory
Depending on interference, retrieval cues, moods, and motives, some things get retrieved, some don't.

FIGURE 25.1
When do we forget? Forgetting can occur at any memory stage. When we process information, we filter, alter, or lose much of it.

anterograde amnesia an inability to form new memories.

retrograde amnesia an inability to remember information from one's past.

Does the unprepared astronaut illustrate a failure of retrospective or prospective memory?[2]

LEIGHTON

"Oh, is that today?"

Careful testing of these unique people reveals something even stranger: Although incapable of recalling new facts or anything they have done recently, Molaison, Jimmie, and others with similar conditions can learn nonverbal tasks. Shown hard-to-find figures in pictures (in the *Where's Waldo?* series), they can quickly spot them again later. They can find their way to the bathroom, though without being able to tell you where it is. They can learn to read mirror-image writing or do a jigsaw puzzle, and they have even learned complicated *procedural* job skills (Schacter, 1992, 1996; Xu & Corkin, 2001). They can be classically conditioned. However, *they do all these things with no awareness of having learned them.* "Well, this is strange," Molaison said, after demonstrating his nondeclarative memory of skillful mirror tracing. "I thought that would be difficult. But it seems as though I've done it quite well" (Shapin, 2013).

Molaison and Jimmie lost their ability to form new explicit memories, but their automatic processing ability remained intact. Like Alzheimer's patients, whose *explicit* memories for new people and events are lost, they could form new *implicit* memories (Lustig & Buckner, 2004). These patients can learn *how* to do something, but they will have no conscious recall of learning their new skill. Such sad case studies confirm that we have two distinct memory systems, controlled by different parts of the brain.

For most of us, forgetting is a less drastic process. Let's consider some of the reasons we forget.

MEMORIES START TO FADE

> 📺 For a helpful tutorial animation about this type of research method, see the ***Video: Case Studies.***

Encoding Failure

Much of what we sense we never notice, and what we fail to encode, we will never remember (**FIGURE 25.2**). The English novelist and critic C. S. Lewis (1967, p. 107) described the enormity of what we never encode:

> [We are] bombarded every second by sensations, emotions, thoughts . . . nine-tenths of which [we] must simply ignore. The past [is] a roaring cataract of billions upon billions of such moments: Any one of them too complex to grasp in its entirety, and the aggregate beyond all imagination. . . . At every tick of the clock, in every inhabited part of the world, an unimaginable richness and variety of "history" falls off the world into total oblivion.

Age can affect encoding efficiency. The brain areas that jump into action when young adults encode new information are less responsive in older adults. This slower encoding helps explain age-related memory decline (Grady et al., 1995). (For more on aging's effect on memory, see Module 16.)

But no matter how young we are, we selectively attend to few of the myriad sights and sounds continually bombarding us. Consider: You have surely seen the Apple logo thousands of times. Can you draw it? In one study, only 1 of 85 UCLA students (including 52 Apple users) could do so accurately (Blake et al., 2015). Most people also struggle to recall details of other familiar objects, such as their country's coins (Nickerson & Adams, 1979; Richardson, 1993). Without encoding effort, many potential memories never form.

⊙ FIGURE 25.2
Forgetting as encoding failure We cannot remember what we have not encoded.

| External event | → | Sensory memory | → Attention → | Working/ short-term memory | → Encoding → | Long-term memory storage |

Encoding failure leads to forgetting

---

[2]It was this astronaut's prospective memory that failed.

FIGURE 25.3
Ebbinghaus' forgetting curve (Data from Ebbinghaus, 1885.)

Storage Decay

Even after encoding something well, we sometimes later forget it. To study the durability of stored memories, Hermann Ebbinghaus (1885) learned lists of nonsense syllables, such as *YOX* and *JIH,* and measured how much he retained when relearning each list, from 20 minutes to 30 days later. The result was his famous forgetting curve: *The course of forgetting is initially rapid, then levels off with time* (**FIGURE 25.3**; Wixted & Ebbesen, 1991). Another study found a similar forgetting curve for Spanish vocabulary learned in school (Bahrick, 1984). Compared with those just completing a high school or college Spanish course, people 3 years out of school had forgotten much of what they had learned (**FIGURE 25.4**). However, what people remembered then, they still basically remembered 25 and more years later. Their forgetting had leveled off.

One explanation for these forgetting curves is a gradual fading of the physical *memory trace.* Cognitive neuroscientists are getting closer to solving the mystery of the physical storage of memory and are increasing our understanding of how memory storage could decay. Like books you can't find in your campus library, memories may be inaccessible for many reasons. Some were never acquired (not encoded). Others were discarded (stored memories decay). And others are out of reach because we can't retrieve them.

Retrieval Failure

Often, forgetting is not memories faded but memories unretrieved. We store in long-term memory what's important to us or what we've rehearsed. But sometimes important events defy our attempts to access them (**FIGURE 25.5**). How frustrating when a name

FIGURE 25.4
The forgetting curve for Spanish learned in school Three years after completing a Spanish course, people remembered much less (on a vocabulary recognition test) than did those just completing the course, but not *much* less than long-ago students. (Data from Bahrick, 1984.)

FIGURE 25.5
Retrieval failure Sometimes even stored information cannot be accessed, which leads to forgetting.

People who are deaf and fluent in sign language experience a parallel "tip of the fingers" phenomenon (Thompson et al., 2005).

lies poised on the tip of our tongue, just beyond reach. Given retrieval cues (*It begins with an M*), we may easily retrieve the elusive memory. Retrieval problems contribute to the occasional memory failures of older adults, who more frequently are frustrated by tip-of-the-tongue forgetting (Abrams, 2008; Salthouse & Mandell, 2013).

Do you recall the gist of the sentence about the attacked swimmer that we asked you to remember? If not, does the word *shark* serve as a retrieval cue? Experiments show that *shark* (likely what you visualized) more readily retrieves the image you stored than does the sentence's actual word, *fish* (Anderson et al., 1976). (The sentence was, *The fish attacked the swimmer.*)

Retrieval problems occasionally stem from interference and even from motivated forgetting.

INTERFERENCE As you collect more and more information, your mental attic never fills, but it does get cluttered. Your brain tries to keep things tidy: Using a new password weakens your memory of competing old passwords (Wimber et al., 2015). But sometimes the clutter wins, and new and old learning collide. **Proactive** *(forward-acting)* **interference** occurs when prior learning disrupts your recall of new information. If you buy a new combination lock, your well-rehearsed old combination may interfere with your retrieval of the new one.

Retroactive *(backward-acting)* **interference** occurs when new learning disrupts your recall of old information. If someone sings new lyrics to the tune of an old song, you may have trouble remembering the original words. Imagine a second stone tossed in a pond, disrupting the waves rippling out from the first.

Information presented in the hour before sleep suffers less retroactive interference because the opportunity for interfering events is minimized (Mercer, 2015). In a classic experiment, two people each learned some nonsense syllables, day after day (Jenkins & Dallenbach, 1924). Then they tried to recall them after a night's sleep or after remaining awake. As **FIGURE 25.6** shows, forgetting occurred more rapidly after being awake and involved with other activities. The investigators surmised that "forgetting is not so much a matter of the decay of old impressions and associations as it is a matter of interference, inhibition, or obliteration of the old by the new" (1924, p. 612).

FIGURE 25.6
Retroactive interference More forgetting occurred when a person stayed awake and experienced other new material. (Data from Jenkins & Dallenbach, 1924.)

The hour before sleep is a good time to commit information to memory (Scullin & McDaniel, 2010), though information presented in the *seconds* just before sleep is seldom remembered (Wyatt & Bootzin, 1994). If you're considering learning *while* sleeping, forget it. We have little memory for information played aloud in the room during sleep, although the ears do register it (Wood et al., 1992).

Old and new learning do not always compete. Knowing Spanish helped me [ND] pick up some Portuguese when at the 2016 Olympics in Brazil. This phenomenon is called *positive transfer*.

> 🎞 To experience a demonstration and explanation of interference effects on memory, visit *Topic Tutorial: PsychSim6, Forgetting.*

MOTIVATED FORGETTING To remember our past is often to revise it. Years ago, the huge cookie jar in my [DM's] kitchen was jammed with freshly baked chocolate chip cookies. Still more were cooling across racks on the counter. Twenty-four hours later, not a crumb was left. Who had taken them? During that time, my wife, three children, and I were the only people in the house. So while memories were still fresh, I conducted a little memory test. Andy admitted wolfing down as many as 20. Peter thought he had eaten 15. Laura guessed she had stuffed her then-6-year-old body with 15 cookies. My wife, Carol, recalled eating 6, and I remembered consuming 15 and taking 18 more to the office. We sheepishly accepted responsibility for 89 cookies. Still, we had not come close; there had been 160.

Why do our memories fail us? This happens in part because memory is an "unreliable, self-serving historian" (Tavris & Aronson, 2007, p. 6). Consider one study, in which researchers told some participants about the benefits of frequent toothbrushing. Those individuals then recalled (more than others did) having frequently brushed their teeth in the preceding two weeks (Ross et al., 1981).

Peter Johansky/Photolibrary/Getty Images

So why were my family and I so far off in our cookie-consumption estimates? Was it an *encoding* problem? (Did we just not notice what we had eaten?) Was it a storage problem? (Might our memories of cookies, like Ebbinghaus' memory of nonsense syllables, have melted away almost as fast as the cookies themselves?) Or was the information still intact but not *retrievable* because it would be embarrassing to remember?[3]

Sigmund Freud might have argued that our memory systems self-censored this information. He proposed that we **repress** painful or unacceptable memories to protect our self-concept and to minimize anxiety. But the repressed memory lingers, he believed, and can be retrieved by some later cue or during therapy. Repression was central to Freud's psychoanalytic theory of personality and remains a popular idea. Indeed, one Norwegian study found that educated people tend to believe in repressed memories more than do those with less formal education (Magnussen et al., 2006). And an American study revealed that 81 percent of university students, and 60 to 90 percent of therapists (depending on their perspective), believe that "traumatic memories are often repressed" (Otgaar et al., 2019; Patihis et al., 2014a,b). However, increasing numbers of memory researchers think repression rarely, if ever, occurs. Consider the words people later remember. People who have experienced sexual assault, for example, succeed in forgetting neutral words *(salt, plant)*, but they struggle to forget trauma-related words *(intercourse, assault)* (Blix & Brennen, 2011). Trauma releases stress hormones, which causes trauma survivors to attend to and remember the threat (Quaedflieg & Schwabe, 2017). Thus, people often have intrusive, persistent memories of the very same traumatic experiences they would most like to forget (Marks et al., 2018).

RETRIEVAL PRACTICE

RP-1 What are three ways we forget, and how does each of these happen?

RP-2 Freud believed (though many researchers doubt) that we _____ unacceptable memories to minimize anxiety.

ANSWERS IN APPENDIX E

> "Memory of traumatic events is stored differently in the brain. Some [parts] . . . can be recalled in excruciating detail, as if the event just occurred, while others may be forgotten." — Jessica Henderson Daniel, president of the American Psychological Association, 2018, in a statement about sexual assault survivors' testimony

---

[3]One of my cookie-scarfing sons, on reading this in his father's textbook years later, confessed he had fibbed "a little."
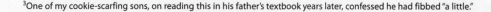

Do people vividly remember—or repress—traumatic experiences? Imagine yourself several hours into Flight AT236 from Toronto to Lisbon. A fractured fuel line begins leaking. Soon the engines go silent and primary electrical power is lost. In the eerie silence, the pilots instruct you and other terrified passengers to don life jackets, and to prepare for ocean impact. Before long, the pilot declares above the passengers' screams and prayers, "About to go into the water." Death awaits.

But no! "We have a runway! Brace! Brace! Brace!" The plane makes a hard landing at an Azores airbase, averting death for all 305 on board.

Among the passengers thinking "I'm going to die" was psychologist Margaret McKinnon. Seizing the opportunity, she tracked down 15 of her fellow passengers to test their trauma memories. Did they repress the experience? No. All exhibited vivid, detailed memories. With trauma comes not repression, but, far more often, "robust" memory (McKinnon et al., 2015).

Stringer/European Pressphoto Agency/Lages/PORTUGAL/Newscom

Memory Construction Errors

LOQ **25-2** How do misinformation, imagination, and source amnesia influence our memory construction? How do we decide whether a memory is real or false?

Nearly two-thirds of Americans agree: "Human memory works like a video camera, accurately recording the events we see and hear so that we can review and inspect them later" (Simons & Chabris, 2011). Actually, memory is not so precise. Like scientists who infer a dinosaur's appearance from its remains, we infer our past from stored information plus what we later imagined, expected, saw, and heard. Memories are constructed: We don't just retrieve memories, we reweave them.

Our memories are like Wikipedia pages, capable of constant revision. When we "replay" a memory, we often replace the original with a slightly modified version, rather like what happens in the telephone game, as a whispered message gets progressively altered when passed from person to person (Hardt et al., 2010). Memory researchers call this **reconsolidation** (Elsey et al., 2018). So, in a sense, said Joseph LeDoux (2009), "your memory is only as good as your last memory. The fewer times you use it, the more pristine it is." This means that, to some degree, "all memory is false" (Bernstein & Loftus, 2009b).

Despite knowing all this, I [DM] rewrote my own past at an international conference, where memory researcher Elizabeth Loftus (2012) spoke. Loftus showed attendees a handful of individual faces that we were later to identify, as if in a police lineup. She then showed us some pairs of faces—one face we had seen earlier and one we had not—and asked us to identify the one we had seen. But one pair she had slipped in included *two* new faces, one of which was rather *like* a face we had seen earlier. Most of us understandably but wrongly identified this face as one we had previously seen. To climax the demonstration, when she showed us the originally seen face and the previously chosen wrong face, most of us picked the wrong face! As a result of our memory reconsolidation, we—an audience of psychologists who should have known better—had replaced the original memory with a false memory.

To understand how to help or hinder memory reconsolidation, neuroscientists are working to identify relevant brain regions and neurochemicals (Bang et al., 2018). And clinical researchers have been experimenting. They ask people to recall a traumatic or negative experience and then disrupt the reconsolidation of that memory with a drug (such as propranolol), a brief, painless electroconvulsive shock, or novel distracting images (Phelps & Hofmann, 2019; Scully et al., 2017; Treanor et al., 2017). Someday it might become possible to use memory reconsolidation in this way to erase specific traumatic memories. Would you wish to erase your troubling memories? If brutally assaulted, would you welcome having your memory of the attack and its associated fears deleted?

reconsolidation a process in which previously stored memories, when retrieved, are potentially altered before being stored again.

misinformation effect occurs when a memory has been corrupted by misleading information.

Leading question:
"About how fast were the cars going when they smashed into each other?"

Image of actual accident

Memory construction

← **FIGURE 25.7**
Memory construction People who viewed a film clip of a car accident and later were asked a leading question recalled a more serious accident than they had witnessed (Loftus & Palmer, 1974).

Misinformation and Imagination Effects

In more than 200 experiments involving more than 20,000 people, Loftus has shown how eyewitnesses reconstruct their memories after a crime or accident. In one important study, two groups of people watched a film clip of a traffic accident and then answered questions about what they had seen (Loftus & Palmer, 1974). Those asked, "About how fast were the cars going when they *smashed* into each other?" gave higher speed estimates than those asked, "About how fast were the cars going when they *hit* each other?" A week later, when asked whether they recalled seeing any broken glass, people who had heard *smashed* were more than twice as likely to report seeing glass fragments (**FIGURE 25.7**). In fact, the clip showed no broken glass.

In many follow-up experiments around the world, others have witnessed an event, received or not received misleading information about it, and then taken a memory test. The repeated result is a **misinformation effect:** Despite feeling confident, we may, when exposed to subtly misleading information, misremember what we've seen or heard (Anglada-Tort et al., 2019; Loftus et al., 1992). Across studies, about half of people show some vulnerability to the misinformation effect (Brewin & Andrews, 2017; Scoboria et al., 2017). A yield sign becomes a stop sign, hammers become screwdrivers, Coke cans become peanut cans, breakfast cereal becomes eggs, and a clean-shaven man morphs into a man with a mustache. Falling for misinformation doesn't mean you have a mushy memory. The misinformation effect is found among people who perform well on other memory measures (Nichols & Loftus, 2019; Patihis et al., 2018). The human mind, it seems, comes naturally equipped with built-in photo-editing software.

So powerful is the misinformation effect that it can influence later attitudes and behaviors (Bernstein & Loftus, 2009a). One experiment falsely suggested to some Dutch university students that, as children, they became ill after eating spoiled egg salad (Geraerts et al., 2008). After absorbing that suggestion, they were less likely to eat egg salad sandwiches, both immediately and 4 months later.

Even repeatedly *imagining* nonexistent actions and events can create false memories. In real life, some people, after suggestive interviews, have even vividly recalled murders or other crimes they didn't commit (Aviv, 2017; Shaw, 2018; Wade et al., 2018).

Misinformation and imagination effects occur partly because visualizing something and actually perceiving it activate similar brain areas (Gonsalves et al., 2004). Imagined events also later seem more familiar, and familiar things seem more real. The more vividly we can imagine things, the more likely they are to become memories (Loftus, 2001; Porter et al., 2000). Telling lies can likewise alter people's memories of the truth (Otgaar & Baker, 2018). Fibbing feeds falsehoods.

"Memory is insubstantial. Things keep replacing it. Your batch of snapshots will both fix and ruin your memory. . . . You can't remember anything from your trip except the wretched collection of snapshots." — Annie Dillard, "To Fashion a Text," 1988

Was Alexander Hamilton a U.S. president? Sometimes our mind tricks us into misremembering dates, places, and names. This often happens because we misuse familiar information. In one study, many Americans mistakenly recalled Alexander Hamilton—whose face appears on the U.S. $10 bill, and who is the subject of Lin-Manuel Miranda's popular Broadway musical—as a U.S. president (Roediger & DeSoto, 2016).

In 2015, *NBC Nightly News* anchor Brian Williams recounted a story about traveling in a military helicopter that was hit with a rocket-propelled grenade. But the event never happened as he described. As memory researcher Christopher Chabris (2015) noted, "A lot of people don't appreciate the extent to which false memories can happen even when we are extremely confident in the memory."

In experiments, researchers have altered photos from a family album to show some family members taking a hot air balloon ride. After viewing these photos (rather than photos showing just the balloon), children reported more false memories of the balloon ride, and indicated high confidence in those memories. When interviewed several days later, *imagination inflation* was evident when they reported even richer details of their false memories (Strange et al., 2008; Wade et al., 2002). Many people—39 percent in one survey—recall improbable first memories from age 2 and before (Akhtar et al., 2018). And in British and Canadian university surveys, nearly one-fourth of students have reported personal memories that they later realized were not accurate (Foley, 2015; Mazzoni et al., 2010). *The bottom line*: Don't believe everything you remember.

Source Amnesia

What is the frailest part of a memory? Its source. We may remember learning something on social media but be uncertain whether it was real or false news. We may dream an event and later be unsure whether it really happened. We may tell a friend some gossip, only to learn we got the news from that friend. Famed child psychologist Jean Piaget was startled as an adult to learn that a vivid, detailed memory from his childhood—a nursemaid's thwarting his kidnapping—was utterly false. He apparently constructed the memory from repeatedly hearing the story (which his nursemaid, after undergoing a religious conversion, later confessed had never happened). In attributing his "memory" to his own experiences, rather than to his nursemaid's stories, Piaget exhibited **source amnesia** (also called *source misattribution*). Misattribution is at the heart of many false memories. Authors, songwriters, and comedians sometimes suffer from it. They think an idea came from their own creative imagination, when in fact they are unintentionally plagiarizing something they earlier read or heard.

Even preschoolers experience source amnesia. In one study, "Mr. Science" engaged preschoolers in activities such as blowing up a balloon with baking soda and vinegar (Poole & Lindsay, 1995, 2001). Three months later, on three successive days, their parents read them a story. It described some things the children had experienced with Mr. Science and some they had not. When asked about an activity that was only in the story—"Did Mr. Science have a machine with ropes to pull?"—4 in 10 children spontaneously recalled engaging in the event.

Source amnesia also helps explain **déjà vu** (French for "already seen"). Two-thirds of us have experienced this fleeting, eerie sense that "I've been in this exact situation before." The key to déjà vu seems to be familiarity with a stimulus and our uncertainty about where we encountered it before (Cleary & Claxton, 2018; Urquhart et al., 2018). Normally, we experience a feeling of *familiarity* (thanks to temporal lobe processing) before we consciously remember details (thanks to hippocampus and frontal lobe processing). When these functions (and brain regions) are out of sync, we may experience a feeling of familiarity without conscious recall. Our amazing brains try to make sense of such an improbable situation, and we get an eerie feeling that we're reliving some earlier part of our life. Our source amnesia forces us to do our best to make sense of an odd moment.

"Do you ever get that strange feeling of vujà dé? Not déjà vu; vujà dé. It's the distinct sense that, somehow, something just happened that has never happened before. Nothing seems familiar. And then suddenly the feeling is gone. Vujà dé." — Comedian George Carlin, *Funny Times*, December 2001

Discerning True and False Memories

Since memory is reconstruction as well as reproduction, we can't be sure whether a memory is real by how real it feels. Much as perceptual illusions may seem like real perceptions, unreal memories *feel* like real memories. Because the misinformation effect and source amnesia happen outside our awareness, it is hard to separate false memories from real ones (Schooler et al., 1986). You can likely recall describing a childhood experience to a friend and filling in memory gaps with reasonable guesses. We all do it. After more retellings, those guessed details—now absorbed into your memory—may feel as real as if you had actually experienced them (Roediger et al., 1993). False memories, like fake diamonds, seem so real.

False memories can be persistent, especially when they align with our beliefs. Such was the case when, in one large experiment, Irish people retained inaccurate memories of false news related to Ireland's 2018 abortion referendum—especially when the false news supported their own views (Murphy et al., 2019).

False memories often retain a false association. Imagine that we were to read aloud a list of words such as *candy, sugar, honey,* and *taste.* Later, we ask you to recognize the presented words from a larger list. If you are at all like the people tested by Henry Roediger and Kathleen McDermott (1995), you would err three out of four times—by falsely remembering a nonpresented similar word, such as *sweet.* We more easily remember the gist than the words themselves.

False memories are socially contagious. When we hear others falsely remember events, we tend to make the same memory mistakes (Roediger et al., 2001). We get confused about where we originally learned about the false event—*Did I already know that or am I learning it from others?*—and adopt others' false memories (Hirst & Echterhoff, 2012). Your Facebook friend may misremember a shy classmate as acting rude, leading you, too, to mistakenly remember the classmate negatively. It's easy to see how false online stories can spread and become false memories.

Memory construction errors also help explain why some people have been sent to prison for crimes they never committed. Of 365 people who were later proven not guilty by DNA testing, 69 percent had been convicted because of faulty eyewitness identification (Innocence Project, 2019; Smalarz & Wells, 2015). It explains why "hypnotically refreshed" memories of crimes so easily incorporate errors, some of which may originate with the hypnotist's leading questions *(Did you hear loud noises?).* Memory construction errors also seem to be at work in many "recovered" memories of childhood abuse. (See Thinking Critically About: Can Memories of Childhood Sexual Abuse Be Repressed and Then Recovered?)

Memory construction errors explain why dating partners who fell in love have *over-estimated* their first impressions of one another *(It was love at first sight),* while those who broke up *underestimated* their earlier liking *(We never really clicked)* (McFarland & Ross, 1987). When we love someone, our memory extinguishes the negative and shines a light on the positive (Cortes et al., 2018). And it explains why people asked how they felt 10 years ago about marijuana or gender issues recalled attitudes closer to their current views than to the views they had actually reported a decade earlier (Markus, 1986). Students who chose to write an essay supporting a higher tuition policy in one experiment constructed a false memory of previously supporting the policy, despite initially opposing it (Rodriguez & Strange, 2015). Ditto for attitudes toward spanking children: People's current views cause them to misremember their previous views (Wolfe & Williams, 2018). People tend to recall having always felt as they feel today (Mazzoni & Vannucci, 2007). As George Vaillant (1977, p. 197) noted after following adult lives through time, "It is all too common for caterpillars to become butterflies and then to maintain that in their youth they had been little butterflies. Maturation makes liars of us all."

ASK YOURSELF

Think of a memory you frequently recall. How might you have changed it without conscious awareness?

> To participate in a simulated experiment on false memory formation, and to review related research, visit *Topic Tutorial: PsychSim6, Can You Trust Your Memory?*

Children's Eyewitness Recall

LOQ 25-4 How reliable are young children's eyewitness descriptions?

If memories can be sincere, yet sincerely wrong, how can jurors decide cases in which children's memories of sexual abuse are the only evidence? "It would be truly awful to ever lose sight of the enormity of child abuse," observed Stephen Ceci (1993). Yet Ceci and Maggie Bruck's (1993, 1995) studies of children's memories have led to awareness of how easily children's memories can be molded. For example, they asked 3-year-olds to show on anatomically correct dolls where a pediatrician had touched them. Of the children who had not received genital examinations, 55 percent pointed to either genital or anal areas.

Eyewitness accuracy is also influenced by our tendency to recall faces of our own race more accurately than faces of other races, known as the *other-race effect.* Among criminal suspects exonerated with DNA evidence after eyewitness misidentification, nearly half were falsely accused after a cross-racial misidentification (Innocence Project, 2019).

source amnesia faulty memory for how, when, or where information was learned or imagined. (Also called *source misattribution.*) Source amnesia, along with the misinformation effect, is at the heart of many false memories.

déjà vu that eerie sense that "I've experienced this before." Cues from the current situation may unconsciously trigger retrieval of an earlier experience.

Can Memories of Childhood Sexual Abuse Be Repressed and Then Recovered?

LOQ 25-3 Why have reports of repressed and recovered memories been so hotly debated?

Two Possible Tragedies:

1. People doubt childhood sexual abuse survivors who tell their secret.

2. Innocent people are falsely accused, as therapists prompt "recovered" memories of childhood sexual abuse:

Well-intentioned therapist

"Victims of sexual abuse often have your symptoms. So maybe you were abused and repressed the memory. Let's see if I can help you recover the memory, by digging back and visualizing your trauma."

Misinformation effect and **source amnesia:** Adult client may form image of threatening person.

With *rehearsal* (repeated therapy sessions), the image grows more vivid.

Client is stunned, angry, and ready to confront or sue the remembered abuser.

Accused person is equally stunned and vigorously denies the accusation of long-ago abuse.

Professional organizations (including the American Medical, American Psychological, and American Psychiatric Associations) are working to find sensible common ground to resolve psychology's "memory war":[1]

- **Childhood sexual abuse happens** and can leave its victims at risk for problems ranging from sexual dysfunction to depression.[2] But there is no "survivor syndrome"—no group of symptoms that lets us spot victims of sexual abuse.[3]
- **Injustice happens.** Innocent people have been falsely convicted. And guilty people have avoided punishment by casting doubt on their truth-telling accusers.
- **Forgetting happens.** Children abused when very young may not have understood the meaning of their experience or remember it. Forgetting long-ago good and bad events is an ordinary part of everyday life.
- **Recovered memories are common.** Cued by a remark or an experience, we may recover pleasant or unpleasant memories of long-forgotten events. But does the unconscious mind forcibly repress painful experiences,

and can these experiences be recovered by therapist-aided techniques?[4] Memories that surface naturally are more likely to be true.[5]
- **Memories of events before age 4 are unreliable.** Infantile amnesia results from not yet developed brain pathways. Most psychologists therefore doubt "recovered" memories of abuse during infancy.[6] The older a child was when suffering sexual abuse, and the more severe the abuse, the more likely it is to be remembered.[7]
- **Memories "recovered" under hypnosis are especially unreliable.**
- **Memories, whether real or false, can be emotionally upsetting.** What was born of mere suggestion can become, like an actual event, a stinging memory that drives bodily stress.[8]

Psychologists question whether *repression* ever occurs.
(See the Personality modules for more on this concept, which is central to Freud's theory.)

Traumatic experiences (witnessing a loved one's murder, being terrorized by a hijacker or rapist, losing everything in a natural disaster) → **TYPICALLY LEAD TO** → vivid, persistent, haunting memories[9]

The Royal College of Psychiatrists Working Group on Reported Recovered Memories of Child Sexual Abuse advised that "when memories are 'recovered' after long periods of amnesia, particularly when extraordinary means were used to secure the recovery of memory, there is a high probability that the memories are false."[10]

---

1. Patihis et al., 2014a. 2. Freyd et al., 2007. 3. Kendall-Tackett et al., 1993. 4. McNally & Geraerts, 2009. 5. Geraerts et al., 2007.
6. Gore-Felton et al., 2000; Knapp & VandeCreek, 2000. 7. Goodman et al., 2003. 8. McNally, 2003, 2007. 9. Porter & Peace, 2007;
Goldfarb et al., 2019. 10. Brandon et al., 1998.

The researchers also studied the effect of suggestive interviewing techniques (Bruck & Ceci, 1999, 2004). In one experiment, children chose a card from a deck of possible happenings, and an adult then read the card to them. For example, "Think real hard, and tell me if this ever happened to you. Can you remember going to the hospital with a mousetrap on your finger?" In interviews, the same adult repeatedly asked children to think about several real and fictitious events. After 10 weeks of this, a new adult asked the same question. The stunning result: 58 percent of preschoolers produced false (often vivid) stories regarding one or more events they had never experienced (Ceci et al., 1994). Here's one:

Darren Matthews/Alamy

> My brother Colin was trying to get Blowtorch [an action figure] from me, and I wouldn't let him take it from me, so he pushed me into the wood pile where the mousetrap was. And then my finger got caught in it. And then we went to the hospital, and my mommy, daddy, and Colin drove me there, to the hospital in our van, because it was far away. And the doctor put a bandage on this finger.

Given such detailed stories, professional psychologists who specialize in interviewing children could not reliably separate the real memories from the false ones. Nor could the children themselves. The above child, reminded that his parents had told him several times that the mousetrap incident never happened—that he had imagined it—protested, "But it really did happen. I remember it!" Unfortunately, this type of error is common. In one analysis of eyewitness data from over 20,000 participants, children regularly identified innocent suspects as guilty (Fitzgerald & Price, 2015). "[The] research," said Ceci (1993), "leads me to worry about the possibility of false allegations. It is not a tribute to one's scientific integrity to walk down the middle of the road if the data are more to one side."

With carefully trained interviewers, both adults and children can, however, be accurate eyewitnesses (Wixted et al., 2018). When questioned about their experiences in neutral words they understand, children often accurately recall what happened and who did it (Brewin & Andrews, 2017; Goodman, 2006). When interviewers have used less suggestive, more effective techniques, even 4- to 5-year-old children have produced more accurate recall (Holliday & Albon, 2004; Pipe et al., 2004). Children are especially accurate when they haven't talked with involved adults prior to the interview and when their disclosure was made in a first interview with a neutral person who asked nonleading questions.

Older adults—especially those whose frontal lobe functioning has declined—are more susceptible than young adults to false memories. This makes older adults more vulnerable to scams, as when a caller falsely claims, "Remember that lottery you entered? You won $4.5 million! To process and deliver your winnings, this lottery requires you to send a $4,500 deposit" (Jacoby & Rhodes, 2006; Roediger & McDaniel, 2007).

RETRIEVAL PRACTICE

RP-3 What—given the commonness of source amnesia—might life be like if we remembered all our waking experiences and all our dreams?

RP-4 Imagine being a jury member in a trial for a parent accused of sexual abuse based on a recovered memory. What insights from memory research should you share with the rest of the jury?

ANSWERS IN APPENDIX E

> Consider how researchers have studied these issues by engaging online with the activity *How Would You Know If People's Memories Are Accurate?*

Improving Memory

LOQ 25-5 How can you use memory research findings to do better in this and other courses?

Biology's findings benefit medicine. Botany's findings benefit agriculture. So, too, can memory researchers' findings benefit education. And they can boost your performance in class and on tests. Here, for easy reference, is a summary of some research-based suggestions that can help you remember information when you need it. The SQ3R—Survey, Question, Read, Retrieve, Review—study technique used in this book incorporates several of these strategies.

Thinking and memory Think actively as you read, by rehearsing and relating ideas, and by making the material personally meaningful. This will yield the best retention.

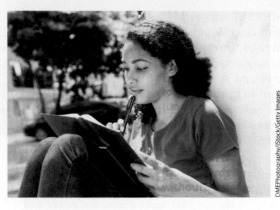

Rehearse repeatedly. To master material, remember the *spacing effect*—use *distributed (spaced) practice.* To learn a concept, give yourself many separate study sessions. Take advantage of life's little intervals—riding a bus, walking across campus, waiting for class to start. New memories are weak; if you exercise them, they will strengthen. Experts recommend retrieving a to-be-remembered item three times before you stop studying it (Miyatsu et al., 2018). Reading complex material with minimal rehearsal yields little retention. Rehearsal and critical reflection help more. As the *testing effect* has shown, it pays to study actively. Mentally saying, writing, or typing information beats silently reading it (MacLeod & Bodner, 2017). This *production effect* explains why we so often learn something best when teaching it, when explaining it to ourselves, or when rehearsing information out loud (Bisra et al., 2018; Forrin & Macleod, 2018; Koh et al., 2018).

The learning power of actively explaining or rehearsing information often goes unnoticed. One experiment randomly assigned students to experience either passive lectures or active learning. The students learned more in the active classroom (but believed they learned less) (Deslauriers et al., 2019). So, you might form a study group where you can verbalize your class material and reap the rewards of social support. But even just taking lecture notes by hand can help you summarize the material in your own words, leading to better retention than typing the lecture verbatim on a laptop. For lectures, "the pen is mightier than the keyboard," note researchers Pam Mueller and Daniel Oppenheimer (2014).

Make the material meaningful. You can build a network of retrieval cues by forming as many associations as possible. Apply the concepts to your own life. Understand and organize information. Form images. Better yet, actually *draw* the concept (Fernandes et al., 2018). Relate the material to what you already know or have experienced. As William James (1890) suggested, "Knit each new thing on to some acquisition already there." Mindlessly repeating someone else's words without taking the time to really understand what they mean won't supply many retrieval cues. On an exam, you may find yourself stuck when a question uses phrasing different from the words you memorized.

Activate retrieval cues. Remember the importance of *context-dependent* and *state-dependent* memory. Mentally re-create the situation and the mood in which your original learning occurred. Jog your memory by allowing one thought to cue the next.

Laptop distraction? In one study of introductory psychology students in a large university course, the average student spent one-third of the class hour browsing online. More time spent online predicted poorer exam performance, even after controlling for aptitude and expressed interest (Ravizza et al., 2017).

Use mnemonic devices. Make up a story that incorporates *vivid images* of the concepts. *Chunk* information. Create a memorable mnemonic. (Did you learn Never Eat Slimy Worms for the four directions clockwise—north, east, south, and west?)

Minimize proactive and retroactive interference. Study before sleep. Do not schedule back-to-back study times for topics that are likely to interfere with each other, such as Spanish and French.

Sleep more. During sleep, the brain reorganizes and *consolidates* information for long-term memory. Sleep deprivation disrupts this process (Frenda et al., 2014; Lo et al., 2016). Even 10 minutes of waking rest enhances memory of what we have read (Dewar et al., 2012). So, after a period of hard study, you might just sit or lie down for a few minutes before tackling the next subject.

Test your own knowledge, both to rehearse it and to find out what you don't yet know. The testing effect is real, and it is powerful. Don't be lulled into overconfidence by your ability to *recognize* information. Test your *recall* using the periodic Retrieval

Practice items, and the numbered Learning Objective and Master the Material questions in the Review sections. Outline sections using a blank page. Define the terms and concepts listed at each section's end before turning back to their definitions. Take practice tests; the online resources that accompany many texts, including this text, are a good source.

ASK YOURSELF

Which three of these study and memory strategies will be most important for you to start using to improve your own learning and retention?

RETRIEVAL PRACTICE

RP-5 Which memory strategies can help you study smarter and retain more information?

ANSWERS IN APPENDIX E

> Evaluate your own memory skills by engaging online with the activity *Assess Your Strengths: How Might You Improve Your Memory?*

---

25 REVIEW Forgetting, Memory Construction, and Improving Memory

LEARNING OBJECTIVES

Test Yourself Answer these repeated Learning Objective Questions on your own (before checking the answers in Appendix D) to improve your retention of the concepts (McDaniel et al., 2009, 2015).

LOQ 25-1 Why do we forget?

LOQ 25-2 How do misinformation, imagination, and source amnesia influence our memory construction? How do we decide whether a memory is real or false?

LOQ 25-3 Why have reports of repressed and recovered memories been so hotly debated?

LOQ 25-4 How reliable are young children's eyewitness descriptions?

LOQ 25-5 How can you use memory research findings to do better in this and other courses?

TERMS AND CONCEPTS TO REMEMBER

Test Yourself Write down the definition in your own words, then check your answer.

anterograde amnesia, p. 311
retrograde amnesia, p. 311
proactive interference, p. 315
retroactive interference, p. 315
repression, p. 315
reconsolidation, p. 316
misinformation effect, p. 316
source amnesia, p. 319
déjà vu, p. 319

MASTER THE MATERIAL

Test Yourself Answer the following questions on your own first, then check your answers in Appendix E.

1. When forgetting is due to encoding failure, information has not been transferred from
   a. the environment into sensory memory.
   b. sensory memory into long-term memory.
   c. long-term memory into short-term memory.
   d. short-term memory into long-term memory.

2. Ebbinghaus' forgetting curve shows that after an initial decline, memory for novel information tends to
   a. increase slightly.
   b. decrease noticeably.
   c. decrease greatly.
   d. level off.

3. You will experience less _____ (proactive/retroactive) interference if you learn new material in the hour before sleep than you will if you learn it before turning to another subject.

4. Freud proposed that painful or unacceptable memories are blocked from consciousness through a mechanism called _____.

5. One reason false memories form is our tendency to fill in memory gaps with our reasonable guesses and assumptions, sometimes based on misleading information. This tendency is an example of
   a. proactive interference.
   b. the misinformation effect.
   c. retroactive interference.
   d. the forgetting curve.

6. Eliza's family loves to tell the story of how she "stole the show" as a 2-year-old, dancing at her aunt's wedding reception. Even though she was so young, Eliza says she can recall the event clearly. How might Eliza have formed this memory?

7. We may recognize a face at a social gathering but be unable to remember how we know that person. This is an example of _____ _____.

8. When a situation triggers the feeling that "I've been here before," you are experiencing _____ _____.

9. Children can be accurate eyewitnesses if
   a. interviewers give the children hints about what really happened.
   b. a neutral person asks nonleading questions soon after the event.
   c. the children have a chance to talk with involved adults before the interview.
   d. interviewers use precise technical and medical terms.

10. Memory researchers involved in the study of memories of abuse tend to *disagree* with some therapists about which of the following statements?
    a. Memories of events that happened before age 4 are not reliable.
    b. We tend to repress extremely upsetting memories.
    c. Memories can be emotionally upsetting.
    d. Sexual abuse happens.

Continue testing yourself with ☒ **LearningCurve** or ☒ **Achieve Read & Practice** to learn and remember most effectively.

fizkes/Shutterstock

Thinking and Language

Throughout history, we humans have both celebrated our wisdom and bemoaned our foolishness. The poet T. S. Eliot was struck by "the hollow men . . . / Headpiece filled with straw." But Shakespeare's Hamlet extolled the human species as "noble in reason! . . . infinite in faculties! . . . in apprehension how like a god!" Throughout this text, we likewise marvel at both our abilities and our errors.

We study the human brain—three pounds of tissue the size of a small meatloaf, yet containing staggeringly complex circuitry. We appreciate the amazing abilities of newborns. We marvel at our visual system, which converts physical stimuli into nerve impulses, distributes them for parallel processing, and reassembles them into colorful perceptions. We ponder our memory's

enormous capacity, and the ease with which our two-track mind processes information, with and without our awareness. Little wonder that our species has had the collective genius to invent the camera, the car, and the computer; to unlock the atom and crack the genetic code; to travel out to space and into our brain's depths.

Yet we also see that in some other ways, we are less than noble in reason. Our species is kin to the other animals, influenced by the same principles that produce learning in rats and pigeons. We note that we not-always-wise humans are easily deceived by perceptual illusions, pseudopsychic claims, and false memories.

In these modules, we encounter further instances of these two aspects of the human condition—the rational and the irrational. We will consider *thinking,* and how we use—and sometimes ignore or misuse—information about the world around us (Module 26). And we

will look at our gift for language and consider how and why it develops (Module 27). Finally, we will reflect on how deserving we are of our species name, *Homo sapiens*—"wise human."

MODULE

26 Thinking

Concepts

(LEARNING OBJECTIVE QUESTION) (LOQ) **26-1** What are *cognition* and *metacognition,* and what are the functions of concepts?

Psychologists who study **cognition** focus on the mental activities associated with thinking, knowing, remembering, and communicating information. One of these activities is **metacognition** (literally "beyond cognition"). Metacognition is cognition about cognition, or thinking about our thinking. Students who use metacognition—who monitor and evaluate their learning—perform better academically (de Boer et al., 2018). (To improve your grades, it helps to figure out what you don't know. Consider using the adaptive quizzing that accompanies this text—LearningCurve in LaunchPad, or Achieve Read & Practice.)

Another of these activities is forming **concepts**—mental groupings of similar objects, events, ideas, or people. The concept *chair* includes many items—a baby's high chair, a reclining chair, a dentist's chair—all for sitting. Concepts simplify our thinking. Imagine life without them. We could not ask a child to "throw the ball" because there would be no concept of *throw* or *ball.* We could not say "I want to earn money," because people aren't born with a concept of *earn* or *money.* Concepts such as *ball* and *money* give us much information with little cognitive effort. And we have a natural bias to separate incoming data into two categories—as when putting people in discrete bins such as "stupid" or "smart," "liberal" or "conservative," "White" or "Black" (Fisher & Keil, 2018).

We often form our concepts by developing a **prototype**—a mental image or best example of a category (Rosch, 1978). People more quickly agree that "a crow is a bird" than that "a penguin is a bird." For most of us, the crow is the birdier bird; it more closely resembles our *bird* prototype. When something closely matches our prototype of a concept, we more readily recognize it as an example of the concept.

When we categorize people, we mentally shift them toward our category prototypes. Such was the experience of Belgian students who viewed ethnically blended faces. When viewing a blended face in which 70 percent of the features were White and 30 percent were Asian, the students categorized the face as White (**FIGURE 26.1**). Later, as their memory shifted toward the White prototype, they were more likely to remember an 80 percent White face than the 70 percent White face they had actually seen (Corneille et al., 2004). Likewise, if shown a 70 percent Asian face, they later remembered a more prototypically Asian face. So, too, with gender: People who viewed 70 percent male faces categorized them as male (no surprise there) and then later misremembered them as even more prototypically male (Huart et al., 2005).

Jeff Kaufman The New Yorker Collection/The Cartoon Bank

"Attention, everyone! I'd like to introduce the newest member of our family."

FIGURE 26.1
Categorizing faces influences recollection Shown a face that was 70 percent White, people tended to classify the person as White and to recollect the face as more White than it was. (Re-creation of experiment courtesy of Olivier Corneille.)

90% WH   80% WH   70% WH   60% WH   50%/50%   60% AS   70% AS   80% AS   90% AS

FaceGen TM

Move away from our prototypes, and category boundaries may blur. Is a tomato a fruit? Is a 16-year-old female a girl or a woman? Is a whale a fish or a mammal? Because a whale fails to match our *mammal* prototype, we are slower to recognize it as a mammal. Similarly, when symptoms don't fit one of our disease prototypes, we are slow to perceive an illness (Bishop, 1991). People whose heart attack symptoms (shortness of breath, exhaustion, a dull weight in the chest) don't match their *heart attack* prototype (sharp chest pain) may not seek help. And when behaviors don't fit our *discrimination* prototypes—of White against Black, male against female, young against old—we often fail to notice prejudice. People more easily detect male prejudice against females than female against males or female against females (Cunningham et al., 2009; Inman & Baron, 1996). Although concepts speed and guide our thinking, they don't always make us wise.

Problem Solving: Strategies and Obstacles

LOQ **26-2** What cognitive strategies assist our problem solving, and what obstacles hinder it?

One tribute to our rationality is our problem-solving skill. What's the best route around this traffic jam? How should we handle a friend's criticism? How, without our keys, can we get into the house?

Some problems we solve through *trial and error*. Thomas Edison tried thousands of light bulb filaments before stumbling upon one that worked. For other problems, we use **algorithms,** step-by-step procedures that guarantee a solution. But step-by-step algorithms can be laborious and exasperating. To find a word using the 10 letters in *SPLOYOCHYG*, for example, you could try each letter in each of the 10 positions—907,200 permutations in all. Rather than give you a computing brain the size of a beach ball, nature resorts to **heuristics,** simpler thinking strategies. Thus, you might reduce the number of options in the *SPLOYOCHYG* example by grouping letters that often appear together (*CH* and *GY*) and excluding rare letter combinations (such as *YY*). By using heuristics and then applying trial and error, you may hit on the answer. Have you guessed it?[1]

Sometimes we puzzle over a problem and the pieces suddenly fall together in a flash of **insight**—an abrupt, true-seeming, and often satisfying solution (Topolinski & Reber, 2010; Webb et al., 2019). Ten-year-old Johnny Appleton had one of these Aha! moments and solved a problem that had stumped construction workers: how to rescue a young robin from a narrow 30-inch-deep hole in a cement-block wall. Johnny's solution: Slowly pour in sand, giving the bird enough time to keep its feet on top of the constantly rising pile (Ruchlis, 1990). Insights aren't perfect, but they often lead to correct solutions (Danek & Salvi, 2018).

What happens in the brain when people experience an Aha! moment? Brain scans (EEGs or fMRIs) show bursts of activity associated with sudden flashes of insight (Kounios & Beeman, 2014). In one study, researchers asked people to think of a word that forms a compound word or phrase with each of three other words in a set (such as *pine, crab,* and *sauce*) and to press a button to sound a bell when they knew the answer. (Need a hint? The word is a fruit.[2]) A sudden Aha! insight led to about half the solutions. Before the Aha! moment, the problem solvers' frontal lobes (involved in focusing attention) were active. At the instant of discovery, there was a burst of activity in the right temporal lobe, just above the ear (**FIGURE 26.2**).

Insight strikes suddenly, with no prior sense of "getting warmer" or feeling close to a solution (Knoblich & Oellinger, 2006; Metcalfe, 1986). When the answer pops into mind (*apple!*), we feel a happy sense of satisfaction. The joy of a joke may similarly lie in our sudden comprehension of an unexpected ending or a double meaning: "You don't need a parachute to skydive. You only need a parachute to skydive twice." Comedian Groucho Marx was a master at this: "I once shot an elephant in my pajamas. How he got in my pajamas I'll never know."

---

[1]Answer to SPLPYOCHYC anagram: PSYCHOLOGY
[2]The word is *apple:* pineapple, crabapple, applesauce.

cognition all the mental activities associated with thinking, knowing, remembering, and communicating.

metacognition cognition about our cognition; keeping track of and evaluating our mental processes.

concept a mental grouping of similar objects, events, ideas, or people.

prototype a mental image or best example of a category. Matching new items to a prototype provides a quick and easy method for sorting items into categories (as when comparing feathered creatures to a prototypical bird, such as a crow).

algorithm a methodical, logical rule or procedure that guarantees solving a particular problem. Contrasts with the usually speedier—but also more error-prone—use of *heuristics.*

heuristic a simple thinking strategy—a mental shortcut—that often allows us to make judgments and solve problems efficiently; usually speedier but also more error-prone than an *algorithm.*

insight a sudden realization of a problem's solution; contrasts with strategy-based solutions.

FIGURE 26.2

The Aha! moment A burst of right temporal lobe activity accompanied insight solutions to word problems (Jung-Beeman et al., 2004). The red dots designate EEG electrodes. The light gray lines show the distribution of high-frequency activity accompanying insight. The insight-related activity is centered in the right temporal lobe (yellow area).

From Mark Jung-Beeman, Northwestern University and John Kounios, Drexel University

S.H. Chambers

"The human understanding, when any proposition has been once laid down . . . forces everything else to add fresh support and confirmation." — Francis Bacon, *Novum Organum*, 1620

Macmillan Learning

⊘ **FIGURE 26.3**

The matchstick problem How would you arrange six matches to form four equilateral triangles?

confirmation bias a tendency to search for information that supports our preconceptions and to ignore or distort contradictory evidence.

fixation in cognition, the inability to see a problem from a new perspective; an obstacle to problem solving.

mental set a tendency to approach a problem in one particular way, often a way that has been successful in the past.

intuition an effortless, immediate, automatic feeling or thought, as contrasted with explicit, conscious reasoning.

Insightful as we are, other cognitive tendencies may lead us astray. **Confirmation bias,** for example, leads us to seek evidence *for* our ideas more eagerly than we seek evidence *against* them (Klayman & Ha, 1987; Skov & Sherman, 1986). In a classic study, Peter Wason (1960) gave British university students a set of three numbers (2-4-6) and told them the series was based on a rule. Their task was to guess the rule. (It was simple: any three ascending numbers.) Before submitting answers, students generated their own three-number sets, and Wason told them whether their sets conformed to his rule. Once *certain* they had the rule, they could announce it. The result? Most students formed a wrong idea (*"Maybe it's counting by twos"*) and then searched only for confirming evidence (by testing 6-8-10, 100-102-104, and so forth). Seldom right but never in doubt.

"Ordinary people," said Wason (1981), "evade facts, become inconsistent, or systematically defend themselves against the threat of new information relevant to the issue." Thus, having formed a belief—that vaccines cause (or do not cause) autism spectrum disorder, that people can (or cannot) change their sexual orientation, that gun control fails (or does not fail) to save lives—we prefer information that supports our belief. And once we get hung up on an incorrect view of a problem, it's hard to approach it from a different angle. This obstacle to problem solving is called **fixation,** an inability to come to a fresh perspective. See if fixation prevents you from solving the matchstick problem in **FIGURE 26.3**. (For the solution, see **FIGURE 26.4**.)

A prime example of fixation is **mental set,** our tendency to approach a problem with the mindset of what has worked for us previously. Indeed, solutions that worked in the past often do work on new problems. Consider:

Given the sequence O-T-T-F-?-?-?, what are the final three letters?

Most people have difficulty recognizing that the three final letters are F(ive), S(ix), and S(even). But solving this problem may make the next one easier:

Given the sequence J-F-M-A-?-?-?, what are the final three letters? (If you don't get this one, ask yourself what month it is.)

As a *perceptual set* predisposes what we perceive, a mental set predisposes how we think. Sometimes this can be an obstacle to problem solving, as when our mental set from our past experiences with matchsticks predisposes us to arrange them in two dimensions.

Forming Good (and Bad) Decisions and Judgments

LOQ 26-3 What is *intuition,* and how can the representativeness and availability heuristics influence our decisions and judgments?

When making each day's hundreds of judgments and decisions (*Should I take a jacket? Can I trust this person? Should I shoot the basketball or pass to the player who's hot?*), we seldom take the time and effort to reason systematically. We follow our **intuition,** our fast, automatic, unreasoned feelings and thoughts. After interviewing policy makers in government, business, and education, social psychologist Irving Janis (1986) concluded that they "often do not use a reflective problem-solving approach. How do they usually arrive at their decisions? If you ask, they are likely to tell you . . . they do it mostly by the *seat of their pants.*"

Two Quick But Risky Shortcuts

When we need to make snap judgments, *heuristics* enable quick thinking that often serves us well (Gigerenzer, 2015). But as cognitive psychologists Amos Tversky and Daniel Kahneman (1974) showed, some intuitive mental shortcuts—the *representativeness* and *availability heuristics*—can lead even the smartest people into dumb decisions.

Few would have predicted Tversky and Kahneman's becoming friends and collaborators (Lewis, 2016; Sunstein & Thaler, 2016). When they met, Tversky was a war hero with a confident swagger who studied decision making; Kahneman was a chronic worrier who studied vision. Setting aside their differences, Tversky and Kahneman would sequester themselves in a small seminar room, where they argued, laughed, and ultimately changed the way that people view thinking and decision making (Dean & Ortoleva, 2019). Their joint efforts earned the ultimate award: a 2002 Nobel Prize. (Sadly,

"In creating these problems, we didn't set out to fool people. All our problems fooled us, too."
—Amos Tversky (1985)

"Intuitive thinking [is] fine most of the time. . . . But sometimes that habit of mind gets us in trouble."
—Daniel Kahneman (2005b)

representativeness heuristic judging the likelihood of events in terms of how well they seem to represent, or match, particular prototypes; may lead us to ignore other relevant information.

availability heuristic judging the likelihood of events based on their availability in memory; if instances come readily to mind (perhaps because of their vividness), we presume such events are common.

only Kahneman was alive to receive the honor.) As Kahneman wrote in a vignette for my [DM's] *Social Psychology* text, "Amos and I shared the wonder of together owning a goose that could lay golden eggs—a joint mind that was better than our separate minds."

THE REPRESENTATIVENESS HEURISTIC To judge the likelihood of something by intuitively comparing it to particular prototypes is to use the **representativeness heuristic.** Imagine someone who is short, slim, and likes to read poetry. Is this person more likely to be an Ivy League university English professor or a truck driver (Nisbett & Ross, 1980)?

Many people guess English professor—because the person better fits their prototype of nerdy professor than of truck driver. In doing so, they fail to consider the *base rate* number of Ivy League English professors (fewer than 400) and truck drivers (3.5 million in the United States alone). Thus, even if the description is 50 times more typical of English professors than of truck drivers, the fact that there are about 7000 times more truck drivers means that the poetry reader is many times more likely to be a truck driver.

Some prototypes have social consequences. One mother of two Black and three White teens asked other parents: "Do store personnel follow your children when they are picking out their Gatorade flavors? They didn't follow my White kids. . . . When your kids trick-or-treat dressed as a ninja and a clown, do they get asked who they are with and where they live, door after door? My White kids didn't get asked" (Roper, 2016). If people have a prototype—a stereotype—of delinquent Black teens, they may unconsciously use the representativeness heuristic when judging individuals. The result, even if unintended, is racism.

THE AVAILABILITY HEURISTIC The **availability heuristic** operates when we estimate the commonality of an event *based on its mental availability*. Anything that makes information pop into mind—its vividness, recency, or distinctiveness—can make it seem commonplace. Casinos know this. They entice us to gamble by broadcasting (infrequent) wins with flashing lights. The (far more frequent) big losses are invisible.

The availability heuristic distorts our judgments of risks. After one celebrity's vaccinated child later developed autism, thousands found her memorable story more persuasive than scientific data disproving any vaccine-autism link (Hoffman, 2019). Or consider who's scarier: toddlers or terrorists? Perhaps you'll change your answer, once you consider that armed toddlers killed more Americans than did feared foreign terrorists in 2015 and 2016 (Ingraham, 2016; LaCapria, 2015). If foreign terrorists were to kill 1000 people in the United States this year, Americans would be mighty afraid. Yet they would have reason to be 30 times more afraid of homicidal, suicidal, and accidental death by guns, which take more than 30,000 lives annually.

"Kahneman and his colleagues and students have changed the way we think about the way people think." — American Psychological Association President Sharon Brehm, 2007

The power of a vivid example An unforgettable (cognitively available) photo of 5-year-old Omran Daqneesh—dazed after being pulled from the rubble of yet another air strike in Aleppo, Syria—helped to awaken Western nations to the plight of Syrian migrants fleeing violence.

Availability heuristic With scenes from school shootings flooding people's minds (including this one from Colorado in 2019), 57 percent of American teens understandably reported feeling "very worried" or "somewhat worried" that a shooting would occur at their school (Graf, 2018). In reality, four times more students were killed in school in the early 1990s than today (Fox et al., 2018). Such hijacking of our rationality (when schools remain comparatively safe places, and other risks, such as driving or influenza, kill so many more) illustrates how we often disproportionately fear the wrong things.

Tom Cooper/Getty Images

"Don't believe everything you think."
— Bumper sticker

To offer a vivid depiction of climate change, Cal Tech scientists created an interactive map of global temperatures over the past 120 years. (See tinyurl.com/TempChange)

Macmillan Learning

⤴ **FIGURE 26.4**
Solution to the matchstick problem
To solve this problem, you must view it from a new perspective, breaking the fixation of limiting solutions to two dimensions.

The bottom line: We often fear the wrong things (see Thinking Critically About: The Fear Factor).

Meanwhile, the lack of available images of future climate change disasters—which some scientists regard as "Armageddon in slow motion"—has left some people unconcerned. Moreover, climate beliefs shift with the day's weather, which, though more cognitively available, tells us nothing about long-term planetary trends (Egan & Mullin, 2012; Kaufmann et al., 2017; Zaval et al., 2014). Unusually hot local weather increases people's worry about global climate warming, while a recent cold day reduces their concern and overwhelms less memorable scientific data (Li et al., 2011). As Stephen Colbert (2014) tweeted, "Global warming isn't real because it was cold today! Also great news: World hunger is over because I just ate."

Dramatic outcomes make us gasp; probabilities we hardly grasp. Over 40 nations have sought to harness the positive power of vivid, memorable images by putting eye-catching warnings and graphic photos on cigarette packages (Riordan, 2013). This campaign has worked because we reason emotionally (Huang et al., 2013). We overfeel and underthink (Slovic, 2007). In 2015, an iconic photo of a Syrian child lying dead on a beach went viral. Red Cross donations to Syrian refugees were 55 times greater in response to that photo than in response to statistics describing the hundreds of thousands of other refugee deaths (Slovic et al., 2017).

ASK YOURSELF

What do you fear? Do some of your fears outweigh their likelihood of happening? How can you use critical thinking to assess the rationality of your fears—and to identify areas of your life where you need to take more precautions?

RETRIEVAL PRACTICE

RP-1   Why can news be described as "something that hardly ever happens"? How does knowing this help us assess our fears?

ANSWERS IN APPENDIX E

Overconfidence

LOQ 26-5 How are our decisions and judgments affected by overconfidence, belief perseverance, and framing?

Sometimes we are more confident than correct. Across various tasks, people overestimate their performance (Metcalfe, 1998). If 60 percent of people correctly answer a factual question, such as "Is absinthe a liqueur or a precious stone?" they will typically average 75 percent confidence (Fischhoff et al., 1977). (It's a licorice-flavored liqueur.) This tendency to overestimate the accuracy of our knowledge and judgments is **overconfidence.**

It is overconfidence that drives stockbrokers and investment managers to market their ability to outperform stock market averages—which, as a group, they cannot do (Malkiel, 2016). A purchase of stock X, recommended by a broker who judges this to be

overconfidence the tendency to be more confident than correct—to overestimate the accuracy of our beliefs and judgments.

Thinking Critically About:
The Fear Factor

LOQ **26-4** What factors exaggerate our fear of unlikely events?

Many people fear flying more than driving.

2001   2008   2017

HOWEVER:
Americans are vastly more likely to die in a vehicle accident than on a scheduled flight.[1]

From 2008 to 2017, for example, **226,565** people died in U.S. car or light truck accidents, and **62** died on scheduled airline flights.

In the three months after 9/11, **FEAR OF FLYING** led more Americans to travel by car, and some to die:[2]

Oct.-Dec. 2001: 353 excess deaths

Number of traffic deaths, 2001

Average number of traffic deaths, 1996-2000

Number of U.S. traffic deaths

3600 3400 3200 3000 2800 2600 2400 2200

Jan Feb Mar Apr May Jun Jul Aug Sep Oct Nov Dec

In the year following 9/11, these researchers estimated, 1500 Americans had "lost their lives on the road by trying to avoid the risk of flying."

WHY DO WE FEAR THE WRONG THINGS?

1. We fear what our ancestral history has prepared us to fear: Snakes, lizards, and spiders combined now kill a tiny fraction of the number killed by modern-day threats, such as cars and cigarettes. Ancestral risks also prepare us to fear confinement and heights, and therefore flying.

2. We fear what we cannot control: Driving we control; flying we do not.

3. We fear what is immediate: Dangers of flying are mostly in the moments of takeoff and landing. Dangers of driving are spread across many moments, each trivially dangerous.

4. Thanks to the availability heuristic, we fear what is most readily available in memory: Vivid images of horrific airline crashes feed our judgments of risk. People may fear sharks more than cigarettes or the effects of an unhealthy diet.[3]

Shark attacks kill ~1 American per year.

"Vivid image!"

Heart disease kills 800,000 Americans per year.

"Harder to visualize"

We remember and fear **disasters** (terrorism, hurricanes, earthquakes) that kill people dramatically, in bunches.

We fear too little the **less dramatic and ongoing threats** that claim lives one by one:

- In an average day, guns kill 92 Americans — in homicides, suicides, and accidents.[4] Yet renewed calls for U.S. gun control tend to follow the well-publicized, mass shootings.

- Worldwide, 500,000 children die each year from diarrhea, with tragically little notice.

"If it's in the news, don't worry about it. The very definition of news is 'something that hardly ever happens.'"[5]

1. National Safety Council, 2019. 2. Gaissmaier & Gigerenzer, 2012; Gigerenzer, 2004, 2006. 3. Daley, 2011. 4. Xu et al., 2016. 5. Schneier, 2007.

Hofstadter's Law: It always takes longer than you expect, even when you take into account Hofstadter's Law. — Douglas Hofstadter, *Gödel, Escher, Bach: The Eternal Golden Braid*, 1979

"When you know a thing, to hold that you know it; and when you do not know a thing, to allow that you do not know it; this is knowledge." — Confucius (551–479 B.C.E.), *Analects*

Predict your own behavior When will you finish reading this module?

"Let me interrupt your expertise with my confidence."

> **belief perseverance** clinging to one's initial conceptions after the basis on which they were formed has been discredited.

the time to buy, is usually balanced by a sale made by someone who judges this to be the time to sell. Despite their confidence, buyer and seller cannot both be right. And it is overconfidence that so often leads us to succumb to a *planning fallacy*—overestimating our future leisure time and income (Zauberman & Lynch, 2005). Students and others often expect to finish assignments ahead of schedule (Buehler et al., 1994, 2002). In fact, such projects generally take about twice the predicted time. Anticipating how much more time we will have next month, we happily accept invitations. And believing we'll surely have more money next year, we take out loans or buy on credit.

Overconfidence—the bias that Kahneman (2015), if given a magic wand, would most like to eliminate—affects life-or-death decisions. History is full of leaders who, when waging war, were more confident than correct. In politics, overconfidence feeds extreme political views. In medicine, overconfidence can lead to incorrect diagnoses (Saposnik et al., 2016).

One research team tested 743 U.S. federal intelligence analysts' ability to predict future events—predictions that typically are overconfident. Those whose predictions most often failed tended to be inflexible and closed-minded (Mellers et al., 2015). Ordinary citizens with a shallow understanding of complex proposals, such as for cap-and-trade carbon emissions or a flat tax, may also express strong views. Sometimes the less we know, the more definite we sound. Asking such people to explain the details of these policies exposes them to their own ignorance, which in turn leads them to express more moderate views (Fernbach et al., 2013). To confront one's own ignorance is to become wiser.

Nevertheless, overconfidence sometimes has adaptive value. Believing that their decisions are right and they have time to spare, self-confident people tend to live more happily. They make tough decisions more easily, and they seem competent (Anderson et al., 2012). Given prompt and clear feedback, we can also learn to be more realistic about the accuracy of our judgments (Fischhoff, 1982). The wisdom to know when we know a thing and when we do not is born of experience.

Belief Perseverance

Our overconfidence is startling. Equally so is our **belief perseverance**—our tendency to cling to our beliefs in the face of contrary evidence. A classic study of belief perseverance engaged people with opposing views of capital punishment (Lord et al., 1979). After studying two supposedly new research findings, one supporting and the other refuting the claim that the death penalty deters crime, each side was more impressed by the study supporting its own beliefs. And each readily disputed the other study. Thus, showing the pro- and anti-capital-punishment groups the *same* mixed evidence actually *increased* their disagreement. Rather than using evidence to draw conclusions, they used their conclusions to assess evidence—a phenomenon also known as *motivated reasoning*.

In other studies and in everyday life, people have similarly welcomed belief-supportive logic and evidence—about climate change, same-sex marriage, or politics—while discounting challenging evidence (Friesen et al., 2015; Gampe et al., 2019; Sunstein et al., 2016). Often, prejudice persists. Beliefs persevere. As an old saying goes, "It's hard to teach an old dogma new tricks."

To rein in belief perseverance, a simple remedy exists: *Consider the opposite.* When the same researchers repeated the capital-punishment study, they asked some participants to be "as *objective* and *unbiased* as possible" (Lord et al., 1984). The plea did nothing to reduce biased evaluations of evidence. They also asked another group to consider "whether you would have made the same high or low evaluations had exactly the same study produced results on the *other* side of the issue." Having imagined and pondered *opposite* findings, these people became much less biased. Newer studies confirm the point: Considering opposing arguments reduces bias (Catapano et al., 2019; Van Boven et al., 2019).

Once beliefs take root, it takes more compelling evidence to change them than it did to create them. Even if we appear open to other perspectives, we might often label belief-contradicting evidence as "weak" (Anglin, 2019). Climate change skeptics, for example, tend to view evidence supporting climate change as inaccurate or untrustworthy (Druckman & McGrath, 2019). As an old Chinese proverb says, "Two-thirds of what we see is behind our eyes."

The Effects of Framing

Framing—the way we present an issue—can be a powerful tool of persuasion, as psychologists and economists have together learned. As a young scholar, behavioral economist Richard Thaler worked closely with cognitive psychologists Amos Tversky and Daniel Kahneman. Thaler and others have shown how the framing of options can **nudge** people toward beneficial decisions (Benartzi et al., 2017; Daniels & Zlatev, 2019; Thaler & Sunstein, 2008).

- *Saving for retirement.* U.S. companies once required employees who wanted to contribute to a retirement plan to choose a lower take-home pay, which few people did. Thanks to a new law, companies can now automatically enroll their employees in the plan but allow them to opt out. Either way, the decision to contribute is the employee's. But under the new opt-out arrangement, enrollments in one analysis of 3.4 million workers soared from 59 to 86 percent (Rosenberg, 2010). Britain's 2012 change to an opt-out framing similarly led to 5 million more retirement savers (Halpern, 2015). Now, researchers are investigating how nudges can help people invest those retirement funds wisely (Camilleri et al., 2019).

- *Making moral decisions.* Imagine an experimenter gives you $5.00 and asks how much, if any, you want to donate. Before you decide, you're asked another question meant to nudge you to adopt a generous frame of mind: "What do you personally think is the morally right thing to do in this situation?" Nudging people to take a moral mindset makes them more generous, increasing charity donations by 44 percent (Capraro et al., 2019).

- *Becoming an organ donor.* In many European countries, as well as in the United States, people renewing their driver's license can decide whether to be organ donors. In some countries, the default option is *Yes,* but people can opt out. Nearly 100 percent of the people in opt-out countries have agreed to be donors. In countries where the default option is *No,* most do *not* agree to be donors (Hajhosseini et al., 2013; Johnson & Goldstein, 2003). Defaulting to donation helps humans.

- *Reducing alcohol consumption.* People who consume alcohol often count their drinks rather than their consumed ounces (or milliliters). By reducing a bar's serving size, one British study reduced alcohol consumption by a third (Kersbergen et al., 2018). In Great Britain, Denmark, Germany, South Korea, and the United States, most people accept policies that, without constraining personal freedom, nudge reduced alcohol consumption (Reynolds et al., 2019; Sunstein et al., 2019).

The point to remember: Framing can nudge our attitudes and decisions.

The Perils and Powers of Intuition

LOQ 26-6 How do smart thinkers use intuition?

We have seen how our unreasoned intuition can plague our efforts to solve problems, assess risks, and make wise decisions. The perils of intuition can persist even when people are offered extra pay for thinking smart, even when they are asked to justify their answers, and even among expert physicians, clinicians, and U.S. federal intelligence agents (Reyna et al., 2014; Shafir & LeBoeuf, 2002; Stanovich et al., 2013). Very smart people can make not-so-smart judgments.

So, are our heads indeed "filled with straw," as T. S. Eliot suggested? Good news: Cognitive scientists are also revealing intuition's powers.

- *Intuition is recognition born of experience.* It is implicit (unconscious) knowledge—what we've recorded in our brains but can't fully explain (Chassy & Gobet, 2011; Gore & Sadler-Smith, 2011). We see it in the smart and quick judgments of experienced nurses, firefighters, art critics, and car mechanics. We see it in skilled athletes who react *without thinking.* Indeed, conscious thinking may disrupt well-practiced movements, leading skilled athletes to choke under pressure, as when shooting free throws (Beilock, 2010). And we would see this instant intuition in you, too, for anything in which you have developed knowledge based on experience.

- *Intuition is usually adaptive.* Our fast and frugal heuristics let us intuitively assume that fuzzy-looking objects are far away—which they usually are, except on foggy

"*The problem is I can't tell the difference between a deeply wise, intuitive nudge from the Universe and one of my own bone-headed ideas!*"

Bradford Veley/CartoonStock

framing the way an issue is posed; how an issue is framed can significantly affect decisions and judgments.

nudge framing choices in a way that encourages people to make beneficial decisions.

mornings. Our learned associations surface as gut feelings, right or wrong: Seeing a stranger who looks like someone who has harmed or threatened us in the past, we may automatically react with distrust. So, intuition aids our survival, and it can also steer us toward satisfying relationship partners: Newlyweds' implicit, gut-level attitudes toward their new spouse predict their marital happiness (McNulty et al., 2017).

- *Intuition is huge.* Unconscious, automatic influences constantly affect our judgments (Custers & Aarts, 2010; Kihlstrom, 2019). Consider: Most people guess that the more complex the choice, the smarter it is to make decisions rationally rather than intuitively (Inbar et al., 2010). Actually, in making complex decisions, we sometimes benefit by letting our brain work on a problem without consciously thinking about it (Strick et al., 2010, 2011). In one series of experiments, three groups of people read complex information (for example, about apartments or European football matches). Those in the first group stated their preference immediately after reading information about four possible options. The second group, given several minutes to analyze the information, made slightly smarter decisions. But wisest of all, in several studies, were those in the third group, whose attention was distracted for a time, enabling their minds to engage in automatic, unconscious processing of the complex information. The practical lesson: Letting a problem incubate while we attend to other things can pay dividends (Dijksterhuis & Strick, 2016). Facing a difficult decision involving a lot of facts, we're wise to gather all the information we can, and then say, "Give me some time *not* to think about this." Even sleeping on it can help. Thanks to our ever-active brain, nonconscious thinking (reasoning, problem solving, decision making, planning) can be surprisingly astute (Creswell et al., 2013; Hassin, 2013; Lin & Murray, 2015).

Critics note that some studies have not found the supposed power of unconscious thought, and they remind us that deliberate, conscious thought also furthers smart thinking (Newell, 2015; Nieuwenstein et al., 2015; Phillips et al., 2016). In challenging situations—making the best chess move, telling the difference between false and real news headlines—superior decision makers take time to think (Moxley et al., 2012; Pennycook & Rand, 2019). And with many sorts of problems, deliberative thinkers are aware of the intuitive option, but know when to override it (Mata et al., 2013). Consider:

1. A bat and a ball together cost 110 cents. The bat costs 100 cents more than the ball. How much does the ball cost?

2. Emily's father has three daughters. The first two are named April and May. What is the third daughter's name?

Most people's intuitive responses—10 cents and June—are wrong, and a few moments of deliberate thinking reveals why.[3]

The bottom line: Our two-track mind makes sweet harmony as smart, critical thinking listens to the creative whispers of our vast unseen mind and then evaluates evidence, tests conclusions, and plans for the future.

ASK YOURSELF

Can you recall a time when contradictory information challenged one of your views? Was it hard for you to consider the opposite view? What caused you to change your thinking or keep your opinion?

Thinking Creatively

LOQ 26-7 What is *creativity*, and what fosters it?

Creativity is the ability to produce ideas that are both novel and valuable (Hennessey & Amabile, 2010). Consider Princeton mathematician Andrew Wiles' incredible, creative moment. Pierre de Fermat, a seventeenth-century mischievous genius, had challenged mathematicians of his day to match his solutions to various number theory problems.

"The heart has its reasons which reason does not know." — Blaise Pascal, *Pensées,* 1670

"It may be, if I may so put it, that you do not know what it is that you know. You are aware only of the result. And that, madam, is your intuition." — Agatha Christie's detective Hercule Poirot, *Dead Man's Folly* (ITV)

creativity the ability to produce new and valuable ideas.

convergent thinking narrowing the available problem solutions to determine the single best solution.

divergent thinking expanding the number of possible problem solutions; creative thinking that diverges in different directions.

---

[3]The first answer is 5 cents. The bat would then cost $1.05, for a $1.10 total. If the ball cost the *intuitive* answer of 10 cents, the bat would then have to cost $1.10 (for a bat-and-ball total of $1.20, not $1.10). The second answer is Emily. If you answered incorrectly, don't feel bad—so do many others (Frederick, 2005; Thomson & Oppenheimer, 2016).

His most famous challenge—*Fermat's last theorem*—baffled the greatest mathematical minds, even after a $2 million prize (in today's dollars) was offered in 1908 to whoever first created a proof.

Wiles had pondered Fermat's theorem for more than 30 years and had come to the brink of a solution. One morning in 1994, out of the blue, the final "incredible revelation" struck him. "It was so indescribably beautiful; it was so simple and so elegant. I couldn't understand how I'd missed it. . . . It was the most important moment of my working life" (Singh, 1997, p. 25). Creative writers and physicists likewise experience many significant ideas, unbidden, during mind wandering (Gable et al., 2019). (Perhaps this is your experience as well?)

Creativity is supported by a certain level of *aptitude* (ability to learn). Those who score exceptionally high in quantitative aptitude as 13-year-olds, for example, are later more likely to create published or patented work (Bernstein et al., 2019; Lubinski et al., 2014). Yet there is more to creativity than aptitude, or what intelligence tests reveal. Indeed, brain activity associated with intelligence differs from that associated with creativity (Jung & Haier, 2013; Shen et al., 2017). Aptitude tests (such as the SAT) typically require **convergent thinking**—an ability to provide a single correct answer.

Creativity tests (*How many uses can you think of for a brick?*) require **divergent thinking**—the ability to consider many different options and to think in novel ways. Injury to certain areas of the frontal lobes can leave reading, writing, and arithmetic skills intact but destroy imagination (Kolb & Whishaw, 2006).

Robert Sternberg and his colleagues believe creativity has five components (Sternberg, 1988, 2003; Sternberg & Lubart, 1991, 1992):

1. **Expertise**—well-developed knowledge—furnishes the ideas, images, and phrases we use as mental building blocks. "Chance favors only the prepared mind," observed Louis Pasteur. The more blocks we have, the more chances we have to combine them in novel ways. Wiles' well-developed knowledge put the needed theorems and methods at his disposal.

2. **Imaginative thinking skills** provide the ability to see things in novel ways, to recognize patterns, and to make connections. Having mastered a problem's basic elements, we can redefine or explore it in a new way. Copernicus first developed expertise regarding the solar system and its planets, and then creatively defined the system as revolving around the Sun, not the Earth. Wiles' imaginative solution combined two partial solutions.

3. A **venturesome, determined personality** seeks new experiences, tolerates ambiguity and risk, and perseveres in overcoming obstacles. Wiles said he labored in near-isolation from the mathematics community partly to stay focused and avoid distraction. Such determination is an enduring trait.

4. **Intrinsic motivation** is the quality of being driven more by interest, satisfaction, and challenge than by external pressures (Amabile & Hennessey, 1992). Creative people focus less on extrinsic motivators—meeting deadlines, impressing people, or making money—than on the pleasure and stimulation of the work itself. Asked how he solved such difficult scientific problems, Isaac Newton reportedly answered, "By thinking about them all the time." Wiles concurred: "I was so obsessed by this problem that . . . I was thinking about it all the time—[from] when I woke up in the morning to when I went to sleep at night" (Singh & Riber, 1997).

5. A **creative environment** sparks, supports, and refines creative ideas. Wiles stood on the shoulders of others and collaborated with a former student. A study of the careers of 2026 prominent scientists and inventors revealed that the most eminent were mentored, challenged, and supported by their colleagues (Simonton, 1992). Creativity-fostering environments support innovation, team building, and communication (Hülsheger et al., 2009). They also minimize anxiety and foster contemplation (Byron & Khazanchi, 2011). While on a retreat in a monastery, Jonas Salk solved a problem that led to the polio vaccine. Later, when he designed the Salk Institute, he provided contemplative spaces where scientists could work without interruption (Sternberg, 2006).

PETER MUHLY/Getty Images

Industrious creativity Researcher Sally Reis (2001) found that notably creative women, such as Nobel laureate geneticist Barbara McClintock, were typically "intelligent, hard working, imaginative, and strong willed" as girls. In her acceptance speech for the 2013 Nobel Prize for Literature, author Alice Munro, shown here, described the creative process as hard work: "The part that's hardest is when you go over the story and realize how bad it is. You know, the first part, excitement, the second, pretty good, but then you pick it up one morning and you think, 'what nonsense,' and that is when you really have to get to work."

Mick Stevens/Cartoon Stock

A creative environment

"For the love of God, is there a doctor in the house?"

WELL, I TOLD YOU TO ADD YEAST TO YOUR SHAMPOO.

Imaginative thinking Cartoonists often display creativity as they see things in new ways or make unusual connections.

For those seeking to boost the creative process, research offers some ideas:

- *Develop your expertise.* Ask yourself what you care about and most enjoy. Follow your passion by broadening your knowledge base and becoming an expert at something.

- *Allow time for incubation.* Think hard on a problem, but then set it aside and come back to it later. For those with enough knowledge—the needed mental building blocks—a period of inattention to a problem ("sleeping on it") allows for automatic processing to form associations (Zhong et al., 2008).

- *Set aside time for the mind to roam freely.* Creativity springs from "defocused attention" (Simonton, 2012a,b). So detach from attention-grabbing television, social networking, and video gaming. Jog, go for a long walk, or meditate. Serenity seeds spontaneity. "Time alone is . . . the font of creativity," says playwright and musician Lin-Manuel Miranda (Hainey, 2016).

- *Experience other cultures and ways of thinking.* Viewing life from a different perspective sometimes sets the creative juices flowing. Students who spend time abroad learn how to blend new norms with those from their home culture, which increases creativity (Godart et al., 2015; Lu et al., 2018). Even getting out of your neighborhood or embracing intercultural friendships fosters flexible thinking (Kim et al., 2013; Ritter et al., 2012).

For a summary of some key ideas from this section, see **TABLE 26.1**.

TABLE 26.1 Comparing Cognitive Processes and Strategies

Process or Strategy	Description	Powers	Perils
Algorithm	Methodical rule or procedure	Guarantees solution	Requires time and effort
Heuristic	Simple thinking shortcut, such as the availability heuristic (which estimates likelihood based on how easily events come to mind)	Lets us act quickly and efficiently	Puts us at risk for errors
Insight	Sudden Aha! reaction	Provides instant realization of solution	May not happen
Confirmation bias	Tendency to search for support for our own views and ignore contradictory evidence	Lets us quickly recognize supporting evidence	Hinders recognition of contradictory evidence
Fixation	Inability to view problems from a new angle	Focuses thinking	Hinders creative problem solving
Intuition	Fast, automatic feelings and thoughts	Is based on our experience; huge and adaptive	Can lead us to overfeel and underthink
Overconfidence	Overestimating the accuracy of our beliefs and judgments	Allows us to be happy and to make decisions easily	Puts us at risk for errors
Belief perseverance	Ignoring evidence that contradicts our beliefs	Supports our enduring beliefs	Closes our mind to new ideas
Framing	Wording a question or statement so that it evokes a desired response	Can influence others' decisions	Can produce a misleading result
Creativity	Ability to innovate valuable ideas	Produces new insights and products	May distract from structured, routine work

ANSWERS IN APPENDIX E

RETRIEVAL PRACTICE

RP-2 Match the process or strategy listed below (i–xi) with its description (a–k).

i.   Algorithm

ii. Intuition

iii. Insight

iv. Heuristic

v.   Fixation

vi. Confirmation bias

vii. Overconfidence

viii. Creativity

ix. Framing

x.   Belief perseverance

xi. Nudge

a. Inability to view problems from a new angle; focuses thinking but hinders creative problem solving

b. Methodological rule or procedure that guarantees a solution but requires time and effort

c. Your fast, automatic, effortless feelings and thoughts based on your experience; huge and adaptive but can lead you to overfeel and underthink

d. Simple thinking shortcut that lets you act quickly and efficiently but puts you at risk for errors

e. Sudden Aha! reaction that instantly reveals the solution

f. Tendency to search for support for your own views and to ignore contradictory evidence

g. Holding on to your beliefs even after they are proven wrong; closing your mind to new ideas

h. Overestimating the accuracy of your beliefs and judgments; allows you to be happier and to make decisions more easily, but puts you at risk for errors

i. Wording a question or statement so that it evokes a desired response; can mislead people and influence their decisions

j. The ability to produce novel and valuable ideas

k. Framing choices to encourage good decisions

Do Other Species Share Our Cognitive Skills?

LOQ 26-8 What do we know about thinking in other species?

Other animals are surprisingly smart (de Waal, 2016). In her 1908 book, *The Animal Mind*, pioneering psychologist Margaret Floy Washburn argued that animal consciousness and intelligence can be inferred from their behavior. In 2012, neuroscientists convening at the University of Cambridge added that animal consciousness can also be inferred from their brains: "Nonhuman animals, including all mammals and birds," possess the *neural networks* "that generate consciousness" (Low, 2012). Consider, then, what animal brains can do.

Using Concepts and Numbers

By touching screens in quest of a food reward, black bears have learned to sort pictures into animal and nonanimal categories, or concepts (Vonk et al., 2012). The great apes—a group that includes chimpanzees and gorillas—also form concepts, such as *cat* and *dog*. After monkeys have learned these concepts, certain frontal lobe neurons in their brain fire in response to new "cat-like" images, others to new "dog-like" images (Freedman et al., 2001). Even pigeons—mere birdbrains—can sort objects (pictures of cars, cats, chairs, flowers) into categories. Shown a picture of a never-before-seen chair, pigeons will reliably peck a key that represents *chairs* (Wasserman, 1995).

Displaying Insight

Psychologist Wolfgang Köhler (1925) showed that humans are not the only creatures to display insight. He placed a piece of fruit and a long stick outside the cage of a chimpanzee named Sultan, beyond his reach. Inside the cage, Köhler placed a short stick, which Sultan grabbed, using it to try to reach the fruit. After several failed attempts, the chimpanzee dropped the stick and seemed to survey the situation. Then suddenly (as if thinking "Aha!"), Sultan jumped up and seized the short stick

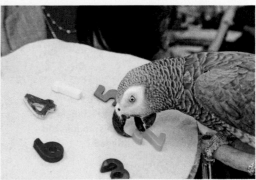

Animal cognition in action Alex, an African Grey parrot, was able to categorize and name objects (Pepperberg, 2009, 2012, 2013). Among his jaw-dropping numerical skills was the ability to comprehend numbers up to 8. He could speak the number of objects. He could add two small clusters of objects and announce the sum. He could indicate which of two numbers was greater. And he gave correct answers when shown various groups of objects. Asked, for example, "What color four?" (meaning "What's the color of the objects of which there are four?"), he could speak the answer.

Mike Lovett

(a)   (b)

⊙ **FIGURE 26.5**

Animal talents (a) One male chimpanzee in Sweden's Furuvik Zoo was observed every morning collecting stones, which later in the day he used as ammunition to pelt visitors (Osvath & Karvonen, 2012). (b) Crows studied by Christopher Bird and Nathan Emery (2009) quickly learned to raise the water level in a tube and nab a floating worm by dropping in stones. Other crows have used twigs to probe for insects, and bent strips of metal to reach food.

again. This time, he used it to pull in the longer stick—which he then used to reach the fruit. Apes have even exhibited foresight by storing a tool they could use to retrieve food the next day (Mulcahy & Call, 2006). (For one example of a chimpanzee's use of foresight, see **FIGURE 26.5a**.) And apes have displayed an ability to read others' minds—by anticipating where a human will look for an object, even if it's no longer there (Krupenye et al., 2016).

Birds, too, have displayed insight. One experiment, by (yes) Christopher Bird and Nathan Emery (2009), brought to life an Aesop fable in which a thirsty crow is unable to reach the water in a partly filled pitcher. See the crow's solution (exactly as in the fable) in Figure 26.5b. Other crows have fashioned wire or sticks for extracting food, such as insects in rotting logs (Jelbert et al., 2018; Rutz et al., 2016). Ravens are similarly adept at inventive tool use, and can plan hours ahead for future events (Kabadayi & Osvath, 2017).

Transmitting Culture

Like humans, other species invent behaviors and transmit cultural patterns to their observing peers and offspring (Boesch-Achermann & Boesch, 1993). Dolphins form coalitions, cooperatively hunt, and learn tool use from one another (Bearzi & Stanford, 2010). In Western Australia, some dolphins learned to use marine sponges as protective nose guards when probing the sea floor for fish—and then taught their offspring (Krützen et al., 2005).

Forest-dwelling chimpanzees select different tools for different purposes—a heavy stick for making holes, a light, flexible stick for fishing for termites, or a pointed stick for roasting marshmallows. (Just kidding: They don't roast marshmallows, but they have surprised us with their sophisticated tool use [Sanz et al., 2004]). Researchers have found at least 39 local customs related to chimpanzee tool use, grooming, and courtship (Claidière & Whiten, 2012; Whiten & Boesch, 2001). One group may slurp termites directly from a stick, while another group may pluck them off individually. One group may break nuts with a stone hammer, while their neighbors use a wooden hammer. One chimpanzee discovered that tree moss could absorb water for drinking from a waterhole, and within six days, seven other observant chimpanzees began doing the same (Hobaiter et al., 2014). These transmitted behaviors, along with differing communication and hunting styles, are the chimpanzee version of cultural diversity.

Other Cognitive Skills

Great apes, dolphins, magpies, and elephants recognize themselves in a mirror, demonstrating self-awareness (Morrison & Reiss, 2018). Elephants also display their abilities to learn, remember, discriminate smells, empathize, cooperate, teach, and spontaneously use tools (Byrne et al., 2009). Chimpanzees show altruism, cooperation, and group aggression. Like humans, they may purposefully kill their neighbor to gain land, and they grieve over dead relatives (Anderson et al., 2010; Biro et al., 2010; Mitani et al., 2010).

* * *

What time is it now? When we asked you (in the section on overconfidence) to estimate how quickly you would finish this module, did you underestimate or overestimate?

Thinking about other species' abilities brings us back to our initial question: How deserving are we of the label *Homo sapiens*—wise human? Let's pause to give our species some midterm grades. On decision making and risk assessment, our smart but error-prone species might rate a B–. On problem solving, where humans are inventive yet vulnerable to confirmation bias and fixation, we would probably receive a better mark, perhaps a B+. And on cognitive efficiency and creativity, our quick (though sometimes faulty) heuristics and divergent thinking would surely earn us an A.

26 REVIEW Thinking

LEARNING OBJECTIVES

Test Yourself Answer these repeated Learning Objective Questions on your own (before checking the answers in Appendix D) to improve your retention of the concepts (McDaniel et al., 2009, 2015).

LOQ 26-1 What are *cognition* and *metacognition*, and what are the functions of concepts?

LOQ 26-2 What cognitive strategies assist our problem solving, and what obstacles hinder it?

LOQ 26-3 What is *intuition*, and how can the representativeness and availability heuristics influence our decisions and judgments?

LOQ 26-4 What factors exaggerate our fear of unlikely events?

LOQ 26-5 How are our decisions and judgments affected by overconfidence, belief perseverance, and framing?

LOQ 26-6 How do smart thinkers use intuition?

LOQ 26-7 What is *creativity*, and what fosters it?

LOQ 26-8 What do we know about thinking in other species?

TERMS AND CONCEPTS TO REMEMBER

Test Yourself Write down the definition in your own words, then check your answer.

cognition, p. 327

metacognition, p. 327

concept, p. 327

prototype, p. 327

algorithm, p. 327

heuristic, p. 327

insight, p. 327

confirmation bias, p. 328

fixation, p. 328

mental set, p. 328

intuition, p. 328

representativeness heuristic, p. 329

availability heuristic, p. 329

overconfidence, p. 330

belief perseverance, p. 332

framing, p. 333

nudge, p. 333

creativity, p. 334

convergent thinking, p. 334

divergent thinking, p. 334

MASTER THE MATERIAL

Test Yourself Answer the following questions on your own first, then check your answers in Appendix E.

1. A mental grouping of similar things is called a
_____.

2. The most systematic procedure for solving a problem is a(n)
_____.

3. Oscar describes his political beliefs as "strongly liberal," but he is interested in exploring opposing viewpoints. How might he be affected by confirmation bias and belief perseverance?

4. A major obstacle to problem solving is fixation, which is a(n)
   a. tendency to base our judgments on vivid memories.
   b. tendency to wait for insight to occur.
   c. inability to view a problem from a new perspective.
   d. rule of thumb for judging the likelihood of an event in terms of our mental image of it.

5. Terrorist attacks made Americans more fearful of being victimized by terrorism than of other, greater threats. Such exaggerated fear after dramatic events illustrates the _____ heuristic.

6. When consumers respond more positively to ground beef described as "75 percent lean" than to the same product labeled "25 percent fat," they have been influenced by
_____.

7. Which of the following is NOT a characteristic of a creative person?
   a. Expertise
   b. Extrinsic motivation
   c. A venturesome personality
   d. Imaginative thinking skills

8. In the early twentieth century, some psychologists noted that animal consciousness can be inferred from their behavior. In the early twenty-first century, other scientists argued that animal consciousness can be inferred from their brain's
_____ _____.

Continue testing yourself with 📚 **LearningCurve** or 📖 **Achieve Read & Practice** to learn and remember most effectively.

27 Language and Thought

Imagine an alien species that could pass thoughts from one head to another merely by pulsating air molecules in the space between them. Perhaps these weird creatures could inhabit a future science fiction movie? Actually, we are those creatures! When we speak, our brain and voice apparatus transmit air pressure waves that we send banging against another's eardrum—enabling us to transfer thoughts from our brain into theirs.

Language transmits knowledge Whether spoken, written, or signed, language—the original wireless communication—enables mind-to-mind information transfer, and with it the transmission of civilization's accumulated knowledge across generations.

"The secret to our ancestors' survival was probably our use of language to develop new modes of cooperation." — David Grinspoon, "Can Humans Outsmart Extinction?" (2016)

STEVE INVALIDATES HIS WEDDING VOWS THROUGH THE CLEVER USE OF HOMOPHONES.

"Eye dew."

As native English speakers, we apologize to the rest of you for some oddities of our language:

· *Extraordinary* does not mean "extra ordinary."
· *Hyphenated* is not hyphenated; *non-hyphenated* is hyphenated.
· *Adjective* is a noun.
· Our spelling of *weird* is weird (not wierd).

As cognitive psychologist Steven Pinker (1998) noted, we sometimes sit for hours "listening to other people make noise as they exhale, because those hisses and squeaks contain *information*." And thanks to all those funny sounds created from the air pressure waves we send out, we get people's attention. We get them to do things. And we maintain relationships (Guerin, 2003). Depending on how you vibrate the air, you may get a scowl or a kiss.

Language is more than vibrating air—it is our spoken, written, or signed words, and the ways we combine them to communicate meaning. When I [DM] created this paragraph, my fingers on the keyboard generated electronic binary numbers that were translated into the squiggles before you. When transmitted by reflected light rays into your retina (or by sound waves into your ear), these squiggles trigger formless nerve impulses that travel to several areas of your brain, which integrate the information, compare it to stored information, and decode meaning. Thanks to language, information is moving from my mind to yours. Many animals know little more than what they sense. Thanks to language, we comprehend much that we've never seen and that our distant ancestors never knew. And thanks to technology, we can use language to communicate across vast distances—through spoken, written, and even pictorial "emoticon" words (including the 2015 *Oxford English Dictionary* "Word" of the Year: 😂). Today, notes Daniel Gilbert (2006), the average taxi driver in Pittsburgh "knows more about the universe than did Galileo, Aristotle, Leonardo, or any of those other guys who were so smart they only needed one name."

Let's begin our study of language by examining some of its components.

Language Structure

LOQ 27-1 What are the structural components of a language?

Consider how we might go about inventing a language. For a spoken language, we would need three building blocks:

- **Phonemes** are the smallest distinctive sound units in a language. To say *bat*, English speakers utter the phonemes *b, a,* and *t.* (Phonemes aren't the same as letters. *That* also has three phonemes—*th, a,* and *t.* And the three *e*'s in *Mercedes* are each a different phoneme.) Linguists surveying nearly 500 languages have identified 869 different phonemes in human speech, but no language uses all of them (Holt, 2002; Maddieson, 1984). Those 800+ sounds "can form all the words in every language of the world," notes child language researcher Patricia Kuhl (2015). English uses about 40 phonemes; other languages use anywhere from half to more than twice as many. As a general rule, consonant phonemes carry more information than do vowel phonemes. *The treth ef thes stetement shed be evedent frem thes bref demenstretien.*

- **Morphemes** are the smallest language units that carry meaning. In English, a few morphemes are also phonemes—the article *a*, for instance. But most morphemes combine two or more phonemes. The word *readers,* for example, contains three morphemes: "read," "er" (signaling that we mean "one who reads"), and "s" (signaling that we mean not one, but multiple readers). Every word in a language contains one or more morphemes.

- **Grammar** is a language's set of rules that enable people to communicate. Grammatical rules guide us in deriving meaning from sounds (*semantics*) and in ordering words into sentences (*syntax*).

Like life constructed from the genetic code's simple alphabet, language is complexity built of simplicity. In English, for example, 40 or so phonemes can be combined to form more than 100,000 morphemes, which alone or in combination produce the 600,000 variations of past and present words in the *Oxford English Dictionary*. Using those words, we can then create an infinite number of sentences, most of which (like this one) are original. We know that you can know why we worry that you think this sentence is starting to get too complex; but that complexity—and our capacity to communicate and comprehend it—is what distinguishes our human language capacity (Hauser et al., 2002; Premack, 2007).

Language Acquisition and Development

We humans have an astonishing knack for language. With remarkable efficiency, we sample tens of thousands of words in our memory, effortlessly assemble them with near-perfect syntax, and spew them out, three words a second (Vigliocco & Hartsuiker, 2002). Seldom do we form sentences in our minds before speaking them. Rather, we organize them on the fly as we speak. And while doing all this, we adapt our utterances to our social and cultural context. We also follow norms for speaking (*How far apart should we stand?*) and listening (*Is it okay to interrupt?*). Given how many ways there are to mess up, it's amazing that we master this social dance. How and when does it happen?

Language Acquisition: How Do We Learn Language?

LOQ **27-2** How do we acquire language, and what is *universal grammar?*

Linguist Noam Chomsky has argued that language is an unlearned human trait, separate from other parts of human cognition. He theorized that a built-in predisposition to learn grammar rules, which he called *universal grammar,* helps explain why preschoolers pick up language so readily and use grammar so well. It happens so naturally—as naturally as birds learn to fly—that training hardly helps. Whether in Indiana or Indonesia, we intuitively follow similar syntax rules (Aryawibawa & Ambridge, 2019). All human languages—and there are more than 6000 of them—have nouns, verbs, and adjectives as grammatical building blocks, and order and utter words in some common ways (Blasi et al., 2016; Futrell et al., 2015).

Other researchers note that children actually learn grammar as they discern patterns in the language they hear (Ibbotson & Tomasello, 2016). And even Chomsky agrees that we are not born with a built-in *specific* language or *specific* set of grammatical rules. The world's languages are structurally very diverse—more so than the universal grammar idea implies (Bergen, 2014). Whatever language we experience as children, whether spoken or signed, we will readily learn its specific grammar and vocabulary (Bavelier et al., 2003). And no matter what language we learn, we start speaking it mostly in nouns (*kitty, da-da*) rather than in verbs and adjectives (Bornstein et al., 2004). Biology and experience work together.

Language Development: When Do We Learn Language?

LOQ **27-3** What are the milestones in language development, and when is the critical period for acquiring language?

Make a quick guess: How many words of your native language did you learn between your first birthday and your high school graduation? Although you use only 150 words for about half of what you say, you probably learned about 60,000 words (Bloom, 2000; McMurray, 2007). That averages (after age 2) nearly 3500 words each year, or nearly 10 each day! How you did it—how those 3500 words could so far outnumber the roughly 200 words your schoolteachers consciously taught you each year—is one of the great human wonders.

Could you even now state the rules of syntax (the correct way to string words together to form sentences) for the language(s) you speak fluently? Most of us cannot. Yet before you were able to add 2+2, you were creating your own original sentences and applying these rules. As a preschooler, you comprehended and spoke with a facility that would put to shame college students struggling to learn a new language.

"Language is a uniquely human gift, central to our experience of being human." — Lera Boroditsky (2009)

"Got idea. Talk better. Combine words. Make sentences."

language our spoken, written, or signed words and the ways we combine them to communicate meaning.

phoneme in a language, the smallest distinctive sound unit.

morpheme in a language, the smallest unit that carries meaning; may be a word or a part of a word (such as a prefix).

grammar in a language, a system of rules that enables us to communicate with and understand others. *Semantics* is the language's set of rules for deriving meaning from sounds, and *syntax* is its set of rules for combining words into grammatically sensible sentences.

© Susan Meiselas/Magnum Photos

Creating a language Brought together as if on a desert island (actually a school), Nicaragua's young deaf children over time drew upon sign gestures from home to create their own Nicaraguan Sign Language, complete with words and intricate grammar. Our biological predisposition for language does not create language in a vacuum. But activated by a social context, nature and nurture work creatively together (Osborne, 1999; Sandler et al., 2005; Senghas & Coppola, 2001).

Care to guess babies' most common first words? (A hint: They tend to be similar across languages.) In English, Croatian, French, Italian, and Kiswahili, they are *mommy* and *daddy* (Frank et al., 2019).

RECEPTIVE LANGUAGE Children's language development moves from simplicity to complexity. Infants start without language (*in fantis* means "not speaking"). Yet by 4 months of age, babies can recognize differences in speech sounds (Stager & Werker, 1997). They can also read lips. We know this because in experiments, babies have preferred looking at a face that matches a sound—an "*ah*" coming from wide open lips and an "*ee*" from a mouth with corners pulled back (Kuhl & Meltzoff, 1982). Recognizing such differences marks the beginning of the development of babies' *receptive language*, their ability to understand what is said to and about them.

Infants' language comprehension greatly outpaces their language production. Even at 6 months, long before speaking, many infants recognize object names (Bergelson & Swingley, 2012, 2013). At 7 months and beyond, they grow in their power to do what adults find difficult when listening to an unfamiliar language: to segment spoken sounds into individual words. When adults listen to an unfamiliar language, the syllables all run together. A young Sudanese couple new to North America and unfamiliar with English might, for example, hear *United Nations* as "Uneye Tednay Shuns." Their 7-month-old daughter would not have this problem. Human infants display a remarkable ability to learn statistical aspects of human speech (Batterink, 2017; Werker et al., 2012). Their brains not only discern word breaks, they statistically analyze which syllables—as in *hap-py-ba-by*—most often go together. After just two minutes of exposure to a computer voice speaking an unbroken, monotone string of nonsense syllables (*bidakupadotigo-labubidaku . . .*), 8-month-olds were able to recognize (as indicated by their attention) three-syllable sequences that appeared repeatedly (Saffran, 2009; Saffran et al., 1996).

PRODUCTIVE LANGUAGE Long after the beginnings of receptive language, babies' *productive language*—their ability to produce words—matures. Before nurture molds babies' speech, nature enables a wide range of possible sounds in the **babbling stage,** beginning around 4 months. Many of these spontaneously uttered sounds are consonant-vowel pairs formed by simply bunching the tongue in the front of the mouth (*da-da, na-na, ta-ta*) or by opening and closing the lips (*ma-ma*), both of which babies do naturally for feeding (MacNeilage & Davis, 2000). Babbling does not imitate the adult speech babies hear—it includes sounds from various languages. From this early babbling, a listener could not identify an infant as being, say, French, Korean, or Ethiopian.

By about 10 months old, infants' babbling has changed so that a trained ear can identify the household language (de Boysson-Bardies et al., 1989). Deaf infants who observe their deaf parents signing begin to babble more with their hands (Petitto & Marentette, 1991). Without exposure to other languages, babies lose their ability to do what we (believe it or not) cannot—to discriminate and produce sounds and tones found outside our native language (Kuhl et al., 2014; Meltzoff et al., 2009). Thus, by adulthood, those who speak only English cannot discriminate certain sounds in Japanese speech. Nor can Japanese adults with no training in English hear the difference between the English *r* and *l*. For a Japanese-speaking adult, "*la-la-ra-ra*" may sound like the same syllable repeated.

Around their first birthday, most children enter the **one-word stage.** They have already learned that sounds carry meanings, and if repeatedly trained to associate, say, *fish* with a picture of a fish, 1-year-olds will look at a fish when a researcher says, "Fish, fish! Look at the fish!" (Schafer, 2005). They begin to use sounds—usually only one barely recognizable syllable, such as *ma* or *da*—to communicate meaning. But family members learn to understand, and gradually the infant's language conforms more to the family's language. Across the world, baby's first words are often nouns that label objects or people (Tardif et al., 2008). At this one-word stage, a single inflected word ("*Doggy!*") may equal a sentence ("*Look at the dog out there!*").

At about 18 months, children's word learning explodes from about a word per week to a word per day. By their second birthday, most have entered the **two-word stage** (**TABLE 27.1**). They start uttering two-word sentences in **telegraphic speech.** Like yesterday's telegrams that charged by the word ("TERMS ACCEPTED. SEND MONEY"), a 2-year-old's speech contains mostly nouns and verbs ("*Want juice*"). Also like telegrams, their speech follows rules of syntax, arranging words in a sensible order. English-speaking children typically place adjectives before nouns—*white house* rather than *house white*. Spanish reverses this order, as in *casa blanca*.

TABLE 27.1 Summary of Language Development

Month (approximate)	Stage
4	Babbles many speech sounds ("ah-goo")
10	Babbling resembles household language ("ma-ma")
12	One-word speech ("Kitty!")
24	Two-word speech ("Get ball.")
24+	Rapid development into complete sentences

Moving out of the two-word stage, children quickly begin uttering longer phrases (Fromkin & Rodman, 1983). By early elementary school, they understand complex sentences and begin to enjoy the humor conveyed by double meanings: "You never starve in the desert because of all the sand-which-is there."

RETRIEVAL PRACTICE

RP-3 What is the difference between *receptive* language and *productive* language, and when do children normally hit these milestones in language development?

ANSWERS IN APPENDIX E

CRITICAL PERIODS Some children—such as those who receive a cochlear implant to enable hearing, or those who are adopted by a family in another country—get a late start on learning a language. For these late bloomers, language development follows the same sequence, although usually at a faster pace (Ertmer et al., 2007; Snedeker et al., 2007). But there is a limit on how long language learning can be delayed. Childhood seems to represent a *critical* (or "sensitive") *period* for mastering certain aspects of language before the language-learning window gradually closes (Hernandez & Li, 2007; Lenneberg, 1967). In one study, Korean language exposure in just the first months of life enabled Korean adoptees in the Netherlands to later do what others could not—to readily learn the consonant sounds of their forgotten language (Choi et al., 2017). Some of what was forgotten was unconsciously retained. But by about age 7, those who have not been exposed to either a spoken or a signed language lose their ability to master *any* language.

Cultural and other environmental variations affect children's language exposure. Among the Tsimane foragers of Bolivia, adults spend less than one minute per daylight hour speaking to children younger than 4 years old (Cristia et al., 2019). Children exposed to low-quality language—such as American 4-year-olds in classrooms with 3-year-olds, or some children from impoverished homes—often display less language skill (Ansari et al., 2015; Hirsh-Pasek et al., 2015). Reading to children is a good way to increase language exposure. Jessica Logan and her colleagues (2019) found that frequent exposure to popular children's books may help children's school readiness. "Kids who hear more vocabulary words are going to be better prepared to see those words in print when they enter school," she suggested.

Language learning ability is universal, but it is easiest when we're children. If we learn a new language as adults, we will usually speak it with the accent of our native language, and with imperfect grammar (Hartshorne et al., 2018). In one experiment, U.S. immigrants from South Korea and China considered 276 English sentences ("*Yesterday the hunter shoots a deer*") and decided whether they were grammatically correct or incorrect (Johnson & Newport, 1991). All had been in the United States for approximately 10 years: Some had arrived in early childhood, others as adults. As **FIGURE 27.1** reveals, those who learned their second language early learned it best.

The older we are when moving to a new country, the harder it is to learn its language and to absorb its culture (Cheung et al., 2011; Hakuta et al., 2003). When I [ND] first went to Japan, I was told not even to bother trying to bow, that there were something like a dozen different bows and I was always going to "bow with an accent."

Purestock/AGE Fotostock

A natural talent
Human infants come with a remarkable capacity to soak up language. But the particular language they learn will reflect their unique interactions with others.

babbling stage the stage in speech development, beginning around 4 months, during which an infant spontaneously utters various sounds that are not all related to the household language.

one-word stage the stage in speech development, from about age 1 to 2, during which a child speaks mostly in single words.

two-word stage the stage in speech development, beginning about age 2, during which a child speaks mostly in two-word sentences.

telegraphic speech the early speech stage in which a child speaks like a telegram—"go car"—using mostly nouns and verbs.

→ **FIGURE 27.1**
Our ability to learn a new language diminishes with age Ten years after coming to the United States, Asian immigrants took an English grammar test. Although there is no sharply defined critical period for second language learning, those who arrived before age 8 understood American English grammar as well as native speakers did. Those who arrived later did not. (Data from Johnson & Newport, 1991.)

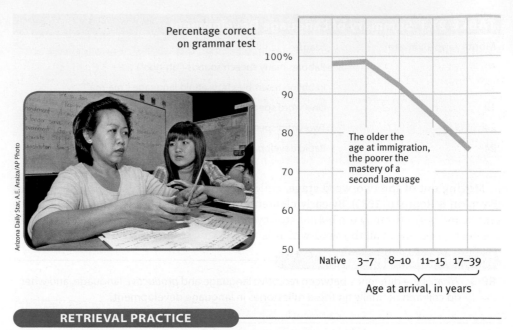

Percentage correct on grammar test

The older the age at immigration, the poorer the mastery of a second language

Native   3–7   8–10   11–15   17–39

Age at arrival, in years

Arizona Daily Star, A.E. Araiza/AP Photo

RETRIEVAL PRACTICE

RP-4 Why is it so difficult to learn a new language in adulthood?

ANSWERS IN APPENDIX E

Deafness and Language Development

The impact of early experiences is evident in language learning in prelingually (before learning language) deaf children born to hearing-nonsigning parents. These children typically do not experience language during their early years. Natively deaf children who learn sign language after age 9 never learn it as well as those who learned it early in life. Those who learn to sign as teens or adults are like immigrants who learn a second language after childhood: They can master basic words and learn to order them, but they never become as fluent as native signers in producing and comprehending subtle grammatical differences (Newport, 1990). As a flower's growth will be stunted without nourishment, so, too, children will typically become linguistically stunted if isolated from language during the critical period for its acquisition.

More than 90 percent of all deaf children are born to hearing parents. Most of these parents want their children to experience their world of sound and talk. Cochlear implants enable this by converting sounds into electrical signals and stimulating the auditory nerve by means of electrodes threaded into the child's cochlea. But if an implant is to help children become proficient in oral communication, parents cannot delay the surgery until their child reaches the age of consent. Giving cochlear implants to children is hotly debated. Deaf culture advocates object to giving implants to children who were deaf prelingually. The National Association of the Deaf, for example, argues that deafness is *not* a disability because native signers are not linguistically disabled. More than five decades ago, Gallaudet University linguist William Stokoe (1960) showed that sign is a complete language with its own grammar, syntax, and meanings. Deaf culture advocates sometimes further contend that deafness could as well be considered "vision enhancement" as "hearing impairment." Close your eyes and immediately you, too, will notice your attention being drawn to your other senses. In one experiment, people who had spent 90 minutes sitting quietly blindfolded became more accurate in their location of sounds (Lewald, 2007). When kissing, lovers minimize distraction and increase sensitivity by closing their eyes.

People who lose one channel of sensation compensate with a slight enhancement of their other sensory abilities (Backman & Dixon, 1992; Levy & Langer, 1992). Those who have been deaf from birth exhibit enhanced visual processing (Almeida et al., 2015). Their auditory cortex, starved for sensory input, remains largely intact but becomes responsive to touch and to visual input (Karns et al., 2012). Once repurposed, the auditory cortex becomes less available for hearing—which helps explain why cochlear implants are most effective when given before age 2 (Geers & Nicholas, 2013; Niparko et al., 2010).

LIVING IN A SILENT WORLD Worldwide, 466 million people live with hearing loss (WHO, 2019). Some are profoundly deaf; most (more men than women) have hearing loss (Agrawal et al., 2008). Some were deaf from birth; others have known the hearing world. Some sign and identify with the language-based Deaf culture. Others, especially those who lost their hearing after speaking a language, are "oral" and converse with the hearing world by reading lips or written notes. Still others move between the two cultures.

The challenges of life without hearing may be greatest for children. Unable to communicate in customary ways, signing playmates may struggle to coordinate their play with speaking playmates. School achievement may also suffer; academic subjects are rooted in *spoken* languages. Adolescents may feel socially excluded, with a resulting low self-confidence. Deaf children who grow up around other deaf people more often identify with Deaf culture and feel positive self-esteem. If raised in a signing household, whether by deaf or hearing parents, they also express higher self-esteem and feel more accepted (Bat-Chava, 1993, 1994).

Adults who lose hearing late in life also face challenges. Expending effort to hear words drains their capacity to perceive, comprehend, and remember them (Wingfield et al., 2005). In several studies, people with hearing loss, especially those not wearing hearing aids, have reported more sadness, less social engagement, and worrying that they irritate others (Kashubeck-West & Meyer, 2008; National Council on Aging, 1999). They also may experience a sort of shyness: "It's almost universal among the deaf to want to cause hearing people as little fuss as possible," observed Henry Kisor (1990, p. 244), a Chicago newspaper editor and columnist who lost his hearing at age 3. "We can be self-effacing and diffident to the point of invisibility. Sometimes this tendency can be crippling. I must fight it all the time." Helen Keller, both blind and deaf, noted that "blindness cuts people off from things. Deafness cuts people off from people."

I [DM] understand. My mother, with whom we communicated by writing notes on an erasable "magic pad," spent her last dozen years in an utterly silent world, largely withdrawn from the stress and strain of trying to interact with people outside a small circle of family and old friends. My own hearing is declining on a trajectory toward hers (with my hearing aids out at night, I cannot understand my wife speaking from her adjacent pillow). Even with hearing aids, I sit front and center at plays and meetings and seek quiet corners in restaurants. I do benefit from cool technology (see HearingLoop.org) that, at the press of a button, can transform my hearing aids into in-the-ear loudspeakers for the broadcast of phone, TV, and public address system sound. Yet I still experience frustration when, with or without hearing aids, I can't hear the joke everyone else is guffawing over; when, after repeated tries, I just can't catch that exasperated person's question and can't fake my way around it; when family members give up and say, "Oh, never mind" after trying three times to tell me something unimportant.

As she aged, my mother came to feel that seeking social interaction was simply not worth the effort. I share newspaper columnist Kisor's belief that communication is worth the effort (p. 246): "So, . . . I will grit my teeth and plunge ahead." To reach out, to connect, to communicate with others, even across a chasm of silence, is to affirm our humanity as social creatures.

Hearing improved A boy in Malawi experiences new hearing aids.

The Brain and Language

LOQ 27-4 What brain areas are involved in language processing and speech?

We think of speaking and reading, or writing and reading, or singing and speaking as merely different examples of the same general ability—language. But consider this curious finding: Damage to any of several cortical areas can produce **aphasia,** impairment of language. Even more curious, some people with aphasia can speak fluently but cannot read (despite good vision). Others can comprehend what they read but cannot speak. Still others can write but not read, read but not write, read numbers but not letters, or sing but not speak. These cases suggest that language is complex, and that different brain areas must serve different language functions.

aphasia impairment of language, usually caused by left hemisphere damage either to Broca's area (impairing speaking) or to Wernicke's area (impairing understanding).

(a)
Speaking words
(Broca's area and
the motor cortex)

(b)
Hearing words
(Wernicke's area and
the auditory cortex)

⑦ FIGURE 27.2
Brain activity when speaking and hearing words

Indeed, in 1865, French physician Paul Broca confirmed a fellow physician's observation that after damage to an area of the left frontal lobe (later called **Broca's area**) a person would struggle to *speak* words, yet could sing familiar songs and comprehend speech. A decade later, German investigator Carl Wernicke discovered that after damage to a specific area of the left temporal lobe (**Wernicke's area**), people were unable to *understand* others' sentences and could speak only meaningless sentences. Asked to describe a picture that showed two boys stealing cookies behind a woman's back, one patient responded: "Mother is away her working her work to get her better, but when she's looking the two boys looking the other part. She's working another time" (Geschwind, 1979).

Today's neuroscience has confirmed brain activity in Broca's and Wernicke's areas during language processing (**FIGURE 27.2**). For people with aphasia, electrical stimulation of Broca's area can help restore their speaking abilities (Marangolo et al., 2016). (For those with a larger-than-average Broca's area, grammar learning is a breeze [Novén et al., 2019].) But we also now know that the brain's processing of language is complex. Broca's area coordinates with the brain's processing of language in other areas as well (Flinker et al., 2015; Tremblay & Dick, 2016). Although you experience language as a single, unified stream, fMRI scans would show that your brain is busily multitasking and networking. Different neural networks are activated by nouns and verbs (or objects and actions); by different vowels; by stories of visual versus motor experiences; by who spoke and what was said; and by many other stimuli (Perrachione et al., 2011; Shapiro et al., 2006; Speer et al., 2009). And these same networks become activated whether you're reading or listening to the words (Deniz et al., 2019).

Moreover, if you're lucky enough to be natively fluent in two languages, your brain processes them in similar areas (Kim et al., 2017). But your brain doesn't use the same areas if you learned a second language after the first or if you sign rather than speak your second language (Berken et al., 2015; Kovelman et al., 2014).

The point to remember: In processing language, as in other forms of information processing, the brain operates by dividing its mental functions—speaking, perceiving, thinking, remembering—into subfunctions. Your conscious experience of reading this page *seems* indivisible, but, thanks to your parallel processing, many different neural networks are pooling their work to give meaning to the words, sentences, and paragraphs (Fedorenko et al., 2016; Snell & Grainger, 2019). *E pluribus unum:* Out of many, one.

Talking hands Human language appears to have evolved from gestured communications (Corballis, 2002, 2003; Pollick & de Waal, 2007). Even today, gestures are naturally associated with spontaneous speech, and similarly so for blind and sighted speakers of a given language (Özçaliskan et al., 2016). Both gesture and speech communicate, and when they convey the same rather than different information (as they do in baseball's sign language), we humans understand faster and more accurately (Dargue et al., 2019; Hostetter, 2011; Kelly et al., 2010). Outfielder William Hoy, the first deaf player to join the major leagues (1892), reportedly helped invent hand signals for "Strike!" "Safe!" (shown here) and "Yerr out!" (Pollard, 1992). Referees in all sports now use invented signs, and fans are fluent in sports sign language.

RETRIEVAL PRACTICE

RP-5 _____ _____ is one part of the brain that, if damaged, might impair your ability to speak words. Damage to _____ _____ might impair your ability to understand language.

ANSWERS IN APPENDIX E

🌊 To review research on left and right hemisphere language processing—and to test your own processing speed—see *Topic Tutorial: PsychSim6, Dueling Hemispheres.*

Jim Cummins/Getty Images

Do Other Species Have Language?

LOQ 27-5 What do we know about other species' capacity for language?

Humans, more than other animals, have a capacity for taking others' perspectives and regulating themselves with a moral sense (Tomasello, 2019). Humans also have long proclaimed that language sets us above other animals. "When we study human language," asserted linguist Noam Chomsky (1972), "we are approaching what some might call the 'human essence,' the qualities of mind that are, so far as we know, unique [to humans]." Is it true that humans, alone, have language?

Some animals display basic language processing. Pigeons can learn the difference between words and nonwords, but they could never read this book (Scarf et al., 2016).

Other animals show impressive comprehension and communication. Various monkey species sound different alarm cries for different predators, such as a barking call for a leopard, a cough for an eagle, and a chuttering for a snake. Hearing the leopard alarm, vervets climb the nearest tree. Hearing the eagle alarm, they rush into the bushes. Hearing the snake alarm, they stand up and scan the ground (Byrne, 1991; Clarke et al., 2015; Coye et al., 2015). To indicate multiple threats (some combination of eagle, leopard, falling tree, neighboring group), monkeys will combine 6 different calls into a 25-call sequence (Balter, 2010). But are such communications language?

In the late 1960s, psychologists Allen Gardner and Beatrix Gardner (1969) aroused enormous scientific and public interest with their work with Washoe, a young chimpanzee. Building on chimpanzees' natural tendencies for gestured communication, they taught Washoe sign language. After four years, Washoe could use 132 signs; by her life's end in 2007, she was using 250 signs (Metzler, 2011; Sanz et al., 1998).

During the 1970s, more and more reports came in. Some chimpanzees were stringing signs together to form sentences. Washoe, for example, signed "You me go out, please." Some word combinations seemed creative—saying *water bird* for "swan" or *apple-which-is-orange* for "orange" (Patterson, 1978; Rumbaugh, 1977).

But by the late 1970s, other psychologists were growing skeptical. Were the chimps language champs or were the researchers chumps? Consider, said the skeptics:

- Ape vocabularies and sentences are simple, rather like those of a 2-year-old child. And unlike children, apes gain their limited vocabularies only with great difficulty (Wynne, 2004, 2008). Speaking or signing children can easily soak up dozens of new words each week, and 60,000 by adulthood.

- Chimpanzees can make signs or push buttons in a sequence to get a reward. The apes' signing might be nothing more than aping their trainers' signs and learning that certain arm movements produce rewards (Terrace, 1979).

- When information is unclear, we are prone to *perceptual set*—a tendency to see what we want or expect to see. Interpreting chimpanzee signs as language may have been little more than the trainers' wishful thinking (Terrace, 1979). When Washoe signed *water bird*, she may have been separately naming *water* and *bird*.

- "Give orange me give eat orange me eat orange . . ." is a far cry from the exquisite syntax of a 3-year-old (Anderson, 2004; Pinker, 1995). Rules of syntax in human language govern the order of words in sentences. So to a child, "You tickle" and "Tickle you" communicate different ideas. A chimpanzee, lacking these rules of syntax, might use the same sequence of signs for both phrases.

Controversy can stimulate progress, and in this case, it triggered more evidence of other species' abilities to think and communicate. One surprising finding was that Washoe trained her adopted son Loulis to use the signs she had learned. Without human assistance, Loulis eventually picked up 68 signs, simply by observing Washoe and three other language-trained chimps signing together. Even more stunning was a later report: Kanzi, a bonobo with a reported 384-word vocabulary, could understand syntax in spoken English (Savage-Rumbaugh et al., 1993, 2009). Kanzi, who appears to have the receptive language ability of a human 2-year-old, has responded appropriately when asked, "Can you show me the light?" and "Can you bring me the [flash]light?" and "Can you turn the light on?" Given stuffed animals and asked—for the first time—to "make the dog bite the snake," he put the snake to the dog's mouth.

So, how should we interpret such studies? Are humans the only language-using species? If by language we mean an ability to communicate through a meaningful sequence of symbols, then apes are indeed

Susanne Baus/AFP/Getty Images/Newscom

Broca's area a frontal lobe brain area, usually in the left hemisphere, that helps control language expression by directing the muscle movements involved in speech.

Wernicke's area a brain area, usually in the left temporal lobe, involved in language comprehension and expression.

Comprehending canine Border collie Rico had a vocabulary of 200 human words. If asked to retrieve a toy with a name he had never heard, Rico would pick out a new toy from a group of familiar items (Kaminski et al., 2004). Hearing that name for the second time four weeks later, Rico more often than not would retrieve the same toy. Another border collie, Chaser, has set an animal record by learning 1000 object names (Pilley, 2013). Like a 3-year-old child, she can also categorize them by function and shape. She can "fetch a ball" or "fetch a doll."

But is this language? Chimpanzees' ability to express themselves in American Sign Language (ASL) raises questions about the very nature of language. Here, the trainer is asking, "What is this?" The sign in response is "Baby." Does the response constitute language?

capable of language. But if we mean a verbal or signed expression of complex grammar that enables us to exchange thoughts, most psychologists would now agree that humans alone possess language (Suddendorf, 2018). Moreover, humans, alone, have a version of a gene (FOXP2) that helps enable the lip, tongue, and vocal cord movements of human speech (Lieberman, 2013). Humans with a mutated form of this gene have difficulty speaking words.

One thing is certain: Studies of animal language and thinking have moved psychologists toward a greater appreciation of other species' remarkable abilities (Friend, 2004; Rumbaugh & Washburn, 2003; Wilson et al., 2015). In the past, many psychologists doubted that other species could plan, form concepts, count, use tools, or show compassion (Thorpe, 1974). Today, thanks to animal researchers, we know better. When communicating, chimps seem to consider what others know—*Does my friend know a snake is nearby?* (Crockford et al., 2017). Nonhuman animals exhibit insight, show family loyalty, care for one another, and transmit cultural patterns across generations. Working out what this means for the moral rights of other animals is an unfinished task.

ASK YOURSELF

Can you think of a time when you believed an animal was communicating with you? How might you put that to a test?

RETRIEVAL PRACTICE

RP-6 If your dog barks at a stranger at the door, does this qualify as language? What if the dog yips in a telltale way to let you know she needs to go out?

ANSWERS IN APPENDIX E

> For examples of intelligent communication and problem solving among orangutans, elephants, and killer whales, see the 6-minute *Video: How Intelligent Are Animals?* See also the *Video: Case Studies* for a helpful tutorial animation on this type of research method.

Thinking and Language

LOQ 27-6 What is the relationship between thinking and language, and what is the value of thinking in images?

Thinking and language—which comes first? This is one of psychology's great chicken-and-egg questions. Do our ideas come first and then the words to name them? Or are our thoughts conceived in words and unthinkable without them?

Linguist Benjamin Lee Whorf (1956) contended that "language itself shapes a [person's] basic ideas." The Hopi, who have no past tense for their verbs, could not readily *think* about the past, he said. Today's psychologists believe that a strong form of Whorf's idea—**linguistic determinism**—is too extreme. We all think about things for which we have no words. (Can you think of a shade of blue you cannot name?) And we routinely have *unsymbolized* (wordless, imageless) thoughts, as when someone, while watching two men carry a load of bricks, wondered whether the men would drop them (Heavey & Hurlburt, 2008; Hurlburt et al., 2013).

A weaker version of linguistic determinism—**linguistic relativism**—recognizes that our words influence our thinking (Gentner, 2016). To those who speak two dissimilar languages, such as English and Japanese, it seems obvious that a person may think differently in different languages (Brown, 1986). Unlike English, which has a rich vocabulary for self-focused emotions such as anger, Japanese has more words for interpersonal emotions such as sympathy (Markus & Kitayama, 1991). Many bilingual individuals report that they have different senses of self—that they feel like different people—depending on which language they are using (Matsumoto, 1994; Pavlenko, 2014). In one series of studies with bilingual Israeli Arabs (who spoke both Arabic and Hebrew), participants thought differently about their social world, with differing automatic associations with Arabs and Jews, depending on which language the testing session used (Danziger & Ward, 2010).

linguistic determinism Whorf's hypothesis that language determines the way we think.

linguistic relativism the idea that language influences the way we think.

Depending on which emotion they want to express, bilingual people often switch languages. "When my mom gets angry at me, she'll speak in Mandarin," explained one Chinese-American student. "If she's really mad, she'll switch to Cantonese" (Chen et al., 2012). Bilingual individuals may even reveal different personality profiles when taking the same test in two languages, with their differing cultural associations (Chen & Bond, 2010; Dinges & Hull, 1992). When China-born, bilingual University of Waterloo students were asked to describe themselves in English, their responses fit typical Canadian profiles, expressing mostly positive self-statements and moods. When responding in Chinese, the same students gave typically Chinese self-descriptions, reporting more agreement with Chinese values and roughly equal positive and negative self-statements and moods (Ross et al., 2002). Similar attitude and personality changes have been shown when bicultural, bilingual people shift between the cultural frames associated with Spanish and English, or Arabic and English (Ogunnaike et al., 2010; Ramírez-Esparza et al., 2006). "Learn a new language and get a new soul," says a Czech proverb. When responding in their second language, bilingual people's moral judgments reflect less emotion—they respond with more "head" than "heart" (Costa et al., 2014).

So our words do influence our thinking (Boroditsky, 2011). Words define our mental categories. In Brazil, the isolated Piraha people have words for the numbers 1 and 2, but numbers above that are simply "many." Thus, if shown 7 nuts in a row, they find it difficult to lay out the same number from their own pile (Gordon, 2004).

Words also influence our thinking about colors. Whether we live in New Mexico, New South Wales, or New Guinea, we *see* colors much the same, but we use our native language to *classify* and *remember* them (Davidoff, 2004; Roberson et al., 2004, 2005). Imagine viewing three colors and calling two of them "yellow" and one of them "blue." Later you would likely see and recall the yellows as being more similar. But if you speak the language of Papua New Guinea's Berinmo tribe, which has words for two different shades of yellow, you would more speedily perceive and better recall the variations between the two yellows. And if your native language is Russian or Greek, which have distinct names for various shades of blue, you would perceive and recall the yellows as more similar and remember the blues better (Maier & Abdel Rahman, 2018). Words matter.

Perceived differences grow as we assign different names. On the color spectrum, blue blends into green—until we draw a dividing line between the portions we call "blue" and "green." Although equally different on the color spectrum, two different items that share the same color name (as the two "blues" do in **FIGURE 27.3**, contrast B) are harder to distinguish than two items with different names ("blue" and "green," as in Figure 27.3, contrast A) (Özgen, 2004). Likewise, $4.99 perceptually differs more from $5.01 than from $4.97. And two places seem closer and more vulnerable to the same natural disaster if labeled as in the same state rather than at an equal distance in adjacent states (Burris & Branscombe, 2005; Mishra & Mishra, 2010). Tornadoes don't know about state lines, but people do.

Given words' subtle influence on thinking, we do well to choose our words carefully. Is "A child learns language as *he* interacts with *his* caregivers" any different from "Children learn language as *they* interact with *their* caregivers"? Many studies have found that it is. When hearing the generic *he* (as in "the artist and his work") people are more likely to picture a male (Henley, 1989; Ng, 1990). If *he* and *his* were truly gender free, we shouldn't skip a beat when hearing that "man, like other mammals, nurses his young." Pronoun usage can also influence how we feel about ourselves. Transgender and gender non-conforming youth report feeling respected and included when their preferred pronouns are used—*he/she, him/her, they/their* (Olson & Gülgöz, 2018; Rae et al., 2019).

Culture and color In Papua New Guinea, Berinmo children have words for different shades of "yellow," which might enable them to spot and recall yellow variations more quickly. Here and everywhere, "the languages we speak profoundly shape the way we think, the way we see the world, the way we live our lives," noted psychologist Lera Boroditsky (2009).

A

B

FIGURE 27.3

Language and perception When people view blocks of equally different colors, they perceive those with different names as more different. Thus the "green" and "blue" in contrast A may appear to differ more than the two equally different blues in contrast B (Özgen, 2004).

To expand language is to expand the ability to think. Young children's thinking develops hand in hand with their language (Gopnik & Meltzoff, 1986). Indeed, it is very difficult to think about or conceptualize certain abstract ideas (*commitment, freedom,* or *rhyming*) without language. And what is true for preschoolers is true for everyone: *It pays to increase your word power.* That's why most textbooks, including this one, introduce new words—to teach new ideas and new ways of thinking. And that's also why Steven Pinker (2007) titled his book on language *The Stuff of Thought.*

Increased word power helps explain what McGill University researcher Wallace Lambert has called the *bilingual advantage* (1992; Lambert et al., 1993). Learning a second language at a young age promotes development of language-related brain regions (Legault et al., 2019; Luo et al., 2019). Some (but not all) studies have shown bilingual people to be skilled at inhibiting one language while using the other—for example, inhibiting "crayón amarillo" while saying "yellow crayon" at school, then doing the reverse at home (Bialystok et al., 2015; Lehtonen et al., 2018; Tsui et al., 2019). Bilingual children also exhibit enhanced social skill, by being better able to shift to understand another's perspective (Fan et al., 2015; Gampe et al., 2019). The bilingual advantage even extends to aging by preserving healthy brain functioning later in life (Li et al., 2017).

Bilingual people's switching between different languages does, however, take a moment (Kleinman & Gollan, 2016; Palomar-García et al., 2015). That's a phenomenon I [DM] failed to realize before speaking to bilingual Chinese colleagues in Beijing. While I spoke in English, my accompanying slides were in Chinese. Alas, I later learned, the translated slides required constant "code switching" from my spoken words, thus making it hard for my audience to process both.

Lambert helped devise a Canadian program that has, since 1981, immersed millions of English-speaking children in French (Statistics Canada, 2013). Not surprisingly, the children attain a natural French fluency unrivaled by other methods of language teaching. Moreover, compared with similarly capable children in control groups, they do so without detriment to their English fluency, and with increased aptitude scores, creativity, and appreciation for French-Canadian culture (Genesee & Gándara, 1999; Lazaruk, 2007).

Whether we are in the linguistic minority or majority, language links us to one another. Language also connects us to the past and the future. "To destroy a people," goes a saying, "destroy their language."

ASK YOURSELF

Consider a language you began to learn *after* learning your first language. How did learning this other language differ from learning your first language? Does speaking it feel different?

RETRIEVAL PRACTICE

RP-7 Benjamin Lee Whorf's controversial hypothesis, called _____ _____, suggested that we cannot think about things unless we have words for those concepts or ideas.

ANSWERS IN APPENDIX E

Play the role of a researcher studying the benefits of learning more than one language by engaging online with *How Would You Know If There Is a Bilingual Advantage?*

Thinking in Images

When you are alone, do you talk to yourself? Is "thinking" simply conversing with yourself? Words do convey ideas. But sometimes ideas precede words. To turn on the cold water in your bathroom, in which direction do you turn the handle? To answer, you probably thought not in words but with *implicit* (nondeclarative, procedural) memory—a mental picture of how you do it.

Indeed, we often think in images. Artists think in images. So do composers, poets, mathematicians, athletes, and scientists. Albert Einstein reported that he achieved some of his greatest insights through visual images and later put them into words. Pianist Liu Chi Kung harnessed the power of thinking in images. One year after placing second in the 1958 Tchaikovsky piano competition, Liu was imprisoned during China's cultural revolution. Soon after his release, after 7 years without touching a piano, he was back on tour. Critics judged Liu's musicianship as better than ever. How did he continue to develop without practice? "I did practice," said Liu, "every day. I rehearsed every piece I had ever played, note by note, in my mind" (Garfield, 1986).

For someone who has learned a skill, such as ballet dancing, even *watching* the activity will activate the brain's internal simulation of it (Calvo-Merino et al., 2004). So, too, will *imagining* a physical experience, which activates some of the same neural networks that are active during the actual experience (Grèzes & Decety, 2001). Small wonder, then, that mental practice has become a standard part of training for Olympic athletes (Blumenstein & Orbach, 2012; Ungerleider, 2005).

One experiment on mental practice and basketball free-throw shooting tracked the University of Tennessee women's team over 35 games (Savoy & Beitel, 1996). During that time, the team's free-throw accuracy increased from approximately 52 percent in games following standard physical practice, to some 65 percent after mental practice. Players had repeatedly imagined making free throws under various conditions, including being "trash-talked" by their opposition. In a dramatic conclusion, Tennessee won the national championship game in overtime, thanks in part to their free-throw shooting.

Mental rehearsal can also help you achieve an academic goal, as researchers demonstrated with two groups of introductory psychology students facing a midterm exam 1 week later (Taylor et al., 1998). (Students who were not engaged in any mental rehearsal formed a third, control group.) The first group spent 5 minutes each day visualizing themselves scanning the posted grade list, seeing their A, beaming with joy, and feeling proud. This daily *outcome simulation* had little effect, adding only 2 points to their exam-score average. The second group spent 5 minutes each day visualizing themselves effectively studying — reading their text, going over notes, eliminating distractions, declining an offer to go out. This daily *process simulation* paid off: The group began studying sooner, spent more time at it, and beat the others' average score by 8 points. *The point to remember*: It's better to spend your fantasy time planning *how* to reach your goal than to focus on your desired destination.

* * *

What, then, should we say about the relationship between thinking and language? As we have seen, language influences our thinking. But if thinking did not also affect language, there would never be any new words. And new words and new combinations of old words express new ideas. The basketball term *slam dunk* was coined after the act itself had become fairly common. *Blogs* became part of our language after "web logs" appeared. So, let us say that *thinking affects our language, which then affects our thought* (**FIGURE 27.4**).

Psychological research on thinking and language mirrors the mixed impressions of our species by those in fields such as literature and religion. The human mind is simultaneously capable of striking intellectual failures and of striking intellectual power. Misjudgments are common and can have disastrous consequences. So we do well to appreciate our capacity for error. Yet our ingenuity at problem solving and our extraordinary power of language mark humankind as (in Shakespeare's words) almost "infinite in faculties."

> "When we see a person walking down the street talking to himself, we generally assume that he is mentally ill. But we all talk to ourselves continuously—we just have the good sense of keeping our mouths shut. . . . It's as though we are having a conversation with an imaginary friend possessed of infinite patience. Who are we talking to?"
>
> — Sam Harris, "We Are Lost in Thought," 2011

Blend Images/Getty Images

JupiterImages/Getty Images

⊖ **FIGURE 27.4**
The interplay of thought and language
The traffic runs both ways between thinking and language. Thinking affects our language, which affects our thought.

Thinking

Language

ASK YOURSELF

How could you use mental practice to improve your performance in some area of your life—for example, in your schoolwork, personal relationships, or hobbies?

RETRIEVAL PRACTICE

RP-8 What is mental practice, and how can it help you to prepare for an upcoming event?

ANSWERS IN APPENDIX E

To experience your own thinking as (a) manipulating words and (b) manipulating images, see *Topic Tutorial: PsychSim6, My Head Is Spinning!*

27 REVIEW Language and Thought

LEARNING OBJECTIVES

Test Yourself Answer these repeated Learning Objective Questions on your own (before checking the answers in Appendix D) to improve your retention of the concepts (McDaniel et al., 2009, 2015).

LOQ 27-1 What are the structural components of a language?

LOQ 27-2 How do we acquire language, and what is *universal grammar*?

LOQ 27-3 What are the milestones in language development, and when is the critical period for acquiring language?

LOQ 27-4 What brain areas are involved in language processing and speech?

LOQ 27-5 What do we know about other species' capacity for language?

LOQ 27-6 What is the relationship between thinking and language, and what is the value of thinking in images?

TERMS AND CONCEPTS TO REMEMBER

Test Yourself Write down the definition in your own words, then check your answer.

language, p. 341
phoneme, p. 341
morpheme, p. 341
grammar, p. 341
babbling stage, p. 343
one-word stage, p. 343
two-word stage, p. 343

telegraphic speech, p. 343
aphasia, p. 345
Broca's area, p. 347
Wernicke's area, p. 347
linguistic determinism, p. 348
linguistic relativism, p. 348

MASTER THE MATERIAL

Test Yourself Answer the following questions on your own first, then check your answers in Appendix E.

1. Children reach the one-word stage of speech development at about
   a. 4 months.
   b. 6 months.
   c. 1 year.
   d. 2 years.

2. The three basic building blocks of language are _____, _____, and _____.

3. When young children speak in short phrases using mostly verbs and nouns, this is referred to as _____ _____.

4. According to Chomsky, humans have a built-in predisposition to learn grammar rules. He calls this trait _____ _____.

5. Most researchers agree that apes can
   a. communicate through symbols.
   b. reproduce most human speech sounds.
   c. master language in adulthood.
   d. surpass a human 3-year-old in language skills.

Continue testing yourself with **LearningCurve** or **Achieve Read & Practice** to learn and remember most effectively.

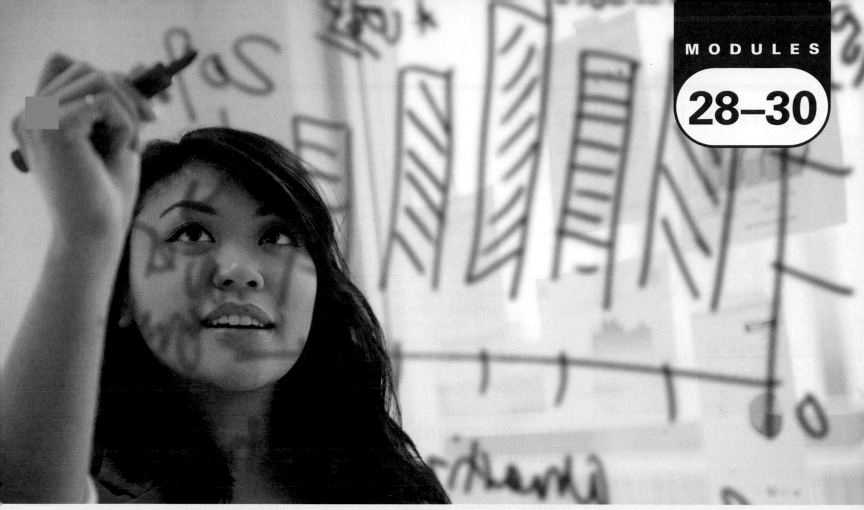

Intelligence

Little Natey's parents never thought he'd excel in the classroom. They were just being realistic: Their son often seemed bored at school. He was never the "smart" kid. Natey overwhelmingly preferred sports to studying. Eventually, he became a skilled musician, learning how to sing and to play multiple instruments. College wasn't in Natey's plans. He definitely wanted a music career. Then Natey's father suggested, "Maybe try a year of college. It can't hurt." So, Natey agreed.

To fill his course schedule, Natey registered for Introduction to Psychology. The assigned text—an earlier edition of the very book you're reading now—left him abuzz with excitement: "I had no idea you could use science to understand people!" Although he did not earn an A, Natey learned something that forever changed his life: Hard work and persistence could grow his knowledge.

With his new mindset, Natey immersed himself in psychology. He read dozens of psychology books and began to excel in his classes. He gained research experience and attended academic conferences. Natey went on to earn two master's degrees and a Ph.D. in psychology and became a professor—and one of your authors. Yes, that's correct: Natey (a family nickname) is me [ND].

In and beyond psychology, few topics have sparked more debate than the *intelligence* controversy: Does each of us have an inborn general mental capacity (intelligence)? Can we quantify this capacity as a meaningful number? How much does intelligence vary within and between groups, and why? How do beliefs about intelligence—whether it is unchangeable or can grow through experience—influence academic achievement?

Modules 28–30 offer answers, by identifying a variety of mental gifts and concluding that the recipe for high achievement blends talent, grit, and life circumstances.

28 What Is Intelligence?

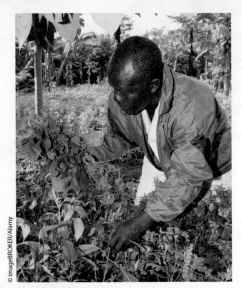

Hands-on healing The socially constructed concept of intelligence varies from culture to culture. This natural healer in Cameroon displays intelligence in his knowledge about medicinal plants and his understanding of the needs of the people he is helping.

LEARNING OBJECTIVE QUESTION **LOQ** **28-1** How do psychologists define *intelligence?*

In many studies, *intelligence* has been defined as whatever *intelligence tests* measure, which has tended to be school smarts. But intelligence is not a quality like height or weight, which has the same meaning to everyone worldwide. People assign this term to the qualities that enable success in their own time and culture (Sternberg & Kaufman, 1998). In Cameroon's equatorial forest, *intelligence* may reflect understanding the medicinal qualities of local plants. In a North American high school, it may reflect mastering difficult concepts in calculus or chemistry. In both places, **intelligence** is the ability to learn from experience, solve problems, and use knowledge to adapt to new situations.

You probably know some people with talents in science, others who excel in the humanities, and still others gifted in athletics, art, music, or dance. You may also know a talented artist who is stumped by the simplest math problem, or a brilliant math student who struggles when discussing literature. Are all these people intelligent? Could you rate their intelligence on a single scale? Or would you need several different scales?

Spearman and Thurstone's Intelligence Theories

LOQ **28-2** What are the arguments for *g?*

Charles Spearman (1863–1945) believed we have one **general intelligence** (often shortened to **g**) that is at the heart of all our intelligent behavior, from navigating the sea to excelling in school. He granted that people often have special, outstanding abilities. But he noted that those who score high in one area, such as verbal intelligence, typically score higher than average in other areas, such as spatial or reasoning ability.

Spearman's (1904) belief stemmed in part from his work with *factor analysis*, a statistical procedure that identifies clusters of related variables. His idea of a general mental capacity expressed by a single intelligence score was controversial in Spearman's day, and so it remains. One of Spearman's early critics was L. L. Thurstone (1887–1955). Thurstone gave 56 different tests to people and mathematically identified seven clusters of *primary mental abilities* (word fluency, verbal comprehension, spatial ability, perceptual speed, numerical ability, inductive reasoning, and memory). Thurstone did not rank people on a single scale of general aptitude. But when other investigators studied these profiles, they detected a persistent tendency: Those who excelled in one of the seven clusters generally scored well on the others. So, the investigators concluded, there was still some evidence of a *g* factor.

We might, then, liken mental abilities to physical abilities: Athleticism is not one thing, but many. The ability to run fast is distinct from the eye-hand coordination required to throw a ball on target. Yet there remains some tendency for good things to come packaged together—for running speed and throwing accuracy to correlate. So, too, with intelligence—for humans worldwide (Warne & Burningham, 2019). Several distinct abilities tend to cluster together and to correlate enough to define a general intelligence factor. Distinct brain networks enable distinct abilities, with *g* explained by their coordinated activity (Cole et al., 2015; Kocevar et al., 2019).

The Cattell-Horn-Carroll Intelligence Theory

LOQ **28-3** How have the concepts of *Gf* and *Gc*, and the *CHC theory,* affected our understanding of intelligence?

Raymond Cattell (1905–1998) and his student, John Horn (1928–2006) simplified Thurstone's primary mental abilities into two factors: **fluid intelligence (Gf)**—our ability to reason speedily and abstractly, as when solving logic problems—and **crystallized intelligence (Gc)**—

"*g* is one of the most reliable and valid measures in the behavioral domain . . . and it predicts important social outcomes such as educational and occupational levels far better than any other trait." — Behavior geneticist Robert Plomin (1999)

intelligence the ability to learn from experience, solve problems, and use knowledge to adapt to new situations.

general intelligence (g) according to Spearman and others, underlies all mental abilities and is therefore measured by every task on an intelligence test.

fluid intelligence (Gf) our ability to reason speedily and abstractly; tends to decrease with age, especially during late adulthood.

crystallized intelligence (Gc) our accumulated knowledge and verbal skills; tends to increase with age.

Cattell-Horn-Carroll (CHC) theory the theory that our intelligence is based on *g* as well as specific abilities, bridged by *Gf* and *Gc*.

our accumulated knowledge as reflected in vocabulary and applied skills (Cattell, 1963). An experienced computer programmer may use her *Gf* to develop creative new theories of computer programming. Her *Gc* may be evident in the way she expertly discusses her work at a conference. Our *Gf* and *Gc* often work together, as when we solve problems by drawing on our accumulated knowledge.

How well did Cattell and Horn's *Gf* and *Gc* research support the idea of a single intelligence factor (*g*)? To answer this question, John Carroll (1993) analyzed hundreds of previous intelligence studies and found support for the following:

- There is a general intelligence factor (*g*).
- We also have more specific abilities.
- *Gf* and *Gc* bridge the gap from general intelligence to specific abilities. We use our *g*-based *fluid intelligence* to learn, and we gain *crystallized intelligence* (specific abilities) in return.

From this work, the **Cattell-Horn-Carroll (CHC) theory** was born. This theory affirmed a general intellectual ability factor. It affirmed the existence of *Gf* and *Gc*. And it identified more specific abilities, such as reading and writing ability, memory capacity, and processing speed (Schneider & McGrew, 2012). The CHC theory continues to influence psychologists, because it recognizes that many abilities comprise intelligence, but that these specific abilities exist under a broader umbrella of general intelligence. Other psychologists, particularly since the mid-1980s, have sought to extend the definition of *intelligence* beyond the idea of academic smarts.

Theories of Multiple Intelligences

Gardner's Multiple Intelligences

LOQ 28-4 How do Gardner's and Sternberg's theories of multiple intelligences differ, and what criticisms have they faced?

Howard Gardner has instead identified eight *relatively independent intelligences*, including the verbal and mathematical aptitudes assessed by standardized tests (**FIGURE 28.1**). Thus, the app developer, the poet, the street-smart adolescent, and the basketball team's play-making point guard exhibit different kinds of intelligence (Gardner, 1998). Gardner (1999a) has also proposed a ninth possible intelligence—*existential intelligence*—the ability "to ponder large questions about life, death, existence." Gardner's notion of multiple intelligences continues to influence many educators' belief that children have different "learning styles," such as visual and auditory (Newton & Miah, 2017). In one study, 93 percent of British teachers agreed that "individuals learn better when they receive

←FIGURE 28.1
Gardner's eight intelligences Gardner has also proposed existential intelligence (the ability to ponder deep questions about life) as a ninth possible intelligence.

Islands of genius: savant syndrome
After a brief helicopter ride over Singapore followed by 5 days of drawing, British savant artist Stephen Wiltshire accurately reproduced an aerial view of the city from memory.

To witness extraordinary savant ability in music, see the *Video: Savant Musical Skills.*

information in their preferred Learning Style" (Dekker et al., 2012). Increasingly, however, research casts doubt on the idea of boosting comprehension in this way (Nancekivell et al., 2019; Papadatou-Pastou et al., 2018).

Gardner (1983, 2006, 2011; Davis et al., 2011) views intelligence domains as multiple abilities that come in different packages. Brain damage, for example, may destroy one ability but leave others intact. One man, Dr. P., had visual brain area damage. He spoke fluently and could walk a straight line. But his facial recognition ability suffered, causing him to mistake his wife for, of all things, a hat (Sacks, 1985). And consider people with **savant syndrome,** who have an island of brilliance but often score low on intelligence tests and may have limited or no language ability (Treffert, 2010). Some can compute complicated calculations almost instantly, or identify the day of the week of any given historical date, or render incredible works of art or music (Miller, 1999).

About 4 in 5 people with savant syndrome are male, and many also have *autism spectrum disorder (ASD)*, a neurodevelopmental disorder. The late memory whiz Kim Peek (who did not have ASD) inspired the 1988 movie *Rain Man*. In 8 to 10 seconds, he could read and remember a page. During his lifetime, he memorized 9000 books, including Shakespeare's works and the Bible. He could provide GPS-like travel directions within any major U.S. city. Yet he could not button his clothes, and he had little capacity for abstract concepts. Asked by his father at a restaurant to lower his voice, he slid down in his chair to lower his voice box. Asked for Lincoln's Gettysburg Address, he responded, "227 North West Front Street. But he only stayed there one night—he gave the speech the next day" (Treffert & Christensen, 2005).

Sternberg's Three Intelligences

Robert Sternberg (1985, 2015, 2017) agrees with Gardner that there is more to success than academic intelligence and that we have multiple intelligences. But Sternberg's *triarchic theory* proposes three, not eight or nine, reliably measured intelligences:

- *Analytical (academic problem-solving) intelligence* is assessed by intelligence tests, which present well-defined problems having a single right answer. Such tests predict school grades reasonably well and vocational success more modestly.

- *Creative intelligence* is demonstrated in innovative smarts: the ability to adapt to new situations and generate novel ideas.

- *Practical intelligence* is required for everyday tasks that may be poorly defined and may have multiple solutions.

Gardner and Sternberg differ in some areas, but they agree on two important points: Multiple abilities can contribute to life success, and differing varieties of giftedness bring both spice to life and challenges for education. Trained to appreciate such variety, many teachers have applied multiple intelligence theories in their classrooms.

Street smarts This child selling candy on the streets of Bogota, Colombia, is developing practical intelligence at a very young age.

ASK YOURSELF

The concept of multiple intelligences assumes that the analytical school smarts measured by traditional intelligence tests are important, but that other abilities are also important. Different people have different gifts. What are yours?

General Intelligence, Grit, and Deliberate Practice

Wouldn't it be nice if the world were so fair that a weakness in one area would be compensated by genius in another? Alas, say critics, the world is not fair (Ferguson, 2009; Scarr, 1989). There is a general intelligence factor: *g* matters (Johnson et al., 2008). It predicts performance on various complex tasks and in various jobs (Gottfredson, 2002a,b, 2003a,b). Studies of nearly 70,000 people from 19 countries find that *g* predicts higher incomes (Ganzach et al., 2018; see also **FIGURE 28.2**). And extremely high cognitive ability scores predict exceptional achievements, such as doctoral degrees and publications (Kuncel & Hezlett, 2010).

savant syndrome a condition in which a person otherwise limited in mental ability has an exceptional specific skill, such as in computation or drawing.

emotional intelligence the ability to perceive, understand, manage, and use emotions.

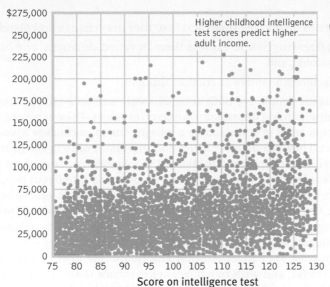

← **FIGURE 28.2**
Smart and rich?
Jay Zagorsky (2007) tracked 7403 participants in the U.S. National Longitudinal Survey of Youth across 25 years. As shown in this illustrative scatterplot, their intelligence scores correlated +.30, a moderate positive correlation, with their later income.

The procrastinator's motto: "Hard work pays off later; laziness pays off now."

Even so, "success" is not a one-ingredient recipe. It also helps to have the luck of an advantaged home and school, and to have been born in a time and place where your talents matter. Adolescents who grow up in a privileged home (lots of space, quiet, well-lit), compared with those who do not, have a more fully developed prefrontal cortex and earn higher reading scores (Uy et al., 2019). And though high academic intelligence will help you get into a profession (via schools and training programs), it alone won't make you successful once there. Success is a combination of talent and grit: Highly successful people tend also to be conscientious, well-connected, and doggedly energetic. Just ask Greek runner Alexi Pappas (2016), a 2016 Olympian who wrote about her time living among the world's best athletes in the Olympic Village. There, the athletes could relax by playing video games, ping pong, or foosball. But these talented and gritty individuals rarely took it easy. "Even when you remove an athlete from competition, you can't take the competition out of them. We can't help it."

Skills that breed success seldom sprout spontaneously. It takes time to cultivate a seedling of talent. K. Anders Ericsson and others proposed a *10-year rule*: A common ingredient of expert performance in chess, dance, sports, computer programming, music, and medicine is "about 10 years of intense, daily practice" (Ericsson & Pool, 2016). Becoming a professional musician, chess player, or elite athlete requires, first, native ability (Macnamara et al., 2014, 2016; Vaci et al., 2019). But it also requires years of *deliberate practice*—about 11,000 hours on average, and a *minimum* of 3000 hours (Campitelli & Gobet, 2011). The recipe for success is a gift of nature plus a whole lot of nurture.

"I happen to have a talent for allocating capital. But my ability to use that talent is completely dependent on the society I was born into. If I'd been born into a tribe of hunters . . . I'd probably end up as some wild animal's dinner." — Warren Buffett, multibillionaire stock investor (2006)

For more on how self-disciplined grit feeds achievement, see Module 35.

Talent + practice After winning the New York State chess championship for kindergarten through third grade, Tanitoluwa ("Tani") Adewumi lugged his trophy to his home—a homeless shelter. In the prior year, after his family fled terrorists in northern Nigeria, Tani learned chess at his elementary school, then began hours of daily practice. "He does 10 times more chess puzzles than the average kid," said his chess teacher, after Tani bested privately tutored children from elite schools (Kristof, 2019).

RETRIEVAL PRACTICE

RP-1 How does the existence of savant syndrome support Gardner's theory of multiple intelligences?

ANSWERS IN APPENDIX E

Emotional Intelligence

LOQ 28-5 What are the four components of emotional intelligence?

Social intelligence is the know-how involved in understanding social situations and managing yourself successfully (Cantor & Kihlstrom, 1987). Psychologist Edward Thorndike first proposed the concept in 1920, noting that "the best mechanic in a factory may fail as a [supervisor] for lack of social intelligence" (Goleman, 2006, p. 83).

A critical part of social intelligence, **emotional intelligence,** consists of four abilities (Mayer et al., 2002, 2012, 2016):

• *Perceiving emotions* (recognizing them in faces, music, and stories, and identifying one's own emotions),

Christopher Lee/The New York Times/Redux Pictures

"You're wise, but you lack tree smarts."

- *Understanding emotions* (predicting them and how they may change and blend),
- *Managing emotions* (knowing how to express them in varied situations, and how to handle others' emotions), and
- *Using emotions* to facilitate adaptive or creative thinking.

Emotionally intelligent people are both socially aware and self-aware. They avoid being hijacked by overwhelming depression, anxiety, or anger. They can read others' emotional cues and know what to say to soothe a grieving friend, encourage a workmate, and manage a conflict. They can delay gratification in pursuit of long-range rewards. Thus, emotionally intelligent people tend to succeed in relationship, career, and parenting situations where academically smarter but less emotionally intelligent people may fail (Cherniss, 2010a,b; Czarna et al., 2016; Miao et al., 2016). They also tend to be happy and healthy (Sánchez-Álvarez et al., 2016; Schutte et al., 2007, 2016). Aware of these benefits, school-based programs have sought to increase teachers' and students' emotional intelligence (Castillo-Gualda et al., 2017; Nathanson et al., 2016).

Some scholars, however, are concerned that emotional intelligence stretches the intelligence concept too far, and with much weaker evidence than for *g* (Brody, 2004; Visser et al., 2006; Waterhouse, 2006). Howard Gardner (1999b) includes interpersonal and intrapersonal intelligences as two of his multiple intelligences. But he notes that we should respect emotional sensitivity, creativity, and motivation as important but different. Stretch *intelligence* to include everything we prize and the word will lose its meaning.

* * *

For a summary of these theories of intelligence, see **TABLE 28.1**.

TABLE 28.1 Comparing Theories of Intelligence

Theory	Summary	Strengths	Other Considerations
Spearman's general intelligence (g)	A basic intelligence predicts our abilities in varied academic areas.	Different abilities, such as verbal and spatial, do have some tendency to correlate.	Human abilities are too diverse to be encapsulated by a single general intelligence factor.
Thurstone's primary mental abilities	Our intelligence may be broken down into seven distinct factors.	A single *g* score is not as informative as scores for seven primary mental abilities.	Even Thurstone's seven mental abilities show a tendency to cluster, suggesting an underlying *g* factor.
Cattell-Horn-Carroll (CHC) theory	Our intelligence is based on a general ability factor as well as other specific abilities, bridged by crystallized and fluid intelligence.	Intelligence is composed of broad and narrow abilities, such as reading ability, memory capacity, and processing speed.	The specific abilities outlined by the CHC theory are too narrowly cognitive.
Gardner's multiple intelligences	Our abilities are best classified into eight or nine independent intelligences, which include a broad range of skills beyond traditional school smarts.	Intelligence is more than just verbal and mathematical skills. Other abilities are equally important to our human adaptability.	Should all our abilities be considered *intelligences*? Shouldn't some be called less vital *talents*?
Sternberg's triarchic theory	Our intelligence is best classified into three areas that predict real-world success: analytical, creative, and practical.	These three domains can be reliably measured.	These three domains may be less independent than the theory suggests, and may actually share an underlying *g* factor.
Emotional intelligence	Social intelligence is an important indicator of life success. Emotional intelligence is a key aspect, consisting of perceiving, understanding, managing, and using emotions.	These four components predict social success and emotional well-being.	Does this stretch the concept of intelligence too far?

📖 Engage online with *Concept Practice: Theories of Intelligence* to review different approaches to intelligence.

RETRIEVAL PRACTICE

RP-2 How does the Cattell-Horn-Carroll theory of intelligence integrate the idea of having general intelligence as well as specific abilities?

ANSWERS IN APPENDIX E

㉘ REVIEW What Is Intelligence?

LEARNING OBJECTIVES

Test Yourself Answer these repeated Learning Objective Questions on your own (before checking the answers in Appendix D) to improve your retention of the concepts (McDaniel et al., 2009, 2015).

LOQ 28-1 How do psychologists define *intelligence*?

LOQ 28-2 What are the arguments for *g*?

LOQ 28-3 How have the concepts of *Gf* and *Gc*, and the CHC theory, affected our understanding of intelligence?

LOQ 28-4 How do Gardner's and Sternberg's theories of multiple intelligences differ, and what criticisms have they faced?

LOQ 28-5 What are the four components of emotional intelligence?

TERMS AND CONCEPTS TO REMEMBER

Test Yourself Write down the definition in your own words, then check your answer.

intelligence, p. 354
general intelligence *(g)*, p. 354
fluid intelligence *(Gf)*, p. 354
crystallized intelligence *(Gc)*, p. 354

Cattell-Horn-Carroll (CHC) theory, p. 354
savant syndrome, p. 356
emotional intelligence, p. 356

MASTER THE MATERIAL

Test Yourself Answer the following questions on your own first, then check your answers in Appendix E.

1. Charles Spearman suggested we have one _____ _____ underlying success across a variety of intellectual abilities.

2. The existence of savant syndrome seems to support
   a. Sternberg's distinction among three types of intelligence.
   b. criticism of multiple intelligence theories.
   c. theories of multiple intelligences.
   d. Thorndike's view of social intelligence.

3. Sternberg's three types of intelligence are _____, _____, and _____.

4. Emotionally intelligent people tend to
   a. seek immediate gratification.
   b. understand their own emotions but not those of others.
   c. understand others' emotions but not their own.
   d. succeed in their careers.

Continue testing yourself with 📚 **LearningCurve** or 📚 **Achieve Read & Practice** to learn and remember most effectively.

㉙ Intelligence Assessment and Dynamics

LOQ 29-1 What is an *intelligence test,* and how do achievement and aptitude tests differ?

An **intelligence test** assesses people's mental aptitudes and compares them with those of others, using numerical scores. How do psychologists design such tests, and what makes them credible?

In your lifetime, you've taken dozens of mental ability tests: school tests of basic reading and math skills, course exams, intelligence tests, driver's license exams. These tests fall under two general categories:

- **Achievement tests,** which are intended to *reflect* what you have learned. Your final exam will measure what you learned in this class.

- **Aptitude tests,** which are intended to *predict* what you will be able to learn. If you took an entrance exam, it was designed to predict your ability to do college or university work.

An aptitude test is a "thinly disguised intelligence test," says Howard Gardner (1999b). Indeed, report Meredith Frey and Douglas Detterman (2004), total scores on the U.S. SAT have correlated +.82 with general intelligence test scores in a national sample of 14- to 21-year-olds (**FIGURE 29.1**). Aptitude also supports achievement: People who learn quickly are also better at retaining information (Zerr et al., 2018).

intelligence test a method for assessing an individual's mental aptitudes and comparing them with those of others, using numerical scores.

achievement test a test designed to assess what a person has learned.

aptitude test a test designed to predict a person's future performance; *aptitude* is the capacity to learn.

FIGURE 29.1
Close cousins: Aptitude and intelligence test scores A scatterplot shows the close correlation that has existed between intelligence test scores and verbal and quantitative SAT scores. (Data from Frey & Detterman, 2004.)

ASK YOURSELF

What achievement or aptitude tests have you taken? In your opinion, how well did these tests assess what you'd learned or predict what you were capable of learning?

Early and Modern Tests of Mental Abilities

LOQ **29-2** When and why were intelligence tests created, and how do today's tests differ from early intelligence tests?

Some societies emphasize the collective welfare of the family, community, and society. Other societies focus on promoting individual opportunity. Plato, a pioneer of the individualist tradition, wrote more than 2000 years ago in *The Republic* that "no two persons are born exactly alike; but each differs from the other in natural endowments, one being suited for one occupation and the other for another." As heirs to Plato's individualism, people in Western societies have pondered how and why individuals differ in mental ability.

Francis Galton: Presuming Hereditary Genius

Western attempts to assess such differences began in earnest with English scientist Francis Galton (1822–1911), who was fascinated with measuring human traits. When his cousin Charles Darwin proposed that nature selects successful traits through the survival of the fittest, Galton wondered if it might be possible to measure "natural ability" and to encourage those of high ability to mate with one another. At the 1884 London Health Exhibition, more than 10,000 visitors received his assessment of their "intellectual strengths" based on such things as reaction time, sensory acuity, muscular power, and body proportions. But alas, on these measures, well-regarded adults and students did not outscore others. Nor did the measures correlate with each other.

Although Galton's quest for a simple intelligence measure failed, he gave us some statistical techniques that we still use (as well as the phrase *nature and nurture*). And his persistent belief in the inheritance of genius—reflected in his book, *Hereditary Genius* (1869)—illustrates an important lesson from both the history of intelligence research and the history of science: Although science itself strives for objectivity, individual scientists are affected by their own assumptions and attitudes.

Alfred Binet: Predicting School Achievement

Modern intelligence testing traces its birth to early twentieth-century France, where a new law required all children to attend school. French officials knew that some children, including many newcomers to Paris, would struggle and need special classes. But how could the schools make fair judgments about children's learning potential? Teachers might assess children who had little prior education as slow learners. Or they might sort children into classes by their social backgrounds. To minimize such bias, France's minister of public education gave psychologist Alfred Binet the task of designing fair tests.

Binet and his student, Théodore Simon, began by assuming that all children follow the same course of intellectual development but that some develop more rapidly (Nicolas & Levine, 2012). A "backward" child should score much like a typical younger child, and a "bright" child like a typical older child. Thus, their goal became measuring each child's **mental age,** the level of performance typically associated with a certain chronological age. The average 8-year-old, then, has a mental age of 8. An 8-year-old with a below-average mental age (perhaps performing at the level of typical 6-year-old) would struggle with age-appropriate schoolwork.

To measure mental age, Binet and Simon theorized that mental aptitude, like athletic aptitude, is a general capacity that shows up in various ways. They tested a variety of reasoning and problem-solving questions on Binet's two daughters, and then on "bright" and "backward" Parisian schoolchildren. Items answered correctly could then predict how well other French children would handle their schoolwork.

Binet and Simon made no assumptions concerning *why* a particular child was slow, average, or precocious. Binet personally leaned toward an environmental explanation. To raise the capacities of low-scoring children, he recommended "mental orthopedics" that would help develop their attention span and self-discipline. He believed his intelligence test did not measure inborn intelligence as a scale measures weight. Rather, it had a single practical purpose: to identify French schoolchildren needing special attention. Binet hoped his test would be used to improve children's education, but he also feared it would be used to label children and limit their opportunities (Gould, 1981).

Alfred Binet (1857–1911) "Some recent philosophers have given their moral approval to the deplorable verdict that an individual's intelligence is a fixed quantity, one which cannot be augmented. We must protest and act against this brutal pessimism" (Binet, 1909, p. 141).

RETRIEVAL PRACTICE

RP-1 What did Binet hope to achieve by establishing a child's mental age?

ANSWERS IN APPENDIX E

Lewis Terman: Measuring Innate Intelligence

After Binet's death in 1911, others adapted his tests for use as a numerical measure of intelligence. Lewis Terman (1877–1956) was an ambitious Stanford University professor who sought to bring intelligence testing to the United States. At a young age, Terman presumed he wasn't destined for an intellectual life (Terman, 1930). He grew up the twelfth of fourteen children, the son of farmers who had little education. Terman overcame being burned in a fire, breaking a hip, and tuberculosis (Boring, 1959). His persistence and unquenchable reading appetite led him out of his one-room schoolhouse to a local college and later to Stanford University to study children who, like him, were born with high general intelligence (*g*).

To achieve his goal, Terman tried the Paris-developed questions and age norms with California kids. Adapting some of Binet's original items, adding others, and establishing new age norms, Terman extended the upper end of the test's range from age 12 to "superior adults." He also gave his revision the name today's version retains—the **Stanford-Binet.**

From such tests, German psychologist William Stern derived the famous term **intelligence quotient,** or **IQ.** The IQ was simply a person's mental age divided by chronological age and multiplied by 100 to get rid of the decimal point. Thus, an average child, whose mental age (8) and chronological age (8) are the same, has an IQ of 100. But an 8-year-old who answers questions as would a typical 10-year-old has an IQ of 125:

$$IQ = \frac{\text{mental age of } 10}{\text{chronological age of } 8} \times 100 = 125$$

The original IQ formula worked fairly well for children but not for adults. (Should a 40-year-old who does as well on the test as an average 20-year-old be assigned an IQ of only 50?) Most current intelligence tests, including the Stanford-Binet, no longer compute an IQ in this manner (though the term IQ still lingers as a shorthand expression

mental age a measure of intelligence test performance devised by Binet; the level of performance typically associated with children of a certain chronological age. Thus, a child who does as well as an average 8-year-old is said to have a mental age of 8.

Stanford-Binet the widely used American revision (by Terman at Stanford University) of Binet's original intelligence test.

intelligence quotient (IQ) defined originally as the ratio of mental age (*ma*) to chronological age (*ca*) multiplied by 100 (thus, IQ = *ma* / *ca* × 100). On contemporary intelligence tests, the average performance for a given age is assigned a score of 100.

Mrs. Randolph takes mother's pride too far.

for "intelligence test score"). Instead, they assign a score that represents a test-taker's performance *relative to the average performance* (which is arbitrarily set at 100) of others the same age. Most people—about 68 percent of those taking an intelligence test—fall between 85 and 115.

Terman inferred that intelligence tests revealed a mental capacity present from birth. He also assumed that some ethnic groups were naturally more intelligent than others. And he supported *eugenics*—the much-criticized nineteenth- and twentieth-century movement that proposed measuring human traits and using the results to encourage only smart and fit people to reproduce.

With Terman's help, the U.S. government developed new tests to evaluate both newly arriving immigrants and World War I army recruits—the world's first mass administration of an intelligence test. To some psychologists, the results indicated the inferiority of people not sharing their Anglo-Saxon heritage.

Binet probably would have been horrified that his test had been adapted and used to draw such conclusions. Indeed, such sweeping judgments became an embarrassment to most of those who championed testing. Even Terman came to appreciate that test scores reflected not only people's innate mental abilities but also their education, native language, and familiarity with the culture assumed by the test. Abuses of the early intelligence tests serve to remind us that science can be value laden. Behind a screen of scientific objectivity, ideology may lurk.

RETRIEVAL PRACTICE

RP-2 What is the IQ score of a 4-year-old with a mental age of 5?

ANSWERS IN APPENDIX E

Matching patterns Block-design puzzles test visual abstract processing ability. Wechsler's individually administered intelligence test comes in forms suited for adults and children.

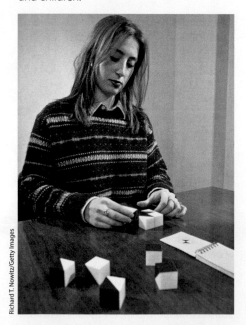

David Wechsler: Testing Separate Strengths

Psychologist David Wechsler created what is now the most widely used individual intelligence test, the **Wechsler Adult Intelligence Scale (WAIS),** together with a version for school-age children (the *Wechsler Intelligence Scale for Children [WISC]*), and another for preschool children (Evers et al., 2012). The 2008 edition of the WAIS (a new version is anticipated in 2021) consists of 15 subtests, including these:

- *Similarities*—reasoning the commonality of two objects or concepts ("In what way are wool and cotton alike?")

- *Vocabulary*—naming pictured objects, or defining words ("What is a guitar?")

- *Block design*—visual abstract processing ("Using the four blocks, make one just like this.")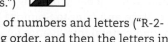

- *Letter-number sequencing*—on hearing a series of numbers and letters ("R-2-C-1-M-3"), repeating the numbers in ascending order, and then the letters in alphabetical order.

The WAIS yields not only an overall intelligence score, as does the Stanford-Binet, but also separate scores for verbal comprehension, perceptual reasoning, *working memory*, and processing speed. In such ways, this test helps realize Binet's aim: to identify those who could benefit from special educational opportunities for improvement.

Intelligence tests also help intelligent people find intelligent friends, sometimes through high-IQ organizations. But not always. Mensa membership, for example, is highest in cultures where IQ testing is most widely adopted: Americans, Britons, and Germans comprise 70 percent of the world's membership (Mensa, 2019).

RETRIEVAL PRACTICE

RP-3 An employer with a pool of applicants for a single available position is interested in testing each applicant's potential. To determine that, she should use an _____ (achievement/aptitude) test. That same employer wishing to test the effectiveness of a new, on-the-job training program would be wise to use an _____ (achievement/aptitude) test.

ANSWERS IN APPENDIX E

To learn more about the promise and perils of intelligence testing, watch the *Video: Locking Away the "Feebleminded"—A Shameful History.* And to test your own performance on simulated WAIS subtasks, see *Concept Practice: Wechsler Intelligence Tasks.*

Principles of Test Construction

LOQ 29-3 What is a *normal curve,* and what does it mean to say that a test has been standardized and is reliable and valid?

To be widely accepted, a psychological test must meet three criteria: It must be *standardized, reliable,* and *valid.* The Stanford-Binet and Wechsler tests meet these requirements.

Standardization

The number of questions you answer correctly on an intelligence test would reveal almost nothing. To know how well you performed, you would need some basis for comparison. That's why test-makers give new tests to a representative sample of people. The scores from this pretested group become the basis for future comparisons. If you then take the test following the same procedures, your score will be meaningful when compared with others. This process is called **standardization.**

If we construct a graph of test-takers' scores, the scores typically form a bell-shaped pattern called the *bell curve,* or **normal curve.** For many human attributes—height, weight, and mental aptitude—the curve's highest point is the average score. On an intelligence test, we give this average score a value of 100 (**FIGURE 29.2**). Moving out from the average, toward either extreme, we find fewer and fewer people. For both the Stanford-Binet and Wechsler tests, a person's score indicates whether that person's performance fell above or below the average. A performance higher than all but 2.5 percent of all scores earns an intelligence score of 130. A performance lower than 97.5 percent of all scores earns an intelligence score of 70.

To keep the average score near 100, the Stanford-Binet and Wechsler scales are periodically restandardized. If you recently took the WAIS, Fourth Edition, your performance was compared with a standardization sample who took the test during 2007, not to David Wechsler's initial 1930s sample. If you compared the performance of the most recent standardization sample with that of the 1930s sample, do you suppose you would find rising or declining test performance? Amazingly—given that college entrance aptitude scores have sometimes dropped, such as during the 1960s and 1970s—intelligence test performance has improved. This worldwide phenomenon is called the *Flynn effect,* in honor of New Zealand researcher James Flynn (1987, 2012, 2018), who first calculated its magnitude. Flynn observed that the average person's intelligence test score rose three points per decade. Thus, an average person in 1920 would—by today's standard—score only a 76! Such rising performance has been observed in 49 countries, from Sweden to Sudan (Dutton et al., 2018; Wongupparaj et al., 2015). Countries that have shown the greatest growth in IQ score over time have also experienced more economic growth (Rindermann et al., 2018). Although there have been some regional reversals, the historic increase is now widely accepted as an important phenomenon (Lynn, 2009; Teasdale & Owen, 2008).

The Flynn effect's cause has been a psychological mystery. Did it result from greater test sophistication? No. Gains appeared before testing was widespread. Perhaps better nutrition? Thanks to improved nutrition, people have gotten taller as well as smarter. But in postwar Britain, notes Flynn (2009), the lower-class children gained the most from improved nutrition, yet the intelligence performance gains were greater among upper-class children. Might the explanation be greater educational opportunities, smaller families, and rising living standards (Pietschnig & Voracek, 2015; Rindermann et al., 2016)? For example, children around the world now have access to educational programs such as *Sesame Street* that increase their intellectual performance and reduce their prejudice toward children from different ethnic backgrounds (Kwauk et al., 2016). Flynn (2012) attributes the IQ score increases to our need to develop new mental skills to cope with modern environments. Regardless of what combination of factors explains the rise in intelligence test scores, the phenomenon counters one concern of some hereditarians—that the higher twentieth-century birthrates among those with lower scores would shove human intelligence scores downward (Lynn & Harvey, 2008).

Wechsler Adult Intelligence Scale (WAIS) the WAIS and its companion versions for children are the most widely used intelligence tests; they contain verbal and performance (nonverbal) subtests.

standardization defining uniform testing procedures and meaningful scores by comparison with the performance of a pretested group.

normal curve the bell-shaped curve that describes the distribution of many physical and psychological attributes. Most scores fall near the average, and fewer and fewer scores lie near the extremes.

FIGURE 29.2

The normal curve Scores on aptitude tests tend to form a normal, or bell-shaped, curve around an average score. For the Wechsler scale, for example, the average score is 100.

Number of scores

About 68 percent of people score within 15 points of 100.

About 95 percent of all people fall within 30 points of 100.

68%

95%

0.1%   2.5% 13.5%   34%   34%   13.5% 2.5%   0.1%

55   70   85   100   115   130   145

Wechsler intelligence score

Reliability

Knowing where you stand in comparison to a standardization group still won't say much about your intelligence unless the test has **reliability.** A reliable test, when retaken, gives consistent scores. To check a test's reliability, researchers test people many times. They may split the test in half (*split-half*: agreement of odd-question scores and even-question scores), test with alternative forms of the test, or retest with the same test (*test-retest*). The higher the *correlation* between the two scores, the higher the test's reliability. The tests we have considered—the Stanford-Binet, the WAIS, and the WISC—are very reliable after early childhood (with *correlation coefficients* of about +.9). In retests, sometimes decades later, people's scores are generally similar to the first score (Deary et al., 2009; Lyons et al., 2017).

Watch the *Video: Correlational Studies* for a helpful tutorial animation.

Validity

High reliability does not ensure a test's **validity**—the extent to which the test actually measures or predicts what it promises. Imagine using a tape measure with faulty markings. If you use it to measure people's heights, your results will be very reliable. No matter how many times you measure, people's heights will be the same. But your faulty height results will not be valid.

We expect intelligence tests to have **predictive validity:** They should predict the criterion of future performance, and to some extent they do. SAT aptitude scores correlate about +.81 with those for the Graduate Record Examination (GRE; an aptitude test similar to the SAT but for those applying to graduate school) (Wai et al., 2018).

Are general aptitude tests as predictive as they are reliable? *No.* Aptitude test scores do predict school grades (Roth et al., 2015). But as critics are fond of noting, the predictive power of aptitude tests peaks in the early school years and weakens later. Academic aptitude test scores are reasonably good predictors of school achievement for children ages 6 to 12, where the correlation between intelligence score and school performance is about +.6 (Jensen, 1980). Intelligence scores correlate even more closely with scores on later achievement tests: +.81 in one comparison of 70,000 English children's intelligence scores at age 11 with their academic achievement in national exams at age 16 (Deary et al., 2007, 2009b). The SAT, used in the United States as a college entrance exam, has been less successful in predicting first-year college grades. (The correlation, less than +.5, has been, however, a bit higher when adjusting for high scorers electing tougher courses [Berry & Sackett, 2009; Willingham et al., 1990].) By the time we get to the GRE, the correlation with graduate school performance is an even more modest but still significant +.4 (Kuncel & Hezlett, 2007).

Why does the predictive power of aptitude scores diminish as students move up the educational ladder? Consider a parallel situation: Among all American and Canadian football linemen, body weight correlates with success. A 300-pound player tends to overwhelm a 200-pound opponent. But within the narrow 280- to 320-pound range typically found at the professional level, the correlation between weight and success becomes negligible (**FIGURE 29.3**). The narrower the *range* of weights, the lower the predictive power of body weight becomes. If an elite university takes only those students who have very high aptitude scores, and then gives them a restricted range of high grades, those scores cannot possibly predict much. This will be true even if the test has excellent predictive validity with a more diverse sample of students. Likewise, modern grade inflation has produced less diverse high school grades. With their diminished range, high school grades now predict college grades no better than have SAT scores (Sackett et al., 2012). So, when we validate a measure using a wide range of scores but then use it with a restricted range of scores, it loses much of its predictive validity.

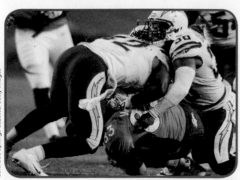

⬇ **FIGURE 29.3**
Diminishing predictive power
Let's imagine a correlation between football linemen's body weight and their success on the field. Note how insignificant the relationship becomes when we narrow the range of weight to 280 to 320 pounds. As the range of data under consideration narrows, its predictive power diminishes.

Football linemen's success

Greater correlation over broad range of body weights

Little correlation within restricted range

Body weight in pounds

RP-4 What are the three criteria that a psychological test must meet in order to be widely accepted? Explain.

RP-5 Correlation coefficients were used in this section. Here's a quick review: Correlations do not indicate cause-effect, but they do tell us whether two things are associated in some way. A correlation of −1.00 represents perfect _____ (agreement/disagreement) between two sets of scores: As one score goes up, the other score goes _____ (up/down). A correlation of _____ represents no association. The highest correlation, +1.00, represents perfect _____ (agreement/disagreement): As the first score goes up, the other score goes _____ (up/down).

ANSWERS IN APPENDIX E

reliability the extent to which a test yields consistent results, as assessed by the consistency of scores on two halves of the test, on alternative forms of the test, or on retesting.

validity the extent to which a test measures or predicts what it is supposed to. (See also *predictive validity*.)

predictive validity the success with which a test predicts the behavior it is designed to predict; it is assessed by computing the correlation between test scores and the criterion behavior. (Also called *criterion-related validity*.)

Extremes of Intelligence

LOQ 29-4 What are the traits of those at the low and high intelligence extremes?

One way to glimpse the validity and significance of any test is to compare people who score at the two extremes of the normal curve. The two groups should differ noticeably, and on intelligence tests, they do.

The Low Extreme

Intellectual disability is a neurodevelopmental disorder that is apparent before age 18, sometimes with a known physical cause. To be diagnosed with an intellectual disability, a person must—among other criteria (see Module 53)—have a test score of 70 or below. For some, intelligence test scores can mean life or death. In the United States (one of the only industrialized countries with the death penalty), the Flynn effect means fewer Americans are now eligible for execution. Why? Because in 2002, the U.S. Supreme Court ruled that the execution of people with an intellectual disability is "cruel and unusual punishment." For Teresa Lewis, that test score cutoff at 70 was high stakes. Lewis, a "dependent personality" with limited intellect (a reported test score of 72), allegedly agreed to a plot in which two men killed her husband and stepson in exchange for a split of a life insurance payout (Eckholm, 2010). The State of Virginia executed Lewis in 2010. If only she had scored 69.

In 2014, the U.S. Supreme Court recognized the imprecision and arbitrariness of a fixed cutoff score of 70, and required states with death row inmates who have scored just above 70 to consider other evidence. Thus, Ted Herring, who had scored 72 and 74 on intelligence tests—but without knowing that summer follows spring or how to transfer between buses—was taken off Florida's death row (Alvarez & Schwartz, 2014).

The High Extreme

Children whose intelligence test scores indicate extraordinary academic gifts mostly thrive. In one famous project begun in 1921, Lewis Terman studied more than 1500 California schoolchildren with IQ scores over 135. These high-scoring children (later called the "Termites")—like those in later studies—were healthy, well-adjusted, and unusually successful academically (Friedman & Martin, 2012; Koenen et al., 2009; Lubinski, 2009, 2016). When restudied over the next seven decades, most people in Terman's group had attained high levels of education (Austin et al., 2002; Holahan & Sears, 1995). Many were doctors, lawyers, professors, scientists, and writers, though none were Nobel Prize winners.

Other studies have followed the lives of precocious youths who had aced the math SAT at age 13—by scoring in the top 1 percent of their age group. By their fifties, these math whizzes had secured 681 patents and many had achieved eminence, often in STEM (science, technology, engineering, and math) fields (Bernstein et al., 2019; Lubinski et al., 2014). About 1 percent of Americans earn doctorates. But for the 12- and 13-year-olds who scored in the top 1 in 10,000 among those of their age taking the SAT, about 40 percent had done so (Kell et al., 2013; Makel et al., 2016). One of psychology's most gifted kids was Jean Piaget, who by age 15 was publishing scientific articles on mollusks and who went on to become the twentieth century's most famous developmental psychologist (Hunt, 1993).

"My dear Adele, I am 4 years old and I can read any English book. I can say all the Latin substantives and adjectives and active verbs besides 52 lines of Latin poetry." — Francis Galton, letter to his sister, 1827

Terman did test two future Nobel laureates in physics, but they failed to score above his gifted sample cutoff (Hulbert, 2005).

Among the high-scoring whiz kids in national searches for precocious youth were Google co-founder Sergey Brin, Facebook's Mark Zuckerberg, and musician Stefani Germanotta (Lady Gaga) (Clynes, 2016). Another became a professional poker player with $100,000+ annual earnings (Lubinski, 2016).

"Zach is in the gifted-and-talented-and-you're-not class."

Schooling and Intelligence

"Gifted child" programs tend to segregate high-scoring children in special classes, often giving them academic enrichment not available to their peers. "Remedial" programs generally mainstream children, but give them access to resources that help them overcome challenges. Critics note that grouping ("tracking") students by aptitude sometimes creates a self-fulfilling prophecy: Implicitly labeling some children as "ungifted" and denying them enrichment opportunities can widen the achievement gap between ability groups (Batruch et al., 2019). Because minority and low-income youth are more often placed in lower academic groups, tracking can also promote segregation and prejudice—hardly, note critics, a healthy preparation for working and living in a modern world.

Critics and proponents of gifted education do, however, agree on this: Children have differing gifts, whether at math, verbal reasoning, art, or social leadership. Educating children as if all were alike is as naive as assuming that giftedness is something, like curly hair, that you either have or do not have. One need not stick labels on children to affirm their special talents or their challenges, and to reach them all at the frontiers of their own ability and understanding. By providing *appropriate placement* suited to each child's talents (as when allowing a math whiz to study math at a higher level, or providing extra resources to children struggling to read), we can promote both equity and excellence for all (Subotnik et al., 2011).

Intelligence Across the Life Span

Researchers are exploring some age-old questions about human intelligence. You know it: You are smarter than some people and not as smart as others. So what in that heart of smarts—the brain—creates this difference? Is it our brain's relative *size?* Our amounts of certain brain *tissue?* Our brain networks' *speed?* These are among the possibilities that researchers have identified.

Here is another question: What happens to our intellectual muscles as we age? Do they gradually decline, as does our body strength? Or do they remain constant? To see how psychologists have studied intelligence—and for an illustration of psychology's self-correcting process—see Thinking Critically About: Cross-Sectional and Longitudinal Studies.

Stability or Change?

LOQ 29-6 How stable are intelligence test scores over the life span?

What can we predict from a child's early-life intelligence scores? Will a precocious 2-year-old mature into a talented college student and a brilliant senior citizen? Maybe—or maybe not. For most children, intelligence assessments before age 3 only modestly predict future aptitudes (Humphreys & Davey, 1988; Tasbihsazan et al., 2003; Yu et al., 2018). Some precocious preschoolers become brilliant adults, but even Albert Einstein was once thought "slow"—as he was in learning to talk (Quasha, 1980).

By age 4, however, children's performance on intelligence tests begins to predict their adolescent and adult scores. The consistency of scores over time increases with the age of the child (Tucker-Drob & Briley, 2014). By age 11, the stability becomes impressive, as Ian Deary and his colleagues (2004, 2009b, 2013) discovered when they retested the same **cohort**—the same group of people—over many years. Their amazing longitudinal studies have been enabled by their country, Scotland, doing something no nation has done before or since. On June 1, 1932, essentially every child in the country born in 1921—87,498 children—took an intelligence test. The aim was to identify working-class children who would benefit from further education. Sixty-five years later to the day, Patricia Whalley, the wife of Deary's co-worker, Lawrence Whalley, discovered the test results on dusty storeroom shelves at the Scottish Council for Research in Education, not far from Deary's Edinburgh University office. "This will change our lives," Deary replied when Whalley told him the news.

And so it has, with dozens of studies of the stability and the predictive capacity of these early test results. One of Deary's studies, for example, retested 542 survivors—now turn-of-the-millennium 80-year-olds—using the same intelligence test they had taken as 11-year-olds in 1932. The correlation between the two sets of scores—after nearly

The stability of intelligence At age 4, James Holzhauer was featured in a *Chicago Tribune* article about his math ability. By age 7, he was in the fifth grade (Jacobs, 2019). At age 34, he won 32 consecutive appearances on the quiz show *Jeopardy!*

LOQ 29-5 What are *cross-sectional studies* and *longitudinal studies*, and why is it important to know which method was used?

Researchers using the **cross-sectional** method study different age groups at one time. They have found that *mental ability declines with age.*[1]

Comparing 70-year-olds and 30-year-olds means not only comparing two different people but also two different eras. These researchers were comparing:

- generally less-educated people (born in the early 1900s) with better-educated people (born after 1950).

- people raised in large families with people raised in smaller families.

- people from less-affluent families with people from more-affluent families.

Researchers using the **longitudinal** method study and restudy the same group at different times in their life span. They have found that *intelligence remains stable, and on some tests it even increases.*[2]

1950

1985

present

But these studies have their own issue. Participants who survive to the end of these studies may be the healthiest and brightest people. When researchers statistically adjust for the loss of less intelligent participants, intelligence does appear to decline somewhat in later life, especially after age 85.[3]

1. Wechsler, 1972. 2. Salthouse, 2010, 2014; Schaie & Geiwitz, 1982. 3. Brayne et al., 1999.

---

70 years of varied life experiences—was striking (**FIGURE 29.4**). Ditto when 106 survivors were retested at age 90 (Deary et al., 2013). Another study that followed Scots born in 1936 from ages 11 to 70 confirmed the remarkable stability of intelligence, independent of life circumstance (Johnson et al., 2010). High-scoring adolescents, 50 years later, even *feel* younger than their age (Stephan et al., 2018).

cross-sectional study research that compares people of different ages at the same point in time.

longitudinal study research that follows and retests the same people over time.

cohort a group of people sharing a common characteristic, such as being from a given time period.

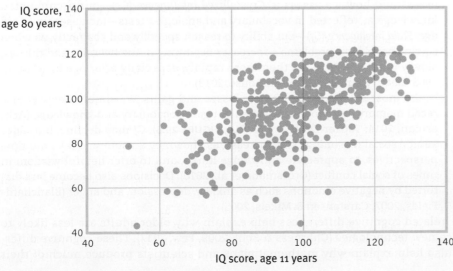

← FIGURE 29.4

Intelligence endures When Ian Deary and his colleagues retested 80-year-old Scots, using an intelligence test they had taken as 11-year-olds, their scores across seven decades correlated +.66, as shown here. (Data from Deary et al., 2004.) When 106 survivors were again retested at age 90, the correlation with their age 11 scores was +.54 (Deary et al., 2013).

"Whether you live to collect your old-age pension depends in part on your IQ at age 11." — Ian Deary, "Intelligence, Health, and Death," 2005

Women scoring in the highest 25 percent on the Scottish national intelligence test at age 11 tended to live longer than those who scored in the lowest 25 percent. "On average," reported Deary (2016), "a girl with a 30-point disadvantage in IQ on this 45-minute test at age 11 was half as likely to be alive" 65 years later.

"In youth we learn, in age we understand." — Marie Von Ebner-Eschenbach, *Aphorisms*, 1883

Children and adults who are more intelligent tend to live healthier and longer lives (Geary, 2019; Stephan et al., 2018). Why might this be the case? Deary (2008) has proposed four possible explanations:

1. Intelligence facilitates more education, better jobs, and a healthier environment.

2. Intelligence encourages healthy living: less smoking, better diet, more exercise.

3. Prenatal events or early childhood illnesses can influence both intelligence and health.

4. A "well-wired body," as evidenced by fast reaction speeds, perhaps fosters both intelligence and longevity.

> Play the role of a researcher studying these issues by engaging online with *How Would You Know If Intelligence Changes With Age?*

Aging and Intelligence

LOQ **29-7** How does aging affect crystallized intelligence *(Gc)* and fluid intelligence *(Gf)*?

It matters what questions psychological scientists ask, but sometimes it matters even more *how* they ask them—the research methods they use. Cross-sectional studies had shown that older adults gave fewer correct answers on intelligence tests than did younger adults. These findings caused WAIS-creator David Wechsler (1972) to conclude that "the decline of mental ability with age is part of the general [aging] process of the organism as a whole." For a long time, this rather dismal view went unchallenged. Many corporations established mandatory retirement policies, assuming the companies would benefit by replacing aging workers with younger, more capable employees. This thinking persists today, with some countries requiring professors to retire by age 60 (Hong Kong) or 65 (the Netherlands). As "everyone knows," you can't teach an old dog new tricks. But after colleges in the 1920s began giving intelligence tests to entering students, psychologists using longitudinal studies (retesting the same cohorts over a period of years) discovered that intelligence remained stable. On some tests, scores even increased, due partly to experience with the tests (Salthouse, 2014) (**FIGURE 29.5**). Methods matter.

The more optimistic results from longitudinal studies challenged the presumption that intelligence sharply declines with age. Famed painter Anna Mary Robertson Moses ("Grandma Moses") took up painting in her seventies, and at age 88 a popular magazine named her "Young Woman of the Year." At age 89, architect Frank Lloyd Wright designed New York City's Guggenheim Museum. At age 101, neuropsychologist Brenda Milner was still conducting research and supervising students. As everyone knows, given good health you're never too old to learn.

So the answers to our age-and-intelligence questions depend on what we assess and how we assess it. *Crystallized intelligence (Gc)*—our accumulated knowledge as reflected in vocabulary and analogies tests—increases up to old age. *Fluid intelligence (Gf)*—our ability to reason speedily and abstractly, as when solving novel logic problems—decreases beginning in the twenties and thirties, slowly up to age 75 or so, then more rapidly, especially after age 85 (Cattell, 1963; Deary & Ritchie, 2016; Salthouse, 2013).

For most people, aging leads to losses and gains. We simultaneously lose recall memory and processing speed but gain vocabulary and knowledge (Ackerman, 2014; Tucker-Drob et al., 2019; **FIGURE 29.6**). *Gf* may decline, but older adults' social reasoning skills increase, as shown by an ability to take multiple perspectives, to appreciate knowledge limits, and to offer helpful wisdom in times of social conflict (Grossmann et al., 2010). Decisions also become less distorted by negative emotions such as anxiety, depression, and anger (Blanchard-Fields, 2007; Carstensen & Mikels, 2005).

Age-related cognitive differences help explain why older adults are less likely to embrace new technologies (Charness & Boot, 2009; Pew, 2017). These cognitive differences also help explain why mathematicians and scientists produce much of their

▼ **FIGURE 29.5**
Cross-sectional versus longitudinal testing of intelligence at various ages In this test of one type of verbal intelligence (inductive reasoning), the cross-sectional method showed declining scores with age. The longitudinal method (in which the same people were retested over a period of years) showed a slight rise in scores well into adulthood. (Data from Schaie, 1994.)

Cross-sectional method suggests decline.

Longitudinal method suggests more stability.

Age in years

■ Cross-sectional method
■ Longitudinal method

FIGURE 29.6
With age, we lose and we win Studies reveal that word power grows with age, while fluid intelligence (*Gf*) declines. (Data from Salthouse, 2010.)

most creative work during their late twenties or early thirties, when *Gf* is at its peak (Jones et al., 2014). In contrast, authors, historians, and philosophers tend to produce their best work in their forties, fifties, and beyond—after accumulating more knowledge (Simonton, 1988, 1990). Poets, who depend on *Gf*, reach their peak output earlier than prose authors, who need the deeper knowledge reservoir that accumulates with age. This finding holds in every major literary tradition, for both living and dead languages.

> "Knowledge is knowing a tomato is a fruit; wisdom is not putting it in a fruit salad."
> — Anonymous

RETRIEVAL PRACTICE

RP-6 Researcher A wants to study how intelligence changes over the life span. Researcher B wants to study the intelligence of people who are now at various life stages. Which researcher should use the cross-sectional method, and which the longitudinal method?

ANSWERS IN APPENDIX E

📺 Watch the *Video: Longitudinal and Cross-Sectional Studies* for a helpful tutorial animation.

"We're looking for someone with the wisdom of a 50-year-old, the experience of a 40-year-old, the drive of a 30-year-old, and the payscale of a 20-year-old."

MODULE

㉙ REVIEW Intelligence Assessment and Dynamics

LEARNING OBJECTIVES

Test Yourself Answer these repeated Learning Objective Questions on your own (before checking the answers in Appendix D) to improve your retention of the concepts (McDaniel et al., 2009, 2015).

LOQ 29-1 What is an *intelligence test,* and how do achievement and aptitude tests differ?

LOQ 29-2 When and why were intelligence tests created, and how do today's tests differ from early intelligence tests?

LOQ 29-3 What is a *normal curve,* and what does it mean to say that a test has been standardized and is reliable and valid?

LOQ 29-4 What are the traits of those at the low and high intelligence extremes?

LOQ 29-5 What are *cross-sectional studies* and *longitudinal studies,* and why is it important to know which method was used?

LOQ 29-6 How stable are intelligence test scores over the life span?

LOQ 29-7 How does aging affect crystallized intelligence *(Gc)* and fluid intelligence *(Gf)*?

TERMS AND CONCEPTS TO REMEMBER

Test Yourself Write down the definition in your own words, then check your answer.

intelligence test, p. 359

achievement test, p. 359

aptitude test, p. 359

mental age, p. 361

Stanford-Binet, p. 361

intelligence quotient (IQ), p. 361

Wechsler Adult Intelligence Scale (WAIS), p. 363

standardization, p. 363

normal curve, p. 363

reliability, p. 365

validity, p. 365

predictive validity, p. 365

cross-sectional study, p. 367

longitudinal study, p. 367

cohort, p. 367

MASTER THE MATERIAL

Test Yourself Answer the following questions on your own first, then check your answers in Appendix E.

1. The IQ of a 6-year-old with a measured mental age of 9 would be
   a. 67.
   b. 133.
   c. 86.
   d. 150.

2. The Wechsler Adult Intelligence Scale (WAIS) is best able to tell us
   a. what part of an individual's intelligence is determined by genetic inheritance.
   b. whether the test-taker will succeed in a job.
   c. how the test-taker compares with other adults in vocabulary and arithmetic reasoning.
   d. whether the test-taker has specific skills for music and the performing arts.

3. The Stanford-Binet, the Wechsler Adult Intelligence Scale, and the Wechsler Intelligence Scale for Children yield consistent results, for example on retesting. In other words, these tests have high _____.

4. Which of the following is NOT a possible explanation for the fact that more intelligent people tend to live longer, healthier lives?
   a. Intelligence facilitates more education, better jobs, and a healthier environment.
   b. Intelligence encourages a more health-promoting lifestyle.
   c. Intelligent people have slower reaction times, so are less likely to put themselves at risk.
   d. Prenatal events or early childhood illnesses could influence both intelligence and health.

5. Use the concepts of *Gc* and *Gf* to explain why writers tend to produce their most creative work later in life, while scientists often hit their peak much earlier.

Continue testing yourself with **LearningCurve** or **Achieve Read & Practice** to learn and remember most effectively.

---

30 Genetic and Environmental Influences on Intelligence

Intelligence runs in families. But why? Are our intellectual abilities mostly inherited? Or are they molded by our environment? Few issues in psychology arouse so much passion. If we mainly inherit our intelligence, then people's socioeconomic standing will correspond to their inborn differences. But if intelligence is mainly nurtured by our environments, then children from disadvantaged backgrounds can expect to lead disadvantaged lives—but with some hope that changing the environment could produce more intelligent and accomplished adults. Let's examine some of the evidence, focusing on these questions:

- What do twin and adoption studies tell us about how heredity and experience influence intelligence?
- Can extreme environmental influences amplify or diminish intelligence?
- What intelligence test score similarities and differences exist among groups, and what accounts for those differences?

Heredity and Intelligence

LOQ 30-1 What is *heritability*, and what do twin and adoption studies tell us about the nature and nurture of intelligence?

Heritability is the portion of variation among individuals in a group that we can attribute to genes. Estimates of the heritability of intelligence—the extent to which intelligence test score variation within a group can be attributed to genetic variation—range from 50 to 80 percent (Madison et al., 2016; Plomin et al., 2016; Plomin & von Stumm, 2018). Does this mean that we can assume that 50–80 percent of *your* intelligence is due to your genes, and the rest to your environment? No. Heritability never applies to an individual, only to *why people in a group differ from one another*.

> **heritability** the proportion of variation among individuals in a group that we can attribute to genes. The heritability of a trait may vary, depending on the range of populations and environments studied.

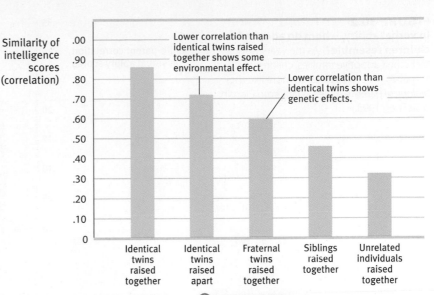

⬆ **FIGURE 30.1**

Intelligence: nature and nurture The most genetically similar people have the most similar intelligence scores. Remember: 1.00 indicates a perfect correlation; zero indicates no correlation at all. (Data from McGue et al., 1993.)

Identical twins share the same genes; do they also share mental abilities? As you can see from **FIGURE 30.1**, which summarizes many studies, the answer is clearly *Yes*. Even when adopted by two different families, their intelligence test scores are very similar. When raised together, their scores are nearly as similar as those of the same person taking the same test twice (Haworth et al., 2009; Lykken, 2006; Plomin et al., 2016). Identical twins also exhibit substantial similarity (and heritability) in specific talents, such as music, math, and sports. Heredity accounts for more than half the variation in the national math and science exam scores of British 16-year-olds (Shakeshaft et al., 2013; Vinkhuyzen et al., 2009).

Scans reveal that identical twins' brains have similar gray- and white-matter volume, and the areas associated with verbal and spatial intelligence are virtually the same (Deary et al., 2009a; Thompson et al., 2001). Their brains also show similar activity while doing mental tasks (Koten et al., 2009).

Are there known genes for genius? When 100 researchers pooled their data on 269,867 people, all of the gene variations analyzed accounted for only about 5 percent of the differences in educational achievement (Savage et al., 2018). Another analysis of genes from 1.1 million people accounted for about 12 percent of their educational attainment differences (Lee et al., 2018). The search for smart genes continues. Some have wondered: Might IVF (in vitro fertilization) physicians screen candidate embryos for intelligence genes? Statistical geneticists report that, for the foreseeable future, the intelligence gain from embryo selection would be minimal (Kaiser, 2019). That's because *intelligence is polygenetic*, involving many genes. Wendy Johnson (2010) likens the polygenetic effect to height: More than 50 specific gene variations together account for 5 percent of our individual height differences, leaving the rest yet to be discovered. What matters for intelligence (as for height, personality, sexual orientation, schizophrenia, or just about any human trait) is the combination of many genes—including 52 intelligence-linked genes identified in one pooling of findings from nearly 80,000 people (Sniekers et al., 2017).

Environment and Intelligence

Fraternal twins are genetically no more alike than other siblings, but they usually share an environment and are often treated similarly. Their intelligence test scores are somewhat more alike than are the scores of nontwin siblings (see Figure 30.1). So environment does have some effect. Adoption studies help us assess the influence of environment. Seeking to untangle genes and environment, researchers have also compared the intelligence test scores of adopted children with those of (a) their *biological parents*, who provided their genes, (b) *adoptive parents*, who provided their home environment, and (c) *adoptive siblings*, who shared that home environment.

➡ **FIGURE 30.2**

In verbal ability, whom do adopted children resemble? As the years went by in their adoptive families, children's verbal ability scores became more like their *biological* parents' scores. (Data from Plomin & DeFries, 1998.)

"Selective breeding has given me an aptitude for the law, but I still love fetching a dead duck out of freezing water."

Several studies suggest that a shared environment exerts a modest influence on intelligence test scores:

- Adoption from poverty into middle-class homes enhances children's intelligence test scores (Nisbett et al., 2012). One large Swedish study looked at this effect among children adopted into wealthier families with more educated parents. The adopted children's IQ scores were higher, by an average of 4.4 points, than those of their non-adopted biological siblings (Kendler et al., 2015a).

- Adoption of mistreated or neglected children also enhances their intelligence scores (Almas et al., 2017).

- The intelligence scores of "virtual twins"—same-age, unrelated children adopted as infants and raised together as siblings—correlate at a level higher than chance: +.28 (Segal et al., 2012).

During childhood, adoptive siblings' test scores correlate modestly. Over time, adopted children accumulate experience in their differing adoptive families. So, would you expect the shared-environment effect to grow with age and the genetic-legacy effect to shrink?

If you would, behavior geneticists have a stunning surprise for you. Adopted children's intelligence scores resemble those of their biological parents much more than their adoptive parents (Loehlin, 2016). And over time, adopted children's verbal ability scores become more like those of their biological parents (**FIGURE 30.2**). Mental ability similarities between adopted children and their adoptive families wane with age (McGue et al., 1993). Who would have guessed?

Genetic influences become more apparent as we accumulate life experience. Identical twins' similarities, for example, continue or increase into their eighties. In one massive study of 11,000 twin pairs in four countries, the heritability of general intelligence (*g*) increased from 41 percent in middle childhood to 55 percent in adolescence to 66 percent in young adulthood (Haworth et al., 2010). Thus, report Ian Deary and his colleagues (2009a, 2012), the heritability of general intelligence increases from "about 30 percent" in early childhood to "well over 50 percent in adulthood."

RETRIEVAL PRACTICE

RP-1 A check on your understanding of heritability: If environments become more equal, the heritability of intelligence will

    a. increase.   **b.** decrease.   **c.** be unchanged.

ANSWERS IN APPENDIX E

📷 For a helpful tutorial animation, watch the *Video: Twin Studies.* Then try to predict the correlation of intelligence scores in *Concept Practice: Studying Twins and Adopted Children.*

Gene–Environment Interactions

LOQ **30-2** How can environmental influences affect cognitive development?

Genes and experience together weave the fabric of intelligence. *Epigenetics* studies part of the dynamic biology of this nature–nurture meeting place. With all our abilities—whether mental or physical—*our genes shape the experiences that shape us*. If you have a natural aptitude for sports, you will probably play more often than others (getting more practice, coaching, and experience). Or, if you have a natural aptitude for academics, you will more likely stay in school, read books, and ask questions—all of which will increase your brain power. The same would be true for your identical twin—who might, not just for genetic reasons, also become a star performer. In these gene–environment interactions, small genetic advantages can trigger social experiences that multiply our original skills (Sauce & Matzel, 2018).

Sometimes, however, environmental conditions work in reverse, depressing physical or cognitive development. Human environments are rarely as impoverished as the dark and barren cages inhabited by deprived rats that develop thinner-than-normal brain cortexes (Rosenzweig, 1984). Yet severe deprivation also leaves footprints on the human brain. Nowhere is the intertwining of biology and experience more apparent than in the most hopeless human environments, such as J. McVicker Hunt (1982) observed in a destitute Iranian orphanage. The typical child Hunt observed there could not sit up unassisted at age 2 or walk at age 4. The little care infants received was not in response to their crying, cooing, or other behaviors, so the children developed little sense of personal control over their environment. They were instead becoming passive "glum lumps." Extreme deprivation was bludgeoning native intelligence—a finding confirmed by other studies of children raised in poorly run orphanages in Romania and elsewhere (Nelson et al., 2009, 2013; van IJzendoorn et al., 2008).

Aware of both the dramatic effects of early experiences and the impact of early intervention, Hunt began a training program for the Iranian caregivers, teaching them to play language-fostering games with 11 infants. They imitated the babies' babbling, engaged them in vocal follow-the-leader, and, finally, they taught the infants sounds from the Persian language. The results were dramatic. By 22 months of age, the infants could name more than 50 objects and body parts, and so charmed visitors that most were adopted—an unprecedented success for the orphanage.

Hunt's findings are an extreme case of a more general finding: The poor environmental conditions that accompany poverty can depress cognitive development and produce stresses that impede cognitive performance (Heberle & Carter, 2015; Tuerk, 2005). And this may help explain another finding: Where environments vary widely, as they do among children of less-educated parents, environmental differences are more predictive of intelligence test scores (Tucker-Drob & Bates, 2016). Like a computer that slows when running multiple operations, impoverished people's worries and distractions consume cognitive bandwidth and can diminish their thinking capacity. On tests of cognitive functioning, sugar cane farmers in India scored better after being paid for their harvest—when their money worries dropped (Mani et al., 2013).

If extreme conditions—sensory deprivation, social isolation, poverty—can slow normal brain development, could the reverse also be true? Could an "enriched" environment amplify normal development and give very young children a superior intellect? Most experts doubt it (DeLoache et al., 2010; Reichert et al., 2010; Vance, 2018). There is no environmental recipe for fast-forwarding a normal infant into a genius. All babies should have normal exposure to sights, sounds, and speech. Beyond that, Sandra Scarr's (1984) verdict still is widely shared: "Parents who are very concerned about providing special educational lessons for their babies are wasting their time."

More encouraging results have come from intensive, post-babyhood enrichment programs (Dodge et al., 2017; Sasser et al., 2017; Tucker-Drob, 2012). This is particularly true of preschool programs for poverty-level children (Gormley et al., 2013; Heckman & Karapakula, 2019; Magnuson et al., 2007). Intelligence scores also rise with nutritional supplements to pregnant mothers and newborns (3.5 points), with quality preschool experiences (4 points), and with interactive reading programs (6 points) (Protzko et al., 2013).

Devastating neglect Some Romanian orphans, such as this child in the Leaganul Pentru Copii orphanage in 1990, had minimal interaction with caregivers, and suffered delayed development.

Josef Polleross/The Image Works

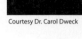

Courtesy Dr. Carol Dweck

It pays to view intelligence as expandable Psychologist Carol Dweck has shown several benefits of adopting a growth mindset—believing that intelligence grows through motivated effort. "No matter what your ability is," Dweck says, "effort is what ignites that ability and turns it into accomplishment" (2006, p. 16).

"It is our choices . . . that show what we truly are, far more than our abilities."
— Professor Dumbledore to Harry Potter in J. K. Rowling's *Harry Potter and the Chamber of Secrets,* 1999

"When you [fail], embrace it; learn from it. Don't think . . . that's going to hinder you from becoming whoever you want to become. . . . I wake up every day telling the world: Come on baby, let's ride. What you got for me?" — Recording artist Pitbull, 2019

A hungry mind

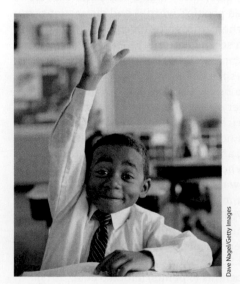

Dave Nagel/Getty Images

growth mindset a focus on learning and growing rather than viewing abilities as fixed.

Growth Mindset

Schooling and intelligence interact, and both enhance later income (Ceci & Williams, 1997, 2009). But what we accomplish with our intelligence depends also on our own beliefs and motivation. One analysis of 72,431 undergraduates found that study motivation and study skills rivaled aptitude and previous grades as predictors of academic achievement (Credé & Kuncel, 2008). Motivation can even affect intelligence test performance. Four dozen studies show that, when promised money for doing well, adolescents score higher on such tests (Duckworth et al., 2011).

These observations would not surprise psychologist Carol Dweck (2018; Dweck & Yeager, 2019). She reports that believing intelligence is changeable fosters a **growth mindset,** a focus on learning and growing. Dweck teaches young teens that the brain is like a muscle, growing stronger with use as neuron connections grow: "Learning how to do a new kind of problem grows your math brain!" Receiving praise for *effort* and for tackling challenges, rather than for being smart or accomplished, helps teens understand the link between hard work and success (Gunderson et al., 2013). Although a growth mindset doesn't alter inborn intelligence, it can make children and youth more resilient when confronted with difficult learning material or frustrating people (Peng & Tullis, 2019; Walton & Wilson, 2018). One national experiment of 6320 lower-achieving U.S. high school students showed that viewing two 25-minute videos fostering a growth mindset modestly improved grades (Yeager et al., 2019). Mindset isn't everything, but it does matter.

More than 300 studies confirm that ability + opportunity + motivation = success in fields from sports to science to music (Ericsson et al., 2007). Extremely high intelligence-test-scoring 12-year-olds are much more likely than the average person to earn doctorates and hold patents—if their ability is "coupled with commitment" (Makel et al., 2016). High school students' math proficiency and college students' grades reflect their aptitude but also their self-discipline, their belief in the power of effort, and a curious, "hungry mind" (Murayama et al., 2013; Richardson et al., 2012; von Stumm et al., 2011). In a study of 168,000 Chilean tenth graders, those from the lowest-income families who had a growth mindset had academic test scores comparable to high-income students who had a fixed mindset (Claro et al., 2016). And consider: Since 2008, youth of South Asian heritage have won most U.S. national spelling bee contests—an incredible achievement likely influenced by a cultural belief that strong effort is energizing and brings success (Rattan et al., 2012; Savani & Job, 2017). To reach your potential, the formula is simple: Believe in your ability to learn, and apply yourself with sustained effort.

These repeated findings—that a growth mindset and disciplined effort enhance achievement—have generated attention. Some researchers caution that applying growth mindset findings in large-scale interventions with at-risk students can have a downside, the social cost of blaming struggling individuals for their circumstances (Ikizer & Blanton, 2016). Others note that researchers and educators sometimes overstate the modest growth mindset benefit (Sisk et al., 2018). Overemphasizing growth mindset power can, as with the motivational concept of *grit,* lead some students to feel that their disappointments reflect a moral flaw. Sometimes people need more than the power of positive thinking to overcome their harsh conditions.

U.S. spelling "octo-champs" The 2019 Scripps National Spelling Bee had eight winners instead of one, six of whom were of South Asian descent.

ASK YOURSELF

Are you working to the potential reflected in your standardized aptitude test scores? What, other than your aptitude, is affecting your school performance?

Group Differences in Intelligence Test Scores

If there were no group differences in intelligence test scores, psychologists would have less debate over hereditary and environmental influences. But there are group differences. What are they? And what shall we make of them?

Gender Similarities and Differences

LOQ 30-3 How and why do the genders differ in mental ability scores?

In science, as in everyday life, it is differences—not similarities—that excite interest. Men's self-estimated intelligence is often higher than women's self-estimated intelligence, which may fuel a false perception that men are smarter than women (Furnham, 2016). In truth, men's and women's intelligence differences are minor. For example, in that 1932 testing of all Scottish 11-year-olds, boys' intelligence scores averaged 100.5 and girls' 100.6 (Deary et al., 2003). As far as *g* is concerned, boys and girls, men and women, are the same.

Yet most people find differences more newsworthy. In cultures where both girls and boys are educated, girls tend to outpace boys in spelling, verbal fluency, reading, and locating objects (Reilly et al., 2019; Voyer & Voyer, 2014). They are better emotion detectors and are more sensitive to touch, taste, and color (Halpern et al., 2007). In math computation and overall math performance, girls and boys hardly differ (Else-Quest et al., 2010; Hyde & Mertz, 2009; Lindberg et al., 2010).

On complex math problems, males outperform females. But the most reliable male edge appears in spatial ability tests like the one shown in **FIGURE 30.3** (Lauer et al., 2019). The solution requires speedy mental rotation of three-dimensional objects. Males' mental ability scores (and brains) also vary more than females'. Worldwide, males outnumber females at both the low and high extremes (Ball et al., 2017; Baye & Monseur, 2016). Males, for example, are more likely than females to need "remedial" math classes. But they are also more likely to earn the highest math scores.

Psychologist Steven Pinker (2005) has argued the evolutionary perspective—that biology affects gender differences in life priorities (women's somewhat greater interest in people versus men's in money and things), in risk-taking (with men more reckless), and in math reasoning and spatial abilities. Such differences are, he noted, observed across cultures, stable over time, influenced by prenatal hormones, and observed in boys raised as girls.

Testosterone therapy for female-to-male sex reassignment results in brain language processing areas that become more male-like, as well as some gray matter loss (Hahn et al., 2016).

FIGURE 30.3

A mental rotation test These kinds of items are often found on spatial abilities tests. See answer below.[1]

Which one of the options below matches the Original?

Original

(a)

(b)   (c)

[1]The correct answer is c.

"That's an excellent suggestion, Miss Triggs. Perhaps one of the men would like to suggest it."

Shrinking the science gap In 2014, Iranian math professor Maryam Mirzakhani (1977–2017) became the first woman to win math's most admired award, the Fields Medal (a). In 2018, physicist Donna Strickland (b) and chemist Frances C. Arnold (c) were each awarded a Nobel Prize in scientific fields where women rarely win. In her acceptance speech, Strickland said, "Not everyone thinks physics is fun, but I do."

But social expectations and opportunities also construct gender by shaping interests and abilities (Crawford et al., 1995; Eccles et al., 1990). Stephen Ceci and Wendy Williams (2010, 2011) report that culturally influenced preferences help explain why American women, more than men, avoid math-intensive vocations. In Asia and Russia, teen girls have outperformed boys in an international science exam; in North America and Britain, boys have scored higher (Fairfield, 2012).

More gender-equal cultures, such as Sweden and Iceland, exhibit little of the gender math gap found in gender-unequal cultures, such as Turkey and Korea (Guiso et al., 2008; Kane & Mertz, 2012). Since the 1970s, as gender equity has increased in the United States, the boy-to-girl ratio among 12- to 14-year-olds with very high SAT math scores (above 700) has declined from 13 to 1 to 3 to 1 (Makel et al., 2016; Nisbett et al., 2012). And in psychology, there's been a dramatic change in the ratio of women to men earning doctorates—from 17 percent women in 1958 to 71 percent in 2018 (Burelli, 2008; NSF, 2019). Experience matters.

(a)

(b)

(c)

Racial and Ethnic Similarities and Differences

LOQ 30-4 How and why do racial and ethnic groups differ in mental ability scores?

Fueling the group-differences debate are two other disturbing but scientifically agreed-upon facts:

- Racial and ethnic groups differ in their average intelligence test scores.
- High-scoring people (and groups) are more likely to attain high levels of education and income.

There are many group differences in average intelligence test scores. New Zealanders of European descent outscore native Maori New Zealanders. Israeli Jews outscore Israeli Arabs. Most Japanese outscore most Burakumin, a stigmatized Japanese minority. And White Americans have outscored Black Americans, although this difference seems to have diminished in recent years, especially among children (Dickens & Flynn, 2006; Nisbett et al., 2012). Such *group* differences provide little basis for judging individuals. Worldwide, women outlive men by five years, but knowing only an individual's gender won't tell us how long that person will live.

We have seen that heredity contributes to *individual* differences in intelligence. But group differences in a heritable trait may be entirely environmental. Consider one of nature's experiments: Allow some children to grow up hearing their culture's dominant language, while others, born deaf, do not. Then give both groups an intelligence test rooted in the dominant language. The result? No surprise, those with expertise in the dominant language will score higher than those who were born deaf (Braden, 1994; Steele, 1990; Zeidner, 1990).

Might the racial and ethnic gap be similarly environmental? Consider:

Genetics research reveals that under the skin, we humans are remarkably alike. Despite some racial variation, such as in health risks, the average genetic difference between two Icelandic villagers or between two Kenyans greatly exceeds the average group difference between Icelanders and Kenyans (Cavalli-Sforza et al., 1994; Rosenberg et al., 2002). Moreover, looks can deceive. Light-skinned Europeans and dark-skinned Africans are genetically closer than are dark-skinned Africans and dark-skinned Aboriginal Australians.

Race is not a neatly defined biological category. Race is primarily a social construction without well-defined physical boundaries; each race blends seamlessly into the race of its geographical neighbors (Helms et al., 2005; Smedley & Smedley, 2005). In one genetic analysis of more than 160,000 people living in the United States, most with less than 28 percent African ancestry said they were White; those with more than 28 percent mostly said they were African American (Byrc et al., 2015). Moreover, with increasingly mixed ancestries, more and more people defy neat racial categorization and self-identify as multiracial (Pauker et al., 2009).

Within the same populations, there are generation-to-generation differences in test scores. Test scores of today's better-fed, better-educated, and more test-prepared populations exceeds those of 1930s populations—by a greater margin than the score difference between today's U.S. Whites and U.S. Blacks (Flynn, 2012; Pietschnig & Voracek, 2015; Trahan et al., 2014). One research review noted that the average intelligence test performance of today's sub-Saharan Africans is the same as that of British adults in 1948 (Wicherts et al., 2010). No one credits genetics for such generation-to-generation differences.

Schools and culture matter. Countries whose economies create a large wealth gap between rich and poor tend also to have a large rich-versus-poor intelligence test score gap (Nisbett, 2009). In China and Turkey, people in poorer regions have the lowest scores, and those in wealthier regions have the highest (Lynn et al., 2015, 2016). Moreover, educational policies (such as kindergarten attendance, school discipline, and instructional time per year) predict national differences in intelligence and knowledge tests (Lynn & Vanhanen, 2012; Rindermann & Ceci, 2009). One analysis of 600,000 students showed that each additional year of school predicted 1 to 5 additional IQ points (Ritchie & Tucker-Drob, 2018). Staying in school secures superior smarts.

Math achievement, aptitude test differences, and especially grades may reflect conscientiousness more than competence (Poropat, 2014). Women in college and university similarly outperform equally able men, thanks partly to their greater conscientiousness (Keiser et al., 2016). Students in Asia, who have largely outperformed North American students on such tests, have also spent more time in school and much more time in and out of school studying (CMEC, 2018; Larson & Verma, 1999; NCEE, 2018). These differences persist within the United States, where Asian-American students devote the most time to studying and earn the highest grades (Hsin & Xie, 2014).

In different eras, different ethnic groups have experienced golden ages—periods of remarkable achievement. Twenty-five hundred years ago, it was the Greeks and the Egyptians, then the Romans. In the eighth and ninth centuries,

World Scrabble champs In 2015, Team Nigeria was the top country in the World Scrabble Championship. Five of its six members finished among the top 50 contestants, including Wellington Jighere, center, the individual world Scrabble champion.

"Do not obtain your slaves from Britain, because they are so stupid and so utterly incapable of being taught." —Cicero, 106–43 B.C.E.

genius seemed to reside in the Arab world. Five hundred years ago, the Aztec Indians and the peoples of Northern Europe were the superachievers. Cultures rise and fall over centuries.

RP-2 The heritability of intelligence scores will be greater in a society marked by equal opportunity than in a society of peasants and aristocrats. Why?

ANSWERS IN APPENDIX E

The Question of Bias

LOQ 30-5 Are intelligence tests biased or unfair? What is *stereotype threat,* and how does it affect test-takers' performance?

Knowing there are group differences in intelligence test scores leads to the question of whether those differences are built into the tests. Is intelligence testing a constructive way to guide people toward suitable opportunities? Or is it a potent, discriminatory weapon camouflaged as science? In short, are intelligence tests biased? The answer depends on which of two very different definitions of bias we use.

The *scientific* meaning of *bias* hinges solely on whether a test predicts future behavior for all groups of test-takers, not just for some. For example, if the SAT accurately predicted the college achievement of women but not that of men, then the test would be biased. In this scientific meaning of the term, the near-consensus among psychologists (as summarized by the U.S. National Research Council's Committee on Ability Testing and the American Psychological Association's Task Force on Intelligence) has been that the major U.S. aptitude tests are *not* biased (Berry & Zhao, 2015; Neisser et al., 1996; Wigdor & Garner, 1982). The tests' predictive validity is roughly the same, regardless of gender, race, ethnicity, or socioeconomic level. If an intelligence test score of 95 predicts slightly below-average grades, that rough prediction usually applies equally to all.

But in everyday language, we may consider a test "biased" if it is unfair—if test scores will be influenced by the test-takers' cultural experiences. This in fact happened to Eastern European immigrants in the early 1900s. Lacking the experience to answer questions about their new culture, many were classified as "feebleminded." If we use *bias* in this popular sense, then yes, intelligence tests may be considered unfair (even if scientifically unbiased). Why? Because they measure the test-takers' developed abilities, which reflect, in part, their education and experiences.

You may have read examples of intelligence test items that make assumptions (for example, that a cup goes with a saucer). Such items bias the test (against those who do not use saucers). Could such questions explain cultural differences in test performance? In such cases, tests can be a vehicle for discrimination, consigning potentially capable children (some of whom may have a different native language) to unchallenging classes and dead-end jobs. Many intelligence researchers therefore recommend culture-neutral questions—such as those that assess people's ability to learn novel words, sayings, and analogies—to enable *culture-fair* aptitude tests (Fagan & Holland, 2007b, 2009).

Defenders of the existing aptitude tests have noted that racial group differences persist on some nonverbal items, such as counting digits backward (Jensen, 1983, 1998). Moreover, they add, blaming the test for a group's lower scores is like blaming a messenger for bad news. Why blame the tests for exposing unequal experiences and opportunities? If, because of malnutrition, people were to suffer stunted growth, would you blame the measuring stick that reveals it? If unequal past experiences predict unequal future achievements, a valid aptitude test will detect such inequalities.

As you have seen in so many contexts throughout this text, expectations and attitudes can influence our perceptions and behaviors. For test-makers, expectations can introduce bias. For test-takers, they can become self-fulfilling prophecies.

RP-3 What is the difference between a test that is culturally biased and a test that is scientifically biased?

ANSWERS IN APPENDIX E

stereotype threat a self-confirming concern that one will be evaluated based on a negative stereotype.

TEST-TAKERS' EXPECTATIONS When Steven Spencer and his colleagues (1997) gave a difficult math test to equally capable men and women, women did not do as well—except when they had been led to expect that women usually do as well as men on the test. Otherwise, something affected their performance. There was a "threat in the air" (Spencer et al., 2016). And with Claude Steele and Joshua Aronson, Spencer (2002) again observed this self-fulfilling **stereotype threat** when Black students performed worse after being reminded of their race just before taking verbal aptitude tests. Follow-up experiments have confirmed that negatively stereotyped minorities and women may have unrealized academic and professional potential (Grand, 2016; Nguyen & Ryan, 2008; Walton & Spencer, 2009). If you worry that your group or "type" often doesn't do well on a certain kind of test or task, your self-doubts and self-monitoring may hijack your working memory and impair attention, performance, and learning (Hutchison et al., 2013; Inzlicht & Kang, 2010; Rydell et al., 2010). Critics argue that stereotype threat effects are weaker than originally thought, because situational factors can reduce or eliminate them (Flore & Wicherts, 2015; Flore et al., 2019).

Stereotype threat helps explain why Blacks in the United States have scored higher when tested by Blacks than when tested by Whites (Danso & Esses, 2001). It implies a possible effect of non-Black teachers having lower expectations for Black students than do Black teachers (Gershenson et al., 2016). It also gives us insight into why women have scored higher on math tests with no test-takers who are men present. And it helps explain why men would rather stay in traditionally feminine jobs (primary school teacher, child protection worker) when they perform their duties without feeling threatened by the presence of highly competent women (Doyle & Voyer, 2016; Kalokerinos et al., 2018). Being shielded from others who are expected to perform better can give you the confidence to do your best.

From such studies, some researchers have concluded that making students believe they probably won't succeed can function as a stereotype and weaken performance. Remedial "minority support" programs may sometimes have this unintended effect (Steele, 1995, 2010).

Other research teams have demonstrated the benefits of self-affirmation exercises that engage students in writing about their most important values (Borman et al., 2019; Ferrer & Cohen, 2018; Logel et al., 2019). When challenged to believe in their potential, think positively about their diverse life experiences, or increase their sense of belonging, disadvantaged university students have earned higher grades and have had lower dropout rates (Broda et al., 2018; Sarrasin et al., 2018; Townsend et al., 2019).

* * *

What, then, can we realistically conclude about aptitude tests and bias? The tests are not biased in the scientific sense of failing to make valid statistical predictions for different groups. But they are indeed biased in one sense—sensitivity to performance differences caused by cultural experience. Are the tests discriminatory? Again, the answer can be *Yes* or *No*. In one sense, *Yes*, their purpose is to discriminate—to distinguish among individuals. In another sense, *No*, their purpose is to reduce discrimination by decreasing reliance on subjective criteria for school and job placement—who you know, how you dress, or whether you are the "right kind of person." Civil service aptitude tests, for example, were devised to discriminate (distinguish) more fairly and objectively by reducing the political, racial, ethnic, and gender discrimination that preceded their use. Banning aptitude tests would lead those who decide on jobs and admissions to rely more on other considerations, such as personal opinion.

Perhaps, then, our goals for tests of mental abilities should be threefold. First, we should realize the benefits that intelligence-testing pioneer Alfred Binet foresaw—to enable schools to recognize who might profit most from early intervention. Second, we must remain alert to Binet's wish that intelligence test scores not be misinterpreted as literal measures of a person's worth and potential. Third, we must remember that the competence that general intelligence tests sample is important; it helps enable success in some life paths. But it reflects only one important aspect of personal competence (Stanovich et al., 2016). Our rationality, practical intelligence, and emotional intelligence matter, too, as do other forms of creativity, talent, and character.

"Math class is tough!" — "Teen Talk" talking Barbie doll (introduced July 1992, recalled three months later)

"Almost all the joyful things of life are outside the measure of IQ tests." — Madeleine L'Engle, *A Circle of Quiet*, 1972

"[Einstein] showed that genius equals brains plus tenacity squared." — Walter Isaacson, "Einstein's Final Quest," 2009

The point to remember: There are many ways of being successful; our differences are variations of human adaptability. Life's great achievements result not only from "can do" abilities (and fair opportunity) but also from "will do" motivation. Competence + Diligence = Accomplishment.

RETRIEVAL PRACTICE

RP-4 What psychological principle may help explain why women tend to score higher on math tests when none of their fellow test-takers are men?

ANSWERS IN APPENDIX E

 To explore how you perceive your own intelligence, engage online with the activity *Assess Your Strengths: What Is Your Theory of Intelligence, and How Is That Affecting Your Success?*

MODULE **30** REVIEW Genetic and Environmental Influences on Intelligence

LEARNING OBJECTIVES

Test Yourself Answer these repeated Learning Objective Questions on your own (before checking the answers in Appendix D) to improve your retention of the concepts (McDaniel et al., 2009, 2015).

LOQ 30-1 What is *heritability,* and what do twin and adoption studies tell us about the nature and nurture of intelligence?

LOQ 30-2 How can environmental influences affect cognitive development?

LOQ 30-3 How and why do the genders differ in mental ability scores?

LOQ 30-4 How and why do racial and ethnic groups differ in mental ability scores?

LOQ 30-5 Are intelligence tests biased or unfair? What is *stereotype threat,* and how does it affect test-takers' performance?

TERMS AND CONCEPTS TO REMEMBER

Test Yourself Write down the definition in your own words, then check your answer.

heritability, p. 370

growth mindset, p. 374

stereotype threat, p. 378

MASTER THE MATERIAL

Test Yourself Answer the following questions on your own first, then check your answers in Appendix E.

1. To say that the heritability of intelligence is about 50 percent means that 50 percent of
   a. an individual's intelligence is due to genetic factors.
   b. the similarities between two groups of people are attributable to genes.
   c. the variation in intelligence within a group of people is attributable to genetic factors.
   d. an individual's intelligence is due to each parent's genes.

2. The strongest support for heredity's influence on intelligence is the finding that
   a. identical twins, but not other siblings, have nearly identical intelligence test scores.
   b. the correlation between intelligence test scores of fraternal twins is not higher than that for other siblings.
   c. similarity of mental abilities between adopted siblings increases with age.
   d. children in impoverished families have similar intelligence scores.

3. The environmental influence that has the clearest, most profound effect on intellectual development is
   a. exposing normal infants to enrichment programs before age 1.
   b. growing up in an economically disadvantaged home.
   c. being raised in conditions of extreme deprivation.
   d. being an identical twin.

4. _____ _____ can lead to poor performance on tests by undermining test-takers' belief that they can do well on the test.

Continue testing yourself with **LearningCurve** or **Achieve Read & Practice** to learn and remember most effectively.

Tomas Rodriguez/Getty Images

What Drives Us: Hunger, Sex, Belonging, and Achievement

How well I [DM] remember asking my first discussion question in a new introductory psychology class. Several hands rose, along with one left foot. The foot belonged to Chris Klein, who was the unlikeliest person to have made it to that class. At birth, Chris suffered oxygen deprivation that required 40 minutes of CPR. "One doctor wanted to let him go," recalled his mother.

The result was severe cerebral palsy. With damage to the brain area that controls muscle movement, Chris can't contain his constantly moving hands. He cannot feed, dress, or care for himself. And he cannot speak. But Chris can control his keen mind and his left foot. With that blessed foot he operates the joystick on his motorized wheelchair. Using his left big toe, he can type sentences, which his communication system can store, send, or speak. And Chris is motivated—very motivated.

When Chris was a high school student in suburban Chicago, three teachers doubted he would be able to leave home for college. Yet he persisted, and, with much support, attended my college called Hope. Five years later, as his left foot drove him across the stage to receive his diploma, his admiring classmates honored his achievement with a spontaneous standing ovation.

Today, Chris is an inspirational speaker for schools, churches, universities, and community events, giving "a voice to those that have none, and a helping hand to those with disabilities." He is writing a book, *Lessons from the Big Toe.* And he has found love and married.

Few of us face Chris Klein's challenges. But we all seek to direct our energy in ways that will produce satisfaction and success. We are pushed by biological motives, such as hunger and sex (Modules 32–33), and social ones, such as the needs to belong and to achieve (Module 34). Chris Klein's fierce will to live, learn, and love highlights the essence of our own *motivations,* which energize and direct our lives.

Let's begin by looking at how psychologists have approached the study of motivation (Module 31).

Basic Motivational Concepts

Katie Green/MLIVE.COM

A motivated man: Chris Klein To see and hear Chris presenting his story, visit tinyurl.com/ChrisPsychStudent.

(**LEARNING OBJECTIVE QUESTION** **LOQ**) **31-1** How do psychologists define *motivation?* What are four key motivation theories?

Our **motivations** arise from the interplay between nature (the bodily "push") and nurture (the "pulls" from our personal experiences, thoughts, and culture). Our motives drive our behavior. That is usually, but not always, for the better. If our motivations get hijacked, our lives go awry. Those with *substance use disorder,* for example, may find their cravings for an addictive substance override their longings for sustenance, safety, and social support.

In their attempts to understand motivated behavior, psychologists have viewed it from four perspectives:

- *Instinct theory* (now replaced by the *evolutionary perspective*) focuses on genetically predisposed behaviors.
- *Drive-reduction theory* focuses on how we respond to inner pushes and external pulls.
- *Arousal theory* focuses on finding the right level of stimulation.
- **Abraham Maslow's** *hierarchy of needs* focuses on the priority of some needs over others.

Instincts and Evolutionary Theory

To qualify as an **instinct,** a complex behavior must have a fixed pattern throughout a species and be unlearned (Tinbergen, 1951). Such unlearned behaviors include *imprinting* in birds and the return of salmon to their birthplace. A few human behaviors, such as infants' innate reflexes to root for a nipple and suck, also exhibit unlearned fixed patterns. *Instinct theory,* popular in the early twentieth century, viewed our instincts as the source of our motivations. But many more behaviors are directed by both physiological needs and psychological wants.

Same motive, different wiring The more complex the nervous system, the more adaptable the organism. Both humans and weaverbirds satisfy their need for shelter in ways that reflect their inherited capacities. Human behavior is flexible; we can learn whatever skills we need to build a house. The bird's behavior pattern is fixed; it can build only this kind of nest.

Annika Erickson/Getty Images

James Warwick/Science Source

Although instincts cannot explain most human motives, the underlying assumption endures in *evolutionary psychology*: Genes do predispose some species-typical behavior. Psychologists might apply this perspective, for example, to explain our human similarities, animals' biological predispositions, and the influence of evolution on our fears, our helping behaviors, and our romantic attractions.

Drives and Incentives

In addition to our predispositions, we have *drives*. **Physiological needs** (such as for food or water) create an aroused, motivated state—a drive (such as hunger or thirst)—that pushes us to reduce the need. **Drive-reduction theory** explains that, with few exceptions, when a physiological need increases, so does our psychological drive to reduce it.

Drive reduction is one way our bodies strive for **homeostasis** (literally "staying the same")—the maintenance of a steady internal state. For example, our body regulates its temperature in a way similar to a room's thermostat. Both systems operate through feedback loops: Sensors feed room temperature to a control device. If the room's temperature cools, the control device switches on the furnace. Likewise, if our body's temperature cools, our blood vessels constrict to conserve warmth, and we feel driven to put on more clothes or seek a warmer environment (**FIGURE 31.1**).

| Need (food, water) | → | Drive (hunger, thirst) | → | Drive-reducing behaviors (eating, drinking) |

⬆ FIGURE 31.1
Drive-reduction theory Drive-reduction motivation arises from *homeostasis*—our body's natural tendency to maintain a steady internal state. Thus, if we are water-deprived, our thirst drives us to drink to restore the body's normal state.

Not only are we *pushed* by our need to reduce drives, we also are *pulled* by **incentives**—positive or negative environmental stimuli that lure or repel us. Such stimuli (when positive) increase our dopamine levels, causing our underlying drives (such as for food or sex) to become active impulses (Hamid et al., 2016). And the more these impulses are satisfied and reinforced, the stronger the drive may become: As Roy Baumeister (2015) noted, "Getting begets wanting." If you are hungry, the aroma of good food will motivate you. Whether that aroma comes from roasted peanuts or toasted tarantula will depend on your culture and experience. Incentives can also be negative: If teasing others on social media results in our being unfollowed or unfriended, that negative incentive may motivate us to change our behavior.

When there is both a need and an incentive, we feel strongly driven. The food-deprived person who smells pizza baking may feel a strong hunger drive, and the baking pizza may become a compelling incentive. For each motive, we can therefore ask, "How is it pushed by our inborn physiological needs and pulled by learned incentives in the environment?"

Arousal Theory

We are much more than calm homeostatic systems, however. Some motivated behaviors actually *increase* rather than decrease arousal. Well-fed animals will leave their shelter to explore and gain information, seemingly in the absence of any need-based drive. Curiosity drives monkeys to monkey around trying to figure out how to unlock a latch that opens nothing or how to open a window that allows them to see outside their room (Butler, 1954). It drives newly mobile infants to investigate every accessible corner of the house. It drove curious students, in one experiment, to click on pens—even when those pens sometimes delivered an electric shock (Hsee & Ruan, 2016). It drives the scientists whose work this text discusses. And it drives explorers and adventurers such as mountaineer George Mallory. Asked why he wanted to climb Mount Everest, Mallory famously answered, "Because it's there." Sometimes uncertainty brings excitement, which amplifies motivation (Shen et al., 2015). Those who, like Mallory, enjoy high arousal are most likely to seek out intense music, novel foods, and risky behaviors and careers (Roberti et al., 2004; Zuckerman, 1979, 2009). Although they have been called *sensation-seekers,* risk takers may also be motivated to master their emotions and actions (Barlow et al., 2013).

So, human motivation aims not to eliminate arousal but to seek optimum levels of arousal. Having all our biological needs satisfied, we feel driven to experience stimulation. Lacking stimulation, we feel bored and look for a way to increase arousal.

motivation a need or desire that energizes and directs behavior.

instinct a complex behavior that is rigidly patterned throughout a species and is unlearned.

physiological need a basic bodily requirement.

drive-reduction theory the idea that a physiological need creates an aroused state (a drive) that motivates an organism to satisfy the need.

homeostasis a tendency to maintain a balanced or constant internal state; the regulation of any aspect of body chemistry, such as blood glucose, around a particular level.

incentive a positive or negative environmental stimulus that motivates behavior.

Driven by curiosity Young monkeys and children are fascinated by the unfamiliar. Their drive to explore maintains an optimum level of arousal and is one of several motives that do not fill any immediate physiological need.

Most people, worldwide, prefer to *do* something—even (when given no other option) to self-administer mild electric shocks (Buttrick et al., 2019; Wilson et al., 2014). Why might people seek to increase their arousal? Moderate arousal and even anxiety can be motivating—leading to higher levels of math achievement, for example (Wang et al., 2015c). Yet *too* much stimulation or stress motivates us to look for ways to decrease arousal. In experiments, people felt less stress when they limited email-checking and phone notifications rather than being continually accessible (Fitz et al., 2019; Kushlev & Dunn, 2015).

Two early twentieth-century psychologists studied the relationship of arousal to performance and identified the **Yerkes-Dodson law:** *moderate arousal leads to optimal performance* (Yerkes & Dodson, 1908). When taking an exam, it pays to be moderately aroused—alert but not trembling with nervousness. (If you're already nervous, it's better not to become further aroused with caffeine.) Between bored low arousal and anxious hyperarousal lies a flourishing life. Optimal arousal levels depend on the task, with more difficult tasks requiring lower arousal for best performance (Hembree, 1988).

ASK YOURSELF

Does boredom ever motivate you to do things just to figure out something new? When was the last time that happened, and what did you find?

RETRIEVAL PRACTICE

RP-1 Performance peaks at lower levels of arousal for difficult tasks, and at higher levels for easy or well-learned tasks. (a) How might this affect marathon runners? (b) How might this affect anxious test-takers facing a difficult exam?

ANSWERS IN APPENDIX E

A Hierarchy of Needs

Some needs take priority. At this moment, with your needs for air and water hopefully satisfied, other motives—such as your desire to learn and achieve—are energizing and directing your behavior. Let your need for water go unsatisfied, however, and your thirst will preoccupy you. Deprived of air, your thirst will disappear.

Abraham Maslow (1970) described these priorities as a **hierarchy of needs,** which others later portrayed as a pyramid (Bridgman et al., 2019; **FIGURE 31.2**). Our physiological needs, such as for food and water, form the pyramid's base. As these needs become met, our focus shifts to our need for safety, and then to satisfying our needs to give and receive love and to enjoy self-esteem. Beyond this, said Maslow (1971), lies the need to actualize one's full potential.

Near the end of his life, Maslow proposed that some people also reach a level of *self-transcendence.* At the self-actualization level, people seek to realize their own potential. At the self-transcendence level, people strive for meaning, purpose, and communion in a way that is transpersonal—beyond the self (Koltko-Rivera, 2006). Maslow's contemporary, psychiatrist Viktor Frankl (1962), a Nazi concentration camp survivor, concurred

"Hunger is the most urgent form of poverty."
— Alliance to End Hunger, 2002

Yerkes-Dodson law the principle that performance increases with arousal only up to a point, beyond which performance decreases.

hierarchy of needs Maslow's pyramid of human needs, beginning at the base with physiological needs that must first be satisfied before people can fulfill their higher-level safety needs and then psychological needs.

Self-transcendence needs
Need to find meaning and identity beyond the self

Self-actualization needs
Need to live up to our fullest and unique potential

Esteem needs
Need for self-esteem, achievement, competence, and independence; need for recognition and respect from others

Belongingness and love needs
Need to love and be loved, to belong and be accepted; need to avoid loneliness and separation

Safety needs
Need to feel that the world is organized and predictable; need to feel safe, secure, and stable

Physiological needs
Need to satisfy hunger and thirst

Lionsgate/Photofest © Lionsgate

◀ FIGURE 31.2

Maslow's hierarchy of needs Reduced to semistarvation by their rulers, inhabitants of Suzanne Collins' fictional nation, Panem, hunger for food and survival. *Hunger Games* heroine Katniss Everdeen (played by Jennifer Lawrence) expresses higher-level needs for actualization and transcendence, and in the process inspires the nation.

that the search for meaning is an important human motive: "Life is never made unbearable by circumstances, but only by lack of meaning and purpose."

"Do you feel your life has an important purpose or meaning?" When Gallup asked this of people in 132 countries, 91 percent answered *Yes* (Oishi & Diener, 2014). People sense meaning when they experience their life as having *purpose* (goals), *significance* (value), and *coherence* (sense)—sentiments that may be nourished by strong social connections, a religious faith, an orderly world, and social status (King et al., 2016; Martela & Steger, 2016). People's sense of life's meaning predicts their psychological and physical well-being, and their capacity to delay gratification (Heine et al., 2006; Van Tongeren et al., 2018). Meaning matters.

The order of Maslow's hierarchy is not universally fixed. American suffragist Alice Paul starved herself to make a political statement (enduring force-feeding by her jailers as a result). Culture also influences our priorities: Self-esteem matters most in individualist nations, whose citizens tend to focus more on personal achievements than on family and community identity (Oishi et al., 1999). And, while agreeing with Maslow's basic levels of need, today's psychologists note that gaining and retaining mates, parenting offspring, and desiring social status are also basic human motives (Anderson et al., 2015; Kenrick et al., 2010).

Nevertheless, the simple idea that some motives are more compelling than others provides a framework for thinking about motivation. Worldwide life-satisfaction surveys support this basic idea (Oishi et al., 1999; Tay & Diener, 2011). In poorer nations that lack easy access to money and the food and shelter it buys, financial satisfaction more strongly predicts feelings of well-being. In wealthy nations, where most are able to meet their basic needs, social connections better predict well-being.

With these classic motivation theories in mind (**TABLE 31.1**), let's now consider four representative motives, beginning at the physiological level with hunger and working up through sexual motivation to the higher-level needs to belong and to achieve. At each level, we shall see how experience interacts with biology.

TABLE 31.1 Classic Motivation Theories

Theory	Its Big Idea
Instincts and evolutionary theory	There is a genetic basis for unlearned, species-typical behavior (such as birds building nests or infants rooting for a nipple).
Drive-reduction theory	Physiological needs (such as hunger and thirst) create an aroused state that drives us to reduce the need (for example, by eating or drinking).
Arousal theory	Our need to maintain an optimal level of arousal motivates behaviors that meet no physiological need (such as our yearning for stimulation and our hunger for information).
Maslow's hierarchy of needs	We prioritize survival-based needs and then social needs more than the needs for esteem and meaning.

ASK YOURSELF

Consider your own experiences in terms of Maslow's hierarchy of needs. Do you remember experiencing hunger or thirst that displaced your concern for other, higher-level needs? Do you usually feel safe? Loved? Confident? How often do you feel you are able to address what Maslow called "self-actualization" needs? What about "self-transcendence" needs?

RETRIEVAL PRACTICE

RP-2 After hours of driving alone in an unfamiliar city, you finally see a diner. Although it looks deserted and a little creepy, you stop because you are *really* hungry and thirsty. How would Maslow's hierarchy of needs explain your behavior?

ANSWERS IN APPENDIX E

MODULE 31

REVIEW Basic Motivational Concepts

LEARNING OBJECTIVES

Test Yourself Answer these repeated Learning Objective Questions on your own (before checking the answers in Appendix D) to improve your retention of the concepts (McDaniel et al., 2009, 2015).

LOQ 31-1 How do psychologists define *motivation?* What are four key motivation theories?

TERMS AND CONCEPTS TO REMEMBER

Test Yourself Write down the definition in your own words, then check your answer.

motivation, p. 383

instinct, p. 383

physiological need, p. 383

drive-reduction theory, p. 383

homeostasis, p. 383

incentive, p. 383

Yerkes-Dodson law, p. 384

hierarchy of needs, p. 384

MASTER THE MATERIAL

Test Yourself Answer the following questions on your own first, then check your answers in Appendix E.

1. Today's evolutionary psychology shares an idea that was an underlying assumption of instinct theory. This idea is that
   a. physiological needs arouse psychological states.
   b. genes predispose species-typical behavior.
   c. physiological needs increase arousal.
   d. external needs energize and direct behavior.

2. An example of a physiological need is _____. An example of a psychological drive is _____.
   a. hunger; a "push" to find food
   b. a "push" to find food; hunger
   c. curiosity; a "push" to reduce arousal
   d. a "push" to reduce arousal; curiosity

3. Danielle walks into a friend's kitchen, smells cookies baking, and begins to feel very hungry. The smell of baking cookies is a(n) _____ (incentive/drive).

4. _____ theory attempts to explain behaviors that do NOT reduce physiological needs.

5. With a challenging task, such as taking a difficult exam, performance is likely to peak when arousal is
   a. very high.
   b. moderate.
   c. very low.
   d. absent.

6. According to Maslow's hierarchy of needs, our most basic needs are physiological, including the need for food and water; just above these are _____ needs.
   a. safety
   b. self-esteem
   c. belongingness
   d. self-transcendence

Continue testing yourself with ■ **LearningCurve** or ■ **Achieve Read & Practice** to learn and remember most effectively.

MODULE 32

Hunger

Physiological needs are powerful. In a vivid demonstration, Ancel Keys and his research team (1950) studied semistarvation among wartime volunteers, who participated as an alternative to military service. After feeding 200 men normally for three months, researchers halved the food intake for 36 of them. These semistarved men became list-less and apathetic as their bodies conserved energy. Eventually, their body weights sta-bilized about 25 percent below their starting weights.

Hunger hijacks the mind World War II survivor Louis Zamperini (protagonist of the book and movie *Unbroken,* shown here) went down with his plane over the Pacific Ocean. He and two other crew members drifted for 47 days, subsisting on an occasional bird or fish. To help pass time, the hunger-driven men recited recipes or recalled their mothers' home cooking.

More dramatic were the psychological effects. Consistent with Abraham Maslow's idea of a needs hierarchy, the men became food obsessed. They talked food. They daydreamed food. They collected recipes, read cookbooks, and feasted their eyes on delectable forbidden foods. Preoccupied with their unfulfilled basic need, they lost interest in sex and social activities. As one participant reported, "If we see a show, the most interesting part of it is contained in scenes where people are eating. I couldn't laugh at the funniest picture in the world, and love scenes are completely dull." The men's preoccupations illustrate how powerful motives can hijack our consciousness.

When you are hungry, thirsty, fatigued, or sexually aroused, little else may seem to matter. In University of Amsterdam studies, Loran Nordgren and his colleagues (2006, 2007) found that people in a motivational "hot" state (from fatigue, hunger, or sexual arousal) easily recalled such feelings in their own past and perceived them as driving forces in others' behavior. (There is a parallel effect of our current good or bad mood on our memories.) When sexually motivated, men more often perceive a smile as flirtation rather than simple friendliness (Howell et al., 2012). *Motives matter mightily.*

"Never hunt when you're hungry."

"The full person does not understand the needs of the hungry." — Irish proverb

The Physiology of Hunger

LOQ **32-1** What physiological factors produce hunger?

Keys' semistarved volunteers felt their hunger because of a homeostatic system that maintains one's normal body weight and an adequate nutrient supply. But what precisely triggers hunger? Is it the pangs of an empty stomach? So it seemed to A. L. Washburn. Working with Walter Cannon, Washburn agreed to swallow a balloon attached to a recording device (Cannon & Washburn, 1912) (**FIGURE 32.1**). When inflated to fill his stomach, the balloon transmitted his stomach contractions. Washburn supplied information about his *feelings* of hunger by pressing a key each time he felt a hunger pang. The discovery: Whenever Washburn felt hungry, he was indeed having stomach contractions.

"Nature often equips life's essentials—sex, eating, nursing—with built-in gratification." — Frans de Waal, "Morals Without God?," 2010

Washburn swallows balloon, which measures stomach contractions.

Washburn presses key each time he feels hungry.

Stomach contractions

Hunger pangs

Time in minutes
0 1 2 3 4 5 6 7 8 9 10

← FIGURE 32.1
Monitoring stomach contractions
(Information from Cannon, 1929.)

glucose the form of sugar that circulates in the blood and provides the major source of energy for body tissues. When its level is low, we feel hunger.

set point the point at which the "weight thermostat" may be set. When the body falls below this weight, increased hunger and a lowered metabolic rate may combine to restore lost weight.

basal metabolic rate the body's resting rate of energy output.

Can hunger exist without stomach pangs? To answer that question, researchers removed some rats' stomachs, creating a direct path to their small intestines (Tsang, 1938). Did the rats continue to eat? Indeed they did. Some hunger similarly persists in humans whose stomachs have been removed due to ulcers or cancer.

If the pangs of an empty stomach are not the only source of hunger, what else matters?

Body Chemistry and the Brain

People and other animals automatically regulate their caloric intake to prevent energy deficits and maintain a stable body weight. This suggests that your body is keeping tabs on its available resources. The blood sugar **glucose** is one such resource. Increases in the hormone *insulin* (secreted by the pancreas) diminish blood glucose, partly by converting it to stored fat. If your blood glucose level drops, you won't consciously feel the lower blood sugar. But your brain, which is automatically monitoring your blood chemistry and your body's internal state, will trigger hunger. Signals from your stomach, intestines, and liver (indicating whether glucose is being deposited or withdrawn) all signal your brain to motivate eating or not.

How does the brain integrate these messages and sound the alarm? The work is done by several neural areas, some housed deep in the hippocampus and within the hypothalamus, a neural traffic intersection (Stevenson & Francis, 2017; **FIGURE 32.2**). For example, one neural network in the hypothalamus (called the *arcuate nucleus*) has a center that secretes appetite-stimulating hormones. When stimulated electrically, well-fed animals begin to eat. If the area is destroyed, even starving animals have no interest in food. Another neural center secretes appetite-suppressing hormones. When electrically stimulated, animals will stop eating. Destroy this area and animals can't stop eating and will become obese (see Figure 32.2b) (Duggan & Booth, 1986; Hoebel & Teitelbaum, 1966).

Blood vessels connect the hypothalamus to the rest of the body, so it can respond to our current blood chemistry and other incoming information. One of its tasks is monitoring levels of appetite hormones, such as *ghrelin*, a hunger-arousing hormone secreted by an empty stomach. During bypass surgery for severe *obesity*, surgeons seal off or remove part of the stomach. The remaining stomach then produces much less ghrelin, reducing the person's appetite and making food less enticing (Ammori, 2013; Lemonick, 2002; Scholtz et al., 2013). Besides ghrelin, other appetite hormones include *orexin, leptin,* and *PYY*; **FIGURE 32.3** describes how they influence our feelings of hunger.

If you lose some extra weight and later find the pounds (or kilograms) creeping back, you can blame your brain for your weight regain (Cornier, 2011). The complex interaction of appetite hormones and brain activity helps explain the body's predisposition to maintain a particular weight. When semistarved rats fall below their normal weight, their "weight thermostat" signals the body to restore the lost weight. It's as though fat cells cry out "Feed me!" and grab glucose from the bloodstream (Ludwig & Friedman, 2014). Hunger increases and energy expenditure decreases. This stable weight toward which semistarved rats return is their **set point** (Keesey & Corbett, 1984; Müller et al., 2010). In rats and humans, heredity influences body type and approximate set point. People with skinny genes tend to wear skinny jeans.

Our bodies regulate weight through the control of food intake, energy output, and **basal metabolic rate**—the resting rate of energy expenditure for maintaining basic body

FIGURE 32.2
The hypothalamus (a) The hypothalamus (colored orange) performs various body maintenance functions, including control of hunger. Blood vessels supply the hypothalamus, enabling it to respond to our current blood chemistry as well as to incoming neural information about the body's state. (b) The fat mouse on the left has nonfunctioning receptors in the appetite-suppressing part of the hypothalamus.

(a)

(b)

FIGURE 32.3
Appetite hormones
Increases appetite
- *Ghrelin:* Hormone secreted by empty stomach; sends "I'm hungry" signals to the brain.
- *Orexin:* Hunger-triggering hormone secreted by hypothalamus.

Decreases appetite
- *Leptin:* Protein hormone secreted by fat cells; when abundant, causes brain to increase metabolism and decrease hunger.
- *PYY:* Digestive tract hormone; sends "I'm *not* hungry" signals to the brain.

functions. By the end of their 6 months of semistarvation, the men who participated in Keys' experiment had stabilized at three-quarters of their normal weight, even though they were taking in only *half* their previous calories. How did they achieve this dieter's nightmare? They reduced their energy expenditure, partly through inactivity but partly because of a 29 percent drop in their basal metabolic rate.

Some researchers, however, doubt that our bodies have a preset tendency to maintain optimum weight (Assanand et al., 1998). They point out that slow, sustained changes in body weight can alter one's set point, and that psychological factors also sometimes drive our feelings of hunger. Given unlimited access to a wide variety of tasty foods, people and other animals tend to overeat and gain weight (Raynor & Epstein, 2001). Thus, many researchers prefer the term *settling point* to indicate the level at which a person's weight settles in response to caloric intake and expenditure (which are influenced by environment as well as biology).

RETRIEVAL PRACTICE

RP-1 Hunger occurs in response to _____ (low/high) blood glucose and _____ (low/high) levels of ghrelin.

ANSWERS IN APPENDIX E

📺 For an interactive and visual tutorial on the brain and eating, visit *Topic Tutorial: PsychSim6, Hunger and the Fat Rat.*

The Psychology of Hunger

LOQ 32-2 What cultural and situational factors influence hunger?

Our internal hunger is pushed by our physiology—our body chemistry and hypothalamic activity. Yet there is more to hunger than meets the stomach. This was strikingly apparent when Paul Rozin and his colleagues (1998) tested two patients with amnesia who had no memory for events occurring more than a minute ago. If, 20 minutes after eating a normal lunch, the patients were offered another, both readily consumed it . . . and usually a third meal offered 20 minutes after the second was finished. This suggests that part of knowing when to eat is our memory of our last meal. As time passes since we last ate, we anticipate eating again and start feeling hungry.

"Never get a tattoo when you're drunk and hungry."

(a)   (b)

An acquired taste People everywhere learn to enjoy the fatty, bitter, or spicy foods common in their culture. (a) For these Alaska Natives, but not for most other North Americans, whale blubber is a tasty treat. (b) For Peruvians, roasted guinea pig is similarly delicious.

Taste Preferences: Biology and Culture

Body cues and environmental factors together influence not only the *when* of hunger, but also the *what*—our taste preferences. When feeling tense or depressed, do you tend to take solace in high-calorie foods, as ardent football fans have done after a big loss (Cornil & Chandon, 2013)? Carbohydrates boost the neurotransmitter serotonin, which has calming effects. When dieting and stressed, both rats and many humans find it extra rewarding to scarf Oreos (Boggiano et al., 2005; Sproesser et al., 2014).

Our preferences for sweet and salty tastes are genetic and universal. Other taste preferences are conditioned, as when people given highly salted foods develop a liking for excess salt (Beauchamp, 1987), or when people who have been sickened by a food develop an aversion to it. (The frequency of children's illnesses provides many chances for them to learn to avoid certain foods.)

Culture affects taste, too. Many Asian people enjoy *durian,* a fruit that's been described as smelling like "turpentine and onions, garnished with a gym sock" (Sterling, 2003). Asians are often repulsed by what many Westerners love—"the rotted bodily fluid of an ungulate" (a.k.a. cheese, some varieties of which have the same bacteria and odor as stinky feet) (Herz, 2012).

Rats tend to avoid unfamiliar foods (Sclafani, 1995). So do we, especially animal-based foods. Such *neophobia* (dislike of unfamiliar things) surely was adaptive for our ancestors, protecting them from potentially toxic substances. We can overcome harmless food dislikes by repeatedly trying small samples of an unfamiliar food or drink. In experiments, this tends to increase people's appreciation for the new taste (Pliner, 1982; Pliner et al., 1993).

Other taste preferences also are adaptive. For example, the spices most commonly used in hot-climate recipes—where food, especially meat, is at risk of spoiling more quickly—inhibit bacteria growth (**FIGURE 32.4**). Pregnancy-related nausea and food aversions peak about the tenth week, when the developing embryo is most vulnerable to toxins. Thus, many pregnant women naturally avoid potentially harmful foods and other substances, such as alcoholic and caffeinated beverages (Forbes et al., 2018; Gaskins et al., 2018).

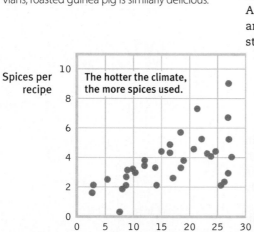

The hotter the climate, the more spices used.

Spices per recipe

Mean annual temperature (degrees Celsius)

⊘ **FIGURE 32.4**

Hot cultures like hot spices Countries with hot climates, in which food historically spoiled more quickly, feature recipes with more bacteria-inhibiting spices (Sherman & Flaxman, 2001). India averages nearly 10 spices per meat recipe; Finland, 2 spices.

Situational Influences on Eating

To a surprising extent, situations also control our eating—a phenomenon psychologists have called the *ecology of eating.* Here are four situational influences you may have noticed but underestimated:

- *Friends and food* Do we tend to eat more when eating with friends? *Yes* (Cummings & Tomiyama, 2019). But when we're trying to impress an attractive date, we often eat less (Baker et al., 2019).

- *Serving size* Researchers studied the effects of portion size by offering people varieties of free snacks (Geier et al., 2006). For example, in an apartment building's lobby, they laid out full or half pretzels, big or little Tootsie Rolls, or a small or large serving scoop by a bowl of M&M'S. Their consistent result: Offered a supersized portion, people put away more calories. Larger portions induce bigger bites, which may increase intake by decreasing oral exposure time (Herman et al., 2015). Children also eat more when using adult-sized (rather than child-sized) dishware (DiSantis et al., 2013). Portion size matters.

- *Stimulating selections* Food variety also stimulates eating. Offered a dessert buffet, people eat more than they do when choosing a portion from one favorite dessert. For our early ancestors, variety was healthy. When foods were abundant and varied, eating more provided a wide range of vitamins and minerals and produced protective fat for winter cold or famine. When a bounty of varied foods was unavailable, eating less extended the food supply until winter or famine ended (Polivy et al., 2008; Remick et al., 2009).

- *Nudging nutrition* By offering schoolchildren carrots before they picked up other foods in a lunch line, one research team quadrupled the carrots taken (Redden et al., 2015). Such "nudges" show how psychological science can improve your everyday life.

ASK YOURSELF

Do you usually eat only when your body sends hunger signals? How much does the sight or smell of delicious food tempt you even when you're full?

RETRIEVAL PRACTICE

RP-2 After an 8-hour hike without food, your long-awaited favorite dish is placed in front of you, and your mouth waters in anticipation. Why?

ANSWERS IN APPENDIX E

* * *

To consider how hunger and other factors affect our risk for **obesity,** see Thinking Critically About: The Challenges of Obesity and Weight Control. And for tips on shedding unwanted weight, see **TABLE 32.1**.

TABLE 32.1 Tips for Weight Management

For those wishing to lose weight, researchers recommend medical guidance, along with these tips:

- *Begin only if you feel motivated and self-disciplined.* Permanent weight loss usually requires a lifelong change in eating habits combined with increased exercise. Those who believe their weight is malleable most often succeed (Ehrlinger et al., 2017).

- *Exercise and get enough sleep.* Especially when supported by 7 to 8 hours of sleep a night, exercise empties fat cells, builds muscle, speeds up metabolism, helps lower your settling point, and reduces stress and stress-induced craving for carbohydrate-rich comfort foods (Bennett, 1995; Ruotsalainen et al., 2015; Thompson et al., 1982). Among TV's *Biggest Loser* competitors, exercise predicted less weight regain (Kerns et al., 2017).

- *Minimize exposure to tempting food cues.* Food-shop on a full stomach. Keep tempting foods out of your home, and tuck away special-occasion foods. You can't eat it if you can't reach it.

- *Limit variety and eat healthy foods.* Given more variety, people consume more. So, eat simple meals with protein, vegetables, fruits, and whole grains. Healthy fats, such as those found in olive oil and fish, help regulate appetite (Taubes, 2001, 2002). Water- and vitamin-rich veggies can fill the stomach with few calories. Better crispy greens than Krispy Kremes.

- *Reduce portion sizes and relabel your portions.* Offered less, people consume less. People also eat less when they think of a portion as a number of items (10 chips) rather than as a general quantity (1 serving of chips) (Lewis & Earl, 2018).

- *Time your intake.* We tend to have a healthier weight (and better sleep) when we eat our last meal in the early evening and then hold off eating or drinking more until the next morning's breakfast (Wilkinson et al., 2020). Eating our heavier meals earlier in the day boosts metabolism, and eating a balanced breakfast helps us to feel more alert and less fatigued by late morning (Spring et al., 1992).

- *Beware of the binge.* Drinking alcohol or feeling anxious or depressed can unleash the urge to eat (Herman & Polivy, 1980). And take note: Eating slowly can lead to eating less (Hurst & Fukuda, 2018; Martin et al., 2007).

- *Before eating with others, decide how much you want to eat.* Eating with friends can distract us from monitoring our own eating (Ward & Mann, 2000).

- *Remember, most people occasionally lapse.* A lapse need not become a collapse.

- *Chart your progress online.* Those who record and publicly disclose their progress toward a goal more often achieve it (Harkin et al., 2016).

- *Connect to a support group.* Join with others, either face-to-face or online, to share goals and progress updates (Freedman, 2011).

---

obesity defined as a body mass index (BMI) measurement of 30 or higher, which is calculated from our weight-to-height ratio. (Individuals who are *overweight* have a BMI of 25 or higher.)

The Challenges of Obesity and Weight Control

LOQ 32-3 How does obesity affect physical and psychological health? What factors are involved in weight management?

Obesity and Its Health Effects

Obesity is associated with:
- **physical health risks**, including diabetes, high blood pressure, heart disease, gallstones, arthritis, and certain types of cancer.[1]
  - **increased depression**, especially among women.[2]
    - **bullying**, outranking race and sexual orientation as the biggest reason for youth bullying in Western cultures.[3]

Percentage Overweight in 195 Countries Studied[4]

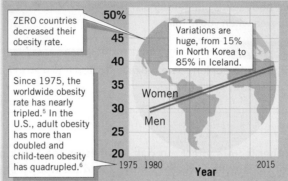

ZERO countries decreased their obesity rate.

Variations are huge, from 15% in North Korea to 85% in Iceland.

Since 1975, the worldwide obesity rate has nearly tripled.[5] In the U.S., adult obesity has more than doubled and child-teen obesity has quadrupled.[6]

Women

Men

1975 1980   2015
Year

Body Mass Index (BMI)

Overweight   *Obese*

25+   30+

See how your BMI compares to others in your country and in the world.

tinyurl.com/GiveMyBMI[6]

How Did We Get Here?

Does obesity reflect a simple lack of willpower, as some people presume?[7]
No. Many factors contribute to obesity.

PHYSIOLOGY FACTORS

Storing fat was adaptive.
- This ideal form of stored energy carried our ancestors through periods of famine. People in some impoverished places still find heavier bodies attractive, as plumpness signals affluence and status.[8]
- In food-rich countries, the drive for fat has become dysfunctional.[9]

fat cell

Set point and metabolism matter.
- Fat (lower metabolic rate than muscle) requires less food intake to maintain than it did to gain.
- If weight drops below *set point/settling point*, the brain triggers more hunger and a slowed metabolism.
  - Body perceives STARVATION; adapts by burning fewer calories. Most dieters in the long run regain what they lose on weight-loss programs.[10]
  - After 30 weeks of competition on TV's *The Biggest Loser*, 6 years later only 1 of 14 contestants had kept the weight off. On average, they regained 70% of what they lost, and their metabolism remained slow.[11]

Genes influence us.
- Lean people seem naturally disposed to move about, burning more calories than energy-conserving overweight people, who tend to sit still longer.[12]
- Adoptive siblings' body weights are uncorrelated with one another or with their adoptive parents, instead resembling their biological parents' weight.[13]
- Identical twins have closely similar weights, even if raised apart.[14] Much lower *fraternal* twin weight correlation suggests genes explain 2/3 of our varying body mass.[15]
- More than 100 genes have been identified as each affecting weight in some small way.[16]

ENVIRONMENTAL FACTORS
- **Sleep loss** makes us more vulnerable to obesity.[17]

Increasing

Decreasing

Sleep deprivation

Ghrelin—appetite-stimulating stomach hormone

Leptin—reports body fat to the brain

NOTE: With weight, as with intelligence and other characteristics, there can be high levels of *heritability* (genetic influence on *individual* differences) without heredity explaining *group* differences. Genes mostly determine why one person is heavier than another. Environment mostly determines why people today are heavier than people were 50 years ago.

- **Social influences:** Our own odds of becoming obese triple if a close friend becomes obese.[18]
- **Food and activity levels:** Worldwide, we eat more energy-dense foods and we move less, with 31% of adults (including 43% of Americans and 25% of Europeans) now sedentary—averaging <20 minutes per day of moderate activity such as walking.[19]

1. Kitahara et al., 2014. 2. Haynes et al., 2019; Jung et al., 2017; Rivera et al., 2017. 3. Puhl et al., 2015. 4. GBD, 2017. 5. NCD, 2016. 6. Flegal et al., 2010, 2012, 2016. 7. NORC, 2016b. 8. Furnham & Baguma, 1994; Nettle et al., 2017; Swami, 2015. 9. Hall, 2016. 10. Mann et al., 2015. 11. Fothergill et al., 2016. 12. Levine et al., 2005. 13. Grilo & Pogue-Geile, 1991. 14. Hjelmborg et al., 2008; Plomin et al., 1997. 15. Maes et al., 1997. 16. Akiyama et al., 2017. 17. Keith et al., 2006; Nedeltcheva et al., 2010; Taheri, 2004; Taheri et al., 2004. 18. Christakis & Fowler, 2007. 19. Hallal et al., 2012.

ASK YOURSELF

Have you or your loved ones ever tried unsuccessfully to lose weight? What happened? What weight-loss strategies might have been more successful?

RETRIEVAL PRACTICE

RP-3 Why can two people of the same height, age, and activity level maintain the same weight, even if one of them eats much less than the other does?

ANSWERS IN APPENDIX E

> For a 7-minute review of hunger, see the *Video: Hunger and Eating.*

MODULE

32 REVIEW Hunger

LEARNING OBJECTIVES

Test Yourself Answer these repeated Learning Objective Questions on your own (before checking the answers in Appendix D) to improve your retention of the concepts (McDaniel et al., 2009, 2015).

LOQ 32-1 What physiological factors produce hunger?

LOQ 32-2 What cultural and situational factors influence hunger?

LOQ 32-3 How does obesity affect physical and psychological health? What factors are involved in weight management?

TERMS AND CONCEPTS TO REMEMBER

Test Yourself Write down the definition in your own words, then check your answer.

glucose, p. 388

set point, p. 388

basal metabolic rate, p. 388

obesity, p. 391

MASTER THE MATERIAL

Test Yourself Answer the following questions on your own first, then check your answers in Appendix E.

1. Journalist Dorothy Dix once remarked, "Nobody wants to kiss when they are hungry." Which motivation theory best supports her statement?

2. According to the concept of _____ point, our body maintains itself at a particular weight level.

3. Which of the following is a genetically predisposed response to food?

   a. An aversion to eating cats and dogs

   b. An interest in novel foods

   c. A preference for sweet and salty foods

   d. An aversion to carbohydrates

4. Blood sugar provides the body with energy. When it is _____ (low/high), we feel hungry.

5. The rate at which your body expends energy while at rest is referred to as the _____ _____ rate.

6. Obese people often struggle to lose weight permanently. This is due to several factors, including the fact that

   a. trying to lose weight triggers neophobia.

   b. the set point of obese people is lower than average.

   c. with food restriction, metabolism increases.

   d. there is a genetic influence on body weight.

7. Sanjay eats a diet high in processed foods, fat, and sugar. He knows he may gain weight, but he figures it's no big deal because he can simply lose it in the future. How would you evaluate Sanjay's plan?

Continue testing yourself with 📚 **LearningCurve** or 📚 **Achieve Read & Practice** to learn and remember most effectively.

MODULE

33 Sexual Motivation

Sex is a part of life. For all but the 1 percent of us considered **asexual** (Bogaert, 2004, 2015), dating and mating become a high priority from puberty on. Biologist Alfred Kinsey (1894–1956) pioneered the study of human sexuality (Kinsey et al., 1948, 1953). Kinsey stumbled into studying sex. Raised in a poor and religious family, he was fascinated by nature (PBS, 2019). He spent the first 20 years of his career as a biologist collecting and categorizing insects, but became concerned that people knew more about insects than about the then-taboo topic of sex. Kinsey's experience teaching a marriage and family course motivated him to spend the rest of his career collecting and categorizing people's sex histories. Kinsey and his colleagues' findings ignited debate and controversy, but they also paved the way for future research on the sexual behavior of men and women. Our sexual feelings and behaviors reflect both physiological and psychological influences.

asexual having no sexual attraction toward others.

"It is a near-universal experience, the invisible clause on one's birth certificate stipulating that one will, upon reaching maturity, feel the urge to engage in activities often associated with the issuance of more birth certificates." — Science writer Natalie Angier, 2007

The Physiology of Sex

Unlike hunger, sex is not an actual *need*. (Without it, we may feel like dying, but we will not.) Yet sex motivates. Had this not been so for all of your biological ancestors, you would not be alive and reading these words. Sexual motivation is nature's clever way of making people procreate, thus enabling our species' survival. Life is sexually transmitted.

Hormones and Sexual Behavior

LOQ **33-1**   How do hormones influence human sexual motivation?

Among the forces driving sexual behavior are the *sex hormones*. The main male sex hormone is **testosterone.** The main female sex hormones are the **estrogens,** such as *estradiol*. Sex hormones influence us at several points in the life span:

- During the prenatal period, they direct our sexual development.
- During puberty, a sex hormone surge ushers us into adolescence.
- After puberty and well into the late adult years, sex hormones facilitate sexual behavior.

In most mammals, nature neatly synchronizes sex with fertility. Females become sexually receptive when their estrogens peak at ovulation, and researchers can cause female animals to become receptive by injecting them with estrogens. Male hormone levels are more constant, and hormone injection does not so easily affect the sexual behavior of male animals. Nevertheless, male hamsters that have had their testosterone-making testes surgically removed will gradually lose much of their interest in receptive females. They gradually regain it if injected with testosterone (Piekarski et al., 2009).

Hormones do influence human sexual behavior, but more loosely. Researchers are exploring and debating whether women's mating preferences change across the menstrual cycle, especially at ovulation, when both estrogens and testosterone rise (Arslan et al., 2018; Marcinkowska et al., 2018; Shirazi et al., 2019). Some evidence suggests that, among women with mates, sexual desire rises slightly at ovulation—a change that men and women can sometimes detect in a woman's scent, behavior, and voice (Gildersleeve et al., 2017; Haselton & Gildersleeve, 2011, 2016).

Women have much less testosterone than men do. But more than other mammalian females, women are responsive to their testosterone level (Davison & Davis, 2011; van Anders, 2012). If a woman's natural testosterone level drops, as happens with removal of the ovaries or adrenal glands, her sexual interest may wane. And as experiments with surgically or naturally menopausal women have demonstrated, testosterone-replacement therapy can often restore diminished sexual activity, arousal, and desire (Braunstein et al., 2005; Buster et al., 2005; Petersen & Hyde, 2011).

In human males with abnormally low testosterone levels, testosterone-replacement therapy often increases sexual desire and also energy and vitality (Khera et al., 2011). But normal fluctuations in testosterone levels, from man to man and hour to hour, have little effect on sexual drive (Byrne, 1982). Indeed, male hormones sometimes vary in *response* to sexual stimulation (Escasa et al., 2011). In one study, Australian skateboarders' testosterone surged in the presence of an attractive female, contributing to riskier moves and more crash landings (Ronay & von Hippel, 2010). Thus, sexual arousal can be a *cause* as well as a consequence of increased testosterone levels.

Large hormonal surges or declines affect sexual desire at two predictable points in the life span, and sometimes at an unpredictable third point:

1. *The pubertal surge in sex hormones triggers the development of sex characteristics and sexual interest.* If puberty's hormonal surge is precluded—as it was during the 1600s and 1700s for prepubertal boys who were castrated to preserve their soprano voices for Italian opera—sex characteristics and sexual desire do not develop normally (Peschel & Peschel, 1987).

2. *In later life, sex hormone levels fall.* Women experience menopause as their estrogen levels decrease; males experience a more gradual change. Sex remains a part of life, but as hormone levels decline, sexual fantasies and intercourse decline as well (Leitenberg & Henning, 1995).

→ **testosterone** the most important male sex hormone. Males and females have it, but the additional testosterone in males stimulates the growth of the male sex organs during the fetal period, and the development of the male sex characteristics during puberty.

estrogens sex hormones, such as estradiol, that contribute to female sex characteristics and are secreted in greater amounts by females than by males. Estrogen levels peak during ovulation. In nonhuman mammals, this promotes sexual receptivity.

sexual response cycle the four stages of sexual responding described by Masters and Johnson—excitement, plateau, orgasm, and resolution.

refractory period in human sexuality, a resting period that occurs after orgasm, during which a person cannot achieve another orgasm.

3. *For some, surgery or drugs may cause hormonal shifts.* When adult men were castrated, their sex drive typically fell as testosterone levels declined sharply (Hucker & Bain, 1990). Male sex offenders who took Depo-Provera, a drug that reduces their testosterone level to that of a prepubertal boy, similarly lost much of their sexual urge (Bilefsky, 2009; Money et al., 1983).

To summarize: We might compare human sex hormones, especially testosterone, to the fuel in a car. Without fuel, a car will not run. But if the fuel level is minimally adequate, adding more won't change how the car runs. The analogy is imperfect, because hormones and sexual motivation interact. However, it correctly suggests that biology is a necessary but incomplete explanation of human sexual behavior. The hormonal fuel is essential, but so are the psychological stimuli that turn on the engine, keep it running, and shift it into high gear.

> ### RETRIEVAL PRACTICE
>
> **RP-1** The primary female sex hormones are the _____.The primary male sex hormone is _____.
>
> *ANSWERS IN APPENDIX E*

The Sexual Response Cycle

LOQ **33-2** What is the human *sexual response cycle,* and how do sexual dysfunctions and paraphilias differ?

The scientific process often begins with careful observations of complex behaviors. When gynecologist-obstetrician William Masters and his collaborator Virginia Johnson (1966) applied this process to human sexual intercourse in the 1960s, they made headlines. They recorded the physiological responses of volunteers who came to their lab to masturbate or have intercourse. (The volunteers—382 women and 312 men—were a somewhat atypical sample, consisting only of people able and willing to display arousal and orgasm while scientists observed.) Masters and Johnson reported observing more than 10,000 sexual "cycles." Their description of the **sexual response cycle** identified four stages:

1. **Excitement:** The genital areas become engorged with blood, causing a woman's clitoris and a man's penis to swell. A woman's vagina expands and secretes lubricant; her breasts and nipples may enlarge.

2. *Plateau:* Excitement peaks as breathing, pulse, and blood pressure rates continue to increase. A man's penis becomes fully engorged—to an average length of 5.6 inches among 1661 men who measured themselves for condom fitting (Herbenick et al., 2014). Some fluid—frequently containing enough live sperm to enable conception—may appear at its tip. A woman's vaginal secretion continues to increase, and her clitoris retracts. Orgasm feels imminent.

3. *Orgasm:* Muscle contractions appear all over the body and are accompanied by further increases in breathing, pulse, and blood pressure rates. The pleasurable feeling of sexual release is much the same for both sexes. One panel of experts could not reliably distinguish between descriptions of orgasm written by men and those written by women (Vance & Wagner, 1976). In another study, PET scans showed that the same subcortical brain regions were active in men and women during orgasm (Holstege et al., 2003a,b).

4. *Resolution:* The body gradually returns to its unaroused state as the genital blood vessels release their accumulated blood. For men, this happens relatively quickly if orgasm has occurred, relatively slowly otherwise. (It's like the nasal tickle that goes away rapidly if you have sneezed, slowly otherwise.) Men then enter a **refractory period** that lasts from a few minutes to a day or more, during which they are incapable of another orgasm. A woman's much shorter refractory period may enable her, if restimulated during or soon after resolution, to have more orgasms.

A nonsmoking 50-year-old male has about a 1-in-a-million chance of a heart attack during any hour. This increases to merely 2-in-a-million in the two hours during and following sex (with no increase for those who exercise regularly). Compared with risks associated with heavy exertion or anger, this risk seems not worth losing sleep (or sex) over (Jackson, 2009; Muller et al., 1996).

There is also a *refractory period* in neural processing—the brief resting pause that occurs after a neuron has fired.

Sexual Dysfunctions and Paraphilias

Masters and Johnson sought not only to describe the human sexual response cycle but also to understand and treat the inability to complete it. **Sexual dysfunctions** are problems that consistently impair sexual arousal or functioning at any point in this cycle. Some involve sexual motivation, especially lack of sexual energy and arousability. For men, others include **erectile disorder** (inability to have or maintain an erection) and *premature ejaculation*. For women, the problem may be pain or **female orgasmic disorder** (distress over infrequently or never experiencing orgasm). In separate surveys of some 3000 Boston women and 32,000 other American women, about 4 in 10 reported a sexual problem, such as orgasmic disorder or low desire. Most women who have experienced sexual distress have related it to their emotional relationship with their partner during sex (Bancroft et al., 2003).

Psychological and medical therapies can help men and women with sexual dysfunctions (Frühauf et al., 2013). In behaviorally oriented therapy, for example, men learn ways to control their urge to ejaculate, and women are trained to bring themselves to orgasm. Starting with the introduction of Viagra in 1998, erectile disorder has been routinely treated by taking a pill. Researchers have struggled to develop reliable drug treatments for *female sexual interest/arousal disorder* (Chivers & Brotto, 2017).

Sexual dysfunction involves problems with arousal or sexual functioning. People with **paraphilias** (mostly men) do experience sexual desire, but they direct it in unusual ways (Baur et al., 2016). The American Psychiatric Association (2013) only classifies such behavior as disordered if

- a person experiences distress from an unusual sexual interest *or*
- it entails harm or risk of harm to others.

The serial killer Jeffrey Dahmer had *necrophilia,* a sexual attraction to corpses. Those with *exhibitionism* derive pleasure from exposing themselves sexually to others, without consent. People with the paraphilic disorder *pedophilia* experience sexual arousal toward children who haven't entered puberty.

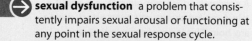

To explore the stories of participants in a drug therapy program for sexual dysfunctions, see the 6-minute *Video: Sexual Dysfunctions and Their Treatments.*

RETRIEVAL PRACTICE

RP-2 Someone who is distressed by impaired sexual arousal may be diagnosed with a
_____ _____. Exhibitionism would be considered a _____.

ANSWERS IN APPENDIX E

Sexually Transmitted Infections

LOQ **33-3** How can sexually transmitted infections be prevented?

Every day, more than 1 million people worldwide acquire a *sexually transmitted infection (STI;* also called *STD,* for *sexually transmitted disease)* (WHO, 2018). Common STIs include chlamydia, gonorrhea, herpes simplex virus (HSV), and human papillomavirus (HPV) infection. "Compared with older adults," reports the Centers for Disease Control and Prevention (CDC, 2016b), "sexually active adolescents aged 15–19 years and young adults aged 20–24 years are at higher risk." Teenage girls, for example, are at heightened risk given their not yet fully mature anatomy and lower levels of protective antibodies (Dehne & Riedner, 2005; Guttmacher Institute, 1994).

Condoms offer only limited protection against certain skin-to-skin STIs, such as herpes, but they do reduce other risks (NIH, 2001). The effects were clear when Thailand promoted condom use by commercial sex workers. Over a four-year period, as condom use soared from 14 to 94 percent, the annual number of bacterial STIs plummeted from 410,406 to 27,362—a 93 percent reduction (WHO, 2000). When used by people with an infected partner, condoms have also been 80 percent effective in preventing transmission of HIV *(human immunodeficiency virus)*—the virus that causes **AIDS** (Weller & Davis-Beaty, 2002; WHO, 2003). Although HIV can be transmitted by other means, such as needle sharing during drug use, its sexual transmission is most common. Half of all those with HIV (and 1 in 5 Americans recently diagnosed with HIV) are women (CDC,

---

sexual dysfunction a problem that consistently impairs sexual arousal or functioning at any point in the sexual response cycle.

erectile disorder inability to develop or maintain an erection due to insufficient blood flow to the penis.

female orgasmic disorder distress due to infrequently or never experiencing orgasm.

paraphilias sexual arousal from fantasies, behaviors, or urges involving nonhuman objects, the suffering of self or others, and/or nonconsenting persons.

AIDS (acquired immune deficiency syndrome) a life-threatening condition caused by the *human immunodeficiency virus* (HIV), a sexually transmitted infection. AIDS depletes the immune system, leaving the person vulnerable to infections.

2018a). Because the virus is spread more easily from men to women than it is from women to men, women's proportion of the worldwide AIDS population is growing.

Half of Americans with AIDS are between ages 30 and 49 (CDC, 2016). AIDS' long incubation period means that many were infected in their teens and twenties. In 2012, the death of 1.6 million people with AIDS worldwide left behind countless grief-stricken loved ones, including millions of orphaned children (UNAIDS, 2013). In sub-Saharan Africa, home to two-thirds of those with HIV, medical treatment to extend life and care for the dying is sapping needed resources.

Having sex with one person means also partnering with that person's past partners—any one of whom might have unknowingly transmitted an STI. So, the first step in preventing STIs is knowing one's status, and sharing it with one's sexual partner.

The Psychology of Sex

LOQ 33-4 How do external and imagined stimuli contribute to sexual arousal?

Biological factors powerfully influence our sexual motivation and behavior. Yet the wide variations over time, across place, and among individuals document the great influence of psychological factors as well (**FIGURE 33.1**). Thus, despite the shared biology that underlies sexual motivation, the 281 reasons study participants expressed for having sex ranged widely—from "to get closer to God" to "to get my boyfriend to shut up" (Buss, 2008; Meston & Buss, 2007).

Biological influences:
• sexual maturity
• sex hormones, especially testosterone

Psychological influences:
• exposure to stimulating conditions
• sexual fantasies

Sexual motivation

Social-cultural influences:
• family and society values
• religious and personal values
• cultural expectations
• media

Digital Vision/Getty Images

◄ FIGURE 33.1
Biopsychosocial influences on sexual motivation Compared with our motivation for eating, our sexual motivation is less influenced by biological factors. Psychological and social-cultural factors play a bigger role.

External Stimuli

Men and women become aroused when they see, hear, or read erotic material (Heiman, 1975; Stockton & Murnen, 1992). In men more than in women, *feelings* of sexual arousal closely mirror their (more obvious) physical genital responses (Chivers et al., 2010).

People may find sexual arousal either pleasing or disturbing. (Those who wish to control their arousal often limit their exposure to arousing materials, just as those wishing to avoid overeating limit their exposure to tempting food cues.) With repeated exposure to any stimulus, including an erotic stimulus, the emotional response lessens, or *habituates*. During the 1920s, when Western women's hemlines rose to the knee, an exposed leg made hearts flutter. Today, many would barely notice.

Can exposure to sexually explicit material have adverse effects? Research indicates that it can, in three ways.

• *Believing rape is acceptable* Although some modern pornography portrays women in powerful roles, mostly it presents women as subservient sexual objects (Fritz & Paul, 2018; Jones, 2018). Depictions of women being sexually coerced—and appearing to enjoy it—have increased viewers' belief in the false idea that women want to be overpowered, and have increased male viewers' expressed willingness to hurt women and to commit rape after viewing such scenes (Allen et al., 1995, 2000; Foubert et al., 2011; Zillmann, 1989).

Robert Mankoff/Cartoon Stock

- *Reducing satisfaction with a partner's appearance or with a relationship* After viewing erotic films of sexually attractive women and men, people have judged their relationship as less satisfying (Perry, 2018). Repeatedly viewing pornography reduces men's and women's sexual satisfaction (Milas et al., 2019; Miller et al., 2019). Perhaps reading or watching erotica's unlikely scenarios creates expectations that few people can fulfill.

- *Desensitization* Extensive online pornography viewing can desensitize young adults to normal sexuality. Repeated exposure to this distorted sexual world may contribute to lowered sexual desire and satisfaction, diminished brain activation in response to sexual images, and, for men, erectile problems (Wright et al., 2018). "Porn is messing with your manhood," argue Philip Zimbardo and colleagues (2016).

Imagined Stimuli

The brain, it has been said, is our most significant sex organ. The stimuli inside our head—our imagination—can influence sexual arousal and desire. Lacking genital sensation because of a spinal-cord injury, people can still feel sexual desire (Willmuth, 1987).

Both men and women report having sexual fantasies and watching pornography, and they have similar brain responses to sexual imagery (Mitricheva et al., 2019; Solano et al., 2018; Wright & Vangeel, 2019). For a few women, sexual fantasies alone can produce orgasms (Komisaruk & Whipple, 2011). Men, regardless of sexual orientation, tend to have more frequent, more physical, and more aggressive sexual fantasies (Apostolou & Khalil, 2019; Schmitt et al., 2012). They also prefer less personal and faster-paced sexual content in books and videos (Leitenberg & Henning, 1995). Fantasizing about sex does *not* indicate a sexual problem or dissatisfaction. If anything, sexually active people have more sexual fantasies.

RETRIEVAL PRACTICE

RP-3 What factors influence our sexual motivation and behavior?

ANSWERS IN APPENDIX E

Sexual Risk Taking and Teen Pregnancy

LOQ **33-5** What factors influence teenagers' sexual behaviors and use of contraceptives?

Sexual attitudes and behaviors vary dramatically across cultures and eras. "Sex between unmarried adults" is "morally unacceptable," agree 97 percent of Indonesians and 6 percent of Germans (Pew, 2014b). And thanks to decreased sexual activity and increased protection, American teen pregnancy rates are declining (CDC, 2016b, 2018f). What environmental factors contribute to teen pregnancy?

COMMUNICATION ABOUT BIRTH CONTROL Many teenagers are uncomfortable discussing contraception with parents, partners, and peers. But teens who talk freely and openly with their parents and with their partner in an exclusive relationship are more likely to use contraceptives (Aspy et al., 2007; Milan & Kilmann, 1987).

IMPULSIVITY Among sexually active 12- to 17-year-old American girls, 72 percent said they regretted having had sex (Reuters, 2000). If passion overwhelms intentions to use contraceptives or to delay having sex, unplanned sexual activity may result in pregnancy (Ariely & Loewenstein, 2006; MacDonald & Hynie, 2008).

ALCOHOL USE Among older teens and young adults, most sexual hook-ups (casual encounters outside of a relationship) occur after alcohol use, often without knowing consent (Fielder et al., 2013; Garcia et al., 2013; Johnson & Chen, 2015). Those who use alcohol prior to sex are less likely to use condoms (Kotchick et al., 2001). By depressing the brain centers that control judgment, inhibition, and self-awareness, alcohol disarms normal restraints—a phenomenon well known to sexually coercive people.

"Condoms should be used on every conceivable occasion." — Anonymous

MASS MEDIA Popular media influence teens by providing *social scripts* for sexual behavior. Media also affect peer perceptions: The more sexual content adolescents and young adults view or read (even when controlling for other predictors of early sexual activity), the more likely they are to perceive their peers as sexually active, to develop sexually permissive attitudes, to experience early intercourse, and to use condoms inconsistently (Escobar-Chaves et al., 2005; O'Hara et al., 2012; Parkes et al., 2013; Ward et al. 2018). Perceived peer norms influence teens' sexual behavior (Lyons, 2015; van de Bongardt et al., 2015).

DELAYING SEX What are the characteristics of teens who delay having sex?

- *High intelligence* Teens with high rather than average intelligence test scores more often delay sex, partly because they consider possible negative consequences and are more focused on future achievement than on here-and-now pleasures (Harden & Mendle, 2011).

- *Religious engagement* Actively religious teens more often reserve sexual activity for adulthood or long-term relationships (Hull et al., 2011; Schmitt & Fuller, 2015; Štulhofer et al., 2011).

- *Father presence* In studies that followed hundreds of New Zealand and U.S. girls from age 5 to 18, having Dad around has reduced the risk of teen pregnancy and of sexual activity before age 16 (Ellis et al., 2003). These associations held even after adjusting for other influences, such as poverty. Close family attachments—as in families that eat together and where parents know their teens' activities and friends—also predict later sexual initiation (Coley et al., 2008).

- *Service-learning participation* American teens volunteering as tutors or teachers' aides, or participating in community projects, have lower pregnancy rates than do comparable teens randomly assigned to control conditions (Kirby, 2002; O'Donnell et al., 2002). Researchers are unsure why. Does service learning promote a sense of personal competence, control, and responsibility? Does it encourage more future-oriented thinking? Or does it simply reduce opportunities for unprotected sex? (After-school activities and later school start times also reduced unplanned pregnancies [Bryan et al., 2016; Steinberg, 2015].)

Keeping abreast of hypersexuality An analysis of the 60 top-selling video games found 489 characters, 86 percent of whom were males (like most of the game players). The female characters were much more likely than the male characters to be "hypersexualized"—partially nude or revealingly clothed, with large breasts and tiny waists (Downs & Smith, 2010). Such depictions can lead to unrealistic expectations about sexuality and body ideals, and contribute to the early sexualization of girls (Karsay et al., 2018). The American Psychological Association suggests countering this by teaching girls to "value themselves for who they are rather than how they look" (APA, 2007).

Father presence

What strategies could your community use to reduce teen pregnancy?

RETRIEVAL PRACTICE

RP-4 Which THREE of the following five factors contribute to unplanned teen pregnancies?

  a. Alcohol use

  b. Higher intelligence level

  c. Father absence

  d. Mass media models

  e. Participating in service-learning programs

ANSWERS IN APPENDIX E

Sexual Orientation

LOQ 33-6 What do we know about sexual orientation?

To motivate is to energize and direct behavior. So far, we have considered the energizing of sexual motivation but not its *direction*, which is our **sexual orientation**—our sexual attraction toward members of the other gender (*heterosexual* orientation), our own gender (*same-sex* orientation), male and female genders (*bisexual* orientation), or to no one

sexual orientation the direction of our sexual attractions, as reflected in our longings and fantasies.

Note that sexual orientation is distinct from *gender identity* (including *transgender* identity).

Driven to suicide In 2010, Rutgers University student Tyler Clementi jumped off this bridge after his roommate secretly filmed, shared, and tweeted about Clementi's intimate encounter with another man. Reports then surfaced of other gay teens who had reacted in a similarly tragic fashion after being taunted. Since 2010, Americans—especially those under 30—have been increasingly supportive of those with same-sex orientations.

at all (*asexual* orientation). For some people, sexual attraction is not restricted to any sex or gender identity (*pansexual* orientation). We experience such attractions in our interests and fantasies (who appears in your imagination?).

Cultures vary in their attitudes toward same-sex attractions. "Should society accept homosexuality?" *Yes,* say 88 percent of Spaniards and 1 percent of Nigerians, with women everywhere being more accepting than men (Pew, 2013a). Yet whether a culture condemns or accepts same-sex unions, heterosexuality is most common and same-sex attraction and other variations exist. In most African countries, same-sex relationships are illegal. Yet the ratio of lesbian, gay, or bisexual people "is no different from other countries in the rest of the world," reports the Academy of Science of South Africa (2015). What is more, same-sex activity spans human history.

How many people have exclusively same-sex attractions? According to more than a dozen national surveys in Europe and the United States, about 3 or 4 percent of men and 2 percent of women (Chandra et al., 2011; Copen et al., 2016; Savin-Williams et al., 2012). But the percentages vary somewhat over time, with the percentage who feel comfortable self-reporting as lesbian, gay, or bisexual gradually increasing with increased social acceptance (Newport, 2018). Percentages are also slightly higher when reporting is anonymous (Copen et al., 2016). A larger number of Americans—17 percent of women and 6 percent of men—say they have had some same-sex sexual contact during their lives (Copen et al., 2016). Psychologists have only begun to research the experiences of those who identify as pansexual (Borgogna et al., 2019; Greaves et al., 2019).

In less tolerant places, people are more likely to hide their sexual orientation. About 3 percent of California men express a same-sex preference on Facebook, for example, as do only about 1 percent in Mississippi. Yet about 5 percent of Google pornography searches in both states are for gay porn. And Craigslist ads for males seeking "casual encounters" with other men tend to be at least as common in less tolerant states, where there are also more Google searches for "gay sex" and "Is my husband gay?" (MacInnis & Hodson, 2015; Stephens-Davidowitz, 2013).

What does it feel like to not be heterosexual in a majority heterosexual culture? If you are heterosexual, imagine that you have found "the one"—a perfect partner of the other sex. How would you feel if you weren't sure who you could trust with knowing you had these feelings? How would you react if you overheard people telling crude jokes about heterosexual people, or if most movies, TV shows, and advertisements showed only same-sex relationships? How would you like hearing that many people wouldn't vote for a political candidate who favors other-sex marriage? And how would you feel if children's organizations and adoption agencies thought you might not be safe or trustworthy because you're attracted to people of the other sex?

Facing such reactions, some people with same-sex attractions may at first try to ignore or deny their desires, hoping they will go away. But they don't. And these people may—particularly if they live in a region or a country that condemns same-sex attractions—conceal their orientation (Pachankis & Bränström, 2018). Especially during adolescence or when feeling rejected by their parents or peers, people may struggle against same-sex attractions. Without supportive parents and friends, gay and lesbian teens express greater anxiety and depression, often related to bullying, and a tripled risk of suicide (Caputi et al., 2017; di Giacomo et al., 2018; NAS, 2019; Ross et al., 2018). Some may try to change their orientation through psychotherapy, willpower, or prayer. But the feelings are typically enduring, as are those of heterosexual people—who are similarly unable to change (Haldeman, 1994, 2002; Myers & Scanzoni, 2005).

Some harmful anti-gay stereotypes have unfortunately persisted. One such stereotype is that people with same-sex attractions are more likely to molest children (Herek, 2016). Is this true? *No.* Measuring men's genital response to various sexual images indicates that sexual orientation is unrelated to pedophilia (Blanchard et al., 2009; Herek, 2016). A Canadian research team led by Ray Blanchard (2012; Dreger, 2011) outfitted 2278 men (mostly sex offenders) with a device that measured their sexual arousal when viewing nude photos of male and female adults and children, accompanied by sexual audio stories. Most of the men responded not to children, but to adult men (if gay) or to adult women (if straight). Some of the men—both straight and gay—exhibited pedophilia, by instead responding mostly to young boys or girls, and much less to adults.

Today's psychologists view sexual orientation as neither willfully chosen nor willfully changed. "Efforts to change sexual orientation are unlikely to be successful and involve some risk of harm," declared a 2009 American Psychological Association report. A consensus of British mental health organizations agreed that such attempts are "unethical and potentially harmful" (Gale et al., 2017). Recognizing this, in 2016, Malta became the first European country to outlaw the controversial practice of "conversion therapy," which aims to change people's *gender identity* or sexual orientation. An increasing number of U.S. states and cities have likewise banned conversion therapy with minors.

Sexual orientation in some ways is like handedness: Most people are one way, some the other. A smaller group experiences some form of ambidexterity. Regardless, the way we are endures, especially in men (Dickson et al., 2013; Norris et al., 2015). Women's sexual orientation tends to be less strongly felt and, for some women, is more fluid and changing. Heterosexual women may experience genital arousal to either male or female sexual stimuli (Chivers, 2017). In general, men are sexually simpler. Men's lesser sexual variability is apparent in many ways (Baumeister, 2000). Across time, cultures, situations, and differing levels of education, religious observance, and peer influence, men's sexual drive and interests have been less flexible and varying than have women's. Women, for example, more often prefer to alternate periods of high sexual activity with periods of almost none (Mosher et al., 2005). Baumeister calls this flexibility *erotic plasticity*.

Origins of Sexual Orientation

So, if we do not choose our sexual orientation and (especially for males) cannot change it, where do these feelings come from? In an early search for possible environmental influences on sexual orientation, Kinsey Institute investigators in the 1980s interviewed nearly 1000 lesbian/gay and 500 heterosexual people. They assessed nearly every imaginable psychological cause of same-sex attraction—parental relationships, childhood sexual experiences, peer relationships, and dating experiences (Bell et al., 1981; Hammersmith, 1982). Their findings: Gay and lesbian people were no more likely than heterosexual people to have been smothered by maternal love or neglected by their father. And consider this: If "distant fathers" were more likely to produce gay sons, then shouldn't boys growing up in father-absent homes more often be gay? (They are not.) And shouldn't the rising number of such homes have led to a noticeable increase in the gay population? (It has not.) Most children raised by gay or lesbian parents display gender-typical behavior and are heterosexual (Farr et al., 2018; Gartrell & Bos, 2010). And they grow up with health and emotional well-being similar to (and sometimes better than) children with straight parents (Bos et al., 2016; Farr, 2017).

So, what else might influence sexual orientation? One theory has proposed that people develop same-sex erotic attachments if segregated by sex at the time their sex drive matures (Storms, 1981). Indeed, gay men tend to recall going through puberty somewhat earlier, when peers are more likely to be all males (Bogaert et al., 2002). But even in tribal cultures in which same-sex sexual behavior is expected of all boys before marriage, most men are still heterosexual (Hammack, 2005; Money, 1987). (As this illustrates, sexual *behavior* is not always indicative of sexual *orientation*.) Moreover, though peers' attitudes predict teens' sexual attitudes and behavior, they do not predict same-sex attraction. "Peer influence has little or no effect" on sexual orientation (Brakefield et al., 2014).

Environment likely contributes to sexual orientation—nature and nurture work together—but the inability to pin down specific environmental influences has led researchers to explore several lines of biological evidence. These include same-sex attraction in other species, brain differences, and genetic and prenatal influences.

SAME-SEX ATTRACTION IN OTHER SPECIES In Boston's Public Gardens, caretakers solved the mystery of why a much-loved swan couple's eggs never hatched. Both swans were female. In New York City's Central Park Zoo, penguins Silo and Roy spent several years as devoted same-sex partners. Same-sex sexual behaviors have also been observed in several hundred other species, including grizzlies, gorillas, giraffes, monkeys, flamingos, and owls (Bagemihl, 1999). Among rams, for example, some 7 to 10 percent display same-sex attraction by shunning ewes and seeking to mount other males (Perkins & Fitzgerald, 1997). Same-sex sexual behavior seems a natural part of the animal world.

"There is no sound scientific evidence that sexual orientation can be changed."
— UK Royal College of Psychiatrists, 2014

In one British survey of 18,876 people (and in other surveys since), about 1 percent identified themselves as asexual, having "never felt sexually attracted to anyone at all" (Bogaert, 2004, 2015). People with an asexual orientation are, however, nearly as likely as others to report masturbating, noting that it feels good, reduces anxiety, or "cleans out the plumbing."

Two penguin dads At Sydney's SEA LIFE Aquarium, Sphen and Magic, a bonded same-sex pair, successfully raised a foster chick (appropriately named "Sphengic").

SEA LIFE Sydney Aquarium

📺 See the *Video: Naturalistic Observation* for a helpful tutorial animation.

BRAIN DIFFERENCES Might the structure and function of gay and straight brains differ? Researcher Simon LeVay (1991) studied sections of the hypothalamus taken from deceased gay and straight people. He found a cell cluster that was indeed reliably larger in straight men than in straight women and gay men.

It should not surprise us that brains differ with sexual orientation (Bao & Swaab, 2011; Savic & Lindström, 2008). Remember our maxim: *Everything psychological is simultaneously biological.* But when did the brain difference begin? At conception? During childhood or adolescence? Did experience produce the difference? Or was it genes or prenatal hormones (or genes activating prenatal hormones)?

LeVay does not view the hypothalamus as a sexual orientation center; rather, he sees it as an important part of the neural pathway engaged in sexual behavior. He acknowledges that sexual behavior patterns may influence the brain's anatomy. In fish, birds, rats, and humans, brain structures vary with experience—including sexual experience, reports sex researcher Marc Breedlove (1997). But LeVay believes it is more likely that brain anatomy influences sexual orientation. His hunch seems confirmed by the discovery of a similar hypothalamic difference between male sheep that do and don't display same-sex attraction (Larkin et al., 2002; Roselli et al., 2002, 2004). Moreover, such differences seem to develop soon after birth, and perhaps even before birth (Rahman & Wilson, 2003).

Since LeVay's brain *structure* discovery, other researchers have reported additional differences in the way that gay and straight brains *function.* One is in an area of the hypothalamus that governs sexual arousal (Savic et al., 2005). When straight women were given a whiff of a scent derived from men's sweat, this area became active. Gay men's brains responded similarly to the men's scent. But straight men's brains showed the arousal response only to a female hormone derivative. In a similar study, lesbians' responses differed from those of straight women (Kranz & Ishai, 2006; Martins et al., 2005). Researcher Qazi Rahman (2015) sums it up: Compared with straight men and women, "gay men appear, on average, more 'female typical' in brain pattern responses and lesbian women are somewhat more 'male typical.'"

On several traits, the average gay man and gay woman fall midway between the average straight man and straight woman. Consider the gay-straight difference in spatial abilities. On mental rotation tasks such as the one in **FIGURE 33.2**, straight men tend to outscore straight women, and the scores of gay men and gay women fall in between (Boone & Hegarty, 2017). But straight women and gay men have both outperformed straight men at remembering objects' spatial locations in memory game tasks (Hassan & Rahman, 2007).

"Gay men simply don't have the brain cells to be attracted to women." — Simon LeVay, *The Sexual Brain*, 1993

⊙ **FIGURE 33.2**
Spatial abilities and sexual orientation Which of the three figures can be rotated to match the Original figure?[1] Straight men tend to find this type of mental rotation task easier than do straight women, with gay men and women falling in between (see graph) (Rahman et al., 2004).

Which one of the options below matches the Original?

Z-score (in standard deviation units)

Original

(a)

(b)

(c)

📺 See the *Video: Twin Studies* for a helpful tutorial animation.

GENETIC INFLUENCES Studies indicate that "about a third of variation in sexual orientation is attributable to genetic influences" (Bailey et al., 2016). A same-sex orientation does tend to run in families. And identical twins are somewhat more likely than fraternal twins to share a same-sex orientation (Alanko et al., 2010; Långström et al., 2010). But

[1]Answer: Figure (c).

because sexual orientations differ in many identical twin pairs, especially female twins, we know that other factors besides genes are also at work—including, it appears, *epigenetic marks* that help distinguish gay and straight twins (Balter, 2015; Gavrilets et al., 2018).

By altering a single gene in fruit flies, experimenters have changed the flies' sexual orientation and behavior (Dickson, 2005). In search of genes that influence human sexual orientation, researchers have analyzed the genomes of 409 pairs of gay brothers, 1231 straight men, and 1077 gay men. They found links between sexual orientation and two genes on chromosomes 13 and 14. The first of those chromosome regions influences a brain area that varies in size with sexual orientation. The second influences thyroid function, which has also been associated with sexual orientation (Sanders et al., 2015, 2017). But we should also recall a familiar lesson: Human traits are influenced by *many genes having small effects*. Indeed, a giant study of nearly 500,000 peoples' genes confirmed that "Same-sex behavior is influenced by not one or a few genes but many" (Ganna et al., 2019).

Researchers have speculated about possible reasons why "gay genes" might exist in the human gene pool, given that same-sex couples cannot naturally reproduce. One possible answer is *kin selection*. Evolutionary psychologists remind us that many of our genes also reside in our biological relatives. Perhaps, then, gay people's genes live on through their supporting the survival and reproductive success of their relatives.

A *fertile females theory* suggests that maternal genetics may also be at work (Bocklandt et al., 2006). Around the world, gay men tend to have more gay relatives on their mother's side than on their father's (Camperio-Ciani et al., 2004, 2009, 2012; VanderLaan et al., 2012; VanderLaan & Vasey, 2011). And the relatives on the mother's side also produce more offspring than do the maternal relatives of heterosexual men. Perhaps the genes that dispose some women to conceive more children with men also dispose some men to be attracted to men (LeVay, 2011). Thus, the decreased reproduction by gay men appears to be offset by the increased reproduction by their maternal extended family.

PRENATAL INFLUENCES Recall that in the womb, sex hormones direct our male and female development. In animals and some human cases, prenatal hormone conditions have altered a fetus' sexual orientation, most clearly so for females (Breedlove, 2017). When pregnant sheep were injected with testosterone during a critical period of fetal development, their female offspring later showed same-sex sexual behavior (Money, 1987). A critical period for the human brain's neural-hormonal control system may exist during the second trimester (Ellis & Ames, 1987; Garcia-Falgueras & Swaab, 2010; Meyer-Bahlburg, 1995). Exposure to the hormone levels typically experienced by female fetuses during this time may predispose females later to become attracted to males. And female fetuses most exposed to testosterone appear most likely later to exhibit gender-atypical traits and to experience same-sex desires.

The mother's immune system may also play a role in the development of sexual orientation. In 35 of 36 samples studied (an amazingly reliable finding), men with older brothers have been somewhat more likely to be gay, reports Ray Blanchard (2004, 2018, 2019)—about one-third more likely for each additional older brother (see also Bogaert, 2003). The odds of same-sex attraction are roughly 2 percent among first sons, and they rise to about 2.6 percent among second sons, 3.5 percent for third sons, and so on for each additional older brother (Bailey et al., 2016). This is called the *older-brother* or *fraternal birth-order effect* (see **FIGURE 33.3**).

> "Modern scientific research indicates that sexual orientation is . . . partly determined by genetics, but more specifically by hormonal activity in the womb." — Glenn Wilson and Qazi Rahman, *Born Gay: The Psychobiology of Sex Orientation*, 2005

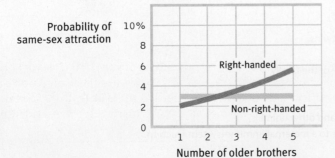

← **FIGURE 33.3**
The older-brother effect These approximate curves depict a man's likelihood of same-sex attraction as a function of the number of biological (not adopted) older brothers he has (Blanchard, 2008a; Bogaert, 2006a). This correlation has been found in several studies, but only among right-handed men (as about 9 in 10 men are).

The reason for this curious phenomenon is unclear. Blanchard suspects a defensive maternal immune response to foreign substances produced by male fetuses. With each pregnancy with a male fetus, the maternal antibodies may become stronger and may prevent the fetus' brain from developing in a male-typical pattern (Bogaert et al., 2018). Consistent with this biological explanation, the fraternal birth-order effect occurs only in men with older brothers born to the same mother (whether raised together or not). Sexual orientation is unaffected by adoptive brothers (Bogaert, 2006a). The birth-order effect on sexual orientation is not found among women with older sisters, women who were womb-mates of twin brothers, and men who are not right-handed (Rose et al., 2002).

Gay-Straight Trait Differences

Comparing the traits of gay and straight people is akin to comparing the heights of men and women. The average man is taller than most women, but many women are taller than most men. And just as knowing someone's height doesn't specify their gender, neither does knowing someone's traits tell you their sexual orientation. Yet on several traits, the average gay female or male is intermediate between straight females and males (**TABLE 33.1**; see also LeVay, 2011; Rahman & Koerting, 2008; Rieger et al., 2016).

The point to remember: Taken together, the brain, genetic, and prenatal findings offer strong support for a biological explanation of sexual orientation, especially for men (LeVay, 2011; Rahman & Koerting, 2008). Our increasing understanding of the greater sexual fluidity of women suggests the need for more research on biopsychosocial influences (Diamond et al., 2017).

* * *

Still, some people wonder: Should the cause of sexual orientation matter? Perhaps it shouldn't, but people's assumptions matter. Those who believe sexual orientation is a lifestyle choice often oppose equal rights for people who are lesbian or gay. For example, in 2014 the president of Uganda signed a bill that made some same-sex sexual acts punishable by life in prison. To justify this, he declared that same-sex attraction is not inborn but rather is a matter of "choice" (Balter, 2014; Landau et al., 2014). Those who understand the inborn nature of sexual orientation—that it is shaped by the biological and prenatal influences outlined in this module—more likely favor "equal rights for homosexual and bisexual people" (Bailey et al., 2016).

> Note that the scientific question is not "What causes same-sex orientation?" (or "What causes heterosexual orientation?") but "What causes differing sexual orientations?" In pursuit of answers, psychological science compares the backgrounds and physiology of people whose sexual orientations *differ*.

TABLE 33.1 Biological Correlates of Sexual Orientation

Gay-straight trait differences

Sexual orientation is part of a package of traits. Studies—some in need of replication—indicate that gay people and straight people differ in the following biological and behavioral traits:

- spatial abilities
- fingerprint ridge counts
- auditory system development
- handedness
- occupational preferences
- relative finger lengths
- gender nonconformity
- age of onset of puberty in males
- face structure and birth size/weight
- sleep length
- physical aggression
- walking style

On average (the evidence is strongest for males), results for gay men and gay women fall between those of straight men and straight women. Three biological influences—brain, genetic, and prenatal—may contribute to these differences.

Brain differences

- One hypothalamic cell cluster is smaller in women and gay men than in straight men.
- Gay men's hypothalamus reacts as does straight women's to the smell of men's sex-related hormones.

Genetic influences

- Shared sexual orientation is higher among identical twins than among fraternal twins.
- Sexual attraction in fruit flies can be genetically manipulated.
- Male same-sex attraction often appears to be transmitted from the mother's side of the family.

Prenatal influences

- Altered prenatal hormone exposure may lead to same-sex attraction in humans and other animals.
- Men with several older biological brothers are more likely to be gay, possibly due to a maternal immune-system reaction.

Our discussion of concepts such as "nonbinary gender identity" (Module 12) and "pansexual" may challenge your understanding. Do these new terms indicate that people have changed? Actually, scientists believe that gender identity and sexual orientation have always varied. In all places and times, some people have not fit neatly into binary male/female or gay/straight categories.

How has learning more about what contributes to sexual orientation and gender identity influenced your views? How might your new knowledge influence your interactions with people who identify as lesbian, gay, bisexual, transgender, or questioning/queer (LGBTQ)?

RETRIEVAL PRACTICE

RP-5 Which THREE of the following five factors have researchers found to have an effect on sexual orientation?

a. A domineering mother

b. The size of a certain cell cluster in the hypothalamus

c. Prenatal hormone exposure

d. A distant or ineffectual father

e. For right-handed men, having multiple older biological brothers

ANSWERS IN APPENDIX E

Sex and Human Relationships

LOQ 33-7 What role do social factors play in our sexuality?

Scientific research on sexual motivation does not aim to define the personal meaning of sex in our own lives. You could know every available fact about sex—that the initial spasms of male and female orgasm come at 0.8-second intervals, that female nipples expand 10 millimeters at the peak of sexual arousal, that systolic blood pressure rises some 60 points and respiration rate reaches 40 breaths per minute—but fail to understand the human significance of sexual intimacy.

Sexual desire motivates people to form intimate, committed relationships, which in turn enable satisfying sex (Birnbaum, 2018). In one national study that followed participants to age 30, later first sex predicted greater satisfaction in one's marriage or partnership (Harden, 2012). Another study asked 2035 married people when they started having sex (while controlling for education, religious engagement, and relationship length). Those whose relationship first developed to a deep commitment, such as marriage, not only reported greater relationship satisfaction and stability but also better sex (Busby et al., 2010; Galinsky & Sonenstein, 2013). For both men and women, but especially for women, sex is more satisfying (with more orgasms and less regret) for those in a committed relationship, rather than a brief sexual hook-up (Armstrong et al., 2012; Benidixen et al., 2017; Dubé et al, 2017). Partners who share regular meals are more likely than one-time dinner companions to understand what seasoning touches suit each other's food tastes; so, too, with the touches of loyal partners who share a bed.

Sex is a socially significant act. Men and women can achieve orgasm alone, yet most people find greater satisfaction—and experience a much greater surge in *prolactin*, the hormone associated with sexual satisfaction and satiety—after intercourse and orgasm with their loved one (Brody & Tillmann, 2006). Among newlyweds in one study, the "sexual afterglow" (lingering satisfaction after sex) lasted 48 hours and increased marital satisfaction (Meltzer et al., 2017). Thanks to their overlapping brain reward areas, sexual desire and love feed each other (Cacioppo et al., 2012). Sex at its human best is life uniting and love renewing.

Increased sex ≠ more happiness
Among married couples, more frequent sex correlates with happiness (Muise et al., 2016). So, would systematically increasing sexual frequency *cause* people to be happier? Alas, heterosexual married couples randomly assigned to double their intercourse frequency over three months became slightly *less* happy (Loewenstein et al., 2015).

MODULE

33 REVIEW Sexual Motivation

LEARNING OBJECTIVES

Test Yourself Answer these repeated Learning Objective Questions on your own (before checking the answers in Appendix D) to improve your retention of the concepts (McDaniel et al., 2009, 2015).

LOQ 33-1 How do hormones influence human sexual motivation?

LOQ 33-2 What is the human *sexual response cycle,* and how do sexual dysfunctions and paraphilias differ?

LOQ 33-3 How can sexually transmitted infections be prevented?

LOQ 33-4 How do external and imagined stimuli contribute to sexual arousal?

LOQ 33-5 What factors influence teenagers' sexual behaviors and use of contraceptives?

LOQ 33-6 What do we know about sexual orientation?

LOQ 33-7 What role do social factors play in our sexuality?

TERMS AND CONCEPTS TO REMEMBER

Test Yourself Write down the definition in your own words, then check your answer.

asexual, p. 393

testosterone, p. 394

estrogens, p. 394

sexual response cycle, p. 394

refractory period, p. 394

sexual dysfunction, p. 396

erectile disorder, p. 396

female orgasmic disorder, p. 396

paraphilias, p. 396

AIDS (acquired immune deficiency syndrome), p. 396

sexual orientation, p. 399

MASTER THE MATERIAL

Test Yourself Answer the following questions on your own first, then check your answers in Appendix E.

1. A striking effect of hormonal changes on human sexual behavior is the

   a. end of sexual desire in men over 60.

   b. sharp rise in sexual interest at puberty.

   c. decrease in women's sexual desire at the time of ovulation.

   d. increase in testosterone levels in castrated males.

2. In describing the sexual response cycle, Masters and Johnson noted that

   a. a plateau phase follows orgasm.

   b. people experience a refractory period during which they cannot experience orgasm.

   c. the feeling that accompanies orgasm is stronger in men than in women.

   d. testosterone is released equally in women and men.

3. What is the difference between sexual dysfunctions and paraphilias?

4. Using condoms during sex _____ (does/doesn't) reduce the risk of getting HIV and _____ (does/doesn't) fully protect against skin-to-skin STIs.

5. An example of an external stimulus that might influence sexual behavior is

   a. the level of testosterone in the bloodstream.

   b. the onset of puberty.

   c. a sexually explicit film.

   d. an erotic fantasy or dream.

6. Which factors have researchers so far found to be *unrelated* to the development of our sexual orientation?

Continue testing yourself with **LearningCurve** or **Achieve Read & Practice** to learn and remember most effectively.

MODULE

34 Affiliation and Achievement

The Need to Belong

LOQ 34-1 What evidence points to our human affiliation need—our need to belong?

Separated from friends or family—at a new school, alone in prison or a foreign land, while "social distancing" to slow the spread of COVID-19—most people feel keenly their lost connections with important others. We are what the ancient Greek philosopher Aristotle called *the social animal.* "Without friends," wrote Aristotle in his *Nicomachean Ethics,* "no one would choose to live, though he had all other goods." This deep *need to belong*—our

Photodisc/Getty Images

affiliation need—is a key human motivation (Baumeister & Leary, 1995). It is normal and healthy to seek some privacy and solitude (Nguyen et al., 2019). But most of us also seek to affiliate—to become strongly attached to certain others in enduring, close relationships. In each of 39 countries studied, those who "often" (rather than rarely) spend time with friends are happier (Ortiz-Ospina, 2019). Human beings, contended personality theorist Alfred Adler, have an "urge to community" (Ferguson, 1989, 2001, 2010).

The Benefits of Belonging

Social bonds boosted our early ancestors' chances of survival. Adults who formed attachments were more likely to survive and reproduce, and to co-nurture their offspring to maturity. Attachment bonds motivated caregivers to keep children close, calming them and protecting them from threats (Esposito et al., 2013). Indeed, to be "wretched" literally means, in its Middle English origin (*wrecched*), to be without kin nearby.

Cooperating with friends and acquaintances also enhanced survival. In solo combat, our ancestors were not the toughest predators. But as hunters, they learned that six hands were better than two. As food gatherers, they gained protection from two-footed and four-footed enemies by traveling in groups. Those who felt a need to belong survived and reproduced most successfully, and their genes now predominate. Our innate need to belong drives us to befriend people who cooperate and to avoid those who exploit (Feinberg et al., 2014; Kashima et al., 2019). People in every society on Earth belong to groups and prefer and favor "us" over "them." Having a *social identity*—feeling part of a group—boosts people's health and well-being (Allen et al., 2015; Haslam et al., 2019).

Do you have close friends—people to whom you freely disclose your ups and downs? Having someone who rejoices with us over good news helps us feel better about both the news and the friendship (Reis, 2018). Such companionship creates connection and cooperation (Canavello & Crocker, 2017). And close friends can literally make us feel warm, as if we are holding a soothing cup of warm tea (Inagaki et al., 2019). The need to belong runs deeper, it seems, than any need to be rich. Very happy university students are distinguished not by their money but by their "strong social relationships" (Diener et al., 2018).

The need to belong colors our thoughts and emotions. We spend a great deal of time thinking about actual and hoped-for relationships. When relationships form, we often feel joy. Falling in mutual love, people have been known to feel their cheeks ache from their irrepressible grins. Asked, "What is necessary for your happiness?" or "What is it that makes your life meaningful?" most people have mentioned—before anything else—close, satisfying relationships with family, friends, or romantic partners (Berscheid, 1985). Happiness hits close to home.

Consider: What was your most satisfying moment in the past week? Researchers asked that question of American and South Korean university students, then asked them to rate how much that moment had satisfied various needs (Sheldon et al., 2001). In both countries, the peak moment had satisfied self-esteem and relatedness-belonging needs. Our affiliation need is universal. According to **self-determination theory,** we strive to satisfy three needs: *competence, autonomy* (a sense of personal control), and *relatedness* (Deci & Ryan, 2012; Ryan & Deci, 2000). Fulfilling these motives increases our health, reduces stress, and boosts our self-esteem (Campbell et al., 2018; Cerasoli et al., 2016; Guertin et al., 2017). One analysis of 200,000 people from nearly 500 studies concluded that "self-determination is key to explaining human motivation" (Howard et al., 2017, p. 1346).

Self-determination theory can help leaders motivate people. Employees who feel empowered perform better. They also feel more autonomous, competent, and socially included (Slemp et al., 2018; Van den Broeck et al., 2016). Ditto for teachers' motivating their students and military leaders motivating their soldiers (Bakadorova & Raufelder, 2018; Chambel et al., 2015; Hagger & Chatzisarantis, 2016). An empowered mindset fuels motivation by giving people the perception that they have unlimited energy (Sieber et al., 2019).

Small wonder, then, that our social behavior often aims to increase our feelings of belonging, and spending more time with friends and family increases happiness (Li & Kanazawa, 2016; Rohrer et al., 2018). To gain acceptance, we generally conform to group

affiliation need the need to build and maintain relationships and to feel part of a group.

self-determination theory the theory that we feel motivated to satisfy our needs for competence, autonomy, and relatedness.

David Ramos/Getty Images

Socially distant As social animals with a need to belong, we seek social connections. During the 2020 COVID-19 pandemic, social distancing slowed the spread of the virus, but it also disrupted our everyday relationships.

standards. We wait in lines and obey laws. We monitor our behavior, hoping to make a good impression. We spend billions on clothes, cosmetics, and diet and fitness aids—all motivated, in part, by our search for love and acceptance.

Thrown together in groups at school or at work, we form bonds. Parting, we feel distress. We promise to stay in touch and return for reunions. By drawing a sharp circle around "us," the need to belong feeds both deep attachments to those inside the circle (loving families, faithful friendships, and team loyalty) and hostilities toward those outside (teen gangs, ethnic rivalries, and fanatic nationalism). Feelings of love activate brain reward and safety systems. In one experiment, deeply in love university students exposed to heat felt less pain when looking at their beloved's picture (Younger et al., 2010). Pictures of our loved ones activate a brain region—the prefrontal cortex—that dampens feelings of physical pain (Eisenberger et al., 2011). Love is a natural painkiller.

Even when bad relationships end, people suffer. In one 16-nation survey, and in repeated U.S. surveys, separated and divorced people have been half as likely as married people to say they are "very happy" (Inglehart, 1990; NORC, 2016a). Is that simply because happy people more often marry and stay married? A national study following British lives through time revealed that, even after controlling for premarital life satisfaction, "the married are still more satisfied, suggesting a causal effect" of marriage (Grover & Helliwell, 2014). Divorce also predicts earlier mortality. Data from more than 600 million(!) people in 24 countries reveal that, compared with married people, separated and divorced people are at greater risk for early death (Shor et al., 2012). As one data scientist noted, "[A happy marriage] is perhaps as important as not smoking, which is to say: huge" (Ungar, 2014).

Children who move through a series of foster homes or through regular family relocations know the fear of being alone. After repeated disruption of budding attachments, they may have difficulty forming deep relationships (Oishi & Schimmack, 2010b). The evidence is clearest at the extremes. Children who grow up in institutions without a sense of belonging to anyone, or who are locked away at home and severely neglected tend to become withdrawn, frightened, even speechless.

No matter how secure our early years were, we all experience anxiety, loneliness, jealousy, or guilt when something threatens or dissolves our social ties. Much as life's best moments occur when close relationships begin—making a new friend, falling in love, having a baby—life's worst moments happen when close relationships end (Beam et al., 2016). Bereaved, we may feel life is empty or pointless, and we may overeat to fill that emptiness (Yang et al., 2016). Even the first months of living on campus can be distressing (English et al., 2017). But our need to belong usually pushes us to form new social connections (Oishi et al., 2013a).

Social isolation can put us at risk for mental decline, ill health, and suicidal thinking (Cacioppo et al., 2015; Cheek et al., 2019). Lonely older adults, for example, make more doctor visits and are at greater risk for dementia (Gerst-Emerson & Jayawardhana, 2015; Holwerda et al., 2014). Social isolation can hurt our health as much as physical inactivity and diabetes do (Yang et al., 2016). To overcome feelings of social isolation and rejection, nurture strong relationships with family or friends, and engage actively in new groups.

Consider your own need to belong by engaging with the activity *Assess Your Strengths: How Strong Is Your Need to Belong, and How Can You Strengthen Your Feelings of Belonging?* And work on improving your relationships with the activity *Assess Your Strengths—How Strong Is Your Relationship, and How Might You Increase Its Strength?*

The Pain of Being Shut Out

Can you recall feeling excluded, ignored, or shunned? Perhaps your texts went unanswered, or you were unfriended or ignored online. Perhaps others gave you the silent treatment, avoided you, looked away, mocked you, or shut you out in some other way. Or perhaps you have felt excluded when among people speaking an unfamiliar language

ostracism deliberate social exclusion of individuals or groups.

(Dotan-Eliaz et al., 2009). We feel the sting even from small-scale exclusions like being *phubbed*—an Australian-coined term meaning *phone-snubbed*—when our conversation partner seems more interested in their phone than in us (Roberts & David, 2016). Frequent phubbing—with partners placing their phone where they can check it during conversational lulls—predicts a less satisfying relationship.

All these experiences are instances of **ostracism**—of social exclusion (Williams, 2007, 2009). Worldwide, humans use many forms of ostracism—exile, imprisonment, solitary confinement—to punish, and therefore control, social behavior. For children, even a brief time-out in isolation can be punishing. Asked to describe personal episodes that made them feel especially *bad* about themselves, people will—about four times in five—describe a broken or painful social relationship (Pillemer et al., 2007). Loneliness is less a matter of being alone than of feeling ignored, dismissed, or not cared about.

Being shunned threatens one's basic need to belong (Vanhalst et al., 2015; Wirth et al., 2010). "It's the meanest thing you can do to someone, especially if you know they can't fight back. I never should have been born," said Lea, a lifelong victim of the silent treatment by her mother and grandmother. Like Lea, people often respond to ostracism with initial efforts to restore social acceptance, followed by depressed mood, and finally withdrawal. Prisoner William Blake (2013) has spent more than a quarter-century in solitary confinement. "I cannot fathom how dying any death could be harder and more terrible than living through all that I have been forced to endure," he observed. To many, social exclusion is a sentence worse than death.

To experience ostracism is to experience real pain, as social psychologists Kipling Williams and his colleagues were surprised to discover in their studies of exclusion on social media (Gonsalkorale & Williams, 2006). Such ostracism elicits increased activity in brain areas, such as the *anterior cingulate cortex,* that also respond to physical pain (Lieberman & Eisenberger, 2015; Rotge et al., 2015).

When people view pictures of romantic partners who broke their heart, their brain and body begin to ache (Kross et al., 2011). That helps explain some other surprising findings. The pain reliever acetaminophen (as in Tylenol) lessens *social* as well as physical pain (DeWall et al., 2010). Ditto for marijuana (Deckman et al., 2014). Across cultures, people use the same words (for example, *hurt, crushed*) for social pain and physical pain (MacDonald & Leary, 2005). Psychologically, we seem to experience social pain with the same emotional unpleasantness that marks physical pain. Compared with collectivist cultures, rejection tends to hurt more in individualist cultures—where people have weaker social support networks (Heu et al., 2019; Uskul & Over, 2017).

Pain, whatever its source, focuses our attention and motivates corrective action. Rejected and powerless, people may relieve stress by seeking new friends, eating calorie-laden comfort foods, or strengthening their religious faith (Aydin et al., 2010; Maner et al., 2007; Sproesser et al., 2014).

Ostracism can also make people disagreeable, uncooperative, and hostile, which leads to further ostracism (Rudert et al., 2019; Walasek et al., 2019). In one series of experiments, researchers told some students that people they had met didn't want them in a group that was forming (Gaertner et al., 2008; Twenge et al., 2001).[2] Others heard good news: "Everyone chose you as someone they'd like to work with." Those who were excluded became much more likely to engage in self-defeating behaviors and to act in disparaging or aggressive ways against those who had excluded them (blasting them with noise, for example).

Enduring the pain of ostracism
White cadets at the U.S. Military Academy at West Point ostracized Henry Flipper for years, hoping he would drop out. Somehow he resisted their cruelty, and in 1877 he became the first African-American West Point graduate.

"How can we subject prisoners to unnecessary solitary confinement, knowing its effects, and then expect them to return to our communities as whole people? It doesn't make us safer. It's an affront to our common humanity." — U.S. President Barack Obama, 2017

Social acceptance and rejection
Successful participants on the reality TV show *Survivor* form alliances and gain acceptance among their peers. The rest receive the ultimate social punishment by being "voted off the island."

CBS/Photofest

---

[2] The researchers later *debriefed* and reassured the participants.

"If no one turned around when we entered, answered when we spoke, or minded what we did, but if every person we met 'cut us dead,' and acted as if we were non-existing things, a kind of rage and impotent despair would ere long well up in us." — William James, *Principles of Psychology*, 1890/1950, pp. 293–294

These findings may help us understand school shooters, who have often experienced social rejection (Leary et al., 2003). One Texas high school student made repeated unwanted sexual advances on a fellow student, leading her to publicly reject him. He responded by shooting and killing her, along with nine other students and teachers (BBC, 2018).

ASK YOURSELF

Have there been times when you felt lonely or ostracized? What are some strategies that might help you to cope the next time you feel this way?

RETRIEVAL PRACTICE

RP-1 How have students reacted in studies when they were made to feel rejected and unwanted? What helps explain these results?

ANSWERS IN APPENDIX E

Connecting and Social Networking

LOQ 34-2 How does social networking influence us?

As social creatures, we live for connection. Researcher George Vaillant (2013) was asked what he had learned from studying 238 Harvard University men from the 1930s to the end of their lives. He replied, "Happiness is love." A South African Zulu saying captures the idea: *Umuntu ngumuntu ngabantu*—"a person is a person through other persons."

MOBILE NETWORKS AND SOCIAL MEDIA Look around and see humans connecting: talking, tweeting, texting, posting, chatting, social gaming, emailing. Walking across campus, you may see students glued to their phones, making little eye contact with passersby (or perhaps that's you?). Today, have you observed more students engaging with each other face-to-face, or silently checking their phones—as one research team's phone app counted students doing 56 times a day (Elias et al., 2016)? The changes in how we connect have been fast and vast:

- *Mobile phones:* By 2018's end, 96 percent of the world's 7.7 billion people lived in an area covered by a mobile-cellular network, and most humans—5.3 billion—had broadband mobile subscriptions (ITU, 2018).

- *Texts and instant messaging:* The average American sends and receives 94 texts/messages per day (Burke, 2018). Half of 18- to 29-year-olds check their phone multiple times per hour, and "can't imagine . . . life without [it]" (Newport, 2015; Saad, 2015).

- *The internet:* In 2018, 81 percent of humans used the internet (ITU, 2018). A survey of 90,000 people from 31 countries found that 6 percent showed signs of "internet addiction" (Cheng & Li, 2014). Among teens, girls more than boys say they use the internet "almost constantly" (Anderson & Jiang, 2018).

- *Social networking:* Half of entering American college students report using social networking sites at least 6 hours per week (Stolzenberg et al., 2019). With our friends online, it's hard to avoid social networks: Check in or miss out.

With increased online time displacing other activities, today's teens spend fewer hours dating, driving, working, drinking, talking face-to-face, and reading books (Livingston et al., 2019; Twenge & Park, 2019; Twenge et al., 2019). Technology has radically changed the teen experience.

THE NET RESULT: SOCIAL EFFECTS OF SOCIAL NETWORKING By connecting like-minded people, the internet serves as a social amplifier. In times of social crisis or personal stress, it provides information and supportive connections. The internet can also function as a matchmaker (as I [ND] can attest: I met my wife online).

But social media also leads people to compare their lives with others. When others seem happier, more popular, or more successful, this can trigger envy and depressed feelings (Verduyn et al., 2017; Whillans et al., 2017). In study after study, most people perceive that others' social lives are more

Ellie Black/The New Yorker Collection/The Cartoon Bank

"All the better to ignore you with."

active than their own (Deri et al., 2017). Perhaps you have noticed? Do others seem to party more, dine out more, and have more friends and fun? Take comfort: Most of your friends are thinking the same.

Smart phones have become pervasive—their number tripled between 2011 and 2018 in the United States, and similarly elsewhere. Simultaneously—and merely coincidentally?—Canadian, British, and American teen depression, anxiety, self-harm, and suicide rates mushroomed. From 2011 to 2018, for example, depressive episodes among 12- to 17-year-old Americans increased from 11 to 14 percent, and from 8 to 14 percent among 18- to 25-year-olds (SAMSHA, 2019). Ditto for college students, whose rates of depression, anxiety, self-injury, and suicidal thinking similarly increased (Duffy et al., 2019).

So, is there a causal connection between these concurrent increases in screen time and mental health problems? Under the leadership of Jonathan Haidt and Jean Twenge (2019), researchers are accumulating and debating findings. They have tentative conclusions from three types of explorations:

- **Correlational studies ask:** *Is social media use associated with teen mental health?* Studies vary, but overall, there is a small positive correlation between adolescents' social media time and their risk of depression, anxiety, and self-harm. The screen time–disorder association is stronger for social media use than for TV and gaming time, the link is greater for females, and it increases only with daily screen time of 3 hours or more.

- **Longitudinal studies ask:** *Does teen social media use predict their future mental health?* In six of eight studies, the answer is Yes.

- **Experiments ask:** *Do volunteers randomly assigned to restricted social media use fare better than those not assigned on outcomes such as loneliness and depression?* On balance, *Yes,* but the few such studies have produced mixed results.

Is screen time the major culprit because it displaces other healthy activities—face-to-face connection, sleep, exercise, reading, and time outdoors? Or is the problem with social media specifically, because it drives envy when comparing one's own mundane life with the lives of cooler-seeming others? What other social forces might be at work? And what can be done to protect and improve youth and young adult well-being? Stay tuned: This important story is still being written.

Online networking is double-edged: It does help us connect with friends, stay in touch with family, and find support when facing challenges (Clark et al., 2018). However, nature has designed us for face-to-face relationships. Even the world's first telephone call, made by Alexander Graham Bell in 1876, was a plea for a face-to-face meeting: "Mr. Watson, come here. I want to see you." Those who spend hours online daily are *less* likely to know and draw help from their real-world neighbors. Yet when used in moderation, social networking supports our face-to-face relationships and therefore predicts longer life (Hobbs et al., 2016; Waytz & Gray, 2018).

Does Electronic Communication Stimulate Healthy Self-Disclosure? *Self-disclosure* is sharing ourselves—our joys, worries, and weaknesses—with others. Confiding can be a healthy way of coping with day-to-day challenges. When communicating electronically rather than face-to-face, we often are less focused on others' reactions. We are less self-conscious and thus less inhibited. Sometimes, disinhibitions may become toxic: political extremists post inflammatory messages, online bullies hound victims, hate groups promote bigotry, and people send selfies they later regret (Frimer et al., 2019). But more often, the increased self-disclosure strengthens friendships (Valkenburg & Peter, 2009).

Does Social Networking Promote Narcissism? **Narcissism** is self-esteem gone wild. Narcissistic people are self-important, self-focused, and self-promoting. To measure your narcissistic tendencies, you might rate your agreement with personality test items such as "I like to be the center of attention." People who agree with such statements tend to have high narcissism scores—and they are especially active on social networking sites (Liu & Baumeister, 2016). They collect more superficial "friends." They offer more staged, glamorous photos. They retaliate more against negative comments. And, not surprisingly, they *seem* more narcissistic to strangers (Buffardi & Campbell, 2008; Weiser, 2015).

"The women on these dating sites don't seem to believe I'm a prince."

narcissism excessive self-love and self-absorption.

Self-esteem or narcissism?
Social networking can help people share self-relevant information and stay connected with family and friends. But social networking can also feed narcissistic tendencies and reward self-glamorizing photo posting.

Guido Mieth/Getty Images

BROOK PIFER/Getty Images

📹 See the *Video: Random Assignment* for a helpful tutorial animation.

For narcissists, social networking sites are more than a gathering place; they are a feeding trough. In one study, college students were *randomly assigned* either to edit and explain their online profiles for 15 minutes, or to use that time to study and explain a Google Maps routing (Freeman & Twenge, 2010). After completing their tasks, all were tested. Who then scored higher on a narcissism measure? Those who had spent the time focused on themselves.

MAINTAINING BALANCE AND FOCUS In both Taiwan and the United States, excessive online socializing and gaming have correlated with lower grades and with increased anxiety and depression (Brooks, 2015; Lepp et al., 2014; Walsh et al., 2013). In one U.S. survey, 47 percent of the heaviest users of the internet and other media were receiving mostly C grades or lower, as were just 23 percent of the lightest users (Kaiser Family Foundation, 2010). In another national survey, young adults who used seven or more social media platforms were three times more likely to be depressed or anxious than those who used two or fewer (Primack et al., 2016). Brain scans reveal a smaller *amygdala* (an emotion-control center) among extremely engaged social media users, making them similar in this way to people with substance use disorder (He et al., 2018).

In today's world, it can be challenging to maintain a healthy balance between our real-world and online time. Experts offer some practical suggestions:

- *Monitor your time.* Use a time-tracking app to measure your time online. Then ask yourself, "Does my time use reflect my priorities? Am I spending more time online than I intended? Does it interfere with my school or work performance or my relationships?"

- *Monitor your feelings.* Ask yourself, "Am I emotionally distracted by my online interests? When I disconnect and move to another activity, how do I feel?"

- *Hide from your incessantly posting online friends when necessary.* And in your own postings, practice the golden rule: Ask yourself, "Is this something I'd care about if someone else posted it?"

- *When studying, get in the habit of checking your devices less often.* Selective attention—the flashlight of your mind—can be in only one place at a time. When we try to do two things at once, we don't do either one of them very well (Willingham, 2010). If you want to study or work productively, resist the temptation to always be available. Disable sound alerts, vibration, and pop-ups. (To reduce distraction, I [ND] am writing this module while using an app that blocks distracting websites.)

- *Refocus by taking a nature walk.* People learn better after a peaceful walk in a park, which—unlike a walk on a busy street—refreshes our capacity for focused attention (Berman et al., 2008). Connecting with nature boosts our spirits and sharpens our minds (Zelenski & Nisbet, 2014).

As psychologist Steven Pinker (2010) said, "The solution is not to bemoan technology but to develop strategies of self-control, as we do with every other temptation in life."

Liam Walsh/Cartoon Stock

"It keeps me from looking at my phone every two seconds."

Do your connections on social media increase your sense of belonging? Sometimes, do they make you feel lonely? Which of the strategies discussed will you find most useful to maintain balance and focus?

RP-2 Social networking tends to _____ (strengthen/weaken) your relationships with people you already know, and _____ (increase/ decrease) your self-disclosure.

ANSWERS IN APPENDIX E

Achievement Motivation

LOQ 34-3 What is *achievement motivation,* and what are some ways to encourage achievement?

Some motives seem to have little obvious survival value. Billionaires may be motivated to make ever more money, internet celebrities to attract ever more social media followers, politicians to achieve ever more power. And motives vary across cultures. In an individualist culture, employees may work to receive an "employee of the month" award; in a collectivist culture, they may strive to join a company's hardest-working team. The more we achieve, the more we may need to achieve. Psychologist Henry Murray (1938) defined **achievement motivation** as a desire for significant accomplishment, for mastering skills or ideas, for control, and for attaining a high standard.

Achievement motivation matters. One famous study followed the lives of 1528 California children whose intelligence test scores were in the top 1 percent. Forty years later, researchers compared those who were most and least successful professionally. What did the researchers discover? A motivational difference. The most successful were more ambitious, energetic, and persistent. As children, they had more active hobbies. As adults, they participated in more groups and sports (Goleman, 1980). Gifted children are able learners. Accomplished adults are tenacious doers. Most of us are energetic doers when starting and when finishing a project. It's easiest—have you noticed?—to get stuck in the middle. That's when high achievers keep going (Bonezzi et al., 2011). Once they get in a groove, their motivation keeps them in an orbit of goal striving (Foulk et al., 2019). It's no wonder that people with high achievement motivation tend to have greater financial success, healthy social relationships, and good physical and mental health (Steptoe & Wardle, 2017).

In some studies of both secondary school and university students, self-discipline has surpassed intelligence test scores in predicting school performance, attendance, and graduation honors. For school performance, "discipline outdoes talent," concluded researchers Angela Duckworth and Martin Seligman (2005, 2017).

Discipline focuses and refines talent. By their early twenties, top violinists have fiddled away thousands of lifetime practice hours—in fact, double the practice time of other violin students aiming to be teachers (Ericsson, 2001, 2006, 2007). A study of outstanding scholars, athletes, and artists found that all were highly motivated and self-disciplined, willing to dedicate hours every day to the pursuit of their goals (Bloom, 1985). But as young Mozart composing at age 8 illustrates, native talent matters, too (Hambrick & Meinz, 2011; Ruthsatz & Urbach, 2012). In sports, music, and chess, people's practice-time differences, while significant, account for a third or less of their performance differences (Hambrick et al., 2014a,b; Macnamara et al., 2014, 2016; Ullén et al., 2016). High achievers benefit from their passion and perseverance, but the superstars among them are also distinguished by their extraordinary natural talent.

Duckworth (2016) has a name for passionate dedication to an ambitious, long-term goal: **grit.** Other researchers see grit as similar to conscientiousness or self-control (Credé, 2018; Schmidt et al., 2018; Vazsonyi et al., 2019). Researchers have begun to sleuth

achievement motivation a desire for significant accomplishment, for mastery of skills or ideas, for control, and for attaining a high standard.

grit in psychology, passion and perseverance in the pursuit of long-term goals.

Calum's road: What grit can accomplish Having spent his life on the Scottish island of Raasay, farming a small patch of land, tending its lighthouse, and fishing, Malcolm ("Calum") MacLeod (1911–1988) felt anguished. His local government repeatedly refused to build a road that would enable vehicles to reach his north end of the island. With the once-flourishing population there having dwindled to two—MacLeod and his wife—he responded with heroic determination. One spring morning in 1964, MacLeod, then in his fifties, gathered an ax, a chopper, a shovel, and a wheelbarrow. By hand, he began to transform the existing footpath into a 1.75-mile road (Miers, 2009).

"With a road," a former neighbor explained, "he hoped new generations of people would return to the north end of Raasay," restoring its culture (Hutchinson, 2006). Day after day he worked through rough hillsides, along hazardous cliff faces, and over peat bogs. Finally, 10 years later, he completed his supreme achievement. The road, which the government has since surfaced, remains a visible example of what vision plus determined grit can accomplish. It bids us each to ponder: What "roads"—what achievements—might we, with sustained effort, build in the years before us?

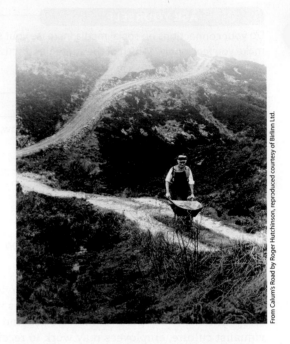

the neural and genetic markers of grit (Nemmi et al., 2016; Rimfeld et al., 2016; Wang et al., 2018). Passion and perseverance fuel gritty goal-striving, which can produce great achievements (Jachimowicz et al., 2018; Muenks et al., 2018). Gritty students are most likely to stay in college rather than drop out (Saunders-Scott et al., 2018). As basketball star, Damian Lillard (2015) has said, "If you want to look good in front of thousands, you have to outwork thousands in front of nobody."

Although intelligence is distributed like a bell curve, achievements are not. This tells us that achievement involves much more than raw ability. That is why it pays to know how best to engage people's motivations to achieve. Promising people a reward for an enjoyable task can backfire. Excessive rewards can destroy **intrinsic motivation**—the desire to perform a behavior effectively for its own sake. In experiments, children have been promised a payoff for playing with an interesting puzzle or toy. Later, they played with the toy *less* than did unpaid children (Deci et al., 1999; Tang & Hall, 1995). Likewise, rewarding children with toys or candy (or money or screen time) for reading diminishes the time they spend reading (Marinak & Gambrell, 2008). It is as if they think, "If I have to be bribed into doing this, it must not be worth doing!"

To sense the difference between intrinsic motivation and **extrinsic motivation** (behaving in certain ways that gain external rewards or avoid threatened punishment), think about your experience in this course. Like most students, you probably want to earn a high grade. But what motivates your actions to achieve your goal? Do you feel pressured to finish this reading before a deadline? Are you worried about your grade? Eager for the credits that will count toward graduation? If *Yes*, then you are extrinsically motivated (as, to some extent, all students must be). Do you also find the material interesting? Does learning it make you feel more competent? If there were no grade at stake, might you be curious enough to want to learn the material for its own sake? If *Yes*, intrinsic motivation also fuels your efforts.

People who focus on their work's meaning and significance not only do better work but ultimately earn more extrinsic rewards (Wrzesniewski et al., 2014). Elementary school students with greater-than-average academic intrinsic motivation—who love learning for its own sake—go on to perform better in school, take more challenging classes, and earn more advanced degrees (Fan & Williams, 2018; Gottfried et al., 2006). Wanting to do something, rather than having to do something, seems to pay off (Converse et al., 2019).

Extrinsic rewards work well when people perform tasks that don't naturally inspire complex, creative thinking (Hewett & Conway, 2015). They're also effective when used to signal a job well done (rather than to bribe or control someone) (Boggiano et al.,

intrinsic motivation a desire to perform a behavior effectively for its own sake.

extrinsic motivation the desire to perform a behavior to receive promised rewards or avoid threatened punishment.

1985). When administered wisely, rewards can improve performance and spark creativity (Eisenberger & Aselage, 2009; Henderlong & Lepper, 2002). "Most improved player" awards, for example, can boost feelings of competence and increase enjoyment of a sport. And the rewards that often follow academic achievement, such as scholarships and job opportunities, can have long-lasting benefits.

Organizational psychologists seek ways to engage and motivate ordinary people doing ordinary jobs (see Appendix C: Psychology at Work).

Goal Setting

Each of us can adopt some research-based strategies for achieving our goals:

1. *Do make that resolution.* Challenging goals motivate achievement (Harkin et al., 2016). SMART goals are specific, measureable, achievable, realistic, and timely. Such goals—"finish my psychology paper by Tuesday"—direct attention and motivate persistence.

2. *Announce the goal to friends or family.* We're more likely to follow through after making a public commitment.

3. *Develop an implementation plan.* Be specific about when, where, and how you'll progress toward your goal. People who flesh out goals with detailed plans become more focused and more likely to succeed (Gollwitzer & Oettingen, 2012). Better to concentrate on small steps—the day's running goal, say—than to fantasize about the marathon.

4. *Create short-term rewards that support long-term goals.* Although delayed rewards motivate us to set goals, immediate rewards best predict our persistence toward those goals (Woolley & Fishbach, 2018).

5. *Monitor and record progress.* If striving for more exercise, use a wearable fitness tracker or enter your activity in a fitness app. It's even more motivating when progress is shared rather than kept secret (Harkin et al., 2016).

6. *Create a supportive environment.* When trying to eat healthily, keep junk food out of the cupboards. When focusing on a project, hole up in the library. When sleeping, stash the phone. Have your gym bag ready the night before. Such "situational self-control strategies" prevent tempting impulses (Duckworth et al., 2016; Schiffer & Roberts, 2018).

7. *Transform the hard-to-do behavior into a must-do habit.* Habits form when we repeat behaviors in a given context. As our behavior becomes linked with the context, our next experience of that context evokes our habitual response. Do something every day for about two months and see it become an ingrained habit.

To achieve important life goals, we often know what to do. We *know* that a full night's sleep boosts our alertness, energy, and mood. We *know* that exercise lessens depression and anxiety, builds muscle, and strengthens our heart and mind. We *know* that what we put into our body—junk food or balanced nutrition, addictive substances or clean air—affects our health and longevity. Alas, as T. S. Eliot foresaw, "Between the idea / And the reality . . . / Falls the Shadow." Nevertheless, by taking these seven steps—resolving, announcing, planning, rewarding, monitoring, controlling, and persistently acting—we can create a bridge between the idea and the reality.

> "Genius is 1% inspiration and 99% perspiration." —Thomas Edison (1847–1931)

ASK YOURSELF

What goal would you like to achieve? How might you use the seven strategies offered in this section to meet that goal?

RETRIEVAL PRACTICE

RP-3 What have researchers found to be an even better predictor of school performance than intelligence test scores?

ANSWERS IN APPENDIX E

MODULE

34 **REVIEW** **Affiliation and Achievement**

LEARNING OBJECTIVES

Test Yourself Answer these repeated Learning Objective Questions on your own (before checking the answers in Appendix D) to improve your retention of the concepts (McDaniel et al., 2009, 2015).

LOQ **34-1** What evidence points to our human affiliation need—our need to belong?

LOQ **34-2** How does social networking influence us?

LOQ **34-3** What is *achievement motivation,* and what are some ways to encourage achievement?

TERMS AND CONCEPTS TO REMEMBER

Test Yourself Write down the definition in your own words, then check your answer.

affiliation need, p. 407

self-determination theory, p. 407

ostracism, p. 408

narcissism, p. 411

achievement motivation, p. 413

grit, p. 413

intrinsic motivation, p. 414

extrinsic motivation, p. 414

MASTER THE MATERIAL

Test Yourself Answer the following questions on your own first, then check your answers in Appendix E.

1. Which of the following is NOT evidence supporting the view that humans are strongly motivated by a need to belong?

    a. Students who rated themselves as "very happy" also tended to have satisfying close relationships.

    b. Social exclusion—such as exile or solitary confinement—is considered a severe form of punishment.

    c. As adults, adopted children tend to resemble their biological parents.

    d. Children who are extremely neglected become withdrawn, frightened, and sometimes even speechless.

2. What are some ways to manage our social networking time successfully?

3. If we want to increase our chance of success in achieving a new goal, such as stopping smoking, we _____ (should/should not) announce the goal publicly, and we _____ (should/should not) share with others our progress toward achieving that goal.

Continue testing yourself with **LearningCurve** or **Achieve Read & Practice** to learn and remember most effectively.

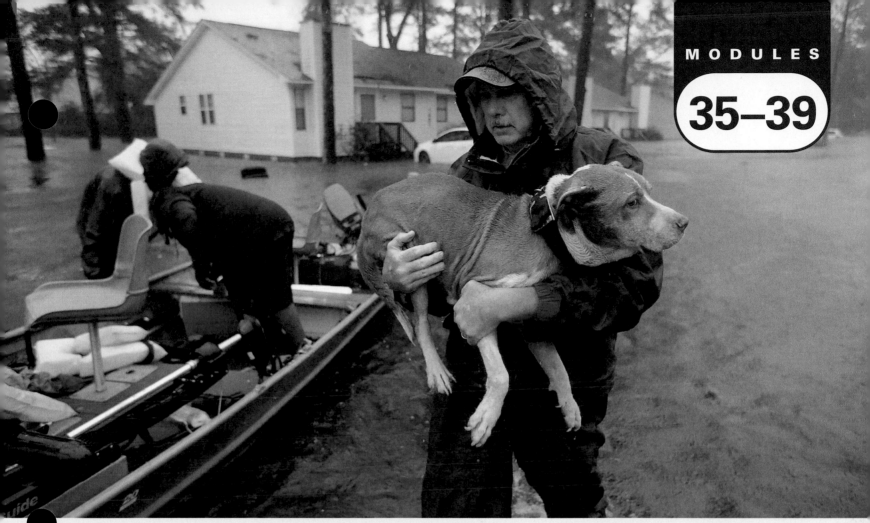

Chip Somodevilla/Getty Images

Emotions, Stress, and Health

No one needs to tell you that feelings add color to your life, or that in times of stress they can disrupt your life, or save it. Fear, anger, sadness, joy, and love are psychological states that also entail physical reactions. Nervous about an important encounter, we feel stomach butterflies. Anxious over public speaking, we frequent the bathroom. Smoldering over a family conflict, we get a splitting headache.

You can surely recall a time when emotion overwhelmed you. I [DM] retain a flashbulb memory of the day I went to a huge store and brought along Peter, my toddler first-born child. As I set Peter down on his feet for a moment to do some paperwork, a passerby warned, "You'd better be careful or you'll lose that boy!" Not more than a few breaths later, I turned and found no Peter beside me.

With mild anxiety, I looked around one end of the customer service counter. No Peter in sight. With slightly more anxiety, I peered around the other side. No Peter there, either. Now, with my heart accelerating, I circled the neighboring counters. Still no Peter anywhere. As anxiety turned to panic, I began racing up and down the store aisles. He was nowhere to be found. The alerted store manager used the intercom to ask customers to assist in looking for a missing child. Soon after, I passed the customer who had warned me. "I told you that you were going to lose him!" he now scolded. With visions of kidnapping (strangers routinely adored that beautiful child), I braced for the unthinkable possibility that my negligence had caused me to lose what I loved above all else, and that I might have to return home and face my wife without our only child.

But then, as I passed the customer service counter yet again, there he was, having been found and returned by some obliging customer. In an instant, the arousal of terror spilled into ecstasy. Clutching my son, with tears suddenly flowing, I found myself unable to speak my thanks and stumbled out of the store awash in grateful joy.

Emotions are subjective. But they are real. As researcher Lisa Feldman Barrett (2012, 2013) notes, "My experience of anger is not an illusion. When I'm angry, I feel angry. That's real." Where do our emotions come from? Why do we have them? What are they made of?

Emotions are our body's adaptive response. They "are our body's way of ensuring we do what is best for us," observes Frans de Waal (2019). When we face challenges, emotions focus our attention and energize our actions (Cyders & Smith, 2008). Our heart races. Our pace quickens. All our senses go on high alert. By integrating data from our environment, our body, and our experiences, we feel emotional stress (Francis, 2018).

But emotions can also be positive. Receiving unexpected good news, we may find our eyes tearing up. We raise our hands triumphantly. We feel exuberance and a newfound confidence. Yet negative and prolonged emotions can harm our health.

In Modules 35, 36, and 37, we explore how psychologists think about and study our emotional expression and experiences. In Modules 38 and 39, we take a close look at the challenges of stress and some ways of coping that help us meet those challenges.

35 Introduction to Emotion

Not only emotion, but most psychological phenomena (vision, sleep, memory, sex, and so forth) can be approached these three ways—physiologically, behaviorally, and cognitively.

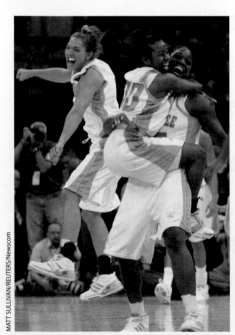

Joy expressed According to the James-Lange theory, we don't just smile because we share our teammates' joy. We also share the joy because we are smiling with them.

Emotion: Arousal, Behavior, and Cognition

LEARNING OBJECTIVE QUESTION **LOQ** **35-1** How do arousal, expressive behavior, and cognition interact in emotion?

As my [DM's] panicked search for Peter illustrates, **emotions** are a mix of

- *bodily arousal* (heart pounding),
- *expressive behaviors* (quickened pace), and
- *conscious experience* (Is this a kidnapping?) *and feelings* (panic, fear, joy).

The puzzle for psychologists is fitting these three pieces together. To do that, the first researchers of emotion considered two big questions:

1. A chicken-and-egg debate: Does your bodily arousal come *before* or *after* your emotional feelings? (Did I first notice my racing heart and faster step, and then feel terror about losing Peter? Or did my sense of fear come first, stirring my heart and legs to respond?)

2. How do *thinking* (cognition) and *feeling* interact? Does cognition always come before emotion? (Did I think about a kidnapping threat before I reacted emotionally?)

Courtesy of David Myers

The psychological study of emotion began with the first question: How do bodily responses relate to emotions? Two of the earliest emotion theories offered different answers.

James-Lange Theory: Arousal Comes Before Emotion

Common sense tells most of us that we cry because we are sad, lash out because we are angry, tremble because we are afraid. But to pioneering psychologist William James, this commonsense view of emotion had things backward. Rather, "We feel sorry because we cry, angry because we strike, afraid because we tremble" (1890, p. 1066). To James, emotions result from attention to our bodily activity. James' idea was also proposed by Danish physiologist Carl Lange, and so is called the **James-Lange theory.** James and Lange would have guessed that I noticed my racing heart and then, shaking with fright, felt the whoosh of emotion—that my feeling of fear *followed* my body's response.

Cannon-Bard Theory: Arousal and Emotion Occur Simultaneously

Physiologist Walter Cannon (1871–1945) disagreed with the James-Lange theory. Does a racing heart signal fear or anger or love? The body's responses—heart rate, perspiration, and body temperature—are too similar, and they change too slowly, to *cause* the different emotions, said Cannon. He, and later another physiologist, Philip Bard, concluded that our bodily responses and experienced emotions occur separately but simultaneously. So, according to the **Cannon-Bard theory,** my heart began pounding *as* I experienced fear. The emotion-triggering stimulus traveled to my sympathetic nervous system, causing my body's arousal. *At the same time,* it traveled to my brain's cortex, causing my awareness of my emotion. My pounding heart did not cause my feeling of fear, nor did my feeling of fear cause my pounding heart.

But are they really independent of each other? Countering the Cannon-Bard theory are studies of people with severed spinal cords, including a survey of 25 World War II soldiers (Hohmann, 1966). Those with *lower-spine injuries,* who had lost sensation only in their legs, reported little change in their emotions' intensity. Those with *high spinal cord injury,* who could feel nothing below the neck, did report changes. Some reactions were much less intense than before the injuries. Anger, one high spinal cord-injured man revealed, "just doesn't have the heat to it that it used to. It's a mental kind of anger." Other emotions, those expressed mostly in body areas above the neck, were felt *more* intensely. These men reported increases in weeping, lumps in the throat, and getting choked up when saying good-bye, worshipping, or watching a touching movie. Such evidence has led some researchers to view feelings as "mostly shadows" of our bodily responses and behaviors (Damasio, 2003).

But our emotions also involve cognition (Averill, 1993; Barrett, 2006, 2017). Here we arrive at psychology's second big emotion question: How do thinking and feeling interact? Whether we fear the man behind us on a dark street depends entirely on whether or not we interpret him as threatening.

RETRIEVAL PRACTICE

RP-1 According to the Cannon-Bard theory, (a) our *physiological response* to a stimulus (for example, a pounding heart), and (b) the *emotion we experience* (for example, fear) occur _____ (simultaneously/sequentially). According to the James-Lange theory, (a) and (b) occur _____ (simultaneously/sequentially).

ANSWERS IN APPENDIX E

Schachter-Singer Two-Factor Theory: Arousal + Label = Emotion

LOQ **35-2** To experience emotions, must we consciously interpret and label them?

Stanley Schachter and Jerome Singer (1962) demonstrated that how we *appraise* (interpret) our experiences also matters. Our physical reactions *and our thoughts* (perceptions, memories, and interpretations) together create emotion. In their **two-factor theory,** emotions have two ingredients: physical arousal and cognitive appraisal. An emotional experience, they argued, requires a conscious interpretation of arousal.

Consider how arousal spills over from one event to the next. Imagine enjoying an invigorating run and then receiving a message that you got your dream job. With arousal lingering from the run, would you feel more elated than if you heard this news after staying awake all night studying?

To explore this *spillover effect,* Schachter and Singer injected college men with the hormone epinephrine, which triggers feelings of arousal. One group of men were told to expect feelings of arousal from the injection. Others were told by the trickster researchers that it would help test their eyesight. Picture yourself as a participant: After receiving the injection, you go to a waiting room, where you find yourself with another person (actually an accomplice of the experimenters) who is acting either euphoric or irritated.

emotion a response of the whole organism, involving (1) physiological arousal, (2) expressive behaviors, and, most importantly, (3) conscious experience resulting from one's interpretations.

James-Lange theory the theory that our experience of emotion occurs when we become aware of our physiological responses to an emotion-arousing stimulus.

Cannon-Bard theory the theory that an emotion-arousing stimulus simultaneously triggers (1) physiological responses and (2) the subjective experience of emotion.

two-factor theory the Schachter-Singer theory that to experience emotion one must (1) be physically aroused and (2) cognitively label the arousal.

The spillover effect Arousal from a soccer match can fuel anger, which can descend into rioting or other violent confrontations.

OLEG POPOV/REUTERS/Newscom

As you observe this person, you begin to feel your heart race, your skin flush, and your breathing become more rapid. If you had been in the group told to expect these effects from the injection, what would you feel? In the experiment, these volunteers felt little emotion—because they correctly attributed their arousal to the drug. But if you had been told the injection would help assess your eyesight, what would you feel? Perhaps you would react as this group of participants did. They "caught" the apparent emotion of the other person in the waiting room. They became happy if the accomplice was acting euphoric, and testy if the accomplice was acting irritated.

This discovery—that a stirred-up state can be experienced as one emotion or another, depending on how we interpret and label it—has been replicated in dozens of experiments and continues to influence modern emotion research (MacCormack & Lindquist, 2016; Reisenzein, 1983; Sinclair et al., 1994). As researcher Daniel Gilbert (2006) noted, "Feelings that one interprets as fear in the presence of a sheer drop may be interpreted as lust in the presence of a sheer blouse."

The point to remember: Arousal fuels emotion; cognition channels it.

> 🎞 For a 4-minute demonstration of the relationship between arousal and cognition, see the *Video: Emotion = Arousal Plus Interpretation.*

RETRIEVAL PRACTICE

RP-2   According to Schachter and Singer, two factors lead to our experience of an emotion: (a) physiological arousal and (b) _____ appraisal.

ANSWERS IN APPENDIX E

Zajonc, LeDoux, and Lazarus: Does Cognition Always Precede Emotion?

But is the heart always subject to the mind? Must we *always* interpret our arousal before we can experience an emotion? Robert Zajonc [ZI-yence] (1923–2008) didn't think so. He contended that we actually have many emotional reactions apart from, or even before, our conscious interpretation of a situation (1980, 1984). Perhaps you can recall liking something or someone immediately, without knowing why.

Even when people repeatedly view stimuli flashed too briefly for them to interpret, they come to prefer those stimuli (Kunst-Wilson & Zajonc, 1980). Unaware of having previously seen them, they nevertheless like them. We also have an acutely sensitive automatic radar for emotionally significant information, such that even a subliminally flashed stimulus can prime us to feel better or worse about a follow-up stimulus (Murphy et al., 1995; Zeelenberg et al., 2006).

Neuroscientists are charting the neural pathways of emotions (Ochsner et al., 2009). Our emotional responses can follow two different brain pathways. Some emotions (especially more complex feelings like hatred and love) travel a "high road." A stimulus following this path would travel (by way of the thalamus) to the brain's cortex (**FIGURE 35.1**).

⊖ FIGURE 35.1

The brain's pathways for emotions In the two-track brain, sensory input may be routed (a) to the cortex (via the thalamus) for analysis and then transmission to the amygdala; or (b) directly to the amygdala (via the thalamus) for an instant emotional reaction.

(a) The thinking high road

(b) The speedy low road

There, it would be analyzed and labeled before the response command is sent out, via the amygdala (an emotion-control center).

But sometimes our emotions (especially simple likes, dislikes, and fears) take what Joseph LeDoux (2002, 2015) has called the more direct "low road," a neural shortcut that bypasses the cortex. Following the low road, a fear-provoking stimulus would travel from the eye or ear (again via the thalamus) directly to the amygdala (Figure 35.1b). This shortcut enables our greased-lightning emotional response before our intellect intervenes. Like speedy reflexes (that also operate separately from the brain's thinking cortex), the amygdala's reactions are so fast that we may be unaware of what's transpired (Dimberg et al., 2000). A conscious fear experience then occurs as we become aware that our brain has detected danger (LeDoux & Brown, 2017).

The amygdala sends more neural projections up to the cortex than it receives back, which makes it easier for our feelings to hijack our thinking than for our thinking to rule our feelings (LeDoux & Armony, 1999). Thus, in the forest, we can jump at the sound of rustling bushes nearby, leaving it to our cortex to decide later whether the sound was made by a snake or by the wind. Such experiences support Zajonc's and LeDoux's belief that *some* of our emotional reactions involve no deliberate thinking.

Emotion researcher Richard Lazarus (1991, 1998) agreed that our brain processes vast amounts of information without our conscious awareness, and that some emotional responses do not require *conscious* thinking. Much of our emotional life operates via the automatic, speedy low road. But he further wondered: How would we *know* what we are reacting to if we did not in some way appraise the situation? The appraisal may be effortless and we may not be conscious of it, but it is still a mental function. To know whether a stimulus is good or bad, the brain must have some idea of what it is (Storbeck et al., 2006). Thus, said Lazarus, emotions arise when we *appraise* an event as harmless or dangerous. We appraise the sound of the rustling bushes as the presence of a threat. Then we realize that it was "just the wind."

So, let's sum up (see also **TABLE 35.1**). As Zajonc and LeDoux have demonstrated, some simple emotional responses involve no conscious thinking. When I [ND] see a big spider trapped behind glass, I experience fear, even though I *know* the spider can't hurt me. Such responses are difficult to alter by changing our thinking. Within a fraction of a second, we may perceive one person as more likable or trustworthy than another (Willis & Todorov, 2006). This instant appeal can even influence our political decisions if we vote (as many people do) for the candidate we *like* over the candidate who expresses positions closer to our own (Westen, 2007).

But other emotions—including depressive moods and complex feelings—are greatly affected by our conscious and unconscious information processing: our memories, expectations, and interpretations. For these emotions, we have more conscious control. When we feel emotionally overwhelmed, we can change our interpretations (Gross, 2013).

TABLE 35.1 Summary of Emotion Theories

Theory	Explanation of Emotions	Example
James-Lange	Emotions arise from our awareness of our specific bodily responses to emotion-arousing stimuli.	We observe our heart racing after a threat and then feel afraid.
Cannon-Bard	Emotion-arousing stimuli trigger our bodily responses and simultaneous subjective experience.	Our heart races at the same time that we feel afraid.
Schachter-Singer	Our experience of emotion depends on two factors: general arousal and a conscious cognitive label.	We may interpret our arousal as fear or excitement, depending on the context.
Zajonc; LeDoux	Some embodied responses happen instantly, without conscious appraisal.	We automatically feel startled by a sound in the forest before labeling it as a threat.
Lazarus	Cognitive appraisal ("Is it dangerous or not?")—sometimes without our awareness—defines emotion.	The sound is "just the wind."

Such *reappraisal* often reduces distress and the corresponding amygdala response (Denny et al., 2015; Troy et al., 2018). Reappraisal not only reduces stress, it also helps students achieve better school performance (Borman et al., 2019). So don't stress about your stress. Embrace it, and approach your next exam with this mindset, "Stress evolved to help maintain my focus and solve problems." Although the emotional low road functions automatically, the thinking high road allows us to retake some control over our emotional life. *The bottom line:* Together, automatic emotion and conscious thinking weave the fabric of our emotional lives.

RETRIEVAL PRACTICE

RP-3 Emotion researchers have disagreed about whether emotional responses occur in the absence of cognitive processing. How would you characterize the approach of each of the following researchers: Zajonc, LeDoux, Lazarus, Schachter, and Singer?

ANSWERS IN APPENDIX E

Embodied Emotion

Whether you are falling in love or grieving a death, you need little convincing that emotions involve the body. Feeling without a body is like breathing without lungs. Some physical responses are easy to notice. Other emotional responses we experience without awareness.

Emotions and the Autonomic Nervous System

LOQ 35-3 What is the link between emotional arousal and the autonomic nervous system?

In a crisis, the *sympathetic division* of your *autonomic nervous system (ANS)* mobilizes your body for action (**FIGURE 35.2**). It directs your adrenal glands to release the stress hormones epinephrine (adrenaline) and norepinephrine (noradrenaline). To provide energy, your liver pours extra sugar (glucose) into your bloodstream. To help burn the sugar, your respiration increases to supply needed oxygen. Your heart rate and blood pressure increase. Your digestion slows, diverting blood from your internal organs to your muscles. With blood sugar driven into the large muscles, action becomes easier. Your pupils dilate, letting in more light. To cool your stirred-up body, you perspire. If wounded, your blood would clot more quickly.

"Fear lends wings to his feet." — Virgil, *Aeneid*, 19 B.C.E.

FIGURE 35.2

Emotional arousal Like a crisis management center, the autonomic nervous system arouses the body in a crisis and calms it when danger passes.

Autonomic Nervous System Controls Physiological Arousal

Sympathetic division (arousing)		Parasympathetic division (calming)
Pupils dilate	EYES	Pupils contract
Decreases	SALIVATION	Increases
Perspires	SKIN	Dries
Increases	RESPIRATION	Decreases
Accelerates	HEART	Slows
Inhibits	DIGESTION	Activates
Secrete stress hormones	ADRENAL GLANDS	Decrease secretion of stress hormones
Reduced	IMMUNE SYSTEM FUNCTIONING	Enhanced

When the crisis passes, the *parasympathetic division* of your ANS gradually calms your body, as stress hormones slowly leave your bloodstream. After your next crisis, think of this: Without any conscious effort, your body's response to danger is wonderfully coordinated and adaptive—preparing you to *fight* or *flee*. So, do the different emotions have distinct arousal fingerprints?

ASK YOURSELF

Can you think of a recent time when you noticed your body's reactions to an emotionally charged situation, such as a tense social setting, or perhaps before an important test or game? How would you describe your sympathetic nervous system's responses?

> To review and then check your understanding of the ANS in action, engage online with *Concept Practice: The Autonomic Nervous System.*

The Physiology of Emotions

LOQ 35-4 How do emotions activate different physiological and brain-pattern responses?

Imagine conducting an experiment measuring the physiological responses of different emotions. In each room, participants watch one of four movies: a horror film, an anger-provoking film, a sexually arousing film, or an utterly boring film. From the control center, you monitor participants' perspiration, pupil size, breathing, and heart rate. Could you tell who is frightened? Who is angry? Who is sexually aroused? Who is bored?

With training, you could probably pick out the bored viewer. But discerning physiological differences among fear, anger, and sexual arousal is much more difficult (Siegel et al., 2018). Different emotions can share common biological signatures.

A single brain region can also serve as the seat of seemingly different emotions. Consider the broad emotional portfolio of the *insula,* a neural center deep inside the brain. The insula is activated when we experience various negative social emotions, such as lusting after another's partner, pridefulness, and disgust. In brain scans, it becomes active when people bite into some disgusting food, smell disgusting food, think about biting into a disgusting cockroach, or feel moral disgust over a sleazy businessperson exploiting a saintly widow (Sapolsky, 2010). Similar multitasking regions are found in other brain areas.

Yet our varying emotions *feel* different to us, and they often *look* different to others. We may appear "paralyzed with fear" or "ready to explode." Fear and joy prompt a similar increased heart rate, but they stimulate different facial muscles. When fearful, your brow muscles tense. When joyful, muscles in your cheeks and under your eyes pull into a smile (Witvliet & Vrana, 1995).

Some of our emotions also have distinct brain circuits (Dixon et al., 2017; Panksepp, 2007). Observers watching fearful faces show more amygdala activity than do other observers who view angry faces (Whalen et al., 2001). Emotions also activate different areas of the brain's cortex. When you experience negative emotions such as disgust, your right prefrontal cortex tends to be more active than the left. Depression-prone people, and those with generally negative perspectives, have also shown more right frontal lobe activity (Harmon-Jones et al., 2002).

Positive moods tend to trigger more left frontal lobe activity. People with positive personalities—from exuberant infants to alert, energized, and persistently goal-directed adults—have also shown more activity in the left frontal lobe than in the right (Davidson et al., 2000; Urry et al., 2004). Indeed, the more a person's baseline frontal lobe activity tilts left—or is made to tilt left by perceptual activity—the more upbeat the person typically is (Drake & Myers, 2006).

To sum up, we can't easily see differences in emotions from tracking heart rate, breathing, and perspiration. But facial expressions and brain activity can vary with the emotion. So, do we, like Pinocchio, give off telltale signs when we lie? (For more on that question, see Thinking Critically About: Lie Detection.)

> To see how skilled you are at lie detection, visit *Topic Tutorial: PsychSim6, Catching Liars.*

"No one ever told me that grief felt so much like fear. I am not afraid, but the sensation is like being afraid. The same fluttering in the stomach, the same restlessness, the yawning. I keep on swallowing." — C. S. Lewis, *A Grief Observed,* 1961

Scary thrills Elated excitement and panicky fear involve similar physiological arousal. That allows us to flip rapidly between the two emotions.

Jacob Lund/Shutterstock

Thinking Critically About:
Lie Detection

LOQ **35-5** How effective are polygraphs in using body states to detect lies?

Polygraphs are not actually lie detectors, but rather arousal detectors. They measure emotion-linked changes in breathing, heart rate, and perspiration. Can we use these results to detect lies?

In the last 20 years, have you ever taken something that didn't belong to you?

No!

Did you ever steal anything from your previous employer?

Uh, no.

EEG

Many people tell a little white lie in response to this *control question*, prompting elevated arousal readings that give the examiner a baseline for comparing responses to other questions.

EEG

This person shows greater arousal in response to the *critical question* than she did to the control question, so the examiner may infer she is lying.

But is it true that *only a thief becomes nervous when denying a theft*?

1. We have similar bodily arousal in response to anxiety, irritation, and guilt. So, is she really guilty, or just anxious?

2. Many innocent people do get tense and nervous when accused of a bad act. (Many of those sexually assaulted, for example, have "failed" these tests because they had strong emotional reactions while telling the truth about the rapist.[1])

About one-third of the time, polygraph test results are *just wrong*.[2]

Innocent people

Guilty people

If these polygraph experts had been the judges, more than one-third of the innocent would have been declared guilty, and nearly one-fourth of the guilty would have gone free.

The CIA and other U.S. agencies have spent millions of dollars testing tens of thousands of employees. Yet the U.S. National Academy of Sciences (2002) has reported that "no spy has ever been caught [by] using the polygraph."

○ Judged innocent by polygraph ● Judged guilty by polygraph

The Concealed Information Test is more effective. Innocent people are seldom wrongly judged to be lying.

Questions focus on specific crime-scene details known only to the police and the guilty person.[3] (If a camera and computer had been stolen, for example, only a guilty person should react strongly to the brand names of the stolen items. A slow response time may also indicate a lie. It typically takes less time to tell the truth than to make up a lie.[4])

1.Lykken, 1991. 2.Kleinmuntz & Szucko, 1984. 3.Ben-Shakhar & Elaad, 2003; Verschuere & Meijer, 2014; Vrij & Fisher, 2016. 4.Suchotzki et al., 2017.

RETRIEVAL PRACTICE

RP-4 How do the two divisions of the autonomic nervous system affect our emotional responses?

ANSWERS IN APPENDIX E

➔ **polygraph** a machine used in attempts to detect lies; measures emotion-linked changes in perspiration, heart rate, and breathing.

MODULE

35 **REVIEW** Introduction to Emotion

LEARNING OBJECTIVES

Test Yourself Answer these repeated Learning Objective Questions on your own (before checking the answers in Appendix D) to improve your retention of the concepts (McDaniel et al., 2009, 2015).

LOQ **35-1** How do arousal, expressive behavior, and cognition interact in emotion?

LOQ **35-2** To experience emotions, must we consciously interpret and label them?

LOQ **35-3** What is the link between emotional arousal and the autonomic nervous system?

LOQ **35-4** How do emotions activate different physiological and brain-pattern responses?

LOQ **35-5** How effective are polygraphs in using body states to detect lies?

TERMS AND CONCEPTS TO REMEMBER

Test Yourself Write down the definition in your own words, then check your answer.

emotion, p. 419

James-Lange theory, p. 419

Cannon-Bard theory, p. 419

two-factor theory, p. 419

polygraph, p. 424

MASTER THE MATERIAL

Test Yourself Answer the following questions on your own first, then check your answers in Appendix E.

1. The _____ - _____ theory of emotion maintains that our emotional experience occurs after our awareness of a physiological response.

2. Assume that after returning from an hour-long run, you receive a letter saying that your scholarship application has been approved. The two-factor theory of emotion would predict that your physical arousal will

   a. weaken your happiness.

   b. intensify your happiness.

   c. transform your happiness into relief.

   d. have no particular effect on your happiness.

3. Zajonc and LeDoux have maintained that some emotional reactions occur before we have had the chance to consciously label or interpret them. Lazarus noted the importance of how we appraise events. These psychologists differ in the emphasis they place on _____ in emotional responses.

   a. physical arousal

   b. the hormone epinephrine

   c. cognitive processing

   d. learning

4. What does a polygraph measure, and why are its results questionable?

Continue testing yourself with **🌊 LearningCurve** or **🌊 Achieve Read & Practice** to learn and remember most effectively.

MODULE

36 Expressing Emotion

Expressive behavior implies emotion. Dolphins, with smiles seemingly plastered on their faces, appear happy. To decipher people's emotions we read their bodies, listen to their vocal tones, and study their faces. Does nonverbal language vary with culture—or is it universal? And do our expressions influence our experienced emotions?

"Your face, my thane, is a book where men may read strange matters." — Lady Macbeth to her husband, in William Shakespeare's *Macbeth*

Detecting Emotion in Others

LOQ 36-1 How do we communicate nonverbally?

To Westerners, a firm handshake conveys an outgoing, expressive personality (Chaplin et al., 2000). A glance can communicate intimacy, while darting eyes may signal anxiety (Kleinke, 1986; Perkins et al., 2012). Passionately in love, people typically spend time—lots of time—gazing into each other's eyes (Bolmont et al., 2014; Rubin, 1970). Would such gazes stir loving feelings between strangers? To find out, researchers have asked unacquainted male-female (and presumed heterosexual) pairs to gaze intently for 2 minutes either at each other's hands or into each other's eyes. After separating, the eye gazers reported feeling a tingle of attraction and affection (Kellerman et al., 1989).

Our brain is an amazing detector of subtle expressions, helping most of us read nonverbal cues well. We are adept at detecting a hint of a smile (Maher et al., 2014). Shown 10 seconds of video from the end of a speed-dating interaction, people can often tell whether one person is attracted to another (Place et al., 2009). Signs of status are also easy to spot. When shown someone with arms raised, chest expanded, and a slight smile, people—from Canadian undergraduates to Fijian villagers—perceive that person as experiencing pride and having high status (Tracy et al., 2013). Even glimpsing a face for one-tenth of a second has enabled viewers to judge people's trustworthiness, or to rate politicians' competence and predict their voter support (Willis & Todorov, 2006). "First impressions . . . occur with astonishing speed," note Christopher Olivola and Alexander Todorov (2010).

We also excel at detecting nonverbal threats. We readily sense subliminally presented negative words, such as *snake* or *bomb* (Gomes et al., 2018). An angry face will "pop out" of a crowd (Öhman et al., 2001; Stjepanovic & LaBar, 2018). Even 2-year-olds attend to angry faces, suggesting that humans are hard-wired to detect threats (Burris et al., 2019).

A silent language of emotion Hindu classical dance uses the face and body to effectively convey 10 different emotions (Hejmadi et al., 2000).

FIGURE 36.1

Experience influences how we perceive emotions Viewing the morphed middle face, evenly mixing anger with fear, physically abused children were more likely than nonabused children to perceive the face as angry (Pollak & Kistler, 2002; Pollak & Tolley-Schell, 2003).

Experience can sensitize us to particular emotions, as shown by experiments using a series of faces (like those in **FIGURE 36.1**) that morph from anger to fear (or sadness). Shown a face that is 50 percent fear and 50 percent anger, physically abused children are more likely than other children to perceive anger. Their perceptions become sensitively attuned to more quickly spot glimmers of danger.

Hard-to-control facial muscles can reveal emotions you may be trying to conceal. Lifting just the inner part of your eyebrows, which few people do consciously, reveals distress or worry. Eyebrows raised and pulled together signal fear. Raised cheeks and activated muscles under the eyes suggest a natural smile. A feigned smile, such as one we make for a photographer, is often frozen in place for several seconds, then suddenly switched off; genuine happy smiles tend to be briefer but to fade less abruptly (Bugental, 1986) (**FIGURE 36.2**). True smiles cause others to perceive us as trustworthy, authentic, and attractive (Gunnery & Ruben, 2016).

Despite our brain's emotion-detecting skill, we find it difficult to discern deceit. The behavioral differences between liars and truth tellers are too minute for most people to detect (Hartwig & Bond, 2011). One digest of 206 studies found that people were just 54 percent accurate in discerning truth from lies—barely better than a coin toss (Bond & DePaulo, 2006). Virtually no one—save perhaps police professionals in high-stakes situations—beats chance by much, not even when detecting children's lies (Gongola et al., 2017; O'Sullivan et al., 2009; ten Brinke et al., 2016).

Some of us more than others are sensitive to the physical cues of various emotions. In one study, people were asked to name the emotion displayed in brief film clips. The clips showed portions of a person's emotionally expressive face or body, sometimes accompanied by a garbled voice (Rosenthal et al., 1979). For example, after a 2-second scene—a "thin slice" of behavior—revealing only the face of an upset woman, viewers were asked if the woman was criticizing someone for being late or was talking about her divorce. Introverts tend to excel at reading others' emotions, while extraverts are generally easier to read (Ambady et al., 1995).

FIGURE 36.2

Which of researcher Paul Ekman's smiles is feigned, which natural? Smile (b) engages the facial muscles of a natural smile.

(a)   (b)

Gestures, facial expressions, and vocal tones, which are absent in written communication, convey important information. The difference was clear when study participants in one group heard 30-second recordings of people describing their marital separations. Participants in the other group read a script of the recording. Those who *heard* the recording were better able to predict the people's current and future adjustment (Mason et al., 2010). Just hearing a stranger say "hello" is enough to give listeners some clue to the speaker's personality.

Online communications often suffer from the absence of vocal and facial nuances. Without the normal expressive cues, we run the risk of what developmental psychologist Jean Piaget called *egocentrism*; we may fail to perceive how others interpret our "just kidding" message (Kruger et al., 2005). So, to help people understand whether our online comment is serious, kidding, or sarcastic, we may insert emojis. 😊

Gender, Emotion, and Nonverbal Behavior

LOQ 36-2 How do men and women differ in nonverbal communication?

Do women have greater sensitivity than men to nonverbal cues? An analysis led by Judith Hall (2016) of 176 "thin slice" studies indicated that women do outperform men at emotion detection. This advantage emerges early in development, even in infants (McClure, 2000). Women's nonverbal sensitivity helps explain their greater emotional literacy. When invited to describe how they would feel in certain situations, men tend to describe simpler emotional reactions (Barrett et al., 2000). You might like to try this yourself: Ask some people how they might feel when saying good-bye to friends after graduation. Research suggests men are more likely to say, simply, "I'll feel bad," and women to express more complex emotions: "It will be bittersweet; I'll feel both happy and sad."

Women's skill at decoding others' emotions may also contribute to their greater emotional responsiveness and expressiveness, especially for positive emotions (Fischer & LaFrance, 2015; McDuff et al., 2017). In studies of 23,000 people from 26 cultures, women more than men reported themselves open to feelings (Costa et al., 2001). Girls also express stronger emotions than boys do, hence the extremely strong perception that emotionality is "more true of women"—a perception expressed by nearly 100 percent of 18- to 29-year-old Americans (Chaplin & Aldao, 2013; Newport, 2001).

One exception: Quickly—imagine an angry face. What gender is the person? If you're like 3 in 4 Arizona State University students, you imagined a man (Becker et al., 2007). And when a gender-neutral face was made to look angry, most people perceived it as a man; if the face was smiling, they were more likely to perceive it as a woman (**FIGURE 36.3**). Anger strikes most people as a more masculine emotion.

The perception of women's emotionality also feeds—and is fed by—people's attributing women's emotionality to their disposition and men's to their circumstances: "She's emotional" versus "He's having a bad day" (Barrett & Bliss-Moreau, 2009). Many factors influence our attributions, including cultural norms (Mason & Morris, 2010). Nevertheless, there are some gender differences in descriptions of emotional experiences. When surveyed, women are also far more likely than men to describe themselves as empathic. If you have *empathy*, you identify with others and imagine being in their skin. You appraise a situation as they do, rejoicing with those who rejoice and weeping with those who weep (Wondra & Ellsworth, 2015). As defense lawyer Atticus Finch explained to his daughter in *To Kill a Mockingbird*, seeing things from another's point of view is a simple way to "get along better with all kinds of folks." But there is a downside to empathy: It focuses us on what we see, and feel, right now—discounting what is unseen or in the future (Bloom, 2016).

Fiction readers, who immerse themselves in other lives, report higher empathy levels (Mar et al., 2009). This may help explain why, compared with men, women also read more fiction (Tepper, 2000). But physiological measures, such as heart rate while seeing another's distress, reveal a much smaller gender gap (Eisenberg & Lennon, 1983; Rueckert et al., 2010).

Women are also more likely to *express* empathy—to display more emotion when observing others' emotions. As **FIGURE 36.4** shows, this gender difference was clear when

⬆ **FIGURE 36.3**
Gendered perceptions? Researchers manipulated a gender-neutral face. People were more likely to see it as a man when it wore an angry expression and as a woman when it wore a smile (Becker et al., 2007).

"Empathy's most important role . . . is to inspire kindness: our tendency to help each other, even at a cost to ourselves."
— Jamil Zaki, *The War for Kindness*, 2019

"Now, that wasn't so hard, was it?"

⬅ **FIGURE 36.4**
Gender and expressiveness Film viewers did not differ dramatically in self-reported emotions or physiological responses, but women's faces *showed* much more emotion than men's. (Data from Kring & Gordon, 1998.)

students watched film clips that were sad (children with a dying parent), happy (slapstick comedy), or frightening (a man nearly falling off the ledge of a tall building) (Kring & Gordon, 1998). Women also tend to experience upsetting emotional events, such as viewing pictures of mutilation, more deeply and with more brain activation in areas sensitive to emotion. And they better remember the scenes three weeks later (Canli et al., 2002).

RETRIEVAL PRACTICE

RP-1 _____ (Women/Men) report experiencing emotions more deeply, and they tend to be more adept at reading nonverbal behavior.

ANSWERS IN APPENDIX E

Culture and Emotional Expression

LOQ 36-3 How are gestures and facial expressions understood within and across cultures?

The meaning of *gestures* varies from culture to culture. I [ND] have taught my preschool children the thumbs-up gesture so they can let me know that something is good. But I will also teach them not to make that gesture if we travel to certain West African and Middle Eastern countries, where it can mean "up yours!" (Koerner, 2003).

Do *facial expressions* also have different meanings in different cultures? To find out, two investigative teams showed photographs of various facial expressions to people in different parts of the world and asked them to guess the emotion (Ekman, 2016; Ekman & Friesen, 1975; Izard, 1994). You can try this matching task yourself by pairing the six emotions with the six faces in **FIGURE 36.5**.

Regardless of your cultural background, you probably did pretty well. A smile's a smile everywhere. Ditto for laughter and sadness. (People around the world can also discriminate real laughs from fake laughs [Bryant et al., 2018].) Other emotional expressions are less universally recognized (Cowen & Keltner, 2019; Crivelli et al., 2016a). But there is no culture where people frown when they are happy.

Data from 182 studies show that we do slightly better when judging emotional displays from our own culture (Crivelli et al., 2016b; Elfenbein & Ambady, 2002; Laukka et al., 2016). Still, the telltale signs of emotion generally cross cultures. The world over, children cry when distressed, shake their heads when defiant, and smile when they are happy. So, too, with blind children who have never seen a face (Eibl-Eibesfeldt, 1971).

→ FIGURE 36.5
Culture-specific or culturally universal expressions? As people of differing cultures, do our faces speak differing languages? Which face expresses disgust? Anger? Fear? Happiness? Sadness? Surprise?[1] (From Matsumoto & Ekman, 1989)

(a)   (b)   (c)   (d)   (e)   (f)

Ekman & Matsumoto, Japanese and Caucasian Facial Expressions of Emotions

[1](a) happiness, (b) surprise, (c) fear, (d) sadness, (e) anger, (f) disgust.

People blind from birth spontaneously exhibit the common facial expressions associated with such emotions as joy, sadness, fear, and anger (Galati et al., 1997).

Do these shared emotional categories reflect shared *cultural* experiences, such as movies and TV shows seen everywhere? Apparently not. Isolated people in New Guinea were asked to respond to such statements as, "Pretend your child has died." When North American undergraduates viewed the recorded responses, they easily read the New Guineans' facial reactions (Ekman & Friesen, 1971).

So we can say that facial muscles speak a universal language. This discovery would not have surprised evolutionary theorist Charles Darwin (1809–1882), who argued that in prehistoric times, before our ancestors communicated in words, they communicated threats, greetings, and submission with facial expressions. Their shared expressions helped them survive (Hess & Thibault, 2009). In confrontations, for example, a human sneer retains elements of an animal baring its teeth in a snarl (**FIGURE 36.6**). Emotional expressions may enhance our survival in other ways, too. Surprise raises the eyebrows and widens the eyes, enabling us to take in more information. Disgust wrinkles the nose, closing it from foul odors.

Smiles are social as well as emotional events. Euphoric Olympic gold-medal winners typically don't smile when they are awaiting their award ceremony. But they wear broad grins when interacting with officials and when facing the crowd and cameras (Fernández-Dols & Ruiz-Belda, 1995). Thus, a glimpse at competitors' spontaneous expressions following Olympic and national judo competitions gives a very good clue to who won, no matter their country (Crivelli et al., 2015; Matsumoto & Willingham, 2006, 2009). Even natively blind athletes, who have never observed smiles, display social smiles in such situations (Matsumoto et al., 2009).

We do tend to smile when happy, frown when sad, and scowl when angry. Yet we also sometimes scowl when concentrating or smile when angry. Moreover, depending on the context and culture, the same facial expression may convey different emotions (Barrett et al., 2019). We judge an angry face set in a frightening situation as afraid, and a fearful face set in a painful situation as pained (Carroll & Russell, 1996). Movie directors harness this phenomenon by creating scenes and soundtracks that amplify our perceptions of particular emotions.

Smiles are also cultural events, with *display rules* on how *much* emotion to express. Consider the many smiling students researchers found on a college campus in a small American city versus far fewer smiling students on a campus in Beijing (Talhelm et al., 2019). Cultures that encourage individuality, as in Western Europe, Australia, New Zealand, and North America, encourage the display of visible emotions (van Hemert et al., 2007). Those that encourage people to adjust to others, as in Japan, China, India, and Korea, often have less visible emotional displays (Cordaro et al., 2018; Matsumoto et al., 2009). In Japan, people infer emotion more from the surrounding context.

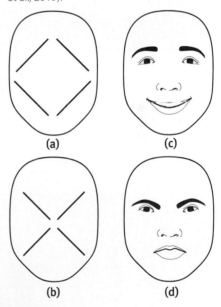

Universal emotions No matter where on Earth you live, you have no trouble recognizing the surprise and joy experienced by Morehouse College graduating students upon unexpectedly learning that a wealthy alum paid off all their educational debt.

"For news of the heart, ask the face."
— Guinean proverb

◆ FIGURE 36.6

Anger expressed Cover up faces (c) and (d) and ask a friend if they would select image (a) or image (b) as the angry one. Even without the obvious facial cues, most people easily choose the correct answer (b) (Franklin et al., 2019).

(a)   (c)

(b)   (d)

(a)

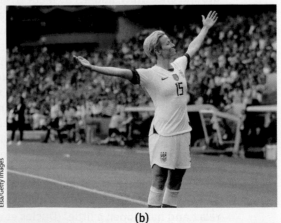
(b)

Display rules differ Soccer players from more collectivist cultures, such as Japanese Yu Kobayashi, tend to celebrate a goal with fellow players in a way that deflects attention from themselves (a). Those from more individualist cultures, such as American Megan Rapinoe—shown here after scoring at the 2019 Women's World Cup—are more comfortable making themselves distinct from others (b).

FIGURE 36.7

Culture and smiling Former U.S. Vice President Joe Biden's broad smile and Chinese President Xi Jinping's more reserved one illustrate a cultural difference in facial expressiveness.

Peter Probst/Alamy

AP Photo

Moreover, the mouth, often so expressive in North Americans, conveys less emotion than do the telltale eyes (Masuda et al., 2008; Yuki et al., 2007). Compared with their counterparts in China, where calmness is emphasized, European-American leaders express broad smiles six times more frequently in their official photos (**FIGURE 36.7**) (Tsai et al., 2006, 2016). If we're happy and we know it, our culture will surely teach us how to show it.

Cultural differences also exist *within* nations. The Irish and their Irish-American descendants have tended to be more expressive than the Scandinavians and their Scandinavian-American descendants (Tsai & Chentsova-Dutton, 2003). And that reminds us of a familiar lesson: Like most psychological events, emotion is best understood not only as a biological and cognitive phenomenon, but also as a social-cultural phenomenon.

RETRIEVAL PRACTICE

RP-2 Are people more likely to differ culturally in their interpretations of facial expressions, or of gestures?

ANSWERS IN APPENDIX E

> For a 4-minute demonstration of our universal facial language, see the *Video: Emotions and Facial Expression.*

The Effects of Facial Expressions

LOQ 36-4 How do our facial expressions influence our feelings?

As William James (1890) struggled with feelings of depression and grief, he came to believe that we can control emotions by going "through the outward movements" of any emotion we want to experience. "To feel cheerful," he advised, "sit up cheerfully, look around cheerfully, and act as if cheerfulness were already there." In *The Expression of the Emotions in Man and Animals,* Charles Darwin (1872) contended that "the free expression by outward signs of an emotion intensifies it. . . . He who gives way to violent gestures will increase his rage."

> "Whenever I feel afraid
> I hold my head erect
> And whistle a happy tune."
> — Richard Rodgers and Oscar Hammerstein,
> *The King and I,* 1958

Were they right? You can test this hypothesis: Fake a big grin. Now scowl. Can you feel the "smile therapy" difference? Participants in dozens of experiments have felt a difference. Researchers subtly induced students to make a frowning expression by asking them to contract certain muscles and pull their brows together (supposedly to help the researchers attach facial electrodes) (Laird, 1974, 1984; Laird & Lacasse, 2014). The results? The students reported feeling a little angry, as do people naturally frowning (by squinting) when facing the Sun (Marzoli et al., 2013). So, too, for other basic emotions. For example, people reported feeling more fear than anger, disgust, or sadness when made to construct a fearful expression: "Raise your eyebrows. And open your eyes wide. Move your whole head back, so that your chin is tucked in a little bit, and let your mouth relax and hang open a little" (Duclos et al., 1989).

RP-3 (a) Based on the *facial feedback effect,* how might students report feeling when the rubber bands raise their cheeks as though in a smile? (b) How might students report feeling when the rubber bands pull their cheeks downward?

A chain of rubber bands

Adhesive bandages

A chain of rubber bands

(a)   (b)   *ANSWERS IN APPENDIX E*

FIGURE 36.8
How to make people smile without telling them to smile Do as Kazuo Mori and Hideko Mori (2009) did with students in Japan: Attach rubber bands to the sides of the face with adhesive bandages, and then run them either over the head or under the chin.

James and Darwin were right; expressions not only communicate emotion, they also amplify and regulate it. This **facial feedback effect** has been found many times, in many places, for many basic emotions (Coles et al., 2019; see **FIGURE 36.8**). We're just a little happier when smiling, angrier when scowling, and sadder when frowning. Merely activating one of the smiling muscles by holding a pen in the teeth (rather than gently between the lips, which produces a neutral expression) makes stressful situations less upsetting (Kraft & Pressman, 2012). A hearty smile—made not just with the mouth but with raised cheeks that crinkle the eyes—enhances positive feelings even more when you are reacting to something pleasant or funny (Soussignan, 2001). When happy we smile, and when smiling we become happier (unless we're distracted by being videotaped [Marsh et al., 2019; Noah et al., 2018; Strack, 2016]).

So, your face is more than a billboard that displays your feelings; it also feeds your feelings. Scowl and the whole world scowls back. No wonder some depressed patients reportedly felt better after Botox injections paralyzed their frowning muscles (Parsaik et al., 2016). Botox paralysis of the frowning muscles slows people's reading of sadness- or anger-related sentences, and it slows activity in emotion-related brain circuits (Havas et al., 2010; Hennenlotter et al., 2008). The opposite happens when Botox paralyzes laughter muscles: People feel more depressed (Lewis, 2018).

Researchers have also observed a broader **behavior feedback effect** (Carney et al., 2015; Flack, 2006). You can duplicate the participants' experience: Walk for a few minutes with short, shuffling steps, keeping your eyes downcast. Now walk around taking long strides, with your arms swinging and your eyes looking straight ahead. Can you feel your mood shift? Or when angry, lean back in a reclined sitting position and feel the anger lessen (Krahé et al., 2018). Going through the motions awakens the emotions.

You can use your understanding of feedback effects to become more empathic: Let your own face mimic another person's expression. Acting as another acts helps us feel what another feels (Vaughn & Lanzetta, 1981). Losing this ability to mimic others can leave us struggling to make emotional connections, as social worker Kathleen Bogart, who has Moebius syndrome (a rare facial paralysis disorder), discovered while working with Hurricane Katrina refugees: When people made a sad expression, "I wasn't able to return it. I tried to do so with words and tone of voice, but it was no use. Stripped of the facial expression, the emotion just dies there, unshared" (Carey, 2010).

Our natural mimicry of others' emotions helps explain why emotions are contagious (Dimberg et al., 2000; Neumann & Strack, 2000; Peters & Kashima, 2015). Positive, upbeat Facebook posts create a ripple effect, leading Facebook friends to also express more positive emotions (Kramer, 2012).

A request from your authors: Smile often as you read this book.

ASK YOURSELF

Imagine a situation in which you would like to change the way you feel. How could you do so by altering your facial expressions or the way you carry yourself? In what other settings could you apply your knowledge of these feedback effects?

facial feedback effect the tendency of facial muscle states to trigger corresponding feelings, such as fear, anger, or happiness.

behavior feedback effect the tendency of behavior to influence our own and others' thoughts, feelings, and actions.

36 REVIEW Expressing Emotion

LEARNING OBJECTIVES

Test Yourself Answer these repeated Learning Objective Questions on your own (before checking the answers in Appendix D) to improve your retention of the concepts (McDaniel et al., 2009, 2015).

LOQ 36-1 How do we communicate nonverbally?

LOQ 36-2 How do men and women differ in nonverbal communication?

LOQ 36-3 How are gestures and facial expressions understood within and across cultures?

LOQ 36-4 How do our facial expressions influence our feelings?

TERMS AND CONCEPTS TO REMEMBER

Test Yourself Write down the definition in your own words, then check your answer.

facial feedback effect, p. 431   behavior feedback effect, p. 431

MASTER THE MATERIAL

Test Yourself Answer the following questions on your own first, then check your answers in Appendix E.

1. When people are induced to assume fearful expressions, they often report feeling some fear. This result is known as the _____ _____ effect.

2. Aiden has a bad cold and finds himself shuffling to class with his head down. How might his posture, as well as his cold, affect his emotional well-being?

Continue testing yourself with 📘 **LearningCurve** or 📘 **Achieve Read & Practice** to learn and remember most effectively.

37 Experiencing Emotion

LOQ 37-1 What are some of the basic emotions?

How many distinct emotions are there? When surveyed, most emotion scientists agreed that anger, fear, disgust, sadness, and happiness are basic human emotions (Ekman, 2016). Carroll Izard (1977) isolated 10 basic emotions (joy, interest-excitement, surprise, sadness, anger, disgust, contempt, fear, shame, and guilt), most present in infancy (**FIGURE 37.1**). Others believe that pride and love are also basic emotions (Shaver et al., 1996; Tracy & Robins, 2004). But Izard has argued that other emotions are combinations of these 10, with love, for example, being a mixture of joy and interest-excitement.

Let's take a closer look at anger and happiness. What functions do they serve? What influences our experience of each?

➡️ **FIGURE 37.1**
Some naturally occurring infant emotions To identify the emotions generally present in infancy, Carroll Izard analyzed the facial expressions of infants.

Joy (mouth forming smile, cheeks lifted, twinkle in eye)

Anger (brows drawn together and downward, eyes fixed, mouth squarish)

Interest (brows raised or knitted, mouth softly rounded, lips may be pursed)

Disgust (nose wrinkled, upper lip raised, tongue pushed outward)

Surprise (brows raised, eyes widened, mouth rounded in oval shape)

Sadness (brows' inner corners raised, mouth corners drawn down)

Fear (brows level, drawn in and up, eyelids lifted, mouth corners retracted)

Anger

LOQ 37-2 What are the causes and consequences of anger?

Anger, the sages have said, is "a short madness" (Horace, 65–8 B.C.E.) that "carries the mind away" (Virgil, 70–19 B.C.E.) and can be "many times more hurtful than the injury that caused it" (Thomas Fuller, 1654–1734). But they have also said that "noble anger" (William Shakespeare, 1564–1616) "makes any coward brave" (Cato, 234–149 B.C.E.) and "brings back . . . strength" (Virgil).

When we face a threat or challenge, fear triggers flight but anger triggers fight—each at times an adaptive behavior. What makes us angry? Sometimes anger is a response to someone's perceived misdeeds, especially when the person's act seems willful, unjustified, and avoidable (Averill, 1983). But small hassles and blameless annoyances—foul odors, high temperatures, a traffic jam, aches and pains—also have the power to make us angry (Berkowitz, 1990).

Anger can harm us, especially when it is chronic. Anger boosts our heart rate, increases *inflammation*—weakening our defenses against disease—and raises our testosterone levels (Barlow et al., 2019; Herrero et al., 2010; Peterson & Harmon-Jones, 2012). How, then, can we manage our anger? Popular media sources sometimes advise that releasing angry feelings can be better than internalizing them. When irritated, should we lash out at the offender? Should we rage at our dead parents, imaginatively curse the boss, or confront our childhood abuser?

Individualist cultures do encourage people to vent their rage. Such advice is seldom heard in cultures where people's identity is centered more on the group. People who keenly sense their *interdependence* see anger as a threat to group harmony (Markus & Kitayama, 1991). In Tahiti, for instance, people learn to be considerate and gentle. In Japan, from infancy on, angry expressions are less common than in Western cultures, where in recent politics and on social media anger seems all the rage.

The Western vent-your-anger advice presumes that aggressive action or fantasy enables emotional release, or **catharsis.** Experimenters report that *sometimes* when people retaliate against a provoker, they may calm down if they direct their counterattack toward the provoker, their retaliation seems justifiable, and their target is not intimidating (Geen & Quanty, 1977; Hokanson & Edelman, 1966; Verona & Sullivan, 2008). In short, expressing anger can be *temporarily* calming *if* it does not leave us feeling guilty or anxious.

Despite this temporary afterglow, catharsis usually fails to cleanse our rage. More often, expressing anger breeds more anger. For one thing, it may provoke further retaliation, causing a minor conflict to escalate into a major confrontation. For another, expressing anger can magnify anger. As *behavior feedback* research demonstrates, *acting* angry can make us *feel* angrier (Flack, 2006; Snodgrass et al., 1986). Anger's backfire potential appeared in a study of people asked to wallop a punching bag while ruminating about a person who had recently angered them (Bushman, 2002). Had the opportunity to "drain off" their anger reduced it? Quite the contrary. Later, when given a chance for revenge, those who vented their anger became even more aggressive.

Anger is often maladaptive. It can fuel aggression and prime prejudice. After the 9/11 terrorist attacks, Americans who responded with anger more than fear displayed intolerance for immigrants and Muslims (DeSteno et al., 2004; Skitka et al., 2004). Angry outbursts that temporarily calm us may also become reinforcing and therefore habit forming. If stressed managers find they can temporarily drain off some of their tension by berating an employee, then the next time they feel irritated and tense they may be more likely to explode again.

What are some better ways to manage your anger? Experts offer three suggestions:

- *Wait.* Doing so will reduce your physiological arousal. "What goes up must come down," noted Carol Tavris (1982). "Any emotional arousal will simmer down if you just wait long enough."

- *Find a healthy distraction or support.* Calm yourself by exercising, playing an instrument, or talking things through with a friend. Brain scans show that ruminating inwardly about why you are angry serves only to increase amygdala blood flow (Fabiansson et al., 2012).

- *Distance yourself.* Try to move away from the situation mentally, as if you are watching it unfold from a distance or the future. Self-distancing reduces rumination, anger, and aggression (Kross & Ayduk, 2011; Mischkowski et al., 2012; White et al., 2015).

Blowing off steam Fans seem to experience a *temporary* release while cheering at World Cup soccer matches, such as this one in South Africa. My [DM's] daughter, a resident, noted, "Every time I got angry at Uruguay, blowing that vuvuzela and joining the chorus of dissent released something in me."

The catharsis idea: Is it true?

catharsis in psychology, the idea that "releasing" aggressive energy (through action or fantasy) relieves aggressive urges.

Anger is not always wrong. Used wisely, it communicates strength and competence (Tiedens, 2001). Anger also motivates people to act courageously and achieve goals (Aarts & Custers, 2012; Halmburger et al., 2015). Controlled expressions of anger are more adaptive than either hostile outbursts or pent-up angry feelings. When angered, people do often react assertively rather than hurtfully (Averill, 1983). Then, to lessen their aggravation, they frequently talk things over with the perpetrator. Civility means not only keeping silent about trivial irritations but also communicating important ones clearly and assertively. A nonaccusing statement of feeling—perhaps letting a roommate know that "I get irritated when I have to clean up your dirty dishes"—can help resolve conflicts. Anger that expresses a grievance in ways that promote reconciliation rather than retaliation can benefit a relationship.

What if someone's behavior really hurts you, and you cannot resolve the conflict? Research commends the age-old response of forgiveness. Without letting the offender off the hook or inviting further harm—sometimes we need to distance ourselves from an abusive person—forgiveness may release anger and calm the body. In a study of the neural effects of forgiveness, German students had their brain scanned while someone thwarted their opportunity to earn money (Strang et al., 2014). Next, the students were asked whether or not they forgave the wrongdoer. Forgiveness increased blood flow to brain regions that help people understand their own emotions and make socially appropriate decisions.

RETRIEVAL PRACTICE

RP-1 Which one of the following is an effective strategy for reducing angry feelings?

a. Retaliate verbally or physically.

b. Wait or "simmer down."

c. Express anger in action or fantasy.

d. Review the grievance silently.

ANSWERS IN APPENDIX E

Happiness

LOQ 37-3 What is the *feel-good, do-good phenomenon,* and what is the focus of positive psychology research?

People aspire to, and wish one another, health and happiness. And for good reason. Our state of happiness or unhappiness colors everything. Happy people perceive the world as safer. Their eyes are drawn toward emotionally positive information (Raila et al., 2015). They are more confident and decisive, and they cooperate more easily. They experience more career success (Walsh et al., 2018). They rate job applicants more favorably, savor their positive past experiences without dwelling on the negative, and are more socially connected. They live healthier and more energized and satisfied lives (Boehm et al., 2015; De Neve et al., 2013; Stellar et al., 2015). And they are more generous (Boenigk & Mayr, 2016).

The simple conclusion: *Moods matter.* When you are gloomy, life as a whole seems depressing and meaningless—and you think more skeptically and attend more critically to your surroundings. Let your mood brighten and your thinking broadens, becoming more playful and creative (Baas et al., 2008; Forgas, 2008; Fredrickson, 2013).

Young adults' happiness helps predict their future life course. One study showed that the happiest 20-year-olds were later more likely to marry and less likely to divorce (Stutzer & Frey, 2006). In another study, which surveyed thousands of U.S. college students in 1976 and restudied them at age 37, happy students had gone on to earn significantly more money than their less-happy-than-average peers (Diener et al., 2002). When we are happy, our relationships, self-image, and hopes for the future also seem more promising.

Moreover—and this is one of psychology's most consistent findings—happiness doesn't just feel good, it *does* good. A mood-boosting experience such as recalling a happy event has made people more likely to give money, pick up someone's dropped papers, volunteer time, and do other good deeds. Psychologists call it the **feel-good, do-good phenomenon** (Salovey, 1990).

To assess your own well-being and consider ways to improve it, engage online with *Assess Your Strengths—How Satisfied Are You With Your Life, and How Could You Be More Satisfied?*

feel-good, do-good phenomenon people's tendency to be helpful when in a good mood.

positive psychology the scientific study of human flourishing, with the goals of discovering and promoting strengths and virtues that help individuals and communities to thrive.

subjective well-being self-perceived happiness or satisfaction with life. Used along with measures of objective well-being (for example, physical and economic indicators) to evaluate people's quality of life.

The reverse is also true: Doing good also promotes good feeling. One survey of more than 200,000 people in 136 countries found that, nearly everywhere, people report feeling happier after spending money on others rather than on themselves (Aknin et al., 2015a). Young children also show more positive emotion when they give, rather than receive, gifts (Aknin et al., 2015b). And in one experiment, helping others caused Spanish workers to experience greater well-being. Moreover, the people they helped also became happier and more helpful (Chancellor et al., 2018). Kidney donation hurts, but it leaves donors feeling good (Brethel-Haurwitz & Marsh, 2014). Even convicted criminals feel good when they do good (Hanniball et al., 2019).

Why does doing good feel so good? One reason is that it strengthens our social relationships (Aknin & Human, 2015; Yamaguchi et al., 2015). Some happiness coaches harness this *do-good, feel-good phenomenon* as they assign people to perform a daily "random act of kindness" and to record the results.

Positive Psychology

William James was writing about the importance of happiness ("the secret motive for all [we] do") as early as 1902. By the 1960s, the *humanistic psychologists* were interested in advancing human fulfillment. In the twenty-first century, under the leadership of American Psychological Association past-president Martin Seligman, **positive psychology** is using scientific methods to study human flourishing. This young subfield includes studies of **subjective well-being**—our feelings of happiness (sometimes defined as a high ratio of positive to negative feelings) or our sense of satisfaction with life.

Taken together, satisfaction with the past, happiness with the present, and optimism about the future define the positive psychology movement's first pillar: *positive well-being*.

Positive psychology is about building not just a pleasant life, says Seligman, but also a good life that engages one's skills, and a meaningful life that points beyond oneself. Thus, the second pillar, *positive traits*, focuses on exploring and enhancing creativity, courage, compassion, integrity, self-control, leadership, wisdom, and spirituality. Happiness is a by-product of a pleasant, engaged, and meaningful life.

The third pillar, *positive groups, communities, and cultures*, seeks to foster a positive social ecology. This includes healthy families, communal neighborhoods, effective schools, socially responsible media, and civil dialogue.

"Positive psychology," Seligman and colleagues have said (2005), "is an umbrella term for the study of positive emotions, positive character traits, and enabling institutions." Its focus differs from psychology's traditional interests in understanding and alleviating negative states—abuse and anxiety, depression and disease, prejudice and poverty. (Psychology articles published since 1887 mentioning "depression" have outnumbered those mentioning "happiness" by 17 to 1.)

In ages past, times of relative peace and prosperity have enabled cultures to turn their attention from repairing weakness and damage to promoting what Seligman (2002) has called "the highest qualities of life." Prosperous fifth-century Athens nurtured philosophy and democracy. Flourishing fifteenth-century Florence nurtured great art. Victorian England, flush with the bounty of the British Empire, nurtured honor, discipline, and duty. In this millennium, Seligman believes, thriving Western cultures have a parallel opportunity to create, as a "humane, scientific monument," a more positive psychology, concerned not only with weakness and damage but also with strength and virtue. Thanks to his leadership, and to more than $200 million in funding, the movement has gained strength, with supporters in 77 countries (IPPA, 2017; Seligman, 2016).

The Short Life of Emotional Ups and Downs

LOQ 37-4 How do time, wealth, adaptation, and comparison affect our happiness levels?

Are some days of the week happier than others? In what may be psychology's biggest-ever data sample, social psychologist Adam Kramer (at my [DM's] request and in cooperation with Facebook) did a *naturalistic observation* of emotion words in *billions of*

Martin E. P. Seligman "The main purpose of a positive psychology is to measure, understand, and then build the human strengths and the civic virtues."

See the *Video: Naturalistic Observation* for a helpful tutorial animation about this type of research design.

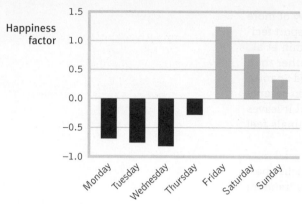

Happiness factor

⑦ FIGURE 37.2

Emotion notification Adam Kramer (2010) tracked positive and negative emotion words in many "billions" (the exact number is proprietary information) of status updates of U.S. Facebook users over a 3-year period.

"No happiness lasts for long." — Seneca, *Agamemnon*, 60 C.E.

"Everything has its wonders, even darkness and silence, and I learn, whatever state I may be in, therein to be content." — Helen Keller, *The Story of My Life*, 1902

status updates. After eliminating exceptional days, such as holidays, he tracked the frequency of positive and negative emotion words by day of the week. The days with the most positive moods? Friday and Saturday (**FIGURE 37.2**). Similar analyses of questionnaire responses and 59 million Twitter messages found Friday to Sunday the week's happiest days (Golder & Macy, 2011; Helliwell & Wang, 2015; Young & Lim, 2014). For you, too?

Over the long run, our emotional ups and downs tend to balance out, even over the course of the day. Positive emotion rises over the early to middle part of most days and then drops off (Kahneman et al., 2004; Watson, 2000). A stressful event—an argument, a sick child, a car problem—can trigger a bad mood. No surprise there. But by the next day, the gloom nearly always lifts (Affleck et al., 1994; Bolger et al., 1989; Stone & Neale, 1984). Our overall judgments of our lives often show lingering effects of good or bad events, but our daily moods typically rebound (Luhmann et al., 2012). If anything, people tend to bounce back from a bad day to a *better*-than-usual good mood the following day.

Worse events—the loss of a spouse or a job—can drag us down for longer periods (Infurna & Luthar, 2016). But eventually, most bad moods end. A romantic breakup feels devastating, but in time the wound heals. In one study, faculty members up for tenure expected their lives would be deflated by a negative decision. Actually, 5 to 10 years later, their happiness level was about the same as for those who received tenure (Gilbert et al., 1998).

Grief over the loss of a loved one or anxiety after severe trauma (such as child abuse, rape, or the terrors of war) can linger. But usually, even tragedy is not permanently depressing. People who become blind or paralyzed may not completely recover their previous well-being, but those with an agreeable personality usually recover near-normal levels of day-to-day happiness (Boyce & Wood, 2011; Hall et al., 1999). Even if you become paralyzed, explained psychologist Daniel Kahneman (2005), "you will gradually start thinking of other things, and the more time you spend thinking of other things the less miserable you are going to be."

The surprising reality: *We overestimate the duration of our emotions and underestimate our resiliency and capacity to adapt.* (As one who inherited hearing loss with a trajectory toward that of my mother, who spent the last 13 years of her life completely deaf, I [DM] take heart from these findings.)

Can Money Buy Happiness?

Would you be happier if you made more money? How important is "being very well off financially"? "Very important" or "essential," say 82 percent of entering U.S. college students (Eagan et al., 2016). But can money truly buy happiness?

EFFECTS OF INCOME AND INEQUALITY

National wealth matters. People in countries where most people have a secure livelihood tend to be happier than those in poor countries (Diener & Tay, 2015).

Personal income (up to a satiation point) predicts happiness. Having enough money to eat, to feel control over your life, and to occasionally treat yourself to something special predicts greater happiness (Fischer & Boer, 2011; Ruberton et al., 2016). As Australian data confirm, the power of more money to increase happiness is strongest at low incomes (Cummins, 2006). A $1000 wage increase does more for someone making $10,000 annually than for someone making $100,000.

Once we have enough money for comfort and security, we reach an "income satiation" point, beyond which piling up more and more matters less and less (Donnelly et al., 2018; Jebb et al., 2018). Experiencing luxury diminishes our savoring of life's simpler pleasures (Cooney et al, 2014; Quoidbach et al., 2010). If you ski the Alps once, your neighborhood sledding hill pales. If you ski the Alps every winter, it becomes an ordinary part of life rather than an experience to treasure (Quoidbach et al., 2015).

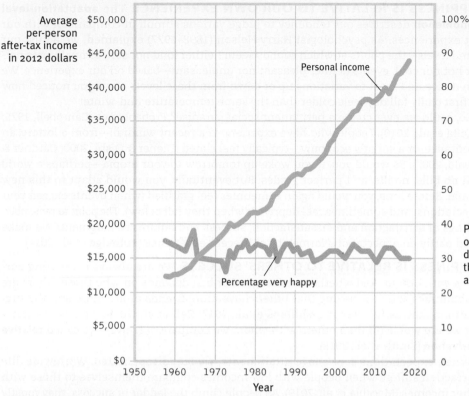

Does money buy happiness? It surely helps us to avoid certain types of pain. But although average buying power has nearly tripled since the 1950s, Americans' reported happiness has remained almost unchanged. (Happiness data from National Opinion Research Center surveys; income data from *Historical Statistics of the United States* and *Economic Indicators*.)

Over time, a rising economic tide has not produced increased happiness or decreased depression. Consider: Since the late 1950s, the average U.S. citizen's buying power almost tripled—enabling larger homes and twice as many cars per person, not to mention tablets and smartphones. Did it also buy more happiness? As **FIGURE 37.3** shows, Americans have become no happier. In 1957, some 35 percent said they were "very happy," as did slightly fewer—33 percent—in 2014. Much the same has been true of Europe, Canada, Australia, and Japan, where increasing real incomes have *not* produced increasing happiness (Australian Unity, 2008; Diener & Biswas-Diener, 2008; Di Tella & MacCulloch, 2010; Zuzanek, 2013). Ditto China, where living standards have risen but happiness and life satisfaction have not (Davey & Rato, 2012; Graham et al., 2018). These findings lob a bombshell at modern materialism: *Economic growth in affluent countries has provided no apparent boost to people's morale or social well-being.*

Extreme inequality is socially toxic. Why has economic growth not made us happier? Economic growth has been accompanied by rising *inequality,* which, across times and places, predicts unhappiness (Cheung & Lucas, 2016; Graafland & Lous, 2019). In countries such as the United States, China, and India, the rising economic tide has lifted the yachts faster than the rowboats (Hasell, 2018). In countries and states with greater inequality, lower income people tend to experience more ill health, social problems, and mental disorders (Payne, 2017; Sommet et al., 2018; Wilkinson & Pickett, 2017a,b). Across the world, we seem to understand this. Regardless of their political party, most people say they would prefer smaller pay gaps between the rich and the poor (Arsenio, 2018; Kiatpongsan & Norton, 2014).

Ironically, in every culture, those who strive hardest for wealth have tended to live with lower well-being, especially when they seek money to prove themselves, gain power, or show off rather than support their families (Donnelly et al., 2016; Niemiec et al., 2009; Srivastava et al., 2001). Those who instead strive for intimacy, personal growth, and community contribution experience a higher quality of life (Kasser, 2018).

Happiness Is Relative: Adaptation and Comparison

Two other psychological principles explain why more money does not, except when scarce, buy more happiness. In its own way, each principle suggests that happiness is relative.

"But on the positive side, money can't buy happiness—so who cares?"

HAPPINESS IS RELATIVE TO OUR OWN EXPERIENCE The **adaptation-level phenomenon** describes our tendency to judge various stimuli in comparison with our past experiences. As psychologist Harry Helson (1898–1977) explained, we adjust our *neutral* levels—the points at which sounds seem neither loud nor soft, temperatures neither hot nor cold, events neither pleasant nor unpleasant—based on our experience. We then notice and react to variations up or down from these levels. Have you noticed how the first chilly fall day feels colder than the same temperature mid-winter?

So, could we ever create a permanent social paradise? Probably not (Campbell, 1975; Di Tella et al., 2010). People who have experienced a recent windfall—from a lottery, an inheritance, or a surging economy—typically feel elated (Diener & Oishi, 2000; Gardner & Oswald, 2007). So would you, if you woke up tomorrow to your utopia—perhaps a world with no bills, no ills, and perfect grades. But eventually, you would adapt to this new normal. Before long, you would again sometimes feel gratified (when events exceed your expectations) and sometimes feel deprived (when they fall below). *The point to remember:* Feelings of satisfaction and dissatisfaction, success and failure are judgments we make based partly on expectations formed by our recent experience (Rutledge et al., 2014).

HAPPINESS IS RELATIVE TO OTHERS' SUCCESS We are always comparing ourselves with others. And whether we feel good or bad depends on who those others are (Lyubomirsky, 2001). Believing that others have more friends or are more socially successful makes us feel worse (Whillans et al., 2017; Zell et al., 2018). This sensation—that we are worse off than others with whom we compare ourselves—is called **relative deprivation** (Smith et al., 2018).

When expectations soar above attainments, we feel disappointed. Worldwide, life satisfaction suffers when people with low incomes compare themselves to those with higher incomes (Macchia et al., 2019). As people climb the ladder of success, they mostly compare themselves with local peers who are at or above their current level (Gruder, 1977; Suls & Tesch, 1978; Zell & Alicke, 2010). As British philosopher Bertrand Russell (1930/1985, pp. 68–69) noted, "Napoleon envied Caesar, Caesar envied Alexander, and Alexander, I daresay, envied Hercules, who never existed. You cannot, therefore, get away from envy by means of success alone, for there will always be in history or legend some person even more successful than you are."

Just as comparing ourselves with those who are better off creates envy, so counting our blessings as we compare ourselves with those worse off boosts our contentment. In one study, university women considered others' deprivation and suffering (Dermer et al., 1979). They viewed vivid depictions of grim city life in 1900. They imagined and then wrote about various personal tragedies, such as being burned and disfigured. Later, the women expressed greater satisfaction with their own lives. Similarly, when mildly depressed people have read about someone who was even more depressed, they felt somewhat better (Gibbons, 1986). "I cried because I had no shoes," states a Persian saying, "until I met a man who had no feet."

> For a 6.5-minute examination of historical and modern views of happiness, see the *Video: The Search for Happiness.*

What Predicts Our Happiness Levels?

LOQ 37-5 What predicts happiness, and how can we be happier?

Happy people share many characteristics (**TABLE 37.1**). But why are some people normally so joyful and others so somber? Here, as in so many other areas, the answer is found in the interplay between nature and nurture.

Genes matter. In one analysis of over 55,000 identical and fraternal twins, 36 percent of the differences among people's happiness ratings was heritable—attributable to genes (Bartels, 2015). Even identical twins raised apart are often similarly happy. The quest for specific genes that influence happiness confirms a familiar lesson: Human traits are influenced by many genes having small effects (Røysamb & Nes, 2019).

But our personal history and our culture matter, too. On the personal level, as we have seen, our emotions tend to balance around a level defined by our experience. On the cultural level, groups vary in the traits they value. Self-esteem and achievement matter

---

"I have a 'fortune cookie maxim' that I'm very proud of: Nothing in life is quite as important as you think it is while you are thinking about it. So, nothing will ever make you as happy as you think it will."
— Nobel laureate psychologist Daniel Kahneman, Gallup interview, "What Were They Thinking?" 2005

Students tend to have a higher academic self-concept if they attend a school where most other students are not exceptionally able (Marsh & Parker, 1984; Rogers & Feller, 2016; Salchegger, 2016). If you were near the top of your graduating class, you might feel inferior or discouraged upon entering a college or university where all students were near the top of their class.

"Comparison is the thief of joy." — Attributed to Theodore Roosevelt

"Researchers say I'm not happier for being richer, but do you know how much researchers make?"

Pat Byrnes The New Yorker Collection/The Cartoon Bank

adaptation-level phenomenon our tendency to form judgments (of sounds, of lights, of income) relative to a neutral level defined by our prior experience.

relative deprivation the perception that we are worse off relative to those with whom we compare ourselves.

TABLE 37.1 Happiness Is . . .

Researchers Have Found That Happy People Tend to	However, Happiness Seems Not Much Related to Other Factors, Such as
Have high self-esteem (in individualist countries).	Age.
Be optimistic, outgoing, agreeable, and humorous.	Gender (women are more often depressed, but also more often joyful).
Have close, positive, and lasting relationships.	Physical attractiveness.
Have work and leisure that engage their skills.	
Have an active religious faith (especially in more religious cultures).	
Sleep well and exercise.	

Information from Batz-Bararich et al., 2018; De Neve & Cooper, 1998; Diener et al., 2003, 2011; Headey et al., 2010; Lucas et al., 2004; Myers, 1993, 2000; Myers & Diener, 1995, 1996; Steel et al., 2008; Veenhoven, 2014, 2015 offers a database of 13,000+ correlates of happiness at WorldDatabaseofHappiness.eur.nl.

more in Western cultures, which value individualism. Social acceptance and harmony matter more in communal cultures such as Japan, which stress family and community (Diener et al., 2003; Fulmer et al., 2010; Uchida & Kitayama, 2009).

Depending on our genes, our outlook, and our recent experiences, our happiness seems to fluctuate around a "happiness set point," which disposes some people to be ever upbeat and others more negative. Even so, after following thousands of lives over two decades, researchers have determined that our satisfaction with life can change (Lucas & Donnellan, 2007). Happiness rises and falls, and can be influenced by factors that are under our control (Layous & Lyubomirsky, 2014; Nes, 2010). See **TABLE 37.2** for research-based suggestions for improving your mood and increasing your satisfaction with life.

RubberBall Selects/Alamy

TABLE 37.2 Evidence-Based Suggestions for a Happier Life

- *Take control of your time.* Happy people feel in control of their lives and less time-stressed (Whillans, 2019). Too little time is stressful, too much is boring. So, set goals and divide them into manageable daily aims. We all tend to overestimate how much we will accomplish in any given day, but the good news is that we generally *underestimate* how much we can accomplish in a year, given just a little daily progress.

- *Act happy.* Research shows that people who are manipulated into a smiling expression feel better. So put on a happy face. Talk *as if* you feel positive self-esteem, are optimistic, and are outgoing. We can often act our way into a happier state of mind.

- *Seek work and leisure that engage your skills.* Happy people often are in a zone called *flow*—absorbed in tasks that challenge but don't overwhelm them. Passive forms of leisure (streaming movies and television shows) often provide less flow experience than exercising, socializing, or expressing artistic interests.

- *Buy experiences rather than things.* For those who are not struggling financially, money buys more happiness when spent on experiences, especially socially shared experiences, that you look forward to, enjoy, remember, and talk about (Caprariello & Reis, 2013; Kumar & Gilovich, 2013, 2015; Lee et al., 2018). As pundit Art Buchwald said, "The best things in life aren't things."

- *Join the "movement" movement.* Aerobic exercise not only promotes health and energy, it also helps prevent or relieve depression (Willis et al., 2018). Sound minds often reside in sound bodies.

- *Give your body the sleep it wants.* Happy people live active lives yet reserve time for renewing, refreshing sleep. Sleep debt results in fatigue, diminished alertness, and gloomy moods. If you sleep now, you'll smile later.

- *Give priority to close relationships.* Compared with unhappy people, happy people engage in more meaningful conversations (Milek et al., 2018). Resolve to nurture your closest relationships by *not* taking your loved ones for granted: Give them the sort of kindness and affirmation you give others. Relationships matter.

- *Focus and find meaning beyond self.* Reach out to those in need. Perform acts of kindness. Happiness increases helpfulness, but doing good also fills us with happiness, meaning, and purpose. And meaning matters mightily: A meaningful life is often a long, active, and healthy life (Alimujiang et al., 2019; Hooker & Masters, 2018).

- *Challenge your negative thinking.* Reframe "I failed" to "I can learn from this." Remind yourself that stuff happens, and that in a month or a year, this bad experience may not seem like that big a deal.

- *Count your blessings and record your gratitude.* Keeping a gratitude journal heightens well-being (Davis et al., 2016). Take time to savor positive experiences and achievements, and to appreciate why they occurred (Sheldon & Lyubomirsky, 2012). Express your gratitude to another and prepare to be surprised at how positively you both feel (Dickens, 2017; Kumar & Epley, 2018).

- *Nurture your spiritual self.* Meditation helps us stay steady, emotionally. And for many people, faith provides a support community, a reason to focus beyond self, and a sense of purpose and hope. That helps explain why, worldwide, people active in faith communities report greater-than-average happiness and often cope well with crises (Pew, 2019).

If we can enhance our happiness on an *individual* level, could we use happiness research to refocus our *national* priorities more on the pursuit of happiness? Many psychologists believe we could. Happy societies are not only prosperous, but also places where people trust one another, feel free, and enjoy close relationships (Helliwell et al., 2013; Oishi & Schimmack, 2010). Thus, in debates about the minimum wage, economic inequality, tax rates, divorce laws, health care, and city planning, people's psychological well-being can be a consideration. Many political leaders agree: 43 nations have begun measuring their citizens' well-being, and many have undertaken interventions to boost national well-being (Diener et al., 2015, 2019). Britain's Annual Population Survey, for example, asks its citizens how satisfied they are with their lives, how worthwhile they judge their lives, and how happy and how anxious they felt yesterday (ONS, 2018).

ASK YOURSELF

Were you surprised by any of the findings related to happiness? What things might you change in your life to increase your happiness?

RETRIEVAL PRACTICE

RP-2 Which of the following factors does NOT predict self-reported happiness?

a. Age

b. Personality traits

c. Sleep and exercise

d. Active religious faith

ANSWERS IN APPENDIX E

MODULE 37 REVIEW Experiencing Emotion

LEARNING OBJECTIVES

Test Yourself Answer these repeated Learning Objective Questions on your own (before checking the answers in Appendix D) to improve your retention of the concepts (McDaniel et al., 2009, 2015).

LOQ 37-1 What are some of the basic emotions?

LOQ 37-2 What are the causes and consequences of anger?

LOQ 37-3 What is the *feel-good, do-good phenomenon,* and what is the focus of positive psychology research?

LOQ 37-4 How do time, wealth, adaptation, and comparison affect our happiness levels?

LOQ 37-5 What predicts happiness, and how can we be happier?

TERMS AND CONCEPTS TO REMEMBER

Test Yourself Write down the definition in your own words, then check your answer.

catharsis, p. 433

feel-good, do-good phenomenon, p. 434

positive psychology, p. 434

subjective well-being, p. 434

adaptation-level phenomenon, p. 438

relative deprivation, p. 438

MASTER THE MATERIAL

Test Yourself Answer the following questions on your own first, then check your answers in Appendix E.

1. One of the most consistent findings of psychological research is that happy people are also

   a. more likely to express anger.

   b. generally luckier than others.

   c. concentrated in the wealthier nations.

   d. more likely to help others.

2. _____ psychology is a scientific field of study focused on how humans thrive and flourish.

3. After moving to a new apartment, you find the street noise irritatingly loud, but after a while it no longer bothers you. This reaction illustrates the

   a. relative deprivation principle.

   b. adaptation-level phenomenon.

   c. feel-good, do-good phenomenon.

   d. catharsis principle.

4. A philosopher observed that we cannot escape envy, because there will always be someone more successful, more accomplished, or richer with whom to compare ourselves. In psychology, this observation is embodied in the _____ _____ principle.

Continue testing yourself with 📚 **LearningCurve** or 📚 **Achieve Read & Practice** to learn and remember most effectively.

38 Stress and Illness

> **stress** the process by which we perceive and respond to certain events, called *stressors,* that we appraise as threatening or challenging.

To live is to experience stress. Worldwide, 35 percent of people reported experiencing "a lot of stress" the day before (Gallup, 2019). (Greeks, at 59 percent, were the most stressed, with Americans, at 55 percent, not far behind.)

Some stresses we anticipate. For those, *trigger warnings* that intend to alert people of, say, graphic video content to come, do little to prevent distress (Sanson et al., 2019). Other stress strikes without warning. Imagine being 21-year-old Ben Carpenter, who experienced the world's wildest and fastest wheelchair ride. As he crossed a street, the light changed and a semitruck moved into the intersection. When they bumped, Carpenter's wheelchair handles got stuck in the truck's grille. The driver, who hadn't seen Carpenter and couldn't hear his cries for help, took off down the highway, pushing the wheelchair at 50 miles per hour until reaching his destination two miles away. As Carpenter tried to cope with his loss of control, his heart raced, his hands sweated, and his breathing sped up: "It was very scary."

How often do you experience stress in your daily life? Do you feel differently about stressful situations that seem imposed on you (assignments, deadlines, tragic events) than about the stress you impose on yourself (adventures, challenges, happy changes)? As we will see, our interpretation of events affects our experience of those events and whether we even consider them stressful. In this section, we take a closer look at stress—what it is and how it affects our health and well-being. Let's begin with some basic terms.

Extreme stress From the audio recording of a 911 caller reporting Ben Carpenter's distress: "You are not going to believe this. There is a semitruck pushing a guy in a wheelchair on Red Arrow highway!"

Michigan State Police

Stress: Some Basic Concepts

LOQ 38-1 How does our appraisal of an event affect our stress reaction, and what are the three main types of stressors?

Stress is the process of appraising and responding to a threatening or challenging event (**FIGURE 38.1**). But stress is a slippery concept. We sometimes use the word informally to describe threats or challenges ("Carpenter was under a lot of stress"), and at other times our responses ("Carpenter experienced acute stress"). To a psychologist, the terrifying truck ride was a *stressor.* Carpenter's physical and emotional responses were a *stress reaction.* And the process by which he related to the threat was *stress.* Stress often arises less from events themselves than from how we appraise them (Lazarus, 1998). One person, alone in a house, ignores its creaking sounds and experiences no stress; someone else suspects an intruder and becomes alarmed. One person regards a new job as a welcome challenge; someone else appraises it as risking failure.

Stressful event
(tough math test)

Appraisal

Threat
("Yikes! This is beyond me!")

Challenge
("I've got to apply all I know.")

Response

Stressed to distraction

Aroused, focused

Fuse/Getty Images

FIGURE 38.1
Stress appraisal The events of our lives flow through a psychological filter. How we appraise an event influences how much stress we experience and how effectively we respond.

⊕ **FIGURE 38.2**
Perceived Stress Scale

Perceived Stress Scale

The questions in this scale ask about your feelings and thoughts *during the last month*. In each case, indicate how often you felt or thought a certain way.

0	1	2	3	4
Never	**Almost never**	**Sometimes**	**Fairly often**	**Very often**

In the last month...

1. ___ ...how often have you been upset because of something that happened unexpectedly?
2. ___ ...how often have you felt that you were unable to control the important things in your life?
3. ___ ...how often have you felt nervous and "stressed"?
4. ___ ...how often have you felt confident about your ability to handle your personal problems?
5. ___ ...how often have you felt that things were going your way?
6. ___ ...how often have you found that you could not cope with all the things you had to do?
7. ___ ...how often have you been able to control irritations in your life?
8. ___ ...how often have you felt that you were on top of things?
9. ___ ...how often have you been angered because of things that were outside of your control?
10. ___ ...how often have you felt difficulties were piling up so high that you could not overcome them?

SCORING:
- First, reverse your scores for questions 4, 5, 7, and 8.
  On these four questions, change the scores like this: 0 = 4, 1 = 3, 2 = 2, 3 = 1, 4 = 0.
- Next, add up your scores to get a **total score**.
- Scores range from 0 to 40, with higher scores indicating higher perceived stress.
- Scores ranging from 0-13 would be considered *low perceived stress*.
- Scores ranging from 14-26 would be considered *moderate perceived stress*.
- Scores ranging from 27-40 would be considered *high perceived stress*.

Scale data from Cohen, S., Kamarck, T., & Mermelstein, R. (1983). A global measure of perceived stress. *Journal of Health and Social Behavior, 24*, 385-396.

When short-lived, or when perceived as challenges, stressors can have positive effects. A momentary stress can mobilize the immune system for fending off infections and healing wounds (Segerstrom, 2007). Stress also arouses and motivates us to conquer problems. In a Gallup World Poll, those who were stressed but not depressed reported being energized and satisfied with their lives. This is the opposite of the lethargy reported by those who were depressed but not stressed (Ng & Feldman, 2009). Championship athletes, successful entertainers, motivated students, and great teachers and leaders all thrive and excel when aroused by a challenge (Blascovich & Mendes, 2010; Wang et al., 2015). In games and athletic contests, the stress of not knowing who will win makes the competition enjoyable (Abuhamdeh et al., 2015). Having conquered cancer or rebounded from a lost job, some people emerge with stronger self-esteem and a deepened spirituality and sense of purpose. Indeed, experiencing some stress early in life builds *resilience* (Seery, 2011). Adversity can produce growth.

But extreme or prolonged stress can harm us. Stress can trigger risky decisions and unhealthy behaviors (Cohen et al., 2016; Starcke & Brand, 2016). And stress can affect health directly, increasing infectious-disease-related deaths (Hamer et al., 2019). Pregnant women with overactive stress systems tend to have shorter pregnancies, which pose health risks for their infants (Guardino et al., 2016). What is your perceived stress level (**FIGURE 38.2**)?

There is an interplay between our head and our health. That isn't surprising: *Mind and body interact; everything psychological is simultaneously physiological*. Before exploring that interplay, let's look more closely at stressors and stress reactions.

Stressors—Things That Push Our Buttons

Stressors fall into three main types: catastrophes, significant life changes, and daily hassles (including social stress). All can be toxic.

CATASTROPHES Catastrophes are large-scale disasters: think earthquakes, hurricanes, wildfires, wars. After such events, damage to emotional and physical health can be significant. In the four months after Hurricane Katrina in 2005, New Orleans' suicide rate reportedly tripled (Saulny, 2006). And in surveys taken in the three weeks after the 9/11 terrorist attacks, 58 percent of Americans said they were experiencing greater-than-average arousal

"Too many parents make life hard for their children by trying, too zealously, to make it easy for them." — German author Johann Wolfgang von Goethe (1749–1832)

and anxiety (Silver et al., 2002). In the New York City area, people were especially likely to report such symptoms, and sleeping pill prescriptions rose by a reported 28 percent (HMHL, 2002; NSF, 2001). Extensively watching 9/11 television footage predicted worse health outcomes 2 to 3 years later (Silver et al., 2013). The 2011 terrorist attacks in Norway triggered a similar uptick in health issues, from heart problems to suicides (Strand et al., 2016).

For those who respond to catastrophes by relocating to another country, the stress may be twofold. The trauma of uprooting and family separation may combine with the challenges of adjusting to a new culture's language, ethnicity, climate, and social norms (Pipher, 2002; Williams & Berry, 1991). Before their morale begins to rebound, newcomers often experience culture shock, leading to stress and inflammation (Gonzales et al., 2018; Scholaske et al., 2018). This *acculturative stress* declines over time, especially when people engage in meaningful activities and connect socially (Bostean & Gillespie, 2018; Kim et al., 2012). In years to come, such relocations may become increasingly common due to climate change.

SIGNIFICANT LIFE CHANGES Life transitions—leaving home, having a loved one die, taking on student debt, losing a job, getting divorced—are often keenly felt. Even happy events, such as graduating or getting married, can be stressful life transitions. Many life changes happen during adolescence and young adulthood. One massive Canadian survey asked people to report whether they were "excellent or good" in their ability to handle unexpected and difficult problems. Adolescents struggled the most (Statistics Canada, 2019). When 650,000 Americans were asked if they had experienced a lot of stress "yesterday," young adults reported the most stress (Newport & Pelham, 2009).

Some psychologists study the health effects of life changes by following people over time. Others compare the life challenges experienced by those who have (or have not) suffered a health problem, such as a heart attack. In such studies, those recently widowed, fired, or divorced have been more vulnerable to disease (Dohrenwend et al., 1982; Sbarra et al., 2015; Strully, 2009). One Finnish study of 96,000 widowed people found that the survivor's risk of death doubled in the week following a partner's death (Kaprio et al., 1987). A cluster of crises—losing a job, home, and partner—puts one even more at risk.

DAILY HASSLES AND SOCIAL STRESS Events don't have to remake our lives to cause stress. Stress also comes from *daily hassles*—aggravating housemates, incessant social media notifications, and too many things to do in too little time (Lazarus, 1990; Pascoe & Richman, 2009; Ruffin, 1993). We might have to give a public speech or do difficult math problems (Balodis et al., 2010; Dickerson & Kemeny, 2004; **FIGURE 38.3**). Some people shrug off such hassles; others cannot. This is especially the case for those who wake up each day facing housing problems, unreliable child care, budgets that won't stretch to the next payday, and poor health. Inequality can likewise take a toll on health and well-being (Piazza et al., 2013; Sapolsky, 2018; Sin et al., 2015). Chronic workplace stress can cause worker "burnout"—feeling ineffective, emotionally depleted, and disconnected (WHO, 2019). Today's stressful feelings can harm your physical health years later—even shortening your life (Chiang et al., 2018; Leger et al., 2018).

Daily pressures may be compounded by prejudice, which—like other stressors—can have both psychological and physical consequences (Benner et al., 2018; Pascoe & Richman, 2009). Thinking that some of the people you encounter each day will dislike, distrust, or doubt you makes daily life stressful. Many transgender and gender-nonconforming people experience the stress of stigma and discrimination (Valentine & Shipherd, 2018). People with a same-sex sexual orientation who face frequent prejudice in their communities die, on average, 12 years earlier than do those who live in more accepting communities (Hatzenbueler, 2014). For many African Americans, the stress of racial discrimination can lead to unhealthy blood pressure and insulin levels, increased risk for brain disease, and sleep deprivation (Beatty et al., 2019; Brody et al., 2018; Levy et al., 2016). And in the aftermath of the 2016 U.S. presidential election, 7 in 10 African Americans and nearly 6 in 10 Asian Americans and Hispanic Americans said the outcome was, for them, a source of stress (APA, 2017).

Stress also arises from the daily conflicts we face between our different **approach and avoidance motives** (Lewin, 1935; Hovland & Sears, 1938). Least stressful are the *approach-approach* conflicts, in which two attractive but incompatible goals pull us—to go to a

Scott Olson/Getty Images

A hurricane of stress and destruction
Unpredictable large-scale events trigger significant levels of stress. Hurricane Michael raged across Central America and the Florida Panhandle in 2018, killing 74 people and destroying thousands of homes and other structures. A year later, school district officials noted that the hurricane continued to damage mental health. "The community at large is suffering from trauma and grief," said officials. "Citizens are fatigued . . . and anxious" (Schneider, 2019). (My [ND's] in-laws were some of those who experienced the Florida devastation firsthand, losing their home and possessions.)

approach and avoidance motives the drive to move toward (approach) or away from (avoid) a stimulus.

FIGURE 38.3

Studying stress Most people experience stress when giving a public speech. To study stress, researchers re-create this type of situation. At the end, they *debrief* and reassure each participant.

Participants chew gum so that collecting saliva is easy.

Researcher takes a saliva sample from each participant at the beginning of the experiment to measure levels of the stress hormone, cortisol.

Participant gives simulated job interview speech to a critical panel.

What is 1223 minus 17?

Next, the participant is asked to complete difficult math problems out loud.

Cortisol (stress hormone) levels

High

Medium

Low

Beginning of experiment | After social stress

(Balodis et al., 2010; Dickerson & Kemeny, 2004.)

Measuring cortisol in participants' saliva before and after tells us that although they enter the lab experiencing some stress, that level goes up 40 percent after they experience social stress.

Research team thanks and *debriefs* the participant—explaining the purpose of the experiment and the role she played.

sporting event or out for pizza, to take a dance or music class, to wear the green or the gray hoodie. Other times, we face an *avoidance-avoidance* conflict between two undesirable alternatives. Do you avoid studying a disliked subject or do you avoid failure by doing your reading? Do you suffer someone's wrath for admitting the truth or feelings of guilt for having lied?

In times of *approach-avoidance* conflict, we feel simultaneously attracted and repelled. You may adore some things about your romantic partner but dislike others. From a distance, the goal—a happy relationship—looks appealing. But as you approach that goal, your avoidance tendency may begin to overtake your approach tendency and you feel an urge to escape. Stepping back, the negative aspects fade and you again feel attracted. Stress multiplies when we face several approach-avoidance conflicts simultaneously—whom to date, which courses to take, which job to accept.

The Stress Response System

LOQ 38-2 How do we respond and adapt to stress?

Medical interest in stress dates back to Hippocrates (460–377 B.C.E.). Centuries later, Walter Cannon (1929) confirmed that the stress response is part of a unified mind-body system. He observed that extreme cold, lack of oxygen, and emotion-arousing events all trigger an outpouring of the adrenal stress hormones epinephrine and norepinephrine. When alerted by any of a number of brain pathways, the sympathetic nervous system arouses us, preparing the body for the wonderfully adaptive response that Cannon called *fight or flight*. It increases heart rate and respiration, diverts blood from digestion to the skeletal muscles, dulls feelings of pain, and releases sugar and fat from the body's stores. The sympathetic nervous system helps more with immediate threats (a poisonous snake nearby) than with distant or looming threats (climate crisis). By fighting or fleeing, we increase our chances of survival.

Since Cannon's time, physiologists have identified an additional stress response system. On orders from the cerebral cortex (via the hypothalamus and pituitary gland), the outer part of the adrenal glands secretes *glucocorticoid* stress hormones such as *cortisol*. The two systems work at different speeds, explained biologist Robert Sapolsky (2003): "In a fight-or-flight scenario, epinephrine is the one handing out guns; glucocorticoids are the ones drawing up blueprints for new aircraft carriers needed for the war effort." The epinephrine guns were firing at high speed during an experiment inadvertently conducted on a British Airways San Francisco to London flight. Three hours after takeoff, a mistakenly played message told passengers the plane was about to crash into the sea. Although the flight crew immediately recognized the error and tried to calm the terrified passengers, several required medical assistance (Associated Press, 1999).

Canadian scientist Hans Selye's (1936, 1976) 40 years of research on stress extended Cannon's findings. His studies of animals' reactions to various stressors, such as electric shock and surgery, helped make stress a major concept in both psychology and medicine. Selye proposed that the body's adaptive response to stress is so general that, like a burglar alarm, it sounds, no matter what intrudes. He named this response the **general adaptation syndrome (GAS),** and he saw it as a three-phase process. Let's say you're suffering physical or emotional trauma:

- In *Phase 1,* you have an *alarm reaction,* as your sympathetic nervous system is suddenly activated. Your heart rate zooms. Blood is diverted to your skeletal muscles. With your resources mobilized, you are now ready to fight back.

- During *Phase 2, resistance,* your temperature, blood pressure, and respiration remain high. Your adrenal glands pump epinephrine and norepinephrine into your bloodstream. You are fully engaged, summoning all your resources to meet the challenge. As time passes, with no relief from stress, your body's reserves begin to dwindle.

- You have reached *Phase 3, exhaustion.* With exhaustion, you become more vulnerable to illness or even, in extreme cases, collapse and death.

Selye's basic point: Although the human body copes well with temporary stress, prolonged stress can damage it. Syria's civil war, for example, has taken a toll on the

general adaptation syndrome (GAS) Selye's concept of the body's adaptive response to stress in three phases—alarm, resistance, exhaustion.

High

The body's resistance to stress can only last so long before exhaustion sets in.

Stress resistance

Stressor occurs

Low

| **Phase 1** | **Phase 2** | **Phase 3** |
| Alarm reaction (mobilize resources) | Resistance (cope with stressor) | Exhaustion (reserves depleted) |

⑦ FIGURE 38.4

Selye's general adaptation syndrome
Due to the ongoing conflict, Syria's White Helmets (volunteer rescuers) are perpetually in "alarm reaction" mode, rushing to pull victims from the rubble after each fresh attack. As their resistance depletes, they risk exhaustion.

"We sleep afraid, we wake up afraid, and leave our homes afraid." — 15-year-old girl's Facebook post, describing her family's daily life in war-torn Yemen (al-Asaadi, 2016).

Friendly foes Kara Goucher and Shalane Flanagan were U.S. marathon rivals, but also good friends. Tending and befriending helped them to cope with stress and to excel. During the 2012 London Olympic Marathon, they battled intense rain and physical pain, finishing within 1 second of each other.

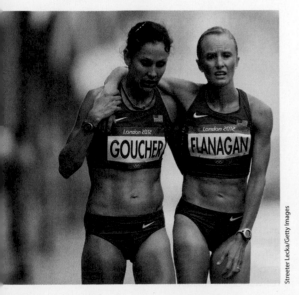

health of its population (Al Ibraheem et al., 2017) (**FIGURE 38.4**). Severe childhood stress gets under the skin, leading to greater adult stress, sleeplessness, and heart disease (Jakubowski et al., 2018; Puterman et al., 2016; Talvitie et al., 2019). In one two-decade-long study, severely stressed Welsh children were three times more likely to develop heart disease as adults (Ashton et al., 2016). Former prisoners of war, who experienced constant stress and suffering, develop shorter *telomeres*—DNA pieces protecting the chromosome ends (Stein et al., 2018). That may explain why, compared with noncaptive soldiers, former war prisoners tend to die sooner (Solomon et al., 2014, 2017). In a study of women who suffered enduring stress as caregivers for children with serious disorders, those who were most stressed had cells that looked a decade older than their chronological age (Epel et al., 2004). Severe stress seems to age people.

We respond to stress in other ways, too. One response is common after a loved one's death: Withdraw. Pull back. Conserve energy. Faced with an extreme disaster, such as a ship sinking, some people become paralyzed by fear. Another response, found often among women, is to give and receive support—what's called the **tend-and-befriend response** (Lim & DeSteno, 2016; Taylor, 2006; von Dawans et al., 2019).

RETRIEVAL PRACTICE

RP-1 The stress response system: When alerted to a negative, uncontrollable event, our _____ nervous system arouses us. Heart rate and respiration _____ (increase/decrease). Blood is diverted from digestion to the skeletal _____. The body releases sugar and fat. All this prepares the body for the _____-_____-_____ response.

ANSWERS IN APPENDIX E

Stress and Vulnerability to Disease

LOQ 38-3 How does stress make us more vulnerable to disease?

It often pays to spend our resources in fighting or fleeing an external threat. But we do so at a cost. When stress is momentary, the cost is small. When stress persists, the cost may be greater, in the form of lowered resistance to infections and other threats to mental and physical well-being.

To study how stress—and healthy and unhealthy behaviors—influence health and illness, psychologists and physicians created the interdisciplinary field of *behavioral medicine,* integrating behavioral and medical knowledge. **Health psychology** provides psychology's contribution to behavioral medicine. A branch of health psychology called **psychoneuroimmunology** focuses on mind-body interactions (Kiecolt-Glaser, 2009; Kipnis, 2018). This awkward name makes sense when said slowly: Your thoughts and

Possible Responses:

Is it a bacterial infection?

Send in:
B lymphocytes, which fight bacterial infections. (This one is shown in front of a macrophage.)

CNRI/Science Source

Intruders!

Is it a cancer cell, virus, or other "foreign substance"?

Send in:
T lymphocytes, which attack cancer cells, viruses, and foreign substances.

NIBSC/Science Source

Is it some other harmful intruder, or perhaps a worn-out cell needing to be cleaned up?

Send in:
macrophage cells ("big eaters"), which attack harmful invaders and worn-out cells. (This one is engulfing tuberculosis bacteria.)

SPL/Science Source

Are there diseased cells (such as those infected by viruses or cancer) that need to be cleared out?

Send in:
natural killer cells (NK cells), which attack diseased cells. (These two are attacking a cancer cell.)

Eye of Science/Science Source

Romariolen/Shutterstock

**⊘ FIGURE 38.5
A simplified view of immune responses** The four types of cells fueling our immune system are the white blood cells *B lymphocytes* and *T lymphocytes,* the *macrophage cells* ("big eaters"), and the *natural killer cells* (NK cells).

feelings *(psycho)* influence your brain *(neuro),* which influences the endocrine hormones that affect your disease-fighting *immune* system. And this subfield is the study *(ology)* of those interactions.

If you've ever had a stress headache, or felt your blood pressure rise with anger, you don't need to be convinced that our psychological states have physiological effects. Stress can even leave you less able to fight off disease because your nervous and endocrine systems influence your immune system (Sternberg, 2009). You can think of the immune system as a complex surveillance system. When it functions properly, it keeps you healthy by isolating and destroying bacteria, viruses, and other invaders. Four types of cells are active in these search-and-destroy missions (**FIGURE 38.5**).

Your age, nutrition, genetics, and stress level all influence your immune system's activity. When your immune system doesn't function properly, it can err in two directions:

1. Responding too strongly, it may attack the body's own tissues, causing an allergic reaction or a self-attacking disease, such as lupus, multiple sclerosis, or some forms of arthritis. Women, who are immunologically stronger than men, are more susceptible to such *autoimmune diseases* (Nussinovitch & Schoenfeld, 2012; Schwartzman-Morris & Putterman, 2012).

2. Underreacting, the immune system may allow a bacterial infection to flare, a dormant virus to erupt, or cancer cells to multiply. To protect transplanted organs, which the recipient's body treats as foreign invaders, a patient's immune system may be deliberately suppressed.

Stress can also trigger immune suppression by reducing the release of disease-fighting lymphocytes. This has been observed in animals stressed by physical restraints, unavoidable electric shocks, noise, crowding, cold water, social defeat, or separation from their mothers (Maier et al., 1994). One study monitored immune responses in 43 monkeys over six months (Cohen et al., 1992). Half were left in stable groups. The rest were stressed by being housed with new roommates—three or four new monkeys each month. By the end of the experiment, the socially disrupted monkeys had weaker immune systems.

tend-and-befriend response under stress, people (especially women) often provide support to others *(tend)* and bond with and seek support from others *(befriend).*

health psychology a subfield of psychology that provides psychology's contribution to behavioral medicine.

psychoneuroimmunology the study of how psychological, neural, and endocrine processes together affect our immune system and resulting health.

⊘ **FIGURE 38.6**
Stress and colds People with the highest life stress scores were also most vulnerable when exposed to an experimentally delivered cold virus (Cohen et al., 1991).

Laurent/Yakou/Science Source

Human immune systems react similarly. Three examples:

- *Surgical wounds heal more slowly in stressed people.* In one experiment, dental students received punch wounds (precise small holes punched in the skin). Compared with wounds placed during summer vacation, those placed three days before a major exam healed 40 percent more slowly (Kiecolt-Glaser et al., 1998). In other studies, marriage conflict has also slowed punch-wound healing (Kiecolt-Glaser et al., 2005).

- *Stressed people are more vulnerable to colds.* Major life stress increases the risk of a respiratory infection (Pedersen et al., 2010). And when researchers dropped a cold virus into people's noses, 47 percent of those living stress-filled lives developed colds (**FIGURE 38.6**). Among those living relatively free of stress, only 27 percent did. In follow-up research, the happiest and most relaxed people were likewise markedly less vulnerable to an experimentally delivered cold virus (Cohen et al., 2003, 2006; Cohen & Pressman, 2006).

- *Stress can hasten the course of disease.* As its name tells us, *AIDS (acquired immune deficiency syndrome)* is an immune disorder, caused by the *human immunodeficiency virus (HIV)*. Stress cannot give people AIDS. But an analysis of 33,252 participants from around the world found that stress and negative emotions sped the transition from HIV infection to AIDS. And stress predicted a faster decline in those with AIDS (Chida & Vedhara, 2009). The greater the stress that HIV-infected people experienced, the faster their disease progressed.

The stress effect on immunity makes physiological sense. It takes energy to track down invaders, produce swelling, and maintain fevers. Thus, when diseased, your body reduces its muscular energy output by decreasing activity (and increasing sleep). Stress does the opposite. It creates a competing energy need. During an aroused fight-or-flight reaction, your stress responses divert energy from your disease-fighting immune system and send it to your muscles and brain. This renders you more vulnerable to illness. Those experiencing the stress of depression tend to age faster and die sooner (McIntosh & Relton, 2018). Even within twin pairs, the less happy twin tends to die first (Saunders et al., 2018). *The point to remember:* Stress gets under the skin. It does not make us sick, but it does alter our immune functioning, which leaves us less able to resist infection.

RETRIEVAL PRACTICE

RP-2 The field of _____ studies mind-body interactions, including the effects of psychological, neural, and endocrine functioning on the immune system and overall health.

RP-3 What general effect does stress have on our health?

ANSWERS IN APPENDIX E

Stress and Cancer

Stress does not create cancer cells. In a healthy, functioning immune system, lymphocytes, macrophages, and NK cells search out and destroy cancer cells and cancer-damaged cells. If stress weakens the immune system, might this weaken a person's ability to fight off cancer? To explore a possible stress-cancer connection, experimenters have implanted tumor cells in rodents or given them *carcinogens* (cancer-producing substances). They then exposed some rodents to uncontrollable stress, such as inescapable shocks, which weakened their immune systems (Sklar & Anisman, 1981). Stressed rodents, compared with their unstressed counterparts, developed cancer more often, experienced tumor growth sooner, and grew larger tumors.

Does this stress-cancer link also hold with humans? The results are generally the same (Lutgendorf & Andersen, 2015). Some studies find that people are at increased risk for cancer within a year after experiencing significant stress or bereavement (Chida et al., 2008; Steptoe et al., 2010). In one large Swedish study, the risk of colon cancer was 5.5 times greater among people with a history of workplace stress than among those who reported no such problems. This difference was not due to group differences in age, smoking, drinking, or physical characteristics (Courtney et al., 1993). Other studies, however, have found no link between stress and human cancer risk (Butow et al., 2018; Petticrew et al., 1999, 2002). Concentration camp survivors and former prisoners of war, for example, do not have elevated cancer rates.

Overstating the link between emotions and cancer may lead some patients to blame themselves for their illness. A corollary danger is a sense of virtuousness among the healthy, who take credit for their "healthy character" and lay a guilt trip on the ill. Dying thus becomes the ultimate failure.

It's important enough to repeat: *Stress does not create cancer cells.* At worst, it may affect their growth by weakening the body's natural defenses against multiplying malignant cells (Lutgendorf et al., 2008; Nausheen et al., 2010; Sood et al., 2010). Although a relaxed, hopeful state may enhance these defenses against the powerful biological processes at work in advanced cancer, we should be aware of the thin line that divides science from wishful thinking (Anderson, 2002). For depressed cancer patients, treating the depression typically improves quality of life—but it does not increase survival rates (Mulick et al., 2018).

> For a 7-minute demonstration of the links between stress, cancer, and the immune system, see the *Video: Fighting Cancer—Mobilizing the Immune System.*

> "I didn't give myself cancer." — Mayor Barbara Boggs Sigmund (1939–1990), Princeton, New Jersey

> When organic causes of illness are unknown, it is tempting to invent psychological explanations. Before the germ that causes tuberculosis was discovered, personality explanations of TB were popular (Sontag, 1978).

Stress and Heart Disease

LOQ 38-4 Why are some of us more prone than others to coronary heart disease?

Imagine a world where you wake up each day, eat your breakfast, and check the news. Among the headlines, you see that four 747 jumbo jets crashed again yesterday, killing another 1642 passengers. You finish your breakfast, grab your bag, and head to class. It's just an average day.

Replace airline crashes with **coronary heart disease,** the United States' leading cause of death, and you have re-entered reality. About 630,000 Americans die annually from heart disease (CDC, 2017). High blood pressure and a family history of the disease increase the risk. So do smoking, obesity, an unhealthy diet, physical inactivity, and a high cholesterol level. Worldwide, coronary heart disease kills more men than women (Bots et al., 2017).

Stress and personality also play a big role in heart disease. The more psychological trauma people experience, the more their bodies generate inflammation, which is associated with heart and other health problems, including depression (Haapakoski et al., 2015; O'Donovan et al., 2012). Plucking a hair and measuring its level of the stress hormone cortisol can help indicate whether a child has experienced prolonged stress or predict whether an adult will have a future heart attack (Karlén et al., 2015; Pereg et al., 2011; Vliegenthart et al., 2016). Cortisol in a fingernail clipping can similarly indicate people's prior stress exposure (Izawa et al., 2017).

coronary heart disease the clogging of the vessels that nourish the heart muscle; a leading cause of death in many developed countries.

Type A Friedman and Rosenman's term for competitive, hard-driving, impatient, verbally aggressive, and anger-prone people.

Type B Friedman and Rosenman's term for easygoing, relaxed people.

In both India and the United States, Type A bus drivers are literally hard-driving: They brake, pass, and honk their horns more often than their more easygoing Type B colleagues (Evans et al., 1987).

"A cheerful heart is a good medicine, but a downcast spirit dries up the bones."
— Proverbs 17:22

◉ FIGURE 38.7

Pessimism and heart disease A Harvard School of Public Health team found pessimistic men at doubled risk of developing heart disease over a 10-year period. (Data from Kubzansky et al., 2001.)

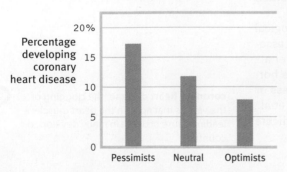

THE EFFECTS OF PERSONALITY, PESSIMISM, AND DEPRESSION In a classic study, Meyer Friedman, Ray Rosenman, and their colleagues tested the idea that stress increases vulnerability to heart disease by measuring at different times of the year the blood cholesterol level and clotting speed of 40 U.S. men who were tax accountants (Friedman & Ulmer, 1984). From January through March, the test results were completely normal. But as the accountants began scrambling to finish their clients' tax returns before the April 15 filing deadline, their cholesterol and clotting measures rose to dangerous levels. In May and June, with the deadline past, the measures returned to normal. For these men, stress predicted heart attack risk.

So, are some of us at high risk of stress-related coronary heart disease? To answer this question, the researchers launched a *longitudinal study* of more than 3000 healthy men, aged 35 to 59. They interviewed each man for 15 minutes, noting his work and eating habits, manner of talking, and other behavior patterns. Those who seemed the most reactive, competitive, hard-driving, impatient, time-conscious, super-motivated, verbally aggressive, and easily angered they called **Type A.** The roughly equal number who were more easygoing they called **Type B.**

Nine years later, 257 men had suffered heart attacks, and 69 percent of them were Type A. Moreover, not one of the "pure" Type Bs—the most mellow and laid-back of their group—had suffered a heart attack.

As often happens in science, this exciting discovery provoked enormous public interest. After that initial honeymoon period, researchers wanted to know more. Was the finding reliable? If so, what was the toxic component of the Type A profile: Time-consciousness? Competitiveness? Anger?

Hundreds of other studies have explored possible psychological correlates or predictors of cardiovascular health (Chida & Hamer, 2008; Chida & Steptoe, 2009). These reveal that Type A's toxic core is negative emotions—especially the anger associated with an aggressively reactive temperament. As their often-active sympathetic nervous system redistributes blood flow to their muscles, it pulls it away from their internal organs. The liver, which normally removes cholesterol and fat from the blood, can't do its job. Thus, excess cholesterol and fat may continue to circulate in the blood and later get deposited around the heart. Hostility also correlates with other risk factors, such as smoking, drinking, and obesity (Bunde & Suls, 2006). Our mind and heart interact.

Hundreds of other studies of young and middle-aged women and men confirm that people who react with anger over little things are the most coronary-prone. In Western cultures, suppressing negative emotions increases depression, relationship problems, and health risks (Cameron & Overall, 2018; Kitayama et al., 2015). Rage "seems to lash back and strike us in the heart muscle" (Spielberger & London, 1982).

Pessimism seems to be similarly toxic (Pänkäläinen et al., 2016). One longitudinal study followed 1306 initially healthy men who a decade earlier had scored as optimists, pessimists, or neither (Kubzansky et al., 2001). Even after adjusting for other risk factors such as smoking, pessimists were more than twice as likely as optimists to develop heart disease (**FIGURE 38.7**). Happy and consistently satisfied people tend to be healthy and to outlive their unhappy peers (Diener et al., 2017; Gana et al., 2016; Martín-María et al., 2017). People with big smiles tend to have extensive social networks, which predict longer life (Hertenstein, 2009). Having a happy spouse also predicts better health. Happy you, healthy me (Chopik & O'Brien, 2017).

As we noted earlier, depressed people tend to age faster and die sooner (Han et al., 2018). In one study, nearly 4000 English adults (ages 52 to 79) provided mood reports from a single day. Compared with those in a good mood, those in a depressed mood were twice as likely to be dead 5 years later (Steptoe & Wardle, 2011). In a U.S. survey of 164,102 adults, those who had experienced a heart attack were twice as likely to report also having been depressed at some point in their lives (Witters & Wood, 2015). And in the years following a heart attack, people with high scores for depression were four times more likely than their low-scoring counterparts to develop further heart problems (Frasure-Smith & Lesperance, 2005). Depression is disheartening.

Do you think you are Type A, Type B, or somewhere in between? In what ways has this been helpful to you, and in what ways has this been a challenge?

See the *Video: Longitudinal and Cross-Sectional Studies* for a helpful tutorial animation. And to play the role of a researcher studying these issues, engage online with *How Would You Know If Stress Increases Risk of Disease?*

STRESS AND INFLAMMATION Depressed people tend to smoke more and exercise less (Whooley et al., 2008). But stress is also disheartening: Work stress, involuntary job loss, and trauma-related stress symptoms increase heart disease risk (Allesøe et al., 2010; Gallo et al., 2006; Kubzansky et al., 2009; Slopen et al., 2010).

Both heart disease and depression may result when chronic stress triggers blood vessel inflammation, disrupting the body's disease-fighting immune system (Miller & Blackwell, 2006; Mommersteeg et al., 2016). People who experience social threats, including children raised in harsh families, are more prone to immune system inflammation responses (Dickerson et al., 2009; Miller & Chen, 2010). So are monkeys that experience the stresses of a low social rank (Snyder-Mackler et al., 2016). Inflammation fights infections. But persistent inflammation can produce problems such as asthma or clogged arteries, and worsen depression (Enache et al., 2019; Sforzini et al., 2019).

Stress can affect our health in many ways. (See Thinking Critically About: Stress and Health.) The stress-illness connection is a price we pay for the benefits of stress. Stress invigorates our lives by arousing and motivating us. An unstressed life would hardly be challenging, productive, or even safe.

A broken heart? Fans were shocked by the unexpected death of Carrie Fisher in 2016 (right), whose most famous role has featured prominently in the latest *Star Wars* reboot. They were shocked again when—the day after the death of her beloved daughter—actress and singer Debbie Reynolds (left) also died. They wondered: Might grief-related depression and stress hormones have contributed to Reynolds' stroke (Carey, 2016)?

Jason LaVeris/Getty Images

Thinking Critically About:
Stress and Health

LOQ 38-5 So, does stress *cause* illness?

- Anger, pessimism, or depression
- ½ empty
- Persistent stressors
- Past due
- pay immediately
- RIP
- You're Fired
- Unhealthy behaviors (smoking, drinking, poor nutrition, sleep loss), which contribute to illness and disease
- Release of stress hormones
- Autonomic nervous system effects (headaches, high blood pressure, inflammation)
- Immune suppression
- 102 F / 39 C
- Heart disease

Stress may not directly cause illness, but it does make us more vulnerable, by influencing our physiology and our behaviors.

* * *

Research on stress and health reminds us that psychological states are physiological events that influence other parts of our physiological system. Just pausing to *think* about biting into an orange wedge—imagine the sweet, tangy juice from the pulpy fruit flooding across your tongue—can trigger salivation. As the ancient Indian text the Mahabharata recognized, "Mental disorders arise from physical causes, and likewise physical disorders arise from mental causes." There is an interplay between our heads and our health. We are biopsychosocial systems.

RETRIEVAL PRACTICE

RP-4 Which component of the Type A personality has been linked most closely to coronary heart disease?

ANSWERS IN APPENDIX E

MODULE 38 REVIEW Stress and Illness

LEARNING OBJECTIVES

Test Yourself Answer these repeated Learning Objective Questions on your own (before checking the answers in Appendix D) to improve your retention of the concepts (McDaniel et al., 2009, 2015).

LOQ 38-1 How does our appraisal of an event affect our stress reaction, and what are the three main types of stressors?

LOQ 38-2 How do we respond and adapt to stress?

LOQ 38-3 How does stress make us more vulnerable to disease?

LOQ 38-4 Why are some of us more prone than others to coronary heart disease?

LOQ 38-5 So, does stress *cause* illness?

TERMS AND CONCEPTS TO REMEMBER

Test Yourself Write down the definition in your own words, then check your answer.

stress, p. 441

approach and avoidance motives, p. 443

general adaptation syndrome (GAS), p. 445

tend-and-befriend response, p. 447

health psychology, p. 447

psychoneuroimmunology, p. 447

coronary heart disease, p. 449

Type A, p. 450

Type B, p. 450

MASTER THE MATERIAL

Test Yourself Answer the following questions on your own first, then check your answers in Appendix E.

1. The number of short-term illnesses and stress-related psychological disorders was higher than usual in the months following an earthquake. Such findings suggest that
   a. daily hassles have adverse health consequences.
   b. experiencing a very stressful event increases a person's vulnerability to illness.
   c. the amount of stress a person feels is directly related to the number of stressors experienced.
   d. daily hassles don't cause stress, but catastrophes can be toxic.

2. Which of the following is NOT one of the three main types of stressors?
   a. Catastrophes
   b. Significant life changes
   c. Daily hassles
   d. Pessimism

3. Selye's general adaptation syndrome (GAS) consists of an alarm reaction followed by _____, then _____.

4. When faced with stress, women are more likely than men to show a _____-and-_____ response.

5. Stress can suppress the _____ _____ by prompting a decrease in the release of lymphocytes, the cells that ordinarily attack bacteria, viruses, cancer cells, and other foreign substances.

6. Research has shown that people are at increased risk for cancer a year or so after experiencing significant stress or bereavement. In describing this link, researchers are quick to point out that
   a. accumulated stress causes cancer.
   b. anger is the negative emotion most closely linked to cancer.
   c. stress does not create cancer cells, but it weakens the body's natural defenses against them.
   d. feeling optimistic about chances of survival increases the likelihood of a cancer patient's recovery.

7. A Chinese proverb warns, "The fire you kindle for your enemy often burns you more than him." How is this true of Type A individuals?

Continue testing yourself with 📚 **LearningCurve** or 📖 **Achieve Read & Practice** to learn and remember most effectively.

MODULE

39 Health and Coping

Promoting health begins with implementing strategies that prevent illness and enhance wellness. Traditionally, people have thought about their health only when something goes wrong and they visit a physician. That, say health psychologists, is like ignoring a car's maintenance and going to a mechanic only when the car breaks down. Health maintenance includes alleviating stress, preventing illness, and promoting well-being.

Coping With Stress

LOQ 39-1 In what two ways do people try to alleviate stress?

Stressors are unavoidable. This fact, coupled with the fact that persistent stress correlates with heart disease, depression, and lowered immunity, gives us a clear message. We need to learn to **cope** with the stress in our lives, alleviating it with emotional, cognitive, or behavioral methods. We address some stressors directly, with **problem-focused coping.** If our impatience leads to a family fight, we may go directly to that family member to work things out. We tend to use problem-focused strategies when we feel a sense of control over a situation and think we can change the circumstances, or at least change ourselves to deal with the circumstances more capably. We turn to **emotion-focused coping** when we believe we cannot change a situation. If, despite our best efforts, we cannot get along with that family member, we may relieve stress by reaching out to friends for support and comfort. Some emotion-focused strategies can harm our health, such as when we respond by eating unhealthy comfort foods. When challenged, some of us tend to respond with cool problem-focused coping, others with emotion-focused coping (Connor-Smith & Flachsbart, 2007). Our feelings of personal control, our explanatory style, our sense of humor, and our supportive connections all influence our ability to cope successfully.

Perceived Lack of Control

LOQ 39-2 How does a perceived lack of control affect health?

Picture the scene: Two rats receive simultaneous shocks. Only one of them can turn a wheel to stop the shocks. The helpless rat, but not the wheel turner, becomes more susceptible to ulcers and lowered immunity to disease (Laudenslager & Reite, 1984). In humans, too, uncontrollable threats trigger the strongest stress responses (Dickerson & Kemeny, 2004).

Any of us may feel helpless, hopeless, and depressed after experiencing a series of bad events beyond our **personal control.** Martin Seligman and his colleagues have shown that for some animals and people, a series of uncontrollable events creates a state of **learned helplessness,** with feelings of passive resignation (**FIGURE 39.1**). In experiments, dogs were strapped in a harness and given repeated shocks, with no opportunity to avoid them (Seligman & Maier, 1967). Later, when placed in another situation where they *could* escape the punishment by simply leaping a hurdle, the dogs displayed learned helplessness; they cowered as if without hope. Other dogs that had been able to escape the first shocks reacted differently. They had learned they were in control and easily escaped the shocks in the new situation (Seligman & Maier, 1967). People have shown similar patterns of learned helplessness (Abramson et al., 1978, 1989; Seligman, 1975).

Perceiving a loss of control, we become more vulnerable to ill health. This is an especially serious problem for older people, who are highly susceptible to health problems and also perceive the greatest loss of control (Drewelies et al., 2017). In a famous study

coping alleviating stress using emotional, cognitive, or behavioral methods.

problem-focused coping attempting to alleviate stress directly—by changing the stressor or the way we interact with that stressor.

emotion-focused coping attempting to alleviate stress by avoiding or ignoring a stressor and attending to emotional needs related to our stress reaction.

personal control our sense of controlling our environment rather than feeling helpless.

learned helplessness the hopelessness and passive resignation humans and other animals learn when unable to avoid repeated aversive events.

Uncontrollable bad events	→	Perceived lack of control	→	Generalized helpless behavior

FIGURE 39.1
Learned helplessness When animals and people experience no control over repeated bad events, they often learn helplessness.

external locus of control the perception that outside forces beyond our personal control determine our fate.

internal locus of control the perception that we control our own fate.

self-control the ability to control impulses and delay short-term gratification for greater long-term rewards.

Loss of control In 2018, new U.S. immigration policies led to thousands of immigrating children being separated from their parents at the southern border. Children taken from parents and held in detention camps lose a sense of control over their own fate. Psychological research suggests that such extreme stress will make these children vulnerable to future physical and psychological problems.

of elderly nursing home residents, those who perceived the least amount of control over their activities declined faster and died sooner than those given more control (Rodin, 1986). Workers able to adjust office furnishings and control interruptions and distractions in their work environment have also experienced less stress (O'Neill, 1993). Such findings help explain why British executives have tended to outlive those in clerical or laboring positions, and why Finnish workers with low job stress have been less than half as likely to die of stroke or heart disease as those with a demanding job and little control. The more control workers have, the longer they live (Bosma et al., 1997, 1998; Kivimaki et al., 2002; Marmot et al., 1997).

Poverty entails less control of one's life, which helps explain a link between economic status and longevity (Jokela et al., 2009). In one study of 843 grave markers in an old cemetery in Glasgow, Scotland, those with the costliest, highest pillars (indicating the most affluence) tended to have lived the longest (Carroll et al., 1994). Likewise, American presidents, who are generally wealthy and well-educated, have had above-average life spans (Olshansky, 2011). Across cultures, high economic status predicts a lower risk of heart and respiratory diseases (Sapolsky, 2005). Wealthy parents also tend to have healthy, advantaged children (Savelieva et al., 2016). With higher economic status come reduced risk of low birth weight, infant mortality, smoking, and violence. Even among other primates, those at the bottom of the social pecking order have been more likely than their higher-status counterparts to become sick when exposed to a cold virus (Cohen et al., 1997).

When rats cannot control shock or when humans or other primates feel unable to control their environment, stress hormone levels rise, blood pressure increases, and immune responses drop (Rodin, 1986; Sapolsky, 2005). Captive animals experience more stress and are more vulnerable to disease than their wild counterparts (Roberts, 1988). Human studies confirm that stress increases when we lack control. The greater nurses' workload, the higher their cortisol level and blood pressure—but only among nurses who reported little control over their environment (Fox et al., 1993). The crowding in high-density neighborhoods, prisons, and college and university dorms is another source of diminished feelings of control—and of elevated levels of stress hormones and blood pressure (Fleming et al., 1987; Ostfeld et al., 1987).

Increasing control—allowing prisoners to move chairs and to control room lights and the TV, having workers participate in decision making, allowing people to personalize their workspace—has noticeably improved health and morale (Humphrey et al., 2007; Ng et al., 2012; Ruback et al., 1986). In the case of nursing home residents, 93 percent of those who were encouraged to exert more control became more alert, active, and happy (Rodin, 1986). As researcher Ellen Langer concluded, "Perceived control is basic to human functioning" (1983, p. 291). "For the young and old alike," she suggested, environments should enhance people's sense of control over their world. No wonder mobile devices and online streaming, which enhance our control of the content and timing of our entertainment, are so popular.

Google has incorporated these principles effectively. Each week, Google employees can spend 20 percent of their working time on projects they find personally interesting. This Innovation Time Off program has increased employees' personal control over their work environment, and it has paid off: Gmail was developed this way.

People thrive when they live in conditions of personal freedom and empowerment. At the national level, citizens of stable democracies report higher levels of happiness (Inglehart et al., 2008). Freedom and personal control foster human flourishing. But does ever-increasing choice breed ever-happier lives? Today's Western cultures may offer an "excess of freedom"—too many choices. The result can be decreased life satisfaction, increased depression, or even behavior paralysis (Schwartz, 2000, 2004). In one study, people offered a choice of one of 30 brands of jam or chocolate were less satisfied with their decision than were others who had chosen from only 6 options (Iyengar & Lepper, 2000). This *tyranny of choice* brings information overload and a greater likelihood that we will feel regret over some of the things we left behind. Do you, too, ever waste time agonizing over too many choices?

Adrees Latif/Reuters/Newscom

INTERNAL VERSUS EXTERNAL LOCUS OF CONTROL Consider your own perceptions of control. Do you believe that your life is beyond your control? That getting a good job depends mainly on being in the right place at the right time? Or do you more strongly believe that you control your own fate? That being a success is a matter of hard work?

Hundreds of studies have compared people who differ in their perceptions of control. On the one side are those who have what psychologist Julian Rotter called an **external locus of control,** the perception that outside forces control their fate. In one study of more than 1200 Israeli individuals exposed to missile attacks, those with an external locus of control experienced the most *posttraumatic stress* symptoms (Hoffman et al., 2016). On the other side are those who perceive an **internal locus of control,** who believe they control their own destiny. In study after study, the "internals" have achieved more in school and work, acted more independently, enjoyed better health, and felt less depressed than did the "externals" (Lefcourt, 1982; Ng et al., 2006). In longitudinal research on more than 7500 people, those who had expressed a more internal locus of control at age 10 exhibited less obesity, lower blood pressure, and less distress at age 30 (Gale et al., 2008). Compared with nonleaders, military and business leaders have lower-than-average levels of stress hormones and report less anxiety, thanks to their greater sense of control (Sherman et al., 2012).

Compared with their parents' generation, today's young Americans more often express an external locus of control (Twenge et al., 2004). This shift may help explain an associated increase in rates of depression and other psychological disorders in young people (Twenge et al., 2010b).

Another way to say that we believe we are in control of our own life is to say we have *free will*. Studies show that people who believe they have free will behave more helpfully, learn better, and persist and perform better at work (Job et al., 2010; Li et al., 2018; Stillman et al., 2010). Across varied cultures, those who believe in free will also experience greater job satisfaction (Feldman et al., 2018). Belief in free will feeds *willpower* or *self-control*—to which we turn next.

Taking control of tragedy Brothers Fatu Matagi (left) and Samoana "Sam" Matagi (right) experienced accidents that resulted in the amputation of one hand for Fatu and both hands for Sam. They took control by learning to live as amputees, which has left them happy and socially connected. "Being an amputee is like being born again—you have to relearn how to do everything," said Sam, whose YouTube tutorials teach others who have lost limbs how to brush their teeth or even play basketball. "I remember that feeling of helplessness and hopelessness. Helping somebody else is good for my soul."

ASK YOURSELF

How much control do you have over your life? What changes could you make to increase your sense of control?

RETRIEVAL PRACTICE

RP-1 To cope with stress when we feel in control of our world, we tend to use _____ (emotion/problem)-focused strategies. To cope with stress when we believe we cannot change a situation, we tend to use _____ (emotion/problem)-focused strategies.

ANSWERS IN APPENDIX E

Extreme self-control Our ability to exert self-control increases with practice, and some of us have practiced more than others! A number of performing artists make their living as very convincing human statues, as does this performer on The Royal Mile in Edinburgh, Scotland.

BUILDING SELF-CONTROL

LOQ 39-3 Why is self-control important, and can our self-control be depleted?

When we have a sense of personal control over our lives, we are more likely to develop **self-control**—the ability to control impulses and delay short-term gratification for longer-term rewards. Self-control predicts good health, higher income, and better school performance (Bub et al., 2016; Keller et al., 2016; Moffitt et al., 2011). In studies of American, Asian, and New Zealander children, self-control outdid intelligence test scores in predicting future academic and life success (Duckworth & Seligman, 2005, 2017; Poulton et al., 2015; Wu et al., 2016).

Strengthening self-control is key to coping effectively with stress. Doing so requires attention and energy—similar to strengthening a muscle. It's easy to form bad habits, but it takes hard work to break them. With frequent practice in overcoming unwanted urges, people have improved their self-management of anger, dishonesty, smoking, and impulsive spending (Beames et al., 2017; Wang et al., 2017a).

Like a muscle, self-control tends to weaken after use, recover after rest, and grow stronger with exercise (Baumeister & Vohs, 2016). Does exercising willpower temporarily gobble up the mental energy we need for self-control on other tasks (Garrison et al., 2019)?

In one famous experiment, hungry people who had spent some of their willpower resisting tempting chocolate chip cookies then abandoned a tedious task sooner than did others (Baumeister et al., 1998a). Although some researchers debate the reliability of this "depletion effect" (Hagger et al., 2016), the big lesson of self-control research remains: Develop self-discipline to help yourself to a healthier, happier, and more successful life (Baumeister et al., 2018; Tuk et al., 2015). Delaying a little fun now can lead to bigger future rewards. And persevering through today's struggles builds an inner strength that enables us to tackle tomorrow's challenges.

Explanatory Style: Optimism Versus Pessimism

LOQ 39-4 How does an optimistic outlook affect health and longevity?

In *The How of Happiness* (2008), psychologist Sonja Lyubomirsky tells the true story of Randy. By any measure, Randy lived a hard life. His dad and best friend both died by suicide. Growing up, his mother's boyfriend treated him poorly. Randy's first wife was unfaithful, and they divorced. Despite these setbacks, Randy is a happy person whose endless optimism can light up a room. He remarried and enjoys being a stepfather to three boys. His work life is rewarding. Randy says he survived his life stressors by seeing the "silver lining in the cloud."

Randy's story illustrates how our outlook—what we expect from the world—influences how we cope with stress. Pessimists expect things to go badly (Aspinwall & Tedeschi, 2010). They attribute their poor performance to a basic lack of ability ("I can't do this") or to situations enduringly beyond their control ("There is nothing I can do about it"). Optimists, such as Randy, do the opposite by expecting more control, coping ability, and better health (Aspinwall & Tedeschi, 2010; Boehm & Kubzansky, 2012; Hernandez et al., 2015). During a semester's final month, optimistic students reported the least fatigue and fewer coughs, aches, and pains. And during the stressful first few weeks of law school, optimists enjoyed better moods and stronger immune systems (Segerstrom et al., 1998). Optimists tend to have optimal health.

Optimists have tended to get better grades because they respond to setbacks with a hopeful attitude that they can improve (Noel et al., 1987; Peterson & Barrett, 1987). Optimists and their romantic partners generally manage conflict constructively, resulting in feeling more supported and satisfied with the resolution and with their relationship (Srivastava et al., 2006). Optimism relates to well-being and success in many places, including in China and Japan (Qin & Piao, 2011).

Consider the consistency and startling magnitude of the optimism and positive emotions factor in several other studies:

- One research team followed 70,021 nurses over time; those scoring in the top quarter on optimism were nearly 30 percent less likely to have died than those scoring in the bottom quarter (Kim et al., 2017). Even greater optimism-longevity differences have been found in studies of Finnish men and American Vietnam War veterans (Everson et al., 1996; Phillips et al., 2009). In long-term studies of nurses and veterans, the most optimistic were 50 to 70 percent more likely than pessimists to live beyond 85 (Lee et al., 2019).

- A classic study followed up on 180 Catholic nuns who had written brief autobiographies at about 22 years of age and had thereafter lived similar lifestyles. Those who had expressed happiness, love, and other positive feelings in their autobiographies lived an average 7 years longer than their more dour counterparts (Danner et al., 2001). By age 80, some 54 percent of those expressing few positive emotions had died, as had only 24 percent of the most positive-spirited.

- Optimists not only live longer lives, they approach their end of life positively. One study followed more than 68,000 American women, ages 50 to 79 years, for nearly two decades (Zaslavsky et al., 2015). As death grew nearer, the optimists tended to feel more life satisfaction than did the pessimists.

Optimism runs in families, so some people are born with a sunny, hopeful outlook. If one identical twin is optimistic, the other typically will be, too (Bates, 2015; Mosing et al.,

---

Test your own self-control with *Assess Your Strengths: How Much Self-Control Do You Have, and Why Is This Worth Working to Increase?* Then consider research-based strategies for improving your self-control by watching my [ND's] 7-minute *Video: Self-Control—Our Greatest Inner Strength* or at tinyurl.com/Self-Control.

"The optimist proclaims we live in the best of all possible worlds; and the pessimist fears this is true." — James Branch Cabell, *The Silver Stallion*, 1926

2009). Optimism also supports healthy genetic expression (Uchida et al., 2018). When encountering stressors, optimists relax rather than get revved up. This leads to lower expression levels of inflammation-producing genes.

The good news is that all of us, even the most pessimistic, can learn to become more optimistic. Compared with a control group of pessimists who simply kept diaries of their daily activities, pessimists in a skill-building group—who learned ways of seeing the bright side of difficult situations and of viewing their goals as achievable—reported lower levels of depression (Sergeant & Mongrain, 2014). In other experiments, people instructed to imagine their best possible future—one where they have worked hard and succeeded in all their life goals—become more optimistic (Malouff & Schutte, 2017). Positive expectations often motivate eventual success: Optimism is the light bulb that can brighten anyone's life.

Social Support

LOQ **39-5** How does social support promote good health?

"We just haven't been flapping them hard enough."

Sam Gross/Cartoon Stock

Social support—feeling liked and encouraged by intimate friends and family—promotes both happiness and health. When randomly prompted by a researcher's phone app, people report more happiness when with others (Quoidbach et al, 2019). In international studies following thousands of people over several years, close relationships have predicted happiness and health in both individualist and collectivist cultures (Brannan et al., 2013; Chu et al., 2010; Rueger et al., 2016). People supported by close relationships tend to live longer (Smith et al., 2018; Whisman et al., 2018). When researchers combined data from 70 studies of 3.4 million people worldwide, they confirmed a striking social support benefit: Compared with those who had ample social connections, socially isolated or lonely people had a 30 percent greater death rate during the 7-year study period (Holt-Lunstad et al., 2010, 2015, 2017). "Loneliness [predicts] a reduction of life span," former U.S. Surgeon General Vivek H. Murthy (2017) bluntly noted, that is "similar to that caused by smoking 15 cigarettes a day."

To combat social isolation, we need to do more than collect lots of acquaintances. We need people who genuinely care about us (Cacioppo et al., 2014; Hawkley et al., 2008). Some fill this need by connecting with friends, family, co-workers, members of a faith community, or support groups. Others connect in positive, supportive marriages. Happy marriages bathe us in social support, leading to less weight gain and a longer life (Chen et al., 2018; VanderWeele, 2017). One seven-decade-long study found that at age 50, healthy aging was better predicted by a good marriage than by a low cholesterol level (Vaillant, 2002). On the flip side, divorce predicts poor health. In one analysis of 600 million people in 24 countries, separated and divorced people were more likely to die early (Shor et al., 2012). But it's less marital status than marital *quality* that predicts health—to about the same extent as a healthy diet and physical activity do (Robles, 2015; Smith & Baucom, 2017).

Jesse Dittmar

Funny business Part of our pleasure in authoring this text—and, we hope, yours in reading it—is finding cartoons that offer comic relief while illustrating and reinforcing psychological concepts. Many have come from the *New Yorker,* whose longtime cartoonist and cartoon editor was Bob Mankoff—a former psychology major who lectures on the psychology of humor and is president of CartoonCollections.com. Mankoff explains: "Humor, like other forms of play, has three main benefits. First, it's physically and psychologically healthy, especially in the way it blocks stress. Second, humor makes us mentally flexible—able to manage change, take risks, and think creatively. And third, humor serves as a social lubricant, making us more effective in dealing with colleagues and clients."

Pets are friends, too Having a pet may increase the odds of survival after a heart attack, relieve depression among people with AIDS, and lower blood pressure and other coronary risk factors (Allen, 2003; McConnell et al., 2011; Wells, 2009). Pets are no substitute for effective drugs and exercise. But for people who enjoy animals, and especially for those who live alone, pets are a healthy pleasure (Reis et al., 2017; Siegel, 1990).

Happy Window/Alamy Stock Photo

What explains the link between social support and health? Are middle-aged and older adults who live alone more likely to smoke, be obese, and have high cholesterol—and therefore to have a doubled risk of heart attacks (Nielsen et al., 2006)? Or are healthy people simply more sociable? Possibly. But research suggests that social support does have health benefits.

Social support calms us, improves our sleep, and reduces blood pressure (Baron et al., 2016; Kent de Grey et al., 2018; Uchino et al., 2017). To see if social support might calm people's response to threats, one research team subjected happily married women, while lying in an fMRI machine, to the threat of electric shock to an ankle (Coan et al., 2006). During the experiment, some women held their husband's hand. Others held the hand of an unknown person or no hand at all. While awaiting the occasional shocks, women holding their husband's hand showed less activity in threat-responsive areas. This soothing benefit was greatest for those reporting the highest-quality marriages. Holding your romantic partner's hand helps you handle stress and improves conflict discussions (Jakubiak & Feeney, 2019).

Social support fosters stronger immune functioning. Stress hampers immune functioning, but social connections strengthen it (Leschak & Eisenberger, 2019). Volunteers exposed to cold viruses showed this effect while being quarantined for 5 days (Cohen, 2004; Cohen et al., 1997). (In these experiments, the more than 600 participants were well-paid volunteers.) Age, race, sex, and health habits being equal, those with close social ties were least likely to catch a cold. People whose daily life included frequent hugs likewise experienced fewer cold symptoms and less symptom severity (Cohen et al., 2015). The cold fact: The effect of social ties is nothing to sneeze at!

Close relationships give us an opportunity for "open heart therapy"—a chance to confide painful feelings (Frattaroli, 2006). Talking about a long-ago stressful event can temporarily arouse us, but in time it calms us (Lieberman et al., 2007; Mendolia & Kleck, 1993; Niles et al., 2015). In one study, 33 Holocaust survivors spent two hours recalling their experiences, many in intimate detail never before disclosed (Pennebaker et al., 1989). Those who disclosed the most had the most improved health 14 months later. In another study, of surviving spouses of people who had died by suicide or in car accidents, those who bore their grief alone had more health problems than those who shared it with others (Pennebaker & O'Heeron, 1984). Confiding is good for the body and the soul.

"Woe to one who is alone and falls and does not have another to help." — Ecclesiastes 4:10

Suppressing emotions can be detrimental to physical health. When psychologist James Pennebaker (1985) surveyed more than 700 undergraduate women, those who had experienced a traumatic sexual experience in childhood reported more headaches and stomach ailments than those who had experienced other traumas—possibly because survivors of sexual abuse are less likely than other trauma survivors to confide in others. Another study, of 437 Australian ambulance drivers, confirmed the ill effects of suppressing one's emotions after witnessing traumas (Wastell, 2002).

Even writing about personal traumas in a diary can help (Burton & King, 2008; Kállay, 2015; Lyubomirsky et al., 2006). In an analysis of 633 trauma victims, writing therapy was as effective as psychotherapy in reducing psychological trauma (van Emmerik et al., 2013). In another experiment, volunteers who wrote trauma diaries had fewer health problems during the ensuing 4 to 6 months (Pennebaker, 1990). As one participant

Laughter among friends is good medicine Laughter arouses us, massages muscles, and leaves us feeling relaxed (Robinson, 1983). Humor (though not hostile sarcasm) may defuse stress, ease pain, and strengthen immune activity (Ayan, 2009; Berk et al., 2001; Dunbar et al., 2011; Kimata, 2001). People who laugh a lot have also tended to have lower rates of heart disease (Clark et al., 2001).

Tim Roberts/Getty Images

explained, "Although I have not talked with anyone about what I wrote, I was finally able to deal with it, work through the pain instead of trying to block it out. Now it doesn't hurt to think about it."

If we are aiming to exercise more, drink less, quit smoking, or be a healthy weight, our social ties can tug us away from or toward our goal. If you are trying to achieve some goal, think about whether your social network can help or hinder you.

ASK YOURSELF

Can you remember a time when you felt better after discussing a problem with a loved one, or even after playing with your pet? How did doing so help you to cope?

Reducing Stress

Having a sense of control, developing more optimistic thinking, and building social support can help us *experience* less stress and thus improve our health. Moreover, these factors interrelate: People who have been upbeat about themselves and their future have tended also to enjoy health-promoting social ties (Stinson et al., 2008). But sometimes we cannot alleviate stress and simply need to *manage* our stress. Aerobic exercise, relaxation, meditation, and spiritual communities have helped people gather inner strength and lessen stress effects.

Aerobic Exercise

LOQ **39-6** How effective is aerobic exercise as a way to manage stress and improve well-being?

It's hard to find a medicine that works for most people most of the time. But **aerobic exercise**—sustained, oxygen-consuming exertion that increases heart and lung fitness—is one of those rare near-perfect "medicines." Estimates vary, but some studies suggest that exercise adds to your quantity of life—about *seven hours longer life for every exercise hour* (Lee et al., 2017; Mandsager et al., 2018; Zahrt & Crum, 2017)—and your quality of life, with more energy, better mood, and stronger relationships (Flueckiger et al., 2016; Hogan et al., 2015; Wiese et al., 2018). Think about it: Nature generously gives a 7-to-1 return for time spent exercising (Myers, 2018). How benevolent!

Exercise helps fight heart disease by strengthening the heart, increasing blood flow, keeping blood vessels open, lowering blood pressure, and reducing the hormone and blood pressure reaction to stress (Ford, 2002; Manson, 2002). Compared with inactive adults, people who exercise suffer about half as many heart attacks (Evenson et al., 2016; Visich & Fletcher, 2009). It's a fact: Fitness predicts longevity (Lee et al., 2011; Moholdt et al., 2018). Dietary fat contributes to clogged arteries, but exercise makes our muscles hungry for those fats and cleans them out of our arteries (Barinaga, 1997). A study of 1.44 million Americans and Europeans found that exercise predicted "lower risks of many cancer types" (Moore et al., 2016). Scottish mail carriers, who spend their days walking, have lower heart disease risk than Scottish mail office workers (Tigbe et al., 2017). Regular exercise in later life also predicts better cognitive functioning and reduced risk of neurocognitive disorder and Alzheimer's disease (Kramer & Erickson, 2007).

"These mountains that you are carrying, you were only supposed to climb." — Poet Najwa Zebian, *The Nectar of Pain*, 2016

aerobic exercise sustained exercise that increases heart and lung fitness; also helps alleviate depression and anxiety.

The genes passed down to us from our distant ancestors enabled the physical activity essential to hunting, foraging, and farming (Raichlen & Polk, 2013; Shave et al., 2019). In muscle cells, those genes, when activated by exercise, respond by producing proteins. We are made for exercise. In the modern inactive person, these genes produce lower quantities of proteins and leave us susceptible to more than 20 chronic diseases, such as type 2 diabetes, coronary heart disease, stroke, and cancer (Booth & Neufer, 2005). Inactivity is thus potentially toxic. Physical activity can weaken the influence of some genetic risk factors. In one analysis of 45 studies, the risk of obesity fell by 27 percent (Kilpeläinen et al., 2012).

Does exercise also boost the spirit? In a 21-country survey of university students, physical exercise was a strong and consistent predictor of life satisfaction (Grant et al., 2009). Americans, Canadians, and Britons who do aerobic exercise at least three times a week manage stress better, exhibit more self-confidence, have more vigor, and feel less depressed and fatigued than their inactive peers (Rebar et al., 2015; Smits et al., 2011). One analysis of 1.2 million Americans compared exercisers with nonexercisers. After controlling for other physical and social differences among them, the exercisers experienced 43 percent "fewer days of poor mental health in the last month" (Chekroud et al., 2018). Exercise has a large antidepressant effect, concluded one digest of 49 controlled studies (Schuch et al., 2018).

But we could state this observation another way: Stressed and depressed people exercise less. Remember, these correlations do not imply causation. To sort out cause and effect, researchers experiment. They *randomly assign* stressed, depressed, or anxious people either to an aerobic exercise group or to a control group. Next, they measure whether aerobic exercise (compared with a control activity not involving exercise) produces a change in stress, depression, anxiety, or some other health-related outcome. One classic experiment randomly assigned mildly depressed female college students to three groups. One-third participated in a program of aerobic exercise. Another third took part in a program of relaxation exercises. The remaining third (the control group) formed a no-treatment group (McCann & Holmes, 1984). As **FIGURE 39.2** shows, 10 weeks later, the women in the aerobic exercise program reported the greatest decrease in depression. Many had, quite literally, run away from their troubles.

> See the *Video: Random Assignment* for a helpful tutorial animation about this important part of effective research design.

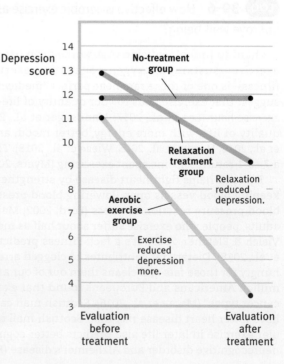

➔ **FIGURE 39.2**
Aerobic exercise reduces mild depression (Data from McCann & Holmes, 1984.)

Dozens of other experiments and longitudinal studies confirm that exercise reduces or prevents depression and anxiety (Catalan-Matamoros et al., 2016; Harvey et al., 2018; Stubbs et al., 2017). When experimenters randomly assigned depressed people to an exercise group, an antidepressant group, or a placebo pill group, exercise diminished depression as effectively as antidepressants—and with longer-lasting effects (Hoffman et al., 2011).

Vigorous exercise provides a substantial and immediate mood boost (Watson, 2000). Even a 10-minute walk stimulates 2 hours of increased well-being by raising energy levels and lowering tension (Thayer, 1987, 1993). Exercise works its magic in several ways. It increases arousal, thus counteracting depression's low arousal state. It enables muscle relaxation and sounder sleep. It produces toned muscles, which filter a depression-causing toxin (Agudelo et al., 2014). Like an antidepressant drug, it orders up mood-boosting chemicals from our body's internal pharmacy—neurotransmitters such as norepinephrine, serotonin, and the endorphins (Jacobs, 1994; Salmon, 2001). Exercise also fosters *neurogenesis*. In mice, exercise causes the brain to produce a molecule that stimulates the production of new, stress-resistant neurons (Hunsberger et al., 2007; Reynolds, 2009; van Praag, 2009).

On a simpler level, the sense of accomplishment and improved physique and body image that often accompany a successful exercise routine may enhance one's self-image, leading to a better emotional state. Frequent exercise is like a drug that prevents and treats disease, increases energy, calms anxiety, and boosts mood—a drug we would all take, if available. Yet few people (only 1 in 4 in the United States) take advantage of it (Mendes, 2010).

The mood boost When energy or spirits are sagging, few things reboot the day better than exercising, as I [DM] can confirm from my noontime biking and basketball, and as I [ND] can confirm from my running.

Relaxation and Meditation

LOQ 39-7 In what ways might relaxation and meditation influence stress and health?

Knowing the damaging effects of stress, could we learn to counteract our stress responses by altering our thinking and lifestyle? In the late 1960s, psychologists began experimenting with *biofeedback,* a system of recording, amplifying, and feeding back information about subtle physiological responses, many controlled by the autonomic nervous system. Biofeedback instruments mirror the results of a person's own efforts, enabling the person to learn which techniques do (or do not) control a particular physiological response. After a decade of study, however, the initial claims for biofeedback seemed overblown and oversold (Miller, 1985). In 1995, a National Institutes of Health panel declared that biofeedback works best on tension headaches.

Simple methods of relaxation, which require no expensive equipment, produce many of the results biofeedback once promised. Massage also helps relax both premature infants and those suffering pain, relaxing muscles and helping to reduce depression (Hou et al., 2010). Figure 39.2 pointed out that aerobic exercise reduces depression. But did you notice in that figure that depression also decreased among women in the relaxation treatment group? More than 60 studies have found that relaxation procedures can also help alleviate headaches, hypertension, anxiety, and insomnia (Nestoriuc et al., 2008; Stetter & Kupper, 2002).

Such findings would not surprise Meyer Friedman, Ray Rosenman, and their colleagues. They tested relaxation in a program designed to help *Type A* heart attack survivors (who are more prone to heart attacks than their *Type B* peers) reduce their risk of future attacks. They randomly assigned hundreds of middle-aged men to one of two groups. The first group received standard advice from cardiologists about medications, diet, and exercise habits. The second group received similar advice, but they also were taught ways of modifying their lifestyles. They learned to slow down and relax by walking, talking, and eating more slowly. They learned to smile at others and laugh

FIGURE 39.3

Recurrent heart attacks and lifestyle modification The San Francisco Recurrent Coronary Prevention Project offered counseling from a cardiologist to survivors of heart attacks. Those who were also guided in modifying their Type A lifestyle suffered fewer repeat heart attacks. (Data from Friedman & Ulmer, 1984.)

at themselves. They learned to admit their mistakes, to take time to enjoy life, and to renew their religious faith. The training paid off (**FIGURE 39.3**). During the next 3 years, those who learned to modify their lifestyle had half as many repeat heart attacks as did the first group. This, wrote the exuberant Friedman, was an unprecedented, spectacular reduction in heart attack recurrence. A smaller-scale British study spanning 13 years similarly showed a halved death rate among high-risk people trained to alter their thinking and lifestyle (Eysenck & Grossarth-Maticek, 1991). After suffering a heart attack at age 55, Friedman started taking his own behavioral medicine—and lived to age 90 (Wargo, 2007).

Time may heal all wounds, but relaxation can help speed that process. In one study, surgery patients were randomly assigned to two groups. Both groups received standard treatment, but the second group also experienced a 45-minute relaxation session and received relaxation recordings to use before and after surgery. A week after surgery, patients in the relaxation group reported lower stress and showed better wound healing (Broadbent et al., 2012).

Meditation is a modern practice with a long history. In many world religions, meditation has been used to reduce suffering and improve awareness, insight, and compassion. Today's technology makes it possible for anyone—regardless of beliefs—to practice meditation. Apps such as Tension Tamer offer users free, guided meditation techniques that can improve their physical health (Adams et al., 2018). Numerous studies have confirmed the psychological benefits of meditation (Goyal et al., 2014; Rosenberg et al., 2015; Sedlmeier et al., 2012). One type, **mindfulness meditation,** has found a new home in stress management programs. If you were taught this practice, you would relax and silently attend to your inner state, without judging it (Goldberg et al., 2018, 2019; Kabat-Zinn, 2001). You would sit down, close your eyes, and mentally scan your body from head to toe. Zooming in on certain body parts and responses, you would remain aware and

"Sit down alone and in silence. Lower your head, shut your eyes, breathe out gently, and imagine yourself looking into your own heart. . . . As you breathe out, say 'Lord Jesus Christ, have mercy on me.' . . . Try to put all other thoughts aside. Be calm, be patient, and repeat the process very frequently." — Gregory of Sinai, died 1346

mindfulness meditation a reflective practice in which people attend to current experiences in a nonjudgmental and accepting manner.

Mellow music Is music a natural anti-stress medicine? One analysis of more than 100 studies showed that listening to music (especially slower tempo music) reduced heart rate, blood pressure, and psychological distress (de Witte et al., 2019). The next time you find yourself stressed, remember that music may help you mellow out.

shapecharge/Getty Images

Furry friends for finals week
Some schools bring cuddly critters on campus for finals week as a way to help students relax and bring disruptive stress levels down. In one study, exam-stressed college students who cuddled with therapy dogs felt less stressed 10 hours later (Ward-Griffin et al., 2018). This student at Emory University is relaxing with dogs and puppies. Other schools offer petting zoos or encourage instructors to bring in their own pets.

accepting. You would also pay attention to your breathing, attending to each breath as if it were a material object.

Practicing mindfulness boosts happiness and lessens anxiety and depression (de Abreu Costa et al., 2019; Lindsay et al., 2018). In one experiment, Korean participants were asked to think about their own mortality. Compared with nonmeditators, those who meditated were less anxious when reminded of their inevitable death (Park & Pyszczynski, 2019). Mindfulness practices have also been linked with improved sleep, helpfulness, and immune system functioning (Donald et al., 2018; Rusch et al., 2019; Villalba et al., 2019). They also increase telomere length, which reduces the risk of cancer and heart disease (Conklin et al., 2018). Just a few minutes of daily mindfulness meditation is enough to improve concentration and decision making (Hafenbrack et al., 2014; Rahl et al., 2017).

Nevertheless, some researchers caution that mindfulness is overhyped (Britton, 2019; Van Dam et al., 2018). Mere solitude can similarly relax us and reduce stress (Nguyen et al., 2018). But the positive results make us wonder: What's going on in the brain as we practice mindfulness? Correlational and experimental studies offer three explanations. Mindfulness

Djomas/Shutterstock

- **strengthens connections among brain regions.** The affected regions are those associated with focusing our attention, processing what we see and hear, and being reflective and aware (Berkovich-Ohana et al., 2014; Ives-Deliperi et al., 2011; Kilpatrick et al., 2011).

- **activates brain regions associated with more reflective awareness** (Davidson et al., 2003; Way et al., 2010). When labeling emotions, mindful people show less activation in the amygdala, a brain region associated with fear, and more activation in the prefrontal cortex, which aids emotion regulation (Creswell et al., 2007; Gotink et al., 2016).

- **calms brain activation in emotional situations.** This lower activation was clear in one study in which participants watched two movies—one sad, one neutral. Those in the control group, who were not trained in mindfulness, showed strong differences in brain activation when watching the two movies. Those who had received mindfulness training showed little change in brain response to the two movies (Farb et al., 2010).

"We don't have a time-out chair in our Classroom Community. That's our mindfulness chair."

And then there are the mystics who seek to use the mind's power to enable Novocain-free cavity repair. Their aim: transcend dental medication.

Emotionally unpleasant images also trigger weaker electrical brain responses in mindful people than in their less mindful counterparts (Brown et al., 2013). A mindful brain is strong, reflective, and calm.

Faith Communities and Health

LOQ 39-8 What is the faith factor, and what are some possible explanations for the link between faith and health?

A wealth of studies—more than 2000 in the twenty-first century's first two decades alone—has revealed another curious correlation, called the *faith factor* (Oman & Syme, 2018; VanderWeele, 2018). Religiously active people tend to live longer than those who are not religiously active. One such study compared the death rates for 3900 people living in two Israeli communities. The first contained 11 religiously orthodox collective settlements; the second contained 11 matched, nonreligious collective settlements (Kark et al., 1996). Over a 16-year period, "belonging to a religious collective was associated with a strong protective effect" not explained by age or economic differences. In every age group, religious community members were about half as likely to have died as were their nonreligious counterparts. This difference is roughly comparable to the gender difference in mortality. Another study followed 74,534 nurses over 20 years. When controlling for various health risk factors, those who attended religious services more than weekly were a third less likely to have died than were nonattenders, and were much less likely to have died by suicide (Li et al., 2016; VanderWeele et al., 2016). In obituaries, mention of a religious affiliation predicted 7.5 years of additional life compared with no religious affiliation (Wallace et al., 2018).

How should we interpret such findings, recalling that researchers cannot randomly assign people to be religiously engaged or not? Correlations are not cause-effect statements, and they leave many factors uncontrolled (Sloan, 2005; Sloan et al., 1999, 2000, 2002). Here is another possible interpretation: Women are more religiously active than men, and women outlive men. Might religious involvement merely reflect this gender-longevity link?

Apparently not. One 8-year National Institutes of Health study followed 92,395 women, ages 50 to 79. After controlling for many factors, researchers found that women attending religious services at least weekly experienced an approximately 20 percent reduced risk of death during the study period (Schnall et al., 2010). Moreover, the association between religious involvement and life expectancy is also found among men (Benjamins et al., 2010; McCullough et al., 2000; McCullough & Laurenceau, 2005). A 28-year study that followed 5286 Californians found that, after controlling for age, gender, ethnicity, and education, frequent religious attenders were 36 percent less likely to have died in any year (**FIGURE 39.4**). In another 8-year controlled study of more than 20,000 people (Hummer et al., 1999), this effect translated into a life expectancy of 83 years for those frequently attending religious services and 75 years for nonattenders.

FIGURE 39.4
Predictors of longer life: Not smoking, frequent exercise, and regular religious attendance One 28-year study followed 5286 Alameda, California, adults (Oman et al., 2002; Strawbridge, 1999; Strawbridge et al., 1997). Controlling for age and education, the researchers found that not smoking, regular exercise, and religious attendance all predicted a lowered risk of death in any given year. Women attending weekly religious services, for example, were only 54 percent as likely to die in a typical study year as were nonattenders.

AlisaNata/Shutterstock   Getty Images/Fuse   Sura Nualpradid/Shutterstock   casejustin/Shutterstock

Georgios Kollidas/Alamy   Georgios Kollidas/Shutterstock   ppart/Shutterstock

Research points to three possible explanations for the religiosity-longevity correlation (**FIGURE 39.5**):

- *Healthy behaviors* Religion promotes self-control (DeWall et al., 2014; McCullough & Willoughby, 2009). This helps explain why religiously active people tend to smoke and drink much less and to have healthier lifestyles (Islam & Johnson, 2003; Koenig & Vaillant, 2009; Masters & Hooker, 2013; Park, 2007). In one Gallup survey of 550,000 Americans, 15 percent of the very religious were smokers, as were 28 percent of the nonreligious (Newport et al., 2010). But such lifestyle differences are not great enough to explain the dramatically reduced mortality in the Israeli religious settlements. In American studies, too, about 75 percent of the longevity difference remained when researchers controlled for unhealthy behaviors, such as inactivity and smoking (Musick et al., 1999).

- *Social support* To belong to a faith community is to participate in a support network. Religiously active people are there for one another when misfortune strikes. In the 20-year nurses study, for example, religious people's social support was the best predictor of their good health. Moreover, religion encourages marriage, another predictor of health and longevity. In the Israeli religious settlements, for example, divorce was almost nonexistent.

- *Positive emotions* Even after controlling for social support, unhealthy behaviors, gender, and preexisting health problems, studies have found that religiously engaged people tend to live longer (Chida et al., 2009). Researchers speculate that religiously active people may benefit from a stable, coherent worldview, a sense of hope for the long-term future, feelings of ultimate acceptance, and the relaxed meditation of prayer or other religious observance. These intervening variables may also help to explain why the religiously active have had healthier immune functioning, fewer hospital admissions, and, for people with AIDS, fewer stress hormones and longer survival (Ironson et al., 2002; Koenig & Larson, 1998; Lutgendorf et al., 2004).

Religious involvement → Healthy behaviors (less smoking, drinking) → Better health (less immune system suppression and fewer stress hormones; greater longevity)

Social support (faith communities, close relationships)

Positive emotions—hope/optimism/coherence (less stress, anxiety)

FIGURE 39.5
Possible explanations for the correlation between religious involvement and health/longevity

📖 To check your understanding of ways to handle stress, engage online with *Concept Practice: Methods of Managing Stress.*

39 REVIEW Health and Coping

LEARNING OBJECTIVES

Test Yourself Answer these repeated Learning Objective Questions on your own (before checking the answers in Appendix D) to improve your retention of the concepts (McDaniel et al., 2009, 2015).

LOQ 39-1 In what two ways do people try to alleviate stress?

LOQ 39-2 How does a perceived lack of control affect health?

LOQ 39-3 Why is self-control important, and can our self-control be depleted?

LOQ 39-4 How does an optimistic outlook affect health and longevity?

LOQ 39-5 How does social support promote good health?

LOQ 39-6 How effective is aerobic exercise as a way to manage stress and improve well-being?

LOQ 39-7 In what ways might relaxation and meditation influence stress and health?

LOQ 39-8 What is the faith factor, and what are some possible explanations for the link between faith and health?

TERMS AND CONCEPTS TO REMEMBER

Test Yourself Write down the definition in your own words, then check your answer.

coping, p. 453

problem-focused coping, p. 453

emotion-focused coping, p. 453

personal control, p. 453

learned helplessness, p. 453

external locus of control, p. 454

internal locus of control, p. 454

self-control, p. 454

aerobic exercise, p. 459

mindfulness meditation, p. 462

MASTER THE MATERIAL

Test Yourself Answer the following questions on your own first, then check your answers in Appendix E.

1. When faced with a situation over which you feel you have little control, you are more likely to turn to _____ (emotion/problem)-focused coping.

2. Seligman's classic research showed that a dog will respond with learned helplessness if it has received repeated shocks and has had

   a. the opportunity to escape.

   b. no control over the shocks.

   c. pain or discomfort.

   d. no food or water prior to the shocks.

3. When elderly patients take an active part in managing their own care and surroundings, their morale and health tend to improve. Such findings indicate that people do better when they experience an _____ (internal/external) locus of control.

4. People who have close relationships are less likely to die prematurely than those who do not, supporting the idea that

   a. social ties can be a source of stress.

   b. gender influences longevity.

   c. Type A behavior is responsible for many premature deaths.

   d. social support has a beneficial effect on health.

5. Because it triggers the release of mood-boosting neurotransmitters such as norepinephrine, serotonin, and the endorphins, _____ exercise raises energy levels and helps alleviate depression and anxiety.

6. Research on the faith factor has found that

   a. pessimists tend to be healthier than optimists.

   b. our expectations influence our feelings of stress.

   c. religiously active people tend to outlive those who are not religiously active.

   d. religious engagement promotes social isolation and repression.

Continue testing yourself with 📖 **LearningCurve** or 📖 **Achieve Read & Practice** to learn and remember most effectively.

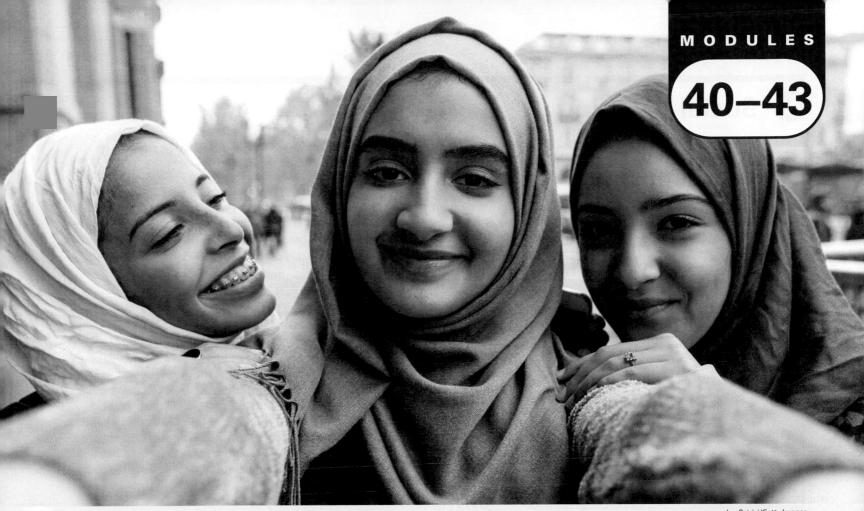

LeoPatrizi/Getty Images

Social Psychology

Dirk Willems faced a moment of decision in 1569. Threatened with torture and death as a member of a persecuted religious minority, he escaped from his Asperen, Holland, prison and fled across an ice-covered pond. His stronger and heavier jailer pursued him but fell through the ice and, unable to climb out, pleaded for help.

With his freedom in front of him, Willems acted with ultimate selflessness. He turned back and rescued his pursuer, who, under orders, took him back to captivity. A few weeks later Willems was condemned to be "executed with fire, until death ensues." For his martyrdom, present-day Asperen has a street named in honor of its folk hero (Toews, 2004).

What drives groups to feel contempt for minority-group members, such as Dirk Willems, and to act so spitefully? What motivates people, such as his jailer, to carry out unfair orders? And what inspired the selflessness of Willems' response, and of so many who have died trying to save others? Indeed, what motivates any of us who volunteer kindness and generosity?

We are social animals. We cannot live for ourselves alone. Many of us felt this keenly with the onset of social distancing during the COVID-19 pandemic. Face-to-face social interaction we'd taken for granted became treasured. *Social psychologists* explore our connections by scientifically studying how we *think about* and *influence* others (Modules 40 and 41), and also how we *relate to* one another (Modules 42 and 43).

40 Social Thinking

Mennonite Library and Archives/Bethel College

An etching of Dirk Willems by Dutch artist Jan Luyken (From *The Martyrs Mirror,* 1685.)

Unlike sociology, which studies societies and social groupings, social psychologists focus more on how *individuals* view and affect one another.

LEARNING OBJECTIVE QUESTION **LOQ** **40-1** What do social psychologists study? How do we tend to explain others' behavior and our own?

Personality psychologists focus on the person. They study the personal traits and dynamics that explain why, in a given situation, *different people* act differently. (Would you have helped your jailer out of the icy water?) **Social psychologists** focus on the situation. They study the social influences that explain why *the same person* acts differently in *different situations*. (Might Willems' jailer have released him under other circumstances?)

The Fundamental Attribution Error

Our social behavior arises from our social cognition. We all want to understand and explain why people act as they do. After studying how people explain others' behavior, Fritz Heider (1958) proposed an **attribution theory:** We can attribute the behavior to the person's stable, enduring traits (a *dispositional attribution*), or we can attribute it to the situation (a *situational attribution*).

For example, in class, we notice that Jill seldom talks. Over coffee, Jack talks nonstop. That must be the sort of people they are, we decide. Jill must be shy and Jack outgoing. Such attributions—to their dispositions—can be valid. People do have enduring personality traits. But sometimes we fall prey to the **fundamental attribution error** (Ross, 1977, 2018): We overestimate the influence of personality and underestimate the influence of situations. In class, Jack may be as quiet as Jill. Catch Jill at a party and you may hardly recognize your quiet classmate.

Researchers demonstrated this tendency in an experiment with college students (Napolitan & Goethals, 1979). Students talked, one at a time, with a woman who acted either cold and critical or warm and friendly. Before the conversations, researchers told half the students that the woman's behavior would be spontaneous. They told the other half the truth—that they had instructed her to *act* friendly or unfriendly.

Did hearing the truth affect students' impressions of the woman? Not at all! If the woman acted friendly, both groups decided she really was a warm person. If she acted unfriendly, both decided she really was a cold person. They attributed her behavior to her personal disposition *even when told that her behavior was situational*—that she was merely acting that way for the purposes of the experiment.

We all commit the fundamental attribution error. Consider: Is your psychology instructor shy or outgoing? If you answer "outgoing," remember that you know your instructor from one situation—the classroom, where teaching demands talking. Your instructor might disagree: "Me, outgoing? It all depends on the situation. In class or with good friends, yes, I'm outgoing. But at professional meetings I'm really rather shy." Outside their assigned roles, professors seem less professorial, presidents less presidential, managers less managerial.

What Factors Affect Our Attributions?

One factor is culture. Westerners more often attribute behavior to people's personal traits. People in China and Japan are more sensitive to the power of the situation (Feinberg, M. et al., 2019; Miyamoto & Kitayama, 2018). In experiments that asked people to view scenes, such as a big fish swimming among smaller fish and plants, Americans focused more on the attributes of the big fish. Japanese viewers focused more on the scene—the situation (Chua et al., 2005; Nisbett, 2003).

Whose behavior also matters. When we explain *our own* behavior, we are sensitive to how behavior changes with the situation (Idson & Mischel, 2001). We also are sensitive to the power of the situation when we explain the behavior of people we have seen

social psychology the scientific study of how we think about, influence, and relate to one another.

attribution theory the theory that we explain someone's behavior by crediting either the situation or the person's disposition.

fundamental attribution error the tendency, when analyzing others' behavior, to underestimate the impact of the situation and to overestimate the impact of personal disposition.

in many different contexts. We more often commit the fundamental attribution error when a stranger acts badly. Having only seen that enraged fan screaming at the referee in the heat of competition, we may assume he is an angry person. But outside the stadium, he may be a good neighbor and a great parent.

Would taking an observer's viewpoint make us more aware of our own behavior? Researchers tested this idea by using separate cameras to film two people interacting. When they showed each person a replay of the interaction—filmed from the other person's perspective—participants credited their own behavior more to their *disposition* (personal character), much as an observer typically would (Lassiter & Irvine, 1986; Storms, 1973). Similarly, when people assess a police officer's actions from the officer's body cam perspective (rather than a dash cam that also shows the officer), they become more attuned to the situation—and become more sympathetic to the officer (Turner et al., 2019).

Two important exceptions to our usual view of our own actions: Our deliberate and *admirable* actions we often attribute to our own good reasons, not to the situation (Malle, 2006; Malle et al., 2007). And as we age, we tend to attribute our younger selves' behavior mostly to our traits (Pronin & Ross, 2006). In 5 or 10 years, your current self may seem like another person.

How Do Our Attributions Matter?

The way we explain others' actions, attributing them to the person or the situation, can have important real-life effects (Fincham & Bradbury, 1993; Fletcher et al., 1990). Does a warm greeting reflect romantic interest or social courtesy? Does a manager's tart-tongued remark reflect a job threat or just a bad day? Was a shooting malicious or an act of self-defense? In one study, 181 U.S. state judges gave lighter sentences to a violent offender who a scientist testified had a gene that altered brain areas related to aggressiveness (Aspinwall et al., 2012). Attributions matter.

Do you attribute poverty and unemployment to social circumstances, or to personal traits and bad choices? In Britain, India, Australia, and the United States, political conservatives have tended to attribute responsibility to the personal dispositions of the poor and unemployed (Dunn, 2018; Furnham, 1982; Pandey et al., 1982; Wagstaff, 1982; Zucker & Weiner, 1993). "People make their own choices. Those who take initiative can still get ahead." In experiments, those who reflect on the power of choice—either by recalling their own choices or by taking note of another's choices—become more likely to think that people get what they deserve (Savani & Rattan, 2012). Political liberals, and those not primed to consider the power of choice, are more likely to blame past and present situations: "If you or I had to live with the same poor education, lack of opportunity, and discrimination, would we be any better off?"

The point to remember: Our attributions—to a person's disposition or to the situation—have real consequences.

> For a quick interactive tutorial, engage online with *Concept Practice: Making Attributions.*

Some 7 in 10 college women report having experienced a man misattributing her friendliness as a sexual come-on (Jacques-Tiura et al., 2007).

"Otis, shout at that man to pull himself together."

An attribution question
Whether we attribute poverty and homelessness to social circumstances or to personal dispositions affects and reflects our political views.

Personal versus situational attributions
Should the 2018 slaughter of 11 Jewish worshippers at Pittsburgh's Tree of Life synagogue be attributed to the shooter's hateful disposition? To social media, where the shooter and like-minded others promoted anti-Semitism and White nationalism? To America's gun culture? (The shooter used four guns.) Or to all of these? And to what should we attribute the compassion of the emergency room nurse—a Jew and the son of a rabbi—who treated the hate-spewing shooter (Flynn, 2018)?

Attitudes and Actions

LOQ **40-2** How do attitudes and actions interact?

Attitudes are feelings, often influenced by our beliefs, that predispose our reactions to objects, people, and events. If we *believe* someone is threatening us, we may *feel* fear and anger toward the person and *act* defensively. The traffic between our attitudes and our actions is two-way. Our attitudes affect our actions. Hateful attitudes feed violent behavior. And our actions affect our attitudes (much as our emotional expressions affect our emotions).

Attitudes Affect Actions

Attitudes affect our behavior. But situational factors, such as strong social pressures, can override the attitude-behavior connection (Wallace et al., 2005). Politicians may vote as their supporters demand, despite privately disagreeing (Nagourney, 2002). Or they may publicly espouse behaviors they don't privately practice (as when one adulterous congressman was said to be "pro-life in the streets, pro-choice in the sheets" [Weiner, 2017]).

Attitudes are especially likely to affect behavior when external influences are minimal, and when the attitude is stable, specific to the behavior, and easily recalled (Glasman & Albarracín, 2006). One experiment used vivid, easily recalled information to convince White sun-tanning college students that repeated tanning put them at risk for future skin cancer. One month later, 72 percent of the participants, and only 16 percent of those in a control group, had lighter skin (McClendon & Prentice-Dunn, 2001). Changed attitudes (about skin cancer risk) changed behavior (less tanning).

Actions Affect Attitudes

Now consider a more surprising principle: Not only will we stand up for what we believe, but we also will more strongly believe in what we have stood up for. Many streams of evidence confirm that *attitudes follow behavior* (**FIGURE 40.1**).

⬄ **FIGURE 40.1**
Attitudes follow behavior Cooperative actions, such as those performed by people on sports teams (including Germany, shown here celebrating a World Cup victory), feed mutual liking. Such attitudes, in turn, promote positive behavior.

Actions

Attitudes

THE FOOT-IN-THE-DOOR PHENOMENON How would you react if someone induced you to act against your beliefs? In many cases, people adjust their attitudes. During the Korean war, many U.S. prisoners were held in Chinese communist war camps. The captors secured prisoners' collaboration in various activities, ranging from simple tasks (running errands to gain privileges) to more serious actions (false confessions, informing on other prisoners, and divulging U.S. military information). After doing so, the prisoners sometimes adjusted their beliefs to be more consistent with their public acts (Lifton, 1961). When the war ended, 21 prisoners chose to stay with the communists. Some others returned home convinced that communism was good for Asia (though not actually "brainwashed," as has often been said).

The Chinese captors succeeded in part thanks to the **foot-in-the-door phenomenon:** They knew that people who agree to a small request will find it easier to comply later with a larger one. The captors began with harmless requests, such as copying a trivial statement, but gradually escalated their demands (Schein, 1956). The next statement to be copied might list flaws of capitalism. Then, to gain privileges, the prisoners would move up to participating in group discussions, writing self-criticisms, and, finally, uttering public confessions. The point is simple: To get people to agree to something big, start small and build (Cialdini, 1993). A trivial act makes the next act easier. A small lie paves the way to a bigger lie. Fibbers may become frauds. Succumb to a temptation and the next temptation becomes harder to resist.

Experiments also reveal a *door-in-the-face* effect: Approach someone with an unreasonable request ("Could you volunteer daily for the next two weeks?"). After you get turned down (the door in the face), a follow-up moderate request becomes more acceptable ("Could you volunteer for the next 30 minutes?").

In dozens of experiments, researchers have coaxed people into acting against their attitudes or violating their moral standards, with the same result: Doing becomes believing. After giving in to an order to harm an innocent victim—by making nasty comments or delivering presumed electric shocks—people begin to disparage their victim. After speaking or writing on behalf of a position they have qualms about, they begin to believe their own words.

Fortunately, the attitudes-follow-behavior principle works with good deeds as well. In one classic experiment, researchers sought permission to place a large "Drive Carefully" sign in people's front yards (Freedman & Fraser, 1966). The 17 percent rate of agreement soared to 76 percent among those who first did a small favor—placing a 3-inch-high "Be a Safe Driver" sign in their window.

The foot-in-the-door tactic has helped boost charitable contributions, blood donations, and U.S. school desegregation. With the passage of the Civil Rights Act of 1964, school desegregation became law. In the years that followed, White Americans expressed diminishing racial prejudice. And as Americans in different regions came to *act* more alike—thanks to more uniform national standards against discrimination—they began to *think* more alike. Experiments confirm the point: *Moral actions strengthen moral convictions.*

ASK YOURSELF

Do you have an attitude or tendency you would like to change? Using the attitudes-follow-behavior principle, how might you go about changing that attitude?

ROLE-PLAYING AFFECTS ATTITUDES When you adopt a new **role**—when you become a college student, marry, or begin a new job—you strive to follow the social prescriptions. At first, your behaviors may feel phony, because you are acting a role. Soldiers may at first feel they are playing war games. Before long, however, what began as play

attitude feelings, often influenced by our beliefs, that predispose us to respond in a particular way to objects, people, and events.

foot-in-the-door phenomenon the tendency for people who have first agreed to a small request to comply later with a larger request.

role a set of expectations (*norms*) about a social position, defining how those in the position ought to behave.

New nurse Pulling on scrubs for the first time can feel like playing dress-up. But over time, that role defines the players, as they jump into the day-to-day work and follow the social cues in their new environment.

"Fake it until you make it."
— Alcoholics Anonymous saying

acting in the theater of life becomes *you*. As *Mad Men*'s Bobbie Barrett advised, "Pick a job and then become the person that does it."

In the real world, step-by-step role playing has even been used to train torturers (Staub, 1989). In the early 1970s, the Greek military government eased men into their roles. First, a trainee played the role of guard outside an interrogation cell. After this foot-in-the-door step, he stood guard inside. Only then was he ready to become actively involved in the questioning-and-torture role. In one study of German men, military training toughened their personalities, leaving them less agreeable even five years later, after leaving the military (Jackson et al., 2012). What we do, we gradually become: Every time we act like the people around us, we slightly change ourselves to be more like them, and less like who we used to be.

Yet people differ. In real-life atrocity-producing situations, some people have succumbed to the situation and others have not (Haslam & Reicher, 2007, 2012; Mastroianni & Reed, 2006; Zimbardo, 2007). Person and situation interact.

COGNITIVE DISSONANCE: RELIEF FROM TENSION We have seen that actions can affect attitudes, sometimes turning prisoners into collaborators and role players into believers. But why? One explanation is that when we become aware that our attitudes and actions don't coincide, we experience tension, or *cognitive dissonance*. To relieve this mental tension, according to Leon Festinger's (1957) **cognitive dissonance theory,** we often bring our attitudes into line with our past actions.

Dozens of experiments have tested cognitive dissonance theory (Levy et al., 2018). Many have made people feel responsible for behavior that clashed with their attitudes and had foreseeable consequences. As a participant in one of these experiments, you might agree for a small sum of money to write an essay supporting something you don't believe in (perhaps a tuition increase). Feeling responsible for your written statements (which are inconsistent with your attitudes), you would probably feel dissonance, especially if you thought your essay might influence an administrator. To reduce the uncomfortable tension, you might start believing your phony words. It's as if we rationalize, "If I chose to do it (or say it), I must believe in it." The less coerced and more responsible we feel for a troubling act, the more dissonance we feel. The more dissonance we feel, the more motivated we are to find and project consistency, such as changing our attitudes to help justify the act.

The attitudes-follow-behavior principle has a heartening implication: We cannot directly control all our feelings, but we can influence them by altering our behavior. If we are depressed, we can alter our attributions and explain events in more positive terms, with more self-acceptance and fewer self-put-downs (Rubenstein et al., 2016). If we are unloving, we can become more loving by behaving *as if* we were—by doing thoughtful things, expressing affection, giving affirmation. "Each time you ask yourself, 'How should I act?,'" observes Robert Levine (2016), "you are also asking, 'Who is the person I want to become?'" That helps explain why teens' doing volunteer work promotes a compassionate identity. Act as if you like someone, and you soon may. Pretense can become reality. Conduct sculpts character. What we do we become.

The point to remember: Not only can we think ourselves into action, we can act ourselves into a way of thinking.

"Sit all day in a moping posture, sigh, and reply to everything with a dismal voice, and your melancholy lingers. . . . If we wish to conquer undesirable emotional tendencies in ourselves, we must . . . go through the outward movements of those contrary dispositions which we prefer to cultivate."
— William James, *Principles of Psychology* (1890)

RP-1 Driving to school one snowy day, Marco narrowly misses a car that slides through a red light. "Slow down! What a terrible driver," he thinks to himself. Moments later, Marco himself slips through an intersection and yelps, "Wow! These roads are awful. The city plows need to get out here." What social psychology principle has Marco just demonstrated? Explain.

RP-2 How do our attitudes and our actions affect each other?

RP-3 When people act in a way that is not in keeping with their attitudes, and then change their attitudes to match those actions, _____ _____ theory attempts to explain why.

ANSWERS IN APPENDIX E

To check your understanding of cognitive dissonance, engage online with *Concept Practice: Cognitive Dissonance.*

Persuasion

LOQ **40-3** How do *peripheral route persuasion* and *central route persuasion* differ?

Often, people may try to influence our actions by *persuading* us to change our attitudes. Persuasion efforts generally take two forms:

- **Peripheral route persuasion** uses attention-getting cues to trigger speedy, emotion-based judgments. One experiment gave some people information that debunked the vaccines-cause-autism myth; others were shown photos of unvaccinated children suffering mumps, measles, or rubella, along with a parent's description of measles. Only those given the vivid photos and description became more supportive of vaccines (Horne et al., 2015). Endorsements by beautiful or famous people can also influence people, whether to choose a political candidate or to buy the latest personal care product. When environmental activist and actor Cate Blanchett urges action to counter climate change disaster, or when Pope Francis (2015) states that "Climate change is a global problem with grave implications," they hope to harness their appeal for peripheral route persuasion. The same is true of advertisements that use heart-tugging imagery to sell products.

- **Central route persuasion** offers evidence and arguments that trigger careful thinking. To persuade buyers to purchase a new gadget, an ad might itemize all the latest features. To marshal support for climate change intervention, effective arguments have focused on the accumulating greenhouse gases, melting arctic ice, rising world temperatures and seas, and increasing extreme weather (van der Linden et al., 2015). Central route persuasion works well for people who are naturally analytical or involved in an issue. And because it is more thoughtful and less superficial, it is more durable. When people actively process a message—when they mentally elaborate on it—they more often retain it (a phenomenon described by the *elaboration likelihood model*).

How can we be more successful at getting others to see our point of view? For more on effective persuasion strategies, see Thinking Critically About: How to Be Persuasive.

Have you found yourself using any of the ineffective persuasive strategies identified in the infographic? How might you improve your approach the next time you are having an important discussion?

RP-4 What are some evidence-based ways to effectively persuade others?

ANSWERS IN APPENDIX E

cognitive dissonance theory the theory that we act to reduce the discomfort (dissonance) we feel when two of our thoughts (cognitions) are inconsistent. For example, when we become aware that our attitudes and our actions clash, we can reduce the resulting dissonance by changing our attitudes.

peripheral route persuasion occurs when people are influenced by incidental cues, such as a speaker's attractiveness.

central route persuasion occurs when interested people's thinking is influenced by considering evidence and arguments.

Thinking Critically About:
How to Be Persuasive

LOQ **40-4** How can we share our views more effectively?

Would you like to be persuasive with those whose views differ from yours?

Do not:

Loudly argue your position before listening. Yelling backfires.

Humiliate people, or imply that they are ignorant. Insults breed defensiveness.

^%*&#!!

idiot

Stupid

#&#!!

Bore people with complex and forgettable information.

Therefore, with that said, direct your attention to this very dull and wonky and boring statistic that you will never remember. Now, however, on the other hand, here are yet more data points that are even more dry and overly complicated than the last... Let us continue...

Do:

Identify your shared values or goals, such as, "We all want to graduate, yes? Find a better job? Let's study for the test before we take time off to hang out."

Appeal to others' admirable motives.
Relate your aims to their yearnings.[1] For example:

"I would like us to **recover the good old days**, when people owned hunting rifles and pistols, but not assault rifles."

"I would prefer to **make a change**, so that in the future people may own hunting rifles and pistols, but no one will have assault rifles."

Political conservatives tend to respond to nostalgia. Those promoting gun safety legislation to this group should frame their message as an affirmation of yesteryear.

Political liberals respond better to future-focused messages.

Make your message vivid. People remember dramatic visual examples well. Pictures of unvaccinated children suffering from preventable diseases, or hungry children starving speak to the heart as well as the head.

Repeat your message. People often come to believe repeated falsehoods, but they also tend to believe oft-repeated truths.

Science
Science
Evidence-based
Science
Evidence-based
Science
Evidence-based
Consider alternatives
Science
Consider alternatives
Evidence-based

Engage your audience in restating your message or, better yet, acting on it. Engage them in actively owning it—not just passively listening.

1. Lammers & Baldwin, 2018.

40 REVIEW Social Thinking

LEARNING OBJECTIVES

Test Yourself Answer these repeated Learning Objective Questions on your own (before checking the answers in Appendix D) to improve your retention of the concepts (McDaniel et al., 2009, 2015).

LOQ 40-1 What do social psychologists study? How do we tend to explain others' behavior and our own?

LOQ 40-2 How do attitudes and actions interact?

LOQ 40-3 How do *peripheral route persuasion* and *central route persuasion* differ?

LOQ 40-4 How can we share our views more effectively?

TERMS AND CONCEPTS TO REMEMBER

Test Yourself Write down the definition in your own words, then check your answer.

social psychology, p. 468

attribution theory, p. 468

fundamental attribution error, p. 468

attitude, p. 471

foot-in-the-door phenomenon, p. 471

role, p. 471

cognitive dissonance theory, p. 473

peripheral route persuasion, p. 473

central route persuasion, p. 473

MASTER THE MATERIAL

Test Yourself Answer the following questions on your own first, then check your answers in Appendix E.

1. A study indicated that most teen boys and girls believe the women they see in online porn are experiencing real sexual pleasure (Jones, 2018). But the situation—being in front of the camera—suggests the women are acting their role. Social psychologists might explain the teens' misperception as the _____ _____ error.

2. We tend to agree to a larger request more readily if we have already agreed to a small request. This tendency is called the _____-_____-_____-_____ phenomenon.

3. Jamala's therapist has suggested that Jamala should "act as if" she is confident, even though she feels insecure and shy. Which social psychological theory would best support this suggestion, and what might the therapist be hoping to achieve?

4. Celebrity endorsements in advertising often lead consumers to purchase products through _____ (central/peripheral) route persuasion.

Continue testing yourself with 📱 **LearningCurve** or 📖 **Achieve Read & Practice** to learn and remember most effectively.

41 Social Influence

Social psychology's great lesson is the enormous power of social influence. This influence stems in part from social **norms**—rules for expected and accepted behavior. On campus, workout clothes are the norm; on New York's Wall Street or London's Bond Street, business attire is expected. When we know how to act, how to groom, how to talk, life functions smoothly.

But sometimes social pressure moves people in dreadful directions. Isolated with others who share their grievances, dissenters may gradually become rebels, and rebels may become terrorists. Shootings, suicides, bomb threats, and airplane hijackings all have a curious tendency to come in clusters. After a mass killing (of four or more people), the probability of another such attack increases for the ensuing 13 days (Towers et al., 2015). Let's examine the pull of these social strings. How strong are they? How do they operate? When do we break them?

> "Have you ever noticed how one example—good or bad—can prompt others to follow? How one illegally parked car can give permission for others to do likewise? How one racial joke can fuel another?" — Marian Wright Edelman, *The Measure of Our Success*, 1992

Conformity: Complying With Social Pressures

LOQ 41-1 How is social contagion a form of conformity, and how do conformity experiments reveal the power of social influence?

Social Contagion

Fish swim in schools. Birds fly in flocks. And humans, too, tend to go with their group, to do what it does and think what it thinks. Behavior is influenced by *social contagion*. If one of us yawns, laughs, coughs, scratches, stares at the sky, or checks our phone, others in our group will often do the same (Holle et al., 2012). Even just reading about yawning increases people's yawning (Provine, 2012), as perhaps you've now noticed?

norms understood rules for accepted and expected behavior. Norms prescribe "proper" behavior.

Tanya Chartrand and John Bargh (1999) call this social contagion the *chameleon effect,* likening it to chameleon lizards' ability to mimic the color of their surroundings. They captured by having students work in a room alongside another person (actually an *accomplice* working for the experimenters). Sometimes the accomplices rubbed their own face. Sometimes they shook their foot. Sure enough, students tended rub their face with the face-rubbing person and shake their foot with the foot-shaking person.

Social contagion is not confined to behavior. We human chameleons also take on the emotional tones of those around us—their expressions, postures, inflections—and even their grammar (Ireland & Pennebaker, 2010). Just hearing someone reading a neutral text in either a happy- or sad-sounding voice creates *mood contagion* in listeners (Neumann & Strack, 2000).

This natural mimicry enables us to *empathize*—to feel what others are feeling. This helps explain why we feel happier around happy people than around depressed people. It also helps explain why studies of groups of British workers have revealed *mood linkage,* or the sharing of moods (Totterdell et al., 1998). Empathic mimicking—as when a conversation partner nods their head as you do—fosters fondness (Chartrand & van Baaren, 2009; Lakin et al., 2008). We tend to mimic those we like, and to like those who mimic us (Kämpf et al., 2018). Just going for a walk with someone—perhaps someone with whom you disagreed—not only synchronizes your movements but increases rapport and empathy (Webb et al., 2017).

Social networks serve as contagious pathways for moods, such as happiness and loneliness, drug use, and even the behavior patterns that lead to obesity and sleep loss (Christakis & Fowler, 2009). On websites, positive ratings generate more positive ratings—a phenomenon called *positive herding* (Muchnik et al., 2013). In a massive experiment on the 2010 U.S. congressional election day, Facebook showed 61 million people a message that encouraged voting, with a link to a local voting place and a clickable "I voted" button. For some recipients, the messages also contained pictures of Facebook friends who had already voted. Those who received "tell your friends you voted" messages were slightly more likely to vote, and that difference generated an estimated 282,000 additional votes.

Suggestibility and mimicry can lead to tragedy. Following highly publicized mass shootings, people are more likely to purchase guns and threaten violence (Cooper, 1999; Porfiri et al., 2019). Spikes in suicide rates sometimes also follow a highly publicized suicide (Phillips et al., 1985, 1989).

What causes behavior clusters? Do people act similarly because of their influence on one another? Or because they are simultaneously exposed to the same events and conditions? Seeking answers to such questions, social psychologists have conducted experiments on conformity.

Conformity and Social Norms

Suggestibility and mimicry are subtle types of **conformity**—adjusting our behavior or thinking toward some group standard. To study conformity, Solomon Asch (1955) devised a simple test. Imagine yourself as a participant in a supposed study of visual perception. You arrive in time to take a seat at a table with five other people. The experimenter asks the group members to state, one by one, which of three comparison lines is identical to a standard line. You see clearly that the answer is Line 2, and you wait your turn to say so. Your boredom begins to show when the next set of lines proves equally easy.

Now comes the third trial, and the correct answer seems just as clear-cut (**FIGURE 41.1**). But the first person gives what strikes you as a wrong answer: "Line 3." When the second person and then the third and fourth give the same wrong answer, you sit up

"When I see synchrony and mimicry—whether it concerns yawning, laughing, dancing, or aping—I see social connection and bonding." — Primatologist Frans de Waal, "The Empathy Instinct," 2009

That contagious laugh Laughter, like yawns, is infectious. That's what "Chewbacca Mom's" (Candace Payne's) viewers discovered after her spontaneous hilarity became, with 164 million views, Facebook Live's most watched 2016 video (tinyurl.com /ThatLaugh).

conformity adjusting our behavior or thinking to coincide with a group standard.

normative social influence influence resulting from a person's desire to gain approval or avoid disapproval.

Tattoos: Yesterday's nonconformity, today's conformity? Steven Pinker (2019) recalls the unnoticed irony of the college administrator who bragged: "Our students are nonconformists. They all have tattoos and piercings."

straight and squint. When the fifth person agrees with the first four, you feel your heart begin to pound. The experimenter then looks to you for your answer. Torn between the unanimity voiced by the five others and the evidence of your own eyes, you feel tense and suddenly unsure. You hesitate before answering, wondering whether you should suffer the discomfort of being the oddball. What answer do you give?

In Asch's experiments, college students, answering questions alone, erred less than 1 percent of the time. But what happened when several others—accomplices—answered incorrectly? Although most people told the truth even when others did not, Asch was disturbed by his result: More than one-third of the time, these "intelligent and well-meaning" college students were "willing to call white black" by going along with the group.

Later investigations have not always found as much conformity as Asch found, but they have revealed that we are more likely to conform when we

- are made to feel incompetent or insecure.
- are in a group with at least three people.
- are in a group in which everyone else agrees. (If just one other person disagrees, the odds of our disagreeing greatly increase.)
- admire the group's status and attractiveness.
- have not made a prior commitment to any response.
- know that others in the group will observe our behavior.
- are from a culture that strongly encourages respect for social standards.

Why do we so often do as others do and think as they think? Why, when asked controversial questions, are students' answers more similar when they raise their hands and more diverse when they use anonymous electronic clickers (Stowell et al., 2010)? Why do we clap when others clap, eat as others eat, believe what others believe, say what others say, even see what others see?

Frequently, we conform to avoid rejection or to gain social approval. In such cases, we are responding to **normative social influence.** We are sensitive to social norms because the price we pay for being different can be severe (Calcutt et al., 2019). We need to

FIGURE 41.1

Asch's conformity experiments Which of the three comparison lines is equal to the standard line? What do you suppose most people would say after hearing five others say, "Line 3"? In this photo from one of Asch's experiments, the student in the center shows the severe discomfort that comes from disagreeing with the responses of other group members (in this case, accomplices of the experimenter).

Standard line   Comparison lines

"I love the little ways you're identical to everyone else."

Like humans, migrating and herding animals conform for both informational and normative reasons (Claidière & Whiten, 2012). Following others is informative; compared with solo geese, a flock of geese migrate more accurately. (There is wisdom in the crowd.) And staying with the herd also sustains group membership.

To review the classic conformity studies and experience a simulated experiment, visit *Topic Tutorial: PsychSim6, Everybody's Doing It!*

belong. People are most conforming to social norms in collectivist cultures, which prize group harmony (Stamkou et al., 2019). People also are responsive to "dynamic norms"—to how norms are *changing,* such as toward eating less meat, consuming less sugary drinks, or supporting gay rights (Sparkman & Walton, 2017, 2019).

At other times, we conform because we want to be accurate. Groups provide information, and only an uncommonly stubborn person will never listen to others. When we accept others' opinions about reality, as when reading online movie and restaurant reviews, we are responding to **informational social influence.** Sometimes it pays to assume others are right and to follow their lead. One Welsh driver set a record for the longest distance driven on the wrong side of a British divided highway—30 miles, with only one minor sideswipe, before the motorway ran out and police were able to puncture her tires. The driver, who was intoxicated, later explained that she thought the hundreds of other drivers coming at her were all on the wrong side of the road (Woolcock, 2004).

Is conformity bad or good? Conformity can be bad—leading people to agree with falsehoods or go along with bullying. Or it can be good—leading people to give more generously after observing others' generosity (Nook et al., 2016). The answer also depends partly on our culturally influenced values. People in many Asian, African, and Latin American countries place a high value on *collectivism* (emphasizing group standards). Western Europeans and people in most English-speaking countries tend to prize *individualism* (emphasizing an independent self). Experiments across 17 countries have found lower conformity rates in individualist cultures (Bond & Smith, 1996). American university students, for example, tend to see themselves as less conforming than others (Pronin et al., 2007). We are, in our own eyes, individuals amid a crowd of sheep.

ASK YOURSELF

How have you found yourself conforming, or perhaps "conforming to nonconformity"? In what ways have you seen others identifying themselves with those of the same culture or subculture?

RETRIEVAL PRACTICE

RP-1 Despite her mother's pleas to use a more ergonomic backpack, Antonia insists on carrying all of her books to school in an oversized purse, the way her fashionable friends do. Antonia is affected by what type of social influence?

ANSWERS IN APPENDIX E

Obedience: Following Orders

LOQ 41-2 What did Milgram's obedience experiments teach us about the power of social influence?

Stanley Milgram (1933–1984) This social psychologist's obedience experiments "belong to the self-understanding of literate people in our age" (Sabini, 1986).

Social psychologist Stanley Milgram (1963, 1974), a student of Solomon Asch, knew that people often give in to social pressures. But what about outright commands? Would they respond as did those who carried out Holocaust atrocities? (Some of Milgram's family members had survived Nazi concentration camps.) To find out, he undertook what have become social psychology's most famous and controversial experiments (Benjamin & Simpson, 2009).

Imagine yourself as one of the nearly 1000 people, mostly men aged 20 to 50, who took part in Milgram's 20 experiments. You respond to an ad for participants in a Yale University psychology study of the effect of punishment on learning. Professor Milgram's assistant asks you and another person to draw slips from a hat to see who will be the "teacher" and who will be the "learner." You draw a "teacher" slip (unknown to you, both slips say "teacher"). The supposed learner, a mild and submissive-seeming man, is led to an adjoining room and strapped into a chair. From the chair, wires run through the wall to a shock machine. You sit down in front of the machine and are given your task: Teach and then test the learner on a list of word pairs. If the learner gives a wrong answer, you are to flip a switch to deliver a brief electric shock. For the first wrong answer, you will flip the switch labeled "15 Volts—Slight Shock." With each succeeding error, you will move to the next higher voltage. With each flip of a switch, lights flash and electronic switches buzz.

The experiment begins, and you deliver the shocks after the first and second wrong answers. If you continue, you hear the learner grunt when you flick the third, fourth, and fifth switches. After you activate the eighth switch ("120 Volts—Moderate Shock"), the learner cries out that the shocks are painful. After the tenth switch ("150 Volts—Strong Shock"), he begins shouting: "Get me out of here! I won't be in the experiment anymore! I refuse to go on!" You draw back, but the stern experimenter prods you: "Please continue—the experiment requires that you continue." You resist, but the experimenter insists, "It is absolutely essential that you continue," or "You have no other choice, you *must* go on."

If you obey, you hear the learner shriek in apparent agony as you continue to raise the shock level after each new error. After the 330-volt level, the learner refuses to answer and falls silent. Still, the experimenter pushes you toward the final, 450-volt switch. "Ask the question," he says, "and if no correct answer is given, administer the next shock level."

Would you follow the experimenter's commands to shock someone? At what level would you refuse to obey? Previously, Milgram had asked nonparticipants what they would do. Most were sure they would stop soon after the learner first indicated pain, certainly before he shrieked in agony. Forty psychiatrists agreed with that prediction. Were the predictions accurate? Not even close. When Milgram actually conducted the experiment, he was astonished. More than 60 percent complied fully—right up to the last switch. When he ran a new study, with 40 new "teachers" and a learner who complained of a "slight heart condition," the results were similar. A full 65 percent of the new teachers obeyed the experimenter, right up to 450 volts (**FIGURE 41.2**). In 10 later studies, women obeyed at rates similar to men's (Blass, 1999).

Were Milgram's results a product of the 1960s American mindset? No. In a more recent replication, 70 percent of the participants obeyed up to the 150-volt point (only a modest reduction from Milgram's 83 percent at that level) (Burger, 2009). A Polish research team found 90 percent obedience to the same level (Doliński et al., 2017). And when a French reality TV show replicated Milgram's study, 81 percent of the teachers, egged on by a cheering audience, obeyed and tortured a screaming victim (Beauvois et al., 2012).

Did Milgram's teachers figure out the hoax—that no real shock was being delivered and the learner was in fact an accomplice pretending to feel pain? Did they realize the experiment was really testing their willingness to comply with commands to inflict punishment? *No.* The teachers typically displayed genuine distress: They perspired, trembled, laughed nervously, and bit their lips.

Milgram's use of deception and stress triggered a debate over his research ethics. In his own defense, Milgram pointed out that, after the participants learned of the deception and actual research purposes, virtually none regretted taking part (though perhaps by then the participants had reduced their *cognitive dissonance*—the discomfort they felt when their actions conflicted with their attitudes). When 40 of the teachers who had agonized most were later interviewed by a psychiatrist, none appeared to be suffering

informational social influence influence resulting from a person's willingness to accept others' opinions about reality.

FIGURE 41.2
Milgram's follow-up obedience experiment In a repeat of the earlier experiment, 65 percent of the adult male "teachers" fully obeyed the experimenter's commands to continue. They did so despite the "learner's" earlier mention of a heart condition and despite hearing increasingly agonized cries of protest after they administered what they thought were greater and greater voltages. (Data from Milgram, 1974.)

Percentage of participants who obeyed experimenter

The majority of participants continued to obey to the end.

| Shock levels in volts |
| "Slight" (15–60) | "Moderate" (75–120) | "Strong" (135–180) | "Very strong" (195–240) | "Intense" (255–300) | "Extreme intensity" (315–360) | "Danger: severe" (375–420) | "XXX" (435–450) |

📖 See the *Video: Research Ethics* for a helpful tutorial animation.

emotional aftereffects. All in all, said Milgram, the experiments provoked less enduring stress than university students experience when facing and failing big exams (Blass, 1996). Other scholars, however, after delving into Milgram's archives, report that his debriefing was less extensive and his participants' distress greater than he had suggested (Nicholson, 2011; Perry, 2013). Critics have also speculated that participants may have been identifying with the researcher and his scientific goals rather than being blindly obedient (Haslam et al., 2014, 2016).

In later experiments, Milgram discovered some conditions that influence people's behavior. When he varied the situation, full obedience ranged from 0 to 93 percent. Obedience was highest when

- *the person giving the orders was close at hand and was perceived to be a legitimate authority figure.* This was the case in 2005 when Temple University's basketball coach sent a 250-pound bench player, Nehemiah Ingram, into a game with instructions to commit "hard fouls." Following orders, Ingram fouled out in 4 minutes after breaking an opposing player's right arm.

- *the authority figure was supported by a powerful or prestigious institution.* Compliance was somewhat lower when Milgram dissociated his experiments from Yale University. People have wondered: Why, during the 1994 Rwandan genocide, did so many Hutu citizens slaughter their Tutsi neighbors? It was partly because they were part of "a culture in which orders from above, even if evil," were understood as having the force of law (Kamatali, 2014).

- *the victim was depersonalized or at a distance, even in another room.* Similarly, many soldiers in combat either have not fired their rifles at an enemy they could see, or have not aimed them properly. Such refusals to kill are rarer among soldiers operating long-distance artillery or aircraft weapons (Padgett, 1989). Those who kill from a distance—by operating remotely piloted drones—also suffer stress, though much less posttraumatic stress than do veterans of on-the-ground conflict in Afghanistan and Iraq (Miller, 2012).

- *there were no role models for defiance.* "Teachers" did not see any other participant disobey the experimenter.

The power of legitimate, close-at-hand authorities was apparent among those who followed orders to carry out the Nazis' Holocaust atrocities. Obedience alone does not explain the Holocaust—anti-Semitic ideology produced eager killers as well (Fenigstein, 2015; Mastroianni, 2015). But obedience was a factor. In the summer of 1942, nearly 500 middle-aged German reserve police officers were dispatched to German-occupied Jozefow, Poland. On July 13, the group's visibly upset commander informed his recruits, mostly family men, of their orders. They were to round up the village's Jews, who were said to be aiding the enemy. Able-bodied men would be sent to work camps, and the rest would be shot on the spot.

The commander gave the recruits a chance to refuse to participate in the executions. Only about a dozen immediately refused. Within 17 hours, the remaining 485 officers killed 1500 helpless citizens, including women, children, and the elderly, shooting them in the back of the head as they lay face down. Hearing the victims' pleas, and seeing the gruesome results, some 20 percent of the officers did eventually dissent, managing either to miss their victims or to slip away and hide until the slaughter was over (Browning, 1992). In real life, as in Milgram's experiments, those who resisted were the minority.

A different story played out in the French village of Le Chambon. There, villagers openly defied orders to cooperate with the "New Order": They sheltered French Jews destined for deportation to Germany, and they sometimes helped them escape across the Swiss border. The villagers' Protestant ancestors had themselves been persecuted, and their pastors taught them to "resist whenever our adversaries will demand of us obedience contrary to the orders of the Gospel" (Rochat, 1993). Ordered by police to give a list of sheltered Jews, the head pastor modeled defiance: "I don't know of Jews, I only know of human beings." At great personal risk, the people of Le Chambon made an initial commitment to resist. They suffered from poverty and were punished for their disobedience. Still, supported by their beliefs, their role models, their interactions with one another, and their own initial acts, they remained defiant to the war's end.

"The Holocaust. . . did not start from gas chambers. This hatred gradually developed from words, stereotypes & prejudice through legal exclusion, dehumanisation & escalating violence." — Auschwitz Museum tweet, 2018

Lest we presume that obedience is always evil and resistance is always good, consider the heroic obedience of British soldiers who, in 1852, were traveling with civilians aboard the steamship *Birkenhead*. As they neared their South African port, the *Birkenhead* became impaled on a rock. The soldiers calmed passengers and helped them onto three available lifeboats—not nearly enough for everyone. "Steady, men!," ordered their officer as the lifeboats filled. Heroically, no one frantically rushed to claim a lifeboat seat. As the boat sank, all left onboard were plunged into the sea, most to be drowned or devoured by sharks. For almost a century, noted James Michener (1978), "the Birkenhead drill remained the measure by which heroic behavior at sea was measured."

Lessons From the Conformity and Obedience Studies

LOQ 41-3 What do the social influence studies teach us about ourselves? How much power do we have as individuals?

How do the laboratory experiments on social influence relate to everyday life? How does judging the length of a line or flicking a shock switch relate to everyday social behavior? Psychology's experiments aim not to re-create the actual, complex behaviors of everyday life but to capture and explore the underlying processes that shape those behaviors. Solomon Asch and Stanley Milgram devised experiments that forced a familiar choice: Do I adhere to my own standards, even when they conflict with the expectations of others?

In Milgram's experiments and their modern replications, participants were torn. Should they respond to the pleas of the victim or the orders of the experimenter? Their moral sense warned them not to harm another, yet it also prompted them to obey the experimenter and to be a good research participant. With kindness and obedience on a collision course, obedience usually won.

These experiments demonstrated that strong social influences induce many people to conform to falsehoods or capitulate to cruelty. Milgram saw this as the fundamental lesson of this work: "Ordinary people, simply doing their jobs, and without any particular hostility on their part, can become agents in a terrible destructive process" (1974, p. 6).

Focusing on the end point—450 volts, or someone's real-life violence—we can hardly comprehend the inhumanity. But Milgram did not entrap his teachers by asking them first to zap learners with enough electricity to make their hair stand on end. Using the *foot-in-the-door* technique, he instead began with a little tickle of electricity and escalated step by step. To those throwing the switches, the small action became justified, making the next act tolerable. So it happens when people succumb, gradually, to evil.

In any society, great evils often grow out of people's compliance with lesser evils. The Nazi leaders suspected that most German civil servants would resist shooting or gassing Jews directly, but they found them willing to handle the paperwork of the Holocaust (Silver & Geller, 1978). Milgram found a similar reaction in his experiments. When he asked 40 men to administer the learning test while someone else did the shocking, 93 percent complied. Cruelty does not require devilish villains. All it takes is ordinary people corrupted by an evil situation. Ordinary students may follow orders to haze initiates into their group. Ordinary employees may follow orders to produce and market harmful products. Ordinary soldiers may follow orders to punish and torture prisoners (Lankford, 2009). Among people abducted into a violent group, those forced to perpetrate violence are most likely to then identify with the group (Littman, 2018). Attitudes follow behavior.

In Jozefow and Le Chambon, as in Milgram's experiments, those who resisted usually did so early. After the first acts of compliance or resistance, attitudes began to follow and justify behavior.

What have social psychologists learned about the power of the individual? *Social control* (the power of the situation) and *personal control* (the power of the individual) interact. Much as water dissolves salt but not sand, so rotten situations turn some people into bad apples while others resist (Johnson, 2007).

"All evil begins with 15 volts."
— Philip Zimbardo, Stanford lecture, 2010

"I was only following orders." — Adolf Eichmann, Director of Nazi deportation of Jews to concentration camps

Minority influence To be August Landmesser, standing defiantly with arms folded as everyone else salutes their allegiance to the Nazi Party and Adolf Hitler, requires extraordinary courage. But sometimes such individuals have inspired others, demonstrating the power of minority influence.

When feeling pressured, some people react by doing the opposite of what is expected (Rosenberg & Siegel, 2018). The power of one or two individuals to sway majorities is *minority influence* (Moscovici, 1985). One research finding repeatedly stands out. When you are the minority, you are far more likely to sway the majority if you hold firmly to your position and don't waffle. This tactic won't make you popular, but it may make you influential, especially if your self-confidence stimulates others to consider why you react as you do. Even when a minority's influence is not yet visible, people may privately develop sympathy for the minority position and rethink their views (Wood et al., 1994).

The power of one In August, 2018, 15-year-old Greta Thunberg sat alone outside the Swedish Parliament—the first school strike protesting climate change. Thirteen months after her act ignited a movement, some 4 million people worldwide joined her for the September, 2019, climate strike, and *Time* magazine honored her as their 2019 Person of the Year.

The powers of social influence are enormous, but so are the powers of the committed individual. Were this not so, communism would have remained an obscure theory, Christianity would be a small Middle Eastern sect, and Rosa Parks' refusal to sit at the back of the bus would not have ignited the U.S. civil rights movement. Social forces matter. But individuals matter, too.

> **RETRIEVAL PRACTICE**

RP-2 Psychology's most famous obedience experiments, in which most participants obeyed an authority figure's demands to inflict presumed painful, dangerous shocks on an innocent participant, were conducted by social psychologist _____ _____.

RP-3 What situations have researchers found to be most likely to encourage obedience in participants?

ANSWERS IN APPENDIX E

Group Behavior

LOQ 41-4 How does the presence of others influence our actions, via social facilitation, social loafing, and deindividuation?

Imagine standing in a room holding a fishing pole. Your task is to wind the reel as fast as you can. On some occasions you wind in the presence of another participant, who is also winding as fast as possible. Will the other's presence affect your own performance?

In one of social psychology's first experiments, Norman Triplett (1898) reported that adolescents would wind a fishing reel faster in the presence of someone doing the same thing. Although a modern reanalysis revealed that the difference was modest (Stroebe, 2012), Triplett inspired later social psychologists to study how others' presence affects our behavior. Group influences operate both in simple groups—one person in the presence of another—and in more complex groups.

Social Facilitation

Triplett's claim—of strengthened performance in others' presence—is called **social facilitation.** But further studies revealed that the truth is more complicated: The presence of others strengthens our most *likely* response—the correct one on an easy task, an incorrect one on a difficult task (Guerin, 1986; Zajonc, 1965). Why? Because when others observe us, we become aroused, and this arousal amplifies our reactions. Perhaps you, like most people, tend to eat more when eating with others (Ruddock et al., 2019)? Or consider the expert pool players who made 71 percent of their shots when alone, and 80 percent when four people came to watch them (Michaels et al., 1982). Poor shooters, who made 36 percent of their shots when alone, made only 25 percent when watched.

The energizing effect of an enthusiastic audience helps explain the home-team advantage. Studies of more than a quarter-million college and professional athletic events in various countries show that the home-team advantage—which has been 54 percent in Major League Baseball games, 60 percent in National Basketball Association games, and 63 percent in English Premier League soccer games—is real (Allen & Jones, 2014; Jamieson, 2010; Moskowitz & Wertheim, 2011).

The point to remember: What you do well, you are likely to do even better in front of an audience, especially a friendly audience. What you normally find difficult may seem all but impossible when you are being watched.

Social facilitation also helps explain a funny effect of crowding. Comedians know that a "good house" is a full one. What they may not know is that crowding triggers arousal. Comedy routines that are mildly amusing in an uncrowded room seem funnier in a densely packed room (Aiello et al., 1983; Freedman & Perlick, 1979). When seated close to one another, people like a friendly person even more and an unfriendly person even less (Schiffenbauer & Schiavo, 1976; Storms & Thomas, 1977). So, to energize your next event, choose a room or set up seating that will just barely accommodate everyone.

Social Loafing

Social facilitation experiments test the effect of others' presence on the performance of an individual task, such as shooting pool. But what happens when people perform as a group—say, in a team tug-of-war? Would you exert more, less, or the same effort as in a one-on-one match?

To find out, a University of Massachusetts research team asked blindfolded students "to pull as hard as [they] can" on a rope. When they fooled the students into believing three others were also pulling behind them, students exerted only 82 percent as much effort as when they knew they were pulling alone (Ingham et al., 1974). And consider what happened when blindfolded people seated in a group clapped or shouted as loudly as they could while hearing (through headphones) other people clapping or shouting loudly (Latané, 1981). When they thought they were part of a group effort, the participants produced about one-third less noise than when clapping or shouting "alone."

This diminished effort is called **social loafing** (Jackson & Williams, 1988; Latané, 1981). Experiments in the United States, India, Thailand, Japan, China, and Taiwan have found

social facilitation in the presence of others, improved performance on simple or well-learned tasks, and worsened performance on difficult tasks.

social loafing the tendency for people in a group to exert less effort when pooling their efforts toward attaining a common goal than when individually accountable.

Social facilitation Skilled athletes often find they are "on" before an audience. What they do well, they do even better when people are watching.

Hope College

social loafing on various tasks, though it was especially common among men in individualist cultures (Karau & Williams, 1993). What causes social loafing? When people act as part of a group, they may

- *feel less accountable* and therefore worry less about what others think.
- *view individual contributions as dispensable* (Harkins & Szymanski, 1989; Kerr & Bruun, 1983).
- *overestimate their own contributions,* downplaying others' efforts (Schroeder et al., 2016).
- *free ride on others' efforts.* Unless highly motivated and strongly identified with the group, people may slack off (as you perhaps have observed on group assignments)—especially when they share equally in the benefits, regardless of how much they contribute.

> **ASK YOURSELF**
>
> What steps could you take to reduce social loafing in your next group project assignment?

Deindividuation

We've seen that the presence of others can arouse people (social facilitation), or it can diminish their feelings of responsibility (social loafing). But sometimes the presence of others does both. The uninhibited behavior that results can range from a food fight to vandalism or rioting. This process of losing self-awareness and self-restraint, called **deindividuation,** often occurs when group participation makes people both *aroused* and *anonymous.* Compared with identifiable women in a control group, New York University women dressed in depersonalizing Ku Klux Klan–style hoods delivered twice as much presumed electric shock to a victim (Zimbardo, 1970).

Deindividuation thrives in many settings. Internet anonymity enables people to feed and freely express their anger, sometimes with bullying and hate speech (Chetty & Alathur, 2018; Kowalski et al., 2018; Zych et al., 2018). Online trolls, illustrating the dark side of free speech, report enjoying their unleashed abuse of others (Buckels et al., 2014; Sest & March, 2017). They might never say "You're disgusting!" to someone's face, but they can hide behind their anonymity online. Tribal warriors wearing face paints or masks are more likely than those with exposed faces to kill, torture, or mutilate captured enemies (Watson, 1973). When we shed self-awareness and self-restraint—whether in a mob, at a concert, at a ball game, or at worship—we become more responsive to the group experience, bad or good. For a comparison of social facilitation, social loafing, and deindividuation, see **TABLE 41.1.**

* * *

We have examined the conditions under which the *presence* of others can motivate people to exert themselves or tempt them to free ride on the efforts of others, make easy tasks easier and difficult tasks harder, and enhance humor or fuel mob violence. Research also shows that *interacting* with others can similarly have both bad and good effects.

Deindividuation In the excitement that followed the Philadelphia Eagles winning their first National Football League Super Bowl in 2018, some fans, disinhibited by social arousal and the anonymity provided by their "underdog" masks, became destructive.

Jessica Kourkounis/Reuters/Newscom

"**Groups tend to be more immoral than individuals.**" — Martin Luther King, Jr., "Letter from Birmingham Jail," 1963

→ **deindividuation** the loss of self-awareness and self-restraint occurring in group situations that foster arousal and anonymity.

group polarization the enhancement of a group's prevailing inclinations through discussion within the group.

TABLE 41.1 Behavior in the Presence of Others: Three Phenomena

Phenomenon	Social context	Psychological effect of others' presence	Behavioral effect
Social facilitation	Individual being observed	Increased arousal	Amplified dominant behavior, such as doing better what one does well, or doing worse what is difficult
Social loafing	Group projects	Diminished feelings of responsibility when not individually accountable	Decreased effort
Deindividuation	Group setting that fosters arousal and anonymity	Reduced self-awareness	Lowered self-restraint

Group Polarization

LOQ 41-5 How can group interaction enable group polarization?

We live in an increasingly polarized world. The Middle East is torn by warring factions. The European Union is struggling with nationalist divisions. In 1990, a one-minute speech in the U.S. Congress would enable you to guess the speaker's party just 55 percent of the time; by 2009, partisanship was evident 83 percent of the time (Gentzkow et al., 2016). In 2016, for the first time in survey history, most U.S. Republicans and Democrats reported having "*very* unfavorable" views of the other party (Doherty & Kiley, 2016). And a record 77 percent of Americans perceived their nation as divided (Jones, 2016).

A powerful principle helps us understand this increasing polarization: The beliefs and attitudes we bring to a group grow stronger as we discuss them with like-minded others. This process, called **group polarization,** can have beneficial results, as when low-prejudice students become even more accepting while discussing racial issues. As George Bishop and I [DM] discovered, it can also be socially toxic, as when high-prejudice students who discuss racial issues together become *more* prejudiced (Myers & Bishop, 1970) (**FIGURE 41.3**). Our repeated finding: Like minds polarize.

Analyses of terrorist organizations reveal that the terrorist mentality emerges slowly among those who share a grievance (McCauley, 2002; McCauley & Segal, 1987; Merari, 2002). As susceptible individuals interact in isolation (sometimes with other "brothers" and "sisters" in camps or in prisons), their views grow more and more extreme. Increasingly, they categorize the world as "us" against "them" (Chulov, 2014; Moghaddam, 2005). Knowing that group polarization occurs when like-minded people segregate, a 2006 U.S. National Intelligence estimate speculated that "the operational threat from self-radicalized cells will grow."

The internet offers us a connected global world, yet also provides an easily accessible medium for group polarization. When I [DM] got my start in social psychology with experiments on group polarization, I never imagined the potential power of polarization in *virtual* groups. Progressives friend progressives and share links to sites that affirm their shared views. Conservatives connect with conservatives and likewise share conservative perspectives. With news feeds and retweets, we fuel one another with information—and misinformation—and click on content we agree with (Hills, 2019). Thus, within the internet's echo chamber of the like-minded, views become more extreme. Suspicion becomes conviction. Disagreements with the other tribe can escalate to demonization. In 2018, an American man sent over a dozen pipe bombs to prominent Democrats and their perceived supporters after venting his partisan resentments on the internet, which "echoed them back. It validated and cultivated them. It took something dark and colored it darker still" (Bruni, 2018).

Mindful of the viral false news phenomenon, tech companies are working on ways to promote media literacy. For more on the internet's role in group polarization—toward ends that are good as well as bad—see Thinking Critically About: The Internet as Social Amplifier.

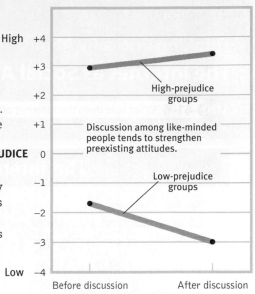

↑ FIGURE 41.3
Group polarization

"Dear Satan, thank you for having my internet news feeds tailored especially for ME!"
— Comedian Steve Martin, 2016

Toxic group polarization As illustrated in this 2017 Charlottesville, Virginia, White nationalist rally, the interaction of like minds—both online and face-to-face—can strengthen preexisting attitudes. The 2019 U.S. Department of Homeland Security's *Strategic Framework for Countering Terrorism and Targeted Violence* declared, "Similar to how ISIS inspired and connected with potential radical Islamist terrorists, white supremacist violent extremists connect with like-minded individuals online."

Thinking Critically About:

The Internet as Social Amplifier

LOQ **41-6** What role does the internet play in group polarization?

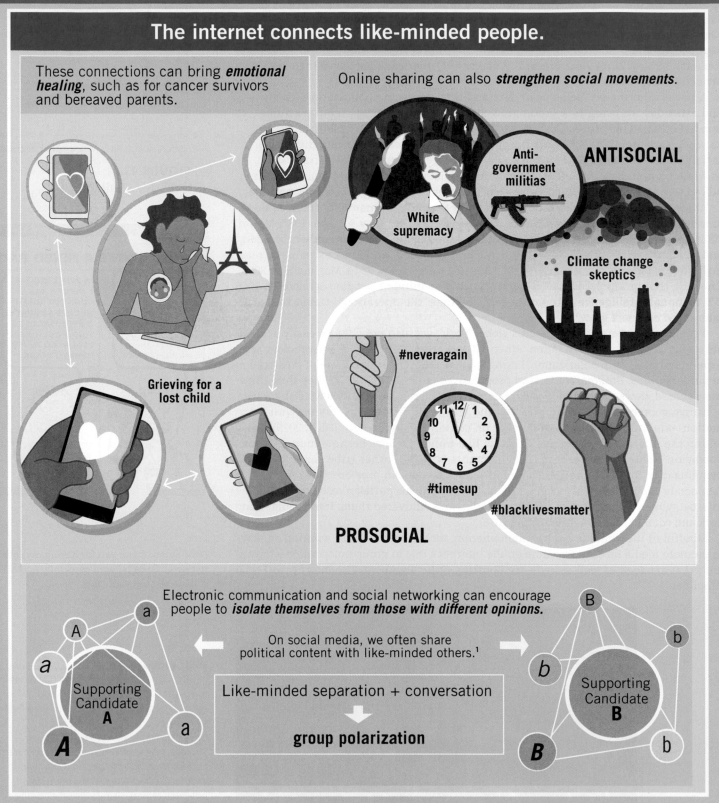

The internet connects like-minded people.

These connections can bring *emotional healing*, such as for cancer survivors and bereaved parents.

Grieving for a lost child

Online sharing can also *strengthen social movements*.

White supremacy

Anti-government militias

ANTISOCIAL

Climate change skeptics

#neveragain

#timesup

#blacklivesmatter

PROSOCIAL

Electronic communication and social networking can encourage people to *isolate themselves from those with different opinions.*

On social media, we often share political content with like-minded others.[1]

Like-minded separation + conversation

group polarization

A a a a A
Supporting Candidate **A**

B b b b B
Supporting Candidate **B**

1. Bakshy et al., 2015; Barberá et al., 2015.

Groupthink

LOQ 41-7 How can group interaction enable groupthink?

Does group influence ever distort important national decisions? Consider the Bay of Pigs fiasco. In 1961, U.S. President John F. Kennedy and his advisers decided to invade Cuba with 1400 CIA-trained Cuban exiles. When the invaders were easily captured and quickly linked to the U.S. government, Kennedy wondered aloud, "How could I have been so stupid?"

Social psychologist Irving Janis (1982) studied the decision-making process leading to the ill-fated invasion. He discovered that the soaring morale of the recently elected president and his advisers fostered undue confidence. To preserve the good feeling, group members suppressed or self-censored their dissenting views, especially after President Kennedy voiced his enthusiasm for the scheme. Since no one spoke strongly against the idea, everyone assumed the support was unanimous. To describe this harmonious but unrealistic group thinking, Janis coined the term **groupthink.**

Later studies showed that groupthink—fed by overconfidence, conformity, self-justification, and group polarization—contributed to other fiascos as well. Among them were the failure to anticipate the 1941 Japanese attack on Pearl Harbor; the escalation of the Vietnam war; the U.S. Watergate cover-up; the Chernobyl nuclear reactor accident (Reason, 1987); the U.S. space shuttle *Challenger* explosion (Esser & Lindoerfer, 1989); and the Iraq war, launched on the false idea that Iraq had weapons of mass destruction (U.S. Senate Intelligence Committee, 2004).

Despite the dangers of groupthink, two heads are often better than one. Great minds often don't think alike. Knowing this, Janis also studied instances in which U.S. presidents and their advisers collectively made good decisions, such as when the Truman administration formulated the Marshall Plan, which offered assistance to Europe after World War II, and when the Kennedy administration successfully prevented the Soviets from installing missiles in Cuba. His conclusion? Groupthink is prevented when a leader—whether in government or in business—welcomes various opinions, invites experts' critiques of developing plans, and assigns people to identify possible problems. Just as the suppression of dissent bends a group toward bad decisions, open debate often shapes good ones. This is especially the case with small but diverse groups, whose varied backgrounds and perspectives often enable creative or superior outcomes (Nemeth & Ormiston, 2007; Wang, J. et al., 2019; Wu et al., 2019). Teams of smart people tend to surpass individual smart people at predicting political events (Mellers et al., 2015). None of us is as smart as all of us.

> "One of the dangers in the White House, based on my reading of history, is that you get wrapped up in groupthink and everybody agrees with everything, and there's no discussion and there are no dissenting views." — Barack Obama, December 1, 2008, press conference

> "If evil is contagious, so is goodness." — Pope Francis tweet, 2017

ASK YOURSELF

How have you been influenced by group polarization on social media recently?

RETRIEVAL PRACTICE

RP-4 What is *social facilitation,* and why does it improve performance with a well-learned task?

RP-5 People tend to exert less effort when working with a group than they would alone, which is called _____ _____.

RP-6 You are organizing a meeting of fiercely competitive political candidates and their supporters. To add to the fun, friends have suggested handing out masks of the candidates' faces for supporters to wear. What phenomenon might these masks engage?

RP-7 When like-minded groups discuss a topic, and the result is the strengthening of the prevailing opinion, this is called _____ _____.

RP-8 When a group's desire for harmony overrides its realistic analysis of other options, _____ has occurred.

ANSWERS IN APPENDIX E

groupthink the mode of thinking that occurs when the desire for harmony in a decision-making group overrides a realistic appraisal of alternatives.

41 REVIEW Social Influence

LEARNING OBJECTIVES

Test Yourself Answer these repeated Learning Objective Questions on your own (before checking the answers in Appendix D) to improve your retention of the concepts (McDaniel et al., 2009, 2015).

LOQ 41-1 How is social contagion a form of conformity, and how do conformity experiments reveal the power of social influence?

LOQ 41-2 What did Milgram's obedience experiments teach us about the power of social influence?

LOQ 41-3 What do the social influence studies teach us about ourselves? How much power do we have as individuals?

LOQ 41-4 How does the presence of others influence our actions, via social facilitation, social loafing, and deindividuation?

LOQ 41-5 How can group interaction enable group polarization?

LOQ 41-6 What role does the internet play in group polarization?

LOQ 41-7 How can group interaction enable groupthink?

TERMS AND CONCEPTS TO REMEMBER

Test Yourself Write down the definition in your own words, then check your answer.

norms, p. 475

conformity, p. 477

normative social influence, p. 477

informational social influence, p. 479

social facilitation, p. 483

social loafing, p. 483

deindividuation, p. 484

group polarization, p. 484

groupthink, p. 487

MASTER THE MATERIAL

Test Yourself Answer the following questions on your own first, then check your answers in Appendix E.

1. Researchers have found that a person is most likely to conform to a group if
   a. the group members have diverse opinions.
   b. the person feels competent and secure.
   c. the person admires the group's status.
   d. no one else will observe the person's behavior.

2. In Milgram's experiments, the rate of obedience was highest when
   a. the "learner" was at a distance from the "teacher."
   b. the "learner" was close at hand.
   c. other "teachers" refused to go along with the experimenter.
   d. the "teacher" disliked the "learner."

3. Dr. Huang, a popular music professor, delivers fascinating lectures on music history but gets nervous and makes mistakes when describing exam statistics in front of the class. Why does his performance vary by task?

4. In a group situation that fosters arousal and anonymity, a person sometimes loses self-consciousness and self-control. This phenomenon is called _____.

5. Sharing our opinions with like-minded others tends to strengthen our views, a phenomenon referred to as _____ _____.

Continue testing yourself with **LearningCurve** or **Achieve Read & Practice** to learn and remember most effectively.

---

42 Antisocial Relations

Social psychology studies how we think about and influence one another, and also how we *relate* to one another. What causes people sometimes to hate and harm, and at other times to love and help? And when destructive conflicts arise, how can we move toward a just peace? In this section we ponder insights into *antisocial* relations gleaned by researchers who have studied prejudice and aggression.

prejudice an unjustifiable and usually negative attitude toward a group and its members. Prejudice generally involves stereotyped beliefs, negative feelings, and a predisposition to discriminatory action.

stereotype a generalized (sometimes accurate but often overgeneralized) belief about a group of people.

discrimination unjustifiable negative behavior toward a group or its members.

Prejudice

LOQ 42-1 What is *prejudice?* How do explicit and implicit prejudice differ?

Prejudice means "prejudgment." It is an unjustifiable and usually negative *attitude* toward a group and its members—who often are people of a particular racial or ethnic group, gender, or sexual orientation. Attitudes are feelings, influenced by beliefs, that predispose us to act in certain ways. The ingredients in prejudice's three-part mixture are

- *negative emotions,* such as hostility or fear.
- **stereotypes,** which are generalized beliefs about a group of people. Our stereotypes sometimes reflect reality. As Texas Senator Ted Cruz (2018) explained, "It's a stereotype that Texans like barbecue. It also happens that pretty much all Texans like barbecue." But stereotypes often overgeneralize or exaggerate. In the U.S., for example, strongly partisan Republicans and Democrats exhibit a "perception gap"—they overestimate the extremism of the other side (Yudkin et al., 2019b).
- a predisposition to **discriminate**—to act in negative and unjustifiable ways toward members of the group. Sometimes prejudice is blatant. People with anti-Black attitudes, for example, are less likely to judge as guilty a White police officer who killed a Black man (Cooley et al., 2019). Other times it is more subtle, taking the form of *microaggressions,* such as race-related traffic stops, a reluctance to choose a train seat next to someone of a different race, or longer Uber wait times and less Airbnb acceptance for people with African American names (Edelman et al., 2017; Ge et al., 2016; Wang et al., 2011).

To believe that obese people are gluttonous, and to feel dislike for an obese person, is to be prejudiced. To pass over obese people on a dating site, or to reject an obese job candidate, is to discriminate.

Explicit and Implicit Prejudice

Again and again, we have seen that our brain processes thoughts, memories, and attitudes on two different tracks. Sometimes that processing is *explicit*—on the radar screen of our awareness. More often, it is *implicit*—an unthinking knee-jerk response operating below the radar, leaving us unaware of how our attitudes are influencing our behavior. In 2015, the U.S. Supreme Court, in upholding the Fair Housing Act, recognized implicit bias research, noting that "unconscious prejudices" can cause discrimination even when people do not consciously intend to discriminate.

Psychologists study implicit prejudice by

- *testing for unconscious group associations.* Tests in which people quickly pair a person's image with a trait demonstrate that even people who deny any racial prejudice may exhibit negative associations (Greenwald & Banaji, 2017). Millions of people have taken the Implicit Association Test (as you can, too, at Implicit.Harvard.edu). Critics question the test's reliability and caution against using it to assess or label individuals (Oswald et al., 2013, 2015). But defenders counter that implicit biases are difficult to change and predict behaviors ranging from simple acts of friendliness to work quality (Forscher et al., 2019; Jost, 2019; Kurdi et al., 2019).
- *considering unconscious patronization.* In one experiment, White university women assessed flawed student essays they believed had been written by either a White or a Black student. The women gave low evaluations, often with harsh comments, to the essays supposedly written by a White student. When the same essay was attributed to a Black student, their assessment was more positive (Harber, 1998). In real-world evaluations, such low expectations and the resulting "inflated praise and insufficient criticism" could hinder minority student achievement, the researcher noted. Thus, many teachers read essays while "blind" to their authors' race.
- *monitoring reflexive bodily responses.* Even people who consciously express little prejudice may give off telltale signals as their body responds selectively to an image of a person from another ethnic group. Neuroscientists can detect signals of implicit prejudice in the viewer's facial-muscle responses and in the activation of the emotion-processing amygdala (Cunningham et al., 2004; Eberhardt, 2005; Stanley et al., 2008).

Body weight bias: In data collected from 4 million U.S. adults, explicit biases against those of a particular sex, disability, age, or race were greatly exceeded by biases in response to body weight (Charlesworth & Banaji, 2019).

Brian Blanco/EPA/Shutterstock

Implicit bias? Does implicit bias research help us understand the 2012 death of Trayvon Martin (shown here 7 months before he was killed)? As he walked alone to his father's fiancée's house in a gated Florida neighborhood, a suspicious resident confronted and shot him. Commentators wondered: Had Martin been an unarmed White teen, would he have been perceived and treated the same way?

"But who can detect their errors? Clear me from hidden faults."
— Psalm 19:12

Targets of Prejudice

LOQ **42-2** What groups are frequent targets of prejudice?

RACIAL AND ETHNIC PREJUDICE Americans' expressed racial attitudes have changed dramatically in the last half-century. Support for interracial marriage between Blacks and Whites, for example, increased from a mere 4 percent approval in 1959 to 87 percent in 2013 (Saad, 2019). Three in four Americans (including nearly 9 in 10 college graduates) now agree that their nation's having "many different races and ethnicities" is good for the country (Horowitz, 2019). The diversity benefit appeared in one analysis of 9 million scientific papers and 6 million scientists: Ethnically diverse scientific teams produced the most influential research (AlShebli et al., 2018).

Yet as overt interracial prejudice wanes, *subtle* prejudice lingers. Black and Hispanic people with darker skin tones experience greater prejudice and discrimination (Gonzales-Barrera, 2019; Landor & Smith, 2019). Black men are judged more harshly than White men when they commit "stereotypically Black" crimes (drive-by shooting, gang violence, street gambling) rather than "stereotypically White" crimes (embezzlement, computer hacking, and insider trading) (Petsko & Bodenhausen, 2019). Medical providers spend more money to treat White patients than to treat equally unhealthy Black patients (Obermeyer et al., 2019).

Many wonder how such prejudice persists. One reason is that few people muster the courage to challenge prejudicial or hate speech. Although many *say* they would feel upset with someone making racist (or homophobic) comments, they often respond indifferently when hearing prejudice-laden language (Kawakami et al., 2009). *The bottom line:* If you disapprove of prejudice, ask yourself, "What message am I sending when I remain silent while others make racist, homophobic, or sexist remarks?"

As noted, prejudice is not just subtle, but often unconscious (implicit). An Implicit Association Test found 9 in 10 White respondents taking longer to identify pleasant words (such as *peace* and *paradise*) as "good" when presented with Black-sounding names (such as *Latisha* and *Darnell*) than when shown White-sounding names (such as *Katie* and *Ian*). Moreover, people who more quickly associate good things with White names or faces also are the quickest to perceive anger and apparent threat in Black faces (Hugenberg & Bodenhausen, 2003). In the 2008 U.S. presidential election, those demonstrating explicit *or* implicit prejudice were less likely to vote for candidate Barack Obama. His election, however, reduced implicit prejudice (Bernstein et al., 2010; Payne et al., 2010; Stephens-Davidowitz, 2014).

Our perceptions can also reflect implicit bias. In 1999, Amadou Diallo, who was Black, was accosted as he approached his doorway by police officers looking for a rapist. When he pulled out his wallet, the officers, perceiving a gun, riddled his body with 19 bullets from 41 shots. In one analysis of 59 unarmed suspect shootings in Philadelphia over seven years, 49 involved the misidentification of an object (such as a phone) or movement (such as pants tugging). Black suspects were more than twice as likely to be misperceived as threatening, even by Black officers (Blow, 2015). Across the United States, about 1 in 1000 Black men have been killed by a police officer—more than double White men's rate (Edwards et al., 2019). One research team analyzed implicit bias scores from more than 2 million Americans, while accounting for several other factors. Their finding: A region's implicit bias toward African Americans predicted its number of African Americans killed by police (Hehman et al., 2018).

To better understand these tragic shootings, researchers have also simulated the situation (Correll et al., 2007, 2015; Plant & Peruche, 2005; Sadler et al., 2012a). They asked viewers to press buttons quickly to "shoot" or not shoot men who suddenly appeared on screen. Some of the on-screen men held a gun. Others held a harmless object, such as a flashlight or bottle. People (both Blacks and Whites, including police officers) more often shot Black men holding the harmless object. Priming people with a flashed Black face rather than a White face also made them more likely to misperceive a flashed tool as a gun (**FIGURE 42.1**). Fatigue, which diminishes one's conscious control and increases automatic reactions, amplifies racial bias in decisions to shoot (Ma et al., 2013).

"Data [show] plunges in extreme poverty, illiteracy, war, violent crime, racism, sexism, homophobia, domestic violence, disease, lethal accidents and just about every other scourge." — Psychologist Steven Pinker, "Scared by the News? Take the Long View," 2018

"If we can't help our latent biases, we can help our behavior in response to those instinctive reactions, which is why we work to design systems and processes that overcome that very human part of us all." — U.S. FBI Director James B. Comey, "Hard Truths: Law Enforcement and Race," 2015

Recognizing the reality of implicit bias, many companies, colleges, and police departments have given their staff implicit bias training—as when Starbucks in 2018 responded to a bias incident by closing its U.S. stores for an afternoon to educate its 175,000 employees. Although such single-session diversity or bias training sessions may modestly change attitudes, behavior is harder to modify (Chang et al., 2019; Forscher et al., 2019).

(a)   (b)   (c)

◆ FIGURE 42.1
Race primes perceptions In experiments by Keith Payne (2006), people viewed (a) a White or Black face, immediately followed by (b) a flashed gun or hand tool, which was then followed by (c) a masking screen. Participants were more likely to misperceive a tool as a gun when it was preceded by a Black rather than a White face.

GENDER PREJUDICE Overt gender prejudice has declined sharply. The one-third of Americans who in 1937 told Gallup pollsters that they would vote for a qualified woman whom their party nominated for president soared to 95 percent in 2012 (Jones, 2012; Newport, 1999). Although women worldwide still represent nearly two-thirds of illiterate adults, and 30 percent have experienced intimate partner violence, 65 percent of all people now say it is very important that women have the same rights as men (UN, 2015; WHO, 2016a; Zainulbhai, 2016).

Nevertheless, both implicit and explicit gender prejudice and discrimination persist. Consider:

- *Pay.* In Western countries, we pay more to those (usually men) who care for our streets than to those (usually women) who care for our children.

- *Leadership.* From 2007 through 2016, male directors of 1000 popular films (the top 100 for each year) outnumbered female directors by 24 to 1 (Smith et al., 2017). Implicit gender bias also contributes to females' not being promoted (Régner et al., 2019).

- *Respect.* People more often refer to men (including male instructors) by their last name and women by their first name (Atir & Ferguson, 2018).

- *Perceived intelligence.* Gender bias even applies to beliefs about intelligence: Despite equality between males and females in intelligence test scores, people tend to perceive their fathers as more intelligent than their mothers and their sons as brighter than their daughters (Furnham, 2016).

Unwanted female infants are no longer left out on a hillside to die of exposure, as was the practice in ancient Greece. Yet the normal male-to-female newborn ratio (105-to-100) doesn't explain what has been estimated as the world's millions of "missing women." In many places, sons are valued more than daughters. In India, there are 3.5 times more Google searches asking how to conceive a boy than how to conceive a girl (Stephens-Davidowitz, 2014). With scientific testing that enables sex-selective abortions, some countries are experiencing a shortfall in female births (**FIGURE 42.2**). India's newborn sex ratio was recently 112 boys for every 100 girls. China's has been 111 to 100, despite China's declaring sex-selective abortions a criminal offense (CIA, 2014). In China and India, which together have 50 million more males than females under age 20, many bachelors will be without mates (Denyer & Gowen, 2018; Gupta, 2017). A shortage of women also contributes to increased crime, violence, prostitution, and trafficking of women (Brooks, 2012).

"Until I was a man, I had no idea how good men had it at work. . . . The first time I spoke up in a meeting in my newly low, quiet voice and noticed that sudden, focused attention, I was so uncomfortable that I found myself unable to finish my sentence." — Thomas Page McBee, 2016, after transitioning from female to male

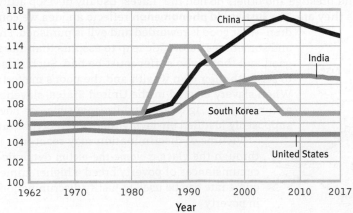

◆ FIGURE 42.2
Boy bias Biologically, the expected sex ratio would be 105 newborn boys for every 100 newborn girls. In reality, most countries show a significant boy bias. (Data from Our World in Data and World Bank/UN.)

LGBTQ PREJUDICE In most of the world, gay, lesbian, and transgender people cannot openly and comfortably disclose who they are and whom they love. Although by 2019, 28 countries allowed same-sex marriage, dozens more had laws criminalizing same-sex relationships. Cultural variation is enormous—ranging from the 98 percent in Ghana to the 6 percent in Spain for whom "homosexuality is morally unacceptable" (Pew, 2014). Worldwide, anti-gay attitudes are most common among men, older adults, and those who are unhappy, unemployed, and less educated (Haney, 2016; Jäckle & Wenzelburger, 2015).

Explicit anti-LGBTQ prejudice persists, even in countries with legal protections in place. When U.S. and U.K. experimenters sent thousands of responses to employment ads, those whose resumes included "Treasurer, Progressive and Socialist Alliance" received more replies than did those whose resumes specified "Treasurer, Gay and Lesbian Alliance" (Agerström et al., 2012; Bertrand & Mullainathan, 2004; Drydakis, 2009, 2015). Other evidence has appeared in national surveys of LGBTQ Americans:

- 39 percent reported having been "rejected by a friend or family member" because of their sexual orientation or gender identity (Pew, 2013b).

- 58 percent reported being "subject to slurs or jokes" (Pew, 2013b).

- 54 percent reported having been harassed at school and at work (Grant et al., 2010; James et al., 2016).

Do attitudes and practices that label, disparage, and discriminate against gay, lesbian, and transgender people increase their risk of psychological disorder and ill health? *Yes.* In U.S. states without protections against LGBTQ hate crime and discrimination, gay and lesbian people experience substantially higher rates of depression and related disorders, even after controlling for income and education differences. In communities where anti-gay prejudice is high, so are gay and lesbian suicide and cardiovascular deaths. In 16 states that banned same-sex marriage between 2001 and 2005, gay and lesbian people (but not straight people) experienced a 37 percent increase in depressive disorder rates, a 42 percent increase in alcohol use disorder, and a 248 percent increase in generalized anxiety disorder. Meanwhile, gay and lesbian people in other states did not experience increased psychiatric disorders (Hatzenbuehler, 2014).

So, do laws that promote acceptance of gay, lesbian, and transgender people *reduce* bias? Again, *Yes.* As happened after the passage of desegregation and civil rights laws, attitudes have followed the newly legislated behavior. In the various U.S. states, people became more gay-supportive when and where same-sex marriages became legal (Ofuso et al., 2019).

Roots of Prejudice

LOQ 42-3 What are some social, emotional, and cognitive roots of prejudice, and what are some ways to reduce prejudice?

Prejudice springs from a culture's divisions, the heart's passions, and the mind's natural workings.

SOCIAL INEQUALITIES AND DIVISIONS When some people have money, power, and prestige and others do not, the "haves" usually develop attitudes that justify things as they are. The **just-world phenomenon** reflects an idea we commonly teach our children—that good is rewarded and evil is punished. From this it is but a short and sometimes automatic leap to assume that those who succeed must be good and those who suffer must be bad. Such reasoning enables the rich to see both their own wealth and the poor's misfortune as justly deserved. When slavery existed in the United States, slaveholders perceived slaves as innately lazy, ignorant, and irresponsible—as having the very traits that supposedly justified enslaving them. Stereotypes rationalize inequalities.

Victims of discrimination may react in ways that feed prejudice through the classic *blame-the-victim* dynamic (Allport, 1954). Do the circumstances of poverty breed a higher crime rate? If so, that higher crime rate can be used to justify discrimination against those who live in poverty.

The ingroup Scotland's famed "Tartan Army" soccer fans, shown here during a match against archrival England, share a social identity that defines "us" (the Scottish ingroup) and "them" (the English outgroup).

Dividing the world into "us" and "them" can result in conflict, racism, and war, but it also provides the benefits of communal solidarity. Thus, we cheer for our groups, kill for them, die for them. Indeed, we define who we are—our *social identity*—partly in terms of our groups (Thomas et al., 2019; Whitehouse, 2018). When Oliver identifies himself as a man, a Brit, a Liverpool native, and a Brexit supporter, he knows who he is, and so do we. Mentally drawing a circle defines "us," the **ingroup.** But the social definition of who we are also states who we are not. People outside that circle are "them," the **outgroup.** An **ingroup bias**—a favoring of our own group—soon follows. In experiments, people, beginning in early childhood, have favored their own group when dividing rewards—even a group that is created by a mere coin toss (Tajfel, 1982; Wilder, 1981; Wynn et al., 2018). Across 17 countries, ingroup bias appears more as ingroup favoritism than as harm to the outgroup (Romano et al., 2017). Discrimination is triggered less by outgroup hostility than by ingroup networking and mutual support—such as hiring a friend's child at the expense of other candidates (Greenwald & Pettigrew, 2014).

We have inherited our Stone Age ancestors' need to belong, to live and love in groups. There was safety in solidarity: Whether hunting, defending, or attacking, 10 hands were better than 2. Evolution prepared us, when encountering strangers, to make instant judgments: friend or foe? This urge to distinguish enemies from friends, and to dehumanize or "otherize" those not like us, predisposes prejudice against strangers (Kteily & Bruneau, 2017; Whitley, 1999). To Greeks of the classical era, all non-Greeks were "barbarians." In our own era, most children believe their school is better than all other schools in town. Many high school students form cliques—jocks, preps, nerds—and disparage those outside their own group. Even chimpanzees have been seen to wipe clean the spot where they were touched by a chimpanzee from another group (Goodall, 1986). They also display ingroup empathy by yawning more after seeing ingroup (rather than outgroup) members yawn (Campbell & de Waal, 2011). Although an ideal world might prioritize justice and love for all, in our real world, ingroup love often outranks universal justice.

IMPRESSIVE RESUMÉ...

ASK YOURSELF

What are some examples of ingroup bias in your own life, and in your community? How can you help break down barriers that you or others may face?

NEGATIVE EMOTIONS Negative emotions nourish prejudice. When facing death, fearing threats, or experiencing frustration, people cling more tightly to their ingroup. When frustrated by extreme inequality, people worldwide wish for a strong leader to restore order (Sprong et al., 2019). When fearing terrorism, patriotism increases, along with loathing and aggression toward those perceived as threats (Pyszczynski et al., 2002, 2008).

Scapegoat theory proposes that when things go wrong, finding someone to blame can provide a target for our negative emotions. During and after the contentious 2016 U.S. presidential election, hate crime reports rose, and in 2019, 7 in 10 Americans perceived race relations as worsening (FBI, 2019; Horowitz, 2019). Why? One reason may be

just-world phenomenon the tendency for people to believe that the world is just and people therefore get what they deserve and deserve what they get.

ingroup "us"—people with whom we share a common identity.

outgroup "them"—those perceived as different or apart from our ingroup.

ingroup bias the tendency to favor our own group.

scapegoat theory the theory that prejudice offers an outlet for anger by providing someone to blame.

David Sipress/Conde Nast/Cartoonbank

"The misfortunes of others are the taste of honey." — Japanese saying

greater acceptance of prejudice toward the groups that then-candidate Donald Trump had targeted during the campaign, such as Muslims and immigrants (Crandall et al., 2018). Counties that hosted Trump rallies in 2016 reportedly experienced a doubled rate of hate crimes thereafter (Feinberg, A. et al., 2019).

In England and Wales, following the 2016 anti-immigrant Brexit referendum, reported hate crimes soared from 52,000 in 2015/2016 to 103,000 in 2018/2019 (Home Office, 2019). There, and in Germany and the United States, anti-Semitic crimes have also been on the increase (ADL, 2019; Statista, 2019). At the outset of the COVID-19 pandemic, some government officials in White-majority countries referred to the "Chinese" virus. Associating the virus with a country fueled prejudice and discrimination, contributing to 650 reported U.S. incidents of discrimination against Asian Americans in just one week (Hong, 2020; Van Bavel et al., 2020). One man was stabbed, others were spit on or told, "You people brought the virus. Go back to China" (Loffman, 2020).

Evidence for the scapegoat theory comes in two forms: (1) *Social trends*—Economically frustrated people often express heightened prejudice, and during economic downturns, racial prejudice intensifies (Bianchi et al., 2018); and (2) *Experiments*—Temporarily frustrating people intensifies their prejudice. Students who experience failure or are made to feel insecure often restore their self-esteem by disparaging a rival school or another person (Cialdini & Richardson, 1980; Crocker et al., 1987). Denigrating others may boost our own sense of status, which explains why a rival's misfortune sometimes provides a twinge of pleasure. (The German language has a word—*Schadenfreude*—for this secret joy that we sometimes take in another's failure.) By contrast, those made to feel loved and supported become more open to and accepting of others who differ (Mikulincer & Shaver, 2001).

COGNITIVE SHORTCUTS Stereotyped beliefs are in part a by-product of how we cognitively simplify the world. To help understand the world around us, we frequently form categories. Chemists categorize molecules as organic and inorganic. Therapists categorize psychological disorders. We all categorize people by gender, ethnicity, race, age, and many other characteristics—including their warmth and their competence (Fiske, 2018). But when we categorize people into groups, we often stereotype. We recognize how greatly *we* differ from other individuals in *our* groups. But we overestimate the extent to which members of other groups are alike (Bothwell et al., 1989). We perceive *outgroup homogeneity*—uniformity of attitudes, personality, and appearance. Our greater recognition for individual own-race faces—called the **other-race effect** (or *cross-race effect* or *own-race bias*)—emerges during infancy, between 3 and 9 months of age (Anzures et al., 2013; Telzer et al., 2013). (We also have an *own-age bias*—better recognition memory for faces of our own age group [Rhodes & Anastasi, 2012]).

© Dave Coverly/speedbump.com

Sometimes, however, people don't fit easily into our racial categories. When that happens, we often assign them to their minority identity. Researchers believe this happens because, after learning the features of a familiar racial group, the observer's *selective attention* is drawn to the distinctive features of the less-familiar minority. Jamin Halberstadt and his colleagues (2011) illustrated this learned-association effect by showing New Zealanders blended Chinese-White faces. Compared with participants of Chinese descent, European-descent New Zealanders more readily classified ambiguous faces as Chinese (**FIGURE 42.3**). With effort and with experience, people get better at recognizing individual faces from another group (Hugenberg et al., 2010; Young et al., 2012).

FIGURE 42.3

Categorizing mixed-race people When New Zealanders quickly classified 104 photos by race, those of European descent more often than those of Chinese descent classified the ambiguous middle two as Chinese (Halberstadt et al., 2011).

| 100% Chinese | 80% Chinese 20% White | 60% Chinese 40% White | 40% Chinese 60% White | 20% Chinese 80% White | 100% White |

Dr. Jamin Halberstadt

REMEMBERING VIVID CASES We also simplify our world by employing *heuristics*—mental shortcuts that enable snap judgments. The *availability heuristic* is the tendency to estimate the frequency of an event by how readily it comes to mind. Vivid cases come to mind easily, so it's no surprise that they feed our stereotypes. In a classic experiment, researchers showed two groups of University of Oregon students' lists containing information about 50 men (Rothbart et al., 1978). The first group's list included 10 men arrested for *nonviolent* crimes, such as forgery. The second group's list included 10 men arrested for *violent* crimes, such as assault. Later, both groups were asked how many men on their list had committed *any* sort of crime. The second group overestimated the number. Violent crimes form vivid memories (FIGURE 42.4).

> To review attribution research and experience a simulation of how stereotypes form, visit *Topic Tutorial: PsychSim6, Not My Type.* And for a 6.5-minute synopsis of the social and cognitive psychology of prejudice, see the *Video: Prejudice.*

VICTIM BLAMING As we noted earlier, people often justify their prejudices by blaming victims. If the world is just, they assume, people must get what they deserve. As one German civilian is said to have remarked when visiting the Bergen-Belsen concentration camp shortly after World War II, "What terrible criminals these prisoners must have been to receive such treatment."

Hindsight bias amplifies victim blaming (Carli & Leonard, 1989). Have you ever heard people say that rape victims, abused spouses, or people with AIDS got what they deserved? In some countries, such as Pakistan, rape victims have been sentenced to severe punishment for violating adultery prohibitions (Mydans, 2002). In one experiment, two groups were given a detailed account of a date (Janoff-Bulman et al., 1985). The first group's account reported that the date ended with the woman being raped. Members of that group perceived the woman's behavior as at least partly to blame, and in hindsight, they thought, "She should have known better." The second group, given the same account with the rape ending deleted, did not perceive the woman's behavior as inviting rape. In the first group, hindsight bias promoted a blame-the-victim mentality. Blaming the victim also serves to reassure people that it couldn't happen to them.

People also have a basic tendency to justify their culture's social systems (Jost, 2019). We're inclined to see the way things are as the way they ought to be and deserve to be: If people are rich, they must be smart (Hussak & Cimpian, 2015). This natural conservatism makes it difficult to legislate major social changes, such as health care improvements or climate change policies. Once policies are in place, our "system justification" tends to preserve them.

* * *

If your own gut-check reveals you sometimes have feelings you would rather not have about other people, remember this: It is what we *do* with our feelings that matters. By monitoring our feelings and actions, by replacing old habits with new ones, and by seeking out new friendships, we can work to free ourselves from prejudice.

RETRIEVAL PRACTICE

RP-1 When prejudice causes us to blame an innocent person for a problem, that person is called a _____.

ANSWERS IN APPENDIX E

Aggression

LOQ 42-4 How does psychology's definition of *aggression* differ from everyday usage? What biological factors make us more prone to hurt one another?

In psychology, **aggression** is any physical or verbal behavior intended to harm someone, whether done out of hostility or as a calculated means to an end. The assertive, persistent salesperson is not aggressive. Nor is the dentist who makes you wince with

FIGURE 42.4
Vivid cases feed stereotypes Global terrorism has created, in many minds, an exaggerated stereotype of Muslims as terrorism-prone. Actually, reported a U.S. National Research Council panel on terrorism (which offered this inexact illustration), most terrorists are *not* Muslim.

Muslims · Terrorism

other-race effect the tendency to recall faces of one's own race more accurately than faces of other races. Also called the *cross-race effect* and the *own-race bias.*

aggression any physical or verbal behavior intended to harm someone physically or emotionally.

Do guns in the home save or take more lives? "Personal safety/protection" is the number one reason Americans have given for gun ownership (Swift, 2013). However, firearm ownership often backfires. Guns in the home are much more often used to kill loved ones or oneself than in self-defense (Kivisto et al., 2019; Stroebe et al., 2017). In 2017, 39,773 Americans died from firearm injuries; 2 in 3 were suicides (CDC, 2019c). Over the last half-century more than 1.5 million Americans have suffered nonwar firearm deaths—more than all war deaths in U.S. history (Jacobson, 2015). Compared with people of the same sex, race, age, and neighborhood, those who keep a gun in the home have been twice as likely to be murdered and three times as likely to die by suicide (Anglemyer et al., 2014; Stroebe, 2013). States and countries with high gun ownership rates also tend to have much higher murder and gun death rates (VPC, 2016). It takes Japan nearly a decade to accumulate as many violent gun deaths as occur in an average U.S. day. More guns → more deaths.

Gilbert Laurie/Getty Images

pain. But the gossip who passes along a vicious rumor about you, the bully who torments you in person or online, and the attacker who robs you are aggressive.

Aggressive behavior emerges from the interaction of biology and experience. For a gun to fire, the trigger must be pulled; with some people, as with hair-trigger guns, it doesn't take much to trip an explosion. Let's look first at some biological factors that influence our thresholds for aggressive behavior, then at the psychological factors that pull the trigger.

The Biology of Aggression

Aggression varies too widely from culture to culture, era to era, and person to person to be considered an unlearned instinct. But biology does *influence* aggression. We can look for biological influences at three levels—genetic, neural, and biochemical.

GENETIC INFLUENCES Genes influence aggression. Animals have been bred for aggressiveness—sometimes for sport, sometimes for research. The effect of genes also appears in human twin studies (Miles & Carey, 1997; Rowe et al., 1999). If one identical twin admits to "having a violent temper," the other twin will often independently admit the same. Fraternal twins are much less likely to respond similarly.

Researchers continue to search for genetic markers in those who commit violent acts. One is already well known and is carried by half the human race: the Y chromosome. Another such marker is the *monoamine oxidase A (MAOA) gene,* which helps break down neurotransmitters such as dopamine and serotonin. Sometimes called the "warrior gene," people who have low MAOA gene expression tend to behave aggressively when provoked. In one experiment, low (compared with high) MAOA gene carriers gave more unpleasant hot sauce to someone who provoked them (McDermott et al., 2009; Tiihonen et al., 2015).

> See the *Video: Twin Studies* for a helpful tutorial animation.

NEURAL INFLUENCES There is no one spot in the brain that controls aggression. Aggression is a complex behavior, and it occurs in particular contexts. But animal and human brains have neural systems that, given provocation, will either inhibit or facilitate aggression (Falkner et al., 2016; Fields, 2019). Consider:

- Researchers implanted a radio-controlled electrode in the brain of the domineering leader of a caged monkey colony. The electrode was in an area that, when stimulated, inhibits aggression. When researchers placed the control button for the electrode in the colony's cage, one small monkey learned to push it every time the boss became threatening.

- A neurosurgeon, seeking to diagnose a disorder, implanted an electrode in the amygdala of a mild-mannered woman. Because the brain has no sensory receptors, she was unable to feel the stimulation. But at the flick of a switch she snarled, "Take my blood pressure. Take it now," then stood up and began to strike the doctor.

- If the frontal lobes are damaged, inactive, disconnected, or not yet fully mature, aggression may be more likely (Amen et al., 1996; Davidson et al., 2000; Raine, 2013). One study of 203 convicted murderers revealed reduced tissue in the impulse-controlling frontal lobes (Sajous-Turner et al., 2019).

BIOCHEMICAL INFLUENCES Our genes engineer our individual nervous systems, which operate electrochemically. The hormone testosterone, for example, circulates in the bloodstream and influences the neural systems that control aggression. A raging bull becomes a gentle giant when castration reduces its testosterone level. Conversely, when injected with testosterone, gentle, castrated mice once again become aggressive.

Donald Reilly The New Yorker Collection/The Cartoon Bank

"It's a guy thing."

Chris Courteau/AGE Fotostock

A lean, mean fighting machine—the testosterone-laden female hyena The hyena's unusual embryology pumps testosterone into female fetuses. The result is revved-up young female hyenas who seem born to fight.

Humans are less sensitive to hormonal changes. But as men's testosterone levels diminish with age, hormonally charged, aggressive 17-year-olds mature into quieter and gentler 70-year-olds. Drugs that sharply reduce testosterone levels subdue men's aggressive tendencies.

Another drug that sometimes circulates in the bloodstream—alcohol—unleashes aggressive responses to frustration. Across police data, prison surveys, and experiments, aggression-prone people are more likely to drink, and to become violent when intoxicated (White et al., 1993). Alcohol is a disinhibitor—it slows the brain activity that controls judgment and inhibitions. Under its influence, people may interpret ambiguous acts (such as being bumped in a crowd) as provocations and react aggressively (Bègue et al., 2010; Giancola & Corman, 2007). Alcohol has been a factor in 73 percent of homicides in Russia and 57 percent in the United States (Landberg & Norström, 2011).

Just *thinking* you've imbibed alcohol can increase aggression (Bègue et al., 2009). But so, too, does unknowingly ingesting alcohol slipped into a drink. Thus, alcohol affects aggression both biologically and psychologically (Bushman, 1993; Ito et al., 1996; Taylor & Chermack, 1993).

> "We could avoid two-thirds of all crime simply by putting all able-bodied young men in cryogenic sleep from the age of 12 through 28." — David T. Lykken, *The Antisocial Personalities*, 1995

Psychological and Social-Cultural Factors in Aggression

LOQ 42-5 What psychological and social-cultural factors may trigger aggressive behavior?

Biological factors influence how easily aggression is triggered. But what psychological and social-cultural factors pull the trigger?

AVERSIVE EVENTS Suffering sometimes builds character. In laboratory experiments, however, those made miserable have often made others miserable (Berkowitz, 1983, 1989). Aversive stimuli—hot temperatures, physical pain, personal insults, foul odors, cigarette smoke, crowding, and a host of others—can evoke hostility. Even hunger can feed anger—making people "hangry" (Bushman et al., 2014). A prime example of this phenomenon is the **frustration-aggression principle**: Frustration creates anger, which can spark aggression.

The frustration-aggression link was illustrated in an analysis of 27,667 hit-by-pitch Major League Baseball incidents between 1960 and 2004 (Timmerman, 2007). Pitchers were most likely to hit batters when the previous batter had hit a home run, the current batter had hit a home run the last time at bat, or the pitcher's teammate had been hit by a pitch in the previous half-inning. A separate study found a similar link between rising temperatures and the number of hit batters (Reifman et al., 1991; see **FIGURE 42.5**). Overheated temperatures → overheated tempers.

In the wider world, violent crime and spousal abuse rates have been higher during hotter years, seasons, months, and days (Anderson et al., 1997; Heilmann & Kahn, 2019). Studies from archaeology, economics, geography, political science, and psychology converge in finding that throughout human history, higher temperatures have predicted increased individual violence, wars, and revolutions (Hsiang et al., 2013). One projection from

frustration-aggression principle the principle that frustration—the blocking of an attempt to achieve some goal—creates anger, which can generate aggression.

FIGURE 42.5

Temperature and retaliation Richard Larrick and his colleagues (2011) looked for occurrences of batters hit by pitches during 4,566,468 pitcher-batter matchups across 57,293 Major League Baseball games since 1952. The probability of a hit batter increased if one or more of the pitcher's teammates had been hit, and also with higher temperatures.

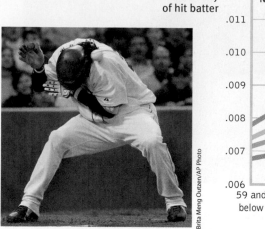

How have researchers studied these concepts? Play the role of a researcher by designing one of these studies in the activity *How Would You Know If Hot Temperatures Cause Aggression?*

available data estimates that global warming of 4 degrees Fahrenheit (about 2 degrees Celsius) could induce tens of thousands of additional assaults and murders (Anderson & Delisi, 2011; Miles-Novelo & Anderson, 2019). And that's before the added violence inducements from climate change–related drought, poverty, food insecurity, and migration.

REINFORCEMENT AND MODELING Aggression may naturally follow aversive events, but learning can alter natural reactions. We learn when our behavior is reinforced, and we learn by watching others.

In situations where experience has taught us that aggression pays, we are likely to act aggressively again. Children whose aggression has successfully intimidated other children may become bullies. Animals that have successfully fought to get food or mates become increasingly ferocious. To foster a kinder, gentler world we had best model and reward sensitivity and cooperation from an early age, perhaps by training parents to discipline without modeling violence. Parent-training programs often advise parents to avoid screaming and hitting; instead, they can reinforce desirable behaviors and frame statements positively. ("When you put your toys away you can go play," rather than "If you don't put your toys away, you'll be in big trouble.")

Different cultures model, reinforce, and evoke different tendencies toward violence. For example, crime rates have been higher and average happiness lower in times and places marked by a great disparity between rich and poor (Messias et al., 2011; Oishi et al., 2011; Wilkinson & Pickett, 2009). And fathers matter (Triandis, 1994). Even after controlling for parental education, race, income, and teen motherhood, American male youths from father-absent homes are incarcerated at twice the rate of their peers (Harper & McLanahan, 2004).

Violence can vary by culture within a country. The American South, for example, has long had a "culture of honor." Richard Nisbett and Dov Cohen (1996) analyzed violence among White Americans in southern towns settled by Scots-Irish herders whose tradition emphasized "manly honor," the use of arms to protect one's flock, and a history of slavery. Compared with their White counterparts in New England towns settled by the more traditionally peaceful Puritan, Quaker, and Dutch farmer-artisans, the cultural descendants of those herders had triple the homicide rates and were more supportive of physically punishing children, of wars, and of uncontrolled gun ownership. Southern culture-of-honor states have had higher rates of students bringing weapons to school and of school shootings (Brown et al., 2009).

MEDIA MODELS FOR VIOLENCE Parents are hardly the only aggression models. Television, films, video games, and the internet offer supersized portions of violence. An adolescent boy faced with a real-life challenge may "act like a man"—at least like an action-film man—by intimidating or eliminating the threat. Media violence teaches us **social scripts**—culturally provided mental files for how to act in certain situations. As more than 100 studies confirm, we sometimes imitate what we've viewed. Watching media depictions of risk-glorifying behaviors (dangerous driving, extreme sports,

social script a culturally modeled guide for how to act in various situations.

unprotected sex) increases real-life risk-taking (Fischer et al., 2011). Watching violent behaviors (murder, robbery) can increase real-life aggressiveness (Anderson et al., 2017).

Music lyrics also write social scripts. In one study, German university men who listened to woman-hating lyrics poured the most hot chili sauce for a woman to consume. They also recalled more negative feelings and beliefs about women. Listening to man-hating lyrics had a similar effect on women (Fischer & Greitemeyer, 2006).

How does repeatedly watching pornographic films affect viewers? As pornography has become more readily available, rates of reported sexual violence have decreased in the United States (though not in Canada, Australia, and Europe). Nevertheless, just as repeated viewing of onscreen violence helps immunize us to aggression, repeated viewing of pornography—even nonviolent pornography—makes sexual aggression seem less serious (Harris, 1994). In one experiment, undergraduates viewed six brief films each week for six weeks (Zillmann & Bryant, 1984). Some viewed sexually explicit films; others viewed films with no sexual content. Three weeks later, both groups, after reading a report about a man convicted of raping a female hitchhiker, suggested an appropriate prison term. Compared with sentences recommended by the control group, the sex film viewers recommended terms that were half as long. In other studies that explored pornography's effects on aggression toward relationship partners, pornography consumption predicted both self-reported aggression and participants' willingness to administer laboratory noise blasts to their partner (Lambert et al., 2011; Peter & Valkenburg, 2016). Pornography acts mostly by adding fuel to a fire: It heightens risk of sexual aggression primarily among aggression-prone men (Malamuth, 2018).

Pornography with violent sexual content can also increase men's readiness to behave aggressively toward women. As a statement by 21 social scientists noted, "Pornography that portrays sexual aggression as pleasurable for the victim increases the acceptance of the use of coercion in sexual relations" (Surgeon General, 1986). Contrary to much popular opinion, viewing such scenes does not provide an outlet for bottled-up impulses. Rather, said the statement, "in laboratory studies measuring short-term effects, exposure to violent pornography increases punitive behavior toward women."

DO VIOLENT VIDEO GAMES TEACH SOCIAL SCRIPTS FOR VIOLENCE? Experiments worldwide indicate that playing positive games produces positive effects (Greitemeyer & Mügge, 2014; Prot et al., 2014). For example, playing the classic video game *Lemmings*, where a goal was to help others, increased real-life helping. So, might a parallel effect occur after playing games that enact violence? Violent video games became an issue for public debate after teenagers in more than a dozen places seemed to mimic the carnage in the shooter games they had so often played (Anderson, 2004, 2013).

Such incidents of violent mimicry make us wonder: What *are* the effects of actively role-playing aggression? Does it cause people to become less sensitive to violence and more open to violent acts? Amid conflicting findings, nearly 400 studies of 130,000 people offer some answers (Calvert et al., 2017). Violent video game playing tends to make us less sensitive to cruelty (Arriaga et al., 2015). Video games can prime aggressive thoughts, decrease empathy, and induce us to respond aggressively when provoked. University men who spend the most hours playing violent video games have also tended to be the most physically aggressive (Anderson & Dill, 2000). For example, they more often acknowledged having hit or attacked someone else. Two dozen longitudinal studies, which followed children and youth for up to 4 years, have found that violent video game playing predicts "greater levels of overt physical violence over time" (Prescott et al., 2018).

In experiments, people who have been randomly assigned to play a game involving bloody murders with groaning victims (rather than to play nonviolent games) became more hostile. On a follow-up task, they have been more likely to blast intense noise at a fellow student. Studies of young adolescents reveal that those who play a lot of violent video games become more aggressive and see the world as more hostile (Bushman, 2016; Exelmans et al., 2015; Gentile, 2009). Compared with nongaming kids, they get into more arguments and fights and earn poorer grades. In another experiment, children who played a video game with gun violence (rather than sword violence or no violence) later became more likely to touch, pick up, and pull the trigger on a real (but disabled) gun (Chang & Bushman, 2019).

Coincidence or cause? In 2011, Norwegian Anders Behring Breivik bombed government buildings in Oslo, and then went to a youth camp where he shot and killed 69 people, mostly teens. As a player of first-person shooter games, Breivik stirred debate when he commented that "I see MW2 [*Modern Warfare 2*] more as a part of my training-simulation than anything else." Did his violent game playing—and that of the 2012 mass murderer of Newtown, Connecticut's first-grade children—contribute to the violence, or was it a merely coincidental association? Psychologists explore such questions with experimental research.

AFP/Getty Images

"Research demonstrates a consistent relation between violent video game use and increases in aggressive behavior, aggressive cognitions and aggressive affect, and decreases in prosocial behavior, empathy and sensitivity to aggression." — American Psychological Association Task Force on Violent Media, 2015

"Study finds exposure to violent children causes increased aggression in video game characters." — The [satirical] Onion, March 6, 2017

Ah, but is this merely because naturally hostile kids are drawn to such games (Greitemeyer et al., 2019)? Apparently not. Comparisons of gamers and nongamers who scored low on hostility measures revealed a difference in the number of fights they reported. Almost 4 in 10 violent-game players had been in fights, compared with only 4 in 100 of the nongaming kids (Anderson, 2004). Some researchers believe that, due partly to the more active participation and rewarded violence of game play, violent video games have even greater effects on aggressive behavior and cognition than do violent TV shows and movies (Anderson & Warburton, 2012).

Other researchers are unimpressed by such findings (Markey & Ferguson, 2018). They note that from 1996 to 2006, video game sales increased, yet youth violence declined. They argue that other factors—depression, family violence, peer influence, and a gun-toting culture—better predict aggression. Although some commentators have tried to blame modern mass shootings on violent video games, most researchers agree that they are, at worst, but one modest contributor to social violence (Mathur & VanderWeele, 2019).

* * *

To sum up, research reveals biological, psychological, and social-cultural influences on aggressive behavior. Complex behaviors, including violence, have many causes, making any single explanation an oversimplification. Asking what causes violence is therefore like asking what causes cancer. Those who study the effects of asbestos exposure on cancer rates may remind us that asbestos is indeed a cancer cause, but it is only one among many. Like so much else, aggression is a biopsychosocial phenomenon (FIGURE 42.6).

A happy concluding note: Historical trends suggest that the world is becoming less violent over time (Pinker, 2011). That people vary across time and place reminds us that environments differ. Yesterday's plundering Vikings have become today's peace-promoting Scandinavians. Like all behavior, aggression arises from the interaction of persons and situations.

→ **FIGURE 42.6**
Biopsychosocial understanding of aggression Because many factors contribute to aggressive behavior, there are many ways to change such behavior, including learning anger management and communication skills, and avoiding violent media and video games.

Biological influences:
• heredity
• biochemical factors, such as testosterone and alcohol
• neural factors, such as a severe head injury

Psychological influences:
• dominating behavior (which boosts testosterone levels in the blood)
• believing that alcohol has been ingested (whether it has or not)
• frustration
• aggressive role models
• rewards for aggressive behavior
• low self-control

Aggressive behavior

Social-cultural influences:
• *deindividuation*, or a loss of self-awareness and self-restraint
• challenging environmental factors, such as crowding, heat, and direct provocations
• parental models of aggression
• minimal father involvement
• rejection from a group
• exposure to violent media

ASK YOURSELF

In what ways have you been affected by social scripts for aggression? Have your viewing and gaming habits influenced these social scripts?

RETRIEVAL PRACTICE

RP-2 What biological, psychological, and social-cultural influences interact to produce aggressive behaviors?

ANSWERS IN APPENDIX E

㊷ REVIEW Antisocial Relations

LEARNING OBJECTIVES

Test Yourself Answer these repeated Learning Objective Questions on your own (before checking the answers in Appendix D) to improve your retention of the concepts (McDaniel et al., 2009, 2015).

LOQ 42-1 What is *prejudice?* How do explicit and implicit prejudice differ?

LOQ 42-2 What groups are frequent targets of prejudice?

LOQ 42-3 What are some social, emotional, and cognitive roots of prejudice, and what are some ways to reduce prejudice?

LOQ 42-4 How does psychology's definition of *aggression* differ from everyday usage? What biological factors make us more prone to hurt one another?

LOQ 42-5 What psychological and social-cultural factors may trigger aggressive behavior?

TERMS AND CONCEPTS TO REMEMBER

Test Yourself Write down the definition in your own words, then check your answer.

prejudice, p. 488
stereotype, p. 488
discrimination, p. 488
just-world phenomenon, p. 493
ingroup, p. 493
outgroup, p. 493
ingroup bias, p. 493

scapegoat theory, p. 493
other-race effect, p. 495
aggression, p. 495
frustration-aggression principle, p. 497
social script, p. 498

MASTER THE MATERIAL

Test Yourself Answer the following questions on your own first, then check your answers in Appendix E.

1. Prejudice toward a group involves negative feelings, a tendency to discriminate, and overly generalized beliefs referred to as _____.

2. If several well-publicized murders are committed by members of a particular group, we may tend to react with fear and suspicion toward all members of that group. In other words, we
   a. blame the victim.
   b. overgeneralize from vivid, memorable cases.

   c. view the world as just.
   d. rationalize inequality.

3. The other-race effect occurs when we assume that other groups are _____ (more/less) homogeneous than our own group.

4. Evidence of a biochemical influence on aggression is the finding that
   a. aggressive behavior varies widely from culture to culture.
   b. animals can be bred for aggressiveness.
   c. stimulation of an area of the brain's limbic system produces aggressive behavior.
   d. a higher-than-average level of the hormone testosterone is associated with violent behavior in males.

5. Studies show that parents of delinquent young people tend to use physical force to enforce discipline. This suggests that aggression can be
   a. learned through direct rewards.
   b. triggered by exposure to violent media.
   c. learned through observation of aggressive models.
   d. caused by hormone changes at puberty.

6. A conference of social scientists studying the effects of pornography unanimously agreed that violent pornography
   a. has little effect on most viewers.
   b. is the primary cause of reported and unreported rapes.
   c. leads viewers to be more accepting of coercion in sexual relations.
   d. has no effect, other than short-term arousal and entertainment.

7. Heterosexual pornography most directly influences men's aggression toward women when the following is true:
   a. Viewing time is lengthy.
   b. Eroticism is portrayed.
   c. Sexual violence is portrayed.
   d. The actors are attractive.

Continue testing yourself with 📘 **LearningCurve** or 📗 **Achieve Read & Practice** to learn and remember most effectively.

㊸ Prosocial Relations

As social animals—as people who need people—we often approach others not with closed fists, but with open arms. Social psychologists focus not only on the dark side of social relationships, but also on the bright side, by studying *prosocial* behavior—behavior that intends to help or benefit someone. Our positive behaviors toward others are evident from explorations of attraction, altruism, and peacemaking.

Familiarity breeds acceptance When this rare white penguin was born in the Sydney, Australia, zoo, his tuxedoed peers ostracized him. Zookeepers thought they would need to dye him black to gain acceptance. But after three weeks of contact, the other penguins came to accept him.

Attraction

Pause a moment and think about your relationships with two people—a close friend, and someone who has stirred your romantic feelings. What psychological chemistry binds us together in friendship or love? Social psychology suggests some answers.

The Psychology of Attraction

LOQ **43-1** Why do we befriend or fall in love with some people but not others?

We endlessly wonder how we can win others' affection and what makes our own affections flourish or fade. Does familiarity breed contempt, or does it amplify affection? Do birds of a feather flock together, or do opposites attract? Is it what's inside that counts, or does physical attractiveness matter, too? To explore these questions, let's consider three ingredients of our liking for one another: proximity, attractiveness, and similarity.

PROXIMITY Before friendships become close, they must begin. *Proximity*—geographic nearness—is friendship's most powerful predictor. Proximity can provide opportunities for aggression. But much more often it breeds liking (and sometimes even marriage) among those who live in the same neighborhood, sit nearby in class, work in the same office, share the same parking lot, or eat in the same dining hall. Look around. Mating starts with meeting.

Proximity breeds liking partly because of the **mere exposure effect.** Repeated exposure to novel visual stimuli increases our liking for them. By age 3 months, infants prefer photos of the race they most often see—usually their own race (Kelly et al., 2007). Familiarity with a face also makes it look happier (Carr et al., 2017). For our ancestors, this mere exposure effect likely had survival value. What was familiar was generally safe and approachable. What was unfamiliar was more often dangerous and threatening. Evolution may therefore have hard-wired into us the tendency to bond with those who look familiar and to be wary of those who look unfamiliar (Sofer et al., 2015; Zajonc, 1998).

Mere exposure increases our liking not only for familiar faces, but also for familiar musical selections, geometric figures, Chinese characters, and for the letters of our own name (Moreland & Zajonc, 1982; Nuttin, 1987; Zajonc, 2001). Mere exposure even increases *unconscious* liking of nonsense syllables—strings of letters presented so quickly our minds don't consciously process them (Van Dessel et al., 2019). So, up to a point (after which the effect wears off), familiarity feeds fondness (Bornstein, 1989, 1999; Montoya et al., 2017). This would come as no surprise to the young Taiwanese man who wrote more than 700 letters to his girlfriend, urging her to marry him. She did marry—the mail carrier (Steinberg, 1993).

No face is more familiar than your own. And that helps explain an interesting finding by Lisa DeBruine (2002, 2004): We like other people when their faces incorporate some morphed features of our own. When McMaster University students played a game with a supposed other player, they were more trusting and cooperative when the other person's image had some of their own facial features morphed into it. In me I trust.

Which is the real Sofía Vergara? The mere exposure effect applies even to ourselves. Because the human face is not perfectly symmetrical, the face we see in the mirror is not the same face our friends see. Most of us prefer the familiar mirror image, while our friends like the reverse (Mita et al., 1977). The person actor Sofía Vergara sees in the mirror each morning is (b), and that's the photo she would probably prefer.

(a)

(b)

MODERN MATCHMAKING Those who have not found a romantic partner in their immediate proximity may cast a wider net. Millions search for love on one of the 8000 online dating sites (Hatfield, 2016). In 2015, 27 percent of 18- to 24-year-old Americans tried an online dating service or mobile dating app (Smith, 2016).

Online matchmaking expands the pool of potential mates, especially for same-sex couples (Finkel et al., 2012a,b; Rosenfeld et al., 2019). How effective is the matchmaking? Compared with those formed in person, internet-formed friendships and romantic relationships are, on average, slightly more likely to last and be satisfying (Bargh & McKenna, 2004; Bargh et al., 2002; Cacioppo et al., 2013). In one study, people disclosed more, with less posturing, to those whom they met online (McKenna et al., 2002). When conversing online with someone for 20 minutes, they felt more liking for that person than they did for someone they had met and talked with face-to-face. This was true even when (unknown to them) it was the same person! Internet friendships often feel as real and important as in-person relationships.

Online connecting comes with some risks. For about half of young women, this includes receiving unwanted sexual messages (Anderson et al., 2020). Nevertheless, some 10 million Americans are using online matchmaking (Statista, 2018). By one estimate, online dating has been responsible for about a fifth of U.S. marriages (Crosier et al., 2012). Among those who met in 2017, 39 percent of straight couples and 65 percent of same-sex couples met online (Rosenfeld et al., 2019; see **FIGURE 43.1**).

"...and if anyone here suspects that the algorithm that put these two together might be flawed, speak now..."

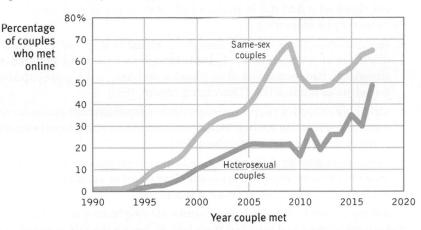

⬅ **FIGURE 43.1**
The changing way we meet our partners The internet's increasing role is clear in American surveys of straight and same-sex couples. (Data from Rosenfeld, 2011; Rosenfeld et al., 2018, 2019.)

Speed dating pushes the search for romance into high gear. In a process pioneered by a matchmaking Jewish rabbi, people meet a succession of prospective partners, either in person or via webcam (Bower, 2009). After a 3- to 8-minute conversation, people move on to the next prospect. (In an in-person meeting of straight daters, one group—usually the women—remains seated while the other group circulates.) Those who want to meet again can arrange for future contact. For many participants, 4 minutes is enough time to form a feeling about a conversational partner and to register whether the partner likes them (Eastwick & Finkel, 2008a,b).

For researchers, speed dating offers a unique opportunity for studying influences on our first impressions of potential romantic partners. Some recent findings:

- *People who fear rejection often elicit rejection.* After a 3-minute speed date, those who most feared rejection were least often selected for a follow-up date (McClure & Lydon, 2014).

- *Given more options, people make more superficial choices.* When people meet lots of potential partners, they focus on more easily assessed characteristics, such as height and weight (Lenton & Francesconi, 2010).

- *Men wish for future contact with more of their speed dates; women tend to be choosier.* But this difference disappears if the conventional roles are reversed, so that men stay seated while women circulate (Finkel & Eastwick, 2009).

- *Compatibility is hard to predict.* In two speed-dating studies, participants answered more than 100 self-report measures beforehand. Alas, nothing predicted successful matches (Joel et al., 2017).

mere exposure effect the tendency for repeated exposure to novel stimuli to increase our liking of them.

PHYSICAL ATTRACTIVENESS Once proximity affords us contact, what most affects our first impressions? The person's sincerity? Intelligence? Personality? Hundreds of experiments reveal that it is something more superficial: physical appearance. This finding is unnerving for those of us taught that "beauty is only skin deep" and "appearances can be deceiving."

In one early study, researchers randomly matched new students for heterosexual blind dates in a Welcome Week dance (Walster et al., 1966). Before the dance, the researchers gave each student a battery of personality and aptitude tests, and they rated each student's physical attractiveness. The couples danced and talked for more than two hours and then took a brief intermission to rate their dates. What predicted whether they liked each other? Only one thing: appearance. Both the men and the women liked good-looking dates best. Women are more likely than men to say that another's looks don't affect them (Lippa, 2007). But studies show that a man's looks do affect women's behavior (Eastwick et al., 2014a,b). In speed-dating experiments, as in Tinder swipes, attractiveness influences first impressions (Belot & Francesconi, 2006; Finkel & Eastwick, 2008).

Physical attractiveness also predicts how often people date and how popular they feel. And it affects initial impressions of people's personalities. We perceive attractive people as healthier, happier, more sensitive, more successful, and more socially skilled (Eagly et al., 1991; Feingold, 1992; Hatfield & Sprecher, 1986).

For those who find the importance of looks unfair and unenlightened, three other findings may be reassuring.

- People's attractiveness is surprisingly unrelated to their self-esteem and happiness (Diener et al., 1995; Major et al., 1984). Unless we have just compared ourselves with superattractive people, few of us (thanks, perhaps, to the mere exposure effect) view ourselves as unattractive (Thornton & Moore, 1993).

- Strikingly attractive people are sometimes suspicious that praise for their work may simply be a reaction to their looks. Less attractive people have been more likely to accept praise as sincere (Berscheid, 1981).

- For couples who were friends before lovers—who became romantically involved long after first meeting—looks matter less (Hunt et al., 2015). With slow-cooked love, shared values and interests matter more.

Beauty is also in the eye of the culture. Hoping to look attractive, people across the globe have pierced and tattooed their bodies, lengthened their necks, bound their feet, artificially lightened or darkened their skin and hair, and bulked up their muscles. They have gorged themselves to achieve a full figure or liposuctioned fat to achieve a slim one, applied chemicals to rid themselves of unwanted hair or to regrow wanted hair, and used undergarments to change the proportions of waists, hips, and breasts. Cultural ideals also change over time. For women in North America, for example, the ultrathin ideal of the Roaring Twenties gave way to the soft, voluptuous Marilyn Monroe ideal of the 1950s, only to be replaced by today's lean yet busty ideal.

Some aspects of heterosexual attractiveness, however, do cross place and time (Cunningham et al., 2005; Langlois et al., 2000). By providing reproductive clues, bodies influence sexual attraction. As evolutionary psychologists explain, men in many cultures, from Australia to Zambia, judge women as more attractive if they have a youthful,

"Personal beauty is a greater recommendation than any letter of introduction."
— Aristotle, *Apothegems*, 330 B.C.E.

Estimated length of human nose removed by U.S. plastic surgeons each year: 5469 feet (*Harper's*, 2009).

What is "attractive"? The answer varies by culture and over time. Yet some adult physical features, such as a healthy appearance and a relatively symmetrical face, seem attractive everywhere.

fertile appearance, suggested by a low waist-to-hip ratio (Karremans et al., 2010; Perilloux et al., 2010; Platek & Singh, 2010). Women feel attracted to healthy-looking men (cues for virility and fertility), but especially to those who seem mature, dominant, masculine, and affluent (Gallup & Frederick, 2010; Gangestad et al., 2010). Faces matter, too. When people rate other-sex faces and bodies separately, the face tends to be the better predictor of overall physical attractiveness (Currie & Little, 2009; Peters et al., 2007).

Our feelings also influence our attractiveness judgments. Imagine two people: One is honest, humorous, and polite. The other is rude, unfair, and abusive. Which one is more attractive? Most people perceive the person with the appealing traits as more physically attractive (Lewandowski et al., 2007). Or imagine being paired with a stranger of the gender you find attractive—someone who listens intently to your self-disclosures. Might you feel a twinge of sexual attraction toward that empathic person? Student volunteers did, in several experiments (Birnbaum & Reis, 2012). Our feelings influence our perceptions. Those we like we find attractive.

In a Rodgers and Hammerstein production of *Cinderella*, Prince Charming asks, "Do I love you because you're beautiful, or are you beautiful because I love you?" Chances are it's both. As we see our loved ones again and again, their physical imperfections grow less noticeable and their attractiveness grows more apparent (Beaman & Klentz, 1983; Gross & Crofton, 1977). Shakespeare said it in *A Midsummer Night's Dream:* "Love looks not with the eyes, but with the mind." Come to love someone and watch beauty grow. Love sees loveliness.

"Cosmetic dentistry changed my life."

Extreme makeover In affluent, beauty-conscious cultures, increasing numbers of people, such as celebrity Kylie Jenner, have turned to cosmetic procedures to change their looks.

SIMILARITY So, proximity has brought you into contact with someone, and your appearance has made an acceptable first impression. What influences whether you will become friends? As you get to know each other, will the chemistry be better if you are opposites or if you are alike?

It makes a good story—extremely different types liking or loving each other: unlikely friends Frog and Toad in Arnold Lobel's books, unlikely couple Hermione and Ron in the Harry Potter series. These stories delight us by expressing what we seldom experience. In real life, opposites retract (Montoya & Horton, 2013; Rosenbaum, 1986). Tall people typically find true love with other tall people; short people show a soft spot for other short people (Yengo et al., 2018). Compared with randomly paired people, friends and couples are far more likely to share—and to like those with whom they share—attitudes, beliefs, and interests (and, for that matter, age, religion, race, education, intelligence, smoking behavior, and economic status). Moreover, the more alike people are, the more their liking endures (Byrne, 1971; Hartl et al., 2015). Journalist Walter Lippmann was right to suppose that love lasts "when the lovers love many things together, and not merely each other." Similarity breeds content.

Proximity, attractiveness, and similarity are not the only determinants of attraction. We also like those who like us. This is especially true when our self-image is low. When we believe someone likes us, we feel good and respond to them warmly, which leads them to like us even more (Curtis & Miller, 1986). To be liked is powerfully rewarding. And good news: more than we tend to suppose (when fretting over our words or looks after meeting someone), most people immediately like us more than we realize (Boothby et al., 2018).

Similarity attracts; perceived dissimilarity does not.

"I like the Pope unless the Pope doesn't like me. Then I don't like the Pope." — Donald Trump, February 18, 2016

Test your own ability to improve your relationships by engaging online with the activity *Assess Your Strengths—Are You a "Skilled Opener," and How Does This Affect Your Relationships?*

Snapshots at jasonlove.com

© Jason Love

Bill looked at Susan, Susan at Bill. Suddenly death didn't seem like an option. This was love at first sight.

passionate love an aroused state of intense positive absorption in another, usually present at the beginning of a romantic relationship.

companionate love the deep affectionate attachment we feel for those with whom our lives are intertwined.

equity a condition in which people receive from a relationship in proportion to what they give to it.

self-disclosure the act of revealing intimate aspects of ourselves to others.

Indeed, all the findings we have considered so far can be explained by a simple *reward theory of attraction*: We will like those whose behavior is rewarding to us, including those who are both able and willing to help us achieve our goals (Montoya & Horton, 2014). When people live or work in close proximity to us, it requires less time and effort to develop the friendship and enjoy its benefits. When people are attractive, they are aesthetically pleasing, and associating with them can be socially rewarding. When people share our views, they reward us by validating our beliefs.

ASK YOURSELF

To what extent have your closest relationships been affected by proximity, physical attractiveness, and similarity?

RETRIEVAL PRACTICE

RP-1 People tend to marry someone who lives or works nearby. This is an example of the _____ _____ _____ in action.

RP-2 How does being physically attractive influence others' perceptions?

ANSWERS IN APPENDIX E

Romantic Love

LOQ 43-2 How does romantic love typically change as time passes?

Sometimes people move from initial impressions to friendship to the more intense, complex, and mysterious state of romantic love. If love endures, temporary *passionate love* will mellow into a lingering *companionate love* (Hatfield, 1988).

PASSIONATE LOVE **Passionate love** mixes something new with something positive (Aron et al., 2000; Coulter & Malouff, 2013). We intensely desire to be with our partner, and seeing our partner stimulates blood flow to a brain region linked to craving and obsession (Acevedo et al., 2012; Hatfield et al., 2015).

The *two-factor theory of emotion* can help us understand the intense positive absorption of passionate love (Hatfield, 1988). That theory assumes that

- emotions have two ingredients—*physical arousal* plus *cognitive appraisal*.
- arousal from any source can enhance one emotion or another, depending on how we interpret and label the arousal.

In one classic experiment, researchers studied men crossing two bridges above British Columbia's rocky Capilano River (Dutton & Aron, 1974, 1989). One, a swaying footbridge, was 230 feet (70 meters) above the rocks; the other was low and solid. As the men came off each bridge, an attractive young woman (working for the researchers) intercepted them and asked them to fill out a short questionnaire. She then offered her phone number in case they wanted to hear more about her project. Far more of the men who had just crossed the high bridge—which left their hearts pounding—accepted the number and later called the woman.

To be revved up and to associate some of that arousal with a desirable person is to feel the pull of passion. Adrenaline makes the heart grow fonder. Sexual desire + a growing attachment = passionate love (Berscheid, 2010).

COMPANIONATE LOVE Although the desire and attachment of romantic love often endure, the intense absorption in the other, the thrill of the romance, the giddy "floating on a cloud" feeling typically fade. Does this mean the French are correct in saying that "love makes the time pass and time makes love pass"? Or can friendship and commitment keep a relationship going after the passion cools?

As love matures, it typically becomes a steadier **companionate love**—a deep, affectionate attachment (Hatfield, 1988). Like a passing storm, the flood of passion-facilitating hormones (testosterone, dopamine, adrenaline) subsides. But another hormone, *oxytocin*, remains, supporting feelings of trust, calmness, and bonding with the mate. This shift from passion to attachment may have adaptive value (Reis & Aron, 2008). Passionate love often produces children; companionate love aids children's survival as the parents lose their obsession with each other.

In the most satisfying marriages, attraction and sexual desire endure, minus the obsession of early romance (Acevedo & Aron, 2009). Recognizing the short duration of obsessive passionate love, some societies deem such feelings an irrational reason for marrying. Better, they say, to seek (or have someone seek for you) a partner with a compatible background and interests. Cultures where people rate love as less important for marriage do have lower divorce rates (Levine et al., 1995).

One key to a gratifying and enduring relationship is **equity.** When equity exists— when both partners receive in proportion to what they give—the chances for sustained and satisfying companionate love have been good (Gray-Little & Burks, 1983; Van Yperen & Buunk, 1990). In one national survey, "sharing household chores" ranked third, after "faithfulness" and a "happy sexual relationship," on a list of nine things people associated with successful marriages. As the Pew Research Center (2007) summarized, "I like hugs. I like kisses. But what I really love is help with the dishes."

Equity's importance extends beyond marriage. Mutually sharing one's self and possessions, making decisions together, giving and getting emotional support, promoting and caring about each other's welfare—all of these acts are at the core of every type of loving relationship (Sternberg & Grajek, 1984). It's true for lovers, for parent and child, and for close friends.

Sharing includes **self-disclosure,** revealing intimate details about ourselves—our likes and dislikes, our dreams and worries, our proud and shameful moments. "When I am with my friend," noted the Roman statesman Seneca, "methinks I am alone, and as much at liberty to speak anything as to think it." Self-disclosure breeds liking, and liking breeds self-disclosure (Collins & Miller, 1994). As one person reveals a little, the other reciprocates, the first then reveals more, and on and on, as friends or lovers move to deeper levels of intimacy (Baumeister & Bratslavsky, 1999).

One experiment marched some student pairs through 45 minutes of increasingly self-disclosing conversation—from "What is the greatest accomplishment of your life?" to "When did you last cry in front of another person? By yourself?" Other pairs spent the time with small-talk questions, such as "What was your high school like?" (Aron et al., 1997). By the experiment's end, those experiencing the escalating intimacy felt much closer to their conversation partner than did the small-talkers. Likewise, after dating couples spent 45 minutes answering such questions, they felt increased love (Welker et al., 2014).

Love is an ancient thing This 5000- to 6000-year-old "Romeo and Juliet" young couple was unearthed locked in embrace, near Rome.

HI & LOIS

In addition to equity and self-disclosure, a third key to enduring love is *positive support.* Relationship conflicts are inevitable, but hurtful communications are not. Do we more often express sarcasm or support, scorn or sympathy, sneers or smiles? For unhappy couples, disagreements, criticisms, and put downs are routine. For happy couples in enduring relationships, positive interactions (compliments, touches, laughing) outnumber negative interactions (sarcasm, disapproval, insults) by at least 5 to 1 (Gottman, 2007; see also Sullivan et al., 2010). Our acute sensitivity to criticism—it takes multiple compliments to equal the attention-getting and emotion-affecting power of one criticism—also applies to all our relationships (Tierney & Baumeister, 2019). Perhaps you have noticed: Hurting words linger long after kind ones have been forgotten.

In the mathematics of love, self-disclosing intimacy + mutually supportive equity = enduring companionate love.

altruism unselfish regard for the welfare of others.

bystander effect the tendency for any given bystander to be less likely to give aid if other bystanders are present.

RP-3 How does the two-factor theory of emotion help explain *passionate love*?

RP-4 Two vital components for maintaining *companionate love* are _____ and _____-_____.

ANSWERS IN APPENDIX E

Altruism

LOQ **43-3** What is *altruism?* When are people most—and least—likely to help?

Altruism is an unselfish concern for the welfare of others. In rescuing his trapped jailer, rather than continuing his escape, Dirk Willems exemplified altruism. Willems fits the definition of a *hero*—moral, courageous, and protective of those in need (Kinsella et al., 2015). Carl Wilkens and Paul Rusesabagina displayed another heroic example of altruism in Kigali, Rwanda. Wilkens, a Seventh-day Adventist missionary, was living there in 1994 with his family when militia from the Hutu ethnic group began to slaughter members of a minority ethnic group, the Tutsis. The U.S. government, church leaders, and friends all implored Wilkens to leave. He refused. After evacuating his family, and after every other American had left Kigali, he alone stayed and contested the 800,000-person genocide. When the militia came to kill him and his Tutsi servants, Wilkens' Hutu neighbors deterred them. Despite repeated death threats, he spent his days running roadblocks to take food and water to orphanages and to negotiate, plead, and bully his way through the bloodshed, saving lives time and again. "It just seemed the right thing to do," he later explained (Kristof, 2004).

Elsewhere in Kigali, Rusesabagina, a Hutu married to a Tutsi and the acting manager of a luxury hotel, was sheltering more than 1200 terrified Tutsis and moderate Hutus. When most international peacekeepers abandoned the city and hostile militia threatened his guests in the "Hotel Rwanda" (as it came to be called in a 2004 movie), the courageous Rusesabagina began cashing in past favors. He bribed the militia and telephoned influential people abroad to exert pressure on local authorities, thereby sparing the lives of the hotel's occupants, despite the surrounding chaos. Both Wilkens and Rusesabagina were displaying altruism.

Altruism became a major concern of social psychologists after an especially vile act. On March 13, 1964, a stalker repeatedly stabbed Kitty Genovese, then raped her as she lay dying outside her Queens, New York, apartment at 3:30 A.M. "Oh, my God, he stabbed me!" Genovese screamed into the early morning stillness. "Please help me!" Windows opened and lights went on as some neighbors heard her screams. Her attacker fled and then returned to stab and rape her again. Until it was too late, no one called police or came to her aid.

Bystander Intervention

Although initial reports of the Genovese murder overestimated the number of witnesses, the reports triggered outrage over the bystanders' apparent "apathy" and "indifference." Rather than blaming the onlookers, social psychologists John Darley and Bibb Latané (1968b) instead attributed their inaction to an important situational factor—the presence of others. Given certain circumstances, they suspected, most of us might behave similarly. To paraphrase the French writer Voltaire, we all are guilty of the good we did not do.

After staging emergencies under various conditions, Darley and Latané assembled their findings into a decision scheme: We will help only if the situation enables us first to *notice* the incident, then to *interpret* it as an emergency, and finally to *assume responsibility* for helping (**FIGURE 43.2**). At each step, the presence of others can turn us away from the path that leads to helping.

One of Darley and Latané's experiments staged a fake emergency as students in separate laboratory rooms took turns talking over an intercom. Only the person whose microphone was switched on could be heard. When his turn came, one student (actually an accomplice) pretended to have an epileptic seizure, and he called for help (1968a).

"Probably no single incident has caused social psychologists to pay as much attention to an aspect of social behavior as Kitty Genovese's murder." — R. Lance Shotland (1984)

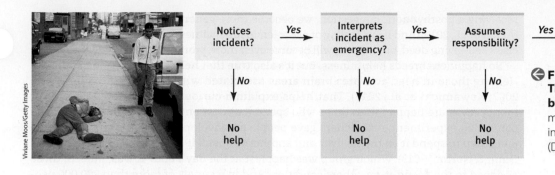

⬅ FIGURE 43.2
The decision-making process for bystander intervention Before helping, one must first notice an emergency, then correctly interpret it, and then assume responsibility. (Data from Darley & Latané, 1968b.)

How did the others react? As **FIGURE 43.3** shows, those who believed only they could hear the victim—and therefore thought they alone were responsible for helping him—usually went to his aid. Students who thought others could also hear the victim's cries were more likely to do nothing. When more people shared responsibility for helping—when there was a *diffusion of responsibility*—any single listener was less likely to help. Indeed, inattention and diffused responsibility contribute to "global bystander nonintervention" as millions of far-away people die of hunger, disease, and genocide (Pittinsky & Diamante, 2015).

Hundreds of additional experiments have confirmed this **bystander effect.** For example, researchers and their assistants took 1497 elevator rides in three cities and "accidentally" dropped coins or pencils in front of 4813 fellow passengers (Latané & Dabbs, 1975). When alone with the person in need, 40 percent helped; in the presence of 5 other bystanders, only 20 percent helped. Ironically, Kitty Genovese's killer, Winston Moseley, was captured thanks to the intervention of a single bystander who confronted him as he later burgled a home. Disbelieving Moseley's explanation that he was helping the owners move, the bystander called another neighbor—who called police—and then pulled wires to disable Moseley's car (Kassin, 2017).

Although the presence of other bystanders reduces the chance that an individual will offer help, sometimes, people *do* help. In CCTV surveillance of arguments and fights caught on the streets of Amsterdam, Lancaster, and Cape Town, 9 times out of 10, at least one bystander and usually more did something to help (Philpot et al., 2019). Another research team planted 17,303 "lost" wallets in 40 countries, walking into public places such as hotels, post offices, and banks and explaining to a clerk: "I found this on the street around the corner. Someone must have lost it. I'm in a hurry and have to go. Can you please take care of it?" Forty percent of those given cashless wallets alerted the owner. Surprisingly to economists surveyed, those receiving wallets with cash were even *more* likely (51 percent) to help (Cohn et al., 2019).

Observations of behavior in thousands of these situations—relaying an emergency phone call, aiding a stranded motorist, donating blood, picking up dropped books, contributing money, giving time—show that the odds of our helping someone depend on the characteristics of that person, the situation, and our own internal state. The odds of helping are highest when

- the person appears to need and deserve help.
- the person is in some way similar to us.
- the person is a woman.
- we have just observed someone else being helpful.
- we are not in a hurry.
- we are in a small town or rural area.
- we are feeling guilty.
- we are focused on others and not preoccupied.
- we are in a good mood.

The "good mood" result—that happy people are helpful people—is one of psychology's most consistent findings. As poet Robert Browning (1868) observed, "Oh, make us happy and you make us good!" It doesn't matter how we are cheered. Whether by being made to feel successful and intelligent, by thinking happy thoughts, by finding money, or even by

⬇ FIGURE 43.3
Responses to a simulated emergency When people thought they alone heard the calls for help from a person they believed to be having an epileptic seizure, they usually helped. But when they thought four others were also hearing the calls, fewer than one-third responded. (Data from Darley & Latané, 1968a.)

Percentage attempting to help

Fewer people help if others seem available.

Number of others presumed available to help

© 2014 Steve Kelley/
Creators Syndicate, Inc.

To test your understanding of emergency helping, engage online with *Concept Practice: When Will People Help Others?*

receiving a posthypnotic suggestion, we become more generous and more eager to help (Aknin et al., 2019). And if our feeling of elevation follows witnessing or learning of someone else's self-giving deed, our helping will become even more pronounced (Schnall et al., 2010).

So happiness breeds helpfulness. But it's also true that helpfulness breeds happiness. Helping those in need activates brain areas associated with reward (Harbaugh et al., 2007; Kawamichi et al., 2015). That helps explain a curious finding: People who give money away are happier than those who spend it almost entirely on themselves. In one controlled experiment, researchers gave people an envelope with cash and instructed one group to spend it on themselves and another to spend it on others (Dunn et al., 2008; Dunn & Norton, 2013). Which group was happiest at the day's end? It was, indeed, those assigned to the spend-it-on-others condition. And in a survey of more than 200,000 people worldwide, people in both rich and poor countries were happier with their lives if they had donated to a charity in the last month. Just reflecting on an instance of spending money on others provides most people with a mood boost (Aknin et al., 2013).

ASK YOURSELF

Imagine being a newcomer needing directions at a busy bus terminal. What could you do to increase the odds that someone will assist you, and what sort of person would be most likely to help?

RETRIEVAL PRACTICE

RP-5 What social psychology principle did the Kitty Genovese incident illustrate?

ANSWERS IN APPENDIX E

Norms for Helping

LOQ 43-4 How do social exchange theory and social norms explain helping behavior?

Why do we help? One widely held view is that self-interest underlies all human interactions, that our constant goal is to maximize rewards and minimize costs. Accountants call it *cost-benefit analysis.* Philosophers call it *utilitarianism.* Social psychologists call it **social exchange theory.** If you are considering donating blood, you may weigh the costs of doing so (time, discomfort, anxiety) against the benefits (reduced guilt, social approval, good feelings). If the rewards exceed the costs, you will help.

Others believe we help because we have been socialized to do so, through norms that prescribe how we *ought* to behave (Everett et al., 2015). Two such norms are the *reciprocity norm* and the *social-responsibility norm.*

The **reciprocity norm** is the expectation that we should return help, not harm, to those who have helped us. Those for whom we do favors will often return favors. (Be kind to others and you may elicit future kindness from them.) With similar others, the reciprocity norm motivates us to give (in favors, gifts, or social invitations) about as much as we receive. Sometimes this means "paying it forward," as happened in one experiment, when people who were treated generously became more likely to be generous to a stranger (Tsvetkova & Macy, 2014). Returning favors feels good, so we tend to find the reciprocity norm a pleasant way to help others (Hein et al., 2016).

The reciprocity norm kicked in after Dave Tally, a Tempe, Arizona, homeless man, found $3300 in a backpack that an Arizona State University student had misplaced on his way to buy a used car (Lacey, 2010). Instead of using the cash for much-needed bike repairs, food, and shelter, Tally turned the backpack in to the social service agency where he volunteered. To reciprocate Tally's help, the backpack's owner thanked him with a cash reward. Hearing about Tally's self-giving deeds, dozens of others also sent him money and job offers.

The **social-responsibility norm** is the expectation that we should help those who need our help—young children and others who cannot give as much as they receive—even if the costs outweigh the benefits. Europeans are most welcoming of asylum seekers who are most vulnerable—those, for example, who have been tortured or have no surviving family (Bansak et al., 2016). This norm was demonstrated during the height of the COVID-19 pandemic. Despite the risk of infection, many brave people continued to help those in need—caring for the sick, grocery shopping for older neighbors, handing out sandwiches to people who are homeless. Construction worker Wesley Autrey exemplified the social-responsibility norm on January 2, 2007. He and his 6- and 4-year-old daughters were awaiting a New York City subway train when, before them, a man collapsed in a seizure, got up, then stumbled to the platform's edge and fell onto the tracks. With train headlights approaching, "I had to make a split-second decision," Autrey later recalled (Buckley, 2007). His decision, as his girls looked on in horror, was to leap from the platform, push the man off the tracks and into a foot-deep space between them, and lay atop him. As the train screeched to a halt, five cars traveled just above his head, leaving grease on his knit cap. When Autrey cried out, "I've got two daughters up there. Let them know their father is okay," onlookers erupted into applause.

Many world religions encourage their followers to practice the social-responsibility norm, and sometimes this leads to prosocial behavior. Between 2006 and 2008, Gallup polls sampled more than 300,000 people across 140 countries, comparing the "highly religious" (who said religion was important to them and who had attended a religious service in the prior week) to those less religious. The highly religious, despite being poorer, were about 50 percent more likely to report having "donated money to a charity in the last month" and to have volunteered time to an organization (Pelham & Crabtree, 2008). New surveys of 32,000 New Zealanders replicate this association of religious engagement with volunteerism (Van Tongeren et al., 2020).

Heroic helping In 2019, when a gunman entered a California synagogue, 60-year-old Lori Gilbert-Kaye selflessly attempted to shield her rabbi, and was murdered. Social psychologists study what prompts people to help.

From Conflict to Peace

Positive social norms encourage generosity and enable group living. But conflicts often divide us. One response to recent global conflict- and scarcity-driven mass migrations has been increasing nationalism and nativism (favoring native-born citizens over newcomers). Moreover, *every day*, the world continues to spend almost $5 billion for arms and armies—money that could be used for needed housing, nutrition, education, and health care. Knowing that wars begin in human minds, psychologists have wondered: What in the human mind causes destructive conflict? How might the perceived threats of social diversity be replaced by a spirit of cooperation?

Elements of Conflict

LOQ 43-5 How do social traps and mirror-image perceptions fuel social conflict?

To a social psychologist, a **conflict** is a perceived incompatibility of actions, goals, or ideas. The elements of conflict are much the same, whether partners sparring, political groups feuding, or nations at war. In each situation, conflict may seed positive change, or it may be a destructive process that can produce unwanted results. Among the destructive processes are *social traps* and *distorted perceptions*.

SOCIAL TRAPS In some situations, pursuing our personal interests also supports our collective well-being. As capitalist Adam Smith wrote in *The Wealth of Nations* (1776), "It is not from the benevolence of the butcher, the brewer, or the baker that we expect our dinner, but from their regard to their own interest." In other situations, we *harm* our collective well-being by pursuing our personal interests. Such situations are **social traps.**

Researchers have created mini social traps in laboratory games that require two participants to choose between pursuing their immediate self-interest, at others' expense, versus cooperating for mutual benefits. Many real-life situations similarly pit our individual interests against our communal well-being. Individual fish trawlers reasoned that the fish they took would not threaten the species and that if they didn't take them, others would anyway. The result: Some fish stocks have been depleted. Anticipating coronavirus shutdowns, people bought and hoarded toilet paper, leaving shelves empty for others. Individual car owners and home owners reason, "Electric cars are more expensive. Besides, the fuel that I burn in my one car doesn't noticeably add to the greenhouse gases." When enough people reason similarly, the collective result threatens disaster—climate change, rising seas, and more extreme weather.

social exchange theory the theory that our social behavior is an exchange process, the aim of which is to maximize benefits and minimize costs.

reciprocity norm an expectation that people will help, not hurt, those who have helped them.

social-responsibility norm an expectation that people will help those needing their help.

conflict a perceived incompatibility of actions, goals, or ideas.

social trap a situation in which two parties, by each pursuing their self-interest rather than the good of the group, become caught in mutually destructive behavior.

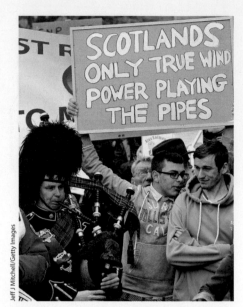

Not in my ocean! Many people support alternative energy sources, including wind turbines. But proposals to construct wind farms in real-world places elicit less support. Wind turbines in the Highlands and off the coast of Scotland have produced heated debate over the benefits of clean energy versus the costs of altering treasured scenic views.

Social traps challenge us to reconcile our right to pursue our personal well-being with our responsibility for the well-being of all. Psychologists have therefore explored ways to convince people to cooperate for their mutual betterment—through agreed-upon *regulations,* through better *communication,* and through promoting *awareness* of our responsibilities toward community, nation, and the whole of humanity (Dawes, 1980; Linder, 1982; Sato, 1987). Given effective regulations, communication, and awareness, people more often cooperate, whether playing a laboratory game or the real game of life.

ENEMY PERCEPTIONS Psychologists have noted that those in conflict have a curious tendency to form diabolical images of one another. These distorted images are, ironically, so similar that we call them **mirror-image perceptions:** As we see "them"—as untrustworthy, with evil intentions—so "they" see us. Each demonizes the other: "My political party, unlike the other party, has the nation's best interests at heart" (Waytz et al., 2014).

Mirror-image perceptions can often feed a vicious cycle of hostility. If Juan believes Maria is annoyed with him, he may snub her, causing her to act in ways that justify his perception. As with individuals, so with countries. Perceptions can become **self-fulfilling prophecies**—beliefs that confirm themselves by influencing the other country to react in ways that seem to justify those beliefs.

Individuals and nations alike tend to see their own actions as responses to provocation, not as the causes of what happens next. Perceiving themselves as returning tit for tat, they often hit back harder, as University College London volunteers did in one experiment (Shergill et al., 2003). Their task: After feeling pressure on their own finger, they were to use a mechanical device to press on another volunteer's finger. Although told to reciprocate with the same amount of pressure, they typically responded with about 40 percent more force than they had just experienced. Despite seeking only to respond in kind, their touches soon escalated to hard presses, much as when each child after a fight claims that "I just touched him, but he hit me!"

Mirror-image perceptions feed similar cycles of hostility on the world stage. To most people, torture seems more justified when done by "us" rather than "them" (Tarrant et al., 2012). In some American media reports, Muslims who kill have been portrayed as fanatical, hateful terrorists, while an American who allegedly killed 16 Afghans was portrayed as stressed out from marriage problems, four tours of duty, and a friend's having had his leg blown off (Greenwald, 2012).

The point is not that truth must lie midway between two such views (one may be more accurate). The point is that enemy perceptions often form mirror images. Moreover, as enemies change, so do perceptions. In American minds and media, the "bloodthirsty, cruel, treacherous" Japanese of World War II later became our "intelligent, hardworking, self-disciplined, resourceful allies" (Gallup, 1972).

RETRIEVAL PRACTICE

RP-6 Why do sports fans tend to feel a sense of satisfaction when their archrival team loses? Do such feelings, in other settings, make conflict resolution more challenging?

ANSWERS IN APPENDIX E

Promoting Peace

LOQ 43-6 What can we do to promote peace?

How can we make peace? Can contact, cooperation, communication, and conciliation transform the antagonisms fed by prejudice and conflicts into attitudes that promote peace? Research indicates that, in some cases, they can.

CONTACT Does it help to put two conflicting parties into close contact? It depends. Negative contact increases *disliking* (Barlow et al., 2019). But positive contact—especially noncompetitive contact between parties of equal status, such as fellow store clerks—typically helps. Initially prejudiced co-workers of different races have, in such circumstances, usually come to accept one another. This finding is confirmed by studies of face-to-face contact between majority people and outgroups, such as ethnic minorities,

---

mirror-image perceptions mutual views often held by conflicting parties, as when each side sees itself as ethical and peaceful and views the other side as evil and aggressive.

self-fulfilling prophecy a belief that leads to its own fulfillment.

superordinate goals shared goals that override differences among people and require their cooperation.

older people, LGBTQ people, and people with disabilities. Among the quarter-million people studied across 38 nations, contact has correlated with (and in experiments has led to) more positive and empathic attitudes (Paluck et al., 2018; Pettigrew & Tropp, 2011; Tropp & Barlow, 2018). Some examples:

- One survey of 116,667 people from 90 countries showed that people from countries with the most immigrants were the most supportive of immigrants; outgroup prejudice was strongest in countries with few immigrants (Shrira, 2020). The same has been true in both Germany and the United States: People in states with few immigrants express more anti-immigrant attitudes (Myers, 2018).

- Straight, cisgender people's attitudes toward gay and transgender people are influenced not only by *what* they know but also by *whom* they know (Brown, 2017; DellaPosta, 2018). In surveys, the reason people most often give for becoming more supportive of same-sex marriage is "having friends, family, or acquaintances who are gay or lesbian" (Pew, 2013a). And in the United States, where 87 percent of people now say they know someone who is gay, attitudes toward same-sex marriage have become much more accepting (McCarthy, 2019; Pew, 2016). Friendly contact—say, between Blacks and Whites as roommates—improves explicit and implicit attitudes toward others of the different race, and even toward other racial groups (Gaither & Sommers, 2013; Meleady et al., 2019; Onyeador et al., 2020).

- More than 100 studies reveal that even "extended contact"—knowing that ingroup friends have outgroup friends—improves attitudes toward the outgroup (Zhou et al., 2019). Straight people often are more gay-accepting if their straight friends have gay friends.

However, contact is not always enough. In most desegregated schools, ethnic groups resegregate themselves in lunchrooms, in classrooms, and elsewhere on school grounds (Alexander & Tredoux, 2010; Clack et al., 2005; Schofield, 1986). People in each group often think that they would welcome more contact with the other group, but they assume the other group does not reciprocate the wish (Richeson & Shelton, 2007). "I don't reach out to them, because I don't want to be rebuffed; they don't reach out to me, because they're just not interested." When such mirror-image misperceptions are corrected, friendships may form and prejudices melt.

COOPERATION To see if enemies could overcome their differences, researcher Muzafer Sherif (1966) set a conflict in motion. He separated 22 Oklahoma City boys into two separate camp areas. Then he had the two groups compete for prizes in a series of activities. Before long, each group became intensely proud of itself and hostile to the other group's "sneaky," "smart-alecky stinkers." Food wars broke out. Cabins were ransacked. Fistfights had to be broken up by camp counselors. Brought together, the two groups avoided each other, except to taunt and threaten. Little did they know that within a few days, they would be friends.

Sherif accomplished this by giving them **superordinate goals**—shared goals that could be achieved only through cooperation. When he arranged for the camp water supply to "fail," all 22 boys had to work together to restore the water. To rent a movie in those pre-Netflix days, they all had to pool their resources. To move a stalled truck, everyone needed to combine their strength, pulling and pushing together. Having used isolation and competition to make strangers into enemies, Sherif used shared predicaments and goals to turn enemies into friends. What reduced conflict was not mere contact, but *cooperative* contact.

Critics suggest that Sherif's research team encouraged the conflict, hoping the study would illustrate their expectations about socially toxic competition and socially beneficial cooperation (Perry, 2018). Yet shared predicaments have powerfully unifying effects. Minority-group members facing rejection or discrimination have developed strong ingroup identification (Bauer et al., 2014; Ramos et al., 2012). Children and youth exposed to war or conflict also develop strong social identities. Israeli children growing up in conflict areas often develop conflict-supportive perceptions, beliefs, and emotions regarding their shared adversary (Nasie et al., 2016). Such interpretations build ingroup solidarity but also insensitivity to the pain experienced by those in the outgroup (Levy et al., 2016).

"Prejudice is learned behavior that can be unlearned." — Desmond & Leah Tutu Legacy Foundation, 2019

Strangers coming together When a family got stuck in a Florida rip current, no less than 80 of their fellow beachgoers formed a human chain, rescuing them. Wrote one of the witnesses, Rosalind Beckton: "All races & ages join[ed] together to save lives" (AP, 2017).

Rosiland Beckton

In the aftermath of a divisive U.S. primary election, party members will usually reunify when facing their shared threat—the opposition party candidate. At such times, cooperation can lead people to define a new, inclusive group that dissolves their former subgroups (Dovidio & Gaertner, 1999). If this were a social psychology experiment, you might seat members of two groups not on opposite sides, but alternately around a table. Give them a new, shared name. Have them work together. Then watch "us" and "them" become "we."

If cooperative contact between rival group members encourages positive attitudes, might this principle bring diverse students together? Could cooperative learning in classrooms create interracial friendships, while also enhancing student achievement? Experiments with adolescents from 11 countries confirm that the answer to both questions is *Yes* (Roseth et al., 2008). In the classroom as in the sports arena, members of multi-ethnic groups who work together on projects typically come to feel friendly toward one another. Knowing this, thousands of teachers have made multi-ethnic cooperative learning part of their classroom experience.

The power of cooperative activity to make friends of former enemies has led psychologists to urge increased international exchange and cooperation. Some experiments have found that just imagining the shared threat of global climate change reduces international hostilities (Pyszczynski et al., 2012). From adjacent Brazilian tribes to European countries, formerly conflicting groups have managed to build interconnections, interdependence, and a shared social identity as they seek common goals (Fry, 2012). As we engage in mutually beneficial trade, as we work to protect our common destiny on this fragile planet, and as we become more aware that our hopes and fears are shared, we can transform misperceptions that feed conflict into feelings of solidarity based on common interests.

> "Me against my brother, my brothers and me against my cousins, then my cousins and me against strangers."— Bedouin proverb

> "Most of us have overlapping identities which unite us with very different groups. We *can* love what we are, without hating what—and who—we are *not*. We can thrive in our own tradition, even as we learn from others." — UN Secretary-General Kofi Annan, Nobel Peace Prize lecture, 2001

Justin Tafoya/Getty Images

Superordinate goals override differences Cooperative efforts to achieve shared goals are an effective way to break down social barriers, as these jubilant Baylor University 2019 U.S. Women's National Champions make clear.

COMMUNICATION When real-life conflicts become intense, a third-party mediator—a marriage counselor, labor mediator, diplomat, community volunteer—may facilitate much-needed communication (Rubin et al., 1994). Mediators help each party voice its viewpoint and understand the other's needs and goals. If successful, mediators can replace a competitive *win-lose* orientation with a cooperative *win-win* orientation that leads to a mutually beneficial resolution. A classic example: Two friends, after quarreling over an orange, agreed to split it. One squeezed his half for juice. The other used the peel from her half to flavor a cake. If only the two had communicated their motives to one another, they could have hit on the win-win solution of one having all the juice, the other all the peel.

CONCILIATION Understanding and cooperative resolution are most needed, yet least likely, in times of anger or crisis (Bodenhausen et al., 1994; Tetlock, 1988). When conflicts intensify, images become more stereotyped, judgments more rigid, and communication more difficult, or even impossible. Each party is likely to threaten, coerce, or retaliate. In the weeks before the 1990 Gulf War, U.S. President George H. W. Bush threatened, in the full glare of publicity, to "kick Saddam's ass." Iraqi president Saddam Hussein communicated in kind, threatening to make Americans "swim in their own blood."

Under such conditions, is there an alternative to war or surrender? Social psychologist Charles Osgood (1962, 1980) advocated a strategy of *Graduated and Reciprocated Initiatives in Tension-Reduction,* nicknamed **GRIT.** In applying GRIT, one side first announces its recognition of mutual interests and its intent to reduce tensions. It then initiates one or more small, conciliatory acts. Without weakening one's retaliatory capability, this modest beginning opens the door for reciprocity by the other party. Should the enemy respond with hostility, one reciprocates in kind. But so, too, with any conciliatory response.

In laboratory experiments, small conciliatory gestures—a smile, a touch, a word of apology—have allowed both parties to begin edging down the tension ladder to a safer rung where communication and mutual understanding can begin (Lindskold, 1978; Lindskold & Han, 1988). In a real-world international conflict, U.S. President John F. Kennedy's gesture of stopping atmospheric nuclear tests began a series of reciprocated conciliatory acts that culminated in the 1963 atmospheric test-ban treaty.

As working toward shared goals reminds us, we are more alike than different. Civilization advances not by conflict and cultural isolation, but by tapping the knowledge, the skills, and the arts that are each culture's legacy to the whole human race. Open societies are enriched by cultural sharing (Sowell, 1991). We have China to thank for paper and printing and for the magnetic compass that opened the great explorations. We have Egypt to thank for trigonometry. We have the Islamic world and India's Hindus to thank for our Arabic numerals. While celebrating and claiming these diverse cultural legacies, we can also welcome the continuing enrichment of today's cultural diversity. We can view ourselves as instruments in a human orchestra. And we can therefore each affirm our own culture's heritage while building bridges of communication, understanding, and cooperation across our cultural traditions.

Polarized Americans finding common ground In local communities across the United States, mediators are helping "red" (conservative) and "blue" (liberal) citizens discover their common ground and form friendships (see Better-Angels.org).

"To begin with, I would like to express my sincere thanks and deep appreciation for the opportunity to meet with you. While there are still profound differences between us, I think the very fact of my presence here today is a major breakthrough."

ASK YOURSELF

Do you regret not getting along with a family member or arguing with a friend? Do you have some ideas now about how you might be able to resolve such conflicts, now or in the future?

RETRIEVAL PRACTICE

RP-7 What are some ways to reconcile conflicts and promote peace?

ANSWERS IN APPENDIX E

GRIT Graduated and Reciprocated Initiatives in Tension-Reduction—a strategy designed to decrease international tensions.

REVIEW Prosocial Relations

LEARNING OBJECTIVES

Test Yourself Answer these repeated Learning Objective Questions on your own (before checking the answers in Appendix D) to improve your retention of the concepts (McDaniel et al., 2009, 2015).

LOQ 43-1 Why do we befriend or fall in love with some people but not others?

LOQ 43-2 How does romantic love typically change as time passes?

LOQ 43-3 What is *altruism?* When are people most—and least—likely to help?

LOQ 43-4 How do social exchange theory and social norms explain helping behavior?

LOQ 43-5 How do social traps and mirror-image perceptions fuel social conflict?

LOQ 43-6 What can we do to promote peace?

TERMS AND CONCEPTS TO REMEMBER

Test Yourself Write down the definition in your own words, then check your answer.

mere exposure effect, p. 503

passionate love, p. 506

companionate love, p. 506

equity, p. 506

self-disclosure, p. 506

altruism, p. 508

bystander effect, p. 508

social exchange theory, p. 511

reciprocity norm, p. 511

social-responsibility norm, p. 511

conflict, p. 511

social trap, p. 511

mirror-image perceptions, p. 512

self-fulfilling prophecy, p. 512

superordinate goals, p. 512

GRIT, p. 515

MASTER THE MATERIAL

Test Yourself Answer the following questions on your own first, then check your answers in Appendix E.

1. The more familiar a stimulus becomes, the more we tend to like it. This exemplifies the _____ _____ effect.

2. A happy couple celebrating their fiftieth wedding anniversary is likely to experience deep _____ love, even though their _____ love has probably decreased over the years.

3. After vigorous exercise, you meet an attractive person, and you are suddenly seized by romantic feelings for that person. This response supports the two-factor theory of emotion, which assumes that emotions, such as passionate love, consist of physical arousal plus

    a. a reward.

    b. proximity.

    c. companionate love.

    d. our interpretation of that arousal.

4. The bystander effect states that a particular bystander is less likely to give aid if

    a. the victim is similar to the bystander in appearance.

    b. no one else is present.

    c. other people are present.

    d. the incident occurs in a deserted or rural area.

5. Our enemies often have many of the same negative impressions of us as we have of them. This exemplifies the concept of _____-_____ perceptions.

6. One way of resolving conflicts and fostering cooperation is by giving rival groups shared goals that help them override their differences. These are called _____ goals.

Continue testing yourself with 📕 **LearningCurve** or 📘 **Achieve Read & Practice** to learn and remember most effectively.

Peathegee Inc/Getty Images

Personality

Lady Gaga dazzles millions with her unique musical arrangements, tantalizing outfits, and provocative performances. Her most predictable feature is her unpredictability. At an MTV Video Music Awards show, she stirred up debate by wearing a meat dress. In 2019, she surprised Academy Award viewers with a stunning duet with actor Bradley Cooper.

Yet even unpredictable Lady Gaga exhibits distinctive and enduring ways of thinking, feeling, and behaving. Her fans and critics alike can depend on her openness to new experiences and the energy she gets from the spotlight. And they can also rely on her painstaking dedication to her performances. She describes her high school self as "very dedicated, very studious, and very disciplined." Now, in adulthood, she shows similar self-discipline: "I'm very detailed—every minute of the show has got to be perfect." Modules 44, 45, and 46 focus on our *personality*—our unique and persistent patterns of thinking, feeling, and behaving.

Much of this book deals with personality. Other modules consider biological influences on personality; personality development across the life span; how personality relates to learning, motivation, emotion, and health; social influences on personality; and disorders of personality. These modules focus on personality itself—what it is and how researchers study it.

We begin with two historically important theories of personality that have become part of Western culture: Sigmund Freud's *psychoanalytic theory* and the *humanistic theories*

517

(Modules 44 and 45). These sweeping perspectives on human nature laid the foundation for later personality theorists and for what Module 46 presents: newer scientific explorations of personality.

Today's personality researchers study the basic dimensions of personality, and the interaction of persons and environments. They also study self-esteem, self-serving bias, and cultural influences on our concept of self—that sense of "Who I am." And they study the unconscious mind—with findings that probably would have surprised even Freud.

MODULE 44 Introduction to Personality and Psychodynamic Theories

Sigmund Freud (1856–1939) "I was the only worker in a new field."

What Is Personality?

LEARNING OBJECTIVE QUESTION LOQ 44-1 What is *personality,* and what theories inform our understanding of personality?

Psychologists have varied ways to view and study **personality**—our characteristic pattern of thinking, feeling, and acting. Sigmund Freud's *psychoanalytic theory* proposed that childhood sexuality and unconscious motivations influence personality. The *humanistic theories* focused on our inner capacities for growth and self-fulfillment. Later theorists built upon these two broad perspectives. *Trait theories* examine characteristic patterns of behavior *(traits). Social-cognitive theories* explore the interaction between people's traits (including their thinking) and their social context. Let's begin with Freud's work, and its modern-day descendant, *psychodynamic theories.*

Psychodynamic Theories

Psychodynamic theories of personality view human behavior as a dynamic interaction between the conscious mind and unconscious mind, including associated motives and conflicts. These theories are descended from Freud's **psychoanalysis**—his theory of personality and the associated treatment techniques. Freud was the first to focus clinical attention on our unconscious mind.

Freud's Psychoanalytic Perspective: Exploring the Unconscious

LOQ 44-2 How did Sigmund Freud's treatment of psychological disorders lead to his view of the unconscious mind?

Ask 100 people on the street to name a notable deceased psychologist, suggested Keith Stanovich (1996, p. 1), and "Freud would be the winner hands down." In the popular mind, he is to psychology what Elvis Presley is to rock music. Freud's influence lingers not only in psychiatry and clinical psychology, but also in literary and film interpretation. Almost 9 in 10 American college courses that reference psychoanalysis have been outside of psychology departments (Cohen, 2007). Freud's early twentieth-century concepts penetrate our twenty-first-century language. Without realizing their source, we may speak of *ego, repression, projection, complex* (as in "inferiority complex"), *sibling rivalry, Freudian slips,* and *fixation.* So, who was Freud, and what did he teach?

Like all of us, Sigmund Freud was a product of his times. The late 1800s, the tail end of the Victorian era, was a time of tremendous discovery and scientific advancement, but also of sexual suppression and men's dominance. Gender roles were clearly defined, with men's superiority assumed and only men's sexuality generally acknowledged (discreetly). These assumptions influenced Freud's thinking about personality. He believed that psychological troubles resulted from men's and women's unresolved conflicts with their expected roles.

"The female . . . acknowledges the fact of her castration, and with it, too, the superiority of the male and her own inferiority; but she rebels against this unwelcome state of affairs." — Sigmund Freud, *Female Sexuality,* 1931

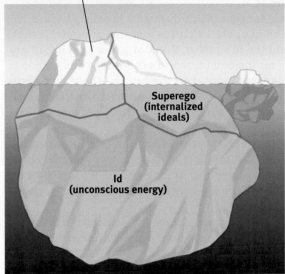

Ego
(mostly conscious; makes peace
between the id and the superego)

Superego
(internalized
ideals)

Id
(unconscious energy)

Conscious mind

Preconscious
(outside
awareness
but accessible)

Unconscious mind

◀ **FIGURE 44.1**
Freud's idea of the mind's
structure Psychologists have used an
iceberg image to illustrate Freud's idea that
the mind is mostly hidden beneath the
conscious surface.

Long before entering the University of Vienna in 1873, young Freud showed signs of independence and brilliance. He so loved reading plays, poetry, and philosophy that he once ran up a bookstore debt beyond his means. As a teen he often took his evening meal in his tiny bedroom in order to lose no time from his studies. After medical school he set up a private practice specializing in nervous disorders. Before long, however, he faced patients whose disorders made no neurological sense. A patient might have lost all feeling in a hand—yet there is no sensory nerve that, if damaged, would numb the entire hand and nothing else. Freud's search for a cause for such disorders set his mind running in a direction destined to change human self-understanding.

Do some neurological disorders have psychological causes? Observing patients led Freud to his "discovery" of the **unconscious.** He speculated that lost feeling in one's hand might be caused by a fear of touching one's genitals; that unexplained blindness or deafness might be caused by not wanting to see or hear something that aroused intense anxiety. After some early unsuccessful trials with hypnosis, Freud turned to **free association,** in which he told the patient to relax and say whatever came to mind, no matter how embarrassing or trivial. He assumed that a line of mental dominoes had fallen from his patients' distant past to their troubled present. Free association, he believed, would allow him to retrace that line, following a chain of thought leading into the patient's unconscious. There, painful unconscious memories, often from childhood, could be retrieved, reviewed, and released.

Basic to Freud's theory was this belief that the mind is mostly hidden (**FIGURE 44.1**). Our *conscious* awareness is like the part of an iceberg that floats above the surface. Beneath this awareness is the larger *unconscious* mind, with its thoughts, wishes, feelings, and memories. Some of these thoughts we store temporarily in a *preconscious* area, from which we can retrieve them into conscious awareness. Of greater interest to Freud was the mass of unacceptable passions and thoughts that he believed we *repress,* or forcibly block from our consciousness because they would be too unsettling to acknowledge. Freud believed that without our awareness, these troublesome feelings and ideas powerfully influence us, sometimes gaining expression in disguised forms—the work we choose, the beliefs we hold, our daily habits, our upsetting symptoms.

PERSONALITY STRUCTURE

LOQ **44-3** What was Freud's view of personality?

Freud believed that human personality, including its emotions and strivings, arises from a conflict between impulse and restraint—between our aggressive, pleasure-seeking biological urges and our internalized social controls over these urges. Freud believed personality springs from our efforts to resolve this basic conflict—to express these

personality an individual's characteristic pattern of thinking, feeling, and acting.

psychodynamic theories theories that view personality with a focus on the unconscious and the importance of childhood experiences.

psychoanalysis Freud's theory of personality that attributes thoughts and actions to unconscious motives and conflicts; the techniques used in treating psychological disorders by seeking to expose and interpret unconscious tensions.

unconscious according to Freud, a reservoir of mostly unacceptable thoughts, wishes, feelings, and memories. According to contemporary psychologists, information processing of which we are unaware.

free association in psychoanalysis, a method of exploring the unconscious in which the person relaxes and says whatever comes to mind, no matter how trivial or embarrassing.

id a reservoir of unconscious psychic energy that, according to Freud, strives to satisfy basic sexual and aggressive drives. The id operates on the *pleasure principle,* demanding immediate gratification.

ego the partly conscious, "executive" part of personality that, according to Freud, mediates among the demands of the id, the superego, and reality. The ego operates on the *reality principle,* satisfying the id's desires in ways that will realistically bring pleasure rather than pain.

superego the partly conscious part of personality that, according to Freud, represents internalized ideals and provides standards for judgment (the conscience) and for future aspirations.

psychosexual stages the childhood stages of development (oral, anal, phallic, latency, genital) during which, according to Freud, the id's pleasure-seeking energies focus on distinct *erogenous zones.*

Oedipus [ED-uh-puss] **complex** according to Freud, a boy's sexual desires toward his mother and feelings of jealousy and hatred for the rival father.

identification the process by which, according to Freud, children incorporate their parents' values into their developing superegos.

fixation in psychoanalytic theory, a lingering focus of pleasure-seeking energies at an earlier psychosexual stage, in which conflicts were unresolved.

defense mechanisms in psychoanalytic theory, the ego's protective methods of reducing anxiety by unconsciously distorting reality.

repression in psychoanalytic theory, the basic defense mechanism that banishes from consciousness anxiety-arousing thoughts, feelings, and memories.

impulses in ways that bring satisfaction without also bringing guilt or punishment. To understand the mind's dynamics during this conflict, Freud proposed three interacting systems: the *id, ego,* and *superego* (Figure 44.1).

The **id**'s entirely unconscious psychic energy constantly strives to satisfy basic drives to survive, reproduce, and aggress. The id operates on the *pleasure principle:* It seeks immediate gratification. To understand the id's power, think of a newborn infant crying out for satisfaction, caring nothing for the outside world's conditions and demands. Or think of people who focus on the present more than the future—those who abuse tobacco, alcohol, or other drugs, and would sooner party now than sacrifice today's temporary pleasure for future success and happiness (Fernie et al., 2013; Friedel et al., 2014; Keough et al., 1999).

As the **ego** develops, a young child responds to the real world. The ego, operating on the *reality principle,* seeks to gratify the id's impulses in realistic ways that will bring long-term pleasure. (Imagine what would happen if, lacking an ego, we acted on our unrestrained sexual or aggressive impulses.) The ego contains our partly conscious perceptions, thoughts, judgments, and memories.

Around age 4 or 5, Freud theorized, a child's ego recognizes the demands of the newly emerging **superego,** the partly conscious voice of our moral compass (conscience) that forces the ego to consider not only the real but also the *ideal.* The superego focuses on how we *ought* to behave. It strives for perfection, judging actions and producing positive feelings of pride or negative feelings of guilt. Someone with an exceptionally strong superego may be virtuous yet guilt ridden; another with a weak superego may be outrageously self-indulgent and remorseless.

Because the superego's demands often oppose the id's, the ego struggles to reconcile the two. The ego is the personality "executive," mediating among the impulsive demands of the id, the restraining demands of the superego, and the real-life demands of the external world. If virtuous Conner feels sexually attracted to Tatiana, his ego may satisfy both his id and superego by joining a volunteer organization that Tatiana attends regularly.

> To review Freud's components of personality, take advantage of the online *Concept Practice: Freud's Personality Structure.*

PERSONALITY DEVELOPMENT

LOQ **44-4** What developmental stages did Freud propose?

Analysis of his patients' histories convinced Freud that personality forms during life's first few years. He concluded that children pass through a series of **psychosexual stages,** during which the id's pleasure-seeking energies focus on distinct pleasure-sensitive areas of the body called *erogenous zones* (**TABLE 44.1**). Each stage offers its own challenges, which Freud saw as conflicting tendencies.

Freud believed that during the *phallic stage,* for example, boys develop both unconscious sexual desires for their mother and jealousy and hatred for their father, whom they consider a rival. He believed these feelings cause boys to feel guilty and to fear punishment, perhaps by castration, from their father. Such was Freud's (1897) own experience: "I have found, in my own case too, [the phenomenon of] being in love with my mother and jealous of my father, and I now consider it a universal event in early childhood." He called this collection of feelings the **Oedipus complex** after the Greek legend of

"I heard that as soon as we become aware of our sexual impulses, whatever they are, we'll have to hide them."

TABLE 44.1 Freud's Psychosexual Stages	
Stage	**Focus**
Oral (0–18 months)	Pleasure centers on the mouth—sucking, biting, chewing
Anal (18–36 months)	Pleasure focuses on bowel and bladder elimination; coping with demands for control
Phallic (3–6 years)	Pleasure zone is the genitals; coping with incestuous sexual feelings
Latency (6 years to puberty)	A phase of dormant sexual feelings
Genital (puberty on)	Maturation of sexual interests

Oedipus, whose failure to understand his unconscious desires led him to unknowingly kill his father and marry his mother. Some psychoanalysts in Freud's era believed that girls experience a parallel *Electra complex* (named after a mythological daughter who helped kill her mother to avenge her father's murder).

Children eventually cope with the threatening feelings, said Freud, by repressing them and by identifying with (trying to become like) the rival parent. It's as though something inside the child decides, "If you can't beat 'em [the same-sex parent], join 'em." Through this **identification** process, children's superegos gain strength as they incorporate many of their parents' values. Freud believed that identification with the same-sex parent provided what psychologists now understand more broadly as our *gender identity*—our sense of being male, female, neither, or some combination of male and female. Freud presumed that our early childhood relations—especially with our parents and other caregivers—influence our developing identity, personality, and frailties.

In Freud's view, conflicts unresolved during earlier psychosexual stages could surface as maladaptive behavior in the adult years. At any point in the oral, anal, or phallic stages, strong conflict could lock, or **fixate,** the person's pleasure-seeking energies in that stage. A person who had been either orally overindulged or deprived (perhaps by abrupt, early weaning) might fixate at the oral stage. This orally fixated adult could exhibit either passive dependence (like that of a nursing infant) or an exaggerated denial of this dependence (by acting tough or uttering biting sarcasm). Or the person might continue to seek oral gratification by smoking or excessive eating. In such ways, Freud suggested, the twig of personality is bent at an early age.

DEFENSE MECHANISMS

LOQ 44-5 How did Freud think people defended themselves against anxiety?

Anxiety, said Freud, is the price we pay for civilization. As members of social groups, we must control our sexual and aggressive impulses, not act them out. But sometimes the ego fears losing control of this inner id-superego war. The presumed result is a dark cloud of unfocused anxiety that leaves us feeling unsettled but unsure why.

Freud proposed that the ego protects itself with **defense mechanisms**—tactics that reduce or redirect anxiety by distorting reality (**TABLE 44.2**). For Freud, *all defense mechanisms functioned indirectly and unconsciously.* Just as the body unconsciously defends itself against disease, so also does the ego unconsciously defend itself against anxiety. For example, **repression** banishes anxiety-arousing wishes and feelings from consciousness.

"Oh, for goodness' sake! Smoke!"

Charles Saxon/The New Yorker Collection/The Cartoon Bank

TABLE 44.2 Six Defense Mechanisms

Freud believed that *repression,* the basic mechanism that banishes anxiety-arousing impulses, enables other defense mechanisms, six of which are listed here.

Defense Mechanism	Unconscious Process Employed to Avoid Anxiety-Arousing Thoughts or Feelings	Example
Regression	Retreating to an earlier psychosexual stage, where some psychic energy remains fixated	A little boy reverts to the oral comfort of thumb sucking in the car on the way to his first day of school.
Reaction formation	Switching unacceptable impulses into their opposites	Repressing angry feelings, a person displays exaggerated friendliness.
Projection	Disguising one's own threatening impulses by attributing them to others	"The thief thinks everyone else is a thief" (an El Salvadoran saying).
Rationalization	Offering self-justifying explanations in place of the real, more threatening unconscious reasons for one's actions	A habitual drinker says she drinks with her friends "just to be sociable."
Displacement	Shifting sexual or aggressive impulses toward a more acceptable or less threatening object or person	A little girl kicks the family dog after her mother puts her in a time-out.
Denial	Refusing to believe or even perceive painful realities	A partner denies evidence of his loved one's affair.

Regression

Nacivet/Getty Images

"Good morning, beheaded—uh, I mean beloved."

"I remember your name perfectly but I just can't think of your face." — Oxford professor W. A. Spooner (1844–1930), famous for his linguistic flip-flops (*spoonerisms*). Spooner rebuked one student for "fighting a liar in the quadrangle" and another who "hissed my mystery lecture," adding, "You have tasted two worms."

According to Freud, *repression underlies all the other defense mechanisms.* However, because repression is often incomplete, repressed urges may appear as symbols in dreams or as slips of the tongue in casual conversation.

Freud believed he could glimpse the unconscious seeping through when a financially stressed patient, not wanting any large pills, said, "Please do not give me any bills, because I cannot swallow them." (Today we call these "Freudian slips.") Freud also viewed jokes as expressions of repressed sexual and aggressive tendencies, and dreams as the "royal road to the unconscious." The remembered content of dreams (their *manifest content*) he believed to be a censored expression of the dreamer's unconscious wishes (the dream's *latent content*). In his dream analyses, Freud searched for patients' inner conflicts.

RETRIEVAL PRACTICE

RP-1 According to Freud's ideas about the three-part personality structure, the _____ operates on the *reality principle* and tries to balance demands in a way that produces long-term pleasure rather than pain; the _____ operates on the *pleasure principle* and seeks immediate gratification; and the _____ represents the voice of our internalized ideals (our *conscience*).

RP-2 In the psychoanalytic view, conflicts unresolved during one of the psychosexual stages may lead to _____ at that stage.

RP-3 Freud believed that our defense mechanisms operate _____ (consciously/unconsciously) and defend us against _____.

ANSWERS IN APPENDIX E

The Neo-Freudian and Later Psychodynamic Theorists

LOQ **44-6** Which of Freud's ideas did his followers accept or reject?

In a historical period when people rarely talked about sex, and certainly not unconscious desires for sex with one's parent, Freud's writings sparked intense debate. "In the Middle Ages, they would have burned me," observed Freud to a friend. "Now they are content with burning my books" (Jones, 1957). Despite the controversy, Freud attracted followers. Several young, ambitious physicians formed an inner circle around their strong-minded leader. These pioneering psychoanalysts, whom we often call *neo-Freudians*, adopted Freud's interviewing techniques and accepted his basic ideas: the personality structures of id, ego, and superego; the importance of the unconscious; the childhood roots of personality; and the dynamics of anxiety and the defense mechanisms. But they broke off from Freud in two important ways. First, they placed more emphasis on the conscious mind's role in interpreting experience and in coping with the environment. And second, they doubted that sex and aggression were all-consuming motivations. Instead, they tended to emphasize loftier motives and social interactions.

Alfred Adler and Karen Horney [HORN-eye], for example, agreed with Freud that childhood is important. But they believed that childhood *social*, not sexual, tensions are crucial for personality formation (Ferguson, 2003, 2015). Adler (who gave us the still popular *inferiority complex* idea) had struggled to overcome childhood illnesses and accidents. He believed that much of our behavior is driven by efforts to conquer childhood inferiority feelings that trigger our strivings for superiority and power. Horney said childhood anxiety triggers our desire for love and security. She also opposed Freud's assumptions that women have weak superegos and suffer "penis envy," and she attempted to balance his masculine bias.

Carl Jung [Yoong], Freud's disciple-turned-dissenter, placed less emphasis on social factors and agreed with Freud that the unconscious exerts a powerful influence. But to Jung, the unconscious contains more than our repressed thoughts and feelings. He believed we also have a **collective unconscious,** a common reservoir of images, or *archetypes,* derived from our species' universal experiences. Jung said that the collective unconscious explains why, for many people, spiritual concerns are deeply rooted and why people in different cultures share certain myths and images. Most of today's psychologists discount the idea of inherited experiences. But they do believe that our shared evolutionary history shaped some universal dispositions, and that experience can leave *epigenetic* marks affecting gene expression.

collective unconscious Carl Jung's concept of a shared, inherited reservoir of memory traces from our species' history.

Alfred Adler (1870–1937) "The individual feels at home in life and feels his existence to be worthwhile just so far as he is useful to others and is overcoming feelings of inferiority" (*Problems of Neurosis,* 1964).

Karen Horney (1885–1952) "The view that women are infantile and emotional creatures, and as such, incapable of responsibility and independence is the work of the masculine tendency to lower women's self-respect" (*Feminine Psychology,* 1932).

Carl Jung (1875–1961) "From the living fountain of instinct flows everything that is creative; hence the unconscious is the very source of the creative impulse" (*The Structure and Dynamics of the Psyche,* 1960).

Freud died in 1939. Since then, some of his ideas have been incorporated into the diverse perspectives that make up modern psychodynamic theory. "Most contemporary [psychodynamic] theorists and therapists are not wedded to the idea that sex is the basis of personality," noted Drew Westen (1996). They "do not talk about ids and egos, and do not go around classifying their patients as oral, anal, or phallic characters." What they do assume, with Freud and with much support from today's psychological science, is that much of our mental life is unconscious. With Freud, they also assume that we often struggle with inner conflicts among our wishes, fears, and values, and that childhood shapes our personality and ways of becoming attached to others.

> For a helpful 9-minute overview, view the *Video: Psychodynamic Theories of Personality.*

Evaluating Freud's Psychoanalytic Perspective and Modern Views of the Unconscious

LOQ **44-7** How do contemporary psychologists view Freud's psychoanalysis?

MODERN RESEARCH CONTRADICTS MANY OF FREUD'S IDEAS We critique Freud from a twenty-first-century perspective. Freud did not have access to neurotransmitter or DNA studies, or to all that we have since learned about human development, thinking, and emotion. To criticize his theory by comparing it with today's thinking is like criticizing the Ford Model T by comparing it with the Tesla Model 3. How tempting it always is to judge the past from the perspective of our present.

Nevertheless, both Freud's devotees and his detractors agree that recent research contradicts many of his specific ideas. Today's developmental psychologists see our *development as lifelong,* not fixed in childhood. They doubt that infants' neural networks are mature enough to sustain as much emotional trauma as Freud assumed. Some think Freud overestimated parental influence and underestimated peer influence. These critics also doubt that conscience and gender identity form as the child resolves the Oedipus (or Electra) complex at age 5 or 6. We gain our gender identity earlier, and those who become strongly masculine or feminine do so even without a same-sex parent present. And they note that Freud's ideas about childhood sexuality arose from stories of childhood sexual abuse told by his female patients—stories that some scholars believe Freud doubted, and attributed to his patients' own childhood sexual wishes and conflicts (Esterson, 2001; Powell & Boer, 1994). Today, we know that *childhood sexual abuse happens,* and we also understand how Freud's questioning might have created false memories of abuse.

Modern dream research disputes Freud's belief that dreams disguise and fulfill wishes. And slips of the tongue can be explained as competition between similar verbal choices in our memory network. Someone who says, "I don't want to do that—it's a lot of brothel" may simply be blending *bother* and *trouble* (Foss & Hakes, 1978). Searching the nearly 300,000 emails I [DM] have received since 2000, I see that friends have written me about their experience on "Wisconsin Pubic Radio" and about accessibility in "pubic venues." And I [ND] have received an email supporting a new policy for the "general pubic."

> "Many aspects of Freudian theory are indeed out of date, and they should be: Freud died in 1939, and he has been slow to undertake further revisions."
> — Psychologist Drew Westen (1998)

Such mistakes are probably random typos, concludes one big data analysis of typing errors (Stephens-Davidowitz, 2017).

History also has failed to support Freud's idea that suppressed sexuality causes psychological disorders. From Freud's time to ours, sexual inhibition has diminished; psychological disorders have not. Psychologists further criticize Freud's theory for its scientific shortcomings. It's important to remember that good scientific theories explain observations and offer testable hypotheses. Freud's theory rests on few objective observations, and parts of it offer few testable hypotheses. For Freud, his own recollections and interpretations of patients' free associations, dreams, and slips—sometimes selected to support his theory—were evidence enough.

What is the most serious problem with Freud's theory? It offers after-the-fact explanations of any characteristic (of one person's smoking, another's fear of horses, another's sexual orientation), yet fails to *predict* such behaviors and traits. If you feel angry at your mother's death, you illustrate Freud's theory because "your unresolved childhood dependency needs are threatened." If you do not feel angry, you again illustrate his theory because "you are repressing your anger." That "is like betting on a horse after the race has been run" (Hall & Lindzey, 1978, p. 68). A good theory makes testable predictions.

So, should psychology post an "Allow Natural Death" order on this old theory? Freud's supporters object. To criticize Freudian theory for not making testable predictions is, they say, like criticizing baseball for not being an aerobic exercise—something it was never intended to be. Freud never claimed that psychoanalysis was predictive science. He merely claimed that, looking back, psychoanalysts could find meaning in our state of mind (Rieff, 1979).

Freud's supporters also note that some of his ideas *are* enduring. It was Freud who drew our attention to the unconscious and the irrational, at a time when such ideas were not popular. Many researchers have since studied our irrationality (Ariely, 2010; Thaler, 2015). Psychologist Daniel Kahneman (in 2002) and behavioral economist Richard Thaler (in 2017) each won Nobel Prizes for their studies of our faulty decision making. Freud also drew our attention to the importance of human sexuality, and to the tension between our biological impulses and our social well-being. It was Freud who challenged our self-righteousness, exposed our self-protective defenses, and reminded us of our potential for evil.

MODERN RESEARCH CHALLENGES THE IDEA OF REPRESSION Psychoanalytic theory hinges on the assumption that our mind often *represses* offending wishes, banishing them into the unconscious until they resurface, like long-lost books in a dusty attic. Recover and resolve childhood's conflicted wishes, and emotional healing should follow. Repression became a widely accepted concept, used to explain hypnotic phenomena and psychological disorders. Some psychodynamic followers extended repression to explain apparently lost and recovered memories of childhood traumas (Boag, 2006; Cheit, 1998; Erdelyi, 2006). In one survey, 88 percent of university students believed that painful experiences commonly get pushed out of awareness and into the unconscious (Garry et al., 1994).

Today's researchers agree that we sometimes preserve our self-esteem by neglecting threatening information (Green et al., 2008). Yet they also find that repression is rare, even in response to terrible trauma. Even those who have witnessed a parent's murder or survived Nazi death camps have retained their unrepressed memories of the horror (Helmreich, 1992, 1994; Malmquist, 1986; Pennebaker, 1990).

Some researchers do believe that extreme, prolonged stress, such as the stress some severely abused children experience, might disrupt memory by damaging the hippocampus (Schacter, 1996). But the far more common reality is that high stress and associated stress hormones *enhance* memory. Indeed, rape, torture, and other traumatic events haunt survivors, who experience unwanted flashbacks. They are seared onto the soul. "You see the babies," said Holocaust survivor Sally H. (1979). "You see the screaming mothers. You see hanging people. You sit and you see that face there. It's something you don't forget."

"Although [Freud] clearly made a number of mistakes in the formulation of his ideas, his understanding of unconscious mental processes was pretty much on target. In fact, it is very consistent with modern neuroscientists' belief that most mental processes are unconscious." — Nobel Prize–winning neuroscientist Eric Kandel (2012)

"During the Holocaust, many children . . . were forced to endure the unendurable. For those who continue to suffer [the] pain is still present, many years later, as real as it was on the day it occurred." — Eric Zillmer, Molly Harrower, Barry Ritzler, and Robert Archer, *The Quest for the Nazi Personality*, 1995

For a helpful 13-minute exploration, see the *Video: Repression—Reality or Myth?*

THE MODERN UNCONSCIOUS MIND

LOQ **44-8** How has modern research developed our understanding of the unconscious?

Freud was right about a big idea that underlies today's psychodynamic thinking: We have limited access to all that goes on in our mind (Erdelyi, 1985, 1988; Norman, 2010). Our two-track mind has a vast unseen realm. Some researchers even argue that "most of a person's everyday life is determined by unconscious thought processes" (Bargh & Chartrand, 1999). (Perhaps, for example, you can recall being sad or mad without consciously knowing why.)

Yet many research psychologists now think of the unconscious not as seething passions and repressive censoring but as information processing that occurs without our awareness. To these researchers, the unconscious also involves

- the *schemas* that automatically control our perceptions and interpretations.
- the *priming* by stimuli to which we have not consciously attended.
- the right-hemisphere activity that enables the *split-brain* patient's left hand to carry out an instruction the patient cannot verbalize.
- the *implicit memories* that operate without conscious recall, even among those with amnesia.
- the *emotions* that activate instantly, before conscious analysis.
- the *stereotypes* and *implicit prejudice* that automatically and unconsciously influence how we process information about others.

More than we realize, we fly on autopilot. Our lives are guided by off-screen, out-of-sight, unconscious information processing. The unconscious mind is vast. However, our current understanding of unconscious information processing is more like the pre-Freudian view, of an underground, unattended stream of thought from which spontaneous behavior and creative ideas surface (Bargh & Morsella, 2008).

Research also supports two of Freud's defense mechanisms. One study demonstrated *reaction formation* (trading unacceptable impulses for their opposite) in men who reported strong anti-gay attitudes. Compared with those who did not report such attitudes, these anti-gay men experienced greater physiological arousal (assessed with a device that measured blood flow to the penis) when watching videos of gay men having sex, even though they said the films did not make them sexually aroused (Adams et al., 1996). Likewise, some evidence suggests that people who have an unconscious same-sex sexual orientation—but who consciously identify as straight—report more negative attitudes toward gay men (Weinstein et al., 2012).

Freud's *projection* (attributing our own threatening impulses to others) has also been confirmed. People do tend to see their traits, attitudes, and goals in others (Baumeister et al., 1998b; Maner et al., 2005). Today's researchers call this the *false consensus effect*—the tendency to overestimate the extent to which others share our beliefs and behaviors. People who binge-drink or break speed limits tend to think many others do the same. However, brain scans show that projection seems motivated less by suppressing our sexual and aggressive impulses, as Freud imagined, than by our need to maintain a positive self-image (Welborn et al., 2017).

Finally, research has supported Freud's idea that we unconsciously defend ourselves against anxiety. Researchers have proposed that one source of anxiety is "the terror resulting from our awareness of vulnerability and death" (Greenberg et al., 1997). Hundreds of experiments testing **terror-management theory** show that thinking about one's mortality—for example, by writing a short essay on dying and its associated emotions—provokes various terror-management defenses (Burke et al., 2010). For example, death anxiety increases aggression toward rivals and heightens esteem for oneself (Cohen & Solomon, 2011; Koole et al., 2006).

Faced with a threatening world, people act not only to enhance their self-esteem but also to adhere more strongly to worldviews that answer questions about life's meaning. The prospect of death promotes religious sentiments, and deep religious convictions

terror-management theory a theory of death-related anxiety; explores people's emotional and behavioral responses to reminders of their impending death.

"It says, 'Someday you will die.'"

enable people to be less defensive—less likely to rise in defense of their worldview—when reminded of death (Jonas & Fischer, 2006; Norenzayan & Hansen, 2006). Moreover, when contemplating death, people prioritize their close relationships (Cox & Arndt, 2012; Mikulincer et al., 2003). The actual death of loved ones can provoke protective responses as well. For years, I [ND] have studied the way people respond to thoughts about death—but it took the shock of my own mother's unexpected death to motivate me to start running again, and to live a healthier lifestyle (Hayasaki, 2014; Kashdan et al., 2014). Facing death can inspire us to affirm life.

ASK YOURSELF

What understandings and impressions of Freud did you bring to this course? Are you surprised to find that some of his ideas have value, or that others have been called into question?

RETRIEVAL PRACTICE

RP-4 What big ideas have survived from Freud's psychoanalytic theory? In what ways has Freud's theory been criticized?

RP-5 Which elements of traditional psychoanalysis have modern-day *psychodynamic* theorists and therapists retained, and which elements have they mostly left behind?

ANSWERS IN APPENDIX E

Assessing Unconscious Processes

LOQ **44-9** What are *projective tests,* how are they used, and what are some criticisms of them?

Personality tests reflect the basic ideas of particular personality theories. So, what might be the assessment tool of choice for someone working in the Freudian tradition? It would need to provide some sort of road into the unconscious—to unearth the residue of early childhood experiences, move beneath surface thoughts, and reveal hidden conflicts and impulses. Objective assessment tools, such as agree-disagree or true-false questionnaires, would be inadequate because they would merely tap the conscious surface.

Henry Murray (1933) demonstrated a possible basis for such a test at a party hosted by his 11-year-old daughter. Murray engaged the children in a frightening game called "Murder." When shown some photographs after the game, the children perceived the photos as more malicious than they had before the game. These children, it seemed to Murray, had *projected* their inner feelings into the pictures.

A few years later, Murray introduced the **Thematic Apperception Test (TAT)**—a **projective test** in which people view ambiguous pictures and then make up stories about them. Shown a daydreaming boy, those who imagine he is fantasizing about an achievement are presumed to be projecting their own goals. "As a rule," said Murray, "the subject leaves the test happily unaware that he has presented the psychologist with what amounts to an X-ray of his inner self" (quoted by Talbot, 1999).

Numerous studies suggest that Murray was right: The TAT provides a valid and reliable map of people's implicit motives (Jenkins, 2017). For example, such storytelling has been used to assess *achievement* and *affiliation motivation* (Drescher & Schultheiss, 2016; Schultheiss et al., 2014). TAT responses also show consistency over time (Lundy, 1985; Schultheiss & Pang, 2007). Show people a picture today, and they'll imagine a story similar to one they will tell when, a month later, they see the same picture.

Swiss psychiatrist Hermann Rorschach [ROAR-shock; 1884–1922] created the most widely used projective test. He based his famous **Rorschach inkblot test** (FIGURE 44.2) on a childhood game. Unlike the TAT's natural life images, Rorschach and his friends would drip ink on a paper, fold it, and then say what they saw in the resulting inkblot (Sdorow, 2005). Do you see predatory animals or weapons? If so, perhaps you have aggressive tendencies. But is this a reasonable assumption, considering that inkblots don't have any real-life meaning? The answer varies.

Some clinicians cherish the Rorschach test, convinced that it projects a client's inner motives to the outside world. Others view the test as a source of suggestive leads, an

FIGURE 44.2

The Rorschach test In this projective test, people tell what they see in a series of symmetrical inkblots. Some who use this test are confident that the interpretation of ambiguous images will reveal unconscious aspects of the test-taker's personality.

icebreaker, or a revealing interview technique. The Society for Personality Assessment (2005) commends the test's "responsible use" when "appropriate and justified" (which would *not* include, for example, using the test to infer past childhood sexual abuse).

But critics insist the Rorschach is no emotional MRI. They argue that only a few of the many Rorschach-derived scores, such as those for cognitive impairment and thought disorder, have demonstrated reliability and validity (Mihura et al., 2013, 2015; Wood et al., 2015). And inkblot assessments have inaccurately diagnosed many healthy adults as pathological (Wood, 2003; Wood et al., 2006). "Even seasoned professionals can be fooled by their intuitions and their faith in tools that lack strong evidence of effectiveness," warned Scott Lilienfeld, James Wood, and Howard Garb (2001, p. 47). "When a substantial body of research demonstrates that old intuitions are wrong, it is time to adopt new ways of thinking."

> **Thematic Apperception Test (TAT)** a projective test in which people express their inner feelings and interests through the stories they make up about ambiguous scenes.
>
> **projective test** a personality test, such as the TAT or Rorschach, that provides ambiguous images designed to trigger projection of people's inner dynamics.
>
> **Rorschach inkblot test** a projective test designed by Hermann Rorschach; seeks to identify people's inner feelings by analyzing how they interpret 10 inkblots.

RETRIEVAL PRACTICE

RP-6 _____ tests ask test-takers to respond to an ambiguous image by describing it or telling a story about it.

ANSWERS IN APPENDIX E

> "The Rorschach [Inkblot Test] has the dubious distinction of being, simultaneously, the most cherished and the most reviled of all psychological assessment tools." — John Hunsley and J. Michael Bailey (1999)

---

44 REVIEW Introduction to Personality and Psychodynamic Theories

LEARNING OBJECTIVES

Test Yourself Answer these repeated Learning Objective Questions on your own (before checking the answers in Appendix D) to improve your retention of the concepts (McDaniel et al., 2009, 2015).

LOQ 44-1 What is *personality,* and what theories inform our understanding of personality?

LOQ 44-2 How did Sigmund Freud's treatment of psychological disorders lead to his view of the unconscious mind?

LOQ 44-3 What was Freud's view of personality?

LOQ 44-4 What developmental stages did Freud propose?

LOQ 44-5 How did Freud think people defended themselves against anxiety?

LOQ 44-6 Which of Freud's ideas did his followers accept or reject?

LOQ 44-7 How do contemporary psychologists view Freud's psychoanalysis?

LOQ 44-8 How has modern research developed our understanding of the unconscious?

LOQ 44-9 What are *projective tests,* how are they used, and what are some criticisms of them?

TERMS AND CONCEPTS TO REMEMBER

Test Yourself Write down the definition in your own words, then check your answer.

personality, p. 519

psychodynamic theories, p. 519

psychoanalysis, p. 519

unconscious, p. 519

free association, p. 519

id, p. 520

ego, p. 520

superego, p. 520

psychosexual stages, p. 520

Oedipus [ED-uh-puss] complex, p. 520

identification, p. 520

fixation, p. 520

defense mechanisms, p. 520

repression, p. 520

collective unconscious, p. 522

terror-management theory, p. 525

Thematic Apperception Test (TAT), p. 527

projective test, p. 527

Rorschach inkblot test, p. 527

MASTER THE MATERIAL

Test Yourself Answer the following questions on your own first, then check your answers in Appendix E.

1. According to Freud's view of personality structure, the "executive" system, the _____, seeks to gratify the impulses of the _____ in more acceptable ways.

   a. id; ego

   b. ego; superego

   c. ego; id

   d. id; superego

2. Freud proposed that the development of the "voice of our moral compass" is related to the _____, which internalizes ideals and provides standards for judgments.

3. According to the psychoanalytic view of development, we all pass through a series of psychosexual stages, including the oral, anal, and phallic stages. Conflicts unresolved at any of these stages may lead to

   a. dormant sexual feelings.

   b. fixation at that stage.

   c. preconscious blocking of impulses.

   d. a distorted gender identity.

4. Freud believed that defense mechanisms are unconscious attempts to distort or disguise reality, all in an effort to reduce our _____.

5. Freud believed that we may block painful or unacceptable thoughts, wishes, feelings, or memories from consciousness through an unconscious process called _____.

6. In general, neo-Freudians such as Adler and Horney accepted many of Freud's views but placed more emphasis than he did on

   a. development throughout the life span.

   b. the collective unconscious.

   c. the role of the id.

   d. social interactions.

7. Modern-day psychodynamic theorists and therapists agree with Freud about

   a. the existence of unconscious mental processes.

   b. the Oedipus complex.

   c. the predictive value of Freudian theory.

   d. the superego's role as the executive part of personality.

8. Which of the following is NOT part of the contemporary view of the unconscious?

   a. Repressed memories of anxiety-provoking events

   b. Schemas that influence our perceptions and interpretations

   c. Stereotypes that affect our information processing

   d. Instantly activated emotions and implicit memories of learned skills

Continue testing yourself with 📖 **LearningCurve** or 📖 **Achieve Read & Practice** to learn and remember most effectively.

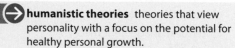

MODULE

45 Humanistic Theories and Trait Theories

➡️ **humanistic theories** theories that view personality with a focus on the potential for healthy personal growth.

hierarchy of needs Maslow's pyramid of human needs, beginning at the base with physiological needs that must first be satisfied before people can fulfill their higher-level safety needs and then psychological needs.

self-actualization according to Maslow, one of the ultimate psychological needs that arises after basic physical and psychological needs are met and self-esteem is achieved; the motivation to fulfill one's potential.

self-transcendence according to Maslow, the striving for identity, meaning, and purpose beyond the self.

unconditional positive regard a caring, accepting, nonjudgmental attitude, which Carl Rogers believed would help people develop self-awareness and self-acceptance.

Humanistic Theories

LOQ **45-1** How did humanistic psychologists view personality, and what was their goal in studying personality?

By the 1960s, some personality psychologists had become discontented with the sometimes bleak focus on drives and conflicts in psychodynamic theory, and the mechanistic psychology of B. F. Skinner's *behaviorism*. Two pioneering theorists—Abraham Maslow and Carl Rogers—offered a *third-force perspective* that emphasized our potential for healthy personal growth. In contrast to Sigmund Freud's emphasis on disorders born out of dark conflicts, these **humanistic theorists** emphasized the ways people strive for self-determination and self-realization. In contrast to behaviorism's scientific objectivity, they studied people through self-reported experiences and feelings.

Abraham Maslow's Self-Actualizing Person

Maslow proposed that we are motivated by a **hierarchy of needs.** If our physiological needs are met, we become concerned with personal safety. If we achieve a sense of security, we then seek to love and to be loved. With our love needs satisfied, we seek self-esteem. Having achieved self-esteem, we ultimately seek **self-actualization** (the process of fulfilling our potential) and **self-transcendence** (meaning, purpose, and identity beyond the self).

Abraham Maslow (1908–1970) "Any theory of motivation that is worthy of attention must deal with the highest capacities of the healthy and strong person as well as with the defensive maneuvers of crippled spirits" (*Motivation and Personality*, 1970, p. 33).

Maslow (1970) developed his ideas by studying healthy, creative people rather than clinical cases of troubled people. His description of self-actualization grew out of his study of people, such as Abraham Lincoln, who seemed notable for their meaningful and productive lives. Maslow reported that such people shared certain characteristics: They were self-aware and self-accepting, open and spontaneous, loving and caring, and not paralyzed by others' opinions (Kaufman, 2018). Secure in their sense of who they were, their interests were task-centered rather than self-centered.

◀ FIGURE 45.1
Characteristics of Self-Actualization Scale (CSAS) This shortened version of the CSAS represents the 10 characteristics studied by Scott Barry Kaufman (2018).

Characteristics of Self-Actualization Scale (CSAS)

Here are a number of characteristics that may or may not describe you. Please select the answer that best indicates the extent to which you agree or disagree with each statement. Be as honest as possible, but rely on your initial feeling and do not think too much.

1	2	3	4	5
Strongly disagree	Disagree	Neutral	Agree	Strongly agree

1. ___I often feel gratitude for the good in my life no matter how many times I encounter it.

2. ___I accept all sides of myself, including my shortcomings.

3. ___I take responsibility for my actions.

4. ___I am often undisturbed and unruffled by things that seem to bother most people.

5. ___I have a purpose in life that will help the good of humankind.

6. ___I often have a clear perception of reality.

7. ___I have a genuine desire to help the human race.

8. ___I often have experiences in which I feel one with all people and things on this planet.

9. ___I have a strong sense of right and wrong in my daily life.

10. ___I bring a generally creative attitude to all of my work.

Scoring Guide:
Add up your scores and divide by 10 for your total score. The items above represent the 10 characteristics of self-actualization studied by Scott Barry Kaufman (2018):
(1) Continued freshness of appreciation, (2) Acceptance, (3) Authenticity, (4) Equanimity (mental calmness), (5) Purpose, (6) Truth seeking, (7) Humanitarianism (concern with human welfare), (8) Peak experiences, 9) Good moral intuition, and (10) Creative spirit.

Kaufman found that those with higher scores experienced "greater life satisfaction, self-acceptance, positive relations, personal growth, purpose in life, and self-transcendent experiences" as well as "creativity across multiple domains of achievement."

Curious about the world, they embraced uncertainties and stretched themselves to seek out new experiences (Compton, 2018; Kashdan, 2009). Once they focused their energies on a particular task, they often regarded it as their life mission, or "calling" (Hall & Chandler, 2005). Most enjoyed a few deep relationships rather than many superficial ones. Many had been moved by spiritual or personal *peak experiences* that surpassed ordinary consciousness. These, said Maslow (1970), are mature adult qualities found in those who have learned enough about life to be compassionate, to have outgrown their mixed feelings toward their parents, to have found their calling, to have "acquired enough courage to be unpopular, to be unashamed about being openly virtuous." (Test your own level of self-actualization in **FIGURE 45.1**.)

Carl Rogers' Person-Centered Perspective

Fellow humanistic psychologist Carl Rogers agreed with much of Maslow's thinking. Rogers' *person-centered perspective* held that people are basically good and are endowed with self-actualizing tendencies. Unless thwarted by an environment that inhibits growth, each of us is like an acorn, primed for growth and fulfillment. Rogers (1980) believed that a growth-promoting social climate provides

- *acceptance.* When people are *accepting,* they offer **unconditional positive regard,** an attitude of grace that values us even knowing our failings. It is a profound relief to drop our pretenses, confess our worst feelings, and discover that we are still accepted. In a good marriage, a close family, or an intimate friendship, we are free to be spontaneous without fearing the loss of others' esteem.

- *genuineness.* When people are *genuine,* they are open with their own feelings, drop their facades, and are transparent and self-disclosing.

Macmillan Learning

Carl Rogers (1902–1987)
"The curious paradox is that when I accept myself just as I am, then I can change" (*On Becoming a Person,* 1961).

A father *not* offering unconditional positive regard:

"Just remember, son, it doesn't matter whether you win or lose—unless you want Daddy's love."

- *empathy.* When people are *empathic*, they share and mirror other's feelings and reflect their meanings. "Rarely do we listen with real understanding, true empathy," said Rogers. "Yet listening, of this very special kind, is one of the most potent forces for change that I know."

Acceptance, genuineness, and empathy are, Rogers believed, the water, Sun, and nutrients that enable people to grow from acorns into vigorous oak trees. For "as persons are accepted and prized, they tend to develop a more caring attitude toward themselves" (Rogers, 1980, p. 116). As persons are empathically heard, "it becomes possible for them to listen more accurately to the flow of inner experiencings."

Writer Calvin Trillin (2006) recalled an example of parental acceptance and genuineness at a camp for children with severe disorders, where his wife, Alice, worked. L., a "magical child," had genetic diseases that meant she had to be tube-fed and could walk only with difficulty. Alice recalled,

> One day, when we were playing duck-duck-goose, I was sitting behind her and she asked me to hold her mail for her while she took her turn to be chased around the circle. It took her a while to make the circuit, and I had time to see that on top of the pile [of mail] was a note from her mom. Then I did something truly awful. . . . I simply had to know what this child's parents could have done to make her so spectacular, to make her the most optimistic, most enthusiastic, most hopeful human being I had ever encountered. I snuck a quick look at the note, and my eyes fell on this sentence: "If God had given us all of the children in the world to choose from, L., we would only have chosen you." Before L. got back to her place in the circle, I showed the note to Bud, who was sitting next to me. "Quick. Read this," I whispered. "It's the secret of life."

The picture of empathy Being open and sharing confidences is easier when the listener shows real understanding. Within such relationships we can relax and fully express our true selves.

Maslow and Rogers would have smiled knowingly. For them, a central feature of personality is one's **self-concept**—all the thoughts and feelings we have in response to the question, "Who am I?" If our self-concept is positive, we tend to act and perceive the world positively. If it is negative—if in our own eyes we fall far short of our *ideal self*—said Rogers, we feel dissatisfied and unhappy. A worthwhile goal for therapists, parents, teachers, and friends is therefore, he said, to help others know, accept, and be true to themselves.

ASK YOURSELF

Think back to a conversation you had when you knew someone was just waiting for their turn to speak instead of listening to you. Now consider the last time someone heard you with empathy. How did those two experiences differ?

To consider how this theory applies to your own life, try the online *Assess Your Strengths: What Is Your Self-Concept?*

Assessing the Self

LOQ 45-2 How did humanistic psychologists assess a person's sense of self?

Humanistic psychologists sometimes assessed personality by asking people to fill out questionnaires that would evaluate their self-concept. One questionnaire, inspired by Carl Rogers, asked people to describe themselves both as they would *ideally* like to be and as they *actually* are. When the ideal and the actual self are nearly alike, said Rogers, the self-concept is positive. Assessing his clients' personal growth during therapy, he looked for successively closer ratings of actual and ideal selves.

Some humanistic psychologists believed that any standardized assessment of personality, even a questionnaire, is depersonalizing. Rather than forcing the person to respond to narrow categories, these humanistic psychologists presumed that

self-concept all our thoughts and feelings about ourselves, in answer to the question, "Who am I?"

interviews and intimate conversation would provide a better understanding of each person's unique experiences. Some researchers today believe our identity may be revealed using the *life story approach*—collecting a rich narrative detailing a person's unique life history (Adler et al., 2016; McAdams & Guo, 2015). A lifetime of stories can show more of a person's complete identity than can the responses to a few questions (Waters et al., 2019).

Evaluating Humanistic Theories

LOQ **45-3** How have humanistic theories influenced psychology? What criticisms have they faced?

One thing said of Freud can also be said of the humanistic psychologists: Their impact has been pervasive. Maslow's and Rogers' ideas have influenced counseling, education, child raising, and management. And they laid the groundwork for today's scientific *positive psychology* subfield.

These theorists have also influenced—sometimes in unintended ways—much of today's popular psychology. Is a positive self-concept the key to happiness and success? Do acceptance and empathy nurture positive feelings about ourselves? Are people basically good and capable of self-improvement? Many people answer *Yes, Yes,* and *Yes.* In 2006, U.S. high school students reported notably higher self-esteem and greater expectations of future career success than did students living in 1975, before humanistic psychology's feel-good philosophy infused American culture (Twenge & Campbell, 2008). Given a choice, North American college students have said they'd rather get a self-esteem boost, such as a compliment or good grade on a paper, than enjoy a favorite food or sexual activity (Bushman et al., 2011). Humanistic psychology's message has been heard.

But the prominence of the humanistic perspective set off a backlash of criticism. First, said the critics, its concepts are vague and subjective. Consider Maslow's description of self-actualizing people as open, spontaneous, loving, self-accepting, and productive. Is this a scientific description? Or is it merely a description of the theorist's own values and ideals? Maslow, noted M. Brewster Smith (1978), offered impressions of his own personal heroes. Imagine another theorist who began with a different set of heroes—perhaps French military conqueror Napoleon and U.S. President Donald Trump. This theorist might describe self-actualizing people as "undeterred by others' opinions," "motivated to achieve," and "comfortable with power."

Critics also objected to the idea that, as Rogers (1985) put it, "The only question which matters is, 'Am I living in a way which is deeply satisfying to me, and which truly expresses me?'" This emphasis on *individualism*—trusting and acting on one's feelings, being true to oneself, fulfilling oneself—could lead to self-indulgence, selfishness, and an erosion of moral restraint (Campbell & Specht, 1985; Wallach & Wallach, 1983). Imagine working on a group project with people who refuse to complete any task that is not deeply satisfying or does not truly express their identity.

Humanistic psychologists have replied that a secure, nondefensive self-acceptance is actually the first step toward loving others. Indeed, people who feel intrinsically liked and accepted—for who they are, not just for their achievements—exhibit less defensive attitudes (Schimel et al., 2001). Those feeling liked and accepted by a romantic partner report being happier in their relationships and acting more kindly toward their partner (Gordon & Chen, 2010).

A final accusation leveled against humanistic psychology is that it is naive—that it fails to appreciate the reality of our human capacity for evil (May, 1982). Faced with climate crisis, overpopulation, terrorism, and the spread of nuclear weapons, we may become apathetic from either of two rationalizations. One is a starry-eyed optimism that denies the threat ("People are basically good; everything will work out"). The other is a dark despair ("It's hopeless; why try?"). Action requires enough realism to fuel concern and enough optimism to provide hope. (Pessimism often fulfills its own predictions, by restraining our efforts at change.) Humanistic psychology, say the critics, encourages the needed hope but not the equally necessary realism about threats.

"We do pretty well when you stop to think that people are basically good."

Dana Fradon/The New Yorker Collection/The Cartoon Bank

> **trait** a characteristic pattern of behavior or a disposition to feel and act in certain ways, as assessed by self-report inventories and peer reports.

RP-1 How did the *humanistic theories* provide a fresh perspective?

RP-2 What does it mean to be *empathic*? How about *self-actualized*? Which humanistic psychologists used these terms?

ANSWERS IN APPENDIX E

Trait Theories

LOQ **45-4** How do psychologists use traits to describe personality?

Rather than focusing on unconscious forces and thwarted growth opportunities, some researchers attempt to define personality in terms of stable and enduring behavior patterns. This perspective can be traced in part to a remarkable meeting in 1919, when Gordon Allport, a curious 22-year-old psychology student, interviewed Sigmund Freud in Vienna. Allport soon discovered just how preoccupied the founder of psychoanalysis was with finding hidden motives, even in Allport's own behavior during the interview. That experience ultimately led Allport to do what Freud did not do: to describe personality in terms of fundamental **traits,** or people's characteristic behaviors and conscious motives (such as the curiosity that actually motivated Allport to see Freud). Meeting Freud, said Allport, "taught me that [psychoanalysis], for all its merits, may plunge too deep, and that psychologists would do well to give full recognition to manifest motives before probing the unconscious." Allport came to define personality in terms of identifiable behavior patterns. He was concerned less with *explaining* individual traits than with *describing* them.

Like Allport, Isabel Briggs Myers (1987) and her mother, Katharine Briggs, wanted to describe important personality differences. They attempted to sort people according to Carl Jung's *personality types*, based on their responses to 126 questions. The *Myers-Briggs Type Indicator (MBTI),* available in 20+ languages, has been taken by millions of people, mostly for counseling, leadership training, and work-team development (CPP, 2017). It offers choices, such as "Do you usually value sentiment more than logic, or value logic more than sentiment?" Then it counts the test-taker's preferences, labels them as indicating, say, a "feeling type" or "thinking type," and feeds them back to the person in complimentary terms. Feeling types, for example, are told they are "sympathetic, appreciative, and tactful"; thinking types are told they are "good at analyzing." (Every type has its strengths, so everyone is affirmed.)

Most people agree with their announced MBTI profile, which mirrors their declared preferences. They may also accept their label as a basis for being matched with work or dating partners, and with tasks that supposedly suit their temperaments. But a National Research Council report noted that despite the test's popularity in business and career counseling, its use has outrun research on its validity as a job performance predictor: "The popularity of this instrument in the absence of proven scientific worth is troublesome" (Druckman & Bjork, 1991, p. 101; see also Pittenger, 1993). Although research on the MBTI has been accumulating since those cautionary words were expressed, the test remains mostly a counseling and coaching tool, not a research instrument. Fortunately, newer research offers reliable and valid tools to explore traits.

Exploring Traits

We are each a unique complex of multiple traits. So how can we describe our personalities in a way that captures our individuality? We might describe an apple by placing it along several trait dimensions—relatively large or small, red or green, sweet or tart. By placing people on several trait dimensions simultaneously, psychologists can describe countless individual personality variations.

What trait dimensions describe personality? If you were looking at profiles on an online dating service, what personality traits would give you the best sense for each person? Allport and his associate H. S. Odbert (1936) counted all the words in an unabridged dictionary with which one could describe people. There were almost 18,000! How, then, could psychologists condense the list to a manageable number of basic traits?

"Hello. This is Dial-a-Grump. What the hell do you want?"

Pictorial Press Ltd/Alamy

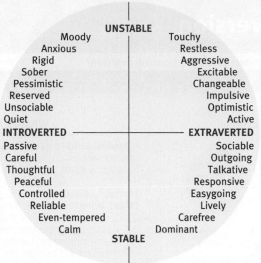

UNSTABLE

Moody | Touchy
Anxious | Restless
Rigid | Aggressive
Sober | Excitable
Pessimistic | Changeable
Reserved | Impulsive
Unsociable | Optimistic
Quiet | Active

INTROVERTED —————— **EXTRAVERTED**

Passive | Sociable
Careful | Outgoing
Thoughtful | Talkative
Peaceful | Responsive
Controlled | Easygoing
Reliable | Lively
Even-tempered | Carefree
Calm | Dominant

STABLE

Abaca Press/AP Images

FIGURE 45.2

Two personality dimensions Mapmakers can tell us a lot by using two axes (north–south and east–west). Two primary personality factors (extraversion–introversion and stability–instability) are similarly useful as axes for describing personality variation. Varying combinations define other, more specific traits (Eysenck & Eysenck, 1963). Although many actors are extraverted, some, such as Emma Watson, are introverts—particularly capable of solitary study to become each character they portray. Professional comedians, such as Jimmy Fallon, are often natural extraverts (Irwing et al., 2020).

FACTOR ANALYSIS One technique is *factor analysis*, a statistical procedure that identifies clusters (factors) of test items that tap basic components of a trait (McCabe & Fleeson, 2016). Imagine that people who describe themselves as outgoing also tend to say that they like excitement and practical jokes and dislike quiet reading. Such a statistically correlated cluster of behaviors reflects a basic factor, or trait—in this case, *extraversion*.

British psychologists Hans Eysenck and Sybil Eysenck [EYE-zink] believed that we can reduce many of our normal individual variations to two dimensions: *extraversion–introversion* and *emotional stability–instability* (**FIGURE 45.2**). People in 35 countries around the world, from China to Uganda to Russia, took the *Eysenck Personality Questionnaire*. When their answers were analyzed, the extraversion and emotionality factors inevitably emerged as basic personality dimensions (Eysenck, 1990, 1992). The Eysencks believed, and research confirms, that these factors are genetically influenced.

BIOLOGY AND PERSONALITY Brain-activity scans of extraverts add to the growing list of traits and mental states now being explored. Such studies indicate that extraverts seek stimulation because their normal brain arousal is relatively low. For example, PET scans have shown that a frontal lobe area involved in behavior inhibition is less active in extraverts than in introverts (Johnson et al., 1999). Dopamine and dopamine-related neural activity tend to be higher in extraverts (Kim et al., 2008; Wacker et al., 2006).

Our biology influences our personality. As we know from twin and adoption studies, compared with fraternal twins, identical twin personalities are more similar (Loehlin & Martin, 2018; Mõttus et al., 2019). What's true of so much of human nature is also true of personality and life outcomes, which are influenced by many genes having small effects (Smith-Wooley et al., 2019; van den Berg et al., 2016). Our genes also influence the *temperament* and behavioral style that shape our personality. Jerome Kagan, for example, has attributed differences in children's shyness and inhibition to their autonomic nervous system reactivity. Those with a reactive autonomic nervous system respond to stress with greater anxiety and inhibition. The fearless, curious child may become the rock-climbing or fast-driving adult. (See Thinking Critically About: The Stigma of Introversion.)

Personality differences among dogs (in energy, affection, reactivity, and curious intelligence) are as evident, and as consistently judged, as personality differences among humans (Gosling et al., 2003; Jones & Gosling, 2005). Monkeys, bonobos, chimpanzees, orangutans, killer whales, sea lions, and even birds and fish also have distinct and stable personalities (Altschul et al., 2018; Úbeda et al., 2018; Weiss, A. et al., 2017). Even conscientiousness varies among individual animals, from chimps to bees (Delgado & Sulloway, 2017). Through selective breeding, researchers can produce bold or shy birds. Both personality types have their place in natural history: In lean years, bold birds are more likely to find food; in abundant years, shy birds feed with less risk.

Octopus personality The real-life Otto the octopus seems to love getting attention from visitors. But when his German aquarium closes during the winter, Otto acts like a bored prankster. He has juggled hermit crabs, squirted water at staff members, and broken his light by spraying it with water.

Thinking Critically About:
The Stigma of Introversion

LOQ **45-5** What are some common misunderstandings about introversion?

Western cultures are hard on introverts:

Superheroes tend to be extraverted. Black Panther unites five tribes of people with his engaging strength of character. Take-charge Elastigirl saves the day in *The Incredibles*.

87% of Westerners want to be more extraverted.[1]

Being introverted seems to imply that we don't have the "right stuff."[2]

What do job interviewers want in their employees? Extraversion outranks most other personality traits.[3]

Attractive, successful people are presumed to be extraverts.[4]

What is introversion?

Introverts tend to gain energy from time alone, and may find social interactions exhausting. Extraverts, by contrast, tend to draw energy from time spent with others.

Introverts are not "shy." (Shy people remain quiet because they fear others will evaluate them negatively.)

Introverted people seek low levels of stimulation from their environment because they have more sensitive nervous systems. For example, when given lemon juice, introverted people salivated more than extraverted people.[5]

Introversion has many benefits:

• Introverted leaders outperform extraverted leaders in some contexts, such as when their employees voice new ideas and challenge existing norms.[6]

• Introverts handle conflict well. In response, they seek solitude rather than revenge.[7]

• Many introverts have flourished, including Bill Gates, Mother Teresa, and Oprah Winfrey. "A true extravert," Winfrey explains, "gets energy,...feeds off people,...and I get sucked dry."[8]

1. Hudson & Roberts, 2014. 2. Cain, 2012. 3. Kluemper et al., 2015; Salgado & Moscoso, 2002. 4. Wilmot et al., 2019. 5. Corcoran, 1964. 6. Grant et al., 2011. 7. Ren et al., 2016. 8. OWN, 2018.

"I come from many tribes—immigrant, introvert, working class, Korean. . . . Growing up, I never knew that people like me could write books or talk in public. . . . Talking is painful because we expose our ideas for evaluation; however, . . . talking is powerful because our ideas . . . have value and require expression." — Writer and lecturer Min Jin Lee, 2019

RETRIEVAL PRACTICE

RP-3 Which two primary dimensions did Hans Eysenck and Sybil Eysenck propose for describing personality variation?

ANSWERS IN APPENDIX E

Assessing Traits

LOQ **45-6** What are *personality inventories,* and what are their strengths and weaknesses as trait-assessment tools?

If stable and enduring traits guide our actions, can we devise valid and reliable tests of them? Several trait-assessment techniques exist—some more valid than others. Some provide quick assessments of a single trait, such as extraversion, anxiety, or self-esteem. **Personality inventories**—longer questionnaires covering a wide range of feelings and behaviors—assess several traits at once.

The classic personality inventory is the **Minnesota Multiphasic Personality Inventory (MMPI).** Although the MMPI was originally developed to identify emotional disorders, it also assesses people's personality traits. One of its creators, Starke Hathaway (1960), compared his effort with that of Alfred Binet. Binet, the founder of modern intelligence testing, developed the first intelligence test by selecting items that identified children who would likely struggle to progress in French schools. Like Binet's items, the MMPI items were **empirically derived:** From a large pool of items, Hathaway and his colleagues selected those on which particular diagnostic groups differed. "My hands and feet are usually warm enough" may seem superficial, but it just so happened that anxious people were more likely to answer *False*. The researchers grouped the questions into 10 clinical scales, including scales that assess depressive tendencies, masculinity–femininity, and introversion–extraversion. Today's MMPI-2 has additional scales that assess work attitudes, family problems, and anger.

Whereas most projective tests (such as the Rorschach) are scored subjectively, personality inventories are scored objectively. Objectivity does not, however, guarantee validity. For example, individuals taking the MMPI for employment purposes can give socially desirable answers to create a good impression. But in so doing they may also score high on a *lie scale* that assesses faking (as when people respond *False* to a universally true statement such as "I get angry sometimes"). In other cases, the MMPI can be used to identify people pretending to have a disorder in order to avoid their responsibilities (Chmielewski et al., 2017). The MMPI's objectivity has contributed to its popularity and its translation into more than 100 languages.

> 🌊 Might astrology hold the secret to our personality traits? Play the role of a researcher testing this question by engaging online with the activity *How Would You Know If Astrologers Can Describe People's Personality?*

People have had fun spoofing the MMPI with their own mock items: "Weeping brings tears to my eyes," "Frantic screams make me nervous," and "I stay in the bathtub until I look like a raisin" (Frankel et al., 1983).

The Big Five Factors

LOQ 45-7 Which traits seem to provide the most useful information about personality variation?

Today's trait researchers believe that simple trait factors, such as the Eysencks' introversion–extraversion and stability–instability dimensions, are important, but they do not tell the whole story. A slightly expanded set of factors—dubbed the **Big Five factors** (also called the *five-factor model*)—does a better job (Costa & McCrae, 2011; Soto & John, 2017). If a test specifies where you are on the five dimensions (*openness, conscientiousness, extraversion, agreeableness,* and *neuroticism*; see **TABLE 45.1**), it has said much of what there is to say about your personality. The Big Five factors can also be used to understand both psychological flourishing and dysfunction (Bleidorn et al., 2019; Ohi et al., 2016; Oltmanns et al., 2018).

Around the world—across 56 nations and 29 languages in one study (Schmitt et al., 2007)—people describe others in terms roughly consistent with this list. The Big Five—today's "common currency for personality psychology" (Funder, 2001)—has been the most active personality research topic since the early 1990s and is currently our best approximation of the basic trait dimensions.

personality inventory a questionnaire (often with *true-false* or *agree-disagree* items) on which people respond to items designed to gauge a wide range of feelings and behaviors; used to assess selected personality traits.

Minnesota Multiphasic Personality Inventory (MMPI) the most widely researched and clinically used of all personality tests. Originally developed to identify emotional disorders (still considered its most appropriate use), this test is now used for many other screening purposes.

empirically derived test a test (such as the MMPI) created by selecting from a pool of items those that discriminate between groups.

Big Five factors researchers identified five factors—*openness, conscientiousness, extraversion, agreeableness,* and *neuroticism*—that describe personality. (Also called the *five-factor model*.)

TABLE 45.3 The "Big Five" Personality Factors

Researchers use a self-report inventory to assess and score the Big Five personality factors.

(*Memory tip:* Picturing an **OCEAN** will help you recall these.)

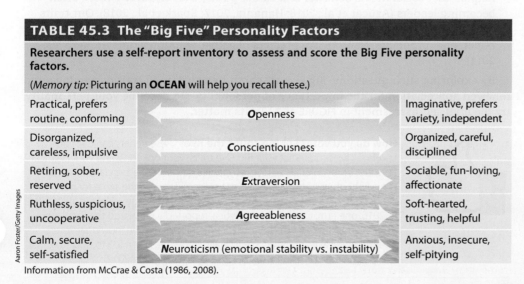

Practical, prefers routine, conforming	←— **O**penness —→	Imaginative, prefers variety, independent
Disorganized, careless, impulsive	←— **C**onscientiousness —→	Organized, careful, disciplined
Retiring, sober, reserved	←— **E**xtraversion —→	Sociable, fun-loving, affectionate
Ruthless, suspicious, uncooperative	←— **A**greeableness —→	Soft-hearted, trusting, helpful
Calm, secure, self-satisfied	←— **N**euroticism (emotional stability vs. instability) —→	Anxious, insecure, self-pitying

Information from McCrae & Costa (1986, 2008).

Aaron Foster/Getty Images

Big Five research has explored various questions:

- *How stable are these traits?* Research teams have analyzed the traits of Americans, Australians, and Germans up to age 50 (Damian et al., 2019; Wagner et al., 2019). Participants' personalities remained generally stable, but most people showed signs of the *maturity principle*: From adolescence onward, they became more conscientious and agreeable, and less neurotic (emotionally unstable) (Allemand et al., 2019; Klimstra et al., 2018; Rohrer et al., 2018). People in Japan also show personality trait stability, but show more variation over time on all Big Five traits because they tend to adapt their personality to their environment (Chopik & Kitayama, 2018).

- *Do self-ratings on these traits match others' ratings?* The ratings of family and friends of our Big Five trait levels resemble the ratings we give ourselves (Finnigan & Vazire, 2018; Luan et al., 2019).

- *Do these traits reflect differing brain structure?* The size and thickness of brain tissue correlates with several Big Five traits (DeYoung & Allen, 2019; Li, T. et al., 2017; Riccelli et al., 2017). For example, those who score high on conscientiousness tend to have a larger frontal lobe area that aids in planning and controlling behavior. Brain connections also influence the Big Five traits (Toschi et al., 2018). People high in neuroticism (emotional instability) have brains that are wired to experience stress intensely (Shackman et al., 2016; Xu & Potenza, 2012).

- *Do these traits reflect birth order?* After controlling for other variables such as family size, are first-born children, for example, more conscientious and agreeable? Contrary to popular opinion, several massive studies failed to find any association between birth order and personality (Damian & Roberts, 2015; Harris, 2009; Rohrer et al., 2015).

- *How well do these traits apply to various cultures?* The Big Five dimensions describe personality in various cultures reasonably well (Fetvadjiev et al., 2017; Kim, H. et al., 2018; Schmitt et al., 2007). From herders in Kenya and Tanzania to gardeners in Mali, these traits help us understand basic features of personality (Thalmayer et al., 2019). After studying people from 50 cultures, Robert McCrae and 79 co-researchers concluded that "features of personality traits are common to all human groups" (2005).

- *Do the Big Five traits predict our actual behaviors?* Yes, Big Five traits reliably predict important life outcomes (Soto, 2019). Conscientiousness and agreeableness predict workplace success (Nickel et al., 2019; Wilmot & Ones, 2019). (Maybe nice people finish first?) Agreeable people tend to be helpful, law-abiding, and unprejudiced (Crawford & Brandt, 2019; Habashi et al., 2016; Walters, 2018). Big Five traits also help predict social media behavior and career paths, with extraverts more often becoming leaders (Azucar et al., 2018; Hanania, 2017; Spark et al., 2018). Our traits also appear in our language patterns. In text messaging, extraversion predicts use of personal pronouns. Neuroticism predicts negative-emotion words (Holtgraves, 2011).

By exploring such questions, Big Five research has sustained trait psychology and renewed appreciation for the importance of personality. (To describe your personality, try the brief self-assessment in **FIGURE 45.3**.) Traits matter.

How do you vote? Let me count the likes Researchers can use your Facebook likes to predict your Big Five traits, your opinions, and your political attitudes (Youyou et al., 2015). Companies gather these "big data" for advertisers (who then personalize the ads you see). They do the same for political candidates, who can target you with persuasive messages (Matz et al., 2017). In 2016, one firm, Cambridge Analytica, reportedly harvested the Facebook profiles and likes of 87 million Americans. Information on individual voters' inferred political leanings and personality types was then fed to door-to-door campaigners for Donald Trump (Grassegger & Krogerus, 2017).[1]

---

[1]Facebook now protects the privacy of user likes.

How Do You Describe Yourself?

Describe yourself as you generally are now, not as you wish to be in the future. Describe yourself as you honestly see yourself, in relation to other people you know of the same sex and roughly the same age. Use the scale below to enter a number for each statement. Then, use the scoring guide at the bottom to see where you fall on the spectrum for each of the Big Five traits.

1	2	3	4	5
Very Inaccurate	Moderately Inaccurate	Neither Accurate Nor Inaccurate	Moderately Accurate	Very Accurate

1. ___Am the life of the party

2. ___Sympathize with others' feelings

3. ___Get stressed out easily

4. ___Am always prepared

5. ___Am full of ideas

6. ___Start conversations

7. ___Take time out for others

8. ___Follow a schedule

9. ___Worry about things

10. ___Have a vivid imagination

SCORING GUIDE SORTED BY BIG FIVE PERSONALITY TRAITS

Openness: statements 5, 10

Conscientiousness: statements 4, 8

Extraversion: statements 1, 6

Agreeableness: statements 2, 7

Neuroticism: statements 3, 9

How to score:

Separate your responses by each Big Five personality trait, as noted at left, and divide by two to obtain your score for each trait. So, for example, for the "Agreeableness" trait let's say you scored 3 for statement 2 ("Sympathize with others' feelings") and 4 for statement 7 ("Take time out for others"). That means on a scale from 1 to 5, your overall score for the "Agreeableness" trait is 3 + 4 = 7 ÷ 2 = **3.5**.

Scale data from: International Personality Item Pool: A Scientific Collaboratory for the Development of Advanced Measures of Personality Traits and Other Individual Differences (ipip.ori.org)

⊘ FIGURE 45.3
The Big Five self-assessment

ASK YOURSELF

Before trying the self-assessment in Figure 45.3, where would you have placed yourself on the Big Five personality dimensions? Where might your family and friends place you? Did the actual results surprise you, and do you think these results would surprise them?

RETRIEVAL PRACTICE

RP-4 What are the *Big Five* personality factors, and why are they scientifically useful?

ANSWERS IN APPENDIX E

⊞ For a review of the Big Five, engage online with *Concept Practice: The Big Five Personality Traits.*

Evaluating Trait Theories

LOQ **45-8** Does research support the consistency of personality traits over time and across situations?

Are our personality traits stable and enduring? Or does our behavior depend on where and with whom we find ourselves? Cheerful, friendly children do tend to become cheerful, friendly adults. At a college reunion, I [DM] was amazed to find that my jovial former classmates were still jovial, the shy ones still shy, the happy-seeming people still smiling and laughing *50 years later*. But it's also true that a fun-loving jokester can suddenly turn serious and respectful at a job interview. New situations and major life events can shift the personality traits we express. Transitioning from high school to university

> "There is as much difference between us and ourselves, as between us and others."
> — Michel de Montaigne, *Essays*, 1588

Roughly speaking, the external influences on behavior are the focus of *social psychology,* and the inner influences are the focus of *personality psychology.* But behavior always depends on the interaction of persons with situations.

my hair over time

childhood

teens and twenties - experimentation

thirties and up

It's not just personality that stabilizes with age.

mitra farmand

FIGURE 45.4

Personality stability With age, personality traits become more stable, as reflected in the stronger correlation of trait scores with follow-up scores 7 years later. (Data from Roberts & DelVecchio, 2000.)

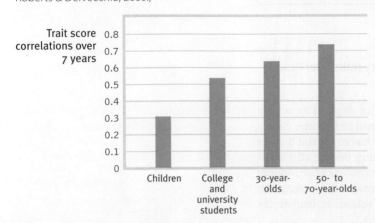

or the workforce, we often become more agreeable, conscientious, and open-minded, and less neurotic (Bleidorn et al., 2018). Losing our job may make us less agreeable and open-minded (Boyce et al., 2015). But when we retire—losing our job *by choice*—we often become more agreeable and open-minded (Schwaba & Bleidorn, 2019).

THE PERSON-SITUATION CONTROVERSY Our behavior is influenced by the interaction of our inner disposition with our environment. Still, the question lingers: Which is more important? When we explore this *person-situation controversy,* we look for genuine personality traits that persist over time and across situations. Are some people dependably conscientious and others unreliable, some cheerful and others dour, some outgoing and others shy? If we are to consider friendliness a trait, friendly people must act friendly at different times and places. Do they?

Longitudinal research follows lives through time. Some scholars (especially those who study infants) are impressed with personality change; others are struck by personality stability during adulthood. As **FIGURE 45.4** illustrates, data from 152 longitudinal studies reveal that personality trait scores are positively correlated with scores obtained 7 years later, and that as people grow older, their personality stabilizes. Interests may change—the avid tropical-fish collector may become an avid gardener. Careers may change—the determined salesperson may become a determined social worker. Relationships may change—the hostile son may become a hostile husband. But most people come to recognize and accept just who they are. As researchers Robert McCrae and Paul Costa (1994) observed, our recognizing the inevitability of our personality is "the culminating wisdom of a lifetime."

So most people—including most psychologists—would probably presume the stability of personality traits. Moreover, our traits are socially significant. They influence our health, our thinking, and our job choices and performance (Hogan, 1998; Jackson et al., 2012; Mueller et al., 2018). Studies that follow thousands of lives through time show that personality traits rival socioeconomic status and cognitive ability as predictors of mortality, divorce, and occupational attainment (Graham et al., 2017; Roberts et al., 2007).

Although our personality *traits* may be both stable and potent, the consistency of our specific *behaviors* from one situation to the next is another matter. What relationship would you expect to find between being conscientious in one situation (say, showing up for class on time) and being conscientious in another (say, avoiding unhealthy foods)? If you've noticed how outgoing you are in some situations and how reserved you are in others, perhaps you said, "Very little." That's what researchers have found—only a small correlation (Mischel, 1968; Sherman et al., 2015). This inconsistency in behaviors also makes personality test scores weak predictors of behaviors. People's scores on an extraversion test, for example, do not neatly predict how sociable they actually will be on any given occasion.

If we remember such results, we will be more cautious about labeling and pigeonholing individuals (Mischel, 1968). Years in advance, science can tell us the Moon's phase for any day. A day in advance, meteorologists can often predict the weather. But we are much further from being able to predict how *you* will feel and act tomorrow.

However, people's *average* outgoingness, happiness, or carelessness over many situations is predictable (Epstein, 1983a,b). This tendency toward trait-consistent actions occurs worldwide, from the United States to Venezuela to Japan (Locke et al., 2017). By collecting snippets of people's daily experience via body-worn recording devices, Matthias Mehl and his colleagues (2006) confirmed that extraverts really do talk more. (I [DM] have repeatedly vowed to cut back on my jabbering and joking during my noontime pickup basketball games with friends. Alas, moments later, the irrepressible chatterbox inevitably reoccupies my body. And I [ND] have a similar experience whenever I buy groceries. Somehow, I always end up chatting with the cashier! As our best friends can verify, we do have persistent (genetically influenced) personality traits. And our personality traits get expressed in our

- *music preferences.* Your playlist reveals something of your personality. Classical, jazz, blues, and folk music lovers tend to be open to experience and verbally intelligent. Extraverts tend to prefer upbeat and energetic music. Country, pop, and religious music lovers tend to be cheerful, outgoing, and conscientious (Langmeyer et al., 2012; Nave et al., 2018; Rentfrow & Gosling, 2003, 2006).

- *written communications.* If you have ever felt you could detect someone's personality from their writing voice, you are right!! What a cool finding!!! ☺ People's writings—even their brief tweets and Facebook posts—often express their extraversion, self-esteem, and agreeableness (Orehek & Human, 2017; Park et al., 2015; Pennebaker, 2011). "Off to meet a friend. Woohoo!!!" posted one Facebook user who had scored high on extraversion (Kern et al., 2014). Extraverts also use more adjectives.

- *online and personal spaces.* Are online profiles, websites, and avatars also a canvas for self-expression? Or are they an opportunity for people to present themselves in false or misleading ways? It's more the former (Akhtar et al., 2018a; Hinds & Joinson, 2019). People who seemed most likable on Facebook or Twitter also seemed most likable in person (Qiu et al., 2012; Weisbuch et al., 2009). Even mere photos, with their associated clothes, expressions, and postures, can give clues to personality and how people act in person (Gunyadin et al., 2017; Naumann et al., 2009). Our living and working spaces also help us express our identity. They all offer clues to our extraversion, agreeableness, conscientiousness, and openness (Back et al., 2010; Fong & Mar, 2015; Gosling, 2008).

"*You tend to overuse the exclamation point.*"

In unfamiliar, formal situations—perhaps as a guest in the home of a person from another culture—our traits remain hidden as we carefully attend to social cues. In familiar, informal situations—just hanging out with friends—we feel less constrained, allowing our traits to emerge (Buss, 1989). In these informal situations, our expressive styles—our animation, manner of speaking, and gestures—are impressively consistent. Viewing "thin slices" of someone's behavior—such as seeing a photo for a mere fraction of a second, or seeing several 2-second clips of a teacher in action—can tell us a lot about the person's basic personality traits (Ambady, 2010; Tackett et al., 2016).

Some people are naturally expressive (and therefore talented at pantomime and charades); others are less expressive (and therefore better poker players). To evaluate people's voluntary control over their expressiveness, Bella DePaulo and her colleagues (1992) asked people to *act* as expressive or inhibited as possible while stating opinions. Their remarkable findings: Inexpressive people, even when feigning expressiveness, were less expressive than expressive people acting naturally. Similarly, expressive people, even when trying to seem inhibited, were less inhibited than inexpressive people acting naturally. It's hard to be someone you're not, or not to be who you are.

To sum up, we can say that at any moment the immediate situation powerfully influences a person's behavior. Social psychologists have learned that this is especially

Room with a cue Even at "zero acquaintance," people can catch a glimpse of others' personality from looking at their online and personal spaces. So, what's your read on the occupants of these two rooms?

so when a "strong situation" makes clear demands (Cooper & Withey, 2009). We can better predict drivers' behavior at traffic lights from knowing the color of the lights than from knowing the drivers' personalities. Thus, professors may perceive certain students as subdued (based on their classroom behavior), but friends may perceive them as pretty wild (based on their party behavior). Averaging our behavior across many occasions does, however, reveal distinct personality traits. Traits exist. We differ. And our differences matter.

ASK YOURSELF

How do you think your own personality traits shine through in your music preferences, communication style, and online and personal spaces?

> For a demonstration of trait research, view the 8-minute *Video: Trait Theories of Personality.*

RETRIEVAL PRACTICE

RP-5 How well do personality test scores predict our behavior? Explain.

ANSWERS IN APPENDIX E

MODULE

45 REVIEW Humanistic Theories and Trait Theories

LEARNING OBJECTIVES

Test Yourself Answer these repeated Learning Objective Questions on your own (before checking the answers in Appendix D) to improve your retention of the concepts (McDaniel et al., 2009, 2015).

LOQ 45-1 How did humanistic psychologists view personality, and what was their goal in studying personality?

LOQ 45-2 How did humanistic psychologists assess a person's sense of self?

LOQ 45-3 How have humanistic theories influenced psychology? What criticisms have they faced?

LOQ 45-4 How do psychologists use traits to describe personality?

LOQ 45-5 What are some common misunderstandings about introversion?

LOQ 45-6 What are *personality inventories,* and what are their strengths and weaknesses as trait-assessment tools?

LOQ 45-7 Which traits seem to provide the most useful information about personality variation?

LOQ 45-8 Does research support the consistency of personality traits over time and across situations?

TERMS AND CONCEPTS TO REMEMBER

Test Yourself Write down the definition in your own words, then check your answer.

humanistic theories, p. 528
hierarchy of needs, p. 528
self-actualization, p. 528
self-transcendence, p. 528
unconditional positive regard, p. 528
self-concept, p. 530

trait, p. 532
personality inventory, p. 535
Minnesota Multiphasic Personality Inventory (MMPI), p. 535
empirically derived test, p. 535
Big Five factors, p. 535

MASTER THE MATERIAL

Test Yourself Answer the following questions on your own first, then check your answers in Appendix E.

1. Maslow's hierarchy of needs proposes that we must satisfy basic physiological and safety needs before we seek ultimate psychological needs, such as self-actualization. Maslow based his ideas on
   a. Freudian theory.
   b. his experiences with patients.
   c. a series of laboratory experiments.
   d. his study of healthy, creative people.

2. How might Rogers explain how environment influences the development of a criminal?

3. The total acceptance Rogers advocated as part of a growth-promoting environment is called _____ _____ _____.

4. _____ theories of personality focus on describing characteristic behavior patterns, such as agreeableness or extraversion.

5. The most widely used personality inventory is the
   a. Extraversion–Introversion Scale.   c. MMPI.
   b. Person-Situation Inventory.   d. Big Five.

6. Which of the following is NOT one of the Big Five personality factors?
   a. Conscientiousness   c. Extraversion
   b. Anxiety   d. Agreeableness

7. Our scores on personality tests best predict
   a. our behavior on a specific occasion.
   b. our average behavior across many situations.
   c. behavior involving a single trait, such as conscientiousness.
   d. behavior that depends on the situation or context.

Continue testing yourself with **LearningCurve** or **Achieve Read & Practice** to learn and remember most effectively.

46 Social-Cognitive Theories and the Self

Social-Cognitive Theories

LOQ 46-1 How do social-cognitive theorists view personality development, and how do they explore behavior?

The **social-cognitive perspective** on personality, proposed by Albert Bandura (1986, 2006, 2008), emphasizes the interaction of our traits with our situations. Much as nature and nurture always work together, so do individuals and their situations.

Social-cognitive theorists believe we learn many of our behaviors either through conditioning or by observing and imitating others. (That's the "social" part.) They also emphasize the importance of mental processes: What we *think* about a situation affects our resulting behavior. (That's the "cognitive" part.) Instead of focusing solely on how our environment *controls* us (behaviorism), social-cognitive theorists focus on how we and our environment *interact*: How do we interpret and respond to external events? How do our schemas, our memories, and our expectations influence our behavior patterns?

Reciprocal Influences

Bandura (1986, 2006) views the person-environment interaction as **reciprocal determinism.** "Behavior, internal personal factors, and environmental influences," he said, "all operate as interlocking determinants of each other" (**FIGURE 46.1**). We can see this interaction in people's relationships. For example, Rosa's past romantic experiences (her behaviors) influence her romantic attitudes (internal factor), which affect how she now responds to Ryan (environmental factor).

Consider three specific ways in which individuals and environments interact:

1. *Different people choose different environments.* The reading we do, the social media we use, the careers we pursue, the music we listen to, the friends we associate with— all are part of an environment we have chosen, based partly on our disposition (Denissen et al., 2018; Funder, 2009). And the environments we choose then shape us. People with inflated self-esteem post frequent selfies in online environments, where they can receive the public attention and praise they crave. This leads to even greater self-love (Halpern et al., 2016).

2. *Our personalities shape how we interpret and react to events.* If we perceive the world as threatening, we will watch for threats and be prepared to defend ourselves. Anxious people often attend to and react strongly to relationship threats (Campbell & Marshall, 2011).

3. *Our personalities help create situations to which we react.* How we view and treat people influences how they then treat us. If we expect that others will not like us, our bragging and other efforts to win their approval might actually cause them to reject us (Scopelliti et al., 2015).

social-cognitive perspective a view of behavior as influenced by the interaction between people's traits (including their thinking) and their social context.

reciprocal determinism the interacting influences of behavior, internal cognition, and environment.

Courtesy of Joslyn Brugh

€ FIGURE 46.1
Reciprocal determinism

Biological influences:
• genetically determined temperament
• autonomic nervous system reactivity
• brain activity

Psychological influences:
• learned responses
• unconscious thought processes
• expectations and interpretations

Personality

Social-cultural influences:
• childhood experiences
• situational factors
• cultural expectations
• social support

FIGURE 46.2
The biopsychosocial approach to the study of personality As with other psychological phenomena, personality is fruitfully studied at multiple levels.

📖 To explore the influence of the person-environment interaction on behavior, engage online with *Concept Practice: Reciprocal Determinism.*

In addition to the interaction of internal personal factors, the environment, and our behaviors, we also experience *gene–environment interaction.* Our genetically influenced traits evoke certain responses from others, which may nudge us in one direction or another. In one well-replicated finding, those with the interacting factors of (1) having a specific gene associated with aggression, and (2) being raised in a difficult environment were most likely to demonstrate adult antisocial behavior (Byrd & Manuck, 2014; Caspi et al., 2002).

In such ways, we are both the products and the architects of our environments: *Behavior emerges from the interplay of external and internal influences.* Boiling water turns an egg hard and a potato soft. A threatening environment turns one person into a hero, another into a scoundrel. Extraverts enjoy greater well-being in an extraverted culture than in an introverted one (Fulmer et al., 2010). At *every moment,* our behavior is influenced by our biology, our social and cultural experiences, and our cognition and dispositions (**FIGURE 46.2**).

ASK YOURSELF

How have your experiences shaped your personality? How has your personality helped shape your environment?

RETRIEVAL PRACTICE

RP-1 Albert Bandura proposed the _____-_____ perspective on personality, which emphasizes the interaction of people with their environment. To describe the interacting influences of behavior, thoughts, and environment, he used the term _____ _____.

ANSWERS IN APPENDIX E

Assessing Behavior in Situations

To predict behavior, social-cognitive psychologists often observe behavior in realistic situations. One ambitious example was the U.S. Army's World War II strategy for assessing candidates for spy missions. Rather than using paper-and-pencil tests, Army psychologists subjected the candidates to simulated undercover conditions. They tested their ability to handle stress, solve problems, maintain leadership, and withstand intense interrogation without blowing their cover. Although time-consuming and expensive, this assessment of behavior in a realistic situation helped predict later success on actual spy missions (OSS Assessment Staff, 1948).

Singing success On the television show *The Voice,* contestants compete against one another in stressful situations. The winner receives a cash prize and music recording contract. The show presumes a valid point: People's behavior in job-relevant situations helps predict their job performance.

Military and educational organizations and many Fortune 500 companies have adopted similar strategies, known as the *assessment center* approach (Bray & Byham, 1991, 1997; Eurich et al., 2009). The U.S. telecommunications giant AT&T has observed prospective managers doing simulated managerial work. Some European universities give student applicants material to study, and then test their learning—thus mimicking the educational program (Niessen & Meijer, 2017). Many colleges assess nursing students' potential by observing their clinical work. And they assess potential faculty members' teaching abilities by observing them teach.

The assessment center approach exploits the principle that the best means of predicting behavior is neither a personality test nor an interviewer's intuition. Rather, *the best predictor of future behavior is the person's past behavior patterns in similar situations* (Lyons et al., 2011; Mischel, 1981; Schmidt & Hunter, 1998). As long as the situation and the person remain much the same, the best predictor of future job performance is past job performance; the best predictor of future grades is past grades; the best predictor of future aggressiveness is past aggressiveness. People who have used marital infidelity websites at home will also be more likely to behave immorally at work (Griffin et al., 2019). If you can't check the person's past behavior, the next best thing is to create an assessment situation that simulates the task so you can see how the person handles it (Lievens et al., 2009; Meriac et al., 2008).

> "What's past is prologue." — William Shakespeare, *The Tempest,* 1611

Evaluating Social-Cognitive Theories

LOQ **46-2** What criticisms have social-cognitive theories faced?

Social-cognitive theories of personality sensitize researchers to how situations affect, and are affected by, individuals. More than other personality theories (see **TABLE 46.1**), they build from psychological research on learning and cognition.

TABLE 46.1 Comparing the Major Personality Theories

Personality Theory	Key Proponents	Assumptions	View of Personality	Personality Assessment Methods
Psychoanalytic	Freud	Emotional disorders spring from unconscious dynamics, such as unresolved sexual and other childhood conflicts, and fixation at various developmental stages. Defense mechanisms fend off anxiety.	Personality consists of pleasure-seeking impulses (the id), a reality-oriented executive (the ego), and an internalized set of ideals (the superego).	Free association, projective tests, dream analysis
Psychodynamic	Adler, Horney, Jung	The unconscious and conscious minds interact. Childhood experiences and defense mechanisms are important.	The dynamic interplay of conscious and unconscious motives and conflicts shapes our personality.	Projective tests, therapy sessions
Humanistic	Maslow, Rogers	Rather than focusing on disorders born of dark conflicts, it's better to emphasize how healthy people may strive for self-realization.	If our basic human needs are met, we will strive toward self-actualization. In a climate of unconditional positive regard, we can develop self-awareness and a more realistic and positive self-concept.	Questionnaires, therapy sessions, life story approach
Trait	Allport; Costa; H. Eysenck; S. Eysenck; McCrae	We have certain stable and enduring characteristics, influenced by genetic predispositions.	Scientific study of traits has isolated important dimensions of personality, such as the Big Five traits (openness, conscientiousness, extraversion, agreeableness, and neuroticism).	Personality inventories
Social-Cognitive	Bandura	Our traits interact with the social context to produce our behaviors.	Conditioning and observational learning interact with cognition to create behavior patterns. Our behavior in one situation is best predicted by considering our past behavior in similar situations.	Observing behavior in realistic situations

Critics charge that social-cognitive theories focus so much on the situation that they fail to appreciate the person's inner traits. Where is the person in this view of personality, ask the dissenters, and where are human emotions? True, the situation does guide our behavior. But in many instances our unconscious motives, our emotions, and our pervasive traits shine through. Personality traits predict behavior at work, in love, and at play. Our biologically influenced traits really do matter. Consider Percy Ray Pridgen and Charles Gill. Each faced the same situation: They had jointly won a $90 million lottery jackpot (Harriston, 1993). When Pridgen learned of the winning numbers, he began trembling uncontrollably, huddled with a friend behind a bathroom door while confirming the win, and then sobbed. When Gill heard the news, he told his wife and then went to sleep.

RETRIEVAL PRACTICE

RP-2 What is the best way to predict a person's future behavior?

ANSWERS IN APPENDIX E

> To review the perspectives and methods of personality psychology, engage online with *Concept Practice: Comparing Personality Theories.*

Exploring the Self

LOQ 46-3 Why has psychology generated so much research on the self? How important is self-esteem to our well-being?

Our personality feeds our sense of self. Asked to consider "Who I am," people draw on their distinctive and enduring ways of thinking, feeling, and acting. Psychology's concern with our sense of self dates back at least to William James, who devoted more than 100 pages of his 1890 *Principles of Psychology* to the topic. By 1943, Gordon Allport lamented that the self had become "lost to view." Although humanistic psychology's later emphasis on the self did not instigate much scientific research, it did help renew the concept of self and keep it alive. Now, more than a century after James, the self is one of Western psychology's most vigorously researched topics. Every year, new studies galore appear on self-esteem, self-disclosure, self-awareness, self-schemas, self-monitoring, and more. Even neuroscientists have searched for the self, by identifying a central frontal lobe region that activates when people respond to self-reflective questions about their traits and dispositions (Damasio, 2010; Mitchell, 2009; Pauly et al., 2013). The **self**, as organizer of our thoughts, feelings, and actions, occupies the center of personality.

Consider the concept of *possible selves* (Markus & Nurius, 1986; Rathbone et al., 2016). Your possible selves include your visions of the self you dream of becoming (the rich self, the successful self, the loved and admired self), and also the self you fear becoming (the unemployed self, the academically failed self, the lonely and unpopular self). Possible selves motivate us to lay out specific goals that direct our energy effectively and efficiently (Landau et al., 2014). Eighth- and ninth-grade students whose families struggle financially are more likely to earn high grades if they have a clear vision of themselves succeeding in school (Duckworth et al., 2013). Dreams do often give birth to achievements.

Our self-focused perspective may motivate us, but it can also lead us to presume too readily that others are noticing and evaluating us, a phenomenon called the **spotlight effect.** In one experiment, university students who were asked to put on an embarrassing T-shirt before meeting other students guessed that nearly half their peers would notice the shirt. But only 23 percent did (Gilovich, 1996). To turn down the spotlight's brightness, we can use two strategies. The first is simply to know and remember the spotlight effect. Public speakers perform better if they understand that their natural nervousness is hardly noticeable (Savitsky & Gilovich, 2003). The second is to take the audience's perspective. When we imagine audience members empathizing with our situation, we usually expect to be judged less harshly (Epley

self in contemporary psychology, assumed to be the center of personality, the organizer of our thoughts, feelings, and actions.

spotlight effect overestimating others' noticing and evaluating our appearance, performance, and blunders (as if we presume a spotlight shines on us).

self-esteem our feelings of high or low self-worth.

self-efficacy our sense of competence and effectiveness.

et al., 2002). The point to remember: *We stand out less than we imagine,* even with dorky clothes and bad hair, and even after a blunder like setting off a library alarm (Gilovich & Savitsky, 1999; Savitsky et al., 2001).

ASK YOURSELF

What possible selves do you dream of—or fear—becoming? To what extent do these imagined selves motivate you now?

The Benefits of Self-Esteem

Self-esteem—our feelings of high or low self-worth—matters. So does **self-efficacy,** our sense of competence on a task (Bandura, 1977, 2018). (A student might feel high self-efficacy in a math course yet low overall self-esteem.) People who feel good about themselves (who strongly agree with self-affirming questionnaire statements, such as "I am fun to be with") have fewer sleepless nights. They tend to be outgoing, responsible, and open to new experiences (Fetvadjiev & He, 2019). Online and in-person, they communicate positively, causing others to like and include them more (Cameron & Granger, 2019; Mahadevan et al., 2019). They feel less shy, anxious, and lonely, and are just plain happier (Greenberg, 2008; Orth & Robins, 2014; Swann et al., 2007). Our self-esteem grows from venturesome experiences and achievement, and therefore changes as we age (Hutteman et al., 2015). Self-esteem often increases dramatically from adolescence to middle adulthood, continuing to climb until peaking between ages 50 and 60 (Bleidorn et al., 2016; Orth et al., 2018; von Soest et al., 2018).

LOW SELF-ESTEEM

Dear diary, Sorry to bother you again.

Mike Twohy/The New Yorker Collection/The Cartoon Bank

But most psychologists doubt that high self-esteem is "the armor that protects kids" from life's problems (Baumeister & Vohs, 2018; McKay, 2000; Seligman, 2002). Children's academic self-efficacy—their confidence that they can do well in a subject—predicts school achievement. But general self-image does not (Marsh & Craven, 2006; Swann et al., 2007; Trautwein et al., 2006). Maybe self-esteem is a side effect of meeting challenges and surmounting difficulties, or a gauge that reports the state of our relationships with others (Reitz et al., 2016). If so, isn't pushing the gauge artificially higher with empty compliments much like forcing a car's low fuel gauge to display "full"?

If feeling good *follows* doing well, then giving praise in the absence of good performance may actually harm people. After receiving weekly self-esteem-boosting messages, struggling students earned *lower*-than-expected grades (Forsyth et al., 2007). Other research showed that giving people random rewards hurt their productivity. Martin Seligman (2012) reported that "when good things occurred that weren't earned, like nickels coming out of slot machines, it did not increase people's well-being. It produced helplessness. People gave up and became passive."

There are, however, important effects when self-esteem is threatened. When researchers temporarily deflated people's self-image (by telling them they did poorly on an aptitude test or by disparaging their personality), those participants became more likely to disparage others or to express heightened racial prejudice (vanDellen et al., 2011; van Dijk et al., 2011; Ybarra, 1999). Self-image threat even increases *unconscious* racial bias (Allen & Sherman, 2011). Those who are negative about themselves have also tended to be oversensitive and judgmental (Baumgardner et al., 1989; Pelham, 1993). Self-esteem threats lead people to spend more time with their online profiles—safe havens in which to rebuild their self-worth (Toma & Hancock, 2013). Such findings are consistent with humanistic psychology's ideas about the benefits of a healthy self-image. Accept yourself and you'll find it easier to accept others. Disparage yourself and you will be prone to the floccinaucinihilipilification[1] of others. People who are down on themselves tend to be down on others.

> "When kids increase in self-control, their grades go up later. But when kids increase their self-esteem, there is no effect on their grades." — Angela Duckworth, *In Character* interview, 2009

> "The enthusiastic claims of the self-esteem movement mostly range from fantasy to hogwash. The effects of self-esteem are small, limited, and not all good." — Roy Baumeister (1996)

---

[1] We couldn't resist throwing that in. But don't worry, you won't be tested on *floccinaucinihilipilification,* which is the act of estimating something as worthless (and was the longest nontechnical word in the first edition of the *Oxford English Dictionary*).

The Costs of Self-Esteem

LOQ 46-4 How do excessive optimism, blindness to one's own incompetence, and self-serving bias reveal the costs of self-esteem, and how do defensive and secure self-esteem differ?

EXCESSIVE OPTIMISM Positive thinking in the face of adversity can pay dividends, but so, too, can a dash of realism (Schneider, 2001). Realistic anxiety over possible future failures can fuel energetic efforts to avoid the dreaded fate (Goodhart, 1986; Norem, 2001; Showers, 1992). Concerned about failing an upcoming exam, students may study thoroughly and outperform their equally able but more confident peers. Asian American students have expressed somewhat greater pessimism than their European American counterparts, which may help explain their often impressive academic achievements (Chang, 2001). Success requires enough optimism to provide hope and enough pessimism to prevent complacency. We want our airline pilots to be mindful of worst-possible outcomes.

Excessive optimism can blind us to real risks (Tenney et al., 2015). More than 1000 studies have shown how our natural positive thinking bias can promote "unrealistic optimism" (Shepperd et al., 2015; Weinstein, 1980). When 56 percent of twelfth graders believed they would earn a graduate degree—though only 9 percent were likely to do so—that was unrealistic optimism (Reynolds et al., 2006). When most people of opposing political views optimistically believed that *their* views would become more widely held, many were in error (Rogers et al., 2017). When students believed they were more likely than their classmates to get a high-paying job and own a nice home, and less likely to have a heart attack or get cancer, that, too, was unrealistic optimism (Waters et al., 2011). If overconfident of our ability to control an impulse such as the urge to smoke, we are more likely to expose ourselves to temptations—and to fail (Nordgren et al., 2009). Blind optimism can be self-defeating, as we can see in those who optimistically deny the addictive toxicity of smoking, venture into ill-fated relationships, and invest money in risky schemes.

Our natural positive thinking bias does seem to vanish, however, when we are awaiting feedback, such as exam results (Carroll et al., 2006). Across many studies in both the real world (awaiting bar exam scores) and laboratory (awaiting intelligence test results), people "brace for the worst" (Sweeny & Falkenstein, 2017). (Perhaps you, too, can recall shifting toward pessimism as a moment of truth approaches?) Positive illusions also vanish after a traumatic personal experience—as they did for victims of a catastrophic California earthquake, who had to give up their illusions of being less vulnerable than others to earthquakes (Helweg-Larsen, 1999).

BLINDNESS TO ONE'S OWN INCOMPETENCE Ironically, people often are most overconfident when most incompetent. That, said Justin Kruger and David Dunning (1999), is because it often takes competence to recognize competence. They found that most students scoring at the low end of grammar and logic tests believed they had scored in the top half. This "ignorance of one's own incompetence" phenomenon—now called the *Dunning-Kruger effect*—can produce overconfidence among political leaders. It also has a parallel among those of us with hearing loss, as I [DM] can confirm. Because we are unaware of what we don't hear, we may overestimate our hearing. If I fail to hear my friend calling my name, the friend notices my inattention. But for me it's a nonevent. I hear what I hear—which, to me, seems pretty normal.

"Our ignorance is invisible to us," summarizes Dunning (2019). "The first rule of the Dunning-Kruger club is you don't know you're a member of the Dunning-Kruger club." Thus, to judge one's competence and predict one's future performance, it pays to invite others' assessments (Dunning, 2006; Grossmann & Kross, 2014). Based on studies in which both individuals and their acquaintances predict their future, we can hazard some advice: Ask your peers for their candid prediction. If you're in love and want to predict whether it will last, don't listen to your heart—ask your roommate.

"What I'd dearly love would be to be able to see [myself] having a Dunning-Kruger moment. But according to my own theory, I'll never have it." — Psychologist David Dunning, NPR, 2016

DOONESBURY

SELF-SERVING BIAS Imagine dashing to class, hoping not to miss the first few minutes. But you arrive five minutes late, huffing and puffing. As you sink into your seat, what sorts of thoughts go through your mind? Do you go through a negative door, thinking "I'm such a loser"? Or do you go through a positive door, telling yourself "At least I made it to class"?

Personality psychologists have found that most people choose the second door because it leads to positive self-thoughts. We have a good reputation with ourselves. We show a **self-serving bias**—a readiness to perceive ourselves favorably (Myers, 2010). Consider:

People accept more responsibility for good deeds than for bad, and for successes than for failures. Athletes often privately credit their victories to their own prowess, and their losses to bad breaks, lousy officiating, or the other team's exceptional performance. Most students who receive poor exam grades criticize the exam or the instructor, not themselves. Drivers filling out insurance forms have explained their accidents in such words as "A pedestrian hit me and went under my car." The question "What have I done to deserve this?" is one we usually ask of our troubles, not our successes. Although a self-serving bias can lead us to avoid uncomfortable truths, it can also motivate us to approach difficult tasks with confidence instead of despair (Tomaka et al., 1992; von Hippel & Trivers, 2011). Indeed, across many studies self-enhancement predicts emotional well-being (Dufner et al., 2019).

Most people see themselves as better than average. Compared with most other people, how moral are you? How easy to get along with? Where would you rank yourself, from the 1st to the 99th percentile? Most people put themselves well above the 50th percentile. This better-than-average effect appears for nearly any subjectively assessed and socially desirable trait or behavior. Most people rate themselves as having better than average intelligence, attractiveness, ethics, job performance, and driving ability (Heck et al., 2018; Myers & Twenge, 2019; Walker & Keller, 2019). Self-serving bias is weaker in Asia, where people tend to value modesty (Church et al., 2014; Falk et al., 2009). Yet in every one of 53 countries surveyed, people expressed self-esteem above the midpoint of the most widely used scale (Schmitt & Allik, 2005). It's normal to think we're above average.

"I never blame myself when I'm not hitting. I just blame the bat and if it keeps up, I change bats." — Baseball great Yogi Berra (1925–2015)

self-serving bias a readiness to perceive ourselves favorably.

PEANUTS

"Fun fact: The average man [thinks] he would be better than 63 percent of other men if he had to survive a zombie apocalypse." — Mathematician Spencer Greenberg and economist Seth Stephens-Davidowitz, 2019

Self-serving bias often underlies conflicts, such as blaming a partner for relationship problems or a colleague for work problems. All of us also tend to see our own *groups*— our school, organization, region, or country—as superior. Although there are 50 U.S. states, Americans on average estimate that their home state made 18 percent of the contributions to U.S. history (Putnam et al., 2018). Such *group*-serving bias—my group is better—fueled Nazi horrors and Rwandan genocide. No wonder literature and religion so often warn against the perils of self-love and pride.

Finding their self-esteem threatened, some people with inflated egos may react violently. Researchers Brad Bushman and Roy Baumeister (1998; Bushman et al., 2009) had undergraduate volunteers write a brief essay, in response to which another supposed student gave them either praise ("Great essay!") or stinging criticism ("One of the worst essays I have read!"). The essay writers were then allowed to lash out at their evaluators by blasting them with unpleasant noise. Can you anticipate the result? After criticism, those with inflated self-esteem were "exceptionally aggressive." They delivered three times the auditory torture than did those with normal self-esteem. Over 80 studies have replicated the dangerous effect of **narcissism** (excessive self-love and self-focus) on aggression (Rasmussen, 2016). Researchers have concluded that "conceited, self-important individuals turn nasty toward those who puncture their bubbles of self-love" (Baumeister, 2001).

After tracking self-importance across several decades, psychologist Jean Twenge (2006; Twenge & Foster, 2010) reported that what she called *Generation Me*—born in the 1980s and 1990s—expressed more narcissism (by agreeing more often with statements such as, "If I ruled the world, it would be a better place," or "I think I am a special person"). Why does a rise in narcissism matter? Narcissists tend to be materialistic, desire fame, have inflated expectations, hook up more often without commitment, and gamble and cheat more—all of which have been increasing as narcissism has increased.

Narcissistic people (more often men) forgive others less, take a game-playing approach to their romantic relationships, and engage in sexually forceful behavior (Blinkhorn et al., 2015; Bushman et al., 2003; Grijalva et al., 2015). They're often charismatic and ambitious, making them popular until others tire of their boastful arrogance (Leckelt et al., 2020; Poorthuis et al., 2019). They crave adulation and often become defensive or enraged when criticized (Geukes et al., 2016; Gnambs & Appel, 2018; Krizan & Herlache, 2018). Many had parents who told them they were superior to others (Brummelman et al., 2015). Reality TV stars are often especially narcissistic (Rubinstein, 2016; Young & Pinsky, 2006).

"The [self-]portraits that we actually believe, when we are given freedom to voice them, are dramatically more positive than reality can sustain." — Shelley Taylor, *Positive Illusions*, 1989

Despite the demonstrated perils of pride, many people object that the idea of self-serving bias overlooks those who feel worthless and unlovable. If self-serving bias prevails, why do so many people disparage themselves? For five reasons: (1) Sometimes self-directed put-downs are *subtly strategic*—they elicit reassuring strokes. Saying "No one likes me" may at least elicit "But not everyone has met you!" (2) Other times, such as before a game or an exam, self-disparaging comments *prepare us for possible failure*. The coach who extols the superior strength of the upcoming opponent makes a loss understandable, a victory noteworthy. (3) A self-disparaging "How could I have been so

narcissism excessive self-love and self-absorption.

stupid!" also helps us *learn from our mistakes*. (4) Sometimes false humility is actually a *humblebrag*: "I barely studied, so I'm amazed I got an A" (Sezer et al., 2018). (5) Self-disparagement frequently *pertains to one's old self*. Asked to remember their really bad behaviors, people recall things from long ago; good behaviors more easily come to mind from their recent past (Escobedo & Adolphs, 2010). Even when they have not changed, people are much more critical of their distant past selves than of their current selves (Wilson & Ross, 2001). Chumps yesterday, but champs today: "At 18, I was a jerk; today I'm more sensitive."

Even so, all of us some of the time (and some of us much of the time) do feel inferior. This is especially true when we compare ourselves with those who are a step or two higher on the ladder of status, looks, income, or ability. The more frequently we feel comparatively inferior, the more unhappy or even depressed we become. But for most people, thinking has a naturally positive bias.

Some researchers identify two types of self-esteem—defensive and secure (Kernis, 2003; Lambird & Mann, 2006; Ryan & Deci, 2004). *Defensive self-esteem* is fragile. It focuses on sustaining itself, which makes failure and criticism feel threatening. Defensive people may respond to such perceived threats with anger or aggression (Crocker & Park, 2004; Donnellan et al., 2005).

Secure self-esteem is less fragile, because it is less contingent on external evaluations. To feel accepted for who we are, and not for our looks, wealth, or acclaim, relieves pressures to succeed and enables us to focus beyond ourselves. By losing ourselves in relationships and purposes larger than ourselves, we may achieve a more secure self-esteem, satisfying relationships, and greater quality of life (Crocker & Park, 2004). Authentic pride, rooted in actual achievement, supports self-confidence and leadership (Tracy et al., 2009; Weidman et al., 2016; Williams & DeSteno, 2009).

> "If you compare yourself with others, you may become vain and bitter; for always there will be greater and lesser persons than yourself." — Max Ehrmann, "Desiderata," 1927

> "True humility is not thinking less of yourself; it is thinking of yourself less." — C. S. Lewis, *Mere Christianity*, 1952

RETRIEVAL PRACTICE

RP-3 What are the positive and negative effects of high self-esteem?

RP-4 The tendency to accept responsibility for success and blame circumstances or bad luck for failure is called _____-_____ _____.

RP-5 _____ (Secure/Defensive) self-esteem is linked to angry and aggressive behavior. _____ (Secure/Defensive) self-esteem is a healthier self-image that allows us to focus beyond ourselves and enjoy a higher quality of life.

ANSWERS IN APPENDIX E

MODULE

46 REVIEW Social-Cognitive Theories and the Self

LEARNING OBJECTIVES

Test Yourself Answer these repeated Learning Objective Questions on your own (before checking the answers in Appendix D) to improve your retention of the concepts (McDaniel et al., 2009, 2015).

LOQ 46-1 How do social-cognitive theorists view personality development, and how do they explore behavior?

LOQ 46-2 What criticisms have social-cognitive theories faced?

LOQ 46-3 Why has psychology generated so much research on the self? How important is self-esteem to our well-being?

LOQ 46-4 How do excessive optimism, blindness to one's own incompetence, and self-serving bias reveal the costs of self-esteem, and how do defensive and secure self-esteem differ?

TERMS AND CONCEPTS TO REMEMBER

Test Yourself Write down the definition in your own words, then check your answer.

social-cognitive perspective, p. 541

reciprocal determinism, p. 541

self, p. 544

spotlight effect, p. 544

self-esteem, p. 544

self-efficacy, p. 544

self-serving bias, p. 547

narcissism, p. 548

MASTER THE MATERIAL

Test Yourself Answer the following questions on your own first, then check your answers in Appendix E.

1. The social-cognitive perspective proposes our personality is shaped by a process called reciprocal determinism, as personal factors, environmental factors, and behaviors interact. An example of an environmental factor is
   a. the presence of books in a home.
   b. a preference for outdoor play.
   c. the ability to read at a fourth-grade level.
   d. the fear of violent action on television.

2. Critics say that _____-_____ personality theories are very sensitive to an individual's interactions with particular situations, but that they give too little attention to the person's enduring traits.

3. The tendency to overestimate others' attention to and evaluation of our appearance, performance, and blunders is called the _____ _____.

4. Researchers have found that low self-esteem tends to be linked with life problems. How should this link be interpreted?
   a. Life problems cause low self-esteem.
   b. The answer isn't clear because the link is correlational and does not indicate cause and effect.
   c. Low self-esteem leads to life problems.
   d. Because of the self-serving bias, we must assume that external factors cause low self-esteem.

5. A fortune cookie advises, "Love yourself and happiness will follow." Is this good advice?

Continue testing yourself with 📖 **LearningCurve** or 📖 **Achieve Read & Practice** to learn and remember most effectively.

baona/Getty Images

Psychological Disorders

I felt the need to clean my room . . . and would spend four to five hours at it. I would take every book out of the bookcase, dust and put it back. . . . I couldn't stop. . . . I made a ritual of touching the wall in my bedroom before I went out because something bad would happen if I didn't do it the right way.

Marc, diagnosed with obsessive-compulsive disorder (from Summers, 1996)

Whenever I get depressed it's because I've lost a sense of self. I can't find reasons to like myself. I think I'm ugly. I think no one likes me.

Greta, diagnosed with depression (from Thorne, 1993, p. 21)

Voices, like the roar of a crowd, came. I felt like Jesus; I was being crucified.

Stuart, diagnosed with schizophrenia (from Emmons et al., 1997)

Now and then, all of us feel, think, or act in ways that may resemble a psychological disorder. We feel anxious, depressed, withdrawn, or suspicious. So it's no wonder that we are drawn to try to understand disturbed psychological states—we sometimes see ourselves in the mental illnesses we study. "To study the abnormal is the best way of understanding the normal," said William James (1842–1910).

Personally or through friends or family, we may experience the bewilderment and pain of unexplained physical symptoms, irrational fears, or a feeling that life is not worth living. In a survey of first-year university students in eight countries, 1 in 3 reported a mental health problem during the prior year (Auerbach et al., 2018).

Worldwide, more than half a billion people live with mental or behavior disorders (WHO, 2017b). Although their rates and symptoms vary by culture, no known society is free of two terrible disorders—major depressive disorder and schizophrenia (Baumeister & Härter, 2007; Jablensky, 1999; Susser & Martínez-Alés, 2018). Modules 47 through 52 examine these and other disorders. The Therapy modules consider their *treatment*.

MODULE

47 Introduction to Psychological Disorders

Most people would agree that someone who is depressed and stays mostly in bed for 3 months has a psychological disorder. But what about a grieving father who can't resume his usual social activities 3 months after his child has died? Where should we draw the line between understandable grief and clinical depression? Between a fear and a phobia? Between normality and abnormality? Let's start with these questions:

- How should we *define* psychological disorders?

- How should we *understand* disorders? How do underlying biological factors contribute to disorder? How do troubling environments influence our well-being? And how do these effects of nature and nurture interact?

- How should we *classify* psychological disorders? And can we do so in a way that allows us to help people without stigmatizing or labeling them?

- Are those with psychological disorders at risk of doing harm to themselves or others?

- What do we know about rates of psychological disorders? How many people have them? Who is vulnerable, and when?

> "Who in the rainbow can draw the line where the violet tint ends and the orange tint begins? Distinctly we see the difference of the colors, but where exactly does the one first blendingly enter into the other? So with sanity and insanity." — Herman Melville, *Billy Budd, Sailor*, 1924

Defining Psychological Disorders

(**LEARNING OBJECTIVE QUESTION** **LOQ** **47-1** How should we draw the line between normality and disorder?

A **psychological disorder** is a syndrome (collection of symptoms) marked by a "clinically significant disturbance in an individual's cognition, emotion regulation, or behavior" (American Psychiatric Association, 2013). Such thoughts, emotions, or behaviors are *dysfunctional* or *maladaptive*—they interfere with normal day-to-day life. Believing your home must be thoroughly cleaned every weekend is not a disorder. But if cleaning rituals interfere with work and leisure, as Marc's uncontrollable rituals did, they may be signs of a disorder. Occasional sad moods that persist and become disabling may likewise signal a psychological disorder.

Distress often accompanies such dysfunction. Marc, Greta, and Stuart were all distressed by their thoughts, emotions, or behaviors.

Over time, definitions of what makes for a "significant disturbance" have varied. From 1952 through December 9, 1973, "homosexuality" was classified as a psychological disorder.

Culture and normality Young American men may plan elaborate invitations for big events, as did this student (a) who appealed (successfully) to his date for prom. Young men of the West African Wodaabe tribe (b) traditionally put on decorative makeup and costumes to attract women. Each culture may view the other's behavior as abnormal.

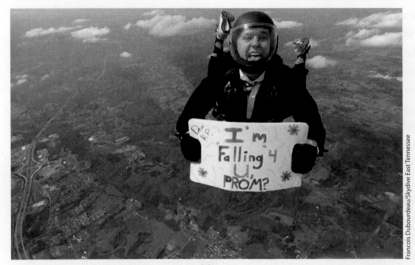
Francois Dubourdeau/Skydive East Tennessee

(a)

Carol Beckwith

(b)

By day's end on December 10, it was not. The American Psychiatric Association made this change because more and more of its members viewed same-sex attraction as a natural biological predisposition and not a psychological problem. Such is the power of shifting societal beliefs. (Despite this cultural progress, American children and adolescents who identify as transgender or gender nonconforming are seven times more likely than their peers to be diagnosed with a psychological disorder [Becerra-Culqui et al., 2018]. This is due largely to the stigma and stress they often experience [Hatzenbuehler et al., 2009; Meyer, 2003]). In the twenty-first century, controversies swirl over other new or altered diagnoses in the most recent edition of the DSM, a common classification tool for describing disorders (Conway et al., 2019; Widiger et al., 2019).

> **psychological disorder** a syndrome marked by a clinically significant disturbance in an individual's cognitions, emotion regulation, or behavior.

RETRIEVAL PRACTICE

RP-1 A lawyer is distressed by feeling the need to wash her hands 100 times a day. She has little time to meet with clients, and her colleagues are wondering about her competence. Her behavior would probably be labeled disordered, because it is _____, that is, it interferes with her day-to-day life.

ANSWERS IN APPENDIX E

Understanding Psychological Disorders

LOQ **47-2** How do the medical model and the biopsychosocial approach influence our understanding of psychological disorders?

The way we view a problem influences how we try to solve it. In earlier times, people often viewed strange behaviors as evidence of strange forces—the movements of the stars, godlike powers, or evil spirits—at work. Had you lived during the Middle Ages, you might have said, "The devil made her do it." Believing that, you might have approved of a harsh cure that would drive out the evil demon. Thus, people considered "mad" were sometimes caged or given "therapies" such as genital mutilation, beatings, removal of teeth or lengths of intestines, or transfusions of animal blood (Farina, 1982).

Reformers, such as Philippe Pinel (1745–1826) in France, opposed such brutal treatments. Madness is not demonic possession, Pinel insisted, but a sickness of the mind caused by severe stress and inhumane conditions. Curing the illness, he said, requires *moral treatment,* including boosting patients' spirits by unchaining them and talking with them. He and others worked to replace brutality with gentleness, isolation with activity, and filth with clean air and sunshine.

In some places, cruel treatments for mental illness—including chaining people to beds or confining them in spaces with wild animals—linger even today. The World Health Organization has launched a reform that aims to transform hospitals worldwide "into patient-friendly and humane places with minimum restraints" (WHO, 2014b).

John W. Verano

Yesterday's "therapy" Through the ages, psychologically disordered people have received brutal treatments, including the trephination evident in this Stone Age patient's skull. Drilling skull holes like these may have been an attempt to release evil spirits and cure those with mental disorders. Did this patient survive the "cure"?

Dance in a Madhouse, 1917 (litho)/Bellows, George Wesley (1882–1925)/SAN DIEGO MUSEUM OF ART/San Diego Museum of Art, USA/Bridgeman Images

Moral treatment Under Philippe Pinel's influence, hospitals sometimes sponsored patient dances, often called "lunatic balls," as depicted in this painting by George Bellows (*Dance in a Madhouse*).

The Medical Model

A medical breakthrough around 1900 prompted further reforms. Researchers discovered that syphilis, a sexually transmitted infection, invades the brain and distorts the mind. This discovery triggered an eager search for physical causes of other mental disorders, and for treatments that would cure them. Hospitals replaced asylums, and the **medical model** of mental disorders was born. Under its influence we still speak of the mental *health* movement. A mental *illness* (also called a psycho*pathology*) needs to be *diagnosed* on the basis of its *symptoms*. It needs to be *treated* through *therapy,* which may include time in a psychiatric *hospital.* The medical perspective has been energized by recent discoveries that many genes together influence the brain and biochemistry abnormalities that contribute to all major disorders (Smoller, 2019). A growing number of clinical psychologists now work in medical hospitals, where they collaborate with physicians to determine how the mind and body operate together.

The Biopsychosocial Approach

To call psychological disorders "sicknesses" tilts research heavily toward the influence of biology. But as in so many other areas, biological, psychological, and social-cultural influences together weave the fabric of our behaviors, thoughts, and feelings. As individuals, we differ in the amount of stress we experience and in the ways we cope with stressors. Cultures also differ in their sources of stress and in their traditional ways of coping. We are physically embodied and socially embedded.

Two disorders—major depressive disorder and schizophrenia—occur worldwide. Other disorders tend to be associated with specific cultures. In Latin America some experience *susto*—severe anxiety or panic in response to an emotional trauma or fear of black magic. In Japanese culture, people may experience *taijin kyofusho*—social anxiety about physical appearance, a readiness to blush, and a fear of eye contact. The eating disorders *anorexia nervosa* and *bulimia nervosa* occur mostly in food-abundant Western cultures. Such disorders may share an underlying dynamic (such as anxiety) while differing in the symptoms (an eating problem or a type of fear) manifested in a particular culture. Even disordered aggression may have varying explanations in different cultures. In Malaysia, *amok* describes a sudden outburst of violent behavior (as in the English phrase "run amok").

The biopsychosocial approach emphasizes that mind and body are inseparable (**FIGURE 47.1**). Negative emotions can trigger physical illness, and physical abnormalities can trigger negative emotions. The biopsychosocial approach gave rise to the *vulnerability-stress model,*[1] which assumes that individual dispositions combine with environmental stressors to influence psychological disorder (Monroe & Simons, 1991; Zuckerman, 1999). Research on **epigenetics** (literally, "in addition to genetics") supports the vulnerability-stress model by showing how our DNA and our environment interact. In one environment, a gene will be *expressed,* but in another, it may lie dormant. For some, that will be the difference between developing a disorder or not developing it.

Biological influences:
- evolution
- individual genes
- brain structure and chemistry

Psychological influences:
- stress
- trauma
- learned helplessness
- mood-related perceptions and memories

Psychological disorder

Social-cultural influences:
- roles
- expectations
- definitions of *normality* and *disorder*

Wavebreakmedia Ltd/
Getty Images

➔ **FIGURE 47.1**

The biopsychosocial approach to psychological disorders Today's psychology studies how biological, psychological, and social-cultural factors interact to produce specific psychological disorders.

---

[1] Also called the *diathesis-stress model*. ("Diathesis"—meaning predisposed vulnerability—derives from a Greek word for predisposition.)

RP-2 Are psychological disorders universal or culture-specific? Explain with examples.

RP-3 What is the biopsychosocial approach, and why is it important in our understanding of psychological disorders?

ANSWERS IN APPENDIX E

Classifying Disorders—and Labeling People

LOQ 47-3 How and why do clinicians classify psychological disorders, and why do some psychologists criticize diagnostic labels?

In biology, classification creates order. To classify an animal as a "mammal" says a great deal—that it is likely warm-blooded, has hair or fur, and produces milk to nourish its young. In psychiatry and psychology, too, classification aims to order and describe symptoms. To classify a person's disorder as "schizophrenia" suggests that the person talks incoherently, has bizarre beliefs, shows either little emotion or inappropriate emotion, or is socially withdrawn. "Schizophrenia" is a quick way to describe a complex disorder.

Moreover, diagnostic classification gives more than a thumbnail sketch of a disorder. In psychiatry and psychology, classification also aims to *predict* a disorder's future course, *suggest* appropriate treatment, and *prompt research* into its causes. To study a disorder, we must first name and describe it.

In many countries, the most common tool for describing disorders is the American Psychiatric Association's *Diagnostic and Statistical Manual of Mental Disorders*, now in its fifth edition (**DSM-5**). Physicians and mental health workers use the detailed DSM-5 to guide diagnoses and treatment. For example, someone who meets all of the criteria in **TABLE 47.1** may be diagnosed with insomnia disorder. The DSM-5 includes diagnostic codes from the World Health Organization's *International Classification of Diseases* (ICD). This also makes it easy to track worldwide trends in psychological disorders.

In real-world tests (*field trials*) assessing the reliability of the DSM-5 categories, some diagnoses fared well and others fared poorly (Freedman et al., 2013). Clinician agreement on adult *posttraumatic stress disorder* and childhood *autism spectrum disorder*, for example, was near 70 percent. (If one psychiatrist or psychologist diagnosed someone with one of these disorders, there was a 70 percent chance that another mental health worker would independently give the same diagnosis.) But for *antisocial personality disorder* and *generalized anxiety disorder*, agreement was closer to 20 percent.

Critics have long faulted the DSM for casting too wide a net and bringing "almost any kind of behavior within the compass of psychiatry" (Eysenck et al., 1983). Some now worry that the DSM-5's even wider net will extend the pathologizing of everyday life. For example, the DSM classifies severe grief following the death of a loved one as a possible *depressive disorder*. Critics suggest that such grief could instead simply be considered a normal reaction to tragic life events.

"I'm always like this, and my family was wondering if you could prescribe a mild depressant."

A book of case illustrations accompanying a previous DSM edition provided several examples for these Psychological Disorders modules.

TABLE 47.1 Insomnia Disorder

* Feeling unsatisfied with amount or quality of sleep (trouble falling asleep, staying asleep, or returning to sleep)

* Sleep disruption causes distress or diminished everyday functioning

* Happens three or more nights each week

* Occurs during at least three consecutive months

* Happens even with sufficient sleep opportunities

* Independent from other sleep disorders (such as narcolepsy)

* Independent from substance use or abuse

* Independent from other mental disorders or medical conditions

Information from: American Psychiatric Association, 2013.

medical model the concept that diseases, in this case psychological disorders, have physical causes that can be *diagnosed, treated,* and, in most cases, *cured,* often through treatment in a *hospital*.

epigenetics "above" or "in addition to" (*epi*) genetics; the study of the molecular mechanisms by which environments can influence genetic expression (without a DNA change).

DSM-5 the American Psychiatric Association's *Diagnostic and Statistical Manual of Mental Disorders,* Fifth Edition; a widely used system for classifying psychological disorders.

A newer classification approach that builds upon the DSM is the U.S. National Institute of Mental Health's Research Domain Criteria (RDoC) project (Insel et al., 2010; NIMH, 2017). The RDoC framework organizes disorders according to behaviors and brain activity, aiming to study them with "the power of modern research approaches in genetics, neuroscience, and behavioral science" (Insel & Lieberman, 2013).

Other critics of classification register a more basic complaint—that diagnostic labels can be subjective, or even value judgments masquerading as science. Once we label a person, we view that person differently (Bathje & Pryor, 2011; Farina, 1982; Sadler et al., 2012b). Labels can change reality by putting us on alert for evidence that confirms our view. If we hear that a new co-worker is mean-spirited, we may treat her suspiciously. She may in turn react to us as a mean-spirited person would. Ditto if we're led to believe that someone is smart. Teachers who were told certain students were "gifted" then acted in ways that elicited the behaviors they expected (Snyder, 1984). Labels can be self-fulfilling, and if negative, they can be stigmatizing.

In one study, people watched recorded interviews. If told the interviewees were job applicants, the viewers perceived them as normal (Langer & Abelson, 1974; Langer & Imber, 1980). Other viewers who were told they were watching cancer or psychiatric patients perceived the same interviewees as "different from most people." Therapists who thought they were watching an interview of a psychiatric patient perceived him as "frightened of his own aggressive impulses," a "passive, dependent type," and so forth. People tend to stigmatize those with psychological disorders (Angermeyer & Dietrich, 2006; Corrigan & Watson, 2002; Pachankis et al., 2018; Weiner et al., 1988). The stigma of mental illness can cause people to hide their symptoms and to avoid seeking treatment (Corrigan, 2004; Nam et al., 2018).

Labels also have power outside the laboratory. Getting a job or finding a place to rent can be a challenge for people recently released from a psychiatric hospital. Label someone as "mentally ill" and people may fear them as potentially violent. That reaction is fading as people come to better understand psychological disorders. Public figures have helped foster this understanding by speaking openly about their own struggles with disorders such as anxiety, depression, and substance abuse—and about how beneficial it was to seek help, receive a diagnosis, and get better through treatment. The more contact we have with people with disorders, the more accepting our attitudes become (Corrigan et al., 2014).

So, labels matter. Yet despite their risks, diagnostic labels have benefits. They help mental health professionals communicate about their cases and study the causes and treatments of disorders. Clients are often relieved to learn that their suffering has a name, and that they are not alone in experiencing their symptoms.

"My sister suffers from a bipolar disorder and my nephew from schizoaffective disorder. There has, in fact, been a lot of depression and alcoholism in my family and, traditionally, no one ever spoke about it. It just wasn't done. The stigma is toxic."
— Actress Glenn Close, "Mental Illness: The Stigma of Silence," 2009

Old stereotypes are slowly being replaced in media portrayals of psychological disorders and disordered behavior. The superhero character of Tony Stark in the *Iron Man* and *Avengers* movies has a backstory of posttraumatic stress disorder. *Black Swan* (2010) dramatized a lead character suffering a delusional disorder. *A Single Man* (2009) depicted depression.

Struggles and recovery During his campaign, Boston Mayor Martin Walsh spoke openly about his past struggles with alcohol. His honesty helped him reduce stigma and win in both 2014 and 2017.

GRETCHEN ERTL/The New York Times/Redux Pictures

To test your ability to form diagnoses, try *Topic Tutorial: PsychSim6, Classifying Disorders.*

ASK YOURSELF

Do you know someone (perhaps even yourself) who has been diagnosed with a psychological disorder? How do you think a diagnostic label has helped or hurt this person?

RETRIEVAL PRACTICE

RP-4 What is the value, and what are the dangers, of labeling individuals with disorders?

ANSWERS IN APPENDIX E

Risk of Harm to Self and Others

People with psychological disorders are more likely to harm themselves. Are they also more likely to harm others?

Understanding Suicide

LOQ **47-4** What factors increase the risk of suicide, and what do we know about nonsuicidal self-injury?

Have you ever, in a moment of despair, considered suicide? If so, you have much company. Among the many who entertain the thought, each year some 800,000 despairing people worldwide will complete the act, electing a permanent solution to what might have been a temporary problem (WHO, 2018e). Someone will likely die by suicide in the 40-odd seconds it takes you to read this paragraph.

For those who have been anxious, the risk of suicide is tripled, and for those who have been depressed, the risk is quintupled (Bostwick & Pankratz, 2000; Kanwar et al., 2013). People seldom elect suicide while in the depths of depression, when energy and initiative are lacking. The risk increases when they begin to rebound and become capable of following through (Chu et al., 2016).

Comparing the suicide rates of different groups, researchers have found

- *national differences:* Russia has double the suicide rate of the United States, which has double that of Spain (WHO, 2018e). Within Europe, Lithuanians have been seven times more likely to die by suicide than Greeks.

- *racial differences:* Within the United States, Whites and Native Americans die by suicide roughly twice as often as Blacks, Hispanics, and Asians (Curtin & Hedegaard, 2019). The rate among Indigenous Canadians is triple that of other Canadians (Kumar & Tjepkema, 2019).

- *gender differences:* Women and girls are much more likely than men to consider or attempt suicide. But worldwide, men are twice as likely to actually die by suicide (ONS, 2019; Ritchie et al., 2019b; WHO, 2018e). The methods men use, such as firing a bullet into the head, are more lethal. In the United States, for example, only 13 percent of all suicide attempts end in death—but for those using firearms, that number mushrooms to 90 percent (Juskalian, 2019).

- *trait differences:* Among Swedes, those with obsessive-compulsive disorder are at higher risk of depression, thereby increasing their risk of suicide (de la Cruz et al., 2017). Suicidal thoughts may also increase when perfectionist people feel driven to reach a goal or standard—to become thin or straight or rich—and find it unattainable (Chatard & Selimbegović, 2011; Smith, M. et al., 2018).

- *age differences:* In late adulthood, rates increase worldwide, with the highest rate among those over 70 (Ritchie et al., 2019a).

- *other group differences:* Suicide rates have been much higher among the rich, the nonreligious, and the unmarried (Norko et al., 2017; Okada & Samreth, 2013; VanderWeele et al., 2016, 2017). Gay, transgender, and gender-nonconforming youth facing an unsupportive environment, including family or peer rejection, are also at increased risk of attempting suicide (Goldfried, 2001; Haas et al., 2011; Hatzenbuehler, 2011; Testa et al., 2017).

- *day-of-the-week and seasonal differences:* Negative emotion tends to go up midweek, which can have tragic consequences (Watson, 2000). A surprising 25 percent of U.S. suicides occur on Wednesdays (Kposowa & D'Auria, 2009). Suicide rates are highest in April and May, and not (as commonly believed) over the winter holidays (Nock, 2016).

- *year-by-year differences:* In most countries, suicides have been increasing (Ritchie et al., 2020). For example, between 1999 and 2017, Americans' suicidal thoughts and suicide rates both increased nearly 40 percent (CDC, 2019e; SAMHSA, 2019).

Social suggestion may trigger suicidal thinking and behavior. One analysis of 17 million Twitter users' data showed that sharing suicidal thoughts had a ripple effect,

> "But life, being weary of these worldly bars, Never lacks power to dismiss itself."
> — William Shakespeare, *Julius Caesar*, 1599

spreading suicidal thinking through one's social network (Cero & Witte, 2019). Following highly publicized suicides and TV programs featuring suicide, rates of suicide sometimes increase (Niederkrotenthaler et al., 2019). So do fatal auto and private airplane "accidents." One six-year study tracked suicide cases among all 1.2 million people who lived in metropolitan Stockholm during the 1990s (Hedström et al., 2008). Men exposed to a co-worker's suicide were 3.5 times more likely to also take their own lives, compared with nonexposed men.

Suicide is usually not an act of hostility or revenge. People—especially older adults—may choose death as an alternative to current or future suffering, a way to switch off unendurable pain and relieve a perceived burden on family members. Suicidal urges typically arise when people feel like they don't belong or are a burden to others, when they feel trapped by a seemingly inescapable situation, or when they feel incapable of experiencing joy (Chu et al., 2018; Ducasse et al., 2018; Taylor et al., 2011). Psychologists worry that suicide rates may increase during the COVID-19 pandemic, which caused widespread unemployment and social isolation (Reger et al., 2020). Compared with cisgender American veterans, transgender veterans, who often feel stigmatized in the military, are also twice as likely to die by suicide (Tucker, 2019).

In hindsight, families and friends may recall signs they believe should have forewarned them—verbal hints, giving possessions away, a sudden mood change, or withdrawal and preoccupation with death (Bagge et al., 2017). To judge from surveys of 84,850 people across 17 nations, about 9 percent of people at some point in their lives have thought seriously of suicide. About 3 in 10 of those who think about it will actually attempt suicide, of whom 3 percent will die (Han et al., 2016; Nock et al., 2008). In one study that followed people for up to 25 years after a first suicide attempt, some 5 percent eventually died by suicide (Bostwick et al., 2016).

As one research team summarized, suicide is hard to predict: "The vast majority of people who possess a specific risk factor [for suicide] will never engage in suicidal behavior" (Franklin et al., 2017, p. 217). But researchers continue to try to solve the suicide puzzle. Using an app that harvests phone data, one investigative team is seeking to predict suicide risk by studying teen volunteers' tone of voice, language, photos, music choice, and sleep disturbances (Servick, 2019). Other research teams are developing suicide-predicting AI (artificial intelligence) algorithms from psychological assessments, health records, or social media posts (Ribeiro et al., 2019; Simon et al., 2018; Walsh et al., 2017).

About 47,000 Americans a year die by suicide, half with guns (CDC, 2019c). (Poison and drug overdoses account for about 80 percent of suicide *attempts,* but only 14 percent of suicide fatalities.) States with high gun ownership, and weaker gun safety laws, are states with high suicide rates, even after controlling for poverty and urbanization (Anestis & Anestis, 2015; Anestis et al., 2015; Miller et al., 2002, 2016; Tavernise, 2013). After Missouri repealed its tough handgun law, its suicide rate went up 15 percent; when Connecticut enacted such a law, its suicide rate dropped 16 percent (Crifasi et al., 2015). Thus, although U.S. gun owners often keep a gun to feel safer, having a gun in the home makes one less safe, because it substantially *increases* the odds of a family member dying by suicide or homicide (Kposowa et al., 2016; VPC, 2015; Vyse, 2016).

How can we be helpful to someone who is talking suicide—who says, for example, "I wish I could just end it all" or "I hate my life; I can't go on"? If people write such things online, you can anonymously contact various social media safety teams (including on Facebook, Twitter, Instagram, YouTube, and Snapchat). If a friend or family member talks suicide, you can

1. *listen* and empathize;

2. *connect* the person with their campus counseling center; with (in the United States) the National Suicide Prevention Lifeline (1-800-273-8255[TALK]) or Crisis Text Line (by texting HOME to 741741), or with their counterparts in other countries (such as CrisisServicesCanada.ca); and

3. *protect* someone who appears at immediate risk by seeking help from a doctor, the nearest hospital emergency room, or 911. Better to share a secret than to attend a funeral.

"People desire death when two fundamental needs are frustrated to the point of extinction: The need to belong with or connect to others, and the need to feel effective with or to influence others." —Thomas Joiner (2006, p. 47)

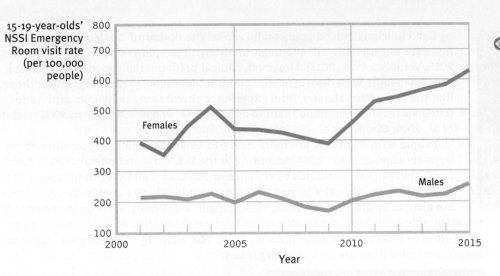

◀ **FIGURE 47.2**
Rates of U.S. nonsuicidal self-injury emergency room visits Self-injury rates peak higher for 15- to 19-year-old females than for same-age males (Mercado et al., 2017). Canada and England have simultaneously experienced the same gender difference and upward trend (CIHI, 2019; McManus et al., 2019).

Nonsuicidal Self-Injury

Self-harm takes many forms. Some people—mostly adolescents and females—may engage in *nonsuicidal self-injury (NSSI)* (Mercado et al., 2017) (**FIGURE 47.2**). They may, for example, cut or burn their skin, hit themselves, or insert objects under their nails or skin.

Those who engage in NSSI often have experienced bullying, harassment, or stress (Miller, A. et al., 2019; van Geel et al., 2015). They are generally less able to tolerate and regulate emotional distress (Hamza et al., 2015). And they are often both self-critical and impulsive (Beauchaine et al., 2019; Cha et al., 2016).

NSSI is often self-reinforcing (Hooley & Franklin, 2018; Selby et al., 2019). People may

- find relief from intense negative thoughts through the distraction of pain.
- attract attention and possibly get help.
- relieve guilt by punishing themselves.
- get others to change their negative behavior (bullying, criticism).
- fit in with a peer group.

Does NSSI lead to suicide? Usually not. Those who engage in NSSI are typically suicide gesturers, not suicide attempters (Evans & Simms, 2019; Nock & Kessler, 2006). Nevertheless, NSSI is a risk factor for suicidal thoughts and future suicide attempts, especially when co-existing with a bipolar disorder (Geulayov et al., 2019). If people do not find help, their nonsuicidal behavior may escalate to suicidal thoughts and, finally, to suicide attempts.

Does Disorder Equal Danger?

LOQ 47-5 Do psychological disorders predict violent behavior?

September 16, 2013, started like any other Monday at the Navy Yard in Washington, DC, with people arriving early to begin work. Then government contractor Aaron Alexis entered the building and began shooting. An hour later, 13 people were dead, including Alexis, who had a history of mental illness and stated that an "ultra low frequency attack is what I've been subject to for the last three months. And to be perfectly honest, that is what has driven me to this." This devastating mass shooting, like many others since, reinforced public perceptions that people with psychological disorders pose a threat (Barry et al., 2013; Jorm et al., 2012). "People with mental illness are getting guns and committing these mass shootings," said U.S. Speaker of the House Paul Ryan (2015). In one survey, 84 percent of Americans agreed that "increased government spending on mental health screening and treatment" would be a "somewhat" or "very" effective "approach to preventing mass shootings at schools" (Newport, 2012). In the aftermath of the 2018 Parkland, Florida, school massacre, U.S. President Donald Trump proposed opening more mental hospitals that could house would-be mass murderers: "When you have some person like this, you can bring them into a mental institution."

Mental health and mass shootings?
Following the 2012 Newtown, Connecticut, slaughter of 20 schoolchildren and 6 adults, and again following the 2018 Parkland, Florida, massacre of 14 youths and 3 adults, people wondered: Could mental health screenings prevent such tragedies? Could the tiny percentage of people with psychological disorders who are violence-prone be identified in advance by mental health workers and prevented from gun ownership? But in 85 percent of U.S. mass killings between 1982 and 2017, the killer had no known prior contact with mental health professionals. Most homicide "is committed by healthy people in the grip of everyday emotions using guns" (Friedman, 2017).

Can clinicians indeed predict who is likely to do harm? *No.* Most violent criminals are not mentally ill, and most mentally ill people are not violent (Leshner, 2019; Verdolini et al., 2018). Moreover, clinical prediction of violence is unreliable. The few people with disorders who commit violent acts tend to be either those, like the Navy Yard shooter, who experience threatening delusions and hallucinated voices that command them to act, or those who abuse substances (Douglas et al., 2009; Elbogen et al., 2016; Fazel et al., 2009, 2010).

People with disorders are more likely to be *victims* than perpetrators of violence (Buchanan et al., 2019). According to the U.S. Surgeon General's Office (1999, p. 7), "there is very little risk of violence or harm to a stranger from casual contact with an individual who has a mental disorder." Better predictors of violence are alcohol or drug use, previous violence, gun availability, and—as in the case of the repeatedly head-injured and ultimately homicidal National Football League player Aaron Hernandez—brain damage (Belson, 2017). Mass-killing shooters have one more thing in common: They are mostly young males.

ASK YOURSELF

Why do you think people often believe those with psychological disorders are dangerous?

Rates of Psychological Disorders

LOQ **47-6** How many people have, or have had, a psychological disorder? What are some of the risk factors?

Who is most vulnerable to psychological disorders? At what times of life? To answer such questions, many countries have conducted lengthy structured interviews of their citizens. After asking hundreds of questions that probed for symptoms—"Has there ever been a period of two weeks or more when you felt like you wanted to die?"—researchers have estimated the current, prior-year, and lifetime prevalence of various disorders.

How many people have a psychological disorder? "Mental and addictive disorders affected more than 1 billion people globally in 2016," reported a major worldwide study (Rehm & Shield, 2019). In the United States, 47 million adults—19 percent—experienced a mental illness within the last year (SAMHSA, 2018) (**TABLE 47.2**).

Do rates of psychological disorder vary by place? A World Health Organization study—based on 90-minute interviews with thousands of people who were representative of their country's population—estimated the number of prior-year mental disorders in 28 countries (Kessler et al., 2009). Cultures vary, and as **FIGURE 47.3** illustrates, the lowest rate of reported mental disorders was in Nigeria, and the highest rate was in the United States. Moreover, immigrants to the United States from Mexico, Africa, and Asia averaged better mental health than their U.S.-born counterparts with the same ethnic heritage (Breslau et al., 2007; Maldonado-Molina et al., 2011). For example, compared with Mexican Americans born in the United States, Mexican Americans who have recently immigrated are less at risk for mental disorders—a phenomenon known as the *immigrant paradox* (Salas-Wright et al., 2018).

TABLE 47.2 Percentage of Americans Reporting Selected Psychological Disorders "in the Past Year"

Psychological Disorder	Percentage
Depressive disorders or bipolar disorders	9.3
Phobia of specific object or situation	8.7
Social anxiety disorder	6.8
Attention-deficit/hyperactivity disorder (ADHD)	4.1
Posttraumatic stress disorder (PTSD)	3.5
Generalized anxiety disorder	3.1
Schizophrenia	1.1
Obsessive-compulsive disorder	1.0

Data from: National Institute of Mental Health, 2015.

What increases vulnerability to mental disorders? As **TABLE 47.3** indicates, there are various risk and protective factors for mental disorders. One predictor—poverty—crosses ethnic and gender lines. The incidence of serious psychological disorders is 2.5 times higher among those below the poverty line (CDC, 2014a). This poverty-disorder correlation raises further questions: Does poverty cause disorders? Or do disorders cause poverty? The answer varies with the disorder. Schizophrenia understandably leads to poverty. Yet the stresses and demoralization of poverty can also precipitate disorders, especially depression in women and substance abuse in men (Dohrenwend et al., 1992). In one natural experiment investigating the poverty-pathology link, researchers tracked rates of behavior problems in North Carolina Native American children as economic development enabled a dramatic reduction in their community's poverty rate. When the study began, children of poverty exhibited more deviant and aggressive behaviors. After four years, children whose families had moved above the poverty line exhibited a 40 percent decrease in behavior problems. Those who maintained their previous positions below or above the poverty line exhibited no change (Costello et al., 2003).

At what times of life do disorders strike? About half of people with a disorder experience their first symptoms by the mid-teens, and three-quarters do so by the mid-twenties (Kessler et al., 2007; Robins & Regier, 1991). Among the earliest to appear are the symptoms of antisocial personality disorder (median age 8) and of phobias (median age 10). Alcohol use disorder, obsessive-compulsive disorder, bipolar disorders, and schizophrenia symptoms appear at a median age near 20. Major depressive disorder often hits somewhat later, at a median age of 25.

RETRIEVAL PRACTICE

RP-5 What is the relationship between poverty and psychological disorders?

ANSWERS IN APPENDIX E

> See the *Video: Correlational Studies* for a helpful tutorial about this research design. For a summary of disorder rates, engage online with *Concept Practice: Risks and Rates of Disorders.*

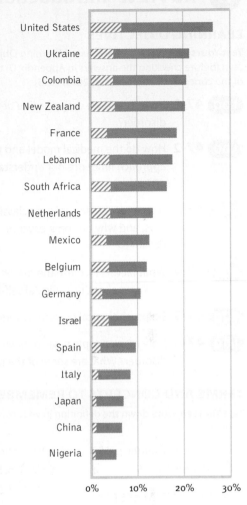

FIGURE 47.3
Prior-year prevalence of disorders in selected areas From interviews in 28 countries. (Data from Kessler et al., 2009.)

TABLE 47.3 Risk and Protective Factors for Mental Disorders

Risk Factors	Protective Factors
Academic failure	Aerobic exercise
Birth complications	Community offering empowerment, opportunity, and security
Caring for those who are chronically ill or who have a neurocognitive disorder	Economic independence
Child abuse and neglect	Effective parenting
Chronic insomnia	Feelings of mastery and control
Chronic pain	Feelings of security
Family disorganization or conflict	High self-esteem
Low birth weight	Literacy
Low socioeconomic status	Positive attachment and early bonding
Medical illness	Positive parent-child relationships
Neurochemical imbalance	Problem-solving skills
Parental mental illness	Resilient coping with stress and adversity
Parental substance abuse	Social and work skills
Personal loss and bereavement	Social support from family and friends
Poor work skills and habits	
Reading disabilities	
Sensory disabilities	
Social incompetence	
Stressful life events	
Substance abuse	
Trauma experiences	

Research from: World Health Organization (WHO, 2004a,b).

LEARNING OBJECTIVES

Test Yourself Answer these repeated Learning Objective Questions on your own (before checking the answers in Appendix D) to improve your retention of the concepts (McDaniel et al., 2009, 2015).

LOQ **47-1** How should we draw the line between normality and disorder?

LOQ **47-2** How do the medical model and the biopsychosocial approach influence our understanding of psychological disorders?

LOQ **47-3** How and why do clinicians classify psychological disorders, and why do some psychologists criticize diagnostic labels?

LOQ **47-4** What factors increase the risk of suicide, and what do we know about nonsuicidal self-injury?

LOQ **47-5** Do psychological disorders predict violent behavior?

LOQ **47-6** How many people have, or have had, a psychological disorder? What are some of the risk factors?

TERMS AND CONCEPTS TO REMEMBER

Test Yourself Write down the definition in your own words, then check your answer.

psychological disorder, p. 553   epigenetics, p. 555
medical model, p. 555   DSM-5, p. 555

MASTER THE MATERIAL

Test Yourself Answer the following questions on your own first, then check your answers in Appendix E.

1. Two major disorders that are found worldwide are schizophrenia and _____ _____ _____.

2. Anna is embarrassed that it takes her several minutes to parallel park her car. She usually gets out of the car once or twice to inspect her distance, both from the curb and from the nearby cars. Should she worry about having a psychological disorder?

3. A therapist says that psychological disorders are sicknesses, and people with these disorders should be treated as patients in a hospital. This therapist's belief reflects the _____ model.

4. What is an example of a culturally-related psychological disorder?

5. Many psychologists reject the disorder-as-illness view and instead contend that other factors may also be involved—for example, the person's level of stress and ways of coping with it. This view represents the _____ approach.
   a. medical
   b. epigenetics
   c. biopsychosocial
   d. diagnostic

6. Why is the DSM, and the DSM-5 in particular, considered controversial?

7. _____ (Women/men) are more likely than _____ (women/men) to die by suicide.

8. One predictor of psychiatric disorders that crosses ethnic and gender lines is _____.

9. The symptoms of _____ appear around age 10; _____ tend[s] to appear later, around age 25.
   a. schizophrenia; bipolar disorders
   b. bipolar disorders; schizophrenia
   c. major depressive disorder; phobias
   d. phobias; major depressive disorder

Continue testing yourself with 📘 **LearningCurve** or 📗 **Achieve Read & Practice** to learn and remember most effectively.

48 Anxiety-Related Disorders

Anxiety is part of life. Speaking in front of a class, peering down from a ladder, or waiting to learn the results of a final exam, any one of us might feel anxious. Anxiety may even cause us to avoid talking or making eye contact—"shyness," we call it. Fortunately for most of us, our uneasiness is not intense and persistent. Some, however, are more prone to fear the unknown and to notice and remember perceived threats—as if living while horror movie background music plays (Gorka et al., 2017; Mitte, 2008). When the brain's danger-detection system becomes hyperactive, we are at greater risk for an *anxiety disorder*, and for three other disorders that involve anxiety: *obsessive-compulsive disorder (OCD)*, *posttraumatic stress disorder (PTSD)*, and the *somatic symptom disorders*.[2]

---

[2]OCD and PTSD were formerly classified as anxiety disorders, but the DSM-5 now classifies them separately.

Anxiety Disorders

LOQ **48-1** How do generalized anxiety disorder, panic disorder, and specific phobias differ?

The **anxiety disorders** are marked by distressing, persistent anxiety or by dysfunctional anxiety-reducing behaviors. For example, people with *social anxiety disorder* become extremely anxious in social settings where others might judge them, such as parties, class presentations, or even eating in public. One university student experienced palpitations, tremors, blushing, and sweating when giving a presentation, taking an exam, or meeting an authority figure, fearing he would embarrass himself. By staying home he avoided the anxious feelings, but it was maladaptive: Avoiding others prevented him from learning to cope and left him feeling lonely (Leichsenring & Leweke, 2017).

Let's take a closer look at three other anxiety disorders:

- *generalized anxiety disorder,* in which a person is, for no obvious reason, continually tense and uneasy;

- *panic disorder,* in which a person experiences *panic attacks*—sudden episodes of intense dread—and fears the next attack; and

- *specific phobias,* in which a person is intensely and irrationally afraid of something.

Generalized Anxiety Disorder

For two years, Tom, a 27-year-old electrician, was bothered by dizziness, sweating palms, and heart palpitations. He felt on edge and sometimes found himself shaking. Tom mostly hid his symptoms from his family and co-workers. But he allowed himself few other social contacts, and occasionally he had to leave work. Neither his family doctor nor a neurologist could find any physical problem.

Tom's unfocused, out-of-control, agitated feelings suggest **generalized anxiety disorder,** which is marked by excessive and uncontrollable worry that persists for six months or more. People with this condition (two-thirds are women) worry continually, and they are often jittery, agitated, and sleep-deprived (McLean & Anderson, 2009). Concentration suffers, as everyday worries demand continual attention. Their *autonomic nervous system* arousal may leak out through furrowed brows, twitching eyelids, trembling, perspiration, or fidgeting.

Those affected usually cannot identify, relieve, or avoid their anxiety. To use Sigmund Freud's term, the anxiety is *free-floating* (not linked to a specific stressor or threat). Generalized anxiety disorder is often accompanied by depressed mood. But even without depression it tends to be disabling. Moreover, it may lead to physical problems, such as high blood pressure. As time passes, however, emotions tend to mellow, and by age 50, generalized anxiety disorder becomes fairly rare (Rubio & López-Ibor, 2007).

Panic Disorder

Some people experience intense anxiety that escalates into a terrifying panic attack—a minutes-long episode of intense fear that something horrible is about to happen. Irregular heartbeat, chest pains, shortness of breath, choking, trembling, or dizziness may accompany the panic. One woman recalled suddenly feeling

> hot and as though I couldn't breathe. My heart was racing and I started to sweat and tremble and I was sure I was going to faint. Then my fingers started to feel numb and tingly and things seemed unreal. It was so bad I wondered if I was dying and asked my husband to take me to the emergency room. By the time we got there (about 10 minutes) the worst of the attack was over and I just felt washed out (Greist et al., 1986).

For the 3 percent of people with **panic disorder,** panic attacks are recurrent. These anxiety tornados strike suddenly, wreak havoc, and disappear, but are not forgotten. Ironically, worries about anxiety—perhaps fearing another panic attack, or fearing anxiety-related symptoms in public—can amplify anxiety symptoms (Olatunji & Wolitzky-Taylor, 2009). After several panic attacks, people may avoid situations where panic might strike. If their fear is intense enough, they may also develop

anxiety disorders psychological disorders characterized by distressing, persistent anxiety or maladaptive behaviors that reduce anxiety.

generalized anxiety disorder an anxiety disorder in which a person is continually tense, apprehensive, and in a state of autonomic nervous system arousal.

panic disorder an anxiety disorder marked by unpredictable, minutes-long episodes of intense dread in which a person may experience terror and accompanying chest pain, choking, or other frightening sensations; often followed by worry over a possible next attack.

Dia Dipasupil/Getty Images

Panic on the prowl As a youthful star in the *Twilight* movies, Kristen Stewart experienced frequent anxiety. "I would have panic attacks," she said. "I literally always had a stomach ache" (Lapidos, 2016). Being open and honest about her anxiety helped. "It opened my life up, and I'm so much happier."

agoraphobia—fear or avoidance of public situations from which escape might be difficult. People with agoraphobia may avoid being outside the home, in a crowd, or in an elevator. Smokers have at least a doubled risk of panic disorder and greater symptoms when they do have an attack (Knuts et al., 2010; Zvolensky & Bernstein, 2005). Because nicotine is a stimulant, lighting up doesn't lighten us up.

Charles Darwin began suffering from panic disorder at age 28, after spending five years sailing the world. He moved to the country, avoided social gatherings, and traveled only in his wife's company. But the relative seclusion did free him to elaborate his evolutionary theory. "Even ill health," he reflected, "has saved me from the distraction of society and its amusements" (quoted in Ma, 1997).

Specific Phobias

We all live with some fears. But people with **specific phobias** are consumed by a persistent, irrational fear and avoidance of some object, activity, or situation—for example, animals, insects, heights, blood, or enclosed spaces (**FIGURE 48.1**). Many people avoid the triggers (such as high places) that arouse their fear, and they manage to live with their phobia. Others are incapacitated. Marilyn, an otherwise healthy and happy 28-year-old, so feared thunderstorms that she felt anxious as soon as a weather forecaster mentioned possible storms later in the week. If her husband was away when a storm was forecast, she often stayed with a close relative. During a storm, she hid from windows and buried her head to avoid seeing the lightning.

Martin Harvey/Getty Images

⊘ **FIGURE 48.1**
Some common specific fears
Researchers surveyed Dutch people to identify the most common events or objects they feared. A strong fear becomes a specific phobia if it provokes a compelling but irrational desire to avoid the dreaded object or situation. (Data from Depla et al., 2008.)

Percentage of people surveyed

	Being alone	Flying	Storms	Water	Blood	Enclosed spaces	Animals	Heights
■ Fear ■ Phobia								

25% / 20 / 15 / 10 / 5 / 0

RETRIEVAL PRACTICE

RP-1 Unfocused tension, apprehension, and arousal are symptoms of _____ _____ disorder.

RP-2 Those who experience unpredictable periods of terror and intense dread, accompanied by frightening physical sensations, may be diagnosed with _____ disorder.

RP-3 If a person is focusing anxiety on specific feared objects, activities, or situations, that person may have a _____ _____.

ANSWERS IN APPENDIX E

Obsessive-Compulsive and Related Disorders

LOQ 48-2   What is *OCD*?

As with the anxiety disorders, we can see aspects of **obsessive-compulsive disorder (OCD)** in our everyday behavior. *Obsessive thoughts* are unwanted and seemingly unending. *Compulsive behaviors* are responses to those thoughts.

We are all at times obsessed with thoughts and we may behave compulsively. Have you ever felt a bit anxious about how your living space will appear to others and found yourself checking and cleaning one last time before your guests arrived? Or, perhaps worried about an upcoming exam, you caught yourself lining up your study materials "just so" before studying? Our everyday lives are full of little rehearsals and fussy

TABLE 48.1 Common Obsessions and Compulsions Among Children and Adolescents With Obsessive-Compulsive Disorder	
Thought or Behavior	**Percentage Reporting Symptom**
Obsessions (repetitive *thoughts*)	
Concern with dirt, germs, or toxins	40
Something terrible happening (fire, death, illness)	24
Symmetry, order, or exactness	17
Compulsions (repetitive *behaviors*)	
Excessive hand washing, bathing, toothbrushing, or grooming	85
Repeating rituals (in/out of a door, up/down from a chair)	51
Checking doors, locks, appliances, car brakes, homework	46

Data from: Rapoport, 1989.

Thriving with OCD Music star Justin Timberlake says support from his family and a sense of humor have helped him cope with the challenges of obsessive-compulsive disorder.

behaviors. They cross the fine line between normality and disorder only when they *persistently interfere* with everyday living and cause distress. Checking that you locked the door is normal; checking 10 times is not. (**TABLE 48.1** offers more examples.) At some time during their lives, often during their late teens or early adulthood, about 2 percent of people cross that line from normal preoccupations and fussiness to debilitating disorder (Kessler et al., 2012). Although people know their anxiety-fueled obsessive thoughts are irrational, the thoughts can become so haunting, and the compulsive rituals so intensely time-consuming, that effective functioning—including school success—becomes near-impossible (Pérez-Vigil et al., 2018).

OCD is more common among teens and young adults than among older people (Samuels & Nestadt, 1997). A 40-year follow-up study of 144 Swedes diagnosed with the disorder found that, for most, the obsessions and compulsions had gradually lessened, though only 1 in 5 had completely recovered (Skoog & Skoog, 1999).

Some people experience other OCD-related disorders, such as *hoarding disorder* (cluttering one's space with acquired possessions one can't part with), *body dysmorphic disorder* (preoccupation with perceived body defects), *trichotillomania* (hair-pulling disorder), or *excoriation* (skin-picking) *disorder*.

> For an eye-opening, 7-minute snapshot of one woman's challenges with compulsive rituals, see the *Video: Obsessive-Compulsive Disorder—A Young Mother's Struggle.*

"Wait—did you wash your hands?"

Posttraumatic Stress Disorder

LOQ 48-3 What is *PTSD*?

While serving overseas, one soldier, Jesse, saw the killing "of children and women. It was just horrible for anyone to experience." Back home, he suffered "real bad flashbacks" (Welch, 2005).

Jesse is not alone. In one study of 104,000 veterans returning from Iraq and Afghanistan, 25 percent were diagnosed with a psychological disorder (Seal et al., 2007). The most frequent was **posttraumatic stress disorder (PTSD).** Survivors of terror, torture, rape, earthquakes, and refugee displacement have also exhibited PTSD (Charlson et al., 2016; Westermeyer, 2018). The hallmark symptom is recurring, vivid, distressing memories and nightmares. PTSD also often entails laser-focused attention on possible threats, social withdrawal, jumpy anxiety, and trouble sleeping (Fried et al., 2018; Lazarov et al., 2019; Malaktaris & Lynn, 2019).

Many of us will experience a traumatic event. And many people will display *survivor resiliency*—by recovering after severe stress (Galatzer-Levy et al., 2018). Although Friedrich Nietzsche's (1889/1990) idea that "what does not kill me makes me stronger" is not true for all, about half of trauma victims report *posttraumatic growth* (Wu, X. et al., 2019). Sometimes, tears become triumphs.

specific phobia an anxiety disorder marked by a persistent, irrational fear and avoidance of a specific object, activity, or situation.

obsessive-compulsive disorder (OCD) a disorder characterized by unwanted repetitive thoughts (obsessions), actions (compulsions), or both.

posttraumatic stress disorder (PTSD) a disorder characterized by haunting memories, nightmares, hypervigilance, avoidance of trauma-related stimuli, social withdrawal, jumpy anxiety, numbness of feeling, and/or insomnia that lingers for four weeks or more after a traumatic experience.

PTSD from Parkland In the 2018 Parkland, Florida, school shooting, Samantha Fuentes (at right) witnessed friends dying, and shrapnel struck her face and legs. She later reported PTSD symptoms, including a fear of returning to the school and jumping at the sound of a slammed door. Two other student survivors died by apparent suicide in 2019, including one who had been diagnosed with PTSD (Mazzei, 2019).

Why do some 5 to 10 percent of people develop PTSD after a traumatic event while others do not (Bonanno et al., 2011)? One factor is the amount of emotional distress: The higher the distress (such as the level of physical torture suffered by prisoners of war), the greater the risk for post-traumatic symptoms (King et al., 2015; Ozer et al., 2003). Among American soldiers in Iraq and Afghanistan, those experiencing both high combat intensity and self-blaming catastrophic thinking were especially vulnerable to PTSD (Seligman et al., 2019). Among survivors of the 9/11 terrorist attack on New York's World Trade Center, the rates of subsequent PTSD diagnoses for those who had been inside were double the rates of those who had been outside (Bonanno et al., 2006).

What else influences PTSD development? Some people may have a more sensitive emotion-processing limbic system that floods their bodies with stress hormones (Duncan et al., 2017; Kosslyn, 2005). Genes and gender also matter. Twins, compared with nontwin siblings, more commonly share PTSD risk factors (Gilbertson et al., 2006). And after a traumatic event, women experience PTSD more often than do men (Olff et al., 2007; Ozer & Weiss, 2004).

Some psychologists believe that PTSD has been overdiagnosed (Dobbs, 2009; McNally, 2003). Too often, say critics, PTSD gets stretched to include normal stress-related bad memories and dreams. And some well-intentioned procedures—such as "debriefing" people by asking them to revisit the experience and vent their emotions—may worsen stress reactions (Bonanno et al., 2010; Wakefield & Spitzer, 2002).

RETRIEVAL PRACTICE

RP-4 Those who express anxiety through unwanted repetitive thoughts or actions may have a(n) _____-_____ disorder.

RP-5 Those with symptoms of recurring memories and nightmares, social withdrawal, jumpy anxiety, numbness of feeling, and/or insomnia for weeks after a traumatic event may be diagnosed with _____ _____disorder.

ANSWERS IN APPENDIX E

Somatic Symptom and Related Disorders

LOQ 48-4 What are *somatic symptom and related disorders*?

Among the common problems bringing people into doctors' offices are "medically unexplained illnesses" (Johnson, 2008). Ellen becomes dizzy and nauseated shortly before she expects her husband home. Neither her primary care physician nor a neurologist can identify a physical cause. They suspect her symptoms have an unconscious psychological origin, possibly triggered by mixed feelings about her husband. Ellen has a **somatic symptom disorder** (formerly known as *somatoform disorder*), in which distressing symptoms take a somatic (bodily) form without apparent physical causes.

We have all experienced inexplicable physical symptoms under stress. Being told the problem is "all in your head" gives no comfort. Although the symptoms may be psychological in origin, they are genuinely felt. One person may have a variety of complaints—vomiting, dizziness, blurred vision, difficulty swallowing. Another may experience severe and prolonged pain. Such symptoms become a disorder when they are associated with significant distress and impaired functioning.

Cultural context has a big effect on people's physical complaints and how they explain them (Kirmayer & Sartorius, 2007). In China, anxiety disorders are the most common psychological disorder (Huang et al., 2019). Yet psychological explanations of anxiety and depression are socially less acceptable there than in many Western countries, so people less often express the emotional aspects of distress. The Chinese appear more sensitive to—and more willing to report—the physical symptoms of their distress (Ryder et al., 2008).

Somatic symptom and related disorders send people not to a psychologist or psychiatrist but to a physician. This is especially true of those who experience **illness anxiety disorder** (previously called *hypochondriasis*). People with this relatively common disorder

somatic symptom disorder a psychological disorder in which the symptoms take a somatic (bodily) form without apparent physical cause.

illness anxiety disorder a disorder in which a person interprets normal physical sensations as symptoms of a disease. (Formerly called *hypochondriasis*.)

interpret normal sensations (a stomach cramp today, a headache tomorrow) as symptoms of a dreaded disease. No amount of reassurance by any physician convinces the patient that the trivial symptoms do not reflect a serious illness. So, the patient moves on to another physician—seeking and receiving more medical attention, but failing to confront the disorder's psychological roots. Sympathy, and temporary relief from everyday demands may reinforce their behaviors.

ASK YOURSELF

Can you recall (as most people can) times when you have fretted needlessly over a normal bodily sensation?

RETRIEVAL PRACTICE

RP-6 What does *somatic* mean, and how does it apply to *somatic symptom disorders?*

ANSWERS IN APPENDIX E

Understanding Anxiety-Related Disorders

LOQ **48-5** How do conditioning, cognition, and biology contribute to the feelings and thoughts that mark anxiety-related disorders?

Anxiety is a feeling. It is also a cognition—a doubt-laden self-appraisal. How do these anxious feelings and cognitions arise? Few psychologists now interpret anxiety the way Sigmund Freud did. His psychoanalytic theory proposed that, beginning in childhood, people *repress* intolerable impulses, ideas, and feelings. Freud believed that this submerged mental energy sometimes leaks out in odd symptoms, such as anxious hand washing. Most psychologists today instead embrace three modern perspectives—conditioning, cognition, and biology.

Conditioning

Through *classical conditioning,* our fear responses can become linked with formerly neutral objects and events. To understand the link between learning and anxiety, researchers have given lab rats unpredictable electric shocks (Schwartz, 1984). The rats, like assault victims who report feeling anxious when returning to the scene of the crime, then become uneasy in their lab environment.

Likewise, anxious or traumatized people learn to associate their anxiety with certain cues (Bar-Haim et al., 2007; Duits et al., 2015). In one survey, 58 percent of those with social anxiety disorder experienced their disorder after a traumatic event (Öst & Hugdahl, 1981). Anxiety or an anxiety-related disorder is more likely to develop when bad events happen unpredictably and uncontrollably (Field, 2006; Mineka & Oehlberg, 2008). Even a single painful and frightening event may trigger a full-blown phobia, thanks to classical conditioning's *stimulus generalization* and operant conditioning's *reinforcement.*

Stimulus generalization occurs when a person experiences a fear-provoking event and later develops a fear of similar events. My [DM's] car was once struck by a driver who missed a stop sign. For months afterward, I felt a twinge of unease when any car approached from a side street. Marilyn's thunderstorm phobia may have similarly generalized after a terrifying or painful experience during a thunderstorm.

Reinforcement helps maintain learned fears and anxieties. Anything that enables us to avoid or escape a feared situation can reinforce maladaptive behaviors. Fearing a panic attack, we may decide not to leave the house. Reinforced by feeling calmer, we are likely to repeat that behavior (Antony et al., 1992). So, too, with compulsive behaviors. If washing our hands relieves our feelings of anxiety, we may wash our hands again when those feelings return.

Cognition

Conditioning influences our feelings of anxiety, but so do our thoughts, memories, interpretations, and expectations. By observing others, we can learn to fear what they fear. Nearly all monkeys raised in the wild fear snakes, yet lab-raised monkeys do not. Surely, most wild

Hemera Technologies/PhotoObjects.net/360/Getty Images

monkeys do not actually suffer snake bites. Do they learn their fear through observation? To find out, Susan Mineka (1985, 2002) experimented with six monkeys raised in the wild (all strongly fearful of snakes) and their lab-raised offspring (virtually none of which feared snakes). After repeatedly observing their parents or peers refusing to reach for food in the presence of a snake, the young monkeys developed a similar strong fear of snakes that persisted when retested three months later. We humans similarly learn fears by observing others (Helsen et al., 2011; Olsson et al., 2007).

Although it pays to be alert to dangers, anxiety is often just a response to self-produced fake news. One study that followed people with anxiety disorder found that more than 9 in 10 worries proved groundless (LaFreniere & Newman, 2019). Such people tend to be *hypervigilant*. They more often *interpret* stimuli as threatening (Everaert et al., 2018). A pounding heart signals a heart attack; a lone spider indicates an infestation; an everyday disagreement with a friend or boss spells doom. And they more often *remember* threatening events (Van Bockstaele et al., 2014). Anxiety is especially common when people cannot switch off such intrusive thoughts and feel helpless (Franklin & Foa, 2011).

> **ASK YOURSELF**
>
> What is a fear that you have learned? How were conditioning or cognition involved?

Biology

Conditioning and cognition can't explain all aspects of anxiety disorders, OCD, and PTSD. Our biology also plays a role.

GENES Among monkeys, fearfulness runs in families. A monkey reacts more strongly to stress if its close biological relatives are anxiously reactive (Suomi, 1986). So, too, with people. Although twins in general are not at higher risk for disorders, if one identical twin has an anxiety disorder, the other is also at risk (Polderman et al., 2015). Even when raised separately, identical twins may develop similar specific phobias (Carey, 1990; Eckert et al., 1981). One pair of separated identical twins independently became so afraid of water that each would wade in the ocean backward and only up to her knees. Another pair of twins with OCD took hours-long showers, used five bottles of disinfecting rubbing alcohol daily, rarely left their house, and, tragically, died together in an apparent suicide pact (Schmidt, 2018).

Given the genetic contribution to anxiety disorders, researchers are sleuthing the culprit genes. One research team identified 17 gene variations associated with typical anxiety disorder symptoms (Hovatta et al., 2005). Other teams have found genes associated specifically with OCD (Mattheisen et al., 2015; Taylor, 2013).

Some genes influence disorders by regulating brain levels of neurotransmitters. These include *serotonin,* which influences sleep, mood, and attending to threats (Canli, 2008; Pergamin-Hight et al., 2012), and *glutamate,* which heightens activity in the brain's alarm centers (Lafleur et al., 2006; Welch et al., 2007).

So genes matter. Some of us have genes that make us like orchids—fragile, yet capable of beauty under favorable circumstances. Others of us are like dandelions—hardy, and able to thrive in varied circumstances (Ellis & Boyce, 2008; Pluess & Belsky, 2013).

But experience affects gene expression. A history of wartime trauma or child abuse can leave long-term *epigenetic marks*. These molecular tags attach to our chromosomes and turn certain genes on or off. Thus, experiences such as abuse can increase the likelihood that a genetic vulnerability to a disorder such as PTSD will be expressed (Mehta et al., 2013; Zannas et al., 2015).

THE BRAIN Our experiences change our brain, paving new pathways. Traumatic fear-learning experiences can leave tracks in the brain, creating fear circuits within the amygdala (Etkin & Wager, 2007; Herringa et al., 2013; Kolassa & Elbert, 2007). These fear pathways create easy inroads for more fear experiences (Armony et al., 1998).

Generalized anxiety disorder, panic attacks, specific phobias, OCD, and PTSD express themselves biologically as overarousal of brain areas involved in impulse control and habitual behaviors. These disorders reflect the brain's danger-detection system gone hyperactive—producing anxiety when little danger exists. In OCD, for example, when the brain detects that something is amiss, it seems to generate a mental hiccup of repeating thoughts (obsessions) or actions (compulsions) (Gehring et al., 2000). Brain scans of people with OCD reveal elevated activity in specific brain areas during behaviors such as compulsive hand washing, checking, organizing, or hoarding (Insel, 2010; Mataix-Cols et al., 2004, 2005). The *anterior cingulate cortex*, a brain region that monitors our actions and checks for errors, is often especially hyperactive (Maltby et al., 2005) **(FIGURE 48.2)**. Scientists are even identifying specific brain cells that contribute to anxiety, with the goal of helping people to control it (Jimenez et al., 2018).

Some antidepressant drugs dampen this fear circuit activity and its associated obsessive-compulsive behavior. Fears can also be blunted by giving people drugs as they recall and then rerecord ("reconsolidate") a traumatic experience (Kindt et al., 2009; Norberg et al., 2008). Although they don't forget the experience, the associated emotion is largely erased.

NATURAL SELECTION We seem biologically prepared to fear threats faced by our ancestors. Our specific phobias focus on specific fears such as spiders, snakes, and other animals; enclosed spaces and heights; storms and darkness. Those fearless about these occasional threats were less likely to survive and leave descendants. Nine-month-old infants attend more to sounds signaling ancient threats (hisses, thunder) than they do to sounds representing modern threats (a bomb exploding, breaking glass) (Erlich et al., 2013). It is easy to condition and hard to extinguish fears of such "evolutionarily relevant" stimuli (Coelho & Purkis, 2009; Davey, 1995; Öhman, 2009). Some of our modern fears (such as of flying) can also have an evolutionary explanation (a biological predisposition to fear confinement and heights).

Just as our specific phobias focus on dangers faced by our ancestors, our compulsive acts typically exaggerate behaviors that contributed to our species' survival. Grooming had survival value. Gone wild, it becomes compulsive hair pulling. Washing up becomes ritual hand washing. And checking territorial boundaries becomes checking and rechecking already locked doors (Rapoport, 1989).

**FIGURE 48.2
An obsessive-compulsive brain** When people engaged in a challenging cognitive task, those with OCD showed the most activity in the anterior cingulate cortex in the brain's frontal area (Maltby et al., 2005).

Anterior cingulate cortex

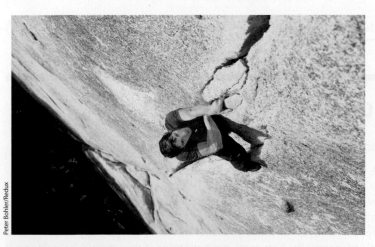

Peter Bohler/Redux

Fearless The biological perspective helps us understand why most people fear heights more than does Alex Honnold, shown here in 2017 becoming the first person to free solo climb (no safety ropes) Yosemite National Park's massive El Capitan granite wall. (*Free Solo*, a documentary about this feat, won a 2019 Oscar.)

RETRIEVAL PRACTICE

RP-7 Researchers believe that conditioning and cognitive processes are aspects of learning that contribute to anxiety-related disorders. What *biological* factors also contribute to these disorders?

ANSWERS IN APPENDIX E

MODULE

48 **REVIEW** Anxiety-Related Disorders

LEARNING OBJECTIVES

Test Yourself Answer these repeated Learning Objective Questions on your own (before checking the answers in Appendix D) to improve your retention of the concepts (McDaniel et al., 2009, 2015).

LOQ 48-1 How do generalized anxiety disorder, panic disorder, and specific phobias differ?

LOQ 48-2 What is *OCD*?

LOQ 48-3 What is *PTSD*?

LOQ 48-4 What are *somatic symptom and related disorders*?

LOQ 48-5 How do conditioning, cognition, and biology contribute to the feelings and thoughts that mark anxiety-related disorders?

TERMS AND CONCEPTS TO REMEMBER

Test Yourself Write down the definition in your own words, then check your answer.

anxiety disorders, p. 563

generalized anxiety disorder, p. 563

panic disorder, p. 563

specific phobia, p. 565

obsessive-compulsive disorder (OCD), p. 565

posttraumatic stress disorder (PTSD), p. 565

somatic symptom disorder, p. 566

illness anxiety disorder, p. 566

MASTER THE MATERIAL

Test Yourself Answer the following questions on your own first, then check your answers in Appendix E.

1. An episode of intense dread that can be accompanied by chest pains, choking, or other frightening sensations is called
   a. an obsession.
   b. a compulsion.
   c. a panic attack.
   d. a specific phobia.

2. Anxiety that takes the form of an irrational and maladaptive fear of a specific object, activity, or situation is called a _____ _____.

3. Marina became consumed with the need to clean the entire house and refused to participate in any other activities. Her family consulted a therapist, who diagnosed her as having _____-_____ disorder.

4. When a person with an anxiety disorder eases anxiety by avoiding or escaping a situation that inspires fear, this is called
   a. free-floating anxiety.
   b. reinforcement.
   c. an epigenetic mark.
   d. hypervigilance.

5. The learning perspective proposes that specific phobias are
   a. the result of individual genetic makeup.
   b. a way of repressing unacceptable impulses.
   c. conditioned fears.
   d. a symptom of having been abused as a child.

Continue testing yourself with **LearningCurve** or **Achieve Read & Practice** to learn and remember most effectively.

MODULE

Depressive Disorders and Bipolar Disorders

LOQ 49-1 How do depressive disorders and bipolar disorders differ?

In the past year, have you at some time "felt so depressed that it was difficult to function"? If so, you were not alone. In one national survey, 31 percent of American college students answered *Yes* (ACHA, 2009). You might feel deeply discouraged about the future, dissatisfied with your life, or socially isolated. You may lack the energy to get things done, to see people, or even to force yourself out of bed. You may be unable to concentrate, eat, or sleep normally. You may even wonder if you would be better off dead. Perhaps academic success came easily to you before, but now you find that disappointing grades jeopardize your goals. Maybe loneliness, discrimination, or a romantic breakup has plunged you into despair. And perhaps low self-esteem increases your brooding, worsening your self-torment (Orth et al., 2016). Likely, seeing on social media your friends having fun, you mistakenly think it's just you feeling this way (Jordan et al., 2011). Most of us will have some direct or indirect experience with depression: Misery has more company than most suppose.

Brad Wenner/Getty Images

As anxiety is a response to the threat of future loss, depression is often a response to past and current stress. To feel bad in reaction to profoundly sad events is to be in touch with reality. In such times, depression is like a car's low-fuel light—a signal to stop and take appropriate measures. As one book title reminds us, there are "good reasons for bad feelings."

People with *major depressive disorder*, however, experience hopelessness and lethargy lasting several weeks or months. *Persistent depressive disorder* (also called *dysthymia*) is similar, but with milder depressive symptoms that last two years or more. Those with *bipolar disorders* (formerly called *manic-depressive disorder*) alternate between depression and overexcited hyperactivity.

Biologically speaking, life's purpose is not happiness but survival and reproduction. Coughing, vomiting, and various sorts of pain protect the body from dangerous toxins and stimuli. Similarly, depression resembles a sort of psychic hibernation: It slows us down, prompting us, when losing a relationship or blocked from a goal, to conserve energy (Beck & Bredemeier, 2016; Gershon et al., 2016). When we grind temporarily to a halt and reassess our life, as depressed people do, we can redirect our energy in more promising ways (Watkins, 2008). There is sense to suffering.

Even mild sadness helps people process and recall faces more accurately (Hills et al., 2011). They also tend to pay more attention to details, think more critically (with less gullibility), and make better decisions (Forgas, 2009, 2013, 2017). Bad moods can serve good purposes. But sometimes depression becomes seriously maladaptive. How do we recognize the fine line between a blue mood and a disorder?

ASK YOURSELF

Has student life ever made you feel depressed or anxious? What advice would you have for new students (perhaps that you wish someone had given to you)?

"My life had come to a sudden stop. I was able to breathe, to eat, to drink, to sleep. I could not, indeed, help doing so; but there was no real life in me." — Leo Tolstoy, *My Confession*, 1887

"[If someone offered you a pill that would make you permanently happy, you would be well advised to run fast and run far. Emotion is a compass that tells us what to do, and a compass that is perpetually stuck on NORTH is worthless." — Daniel Gilbert, "The Science of Happiness," 2006

"Depression is a silent, slow motion tsunami of dark breaking over me." — Effy Redman, "Waiting for Depression to Lift," 2017

Major Depressive Disorder

Joy, contentment, sadness, and despair are different points on a continuum—points at which any of us may be found at any given moment. The difference between a blue mood after bad news and **major depressive disorder** is like the difference between breathlessness after a hard run and chronic breathing problems (**TABLE 49.1**).

TABLE 49.1 Diagnosing Major Depressive Disorder

The DSM-5 classifies major depressive disorder as the presence of at least five of the following symptoms over a 2-week period of time (minimally including depressed mood or reduced interest) (American Psychiatric Association, 2013).

- Depressed mood most of the time
- Dramatically reduced interest or enjoyment in most activities most of the time
- Significant challenges regulating appetite and weight
- Significant challenges regulating sleep
- Physical agitation or lethargy
- Feeling listless or with much less energy
- Feeling worthless, or feeling unwarranted guilt
- Problems in thinking, concentrating, or making decisions
- Thinking repetitively of death and suicide

major depressive disorder a disorder in which a person experiences, in the absence of drug use or a medical condition, two or more weeks with five or more symptoms, at least one of which must be either (1) depressed mood or (2) loss of interest or pleasure.

bipolar disorders a group of disorders in which a person alternates between the hopelessness and lethargy of depression and the overexcited state of mania. (Formerly called *manic-depressive disorder*.)

mania a hyperactive, wildly optimistic state in which dangerously poor judgment is common.

Depression is the number-one reason people seek mental health services. Indeed, the World Health Organization declared depression "the leading cause of disability worldwide" (WHO, 2017a). In one survey conducted in 21 countries, 4.6 percent of people interviewed were experiencing moderate or severe depression (Thornicroft et al., 2017), as have 1 in 10 U.S. adults, at some point during the prior year (Hasin et al., 2018).

Some people's depression seems to have a *seasonal pattern,* returning each winter, when antidepressant prescriptions increase (Lansdall-Welfare et al., 2019). Although the DSM-5 recognizes a seasonal pattern in major depressive disorder and bipolar disorders, some researchers challenge the presumption of widespread "seasonal affective disorder." They report that people in northerly or cloudier places do *not* experience more wintertime depression (LoBello & Mehta, 2019; Traffanstedt et al., 2016). So stay tuned.

Bipolar Disorders

Our genes dispose some of us, more than others, to respond emotionally to good and bad events (Whisman et al., 2014). People with a **bipolar disorder** bounce from one emotional extreme to the other (week to week, rather than day to day or moment to moment). When a depressive episode ends, a euphoric, overly talkative, wildly energetic, and excessively optimistic state called **mania** follows. But before long, the mood either returns to normal or plunges again into depression, sometimes with back-and-forth *bipolar cycling.* Instead of these extreme swings (called *bipolar I disorder*), others (with *bipolar II disorder*) move between depression and a milder *hypomania.*

During the manic phase, people with bipolar disorders typically have less need for sleep. They show fewer sexual inhibitions. Their positive emotions persist abnormally (Gruber et al., 2019; Stanton et al., 2019). Their speech is loud, flighty, and hard to interrupt. They find advice irritating. Yet they need protection from their own poor judgment, which may lead to reckless spending or unsafe sex. Thinking fast feels good, but it also increases risk taking (Chandler & Pronin, 2012; Pronin, 2013).

Mania's energy and flood of ideas can fuel creativity. Genes associated with high creativity increase the likelihood of a bipolar disorder, and risk factors for developing a bipolar disorder predict greater creativity (Taylor, 2017). George Frideric Handel, who may have suffered from a mild form of bipolar disorder, composed his nearly three-hourlong *Messiah* (1742) during three weeks of intense, creative energy (Keynes, 1980). Robert Schumann composed 51 musical works during two years of mania (1840 and 1849) but none during 1844, when he was severely depressed (Slater & Meyer, 1959). Those who rely on precision and logic, such as architects, designers, and journalists, suffer bipolar disorders less often than do those who rely on emotional expression and vivid imagery. Composers, artists, poets, novelists, and entertainers seem especially prone (Jamison, 1993, 1995; Kaufman & Baer, 2002; Ludwig, 1995). Indeed, one analysis of over a million individuals showed that the only psychiatric condition linked to working in a creative profession was a bipolar disorder (Kyaga et al., 2013).

Bipolar disorders Artist Abigail Southworth illustrated her experience of a bipolar disorder.

Life as a Two-Headed Beast: Bipolar, Abigail Southworth

Though bipolar disorders are much less common than major depressive disorder, they are often more dysfunctional, claiming twice as many lost workdays yearly (Kessler et al., 2006). It is also a predictor of suicide (Schaffer et al., 2015). Unlike major depressive disorder, for which women are at highest risk, bipolar disorders afflict as many men as women. The diagnosis has risen among adolescents, whose mood swings, sometimes prolonged, may vary from raging to bubbly. In the decade between 1994 and 2003, bipolar diagnoses in Americans under age 20 revealed an astonishing 40-fold increase—from an estimated 20,000 to 800,000 (Carey, 2007; Flora & Bobby, 2008; Moreno et al., 2007). Americans are twice as likely as people of other countries to have ever been diagnosed with a bipolar disorder (Merikangas et al., 2011). The new DSM-5 classifications have, however, begun to reduce the number of child and adolescent bipolar diagnoses: Some of those who are persistently irritable and who have frequent and recurring behavior outbursts are now instead diagnosed with *disruptive mood dysregulation disorder* (Faheem et al., 2017).

Actor Russell Brand

Recording artist Mariah Carey

Creativity and bipolar disorders There have been many creative artists, composers, writers, and musical performers with a bipolar disorder. Some, like Russell Brand, have developed a substance abuse disorder as well. Others struggle secretly, as did Mariah Carey for 17 years.

Understanding Depressive Disorders and Bipolar Disorders

LOQ 49-2 How can the biological and social-cognitive perspectives help us understand depressive disorders and bipolar disorders?

Today's psychologists continue to sleuth why people have major depressive disorder and bipolar disorders, and to design more effective ways to treat and prevent them. Here, we focus primarily on major depressive disorder. One research group summarized the facts that any theory of depression must explain (Lewinsohn et al., 1985, 1998, 2003):

- *Behavioral and cognitive changes accompany depression.* People trapped in a depressed mood become inactive and feel alone, empty, and without a meaningful future (Bullock & Murray, 2014; Khazanov & Ruscio, 2016; Smith & Rhodes, 2014). Although it's normal to feel sad when bad things happen, people with depression feel a heavy sadness when nothing bad happens. They also more often recall and expect negative happenings (my team will lose, my grades will fall, my love will fail) (Zetsche et al., 2019).

- *Depression is widespread, with women everywhere at greater risk.* Worldwide, 350 million people have major depressive disorder and 60 million people have a bipolar disorder (WHO, 2017a). Globally, women's risk for major depressive disorder is roughly double men's (Kuehner, 2017; see also **FIGURE 49.1**). The depression gender gap fits a bigger pattern: Women are generally more vulnerable to disorders involving internal states, such as depression, anxiety, and inhibited sexual desire. Women also experience more situations that increase their risk for depression, such as receiving less pay for equal work, juggling multiple roles, and caring for children and elderly family members (Freeman & Freeman, 2013). Men's disorders tend to be more external—alcohol use disorder, and disorders related to antisocial conduct and lack of impulse control. Women often get sadder than men do; men often get madder than women do.

- *Most major depressive episodes self-terminate.* Therapy often speeds recovery. But even without professional help, most people recover from depression. Some do so without future depression and with "optimal well-being" (Rottenberg et al., 2019). The plague of depression comes and, after sustained struggle, it often goes. But for about half of these people, depression returns (Curry et al., 2011; Klein & Kotov, 2016). For some 20 percent, the condition will be chronic (Klein, 2010). An enduring recovery is more likely if: The first episode strikes later in life, there were no previous episodes, the person experiences minimal physical or psychological stress, and there is ample social support (Fuller-Thomson et al., 2016).

FIGURE 49.1
Female-to-male depression ratio, worldwide Researchers Rachel Salk, Janet Hyde, and Lyn Abramson (2017) found that, compared with males, females have twice the risk of depression, and a tripled rate during early adolescence. For many girls, the early teen years are a tough time.

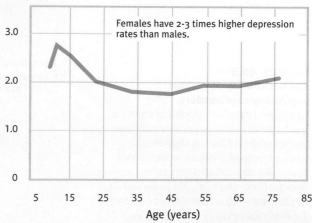

Female-to-male depression ratio

Females have 2-3 times higher depression rates than males.

Age (years)

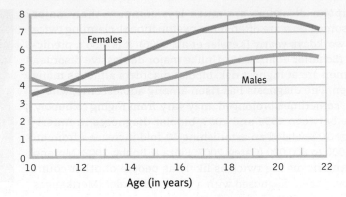

⊘ **FIGURE 49.2**
Depression's developmental trajectory Among nearly 10,000 British teens and young adults, depression symptoms increased during the teen years (Kwong et al., 2019).

- *Work and relationship stresses often precede depression.* About 1 person in 4 diagnosed with depression has been brought down by a significant loss or trauma, such as a loved one's death, a ruptured marriage, a physical assault, or a lost job (Kendler et al., 2008; Monroe & Reid, 2009; Orth et al., 2009; Wakefield et al., 2007). Moving to a new culture also increases risk for depression, especially among younger people who have not yet formed their identities (Zhang et al., 2013). And childhood abuse doubles a person's risk of adult depression (Nelson et al., 2017).

- *Compared with generations past, depression strikes earlier and more often, with the highest rates among older teens and young adults* (Cross-National Collaborative Group, 1992; Kessler et al., 2010; Olfson et al., 2015; see **FIGURE 49.2**).

Armed with these facts, today's researchers propose biological and cognitive explanations of depression, often combined in a biopsychosocial perspective.

> ⧉ For a 9-minute story about one young man's struggle with depression, see the *Video: Depression.*

The Biological Perspective

Depression is a whole-body disorder. It involves genetic predispositions and biochemical imbalances, as well as negative thoughts and a gloomy mood.

GENETIC INFLUENCES Major depressive disorder and bipolar disorders run in families. As one researcher noted, emotions are "postcards from our genes" (Plotkin, 1994). The risk of being diagnosed with one of these disorders increases if your parent or sibling has the disorder (Sullivan et al., 2000; Weissman et al., 2016). If one identical twin is diagnosed with major depressive disorder, the chances are about 1 in 2 that at some time the other twin will be, too. If one identical twin has a bipolar disorder, the chances of a similar diagnosis for the co-twin are even higher—7 in 10—even for twins raised apart (DiLalla et al., 1996). Summarizing the major twin studies, two research teams independently estimated the *heritability*—the extent to which individual differences are attributable to genes—of major depressive disorder at 40 percent (Kendler et al., 2018; Polderman et al., 2015; see also **FIGURE 49.3**).

⊘ **FIGURE 49.3**
The heritability of various psychological disorders Using aggregated data from studies of identical and fraternal twins, researchers estimated the heritability of bipolar disorders, schizophrenia, anorexia nervosa, major depressive disorder, and generalized anxiety disorder (Bienvenu et al., 2011). (Heritability was calculated by a formula that compares the extent of similarity among identical versus fraternal twins.)

To tease out the genes that put people at risk for depression, researchers may use *linkage analysis*. First, geneticists find families in which the disorder appears across several generations. Next, the researchers look for differences in DNA from affected and unaffected family members. Linkage analysis points them to a chromosome neighborhood; "A house-to-house search is then needed to find the culprit gene" (Plomin & McGuffin, 2003). But depression is a complex condition. Many genes work together, producing a mosaic of small effects that interact with other factors to put some people at greater risk. Nevertheless, researchers are identifying culprit gene variations in depressive and bipolar disorders that may open the door to more effective drug therapy (Halldorsdottir et al., 2019; Stahl et al., 2019).

BRAIN ACTIVITY Scanning devices offer a window into the brain's activity during depressed and manic states. One study gave 13 elite Canadian swimmers the wrenching experience of watching a video of the swim in which they failed to make the Olympic team or failed at the Olympic games (Davis et al., 2008). Functional MRI scans showed the disappointed swimmers experiencing brain activity patterns similar to those of people with depressed moods.

Many studies have found diminished brain activity during slowed-down depressive states, and more activity during periods of mania (**FIGURE 49.4**). Depression can cause the brain's reward centers to become less active (Pizzagalli et al., 2019). During positive emotions, the left frontal lobe and an adjacent reward center become more active (Davidson et al., 2002; Heller et al., 2009; Robinson et al., 2012). Neuroscientists have also discovered altered brain structures in people with a bipolar disorder, including decreased white matter (myelinated axons) and enlarged fluid-filled ventricles (Arnone et al., 2009; Hibar et al., 2016).

Courtesy of Drs. Lewis Baxter and Michael E. Phelps, UCLA School of Medicine

Depressed state
(May 17)

Manic state
(May 18)

Depressed state
(May 27)

⬅ **FIGURE 49.4**
The ups and downs of a bipolar disorder These top-facing PET scans show that brain energy consumption rises and falls with the patient's emotional changes. Red areas are where the brain rapidly consumes *glucose,* an important energy source.

At least two neurotransmitter systems are at work during the periods of brain inactivity and hyperactivity that accompany major depressive disorder and bipolar disorders. *Norepinephrine,* which increases arousal and boosts mood, is scarce during depression and overabundant during mania. Drugs that decrease mania reduce norepinephrine. *Serotonin* is also scarce or inactive during depression (Carver et al., 2008). One well-publicized study of New Zealand young adults found that the recipe for depression combined two necessary ingredients—significant life stress plus a variation of a serotonin-controlling gene (Caspi et al., 2003; Moffitt et al., 2006). Depression arose from the combination of an adverse environment plus a genetic susceptibility, but not from either alone. But stay tuned: The story of gene–environment interactions is still being written, as other researchers debate the reliability of this result (Border et al., 2019).

Drugs that relieve depression tend to increase norepinephrine or serotonin supplies by blocking either their reuptake (as Prozac, Zoloft, and Paxil do with serotonin) or their chemical breakdown. Repetitive physical exercise, such as jogging, reduces depression in part because it increases serotonin, which affects mood and arousal (Airan et al., 2007; Harvey et al., 2018; Ilardi, 2009). In one study, running for 2 hours increased brain activation in regions associated with euphoria (Boecker et al., 2008). To get away from a bad mood, some people have used their own two feet.

NUTRITIONAL EFFECTS What's good for the heart is also good for the brain and mind. People who eat a heart-healthy "Mediterranean diet" (heavy on vegetables, fish, whole grains, and olive oil) have a comparatively low risk of developing heart disease, stroke,

Minding the gut Does food modify mood? Digestive system bacteria produce neurotransmitters that influence emotions. Although some researchers think the happy gut/happy brain relationship is over-hyped, healthy, diverse gut microbes do at least correlate with a reduced risk of anxiety, depression, and PTSD (Hooks et al., 2019; Smith & Wissel, 2019).

late-life cognitive decline, and depression—all of which are associated with inflammation in the body (Kaplan et al., 2015; Psaltopoulou et al., 2013; Rechenberg, 2016). Excessive alcohol use also correlates with depression, partly because depression can increase alcohol use but mostly because alcohol misuse *leads* to depression (Fergusson et al., 2009).

The Social-Cognitive Perspective

Biological influences contribute to depression, but in the nature–nurture dance, our life experiences also play a part. Diet, drugs, stress, and other environmental influences lay down epigenetic marks, those molecular genetic tags that can turn certain genes on or off. Animal studies suggest that long-lasting epigenetic influences may play a role in depression (Nestler, 2011).

Thinking matters, too. The *social-cognitive perspective* explores how people's assumptions and expectations influence what they perceive. Many depressed people view life through the dark glasses of low self-esteem (Orth et al., 2016). They have intensely negative assumptions about themselves, their situation, and their future. Norman, a Canadian university professor, recalled his depression this way:

> I [despaired] of ever being human again. I honestly felt subhuman, lower than the lowest vermin. Furthermore, I was self-deprecatory and could not understand why anyone would want to associate with me, let alone love me. . . . I was positive that I was a fraud and a phony and that I didn't deserve my Ph.D. . . . I didn't deserve the research grants I had been awarded; I couldn't understand how I had written books and journal articles. . . . I must have conned a lot of people. (Endler, 1982, pp. 45–49)

Expecting the worst, depressed people magnify bad experiences and minimize good ones (Wenze et al., 2012). Their *self-defeating beliefs* and their *negative explanatory style* feed their depression.

NEGATIVE THOUGHTS, NEGATIVE MOODS, AND GENDER Why are women nearly twice as vulnerable as men to depression, and twice as likely to take antidepressant drugs (Pratt et al., 2017)? Women may respond more strongly to stress (Hankin & Abramson, 2001; Mazure et al., 2002; Nolen-Hoeksema, 2001, 2003). For example, 38 percent of women and 17 percent of men entering American colleges and universities have reported feeling at least occasionally "overwhelmed by all I have to do" (Pryor et al., 2006). Relationship stresses also affect teen girls more than boys (Hamilton et al., 2015).

Susan Nolen-Hoeksema (2003) related women's higher risk of depression to what she described as their tendency to ruminate or *overthink*. Staying focused on a problem—thanks to the continuous activation of an attention-sustaining frontal lobe area—can be adaptive (Altamirano et al., 2010; Andrews & Thomson, 2009a,b). But relentless, self-focused **rumination** can distract us, increase negative emotion, and disrupt daily activities (Johnson et al., 2016; Leary, 2018; Yang et al., 2017). Comparisons can also feed misery. While Elijah is happily playing video games, lonely Lori scrolls through her social media feed and sees Maria having a blast at a party, Angelique enjoying a family vacation, and Amira looking super in a swimsuit. In response, Lori broods: "My life is terrible."

But why do life's unavoidable failures lead only some people to become depressed? The answer lies partly in their *explanatory style*—who or what they blame for their failures. Think of how you might feel if you failed a test. If you can externalize the blame ("What an unfair test!"), you are more likely to feel angry. If you blame yourself, you probably will feel stupid and depressed.

Depression-prone people respond to bad events in an especially self-focused, self-blaming way (Huang, 2015; LeMoult & Gotlib, 2019; Mor & Winquist, 2002). As **FIGURE 49.5** illustrates, they explain bad events in terms that are *stable*, *global*, and *internal*.

Rumination runs wild It's normal to think about our flaws. But dwelling constantly on negative thoughts—particularly negative thoughts about ourselves—makes it difficult to believe in ourselves and solve problems. People sometimes seek therapy to reduce their rumination.

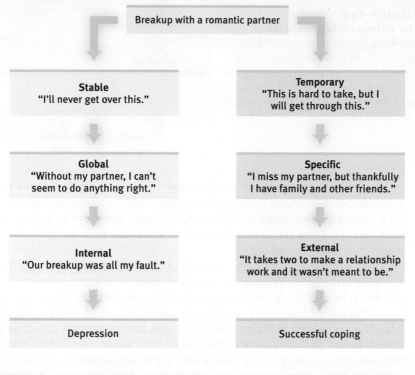

⬅ **FIGURE 49.5**
Explanatory style and depression

"You should never engage in unsupervised introspection."

Self-defeating beliefs may arise from *learned helplessness,* the hopelessness and passive resignation that humans and other animals learn when they experience uncontrollable painful events (Maier & Seligman, 2016). Pessimistic, overgeneralized, self-blaming attributions may create a depressing sense of hopelessness (Abramson et al., 1989; Groß et al., 2017). As researcher Martin Seligman has noted, "A recipe for severe depression is preexisting pessimism encountering failure" (1991, p. 78). What, then, might we expect of new college students who exhibit a pessimistic explanatory style? Lauren Alloy and her colleagues (1999) monitored several hundred students every 6 weeks for 2.5 years. Among those identified as having a pessimistic thinking style, 17 percent had a first episode of major depression, as did only 1 percent of those who began college with an optimistic thinking style.

Why is depression so common among young Westerners? Seligman (1991, 1995) pointed to the rise of individualism and the decline of commitment to religion and family. In non-Western cultures, where close-knit relationships and cooperation are the norm, major depressive disorder is less common and less tied to self-blame for failure (De Vaus et al., 2018; Ferrari et al., 2013). In Japan, for example, depressed people instead tend to report feeling shame over letting others down (Draguns, 1990).

Critics note a chicken-and-egg problem nesting in the social-cognitive explanation of depression. Which comes first? The pessimistic explanatory style, or the depressed mood? The negative explanations *coincide* with a depressed mood, and they are *indicators* of depression. But do negative thoughts *cause* depression, any more than a speedometer's reading causes a car's speed? Temporarily putting people in a bad or sad mood does make their memories, judgments, and expectations more pessimistic. Memory researchers call this tendency to recall experiences that fit our current good or bad mood *state-dependent memory.*

DEPRESSION'S VICIOUS CYCLE Depression is both a cause and an effect of stressful experiences that disrupt our sense of who we are and why we matter. Such disruptions can lead to brooding, which amplifies negative feelings. Being withdrawn, self-focused, and complaining can in turn elicit rejection (Furr & Funder, 1998; Gotlib & Hammen, 1992). Indeed, people in the throes of depression are at high risk for divorce, job loss, and other stressful life events. Weary of the person's fatigue, hopeless attitude, and negativity, a spouse may threaten to leave or a boss may begin to question the person's competence. (This provides another example of gene–environment interaction: People genetically predisposed to depression more often experience depressing events.) Rejection and depression feed each other. Misery may love another's company, but company does not love another's misery.

To explore your own thinking style, engage online with *Assess Your Strengths: How Hopeful Are You? Why Is This Important?*

"Some cause happiness wherever they go; others, whenever they go." — Irish writer Oscar Wilde (1854–1900)

→ **FIGURE 49.6**
The vicious cycle of depressed thinking Therapists recognize this cycle, and they work to help depressed people break out of it by changing their negative thinking, turning their attention outward, and engaging them in more pleasant and competent behavior.

> "Man never reasons so much and becomes so introspective as when he suffers, since he is anxious to get at the cause of his sufferings." — Luigi Pirandello, *Six Characters in Search of an Author*, 1922

We can now assemble the pieces of the depression puzzle (**FIGURE 49.6**): (1) Stressful experiences interpreted through (2) a ruminating, pessimistic explanatory style create (3) a hopeless, depressed state that (4) hampers the way the person thinks and acts. This, in turn, fuels (1) further stressful experiences such as rejection. Depression is a snake that bites its own tail.

None of us are immune to the dejection, diminished self-esteem, and negative thinking brought on by rejection or defeat. Even small losses can temporarily sour our thinking. In one study, researchers studied some avid Indiana University basketball fans who seemed to regard the team as an extension of themselves (Hirt et al., 1992). After the fans watched their team lose or win, the researchers asked them to predict the team's future performance and their own. After a loss, the morose fans offered bleaker assessments not only of the team's future but also of their own likely performance at throwing darts, solving anagrams, and getting a date. When things aren't going our way, it may seem as though they never will.

It is a cycle we can all recognize. Bad moods feed on themselves: When we feel down, we think negatively and remember bad experiences. Britain's Prime Minister Winston Churchill called depression a "black dog" that periodically hounded him. U.S. President Abraham Lincoln was so withdrawn and brooding as a young man that his friends feared he might take his own life (Kline, 1974). Poet Emily Dickinson was so afraid of bursting into tears in public that she spent much of her adult life in seclusion (Patterson, 1951). J. K. Rowling wrote the first Harry Potter book as she fought depression. As their lives remind us, "depression" can be a living anagram for "I pressed on." Many people struggle through depression and regain their capacity to love, to work, and to succeed.

Life after depression J. K. Rowling, author of the Harry Potter books, reported suffering acute depression—a "dark time," with suicidal thoughts—between ages 25 and 28. It was a "terrible place," she said, but it formed a foundation that allowed her "to come back stronger" (McLaughlin, 2010).

RETRIEVAL PRACTICE

RP-1 What does it mean to say that "depression is a whole-body disorder"?

ANSWERS IN APPENDIX E

MODULE

49 REVIEW Depressive Disorders and Bipolar Disorders

LEARNING OBJECTIVES

Test Yourself Answer these repeated Learning Objective Questions on your own (before checking the answers in Appendix D) to improve your retention of the concepts (McDaniel et al., 2009, 2015).

LOQ 49-1 How do major depressive disorders and bipolar disorders differ?

LOQ 49-2 How can the biological and social-cognitive perspectives help us understand depressive disorders and bipolar disorders?

TERMS AND CONCEPTS TO REMEMBER

Test Yourself Write down the definition in your own words, then check your answer.

major depressive disorder, p. 571

bipolar disorders, p. 572

mania, p. 572

rumination, p. 577

MASTER THE MATERIAL

Test Yourself Answer the following questions on your own first, then check your answers in Appendix E.

1. The gender gap in depression refers to the finding that _____ (men's/women's) risk of depression is roughly double that of _____ (men's/women's).

2. Rates of bipolar disorders in the United States rose dramatically between 1994 and 2003, especially among

   a. middle-aged women.

   b. middle-aged men.

   c. people 20 and over.

   d. people 19 and under.

3. Treatment for depression often includes drugs that increase supplies of the neurotransmitters _____ and _____.

4. Psychologists who emphasize the importance of negative perceptions, beliefs, and thoughts in depression are working within the _____-_____ perspective.

Continue testing yourself with 📚 **LearningCurve** or 📖 **Achieve Read & Practice** to learn and remember most effectively.

MODULE

50 Schizophrenia

During their most severe periods, people with **schizophrenia** live in a private inner world, preoccupied with the strange ideas and images that haunt them. The word itself means "split" (*schizo*) "mind" (*phrenia*). It refers *not* to a multiple identity split but rather to the mind's split from reality. People with schizophrenia have disturbed perceptions and beliefs, disorganized speech, and diminished, inappropriate emotions (and actions). Schizophrenia is the chief example of a **psychotic disorder,** a group of disorders marked by irrationality, distorted perceptions, and lost contact with reality.

Symptoms of Schizophrenia

LOQ 50-1 What patterns of perceiving, thinking, and feeling characterize schizophrenia?

Schizophrenia comes in varied forms. People with schizophrenia display symptoms that are *positive* (*inappropriate* behaviors are *present*) or *negative* (*appropriate* behaviors are *absent*). Those with *positive* symptoms may experience disturbed perceptions, talk in disorganized and deluded ways, or exhibit inappropriate laughter, tears, or rage. Those with negative symptoms may exhibit an absence of emotion in their voices, expressionless faces, or mute and rigid bodies.

Disturbed Perceptions and Beliefs

People with schizophrenia sometimes *hallucinate*—they see, hear, feel, taste, or smell things that exist only in their minds. Most often, the hallucinations are voices, which sometimes

schizophrenia a disorder characterized by delusions, hallucinations, disorganized speech, and/or diminished, inappropriate emotional expression.

psychotic disorders a group of disorders marked by irrational ideas, distorted perceptions, and a loss of contact with reality.

Art by someone diagnosed with schizophrenia
Commenting on the kind of artwork shown here (from Craig Geiser's 2010 art exhibit in Michigan), poet and art critic John Ashbery wrote: "The lure of the work is strong, but so is the terror of the unanswerable riddles it proposes."

"Now consider this: The regulator that funnels certain information to you and filters out other information suddenly shuts off. Immediately, every sight, every sound, every smell coming at you carries equal weight; every thought, feeling, memory, and idea presents itself to you with an equally strong and demanding intensity."

— Elyn R. Saks, *The Center Cannot Hold*, 2007

make insulting remarks or give orders. The voices may tell the person that she is bad or that she must burn herself with a cigarette lighter. Imagine your own reaction if a dream broke into your waking consciousness, making it hard to separate your experience from your imagination. When the unreal seems real, the resulting perceptions are at best bizarre, at worst terrifying.

Hallucinations are false *perceptions*. People with schizophrenia also have disorganized, fragmented thinking, often distorted by false *beliefs* called **delusions.** If they have *paranoid* delusions, they may believe they are being threatened or pursued.

One cause of disorganized thinking may be a breakdown in *selective attention.* Normally, we have a remarkable capacity to give our undivided attention to one set of sensory stimuli while filtering out others. People with schizophrenia are easily distracted by tiny unrelated stimuli, such as the grooves on a brick or tones in a voice. This selective-attention difficulty is but one of dozens of cognitive differences associated with schizophrenia (Reichenberg & Harvey, 2007).

Disorganized Speech

Maxine, a young woman with schizophrenia, believed she was Mary Poppins. Communicating with Maxine was difficult because her thoughts spilled out in no logical order. Her biographer, Susan Sheehan (1982, p. 25), observed her saying aloud to no one in particular, "This morning, when I was at Hillside [Hospital], I was making a movie. I was surrounded by movie stars. . . . Is this room painted blue to get me upset? My grandmother died four weeks after my eighteenth birthday."

Jumbled ideas may make no sense even within sentences, forming what is known as *word salad.* One young man begged for "a little more allegro in the treatment," and suggested that "liberationary movement with a view to the widening of the horizon" will "ergo extort some wit in lectures."

Diminished and Inappropriate Emotions

The expressed emotions of schizophrenia are often utterly inappropriate, split off from reality (Kring & Caponigro, 2010). Maxine laughed after recalling her grandmother's death. On other occasions, she cried when others laughed, or became angry for no apparent reason. Others with schizophrenia lapse into an emotionless *flat affect* state of no apparent feeling.

Most also have an *impaired theory of mind*—they have difficulty reading other peoples' facial expressions and states of mind (Bora & Pantelis, 2016). Unable to understand others' mental states, those with schizophrenia struggle to feel sympathy and compassion (Bonfils et al., 2016). These emotional deficiencies occur early in the illness and have a genetic basis (Bora & Pantelis, 2013). *Motor behavior* may also be inappropriate and disruptive. Those with schizophrenia may experience *catatonia,* characterized by motor behaviors ranging from a physical stupor (remaining motionless for hours), to senseless, compulsive actions (such as continually rocking or rubbing an arm), to severe and dangerous agitation.

As you can imagine, such disturbed perceptions and beliefs, disorganized speech, and out of place emotions profoundly disrupt social and work relationships. During their most severe periods, people with schizophrenia live in a private inner world, preoccupied with illogical ideas and unreal images. As with other disorders, many have sleep problems, which can increase night eating and obesity (Baglioni et al., 2016; Palmese et al., 2011). Given a supportive environment and medication, over 40 percent of people with schizophrenia will have periods of a year or more of normal life experience (Jobe & Harrow, 2010). But only 1 in 7 will have a full and enduring recovery (Jääskeläinen et al., 2013).

delusion a false belief, often of persecution or grandeur, that may accompany psychotic disorders.

chronic schizophrenia (also called *process schizophrenia*) a form of schizophrenia in which symptoms usually appear by late adolescence or early adulthood. As people age, psychotic episodes last longer and recovery periods shorten.

acute schizophrenia (also called *reactive schizophrenia*) a form of schizophrenia that can begin at any age, frequently occurs in response to a traumatic event, and from which recovery is much more likely.

Onset and Development of Schizophrenia

LOQ 50-2 How do *chronic schizophrenia* and *acute schizophrenia* differ?

This year, 1 in 100 people will join an estimated 21 million others worldwide who have schizophrenia (WHO, 2017b). This disorder knows no national boundaries and it typically strikes as young people are maturing into adulthood. Men tend to be diagnosed more often than women, and to be struck earlier and more severely (Aleman et al., 2003; Eranti et al., 2013; Picchioni & Murray, 2007).

When schizophrenia is a slow-developing process, called **chronic schizophrenia,** recovery is doubtful (Harrison et al., 2001; Jääskeläinen et al., 2013). This was the case with Maxine, whose schizophrenia took a slow course, emerging after a long history of social inadequacy and poor school performance (MacCabe et al., 2008). Social withdrawal, a negative symptom, is often found among those with chronic schizophrenia (Kirkpatrick et al., 2006). Men more often exhibit negative symptoms and chronic schizophrenia (Räsänen et al., 2000).

When previously well-adjusted people develop schizophrenia rapidly following particular life stresses, this is called **acute schizophrenia,** and recovery is much more likely. They more often have positive symptoms that respond to drug therapy (Fenton & McGlashan, 1991, 1994; Fowles, 1992).

Understanding Schizophrenia

Schizophrenia is one of the most heavily researched psychological disorders. Most studies now link it with abnormal brain tissue and genetic predispositions. Schizophrenia is a disease of the brain manifested in symptoms of the mind.

Brain Abnormalities

LOQ **50-3** What brain abnormalities are associated with schizophrenia?

Might chemical imbalances in the brain underlie schizophrenia? Scientists have long known that strange behavior can have strange chemical causes. The saying "as mad as a hatter" is often thought to refer to the psychological deterioration of British hatmakers whose brains, it was later discovered, were slowly poisoned by the mercury-laden felt material (Smith, 1983). Could schizophrenia symptoms have a similar biochemical key? Scientists are searching for blood proteins that might predict schizophrenia onset (Chan et al., 2015). And they are tracking the mechanisms by which chemicals produce hallucinations and other symptoms.

DOPAMINE OVERACTIVITY One possible answer emerged when researchers examined schizophrenia patients' brains after death. They found an excess number of *dopamine* receptors, including a sixfold excess for the dopamine receptor D4 (Seeman et al., 1993; Wong et al., 1986). Such a hyper-responsive dopamine system may intensify brain signals in schizophrenia, creating positive symptoms such as hallucinations and paranoia (Maia & Frank, 2017). Drugs that block dopamine receptors often lessen these symptoms. Drugs that increase dopamine levels, such as nicotine, amphetamines, and cocaine, sometimes intensify them (Basu & Basu, 2015; Farnia et al., 2014).

ABNORMAL BRAIN ACTIVITY AND ANATOMY Abnormal brain activity and brain structures accompany schizophrenia. Some people diagnosed with schizophrenia have abnormally low brain activity in the frontal lobes, areas that help us reason, plan, and solve problems (Morey et al., 2005; Pettegrew et al., 1993; Resnick, 1992). Brain scans also show a noticeable decline in the brain waves that reflect synchronized neural firing in the frontal lobes (Spencer et al., 2004; Symond et al., 2005).

One study took PET scans of brain activity while people with schizophrenia were hallucinating (Silbersweig et al., 1995). When participants heard a voice or saw something, their brain became vigorously active in several core regions. One was the thalamus, the structure that filters incoming sensory signals and transmits them to the brain's cortex. Another PET scan study of people with paranoia found increased activity in the amygdala, a fear-processing center (Epstein et al., 1998).

Many studies have also found enlarged, fluid-filled ventricles and a corresponding shrinkage and thinning of cerebral tissue (Goldman et al., 2009; van Haren et al., 2016). People often inherit these brain differences. If one affected identical twin shows brain abnormalities, the odds are at least 1 in 2 that the other twin's brain will have them (van Haren et al., 2012). Some studies have even found these abnormalities in people who *later* developed the disorder (Karlsgodt et al., 2010). The greater the brain shrinkage, the more severe the thought disorder (Collinson et al., 2003; Nelson et al., 1998; Shenton, 1992).

Storing and studying brains Psychiatrist E. Fuller Torrey has collected the brains of hundreds of people who died as young adults and suffered disorders such as schizophrenia and bipolar disorders.

© Chris Mueller/Redux Pictures

Smaller-than-normal areas may include the cortex, the hippocampus, and the corpus callosum connecting the brain's two hemispheres (Arnone et al., 2008; Bois et al., 2016). Often, the thalamus is also smaller than normal, which may explain why people with schizophrenia have difficulty filtering sensory input and focusing attention (Andreasen et al., 1994; Ellison-Wright et al., 2008). Schizophrenia also tends to involve a loss of neural connections across the brain network (Bohlken et al., 2016; Kambeitz et al., 2016). *The bottom line:* Schizophrenia involves not one isolated brain abnormality but problems with several brain regions and their interconnections (Andreasen, 1997, 2001; Arnedo et al., 2015).

Prenatal Environment and Risk

LOQ **50-4** What prenatal events are associated with increased risk of developing schizophrenia?

What causes these brain abnormalities in people with schizophrenia? Some scientists point to prenatal development or delivery (Fatemi & Folsom, 2009; Walker et al., 2010). Risk factors include low birth weight, maternal diabetes, older paternal age, and oxygen deprivation during delivery (King et al., 2010). Famine may also increase risks. People conceived during the peak of World War II's Dutch famine, as well as during the famine of 1959 to 1961 in eastern China, later developed schizophrenia at twice the normal rate (St. Clair et al., 2005; Susser et al., 1996). And extreme maternal stress may be a culprit: A study of 200,000 Israeli mothers showed that exposure to terror attacks during pregnancy doubled their children's risk of schizophrenia (Weinstein et al., 2018b).

Let's consider another possible culprit. Might a midpregnancy viral infection impair fetal brain development (Brown & Patterson, 2011)? Can you imagine some ways to test this fetal-virus idea? Scientists have asked the following:

- *Are people at increased risk of schizophrenia if, during the middle of their fetal development, their country experienced a flu epidemic?* The repeated answer has been *Yes* (Mednick et al., 1994; Murray et al., 1992; Wright et al., 1995).

- *Are people born in densely populated areas, where viral diseases spread more readily, at greater risk for schizophrenia?* The answer, confirmed in a study of 1.75 million Danes, has again been *Yes* (Jablensky, 1999; Mortensen, 1999).

- *Are those born during the winter and spring months—those who were in utero during the fall-winter flu season—also at increased risk?* The answer is again *Yes* (Fox, 2010; Schwartz, 2011; Torrey & Miller, 2002; Torrey et al., 1997).

- *In the Southern Hemisphere, where the seasons are the reverse of the Northern Hemisphere, are the months of above-average pre-schizophrenia births similarly reversed?* Again, the answer has been *Yes*. In Australia, people born between August and October are at greater risk. But people born in the Northern Hemisphere who later moved to Australia still have a greater risk if they were born between January and March (McGrath et al., 1995; McGrath & Welham, 1999).

- *Are mothers who report being sick with influenza during pregnancy more likely to bear children who develop schizophrenia?* In one study of nearly 8000 women, the answer was *Yes*. The schizophrenia risk increased from the customary 1 percent to about 2 percent—but only when infections occurred during the second trimester (Brown et al., 2000). Maternal influenza infection during pregnancy affects brain development in monkeys as well (Short et al., 2010).

- *Does blood drawn from pregnant women whose offspring develop schizophrenia show higher-than-normal levels of antibodies that suggest a viral infection?* In several studies—including one that collected blood samples from some 20,000 pregnant women—the answer has again been *Yes* (Brown et al., 2004; Buka et al., 2001; Canetta et al., 2014).

These converging lines of evidence suggest that fetal-virus infections contribute to the development of schizophrenia. They also strengthen the World Health Organization's (2012b) recommendation that pregnant women be given highest priority for seasonal flu vaccine.

Genetic Factors

LOQ **50-5** How do genes influence schizophrenia? What factors may be early warning signs of schizophrenia in children?

Fetal-virus infections may increase the odds that a child will develop schizophrenia. But many women get the flu during their second trimester of pregnancy, and only 2 percent of them bear children who develop schizophrenia. Why are only some children at risk? Might some people be more genetically vulnerable to schizophrenia? *Yes.* The 1-in-100 odds of any person's being diagnosed with schizophrenia become about 1 in 10 among those who have a sibling or parent with the disorder. If the affected sibling is an identical twin, the odds increase to nearly 1 in 2 (**FIGURE 50.1**). Those odds remain the same even when the twins are raised apart (Plomin et al., 1997). (Only about a dozen such cases are on record.)

Remember, though, that identical twins share more than their genes. They also share a prenatal environment. About two-thirds share a placenta and the blood it supplies; the other third have separate placentas. Shared placentas matter. If the co-twin of an identical twin with schizophrenia shared the placenta, the chances of developing the disorder are 6 in 10. If the identical twins had separate placentas, the co-twin's chances of developing schizophrenia drop to 1 in 10 (Davis et al., 1995; Davis & Phelps, 1995; Phelps et al., 1997). Twins who share a placenta are more likely to share the same prenatal viruses. So perhaps shared germs as well as shared genes produce identical twin similarities (**FIGURE 50.2**).

Adoption studies help untangle genetic and environmental influences. Children adopted by someone who develops schizophrenia do not "catch" the disorder. Rather, adopted children have an elevated risk if a *biological* parent is diagnosed with schizophrenia (Gottesman, 1991). Genes indeed matter.

Although genes matter, the genetic formula is not straightforward as with inheritance of eye color. Schizophrenia is influenced by (no surprise by now) many genes, each with small effects (Binder, 2019; Weinberger, 2019). The search is on for specific genes that, in some combination, predispose schizophrenia-inducing brain abnormalities. In the largest genetic studies of schizophrenia, scientists analyze worldwide data from the genomes of tens of thousands of people with and without schizophrenia (Lam et al., 2019; Pardiñas et al., 2018). One analysis found 176 genome locations linked with this disorder, some affecting dopamine and other neurotransmitters. Another study of more than 100,000 people—nearly half with schizophrenia and the rest without—identified 413 schizophrenia-associated genes (Huckins et al., 2019).

Moreover, as we have so often seen, nature and nurture interact. *Epigenetic* factors influence whether genes will be expressed. Like hot water activating a tea bag, environmental factors such as viral infections, nutritional deprivation, and maternal or severe life stress can "turn on" the genes that put some of us at higher risk for schizophrenia. Identical twins' differing histories in the womb and beyond explain why they may show differing gene expressions (Dempster et al., 2013; Walker et al., 2010). Our heredity and our life experiences work together. Neither hand claps alone.

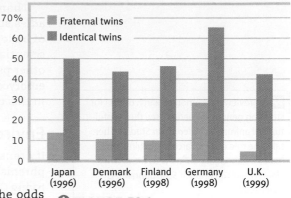

Schizophrenia risk for twins of those diagnosed with schizophrenia

FIGURE 50.1
Risk of developing schizophrenia The lifetime risk of developing schizophrenia varies with one's genetic relatedness to someone having this disorder. Across countries, barely more than 1 in 10 fraternal twins, but some 5 in 10 identical twins, share a schizophrenia diagnosis. (Data from Gottesman, 2001; Hilker et al., 2018.)

No schizophrenia
(a)

Schizophrenia
(b)

Daniel Weinberger, M.D., CBDB, NIMH

FIGURE 50.2
Schizophrenia in only one identical twin When twins differ, only the brain of the twin with schizophrenia typically has enlarged, fluid-filled cranial cavities (b) (Suddath et al., 1990). The difference between the twins implies some nongenetic factor, such as a virus, is also at work.

Thanks to our expanding understanding of genetic and brain influences on maladies such as schizophrenia, the general public increasingly recognizes the potency of biological factors in psychiatric disorders (Pescosolido et al., 2010). So, will future scientists develop genetic tests that reveal who is at risk—for schizophrenia, or for other psychological disorders? If so, will people undergo testing for themselves, their embryos, or their children to determine risk? And how will they use that information? In this twenty-first-century world, such questions await answers.

Environmental Triggers for Schizophrenia

If prenatal viruses and genetic predispositions do not, by themselves, cause schizophrenia, neither do family or social factors alone. It remains true, as Susan Nicol and Irving Gottesman (1983) noted over three decades ago, that "no environmental causes have been discovered that will invariably, or even with moderate probability, produce schizophrenia in persons who are not related to" a person with schizophrenia.

Hoping to identify environmental triggers of schizophrenia, researchers have compared the experiences of high-risk children (for example, those with relatives with schizophrenia) and low-risk children. In one 2.5-year study that followed 163 teens and early-twenties adults who had two relatives with schizophrenia, the 20 percent of participants who developed schizophrenia showed social withdrawal or other abnormal behavior before the onset of the disorder (Johnstone et al., 2005). Researchers identified other possible early warning signs, including a mother whose schizophrenia was severe and long-lasting; birth complications (often involving oxygen deprivation and low birth weight); frequent childhood hospitalizations for viral and other infections; separation from parents; short attention span and poor muscle coordination; disruptive or withdrawn behavior; emotional unpredictability; poor peer relations and solo play; and childhood physical, sexual, or emotional abuse (Abel et al., 2010; Debost et al., 2019; Freedman et al., 1998; Schiffman et al., 2001; Susser, 1999; Welham et al., 2009).

* * *

Few of us can relate to the strange thoughts, perceptions, and behaviors of schizophrenia. Sometimes our thoughts jump around, but we rarely talk nonsensically. Occasionally we feel unjustly suspicious of someone, but we do not fear that the world is plotting against us. Often our perceptions err, but rarely do we see or hear things that are not there. We feel regret after laughing at someone's misfortune, but we rarely giggle in response to our own bad news. At times we just want to be alone, but we do not retreat into fantasy worlds. However, millions of people around the world do talk strangely, suffer delusions, hear nonexistent voices, see things that are not there, laugh or cry at inappropriate times, or withdraw into private imaginary worlds. The quest to solve the cruel puzzle of schizophrenia continues, more vigorously than ever.

> To review a common research design for studying genetic influences, see the helpful tutorial animation *Video: Twin Studies*. Then take the role of a researcher studying these issues by engaging online with the activity *How Would You Know If Schizophrenia Is Inherited?*

> For an 8-minute description of how clinicians define and treat schizophrenia, see the *Video: Schizophrenia—New Definitions, New Therapies.*

ASK YOURSELF

Can you recall a time when you heard something or someone casually (and inaccurately) described as "schizophrenic"? Now that you know more about this disorder, how might you correct such descriptions?

RETRIEVAL PRACTICE

RP-1 A person with schizophrenia who has _____ (positive/negative) symptoms may have an expressionless face and toneless voice. These symptoms are most common with _____ (chronic/acute) schizophrenia and are not likely to respond to drug therapy. Those with _____ (positive/negative) symptoms are likely to experience delusions and to be diagnosed with _____ (chronic/acute) schizophrenia, which is much more likely to respond to drug therapy.

RP-2 What factors contribute to the onset and development of schizophrenia?

ANSWERS IN APPENDIX E

50 REVIEW Schizophrenia

LEARNING OBJECTIVES

Test Yourself Answer these repeated Learning Objective Questions on your own (before checking the answers in Appendix D) to improve your retention of the concepts (McDaniel et al., 2009, 2015).

LOQ 50-1 What patterns of perceiving, thinking, and feeling characterize schizophrenia?

LOQ 50-2 How do *chronic schizophrenia* and *acute schizophrenia* differ?

LOQ 50-3 What brain abnormalities are associated with schizophrenia?

LOQ 50-4 What prenatal events are associated with increased risk of developing schizophrenia?

LOQ 50-5 How do genes influence schizophrenia? What factors may be early warning signs of schizophrenia in children?

TERMS AND CONCEPTS TO REMEMBER

Test Yourself Write down the definition in your own words, then check your answer.

schizophrenia, p. 579

psychotic disorders, p. 579

delusion, p. 580

chronic schizophrenia, p. 580

acute schizophrenia, p. 580

MASTER THE MATERIAL

Test Yourself Answer the following questions on your own first, then check your answers in Appendix E.

1. Valencia exclaimed, "The weather has been so schizophrenic lately: It's hot one day and freezing the next!" In addition to being insensitive, this comparison is inaccurate. Explain.

2. A person with positive symptoms of schizophrenia is most likely to experience
   a. catatonia.
   b. delusions.
   c. withdrawal.
   d. flat emotion.

3. People with schizophrenia may hear voices urging self-destruction, an example of a(n) _____.

4. Chances for recovery from schizophrenia are best when
   a. onset is sudden, in response to stress.
   b. deterioration occurs gradually, during childhood.
   c. no environmental causes can be identified.
   d. there is a detectable brain abnormality.

Continue testing yourself with 📚 **LearningCurve** or 📖 **Achieve Read & Practice** to learn and remember most effectively.

51 Dissociative, Personality, and Eating Disorders

Dissociative Disorders

LOQ 51-1 What are *dissociative disorders*, and why are they controversial?

Among the most bewildering disorders are the rare **dissociative disorders,** in which a person's conscious awareness *dissociates* (separates) from painful memories, thoughts, and feelings. The result may be a *dissociative fugue state*, a sudden loss of memory or change in identity, often in response to an overwhelmingly stressful situation (Harrison et al., 2017). Such was the case for one Vietnam veteran who was haunted by his comrades' deaths, and who had left his World Trade Center office shortly before the 9/11 terrorist attack. Later, he disappeared. Six months later, when he was discovered in a Chicago homeless shelter, he reported no memory of his identity or family (Stone, 2006).

Dissociation itself is not so rare. Any one of us may have a sense of being unreal, of being separated from our body, of watching ourselves as if in a movie. Sometimes we may say, "I was not myself at the time." Perhaps you can recall getting up to go somewhere and ending up at some unintended location while your mind was preoccupied. Or perhaps you can play a well-practiced tune on a guitar or piano while talking to someone. When we face trauma, dissociative detachment may protect us from being overwhelmed by emotion.

dissociative disorders controversial, rare disorders in which conscious awareness becomes separated (dissociated) from previous memories, thoughts, and feelings.

Multiple identities in the movies Chris Sizemore's story, told in the book and movie *The Three Faces of Eve,* gave early visibility to what is now called dissociative identity disorder. This controversial disorder continues to influence modern media, as in the 2019 movie *Glass,* where James McAvoy's character displays 24 different identities.

"Pretense may become reality."

— Chinese proverb

Dissociative Identity Disorder

A massive dissociation of self from ordinary consciousness is said to occur in **dissociative identity disorder (DID),** in which two or more distinct identities—each with its own voice and mannerisms—seem to control a person's behavior at different times. Thus, the person may be prim and proper one moment, loud and flirtatious the next. Typically, the original identity denies any awareness of the other(s).

UNDERSTANDING DISSOCIATIVE IDENTITY DISORDER Skeptics question DID. First, instead of being a true disorder, could DID be an extension of our normal capacity for identity shifts? Nicholas Spanos (1986, 1994, 1996) asked college students to pretend they were accused murderers being examined by a psychiatrist. Given a hypnotic treatment—as has been used in some famous cases of DID—most spontaneously expressed a second identity. This discovery made Spanos wonder: Perhaps dissociative identities are simply a more extreme version of the varied "selves" we normally present—a goofy self around our friends, a subdued self around our employer. Are clinicians who discover multiple identities merely triggering role playing by fantasy-prone people in a particular social context (Giesbrecht et al., 2008, 2010; Lynn et al., 2014; Merskey, 1992)? After all, clients do not enter therapy saying "Allow me to introduce myselves." Instead, charge the critics, some therapists go fishing for multiple identities: "Have you ever felt like another part of you does things you can't control?" "Does this part of you have a name? Can I talk to the angry part of you?" Once clients permit a therapist to talk, by name, "to the part of you that says those angry things," they begin acting out the fantasy. Like actors who lose themselves in their roles, vulnerable patients may "become" the parts they are acting out. The result may be the experience of another self.

Skeptics also find it suspicious that the disorder has such a short and localized history. Between 1930 and 1960, the number of North American DID diagnoses averaged 2 per decade. By the 1980s, when the American Psychiatric Association's *Diagnostic and Statistical Manual of Mental Disorders* (DSM) contained the first formal code for this disorder, the number had exploded to more than 20,000 (McHugh, 1995). The average number of displayed identities also mushroomed—from 3 to 12 per patient (Goff & Simms, 1993). And although diagnoses have been increasing in countries where DID has been publicized, the disorder is much less prevalent outside North America (Lilienfeld, 2017).

Despite some hoaxes, other researchers and clinicians believe DID is a real disorder. They cite findings of distinct body and brain states associated with differing identities (Putnam, 1991). Abnormal brain anatomy and activity can also accompany DID. Brain scans show shrinkage in areas that aid memory and detection of threat (Vermetten et al., 2006). Heightened activity appears in brain areas associated with the control and inhibition of traumatic memories (Elzinga et al., 2007).

Both the psychodynamic and learning perspectives have interpreted DID symptoms as ways of coping with anxiety. Some psychodynamic theorists see them as defenses against the anxiety caused by the eruption of unacceptable impulses. In this view, a second identity enables the discharge of forbidden impulses. Learning theorists see dissociative disorders as behaviors reinforced by anxiety reduction.

Widespread dissociation Shirley Mason was a psychiatric patient diagnosed with dissociative identity disorder. Her life formed the basis of the bestselling book, *Sybil* (Schreiber, 1973), and of two movies. The book and movies' popularity contributed to increased DID diagnoses. Audio recordings revealed that Mason's psychiatrist manipulated her and that she did not actually have the disorder (Nathan, 2011).

Some clinicians include dissociative disorders under the umbrella of posttraumatic stress disorder as a natural, protective response to traumatic experiences during childhood (Brand et al., 2016; Spiegel, 2008). Many people being treated for DID recall being physically, sexually, or emotionally abused as children (Gleaves, 1996; Lilienfeld et al., 1999). Critics wonder, however, whether vivid imagination or therapist suggestion contributed to such recollections (Kihlstrom, 2005). So the scientific debate continues.

> "Though this be madness, yet there is method in 't." —William Shakespeare, *Hamlet*, 1600

ASK YOURSELF
Do you ever flip between displays of different aspects of your identity depending on the situation? How is your experience similar to and different from the described symptoms of dissociative identity disorder?

RETRIEVAL PRACTICE

RP-1 The psychodynamic and learning perspectives agree that dissociative identity disorder symptoms are ways of dealing with anxiety. How do their explanations differ?

ANSWERS IN APPENDIX E

Personality Disorders

LOQ 51-2 What are the three clusters of personality disorders? What behaviors and brain activity characterize antisocial personality disorder?

The inflexible and enduring behavior patterns of **personality disorders** interfere with social functioning. These 10 disorders in DSM-5 tend to form three clusters, characterized by

- *anxiety,* such as a fearful sensitivity to rejection that predisposes the withdrawn *avoidant personality disorder.*

- *eccentric or odd behaviors,* such as those prompted by the magical thinking of *schizotypal personality disorder.*

- *dramatic or impulsive behaviors,* such as the unstable, attention-getting *borderline personality disorder,* the self-focused and self-inflating *narcissistic personality disorder,* and—what we next discuss as an in-depth example—the callous, and often dangerous, *antisocial personality disorder.*

Antisocial Personality Disorder

People with **antisocial personality disorder,** usually male, can display symptoms by age 8. Their lack of conscience becomes plain before age 15, as they begin to lie, steal, fight, or display unrestrained sexual behavior (Cale & Lilienfeld, 2002). Not all children with these traits become antisocial adults, and for many males, antisocial behavior often subsides after adolescence (Moffitt, 2018). (Note that *antisocial* means socially harmful and remorseless, not merely unsociable.) Those who do develop the disorder—about half—will generally act in violent or otherwise criminal ways, be unable to keep a job, and behave irresponsibly toward family members (Farrington, 1991).

No remorse Bruce McArthur, a 66-year-old landscaper in Toronto, shown here in a courtroom sketch, was convicted in 2019 of killing eight people over an eight-year span. He often targeted men who were gay, homeless, or immigrants, storing their remains in boxes at his job sites. McArthur exhibited the extreme lack of remorse that marks antisocial personality disorder.

Stringer/Reuters/Newscom

dissociative identity disorder (DID) a rare dissociative disorder in which a person exhibits two or more distinct and alternating identities. (Formerly called *multiple personality disorder.*)

personality disorders inflexible and enduring behavior patterns that impair social functioning.

antisocial personality disorder a personality disorder in which a person (usually a man) exhibits a lack of conscience for wrongdoing, even toward friends and family members; may be aggressive and ruthless or a clever con artist.

"Thursday is out. I have jury duty."

Many criminals, like this one, display a sense of conscience and responsibility in other areas of their life, and thus do not exhibit antisocial personality disorder.

But criminality is not an essential component of antisocial behavior (Skeem & Cooke, 2010). And many criminals do not exhibit antisocial personality disorder; rather, they show responsible concern for their friends and family members. In contrast with most criminals, people with antisocial personality disorder (sometimes called *sociopaths* or *psychopaths*) are more socially deficient. They often exhibit less *emotional intelligence*—the ability to understand, manage, and perceive emotions (Ermer et al., 2012b; Gillespie et al., 2019).

Antisocial personalities behave impulsively, and then feel and fear little (Fowles & Dindo, 2009). Their impulsivity can have horrific consequences, including homicide (Camp et al., 2013; Fox & DeLisi, 2019). Consider the case of Henry Lee Lucas. He killed his first victim when he was 13. He felt little regret then or later. During his years of crime, he brutally murdered 157 women, men, and children. For the last six years of his reign of terror, Lucas teamed with Ottis Elwood Toole, who reportedly slaughtered people he "didn't think was worth living anyhow" (Darrach & Norris, 1984).

UNDERSTANDING ANTISOCIAL PERSONALITY DISORDER Antisocial personality disorder is woven of both biological and psychological strands. Twin and adoption studies reveal that biological relatives of people with antisocial and unemotional tendencies are at increased risk for antisocial behavior (Frisell et al., 2012; Kendler et al., 2015a). People with antisocial personalities sometimes spread their genes to future generations by marrying others who have antisocial personalities (Weiss, B. et al., 2017). No single gene codes for a complex behavior such as crime. But genes that dispose lower mental ability and self-control predict a higher crime risk (Wertz et al., 2018). As with other disorders, geneticists have also identified specific genes that are more common in those with antisocial personality disorder (Gunter et al., 2010; Tielbeek et al., 2017).

The genetic vulnerability of people with antisocial tendencies appears as low arousal in response to threats. Awaiting aversive events, such as electric shocks or loud noises, they show little autonomic nervous system arousal (Hare, 1975; Ling et al., 2019). Long-term studies show that their stress hormone levels were lower than average as teenagers, before committing any crime (**FIGURE 51.1**). And those who were slow to develop conditioned fears at age 3 were also more likely to commit a crime later in life (Gao et al., 2010). Likewise, preschool boys who later become aggressive or antisocial adolescents tend to be impulsive, uninhibited, unconcerned with social rewards, and low in anxiety (Caspi et al., 1996; Tremblay et al., 1994).

Traits such as fearlessness and dominance can be adaptive. If channeled in more productive directions, fearlessness may lead to athletic stardom, adventurism, or courageous heroism (Costello et al., 2018; Patton et al., 2018). Indeed, 42 American presidents exhibited higher than usual fearlessness and dominance (Lilienfeld et al., 2012, 2016). Patient S. M., a 49-year-old woman with amygdala damage, showed fearlessness and impulsivity but also heroism: She gave a man in need her only coat and scarf, and donated her hair to the Locks of Love charity after befriending a child with cancer (Lilienfeld et al., 2017). Lacking a sense of social responsibility, however, the same disposition may produce a cool con artist or killer (Lykken, 1995).

Genetic influences, often in combination with negative environmental factors such as childhood abuse, family instability, or poverty, help wire the brain (Dodge, 2009). This gene–environment combination also occurs in chimpanzees, which, like humans, vary in antisocial (mean/bold/disinhibited) tendencies (Latzman et al., 2017). In people with antisocial criminal tendencies, the emotion-controlling amygdala is often smaller (Pardini et al., 2014).

The frontal lobes are also less active, as shown by PET scans of 41 murderers' brains compared with those from people of similar age and sex (Raine, 1999, 2005; **FIGURE 51.2**). The frontal lobes help control impulses. The reduced activation was especially apparent in those who murdered impulsively. In a follow-up study, Adrian Raine and his team (2000) found that violent repeat offenders had 11 percent less frontal lobe tissue than normal. This helps explain why people with antisocial personality disorder exhibit marked deficits in frontal lobe cognitive functions, such as planning, organization, and inhibition (Morgan & Lilienfeld, 2000). Compared with people who feel and display empathy, their brains also respond less to facial displays of others' distress, which may contribute to their lower emotional intelligence (Deeley et al., 2006).

FIGURE 51.1

Cold-blooded arousability and risk of crime Levels of the stress hormone adrenaline were measured in two groups of 13-year-old Swedish boys. In both stressful and nonstressful situations, those who would later be convicted of a crime as 18- to 26-year-olds showed relatively low arousal. (Data from Magnusson, 1990.)

Adrenaline excretion (ng/min.)

Males with criminal convictions as adults had lower levels of arousal as 13-year-olds.

- No criminal conviction
- Criminal conviction

Nonstressful situation / Stressful situation

A biologically based fearlessness, as well as early environment, helped explain an unusual family reunion. Long-separated sisters Joyce Lott, 27, and Mary Jones, 29, came together at a place that normally separates family members rather than brings them together—a South Carolina prison where both were sent on drug charges. After a newspaper story about their reunion, their long-lost half-brother Frank Strickland called. But he had his own problem: He was stuck in jail on drug, burglary, and larceny charges (Shepherd et al., 1990).

The genes that put people at risk for antisocial behavior also put people at risk for substance use disorders (Dick, 2007). Disorders often do appear together—for example, depressive disorders and anxiety disorders (Jacobson & Newman, 2017; Plana-Ripoll et al., 2019). People diagnosed with one disorder are at higher risk for being diagnosed with another. Such *comorbidity* results from overlapping genes that predispose different disorders (Brainstorm Consortium, 2018; Gandal et al., 2018).

Genetics alone do not tell the whole story of antisocial crime, however. In another Raine-led study (1996), researchers checked criminal records on nearly 400 Danish men at ages 20 to 22. All these men either had experienced biological risk factors at birth (such as premature birth) or came from family backgrounds marked by poverty and family instability. The researchers then compared each of these two groups with a third *biosocial* group (people whose lives were marked by *both* those biological and social risk factors). The biosocial group had double the risk of committing a crime. Similar findings emerged from a famous study that followed 1037 children for a quarter-century: Two combined factors—childhood maltreatment and a gene that altered neurotransmitter balance—predicted antisocial problems (Caspi et al., 2002). Neither "bad" genes alone nor a "bad" environment alone predisposed later antisocial behavior. Rather, genes predisposed some children to be more sensitive to maltreatment. Within "genetically vulnerable segments of the population," environmental influences matter—for better or for worse (Belsky & Pluess, 2009; Moffitt, 2005).

So, with antisocial behavior—as with so much else—nature and nurture interact. Once again, the biopsychosocial perspective helps us understand the whole story. To further explore the neural basis of antisocial personality disorder, neuroscientists are trying to identify brain activity differences in criminals who display antisocial symptoms. Shown emotionally evocative photographs, such as a man holding a knife to a woman's throat, criminals with antisocial personality disorder display blunted heart rate and perspiration responses, and less activity in brain areas that typically respond to emotional stimuli (Harenski et al., 2010; Kiehl & Buckholtz, 2010). They also have a larger and hyperreactive dopamine reward system, which predisposes their impulsive drive to do something rewarding despite the consequences (Buckholtz et al., 2010; Glenn et al., 2010). Such data provide another reminder: Everything psychological is also biological.

← FIGURE 51.2 Murderous minds Researchers have found reduced activation in a murderer's frontal lobes. This brain area (shown in a left-facing brain) helps brake impulsive, aggressive behavior (Raine, 1999).

Frontal lobes

Does a full Moon trigger "madness" in some people? Researchers examined data from 37 studies that related lunar phase to crime (homicides specifically), crisis calls, and psychiatric hospital admissions (Rotton & Kelley, 1985). Their conclusion: There is virtually no evidence of "Moon madness." Nor does lunar phase correlate with suicides, assaults, emergency room visits, or traffic disasters (Martin et al., 1992; Raison et al., 1999).

RETRIEVAL PRACTICE

RP-2 How do biological and psychological factors contribute to antisocial personality disorder?

ANSWERS IN APPENDIX E

Eating Disorders

LOQ 51-3 What are the three main eating disorders, and how do biological, psychological, and social-cultural influences make people more vulnerable to them?

Our bodies are naturally disposed to maintain a steady weight, including storing energy for times when food becomes unavailable. But sometimes psychological influences overwhelm biological wisdom. This becomes painfully clear in three eating disorders.

- In **anorexia nervosa,** people—usually female adolescents, but some women, men, and boys as well—starve themselves. Anorexia often begins as an attempt to lose weight, but the dieting becomes a habit (Steinglass et al., 2018). Even when far below normal weight, the self-starved person feels fat, fears being fat, and focuses obsessively on losing weight, sometimes exercising excessively.

anorexia nervosa an eating disorder in which a person (usually an adolescent female) maintains a starvation diet despite being significantly underweight, and has an inaccurate self-perception; sometimes accompanied by excessive exercise.

A distorted body image underlies anorexia.

- In **bulimia nervosa,** a cycle of repeated episodes of binge eating alternates with behaviors to compensate, such as vomiting, laxative use, fasting, or excessive exercise (Wonderlich et al., 2007). Unlike anorexia, bulimia is marked by weight fluctuations within or above normal ranges, making the disorder easier to hide. Bulimia may also be triggered by a weight-loss diet that is broken by gorging on forbidden foods. People with this disorder—mostly women in their late teens or early twenties (but also some men)—eat in spurts, sometimes influenced by negative emotion or by friends who are bingeing (Crandall, 1988; Haedt-Matt & Keel, 2011). Preoccupied with food (craving sweet and high-fat foods), and fearful of becoming overweight, binge-purge eaters experience bouts of depression, guilt, and anxiety during and following binges (Hinz & Williamson, 1987; Johnson et al., 2002).

- Those with **binge-eating disorder** engage in significant bouts of bingeing, followed by remorse. But they do not purge, fast, or exercise excessively.

At some point during their lifetime, about 2.6 million Americans (.8 percent) meet DSM-5-defined criteria for anorexia, 2.6 million for bulimia, and 2.7 million for binge-eating disorder (Udo & Grilo, 2019). All three disorders can be deadly. They harm the body and mind, resulting in shorter life expectancy and greater risk of suicide and nonsuicidal self-injury (Cucchi et al., 2016; Fichter & Quadflieg, 2016; Mandelli et al., 2019).

Understanding Eating Disorders

Eating disorders are *not* (as some have speculated) a telltale sign of childhood sexual abuse (Smolak & Murnen, 2002; Stice, 2002). The family environment may influence eating disorders in other ways, however. For example, the families of those with anorexia tend to be competitive, high-achieving, and protective (Ahrén et al., 2013; Berg et al., 2014; Yates, 1989, 1990). Those with eating disorders often have low body satisfaction, set perfectionist standards, and ruminate about falling short of expectations and how others perceive them (Farstad et al., 2016; Smith, M. et al., 2018; Wang, S. et al., 2019). Some of these factors also predict teen boys' pursuit of unrealistic muscularity (Karazsia et al., 2017; Ricciardelli & McCabe, 2004).

Heredity also matters. Identical twins share these disorders more often than do fraternal twins—to an extent indicating 50 to 60 percent heritability for anorexia (Yilmaz et al., 2015). Scientists are searching for culprit genes. The largest study identified gene differences by comparing the genomes of nearly 17,000 anorexia patients with 56,000 others (Watson et al., 2019).

But eating disorders also have cultural and gender components. Ideal shapes vary across culture and time. Plump may mean prosperity and thin may signal poverty or illness in countries with high poverty rates (Knickmeyer, 2001; Swami et al., 2010). Not so in wealthy Western cultures. In one analysis of 222 studies, the rise in eating disorders in the last half of the twentieth century coincided with a dramatic decline in Western women's body image (Feingold & Mazzella, 1998).

Those most vulnerable to eating disorders have also been those (usually women or gay men) who most idealize thinness and have the greatest body dissatisfaction (Feldman & Meyer, 2010; Kane, 2010; Stice et al., 2010). Should it surprise us, then, that women who view real and doctored images of unnaturally thin models and celebrities often feel ashamed, depressed, and dissatisfied with their own bodies—the very attitudes that predispose eating disorders (Bould et al., 2018; Tiggemann & Miller, 2010)? Eric Stice and his colleagues (2001) tested this modeling idea by giving some adolescent girls (but not others) a 15-month subscription to an American teen-fashion magazine. Compared with those who had not received the magazine, vulnerable girls—defined as those who were already dissatisfied, idealizing thinness, and lacking social support—exhibited increased body dissatisfaction and eating disorder tendencies. Even ultra-thin models do not reflect the impossible standard of the original Barbie doll, who had, when adjusted to a height of 5 feet 7 inches, a 32–16–29 figure (in centimeters, 81–41–74) (Norton et al., 1996).

There is, however, more to body dissatisfaction and anorexia than media effects (Ferguson et al., 2011). Peer influences, such as teasing and harassment, also matter. Nevertheless, the sickness of today's eating disorders stems in part from today's

bulimia nervosa an eating disorder in which a person's binge eating (usually of high-calorie foods) is followed by inappropriate weight-loss-promoting behavior, such as vomiting, laxative use, fasting, or excessive exercise.

binge-eating disorder significant binge-eating episodes, followed by distress, disgust, or guilt, but without the compensatory behavior that marks bulimia nervosa.

weight-obsessed culture—a culture that says "fat is bad" in countless ways, that motivates millions of women to diet constantly, and that invites eating binges by pressuring women to live in a constant state of semistarvation. One former model recalled walking into a meeting with her agent, starving and with her organs failing due to anorexia (Carroll, 2013). Her agent's greeting: "Whatever you are doing, keep doing it."

Most people diagnosed with an eating disorder do improve. In one 22-year study, 2 in 3 women with anorexia nervosa or bulimia nervosa had recovered (Eddy et al., 2017). Prevention is also possible. Interactive programs that teach teen girls to accept their bodies have reduced the risk of eating disorders (Beintner et al., 2012; Melioli et al., 2016; Vocks et al., 2010). By combating cultural learning, those at risk may instead live long and healthy lives.

"Up until that point, Bernice had never once had a problem with low self-esteem."

"Why do women have such low self-esteem? There are many complex psychological and societal reasons, by which I mean Barbie."
— Humorist Dave Barry, 1999

RETRIEVAL PRACTICE

RP-3 People with _____ _____ (anorexia nervosa/ bulimia nervosa) continue to want to lose weight even when they are underweight. Those with _____ _____ (anorexia nervosa/ bulimia nervosa) tend to have a weight that fluctuates within or above normal ranges.

ANSWERS IN APPENDIX E

MODULE 51 REVIEW Dissociative, Personality, and Eating Disorders

LEARNING OBJECTIVES

Test Yourself Answer these repeated Learning Objective Questions on your own (before checking the answers in Appendix D) to improve your retention of the concepts (McDaniel et al., 2009, 2015).

LOQ 51-1 What are *dissociative disorders,* and why are they controversial?

LOQ 51-2 What are the three clusters of personality disorders? What behaviors and brain activity characterize antisocial personality disorder?

LOQ 51-3 What are the three main eating disorders, and how do biological, psychological, and social-cultural influences make people more vulnerable to them?

TERMS AND CONCEPTS TO REMEMBER

Test Yourself Write down the definition in your own words, then check your answer.

dissociative disorders, p. 585
dissociative identity disorder (DID), p. 587

personality disorders, p. 587
antisocial personality disorder, p. 587

anorexia nervosa, p. 589
bulimia nervosa, p. 590

binge-eating disorder, p. 590

MASTER THE MATERIAL

Test Yourself Answer the following questions on your own first, then check your answers in Appendix E.

1. Dissociative identity disorder is controversial because
   a. dissociation is quite rare.
   b. it was reported frequently in the 1920s but is rarely reported today.
   c. it is almost never reported outside North America.
   d. its symptoms are nearly identical to those of obsessive-compulsive disorder.

2. A personality disorder, such as antisocial personality, is characterized by
   a. depression.
   b. hallucinations.
   c. inflexible and enduring behavior patterns that impair social functioning.
   d. an elevated level of autonomic nervous system arousal.

3. PET scans of murderers' brains have revealed

   a. higher-than-normal activation in the frontal lobes.

   b. lower-than-normal activation in the frontal lobes.

   c. more frontal lobe tissue than normal.

   d. no differences in brain structures or activity.

4. Which of the following statements is true of bulimia nervosa?

   a. People with bulimia continue to want to lose weight even when they are underweight.

   b. Bulimia is marked by weight fluctuations within or above normal ranges.

   c. Those with bulimia are equally likely to be male or female.

   d. If one twin is diagnosed with bulimia, the chances of the other twin sharing the disorder are greater if they are fraternal rather than identical twins.

Continue testing yourself with ⚞ **LearningCurve** or ⚞ **Achieve Read & Practice** to learn and remember most effectively.

MODULE 52 Neurodevelopmental Disorders

Neurodevelopmental disorders are defined by central nervous system abnormalities, typically in the brain. The result is altered thinking and behavior, starting in childhood, that can manifest as intellectual limitations or as psychological disorders.

Intellectual Disability

LOQ 52-1 What is an *intellectual disability*?

Intellectual disability is apparent before age 18, often with a known physical cause. (*Down syndrome*, for example, is a disorder of varying intellectual and physical severity caused by an extra copy of chromosome 21 in the person's genetic makeup.) To be diagnosed with an intellectual disability, a person must meet two criteria. The first is low intellectual functioning as reflected in a low intelligence test score. Guidelines specify test score performance that is in the lowest 3 percent of the general population, or about 70 or below (Schalock et al., 2010). The second criterion is that the person must have difficulty adapting to the normal demands of independent living, as expressed in three areas, or skills: conceptual (language, reading, and concepts of money, time, and number); social (interpersonal skills, being socially responsible, following basic rules and laws, avoiding being victimized); and practical (health and personal care, occupational skill, and travel). In mild forms, intellectual disability, like normal intelligence, results from a combination of genetic and environmental factors (Reichenberg et al., 2016).

RETRIEVAL PRACTICE

RP-1 What criteria must be met for someone to be diagnosed with an intellectual disability?

ANSWERS IN APPENDIX E

Autism Spectrum Disorder

LOQ 52-2 What is *autism spectrum disorder*?

Autism spectrum disorder (ASD) is a cognitive and social-emotional disorder that is marked by social deficiencies and repetitive behaviors. Once believed to affect 1 in 2500 children (and referred to simply as *autism*), ASD is now diagnosed in 1 in 38 children in South Korea, 1 in 59 in the United States, 1 in 66 in Canada, and 1 in 100 in Britain (Baio et al., 2018; CDC, 2014b; Kim et al., 2011; NAS, 2011; Offner et al., 2018). The increase in ASD diagnoses has been offset by a decrease in the number of children with a "cognitive disability" or "learning disability," which suggests a relabeling of children's disorders (Gernsbacher et al., 2005; Grinker, 2007; Shattuck, 2006).

 neurodevelopmental disorder central nervous system abnormalities (usually in the brain) that start in childhood and alter thinking and behavior (as in intellectual limitations or a psychological disorder).

intellectual disability a condition of limited mental ability, indicated by an intelligence test score of 70 or below and difficulty adapting to the demands of life. (Formerly referred to as *mental retardation*.)

autism spectrum disorder (ASD) a disorder that appears in childhood and is marked by significant limitations in communication and social interaction, and by rigidly fixated interests and repetitive behaviors.

Autism spectrum disorder This speech-language pathologist is helping a boy with ASD learn to form sounds and words. ASD is marked by limited communication ability and difficulty grasping others' states of mind.

The underlying source of ASD's symptoms seems to be poor communication among brain regions that normally work together to let us take another's viewpoint. From age 2 months on, children typically spend more and more time looking into others' eyes; those who later develop ASD do so less and less (Baron-Cohen, 2017; Wang et al., 2020). People with ASD have an *impaired theory of mind* (Matthews & Goldberg, 2018; Velikonja et al., 2019). Mind reading that most of us find intuitive *(Is that face conveying a smile or a sneer?)* is difficult for those with ASD. They have difficulty inferring and remembering others' thoughts and feelings, appreciating that playmates and parents might view things differently, and understanding that their teachers know more than they do (Boucher et al., 2012; Frith & Frith, 2001; Knutsen et al., 2015). Partly for such reasons, a national survey of parents and school staff reported that 46 percent of adolescents with ASD had suffered the taunts and torments of bullying—four times the 11 percent rate for other children (Sterzing et al., 2012). Children with ASD do make friends, but their peers often find such relationships emotionally unsatisfying (Mendelson et al., 2016). This helps explain why "individuals with ASD are 4-times more likely to experience depression in their lifetime" (Hudson et al., 2019).

ASD has differing levels of severity. About half of people with ASD experience a "fair" or even "good" outcome (Steinhausen et al., 2016). Some (those diagnosed with what used to be called *Asperger syndrome*) generally function at a high level. They have normal intelligence, often accompanied by exceptional skill or talent in a specific area. One study of 6500 people in 104 countries found that people with autistic traits displayed a slightly better than average understanding of social psychological phenomena, such as social loafing and groupthink (Gollwitzer et al., 2019). But those with ASD may lack the motivation and ability to interact and communicate socially, and they tend to become distracted by irrelevant stimuli (Clements et al., 2018; Remington et al., 2009). Those at the spectrum's more severe end struggle to use language.

ASD gets diagnosed in about three boys for every girl, perhaps partly because girls may be more skilled in hiding ASD-related traits (Dean et al., 2017; Loomes et al., 2017). Psychologist Simon Baron-Cohen (2010) believes the imbalance is because boys, more often than girls, are "systemizers." They tend to understand things according to rules or laws, as in mathematical and mechanical systems. Girls, he contends, are more often predisposed to be "empathizers." They tend to excel at reading facial expressions and gestures (van Honk et al., 2011). Whether male or female, those with ASD are systemizers who have more difficulty reading facial expressions (Baron-Cohen et al., 2015). People working in STEM (science, technology, engineering, or mathematics) careers are also somewhat more likely than others to exhibit some ASD-like traits (Ruzich et al., 2015).

Biological factors contribute to ASD (Zhou et al., 2019). Prenatal environment matters, especially when altered by maternal infection, psychiatric drug use, or stress hormones (NIH, 2013; Wang, 2014). Genes also matter. One five-nation study of 2 million individuals found the heritability of ASD was near 80 percent (Bai et al., 2019). If one identical twin is diagnosed with ASD, the chances are 50 to 70 percent that the co-twin will be as well (Tick et al., 2016). No one "autism gene" accounts for the disorder. Rather, many

"I'm autistic, which means everyone around me has a disorder that makes them . . . creepily stare into my eyeballs." — Facebook. com/autisticnotweird, 2020

"Autism makes my life difficult, but it also makes my life beautiful. When everything is more intense, then the everyday, the mundane, the typical, the normal — those things become outstanding." — Erin McKinney, "The Best Way I Can Describe What It's Like to Have Autism," 2015

"Autism" case number 1 In 1943, Donald Gray Triplett, an "odd" child with unusual gifts and social limitations, was the first person to receive the diagnosis of "autism." (After a 2013 change in the diagnosis manual, his condition is now called *autism spectrum disorder.*) In 2016, at age 82, Triplett was still living in his family home and Mississippi town, where he often played golf (Atlas, 2016).

genes—with more than 400 identified so far—appear to contribute (Krishnan et al., 2016; Yuen et al., 2016). Random genetic mutations in sperm cells may also play a role. As men age, these mutations become more frequent, which may help explain why an over-40 man has a much higher risk of fathering a child with ASD than does a man under 30 (Wu et al., 2017).

Researchers are also sleuthing ASD's telltale signs in the brain's structure. Several studies have revealed "underconnectivity"—fewer-than-normal fiber tracts connecting the front of the brain to the back (Picci et al., 2016). With underconnectivity, there is less of the whole-brain synchrony that, for example, integrates visual and emotional information. In children as young as 3 months, EEG-recorded brain activity can foretell ASD (Bosl et al., 2018).

Biology's role in ASD also appears in the brain's functioning. People without ASD often yawn after seeing others yawn. And as they view and imitate another's smiling or frowning, they feel something of what the other is feeling. Not so among those with ASD, who are less imitative and show less activity in brain areas involved in mirroring others' actions (Edwards, 2014; Yang & Hofmann, 2015). When people with ASD watch another person's hand movements, for example, their brain displays less-than-normal mirroring activity (Oberman & Ramachandran, 2007; Théoret et al., 2005). Scientists are exploring and debating this idea that the brains of people with ASD have "broken mirrors" (Gallese et al., 2011; Schulte-Rüther et al., 2016). And they are exploring whether treatment with oxytocin, the hormone that promotes social bonding, might improve social understanding in those with ASD (Gordon et al., 2013; Lange & McDougle, 2013).

What does *not* contribute to ASD? Childhood vaccinations, which—despite a fraudulent 1998 study claiming otherwise—have *no* relationship to the disorder (Taylor et al., 2014). For example, in one recent study following nearly 700,000 Danish children, those receiving the measles/mumps/rubella vaccine were actually slightly *less* likely to later be among the 6517 children diagnosed with ASD (Hviid et al., 2019).

Attention-Deficit/Hyperactivity Disorder

For children who experience the challenging symptoms of **attention-deficit/hyperactivity disorder (ADHD),** diagnosis and treatment can help (Kupfer, 2012; Maciejewski et al., 2016). The DSM has broadened the diagnostic criteria for this disorder. However, critics suggest that these criteria are now too broad and may turn normal, childish rambunctiousness into a disorder (Frances, 2013, 2014). Shall we say such a child is hyperactive—or energetic? Impulsive—or spontaneous? Excessively talkative—or excited? One 10-year study in Sweden found children's attentional behaviors unchanging, while national ADHD diagnoses increased fivefold (Rydell et al., 2018). (See Thinking Critically About: ADHD—Normal High Energy or Disordered Behavior?)

* * *

The bewilderment, fear, and sorrow caused by psychological disorders are real. But, as the Therapy modules show, hope, too, is real.

attention-deficit/hyperactivity disorder (ADHD) a psychological disorder marked by extreme inattention and/or hyperactivity and impulsivity.

Thinking Critically About:

ADHD—Normal High Energy or Disordered Behavior?

LOQ 52-3 Why is there controversy over attention-deficit/hyperactivity disorder?

Diagnosis in the U.S.

9.4%[1] 2- to 17-year-olds

2.5%[2] adults

Less often in many other countries, such as Norway and Sweden[3]

Twice as often in BOYS as in girls

Symptoms

- inattention and distractibility[4]
- hyperactivity[5]
- impulsivity

SKEPTICS note:

Energetic child + boring school = ADHD overdiagnosis

- Children are not designed to sit for hours in chairs inside.
- The youngest children in a class tend to be more fidgety—and more often diagnosed.[6]
- Older students may seek out stimulant ADHD prescription drugs–"good-grade pills."[7]
- What are the long-term effects of drug treatment?
- Why the increase in ADHD diagnoses and drugs?[8]

SUPPORTERS note:

- More diagnoses reflect increased awareness.
- "ADHD is a real neurobiological disorder whose existence should no longer be debated."[9]
- ADHD is associated with abnormal brain structure, abnormal brain activity patterns, and future risky or antisocial behavior.[10]

Causes?

- May co-exist with a learning disorder or with defiant and temper-prone behavior.
- May be genetic.[11]

Treatment

- Stimulant drugs (Ritalin and Adderall) calm hyperactivity, and increase ability to sit and focus.[12] So do behavior therapy and aerobic exercise.[13]
- Psychological therapies help with the distress of ADHD.[14]

The bottom line:

Extreme inattention, hyperactivity, and impulsivity can derail social, academic, and work achievements. These symptoms can be treated with medication and other therapies. But the debate continues over whether normal high energy is too often diagnosed as a psychiatric disorder, and whether there is a cost to the long-term use of stimulant drugs in treating ADHD.

1. CDC, 2019a. 2. Simon et al., 2009. 3. MacDonald et al., 2019; Smith, 2017. 4. Martel et al., 2016. 5. Kofler et al., 2016. 6. Chen, M. et al., 2016. 7. Schwarz, 2012. 8. Ellison, 2015. Hales et al., 2018; Sayal et al., 2017. 9. World Federation for Mental Health, 2005. 10. Ball et al, 2019; Hoogman et al., 2019. 11. Nikolas & Burt, 2010; Poelmans et al., 2011; Volkow et al., 2009; Williams et al., 2010. 12. Barbaresi et al., 2007. 13. Cerrillo-Urbina et al., 2015; Pelham et al., 2016. 14. Fabiano et al., 2008.

MODULE

52 REVIEW Neurodevelopmental Disorders

LEARNING OBJECTIVES

Test Yourself Answer these repeated Learning Objective Questions on your own (before checking the answers in Appendix D) to improve your retention of the concepts (McDaniel et al., 2009, 2015).

LOQ 52-1 What is an *intellectual disability*?

LOQ 52-2 What is *autism spectrum disorder*?

LOQ 52-3 Why is there controversy over attention-deficit/ hyperactivity disorder?

TERMS AND CONCEPTS TO REMEMBER

Test Yourself Write down the definition in your own words, then check your answer.

neurodevelopmental disorders, p. 592

intellectual disability, p. 592

autism spectrum disorder (ASD), p. 592

attention-deficit/hyperactivity disorder (ADHD), p. 594

MASTER THE MATERIAL

Test Yourself Answer the following questions on your own first, then check your answers in Appendix E.

1. Which of the following statements is true of intellectual disability?

    a. People with this condition can generally adapt to the normal demands of independent living.

    b. This condition typically presents with no known physical cause.

    c. People with this condition have an intelligence test score of about 70 or below.

    d. People with this condition are systemizers who tend to have difficulty reading facial expressions.

2. Some researchers have suggested that the brains of people with ASD have "broken mirrors." What do they mean by this?

3. Some critics believe that the DSM-5 may pathologize everyday life and normal behaviors. How does the ADHD controversy relate to this concern?

Continue testing yourself with 📖 **LearningCurve** or 📖 **Achieve Read & Practice** to learn and remember most effectively.

Caiaimage/Tom Merton/Getty Images

Therapy

Kay Redfield Jamison is both an award-winning clinical psychologist and a world expert on the emotional extremes of bipolar disorders. She knows her subject firsthand, as she recalled in *An Unquiet Mind:*

> For as long as I can remember, I was frighteningly, although often wonderfully, beholden to moods. Intensely emotional as a child, mercurial as a young girl, first severely depressed as an adolescent, and then unrelentingly caught up in the cycles of manic-depressive illness [now known as bipolar disorder I] by the time I began my professional life, I became, both by necessity and intellectual inclination, a student of moods. (1995, pp. 4–5)

Jamison's life was blessed with times of intense sensitivity and passionate energy. But like her father's, it was also sometimes plagued by reckless spending, racing conversation, and sleeplessness, alternating with swings into "the blackest caves of the mind."

Then, "in the midst of utter confusion," she made a life-changing decision. Risking professional embarrassment, she made an appointment with a therapist, a psychiatrist she would visit weekly for years to come.

> He kept me alive a thousand times over. He saw me through madness, despair, wonderful and terrible love affairs, disillusionments and triumphs, recurrences of illness, an almost fatal suicide attempt, the death of a man I greatly loved, and the enormous pleasures and aggravations of my professional life. . . . He was very tough, as well as very kind, and even though he understood more than anyone how much I felt I was losing—in energy, vivacity, and originality—by taking medication, he never [lost] sight of the overall perspective of how costly, damaging, and life threatening my illness was. . . . Although I went to him to be treated for an illness, he taught me . . . the total beholdenness of brain to mind and mind to brain. (pp. 87–88)

597

Actor Kerry Washington and singer Katy Perry have also shared openly about the benefits of psychotherapy. "I've been going to therapy for about five years," Perry says, "and I think it has really helped my mental health incredibly" (Chen, 2017). Catherine, Duchess of Cambridge (a.k.a. Kate Middleton), has worked on reducing the stigma surrounding mental illness and therapy: "We need to help young people and their parents understand that it's not a sign of weakness to ask for help" (Holmes, 2015).

These modules explore some of the healing options available to therapists and the people who seek their help. We begin by exploring and evaluating *psychotherapies* (Modules 53 and 54), and then focus on *biomedical therapies* and preventing disorders (Module 55).

53 Introduction to Therapy and the Psychological Therapies

Dorothea Dix "I . . . call your attention to the state of the Insane Persons confined within this Commonwealth, in cages." *(Memorial to the Legislature of Massachusetts, 1843)*

The long history of efforts to treat psychological disorders has included a bewildering mix of harsh and gentle methods. Would-be healers have cut holes in people's heads and restrained, bled, or "beat the devil" out of them. But they also have given warm baths and massages and placed people in sunny, serene environments. They have given them drugs. And they have talked with them about childhood experiences, current feelings, and maladaptive thoughts and behaviors.

Reformers Philippe Pinel (1745–1826) and Dorothea Dix (1802–1887) pushed for gentler, more humane treatments and for constructing psychiatric hospitals. Their efforts largely paid off. Since the 1950s, the introduction of effective drug therapies and community-based treatment programs has emptied most of those hospitals. Unfortunately, this *deinstitutionalization* has contributed to increased homelessness and incarceration. Today, 1 in 5 Americans receives some form of outpatient mental health therapy (Olfson et al., 2019).

The history of treatment Visitors to eighteenth-century psychiatric hospitals paid to gawk at patients, as though they were viewing zoo animals. William Hogarth's (1697–1764) painting captured one of these visits to London's St. Mary of Bethlehem hospital (commonly called Bedlam).

Treating Psychological Disorders

LEARNING OBJECTIVE QUESTION **LOQ** **53-1** How do *psychotherapy* and the *biomedical therapies* differ?

Modern Western therapies can be classified into two main categories.

- In **psychotherapy,** a trained therapist uses psychological techniques to assist someone seeking to overcome difficulties and achieve personal growth. The therapist may explore a client's early relationships, encourage the client to adopt new ways of thinking, or coach the client in replacing old behaviors with new ones.

- **Biomedical therapy** offers medications and other biological treatments. For example, a person with severe depression may receive antidepressants, electroconvulsive shock therapy (ECT), or deep brain stimulation.

The care provider's training and expertise, as well as the disorder itself, influence the choice of treatment. Psychotherapy and medication are often combined. Kay Redfield Jamison received psychotherapy in her meetings with her psychiatrist, and she took medications to control her wild mood swings.

Let's look first at some influential psychotherapy options for those treated with "talk therapies." Each is built on one or more of psychology's major theories: psychodynamic, humanistic, behavioral, and cognitive. Most of these techniques can be used one-on-one or in groups, in person or online. Some therapists combine techniques. Indeed, many psychotherapists describe their approach as **eclectic,** using a blend of therapies.

Psychoanalysis and Psychodynamic Therapies

LOQ **53-2** What are the goals and techniques of psychoanalysis, and how have they been adapted in psychodynamic therapy?

The first major psychological therapy was Sigmund Freud's **psychoanalysis.** Although few clinicians today practice therapy as Freud did, his work deserves discussion. It helped form the foundation for treating psychological disorders, and it continues to influence modern therapists working from the *psychodynamic* perspective.

The Goals of Psychoanalysis

Freud believed that in therapy, people could achieve healthier, less anxious living by releasing the energy they had previously devoted to id-ego-superego conflicts. Freud assumed that we do not fully know ourselves. He believed that there are threatening things we *repress*—things we do not want to know, so we disavow or deny them. Psychoanalysis was Freud's method of helping people to bring these repressed feelings into conscious awareness. By helping them reclaim their unconscious thoughts and feelings, and by giving them *insight* into the origins of their disorders, the therapist (*analyst*) could help them reduce growth-impeding inner conflicts.

The Techniques of Psychoanalysis

Psychoanalytic theory emphasizes the power of childhood experiences to mold the adult. Thus, psychoanalysis is historical reconstruction. It aims to unearth the past in the hope of loosening its bonds on the present. After discarding hypnosis as an unreliable excavator, Freud turned to *free association*.

Imagine yourself as a patient using free association. You begin by relaxing, perhaps by lying on a couch. The psychoanalyst, who sits out of your line of vision, asks you to say aloud whatever comes to mind. At one moment, you're relating a childhood memory. At another, you're describing a dream or recent experience. It sounds easy, but soon you notice how often you edit your thoughts as you speak. You pause for a second before uttering an embarrassing thought. You omit what seems trivial, irrelevant, or shameful. Sometimes your mind goes blank or you clutch up, unable to remember important details. You may joke or change the subject to something less threatening.

To the analyst, these mental blocks indicate **resistance.** They hint that anxiety lurks and you are defending against sensitive material. The analyst will note your resistance and then provide insight into its meaning. If offered at the right moment, this **interpretation**—of, say, your reluctance to call or message your mother—may illuminate the underlying wishes, feelings, and conflicts you are avoiding. The analyst may also offer an explanation of how this resistance fits with other pieces of your psychological puzzle, including those based on analysis of your dream content.

Over many such sessions, your relationship patterns surface in your interaction with your analyst. You may find yourself experiencing strong positive or negative feelings for this confidant. The analyst may suggest you are **transferring** feelings, such as dependency or mingled love and anger, that you experienced in earlier relationships with family members or other important people. By exposing such feelings, you may gain insight into your current relationships.

Relatively few North American therapists now offer traditional psychoanalysis. Much of its underlying theory is not supported by scientific research. Analysts' interpretations cannot be proven or disproven. And psychoanalysis takes considerable time and money, often years of several sessions per week. Some of these problems have been addressed in the modern *psychodynamic perspective* that has evolved from psychoanalysis.

psychotherapy treatment involving psychological techniques; consists of interactions between a trained therapist and someone seeking to overcome psychological difficulties or achieve personal growth.

biomedical therapy prescribed medications or procedures that act directly on the person's physiology.

eclectic approach an approach to psychotherapy that uses techniques from various forms of therapy.

psychoanalysis Sigmund Freud's therapeutic technique. Freud believed the patient's free associations, resistances, dreams, and transferences—and the analyst's interpretations of them—released previously repressed feelings, allowing the patient to gain self-insight.

resistance in psychoanalysis, the blocking from consciousness of anxiety-laden material.

interpretation in psychoanalysis, the analyst's noting of supposed dream meanings, resistances, and other significant behaviors and events in order to promote insight.

transference in psychoanalysis, the patient's transfer to the analyst of emotions linked with other relationships (such as love or hatred for a parent).

"I'm more interested in hearing about the eggs you're hiding from yourself."

Paul Noth/The New Yorker Collection/ The Cartoon Bank

"Freud is the father of psychoanalysis. It had no mother." — Germaine Greer, *The Female Eunuch*, 1970

Psychodynamic Therapy

Although influenced by Freud's ideas, **psychodynamic therapists** don't talk much about id-ego-superego conflicts. Instead they try to help people understand their current symptoms by focusing on important relationships and events, including childhood experiences and the therapist-client relationship. "We can have loving feelings and hateful feelings toward the same person," observed psychodynamic therapist Jonathan Shedler (2009), and "we can desire something and also fear it." Client-therapist meetings take place once or twice a week (rather than several times weekly) and often for only a few weeks or months. Rather than lying on a couch, out of the therapist's line of vision, clients meet with their therapist face-to-face (or online) and gain perspective by exploring defended-against thoughts and feelings.

Therapist David Shapiro (1999, p. 8) illustrated this with the case of a young man who had told women that he loved them but knew that he didn't. The client's explanation: They expected it, so he said it. But later, with his wife, who wished he would say that he loved her, he found himself unable—"I don't know why, but I can't."

> *Therapist: Do you mean, then, that if you could, you would like to?*
>
> *Patient: Well, I don't know. . . . Maybe I can't say it because I'm not sure it's true. Maybe I don't love her.*

Further interactions revealed that the client could not express real love because it would feel "mushy" and "soft" and therefore unmanly. He was "in conflict with himself, and . . . cut off from the nature of that conflict." Shapiro noted that with such patients, who are estranged from themselves, therapists using psychodynamic techniques "are in a position to introduce them to themselves. We can restore their awareness of their own wishes and feelings, and their awareness, as well, of their reactions against those wishes and feelings." Thus, without embracing all of Freud's theory, psychodynamic therapists aim to help people gain insight into unconscious dynamics that arise from their life experience.

Humanistic Therapies

 LOQ **53-3** What are the basic themes of humanistic therapy? What are the goals and techniques of Rogers' person-centered approach?

The *humanistic* perspective emphasizes people's innate potential for self-fulfillment. Not surprisingly, humanistic therapies attempt to reduce the inner conflicts that interfere with natural development and growth. To achieve this goal, humanistic therapists try to help clients discover new insights. Indeed, because they share this goal, the psychodynamic and humanistic therapies are often referred to as **insight therapies.** But humanistic therapies differ from psychodynamic therapies in many ways:

- Humanistic therapists aim to boost people's self-fulfillment by helping them grow in self-awareness and self-acceptance.

- Promoting this growth, not curing illness, is the therapy focus. Thus, those in therapy are called "persons" or "clients" rather than "patients" (a change many other therapists have adopted).

- The path to growth is taking immediate responsibility for one's feelings and actions, rather than uncovering hidden determinants.

psychodynamic therapy therapy deriving from the psychoanalytic tradition; views individuals as responding to unconscious forces and childhood experiences, and seeks to enhance self-insight.

insight therapies therapies that aim to improve psychological functioning by increasing a person's awareness of underlying motives and defenses.

person-centered therapy a humanistic therapy, developed by Carl Rogers, in which the therapist uses techniques such as *active listening* within an accepting, genuine, empathic environment to facilitate clients' growth. (Also called *client-centered therapy.*)

active listening empathic listening in which the listener echoes, restates, and seeks clarification. A feature of Rogers' person-centered therapy.

- Conscious thoughts are more important than unconscious thoughts.
- The present and future are more important than the past. Therapy thus focuses on exploring feelings as they occur, rather than on achieving insights into the childhood origins of those feelings.

All these themes are present in the widely used humanistic technique that Carl Rogers (1902–1987) developed and called **person-centered therapy.** In this *nondirective therapy*, the client leads the discussion. The therapist listens, without judging or interpreting, and refrains from directing the client toward certain insights. Believing that most people possess the resources for growth, Rogers (1961, 1980) encouraged therapists to foster that growth by exhibiting acceptance, genuineness, and empathy. By being *accepting*, therapists may help clients feel freer and more open to change. By being *genuine*, therapists hope to encourage clients to likewise express their true feelings. By being *empathic*, therapists try to sense and reflect their clients' feelings, helping them experience a deeper self-understanding and self-acceptance (Hill & Nakayama, 2000). As Rogers (1980) explained,

> Hearing has consequences. When I truly hear a person and the meanings that are important to him at that moment, hearing not simply his words, but him, and when I let him know that I have heard his own private personal meanings, many things happen. There is first of all a grateful look. He feels released. He wants to tell me more about his world. He surges forth in a new sense of freedom. He becomes more open to the process of change.
>
> I have often noticed that the more deeply I hear the meanings of the person, the more there is that happens. Almost always, when a person realizes he has been deeply heard, his eyes moisten. I think in some real sense he is weeping for joy. It is as though he were saying, "Thank God, somebody heard me. Someone knows what it's like to be me." (p. 10)

To Rogers, "hearing" was **active listening.** The therapist echoes, restates, and seeks clarification of what the person expresses (verbally or nonverbally). The therapist also acknowledges those expressed feelings. Active listening is now an accepted part of counseling practices in many schools, colleges, and clinics. Counselors listen attentively. They interrupt only to restate and confirm feelings, to accept what is being expressed, or to seek clarification. In the following brief excerpt, note how Rogers tried to provide a psychological mirror that would help the client see himself more clearly (Meador & Rogers, 1984, p. 167):

Rogers: Feeling that now, hm? That you're just no good to yourself, no good to anybody. Never will be any good to anybody. Just that you're completely worthless, huh?—Those really are lousy feelings. Just feel that you're no good at all, hm?

Client: Yeah. (*Muttering in low, discouraged voice*) That's what this guy I went to town with just the other day told me.

Rogers: This guy that you went to town with really told you that you were no good? Is that what you're saying? Did I get that right?

Client: M-hm.

Active listening Carl Rogers (right) empathized with a client during this group therapy session.

Michael Rougier/Getty Images

Rogers: I guess the meaning of that if I get it right is that here's somebody that— meant something to you and what does he think of you? Why, he's told you that he thinks you're no good at all. And that just really knocks the props out from under you. *(Client weeps quietly.)* It just brings the tears. *(Silence of 20 seconds)*

Client: (Rather defiantly) I don't care though.

Rogers: You tell yourself you don't care at all, but somehow I guess some part of you cares because some part of you weeps over it.

> "We have two ears and one mouth that we may listen the more and talk the less."
> — Zeno, 335–263 B.C.E., *Diogenes Laertius*

Can a therapist be a perfect mirror, without selecting and interpreting what is reflected? Rogers conceded that one cannot be *totally* nondirective. Nevertheless, he said, the therapist's most important contribution is to accept and understand the client. Given a nonjudgmental, grace-filled environment that provides **unconditional positive regard,** people may accept even their worst traits and feel valued and whole.

How can we improve communication in our own relationships by listening more actively? Three Rogers-inspired hints may help:

1. *Paraphrase.* Check your understanding by summarizing the person's words out loud, in your own words.

2. *Invite clarification.* "What might be an example of that?" may encourage the person to say more.

3. *Reflect feelings.* "It sounds frustrating" might mirror what you're sensing from the person's body language and intensity.

ASK YOURSELF

Think of your closest friends. Do they tend to express more empathy than those you feel less close to? How might *you* more deeply and actively listen to your friends?

> To learn more about how therapists use these approaches, see the *Video: Psychodynamic and Humanistic Therapies.*

Behavior Therapies

LOQ **53-4** How does the basic assumption of behavior therapy differ from the assumptions of psychodynamic and humanistic therapies? What classical conditioning techniques are used in exposure therapies and aversive conditioning?

The insight therapies assume that self-awareness and psychological well-being go hand in hand. Psychodynamic therapists expect people's problems to diminish as they gain insight into their unresolved and unconscious tensions. Humanistic therapists expect problems to diminish as people get in touch with their feelings. **Behavior therapists,** however, doubt the healing power of self-awareness. Rather than delving deeply below the surface looking for inner causes, behavior therapists assume that problem behaviors *are* the problems. (You can become aware of why you are highly anxious during exams and still be anxious.) If specific phobias, sexual dysfunctions, or other maladaptive symptoms are learned behaviors, why not apply the learning principles of classical and operant conditioning to replace them with new, constructive behaviors?

Classical Conditioning Techniques

One cluster of behavior therapies derives from principles developed in Ivan Pavlov's early twentieth-century conditioning experiments. As Pavlov and others showed, we learn various behaviors and emotions through classical conditioning. If we're attacked by a dog, we may thereafter have a conditioned fear response when other dogs approach. (Our fear generalizes, and all dogs become conditioned stimuli.)

Could maladaptive symptoms be examples of conditioned responses? If so, might reconditioning be a solution? Learning theorist O. H. Mowrer thought so. He developed a successful conditioning therapy for chronic bed-wetting, using a liquid-sensitive pad connected to an alarm. If the sleeping child wets the bed pad, moisture triggers the alarm, waking the child. After a number of trials, the child associates bladder relaxation with waking. In three out of four cases, the treatment has been effective and the success has boosted the child's self-image (Christophersen & Edwards, 1992; Houts et al., 1994).

Can we unlearn fear responses, such as to public speaking or flying, through new conditioning? Many people have. An example: The fear of riding in an elevator is often a learned aversion to being in a confined space. **Counterconditioning,** such as with *exposure therapy,* pairs the trigger stimulus (in this case, the enclosed space of the elevator) with a new response (relaxation) that is incompatible with fear.

> **RETRIEVAL PRACTICE**
>
> **RP-2** What might a psychodynamic therapist say about Mowrer's therapy for bed-wetting? How might a behavior therapist defend it?
>
> *ANSWERS IN APPENDIX E*

EXPOSURE THERAPIES Picture this scene: Behavioral psychologist Mary Cover Jones is working with 3-year-old Peter, who is petrified of rabbits and other furry objects. To rid Peter of his fear, Jones plans to associate the fear-evoking rabbit with the pleasurable, relaxed response associated with eating. As Peter begins his midafternoon snack, she introduces a caged rabbit on the other side of the huge room. Peter, eagerly munching away on his crackers and drinking his milk, hardly notices. On succeeding days, she gradually moves the rabbit closer and closer. Within two months, Peter is holding the rabbit in his lap, even stroking it while he eats. Moreover, his fear of other furry objects subsides as well, having been *countered,* or replaced, by a relaxed state that cannot coexist with fear (Fisher, 1984; Jones, 1924).

Unfortunately for many who might have been helped by Jones' counterconditioning procedures, her story of Peter and the rabbit didn't become well-known when it was reported in 1924. It was more than 30 years before psychiatrist Joseph Wolpe (1958; Wolpe & Plaud, 1997) refined Jones' counterconditioning technique into the **exposure therapies** used today. These therapies, in a variety of ways, try to change people's reactions by repeatedly exposing them to stimuli that trigger unwanted reactions. We all experience this process in everyday life. A person moving to a new apartment may be annoyed by nearby loud traffic noise, but only for a while. With repeated exposure, the person adapts. So, too, with people who have fear reactions to specific events, such as people with PTSD (Thompson-Hollands et al., 2018). Exposed repeatedly to the situation that once petrified them, with support from talk therapy, they can learn to react less anxiously (Langkaas et al., 2017; Stein & Rothbaum, 2018). Exposure therapy is neither pleasant nor easy, so it helps to have supportive family and friends (Meis et al., 2019).

One exposure therapy used to treat specific phobias is **systematic desensitization.** You cannot simultaneously be anxious and relaxed. Therefore, if you can repeatedly relax when facing anxiety-provoking stimuli, you can gradually eliminate your anxiety. The trick is to proceed gradually. If you fear public speaking, a behavior therapist might first help you construct an *anxiety hierarchy*—a kind of ladder of speaking situations that trigger increasing levels of anxiety. Yours might range from mildly anxiety-provoking situations (perhaps speaking up in a small group of friends) to panic-provoking situations (having to address a large audience).

Next, the therapist would train you in *progressive relaxation.* You would learn to release tension in one muscle group after another, until you achieve a comfortable, complete state of relaxation. Then the therapist might ask you to imagine, with your eyes closed, a mildly anxiety-arousing situation: You are having coffee with a group of friends and are trying to decide whether to speak up. If imagining the scene causes you to feel any anxiety, you are told to signal by raising your finger. Seeing the signal, the therapist will instruct you to switch off the mental image and go back to deep relaxation. This imagined scene is repeatedly paired with relaxation until you feel no trace of anxiety.

The therapist will then move to the next item in your anxiety hierarchy, again using relaxation techniques to desensitize you to each imagined situation. After several

unconditional positive regard a caring, accepting, nonjudgmental attitude, which Carl Rogers believed would help clients develop self-awareness and self-acceptance.

behavior therapy therapy that applies learning principles to the elimination of unwanted behaviors.

counterconditioning behavior therapy procedures that use classical conditioning to evoke new responses to stimuli that are triggering unwanted behaviors; include *exposure therapies* and *aversive conditioning.*

exposure therapies behavioral techniques, such as *systematic desensitization* and *virtual reality exposure therapy,* that treat anxieties by exposing people (in imaginary or actual situations) to the things they fear and avoid.

systematic desensitization a type of exposure therapy that associates a pleasant relaxed state with gradually increasing anxiety-triggering stimuli. Commonly used to treat specific phobias.

FIGURE 53.1
Terrifying tarantula Within the confines of a room, virtual reality technology exposes people to vivid simulations of feared stimuli, such as spiders, and helps them gradually overcome their fear.

"The only thing we have to fear is fear itself." — U.S. President Franklin D. Roosevelt's First Inaugural Address, 1933

sessions, you move to actual situations and practice what you had only imagined before, beginning with relatively easy tasks and gradually moving to more anxiety-filled ones. Conquering your anxiety in an actual situation, not just in your imagination, will increase your self-confidence (Foa & Kozak, 1986; Williams, 1987). Eventually, you may even become a confident public speaker. Often people fear not just a situation, such as public speaking, but also being incapacitated by their own fear response. As their fear subsides, so also does their fear of the fear.

If anxiety-arousing situations (such as flying, heights, particular animals, and public speaking) are too expensive, difficult, or embarrassing to re-create, the therapist may recommend **virtual reality exposure therapy.** In this therapy, you don a head-mounted display unit that projects a lifelike three-dimensional virtual world tailored to your particular fear. If you fear spiders, for example, you could look at a computer-generated, three-dimensional tarantula located on a table, and step-by-step over time walk toward it, place your hand on the table, and ultimately experience the "crawling" sensations as you "hold" the spider (**FIGURE 53.1**). If you fear social interactions, you could experience simulated stressful situations, such as entering a roomful of people. In controlled studies, people treated with virtual reality exposure therapy have experienced relief from real-life fear and social anxiety (Anderson et al., 2017; Freeman et al., 2018; Minns et al., 2019).

AVERSIVE CONDITIONING Exposure therapy helps you learn what you *should* do; it enables a more relaxed, positive response to an upsetting *harmless* stimulus. **Aversive conditioning** helps you learn what you *should not* do; it creates a negative (aversive) response to a *harmful* stimulus (such as alcohol). The aversive conditioning procedure is simple: It associates the unwanted behavior with unpleasant feelings. To treat compulsive nail biting, the therapist may suggest painting the fingernails with a nasty-tasting nail polish (Baskind, 1997). To treat alcohol use disorder, the therapist may offer the client appealing alcoholic drinks laced with a drug that produces severe nausea. If that therapy links alcohol with violent nausea, the person's reaction to alcohol may change from positive to negative (**FIGURE 53.2**).

FIGURE 53.2
Aversion therapy for alcohol use disorder After repeatedly imbibing an alcoholic drink mixed with a drug that produces severe nausea, some people with a history of alcohol use disorder develop at least a temporary conditioned aversion to alcohol. (Remember: US is unconditioned stimulus, UR is unconditioned response, NS is neutral stimulus, CS is conditioned stimulus, and CR is conditioned response.)

US (drug) → UR (nausea)

NS (alcohol) + US (drug) → UR (nausea)

CS (alcohol) → CR (nausea)

Taste aversion learning has been a successful alternative to killing predators in some animal protection programs (Dingfelder, 2010; Garcia & Gustavson, 1997). After being sickened by eating a tainted sheep, wolves may later avoid sheep. Does aversive conditioning also transform humans' reactions to alcohol? In the short run it may. In one classic study, 685 hospital patients with alcohol use disorder completed an aversion therapy program (Wiens & Menustik, 1983). Over the next year, they returned for several booster treatments that paired alcohol with sickness. At the end of that year, 63 percent were not drinking alcohol. But after three years, only 33 percent were alcohol free.

In therapy, as in research, cognition influences conditioning. People know that outside the therapist's office they can drink without fear of nausea. This ability to discriminate between the therapy situation and all others can limit aversive conditioning's effectiveness. Thus, therapists often combine aversive conditioning with other treatments.

Operant Conditioning Techniques

LOQ **53-5** What is the main premise of behavior therapy based on operant conditioning principles, and what are the views of its proponents and critics?

If you have learned to swim, you learned how to hold your breath with your head under water, how to pull your body through the water, and perhaps even how to dive safely. Operant conditioning shaped your swimming. You were reinforced for safe, effective behaviors. And you were naturally punished, as when you swallowed water, for improper swimming behaviors.

Consequences strongly influence our voluntary behaviors. Knowing this basic principle of operant conditioning, behavior therapists can practice *behavior modification*. They reinforce desirable behaviors, and they fail to reinforce—or sometimes punish—undesirable behaviors.

Using operant conditioning to solve specific behavior problems has raised hopes for some seemingly hopeless cases. Children with intellectual disabilities have been taught to care for themselves. Socially withdrawn children with autism spectrum disorder (ASD) have learned to interact. People with schizophrenia have been helped to behave more rationally in their hospital ward. In such cases, therapists use positive reinforcers to *shape* behavior. In a step-by-step manner, they reward closer and closer approximations of the desired behavior.

In extreme cases, treatment must be intensive. One study worked with 19 withdrawn, uncommunicative 3-year-olds with ASD. For two years, 40 hours each week, the children's parents attempted to shape their behavior (Lovaas, 1987). They positively reinforced desired behaviors and ignored or punished aggressive and self-abusive behaviors. The combination worked wonders for some children. By first grade, 9 of the 19 were functioning successfully in school and exhibiting normal intelligence. In a control group of 40 comparable children not undergoing this effortful treatment, only one showed similar improvement. Later studies focused on positive reinforcement—which turned out to be the effective aspect of this early intensive behavioral intervention (Reichow, 2012).

Rewards used to modify behavior vary. For some people, the reinforcing power of attention or praise is sufficient. Others require concrete rewards, such as food. In institutional settings, therapists may create a **token economy.** When people display a desired behavior, such as getting out of bed, washing, dressing, eating, talking coherently, cleaning up their rooms, or playing cooperatively, they receive a token or plastic coin. Later, they can exchange a number of these tokens for rewards, such as candy, TV time, day trips, or better living quarters. Token economies have been used successfully in group homes, classrooms, and correctional institutions, and among people with various disabilities (Matson & Boisjoli, 2009).

Behavior modification critics express two concerns:

- *How durable are the behaviors?* Will people become so dependent on extrinsic rewards that the desired behaviors will stop when reinforcers stop? Behavior modification advocates believe the behaviors will endure if therapists wean people from the tokens by shifting them toward other, real-life rewards, such as social approval. Further, they point out, the desired behaviors themselves can be rewarding. As people become more socially competent, the intrinsic satisfactions of social interaction may sustain the behaviors.

virtual reality exposure therapy a counterconditioning technique that treats anxiety through creative electronic simulations in which people can safely face their greatest fears, such as airplane flying, spiders, or public speaking.

aversive conditioning associates an unpleasant state (such as nausea) with an unwanted behavior (such as drinking alcohol).

token economy an operant conditioning procedure in which people earn a token for exhibiting a desired behavior and can later exchange tokens for privileges or treats.

- *Is it right for one human to control another's behavior?* Those who set up token economies deprive people of something they desire and decide which behaviors to reinforce. To critics, this whole process feels too authoritarian. Advocates reply that control already exists: People's destructive behavior patterns are being maintained and perpetuated by natural reinforcers and punishers in their environments. Isn't using positive rewards to reinforce adaptive behavior more humane than institutionalizing or punishing people? Advocates also argue that the right to effective treatment and an improved life justifies temporary deprivation.

RETRIEVAL PRACTICE

RP-3 What are the *insight therapies*, and how do they differ from behavior therapies?

RP-4 Some maladaptive behaviors are learned. What hope does this fact provide?

RP-5 Exposure therapies and aversive conditioning are applications of _____ conditioning. Token economies are an application of _____ conditioning.

ANSWERS IN APPENDIX E

ASK YOURSELF

What is your judgment of behavior modification techniques, such as those used in token economies? Do you agree or disagree with this approach?

Cognitive Therapies

LOQ 53-6 What are the goals and techniques of the cognitive therapies and of cognitive-behavioral therapy?

People with specific fears and problem behaviors may respond to behavior therapy. But how might behavior therapists modify the wide assortment of behaviors that accompany depressive disorders? Or treat people with generalized anxiety disorder, where unfocused anxiety doesn't lend itself to a neat list of anxiety-triggering situations? The *cognitive revolution* that has profoundly changed other areas of psychology since the 1960s has influenced therapy as well.

The **cognitive therapies** assume that our *thinking* colors our *feelings* (**FIGURE 53.3**). Between an event and our response lies the mind. Anxiety, for example, can arise from an "attention bias to threat" (MacLeod & Clarke, 2015). Self-blaming and overgeneralized explanations of bad events feed depression. If depressed, we may interpret a suggestion as criticism, disagreement as dislike, praise as flattery, friendliness as pity. Dwelling on such thoughts sustains negative thinking. Cognitive therapies help people change their mind with new, more constructive ways of perceiving and interpreting events (Schmidt et al., 2019).

Beck's Therapy for Depression

In the late 1960s, a woman left a party early. Things had not gone well. She felt disconnected from the other partygoers and assumed no one liked her. A few days later, she visited cognitive therapist Aaron Beck. Rather than go down the traditional path to her childhood, Beck challenged her thinking. After she then listed a dozen people who *did* like her, Beck realized that challenging people's automatic negative thoughts could be therapeutic. And thus was born his cognitive therapy, which assumes that changing people's thinking can change their functioning (Spiegel, 2015).

> "Life does not consist mainly, or even largely, of facts and happenings. It consists mainly of the storm of thoughts that are forever blowing through one's mind."
> — Author and humorist Mark Twain

➔ **FIGURE 53.3**
A cognitive perspective on psychological disorders The person's emotional reactions are produced not directly by the event, but by the person's thoughts in response to the event.

Depressed people, Beck found, often reported dreams with negative themes of loss, rejection, and abandonment. These themes extended into their waking thoughts, and even into therapy, as clients recalled and rehearsed their failings and worst impulses (Kelly, 2000). With cognitive therapy, Beck and his colleagues (1979) sought to reverse clients' negativity about themselves, their situations, and their futures. With this technique, gentle questioning seeks to reveal irrational thinking, and then to persuade people to remove the dark glasses through which they view life (Beck et al., 1979, pp. 145–146):

> **Client:** *I agree with the descriptions of me but I guess I don't agree that the way I think makes me depressed.*
>
> **Beck:** *How do you understand it?*
>
> **Client:** *I get depressed when things go wrong. Like when I fail a test.*
>
> **Beck:** *How can failing a test make you depressed?*
>
> **Client:** *Well, if I fail I'll never get into law school.*
>
> **Beck:** *So failing the test means a lot to you. But if failing a test could drive people into clinical depression, wouldn't you expect everyone who failed the test to have a depression? . . . Did everyone who failed get depressed enough to require treatment?*
>
> **Client:** *No, but it depends on how important the test was to the person.*
>
> **Beck:** *Right, and who decides the importance?*
>
> **Client:** *I do.*
>
> **Beck:** *And so, what we have to examine is your way of viewing the test (or the way that you think about the test) and how it affects your chances of getting into law school. Do you agree?*
>
> **Client:** *Right.*
>
> **Beck:** *Do you agree that the way you interpret the results of the test will affect you? You might feel depressed, you might have trouble sleeping, not feel like eating, and you might even wonder if you should drop out of the course.*
>
> **Client:** *I have been thinking that I wasn't going to make it. Yes, I agree.*
>
> **Beck:** *Now what did failing mean?*
>
> **Client:** *(tearful) That I couldn't get into law school.*
>
> **Beck:** *And what does that mean to you?*
>
> **Client:** *That I'm just not smart enough.*
>
> **Beck:** *Anything else?*
>
> **Client:** *That I can never be happy.*
>
> **Beck:** *And how do these thoughts make you feel?*
>
> **Client:** *Very unhappy.*
>
> **Beck:** *So it is the meaning of failing a test that makes you very unhappy. In fact, believing that you can never be happy is a powerful factor in producing unhappiness. So, you get yourself into a trap—by definition, failure to get into law school equals "I can never be happy."*

We often think in words. Therefore, getting people to change what they say to themselves is an effective way to change their thinking. Perhaps you can identify with the anxious students who, before an exam, make matters worse with self-defeating thoughts: "This exam's probably going to be impossible. Everyone seems so relaxed and confident. I wish I were better prepared. I'm so nervous I'll forget everything." Psychologists call this sort of relentless, overgeneralized, self-blaming behavior *catastrophizing*.

To change such negative self-talk, cognitive therapists have offered *stress inoculation training*: teaching people to restructure their thinking in stressful situations (Meichenbaum, 1977, 1985). Sometimes it may be enough simply to say more positive things to oneself: "Relax. The exam may be hard, but it will be hard for everyone else, too. I studied harder than most people. Besides, I don't need a perfect score to get a good grade." After learning to "talk back" to negative thoughts, depression-prone children, teens, and college students have shown a greatly reduced rate of future depression (Reivich et al., 2013; Seligman et al., 2009). Ditto for anxiety (Krueze et al., 2018). To a

Aaron Beck "Cognitive therapy seeks to alleviate psychological stresses by correcting faulty conceptions and beliefs. By correcting erroneous beliefs we can lower excessive reactions" (Beck, 1978).

© Macmillan Learning

cognitive therapy therapy that teaches people new, more adaptive ways of thinking; based on the assumption that thoughts intervene between events and our emotional reactions.

TABLE 53.1 Selected Cognitive Therapy Techniques

Aim of Technique	Technique	Therapists' Directives
Reveal beliefs	Question your interpretations	Explore your beliefs, revealing faulty assumptions such as "I must be liked by everyone."
	Rank thoughts and emotions	Gain perspective by ranking your thoughts and emotions from mildly to extremely upsetting.
Test beliefs	Examine consequences	Explore difficult situations, assessing possible consequences and challenging faulty reasoning.
	Decatastrophize thinking	Work through the actual worst-case consequences of the situation you face (it is often not as bad as imagined). Then determine how to cope with the real situation you face.
Change beliefs	Take appropriate responsibility	Challenge total self-blame and negative thinking, noting aspects for which you may be truly responsible, as well as aspects that aren't your responsibility.
	Resist extremes	Develop new ways of thinking and feeling to replace maladaptive habits. For example, change from thinking "I am a total failure" to "I got a failing grade on that paper, and I can make these changes to succeed next time."

PEANUTS

large extent, it is the thought that counts. For a sampling of commonly used cognitive therapy techniques, see **TABLE 53.1**.

It's not just depressed people who can benefit from positive self-talk. We all talk to ourselves (thinking "I wish I hadn't said that" can protect us from repeating the blunder). The findings of nearly three dozen sport psychology studies show that self-talk interventions can enhance the learning of athletic skills, too (Hatzigeorgiadis et al., 2011). For example, novice basketball players may be trained to think "focus" and "follow through," swimmers to think "high elbow," and tennis players to think "look at the ball." People anxious about public speaking have grown in confidence if asked to recall a speaking success and then asked this: "Explain WHY you were able to achieve such a successful performance" (Zunick et al., 2015).

ASK YOURSELF

Have you ever struggled to reach a goal at school or work because of your own self-defeating thoughts? How could you challenge those thoughts?

> To learn more about how cognitive therapy can be used to help those with anxiety, see the *Video: Cognitive Therapies.*

Cognitive-Behavioral Therapy

"The trouble with most therapy," said therapist Albert Ellis (1913–2007), "is that it helps you to feel better. But you don't get better. You have to back it up with action, action, action." **Cognitive-behavioral therapy (CBT)** takes a combined approach to treating depressive and other disorders. This widely practiced *integrative* therapy aims to alter not only the way people *think* but also the way they *act*. Like other cognitive therapies, CBT seeks to make people aware of their irrational negative thinking and to replace it with new ways of thinking. And like other behavior therapies, it trains people to *practice* the more positive approach in everyday settings.

Anxiety, depressive, and bipolar disorders share a common problem: unhealthy emotion regulation (Aldao & Nolen-Hoeksema, 2010; Szkodny et al., 2014). An effective CBT program for these emotional disorders trains people both to replace their catastrophizing thinking with more realistic appraisals, and, as homework, to practice behaviors that are incompatible with their problem (Kazantzis et al., 2010; Moses & Barlow, 2006). A person might keep a log of daily situations associated with negative and positive emotions, and engage more in activities that lead to feeling good. Those who fear social situations might learn to restrain the negative thoughts surrounding their social anxiety and practice approaching people.

CBT effectively treats people with obsessive-compulsive and related disorders (Öst et al., 2015; Tolin et al., 2019). In one classic study, people learned to prevent their compulsive behaviors by relabeling their obsessive thoughts (Schwartz et al., 1996). Feeling the urge to wash their hands again, they would tell themselves, "I'm having a compulsive urge." They would explain to themselves that the hand-washing urge was a result of their brain's abnormal activity, which they had previously viewed in PET scans. Then, instead of giving in, they would spend 15 minutes in an enjoyable, alternative behavior—practicing an instrument, taking a walk, gardening. This helped "unstick" the brain by shifting attention and engaging other brain areas. For two or three months, the weekly therapy sessions continued, with relabeling and refocusing practice at home. By the study's end, most participants' symptoms had diminished and their PET scans revealed normalized brain activity. Many other studies confirm CBT's effectiveness for treating anxiety, depression, eating disorders, ADHD, and alcohol or other substance use disorders (Brown et al., 2018; Knouse et al., 2017; Linardon et al., 2017; Magill et al., 2019).

Online and app-guided CBT quizzes and exercises—therapies without a face-to-face therapist—have also helped alleviate insomnia, depression, and anxiety (Andrews et al., 2018; Carlbring et al., 2018; Ebert et al., 2018). By offering flexible, affordable, and effective treatment, online CBT can reach people who—because of rural location, low income, or embarrassment, for example—will seldom attend face-to-face therapy sessions (Dadds et al., 2019; Sheeber et al., 2017).

A newer CBT variation, *dialectical behavior therapy (DBT)*, helps change harmful and even suicidal behavior patterns (Linehan et al., 2015; McCauley et al., 2018; Tebbett-Mock et al., 2019). *Dialectical* means "opposing," and this therapy attempts to make peace between two opposing forces—acceptance and change. Therapists create an accepting and encouraging environment, helping clients feel they have an ally who will offer them constructive feedback and guidance. In individual sessions, clients learn new ways of thinking that help them tolerate distress and regulate their emotions. They also receive training in social skills and in *mindfulness meditation,* which helps alleviate depression (Gu, J. et al., 2015; Wielgosz et al., 2019). Group training sessions offer additional opportunities to practice new skills in a social context, with further practice as homework.

Cognitive-behavioral therapy for eating disorders aided by journaling Cognitive-behavioral therapists guide people with eating disorders toward new ways of explaining their good and bad food-related experiences (Linardon et al., 2017). By recording positive events and how she has enabled them, this woman may become more mindful of her self-control and more optimistic.

RETRIEVAL PRACTICE

RP-6 How do the humanistic and cognitive therapies differ?

RP-7 A critical attribute of the _____ _____ developed by Aaron Beck focuses on the belief that changing people's thinking can change their functioning.

RP-8 What is *cognitive-behavioral therapy,* and what sorts of problems does this therapy best address?

ANSWERS IN APPENDIX E

Group and Family Therapies

LOQ 53-7 What are the aims and benefits of group and family therapies?

Group Therapy

Except for traditional psychoanalysis, most therapies may also occur in small groups. **Group therapy** does not provide the same degree of therapist involvement with each client. However, it offers other benefits:

- *It saves therapists' time and clients' money,* and often is no less effective than individual therapy (Burlingame et al., 2016).

- *It offers a social laboratory for exploring social behaviors and developing social skills.* Therapists frequently suggest group therapy for people experiencing frequent conflicts or whose behavior distresses others. The therapist guides people's interactions as they discuss issues and try out new behaviors.

- *It enables people to see that others share their problems.* It can be a relief to discover that others have experienced similar stressors, troublesome feelings, and behaviors (Rahman et al., 2019).

- *It provides feedback as clients try out new ways of behaving.* Hearing that you look or sound poised, even though you feel anxious and self-conscious, can be very reassuring.

cognitive-behavioral therapy (CBT) a popular integrative therapy that combines cognitive therapy (changing self-defeating thinking) with behavior therapy (changing behavior).

group therapy therapy conducted with groups rather than individuals, providing benefits from group interaction.

Family therapy As a preventive mental health strategy, family therapy includes *couples therapy*, as shown here at a retreat for U.S. military families. The therapist helps family members understand how their ways of relating to one another create problems. The treatment's emphasis is not only on changing the individuals, but also on changing their relationships and interactions.

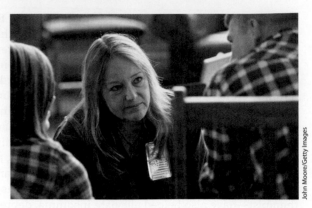

Family Therapy

One special type of group interaction, **family therapy,** assumes that no person is an island: We live and grow in relation to others, especially our family. We struggle to differentiate ourselves from our families, but we also need to connect with them emotionally. These two opposing tendencies can create stress for both the individual and the family.

Family therapists tend to view families as systems, in which each person's actions trigger reactions from others. A child's rebellion, for example, affects and is affected by other family tensions. Therapists are often successful in helping family members identify their roles within the family's social system, improve communication, and discover new ways of preventing or resolving conflicts (Hazelrigg et al., 1987; Shadish et al., 1993).

Self-Help Groups

More than 100 million Americans have belonged to religious, special-interest, or support groups that meet regularly—with 9 in 10 reporting that group members "support each other emotionally" (Gallup, 1994). Self-help groups often provide support to people who struggle to find it elsewhere. One analysis of more than 14,000 self-help groups reported that most focus on stigmatized, hard-to-discuss problems (Davison et al., 2000). AIDS patients were 250 times more likely than hypertension patients to be in support groups. People with anorexia and alcohol use disorder often join groups; those with migraines and ulcers usually do not.

With more than 2 million members in 180 countries, AA is said to be "the largest organization on Earth that nobody wanted to join" (Finlay, 2000).

The famous 12-step program of that grandparent of support groups, Alcoholics Anonymous (AA), has been emulated by many other self-help groups. It asks members to admit their powerlessness, to seek help from a higher power and from one another, and (the twelfth step) to take the message to others in need of it (Galanter, 2016). Studies of 12-step programs such as AA have found that they help reduce alcohol use disorder at rates comparable to other treatment interventions (Ferri et al., 2006; Moos & Moos, 2005). An eight-year, $27 million investigation found that AA participants reduced their drinking sharply, as did those assigned to CBT or an alternative therapy (Project Match, 1997). Another study of 2300 veterans who sought treatment for alcohol use disorder found that a high level of AA involvement was followed by diminished alcohol problems (McKellar et al., 2003). The more meetings AA members attend, the greater their alcohol abstinence (Moos & Moos, 2006). Those whose personal stories include a "redemptive narrative"—who see something good as having come from their struggles—more often sustain sobriety (Dunlop & Tracy, 2013).

In an individualist age, with more and more people living alone or feeling isolated, the popularity of support groups—for the addicted, the bereaved, the divorced, or simply those seeking fellowship and growth—may reflect a longing for community and connectedness.

* * *

For a synopsis of these modern psychotherapies, see **TABLE 53.2.**

family therapy therapy that treats people in the context of their family system. Views an individual's unwanted behaviors as influenced by, or directed at, other family members.

To study and remember the aims and techniques of different psychotherapies, review *Concept Practice: Types of Therapies and Therapists.* Assess your ability to recognize excerpts from each type with *Topic Tutorial: PsychSim6, Mystery Therapist.*

TABLE 53.2 Comparing Modern Psychotherapies

Therapy	Presumed Problem	Therapy Aim	Therapy Technique
Psychodynamic	Unconscious conflicts from childhood experiences	Reduce anxiety through self-insight.	Interpret clients' memories, dreams, and feelings.
Person-centered	Barriers to self-understanding and self-acceptance	Enable growth via unconditional positive regard, acceptance, genuineness, and empathy.	Listen actively and reflect clients' feelings.
Behavior	Dysfunctional behaviors	Learn adaptive behaviors; extinguish problem ones.	Use classical conditioning (via exposure or aversion therapy) or operant conditioning (as in token economies).
Cognitive	Negative, self-defeating thinking	Promote healthier thinking and self-talk.	Train people to dispute negative thoughts and attributions.
Cognitive-behavioral	Self-harmful thoughts and behaviors	Promote healthier thinking and adaptive behaviors.	Train people to counter self-harmful thoughts and to act out their new ways of thinking.
Group and family	Stressful relationships	Heal relationships.	Develop an understanding of family and other social systems, explore roles, and improve communication.

MODULE

53 REVIEW Introduction to Therapy and the Psychological Therapies

LEARNING OBJECTIVES

Test Yourself Answer these repeated Learning Objective Questions on your own (before checking the answers in Appendix D) to improve your retention of the concepts (McDaniel et al., 2009, 2015).

LOQ 53-1 How do *psychotherapy* and the *biomedical therapies* differ?

LOQ 53-2 What are the goals and techniques of psychoanalysis, and how have they been adapted in psychodynamic therapy?

LOQ 53-3 What are the basic themes of humanistic therapy? What are the goals and techniques of Rogers' person-centered approach?

LOQ 53-4 How does the basic assumption of behavior therapy differ from the assumptions of psychodynamic and humanistic therapies? What classical conditioning techniques are used in exposure therapies and aversive conditioning?

LOQ 53-5 What is the main premise of behavior therapy based on operant conditioning principles, and what are the views of its proponents and critics?

LOQ 53-6 What are the goals and techniques of the cognitive therapies and of cognitive-behavioral therapy?

LOQ 53-7 What are the aims and benefits of group and family therapies?

TERMS AND CONCEPTS TO REMEMBER

Test Yourself Write down the definition in your own words, then check your answer.

psychotherapy, p. 599

biomedical therapy, p. 599

eclectic approach, p. 599

psychoanalysis, p. 599

resistance, p. 599

interpretation, p. 599

transference, p. 599

psychodynamic therapy, p. 600

insight therapies, p. 600

person-centered therapy, p. 600

active listening, p. 600

unconditional positive regard, p. 603

behavior therapy, p. 603

counterconditioning, p. 603

exposure therapies, p. 603

systematic desensitization, p. 603

virtual reality exposure therapy, p. 605

aversive conditioning, p. 605

token economy, p. 605

cognitive therapy, p. 607

cognitive-behavioral therapy (CBT), p. 609

group therapy, p. 609

family therapy, p. 610

MASTER THE MATERIAL

Test Yourself Answer the following questions on your own first, then check your answers in Appendix E.

1. A therapist who helps clients search for the unconscious roots of their problem and offers interpretations of their behaviors, feelings, and dreams, is drawing from

   a. psychoanalysis.

   b. humanistic therapies.

   c. person-centered therapy.

   d. behavior therapy.

2. _____ therapies are designed to help individuals discover the unconscious thoughts and feelings that guide their motivation and behavior.

3. Compared with psychoanalysts, humanistic therapists are more likely to emphasize

   a. hidden or repressed feelings.

   b. childhood experiences.

   c. psychological disorders.

   d. self-fulfillment and growth.

4. A therapist who restates and clarifies the client's statements is practicing the technique of _____ _____.

5. The goal of behavior therapy is to

   a. identify and treat the underlying causes of the problem.

   b. improve learning and insight.

   c. eliminate the unwanted behavior.

   d. improve communication and social sensitivity.

6. Behavior therapies often use _____ techniques, such as systematic desensitization and aversive conditioning, to encourage clients to produce new responses to old stimuli.

7. The technique of _____ _____ teaches people to relax in the presence of progressively more anxiety-provoking stimuli.

8. After a near-fatal car accident, Rico developed such an intense fear of driving on the highway that he takes lengthy alternative routes to work each day. Which psychological therapy might best help Rico overcome his specific phobia, and why?

9. At a treatment center, people who display a desired behavior receive coins that they can later exchange for other rewards. This is an example of a(n) _____ _____.

10. Cognitive therapy has been especially effective in treating

    a. nail biting.

    b. specific phobias.

    c. alcohol use disorder.

    d. depressive disorders.

11. _____-_____ therapy helps people to change their self-defeating ways of thinking and to act out those changes in their daily behavior.

12. In family therapy, the therapist assumes that

    a. only one family member needs to change.

    b. each person's actions trigger reactions from other family members.

    c. dysfunctional family behaviors are based largely on genetic factors.

    d. therapy is most effective when clients are treated apart from the family unit.

Continue testing yourself with 📖 **LearningCurve** or 📖 **Achieve Read & Practice** to learn and remember most effectively.

🔴54 Evaluating Psychotherapies

Many people presume **psychotherapy's** effectiveness. "Seek counseling" or "Ask your mate to find a therapist," advice columnists often urge. Before 1950, psychiatrists were the primary providers of mental health care. Today's providers include clinical and counseling psychologists; clinical social workers; pastoral, marital, abuse, and school counselors; and psychiatric nurses. With such an enormous outlay of time as well as money and effort, it is important to ask: Are the millions of people worldwide justified in placing their hopes in psychotherapy?

Is Psychotherapy Effective?

LOQ 54-1 Does psychotherapy work? How can we know?

The question, though simply put, is not simply answered. If an infection quickly clears, we may assume an antibiotic has been effective. But how can we assess psychotherapy's effectiveness? By how we feel about our progress? By how our therapist feels about it? By how our friends and family feel about it? By how our behavior has changed?

SO HOW LONG HAVE YOU WANTED TO BE A THERAPIST?

THAT'S WHAT I WOULD LIKE TO ASK YOU.

ED WAS IN THERAPY FOR BELIEVING HE WAS A THERAPIST.

Client Perceptions

If client testimonials were the only measuring stick, we could strongly affirm psycho-therapy's effectiveness. Consider the 2900 *Consumer Reports* readers who related their experiences with mental health professionals (1995; Kotkin et al., 1996; Seligman, 1995). How many were at least "fairly well satisfied"? Almost 90 percent. Among those who recalled feeling *fair* or *very poor* when beginning therapy, 9 in 10 now were feeling *very good, good,* or at least *so-so*. We have their word for it—and who should know better?

We should not dismiss these testimonials. But critics note reasons for skepticism:

- *People often enter therapy in crisis.* When, with the normal ebb and flow of events, the crisis passes, people may attribute their improvement to the therapy. Depressed people often get better no matter what they do.

- *Clients believe that treatment will be effective.* The *placebo effect* is the healing power of positive expectations.

- *Clients generally speak kindly of their therapists.* Even if the problems remain, clients "work hard to find something positive to say. The therapist had been very under-standing, the client had gained a new perspective, he learned to communicate better, his mind was eased, anything at all so as not to have to say treatment was a failure" (Zilbergeld, 1983, p. 117).

- *Clients want to believe the therapy was worth the effort.* If you invested time and money in something, wouldn't you be motivated to find something positive about it? Psychologists call this *effort justification*.

Consider the testimonials gathered in a massive experiment with over 500 Massa-chusetts boys, aged 5 to 13 years, many of whom seemed bound for delinquency. By the toss of a coin, half the boys were assigned to a 5-year treatment program. The treated boys were visited by counselors twice a month. They participated in community pro-grams, and they received academic tutoring, medical attention, and family assistance as needed. Some 30 years later, Joan McCord (1978, 1979) located 485 participants, sent them questionnaires, and checked public records from courts, psychiatric hospitals, and other sources. Was the treatment successful?

Client testimonials were glowing. Some men noted that, had it not been for their counselors, "I would probably be in jail," "My life would have gone the other way," or "I think I would have ended up in a life of crime." Court records offered apparent support: Even among the "difficult" boys in the treatment group, 66 percent had no official juve-nile crime record.

But recall psychology's most powerful tool for sorting reality from wishful think-ing: the *control group*. For every boy in the treatment group, there was a similar boy in a control group receiving no counseling. Of these untreated men, *70 percent* had no juve-nile record. On several other measures, such as a record of having committed a second crime, alcohol use disorder, death rate, and job satisfaction, the untreated men exhib-ited slightly *fewer* problems. Unfortunately, the glowing testimonials of those treated were misleading.

Clinician Perceptions

If clinician perceptions were proof of therapy's effectiveness, we would have even more reason to celebrate. Case studies of successful treatment abound. The problem is that clients enter psychotherapy focused on their unhappiness and leave it focused on their well-being. Therapists treasure compliments from those clients saying good-bye or later expressing their gratitude. But they hear little from clients who experience only temporary relief and seek out new therapists for their recurring problems. Thus, thera-pists are most aware of the failures of *other* therapists. The same person, with the same recurring anxieties, depression, or marital difficulty, may be a "success" story in sev-eral therapists' files. Moreover, therapists, like the rest of us, are vulnerable to cognitive errors. **Confirmation bias** can lead them to unconsciously seek evidence that confirms their beliefs and to ignore contradictory evidence, and *illusory correlations* can lead them to perceive associations that don't really exist (Lilienfeld et al., 2015b).

To consider the impact of clients' belief in the treatment, see *Video: Therapeutic Effectiveness—The Placebo Effect.*

psychotherapy treatment involving psychological techniques; consists of inter-actions between a trained therapist and someone seeking to overcome psychological difficulties or achieve personal growth.

confirmation bias a tendency to search for information that supports our preconcep-tions and to ignore or distort contradictory evidence.

Outcome Research

How, then, can we objectively measure the effectiveness of psychotherapy? What *outcomes* can we expect—what types of people and problems are helped, and by what type of psychotherapy?

In search of answers, psychologists have turned to the well-traveled path of controlled research. Similar research in the 1800s transformed the field of medicine when skeptical physicians began to realize that many patients were dying despite receiving then-mainstream treatments (bloodletting), and many others were getting better on their own. Sorting fact from superstition required observing patients and recording outcomes with and without a particular treatment. Typhoid fever patients, for example, often improved after being bled, convincing most physicians that the treatment worked. Then came the shock. A control group was given mere bed rest, and after five weeks of fever, 70 percent improved, showing that the bleeding was worthless (Thomas, 1992).

A similar shock—and spirited debate—followed in the twentieth century, when British psychologist Hans Eysenck (1952) summarized 24 studies of psychotherapy outcomes. He found that two-thirds of those receiving psychotherapy for disorders not involving hallucinations or delusions improved markedly. To this day, no one disputes that optimistic estimate. But there was a catch. Eysenck also reported similar improvement among people who were *untreated*, such as those on treatment waiting lists. With or without psychotherapy, he said, roughly two-thirds improved noticeably. Time was a great healer.

Later research revealed shortcomings in Eysenck's analyses. His sample was small—only 24 outcome studies in 1952, compared with the thousands available today. The best of these are *randomized clinical trials,* in which researchers randomly assign people on a waiting list to therapy or to no therapy. Later, they evaluate everyone and compare outcomes, with tests and assessments by others who don't know whether therapy was given.

A glimpse of psychotherapy's overall effectiveness can then be provided by means of a **meta-analysis,** a statistical procedure that combines the conclusions of a large number of different studies. Simply said, a meta-analysis summarizes the bottom-line result of lots of studies. Therapists welcomed the first meta-analysis of some 475 psychotherapy outcome studies (Smith et al., 1980). It showed that the average therapy client ends up better off than 80 percent of the untreated individuals on waiting lists (**FIGURE 54.1**). Mary Lee Smith and her colleagues summed it up: "Psychotherapy benefits people of all ages as reliably as schooling educates them, medicine cures them, or business turns a profit" (p. 183).

Dozens of subsequent summaries have now examined psychotherapy's effectiveness. Their verdict echoes earlier results: *Those not undergoing therapy often improve, but those undergoing therapy are more likely to improve—and to improve more quickly and with less risk of relapse* (Eckshtain et al., 2019; Weisz et al., 2017). (One qualification: Compared with studies that find no therapy benefit, those that do find a positive therapy effect are more likely to get published [Driessen et al., 2015].) After therapy, many people exhibit

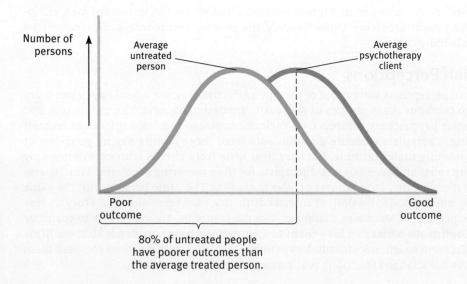

FIGURE 54.1
Treatment versus no treatment These two normal distribution curves based on data from 475 studies show the improvement of untreated people and psychotherapy clients. The outcome for the average therapy client surpassed the outcome for 80 percent of the untreated people. (Data from Smith et al., 1980.)

Number of persons

Average untreated person

Average psychotherapy client

Poor outcome

Good outcome

80% of untreated people have poorer outcomes than the average treated person.

improved insight and emotional awareness, with a more patient, outgoing personality (Høglend & Hagtvet, 2019; Roberts et al., 2017). Some people with depression or anxiety also experience sudden symptom reductions between their treatment sessions (Aderka et al., 2012). Those "sudden gains"—experienced by about 12 percent of people in therapy—bode well for long-term improvement (Wucherpfennig et al., 2017; Zilcha-Mano et al., 2019).

Psychotherapy also can be cost-effective. Studies show that when people seek psychological treatment, their search for other medical treatment drops substantially—by 16 percent in one digest of 91 studies (Chiles et al., 1999). Substance abuse and other psychological disorders cost society in accidents, lost work, and treatment. By one estimate, the opioid epidemic cost the United States more than $1 trillion between 2001 and 2017 (Altarum, 2018). Given such staggering costs, psychotherapy is a good investment, much like money spent on prenatal and well-baby care (Chisholm et al., 2016; Johnson et al., 2019). Both reduce long-term costs. Boosting employees' psychological well-being can lower medical costs, improve work efficiency, and diminish absenteeism. It's no wonder that U.S. health insurers and the National Health Service in Britain have increasingly funded therapy (Hockenberry et al., 2019; NHS, 2020).

But note that the claim—that psychotherapy, *on average*, is somewhat effective—refers to no one therapy in particular. It is like reassuring lung-cancer patients that "on average," medical treatment of health problems is effective. But what distressed people—and those paying for their therapy—want to know is whether a *particular* treatment is effective for their specific problems.

Feng Li/Getty Images

Trauma Those who suffer trauma, such as these women in China mourning the devastating loss of lives and homes in the 2010 Yushu earthquake, may benefit from counseling. But many people recover on their own or with the help of supportive relationships with family and friends. "Life itself still remains a very effective therapist," noted psychodynamic therapist Karen Horney (*Our Inner Conflicts,* 1945).

> **RETRIEVAL PRACTICE**

RP-1 How might the *placebo effect* bias clients' and clinicians' appraisals of the effectiveness of psychotherapies?

ANSWERS IN APPENDIX E

Which Psychotherapies Work Best?

LOQ 54-2 Are some psychotherapies more effective than others for specific disorders?

The early statistical summaries and surveys did not find that any one type of psychotherapy is generally superior (Smith & Glass, 1977; Smith et al., 1980). Later studies have similarly found that clients can benefit from psychotherapy regardless of their clinicians' experience, training, supervision, and licensing (Cuijpers, 2017; Kivlighan et al., 2015; Wampold et al., 2017). A *Consumer Reports* survey found the same result (Seligman, 1995). Were clients treated by a psychiatrist, psychologist, or social worker? Were they seen in a group or individual context? Did the therapist have extensive or relatively limited training and experience? It didn't matter.

So, was the dodo bird in *Alice in Wonderland* right: "Everyone has won and all must have prizes"? Not quite. One general finding emerges from the studies: The more specific the problem, the greater the hope that psychotherapy might solve it (Singer, 1981; Westen & Morrison, 2001). Those who experience panic or specific phobias, who are unassertive, or who are frustrated by sexual performance problems can hope for improvement. Those with less-focused problems, such as depression and anxiety, usually benefit in the short term but often relapse later. There often is also an overlapping of disorders (known as *comorbidity*).

Nevertheless, some forms of therapy do get prizes for effectively treating *particular* problems:

- *Cognitive and cognitive-behavioral therapies*—primarily anxiety, posttraumatic stress disorder, insomnia, and depression (Qaseem et al., 2016; Scaini et al., 2016; Tolin, 2010).

- *Behavioral conditioning therapies*—behavior problems such as bed-wetting, specific phobias, compulsions, marital difficulties, and sexual dysfunctions (Baker et al., 2008; Hunsley & DiGiulio, 2002; Shadish & Baldwin, 2005).

"Different sores have different salves."
— English proverb

meta-analysis a statistical procedure for analyzing the results of multiple studies to reach an overall conclusion.

- *Psychodynamic therapy*—depression and anxiety (Driessen et al., 2010; Leichsenring & Rabung, 2008; Shedler, 2010). Some analyses suggest that psychodynamic therapy and cognitive-behavioral therapy are equally effective in reducing depression (Driessen et al., 2017; Steinert et al., 2017).

- *Nondirective (person-centered) counseling*—mild to moderate depression (Cuijpers et al., 2012).

The tendency of many abnormal states of mind to return to normal, combined with the placebo effect (the healing power of mere belief in a treatment), creates fertile soil for pseudotherapies. But no prizes—and no scientific support—go to certain alternative therapies (Arkowitz & Lilienfeld, 2006; Lilienfeld et al., 2015a). We would all be wise to avoid therapies that propose to manipulate invisible "energy fields," therapies that reenact the supposed trauma of a client's birth, and therapies that "facilitate" hand-guided communication to reach uncommunicative people.

As with some medical treatments, some psychological treatments are not only ineffective but also harmful. The American Psychiatric Association, the Canadian Psychological Association, and the British Psychological Society have warned against conversion therapies that purport to change people's gender identity or sexual orientation. These therapies aim to "repair . . . something that is not a mental illness and therefore does not require therapy," declared American Psychological Association president Barry Anton (2015). Indeed, conversion therapy entails "a significant risk of harm" (APA, 2018a; Turban et al., 2020). Such evidence has led to many bans of this practice, especially for minors. Other initiatives—the Scared Straight program designed to tame teenage violence, the police-promoted D.A.R.E. anti-drug effort, and numerous weight-reduction and pedophile rehabilitation efforts—have also been found ineffective or even harmful (Walton & Wilson, 2018).

The evaluation question—which therapies get prizes and which do not?—lies at the heart of what some call psychology's civil war. To what extent should science guide both clinical practice and the willingness of health care providers and insurers to pay for psychotherapy? On one side are research psychologists using scientific methods to extend the list of well-defined and validated therapies for various disorders. They decry clinicians who seem to "give more weight to their personal experience than to science" (Baker et al., 2008). On the other side are some nonscientist therapists who view their practice as more art than science: People are too complex and psychotherapy is too intuitive to describe in a manual or test in an experiment.

Between these two factions stand the science-oriented clinicians calling for **evidence-based practice,** which has been endorsed by the American Psychological Association and others (2006; Holmes et al., 2018; Sakaluk et al., 2019). Therapists using this approach integrate the best available research with clinical expertise and with client preferences and characteristics (**FIGURE 54.2**). After rigorous evaluation, clinicians apply therapies suited to their own skills and their clients' unique situations. Some are using technology, too. By analyzing many pieces of client information, computer programs can help clinicians offer personalized therapeutic solutions (Ewbank et al., 2019; Webb et al., 2020). Increasingly, insurer and government support for mental health services require evidence-based practice.

◳ **FIGURE 54.2**
Evidence-based practice Ideal clinical decision making can be visualized as a three-legged stool, upheld by research evidence, clinical expertise, and knowledge of the client.

Client's culture, values, personal identity, preferences, circumstances

Clinical expertise

Best available research evidence

RETRIEVAL PRACTICE

RP-2 Therapy is most likely to be helpful for those with problems that _____ (are/are not) well-defined.

RP-3 What is *evidence-based practice*?

ANSWERS IN APPENDIX E

---

evidence-based practice clinical decision making that integrates the best available research with clinical expertise and patient characteristics and preferences.

therapeutic alliance a bond of trust and mutual understanding between a therapist and client, who work together constructively to overcome the client's problem.

How Do Psychotherapies Help People?

LOQ 54-3 What three elements are shared by all forms of psychotherapy?

Why have studies found little correlation between therapists' training and experience and clients' outcomes? One answer seems to be that all psychotherapies share three basic benefits (Cuijpers et al., 2019; Frank, 1982; Wampold, 2007):

- *Hope for demoralized people* People seeking therapy typically feel anxious, depressed, self-disapproving, and incapable of turning things around. What any psychotherapy offers is the expectation that, with commitment from the therapy seeker, things can and will get better. This belief, apart from any therapeutic technique, may improve morale, create feelings of self-efficacy, and diminish symptoms (Corrigan, 2014; Meyerhoff & Rohan, 2016).

- *A new perspective* Every therapy offers people a plausible explanation of their symptoms. Armed with a believable fresh perspective, they may approach life with a new attitude, open to making changes in their behaviors and their views of themselves.

- *An empathic, trusting, caring relationship* No matter what technique they use, effective therapists are empathic. They seek to understand the client's experience. They communicate care and concern, and they earn trust through respectful listening, reassurance, and guidance. These qualities were clear in recorded therapy sessions from 36 recognized master therapists (Goldfried et al., 1998). Some took a cognitive-behavioral approach. Others used psychodynamic principles. Although the master therapists used different approaches, they showed some striking *similarities*. They helped clients evaluate themselves, link one aspect of their life with another, and gain insight into their interactions with others. The emotional bond between therapist and client—the **therapeutic alliance**—helps explain why empathic, caring therapists are especially effective (Atzil-Slonim et al., 2019; Rubel et al., 2019). Whether experienced in Canada or Cambodia, a strong therapeutic alliance fosters psychological health (Falkenström et al., 2019; Gold, 2019). A therapeutic alliance may even save lives. In one analysis of a dozen studies, a strong therapeutic alliance predicted less frequent suicidal thoughts, self-harming behaviors, and suicide attempts (Dunster-Page et al., 2017).

"The thing is, you have to really want to change."

These three common elements—hope, a fresh perspective, and an empathic, caring relationship—help us understand why *paraprofessionals* (briefly trained caregivers, who may be recovered former clients) can assist many troubled people so effectively (Bryan & Arkowitz, 2015; Christensen & Jacobson, 1994). They are also part of what the growing numbers of in-person and online self-help and support groups offer their members. And they are part of what traditional healers have offered (Jackson, 1992). Healers everywhere— special people to whom others disclose their suffering, whether psychiatrists or shamans—have listened in order to understand and to empathize, reassure, advise, console, interpret, or explain (Torrey, 1986). Such qualities may explain why people who feel supported by close relationships—who enjoy the fellowship and friendship of caring people—have been less likely to seek therapy (Frank, 1982; O'Connor & Brown, 1984).

Friendship bench Some Zimbabwe health clinics have added outdoor "friendship benches," where paraprofessional community health workers offer therapy (Chibanda, 2016). Psychiatrist Dixon Chibanda created this free therapy for rural communities after a client without bus fare to get to his office died by suicide. "We have to take [psychiatry] to the community," he said (Rosenberg, 2019).

* * *

To recap, people who seek help usually improve. So do many of those who do not undergo psychotherapy, and that is a tribute to our human resourcefulness and our capacity to care for one another. Nevertheless, though the therapist's orientation and experience appear not to matter much, people who receive some psychotherapy usually improve more than those who do not. People with clear-cut, specific problems tend to improve the most.

ASK YOURSELF

Based on what you've read, would you seek therapy if you were struggling with a problem? Why or why not? If you've experienced therapy, does what you've learned influence your feelings about the experience?

RETRIEVAL PRACTICE

RP-4 Those who undergo psychotherapy are _____ (more/less) likely to show improvement than those who do not undergo psychotherapy.

ANSWERS IN APPENDIX E

How Does Human Diversity Influence Psychotherapy?

LOQ 54-4 What personal factors influence the therapist-client relationship?

All psychotherapies offer hope, and nearly all psychotherapists attempt to enhance their clients' sensitivity, openness, personal responsibility, and sense of purpose (Jensen & Bergin, 1988). But in matters of culture, values, and personal identity, psychotherapists differ from one another and may differ from their clients (Delaney et al., 2007; Kelly, 1990).

These differences can create a mismatch—for example, when a therapist from one culture interacts with a client from another. In North America, Europe, and Australia, most psychotherapists reflect their culture's *individualism,* which often gives priority to personal desires and identity. Clients with a *collectivist* perspective, as with many from Asian cultures, may assume people will be more mindful of social and family responsibilities, harmony, and group goals. These clients may have trouble relating to therapists who ask them to think only of their own well-being (Markus & Kitayama, 1991).

Cultural differences help explain some groups' reluctance to use mental health services. People living in "cultures of honor" prize being strong and tough. They may feel that seeking mental health care is an admission of weakness rather than an opportunity for growth (Brown et al., 2014). And some minority groups tend to be both reluctant to seek therapy and quick to leave it (Chen et al., 2009; Sue et al., 2009). In one experiment, Asian American clients matched with counselors who shared their cultural values (rather than mismatched with those who did not) perceived more counselor empathy and felt a stronger alliance with the counselor (Kim et al., 2005). Apparent mismatches can have life or death consequences: U.S. military personnel who have perceived greater barriers to treatment have been most likely to die by suicide (Zuromski et al., 2019).

Client-psychotherapist mismatches may also stem from other personal differences. Highly religious people may prefer and benefit from religiously similar therapists who share their values and beliefs (Masters, 2010; Pearce et al., 2015). Likewise, therapists' attitudes toward people who identify as lesbian, gay, bisexual, transgender, or questioning/queer (LGBTQ) can affect the client-therapist relationship. Transgender people, for example, may understandably seek out therapists who affirm them (Bettergarcia & Israel, 2018).

Who Seeks Psychotherapy and Who Provides It?

LOQ 54-5 When should a person seek therapy, and what should people look for when selecting a therapist?

Life for everyone is marked by a mix of serenity and stress, blessing and bereavement, good moods and bad. So, when should we seek a mental health professional's help? The American Psychological Association offers these common trouble signals:

- Feelings of hopelessness
- Deep and lasting depression
- Self-destructive behavior, such as substance abuse
- Disruptive fears
- Sudden mood shifts
- Thoughts of suicide
- Compulsive rituals, such as lock checking
- Sexual difficulties
- Hearing voices or seeing things that others don't experience

In looking for a psychotherapist, you may want to have a preliminary consultation with two or three. Meeting with more than one therapist gives you more opportunities to find someone with whom you feel comfortable sharing. College and university health centers are generally good starting points; you may be able to access qualified therapists and some free services by browsing their web page or visiting in person. You may also

TABLE 54.1 Therapists and Their Training

Type	Description
Clinical psychologists	Most are psychologists with a Ph.D. (includes research training) or Psy.D. (focuses on therapy) supplemented by a supervised internship and, often, postdoctoral training. About half work in agencies and institutions, half in private practice.
Psychiatrists	Psychiatrists are physicians who specialize in the treatment of psychological disorders. Not all psychiatrists have had extensive training in psychotherapy, but as M.D.s or D.O.s they can prescribe medications. Thus, they tend to see those with the most serious problems. Many have their own private practice.
Clinical or psychiatric social workers	A two-year master of social work graduate program plus postgraduate supervision prepares some social workers to offer psychotherapy, mostly to people with everyday personal and family problems. About half in the United States have earned the National Association of Social Workers' designation of clinical social worker.
Counselors	Family and couples counselors specialize in problems arising from family relations. Clergy provide counseling to countless people. Abuse counselors work with substance abusers and with spouse and child abusers and victims of abuse. Mental health and other counselors may be required to have a two-year master's degree.

get a referral from a physician or walk-in clinic. If you have insurance coverage, your provider may supply a listing of participating therapists. Many people also use the internet to search for therapists and to receive help online or via one of the more than 10,000 mental health apps (Kocsis, 2018; Levin et al., 2018; Nielssen et al., 2019). Online and app-based therapy can help reduce depression, anxiety, and insomnia (Espie et al., 2019; Firth et al., 2017a,b; Linardon et al., 2019).

In your in-person or online meetings, you can describe your problem and learn each therapist's treatment approach. You can ask questions about the therapist's values, credentials (**TABLE 54.1**), and fees. And you can assess your own feelings about each of them. The emotional bond between therapist and client is perhaps the most important factor in effective therapy.

The American Psychological Association recognizes the importance of a strong therapeutic alliance and it welcomes diverse therapists who can relate well to diverse clients. It accredits programs that provide training in cultural sensitivity (for example, to differing values, communication styles, and languages) and that recruit underrepresented cultural groups.

What Are Some Important Ethical Principles in Psychotherapy?

LOQ 54-6 What ethical principles guide psychotherapy and psychological research on mental illness?

Psychotherapists use different approaches to help reduce their clients' suffering. Likewise, researchers apply many methods to understand how to lessen people's disordered thoughts, feelings, and behaviors. But before psychotherapists or researchers begin their treatment or investigation, they must follow their country's ethical principles and code of conduct (APA, 2017a).

According to the American Psychological Association, your therapist should follow these principles:

- Seek to benefit you and do you no harm
- Establish a feeling of trust and a defined role as your therapist, as well as be of service to the therapeutic community
- Be honest, truthful, and accurate
- Be fair and promote justice for you and others, helping everyone to have access to the benefits of therapy
- Respect the dignity and worth of you and others, recognizing the right to privacy, confidentiality, and self-determination

Psychological researchers use the same ethical guidelines when studying how to lessen mental illness. They aim to benefit others, to be honest and truthful, and to never expose people to experiences that pose greater than a *minimal risk*—to more than what people may encounter in their daily lives.

RETRIEVAL PRACTICE

RP-5 There are many acceptable mental health treatment and study approaches, but all therapists and psychological researchers must follow _____ principles.

ANSWERS IN APPENDIX E

MODULE

54 **REVIEW** Evaluating Psychotherapies

LEARNING OBJECTIVES

Test Yourself Answer these repeated Learning Objective Questions on your own (before checking the answers in Appendix D) to improve your retention of the concepts (McDaniel et al., 2009, 2015).

LOQ 54-1 Does psychotherapy work? How can we know?

LOQ 54-2 Are some psychotherapies more effective than others for specific disorders?

LOQ 54-3 What three elements are shared by all forms of psychotherapy?

LOQ 54-4 What personal factors influence the therapist-client relationship?

LOQ 54-5 When should a person seek therapy, and what should people look for when selecting a therapist?

LOQ 54-6 What ethical principles guide psychotherapy and psychological research on mental illness?

TERMS AND CONCEPTS TO REMEMBER

Test Yourself Write down the definition in your own words, then check your answer.

psychotherapy, p. 613

confirmation bias, p. 613

meta-analysis, p. 615

evidence-based practice, p. 616

therapeutic alliance, p. 616

MASTER THE MATERIAL

Test Yourself Answer the following questions on your own first, then check your answers in Appendix E.

1. The most enthusiastic or optimistic view of the effectiveness of psychotherapy comes from

   a. outcome research.

   b. randomized clinical trials.

   c. reports of clinicians and clients.

   d. a government study of treatment for depression.

2. Studies show that _____ therapy is the most effective treatment for most psychological disorders.

   a. behavior

   b. humanistic

   c. psychodynamic

   d. no one type of

3. What are the three components of evidence-based practice?

4. Psychotherapies help people by providing _____, a new perspective, and an empathic, trusting, caring relationship.

Continue testing yourself with 📖 **LearningCurve** or 📖 **Achieve Read & Practice** to learn and remember most effectively.

MODULE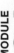

55 The Biomedical Therapies and Preventing Psychological Disorders

"No twisted thought without a twisted molecule." — Attributed to psychologist Ralph Gerard (1900–1974)

> **biomedical therapy** prescribed medications or procedures that act directly on the person's physiology.

Psychotherapy is one way to treat psychological disorders. The other is **biomedical therapy**. Biomedical treatments can change the brain's chemistry with drugs; affect its circuitry with electrical stimulation, magnetic impulses, or psychosurgery; or influence its responses with lifestyle changes.

Are you surprised to find *lifestyle changes* in this list? We find it convenient to talk of separate psychological and biological influences, but everything psychological is also biological. Thus, our lifestyle—exercise, nutrition, relationships, recreation, relaxation, religious or spiritual engagement, and our service to others—affects our mental health (Schuch et al., 2016; Walsh, 2011). (See Thinking Critically About: Therapeutic Lifestyle Change.)

Thinking Critically About:
Therapeutic Lifestyle Change

LOQ 55-1 Why is therapeutic lifestyle change considered an effective biomedical therapy, and how does it work?

LIFESTYLE
(exercise, nutrition, relationships, recreation, service to others, relaxation, and religious or spiritual engagement) → influences our **BRAIN AND BODY** → affects our **MENTAL HEALTH**[1]

Our shared history has prepared us to be physically active and socially engaged.

Our ancestors hunted, gathered, and built in groups.

Modern researchers have found that outdoor activity in a natural environment reduces stress and promotes health.[2]

APPLICATION TO THERAPY

Training seminars promote therapeutic lifestyle change.[3] Small groups of people with depression undergo a 12-week training program with the following goals:

Aerobic exercise, 30 minutes a day, at least three times weekly (increases fitness and vitality, stimulates endorphins)

Regular aerobic exercise rivals the healing power of antidepressant drugs.[4]

Light exposure, 15 to 30 minutes each morning with a light box (amplifies arousal, influences hormones)

Reducing rumination, by identifying and redirecting negative thoughts (enhances positive thinking)

Adequate sleep, with a goal of 7 to 8 hours per night.

A complete night's sleep boosts immunity and increases energy, alertness, and mood.[5]

ZZZZZZZZZZZZZZZZZZZZZZZZ

Social connection, with less alone time and at least two meaningful social engagements weekly (helps satisfy the human need to belong)

Nutritional supplements, including a daily supplement with omega-3 fatty acids (reduces aggressive behavior)[6]

Initial small study (74 participants)[7]

77% of those who completed the program experienced relief from depressive symptoms.

Only 19% of those assigned to a treatment-as-usual control group showed similar results.

Future research will try to identify which parts of the treatment produce the therapeutic effect.

The biomedical therapies assume that mind and body are a unit:

Affect one and you will affect the other.

1. Sánchez-Villegas et al., 2015; Walsh, 2011. 2. MacKerron & Mourato, 2013; NEEF, 2015; Phillips, 2011. 3. Ilardi, 2009. 4. Babyak et al., 2000; Salmon, 2001; Schuch et al., 2016. 5. Gregory et al., 2009; Walker & van der Helm, 2009. 6. Bègue et al., 2017; Raine et al., 2018. 7. Ilardi, 2009, 2016.

Every thought and feeling depends on the functioning brain. Every creative idea, every moment of joy or anger, every period of depression emerges from the electrochemical activity of the living brain. Anxiety disorders, obsessive-compulsive and related disorders, posttraumatic stress disorder, depressive disorders, bipolar disorders, and schizophrenia are all biological events. Some psychologists consider even psychotherapy to be a biological treatment, because changing the way we think and behave is a brain-changing experience (Kandel, 2013). When psychotherapy relieves behaviors associated with obsessive-compulsive disorder or schizophrenia, PET scans reveal a calmer brain (Habel et al., 2010; Schwartz et al., 1996). As we have seen over and over, *a human being is an integrated biopsychosocial system.*

> **RETRIEVAL PRACTICE**
>
> **RP-1** What are some examples of lifestyle changes people can make to enhance their mental health?
>
> *ANSWERS IN APPENDIX E*

Drug Therapies

LOQ 55-2 What are the drug therapies? How do double-blind studies help researchers evaluate a drug's effectiveness?

By far the most widely used biomedical treatments today are the drug therapies. Most drugs for anxiety and depression are prescribed by primary care providers, followed by psychiatrists and, in some U.S. states, psychologists. As is the case for most medical treatment, people can choose whether to take prescribed mental health medications—except in rare cases of risk of great harm to self or others.

Since the 1950s, discoveries in **psychopharmacology** (the study of drug effects on mind and behavior) have revolutionized the treatment of people with severe disorders, liberating hundreds of thousands from hospital confinement. Thanks to drug therapies and local community mental health programs, today's resident population of psychiatric hospitals has dropped to a small fraction of what it once was. For some who are unable to care for themselves, however, release from hospitals has meant homelessness, not liberation.

"Our psychopharmacologist is a genius."

Almost any new treatment, including drug therapy, is greeted by an initial wave of enthusiasm as many people apparently improve. But that enthusiasm often diminishes on closer examination. To evaluate the effectiveness of any new drug, researchers also need to know normal recovery rates:

- How many people recover without treatment, and how quickly?

- Is recovery due to the drug or to the placebo effect? When patients or mental health workers expect positive results, they may see what they expect, not what really happens. Even mere exposure to advertising about a drug's supposed effectiveness can increase its effect (Kamenica et al., 2013).

To control for these influences, drug researchers give half the patients the drug, and the other half a similar-appearing placebo. Because neither the staff nor the patients know who gets which, this is called a *double-blind procedure*. The good news: In double-blind studies, several types of drugs effectively treat psychological disorders.

Antipsychotic Drugs

An accidental discovery launched a treatment revolution for people with *psychoses*. The discovery: Certain drugs, used for other medical purposes, calmed the hallucinations or delusions that are part of these patients' split from reality. First-generation **antipsychotic drugs,** such as chlorpromazine (Thorazine), dampened responsiveness to irrelevant stimuli. Thus, they provided the most help to patients experiencing positive (actively inappropriate) symptoms of schizophrenia, such as auditory hallucinations and paranoia (Leucht et al., 2018). (Antipsychotic drugs are less effective in changing negative symptoms, such as apathy and withdrawal.)

The molecules of most conventional antipsychotic drugs are similar enough to molecules of the neurotransmitter dopamine to occupy its receptor sites and block its activity. This finding reinforces the idea that an overactive dopamine system contributes to schizophrenia.

Antipsychotics also have powerful side effects. Some produce sluggishness, tremors, and twitches similar to those of Parkinson's disease (Kaplan & Saddock, 1989). Long-term use of antipsychotics can produce *tardive dyskinesia,* with involuntary movements of the facial muscles (such as grimacing), tongue, and limbs. Although not more effective in controlling schizophrenia symptoms, many of the newer-generation antipsychotics, such as risperidone (Risperdal) and olanzapine (Zyprexa), work best for those with severe symptoms and have fewer of these effects (Furukawa et al., 2015). These drugs may, however, increase the risk of obesity and diabetes (Buchanan et al., 2010; Tiihonen et al., 2009). Researchers have combed through historical data to identify the most effective and safe dose for more than 20 antipsychotic medications (Leucht et al., 2020).

Antipsychotics, combined with life-skills programs and family support, have given new hope to many people with schizophrenia (Goff et al., 2017; Guo et al., 2010). Computer programs are now helping clinicians identify which people with schizophrenia will benefit from specific antipsychotic medications (Lee, B. et al., 2018; Yu et al., 2018b). Hundreds of thousands of patients have returned to work and to near-normal lives (Leucht et al., 2003). Elyn Saks (2007), a University of Southern California law professor, knows what it means to live with schizophrenia. Thanks to her treatment, which combines an antipsychotic drug and psychotherapy, she noted, "Now I'm mostly well. I'm mostly thinking clearly. I do have episodes, but it's not like I'm struggling all of the time to stay on the right side of the line."

Antianxiety Drugs

Like alcohol, **antianxiety drugs,** such as Xanax or Ativan, depress central nervous system activity (and so should not be used in combination with alcohol). Some antianxiety drugs have been successfully used in combination with psychological therapy to enhance exposure therapy's extinction of learned fears and to help relieve the symptoms of posttraumatic stress disorder and obsessive-compulsive disorder (Davis, 2005; Kushner et al., 2007).

Some critics fear that antianxiety drugs may reduce symptoms without resolving underlying problems, especially when used as an ongoing treatment. "Popping a Xanax" at the first sign of tension can create a learned response: The immediate relief reinforces a person's tendency to take drugs when anxious. Antianxiety drugs can also be addictive. Regular users who stop taking these drugs may experience increased anxiety, insomnia, and other withdrawal symptoms.

Antidepressant Drugs

The **antidepressant drugs** were named for their ability to lift people up from a state of depression, and this was their main use until recently. These drugs are now also increasingly used to treat anxiety disorders, obsessive-compulsive and related disorders, and posttraumatic stress disorder (Beaulieu et al., 2019; Merz et al., 2019; Slee et al., 2019). Many work by increasing the availability of neurotransmitters, such as norepinephrine or serotonin, which elevate arousal and mood and are scarce when a person experiences feelings of depression or anxiety. The most commonly prescribed drugs in this group, including Prozac and its cousins Zoloft and Paxil, work by prolonging the time serotonin molecules remain in the brain's synapses. They do this by partially blocking the normal reuptake process. Given their use in treating disorders other than depressive ones—from anxiety to strokes—these drugs are most often called *SSRIs—selective serotonin reuptake inhibitors* (rather than antidepressants) (Kramer, 2011).

Some of the older antidepressant drugs work by blocking the reabsorption or breakdown of both norepinephrine and serotonin. Though effective, these dual-action drugs have more potential side effects, such as dry mouth, weight gain, hypertension, or dizzy spells (Anderson, 2000; Mulrow, 1999). Administering them by means of a patch, which bypasses the intestines and liver, helps reduce such side effects (Bodkin & Amsterdam, 2002).

Perhaps you can guess an occasional side effect of L-dopa, a drug that raises dopamine levels for Parkinson's patients: hallucinations.

psychopharmacology the study of the effects of drugs on mind and behavior.

antipsychotic drugs drugs used to treat schizophrenia and other forms of severe thought disorders.

antianxiety drugs drugs used to control anxiety and agitation.

antidepressant drugs drugs used to treat depressive disorders, anxiety disorders, obsessive-compulsive and related disorders, and posttraumatic stress disorder. (Several widely used antidepressant drugs are *selective serotonin reuptake inhibitors—SSRIs.*)

But be advised: Patients with depression who begin taking antidepressants do not wake up the next morning singing, "It's a beautiful day!" SSRIs begin to influence neurotransmission within hours, but their full psychological effect may take four weeks (and may involve a side effect of diminished sexual desire). One possible reason for the delay is that increased serotonin promotes new synapses plus *neurogenesis*—the birth of new brain cells—perhaps reversing stress-induced loss of neurons (Launay et al., 2011). With those at risk of suicide, researchers are also exploring the possibility of quicker-acting antidepressants. One, ketamine, which is also an anesthetic that is sometimes used as a risky, psychedelic party drug, blocks hyperactive receptors for glutamate, a neurotransmitter. It can provide relief from depression in as little as an hour (Domany et al., 2019; Phillips et al., 2019; Popova, V. et al., 2019). But the relief often dissipates in a week, which raises questions about the risks of repeated use (Nemeroff, 2018; Schatzberg, 2019). Given that ketamine acts as an opioid, one skeptic wonders if ketamine clinics are "nothing more than modern opium dens" (George, 2018). But others note that ketamine stimulates new synapses (Beyeler, 2019).

Some drug companies are hoping to develop ketamine-like, fast-acting drugs with fewer side effects (Kirby, 2015). Researchers are also exploring possible therapeutic benefits of microdosing psychedelic drugs such as psilocybin (Carey, 2019b; Kuypers et al., 2019). Antidepressant drugs are not the only way to give the body a lift. Aerobic exercise often calms people who feel anxious and energizes those who feel depressed. Regular physical activity boosts teen mental health (Beauchamp et al., 2018). And for adults worldwide, three or more weekly exercise hours predicts a lower risk of future depression (Choi et al., 2019; Schuch et al., 2018).

Cognitive therapy, by helping people reverse their habitual negative thinking style, can boost drug-aided relief from depression and reduce posttreatment relapses (Amick et al., 2015). Some clinicians attack depression (and anxiety) from both below and above (Cuijpers et al., 2010; Hollon et al., 2014; Kennard et al., 2014): They use antidepressant drugs (which work, bottom-up, on the emotion-forming limbic system) in conjunction with cognitive-behavioral therapy (which works, top-down, to alter frontal lobe activity and change thought processes).

Researchers generally agree that people with depression often improve after a month on antidepressant drugs. But after allowing for natural recovery and the placebo effect, how big is the drug effect? The effect is consistent but, critics argue, not very big (Cipriani et al., 2018; Kirsch et al., 1998, 2014). In double-blind clinical trials,

"If this doesn't help you don't worry, it's a placebo."

placebos produced improvement comparable to about 75 percent of the active drug's effect. For those with severe depression, there is less of a placebo effect and the added drug benefit is somewhat greater (Fournier et al., 2010; Kirsch et al., 2008; Olfson & Marcus, 2009). Given the negative side effects of antidepressant drugs, some clinicians advise beginning with psychotherapy before introducing antidepressants (Strayhorn, 2019; Svaldi et al., 2019). "If [drugs] are to be used at all," notes Irving Kirsch (2016), "it should be as a last resort." *The point to remember:* If you're concerned about your mental health, consult with a mental health professional to determine the best treatment for you.

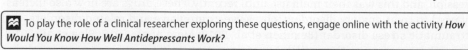

To play the role of a clinical researcher exploring these questions, engage online with the activity *How Would You Know How Well Antidepressants Work?*

Mood-Stabilizing Medications

In addition to antipsychotic, antianxiety, and antidepressant drugs, psychiatrists have *mood-stabilizing drugs* in their arsenal. One of them, Depakote, was originally used to treat epilepsy. It was also found effective in controlling the manic episodes associated with bipolar disorders. Another, the simple salt *lithium,* effectively levels the emotional highs and lows of these disorders.

In the 1940s, Australian physician John Cade discovered that lithium calmed guinea pigs. Wondering if it might do the same for humans, he first tried it himself (to confirm its safety), and then on 10 people with mania—all of whom dramatically improved (Brown, 2019). About 7 in 10 people with bipolar disorders benefit from a long-term daily dose of this cheap salt, which helps prevent or ease manic episodes and, to a lesser extent, lifts depression (Solomon et al., 1995). Kay Redfield Jamison (1995) described the effect:

electroconvulsive therapy (ECT) a biomedical therapy for severely depressed patients in which a brief electric current is sent through the brain of an anesthetized patient.

Lithium prevents my seductive but disastrous highs, diminishes my depressions, clears out the wool and webbing from my disordered thinking, slows me down, gentles me out, keeps me from ruining my career and relationships, keeps me out of a hospital, alive, and makes psychotherapy possible. (pp. 88–89)

Taking lithium also correlates with a lower risk of suicide among people with bipolar disorders—to about one-sixth the risk of those not taking lithium (Oquendo et al., 2011). Naturally occurring lithium in drinking water has also correlated with lower suicide rates (across 18 Japanese cities and towns) and lower crime rates (across 27 Texas counties) (Ohgami et al., 2009; Schrauzer & Shrestha, 1990, 2010; Terao et al., 2010). Lithium works.

RETRIEVAL PRACTICE

RP-2 How do researchers determine if particular drug therapies are effective?

RP-3 The drugs given most often to treat depression are called _____.
Schizophrenia is often treated with _____ drugs.

ANSWERS IN APPENDIX E

Brain Stimulation

LOQ 55-3 How are brain stimulation and psychosurgery used in treating specific disorders?

Electroconvulsive Therapy

Another biomedical treatment, **electroconvulsive therapy (ECT),** manipulates the brain by shocking it. When ECT was first introduced in 1938, the wide-awake patient was strapped to a table and jolted with electricity to the brain. The procedure, which produced convulsions and brief unconsciousness, gained a barbaric image. Although that image lingers, today's ECT is much kinder and gentler, and no longer "convulsive." The patient receives a general anesthetic and a muscle relaxant (to prevent bodily convulsions). A psychiatrist then delivers a brief electrical pulse, sometimes only to the brain's right side, which triggers a 30- to 60-second brain seizure (McCall et al., 2017). Within 30 minutes, the patient awakens and remembers nothing of the treatment or of the preceding hours. The mysteriously effective treatment is similar to rebooting a computer, or interrupting an orchestra and sending the musicians home for a short nap.

Study after study confirms that ECT can effectively treat severe depression in "treatment-resistant" patients who have not responded to drug therapy (Fink, 2009; Giacobbe et al., 2018; Ross, E. et al., 2018). After three such sessions each week for two to four weeks, 70 percent or more of those receiving today's ECT improve markedly, with less memory loss than with earlier versions of ECT and without discernible brain damage or increased dementia risk (Osler et al., 2018). ECT also reduces suicidal thoughts and has been credited with saving many from suicide (Kellner et al., 2006). A *Journal of the American Medical Association* editorial concluded that "the results of ECT in treating severe depression are among the most positive treatment effects in all of medicine" (Glass, 2001).

How does ECT alleviate severe depression? After more than 70 years, no one knows for sure. One recipient likened ECT to the smallpox vaccine, which was saving lives before we knew how it worked. Perhaps the brief electric current calms neural centers where overactivity produces depression. Some research indicates that ECT stimulates neurogenesis (new neurons) and new synaptic connections (Joshi et al., 2016; Rothene-ichner et al., 2014; Wang et al., 2017b).

No matter how impressive the results, the idea of electrically shocking a person's brain still strikes many as barbaric, especially given our ignorance about why ECT works. Moreover, the mood boost may not last long. Many ECT-treated patients eventually relapse back into depression, although relapses are somewhat fewer for those who also receive antidepressant drugs or who do aerobic exercise (Rosenquist et al., 2016; Salehi et al., 2016). *The bottom line:* In the minds of many psychiatrists and patients, ECT is a lesser evil than severe depression's anguish and risk of suicide. As research psychologist Norman Endler (1982) reported after ECT alleviated his deep depression, "A miracle had happened in two weeks."

The medical use of electricity is an ancient practice. Physicians treated the Roman Emperor Claudius (10 B.C.E.–54 C.E.) for headaches by pressing electric eels to his temples. Today, about 17 people per 100,000—people whose depression has not responded to other treatments—have received ECT (Lesage et al., 2016).

To witness the powerful effects of ECT, see the *Video: Electroconvulsive Therapy.*

Electroconvulsive therapy (ECT)
Psychiatrist administers a strong current, which triggers a seizure in the anesthetized patient.

Transcranial direct current stimulation (tDCS)
Psychiatrist applies a weak current to the scalp.

Transcranial magnetic stimulation (TMS)
Psychiatrist sends a painless magnetic field through the skull to the surface of the cortex to alter brain activity.

Deep brain stimulation (DBS)
Psychiatrist stimulates electrodes implanted in "sadness centers" to calm those areas.

⏱ FIGURE 55.1

A stimulating experience Today's neurostimulation therapies apply strong or mild electricity, or magnetic energy, either to the skull's surface or directly to brain neurons.

A depression switch? By comparing the brains of patients with and without depression, researcher Helen Mayberg identified a brain area (highlighted in red) that appears active in people who are depressed or sad, and whose activity may be calmed by deep brain stimulation.

Alternative Neurostimulation Therapies

Three other neural stimulation techniques—mild cranial electrical stimulation, magnetic stimulation, and deep brain stimulation—also aim to treat the depressed brain (**FIGURE 55.1**).

TRANSCRANIAL ELECTRICAL STIMULATION In contrast to ECT, which produces a brain seizure with about 800 milliamps of electricity, *transcranial direct current stimulation* (tDCS) administers a weak 1- to 2-milliamp current to the scalp. Skeptics argue that such a current is too weak to penetrate the brain (Underwood, 2016). But research suggests that tDCS is a modestly effective depression, schizophrenia, and obsessive-compulsive disorder treatment (Brunelin et al., 2018; Jeon et al., 2018; Koops et al., 2018).

MAGNETIC STIMULATION Depressed moods also sometimes improve when a painless procedure called **transcranial magnetic stimulation (TMS)** is performed on wide-awake patients in sessions over several weeks. Repeated pulses surging through a magnetic coil held close to the skull can stimulate or suppress activity in areas of the cortex. Like tDCS (and unlike ECT), the TMS procedure produces no memory loss or other serious side effects, aside from possible headaches.

Results are mixed. Some studies have found that, for 30 to 40 percent of people with depression, TMS works, although less effectively than ECT (Carmi et al, 2019; Mutz et al., 2019). TMS also reduces some symptoms of schizophrenia, such as loss of motivation and social interest (Osoegawa et al., 2018). How it works is unclear. One possible explanation is that the stimulation energizes the brain's left frontal lobe, which is relatively inactive during depression (Helmuth, 2001). Repeated stimulation may cause nerve cells to form new functioning circuits through the process of *long-term potentiation*. Another possible explanation is a placebo effect—people benefit when, after being given a credible rationale, they *believe* TMS will work (Geers et al., 2019; Yesavage et al., 2018).

DEEP BRAIN STIMULATION Other patients whose depression has resisted both drugs and ECT have benefited from an experimental treatment pinpointing a neural hub that bridges the thinking frontal lobes to the limbic system (Becker et al., 2016; Brunoni et al., 2017; Ryder & Holtzheimer, 2016). This area, which is overactive in the brain of a depressed or temporarily sad person, typically calms when treated by ECT or antidepressants. To experimentally activate neurons that inhibit this negative activity, neuroscientist Helen Mayberg drew upon *deep brain stimulation (DBS)* technology, sometimes used to treat Parkinson's tremors. Since 2003, she and her colleagues have used DBS to treat some 200 depressed patients via implanted electrodes in a brain area that functions as the neural "sadness center" (Lozano & Mayberg, 2015). Does DBS work? Studies show that, for some patients, DBS produces large and enduring reductions in depression (Crowell et al., 2019; Kisely et al., 2018). "The bottom line," notes Mayberg, "is that if you get better, you stay better" (Carey, 2019a).

Psychosurgery

Because its effects are irreversible, **psychosurgery**—surgery that removes or destroys brain tissue—is the most drastic and least-used biomedical intervention for changing behavior. In the 1930s, Portuguese physician Egas Moniz developed what would become the best-known psychosurgical operation: the **lobotomy.** Moniz found that cutting the nerves connecting the frontal lobes with the emotion-controlling centers of the inner brain calmed uncontrollably emotional and violent patients. In what would later become, in others' hands, a crude but quick and easy procedure, a neurosurgeon would shock the patient into a coma, hammer an icepick-like instrument through the top of each eye socket into the brain, and then wiggle it to sever connections running up to the frontal lobes. Between 1936 and 1954, tens of thousands of severely disturbed people were "lobotomized" (Valenstein, 1986).

Although the intention was simply to disconnect emotion from thought, the effect was often more drastic. A lobotomy usually decreased the person's misery or tension, but also produced a permanently lethargic, immature, uncreative person. During the 1950s, after some 35,000 people had been lobotomized in the United States alone, calming drugs became available and psychosurgery became scorned, as in the saying sometimes attributed to satirist Dorothy Parker that "I'd rather have a bottle in front of me than a frontal lobotomy."

Today, lobotomies are history. More precise, microscale psychosurgery is sometimes used in extreme cases. For example, if a patient suffers uncontrollable seizures, surgeons can deactivate the specific nerve clusters that cause or transmit the convulsions. MRI-guided precision surgery is also occasionally done to cut the circuits involved in severe major depressive disorder and obsessive-compulsive disorder (Carey, 2009, 2011; Kim, M. et al., 2018; Sachdev & Sachdev, 1997). Because these procedures are irreversible, neurosurgeons perform them only as a last resort.

Failed lobotomy This 1940 photo shows Rosemary Kennedy (center) at age 22 with brother (and future U.S. president) John and sister Jean. A year later, her father approved a lobotomy that doctors suggested would control her reportedly violent mood swings. The procedure left her confined to a hospital with an infantile mentality for the next 63 years, until her death in 2005.

RETRIEVAL PRACTICE

RP-4 Severe depression that has not responded to other therapy may be treated with _____ _____, which can cause some memory loss of the preceding hours. More moderate neural stimulation techniques designed to help alleviate depression include _____ direct current stimulation, _____ magnetic stimulation, and _____ stimulation.

ANSWERS IN APPENDIX E

---

* * *

TABLE 55.1 summarizes some aspects of the biomedical therapies we've discussed.

ASK YOURSELF

What were your impressions of biomedical therapies before reading this section? Are any of your views different now? Why or why not?

TABLE 55.1 Comparing Biomedical Therapies

Therapy	Presumed Problem	Therapy Aim	Therapy Technique
Therapeutic lifestyle change	Stress and unhealthy lifestyle	Restore healthy biological state.	Alter lifestyle through adequate exercise, sleep, nutrition, and other changes.
Drug therapies	Neurotransmitter malfunction	Control symptoms of psychological disorders.	Alter brain chemistry through drugs.
Brain stimulation	Depressive disorders (ECT is used only for severe, treatment-resistant depressive disorders)	Alleviate depression, especially when it is unresponsive to drugs or other forms of therapy.	Stimulate brain through electroconvulsive shock, mild electrical stimulation, magnetic pulses, or deep brain stimulation.
Psychosurgery	Brain malfunction	Relieve severe disorders.	Remove or destroy brain tissue.

transcranial magnetic stimulation (TMS) the application of repeated pulses of magnetic energy to the brain; used to stimulate or suppress brain activity.

psychosurgery surgery that removes or destroys brain tissue in an effort to change behavior.

lobotomy a psychosurgical procedure once used to calm uncontrollably emotional or violent patients. The procedure cut the nerves connecting the frontal lobes to the emotion-controlling centers of the inner brain.

THIS ANTI-DEPRESSANT WORKS BEST IF YOU TAKE IT WITH WATER LAPPING NEAR YOUR HAMMOCK ON A CARIBBEAN BEACH.

Dave Coverly/Speed Bump

Preventing Psychological Disorders and Building Resilience

LOQ **55-4** What may help prevent psychological disorders, and why is it important to develop resilience?

Psychotherapies and biomedical therapies tend to locate the cause of psychological disorders within the person. We infer that people who act cruelly must be cruel and that people who act "crazy" must be "sick." We attach labels to such people, thereby distinguishing them from "normal" folks. It follows, then, that we try to treat "abnormal" people by giving them insight into their problems, by changing their thinking, by helping them gain control with drugs.

There is an alternative viewpoint: We could interpret many psychological disorders as understandable responses to a disturbing and stressful world. According to this view, it is not just the person who needs treatment, but also the person's social context. Better to prevent a problem by reforming an unhealthy situation and by developing people's coping competencies than to wait for and treat problems.

Preventive Mental Health

A story about the rescue of a drowning person from a rushing river illustrates this viewpoint: Having successfully administered first aid to the victim, the rescuer spots another struggling person and pulls her out, too. After a half-dozen repetitions, the rescuer suddenly turns and starts running away while the river sweeps yet another floundering person into view. "Aren't you going to rescue that guy?" asks a bystander. "Nope," the rescuer replies. "I'm going upstream to find out what's pushing all these people in."

Preventive mental health is upstream work. It seeks to prevent psychological casualties by identifying and alleviating the conditions that cause them. As George Albee (1986, 2006) pointed out, there is abundant evidence that poverty, meaningless work, constant criticism, unemployment, and discrimination undermine people's sense of competence, personal control, and self-esteem. Such stresses increase their risk of depression, alcohol use disorder, and suicide. To prevent psychological casualties we should, Albee contended, support programs that work to improve these demoralizing situations. We eliminated smallpox not by treating the afflicted but by inoculating the unafflicted.

Preventing psychological problems means empowering those who have learned an attitude of helplessness and changing environments that breed loneliness. It means renewing fragile family ties and boosting parents' and teachers' skills at nurturing children's competence and belief in their abilities. It means harnessing positive psychology interventions to enhance human flourishing. One intervention taught adolescents that personality isn't fixed—people can change—and reduced their incidence of future depression by 40 percent (Miu & Yeager, 2015). This result is no fluke: Preventive therapies have consistently reduced the risk for depression (Breedvelt et al., 2018).

In short, "everything aimed at improving the human condition, at making life more fulfilling and meaningful, may be considered part of primary prevention of mental or emotional disturbance" (Kessler & Albee, 1975, p. 557). Prevention can sometimes provide a double payoff. People with a strong sense of life's meaning are more engaging socially (Stillman et al., 2011). By strengthening people's sense of meaning in life, we may also lessen their loneliness as they become more engaging companions.

Among the upstream prevention workers are *community psychologists*. Mindful of how people interact with their environment, they focus on creating environments that support psychological health. Through their research and social action, community psychologists aim to empower people and to enhance their competence, health, and well-being.

Building Resilience

Preventive mental health includes efforts to build individuals' **resilience**—the ability to cope with stress and recover from adversity.

Faced with extreme suffering or trauma, some people experience lasting harm, some experience stable resilience, and some actually experience growth (Myers, 2019). In the aftermath of the September 11 terror attacks, many New Yorkers exhibited resilience.

"It is better to prevent than to cure."
— Peruvian folk wisdom

"Mental disorders arise from physical ones, and likewise physical disorders arise from mental ones." — *The Mahabharata*, 200 B.C.E.

Resilient growth from prisoner to politician Before becoming a U.S. senator, the late John McCain spent more than five years as a Vietnam War prisoner. He was regularly beaten and tortured, which left him permanently unable to lift his arms above his head. Yet he was resilient: "I put the war behind me when I left," he said. "The memories I have are of the wonderful people I had the privilege of serving with" (Myre, 2000). When McCain was diagnosed with brain cancer in 2017 (he died the following year), his daughter Meghan tweeted that "the one of us who is most confident and calm is my father."

This was especially true for those who enjoyed supportive close relationships and who had not recently experienced other stressful events (Bonanno et al., 2007). More than 9 in 10 New Yorkers, although stunned and grief-stricken by 9/11, did *not* have a dysfunctional stress reaction. Among those who did, the stress symptoms were mostly gone by the following January (Person et al., 2006). Even most combat-stressed veterans, most political rebels who have survived torture, and most people with spinal cord injuries do not later exhibit posttraumatic stress disorder (Bonanno et al., 2012; Mineka & Zinbarg, 1996).

Struggling with challenging crises can lead to **posttraumatic growth.** Many cancer survivors have reported a greater appreciation for life, more meaningful relationships, increased personal strength, changed priorities, and a richer spiritual life (Tedeschi & Calhoun, 2004). Out of even our worst experiences, some good can come, especially when we can imagine new possibilities (Mangelsdorf et al., 2019; Roepke, 2015). As with positive experiences, suffering can beget new sensitivity and strength.

RETRIEVAL PRACTICE

RP-5 What is the difference between preventive mental health and the psychological or biomedical therapies?

ANSWERS IN APPENDIX E

> 📖 Consider ways to build your own resilience by engaging with *Assess Your Strengths—How Resilient Are You, and Why Should You Build More Resilience?*

* * *

If you just finished reading this book, your introduction to psychological science is completed. Our tour of psychological science has taught us much—and you, too?—about our moods and memories, about the reach of our unconscious, about how we flourish and struggle, about how we perceive our physical and social worlds, and about how our biology and culture together weave us. As your guides on this tour, we hope that you have shared our fascination, grown in your understanding and compassion, and sharpened your critical thinking. And we hope you enjoyed the ride.

With every good wish in your life journey ahead,

David G. Myers
DavidMyers.org

Nathan DeWall
NathanDeWall.com

resilience the personal strength that helps people cope with stress and recover from adversity and even trauma.

posttraumatic growth positive psychological changes following a struggle with extremely challenging circumstances and life crises.

55 REVIEW The Biomedical Therapies and Preventing Psychological Disorders

LEARNING OBJECTIVES

Test Yourself Answer these repeated Learning Objective Questions on your own (before checking the answers in Appendix D) to improve your retention of the concepts (McDaniel et al., 2009, 2015).

LOQ 55-1 Why is therapeutic lifestyle change considered an effective biomedical therapy, and how does it work?

LOQ 55-2 What are the drug therapies? How do double-blind studies help researchers evaluate a drug's effectiveness?

LOQ 55-3 How are brain stimulation and psychosurgery used in treating specific disorders?

LOQ 55-4 What may help prevent psychological disorders, and why is it important to develop resilience?

TERMS AND CONCEPTS TO REMEMBER

Test Yourself Write down the definition in your own words, then check your answer.

biomedical therapy, p. 620

psychopharmacology, p. 623

antipsychotic drugs, p. 623

antianxiety drugs, p. 623

antidepressant drugs, p. 623

electroconvulsive therapy (ECT), p. 624

transcranial magnetic stimulation (TMS), p. 627

psychosurgery, p. 627

lobotomy, p. 627

resilience, p. 629

posttraumatic growth, p. 629

MASTER THE MATERIAL

Test Yourself Answer the following questions on your own first, then check your answers in Appendix E.

1. Some antipsychotic drugs, used to calm people with schizophrenia, can have unpleasant side effects, most notably
   a. hyperactivity.
   b. momentary memory loss.
   c. sluggishness, tremors, and twitches.
   d. paranoia.

2. Drugs such as Xanax and Ativan, which depress central nervous system activity, can become addictive when used as ongoing treatment. These drugs are referred to as _____ drugs.

3. A simple salt that often brings relief to patients suffering the highs and lows of a bipolar disorder is _____.

4. When drug therapies have not been effective, electroconvulsive therapy (ECT) may be used as a treatment for people with
   a. severe obsessive-compulsive disorder.
   b. severe depression.
   c. schizophrenia.
   d. anxiety disorders.

5. An approach that seeks to identify and alleviate conditions that put people at higher risk for developing psychological disorders is called
   a. deep brain stimulation.
   b. the mood-stabilizing perspective.
   c. spontaneous recovery.
   d. preventive mental health.

Continue testing yourself with 🎓 **LearningCurve** or 🎓 **Achieve Read & Practice** to learn and remember most effectively.

The Story of Psychology: A Timeline

Charles L. Brewer, *Furman University* and **Salena Brody,** *University of Texas, Dallas*

B.C.E.

387— Plato, who believed in innate ideas, suggests that the brain is the seat of mental processes.

335— Aristotle, who denied the existence of innate ideas, suggests that the heart is the seat of mental processes.

C.E.

1604— Johannes Kepler describes inverted image on the retina.

Inverted image on the retina

1605— Francis Bacon publishes *The Proficiency and Advancement of Learning.*

1636— Harvard College is founded.

1637— René Descartes, the French philosopher and mathematician who proposed mind–body interaction and the doctrine of innate ideas, publishes *A Discourse on Method.*

1690— John Locke, the British philosopher who rejected Descartes' notion of innate ideas and insisted that the mind at birth is a "blank slate" *(tabula rasa),* publishes *An Essay Concerning Human Understanding,* which stresses empiricism over speculation.

1774— Franz Mesmer, an Austrian physician, performs his first supposed cure using "animal magnetism" (later called mesmerism and hypnosis). In 1777 he was expelled from the practice of medicine in Vienna.

1793— Philippe Pinel releases the first mental patients from their chains at the Bicêtre Asylum in France and advocates for more humane treatment of mental patients.

1802— Thomas Young publishes *A Theory of Color Vision* in England. (His theory was later called the trichromatic theory.)

1808— Franz Joseph Gall, a German physician, describes phrenology, the belief that the shape of a person's skull reveals mental faculties and character traits.

1813— The first private psychiatric hospital in the United States opens in Philadelphia.

1834— Ernst Heinrich Weber publishes *The Sense of Touch,* in which he discusses the "just noticeable difference *(jnd)"* and what we now call Weber's law.

1844— In Philadelphia, 13 superintendents form *The Association of Medical Superintendents of American Institutions for the Insane* (now known as the American Psychiatric Association).

1848— Phineas Gage suffers massive brain damage when a large iron rod accidentally pierces his brain, leaving his intellect and memory intact but altering his personality.

Phineas Gage

1850— Hermann von Helmholtz measures the speed of the nerve impulse.

1859— Charles Darwin publishes *On the Origin of Species by Means of Natural Selection,* synthesizing much previous work on the theory of evolution, including that of Herbert Spencer, who coined the phrase "survival of the fittest."

1861— Paul Broca, a French physician, discovers an area in the left frontal lobe of the brain (now called Broca's area) that is critical for the production of spoken language.

1869— Francis Galton, Charles Darwin's cousin, publishes *Hereditary Genius,* in which he claims that intelligence is inherited. In 1876 he coins the expression "nature and nurture" to correspond with "heredity and environment."

1874— Carl Wernicke, a German neurologist and psychiatrist, shows that damage to a specific area in the left temporal lobe (now called Wernicke's area) disrupts ability to comprehend or produce spoken or written language.

1878— G. Stanley Hall receives from Harvard University's Department of Philosophy the first U.S. Ph.D. degree based on psychological research.

1879 — Wilhelm Wundt establishes at the University of Leipzig, Germany, the first psychology laboratory, which becomes a mecca for psychology students from all over the world.

Wilhelm Wundt
(1832–1920)

1883 — G. Stanley Hall, student of Wilhelm Wundt, establishes the first formal U.S. psychology laboratory at Johns Hopkins University.

1885 — Hermann Ebbinghaus publishes *On Memory*, summarizing his extensive research on learning and memory, including the "forgetting curve."

1886 — Joseph Jastrow receives from Johns Hopkins University the first Ph.D. degree in psychology awarded by a Department of Psychology in the United States.

1889 — Henri-Étienne Beaunis and Alfred Binet establish the first psychology laboratory in France at the Sorbonne, and the first International Congress of Psychology meets in Paris.

Alfred Binet
(1857–1911)

1890 — William James, Harvard University philosopher and psychologist, publishes *The Principles of Psychology*, describing psychology as "the science of mental life."

William James
(1842–1910)

1891 — James Mark Baldwin establishes the first psychology laboratory in the British Commonwealth at the University of Toronto.

1892 — G. Stanley Hall spearheads the founding of the American Psychological Association (APA) and becomes its first president.

1893 — Mary Whiton Calkins and Christine Ladd-Franklin are the first women elected to membership in the APA.

Mary Whiton Calkins   Christine Ladd-Franklin
(1863–1930)   (1847–1930)

1894 — Margaret Floy Washburn is the first woman to receive a Ph.D. degree in psychology (Cornell University).

— Harvard University denies Mary Whiton Calkins admission to doctoral candidacy because of her gender, despite Hugo Münsterberg's claim that she was the best student he had ever had there.

All Portraits: Macmillan Learning

1896 — John Dewey publishes "The Reflex Arc Concept in Psychology," helping to formalize the school of psychology called functionalism.

1898 — In *Animal Intelligence,* Edward L. Thorndike, Columbia University, describes his learning experiments with cats in "puzzle boxes." In 1905, he proposes the "law of effect."

— Doctoral student Alice Lee uses published data from the *Journal of Anatomy* to debunk the popular eugenics argument that skull size is related to intelligence.

1900 — Sigmund Freud publishes *The Interpretation of Dreams*, his major theoretical work on psychoanalysis.

1901 — Ten founders establish the British Psychological Society.

1904 — Ivan Pavlov is awarded the Nobel Prize for Physiology or Medicine for his studies on the physiology of digestion.

1905 — Mary Whiton Calkins becomes the first woman president of the APA.

— Ivan Petrovich Pavlov begins publishing studies of conditioning in animals.

Ivan Pavlov
(1849–1936)

— Alfred Binet and Théodore Simon produce the first intelligence test for assessing the abilities and academic progress of Parisian schoolchildren.

1909 — Sigmund Freud makes his only trip to America to deliver a series of lectures at Clark University.

Sigmund Freud
(1856–1939)

1913 — John B. Watson outlines the tenets of behaviorism in a *Psychological Review* article, "Psychology as the Behaviorist Views It."

John Watson
(1878–1958)

1914 — During World War I, Robert Yerkes and his staff develop a group intelligence test for evaluating U.S. military personnel, which increases the U.S. public's acceptance of psychological testing.

— Lilian Gilbreth publishes *Principles of Management*, a foundational text for the field of industrial-organizational psychology.

1920— 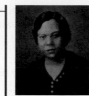 Leta Stetter Hollingworth publishes *The Psychology of Subnormal Children*, an early classic. In 1921 she is cited in *American Men of Science* for her research on the psychology of women.

Leta Stetter Hollingworth
(1886–1939)

 Francis Cecil Sumner receives a Ph.D. degree in psychology from Clark University, becoming the first African-American to earn a psychology doctorate.

Francis Cecil Sumner
(1895–1954)

John B. Watson and Rosalie Rayner report conditioning a fear reaction in a child called "Little Albert."

1921— Hermann Rorschach, a Swiss psychiatrist, introduces the Rorschach Inkblot Test.

1923— Developmental psychologist Jean Piaget publishes *The Language and Thought of the Child*.

1924— Mary Cover Jones reports reconditioning a fear reaction in a child (Peter), a forerunner of systematic desensitization developed by Joseph Wolpe.

1927— In *Introduction to the Technique of Child Analysis*, Anna Freud discusses psychoanalysis in the treatment of children.

1929— Wolfgang Köhler publishes *Gestalt Psychology*, which criticizes behaviorism and outlines essential elements of the gestalt position and approach.

1931— Margaret Floy Washburn becomes the first female psychologist (and the second female scientist in any discipline) elected to the U.S. National Academy of Sciences.

Margaret Floy Washburn
(1871–1939)

1932— In *The Wisdom of the Body*, Walter B. Cannon coins the term *homeostasis*, discusses the fight-or-flight response, and identifies hormonal changes associated with stress.

1933— Inez Beverly Prosser becomes the first African-American woman to receive a doctoral degree in psychology from a U.S. institution (Ph.D., University of Cincinnati).

Inez Beverly Prosser
(1895–1934)

1934— Ruth Winifred Howard becomes the second African-American woman to receive a doctoral degree in psychology (Ph.D., University of Minnesota).

Ruth Winifred Howard
(1900–1997)

1935— Christiana Morgan and Henry Murray introduce the Thematic Apperception Test to elicit fantasies from people undergoing psychoanalysis.

1936— Egas Moniz, a Portuguese physician, publishes work on the first frontal lobotomies performed on humans.

1938— B. F. Skinner publishes *The Behavior of Organisms*, which describes operant conditioning of animals.

In *Primary Mental Abilities*, Louis L. Thurstone proposes seven such abilities.

Ugo Cerletti and Lucio Bini use electroshock treatment with a human patient.

1939— David Wechsler publishes the Wechsler–Bellevue intelligence test, forerunner of the Wechsler Intelligence Scale for Children (WISC) and the Wechsler Adult Intelligence Scale (WAIS).

 Mamie Phipps Clark receives a master's degree from Howard University. In collaboration with Kenneth B. Clark, she later extends her thesis, "The Development of Consciousness of Self in Negro Preschool Children," providing joint research cited in the U.S. Supreme Court's 1954 decision to end racial segregation in public schools.

Mamie Phipps Clark
(1917–1983)

Edward Alexander Bott helps found the Canadian Psychological Association. He becomes its first president in 1940.

World War II provides many opportunities for psychologists to enhance the popularity and influence of psychology, especially in applied areas.

1943— Psychologist Starke Hathaway and physician J. Charnley McKinley publish the Minnesota Multiphasic Personality Inventory (MMPI).

1945— Karen Horney, who criticized Freud's theory of female sexual development, publishes *Our Inner Conflicts*.

Karen Horney
(1885–1952)

1946— Benjamin Spock's first edition of *The Commonsense Book of Baby and Child Care* appears; the book will influence child raising in North America for several decades.

1948 — Alfred Kinsey and his colleagues publish *Sexual Behavior in the Human Male*, and they publish *Sexual Behavior in the Human Female* in **1953**.

B. F. Skinner's novel, *Walden Two*, describes a Utopian community based on positive reinforcement, which becomes a clarion call for applying psychological principles in everyday living, especially communal living.

B. F. Skinner
(1904–1990)

— Ernest R. Hilgard publishes *Theories of Learning*, which was required reading for several generations of psychology students in North America.

1949 — Raymond B. Cattell publishes the Sixteen Personality Factor Questionnaire (16PF).

— The scientist-practitioner model of training is approved at The Boulder Conference on Graduate Education in Clinical Psychology.

— In *The Organization of Behavior: A Neuropsychological Theory*, Canadian psychologist Donald O. Hebb outlines a new and influential conceptualization of how the nervous system functions.

1950 — Solomon Asch publishes studies of effects of conformity on judgments of line length.

— In *Childhood and Society*, Erik Erikson outlines his stages of psychosocial development.

1951 — Carl Rogers publishes *Client-Centered Therapy*.

1952 — The American Psychiatric Association publishes the *Diagnostic and Statistical Manual of Mental Disorders,* an influential book that will be updated periodically.

1953 — Eugene Aserinski and Nathaniel Kleitman describe rapid eye movements (REM) that occur during sleep.

— Janet Taylor's Manifest Anxiety Scale appears in the *Journal of Abnormal Psychology*.

1954 — In *Motivation and Personality*, Abraham Maslow proposes a hierarchy of motives ranging from physiological needs to self-actualization. (Maslow later updates the hierarchy to include self-transcendence needs.)

— James Olds and Peter Milner, McGill University neuropsychologists, describe the rewarding effects of electrical stimulation of the hypothalamus in rats.

— Gordon Allport publishes *The Nature of Prejudice*.

1956 — In his *Psychological Review* article titled "The Magical Number Seven, Plus or Minus Two: Some Limits on Our Capacity for Processing Information," George Miller coins the term *chunk* for memory researchers.

1957 — Robert Sears, Eleanor Maccoby, and Harry Levin publish *Patterns of Child Rearing*.

— Charles Ferster and B. F. Skinner publish *Schedules of Reinforcement*.

1958 — Harry Harlow publishes "The Nature of Love," outlining his work on attachment in monkeys.

1959 — Noam Chomsky's critical review of B. F. Skinner's *Verbal Behavior* appears in the journal *Language*.

Keturah Whitehurst becomes the first African-American to be licensed as a psychologist, in Virginia.

Keturah Whitehurst
(1912–2000)

— Eleanor Gibson and Richard Walk report their research on infants' depth perception in "The Visual Cliff."

— Lloyd Peterson and Margaret Peterson, in the *Journal of Experimental Psychology* article, "Short-Term Retention of Individual Verbal Items," highlight the importance of rehearsal in memory.

— John Thibaut and Harold Kelley publish *The Social Psychology of Groups*.

1960 — George Sperling publishes "The Information Available in Brief Visual Presentations."

1961 — Georg von Békésy receives a Nobel Prize for research on the physiology of hearing.

— David McClelland publishes *The Achieving Society*.

1962 — Jerome Kagan and Howard Moss publish *Birth to Maturity*.

Martha E. Bernal becomes the first Latina to earn a U.S. doctoral degree (Ph.D., Indiana University).

Martha E. Bernal
(1931–2001)

— Stanley Schachter and Jerome Singer publish findings that support the two-factor theory of emotion.

— Albert Ellis' *Reason and Emotion in Psychotherapy* is published; it is a milestone in the development of rational-emotive therapy (RET).

1963 — Raymond B. Cattell distinguishes between *fluid* and *crystallized* intelligence.

— Stanley Milgram's "Behavioral Study of Obedience" appears in the *Journal of Abnormal and Social Psychology*.

1964 — Marigold Linton becomes the first Native American to receive a doctoral degree in psychology (University of California, Los Angeles). She is a founding member of both the Society for Advancement of Chicanos and Native Americans in Science, and the National Indian Education Association.

Marigold Linton
(born 1936)

1965— Canadian researcher Ronald Melzack and British researcher Patrick Wall propose the gate-control theory of pain.

— Robert Zajonc's "Social Facilitation" is published in *Science*.

— The Archives of the History of American Psychology is founded at the University of Akron.

1966— Nancy Bayley becomes the first woman to receive the APA's Distinguished Scientific Contribution Award.

— Jerome Bruner and colleagues at Harvard University's Center for Cognitive Studies publish *Studies in Cognitive Growth*.

— William Masters and Virginia Johnson publish results of their research in *Human Sexual Responses*.

— Allen Gardner and Beatrix Gardner begin training a chimpanzee (Washoe) in American Sign Language at the University of Nevada, Reno. Washoe dies in 2007.

John Garcia and Robert Koelling publish a study on taste aversion in rats.

John Garcia
(1917–1983)

— David M. Green and John A. Swets publish *Signal Detection Theory and Psychophysics*.

— Julian Rotter publishes research on locus of control.

1967— Ulric Neisser's *Cognitive Psychology* helps to steer psychology away from behaviorism and toward cognitive processes.

— Martin Seligman and Steven Maier publish the results of their research with "learned helplessness" in dogs.

1968— Richard Atkinson and Richard Shiffrin's influential three-stage memory model appears in *The Psychology of Learning and Motivation*.

— Neal E. Miller's article in *Science*, describing instrumental conditioning of autonomic responses, stimulates research on biofeedback.

1969— Albert Bandura publishes *Principles of Behavior Modification*.

— The Association for Women in Psychology is founded. E. Kitch Childs was instrumental in this effort, and pioneered therapy techniques grounded in *intersectionality* (considering how race, class, and other aspects of identity may combine to create discrimination or disadvantage).

— George Miller, in his APA presidential address, "Psychology as a Means of Promoting Human Welfare," emphasizes the importance of "giving psychology away."

1970—

Psychologist Reiko Homma True lobbies successfully to open the Asian American Community Mental Health program—the first to focus on a minority population.

Reiko Homma True
(born 1933)

1971—

Kenneth B. Clark becomes the first African-American president of the American Psychological Association.

Kenneth B. Clark
(1914–2005)

— Albert Bandura publishes *Social Learning Theory*.

— B. F. Skinner publishes *Beyond Freedom and Dignity*.

1972— Elliot Aronson publishes *The Social Animal*.

— Fergus Craik and Robert Lockhart's "Levels of Processing: A Framework for Memory Research" appears in the *Journal of Verbal Learning and Verbal Behavior*.

— Robert Rescorla and Allan Wagner publish their associative model of Pavlovian conditioning.

— Under the leadership of Derald Wing Sue and Stanley Sue, the Asian American Psychological Association is founded.

Derald Wing Sue   Stanley Sue
(born 1942)   (born 1944)

1973— Ethologists Karl von Frisch, Konrad Lorenz, and Nikolaas Tinbergen receive the Nobel Prize for their research on animal behavior.

1974— APA's Division 2 first publishes its journal, *Teaching of Psychology*, with Robert S. Daniel as editor.

— Eleanor Maccoby and Carol Jacklin publish *The Psychology of Sex Differences*.

1975— Biologist Edward O. Wilson's *Sociobiology* is published; it will be a controversial precursor to evolutionary psychology.

1976— Sandra Wood Scarr and Richard A. Weinberg publish "IQ Test Performance of Black Children Adopted by White Families" in *American Psychologist*.

Psychologist Robert V. Guthrie publishes *Even the Rat Was White*, the first history of African-American psychologists in America.

— Saundra Murray Nettles chairs the Task Force on Black Women's Priorities, which leads to the creation of APA's Division 35, Section 1: The Psychology of Black Women.

All Portraits: Macmillan Learning

Psychologist Carolyn Payton becomes the first African-American and first woman Director of the U.S. Peace Corps.

1978 — Psychologist Herbert A. Simon, Carnegie-Mellon University, wins a Nobel Prize for pioneering research on computer simulations of human thinking and problem solving.

1979 — James J. Gibson publishes *The Ecological Approach to Visual Perception.*

Elizabeth Loftus publishes *Eyewitness Testimony.*

1981 — David Hubel and Torsten Wiesel receive a Nobel Prize for research on single-cell recordings that identified feature detector cells in the visual cortex.

Roger Sperry receives a Nobel Prize for research on split-brain patients.

Sociologist Harriette Pipe McAdoo publishes *Black Families*, an anthology of work done with John Lewis McAdoo on middle class African-American families. Previous studies had focused on dysfunctional families, such as those in contact with prison and drug treatment programs.

Paleontologist Stephen Jay Gould publishes *The Mismeasure of Man*, highlighting the debate concerning biological determination of intelligence.

1983 — In his *Frames of Mind*, Howard Gardner outlines his theory of multiple intelligences.

1984 — **44**))) Society for the **Psychology** of Sexual Orientation and Gender Diversity   The American Psychological Association creates Division 44 (Society for the Psychology of Sexual Orientation and Gender Diversity).

Robert Sternberg proposes the triarchic theory of human intelligence in *Behavioral and Brain Sciences.*

1987 — Elizabeth Scarborough and Laurel Furumoto publish *Untold Lives: The First Generation of American Women Psychologists.*

Fluoxetine (Prozac) is introduced as a treatment for depression.

Wilbert J. McKeachie, University of Michigan, receives the first APA Award for Distinguished Career Contributions to Education and Training in Psychology.

1988 — The American Psychological Society is founded. It changes its name to Association for Psychological Science in 2006.

1990 — Psychiatrist Aaron Beck receives the Distinguished Scientific Award for the Applications of Psychology for advancing understanding and treatment of psychopathology, including pivotal contributions to the development of cognitive therapy.

B. F. Skinner receives APA's first Citation for Outstanding Lifetime Contributions to Psychology and presents his last public address, "Can Psychology Be a Science of Mind?" (He died a few days later at age 86.)

1991 — Martin Seligman publishes *Learned Optimism*, which foreshadows the "positive psychology" movement.

1992 — Teachers of Psychology in Secondary Schools (TOPSS) is established as part of the APA.

About 3,000 U.S. secondary school students take the first Advanced Placement (AP) Examination in Psychology, hoping to earn exemption from an introductory psychology course at the postsecondary level.

1993 — Psychologist Judith Rodin is elected president of the University of Pennsylvania, becoming the first female president of an Ivy League school.

1996 — Dorothy Cantor becomes the first president of the APA with a Psy.D. degree.

1998 — *The Handbook of Asian American Psychology* is published.

2002 — New Mexico becomes the first U.S. state to allow qualified clinical psychologists to prescribe certain drugs.

Psychologist Daniel Kahneman, Princeton University, receives a Nobel Prize for research on decision making.

2009 — Psychologist Judy Chu becomes the first Chinese-American woman elected to the U.S. Congress.

2011 — Proposed by participants at the 2008 national conference at the University of Puget Sound, the document, "Principles for Quality Undergraduate Education in Psychology," is approved as official APA policy.

Melba J. T. Vasquez is the first Latina president of the American Psychological Association.

Melba J. T. Vasquez
(born 1951)

2013 — U.S. President Barack Obama announces $100 million in funding for an interdisciplinary project to advance understanding of the human brain.

2014 — Social psychologist Jennifer L. Eberhardt is awarded the MacArthur Fellowship ("Genius Grant") to support her implicit bias research.

2015 — The *Independent Review Relating to APA Ethics Guidelines, National Security Interrogations, and Torture* is presented to the American Psychological Association.

2018 — Kristina Olson becomes the first psychologist to receive the National Science Foundation's Waterman Award. She also receives a 2018 MacArthur Fellowship for her work studying the social and cognitive development of transgender and gender-nonconforming youth.

Career Fields in Psychology

Jennifer Zwolinski, *University of San Diego*

What can you do with a degree in psychology? Lots!

As a psychology major, you will graduate with a scientific mindset and an awareness of basic principles of human behavior (biological mechanisms, nature–nurture interactions, life-span development, cognition, psychological disorders, social interaction). This background will prepare you for success in many areas, including business, the helping professions, health services, marketing, law, sales, and teaching. You may even go on to graduate school for specialized training to become a psychology professional. This appendix provides an overview of some of psychology's key career fields.[1] For more detailed information, see *Pursuing a Psychology Career* in LaunchPad (LaunchPadWorks.com), where you can learn more about the many interesting options available to those with bachelor's, master's, and doctoral degrees in psychology.

If you are like most psychology students, you may be unaware of the wide variety of specialties and work settings available in psychology (Terre & Stoddart, 2000). To date, the American Psychological Association (APA) has 54 divisions (apa.org/about/division/index.aspx) that represent the popular subfields and interest groups of APA members (**TABLE B.1**). For example, Division 2 (Society for the Teaching of Psychology) offers an excellent career exploration resource for those interested in learning about the hundreds of career options available for students with an undergraduate degree in psychology (teachpsych.org/psycareer).

---

[1] Although this text covers the world of psychology for students in many countries, this appendix draws primarily from available U.S. data. These descriptions of career fields in psychology do, however, apply to many other countries as well.

TABLE B.1 APA Divisions by Number and Name

1. Society for General Psychology	31. State, Provincial, and Territorial Psychological Association Affairs
2. Society for the Teaching of Psychology	32. Society for Humanistic Psychology
3. Society for Experimental Psychology and Cognitive Science	33. Intellectual and Developmental Disabilities/Autism Spectrum Disorder
4. *There is no active Division 4.*	34. Society for Environmental, Population, and Conservation Psychology
5. Quantitative and Qualitative Methods	35. Society for the Psychology of Women
6. Society for Behavioral Neuroscience and Comparative Psychology	36. Society for the Psychology of Religion and Spirituality
7. Developmental Psychology	37. Society for Child and Family Policy and Practice
8. Society for Personality and Social Psychology	
9. Society for the Psychological Study of Social Issues (SPSSI)	38. Society for Health Psychology
10. Society for the Psychology of Aesthetics, Creativity, and the Arts	39. Society for Psychoanalysis and Psychoanalytic Psychology
11. *There is no active Division 11.*	40. Society for Clinical Neuropsychology
12. Society of Clinical Psychology	41. American Psychology-Law Society
13. Society of Consulting Psychology	42. Psychologists in Independent Practice
14. Society for Industrial and Organizational Psychology	43. Society for Couple and Family Psychology
15. Educational Psychology	44. Society for the Psychology of Sexual Orientation and Gender Diversity
16. School Psychology	
17. Society of Counseling Psychology	45. Society for the Psychological Study of Culture, Ethnicity, and Race
18. Psychologists in Public Service	46. Society for Media Psychology and Technology
19. Society for Military Psychology	47. Society for Sport, Exercise, and Performance Psychology
20. Adult Development and Aging	
21. Applied Experimental and Engineering Psychology	48. Society for the Study of Peace, Conflict and Violence: Peace Psychology Division
22. Rehabilitation Psychology	49. Society of Group Psychology and Group Psychotherapy
23. Society for Consumer Psychology	
24. Society for Theoretical and Philosophical Psychology	50. Society of Addiction Psychology
25. Behavior Analysis	51. Society for the Psychological Study of Men and Masculinities
26. Society for the History of Psychology	52. International Psychology
27. Society for Community Research and Action: Division of Community Psychology	53. Society of Clinical Child and Adolescent Psychology
28. Psychopharmacology and Substance Abuse	54. Society of Pediatric Psychology
29. Society for the Advancement of Psychotherapy	55. American Society for the Advancement of Pharmacotherapy
30. Society of Psychological Hypnosis	56. Trauma Psychology

Source: American Psychological Association (2020)

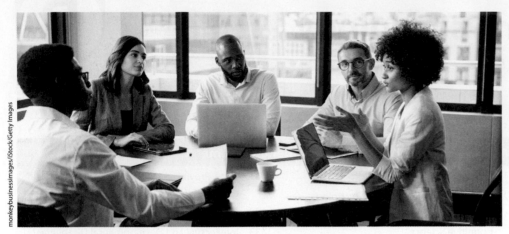

monkeybusinessimages/iStock/Getty Images

Cognitive consulting Cognitive psychologists may advise businesses on how to operate more effectively by understanding the human factors involved.

The following paragraphs (arranged alphabetically) describe some of psychology's main career fields, most of which require a graduate degree.

CLINICAL PSYCHOLOGISTS promote psychological health in individuals, groups, and organizations. Some clinical psychologists specialize in specific psychological disorders. Others treat a range of disorders, from adjustment difficulties to severe psychopathology. Clinical psychologists often provide therapy but may also engage in research, teaching, assessment, and consultation. Clinical psychologists work in a variety of settings, including private practice, mental health service organizations, schools, universities, industries, legal systems, medical systems, counseling centers, government agencies, correctional facilities, nonprofit organizations, and military services.

To become a clinical psychologist, you will need to earn a doctorate from a clinical psychology program. The APA sets the standards for clinical psychology graduate programs, offering *accreditation* (official recognition) to those who meet their standards. In all U.S. states, clinical psychologists working in independent practice must obtain a license to offer services such as therapy and testing.

COGNITIVE PSYCHOLOGISTS study thought processes and focus on such topics as perception, language, attention, problem solving, memory, judgment and decision making, and intelligence. Research interests include designing computer-based models of thought processes and identifying biological correlates of cognition. As a cognitive psychologist, you might work as a professor, industrial consultant, or human factors specialist in an educational or business setting.

COMMUNITY PSYCHOLOGISTS move beyond focusing on specific individuals or families and deal with broad problems of mental health in community settings. These psychologists believe that human behavior is powerfully influenced by the interaction between people and their physical, social, political, and economic environments. They seek to promote psychological health by enhancing environmental settings—focusing on preventive measures and crisis intervention, with special attention to the problems of underserved groups and minority groups. Some community psychologists collaborate with professionals in other areas, such as public health, with a shared emphasis on prevention. As a community psychologist, your work settings could include federal, state, and local departments of mental health, corrections, and welfare. You might conduct research or help evaluate research in health service settings, serve as an independent consultant for a private or government agency, or teach and consult as a college or university faculty member.

Community care Community psychologists in Haiti have helped residents work through the ongoing emotional challenges that followed the devastating 2010 earthquake and, more recently, the widely destructive 2016 hurricane.

AP Photo

COUNSELING PSYCHOLOGISTS help people adjust to life transitions or make lifestyle changes. Although similar to clinical psychologists, counseling psychologists typically help people with adjustment problems rather than severe psychopathology. Like clinical psychologists, counseling psychologists conduct therapy and provide assessments to individuals and groups. As a counseling psychologist, you would likely emphasize your clients' strengths, helping them to use their own skills, interests, and abilities to cope during transitions. You might find yourself working in an academic setting as a faculty member or administrator or in a university counseling center, community mental health center, business, or private practice. As with clinical psychology, if you plan to work in independent practice you will need to obtain a state license to provide counseling services to the public.

DEVELOPMENTAL PSYCHOLOGISTS conduct research on age-related behavioral changes and apply their scientific knowledge to educational, child-care, policy, and related settings. As a developmental psychologist, you would investigate change across a broad range of topics, including the biological, psychological, cognitive, and social aspects of development. Developmental psychology informs a number of applied fields, including educational psychology, school psychology, child psychopathology, and gerontology. The field also informs public policy in areas such as education and child-care reform, maternal and child health, and attachment and adoption. You would probably specialize in a specific stage of the life span, such as infancy, childhood, adolescence, or middle or late adulthood. Your work setting could be an educational institution, day-care center, youth group program, or senior center.

EDUCATIONAL PSYCHOLOGISTS are interested in the psychological processes involved in learning. They study the relationship between learning and the physical and social environments, and they develop strategies for enhancing the learning process. As an educational psychologist, working in a university psychology department or school of education, you might conduct basic research on topics related to learning, or develop innovative methods of teaching to enhance the learning process. You might design effective tests, including measures of aptitude and achievement. You might be employed by a school or government agency or charged with designing and implementing effective employee-training programs in a business setting.

ENVIRONMENTAL PSYCHOLOGISTS study the interaction of individuals with their natural and built (urban) environments. They are interested in how we influence and are affected by these environments. As an environmental psychologist, you might study wildlife conservation, the impact of urbanization on health, or cognitive factors involved in sustainable lifestyle choices. Environmental psychologists tend to address these kinds of questions by working with other professionals as part of an interdisciplinary team. As an environmental psychologist, you might work in a consulting firm, an academic setting, the nonprofit sector, or the government.

EXPERIMENTAL PSYCHOLOGISTS are a diverse group of scientists who investigate a variety of basic behavioral processes in humans and other animals. Prominent areas of experimental research include comparative methods of science, motivation, learning, thought, attention, memory, perception, and language. Most experimental psychologists identify with a particular subfield, such as cognitive psychology, depending on their interests and training. Experimental research methods are not limited to the field of experimental psychology; many other subfields rely on experimental methodology to conduct studies. As an experimental psychologist, you would most likely work in an academic setting, teaching courses and supervising students' research in addition to conducting your own research. Or you might be employed by a research institution, zoo, business, or government agency.

FORENSIC PSYCHOLOGISTS apply psychological principles to legal issues. They conduct research on the interface of law and psychology, help to create public policies related to mental health, help law-enforcement agencies in criminal investigations, or consult on jury selection and deliberation processes. They also provide assessment to assist the legal community. Although most forensic

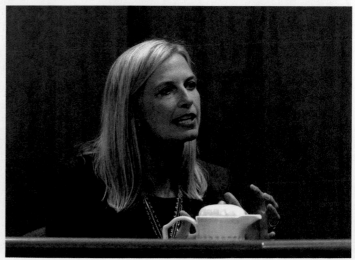

Forensics in court Forensic psychologists may be called on to assist police officers investigating a crime scene, but most forensic work occurs in the lab and for the judicial system.

psychologists are clinical psychologists, many have expertise in other areas of psychology, such as social or cognitive psychology. Some also hold law degrees. As a forensic psychologist, you might work in a university psychology department, law school, research organization, community mental health agency, law-enforcement agency, court, or correctional setting.

HEALTH PSYCHOLOGISTS are researchers and practitioners concerned with psychology's contribution to promoting health and preventing disease. As applied psychologists or clinicians, they may help individuals lead healthier lives by designing, conducting, and evaluating programs to stop smoking, lose weight, improve sleep, manage pain, prevent the spread of sexually transmitted infections, or treat psychosocial problems associated with chronic and terminal illnesses. As researchers and clinicians, they identify conditions and practices associated with health and illness to help create effective interventions. In public service, health psychologists study and work to improve government policies and health care systems. As a health psychologist, you could be employed in a hospital, medical school, rehabilitation center, public health agency, college or university, or, if you are also a clinical psychologist, in private practice.

INDUSTRIAL-ORGANIZATIONAL (I/O) PSYCHOLOGISTS study the relationship between people and their working environments. They may develop new ways to increase productivity, improve personnel selection, or promote job satisfaction in an organizational setting. Their interests include organizational structure and change, consumer behavior, and personnel selection and training. As an I/O psychologist, you might conduct workplace training or provide organizational analysis and development. You may find yourself working in business, industry, the government, or a college or university. Or you may be self-employed as a consultant or work for a management consulting firm. (For more on I/O psychology, see Appendix C, "Psychology at Work.")

NEUROPSYCHOLOGISTS investigate the relationship between neurological processes (structure and function of the brain) and behavior. As a neuropsychologist you might assess, diagnose, or treat central nervous system disorders, such as Alzheimer's disease or stroke. You might also evaluate individuals for evidence of head injuries; learning and developmental disabilities, such as autism spectrum disorder; and other psychiatric disorders, such as attention-deficit/hyperactivity disorder (ADHD). If you are a *clinical neuropsychologist*, you might work in a hospital's neurology, neurosurgery, or psychiatric unit. Neuropsychologists also work in academic settings, where they conduct research and teach.

Evaluating cognitive functioning The American Psychological Association projects that by 2030, those age 65 and older will be the U.S. age group demanding the most psychological care (APA, 2018). We will need more psychologists trained to use neuropsychological assessments to evaluate cognitive capacities in our aging population. Mental health professionals can use such test results to help diagnose, treat, and manage psychological disorders, such as Alzheimer's disease.

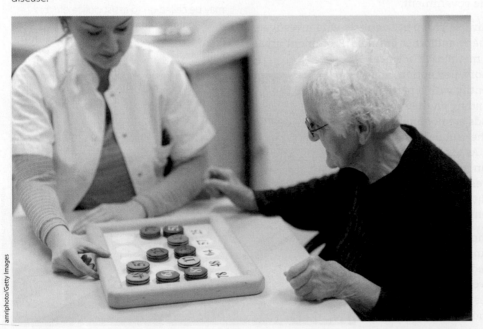

amriphoto/Getty Images

PSYCHOMETRIC AND QUANTITATIVE PSYCHOLOGISTS study the methods and techniques used to acquire psychological knowledge. A psychometric psychologist may update existing neurocognitive or personality tests or devise new tests for use in clinical and school settings or in business and industry. These psychologists also administer, score, and interpret such tests. Quantitative psychologists collaborate with researchers to design, analyze, and interpret the results of research programs. As a psychometric or quantitative psychologist, you will need to be well trained in research methods, statistics, and computer technology. You will most likely be employed by a university or college, a testing company, a private research firm, or a government agency.

REHABILITATION PSYCHOLOGISTS are researchers and practitioners who work with people who have lost optimal functioning after an accident, illness, or other event. As a rehabilitation psychologist, you would probably work in a medical rehabilitation institution or hospital. You might also work in a medical school, university, state or federal vocational rehabilitation agency, or in private practice serving people with physical disabilities.

SCHOOL PSYCHOLOGISTS are involved in the assessment of and intervention for children in educational settings. They diagnose and treat cognitive, social, and emotional problems that may negatively influence children's learning or overall functioning at school. As a school psychologist, you would collaborate with teachers, parents, and administrators, making recommendations to improve student learning. You would work in an academic setting, a federal or state government agency, a child guidance center, or a behavioral research laboratory.

SOCIAL PSYCHOLOGISTS are interested in our interactions with others. Social psychologists study how our beliefs, feelings, and behaviors are affected by and influence other people. They study topics such as attitudes, aggression, prejudice, interpersonal attraction, group behavior, and leadership. As a social psychologist, you would probably be a college or university faculty member. You might also work in organizational consultation, market research, or other applied psychology fields, including social neuroscience. Some social psychologists work for hospitals, federal agencies, social networking sites, or businesses performing applied research.

SPORT PSYCHOLOGISTS study the psychological factors that influence, and are influenced by, participation in sports and other physical activities. Their professional activities include coach education and athlete preparation, as well as research and teaching. Sport psychologists who also have a clinical or counseling degree can apply those skills to working with individuals with psychological problems, such as anxiety or substance abuse, that might interfere with optimal performance. As a sport psychologist, if you were not working in an academic or research setting, you would most likely work as part of a team or an organization or in a private capacity.

* * *

So, the next time someone asks you what you will do with your psychology degree, tell them you have a lot of options. You might use your acquired skills and understanding to get a job and succeed in any number of fields, or you might pursue graduate school and then career opportunities in associated professions. In any case, what you have learned about behavior and mental processes will surely enrich your life (Hammer, 2003)

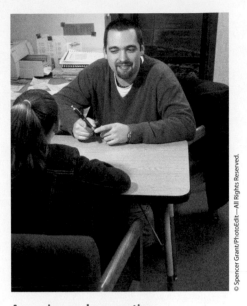

Assessing and supporting children School psychologists may find themselves working with children individually or in groups. They receive interdisciplinary training in mental health assessment and behavior analysis, research methods and design, and special needs education. They work primarily in schools, but also in a range of other settings, including pediatric hospitals, mental health centers, and correctional facilities.

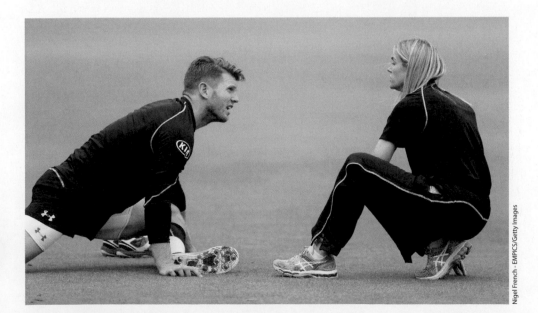

Improving athletic achievement Sussex cricket player Stuart Meaker gathers input from his team's sport psychologist during warmup.

Psychology at Work

For many people, to live is to work. Work supports us, enabling food, water, and shelter. Work connects us, meeting our social needs. Work helps define us. Meeting people and wondering about their identity, we may ask, "So, what do you do?"

We vary in our job satisfaction. On the day we leave the workforce, some of us will sadly bid our former employer farewell; others will gladly bid our former employer good riddance.

Few of us will look back and say we have followed a predictable career path. We will have changed jobs, some of us often. The trigger for those changes may have been shifting needs in the economy. Rapid technological change has made some jobs disappear, with new ones taking their place—and not always smoothly. Or it may have been a desire for better pay, happier on-the-job relationships, or more fulfilling work.

You might view your job as a necessary chore or a meaningful calling. You may also approach your job as an opportunity to do the bare minimum or to maximize your potential. And you may find your job to be an experience of either tedious boredom or of absorbing *flow*. Let's take a look at how psychologists can help explain why some jobs are more rewarding than others.

Work and Life Satisfaction

Flow at Work

LEARNING OBJECTIVE QUESTION **LOQ** **C-1** What is *flow*?

Individuals across various occupations vary in their attitudes toward their work. Some view their work as a *job,* an unfulfilling but necessary way to make money. Others view their work as a *career,* an opportunity to advance from one position to a better position. The rest—those who view their work as a *calling,* a fulfilling and socially useful activity— report the highest satisfaction with their work and with their lives (Dik & Duffy, 2012; Wrzesniewski & Dutton, 2001).

These findings would not surprise Mihaly Csikszentmihalyi [chick-SENT-me-hi] (1990, 1999). He observed that our quality of life increases when we are purposefully engaged. Between the anxiety of being overwhelmed and stressed, and the apathy of being underwhelmed and bored, lies a zone in which we experience **flow**. Perhaps you can recall being in a zoned-out flow state while online. If so, then perhaps you can sympathize with the two airline pilots who in 2009 were so focused on their laptops that they missed their control tower's messages. The pilots flew 150 miles past their Minneapolis destination—and lost their jobs.

Csikszentmihalyi formulated the flow concept after studying artists who spent hour after hour painting or sculpting with focused concentration. Immersed in a project, they worked as if nothing else mattered, and then, when finished, they promptly moved on. The artists seemed driven less by external rewards—money, praise, promotion—than by the intrinsic rewards of creating their art. Nearly 200 other studies confirm that *intrinsic motivation* enhances performance (Cerasoli et al., 2014).

Csikszentmihalyi studied dancers, chess players, surgeons, writers, parents, mountain climbers, sailors, and farmers. His research included Australians, North Americans,

The jobs people do: Columnist Gene Weingarten (2002) noted that sometimes a humorist knows "when to just get out of the way." Here are some sample job titles from the U.S. Department of Labor's *Dictionary of Occupational Titles:* animal impersonator, human projectile, banana ripening-room supervisor, impregnator, impregnator helper, dope sprayer, finger waver, rug scratcher, egg smeller, bottom buffer, cookie breaker, brain picker, hand pouncer, bosom presser, and mother repairer.

flow a completely involved, focused state, with diminished awareness of self and time; results from full engagement of our skills.

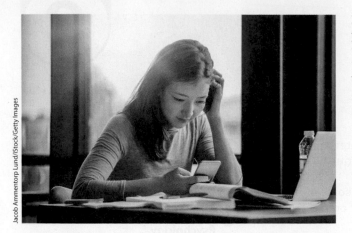

Jacob Ammentorp Lund/iStock/Getty Images

Koreans, Japanese, and Italians. Participants ranged in age from the teen years to the golden years. A clear principle emerged: It's exhilarating to flow with an activity that fully engages our skills (Fong et al., 2015). Flow experiences boost our sense of self-esteem, competence, and well-being. One research team studied 10,000 Swedish twins and found that frequent flow experiences reduced their risk of depression and burnout (Mosing et al., 2018). A focused mind is a happy mind.

Idleness may sound like bliss. You may dream of a future filled with streaming movies, sleeping in, and no responsibilities. In reality, purposeful work enriches our lives. People who leave the workforce tend to become unhappy, but rejoining the workforce rapidly improves their mood (Zhou, Y. et al., 2019). Busy people are often happy people (Hsee et al., 2010; Robinson & Martin, 2008).

Life disrupted Playing and socializing online are ever-present sources of distraction. It takes energy to resist checking our phones, and time to refocus mental concentration after each disruption. Such frequent interruptions disrupt flow, so it's a good idea to instead schedule regular breaks for checking our devices.

Have you ever noticed that when you are immersed in an activity, time flies? And that when you are watching the clock, it seems to move more slowly? French researchers have confirmed that the more we attend to an event's duration, the longer it seems to last (Couli et al., 2004).

Finding Your Own Flow, and Matching Interests to Work

Want to identify your own path to flow? You can start by pinpointing your strengths and the types of work that may prove satisfying and successful. Marcus Buckingham and Donald Clifton (2001) suggested asking yourself four questions:

1. What activities give me pleasure? Bringing order out of chaos? Playing host? Helping others? Challenging sloppy thinking?

2. What activities leave me wondering, "When can I do this again?" rather than, "When will this be over?"

3. What sorts of challenges do I relish? And which do I dread?

4. What sorts of tasks do I learn easily? And which do I struggle with?

You may find your skills engaged and time flying when teaching or selling or writing or cleaning or consoling or creating or repairing. If an activity feels good, if it comes easily, if you look forward to it, then look deeper. You'll see your strengths at work (Buckingham, 2007). For a free (requires registration) assessment of your own strengths, take the "Brief Strengths Test" at AuthenticHappiness.sas.upenn.edu.

The U.S. Department of Labor also offers a career interest questionnaire through its Occupational Information Network (O*NET). At MyNextMove.org/explore/ip you will need about 10 minutes to respond to 60 items, indicating how much you would like or dislike activities ranging from building kitchen cabinets to playing a musical instrument. You will then receive feedback on how strongly your responses reflect six interest types (Holland, 1996):

Michael Maslin/The Cartoon Bank/Conde Nast Publications

"Let's face it: you and this organization have never been a good fit."

- *Realistic* (hands-on doers)
- *Investigative* (thinkers)
- *Artistic* (creators)
- *Social* (helpers, teachers)
- *Enterprising* (persuaders, deciders)
- *Conventional* (organizers)

Finally, depending on how much training you are willing to complete, you will be shown occupations that fit your interest pattern (selected from a national database of 900+ occupations).

Do what you love and you will love what you do. A career counseling science aims, first, to assess people's differing values, personalities, and, especially, *interests,* which are remarkably stable and predictive of future life choices and outcomes (Dik & Rottinghaus, 2013; Stoll et al., 2017). (Your job may change, but your interests today will likely still be your interests in 10 years.) Second, it aims to alert people to well-matched

"Find a job you love, and you'll never work another day of your life." — Popular saying expressed in a Facebook hiring video, 2016

vocations—vocations with a good *person-environment fit*. It pays to have a job that fits your personality. People who are highly open earn more if they hold jobs that demand openness (actors); people who are highly conscientious earn more if they work in jobs that require conscientiousness (financial managers) (Denissen et al., 2018).

One study assessed 400,000 high school students' interests and then followed them over time. The take-home finding: "Interests uniquely predict academic and career success over and above cognitive ability and personality" (Rounds & Su, 2014). Sixty other studies confirm the point both for students in school and workers on the job: Interests predict both performance and persistence (Nye et al., 2012). Lack of job fit can fuel frustration, resulting in unproductive and even hostile work behavior (Harold et al., 2016). One fee-based online service, jobZology.com, was developed by *industrial-organizational psychologists* to put career counseling science into action. First, it assesses people's interests, values, personalities, and workplace culture preferences. It then suggests occupations and connects them to job listings.

Column 1: Hope College; Kathryn Brownson; Anna Munroe; Steven McIntosh. Column 2: Lorie Hailey; Trish Morgar; Stephanie Ellis; Laura Burden. Column 3: Danielle Slevens; Don Probert; Jeff Brune.

ASK YOURSELF

What have you discovered about your own strengths and about the kind of career you might see yourself pursuing?

RETRIEVAL PRACTICE

RP-1 What is the value of finding flow in our work?

The modern workforce The editorial and production team that guides the development of this book and its resources works from far-flung places. In column 1: Nancy Fleming in Massachusetts, Kathryn Brownson in Michigan, Anna Munroe in New York, and Won McIntosh in New York. In column 2: Lorie Hailey in Kentucky, Trish Morgan in Alberta, Carlise Stembridge in Minnesota, and Laura Burden in New York. In column 3: Danielle Slevens in Massachusetts, Betty Probert in Florida, and Christine Brune in Washington, DC.

 # Industrial-Organizational Psychology

LOQ C-2 What are industrial-organizational psychology's three key areas of study?

In developed nations work has expanded, from farming to manufacturing to *knowledge work*. More and more work is *outsourced* to temporary employees and consultants, or to workers telecommuting from off-site workplaces (Gallup, 2020). (The two-author team for this book and its teaching package is aided immeasurably by a team of people in a dozen cities, from Alberta to Florida.)

As work has changed, have our attitudes toward our work also changed? Has our satisfaction with work increased or decreased? Has the *psychological contract*—the sense of mutual obligation between workers and employers—become more or less trusting and secure? How can psychologists help organizations make work more satisfying and productive? These are among the questions that fascinate **industrial-organizational (I/O) psychologists** as they apply psychology's principles to the workplace (**TABLE C.1**).

- The I/O psychology subfield of **personnel psychology** applies psychology's methods and principles to selecting, placing, training, and evaluating workers. Personnel psychologists match people with jobs by identifying and placing well-suited candidates. The **organizational psychology** subfield considers how work environments and management styles influence worker motivation, satisfaction, and productivity. It focuses on modifying jobs and supervision in ways that boost morale and productivity.

- **Human factors psychology,** now a distinct field allied with I/O psychology, explores how machines and environments can be optimally designed to fit human abilities. Human factors psychologists study people's natural perceptions and inclinations, using this research to create user-friendly machines and work settings.

industrial-organizational (I/O) psychology the application of psychological concepts and methods to human behavior in workplaces.

personnel psychology an I/O psychology subfield that helps with job seeking, and with employee recruitment, selection, placement, training, appraisal, and development.

organizational psychology an I/O psychology subfield that examines organizational influences on worker satisfaction and productivity and facilitates organizational change.

human factors psychology a field of psychology allied with I/O psychology that explores how people and machines interact and how machines and physical environments can be made safe and easy to use.

TABLE C.1 I/O Psychology and Human Factors Psychology at Work

As scientists, consultants, and management professionals, industrial-organizational (I/O) psychologists may be found helping organizations to resolve work-family conflicts, build employee retention, improve organizational spirit, or promote teamwork. Human factors psychologists contribute to human safety and improved designs.

Personnel Psychology: Maximizing Human Potential	Organizational Psychology: Building Better Organizations
Developing training programs to increase job seekers' success	**Developing organizations**
Selecting and placing employees	• Analyzing organizational structures
• Developing and testing assessment tools for selecting, placing, and promoting workers	• Maximizing worker satisfaction and productivity
• Analyzing job content	• Facilitating organizational change
• Optimizing worker placement	**Enhancing quality of work life**
Training and developing employees	• Expanding individual productivity
• Identifying needs	• Identifying elements of satisfaction
• Designing training programs, including for ethical and diverse workplaces	• Redesigning jobs
• Evaluating training programs	• Balancing work and nonwork life in an era of social media, smart phones, and rapid technological change
Appraising performance	**Human Factors Psychology: Optimizing Machines and Environments**
• Developing guidelines	
• Measuring individual performance	• Designing optimum work environments
• Measuring organizational performance	• Optimizing person-machine interactions
	• Developing systems technologies

Information from the Society of Industrial and Organizational Psychology. For more information about I/O psychology, more than 500 North American I/O graduate programs, and related job opportunities, visit SIOP.org.

Personnel Psychology

LOQ C-3 How do personnel psychologists facilitate job seeking, employee selection, work placement, and performance appraisal?

Psychologists assist organizations at various stages of selecting and assessing employees. They may help identify needed job skills, develop effective selection methods, recruit and evaluate diverse applicants, introduce and train new employees, appraise performance, and facilitate team building among people with differing cultural backgrounds. They also seek to enhance the well-being and productivity of "neurodiverse" workers—those on the autism spectrum, or those challenged by ADHD, a learning disorder, or brain injury (Weinberg & Doyle, 2017).

And they assist job seekers. Across four dozen studies, training programs (which teach job-search skills, improve self-presentation, boost self-confidence, promote goal setting, and enlist support) have nearly tripled job seekers' success (Liu et al., 2014).

Using Strengths for Successful Selection

As a new AT&T human resources executive, psychologist Mary Tenopyr (1997), was assigned to solve a problem: Customer-service representatives were failing at a high rate. After concluding that many of the hires were ill-matched to the demands of their new job, Tenopyr developed a new selection instrument:

1. She asked new applicants to respond to various test questions (without as yet making any use of their responses).

2. She followed up later to assess which of the applicants excelled on the job.

3. She identified the earlier test questions that best predicted success.

JOB RECRUITER: "Why did you leave your last job?"

JOB CANDIDATE: "It was something my boss said."

RECRUITER: "What did he say?"

CANDIDATE: "You're fired."

—Joke adapted from ZoomInfo blog

The happy result of her data-driven work was a new test that enabled AT&T to identify likely-to-succeed representatives. Personnel selection techniques such as this one aim to recruit people with the kind of strengths that will enable them and their organization to flourish. Marry the strengths of people with the tasks of organizations and the result is often prosperity and profit.

Do Interviews Predict Performance?

Employee selection usually includes an interview, and many interviewers feel confident of their ability to predict long-term job performance from a get-acquainted (*unstructured*) interview. What's therefore shocking is how error-prone interviewers' predictions may be when predicting job or graduate school success. General mental ability has been a better predictor, especially for complex jobs—for which it indicates people's ability to learn new skills (Schmidt & Hunter, 2004). Informal interviews are less informative than aptitude tests, work samples, job knowledge tests, and past job performance. After studying thousands of informal interviews and later job success, Google found "zero relationship. It's a complete random mess" (Bock, 2013).

Unstructured Interviews and the Interviewer Illusion

Traditional, unstructured interviews can provide a sense of someone's personality—their expressiveness, warmth, and verbal ability, for example. But these informal interviews also give interviewees considerable power to control the impression they are making in the interview situation (Barrick et al., 2009). Why, then, do many interviewers have such faith in their ability to discern interviewees' fitness for a job? "I have excellent interviewing skills," I/O psychology consultants often hear, "so I don't need reference checking as much as someone who doesn't have my ability to read people." Overrating one's ability to predict people's futures is called the *interviewer illusion* (Dana et al., 2013; Nisbett, 1987). Five factors explain interviewers' overconfidence:

- *Interviewers presume that people are what they seem to be in the interview situation.* An unstructured interview may create a false impression of a person's behavior toward others in different situations. Some interviewees may feign desired attitudes; others may be nervous. As social psychologists explain, when meeting others, we commit the *fundamental attribution error*: We discount the enormous influence of varying situations and mistakenly presume that what we see is what we will get. But research on everything from chattiness to conscientiousness reveals that how we behave reflects not only our enduring traits, but also the details of the particular situation (such as wanting to impress in a job interview).

- *Interviewers' preconceptions and moods color how they perceive interviewees' responses* (Cable & Gilovich, 1998; Macan & Dipboye, 1994). If interviewers instantly like a person who perhaps is similar to themselves (opening the door to unintended racial bias), they may interpret the person's assertiveness as indicating "confidence" rather than "arrogance." If told certain applicants have been prescreened, interviewers are disposed to judge them more favorably. Such interviewers are showing *confirmation bias*: They search for information that supports their preconceptions about a job candidate and ignore or distort contradictory evidence (Skov & Sherman, 1986).

- *Interviewers judge people relative to those interviewed just before and after them* (Simonsohn & Gino, 2013). If you are being interviewed for a job or graduate program, hope for a day when the other interviewees have been weak.

- *Interviewers more often follow the successful careers of those they have hired than the successful careers of those they have rejected.* This missing feedback prevents interviewers from getting a reality check on their hiring ability.

- *Interviews disclose the interviewee's good intentions, which are less revealing than habitual behaviors* (Ouellette & Wood, 1998). Intentions matter. People can change. But the best predictor of the person we will be is the person we have been.

"Between the idea / And the reality . . . /
Falls the Shadow." — T. S. Eliot, *The Hollow
Men*, 1925

Compared with work-avoiding university students, those who engage in their tasks are more likely, a decade and more later, to be engaged workers (Salmela-Aro et al., 2009). Wherever we go, we take ourselves along.

Hoping to improve prediction and selection, personnel psychologists have put people in simulated work situations, sought information on past performance, aggregated evaluations from multiple interviews, administered tests, and developed job-specific interviews.

Structured Interviews

Unlike casual conversation aimed at getting a feel for someone, **structured interviews** offer a disciplined method of collecting information. A personnel psychologist may analyze a job, script questions, and train interviewers. The interviewers then ask all applicants the same questions, in the same order, and rate each applicant on established scales.

In an unstructured interview, someone might ask, "How organized are you?" "How well do you get along with people?" or "How do you handle stress?" Street-smart applicants know how to score high: "Although I sometimes drive myself too hard, I handle stress by prioritizing and delegating, and leaving time for sleep and exercise."

By contrast, structured interviews pinpoint strengths (attitudes, behaviors, knowledge, and skills) that distinguish high performers in a particular line of work. The process includes outlining job-specific situations and asking candidates to explain how they would handle them, and how they handled similar situations in their prior employment. "Tell me about a time when you were caught between conflicting demands, without time to accomplish both. How did you handle that?" In its interviews, Google has asked, "Give me an example of a time when you solved an analytically difficult problem" (Bock, 2013).

To reduce memory distortions and bias, the interviewer takes notes and makes ratings as the interview proceeds and avoids irrelevant and follow-up questions. The structured interview therefore feels less warm, but that can be explained to the applicant: "This conversation won't typify how we relate to each other in this organization."

A review of 150 findings revealed that structured interviews had double the predictive accuracy of unstructured interviews (Schmidt & Hunter, 1998; Wiesner & Cronshaw, 1988). Structured interviews also reduce bias, such as against overweight applicants (Kutcher & Bragger, 2004).

If, instead, we let our intuitions bias the hiring process, noted Malcolm Gladwell (2000, p. 86), then "all we will have done is replace the old-boy network, where you hired your nephew, with the new-boy network, where you hire whoever impressed you most when you shook his hand. Social progress, unless we're careful, can merely be the means by which we replace the obviously arbitrary with the not so obviously arbitrary."

To recap, personnel psychologists help train job seekers, and they assist organizations in analyzing jobs, recruiting well-suited applicants, and selecting and placing employees. They also appraise employees' performance (**FIGURE C.1**)—our next topic.

> **structured interview** an interview process that asks the same job-relevant questions of all applicants, each of whom is rated on established scales.

FIGURE C.1 ⊜
Personnel psychologists at work Personnel psychologists consult in human resources activities, from job definition to recruitment to employee appraisal. The *assessment center* approach may be used to evaluate potential and existing employees.

Appraising Performance

Performance appraisal serves organizational purposes: It helps decide who to keep on staff, how to appropriately reward and pay people, and how to better harness employee strengths, sometimes with job shifts or promotions. Performance appraisal also serves individual purposes: Feedback affirms workers' strengths and helps motivate needed improvements.

Performance appraisal methods include

- *checklists* on which supervisors simply check specific behaviors that describe the worker ("always attends to customers' needs"; "takes long breaks").

- *graphic rating scales* on which a supervisor checks, perhaps on a five-point scale, how often a worker is dependable, productive, and so forth.

- *behavior rating scales* on which a supervisor checks scaled behaviors that describe a worker's performance. If rating the extent to which a worker "follows procedures," the supervisor might mark the employee somewhere between "often takes shortcuts" and "always follows established procedures" (Levy, 2003).

In some organizations, performance feedback comes not only from supervisors but also from all organizational levels. If you join an organization that practices *360-degree feedback* (**FIGURE C.2**), you will rate yourself, your manager, and your other colleagues, and you will be rated by your manager, other colleagues, and customers (Green, 2002). The net result is often more open communication and more complete appraisal.

Performance appraisal, like other social judgments, is vulnerable to bias (Murphy & Cleveland, 1995). *Halo errors* occur when one's overall evaluation of an employee, or of a personal trait such as their friendliness, biases ratings of their specific work-related behaviors, such as their reliability. *Leniency* and *severity errors* reflect evaluators' tendencies to be either too easy or too harsh on everyone. *Recency errors* occur when raters focus only on easily remembered recent behavior. By using multiple raters and developing objective, job-relevant performance measures, personnel psychologists seek to support their organizations while also helping employees perceive the appraisal process as fair.

FIGURE C.2
360-degree feedback With multisource 360-degree feedback, our knowledge, skills, and behaviors are rated by ourselves and surrounding others. Professors, for example, may be rated by their department chairs, their students, and their colleagues. After receiving all these ratings, professors discuss the 360-degree feedback with their department chair.

RETRIEVAL PRACTICE

RP-2 A human resources director explains to you that "I don't bother with tests or references. It's all about the interview." Based on I/O psychology research, what concerns does this raise?

 # Organizational Psychology

Recruiting, hiring, training, and appraising capable and diverse workers matters, but so does employee motivation and morale. Organizational psychologists assist with efforts to motivate and engage employees, and they also explore effective leadership.

Satisfaction and Engagement at Work

LOQ C-4 Why are organizational psychologists interested in employee satisfaction and engagement?

I/O psychologists have found that satisfaction with work, and with work-life balance, feeds overall satisfaction with life (Bowling et al., 2010). Lower job stress (sometimes enabled by telecommuting) supports better health (Allen et al., 2015).

Satisfied employees also contribute to successful organizations. Positive moods at work enhance creativity, persistence, and helpfulness (Ford et al., 2011; Jeffrey et al., 2014; Shockley et al., 2012). Are engaged, happy workers also less often absent? Less likely to quit? Less prone to theft? More punctual? More productive? Statistical digests of prior research have found a modest positive correlation between individual job satisfaction and performance (Judge et al., 2001; Ng et al., 2009). In one analysis of 4500

Doing well while doing good—"The Great Experiment" At the end of the 1700s, the New Lanark, Scotland, cotton mill had more than 1000 workers. Many were children drawn from Glasgow's poorhouses. They worked 13-hour days and lived in grim conditions.

On a visit to Glasgow, Welsh-born Robert Owen—an idealistic young cotton-mill manager—met and married the mill owner's daughter. Owen and some partners purchased the mill and on the first day of the 1800s began what he called "the most important experiment for the happiness of the human race that had yet been instituted at any time in any part of the world" (Owen, 1814). The exploitation of child and adult labor was, he observed, producing unhappy and inefficient workers. Owen showed *transformational leadership* (discussed later in this appendix) when he undertook numerous innovations: a nursery for preschool children, education for older children (with encouragement rather than corporal punishment), Sundays off, health care, paid sick days, unemployment pay for days when the mill could not operate, and a company store selling goods at reduced prices. He also innovated a goals- and worker-assessment program that included detailed records of daily productivity and costs but with "no beating, no abusive language."

The ensuing commercial success fueled a humanitarian reform movement. By 1816, with decades of profitability still ahead, Owen believed he had demonstrated "that society may be formed so as to exist without crime, without poverty, with health greatly improved, with little if any misery, and with intelligence and happiness increased a hundredfold." Although his utopian vision has not been fulfilled, Owen's great experiment laid the groundwork for employment practices that have today become accepted in much of the world.

Courtesy of New Lanark Trust

An engaged employee Mohamed Mamow, left, was joined by his employer in saying the Pledge of Allegiance as he became a U.S. citizen. Mamow and his wife met in a Somali refugee camp. Since then, he has supported his family by working as a machine operator. Mindful of his responsibility—"I don't like to lose my job. I have a responsibility for my children and my family"—he would arrive for work a half hour early and tend to every detail on his shift. "He is an extremely hard-working employee," noted his employer, and "a reminder to all of us that we are really blessed" (Roelofs, 2010).

Advance/MLive.com

employees at 42 British manufacturing companies, the most productive workers were those who found their work environment satisfying (Patterson et al., 2004).

Some organizations seem to have a knack for cultivating more engaged and productive employees. In the United States, *Fortune's* "100 Best Companies to Work For" have also produced markedly higher-than-average returns for their investors (Yoshimoto & Frauenheim, 2018). And consider a huge study of more than 198,000 employees in nearly 8000 business units of 36 large companies (including some 1100 bank branches, 1200 stores, and 4200 teams or departments). James Harter, Frank Schmidt, and Theodore Hayes (2002) explored correlations between various measures of organizational success and *employee engagement*—the extent of workers' involvement, enthusiasm, and identification with their organizations (**TABLE C.2**). They found that engaged workers (compared with not-engaged workers who are just putting in their time) knew what was expected of them, had what they needed to do their work, felt fulfilled in their work, had regular opportunities to do what they do best, perceived that they were part of something significant, and had opportunities to learn and develop. They also found that business units with engaged employees had more loyal customers, lower turnover rates, higher productivity, and greater profits.

What percentage of employees are engaged? One massive study of 6.4 million people in 159 countries showed that only about 15 percent of workers reported being engaged (Gallup, 2017, 2020). Engagement—feeling involved in and enthusiastic about one's work—is highest among people who have knowledge-based jobs, flexible hours, and freedom to work remotely. More organizations now offer such benefits in the hopes of increasing employee engagement (Eisenberger et al., 2019).

But what causal arrows explain this correlation between business success and employee morale and engagement? Does success boost morale, or does high morale boost success? In a follow-up longitudinal study of 142,000 workers, researchers found that, over time, employee attitudes predicted future business success (more than the other way around) (Harter et al., 2010). Many other studies confirm that happy workers tend to be good workers (Ford et al., 2011; Seibert et al., 2011; Shockley et al., 2012). One analysis compared companies with top-quartile versus below-average employee engagement levels. Over a three-year period, earnings grew 2.6 times faster for the companies with highly engaged workers (Ott, 2007). It pays to have engaged employees.

Task significance People find their work meaningful and engaging when it has *task significance*—when they view their work as benefiting others (Allan, 2017).

TABLE C.2 Three Types of Employees
• *Engaged:* working with commitment and energy, and feeling connected to their company or organization.
• *Not engaged:* putting In the time but investing little passion or energy in their work.
• *Actively disengaged:* unhappy workers undermining what their colleagues accomplish.

Information from Gallup via Crabtree, 2005.

Effective Leadership

LOQ C-5 How can leaders be most effective?

Engaged employees don't just happen. Most have effective **leaders**—people who motivate and influence them to enable their group's success, and who engage their interests and loyalty (Royal, 2019). Great managers support employees' well-being, articulate goals clearly, and lead in ways that suit the situation and consider the cultural context.

Setting Specific, Challenging Goals

Measurable objectives, such as "finish gathering the history paper information by Friday," focus our attention and stimulate us to persist and to be creative. Goals motivate achievement, especially when combined with progress reports (Harkin et al., 2016). For many people, a landmark in time—a special birthday, the new year or new school term, graduation, a new job, a new decade of life—spurs personal goal setting (Alter & Hershfield, 2014; Dai et al., 2014). Action plans that break large goals into smaller steps (subgoals) and that specify *implementation intentions*—when, where, and how to achieve those steps—increase the chances of completing a project on time (Fishbach et al., 2006; Gollwitzer & Sheeran, 2006). Through a task's ups and downs, we best sustain our mood and motivation when we focus on immediate goals (such as daily study) rather than distant goals (such as a course grade). Better to have our nose to the grindstone than our eye on the ultimate prize (Houser-Marko & Sheldon, 2008).

Thus, before beginning each new edition of this book, our author-editor team *manages by objectives*—we agree on target dates for completion of each draft. If we focus on achieving each of these short-term goals, then the prize—an on-time book—takes care of itself. So, to motivate high productivity, effective leaders work with people to define explicit goals, subgoals, and implementation plans, and then provide feedback on progress. Such goals are SMART goals—specific, measurable, actionable, realistic, and time-bound (SIOP, 2018).

Choosing an Appropriate Leadership Style

Effective leaders of laboratory groups, work teams, and large corporations often exude *charisma*—an ability to influence others while making them comfortable (Goethals &

"Good leaders don't ask more than their constituents can give, but they often ask—and get—more than their constituents intended to give or thought it was possible to give." — John W. Gardner, *Excellence*, 1984

leadership an individual's ability to motivate and influence others to contribute to their group's success.

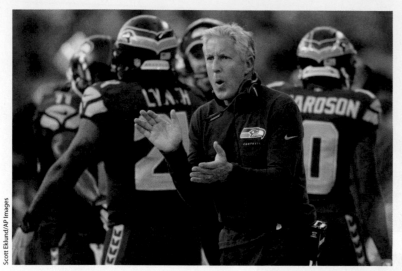

Scott Eklund/AP Images

The power of positive coaching Football coach Pete Carroll, who led the University of Southern California to two national championships and the Seattle Seahawks to a Super Bowl championship, has combined positive enthusiasm and fun workouts with "a commitment to a nurturing environment that allows people to be themselves while still being accountable to the team" (Trotter, 2014). "It shows you can win with positivity," noted former Seahawks defensive star Richard Sherman. "It's literally all positive reinforcement," said teammate Jimmy Graham (Belson, 2015).

Allison, 2014; Tskhay et al., 2018). Charismatic people have the ability to inspire others' loyalty and to focus their enthusiasm (Grabo & van Vugt, 2016).

Charisma can bolster leadership, especially when combined with practical managerial skills (Vergauwe et al., 2018). What other qualities help? Leadership styles vary, depending on both the qualities of the leader and the demands of the situation (Badura et al., 2019). In some situations (think of a commander leading troops into battle), a *directive* style may be needed (Fiedler, 1981). In other situations—developing a comedy show, for example—a leader might get better results using a *democratic* style that welcomes team member creativity.

Leaders differ in the personal qualities they bring to the job. Some excel at **task leadership**—by setting standards, organizing work, and focusing attention on goals. To keep the group centered on its mission, task leaders typically use a directive style, which can work well if the leader gives good directions (Fiedler, 1987).

Other managers excel at **social leadership**. They explain decisions, help group members solve conflicts, and build teams that work well together (Bisbey et al., 2019; Pfaff et al., 2013). Social leaders, many of whom are women, often have a democratic style. They share authority and welcome team members' opinions. Social leadership and team-building increases morale and productivity (Shuffler et al., 2011, 2013). We usually feel more satisfied and motivated, and perform better, when we can participate in decision making (Cawley et al., 1998; Pereira & Osburn, 2007). Moreover, when members are sensitive to one another and participate equally, groups solve problems with greater "collective intelligence" (Woolley et al., 2010).

In one study of 50 Dutch companies, the firms with the highest morale had chief executives who most inspired their colleagues "to transcend their own self-interests for the sake of the collective" (de Hoogh et al., 2004). *Transformational leadership* of this kind motivates others to identify with and fully commit themselves to the group's mission. Transformational leaders, many of whom are natural extraverts, articulate high standards, inspire people to share their vision, and offer personal attention (Bono & Judge, 2004). The frequent result is more engaged, trusting, and effective workers (Turner et al., 2002). Women more than men tend to exhibit transformational leadership qualities (Wang, G. et al., 2018).

Studies in India, Taiwan, and Iran suggest that effective managers—whether in coal mines, banks, or government offices—often exhibit a high degree of *both* task and social leadership (Smith & Tayeb, 1989). As achievement-minded people, effective managers care about how well work is done, yet they are sensitive to their subordinates' needs. Workers in family-friendly organizations that offer flexible hours report feeling greater job satisfaction and loyalty to their employers (Butts et al., 2013; Roehling et al., 2001). Over time, U.S. senators who practice common virtues (humility, wisdom, courage) become more influential in leadership roles than do those who practice manipulation and intimidation (ten Brinke et al., 2016). Social virtues work.

POSITIVE REINFORCEMENT Effective leadership often builds on a basic principle of *operant conditioning*: To teach a behavior, catch a person doing something right and reinforce it. It sounds simple, but many managers are like parents who, when a child brings home a near-perfect school report card, focus on the one low grade in a troublesome class and ignore the rest. "Sixty-five percent of Americans received NO praise or recognition in the workplace last year," reported the Gallup organization (2004).

FULFILLING THE NEED TO BELONG A work environment that satisfies employees' need to belong is energizing. Employees who enjoy high-quality colleague relationships engage their work with more vigor (Carmeli et al., 2009). Gallup researchers have asked more than 15 million employees worldwide if they have a "best friend at work." The 30 percent who do "are *seven times* as likely to be engaged in their jobs" as those who don't, report Tom Rath and James Harter (2010). And, as we noted earlier, positive, engaged employees are a mark of thriving organizations.

task leadership goal-oriented leadership that sets standards, organizes work, and focuses attention on goals.

social leadership group-oriented leadership that builds teamwork, mediates conflict, and offers support.

PARTICIPATIVE MANAGEMENT Employee participation in decision making is common in Sweden, Japan, the United States, and elsewhere (Cawley et al., 1998; Sundstrom et al., 1990). Workers given a chance to voice their opinion and be part of the decision-making process have responded more positively to the final decision (van den Bos & Spruijt, 2002). They also feel more empowered, and are likely, therefore, to be more creative and committed (Hennessey & Amabile, 2010; Seibert et al., 2011).

The ultimate in employee participation is the employee-owned company, of which there are said to be some 2000 in the United States—including Publix Supermarkets with its nearly 200,000 employees (Lapp, 2019). One such company in my [DM's] town is the Fleetwood Group, a thriving 165-employee manufacturer of educational furniture and wireless communication devices. Every employee owns part of the company, and as a group they own 100 percent. The more years employees work, the more they own, yet no one owns more than 5 percent. Like every corporate president, Fleetwood's president works for his stockholders—who also just happen to be his employees.

As a company that endorses faith-inspired "respect and care for each team member-owner," Fleetwood is free to place people above profits. Thus, when orders lagged during a recession, the employee-owners decided that job security meant more to them than profits. So the company paid otherwise idle workers to do community service, such as answering phones at nonprofit agencies and building Habitat for Humanity houses. Employee ownership attracts and retains talented people, which for Fleetwood has meant company success.

Cultural Influences on Leadership Styles

LOQ **C-6** What cultural influences need to be considered when choosing an effective leadership style?

I/O psychology sprang from North American roots. So, how well do its leadership principles apply to cultures worldwide?

One worldwide investigation, Project GLOBE (Global Leadership and Organizational Behavior Effectiveness), has studied cultural variations in leadership expectations (House et al., 2001). Some cultures, for example, encourage collective sharing of resources and rewards; others are more individualist. Some cultures minimize and others accentuate traditional gender roles. Some cultures prioritize being friendly, caring, and kind, and others encourage a "me-first" attitude. The program's first research phase studied 17,300 leaders of 950 organizations in 61 countries (Brodbeck et al., 2008; Dorfman et al., 2012). One finding: Leaders who fulfill expectations, such as by being directive in some cultures or participative in others, tend to be successful. Cultures shape leadership and what makes for leadership success.

Nevertheless, some leader behaviors are universally effective. From its massive study of nearly 50,000 business units in 45 countries, Gallup observed that thriving companies tend to focus on identifying and enhancing employee *strengths* (rather than punishing their deficiencies). Doing so predicts increased employee engagement, customer satisfaction, and profitability (Rigoni & Asplund, 2016a,b). *Strengths-based* leadership pays dividends, supporting happier, more creative, more productive employees in workplaces with less absenteeism and turnover (Amabile & Kramer, 2011; De Neve et al., 2013).

Moreover, the same principles affect student satisfaction, retention, and future success (Larkin et al., 2013; Ray & Kafka, 2014). Students who feel supported by caring friends and mentors tend to persist and ultimately succeed during school and after graduation.

Effective leaders + satisfying work = engaged employees

* * *

We have considered *personnel psychology* (the I/O psychology subfield that focuses on training job seekers, and assisting with employee selection, placement, appraisal, and development). And we have considered *organizational psychology* (the I/O psychology subfield that focuses on worker satisfaction and productivity, and on organizational change). Finally, we turn to *human factors psychology,* which explores the human-machine interface.

ASK YOURSELF

In what type of leadership role do you think you would most excel? If you already have leadership experience, how could you grow to become a more effective leader?

RETRIEVAL PRACTICE

RP-3   What characteristics are important for *transformational leaders*?

→ Human Factors Psychology

LOQ **C-7** How do human factors psychologists work to create user-friendly machines and work settings?

Designs sometimes neglect the human factor. Cognitive scientist Donald Norman (2001) bemoaned the complexity of assembling his new HDTV, related components, and seven remotes into a usable home theater system: "I was VP of Advanced Technology at Apple. I can program dozens of computers in dozens of languages. I understand television, really, I do. . . . It doesn't matter: I am overwhelmed."

Human factors psychologists work with designers and engineers to tailor appliances, machines, and work settings to our natural perceptions and inclinations. Bank ATM machines are internally more complex than remote controls ever were, yet thanks to human factors engineering, ATMs are easier to operate. Digital recorders have solved the TV recording problem with a simple select-and-click menu system ("record that one"). Apple similarly engineered easy usability with the iPhone and iPad. Handheld and wearable technologies are increasingly making use of *haptic* (touch-based) feedback—opening a phone with a thumbprint, sharing your heartbeat via a smartwatch, or having GPS directional instructions ("turn left" arrow) "drawn" on your skin with other wrist-worn devices.

Norman hosts a website (jnd.org) that illustrates good designs that fit people (**FIGURE C.3**). Human factors psychologists also help design efficient environments. An ideal kitchen layout, researchers have found, puts needed items close to their usage point and near eye level. It locates work areas to enable doing tasks in order, such as placing the refrigerator, stove, and sink in a triangle. It creates counters that enable hands to work at or slightly below elbow height (Boehm-Davis, 2005).

Understanding human factors can help prevent accidents. By studying the human factor in driving accidents, psychologists seek to devise ways to reduce the distractions, fatigue, and inattention that contribute to 1.25 million annual worldwide traffic fatalities (WHO, 2016). At least two-thirds of commercial air accidents have been caused by human error (Shappell et al., 2007). After beginning commercial flights in the 1960s, the Boeing 727 was involved in several landing accidents caused by pilot error. Psychologist Conrad Kraft (1978) noted a common context for these accidents: All took place at night, and all involved landing short of the runway after crossing a dark stretch of water or unilluminated ground. Kraft reasoned that, on rising terrain, city lights beyond the runway would project a larger retinal image, making the ground seem farther away than it was. By re-creating these conditions in flight simulations, Kraft discovered that pilots were deceived into thinking they were flying higher than their actual altitudes (**FIGURE C.4**). Aided by Kraft's finding, airlines began requiring the co-pilot to monitor the altimeter—calling out altitudes during the descent—and the accidents diminished.

Ride On Carry On

OXO Good Grips

⊘ FIGURE C.3
Designing products that fit people
Human factors expert Donald Norman offers these and other examples of effectively designed products. The Ride On Carry On foldable chair attachment, "designed by a flight attendant mom," enables a small suitcase to double as a stroller. The OXO measuring cup allows the user to see the quantity from above.

Human factors psychologists can also help us to function in other settings. Consider the available *assistive listening* technologies in various theaters, auditoriums, and places of worship. One technology, commonly available in the United States, requires a headset attached to a pocket-sized receiver. The well-meaning people who provide these systems correctly understand that the technology puts sound directly into the user's ears. Alas, few people with hearing loss elect the hassle and embarrassment of locating, requesting, wearing, and returning a conspicuous headset. Most such units therefore sit in closets. Britain, the Scandinavian countries, Australia, and now many parts of the United States have instead installed *loop systems* (see HearingLoop.org) that broadcast customized sound directly through a person's own hearing aid. When suitably equipped, a hearing aid can be transformed by a discreet touch of a switch into a customized in-the-ear speaker. When offered convenient, inconspicuous, personalized sound, many more people elect to use assistive listening.

Designs that enable safe, easy, and effective interactions between people and technology often seem obvious after the fact. Why, then, aren't they more common? Technology developers, like all of us, sometimes mistakenly assume that others share their expertise—that what's clear to them will similarly be clear to others (Camerer et al., 1989; Nickerson, 1999). When people rap their knuckles on a table to convey a familiar tune (try this with a friend), they often expect their listener to recognize it. But for the listener, this is a near-impossible task (Newton, 1991). When you know a thing, it's hard to mentally simulate what it's like not to know, and that is called the *curse of knowledge*.

The point to remember: Everyone benefits when designers and engineers tailor machines, technologies, and environments to fit human abilities and behaviors, when they user-test their work before production and distribution, and when they remain mindful of the curse of knowledge.

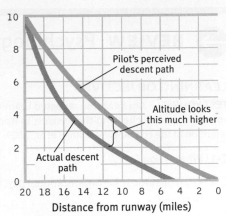

⬆ **FIGURE C.4**
The human factor in accidents Lacking distance cues when approaching a runway from over a dark surface, pilots simulating a night landing tended to fly too low. (Data from Kraft, 1978.)

"The better you know something, the less you remember about how hard it was to learn." — Psychologist Steven Pinker, *The Sense of Style*, 2014

The human factor in safe landings
Advanced cockpit design and rehearsed emergency procedures aided pilot Chesley "Sully" Sullenberger, a U.S. Air Force Academy graduate who earned a Master's degree in industrial psychology. In 2009, Sullenberger's instantaneous decisions safely guided his disabled airplane onto New York City's Hudson River, where all 155 of the passengers and crew were safely evacuated.

Steven Day/AP Images

ASK YOURSELF

What situations have you experienced (using new technology, visiting buildings, using transportation) in which the design did not work well? What situations have you experienced in which planners did a particularly good job matching machines and physical environments to abilities and expectations?

RETRIEVAL PRACTICE

RP-4   What is the *curse of knowledge*, and what does it have to do with the work of human factors psychologists?

REVIEW Psychology at Work

LEARNING OBJECTIVES

TEST YOURSELF Answer these repeated Learning Objective Questions on your own (before checking the answers in Appendix D) to improve your retention of the concepts (McDaniel et al., 2009, 2015).

C-1 What is *flow?*

C-2 What are industrial-organizational psychology's three key areas of study?

C-3 How do personnel psychologists facilitate job seeking, employee selection, work placement, and performance appraisal?

C-4 Why are organizational psychologists interested in employee satisfaction and engagement?

C-5 How can leaders be most effective?

C-6 What cultural influences need to be considered when choosing an effective leadership style?

C-7 How do human factors psychologists work to create user-friendly machines and work settings?

TERMS AND CONCEPTS TO REMEMBER

TEST YOURSELF Write down the definition in your own words, then check your answer.

flow, p. C-1

industrial-organizational (I/O) psychology, p. C-3

personnel psychology, p. C-3

organizational psychology, p. C-3

human factors psychology, p. C-3

structured interview, p. C-6

leadership, p. C-9

task leadership, p. C-10

social leadership, p. C-10

MASTER THE MATERIAL

TEST YOURSELF Answer the following questions on your own first, then check your answers in Appendix E.

1. People who view their work as a calling often experience _____, a focused state of consciousness, with diminished awareness of themselves and of time.

2. _____ psychologists assist with job seeking, and the recruitment, selection, placement, training, appraisal,

and development of employees; _____ _____ psychologists focus on how people and machines interact, and on optimizing devices and work environments.

3. A personnel psychologist scripted a set of questions to ask all applicants for a job opening. She then trained the firm's interviewers to ask only those questions, to take notes, and to rate applicants' responses. This technique is known as a(n)

   a. structured interview.

   b. unstructured interview.

   c. performance appraisal checklist.

   d. behavior rating scale.

4. In your job, you rate your own performance, your manager's, and your peers'. Your manager, your peers, and your customers also rate your performance. Your organization is using a form of performance appraisal called

   a. the assessment center approach.

   b. graphic feedback.

   c. structured interviews.

   d. 360-degree feedback.

5. What type of goals will best help you stay focused and motivated to do your finest work in this class?

6. Research indicates that women are often social leaders. They are also more likely than men to have a _____ leadership style.

7. Effective managers often exhibit

   a. only task leadership.

   b. only social leadership.

   c. both task and social leadership, depending on the situation and the person.

   d. task leadership for building teams and social leadership for setting standards.

8. Human factors psychologists focus primarily on

   a. training and developing employees.

   b. appraising employee performance.

   c. maximizing worker satisfaction.

   d. improving the design of machines and environments.

Continue testing yourself with **LearningCurve** or **Achieve Read & Practice** to learn and remember most effectively.

Complete Module Reviews

The Story of Psychology

MODULE 1: What Is Psychology?

1-1 How is psychology a science?
Psychology's findings, based on an *empirical approach,* are the result of careful observation and testing. Sifting sense from nonsense requires a scientific attitude, as seen in one of psychology's early mottos: "The rat is always right."

1-2 What are the three key elements of the scientific attitude, and how do they support scientific inquiry?
The scientific attitude equips us to be curious, skeptical, and humble in scrutinizing competing ideas or our own observations. Curiosity triggers new ideas, skepticism encourages attention to the facts, and humility helps us discard predictions that can't be verified by research. Together, these three key elements make modern science possible.

1-3 How does critical thinking feed a scientific attitude, and smarter thinking for everyday life?
Critical thinking puts ideas to the test by examining assumptions, appraising the source, discerning hidden biases, evaluating evidence, and assessing conclusions.

1-4 What were some important milestones in psychology's early history?
Wilhelm Wundt established the first psychological laboratory in 1879 in Germany. Two early schools of thought in psychology were *structuralism* and *functionalism.* Mary Whiton Calkins and Margaret Floy Washburn were two of the first women in the field.

1-5 How did behaviorism, Freudian psychology, and humanistic psychology further the development of psychological science?
Early researchers defined *psychology* as "the science of mental life." In the 1920s, under the influence of John B. Watson and the behaviorists, the field's focus changed to the "scientific study of observable behavior." *Behaviorism* became one of psychology's two major forces well into the 1960s. However, the second major force of Freudian (psychoanalytic) psychology, along with the influence of *humanistic psychology,* revived interest in the study of mental processes.

1-6 How has contemporary psychology focused on cognition, on biology and experience, on culture and gender, and on human flourishing?
The *cognitive* revolution in the 1960s led psychology back to its early interest in the mind, and to its current definition as the science of behavior and mental processes. The field of *cognitive neuroscience* now examines the brain activity underlying mental activity. Our growing understanding of biology and experience has fed psychology's most enduring debate. The *nature–nurture issue* centers on the relative contributions of genes and experience, and their interaction in specific environments. Charles Darwin's view that *natural selection* shapes behaviors as well as bodies led to *evolutionary psychology's* study of our similarities because of our common biology and evolutionary history, and *behavior genetics'* focus on the relative power and limits of genetic and environmental influences on behavior. Cross-cultural and gender studies have diversified psychology's assumptions while also reminding us of our similarities. Attitudes and behaviors may vary somewhat by gender or across *cultures,* but because of our shared human kinship, the underlying processes and principles are more similar than different. Psychology's traditional focus on understanding and treating troubles has expanded with *positive psychology's* call for more research on human flourishing and its attempt to discover and promote traits that help people to thrive.

1-7 How do psychologists use the biopsychosocial approach, and how can it help us understand our diverse world?
The *biopsychosocial approach* integrates information from three differing but complementary *levels of analysis:* biological, psychological, and social-cultural. This approach offers a more complete understanding than could usually be reached by relying on only one of psychology's current theoretical perspectives (neuroscience, evolutionary, behavior genetics, psychodynamic, behavioral, cognitive, and social-cultural).

1-8 What are psychology's main subfields?
Within the science of psychology, researchers may conduct *basic research* to increase the field's knowledge base (often in biological, developmental, cognitive, personality, and social psychology) or *applied research* to solve practical problems (in industrial-organizational psychology and other areas). Those who engage in psychology as a helping profession may assist people as *counseling psychologists,* helping people with challenges and crises (including academic, vocational, and relationship issues) and to improve their personal and social functioning, or as *clinical psychologists,* assessing and treating people with mental, emotional, and behavior disorders. (*Psychiatrists* also assess and treat people with disorders, but as medical doctors, they may prescribe drugs in addition to psychotherapy.) *Community psychologists* work to create healthy social and physical environments (in schools and neighborhoods, for example).

1-9 How can psychological principles help you learn, remember, and thrive?
The *testing effect* shows that learning and memory are enhanced by actively retrieving, rather than simply rereading, previously studied material. The SQ3R study method—survey, question, read, retrieve, and review—applies principles derived from memory research and can help you

learn and remember material. Four additional tips are (1) distribute your study time; (2) learn to think critically; (3) process class information actively; and (4) overlearn. Psychological research has shown that people who live happy, thriving lives manage their time to get a full night's sleep; make space for exercise; set long-term goals, with daily aims; have a growth mindset; and prioritize relationships.

Thinking Critically With Psychological Science

MODULE 2: Research Strategies: How Psychologists Ask and Answer Questions

2-1 How does our everyday thinking sometimes lead us to a wrong conclusion?

Our everyday thinking can lead us astray because of three phenomena. *Hindsight bias* (the "I-knew-it-all-along phenomenon") is the tendency to believe, after learning an outcome, that we would have foreseen it. Overconfidence is often the result of our readiness to be more confident than correct. These tendencies, along with our eagerness to perceive patterns in random events, lead us to overestimate the weight of commonsense thinking. Although limited by the testable questions it can address, scientific inquiry can help us overcome such biases and shortcomings.

2-2 Why are we so vulnerable to believing untruths?

In our modern "post-truth" culture, our emotions, beliefs, and group affiliations may color our judgments, prevent our acknowledgement of objective facts, and prompt us to accept only the information that confirms our views. Misinformation may spread as a result of repetition and memorable examples, contributing to the post-truth culture. Critical evaluation of information and a scientific mindset can help to combat our biases and distorted thinking.

2-3 How do theories advance psychological science?

Psychological *theories* apply an integrated set of principles to organize observations and to generate *hypotheses*. By testing their hypotheses, researchers can confirm, reject, or revise their theories. To enable other researchers to *replicate* the studies, researchers report them using precise *operational definitions* of their procedures and concepts. If others achieve similar results, confidence in the conclusion will be greater. More and more psychologists use *preregistration* to publicly communicate their planned study design, hypotheses, data collection, and analyses, which promotes openness and transparency. By combining the results of many studies, *meta-analysis* helps increase researchers' confidence in their results by avoiding the problem of small sample sizes.

2-4 How do psychologists use case studies, naturalistic observations, and surveys to observe and describe behavior, and why is random sampling important?

Descriptive methods, which include *case studies* (in-depth analyses of individuals or groups), *naturalistic observations* (recording many individuals' natural behavior), and *surveys* (asking people questions), show us what can happen, and they may offer ideas for further study. The best basis for generalizing about a *population* is a representative sample; in a *random sample*, every person in the entire population being studied has an equal chance of participating. Descriptive methods describe but do not *explain* behavior; they cannot show cause and effect because researchers cannot control variables.

2-5 What does it mean when we say two things are correlated, and what are positive and negative correlations?

Correlation is the degree to which two *variables* are related, and how well one predicts the other. In a positive correlation, two variables increase or decrease together; in a negative correlation, one variable increases as the other decreases. The strength and direction of their relationship is expressed as a *correlation coefficient*, which ranges from +1.00 (a perfect positive correlation) through 0 (no correlation) to –1.00 (a perfect negative correlation). The relationship may be displayed in a *scatterplot*, in which each dot represents a value for the two variables.

2-6 What are *illusory correlations*, and what is *regression toward the mean*?

Illusory correlations are random events that we notice and falsely assume are related. *Regression toward the mean* is the tendency for extreme or unusual scores to fall back (regress) toward their average.

2-7 Why do correlations enable prediction but not cause-effect explanation?

Correlations enable prediction because they show how two factors are related—either positively or negatively. A correlation can indicate the possibility of a cause-effect relationship, but it does not prove the direction of the influence, or whether an underlying third factor may explain the correlation.

2-8 What are the characteristics of experimentation that make it possible to isolate cause and effect?

To discover cause-effect relationships, psychologists conduct *experiments*, manipulating one or more variables of interest and controlling other variables. Using *random assignment*, they can minimize *confounding variables*, such as preexisting differences between the *experimental group* (exposed to the treatment) and the *control group* (not given the treatment). The *independent variable* is the factor the experimenter manipulates to study its effect; the *dependent variable* is the factor the experimenter measures to discover any changes occurring in response to the manipulation of the independent variable. Studies may use a *double-blind procedure* to avoid the *placebo effect* and researcher bias.

2-9 How would you know which research design to use?

Psychological scientists design studies and choose research methods that will best provide meaningful results. Researchers generate testable questions, and then carefully consider the best design to use in studying those questions (experimental, correlational, case study, naturalistic observation, twin study, longitudinal, or cross-sectional). Next, psychologists measure the variables they are studying, and finally they interpret their results, keeping possible confounding variables in mind. (The online *How Would You Know?* research activities allow you to play the role of the researcher, making choices about the best ways to test interesting questions.)

2-10 How can simplified laboratory conditions illuminate everyday life?

Researchers intentionally create a controlled, artificial environment in the laboratory to test general theoretical principles. It is the general principles—not the specific findings—that help explain everyday behaviors.

2-11 Why do psychologists study animals, and what ethical research guidelines safeguard human and animal welfare? How do psychologists' values influence what they study and how they apply their results?

Some psychologists are primarily interested in animal behavior; others want to better understand the physiological and psychological processes shared by humans and other species. Government agencies have established standards for animal care and housing. Professional associations and funding agencies also have guidelines for protecting animals' well-being. The ethics codes of the American Psychological Association (APA) and the British Psychological Society (BPS) outline standards for safeguarding human participants' well-being, including obtaining their *informed consent* and *debriefing* them later. Scientific scrutiny and replication help to guard against the fabrication of data, which has the potential to cause great harm. Psychologists' values influence their choice of research topics, their theories and observations, and their labels for behavior. Applications of psychology's principles have been used mainly in the service of humanity.

MODULE 3: Statistical Reasoning in Everyday Life

3-1 How do we describe data using three measures of central tendency, and what is the relative usefulness of the two measures of variation?

Researchers use descriptive statistics to measure and describe characteristics of groups under study. A measure of central tendency is a single score that represents a whole set of scores. Three such measures that we use to describe data are the *mode* (the most frequently occurring score), the *mean* (the arithmetic average), and the *median* (the middle score in a group of data). Measures of central tendency neatly summarize data; measures of variation tell us how diverse data are. Two measures of variation are the *range* (which describes the gap between the highest and lowest scores) and the *standard deviation* (which states how much scores vary around the mean, or average, score). Scores often form a *normal* (or bell-shaped) *curve.*

3-2 How do we know whether an observed difference can be generalized to other populations?

Researchers use inferential statistics (which include ways of determining the reliability and significance of an observed difference between the results for different groups) to determine if results can be generalized to a larger population. Reliable differences are based on samples that are representative of the larger population being studied, that demonstrate low variability, on average, and that consist of many cases. The *effect size*—the size of the difference between groups—helps determine *statistical significance:* When the sample averages are reliable and the difference between them is large, we can reject the null hypothesis of no existing differences. Many psychological tests provide *p*-values, which indicate the probability of the null hypothesis given the sample data.

The Biology of Mind

MODULE 4: Neural and Hormonal Systems

4-1 Why are psychologists concerned with human biology?

Psychologists working from a *biological* perspective study the links between biological processes and psychological processes. We are biopsychosocial systems, in which biological, psychological, and social-cultural factors interact to influence behavior.

4-2 How do biology and experience together enable neuroplasticity?

Neuroplasticity enables our brain to build new neural pathways as we adjust to new experiences, thereby being sculpted by both genes and life. While this is a lifelong ability, neuroplasticity is greatest in childhood. With practice, our brain develops unique patterns that reflect our life experiences.

4-3 What are *neurons,* and how do they transmit information?

Neurons are the elementary components of the nervous system, the body's speedy electrochemical information system. A neuron (a *cell body* and its branching fibers) receives signals through its often bushy, branching *dendrites* and sends signals through its *axons*. Some axons are encased in a *myelin sheath*, which enables faster transmission. *Glial cells* support, nourish, and protect neurons and also play a role in learning, thinking, and memory. If the combined signals received by a neuron exceed a minimum *threshold,* the neuron fires, transmitting an electrical impulse (the *action potential*) down its axon by means of a chemistry-to-electricity process. Neurons need a short rest called the *refractory period,* after which they can fire again. The neuron's reaction is an *all-or-none response.*

4-4 How do nerve cells communicate with other nerve cells?

When action potentials reach the end of an axon (the button-like axon terminals), they stimulate the release of *neurotransmitters*. These chemical messengers carry a message from the sending neuron across a *synapse* to receptor sites on a receiving neuron. The sending neuron, in a process called *reuptake,* then normally reabsorbs the excess neurotransmitter molecules in the synaptic gap. If incoming signals are strong enough, the receiving neuron generates its own action potential and relays the message to other cells.

4-5 How do neurotransmitters influence behavior, and how do drugs and other chemicals affect neurotransmission?

Neurotransmitters travel designated pathways in the brain and influence specific behaviors and emotions. Acetylcholine (ACh) enables muscle action, learning, and memory. *Endorphins* are natural opiates released in response to pain and exercise. Drugs and other chemicals affect brain chemistry at synapses. *Agonists* increase a neurotransmitter's action, and may do so in various ways. *Antagonists* decrease a neurotransmitter's action by blocking production or release.

4-6 What are the functions of the nervous system's main divisions, and what are the three main types of neurons?

The *central nervous system* (CNS)—the brain and the spinal cord—is the *nervous system's* decision maker. The *peripheral nervous system* (PNS), which connects the CNS to the rest of the body by means of *nerves*, gathers information and transmits CNS decisions to the rest of the body. The two main PNS divisions are the *somatic nervous system* (which enables voluntary control of the skeletal muscles) and the *autonomic nervous system* (which controls involuntary muscles and glands by means of its *sympathetic* and *parasympathetic* divisions). The three types of neurons cluster into working networks: (1) *Sensory (afferent) neurons* carry incoming information from the body's tissues and sensory receptors to the brain and spinal cord. (2) *Motor (efferent) neurons* carry outgoing information from the brain and spinal cord to the muscles and glands. (3) *Interneurons* communicate within the brain and spinal cord and process information between the sensory inputs and motor outputs.

4-7 How does the endocrine system transmit information and interact with the nervous system?

The *endocrine system* secretes *hormones* into the bloodstream, where they travel through the body and affect other tissues, including the brain. The endocrine system's master gland, the *pituitary*, influences hormone release by other glands, including the *adrenal glands*. In an intricate feedback system, the brain's hypothalamus influences the pituitary gland, which influences other glands, which release hormones, which in turn influence the brain.

MODULE 5: Tools of Discovery, Older Brain Structures, and the Limbic System

5-1 How do neuroscientists study the brain's connections to behavior and mind?

Clinical observations and *lesioning* reveal the general effects of brain damage. Electrical, chemical, or magnetic stimulation can also reveal aspects of information processing in the brain. *MRI* scans show anatomy. *EEG, MEG, PET,* and *fMRI (functional MRI)* recordings reveal brain function. Other revealing techniques include optogenetics and fNIRS.

5-2 What structures make up the brainstem, and what are the functions of the brainstem, thalamus, reticular formation, and cerebellum?

The *brainstem*, the oldest part of the brain, is responsible for automatic survival functions. It includes the *medulla* (which controls heartbeat and breathing), the pons (which helps coordinate movements and control sleep), and the *reticular formation* (which filters incoming stimuli, relays information to other brain areas, and affects arousal). The *thalamus*, sitting above the brainstem, acts as the brain's sensory control center. The *cerebellum*, attached to the rear of the brainstem, coordinates muscle movement and

balance and enables nonverbal learning and memory.

5-3 What are the limbic system's structures and functions?

The *limbic system* is linked to emotions, memory, and drives. Its neural centers include the *amygdala* (involved in behavioral and emotional responses, such as aggression and fear); the *hypothalamus* (directs various bodily maintenance functions, helps govern the endocrine system, and is linked to emotion and reward); and the *hippocampus* (helps process explicit, conscious memories). The hypothalamus controls the pituitary (the "master gland") by stimulating it to trigger the release of hormones.

MODULE 6: The Cerebral Cortex

6-1 What four lobes make up the cerebral cortex, and what are the functions of the motor cortex, somatosensory cortex, and association areas?

The *cerebral cortex* has two hemispheres, and each hemisphere has four lobes: the *frontal, parietal, occipital,* and *temporal.* Each lobe performs many functions and interacts with other areas of the cortex. The *motor cortex*, at the rear of the frontal lobes, controls voluntary movements. The *somatosensory cortex*, at the front of the parietal lobes, registers and processes body touch and movement sensations. Body parts requiring precise control (in the motor cortex) or those that are especially sensitive (in the somatosensory cortex) occupy the greatest amount of space. Most of the brain's cortex—the major portion of each of the four lobes—is devoted to uncommitted *association areas*, which integrate information involved in higher mental functions such as learning, remembering, thinking, and speaking. Our mental experiences arise from coordinated brain activity.

6-2 Is it true that 90 percent of our brain isn't really used?

The unresponsiveness of our association areas to electrical probing led to the false claim that we only use 10 percent of our brain. But these vast areas of the brain are responsible for interpreting, integrating, and acting on sensory information and linking it with stored memories. Evidence from brain damage shows that the neurons in association areas are busy with higher mental functions; a bullet would not land in an "unused" area.

6-3 To what extent can a damaged brain reorganize itself, and what is *neurogenesis*?

While brain and spinal cord neurons usually do not regenerate, some neural tissue can reorganize in response to damage. The damaged brain may demonstrate neuroplasticity, especially in young children, as new pathways are built and functions migrate to other brain regions. Reassignment of functions to different areas of the brain may also occur in blindness and deafness, or as a result of damage and disease. Some research suggests that the brain may sometimes mend itself by forming new neurons, a process known as *neurogenesis*.

6-4 What do split brains reveal about the functions of our two brain hemispheres?

Split-brain research (experiments on people with a severed *corpus callosum*) has confirmed that in most people, the left hemisphere is the more verbal. The right hemisphere excels in visual perception and making inferences, and helps us modulate our speech and orchestrate our self-awareness. Studies of the intact brain in healthy people confirm that each hemisphere makes unique contributions to the integrated functioning of the whole brain.

Consciousness and The Two-Track Mind

MODULE 7: Basic Consciousness Concepts

7-1 What is the place of consciousness in psychology's history?

After initially claiming consciousness as their area of study in the nineteenth century, psychologists abandoned it in the first half of the twentieth century, turning instead to the study of observable behavior because they believed consciousness was too difficult to study scientifically. Since 1960, under the influence of cognitive psychology, neuroscience, and *cognitive neuroscience*, our awareness of ourselves and our environment—our *consciousness*—has reclaimed its place as an important area of research.

7-2 How does selective attention direct our perceptions?

We *selectively attend* to, and process, a very limited portion of incoming information, blocking out much and often shifting the spotlight of our attention from one thing to another. Focused intently on one task, we often display *inattentional blindness* to other events, including *change blindness* to changes around us.

7-3 What is the *dual processing* being revealed by today's cognitive neuroscience?

Scientists studying the brain mechanisms underlying consciousness and cognition have discovered that the mind processes information on two separate tracks, one operating at a conscious level (*sequential processing*) and the other at an unconscious level (*parallel processing*). Parallel processing takes care of the routine business, while sequential processing is best for solving new problems that require our attention. Together, this *dual processing*—conscious and unconscious—affects our perception, memory, attitudes, and other cognitions.

MODULE 8: Sleep and Dreams

8-1 What is *sleep*?

Sleep is the periodic, natural loss of normal consciousness—as distinct from unconsciousness resulting from a coma, general anesthesia, or hibernation.

8-2 How do our biological rhythms influence our daily functioning?

Our bodies have an internal biological clock, roughly synchronized with the 24-hour cycle of night and day. This *circadian rhythm* appears in our daily patterns of body temperature, arousal, sleeping, and waking. Age and experience can alter these patterns, resetting our biological clock.

8-3 What is the biological rhythm of our sleeping and dreaming stages?

Younger adults cycle through four distinct sleep stages about every 90 minutes. (The sleep cycle repeats more frequently for older adults.) Leaving the *alpha waves* of the awake, relaxed stage, we descend into the irregular brain waves of non-REM stage 1 (N1) sleep, often with *hallucinations*. N2 sleep (in which we spend about half our sleep time) follows, lasting about 20 minutes, with its characteristic sleep spindles. We then enter N3 sleep, lasting about 30 minutes, with large, slow *delta waves*. About an hour after falling asleep, we ascend from our initial sleep dive and begin periods of *REM* (rapid eye movement or R) *sleep*. REM sleep, which includes most dreaming, is described as a paradoxical sleep stage because of internal arousal but external calm (near paralysis). During a normal night's sleep, N3 sleep shortens and REM and N2 sleep lengthens.

8-4 How do biology and environment interact in our sleep patterns?

Our biology—our circadian rhythm as well as our age and our body's production of melatonin (influenced by the brain's *suprachiasmatic nucleus*)—interacts with social, cultural, and economic influences and individual behaviors to determine our sleeping and waking patterns. Being bathed in (or deprived of) light disrupts our 24-hour biological clock. Those who are chronically deprived of natural sunlight, such as night-shift workers, may experience desynchronization.

8-5 What are sleep's functions?

Sleep may have played a protective role in human evolution by keeping people safe during potentially dangerous periods. Sleep also helps restore and repair damaged neurons. Sleep consolidates our memories by replaying recent learning and strengthening neural connections. Sleep promotes creative problem solving the next day. During slow-wave sleep, the pituitary gland secretes a growth hormone necessary for muscle development. As a result of these benefits, a regular full night's sleep can greatly enhance athletic performance.

8-6 How does sleep loss affect us, and what are the major sleep disorders?

Sleep deprivation causes fatigue and irritability, and it impairs concentration and memory consolidation. It can also lead to depression, obesity, joint inflammation, a suppressed immune system, and slowed performance (with greater vulnerability to accidents). Sleep disorders include *insomnia* (recurring problems in falling or staying asleep); *narcolepsy* (sudden uncontrollable sleepiness, sometimes lapsing directly into REM sleep); *sleep apnea* (the repeated stopping of breathing while asleep; associated with obesity, especially in men); *night terrors* (high arousal and the appearance of being terrified; N3 disorder found mainly in children); sleepwalking; and sleeptalking.

8-7 What do we dream, and what functions have theorists proposed for dreams?

We usually *dream* of ordinary events and everyday experiences, most involving some anxiety or misfortune. Fewer than 10 percent of dreams among men (and fewer still among women) have any sexual content. Most dreams occur during REM sleep. There are five major views of the function of dreams. (1) Freud's wish-fulfillment: Dreams provide a psychic "safety valve," with *manifest content* (story line) acting as a censored version of *latent content* (underlying meaning that gratifies our unconscious wishes). (2) Information-processing: Dreams help us sort out the day's events and consolidate them in memory. (3) Physiological function: Regular brain stimulation may help develop and preserve neural pathways in the brain. (4) Neural activation: The brain attempts to make sense of neural static by weaving it into a story line. (5) Cognitive development: Dreams reflect the dreamers' level of development—their knowledge and understanding. Most sleep theorists agree that REM sleep and its associated dreams serve an important function, as shown by the REM *rebound* that occurs following REM deprivation in humans and other species.

MODULE 9: Drugs and Consciousness

9-1 What are *substance use disorders*?

Those with a *substance use disorder* experience continued substance craving and use despite significant life disruption and/or physical risk. *Psychoactive drugs* alter perceptions and moods.

9-2 What roles do tolerance and addiction play in substance use disorders, and how has the concept of *addiction* changed?

Psychoactive drugs may produce *tolerance*—requiring larger doses to achieve the desired effect—and *withdrawal*—significant discomfort, due to strong addictive cravings, accompanying attempts to quit. Addiction prompts users to crave the drug and to continue use despite known adverse consequences. Therapy or group support may help; it helps to believe that addictions are controllable and that people can change. Although psychologists try to avoid overuse of the term *addiction* to label driven, excessive behaviors, there are some behavior addictions (such as gambling disorder and internet gaming disorder) in which behaviors become compulsive and dysfunctional.

9-3 What are *depressants,* and what are their effects?

Depressants, such as alcohol, *barbiturates,* and the *opiates,* reduce neural activity and slow body functions. Alcohol disinhibits, increasing the likelihood that we will act on our impulses, whether harmful or helpful. It also impairs judgment by slowing neural processing, disrupts memory processes by suppressing REM sleep, and reduces self-awareness and self-control. User expectations strongly influence alcohol's behavioral effects. Alcohol can shrink the brain in those with *alcohol use disorder* (marked by tolerance, withdrawal if use is suspended, and a drive to continue problematic use).

9-4 What are *stimulants,* and what are their effects?

Stimulants—including caffeine, nicotine, cocaine, the amphetamines, methamphetamine, and *Ecstasy*—excite neural activity and speed up body functions, triggering energy and mood changes. All are highly addictive. *Nicotine's* effects make tobacco product use a difficult habit to kick, yet repeated attempts to quit seem to pay off. *Cocaine* gives users a fast high, followed shortly by a crash. Its risks include cardiac arrest, respiratory failure, convulsions, and emotional disturbances. *Amphetamines* stimulate neural activity, leading to heightened energy and mood. *Methamphetamine* use may permanently reduce dopamine production. *Ecstasy* (*MDMA*) is a combined stimulant and mild hallucinogen that produces euphoria and feelings of intimacy. Its users risk immune system suppression, permanent damage to mood and memory, and (if taken during physical activity) dehydration and escalating body temperatures.

9-5 What are *hallucinogens,* and what are their effects?

Hallucinogens, such as *LSD* and marijuana, distort perceptions and evoke hallucinations. The user's mood and expectations influence the effects of LSD, but common experiences are hallucinations and emotions varying from euphoria to panic. Marijuana's main ingredient, *THC,* may trigger feelings of disinhibition, euphoria,

relaxation, relief from pain, and intense sensitivity to sensory stimuli, but may increase the risk of psychological disorders and lead to impaired learning and memory.

9-6 Why do some people become regular users of consciousness-altering drugs?

Some people may be biologically vulnerable to particular drugs. Psychological factors (such as stress, depression, and hopelessness) and social factors (such as peer pressure and cultural influences) combine to lead many people to experiment with—and sometimes become addicted to—drugs. Cultural and ethnic groups have differing rates of drug use. Each type of influence—biological, psychological, and social-cultural—offers a possible path for drug misuse prevention and treatment programs.

Nature, Nurture, and Human Diversity

MODULE 10: Behavior Genetics: Predicting Individual Differences

10-1 What are *chromosomes, DNA, genes,* and the human *genome?* How do behavior geneticists explain our individual differences?

Genes are the biochemical units of heredity that make up *chromosomes,* the threadlike coils of *DNA.* When genes are expressed, they provide the code for creating the proteins that form our body's building blocks. The human *genome* is the shared genetic profile that distinguishes humans from other species, consisting at an individual level of all the genetic material in an organism's chromosomes. *Behavior geneticists* study the relative power and limits of genetic and *environmental* influences on behavior. Most of our differing traits are polygenetic, and are influenced by the interaction of our individual environments with these genetic predispositions.

10-2 How do twin and adoption studies help us understand the effects and interactions of nature and nurture?

Studies of *identical (monozygotic) twins* versus *fraternal (dizygotic) twins,* separated twins, and biological versus adoptive

relatives allow researchers to consider the effects of shared environment and shared genes, which sheds light on how nature and nurture influence our traits. Shared family environments have surprisingly little effect on personality, though parenting does influence other factors.

10-3 What have psychologists learned about temperament?

The stability of *temperament,* a person's characteristic emotional reactivity and intensity, from the first weeks of life suggests a genetic predisposition. The genetic effect appears in physiological differences such as heart rate and nervous system reactivity.

10-4 What is *heritability,* and how does it relate to individuals and groups?

Heritability describes the extent to which variation among members of a group can be attributed to genes. Heritable individual differences (in traits such as height or intelligence) need not imply heritable group differences. Genes mostly explain why some people are taller than others, but not why people are taller today than they were a century ago.

10-5 How is molecular genetics research changing our understanding of the effects of nature and nurture?

Our genetic predispositions and our specific environments *interact.* Environments can trigger genetic expression, and genetically influenced traits can influence the experiences we seek and the responses we evoke from others. *Molecular geneticists* study the molecular structure and function of genes, including those that affect behavior. One goal of *molecular behavior genetics* is to identify specific genes—or, more often, teams of genes—that together orchestrate complex traits (such as body weight, sexual orientation, and impulsivity) or put people at risk for disorders. The field of *epigenetics* studies the molecular mechanisms by which environments can trigger or block genetic expression.

MODULE 11: Evolutionary Psychology: Explaining Human Nature and Nurture

11-1 How do evolutionary psychologists use natural selection to explain behavior tendencies?

Evolutionary psychologists attempt to understand how *natural selection* has shaped traits and behavior tendencies found in all people. Genetic variations that increase the odds of reproducing and surviving in a particular environment are most likely to be passed on to future generations. Some variations arise from *mutations,* others from new gene combinations at conception. Humans share a genetic legacy and are predisposed to behaviors that promoted our ancestors' survival and reproduction. Charles Darwin's theory of evolution is one of biology's fundamental organizing principles. He anticipated today's application of evolutionary principles in psychology.

11-2 How might an evolutionary psychologist explain male-female differences in sexuality and mating preferences?

Women tend to be more selective than men when choosing sexual partners. Evolutionary psychologists reason that men's attraction to multiple fertile-appearing partners increases their chances of spreading their genes widely. Because women incubate and nurse babies, they increase their own and their children's chances of survival by searching for mates with the potential for long-term investment in their joint offspring.

11-3 What are the key criticisms of evolutionary explanations of human sexuality, and how do evolutionary psychologists respond?

Critics argue that evolutionary psychologists start with an effect and work backward to an explanation, minimize contemporary social and cultural influences (including learned *social scripts*), and relieve people from taking responsibility for their sexual behavior, including men's sexual aggression. Evolutionary psychologists respond that they recognize the importance of social and cultural influences, but note the value in testable predictions based on evolutionary principles: Understanding our predispositions can help us overcome them.

MODULE 12: Cultural and Gender Diversity: Understanding Nature and Nurture

12-1 How do early experiences modify the brain?

As a child's brain develops, neural connections grow more numerous and complex. Experiences then prompt a pruning process, in which unused connections weaken and heavily used ones

strengthen. Early childhood is an important period for shaping the brain, but thanks to neuroplasticity the brain modifies itself throughout our lives in response to our learning.

12-2 In what ways do parents and peers shape children's development?

Family environment and parental expectations can affect children's motivation and future success. Personality, however, is mostly not attributable to the effects of nurture. As children attempt to fit in with their peers, they tend to adopt their culture—styles, accents, slang. By choosing their children's neighborhoods and schools, parents exert some influence over peer group culture.

12-3 How does culture affect our behavior?

A *culture* is an enduring set of behaviors, ideas, attitudes, values, and traditions shared by a group and transmitted from one generation to the next. Cultural *norms* are understood rules that inform members of a culture about accepted and expected behaviors. Cultures differ across time and space.

12-4 How do individualist and collectivist cultures differ in their values and goals?

Although individuals vary, different cultures tend to emphasize either individualism or collectivism. Cultures based on self-reliant *individualism* tend to value personal independence and individual achievement. They define identity in terms of self-esteem, personal goals and attributes, and personal rights and liberties. Cultures based on socially connected *collectivism* tend to value group goals, social identity, and commitments. They define identity in terms of interdependence, tradition, and harmony.

12-5 How does the meaning of *gender* differ from the meaning of *sex*?

In psychology, *gender* refers to the behavioral characteristics that people associate with *boy, girl, man,* and *woman. Sex* refers to the biologically influenced characteristics by which people define *male, female,* and *intersex.* Our understanding of gender arises from the interplay between our biology and our experiences.

12-6 What are some of the ways in which males and females tend to be alike and to differ?

Whether male, female, or intersex, most of us receive 23 chromosomes from

our mother and 23 from our father, of which 45 are *unisex*—the same for everyone. Males and females are more alike than different, thanks to similar genetic makeup—they see, learn, and remember similarly, with comparable creativity, intelligence, and emotions. Male-female differences include age of onset of puberty, life expectancy, emotional expressiveness, and vulnerability to certain disorders. Men admit to more *aggression* than women do, and they are more likely to be physically (rather than *relationally*) aggressive. In most societies, men have more social power. Men tend to be more independent, while women tend to be more interdependent. Women often focus more on social connectedness than do men, and they tend and befriend.

12-7 What factors contribute to gender bias in the workplace?

Gender bias in the workplace is seen in such differences as perception, compensation, and child-care responsibility. Social norms, interaction styles, and everyday behaviors also contribute. Men's leadership style tends to be directive, whereas women's tends to be more democratic. In their everyday behaviors and interactions, men tend to act more assertive and opinionated; women tend to act more supportive and apologetic.

12-8 How do sex hormones influence prenatal and adolescent sexual development?

Both sex chromosomes and sex hormones influence development. About seven weeks after conception, a gene on the Y *chromosome* from the father—who can contribute either this or an X *chromosome* (the mother always contributes the latter)—triggers the production of *testosterone.* This promotes male sex organ development. *Estrogens* contribute to female sex characteristics and are secreted in greater amounts by females than by males. During the fourth and fifth prenatal months, sex hormones bathe the fetal brain, with different patterns developing due to the male's greater testosterone and the female's estrogens. Prenatal exposure of females to unusually high levels of male hormones can later dispose them to more male-typical interests. Another flood of hormones occurs in *puberty,* triggering a growth spurt, the development of *primary* and *secondary sex characteristics,* and the landmark events of *menarche* and *spermarche.* Sexual development variations may occur through unusual combinations of male and female chromosomes, hormones, and anatomy.

12-9 What are some cultural influences on gender roles?

Gender roles, the expected behaviors, attitudes, and traits a culture expects from its men and women, vary across place and time. Gender roles in many parts of the world have changed dramatically in the last century. Expectations about gender roles also influence cultural attitudes about *sexual aggression.*

12-10 What are the effects of sexual aggression? How have cultural views changed, and how can we reduce sexual aggression?

Sexual aggression, which includes sexual harassment and sexual assault, can disrupt sleep, harm health, and make it difficult to trust new relationship partners. Cultural views of sexual aggression differ across time and place, with some cultures continuing to blame victims, but changes in the United States and elsewhere over the last half-century have made victim-blaming less acceptable. Therapy for sexual aggressors has not proven effective, but we may reduce sexual aggression by encouraging people to report and share their experiences, empowering those victimized, and educating people about preventive bystander intervention strategies.

12-11 How do we form our gender identity?

Social learning theory proposes that we learn our *gender identity*—our sense of being male, female, neither, or some combination of male and female—as we learn other things: through reinforcement, punishment, and observation. But critics argue that cognition also plays a role, because modeling and rewards cannot explain variation in *gender typing.* Some children organize themselves into "boy worlds" and "girl worlds"; others prefer *androgyny.* For people who identify as cisgender, gender identity corresponds with birth-assigned sex. For those who identify as *transgender,* gender identity differs from what's typical for that person's birth-assigned sex. Transgender people may be sexually attracted to people of the other gender, the same gender, all genders, or to no one at all.

12-12 How do nature, nurture, and our own choices influence gender roles and other aspects of our lives?

Individual development results from the interaction of biological, psychological, and social-cultural influences. Biological influences include our shared human genome; individual variations; prenatal environment; and sex-related genes, hormones, and physiology. Psychological influences include gene–environment interactions; the effect of early experiences on neural networks; responses evoked by our own characteristics, such as gender and temperament; and personal beliefs, feelings, and expectations. Social-cultural influences include parental and peer influences; cultural traditions and values; and cultural gender norms. And our individual choices affect the way all of these influences interact.

Developing Through The Life Span

MODULE 13: Developmental Issues, Prenatal Development, and the Newborn

13-1 What three issues have engaged developmental psychologists?

Developmental psychologists study physical, cognitive, and social changes across the life span. They often use *cross-sectional* (comparing people of different ages at one point in time) and *longitudinal studies* (retesting the same people over a period of years) to explore three issues: nature and nurture (the interaction between our genetic inheritance and our experiences); continuity and stages (which aspects of development are gradual and continuous and which change relatively abruptly); and stability and change (whether our traits endure or change as we age).

13-2 What is the course of prenatal development, and how do teratogens affect that development?

The life cycle begins at conception, when one sperm cell unites with an egg to form a *zygote.* The zygote's inner cells become the *embryo,* and the outer cells become the placenta. In the next 6 weeks, body organs begin to form and function, and by 9 weeks, the *fetus* is recognizably human. *Teratogens* are potentially harmful agents that can pass through the placenta and harm the developing embryo or fetus, as happens with *fetal alcohol syndrome.*

13-3 What are some newborn abilities, and how do researchers explore infants' mental abilities?

Babies are born with sensory equipment and reflexes that facilitate their survival and their social interactions with adults. For example, they quickly learn to discriminate their mother's smell, and they prefer the sound of human voices. Researchers use techniques that test *habituation* to explore infants' abilities.

MODULE 14: Infancy and Childhood

14-1 During infancy and childhood, how do the brain and motor skills develop?

The brain's nerve cells are sculpted by heredity and experience. As a child's brain develops, neural connections grow more numerous and complex. Experiences then trigger a pruning process, in which unused connections weaken and heavily used ones strengthen. In childhood, complex motor skills—sitting, standing, walking—develop in a predictable sequence, though the timing of that sequence is a function of individual *maturation* and culture. We have few or no conscious memories of events occurring before about age 4. This infantile amnesia occurs in part because major brain areas have not yet matured.

14-2 How did Piaget broaden our understanding of the way a child's mind develops, and how have today's researchers built on his work?

As he studied children's *cognitive* development, Jean Piaget proposed that they actively construct and modify their understanding of the world through the processes of *assimilation* and *accommodation.* They form *schemas* that help them organize their experiences. Progressing from the simplicity of the *sensorimotor stage* of the first two years, in which they develop *object permanence,* children move to more complex ways of thinking. In the *preoperational stage* (about age 2 to about 6 or 7), they develop a *theory of mind.* In the preoperational stage, children are *egocentric* and unable to perform simple logical operations. By about age 7, they enter the *concrete operational stage* and are able to comprehend the principle of *conservation*. By age 12, children enter the *formal operational stage* and can reason systematically. Research supports the sequence Piaget proposed, but it also shows that young children are more capable, and their development more continuous, than he believed.

14-3 How did Vygotsky view children's cognitive development?

Lev Vygotsky's studies of child development focused on the ways a child's mind grows by interacting with the social environment. In his view, parents, teachers, and other children provide temporary *scaffolds* enabling children to step to higher levels of thinking.

14-4 What does it mean to develop a *theory of mind,* and how is this impaired in those with autism spectrum disorder?

Our *theory of mind*—our ideas about our own and others' mental states—develops during early childhood. Children with *autism spectrum disorder (ASD)* have an impaired theory of mind: They have difficulty understanding others' state of mind, as well as reflecting on their own.

14-5 How do caregiver-infant attachment bonds form?

At about 8 months, soon after object permanence develops, children separated from their caregivers display *stranger anxiety*. Infants form *attachments* with caregivers who gratify biological needs but, more importantly, who are comfortable, familiar, and responsive. Many birds and other animals have a more rigid attachment process, called *imprinting*, that occurs during a *critical period*.

14-6 How have psychologists studied attachment differences, and what have they learned?

Attachment has been studied in strange situation experiments, which show that some children are securely attached and others are insecurely (anxiously or avoidantly) attached. Infants' differing attachment styles reflect both their individual temperament and the responsiveness of their parents and child-care providers. Adult relationships seem to reflect the attachment styles of early childhood, lending support to Erik Erikson's idea that *basic trust* is formed in infancy by our experiences with responsive caregivers.

14-7 How does childhood neglect or abuse affect children's attachments?

Most children are resilient, but those who are abused or severely neglected by their caregivers, or otherwise prevented from forming attachments at an early age, may be at risk for attachment problems. Extreme trauma in childhood may alter the brain, affecting our stress responses or leaving epigenetic marks.

14-8 How do children's self-concepts develop?

Self-concept, an understanding and evaluation of who we are, emerges gradually. By 15 to 18 months, children recognize themselves in a mirror. By school age, they can describe many of their own traits and by age 8 or 10 their self-image is stable.

14-9 What are the four main parenting styles?

The main parenting styles are authoritarian (coercive), permissive (unrestraining), neglectful (uninvolved), and authoritative (confrontive).

14-10 What outcomes are associated with each parenting style?

Authoritative parenting is associated with greater self-esteem, self-reliance, self-regulation, and social competence; authoritarian parenting with lower self-esteem, less social skill, and a brain that overreacts to mistakes; permissive parenting with greater aggression and immaturity; and neglectful parenting with poor academic and social outcomes. However, correlation does not equal causation (it's possible that children with positive characteristics are more likely to bring out positive parenting methods).

MODULE 15: Adolescence

15-1 How is *adolescence* defined, and how do physical changes affect developing teens?

Adolescence is the transition period from childhood to adulthood, extending from *puberty* to social independence. Early maturation can be a challenge for developing adolescents. The brain's frontal lobes mature and myelin growth increases during adolescence and the early twenties, enabling improved judgment, impulse control, and long-term planning.

15-2 How did Piaget, Kohlberg, and later researchers describe adolescent cognitive and moral development?

Piaget theorized that adolescents develop a capacity for formal operations and that this development is the foundation for moral judgment. Lawrence Kohlberg proposed a stage theory of moral reasoning, from a preconventional morality of self-interest, to a conventional morality concerned with upholding laws and social rules, to (in some people) a postconventional morality of basic rights and self-defined ethical principles. Other researchers believe that morality lies in moral intuition and moral action as well as thinking. Kohlberg's critics note that the postconventional level is culturally limited (representing morality only from the perspective of an individualist society), and male-focused (since women more often emphasize care for those in need over what is "fair"). Life success can grow from the ability to delay gratification.

15-3 What are the social tasks and challenges of adolescence?

Erik Erikson proposed eight stages of psychosocial development across the life span. He believed we need to achieve trust, autonomy, initiative, competency, *identity* (in adolescence), *intimacy* (in young adulthood), generativity, and integrity. Each life stage has its own psychosocial task. Solidifying one's sense of self in adolescence means trying out a number of different roles. *Social identity* is the part of the self-concept that comes from a person's group memberships.

15-4 How do parents and peers influence adolescents?

During adolescence, parental influence diminishes and peer influence increases. Adolescents adopt their peers' ways of dressing, acting, and communicating. Positive parent-teen relationships correlate with positive peer relationships, however. Personalities and temperaments are shaped by both nature and nurture, including parental and peer influences.

15-5 What is *emerging adulthood?*

Due to earlier sexual maturity and later independence, the transition from adolescence to adulthood is taking longer than it once did. *Emerging adulthood* is the period from age 18 to the mid-twenties, when many young people are not yet fully independent. This stage is found mostly in today's Western cultures.

MODULE 16: Adulthood

16-1 What physical changes occur during middle and late adulthood?

Muscular strength, reaction time, sensory abilities, and cardiac output begin to almost imperceptibly decline in the mid-twenties; this downward trajectory accelerates through middle and late adulthood, varying considerably with personal health and exercise habits. Women's period of fertility ends with *menopause* around age 50; men experience a more gradual decline. In late adulthood, the immune system weakens, increasing susceptibility to life-threatening illnesses. But longevity-supporting genes, low stress, and healthful habits may enable good health even in late life.

16-2 How does memory change with age?

Recall begins to decline, especially for meaningless information, but recognition memory remains strong. Developmental researchers study age-related changes such as in memory with cross-sectional studies and longitudinal studies. "Terminal decline" describes the cognitive decline in the final few years of life.

16-3 How do neurocognitive disorders and Alzheimer's disease affect cognitive ability?

Neurocognitive disorders (NCDs) are acquired (not lifelong) disorders marked by cognitive deficits, which are often related to Alzheimer's disease, brain injury or disease, or substance abuse. This damage to brain cells results in the erosion of mental abilities that is not typical of normal aging. *Alzheimer's disease* causes the deterioration of memory, then reasoning. After 5 to 20 years, the person becomes emotionally flat, disoriented, disinhibited, incontinent, and finally mentally vacant.

16-4 What themes and influences mark our social journey from early adulthood to death?

Adults do not progress through an orderly sequence of age-related social stages. Chance events can determine life choices. The *social clock* is a culture's preferred timing for events such as marriage, parenthood, and retirement. Many people in Western cultures today feel freer about setting their own timing. Adulthood's dominant themes are love and work (Erikson's intimacy and generativity).

16-5 How does our well-being change across the life span?

Surveys show that life satisfaction is unrelated to age until the terminal decline phase. Positive emotions increase after midlife and negative ones decrease; with age come fewer extremes of emotion and mood.

16-6 What range of reactions does a loved one's death trigger?

People do not grieve in predictable stages, as was once supposed, and bereavement therapy is not significantly more effective than grieving without such aid. Life can be affirmed even at death, especially for those who experience what Erikson called a sense of integrity—a feeling that one's life has been meaningful.

Sensation and Perception

MODULE 17: Basic Concepts of Sensation and Perception

17-1 What are *sensation* and *perception*? What do we mean by *bottom-up processing* and *top-down processing*?

Sensation is the process by which our *sensory receptors* and nervous system receive and represent stimulus energies from our environment. *Perception* is the process of organizing and interpreting this information, enabling recognition of meaningful objects and events. Sensation and perception are one continuous process. *Bottom-up processing* is sensory analysis that begins at the entry level, with information flowing from the sensory receptors to the brain. *Top-down processing* is information processing guided by high-level mental processes, as when we construct perceptions by filtering information through our experience and expectations.

17-2 What three steps are basic to all of our sensory systems?

Our senses (1) receive sensory stimulation, often using specialized receptor cells; (2) transform that stimulation into neural impulses; and (3) deliver the neural information to the brain. *Transduction* is the process of converting one form of energy into another. Researchers in *psychophysics* study the relationships between stimuli's physical characteristics and our psychological experience of them.

17-3 How do *absolute thresholds* and *difference thresholds* differ?

Our *absolute threshold* for any stimulus is the minimum stimulation necessary for us to be consciously aware of it 50 percent of the time. *Signal detection theory* predicts how and when we will detect a faint stimulus amid background noise. Individual absolute thresholds vary, depending on the strength of the signal and also on our experience, expectations, motivation, and alertness. Our *difference threshold* (also called the *just noticeable difference*, or *jnd*) is the minimum difference we can discern between two stimuli 50 percent of the time. *Weber's law* states that two stimuli must differ by a constant minimum percentage (not a constant amount) to be perceived as different.

17-4 How are we affected by subliminal stimuli?

We do sense some stimuli *subliminally*—less than 50 percent of the time—and can be affected by these sensations. But although we can be *primed*, subliminal sensations have no powerful, enduring influence.

17-5 What is the function of sensory adaptation?

Sensory adaptation (our diminished sensitivity to constant or routine odors, sounds, and touches) focuses our attention on informative changes in our environment.

17-6 How do our expectations, contexts, motivation, and emotions influence our perceptions?

Perceptual set is a mental predisposition that functions as a lens through which we perceive the world. Our learned concepts (schemas) prime us to organize and interpret ambiguous stimuli in certain ways. Our expectations, contexts, motivation, and emotions can color our interpretation of events and behaviors.

MODULE 18: Vision: Sensory and Perceptual Processing

18-1 What are the characteristics of the energy that we see as visible light? What structures in the eye help focus that energy?

What we see as light is only a thin slice of the broad spectrum of electromagnetic energy. The portion visible to humans extends from the shorter blue-violet wavelengths to the longer red light wavelengths. After entering the eye through the cornea, passing through the pupil and iris, and being focused by a lens, light energy particles strike the eye's inner surface, the *retina*. The *hue* we perceive in a light depends on its *wavelength,* and its brightness depends on its *intensity.*

18-2 How do the rods and cones process information, and what is the path information travels from the eye to the brain?

Light entering the eye triggers chemical changes that convert light energy into neural impulses. Photoreceptors called *cones* and *rods* at the back of the retina each provide a special sensitivity—cones to detail and color, rods to faint light and peripheral motion. After processing by bipolar and ganglion cells, neural impulses travel from the retina through the *optic nerve* to the thalamus, and on to the visual cortex.

18-3 How do we perceive color in the world around us?

According to the *Young-Helmholtz trichromatic (three-color) theory,* the retina contains three types of color receptors. Contemporary research has found three types of cones, each most sensitive to the wavelengths of one of the three primary colors of light (red, green, or blue). According to Hering's *opponent-process theory,* there are three additional sets of opposing retinal processes (red-green, blue-yellow, black-white). Research has confirmed that, en route to the brain, neurons in the retina and the thalamus code the color-related information from the cones into pairs of opponent colors. These two theories, and the research supporting them, show that color processing occurs in two stages.

18-4 Where are feature detectors located, and what do they do?

Feature detectors, specialized nerve cells in the visual cortex, respond to specific features of the visual stimulus, such as shape, angle, or movement. Feature detectors pass information on to other cortical areas, where supercell clusters respond to more complex patterns.

18-5 How does the brain use parallel processing to construct visual perceptions?

Through *parallel processing,* the brain handles many aspects of vision (color, movement, form, and depth) simultaneously. Other neural teams integrate the results, comparing them with stored information and enabling perceptions.

18-6 How did the Gestalt psychologists understand perceptual organization, and how do figure-ground and grouping principles contribute to our perceptions?

Gestalt psychologists searched for rules by which the brain organizes fragments of sensory data into *gestalts,* or meaningful forms. In pointing out that the whole may exceed the sum of its parts, they noted that we filter sensory information and construct our perceptions. To recognize an object, we must first perceive it (see it as a *figure*) as distinct from its surroundings (the *ground*). We bring order and form to stimuli by organizing them into meaningful *groups,* following such rules as proximity, continuity, and closure.

18-7 How do we use binocular and monocular cues to see the world in three dimensions, and how do we perceive motion?

Depth perception is our ability to see objects in three dimensions and to judge distance. The *visual cliff* and other research demonstrate that many species perceive the world in three dimensions at, or very soon after, birth. *Binocular cues,* such as *retinal disparity,* are depth cues that rely on information from both eyes. *Monocular cues* (such as relative height, relative size, relative motion, linear perspective, and interposition) let us judge depth using information transmitted by only one eye. As objects move, we assume that shrinking objects are retreating and enlarging objects are approaching. The brain computes motion imperfectly, with young children especially at risk of incorrectly perceiving approaching hazards such as vehicles. A quick succession of images on the retina can create an illusion of movement, as in stroboscopic movement or the *phi phenomenon.*

18-8 How do perceptual constancies help us construct meaningful perceptions?

Perceptual constancies, such as in color, brightness (or lightness), shape, or size, enable us to perceive objects as stable despite the changing image they cast on our retinas. Our brain constructs our experience of an object's color or brightness through comparisons with other surrounding objects. Knowing an object's size gives us clues to its distance; knowing its distance gives clues about its size, but we sometimes misread monocular distance cues and reach the wrong conclusions, as in the Moon illusion.

18-9 What does research on restored vision, sensory restriction, and perceptual adaptation reveal about the effects of experience on perception?

Experience guides our perceptual interpretations. People blind from birth who gain sight after surgery lack the experience to visually recognize shapes and forms. Sensory restriction research indicates that there is a critical period for some aspects of sensory and perceptual development. Without early stimulation, the brain's neural organization does not develop normally. People given glasses that shift the world slightly to the left or right, or even upside down, experience *perceptual adaptation.* They are initially disoriented, but they manage to adapt to their new context.

MODULE 19: The Nonvisual Senses

19-1 What are the characteristics of the air pressure waves that we hear as sound?

Sound waves are bands of compressed and expanded air. Our ears detect these changes in air pressure and transform them into neural impulses, which the brain decodes as sound. Sound waves vary in amplitude, which we perceive as differing loudness (with sound intensity measured in decibels), and in *frequency* (measured in hertz), which we experience as differing *pitch.*

19-2 How does the ear transform sound energy into neural messages?

The *middle ear* is the chamber between the eardrum and *cochlea;* the *inner ear* consists of the cochlea, semicircular canals, and vestibular sacs. Sound waves traveling through the auditory canal cause tiny vibrations in the eardrum. The bones of the middle ear amplify the vibrations and relay them to the fluid-filled cochlea. Rippling of the basilar membrane, caused by pressure changes in the cochlear fluid, causes movement of the tiny hair cells, triggering neural messages to be sent (via the thalamus) to the auditory cortex in the brain. *Sensorineural hearing loss* (or nerve deafness) results from damage to the cochlea's hair cells or their associated nerves. *Conduction hearing loss* results from damage to the mechanical system that transmits sound waves to the cochlea. *Cochlear implants* can restore hearing for some people.

19-3 How do we detect loudness, discriminate pitch, and locate sounds?

Loudness is not related to the intensity of a hair cell's response, but rather to the number of activated hair cells. *Place theory* (place coding) explains how we hear high-pitched sounds, and *frequency theory* (temporal coding) extended by the volley principle explains how we hear low-pitched sounds. A combination of the two theories explains how we hear pitches in the middle range. Sound waves strike one ear sooner and more intensely than the other. To locate sounds, the brain analyzes the minute differences in the sounds received by the two ears and computes the sound's source.

19-4 What are the four basic touch sensations, and how do we sense touch?

Our sense of touch is four basic sensations—pressure, warmth, cold, and pain—that combine to produce other sensations, such as "itchy" or "wet."

19-5 What biological, psychological, and social-cultural influences affect our experience of pain? How do placebos, distraction, and hypnosis help control pain?

The biopsychosocial perspective views our perception of pain as the sum of biological, psychological, and social-cultural influences. Pain reflects bottom-up sensations and top-down processes. One theory of pain is that a "gate" in the spinal cord either opens to permit pain signals traveling up small nerve fibers to reach the brain, or closes to prevent their passage. Pain treatments often combine physical and psychological elements. Combining a placebo with distraction, and amplifying the effect with *hypnosis* (which increases our response to suggestions), can help relieve pain. *Posthypnotic suggestion* is used by some clinicians to control undesired symptoms and behavior.

19-6 In what ways are our senses of taste and smell similar, and how do they differ?

Taste and smell are both chemical senses. Taste (*gustation*) is a composite of five basic sensations—sweet, sour, salty, bitter, and umami—and of the aromas that interact with information from the taste receptor cells of the taste buds. There are no basic sensations for smell (*olfaction*). From the top of each nasal cavity, some 20 million olfactory receptor cells for smell send messages to the brain's olfactory bulb and then onward to the temporal lobe's primary smell cortex and to the parts of the limbic system involved in memory and emotion.

19-7 How do we sense our body's position and movement?

Position and motion sensors in muscles, tendons, and joints called proprioceptors enable *kinesthesia*, our sense of the position and movement of our body parts. We monitor our head's (and thus our body's) position and movement, and maintain our balance, with our *vestibular sense*, which relies on the semicircular canals and vestibular sacs to sense the tilt or rotation of our head.

19-8 How does sensory interaction influence our perceptions, and what is *embodied cognition*?

Our senses influence one another. This *sensory interaction* occurs, for example, when the smell of a favorite food amplifies its taste. *Embodied cognition* is the influence of bodily sensations, gestures, and other states on cognitive preferences and judgments.

19-9 What are the claims of ESP, and what have most research psychologists concluded after putting these claims to the test?

Parapsychology is the study of paranormal phenomena, including *extrasensory perception (ESP)* and psychokinesis. The three most testable forms of ESP are telepathy (mind-to-mind communication), clairvoyance (perceiving remote events), and precognition (perceiving future events). To refute those who say there is no ESP, one need only produce a single person who can demonstrate a single, reproducible ESP event. Although study continues, researchers have been unable to replicate ESP phenomena under controlled conditions.

Learning

MODULE 20: Basic Learning Concepts and Classical Conditioning

20-1 How do we define *learning*, and what are some basic forms of learning?

Learning is the process of acquiring through experience new information or behaviors. In *associative learning*, we learn that certain events occur together. In classical conditioning, we learn to associate two or more *stimuli*. Automatically responding to stimuli we do not control is called *respondent behavior*. In operant conditioning, we learn to associate a response and its consequence. These associations produce *operant behaviors*. Through *cognitive learning*, we acquire mental information that guides our behavior. For example, in observational learning, we learn new behaviors by observing events and watching others.

20-2 What is behaviorism's view of learning?

Ivan Pavlov's work on classical conditioning laid the foundation for *behaviorism*, the view that psychology should be an objective science that studies behavior without reference to mental processes. The behaviorists believed that the basic laws of learning are the same for all species, including humans.

20-3 Who was Pavlov, and what are the basic components of classical conditioning?

Ivan Pavlov, a Russian physiologist, created novel experiments on learning. His early twentieth-century research over the last three decades of his life demonstrated that classical conditioning is a basic form of learning. *Classical conditioning* is a type of learning in which an organism comes to associate stimuli and anticipate events. A *UR* (unconditioned response) is an event that occurs naturally (such as salivation), in response to some stimulus. A *US* (unconditioned stimulus) is something that naturally and automatically (without learning) triggers the unlearned response (as food in the mouth triggers salivation). A *CS* (conditioned stimulus) is originally an *NS* (neutral stimulus, such as a tone) that, after association with a US (such as food) comes to trigger a CR. A *CR* (conditioned response) is the learned response (salivating) to the originally neutral (but now conditioned) stimulus.

20-4 In classical conditioning, what are the processes of *acquisition, extinction, spontaneous recovery, generalization,* and *discrimination*?

In classical conditioning, the first stage is *acquisition*, associating an NS with the US so that the NS begins triggering the CR. Acquisition occurs most readily when the NS is presented just before (ideally, about a half-second before) a US, preparing the organism for the upcoming event. This finding supports the view that classical conditioning is biologically adaptive. *Extinction* is diminished responding, which occurs if the CS appears repeatedly by itself without the US. *Spontaneous recovery* is the reappearance of a weakened conditioned response, following a rest period. *Generalization* is the tendency to respond to stimuli that are similar to a CS. *Discrimination* is the learned ability to distinguish between a CS and other irrelevant stimuli.

20-5 Why does Pavlov's work remain so important?

Pavlov taught us that significant psychological phenomena can be studied objectively, and that classical conditioning is a basic form of learning that applies to all species.

20-6 What have been some applications of Pavlov's work to human health and well-being? How did Watson apply Pavlov's principles to learned fears?

Classical conditioning techniques are used to improve human health and well-being in many areas, including behavioral therapy for some types of psychological disorders. The body's immune system may also respond to classical conditioning. Pavlov's work also provided a basis for Watson's idea that human emotions and behaviors, though biologically influenced, are mainly a bundle of conditioned responses. Watson applied classical conditioning principles in his studies of "Little Albert" to demonstrate how specific fears might be conditioned.

MODULE 21: Operant Conditioning

21-1 What is *operant conditioning*?

Operant conditioning is a type of learning in which behavior becomes more likely to recur if followed by a reinforcer or less likely to recur if followed by a punisher.

21-2 Who was Skinner, and how is operant behavior reinforced and shaped?

B. F. Skinner was a college English major and aspiring writer who later entered psychology graduate school. He became modern behaviorism's most influential and controversial figure. Expanding on Edward Thorndike's *law of effect*, Skinner and others found that the behavior of rats or pigeons placed in an *operant chamber*

(Skinner box) can be *shaped* by using reinforcers to guide successive approximations of the desired behavior.

21-3 How do positive and negative reinforcement differ, and what are the basic types of reinforcers?

Reinforcement is any event that strengthens the behavior it follows. *Positive reinforcement* adds a desirable stimulus to increase the frequency of a behavior. *Negative reinforcement* reduces or removes an aversive stimulus to increase the frequency of a behavior. *Primary reinforcers* (such as receiving food when hungry or having nausea end during an illness) are innately satisfying—no learning is required. *Conditioned* (or secondary) *reinforcers* (such as cash) are satisfying because we have learned to associate them with more basic rewards (such as the food or medicine we buy with them). Immediate reinforcers (such as a food reward given right after a desired behavior) offer immediate payback; delayed reinforcers (such as a paycheck) require the ability to delay gratification.

21-4 How do different reinforcement schedules affect behavior?

A *reinforcement schedule* defines how often a response will be reinforced. In *continuous reinforcement* (reinforcing desired responses every time they occur), learning is rapid, but so is extinction if rewards cease. In *partial (intermittent) reinforcement* (reinforcing responses only sometimes), initial learning is slower, but the behavior is much more resistant to extinction. *Fixed-ratio schedules* reinforce behaviors after a set number of responses; *variable-ratio schedules*, after an unpredictable number. *Fixed-interval schedules* reinforce behaviors after set time periods; *variable-interval schedules*, after unpredictable time periods.

21-5 How does punishment differ from negative reinforcement, and how does punishment affect behavior?

Punishment administers an undesirable consequence (such as a time-out) or withdraws something desirable (such as taking away a favorite toy) to decrease the frequency of a behavior (a child's disobedience). Negative reinforcement (taking an aspirin) removes an aversive stimulus (a headache). This desired consequence (freedom from pain) increases the

likelihood that the behavior (taking aspirin to end pain) will be repeated. Physical punishment can have undesirable side effects, such as suppressing rather than changing unwanted behaviors, failing to provide a direction for appropriate behavior, encouraging discrimination (so that the undesirable behavior appears when the punisher is not present), creating fear, and teaching aggression.

21-6 Why did Skinner's ideas provoke controversy, and how might his operant conditioning principles be applied?

Critics of Skinner's principles believed the approach dehumanized people by neglecting their personal freedom and seeking to control their actions. Skinner replied that people's actions are already controlled by external consequences, and that reinforcement is more humane than punishment as a means for controlling behavior. Teachers can use shaping techniques to guide students' behaviors, and use interactive media such as online adaptive quizzing to provide immediate feedback. (The LearningCurve and Achieve Read & Practice systems available with this text provide such feedback, and allow students to direct the pace of their own learning.) Coaches can build players' skills and self-confidence by rewarding small improvements. Artificial intelligence (AI) programs developed using reinforcement principles are teaching us about the limits of human learning. Managers can boost productivity and morale by rewarding well-defined and achievable behaviors. Parents can reward desired behaviors but not undesirable ones. We can shape our own behaviors by stating realistic goals, planning how to work toward those goals, monitoring the frequency of desired behaviors, reinforcing desired behaviors, and gradually reducing rewards as behaviors become habitual.

21-7 How does operant conditioning differ from classical conditioning?

In operant conditioning, an organism learns associations between its own behavior and resulting events; this form of conditioning involves operant behavior (behavior that operates on the environment, producing rewarding or punishing consequences). In classical conditioning, the organism forms associations between stimuli—events it does not control; this form of conditioning involves respondent behavior (automatic responses to some stimulus).

MODULE 22: Biology, Cognition, and Learning

22-1 How do biological constraints affect classical and operant conditioning?

An animal's capacity for conditioning is limited by biological constraints, so some associations are easier to learn. Each species learns behaviors that aid its survival—a phenomenon called *preparedness*. Those who readily learned taste aversions were unlikely to eat the same toxic food again and were more likely to survive and leave descendants. Nature constrains each species' capacity for both classical conditioning and operant conditioning. Our preparedness to associate a CS with a US that follows predictably and immediately is often (but not always) adaptive. During operant training, animals may display *instinctive drift* by reverting to biologically predisposed patterns.

22-2 How do cognitive processes affect classical and operant conditioning?

In classical conditioning, animals may learn when to expect a US and may be aware of the link between stimuli and responses. In operant conditioning, *cognitive mapping* and *latent learning* research demonstrate the importance of cognitive processes in learning.

22-3 What is *observational learning?*

Observational learning (also called *social learning*) involves learning by watching and imitating, rather than through direct experience.

22-4 How may observational learning be enabled by neural mirroring?

Our brain's frontal lobes have a demonstrated ability to mirror the activity of another's brain, which may enable imitation and observational learning. Some scientists argue that *mirror neurons* are responsible for this ability, while others attribute it to distributed brain networks.

22-5 What is the impact of prosocial modeling and of antisocial modeling?

Children tend to imitate what a model does and says, whether the behavior being *modeled* is *prosocial* (positive, constructive, and helpful) or antisocial. If a model's actions and words are inconsistent, children may imitate the hypocrisy they observe.

22-6 What is the violence-viewing effect?

Media violence can contribute to aggression. This violence-viewing effect may be prompted by imitation and desensitization. Correlation does not equal causation, but study participants have reacted more cruelly to provocations when they have viewed violence (instead of entertaining nonviolence).

Memory

MODULE 23: Studying and Encoding Memories

23-1 What is *memory,* and how is it measured?

Memory is learning that has persisted over time, through the encoding, storage, and retrieval of information. Evidence of memory may be seen in an ability to *recall* information, *recognize* it, or *relearn* it more easily on a later attempt. Psychologists can measure these different forms of memory separately.

23-2 How do memory models help us study memory, and how has later research updated the three-stage information-processing model?

Psychologists use memory models to think about and explain how our brain forms and retrieves memories. Information-processing models involve three processes: *encoding, storage,* and *retrieval.* Our agile brain processes many things simultaneously by means of *parallel processing.* The connectionism information-processing model focuses on this multitrack processing, viewing memories as products of interconnected neural networks. The three processing stages in the Atkinson-Shiffrin model are *sensory memory, short-term memory,* and *long-term memory.* This model has since been updated to include two important concepts: (1) *automatic processing,* which occurs behind the scenes to allow information to slip into long-term memory without the need to consciously attend to it; and (2) *working memory,* the active "scratch pad" processing that occurs in the short-term memory stage.

23-3 How do explicit and implicit memories differ?

The human brain processes information on dual tracks, consciously and unconsciously. Many *explicit (declarative) memories*—our conscious memories of facts and experiences—form through *effortful processing,* which requires conscious effort and attention. *Implicit (non-declarative) memories*—of learned skills and classically conditioned associations—happen without our awareness, through *automatic processing.*

23-4 What information do we process automatically?

In addition to skills and classically conditioned associations, we automatically process incidental information about space, time, and frequency.

23-5 How does sensory memory work?

Sensory memory feeds some information into working memory for active processing there. An *iconic memory* is a very brief (a few tenths of a second) sensory memory of visual stimuli; an *echoic memory* is a three- or four-second sensory memory of auditory stimuli.

23-6 What is our short-term memory capacity?

Short-term memory capacity is about seven bits of information, plus or minus two, but this information disappears from memory quickly without rehearsal. Our working memory capacity for active processing varies, depending on age and other factors, but everyone does better and more efficient work by avoiding task-switching.

23-7 What are some effortful processing strategies that can help us remember new information?

Effective effortful processing strategies include *chunking, mnemonics,* and hierarchies. Each boosts our ability to form new memories.

23-8 How do distributed practice, deep processing, and making new material personally meaningful aid memory?

Distributed practice sessions (the *spacing effect*) produce better long-term recall. The *testing effect* is the finding that consciously retrieving, rather than simply rereading, information enhances memory. Depth of processing also affects long-term retention. In *shallow processing,* we encode words based on their structure or appearance. Retention is best when we use *deep processing,* encoding words based on their meaning. We also more easily remember material when we learn and rephrase it into personally meaningful terms—the self-reference effect.

MODULE 24: Storing and Retrieving Memories

24-1 What is the capacity of long-term memory? Are our long-term memories processed and stored in specific locations?

Our long-term memory capacity is essentially unlimited. Memories are not stored intact in the brain in single spots. Many parts of the brain interact as we encode, store, and retrieve memories.

24-2 What roles do the frontal lobes and hippocampus play in memory processing?

The frontal lobes and *hippocampus* are parts of the brain network dedicated to explicit memory formation. Many brain regions send information to the frontal lobes for processing. The hippocampus, with the help of nearby brain networks, registers and temporarily holds elements of explicit memories (which are either *semantic* or *episodic*) before moving them to other brain regions for long-term storage. The neural storage of long-term memories, which is supported by sleep, is called *memory consolidation*.

24-3 What roles do the cerebellum and basal ganglia play in memory processing?

The cerebellum and basal ganglia are parts of the brain network dedicated to implicit memory formation. The cerebellum is important for storing classically conditioned memories. The basal ganglia are involved in motor movement and help form procedural memories for skills. Many reactions and skills learned during our first four years continue into our adult lives, though we cannot consciously remember learning these associations and skills (infantile amnesia).

24-4 How do emotions affect our memory processing?

Emotional arousal causes an outpouring of stress hormones, which leads the amygdala to boost activity in the brain's memory-forming areas. Significantly stressful events can trigger very clear *flashbulb memories*. Through rehearsal, memory of personally important experiences largely endures.

24-5 How do changes at the synapse level affect our memory processing?

Long-term potentiation (LTP) is the neural basis for learning and memory. In LTP, neurons become more efficient at releasing and sensing the presence of neurotransmitters, and more connections develop between neurons.

24-6 How do external cues, internal emotions, and order of appearance influence memory retrieval?

External cues activate associations that help us retrieve memories; this process may occur without our awareness, as it does in *priming*. The *encoding specificity principle* is the idea that cues and contexts specific to a particular memory will be most effective in helping us recall it. Returning to the same physical context or emotional state (*mood congruency*) in which we formed a memory can help us retrieve it. The *serial position effect* is our tendency to recall best the last items (which may still be in working memory) and the first items (which we've spent more time rehearsing) in a list.

MODULE 25: Forgetting, Memory Construction, and Improving Memory

25-1 Why do we forget?

Some people experience *anterograde amnesia*, an inability to form new memories, or *retrograde amnesia*, an inability to retrieve old memories. Normal forgetting can happen because we have never encoded information (encoding failure); because the physical memory trace has decayed (storage decay); or because we cannot retrieve what we have encoded and stored (retrieval failure). Retrieval problems may result from *proactive* (forward-acting) *interference*, when prior learning interferes with recall of new information, or from *retroactive* (backward-acting) *interference*, when new learning disrupts recall of old information. Motivated forgetting occurs, but researchers have found little evidence of *repression*.

25-2 How do misinformation, imagination, and source amnesia influence our memory construction? How do we decide whether a memory is real or false?

Memories can be continually revised when retrieved, a process memory researchers call *reconsolidation*. *Misinformation* (exposure to misleading information) and imagination effects corrupt our stored memories of what actually happened. When we reassemble a memory during retrieval, we may attribute it to the wrong source (*source amnesia*). Source

amnesia may help explain *déjà vu*. False memories feel like real memories and can be persistent but are usually limited to the gist of the event.

25-3 Why have reports of repressed and recovered memories been so hotly debated?

The debate focuses on whether memories of early childhood abuse are repressed and can be recovered during therapy. Unless the victim was a child too young to remember, such traumas are usually remembered vividly, not repressed. Psychologists agree that childhood sexual abuse happens; injustice happens; forgetting happens; recovered memories are common; memories of events that happened before age 4 are unreliable; memories "recovered" under hypnosis are especially unreliable; and memories, whether real or false, can be emotionally upsetting.

25-4 How reliable are young children's eyewitness descriptions?

Children's eyewitness descriptions are subject to the same memory influences that distort adult reports. If questioned soon after an event in neutral words they understand, children can accurately recall events and people involved in them.

25-5 How can you use memory research findings to do better in this and other courses?

Memory research findings suggest the following strategies for improving memory: Rehearse repeatedly, make the material meaningful, activate retrieval cues, use mnemonic devices, minimize proactive and retroactive interference, sleep more, and test yourself to be sure you can retrieve, as well as recognize, material.

Thinking and Language

MODULE 26: Thinking

26-1 What are *cognition* and *metacognition*, and what are the functions of concepts?

Cognition refers to all the mental activities associated with thinking, knowing, remembering, and communicating. *Metacognition* is cognition about our cognition, or keeping track of and evaluating our mental processes. We use *concepts*, mental groupings of similar objects, events, ideas, or people, to simplify and order the world around us. We form most concepts around *prototypes*, or best examples of a category.

26-2 What cognitive strategies assist our problem solving, and what obstacles hinder it?

An *algorithm* is a methodical, logical rule or procedure (such as a step-by-step description for evacuating a building during a fire) that guarantees a solution to a problem. A *heuristic* is a simpler strategy (such as running for an exit if you smell smoke) that is usually speedier than an algorithm but is also more error prone. *Insight* is not a strategy-based solution, but rather a sudden flash of inspiration that solves a problem. Obstacles to problem solving include *confirmation bias*, which predisposes us to verify rather than challenge our hypotheses, and *fixation*, such as *mental set*, which may prevent us from taking the fresh perspective that would lead to a solution.

26-3 What is *intuition*, and how can the representativeness and availability heuristics influence our decisions and judgments?

Intuition is the effortless, immediate, automatic feelings or thoughts we often use instead of systematic reasoning. Heuristics enable snap judgments. Using the *representativeness heuristic*, we judge the likelihood of events based on how well they seem to represent particular prototypes. Using the *availability heuristic*, we judge the likelihood of things based on how readily they come to mind.

26-4 What factors exaggerate our fear of unlikely events?

We tend to be afraid of what our ancestral history has prepared us to fear, what we cannot control, what is immediate, and what is most readily available. We fear too little the ongoing threats that claim lives one by one, such as traffic accidents and diseases.

26-5 How are our decisions and judgments affected by overconfidence, belief perseverance, and framing?

Overconfidence can lead us to overestimate the accuracy of our beliefs. When a belief we have formed and explained has been discredited, *belief perseverance* may cause us to cling to that belief. A remedy for belief perseverance is to consider how we might have explained an opposite result. *Framing* is the way an issue is posed. Subtle differences in presentation can dramatically alter our responses and *nudge* us toward beneficial decisions.

26-6 How do smart thinkers use intuition?

Smart thinkers welcome their intuitions (which are usually adaptive), but also know when to override them. When making complex decisions we may benefit from gathering as much information as possible and then taking time to let our two-track mind process it.

26-7 What is *creativity*, and what fosters it?

Creativity, the ability to produce novel and valuable ideas, correlates somewhat with aptitude, but is more than school smarts. Aptitude tests require *convergent thinking*, but creativity requires *divergent thinking*. Robert Sternberg has proposed that creativity involves expertise; imaginative thinking skills; a venturesome personality; intrinsic motivation; and a creative environment that sparks, supports, and refines creative ideas.

26-8 What do we know about thinking in other species?

Researchers make inferences about other species' consciousness and intelligence based on behavior and neural activity. Evidence from studies of various species shows that many other animals use concepts, numbers, and tools and that they transmit learning from one generation to the next (cultural transmission). And, like humans, some other species show insight, self-awareness, altruism, cooperation, and grief.

MODULE 27: Language and Thought

27-1 What are the structural components of a language?

Phonemes are a *language's* basic units of sound. *Morphemes* are the elementary units of meaning. *Grammar*—the system of rules that enables us to communicate—includes semantics (rules for deriving meaning) and syntax (rules for ordering words into sentences).

27-2 How do we acquire language, and what is *universal grammar*?

As our biology and experience interact, we readily learn the specific grammar and vocabulary of the language we experience as children. Linguist Noam Chomsky has proposed that humans are born with a built-in predisposition to learn grammar rules, which he called universal grammar. Human languages do share some commonalities, but other researchers note that children learn grammar as they discern language patterns.

27-3 What are the milestones in language development, and when is the critical period for acquiring language?

Language development's timing varies, but all children follow the same sequence. Receptive language (the ability to understand what is said to or about you) develops before productive language (the ability to produce words). At about 4 months of age, infants *babble*, making sounds found in languages from all over the world, which by about 10 months includes only the sounds found in their household language. Around 12 months of age, children begin to speak in single words. This *one-word stage* evolves into *two-word (telegraphic)* utterances before their second birthday, after which they begin speaking in full sentences. Childhood is a critical period for learning language. Children who get a late start on language learning follow the usual developmental sequence, though at a faster pace. But children not exposed to either a spoken or a signed language until age 7 will never master any language. The importance of early language experiences is often evident in deaf children born to hearing-nonsigning parents.

27-4 What brain areas are involved in language processing and speech?

Aphasia is an impairment of language, usually caused by left-hemisphere damage. Two important language- and speech-processing areas are *Broca's area*, a region of the left frontal lobe that controls language expression, and *Wernicke's area*, a region in the left temporal lobe that controls language reception. Language processing is spread across other brain areas as well, with different neural networks handling specific linguistic subtasks.

27-5 What do we know about other species' capacity for language?

Chimpanzees and bonobos have learned to communicate with humans by signing or by pushing buttons. Some have developed vocabularies of nearly 400 words, communicated by stringing these words together, and have demonstrated some understanding of syntax. While only humans communicate in complex sentences, other animals' impressive abilities to think and communicate challenge humans to consider what this means about the moral rights of other species.

27-6 What is the relationship between thinking and language, and what is the value of thinking in images?

Although Benjamin Lee Whorf's *linguistic determinism* hypothesis suggested that language determines thought, it is more accurate to say that language influences thought *(linguistic relativism)*. Different languages embody different ways of thinking, and immersion in bilingual education can enhance thinking. We often think in images when we use implicit (nondeclarative, procedural) memory—our automatic memory system for learned skills and classically conditioned associations. Thinking in images can increase our skills when we mentally practice upcoming events. Process simulation (focusing on the steps needed to reach a goal) is effective, but outcome simulation (fantasizing about having achieved the goal) does little.

Intelligence

MODULE 28: What Is Intelligence?

28-1 How do psychologists define *intelligence?*

Intelligence is the ability to learn from experience, solve problems, and use knowledge to adapt to new situations.

28-2 What are the arguments for *g?*

Charles Spearman proposed that we have one *general intelligence* (g) underlying all mental abilities. Through his work with factor analysis, a statistical procedure that identifies clusters of related abilities, he noted that those who score high in one area typically score higher than average in other areas. L. L. Thurstone disagreed and identified seven different clusters of mental abilities. Yet a tendency remained for high scorers in one cluster to score high in other clusters, providing further evidence of a *g* factor.

28-3 How have the concepts of *Gf* and *Gc,* and the CHC theory, affected our understanding of intelligence?

Raymond Cattell and John Horn simplified Thurstone's primary mental abilities into *fluid intelligence* (Gf) and *crystallized intelligence* (Gc). The *Cattell-Horn-Carroll (CHC) theory* affirms a general intellectual ability factor, but also identifies more specific abilities (such as reading and writing ability, memory capacity, and processing speed).

28-4 How do Gardner's and Sternberg's theories of multiple intelligences differ, and what criticisms have they faced?

Howard Gardner proposed eight relatively independent intelligences (linguistic, logical-mathematical, musical, spatial, bodily-kinesthetic, intrapersonal, interpersonal, and naturalist), as well as a possible ninth (existential intelligence). The different intelligences of people with *savant syndrome,* autism spectrum disorder (ASD), and certain kinds of brain damage seem to support this view. Robert Sternberg's triarchic theory proposes three intelligence areas that predict real-world skills: analytical (academic problem solving), creative (innovative smarts), and practical (street smarts). Critics note that research has confirmed a general intelligence factor, which widely predicts performance. Highly successful people also tend to be conscientious, well-connected, and doggedly energetic; their achievements arise from both ability *and* deliberate practice. Also important is an advantaged home and school, and living in a time and place where your talents matter.

28-5 What are the four components of emotional intelligence?

Emotional intelligence, which is an aspect of social intelligence, includes the abilities to perceive, understand, manage, and use emotions. Emotionally intelligent people tend to be happy, healthy, and more successful personally and professionally. Some critics question whether calling these abilities "intelligence" stretches that concept too far.

MODULE 29: Intelligence Assessment and Dynamics

29-1 What is an *intelligence test,* and how do achievement and aptitude tests differ?

An *intelligence test* assesses an individual's mental aptitudes and compares them with those of others, using numerical scores. *Aptitude* tests measure the ability to learn, while *achievement* tests measure what we have already learned.

29-2 When and why were intelligence tests created, and how do today's tests differ from early intelligence tests?

Francis Galton, who was fascinated with measuring what he believed to be hereditary genius (so that those with exceptional abilities might be encouraged to reproduce), attempted but failed to construct a simple

intelligence test in the late 1800s. Alfred Binet, who tended toward an environmental explanation of intelligence differences, started the modern intelligence-testing movement in France in the early 1900s, when he developed questions to help predict children's future progress in the Paris school system. Binet hoped his test, which measured children's *mental age,* would improve their education but feared it might also be used to label children. During the early twentieth century, Lewis Terman of Stanford University revised Binet's work for use in the United States. Terman thought his *Stanford-Binet* could help guide people toward appropriate opportunities, but his belief in an intelligence that was fixed at birth and differed among ethnic groups realized Binet's fear that intelligence tests would be used to limit children's opportunities. William Stern contributed the concept of the *IQ* (intelligence quotient). The most widely used intelligence tests today are the *Wechsler Adult Intelligence Scale* (WAIS) and Wechsler's tests for children. These tests differ from their predecessors in the way they offer an overall intelligence score as well as scores for verbal comprehension, perceptual reasoning, working memory, and processing speed.

29-3 What is a *normal curve,* and what does it mean to say that a test has been standardized and is reliable and valid?

The distribution of test scores often forms a *normal* (bell-shaped) *curve* around the central average score, with fewer and fewer scores at the extremes. *Standardization* establishes a basis for meaningful score comparisons by giving a test to a representative sample of future test-takers. *Reliability* is the extent to which a test yields consistent results (on two halves of the test, on alternative forms of the test, or on retesting). *Validity* is the extent to which a test measures or predicts what it is supposed to. A test has *predictive validity* if it predicts a behavior it was designed to predict. (Aptitude tests have predictive validity if they can predict future achievements; their predictive power is best for the early school years.)

29-4 What are the traits of those at the low and high intelligence extremes?

People who score at the two extremes of the normal curve should differ noticeably, and they do. An intelligence test score of or below 70 is one diagnostic criterion for the diagnosis of intellectual disability. People at the high intelligence extreme—such as those with IQ scores of over 135 whom Terman studied—tend to be healthy and well-adjusted, as well as unusually successful academically. "Gifted" and "remedial" programs may create self-fulfilling prophecies, but can be effective when students are appropriately placed.

29-5 What are *cross-sectional studies* and *longitudinal studies,* and why is it important to know which method was used?

Cross-sectional studies compare people of different eras and life circumstances. This can provide an excellent snapshot of a particular point in time, but *longitudinal studies* are superior for tracing the evolution of traits over a longer period. Psychologists using the cross-sectional method concluded that mental ability declines with age, but those using the longitudinal method learned that it remains stable (or even increases).

29-6 How stable are intelligence test scores over the life span?

The stability of intelligence test scores increases with age. At age 4, scores begin to predict adolescent and adult scores. By age 11, scores are very stable and predictive.

29-7 How does aging affect crystallized intelligence *(Gc)* and fluid intelligence *(Gf)*?

The answers to age-and-intelligence questions depend on what we assess and how we assess it. Fluid intelligence (*Gf*) declines in older adults, in part because neural processing slows. However, crystallized intelligence (*Gc*) tends to increase with age.

MODULE 30: Genetic and Environmental Influences on Intelligence

30-1 What is *heritability,* and what do twin and adoption studies tell us about the nature and nurture of intelligence?

Heritability is the proportion of variation among individuals in a group that can be attributed to genes. Studies of twins, family members, and adoptive parents and siblings indicate a significant hereditary contribution to intelligence scores. Intelligence is polygenetic.

30-2 How can environmental influences affect cognitive development?

Studies of children raised in impoverished environments with minimal social interaction indicate that life experiences significantly influence cognitive development. No evidence supports the idea that normal, healthy children can be molded into geniuses by growing up in an exceptionally enriched environment. Environments that foster a *growth mindset* do not alter intelligence, but can positively impact achievement.

30-3 How and why do the genders differ in mental ability scores?

Boys and girls have the same average intelligence test scores, but they tend to differ in some specific abilities. Girls, on average, are better spellers, more verbally fluent, better at reading and at locating objects, better at detecting emotions, and more sensitive to touch, taste, and color. Boys outperform girls at spatial ability and complex mathematics, though boys and girls hardly differ in math computation and overall math performance. Boys also outnumber girls at the low and high extremes of mental abilities. Evolutionary and cultural explanations have been proposed for these gender differences.

30-4 How and why do racial and ethnic groups differ in mental ability scores?

Racial and ethnic groups differ in their average intelligence test scores. Evidence suggests that environmental differences are responsible for these group differences.

30-5 Are intelligence tests biased or unfair? What is *stereotype threat,* and how does it affect test-takers' performance?

The scientific meaning of bias hinges on a test's ability to predict future behavior for all test-takers, not just for some. In this sense, most experts consider the major aptitude tests unbiased. However, if we consider bias to mean that a test may be influenced by the test-taker's cultural experience, then intelligence tests, by that definition, may be considered unfair. *Stereotype threat,* a self-confirming concern that one will be evaluated based on a negative stereotype, affects performance on all kinds of tests; some research findings suggest effective reduction strategies.

What Drives Us: Hunger, Sex, Belonging, and Achievement

MODULE 31: Basic Motivational Concepts

31-1 How do psychologists define *motivation?* What are four key motivation theories?

Motivation is a need or desire that energizes and directs behavior. The *instinct/ evolutionary* perspective explores genetic influences on complex behaviors. *Drive-reduction theory* explores how *physiological needs* create aroused tension states (drives) that direct us to satisfy those needs. Environmental *incentives* can intensify drives. Drive-reduction's goal is *homeostasis,* maintaining a steady internal state. Arousal theory proposes that some behaviors (such as those driven by curiosity) do not reduce physiological needs but rather are prompted by a search for an optimum level of arousal. The *Yerkes-Dodson law* describes the relationship between arousal and performance. Abraham Maslow's *hierarchy of needs* proposes a pyramid of human needs, from basic needs up to higher-level needs.

MODULE 32: Hunger

32-1 What physiological factors produce hunger?

Hunger pangs correspond to stomach contractions, but hunger also has other causes. Neural areas in the brain, some within the hypothalamus, monitor blood chemistry (including level of *glucose*) and incoming information about the body's state. Appetite hormones include ghrelin (secreted by an empty stomach); orexin (secreted by the hypothalamus); leptin (secreted by fat cells); and PYY (secreted by the digestive tract). *Basal metabolic rate* is the body's resting rate of energy expenditure. The body may have a *set point* (a biologically fixed tendency to maintain an optimum weight) or a looser settling point (also influenced by the environment).

32-2 What cultural and situational factors influence hunger?

Hunger reflects our memory of when we last ate and our expectation of when we should eat again. Humans as a species prefer certain tastes (such as sweet and salty), but our individual preferences are also influenced by conditioning, culture, and situation. Some taste preferences have survival value. Situational influences include the presence of others, serving size, and the variety of foods offered.

32-3 How does obesity affect physical and psychological health? What factors are involved in weight management?

Obesity, defined by a body mass index (BMI) of 30 or above, is associated with increased depression (especially among women) and bullying, and with many physical health risks. Genes and environment interact to produce obesity. Storing fat was adaptive to our ancestors, and fat requires less food intake to maintain than it did to gain. Set point and metabolism matter. Twin and adoption studies indicate that body weight is also genetically influenced. Environmental influences include sleep loss, social influence, and food and activity levels. Those wishing to lose weight are advised to make a lifelong change in habits: Begin only if you feel motivated and self-disciplined; exercise and get enough sleep; minimize exposure to tempting food cues; limit variety and eat healthy foods; reduce portion sizes; relabel portions; time intake to avoid nighttime eating and eat heavier meals earlier in the day; beware of the binge; plan ahead to control eating during social events; forgive the occasional lapse; publicly chart your progress; and connect to a support group.

MODULE 33: Sexual Motivation

33-1 How do hormones influence human sexual motivation?

For all but those few of us considered *asexual,* dating and mating become a high priority from puberty on. The female *estrogen* and male *testosterone* hormones influence human sexual behavior less directly than they influence sexual behavior in other species. Women's sexuality is more responsive to testosterone level than to estrogen level. Short-term shifts in testosterone level are normal in men, partly in response to stimulation.

33-2 What is the human *sexual response cycle,* and how do sexual dysfunctions and paraphilias differ?

William Masters and Virginia Johnson described four stages in the human *sexual response cycle:* excitement, plateau, orgasm, and resolution. During resolution there is a *refractory period* in which renewed arousal and orgasm are impossible. *Sexual dysfunctions* are problems that consistently impair sexual arousal or functioning. They include *erectile disorder* and *female orgasmic disorder,* and can often be successfully treated by behaviorally oriented therapy or drug therapy. *Paraphilias* are considered disordered if a person experiences distress from an unusual sexual interest or if it entails harm or risk of harm to others.

33-3 How can sexually transmitted infections be prevented?

Safe-sex practices help prevent sexually transmitted infections (STIs). Condoms are especially effective in preventing transmission of HIV, the virus that causes *AIDS.* Knowing one's STI status, and sharing it with one's sexual partner, is an important first step in STI prevention.

33-4 How do external and imagined stimuli contribute to sexual arousal?

External stimuli can trigger sexual arousal. Sexually explicit material may lead people to perceive their partners as comparatively less appealing and to devalue their relationships. Viewing sexually coercive material can lead to increased acceptance of violence toward women. Extensive online pornography exposure may desensitize young adults to real-life sexuality, leading to lowered sexual desire and satisfaction, and to erectile problems for men. Imagined stimuli (dreams and fantasies) also influence sexual arousal.

33-5 What factors influence teenagers' sexual behaviors and use of contraceptives?

Teen sexuality varies from culture to culture and era to era. Factors contributing to these variations include communication about birth control; impulsivity; alcohol use; and mass media. High intelligence, religious engagement, father presence, and service-learning participation predict teen sexual restraint.

33-6 What do we know about sexual orientation?

Sexual orientation is the direction of our sexual attractions, as reflected in our longings and fantasies. We may have sexual attraction toward members of the other gender (heterosexual orientation), our own gender (same-sex orientation), male and female genders (bisexual orientation), or no one at all (asexual orientation). Some people report experiencing sexual attraction unrestricted to any sex or gender identity (pansexual orientation). About 3 or 4 percent of men and 2 percent of women in Europe and the United States have exclusively same-sex attractions. Scientists have been unable to find specific environmental influences that contribute to sexual orientation. Evidence for biological influences includes same-sex attraction in other species; gay-straight trait and brain differences; genetic influences; and prenatal influences.

33-7 What role do social factors play in our sexuality?

Scientific research on sexual motivation does not attempt to define the personal meaning of sex in our lives, which is influenced by many social factors. Sex is a socially significant act. Sexual desire motivates people to form intimate, committed relationships, which in turn enable satisfying sex. Sex at its human best is life uniting and love renewing.

MODULE 34: Affiliation and Achievement

34-1 What evidence points to our human affiliation need—our need to belong?

Our *affiliation need*—to feel connected and identified with others—had survival value for our ancestors, which may explain why humans in every society live in groups. According to *self-determination theory,* we strive to satisfy our needs for competence, autonomy, and relatedness. Social bonds help us to be healthier and happier, and feeling loved activates brain regions associated with reward and safety systems. *Ostracism* is the deliberate social exclusion of individuals or groups. Social isolation can put us at risk mentally and physically.

34-2 How does social networking influence us?

We connect with others through social networking, strengthening our relationships, meeting new friends or romantic partners, and finding support at difficult times. But increased online time displaces other activities, and social media use increases people's comparing their lives with others. Researchers are investigating possible connections between increasing screen time and a rise in teen mental health problems. When networking, people tend toward increased self-disclosure. People with high *narcissism* are especially active on social networking sites. Working out strategies for self-control and disciplined usage can help people maintain a healthy balance between their real-world and online time.

34-3 What is *achievement motivation,* and what are some ways to encourage achievement?

Achievement motivation is a desire for significant accomplishment, for mastery of skills or ideas, for control, and for attaining a high standard. High achievement motivation leads to greater success, especially when combined with determined, persistent *grit.* Research shows that excessive rewards (driving *extrinsic motivation*) can undermine *intrinsic motivation.* To achieve our own goals, we can make a resolution; announce the goal; develop an implementation plan; create short-term rewards; monitor and record progress; create a supportive environment; and transform the behavior into a habit.

Emotions, Stress, and Health

MODULE 35: Introduction to Emotion

35-1 How do arousal, expressive behavior, and cognition interact in emotion?

Emotions are responses of the whole organism, involving physiological arousal, expressive behaviors, and, most importantly, conscious experience resulting from one's interpretations. Theories of emotion generally address two major questions: (1) Does physiological arousal come before or after emotional feelings? and (2) How do feeling and cognition interact? The *James-Lange theory* maintains that emotion occurs when we become aware of our body's response to emotion-inducing stimuli (we observe our heart pounding and feel fear). The *Cannon-Bard theory* proposes that our physiological response to an emotion-inducing stimulus occurs at the same time as our subjective feeling of the emotion (one does not cause the other).

35-2 To experience emotions, must we consciously interpret and label them?

The Schachter-Singer *two-factor theory* holds that our emotions have two ingredients, physical arousal and a cognitive label; the cognitive labels we put on our states of arousal are an essential ingredient of emotion. Lazarus agreed that many important emotions arise from our interpretations or inferences. But Zajonc and LeDoux have contended that some simple emotional responses occur instantly, not only outside our conscious awareness, but before any cognitive processing occurs. This interplay between emotion and cognition illustrates our two-track mind.

35-3 What is the link between emotional arousal and the autonomic nervous system?

The arousal component of emotion is regulated by the autonomic nervous system's sympathetic (arousing) and parasympathetic (calming) divisions. In a crisis, the fight-or-flight response automatically mobilizes your body for action.

35-4 How do emotions activate different physiological and brain-pattern responses?

The large-scale body changes that accompany fear, anger, and sexual arousal are very similar (increased perspiration, breathing, and heart rate), though they feel different. Emotions may be similarly arousing, but some subtle physiological responses (such as facial muscle movements) distinguish them. More meaningful differences have been found in activity in some brain pathways and cortical areas.

35-5 How effective are polygraphs in using body states to detect lies?

Polygraphs (lie detectors) attempt to detect lies by measuring several emotion-linked physiological changes, but are not accurate enough to justify widespread use in business and law enforcement. The Concealed Information Test produces better indications of lying.

MODULE 36: Expressing Emotion

36-1 How do we communicate nonverbally?

Much of our communication is through body movements, facial expressions, and vocal tones. Even seconds-long filmed slices of behavior can reveal feelings.

36-2 How do men and women differ in nonverbal communication?

Women tend to read emotional cues more easily and to be more empathic. Their faces also express more emotion.

36-3 How are gestures and facial expressions understood within and across cultures?

The meaning of gestures varies with culture, but facial expressions, such as those of happiness and sadness, are roughly similar the world over. Context and culture can influence the interpretation of facial expressions; cultural display rules also influence the amount of emotion expressed.

36-4 How do our facial expressions influence our feelings?

Research on the *facial feedback effect* shows that our facial expressions can trigger emotional feelings and signal our body to respond accordingly. We also mimic others' expressions, which helps us empathize. A similar *behavior feedback effect* is the tendency of behavior to influence our

own and others' thoughts, feelings, and actions.

MODULE 37: Experiencing Emotion

37-1 What are some of the basic emotions?

Most emotion scientists agree that anger, fear, disgust, sadness, and happiness are basic human emotions. Carroll Izard's 10 basic emotions are joy, interest-excitement, surprise, sadness, anger, disgust, contempt, fear, shame, and guilt.

37-2 What are the causes and consequences of anger?

Anger is often evoked by misdeeds that we interpret as willful, unjustified, and avoidable. But smaller frustrations and blameless annoyances can also trigger anger, and our culture can influence how we express that anger. Anger boosts our heart rate and increases inflammation. Emotional *catharsis* may be temporarily calming, but it does not reduce anger; expressing anger can make us angrier. Experts suggest reducing the level of physiological arousal of anger by waiting, finding a healthy distraction or support, and trying to move away from the situation mentally. Controlled assertions of feelings may resolve conflicts, and forgiveness may rid us of angry feelings.

37-3 What is the *feel-good, do-good phenomenon,* and what is the focus of positive psychology research?

Happy people tend to be healthy, energized, and satisfied with life, making them more willing to help others (the *feel-good, do-good phenomenon*). *Positive psychologists* use scientific methods to study human flourishing, aiming to discover and promote strengths and virtues that help individuals and communities to thrive.

37-4 How do time, wealth, adaptation, and comparison affect our happiness levels?

The moods triggered by good or bad events seldom last beyond that day. Even significant good events seldom increase happiness for long. Having enough money to assure comfort, security, and a sense of control predicts happiness; having more than enough does not increase it. Economic growth in many countries has produced rising inequality, which predicts unhappiness; in countries and states with greater inequality, lower-income people experience more ill health, social problems, and mental disorders. Happiness is relative to our own experiences (the *adaptation-level phenomenon*) and to others' success (the *relative deprivation* principle).

37-5 What predicts happiness, and how can we be happier?

Some individuals, because of their genetic predispositions and personal histories, are happier than others. Cultures, which vary in the traits they value and the behaviors they expect and reward, also influence personal levels of happiness. Tips for increasing happiness levels: Take charge of your schedule, act happy, seek meaningful work and leisure, buy experiences rather than things, exercise, sleep enough, foster friendships, focus and find meaning beyond the self, challenge negative thinking, and nurture gratitude and spirituality.

MODULE 38: Stress and Illness

38-1 How does our appraisal of an event affect our stress reaction, and what are the three main types of stressors?

Stress is the process by which we appraise and respond to stressors that challenge or threaten us. If we appraise an event as challenging, we will be aroused and focused in preparation for success; if we appraise it as a threat, we will experience a stress reaction, and our health may suffer. The three main types of stressors are catastrophes, significant life changes, and daily hassles and social stress. Daily hassles and social stress may include inequality and prejudice, chronic workplace stress (which may lead to worker "burnout"), and the conflicts we face between our different *approach and avoidance motives*.

38-2 How do we respond and adapt to stress?

Walter Cannon viewed the stress response as a fight-or-flight system. Hans Selye proposed a three-phase (alarm, resistance, exhaustion) *general adaptation syndrome (GAS)*. People may react to stress by withdrawing. They may also show a *tend-and-befriend response* (more common in women).

38-3 How does stress make us more vulnerable to disease?

Psychoneuroimmunology is the study of how psychological, neural, and endocrine processes together affect our immune system

and resulting health. Stress diverts energy from the immune system, inhibiting the activities of its B and T lymphocytes, macrophages, and NK cells. Stress does not cause illness, but by altering our immune functioning it may make us more vulnerable to diseases and influence their progression.

38-4 Why are some of us more prone than others to coronary heart disease?

Coronary heart disease has been linked with the reactive, anger-prone *Type A* personality. Compared with relaxed, easygoing *Type B* personalities, who are less likely to experience heart disease, Type A people's more active sympathetic nervous system may divert blood flow from the liver to the muscles, leaving excess cholesterol and fat circulating in the bloodstream. Chronic stress also contributes to persistent inflammation, which is associated with heart and other health problems, including depression.

38-5 So, does stress *cause* illness?

Stress may not directly cause illness, but it does make us more vulnerable, by influencing our physiology and our behaviors.

MODULE 39: Health and Coping

39-1 In what two ways do people try to alleviate stress?

We use *problem-focused coping* to change the stressor or the way we interact with it. We use *emotion-focused coping* to avoid or ignore stressors and attend to emotional needs related to stress reactions.

39-2 How does a perceived lack of control affect health?

A perceived lack of *personal control* provokes an outpouring of hormones that put people's health at risk. Being unable to avoid repeated aversive events can lead to *learned helplessness*. People who perceive an *internal locus of control* achieve more, enjoy better health, and are happier than those who perceive an *external locus of control*. Belief in free will is linked to more helpful behavior, better learning, and greater work persistence, performance, and satisfaction.

39-3 Why is self-control important, and can our self-control be depleted?

Self-control requires attention and energy, but predicts good health, higher income, and better school performance; it does better than an intelligence test score

in predicting future academic and life success. Self-control varies over time. Researchers disagree about the factors influencing self-control, but strengthening it can lead to a healthier, happier, and more successful life.

39-4 How does an optimistic outlook affect health and longevity?

Studies of people with an optimistic outlook show that they are more likely than pessimists to have optimal health, to be successful, and to have a longer life expectancy.

39-5 How does social support promote good health?

Social support promotes health by calming us, improving our sleep, and reducing blood pressure, and it fosters stronger immune functioning. We can significantly reduce our stress and increase our health by building and maintaining relationships, and by confiding rather than suppressing painful feelings.

39-6 How effective is aerobic exercise as a way to manage stress and improve well-being?

Aerobic exercise increases arousal, leads to muscle relaxation and sounder sleep, triggers the production of neurotransmitters, fosters neurogenesis, and enhances self-image. It can reduce or prevent depression and anxiety. In later life, regular exercise is associated with better cognitive functioning and longer life.

39-7 In what ways might relaxation and meditation influence stress and health?

Relaxation and meditation have been shown to lower stress, reduce blood pressure, improve immune functioning, and lessen anxiety and depression. *Mindfulness meditation* is a reflective practice of attending to current experiences in a nonjudgmental and accepting manner. Massage therapy also promotes relaxation and reduces depression.

39-8 What is the faith factor, and what are some possible explanations for the link between faith and health?

The faith factor is the finding that religiously active people tend to live longer than those who are not religiously active. Possible explanations may include intervening variables such as the healthy behaviors, social support, or positive emotions often found among people who regularly attend religious services.

Social Psychology

MODULE 40: Social Thinking

40-1 What do social psychologists study? How do we tend to explain others' behavior and our own?

Social psychologists use scientific methods to study how people think about, influence, and relate to one another. They study the social influences that explain why the same person will act differently in different situations. When explaining others' behavior, we may—especially if we come from an individualist Western culture—commit the *fundamental attribution error,* by underestimating the influence of the situation and overestimating the effects of stable, enduring traits. When explaining our own behavior, we more readily attribute it to the influence of the situation.

40-2 How do attitudes and actions interact?

Our *attitudes* and our actions influence one another. When other influences are minimal, attitudes that are stable, specific, and easily recalled can affect our actions. Actions can modify attitudes, as in the *foot-in-the-door phenomenon* and *role* playing. When our attitudes don't fit with our actions, *cognitive dissonance theory* suggests that we will reduce tension by changing our attitudes to match our actions.

40-3 How do *peripheral route persuasion* and *central route persuasion* differ?

Peripheral route persuasion uses attention-getting cues (such as celebrity endorsement) to trigger fast but relatively thoughtless judgments. *Central route persuasion* offers evidence and arguments to trigger thoughtful responses.

40-4 How can we share our views more effectively?

To persuade people with views that differ from your own, avoid yelling at, humiliating, or boring them with complicated or forgettable information. Instead, identify shared goals and relate your aim to their motives. It also helps to make your message vivid, to repeat it, and to engage others in restating it.

MODULE 41: Social Influence

41-1 How is social contagion a form of conformity, and how do conformity experiments reveal the power of social influence?

Social contagion (the chameleon effect)—our tendency to unconsciously imitate others' behavior, expressions, postures, voice tones, and moods—is a form of *conformity.* Social networks serve as contagious pathways for moods, both good and bad. Solomon Asch and others found that we are most likely to adjust our behavior or thinking to coincide with a group standard when we feel incompetent or insecure, our group has at least three people, everyone else agrees, we admire the group's status and attractiveness, we have not already committed to another response, we know we are being observed, and our culture encourages respect for social standards. We may conform to gain approval *(normative social influence)* or because we are willing to accept others' opinions as new information *(informational social influence).*

41-2 What did Milgram's obedience experiments teach us about the power of social influence?

Stanley Milgram's experiments—in which people obeyed orders even when they thought they were harming another person—demonstrated that strong social influences can make ordinary people conform to falsehoods or capitulate to cruelty. Obedience was highest when the person giving orders was nearby and was perceived as a legitimate authority figure, the research was supported by a prestigious institution, the victim was depersonalized or at a distance, and there were no role models for defiance.

41-3 What do the social influence studies teach us about ourselves? How much power do we have as individuals?

These experiments have demonstrated that strong social influences can influence behavior. The power of the individual (personal control) and the power of the situation (social control) interact. A small minority that consistently expresses its views may sway the majority, as may even a single committed individual.

41-4 How does the presence of others influence our actions, via social facilitation, social loafing, and deindividuation?

In *social facilitation,* the mere presence of others arouses us, improving our performance on easy or well-learned tasks but decreasing it on difficult ones. In *social loafing,* group work makes us feel less responsible, and we may free ride on others' efforts. When the presence of others both arouses us and makes us feel anonymous, we may experience *deindividuation*—loss of self-awareness and self-restraint.

41-5 How can group interaction enable group polarization?

In *group polarization,* group discussions with like-minded others strengthen members' prevailing beliefs and attitudes.

41-6 What role does the internet play in group polarization?

Internet communication magnifies the effect of connecting like-minded people, for better and for worse. People find support, which strengthens their ideas, but also often isolation from those with different opinions. Separation plus conversation may thus lead to group polarization.

41-7 How can group interaction enable groupthink?

Groupthink is driven by a desire for harmony within a decision-making group, overriding realistic appraisal of alternatives. Group leaders can harness the benefits of group interaction by assigning people to identify possible problems, and by welcoming various opinions and expert critique.

MODULE 42: Antisocial Relations

42-1 What is *prejudice*? How do explicit and implicit prejudice differ?

Prejudice is an unjustifiable, usually negative attitude toward a group and its members. Prejudice's three components are beliefs (often *stereotypes*), emotions, and predispositions to action (*discrimination*). Prejudice may be explicit (overt), or it may be implicit—an unthinking knee-jerk response operating below conscious awareness. Implicit prejudice can cause discrimination even when people do not consciously intend to discriminate.

42-2 What groups are frequent targets of prejudice?

Prejudice involves explicit and implicit negative attitudes toward people of a particular racial or ethnic group, gender, or sexual orientation. In the United States, frequently targeted groups include Black Americans, women, and LGBTQ people.

42-3 What are some social, emotional, and cognitive roots of prejudice, and what are some ways to reduce prejudice?

The social roots of prejudice include social inequalities and divisions. Higher-status groups often justify their privileged position with the *just-world phenomenon*. We tend to favor our own group (*ingroup bias*) as we divide ourselves into "us" (the *ingroup*) and "them" (the *outgroup*). Prejudice can also be a tool for protecting our emotional well-being, as when we focus our anger by blaming events on a *scapegoat*. The cognitive roots of prejudice grow from our natural ways of processing information: forming categories, remembering vivid cases, and believing that the world is just (and that our own and our group's ways of doing things are the right ways). Monitoring our feelings and actions, as well as developing new friendships, can help us free ourselves from prejudice.

42-4 How does psychology's definition of *aggression* differ from everyday usage? What biological factors make us more prone to hurt one another?

In psychology's more specific meaning, *aggression* is any physical or verbal behavior intended to harm someone physically or emotionally. Biology influences our threshold for aggressive behaviors at three levels: genetic (inherited traits), neural (activity in key brain areas), and biochemical (such as alcohol or excess testosterone in the bloodstream). Aggression is a complex behavior resulting from the interaction of biology and experience.

42-5 What psychological and social-cultural factors may trigger aggressive behavior?

Frustration (the *frustration-aggression principle*), previous reinforcement for aggressive behavior, and observing aggressive role models all contribute to aggression. Media violence provides *social scripts* that children learn to follow. Viewing sexual violence contributes to greater aggression toward women. Playing violent video games can increase aggressive thoughts, emotions, and behaviors.

MODULE 43: Prosocial Relations

43-1 Why do we befriend or fall in love with some people but not others?

Proximity (geographical nearness) increases liking, in part because of the *mere exposure effect*—exposure to novel stimuli increases liking of those stimuli. Physical attractiveness increases social opportunities and improves the way we are perceived. Similarity of attitudes and interests greatly increases liking, especially as relationships develop. We also like those who like us.

43-2 How does romantic love typically change as time passes?

Intimate love relationships start with *passionate love*—an intensely aroused state. Over time, the strong affection of *companionate love* may develop, especially if enhanced by an *equitable* relationship, intimate *self-disclosure*, and positive support.

43-3 What is *altruism?* When are people most—and least—likely to help?

Altruism is unselfish regard for the well-being of others. We are most likely to help when we notice an incident, interpret it as an emergency, and assume responsibility for helping. Other factors, including our mood and our similarity to the victim, also affect our willingness to help. We are least likely to help if other bystanders are present (the *bystander effect*).

43-4 How do social exchange theory and social norms explain helping behavior?

Social exchange theory is the view that we help others because it is in our own self-interest; in this view, the goal of social behavior is maximizing personal benefits and minimizing costs. Others believe that helping results from socialization, in which we are taught guidelines for expected behaviors in social situations, such as the *reciprocity norm* and the *social-responsibility norm*.

43-5 How do social traps and mirror-image perceptions fuel social conflict?

Social traps are situations in which people in *conflict* pursue their own individual self-interest, harming the collective well-being. Individuals and cultures in conflict also tend to form *mirror-image perceptions*: Each party views the opponent as untrustworthy and evil-intentioned, and itself as an ethical, peaceful victim. Perceptions can become *self-fulfilling prophecies*.

43-6 What can we do to promote peace?

Peace can result when individuals or groups work together to achieve *superordinate* (shared) *goals*. Research indicates that contact, cooperation, communication, and conciliation—such as the Graduated and Reciprocated Initiatives in Tension-Reduction (*GRIT*) strategy—help promote peace.

Personality

MODULE 44: Introduction to Personality and Psychodynamic Theories

44-1 What is *personality,* and what theories inform our understanding of personality?

Personality is an individual's characteristic pattern of thinking, feeling, and acting. Psychoanalytic (and later psychodynamic) theory and humanistic theory have become part of Western culture. They also laid the foundation for later theories, such as trait and social-cognitive theories of personality.

44-2 How did Sigmund Freud's treatment of psychological disorders lead to his view of the unconscious mind?

Psychodynamic theories of personality view behavior as a dynamic interaction between the conscious and unconscious mind. These theories trace their origin to Sigmund Freud's theory of *psychoanalysis*. In treating patients whose disorders had no clear physical explanation, Freud concluded that these problems reflected unacceptable thoughts and feelings, hidden away in the *unconscious* mind. To explore this hidden part of a patient's mind, Freud used *free association* and dream analysis.

44-3 What was Freud's view of personality?

Freud believed that personality results from conflict arising from the interaction among the mind's three systems:

the id (pleasure-seeking impulses), *ego* (reality-oriented executive), and *superego* (internalized set of ideals, or conscience).

44-4 What developmental stages did Freud propose?

He believed children pass through five *psychosexual stages* (oral, anal, phallic, latency, and genital). According to this view, unresolved conflicts at any stage can leave a person's pleasure-seeking impulses *fixated* (stalled) at that stage.

44-5 How did Freud think people defended themselves against anxiety?

For Freud, anxiety was the product of tensions between the demands of the id and superego. The ego copes by using unconscious *defense mechanisms,* such as *repression,* which he viewed as the basic mechanism underlying and enabling all the others.

44-6 Which of Freud's ideas did his followers accept or reject?

Freud's early followers, the neo-Freudians, accepted many of his ideas. They differed in placing more emphasis on the conscious mind and in stressing social motives more than sex or aggression. Most contemporary psychodynamic theorists and therapists reject Freud's emphasis on sexual motivation. They stress, with support from modern research findings, that much of our mental life is unconscious, and they believe that our childhood experiences influence our adult personality and attachment patterns. Many also believe that our species' shared evolutionary history shaped some universal predispositions.

44-7 How do contemporary psychologists view Freud's psychoanalysis?

Freud is credited with drawing attention to the vast unconscious and our irrationality, to the importance of human sexuality and to the conflict between biological impulses and social restraints, and for formulating some science-backed defense mechanisms. But his concept of repression, and his view of the unconscious as a collection of repressed and unacceptable thoughts, wishes, feelings, and memories, cannot survive scientific scrutiny. Freud offered after-the-fact explanations, which are hard to test scientifically. Research does not support many of Freud's specific ideas, such as the view that development is fixed in childhood. (We now know it is lifelong.)

44-8 How has modern research developed our understanding of the unconscious?

Research confirms that we do not have full access to all that goes on in our mind, though today's science views the unconscious as a separate and parallel track of information processing that occurs outside our awareness. This processing includes schemas that control our perceptions, priming, implicit memories of learned skills, instantly activated emotions, and the implicit prejudice and stereotypes that filter our information processing of others' traits and characteristics. Research also supports reaction formation and projection (the false consensus effect), and the idea that we unconsciously defend ourselves from anxiety (as seen in experiments testing *terror-management theory*).

44-9 What are *projective tests,* how are they used, and what are some criticisms of them?

Projective tests show people stimuli that are open to many possible interpretations, treating their answers as revelations of inner dynamics. The *Thematic Apperception Test (TAT)* and the *Rorschach inkblot test* are two such tests. The TAT provides a valid and reliable map of people's implicit motives that is consistent over time. The Rorschach has low reliability and validity, but some clinicians value it as a source of suggestive leads, an icebreaker, or a revealing interview technique.

MODULE 45: Humanistic Theories and Trait Theories

45-1 How did humanistic psychologists view personality, and what was their goal in studying personality?

The *humanistic* psychologists' view of personality focused on the potential for healthy personal growth and people's striving for self-determination and self-realization. Abraham Maslow proposed that human motivations form a *hierarchy of needs;* if basic needs are fulfilled, people will strive toward *self-actualization* and *self-transcendence.* Carl Rogers believed that the ingredients of a growth-promoting environment are acceptance (including *unconditional positive regard*), genuineness, and empathy. *Self-concept* was a central feature of personality for both Maslow and Rogers.

45-2 How did humanistic psychologists assess a person's sense of self?

Some rejected any standardized assessments and relied on interviews and conversations. Others, like Rogers, sometimes used questionnaires in which people described their ideal and actual selves; these were later used to judge progress during therapy. Some now use the life story approach, enabling a rich narrative detailing each person's unique life history.

45-3 How have humanistic theories influenced psychology? What criticisms have they faced?

Humanistic psychology has had pervasive cultural impact and helped renew interest in the concept of self; it also laid the groundwork for today's scientific subfield of positive psychology. Critics have said that humanistic psychology's concepts are vague and subjective, its values self-centered, and its assumptions naively optimistic.

45-4 How do psychologists use traits to describe personality?

Trait theorists see personality as a stable and enduring pattern of behavior. They have been more interested in trying to describe our differences than in explaining them. Using factor analysis, they identify clusters of behavior tendencies that occur together. Genetic predispositions influence many traits.

45-5 What are some common misunderstandings about introversion?

Western cultures prize extraversion, but introverts have different, equally important skills. Introversion does not equal shyness, and extraverts don't always outperform introverts as leaders. Introverts handle conflict well, seeking solitude rather than revenge.

45-6 What are *personality inventories,* and what are their strengths and weaknesses as trait-assessment tools?

Personality inventories (such as the MMPI) are questionnaires on which people respond to items designed to gauge a wide range of feelings and behaviors. Test items are *empirically derived,* and the tests are objectively scored. Objectivity does not guarantee validity; people can fake their answers to create a good impression (but may then score high on a lie scale that assesses faking).

45-7 Which traits seem to provide the most useful information about personality variation?

The *Big Five* personality factors—openness, conscientiousness, extraversion, agreeableness, and neuroticism (OCEAN)—currently offer our best approximation of the basic trait dimensions. These factors are generally stable and describe people in various cultures reasonably well. Many genes, each having small effects, combine to influence our traits.

45-8 Does research support the consistency of personality traits over time and across situations?

A person's average traits persist over time and are predictable over many different situations. But traits cannot predict behavior in any one situation.

MODULE 46: Social-Cognitive Theories and the Self

46-1 How do social-cognitive theorists view personality development, and how do they explore behavior?

Albert Bandura's *social-cognitive perspective* emphasizes the interaction of our traits with our situations. Social-cognitive researchers apply principles of learning, cognition, and social behavior to personality. *Reciprocal determinism* describes the interaction and mutual influence of behavior, internal cognition, and environment. Assessment situations involving simulated conditions exploit the principle that the best predictor of future behavior is a person's actions in similar situations.

46-2 What criticisms have social-cognitive theories faced?

Social-cognitive theories build on well-established concepts of learning and cognition, sensitizing researchers to the ways situations affect, and are affected by, individuals. They have been faulted for underemphasizing the importance of unconscious motives, emotions, and biologically influenced traits.

46-3 Why has psychology generated so much research on the self? How important is self-esteem to our well-being?

The *self* is vigorously researched as the center of personality, organizing our thoughts, feelings, and actions. Considering possible selves helps motivate us toward positive development, but

focusing too intensely on ourselves can lead to the *spotlight effect*. High *self-esteem* and self-efficacy correlate with benefits such as higher school achievement and with being able to meet challenges. But the direction of the correlation is unclear. Rather than unrealistically promoting self-worth, it's better to reward achievements, thus promoting feelings of competence.

46-4 How do excessive optimism, blindness to one's own incompetence, and self-serving bias reveal the costs of self-esteem, and how do defensive and secure self-esteem differ?

Excessive optimism can lead to complacency and prevent us from seeing real risks, while blindness to one's own incompetence may lead us to make the same mistakes repeatedly. *Self-serving bias* is our tendency to perceive ourselves favorably, as when viewing ourselves as better than average or when accepting credit for our successes but not blame for our failures. Defensive self-esteem is fragile, focuses on sustaining itself, and views failure or criticism as a threat. Secure self-esteem enables us to feel accepted for who we are.

Psychological Disorders

MODULE 47: Introduction to Psychological Disorders

47-1 How should we draw the line between normality and disorder?

According to psychologists and psychiatrists, *psychological disorders* are marked by a clinically significant disturbance in an individual's cognition, emotion regulation, or behavior. Such dysfunctional or maladaptive thoughts, emotions, or behaviors interfere with daily life, and thus are disordered.

47-2 How do the medical model and the biopsychosocial approach influence our understanding of psychological disorders?

The *medical model* assumes that psychological disorders have physical causes that can be diagnosed, treated, and often cured through therapy, sometimes in a hospital. The biopsychosocial perspective assumes that disordered behavior comes from the interaction of biological characteristics, psychological dynamics, and social-cultural circumstances. This approach has given rise to the vulnerability-stress

model, in which individual characteristics and environmental stressors combine to increase or decrease the likelihood of developing a psychological disorder, a model supported by *epigenetics* research.

47-3 How and why do clinicians classify psychological disorders, and why do some psychologists criticize diagnostic labels?

The American Psychiatric Association's *DSM-5* (*Diagnostic and Statistical Manual of Mental Disorders*, Fifth Edition) contains diagnostic labels and descriptions that provide a common language and shared concepts for communication and research. Critics of the DSM say it casts too wide a net, pathologizing normal behaviors. A complementary approach to classification is the U.S. National Institute of Mental Health's Research Domain Criteria (RDoC) project, a framework that organizes disorders according to behaviors and brain activity along several dimensions. Any classification attempt produces diagnostic labels that may create preconceptions, which bias perceptions of the labeled person's past and present behavior.

47-4 What factors increase the risk of suicide, and what do we know about nonsuicidal self-injury?

Suicide rates differ by nation, race, gender, age group, income, religious involvement, marital status, and other factors. In most countries, suicide rates have been increasing. Those lacking social support, such as many gay, transgender, and gender nonconforming youth, are at increased risk, as are people who have been anxious or depressed. Isolation and unemployment can also heighten risk. Forewarnings of suicide may include verbal hints, giving away possessions, withdrawal, and preoccupation with death. People who talk about suicide should be taken seriously: Listen and empathize, connect them to help, and protect those who appear at immediate risk. Nonsuicidal self-injury (NSSI) does not usually lead to suicide but may escalate to suicidal thoughts and acts if untreated. People who engage in NSSI do not tolerate stress well and tend to be self-critical and impulsive.

47-5 Do psychological disorders predict violent behavior?

Mental disorders seldom lead to violence, and clinicians cannot predict who is likely to harm others. Most people with disorders are nonviolent and are more likely to be victims than attackers. Better predictors of violence are alcohol or drug use, previous violence, gun availability, and brain damage.

47-6 How many people have, or have had, a psychological disorder? What are some of the risk factors?

Psychological disorder rates vary, depending on the time and place of the survey. In one multinational survey, the lowest rate of reported mental disorders was in Nigeria, and the highest rate in the United States. Poverty is a risk factor. But some disorders, such as schizophrenia, can also drive people into poverty. Immigrants to the United States may average better mental health than their U.S. counterparts with the same ethnic heritage (a phenomenon known as the immigrant paradox).

MODULE 48: Anxiety-Related Disorders

48-1 How do generalized anxiety disorder, panic disorder, and specific phobias differ?

Anxiety disorders are psychological disorders characterized by distressing, persistent anxiety or maladaptive behaviors that reduce anxiety. People with *generalized anxiety disorder* feel persistently and uncontrollably tense and apprehensive, for no apparent reason. In the more extreme *panic disorder,* anxiety escalates into periodic episodes of intense dread. Those with a *specific phobia* may be irrationally afraid of some object, activity, or situation.

48-2 What is *OCD*?

Persistent and repetitive thoughts (obsessions), actions (compulsions), or both characterize *obsessive-compulsive disorder (OCD)*.

48-3 What is *PTSD*?

Symptoms of *posttraumatic stress disorder (PTSD)* include four or more weeks of haunting memories, nightmares, hypervigilance, avoidance of trauma-related stimuli, social withdrawal, jumpy anxiety, numbness of feeling, and/or sleep problems following some traumatic experience.

48-4 What are *somatic symptom* and related disorders?

In *somatic symptom* and related disorders, including *illness anxiety disorder,* symptoms take a somatic (bodily) form without apparent physical cause.

48-5 How do conditioning, cognition, and biology contribute to the feelings and thoughts that mark anxiety-related disorders?

The learning perspective views anxiety-related disorders as products of fear conditioning, stimulus generalization, fearful-behavior reinforcement, and observational learning of others' fears and cognitions. The biological perspective considers genetic predispositions for high levels of emotional reactivity and neurotransmitter production; abnormal responses in the brain's fear circuits; and the role that fears of life-threatening dangers played in natural selection and evolution.

MODULE 49: Depressive Disorders and Bipolar Disorders

49-1 How do depressive disorders and bipolar disorders differ?

A person with *major depressive disorder* experiences at least five symptoms of depression (including either depressed mood or loss of interest or pleasure) for two or more weeks. Persistent depressive disorder includes a long-lasting mildly depressed mood. A person with a *bipolar disorder* experiences not only depression but also *mania*—episodes of hyperactive and wildly optimistic, impulsive behavior.

49-2 How can the biological and social-cognitive perspectives help us understand depressive disorders and bipolar disorders?

The biological perspective on depressive disorders and bipolar disorders focuses on genetic predispositions, abnormalities in brain structures and function (including those found in neurotransmitter systems), and nutritional (and drug) effects. The social-cognitive perspective views depression as an ongoing cycle of stressful experiences (interpreted through negative beliefs, attributions, and memories, often with relentless *rumination*) leading to negative moods, thoughts, and actions, thereby fueling new stressful experiences.

MODULE 50: Schizophrenia

50-1 What patterns of perceiving, thinking, and feeling characterize schizophrenia?

Schizophrenia is a *psychotic disorder* characterized by delusions, hallucinations, disorganized speech, and/or diminished, inappropriate emotional expression. Hallucinations are sensory experiences without sensory stimulation; *delusions* are false beliefs. Schizophrenia symptoms may be positive (the presence of inappropriate behaviors) or negative (the absence of appropriate behaviors).

50-2 How do *chronic schizophrenia* and *acute schizophrenia* differ?

Schizophrenia typically strikes during late adolescence, affects males slightly more often, and occurs in all cultures. In *chronic* (or process) *schizophrenia,* development is gradual and recovery is doubtful. In *acute* (or reactive) *schizophrenia,* onset is sudden—in reaction to stress—and prospects for recovery are brighter.

50-3 What brain abnormalities are associated with schizophrenia?

People with schizophrenia have an excess number of dopamine receptors, which may intensify brain signals, creating positive symptoms such as hallucinations and paranoia. Brain scans have revealed abnormal activity in the frontal lobes, thalamus, and amygdala, as well as a loss of neural connections across the brain network. Brain abnormalities associated with schizophrenia include enlarged, fluid-filled areas and corresponding shrinkage and thinning of cerebral tissue. Smaller-than-normal areas may include the cortex, the hippocampus, the corpus callosum, and the thalamus.

50-4 What prenatal events are associated with increased risk of developing schizophrenia?

Possible contributing factors include maternal diabetes, older paternal age, viral infections or famine conditions during the mother's pregnancy, and low weight or oxygen deprivation at birth.

50-5 How do genes influence schizophrenia? What factors may be early warning signs of schizophrenia in children?

Twin and adoption studies indicate that the predisposition to schizophrenia is inherited. Multiple genes interact to produce schizophrenia. No environmental causes invariably produce schizophrenia, but environmental events (such as prenatal viruses or maternal stress) may "turn on" genes in those who are predisposed to this disorder. Possible early warning signs include social withdrawal; a mother with severe and long-lasting schizophrenia;

birth complications; separation from parents; short attention span; poor muscle coordination; emotional unpredictability; poor peer relations and solo play; separation from parents; and childhood abuse.

MODULE 51: Dissociative, Personality, and Eating Disorders

51-1 What are *dissociative disorders,* and why are they controversial?

Dissociative disorders are controversial, rare conditions in which conscious awareness seems to become separated from previous memories, thoughts, and feelings. Skeptics note that *dissociative identity disorder (DID)* increased dramatically in the late twentieth century; is rarely found outside North America; and may reflect role playing by people vulnerable to therapists' suggestions. Others view DID as a manifestation of feelings of anxiety, or as a response learned when behaviors are reinforced by anxiety-reduction.

51-2 What are the three clusters of personality disorders? What behaviors and brain activity characterize antisocial personality disorder?

Personality disorders are inflexible and enduring behavior patterns that impair social functioning. The ten DSM-5 disorders tend to form three clusters, characterized by (1) anxiety, (2) eccentric or odd behaviors, and (3) dramatic or impulsive behaviors. *Antisocial personality disorder* (one of those in the third cluster) is characterized by a lack of conscience and, sometimes, by aggressive and fearless behavior. The amygdala is often smaller and the frontal lobes less active in people with this disorder, leading to impaired frontal lobe cognitive functions and decreased responsiveness to others' distress. Genetic predispositions may interact with the environment to produce these characteristics.

51-3 What are the three main eating disorders, and how do biological, psychological, and social-cultural influences make people more vulnerable to them?

In those with eating disorders (most often women or gay men), psychological factors overwhelm the body's tendency to maintain a normal weight. Despite being significantly underweight, people with *anorexia nervosa* (usually adolescent females) maintain a starvation diet, sometimes exercising excessively, and have an inaccurate self-perception. Those with *bulimia nervosa* (usually women in their late teens and early twenties) binge and then compensate by purging, fasting, or excessively exercising. Those with *binge-eating disorder* binge but do not follow with purging, fasting, and exercising. Cultural pressures, low self-esteem, and negative emotions interact with stressful life experiences and genetics to produce eating disorders.

MODULE 52: Neurodevelopmental Disorders

Neurodevelopmental disorders are central nervous system abnormalities (usually in the brain) that start in childhood and alter thinking and behavior (as in intellectual limitations or a psychological disorder).

52-1 What is an *intellectual disability?*

An *intellectual disability* is a condition of limited mental ability, indicated by an intelligence test score of 70 or below and difficulty adapting to the demands of life in three skill areas (conceptual, social, and practical).

52-2 What is *autism spectrum disorder?*

Autism spectrum disorder appears in childhood and is marked by significant limitations in communication and social interaction, as well as rigidly fixated interests and repetitive behaviors.

52-3 Why is there controversy over attention-deficit/hyperactivity disorder?

A child (or, less commonly, an adult) who displays extreme inattention and/or hyperactivity and impulsivity may be diagnosed with *attention-deficit/hyperactivity disorder (ADHD)*. Controversies center on whether the growing number of ADHD cases reflect overdiagnosis or increased awareness of the disorder, and on the long-term effects of stimulant-drug treatment.

Therapy

MODULE 53: Introduction to Therapy and the Psychological Therapies

53-1 How do *psychotherapy* and the *biomedical therapies* differ?

Psychotherapy is treatment involving psychological techniques that consists of interactions between a trained therapist and someone seeking to overcome psychological difficulties or achieve personal growth. The major psychotherapies derive from psychology's psychodynamic, humanistic, behavioral, and cognitive perspectives. *Biomedical therapy* treats psychological disorders with medications or procedures that act directly on a patient's physiology. An *eclectic approach* combines techniques from various forms of psychotherapy.

53-2 What are the goals and techniques of psychoanalysis, and how have they been adapted in psychodynamic therapy?

Through *psychoanalysis,* Sigmund Freud tried to give people self-insight and relief from their disorders by bringing anxiety-laden feelings and thoughts into conscious awareness. Psychoanalytic techniques included using free association and *interpretation* of instances of *resistance* and *transference.* *Psychodynamic therapy* has been influenced by traditional psychoanalysis but differs from it in many ways, including little attention to the concepts of id, ego, and superego. This contemporary therapy is briefer, less expensive, and more focused on helping the client find relief from current symptoms. Psychodynamic therapists help clients understand how past relationships create themes that may be acted out in present relationships.

53-3 What are the basic themes of humanistic therapy? What are the goals and techniques of Rogers' person-centered approach?

Both psychodynamic and humanistic therapies are *insight therapies*—they attempt to improve functioning by increasing people's awareness of motives and defenses. Humanistic therapy's goals include helping people grow in self-awareness and self-acceptance; promoting personal growth rather than curing illness; helping people take responsibility for their own growth; focusing on conscious thoughts rather than unconscious motivations; and seeing the present and future as more important than the past. Carl Rogers' *person-centered therapy* proposed that therapists' most important contribution is to function as a psychological mirror through *active listening* and to provide a growth-fostering environment of *unconditional positive regard.*

53-4 How does the basic assumption of behavior therapy differ from the assumptions of psychodynamic and humanistic therapies? What classical conditioning techniques are used in exposure therapies and aversive conditioning?

Behavior therapies are not insight therapies, and instead assume that problem behaviors *are* the problem. Their goal is to apply learning principles to modify these problem behaviors. Classical conditioning techniques, including *exposure therapies* (such as *systematic desensitization* or *virtual reality exposure therapy*) and *aversive conditioning,* attempt to change behaviors through *counterconditioning*—evoking new responses to old stimuli that trigger unwanted behaviors.

53-5 What is the main premise of therapy based on operant conditioning principles, and what are the views of its proponents and critics?

Operant conditioning operates under the premise that voluntary behaviors are strongly influenced by their consequences. Therapy based on operant conditioning principles therefore uses behavior modification techniques to change unwanted behaviors by positively reinforcing desired behaviors and ignoring or punishing undesirable behaviors. Critics maintain that (1) techniques such as those used in *token economies* may produce behavior changes that disappear when rewards end, and (2) deciding which behaviors should change is authoritarian and unethical. Proponents argue that treatment with positive rewards is more humane than punishing people or institutionalizing them for undesired behaviors.

53-6 What are the goals and techniques of the cognitive therapies and of cognitive-behavioral therapy?

The *cognitive therapies,* such as Aaron Beck's cognitive therapy for depression, assume that our thinking colors our feelings, and that the therapist's role is to change clients' self-defeating thinking by training them to perceive and interpret events in more constructive ways. The widely researched and practiced *cognitive-behavioral therapy (CBT)* combines cognitive therapy and behavior therapy by helping clients regularly try out their new ways of thinking and behaving in their everyday life. A newer CBT variation, dialectical behavior therapy (DBT), combines cognitive tactics for tolerating distress and regulating emotions with social skills training and mindfulness meditation.

53-7 What are the aims and benefits of group and family therapies?

Group therapy sessions can help more people with less cost than individual therapy. Clients may benefit in person or online from exploring feelings and developing social skills in a group situation, from learning that others have similar problems, and from getting feedback on new ways of behaving. *Family therapy* aims to help family members discover the roles they play within the family's interactive social system, improve communication, and learn new ways to prevent or resolve conflicts.

MODULE 54: Evaluating Psychotherapies

54-1 Does psychotherapy work? How can we know?

Clients' and therapists' positive testimonials cannot prove that psychotherapy is effective, and the placebo effect and *confirmation bias* make it difficult to judge whether improvement occurred because of the treatment. Using *meta-analyses* to statistically combine the results of hundreds of randomized psychotherapy outcome studies, researchers have found that those not undergoing treatment often improve, but those undergoing psychotherapy are more likely to improve—and to improve more quickly and with less risk of relapse.

54-2 Are some psychotherapies more effective than others for specific disorders?

No one type of psychotherapy is generally superior to all others. Therapy is most effective for those with clear-cut, specific problems. Some therapies—such as behavior conditioning for treating specific phobias and compulsions—are more effective for particular disorders. Cognitive and cognitive-behavioral therapies have been effective in coping with anxiety, posttraumatic stress disorder, insomnia, and depression; behavioral conditioning therapies with specific behavior problems; psychodynamic therapy for depression and anxiety; and nondirective (client-centered) counseling for mild to moderate depression. Abnormal states tend to return to normal on their own, and the placebo effect can create the impression that a treatment has been effective. *Evidence-based practice* integrates the best available research with clinicians' expertise and clients' culture, values, personality identity, and circumstances.

54-3 What three elements are shared by all forms of psychotherapy?

All psychotherapies offer new hope for demoralized people; a fresh perspective; and (if the therapist is effective) an empathic, trusting, and caring relationship. The emotional bond of trust and understanding between therapist and client—the *therapeutic alliance*—is an important element in effective therapy.

54-4 What personal factors influence the client-therapist relationship?

Therapists differ in the values that influence their goals in therapy and their views of progress. They may also differ from their clients. These differences may create problems if therapists and clients differ in their cultural, religious, or personal values and perspectives.

54-5 When should a person seek therapy, and what should people look for when selecting a therapist?

Campus health centers are generally good starting points for counseling options, and they may offer some free services. A person seeking therapy may want to ask about the therapist's treatment approach, values, credentials, and fees. An important consideration is whether the therapy seeker feels comfortable and able to establish a bond with the therapist. Recognizing the importance of a strong therapeutic alliance, the American Psychological Association accredits programs that provide training in cultural sensitivity and that recruit underrepresented cultural groups.

54-6 What ethical principles guide psychotherapy and psychological research on mental illness?

Psychotherapists and psychological researchers on mental health must follow their country's ethical principles and code of conduct, aiming to benefit others, to be honest and truthful, and to never expose people to greater risks than would be encountered in everyday life.

MODULE 55: The Biomedical Therapies and Preventing Psychological Disorders

55-1 Why is therapeutic lifestyle change considered an effective biomedical therapy, and how does it work?

Therapeutic lifestyle change is considered a biomedical therapy because it influences the way the brain responds. Mind and body are a unit; affect one and you will affect the other. Our exercise, nutrition, relationships, recreation, relaxation, and religious or spiritual engagement affect our mental health. People who undergo a program of aerobic exercise, adequate sleep, light exposure, social engagement, rumination reduction, and better nutrition have gained relief from depressive symptoms.

55-2 What are the drug therapies? How do double-blind studies help researchers evaluate a drug's effectiveness?

Psychopharmacology has helped make drug therapy the most widely used biomedical therapy. *Antipsychotic drugs* are used in treating schizophrenia; some block dopamine activity. Side effects may include tardive dyskinesia (involuntary movements of facial muscles, tongue, and limbs) or increased risk of obesity and diabetes. *Antianxiety drugs,* which depress central nervous system activity, are used to treat anxiety disorders, obsessive-compulsive disorder, and posttraumatic stress disorder, and can be addictive. *Antidepressant drugs,* which often increase the availability of serotonin and norepinephrine, are used to treat depression, anxiety disorders, obsessive-compulsive and related disorders, and posttraumatic stress disorder with modest effectiveness. Given their use in treating disorders other than depressive ones (from anxiety to strokes), these drugs are more often called SSRIs (selective serotonin reuptake inhibitors) rather than antidepressants. Quicker-acting antidepressants may include ketamine and microdoses of psychedelic drugs such as psilocybin. Lithium and Depakote are mood stabilizers prescribed for those with bipolar disorder. Studies may use a double-blind procedure to avoid the placebo effect and researcher bias.

55-3 How are brain stimulation and psychosurgery used in treating specific disorders?

Electroconvulsive therapy (ECT), in which a brief electric current is sent through the brain of an anesthetized patient, is an effective treatment for severe depression in people who have not responded to other therapy. Newer alternative treatments for depression include transcranial direct current stimulation (tDCS), *transcranial magnetic stimulation (TMS),* and deep-brain stimulation (DBS; may calm an overactive brain region linked with negative emotions in some patients). *Psychosurgery* removes or destroys brain tissue in hopes of modifying behavior. Radical psychosurgical procedures such as *lobotomy* are no longer performed. Today's microscale psychosurgery and MRI-guided precision brain surgery are rare, last-resort treatments because the effects are irreversible.

55-4 What may help prevent psychological disorders, and why is it important to develop resilience?

Preventive mental health programs are based on the idea that many psychological disorders could be prevented by transforming stressful and negative social contexts into more benevolent, nurturing environments that foster growth, self-confidence, and *resilience.* Struggling with challenges can lead to *posttraumatic growth.* Community psychologists work to prevent psychological disorders by turning destructive environments into more nurturing places that foster competence, health, and well-being.

(There are no learning objective questions in Appendix A, The Story of Psychology: A Timeline, and Appendix B, Career Fields in Psychology.)

APPENDIX C

Psychology at Work

WORK AND LIFE SATISFACTION

C-1 What is *flow*?

Flow is a completely involved, focused state of consciousness with diminished awareness of self and time. It results from fully engaging one's skills. Interests predict both performance and persistence, so people should find vocations with a strong person-environment fit.

INDUSTRIAL-ORGANIZATIONAL PSYCHOLOGY

C-2 What are industrial-organizational psychology's three key areas of study?

Three key areas of study related to *industrial-organizational (I/O) psychology* are *personnel, organizational,* and *human factors psychology.* Each uses psychological principles to study and benefit the wide range of today's workers, workplaces, and work activities.

PERSONNEL PSYCHOLOGY

C-3 How do personnel psychologists facilitate job seeking, employee selection, work placement, and performance appraisal?

Personnel psychologists work to provide training programs for job seekers, devise selection methods for new employees, recruit and evaluate diverse applicants, design and evaluate training programs, identify people's interests and strengths, analyze job content, appraise individual and organizational performance, and facilitate team building. Unstructured, subjective interviews foster the interviewer illusion; *structured interviews* pinpoint job-relevant strengths and are better predictors of performance. Checklists, graphic rating scales, and behavior rating scales are useful performance appraisal methods.

ORGANIZATIONAL PSYCHOLOGY

C-4 Why are organizational psychologists interested in employee satisfaction and engagement?

Organizational psychologists examine influences on worker satisfaction and productivity and facilitate organizational change. Employee satisfaction and engagement tend to correlate with organizational success; in fact, employee attitudes predict future business success.

C-5 How can leaders be most effective?

Effective leaders set specific, challenging goals and choose an appropriate *leadership* style. Leadership style may be goal-oriented (*task leadership*), group-oriented (*social leadership*), or some combination of the two. Effective management often involves positive reinforcement, fulfilling the need to belong, and participative management.

C-6 What cultural influences need to be considered when choosing an effective leadership style?

Project GLOBE studies cultural variations in leadership expectations. Leaders who fulfill expectations (being directive in some cultures or participative in others) tend to be successful. But thriving companies worldwide tend to focus on identifying and enhancing employee strengths; strengths-based leadership pays dividends everywhere.

HUMAN FACTORS PSYCHOLOGY

C-7 How do human factors psychologists work to create user-friendly machines and work settings?

Human factors psychologists contribute to human safety and improved design by encouraging developers and designers to consider human abilities and behaviors, to user-test their work before production and distribution, and to remain mindful of the curse of knowledge.

Answers to the *Retrieval Practice* and *Master the Material* Questions

The Story of Psychology

MODULE 1: What Is Psychology?

RETRIEVAL PRACTICE ANSWERS

RP-1 Evaluating evidence, appraising the source, assessing conclusions, and examining our own assumptions are essential parts of critical thinking. **RP-2** Scientific psychology began in Germany in 1879, when Wilhelm Wundt opened the first psychology laboratory. **RP-3** People's self-reports varied, depending on the experience and the person's intelligence and verbal ability. **RP-4** structuralism; functionalism. **RP-5** behaviorism; Freudian. **RP-6** It recaptured the field's early interest in mental processes and made them legitimate topics for scientific study. **RP-7** This is the process by which nature selects from chance variations the traits that best enable an organism to survive and reproduce in a particular environment. **RP-8** Psychological events stem from the interaction of nature and nurture, rather than from either of them acting alone. **RP-9** By incorporating three different levels of analysis, the biopsychosocial approach can provide a more complete view than any one perspective could offer. **RP-10** social-cultural; behavioral. **RP-11** i. b, ii. c, iii. a. **RP-12** testing effect. **RP-13** Survey, Question, Read, Retrieve, Review.

MASTER THE MATERIAL ANSWERS

1. Critical thinking is smart thinking. When evaluating media claims (even about topics you might not know much about), look for empirical evidence. Ask the following questions in your analysis: Are the claims based on anecdote, or on evidence? Are sources cited? If so, are they credible (are they affiliated with a credible institution, and have they conducted or written about scientific research)? What agenda might the author have? What alternative explanations are possible? **2.** Wilhelm Wundt. **3.** a. **4.** a. **5.** b. **6.** The environment (nurture) has an influence on us, but that influence is constrained by our biology (nature). Nature and nurture interact. People predisposed to be very tall (nature), for example, are unlikely to become Olympic gymnasts, no matter how hard they work (nurture). **7.** b. **8.** positive psychology. **9.** d. **10.** psychiatrist. **11.** c.

Thinking Critically With Psychological Science

MODULE 2: Research Strategies: How Psychologists Ask and Answer Questions

RETRIEVAL PRACTICE ANSWERS

RP-1 We often suffer from hindsight bias—after we've learned a situation's outcome, that outcome seems familiar and therefore obvious. **RP-2** A good theory *organizes* observed facts and implies hypotheses that offer testable *predictions* and, sometimes, practical applications. It also often stimulates further research. **RP-3** When other investigators are able to replicate an experiment with the same (or stronger) results, scientists can confirm the result and become more confident of its reliability. **RP-4** Case studies involve only one individual or group, so we can't know for sure whether the principles observed would apply to a larger population. **RP-5** Naturalistic observation does not explain behavior, and it does not control for all the factors that may influence behavior. Nevertheless, the descriptions it provides can be revealing, expanding our understanding and paving the way for future studies. **RP-6** An unrepresentative sample is a group that does not represent the entire population being studied. *Random sampling* helps researchers form a representative sample, because each member of the population has an equal chance of being included. **RP-7** 1. Negative, 2. Positive, 3. Positive, 4. Negative. **RP-8** The team's poor performance was not their typical behavior. The return to their normal—their winning streak—may just have been a case of regression toward the mean. **RP-9** In this case, as in many others, a third factor may explain the correlation: Golden anniversaries and baldness both accompany aging. **RP-10** Research designed to prevent the placebo effect randomly assigns participants to an *experimental group* (which receives the real treatment) or to a *control group* (which receives a placebo). A double-blind procedure prevents people's beliefs and hopes from affecting the results, because neither the participants nor those collecting the data know who receives the placebo. A comparison of the results will demonstrate whether the real treatment produces better results than *belief* in that

treatment. **RP-11** confounding variables. **RP-12** i. c, ii. a, iii. b. **RP-13** We learn more about the drug's effectiveness when we can compare the results of those who took the drug (the experimental group) with the results of those who did not (the control group). If we gave the drug to all 1000 participants, we would have no way of knowing whether the drug is serving as a placebo or is actually medically effective. **RP-14** Animal protection legislation, laboratory regulation and inspection, and local and university ethics committees (which screen research proposals) attempt to safeguard animal welfare. International psychological organizations urge researchers involving human participants to obtain *informed consent*, protect them from greater-than-usual harm and discomfort, treat their personal information confidentially, and *debrief* them fully at the end of the experiment. Institutional Review Boards serve to enforce these standards.

MASTER THE MATERIAL ANSWERS

1. Hindsight bias. **2.** d. **3.** hypothesis. **4.** c. **5.** representative. **6.** negative. **7.** scatterplot. **8.** a. **9.** Regression toward the mean is a statistical phenomenon describing the tendency of extreme scores or outcomes to return to normal after an unusual event. Without knowing this, we may inaccurately decide the return to normal was a result of our own behavior. **10.** a. **11.** (a) *Alcohol use is associated with violence. (One interpretation: Drinking triggers or unleashes aggressive behavior.)* Perhaps anger triggers drinking, or perhaps the same genes or child-raising practices are predisposing both drinking and aggression. (Here researchers have learned that drinking does indeed trigger aggressive behavior.) (b) *Educated people live longer, on average, than less-educated people. (One interpretation: Education lengthens life and enhances health.)* Perhaps richer people can afford more education and better health care. (Research supports this conclusion.) (c) *Teens engaged in team sports are less likely to use drugs, smoke, have sex, carry weapons, and eat junk food than are teens who do not engage in team sports. (One interpretation: Team sports encourage healthy living.)* Perhaps some third factor explains this correlation—teens who use drugs, smoke, have sex, carry weapons, and eat junk food may be "loners" who do not enjoy playing on any team.

(d) *Adolescents who frequently see smoking in movies are more likely to smoke. (One interpretation: Movie stars' behavior influences impressionable teens.)* Perhaps adolescents who smoke and attend movies frequently have less parental supervision and more access to spending money than other adolescents. **12.** experiments. **13.** placebo. **14.** c. **15.** independent variable. **16.** b. **17.** d.

MODULE 3: Statistical Reasoning in Everyday Life

RETRIEVAL PRACTICE ANSWERS

RP-1 Note how the y-axis of each graph is labeled. The range for the y-axis label in graph (a) is only from 95 to 100. The range for graph (b) is from 0 to 100. All the trucks rank as 95 percent and up, so almost all are still functioning after 10 years, which graph (b) makes clear. **RP-2** mean; mode; median; range; standard deviation. **RP-3** Averages based on fewer courses are more variable, which guarantees a greater number of extremely low and high marks at the end of the first term. **RP-4** Descriptive; inferential.

MASTER THE MATERIAL ANSWERS

1. b. **2.** d. **3.** normal curve. **4.** a.

The Biology of Mind

MODULE 4: Neural and Hormonal Systems

RETRIEVAL PRACTICE ANSWERS

RP-1 They share a focus on the links between the brain and behavior. Phrenology faded because it had no scientific basis—skull bumps don't reveal mental traits and abilities. **RP-2** Thanks to its *neuroplasticity*, our brain changes in response to the experiences we have. Learning and practicing a new skill, like playing an instrument, can promote the development of new neural pathways and cause lasting changes in brain organization. **RP-3** dendrites, cell body, axon. **RP-4** Stronger stimuli (the slap) cause more neurons to fire and to fire more frequently than happens with weaker stimuli (the tap). **RP-5** Neurons send neurotransmitters (chemical messengers) across this tiny space between one neuron's terminal branch and the next neuron's dendrite or cell body. **RP-6** Reuptake occurs when excess neurotransmitters are reabsorbed by the sending neuron. Neurotransmitters can also drift away or be broken down by enzymes. **RP-7** neurotransmitters. **RP-8** Morphine is an agonist; curare is an antagonist. **RP-9** i. c, ii. a, iii. b. **RP-10** The sympathetic division of the autonomic nervous system would have directed arousal (accelerated heartbeat, inhibited digestion, and so forth), and the parasympathetic division would have directed calming. **RP-11** Responding to signals from the hypothalamus, the pituitary releases hormones that trigger other endocrine glands to secrete hormones, which in turn influence brain and behavior. **RP-12** Both of these communication systems produce chemical molecules that act on the body's receptors to influence our behavior and emotions. The endocrine system, which secretes hormones into the bloodstream, delivers its messages much more slowly than the speedy nervous system, and the effects of the endocrine system's messages tend to linger much longer than those of the nervous system.

MASTER THE MATERIAL ANSWERS

1. The human brain is uniquely designed to be flexible; it can reorganize after damage and it can build new pathways based on experience. This plasticity enables us to adapt to our changing world. **2.** axon. **3.** c. **4.** a. **5.** neurotransmitters. **6.** b. **7.** c. **8.** autonomic. **9.** central. **10.** a. **11.** adrenal glands.

MODULE 5: Tools of Discovery, Older Brain Structures, and the Limbic System

RETRIEVAL PRACTICE ANSWERS

RP-1 i. b, ii. a, iii. c. **RP-2** brainstem. **RP-3** (a) cerebellum, (b) thalamus, (c) reticular formation, (d) medulla. **RP-4** The sympathetic nervous system. **RP-5** (a) The *amygdala* is involved in aggression and fear responses. (b) The *hypothalamus* is involved in bodily maintenance, pleasurable rewards, and control of the hormonal systems. (c) The *hippocampus* processes memories of facts and events.

MASTER THE MATERIAL ANSWERS

1. b. **2.** d. **3.** c. **4.** cerebellum. **5.** b. **6.** amygdala. **7.** b. **8.** hypothalamus.

MODULE 6: The Cerebral Cortex

RETRIEVAL PRACTICE ANSWERS

RP-1 the brainstem; the cerebral cortex. **RP-2** (a) The right limbs' opposed activities interfere with each other because both are controlled by the same (left) side of your brain. (b) Opposite sides of your brain control your left and right limbs, so the reversed motion causes less interference. **RP-3** somatosensory; motor. **RP-4** Association areas are involved in higher mental functions—interpreting, integrating, and acting on information processed in other areas. **RP-5** (a) yes, (b) no, (c) green.

MASTER THE MATERIAL ANSWERS

1. d. **2.** The visual cortex is a neural network of sensory neurons connected via interneurons to other neural networks, including auditory networks. If you can see and hear, this allows you to integrate visual and auditory information to respond when a friend you recognize greets you at a party. **3.** c. **4.** frontal. **5.** association areas. **6.** c. **7.** ON; HER. **8.** a. **9.** b.

Consciousness and the Two-Track Mind

MODULE 7: Basic Consciousness Concepts

RETRIEVAL PRACTICE ANSWERS

RP-1 cognitive neuroscience. **RP-2** Our *selective attention* allows us to focus on only a limited portion of our surroundings. *Inattentional blindness* explains why we don't perceive some things when we are distracted. *Change blindness,* for example, happens when we fail to notice a relatively unimportant change in our environment. These principles help magicians fool us, as they direct our attention elsewhere to perform their tricks. **RP-3** Our mind simultaneously processes information on a conscious track and an unconscious track (dual processing) as we organize and interpret information.

MASTER THE MATERIAL ANSWERS

1. inattentional blindness. **2.** unconscious; conscious. **3.** selective.

MODULE 8: Sleep and Dreams

RETRIEVAL PRACTICE ANSWERS

RP-1 With each refugee cycling through the sleep stages independently, at any given time at least one likely will be in an easily awakened stage. **RP-2** REM, N1, N2, N3; normally we move through N1, then N2, then N3, then back up through N2 before we experience REM sleep. **RP-3** i. b, ii. c, iii. a. **RP-4** suprachiasmatic; circadian. **RP-5** (1) Sleep has survival value. (2) Sleep helps us restore the immune system, heal from infection, and repair brain tissue. (3) During sleep we consolidate memories. (4) Sleep fuels creativity. (5) Sleep plays a role in the growth process. **RP-6** quick reaction times; gain weight. **RP-7** (1) Freud's wish-fulfillment (dreams as a psychic safety valve), (2) information-processing (dreams sort the day's events and consolidate memories), (3) physiological function (dreams pave neural pathways), (4) activation-synthesis (REM sleep triggers random neural activity that the mind weaves into stories), and

(5) cognitive development (dreams reflect the dreamer's developmental stage).

MASTER THE MATERIAL ANSWERS

1. circadian rhythm. **2.** b. **3.** N3. **4.** It increases in duration. **5.** c. **6.** With narcolepsy, the person periodically falls directly into REM sleep, with no warning; with sleep apnea, the person repeatedly awakens during the night. **7.** d. **8.** The activation-synthesis theory suggests that dreams are the brain's attempt to synthesize random neural activity. **9.** The information-processing explanation of dreaming proposes that brain activity during REM sleep enables us to sift through the daily events and activities we have been thinking about (*what one has dwelt on by day*). **10.** REM rebound.

MODULE 9: Drugs and Consciousness

RETRIEVAL PRACTICE ANSWERS

RP-1 With repeated exposure to a psychoactive drug, the user's brain chemistry adapts and the drug's effect lessens. Thus, it takes bigger doses to get the desired effect. **RP-2** Unless it becomes compulsive or dysfunctional, simply having a strong interest in shopping is not the same as having a physical addiction to a drug. It typically does not involve obsessive craving in spite of known negative consequences. **RP-3** depressants. **RP-4** Nicotine-withdrawal symptoms include strong cravings, insomnia, anxiety, irritability, and distractibility. However, if your friend sticks with it, the craving and withdrawal symptoms will gradually dissipate over about 6 months. **RP-5** Psychoactive drugs create pleasure by altering brain chemistry. With repeated use of the drug, the user develops tolerance and needs more of the drug to achieve the desired effect. (Marijuana is an exception.) Discontinuing use of the substance then produces painful or psychologically unpleasant withdrawal symptoms. **RP-6** Nicotine is powerfully addictive, and those who start paving the neural pathways when young may find it very hard to stop using it. As a result, tobacco companies may have lifelong customers. Moreover, evidence suggests that if cigarette manufacturers haven't hooked customers by early adulthood, they most likely won't. **RP-7** Possible explanations include (a) biological factors (a person could have a biological predisposition to both early use and later abuse, or alcohol use could modify a person's neural pathways); (b) psychological factors (early use could establish taste preferences for alcohol); and (c) social-cultural factors (early use could influence enduring habits, attitudes, activities, or peer relationships that could foster alcohol use disorder).

MASTER THE MATERIAL ANSWERS

1. tolerance. **2.** a. **3.** Alcohol is a disinhibitor—it makes us more likely to do what we would have done when sober, whether that is being helpful or being aggressive. **4.** d. **5.** hallucinogenic. **6.** a. **7.** b.

Nature, Nurture, and Human Diversity

MODULE 10: Behavior Genetics: Predicting Individual Differences

RETRIEVAL PRACTICE ANSWERS

RP-1 gene, chromosome, nucleus. **RP-2** Researchers use twin and adoption studies to understand how much variation among individuals is due to genetic makeup and how much is due to environmental factors. Some studies compare the traits and behaviors of identical twins (same genes) and fraternal twins (different genes, as in any two siblings). They also compare adopted children with their adoptive and biological parents. Some studies compare traits and behaviors of twins raised together or separately. **RP-3** genes. **RP-4** i. c, ii. b, iii. a.

MASTER THE MATERIAL ANSWERS

1. chromosomes. **2.** gene. **3.** b. **4.** c. **5.** Identical (monozygotic). **6.** b. **7.** temperament. **8.** Heritability. **9.** environments.

MODULE 11: Evolutionary Psychology: Understanding Human Nature

RETRIEVAL PRACTICE ANSWERS

RP-1 Over many generations, Belyaev and Trut selected and bred foxes that exhibited a trait they desired: tameness. This process is similar to naturally occurring selection, but it differs in that natural selection is much slower, and normally favors traits (including those arising from mutations) that contribute to reproduction and survival. **RP-2** Evolutionary psychologists theorize that females have inherited their ancestors' tendencies to be more cautious sexually because of the challenges associated with incubating and nurturing offspring. Males have inherited a tendency to be more casual about sex, because their act of fathering requires a smaller investment. **RP-3** First, it starts with an effect and works backward to propose an explanation. Second, this explanation may overlook the effects of cultural expectations and socialization. Third, men could use such explanations to rationalize irresponsible behavior toward women.

MASTER THE MATERIAL ANSWERS

1. differences; commonalities. **2.** c. **3.** *Natural selection* favors traits and behaviors that enable survival and reproduction. Evolutionary psychologists argue that women are choosier about their mates because of the investment required to incubate, birth, protect, and nurse children. Straight women tend to prefer men who seem capable of supporting and protecting their joint offspring. Men, who have less at stake, tend to be more casual about sex, and straight men tend to prefer women whose traits convey health and fertility.

MODULE 12: Cultural and Gender Diversity: Understanding Nature and Nurture

RETRIEVAL PRACTICE ANSWERS

RP-1 Adolescents tend to *select* similar others and to sort themselves into like-minded groups. For an athletic teen, this could lead to finding other athletic teens and joining school teams together. **RP-2** Individualists give priority to personal goals over group goals and tend to define their identity in terms of their own personal attributes. Collectivists give priority to group goals over individual goals and tend to define their identity in terms of group identifications. **RP-3** Women; men. **RP-4** seven; puberty. **RP-5** *Gender roles* are social rules or norms for expected behaviors for women and men. The norms associated with various roles, including gender roles, vary widely in different cultural contexts, which is proof that we are able to learn and adapt to the social demands of different environments. **RP-6** The biopsychosocial approach considers all the factors that influence our individual development: biological factors (including evolution and our genes, hormones, and brain), psychological factors (including our experiences, beliefs, feelings, and expectations), and social-cultural factors (including parental and peer influences, cultural individualism or collectivism, and gender norms).

MASTER THE MATERIAL ANSWERS

1. b. **2.** sex; gender. **3.** c. **4.** Y. **5.** d. **6.** 10; 12. **7.** intersex. **8.** b. **9.** gender identity.

Developing Through the Life Span

MODULE 13: Developmental Issues, Prenatal Development, and the Newborn

RETRIEVAL PRACTICE ANSWERS

RP-1 continuity; stages. **RP-2** (1) Stage theory is supported by the work of Piaget (cognitive development), Kohlberg (moral development), and Erikson (psychosocial development). (2) Some traits, such as temperament, exhibit remarkable stability across many years. **RP-3** zygote; fetus; embryo. **RP-4** habituation.

MASTER THE MATERIAL ANSWERS

1. Cross-sectional studies compare people of different ages at one point in time. Longitudinal studies restudy and retest the same people over a long period of time. **2.** continuity/stages. **3.** b. **4.** c. **5.** teratogens.

MODULE 14: Infancy and Childhood

RETRIEVAL PRACTICE ANSWERS

RP-1 maturation. **RP-2** Object permanence for the sensorimotor stage, pretend play for the preoperational stage, conservation for the concrete operational stage, and abstract logic for the formal operational stage. **RP-3** i. d, ii. b, iii. c, iv. c, v. a, vi. b. **RP-4** Theory of mind focuses on our ability to understand our own and others' mental states. Those with autism spectrum disorder struggle with this ability. **RP-5** Attachment is the normal process by which we form emotional ties with important others. Imprinting occurs only in certain animals that have a critical period very early in their development during which they must form their attachments, and they do so in an inflexible manner. **RP-6** The authoritarian style would be described as too hard, the permissive style too soft, the neglectful style too uncaring, and the authoritative style just right. Parents using the authoritative style tend to have children with high self-esteem, self-reliance, self-regulation, and social competence.

MASTER THE MATERIAL ANSWERS

1. a. **2.** frontal. **3.** b. **4.** We consciously recall little from before age 4, in part because major brain areas have not yet matured. **5.** Infants in Piaget's *sensorimotor stage* tend to be focused only on their own perceptions of the world and may, for example, be unaware that objects continue to exist when unseen. A child in the *preoperational stage* is still egocentric and incapable of appreciating simple logic, such as the reversibility of operations. A preteen in the *concrete operational stage* is beginning to think logically about concrete events but not about abstract concepts. **6.** a. **7.** stranger anxiety. **8.** Before these studies, many psychologists believed that infants simply became attached to those who nourished them.

MODULE 15: Adolescence

RETRIEVAL PRACTICE ANSWERS

RP-1 preconventional; postconventional; conventional. **RP-2** Kohlberg's work reflected an individualist worldview, so his theory is less culturally universal than he supposed. **RP-3** i. g, ii. h, iii. c, iv. f, v. e, vi. d, vii. a, viii. b.

MASTER THE MATERIAL ANSWERS

1. b. **2.** formal operational. **3.** b. **4.** emerging adulthood.

MODULE 16: Adulthood

RETRIEVAL PRACTICE ANSWERS

RP-1 love; work. **RP-2** Challenges: decline of muscular strength, reaction times, stamina, sensory keenness, cardiac output, and immune system functioning. Risk of cognitive decline increases. Rewards: positive feelings tend to grow; negative emotions subside; and anger, stress, worry, and social-relationship problems decrease.

MASTER THE MATERIAL ANSWERS

1. a. **2.** generativity. **3.** c.

Sensation and Perception

MODULE 17: Basic Concepts of Sensation and Perception

RETRIEVAL PRACTICE ANSWERS

RP-1 *Sensation* is the bottom-up process by which your sensory receptors and your nervous system receive and represent stimuli. *Perception* is the top-down process by which your brain creates meaning by organizing and interpreting what your senses detect. **RP-2** *Absolute threshold* is the minimum stimulation needed to detect a particular sound (such as an approaching bike on the sidewalk behind you) 50 percent of the time. *Subliminal* stimulation happens when, without your awareness, your sensory system processes a sound that is below your absolute threshold. A *difference threshold* is the minimum difference needed to distinguish between two stimuli (such as between the sound of a bike and the sound of a runner coming up behind you) 50 percent of the time. **RP-3** The shoes provide constant stimulation. Thanks to *sensory adaptation,* we tend to focus primarily on changing stimuli. **RP-4** *Perceptual set* involves top-down processing, because it draws on your experiences, assumptions, and expectations when interpreting stimuli.

MASTER THE MATERIAL ANSWERS

1. b. **2.** perception. **3.** d. **4.** just noticeable difference. **5.** b. **6.** d. **7.** a.

MODULE 18: Vision: Sensory and Perceptual Processing

RETRIEVAL PRACTICE ANSWERS

RP-1 Your blind spot is on the nose side of each retina, which means that objects to your right may fall onto the right eye's blind spot. Objects to your left may fall on the left eye's blind spot. The blind spot does not normally impair your vision, because your eyes are moving and because one eye catches what the other misses. Moreover, even with only one eye open, your brain gives you a perception without a hole in it. **RP-2** rods; cones; color. **RP-3** pupils. **RP-4** The *Young-Helmholtz trichromatic theory* shows that the retina contains color receptors for red, green, and blue. The *opponent-process theory* shows that we have opponent-process cells in the retina and thalamus for red-green, blue-yellow, and white-black. These theories are complementary and outline the two stages of color vision. First, the retina's receptors for red, green, and blue respond to different color stimuli. Second, the receptors' signals are then processed by the opponent-process cells on their way to the visual cortex in the brain. **RP-5** Light waves reflect off the person and travel into your eyes. Receptor cells in your retina convert the light waves' energy into neural impulses sent to your brain. Your brain detector cells and work teams process the subdimensions of this visual input—including color, movement, form, and depth—separately but simultaneously. Your brain interprets this information, based on previously stored information and your expectations, and forms a conscious perception of your friend. **RP-6** figure; ground. **RP-7** Gestalt psychologists used this saying to describe our perceptual tendency to organize clusters of sensations into meaningful forms or coherent groups. **RP-8** We are normally able to perceive depth thanks to both binocular cues (such as retinal disparity) and monocular cues (which include relative height, relative size, relative motion, linear perspective, and interposition).

MASTER THE MATERIAL ANSWERS

1. wavelength. **2.** a. **3.** c. **4.** c. **5.** d. **6.** Your brain constructs this perception of color in two stages. In the first stage, the lemon reflects light energy into your eyes, where it is transformed into neural messages. Three sets of cones, each sensitive to a different light frequency (red, blue, and green) process color. In this case, the light energy stimulates both red-sensitive and green-sensitive cones. In the second stage, opponent-process cells sensitive to paired opposites of color (red/green, blue/yellow, and black/white) evaluate the incoming neural messages as they pass through your optic nerve to the thalamus and visual cortex. When the yellow-sensitive opponent-process cells are stimulated, you identify the lemon as yellow. **7.** feature detectors. **8.** parallel processing. **9.** a. **10.** d. **11.** b. **12.** c. **13.** monocular. **14.** b. **15.** b. **16.** perceptual adaptation.

MODULE 19: The Nonvisual Senses

RETRIEVAL PRACTICE ANSWERS

RP-1 The outer ear collects sound waves, which are translated into mechanical waves by the *middle ear* and turned into fluid waves in the *inner ear*. The *auditory nerve* then translates the energy into electrical waves and sends them to the brain, which perceives and interprets the sound. **RP-2** loudness. **RP-3** lower; lower. **RP-4** place theory; frequency theory. **RP-5** c. **RP-6** We have four basic touch senses and five basic taste sensations. But we have no specific smell receptors. Instead, different combinations of odor receptors send messages to the brain, enabling us to recognize some 1 trillion different smells. **RP-7** Kinesthetic receptors, called proprioceptors, are located in our joints, tendons, and muscles. Vestibular sense receptors are located in our inner ear. **RP-8** The ESP event would need to be replicated in other scientific studies.

MASTER THE MATERIAL ANSWERS

1. cochlea. **2.** Sound waves are collected by the outer ear, translated into mechanical waves by the *middle ear,* and turned into fluid waves in the *inner ear.* The *auditory nerve* then translates this energy into electrical waves and sends them to the brain, which interprets the sound. **3.** Place; frequency; volley. **4.** nociceptors. **5.** c. **6.** Our experience of pain is influenced by biological factors (such as genetic differences in endorphin production), psychological factors (such as our attention), and social-cultural factors (such as the presence of others). **7.** We have specialized receptors for detecting sweet, salty, sour, bitter, and umami tastes. Being able to detect pleasurable tastes enabled our ancestors to seek out energy- or protein-rich foods. Detecting aversive tastes deterred them from eating toxic substances, increasing their chances of survival. **8.** Kinesthesia; vestibular sense. **9.** Your vestibular sense regulates balance and body positioning through kinesthetic receptors triggered by fluid in your inner ear. Wobbly legs and a spinning world are signs that these receptors are still responding to the ride's turbulence. As your vestibular sense adjusts to solid ground, your balance will be restored. **10.** d. **11.** d.

Learning

MODULE 20: Basic Learning Concepts and Classical Conditioning

RETRIEVAL PRACTICE ANSWERS

RP-1 Habits form when we repeat behaviors in a given context and, as a result, learn associations—often without our awareness. For example, we may have eaten a sweet pastry with a cup of coffee often enough to associate the flavor of the coffee with the treat, so that the cup of coffee alone just doesn't seem right anymore! **RP-2** NS = tone before conditioning; US = air puff; UR = blink to air puff; CS = tone after conditioning; CR = blink to tone. **RP-3** The cake (including its taste) is the US. The associated aroma is the CS. Salivation to the aroma is the CR. **RP-4** acquisition; extinction. **RP-5** generalization. **RP-6** If viewing an admired actor (a US) elicits a positive response (a UR), then pairing the US with a new NS (the beverage) could turn the beverage into a conditioned stimulus (CS) that also becomes positive, a conditioned response (CR). **RP-7** The US was the loud noise; the UR was the fear response to the noise; the NS was the rat before it was paired with the noise; the CS was the rat after pairing; the CR was fear of the rat.

MASTER THE MATERIAL ANSWERS

1. information; behaviors. **2.** c. **3.** conditioned. **4.** discrimination. **5.** b. **6.** A sexual image is a US that triggers a UR of interest or arousal. Before the ad pairs a product with a sexual image, the product is an NS. Over time the product can become a CS that triggers the CR of interest or arousal.

MODULE 21: Operant Conditioning

RETRIEVAL PRACTICE ANSWERS

RP-1 do not; resulting. **RP-2** The baby negatively reinforces her parents' behavior when she stops crying once they grant her wish. Her parents positively reinforce her cries by letting her sleep with them. **RP-3** Spammers are reinforced on a variable-ratio schedule (after sending a varying number of emails). Cookie checkers are reinforced on a fixed-interval schedule. Sandwich shop rewards programs use a fixed-ratio schedule. **RP-4** 1. PR (positive reinforcement); 2. NP (negative punishment); 3. PP (positive punishment); 4. NR (negative reinforcement). **RP-5** If Joslyn is seeking attention, the teacher's scolding may be reinforcing rather than punishing. To change Joslyn's behavior, her teacher could offer reinforcement (such as praise) each time she behaves well. The teacher might encourage Joslyn toward increasingly appropriate behavior through shaping, or by rephrasing rules as rewards instead of punishments. ("You can use the blocks if you play nicely with the other children" [reward] rather than "You may not use the blocks if you misbehave!" [punishment].) **RP-6** respondent; operant.

MASTER THE MATERIAL ANSWERS

1. Skinner. **2.** shaping. **3.** b. **4.** Your instructor could reinforce your attentive behavior by taking away something you dislike. For example, your instructor could offer to shorten the length of an assigned paper or replace standard lecture time with an interesting in-class activity. In both cases, the instructor would remove something aversive in order to negatively reinforce your focused attention. **5.** partial (intermittent). **6.** a. **7.** variable-interval. **8.** c.

MODULE 22: Biology, Cognition, and Learning

RETRIEVAL PRACTICE ANSWERS

RP-1 Garcia and Koelling demonstrated that rats may learn an aversion to tastes, on which their survival depends, but not to sights or sounds. **RP-2** The success of operant conditioning is affected not just by environmental cues, but also by biological and cognitive factors. **RP-3** Emily may be more likely to speed. Observational learning studies suggest that children tend to do as others do and say what they say. **RP-4** i. c, ii. d, iii. a, iv. e, v. b.

MASTER THE MATERIAL ANSWERS

1. taste-aversion. **2.** This finding supports Darwin's principle that natural selection favors traits that aid survival. **3.** cognitive map. **4.** latent learning. **5.** observational learning. **6.** vicarious; vicarious. **7.** a. **8.** mirror. **9.** c.

Memory

MODULE 23: Studying and Encoding Memories

RETRIEVAL PRACTICE ANSWERS

RP-1 recognition; recall. **RP-2** It would be better to test your memory with *recall* (such as with short-answer or fill-in-the-blank self-test questions) rather than *recognition* (such as with multiple-choice questions). Recalling information is harder than recognizing it. So if you can recall it, that means your retention of the material is better than if you could only recognize it. Your chances of test success are therefore greater. **RP-3** The Atkinson-Shiffrin model viewed short-term memory as a temporary holding space for briefly storing recent thoughts and experiences. The newer idea of *working memory* expands our understanding of Atkinson-Shiffrin's short-term memory stage, emphasizing the conscious, active processing that takes place as the brain makes sense of new experiences and links them with our long-term memories. **RP-4** Working memory's two basic functions are active integration of new information with existing long-term memories and focusing of our spotlight of attention. **RP-5** *Automatic* processing occurs unconsciously (automatically) for such things as the sequence and frequency of a day's events, and reading and comprehending words in our own language(s). *Effortful* processing requires attentive awareness and happens, for example, when we work hard to learn new material in class, or new lines for a play. **RP-6** sensory memory. **RP-7** Although cramming and rereading may lead to short-term gains in knowledge, distributed practice and repeated self-testing will result in the greatest long-term retention. **RP-8** Making material personally meaningful involves processing at a deep level, because you are processing *semantically*—based on the meaning of the words. Deep processing leads to greater retention.

MASTER THE MATERIAL ANSWERS

1. recall. **2.** encoding; storage; retrieval. **3.** a. **4.** iconic; echoic. **5.** seven. **6.** mnemonics.

MODULE 24: Storing and Retrieving Memories

RETRIEVAL PRACTICE ANSWERS

RP-1 The cerebellum and basal ganglia are important for *implicit* memory processing, and the frontal lobes and hippocampus are key to *explicit* memory formation. **RP-2** Our *explicit* conscious memories of facts and episodes differ from our *implicit* memories of skills (such as tying shoelaces) and classically conditioned responses. The parts of the brain involved in explicit memory processing (the frontal lobes and hippocampus) may have sustained damage in the accident, while the parts involved in implicit memory processing (the cerebellum and basal ganglia) appear to have escaped harm. **RP-3** the amygdala. **RP-4** long-term potentiation. **RP-5** *Priming* is the activation (often without our awareness) of associations. Seeing a gun, for example, might temporarily predispose someone to interpret an ambiguous face as threatening or to recall a boss as nasty. **RP-6** serial position.

MASTER THE MATERIAL ANSWERS

1. a. **2.** implicit. **3.** c. **4.** retrieval cues. **5.** Memories are stored within a web of many associations, one of which is mood. When you recall happy moments from your past, you activate these positive links. You may then experience mood-congruent memory and recall other happy moments, which could improve your mood and brighten your interpretation of current events. **6.** a.

MODULE 25: Forgetting, Memory Construction, and Improving Memory

RETRIEVAL PRAPCTICE ANSWERS

RP-1 First, through *encoding failure*: Unattended information never entered our memory system. Second, through *storage decay*: Information fades from our memory. Third, through *retrieval failure*: We cannot access stored information accurately, sometimes due to interference or motivated forgetting. **RP-2** repress. **RP-3** Real experiences would be confused with those we dreamed. When seeing people we know, we might therefore be unsure whether we were reacting to something they previously did or to something we dreamed they did. **RP-4** It will be important to remember the key points agreed upon by most researchers and professional associations: Sexual abuse, injustice, forgetting, and memory construction all happen; recovered memories are common; memories from before age 4 are unreliable; memories claimed to be recovered through hypnosis are especially unreliable; and memories, whether real or false, can be emotionally upsetting. **RP-5** Spend more time rehearsing or actively thinking about the material to boost long-term recall. Consider a study group so you can verbalize your learning. Schedule spaced (not crammed) study times. Make the material personally meaningful, with well-organized and vivid associations. Refresh your memory by returning to contexts and moods to activate retrieval cues. Use mnemonic devices. Minimize proactive and retroactive interference. Plan ahead to ensure a complete night's sleep. Test yourself repeatedly—retrieval practice is a proven retention strategy.

MASTER THE MATERIAL ANSWERS

1. d. **2.** d. **3.** retroactive. **4.** repression. **5.** b. **6.** Eliza's immature hippocampus and minimal verbal skills made it impossible for her to encode an explicit memory of the wedding reception at the age of two. It's more likely that Eliza learned information (from hearing the story repeatedly) that she eventually constructed into a memory that feels very real. **7.** source amnesia. **8.** déjà vu. **9.** b. **10.** b.

Thinking and Language

MODULE 26: Thinking

RETRIEVAL PRACTICE ANSWERS

RP-1 If a tragic event such as a plane crash makes the news, it is noteworthy and unusual, unlike much more common bad events, such as traffic accidents. Knowing this, we can worry less about unlikely events and think more about improving the safety of our everyday activities. (For example, we can wear a seat belt when in a vehicle and use the crosswalk when walking.) **RP-2** i. b, ii. c, iii. e, iv. d, v. a, vi. f, vii. h, viii. j, ix. i, x. g, xi. k.

MASTER THE MATERIAL ANSWERS

1. concept. **2.** algorithm. **3.** Oscar will need to guard against *confirmation bias* (searching for support for his own views and ignoring contradictory evidence) as he seeks out opposing viewpoints. Even if Oscar encounters new information that disproves his beliefs, *belief perseverance* may lead him to cling to these views anyway. It will take more compelling evidence to change his political beliefs than it took to create them. **4.** c. **5.** availability. **6.** framing. **7.** b. **8.** neural networks.

MODULE 27: Language and Thought

RETRIEVAL PRACTICE ANSWERS

RP-1 Two morphemes—*cat* and *s*, and four phonemes—*c*, *a*, *t*, and *s*. **RP-2** Chomsky maintained that humans are biologically predisposed to learn the grammar rules of language. **RP-3** Infants normally start developing *receptive language* skills (ability to understand what is said to and about them) around 4 months of age. Then, starting with babbling at 4 months and beyond, infants normally start building *productive language* skills (ability to produce sounds and eventually words). **RP-4** Our brain's *critical period* for language learning is in childhood, when we can absorb language structure almost effortlessly. As we move past that stage in our brain's development, our ability to learn a new language diminishes dramatically. **RP-5** Broca's area; Wernicke's area. **RP-6** These are definitely communications. But if language consists of words and the grammatical rules we use to combine them to communicate meaning, few scientists would label a dog's barking and yipping as language. **RP-7** linguistic determinism. **RP-8** Mental practice uses visual imagery to mentally rehearse future behaviors, activating some of the same brain areas used during the actual behaviors. Visualizing the details of the process is more effective than visualizing only your end goal.

MASTER THE MATERIAL ANSWERS

1. c. **2.** phonemes; morphemes; grammar. **3.** telegraphic speech. **4.** universal grammar. **5.** a.

Intelligence

MODULE 28: What Is Intelligence?

RETRIEVAL PRACTICE ANSWERS

RP-1 People with savant syndrome have limited mental ability overall but possess one or more exceptional skills. According to Howard Gardner, this suggests that our abilities come in separate packages rather than being fully expressed by one general intelligence that encompasses all of our talents. **RP-2** Intelligence is composed of both a broad ability factor as well as other specific abilities, such as reading ability, memory capacity, and processing speed.

MASTER THE MATERIAL ANSWERS

1. general intelligence. **2.** c. **3.** analytical; creative; practical. **4.** d.

MODULE 29: Intelligence Assessment and Dynamics

RETRIEVAL PRACTICE ANSWERS

RP-1 Binet hoped that determining the child's mental age (the age that typically corresponds to a certain level of performance) would help identify appropriate school placements. **RP-2** 125 (5/4 × 100 = 125). **RP-3** aptitude; achievement. **RP-4** A psychological test must be *standardized* (pretested on a representative sample of people), *reliable* (yielding consistent results), and *valid* (measuring and predicting what it is supposed to). **RP-5** disagreement; down; zero; agreement; up. **RP-6** Researcher A should develop a *longitudinal study* to examine how intelligence changes in the same people over the life span. Researcher B should develop a *cross-sectional study* to examine the intelligence of people now at various life stages.

MASTER THE MATERIAL ANSWERS

1. d (9/6 × 100 = 150). **2.** c. **3.** reliability. **4.** c. **5.** Writers' work relies more on Gc (crystallized intelligence)—accumulated knowledge that increases with age. For top performance, scientists doing research may need more Gf (the speedy and abstract reasoning of fluid intelligence), which tends to decrease with age.

MODULE 30: Genetic and Environmental Influences on Intelligence

RETRIEVAL PRACTICE ANSWERS

RP-1 a. (Heritability—variation explained by genetic influences—will increase as environmental variation decreases.) **RP-2** Perfectly equal opportunity would create 100 percent heritability, because genes alone would account for any human differences. **RP-3** A test may be *culturally* "biased" (unfair) if higher scores are achieved by those with certain cultural experiences. That same test is not scientifically biased as long as it has *predictive validity*—if it predicts what it is supposed to predict. For example, the SAT may favor those with experience in the U.S. school system, but it does still accurately predict U.S. college success. **RP-4** stereotype threat.

MASTER THE MATERIAL ANSWERS

1. c. **2.** a. **3.** c. **4.** Stereotype threat.

What Drives Us: Hunger, Sex, Belonging, and Achievement

MODULE 31: Basic Motivational Concepts

RETRIEVAL PRACTICE ANSWERS

RP-1 (a) Well-practiced runners tend to excel when aroused by competition. (b) High anxiety about a difficult exam may disrupt test-takers' performance. **RP-2** According to Maslow, our drive to meet the physiological needs of hunger and thirst takes priority over our safety needs, prompting us to take risks at times.

MASTER THE MATERIAL ANSWERS

1. b. **2.** a. **3.** incentive. **4.** Arousal. **5.** b. **6.** a.

MODULE 32: Hunger

RETRIEVAL PRACTICE ANSWERS

RP-1 low; high. **RP-2** You have learned to respond to the sight and aroma that signal the food about to enter your mouth. Both *physiological* cues (low blood sugar) and *psychological* cues (anticipation of the tasty meal) heighten your experienced hunger. **RP-3** Genetically influenced set/settling points, metabolism, and other factors (such as adequate sleep) influence the way our body burns calories.

MASTER THE MATERIAL ANSWERS

1. Maslow's hierarchy of needs supports this statement because it addresses the primacy of some motives over others. Once our basic physiological needs are met, safety concerns are addressed next, followed by belongingness and love needs (such as the desire to kiss). **2.** set. **3.** c. **4.** low. **5.** basal metabolic. **6.** d. **7.** Sanjay's plan is problematic. After he gains weight, the extra fat will require less energy to maintain than it did to gain in the first place. Sanjay may have a hard time getting rid of it later, when his metabolism slows down in an effort to retain his body weight.

MODULE 33: Sexual Motivation

RETRIEVAL PRACTICE ANSWERS

RP-1 estrogens; testosterone. **RP-2** sexual dysfunction; paraphilia. **RP-3** Influences include biological factors such as sexual maturity and sex hormones, psychological factors such as environmental stimuli and fantasies, and social-cultural factors such as the values and expectations absorbed from family and the surrounding culture. **RP-4** a, c, d. **RP-5** b, c, e.

MASTER THE MATERIAL ANSWERS

1. b. **2.** b. **3.** Sexual dysfunctions are problems that consistently impair sexual arousal or sexual function. Paraphilias are conditions, which may be classified as psychological disorders, in which sexual arousal is associated with nonhuman objects, the suffering of self or others, and/or nonconsenting persons. **4.** does; doesn't. **5.** c. **6.** Researchers have found no evidence that any environmental factor (parental relationships, childhood experiences, peer relationships, or dating experiences) influences the development of our sexual orientation.

MODULE 34: Affiliation and Achievement

RETRIEVAL PRACTICE ANSWERS

RP-1 They engaged in more self-defeating behaviors and displayed more disparaging and aggressive behavior. These students' basic *need to belong* seems to have been disrupted. **RP-2** strengthen; increase. **RP-3** self-discipline (*grit*).

MASTER THE MATERIAL ANSWERS

1. c. **2.** Monitor our time spent online, as well as our feelings about that time. Hide from distracting online friends when necessary. Check our devices less often. Get outside and away from technology regularly. **3.** should; should.

Emotions, Stress, and Health

MODULE 35: Introduction to Emotion

RETRIEVAL PRACTICE ANSWERS

RP-1 simultaneously; sequentially (first the physiological response, and then the experienced emotion). **RP-2** cognitive. **RP-3** Zajonc and LeDoux suggested that we experience some emotions without any conscious, cognitive appraisal. Lazarus, Schachter, and Singer emphasized the importance of appraisal and cognitive labeling in our experience of emotion. **RP-4** The *sympathetic division* of the ANS arouses us for more intense experiences of emotion, pumping out the stress hormones epinephrine and norepinephrine to prepare our body for fight or flight. The *parasympathetic division* of the ANS takes over when a crisis passes, restoring our body to a calm physiological and emotional state.

MASTER THE MATERIAL ANSWERS

1. James-Lange. **2.** b. **3.** c. **4.** A polygraph measures emotion-linked physiological changes, such as in perspiration, heart rate, and breathing. But the measure cannot distinguish between emotions with similar physiology (such as anxiety and guilt).

MODULE 36: Expressing Emotion

RETRIEVAL PRACTICE ANSWERS

RP-1 Women. **RP-2** gestures. **RP-3** (a) Most students report feeling more happy than sad when their cheeks are raised upward. (b) Most students report feeling more sad than happy when their cheeks are pulled downward.

MASTER THE MATERIAL ANSWERS

1. facial feedback. **2.** Aiden's droopy posture could negatively affect his mood thanks to the behavior feedback effect, which tends to make us feel the way we act.

MODULE 37: Experiencing Emotion

RETRIEVAL PRACTICE ANSWERS

RP-1 b. **RP-2** a. (Age does NOT effectively predict happiness levels. Better predictors are personality traits, sleep and exercise, and religious faith.)

MASTER THE MATERIAL ANSWERS

1. d. **2.** Positive. **3.** b. **4.** relative deprivation.

MODULE 38: Stress and Illness

RETRIEVAL PRACTICE ANSWERS

RP-1 sympathetic; increase; muscles; fight-or-flight. **RP-2** psychoneuroimmunology. **RP-3** Stress tends to reduce our immune system's ability to function properly, so that higher stress generally leads to greater risk of physical illness. **RP-4** Feeling angry and negative much of the time.

MASTER THE MATERIAL ANSWERS

1. b. **2.** d. **3.** resistance; exhaustion. **4.** tend; befriend. **5.** immune system. **6.** c. **7.** Type A individuals frequently experience negative emotions (anger, impatience), during which the sympathetic nervous system diverts blood away from the liver. This leaves fat and cholesterol circulating in the bloodstream for deposit near the heart and other organs, increasing the risk of heart disease and other health problems. Thus, Type A individuals actually harm themselves by directing anger at others.

MODULE 39: Health and Coping

RETRIEVAL PRACTICE ANSWERS

RP-1 problem; emotion. **RP-2** Aerobic exercise, relaxation procedures, relaxation and meditation, and religious engagement.

MASTER THE MATERIAL ANSWERS

1. emotion. **2.** b. **3.** internal. **4.** d. **5.** aerobic. **6.** c.

Social Psychology

MODULE 40: Social Thinking

RETRIEVAL PRACTICE ANSWERS

RP-1 By attributing the other person's behavior to the person ("What a terrible driver") and his own to the situation ("These roads are awful"), Marco has exhibited the *fundamental attribution error.* **RP-2** Our attitudes often influence our actions as we behave in ways consistent with our beliefs. However, our actions also influence our attitudes; we come to believe in what we have done. **RP-3** cognitive dissonance. **RP-4** Avoid yelling at, humiliating, or boring your audience. It's more effective to identify shared values, appeal to others' admirable motives, make your message vivid and repeat it, and get your audience to actively engage with your message.

MASTER THE MATERIAL ANSWERS

1. fundamental attribution. **2.** foot-in-the-door. **3.** Cognitive dissonance theory best supports this suggestion. If Jamala acts confident, her behavior will contradict her negative self-thoughts, creating cognitive dissonance. To relieve the tension, Jamala may realign her attitudes with her actions by viewing herself as more outgoing and confident. **4.** peripheral.

MODULE 41: Social Influence

RETRIEVAL PRACTICE ANSWERS

RP-1 normative social influence. **RP-2** Stanley Milgram. **RP-3** The Milgram studies showed that people were most likely to follow orders when the experimenter was nearby and was perceived to be a legitimate authority figure, the authority figure was supported by a powerful or prestigious institution, the victim was depersonalized or at a distance, and there were no models for defiance. **RP-4** This improved performance in the presence of others is most likely to occur with a well-learned task, because the added arousal caused by an audience tends to strengthen the most likely response. This also predicts poorer performance on a difficult task in others' presence. **RP-5** social loafing. **RP-6** The anonymity provided by the masks, combined with the arousal of the contentious setting, might create deindividuation (lessened self-awareness and self-restraint). **RP-7** group polarization. **RP-8** groupthink.

MASTER THE MATERIAL ANSWERS

1. c. **2.** a. **3.** The presence of a large audience generates arousal and strengthens Dr. Huang's most likely response: enhanced performance on a task he has mastered (teaching music history) and impaired performance on a task he finds difficult (statistics). **4.** deindividuation. **5.** group polarization.

MODULE 42: Antisocial Relations

RETRIEVAL PRACTICE ANSWERS

RP-1 scapegoat. **RP-2** Our biology (our genes, neural systems, and biochemistry—including testosterone and alcohol levels) influences our aggressive tendencies. Psychological factors (such as frustration, previous rewards for aggressive acts, and observation of others' aggression) can trigger any aggressive tendencies we may have. Social influences, such as exposure to violent media or being ostracized from a group, and cultural influences, such as whether we've grown up in a "culture of honor" or a father-absent home, can also affect our aggressive responses.

MASTER THE MATERIAL ANSWERS

1. stereotypes. **2.** b. **3.** more. **4.** d. **5.** c. **6.** c. **7.** c.

MODULE 43: Prosocial Relations

RETRIEVAL PRACTICE ANSWERS

RP-1 mere exposure effect. **RP-2** Being physically attractive tends to elicit positive first impressions. People tend to assume that attractive people are healthier, happier, more sensitive, more successful, and more socially skilled than others are. **RP-3** Emotions consist of (1) physical arousal and (2) our interpretation of that arousal. Researchers have found that any source of arousal may be interpreted as passion in the presence of a desirable person. **RP-4** equity; self-disclosure. **RP-5** In the presence of others, an individual is less likely to notice a situation, correctly interpret it as an emergency, and take responsibility for offering help. The Kitty Genovese case demonstrated this *bystander effect,* as each witness assumed many others were also aware of the event. **RP-6** Sports fans may feel they are a part of an *ingroup* that sets itself apart from an *outgroup* (fans of the archrival team). Ingroup bias tends to develop, leading to prejudice and the view that the outgroup "deserves" misfortune. So, the archrival team's loss may seem justified. In conflicts, this kind of thinking is problematic, especially when each side in the conflict develops *mirror-image perceptions* of the other (distorted, negative images that are ironically similar). **RP-7** Peacemakers should encourage equal-status contact, cooperation to achieve *superordinate goals* (shared goals that override differences), understanding through communication, and reciprocated conciliatory gestures (each side gives a little).

MASTER THE MATERIAL ANSWERS

1. mere exposure. 2. companionate; passionate. 3. d. 4. c. 5. mirror-image. 6. superordinate.

Personality

MODULE 44: Introduction to Personality and Psychodynamic Theories

RETRIEVAL PRACTICE ANSWERS

RP-1 ego; id; superego. **RP-2** fixation. **RP-3** unconsciously; anxiety. **RP-4** Freud is credited with first drawing attention to the importance of childhood experiences, to the existence of the unconscious mind, and to our self-protective defense mechanisms. Freud's theory has been criticized as not scientifically testable and offering after-the-fact explanations, focusing too much on sexual conflicts in childhood, and being based on the idea of repression, which has not been supported by modern research. **RP-5** Today's psychodynamic theorists and therapists still use Freud's interviewing techniques, and they still tend to focus on childhood experiences and attachments, unresolved conflicts, and unconscious influences. However, they are not likely to dwell on fixation at any psychosexual stage, or the idea that sexual issues are the basis of our personality. **RP-6** Projective.

MASTER THE MATERIAL ANSWERS

1. c. 2. superego. 3. b. 4. anxiety. 5. repression. 6. d. 7. a. 8. a.

MODULE 45: Humanistic Theories and Trait Theories

RETRIEVAL PRACTICE ANSWERS

RP-1 The humanistic theories sought to turn psychology's attention away from drives and conflicts and toward our growth potential. This movement's focus on the way people strive for self-determination and self-realization was in contrast to Freudian theory and strict behaviorism. **RP-2** To be *empathic* is to share and mirror another person's feelings. Carl Rogers believed that people nurture growth in others by being empathic. Abraham Maslow proposed that *self-actualization* is the motivation to fulfill one's potential, and one of the ultimate psychological needs (another is self-transcendence). **RP-3** extraversion–introversion and emotional stability–instability. **RP-4** The Big Five personality factors are openness, conscientiousness, extraversion, agreeableness, and neuroticism (emotional stability vs.

instability): OCEAN. These factors may be objectively measured, they are relatively stable over the life span, and they apply fairly well to all cultures in which they have been studied. **RP-5** Our scores on personality tests predict our *average* behavior across many situations much better than they predict our specific behavior in any given situation.

MASTER THE MATERIAL ANSWERS

1. d. 2. Rogers might assert that the criminal was raised in an environment lacking acceptance (unconditional positive regard), genuineness, and empathy, which inhibited psychological growth and led to a negative self-concept. 3. unconditional positive regard. 4. Trait. 5. c. 6. b. 7. b.

MODULE 46: Social-Cognitive Theories and the Self

RETRIEVAL PRACTICE ANSWERS

RP-1 social-cognitive; reciprocal determinism. **RP-2** To predict someone's future behavior, examine the person's past behavior patterns in similar situations. **RP-3** People who feel confident in their abilities tend to be outgoing, responsible, and open to new experiences, and are often happier, less anxious, and less lonely. Inflated self-esteem can lead to self-serving bias, aggression, and narcissism. **RP-4** self-serving bias. **RP-5** Defensive; Secure.

MASTER THE MATERIAL ANSWERS

1. a. 2. social-cognitive. 3. spotlight effect. 4. b. 5. Yes, if that self-love is of the *secure* type. Secure self-esteem promotes a focus beyond the self and a higher quality of life. Excessive self-love may promote artificially high or defensive self-esteem, which is fragile; perceived threats may be met with anger or aggression.

Psychological Disorders

MODULE 47: Introduction to Psychological Disorders

RETRIEVAL PRACTICE ANSWERS

RP-1 dysfunctional or maladaptive. **RP-2** Some psychological disorders are culture-specific. For example, anorexia nervosa occurs mostly in Western cultures, and *taijin kyofusho* appears largely in Japan. Other disorders, such as major depressive disorder and schizophrenia, are universal—they occur in all cultures. **RP-3** Biological, psychological, and social-cultural influences combine to produce psychological disorders. This approach helps us understand that our well-being is

affected by our genes, brain functioning, inner thoughts and feelings, and the influences of our social and cultural environment. **RP-4** Therapists and others apply disorder labels to communicate with one another using a common language, and to share concepts during research. Clients may benefit from knowing that they are not the only ones with these symptoms. The dangers of labeling people are that (1) overly broad classifications may pathologize normal behavior, and (2) the labels can trigger assumptions that will change people's behavior toward those labeled. **RP-5** Poverty-related stresses can help trigger disorders, but disabling disorders can also contribute to poverty. Thus, poverty and disorder are often a chicken-and-egg situation; it's hard to know which came first.

MASTER THE MATERIAL ANSWERS

1. major depressive disorder. 2. No. Anna's behavior is unusual, causes her distress, and may make her a few minutes late on occasion, but it does not appear to significantly disrupt her ability to function. Like most of us, Anna demonstrates some unusual behaviors. Since they are not disabling or dysfunctional, they do not suggest a psychological disorder. 3. medical. 4. There are various culture-linked disorders, including *susto* (in Latin America), *taijin kyofusho* (in Japan), *amok* (in Malaysia), and eating disorders (in food-abundant Western cultures). 5. c. 6. Critics have expressed concerns about the negative effects of labeling by the DSM and other classification systems. Labels have the potential to be both subjective and stigmatizing. Further, critics suggest that the DSM-5 casts too wide a net on disorders, pathologizing normal behavior. 7. poverty. 8. d.

MODULE 48: Anxiety-Related Disorders

RETRIEVAL PRACTICE ANSWERS

RP-1 generalized anxiety. **RP-2** panic. **RP-3** specific phobia. **RP-4** obsessive-compulsive. **RP-5** posttraumatic stress. **RP-6** *Somatic* means "relating to the body"; *somatic symptom disorders* produce distressing bodily symptoms that have no apparent physical cause. **RP-7** Biological factors include inherited temperament differences and other gene variations; experience-altered brain pathways; and outdated, inherited responses that had survival value for our distant ancestors.

MASTER THE MATERIAL ANSWERS

1. c. 2. specific phobia. 3. obsessive-compulsive. 4. b. 5. c.

MODULE 49: Depressive Disorders and Bipolar Disorders

RETRIEVAL PRACTICE ANSWERS

RP-1 Many factors contribute to depression, including the biological influences of genetics and brain function. Social-cognitive factors also matter, including the interaction of explanatory style, mood, our responses to stressful experiences, changes in our patterns of thinking and behaving, and cultural influences. Depression involves the whole body and may disrupt sleep, energy levels, and concentration.

MASTER THE MATERIAL ANSWERS

1. women's; men's. **2.** d. **3.** norepinephrine; serotonin. **4.** social-cognitive.

MODULE 50: Schizophrenia

RETRIEVAL PRACTICE ANSWERS

RP-1 negative; chronic; positive; acute.
RP-2 Biological factors include abnormalities in brain structure and function and a genetic predisposition to the disorder. Environmental factors such as nutritional deprivation, exposure to virus, and maternal stress contribute by activating the genes that increase risk. Exposure to many environmental triggers can increase the odds of developing schizophrenia.

MASTER THE MATERIAL ANSWERS

1. Schizophrenia involves the altered perceptions, emotions, and behaviors of a mind split from reality. It does not involve the rapid changes in mood or identity suggested by this comparison. **2.** b. **3.** hallucination. **4.** a.

MODULE 51: Dissociative, Personality, and Eating Disorders

RETRIEVAL PRACTICE ANSWERS

RP-1 The psychodynamic explanation of DID symptoms is that they are defenses against anxiety generated by unacceptable urges. The learning perspective attempts to explain these symptoms as behaviors that have been reinforced by relieving anxiety. **RP-2** Twin and adoption studies show that biological relatives of people with antisocial personality disorder are at increased risk for antisocial behavior. Researchers have also observed differences in the brain activity and structure of antisocial criminals. Negative environmental factors, such as poverty or childhood abuse, may channel genetic traits such as fearlessness in more dangerous directions—toward aggression and away from social responsibility.
RP-3 anorexia nervosa; bulimia nervosa.

MASTER THE MATERIAL ANSWERS

1. c. **2.** c. **3.** b. **4.** b.

MODULE 52: Neurodevelopmental Disorders

RETRIEVAL PRACTICE ANSWERS

RP-1 To be diagnosed with an intellectual disability, a person's intelligence test score must be in the lowest 3 percent of the general population, or about 70 or below. Second, the person must have difficulty adapting to the normal demands of independent living: conceptual (language, reading, and concepts of money, time, and number); social (interpersonal skills, being socially responsible, following basic rules and laws, avoiding being victimized); and practical (health and personal care, occupational skill, and travel).

MASTER THE MATERIAL ANSWERS

1. c. **2.** People with ASD are less imitative and show less activity in brain areas involved in mirroring others' actions. When people with ASD watch another person's hand movements, for example, their brain displays less-than-normal mirroring activity. **3.** The DSM has broadened the diagnostic criteria for ADHD, leading to an increase in diagnoses without concurrent changes in children's attentional behavior. Critics suggest that these criteria are now too broad and may pathologize normal behaviors, turning everyday childish rambunctiousness into a disorder.

Therapy

MODULE 53: Introduction to Therapy and the Psychological Therapies

RETRIEVAL PRACTICE ANSWERS

RP-1 transference; resistance; interpretation. **RP-2** A psychodynamic therapist might be more interested in helping the child develop insight about the underlying problems that have caused the bed-wetting response. A behavior therapist would be more likely to agree with Mowrer that the bed-wetting symptom *is* the problem, and that counterconditioning the unwanted behavior would indeed bring emotional relief. **RP-3** The *insight therapies*—psychodynamic and humanistic therapies—seek to relieve problems by providing an understanding of their origins. *Behavior therapies* assume the problem behavior is the problem and treat it directly, paying less attention to its origins. **RP-4** If a behavior can be learned, it can be *unlearned* and replaced by other, more adaptive responses. **RP-5** classical;

operant. **RP-6** By reflecting people's feelings in a nondirective setting, the *humanistic therapies* attempt to foster personal growth by helping people become more self-aware and self-accepting. By making people aware of self-defeating patterns of thinking, *cognitive therapies* guide them toward more adaptive ways of thinking about themselves and their world. **RP-7** cognitive therapy. **RP-8** This integrative therapy helps people change self-defeating thinking and behavior. It has been shown to be effective for those with anxiety disorders, obsessive-compulsive and related disorders, depressive disorders, bipolar disorders, ADHD, eating disorders, and alcohol or other substance use disorders.

MASTER THE MATERIAL ANSWERS

1. a. **2.** Insight. **3.** d. **4.** active listening. **5.** c. **6.** counterconditioning. **7.** systematic desensitization. **8.** Behavior therapies are often the best choice for treating specific phobias. Viewing Rico's fear of the highway as a learned response, a behavior therapist might help Rico learn to replace his anxious response to highway driving with a relaxation response. **9.** token economy. **10.** d. **11.** Cognitive-behavioral. **12.** b.

MODULE 54: Evaluating Psychotherapies

RETRIEVAL PRACTICE ANSWERS

RP-1 The *placebo effect* is the healing power of *belief* in a treatment. Patients and therapists who expect a treatment to be effective may believe it was. **RP-2** are. **RP-3** When using an evidence-based approach, therapists make decisions about treatment based on research evidence, clinical expertise, and knowledge of the client. **RP-4** more. **RP-5** ethical.

MASTER THE MATERIAL ANSWERS

1. c. **2.** d. **3.** research evidence, clinical expertise, and knowledge of the patient. **4.** hope.

MODULE 55: The Biomedical Therapies and Preventing Psychological Disorders

RETRIEVAL PRACTICE ANSWERS

RP-1 Exercise regularly, get enough sleep, get more exposure to light (get outside or use a light box), nurture important relationships, redirect negative thinking, and eat a diet rich in omega-3 fatty acids. **RP-2** Researchers assign people to treatment and no-treatment conditions to see if those who receive the drug therapy improve more than those who don't. Double-blind controlled studies are most effective. If neither the therapist nor the client knows which participants have received the drug treatment, then any difference between the treated and untreated groups will reflect the drug treatment's actual effect. **RP-3** antidepressants; antipsychotic. **RP-4** electroconvulsive therapy; transcranial; transcranial; deep brain. **RP-5** Psychological or biomedical therapies attempt to relieve people's suffering from psychological disorders. Preventive mental health attempts to prevent suffering by identifying and eliminating the conditions that cause disorders, as well as by building resilience.

MASTER THE MATERIAL ANSWERS

1. c. **2.** antianxiety. **3.** lithium. **4.** b. **5.** d.

APPENDIX C

Psychology at Work

RETRIEVAL PRACTICE ANSWERS

RP-1 We become more likely to view our work as fulfilling and socially useful, and we experience higher self-esteem, feelings of competence, and overall well-being. **RP-2** (1) Interviewers may presume people are what they seem to be in interviews. (2) Interviewers' preconceptions and moods color how they perceive interviewees' responses. (3) Interviewers judge people relative to other recent interviewees. (4) Interviewers tend to track the successful careers of those they hire, not the successful careers of those they reject. (5) Interviews tend to disclose prospective workers' good intentions, not their habitual behaviors.

RP-3 *Transformational leaders* are able to inspire others to share a vision and commit themselves to a group's mission. They tend to be naturally extraverted and set high standards. **RP-4** To develop safer machines and work environments, human factors psychologists stay mindful of the curse of knowledge—the tendency for experts to mistakenly assume that others share their knowledge.

MASTER THE MATERIAL ANSWERS

1. flow. **2.** Personnel; human factors. **3.** a. **4.** d. **5.** Focusing on SMART goals—goals that are *specific, measurable, actionable, realistic,* and *time-bound* (such as maintaining a regular study schedule)—will be more helpful than focusing on more distant general goals (such as earning a good grade in this class). **6.** transformational. **7.** c. **8.** d.

Glossary

absolute threshold the minimum stimulus energy needed to detect a particular stimulus 50 percent of the time. (p. 213)

accommodation (1) in developmental psychology, adapting our current understandings (schemas) to incorporate new information. (2) in sensation and perception, the process by which the eye's lens changes shape to focus near or far objects on the retina. (pp. 175, 222)

achievement motivation a desire for significant accomplishment, for mastery of skills or ideas, for control, and for attaining a high standard. (p. 413)

achievement test a test designed to assess what a person has learned. (p. 359)

acquisition in classical conditioning, the initial stage—when one links a neutral stimulus and an unconditioned stimulus so that the neutral stimulus begins triggering the conditioned response. (In operant conditioning, the strengthening of a reinforced response.) (p. 262)

action potential a neural impulse; a brief electrical charge that travels down an axon. (p. 55)

active listening empathic listening in which the listener echoes, restates, and seeks clarification. A feature of Rogers' person-centered therapy. (p. 600)

acute schizophrenia (also called *reactive schizophrenia*) a form of schizophrenia that can begin at any age, frequently occurs in response to a traumatic event, and from which recovery is much more likely. (p. 580)

adaptation-level phenomenon our tendency to form judgments (of sounds, of lights, of income) relative to a neutral level defined by our prior experience. (p. 438)

adolescence the transition period from childhood to adulthood, extending from puberty to independence. (p. 189)

adrenal [ah-DREEN-el] **glands** a pair of endocrine glands that sits just above the kidneys and secretes hormones (epinephrine and norepinephrine) that help arouse the body in times of stress. (p. 64)

aerobic exercise sustained exercise that increases heart and lung fitness; also helps alleviate depression and anxiety. (p. 459)

affiliation need the need to build and maintain relationships and to feel part of a group. (p. 407)

aggression any physical or verbal behavior intended to harm someone physically or emotionally. (pp. 151, 495)

agonist a molecule that increases a neurotransmitter's action. (p. 59)

AIDS (acquired immune deficiency syndrome) a life-threatening condition caused by the *human immunodeficiency virus* (HIV), a sexually transmitted infection. AIDS depletes the immune system, leaving the person vulnerable to infections. (p. 396)

alcohol use disorder (popularly known as *alcoholism*) alcohol use marked by tolerance, withdrawal, and a drive to continue problematic use. (p. 112)

algorithm a methodical, logical rule or procedure that guarantees solving a particular problem. Contrasts with the usually speedier—but also more error-prone—use of *heuristics*. (p. 327)

all-or-none response a neuron's reaction of either firing (with a full-strength response) or not firing. (p. 57)

alpha waves the relatively slow brain waves of a relaxed, awake state. (p. 97)

altruism unselfish regard for the welfare of others. (p. 508)

Alzheimer's disease a neurocognitive disorder marked by neural plaques, often with onset after age 80, and entailing a progressive decline in memory and other cognitive abilities. (p. 205)

amphetamines drugs (such as *methamphetamine*) that stimulate neural activity, causing accelerated body functions and associated energy and mood changes. (p. 114)

amygdala [uh-MIG-duh-la] two lima-bean-sized neural clusters in the limbic system; linked to emotion. (p. 71)

androgyny displaying both traditionally masculine and traditionally feminine psychological characteristics. (p. 158)

anorexia nervosa an eating disorder in which a person (usually an adolescent female) maintains a starvation diet despite being significantly underweight, and has an inaccurate self-perception; sometimes accompanied by excessive exercise. (p. 589)

antagonist a molecule that inhibits or blocks a neurotransmitter's action. (p. 61)

anterograde amnesia an inability to form new memories. (p. 311)

antianxiety drugs drugs used to control anxiety and agitation. (p. 623)

antidepressant drugs drugs used to treat depressive disorders, anxiety disorders, obsessive-compulsive and related disorders, and post-traumatic stress disorder. (Several widely used antidepressant drugs are *selective serotonin reuptake inhibitors*—SSRIs.) (p. 623)

antipsychotic drugs drugs used to treat schizophrenia and other forms of severe thought disorders. (p. 623)

antisocial personality disorder a personality disorder in which a person (usually a man) exhibits a lack of conscience for wrongdoing, even toward friends and family members; may be aggressive and ruthless or a clever con artist. (p. 587)

anxiety disorders psychological disorders characterized by distressing, persistent anxiety or maladaptive behaviors that reduce anxiety. (p. 563)

aphasia impairment of language, usually caused by left hemisphere damage either to Broca's area (impairing speaking) or to Wernicke's area (impairing understanding). (p. 345)

applied research a scientific study that aims to solve practical problems. (p. 14)

approach and avoidance motives the drive to move toward (approach) or away from (avoid) a stimulus. (p. 443)

aptitude test a test designed to predict a person's future performance; *aptitude* is the capacity to learn. (p. 359)

asexual having no sexual attraction toward others. (p. 393)

assimilation interpreting our new experiences in terms of our existing schemas. (p. 175)

association areas areas of the cerebral cortex that are not involved in primary motor or sensory functions; rather, they are involved in higher mental functions such as learning, remembering, thinking, and speaking. (p. 79)

associative learning learning that certain events occur together. The events may be two stimuli (as in classical conditioning) or a response and its consequence (as in operant conditioning). (pp. 258, 267)

attachment an emotional tie with others; shown in young children by their seeking closeness to caregivers and showing distress on separation. (p. 180)

attention-deficit/hyperactivity disorder (ADHD) a psychological disorder marked by extreme inattention and/or hyperactivity and impulsivity. (p. 594)

attitude feelings, often influenced by our beliefs, that predispose us to respond in a particular way to objects, people, and events. (p. 471)

attribution theory the theory that we explain someone's behavior by crediting either the situation or the person's disposition. (p. 468)

audition the sense or act of hearing. (p. 239)

autism spectrum disorder (ASD) a disorder that appears in childhood and is marked by significant limitations in communication and social interaction, and by rigidly fixated interests and repetitive behaviors. (p. 592)

automatic processing unconscious encoding of incidental information, such as space, time, and frequency, and of familiar or well-learned information, such as sounds, smells, and word meanings. (p. 296)

autonomic [aw-tuh-NAHM-ik] **nervous system (ANS)** the part of the peripheral nervous system that controls the glands and the muscles of the internal organs (such as the heart). Its *sympathetic* division arouses; its *parasympathetic* division calms. (p. 61)

availability heuristic judging the likelihood of events based on their availability in memory; if instances come readily to mind (perhaps because of their vividness), we presume such events are common. (p. 329)

aversive conditioning associates an unpleasant state (such as nausea) with an unwanted behavior (such as drinking alcohol). (p. 605)

axon the segmented neuron extension that passes messages through its branches to other neurons or to muscles or glands. (p. 55)

babbling stage the stage in speech development, beginning around 4 months, during which an infant spontaneously utters various sounds that are not all related to the household language. (p. 343)

barbiturates drugs that depress central nervous system activity, reducing anxiety but impairing memory and judgment. (p. 114)

basal metabolic rate the body's resting rate of energy output. (p. 388)

basic research pure science that aims to increase the scientific knowledge base. (p. 14)

basic trust according to Erik Erikson, a sense that the world is predictable and trustworthy; said to be formed during infancy by appropriate experiences with responsive caregivers. (p. 182)

behavior feedback effect the tendency of behavior to influence our own and others' thoughts, feelings, and actions. (p. 431)

behavior genetics the study of the relative power and limits of genetic and environmental influences on behavior. (pp. 10, 127)

behavior therapy therapy that applies learning principles to the elimination of unwanted behaviors. (p. 603)

behaviorism the view that psychology (1) should be an objective science that (2) studies behavior without reference to mental processes. Most research psychologists today agree with (1) but not with (2). (pp. 8, 261)

belief perseverance clinging to one's initial conceptions after the basis on which they were formed has been discredited. (p. 332)

Big Five factors researchers identified five factors—*openness, conscientiousness, extraversion, agreeableness,* and *neuroticism*—that describe personality. (Also called the *five-factor model.*) (p. 535)

binge-eating disorder significant binge-eating episodes, followed by distress, disgust, or guilt, but without the compensatory behavior that marks bulimia nervosa. (p. 590)

binocular cue a depth cue, such as retinal disparity, that depends on the use of two eyes. (p. 231)

biological psychology the scientific study of the links between biological (genetic, neural, hormonal) and psychological processes. Some biological psychologists call themselves *behavioral neuroscientists, neuropsychologists, behavior geneticists, physiological psychologists,* or *biopsychologists.* (p. 52)

biomedical therapy prescribed medications or procedures that act directly on the person's physiology. (p. 599)

biopsychosocial approach an integrated approach that incorporates biological, psychological, and social-cultural levels of analysis. (p. 12)

bipolar disorders a group of disorders in which a person alternates between the hopelessness and lethargy of depression and the overexcited state of mania. (Formerly called *manic-depressive disorder.*) (p. 572)

blindsight a condition in which a person can respond to a visual stimulus without consciously experiencing it. (p. 93)

blind spot the point at which the optic nerve leaves the eye, creating a "blind" spot because no receptor cells are located there. (p. 222)

bottom-up processing analysis that begins with the sensory receptors and works up to the brain's integration of sensory information. (p. 213)

brainstem the oldest part and central core of the brain, beginning where the spinal cord swells as it enters the skull; the brainstem is responsible for automatic survival functions. (p. 69)

Broca's area a frontal lobe brain area, usually in the left hemisphere, that helps control language expression by directing the muscle movements involved in speech. (p. 347)

bulimia nervosa an eating disorder in which a person's binge eating (usually of high-calorie foods) is followed by inappropriate weight-loss-promoting behavior, such as vomiting, laxative use, fasting, or excessive exercise. (p. 590)

bystander effect the tendency for any given bystander to be less likely to give aid if other bystanders are present. (p. 508)

Cannon-Bard theory the theory that an emotion-arousing stimulus simultaneously triggers (1) physiological responses and (2) the subjective experience of emotion. (p. 419)

case study a descriptive technique in which one individual or group is studied in depth in the hope of revealing universal principles. (p. 27)

catharsis in psychology, the idea that "releasing" aggressive energy (through action or fantasy) relieves aggressive urges. (p. 433)

cell body the part of a neuron that contains the nucleus; the cell's life-support center. (p. 55)

central nervous system (CNS) the brain and spinal cord. (p. 61)

central route persuasion occurs when interested people's thinking is influenced by considering evidence and arguments. (p. 473)

cerebellum [sehr-uh-BELL-um] the "little brain" at the rear of the brainstem; functions include processing sensory input, coordinating movement output and balance, and enabling nonverbal learning and memory. (p. 71)

cerebral [seh-REE-bruhl] **cortex** the intricate fabric of interconnected neural cells covering the cerebral hemispheres; the body's ultimate control and information-processing center. (p. 75)

change blindness failing to notice changes in the environment; a form of *inattentional blindness.* (p. 92)

chromosomes threadlike structures made of DNA molecules that contain the genes. (p. 127)

chronic schizophrenia (also called *process schizophrenia*) a form of schizophrenia in which symptoms usually appear by late adolescence or early adulthood. As people age, psychotic episodes last longer and recovery periods shorten. (p. 580)

chunking organizing items into familiar, manageable units; often occurs automatically. (p. 298)

circadian [ser-KAY-dee-an] **rhythm** our biological clock; regular bodily rhythms (for example, of temperature and wakefulness) that occur on a 24-hour cycle. (p. 95)

classical conditioning a type of learning in which we link two or more stimuli; as a result, to illustrate with Pavlov's classic experiment, the first stimulus (a tone) comes to elicit behavior (drooling) in anticipation of the second stimulus (food). (p. 261)

clinical psychology a branch of psychology that studies, assesses, and treats people with psychological disorders. (p. 14)

cocaine a powerful and addictive stimulant derived from the coca plant; produces temporarily increased alertness and euphoria. (p. 116)

cochlea [KOHK-lee-uh] a coiled, bony, fluid-filled tube in the inner ear; sound waves traveling through the cochlear fluid trigger nerve impulses. (p. 239)

cochlear implant a device for converting sounds into electrical signals and stimulating the auditory nerve through electrodes threaded into the cochlea. (p. 240)

cognition all the mental activities associated with thinking, knowing, remembering, and communicating. (pp. 175, 327)

cognitive-behavioral therapy (CBT) a popular integrative therapy that combines cognitive therapy (changing self-defeating thinking) with behavior therapy (changing behavior). (p. 609)

cognitive dissonance theory the theory that we act to reduce the discomfort (dissonance) we feel when two of our thoughts (cognitions) are inconsistent. For example, when we become aware that our attitudes and our actions clash, we can reduce the resulting dissonance by changing our attitudes. (p. 473)

cognitive learning the acquisition of mental information, whether by observing events, by watching others, or through language. (p. 261)

cognitive map a mental representation of the layout of one's environment. For example, after exploring a maze, rats act as if they have learned a cognitive map of it. (p. 282)

cognitive neuroscience the interdisciplinary study of the brain activity linked with cognition (including perception, thinking, memory, and language). (pp. 9, 88)

cognitive psychology the study of mental processes, such as occur when we perceive, learn, remember, think, communicate, and solve problems. (p. 9)

cognitive therapy therapy that teaches people new, more adaptive ways of thinking; based on the assumption that thoughts intervene between events and our emotional reactions. (p. 607)

cohort a group of people sharing a common characteristic, such as being from a given time period. (p. 367)

collective unconscious Carl Jung's concept of a shared, inherited reservoir of memory traces from our species' history. (p. 522)

collectivism giving priority to the goals of one's group (often one's extended family or work group) and defining one's identity accordingly. (p. 146)

community psychology a branch of psychology that studies how people interact with their social environments and how social institutions (such as schools and neighborhoods) affect individuals and groups. (p. 14)

companionate love the deep affectionate attachment we feel for those with whom our lives are intertwined. (p. 506)

concept a mental grouping of similar objects, events, ideas, or people. (p. 327)

concrete operational stage in Piaget's theory, the stage of cognitive development (from about 7 to 11 years of age) at which children gain the mental operations that enable them to think logically about concrete events. (p. 179)

conditioned reinforcer a stimulus that gains its reinforcing power through its association with a primary reinforcer. (Also known as a *secondary reinforcer.*) (p. 270)

conditioned response (CR) in classical conditioning, a learned response to a previously neutral (but now conditioned) stimulus (CS). (p. 262)

conditioned stimulus (CS) in classical conditioning, an originally neutral stimulus that, after association with an unconditioned stimulus (US), comes to trigger a conditioned response (CR). (p. 262)

conduction hearing loss a less common form of hearing loss, caused by damage to the mechanical system that conducts sound waves to the cochlea. (p. 240)

cones retinal receptors that are concentrated near the center of the retina and that function in daylight or in well-lit conditions. Cones detect fine detail and give rise to color sensations. (p. 222)

confirmation bias a tendency to search for information that supports our preconceptions and to ignore or distort contradictory evidence. (pp. 328, 613)

conflict a perceived incompatibility of actions, goals, or ideas. (p. 511)

conformity adjusting our behavior or thinking to coincide with a group standard. (p. 477)

confounding variable in an experiment, a factor other than the factor being studied that might influence a study's results. (p. 36)

consciousness our subjective awareness of ourselves and our environment. (p. 88)

conservation the principle (which Piaget believed to be a part of concrete operational reasoning) that properties such as mass, volume, and number remain the same despite changes in the forms of objects. (p. 177)

continuous reinforcement schedule reinforcing the desired response every time it occurs. (p. 270)

control group in an experiment, the group *not* exposed to the treatment; contrasts with the experimental group and serves as a comparison for evaluating the effect of the treatment. (p. 35)

convergent thinking narrowing the available problem solutions to determine the single best solution. (p. 334)

coping alleviating stress using emotional, cognitive, or behavioral methods. (p. 453)

coronary heart disease the clogging of the vessels that nourish the heart muscle; a leading cause of death in many developed countries. (p. 449)

corpus callosum [KOR-pus kah-LOW-sum] the large band of neural fibers connecting the two brain hemispheres and carrying messages between them. (p. 82)

correlation a measure of the extent to which two factors vary together, and thus of how well either factor predicts the other. (p. 30)

correlation coefficient a statistical index of the relationship between two things (from –1.00 to +1.00). (p. 30)

counseling psychology a branch of psychology that assists people with problems in living (often related to school, work, or relationships) and in achieving greater well-being. (p. 14)

counterconditioning behavior therapy procedures that use classical conditioning to evoke new responses to stimuli that are triggering unwanted behaviors; include *exposure therapies* and *aversive conditioning*. (p. 603)

creativity the ability to produce new and valuable ideas. (p. 334)

critical period an optimal period early in the life of an organism when exposure to certain stimuli or experiences produces normal development. (p. 180)

critical thinking thinking that does not automatically accept arguments and conclusions. Rather, it examines assumptions, appraises the source, discerns hidden biases, evaluates evidence, and assesses conclusions. (p. 3)

cross-sectional study research that compares people of different ages at the same point in time. (pp. 166, 367)

crystallized intelligence (Gc) our accumulated knowledge and verbal skills; tends to increase with age. (p. 354)

culture the enduring behaviors, ideas, attitudes, values, and traditions shared by a group of people and transmitted from one generation to the next. (pp. 11, 145)

debriefing the postexperimental explanation of a study, including its purpose and any deceptions, to its participants. (p. 41)

deep processing encoding semantically, based on the meaning of the words; tends to yield the best retention. (p. 301)

defense mechanisms in psychoanalytic theory, the ego's protective methods of reducing anxiety by unconsciously distorting reality. (p. 520)

deindividuation the loss of self-awareness and self-restraint occurring in group situations that foster arousal and anonymity. (p. 484)

déjà vu that eerie sense that "I've experienced this before." Cues from the current situation may unconsciously trigger retrieval of an earlier experience. (p. 319)

delta waves the large, slow brain waves associated with deep sleep. (p. 97)

delusion a false belief, often of persecution or grandeur, that may accompany psychotic disorders. (p. 580)

dendrites a neuron's often bushy, branching extensions that receive and integrate messages, conducting impulses toward the cell body. (p. 55)

dependent variable in an experiment, the outcome that is measured; the variable that may change when the independent variable is manipulated. (p. 36)

depressants drugs (such as alcohol, barbiturates, and opiates) that reduce neural activity and slow body functions. (p. 112)

depth perception the ability to see objects in three dimensions, although the images that strike the retina are two-dimensional; allows us to judge distance. (p. 230)

developmental psychology a branch of psychology that studies physical, cognitive, and social development throughout the life span. (p. 166)

difference threshold the minimum difference between two stimuli required for detection 50 percent of the time. We experience the difference threshold as a *just noticeable difference* (or *jnd*). (p. 214)

discrimination (1) in classical conditioning, the learned ability to distinguish between a conditioned stimulus and similar stimuli that do not signal an unconditioned stimulus; in operant conditioning, the ability to distinguish responses that are reinforced from similar responses that are not reinforced. (2) in social psychology, unjustifiable negative behavior toward a group or its members. (pp. 264, 488)

dissociation a split in consciousness, which allows some thoughts and behaviors to occur simultaneously with others. (p. 247)

dissociative disorders controversial, rare disorders in which conscious awareness becomes separated (dissociated) from previous memories, thoughts, and feelings. (p. 585)

dissociative identity disorder (DID) a rare dissociative disorder in which a person exhibits two or more distinct and alternating identities. (Formerly called *multiple personality disorder*.) (p. 587)

divergent thinking expanding the number of possible problem solutions; creative thinking that diverges in different directions. (p. 334)

DNA (deoxyribonucleic acid) a complex molecule containing the genetic information that makes up the chromosomes. (p. 127)

double-blind procedure an experimental procedure in which both the research participants and the research staff are ignorant (blind) about whether the research participants have received the treatment or a placebo. Commonly used in drug-evaluation studies. (p. 36)

dream a sequence of images, emotions, and thoughts passing through a sleeping person's mind. (p. 105)

drive-reduction theory the idea that a physiological need creates an aroused state (a drive) that motivates an organism to satisfy the need. (p. 383)

DSM-5 the American Psychiatric Association's *Diagnostic and Statistical Manual of Mental Disorders*, Fifth Edition; a widely used system for classifying psychological disorders. (p. 555)

dual processing the principle that information is often simultaneously processed on separate conscious and unconscious tracks. (p. 92)

echoic memory a momentary sensory memory of auditory stimuli; if attention is elsewhere, sounds and words can still be recalled within 3 or 4 seconds. (p. 296)

eclectic approach an approach to psychotherapy that uses techniques from various forms of therapy. (p. 599)

Ecstasy (MDMA) a synthetic stimulant and mild hallucinogen. Produces euphoria and social intimacy, but with short-term health risks and longer-term harm to serotonin-producing neurons and to mood and cognition. (p. 116)

EEG (electroencephalogram) an amplified recording of the waves of electrical activity sweeping across the brain's surface. These waves are measured by electrodes placed on the scalp. (p. 67)

effortful processing encoding that requires attention and conscious effort. (p. 296)

ego the partly conscious, "executive" part of personality that, according to Freud, mediates among the demands of the id, the superego, and reality. The ego operates on the *reality principle*, satisfying the id's desires in ways that will realistically bring pleasure rather than pain. (p. 520)

egocentrism in Piaget's theory, the preoperational child's difficulty taking another's point of view. (p. 177)

electroconvulsive therapy (ECT) a biomedical therapy for severely depressed patients in which a brief electric current is sent through the brain of an anesthetized patient. (p. 624)

embodied cognition the influence of bodily sensations, gestures, and other states on cognitive preferences and judgments. (p. 252)

embryo the developing human organism from about 2 weeks after fertilization through the second month. (p. 168)

emerging adulthood a period from about age 18 to the mid-twenties, when many in Western cultures are no longer adolescents but have not yet achieved full independence as adults. (p. 196)

emotion a response of the whole organism, involving (1) physiological arousal, (2) expressive behaviors, and, most importantly, (3) conscious experience resulting from one's interpretations. (p. 419)

emotional intelligence the ability to perceive, understand, manage, and use emotions. (p. 356)

emotion-focused coping attempting to alleviate stress by avoiding or ignoring a stressor and attending to emotional needs related to our stress reaction. (p. 453)

empirical approach an evidence-based method that draws on observation and experimentation. (p. 2)

empirically derived test a test (such as the MMPI) created by selecting from a pool of items those that discriminate between groups. (p. 535)

encoding the process of getting information into the memory system—for example, by extracting meaning. (p. 294)

encoding specificity principle the idea that cues and contexts specific to a particular memory will be most effective in helping us recall it. (p. 309)

endocrine [EN-duh-krin] **system** the body's "slow" chemical communication system; glands and fat tissue that secrete hormones into the bloodstream. (p. 62)

endorphins [en-DOR-fins] "morphine within"— natural, opiate-like neurotransmitters linked to pain control and to pleasure. (p. 59)

environment every nongenetic influence, from prenatal nutrition to the people and things around us. (p. 127)

epigenetics "above" or "in addition to" (*epi*) genetics; the study of the molecular mechanisms by which environments can influence genetic expression (without a DNA change). (pp. 133, 555)

episodic memory explicit memory of personally experienced events; one of our two conscious memory systems (the other is *semantic memory*). (p. 302)

equity a condition in which people receive from a relationship in proportion to what they give to it. (p. 506)

erectile disorder inability to develop or maintain an erection due to insufficient blood flow to the penis. (p. 396)

estrogens sex hormones, such as estradiol, that contribute to female sex characteristics and are secreted in greater amounts by females than by males. (pp. 155, 394)

evidence-based practice clinical decision making that integrates the best available research with clinical expertise and patient characteristics and preferences. (p. 616)

evolutionary psychology the study of the evolution of behavior and the mind, using principles of natural selection. (pp. 10, 135)

experiment a research method in which an investigator manipulates one or more factors (independent variables) to observe the effect on some behavior or mental process (the dependent variable). By *random assignment* of participants, the experimenter aims to control other relevant factors. (p. 35)

experimental group in an experiment, the group exposed to the treatment, that is, to one version of the independent variable. (p. 35)

explicit memory retention of facts and experiences that we can consciously know and "declare." (Also called *declarative memory*.) (p. 296)

exposure therapies behavioral techniques, such as *systematic desensitization* and *virtual reality exposure therapy*, that treat anxieties by exposing people (in imaginary or actual situations) to the things they fear and avoid. (p. 603)

external locus of control the perception that outside forces beyond our personal control determine our fate. (p. 454)

extinction the diminishing of a conditioned response; occurs in classical conditioning when an unconditioned stimulus (US) does not follow a conditioned stimulus (CS); occurs in operant conditioning when a response is no longer reinforced. (p. 262)

extrasensory perception (ESP) the controversial claim that perception can occur apart from sensory input; includes telepathy, clairvoyance, and precognition. (p. 252)

extrinsic motivation the desire to perform a behavior to receive promised rewards or avoid threatened punishment. (p. 414)

facial feedback effect the tendency of facial muscle states to trigger corresponding feelings such as fear, anger, or happiness. (p. 431)

family therapy therapy that treats people in the context of their family system. Views an individual's unwanted behaviors as influenced by, or directed at, other family members. (p. 610)

feature detectors nerve cells in the brain's visual cortex that respond to specific features of the stimulus, such as shape, angle, or movement. (p. 227)

feel-good, do-good phenomenon people's tendency to be helpful when in a good mood. (p. 434)

female orgasmic disorder distress due to infrequently or never experiencing orgasm. (p. 396)

fetal alcohol syndrome (FAS) physical and cognitive abnormalities in children caused by a pregnant woman's heavy drinking. In severe cases, signs include a small, out-of-proportion head and abnormal facial features. (p. 171)

fetus the developing human organism from 9 weeks after conception to birth. (p. 168)

figure-ground the organization of the visual field into objects (the *figures*) that stand out from their surroundings (the *ground*). (p. 228)

fixation (1) in cognition, the inability to see a problem from a new perspective; an obstacle to problem solving. (2) in psychoanalytic theory, a lingering focus of pleasure-seeking energies at an earlier psychosexual stage, in which conflicts were unresolved. (pp. 328, 520)

fixed-interval schedule in operant conditioning, a reinforcement schedule that reinforces a response only after a specified time has elapsed. (p. 273)

fixed-ratio schedule in operant conditioning, a reinforcement schedule that reinforces a response only after a specified number of responses. (p. 270)

flashbulb memory a clear memory of an emotionally significant moment or event. (p. 304)

fluid intelligence (*Gf*) our ability to reason speedily and abstractly; tends to decrease with age, especially during late adulthood. (p. 354)

fMRI (functional MRI) a technique for revealing blood flow and, therefore, brain activity by comparing successive MRI scans. fMRI scans show brain function as well as structure. (p. 67)

foot-in-the-door phenomenon the tendency for people who have first agreed to a small request to comply later with a larger request. (p. 471)

formal operational stage in Piaget's theory, the stage of cognitive development (normally beginning about age 12) at which people begin to think logically about abstract concepts. (p. 179)

fovea the central focal point in the retina, around which the eye's cones cluster. (p. 222)

framing the way an issue is posed; how an issue is framed can significantly affect decisions and judgments. (p. 333)

fraternal (dizygotic) twins individuals who developed from separate fertilized eggs. They are genetically no closer than ordinary siblings, but shared a prenatal environment. (p. 129)

free association in psychoanalysis, a method of exploring the unconscious in which the person relaxes and says whatever comes to mind, no matter how trivial or embarrassing. (p. 519)

frequency the number of complete wavelengths that pass a point in a given time (for example, per second). (p. 239)

frequency theory in hearing, the theory that the rate of nerve impulses traveling up the auditory nerve matches the frequency of a tone, thus enabling us to sense its pitch. (Also called *temporal coding*.) (p. 242)

frontal lobes the portion of the cerebral cortex lying just behind the forehead; involved in speaking and muscle movements and in making plans and judgments. (p. 76)

frustration-aggression principle the principle that frustration—the blocking of an attempt to achieve some goal—creates anger, which can generate aggression. (p. 497)

functionalism an early school of thought promoted by James and influenced by Darwin; explored how mental and behavioral processes function—how they enable the organism to adapt, survive, and flourish. (p. 6)

fundamental attribution error the tendency, when analyzing others' behavior, to underestimate the impact of the situation and to overestimate the impact of personal disposition. (p. 468)

gate-control theory the theory that the spinal cord contains a neurological "gate" that blocks pain signals or allows them to pass on to the brain. The "gate" is opened by the activity of pain signals traveling up small nerve fibers and is closed by activity in larger fibers or by information coming from the brain. (p. 245)

gender in psychology, the behavioral characteristics that people associate with *boy, girl, man,* and *woman*. (See also *gender identity*.) (p. 151)

gender identity our sense of being male, female, neither, or some combination of male and female. (p. 158)

gender role a set of expected behaviors, attitudes, and traits for men and for women. (p. 157)

gender typing the acquisition of a traditional masculine or feminine role. (p. 158)

general adaptation syndrome (GAS) Selye's concept of the body's adaptive response to stress in three phases—alarm, resistance, exhaustion. (p. 445)

general intelligence (*g*) according to Spearman and others, underlies all mental abilities and is therefore measured by every task on an intelligence test. (p. 354)

generalization (also called *stimulus generalization*) in classical conditioning, the tendency, once a response has been conditioned, for stimuli similar to the conditioned stimulus to elicit similar responses. (In operant conditioning, generalization occurs when responses learned in one situation occur in other, similar situations.) (p. 264)

generalized anxiety disorder an anxiety disorder in which a person is continually tense, apprehensive, and in a state of autonomic nervous system arousal. (p. 563)

genes the biochemical units of heredity that make up the chromosomes; small segments of DNA capable of synthesizing proteins. (p. 127)

genome the complete instructions for making an organism, consisting of all the genetic material in that organism's chromosomes. (p. 127)

gestalt an organized whole. Gestalt psychologists emphasized our tendency to integrate pieces of information into meaningful wholes. (p. 228)

glial cells (glia) cells in the nervous system that support, nourish, and protect neurons; they also play a role in learning, thinking, and memory. (p. 55)

glucose the form of sugar that circulates in the blood and provides the major source of energy for body tissues. When its level is low, we feel hunger. (p. 388)

grammar in a language, a system of rules that enables us to communicate with and understand others. *Semantics* is the language's set of rules for deriving meaning from sounds, and *syntax* is its set of rules for combining words into grammatically sensible sentences. (p. 341)

GRIT Graduated and Reciprocated Initiatives in Tension-Reduction—a strategy designed to decrease international tensions. (p. 515)

grit in psychology, passion and perseverance in the pursuit of long-term goals. (p. 413)

grouping the perceptual tendency to organize stimuli into coherent groups. (p. 228)

group polarization the enhancement of a group's prevailing inclinations through discussion within the group. (p. 484)

group therapy therapy conducted with groups rather than individuals, providing benefits from group interaction. (p. 609)

groupthink the mode of thinking that occurs when the desire for harmony in a decision-making group overrides a realistic appraisal of alternatives. (p. 487)

growth mindset a focus on learning and growing rather than viewing abilities as fixed. (p. 374)

gustation our sense of taste. (p. 247)

habituation decreasing responsiveness with repeated stimulation. As infants gain familiarity with repeated exposure to a stimulus, their interest wanes and they look away sooner. (p. 171)

hallucinations false sensory experiences, such as seeing something in the absence of an external visual stimulus. (p. 97)

hallucinogens psychedelic ("mind-manifesting") drugs, such as LSD, that distort perceptions and evoke sensory images in the absence of sensory input. (p. 119)

health psychology a subfield of psychology that provides psychology's contribution to behavioral medicine. (p. 447)

heredity the genetic transfer of characteristics from parents to offspring. (p. 127)

heritability the proportion of variation among individuals in a group that we can attribute to genes. The heritability of a trait may vary, depending on the range of populations and environments studied. (pp. 133, 370)

heuristic a simple thinking strategy—a mental shortcut—that often allows us to make judgments and solve problems efficiently; usually speedier but also more error-prone than an *algorithm*. (p. 327)

hierarchy of needs Maslow's pyramid of human needs, beginning at the base with physiological needs that must first be satisfied before people can fulfill their higher-level safety needs and then psychological needs. (pp. 384, 528)

higher-order conditioning a procedure in which the conditioned stimulus in one conditioning experience is paired with a new neutral stimulus, creating a second (often weaker) conditioned stimulus. For example, an animal that has learned that a tone predicts food might then learn that a light predicts the tone and begin responding to the light alone. (Also called *second-order conditioning*.) (p. 262)

hindsight bias the tendency to believe, after learning an outcome, that one would have foreseen it. (Also known as the *I-knew-it-all-along phenomenon*.) (p. 22)

hippocampus a neural center located in the limbic system; helps process explicit (conscious) memories—of facts and events—for storage. (pp. 73, 302)

homeostasis a tendency to maintain a balanced or constant internal state; the regulation of any aspect of body chemistry, such as blood glucose, around a particular level. (p. 383)

hormones chemical messengers that are manufactured by the endocrine glands, travel through the bloodstream, and affect other tissues. (p. 62)

hue the dimension of color that is determined by the wavelength of light; what we know as the color names *blue, green,* and so forth. (p. 221)

humanistic psychology a historically significant perspective that emphasized human growth potential. (p. 9)

humanistic theories theories that view personality with a focus on the potential for healthy personal growth. (p. 528)

hypnosis a social interaction in which one person (the hypnotist) suggests to another (the subject) that certain perceptions, feelings, thoughts, or behaviors will spontaneously occur. (pp. 88, 247)

hypothalamus [hi-po-THAL-uh-muss] a neural structure in the limbic system lying below (*hypo*) the thalamus; it directs several maintenance activities (eating, drinking, body temperature), helps govern the endocrine system via the pituitary gland, and is linked to emotion and reward. (p. 72)

hypothesis a testable prediction, often implied by a theory. (p. 26)

iconic memory a momentary sensory memory of visual stimuli; a photographic or picture-image memory lasting no more than a few tenths of a second. (p. 296)

id a reservoir of unconscious psychic energy that, according to Freud, strives to satisfy basic sexual and aggressive drives. The id operates on the *pleasure principle*, demanding immediate gratification. (p. 520)

identical (monozygotic) twins individuals who developed from a single fertilized egg that split in two, creating two genetically identical organisms. (p. 129)

identification the process by which, according to Freud, children incorporate their parents' values into their developing superegos. (p. 520)

identity our sense of self; according to Erikson, the adolescent's task is to solidify a sense of self by testing and integrating various roles. (p. 194)

illness anxiety disorder a disorder in which a person interprets normal physical sensations as symptoms of a disease. (Formerly called *hypochondriasis*.) (p. 566)

illusory correlation perceiving a relationship where none exists, or perceiving a stronger-than-actual relationship. (p. 33)

implicit memory retention of learned skills or classically conditioned associations independent of conscious recollection. (Also called *nondeclarative memory*.) (p. 296)

imprinting the process by which certain animals form strong attachments during early life. (p. 180)

inattentional blindness failing to see visible objects when our attention is directed elsewhere. (p. 90)

incentive a positive or negative environmental stimulus that motivates behavior. (p. 383)

independent variable in an experiment, the factor that is manipulated; the variable whose effect is being studied. (p. 36)

individualism giving priority to one's own goals over group goals and defining one's identity in terms of personal attributes rather than group identifications. (p. 146)

informational social influence influence resulting from a person's willingness to accept others' opinions about reality. (p. 479)

informed consent giving potential participants enough information about a study to enable them to choose whether they wish to participate. (p. 41)

ingroup "us"—people with whom we share a common identity. (p. 493)

ingroup bias the tendency to favor our own group. (p. 493)

inner ear the innermost part of the ear, containing the cochlea, semicircular canals, and vestibular sacs. (p. 239)

insight a sudden realization of a problem's solution; contrasts with strategy-based solutions. (p. 327)

insight therapies therapies that aim to improve psychological functioning by increasing a person's awareness of underlying motives and defenses. (p. 600)

insomnia recurring problems in falling or staying asleep. (p. 105)

instinct a complex behavior that is rigidly patterned throughout a species and is unlearned. (p. 383)

instinctive drift the tendency of learned behavior to gradually revert to biologically predisposed patterns. (p. 281)

intellectual disability a condition of limited mental ability, indicated by an intelligence test score of 70 or below and difficulty adapting to the demands of life. (Formerly referred to as *mental retardation*.) (p. 592)

intelligence the ability to learn from experience, solve problems, and use knowledge to adapt to new situations. (p. 354)

intelligence quotient (IQ) defined originally as the ratio of mental age (*ma*) to chronological age (*ca*) multiplied by 100 (thus, IQ = *ma* / *ca* × 100). On contemporary intelligence tests, the average performance for a given age is assigned a score of 100. (p. 361)

intelligence test a method for assessing an individual's mental aptitudes and comparing them with those of others, using numerical scores. (p. 359)

intensity the amount of energy in a light wave or sound wave, which influences what we perceive as brightness or loudness. Intensity is determined by the wave's amplitude (height). (p. 221)

interaction the interplay that occurs when the effect of one factor (such as environment) depends on another factor (such as heredity). (p. 133)

internal locus of control the perception that we control our own fate. (p. 454)

interneurons neurons within the brain and spinal cord; they communicate internally and process information between the sensory inputs and motor outputs. (p. 61)

interpretation in psychoanalysis, the analyst's noting of supposed dream meanings, resistances, and other significant behaviors and events in order to promote insight. (p. 599)

intersex possessing male and female biological sexual characteristics at birth. (p. 151)

intimacy in Erikson's theory, the ability to form close, loving relationships; a primary developmental task in young adulthood. (p. 196)

intrinsic motivation a desire to perform a behavior effectively for its own sake. (p. 414)

intuition an effortless, immediate, automatic feeling or thought, as contrasted with explicit, conscious reasoning. (p. 328)

James-Lange theory the theory that our experience of emotion occurs when we become aware of our physiological responses to an emotion-arousing stimulus. (p. 419)

just-world phenomenon the tendency for people to believe that the world is just and people therefore get what they deserve and deserve what they get. (p. 493)

kinesthesia [kin-ehs-THEE-zhuh] our movement sense—our system for sensing the position and movement of individual body parts. (p. 250)

language our spoken, written, or signed words and the ways we combine them to communicate meaning. (p. 341)

latent content according to Freud, the underlying meaning of a dream (as distinct from its manifest content). (p. 106)

latent learning learning that occurs but is not apparent until there is an incentive to demonstrate it. (p. 282)

law of effect Thorndike's principle that behaviors followed by favorable consequences become more likely, and that behaviors followed by unfavorable consequences become less likely. (p. 268)

learned helplessness the hopelessness and passive resignation humans and other animals learn when unable to avoid repeated aversive events. (p. 453)

learning the process of acquiring through experience new and relatively enduring information or behaviors. (pp. 258, 267, 278)

lesion [LEE-zhuhn] tissue destruction. A brain lesion is a naturally or experimentally caused destruction of brain tissue. (p. 67)

levels of analysis the differing complementary views, from biological to psychological to social-cultural, for analyzing any given phenomenon. (p. 12)

limbic system neural system (including the *amygdala, hypothalamus,* and *hippocampus*) located below the cerebral hemispheres; associated with emotions and drives. (p. 71)

linguistic determinism Whorf's hypothesis that language determines the way we think. (p. 348)

linguistic relativism the idea that language influences the way we think. (p. 348)

lobotomy a psychosurgical procedure once used to calm uncontrollably emotional or violent patients. The procedure cut the nerves connecting the frontal lobes to the emotion-controlling centers of the inner brain. (p. 627)

longitudinal study research that follows and retests the same people over time. (pp. 166, 367)

long-term memory the relatively permanent and limitless archive of the memory system. Includes knowledge, skills, and experiences. (p. 294)

long-term potentiation (LTP) an increase in a nerve cell's firing potential after brief, rapid stimulation; a neural basis for learning and memory. (p. 304)

LSD (*lysergic acid diethylamide*) a powerful hallucinogenic drug; also known as *acid*. (p. 119)

magnetoencephalography (MEG) a brain-imaging technique that measures magnetic fields from the brain's natural electrical activity. (p. 67)

major depressive disorder a disorder in which a person experiences, in the absence of drug use or a medical condition, two or more weeks with five or more symptoms, at least one of which must be either (1) depressed mood or (2) loss of interest or pleasure. (p. 571)

mania a hyperactive, wildly optimistic state in which dangerously poor judgment is common. (p. 572)

manifest content according to Freud, the symbolic, remembered story line of a dream (as distinct from its latent, or hidden, content). (p. 106)

maturation biological growth processes that enable orderly changes in behavior, relatively uninfluenced by experience. (p. 172)

mean the arithmetic average of a distribution, obtained by adding the scores and then dividing by the number of scores. (p. 44)

median the middle score in a distribution; half the scores are above it and half are below it. (p. 44)

medical model the concept that diseases, in this case psychological disorders, have physical causes that can be *diagnosed, treated,* and, in most cases, *cured,* often through treatment in a *hospital.* (p. 555)

medulla [muh-DUL-uh] the base of the brainstem; controls heartbeat and breathing. (p. 69)

memory the persistence of learning over time through the encoding, storage, and retrieval of information. (p. 293)

memory consolidation the neural storage of a long-term memory. (p. 302)

menarche [meh-NAR-key] the first menstrual period. (p. 155)

menopause the time of natural cessation of menstruation; also refers to the biological changes a woman experiences as her ability to reproduce declines. (p. 199)

mental age a measure of intelligence test performance devised by Binet; the level of performance typically associated with children of a certain chronological age. Thus, a child who does as well as an average 8-year-old is said to have a mental age of 8. (p. 361)

mental set a tendency to approach a problem in one particular way, often a way that has been successful in the past. (p. 328)

mere exposure effect the tendency for repeated exposure to novel stimuli to increase our liking of them. (p. 503)

meta-analysis a statistical procedure for analyzing the results of multiple studies to reach an overall conclusion. (pp. 27, 615)

metacognition cognition about our cognition; keeping track of and evaluating our mental processes. (p. 327)

methamphetamine a powerfully addictive drug that stimulates the central nervous system, with accelerated body functions and associated energy and mood changes; over time, reduces baseline dopamine levels. (p. 116)

middle ear the chamber between the eardrum and cochlea containing three tiny bones—hammer (malleus), anvil (incus), and stirrup (stapes)—that concentrate the vibrations of the eardrum on the cochlea's oval window. (p. 239)

mindfulness meditation a reflective practice in which people attend to current experiences in a nonjudgmental and accepting manner. (p. 462)

Minnesota Multiphasic Personality Inventory (MMPI) the most widely researched and clinically used of all personality tests. Originally developed to identify emotional disorders (still considered its most appropriate use), this test is now used for many other screening purposes. (p. 535)

mirror-image perceptions mutual views often held by conflicting parties, as when each side sees itself as ethical and peaceful and views the other side as evil and aggressive. (p. 512)

mirror neurons frontal lobe neurons that some scientists believe fire when we perform certain actions or observe another doing so. The brain's mirroring of another's action may enable imitation and empathy. (p. 284)

misinformation effect occurs when a memory has been corrupted by misleading information. (p. 316)

mnemonics [nih-MON-iks] memory aids, especially those techniques that use vivid imagery and organizational devices. (p. 298)

mode the most frequently occurring score(s) in a distribution. (p. 44)

modeling the process of observing and imitating a specific behavior. (p. 282)

molecular behavior genetics the study of how the structure and function of genes interact with our environment to influence behavior. (p. 133)

molecular genetics the subfield of biology that studies the molecular structure and function of genes. (p. 133)

monocular cue a depth cue, such as interposition or linear perspective, available to either eye alone. (p. 232)

mood-congruent memory the tendency to recall experiences that are consistent with one's current good or bad mood. (p. 309)

morpheme in a language, the smallest unit that carries meaning; may be a word or a part of a word (such as a prefix). (p. 341)

motivation a need or desire that energizes and directs behavior. (p. 383)

motor (efferent) neurons neurons that carry outgoing information from the brain and spinal cord to the muscles and glands. (p. 61)

motor cortex a cerebral cortex area at the rear of the frontal lobes that controls voluntary movements. (p. 76)

MRI (magnetic resonance imaging) a technique that uses magnetic fields and radio waves to produce computer-generated images of soft tissue. MRI scans show brain anatomy. (p. 67)

mutation a random error in gene replication that leads to a change. (p. 136)

myelin [MY-uh-lin] **sheath** a fatty tissue layer segmentally encasing the axons of some neurons; enables vastly greater transmission speed as neural impulses hop from one node to the next. (p. 55)

narcissism excessive self-love and self-absorption. (pp. 411, 548)

narcolepsy a sleep disorder characterized by uncontrollable sleep attacks. The sufferer may lapse directly into REM sleep, often at inopportune times. (p. 105)

naturalistic observation a descriptive technique of observing and recording behavior in naturally occurring situations without trying to manipulate and control the situation. (p. 28)

natural selection the principle that inherited traits that better enable an organism to survive and reproduce in a particular environment will (in competition with other trait variations) most likely be passed on to succeeding generations. (pp. 10, 135)

nature–nurture issue the longstanding controversy over the relative contributions that genes and experience make to the development of psychological traits and behaviors. Today's science sees traits and behaviors arising from the interaction of nature and nurture. (p. 10)

near-death experience an altered state of consciousness reported after a close brush with death (such as cardiac arrest); often similar to drug-induced hallucinations. (p. 119)

negative reinforcement increasing behaviors by stopping or reducing an aversive stimulus. A negative reinforcer is any stimulus that, when *removed* after a response, strengthens the response. (*Note:* Negative reinforcement is not punishment.) (p. 270)

nerves bundled axons that form neural cables connecting the central nervous system with muscles, glands, and sensory organs. (p. 61)

nervous system the body's speedy, electrochemical communication network, consisting of all the nerve cells of the peripheral and central nervous systems. (p. 61)

neurocognitive disorders (NCDs) acquired (not lifelong) disorders marked by cognitive deficits; often related to Alzheimer's disease, brain injury or disease, or substance abuse. In older adults, neurocognitive disorders are also called *dementia*. (p. 205)

neurodevelopmental disorder central nervous system abnormalities (usually in the brain) that start in childhood and alter thinking and behavior (as in intellectual limitations or a psychological disorder). (p. 592)

neurogenesis the formation of new neurons. (p. 82)

neuron a nerve cell; the basic building block of the nervous system. (p. 55)

neuroplasticity the brain's ability to change, especially during childhood, by reorganizing after damage or by building new pathways based on experience. (pp. 52, 81)

neurotransmitters chemical messengers that cross the synaptic gap between neurons. When released by the sending neuron, neurotransmitters travel across the synapse and bind to receptor sites

on the receiving neuron, thereby influencing whether that neuron will generate a neural impulse. (p. 57)

neutral stimulus (NS) in classical conditioning, a stimulus that elicits no response before conditioning. (p. 261)

nicotine a stimulating and highly addictive psychoactive drug in tobacco products. (p. 114)

night terrors a sleep disorder characterized by high arousal and an appearance of being terrified; unlike nightmares, night terrors occur during N3 sleep, within 2 or 3 hours of falling asleep, and are seldom remembered. (p. 105)

norm an understood rule for accepted and expected behavior. Norms prescribe "proper" behavior. (p. 145)

normal curve a symmetrical, bell-shaped curve that describes the distribution of many types of data; most scores fall near the mean (about 68 percent fall within one standard deviation of it) and fewer and fewer near the extremes. (Also called a *normal distribution*.) (pp. 47, 363)

normative social influence influence resulting from a person's desire to gain approval or avoid disapproval. (p. 477)

norms understood rules for accepted and expected behavior. Norms prescribe "proper" behavior. (p. 475)

nudge framing choices in a way that encourages people to make beneficial decisions. (p. 333)

obesity defined as a body mass index (BMI) measurement of 30 or higher, which is calculated from our weight-to-height ratio. (Individuals who are *overweight* have a BMI of 25 or higher.) (p. 391)

object permanence the awareness that things continue to exist even when not perceived. (p. 175)

observational learning learning by observing others. (p. 282)

obsessive-compulsive disorder (OCD) a disorder characterized by unwanted repetitive thoughts (obsessions), actions (compulsions), or both. (p. 565)

occipital [ahk-SIP-uh-tuhl] **lobes** the portion of the cerebral cortex lying at the back of the head; includes areas that receive information from the visual fields. (p. 76)

Oedipus [ED-uh-puss] **complex** according to Freud, a boy's sexual desires toward his mother and feelings of jealousy and hatred for the rival father. (p. 520)

olfaction our sense of smell. (p. 248)

one-word stage the stage in speech development, from about age 1 to 2, during which a child speaks mostly in single words. (p. 343)

operant behavior behavior that operates on the environment, producing a consequence. (pp. 258, 268)

operant chamber in operant conditioning research, a chamber (also known as a *Skinner box*) containing a bar or key that an animal can manipulate to obtain a food or water reinforcer; attached devices record the animal's rate of bar pressing or key pecking. (p. 268)

operant conditioning a type of learning in which a behavior becomes more likely to recur if followed by a reinforcer or less likely to recur if followed by a punisher. (p. 268)

operational definition a carefully worded statement of the exact procedures (operations) used in a research study. For example, *human intelligence* may be operationally defined as what an intelligence test measures. (Also known as *operationalization*.) (p. 26)

opiates opium and its derivatives, such as morphine and heroin; depress neural activity, temporarily lessening pain and anxiety. (p. 114)

opponent-process theory the theory that opposing retinal processes (red-green, blue-yellow, white-black) enable color vision. For example, some cells are stimulated by green and inhibited by red; others are stimulated by red and inhibited by green. (p. 227)

optic nerve the nerve that carries neural impulses from the eye to the brain. (p. 222)

ostracism deliberate social exclusion of individuals or groups. (p. 408)

other-race effect the tendency to recall faces of one's own race more accurately than faces of other races. Also called the *cross-race effect* and the *own-race bias*. (p. 495)

outgroup "them"—those perceived as different or apart from our ingroup. (p. 493)

overconfidence the tendency to be more confident than correct—to overestimate the accuracy of our beliefs and judgments. (p. 330)

panic disorder an anxiety disorder marked by unpredictable, minutes-long episodes of intense dread in which a person may experience terror and accompanying chest pain, choking, or other frightening sensations; often followed by worry over a possible next attack. (p. 563)

parallel processing processing many aspects of a stimulus or problem simultaneously. (pp. 93, 228, 294)

paraphilias sexual arousal from fantasies, behaviors, or urges involving nonhuman objects, the suffering of self or others, and/or nonconsenting persons. (p. 396)

parapsychology the study of paranormal phenomena, including ESP and psychokinesis (also called *telekinesis*). (p. 254)

parasympathetic nervous system the division of the autonomic nervous system that calms the body, conserving its energy. (p. 61)

parietal [puh-RYE-uh-tuhl] **lobes** the portion of the cerebral cortex lying at the top of the head and toward the rear; receives sensory input for touch and body position. (p. 76)

partial (intermittent) reinforcement schedule reinforcing a response only part of the time; results in slower acquisition of a response but much greater resistance to extinction than does continuous reinforcement. (p. 270)

passionate love an aroused state of intense positive absorption in another, usually present at the beginning of a romantic relationship. (p. 506)

perception the process by which our brain organizes and interprets sensory information, enabling us to recognize meaningful objects and events. (p. 213)

perceptual adaptation the ability to adjust to changed sensory input, including an artificially displaced or even inverted visual field. (p. 236)

perceptual constancy perceiving objects as unchanging (having consistent color, brightness, shape, and size) even as illumination and retinal images change. (p. 232)

perceptual set a mental predisposition to perceive one thing and not another. (p. 217)

peripheral nervous system (PNS) the sensory and motor neurons that connect the central nervous system (CNS) to the rest of the body. (p. 61)

peripheral route persuasion occurs when people are influenced by incidental cues, such as a speaker's attractiveness. (p. 473)

personal control our sense of controlling our environment rather than feeling helpless. (p. 453)

personality an individual's characteristic pattern of thinking, feeling, and acting. (p. 519)

personality disorders inflexible and enduring behavior patterns that impair social functioning. (p. 587)

personality inventory a questionnaire (often with *true-false* or *agree-disagree* items) on which people respond to items designed to gauge a wide range of feelings and behaviors; used to assess selected personality traits. (p. 535)

person-centered therapy a humanistic therapy, developed by Carl Rogers, in which the therapist uses techniques such as *active listening* within an accepting, genuine, empathic environment to facilitate clients' growth. (Also called *client-centered therapy*.) (p. 600)

PET (positron emission tomography) a technique for detecting brain activity that displays where a radioactive form of glucose goes while the brain performs a given task. (p. 67)

phi phenomenon an illusion of movement created when two or more adjacent lights blink on and off in quick succession. (p. 232)

phoneme in a language, the smallest distinctive sound unit. (p. 341)

physiological need a basic bodily requirement. (p. 383)

pitch a tone's experienced highness or lowness; depends on frequency. (p. 239)

pituitary gland the endocrine system's most influential gland. Under the influence of the hypothalamus, the pituitary regulates growth and controls other endocrine glands. (p. 64)

place theory in hearing, the theory that links the pitch we hear with the place where the cochlea's membrane is stimulated. (Also called *place coding*.) (p. 242)

placebo [pluh-SEE-bo; Latin for "I shall please"] **effect** experimental results caused by expectations alone; any effect on behavior caused by the administration of an inert substance or condition, which the recipient assumes is an active agent. (p. 36)

polygraph a machine used in attempts to detect lies; measures emotion-linked changes in perspiration, heart rate, and breathing. (p. 424)

population all those in a group being studied, from which random samples may be drawn. (*Note:* Except for national studies, this does *not* refer to a country's whole population.) (p. 30)

positive psychology the scientific study of human flourishing, with the goals of discovering and promoting strengths and virtues that help individuals and communities to thrive. (pp. 12, 434)

positive reinforcement increasing behaviors by presenting a pleasurable stimulus. A positive reinforcer is any stimulus that, when presented after a response, strengthens the response. (p. 268)

posthypnotic suggestion a suggestion, made during a hypnosis session, to be carried out after the subject is no longer hypnotized; used by some clinicians to help control undesired symptoms and behaviors. (p. 247)

posttraumatic growth positive psychological changes following a struggle with extremely challenging circumstances and life crises. (p. 629)

posttraumatic stress disorder (PTSD) a disorder characterized by haunting memories, nightmares, hypervigilance, avoidance of trauma-related stimuli, social withdrawal, jumpy anxiety, numbness of feeling, and/or insomnia that lingers for four weeks or more after a traumatic experience. (p. 565)

predictive validity the success with which a test predicts the behavior it is designed to predict; it is assessed by computing the correlation between test scores and the criterion behavior. (Also called *criterion-related validity*.) (p. 365)

prejudice an unjustifiable and usually negative attitude toward a group and its members. Prejudice generally involves stereotyped beliefs, negative feelings, and a predisposition to discriminatory action. (p. 488)

preoperational stage in Piaget's theory, the stage (from about 2 to 6 or 7 years of age) at which a child learns to use language but does not yet comprehend the mental operations of concrete logic. (p. 177)

preparedness a biological predisposition to learn associations, such as between taste and nausea, that have survival value. (p. 278)

preregistration publicly communicating planned study design, hypotheses, data collection, and analyses. (p. 27)

primary reinforcer an innately reinforcing stimulus, such as one that satisfies a biological need. (p. 270)

primary sex characteristics the body structures (ovaries, testes, and external genitalia) that make sexual reproduction possible. (p. 155)

priming the activation, often unconsciously, of certain associations, thus predisposing one's perception, memory, or response. (pp. 214, 307)

proactive interference the forward-acting disruptive effect of older learning on the recall of *new* information. (p. 315)

problem-focused coping attempting to alleviate stress directly—by changing the stressor or the way we interact with that stressor. (p. 453)

projective test a personality test, such as the TAT or Rorschach, that provides ambiguous images designed to trigger projection of people's inner dynamics. (p. 527)

prosocial behavior positive, constructive, helpful behavior. The opposite of antisocial behavior. (p. 287)

prototype a mental image or best example of a category. Matching new items to a prototype provides a quick and easy method for sorting items into categories (as when comparing feathered creatures to a prototypical bird, such as a crow). (p. 327)

psychiatry a branch of medicine dealing with psychological disorders; practiced by physicians who sometimes provide medical (for example, drug) treatments as well as psychological therapy. (p. 14)

psychoactive drug a chemical substance that alters perceptions and moods. (p. 110)

psychoanalysis (1) Freud's theory of personality that attributes thoughts and actions to unconscious motives and conflicts. (2) Freud's therapeutic technique. Freud believed the patient's free associations, resistances, dreams, and transferences—and the analyst's interpretations of them—released previously repressed feelings, allowing the patient to gain self-insight. (pp. 519, 599)

psychodynamic theories theories that view personality with a focus on the unconscious and the importance of childhood experiences. (p. 519)

psychodynamic therapy therapy deriving from the psychoanalytic tradition; views individuals as responding to unconscious forces and childhood experiences, and seeks to enhance self-insight. (p. 600)

psychological disorder a syndrome marked by a clinically significant disturbance in an individual's cognitions, emotion regulation, or behavior. (p. 553)

psychology the science of behavior and mental processes. (p. 9)

psychoneuroimmunology the study of how psychological, neural, and endocrine processes together affect our immune system and resulting health. (p. 447)

psychopharmacology the study of the effects of drugs on mind and behavior. (p. 623)

psychophysics the study of relationships between the physical characteristics of stimuli, such as their intensity, and our psychological experience of them. (p. 213)

psychosexual stages the childhood stages of development (oral, anal, phallic, latency, genital) during which, according to Freud, the id's pleasure-seeking energies focus on distinct *erogenous zones*. (p. 520)

psychosurgery surgery that removes or destroys brain tissue in an effort to change behavior. (p. 627)

psychotherapy treatment involving psychological techniques; consists of interactions between a trained therapist and someone seeking to overcome psychological difficulties or achieve personal growth. (pp. 599, 613)

psychotic disorders a group of disorders marked by irrational ideas, distorted perceptions, and a loss of contact with reality. (p. 579)

puberty the period of sexual maturation, during which a person usually becomes capable of reproducing. (pp. 155, 190)

punishment an event that tends to *decrease* the behavior that it follows. (p. 273)

random assignment assigning participants to experimental and control groups by chance, thus minimizing preexisting differences between the different groups. (p. 35)

random sample a sample that fairly represents a population because each member has an equal chance of inclusion. (p. 30)

range the difference between the highest and lowest scores in a distribution. (p. 47)

recall a measure of memory in which the person must retrieve information learned earlier, as on a fill-in-the-blank test. (p. 293)

reciprocal determinism the interacting influences of behavior, internal cognition, and environment. (p. 541)

reciprocity norm an expectation that people will help, not hurt, those who have helped them. (p. 511)

recognition a measure of memory in which the person identifies items previously learned, as on a multiple-choice test. (p. 293)

reconsolidation a process in which previously stored memories, when retrieved, are potentially altered before being stored again. (p. 316)

reflex a simple, automatic response to a sensory stimulus, such as the knee-jerk reflex. (p. 62)

refractory period (1) in neural processing, a brief resting pause that occurs after a neuron has fired; subsequent action potentials cannot occur until the axon returns to its resting state. (2) in human sexuality, a resting period that occurs after orgasm, during which a person cannot achieve another orgasm. (pp. 57, 394)

regression toward the mean the tendency for extreme or unusual scores or events to fall back (regress) toward the average. (p. 33)

reinforcement in operant conditioning, any event that *strengthens* the behavior it follows. (p. 268)

reinforcement schedule a pattern that defines how often a desired response will be reinforced. (p. 270)

relational aggression an act of aggression (physical or verbal) intended to harm a person's relationship or social standing. (p. 151)

relative deprivation the perception that we are worse off relative to those with whom we compare ourselves. (p. 438)

relearning a measure of memory that assesses the amount of time saved when learning material again. (p. 293)

reliability the extent to which a test yields consistent results, as assessed by the consistency of scores on two halves of the test, on alternative forms of the test, or on retesting. (p. 365)

REM rebound the tendency for REM sleep to increase following REM sleep deprivation. (p. 109)

REM (R) sleep rapid eye movement sleep; a recurring sleep stage during which vivid dreams commonly occur. Also known as *paradoxical sleep*, because the muscles are relaxed (except for minor twitches) but other body systems are active. (p. 97)

replication repeating the essence of a research study, usually with different participants in different situations, to see whether the basic finding can be reproduced. (p. 26)

representativeness heuristic judging the likelihood of events in terms of how well they seem to represent, or match, particular prototypes; may lead us to ignore other relevant information. (p. 329)

repression in psychoanalytic theory, the basic defense mechanism that banishes from consciousness anxiety-arousing thoughts, feelings, and memories. (pp. 315, 520)

resilience the personal strength that helps people cope with stress and recover from adversity and even trauma. (p. 629)

resistance in psychoanalysis, the blocking from consciousness of anxiety-laden material. (p. 599)

respondent behavior behavior that occurs as an automatic response to some stimulus. (pp. 258, 267)

reticular formation a nerve network that travels through the brainstem into the thalamus; filters information and plays an important role in controlling arousal. (p. 71)

retina the light-sensitive inner surface of the eye, containing the receptor rods and cones plus layers of neurons that begin the processing of visual information. (p. 222)

retinal disparity a binocular cue for perceiving depth. By comparing retinal images from the two eyes, the brain computes distance—the greater the disparity (difference) between the two images, the closer the object. (p. 231)

retrieval the process of getting information out of memory storage. (p. 294)

retroactive interference the backward-acting disruptive effect of newer learning on the recall of old information. (p. 315)

retrograde amnesia an inability to remember information from one's past. (p. 311)

reuptake a neurotransmitter's reabsorption by the sending neuron. (p. 59)

rods retinal receptors that detect black, white, and gray, and are sensitive to movement. Rods are necessary for peripheral and twilight vision, when cones don't respond. (p. 222)

role a set of expectations (*norms*) about a social position, defining how those in the position ought to behave. (pp. 157, 471)

Rorschach inkblot test the most widely used projective test. Designed by Hermann Rorschach, the test seeks to identify people's inner feelings by analyzing how they interpret 10 inkblots. (p. 527)

rumination compulsive fretting; *overthinking* our problems and their causes. (p. 577)

savant syndrome a condition in which a person otherwise limited in mental ability has an exceptional specific skill, such as in computation or drawing. (p. 356)

scaffold in Vygotsky's theory, a framework that offers children temporary support as they develop higher levels of thinking. (p. 179)

scapegoat theory the theory that prejudice offers an outlet for anger by providing someone to blame. (p. 493)

scatterplot a graphed cluster of dots, each of which represents the values of two variables. The slope of the points suggests the direction of the relationship between the two variables. The amount of scatter suggests the strength of the correlation (little scatter indicates high correlation). (p. 30)

schema a concept or framework that organizes and interprets information. (p. 175)

schizophrenia a disorder characterized by delusions, hallucinations, disorganized speech, and/or diminished, inappropriate emotional expression. (p. 579)

secondary sex characteristics nonreproductive sexual traits, such as female breasts and hips, male voice quality, and body hair. (p. 155)

selective attention focusing conscious awareness on a particular stimulus. (p. 90)

self in contemporary psychology, assumed to be the center of personality, the organizer of our thoughts, feelings, and actions. (p. 544)

self-actualization according to Maslow, one of the ultimate psychological needs that arises after basic physical and psychological needs are met and self-esteem is achieved; the motivation to fulfill one's potential. (p. 528)

self-concept all our thoughts and feelings about ourselves, in answer to the question, "Who am I?" (pp. 186, 530)

self-control the ability to control impulses and delay short-term gratification for greater long-term rewards. (p. 454)

self-determination theory the theory that we feel motivated to satisfy our needs for competence, autonomy, and relatedness. (p. 407)

self-disclosure the act of revealing intimate aspects of ourselves to others. (p. 506)

self-efficacy our sense of competence and effectiveness. (p. 544)

self-esteem our feelings of high or low self-worth. (p. 544)

self-fulfilling prophecy a belief that leads to its own fulfillment. (p. 512)

self-serving bias a readiness to perceive ourselves favorably. (p. 547)

self-transcendence according to Maslow, the striving for identity, meaning, and purpose beyond the self. (p. 528)

semantic memory explicit memory of facts and general knowledge; one of our two conscious memory systems (the other is *episodic memory*). (p. 302)

sensation the process by which our sensory receptors and nervous system receive and represent stimulus energies from our environment. (p. 213)

sensorimotor stage in Piaget's theory, the stage (from birth to nearly 2 years of age) at which infants know the world mostly in terms of their sensory impressions and motor activities. (p. 175)

sensorineural hearing loss the most common form of hearing loss, caused by damage to the cochlea's receptor cells or to the auditory nerve; also called *nerve deafness*. (p. 240)

sensory adaptation diminished sensitivity as a consequence of constant stimulation. (p. 217)

sensory interaction the principle that one sense can influence another, as when the smell of food influences its taste. (p. 252)

sensory memory the immediate, very brief recording of sensory information in the memory system. (p. 294)

sensory (afferent) neurons neurons that carry incoming information from the body's tissues and sensory receptors to the brain and spinal cord. (p. 61)

sensory receptors sensory nerve endings that respond to stimuli. (p. 213)

sequential processing processing one aspect of a stimulus or problem at a time; generally used to process new information or to solve difficult problems. (p. 93)

serial position effect our tendency to recall best the last (*recency effect*) and first (*primacy effect*) items in a list. (p. 309)

set point the point at which your "weight thermostat" may be set. When your body falls below this weight, increased hunger and a lowered metabolic rate may combine to restore lost weight. (p. 388)

sex in psychology, the biologically influenced characteristics by which people define *male, female,* and *intersex*. (p. 151)

sexual aggression any physical or verbal behavior of a sexual nature that is unwanted or intended to harm someone physically or emotionally. Can be expressed as either *sexual harassment* or *sexual assault*. (p. 158)

sexual dysfunction a problem that consistently impairs sexual arousal or functioning at any point in the sexual response cycle. (p. 396)

sexual orientation the direction of our sexual attractions, as reflected in our longings and fantasies. (p. 399)

sexual response cycle the four stages of sexual responding described by Masters and Johnson—excitement, plateau, orgasm, and resolution. (p. 394)

shallow processing encoding on a basic level, based on the structure or appearance of words. (p. 301)

shaping an operant conditioning procedure in which reinforcers guide behavior toward closer and closer approximations of the desired behavior. (p. 268)

short-term memory briefly activated memory of a few items (such as digits of a phone number while calling) that is later stored or forgotten. (p. 294)

signal detection theory a theory predicting how and when we detect the presence of a faint stimulus (*signal*) amid background stimulation (*noise*). Assumes there is no single absolute threshold and that detection depends partly on a person's experience, expectations, motivation, and alertness. (p. 213)

sleep a periodic, natural loss of consciousness—as distinct from unconsciousness resulting from a coma, general anesthesia, or hibernation. (Adapted from Dement, 1999.) (p. 95)

sleep apnea a sleep disorder characterized by temporary cessations of breathing during sleep and repeated momentary awakenings. (p. 105)

social clock the culturally preferred timing of social events such as marriage, parenthood, and retirement. (p. 205)

social-cognitive perspective a view of behavior as influenced by the interaction between people's traits (including their thinking) and their social context. (p. 541)

social exchange theory the theory that our social behavior is an exchange process, the aim of which is to maximize benefits and minimize costs. (p. 511)

social facilitation in the presence of others, improved performance on simple or well-learned tasks, and worsened performance on difficult tasks. (p. 483)

social identity the "we" aspect of our self-concept; the part of our answer to "Who am I?" that comes from our group memberships. (p. 194)

social learning theory the theory that we learn social behavior by observing and imitating and by being rewarded or punished. (p. 158)

social loafing the tendency for people in a group to exert less effort when pooling their efforts toward attaining a common goal than when individually accountable. (p. 483)

social psychology the scientific study of how we think about, influence, and relate to one another. (p. 468)

social-responsibility norm an expectation that people will help those needing their help. (p. 511)

social script a culturally modeled guide for how to act in various situations. (pp. 140, 498)

social trap a situation in which the conflicting parties, by each pursuing their self-interest rather than the good of the group, become caught in mutually destructive behavior. (p. 511)

somatic nervous system the division of the peripheral nervous system that controls the body's skeletal muscles. Also called the *skeletal nervous system*. (p. 61)

somatic symptom disorder a psychological disorder in which the symptoms take a somatic (bodily) form without apparent physical cause. (p. 566)

somatosensory cortex a cerebral cortex area at the front of the parietal lobes that registers and processes body touch and movement sensations. (p. 78)

source amnesia faulty memory for how, when, or where information was learned or imagined. (Also called *source misattribution*.) Source amnesia, along with the misinformation effect, is at the heart of many false memories. (p. 319)

spacing effect the tendency for distributed study or practice to yield better long-term retention than

is achieved through massed study or practice. (p. 298)

specific phobia an anxiety disorder marked by a persistent, irrational fear and avoidance of a specific object, activity, or situation. (p. 565)

spermarche [sper-MAR-key] the first ejaculation. (p. 155)

split brain a condition resulting from surgery that separates the brain's two hemispheres by cutting the fibers (mainly those of the corpus callosum) connecting them. (p. 82)

spontaneous recovery the reappearance, after a pause, of an extinguished conditioned response. (p. 262)

spotlight effect overestimating others' noticing and evaluating our appearance, performance, and blunders (as if we presume a spotlight shines on us). (p. 544)

SQ3R a study method incorporating five steps: Survey, Question, Read, Retrieve, Review. (p. 17)

standard deviation a computed measure of how much scores vary around the mean score. (p. 47)

standardization defining uniform testing procedures and meaningful scores by comparison with the performance of a pretested group. (p. 363)

Stanford-Binet the widely used American revision (by Terman at Stanford University) of Binet's original intelligence test. (p. 361)

statistical significance a statistical statement of how likely it is that an obtained result occurred by chance. (p. 48)

stereotype a generalized (sometimes accurate but often overgeneralized) belief about a group of people. (p. 488)

stereotype threat a self-confirming concern that one will be evaluated based on a negative stereotype. (p. 378)

stimulants drugs (such as caffeine, nicotine, and the more powerful cocaine, amphetamines, methamphetamine, and Ecstasy) that excite neural activity and speed up body functions. (p. 114)

stimulus any event or situation that evokes a response. (pp. 258, 267)

storage the process of retaining encoded information over time. (p. 294)

stranger anxiety the fear of strangers that infants commonly display, beginning by about 8 months of age. (p. 180)

stress the process by which we perceive and respond to certain events, called *stressors*, that we appraise as threatening or challenging. (p. 441)

structuralism an early school of thought promoted by Wundt and Titchener; used introspection to reveal the structure of the human mind. (p. 6)

subjective well-being self-perceived happiness or satisfaction with life. Used along with measures of objective well-being (for example, physical and economic indicators) to evaluate people's quality of life. (p. 434)

subliminal below one's absolute threshold for conscious awareness. (p. 214)

substance use disorder a disorder characterized by continued substance craving and use despite significant life disruption and/or physical risk. (p. 110)

superego the partly conscious part of personality that, according to Freud, represents internalized

ideals and provides standards for judgment (the conscience) and for future aspirations. (p. 520)

superordinate goals shared goals that override differences among people and require their cooperation. (p. 512)

suprachiasmatic nucleus (SCN) a pair of cell clusters in the hypothalamus that controls circadian rhythm. In response to light, the SCN causes the pineal gland to adjust melatonin production, thus modifying our feelings of sleepiness. (p. 99)

survey a descriptive technique for obtaining the self-reported attitudes or behaviors of a particular group, usually by questioning a representative, *random sample* of the group. (p. 30)

sympathetic nervous system the division of the autonomic nervous system that arouses the body, mobilizing its energy. (p. 61)

synapse [SIN-aps] the junction between the axon tip of the sending neuron and the dendrite or cell body of the receiving neuron. The tiny gap at this junction is called the *synaptic gap* (or *synaptic cleft*). (p. 57)

systematic desensitization a type of exposure therapy that associates a pleasant relaxed state with gradually increasing anxiety-triggering stimuli. Commonly used to treat specific phobias. (p. 603)

telegraphic speech the early speech stage in which a child speaks like a telegram—"go car"—using mostly nouns and verbs. (p. 343)

temperament a person's characteristic emotional reactivity and intensity. (p. 131)

temporal lobes the portion of the cerebral cortex lying roughly above the ears; includes the auditory areas, each receiving information primarily from the opposite ear. (p. 76)

tend-and-befriend response under stress, people (especially women) often provide support to others (*tend*) and bond with and seek support from others (*befriend*). (p. 447)

teratogens agents, such as chemicals and viruses, that can reach the embryo or fetus during prenatal development and cause harm. (p. 171)

terror-management theory a theory of death-related anxiety; explores people's emotional and behavioral responses to reminders of their impending death. (p. 525)

testing effect enhanced memory after retrieving, rather than simply rereading, information. Also referred to as a *retrieval practice effect* or *test-enhanced learning*. (pp. 17, 298)

testosterone the most important male sex hormone. Males and females have it, but the additional testosterone in males stimulates the growth of the male sex organs during the fetal period, and the development of the male sex characteristics during puberty. (pp. 155, 394)

thalamus [THAL-uh-muss] the brain's sensory control center, located on top of the brainstem; it directs messages to the sensory receiving areas in the cortex and transmits replies to the cerebellum and medulla. (p. 71)

THC the major active ingredient in marijuana; triggers a variety of effects, including mild hallucinations. (p. 119)

Thematic Apperception Test (TAT) a projective test in which people express their inner feelings and interests through the stories they make up about ambiguous scenes. (p. 527)

theory an explanation using an integrated set of principles that organizes observations and predicts behaviors or events. (p. 24)

theory of mind people's ideas about their own and others' mental states—about their feelings, perceptions, and thoughts, and the behaviors these might predict. (p. 179)

therapeutic alliance a bond of trust and mutual understanding between a therapist and client, who work together constructively to overcome the client's problem. (p. 616)

threshold the level of stimulation required to trigger a neural impulse. (p. 57)

token economy an operant conditioning procedure in which people earn a token for exhibiting a desired behavior and can later exchange tokens for privileges or treats. (p. 605)

tolerance the diminishing effect with regular use of the same dose of a drug, requiring the user to take larger and larger doses before experiencing the drug's effect. (p. 110)

top-down processing information processing guided by higher-level mental processes, as when we construct perceptions drawing on our experience and expectations. (p. 213)

trait a characteristic pattern of behavior or a disposition to feel and act in certain ways, as assessed by self-report inventories and peer reports. (p. 532)

transcranial magnetic stimulation (TMS) the application of repeated pulses of magnetic energy to the brain; used to stimulate or suppress brain activity. (p. 627)

transduction conversion of one form of energy into another. In sensation, the transforming of stimulus energies, such as sights, sounds, and smells, into neural impulses our brain can interpret. (p. 213)

transference in psychoanalysis, the patient's transfer to the analyst of emotions linked with other relationships (such as love or hatred for a parent). (p. 599)

transgender an umbrella term describing people whose gender identity or expression differs from that associated with their birth-assigned sex. (p. 160)

two-factor theory the Schachter-Singer theory that to experience emotion one must (1) be physically aroused and (2) cognitively label the arousal. (p. 419)

two-word stage the stage in speech development, beginning about age 2, during which a child speaks mostly in two-word statements. (p. 343)

Type A Friedman and Rosenman's term for competitive, hard-driving, impatient, verbally aggressive, and anger-prone people. (p. 450)

Type B Friedman and Rosenman's term for easygoing, relaxed people. (p. 450)

unconditional positive regard a caring, accepting, nonjudgmental attitude, which Carl Rogers believed would help people develop self-awareness and self-acceptance. (pp. 528, 603)

unconditioned response (UR) in classical conditioning, an unlearned, naturally occurring response (such as salivation) to an unconditioned stimulus (US) (such as food in the mouth). (p. 261)

unconditioned stimulus (US) in classical conditioning, a stimulus that unconditionally—naturally and automatically—triggers an unconditioned response (UR). (p. 261)

unconscious according to Freud, a reservoir of mostly unacceptable thoughts, wishes, feelings, and memories. According to contemporary psychologists, information processing of which we are unaware. (p. 519)

validity the extent to which a test measures or predicts what it is supposed to. (See also *predictive validity*.) (p. 365)

variable anything that can vary and is feasible and ethical to measure. (p. 30)

variable-interval schedule in operant conditioning, a reinforcement schedule that reinforces a response at unpredictable time intervals. (p. 273)

variable-ratio schedule in operant conditioning, a reinforcement schedule that reinforces a response after an unpredictable number of responses. (p. 273)

vestibular sense our balance sense—our sense of body movement and position that enables our sense of balance. (p. 250)

virtual reality exposure therapy a counterconditioning technique that treats anxiety through creative electronic simulations in which people can safely face their greatest fears, such as airplane flying, spiders, or public speaking. (p. 605)

visual cliff a laboratory device for testing depth perception in infants and young animals. (p. 230)

wavelength the distance from the peak of one light or sound wave to the peak of the next. Electromagnetic wavelengths vary from the short blips of gamma rays to the long pulses of radio transmission. (p. 221)

Weber's law the principle that, to be perceived as different, two stimuli must differ by a constant minimum percentage (rather than a constant amount). (p. 214)

Wechsler Adult Intelligence Scale (WAIS) the WAIS and its companion versions for children are the most widely used intelligence tests; they contain verbal and performance (nonverbal) subtests. (p. 363)

Wernicke's area a brain area, usually in the left temporal lobe, involved in language comprehension and expression. (p. 347)

withdrawal the discomfort and distress that follow discontinuing an addictive drug or behavior. (p. 110)

working memory a newer understanding of short-term memory that adds conscious, active processing of both incoming sensory information and of information retrieved from long-term memory. (p. 295)

X chromosome the sex chromosome found in males and females. Females typically have two X chromosomes; males typically have one. An X chromosome from each parent produces a female child. (p. 155)

Y chromosome the sex chromosome typically found only in males. When paired with an X chromosome from the mother, it produces a male child. (p. 155)

Yerkes-Dodson law the principle that performance increases with arousal only up to a point, beyond which performance decreases. (p. 384)

Young-Helmholtz trichromatic (three-color) theory the theory that the retina contains three different types of color receptors—one most sensitive to red, one to green, one to blue—which, when stimulated in combination, can produce the perception of any color. (p. 225)

zygote the fertilized egg; it enters a 2-week period of rapid cell division and develops into an embryo. (p. 168)

References

Note: As your authors, we aim to report psychology's current state, including each sub-discipline's latest research insights. We've incorporated 2100 citations dated 2015–2020, highlighted here in blue. For more on our Research and Critical Thinking Story, see p. xii of the Preface at the beginning of the text.

AAA. (2010). *Asleep at the wheel: The prevalence and impact of drowsy driving* [PDF file]. https://aaafoundation.org/wp-content/uploads/2018/02/2010DrowsyDrivingReport.pdf

AAA. (2015). *Teen driver safety: Environmental factors and driver behaviors in teen driver crashes.* AAA Foundation for Traffic Safety.

AAMC. (2014). *Medical students, selected years, 1965–2013.* https://www.aamc.org/download/411782/data/2014_table1.pdf

AAMC. (2018). *Total enrollment by U.S. medical school and sex, 2014–2015 through 2018–2019.* American Association of Medical Colleges (aamc.org).

Aarts, H., & Custers, R. (2012). Unconscious goal pursuit: Nonconscious goal regulation and motivation. In R. M. Ryan (Ed.), *The Oxford handbook of human motivation* (pp. 232–247). Oxford University Press.

Abbey, A. (1987). Misperceptions of friendly behavior as sexual interest: A survey of naturally occurring incidents. *Psychology of Women Quarterly, 11,* 173–194.

Abel, K. M., Drake, R., & Goldstein, J. M. (2010). Sex differences in schizophrenia. *International Review of Psychiatry, 22,* 417–428.

Abrams, D. B., & Wilson, G. T. (1983). Alcohol, sexual arousal, and self-control. *Journal of Personality and Social Psychology, 45,* 188–198.

Abrams, L. (2008). Tip-of-the-tongue states yield language insights. *American Scientist, 96,* 234–239.

Abrams, M. (2002, June). Sight unseen—Restoring a blind man's vision is now a real possibility through stem-cell surgery. But even perfect eyes cannot see unless the brain has been taught to use them. *Discover, 23,* 54–60.

Abramson, L. Y., Metalsky, G. I., & Alloy, L. B. (1989). Hopelessness depression: A theory-based subtype. *Psychological Review, 96,* 358–372.

Abramson, L. Y., Seligman, M. E. P., & Teasdale, J. D. (1978). Learned helplessness in humans: Critique and reformulation. *Journal of Abnormal Psychology, 87,* 49–74.

Abuhamdeh, S., Csikszentmihalyi, M., & Jalal, B. (2015). Enjoying the possibility of defeat: Outcome uncertainty, suspense, and intrinsic motivation. *Motivation and Emotion, 39,* 1–10.

Academy of Science of South Africa. (2015). *Diversity in human sexuality: Implications for policy in Africa.* http://research.assaf.org.za/handle/20.500.11911/38

Acevedo, B. P., & Aron, A. (2009). Does a long-term relationship kill romantic love? *Review of General Psychology, 13,* 59–65.

Acevedo, B. P., Aron, A., Fisher, H. E., & Brown, L. L. (2012). Neural correlates of long-term intense romantic love. *Social Cognitive and Affective Neuroscience, 7,* 145–159.

ACHA. (2009). *American College Health Association-National College Health Assessment II: Reference group executive summary Fall 2008.* American College Health Association.

Ackerman, D. (2004). *An alchemy of mind: The marvel and mystery of the brain.* Scribner.

Ackerman, P. L. (2014). Adolescent and adult intellectual development. *Current Directions in Psychological Science, 23,* 246–251.

ACMD. (2009). *MDMA ('Ecstasy'): A review of its harms and classification under the Misuse of Drugs Act 1971* [PDF file]. https://assets.publishing.service.gov.uk/government/uploads/system/uploads/attachment_data/file/119088/mdma-report.pdf

Adachi, T., Fujino, H., Nakae, A., Mashimo, T., & Sasaki, J. (2014). A meta-analysis of hypnosis for chronic pain problems: A comparison between hypnosis, standard care, and other psychological interventions. *International Journal of Clinical and Experimental Hypnosis, 62,* 1–28.

Adams, H. E., Wright, L. W., Jr., & Lohr, B. A. (1996). Is homophobia associated with homosexual arousal? *Journal of Abnormal Psychology, 105,* 440–446.

Adams, Z. W., Sieverdes, J. C., Brunner-Jackson, B., Mueller, M., Chandler, J., Diaz, V., Patel, S., Sox, L. R., Wilder, S., & Treiber, F. A. (2018). Meditation smartphone application effects on prehypertensive adults' blood pressure: Dose-response feasibility trial. *Health Psychology, 37,* 850–860.

Addis, D. R., Leclerc, C. M., Muscatell, K. A., & Kensinger, E. A. (2010). There are age-related changes in neural connectivity during the encoding of positive, but not negative, information. *Cortex, 46,* 425–433.

Adelmann, P. K., Antonucci, T. C., Crohan, S. F., & Coleman, L. M. (1989). Empty nest, cohort, and employment in the well-being of midlife women. *Sex Roles, 20,* 173–189.

Ader, R., & Cohen, N. (1985). CNS-immune system interactions: Conditioning phenomena. *Behavioral and Brain Sciences, 8,* 379–394.

Aderka, I. M., Nickerson, A., Bøe, H. J., & Hofmann, S. G. (2012). Sudden gains during psychological treatments of anxiety and depression: A meta-analysis. *Journal of Consulting and Clinical Psychology, 80,* 93–101.

Adetunji, J. (2014, February 17). Genes predispose obesity but it's fullness that makes you fat. The Conversation. https://theconversation.com/genes-predispose-obesity-but-its-fullness-that-makes-you-fat-23335

ADL. (2019, accessed November 14). *Anti-Semitism in the US.* Anti-Defamation League. Retrieved from https://www.adl.org/what-we-do/anti-semitism/anti-semitism-in-the-us

Adler, J. (2012). Erasing painful memories. *Scientific American, 306,* 56–61.

Adler, J. M., Lodi-Smith, J., Philippe, F. L., & Houle, I. (2016). The incremental validity of narrative identity in predicting well-being: A review of the field and recommendations for the future. *Personality and Social Psychology Review, 20,* 142–175.

Admon, R., Vaisvaser, S., Erlich, N., Lin, T., Shapira-Lichter, I., Fruchter, E., Gazit, T., & Hendler, T. (2018). The role of the amygdala in enhanced remembrance of negative episodes and acquired negativity of related neutral cues. *Biological Psychology, 139,* 17–24.

Adolph, K. E., & Hoch, J. E. (2019). Motor development: Embodied, embedded, encultured, and enabling. *Annual Review of Psychology, 70,* 141–164.

Adolph, K. E., Kretch, K. S., & LoBue, V. (2014). Fear of heights in infants? *Current Directions in Psychological Science, 23,* 60–66.

Affleck, G., Tennen, H., Urrows, S., & Higgins, P. (1994). Person and contextual features of daily stress reactivity: Individual differences in relations of undesirable daily events with mood disturbance and chronic pain intensity. *Journal of Personality and Social Psychology, 66,* 329–340.

Afzali, M. H., Sunderland, M., Stewart, S., Masse, B., Seguin, J., Newton, N., Teesson, M., & Conrod, P. (2019). Machine-learning prediction of adolescent alcohol use: a cross-study, cross-cultural validation. *Addiction, 114,* 662–671.

Agerström, J., Björklund, F., Carlsson, R., & Rooth, D.-O. (2012). Warm and competent Hassan = cold and incompetent Eric: A harsh equation of real-life hiring discrimination. *Basic and Applied Social Psychology, 34,* 359–366.

Agrawal, Y., Platz, E. A., & Niparko, J. K. (2008). Prevalence of hearing loss and differences by demographic characteristics among US adults: Data from the National Health and Nutrition Examination Survey, 1999–2004. *Archives of Internal Medicine, 168,* 1522–1530.

Agrigoroaei, S., & Lachman, M. E. (2011). Cognitive functioning in midlife and old age: Combined effects of psychosocial and behavioral factors. *The Journals of Gerontology. Series B: Psychological Sciences and Social Sciences, 66* (suppl 1), 1130–1140.

Agrillo, C. (2011). Near-death experience: Out-of-body and out-of-brain? *Review of General Psychology, 15,* 1–10.

Agudelo, L. Z., Femenía, T., Orhan, F., Porsmyr-Palmertz, M., Goiny, M., Martinez-Redondo, V., Correia, J. C., Izadi, M., Bhat, M., Schuppe-Koistinen, I., Pettersson, A. T., Ferreira, D. M. S., Krook, A., Barres, R., Zierath, J. R., Erhardt, S., & Ruas, J. L. (2014). Skeletal muscle PGC-1α1 modulates kynurenine metabolism and mediates resilience to stress-induced depression. *Cell, 159,* 33–45.

Ahrén, J. C., Chiesa, F., Koupil, I., Magnusson, C., Dalman, C., & Goodman, A. (2013). We are family—parents, siblings, and eating disorders in a prospective total-population study of 250,000 Swedish males and females. *International Journal of Eating Disorders, 46,* 693–700.

Aichele, S., Rabbitt, P., & Ghisletta, P. (2016). Think fast, feel fine, live long: A 29-year study of cognition, health, and survival in middle-aged and older adults. *Psychological Science, 27,* 518–529.

Aiello, J. R., Thompson, D. D., & Brodzinsky, D. M. (1983). How funny is crowding anyway? Effects of room size, group size, and the introduction of humor. *Basic and Applied Social Psychology, 4,* 193–207.

Ainsworth, M. D. S. (1973). The development of infant-mother attachment. In B. Caldwell & H. Ricciuti (Eds.), *Review of child development research* (Vol. 3). University of Chicago Press.

Ainsworth, M. D. S. (1979). Infant-mother attachment. *American Psychologist, 34,* 932–937.

Ainsworth, M. D. S. (1989). Attachments beyond infancy. *American Psychologist, 44,* 709–716.

Airan, R. D., Meltzer, L. A., Roy, M., Gong, Y., Chen, H., & Deisseroth, K. (2007). High-speed imaging reveals neurophysiological links to behavior in an animal model of depression. *Science, 317,* 819–823.

Ajiboye, A. B., Willett, F. R., Young, D. R., Memberg, W. D., Murphy, B. A., Miller, J. P., Walter, B. L., Sweet, J. A., Hoyen, H. A., Keith, M. W., Peckham, P. H., Simeral, J. D., Donoghue, J. P., Hochberg, L. R., & Kirsch, R. F. (2017). Restoration of reaching and grasping in a person with tetraplegia through brain-controlled muscle stimulation: A proof-of-concept demonstration. *Lancet, 389,* 1821–1830.

Akanbi, M. O., Carroll, A. J., Achenbach, C., O'Dwyer, L. C., Jordan, N., Hitsman, B., Bilaver, L. A., McHugh, M. C., & Murphy, R. (2019). The efficacy of smoking cessation interventions in low- and middle-income countries: a systematic review and meta-analysis. *Addiction, 114,* 620–635.

Åkerlund, D., Golsteyn, B. H., Grönqvist, H., & Lindahl, L. (2016). Time discounting and criminal behavior. PNAS, 113, 6160–6165.

Akers, K. G., Martinez-Canabal, A., Restivo, L., Yiu, A. P., De Cristofara, A., Hsiang, H.-L., Wheeler, A. L., Guskjolen, A., Niibori, Y., Shoji, H., Richards, B. A., Miyakawa, T., Josselin, S. A., & Frankland, P. W. (2014). Hippocampal neurogenesis regulates forgetting during adulthood and infancy. *Science, 344,* 598–602.

Akhtar, R., Winsborough, D., Ort, U., Johnson, A., & Chamorro-Premuzic, T. (2018a). Detecting the dark side of personality using social media status updates. *Personality and Individual Differences, 132,* 90–97.

Akhtar, S., Justice, L. V., Morrison, C. M., & Conway, M. A. (2018). Fictional first memories. *Psychological Science, 29,* 1612–1619.

Akiyama, M., Okada, Y., Kanai, M., Takahashi, A., Momozawa, Y., Ikeda, M., Iwata, N., Ikegawa, S., Hirata, M., Matsuda, K., & Iwasaki, M. (2017). Genome-wide association study identifies 112 new loci for body mass index in the Japanese population. *Nature Genetics, 49,* 1458–1467.

Aknin, L. B., & Human, L. J. (2015). Give a piece of you: Gifts that reflect givers promote closeness. *Journal of Experimental Social Psychology, 60,* 8–16.

Aknin, L. B., Barrington-Leigh, C., Dunn, E. W., Helliwell, J. F., Burns, J., Biswas-Diener, R., Kemeza, I., Nyende, P., Ashton-James, C. E., & Norton, M. I. (2013). Prosocial spending and well-being: Cross-cultural evidence for a psychological universal. *Journal of Personality and Social Psychology, 104,* 635–652.

Aknin, L. B., Broesch, T., Kiley Hamlin, J., & Van de Vondervoort, J. W. (2015a). Prosocial behavior leads to happiness in a small-scale rural society. *Journal of Experimental Psychology: General, 144,* 788–795.

Aknin, L. B., Whillans, A. V., Norton, M. I., & Dunn, E. W. (2019). Happiness and prosocial behavior: An evaluation of the evidence (Chapter 4). In J. Helliwell, R. Layard, & J. Sachs (Eds.), *World happiness report 2019.* Sustainable Development Solutions Network.

Akpinar, E., & Berger, J. (2015). Drivers of cultural success: The case of sensory metaphors. *Journal of Personality and Social Psychology, 109,* 20–34.

Al Aïn, S., Poupon, D., Hétu, S., Mercier, N., Steffener, J., & Frasnelli, J. (2019). Smell training improves olfactory function and alters brain structure. *NeuroImage, 189,* 45–54.

al-Asaadi, M. (2016). "We sleep afraid, we wake up afraid": A child's life in Yemen. *The New York Times.* https://www.nytimes.com/2016/10/12/world/middleeast/yemen-children-in-a-war-zone.html

Al Ibraheem, B., Kira, I. A., Aljakoub, J., & Al Ibraheem, A. (2017). The health effect of the Syrian conflict on IDPs and refugees. *Peace and Conflict: Journal of Peace Psychology, 23,* 140–152.

al-Sharif, M. (2019, April 10). We finally won the right to drive in Saudi Arabia. But the kingdom's war on women is only getting worse. *Time Magazine.* https://time.com/5567330/saudi-arabia-women-rights-drive/

Alanko, K., Santtila, P., Harlaar, N., Witting, K., Varjonen, M., Jern, P., Johansson, A., von der Pahlen, B., & Sandnabba, N. K. (2010). Common genetic effects of gender atypical behavior in childhood and sexual orientation in adulthood: A study of Finnish twins. *Archives of Sexual Behavior, 39,* 81–92.

Albee, G. W. (1986). Toward a just society: Lessons from observations on the primary prevention of psychopathology. *American Psychologist, 41,* 891–898.

Albee, G. W. (2006). Historical overview of primary prevention of psychopathology: Address to the 3rd world conference on the promotion of mental health and prevention of mental and behavioral disorders. September 15–17, 2004, Auckland, New Zealand. *The Journal of Primary Prevention, 27,* 449–456.

Alcock, J. E. (2011, March/April). Back from the future: Parapsychology and the Bem affair. *Skeptical Inquirer,* pp. 31–39.

Aldao, A., & Nolen-Hoeksema, S. (2010). Emotion-regulation strategies across psychopathology: A meta-analytic review. *Clinical Psychology Review, 30,* 217–237.

Aleman, A., Kahn, R. S., & Selten, J.-P. (2003). Sex differences in the risk of schizophrenia: Evidence from meta-analysis. *Archives of General Psychiatry, 60,* 565–571.

Alexander, L., & Tredoux, C. (2010). The spaces between us: A spatial analysis of informal segregation. *Journal of Social Issues, 66,* 367–386.

Alimujiang, A., Wiensch, A., Boss, J., Fleischer, N. L., Mondul, A. M., McLean, K., Mukherjee, B., & Pearce, C. L. (2019). Association between life purpose and mortality among U.S. adults older than 50 years. *JAMA Network Open, 2,* e194270.

Allan, B. A. (2017). Task significance and meaningful work: A longitudinal study. *Journal of Vocational Behavior, 102,* 174–182.

Allard, F., & Burnett, N. (1985). Skill in sport. *Canadian Journal of Psychology, 39,* 294–312.

Allcott, H., Braghieri, L., Eichmeyer, S., & Gentzkow, M. (2019). *The welfare effects of social media.* NBER working paper 25514. http://www.nber.org/papers/w25514

Allemand, M., Job, V., & Mroczek, D. K. (2019). Self-control development in adolescence predicts love and work in adulthood. *Journal of Personality and Social Psychology, 117,* 621–634.

Allen, J. P., Uchino, B. N., & Hafen, C. A. (2015). Running with the pack: Teen peer-relationship qualities as predictors of adult physical health. *Psychological Science, 26,* 1574–1583.

Allen, J., Weinrich, M., Hoppitt, W., & Rendell, L. (2013). Network-based diffusion analysis reveals cultural transmission of lobtail feeding in humpback whales. *Science, 340,* 485–488.

Allen, K. (2003). Are pets a healthy pleasure? The influence of pets on blood pressure. *Current Directions in Psychological Science, 12,* 236–239.

Allen, M., D'Alessio, D., & Emmers-Sommer, T. M. (2000). Reactions of criminal sexual offenders to pornography: A meta-analytic summary. In M. Roloff (Ed.), *Communication Yearbook 22* (pp. 139–169). Sage.

Allen, M., Emmers, T. M., Gebhardt, L., & Giery, M. (1995). Pornography and rape myth acceptance. *Journal of Communication, 45,* 5–26.

Allen, M. S., & Jones, M. V. (2014). The "home advantage" in athletic competitions. *Current Directions in Psychological Science, 23,* 48–53.

Allen, M. W., Gupta, R., & Monnier, A. (2008). The interactive effect of cultural symbols and human values on taste evaluation. *Journal of Consumer Research, 35,* 294–308.

Allen, T., & Sherman, J. (2011). Ego threat and intergroup bias: A test of motivated-activation versus self-regulatory accounts. *Psychological Science, 22,* 331–333.

Allesøe, K., Hundrup, V. A., Thomsen, J. F., & Osler, M. (2010). Psychosocial work environment and risk of ischaemic heart disease in women: The Danish Nurse Cohort Study. *Occupational and Environmental Medicine, 67,* 318–322.

Alloy, L. B., Abramson, L. Y., Whitehouse, W. G., Hogan, M. E., Tashman, N. A., Steinberg, D. L., Rose, D. T., & Donovan, P. (1999). Depressogenic cognitive styles: Predictive validity, information processing and personality characteristics, and developmental origins. *Behaviour Research and Therapy, 37,* 503–531.

Alloy, L. B., Hamilton, J. L., Hamlat, E. J., & Abramson, L. Y. (2016). Pubertal development, emotion regulatory styles, and the emergence of sex differences in internalizing disorders and symptoms in adolescence. *Clinical Psychological Science, 4,* 867–881.

Allport, G. W. (1954). *The nature of prejudice.* Addison-Wesley.

Allport, G. W., & Odbert, H. S. (1936). Trait-names: A psycho-lexical study. *Psychological Monographs, 47.*

Almas, A. N., Degnan, K. A., Nelson, C. A., Zeanah, C. H., & Fox, N. A. (2017). IQ at age 12 following a history of institutional care: Findings from the Bucharest Early Intervention Project. *Developmental Psychology, 52,* 1858–1866.

Almås, I., Cappelen, A. W., Sørensen, E. Ø., & Tungodden, B. (2010). Fairness and the development of inequality acceptance. *Science, 328,* 1176–1178.

Almeida, J., He, D., Chen, Q., Mahon, B. Z., Zhang, F., Gonçalves, Ó. F., Fang, F., & Bi, Y. (2015). Decoding visual location from neural patterns in the auditory cortex of the congenitally deaf. *Psychological Science, 26,* 1771–1782.

AlShebli, B. K., Rahwan, T., & Woon, W. L. (2018). The preeminence of ethnic diversity in scientific collaboration. *Nature Communications, 9,* 5163.

Altamirano, L. J., Miyake, A., & Whitmer, A. J. (2010). When mental inflexibility facilitates executive control: Beneficial side effects of ruminative tendencies on goal maintenance. *Psychological Science, 21,* 1377–1382.

Altarum. (2018). *Economic toll of opioid crisis in U.S. exceeded $1 trillion since 2001.* https://altarum.org/news/economic-toll-opioid-crisis-us-exceeded-1-trillion-2001

Alter, A. (2017). *Irresistible: The rise of addictive technology and the business of keeping us hooked.* Penguin.

Alter, A. L., & Hershfield, H. E. (2014). People search for meaning when they approach a new decade in chronological age. PNAS, 111, 17066–17070.

Altschul, D. M., Hopkins, W. D., Herrelko, E. S., Inoue-Murayama, M., Matsuzawa, T., King, J. E., Ross, S. R., & Weiss, A. (2018). Personality links with lifespan in chimpanzees. *eLife, 7,* e33781.

Alvarez, L., & Schwartz, J. (2014, May 30). On death row with low I.Q., and new hope for a reprieve. *The New York Times.* https://www.nytimes.com/2010/09/22/us/22execute.html

Alving, C. R. (2011, March 2). *Carl Alving: Idea for vaccine patch came to me in dream* [Podcast]. American Association for the Advancement of Science. (membercentral.aas.org).

Alwin, D. F. (1990). Historical changes in parental orientations to children. In N. Mandell (Ed.), *Sociological studies of child development* (Vol. 3). JAI Press.

Amabile, T. M., & Hennessey, B. A. (1992). The motivation for creativity in children. In A. K. Boggiano & T. S. Pittman (Eds.), *Achievement and motivation: A social-developmental perspective.* Cambridge University Press.

Amabile, T. M., & Kramer, S. J. (2011). *The progress principle: Using small wins to ignite joy, engagement, and creativity at work.* Harvard Business Review Press.

Amalric, M., & Dehaene, S. (2019). A distinct cortical network for mathematical knowledge in the human brain. *NeuroImage, 189,* 19–31.

Ambady, N. (2010). The perils of pondering: Intuition and thin slice judgments. *Psychological Inquiry, 21,* 271–278.

Ambady, N., Hallahan, M., & Rosenthal, R. (1995). On judging and being judged accurately in zero-acquaintance situations. *Journal of Personality and Social Psychology, 69,* 518–529.

Ambrose, C. T. (2010). The widening gyrus. *American Scientist, 98,* 270–274.

Amedi, A., Merabet, L. B., Bermpohl, F., & Pascual-Leone, A. (2005). The occipital cortex in the blind: Lessons about plasticity and vision. *Current Directions in Psychological Science, 14,* 306–311.

Amen, D. G., Stubblefield, M., Carmichael, B., & Thisted, R. (1996). BrainSPECT findings and aggressiveness. *Annals of Clinical Psychiatry, 8,* 129–137.

American Academy of Pediatrics. (2013). *Promoting the well-being of children whose parents are gay or lesbian.* https://pediatrics.aappublications.org/content/131/4/827

American Academy of Pediatrics. (2014). Policy statement: School start times for adolescents. *Pediatrics, 134,* 642–649.

American Psychiatric Association. (2013). *Diagnostic and statistical manual of mental disorders* (Fifth ed.). American Psychiatric Publishing.

American Psychological Association. (2020). APA divisions. *Professional homes organized by members of APA.* https://www.apa.org/about/division/

American Sociological Association. (2013, February 28). *Brief of Amicus Curiae American Sociological Association in support of respondent Kristin M. Perry and respondent Edith Schlain Windsor.* Supreme Court of the United States, Nos. 12–144, 12–307.

Amick, H. R., Gartlehner, G., Gaynes, B. N., Forneris, C., Asher, G. N., Morgan, L. C., Coker-Schwimmer, E., Boland, E., Lux, L. J., Gaylord, S., Bann, C., Pieri, C. B., & Lohr, K. N. (2015). Comparative benefits and harms of second generation antidepressants and cognitive behavioral therapies in initial treatment of major depressive disorder: Systematic review and meta-analysis. *BMJ, 351,* h6019.

Ammori, B. (2013, January 4). Viewpoint: Benefits of bariatric surgery. *GP.* https://www.gponline.com/viewpoint-benefits-bariatric-surgery/obesity/bariatric-surgery/article/1164873

Amnesty International. (2018). *Amnesty International Report 2017/18: The state of world's human rights* [PDF file]. https://www.amnesty.org/download/Documents/POL1067002018ENGLISH.PDF

Amrhein, V., Greenland, S., & McShane, B. (2019). Scientists rise up against statistical significance. *Nature, 567,* 305–307.

Ananth, M., Hetelekides, E. M., Hamilton, J., & Thanos, P. K. (2019). Dopamine D4 receptor gene expression plays important role in extinction and reinstatement of cocaine-seeking behavior in mice. *Behavioural Brain Research, 365,* 1–6.

Andersen, R. (2019, April). The intention machine. *Scientific American,* pp. 25–31.

Andersen, R. A., Hwang, E. J., & Mulliken, G. H. (2010). Cognitive neural prosthetics. *Annual Review of Psychology, 61,* 169–190.

Andersen, S. M. (1998, September). *Service learning: A national strategy for youth development.* Washington, DC: Institute for Communitarian Policy Studies, George Washington University.

Anderson, B. L. (2002). Biobehavioral outcomes following psychological interventions for cancer patients. *Journal of Consulting and Clinical Psychology, 70,* 590–610.

Anderson, C., Hildreth, J. A. D., & Howland, L. (2015). Is the desire for status a fundamental human motive? A review of the empirical literature. *Psychological Bulletin, 141,* 574–601.

Anderson, C. A. (2004). An update on the effects of playing violent video games. *Journal of Adolescence, 27,* 113–122.

Anderson, C. A. (2013, June). Guns, games, and mass shootings in the U.S. *Bulletin of the International Society for Research on Aggression, 35,* 14–19.

Anderson, C. A., & Delisi, M. (2011). Implications of global climate change for violence in developed and developing countries. In J. Forgas, A. Kruglanski., & K. Williams (Eds.), *The psychology of social conflict and aggression* (pp. 249–265). Psychology Press.

Anderson, C. A., & Dill, K. E. (2000). Video games and aggressive thoughts, feelings, and behavior in the laboratory and in life. *Journal of Personality and Social Psychology, 78,* 772–790.

Anderson, C. A., & Warburton, W. A. (2012). The impact of violent video games: An overview. In W. Warburton & D. Braunstein (Eds.), *Growing up fast and furious: Reviewing the impacts of violent and sexualized media on children* (pp. 56–84). Federation Press.

Anderson, C. A., Brion, S., Moore, D. A., & Kennedy, J. A. (2012). A status-enhancement account of overconfidence. *Journal of Personality and Social Psychology, 103,* 718–735.

Anderson, C. A., Bushman, B. J., & Groom, R. W. (1997). Hot years and serious and deadly assault: Empirical tests of the heat hypothesis. *Journal of Personality and Social Psychology, 73,* 1213–1223.

Anderson, C. A., Suzuki, K., Swing, E. L., Groves, C. L., Gentile, D. A., Prot, S., Lam, C. P., Sakamoto, A., Horiuchi, Y., Krahé, B., Jelic, M., Liuqing, W., Toma, R., Warburton, W. A., Zhang, X. M., Tajima, S., Qing, F., & Petrescu, P. (2017). Media violence and other aggression risk factors in seven nations. *Personality and Social Psychology Bulletin, 43,* 986–998.

Anderson, E., Siegel, E., White, D., & Barrett, L. F. (2012). Out of sight but not out of mind: Unseen affective faces influence evaluations and social impressions. *Emotion, 12,* 1210–1221.

Anderson, F. T., & McDaniel, M. A. (2019). Hey buddy, why don't we take it outside: An experience sampling study of prospective memory. *Memory & Cognition, 47,* 47–62.

Anderson, I. M. (2000). Selective serotonin reuptake inhibitors versus tricyclic antidepressants: A meta-analysis of efficacy and tolerability. *Journal of Affective Disorders, 58,* 19–36.

Anderson, J. R., Gillies, A., & Lock, L. C. (2010). Pan thanatology. *Current Biology, 20,* R349–R351.

Anderson, M. & Jiang, J. (2018). *Teens, social media and technology 2018.* Pew Research Center, Internet & Technology. https://infogram.com/teens-social-media-and-technology-2018-1hxr4zngvexy4yo

Anderson, M., Vogels, E. A., & Turner, E. (2020, February 6). *The virtues and downsides of online dating.* Pew Research Center. https://www.pewresearch.org/internet/2020/02/06/the-virtues-and-downsides-of-online-dating/

Anderson, P. L., Edwards, S. M., & Goodnight, J. R. (2017). Virtual reality and exposure group therapy for social anxiety disorder: Results from a 4-6 year follow-up. *Cognitive Therapy and Research, 41,* 230–236.

Anderson, R. C., Pichert, J. W., Goetz, E. T., Schallert, D. L., Stevens, K. V., & Trollip, S. R. (1976). Instantiation of general terms. *Journal of Verbal Learning and Verbal Behavior, 15,* 667–679.

Anderson, S. E., Dallal, G. E., & Must, A. (2003). Relative weight and race influence average age at menarche: Results from two nationally representative surveys of U.S. girls studied 25 years apart. *Pediatrics, 111,* 844–850.

Andics, A., Gábor, A., Gácsi, M., Faragó, T., Szabó, D., & Miklósi, Á. (2016). Neural mechanisms for lexical processing in dogs. *Science, 353,* 1030–1032.

Andreasen, N. C. (1997). Linking mind and brain in the study of mental illnesses: A project for a scientific psychopathology. *Science, 275,* 1586–1593.

Andreasen, N. C. (2001). *Brave new brain: Conquering mental illness in the era of the genome.* Oxford University Press.

Andreasen, N. C., Arndt, S., Swayze, V., II, Cizadlo, T., & Flaum, M. (1994). Thalamic abnormalities in schizophrenia visualized through magnetic resonance image averaging. *Science, 266,* 294–298.

Andrews, G., Basu, A., Cuijpers, P., Craske, M. G., McEvoy, P., English, C. L., & Newby, J. M. (2018). Computer therapy for the anxiety and depression disorders is effective, acceptable and practical health care: An updated meta-analysis. *Journal of Anxiety Disorders, 55,* 70–78.

Andrews, P. W., & Thomson, J. A., Jr. (2009a). The bright side of being blue: Depression as an adaptation for analyzing complex problems. *Psychological Review, 116,* 620–654.

Andrews, P. W., & Thomson, J. A., Jr. (2009b). Depression's evolutionary roots. *Scientific American Mind, 20,* 56–61.

Andrillon, T., Nir, Y., Cirelli, C., Tononi, G., & Fried, I. (2015). Single-neuron activity and eye movements during human REM sleep and awake vision. *Nature Communications, 6,* Article 7884.

Anestis, M. D., & Anestis, J. C. (2015). Suicide rates and state laws regulating access and exposure to handguns. *American Journal of Public Health, 105,* 2049–2058.

Anestis, M. D., Khazem, L. R., Law, K. C., Houtsma, C., LeTard, R., Moberg, F., & Martin, R. (2015). The association between state laws regulating handgun ownership and statewide suicide rates. *American Journal of Public Health, 105,* 2059–2067.

Angelakis, I., Gillespie, E. L., & Panagioti, M. (2019). Childhood maltreatment and adult suicidality: A comprehensive systematic review with meta-analysis. *Psychological Medicine, 49,* 1057–1078.

Angermeyer, M. C., & Dietrich, S. (2006). Public beliefs about and attitudes towards people with mental illness: a review of population studies. *Acta Psychiatrica Scandinavica, 113,* 163–179.

Anglada-Tort, M., Baker, T., & Müllensiefen, D. (2019). False memories in music listening: Exploring the misinformation effect and individual difference factors in auditory memory. *Memory, 27,* 612–627.

Anglemyer, A., Horvath, T., & Rutherford, G. (2014). The accessibility of firearms and risk for suicide and homicide victimization among household members. *Annals of Internal Medicine, 160,* 101–112.

Anglin, S. M. (2019). Do beliefs yield to evidence? Examining belief perseverance vs. change in response to congruent empirical findings. *Journal of Experimental Social Psychology, 82,* 176–199.

Annese, J., Schenker-Ahmed, N. M., Bartsch, H., Maechler, P., Sheh, C., Thomas, N., Kayano, J., Ghatan, A., Bresler, N., Frosch, M. P., Klaming, R., & Corkin, S. (2014). Postmortem examination of patient H. M.'s brain based on histological sectioning and digital 3D reconstruction. *Nature Communications, 5,* Article 3122.

Ansari, A., Purtell, K., & Gershoff, E. (2015). Classroom age composition and the school readiness of 3- and 4-year-olds in the Head Start program. *Psychological Science, 27,* 53–63.

Anton, B. S. (2015, June). Quoted in, "APA applauds President Obama's call to end use of therapies intended to change sexual orientation." *Monitor, 46,* p. 10.

Antonaccio, O., Botchkovar, E. V., & Tittle, C. R. (2011). Attracted to crime: Exploration of criminal motivation among respondents in three European cities. *Criminal Justice and Behavior, 38,* 1200–1221.

Antony, M. M., Brown, T. A., & Barlow, D. H. (1992). Current perspectives on panic and panic disorder. *Current Directions in Psychological Science, 1,* 79–82.

Antrobus, J. (1991). Dreaming: Cognitive processes during cortical activation and high afferent thresholds. *Psychological Review, 98,* 96–121.

Anumanchipalli, G. K., Chartier, J., & Chang, E. F. (2019). Speech synthesis from neural decoding of spoken sentences. *Nature, 568,* 493–498.

Anzures, G., Quinn, P. C., Pascalis, O., Slater, A. M., Tanaka, J. W., & Lee, K. (2013). Developmental origins of the other-race effect. *Current Directions in Psychological Science, 22,* 173–178.

Aonuma, H., Totani, Y., Kaneda, M., Nakamura, R., Watanabe, T., Hatakeyama, D., Dyakonova, V. E., Lukowiak, K., & Ito, E. (2018). Effects of 5-HT and insulin on learning and memory formation in food-deprived snails. *Neurobiology of Learning and Memory, 148,* 20–29.

AP. (2009, May 9). *AP-mtvU poll: Financial worries, stress and depression on college campus* [PDF file]. http://surveys.associatedpress.com/data/Edison/APMTV%20Topline%20marginals.pdf

AP. (2017). *Strangers on beach form 80-link human chain, rescue family from rip current.* CBC. https://www.cbc.ca/news/world/human-chain-saves-family-in-water-1.4199181

APA. (2006). Evidence-based practice in psychology (from APA Presidential Task Force on Evidence-Based Practice). *American Psychologist, 61,* 271–285.

APA. (2007). *Report of the task force on the sexualization of girls.* https://www.apa.org/pi/women/programs/girls/report

APA. (2010, accessed July 31). *Answers to your questions about transgender individuals and gender identity.* American Psychological Association.

APA. (2012). *Guidelines for ethical conduct in the care and use of nonhuman animals in research.* American Psychological Association.

APA. (2017). *Stress in America: Coping with change.* American Psychological Association.

APA. (2017a). *Ethical principles of psychologists and code of conduct* [PDF file]. American Psychological Association. https://www.apa.org/ethics/code/ethics-code-2017.pdf

APA. (2018). *APA fact sheet series on psychologist supply and demand projections 2015–2030: Demand across age groups* [PDF file]. https://www.apa.org/workforce/publications/supply-demand/demand-age-groups.pdf

APA. (2018). *Supplement to diagnostic and statistical manual of mental disorders* (Fifth ed.). American Psychiatric Publishing.

APA. (2018a). *APA reiterates strong opposition to conversion therapy.* American Psychiatric Association. https://www.psychiatry.org/newsroom/news-releases/apa-reiterates-strong-opposition-to-conversion-therapy

APA. (2019, February). *Resolution on physical discipline of children by parents* [PDF file]. American Psychological Association. https://www.apa.org/about/policy/physical-discipline.pdf

Apostolou, M., & Khalil, M. (2019). Aggressive and humiliating sexual play: Occurrence rates and discordance between the sexes. *Archives of Sexual Behavior, 48,* 2187–2200.

Apostolova, L. G., Dutton, R. A., Dinov, I. D., Hayashi, K. M., Toga, A. W., Cummings, J. L., & Thompson, P. M. (2006). Conversion of mild cognitive impairment to Alzheimer disease predicted by hippocampal atrophy maps. *Archives of Neurology, 63,* 693–699.

Archer, J. (2000). Sex differences in aggression between heterosexual partners: A meta-analytic review. *Psychological Bulletin, 126,* 651–680.

Archer, J. (2004). Sex differences in aggression in real-world settings: A meta-analytic review. *Review of General Psychology, 8,* 291–322.

Archer, J. (2007). A cross-cultural perspective on physical aggression between partners. *Issues in Forensic Psychology, No. 6,* 125–131.

Archer, J. (2009). Does sexual selection explain human sex differences in aggression? *Behavioral and Brain Sciences, 32,* 249–311.

Arendt, H. (1963). *Eichmann in Jerusalem: A report on the banality of evil.* Viking.

Ariel, R., & Karpicke, J. D. (2018). Improving self-regulated learning with a retrieval practice intervention. *Journal of Experimental Psychology: Applied, 24,* 43–56.

Ariely, D. (2010). *Predictably irrational, revised and expanded edition: The hidden forces that shape our decisions.* Harper Perennial.

Ariely, D., & Loewenstein, G. (2006). The heat of the moment: The effect of sexual arousal on sexual decision making. *Journal of Behavioral Decision Making, 19,* 87–98.

Aries, E. (1987). Gender and communication. In P. Shaver & C. Henrick (Eds.), *Review of Personality and Social Psychology, 7,* 149–176.

Arkowitz, H., & Lilienfeld, S. O. (2006, April/May). Psychotherapy on trial. *Scientific American: Mind,* pp. 42–49.

Armony, J. L., Quirk, G. J., & LeDoux, J. E. (1998). Differential effects of amygdala lesions on early and late plastic components of auditory cortex spike trains during fear conditioning. *Journal of Neuroscience, 18,* 2592–2601.

Armstrong, E. A., England, P., & Fogarty, A. C. K. (2012). Accounting for women's orgasm and sexual enjoyment in college hookups and relationships. *American Sociological Review, 77,* 435–462.

Arnedo, J., Mamah, D., Baranger, D. A., Harms, M. P., Barch, D. M., Svrakic, D. M., de Erausquin, G. A., Cloninger, C. R., & Zwir, I. (2015). Decomposition of brain diffusion imaging data uncovers latent schizophrenias with distinct patterns of white matter anisotropy. *NeuroImage, 120,* 43–54.

Arnett, J. J. (1999). Adolescent storm and stress, reconsidered. *American Psychologist, 54,* 317–326.

Arnett, J. J. (2006). Emerging adulthood: Understanding the new way of coming of age. In J. J. Arnett & J. L. Tanner (Eds.), *Emerging adults in America: Coming of age in the 21st century* (pp. 3–19). American Psychological Association.

Arnett, J. J. (2007). Socialization in emerging adulthood: From the family to the wider world, from socialization to self-socialization. In J. E. Grusec & P. D. Hastings (Eds.), *Handbook of socialization: Theory and research* (pp. 208–230). Guilford Press.

Arnold, K. M., Umanath, S., Thio, K., Reilly, W. B., McDaniel, M. A., & Marsh, E. J. (2017). Understanding the cognitive processes involved in writing to learn. *Journal of Experimental Psychology: Applied, 23,* 115–127.

Arnone, D., Cavanagh, J., Gerber, D., Lawrie, S. M., Ebmeier, K. P., & McIntosh, A. M. (2009). Magnetic resonance imaging studies in bipolar disorder and schizophrenia: Meta-analysis. *British Journal of Psychiatry, 195,* 194–201.

Arnone, D., McIntosh, A. M., Tan, G. M. Y., & Ebmeier, K. P. (2008). Meta-analysis of magnetic resonance imaging studies of the corpus callosum in schizophrenia. *Schizophrenia Research, 101,* 124–132.

Aron, A., Norman, C. C., Aron, E. N., McKenna, C., & Heyman, R. E. (2000). Couples' shared participation in novel and arousing activities and experienced relationship quality. *Journal of Personality and Social Psychology, 78,* 273–284.

Aron, A. P., Melinat, E., Aron, E. N., Vallone, R. D., & Bator, R. J. (1997). The experimental generation of interpersonal closeness: A procedure and some preliminary findings. *Personality and Social Psychology Bulletin, 23,* 363–377.

Aronson, E. (2001, April 13). *Newsworthy violence* [e-mail to Society for Personality and Social Psychology discussion list], drawing from *Nobody left to hate: Teaching compassion after Columbine.* (2000). Freeman.

Arriaga, P., Adrião, J., Madeira, F., Cavaleiro, I., Maia e Silva, A., Barahona, I., & Esteves, F. (2015). A "dry eye" for victims of violence: Effects of playing a violent video game on pupillary dilation to victims and on aggressive behavior. *Psychology of Violence, 5,* 199–208.

Arsenio, W. F. (2018). The wealth of nations: International judgments regarding actual and ideal resource distributions. *Current Directions in Psychological Science, 27,* 357–362.

Arslan, R. C., Schilling, K. M., Gerlach, T. M., & Penke, L. (2018). Using 26,000 diary entries to show ovulatory changes in sexual desire and behavior. *Journal of Personality and Social Psychology.* doi: 10.1037/pspp0000208

Aryawibawa, I. N., & Ambridge, B. (2018). Is syntax semantically constrained? Evidence from a grammaticality judgment study of Indonesian. *Cognitive Science, 42,* 3135–3148.

Arzi, A., Shedlesky, L., Ben-Shaul, M., Nasser, K., Oksenberg, A., Hairston I. S., & Sobel, N. (2012). Humans can learn new information during sleep. *Nature Neuroscience, 15,* 1460–1465.

Ascády, L., & Harris, K. D. (2017). Synaptic scaling in sleep. *Science, 355,* 457.

Asch, S. E. (1955). Opinions and social pressure. *Scientific American, 193,* 31–35.

Aserinsky, E. (1988, January 17). Personal communication.

Ashton, K., Bellis, M., Davies, A., Hardcastle, K., & Hughes, K. (2016). *Adverse childhood experiences and their association with chronic disease and health service use in the Welsh adult population.* Welsh Adverse Childhood Experiences (ACE) Study, NHS Wales Public Trust.

Askay, S. W., & Patterson, D. R. (2007). Hypnotic analgesia. *Expert Review of Neurotherapeutics, 7,* 1675–1683.

Asperholm, M., Högman, N., Rafi, J., & Herlitz, A. (2019). What did you do yesterday? A meta-analysis of sex differences in episodic memory. *Psychological Bulletin, 145,* 785–821.

Aspinwall, L. G., & Tedeschi, R. G. (2010). The value of positive psychology for health psychology: Progress and pitfalls in examining the relation of positive phenomena to health. *Annals of Behavioral Medicine, 39,* 4–15.

Aspinwall, L. G., Brown, T. R., & Tabery, J. (2012). The double-edged sword: Does biomechanism increase or decrease judges' sentencing of psychopaths? *Science, 337,* 846–849.

Aspy, C. B., Vesely, S. K., Oman, R. F., Rodine, S., Marshall, L., & McLeroy, K. (2007). Parental communication and youth sexual behaviour. *Journal of Adolescence, 30,* 449–466.

Assanand, S., Pinel, J. P. J., & Lehman, D. R. (1998). Personal theories of hunger and eating. *Journal of Applied Social Psychology, 28,* 998–1015.

Associated Press. (1999, April 26). Airline passengers mistakenly told plane would crash. *Grand Rapids Press,* p. A3.

Astin, A. W., Astin, H. S., & Lindholm, J. A. (2004). *Spirituality in higher education: A national study of college students' search for meaning and purpose.* Higher Education Research Institute, University of California, Los Angeles.

Atir, S., & Ferguson, M. J. (2018). How gender determines the way we speak about professionals. *PNAS*, 115, 7278–7283.

Atkinson, R. C., & Shiffrin, R. M. (1968). Human memory: A control system and its control processes. In K. Spence (Ed.), *The psychology of learning and motivation* (Vol. 2). Academic Press.

Atkinson, R. C., & Shiffrin, R. M. (2016). Human memory: A proposed system and its control processes. In R. J. Sternberg, S. T. Fiske, & D. J. Foss (Eds.), *Scientists making a difference: One hundred eminent behavioral and brain scientists talk about their most important contributions*. Cambridge University Press.

Atlas, D. (2016, January 29). Autism's first-ever patient, now 82, "has continued to grow his whole life." *People*. https://people.com/celebrity/donald-triplett-autisms-first-ever-patient-now-82-has-continued-to-grow/

Attard-Johnson, J., Bindemann, M., & Ciardha, C. Ó. (2016). Pupillary response as an age-specific measure of sexual interest. *Archives of Sexual Behavior*, 45, 855–870.

Attard-Johnson, J., Bindemann, M., & Ciardha, C. Ó. (2017). Heterosexual, homosexual, and bisexual men's pupillary responses to persons at different stages of sexual development. *The Journal of Sex Research*, 54, 1085–1096.

Atzil-Slonim, D., Bar-Kalifa, E., Fisher, H., Lazarus, G., Hasson-Ohayon, I., Lutz, W., Rubel, J., & Rafaeli, E. (2019). Therapists' empathic accuracy toward their clients' emotions. *Journal of Consulting and Clinical Psychology*, 87, 33–45.

Aubrey, A. (2019, August 29). *Surgeon General sounds alarm on risk of marijuana addiction and harm*. National Public Radio. https://www.npr.org/sections/health-shots/2019/08/29/755423290/

Auerbach, R. P., Mortier, P., Bruffaerts, R., Alonso, J., Benjet, C., Cuijpers, P., Demyttenaere, K., Ebert, D. D., Green, J. G., Hasking, P., Murray, E., Nock, M. K., Pinder-Amaker, S., Sampson, N. A., Stein, D. J., Vilagut, G., Zaslavsky, A. M., Kessler, R. C., & WHO WMH-ICS Collaborators. (2018). WHO world mental health surveys international college student project: Prevalence and distribution of mental disorders. *Journal of Abnormal Psychology*, 127, 623–638.

Austen, J. M., & Sanderson, D. J. (2019). Delay of reinforcement versus rate of reinforcement in Pavlovian conditioning. *Journal of Experimental Psychology: Animal Learning and Cognition*, 45, 203–221.

Austin, E. J., Deary, I. J., Whiteman, M. C., Fowkes, F. G. R., Pedersen, N. L., Rabbitt, P., Bent, N., & McInnes, L. (2002). Relationships between ability and personality: Does intelligence contribute positively to personal and social adjustment? *Personality and Individual Differences*, 32, 1391–1411.

Australian Unity. (2008). *What makes us happy? The Australian Unity Wellbeing Index*. Australian Unity.

Averill, J. R. (1983). Studies on anger and aggression: Implications for theories of emotion. *American Psychologist*, 38, 1145–1160.

Averill, J. R. (1993). William James's other theory of emotion. In M. E. Donnelly (Ed.), *Reinterpreting the legacy of William James*. American Psychological Association.

Aviv, R. (2017, June 19). Remembering the murder you didn't commit. *The New Yorker*. https://www.newyorker.com/magazine/2017/06/19/remembering-the-murder-you-didnt-commit

Ayan, S. (2009). Laughing matters. *Scientific American Mind*, 20, 24–31.

Aydin, N., Fischer, P., & Frey, D. (2010). Turning to God in the face of ostracism: Effects of social exclusion on religiousness. *Personality and Social Psychology Bulletin*, 36, 742–753.

Azevedo, F. A., Carvalho, L. R., Grinberg, L. T., Farfel, J. M., Ferretti, R. E., Leite, R. E., Filho, J., Lent, R., & Herculano-Houzel, S. (2009). Equal numbers of neuronal and nonneuronal cells make the human brain an isometrically scaled-up primate brain. *Journal of Comparative Neurology*, 513, 532–541.

Azucar, D., Marengo, D., & Settanni, M. (2018). Predicting the Big 5 personality traits from digital footprints on social media: A meta-analysis. *Personality and Individual Differences*, 124, 150–159.

Baas, M., De Dreu, C. K. W., & Nijstad, B. A. (2008). A meta-analysis of 25 years of mood-creativity research: Hedonic tone, activation, or regulatory focus? *Psychological Bulletin*, 134, 779–806.

Babyak, M., Blumenthal, J. A., Herman, S., Khatri, P., Doraiswamy, M., Moore, K., Craighead, W. E., Baldewicz, T. T., & Krishnan, K. R. (2000). Exercise treatment for major depression: Maintenance of therapeutic benefit at ten months. *Psychosomatic Medicine*, 62, 633–638.

Bachman, J., O'Malley, P. M., Schulenberg, J. E., Johnston, L. D., Freedman-Doan, P., & Messersmith, E. E. (2007). *The education-drug use connection: How successes and failures in school relate to adolescent smoking, drinking, drug use, and delinquency*. Earlbaum.

Back, M. D., Stopfer, J. M., Vazire, S., Gaddis, S., Schmukle, S. C., Egloff, B., & Gosling, S. D. (2010). Facebook profiles reflect actual personality, not self-idealization. *Psychological Science*, 21, 372–374.

Backman, L., & Dixon, R. A. (1992). Psychological compensation: A theoretical framework. *Psychological Bulletin*, 112, 259–283.

Backman, L., & MacDonald, S. W. S. (2006). Death and cognition: Synthesis and outlook. *European Psychologist*, 11, 224–235.

Baddeley, A. D. (1982). *Your memory: A user's guide*. Macmillan.

Baddeley, A. D. (2002, June). Is working memory still working? *European Psychologist*, 7, 85–97.

Baddeley, A. D., Thomson, N., & Buchanan, M. (1975). Word length and the structure of short-term memory. *Journal of Verbal Learning and Verbal Behavior*, 14, 575–589.

Baddeley, J. L., & Singer, J. A. (2009). A social interactional model of bereavement narrative disclosure. *Review of General Psychology*, 13, 202–218.

Badura, K. L., Grijalva, E., Galvin, B. M., Owens, B. P., & Joseph, D. L. (2019). Motivation to lead: A meta-analysis and distal-proximal model of motivation and leadership. *Journal of Applied Psychology*, 105, 331–354.

Bagemihl, B. (1999). *Biological exuberance: Animal homosexuality and natural diversity*. St. Martins.

Bagge, C. L., Littlefield, A. K., & Glenn, C. R. (2017). Trajectories of affective response as warning signs for suicide attempts: An examination of the 48 hours prior to a recent suicide attempt. *Clinical Psychological Science*, 5, 259–271.

Baglioni, C., Nanovska, S., Regen, W., Spiegelhalder, K., Feige, B., Nissen, C., Reynolds, C. F., & Riemann, D. (2016). Sleep and mental disorders: A meta-analysis of polysomnographic research. *Psychological Bulletin*, 142, 969–990.

Bahrick, H. P. (1984). Semantic memory content in permastore: 50 years of memory for Spanish learned in school. *Journal of Experimental Psychology: General*, 111, 1–29.

Bahrick, H. P., Bahrick, P. O., & Wittlinger, R. P. (1975). Fifty years of memory for names and faces: A cross-sectional approach. *Journal of Experimental Psychology: General*, 104, 54–75.

Bai, D., Yip, B. H. K., & Windham, G. C. (2019). Association of genetic and environmental factors with autism in a 5-country cohort. *JAMA Psychiatry*, 76, 1035–1043.

Bailey, J. M., Gaulin, S., Agyei, Y., & Gladue, B. A. (1994). Effects of gender and sexual orientation on evolutionary relevant aspects of human mating psychology. *Journal of Personality and Social Psychology*, 66, 1081–1093.

Bailey, J. M., Vasey, P. L., Diamond, L. M., Breedlove, S. M., Vilain, E., & Epprecht, M. (2016). Sexual orientation, controversy, and science. *Psychological Science in the Public Interest*, 17, 45–101.

Bailey, P. E., & Leon, T. (2019). A systematic review and meta-analysis of age-related differences in trust. *Psychology and Aging*, 34, 674–685.

Bailey, R. E., & Gillaspy, J. A., Jr. (2005). Operant psychology goes to the fair: Marian and Keller Breland in the popular press, 1947–1966. *The Behavior Analyst*, 28, 143–159.

Baillargeon, R., Scott, R. M., & Bian, L. (2016). Psychological reasoning in infancy. *Annual Review of Psychology*, 67, 159–186.

Baio, J., Wiggins, L., Christensen, D. L., Maenner, M. J., Daniels, J., Warren, Z., Kurzius-Spencer, M., Zahorodny, W., Rosenberg, C. R., White, T., Durkin, M. S., Imm, P., Nikolaou, L., Yeargin-Allsopp, M., Lee, L.-C., Harrington, R., Lopez, M., Fitzgerald, R. T., Hewitt, A., . . . Dowling, N. F. (2018). Prevalence of autism spectrum disorder among children aged 8 years—Autism and Developmental Disabilities Monitoring Network, 11 Sites, United States, 2014. *MMWR Surveillance Summaries*, 67, 1.

Bakadorova, O., & Raufelder, D. (2018). The essential role of the teacher-student relationship in students' need satisfaction during adolescence. *Journal of Applied Developmental Psychology*, 58, 57–65.

Baker, D. H., & Cass, J. R. (2013). A dissociation of performance and awareness during binocular rivalry. *Psychological Science*, 24, 2563–2568.

Baker, J. T., Dillon, D. G., Patrick, L. M., Roffman, J. L., Brady, R. O., Pizzagalli, D. A., Öngür, D., & Holmes, A. J. (2019). Functional connectomics of affective and psychotic pathology. *PNAS*, 116, 9050–9059.

Baker, M., Strickland, A., & Fox, N. D. (2019). Choosing a meal to increase your appeal: How relationship status, sexual orientation, dining partner sex, and attractiveness impact nutritional choices in social dining scenarios. *Appetite*, 133, 262–269.

Baker, T. B., McFall, R. M., & Shoham, V. (2008). Current status and future prospects of clinical psychology: Toward a scientifically principled approach to mental and behavioral health care. *Psychological Science in the Public Interest*, 9, 67–103.

Baker, T. B., Piper, M. E., McCarthy, D. E., Majeskie, M. R., & Fiore, M. C. (2004). Addiction motivation reformulated: An affective processing model of negative reinforcement. *Psychological Review*, 111, 33–51.

Bakermans-Kranenburg, M. J., van IJzendoorn, M. H., & Juffer, F. (2003). Less is more: Meta-analyses of sensitivity and attachment interventions in early childhood. *Psychological Bulletin*, 129, 195–215.

Bakshy, E., Messing, S., & Adamic, L. A. (2015). Exposure to ideologically diverse news and opinion on Facebook. *Science*, 348, 1130–1132.

Balaban, H., Fukuda, K., & Luria, R. (2019). What can half a million change detection trials tell us about visual working memory? *Cognition*, 191, 103984.

Balcetis, E., & Dunning, D. (2010). Wishful seeing: More desire objects are seen as closer. *Psychological Science*, 21, 147–152.

Ball, G., Adamson, C., Beare, R., & Seal, M. L. (2017). *Modelling neuroanatomical variation due to age and sex during childhood and adolescence*. Unpublished manuscript. biorxiv.org/content/early/2017/07/16/126441

Ball, G., Malpas, C. B., Genc, S., Efron, D., Sciberras, E., Anderson, V., Nicholson, J. M., & Silk, T. J. (2019). Multimodal structural neuroimaging markers of brain development and ADHD symptoms. *The American Journal of Psychiatry, 176,* 57–66.

Balodis, I. M., Wynne-Edwards, K. E., & Olmstead, M. C. (2010). The other side of the curve: Examining the relationship between pre-stressor physiological responses and stress reactivity. *Psychoneuroendocrinology, 35,* 1363–1373.

Balsam, K. F., Beauchaine, T. P., Rothblum, E. S., & Solomon, S. E. (2008). Three-year follow-up of same-sex couples who had civil unions in Vermont, same-sex couples not in civil unions, and heterosexual married couples. *Developmental Psychology, 44,* 102–116.

Balter, M. (2010). Animal communication helps reveal roots of language. *Science, 328,* 969–970.

Balter, M. (2014). Science misused to justify Ugandan antigay law. *Science, 343,* 956.

Balter, M. (2015). Can epigenetics explain homosexuality puzzle? *Science, 350,* 148.

Bancroft, J., Loftus, J., & Long, J. S. (2003). Distress about sex: A national survey of women in heterosexual relationships. *Archives of Sexual Behavior, 32,* 193–208.

Bandura, A. (1977). Self-efficacy: Toward a unifying theory of behavior. *Psychological Review, 84,* 191–215.

Bandura, A. (1982). The psychology of chance encounters and life paths. *American Psychologist, 37,* 747–755.

Bandura, A. (1986). *Social foundations of thought and action: A social-cognitive theory.* Prentice-Hall.

Bandura, A. (2005). The evolution of social cognitive theory. In K. G. Smith & M. A. Hitt (Eds.), *Great minds in management: The process of theory development.* Oxford University Press.

Bandura, A. (2006). Toward a psychology of human agency. *Perspectives on Psychological Science, 1,* 164–180.

Bandura, A. (2008). An agentic perspective on positive psychology. In S. J. Lopez (Ed.), *The science of human flourishing.* Praeger.

Bandura, A. (2016). The power of observational learning through social modeling. In R. J. Sternberg, S. T. Fiske, & D. J. Foss (Eds.), *Scientists making a difference: One hundred eminent behavioral and brain scientists talk about their most important contributions* (pp. 235–239). Cambridge University Press.

Bandura, A. (2017). The Bobo Doll legacy. *Psychology Review, 22*(3), 2–6.

Bandura, A. (2018). Toward a psychology of human agency: Pathways and reflections. *Perspectives on Psychological Science, 13,* 130–136.

Bandura, A., Ross, D., & Ross, S. A. (1961). Transmission of aggression through imitation of aggressive models. *Journal of Abnormal and Social Psychology, 63,* 575–582.

Bang, J. W., Shibata, K., Frank, S. M., Walsh, E. G., Greenlee, M. W., Watanabe, T., & Sasaki, Y. (2018). Consolidation and reconsolidation share behavioural and neurochemical mechanisms. *Nature Human Behaviour, 2,* 507–513.

Bansak, K., Hainmueller, J., & Hangartner, D. (2016). How economic, humanitarian, and religious concerns shape European attitudes toward asylum seekers. *Science, 354,* 217–222.

Banville, J. (2012, April). APA weighs in on the constitutionality of life without parole for juvenile offenders. *Monitor on Psychology,* p. 12.

Bao, A.-M., & Swaab, D. F. (2011). Sexual differentiation of the human brain: Relation to gender identity, sexual orientation and neuropsychiatric disorders. *Frontiers in Neuroendocrinology, 32,* 214–226.

Barash, D. P. (2012). *Homo mysterius: Evolutionary puzzles of human nature.* Oxford University Press.

Barbaresi, W. J., Katusic, S. K., Colligan, R. C., Weaver, A. L., & Jacobsen, S. J. (2007). Modifiers of long-term school outcomes for children with attention deficit/hyperactivity disorder: Does treatment with stimulant medication make a difference? Results from a population-based study. *Journal of Developmental and Behavioral Pediatrics, 28,* 274–287.

Barberá, P., Jost, J. T., Nagler, J., Tucker, J. A., & Bonneau, R. (2015). Tweeting from left to right: Is online political communication more than an echo chamber? *Psychological Science, 26,* 1531–1542.

Bargh, J. A., & Chartrand, T. L. (1999). The unbearable automaticity of being. *American Psychologist, 54,* 462–479.

Bargh, J. A., & McKenna, K. Y. A. (2004). The internet and social life. *Annual Review of Psychology, 55,* 573–590.

Bargh, J. A., & Morsella, E. (2008). The unconscious mind. *Perspectives on Psychological Science, 3,* 73–79.

Bargh, J. A., McKenna, K. Y. A., & Fitzsimons, G. M. (2002). Can you see the real me? Activation and expression of the "true self" on the internet. *Journal of Social Issues, 58,* 33–48.

Bar-Haim, Y., Lamy, D., Pergamin, L., Bakermans-Kranenburg, M. J., & van IJzendoorn, M. H. (2007). Threat-related attentional bias in anxious and nonanxious individuals: A meta-analytic study. *Psychological Bulletin, 133,* 1–24.

Barinaga, M. B. (1992). The brain remaps its own contours. *Science, 258,* 216–218.

Barinaga, M. B. (1997). How exercise works its magic. *Science, 276,* 1325.

Barinaga, M. B. (1999). Salmon follow watery odors home. *Science, 286,* 705–706.

Barkley-Levenson, E., & Galván, A. (2014). Neural representation of expected value in the adolescent brain. *PNAS, 111,* 1646–1651.

Barlow, F. K. (2019). Nature vs. nurture is nonsense: On the necessity of an integrated genetic, social, developmental, and personality psychology. *Australian Journal of Psychology, 71,* 68–79.

Barlow, F. K., Hornsey, M. J., Hayward, L. E., Houkamau, C. A., Kang, J., Milojev, P., & Sibley, C. G. (2019). Why do we hold mixed emotions about racial out-groups? A case for affect matching. *Psychological Science, 30,* 917–929.

Barlow, M., Woodman, T., & Hardy, L. (2013). Great expectations: Different high-risk activities satisfy different motives. *Journal of Personality and Social Psychology, 105,* 458–475.

Barlow, M. A., Wrosch, C., Gouin, J. P., & Kunzmann, U. (2019). Is anger, but not sadness, associated with chronic inflammation and illness in older adulthood? *Psychology and Aging, 34,* 330–340.

Barnier, A. J., & McConkey, K. M. (2004). Defining and identifying the highly hypnotizable person. In M. Heap, R. J. Brown, & D. A. Oakley (Eds.), *The highly hypnotizable person: Theoretical, experimental and clinical issues* (pp. 30–60). Brunner-Routledge.

Baron, C. E., Smith, T. W., Uchino, B. N., Baucom, B. R., & Birmingham, W. C. (2016). Getting along and getting ahead: Affiliation and dominance predict ambulatory blood pressure. *Health Psychology, 35,* 253–261.

Baron-Cohen, S. (2010). Autism and the empathizing-systemizing (E-S) theory. In P. D. Zelazo, M. Chandler & E. Crone (Eds.), *Developmental social cognitive neuroscience* (pp. 125–138). Psychology Press.

Baron-Cohen, S. (2017). The eyes as window to the mind. *American Journal of Psychiatry, 174,* 1–2.

Baron-Cohen, S., Bowen, D. C., Rosemary, J. H., Allison, C., Auyeung, B., Lombardo, M. V., & Lai, M.-C. (2015). The "reading the mind in the eyes" test: Complete absence of typical difference in ~400 men and women with autism. *PLOS ONE, 10,* e0136521.

Baron-Cohen, S., Leslie, A. M., & Frith, U. (1985). Does the autistic child have a "theory of mind"? *Cognition, 21,* 37–46.

Barr, S. M., Budge, S. L., & Adelson, J. L. (2016). Transgender community belongingness as a mediator between strength of transgender identity and well-being. *Journal of Counseling Psychology, 63,* 87.

Barrett, D. (2011). Answers in your dreams. *Scientific American Mind, 22,* 26–33.

Barrett, H. C., Bolyanatz, A., Crittenden, A. N., Fessler, D. M., Fitzpatrick, S., Gurven, M., Henrich, J., Kanovsky, M., Kushnick, G., Pisor, A., Scelza, B. A., Stich, S., von Rueden, C., Zhao, W., & Laurence, S. (2016). Small-scale societies exhibit fundamental variation in the role of intentions in moral judgment. *PNAS, 113,* 4688–4693.

Barrett, L. F. (2006). Are emotions natural kinds? *Perspectives on Psychological Science, 1,* 28–58.

Barrett, L. F. (2012). Emotions are real. *Emotion, 12,* 413–429.

Barrett, L. F. (2013). Quoted by Fischer, S. About face: Emotions and facial expressions may not be directly related. *Boston Magazine.* https://www.bostonmagazine.com/news/2013/06/25/emotions-facial-expressions-not-related/

Barrett, L. F. (2017). *How emotions are made: The secret life of the brain.* Houghton Mifflin Harcourt.

Barrett, L. F., Adolphs, R., Marsella, S., Martinez, A. M., & Pollak, S. D. (2019). Emotional expressions reconsidered: Challenges to inferring emotion from human facial movements. *Psychological Science in the Public Interest, 20,* 1–68.

Barrett, L. F., & Bliss-Moreau, E. (2009). She's emotional. He's having a bad day: Attributional explanations for emotion stereotypes. *Emotion, 9,* 649–658.

Barrett, L. F., Lane, R. D., Sechrest, L., & Schwartz, G. E. (2000). Sex differences in emotional awareness. *Personality and Social Psychology Bulletin, 26,* 1027–1035.

Barretto, R. P., Gillis-Smith, S., Chandrashekar, J., Yarmolinsky, D. A., Schnitzer, M. J., Ryba, N. J., & Zuker, C. S. (2015). The neural representation of taste quality at the periphery. *Nature, 517,* 373–376.

Barrick, M. R., Shaffer, J. A., & DeGrassi, S. W. (2009). What you see may not be what you get: Relationships among self-presentation tactics and ratings of interview and job performance. *Journal of Applied Psychology, 94,* 1304–1411.

Barrouillet, P., Portrat, S., & Camos, V. (2011). On the law relating processing to storage in working memory. *Psychological Review, 118,* 175–192.

Barry, C. L., McGinty, E. E., Vernick, J. S., & Webster, D. W. (2013). After Newtown—Public opinion on gun policy and mental illness. *New England Journal of Medicine, 368,* 1077–1081.

Barry, D. (1985). *Dave Barry's stay fit and healthy until you're dead.* Rodale.

Barry, D. (1995, September 17). Teen smokers, too, get cool, toxic, waste-blackened lungs. *Asbury Park Press,* p. D3.

Bartels, M. (2015). Genetics of wellbeing and its components with life, happiness, and quality of life: A review of meta-analysis of heritability studies. *Behavior Genetics, 45,* 137–156.

Bartoshuk, L. (2010, June 18). Quoted by K. Travis, Interview: Linda Bartoshuk. *Science.* https://blogs.sciencemag.org/sciencecareers/2010/06/linda-bartoshuk.html

Bartoshuk, L. M. (2000). Comparing sensory experiences across individuals: Recent psychophysical advances illuminate genetic variation in taste perception. *Chemical Senses, 25,* 447–460.

Bartz, J. A., Nitschke, J. P., Krol, S. A., & Tellier, P. P. (2019). Oxytocin selectively improves empathic accuracy: A replication in men and novel insights in women. *Biological Psychiatry: Cognitive Neuroscience and Neuroimaging, 4*, 1042–1048.

Bashore, T. R., Ridderinkhof, K. R., & van der Molen, M. W. (1997). The decline of cognitive processing speed in old age. *Current Directions in Psychological Science, 6*, 163–169.

Baskind, D. E. (1997, December 14). Personal communication, from Delta College.

Basner, M., Dinges, D. F., Mollicone, D., Ecker, A., Jones, C. W., Hyder, E. C., Di Antonio, A., Savelev, I., Kan, K., Goel, N., Morukov, B. V., & Sutton, J. P. (2013). Mars 520-d mission simulation reveals protracted crew hypokinesis and alterations of sleep duration and timing. *PNAS, 110*, 2635–2640.

Bassett, D. S., Zurn, P., & Gold, J. I. (2018). On the nature and use of models in network neuroscience. *Nature Reviews Neuroscience, 19*, 566–578.

Bastian, B., Jetten, J., Hornsey, M. J., & Leknes, S. (2014). The positive consequences of pain: A biopsychosocial approach. *Personality and Social Psychology Review, 18*, 256–279.

Basu, S., & Basu, D. (2015). The relationship between psychoactive drugs, the brain and psychosis. *International Archives of Addiction Research and Medicine, 1*, 1.

Bat-Chava, Y. (1993). Antecedents of self-esteem in deaf people: A meta-analytic review. *Rehabilitation Psychology, 38*, 221–234.

Bat-Chava, Y. (1994). Group identification and self-esteem of deaf adults. *Personality and Social Psychology Bulletin, 20*, 494–502.

Bates, T. C. (2015). The glass is half full and half empty: A population-representative twin study testing if optimism and pessimism are distinct systems. *Journal of Positive Psychology, 10*, 533–542.

Bathje, G. J., & Pryor, J. B. (2011). The relationships of public and self-stigma to seeking mental health services. *Journal of Mental Health Counseling, 33*, 161–177.

Batruch, A., Autin, F., Bataillard, F., & Butera, F. (2019). School selection and the social class divide: How tracking contributes to the reproduction of inequalities. *Personality and Social Psychology Bulletin, 45*, 477–490.

Batsell, W. R., Perry, J. L., Hanley, E., & Hostetter, A. B. (2017). Ecological validity of the testing effect: The use of daily quizzes in introductory psychology. *Teaching of Psychology, 44*, 18–23.

Batterink, L. J. (2017). Rapid statistical learning supporting word extraction from continuous speech. *Psychological Science, 28*, 921–928.

Batz-Barbarich, C., Tay, L., Kuykendall, L., & Cheung, H. K. (2018). A meta-analysis of gender differences in subjective well-being: Estimating effect sizes and associations with gender inequality. *Psychological Science, 29*, 1491–1503.

Bauer, C. M., Hirsch, G. V., Zajac, L., Koo, B-B., Collignon, O., & Merabet, L. B. (2017). Multimodal MR-imaging reveals large-scale structural and functional connectivity changes in profound early blindness. *PLOS ONE, 12*, e0173064.

Bauer, M., Cassar, A., Chytilová, J., & Henrich, J. (2014). War's enduring effects on the development of egalitarian motivations and in-group biases. *Psychological Science, 25*, 47–57.

Bauer, P. J., & Larkina, M. (2014). The onset of childhood amnesia in childhood: A prospective investigation of the course and determinants of forgetting of early-life events. *Memory, 22*, 907–924.

Bault, N., di Pellegrino, G., Puppi, M., Opolczynski, G., Monti, A., Braghittoni, D., Thibaut, F., Rustichini, A., & Coricelli, G. (2019). Dissociation between private and social counterfactual value signals following ventromedial prefrontal cortex damage. *Journal of Cognitive Neuroscience, 31*, 639–656.

Baumann, J., & DeSteno, D. (2010). Emotion guided threat detection: Expecting guns where there are none. *Journal of Personality and Social Psychology, 99*, 595–610.

Baumeister, H., & Härter, M. (2007). Prevalence of mental disorders based on general population surveys. *Social Psychiatry and Psychiatric Epidemiology, 42*, 537–546.

Baumeister, R. F. (1996). Should schools try to boost self-esteem? Beware the dark side. *American Educator, 20*, 43.

Baumeister, R. F. (2000). Gender differences in erotic plasticity: The female sex drive as socially flexible and responsive. *Psychological Bulletin, 126*, 347–374.

Baumeister, R. F. (2001). Violent pride: Do people turn violent because of self-hate, or self-love? *Scientific American, 17*, 96–101.

Baumeister, R. F. (2005). *The cultural animal: Human nature, meaning, and social life.* Oxford University Press.

Baumeister, R. F. (2010). *Is there anything good about men?: How cultures flourish by exploiting men.* Oxford.

Baumeister, R. F. (2015). Toward a general theory of motivation: Problems, challenges, opportunities, and the big picture. *Motivation and Emotion, 40*, 1–10.

Baumeister, R. F., & Bratslavsky, E. (1999). Passion, intimacy, and time: Passionate love as a function of change in intimacy. *Personality and Social Psychology Review, 3*, 49–67.

Baumeister, R. F., Bratslavsky, E., Muraven, M., & Tice, D. M. (1998a). Ego depletion: Is the active self a limited resource? *Journal of Personality and Social Psychology, 74*, 1252–1265.

Baumeister, R. F., Catanese, K. R., & Vohs, K. D. (2001). Is there a gender difference in strength of sex drive? Theoretical views, conceptual distinctions, and a review of relevant evidence. *Personality and Social Psychology Review, 5*, 242–273.

Baumeister, R. F., Dale, K., & Sommer, K. L. (1998b). Freudian defense mechanisms and empirical findings in modern personality and social psychology: Reaction formation, projection, displacement, undoing, isolation, sublimation, and denial. *Journal of Personality, 66*, 1081–1125.

Baumeister, R. F., & Leary, M. R. (1995). The need to belong: Desire for interpersonal attachments as a fundamental human motivation. *Psychological Bulletin, 117*, 497–529.

Baumeister, R. F., & Tice, D. M. (1986). How adolescence became the struggle for self: A historical transformation of psychological development. In J. Suls & A. G. Greenwald (Eds.), *Psychological perspectives on the self* (Vol. 3, pp. 183–201). Erlbaum.

Baumeister, R. F., Tice, D. M., & Vohs, K. D. (2018). The strength model of self-regulation: Conclusions from the second decade of willpower research. *Perspectives on Psychological Science, 13*, 141–145.

Baumeister, R. F., & Vohs, K. D. (2016). Strength model of self-regulation as limited resource: Assessment, controversies, update. *Advances in Experimental Social Psychology, 54*, 67–127.

Baumeister, R. F., & Vohs, K. D. (2018). Revisiting our reappraisal of the (surprisingly few) benefits of high self-esteem. *Perspectives on Psychological Science, 13*, 137–140.

Baumgardner, A. H., Kaufman, C. M., & Levy, P. E. (1989). Regulating affect interpersonally: When low esteem leads to greater enhancement. *Journal of Personality and Social Psychology, 56*, 907–921.

Baumrind, D. (1966). Effects of authoritative parental control on child behavior. *Child Development, 37*, 887–907.

Baumrind, D. (1989). Rearing competent children. In W. Damon (Ed.), *Child Development Today and Tomorrow* (pp. 349–378). Jossey-Bass.

Baumrind, D. (1991). The influence of parenting style on adolescent competence and substance abuse. *Journal of Early Adolescence, 11*, 56–95.

Baumrind, D. (1996). The discipline controversy revisited. *Family Relations, 45*, 405–414.

Baumrind, D. (2013). Is a pejorative view of power assertion in the socialization process justified? *Review of General Psychology, 17*, 420–427.

Baur, E., Forsman, M., Santtila, P., Johansson, A., Sandnabba, K., & Långström, N. (2016). Paraphilic sexual interests and sexually coercive behavior: A population-based twin study. *Archives of Sexual Behavior, 45*, 1163–1172.

Bavelier, D., Newport, E. L., & Supalla, T. (2003). Children need natural languages, signed or spoken. *Cerebrum, 5*, 19–32.

Bavelier, D., Tomann, A., Hutton, C., Mitchell, T., Corina, D., Liu, G., & Neville, H. (2000). Visual attention to the periphery is enhanced in congenitally deaf individuals. *Journal of Neuroscience, 20*, 1–6.

Baye, A., & Monseur, C. (2016). Gender differences in variability and extreme scores in an international context. *Large-scale Assessments in Education, 4*, 1.

BBC. (2018, May 21). *Santa Fe school shooting: Suspect 'was rejected' by victim Shana Fisher.* https://www.bbc.com/news/world-us-canada-44194074

Beam, C. R., Emery, R. E., Reynolds, C. A., Gatz, M., Turkheimer, R., & Pedersen, N. L. (2016). Widowhood and the stability of late life depressive symptomatology in the Swedish Adoption Twin Study of Aging. *Behavior Genetics, 46*, 100–113.

Beaman, A. L., & Klentz, B. (1983). The supposed physical attractiveness bias against supporters of the women's movement: A meta-analysis. *Personality and Social Psychology Bulletin, 9*, 544–550.

Beames, J. R., Schofield, T. P., & Denson, T. F. (2017). A meta-analysis of improving self-control with practice. In D. T. D. de Ridder, M. A. Adriaanse, & K. Fujita (Eds.), *Handbook of self-control in health and well-being.* Routledge.

Bearzi, M., & Stanford, C. (2010). A bigger, better brain. *American Scientist, 98*, 402–409.

Beatty Moody, D. L., Taylor, A. D., Leibel, D. K., Al-Najjar, E., Katzel, L. I., Davatzikos, C., Gullapalli, R. P., Seliger, S. L., Kouo, T., Erus, G., Rosenberger, W. F., Evans, M. K., Zonderman, A. B., & Waldstein, S. R. (2019). Lifetime discrimination burden, racial discrimination, and subclinical cerebrovascular disease among African Americans. *Health Psychology, 38*, 63–74.

Beauchaine, T. P., Hinshaw, S. P., & Bridge, J. A. (2019). Nonsuicidal self-injury and suicidal behaviors in girls: The case for targeted prevention in preadolescence. *Clinical Psychological Science, 7*, 643–667.

Beauchamp, G. K. (1987). The human preference for excess salt. *American Scientist, 75*, 27–33.

Beauchamp, M. R., Puterman, E., & Lubans, D. R. (2018). Physical inactivity and mental health in late adolescence. *JAMA Psychiatry, 75*, 543–544.

Beaulieu, A. M., Tabasky, E., & Osser, D. N. (2019). The psychopharmacology algorithm project at the Harvard South Shore Program: an algorithm for adults with obsessive-compulsive disorder. *Psychiatry Research, 281*, 112583.

Beauvois, J.-L., Courbet, D., & Oberlé, D. (2012). The prescriptive power of the television host: A transposition of Milgram's obedience paradigm to the context of TV game show. *European Review of Applied Psychology/Revue Européenne de Psychologie Appliquée, 62*, 111–119.

Becerra-Culqui, T. A., Liu, Y., Nash, R., Cromwell, L., Flanders, W. D., Getahun, D., Giammattei, S. V.,

Hunkeler, E. M., Lash, T. L., Millman, A., Quinn, V. P., Robinson, B., Roblin, D., Sandberg, D. E., Silverberg, M. J., Tangpricha, V., & Goodman, M. (2018). Mental health of transgender and gender nonconforming youth compared with their peers. *Pediatrics, 141,* e20173845.

Bechara, A., Berridge, K. C., Bickel, W. K., Morón, J. A., Williams, S. B., & Stein, J. S. (2019). A neurobehavioral approach to addiction: Implications for the opioid epidemic and the psychology of addiction. *Psychological Science in the Public Interest, 20,* 96–127.

Beck, A. T. (1978). *Cognitive therapy and the emotional disorders.* Penguin.

Beck, A. T., & Bredemeier, K. (2016). A unified model of depression: Integrating clinical, cognitive, biological, and evolutionary perspectives. *Clinical Psychological Science, 4,* 596–619.

Beck, A. T., Rush, A. J., Shaw, B. F., & Emery, G. (1979). *Cognitive therapy of depression.* Guilford Press.

Beck, D. M. (2010). The appeal of the brain in the popular press. *Perspectives on Psychological Science, 5,* 762–766.

Becker, D. V., Kenrick, D. T., Neuberg, S. L., Blackwell, K. C., & Smith, D. M. (2007). The confounded nature of angry men and happy women. *Journal of Personality and Social Psychology, 92,* 179–190.

Becker, J. E., Maley, C., Shultz, E., & Taylor, W. D. (2016). Update on transcranial magnetic stimulation for depression and other neuropsychiatric illnesses. *Psychiatric Annals, 46,* 637–641.

Becklen, R., & Cervone, D. (1983). Selective looking and the noticing of unexpected events. *Memory and Cognition, 11,* 601–608.

Bediou, B., Adams, D. M., Mayer, R. E., Tipton, E., Green, C. S., & Bavelier, D. (2018). Meta-analysis of action video game impact on perceptual, attentional, and cognitive skills. *Psychological Bulletin, 144,* 77–110.

Beeman, M. J., & Chiarello, C. (1998). Complementary right- and left-hemisphere language comprehension. *Current Directions in Psychological Science, 7,* 2–8.

Bègue, L., Bushman, B. J., Giancola, P. R., Subra, B., & Rosset, E. (2010). "There is no such thing as an accident," especially when people are drunk. *Personality and Social Psychology Bulletin, 36,* 1301–1304.

Bègue, L., Subra, B., Arvers, P., Muller, D., Bricout, V., & Zorman, M. (2009). A message in a bottle: Extra-pharmacological effects of alcohol on aggression. *Journal of Experimental Social Psychology, 45,* 137–142.

Bègue, L., Zaalberg, A., Shankland, R., Duke, A., Jacquet, J., Kaliman, P., Pennel, L., Chanove, M., Arvers, P., & Bushman, B. J. (2017). Omega-3 supplements reduce self-reported physical aggression in healthy adults. *Psychiatry Research.* Advance online publication. doi: 10.1016/j.psychres.2017.12.038

Beil, L. (2018, July 21). The clean cycle. *Science News,* pp. 22–26.

Beilin, H. (1992). Piaget's enduring contribution to developmental psychology. *Developmental Psychology, 28,* 191–204.

Beilock, S. (2010). *Choke: What the secrets of the brain reveal about getting it right when you have to.* Free Press.

Beintner, I., Jacobi, C., & Taylor, C. B. (2012). Effects of an Internet-based prevention programme for eating disorders in the USA and Germany: A meta-analytic review. *European Eating Disorders Review, 20,* 1–8.

Bell, A. P., Weinberg, M. S., & Hammersmith, S. K. (1981). *Sexual preference: Its development in men and women.* Indiana University Press.

Belluck, P. (2012, July 16). Footprints to cognitive decline and Alzheimer's are seen in gait. *The New York Times.* https://www.nytimes.com/2012/07/17/health/research/signs-of-cognitive-decline-and-alzheimers-are-seen-in-gait.html?

Belluck, P. (2013, February 5). People with mental illness more likely to be smokers, study finds. *The New York Times.* https://www.nytimes.com/2013/02/06/health/more-smoking-found-by-mentally-ill-people.html?

Belot, M., & Francesconi, M. (2006, November). *Can anyone be "the one"? Evidence on mate selection from speed dating.* Centre for Economic Policy Research.

Belsky, J., & Pluess, M. (2009). Beyond diathesis stress: Differential susceptibility to environmental influences. *Psychological Bulletin, 135,* 885–908.

Belson, K. (2015, September 6). No foul mouths on this field: Football with a New Age twist. *The New York Times.* https://www.nytimes.com/2015/09/07/sports/football/no-foul-mouths-on-pete-carrolls-field-football-with-a-new-age-twist.html?

Belson, K. (2017, September 21). Aaron Hernandez had severe C.T.E. when he died at age 27. *The New York Times.* https://www.nytimes.com/2017/09/21/sports/aaron-hernandez-cte-brain.html?

Bem, D., Tressoldi, P., Rabeyron, T., & Duggan, M. (2015). Feeling the future: A meta-analysis of 90 experiments on the anomalous anticipation of random future events. *F1000Research, 4,* 1188.

Bem, D. J. (1984). Quoted in *The Skeptical Inquirer, 8,* 194.

Bem, D. J. (2011). Feeling the future: Experimental evidence for anomalous retroactive influences on cognition and affect. *Journal of Personality and Social Psychology, 100,* 407–425.

Bem, S. L. (1987). Masculinity and femininity exist only in the mind of the perceiver. In J. M. Reinisch, L. A. Rosenblum, & S. A. Sanders (Eds.), *Masculinity/femininity: Basic perspectives.* Oxford University Press.

Bem, S. L. (1993). *The lenses of gender.* Yale University Press.

Ben Malek, B. H., Philippi, H., Botzung, A., Cretin, B., Berna, F., Manning, L., & Blanc, F. (2019). Memories defining the self in Alzheimer's disease. *Memory, 27,* 698–704.

Ben-Shakhar, G., & Elaad, E. (2003). The validity of psychophysiological detection of information with the guilty knowledge test: A meta-analytic review. *Journal of Applied Psychology, 88,* 131–151.

Benartzi, S., Beshears, J., Milkman, K. L., Sunstein, C. R., Thaler, R. H., Shankar, M., Tucker-Ray, W., Congdon, W. J., & Galing, S. (2017). Should governments invest more in nudging? *Psychological Science, 28,* 1041–1055.

Bendixen, M., Asao, K., Wyckoff, J. P., Buss, D. M., & Kennair, L. E. O. (2017). Sexual regret in US and Norway: Effects of culture and individual differences in religiosity and mating strategy. *Personality and Individual Differences, 116,* 246–251.

Benedict, C., Brooks, S. J., O'Daly, O. G., Almén, M. S., Morell, A., Åberg, K., Gingnell, M., Schultes, B., Hallschmid, M., Broman, J. E., Larsson, E. M., & Schiöth, H. B. (2012). Acute sleep deprivation enhances the brain's response to hedonic food stimuli: An fMRI study. *Journal of Clinical Endocrinology and Metabolism, 97,* 2011–2759.

Benenson, J. F., Markovits, H., Fitzgerald, C., Geoffroy, D., Flemming, J., Kahlenberg, S. M., & Wrangham, R. W. (2009). Males' greater tolerance of same-sex peers. *Psychological Science, 20,* 184–190.

Benjamin, L. T., Jr., & Simpson, J. A. (2009). The power of the situation: The impact of Milgram's obedience studies on personality and social psychology. *American Psychologist, 64,* 12–19.

Benjamins, M. R., Ellison, C. G., & Rogers, R. G. (2010). Religious involvement and mortality risk among pre-retirement aged U.S. adults. In C. E. Ellison & R. A. Hummer (Eds.), *Religion, families, and health: Population-based research in the United States.* Rutgers University Press.

Benner, A. D., Wang, Y., Shen, Y., Boyle, A. E., Polk, R., & Cheng, Y. P. (2018). Racial/ethnic discrimination and well-being during adolescence: A meta-analytic review. *American Psychologist, 73,* 855–883.

Bennett, W. I. (1995). Beyond overeating. *New England Journal of Medicine, 332,* 673–674.

Berg, J. M., Wall, M., Larson, N., Eisenberg, M. E., Loth, K. A., & Neumark-Sztainer, D. (2014). The unique and additive associations of family functioning and parenting practices with disordered eating behaviors in diverse adolescents. *Journal of Behavioral Medicine, 37,* 205–217.

Bergelson, E., & Swingley, D. (2012). At 6–9 months, human infants know the meanings of many common nouns. *PNAS, 109,* 3253–3258.

Bergelson, E., & Swingley, D. (2013). The acquisition of abstract words by young infants. *Cognition, 127,* 391–397.

Bergen, B. K. (2014). *Universal grammar.* Response to 2014 Edge question: What scientific idea is ready for retirement? Edge. https://www.edge.org/response-detail/25539

Berk, L. E. (1994, November). Why children talk to themselves. *Scientific American,* pp. 78–83.

Berk, L. S., Felten, D. L., Tan, S. A., Bittman, B. B., & Westengard, J. (2001). Modulation of neuroimmune parameters during the eustress of humor-associated mirthful laughter. *Alternative Therapies, 7,* 62–76.

Berken, J. A., Gracco, V. L., Chen, J., Soles, J., Watkins, K. E., Baum, S., Callahan, M., & Klein, D. (2015). Neural activation in speech production and reading aloud in native and non-native languages. *NeuroImage, 112,* 208–217.

Berkovich-Ohana, A., Glickson, J., & Goldstein, A. (2014). Studying the default mode and its mindfulness-induced changes using EEF functional connectivity. *Social Cognitive and Affective Neuroscience, 9,* 1616–1624.

Berkowitz, L. (1983). Aversively stimulated aggression: Some parallels and differences in research with animals and humans. *American Psychologist, 38,* 1135–1144.

Berkowitz, L. (1989). Frustration-aggression hypothesis: Examination and reformulation. *Psychological Bulletin, 106,* 59–73.

Berkowitz, L. (1990). On the formation and regulation of anger and aggression: A cognitive-neoassociationistic analysis. *American Psychologist, 45,* 494–503.

Berman, M. G., Jonides, J., & Kaplan, S. (2008). The cognitive benefits of interacting with nature. *Psychological Science, 19,* 1207–1212.

Bernal-Gamboa, R., Rosas, J. M., & Nieto, J. (2018). Extinction makes acquisition context-specific in conditioned taste aversion regardless of the context where acquisition and testing take place. *Journal of Experimental Psychology: Animal Learning and Cognition, 44,* 385–395.

Berndt, T. J. (1992). Friendship and friends' influence in adolescence. *Current Directions in Psychological Science, 1,* 156–159.

Bernieri, F., Davis, J., Rosenthal, R., & Knee, C. (1994). Interactional synchrony and rapport: Measuring synchrony in displays devoid of sound and facial affect. *Personality and Social Psychology Bulletin, 20,* 303–311.

Bernstein, B. O., Lubinski, D., & Benbow, C. P. (2019). Psychological constellations assessed at age 13 predict distinct forms of eminence 35 years later. *Psychological Science, 30,* 444–454.

Bernstein, D. M., & Loftus, E. F. (2009a). The consequences of false memories for food preferences and choices. *Perspectives on Psychological Science, 4,* 135–139.

Bernstein, D. M., & Loftus, E. F. (2009b). How to tell if a particular memory is true or false. *Perspectives on Psychological Science, 4,* 370–374.

Bernstein, M. J., Young, S. G., & Claypool, H. M. (2010). Is Obama's win a gain for Blacks? Changes in implicit racial prejudice following the 2008 election. *Social Psychology, 41,* 147–151.

Berridge, K. C., Robinson, T. E., & Aldridge, J. W. (2009). Dissecting components of reward: "liking", "wanting", and learning. *Current Opinion in Pharmacology, 9,* 65–73.

Berry, C. M., & Sackett, P. R. (2009). Individual differences in course choice result in underestimation of the validity of college admissions systems. *Psychological Science, 20,* 822–830.

Berry, C. M., & Zhao, P. (2015). Addressing criticisms of existing predictive bias research: Cognitive ability test scores still overpredict African Americans' job performance. *Journal of Applied Psychology, 100,* 162–179.

Berscheid, E. (1981) An overview of the psychological effects of physical attractiveness and some comments upon the psychological effects of knowledge of the effects of physical attractiveness. In G. W. Lucker, K. Ribbens, & J. A. McNamara (Eds.), *Psychological aspects of facial form* (Craniofacial Growth Series). Center for Human Growth and Development, University of Michigan.

Berscheid, E. (1985). Interpersonal attraction. In G. Lindzey & E. Aronson (Eds.), *The handbook of social psychology.* Random House.

Berscheid, E. (2010). Love in the fourth dimension. *Annual Review of Psychology, 61,* 1–25.

Berti, A., Cottini, G., Gandola, M., Pia, L., Smania, N., Stracciari, A., Castiglioni, I., Vallar, G., & Paulesu, E. (2005). Shared cortical anatomy for motor awareness and motor control. *Science, 309,* 488–491.

Bértolo, H. (2005). Visual imagery without visual perception? *Psicológica, 26,* 173–188.

Bertrand, M., & Mullainathan, S. (2004). Are Emily and Greg more employable than Lakisha and Jamal? A field experiment on labor market discrimination. *American Economic Review, 94,* 991–1013.

Bettergarcia, J. N., & Israel, T. (2018). Therapist reactions to transgender identity exploration: Effects on the therapeutic relationship in an analogue study. *Psychology of Sexual Orientation and Gender Diversity, 5,* 423–431.

Beyeler, A. (2019). Do antidepressants restore lost synapses? *Science, 364,* 129–130.

Bhatt, R. S., Wasserman, E. A., Reynolds, W. F., Jr., & Knauss, K. S. (1988). Conceptual behavior in pigeons: Categorization of both familiar and novel examples from four classes of natural and artificial stimuli. *Journal of Experimental Psychology: Animal Behavior Processes, 14,* 219–234.

Bialik, K. (2018, December 6). *How asking about your sleep, smoking or yoga habits can help pollsters verify their findings.* Pew Research Center. https://tinyurl.com/skp7f96

Bialystok, E., Kroll, J. F., Green, D. W., MacWhinney, B., & Craik, F. I. M. (2015). Publication bias and the validity of evidence: What's the connection? *Psychological Science, 26,* 944–946.

Bianchi, E. C., Hall, E. V., & Lee, S. (2018). Reexamining the link between economic downturns and racial antipathy: Evidence that prejudice against blacks rises during recessions. *Psychological Science, 29,* 1584–1597.

Bianconi, E., Piovesan, A., Facchin, F., Beraudi, A., Casadei, R., Frabetti, F., Vitale, L., Pelleri, M. C., Tassani, S., Piva, F., Perez-Amodio, S., Strippoli, P., & Canaider, S. (2013). An estimation of the number of cells in the human body. *Annals of Human Biology, 40,* 463–471.

Bick, J., Fox, N., Zeanah, C., & Nelson, C. A. (2015). Early deprivation, atypical brain development, and internalizing symptoms in late childhood. *Neuroscience, 342,* 140–153.

Bienvenu, O. J., Davydow, D. S., & Kendler, K. S. (2011). Psychiatric "diseases" versus behavioral disorders and degree of genetic influence. *Psychological Medicine, 41,* 33–40.

Bilefsky, D. (2009, March 11). Europeans debate castration of sex offenders. *The New York Times.* https://www.nytimes.com/2009/03/11/world/europe/11castrate.html?

Billock, V. A., & Tsou, B. H. (2012). Elementary visual hallucinations and their relationships to neural pattern-forming mechanisms. *Psychological Bulletin, 138,* 744–774.

Binder, E. B. (2019). Polygenic risk scores in schizophrenia: Ready for the real world? *American Journal of Psychiatry, 176,* 783–784.

Binet, A. (1909). *Les idées modernes sur les enfants* [Modern ideas about children]. Flammarion. Quoted in Clarke, A., & Clarke A. (2006), Born to be bright. *The Psychologist, 19,* 409.

Bird, C. D., & Emery, N. J. (2009). Rooks use stones to raise the water level to reach a floating worm. *Current Biology, 19,* 1410–1414.

Birnbaum, G. E. (2018). The fragile spell of desire: A functional perspective on changes in sexual desire across relationship development. *Personality and Social Psychology Review, 22,* 101–127.

Birnbaum, G. E., & Reis, H. T. (2012). When does responsiveness pique sexual interest? Attachment and sexual desire in initial acquaintanceships. *Personality and Social Psychology Bulletin, 38,* 946–958.

Birnbaum, G. E., Reis, H. T., Mikulincer, M., Gillath, O., & Orpaz, A. (2006). When sex is more than just sex: Attachment orientations, sexual experience, and relationship quality. *Journal of Personality and Social Psychology, 91,* 929–943.

Biro, D., Humle, T., Koops, K., Sousa, C., Hayashi, M., & Matsuzawa, T. (2010). Chimpanzee mothers at Bossou, Guinea carry the mummified remains of their dead infants. *Current Biology, 20,* R351–R352.

Biro, F. M., Galvez, M. P., Greenspan, L. C., Succop, P. A., Vangeepuram, N., Pinney, S. M., Teitelbaum, S., Windham, G. C., Kushi, L. H., & Wolff, M. S. (2010). Pubertal assessment method and baseline characteristics in a mixed longitudinal study of girls. *Pediatrics, 126,* e583–e590.

Biro, F. M., Greenspan, L. C., & Galvez, M. P. (2012). Puberty in girls of the 21st century. *Journal of Pediatric and Adolescent Gynecology, 25,* 289–294.

Bisbey, T. M., Reyes, D. L., Traylor, A. M., & Salas, E. (2019). Teams of psychologists helping teams: The evolution of the science of team training. *American Psychologist, 74,* 278–289.

Bishop, D. I., Weisgram, E. S., Holleque, K. M., Lund, K. E., & Wheeler, J. R. (2005). Identity development and alcohol consumption: Current and retrospective self-reports by college students. *Journal of Adolescence, 28,* 523–533.

Bishop, G. D. (1991). Understanding the understanding of illness: Lay disease representations. In J. A. Skelton & R. T. Croyle (Eds.), *Mental representation in health and illness.* Springer-Verlag.

Bisra, K., Liu, Q., Nesbit, J. C., Salimi, F., & Winne, P. H. (2018). Inducing self-explanation: A meta-analysis. *Educational Psychology Review, 30,* 703–725.

Bjork, E. L., & Bjork, R. A. (2011). Making things hard on yourself, but in a good way: Creating desirable difficulties to enhance learning. In M. A. Gernsbacher, M. A. Pew, L. M. Hough, & J. R. Pomerantz (Eds.), *Psychology and the real world.* Worth Publishers.

Bjork, R. (2011, January 20). Quoted by P. Belluck, To really learn, quit studying and take a test. *The New York Times.* https://www.nytimes.com/2011/01/21/science/21memory.html?

Bjork, R. A., & Bjork, E. L. (2019). Forgetting as the friend of learning: implications for teaching and self-regulated learning. *Advances in Physiology Education, 43,* 164–167.

Bjorklund, D. F., & Green, B. L. (1992). The adaptive nature of cognitive immaturity. *American Psychologist, 47,* 46–54.

BJS. (2017). *Data collection: National Crime Victimization Survey (NCVS).* https://www.bjs.gov/index.cfm?ty=dcdetail&iid=245

Black, M. C., Basile, K. C., Breiding, M. J., Smith, S. G., Walters, M. L., Merrick, M. T., Chen, J., & Stevens, M. R. (2011). *The National Intimate Partner and Sexual Violence Survey (NISVS): 2010 summary report.* National Center for Injury Prevention and Control, Centers for Disease Control and Prevention.

Blake, A., Nazarian, M., & Castel, A. (2015). The Apple of the mind's eye: Everyday attention, metamemory, and reconstructive memory for the Apple logo. *Quarterly Journal of Experimental Psychology, 68,* 858–865.

Blake, W. (2013, March). *Voices from solitary: A sentence worse than death* [Essay]. Published at Solitary Watch, News from a Nation in Lockdown. https://www.huffpost.com/entry/voices-from-solitary-a-se_n_2890157

Blakemore, S. (2018). Avoiding social risk in adolescence. *Current Directions in Psychological Science, 27,* 116–122.

Blakemore, S.-J. (2008). Development of the social brain during adolescence. *Quarterly Journal of Experimental Psychology, 61,* 40–49.

Blakemore, S.-J., Wolpert, D. M., & Frith, C. D. (1998). Central cancellation of self-produced tickle sensation. *Nature Neuroscience, 1,* 635–640.

Blakeslee, S. (2006, January 10). Cells that read minds. *The New York Times.* https://www.nytimes.com/2006/01/10/science/cells-that-read-minds.html?

Blanchard, R. (2004). Quantitative and theoretical analyses of the relation between older brothers and homosexuality in men. *Journal of Theoretical Biology, 230,* 173–187.

Blanchard, R. (2008). Review and theory of handedness, birth order, and homosexuality in men. *Laterality, 13,* 51–70.

Blanchard, R. (2018). Fraternal birth order, family size, and male homosexuality: Meta-analysis of studies spanning 25 years. *Archives of Sexual Behavior, 47,* 1–15.

Blanchard, R. (2019). Recent findings on fraternal birth order and homosexuality in males. *Archives of Sexual Behavior, 48,* 1899–1900.

Blanchard, R., Kuban, M. E., Blak, T., Klassen, P. E., Dickey, R., & Cantor, J. M. (2012). Sexual attraction to others: A comparison of two models of alloerotic responding in men. *Archives of Sexual Behavior, 41,* 13–29.

Blanchard, R., Lykins, A. D., Wherrett, D., Kuban, M. E., Cantor, J. M., Blak, T., Dickey, R., & Klassen, P. E. (2009). Pedophilia, hebephilia, and the DSM-V. *Archives of Sexual Behavior, 38,* 335–350.

Blanchard-Fields, F. (2007). Everyday problem solving and emotion: An adult developmental perspective. *Current Directions in Psychological Science, 16,* 26–31.

Blascovich, J., & Mendes, W. B. (2010). Social psychophysiology and embodiment. In S. T. Fiske, D. T. Gilbert, & G. Lindzey (Eds.), *The handbook of social psychology,* 5th ed. (pp. 194–227). Wiley.

Blasi, D. E., Wichmann, S., Hammarström, H., Stadler, P. F., & Christiansen, M. H. (2016). Sound-meaning association biases evidenced across thousands of languages. *PNAS, 113,* 10818–10823.

Blass, T. (1996). Stanley Milgram: A life of inventiveness and controversy. In G. A. Kimble, C. A. Boneau, & M. Wertheimer (Eds.), *Portraits of pioneers in psychology* (Vol. II). American Psychological Association and Lawrence Erlbaum.

Blass, T. (1999). The Milgram paradigm after 35 years: Some things we now know about obedience to authority. *Journal of Applied Social Psychology, 29,* 955–978.

Blazer, D. G., & Tucci, D. L. (2019). Hearing loss and psychiatric disorders: a review. *Psychological Medicine, 49,* 891–897.

Blechert, J., Testa, G., Georgii, C., Klimesch, W., & Wilhelm, F. H. (2016). The Pavlovian craver: Neural and experiential correlates of single trial naturalistic food conditioning in humans. *Physiology & Behavior, 158,* 18–25.

Bleidorn, W., Arslan, R. C., Denissen, J. J. A., Rentfrow, P. J., Gebauer, J. E., Potter, J., & Gosling, S. D. (2016). Age and gender differences in self-esteem—A cross-cultural window. *Journal of Personality and Social Psychology, 111,* 396–410.

Bleidorn, W., Hopwood, C. J., Ackerman, R. A., Witt, E. A., Kandler, C., Riemann, R., Samuel, D. B., & Donnellan, M. B. (2019). The healthy personality from a basic trait perspective. *Journal of Personality and Social Psychology.* Advance online publication. https://doi.org/10.1037/pspp0000231

Bleidorn, W., Hopwood, C. J., & Lucas, R. E. (2018). Life events and personality trait change. *Journal of Personality, 86,* 83–96.

Blinkhorn, V., Lyons, M., & Almond, L. (2015). The ultimate femme fatale: Narcissism predicts serious and aggressive sexually coercive behavior in females. *Personality and Individual Differences, 87,* 219–223.

Blix, I., & Brennen, T. (2011). Mental time travel after trauma: The specificity and temporal distribution of autobiographical memories and future-directed thoughts. *Memory, 19,* 956–967.

Blokland, G. A., McMahon, K. L., Thompson, P. M., Martin, N. G., de Zubicaray, G. I., & Wright, M. J. (2011). Heritability of working memory brain activation. *Journal of Neuroscience, 31,* 10882–10890.

Bloom, B. C. (Ed.). (1985). *Developing talent in young people.* Ballantine.

Bloom, F. E. (1993, January/February). What's new in neurotransmitters. *Brain-Work,* pp. 7–9.

Bloom, P. (2000). *How children learn the meanings of words.* MIT Press.

Bloom, P. (2016). *Against empathy: The case for rational compassion.* HarperCollins

Blow, C. M. (2015, March 26). Officers' race matters less than you think. *The New York Times.* https://www.nytimes.com/2015/03/26/opinion/charles-blow-officer-race-matters-less-than-you-think.html?

BLS. (2011, June 22). *American time use survey summary.* https://www.scribd.com/document/154489647/American-Time-Use-Survey-Summary

BLS. (2019). *Labor force statistics from the current population survey.* Bureau of Labor Statistics. https://www.bls.gov/cps/

Blum, D. (2011). *Love at Goon Park: Harry Harlow and the science of affection* (2nd edition). Perseus.

Blum, K., Cull, J. G., Braverman, E. R., & Comings, D. E. (1996). Reward deficiency syndrome. *American Scientist, 84,* 132–145.

Blum, K., Thanos, P. K., & Gold, M. S. (2014). Dopamine and glucose, obesity, and reward deficiency syndrome. *Frontiers in Psychology, 5,* 919.

Blumenstein, B., & Orbach, I. (2012). *Mental practice in sport: Twenty case studies.* Novinka/Nova Science Publishers.

Boag, S. (2006). Freudian repression, the common view, and pathological science. *Review of General Psychology, 10,* 74–86.

Bock, L. (2013, June 19). Interview by Adam Bryant, "In head-hunting, big data may not be such a big deal." *The New York Times.* https://www.nytimes.com/2013/06/20/business/in-head-hunting-big-data-may-not-be-such-a-big-deal.html?

Bocklandt, S., Horvath, S., Vilain, E., & Hamer, D. H. (2006). Extreme skewing of X chromosome inactivation in mothers of homosexual men. *Human Genetics, 118,* 691–694.

Bockting, W. O. (2014). Transgender identity development. In W. O. Bockting (Ed.), *APA handbook of sexuality and psychology* (Vol. 1, pp. 739–758). American Psychological Association.

Bodenhausen, G. V., Sheppard, L. A., & Kramer, G. P. (1994). Negative affect and social judgment: The differential impact of anger and sadness. *European Journal of Social Psychology, 24,* 45–62.

Bodkin, J. A., & Amsterdam, J. D. (2002). Transdermal selegiline in major depression: A double-blind, placebo-controlled, parallel-group study in outpatients. *American Journal of Psychiatry, 159,* 1869–1875.

Boecker, H., Sprenger, T., Spilker, M. E., Henriksen, G., Koppenhoefer, M., Wagner, K. J., Valet, M., Berthele, A., & Tolle, T. R. (2008). The runner's high: Opioidergic mechanisms in the human brain. *Cerebral Cortex, 18,* 2523–2531.

Boehm, J. K., & Kubzansky, L. D. (2012). The heart's content: The association between positive psychological well-being and cardiovascular health. *Psychological Bulletin, 138,* 655–691.

Boehm, J. K., Winning, A., Segerstrom, S., & Kubzansky, L. D. (2015). Variability modifies life satisfaction's association with mortality risk in older adults. *Psychological Science, 26,* 1063–1070.

Boehm-Davis, D. A. (2005). Improving product safety and effectiveness in the home. In R. S. Nickerson (Ed.), *Reviews of human factors and ergonomics.* Volume 1 (pp. 219–253). Human Factors and Ergonomics Society.

Boenigk, S., & Mayr, M. L. (2016). The happiness of giving: Evidence from the German socioeconomic panel that happier people are more generous. *Journal of Happiness Studies, 17,* 1825–1846.

Boesch-Achermann, H., & Boesch, C. (1993). Tool use in wild chimpanzees: New light from dark forests. *Current Directions in Psychological Science, 2,* 18–21.

Bogaert, A. F. (2003). Number of older brothers and sexual orientation: New texts and the attraction/behavior distinction in two national probability samples. *Journal of Personality and Social Psychology, 84,* 644–652.

Bogaert, A. F. (2004). Asexuality: Prevalence and associated factors in a national probability sample. *Journal of Sex Research, 41,* 279–287.

Bogaert, A. F. (2006). Biological versus nonbiological older brothers and men's sexual orientation. *PNAS, 103,* 10771–10774.

Bogaert, A. F. (2015). Asexuality: What it is and why it matters. *Journal of Sex Research, 52,* 362–379.

Bogaert, A. F., Friesen, C., & Klentrou, P. (2002). Age of puberty and sexual orientation in a national probability sample. *Archives of Sexual Behavior, 31,* 73–81.

Bogaert, A. F., Skorska, M. N., Wang, C., Gabrie, J., MacNeil, A. J., Hoffarth, M. R., VanderLaan, D. P., Zucker, K. J., & Blanchard, R. (2018). Male homosexuality and maternal immune responsivity to the Y-linked protein NLGN4Y. *PNAS, 115,* 302–306.

Bogen, J. E. & Vogel, P. J. (1962). Cerebral commissurotomy in man: Preliminary case report. *Bulletin Los Angeles Neurological Society, 27,* 169-172.

Boggiano, A. K., Harackiewicz, J. M., Bessette, M. M., & Main, D. S. (1985). Increasing children's interest through performance-contingent reward. *Social Cognition, 3,* 400–411.

Boggiano, M. M., Chandler, P. C., Viana, J. B., Oswald, K. D., Maldonado, C. R., & Wauford, P. K. (2005). Combined dieting and stress evoke exaggerated responses to opioids in binge-eating rats. *Behavioral Neuroscience, 119,* 1207–1214.

Bohlken, M. M., Brouwer, R. M., Mandl, R. C. W., Van, d. H., Hedman, A. M., De Hert, M., Cahn, W., Kahn, R. S., & Pol, H. E. H. (2016). Structural brain connectivity as a genetic marker for schizophrenia. *JAMA Psychiatry, 73,* 11–19.

Bohman, M., & Sigvardsson, S. (1990). Outcome in adoption: Lessons from longitudinal studies. In D. Brodzinsky & M. Schechter (Eds.), *The psychology of adoption* (pp. 93–106). Oxford University Press.

Bois, C., Levita, L., Ripp, I., Owens, D. C. G., Johnstone, E. C., Whalley, H. C., & Lawrie, S. M. (2016). Longitudinal changes in hippocampal volume in the Edinburgh High Risk Study of Schizophrenia. *Schizophrenia Research, 173,* 146–151.

Boldrini, M., Fulmore, C. A., Tartt, A. N., Simeon, L. R., Pavlova, I, Poposka, V., Rosoklija, G. B., Stankov, A., Arango, V., Dwork, A. J., Hen, R., & Mann, J. J. (2018). Human hippocampal neurogenesis persists throughout aging. *Cell Stem Cell, 22,* 589–599.

Bolger, N., DeLongis, A., Kessler, R. C., & Schilling, E. A. (1989). Effects of daily stress on negative mood. *Journal of Personality and Social Psychology, 57,* 808–818.

Bolmont, M., Cacioppo, J. T., & Cacioppo, S. (2014). Love is in the gaze: An eye-tracking study of love and sexual desire. *Psychological Science, 25,* 1748–1756.

Boly, M., Garrido, M. I., Gosseries, O., Bruno, M.-A., Boveroux, P., Schnakers, C., Massimini, M., Litvak, V., Laureys, S., & Friston, K. (2011). Preserved feed-forward but impaired top-down processes in the vegetative state. *Science, 332,* 858–862.

Bonanno, G. A. (2004). Loss, trauma, and human resilience: Have we underestimated the human capacity to thrive after extremely aversive events? *American Psychologist, 59,* 20–28.

Bonanno, G. A., Brewin, C. R., Kaniasty, K., & La Greca, A. M. (2010). Weighing the costs of disaster: Consequences, risks, and resilience in individuals, families, and communities. *Psychological Science in the Public Interest, 11,* 1–49.

Bonanno, G. A., Galea, S., Bucciarelli, A., & Vlahov, D. (2006). Psychological resilience after disaster. *Psychological Science, 17,* 181–186.

Bonanno, G. A., Galea, S., Bucciarelli, A., & Vlahov, D. (2007). What predicts psychological resilience after disaster? The role of demographics, resources, and life stress. *Journal of Consulting and Clinical Psychology, 75,* 671–682.

Bonanno, G. A., & Kaltman, S. (1999). Toward an integrative perspective on bereavement. *Psychological Bulletin, 125,* 760–777.

Bonanno, G. A., Kennedy, P., Galatzer-Levy, I. R., Lude, P., & Elfström, M. L. (2012). Trajectories of resilience, depression, and anxiety following spinal cord injury. *Rehabilitation Psychology, 57,* 236–247.

Bonanno, G. A., Westphal, M., & Mancini, A. D. (2011). Resilience to loss and potential trauma. *Annual Review of Clinical Psychology, 11,* 511–535.

Bond, C. F., Jr., & DePaulo, B. M. (2006). Accuracy of deception judgments. *Personality and Social Psychology Review, 10,* 214–234.

Bond, M. H., Lun, V. M.-C., Chan, J., Chan, W. W.-Y., & Wong, D. (2012). Enacting modesty in Chinese culture: The joint contribution of personal characteristics and contextual features. *Asian Journal of Social Psychology, 15,* 14–25.

Bond, R., & Smith, P. B. (1996). Culture and conformity: A meta-analysis of studies using Asch's (1952, 1956) line judgment task. *Psychological Bulletin, 119,* 111–137.

Bonezzi, A., Brendl, C. M., & DeAngelis, M. (2011). Stuck in the middle: The psychophysics of goal pursuit. *Psychological Science, 22,* 607–612.

Bonfils, K. A., Lysaker, P. H., Minor, K. S., & Salyers, M. P. (2016). Affective empathy in schizophrenia: A meta-analysis. *Schizophrenia Research, 175,* 109–117.

Bono, J. E., & Judge, T. A. (2004). Personality and transformational and transactional leadership: A meta-analysis. *Journal of Applied Psychology, 89,* 901–910.

Bookheimer, S. H., Strojwas, M. H., Cohen, M. S., Saunders, A. M., Pericak-Vance, M. A., Mazziotta, J. C., & Small, G. W. (2000). Patterns of brain activation in people at risk for Alzheimer's disease. *New England Journal of Medicine, 343,* 450–456.

Bookheimer, S. Y., Salat, D. H., Terpstra, M., Ances, B. M., Barch, D. M., Buckner, R. L., Fischl, B. (2019). The Lifespan Human Connectome Project in Aging: An overview. *NeuroImage, 185,* 335–348.

Boone, A. P., & Hegarty, M. (2017). Sex differences in mental rotation tasks: Not just in the mental rotation process! *Journal of Experimental Psychology: Learning, Memory, and Cognition, 43,* 1005–1019.

Booth, F. W., & Neufer, P. D. (2005). Exercise controls gene expression. *American Scientist, 93,* 28–35.

Boothby, E. J., Cooney, G., Sandstrom, G. M., & Clark, M. S. (2018). The liking gap in conversations: Do people like us more than we think? *Psychological Science, 29,* 1742–1756.

Bopp, K. L., & Verhaeghen, P. (2020). Aging and n-back performance: A meta-analysis. *The Journals of Gerontology: Series B, 75*(2), 229–240.

Bor, D. (2010). The mechanics of mind reading. *Scientific American, 21,* 52–57.

Bora, E., & Pantelis, C. (2013). Theory of mind impairments in first-episode psychosis, individuals at ultra-high risk for psychosis and in first-degree relatives of schizophrenia: Systematic review and meta-analysis. *Schizophrenia Research, 144,* 31–36.

Bora, E., & Pantelis, C. (2016). Social cognitive in schizophrenia in comparison to bipolar disorder: A meta-analysis. *Schizophrenia Research, 175,* 72–78.

Border, R., Johnson, E. C., Evans, L. M., Smolen, A., Berley, N., Sullivan, P. F., & Keller, M. C. (2019). No support for historical candidate gene or candidate gene-by-interaction hypotheses for major depression across multiple large samples. *American Journal of Psychiatry, 176,* 376–387.

Borgogna, N. C., McDermott, R. C., Aita, S. L., & Kridel, M. M. (2018). Anxiety and depression across gender and sexual minorities: Implications for transgender, gender nonconforming, pansexual, demisexual, asexual, queer, and questioning individuals. *Psychology of Sexual Orientation and Gender Diversity, 6,* 54–63

Boring, E. G. (1930). A new ambiguous figure. *American Journal of Psychology, 42,* 444–445.

Boring, E. G. (1959). *Lewis Madison Terman, 1877–1956.* National Academy of Sciences.

Borman, G. D., Rozek, C. S., Pyne, J., & Hanselman, P. (2019). Reappraising academic and social adversity improves middle school students' academic achievement, behavior, and well-being. *PNAS, 116,* 16286–16291.

Bornstein, M. H., Cote, L. R., Maital, S., Painter, K., Park, S.-Y., Pascual, L., Pêcheux, M. G., Ruel, J., Venuti, P., & Vyt, A. (2004). Cross-linguistic analysis of vocabulary in young children: Spanish, Dutch, French, Hebrew, Italian, Korean, and American English. *Child Development, 75,* 1115–1139.

Bornstein, M. H., Tal, J., Rahn, C., Galperin, C. Z., Pecheux, M.-G., Lamour, M., Toda, S., Azuma, H., Ogino, M., & Tamis-LeMonda, C. S. (1992a). Functional analysis of the contents of maternal speech to infants of 5 and 13 months in four cultures: Argentina, France, Japan, and the United States. *Developmental Psychology, 28,* 593–603.

Bornstein, M. H., Tamis-LeMonda, C. S., Tal, J., Ludemann, P., Toda, S., Rahn, C. W., Pêcheux, M. G., Azuma, H., & Vardi, D. (1992b). Maternal responsiveness to infants in three societies: The United States, France, and Japan. *Child Development, 63,* 808–821.

Bornstein, R. F. (1989). Exposure and affect: Overview and meta-analysis of research, 1968–1987. *Psychological Bulletin, 106,* 265–289.

Bornstein, R. F. (1999). Source amnesia, misattribution, and the power of unconscious perceptions and memories. *Psychoanalytic Psychology, 16,* 155–178.

Bornstein, R. F., Galley, D. J., Leone, D. R., & Kale, A. R. (1991). The temporal stability of ratings of parents: Test-retest reliability and influence of parental contact. *Journal of Social Behavior and Personality, 6,* 641–649.

Boroditsky, L. (2009, June 12). *How does our language shape the way we think?* Edge. https://www.edge.org/conversation/lera_boroditsky-how-does-our-language-shape-the-way-we-think

Boroditsky, L. (2011, February). How language shapes thought. *Scientific American,* pp. 63–65.

Bos, H. M. W., Knox, J. R., van Rijn-van Gelderen, L., & Gartrell, N. K. (2016). Same-sex and different-sex parent households and child health outcomes: Findings from the National Survey of Children's Health. *Journal of Developmental and Behavioral Pediatrics, 37,* 179–187.

Bosl, W. J., Tager-Flusberg, H. & Nelson, C. A. (2018). EEG analytics for early detection of autism spectrum disorder: A data-driven approach. *Scientific Reports, 8,* 6828.

Bosma, H., Marmot, M. G., Hemingway, H., Nicolson, A. C., Brunner, E., & Stansfeld, S. A. (1997). Low job control and risk of coronary heart disease in Whitehall II (prospective cohort) study. *British Medical Journal, 314,* 558–565.

Bosma, H., Peter, R., Siegrist, J., & Marmot, M. (1998). Two alternative job stress models and the risk of coronary heart disease. *American Journal of Public Health, 88,* 68–74.

Bostean, G., & Gillespie, B. J. (2018). Acculturation, acculturative stressors, and family relationships among Latina/o immigrants. *Cultural Diversity and Ethnic Minority Psychology, 24,* 126–138.

Bostwick, J. M., Pabbati, C., Geske, J. R., & McKean, A. J. (2016). Suicide attempt as a risk factor for completed suicide: Even more lethal than we knew. *The American Journal of Psychiatry, 173,* 1094–1100.

Bostwick, J. M., & Pankratz, V. S. (2000). Affective disorders and suicide risk: A re-examination. *American Journal of Psychiatry, 157,* 1925–1932.

Bosworth, R. G., & Dobkins, K. R. (1999). Left-hemisphere dominance for motion processing in deaf signers. *Psychological Science, 10,* 256–262.

Bothwell, R. K., Brigham, J. C., & Malpass, R. S. (1989). Cross-racial identification. *Personality and Social Psychology Bulletin, 15,* 19–25.

Bots, S. H., Peters, S. A., & Woodward, M. (2017). Sex differences in coronary heart disease and stroke mortality: a global assessment of the effect of ageing between 1980 and 2010. *BMJ Global Health, 2,* e000298.

Botvinick, M., Ritter, S., Wang, J. X., Kurth-Nelson, Z., Blundell, C., Hassabis, D. (2019). Reinforcement learning, fast and slow. *Trends in Cognitive Sciences, 23,* 408–422.

Bouchard, T. J., Jr. (2009). Genetic influences on human intelligence (Spearman's *g*): How much? *Annals of Human Biology, 36,* 527–544.

Boucher, J., Mayes, A., & Bigham, S. (2012). Memory in autistic spectrum disorder. *Psychological Bulletin, 138,* 458–496.

Bould, H., Carnegie, R., Allward, H., Bacon, E., Lambe, Sapseid, M., Button, K. S., Lewis, G., Skinner, A., Broome, M. R., Park, R., Harmer, C. J., Penton-Boak, I. S., & Munafó, M. R. (2018). Effects of exposure to bodies of different sizes on perception of and satisfaction with own body size: Two randomized studies. *Royal Society Open Science, 5,* 171387.

Bowden, E. M., & Beeman, M. J. (1998). Getting the right idea: Semantic activation in the right hemisphere may help solve insight problems. *Psychological Science, 9,* 435–440.

Bowdring, M. A., & Sayette, M. A. (2018). Perception of physical attractiveness when consuming and not consuming alcohol: A meta-analysis. *Addiction, 113,* 1585–1597.

Bower, B. (2009, February 14). The dating go round. *Science News,* pp. 22–25.

Bower, G. H. (1986). Prime time in cognitive psychology. In P. Eelen (Ed.), *Cognitive research and behavior therapy: Beyond the conditioning paradigm.* North Holland Publishers.

Bower, G. H., Clark, M. C., Lesgold, A. M., & Winzenz, D. (1969). Hierarchical retrieval schemes in recall of categorized word lists. *Journal of Verbal Learning and Verbal Behavior, 8,* 323–343.

Bower, G. H., & Morrow, D. G. (1990). Mental models in narrative comprehension. *Science, 247,* 44–48.

Bower, J. M., & Parsons, L. M. (2003, August). Rethinking the "lesser brain." *Scientific American,* pp. 50–57.

Bowers, J. M., & Moyer, A. (2017). Effects of school start time on students' sleep duration, daytime sleepiness, and attendance: a meta-analysis. *Sleep Health, 3,* 423–431.

Bowers, J. S. (2009). On the biological plausibility of grandmother cells: Implications for neural network theories in psychology and neuroscience. *Psychological Review, 116,* 220–251.

Bowker, E., & Dorstyn, D. (2016). Hypnotherapy for disability-related pain: A meta-analysis. *Journal of Health Psychology, 21,* 526–539.

Bowling, N. A., Eschleman, K. J., & Wang, Q. (2010). A meta-analytic examination of the relationship between job satisfaction and subjective well-being. *Journal of Occupational and Organizational Psychology, 83,* 915–934.

Boxer, P., Huesmann, L. R., Bushman, B. J., O'Brien, M., & Moceri, D. (2009). The role of violent media preference in cumulative developmental risk for violence and general aggression. *Journal of Youth and Adolescence, 38,* 417–428.

Boyatzis, C. J. (2012). Spiritual development during childhood and adolescence. In L. J. Miller (Ed.), *The Oxford handbook of psychology and spirituality* (pp. 151–164). Oxford University Press.

Boyatzis, C. J., Matillo, G. M., & Nesbitt, K. M. (1995). Effects of the "Mighty Morphin Power Rangers" on children's aggression with peers. *Child Study Journal, 25,* 45–55.

Boyce, C. J., & Wood, A. M. (2011). Personality prior to disability determines adaptation: Agreeable individuals recover lost life satisfaction faster and more completely. *Psychological Science, 22,* 1397–1402.

Boyce, C. J., Wood, A. M., Daly, M., & Sedikides, C. (2015). Personality change following unemployment. *Journal of Applied Psychology, 100*, 991–1011.

Boyce, R., Glasgow, S. D., Williams, S., & Adamantidis, A. (2016). Causal evidence for the role of REM sleep theta rhythm in contextual memory consolidation. *Science, 352*, 812–816.

Boyden, E. S. (2014). Let there be light. *Scientific American, 25*, 62–69.

Boynton, R. M. (1979). *Human color vision.* Holt, Rinehart & Winston.

Braden, J. P. (1994). *Deafness, deprivation, and IQ.* Plenum.

Bradley, D. R., Dumais, S. T., & Petry, H. M. (1976). Reply to Cavonius. *Nature, 261*, 78.

Bradley, R. B., Binder, E. B., Epstein, M. P., Tan, Y.-L., Nair, H. P., Liu, W., Gillespie, C. F., Berg, T., Evces, M., Newport, D. J., Stowe, Z. N., Heim, C. M., Nemeroff, C. B., Schwartz, A., Cubells, J. F., & Ressler, K. (2008). Influence of child abuse on adult depression: Moderation by the corticotropin-releasing hormone receptor gene. *Archives of General Psychiatry, 65*, 190–200.

Bradshaw, C., Sawyer, A., & O'Brennan, L. (2009). A social disorganization perspective on bullying-related attitudes and behaviors: The influence of school context. *American Journal of Community Psychology, 43*, 204–220.

Brady, W. J., Wills, J. A., Jost, J. T., Tucker, J. A., & Van Bavel, J. J. (2017). Emotion shapes the diffusion of moralized content in social networks. *PNAS, 114*, 7313–7318.

Braiker, B. (2005, October 18). A quiet revolt against the rules on SIDS. *The New York Times.* https://www.nytimes.com/2005/10/18/health/a-quiet-revolt-against-the-rules-on-sids.html?

Brainerd, C. J. (1996). Piaget: A centennial celebration. *Psychological Science, 7*, 191–195.

Brainstorm Consortium. (2018). Analysis of shared heritability in common disorders of the brain. *Science, 360*, 1313.

Brakefield, T. A., Mednick, S. C., Wilson, H. W., De Neve, J., Christakis, N. A., & Fowler, J. H. (2014). Same-sex sexual attraction does not spread in adolescent social networks. *Archives of Sexual Behavior, 43*, 335–344.

Brand, B. L., Sar, V., Stavropoulos, P., Krüger, C., Korzekwa, M., Martínez-Taboas, A., & Middleton, W. (2016). Separating fact from fiction: An empirical examination of six myths about dissociative identity disorder. *Harvard Review of Psychiatry, 24*, 257–270.

Brandon, S., Boakes, J., Glaser, & Green, R. (1998). Recovered memories of childhood sexual abuse: Implications for clinical practice. *British Journal of Psychiatry, 172*, 294–307.

Brang, D., Edwards, L., Ramachandran, V. S., & Coulson, S. (2008). Is the sky 2? Contextual priming in grapheme-color synaesthesia. *Psychological Science, 19*, 421–428.

Brannan, D., Biswas-Diener, R., Mohr, C., Mortazavi, S., & Stein, N. (2013). Friends and family: A cross-cultural investigation of social support and subjective well-being among college students. *Journal of Positive Psychology, 8*, 65–75.

Bransford, J. D., & Johnson, M. K. (1972). Contextual prerequisites for understanding: Some investigations of comprehension and recall. *Journal of Verbal Learning and Verbal Behavior, 11*, 717–726.

Brasel, S. A., & Gips, J. (2011). Media multitasking behavior: Concurrent television and computer usage. *Cyberpsychology, Behavior, and Social Networking, 14*, 527–534.

Braun, S. (2001, Spring). Seeking insight by prescription. *Cerebrum*, pp. 10–21.

Braunstein, G. D., Sundwall, D. A., Katz, M., Shifren, J. L., Buster, J. E., Simon, J. A., Bachman, G., Aguirre, O. A., Lucas, J. D., Rodenberg, C., Buch, A., & Watts, N. B. (2005). Safety and efficacy of a testosterone patch for the treatment of hypoactive sexual desire disorder in surgically menopausal women: A randomized, placebo-controlled trial. *Archives of Internal Medicine, 165*, 1582–1589.

Bray, D. W., & Byham, W. C. (1991, Winter). Assessment centers and their derivatives. *Journal of Continuing Higher Education, 39*, 8–11.

Bray, D. W., & Byham, W. C. (1997). Interviewed by Mayes, B. T. Insights into the history and future of assessment centers: An interview with Dr. Douglas W. Bray and Dr. William Byham. *Journal of Social Behavior and Personality, 12*, 3–12.

Brayne, C., Spiegelhalter, D. J., Dufouil, C., Chi, L. Y., Dening, T. R., Paykel, E. S., O'Connor, D. W., Ahmed, A., McGee, M. A., & Huppert, F. A. (1999). Estimating the true extent of cognitive decline in the old old. *Journal of the American Geriatrics Society, 47*, 1283–1288.

Breedlove, S. M. (1997). Sex on the brain. *Nature, 389*, 801.

Breedlove, S. M. (2017). Prenatal influences on human sexual orientation: Expectations versus data. *Archives of Sexual Behavior, 46*, 1583–1592.

Breedvelt, J. J. F., Kandola, A., Kousoulis, A. A., Brouwer, M. E., Karyotaki, E., Bockting, C. L. H., & Cuijpers, P. M. W. (2018). What are the effects of preventative interventions on major depressive disorder (MDD) in young adults? A systematic review and meta-analysis of randomized controlled trials. *Journal of Affective Disorders, 239*, 18–29.

Brennan, Z. (2010, April 8). The Goering who saved Jews: While Hermann masterminded the Final Solution his brother Albert rescued Gestapo victims. *Daily Mail.* https://www.dailymail.co.uk/news/article-1264738/The-Goering-saved-Jews-A-new-book-reveals-Hermann-masterminded-Final-Solution-brother-Albert-rescued-Gestapo-victims.html

Bresin, K., Mekawi, Y., & Verona, E. (2018). The effect of laboratory manipulations of negative affect on alcohol craving and use: A meta-analysis. *Psychology of Addictive Behaviors, 32*, 617–627.

Breslau, J., Aguilar-Gaxiola, S., Borges, G., Kendler, K. S., Su, M., & Kessler, R. C. (2007). Risk for psychiatric disorder among immigrants and their US-born descendants. *Journal of Nervous and Mental Disease, 195*, 189–195.

Brethel-Haurwitz, K. M., & Marsh, A. A. (2014, March). Geographical differences in subjective well-being predict extraordinary altruism. *Psychological Science, 25*, 762–771.

Brewer, M. B., & Chen, Y.-R. (2007). Where (who) are collectives in collectivism? Toward conceptual clarification of individualism and collectivism. *Psychological Review, 114*, 133–151.

Brewer, W. F. (1977). Memory for the pragmatic implications of sentences. *Memory & Cognition, 5*, 673–678.

Brewin, C. R., & Andrews, B. (2017). Creating memories for false autobiographical events in childhood: A systematic review. *Applied Cognitive Psychology, 31*, 2–23.

Brewin, C. R., Kleiner, J. S., Vasterling, J. J., & Field, A. P. (2007). Memory for emotionally neutral information in posttraumatic stress disorder: A meta-analytic investigation. *Journal of Abnormal Psychology, 116*, 448–463.

Bridgman, T., Cummings, S., & Ballard, J. (2019). Who built Maslow's pyramid? A history of the creation of management studies' most famous symbol and its implications for management education. *Academy of Management Learning & Education, 18*, 81–98.

Briscoe, D. (1997, February 16). Women lawmakers still not in charge. *Grand Rapids Press*, p. A23.

Brislin, R. W. (1988). Increasing awareness of class, ethnicity, culture, and race by expanding on students' own experiences. In I. Cohen (Ed.), *The G. Stanley Hall lecture series.* American Psychological Association.

Britto, P. R., Lye, S. J., Proulx, K., Yousafzai, A. K., Matthews, S. G., Vaivada, T., Perez-Escamilla, R., Rao, N., Ip, P., Fernald, L. C. H., MacMillan, H., Hanson, M., Wachs, T. D., Yao, H., Yoshikawa, H., Cerezo, A., Leckman, J. F., Bhutta, Z. A., & Early Childhood Development Interventions Review Group. (2017). Nurturing care: promoting early childhood development. *The Lancet, 389*, 91–102.

Britton, W. B. (2019). Can mindfulness be too much of a good thing? The value of a middle way. *Current Opinion in Psychology, 28*, 159–165.

Broadbent, E., Kakokehr, A., Booth, R. J., Thomas, J., Windsor, J. A., Buchanan, C. M., Wheeler, B. R., Sammour, T., & Hill, A. G. (2012). A brief relaxation intervention reduces stress and improves surgical wound healing response: A randomized trial. *Brain, Behavior, and Immunity, 26*, 212–217.

Broda, M., Yun, J., Schneider, B., Yeager, D. S., Walton, G. M., & Diemer, M. (2018). Reducing inequality in academic success for incoming college students: A randomized trial of growth mindset and belonging interventions. *Journal of Research on Educational Effectiveness, 11*, 317–338.

Brodbeck, F. C., Chhokar, J. S., & House, R. J. (2008). Culture and leadership in 25 societies: Integration, conclusions, and future directions. In J. S. Chhokar, F. C. Brodbeck & R. J. House (Eds.), *Culture and leadership across the world: The GLOBE book of in-depth studies of 25 societies* (pp. 1023–1099). Erlbaum.

Brodt, S., Gais, S., Beck, J., Erb, M., Scheffler, K., & Schönauer, M. (2018). Fast track to the neocortex: A memory engram in the posterior parietal cortex. *Science, 362*, 1045–1048.

Brody, G. H., Yu, T., Chen, E., Ehrlich, K. B., & Miller, G. E. (2018). Racial discrimination, body mass index, and insulin resistance: A longitudinal analysis. *Health Psychology, 37*, 1107–1114.

Brody, J. E. (2018, August 13). An underappreciated key to college success: Sleep. *The New York Times.* https://www.nytimes.com/2018/08/13/well/an-underappreciated-key-to-college-success-sleep.html?

Brody, J. E. (2019, April 29). Virtual reality as therapy for pain. *The New York Times.* https://www.nytimes.com/2019/04/29/well/live/virtual-reality-as-therapy-for-pain.html?

Brody, N. (2004). What cognitive intelligence is and what emotional intelligence is not. *Psychological Inquiry, 15*, 234–238.

Brody, S., & Tillmann, H. C. (2006). The post-orgasmic prolactin increase following intercourse is greater than following masturbation and suggests greater satiety. *Biological Psychology, 71*, 312–315.

Broks, P. (2007, April). *The mystery of consciousness.* Prospect. https://www.prospectmagazine.co.uk/magazine/themysteryofconsciousness

Brooks, R. (2012). "Asia's missing women" as a problem in applied evolutionary psychology? *Evolutionary Psychology, 12*, 910–925.

Brooks, S. (2015). Does personal social media usage affect efficiency and well-being? *Computers in Human Behavior, 46*, 26–37.

Brose, A., de Roover, K., Ceulemans, E., & Kuppens, P. (2015). Older adults' affective experiences across 100 days are less variable and less complex than younger adults'. *Psychology and Aging, 30*, 194–208.

Brown, A. (2017, November 8). *Republicans, Democrats have starkly different views on transgender issues.*

Pew Research Center. https://www.pewresearch.org/fact-tank/2017/11/08/transgender-issues-divide-republicans-and-democrats/

Brown, A. S., Begg, M. D., Gravenstein, S., Schaefer, C. A., Wyatt, R. J., Bresnahan, M., Babulas, V. P., & Susser, E. S. (2004). Serologic evidence of prenatal influenza in the etiology of schizophrenia. *Archives of General Psychiatry, 61,* 774–780.

Brown, A. S., & Patterson, P. H. (2011). Maternal infection and schizophrenia: Implications for prevention. *Schizophrenia Bulletin, 37,* 284–290.

Brown, A. S., Schaefer, C. A., Wyatt, R. J., Goetz, R., Begg, M. D., Gorman, J. M., & Susser, E. S. (2000). Maternal exposure to respiratory infections and adult schizophrenia spectrum disorders: A prospective birth cohort study. *Schizophrenia Bulletin, 26,* 287–295.

Brown, E. L., & Deffenbacher, K. (1979). *Perception and the senses.* Oxford University Press.

Brown, J. A. (1958). Some tests of the decay theory of immediate memory. *Quarterly Journal of Experimental Psychology, 10,* 12–21.

Brown, K. W., Goodman, R. J., & Inzlicht, M. (2013). Dispositional mindfulness and the attenuation of neural responses to emotional stimuli. *Social Cognitive and Affective Neuroscience, 8,* 93–99.

Brown, L. A., Gallagher, T., Petersen, J., Benhamou, K., Foa, E. B., & Asnaani, A. (2018). Does CBT for anxiety-related disorders alter suicidal ideation? Findings from a naturalistic sample. *Journal of Anxiety Disorders, 59,* 10–16.

Brown, R. (1986). Linguistic relativity. In S. H. Hulse & B. F. Green, Jr. (Eds.), *One hundred years of psychological research in America.* Johns Hopkins University Press.

Brown, R. P., Imura, M., & Mayeux, L. (2014). Honor and the stigma of mental healthcare. *Personality and Social Psychology Bulletin, 40,* 1119–1131.

Brown, R. P., Osterman, L. L., & Barnes, C. D. (2009). School violence and the culture of honor. *Psychological Science, 20,* 1400–1405.

Brown, S., Cockett, P., & Yuan, Y. (2019). The neuroscience of Romeo and Juliet: An fMRI study of acting. *Royal Society Open Science, 6,* 181908.

Brown, S. L., Brown, R. M., House, J. S., & Smith, D. M. (2008). Coping with spousal loss: Potential buffering effects of self-reported helping behavior. *Personality and Social Psychology Bulletin, 34,* 849–861.

Brown, S. L., Stykes, J. B., & Manning, W. D. (2016). Trends in children's family instability, 1995–2010. *Journal of Marriage and Family, 78,* 1173–1183.

Brown, W. A. (2019). *Lithium: A doctor, a drug, and a breakthrough.* Liveright.

Browning, C. (1992). *Ordinary men: Reserve Police Battalion 101 and the final solution in Poland.* HarperCollins.

Browning, R. (1868). *The ring and the book. IV—Tertium quid.* Thomas Y. Crowell.

Bruck, M., & Ceci, S. J. (1999). The suggestibility of children's memory. *Annual Review of Psychology, 50,* 419–439.

Bruck, M., & Ceci, S. J. (2004). Forensic developmental psychology: Unveiling four common misconceptions. *Current Directions in Psychological Science, 15,* 229–232.

Brummelman, E., Thomaes, S., Nelemans, S. A., Orobio de Castro, B., Overbeek, G., & Bushman, B. J. (2015). Origins of narcissism in children. *PNAS, 112,* 3659–3662.

Brunelin, J., Mondino, M., Bation, R., Palm, U., Saoud, M., & Poulet, E. (2018). Transcranial direct current stimulation for obsessive-compulsive disorder: a systematic review. *Brain Sciences, 8,* 37.

Brunet, A., Saumier, D., Liu, A., Streiner, D. L., Tremblay, J., & Pitman, R. K. (2018). Reduction of PTSD symptoms with pre-reactivation propranolol therapy: A randomized controlled trial. *The American Journal of Psychiatry, 175,* 427–433.

Bruni, F. (2018, October 30). The internet will be the death of us. *The New York Times.* https://www.nytimes.com/2018/10/30/opinion/internet-violence-hate-prejudice.html?

Brunoni, A. R., Chaimani, A., Moffa, A. H., Razza, L. B., Gattaz, W. F., Daskalakis, Z. J., & Carvalho, A. F. (2017). Repetitive transcranial magnetic stimulation for the acute treatment of major depressive episodes: A systematic review with network meta-analysis. *JAMA Psychiatry, 74,* 143–152.

Bryan, A. D., Gillman, A. S., & Hansen, N. S. (2016). Changing the context is important and necessary, but not sufficient, for reducing adolescent risky sexual behavior: A reply to Steinberg (2015). *Perspectives on Psychological Science, 11,* 535–538.

Bryan, A. E. B., & Arkowitz, H. (2015). Meta-analysis of the effects of peer-administered psychosocial interventions on symptoms of depression. *American Journal of Community Psychology, 55,* 455–471.

Bryant, A. N., & Astin, H. A. (2008). The correlates of spiritual struggle during the college years. *Journal of Higher Education, 79,* 1–27.

Bryant, G. A., Fessler, D. M. T., Fusaroli, R., Clint, E., Amir, D., Chávez, B., Denton, K. K., Diaz, C., Duran, L. T., Fančovićová, J., Fux, M., Ginting, E. F., Hasan, Y., Hu, A., Kamble, S. V., Kameda, T., Kuroda, K., Li, N. P., Luberti, F. R., . . . Zhou, Y. (2018). The perception of spontaneous and volitional laughter across 21 societies. *Psychological Science, 29,* 1515–1525.

Bub, K. L., Robinson, L. E., & Curtis, D. S. (2016). Longitudinal associations between self-regulation and health across childhood and adolescence. *Health Psychology, 35,* 1235–1245.

Buchanan, A., Sint, K., Swanson, J., & Rosenheck, R. (2019). Correlates of future violence in people being treated for schizophrenia. *American Journal of Psychiatry, 176,* 694–701.

Buchanan, R. W., Kreyenbuhl, J., Kelly, D. L., Noel, J. M., Boggs, D. L., Fischer, B. A., Himelhoch, S., Fang, B., Peterson, E., Aquino, P. R., Keller, W., & Schizophrenia Patient Outcomes Research Team (PORT). (2010). The 2009 schizophrenia PORT psychopharmacological treatment recommendations and summary statements. *Schizophrenia Bulletin, 36,* 71–93.

Buchanan, T. W. (2007). Retrieval of emotional memories. *Psychological Bulletin, 133,* 761–779.

Buck, L. B., & Axel, R. (1991). A novel multigene family may encode odorant receptors: A molecular basis for odor recognition. *Cell, 65,* 175–187.

Buckell, J., & Sindelar, J. L. (2019). The impact of flavors, health risks, secondhand smoke and prices on young adults' cigarette and e-cigarette choices: a discrete choice experiment. *Addiction, 114,* 1427–1435.

Buckels, E. E., Trapnell, P. D., & Paulhus, D. L. (2014). Trolls just want to have fun. *Personality and Individual Differences, 67,* 97–102.

Buckholtz, J. W., Treadway, M. T., Cowan, R. L., Woodward, N. D., Benning, S. D., Li, R., Ansari, M. S., Baldwin, R. M., Schwartzman, A. N., Shelby, E. S., Smith, C. E., Cole, D., Kessler, R. M., & Zald, D. H. (2010). Mesolimbic dopamine reward system hypersensitivity in individuals with psychopathic traits. *Nature Neuroscience, 13,* 419–421.

Buckingham, M. (2007). *Go put your strengths to work: 6 powerful steps to achieve outstanding performance.* Free Press.

Buckingham, M., & Clifton, D. O. (2001). *Now, discover your strengths.* Free Press.

Buckley, C. (2007, January 3). Man is rescued by stranger on subway tracks. *The New York Times.* https://www.nytimes.com/2007/01/03/nyregion/03life.html?

Buckner, J. D., Walukevich Dienst, K., & Zvolensky, M. J. (2019). Distress tolerance and cannabis craving: The impact of laboratory-induced distress. *Experimental and Clinical Psychopharmacology, 27,* 38–44.

Buehler, R., Griffin, D., & Ross, M. (1994). Exploring the "planning fallacy": Why people underestimate their task completion times. *Journal of Personality and Social Psychology, 67,* 366–381.

Buehler, R., Griffin, D., & Ross, M. (2002). Inside the planning fallacy: The causes and consequences of optimistic time predictions. In T. Gilovich, D. Griffin, & D. Kahneman (Eds.), *Heuristics and biases: The psychology of intuitive judgment.* Cambridge University Press.

Buffardi, L. E., & Campbell, W. K. (2008). Narcissism and social networking web sites. *Personality and Social Psychology Bulletin, 34,* 1303–1314.

Buffett, W. (2006). Quoted by B. Obama in *The audacity of hope: Thoughts on reclaiming the American dream.* Penguin.

Bugental, D. B. (1986). Unmasking the "polite smile": Situational and personal determinants of managed affect in adult-child interaction. *Personality and Social Psychology Bulletin, 12,* 7–16.

Buhle, J. T., Stevens, B. L., Friedman, J. J., & Wager, T. D. (2012). Distraction and placebo: Two separate routes to pain control. *Psychological Science, 23,* 246–253.

Buka, S. L., Tsuang, M. T., Torrey, E. F., Klebanoff, M. A., Wagner, R. L., & Yolken, R. H. (2001). Maternal infections and subsequent psychosis among offspring. *Archives of General Psychiatry, 58,* 1032–1037.

Bullock, B., & Murray, G. (2014). Reduced amplitude of the 24-hour activity rhythm: A biomarker of vulnerability to bipolar disorder? *Clinical Psychological Science, 2,* 86–96.

Bunde, J., & Suls, J. (2006). A quantitative analysis of the relationship between the Cook-Medley Hostility Scale and traditional coronary artery disease risk factors. *Health Psychology, 25,* 493–500.

Buquet, R. (1988). Le reve et les deficients visuels [Dreams and the visually impaired]. *Psychanalyse-a-l'Universite, 13,* 319–321.

Burelli, J. (2008). *Thirty-three years of women in S&E faculty positions* (Publication No. NSF 08-308). National Science Foundation. wayback.archive-it.org/5902/20160210152800/http://www.nsf.gov/statistics/infbrief/nsf08308/

Burger, J. M. (2009). Replicating Milgram: Would people still obey today? *American Psychologist, 64,* 1–11.

Burger, J. M., Bender, T. J., Day, L., DeBolt, J. A., Guthridge, L., How, H. W., Meyer, M., Russell, K. A., & Taylor, S. (2015). The power of one: The relative influence of helpful and selfish models. *Social Influence, 10,* 77–84.

Buri, J. R., Louiselle, P. A., Misukanis, T. M., & Mueller, R. A. (1988). Effects of parental authoritarianism and authoritativeness on self-esteem. *Personality and Social Psychology Bulletin, 14,* 271–282.

Burish, T. G., & Carey, M. P. (1986). Conditioned aversive responses in cancer chemotherapy patients: Theoretical and developmental analysis. *Journal of Counseling and Clinical Psychology, 54,* 593–600.

Burk, W. J., Denissen, J., Van Doorn, M. D., Branje, S. J. T., & Laursen, B. (2009). The vicissitudes of conflict measurement: Stability and reliability in the frequency of disagreements. *European Psychologist, 14,* 153–159.

Burke, B. L., Martens, A., & Faucher, E. H. (2010). Two decades of terror management theory: A meta-analysis of mortality salience research. *Personality and Social Psychology Review, 14,* 155–195.

Burke, D. M., & Shafto, M. A. (2004). Aging and language production. *Current Directions in Psychological Science, 13,* 21–24.

Burke, K. (2018). *How many texts do people send every day (2018)?* Text Request. textrequest.com/blog/how-many-texts-people-send-per-day/

Burlingame, G. M., Seebeck, J. D., Janis, R. A., Whitcomb, K. E., Barkowski, S., Rosendahl, J., & Strauss, B. (2016). Outcome differences between individual and group formats when identical and nonidentical treatments, patients, and doses are compared: A 25-year meta-analytic perspective. *Psychotherapy, 53,* 446–461.

Burns, S. M., Barnes, L. N., McCulloh, I. A., Dagher, M. M., Falk, E. B., Storey, J. D., & Lieberman, M. D. (2019). Making social neuroscience less WEIRD: Using fNIRS to measure neural signatures of persuasive influence in a Middle East participant sample. *Journal of Personality and Social Psychology, 116,* e1–e11.

Burris, C. T., & Branscombe, N. R. (2005). Distorted distance estimation induced by a self-relevant national boundary. *Journal of Experimental Social Psychology, 41,* 305–312.

Burris, J. L., Oleas, D., Reider, L., Buss, K. A., Pérez-Edgar, K., & LoBue, V. (2019). Biased attention to threat: Answering old questions with young infants. *Current Directions in Psychological Science, 28*(6), 534–539.

Burrow, A. L., Hill, P. L., & Sumner, R. (2016). Leveling mountains: Purpose attenuates links between perceptions of effort and steepness. *Personality and Social Psychology Bulletin, 42,* 94–103.

Burton, C. M., & King, L. A. (2008). Effects of (very) brief writing on health: The two-minute miracle. *British Journal of Health Psychology, 13,* 9–14.

Busby, D. M., Carroll, J. S., & Willoughby, B. J. (2010). Compatibility or restraint? The effects of sexual timing on marriage relationships. *Journal of Family Psychology, 24,* 766–774.

Bushdid, C., Magnasco, M. O., Vosshall, L. B., & Keller, A. (2014). Humans can discriminate more than 1 trillion olfactory stimuli. *Science, 343,* 1370–1372.

Bushman, B. J. (1993). Human aggression while under the influence of alcohol and other drugs: An integrative research review. *Current Directions in Psychological Science, 2,* 148–152.

Bushman, B. J. (2002). Does venting anger feed or extinguish the flame? Catharsis, rumination, distraction, anger, and aggressive responding. *Personality and Social Psychology Bulletin, 28,* 724–731.

Bushman, B. J. (2016). Violent media and hostile appraisals: A meta-analytic review. *Aggressive Behavior, 42,* 605–613.

Bushman, B. J. (2018). Teaching students about violent media effects. *Teaching of Psychological Science, 45,* 200–206.

Bushman, B. J., & Anderson, C. A. (2009). Comfortably numb: Desensitizing effects of violent media on helping others. *Psychological Science, 20,* 273–277.

Bushman, B. J., & Baumeister, R. F. (1998). Threatened egotism, narcissism, self-esteem, and direct and displaced aggression: Does self-love or self-hate lead to violence? *Journal of Personality and Social Psychology, 75,* 219–229.

Bushman, B. J., Baumeister, R. F., Thomaes, S., Ryu, E., Begeer, S., & West, S. G. (2009). Looking again, and harder, for a link between low self-esteem and aggression. *Journal of Personality, 77,* 427–446.

Bushman, B. J., Bonacci, A. M., van Dijk, M., & Baumeister, R. F. (2003). Narcissism, sexual refusal, and aggression: Testing a narcissistic reactance model of sexual coercion. *Journal of Personality and Social Psychology, 84,* 1027–1040.

Bushman, B. J., DeWall, C. N., Pond, R. S., Jr., & Hanus, M. D. (2014). Low glucose relates to greater aggression in married couples. *PNAS, 111,* 6254–6257.

Bushman, B. J., & Huesmann, L. R. (2010). Aggression. In S. T. Fiske, D. T. Gilbert, & G. Lindzey (Eds.), *Handbook of social psychology* (5th ed., Ch. 23, pp. 833–863). John Wiley & Sons.

Bushman, B. J., Moeller, S. J., & Crocker, J. (2011). Sweets, sex, or self-esteem? Comparing the value of self-esteem boosts with other pleasant rewards. *Journal of Personality, 79,* 993–1012.

Bushman, B. J., Ridge, R. D., Das, E., Key, C. W., & Busath, G. L. (2007). When God sanctions killing: Effects of scriptural violence on aggression. *Psychological Science, 18,* 204–207.

Buss, A. H. (1989). Personality as traits. *American Psychologist, 44,* 1378–1388.

Buss, D. M. (1991). Evolutionary personality psychology. *Annual Review of Psychology, 42,* 459–491.

Buss, D. M. (2008). *Female sexual psychology.* https://www.edge.org/response-detail/10356

Buss, D. M., & Schmitt, D. P. (2019). Mate preferences and their behavioral manifestations. *Annual Review of Psychology, 70,* 77–110.

Buss, D. M., & von Hippel, W. (2018). Psychological barriers to evolutionary psychology: Ideological bias and coalitional adaptations. *Archives of Scientific Psychology, 6,* 148–158.

Buster, J. E., Kingsberg, S. A., Aguirre, O., Brown, C., Breaux, J. G., Buch, A., Rodenberg, C. A., Wekselman, K., & Casson, P. (2005). Testosterone patch for low sexual desire in surgically menopausal women: A randomized trial. *Obstetrics and Gynecology, 105,* 944–952.

Butler, J. D. (2017). The complex intersection of education and therapy in the drama therapy classroom. *The Arts in Psychotherapy, 53,* 28–35.

Butler, R. A. (1954, February). Curiosity in monkeys. *Scientific American,* pp. 70–75.

Butow, P., Price, M., Coll, J., Tucker, K., Meiser, B., Milne, R., Wilson, J., Heiniger, L., Baylock, B., Bullen, T., Weideman, P., Phillips, K. A., kConFab investigators, kConFab Clinical Follow-Up investigators, & kConFab psychosocial investigators. (2018). Does stress increase risk of breast cancer? A 15-year prospective study. *Psycho-Oncology, 27,* 1908–1914.

Butterworth, G. (1992). Origins of self-perception in infancy. *Psychological Inquiry, 3,* 103–111.

Buttrick, N., Choi, H., Wilson, T. D., Oishi, S., Boker, S. M., Gilbert, D. T., Alper, S., Aveyard, M., Cheong, W., Čolić, M. V., Dalgar, I., Doğulu, C., Karabati, S., Kim, E., Knežević, G., Komiya, A., Laclé, C. O., Ambrosio Lage, C., Lazarević, L. B., . . . Wilks, D. C. (2018). Cross-cultural consistency and relativity in the enjoyment of thinking versus doing. *Journal of Personality and Social Psychology, 117*(5), e71–e83.

Butts, M. M., Casper, W. J., & Yang, T. S. (2013). How important are work-family support policies? A meta-analytic investigation of their effects on employee outcomes. *Journal of Applied Psychology, 98,* 1–25.

Byers-Heinlein, K., Burns, T. C., & Werker, J. F. (2010). The roots of bilingualism in newborns. *Psychological Science, 21,* 343–348.

Byrc, K., Durand, E. Y., Macpherson, J. M., Reich, D., & Mountain, J. L. (2015). The genetic ancestry of African Americans, Latinos, and European Americans across the United States. *American Journal of Human Genetics 96,* 37–53.

Byrd, A. L., & Manuck, S. B. (2014). MAOA, childhood maltreatment, and antisocial behavior: Meta-analysis of a gene-environment interaction. *Biological Psychiatry, 75,* 9–17.

Byrd, A. L., Manuck, S. B., Hawes, S. W., Vebares, T. J., Nimgaonkar, V., Chowdari, K. V., Hipwell, A. E.,

Keenan, K., & Stepp, S. D. (2019). The interaction between monoamine oxidase A (MAOA) and childhood maltreatment as a predictor of personality pathology in females: Emotional reactivity as a potential mediating mechanism. *Development and Psychopathology, 31,* 361–377.

Byrne, D. (1971). *The attraction paradigm.* Academic Press.

Byrne, D. (1982). Predicting human sexual behavior. In A. G. Kraut (Ed.), *The G. Stanley Hall Lecture Series* (Vol. 2, pp. 211–254). American Psychological Association.

Byrne, R. W. (1991, May/June). Brute intellect. *The Sciences,* pp. 42–47.

Byrne, R. W., Bates, L. A., & Moss, C. J. (2009). Elephant cognition in primate perspective. *Comparative Cognition & Behavior Reviews, 4,* 1–15.

Byron, K., & Khazanchi, S. (2011). A meta-analytic investigation of the relationship of state and trait anxiety to performance on figural and verbal creative tasks. *Personality and Social Psychology Bulletin, 37,* 269–283.

Cable, D. M., & Gilovich, T. (1998). Looked over or overlooked? Prescreening decisions and post-interview evaluations. *Journal of Personality and Social Psychology, 83,* 501–508.

Cacioppo, J. T., Cacioppo, S., Capitanio, J. P., & Cole, S. W. (2015). The neuroendocrinology of social isolation. *Annual Review of Psychology, 66,* 733–767.

Cacioppo, J. T., Cacioppo, S., Gonzaga, G. C., Ogburn, E. L., & VanderWeele, T. J. (2013). Marital satisfaction and break-ups differ across on-line and off-line meeting venues. *PNAS, 110,* 10135–10140.

Cacioppo, S., Bianchi-Demicheli, F., Frum, C., Pfaus, J. G., & Lewis, J. W. (2012). The common neural bases between sexual desire and love: A multilevel kernel density fMRI analysis. *Journal of Sexual Medicine, 12,* 1048–1054.

Cacioppo, S., Capitanio, J. P., & Cacioppo, J. T. (2014). Toward a neurology of loneliness. *Psychological Bulletin, 140,* 1464–1504.

Caddick, A., & Porter, L. E. (2012). Exploring a model of professionalism in multiple perpetrator violent crime in the UK. *Criminological & Criminal Justice: An International Journal, 12,* 61–82.

Cain, S. (2012). *Quiet: The power of introverts in a world that can't stop talking.* Crown.

Calcutt, S. E., Proctor, D., Berman, S. M., & de Waal, F. B. (2019). Chimpanzees (Pan troglodytes) are more averse to social than nonsocial risk. *Psychological Science, 30,* 105–115.

Caldwell, J. A. (2012). Crew schedules, sleep deprivation, and aviation performance. *Current Directions in Psychological Science, 21,* 85–89.

Cale, E. M., & Lilienfeld, S. O. (2002). Sex differences in psychopathy and antisocial personality disorder: A review and integration. *Clinical Psychology Review, 22,* 1179–1207.

Callaghan, T., Rochat, P., Lillard, A., Claux, M. L., Odden, H., Itakura, S., Tapanya, S., & Singh, S. (2005). Synchrony in the onset of mental-state reasoning. *Psychological Science, 16,* 378–384.

Callan, M. J., Shead, N. W., & Olson, J. M. (2011). Personal relative deprivation, delay discounting, and gambling. *Journal of Personality and Social Psychology, 101,* 955–973.

Calvert, S. L., Appelbaum, M., Dodge, K. A., Graham, S., Nagayama Hall, G. C., Hamby, S., Fasig-Caldwell, L. G., Citkowicz, M., Galloway, D. P., & Hedges, L. V. (2017). The American Psychological Association Task Force assessment of violent video games: Science in the service of public interest. *American Psychologist, 72,* 126–143.

Calvo-Merino, B., Glaser, D. E., Grèzes, J., Passingham, R. E., & Haggard, P. (2004). Action observation and acquired motor skills: An fMRI study with expert dancers. *Cerebral Cortex, 15,* 1243–1249.

Calzo, J. P., Mays, V. M., Björkenstam, C., Björkenstam, E., Kosidou, K., & Cochran, S. D. (2019). Parental sexual orientation and children's psychological well-being: 2013–2015 National Health Interview Survey. *Child Development, 90,* 1097–1108.

Camerer, C. F., Dreber, A., Holzmeister, F., Ho, T. H., Huber, J., Johannesson, M., Kirchler, M., Nave, G., Nosek, B. A., Pfeiffer, T., Altmejd, A., Buttrick, N., Chan, T., Chen, Y., Forsell, E., Gampa, A., Heikensten, E., Hummer, L., Imai, T., . . . Wu, H. (2018). Evaluating the replicability of social science experiments in *Nature* and *Science* between 2010 and 2015. *Nature Human Behaviour, 2,* 637–644.

Camerer, C. F., Loewenstein, G., & Weber, M. (1989). The curse of knowledge in economic settings: An experimental analysis. *Journal of Political Economy, 97,* 1232–1254.

Cameron, J. J., & Granger, S. (2019). Does self-esteem have an interpersonal imprint beyond self-reports? A meta-analysis of self-esteem and objective interpersonal indicators. *Personality and Social Psychology Review, 23,* 73–102.

Cameron, L. D., & Overall, N. C. (2018). Suppression and expression as distinct emotion-regulation processes in daily interactions: Longitudinal and meta-analyses. *Emotion, 18,* 465–480.

Camilleri, A. R., Cam, M. A., & Hoffmann, R. (2019). Nudges and signposts: The effect of smart defaults and pictographic risk information on retirement saving investment choices. *Journal of Behavioral Decision Making, 32,* 431–449.

Camp, J. P., Skeem, J. L., Barchard, K., Lilienfeld, S. O., & Poythress, N. G. (2013). Psychopathic predators? Getting specific about the relation between psychopathy and violence. *Journal of Consulting and Clinical Psychology, 81,* 467–480.

Campbell, D. T. (1975). On the conflicts between biological and social evolution and between psychology and moral tradition. *American Psychologist, 30,* 1103–1126.

Campbell, D. T., & Specht, J. C. (1985). Altruism: Biology, culture, and religion. *Journal of Social and Clinical Psychology, 3,* 33–42.

Campbell, L., & Marshall, T. (2011). Anxious attachment and relationship processes: An interactionist perspective. *Journal of Personality, 79,* 1219–1249.

Campbell, M. W., & de Waal, F. B. M. (2011). Ingroup-outgroup bias in contagious yawning by chimpanzees supports link to empathy. *PLOS ONE, 6,* e18283.

Campbell, R., Soenens, B., Beyers, W., & Vansteenkiste, M. (2018). University students' sleep during an exam period: the role of basic psychological needs and stress. *Motivation and Emotion, 42,* 671–681.

Campbell, S. (1986). *The Loch Ness Monster: The evidence.* Aquarian Press.

Camper, J. (1990, February 7). "Drop pompom squad, U. of I. rape study says." *Chicago Tribune,* p. 1.

Camperio-Ciani, A., Corna, F., & Capiluppi, C. (2004). Evidence for maternally inherited factors favouring male homosexuality and promoting female fecundity. *Proceedings of the Royal Society of London B, 271,* 2217–2221.

Camperio-Ciani, A., Lemmola, F., & Blecher, S. R. (2009). Genetic factors increase fecundity in female maternal relatives of bisexual men as in homosexuals. *Journal of Sexual Medicine, 6,* 449–455.

Camperio-Ciani, A., & Pellizzari, E. (2012). Fecundity of paternal and maternal non-parental female relatives of homosexual and heterosexual men. *PLOS ONE, 7,* e51088.

Campitelli, G., & Gobet, F. (2011). Deliberate practice: Necessary but not sufficient. *Current Directions in Psychological Science, 20,* 280–285.

Campos, B., Schoebi, D., Gonzaga, G. C., Gable, S. L., & Keltner, D. (2015). Attuned to the positive? Awareness and responsiveness to others' positive emotion experience and display. *Motivation and Emotion, 39,* 780–794.

Campos, J. J., Bertenthal, B. I., & Kermoian, R. (1992). Early experience and emotional development: The emergence of wariness and heights. *Psychological Science, 3,* 61–64.

Canadian Press. (2018, March 14). *Calgary researchers develop tool to literally shine light on concussions.* https://www.cbc.ca/news/canada/calgary/calgary-university-concussions-brain-imaging-research-dunn-1.4575645

Canavello, A., & Crocker, J. (2017). Compassionate goals and affect in social situations. *Motivation and Emotion, 41,* 158–179.

Canetta, S., Sourander, A., Surcel, H., Hinkka-Yli-Salomäki, S., Leiviskä, J., Kellendonk, C., McKeague, I. W., & Brown, A. S. (2014). Elevated maternal C-reactive protein and increased risk of schizophrenia in a national birth cohort. *American Journal of Psychiatry, 171,* 960–968.

Canli, T. (2008). The character code. *Scientific American Mind, 19,* 52–57.

Canli, T., Desmond, J. E., Zhao, Z., & Gabrieli, J. D. E. (2002). Sex differences in the neural basis of emotional memories. *PNAS, 99,* 10789–10794.

Cannon, W. B. (1929). *Bodily changes in pain, hunger, fear, and rage.* Branford.

Cannon, W. B., & Washburn, A. L. (1912). An explanation of hunger. *American Journal of Physiology, 29,* 441–454.

Cantor, N., & Kihlstrom, J. F. (1987). *Personality and social intelligence.* Prentice-Hall.

Caplan, N., Choy, M. H., & Whitmore, J. K. (1992, February). Indochinese refugee families and academic achievement. *Scientific American,* pp. 36–42.

Caprariello, P. A., & Reis, H. T. (2013). To do, to have, or to share? Valuing experiences over material possessions depends on the involvement of others. *Journal of Personality and Social Psychology, 104,* 199–215.

Capraro, V., Jagfeld, G., Klein, R., Mul, M., & van de Pol, I. (2019). Increasing altruistic and cooperative behaviour with simple moral nudges. *Scientific Reports, 9,* 1–11.

Caputi, T. L., Smith, D., & Ayers, J. W. (2017). Suicide risk behaviors among sexual minority adolescents in the United States, 2015. *JAMA, 318,* 2349–2351.

Cardeña, E. (2018). The experimental evidence for parapsychological phenomena: A review. *American Psychologist, 73,* 663–677.

Carey, B. (2007, September 4). Bipolar illness soars as a diagnosis for the young. *The New York Times.* https://www.nytimes.com/2007/09/04/health/04psych.html?

Carey, B. (2009, November 27). Surgery for mental ills offers both hope and risk. *The New York Times.* https://www.nytimes.com/2009/11/27/health/research/27brain.html?

Carey, B. (2010). Seeking emotional clues without facial cues. *The New York Times.* https://www.nytimes.com/2010/04/06/health/06mind.html?

Carey, B. (2011, February 14). Wariness on surgery of the mind. *The New York Times.* https://www.nytimes.com/2011/02/15/health/15brain.html?

Carey, B. (2016, December 29). Did Debbie Reynolds die of a broken heart? *The New York Times.* https://www.nytimes.com/2016/12/29/health/did-debbie-reynolds-die-of-a-broken-heart.html?

Carey, B. (2019a). Brain stimulation shows promise in treating severe depression. *The New York Times.* https://www.nytimes.com/2019/10/04/health/deep-brain-stimulation-depression.html?

Carey, B. (2019b, September 4). Johns Hopkins opens new center for psychedelic research. *The New York Times.* https://www.nytimes.com/2019/09/04/science/psychedelic-drugs-hopkins-depression.html?

Carey, G. (1990). Genes, fears, phobias, and phobic disorders. *Journal of Counseling and Development, 68,* 628–632.

Carhart-Harris, R. L., Muthukumaraswamy, S., Roseman, L., Kaelen, M., Droog, W., Murphy, K., Tagliazucchi, E., Schenberg, T. N., Nest, T., Orban, C., Leech, R., Williams, L. T., Williams, T. M., Bolstridge, M., Sessa, B., McGonigle, J., Sereno, M. I., Nichols, D., Hellyer, P. J., . . . Nutt, D. J. (2016). Neural correlates of the LSD experience revealed by multimodal neuroimaging. *PNAS, 113,* 4853–4858.

Carlbring, P., Andersson, G., Cuijpers, P., Riper, H., & Hedman-Lagerlöf, E. (2018). Internet-based vs. face-to-face cognitive behavior therapy for psychiatric and somatic disorders: An updated systematic review and meta-analysis. *Cognitive Behaviour Therapy, 47,* 1–18.

Carli, L. L., & Leonard, J. B. (1989). The effect of hindsight on victim derogation. *Journal of Social and Clinical Psychology, 8,* 331–343.

Carmeli, A., Ben-Hador, B., Waldman, D. A., & Rupp, D. E. (2009). How leaders cultivate social capital and nurture employee vigor: Implications for job performance. *Journal of Applied Psychology, 94,* 1553–1561.

Carmi, L., Tendler, A., Bystritsky, A., Hollander, E., Blumberger, D. M., Daskalakis, J., Ward, H., Lapidus, K., Goodman, W., Casuto, L., Feifel, D., Barnea-Ygael, N., Roth, Y., Zangen, A., & Zohar, J. (2019). Efficacy and safety of deep transcranial magnetic stimulation for obsessive-compulsive disorder: A prospective multicenter randomized double-blind place-controlled trial. *American Journal of Psychiatry, 176,* 931–938.

Carney, D. R., Cuddy, A. J. C., & Yap, A. J. (2015). Review and summary of research on the embodied effects of expansive (vs. contractive) nonverbal displays. *Psychological Science, 26,* 657–663.

Carpusor, A., & Loges, W. E. (2006). Rental discrimination and ethnicity in names. *Journal of Applied Social Psychology, 36,* 934–952.

Carr, E. W., Brady, T. F., & Winkielman, P. (2017). Are you smiling, or have I seen you before? Familiarity makes faces look happier. *Psychological Science, 28,* 1087–1102.

Carragan, R. C., & Dweck, C. S. (2014). Rethinking natural altruism: Simple reciprocal interactions trigger children's benevolence. *PNAS, 111,* 17071–17074.

Carroll, D., Davey Smith, G., & Bennett, P. (1994, March). Health and socioeconomic status. *The Psychologist,* pp. 122–125.

Carroll, H. (2013, October). Teen fashion model Georgina got so thin her organs were failing. But fashion designers still queued up to book her. Now she's telling her story to shame the whole industry. The Daily Mail. https://www.dailymail.co.uk/femail/article-2442084/Anorexic-model-Georgina-Wilkin-organs-failing-designers-booked-her.html

Carroll, J. M., & Russell, J. A. (1996). Do facial expressions signal specific emotions? Judging emotion from the face in context. *Journal of Personality and Social Psychology, 70,* 205–218.

Carroll, P., Sweeny, K., & Shepperd, J. A. (2006). Forsaking optimism. *Review of General Psychology, 10,* 56–73.

Carstensen, L. L. (2011). *A long bright future: Happiness, health and financial security in an age of increased longevity.* PublicAffairs.

Carstensen, L. L., & Mikels, J. A. (2005). At the intersection of emotion and cognition: Aging and the positivity effect. *Current Directions in Psychological Science, 14,* 117–121.

Carta, I., Chen, C. H., Schott, A. L., Dorizan, S., & Khodakhah, K. (2019). Cerebellar modulation of the reward circuitry and social behavior. *Science, 363,* 248.

Carver, C. S., Johnson, S. L., & Joormann, J. (2008). Serotonergic function, two-mode models of self-regulation, and vulnerability to depression: What depression has in common with impulsive aggression. *Psychological Bulletin, 134,* 912–943.

CASA. (2003). *The formative years: Pathways to substance abuse among girls and young women ages 8–22.* National Center on Addiction and Substance Use. https://www.centeronaddiction.org/addiction -research/reports/formative-years-pathways-substance-abuse-among-girls-and-young-women-ages

Casey, B. J., & Caudle, K. (2013). The teenage brain: Self-control. *Current Directions in Psychological Science, 22,* 82–87.

Caspi, A., Harrington, H., Milne, B., Amell, J. W., Theodore, R. F., & Moffitt, T. E. (2003). Children's behavioral styles at age 3 are linked to their adult personality traits at age 26. *Journal of Personality, 71,* 496–513.

Caspi, A., Houts, R. M., Belsky, D. W., Harrington, H., Hogan, S., Ramrakha, S., Poulton, R., & Moffitt, T. E. (2016). Childhood forecasting of a small segment of the population with large economic burden. *Nature Human Behavior, 1,* article 0005.

Caspi, A., McClay, J., Moffitt, T., Mill, J., Martin, J., Craig, I. W., Taylor, A., & Poulton, R. (2002). Role of genotype in the cycle of violence in maltreated children. *Science, 297,* 851–854.

Caspi, A., Moffitt, T. E., Newman, D. L., & Silva, P. A. (1996). Behavioral observations at age 3 years predict adult psychiatric disorders: Longitudinal evidence from a birth cohort. *Archives of General Psychiatry, 53,* 1033–1039.

Cassidy, J., & Shaver, P. R. (1999). *Handbook of attachment.* Guilford.

Castillo-Gualda, R., Cabello, R., Herrero, M., Rodríguez-Carvajal, R., & Fernández-Berrocal, P. (2017). A three-year emotional intelligence intervention to reduce adolescent aggression: The mediating role of unpleasant affectivity. *Journal of Research on Adolescence, 28,* 286–198.

Catalan-Matamoros, D., Gomez-Conesa, A., Stubbs, B., & Vancampfort, D. (2016). Exercise improves depressive symptoms in older adults: An umbrella review of systematic reviews and meta-analyses. *Psychiatry Research, 244,* 202–209.

Catapano, R., Tormala, Z. L., & Rucker, D. D. (2019). Perspective taking and self-persuasion: Why "putting yourself in their shoes" reduces openness to attitude change. *Psychological Science, 30,* 424–435.

CATO Institute. (2017). *Criminal immigrants: Their numbers, demographics, and countries of origin.* https://www.cato.org/publications/immigration-reform -bulletin/criminal-immigrants-their-numbers-demographics-countries

Cattell, R. B. (1963). Theory of fluid and crystallized intelligence: A critical experiment. *Journal of Educational Psychology, 54,* 1–22.

Cavalli-Sforza, L., Menozzi, P., & Piazza, A. (1994). *The history and geography of human genes.* Princeton University Press.

Cawley, B. D., Keeping, L. M., & Levy, P. E. (1998). Participation in the performance appraisal process and employee reactions: A meta-analytic review of field investigations. *Journal of Applied Psychology, 83,* 615–633.

CBC News. (2014, March 19). *Distracted driving laws across Canada.* https://www.cbc.ca/news/canada /distracted-driving-laws-across-canada-1.2576880

CCSA. (2017, August). *Canadian drug use summary: Cannabis* [PDF file]. https://www.cpha.ca/sites /default/files/uploads/resources/cannabis/ccsa -canadian-drug-summary-cannabis-2017-en.pdf

CDC. (2011). *Who's at risk? Tobacco use—smoking.* (cdc.gov)

CDC. (2013b). *Tobacco-related mortality.* (cdc.gov)

CDC. (2014a, December). *Depression in the U.S. household population, 2009–2012.* NCHS Data Brief No. 172.

CDC. (2014b, March 28). Prevalence of autism spectrum disorder among children aged 8 years— Autism and developmental disabilities monitoring network, 11 sites. United States, 2010. *Morbidity and Mortality Weekly Report (MMWR), 63*(SS02), 1–21.

CDC. (2016, accessed August 23, 2018). *HIV surveillance report: Diagnoses of HIV infection in the United States and dependent areas* (Vol. 28) [PDF file]. https: //www.cdc.gov/hiv/pdf/library/reports/surveillance /cdc-hiv-surveillance-report-2016-vol-28.pdf

CDC. (2016b, accessed January 21). *Reproductive health: Teen pregnancy.* https://www.cdc.gov/teenpregnancy

CDC. (2017). *Heart disease fact sheet.* cdc.gov/dhdsp /data_statistics/fact_sheets/fs_heart_disease.htm

CDC. (2018). *What you need to know about marijuana use and pregnancy.* https://www.cdc.gov/marijuana /factsheets/pregnancy.htm

CDC. (2018a). Estimated HIV incidence and prevalence in the United States, 2010–2015. *HIV Surveillance Supplemental Report, 23.*

CDC. (2018b). *Distracted driving.* https://www.cdc.gov /motorvehiclesafety/distracted_driving/index.html

CDC. (2018b). Notes from the field: Use of electronic cigarettes and any tobacco product among middle and high school students—United States, 2011–2018. https://www.cdc.gov/mmwr/volumes/67/wr /mm6745a5.htm

CDC. (2018f). *Youth risk behavior survey: Data summary and trends report 2007–2017* [PDF file]. https://www.cdc.gov/healthyyouth/data/yrbs/pdf /trendsreport.pdf

CDC. (2019, May 3). *Increase in measles cases—United States, January 1–April 26, 2019.* https://www.cdc .gov/mmwr/volumes/68/wr/mm6817e1.htm

CDC. (2019). "Did not get 8 or more hours of sleep." Retrieved on May 31, 2019, from High School Youth Risk Behavior Survey, 2017. https://tinyurl.com /s2ck2zs

CDC. (2019a, October 15). *Attention-deficit/hyperactivity disorder.* https://www.cdc.gov/ncbddd/adhd /data.html

CDC. (2019c). *Fatal injury reports, national, regional and state (restricted), 1999–2017.* https://webappa .cdc.gov/sasweb/ncipc/mortrate.html

CDC. (2019e, accessed November 29). *Suicide and self-inflicted injury.* Retrieved from https://www.cdc .gov/nchs/fastats/suicide.htm

CEA. (2014). *Nine facts about American families and work.* Office of the President of the United States: Council of Economic Advisers. https://obamawhite house.archives.gov/the-press-office/2014/06/20 /white-house-report-nine-facts-about-american -families-and-work

Ceci, S. J. (1993). *Cognitive and social factors in children's testimony.* Master lecture presented at the Annual Convention of the American Psychological Association.

Ceci, S. J., & Bruck, M. (1993). Child witnesses: Translating research into policy. *Social Policy Report (Society for Research in Child Development), 7,* 1–30.

Ceci, S. J., & Bruck, M. (1995). *Jeopardy in the courtroom: A scientific analysis of children's testimony.* American Psychological Association.

Ceci, S. J., Huffman, M. L. C., Smith, E., & Loftus, E. F. (1994). Repeatedly thinking about a non-event: Source misattributions among preschoolers. *Consciousness and Cognition, 3,* 388–407.

Ceci, S. J., & Williams, W. M. (1997). Schooling, intelligence, and income. *American Psychologist, 52,* 1051–1058.

Ceci, S. J., & Williams, W. M. (2009). *The mathematics of sex: How biology and society conspire to limit talented women and girls.* Oxford University Press.

Ceci, S. J., & Williams, W. M. (2010). Sex differences in math-intensive fields. *Current Directions in Psychological Science, 19,* 275–279.

Ceci, S. J., & Williams, W. M. (2011). Understanding current causes of women's underrepresentation in science. *PNAS, 108,* 3157–3162.

Census Bureau. (2018). *Full-time, year-round workers and median earnings: 2000 and 2013–2017.* https: //www.census.gov/data/tables/time-series/demo /industry-occupation/median-earnings.html

Centerwall, B. S. (1989). Exposure to television as a risk factor for violence. *American Journal of Epidemiology, 129,* 643–652.

Cepeda, N. J., Pashler, H., Vul, E., Wixted, J. T., & Rohrer, D. (2006). Distributed practice in verbal recall tasks: A review and quantitative synthesis. *Psychological Bulletin, 132,* 354–380.

Cepeda, N. J., Vul, E., Rohrer, D., Wixed, J. T., & Pashler, H. (2008). Spacing effects in learning: A temporal ridgeline of optimal retention. *Psychological Science, 19,* 1095–1102.

Cerasoli, C. P., Nicklin, J. M., & Ford, M. T. (2014). Intrinsic motivation and extrinsic incentives jointly predict performance: A 40-year meta-analysis. *Psychological Bulletin, 140,* 980–1008.

Cerasoli, C. P., Nicklin, J. M., & Nassrelgrgawi, A. S. (2016). Performance, incentives, and needs for autonomy, competence, and relatedness: A meta-analysis. *Motivation and Emotion, 40,* 781–813.

Cero, I., & Witte, T. K. (2019). Assortativity of suicide-related posting on social media. *American Psychologist.* Advance online publication. doi: 10.1037 /amp0000477

Cerrillo-Urbina, A. J., García-Hermoso, A., Sánchez-López, M., Pardo-Guijarro, M. J., Santos Gómez, J. L., & Martínez-Vizcaíno, V. (2015). The effects of physical exercise in children with attention deficit hyperactivity disorder: A systematic review and meta-analysis of randomized control trials. *Child: Care, Health and Development, 41,* 779–788.

CFI. (2003, July). *International developments.* Report. Center for Inquiry International.

Cha, C. B., Augenstein, T. M., Frost, K. H., Gallagher, K., D'Angelo, E. J., & Nock, M. K. (2016). Using implicit and explicit measures to predict nonsuicidal self-injury among adolescent inpatients. *Journal of the American Academy of Child & Adolescent Psychiatry, 55,* 62–68.

Chabris, C. (2015, February 9). Quoted by Parker-Pope in Was Brian Williams a victim of false memory? *The New York Times.* https://well.blogs .nytimes.com/2015/02/09/was-brian-williams-a -victim-of-false-memory/?

Chabris, C. F., & Simons, D. (2010). *The invisible gorilla: And other ways our intuitions deceive us.* Crown.

Chajut, E., Caspi, A., Chen, R., Hod, M., & Ariely, D. (2014). In pain thou shalt bring forth children: The peak-and-end rule in recall of labor pain. *Psychological Science, 25,* 2266–2271.

Chambel, M. J., Castanheira, F., Oliveira-Cruz, F., & Lopes, S. (2015). Work context support and Portuguese soldiers' well-being: The mediating role of autonomous motivation. *Military Psychology, 27,* 297–310.

Chamove, A. S. (1980). Nongenetic induction of acquired levels of aggression. *Journal of Abnormal Psychology, 89,* 469–488.

Champagne, F. A. (2010). Early adversity and developmental outcomes: Interaction between genetics, epigenetics, and social experiences across the life span. *Perspectives on Psychological Science, 5,* 564–574.

Champagne, F. A., Francis, D. D., Mar, A, & Meaney, M. J. (2003). Naturally-occurring variations in maternal care in the rat as a mediating influence for the effects of environment on the development of individual differences in stress reactivity. *Physiology & Behavior, 79,* 359–371.

Champagne, F. A., & Mashoodh, R. (2009). Genes in context: Gene-environment interplay and the origins of individual differences in behavior. *Current Directions in Psychological Science, 18,* 127–131.

Chan, E. Y., & Maglio, S. J. (2019). Coffee cues elevate arousal and reduce level of construal. *Consciousness and Cognition, 70,* 57–69.

Chan, M. K., Krebs, M. O., Cox, D., Guest, P. C., Yolken, R. H., Rahmoune, H., Rothermundt, M., Steiner, J., Leweke, F. M., Van Beveren, N. J. M., Niebuhr, D., Weber, N. S., Cowan, D. N., Suarez-Pinilla, P., Crespo-Facorro, B., Mam-Lam-Fook, C., Bourgin, J., Wenstrup, R. J., Kaldate, R. R., . . . Bahn, S. (2015, July 14). Development of a blood-based molecular biomarker test for identification of schizophrenia before disease onset. *Translational Psychiatry, 5,* e601.

Chance News. (1997, 25 November). *More on the frequency of letters in texts.* Dart.Chance@Dartmouth.edu

Chancellor, J., Margolis, S., Jacobs Bao, K., & Lyubomirsky, S. (2018). Everyday prosociality in the workplace: The reinforcing benefits of giving, getting, and glimpsing. *Emotion, 18,* 507–517.

Chandler, J. J., & Pronin, E. (2012). Fast thought speed induces risk taking. *Psychological Science, 23,* 370–374.

Chandra, A., Mosher, W. D., & Copen, C. (2011, March 3). *Sexual behavior, sexual attraction, and sexual identity in the United States: Data from the 2006–2008 National Survey of Family Growth* (National Health Statistics Report No. 36). https://www.cdc.gov/nchs/data/nhsr/nhsr036.pdf

Chang, A.-M., Aeschbach, D., Duggy, J. F., & Czeisler, C. A. (2015). Evening use of light-emitting eReaders negatively affects sleep, circadian timing, and next-morning alertness. *PNAS, 112,* 1232–1237.

Chang, E. C. (2001). Cultural influences on optimism and pessimism: Differences in Western and Eastern construals of the self. In E. C. Chang (Ed.), *Optimism and pessimism* (pp. 257–280). APA Books.

Chang, E. H., Milkman, K. L., Gromet, D. M., Rebele, R. W., Massey, C., Duckworth, A. L., & Grant, A. M. (2019). The mixed effects of online diversity training. *PNAS, 116,* 7778–7783.

Chang, J. H., & Bushman, B. J. (2019). Effect of exposure to fun violence in video games on children's dangerous behavior with real guns: A randomized clinical trial. *JAMA Network Open, 2,* e194319.

Chaplin, T. M. (2015). Gender and emotion expression: A developmental contextual perspective. *Emotion Review, 7,* 14–21.

Chaplin, T. M., & Aldao, A. (2013). Gender differences in emotion expression in children: A meta-analytic review. *Psychological Bulletin, 139,* 735–765.

Chaplin, W. F., Phillips, J. B., Brown, J. D., Clanton, N. R., & Stein, J. L. (2000). Handshaking, gender, personality, and first impressions. *Journal of Personality and Social Psychology, 79,* 110–117.

Charlesworth, T. E. S., & Banaji, M. R. (2019). Patterns of implicit and explicit attitudes: I. long-term change and stability from 2007 to 2016. *Psychological Science, 30,* 174–192.

Charlson, F. J., Flaxman, A., Ferrari, A. J., Vos, T., Steel, Z., & Whiteford, H. A. (2016). Post-traumatic stress disorder and major depression in conflict-affected populations: An epidemiologic analysis. *Global Mental Health (Cambridge Core), 3,* e4.

Charness, N., & Boot, W. R. (2009). Aging and information technology use. *Current Directions in Psychological Science, 18,* 253–258.

Charpak, G., & Broch, H. (2004). *Debunked! ESP, telekinesis, and other pseudoscience.* Johns Hopkins University Press.

Chartrand, T. L., & Bargh, J. A. (1999). The chameleon effect: The perception-behavior link and social interaction. *Journal of Personality and Social Psychology, 76,* 893–910.

Chartrand, T. L., & Lakin, J. (2013). The antecedents and consequences of human behavioral mimicry. *Annual Review of Psychology, 64,* 285–308.

Chartrand, T. L., & van Baaren, R. (2009). Human mimicry. In M. P. Zanna (Ed.), *Advances in experimental social psychology* (pp. 219–274). Elsevier Academic Press.

Chassin, M. R. L., & MacKinnon, D. P. (2015). Role transitions and young adult maturing out of heavy drinking: Evidence for larger effects of marriage among more severe premarriage problem drinkers. *Alcoholism: Clinical and Experimental Research, 39,* 1064–1074.

Chassy, P., & Gobet, F. (2011). A hypothesis about the biological basis of expert intuition. *Review of General Psychology, 15,* 198–212.

Chatard, A., & Selimbegović, L. (2011). When self-destructive thoughts flash through the mind: Failure to meet standards affects the accessibility of suicide-related thoughts. *Journal of Personality and Social Psychology, 100,* 587–605.

Chatterjee, R. (2015, October 3). Out of the darkness. *Science, 350,* 372–375.

Cheek, J. M., & Melchior, L. A. (1990). Shyness, self-esteem, and self-consciousness. In H. Leitenberg (Ed.), *Handbook of social and evaluation anxiety.* Plenum.

Cheek, S. M., Goldston, D. B., Erkanli, A., Massing-Schaffer, M., & Liu, R. T. (2019). Social rejection and suicidal ideation and attempts among adolescents following hospitalization: a prospective study. *Journal of Abnormal Child Psychology, 48*(1), 123–133.

Chein, J. M., & Schneider, W. (2012). The brain's learning and control architecture. *Current Directions in Psychological Science, 21,* 78–84.

Cheit, R. E. (1998). Consider this, skeptics of recovered memory. *Ethics & Behavior, 8,* 141–160.

Chekroud, S. R., Gueorguieva, R., Zheutlin, A. B., Paulus, M., Krumholz, H. M., Krystal, J. H., & Chekroud, A. M. (2018). Association between physical exercise and mental health in 1.2 million individuals in the USA between 2011 and 2015: A cross-sectional study. *The Lancet Psychiatry, 5,* 739–746.

Chen, A. W., Kazanjian, A., & Wong, H. (2009). Why do Chinese Canadians not consult mental health services: Health status, language or culture? *Transcultural Psychiatry, 46,* 623–640.

Chen, E., Turiano, N. A., Mroczek, D. K., & Miller, G. E. (2016). Association of reports of childhood abuse and all-cause mortality rates in women. *JAMA Psychiatry, 73,* 920–927.

Chen, G., Wu, Z., Guo, Z., & Gearing, M. (2014). Tonic inhibition in dentate gyrus impairs long-term potentiation and memory in an Alzheimer's disease model. *Nature Communications, 5,* 4159.

Chen, J. (2017, June 28). *Katy Perry defends her livestream therapy session: 'People think it's weird'.* Rolling Stone. https://www.rollingstone.com/music/music-news/katy-perry-defends-her-livestream-therapy-session-people-think-its-weird-194530/

Chen, M.-H., Lan, W.-H., Bai, Y.-M., Huang, K.-L., Su, T.-P., Tsai, S.-J., Li, C. T., Lin, W. C., Chang, W. H., Pan, T. L., Chen, T. J., & Hsu, J.-W. (2016). Influence of relative age on diagnosis and treatment of attention-deficit hyperactivity disorder in Taiwanese children. *Journal of Pediatrics, 172,* 162–167.

Chen, S. H., Kennedy, M., & Zhou, Q. (2012). Parents' expression and discussion of emotion in the multilingual family: Does language matter? *Perspectives on Psychological Science, 7,* 365–383.

Chen, S. X., & Bond, M. H. (2010). Two languages, two personalities? Examining language effects on the expression of personality in a bilingual context. *Personality and Social Psychology Bulletin, 36,* 1514–1528.

Chen, Y., Kawachi, I., Berkman, L. F., Trudel-Fitzgerald, C., & Kubzansky, L. D. (2018). A prospective study of marital quality and body weight in midlife. *Health Psychology, 37,* 247–256.

Cheng, C., & Li, A. Y. L. (2014). Internet addiction prevalence and quality of (real) life: A meta-analysis of 31 nations across seven world regions. *Cyberpsychology, Behavior, and Social Networking, 17,* 755–760.

Chennu, S., Pinoia, P., Kamau, E. Allanson, J., Williams, G. B., Monti, M. M., Noreika, V., Arnatkeviciute, A., Canales-Johnson, A., Olivares, F., Cabezas-Soto, D., Menon, D. K., Pickard, J. D., Owen, A. M., & Bekinschtein, T. A. (2014). Spectral signatures of reorganised brain network in disorders of consciousness. *PLOS Computational Biology, 10,* e1003887.

Cheon, B. K., Im, D.-M., Harada, T., Kim, J.-S., Mathur, V. A., Scimeca, J. M., Parrish, T. B., Park, H., & Chiao, J. Y. (2013). Cultural modulation of the neural correlates of emotional pain perception: The role of other-focusedness. *Neuropsychologia, 51,* 1177–1186.

Cherniss, C. (2010a). Emotional intelligence: New insights and further clarifications. *Industrial and Organizational Psychology, 3,* 183–191.

Cherniss, C. (2010b). Emotional intelligence: Toward clarification of a concept. *Industrial and Organizational Psychology, 3,* 110–126.

Chernyak, N., Kang, C., & Kushnir, T. (2019). The cultural roots of free will beliefs: How Singaporean and U.S. children judge and explain possibilities for action in interpersonal contexts. *Developmental Psychology, 55,* 866–876.

Chess, S., & Thomas, A. (1987). *Know your child: An authoritative guide for today's parents.* Basic Books.

Chester, D. S., & DeWall, C. N. (2016). The pleasure of revenge: Retaliatory aggression arises from a neural imbalance toward reward. *Social Cognitive and Affective Neuroscience, 11,* 1173–1182.

Chester, D. S., DeWall, C. N., Derefinko, K. J., Estus, S., Lynam, D. R., Peters, J. R., & Jiang, Y. (2016). Looking for reward in all the wrong places: Dopamine receptor gene polymorphisms indirectly affect aggression through sensation-seeking. *Social Neuroscience, 11,* 487–494.

Chetty, N., & Alathur, S. (2018). Hate speech review in the context of online social networks. *Aggression and Violent Behavior, 40,* 108–118.

Cheung, B. Y., Chudek, M., & Heine, S. J. (2011). Evidence for a sensitive period for acculturation: Younger immigrants report acculturating at a faster rate. *Psychological Science, 22,* 147–152.

Cheung, F., & Lucas, R. E. (2016). Income inequality is associated with stronger social comparison effects: The effect of relative income on life satisfaction. *Journal of Personality and Social Psychology, 110,* 332–341.

Chiang, J. J., Turiano, N. A., Mroczek, D. K., & Miller, G. E. (2018). Affective reactivity to daily stress and 20-year mortality risk in adults with chronic illness: Findings from the National Study of Daily Experiences. *Health Psychology, 37,* 170–178.

Chibanda, D., Weiss, H. A., Verhey, R., Simms, V., Munjoma, R., Rusakaniko, S., Chingono, A., Munetsi, E., Bere, T., Manda, E., Abas, M., & Araya, R. (2016). Effect of a primary care-based psychological intervention on symptoms of common mental disorders in Zimbabwe: a randomized clinical trial. *JAMA, 316*, 2618–2626.

Chida, Y., & Hamer, M. (2008). Chronic psychosocial factors and acute physiological responses to laboratory-induced stress in healthy populations: A quantitative review of 30 years of investigations. *Psychological Bulletin, 134*, 829–885.

Chida, Y., Hamer, M., Wardle, J., & Steptoe, A. (2008). Do stress-related psychosocial factors contribute to cancer incidence and survival? *Nature Reviews: Clinical Oncology, 5*, 466–475.

Chida, Y., & Steptoe, A. (2009). The association of anger and hostility with future coronary heart disease: A meta-analytic review of prospective evidence. *Journal of the American College of Cardiology, 17*, 936–946.

Chida, Y., Steptoe, A., & Powell, L. H. (2009). Religiosity/spirituality and mortality. *Psychotherapy and Psychosomatics, 78*, 81–90.

Chida, Y., & Vedhara, K. (2009). Adverse psychosocial factors predict poorer prognosis in HIV disease: A meta-analytic review of prospective investigations. *Brain, Behavior, and Immunity, 23*, 434–445.

Chiles, J. A., Lambert, M. J., & Hatch, A. L. (1999). The impact of psychological interventions on medical cost offset: A meta-analytic review. *Clinical Psychology: Science and Practice, 6*, 204–220.

Chisholm, D., Sweeny, K., Sheehan, P., Rasmussen, B., Smit, F., Cuijpers, P., & Saxena, S. (2016). Scaling-up treatment of depression and anxiety: A global return on investment analysis. *The Lancet Psychiatry, 3*, 415–424.

Chivers, M. L. (2017). The specificity of women's sexual response and its relationship with sexual orientations: A review and ten hypotheses. *Archives of Sexual Behavior, 46*, 1161–1179.

Chivers, M. L., & Brotto, L. A. (2017). Controversies of women's sexual arousal and desire. *European Psychologist, 22*, 5–26.

Chivers, M. L., Seto, M. C., Lalumière, M. L., Laan, E., & Grimbos, T. (2010). Agreement of self-reported and genital measures of sexual arousal in men and women: A meta-analysis. *Archives of Sexual Behavior, 39*, 5–56.

Chmielewski, M., Zhu, J., Burchett, D., Bury, A. S., & Bagby, R. M. (2017). The comparative capacity of the Minnesota Multiphasic Personality Inventory–2 (MMPI–2) and MMPI–2 Restructured Form (MMPI-2-RF) validity scales to detect suspected malingering in a disability claimant sample. *Psychological Assessment, 29*, 199–208.

Cho, K. W., Neely, J. H., Crocco, S., & Vitrano, D. (2017). Testing enhances both encoding and retrieval for both tested and untested items. *The Quarterly Journal of Experimental Psychology, 70*, 1211–1235.

Choi, C. Q. (2008, March). Do you need only half your brain? *Scientific American*. https://www.scientific american.com/article/do-you-need-only-half-your -brain/

Choi, J., Broersma, M., & Cutler, A. (2017). Early phonology revealed by international adoptees' birth language retention. *PNAS, 114*, 7307–7312.

Choi, K. W., Zheutlin, A. B., Karlson, R. A., Wang, M. J., Dunn, E. C., Stein, M. B., Karlson, E. W., & Smoller, J. W. (2019). Physical activity offsets genetic risk for incident depression assessed via electronic health records in a biobank cohort study. *Depression and Anxiety, 37*(2), 106–114.

Chomsky, N. (1972). *Language and mind*. Harcourt Brace.

Chopik, W., & O'Brien, E. (2017). Happy you, healthy me? Having a happy partner is independently associated with better health in oneself. *Health Psychology, 36*, 21–30.

Chopik, W. J., Edelstein, R. S., & Fraley, R. C. (2013). From the cradle to the grave: Age differences in attachment from early adulthood to old age. *Journal of Personality, 81*, 171–183.

Chopik, W. J., & Kitayama, S. (2018). Personality change across the life span: Insights from a cross-cultural, longitudinal study. *Journal of Personality, 86*, 508–521.

Christakis, D. A., Garrison, M. M., Herrenkohl, T., Haggerty, K., Rivara, K. P., Zhou, C., & Liekweg, K. (2013). Modifying media content for preschool children: A randomized control trial. *Pediatrics, 131*, 431–438.

Christakis, N. (2019, March 24). We are one: Obsession with human difference is out of step with scientific evidence on universals that connect us. *New York Daily News*. https://www.nydailynews.com /opinion/ny-oped-we-are-one-20190324-nmngbhbs 3fcelfwawh3iibhpwu-story.html

Christakis, N. A., & Fowler, J. H. (2007). The spread of obesity in a large social network over 32 years. *New England Journal of Medicine, 357*, 370–379.

Christakis, N. A., & Fowler, J. H. (2008, May). The collective dynamics of smoking in a large social network. *New England Journal of Medicine, 358*, 2249–2258.

Christakis, N. A., & Fowler, J. H. (2009). *Connected: The surprising power of social networks and how they shape our lives*. Little, Brown.

Christensen, A., & Jacobson, N. S. (1994). Who (or what) can do psychotherapy: The status and challenge of nonprofessional therapies. *Psychological Science, 5*, 8–14.

Christiansen, P., Jennings, E., & Rose, A. K. (2016). Anticipated effects of alcohol stimulate craving and impair inhibitory control. *Psychology of Addictive Behaviors, 30*, 383–388.

Christophersen, E. R., & Edwards, K. J. (1992). Treatment of elimination disorders: State of the art 1991. *Applied & Preventive Psychology, 1*, 15–22.

Chu, C., Podlogar, M. C., Hagan, C. R., Buchman-Schmitt, J. M., Silva, C., Chiurliza, B., Hames, J. L., Stanley, I. H., Lim, L. I., & Joiner, T. E. (2016). The interactive effects of the capability for suicide and major depressive episodes on suicidal behavior in a military sample. *Cognitive Therapy and Research, 40*, 22–30.

Chu, C., Walker, K. L., Stanley, I. H., Hirsch, J. K., Greenberg, J. H., Rudd, M. D., & Joiner, T. E. (2018). Perceived problem-solving deficits and suicidal ideation: Evidence for the explanatory roles of thwarted belongingness and perceived burdensomeness in five samples. *Journal of Personality and Social Psychology, 115*, 137–160.

Chu, P. S., Saucier, D. A., & Hafner, E. (2010). Meta-analysis of the relationships between social support and well-being in children and adolescents. *Journal of Social and Clinical Psychology, 29*, 624–645.

Chua, A. (2011). *Battle hymn of the tiger mother*. Bloomsbury.

Chua, H. F., Boland, J. E., & Nisbett, R. E. (2005). Cultural variation in eye movements during scene perception. *PNAS, 102*, 12629–12633.

Chugani, H. T., & Phelps, M. E. (1986). Maturational changes in cerebral function in infants determined by 18FDG positron emission tomography. *Science, 231*, 840–843.

Chulov, M. (2014, December 11). ISIS: The inside story. *The Guardian*. https://www.theguardian.com /world/2014/dec/11/-sp-isis-the-inside-story

Chung, T., Tittgemeyer, M., & Ewing, S. W. F. (2017). Introduction to the Special Issue: Using neuroimaging to probe mechanisms of behavior change. *Neuroimage, 151*, 1–3.

Church, A. T., Katigbak, M. S., Mazuera Arias, R., Rincon, B. C., Vargas-Flores, J., Ibáñez-Reyes, J., Wang, L., Alvarez, J. M., Wang, C., & Ortiz, F. A. (2014). A four-culture study of self-enhancement and adjustment using the social relations model: Do alternative conceptualizations and indices make a difference? *Journal of Personality and Social Psychology, 106*, 997–1014.

Churchland, P. S. (2013). *Touching a nerve: The self as brain*. Norton.

CIA. (2014, accessed April 23). Sex ratio. *The world factbook*. Retrieved from https://www.cia.gov /library/publications/the-world-factbook/geos /print_ch.html

Cialdini, R. B. (1993). *Influence: Science and practice* (3rd ed.). HarperCollins.

Cialdini, R. B., & Richardson, K. D. (1980). Two indirect tactics of image management: Basking and blasting. *Journal of Personality and Social Psychology, 39*, 406–415.

CIHI. (2019, accessed December 2). *Intentional self-harm among youth in Canada* [PDF file]. Retrieved from https://www.cihi.ca/sites/default/files /info_child_harm_en.pdf

Cin, S. D., Gibson, B., Zanna, M. P., Shumate, R., & Fong, G. T. (2007). Smoking in movies, implicit associations of smoking with the self, and intentions to smoke. *Psychological Science, 18*, 559–563.

Cipriani, A., Furukawa, T. A., Salanti, G., Chaimani, A., Atkinson, L. Z., Ogawa, Y., Leucht, S., Ruhe, H. G., Turner, E. H., Higgins, J. P., Egger, M., Takeshima, N., Hayasaka, Y., Imai, H., Shinohara, K., Tajika, A., Ioannidis, J. P. A., & Geddes, J. R. (2018). Comparative efficacy and acceptability of 21 antidepressant drugs for the acute treatment of adults with major depressive disorder: A systematic review and network meta-analysis. *The Lancet, 391*, 1357–1366.

Clack, B., Dixon, J., & Tredoux, C. (2005). Eating together apart: Patterns of segregation in a multi-ethnic cafeteria. *Journal of Community and Applied Social Psychology, 15*, 1–16.

Claidière, N., & Whiten, A. (2012). Integrating the study of conformity and culture in humans and non-human animals. *Psychological Bulletin, 138*, 126–145.

Clancy, S. A. (2005). *Abducted: How people come to believe they were kidnapped by aliens*. Harvard University Press.

Clancy, S. A. (2010). *The trauma myth: The truth about the sexual abuse of children—and its aftermath*. Basic Books.

Clark, A., Seidler, A., & Miller, M. (2001). Inverse association between sense of humor and coronary heart disease. *International Journal of Cardiology, 80*, 87–88.

Clark, I. A., & Maguire, E. A. (2016). Remembering preservation in hippocampal amnesia. *Annual Review of Psychology, 67*, 51–82.

Clark, J. L., Algoe, S. B., & Green, M. C. (2018). Social network sites and well-being: The role of social connection. *Current Directions in Psychological Science, 27*, 32–37.

Clark, K. B., & Clark, M. P. (1947). Racial identification and preference in Negro children. In T. M. Newcomb & E. L. Hartley (Eds.), *Readings in social psychology*. Holt.

Clark, R., & Gilchrist, I. D. (2018). The relationship between reward and probability: Evidence that exploration may be intrinsically rewarding. *Visual Cognition, 26*, 672–694.

Clark, R. D., III, & Hatfield, E. (1989). Gender differences in willingness to engage in casual sex. *Journal of Psychology and Human Sexuality, 2*, 39–55.

Clarke, E., Reichard, U. H., & Zuberbuehler, K. (2015). Context-specific close-range "hoo" calls in wild gibbons (Hylobates lar). *BMC Evolutionary Biology, 15*, 56.

Claro, S., Paunesku, D., & Dweck, C. S. (2016). Growth mindset tempers the effects of poverty on academic achievement. *PNAS, 113*, 8664–8668.

Clausen, J., Fetz, E., Donoghue, J., Ushiba, J., Spöhase, J., Birbaummer, N., & Soekadar, S. R. (2017). Help, hope, and hype: Ethical dimensions of neuroprosthetics. *Science, 356,* 1338–1339.

Cleary, A. M., & Claxton, A. B. (2018). Déjà vu: An illusion of prediction. *Psychological Science, 29,* 635–644.

Clements, C. C., Zoltowski, A. R., Yankowitz, L. D., Yerys, B. E., Schultz, R. T., & Herrington, J. D. (2018). Evaluation of the social motivation hypothesis of autism: A systematic review and meta-analysis. *JAMA Psychiatry, 75,* 797–808.

Clynes, T. (2016). How to raise a genius. *Nature, 537,* 152–155.

CMEC. (2018). *Measuring up: Canadian results of the OECD PISA Study. The performance of Canada's youth in science, reading and mathematics* [PDF file]. Council of Ministers of Education, Canada. https://www.cmec.ca/Publications/Lists/Publications/Attachments/396/PISA2018_PublicReport_EN.pdf

Coan, J. A., Schaefer, H. S., & Davidson, R. J. (2006). Lending a hand: Social regulation of the neural response to threat. *Psychological Science, 17,* 1032–1039.

Coelho, C. M., & Purkis, H. (2009). The origins of specific phobias: Influential theories and current perspectives. *Review of General Psychology, 13,* 335–348.

Cohen, A. B. (2009). Many forms of culture. *American Psychologist, 64,* 194–204.

Cohen, A. O., Breiner, K., Steinberg, L., Bonnie, R. J., Scott, E. S., Taylor-Thompson, K. A., Rudolph, M. D., Chein, J., Richeson, J. A., Heller, A. S., Silverman, M. R. Dellarco, D. V., Fair, D. A., Galván, A., & Casey, B. J. (2016). When is an adolescent an adult? Assessing cognitive control in emotional and nonemotional contexts. *Psychological Science, 27,* 549–562.

Cohen, F., & Solomon, S. (2011). The politics of mortal terror. *Current Directions in Psychological Science, 20,* 316–320.

Cohen, G. (1990). Why is it difficult to put names to faces? *British Journal of Psychology, 81,* 287–297.

Cohen, P. (2007, November 15). Freud is widely taught at universities, except in the psychology department. *The New York Times.* https://www.nytimes.com/2007/11/25/weekinreview/25cohen.html

Cohen, P. (2010, June 11). Long road to adulthood is growing even longer. *The New York Times.* https://www.nytimes.com/2010/06/13/us/13generations.html?

Cohen, S. (2004). Social relationships and health. *American Psychologist, 59,* 676–684.

Cohen, S., Alper, C. M., Doyle, W. J., Treanor, J. J., & Turner, R. B. (2006). Positive emotional style predicts resistance to illness after experimental exposure to rhinovirus or influenza A virus. *Psychosomatic Medicine, 68,* 809–815.

Cohen, S., Doyle, W. J., Skoner, D. P., Rabin, B. S., & Gwaltney, J. M., Jr. (1997). Social ties and susceptibility to the common cold. *Journal of the American Medical Association, 277,* 1940–1944.

Cohen, S., Doyle, W. J., Turner, R., Alper, C. M., & Skoner, D. P. (2003). Sociability and susceptibility to the common cold. *Psychological Science, 14,* 389–395.

Cohen, S., Janicki-Deverts, D., Turner, R. B., & Doyle, W. J. (2015). Does hugging provide stress-buffering social support? A study of susceptibility to upper respiratory infection and illness. *Psychological Science, 26,* 135–147.

Cohen, S., Kaplan, J. R., Cunnick, J. E., Manuck, S. B., & Rabin, B. S. (1992). Chronic social stress, affiliation, and cellular immune response in nonhuman primates. *Psychological Science, 3,* 301–304.

Cohen, S., & Pressman, S. D. (2006). Positive affect and health. *Current Directions in Psychological Science, 15,* 122–125.

Cohen, S., Tyrrell, D. A. J., & Smith, A. P. (1991). Psychological stress and susceptibility to the common cold. *New England Journal of Medicine, 325,* 606–612.

Cohn, A., Maréchal, M. A., Tannenbaum, D., & Zünd, C. L. (2019). Civic honesty around the globe. *Science, 365,* 70–73.

Cohn, D. (2013, February 13). *Love and marriage.* https://www.pewsocialtrends.org/2013/02/13/love-and-marriage/

Coker, A. L., Bush, H. M., Cook-Craig, P. G., DeGue, S. A., Clear, E. R., Brancato, C. J., Fisher, B. S., & Recktenwald, E. A. (2017). RCT testing bystander effectiveness to reduce violence. *American Journal of Preventative Medicine, 52,* 566–578.

Colapinto, J. (2000). *As nature made him: The boy who was raised as a girl.* HarperCollins.

Colarelli, S. M., Spranger, J. L., & Hechanova, M. R. (2006). Women, power, and sex composition in small groups: An evolutionary perspective. *Journal of Organizational Behavior, 27,* 163–184.

Colbert, S. (2014, November 18). Tweet. Twitter: @StephenAtHome

Cole, K. C. (1998). *The universe and the teacup: The mathematics of truth and beauty.* Harcourt Brace.

Cole, M. W., Ito, T., & Braver, T. S. (2015). Lateral prefrontal cortex contributes to fluid intelligence through multinetwork connectivity. *Brain Connectivity, 5,* 497–504.

Coles, N. A., Larsen, J. T., & Lench, H. C. (2019). A meta-analysis of the facial feedback literature: Effects of facial feedback on emotional experience are small and variable. *Psychological Bulletin, 145,* 610–651.

Coley, R. L., Medeiros, B. L., & Schindler, H. (2008). Using sibling differences to estimate effects of parenting on adolescent sexual risk behaviors. *Journal of Adolescent Health, 43,* 133–140.

Collins, F. (2006). *The language of God.* Free Press.

Collins, N. L., & Miller, L. C. (1994). Self-disclosure and liking: A meta-analytic review. *Psychological Bulletin, 116,* 457–475.

Collins, W. A., Welsh, D. P., & Furman, W. (2009). Adolescent romantic relationships. *Annual Review of Psychology, 60,* 631–652.

Collinson, S. L., MacKay, C. E., James, A. C., Quested, D. J., Phillips, T., Roberts, N., & Crow, T. J. (2003). Brain volume, asymmetry and intellectual impairment in relation to sex in early-onset schizophrenia. *British Journal of Psychiatry, 183,* 114–120.

Colombo, J. (1982). The critical period concept: Research, methodology, and theoretical issues. *Psychological Bulletin, 91,* 260–275.

Compton, W. C. (2018). Self-actualization myths: What did Maslow really say? *Journal of Humanistic Psychology.* Advance online publication. doi.org/10.1177/0022167818761929

Confer, J. C., Easton, J. A., Fleischman, D. S., Goetz, C. D., Lewis, D. M. G., Perilloux, C., & Buss, D. M. (2010). Evolutionary psychology: Controversies, questions, prospects, and limitations. *American Psychologist, 65,* 110–126.

Conklin, Q. A., King, B. G., Zanesco, A. P., Lin, J., Hamidi, A. B., Pokorny, J. J., Álvarez-López, M. J., Cosin-Tomás, M., Huang, C., Kaliman, P., Epel, E. S., & Saron, C. D. (2018). Insight meditation and telomere biology: The effects of intensive retreat and the moderating role of personality. *Brain, Behavior, and Immunity, 70,* 233–245.

Conley, T. D. (2011). Perceived proposer personality characteristics and gender differences in acceptance of casual sex offers. *Journal of Personality and Social Psychology, 100,* 300–329.

Connor, C. E. (2010). A new viewpoint on faces. *Science, 330,* 764–765.

Connor-Smith, J. K., & Flachsbart, C. (2007). Relations between personality and coping: A meta-analysis. *Journal of Personality and Social Psychology, 93,* 1080–1107.

Consumer Reports. (1995, November). Does therapy help? pp. 734–739.

Converse, B. A., Juarez, L., & Hennecke, M. (2019). Self-control and the reasons behind our goals. *Journal of Personality and Social Psychology, 116,* 860–883.

Conway, C. C., Forbes, M. K., Forbush, K. T., Fried, E. I., Hallquist, M. N., Kotov, R., Mullins-Sweatt, S. N., Shackman, A. J., Skodol, A. E., South, S. C., Sunderland, M., Waszczuk, M. A., Zald, D. H., Afzali, M. H., Bornovalova, M. A., Carragher, N., Docherty, A. R., Jonas, K. G., Krueger, R. F., . . . Eaton, N. R. (2019). A hierarchical taxonomy of psychopathology can transform mental health research. *Perspectives on Psychological Science, 14,* 419–436.

Conway, M. A., Wang, Q., Hanyu, K., & Haque, S. (2005). A cross-cultural investigation of autobiographical memory. On the universality and cultural variation of the reminiscence bump. *Journal of Cross-Cultural Psychology, 36,* 739–749.

Cook, S., Kokmotou, K., Soto, V., Fallon, N., Tyson-Carr, J., Thomas, A., Giesbrecht, T., Field, M., & Stancak, A. (2017). Pleasant and unpleasant odour-face combinations influence face and odour perception: An event-related potential study. *Behavioural Brain Research, 333,* 304–313.

Cooke, L. J., Wardle, J., & Gibson, E. L. (2003). Relationship between parental report of food neophobia and everyday food consumption in 2–6-year-old children. *Appetite, 41,* 205–206.

Cooley, E., Lei, R., Brown-Iannuzzi, J., & Ellerkamp, T. (2019). Personal prejudice, other guilt: explicit prejudice toward Black people predicts guilty verdicts for White officers who kill Black men. *Personality and Social Psychology Bulletin, 45,* 754–766.

Cooney, G., Gilbert, D. T., & Wilson, T. D. (2014). The unforeseen costs of extraordinary experience. *Psychological Science, 25,* 2259–2265.

Cooper, K. J. (1999, May 1). This time, copycat wave is broader. *The Washington Post.* https://www.washingtonpost.com/wp-srv/national/longterm/juvmurders/stories/copycat050199.htm

Cooper, N., Garcia, J. O., Tompson, S. H., O'Donnell, M. B., Falk, E. B., & Vettel, J. M. (2019). Time-evolving dynamics in brain networks forecast responses to health messaging. *Network Neuroscience, 3,* 138–156.

Cooper, W. H., & Withey, M. J. (2009). The strong situation hypothesis. *Personality and Social Psychology Review, 13,* 62–72.

Coopersmith, S. (1967). *The antecedents of self-esteem.* Freeman.

Copen, C. E., Chandra, A., & Febo-Vazquez, I. (2016, January 7). Sexual behavior, sexual attraction, and sexual orientation among adults aged 18–44 in the United States: Data from the 2011–2013 National Survey of Family Growth. Centers for Disease Control and Prevention, *National Health Statistics Reports,* Number 88.

Corballis, M. C. (2002). *From hand to mouth: The origins of language.* Princeton University Press.

Corballis, M. C. (2003). From mouth to hand: Gesture, speech, and the evolution of right-handedness. *Behavioral and Brain Sciences, 26,* 199–260.

Corcoran, D. W. J. (1964). The relation between introversion and salivation. *The American Journal of Psychology, 77,* 298–300.

Cordaro, D. T., Sun, R., Keltner, D., Kamble, S., Huddar, N., & McNeil, G. (2018). Universals and cultural variations in 22 emotional expressions across five cultures. *Emotion, 18,* 75–93.

Coren, S. (1996). *Sleep thieves: An eye-opening exploration into the science and mysteries of sleep.* Free Press.

Corey, D. P., García-Añoveros, J., Holt, J. R., Kwan, K. Y., Lin, S.-Y., Vollrath, M. A., Amalfitano, A., Cheung, E. L., Derfler, B. H., Duggan, A., Géléoc, G. S., Gray, P. A., Hoffman, M. P., Rehm, H. L., Tamasauskas, D., & Zhang, D.-S. (2004). TRPA1 is a candidate for the mechanosensitive transduction channel of vertebrate hair cells. *Nature, 432,* 723–730.

Corina, D. P. (1998). The processing of sign language: Evidence from aphasia. In B. Stemmer & H. A. Whittaker (Eds.), *Handbook of neurolinguistics* (pp. 313–329). Academic Press.

Corina, D. P., Vaid, J., & Bellugi, U. (1992). The linguistic basis of left hemisphere specialization. *Science, 255,* 1258–1260.

Corkin, S. (2005, September). Quoted by R. Adelson in Lessons from H. M. *Monitor on Psychology,* p. 59.

Corkin, S. (2013). *Permanent present tense: The unforgettable life of the amnesic patient.* Basic Books.

Corneille, O., Huart, J., Becquart, E., & Brédart, S. (2004). When memory shifts toward more typical category exemplars: Accentuation effects in the recollection of ethnically ambiguous faces. *Journal of Personality and Social Psychology, 86,* 236–250.

Cornier, M.-A. (2011). Is your brain to blame for weight regain? *Physiology & Behavior, 104,* 608–612.

Cornil, Y., & Chandon, P. (2013). From fan to fat? Vicarious losing increases unhealthy eating, but self-affirmation is an effective remedy. *Psychological Science, 24,* 1936–1946.

Correll, J., Park, B., Judd, C. M., Wittenbrink, B., Sadler, M. S., & Keesee, T. (2007). Across the thin blue line: Police officers and racial bias in the decision to shoot. *Journal of Personality and Social Psychology, 92,* 1006–1023.

Correll, J., Wittenbrink, B., Crawford, M. T., & Sadler, M. S. (2015). Stereotypic vision: How stereotypes disambiguate visual stimuli. *Journal of Personality and Social Psychology, 108,* 219–233.

Corrigan, P. (2004). How stigma interferes with mental health care. *American Psychologist, 59,* 614–625.

Corrigan, P. W. (2014). Can there be false hope in recovery? *British Journal of Psychiatry, 205,* 423–424.

Corrigan, P. W., Druss, B. G., & Perlick, D. A. (2014). The impact of mental illness stigma on seeking and participating in mental health care. *Psychological Science in the Public Interest, 15,* 37–70.

Corrigan, P. W., & Watson, A. C. (2002). Understanding the impact of stigma on people with mental illness. *World Psychiatry, 1,* 16–20.

Cortes, K., Leith, S., & Wilson, A. E. (2018). Relationship satisfaction and the subjective distance of past relational events. *Journal of Social and Personal Relationships, 35,* 1092–1117.

Costa, A., Foucart, A., Hayakawa, S., Aparici, M., Apesteguia, J., Heafner, J., & Keysar, B. (2014). Your morals depend on language. *PLOS ONE, 9,* e94842.

Costa, D. L., Yetter, N., & DeSomer, H. (2018). Intergenerational transmission of paternal trauma among US Civil War ex-POWs. *PNAS, 115,* 11215–11220.

Costa, P. T., Jr., & McCrae, R. R. (2011). The five-factor model, five-factor theory, and interpersonal psychology. In L. M. Horowitz & S. Strack (Eds.), *Handbook of interpersonal psychology: Theory, research, assessment, and therapeutic interventions* (pp. 91–104). John Wiley & Sons.

Costa, P. T., Jr., Terracciano, A., & McCrae, R. R. (2001). Gender differences in personality traits across cultures: Robust and surprising findings. *Journal of Personality and Social Psychology, 81,* 322–331.

Costello, E. J., Compton, S. N., Keeler, G., & Angold, A. (2003). Relationships between poverty and psychopathology: A natural experiment. *Journal of the American Medical Association, 290,* 2023–2029.

Costello, T. H., Unterberger, A., Watts, A. L., & Lilienfeld, S. O. (2018). Psychopathy and pride: Testing Lykken's hypothesis regarding the implications of fearlessness for prosocial and antisocial behavior. *Frontiers in Psychology, 9,* 185.

Coudé, G., Toschi, G., Festante, F., Bimbi, M., Bonaiuto, J., & Ferrari, P. F. (2019). Grasping neurons in the ventral premotor cortex of macaques are modulated by social goals. *Journal of Cognitive Neuroscience, 31,* 299–313.

Couli, J. T., Vidal, F., Nazarian, B., & Macar, F. (2004). Functional anatomy of the attentional modulation of time estimation. *Science, 303,* 1506–1508.

Coulter, K. C., & Malouff, J. M. (2013). Effects of an intervention designed to enhance romantic relationship excitement: A randomized-control trial. *Couple and Family Psychology: Research and Practice, 2,* 34–44.

Courage, M. L., & Howe, M. L. (2002). From infant to child: The dynamics of cognitive change in the second year of life. *Psychological Bulletin, 128,* 250–277.

Courtney, J. G., Longnecker, M. P., Theorell, T., & de Verdier, M. G. (1993). Stressful life events and the risk of colorectal cancer. *Epidemiology, 4,* 407–414.

Cowan, N. (1988). Evolving conceptions of memory storage, selective attention, and their mutual constraints within the human information-processing system. *Psychological Bulletin, 104,* 163–191.

Cowan, N. (2008). What are the differences between long-term, short-term, and working memory? *Progress in Brain Research, 169,* 323–338.

Cowan, N. (2010). The magical mystery four: How is working memory capacity limited, and why? *Current Directions in Psychological Science, 19,* 51–57.

Cowan, N. (2015). George Miller's magical number of immediate memory in retrospect: Observations on the faltering progression of science. *Psychological Review, 122,* 536–541

Cowan, N. (2016). Working memory maturation: Can we get at the essence of cognitive growth? *Perspectives on Psychological Science, 11,* 239–264.

Cowart, B. J. (1981). Development of taste perception in humans: Sensitivity and preference throughout the life span. *Psychological Bulletin, 90,* 43–73.

Cowart, B. J. (2005). Taste, our body's gustatory gatekeeper. *Cerebrum, 7,* 7–22.

Cowell, J. M., & Decety, J. (2015). Precursors to morality in development as a complex interplay between neural, socioenvironmental, and behavioral facets. *PNAS, 112,* 12657–12662.

Cowen, A. S., & Keltner, D. (2019). What the face displays: Mapping 28 emotions conveyed by naturalistic expression. *American Psychologist.* Advance online publication. https://doi.org/10.1037/amp0000488

Cox, C. R., & Arndt, J. (2012). How sweet it is to be loved by you: The role of perceived regard in the terror management of close relationships. *Journal of Personality and Social Psychology, 102,* 616–632.

Cox, J. J., Reimann, F. Nicholas, A. K., Thornton, G., Roberts, E., Springell, K., & Woods, C. G. (2006). An SCN9A channelopathy causes congenital inability to experience pain. *Nature, 444,* 894–898.

Coye, C., Ouattara, K., Zuberbühler, K., & Lemasson, A. (2015). Suffixation influences receivers' behaviour in non-human primates. *Proceedings of the Royal Society B, 282,* 1807.

Coyne, S. M., Padilla-Walker, L., Holmgren, H. G., Davis, E. J., Collier, K. M., Memmott-Elison, M., & Hawkins, A. J. (2018). A meta-analysis of prosocial media on prosocial behavior, aggression, and empathic concern: A multidimensional approach. *Developmental Psychology, 54,* 331–347.

CPP. (2017). Myers-Briggs Type Indicator® (MBTI®). CPP, Inc. (cpp.com).

Crabbe, J. C. (2002). Genetic contributions to addiction. *Annual Review of Psychology, 53,* 435–462.

Crabtree, S. (2011, December 12). *U.S. seniors maintain happiness highs with less social time.* Gallup poll (gallup.com).

Craik, F. I. M., & Tulving, E. (1975). Depth of processing and the retention of words in episodic memory. *Journal of Experimental Psychology: General, 104,* 268–294.

Crandall, C., & White, M. (2016, November 17). *Trump and the social psychology of prejudice.* Undark. https://undark.org/2016/11/17/trump-social-psychology-prejudice-unleashed/

Crandall, C. S. (1988). Social contagion of binge eating. *Journal of Personality and Social Psychology, 55,* 588–598.

Crandall, C. S., Miller, J. M., & White, M. H. (2018). Changing norms following the 2016 US presidential election: The Trump effect on prejudice. *Social Psychological and Personality Science, 9,* 186–192.

Crawford, J. T., & Brandt, M. J. (2019). Who is prejudiced, and toward whom? The Big Five traits and generalized prejudice. *Personality and Social Psychology Bulletin, 45,* 1455–1467.

Crawford, M., Chaffin, R., & Fitton, L. (1995). Cognition in social context. Learning and individual differences, special issue: Psychological and psychobiological perspectives on sex differences in cognition: 1. *Theory and Research, 7,* 341–362.

Credé, M. (2018). What shall we do about grit? A critical review of what we know and what we don't know. *Educational Researcher, 47,* 606–611.

Credé, M., & Kuncel, N. R. (2008). Study habits, skills, and attitudes: The third pillar supporting collegiate academic performance. *Perspectives on Psychological Science, 3,* 425–453.

Creswell, J. D., Bursley, J. K., & Satpute, A. B. (2013). Neural reactivation links unconscious thought to decision making performance. *Social Cognitive and Affective Neuroscience, 8,* 863–869.

Creswell, J. D., Way, B. M., Eisenberger, N. I., & Lieberman, M. D. (2007). Neural correlates of dispositional mindfulness during affect labeling. *Psychosomatic Medicine, 69,* 560–565.

Creswell, K. G., Chung, T., Clark, D., & Martin, C. (2014). Solitary alcohol use in teens is associated with drinking in response to negative affect and predicts alcohol problems in young adulthood. *Clinical Psychological Science, 2,* 602–610.

Crews, F. T., He, J., & Hodge, C. (2007). Adolescent cortical development: A critical period of vulnerability for addiction. *Pharmacology, Biochemistry and Behavior, 86,* 189–199.

Crews, F. T., Mdzinarishvilli, A., Kim, D., He, J., & Nixon, K. (2006). Neurogenesis in adolescent brain is potently inhibited by ethanol. *Neuroscience, 137,* 437–445.

Crifasi, C. K., Meyers, J. S., Vernick, J. S., & Webster, D. W. (2015). Effects of changes in permit-to-purchase handgun laws in Connecticut and Missouri on suicide rates. *Preventive Medicine: An International Journal Devoted to Practice and Theory, 79,* 43–49.

Cristia, A., Dupoux, E., Gurven, M., & Stieglitz, J. (2019). Child-directed speech is infrequent in a forager-farmer population: A time allocation study. *Child Development, 90,* 759–773.

Crivelli, C., Carrera, P., & Fernández-Dols, J. (2015). Are smiles a sign of happiness? Spontaneous expressions of judo winners. *Evolution and Human Behavior, 36,* 52–58.

Crivelli, C., Jarillo, S., Russell, J. A., & Fernández-Dols, J. M. (2016a). Reading emotions from faces in two indigenous societies. *Journal of Experimental Psychology: General, 145,* 830–843.

Crivelli, C., Russell, J. A., Jarillo, S., & Fernández-Dols, J. M. (2016b). The fear gasping face as a threat display in a Melanesian society. *PNAS, 113,* 12403–12407.

Crocker, J., & Park, L. E. (2004). The costly pursuit of self-esteem. *Psychological Bulletin, 130,* 392–414.

Crocker, J., Thompson, L. L., McGraw, K. M., & Ingerman, C. (1987). Downward comparison, prejudice, and evaluation of others: Effects of self-esteem and threat. *Journal of Personality and Social Psychology, 52,* 907–916.

Crockett, M. J., Kurth-Nelson, Z., Siegel, J. Z., Dayan, P., & Dolan, R. J. (2014). Harm to others outweighs harm to self in moral decision making. *PNAS, 111,* 17320–17325.

Crockford, C., Wittig, R. M., & Zuberbühler, K. (2017). Vocalizing in chimpanzees is influenced by social-cognitive processes. *Science Advances, 3,* e1701742.

Croft, A., Schmader, T., Block, K., & Baron, A. S. (2014). The second shift reflected in the second generation: Do parents' gender roles at home predict children's aspirations? *Psychological Science, 25,* 1418–1428.

Croft, R. J., Klugman, A., Baldeweg, T., & Gruzelier, J. H. (2001). Electrophysiological evidence of serotonergic impairment in long-term MDMA ("Ecstasy") users. *American Journal of Psychiatry, 158,* 1687–1692.

Crombie, A. C. (1964, May). Early concepts of the senses and the mind. *Scientific American,* pp. 108–116.

Crook, T. H., & West, R. L. (1990). Name recall performance across the adult lifespan. *British Journal of Psychology, 81,* 335–340.

Crosier, B. S., Webster, G. D., & Dillon, H. M. (2012). Wired to connect: Evolutionary psychology and social networks. *Review of General Psychology, 16,* 230–239.

Cross-National Collaborative Group. (1992). The changing rate of major depression. *Journal of the American Medical Association, 268,* 3098–3105.

Crowell, A. L., Riva-Posse, P., Holtzheimer, P. E., Garlow, S. J., Kelley, M. E., Gross, R. E., Denison, L., Quinn, S., & Mayberg, H. S. (2019). Long-term outcomes of subcallosal cingulate deep brain stimulation for treatment-resistant depression. *American Journal of Psychiatry, 176,* 949–956.

Crowell, J. A., & Waters, E. (1994). Bowlby's theory grown up: The role of attachment in adult love relationships. *Psychological Inquiry, 5,* 1–22.

Croy, I., Bojanowski, V., & Hummel, T. (2013). Men without a sense of smell exhibit a strongly reduced number of sexual relationships, women exhibit reduced partnership security: A reanalysis of previously published data. *Biological Psychology, 92,* 292–294.

Croy, I., Negoias, S., Novakova, L., Landis, B. N., & Hummel, T. (2012). Learning about the functions of the olfactory system from people without a sense of smell. *PLOS ONE 7,* e33365.

Csikszentmihalyi, M. (1990). *Flow: The psychology of optimal experience.* Harper & Row.

Csikszentmihalyi, M. (1999). If we are so rich, why aren't we happy? *American Psychologist, 54,* 821–827.

Csikszentmihalyi, M., & Hunter, J. (2003). Happiness in everyday life: The uses of experience sampling. *Journal of Happiness Studies, 4,* 185–199.

Csikszentmihalyi, M., & Larson, R. (1984). *Being adolescent: Conflict and growth in the teenage years.* Basic Books.

Cucchi, A., Ryan, D., Konstantakopoulos, G., Stroumpa, S., Kaçar, A. Ş., Renshaw, S., Landau, S., & Kravariti, E. (2016). Lifetime prevalence of non-suicidal self-injury in patients with eating disorders: A systematic review and meta-analysis. *Psychological Medicine, 46,* 1345–1358.

Cuijpers, P. (2017). Four decades of outcome research on psychotherapies for adult depression: An overview of a series of meta-analyses. *Canadian Psychology/Psychologie Canadienne, 58,* 7–19.

Cuijpers, P., Driessen, E., Hollon, S. D., van Oppen, P., Barth, J., & Andersson, G. (2012). The efficacy of non-directive supportive therapy for adult depression: A meta-analysis. *Clinical Psychology Review, 32,* 280–291.

Cuijpers, P., Reijnders, M., & Huibers, M. J. H. (2019). The role of common factors in psychotherapy outcomes. *Annual Review of Clinical Psychology, 15,* 207-231.

Cuijpers, P., van Straten, A., Schuurmans, J., van Oppen, P., Hollon, S. D., & Andersson, G. (2010). Psychotherapy for chronic major depression and dysthymia: A meta-analysis. *Clinical Psychology Review, 30,* 51–62.

Cummings, J. R., & Tomiyama, A. J. (2019). Food loves company: Risky eating with friends increases interpersonal closeness. *Journal of Experimental Social Psychology, 81,* 61–69.

Cummins, R. A. (2006, April 4). *Australian Unity Wellbeing Index: Survey 14.1.* Australian Centre on Quality of Life, Deakin University.

Cunningham, G. B., Ferreira, M., & Fink, J. S. (2009). Reactions to prejudicial statements: The influence of statement content and characteristics of the commenter. *Group Dynamics: Theory, Research, and Practice, 13,* 59–73.

Cunningham, M. R., Roberts, A., Barbee, A. P., Druen, P. B., & Wu, C.-H. (2005). "Their ideas of beauty are, on the whole, the same as ours": Consistency and variability in the cross-cultural perception of female physical attractiveness. *Journal of Personality and Social Psychology, 68,* 261–279.

Cunningham, P. J., & Shahan, T. A. (2019). Rats engage in suboptimal choice when the delay to food is sufficiently long. *Journal of Experimental Psychology: Animal Learning and Cognition, 45,* 301–310.

Cunningham, W. A., Johnson, M. K., Raye, C. L., Gatenby, J. C., Gore, J. C., & Banaji, M. R. (2004). Separable neural components in the processing of Black and White faces. *Psychological Science, 15,* 806–813.

Curci, A., Lanciano, T., Mastandrea, S., & Sartori, G. (2015). Flashbulb memories of the Pope's resignation: Explicit and implicit measure across different religious groups. *Memory, 23,* 529–544.

Currie, T. E., & Little, A. C. (2009). The relative importance of the face and body in judgments of human physical attractiveness. *Evolution and Human Behavior, 30,* 409–416.

Curry, J., Silva, S., Rohde, P., Ginsburg, G., Kratochvil, C., Simons, A., Kirchner, J., May, D., Kennard, B., Mayes, T., Feeny, N., Albano, A. M., Lavanier, S., Reinecke, M., Jacobs, R., Becker-Weidman, E., Weller, E., Emslie, G., Walkup, J., . . . March, J. (2011). Recovery and recurrence following treatment for adolescent major depression. *Archives of General Psychiatry, 68,* 263–269.

Curtin, S. C., & Hedegaard, H. (2019). *Suicide rates for females and males by race and ethnicity: United States, 1999 and 2017.* NCHS Health Statistics. https://www.cdc.gov/nchs/data/hestat/suicide /rates_1999_2017.htm

Curtis, R. C., & Miller, K. (1986). Believing another likes or dislikes you: Behaviors making the beliefs come true. *Journal of Personality and Social Psychology, 51,* 284–290.

Custers, R., & Aarts, H. (2010). The unconscious will: How the pursuit of goals operates outside of conscious awareness. *Science, 329,* 47–50.

Cyders, M. A., & Smith, G. T. (2008). Emotion-based dispositions to rash action: Positive and negative urgency. *Psychological Bulletin, 134,* 807–828.

Czarna, A. Z., Leifeld, P., Śmieja, M., Dufner, M., & Salovey, P. (2016). Do narcissism and emotional intelligence win us friends? Modeling dynamics of peer popularity using inferential network analysis. *Personality and Social Psychology Bulletin, 42,* 1588–1599.

Czeisler, C. A., Allan, J. S., Strogatz, S. H., Ronda, J. M., Sanchez, R., & Rios, C. D. (1986). Bright light resets the human circadian pacemaker independent of the timing of the sleep-wake cycle. *Science, 233,* 667–671.

Czeisler, C. A., Duffy, J. F., Shanahan, T. L., Brown, E. N., Mitchell, J. F., Rimmer, D. W., Ronda, J. M., Silva, E. J., Allan, J. S., Emens, J. S., Dijk, D. J., & Kronauer, R. E. (1999). Stability, precision, and near-24-hour period of the human circadian pacemaker. *Science, 284,* 2177–2181.

Czeisler, C. A., Kronauer, R. E., Allan, J. S., & Duffy, J. F. (1989). Bright light induction of strong (Type O) resetting of the human circadian pacemaker. *Science, 244,* 1328–1333.

da Cunha-Bang, S., Fisher, P. M., Hjordt, L. V., Perfalk, E., Persson Skibsted, A., Bock, C., Ohlhues, B. A., Deen, M., Thomsen, C., Sestoft, D. M., & Knudsen, G. M. (2017). Violent offenders respond to provocations with high amygdala and striatal reactivity. *Social Cognitive and Affective Neuroscience, 12,* 802–810.

Dadds, M. R., Thai, C., Mendoza Diaz, A., Broderick, J., Moul, C., Tully, L. A., Hawes, D. J., Davies, S., Burchfield, K., & Cane, L. (2019). Therapist-assisted online treatment for child conduct problems in rural and urban families: Two randomized controlled trials. *Journal of Consulting and Clinical Psychology, 87,* 706–719.

Dadds, M. R., & Tully, L. A. (2019). What is it to discipline a child: What should it be? A reanalysis of time-out from the perspective of child mental health, attachment, and trauma. *American Psychologist, 74*(7), 794–808.

Dahl, R. E., Allen, N. B., Wilbrecht, L., & Suleiman, A. B. (2018). Importance of investing in adolescence from a developmental science perspective. *Nature, 554,* 441–450.

Dai, H., Milkman, K. L., & Riis, J. (2014). The fresh start effect: Temporal landmarks motivate aspirational behavior. *Management Science, 60,* 2563–2582.

Daley, J. (2011, July/August). What you don't know can kill you. *Discover.* https://www.discovermagazine .com/mind/what-you-dont-know-can-kill-you

Daly, M., Delaney, L., Egan, R. F., & Baumeister, R. F. (2015). Childhood self-control and unemployment throughout the life span: Evidence from two British cohort studies. *Psychological Science, 26,* 709–723.

Damasio, A. R. (2003). *Looking for Spinoza: Joy, sorrow, and the feeling brain.* Harcourt.

Damasio, A. R. (2010). *Self comes to mind: Constructing the conscious brain.* Pantheon.

Damian, R. I., & Roberts, B. W. (2015). The associations of birth order with personality and intelligence in a representative sample of U.S. high school students. *Journal of Research in Personality, 58,* 96–105.

Damian, R. I., Spengler, M., Sutu, A., & Roberts, B. W. (2019). Sixteen going on sixty-six: A longitudinal study of personality stability and change across 50 years. *Journal of Personality and Social Psychology, 117,* 674–695.

Damon, W., & Hart, D. (1982). The development of self-understanding from infancy through adolescence. *Child Development, 53,* 841–864.

Damon, W., & Hart, D. (1988). *Self-understanding in childhood and adolescence.* Cambridge University Press.

Damon, W., & Hart, D. (1992). Self-understanding and its role in social and moral development. In M. H. Bornstein & M. E. Lamb (Eds.), *Developmental psychology: An advanced textbook* (3rd ed.). Lawrence Erlbaum.

Damon, W., Menon, J., & Bronk, K. (2003). The development of purpose during adolescence. *Applied Developmental Science, 7,* 119–128.

Dana, J., Dawes, R., & Peterson, N. (2013). Belief in the unstructured interview: The persistence of an illusion. *Judgment and Decision Making, 8,* 512–520.

Dandine-Roulland, C., Laurent, R., Dall'Ara, I., Toupance, B., & Chaix, R. (2019). Genomic evidence for MHC disassortative mating in humans. *Proceedings of the Royal Society B, 286*(1899), 20182664.

Danek, A. H., & Salvi, C. (2018). Moment of truth: Why aha! experiences are correct. *The Journal of Creative Behavior.* Advance online publication. doi.org/10.1002/jocb.380

Danelli, L., Cossu, G., Berlingeri, M., Bottini, G., Sberna, M., & Paulesu, E. (2013). Is a lone right hemisphere enough? Neurolinguistic architecture in a case with a very early left hemispherectomy. *Neurocase, 19,* 209–231.

Daniel, T. A., & Katz, J. S. (2018). Primacy and recency effects for taste. *Journal of Experimental Psychology: Learning, Memory, and Cognition, 44,* 399–405.

Daniels, D. P., & Zlatev, J. J. (2019). Choice architects reveal a bias toward positivity and certainty. *Organizational Behavior and Human Decision Processes, 151,* 132–149.

Danner, D. D., Snowdon, D. A., & Friesen, W. V. (2001). Positive emotions in early life and longevity: Findings from the Nun Study. *Journal of Personality and Social Psychology, 80,* 804–813.

Danso, H., & Esses, V. (2001). Black experimenters and the intellectual test performance of white participants: The tables are turned. *Journal of Experimental Social Psychology, 37,* 158–165.

Danziger, S., & Ward, R. (2010). Language changes implicit associations between ethnic groups and evaluation in bilinguals. *Psychological Science, 21,* 799–800.

Dargue, N., Sweller, N., & Jones, M. P. (2019). When our hands help us understand: A meta-analysis into the effects of gesture on comprehension. *Psychological Bulletin, 145,* 765–784.

Darley, J. M. (2009). Morality in the law: The psychological foundations of citizens' desires to punish transgressions. *Annual Review of Law and Social Science, 5,* 1–23.

Darley, J. M., & Alter, A. (2013). Behavioral issues of punishment, retribution, and deterrence. In E. Shafir (Ed.), *The behavioral foundations of public policy* (pp. 181–194). Princeton University Press.

Darley, J. M., & Latané, B. (1968a). Bystander intervention in emergencies: Diffusion of responsibility. *Journal of Personality and Social Psychology, 8,* 377–383.

Darley, J. M., & Latané, B. (1968b, December). When will people help in a crisis? *Psychology Today,* pp. 54–57, 70–71.

Darrach, B., & Norris, J. (1984, August). An American tragedy. *Life,* pp. 58–74.

Darwin, C. (1859). *On the origin of species by means of natural selection.* John Murray.

Darwin, C. (1872). *The expression of the emotions in man and animals.* John Murray.

Daum, I., & Schugens, M. M. (1996). On the cerebellum and classical conditioning. *Psychological Science, 5,* 58–61.

Davey, G., & Rato, R. (2012). Subjective well-being in China: A review. *Journal of Happiness Studies, 13,* 333–346.

Davey, G. C. L. (1992). Classical conditioning and the acquisition of human fears and phobias: A review and synthesis of the literature. *Advances in Behavior Research and Therapy, 14,* 29–66.

Davey, G. C. L. (1995). Preparedness and phobias: Specific evolved associations or a generalized expectancy bias? *Behavioral and Brain Sciences, 18,* 289–297.

Davidoff, J. (2004). Coloured thinking. *The Psychologist, 17,* 570–572.

Davidson, R. J., Kabat-Zinn, J., Schumacher, J., Rosenkranz, M., Muller, D., Santorelli, S. F., Urbanowski, F., Harrington, A., Bonus, K., & Sheridan, J. F. (2003). Alterations in brain and immune function produced by mindfulness meditation. *Psychosomatic Medicine, 65,* 564–570.

Davidson, R. J., Pizzagalli, D., Nitschke, J. B., & Putnam, K. (2002). Depression: Perspectives from affective neuroscience. *Annual Review of Psychology, 53,* 545–574.

Davidson, R. J., Putnam, K. M., & Larson, C. L. (2000). Dysfunction in the neural circuitry of emotion regulation—a possible prelude to violence. *Science, 289,* 591–594.

Davidson, T. L., & Riley, A. L. (2015). Taste, sickness, and learning. *American Scientist, 103,* 204–211.

Davies, P. (2007). *Cosmic jackpot: Why our universe is just right for life.* Houghton Mifflin.

Davis, B. E., Moon, R. Y., Sachs, H. C., & Ottolini, M. C. (1998). Effects of sleep position on infant motor development. *Pediatrics, 102,* 1135–1140.

Davis, D. E., Choe, E., Meyers, J., Wade, N., Varias, K., Gifford, A., Quinn, A., Hook, J. N., Van Tongeren, D. R., Griffin, B. J., & Worthington, E. L. (2016). Thankful for the little things: A meta-analysis of gratitude interventions. *Journal of Counseling Psychology, 63,* 20–31.

Davis, E. P., Stout, S. A., Molet, J., Vegetabile, B., Glynn, L. M., Sandman, C. A., Heins, K., Stern, H., & Baram, T. Z. (2017). Exposure to unpredictable maternal sensory signals influences cognitive development across species. *PNAS, 114,* 10390–10395.

Davis, H., IV, Liotti, M., Ngan, E. T., Woodward, T. S., Van Sellenberg, J. X., van Anders, S. M., Smith, A., & Mayberg, H. S. (2008). fMRI BOLD signal changes in elite swimmers while viewing videos of personal failure. *Brain Imaging and Behavior, 2,* 84–93.

Davis, J. O., & Phelps, J. A. (1995). Twins with schizophrenia: Genes or germs? *Schizophrenia Bulletin, 21,* 13–18.

Davis, J. O., Phelps, J. A., & Bracha, H. S. (1995). Prenatal development of monozygotic twins and concordance for schizophrenia. *Schizophrenia Bulletin, 21,* 357–366.

Davis, J. P., Lander, K., & Jansari, A. (2013). I never forget a face. *The Psychologist, 26,* 726–729.

Davis, K., Christodoulou, J., Seider, S., & Gardner, H. (2011). The theory of multiple intelligences. In R. J. Sternberg & S. B. Kaufman (Eds.), *Cambridge handbook of intelligence.* Cambridge University Press.

Davis, M. (2005). Searching for a drug to extinguish fear. *Cerebrum, 7,* 47–58.

Davison, K. P., Pennebaker, J. W., & Dickerson, S. S. (2000). Who talks? The social psychology of illness support groups. *American Psychologist, 55,* 205–217.

Davison, S. L., & Davis, S. R. (2011). Androgenic hormones and aging—The link with female function. *Hormones and Behavior, 59,* 745–753.

Dawes, R. M. (1980). Social dilemmas. *Annual Review of Psychology, 31,* 169–193.

Dawkins, L., Shahzad, F.-Z., Ahmed, S. S., & Edmonds, C. J. (2011). Expectation of having consumed caffeine can improve performance and moods. *Appetite, 57,* 597–600.

Dawkins, R. (1998). *Unweaving the rainbow.* Houghton Mifflin.

Dawkins, R. (2007, July 1). Inferior design. *The New York Times.* https://www.nytimes.com/2007/07/01/books/review/Dawkins-t.html?

Day, F. R., Thompson, D. J., Helgason, H., Chasman, D. I., Finucane, H., Sulem, P., Ruth, K. S., Whalen, S., Sarkar, A. K., Albrecht, E., Altmaier, E., Amini, M., Barbieri, C. M., Boutin, T., Campbell, A., Demerath, E., Giri, A., He, C., Hottenga, J. J., . . . Perry, J. R. B. (2017). Genomic analyses identify hundreds of variants associated with age at menarche and support a role for puberty timing in cancer risk. *Nature Genetics, 49,* 834–841.

de Abreu Costa, M., de Oliveira, G. S. D. A., Tatton-Ramos, T., Manfro, G. G., & Salum, G. A. (2019). Anxiety and stress-related disorders and mindfulness-based interventions: a systematic review and multilevel meta-analysis and meta-regression of multiple outcomes. *Mindfulness, 10,* 996–1005.

de Boer, H., Donker, A. S., Kostons, D. D., & van der Werf, G. P. (2018). Long-term effects of metacognitive strategy instruction on student academic performance: A meta-analysis. *Educational Research Review, 24,* 98–115.

de Boysson-Bardies, B., Halle, P., Sagart, L., & Durand, C. (1989). A cross linguistic investigation of vowel formats in babbling. *Journal of Child Language, 16,* 1–17.

de Chastelaine, M., Mattson, J. T., Wang, T. H., Donley, B. E., & Rugg, M. D. (2016). The neural correlates of recollection and retrieval monitoring: Relationships with age and recollection performance. *NeuroImage, 138,* 164–175.

de Courten-Myers, G. M. (2005, February 4). Personal communication.

De Dreu, C. K. W., Nijstad, B. A., Baas, M., Wolsink, I., & Roskes, M. (2012). Working memory benefits creative insight, musical improvisation, and original ideation through maintained task-focused attention. *Personality and Social Psychology Bulletin, 38,* 656–669.

de Gee, J., Knapen, T., & Donner, T. H. (2014). Decision-related pupil dilation reflects upcoming choice and individual bias. *PNAS, 111,* E618–E625.

de Gelder, B. (2010). Uncanny sight in the blind. *Scientific American, 302,* 60–65.

de Hoogh, A. H. B., den Hartog, D. N., Koopman, P. L., Thierry, H., van den Berg, P. T., van der Weide, J. G., & Wilderom, C. P. M. (2004). Charismatic leadership, environmental dynamism, and performance. *European Journal of Work and Organisational Psychology, 13,* 447–471.

De keersmaecker, J., Dunning, D., Pennycook, G., Rand, D. G., Sanchez, C., Unkelbach, C., & Roets, A. (2019). Investigating the robustness of the illusory truth effect across individual differences in cognitive ability, need for cognitive closure, and cognitive style. *Personality and Social Psychology Bulletin, 46*(2), 204–215.

de la Cruz, L. F., Rydell, M., Runeson, B., D'Onofrio, B. M., Brander, G., Rück, C., Lichtenstein, P., Larsson, H., & Mataix-Cols, D. (2017). Suicide in obsessive-compulsive disorder: A population-based study of 36,788 Swedish patients. *Molecular Psychiatry, 22,* 1626–1632.

de Lange, M., Debets, L., Ruitenberg, K., & Holland, R. (2012). Making less of a mess: Scent exposure as a tool for behavioral change. *Social Influence, 7,* 90–97.

de la Vega, A., Chang, L. J., Banich, M. T., Wager, T. D., & Yarkoni, T. (2016). Large-scale meta-analysis of human medial frontal cortex reveals tripartite functional organization. *The Journal of Neuroscience, 36,* 6553–6562.

De Meyer, G., Shapiro, F., Vanderstichele, H., Vanmechelen, E., Engelborghs, S., De Deyn, P. P., & Trojanowski, J. Q. (2010). Diagnosis-independent Alzheimer disease biomarker signature in cognitively normal elderly people. *Archives of Neurology, 67,* 949–956.

De Neve, J.-E., Diener, E., Tay, L., & Xuereb, C. (2013). The objective benefits of subjective well-being. In J. F. Helliwell, R. Layard, & J. Sachs (Eds.), *World happiness report 2013.* Volume 2. (pp. 54–79). UN Sustainable Network Development Solutions Network.

De Neve, K. M., & Cooper, H. (1998). The happy personality: A meta-analysis of 137 personality traits and subjective well-being. *Psychological Bulletin, 124,* 197–229.

De Pinto, J. (2019, April 19). *Support for marijuana legalization hits new high, CBS News poll finds.* CBS News. https://www.cbsnews.com/news/support-for-marijuana-legalization-hits-new-high-cbs-news-poll-finds/

De Vaus, J., Hornsey, M. J., Kuppens, P., & Bastian, B. (2018). Exploring the East-West divide in prevalence of affective disorder: A case for cultural differences in coping with negative emotion. *Personality and Social Psychology Review, 22,* 285–304.

de Waal, F. (2016). *Are we smart enough to know how smart animals are?* Norton.

de Waal, F. (2019). *Mama's last hug: Animal emotions and what they tell us about ourselves* (p. 85). Norton.

de Witte, M., Spruit, A., van Hooren, S., Moonen, X., & Stams, G. J. (2019). Effects of music interventions on stress-related outcomes: a systematic review and two meta-analyses. *Health Psychology Review, 15,* 1–31.

De Wolff, M. S., & van IJzendoorn, M. H. (1997). Sensitivity and attachment: A meta-analysis on parental antecedents of infant attachment. *Child Development, 68,* 571–591.

Deal, G. (2011, January 14). Chinese parenting: Thanks, I'll pass. *The Wall Street Journal.* https://blogs.wsj.com/wsjam/2011/01/14/chinese-parenting-thanks-ill-pass/

Dean, G. (2012, November/December). Phrenology and the grand delusion of experience. *Skeptical Inquirer,* pp. 31–38.

Dean, M., Harwood, R., & Kasari, C. (2017). The art of camouflage: Gender differences in the social behaviors of girls and boys with autism spectrum disorder. *Autism, 21,* 678–689.

Dean, M., & Ortoleva, P. (2019). The empirical relationship between nonstandard economic behaviors. *PNAS, 116,* 16262–16267.

Deary, I. J. (2008). Why do intelligent people live longer? *Nature, 456,* 175–176.

Deary, I. J. (2016, February). Intelligence over time. Quoted in APS Award Address. Association for Psychological Science *Observer,* p. 15.

Deary, I. J., Johnson, W., & Houlihan, L. M. (2009a). Genetic foundations of human intelligence. *Human Genetics, 126,* 215–232.

Deary, I. J., Pattie, A., & Starr, J. M. (2013). The stability of intelligence from age 11 to age 90 years: The Lothian birth cohort of 1921. *Psychological Science, 24,* 2361–2368.

Deary, I. J., & Ritchie, S. J. (2016). Processing speed differences between 70- and 83-year-olds matched on childhood IQ. *Intelligence, 55,* 28–33.

Deary, I. J., Strand, S., Smith, P., & Fernandes, C. (2007). Intelligence and educational achievement. *Intelligence, 35,* 13–21.

Deary, I. J., Thorpe, G., Wilson, V., Starr, J. M., & Whalley, L. J. (2003). Population sex differences in IQ at age 11: The Scottish mental survey 1932. *Intelligence, 31,* 533–541.

Deary, I. J., Whalley, L. J., & Starr, J. M. (2009). *A lifetime of intelligence: Follow-up studies of the Scottish Mental Surveys of 1932 and 1947.* American Psychological Association.

Deary, I. J., Whiteman, M. C., Starr, J. M., Whalley, L. J., & Fox, H. C. (2004). The impact of childhood intelligence on later life: Following up the Scottish mental surveys of 1932 and 1947. *Journal of Personality and Social Psychology, 86,* 130–147.

Deary, I. J., Yang, J., Davies, G., Harris, S. E., Tenesa, A., Liewald, D., Luciano, M., Lopez, L. M., Gow, A. J., Corley, J., Redmond, P., Fox, H. C., Rowe, S. J., Haggarty, P., McNeill, G., Goddard, M. E., Porteous, D. J., Whalley, L., J., Starr, J. M., & Visscher, P. M. (2012). Genetic contributions to stability and change in intelligence from childhood to old age. *Nature, 481,* 212–215.

deBettencourt, M. T., Keene, P. A., Awh, E., & Vogel, E. K. (2019). Real-time triggering reveals concurrent lapses of attention and working memory. *Nature Human Behaviour, 3,* 808–816.

Debost, J. C., Larsen, J. T., Munk-Olsen, T., Mortensen, P. B., Agerbo, E., & Petersen, L. V. (2019). Childhood infections and schizophrenia: The impact of parental SES and mental illness, and childhood adversities. *Brain, Behavior, and Immunity, 81,* 341–347.

DeBruine, L. M. (2002). Facial resemblance enhances trust. *Proceedings of the Royal Society of London, 269,* 1307–1312.

DeBruine, L. M. (2004). Facial resemblance increases the attractiveness of same-sex faces more than other-sex faces. *Proceedings of the Royal Society of London B, 271,* 2085–2090.

DeCasper, A. J., & Spence, M. J. (1986). Prenatal maternal speech influences newborns' perception of speech sounds. *Infant Behavior and Development, 9,* 133–150.

DeCasper, A. J., Lecanuet, J.-P., Busnel, M.-C., Granier-Deferre, C., & Maugeais, R. (1994). Fetal reactions to recurrent maternal speech. *Infant Behavior and Development, 17,* 159–164.

Dechêne, A., Stahl, C., Hansen, J., & Wänke, M. (2010). The truth about the truth: A meta-analytic review of the truth effect. *Personality and Social Psychology Review, 14,* 238–257.

Dechesne, M., Pyszczynski, T., Arndt, J., Ransom, S., Sheldon, K. M., van Knippenberg, A., & Janssen, J. (2003). Literal and symbolic immortality: The effect of evidence of literal immortality on self-esteem striving in response to mortality salience. *Journal of Personality and Social Psychology, 84,* 722–737.

Deci, E. L., Koestner, R., & Ryan, R. M. (1999, November). A meta-analytic review of experiments examining the effects of extrinsic rewards on intrinsic motivation. *Psychological Bulletin, 125,* 627–668.

Deci, E. L., & Ryan, R. M. (2012). Motivation, personality, and development within embedded social contexts: An overview of self-determination theory. In R. M. Ryan (Ed.), *Oxford handbook of human motivation* (pp. 85–107). Oxford University Press.

Deckman, T., DeWall, C. N., Way, B., Gilman, R., & Richman, S. (2014). Can marijuana reduce social pain? *Social Psychological and Personality Science, 5,* 131–139.

Deeley, Q., Daly, E., Surguladze, S., Tunstall, N., Mezey, G., Beer, D., Ambikapathy, A., Robertson, D., Giampietro, V., Brammer, M. J., & Clark, A. (2006). Facial emotion processing in criminal psychopathy. *British Journal of Psychiatry, 189,* 533–539.

Deer, L. K., Shields, G. S., Ivory, S. L., Hostinar, C. E., & Telzer, E. H. (2018). Racial/ethnic disparities in cortisol diurnal patterns and affect in adolescence. *Development and Psychopathology, 30,* 1977–1993.

Dehaene, S. (2014). *Consciousness and the brain: Deciphering how the brain codes our thoughts.* Viking.

Dehne, K. L., & Riedner, G. (2005). *Sexually transmitted infections among adolescents: The need for adequate health services.* World Health Organization.

Dekker, S., Lee, N. C., Howard-Jones, P., & Jolles, J. (2012). Neuromyths in education: Prevalence and predictors of misconceptions among teachers. *Frontiers in Psychology, 3,* 429.

DeLamater, J. (2012). Sexual expression in later life: A review and synthesis. *Journal of Sex Research, 49,* 125–141.

DeLamater, J. D., & Sill, M. (2005). Sexual desire in later life. *Journal of Sex Research, 42,* 138–149.

Delaney, H. D., Miller, W. R., & Bisonó, A. M. (2007). Religiosity and spirituality among psychologists: A survey of clinician members of the American Psychological Association. *Professional Psychology: Research and Practice, 38,* 538–546.

Delaunay-El Allam, M., Soussignan, R., Patris, B., Marlier, L., & Schaal, B. (2010). Long-lasting memory for an odor acquired at the mother's breast. *Developmental Science, 13,* 849–863.

Delgado, J. M. R. (1969). *Physical control of the mind: Toward a psychocivilized society.* Harper & Row.

Delgado, M. M., & Sulloway, F. J. (2017). Attributes of conscientiousness throughout the animal kingdom: An empirical and evolutionary overview. *Psychological Bulletin, 143,* 823–867.

DellaPosta, D. (2018). Gay acquaintanceship and attitudes toward homosexuality: A conservative test. *Socius: Sociological Research for a Dynamic World, 4,* 1–12.

DeLoache, J. S. (1987). Rapid change in the symbolic functioning of very young children. *Science, 238,* 1556–1557.

DeLoache, J. S., Chiong, C., Sherman, K., Islam, N., Vanderborght, M., Troseth, G. L., Strouse, G. A., & O'Doherty, K. (2010). Do babies learn from baby media? *Psychological Science, 21,* 1570–1574.

DelPriore, D. J., Schlomer, G. L., & Ellis, B. J. (2017). Impact of fathers on parental monitoring of daughters and their affiliation with sexually promiscuous peers: A genetically and environmentally controlled sibling study. *Developmental Psychology, 53,* 1330–1343.

DelPriore, D. J., Shakiba, N., Schlomer, G. L., Hill, S. E., & Ellis, B. J. (2019). The effects of fathers on daughters' expectations for men. *Developmental Psychology, 55,* 1523–1536.

Dement, W. C. (1978). *Some must watch while some must sleep.* Norton.

Dement, W. C., & Wolpert, E. A. (1958). The relation of eye movements, body mobility, and external stimuli to dream content. *Journal of Experimental Psychology, 55,* 543–553.

Demertzi A., Tagliazucchi, E., Dehaene, S., Deco, G., Bartfield, P., Raimondo, F., Martial, C., Fernández-Espejo, D., Rohaut, B., Voss, H. U., Schiff, N. D., Owen, A. M., Laureys, S., Naccache, L., & Sitt, J. D. Human consciousness is supported by dynamic complex patterns of brain signal coordination. *Science Advances, 5,* eaat7603.

Dempster, E., Viana, J., Pidsley, R., & Mill, J. (2013). Epigenetic studies of schizophrenia: Progress, predicaments, and promises for the future. *Schizophrenia Bulletin, 39,* 11–16.

Denissen, J. J. A., Bleidorn, W., Hennecke, M., Luhmann, M., Orth, U., Specht, J., & Zimmermann, J. (2018). Uncovering the power of personality to shape income. *Psychological Science, 29,* 3–13.

Deniz, F., Nunez-Elizalde, A. O., Huth, A. G., & Gallant, J. L. (2019). The representation of semantic information across human cerebral cortex during listening versus reading is invariant to stimulus modality. *Journal of Neuroscience, 39,* 7722–7736.

Dennehy, T. C., & Dasgupta, N. (2017). Female peer mentors early in college increase women's positive academic experiences and retention in engineering. *PNAS, 114*, 5964–5969.

Dennett, D. C. (1996, September 9). Quoted by Ian Parker in Richard Dawkins' evolution. *The New Yorker*, pp. 41–45.

Denny, B. T., Inhoff, M. C., Zerubavel, N., Davachi, L., & Ochsner, K. N. (2015). Getting over it: Long-lasting effects of emotion regulation on amygdala response. *Psychological Science, 26*, 1377–1388.

Denton, K., & Krebs, D. (1990). From the scene to the crime: The effect of alcohol and social context on moral judgment. *Journal of Personality and Social Psychology, 59*, 242–248.

Denyer, S., & Gowen, A. (2018, April 18). Too many men. *The Washington Post*. https://www.washingtonpost.com/graphics/2018/world/too-many-men/

DePaulo, B. M., Blank, A. L., Swaim, G. W., & Hairfield, J. G. (1992). Expressiveness and expressive control. *Personality and Social Psychology Bulletin, 18*, 276–285.

Depla, M. F. I. A., ten Have, M. L., van Balkom, A. J. L. M., & de Graaf, R. (2008). Specific fears and phobias in the general population: Results from the Netherlands Mental Health Survey and Incidence Study (NEMESIS). *Social Psychiatry and Psychiatric Epidemiology, 43*, 200–208.

Derebery, M. J., Vermiglio, A., Berliner, K. I., Potthoff, M., & Holguin, K. (2012). Facing the music: Pre- and postconcert assessment of hearing in teenagers. *Otology & Neurotology, 33*, 1136–1141.

Deri, S., Davidai, S., & Gilovich, T. (2017). Home alone: Why people believe others' social lives are richer than their own. *Journal of Personality and Social Psychology, 113*, 858–877.

Dermer, M., Cohen, S. J., Jacobsen, E., & Anderson, E. A. (1979). Evaluative judgments of aspects of life as a function of vicarious exposure to hedonic extremes. *Journal of Personality and Social Psychology, 37*, 247–260.

Desikan, R. S., Cabral, H. J., Hess, C. P., Dillon, W. P., Glastonbury, C. M., Weiner, M. W., & Fischl, B. (2009). Automated MRI measures identify individuals with mild cognitive impairment and Alzheimer's disease. *Brain, 132*, 2048–2057.

Deslauriers, L., McCarthy, L. S., Miller, K., Callaghan, K., & Kestin, G. (2019). Measuring actual learning versus feeling of learning in response to being actively engaged in the classroom. *PNAS, 116*, 19251–19257.

Desmurget, M., Reilly, K. T., Richard, N., Szathmari, A., Mottolese, C., & Sirigu, A. (2009). Movement intention after parietal cortex stimulation in humans. *Science, 324*, 811–813.

DeSteno, D., Dasgupta, N., Bartlett, M. Y., & Cajdric, A. (2004). Prejudice from thin air: The effect of emotion on automatic intergroup attitudes. *Psychological Science, 15*, 319–324.

DeSteno, D., Petty, R. E., Wegener, D. T., & Rucker, D. D. (2000). Beyond valence in the perception of likelihood: The role of emotion specificity. *Journal of Personality and Social Psychology, 78*, 397–416.

Dettman, S. J., Pinder, D., Briggs, R. J. S., Dowell, R. C., & Leigh, J. R. (2007). Communication development in children who receive the cochlear implant younger than 12 months: Risk versus benefits. *Ear and Hearing, 28*(2, Suppl.), 11S–18S.

Deutsch, J. A. (1972, July). Brain reward: ESP and ecstasy. *Psychology Today*, 46–48.

DeValois, R. L., & DeValois, K. K. (1975). Neural coding of color. In E. C. Carterette & M. P. Friedman (Eds.), *Handbook of perception: Vol. 5. Seeing* (pp. 117–166). Academic Press.

Dew, M. A., Hoch, C. C., Buysse, D. J., Monk, T. H., Begley, A. E., Houck, P. R., Hall, M., Kupfer, D. J., & Reynolds, C. F., III. (2003). Healthy older adults' sleep predicts all-cause mortality at 4 to 19 years of follow-up. *Psychosomatic Medicine, 65*, 63–73.

DeWall, C. N., MacDonald, G., Webster, G. D., Masten, C. L., Baumeister, R. F., Powell, C., Combs, D., Schurtz, D. R., Stillman, T. F., Tice, D. M., & Eisenberger, N. I. (2010). Acetaminophen reduces social pain: Behavioral and neural evidence. *Psychological Science, 21*, 931–937.

DeWall, C. N., & Pond, R. S., Jr. (2011). Loneliness and smoking: The costs of the desire to reconnect. *Self and Identity, 10*, 375–385.

DeWall, C. N., Pond, R. S., Jr., Carter, E. C., McCullough, M. E., Lambert, N. M., Fincham, F. D., & Nezlek, J. B. (2014). Explaining the relationship between religiousness and substance use: Self-control matters. *Journal of Personality and Social Psychology, 107*, 339–351.

Dewar, M., Alber, J., Butler, C., Cowan, N., & Sala, S. D. (2012). Brief wakeful resting boosts new memories over the long term. *Psychological Science, 23*, 955–960.

DeYoung, C. G., Allen, T. A. (2019). Personality neuroscience: A developmental perspective. In. D. P. McAdams, Rebecca L. Shiner & Jennifer L. Tackett (Eds.), *Handbook of personality development*. Guilford Press.

Di Carlo, D., Schulte-Cloos, J., & Saudelli, G. (2018, March 3). *Has immigration really led to an increase in crime in Italy?* London School of Economics and Political Science. https://blogs.lse.ac.uk/europpblog/2018/03/03/has-immigration-really-led-to-an-increase-in-crime-in-italy/

di Giacomo, E., Krausz, M., Colmegna, F., Aspesi, F., & Clerici, M. (2018). Estimating the risk of attempted suicide among sexual minority youths: A systematic review and meta-analysis. *JAMA Pediatrics, 172*, 1145–1152.

Di Tella, R., Haisken-De New, J., & MacCulloch, R. (2010). Happiness adaptation to income and to status in an individual panel. *Journal of Economic Behavior & Organization, 76*, 834–852.

Di Tella, R., & MacCulloch, R. (2010). Happiness adaptation to income beyond "basic needs." In E. Diener, J. Helliwell, & D. Kahneman (Eds.), *International differences in well-being* (pp. 217–247). Oxford University Press.

Diaconis, P. (2002, August 11). Quoted by L. Belkin in The odds of that. *The New York Times*. https://www.nytimes.com/2002/08/11/magazine/the-odds-of-that.html

Diaconis, P., & Mosteller, F. (1989). Methods for studying coincidences. *Journal of the American Statistical Association, 84*, 853–861.

Diamond, L. M., Dickenson, J. A., & Blair, K. L. (2017). Stability of sexual attractions across different timescales: The roles of bisexuality and gender. *Archives of Sexual Behavior, 46*, 193–204.

Diamond, M. (2016). Quoted in *My love affair with the brain: The life and science of Dr. Marian Diamond* [Video]. Luna Productions. http://lunaproductions.com/marian-diamond/

Dick, D. M. (2007). Identification of genes influencing a spectrum of externalizing psychopathology. *Current Directions in Psychological Science, 16*, 331–335.

Dickens, L. R. (2017). Using gratitude to promote positive change: A series of meta-analyses investigating the effectiveness of gratitude interventions. *Basic and Applied Social Psychology, 39*, 193–208.

Dickens, W. T., & Flynn, J. R. (2006). Black Americans reduce the racial IQ gap: Evidence from standardization samples. *Psychological Science, 17*, 913–920.

Dicker, D., Murray, C. J. L., & Gakidou, E. (2018). Global, regional, and national age-sex-specific mortality and life expectancy, 1950–2017: A systematic analysis for the Global Burden of Disease Study 2017. *Lancet, 392*, 1684–1735.

Dickerson, S. S., Gable, S. L., Irwin, M. R., Aziz, N., & Kemeny, M. E. (2009). Social-evaluative threat and proinflammatory cytokine regulation: An experimental laboratory investigation. *Psychological Science, 20*, 1237–1243.

Dickerson, S. S., & Kemeny, M. E. (2004). Acute stressors and cortisol responses: A theoretical integration and synthesis of laboratory research. *Psychological Bulletin, 130*, 355–391.

Dickson, B. J. (2005, June 3). Quoted in E. Rosenthal, For fruit flies, gene shift tilts sex orientation. *The New York Times*. https://www.nytimes.com/2005/06/03/science/for-fruit-flies-gene-shift-tilts-sex-orientation.html?

Dickson, N., van Roode, T., Cameron, C., & Paul, C. (2013). Stability and change in same-sex attraction, experience, and identity by sex and age in a New Zealand birth cohort. *Archives of Sexual Behavior, 42*, 753–763.

Diener, E., & Biswas-Diener, R. (2008). *Happiness: Unlocking the mysteries of psychological wealth*. Blackwell.

Diener, E., Biswas-Diener, R., & Personal Happiness Committee. (2019). Well-being interventions to improve societies [PDF file]. In J. Sachs, R. Layard, & J. F. Helliwell (Eds.), *Global happiness policy report 2019*. Global Happiness Council. https://s3.amazonaws.com/ghwbpr-2019/UAE/GH19_Ch6.pdf

Diener, E., Nickerson, C., Lucas, R. E., & Sandvik, E. (2002). Dispositional affect and job outcomes. *Social Indicators Research, 59*, 229–259.

Diener, E., & Oishi, S. (2000). Money and happiness: Income and subjective well-being across nations. In E. Diener & E. M. Suh (Eds.), *Subjective well-being across cultures*. MIT Press.

Diener, E., Oishi, S., & Lucas, R. E. (2003). Personality, culture, and subjective well-being: Emotional and cognitive evaluations of life. *Annual Review of Psychology, 54*, 403–425.

Diener, E., Oishi, S., & Lucas, R. E. (2015). National accounts of subjective well-being. *American Psychologist, 70*, 234–242.

Diener, E., Oishi, S., & Park, J. Y. (2014). An incomplete list of eminent psychologists of the modern era. *Archives of Scientific Psychology, 21*, 20–31.

Diener, E., Pressman, S. D., Hunter, J., & Delgadillo-Chase, D. (2017). If, why, and when subjective well-being influences health, and future needed research. *Applied Psychology: Health and Well-Being, 9*, 133–167.

Diener, E., & Tay, L. (2015). Subjective well-being and human welfare around the world as reflected in the Gallup world poll. *International Journal of Psychology, 50*, 135–149.

Diener, E., Tay, L., & Myers, D. G. (2011). The religion paradox: If religion makes people happy, why are so many dropping out? *Journal of Personality and Social Psychology, 101*, 1278–1290.

Diener, E., Wolsic, B., & Fujita, F. (1995). Physical attractiveness and subjective well-being. *Journal of Personality and Social Psychology, 69*, 120–129.

DiFranza, J. R. (2008). Hooked from the first cigarette. *Scientific American, 298*, 82–87.

Dijksterhuis, A., & Strick, M. (2016). A case for thinking without consciousness. *Perspectives on Psychological Science, 11*, 117–132.

Dik, B. J., & Duffy, R. D. (2012). *Make your job a calling: How the psychology of vocation can change your life at work*. Templeton Press.

Dik, B. J., & Rottinghaus, P. J. (2013). Assessments of interests. In K. F. Geisinger & six others (Eds.), *APA handbook of testing and assessment in psychology*, Vol. 2. American Psychological Association.

DiLalla, D. L., Carey, G., Gottesman, I. I., & Bouchard, T. J., Jr. (1996). Heritability of MMPI personality indicators of psychopathology in twins reared apart. *Journal of Abnormal Psychology, 105*, 491–499.

Dimberg, U., Thunberg, M., & Elmehed, K. (2000). Unconscious facial reactions to emotional facial expressions. *Psychological Science, 11*, 86–89.

Dimitrov, S., Lange, T., Gouttefangeas, C., Jensen, A. T. R., Szczepanski, M., Lehnnolz, J., Soekadar, S., Rammensee, H. G., Born, J., & Besedovsky, L. (2019). Gα$_s$-coupled receptor signaling and sleep regulate integrin activation of human antigen-specific T cells. *Journal of Experimental Medicine, 216*, 517–526.

Dimsdale-Zucker, H. R., Flegal, K. E., Atkins, A. S., & Reuter-Lorenz, P. A. (2019). Serial position-dependent false memory effects. *Memory, 27*, 397–409.

Dindia, K., & Allen, M. (1992). Sex differences in self-disclosure: A meta-analysis. *Psychological Bulletin, 112*, 106–124.

Ding, F., O'Donnell, J., Xu, Q., Kang, N., Goldman, N., & Nedergaard, M. (2016). Changes in the composition of brain interstitial ions control the sleep-wake cycle. *Science, 352*, 550–555.

Dinges, C. W., Varnon, C. A., Cota, L. D., Slykerman, S., & Abramson, C. I. (2017). Studies of learned helplessness in honey bees (*Apis mellifera ligustica*). *Journal of Experimental Psychology: Animal Learning and Cognition, 43*, 147–158.

Dinges, N. G., & Hull, P. (1992). Personality, culture, and international studies. In D. Lieberman (Ed.), *Revealing the world: An interdisciplinary reader for international studies*. Kendall-Hunt.

Dingfelder, S. F. (2010, November). A second chance for the Mexican wolf. *Monitor on Psychology*, pp. 20–21.

Dion, K. K., & Dion, K. L. (1993). Individualistic and collectivistic perspectives on gender and the cultural context of love and intimacy. *Journal of Social Issues, 49*, 53–69.

Dirix, C. E. H., Nijhuis, J. G., Jongsma, H. W., & Hornstra, G. (2009). Aspects of fetal learning and memory. *Child Development, 80*, 1251–1258.

DiSantis, K. I., Birch, L. L., Davey, A., Serrano, E. L., Zhang, J., Bruton, Y., & Fisher, J. O. (2013). Plate size and children's appetite: Effects of larger dishware on self-served portions and intake. *Pediatrics, 131*, e1451–e1458.

Discover. (1996, May). A fistful of risks. pp. 82–83.

Ditre, J. W., Brandon, T. H., Zale, E. L., & Meagher, M. M. (2011). Pain, nicotine, and smoking: Research findings and mechanistic considerations. *Psychological Bulletin, 137*, 1065–1093.

Ditto, P. H., Clark, C. J., Liu, B. S., Wojcik, S. P., Chen, E. E., Grady, R. H., Celniker, J. B., & Zinger, J. F. (2019b). Partisan bias and its discontents. *Perspectives on Psychological Science, 14*, 304–316.

Ditto, P. H., Liu, B. S., Clark, C. J., Wojcik, S. P., Chen, E. E., Grady, R. H., Celniker, J. B., & Zinger, J. F. (2019a). At least bias is bipartisan: A meta-analytic comparison of partisan bias in liberals and conservatives. *Perspectives on Psychological Science, 14*, 273–291.

Dixon, M. L., Thiruchselvam, R., Todd, R., & Christoff, K. (2017). Emotion and the prefrontal cortex: An integrative review. *Psychological Bulletin, 143*, 1033–1081.

Dobbs, D. (2009). The post-traumatic stress trap. *Scientific American, 300*, 64–69.

Dobson, K., Campbell, L., & Stanton, S. C. E. (2018). Are you coming on to me? Bias and accuracy in couples' perceptions of sexual advances. *Journal of Social and Personal Relationships, 35*, 460–484.

Dodge, K. A. (2009). Mechanisms of gene-environment interaction effects in the development of conduct disorder. *Perspectives on Psychological Science, 4*, 408–414.

Dodge, K. A., Bai, Y., Ladd, H. F., & Muschkin, C. G. (2017). Impact of North Carolina's early childhood programs and policies on educational outcomes in elementary school. *Child Development, 88*, 996–1014.

Doherty, C., & Kiley, J. (2016, June 22). *Key facts about partisanship and political animosity in America*. Pew Research. https://www.pewresearch.org/fact-tank/2016/06/22/key-facts-partisanship/

Doherty, E. W., & Doherty, W. J. (1998). Smoke gets in your eyes: Cigarette smoking and divorce in a national sample of American adults. *Families, Systems, and Health, 16*, 393–400.

Dohrenwend, B. P., Levav, I., Shrout, P. E., Schwartz, S., Naveh, G., Link, B. G., Skodol, A., & Stueve, A. (1992). Socioeconomic status and psychiatric disorders: The causation-selection issue. *Science, 255*, 946–952.

Dohrenwend, B. P., Pearlin, L., Clayton, P., Hamburg, B., Dohrenwend, B. S., Riley, M., & Rose, R. (1982). Report on stress and life events. In G. R. Elliott & C. Eisdorfer (Eds.), *Stress and human health: Analysis and implications of research* (A study by the Institute of Medicine/National Academy of Sciences). Springer.

Doidge, N. (2007). *The brain that changes itself*. Viking.

Dolezal, H. (1982). *Living in a world transformed*. Academic Press.

Dolinoy, D. C., Huang, D., Jirtle, R. L. (2007). Maternal nutrient supplementation counteracts bisphenol A-induced DNA hypomethylation in early development. *PNAS, 104*, 13056–13061.

Doliński, D., Grzyb, T., Folwarczny, M., Grzybała, P., Krzyszycha, K., Martynowska, K., & Trojanowski, J. (2017). Would you deliver an electric shock in 2015? Obedience in the experimental paradigm developed by Stanley Milgram in the 50 years following the original studies. *Social Psychological and Personality Science, 8*, 927–933.

Dollfus, S., Lecardeur, L., Morello, R., & Etard, O. (2016). Placebo response in repetitive transcranial magnetic stimulation trials of auditory hallucinations in schizophrenia: A meta-analysis. *Schizophrenia Bulletin, 42*, 301–308.

Domany, Y., Bleich-Cohen, M., Tarrasch, R., Meidan, R., Litvak-Lazar, O., Stoppleman, N., Schreiber, S., Bloch, M., Hendler, T., & Sharon, H. (2019). Repeated oral ketamine for out-patient treatment of resistant depression: Randomised, double-blind, placebo-controlled, proof-of-concept study. *The British Journal of Psychiatry, 214*, 20–26.

Domhoff, G. W. (1996). *Finding meaning in dreams: A quantitative approach*. Plenum.

Domhoff, G. W. (2003). *The scientific study of dreams: Neural networks, cognitive development, and content analysis*. APA Books.

Domhoff, G. W. (2007). Realistic simulations and bizarreness in dream content: Past findings and suggestions for future research. In D. Barrett & P. McNamara (Eds.), *The new science of dreaming: Content, recall, and personality characteristics*. Praeger.

Domhoff, G. W. (2010). *The case for a cognitive theory of dreams* [Unpublished manuscript]. University of California at Santa Cruz. https://dreams.ucsc.edu/Library/domhoff_2010a.html

Domhoff, G. W. (2011). The neural substrate for dreaming: Is it a subsystem of the default network? *Consciousness and Cognition, 20*, 1163–1174.

Domhoff, G. W. (2014, January 5). Personal communication.

Domingue, B. W., Belsky, D. W., Fletcher, J. M., Conley, D., Boardman, J. D., & Harris, K. M. (2018). The social genome of friends and schoolmates in the National Longitudinal Study of Adolescent to Adult Health. *PNAS, 115*, 702–707.

Dominus, S. (2015, July 9). The mixed-up brothers of Bogotá. *The New York Times Magazine*. https://www.nytimes.com/interactive/2015/07/09/magazine/twins-promo.html?

Domjan, M. (1992). Adult learning and mate choice: Possibilities and experimental evidence. *American Zoologist, 32*, 48–61.

Domjan, M. (1994). Formulation of a behavior system for sexual conditioning. *Psychonomic Bulletin & Review, 1*, 421–428.

Domjan, M. (2005). Pavlovian conditioning: A functional perspective. *Annual Review of Psychology, 56*, 179–206.

Donahue, C. J., Glasser, M. F., Preuss, T. M., Rilling, J. K., & Van Essen, D. C. (2018). Quantitative assessment of prefrontal cortex in humans relative to nonhuman primates. *PNAS, 115*, E5183–E5192.

Donald, J. N., Sahdra, B. K., Van Zanden, B., Duineveld, J. J., Atkins, P. W., Marshall, S. L., & Ciarrochi, J. (2018). Does your mindfulness benefit others? A systematic review and meta analysis of the link between mindfulness and prosocial behaviour. *British Journal of Psychology, 110*, 101–125.

Dong, X., Talhelm, T., & Ren, X. (2019). Teens in Rice County are more interdependent and think more holistically than nearby Wheat County. *Social Psychological and Personality Science, 10*, 966–976.

Donnellan, M. B., Trzesniewski, K. H., Robins, R. W., Moffitt, T. E., & Caspi, A. (2005). Low self-esteem is related to aggression, antisocial behavior, and delinquency. *Psychological Science, 16*, 328–335.

Donnelly, G. E., Ksendzova, M., Howell, R. T., Vohs, K. D., & Baumeister, R. F. (2016). Buying to blunt negative feelings: Materialistic escape from the self. *Review of General Psychology, 20*, 272–316.

Donnelly, G. E., Zheng, T., Haisley, E., & Norton, M. I. (2018). The amount and source of millionaires' wealth (moderately) predict their happiness. *Personality and Social Psychology Bulletin, 44*, 684–699.

Dorfman, P., Javidan, M., Hanges, P., Dastmalchian, A., & House, R. (2012). GLOBE: A twenty-year journey into the intriguing world of culture and leadership. *Journal of World Business, 47*, 504–518.

Doss, B. D., Rhoades, G. K., Stanley, S. M., & Markman, H. J. (2009). The effect of the transition to parenthood on relationship quality: An 8-year prospective study. *Journal of Personality and Social Psychology, 96*, 601–619.

Dotan-Eliaz, O., Sommer, K. L., & Rubin, S. (2009). Multilingual groups: Effects of linguistic ostracism on felt rejection and anger, coworker attraction, perceived team potency, and creative performance. *Basic and Applied Social Psychology, 31*, 363–375.

Dotterer, H. L., Hyde, L. W., Swartz, J. R., Hariri, A. R., & Williamson, D. E. (2017). Amygdala reactivity predicts adolescent antisocial behavior but not callous-unemotional traits. *Developmental Cognitive Neuroscience, 24*, 84–92.

Doty, R. L. (2001). Olfaction. *Annual Review of Psychology, 52*, 423–452.

Dougherty, M. R., Slevc, L. R., & Grand, J. A. (2018). Making research evaluation more transparent: Aligning research philosophy, institutional values, and reporting. *Perspectives on Psychological Science, 14*(3), 361–375.

Douglas, K. S., Guy, L. S., & Hart, S. D. (2009). Psychosis as a risk factor for violence to others: A meta-analysis. *Psychological Bulletin, 135*, 679–706.

Dovidio, J. F., & Gaertner, S. L. (1999). Reducing prejudice: Combating intergroup biases. *Current Directions in Psychological Science, 8*, 101–105.

Downing, P. E., Jiang, Y., & Shuman, M. (2001). A cortical area selective for visual processing of the human body. *Science, 293,* 2470–2473.

Downs, E., & Smith, S. L. (2010). Keeping abreast of hypersexuality: A video game character content analysis. *Sex Roles, 62,* 721–733.

Doyle, R. (2005, March). Gay and lesbian census. *Scientific American,* p. 28.

Doyle, R. A., & Voyer, R. A. (2016). Stereotype manipulation effects on math and spatial test performance: A meta-analysis. *Learning and Individual Differences, 47,* 103–116.

Draganski, B., Gaser, C., Busch, V., Schuierer, G., Bogdahn, U., & May, A. (2004). Neuroplasticity: Changes in grey matter induced by training. *Nature, 427,* 311–312.

Draguns, J. G. (1990). Applications of cross-cultural psychology in the field of mental health. In R. W. Brislin (Ed.), *Applied cross-cultural psychology* (pp. 302–324). Sage.

Drake, R. A., & Myers, L. R. (2006). Visual attention, emotion, and action tendency: Feeling active or passive. *Cognition and Emotion, 20,* 608–622.

Dreger, A. (2011, February 28). Do gay men have more sexual interest in children than straight men do? *Psychology Today.* Retrieved from https://www.psychologytoday.com/us/blog/fetishes-i-dont-get/201102/do-gay-men-have-more-sexual-interest-in-children

Drescher, A., & Schultheiss, O. C. (2016). Meta-analytic evidence for higher implicit affiliation and intimacy motivation scores in women, compared to men. *Journal of Research in Personality, 64,* 1–10.

Drew, T., Võ, M. L.-H., & Wolfe, J. M. (2013). Sustained inattentional blindness in expert observers. *Psychological Science, 24,* 1848–1853.

Drewelies, J., Wagner, J., Tesch-Römer, C., Heckhausen, J., & Gerstorf, D. (2017). Perceived control across the second half of life: The role of physical health and social integration. *Psychology and Aging, 32,* 76–92.

Driessen, E., Cuijpers, P., de Maat, S. C. M., Abbas, A. A., de Jonghe, F., & Dekker, J. J. M. (2010). The efficacy of short-term psychodynamic psychotherapy for depression: A meta-analysis. *Clinical Psychology Review, 30,* 25–36.

Driessen, E., Hollon, S. D., Bockting, C. L. H., Cuijpers, P., & Turner, E. H. (2015, September 30). Does publican bias inflate the apparent efficacy of psychological treatment for major depressive disorder? A systematic review and meta-analysis of U.S. National Institutes of Health-funded trials. *PLOS ONE, 10,* e0137864.

Driessen, E., Van, H. L., Peen, J., Don, F. J., Twisk, J. W. R., Cuijpers, P., & Dekker, J. J. M. (2017). Cognitive-behavioral versus psychodynamic therapy for major depression: Secondary outcomes of a randomized clinical trial. *Journal of Consulting and Clinical Psychology, 85,* 653–663.

Druckman, D., & Bjork, R. A. (1991). *In the mind's eye: Enhancing human performance.* National Academy Press.

Druckman, J. N., & McGrath, M. C. (2019). The evidence for motivated reasoning in climate change preference formation. *Nature Climate Change, 9,* 111–119.

Drydakis, N. (2009). Sexual orientation discrimination in the labour market. *Labour Economics, 16,* 364–372.

Drydakis, N. (2015). Sexual orientation discrimination in the United Kingdom's labour market: A field experiment. *Human Relations, 68,* 1769–1796.

Dubé, S., Lavoie, F., Blais, M., & Hébert, M. (2017). Consequences of casual sex relationships and experiences on adolescents' psychological well-being: A prospective study. *Journal of Sex Research, 54,* 1006–1017.

Ducasse, D., Loas, G., Dassa, D., Gramaglia, C., Zeppegno, P., Guillaume, S., Olié, E., & Courtet, P. (2018). Anhedonia is associated with suicidal ideation independently of depression: A meta-analysis. *Depression and Anxiety, 35,* 382–392.

Duckworth, A. (2016). *Grit: The power of passion and perseverance.* Scribner.

Duckworth, A. L., Gendler, T. S., & Gross, J. J. (2016). Situational strategies for self-control. *Perspectives on Psychological Science, 11,* 35–55.

Duckworth, A. L., Quinn, P. D., Lynam, D. R., Loeber, R., & Stouthamer-Loeber, M. (2011). Role of test motivation in intelligence testing. *PNAS, 108,* 7716–7720.

Duckworth, A. L., & Seligman, M. E. P. (2005). Discipline outdoes talent: Self-discipline predicts academic performance in adolescents. *Psychological Science, 12,* 939–944.

Duckworth, A. L., & Seligman, M. E. P. (2017). The science and practice of self-control. *Perspectives on Psychological Science, 12,* 715–718.

Duckworth, A. L., Tsukayama, E., & Kirby, T. A. (2013). Is it really self-control? Examining the predictive power of the delay of gratification task. *Personality and Social Psychology Bulletin, 39,* 843–855.

Duclos, S. E., Laird, J. D., Sexter, M., Stern, L., & Van Lighten, O. (1989). Emotion-specific effects of facial expressions and postures on emotional experience. *Journal of Personality and Social Psychology, 57,* 100–108.

Duffy, M. E., Twenge, J. M., & Joiner, T. E. (2019). Trends in mood and anxiety symptoms and suicide-related outcomes among U.S. undergraduates, 2007–2018: Evidence from two national surveys. *Journal of Adolescent Health, 65,* 590–598.

Dufner, M., Gebauer, J. E., Sedikides, C., & Denissen, J. J. A. (2019). Self-enhancement and psychological adjustment: A meta-analytic review. *Personality and Social Psychology Review, 23,* 48–72.

Dugatkin, L. A., & Trut, L. (2017). How to take a fox and build a dog. *American Scientist, 105,* 240–247.

Duggan, J. P., & Booth, D. A. (1986). Obesity, overeating, and rapid gastric emptying in rats with ventromedial hypothalamic lesions. *Science, 231,* 609–611.

Duits, P., Cath, D. C., Lissek, S., Hox, J. J., Hamm, A. O., Engelhard, I. M., Van Den Hout, M.A., & Baas, J. M. P. (2015). Updated meta-analysis of classical fear conditioning in the anxiety disorders. *Depression and Anxiety, 32,* 239–253.

Dumont, K. A., Widom, C. S., & Czaja, S. J. (2007). Predictors of resilience in abused and neglected children grown-up: The role of individual and neighborhood characteristics. *Child Abuse & Neglect, 31,* 255–274.

Dunbar, R. I. M., Baron, R., Frangou, A., Pearce, E., van Leeuwin, E. J. C., Stow, J., Partridge, G., MacDonald, I., Barra, V., & van Vugt, M. (2011). Social laughter is correlated with an elevated pain threshold. *Proceedings of the Royal Society B, 279,* 1161–1167.

Duncan, L., Yilmaz, Z., Gaspar, H., Walters, R., Goldstein, J., Anttila, V., Bulik-Sullivan, B., Ripke, S., Eating Disorders Working Group of the Psychiatric Genomics Consortium, Thornton, L., Hinney, A., Daly, M., Sullivan, P. F., Zeggini, E., Breen, G., & Bulik, C. M. (2017). Significant locus and metabolic genetic correlations revealed in genome-wide association study of anorexia nervosa. *The American Journal of Psychiatry, 174,* 850–858.

Dunlop, W. L., & Tracy, J. L. (2013). Sobering stories: Narratives of self-redemption predict behavioral change and improved health among recovering alcoholics. *Journal of Personality and Social Psychology, 104,* 576–590.

Dunn, A. (2018, October 4). *Partisans are divided over the fairness of the U.S. economy—and why people are rich or poor.* Pew Research Center. https://pewrsr.ch/39o8yIL

Dunn, E., & Norton, M. (2013). *Happy money: The science of smarter spending.* Simon & Schuster.

Dunn, E. W., Aknin, L. B., & Norton, M. I. (2008). Spending money on others promotes happiness. *Science, 319,* 1687–1688.

Dunn, M., & Searle, R. (2010). Effect of manipulated prestige-car ownership on both sex attractiveness ratings. *British Journal of Psychology, 101,* 69–80.

Dunn, M. J., & Hill, A. (2014). Manipulated luxury-apartment ownership enhances opposite-sex attraction in females but not males. *Journal of Evolutionary Psychology, 12,* 1–17.

Dunning, D. (2006). Strangers to ourselves? *The Psychologist, 19,* 600–603.

Dunning, D. (2019, January 31). *An expert on human blind spots gives advice on how to think* [Interview with Brian Resnick]. Vox. https://lsa.umich.edu/psych/news-events/all-news/faculty-news/an-expert-on-human-blind-spots-gives-advice-on-how-to-think.html

Dunsmoor, J. E., Murty, V. P., Davachi, L., & Phelps, E. A. (2015). Emotional learning selectively and retroactively strengthens memories for related events. *Nature, 520,* 345–348.

Dunson, D. B., Colombo, B., & Baird, D. D. (2002). Changes with age in the level and duration of fertility in the menstrual cycle. *Human Reproduction, 17,* 1399–1403.

Dunster, G. P., de la Iglesia, L., Ben-Hamo, M., Nave, C., Fleischer, J. G., Panda, S., & Horacio, O. (2018). Sleepmore in Seattle: Later school start times are associated with more sleep and better performance in high school students. *Science Advances, 4*(12), eaau6200.

Dunster-Page, C., Haddock, G., Wainwright, L., & Berry, K. (2017). The relationship between therapeutic alliance and patient's suicidal thoughts, self-harming behaviours and suicide attempts: A systematic review. *Journal of Affective Disorders, 223,* 165–174.

Dutton, D. G., & Aron, A. P. (1974). Some evidence for heightened sexual attraction under conditions of high anxiety. *Journal of Personality and Social Psychology, 30,* 510–517.

Dutton, D. G., & Aron, A. P. (1989). Romantic attraction and generalized liking for others who are sources of conflict-based arousal. *Canadian Journal of Behavioural Sciences, 21,* 246–257.

Dutton, E., Bakhiet, S. F. A., Osman, H. A., Becker, D., Essa, Y. A. S., Blahmar, T. A. M., Lynn, R., & Hakami, S. M. (2018). A Flynn effect in Khartoum, the Sudanese capital, 2004–2016. *Intelligence, 68,* 82–86.

Dutton, J. (2018, April). 'She's afflicted by these memories. . . they flood her.' *The Psychologist,* pp. 28–30.

Dweck, C. (2018, August 20). Growth mindset interventions yield impressive results. *Character & Context.* http://www.spsp.org/news-center/blog/growth-mindset-interventions-results

Dweck, C. S. (2006). *Mindset: The new psychology of success.* Random House.

Dweck, C. S., & Yeager, D. S. (2019). Mindsets: A view from two eras. *Perspectives on Psychological Science, 14,* 481–496.

Dygalo, N. N., & Shishkina, G. T. (2019). Optogenetic studies of the pathophysiological mechanisms and treatment of depression. *Neuroscience and Behavioral Physiology, 49,* 178–183.

Dyrdal, G. M., & Lucas, R. E. (2011). *Reaction and adaptation to the birth of a child: A couple level analysis* [Unpublished manuscript]. Michigan State University.

Eagan, K., Stolzenberg, E. B., Bates, A. K., Aragon, M. C. Suchard, M. R., & Rios-Aguilar, C. R. (2016). *The American freshman: National norms 2015.* Higher Education Research Institute, UCLA.

Eagleman, D. (2011, September). Secret life of the mind. *Discover,* pp. 50–53.

Eagly, A. H., Ashmore, R. D., Makhijani, M. G., & Kennedy, L. C. (1991). What is beautiful is good, but . . .: A meta-analytic review of research on the physical attractiveness stereotype. *Psychological Bulletin, 110,* 109–128.

Eagly, A. H., & Carli, L. (2007). *Through the labyrinth: The truth about how women become leaders.* Harvard University Press.

Eagly, A. H., & Wood, W. (1999). The origins of sex differences in human behavior: Evolved dispositions versus social roles. *American Psychologist, 54,* 408–423.

Eagly, A. H., & Wood, W. (2013). The nature-nurture debates: 25 years of challenges in understanding the psychology of gender. *Perspectives on Psychological Science, 8,* 340–357.

Eastman, C. L., Boulos, Z., Terman, M., Campbell, S. S., Dijk, D.-J., & Lewy, A. J. (1995). Light treatment for sleep disorders: Consensus report. VI. Shift work. *Journal of Biological Rhythms, 10,* 157–164.

Eastwick, P. W., & Finkel, E. J. (2008a). Speed-dating as a methodological innovation. *The Psychologist, 21,* 402–403.

Eastwick, P. W., & Finkel, E. J. (2008b). Sex differences in mate preferences revisited: Do people know what they initially desire in a romantic partner? *Journal of Personality and Social Psychology, 94,* 245–264.

Eastwick, P. W., Luchies, L. B., Finkel, E. J., & Hunt, L. L. (2014a). The many voices of Darwin's descendants: Reply to Schmitt (2014). *Psychological Bulletin, 140,* 673–681.

Eastwick, P. W., Luchies, L. B., Finkel, E. J., & Hunt, L. L. (2014b). The predictive validity of ideal partner preferences: A review and meta-analysis. *Psychological Bulletin, 140,* 623–665.

Ebbinghaus, H. (1885/1964). *Memory: A contribution to experimental psychology* (H. A. Ruger & C. E. Bussenius, Trans.). Dover.

Eberhardt, J. L. (2005). Imaging race. *American Psychologist, 60,* 181–190.

Ebert, D. D., Van Daele, T., Nordgreen, T., Karekla, M., Compare, A., Zarbo, C., Brugnera, A., Øverland, S., Trebbi, G., Jensen, K. L., Kaehlke, F., Baumeister, H., & Taylor, J. (2018). Internet- and mobile-based psychological interventions: Applications, efficacy, and potential for improving mental health: A report of the EFPA E-health taskforce. *European Psychologist, 23,* 167–187.

Eccles, J. S., Jacobs, J. E., & Harold, R. D. (1990). Gender role stereotypes, expectancy effects, and parents' socialization of gender differences. *Journal of Social Issues, 46,* 183–201.

Eckensberger, L. H. (1994). Moral development and its measurement across cultures. In W. J. Lonner & R. Malpass (Eds.), *Psychology and culture* (pp. 71–78). Allyn & Bacon.

Eckert, E. D., Heston, L. L., & Bouchard, T. J., Jr. (1981). MZ twins reared apart: Preliminary findings of psychiatric disturbances and traits. In L. Gedda, P. Paris, & W. D. Nance (Eds.), *Twin research: Intelligence, personality, and development* (Vol. 3. Pt. B.). Alan Liss.

Eckholm, E. (2010, September 21). Woman on death row runs out of appeals. *The New York Times* (nytimes.com).

Ecklund-Flores, L. (1992). *The infant as a model for the teaching of introductory psychology* [Paper]. Presented at the American Psychological Association annual convention.

Eckshtain, D., Kuppens, S., Ugueto, A., Ng, M. Y., Vaughn-Coaxum, R., Corteselli, K., & Weisz, J. R. (2019). Meta-analysis: 13-year follow-up of psychotherapy effects on youth depression. *Journal of the American Academy of Child & Adolescent Psychiatry, 59,* 45–63.

Economist. (2001, December 20). An anthropology of happiness. *The Economist.* https://www.economist .com/christmas-specials/2001/12/20/an-anthropology-of-happiness

Eddy, K. T., Tabri, N., Thomas, J. J., Murray, H. B., Keshaviah, A., Hastings, E., Edkins, K., Krishna, M., Herzog, D. B., Keel, P. K., & Franko, D. L. (2017). Recovery from anorexia nervosa and bulimia nervosa at 22-year follow-up. *Journal of Clinical Psychiatry, 78,* 184–189.

Edelman, B., Luca, M., & Svirsky, D. (2017). Racial discrimination in the sharing economy: Evidence from a field experiment. *American Economic Journal: Applied Economics, 9,* 1–22.

Edsinger, E., & Dölen, G. (2018). A conserved role for serotonergic neurotransmission in mediating social behavior in octopus. *Current Biology, 28,* 3136–3142.

Edwards, A. C., & Kendler, K. S. (2012). A twin study of depression and nicotine dependence: Shared liability or causal relationship? *Journal of Affective Disorders, 142,* 90–97.

Edwards, F., Lee, H., & Esposito, M. (2019). Risk of being killed by police use of force in the United States by age, race–ethnicity, and sex. *PNAS, 116,* 16793–16798.

Edwards, L. A. (2014). A meta-analysis of imitation abilities in individuals with autism spectrum disorders. *Autism Research, 7,* 363–380.

Edwards, R. R., Campbell, C., Jamison, R. N., & Wiech, K. (2009). The neurobiological underpinnings of coping with pain. *Current Directions in Psychological Science, 18,* 237–241.

Egan, P. J., & Mullin, M. (2012). Turning personal experience into political attitudes: The effects of local weather on Americans' perceptions about global warming. *Journal of Politics, 74,* 796–809.

Ehrlinger, J., Burnette, J. L., Park, J., Harrold, M. L., & Orvidas, K. (2017). Incremental theories of weight and healthy eating behavior. *Journal of Applied Social Psychology, 47,* 320–330.

Eibl-Eibesfeldt, I. (1971). *Love and hate: The natural history of behavior patterns.* Holt, Rinehart & Winston.

Eich, E. (1990). Learning during sleep. In R. B. Bootzin, J. F. Kihlstrom, & D. L. Schacter (Eds.), *Sleep and cognition.* American Psychological Association.

Eichstaedt, J. C., Schwartz, H. A., Kern, M. L., Park, G., Labarthe, D. R., Merchant, R. M., Jha, S., Agrawal, M., Dziurzynski, L. A., Sap, M., Weeg, C., Larson, E. E., Ungar, L. H., & Seligman, M. E. P. (2015). Psychological language on Twitter predicts county-level heart disease mortality. *Psychological Science, 26,* 159–169.

Ein-Dor, T., & Perry, A. (2012). Scared saviors: Evidence that people high in attachment anxiety are more effective in alerting others to threat. *European Journal of Social Psychology, 42,* 667–671.

Ein-Dor, T., & Perry, A. (2013, April). Full house of fears: Evidence that people high in attachment anxiety are more accurate in detecting deceit. *Journal of Personality, 82,* 83–92.

Einstein, G. O., & McDaniel, M. A. (1990). Normal aging and prospective memory. *Journal of Experimental Psychology: Learning, Memory, and Cognition, 16,* 717–726.

Einstein, G. O., McDaniel, M. A., Richardson, S. L., Guynn, M. J., & Cunfer, A. R. (1995). Aging and prospective memory: Examining the influences of self-initiated retrieval processes. *Journal of Experimental*

Psychology: Learning, Memory, and Cognition, 21, 996–1007.

Einstein, G. O., McDaniel, M. A., Smith, R. E., & Shaw, P. (1998). Habitual prospective memory and aging: Remembering intentions and forgetting actions. *Psychological Science, 9,* 284–288.

Eippert, F., Finsterbush, J., Bingel, U., & Büchel, C. (2009). Direct evidence for spinal cord involvement in placebo analgesia. *Science, 326,* 404.

Eisenberg, N., & Lennon, R. (1983). Sex differences in empathy and related capacities. *Psychological Bulletin, 94,* 100–131.

Eisenberger, N. I., Master, S. L., Inagaki, T. K., Taylor, S. E., Shirinyan, D., Lieberman, M. D., & Naliboff, B. D. (2011). Attachment figures activate a safety signal-related neural region and reduce pain experience. *PNAS, 108,* 11721–11726.

Eisenberger, R., & Aselage, J. (2009). Incremental effects of reward on experienced performance pressure: Positive outcomes for intrinsic interest and creativity. *Journal of Organizational Behavior, 30,* 95–117.

Eisenberger, R., Rockstuhl, T., Shoss, M. K., Wen, X., & Dulebohn, J. (2019). Is the employee–organization relationship dying or thriving? A temporal meta-analysis. *Journal of Applied Psychology, 104,* 1036–1057.

Ekman, P. (2016). What scientists who study emotion agree about. *Perspectives on Psychological Science, 11,* 31–34.

Ekman, P., & Friesen, W. V. (1971). Constants across cultures in the face and emotion. *Journal of Personality and Social Psychology, 17,* 124–129.

Ekman, P., & Friesen, W. V. (1975). *Unmasking the face.* Prentice-Hall.

Elbert, T., Pantev, C., Wienbruch, C., Rockstroh, B., & Taub, E. (1995). Increased cortical representation of the fingers of the left hand in string players. *Science, 270,* 305–307.

Elbogen, E. B., Dennis, P. A., & Johnson, S. C. (2016). Beyond mental illness: Targeting stronger and more direct pathways to violence. *Clinical Psychological Science, 4,* 747–759.

Eldar, E., Bae, G. J., Kurth-Nelson, Z., Dayan, P., & Dolan, R. J. (2018). Magnetoencephalography decoding reveals structural differences within integrative decision processes. *Nature Human Behaviour, 2,* 670–681.

Elenbaas, L. (2019). Against unfairness: Young children's judgments about merit, equity, and equality. *Journal of Experimental Child Psychology, 186,* 73–82.

Elfenbein, H. A., & Ambady, N. (2002). On the universality and cultural specificity of emotion recognition: A meta-analysis. *Psychological Bulletin, 128,* 203–235.

Elias, S., Lozano, J., & Bentley, J. (2016). *How executive functioning, anxiety, and technology use impact university students' course performance* [Paper]. Presented at the Western Psychological Association Convention.

Elkind, D. (1970). The origins of religion in the child. *Review of Religious Research, 12,* 35–42.

Elkins, G., Johnson, A., & Fisher, W. (2012). Cognitive hypnotherapy for pain management. *American Journal of Clinical Hypnosis, 54,* 294–310.

Ellenbogen, J. M., Hu, P. T., Payne, J. D., Titone, D., & Walker, M. P. (2007). Human relational memory requires time and sleep. *PNAS, 104,* 7723–7728.

Ellis, A., & Becker, I. M. (1982). *A guide to personal happiness.* Wilshire.

Ellis, B. J., Bates, J. E., Dodge, K. A., Fergusson, D. M., John, H. L., Pettit, G. S., & Woodward, L. (2003). Does father absence place daughters at special risk for early sexual activity and teenage pregnancy? *Child Development, 74,* 801–821.

Ellis, B. J., Bianchi, J., Griskevicius, V., & Frankenhuis, W. E. (2017). Beyond risk and protective factors: An adaptation-based approach to resilience. *Perspectives on Psychological Science, 12*, 561–587.

Ellis, B. J., & Boyce, W. T. (2008). Biological sensitivity to context. *Current Directions in Psychological Science, 17*, 183–187.

Ellis, B. J., Schlomer, G. L., Tilley, E. H., & Butler, E. A. (2012). Impact of fathers on risky sexual behavior in daughters: A genetically and environmentally controlled sibling study. *Development and Psychopathology, 24*, 317–332.

Ellis, L., & Ames, M. A. (1987). Neurohormonal functioning and sexual orientation: A theory of homosexuality-heterosexuality. *Psychological Bulletin, 101*, 233–258.

Ellison, K. (2015, November 9). A.D.H.D. rates rise around globe, but sympathy often lags. *The New York Times.* https://well.blogs.nytimes.com/2015/11/09/a-d-h-d-rates-rise-around-globe-but-sympathy-often-lags/?

Ellison-Wright, I., Glahn, D. C., Laird, A. R., Thelen, S. M., & Bullmore, E. (2008). The anatomy of first-episode and chronic schizophrenia: An anatomical likelihood estimation meta-analysis. *American Journal of Psychiatry, 165*, 1015–1023.

Else-Quest, N. M., Hyde, J. S., & Linn, M. C. (2010). Cross-national patterns of gender differences in mathematics: A meta-analysis. *Psychological Bulletin, 136*, 103–127.

Elsey, J. W. B., Van Ast, V. A., & Kindt, M. (2018). Human memory reconsolidation: A guiding framework and critical review of the evidence. *Psychological Bulletin, 144*, 797–848.

Elson, M., Ferguson, C. J., Gregerson, M., Hogg, J. L., Ivory, J., Klisanin, D., Markey, P. M., Nichols, D., Siddiqui, S., & Wilson, J. (2019). Do policy statements on media effects faithfully represent the science? *Advances in Methods and Practices in Psychological Science, 2*, 12–25.

Elzinga, B. M., Ardon, A. M., Heijnis, M. K., De Ruiter, M. B., Van Dyck, R., & Veltman, D. J. (2007). Neural correlates of enhanced working-memory performance in dissociative disorder: A functional MRI study. *Psychological Medicine, 37*, 235–245.

Emmons, S., Geisler, C., Kaplan, K. J., & Harrow, M. (1997). *Living with schizophrenia.* Taylor and Francis.

Empson, J. A. C., & Clarke, P. R. F. (1970). Rapid eye movements and remembering. *Nature, 227*, 287–288.

Enache, D., Pariante, C., & Mondelli, V. (2019). Markers of central inflammation in major depressive disorder: A systematic review and meta-analysis of studies examining cerebrospinal fluid, positron emission tomography and post-mortem brain tissue. *Brain, Behavior, and Immunity, 81*, 24–40.

Endendijk, J. J., Beltz, A. M., McHale, S. M., Bryk, K., & Berenbaum, S. A. (2016). Linking prenatal androgens to gender-related attitudes, identity, and activities: Evidence from girls with congenital adrenal hyperplasia. *Archives of Sexual Behavior, 45*, 1807–1815.

Endler, N. S. (1982). *Holiday of darkness: A psychologist's personal journey out of his depression.* Wiley.

Engeler, I., & Raghubir, P. (2018). Decomposing the cross-sex misprediction bias of dating behaviors: Do men overestimate or women underreport their sexual intentions? *Journal of Personality and Social Psychology, 114*, 95–109.

Engen, T. (1987). Remembering odors and their names. *American Scientist, 75*, 497–503.

Engle, R. W. (2002). Working memory capacity as executive attention. *Current Directions in Psychological Science, 11*, 19–23.

English, T., Davis, J., Wei, M., & Gross, J. J. (2017). Homesickness and adjustment across the first year of college: A longitudinal study. *Emotion, 17*, 1–5.

Epel, E. S. (2009). Telomeres in a life-span perspective: A new "psychobiomarker"? *Current Directions in Psychological Science, 18*, 6–9.

Epel, E. S., Blackburn, E. H., Lin, J., Dhabhar, F. S., Adler, N. E., Morrow, J. D., & Cawthon, R. M. (2004). Accelerated telomere shortening in response to life stress. *PNAS, 101*, 17312–17315.

Epley, N., Keysar, B., Van Boven, L., & Gilovich, T. (2004). Perspective taking as egocentric anchoring and adjustment. *Journal of Personality and Social Psychology, 87*, 327–339.

Epley, N., Savitsky, K., & Gilovich, T. (2002). Empathy neglect: Reconciling the spotlight effect and the correspondence bias. *Journal of Personality and Social Psychology, 83*, 300–312.

Epstein, J., Stern, E., & Silbersweig, D. (1998). Mesolimbic activity associated with psychosis in schizophrenia: Symptom-specific PET studies. In J. F. McGinty (Ed.), *Advancing from the ventral striatum to the extended amygdala: Implications for neuropsychiatry and drug use: In honor of Lennart Heimer. Annals of the New York Academy of Sciences, 877*, 562–574.

Epstein, S. (1983a). Aggregation and beyond: Some basic issues on the prediction of behavior. *Journal of Personality, 51*, 360–392.

Epstein, S. (1983b). The stability of behavior across time and situations. In R. Zucker, J. Aronoff, & A. I. Rabin (Eds.), *Personality and the prediction of behavior.* Academic Press.

Eranti, S. V., MacCabe, J. H., Bundy, H., & Murray, R. M. (2013). Gender difference in age at onset of schizophrenia: A meta-analysis. *Psychological Medicine, 43*, 155–167.

Erdelyi, M. H. (1985). *Psychoanalysis: Freud's cognitive psychology.* Freeman.

Erdelyi, M. H. (1988). Repression, reconstruction, and defense: History and integration of the psychoanalytic and experimental frameworks. In J. Singer (Ed.), *Repression: Defense mechanism and cognitive style.* University of Chicago Press.

Erdelyi, M. H. (2006). The unified theory of repression. *Behavioral and Brain Sciences, 29*, 499–551.

Erel, O., & Burman, B. (1995). Interrelatedness of marital relations and parent–child relations: A meta-analytic review. *Psychological Bulletin, 118*, 108–132.

Erickson, K. I., Raji, C. A., Lopez, O. L., Becker, J. T., Rosano, C., Newman, A. B., Gach, H. M., Thompson, P. M., Ho, A. J., & Kuller, L. H. (2010). Physical activity predicts gray matter volume in late adulthood: The Cardiovascular Health Study. *Neurology, 75*, 1415–1422.

Erickson, M. F., & Aird, E. G. (2005). *The motherhood study: Fresh insights on mothers' attitudes and concerns.* The Motherhood Project, Institute for American Values.

Ericsson, K. A. (2001). Attaining excellence through deliberate practice: Insights from the study of expert performance. In M. Ferrari (Ed.), *The pursuit of excellence in education.* Erlbaum.

Ericsson, K. A. (2006). The influence of experience and deliberate practice on the development of superior expert performance. In K. A. Ericsson, N. Charness, P. J. Feltovich, & R. R. Hoffman (Eds.), *The Cambridge handbook of expertise and expert performance.* Cambridge University Press.

Ericsson, K. A. (2007). Deliberate practice and the modifiability of body and mind: Toward a science of the structure and acquisition of expert and elite performance. *International Journal of Sport Psychology, 38*, 4–34.

Ericsson, K. A., Cheng, X., Pan, Y., Ku, Y., Ge, Y., & Hu, Y. (2017). Memory skills mediating superior memory in a world-class memorist. *Memory, 25*, 1294–1302.

Ericsson, K. A., & Pool, R. (2016). *PEAK: Secrets from the New Science of Expertise.* Houghton Mifflin.

Ericsson, K. A., Roring, R. W., & Nandagopal, K. (2007). Giftedness and evidence for reproducibly superior performance: An account based on the expert performance framework. *High Ability Studies, 18*, 3–56.

Erikson, E. H. (1963). *Childhood and society.* Norton.

Erikson, E. H. (1983, June). A conversation with Erikson (by E. Hall). *Psychology Today,* pp. 22–30.

Erlandsson, A., Nilsson, A., Tinghög, G., & Västfjäll, D. (2018). Bullshit-sensitivity predicts prosocial behavior. *PLOS ONE, 13*, e0201474.

Erlich, N., Lipp, O. V., & Slaughter, V. (2013). Of hissing snakes and angry voices: Human infants are differentially responsive to evolutionary fear-relevant sounds. *Developmental Science, 16*, 894–904.

Ermer, E., Cope, L. M., Nyalakanti, P. K., Calhoun, V. D., & Kiehl, K. A. (2012). Aberrant paralimbic gray matter in criminal psychopathy. *Journal of Abnormal Psychology, 121*, 649–658.

Ermer, E., Kahn, R. E., Salovey, P., & Kiehl, K. A. (2012b). Emotional intelligence in incarcerated men with psychopathic traits. *Journal of Personality and Social Psychology, 103*, 194–204.

Ert, E., Yechiam, E., & Arshavsky, O. (2013). Smokers' decision making: More than mere risk taking. *PLOS ONE, 8*(7), e68064.

Ertmer, D. J., Young, N. M., & Nathani, S. (2007). Profiles of focal development in young cochlear implant recipients. *Journal of Speech, Language, and Hearing Research, 50*, 393–407.

Escasa, M. J., Casey, J. F., & Gray, P. B. (2011). Salivary testosterone levels in men at a U.S. sex club. *Archives of Sexual Behavior, 40*, 921–926.

Escobar-Chaves, S. L., Tortolero, S. R., Markham, C. M., Low, B. J., Eitel, P., & Thickstun, P. (2005). Impact of the media on adolescent sexual attitudes and behaviors. *Pediatrics, 116*, 303–326.

Escobedo, J. R., & Adolphs, R. (2010). Becoming a better person: Temporal remoteness biases autobiographical memories for moral events. *Emotion, 10*, 511–518.

Espie, C. A., Emsley, R., Kyle, S. D., Gordon, C., Drake, C. L., Siriwardena, A. N., Cape, J., Ong, J. C., Sheaves, B., Foster, R., Freeman, D., Costa-Font, J., Marsden, A., & Luik, A. I. (2019). Effect of digital cognitive behavioral therapy for insomnia on health, psychological well-being, and sleep-related quality of life: a randomized clinical trial. *JAMA Psychiatry, 76*, 21–30.

Esposito, G., Yoshida, S., Ohnishi, R., Tsuneoka, Y., Rostagno, M., Yokoto, S., Okabe, S., Kamiya, K., Hoshino, M., Shimizu, M., Venuti, P., Kikusui, T., Kato, T., & Kuroda, K. O. (2013). Infant calming responses during maternal carrying in humans and mice. *Current Biology, 23*, 739–745.

Esser, J. K., & Lindoerfer, J. S. (1989). Groupthink and the space shuttle *Challenger* accident: Toward a quantitative case analysis. *Journal of Behavioral Decision Making, 2*, 167–177.

Esterson, A. (2001). The mythologizing of psychoanalytic history: Deception and self-deception in Freud's accounts of the seduction theory episode. *History of Psychiatry, 12*, 329–352.

Etkin, A., & Wager, T. D. (2007). Functional neuroimaging of anxiety: A meta-analysis of emotional processing in PTSD, social anxiety disorder, and specific phobia. *American Journal of Psychiatry, 164*, 1476–1488.

Eurich, T. L., Krause, D. E., Cigularov, K., & Thornton, G. C., III. (2009). Assessment centers: Current practices in the United States. *Journal of Business Psychology, 24*, 387–407.

Euston, D. R., Tatsuno, M., & McNaughton, B. L. (2007). Fast-forward playback of recent memory sequences in prefrontal cortex during sleep. *Science, 318,* 1147–1150.

Evans, C. M., & Simms, L. J. (2019). The latent structure of self-harm. *Journal of Abnormal Psychology, 128,* 12–24.

Evans, G. W., Palsane, M. N., & Carrere, S. (1987). Type A behavior and occupational stress: A cross-cultural study of blue-collar workers. *Journal of Personality and Social Psychology, 52,* 1002–1007.

Evenson, K. R., Wen, F., & Herring, A. H. (2016). Associations of accelerometry-assessed and self-reported physical activity and sedentary behavior with all-cause and cardiovascular mortality among U.S. adults. *American Journal of Epidemiology, 184,* 621–632.

Everaert, J., Bronstein, M. V., Cannon, T. D., & Joormann, J. (2018). Looking through tinted glasses: Depression and social anxiety are related to both interpretation biases and inflexible negative interpretations. *Clinical Psychological Science, 6,* 517–528.

Everett, J. A. C., Caviola, L., Kahane, G., Savulescu, J., & Faber, N. S. (2015). Doing good by doing nothing? The role of social norms in explaining default effects in altruistic contexts. *European Journal of Social Psychology, 45,* 230–241.

Evers, A., Muñiz, J., Bartram, D., Boben, D., Egeland, J., Fernández-Hermida, J. R., Frans, Ö., Gintilienė, G., Hagemeister, C., Halama, P., Iliescu, D., Jaworowska, A., Jimenez, P., Manthouli, M., Matešić, K., Schittekatte, M., Sümer, H. C., & Urbánek, T. (2012). Testing practices in the 21st century: Developments and European psychologists' opinions. *European Psychologist, 17,* 300–319.

Everson, S. A., Goldberg, D. E., Kaplan, G. A., Cohen, R. D., Pukkala, E., Tuomilehto, J., & Salonen, J. T. (1996). Hopelessness and risk of mortality and incidence of myocardial infarction and cancer. *Psychosomatic Medicine, 58,* 113–121.

Ewbank, M. P., Cummins, R., Tablan, V., Bateup, S., Catarino, A., Martin, A. J., & Blackwell, A. D. (2019). Quantifying the association between psychotherapy content and clinical outcomes using deep learning. *JAMA Psychiatry, 77,* 35–43.

Exelmans, L., Custers, K., & Van den Bulck, J. (2015). Violent video games and delinquent behavior in adolescents: A risk factor perspective. *Aggressive Behavior, 41,* 267–279.

Exelmans, L., & Van den Bulck, J. (2018). Self-control depletion and sleep duration: the mediating role of television viewing. *Psychology & Health, 33,* 1251–1268.

Eysenck, H. J. (1952). The effects of psychotherapy: An evaluation. *Journal of Consulting Psychology, 16,* 319–324.

Eysenck, H. J. (1990, April 30). An improvement on personality inventory. *Current Contents: Social and Behavioral Sciences, 22,* 20.

Eysenck, H. J. (1992). Four ways five factors are not basic. *Personality and Individual Differences, 13,* 667–673.

Eysenck, H. J., & Grossarth-Maticek, R. (1991). Creative novation behavior therapy as a prophylactic treatment for cancer and coronary heart disease: Part II—Effects of treatment. *Behaviour Research and Therapy, 29,* 17–31.

Eysenck, H. J., Wakefield, J. A., Jr., & Friedman, A. F. (1983). Diagnosis and clinical assessment: The DSM-III. *Annual Review of Psychology, 34,* 167–193.

Eysenck, S. B. G., & Eysenck, H. J. (1963). The validity of questionnaire and rating assessments of extraversion and neuroticism, and their factorial stability. *British Journal of Psychology, 54,* 51–62.

Fabiano, G. A., Pelham, W. E., Jr., Coles, E. K., Gnagy, E. M., Chronis-Tuscano, A., & O'Connor, B. C. (2008). A meta-analysis of behavioral treatments for attention-deficit/hyperactivity disorder. *Clinical Psychology Review, 29,* 129–140.

Fabiansson, E. C., Denson, T. F., Moulds, M. L., Grisham, J. R., & Schira, M. M. (2012). Don't look back in anger: Neural correlates of reappraisal, analytical rumination, and angry rumination during a recall of an anger-inducing autobiographical memory. *NeuroImage, 59,* 2974–2981.

Facco, E. (2016). Hypnosis and anesthesia: back to the future. *Minerva Anestesiologica, 82,* 1343–1356.

Fagan, J. F., & Holland, C. R. (2007). Racial equality in intelligence: Predictions from a theory of intelligence as processing. *Intelligence, 35,* 319–334.

Fagan, J. F., & Holland, C. R. (2009). Culture-fair prediction of academic achievement. *Intelligence, 37,* 62–67.

Fagundes, C. P., & Way, B. (2014). Early-life stress and adult inflammation. *Current Directions in Psychological Science, 23,* 277–283.

Faheem, S., Petti, V., & Mellos, G. (2017). Disruptive mood dysregulation disorder and its effect on bipolar disorder. *Annals of Clinical Psychiatry, 29,* e1–e8.

Fairbairn, C. E., Briley, D. A., Kang, D., Fraley, R. C., Hankin, B. L., & Ariss, T. (2018). A meta-analysis of longitudinal associations between substance use and interpersonal attachment security. *Psychological Bulletin, 144,* 532–555.

Fairbairn, C. E., & Sayette, M. A. (2014). A social-attributional analysis of alcohol response. *Psychological Bulletin, 140,* 1361–1382.

Fairfield, H. (2012, February 4). Girls lead in science exam, but NOT in the United States. *The New York Times.* https://archive.nytimes.com/www.nytimes.com/interactive/2013/02/04/science/girls-lead-in-science-exam-but-not-in-the-united-states.html

Falk, C. F., Heine, S. J., Yuki, M., & Takemura, K. (2009). Why do Westerners self-enhance more than East Asians? *European Journal of Personality, 23,* 183–203.

Falk, E. B., Hyde, L. W., Mitchell, C., Faul, J., Gonzalez, R., Heitzeg, M. M., Keating, D. P., Langa, K. M., Martz, M. E., Maslowsky, J., Morrison, F. J., Noll, D. C., Patrick, M. E., Pfeffer, F. T., Reuter-Lorenz, P. A., Thomason, M. E., Davis-Kean, P., Monk, C. D., & Schulenberg, J. (2013). What is a representative brain? Neuroscience meets population science. *PNAS, 110,* 17615–17622.

Falkenström, F., Kuria, M., Othieno, C., & Kumar, M. (2019). Working alliance predicts symptomatic improvement in public hospital–delivered psychotherapy in Nairobi, Kenya. *Journal of Consulting and Clinical Psychology, 87,* 46–55.

Falkner, A. L., Grosenick, L., Davidson, T. J., Deisseroth, K., & Lin, D. (2016). Hypothalamic control of male aggression-seeking behavior. *Nature Neuroscience, 19,* 596–604.

Fan, S. P., Liberman, Z., Keysar, B., & Kinzler, K. D. (2015). The exposure advantage: Early exposure to a multilingual environment promotes effective communication. *Psychological Science, 26,* 1090–1097.

Fan, W., & Williams, C. (2018). The mediating role of student motivation in the linking of perceived school climate and academic achievement in reading and mathematics. *Frontiers in Education, 3,* 50.

Fang, Z., Spaeth, A. M., Ma, N., Zhu, S., Hu, S., Goel, N., Detre, J. A., Dinges, D. F., & Rao, H. (2015). Altered salience network connectivity predicts macronutrient intake after sleep deprivation. *Scientific Reports, 5,* Article 8215.

Fanti, K. A., Vanman, E., Henrich, C. C., & Avraamides, M. N. (2009). Desensitization to media violence over a short period of time. *Aggressive Behavior, 35,* 179–187.

Farah, M. J. (2017). The neuroscience of socioeconomic status: Correlates, causes, and consequences. *Neuron, 96,* 56–71.

Farah, M. J., Rabinowitz, C., Quinn, G. E., & Liu, G. T. (2000). Early commitment of neural substrates for face recognition. *Cognitive Neuropsychology, 17,* 117–124.

Farb, N. A. S., Anderson, A. K., Mayberg, H., Bean, J., McKeon, D., & Segal, Z. V. (2010). Minding one's emotions: Mindfulness training alters the neural expression of sadness. *Emotion, 10,* 25–33.

Farina, A. (1982). The stigma of mental disorders. In A. G. Miller (Ed.), *In the eye of the beholder.* Praeger.

Farnia, V., Shakeri, J., Tatari, F., Juibari, T. A., Yazdchi, K., Bajoghli, H., Brand, S., Abdoli, N., & Aghaei, A. (2014). Randomized controlled trial of aripiprazole versus risperidone for the treatment of amphetamine-induced psychosis. *The American Journal of Drug and Alcohol Abuse, 40,* 10–15.

Farr, R. H. (2017). Does parental sexual orientation matter? A longitudinal follow-up of adoptive families with school-age children. *Developmental Psychology, 53,* 252–264.

Farr, R. H., Bruun, S. T., Doss, K. M., & Patterson, C. J. (2018). Children's gender-typed behavior from early to middle childhood in adoptive families with lesbian, gay, and heterosexual parents. *Sex Roles, 78,* 528–541.

Farrington, D. P. (1991). Antisocial personality from childhood to adulthood. *The Psychologist: Bulletin of the British Psychological Society, 4,* 389–394.

Farstad, S. M., McGeown, L. M., & von Ranson, K. M. (2016). Eating disorders and personality, 2004–2016: A systematic review and meta-analysis. *Clinical Psychology Review, 46,* 91–105.

Fatemi, S. H., & Folsom, T. D. (2009). The neurodevelopmental hypothesis of schizophrenia, revisted. *Schizophrenia Bulletin, 35,* 528–548.

Fattore, L. (2016). Synthetic cannabinoids—further evidence supporting the relationship between cannabinoids and psychosis. *Biological Psychiatry, 79,* 539–548.

Fazel, S., Langstrom, N., Hjern, A., Grann, M., & Lichtenstein, P. (2009). Schizophrenia, substance abuse, and violent crime. *JAMA, 301,* 2016–2023.

Fazel, S., Lichtenstein, P., Grann, M., Goodwin, G. M., & Långström, N. (2010). Bipolar disorder and violent crime: New evidence from population-based longitudinal studies and systematic review. *Archives of General Psychiatry, 67,* 931–938.

Fazio, L. K., Brashier, N. M., Payne, B. K., & Marsh, E. J. (2015). Knowledge does not protect against illusory truth. *Journal of Experimental Psychology: General, 144,* 993–1002.

FBI. (2019). *Hate crime statistics.* Retrieved from ucr.fbi.gov/hate-crime

Fecher, N., & Johnson, E. K. (2019). By 4.5 months, linguistic experience already affects infants' talker processing abilities. *Child Development, 90,* 1535–1543.

Fedorenko, E., Scott, T. L., Brunner, P., Coon, W. G., Pritchett, B., Schalk, G., & Kanwisher, N. (2016). Neural correlate of the construction of sentence meaning. *PNAS, 113,* E6256–E6262.

Fedotova, N. O., & Rozin, P. (2018). Contamination, association, or social communication: An examination of alternative accounts for contagion effects. *Judgment & Decision Making, 13,* 150–162.

Feeney, D. M. (1987). Human rights and animal welfare. *American Psychologist, 42,* 593–599.

Feigenson, L., Carey, S., & Spelke, E. (2002). Infants' discrimination of number vs. continuous extent. *Cognitive Psychology, 44,* 33–66.

Feinberg, A. Branton, R., & Martinez-Ebers, V. (2019, March 22). Counties that hosted a 2016 Trump rally saw a 226 percent increase in hate crimes. *The Washington Post* (washingtonpost.com).

Feinberg, M., Fang, R., Liu, S., & Peng, K. (2019). A world of blame to go around: Cross-cultural determinants of responsibility and punishment judgments. *Personality and Social Psychology Bulletin, 45,* 634–651.

Feinberg, M., Willer, R., Antonenko, O., & John, O. P. (2012). Liberating reason from the passions: Overriding intuitionist moral judgments through emotion reappraisal. *Psychological Science, 23,* 788–795.

Feinberg, M., Willer, R., & Schultz, M. (2014). Gossip and ostracism promote cooperation in groups. *Psychological Science, 25,* 656–664.

Feinberg, T. E., & Mallatt, J. (2016). The nature of primary consciousness: A new synthesis. *Consciousness and Cognition, 43,* 113–127.

Feingold, A. (1992). Good-looking people are not what we think. *Psychological Bulletin, 111,* 304–341.

Feingold, A., & Mazzella, R. (1998). Gender differences in body image are increasing. *Psychological Science, 9,* 190–195.

Feinstein, J. S., Buzza, C., Hurlemann, R., Follmer, R. L., Dahdaleh, N. S., Coryell, W. H., Welsh, M. J., Tranel, D., & Wemmie, J. A. (2013). Fear and panic in humans with bilateral amygdala damage. *Nature Neuroscience, 16,* 270–272.

Feinstein, J. S., Duff, M. C., & Tranel, D. (2010, April 27). Sustained experiences of emotion after loss of memory in patients with amnesia. *PNAS, 107,* 7674–7679.

Feldman, G., Farh, J. L., & Wong, K. F. E. (2018). Agency beliefs over time and across cultures: Free will beliefs predict higher job satisfaction. *Personality and Social Psychology Bulletin, 44,* 304–317.

Feldman, M. B., & Meyer, I. H. (2010). Comorbidity and age of onset of eating disorders in gay men, lesbians, and bisexuals. *Psychiatry Research, 180,* 126–131.

Feldman, R., Rosenthal, Z., & Eidelman, A. I. (2014). Maternal-preterm skin-to-skin contact enhances child physiologic organization and cognitive control across the first 10 years of life. *Biological Psychiatry, 75,* 56–64.

Fenigstein, A. (2015). Milgram's shock experiments and the Nazi perpetrators: A contrarian perspective on the role of obedience pressures during the Holocaust. *Theory and Psychology, 25,* 581–598.

Fenn, K. M., & Hambrick, D. Z. (2012). Individual differences in working memory capacity predict sleep-dependent memory consolidation. *Journal of Experimental Psychology: General, 141,* 404–410.

Fenton, W. S., & McGlashan, T. H. (1991). Natural history of schizophrenia subtypes: II. Positive and negative symptoms and long-term course. *Archives of General Psychiatry, 48,* 978–986.

Fenton, W. S., & McGlashan, T. H. (1994). Antecedents, symptom progression, and long-term outcome of the deficit syndrome in schizophrenia. *American Journal of Psychiatry, 151,* 351–356.

Ferguson, C. J. (2009, June 14). Not every child is secretly a genius. *The Chronicle Review.* https://www.chronicle.com/article/Not-Every-Child-Is-Secretly-a/48001

Ferguson, C. J. (2013a). Spanking, corporal punishment and negative long-term outcomes: A meta-analytic review of longitudinal studies. *Clinical Psychology Review, 33,* 196–208.

Ferguson, C. J. (2015). Do angry birds make for angry children? A meta-analysis of video game influences on children's and adolescents' aggression, mental health, prosocial behavior, and academic performance. *Perspectives on Psychological Science, 10,* 646–666.

Ferguson, C. J., Winegard, B., & Winegard, B. M. (2011). Who is the fairest one of all? How evolution guides peer and media influences on female body dissatisfaction. *Review of General Psychology, 15,* 11–28.

Ferguson, E. D. (1989). Adler's motivational theory: An historical perspective on belonging and the fundamental human striving. *Individual Psychology, 45,* 354–361.

Ferguson, E. D. (2001). Adler and Dreikurs: Cognitive-social dynamic innovators. *Journal of Individual Psychology, 57,* 324–341.

Ferguson, E. D. (2003). Social processes, personal goals, and their intertwining: Their importance in Adlerian theory and practice. *Journal of Individual Psychology, 59,* 136–144.

Ferguson, E. D. (2010). Editor's notes: Adler's innovative contributions regarding the need to belong. *Journal of Individual Psychology, 66,* 1–7.

Ferguson, M. J., & Zayas, V. (2009). Automatic evaluation. *Current Directions in Psychological Science, 18,* 362–366.

Fergusson, D. M., Boden, J. M., & Horwood, L. J. (2009). Tests of causal links between alcohol abuse or dependence and major depression. *Archives of General Psychiatry, 66,* 260–266.

Fernandes, M. A., Wammes, J. D., & Meade, M. E. (2018). The surprisingly powerful influence of drawing on memory. *Current Directions in Psychological Science, 27,* 302–308.

Fernández-Dols, J.-M., & Ruiz-Belda, M.-A. (1995). Are smiles a sign of happiness? Gold medal winners at the Olympic Games. *Journal of Personality and Social Psychology, 69,* 1113–1119.

Fernandez-Duque, E., Evans, J., Christian, C., & Hodges, S. D. (2015). Superfluous neuroscience information makes explanations of psychological phenomena more appealing. *Journal of Cognitive Neuroscience, 27,* 926–944.

Fernbach, P. M., Rogers, T., Fox, C. R., & Sloman, S. A. (2013). Political extremism is supported by an illusion of understanding. *Psychological Science, 24,* 939–946.

Fernie, G., Peeters, M., Gullo, M. J., Christianson, P., Cole, J. C., Sumnall, H., & Field, M. (2013). Multiple behavioral impulsivity tasks predict prospective alcohol involvement in adolescents. *Addiction, 108,* 1916–1923.

Fernyhough, C. (2008). Getting Vygotskian about theory of mind: Mediation, dialogue, and the development of social understanding. *Developmental Review, 28,* 225–262.

Ferrari, A. J., Charlson, F. J., Norman, R. E., Patten, S. B., Freedman, G., Murray, C. J. L., Vos, T., & Whiteford, H. A. (2013). Burden of depressive disorders by country, sex, age, and year: Findings from the Global Burden of Disease Study 2010. *PLOS Medicine, 10,* e1001547.

Ferrer, R. A., & Cohen, G. L. (2018). Reconceptualizing self-affirmation with the trigger and channel framework: Lessons from the health domain. *Personality and Social Psychology Review, 23(3),* 285–304.

Ferreri, L., Mas-Herrero, E., Zatorre, R. J., Ripollés, P., Gomez-Andres, A., Alicart, H., Olivé, G., Marco-Pallarés, J., Antonijoan, R. M., Valle, M., Riba, J., & Rodriguez-Fornelis, A. (2019). Dopamine modulates the reward experiences elicited by music. *PNAS, 116,* 3793–3798.

Ferri, M., Amato, L., & Davoli, M. (2006). Alcoholics Anonymous and other 12-step programmes for alcohol dependence. *Cochrane Database of Systematic Reviews, 3,* Art. No. CD005032.

Ferriman, K., Lubinski, D., & Benbow, C. P. (2009). Work preferences, life values, and personal views of top math/science graduate students and the profoundly gifted: Developmental changes and gender differences during emerging adulthood and parenthood. *Journal of Personality and Social Psychology, 97,* 517–522.

Ferris, C. F. (1996, March). The rage of innocents. *The Sciences,* pp. 22–26.

Festinger, L. (1957). *A theory of cognitive dissonance.* Stanford University Press.

Fetterman, A. K., Wilkowski, B. M., & Robinson, M. D. (2018). On feeling warm and being warm: Daily perceptions of physical warmth fluctuate with interpersonal warmth. *Social Psychological and Personality Science, 9,* 560–567.

Fetterolf, J. (2017, March 7). *In many countries, at least four-in-ten in the labor force are women.* Pew Research Center. https://www.pewresearch.org/fact-tank/2017/03/07/in-many-countries-at-least-four-in-ten-in-the-labor-force-are-women/

Fetvadjiev, V. H., & He, J. (2019). The longitudinal links of personality traits, values, and well-being and self-esteem: A five-wave study of a nationally representative sample. *Journal of Personality and Social Psychology, 117,* 448–464.

Fetvadjiev, V. H., Meiring, D., van de Vijver, F. J., Nel, J. A., Sekaja, L., & Laher, S. (2017). Personality and behavior prediction and consistency across cultures: A multimethod study of Blacks and Whites in South Africa. *Journal of Personality and Social Psychology, 114,* 465–481.

Fichter, M. M., & Quadflieg, N. (2016). Mortality in eating disorders—results of a large prospective clinical longitudinal study. *International Journal of Eating Disorders, 49,* 391–401.

Fiedler, F. E. (1981). Leadership effectiveness. *American Behavioral Scientist, 24,* 619–632.

Fiedler, F. E. (1987, September). When to lead, when to stand back. *Psychology Today,* pp. 26–27.

Field, A. P. (2006). Is conditioning a useful framework for understanding the development and treatment of phobias? *Clinical Psychology Review, 26,* 857–875.

Field, T., Diego, M., & Hernandez-Reif, M. (2007). Massage therapy research. *Developmental Review, 27,* 75–89.

Field, T., Hernandez-Reif, M., Feijo, L., & Freedman, J. (2006). Prenatal, perinatal and neonatal stimulation: A survey of neonatal nurseries. *Infant Behavior & Development, 29,* 24–31.

Fielder, R. L., Walsh, J. L., Carey, K. B., & Carey, M. P. (2013). Predictors of sexual hookups: A theory-based, prospective study of first-year college women. *Archives of Sexual Behavior, 42,* 1425–1441.

Fields, R. D. (2004, April). The other half of the brain. *Scientific American,* pp. 54–61.

Fields, R. D. (2005). Making memories stick. *Scientific American, 292,* 74–81.

Fields, R. D. (2008, March). White matter matters. *Scientific American,* pp. 54–61.

Fields, R. D. (2011, May/June). The hidden brain. *Scientific American,* pp. 53–59.

Fields, R. D. (2013). Neuroscience: Map the other brain. *Nature, 501,* 25–27.

Fields, R. D. (2019, May). The roots of human aggression. *Scientific American,* pp. 65–71.

Fincham, F. D., & Bradbury, T. N. (1993). Marital satisfaction, depression, and attributions: A longitudinal analysis. *Journal of Personality and Social Psychology, 64,* 442–452.

Finer, L. B., & Philbin, J. M. (2014). Trends in ages at key reproductive transitions in the United States, 1951–2010. *Women's Health Issues, 24,* e271–279.

Fingerman, K. L., & Charles, S. T. (2010). It takes two to tango: Why older people have the best relationships. *Current Directions in Psychological Science, 19,* 172–176.

Fink, A., Bay, J. U., Koschutnig, K., Prettenthaler, K., Rominger, C., Benedek, M., Papousek, I., Weiss, E. M., Seidel, A., & Memmert, D. (2019). Brain and soccer: Functional patterns of brain activity during the generation of creative moves in real soccer decision-making situations. *Human Brain Mapping*, 40, 755–764.

Fink, M. (2009). *Electroconvulsive therapy: A guide for professionals and their patients*. Oxford University Press.

Finkel, E. J. (2017). *The all-or-nothing marriage*. Dutton.

Finkel, E. J., DeWall, C. N., Slotter, E. B., McNulty, J. K., Pond, R. S., Jr., & Atkins, D. C. (2012a). Using I3 theory to clarify when dispositional aggressiveness predicts intimate partner violence perpetration. *Journal of Personality and Social Psychology*, 102, 533–549.

Finkel, E. J., & Eastwick, P. W. (2008). Speed-dating. *Current Directions in Psychological Science*, 17, 193–197.

Finkel, E. J., & Eastwick, P. W. (2009). Arbitrary social norms influence sex differences in romantic selectivity. *Psychological Science*, 20, 1290–1295.

Finkel, E. J., Eastwick, P. W., Karney, B. R., Reis, H. T., & Sprecher, S. (2012b, September/October). Dating in a digital world. *Scientific American Mind*, pp. 26–33.

Finkenauer, C., Buyukcan-Tetik, A., Baumeister, R. F., Schoemaker, K., Bartels, M., & Vohs, K. D. (2015). Out of control: Identifying the role of self-control strength in family violence. *Current Directions in Psychological Science*, 24, 261–266.

Finlay, S. W. (2000). Influence of Carl Jung and William James on the origin of alcoholics anonymous. *Review of General Psychology*, 4, 3–12.

Finnigan, K. M., & Vazire, S. (2018). The incremental validity of average state self-reports over global self-reports of personality. *Journal of Personality and Social Psychology*, 115, 321–337.

Fiore, M. C., Jaén, C. R., Baker, T. B., Bailey, W. C., Benowitz, N. L., Curry, S. J., Dorfman, S. F., Froelicher, E. S., Goldstein, M. G., Healton, C. G., Henderson, P. N., Heyman, R. B., Koh, H. K., Kottke, T. E., Lando, H. A., Mecklenburg, R. E., Mullen, P. D., Orleans, C. T., Robinson, L., . . . Wewers, M. E. (2008). *Treating tobacco use and dependence: 2008 update. Clinical practice guideline*. U.S. Department of Health and Human Services, Public Health Service.

Firsov, M. L. (2019). Perspectives for the optogenetic prosthetization of the retina. *Neuroscience and Behavioral Physiology*, 49, 192–198.

Firth, J., Torous, J., Nicholas, J., Carney, R., Pratap, A., Rosenbaum, S., & Sarris, J. (2017a). The efficacy of smartphone-based mental health interventions for depressive symptoms: A meta-analysis of randomized controlled trials. *World Psychiatry*, 16, 287–298.

Firth, J., Torous, J., Nicholas, J., Carney, R., Rosenbaum, S., & Sarris, J. (2017b). Can smartphone mental health interventions reduce symptoms of anxiety? A meta-analysis of randomized controlled trials. *Journal of Affective Disorders*, 218, 15–22.

Fischer, A., & LaFrance, M. (2015). What drives the smile and the tear: Why women are more emotionally expressive than men. *Emotion Review*, 7, 22–29.

Fischer, P., & Greitemeyer, T. (2006). Music and aggression: The impact of sexual-aggressive song lyrics on aggression-related thoughts, emotions, and behavior toward the same and the opposite sex. *Personality and Social Psychology Bulletin*, 32, 1165–1176.

Fischer, P., Greitemeyer, T., Kastenmüller, A., Vogrincic, C., & Sauer, A. (2011). The effects of risk-glorifying media exposure on risk-positive cognitions, emotions, and behaviors: A meta-analytic review. *Psychological Bulletin*, 137, 367–390.

Fischer, R., & Boer, D. (2011). What is more important for national well-being: money or autonomy?

A meta-analysis of well-being, burnout, and anxiety across 63 societies. *Journal of Personality and Social Psychology*, 101, 164–184.

Fischetti, M. (2014). Sleeping through high school. *Scientific American*, 311, 27.

Fischhoff, B. (1982). Debiasing. In D. Kahneman, P. Slovic, & A. Tversky (Eds.), *Judgment under uncertainty: Heuristics and biases*. Cambridge University Press.

Fischhoff, B., Slovic, P., & Lichtenstein, S. (1977). Knowing with certainty: The appropriateness of extreme confidence. *Journal of Experimental Psychology: Human Perception and Performance*, 3, 552–564.

Fishbach, A., Dhar, R., & Zhang, Y. (2006). Subgoals as substitutes or complements: The role of goal accessibility. *Journal of Personality and Social Psychology*, 91, 232–242.

Fisher, H. E. (1993, March/April). After all, maybe it's biology. *Psychology Today*, pp. 40–45.

Fisher, H. T. (1984). Little Albert and Little Peter. *Bulletin of the British Psychological Society*, 37, 269.

Fisher, M., & Keil, F. C. (2018). The binary bias: A systematic distortion in the integration of information. *Psychological Science*, 29, 1846–1858.

Fiske, S. T. (2018). Stereotype content: Warmth and competence endure. *Current Directions in Psychological Science*, 27, 67–73.

Fitz, N., Kushlev, K., Jagannathan, R., Lewis, T., Paliwal, D., & Ariely, D. (2019). Batching smartphone notifications can improve well-being. *Computers in Human Behavior*, 101, 84–94.

Fitzgerald, R. J., & Price, H. L. (2015). Eyewitness identification across the life span: A meta-analysis of age differences. *Psychological Bulletin*, 141, 1228–1265.

Flack, W. F. (2006). Peripheral feedback effects of facial expressions, bodily postures, and vocal expressions on emotional feelings. *Cognition and Emotion*, 20, 177–195.

Flagg, A. (2018, March 30). The myth of the criminal immigrant. *The New York Times*. https://www.nytimes.com/interactive/2018/03/30/upshot/crime-immigration-myth.html?

Flagg, A. (2019, May 13). Is there a connection between undocumented immigrants and crime? *The New York Times*. https://www.nytimes.com/2019/05/13/upshot/illegal-immigration-crime-rates-research.html?

Flaherty, D. K. (2011). The vaccine-autism connection: A public health crisis caused by unethical medical practices and fraudulent science. *Annals of Pharmacotherapy*, 45, 1302–1304.

Flegal, K. M., Carroll, M. D., Kit, B. K., & Ogden, C. L. (2012). Prevalence of obesity and trends in the distribution of body mass index among US adults, 1999–2010. *JAMA*, 307, 491–497.

Flegal, K. M., Carroll, M. D., Ogden, C. L., & Curtin, L. R. (2010). Prevalence and trends in obesity among US adults, 1999–2008. *JAMA*, 303, 235–241.

Flegal, K. M., Kruszon-Moran, D., Carroll, M. D., Fryar, C. D., & Ogden, C. L. (2016). Trends in obesity among adults in the United States, 2005 to 2014. *JAMA*, 315, 2284–2291.

Flegenheimer, M. (2018). Beto O'Rourke dreams of one Texas. Ted Cruz sees another clearly. *The New York Times*. https://www.nytimes.com/2018/08/31/us/politics/beto-orourke-dreams-of-one-texas-ted-cruz-sees-another-clearly.html

Fleming, I., Baum, A., & Weiss, L. (1987). Social density and perceived control as mediator of crowding stress in high-density residential neighborhoods. *Journal of Personality and Social Psychology*, 52, 899–906.

Fletcher, G. J. O., Fitness, J., & Blampied, N. M. (1990). The link between attributions and happiness in

close relationships: The roles of depression and explanatory style. *Journal of Social and Clinical Psychology*, 9, 243–255.

Flinker, A., Korzeniewska, A., Shestyuk, A. Y., Franaszczuk, P. J., Dronkers, N. F., Knight, R. T., & Crone, N. E. (2015). Redefining the role of Broca's area in speech. *PNAS*, 112, 2871–2875.

Flora, S. R. (2004). *The power of reinforcement*. SUNY Press.

Flora, S. R., & Bobby, S. E. (2008, September/October). The bipolar bamboozle. *Skeptical Inquirer*, pp. 41–45.

Flore, P. C., Mulder, J., & Wicherts, J. M. (2019). The influence of gender stereotype threat on mathematics test scores of Dutch high school students: a registered report. *Comprehensive Results in Social Psychology*. https://www.tandfonline.com/doi/full/10.1080/23743603.2018.1559647?scroll=top&needAccess=true

Flore, P. C., & Wicherts, J. M. (2015). Does stereotype threat influence performance of girls in stereotyped domains? A meta-analysis. *Journal of School Psychology*, 53, 25–44.

Floud, R., Fogel, R. W., Harris, B., & Hong, S. C. (2011). *The changing body: Health, nutrition, and human development in the western world since 1700*. Cambridge University Press.

Flouri, E., & Buchanan, A. (2004). Early father's and mother's involvement and child's later educational outcomes. *British Journal of Educational Psychology*, 74, 141–153.

Flueckiger, L., Lieb, R., Meyer, A., Witthauer, C., & Mata, J. (2016). The importance of physical activity and sleep for affect on stressful days: Two intensive longitudinal studies. *Emotion*, 16, 488–497.

Flynn, J. R. (1987). Massive IQ gains in 14 nations: What IQ tests really measure. *Psychological Bulletin*, 101, 171–191.

Flynn, J. R. (2009). Requiem for nutrition as the cause of IQ gains: Raven's gains in Britain 1938–2008. *Economics and Human Biology*, 7, 18–27.

Flynn, J. R. (2012). *Are we getting smarter? Rising IQ in the twenty-first century*. Cambridge University Press.

Flynn, J. R. (2018). Reflections about intelligence over 40 years. *Intelligence*, 70, 73–83.

Flynn, M. (2018, November 5). 'I wanted him to feel compassion': The Jewish nurse who treated the synagogue shooting suspect tells his story. *The Washington Post* (washingtonpost.com).

Foa, E. B., & Kozak, M. J. (1986). Emotional processing of fear: Exposure to corrective information. *Psychological Bulletin*, 99, 20–35.

Fodor, J. D. (1999). Let your brain alone. *London Review of Books*, 21.

Foell, J., Palumbo, I. M., Yancey, J. R., Vizueta, N., Demirakca, T., & Patrick, C. J. (2019). Biobehavioral threat sensitivity and amygdala volume: A twin neuroimaging study. *NeuroImage*, 186, 14–21.

Foer, J. (2011). *Moonwalking with Einstein: The art and science of remembering everything*. Penguin.

Foley, M. A. (2015). Setting the records straight: Impossible memories and the persistence of their phenomenological qualities. *Review of General Psychology*, 19, 230–248.

Foley, R. T., Whitwell, R. L., & Goodale, M. A. (2015). The two-visual-systems hypothesis and the perspectival features of visual experience. *Consciousness and Cognition*, 35, 225–233.

Fong, C. J., Zaleski, D. J., & Leach, J. K. (2015). The challenge–skill balance and antecedents of flow: A meta-analytic investigation. *Journal of Positive Psychology*, 10, 425–446.

Fong, K., & Mar, R. A. (2015). What does my avatar say about me? Inferring personality from avatars. *Personality and Social Psychology Bulletin*, 41, 237–249.

Forbes, L., Graham, J., Berglund, C., & Bell, R. (2018). Dietary change during pregnancy and women's reasons for change. *Nutrients, 10,* 1032.

Forbes, M. K., Eaton, N. R., & Krueger, R. F. (2017). Sexual quality of life and aging: A prospective study of a nationally representative sample. *Journal of Sex Research, 54,* 137–148.

Ford, E. S. (2002). Does exercise reduce inflammation? Physical activity and B-reactive protein among U.S. adults. *Epidemiology, 13,* 561–569.

Ford, M. T., Cerasoli, C. P., Higgins, J. A., & Deccesare, A. L. (2011). Relationships between psychological, physical, and behavioural health and work performance: A review and meta-analysis. *Work & Stress, 25,* 185–204.

Foree, D. D., & LoLordo, V. M. (1973). Attention in the pigeon: Differential effects of food-getting versus shock-avoidance procedures. *Journal of Comparative and Physiological Psychology, 85,* 551–558.

Forest, A. L., Kille, D. R, Wood, J. V., & Stehouwer, L. R. (2015). Turbulent times, rocky relationships: Relational consequences of experiencing physical instability. *Psychological Science, 26,* 1261–1271.

Forgas, J. (2017, May 14). *Why bad moods are good for you: The surprising benefits of sadness.* The Conversation. https://theconversation.com/why-bad-moods-are-good-for-you-the-surprising-benefits-of-sadness-75402

Forgas, J. P. (2008). Affect and cognition. *Perspectives on Psychological Science, 3,* 94–101.

Forgas, J. P. (2009, November/December). Think negative! *Australian Science,* pp. 14–17.

Forgas, J. P. (2013). Don't worry, be sad! On the cognitive, motivational, and interpersonal benefits of negative mood. *Current Directions in Psychological Science, 22,* 225–232.

Forgas, J. P., Bower, G. H., & Krantz, S. E. (1984). The influence of mood on perceptions of social interactions. *Journal of Experimental Social Psychology, 20,* 497–513.

Forman, D. R., Aksan, N., & Kochanska, G. (2004). Toddlers' responsive imitation predicts preschool-age conscience. *Psychological Science, 15,* 699–704.

Forrin, N. D., & MacLeod, C. M. (2018). This time it's personal: The memory benefit of hearing oneself. *Memory, 26,* 574–579.

Forscher, P. S., Lai, C. K., Axt, J. R., Ebersole, C. R., Herman, M., Devine, P. G., & Nosek, B. A. (2019). A meta-analysis of procedures to change implicit measures. *Journal of Personality and Social Psychology, 117,* 522–559.

Forster, S., & Spence, C. (2018). "What smell?" Temporarily loading visual attention induces a prolonged loss of olfactory awareness. *Psychological Science, 29,* 1642–1652.

Forsyth, D. R., Lawrence, N. K., Burnette, J. L., & Baumeister, R. F. (2007). Attempting to improve academic performance of struggling college students by bolstering their self-esteem: An intervention that backfired. *Journal of Social and Clinical Psychology, 26,* 447–459.

Foss, D. J., & Hakes, D. T. (1978). *Psycholinguistics: An introduction to the psychology of language.* Prentice-Hall.

Foss, D. J., & Pirozzolo, J. W. (2017). Four semesters investigating frequency of testing, the testing effect, and transfer of training. *Journal of Educational Psychology, 109,* 1067.

Foss, R. D., Smith, R. L., & O'Brien, N. P. (2019). School start times and teenage driver motor vehicle crashes. *Accident Analysis & Prevention, 126,* 54–63.

Fothergill, E., Guo, J., Howard, L., Kerns, J. C., Knuth, J. D., Brychta, R., Chen, K. Y., Skarulis, M. C., Walter, M., Walter, P. J., & Hall, K. D. (2016). Persistent metabolic adaptation 6 years after "The Biggest Loser" competition. *Obesity, 24,* 1612–1619.

Foubert, J. D., Brosi, M. W., & Bannon, R. S. (2011). Pornography viewing among fraternity men: Effects on bystander intervention, rape myth acceptance, and behavioral intent to commit sexual assault. *Sexual Addiction & Compulsivity, 18,* 212–231.

Foulk, T. A., Lanaj, K., & Krishnan, S. (2019). The virtuous cycle of daily motivation: Effects of daily strivings on work behaviors, need satisfaction, and next-day strivings. *Journal of Applied Psychology, 104,* 755–775.

Foulkes, D. (1999). *Children's dreaming and the development of consciousness.* Harvard University Press.

Fournier, J. C., DeRubeis, R. J., Hollon, S. D., Dimidjian, S., Amsterdam, J. D., Shelton, R. C., & Fawcett, J. (2010). Antidepressant drug effects and depression severity: A patient-level meta-analysis. *Journal of the American Medical Association, 303,* 47–53.

Fowles, D. C. (1992). Schizophrenia: Diathesis-stress revisited. *Annual Review of Psychology, 43,* 303–336.

Fowles, D. C., & Dindo, L. (2009). Temperament and psychopathy: A dual-pathway model. *Current Directions in Psychological Science, 18,* 179–183.

Fox, A. S., Oler, J. A., Shackman, A. J., Shelton, S. E., Raveendran, M., McKay, D. R., Converse, A. K., Alexander, A., Davidson, R. J., Blangero, J., Rogers, J., & Kalin, N. H. (2015). Intergenerational neural mediators of early-life anxious temperament. *PNAS, 112,* 9118–9122.

Fox, B., & DeLisi, M. (2019). Psychopathic killers: A meta-analytic review of the psychopathy-homicide nexus. *Aggression and Violent Behavior, 44,* 67–79.

Fox, D. (2010, June). The insanity virus. *Discover,* pp. 58–64.

Fox, J. A., & Fridel, E. E. (2018). The menace of school shootings in America. In H. Shapiro (Ed.) *The Wiley Handbook on Violence in Education: Forms, Factors, and Preventions* (pp. 15–35). John Wiley & Sons.

Fox, K. C. R., Nijeboer, S., Solomonova, E., Domhoff, G. W., & Christoff, K. (2013). Dreaming as mind wandering: Evidence from functional neuroimaging and first-person content reports. *Frontiers in Human Neuroscience, 7,* 412.

Fox, M. L., Dwyer, D. J., & Ganster, D. C. (1993). Effects of stressful job demands and control on physiological and attitudinal outcomes in a hospital setting. *Academy of Management Journal, 36,* 289–318.

Fox, N. A., Bakermans-Kranenburg, M., Yoo, K. H., Bowman, L. C., Cannon, E. N., Vanderwert, R. E., Ferrari, P. F., & van IJzendoorn, M. H. (2016). Assessing human mirror activity with EEG mu rhythm: A meta-analysis. *Psychological Bulletin, 142,* 291–313.

Fozard, J. L., & Popkin, S. J. (1978). Optimizing adult development: Ends and means of an applied psychology of aging. *American Psychologist, 33,* 975–989.

Fragaszy, D. M., Eshchar, Y., Visalberghi, E., Resende, B., Laity, K., & Izar, P. (2017). Synchronized practice helps bearded capuchin monkeys learn to extend attention while learning a tradition. *PNAS, 114,* 7798–7805.

Fraley, R. C., Roisman, G. I., Booth-LaForce, C., Owen, M. T., & Holland, A. S. (2013). Interpersonal and genetic origins of adult attachment styles: A longitudinal study from infancy to early adulthood. *Journal of Personality and Social Psychology, 104,* 817–838.

Fraley, R. C., & Tancredy, C. M. (2012). Twin and sibling attachment in a nationally representative sample. *Personality and Social Psychology Bulletin, 38,* 308–316.

Fraley, R. C., Vicary, A. M., Brumbaugh, C. C., & Roisman, G. I. (2011). Patterns of stability in adult attachment: An empirical test of two models of continuity and change. *Journal of Personality and Social Psychology, 101,* 974–992.

Frances, A. J. (2013). *Saving normal: An insider's revolt against out-of-control psychiatric diagnosis, DSM-5, Big Pharma, and the medicalization of ordinary life.* HarperCollins.

Frances, A. J. (2014, September/October). No child left undiagnosed. *Psychology Today,* pp. 49–50.

Francis, A. L. (2018). The embodied theory of stress: A constructionist perspective on the experience of stress. *Review of General Psychology, 22,* 398–405.

Frank, J. D. (1982). Therapeutic components shared by all psychotherapies. In J. H. Harvey & M. M. Parks (Eds.), *The Master Lecture Series: Vol. 1. Psychotherapy research and behavior change.* American Psychological Association.

Frank, M., Braginsky, M., Marchman, V., & Yurovsky, D. (2019). Chapter 8, Consistency in early vocabulary comprehension, in *Variability and consistency in early language learning.* The Wordbank Project. https://langcog.github.io/wordbank-book/items-consistency.html

Frankel, A., Strange, D. R., & Schoonover, R. (1983). CRAP: Consumer rated assessment procedure. In G. H. Scherr & R. Liebmann-Smith (Eds.), *The best of The Journal of Irreproducible Results.* Workman.

Frankenburg, W., Dodds, J., Archer, P., Shapiro, H., & Bresnick, B. (1992). The Denver II: A major revision and restandardization of the Denver Developmental Screening Test. *Pediatrics, 89,* 91–97.

Frankl, V. E. (1962). *Man's search for meaning: An introduction to logotherapy.* Beacon Press.

Franklin, J. C., Ribeiro, J. D., Fox, K. R., Bentley, K. H., Kleiman, E. M., Huang, X., Musacchio, K. M., Jaroszewski, A. C., Chang, B. P., & Nock, M. K. (2017). Risk factors for suicidal thoughts and behaviors: A meta-analysis of 50 years of research. *Psychological Bulletin, 143,* 187–232.

Franklin, M., & Foa, E. B. (2011). Treatment of obsessive-compulsive disorder. *Annual Review of Clinical Psychology, 7,* 229–243.

Franklin, R. G., Adams, R. B., Steiner, T. G., Zebrowitz, L. A. (2019). Reading the lines in the face: The contribution of angularity and roundness to perceptions of facial anger and joy. *Emotion, 19*(2), 209–218.

Franz, E. A., Waldie, K. E., & Smith, M. J. (2000). The effect of callosotomy on novel versus familiar bimanual actions: A neural dissociation between controlled and automatic processes? *Psychological Science, 11,* 82–85.

Fraser, M. A., Shaw, M. E., & Cherubin, N. (2015). A systematic review and meta-analysis of longitudinal hippocampal atrophy in healthy human ageing. *NeuroImage, 112,* 364–374.

Frassanito, P., & Pettorini, B. (2008). Pink and blue: The color of gender. *Child's Nervous System, 24,* 881–882.

Frasure-Smith, N., & Lesperance, F. (2005). Depression and coronary heart disease: Complex synergism of mind, body, and environment. *Current Directions in Psychological Science, 14,* 39–43.

Frattaroli, J. (2006). Experimental disclosure and its moderators: A meta-analysis. *Psychological Bulletin, 132,* 823–865.

Frederick, S. (2005). Cognitive reflection and decision making. *Journal of Economic Perspectives, 4,* 25–42.

Fredrickson, B. L. (2013). Updated thinking on positivity ratios. *American Psychologist, 68,* 814–822.

Freedman, D. H. (2011, February). How to fix the obesity crisis. *Scientific American,* pp. 40–47.

Freedman, D. J., Riesenhuber, M., Poggio, T., & Miller, E. K. (2001). Categorical representation of visual stimuli in the primate prefrontal cortex. *Science, 291,* 312–316.

Freedman, J. L., & Fraser, S. C. (1966). Compliance without pressure: The foot-in-the-door technique.

Journal of Personality and Social Psychology, 4, 195–202.

Freedman, J. L., & Perlick, D. (1979). Crowding, contagion, and laughter. *Journal of Experimental Social Psychology, 15,* 295–303.

Freedman, L. R., Rock, D., Roberts, S. A., Cornblatt, B. A., & Erlenmeyer-Kimling, L. (1998). The New York high-risk project: Attention, anhedonia and social outcome. *Schizophrenia Research, 30,* 1–9.

Freedman, R., Lewis, D. A., Michels, R., Pine, D. S., Schultz, S. K., Tamminga, C. A., Gabbard, G. O., Gau, S. S., Javitt, D. C., Oquendo, M. A., Shrout, P. E., Vieta, E., & Yager, J. (2013). The initial field trials of DSM-5: New blooms and old thorns. *American Journal of Psychiatry, 170,* 1–5.

Freeman, D., & Freeman, J. (2013). *The stressed sex: Uncovering the truth about men, women, and mental health.* Oxford University Press.

Freeman, D., Haselton, P., Freeman, J., Spanlang, B., Kishore, S., Albery, E., Denne, M., Brown, P., Slater, M., & Nickless, A. (2018). Automated psychological therapy using immersive virtual reality for treatment of fear of heights: A single-blind, parallel-group, randomised controlled trial. *The Lancet Psychiatry, 5,* 625–632.

Freeman, E. C., & Twenge, J. M. (2010, January). *Using MySpace increases the endorsement of narcissistic personality traits* [Poster]. Presented at the annual conference of the Society for Personality and Social Psychology, Las Vegas, NV.

Freeman, S., Eddy, S. L., McDonough, M., Smith, M. K., Okoroafor, N., Jordt, H., & Wenderoth, M. P. (2014). Active learning increases student performance in science, engineering, and mathematics. *PNAS, 111,* 8410–8415.

Freeman, W. J. (1991, February). The physiology of perception. *Scientific American,* pp. 78–85.

Frenda, S. J., Patihis, L., Loftus, E. F., Lewis, H. C., & Fenn, K. M. (2014). Sleep deprivation and false memories. *Clinical Psychological Science, 25,* 1674–1681.

Freud, S. (1897, October 15). Letter of Freud to Fleiss. In J. M. Masson (Ed.) (1985), *The complete letters of Sigmund Freud to Wilhelm Fleiss, 1887–1904.* Harvard University Press.

Freud, S. (1935; reprinted 1960). *A general introduction to psychoanalysis.* Washington Square Press.

Frey, M. C., & Detterman, D. K. (2004). Scholastic assessment or *g*? The relationship between the Scholastic Assessment Test and general cognitive ability. *Psychological Science, 15,* 373–378.

Freyd, J. J., DePrince, A. P., & Gleaves, D. H. (2007). The state of betrayal trauma theory: Reply to McNally—Conceptual issues and future directions. *Memory, 15,* 295–311.

Fried, E. I., Eidhof, M. B., Palic, S., Costantini, G., Huisman-van Dijk, H. M., Bockting, C. L. H., Engelhard, I., Armour, C., Nielsen, A. B., & Karstoft, K.-I. (2018). Replicability and generalizability of posttraumatic stress disorder (PTSD) networks: A cross-cultural multisite study of PTSD symptoms in four trauma patient samples. *Clinical Psychological Science, 6,* 335–351.

Friedel, J. E., DeHart, W. B., Madden, G. J., & Odum, A. L. (2014). Impulsivity and cigarette smoking: Discounting of monetary and consumable outcomes in current and non-smokers. *Psychopharmacology, 231,* 4517–4526.

Friedman, H. S., & Martin, L. R. (2012). *The longevity project.* Penguin (Plume).

Friedman, M., & Ulmer, D. (1984). *Treating Type A behavior—and your heart.* Knopf.

Friedman, R., & James, J. W. (2008). The myth of the stages of dying, death and grief. *Skeptic, 14,* 37–41.

Friedman, R. A. (2017, October 11). Psychiatrists can't stop mass killers. *The New York Times.* https://www.nytimes.com/2017/10/11/opinion/psychiatrists-mass-killers.html?

Friedrich, M., Wilhelm, I., Born, J., & Friederici, A. D. (2015). Generalization of word meanings during infant sleep. *Nature Communications, 6,* Article 6004.

Friend, T. (2004). *Animal talk: Breaking the codes of animal language.* Free Press.

Friesen, J. P., Campbell, T. H., & Kay, A. C. (2015). The psychological advantage of unfalsifiability: The appeal of untestable religious and political ideologies. *Journal of Personality and Social Psychology, 108,* 515–529.

Frimer, J. A., Brandt, M. J., Melton, Z., & Motyl, M. (2019). Extremists on the left and right use angry, negative language. *Personality and Social Psychology Bulletin, 45,* 1216–1231.

Frisell, T., Pawitan, Y., Långström, N., & Lichtenstein, P. (2012). Heritability, assortative mating and gender differences in violent crime: Results from a total population sample using twin, adoption, and sibling models. *Behavior Genetics, 42,* 3–18.

Frith, U., & Frith, C. (2001). The biological basis of social interaction. *Current Directions in Psychological Science, 10,* 151–155.

Frithsen, A., Stark, S. M., & Stark, C. E. (2019). Response bias, recollection, and familiarity in individuals with Highly Superior Autobiographical Memory (HSAM). *Memory, 27,* 739–749.

Fritz, C., Curtin, J., Poitevineau, J., & Tao, F.-C. (2017). Listener evaluations of new and Old Italian violins. *PNAS, 114,* 5395–5400.

Fritz, N., & Paul, B. (2018). From orgasms to spanking: A content analysis of the agentic and objectifying sexual scripts in feminist, for women, and mainstream pornography, *Sex Roles, 77,* 639–652.

Fromkin, V., & Rodman, R. (1983). *An introduction to language* (3rd ed.). Holt, Rinehart & Winston.

Frühauf, S., Gerger, H., Schmidt, H. M., Munder, T., & Barth, J. (2013). Efficacy of psychological interventions for sexual dysfunction: A systematic review and meta-analysis. *Archives of Sexual Behavior, 42,* 915–933.

Fry, A. F., & Hale, S. (1996). Processing speed, working memory, and fluid intelligence: Evidence for a developmental cascade. *Psychological Science, 7,* 237–241.

Fry, D. P. (2012). Life without war. *Science, 336,* 879–884.

Fry, R. (2017, May 5). *It's becoming more common for young adults to live at home—and for longer stretches.* Pew Research Center. https://www.pewresearch.org/fact-tank/2017/05/05/its-becoming-more-common-for-young-adults-to-live-at-home-and-for-longer-stretches/

Fu, A., & Markus, H. R. (2014). My mother and me: Why tiger mothers motivate Asian Americans but not European Americans. *Personality and Social Psychology Bulletin, 40,* 739–749.

Fuhrmann, D., Knoll, L. J., & Blakemore, S. J. (2015). Adolescence as a sensitive period of brain development. *Trends in Cognitive Sciences, 19,* 558–566.

Fuller-Thomson, E., Agbeyaka, S., LaFond, D. M., & Bern-Klug, M. (2016). Flourishing after depression: Factors associated with achieving complete mental health among those with a history of depression. *Psychiatry Research, 242,* 111–120.

Fulmer, C. A., Gelfand, M. J., Kruglanski, A. W., Kim-Prieto, C., Diener, E., Pierro, A., & Higgins, E. T. (2010). On "feeling right" in cultural contexts: How person–culture match affects self-esteem and subjective well-being. *Psychological Science, 21,* 1563–1569.

Funder, D. C. (2001). Personality. *Annual Review of Psychology, 52,* 197–221.

Funder, D. C. (2009). Persons, behaviors and situations: An agenda for personality psychology in the postwar era. *Journal of Research in Personality, 43,* 155–162.

Funder, D. C., & Block, J. (1989). The role of ego-control, ego-resiliency, and IQ in delay of gratification in adolescence. *Journal of Personality and Social Psychology, 57,* 1041–1050.

Funk, C. (2019, February 6). *How highly religious Americans view evolution depends on how they're asked about it.* Pew Research Center. https://tinyurl.com/qszpfzc

Furnham, A. (1982). Explanations for unemployment in Britain. *European Journal of Social Psychology, 12,* 335–352.

Furnham, A. (2016). Whether you think you can, or you think you can't—you're right. In R. J. Sternberg, S. T. Fiske, & D. J. Foss (Eds.), *Scientists making a difference: One hundred eminent behavioral and brain scientists talk about their most important contributions.* Cambridge University Press.

Furnham, A. (2018). Myths and misconceptions in developmental and neuro-psychology. *Psychology, 9,* 249–259.

Furnham, A., & Baguma, P. (1994). Cross-cultural differences in the evaluation of male and female body shapes. *International Journal of Eating Disorders, 15,* 81–89.

Furr, R. M., & Funder, D. C. (1998). A multimodal analysis of personal negativity. *Journal of Personality and Social Psychology, 74,* 1580–1591.

Furukawa, T. A., Levine, S. Z., Tanaka, S., Goldberg, Y., Samara, M., Davis, J. M., Cipriani, A., & Leucht, S. (2015). Initial severity of schizophrenia and efficacy of antipsychotics: Participant-level meta-analysis of 6 placebo-controlled studies. *JAMA Psychiatry, 72,* 14–21.

Fuss, J., Steinle, J., Bindila, L., Auer, M. K., Kirchherr, H., Lutz, B., & Gass, P. (2015). A runner's high depends on cannabinoid receptors in mice. *PNAS, 112,* 13105–13108.

Futrell, R., Mahowald, K., & Gibson, E. (2015). Large-scale evidence of dependency length minimization in 37 languages. *PNAS, 112,* 10336–10341.

Gable, S. L., Hopper, E. A., & Schooler, J. W. (2019). When the muses strike: Creative ideas of physicists and writers routinely occur during mind wandering. *Psychological Science, 30,* 396–404.

Gaddy, M. A., & Ingram, R. E. (2014). A meta-analytic review of mood-congruent implicit memory in depressed mood. *Clinical Psychology Review, 34,* 402–416.

Gaertner, L., Iuzzini, J., & O'Mara, E. M. (2008). When rejection by one fosters aggression against many: Multiple-victim aggression as a consequence of social rejection and perceived groupness. *Journal of Experimental Social Psychology, 44,* 958–970.

Gage, S. (2019). Cannabis and psychosis: Triangulating the evidence. *The Lancet, 6,* 364–365.

Gaissmaier, W., & Gigerenzer, G. (2012). 9/11, Act II: A fine-grained analysis of regional variations in traffic fatalities in the aftermath of the terrorist attacks. *Psychological Science, 23,* 1449–1454.

Gaither, S. E., & Sommers, S. R. (2013). Living with another-race roommate shapes whites' behavior in subsequent diverse settings. *Journal of Experimental Social Psychology, 49,* 272–276.

Galambos, N. L. (1992). Parent–adolescent relations. *Current Directions in Psychological Science, 1,* 146–149.

Galanter, E. (1962). Contemporary psychophysics. In R. Brown, E. Galanter, E. H. Hess, & G. Mandler (Eds.), *New directions in psychology* (pp. 87–156). Holt, Rinehart & Winston.

Galanter, M. (2016). *What is Alcoholics Anonymous?* Oxford University Press.

Galati, D., Scherer, K. R., & Ricci-Bitti, P. E. (1997). Voluntary facial expression of emotion: Comparing congenitally blind with normally sighted encoders. *Journal of Personality and Social Psychology, 73,* 1363–1379.

Galatzer-Levy, I., Huang, S. H., & Bonanno, G. A. (2018). Trajectories of resilience and dysfunction following potential trauma: A review and statistical evaluation. *Clinical Psychology Review, 63,* 41–55.

Gale, C. R., Batty, G. D., & Deary, I. J. (2008). Locus of control at age 10 years and health outcomes and behaviors at age 30 years: The 1970 British Cohort Study. *Psychosomatic Medicine, 70,* 397–403.

Gale, N., Swaine, T., Morgan, H., Parkinson, V., Bagnall-Oakeley, R., Clarke, J., Williams, C., Ross, M., Keogh, B., Wilson, S., Singh, R., Reeves, A., Saddington, P., Calderwood, C., Mathers, N., Ruddle, A., Andersen-Warren, M., Stewart, J., Davis, D., & Pollecoff, M. (2017). *Memorandum of understanding on conversion therapy in the UK, Version 2* [PDF file]. https://www.psychotherapy.org.uk/wp-content/uploads/2017/10/UKCP-Memorandum-of-Understanding-on-Conversion-Therapy-in-the-UK.pdf

Galinsky, A. M., & Sonenstein, F. L. (2013). Relationship commitment, perceived equity, and sexual enjoyment among young adults in the United States. *Archives of Sexual Behavior, 42,* 93–104.

Galla, B. M., & Duckworth, A. L. (2015). More than resisting temptation: Beneficial habits mediate the relationship between self-control and positive life outcomes. *Journal of Personality and Social Psychology, 109,* 508–525.

Gallace, A. (2012). Living with touch. *Psychologist, 25,* 896–899.

Gallace, A., & Spence, C. (2011). To what extent do Gestalt grouping principles influence tactile perception? *Psychological Bulletin, 137,* 538–561.

Gallese, V., Gernsbacher, M. A., Heyes, C., Hickok, G., & Iacoboni, M. (2011). Mirror neuron forum. *Perspectives on Psychological Science, 6,* 369–407.

Gallo, W. T., Teng, H. M., Falba, T. A., Kasl, S. V., Krumholz, H. M., & Bradley, E. H. (2006). The impact of late career job loss on myocardial infarction and stroke: A 10-year follow up using the health and retirement survey. *Occupational and Environmental Medicine, 63,* 683–687.

Gallup, G. G., Jr., & Frederick, D. A. (2010). The science of sex appeal: An evolutionary perspective. *Review of General Psychology, 14,* 240–250.

Gallup, G. G., Jr., & Suarez, S. D. (1986). Self-awareness and the emergence of mind in humans and other primates. In J. Suls & A. G. Greenwald (Eds.), *Psychological perspectives on the self* (Vol. 3.). Erlbaum.

Gallup, G. H. (1972). *The Gallup poll: Public opinion 1935–1971* (Vol. 3). Random House.

Gallup, G. H., Jr. (1994, October). Millions finding care and support in small groups. *Emerging Trends,* pp. 2–5.

Gallup. (2004, August 16). 65% of Americans receive NO praise or recognition in the workplace. E-mail from Tom Rath: bucketbook@gallup.com

Gallup. (2017). *State of the global workplace.* Gallup. https://www.gallup.com/workplace/238079/state-global-workplace-2017.aspx

Gallup. (2019). *Gallup global emotions report.* https://www.gallup.com/analytics/248906/gallup-global-emotions-report-2019.aspx

Gallup. (2019). *Illegal drugs.* Gallup News. https://news.gallup.com/poll/1657/illegal-drugs.aspx

Gallup. (2020, February 4). *Is working remotely effective? Gallup research says yes.* https://gallup.com/workplace/283985/working-remotely-effective-gallup-research-says-yes.aspx

Gampe, A., Wermelinger, S., & Daum, M. M. (2019). Bilingual children adapt to the needs of their communication partners, monolinguals do not. *Child Development, 90,* 98–107.

Gana, K., Broc, G., Saada, Y., Amieva, H., & Quintard, B. (2016). Subjective wellbeing and longevity: Findings from a 22-year cohort study. *Journal of Psychosomatic Research, 85,* 28–34.

Gandal, M. J., Haney, J. R., Parikshak, N. N., Leppa, V., Ramaswami, G., Hartl, C., Schork, A. J., Appadurai, V., Buil, A., Werge, T. M., Liu, C., White, K. P., CommonMind Consortium, PsychENCODE Consortium; iPSYCH-BROAD Working Group, Horvath, S., & Geschwind, D. H. (2018). Shared molecular neuropathology across major psychiatric disorders parallels polygenic overlap. *Science, 359,* 693–697.

Gandhi, A. V., Mosser, E. A., Oikonomou, G., & Prober, D. A. (2015). Melatonin is required for the circadian regulation of sleep. *Neuron, 85,* 1193–1199.

Gandhi, T. K., Ganesh, S., & Sinha, P. (2014). Improvement in spatial imagery following sight onset late in childhood. *Psychological Science, 25,* 693–701.

Gandhi, T. K., Singh, A. K., Swami, P., Ganesh, S., & Sinha, P. (2017). Emergence of categorical face perception after extended early-onset blindness. *PNAS, 114,* 6139–6143.

Gangestad, S. W., Thornhill, R., & Garver-Apgar, C. E. (2010). Men's facial masculinity predicts changes in their female partners' sexual interests across the ovulatory cycle, whereas men's intelligence does not. *Evolution and Human Behavior, 31,* 412–424.

Gangwisch, J. E., Babiss, L. A., Malaspina, D., Turner, J. B., Zammit, G. K., & Posner, K. (2010). Earlier parental set bedtimes as a protective factor against depression and suicidal ideation. *Sleep, 33,* 97–106.

Ganna, A., Verweij, K. J., Nivard, M. G., Maier, R., Wedow, R., Busch, A. S., Abdellaoui, A., Guo, S., Sathirapongsasuti, J. F., 23andMe Research Team, Lichtenstein, P., Lundström, S., Långström, N., Auton, A., Harris, K. M., Beecham, G. W., Martin, E. R., Sanders, A. R., Perry, J. R. B., Neale, B. M., & Zietsch, B. P. (2019). Large-scale GWAS reveals insights into the genetic architecture of same-sex sexual behavior. *Science, 365*(6456), eaat7693.

Ganzach, Y., & Patel, P. (2018). Wages, mental abilities and assessments in large scale international surveys: Still not much more than *g. Intelligence, 69,* 1–7.

Gao, Y., Raine, A., Venables, P. H., Dawson, M. E., & Mednick, S. A. (2010). Association of poor child fear conditioning and adult crime. *American Journal of Psychiatry, 167,* 56–60.

Garcia, J., & Gustavson, A. R. (1997, January). Carl R. Gustavson (1946–1996): Pioneering wildlife psychologist. *APS Observer,* pp. 34–35.

Garcia, J., & Koelling, R. A. (1966). Relation of cue to consequence in avoidance learning. *Psychonomic Science, 4,* 123–124.

Garcia, J. R., Reiber, C., Massey, S. G., & Merriwether, A. M. (2013, February). Sexual hook-up culture. *Monitor on Psychology,* pp. 60–66.

Garcia-Falgueras, A., & Swaab, D. F. (2010). Sexual hormones and the brain: An essential alliance for sexual identity and sexual orientation. *Endocrine Development, 17,* 22–35.

Gardner, H. (1983). *Frames of mind: The theory of multiple intelligences.* Basic Books.

Gardner, H. (1998, March 19). An intelligent way to progress. *The Independent* (London), p. E4.

Gardner, H. (1999a). *Multiple views of multiple intelligence.* Basic Books.

Gardner, H. (1999b, February). Who owns intelligence? *Atlantic Monthly,* pp. 67–76.

Gardner, H. (2006). *The development and education of the mind: The selected works of Howard Gardner.* Routledge/Taylor & Francis.

Gardner, H. (2011). *The theory of multiple intelligences: As psychology, as education, as social science* [Address]. Upon the receipt of an honorary degree from José Cela University in Madrid and the Prince of Asturias Prize for Social Science.

Gardner, J., & Oswald, A. J. (2007). Money and mental well-being: A longitudinal study of medium–sized lottery wins. *Journal of Health Economics, 6,* 49–60.

Gardner, R. A., & Gardner, B. I. (1969). Teaching sign language to a chimpanzee. *Science, 165,* 664–672.

Garfield, C. (1986). *Peak performers: The new heroes of American business.* Morrow.

Garon, N., Bryson, S. E., & Smith, I. M. (2008). Executive function in preschoolers: A review using an integrative framework. *Psychological Bulletin, 134,* 31–60.

Garrett-Bakelman, F. E., Darshi, M., Green, S. J., Gur, R. C., Lin, L., Macias, B. R., McKenna, M. J., Meydan, C., Mishra, T., Nasrini, J., Piening, B. D., Rizzardi, L. F., Sharma, K., Siamwala, J. H., Taylor, L., Vitaterna, M. H., Afkarian, M., Afshinnekoo, E., Ahadi, S., Turek, F. W. (2019). The NASA Twins Study: A multidimensional analysis of a year-long human spaceflight. *Science, 364*(6436), eaau8650.

Garrison, K. E., Finley, A. J., & Schmeichel, B. J. (2019). Ego depletion reduces attention control: Evidence from two high-powered preregistered experiments. *Personality and Social Psychology Bulletin, 45,* 728–739.

Garry, M., Loftus, E. F., & Brown, S. W. (1994). Memory: A river runs through it. *Consciousness and Cognition, 3,* 438–451.

Gartrell, N., & Bos, H. (2010). U.S. national longitudinal lesbian family study: Psychological adjustment of 17-year-old adolescents. *Pediatrics, 126,* 28–36.

Gasiorowska, A., Chaplin, L. N., Zaleskiewicz, T., Wygrab, S., & Vohs, K. D. (2016). Money cues increase agency and decrease prosociality among children: Early signs of market-mode behaviors. *Psychological Science, 27,* 331–344.

Gaskins, A. J., Rich-Edwards, J. W., Williams, P. L., Toth, T. L., Missmer, S. A., & Chavarro, J. E. (2018). Pre-pregnancy caffeine and caffeinated beverage intake and risk of spontaneous abortion. *European Journal of Nutrition, 57,* 107–117.

Gatchel, R. J., Peng, Y. B., Peters, M. L., Fuchs, P. N., & Turk, D. C. (2007). The biopsychosocial approach to chronic pain: Scientific advances and future directions. *Psychological Bulletin, 133,* 581–624.

Gavin, K. (2004, November 9). *U-M team reports evidence that smoking affects human brain's natural "feel good" chemical system* [Press release]. med.umich.edu/

Gavrilets, S., Friberg, U., & Rice, W. R. (2018). Understanding homosexuality: Moving on from patterns to mechanisms. *Archives of Sexual Behavior, 47,* 27–31.

Gawande, A. (1998, September 21). The pain perplex. *The New Yorker,* pp. 86–94.

Gawin, F. H. (1991). Cocaine addiction: Psychology and neurophysiology. *Science, 251,* 1580–1586.

Gazzaniga, M. S. (1967, August). The split brain in man. *Scientific American,* pp. 24–29.

Gazzaniga, M. S. (1983). Right hemisphere language following brain bisection: A 20-year perspective. *American Psychologist, 38,* 525–537.

Gazzaniga, M. S. (1988). Organization of the human brain. *Science, 245,* 947–952.

Gazzola, V., Spezio, M. L., Etzel, J. A., Catelli, F., Adolphs, R., & Keysers, C. (2012). Primary somatosensory cortex discriminates affective significance in social touch. *PNAS, 109,* E1657–E1666.

GBD (Global Burden of Disease). (2017). Smoking prevalence and attributable disease burden in 195 countries and territories, 1990–2015: A systematic analysis from the Global Burden of Disease Study 2015. *The Lancet, 389*, 1885–1906.

Ge, X., & Natsuaki, M. N. (2009). In search of explanations for early pubertal timing effects on developmental psychopathology. *Current Directions in Psychological Science, 18*, 327–441.

Ge, Y., Knittel, C. R., MacKenzie, D., & Zoepf, S. (2016, October). *Racial and gender discrimination in transportation network companies* (NBER Working Paper No. 22776). https://www.nber.org/papers/w22776

Geary, D. C. (2010). *Male, female: The evolution of human sex differences* (2nd ed.). American Psychological Association.

Geary, D. C. (2019). The spark of life and the unification of intelligence, health, and aging. *Current Directions in Psychological Science, 28*, 223–228.

Gecewicz, C. (2018, October 1). *'New Age' beliefs common among both religious and nonreligious Americans.* Pew Research Center. https://www.pewresearch.org/fact-tank/2018/10/01/new-age-beliefs-common-among-both-religious-and-nonreligious-americans/

Geen, R. G., & Quanty, M. B. (1977). The catharsis of aggression: An evaluation of a hypothesis. In L. Berkowitz (Ed.), *Advances in experimental social psychology* (Vol. 10). Academic Press.

Geers, A. E., & Nicholas, J. G. (2013). Enduring advantages of early cochlear implantation for spoken language development. *Journal of Speech, Language, and Hearing Research, 56*, 643–653.

Geers, A. L., Briñol, P., & Petty, R. E. (2019). An analysis of the basic processes of formation and change of placebo expectations. *Review of General Psychology, 23*, 211–229.

Gehring, W. J., Wimke, J., & Nisenson, L. G. (2000). Action monitoring dysfunction in obsessive-compulsive disorder. *Psychological Science, 11*, 1–6.

Geier, A. B., Rozin, P., & Doros, G. (2006). Unit bias: A new heuristic that helps explain the effects of portion size on food intake. *Psychological Science, 17*, 521–525.

Gellis, L. A., Arigo, D., & Elliott, J. C. (2013). Cognitive refocusing treatment for insomnia: A randomized controlled trial in university students. *Behavior Therapy, 44*, 100–110.

Gelman, A. (2009, April 16). *Red and blue economies?* https://fivethirtyeight.com/features/red-and-blue-economies/

Genesee, F., & Gándara, P. (1999). Bilingual education programs: A cross-national perspective. *Journal of Social Issues, 55*, 665–685.

Gentile, D. A. (2009). Pathological video-game use among youth ages 8 to 18: A national study. *Psychological Science, 20*, 594–602.

Gentile, D. A., & Bushman, B. J. (2012). Reassessing media violence effects using a risk and resilience approach to understanding aggression. *Psychology of Popular Media Culture, 1*, 138–151.

Gentile, D. A., Coyne, S., & Walsh, D. A. (2011). Media violence, physical aggression and relational aggression in school age children: A short-term longitudinal study. *Aggressive Behavior, 37*, 193–206.

Gentner, D. (2016). Language as cognitive tool kit: How language supports relational thought. *American Psychologist, 71*, 650–657.

Gentzkow, M., Shapiro, J. M., & Taddy, M. (2016, July). *Measuring polarization in high-dimensional data: Method and application to congressional speech* (NBER Working Paper 22423). Stanford Institute for Economic Policy Research.

George, M. S. (2018). Is there really nothing new under the sun? Is low-dose ketamine a fast-acting antidepressant simply because it is an opioid? *The American Journal of Psychiatry, 175*, 1157–1158.

Geraerts, E., Bernstein, D. M., Merckelbach, H., Linders, C., Raymaekers, L., & Loftus, E. F. (2008). Lasting false beliefs and their behavioral consequences. *Psychological Science, 19*, 749–753.

Geraerts, E., Schooler, J. W., Merckelbach, H., Jelicic, M., Hauer, B. J. A., & Ambadar, Z. (2007). The reality of recovered memories: Corroborating continuous and discontinuous memories of childhood sexual abuse. *Psychological Science, 18*, 564–568.

Gernsbacher, M. A., Dawson, M., & Goldsmith, H. H. (2005). Three reasons not to believe in an autism epidemic. *Current Directions in Psychological Science, 14*, 55–58.

Gershenson, S., Holt, S. B., & Papageorge, N. W. (2016). Who believes in me? The effect of student-teacher demographic match on teacher expectations. *Economics of Education Review, 52*, 209–224.

Gershoff, E. T., & Grogan-Kaylor, A. (2016). Spanking and child outcomes: Old controversies and new meta-analyses. *Journal of Family Psychology, 30*, 453–469.

Gershoff, E. T., Grogan-Kaylor, A., Lansford, J. E., Chang, L., Zelli, A., Deater-Deckard, K., & Dodge, K. A. (2010). Parent discipline practices in an international sample: Associations with child behaviors and moderation by perceived normativeness. *Child Development, 81*, 487–502.

Gershoff, E. T., Sattler, K. M. P., & Ansari, A. (2018). Strengthening causal estimates for links between spanking and children's externalizing behavior problems. *Psychological Science, 29*, 110–120.

Gershon, A., Ram, N., Johnson, S. L., Harvey, A. G., & Zeitzer, J. M. (2016). Daily actigraphy profiles distinguish depressive and interepisode states in bipolar disorder. *Clinical Psychological Science, 4*, 641–650.

Gerst-Emerson, K., & Jayawardhana, J. (2015). Loneliness as a public health issue: The impact of loneliness on health care utilization among older adults. *American Journal of Public Health, 105*, 1013–1019.

Geschwind, N. (1979, September). Specializations of the human brain. *Scientific American, 241*, 180–199.

Geukes, K., Nestler, S., Hutteman, R., Dufner, M., Küfner, A. C., Egloff, B., Denissen, J. J. A., & Back, M. D. (2016). Puffed-up but shaky selves: State self-esteem level and variability in narcissists. *Journal of Personality and Social Psychology, 11*, 769–786.

Geulayov, G., Casey, D., Bale, L., Brand, F., Clements, C., Farooq, B., Kapur, N., Ness, J., Waters, K., Tsiachristas, A., & Hawton, K. (2019). Suicide following presentation to hospital for non-fatal self-harm in the Multicentre Study of Self-Harm: A long-term follow-up study. *The Lancet Psychiatry, 6*, 1021–1030.

Ghazi Sherbaf, F., Aarabi, M. H., Hosein Yazdi, M., & Haghshomar, M. (2019). White matter microstructure in fetal alcohol spectrum disorders: A systematic review of diffusion tensor imaging studies. *Human Brain Mapping, 40*, 1017–1036.

Giacobbe, P., Rakita, U., Penner-Goeke, K., Feffer, K., Flint, A. J., Kennedy, S. H., & Downar, J. (2018). Improvements in health-related quality of life with electroconvulsive therapy: A meta-analysis. *Journal of ECT, 34*, 87–94.

Giampietro, M., & Cavallera, G. M. (2007). Morning and evening types and creative thinking. *Personality and Individual Differences, 42*, 453–463.

Giancola, P. R., & Corman, M. D. (2007). Alcohol and aggression: A test of the attention-allocation model. *Psychological Science, 18*, 649–655.

Giancola, P. R., Josephs, R. A., Parrott, D. J., & Duke, A. A. (2010). Alcohol myopia revisited: Clarifying aggression and other acts of disinhibition through a distorted lens. *Perspectives on Psychological Science, 5*, 265–278.

Gibbons, F. X. (1986). Social comparison and depression: Company's effect on misery. *Journal of Personality and Social Psychology, 51*, 140–148.

Gibson, E. J., & Walk, R. D. (1960, April). The "visual cliff." *Scientific American*, pp. 64–71.

Gibson, J. J. (1979). *The ecological approach to visual perception*. Houghton Mifflin.

Giedd, J. N. (2015, June). The amazing teen brain. *Scientific American*, pp. 33–37.

Giesbrecht, T., Lynn, S. J., Lilienfeld, S. O., & Merckelbach, H. (2008). Cognitive processes in dissociation: An analysis of core theoretical assumptions. *Psychological Bulletin, 134*, 617–647.

Giesbrecht, T., Lynn, S. J., Lilienfeld, S. O., & Merckelbach, H. (2010). Cognitive processes, trauma, and dissociation—Misconceptions and misrepresentations: Reply to Bremmer (2010). *Psychological Bulletin, 136*, 7–11.

Gigerenzer, G. (2004). Dread risk, September 11, and fatal traffic accidents. *Psychological Science, 15*, 286–287.

Gigerenzer, G. (2006). Out of the frying pan into the fire: Behavioral reactions to terrorist attacks. *Risk Analysis, 26*, 347–351.

Gigerenzer, G. (2010). *Rationality for mortals: How people cope with uncertainty*. Oxford University Press.

Gigerenzer, G. (2015). *Simply rational: Decision making in the real world*. Oxford University Press.

Gilbert, D. T. (2006). *Stumbling on happiness*. Knopf.

Gilbert, D. T., Pinel, E. C., Wilson, T. D., Blumberg, S. J., & Wheatley, T. P. (1998). Immune neglect: A source of durability bias in affective forecasting. *Journal of Personality and Social Psychology, 75*, 617–638.

Gilbertson, M. W., Paulus, L. A., Williston, S. K., Gurvits, T. V., Lasko, N. B., Pitman, R. K., & Orr, S. P. (2006). Neurocognitive function in monozygotic twins discordant for combat exposure: Relationship to posttraumatic stress disorder. *Journal of Abnormal Psychology, 115*, 484–495.

Gildersleeve, K. A., Fales, M. R., & Haselton, M. G. (2017). Women's evaluations of other women's natural body odor depend on target's fertility status. *Evolution and Human Behavior, 38*, 155–163.

Gillen-O'Neel, C., Huynh, V. W., & Fuligni, A. J. (2013). To study or to sleep? The academic costs of extra studying at the expense of sleep. *Child Development, 84*, 133–142.

Gillespie, S. M., Rotshtein, P., Chapman, H., Brown, E., Beech, A. R., & Mitchell, I. J. (2019). Pupil reactivity to emotional faces among convicted violent offenders: The role of psychopathic traits. *Journal of Abnormal Psychology, 128*, 622–632.

Gilligan, C. (1982). *In a different voice: Psychological theory and women's development*. Harvard University Press

Gilligan, C. (2015). In a different voice: Women's conceptions of self and morality. In V. Burr (Ed.), *Gender and psychology* (Vol. II, pp. 33–74). Routledge/Taylor & Francis Group.

Gilovich, T. (1991). *How we know what isn't so: The fallibility of human reason in everyday life*. Free Press.

Gilovich, T. D. (1996). *The spotlight effect: Exaggerated impressions of the self as a social stimulus* [Unpublished manuscript]. Cornell University.

Gilovich, T. D., & Medvec, V. H. (1995). The experience of regret: What, when, and why. *Psychological Review, 102*, 379–395.

Gilovich, T. D., & Savitsky, K. (1999). The spotlight effect and the illusion of transparency: Egocentric assessments of how we are seen by others. *Current Directions in Psychological Science, 8*, 165–168.

Gingerich, O. (1999, February 6). *Is there a role for natural theology today?* http://faculty.smu.edu/jclam/science_religion/gingerich.html

Gingerich, O. (2006). *God's universe*. Belknap Press.

Gino, G., Wilmuth, C. A., & Brooks, A. W. (2015). Compared to men, women view professional advancement as equally attainable, but less desirable. *PNAS, 112*, 12354–12359.

Giuliano, T. A., Barnes, L. C., Fiala, S. E., & Davis D. M. (1998). *An empirical investigation of male answer syndrome.* Paper presented at the Southwestern Psychological Association convention.

Gladwell, M. (2000, May 9). The new-boy network: What do job interviews really tell us? *The New Yorker*, pp. 68–86.

Glasman, L. R., & Albarracín, D. (2006). Forming attitudes that predict future behavior: A meta-analysis of the attitude-behavior relation. *Psychological Bulletin, 132,* 778–822.

Glass, R. M. (2001). Electroconvulsive therapy: Time to bring it out of the shadows. *Journal of the American Medical Association, 285,* 1346–1348.

Glasser, M. F., Coalson, T. S., Robinson, E. C., Hacker, C. D., Harwell, J., Yacoub, E., Ugurbil, K., Andersson, J., Beckmann, C. F., Jenkinson, M., Smith, S. M., & Van Essen, D. C. (2016). A multi-modal parcellation of human cerebral cortex. *Nature, 536,* 171–178.

Gleaves, D. H. (1996). The sociocognitive model of dissociative identity disorder: A reexamination of the evidence. *Psychological Bulletin, 120,* 42–59.

Glenn, A. L., Raine, A. (2014). Neurocriminology: Implications for the punishment, prediction and prevention of criminal behavior. *Nature Reviews Neuroscience, 15,* 54–63.

Glenn, A. L., Raine, A., Yaralian, P.S., & Yang, Y. (2010). Increased volume of the striatum in psychopathic individuals. *Biological Psychiatry, 67,* 52–58.

Gliklich, E., Guo, R., & Bergmark, R. W. (2016). Texting while driving: A study of 1211 U.S. adults with the Distracted Driving Survey. *Preventive Medicine Reports, 4,* 486–489.

Global Burden of Disease Study, 2013 collaborators. (2015). Global, regional, and national incidence, prevalence, and years lived with disability for 301 acute and chronic diseases and injuries in 188 countries, 1990–2013: A systematic analysis for the Global Burden of Disease Study 2013. *The Lancet, 386,* 743–800.

GLSEN. (2012). *The 2011 national school climate survey.* Gay, Lesbian & Straight Education Network. https://www.glsen.org/news/2011-national-school-climate-survey

Glynn, L. M., & Sandman, C. A. (2011). Prenatal origins of neurological development: A critical period for fetus and mothers. *Current Directions in Psychological Science, 20,* 384–389.

Glynn, T. R., Gamarel, K. E., Kahler, C. W., Iwamoto, M., Operario, D., & Nemoto, T. (2017). The role of gender affirmation in psychological well-being among transgender women. *Psychology of Sexual Orientation and Gender Diversity, 3,* 336–344.

Gnambs, T., & Appel, M. (2018). Narcissism and social networking behavior: A meta-analysis. *Journal of Personality, 86,* 200–212.

Gobbi, G., Atkin, T., Zytynski, T., Wang, S., Askari, S., Boruff, J., Ware, M., Marmorstein, N., Cipriani, A., Dendukuri, N., & Mayo, N. (2019). Association of cannabis use in adolescence and risk of depression, anxiety, and suicidality in young adulthood: a systematic review and meta-analysis. *JAMA Psychiatry, 76,* 426–434.

Godart, F. C., Maddux, W. W., Shipilov, A. V., & Galinsky, A. D. (2015). Fashion with a foreign flair: Professional experiences abroad facilitate the creative innovations of organizations. *Academy of Management Journal, 58,* 195–220.

Goddard, M. J. (2018). Extending B.F. Skinner's selection by consequences to personality change, implicit theories of intelligence, skill learning, and language. *Review of General Psychology, 22,* 421–426.

Godden, D. R., & Baddeley, A. D. (1975). Context-dependent memory in two natural environments: On land and underwater. *British Journal of Psychology, 66,* 325–331

Godlee, F. (2011). Wakefield's article linking MMR vaccine and autism was fraudulent. *BMJ, 342,* c7452.

Goethals, G. R., & Allison, S. T. (2014). Kings and charisma, Lincoln and leadership: An evolutionary perspective. In G. R. Goethals, S. T. Allison, R. M. Kramer, & D. M. Messick (Eds.), *Conceptions of leadership: Enduring ideas and emerging insights* (pp. 111–124). Palgrave Macmillan.

Goetz, S. M. M., Tang, L., Thomason, M. E., Diamond, M. P., Hariri, A. R., & Carré, J. (2014). Testosterone rapidly increases neural reactivity to threat in healthy men: A novel two-step pharmacological challenge paradigm. *Biological Psychiatry, 76,* 324–331.

Goff, D. C., Falkai, P., Fleischhacker, W. W., Girgis, R. R., Kahn, R. M., Uchida, H., Zhao, J., & Lieberman, J. A. (2017). The long-term effects of antipsychotic medication on clinical course in schizophrenia. *The American Journal of Psychiatry, 174,* 840–849.

Goff, D. C., & Simms, C. A. (1993). Has multiple personality disorder remained consistent over time? *Journal of Nervous and Mental Disease, 181,* 595–600.

Gold, M. (2019, Jan. 21). New York passes a ban on 'conversion therapy' after years-long efforts. *The New York Times.* https://www.nytimes.com/2019/01/21/nyregion/conversion-therapy-ban.html?

Gold, M., & Yanof, D. S. (1985). Mothers, daughters, and girlfriends. *Journal of Personality and Social Psychology, 49,* 654–659.

Goldberg, J. (2007). *Quivering bundles that let us hear.* hhmi.org/senses/c120.html

Goldberg, S. B., Tucker, R. P., Greene, P. A., Davidson, R. J., Kearney, D. J., & Simpson, T. L. (2019). Mindfulness-based cognitive therapy for the treatment of current depressive symptoms: A meta-analysis. *Cognitive Behaviour Therapy, 48,* 445–462.

Goldberg, S. B., Tucker, R. P., Greene, P. A., Davidson, R. J., Wampold, B. E., Kearney, D. J., & Simpson, T. L. (2018). Mindfulness-based interventions for psychiatric disorders: A systematic review and meta-analysis. *Clinical Psychology Review, 59,* 52–60.

Golder, S. A., & Macy, M. W. (2011). Diurnal and seasonal mood vary with work, sleep, and day-length across diverse cultures. *Science, 333,* 1878–1881.

Goldfarb, D., Goodman, G. S., Larson, R. P., Eisen, M. L., & Qin, J. (2019). Long-term memory in adults exposed to childhood violence: Remembering genital contact nearly 20 years later. *Clinical Psychological Science, 7,* 381–396.

Goldfried, M. R. (2001). Integrating gay, lesbian, and bisexual issues into mainstream psychology. *American Psychologist, 56,* 977–988.

Goldfried, M. R., Raue, P. J., & Castonguay, L. G. (1998). The therapeutic focus in significant sessions of master therapists: A comparison of cognitive–behavioral and psychodynamic–interpersonal interventions. *Journal of Consulting and Clinical Psychology, 66,* 803–810.

Goldinger, S. D., & Papesh, M. H. (2012). Pupil dilation reflects the creation and retrieval of memories. *Current Directions in Psychological Science, 21,* 90–95.

Goldman, A. L., Pezawas, L., Mattay, V. S., Fischl, B., Verchinski, B. A., Chen, Q., Weinberger, D. R., & Meyer-Lindenberg, A. (2009). Widespread reductions of cortical thickness in schizophrenia and spectrum disorders and evidence of heritability. *Archives of General Psychiatry, 66,* 467–477.

Goldstein, A. P., Glick, B., & Gibbs, J. C. (1998). *Aggression replacement training: A comprehensive intervention for aggressive youth* (rev. ed.). Research Press.

Goleman, D. (1980, February). 1,528 little geniuses and how they grew. *Psychology Today,* pp. 28–53.

Goleman, D. (2006). *Social intelligence.* Bantam Books.

Golkar, A., Selbing, I., Flygare, O., Öhman, A., & Olsson, A. (2013). Other people as means to a safe end: Vicarious extinction blocks the return of learned fear. *Psychological Science, 24,* 2182–2190.

Gollwitzer, A., Martel, C., McPartland, J. C., & Bargh, J. A. (2019). Autism spectrum traits predict higher social psychological skill. *PNAS, 116,* 19245–19247.

Gollwitzer, P. M., & Oettingen, G. (2012). Goal pursuit. In P. M. Gollwitzer & G. Oettingen (Eds.), *The Oxford handbook of human motivation* (pp. 208–231). Oxford University Press.

Gollwitzer, P. M., & Sheeran, P. (2006). Implementation intentions and goal achievement: A meta-analysis of effects and processes. *Advances in Experimental Social Psychology, 38,* 69–119.

Gomes, C. M., Miranda, E. P., de Bessa Jr., J., Bellucci, C. H. S., Battistella, L. R., Abdo, C. H. N., Bruschini, H., Srougi, M., & Mulhall, J. P. (2017). Erectile function predicts sexual satisfaction in men with spinal cord injury. *Sexual Medicine, 5,* e148–e155.

Gomes, N., Soares, S. C., Silva, S., & Silva, C. F. (2018). Mind the snake: Fear detection relies on low spatial frequencies. *Emotion, 18,* 886–895.

Gómez-Robles, A., Hopkins, W. D., Schapiro, S. J., & Sherwood, C. C. (2015). Relaxed genetic control of cortical organization in human brains compared with chimpanzees. *PNAS, 112,* 14799–14804.

Gongola, J., Scurich, N., & Quas, J. A. (2017). Detecting deception in children: A meta-analysis. *Law and Human Behavior, 41,* 44–54.

Gonsalkorale, K., & Williams, K. D. (2006). The KKK would not let me play: Ostracism even by a despised outgroup hurts. *European Journal of Social Psychology, 36,* 1–11.

Gonsalves, B., Reber, P. J., Gitelman, D. R., Parrish, T. B., Mesulam, M.-M., & Paller, K. A. (2004). Neural evidence that vivid imagining can lead to false remembering. *Psychological Science, 15,* 655–659.

Gonzales, N. A., Johnson, M., Shirtcliff, E. A., Tein, J. Y., Eskenazi, B., & Deardorff, J. (2018). The role of bicultural adaptation, familism, and family conflict in Mexican American adolescents' cortisol reactivity. *Development and Psychopathology, 30,* 1571–1587.

Gonzalez, R. (2018, June 8). *How science helps the warriors sleep their way to success.* Wired Magazine. https://www.wired.com/story/how-science-helps-the-warriors-sleep-their-way-to-success/

Gonzalez-Barrera, A. (2019, July 2). *Hispanics with darker skin are more likely to experience discrimination than those with lighter skin.* Pew Research Center. https://pewrsr.ch/2wH7PoH

Goodall, J. (1986). *The chimpanzees of Gombe: Patterns of behavior.* Harvard University Press.

Goodall, J. (1998). Learning from the chimpanzees: A message humans can understand. *Science, 282,* 2184–2185.

Goode, E. (1999, April 13). If things taste bad, "phantoms" may be at work. *The New York Times.* https://www.nytimes.com/1999/04/13/science/if-things-taste-bad-phantoms-may-be-at-work.html?

Goodhart, D. E. (1986). The effects of positive and negative thinking on performance in an achievement situation. *Journal of Personality and Social Psychology, 51,* 117–124.

Goodman, G. S. (2006). Children's eyewitness memory: A modern history and contemporary commentary. *Journal of Social Issues, 62,* 811–832.

Goodman, G. S., Ghetti, S., Quas, J. A., Edelstein, R. S., Alexander, K. W., Redlich, A. D., Cordon, I. M., & Jones, D. P. H. (2003). A prospective study of memory for child sexual abuse: New findings relevant to the repressed-memory controversy. *Psychological Science, 14,* 113–118.

Goodman, J. B., Freeman, E. E., & Chalmers, K. A. (2019). The relationship between early life stress and working memory in adulthood: A systematic review and meta-analysis. *Memory, 27,* 868–880.

Goodwin, P. Y., Mosher, W. D., & Chandra, A. (2010, February). *Marriage and cohabitation in the United States: A statistical portrait based on Cycle 6 (2002) of the National Survey of Family Growth* (Vital Health Statistics Series 23, No. 28). U.S. Department of Health and Human Service, Centers for Disease Control and Prevention, National Center for Health Statistics.

Gopnik, A. (2016). *The carpenter and the gardener.* Farrar, Straus, and Giroux.

Gopnik, A., Griffiths, T. L., & Lucas, C. G. (2015). When younger learners can be better (or at least more open-minded) than older ones. *Current Directions in Psychological Science, 24,* 87–92.

Gopnik, A., & Meltzoff, A. N. (1986). Relations between semantic and cognitive development in the one-word stage: The specificity hypothesis. *Child Development, 57,* 1040–1053.

Goranson, A., Ritter, R. S., Waytz, A., Norton, M. I., & Gray, K. (2017). Dying is unexpectedly positive. *Psychological Science, 28,* 988–999.

Goranson, R. E. (1978). *The hindsight effect in problem solving.* Unpublished manuscript cited in G. Wood (1984), Research methodology: A decision-making perspective. In A. M. Rogers & C. J. Scheirer (Eds.), *The G. Stanley Hall Lecture Series* (Vol. 4, pp. 193–217). American Psychological Association.

Gorchoff, S. M., John, O. P., & Helson, R. (2008). Contextualizing change in marital satisfaction during middle age. *Psychological Science, 19,* 1194–1200.

Gordon, A. M., & Chen, S. (2010). When you accept me for me: The relational benefits of intrinsic affirmations from one's relationship partner. *Personality and Social Psychology Bulletin, 36,* 1439–1453.

Gordon, I., Vander Wyk, B. C., Bennett, R. H., Cordeaux, C., Lucas, M. V., Eilbott, J. A., Zagoory-Sharon, O., Leckman, J. F., Feldman, R., & Pelphrey, K. A. (2013). Oxytocin enhances brain function in children with autism. PNAS, 110, 20953–20958.

Gordon, P. (2004). Numerical cognition without words: Evidence from Amazonia. *Science, 306,* 496–499.

Gore, J., & Sadler-Smith, E. (2011). Unpacking intuition: A process and outcome framework. *Review of General Psychology, 15,* 304–316.

Gore-Felton, C., Koopman, C., Thoresen, C., Arnow, B., Bridges, E., & Spiegel, D. (2000). Psychologists' beliefs and clinical characteristics: Judging the veracity of childhood sexual abuse memories. *Professional Psychology: Research and Practice, 31,* 372–377.

Gorka, S. M., Lieberman, L., Shankman, S. A., & Phan, K. L. (2017). Startle potentiation to uncertain threat as a psychophysiological indicator of fear-based psychopathology: An examination across multiple internalizing disorders. *Journal of Abnormal Psychology, 126,* 8.

Gorlick, A. (2010, January 13). Stanford scientists link brain development to chances of recovering vision after blindness. *Stanford Report* (news.stanford.edu).

Gorman, J. (2019, December 3). Why are these foxes tame? Maybe they weren't so wild to begin with. *The New York Times.* https://www.nytimes.com/2019/12/03/science/foxes-tame-belyaev.html

Gormley, W., Kitchens, K., & Adelstein, S. (2013). Do middle-class families benefit from high-quality pre-K? CROCUS Policy Brief, July. Center for Research on Children in the U.S., Georgetown University.

Gorno-Tempini, M. L., & Price, C. J. (2001). Identification of famous faces and buildings: A functional neuroimaging study of semantically unique items. *Brain, 124,* 2087–2097.

Gorrese, A., & Ruggieri, R. (2012). Peer attachment: A meta-analytic review of gender and age differences and associations with parent attachment. *Journal of Youth and Adolescence, 41,* 650–672.

Gosling, S. D. (2008). *Snoop: What your stuff says about you.* Basic Books.

Gosling, S. D., Kwan, V. S. Y., & John, O. P. (2003). A dog's got personality: A cross-species comparative approach to personality judgments in dogs and humans. *Journal of Personality and Social Psychology, 85,* 1161–1169.

Gotink, R. A., Meijboom, R., Vernooij, M. W., Smits, M., & Hunink, M. G. M. (2016). 8-week mindfulness based stress reduction induces brain changes similar to traditional long-term meditation practice—A systematic review. *Brain and Cognition, 108,* 32–41.

Gotlib, I. H., & Hammen, C. L. (1992). *Psychological aspects of depression: Toward a cognitive-interpersonal integration.* Wiley.

Gottesman, I. I. (1991). *Schizophrenia genesis: The origins of madness.* Freeman.

Gottesman, I. I. (2001). Psychopathology through a life span—genetic prism. *American Psychologist, 56,* 867–881.

Gottfredson, L. S. (2002a). Where and why g matters: Not a mystery. *Human Performance, 15,* 25–46.

Gottfredson, L. S. (2002b). g: Highly general and highly practical. In R. J. Sternberg & E. L. Grigorenko (Eds.), *The general factor of intelligence: How general is it?* (pp. 331–380). Erlbaum.

Gottfredson, L. S. (2003a). Dissecting practical intelligence theory: Its claims and evidence. *Intelligence, 31,* 343–397.

Gottfredson, L. S. (2003b). On Sternberg's "Reply to Gottfredson." *Intelligence, 31,* 415–424.

Gottfried, A. W., Gottfried, A. E., & Guerin, D. W. (2006). The Fullerton Longitudinal Study: A long-term investigation of intellectual and motivational giftedness. *Journal for the Education of the Gifted, 29,* 430–450.

Gottman, J. (2007). *Why marriages succeed or fail.* Bloomsbury.

Gottman, J. M., & Gottman, J. S. (2018). *The science of couples and family therapy: Behind the scenes at the "love lab."* W. W. Norton.

Gould, E. (2007). How widespread is adult neurogenesis in mammals? *Nature Neuroscience, 8,* 481–488.

Gould, E., Simhon, A., & Weinberg, B. A. (2019, January). *Does parental quality matter? Evidence on the transmission of human capital using variation in parental influence from death, divorce, and family size.* NBER Working Paper No. 25495. https://www.nber.org/papers/w25495

Gould, K. L., Gilbertson, K. E., Hrvol, A. J., Nelson, J. C., Seyfer, A. L., Brantner, R. M., & Kamil, A. C. (2013). Differences in relative hippocampus volume and number of hippocampus neurons among five corvid species. *Brain, Behavior and Evolution, 81,* 56–70.

Gould, S. J. (1981). *The mismeasure of man.* Norton.

Gow, A. J., Bastin, M. E., Maniega, S. M., Hernández, M. C. V., Morris, Z., Murray, C., Royle, N. A., Starr, J. M., Deary, I. J., & Wardlaw, J. M. (2012). Neuroprotective lifestyles and the aging brain: Activity, atrophy, and white matter integrity. *Neurology, 79,* 1802–1808.

Goyal, M., Singh, S., Sibinga, E. S., Gould, N. F., Rowland-Seymour, A., Sharma, R., Berger, Z., Sleicher, D., Maron, D. D., Shihab, H. M., Ranasinghe, P. D., Linn, S., Saha, S., Bass, E. B., & Haythornthwaite, J. A. (2014). Meditation programs for psychological stress and well-being: A systematic review and meta-analysis. *JAMA Internal Medicine, 174,* 357–368.

Graafland, J., & Lous, B. (2019). Income Inequality, Life Satisfaction Inequality and Trust: A Cross Country Panel Analysis. *Journal of Happiness Studies, 20,* 1717–1737.

Grabo, A., & van Vugt, M. (2016). Charismatic leadership and the evolution of cooperation. *Evolution and Human Behavior, 37,* 399–406.

Grady, C. L., McIntosh, A. R., Horwitz, B., Maisog, J. M., Ungeleider, L. G., Mentis, M. J., Pietrini, P., Schapiro, M. B., & Haxby, J. V. (1995). Age-related reductions in human recognition memory due to impaired encoding. *Science, 269,* 218–221.

Graf, N. (2018, April 18). *A majority of U.S. teens fear a shooting could happen at their school, and most parents share their concern.* Pew Research Center. https://www.pewresearch.org/fact-ank/2018/04/18/a-majority-of-u-s-teens-fear-a-shooting-could-happen-at-their-school-and-most-parents-share-their-concern/

Graham, A. M., Fisher, P. A., & Pfeifer, J. H. (2013). What sleeping babies hear: A functional MRI study of interparental conflict and infants' emotion processing. *Psychological Science, 24,* 782–789.

Graham, C., Laffan, K., & Pinto, S. (2018). Well-being in metrics and policy. *Science, 362,* 287–288.

Graham, E. K., Rutsohn, J. P., Turiano, N. A., Bendayan, R., Batterham, P. J., Gerstorf, D., Katz, M. J., Reynolds, C. A., Sharp, E. S., Yoneda, T. B., Bastarache, E. D., Elleman, L. G., Zelinski, E. M., Johansson, B., Kuh, D., Barnes, L. L., Bennett, D. A., Deeg, D. J. H., Lipton, R. B., . . . Mroczek, D. K. (2017). Personality predicts mortality risk: An integrative data analysis of 15 international longitudinal studies. *Journal of Research in Personality, 70,* 174–186.

Graham, M., Winter, A. K., Ferrari, M., Grenfell, B., Moss, W. J., Azman, A. S., Metcalf, J. E., & Lessler, J. (2019). Measles and the canonical path to elimination. *Science, 364,* 584–587.

Gramlich, J. (2018, October 24). *8 facts about Americans and Facebook.* Pew Research Center. https://www.pewresearch.org/fact-tank/2018/10/24/facts-about-americans-and-facebook/

Grand, J. A. (2016). Brain drain? An examination of stereotype threat effects during training on knowledge acquisition and organizational effectiveness. *Journal of Applied Psychology, 102,* 115–150.

Granqvist, P., Mikulincer, M., & Shaver, P. R. (2010). Religion as attachment: Normative processes and individual differences. *Personality and Social Psychology Review, 14,* 49–59.

Granqvist, P., Vestbrant, K., Döllinger, L., Liuzza, M. T., Olsson, M. J., Blomkvist, A., & Lundström, J. N. (2019). The scent of security: Odor of romantic partner alters subjective discomfort and autonomic stress responses in an adult attachment-dependent manner. *Physiology & Behavior, 198,* 144–150.

Grant, A. M., Gino, F., & Hofmann, D. A. (2011). Reversing the extraverted leadership advantage: The role of employee proactivity. *Academy of Management Journal, 54,* 528–550.

Grant, J. M., Mottet, L. A., Tanis, J., Herman, J. L., Harrison, J., & Keisling, M. (2010). *National transgender discrimination survey report on health and health care.* National Center for Transgender Equality and National Gay and Lesbian Task Force.

Grant, N., Wardle, J., & Steptoe, A. (2009). The relationship between life satisfaction and health behavior: A cross-cultural analysis of young adults. *International Journal of Behavioral Medicine, 16,* 259–268.

Grassegger, H., & Krogerus, M. (2017, January 28). *The data that turned the world upside down.* Motherboard. https://www.vice.com/en_us/article/mg9vvn/how-our-likes-helped-trump-win

Gray-Little, B., & Burks, N. (1983). Power and satisfaction in marriage: A review and critique. *Psychological Bulletin, 93,* 513–538.

Graybiel, A. M., & Smith, K. S. (2014, June). Good habits, bad habits. *Scientific American, 310,* 38–43.

Greaves, L. M., Sibley, C. G., Fraser, G., & Barlow, F. K. (2019). Comparing pansexual- and bisexual-identified participants on demographics, psychological well-being, and political ideology in a New Zealand National Sample. *The Journal of Sex Research, 56*(9), 1083–1090.

Green, B. (2002). Listening to leaders: Feedback on 360-degree feedback one year later. *Organizational Development Journal, 20,* 8–16.

Green, J. D., Sedikides, C., & Gregg, A. P. (2008). Forgotten but not gone: The recall and recognition of self-threatening memories. *Journal of Experimental Social Psychology, 44,* 547–561.

Green, J. T., & Woodruff-Pak, D. S. (2000). Eyeblink classical conditioning: Hippocampal formation is for neutral stimulus associations as cerebellum is for association-response. *Psychological Bulletin, 126,* 138–158.

Greenberg, J. (2008). Understanding the vital human quest for self-esteem. *Perspectives on Psychological Science, 3,* 48–55.

Greenberg, J., Solomon, S., & Pyszczynski, T. (1997). Terror management theory of self-esteem and cultural worldviews: Empirical assessments and conceptual refinements. *Advances in Social Psychology, 29,* 61–142.

Greene, J. (2010). Remarks to an Edge conference: *The new science of morality.* Edge. https://www.edge.org/event/the-new-science-of-morality

Greene, J. D., Sommerville, R. B., Nystrom, L. E., Darley, J. M., & Cohen, J. D. (2001). An fMRI investigation of emotional engagement in moral judgment. *Science, 293,* 2105–2108.

Greenwald, A. G. (1992). *Subliminal semantic activation and subliminal snake oil* [Paper]. Presented to the American Psychological Association Convention, Washington, DC.

Greenwald, A. G., & Banaji, M. R. (2017). The implicit revolution: Reconceiving the relation between conscious and unconscious. *American Psychologist, 72,* 861–871.

Greenwald, A. G., & Pettigrew, T. F. (2014). With malice toward none and charity for some: Ingroup favoritism enables discrimination. *American Psychologist, 69,* 645–655.

Greenwald, A. G., Spangenberg, E. R., Pratkanis, A. R., & Eskenazi, J. (1991). Double-blind tests of subliminal self-help audiotapes. *Psychological Science, 2,* 119–122.

Greenwald, G. (2012, March 19). *Discussing the motives of the Afghan shooter.* Salon. https://www.salon.com/2012/03/19/discussing_the_motives_of_the_afghan_shooter/

Greer, S. G., Goldstein, A. N., & Walker, M. P. (2013). The impact of sleep deprivation on food desire in the human brain. *Nature Communications, 4,* 2259.

Gregory, A. M., Rijksdijk, F. V., Lau, J. Y., Dahl, R. E., & Eley, T. C. (2009). The direction of longitudinal associations between sleep problems and depression symptoms: A study of twins aged 8 and 10 years. *Sleep, 32,* 189–199.

Gregory, R. L. (1978). *Eye and brain: The psychology of seeing* (3rd ed.). McGraw-Hill.

Gregory, R. L., & Gombrich, E. H. (Eds.). (1973). *Illusion in nature and art.* Charles Scribner's Sons.

Greist, J. H., Jefferson, J. W., & Marks, I. M. (1986). *Anxiety and its treatment: Help is available.* American Psychiatric Press.

Greitemeyer, T., & Mügge, D. O. (2014). Video games do affect social outcomes: A meta-analytic review of the effects of violent and prosocial video game play. *Personality and Social Psychology Bulletin, 40,* 578–589.

Greitemeyer, T., Weiß, N., & Heuberger, T. (2019). Are everyday sadists specifically attracted to violent video games and do they emotionally benefit from playing those games? *Aggressive Behavior, 45,* 206–213.

Greyson, B. (2010). Implications of near-death experiences for a postmaterialist psychology. *Review of Religion and Spirituality, 2,* 37–45.

Grèzes, J., & Decety, J. (2001). Function anatomy of execution, mental simulation, observation, and verb generation of actions: A meta-analysis. *Human Brain Mapping, 12,* 1–19.

Griesler, P. C., Hu, M. C., Wall, M. M., & Kandel, D. B. (2019). Nonmedical prescription opioid use by parents and adolescents in the US. *Pediatrics, 143,* e20182354.

Griffin, J. M., Kruger, S., & Maturana, G. (2019). Personal infidelity and professional conduct in 4 settings. PNAS, 116, 16268–16273.

Griffin, E. A., Jr., Melas, P. A., Zhou, R., Li, Y., Mercado, P., & Kemp, K. A. (2017). Prior alcohol use enhances vulnerability to compulsive cocaine self-administration by promoting degradation of HDAC4 and HDAC5. *Science Advances, 3*(11), e1701682.

Griffiths, M. (2001). Sex on the internet: Observations and implications for internet sex addiction. *Journal of Sex Research, 38,* 333–342.

Grijalva, E., Newman, D. A., Tay, L., Donnellan, M. B., Harms, P. D., Robins, R. W., & Yan, T. (2015). Gender differences in narcissism: A meta-analytic review. *Psychological Bulletin, 141,* 261–310.

Grilo, C. M., & Pogue-Geile, M. F. (1991). The nature of environmental influences on weight and obesity: A behavior genetic analysis. *Psychological Bulletin, 110,* 520–537.

Grinberg, N., Joseph, K., Friedland, L., Swire-Thompson, B., & Lazer, D. (2019). Fake news on Twitter during the 2016 U.S. presidential election. *Science, 363,* 374–378.

Grinker, R. R. (2007). *Unstrange minds: Remapping the world of autism.* Basic Books.

Grinker, R. R. (2018, December 6). Being trans is not a mental disorder. *The New York Times.* https://www.nytimes.com/2018/12/06/opinion/trans-gender-dysphoria-mental-disorder.html

Grinspoon, D. (2016, September 1). Can humans outsmart extinction? *Scientific American, 315*(3).

Grobstein, C. (1979, June). External human fertilization. *Scientific American,* pp. 57–67.

Grønnerød, C., Grønnerød, J. S., & Grøndahl, P. (2015). Psychological treatment of sexual offenders against children: A meta-analytic review of treatment outcome studies. *Trauma, Violence, & Abuse, 16,* 280–290.

Gross, A. E., & Crofton, C. (1977). What is good is beautiful. *Sociometry, 40,* 85–90.

Groß, J., Blank, H., & Bayen U. J. (2017). Hindsight bias in depression. *Clinical Psychological Science, 5,* 771–788.

Gross, J. J. (2013). Emotion regulation: Taking stock and moving forward. *Emotion, 13,* 359–365.

Grossberg, S. (1995). The attentive brain. *American Scientist, 83,* 438–449.

Grossmann, I., & Kross, E. (2014). Exploring Solomon's paradox: Self-distancing eliminates the self-other asymmetry in wise reasoning about close relationships in younger and older adults. *Psychological Science, 25,* 1571–1580.

Grossmann, I., Na, J., Varnum, M. E. W., Park, D. C., Kitayama, S., & Nisbett, R. E. (2010). Reasoning about social conflicts improves into old age. PNAS, 107, 7246–7250.

Grossmann, I., & Varnum, M. E. W. (2015). Social structure, infectious diseases, disasters, secularism, and cultural change in America. *Psychological Science, 26,* 311–324.

Grover, S. & Helliwell, J. F. (2014, December). *How's life at home? New evidence on marriage and the set point for happiness.* NBER Working Paper No. 20794. https://www.nber.org/papers/w20794

Gruber, J., Villanueva, C., Burr, E., Purcell, J. R., & Karoly, H. (2019). Understanding and taking stock of positive emotion disturbance. *Social and Personality Psychology Compass, 14,* e12515.

Gruder, C. L. (1977). Choice of comparison persons in evaluating oneself. In J. M. Suls & R. L. Miller (Eds.), *Social comparison processes.* Hemisphere.

Gu, J., Strauss, C., Bond, R., & Cavanagh, K. (2015). How do mindfulness-based cognitive therapy and mindfulness-based stress reduction improve mental health and wellbeing? A systematic review and meta-analysis of mediation studies. *Clinical Psychology Review, 37,* 1–12.

Gu, X., Lohrenz, T., Salas, R., Baldwin, P. R., Soltani, A., Kirk, U., Cinciripini, P. M., & Montague, P. R. (2015). Belief about nicotine selectively modulates value and reward prediction error signals in smokers. PNAS, 112, 2539–2544.

Guardino, C. M., Schetter, C. D., Saxbe, D. E., Adam, E. K., Ramey, S. L., & Shalowitz, M. U. (2016). Diurnal salivary cortisol patterns prior to pregnancy predict infant birth weight. *Health Psychology, 35,* 625–633.

Guéguen, N. (2011). Effects of solicitor sex and attractiveness on receptivity to sexual offers: A field study. *Archives of Sexual Behavior, 40,* 915–919.

Guerin, B. (1986). Mere presence effects in humans: A review. *Journal of Personality and Social Psychology, 22,* 38–77.

Guerin, B. (2003). Language use as social strategy: A review and an analytic framework for the social sciences. *Review of General Psychology, 7,* 251–298.

Guertin, C., Pelletier, L. G., Émond, C., & Lalande, G. (2017). Change in physical and psychological health over time in patients with cardiovascular disease: On the benefits of being self-determined, physically active, and eating well. *Motivation and Emotion, 41*(3), 294–307.

Guinness World Records. (2019). *Guinness world records 2019.* Guinness World Records Limited.

Guiso, L., Monte, F., Sapienza, P., & Zingales, L. (2008). Culture, gender, and math. *Science, 320,* 1164–1165.

Gülgöz, S., Glazier, J. J., Enright, E. A., Alonso, D. J, Durwood, L. J., Fast, A. A., Lowe, R., Ji, C., Heer, J., Martin, C. L., & Olson, K. R. (2019). Similarity in transgender and cisgender children's gender development. PNAS, 116, 24480–24485.

Gunderson, E. A., Gripshover, S. J., Romero, C., Dweck, C. S., Goldin-Meadow, S., & Levine, S. C. (2013). Parent praise to 1- to 3-year-olds predicts children's motivational frameworks 5 years later. *Child Development, 84,* 1526–1541.

Gunn, R. L., Norris, A. L., Sokolovsky, A., Micalizzi, L., Merrill, J. E., & Barnett, N. P. (2018). Marijuana use is associated with alcohol use and consequences across the first 2 years of college. *Psychology of Addictive Behaviors, 32,* 885–894.

Gunnery, S. D., & Ruben, M. A. (2016). Perceptions of Duchenne and non-Duchenne smiles: A meta-analysis. *Cognition and Emotion, 30,* 501–515.

Gunter, T. D., Vaughn, M. G., & Philibert, R. A. (2010). Behavioral genetics in antisocial spectrum disorders and psychopathy: A review of the recent literature. *Behavioral Sciences and the Law, 28,* 148–173.

Gunyadin, G., Selcuk, E., & Zayas, V. (2017). Impressions based on a portrait predict, 1-month later, impressions following a live interaction. *Social Psychological and Personality Science, 8,* 36–44.

Guo, X., Zhai, J., Liu, Z., Fang, M., Wang, B., Wang, C., Hu, B., Sun, X., Lv, L., Lu, Z., Ma, C., He, X., Gui, T., Xie, S., Wu, R., Xue, Z., Chen, J., Twamley, E. W.,

Jin, H., & Zhao, J. (2010). Effect of antipsychotic medication alone vs combined with psychosocial intervention on outcomes of early-stage schizophrenia. *Archives of General Psychiatry, 67,* 895–904.

Gupta, M. D. (2017, September). Return of the missing daughters. *Scientific American,* pp. 78–85.

Gustavson, C. R., Garcia, J., Hankins, W. G., & Rusiniak, K. W. (1974). Coyote predation control by aversive conditioning. *Science, 184,* 581–583.

Gustavson, C. R., Kelly, D. J., & Sweeney, M. (1976). Prey-lithium aversions I: Coyotes and wolves. *Behavioral Biology, 17,* 61–72.

Gutchess, A. (2014). Plasticity in the aging brain: New directions in cognitive neuroscience. *Science, 346,* 579–582.

Guttmacher Institute. (1994). *Sex and America's teenagers.* Alan Guttmacher Institute.

H., Sally. (1979, August). [Videotape.] Recording number T–3, Fortunoff Video Archive of Holocaust Testimonies. Yale University Library.

Haaker, J., Yi, J., Petrovic, P., & Olsson, A. (2017). Endogenous opioids regulate social threat learning in humans. *Nature Communications, 8,* 15495.

Haapakoski, R., Mathieu, J., Ebmeier, K. P., Alenius, H., & Kivimäki, M. (2015). Cumulative meta-analysis of interleukins 6 and 1b, tumour necrosis factor a and C-reactive protein in patients with major depressive disorder. *Brain, Behavior, and Immunity, 49,* 206–215.

Haas, A. P., Eliason, M., Mays, V. M., Mathy, R. M., Cochran, S. D., D'Augelli, A. R., Silverman, M. M., Fisher, P. W., Hughes, T., Rosario, M., Russell, S. T., Malley, E., Reed, J., Litts, D. A., Haller, E., Sell, R. L., Remafedi, G., Bradford, J., Beautrais, A. L., . . . Clayton, P. J. (2011). Suicide and suicide risk in lesbian, gay, bisexual, and transgender populations: Review and recommendations. *Journal of Homosexuality, 58,* 10–51.

Habashi, M. M., Graziano, W. G., & Hoover, A. E. (2016). Searching for the prosocial personality: A big five approach to linking personality and prosocial behavior. *Personality and Social Psychology Bulletin, 42,* 1177–1192.

Habel, U., Koch, K., Kellerman, T., Reske, M., Frommann, N., Wölwer, W., Zilles, K., Shah, N. J., & Schneider, F. (2010). Training of affect recognition in schizophrenia: Neurobiological correlates. *Social Neuroscience, 5,* 92–104.

Haber, R. N. (1970). How we remember what we see. *Scientific American,* pp. 104–112.

Habib, A. M., Okorkov, A. L., Hill, M. N., Bras, J. T., Lee, M-C., Li, S., Gossage, S. J., van Drimmelen, M., Morena, M., Houlden, H., Ramirez, J. D., Bennett, D. L. H., Srivastava, D., & Cox, J. J. (2019). Microdeletion in a *FAAH* pseudogene identified in a patient with high anandamide concentrations and pain insensitivity. *British Journal of Anaesthesia, 123,* e249–e253.

Hadjistavropoulos, T., Craig, K. D., Duck, S. Cano, A., Goubert, L., Jackson, P. L., Mogil, J. S., Rainville, P., Sullivan, M. J. L., Williams, A. C. C., Vervoort, T., & Fitzgerald, T. D. (2011). A biopsychosocial formulation of pain communication. *Psychological Bulletin, 137,* 910–939.

Haedt-Matt, A. A., & Keel, P. K. (2011). Revisiting the affect regulation model of binge eating: A meta-analysis of studies using ecological momentary assessment. *Psychological Bulletin, 137,* 660–681.

Hafenbrack, A. C., Kinias, Z., & Barsade, S. G. (2014). Debiasing the mind through meditation: Mindfulness and the sunk-cost bias. *Psychological Science, 25,* 369–376.

Hagger, M. S., & Chatzisarantis, N. L. (2016). The trans-contextual model of autonomous motivation in education: Conceptual and empirical issues and meta-analysis. *Review of Educational Research, 86,* 360–407.

Hagger, M. S., Chatzisarantis, N. L. D., Alberts, H., Anggono, C. O., Birt, A., Brand, R., Brandt, M. J., Brewer, G., Bruyneel, S., Calvillo, D., Campbell, W., Cannon, P., Carlucci, M., Carruth, N., Cheung, T., Crowell, A., Ridder, D., Dewitte, S., & Elson, M. (2016). A multi-lab pre-registered replication of the ego-depletion effect. *Perspectives on Psychological Science, 11,* 546–573.

Hahn, A., Kranz, G., Sladky, R., Kaufmann, U., Ganger, S., Hummer, A., Seiger, R., Spies, M., Vanicek, T., Winkler, D., Kasper, S., Windischberger, C., Swabb, D. F., & Lanzenberger, R. (2016). Testosterone affects language areas of the adult human brain. *Human Brain Mapping, 37,* 1738–1748.

Haidt, J. (2000). The positive emotion of elevation. *Prevention and Treatment, 3,* article 3.

Haidt, J. (2002). The moral emotions. In R. J. Davidson, K. Scherer, & H. H. Goldsmith (Eds.), *Handbook of affective sciences.* Oxford University Press.

Haidt, J. (2012). *The righteous mind: Why good people are divided by politics and religion.* Pantheon.

Haidt, J. (2019, accessed May 7). *Social media use and mental health: A review.* Working document. https://tinyurl.com/y2noowlr

Haidt, J., & Twenge, J. M. (2019). *Social media use and mental health: A review.* https://bit.ly/2OoPUsJ

Hainey, M. (2016). Lin-Manuel Miranda thinks the key to parenting is a little less parenting. *GQ Magazine.* https://www.gq.com/story/unexpected-lin-manuel-miranda

Hajhosseini, B., Stewart, B., Tan, J. C., Busque, S., & Melcher, M. L. (2013). Evaluating deceased donor registries: Identifying predictive factors of donor designation. *American Surgeon, 79,* 235–241.

Hakuta, K., Bialystok, E., & Wiley, E. (2003). Critical evidence: A test of the critical-period hypothesis for second-language acquisition. *Psychological Science, 14,* 31–38.

Halberstadt, J., Sherman, S. J., & Sherman, J. W. (2011). Why Barack Obama is Black. *Psychological Science, 22,* 29–33.

Halberstadt, J. B., Niedenthal, P. M., & Kushner, J. (1995). Resolution of lexical ambiguity by emotional state. *Psychological Science, 6,* 278–281.

Haldeman, D. C. (1994). The practice and ethics of sexual orientation conversion therapy. *Journal of Consulting and Clinical Psychology, 62,* 221–227.

Haldeman, D. C. (2002). Gay rights, patient rights: The implications of sexual orientation conversion therapy. *Professional Psychology: Research and Practice, 33,* 260–264.

Hales, C. M., Kit, B. K., Gu, Q., & Ogden, C. L. (2018). Trends in prescription medication use among children and adolescents—United States, 1999–2014. *JAMA, 319*(19), 2009–2020.

Hall, C. S., Dornhoff, W., Blick, K. A., & Weesner, K. E. (1982). The dreams of college men and women in 1950 and 1980: A comparison of dream contents and sex differences. *Sleep, 5,* 188–194.

Hall, C. S., & Lindzey, G. (1978). *Theories of personality* (2nd ed.). Wiley.

Hall, D. T., & Chandler, D. E. (2005). Psychological success: When the career is a calling. *Journal of Organizational Behavior, 26,* 155–176.

Hall, G. (1997). Context aversion, Pavlovian conditioning, and the psychological side effects of chemotherapy. *European Psychologist, 2,* 118–124.

Hall, G. S. (1904). *Adolescence: Its psychology and its relations to physiology, anthropology, sex, crime, religion and education* (Vol. 1). Appleton-Century-Crofts.

Hall, J. A., Gunnery, S. D., & Horgan, T. G. (2016). Gender differences in interpersonal accuracy. In J. A. Hall, M. S. Mast & T. V. West (Eds.), *The social psychology of perceiving others accurately* (pp. 309–327). Cambridge University Press.

Hall, K. M., Knudson, S. T., Wright, J., Charlifue, S. W., Graves, D. E., & Warner, P. (1999). Follow-up study of individuals with high tetraplegia (C1-C4) 14 to 24 years postinjury. *Archives of Physical Medicine and Rehabilitation, 80,* 1507–1513.

Hall, M. H., Brindle, R. C., & Buysse, D. J. (2018). Sleep and cardiovascular disease: Emerging opportunities for psychology. *American Psychologist, 73,* 994–1006.

Hall, P. A. (2016). Executive-control processes in high-calorie food consumption. *Current Directions in Psychological Science, 25,* 91–98.

Hall, S. S. (2004, May). The good egg. *Discover,* pp. 30–39.

Hall, S. S., Knox, D., & Shapiro, K. (2017). "I have," "I would," "I won't": Hooking up among sexually diverse groups of college students. *Psychology of Sexual Orientation and Gender Diversity, 4,* 233–240.

Hallal, P. C., Andersen, L. B., Bull, F. C., Guthold, R., Haskell, W., & Ekelund, U. (2012). Global physical activity levels: Surveillance progress, pitfalls, and prospects. *The Lancet, 380,* 247–257.

Halldorsdottir, T., Piechaczek, C., Soares, d. M., Czamara, D., Pehl, V., Wagenbuechler, P., Feldmann, L., Quickenstedt-Reinhardt, P., Allgaier, A. K., Freisleder, F. J., Greimel, E., Kvist, T., Lahti, J., Räikkönen, K., Rex-Haffner, M., Arnarson, E. Ö., Craighead, W. E., Schulte-Körne, G., & Binder, E. B. (2019). Polygenic risk: Predicting depression outcomes in clinical and epidemiological cohorts of youths. *The American Journal of Psychiatry, 176,* 615–625.

Haller, R., Rummel, C., Henneberg, S., Pollmer, U., & Köster, E. P. (1999). The influence of early experience with vanillin on food preference later in life. *Chemical Senses, 24,* 465–467.

Halmburger, A., Baumert, A., & Schmitt, M. (2015). Anger as driving factor of moral courage in comparison with guilt and global mood: A multimethod approach. *European Journal of Social Psychology, 45,* 39–51.

Halpern, D. (2015). The rise of psychology in policy: The UK's de facto council of psychological science advisers. *Perspectives on Psychological Science, 10,* 768–771.

Halpern, D., Valenzuela, S., & Katz, J. E. (2016). "Selfie-ists" or "Narci-selfiers"?: A cross-lagged panel analysis of selfie taking and narcissism. *Personality and Individual Differences, 97,* 98–101.

Halpern, D. F., Benbow, C. P., Geary, D. C., Gur, R. C., Hyde, J. S., & Gernsbacher, M. A. (2007). The science of sex differences in science and mathematics. *Psychological Science in the Public Interest, 8,* 1–51.

Hambrick, D. Z. (2014, December 2). Brain training doesn't make you smarter. *Scientific American.* https://www.scientificamerican.com/article/brain-training-doesn-t-make-you-smarter/

Hambrick, D. Z., Altmann, E. M., Oswald, F. L., Meinz, E. J., Gobet, F., & Campitelli, G. (2014a). Accounting for expert performance: The devil is in the details. *Intelligence, 45,* 112–114.

Hambrick, D. Z., & Meinz, E. J. (2011). Limits on the predictive power of domain-specific experience and knowledge in skilled performance. *Current Directions in Psychological Science, 20,* 275–279.

Hambrick, D. Z., Oswald, F. L., Altmann, E. M., Meinz, E. J., Gobet, F., & Campitelli, G. (2014b). Deliberate practice: Is that all it takes to become an expert? *Intelligence, 45,* 34–45.

Hamer, M., Kivimaki, M., Stamatakis, E., & Batty, G. D. (2019). Psychological distress and infectious disease mortality in the general population. *Brain, Behavior, and Immunity, 76,* 280–283.

Hamid, A. A., Pettibone, J. R., Mabrouk, O. S., Hetrick, V. L., Schmidt, R., Vander Weele, C. M., Kennedy, R. T., Aragona, B. J., & Berke, J. D. (2016). Mesolimbic dopamine signals the value of work. *Nature Neuroscience, 19,* 117–126.

Hamilton, J. L., Stange, J. P., Abramson, L. Y., & Alloy, L. B. (2015). Stress and the development of cognitive vulnerabilities to depression explain sex differences in depressive symptoms during adolescence. *Clinical Psychological Science, 3*, 702–714.

Hamlin, J. K., Wynn, K., Bloom, P., & Mahajan, N. (2011). How infants and toddlers reach to antisocial others. *PNAS, 108*, 19931–19936.

Hammack, P. L. (2005). The life course development of human sexual orientation: An integrative paradigm. *Human Development, 48*, 267–290.

Hammer, E. (2003). How lucky you are to be a psychology major. *Eye on Psi Chi*, 4–5.

Hammersmith, S. K. (1982, August). *Sexual preference: An empirical study from the Alfred C. Kinsey Institute for Sex Research* [Paper]. Presented at the meeting of the American Psychological Association, Washington, DC.

Hammond, D. C. (2008). Hypnosis as sole anesthesia for major surgeries: Historical and contemporary perspectives. *American Journal of Clinical Hypnosis, 51*, 101–121.

Hamza, C. A., Willoughby, T., & Heffer, T. (2015). Impulsivity and nonsuicidal self-injury: A review and meta-analysis. *Clinical Psychology Review, 38*, 13–24.

Han, B., Kott, P. S., Hughes, A., McKeon, R., Blanco, C., & Compton, W. M. (2016). Estimating the rates of deaths by suicide among adults who attempt suicide in the United States. *Journal of Psychiatric Research, 77*, 125–133.

Han, L. K. M., Aghajani, M., Clark, S. L., Chan, R. F., Hattab, M. W., Shabalin, A. A., Zhao, M., Kumar, G., Xie, L. Y., Jansen, R., Milaneschi, Y., Den, B., Aberg, K. A., van den Oord, D. J. C. G., & Penninx, B. W. J. H. (2018). Epigenetic aging in major depressive disorder. *The American Journal of Psychiatry, 175*, 774–782.

Hanania, R. (2017). The personalities of politicians: A big five survey of American legislators. *Personality and Individual Differences, 108*, 164–167.

Haney, J. L. (2016). Predictors of homonegativity in the United States and the Netherlands using the fifth wave of the World Values Survey. *Journal of Homosexuality, 63*, 1355–1377.

Hänggi, J., Koeneke, S., Bezzola, L., Jäncke, L. (2010). Structural neuroplasticity in the sensorimotor network of professional female ballet dancers. *Human Brain Mapping, 31*, 1196–1206.

Hankin, B. L., & Abramson, L. Y. (2001). Development of gender differences in depression: An elaborated cognitive vulnerability-transactional stress theory. *Psychological Bulletin, 127*, 773–796.

Hanlon, E. C., Tasali, E., Leproult, R., Stuhr, K. L., Doncheck, E., de Wit, H., Hillard, C. J., & Van Cauter, E. (2015). Sleep restriction enhances the daily rhythm of circulating levels of endocannabinoid 2-arachidonoylglycerol. *Sleep, 39*, 653–664.

Hanniball, K. B., Aknin, L. B., Douglas, K. S., & Viljoen, J. L. (2019). Does helping promote well-being in at-risk youth and ex-offender samples? *Journal of Experimental Social Psychology, 82*, 307–317.

Hansen, A., Turpyn, C. C., Mauro, K., Thompson, J. C., & Chaplin, T. M. (2019). Adolescent brain response to reward is associated with a bias toward immediate reward. *Developmental Neuropsychology*, 1–12.

Harari, G. M., Lane, N. D., Wang, R., Crosier, B. S., Campbell, A. T., & Gosling, S. D. (2016). Using smartphones to collect behavioral data in psychological science: Opportunities, practical considerations, and challenges. *Perspectives on Psychological Science, 11*, 838–854.

Harbaugh, W. T., Mayr, U., & Burghart, D. R. (2007). Neural responses to taxation and voluntary giving reveal motives for charitable donations. *Science, 316*, 1622–1625.

Harber, K. D. (1998). Feedback to minorities: Evidence of a positive bias. *Journal of Personality and Social Psychology, 74*, 622–628.

Harden, K. P. (2012). True love waits? A sibling-comparison study of age at first sexual intercourse and romantic relationships in young adulthood. *Psychological Science, 23*, 1324–1336.

Harden, K. P., & Mendle, J. (2011). Why don't smart teens have sex? A behavioral genetic approach. *Child Development, 82*, 1327–1344.

Hards, E., Ellis, J., Fisk, J., & Reynolds, S. (2019). Memories of the self in adolescence: Examining 6558 self-image norms. *Memory, 27*, 1–7.

Hardt, O., Einarsson, E. O., & Nader, K. (2010). A bridge over troubled water: Reconsolidation as a link between cognitive and neuroscientific memory research traditions. *Annual Review of Psychology, 61*, 141–167.

Hare, R. D. (1975). Psychophysiological studies of psychopathy. In D. C. Fowles (Ed.), *Clinical applications of psychophysiology*. Columbia University Press.

Harenski, C. L., Harenski, K. A., Shane, M. W., & Kiehl, K. A. (2010). Aberrant neural processing of moral violations in criminal psychopaths. *Journal of Abnormal Psychology, 119*, 863–874.

Harkin, B., Webb, T. L., Chang, B. P. I., Prestwich, A., Conner, M., Kellar, I., Benn, Y., & Sheeran, P. (2016). Does monitoring goal progress promote goal attainment? A meta-analysis of the experimental evidence. *Psychological Bulletin, 142*, 198–229.

Harkins, S. G., & Szymanski, K. (1989). Social loafing and group evaluation. *Journal of Personality and Social Psychology, 56*, 934–941.

Harlow, H. F., Harlow, M. K., & Suomi, S. J. (1971). From thought to therapy: Lessons from a primate laboratory. *American Scientist, 59*, 538–549.

Harmon-Jones, E., Abramson, L. Y., Sigelman, J., Bohlig, A., Hogan, M. E., & Harmon-Jones, C. (2002). Proneness to hypomania/mania symptoms or depression symptoms and asymmetrical frontal cortical responses to an anger-evoking event. *Journal of Personality and Social Psychology, 82*, 610–618.

Harnett, N. G., Shumen, J. R., Wagle, P. A., Wood, K. H., Wheelock, M. D., Baños, J. H., & Knight, D. C. (2016). Neural mechanisms of human temporal fear conditioning. *Neurobiology of Learning and Memory, 136*, 97–104.

Harold, C. M., Oh, I.-S., Holtz, B. C., Han, S., & Giacalone, R. A. (2016). Fit and frustration as drivers of targeted counterproductive work behaviors: A multifoci perspective. *Journal of Applied Psychology, 101*, 1513–1535.

Harper, C., & McLanahan, S. (2004). Father absence and youth incarceration. *Journal of Research on Adolescence, 14*, 369–397.

Harper's. (2009, November). Harper's index. *Harper's*, p. 13.

Harris, B. (1979). Whatever happened to Little Albert? *American Psychologist, 34*, 151–160.

Harris, J. R. (1998). *The nurture assumption*. Free Press.

Harris, J. R. (2000). Beyond the nurture assumption: Testing hypotheses about the child's environment. In J. G. Borkowski & S. L. Ramey (Eds.), *Parenting and the child's world: Influences on academic, intellectual, and social-emotional development*. APA Books.

Harris, J. R. (2007, August 8). Do pals matter more than parents? [PDF]. *The Times*. https://www.nyman.org/Judith%20Rich%20Harris.pdf

Harris, J. R. (2009). *The nurture assumption: Why children turn out the way they do, revised and updated*. Free Press.

Harris, M. A., Brett, C. E., Johnson, W., & Deary, I. J. (2016). Personality stability from age 14 to age 77 years. *Psychology and Aging, 31*, 862–874.

Harris, R. J. (1994). The impact of sexually explicit media. In J. Brant & D. Zillmann (Eds.), *Media effects: Advances in theory and research*. Erlbaum.

Harrison, G., Hopper, K. I. M., Craig, T., Laska, E., Siegel, C., Wanderling, J., Dube, K. C., Ganev, K, Giel, R., Der Heiden, W. A., Holmberg, S. K., Janca, A., Lee, P. W., León, C. A., Malhotra, S., Marsella, A. J., Nakane, Y., Sartorius, N., Shen, Y., . . . Wiersma, D. (2001). Recovery from psychotic illness: A 15-and 25-year international follow-up study. *The British Journal of Psychiatry, 178*, 506–517.

Harrison, L. A., Hurlemann, R., & Adolphs, R. (2015). An enhanced default approach bias following amygdala lesions in humans. *Psychological Science, 26*, 1543–1555.

Harrison, N. A., Johnston, K., Corno, F., Casey, S. J., Friedner, K., Humphreys, K., Jaldow, E. J., Pitkanen, M., & Kopelman, M. D. (2017). Psychogenic amnesia: Syndromes, outcome, and patterns of retrograde amnesia. *Brain: A Journal of Neurology, 140*, 2498–2510.

Harriston, K. A. (1993, December 24). 1 shakes, 1 snoozes: Both win $45 million. *Washington Post* release in *Tacoma News Tribune*, pp. A1, A2.

Harter, J. K., Schmidt, F. L., Asplund, J. W., Killham, E. A., & Agrawal, S. (2010). Causal impact of employee work perceptions on the bottom line of organizations. *Perspectives on Psychological Science, 5*, 378–389.

Harter, J. K., Schmidt, F. L., & Hayes, T. L. (2002). Business-unit-level relationship between employee satisfaction, employee engagement, and business outcomes: A meta-analysis. *Journal of Applied Psychology, 87*, 268–279.

Hartl, A. C., Laursen, B., & Cillessen, A. H. (2015). A survival analysis of adolescent friendships: The downside of dissimilarity. *Psychological Science, 26*, 1304–1315.

Hartshorne, J. K., Tenenbaum, J. B., & Pinker, S. (2018). A critical period for second language acquisition: Evidence from 2/3 million English speakers. *Cognition, 177*, 263–277.

Hartwig, M., & Bond, C. F., Jr. (2011). Why do lie-catchers fail? A lens model meta-analysis of human lie judgments. *Psychological Bulletin, 137*, 643–659.

Harvard Business School. (2019). Admissions—Class of 2020 profile. (hbs.edu).

Harvey, A. G., & Tang, N. K. Y. (2012). (Mis)perception of sleep in insomnia: A puzzle and a resolution. *Psychological Bulletin, 138*, 77–101.

Harvey, P. D. (2019). Smoking cannabis and acquired impairments I cognition: Starting early seems like a really bad idea. *American Journal of Psychiatry, 176*, 90–91.

Harvey, S. B., Øverland, S., Hatch, S. L., Wessely, S., Mykletun, A., & Hotopf, M. (2018). Exercise and the prevention of depression: Results of the HUNT Cohort Study. *American Journal of Psychiatry, 175*, 28–36.

Harward, S. C., Hedrick, N. G., Hall, C. E., Parra-Bueno, P., Milner, T. A., Pan, E., Laviv, T., Hempstead, B. L., Yasuda, R., & McNamara, J. O. (2016). Autocrine BDNF–TrkB signalling within a single dendritic spine. *Nature, 538*, 99–103.

Hasell, J. (2018). *Is income inequality rising around the world?* Our World in Data. https://ourworldindata.org/income-inequality-since-1990

Haselton, M. G., & Gildersleeve, K. (2011). Can men detect ovulation? *Current Directions in Psychological Science, 20*, 87–92.

Haselton, M. G., & Gildersleeve, K. (2016). Human ovulation cues. *Current Opinion in Psychology, 7*, 120–125.

Hasin, D. S., Sarvet, A. L., Meyers, J. L. (2018). Epidemiology of adult DSM-5 major depressive disorder and its specifiers in the United States. *JAMA Psychiatry, 75,* 334–336.

Haslam, C., Cruwys, T., Chang, M. X. L., Bentley, S. V., Haslam, S. A., Dingle, G. A., & Jetten, J. (2019). GROUPS 4 HEALTH reduces loneliness and social anxiety in adults with psychological distress: Findings from a randomized controlled trial. *Journal of Consulting and Clinical Psychology, 87,* 787–801.

Haslam, S. A., & Reicher, S. (2007). Beyond the banality of evil: Three dynamics of an interactionist social psychology of tyranny. *Personality and Social Psychology Bulletin, 33,* 615–622.

Haslam, S. A., & Reicher, S. D. (2012). Contesting the "nature" of conformity: What Milgram and Zimbardo's studies really show. *PLOS Biology, 10,* e1001426.

Haslam, S. A., Reicher, S. D., & Birney, M. E. (2014). Nothing by mere authority: Evidence that in an experimental analogue of the Milgram paradigm participants are motivated not by orders but by appeals to science. *Journal of Social Issues, 70,* 473–488.

Haslam, S. A., Reicher, S. D., & Birney, M. E. (2016). Questioning authority: New perspectives on Milgram's "obedience" research and its implications for intergroup relations. *Current Opinion in Psychology, 11,* 6–9.

Hassan, B., & Rahman, Q. (2007). Selective sexual orientation-related differences in object location memory. *Behavioral Neuroscience, 121,* 625–633.

Hassin, R. R. (2013). Yes it can: On the functional abilities of the human unconscious. *Perspectives on Psychological Science, 8,* 195–207.

Hatfield, E. (1988). Passionate and companionate love. In R. J. Sternberg & M. L. Barnes (Eds.), *The psychology of love* (pp. 191–217). Yale University Press.

Hatfield, E. (2016). Love and sex in the marketplace. In R. J. Sternberg, S. T. Fiske, & D. J. Foss (Eds.), *Scientists making a difference: One hundred eminent behavioral and brain scientists talk about their most important contributions.* Cambridge University Press.

Hatfield, E., Mo, Y., & Rapson, R. L. (2015). Love, sex, and marriage across cultures. In L. A. Jensen (Ed.), *The Oxford handbook of human development and culture: An interdisciplinary perspective* (pp. 570–585). Oxford University Press.

Hatfield, E., & Sprecher, S. (1986). *Mirror, mirror . . . The importance of looks in everyday life.* State University of New York.

Hathaway, S. R. (1960). An MMPI Handbook (Vol. 1, Foreword). University of Minnesota Press (rev. ed.), 1972.

Hatzenbuehler, M. L. (2011). The social environment and suicide attempts in lesbian, gay, and bisexual youth. *Pediatrics, 127,* 896–903.

Hatzenbuehler, M. L. (2014). Structural stigma and the health of lesbian, gay, and bisexual populations. *Current Directions in Psychological Science, 23,* 127–132.

Hatzenbuehler, M. L., Nolen-Hoeksema, S., & Dovidio, J. (2009). How does stigma "get under the skin?" The mediating role of emotion regulation. *Psychological Science, 20,* 1282–1289.

Hatzigeorgiadis, A., Zourbanos, N., Galanis, E., & Theodorakis, Y. (2011). Self-talk and sports performance: A meta-analysis. *Perspectives on Psychological Science, 6,* 348–356.

Hauser, M. D., Chomsky, N., & Fitch, W. T. (2002). The faculty of language: What is it, who has it, and how did it evolve? *Science, 298,* 1569–1579.

Havas, D. A., Glenberg, A. M., Gutowski, K. A., Lucarelli, M. J., & Davidson, R. J. (2010). Cosmetic use of Botulinum Toxin-A affects processing of emotional language. *Psychological Science, 21,* 895–900.

Hawkley, L. C., Hughes, M. E., Waite, L. J., Masi, C. M., Thisted, R. A., & Cacioppo, J. T. (2008). From social structure factors to perceptions of relationship quality and loneliness: The Chicago Health, Aging, and Social Relations Study. *Journal of Gerontology: Series B, 63,* S375–S384.

Haworth, C. M. A., Wright, M. J., Luciano, M., Martin, N. G., de Geus, E. J., van Beijsterveldt, C. E., Bartels, M., Posthuma, D., Boomsma, D. I., Davis, O. S., Kovas, Y., Corley, R. P., Defries, J. C. Hewitt, J. K., Olson, R. K., Rhea, S. A., Wadsworth, S. J., Iacono, W. G., McGue, M., . . . Plomin, R. (2010). The heritability of general cognitive ability increases linearly from childhood to young adulthood. *Molecular Psychiatry, 15,* 1112–1120.

Haworth, C. M. A., Wright, M. J., Martin, N. W., Martin, N. G., Boomsma, D. I., Bartels, M., Posthuma, D., Davis, O. S., Brant, A. M., Corley, R. P., Hewitt, J. K., Iacono, W. G., McGue, M., Thompson, L. A., Hart, S. A., Petrill, S. A., Lubinski, D., & Plomin, R. (2009). A twin study of the genetics of high cognitive ability selected from 11,000 twin pairs in six studies from four countries. *Behavior Genetics, 39,* 359–370.

Haxby, J. V. (2001, July 7). Quoted in B. Bower, Faces of perception. *Science News,* pp. 10–12. See also J. V. Haxby, M. I. Gobbini, M. L. Furey, A. Ishai, J. L. Schouten & P. Pietrini (2001), Distributed and overlapping representations of faces and objects in ventral temporal cortex. *Science, 293,* 2425–2430.

Hayasaki, E. (2014, July). Want to know when you'll die? 'Big data' could tell you. *Newsweek.* https://www.newsweek.com/2014/08/01/want-know-when-youll-die-big-data-could-tell-you-260883.html

Hayashi, Y., Kashiwagi, M., Yasuda, K., Ando, R., Kanuka, M., Sakai, K., & Itohara, S. (2015). Cells of a common developmental origin regulate REM/non-REM sleep and wakefulness in mice. *Science, 350,* 957–961.

Haynes, A., Kersbergen, I., Sutin, A., Daly, M., & Robinson, E. (2019). Does perceived overweight increase risk of depressive symptoms and suicidability beyond objective weight status? A systematic review and meta-analysis. *Clinical Psychology Review, 73,* 101753.

Hays, C., & Carver, L. J. (2014). Follow the liar: The effects of adult lies on children's honesty. *Developmental Science, 17,* 977–983.

Hazan, C., & Shaver, P. R. (1994). Attachment as an organizational framework for research on close relationships. *Psychological Inquiry, 5,* 1–22.

Hazelrigg, M. D., Cooper, H. M., & Borduin, C. M. (1987). Evaluating the effectiveness of family therapies: An integrative review and analysis. *Psychological Bulletin, 101,* 428–442.

HBVA. (2018). *Honour killings by region, South and Central Asia.* Honour Based Violence Awareness Network. Retrieved on February 20, 2018, from http://hbv-awareness.com/regions/

He, Q., Turel, O., & Bechara, A. (2018). Association of excessive social media use with abnormal white matter integrity of the corpus callosum. *Psychiatry Research: Neuroimaging, 278,* 42–47.

He, Z., & Jin, Y. (2016). Intrinsic control of axon regeneration. *Neuron, 90,* 437–451.

Headey, B., Muffels, R., & Wagner, G. G. (2010). Long-running German panel survey shows that personal and economic choices, not just genes, matter for happiness. *PNAS, 107,* 17922–17926.

Healy, A. F., Jones, M., Lalchandani, L. A., & Tack, L. A. (2017). Timing of quizzes during learning: Effects on motivation and retention. *Journal of Experimental Psychology: Applied, 23,* 128–137.

Heavey, C. L., & Hurlburt, R. T. (2008). The phenomena of inner experience. *Consciousness and Cognition, 17,* 798–810.

Hebb, D. O. (1949). *The organization of behavior: A neuropsychological theory.* Psychology Press.

Heberle, A. E., & Carter, A. S. (2015). Cognitive aspects of young children's experience of economic disadvantage. *Psychological Bulletin, 141,* 723–746.

Heck, P. R., Simons, D. J., & Chabris, C. F. (2018). 65% of Americans believe they are above average in intelligence: Results of two nationally representative surveys. *PLOS ONE, 13,* e0200103.

Heckert, J. (2012, November 15). The hazards of growing up painlessly. *The New York Times.* https://www.nytimes.com/2012/11/18/magazine/ashlyn-blocker-feels-no-pain.html?

Heckman, J. J., & Karapakula, G. (2019). *Intergenerational and intragenerational externalities of the Perry Preschool Project* (No. w25889). National Bureau of Economic Research.

Hedström, P., Liu, K.-Y., & Nordvik, M. K. (2008). Interaction domains and suicides: A population-based panel study of suicides in the Stockholm metropolitan area, 1991–1999. *Social Forces, 2,* 713–740.

Hehman, E., Flake, J. K., & Calanchini, J. (2018). Disproportionate use of lethal force in policing is associated with regional racial biases of residents. *Social Psychological Personality Science, 9(4),* 393–401.

Heider, F. (1958). *The psychology of interpersonal relations.* Wiley.

Heilmann, K., & Kahn, M. E. (2019, June) *The urban crime and heat gradient in high and low poverty areas* (NBER Working Paper No. 25961). https://www.nber.org/papers/w25961

Heiman, J. R. (1975, April). The physiology of erotica: Women's sexual arousal. *Psychology Today,* pp. 90–94.

Hein, G., Morishima, Y., Leiberg, S., Sul, S., & Fehr, E. (2016). The brain's functional network architecture reveals human motives. *Science, 351,* 1074–1078.

Heine, S. J., Proulx, T., & Vohs, K. D. (2006). Meaning maintenance model: On the coherence of human motivations. *Personality and Social Psychology Review, 10,* 88–110.

Hejmadi, A., Davidson, R. J., & Rozin, P. (2000). Exploring Hindu Indian emotion expressions: Evidence for accurate recognition by Americans and Indians. *Psychological Science, 11,* 183–187.

Helfand, D. (2011, January 7). An assault on rationality. *The New York Times* (nytimes.com).

Heller, A. S., Johnstone, T., Schackman, A. J., Light, S. N., Peterson, M. J., Kolden, G. G., Kalin, N. H., & Davidson, R. J. (2009). Reduced capacity to sustain positive emotion in major depression reflects diminished maintenance of fronto-striatal brain activation. *PNAS, 106,* 22445–22450.

Heller, S. B. (2014). Summer jobs reduce violence among disadvantaged youth. *Science, 346,* 1219–1222.

Heller, W. (1990, May/June). Of one mind: Second thoughts about the brain's dual nature. *The Sciences,* pp. 38–44.

Helliwell, J., Layard, R., & Sachs, J. (Eds.) (2013). *World happiness report.* The Earth Institute, Columbia University.

Helliwell, J. F., & Wang, S. (2015). How was the weekend? How the social context underlies weekend effects in happiness and other emotions for US workers. *PLOS ONE, 10,* e0145123.

Helmreich, W. B. (1992). *Against all odds: Holocaust survivors and the successful lives they made in America.* Simon & Schuster.

Helmreich, W. B. (1994). Personal correspondence. Department of Sociology, City University of New York.

Helms, J. E., Jernigan, M., & Mascher, J. (2005). The meaning of race in psychology and how to change it: A methodological perspective. *American Psychologist, 60,* 27–36.

Helmuth, L. (2001). Boosting brain activity from the outside in. *Science, 292,* 1284–1286.

Helsen, K., Goubert, L., Peters, M. L., & Vlaeyen, J. W. S. (2011). Observational learning and pain-related fear: An experimental study with colored cold pressor tasks. *The Journal of Pain, 12,* 1230–1239.

Helweg-Larsen, M. (1999). (The lack of) optimistic biases in response to the 1994 Northridge earthquake: The role of personal experience. *Basic and Applied Social Psychology, 21,* 119–129.

Hembree, R. (1988). Correlates, causes, effects, and treatment of test anxiety. *Review of Educational Research, 58,* 47–77.

Henderlong, J., & Lepper, M. R. (2002). The effects of praise on children's intrinsic motivation: A review and synthesis. *Psychological Bulletin, 128,* 774–795.

Henderson, J. M. (2007). Regarding scenes. *Current Directions in Psychological Science, 16,* 219–222.

Henig, R. M. (2010, August 18). What is it about 20-somethings? *The New York Times Magazine.* https://www.nytimes.com/2010/08/22/magazine/22Adulthood-t.html?

Henley, N. M. (1989). Molehill or mountain? What we know and don't know about sex bias in language. In M. Crawford & M. Gentry (Eds.), *Gender and thought: Psychological perspectives* (pp. 59–78). Springer-Verlag.

Hennenlotter, A., Dresel, C., Castrop, F., Ceballos Baumann, A., Wohschlager, A., & Haslinger, B. (2008). The link between facial feedback and neural activity within central circuitries of emotion: New insights from Botulinum Toxin-induced denervation of frown muscles. *Cerebral Cortex, 19,* 537–542.

Hennessey, B. A., & Amabile, T. M. (2010). Creativity. *Annual Review of Psychology, 61,* 569–598.

Henrich, J., Heine, S. J., & Norenzayan, A. (2010). The weirdest people in the world? *Behavioral and Brain Sciences, 33,* 61–135.

Henry, J. D., MacLeod, M. S., Phillips, L. H., & Crawford, J. R. (2004). A meta-analytic review of prospective memory and aging. *Psychology and Aging, 19,* 27–39.

Hensley, C., Browne, J. A., & Trentham, C. E. (2018). Exploring the social and emotional context of childhood animal cruelty and its potential link to adult human violence. *Psychology, Crime & Law, 24,* 489–499.

Hepper, P. (2005). Unravelling our beginnings. *The Psychologist, 18,* 474–477.

Herbenick, D., Reece, M., Schick, V., & Sanders, S. A. (2014). Erect penile length and circumference dimensions of 1,661 sexually active men in the United States. *Journal of Sexual Medicine, 11,* 93–101.

Herculano-Houzel, S. (2012). The remarkable, yet not extraordinary, human brain as a scaled-up primate brain and its associated cost. *PNAS, 109* (suppl 1), 10661–10668.

Herek, G. M. (2016, accessed December 27). *Facts about homosexuality and child molestation.* Retrieved from https://psychology.ucdavis.edu/rainbow/html/facts_molestation.html

Herman, C. P., & Polivy, J. (1980). Restrained eating. In A. J. Stunkard (Ed.), *Obesity.* Saunders.

Herman, C. P., Polivy, J., Pliner, P., & Vartanian, L. R. (2015). Mechanisms underlying the portion-size effect. *Physiology & Behavior, 144,* 129–136.

Herman-Giddens, M. E. (2013). The enigmatic pursuit of puberty in girls. *Pediatrics, 132,* 1125–1126.

Herman-Giddens, M. E., Steffes, J., Harris, D., Slora, E., Hussey, M., Dowshen, S. A., Wasserman, R., Serwint, J. F., Smitherman, L., & Reiter, E. O. (2012). Secondary sexual characteristics in boys: Data from the pediatric research in office settings network. *Pediatrics, 130,* 1058–1068.

Hernandez, A. E., & Li, P. (2007). Age of acquisition: Its neural and computational mechanisms. *Psychological Bulletin, 133,* 638–650.

Hernandez, R., Kershaw, K. N., Siddique, J., Boehm, J. K., Kubzansky, L. D., Diez-Roux, A., Ning, H., & Lloyd-Jones, D. M. (2015). Optimism and cardiovascular health: Multi-Ethnic Study of Atherosclerosis (MESA). *Health Behavior and Policy Review, 2,* 62–73.

Herrero, N., Gadea, M., Rodríguez-Alarcón, G., Espert, R., & Salvador, A. (2010). What happens when we get angry? Hormonal, cardiovascular and asymmetrical brain responses. *Hormones and Behavior, 57,* 276–283.

Herringa, R. J., Phillips, M. L., Fournier, J. C., Kronhaus, D. M., & Germain, A. (2013). Childhood and adult trauma both correlate with dorsal anterior cingulate activation to threat in combat veterans. *Psychological Medicine, 43,* 1533–1542.

Herrmann, E., Call, J., Hernández-Lloreda, M. V., Hare, B., & Tomasello, M. (2007). Humans have evolved specialized skills of social cognition: The cultural intelligence hypothesis. *Science, 317,* 1360–1365.

Herrnstein, R. J., & Loveland, D. H. (1964). Complex visual concept in the pigeon. *Science, 146,* 549–551.

Hershenson, M. (1989). *The moon illusion.* Erlbaum.

Hertenstein, M. J., Hansel, C., Butts, S., Hile, S. (2009). Smile intensity in photographs predicts divorce later in life. *Motivation & Emotion, 33,* 99–105.

Hertenstein, M. J., Keltner, D., App, B., Bulleit, B., & Jaskolka, A. (2006). Touch communicates distinct emotions. *Emotion, 6,* 528–533.

Herz, R. (2007). *The scent of desire: Discovering our enigmatic sense of smell.* Morrow/HarperCollins.

Herz, R. (2012, January 28). You eat that? *The Wall Street Journal.* https://www.wsj.com/articles/SB10001424052970204661604577186843056231170

Herz, R. S. (2001, October). Ah, sweet skunk! Why we like or dislike what we smell. *Cerebrum,* pp. 31–47.

Herz, R. S., Beland, S. L., & Hellerstein, M. (2004). Changing odor hedonic perception through emotional associations in humans. *International Journal of Comparative Psychology, 17,* 315–339.

Hess, E. H. (1956, July). Space perception in the chick. *Scientific American,* pp. 71–80.

Hess, M. J., & Hough, S. (2012). Impact of spinal cord injury on sexuality: broad-based clinical practice intervention and practical application. *The Journal of Spinal Cord Medicine, 35,* 211–218.

Hess, U., & Thibault, P. (2009). Darwin and emotion expression. *American Psychologist, 64,* 120–128.

Heu, L. C., van Zomeren, M., & Hansen, N. (2019). Lonely alone or lonely together? A Cultural-psychological examination of individualism–Collectivism and loneliness in five European countries. *Personality and Social Psychology Bulletin, 45,* 780–793.

HEUNI. (2015). *Homicide and gender* [PDF file]. United Nations Office on Drugs and Crime data summarized by the European Institute for Crime Prevention and Control, affiliated with the United Nations. https://www.heuni.fi/material/attachments/heuni/projects/wd2vDSKcZ/Homicide_and_Gender.pdf

Hewett, R., & Conway, N. (2015). The undermining effect revisited: The salience of everyday verbal rewards and self-determined motivation. *Journal of Organizational Behavior, 37,* 436–455.

Hewlett, B. S. (1991). Demography and childcare in preindustrial societies. *Journal of Anthropological Research, 47,* 1–37.

Hibar, D. P., Westlye, L. T., van Erp, T. G., Rasmussen, J., Leonardo, C. D., Faskowitz, J., Hauvick, U. K., Hartberg, C. B., Doan, N. T., Agartz, I., Dale, A. M., Gruber, O., Krämer, B., Trost, S., Liberg, B., Abé, C., Ekman, C. J., Ingvar, M., Landén, M., . . . Andreassen, O. A. (2016). Subcortical volumetric abnormalities in bipolar disorder. *Molecular Psychiatry, 21,* 1710–1716.

Hickok, G. (2014). *The myth of mirror neurons: The real neuroscience of communication and cognition.* Norton.

Hickok, G., Bellugi, U., & Klima, E. S. (2001, June). Sign language in the brain. *Scientific American,* pp. 58–65.

Hilgard, E. R. (1986). *Divided consciousness: Multiple controls in human thought and action.* Wiley.

Hilgard, E. R. (1992). Dissociation and theories of hypnosis. In E. Fromm & M. R. Nash (Eds.), *Contemporary hypnosis research.* Guilford.

Hilker, R., Helenius, D., Fagerlund, B., Skytthe, A., Christensen, K., Werge, T. M., Nordentoft, N., & Glenthøj, B. (2018). Heritability of schizophrenia and schizophrenia spectrum based on the nationwide Danish twin register. *Biological Psychiatry, 83,* 492–498.

Hill, A. J. (2007). The psychology of food craving. *Proceedings of the Nutrition Society, 66,* 277–285.

Hill, C. E., & Nakayama, E. Y. (2000). Client-centered therapy: Where has it been and where is it going? A comment on Hathaway. *Journal of Clinical Psychology, 56,* 961–875.

Hill, D. B. (2019). Andocentrism and the great man narrative in psychology textbooks. *Journal of Research in Gender Studies, 9,* 9–37.

Hills, P. J., Werno, M. A., & Lewis, M. B. (2011). Sad people are more accurate at face recognition than happy people. *Consciousness and Cognition, 20,* 1502–1517.

Hills, T. T. (2019). The dark side of information proliferation. *Perspectives on Psychological Science, 14,* 323–330.

Hinds, J., & Joinson, A. (2019). Human and computer personality prediction from digital footprints. *Current Directions in Psychological Science, 28,* 204–211.

Hines, M. (2004). *Brain gender.* Oxford University Press.

Hingson, R. W., Heeren, T., & Winter, M. R. (2006). Age at drinking onset and alcohol dependence. *Archives of Pediatrics & Adolescent Medicine, 160,* 739–746.

Hinnant, J. B., McConnell, L. M., Yanes, J. A., McCormick, M. J., Murphy, J. E., Erath, S. A., & Robinson, J. L. (2019). Rewarding safe choices in peer contexts: Adolescent brain activity during decision making. *Biological Psychology, 142,* 45–53.

Hintzman, D. L. (1978). *The psychology of learning and memory.* Freeman.

Hinz, L. D., & Williamson, D. A. (1987). Bulimia and depression: A review of the affective variant hypothesis. *Psychological Bulletin, 102,* 150–158.

Hirad, A. A., Bazarian, J. J., Merchant-Borna, K., Garcea, F. E., Heilbronner, S., Paul, D., Hintz, E. B., van Wijngaarden, E., Schifitto, G., Wright, D. W., Espinoza, T. R., & Mahon, B. Z. (2019). A common neural signature of brain injury in concussion and subconcussion. *Science Advances, 5,* 1–11.

Hirsh-Pasek, K., Adamson, L. B., Bakeman, R., Owen, M. T., Golinkoff, R. M., Pace, A., Yust, P. K., & Suma, K. (2015). The contribution of early communication quality to low-income children's language success. *Psychological Science, 26,* 1071–1083.

Hirst, W., & Echterhoff, G. (2012). Remembering in conversations: The social sharing and reshaping of memories. *Annual Review of Psychology, 63,* 55–79.

Hirst, W., & Phelps, E. A. (2016). Flashbulb memories. *Current Directions in Psychological Science, 25,* 36–41.

Hirst, W., Phelps, E. A., Meksin, R., Vaidya, C. J., Johnson, M. K., Mitchell, K. J., Buckner, R. L., Budson, A. E., Gabrieli, J. D., Lustig, C., Mather, M., Ochsner, K. N., Schacter, D., Simons, J. S., Lyle, K. B., Cuc, A. F., & Olsson, A. (2015). A ten-year follow-up of a study of memory for the attack of September 11, 2001: Flashbulb memories and memories for flashbulb events. *Journal of Experimental Psychology: General*, 144, 604.

Hirt, E. R., Zillmann, D., Erickson, G. A., & Kennedy, C. (1992). Costs and benefits of allegiance: Changes in fans' self-ascribed competencies after team victory versus defeat. *Journal of Personality and Social Psychology*, 63, 724–738.

Hjelmborg, J. V. B., Fagnani, C., Silventoinen, K., McGue, M., Korkeila, M., Christensen, K., Rissanen, A., & Kaprio, J. (2008). Genetic influences on growth traits of BMI: A longitudinal study of adult twins. *Obesity*, 16, 847–852.

Hjelmgaard, K. (2019, March 27). Head transplant doctors Xiaoping Ren and Sergio Canavero claim spinal cord progress. *USA Today*. https://conspiracy411.info/head-transplant-doctors-xiaoping-ren-and-sergio-canavero-claim-spinal-cord-progress/

HMHL. (2002, January). Disaster and trauma. *Harvard Mental Health Letter*, pp. 1–5.

Ho, T., Chong, J. K., & Xia, X. (2017). Yellow taxis have fewer accidents than blue taxis because yellow is more visible than blue. *PNAS*, 114, 3074–3078.

Hobaiter, C., Poisot, T., Zuberbühler, K., Hoppitt, W., & Gruber, T. (2014). Social network analysis shows direct evidence for social transmission of tool use in wild chimpanzees. *PLOS Biology*, 12, e1001960.

Hobbs, W. R., Burke, M., Christakis, N. A., & Fowler, J. H. (2016). Online social integration is associated with reduced mortality risk. *PNAS*, 113, 12980–12984.

Hobson, J. A. (1995, September). Quoted by C. H. Colt in The power of dreams. *Life*, pp. 36–49.

Hobson, J. A. (2003). *Dreaming: An introduction to the science of sleep*. Oxford.

Hobson, J. A. (2004). *13 dreams Freud never had: The new mind science*. Pi Press.

Hobson, J. A. (2009). REM sleep and dreaming: Towards a theory of protoconsciousness. *Nature Reviews*, 10, 803–814.

Hochberg, L. R., Serruya, M. D., Friehs, G. M., Mukand, J. A., Saleh, M., Caplan, A. H., Branner, A., Chen, D., Penn, R. D., & Donoghue, J. P. (2006). Neuronal ensemble control of prosthetic devices by a human with tetraplegia. *Nature*, 442, 164–171.

Hochmair, I. (2013, September). *Cochlear implants: The size of the task concerning children born deaf*. www.medel.com

Hockenberry, J. M., Joski, P., Yarbrough, C., & Druss, B. G. (2019). Trends in treatment and spending for patients receiving outpatient treatment of depression in the United States, 1998–2015. *JAMA Psychiatry*, 76, 810–817.

Hoebel, B. G., & Teitelbaum, P. (1966). Effects of forcefeeding and starvation on food intake and body weight in a rat with ventromedial hypothalamic lesions. *Journal of Comparative and Physiological Psychology*, 61, 189–193.

Hoeft, F., Watson, C. L., Kesler, S. R., Bettinger, K. E., & Reiss, A. L. (2008). Gender differences in the mesocorticolimbic system during computer gameplay. *Journal of Psychiatric Research*, 42, 253–258.

Hofer, M. K., Whillans, A. V., & Chen, F. S. (2018). Olfactory cues from romantic partners and strangers influence women's responses to stress. *Journal of Personality and Social Psychology*, 114, 1–9.

Hoff, K. A., Briley, D. A., Wee, C. J. M., & Rounds, J. (2018). Normative changes in interests from adolescence to adulthood: A meta-analysis of longitudinal studies. *Psychological Bulletin*, 144, 426–451.

Hoffman, B. M., Babyak, M. A., Craighead, W. E., Sherwood, A., Doraiswamy, P. M., Coons, M. J., & Blumenthal, J. A. (2011). Exercise and pharmacotherapy in patients with major depression: One-year follow-up of the SMILE study. *Psychosomatic Medicine*, 73, 127–133.

Hoffman, D. D. (1998). *Visual intelligence: How we create what we see*. Norton.

Hoffman, H. (2012). Considering the role of conditioning in sexual orientation. *Archives of Sexual Behavior*, 41, 63–71.

Hoffman, H. G. (2004, August). Virtual-reality therapy. *Scientific American*, pp. 58–65.

Hoffman, J. (2019, Aug. 26). Johnson & Johnson ordered to pay $572 million in landmark opioid trial. *The New York Times*. https://www.nytimes.com/2019/08/26/health/oklahoma-opioids-johnson-and-johnson.html?

Hoffman, J. (2019, September). How anti-vaccine sentiment took hold in the United States. *The New York Times*. https://www.nytimes.com/2019/09/23/health/anti-vaccination-movement-us.html?

Hoffman, Y. S. G., Shrira, A., Cohen-Fridel, S., Grossman, E. S., & Bodner, E. (2016). The effect of exposure to missile attacks on posttraumatic stress disorder symptoms as a function of perceived media control and locus of control. *Psychiatry Research*, 244, 51–56.

Hoffmann, H. (2017). Situating human sexual conditioning. *Archives of Sexual Behavior*, 46, 2213–2229.

Hogan, C. L., Catalino, L. I., Mata, J., & Fredrickson, B. L. (2015). Beyond emotional benefits: Physical activity and sedentary behavior affect psychosocial resources through emotions. *Psychology & Health*, 30, 354–369.

Hogan, R. (1998). Reinventing personality. *Journal of Social and Clinical Psychology*, 17, 1–10.

Høglend, P., & Hagtvet, K. (2019). Change mechanisms in psychotherapy: Both improved insight and improved affective awareness are necessary. *Journal of Consulting and Clinical Psychology*, 87, 332–344.

Hohmann, G. W. (1966). Some effects of spinal cord lesions on experienced emotional feelings. *Psychophysiology*, 3, 143–156.

Hokanson, J. E., & Edelman, R. (1966). Effects of three social responses on vascular processes. *Journal of Personality and Social Psychology*, 3, 442–447.

Holahan, C. K., & Sears, R. R. (1995). *The gifted group in later maturity*. Stanford University Press.

Holden, C. (2008). Poles apart. *Science*, 321, 193–195.

Holden, G. W., & Miller, P. C. (1999). Enduring and different: A meta-analysis of the similarity in parents' child rearing. *Psychological Bulletin*, 125, 223–254.

Holland, D., Chang, L., Ernst, T. M., Curran, M., Buchthal, S. D., Alicata, D., Skranes, J., Johansen, H., Hernandez, A., Yamakawa, R., Kuperman, J. M., & Dale, A. M. (2014). Structural growth trajectories and rates of change in the first 3 months of infant brain development. *JAMA Neurology*, 71, 1266–1274.

Holland, J. L. (1996). Exploring careers with a typology: What we have learned and some new directions. *American Psychologist*, 51, 397–406.

Holle, H., Warne, K., Seth, A. K., Critchley, H. D., & Ward, J. (2012). Neural basis of contagious itch and why some people are more prone to it. *PNAS*, 109, 19816–19821.

Holliday, R. E., & Albon, A. J. (2004). Minimizing misinformation effects in young children with cognitive interview mnemonics. *Applied Cognitive Psychology*, 18, 263–281.

Hollis, K. L. (1997). Contemporary research on Pavlovian conditioning: A "new" functional analysis. *American Psychologist*, 52, 956–965.

Hollon, S. D., DeRubeis, R. J., Fawcett, J., Amsterdam, J. D., Shelton, R. C., Zajecka, J., Young, P. R., & Gallop, R. (2014). Effect of cognitive therapy with antidepressant medications vs. antidepressants alone on the rate of recovery in major depressive disorder. *JAMA Psychiatry*, 71, 1157–1164.

Holmes, E. A., Ghaderi, A., Harmer, C. J., Ramchandani, P. G., Cuijpers, P., Morrison, A. P., Roiser, J. P., Bockting, C. L., O'Connor, R. C., Shafran, R., Moulds, M. L., & Craske, M. G. (2018). The *Lancet Psychiatry* Commission on psychological treatments research in tomorrow's science. *The Lancet Psychiatry*, 5, 237–286.

Holmes, L. (2015, February 18). Kate Middleton has an empowering message for those facing mental health stigma. *The New York Times* (nytimes.com).

Holstege, G., Georgiadis, J. R., Paans, A. M. J., Meiners, L. C., van der Graaf, F. H. C. E., & Reinders, A. A. T. S. (2003a). Brain activation during male ejaculation. *Journal of Neuroscience*, 23, 9185–9193.

Holstege, G., Reinders, A. A. T., Paans, A. M. J., Meiners, L. C., Pruim, J., & Georgiadis, J. R. (2003b). *Brain activation during female sexual orgasm* (Annual Conference Abstract Viewer/Itinerary Planner Program No. 727.7). Washington, DC: Society for Neuroscience.

Holt-Lunstad, J., Robles, T. F., & Sbarra, D. A. (2017). Advancing social connection as a public health priority in the United States. *American Psychologist*, 72, 517-530.

Holt-Lunstad, J., Smith, T. B., Baker, M., Harris, T., & Stephenson, D. (2015). Loneliness and social isolation as risk factors for mortality: A meta-analytic review. *Perspectives on Psychological Science*, 10, 227–237.

Holt-Lunstad, J., Smith, T. B., & Layton, J. B. (2010). Social relationships and mortality risk: A meta-analytic review. *PLOS Medicine*, 7, e1000316.

Holt, L. (2002, August). Reported in "Sounds of speech," p. 26, and in personal correspondence, July 18, 2002.

Holtgraves, T. (2011). Text messaging, personality, and the social context. *Journal of Research in Personality*, 45, 92–99.

Holwerda, T. J., Deeg, D. J., Beekman, A. T., van Tilburg, T. G., Stek, M. L., Jonker, C., Schoevers, R. A. (2014). Feelings of loneliness, but not social isolation, predict dementia onset: Results from the Amsterdam Study of the Elderly (AMSTEL). *Journal of Neurology, Neurosurgery, and Psychiatry*, 85, 135–142.

Home Office. (2019). *Hate crime, England and Wales, 2018 to 2019*. https://www.gov.uk/government/statistics/hate-crime-england-and-wales-2018-to-2019

Homer, B. D., Solomon, T. M., Moeller, R. W., Mascia, A., DeRaleau, L., & Halkitis, P. N. (2008). Methamphetamine abuse and impairment of social functioning: A review of the underlying neurophysiological causes and behavioral implications. *Psychological Bulletin*, 134, 301–310.

Hong, C. P. (2020, April 12). The slur I never expected to hear in 2020. *The New York Times*. https://www.nytimes.com/2020/04/12/magazine/asian-american-discrimination-coronavirus.html?

Hoogman, M., Muetzel, R., Guimaraes, J. P., Shumskaya, E., Mennes, M., Zwiers, M. P., Jahanshad, N., Sudre, G., Wolfers, T., Earl, E. A., Soliva Vila, J. C., Vives-Gilabert, Y., Khadka, S., Novotny, S. E., Hartman, C., Heslenfeld, D. J., Schweren, L. J. S., Ambrosino, S., Oranje, B., . . . Franke, B. (2019). Brain imaging of the cortex in ADHD: A coordinated analysis of large-scale clinical and population-based samples. *The American Journal of Psychiatry*, 176, 531–542.

Hooker, S. A., & Masters, K. S. (2018). Daily meaning salience and physical activity in previously inactive exercise initiates. *Health Psychology*, 37, 344–354.

Hooks, K. B., Konsman, J. P., & O'Malley, M. A. (2019). Microbiota-gut-brain research: A critical analysis. *Behavioral and Brain Sciences, 42*, e60.

Hooley, J. M., & Franklin, J. C. (2018). Why do people hurt themselves? A new conceptual model of nonsuicidal self-injury. *Clinical Psychological Science, 6*, 428–451.

Hooper, J., & Teresi, D. (1986). *The three-pound universe*. Macmillan.

Hopkins, E. D., & Cantalupo, C. (2008). Theoretical speculations on the evolutionary origins of hemispheric specialization. *Current Directions in Psychological Science, 17*, 233–237.

Hopman, E. W. M., & MacDonald, M. C. (2018). Production practice during language learning improves comprehension. *Psychological Science, 29*, 961–971.

Hopper, L. M., Lambeth, S. P., Schapiro, S. J., & Whiten, A. (2008). Observational learning in chimpanzees and children studied through "ghost" conditions. *Proceedings of the Royal Society, 275*, 835–840.

Hörder, H., Johansson, L., Guo, X., Grimby, G., Kern, S., Östling, S., & Skoog, I. (2018). Midlife cardiovascular fitness and dementia: A 44-year longitudinal population study in women. *Neurology, 90*, e1298–e1305.

Horne, J. (2011). The end of sleep: "Sleep debt" versus biological adaptation of human sleep to waking needs. *Biological Psychology, 87*, 1–14.

Horne, Z., Powell, D., Hummel, J. E., & Holyoak, K. J. (2015). Countering antivaccination attitudes. *PNAS, 112*, 10321–10324.

Horowitz, J. M. (2019, April 9). *How Americans see the state of race relations*. Pew Research Center. https://www.pewsocialtrends.org/2019/04/09/how-americans-see-the-state-of-race-relations/

Horowitz, S. S. (2012, November 9). The science and art of listening. *The New York Times*. https://www.nytimes.com/2012/11/11/opinion/sunday/why-listening-is-so-much-more-than-hearing.html?

Horsthemke, B. (2018). A critical view on transgenerational epigenetic inheritance in humans. *Nature Communications, 9*, 2973.

Horváth, K., Hannon, B., Ujma, P. P., Gombos, F., & Plunkett, K. (2017). Memory in 3-month-old infants benefits from a short nap. *Developmental Science, 21*, e12587.

Horwood, L. J., & Fergusson, D. M. (1998). Breastfeeding and later cognitive and academic outcomes. *Pediatrics, 101*(1), e9.

Hostetter, A. B. (2011). When do gestures communicate? A meta-analysis. *Psychological Bulletin, 137*, 297–315.

Hou, W.-H., Chiang, P.-T., Hsu, T.-Y., Chiu, S.-Y., & Yen, Y.-C. (2010). Treatment effects of massage therapy in depressed people: A meta-analysis. *Journal of Clinical Psychiatry, 71*, 894–901.

House, R., Javidan, M., & Dorfman, P. (2001). Project GLOBE: An introduction. *Applied Psychology: An International Review, 50*, 489–505.

Houser-Marko, L., & Sheldon, K. M. (2008). Eyes on the prize or nose to the grindstone? The effects of level of goal evaluation on mood and motivation. *Personality and Social Psychology Bulletin, 34*, 1556–1569.

Houts, A. C., Berman, J. S., & Abramson, H. (1994). Effectiveness of psychological and pharmacological treatments for nocturnal enuresis. *Journal of Consulting and Clinical Psychology, 62*, 737–745.

Hovatta, I., Tennant, R. S., Helton, R., Marr, R. A., Singer, O., Redwine, J. M., Ellison, J. A., Schadt, E. E., Verman, I. M., Lockhart, D. J., & Barlow, C. (2005). Glyoxalase 1 and glutathione reductase 1 regulate anxiety in mice. *Nature, 438*, 662–666.

Hovland, C. I., & Sears, R. R. (1938). Experiments on motor conflict. I. Types of conflict and their modes of resolution. *Journal of Experimental Psychology, 23*, 477–493.

Howard, D. M., Adams, M. J., Clarke, T.-K., Hafferty, J. D., Gibson, J., Shirali, M., Coleman, J. R. I., Hagenaars, S. P., Ward, J., Wigmore, E. M., Alloza, C., Shen, X., Barbu, M. C.. Xu, E. Y., Whalley, H. C., Marioni, R. E., Porteous, D. J., Davies, G., Deary, I. J., . . . McIntosh, A. M. (2019). Genome-wide meta-analysis of depression identifies 102 independent variants and highlights the importance of the prefrontal brain regions. *Nature Neuroscience, 22*, 343–352.

Howard, J. L., Gagné, M., & Bureau, J. S. (2017). Testing a continuum structure of self-determined motivation: A meta-analysis. *Psychological Bulletin, 143*, 1346–1377.

Howell, E. C., Etchells, P. J., & Penton-Voak, I. S. (2012). The sexual overperception bias is associated with sociosexuality. *Personality and Individual Differences, 53*, 1012–1016.

Hruschka, D. J., Medin, D. L., Rogoff, B., & Henrich, J. (2018). Pressing questions in the study of psychological and behavioral diversity. *PNAS, 115*, 11366–11368.

Hsee, C. K., & Ruan, B. (2016). The Pandora effect: The power and peril of curiosity. *Psychological Science, 27*, 659–666.

Hsee, C. K., Yang, A. X., & Wang, L. (2010). Idleness aversion and the need for justifiable busyness. *Psychological Science, 21*, 926–930.

Hsiang, S. M., Burke, M., & Miguel, E. (2013). Quantifying the influence of climate on human conflict. *Science, 341*, 1212.

Hsin, A., & Xie, Y. (2014). Explaining Asian Americans' academic advantage over Whites. *PNAS, 111*, 8416–8421.

Huang, C. (2015). Relation between attributional style and subsequent depressive symptoms: A systematic review and meta-analysis of longitudinal studies. *Cognitive Therapy and Research, 39*, 721–735.

Huang, J., Chaloupka, F. J., & Fong, G. T. (2013). Cigarette graphic warning labels and smoking prevalence in Canada: A critical examination and reformulation of the FDA regulatory impact analysis. *Tobacco Control*. https://www.ncbi.nlm.nih.gov/pmc/articles/PMC4254709/

Huang, Y., Wang, Y., Wang, H., Liu, Z., Yu, X., Yan, J., Yu, Y., Kou, C., Xu, X., Lu, J., Wang, Z., He, S., Xu, Y., He, Y., Li, T., Guo, W., Tian, H., Xu, G., Xu, X., . . . Wu, Y. (2019). Prevalence of mental disorders in China: A cross-sectional epidemiological study. *The Lancet Psychiatry, 6*, 211–224.

Huart, J., Corneille, O., & Becquart, E. (2005). Face-based categorization, context-based categorization, and distortions in the recollection of gender ambiguous faces. *Journal of Experimental Social Psychology, 41*, 598–608.

Hubbard, E. M., Arman, A. C., Ramachandran, V. S., & Boynton, G. M. (2005). Individual differences among grapheme-color synesthetes: Brain-behavior correlations. *Neuron, 45*, 975–985.

Hubel, D. H. (1979, September). The brain. *Scientific American*, pp. 45–53.

Hubel, D. H., & Wiesel, T. N. (1963). Receptive fields of cells in striate cortex of very young, visually inexperienced kittens. *Journal of Neurophysiology, 26*, 994–1002.

Hubel, D. H., & Wiesel, T. N. (1979, September). Brian mechanisms of vision. *Scientific American*, pp. 150–162.

Huber, E., Webster, J. M., Brewer, A. A., MacLeod, D. I. A., Wandell, B. A., Boynton, G. M., Wade, A. R., & Fine, I. (2015). A lack of experience-dependent plasticity after more than a decade of recovered sight. *Psychological Science, 26*, 393–401.

Hucker, S. J., & Bain, J. (1990). Androgenic hormones and sexual assault. In W. L. Marshall, D. R. Laws, & H. E. Barbaree (Eds.), *Handbook of sexual assault: Issues, theories, and treatment of the offender* (pp. 209–229). Plenum Press.

Huckins, L. M. (2017). Linking cannabis use to depression and suicidal thoughts and behaviours. *Lancet Psychiatry, 4*, P654–656.

Huckins, L. M., Dobbyn, A., Ruderfer, D. M., Hoffman, Wang, W., Pardiñas, A. F., Rajagopal, V. M., Als, T. D., Nguyen, H. T., Girdhar, K., Boocock, J., Roussos, P., Fromer, M., Kramer, R., Domenici, E., Gamazon, E. R., Purcell, S., CommonMind Consortium, Schizophrenia Working Group of the Psychiatric Genomis Consortium, iPSYCH-GEMS Schizophrenia Working Group, . . . Stahl, E. A. (2019). Gene expression imputation across multiple brain regions provides insights into schizophrenia risk. *Nature Genetics, 51*, 659–674.

Hudson, C. C., Hall, L., & Harkness, K. L. (2019). Prevalence of depressive disorders in individuals with autism spectrum disorder: A meta-analysis. *Journal of Abnormal Child Psychology, 47*, 165–175.

Hudson, N. W., & Roberts, B. W. (2014). Goals to change personality traits: Concurrent links between personality traits, daily behavior, and goals to change oneself. *Journal of Research in Personality, 53*, 68–83.

Huey, E. D., Krueger, F., & Grafman, J. (2006). Representations in the human prefrontal cortex. *Current Directions in Psychological Science, 15*, 167–171.

Hugenberg, K., & Bodenhausen, G. V. (2003). Facing prejudice: Implicit prejudice and the perception of facial threat. *Psychological Science, 14*, 640–643.

Hugenberg, K., Young, S. G., Bernstein, M. J., & Sacco, D. F. (2010). The categorization–individuation model: An integrative account of the other-race recognition deficit. *Psychological Review, 117*, 1168–1187.

Hughes, B. L., Camp, N. P., Gomez, J., Natu, V. S., Grill-Spector, K., & Eberhardt, J. L. (2019). Neural adaptation to faces reveals racial outgroup homogeneity effects in early perception. *PNAS, 116*, 14532–14537.

Hughes, J. R. (2010). Craving among long-abstinent smokers: An Internet survey. *Nicotine & Tobacco Research, 12*, 459–462.

Hughes, M. L., Geraci, L., & De Forrest, R. L. (2013). Aging 5 years in 5 minutes: The effect of taking a memory test on older adults' subjective age. *Psychological Science, 24*, 2481–2488.

Hulbert, A. (2005, November 20). The prodigy puzzle. *The New York Times Magazine*. https://www.nytimes.com/2005/11/20/magazine/the-prodigy-puzzle.html

Hull, H. R., Morrow, M. L., Dinger, M. K., Han, J. L., & Fields, D. A. (2007, November 20). Characterization of body weight and composition changes during the sophomore year of college. *BMC Women's Health, 7*, 21.

Hull, J. G., & Bond, C. F., Jr. (1986). Social and behavioral consequences of alcohol consumption and expectancy: A meta-analysis. *Psychological Bulletin, 99*, 347–360.

Hull, J. M. (1990). *Touching the rock: An experience of blindness*. Vintage Books.

Hull, S. J., Hennessy, M., Bleakley, A., Fishbein, M., & Jordan, A. (2011). Identifying the causal pathways from religiosity to delayed adolescent sexual behavior. *Journal of Sex Research, 48*, 543–553.

Hülsheger, U. R., Anderson, N., & Salgado, J. F. (2009). Team-level predictors of innovation at work: A comprehensive meta-analysis spanning three decades of research. *Journal of Applied Psychology, 94*, 1128–1145.

Hummer, R. A., Rogers, R. G., Nam, C. B., & Ellison, C. G. (1999). Religious involvement and U.S. adult mortality. *Demography, 36*, 273–285.

Humphrey, S. E., Nahrgang, J. D., & Morgeson, F. P. (2007). Integrating motivational, social, and contextual work design features: A meta-analytic summary and theoretical extension of the work design literature. *Journal of Applied Psychology, 92,* 1332–1356.

Humphreys, L. G., & Davey, T. C. (1988). Continuity in intellectual growth from 12 months to 9 years. *Intelligence, 12,* 183–197.

Hunsberger, J. G., Newton, S. S., Bennett, A. H., Duman, C. H., Russell, D. S., Salton, S. R., & Duman, R. S. (2007). Antidepressant actions of the exercise-regulated gene VGF. *Nature Medicine, 13,* 1476–1482.

Hunsley, J., & Bailey, J. M. (1999). The clinical utility of the Rorschach: Unfulfilled promises and an uncertain future. *Psychological Assessment, 11,* 266–277.

Hunsley, J., & Di Giulio, G. (2002). Dodo bird, phoenix, or urban legend? The question of psychotherapy equivalence. *Scientific Review of Mental Health Practice, 1,* 11–22.

Hunt, J. M. (1982). Toward equalizing the developmental opportunities of infants and preschool children. *Journal of Social Issues, 38,* 163–191.

Hunt, L. L., Eastwick, P. W., & Finkel, E. J. (2015). Leveling the playing field: Longer acquaintance predicts reduced assortative mating on attractiveness. *Psychological Science, 26,* 1046–1053.

Hunt, M. (1990). *The compassionate beast: What science is discovering about the humane side of humankind.* William Morrow.

Hunt, M. (1993). *The story of psychology.* Doubleday.

Hunter, S., & Sundel, M. (Eds.). (1989). *Midlife myths: Issues, findings, and practice implications.* Sage.

Hurlburt, R. T., Heavey, C. L., & Kelsey, J. M. (2013). Toward a phenomenology of inner speaking. *Consciousness and Cognition: An International Journal, 22,* 1477–1494.

Hurst, Y., & Fukuda, H. (2018). Effects of changes in eating speed on obesity in patients with diabetes: A secondary analysis of longitudinal health check-up data. *BMJ Open, 8*(1), e019589.

Hussak, L. J., & Cimpian, A. (2015). An early-emerging explanatory heuristic promotes support for the status quo. *Journal of Personality and Social Psychology, 109,* 739–752.

Hussong, A. M., Ennett, S. T., McNeish, D. M., Cole, V. T., Gottfredson, N. C., Rothenberg, W. A., & Faris, R. W. (2019). Social network isolation mediates associations between risky symptoms and substance use in the high school transition. *Development and Psychopathology,* 1–16.

Hutchinson, R. (2006). *Calum's road.* Burlinn Limited.

Hutchison, K. A., Smith, J. L., & Ferris, A. (2013). Goals can be threatened to extinction using the Stroop task to clarify working memory depletion under stereotype threat. *Social and Personality Psychological Science, 4,* 74–81.

Hutteman, R., Nestler, S., Wagner, J., Egloff, B., & Back, M. D. (2015). Wherever I may roam: Processes of self-esteem development from adolescence to emerging adulthood in the context of international student exchange. *Journal of Personality and Social Psychology, 108,* 767–783.

Hviid, A., Hansen, J. V., Frisch, M., & Melbye, M. (2019). Measles, mumps, rubella vaccination and autism: A nationwide cohort study. *Annals of Internal Medicine, 170,* 513–520.

Hyde, J. S. (2014). Gender similarities and differences. *Annual Review of Psychology, 65,* 373–398.

Hyde, J. S., Bigler, R. S., Joel, D., Tate, C. C., & van Anders, S. M. (2019). The future of sex and gender in psychology: Five challenges to the gender binary. *American Psychologist, 74,* 171–193.

Hyde, J. S., & Mertz, J. E. (2009). Gender, culture, and mathematics performance. *PNAS, 106,* 8801–8807.

Hymowitz, K., Carroll, J. S., Wilcox, W. B., & Kaye, K. (2013). *Knot yet: The benefits and costs of delayed marriage in America.* National Marriage Project, University of Virginia.

Iacoboni, M. (2008). *Mirroring people: The new science of how we connect with others.* Farrar, Straus & Giroux.

Iacoboni, M. (2009). Imitation, empathy, and mirror neurons. *Annual Review of Psychology, 60,* 653–670.

Ibbotson, P., & Tomasello, M. (2016, November). Language in a new key. *Scientific American,* pp. 71–75.

Idson, L. C., & Mischel, W. (2001). The personality of familiar and significant people: The lay perceiver as a social-cognitive theorist. *Journal of Personality and Social Psychology, 80,* 585–596.

Ikizer, E. G., & Blanton, H. (2016). Media coverage of "wise" interventions can reduce concern for the disadvantaged. *Journal of Experimental Psychology: Applied, 22,* 135–147.

Ilardi, S. (2016). *Therapeutic lifestyle change (TLC).* University of Kansas. tlc.ku.edu

Ilardi, S. S. (2009). *The depression cure: The six-step program to beat depression without drugs.* De Capo Lifelong Books.

Iliescu, A. F., Hall, J., Wilkinson, L. S., Dwyer, D. M., & Honey, R. C. (2018). The nature of phenotypic variation in Pavlovian conditioning. *Journal of Experimental Psychology: Animal Learning and Cognition, 44,* 358–369.

Ilieva, I. P., Hook, C. J., & Farah, M. J. (2015). Prescription stimulants' effects on healthy inhibitory control, working memory, and episodic memory: A meta-analysis. *Journal of Cognitive Neuroscience, 27,* 1069–1089.

Illes, J., & McDonald, P. J. (2017). Head transplants: Ghoulish takes on new definition. *AJOB Neuroscience, 8,* 211–212.

Im, S., Varma, K., & Varma, S. (2017). Extending the seductive allure of neuroscience explanations effect to popular articles about educational topics. *British Journal of Educational Psychology, 87,* 518–534.

Inagaki, T. K., Hazlett, L. I., & Andreescu, C. (2019). Naltrexone alters responses to social and physical warmth: implications for social bonding. *Social Cognitive and Affective Neuroscience, 14,* 471–479.

Inbar, Y., Cone, J., & Gilovich, T. (2010). People's intuitions about intuitive insight and intuitive choice. *Journal of Personality and Social Psychology, 99,* 232–247.

Inbar, Y., Pizarro, D., & Bloom, P. (2012). Disgusting smells cause decreased liking of gay men. *Emotion, 12*(1), 23–27.

İnel Manav, A., & Simsek, N. (2019). The effect of reminiscence therapy with Internet-based videos on cognitive status and apathy of older people with mild dementia. *Journal of Geriatric Psychiatry and Neurology, 32,* 104–113.

Infurna, F. J., & Luthar, S. S. (2016). The multidimensional nature of resilience to spousal loss. *Journal of Personality and Social Psychology, 112,* 926–947.

Ingalhalikar, M., Smith, A., Parker, D., Satterthwaite, T. D., Elliott, M. A., Ruparel, K., Hakonarson, H., Gur, R. E., Gur, R. C., & Verma, R. (2013). Sex differences in the structural connectome of the human brain. *PNAS, 111,* 823–828.

Ingham, A. G., Levinger, G., Graves, J., & Peckham, V. (1974). The Ringelmann effect: Studies of group size and group performance. *Journal of Experimental Social Psychology, 10,* 371–384.

Inglehart, R. (1990). *Culture shift in advanced industrial society.* Princeton University Press.

Inglehart, R., Foa, R., Peterson, C., & Welzel, C. (2008). Development, freedom, and rising happiness: A global perspective (1981–2007). *Perspectives on Psychological Science, 3,* 264–285.

Ingraham, C. (2016, May 1). Toddlers have shot at least 23 people this year. *The Washington Post.* https://www.washingtonpost.com/

Inman, M. L., & Baron, R. S. (1996). Influence of prototypes on perceptions of prejudice. *Journal of Personality and Social Psychology, 70,* 727–739.

Innocence Project. (2019, accessed September 30). *DNA exonerations in the United States.* https://www.innocenceproject.org/dna-exonerations-in-the-united-states/

Insel, T., Cuthbert, B., Garvey, M., Heinssen, R., Pine, D. S., Quinn, K., Sanislow, C., & Wang, P. (2010). Research Domain Criteria (RDoC): Toward a new classification framework for research on mental disorders. *American Journal of Psychiatry, 167,* 748–751.

Insel, T. R. (2010). Faulty circuits. *Scientific American, 302,* 44–51.

Insel, T. R., & Lieberman, J. A. (2013, May 13). *DSM-5 and RDoC: Shared interests* [PDF file]. National Institute of Mental Health. http://publichealthunited.org/pressreleases/DSM5andRDoCSharedInterests.pdf

Inzlicht, M., & Kang, S. K. (2010). Stereotype threat spillover: How coping with threats to social identity affects aggression, eating, decision making, and attention. *Journal of Personality and Social Psychology, 99,* 467–481.

IPPA. (2017, January 27). Communication from International Positive Psychology Association.

IPU. (2018). *Women in parliament in 2017: The year in review.* Inter-Parliamentary Union. https://www.ipu.org/resources/publications/reports/2018-03/women-in-parliament-in-2017-year-in-review

Ireland, M. E., & Pennebaker, J. W. (2010). Language style matching in writing: Synchrony in essays, correspondence, and poetry. *Journal of Personality and Social Psychology, 99,* 549–571.

Ironson, G., Solomon, G. F., Balbin, E. G., O'Cleirigh, C., George, A., Kumar, M., Larson, D., & Woods, T. E. (2002). The Ironson-Woods spiritual/religiousness index is associated with long survival, health behaviors, less distress, and low cortisol in people with HIV/AIDS. *Annals of Behavioral Medicine, 24,* 34–48.

Irwin, M. R., Cole, J. C., & Nicassio, P. M. (2006). Comparative meta-analysis of behavioral interventions for insomnia and their efficacy in middle-aged adults and in older adults 55+ years of age. *Health Psychology, 25,* 3–14.

Irwing, P., Cook, C., Pollet, T. V., & Hughes, D. J. (2020). Comedians' trait level and stage personalities: Evidence for goal-directed personality adaptation. *Personality and Social Psychology Bulletin, 46*(4), 590–602.

Isaacowitz, D. M. (2012). Mood regulation in real time: Age differences in the role of looking. *Current Directions in Psychological Science, 21,* 237–242.

Ishiyama, S., & Brecht, M. (2017). Neural correlates of ticklishness in the rat somatosensory cortex. *Science, 354,* 757–760.

Islam, S. S., & Johnson, C. (2003). Correlates of smoking behavior among Muslim Arab-American adolescents. *Ethnicity & Health, 8,* 319–337.

Iso-Markku, P., Waller, K., Vuoksimaa, E., Heikkilä, K., Rinne, J., Kaprio, J., & Kujala, U. M. (2016). Midlife physical activity and cognition later in life: A prospective twin study. *Journal of Alzheimer's Disease, 54,* 1303–1317.

Ito, T. A., Miller, N., & Pollock, V. E. (1996). Alcohol and aggression: A meta-analysis on the moderating effects of inhibitory cues, triggering events, and self-focused attention. *Psychological Bulletin, 120,* 60–82.

ITU. (2018, December 7). *ITU releases 2018 global and regional ICT estimates.* International Telecommunications Union. https://www.itu.int/en/mediacentre/Pages/2018-PR40.aspx

Ives-Deliperi, V. L., Solms, M., & Meintjes, E. M. (2011). The neural substrates of mindfulness: An fMRI investigation. *Social Neuroscience, 6*, 231–242.

Iyengar, S., & Westwood, S. J. (2015). Fear and loathing across party lines: New evidence on group polarization. *American Journal of Political Science, 59*, 690–707.

Iyengar, S. S., & Lepper, M. R. (2000). When choice is demotivating: Can one desire too much of a good thing? *Journal of Personality and Social Psychology, 79*, 995–1006.

Izard, C. E. (1977). *Human emotions.* Plenum Press.

Izard, C. E. (1994). Innate and universal facial expressions: Evidence from developmental and cross-cultural research. *Psychological Bulletin, 114*, 288–299.

Izawa, S., Matsudaira, K., Miki, K., Arisaka, M., & Tsuchiya, M. (2017). Psychosocial correlates of cortisol levels in fingernails among middle-aged workers. *The International Journal on the Biology of Stress, 20*, 386–389.

Jääskeläinen, E., Juola, P., Hirvonen, N., McGrath, J. J., Saha, S., Isohanni, M. , Veijola, J., & Miettunen, J. (2013). A systematic review and meta-analysis of recovery in schizophrenia. *Schizophrenia Bulletin, 39*, 1296–1306.

Jablensky, A. (1999). Schizophrenia: Epidemiology. *Current Opinion in Psychiatry, 12*, 19–28.

Jachimowicz, J., Wihler, A., Bailey, E., & Galinsky, A. (2018). Why grit requires perseverance and passion to positively predict performance. *PNAS, 115*, 9980–9985.

Jäckle, S., & Wenzelburger, G. (2015). Religion, religiosity, and the attitudes toward homosexuality—A multilevel analysis of 79 countries. *Journal of Homosexuality, 62*, 207–241.

Jackson, G. (2009). Sexual response in cardiovascular disease. *Journal of Sex Research, 46*, 233–236.

Jackson, J. J., Thoemmes, F., Jonkmann, K., Lüdtke, O., & Trautwien, U. (2012). Military training and personality trait development: Does the military make the man, or does the man make the military? *Psychological Science, 23*, 270–277.

Jackson, J. M., & Williams, K. D. (1988). *Social loafing: A review and theoretical analysis* [Unpublished manuscript]. Fordham University.

Jackson, S. W. (1992). The listening healer in the history of psychological healing. *American Journal Psychiatry, 149*, 1623–1632.

Jacobs, B. L. (1994). Serotonin, motor activity, and depression-related disorders. *American Scientist, 82*, 456–463.

Jacobs, J. (2019, May 7). James Holzhauer was told to smile to get on 'Jeopardy!' He's smiling now. *The New York Times.* https://www.nytimes.com/2019/05/07/arts/television/james-holzhauer-jeopardy.html

Jacobson, L. (2015, August 27). *Nicholas Kristof stated on August 27, 2015 in his column in The New York Times: "More Americans have died from guns in the United States since 1968 than on battlefields of all the wars in American history."* Politifact. https://bit.ly/2JlMDYg

Jacobson, N. C., & Newman, M. G. (2017). Anxiety and depression as bidirectional risk factors for one another: A meta-analysis of longitudinal studies. *Psychological Bulletin, 143*, 1155–1200.

Jacoby, L. L., & Rhodes, M. G. (2006). False remembering in the aged. *Current Directions in Psychological Science, 15*, 49–53.

Jacques, C., & Rossion, B. (2006). The speed of individual face categorization. *Psychological Science, 17*, 485–492.

Jacques-Tiura, A. J., Abbey, A., Parkhill, M. R., & Zawacki, T. (2007). Why do some men misperceive women's sexual intentions more frequently than others do? An application of the confluence model. *Personality and Social Psychology Bulletin, 33*, 1467–1480.

Jaderberg, M., Czarnecki, W. M., Dunning, I., Marris, L., Lever, G., Castañeda, A. G., Beattie, C., Rabinowitz, N. C., Morcos, A. S., Ruderman, A., Sonnerat, N., Green, T., Deason, L., Leibo, J. Z., Silver, D., Hassabis, D., Kavukcuoglu, K., & Graepel, T. (2019). Human-level performance in 3D multiplayer games with population-based reinforcement learning. *Science, 364*, 859–865.

Jaffe, E. (2004, October). Peace in the Middle East may be impossible: Lee D. Ross on naive realism and conflict resolution. *APS Observer,* pp. 9–11.

Jakubiak, B. K., & Feeney, B. C. (2017). Affectionate touch to promote relational, psychological, and physical well-being in adulthood: A theoretical model and review of the research. *Personality and Social Psychology Review, 21*, 228–252.

Jakubiak, B. K., & Feeney, B. C. (2019). Hand-in-hand combat: Affectionate touch promotes relational well-being and buffers stress during conflict. *Personality and Social Psychology Bulletin, 45*, 431–446.

Jakubowski, K. P., Cundiff, J. M., & Matthews, K. A. (2018). Cumulative childhood adversity and adult cardiometabolic disease: A meta-analysis. *Health Psychology, 37*, 701–715.

James, K. (1986). Priming and social categorizational factors: Impact on awareness of emergency situations. *Personality and Social Psychology Bulletin, 12*, 462–467.

James, S. E., Herman, J. L., Rankin, S., Keisling, M., Mottet, L., & Anafi, M. (2016). *The report of the 2015 U.S. Transgender Survey* [PDF file]. National Center for Transgender Equality. https://transequality.org/sites/default/files/docs/usts/USTS-Full-Report-Dec17.pdf

James, W. (1890). *The principles of psychology* (Vol. 2). Holt.

Jameson, D. (1985). Opponent-colors theory in light of physiological findings. In D. Ottoson & S. Zeki (Eds.), *Central and peripheral mechanisms of color vision* (pp. 83–102). Macmillan.

Jamieson, J. P. (2010). The home field advantage in athletics: A meta-analysis. *Journal of Applied Social Psychology, 40*, 1819–1848.

Jamison, K. R. (1993). *Touched with fire: Manic-depressive illness and the artistic temperament.* Free Press.

Jamison, K. R. (1995). *An unquiet mind.* Knopf.

Janis, I. L. (1982). *Groupthink: Psychological studies of policy decisions and fiascoes.* Houghton Mifflin.

Janis, I. L. (1986). Problems of international crisis management in the nuclear age. *Journal of Social Issues, 42*, 201–220.

Janoff-Bulman, R., Timko, C., & Carli, L. L. (1985). Cognitive biases in blaming the victim. *Journal of Experimental Social Psychology, 21*, 161–177.

Jansen, P. R., Watanabe, K., Stringer, S., Skene, N., Bryois, J., Hammerschlag, A. R., de Leeuw, C. A., Benjamins, J. S., Muñoz-Manchado, A. B., Nagel, M., Savage, J. E., Tiemeier, H., White, T., 23andMe Research Team, Tung, J. Y., Hinds, D. A., Vacic, V., Wang, X., Sullivan, P. F., & Posthuma, D. (2019). Genome-wide analysis of insomnia in 1,331,010 individuals identifies new risk loci and functional pathways. *Nature Genetics, 51*, 394–403.

Janssen, S. M. J., Rubin, D. C., & Conway, M. A. (2012). The reminiscence bump in the temporal distribution of the best football players of all time: Pelé, Cruijff or Maradona? *The Quarterly Journal of Experimental Psychology, 65*, 165–178.

Jansson-Fröjmark, M., Evander, J., & Alfonsson, S. (2019). Are sleep hygiene practices related to the incidence, persistence and remission of insomnia? Findings from a prospective community study. *Journal of Behavioral Medicine, 42*, 128–138.

Jaroslawska, A. J., & Rhodes, S. (2019). Adult age differences in the effects of processing on storage in working memory: A meta-analysis. *Psychology and Aging, 34*, 512–530.

Jayakar, R., King, T. Z., Morris, R., & Na, S. (2015). Hippocampal volume and auditory attention on a verbal memory task with adult survivors of pediatric brain tumor. *Neuropsychology, 29*, 303–319.

Jebb, A. T., Tay, L., Diener, E., & Oishi, S. (2018). Happiness, income satiation and turning points around the world. *Nature: Human Behaviour, 2*, 33–38.

Jeffrey, K., Mahoney, S., Michaelson, J., & Abdallah, S. (2014). *Well-being at work: A review of the literature.* https://neweconomics.org/2014/03/wellbeing-at-work

Jelbert, S. A., Hosking, R. J., Taylor, A. H., & Gray, R. D. (2018). Mental template matching is a potential cultural transmission mechanism for New Caledonian crow tool manufacturing traditions. *Scientific Reports, 8*, article number 8956.

Jena, A. B., Jain, A., & Hicks, T. R. (2018). Do 'Fast and Furious' movies cause a rise in speeding? *The New York Times.* https://www.nytimes.com/2018/01/30/upshot/do-fast-and-furious-movies-cause-a-rise-in-speeding.html?

Jenkins, J. G., & Dallenbach, K. M. (1924). Oblivescence during sleep and waking. *American Journal of Psychology, 35*, 605–612.

Jenkins, J. M., & Astington, J. W. (1996). Cognitive factors and family structure associated with theory of mind development in young children. *Developmental Psychology, 32*, 70–78.

Jenkins, R., Dowsett, A. J., Burton, A. M. (2018) How many faces do people know? *Proceedings of the Royal Society, B285,* 20181319.

Jenkins, S. R. (2017). Not your same old story: New rules for Thematic Apperceptive Techniques (TATs). *Journal of Personality Assessment, 99*, 238–253.

Jennings, W., & Wlezien, C. (2018). Election polling errors across time and space. *Nature Human Behaviour, 2*, 276–283.

Jensen, A. R. (1980). *Bias in mental testing.* Free Press.

Jensen, A. R. (1983, August). *The nature of the Black-White difference on various psychometric tests: Spearman's hypothesis* [Paper]. Presented at the meeting of the American Psychological Association, Anaheim, CA.

Jensen, A. R. (1998). *The g factor: The science of mental ability.* Praeger/Greenwood.

Jensen, J. P., & Bergin, A. E. (1988). Mental health values of professional therapists: A national interdisciplinary survey. *Professional Psychology: Research and Practice, 19*, 290–297.

Jensen, M. P. (2008). The neurophysiology of pain perception and hypnotic analgesia: Implications for clinical practice. *American Journal of Clinical Hypnosis, 51*, 123–147.

Jeon, D.-W., Jung, D.-U., Kim, S.-J., Shim, J.-C., Moon, J. J., Seo, Y.-S., Jung, S.-S., Seo, B.-J., Kim, J.-E., Oh, M., & Kim, Y.-N. (2018). Adjunct transcranial direct current stimulation improves cognitive function in patients with schizophrenia: A double-blind 12-week study. *Schizophrenia Research, 197*, 378–385.

Jepson, C., Krantz, D. H., & Nisbett, R. E. (1983). Inductive reasoning: Competence or skill? *The Behavioral and Brain Sciences, 3*, 494–501.

Jerrim, J., Parker, P., & Shure, N. (2019, April). *Bullshitters. Who are they and what do we know about their lives?* Discussion Paper Series. Institute of Labor Economics, Bonn, Germany.

Jessberger, S., Aimone, J. B., & Gage, F. H. (2008). Neurogenesis. In J. H. Byrne (Ed.), *Learning and* memory: A comprehensive reference: Vol. 4. Molecular mechanisms of memory (pp. 839–858). Elsevier.

Jesse, D. (2019, February 8). Second wave of more than 160 Nassar survivors fight for acknowledgement. *Detroit Free Press*. https://www.freep.com/story/news/education/2019/02/08/second-wave-nassar-survivors-fight-acknowledgement/2794436002/

Jiang, H., White, M. P., Greicius, M. D., Waelde, L. C., & Spiegel, D. (2016). Brain activity and functional connectivity associated with hypnosis. *Cerebral Cortex, 27*, 4083–4093.

Jiang, M., Wong, S., Chung, H., Hsiao, J., Sui, J., & Humphreys, G. (2019). Cultural orientation of self bias in perceptual matching. *Frontiers in Psychology, 10*, 1469.

Jiang, Y., Costello, P., Fang, F., Huang, M., & He, S. (2006). A gender- and sexual orientation-dependent spatial attentional effect of invisible things. *PNAS, 103*, 17048–17052.

Jimenez, J. C., Su, K., Goldberg, A. R., Luna, V. M., Biane, J. S., Ordek, G., Zhou, P., Ong, S. K., Wright, M. A., Zweifel, L., Paninski, L., Hen, R., & Kheirbek, M. A. (2018). Anxiety cells in a hippocampal-hypothalamic circuit. *Neuron, 97*, 670–683.

Jin, M., Onie, S., Curby, K. M., & Most, S. B. (2018). Aversive images cause less perceptual interference among violent video game players: evidence from emotion-induced blindness. *Visual Cognition, 26*, 753–763.

Job, V., Dweck, C. S., & Walton, G. M. (2010). Ego depletion—Is it all in your head?: Implicit theories about willpower affect self-regulation. *Psychological Science, 21*, 1686–1693.

Jobe, T. H., & Harrow, M. (2010). Schizophrenia course, long-term outcome, recovery, and prognosis. *Current Directions in Psychological Science, 19*, 220–225.

Jobson, L., & Cheraghi, S. (2016). Influence of memory theme and posttraumatic stress disorder on memory specificity in British and Iranian trauma survivors. *Memory, 24*, 1015–1022.

Joel, D., Berman, Z., Tavor, I., Wexler, N., Gaber, O., Stein, Y., Shefi, N., Pool, J., Urchs, S., Margulies, D. S., Liem, F., Hänggi, J., Jäncke, L., & Assaf, Y. (2015, December). Sex beyond the genitalia: The human brain mosaic. *PNAS, 112*, 15468–15473.

Joel, S., Eastwick, P. W., & Finkel, E. J. (2017). Is romantic desire predictable? Machine learning applied to initial romantic attraction. *Psychological Science, 28*, 1478–1489.

Johnson, D., Thorpe, R., McGrath, J., Jackson, W., & Jackson, C. (2018). Black–white differences in housing type and sleep duration as well as sleep difficulties in the United States. *International Journal of Environmental Research and Public Health, 15*, 564.

Johnson, D. F. (1997). Margaret Floy Washburn. *Psychology of Women Newsletter*, pp. 17, 22.

Johnson, D. J., Cesario, J., & Pleskac, T. J. (2018). How prior information and police experience impact decisions to shoot. *Journal of Personality and Social Psychology, 115*, 601–623.

Johnson, D. L., Wiebe, J. S., Gold, S. M., Andreasen, N. C., Hichwa, R. D., Watkins, G. L., & Ponto, L. L. B. (1999). Cerebral blood flow and personality: A positron emission tomography study. *American Journal of Psychiatry, 156*, 252–257.

Johnson, D. P., Rhee, S. H., Friedman, N. P., Corley, R. P., Munn-Chernoff, M., Hewitt, J. K., & Whisman, M. A. (2016). A twin study examining rumination as a transdiagnostic correlate of psychopathology. *Clinical Psychological Science, 4*, 971–987.

Johnson, E. J., & Goldstein, D. (2003). Do defaults save lives? *Science, 302*, 1338–1339.

Johnson, J. A. (2007, June 26). Not so situational. Commentary on the SPSP listserv. https://www.psychologicalscience.org/observer/not-so-situational

Johnson, J. E., Stout, R. L., Miller, T. R., Zlotnick, C., Cerbo, L. A., Andrade, J. T., Nargiso, J., Bonner, J., & Wiltsey-Stirman, S. (2019). Randomized cost-effectiveness trial of group interpersonal psychotherapy (IPT) for prisoners with major depression. *Journal of Consulting and Clinical Psychology, 87*, 392–406.

Johnson, J. G., Cohen, P., Kotler, L., Kasen, S., & Brook, J. S. (2002). Psychiatric disorders associated with risk for the development of eating disorders during adolescence and early adulthood. *Journal of Consulting and Clinical Psychology, 70*, 1119–1128.

Johnson, J. S., & Newport, E. L. (1991). Critical period affects on universal properties of language: The status of subjacency in the acquisition of a second language. *Cognition, 39*, 215–258.

Johnson, M. D., & Chen, J. (2015). Blame it on the alcohol: The influence of alcohol consumption during adolescence, the transition to adulthood, and young adulthood on one-time sexual hookups. *Journal of Sex Research, 52*, 570–579.

Johnson, M. H. (1992). Imprinting and the development of face recognition: From chick to man. *Current Directions in Psychological Science, 1*, 52–55.

Johnson, M. P. (2008). *A typology of domestic violence: Intimate terrorism, violent resistance, and situational couple violence.* Northeastern University Press.

Johnson, R. (2017, August 12). The mystery of S. The man with an impossible memory. *The New Yorker*. https://www.newyorker.com/books/page-turner/the-mystery-of-s-the-man-with-an-impossible-memory

Johnson, S. C., Schmitz, T. W., Moritz, C. H., Meyerand, M. E., Rowley, H. A., Alexander, A. L., Hansen, K. W., Gleason, C. E., Carlsson, C. M., Ries, M. L., Asthana, S., Chen, K., Reiman, E. M., & Alexander, G. E. (2006). Activation of brain regions vulnerable to Alzheimer's disease: The effect of mild cognitive impairment. *Neurobiology of Aging, 27*, 1604–1612.

Johnson, W. (2010). Understanding the genetics of intelligence: Can height help? Can corn oil? *Current Directions in Psychological Science, 19*, 177–182.

Johnson, W., Carothers, A., & Deary, I. J. (2008). Sex differences in variability in general intelligence: A new look at the old question. *Perspectives on Psychological Science, 3*, 518–531.

Johnson, W., Gow, A. J., Corley, J., Starr, J. M., & Deary, I. J. (2010). Location in cognitive and residential space at age 70 reflects a lifelong trait over parental and environmental circumstances: The Lothian Birth Cohort 1936. *Intelligence, 38*, 403–411.

Johnson, W., Turkheimer, E., Gottesman, I. I., & Bouchard, Jr., T. J. (2009). Beyond heritability: Twin studies in behavioral research. *Current Directions in Psychological Science, 18*, 217–220.

Johnstone, E. C., Ebmeier, K. P., Miller, P., Owens, D. G. C., & Lawrie, S. M. (2005). Predicting schizophrenia: Findings from the Edinburgh High-Risk Study. *British Journal of Psychiatry, 186*, 18–25.

Joiner, T. E., Jr. (2006). *Why people die by suicide.* Harvard University Press.

Jokela, M., Elovainio, M., Archana, S.-M., & Kivimäki, M. (2009). IQ, socioeconomic status, and early death: The U.S. National Longitudinal Survey of Youth. *Psychosomatic Medicine, 71*, 322–328.

Jonas, E., & Fischer, P. (2006). Terror management and religion: Evidence that intrinsic religiousness mitigates worldview defense following mortality salience. *Journal of Personality and Social Psychology, 91*, 553–567.

Jones, A. C., & Gosling, S. D. (2005). Temperament and personality in dogs (Canis familiaris): A review and evaluation of past research. *Applied Animal Behaviour Science, 95*, 1–53.

Jones, B., Reedy, E. J., & Weinberg, B. A. (2014, January). *Age and scientific genius.* NBER Working Paper Series. nber.org/papers/w19866

Jones, E. (1957). *Sigmund Freud: Life and work*, Vol. 3, Pt. 1., Ch. 4. Basic Books.

Jones, J. M. (2012, June 21). *Atheists, Muslims see most bias as presidential candidates.* Gallup. https://news.gallup.com/poll/155285/atheists-muslims-bias-presidential-candidates.aspx

Jones, J. M. (2016, November 21). *Record-high 77% of Americans perceive nation as divided.* Gallup. https://news.gallup.com/poll/197828/record-high-americans-perceive-nation-divided.aspx

Jones, M. (2018, February 7). What teenagers are learning from online porn. *The New York Times Magazine*. https://www.nytimes.com/2018/02/07/magazine/teenagers-learning-online-porn-literacy-sex-education.html?

Jones, M. C. (1924). A laboratory study of fear: The case of Peter. *Journal of Genetic Psychology, 31*, 308–315.

Jones, S. (2017). Can newborn infants imitate? *WIREs Cognitive Science, 8*(1–2), 1–13.

Jones, S. E., Lane, J. M., Wood, A. R., van Hees, V. T., Tyrell, J., Beaumont, R. N., Jeffries, A. R., Dashti, H. S., Hillsdon, M., Ruth, K. S., Tuke, M. A., Yaghootkar, H., Sharp, S. A., Jie, Y., Thompson, W. D., Harrison, J. W., Dawes, A., Dyrne, E. M., Tiemeier, H., . . . Weedon, M. N. (2019). Genome-wide association analyses of chronotype in 697,828 individuals provides insights into circadian rhythms. *Nature Communications, 10*, 343.

Jones, S. S. (2007). Imitation in infancy: The development of mimicry. *Psychological Science, 18*, 593–599.

Jones, W. H., Carpenter, B. N., & Quintana, D. (1985). Personality and interpersonal predictors of loneliness in two cultures. *Journal of Personality and Social Psychology, 48*, 1503–1511.

Joo, M., Terzino, K. A., Cross, S. E., Yamaguchi, N., & Ohbuchi, K. I. (2019). How does culture shape conceptions of forgiveness? Evidence from Japan and the United States. *Journal of Cross-Cultural Psychology, 50*, 676–702.

Jordan, A. H., Monin, B., Dweck, C. S., Lovett, B. J., John, O. P., & Gross, J. J. (2011). Misery has more company than people think: Underestimating the prevalence of others' negative emotions. *Personality and Social Psychology Bulletin, 37*, 120–135.

Jordan, G., Deeb, S. S., Bosten, J. M., & Mollon, J. D. (2010). The dimensionality of color vision in carriers of anomalous trichromacy. *Journal of Vision, 10*, ArtID: 12.

Jorm, A. F., Reavley, N. J., & Ross, A. M. (2012). Belief in the dangerousness of people with mental disorders: A review. *Australian and New Zealand Journal of Psychiatry, 46*, 1029–1045.

Jose, A., O'Leary, D., & Moyer, A. (2010). Does premarital cohabitation predict subsequent marital stability and marital quality? A meta-analysis. *Journal of Marriage and Family, 72*, 105–116.

Joseph, J. (2001). Separated twins and the genetics of personality differences: A critique. *American Journal of Psychology, 114*, 1–30.

Joshi, S. H., Espinoza, R. T., Pirnia, T., Shi, J., Wang, Y., Ayers, B., Leaver, A., Woods, R. P., & Narr, K. L. (2016). Structural plasticity of the hippocampus and amygdala induced by electroconvulsive therapy in major depression. *Biological Psychiatry, 79*, 282–292.

Jost, J. T. (2019). A quarter century of system justification theory: Questions, answers, criticisms, and societal applications. *British Journal of Social Psychology, 58*, 263–314.

Jovanovic, T., Blanding, N. Q., Norrholm, S. D., Duncan, E., Bradley, B., & Ressler, K. J. (2009). Childhood abuse is associated with increased startle reactivity in adulthood. *Depression and Anxiety, 26*, 1018–1026.

Juarez, B., Liu, Y., Zhang, L., & Han, M. H. (2019). Optogenetic investigation of neural mechanisms for alcohol use disorders. *Alcohol, 74,* 29–38.

Judge, T. A., Thoresen, C. J., Bono, J. E., & Patton, G. K. (2001). The job satisfaction/job performance relationship: A qualitative and quantitative review. *Psychological Bulletin, 127,* 376–407.

Julian, K. (2018, December). Why are young people having so little sex? *The Atlantic.* https://www.realclearpolitics.com/2018/11/13/why_are_young_people_having_so_little_sex_458984.html

Jung, H., Herrenkohl, T. I., Skinner, M. L., Lee, J. O., Klika, J. B., & Rousson, A. N. (2019). Gender differences in intimate partner violence: a predictive analysis of IPV by child abuse and domestic violence exposure during early childhood. *Violence Against Women, 25,* 903–924.

Jung, R. E., & Haier, R. J. (2013). Creativity and intelligence: Brain networks that link and differentiate the expression of genius. In O. Vartanian, A. S. Bristol, & J. C. Kaufman (Eds.), *Neuroscience of creativity.* MIT Press.

Jung, S. J., Woo, H., Cho, S., Park, K., Jeong, S., Lee, Y. J., Kang, D., & Shin, A. (2017). Association between body size, weight change and depression: Systematic review and meta-analysis. *The British Journal of Psychiatry, 211,* 14–21.

Jung-Beeman, M., Bowden, E. M., Haberman, J., Frymiare, J. L., Arambel-Liu, S., Greenblatt, R., Reber, P. J., & Kounios, J. (2004). Neural activity when people solve verbal problems with insight. *PLOS Biology, 2,* e111.

Juskalian, R. (2019, September/October). The science of fun violence. *Discover,* pp. 31–37.

Just, M. A., Keller, T. A., & Cynkar, J. (2008). A decrease in brain activation associated with driving when listening to someone speak. *Brain Research, 1205,* 70–80.

Kabadayi, C., & Osvath, M. (2017). Ravens parallel great apes in flexible planning for tool-use and bartering. *Science, 357,* 202–203.

Kabat-Zinn, J. (2001). Mindfulness-based interventions in context: Past, present, and future. *Clinical Psychology: Science and Practice, 10,* 144–156.

Kable, J. W., Caulfield, M. K., Falcone, M., McConnell, M., Bernardo, L., Parthasarathi, T., Cooper, N., Ashare, R., Audrain-McGovern, J., Hornik, R., Diefenbach, P., Lee, F. J., & Lerman, C. (2017). No effect of commercial cognitive training on brain activity, choice behavior, or cognitive performance. *Journal of Neuroscience, 37,* 7390–7402.

Kadohisa, M. (2013). Effects of odor on emotion, with implications. *Frontiers in Systems Neuroscience, 7,* 6.

Kagan, J. (1976). Emergent themes in human development. *American Scientist, 64,* 186–196.

Kagan, J. (1984). *The nature of the child.* Basic Books.

Kagan, J. (1995). On attachment. *Harvard Review of Psychiatry, 3,* 104–106.

Kagan, J. (1998). *Three seductive ideas.* Harvard University Press.

Kagan, J., & Snidman, N. (2004). *The long shadow of temperament.* Belknap Press.

Kahneman, D. (1985, June). Quoted by K. McKean in Decisions, decisions [PDF file]. *Discover.* http://d1m3qhodv9fjlf.cloudfront.net/wp-content/uploads/2013/01/Decisions_Decisions.pdf

Kahneman, D. (1999). Assessments of objective happiness: A bottom-up approach. In D. Kahneman, E. Diener, & N. Schwartz (Eds.), *Understanding well-being: Scientific perspectives on enjoyment and suffering.* Russell Sage Foundation.

Kahneman, D. (2005, January 13). What were they thinking? Q&A with Daniel Kahneman. *Gallup Management Journal.* https://news.gallup.com/businessjournal/14503/what-were-they-thinking.aspx

Kahneman, D. (2011). *Thinking, fast and slow.* Farrar, Straus and Giroux.

Kahneman, D. (2015, July 18). Quoted by D. Shariatmadari in Daniel Kahneman: 'What would I eliminate if I had a magic wand? Overconfidence.' *The Guardian.* https://www.theguardian.com/books/2015/jul/18/daniel-kahneman-books-interview

Kahneman, D., Fredrickson, B. L., Schreiber, C. A., & Redelmeier, D. A. (1993). When more pain is preferred to less: Adding a better end. *Psychological Science, 4,* 401–405.

Kahneman, D., Krueger, A. B., Schkade, D. A., Schwarz, N., & Stone, A. A. (2004). A survey method for characterizing daily life experience: The day reconstruction method. *Science, 306,* 1776–1780.

Kail, R. (1991). Developmental change in speed of processing during childhood and adolescence. *Psychological Bulletin, 109,* 490–501.

Kaiser, J. (2019). Screen embryos for complex genetic traits called premature. *Science, 366,* 405–406.

Kaiser Family Foundation. (2010, January). *Generation M2: Media in the lives of 8- to 18-year-olds* (by V. J. Rideout, U. G. Foeher, & D. F. Roberts). Henry J. Kaiser Family Foundation.

Kakinami, L., Barnett, T. A., Séguin, L., & Paradis, G. (2015). Parenting style and obesity risk in children. *Preventive Medicine, 75,* 18–22.

Kállay, É. (2015). Physical and psychological benefits of written emotional expression: Review of meta-analyses and recommendations. *European Psychologist, 20,* 242–251.

Kalokerinos, E. K., Kjelsaas, K., Bennetts, S., & von Hippel, C. (2018). Men in pink-collars: Stereotype threat and disengagement among male teachers and child protection workers. *European Journal of Social Psychology, 47,* 553–565.

Kamatali, J.-M. (2014, April 4). Following orders in Rwanda. *The New York Times.* https://www.nytimes.com/2014/04/05/opinion/following-orders-in-rwanda.html?

Kambeitz, J., Kambelitz-Ilankovic, L., Cabral, C., Dwyer, D. B., Calhoun, V. C., van den Heuvel, M. P., Falkai, P., Koutsouleris, N., & Malchow, B. (2016). Aberrant functional whole-brain network architecture in patients with schizophrenia: A meta-analysis. *Schizophrenia Bulletin, 42,* Suppl. no. 1, S13–S21.

Kamel, N. S., & Gammack, J. K. (2006). Insomnia in the elderly: Cause, approach, and treatment. *American Journal of Medicine, 119,* 463–469.

Kamenica, E., Naclerio, R., & Malani, A. (2013). Advertisements impact the physiological efficacy of a branded drug. *PNAS, 110,* 12931–12935.

Kamil, A. C., & Cheng, K. (2001). Way-finding and landmarks: The multiple-bearings hypothesis. *Journal of Experimental Biology, 204,* 103–113.

Kaminski, J., Cali, J., & Fischer, J. (2004). Word learning in a domestic dog: Evidence for "fast mapping." *Science, 304,* 1682–1683.

Kämpf, M. S., Liebermann, H., Kerschreiter, R., Krause, S., Nestler, S., & Schmukle, S. C. (2018). Disentangling the sources of mimicry: Social relations analyses of the link between mimicry and liking. *Psychological Science, 29,* 131–138.

Kandel, E. (2008, October/November). Quoted by S. Avan in Speaking of memory. *Scientific American Mind,* pp. 16–17.

Kandel, E. (2012, March 5). Interview by Claudia Dreifus: A quest to understand how memory works. *The New York Times.* https://www.nytimes.com/2012/03/06/science/a-quest-to-understand-how-memory-works.html?

Kandel, E. (2013, September 6). The new science of mind. *The New York Times.* https://www.nytimes.com/2013/09/08/opinion/sunday/the-new-science-of-mind.html?

Kandel, E. R. (2012, March 5). A quest to understand how memory works [Interview with Claudia Dreifus]. *The New York Times.* https://www.nytimes.com/2012/03/06/science/a-quest-to-understand-how-memory-works.html?

Kandel, E. R., & Schwartz, J. H. (1982). Molecular biology of learning: Modulation of transmitter release. *Science, 218,* 433–443.

Kandler, C., Bleidorn, W., Riemann, R., Angleitner, A., & Spinath, F. M. (2012). Life events as environmental states and genetic traits and the role of personality: A longitudinal twin study. *Behavior Genetics, 42,* 57–72.

Kandler, C., & Riemann, R. (2013). Genetic and environmental sources of individual religiousness: The roles of individual personality traits and perceived environmental religiousness. *Behavior Genetics, 43,* 297–313.

Kandler, C., Riemann, R., & Angleitner, A. (2013). Patterns and sources of continuity and change of energetic and temporal aspects of temperament in adulthood: A longitudinal twin study of self- and peer reports. *Developmental Psychology, 49,* 1739–1753.

Kane, G. D. (2010). Revisiting gay men's body image issues: Exposing the fault lines. *Review of General Psychology, 14,* 311–317.

Kane, J. M., & Mertz, J. E. (2012). Debunking myths about gender and mathematics performance. *Notices of the American Mathematical Society, 59,* 10–21.

Kane, M. J., Brown, L. H., McVay, J. C., Silvia, P. J., Myin-Germeys, I., & Kwapil, T. R. (2007). For whom the mind wanders, and when: An experience-sampling study of working memory and executive control in daily life. *Psychological Science, 18,* 614–621.

Kanwar, A., Malik, S., Prokop, L. J., Sim, L. A., Feldstein, D., Wang, Z., & Murad, M. H. (2013). The association between anxiety disorders and suicidal behaviors: A systematic review and meta-analysis. *Depression and Anxiety, 30,* 917–929.

Kaplan, B. J., Rucklidge, J. J., Romijn, A., & McLeod, K. (2015). The emerging field of nutritional mental health: Inflammation, the microbiome, oxidative stress, and mitochondrial function. *Clinical Psychological Science, 3,* 964–980.

Kaplan, H. I., & Saddock, B. J. (Eds.). (1989). *Comprehensive textbook of psychiatry,* V. Williams and Wilkins.

Kaprio, J., Koskenvuo, M., & Rita, H. (1987). Mortality after bereavement: A prospective study of 95,647 widowed persons. *American Journal of Public Health, 77,* 283–287.

Kaptchuk, T. J., Stason, W. B., Davis, R. B., Legedza, A. R. T., Schnyer, R. N., Kerr, C. E., Stone, D. A., Nam, B. H., Kirsch, I., & Goldman, R. H. (2006). Sham device v inert pill: Randomised controlled trial of two placebo treatments. *British Medical Journal, 332,* 391–397.

Karacan, I., Goodenough, D. R., Shapiro, A., & Starker, S. (1966). Erection cycle during sleep in relation to dream anxiety. *Archives of General Psychiatry, 15,* 183–189.

Karasik, L. B., Adolph, K. E., Tamis-LeMonda, C. S., & Bornstein, M. H. (2010). WEIRD walking: Cross-cultural research on motor development. *Behavioral and Brain Sciences, 33,* 95–96.

Karau, S. J., & Williams, K. D. (1993). Social loafing: A meta-analytic review and theoretical integration. *Journal of Personality and Social Psychology, 65,* 681–706.

Karazsia, B. T., Murnen, S. K., & Tylka, T. L. (2017). Is body dissatisfaction changing across time? A cross-temporal meta-analysis. *Psychological Bulletin, 143,* 293–320.

Kark, J. D., Shemi, G., Friedlander, Y., Martin, O., Manor, O., & Blondheim, S. H. (1996). Does religious observance promote health? Mortality in secular vs. religious kibbutzim in Israel. *American Journal of Public Health, 86,* 341–346.

Karlén, J., Ludvigsson, J., Hedmark, M., Faresjö, Å., Theodorsson, E., & Faresjö, T. (2015). Early psychosocial exposures, hair cortisol levels, and disease risk. *Pediatrics, 135,* e1450–e1457.

Karlsgodt, K. H., Sun, D., & Cannon, T. D. (2010). Structural and functional brain abnormalities in schizophrenia. *Current Directions in Psychological Science, 19,* 226–231.

Karni, A., Meyer, G., Rey-Hipolito, C., Jezzard, P., Adams, M. M., Turner, R., & Ungerleider, L. G. (1998). The acquisition of skilled motor performance: Fast and slow experience-driven changes in primary motor cortex. *PNAS, 95,* 861–868.

Karni, A., & Sagi, D. (1994). Dependence on REM sleep for overnight improvement of perceptual skills. *Science, 265,* 679–682.

Karns, C. M., Dow, M. W., & Neville, H. J. (2012). Altered cross-modal processing in the primary auditory cortex of congenitally deaf adults: A visual-somatosensory fMRI study with a double-flash illusion. *The Journal of Neuroscience, 32,* 9626–9638.

Karpicke, J. D. (2012). Retrieval-based learning: Active retrieval promotes meaningful learning. *Current Directions in Psychological Science, 21,* 157–163.

Karremans, J. C., Frankenhis, W. E., & Arons, S. (2010). Blind men prefer a low waist-to-hip ratio. *Evolution and Human Behavior, 31,* 182–186.

Karsay, K., Knoll, J., & Matthes, J. (2018). Sexualizing media use and self-objectification: A meta-analysis. *Psychology of Women Quarterly, 42,* 9–28.

Kasen, S., Chen, H., Sneed, J., Crawford, T., & Cohen, P. (2006). Social role and birth cohort influences on gender-linked personality traits in women: A 20-year longitudinal analysis. *Journal of Personality and Social Psychology, 91,* 944–958.

Kashdan, T., DeWall, C. N., Schurtz, D., Deckman, T., Lykins, E. L. B., Evans, D., McKenzie, J., Segerstrom, S. C., Gailliot, M. T., & Brown, K. (2014). More than words: Contemplating death enhances positive emotional word use. *Personality and Individual Differences, 71,* 171–175.

Kashdan, T. B. (2009). *Curious? Discover the missing ingredient to a fulfilling life.* William Morrow.

Kashima, Y., Bain, P. G., & Perfors, A. (2019). The psychology of cultural dynamics: What is it, what do we know, and what is yet to be known? *Annual Review of Psychology, 70,* 499–529.

Kashubeck-West, S., & Meyer, J. (2008). The well-being of women who are late deafened. *Journal of Counseling Psychology, 55,* 463–472.

Kasser, T. (2018). Materialism and living well. In E. Diener, S. Oishi, & L. Tay (Eds.), *Handbook of well-being.* DEF Publishers.

Kassin, S. M. (2017). The killing of Kitty Genovese: What else does this case tell us? *Perspectives on Psychological Science, 12,* 374–381.

Kassing, F., Godwin, J., Lochman, J. E., Coie, J. D., & Conduct Problems Prevention Research Group. (2019). Using early childhood behavior problems to predict adult convictions. *Journal of Abnormal Child Psychology, 47,* 765–778.

Katz-Wise, S. L., Priess, H. A., & Hyde, J. S. (2010). Gender-role attitudes and behavior across the transition to parenthood. *Developmental Psychology, 46,* 18–28.

Kaufman, J., & Zigler, E. (1987). Do abused children become abusive parents? *American Journal of Orthopsychiatry, 57,* 186–192.

Kaufman, J. C., & Baer, J. (2002). I bask in dreams of suicide: Mental illness, poetry, and women. *Review of General Psychology, 6,* 271–286.

Kaufman, L., & Kaufman, J. H. (2000). Explaining the moon illusion. *PNAS, 97,* 500–505.

Kaufman, S. B. (2018). Self-actualizing people in the 21st century: Integration with contemporary theory and research on personality and well-being. *Journal of Humanistic Psychology.* Advance online publication. doi: 10.1177/0022167818809187

Kaufmann, R. K., Mann, M. L., Gopal, S., Liederman, J. A., Howe, P. D., Pretis, F., Tang, X., & Gilmore, M. (2017). Spatial heterogeneity of climate change as an experiential basis for skepticism. *PNAS, 114,* 67–71.

Kaunitz, L. N., Rowe, E. G., & Tsuchiya, N. (2016). Large capacity of conscious access for incidental memories in natural scenes. *Psychological Science, 27,* 1266–1277.

Kawakami, K., Dunn, E., Karmali, F., & Dovidio, J. F. (2009). Mispredicting affective and behavioral responses to racism. *Science, 323,* 276–278.

Kawamichi, H., Yoshihara, K., Sugawara, S. K., Matsunaga, M., Makita, K., Hamano, Y. H., Tanabe, H. C., & Sadato, N. (2015). Helping behavior induced by empathic concern attenuates anterior cingulate activation in response to others' distress. *Social Neuroscience, 11,* 109–122.

Kayser, C. (2007, April/May). Listening with your eyes. *Scientific American Mind,* pp. 24–29.

Kazantzis, N., Whittington, C., & Dattilio, F. M. (2010). Meta-analysis of homework effects in cognitive and behavioral therapy: A replication and extension. *Clinical Psychology: Science and Practice, 17,* 144–156.

Kean, S. (2016, September). The audacious plan to save this man's life by transplanting his head. *The Atlantic.* https://www.theatlantic.com/magazine/archive/2016/09/the-audacious-plan-to-save-this-mans-life-by-transplanting-his-head/492755/

Kearns, M. C., Ressler, K. J., Zatzick, D., & Rothbaum, B. O. (2012). Early interventions for PTSD: A review. *Depression and Anxiety, 29,* 833–842.

Keefe, P. R. (2016, August 15). *The detectives who never forget a face.* NPR. https://www.npr.org/2016/08/17/490314062/new-yorker-the-detectives-who-never-forget-a-face

Keesey, R. E., & Corbett, S. W. (1984). Metabolic defense of the body weight set-point. In A. J. Stunkard & E. Stellar (Eds.), *Eating and its disorders* (pp. 87–96). Raven Press.

Keiser, H. N., Sackett, P. R., Kuncel, N. R., & Brothen, T. (2016). Why women perform better in college than admission scores would predict: Exploring the roles of conscientiousness and course-taking patterns. *Journal of Applied Psychology, 101,* 569–581.

Keith, S. W., Redden, D. T., Katzmarzyk, P. T., Boggiano, M. M., Hanlon, E. C., Benca, R. M., Ruden, D., Pietrobelli, A., Barger, J. L., Fontaine, K. R., Wang, C., Aronne, L. J. Wright, S. M., Baskin, M., Dhurandhar, N. V., Lijoi, M. C., Grilo, C. M., DeLuca, M., Westfall, A. O., & Allison, D. B. (2006). Putative contributors to the secular increase in obesity: Exploring the roads less traveled. *International Journal of Obesity, 30,* 1585–1594.

Kell, H. J., Lubinski, D., & Benbow, C. P. (2013). Who rises to the top? Early indicators. *Psychological Science, 24,* 648–659.

Keller, C., Hartmann, C., & Siegrist, M. (2016). The association between dispositional self-control and longitudinal changes in eating behaviors, diet quality, and BMI. *Psychology & Health, 31,* 1311–1327.

Keller, P. S., Haak, E. A., DeWall, C. N., & Renzetti, C. (2019). Poor sleep is associated with greater marital aggression: The role of self-control. *Behavioral Sleep Medicine, 17,* 174–180.

Kellerman, J., Lewis, J., & Laird, J. D. (1989). Looking and loving: The effects of mutual gaze on feelings of romantic love. *Journal of Research in Personality, 23,* 145–161.

Kelling, S. T., & Halpern, B. P. (1983). Taste flashes: Reaction times, intensity, and quality. *Science, 219,* 412–414.

Kellner, C. H., Knapp, R. G., Petrides, G., Rummans, T. A., Husain, M. M., Rasmussen, K., Mueller, M., Bernstein, H. J., O'Connor, K., Smith, G., Biggs, M., Bailine, S. H., Malur, C., Yim, E., McClintock, S., Sampson, S., & Fink, M. (2006). Continuation electroconvulsive therapy vs. pharmacotherapy for relapse prevention in major depression: A multisite study from the Consortium for Research in Electroconvulsive Therapy (CORE). *Archives of General Psychiatry, 63,* 1337–1344.

Kelly, A. E. (2000). Helping construct desirable identities: A self-presentational view of psychotherapy. *Psychological Bulletin, 126,* 475–494.

Kelly, D. J., Quinn, P. C., Slater, A. M., Lee, K., Ge, L., & Pascalis, O. (2007). The other-race effect develops during infancy: Evidence of perceptual narrowing. *Psychological Science, 18,* 1084–1089.

Kelly, S. D., Özyürek, A., & Maris, E. (2010). Two sides of the same coin: Speech and gesture mutually interact to enhance comprehension. *Psychological Science, 21,* 260–267.

Kelly, T. A. (1990). The role of values in psychotherapy: A critical review of process and outcome effects. *Clinical Psychology Review, 10,* 171–186.

Kelly, Y., Zilanawala, A., Booker, C. & Sacker, A. (2018). Social media use and adolescent mental health: Findings from the UK Millennium Cohort Study. *EClinicalMedicine (The Lancet), 6,* 59–68.

Kempe, R. S., & Kempe, C. C. (1978). *Child abuse.* Harvard University Press.

Kempermann, G. (2019). Environmental enrichment, new neurons and the neurobiology of individuality. *Nature Reviews Neuroscience, 20,* 235–245.

Kempermann, G., Gage, F. H., Aigner, L., Song, H., Curtis, M. A., Thuret, S., Kuhn, H. G., Jessberger, S., Frankland, P. W., Cameron, H. A., Gould, E., Hen, R., Abrous, D. N., Toni, N., Schinder, A. F., Zhao, X., Lucassen, P. J., & Frisén, J. (2018). Human adult neurogenesis: Evidence and remaining questions. *Cell Stem Cell, 23,* 25–30.

Kendall-Tackett, K. A., Williams, L. M., & Finkelhor, D. (1993). Impact of sexual abuse on children: A review and synthesis of recent empirical studies. *Psychological Bulletin, 113,* 164–180.

Kendler, K. S. (1996). Parenting: A genetic-epidemiologic perspective. *The American Journal of Psychiatry, 153,* 11–20.

Kendler, K. S., Maes, H. H., Lönn, S. L., Morris, N. A., Lichtenstein, P., Sundquist, J., & Sundquist, K. (2015a). A Swedish national twin study of criminal behavior and its violent, white-collar and property subtypes. *Psychological Medicine, 45,* 2253–2262.

Kendler, K. S., Morris, N. A., Ohlsson, H., Lönn, S. L., Sundquist, J., & Sundquist, K. (2016). Criminal offending and the family environment: Swedish national high-risk home-reared and adopted-away co-sibling control study. *The British Journal of Psychiatry, 209,* 294–299.

Kendler, K. S., Myers, J., & Zisook, S. (2008). Does bereavement-related major depression differ from major depression associated with other stressful life events? *American Journal of Psychiatry, 165,* 1449–1455.

Kendler, K. S., Neale, M. C., Kessler, R. C., Heath, A. C., & Eaves, L. J. (1994). Parent treatment and the equal environment assumption in twin studies of psychiatric illness. *Psychological Medicine, 24*, 579–590.

Kendler, K. S., Neale, M. C., Thornton, L. M., Aggen, S. H., Gilman, S. E., & Kessler, R. C. (2002). Cannabis use in the last year in a U.S. national sample of twin and sibling pairs. *Psychological Medicine, 32*, 551–554.

Kendler, K. S., Ohlsson, H., Lichtenstein, P., Sundquist, J., & Sundquist, K. (2018) The genetic epidemiology of treated major depression in Sweden. *The American Journal of Psychiatry, 175*, 1137–1144.

Kendler, K. S., Ohlsson, H., Sundquist, J., & Sundquist, K. (2016). Alcohol use disorder and mortality across the lifespan: A longitudinal cohort and corelative analysis. *JAMA Psychiatry, 73*, 575–581.

Kendler, K. S., Sundquist, K., Ohlsson, H., Palmer, K., Maes, H., Winkleby, M. A., & Sundquist, J. (2012). Genetic and familiar environmental influences on the risk for drug abuse: A Swedish adoption study. *Archives of General Psychiatry, 69*, 690–697.

Kendler, K. S., Turkheimer, E., Ohlsson, H., Sundquist, J., & Sundquist, K. (2015b). Family environment and the malleability of cognitive ability: A Swedish national home-reared and adopted-away cosibling control study. *PNAS, 112*, 4612–4617.

Kendrick, K. M., & Feng, J. (2011). Neural encoding principles in face perception revealed using non-primate models. In G. Rhodes, A. Calder, M. Johnson, & J. V. Haxby (Eds.), *The Oxford handbook of face perception.* Oxford University Press.

Kennard, B. D., Emslie, G. J., Mayes, T. L., Nakonezny, P. A., Jones, J. M., Foxwell, A. A., & King, J. (2014). Sequential treatment of fluoxetine and relapse-prevention CBT to improve outcomes in pediatric depression. *American Journal of Psychiatry, 171*, 1083–1090.

Kennedy, M., Kreppner, J., Knights, N., Kumsta, R., Maughan, B., Golm, D., Rutter, M., Schlotz, W., & Sonuga-Barke, E. J. (2016). Early severe institutional deprivation is associated with a persistent variant of adult attention-deficit/hyperactivity disorder: Clinical presentation, developmental continuities and life circumstances in the English and Romanian Adoptees study. *Journal of Child Psychology and Psychiatry, 57*, 1113–1125.

Kennedy, S., & Over, R. (1990). Psychophysiological assessment of male sexual arousal following spinal cord injury. *Archives of Sexual Behavior, 19*, 15–27.

Kenrick, D. T., Griskevicious, V., Neuberg, S. L., & Schaller, M. (2010). Renovating the pyramid of needs: Contemporary extensions build upon ancient foundations. *Perspectives on Psychological Science, 5*, 292–314.

Kenrick, D. T., Nieuweboer, S., & Buunk, A. P. (2009). Universal mechanisms and cultural diversity: Replacing the blank slate with a coloring book. In M. Schaller, A. Norenzayan, S. Heine, A. Norenzayan, T. Yamagishi, & T. Kameda (Eds.), *Evolution, culture, and the human mind.* Erlbaum.

Kensinger, E. A. (2007). Negative emotion enhances memory accuracy: Behavioral and neuroimaging evidence. *Current Directions in Psychological Science, 16*, 213–218.

Kent de Grey, R. G., Uchino, B. N., Trettevik, R., Cronan, S., & Hogan, J. N. (2018). Social support and sleep: A meta-analysis. *Health Psychology, 37*, 787–798.

Keough, K. A., Zimbardo, P. G., & Boyd, J. N. (1999). Who's smoking, drinking, and using drugs? Time perspective as a predictor of substance use. *Basic and Applied Social Psychology, 2*, 149–164.

Keramati, M., Durand, A., Girardeau, P., Gutkin, B., & Ahmed, S. H. (2017). Cocaine addiction as a homeostatic reinforcement learning disorder. *Psychological Review, 124*, 130–153.

Keresztes, A., Bender, A. R., Bodammer, N. C., Lindenberger, U., Shing, Y. L., & Werkle-Bergner, M. (2017). Hippocampal maturity promotes memory distinctiveness in childhood and adolescence. *PNAS, 114*, 9212–9217.

Kern, M. L., Eichstaedt, J. C., Schwartz, H. A., Dziurzynski, L., Ungar, L. H., Stillwell, D. J., Kosinski, M., Ramones, S. M., & Seligman, M. E. P. (2014). The online social self: An open vocabulary approach to personality. *Assessment, 21*, 158–169.

Kernis, M. H. (2003). Toward a conceptualization of optimal self-esteem. *Psychological Inquiry, 14*, 1–26.

Kerns, J. C., Guo, J., Fothergill, E., Howard, L., Knuth, N. D., Brychta, R., Chen, K. Y., Skaruli, M. C., Walter, P. J., & Hall, K. D. (2017). Increased physical activity associated with less weight regain six years after "The Biggest Loser" competition. *Obesity, 25*, 1838–1843.

Kerr, N. L., & Bruun, S. E. (1983). Dispensability of member effort and group motivation losses: Free-rider effects. *Journal of Personality and Social Psychology, 44*, 78–94.

Kersbergen, I., Oldham, M., Jones, A., Field, M., Angus, C., & Robinson, E. (2018). Reducing the standard serving size of alcoholic beverages prompts reductions in alcohol consumption. *Addiction, 113*, 1598–1608.

Kessler, M., & Albee, G. (1975). Primary prevention. *Annual Review of Psychology, 26*, 557–591.

Kessler, R. C., Aguilar-Gaxiola, S., Alonso, J., Chatterji, S., Lee, S., Ormel, J., Üstün, T. B., & Wang, P. S. (2009). The global burden of mental disorders: An update from the WHO World Mental Health (WMH) Surveys. *Epidemiology and Psychiatric Services, 18*, 23–33.

Kessler, R. C., Akiskal, H. S., Ames, M., Birnbaum, H., Greenberg, P., Hirschfeld, R. M. A., Jin, R., Merikangas, K., Simon, G., & Wang, P. S. (2006). Prevalence and effects of mood disorders on work performance in a nationally representative sample of U.S. workers. *American Journal of Psychiatry, 163*, 1561–1568.

Kessler, R. C., Amminger, G. P., Aguilar-Gaxiola, S., Alonso, J., Lee, S., & Üstün, T. B. (2007). Age of onset of mental disorders: A review of recent literature. *Current Opinion in Psychiatry, 20*, 359–364.

Kessler, R. C., Brinbaum, H. G., Shahly, V., Bromet, E., Hwang, I., McLaughlin, K. A., Sampson, N., Andrade, L. H., De Girolamo, G., Demyttenaere, K., Haro, J. M., Karam, A. N., Kostyuchenko, S., Kovess, V., Lara, C., Levinson, D., Matschinger, H., Nakane, Y., Oakley, B., . . . Stein, D. J. (2010). Age differences in the prevalence and co-morbidity of DSM-IV major depressive episodes: Results from the WHO World Mental Health Survey Initiative. *Depression and Anxiety, 27*, 351–364.

Kessler, R. C., Petukhova, M., Sampson, N. A., Zaslavsky, A. M., & Wittchen, H.-A. (2012). Twelve-month and lifetime morbid risk of anxiety and mood disorders in the United States. *International Journal of Methods in Psychiatric Research, 21*, 169–184.

Keyes, K. M., Cerdá, M., Brady, J. E., Havens, J. R., & Galea, S. (2014). Understanding the rural–urban differences in nonmedical prescription opioid use and abuse in the United States. *American Journal of Public Health, 104*, e52–e59.

Keyes, K. M., Maslowsky, J., Hamilton, A., & Schulenberg, J. (2015). The great sleep recession: Changes in sleep duration among U.S. adolescents, 1991–2012. *Pediatrics, 135*, 460–468.

Keynes, M. (1980, December 20/27). Handel's illnesses. *The Lancet,* pp. 1354–1355.

Keys, A., Brozek, J., Henschel, A., Mickelsen, O., & Taylor, H. L. (1950). *The biology of human starvation.* University of Minnesota Press.

Khaldun, I. (1377/1967). *Muqaddimah: An introduction to history. Abridged.* Princeton University Press.

Khanna, S., & Greyson, B. (2014). Daily spiritual experiences before and after near-death experiences. *Psychology of Religion and Spirituality, 6*, 302–309.

Khanna, S., & Greyson, B. (2015). Near-death experiences and posttraumatic growth. *Journal of Nervous and Mental Disease, 203*, 749–755.

Khazanoy, G. K., & Ruscio, A. M. (2016). Is low positive emotionality a specific risk factor for depression? A meta-analysis of longitudinal studies. *Psychological Bulletin, 142*, 991–1015.

Khera, M., Bhattacharya, R. K., Blick, G., Kushner, H., Nguyen, D., & Miner, M. M. (2011). Improved sexual function with testosterone replacement therapy in hypogonadal men: Real-world data from the Testim Registry in the United States (TriUS). *Journal of Sexual Medicine, 8*, 3204–3213.

Khodagholy, D., Gelinas, J. N., & Buzsáki, G. (2017). Learning-enhanced coupling between ripple oscillations in association cortices and hippocampus. *Science, 358*, 369–372.

Kiatpongsan, S., & Norton, M. (2014). How much (more) should CEOs make? A universal desire for more equal pay. *Perspectives on Psychological Science, 9*, 587–593.

Kiecolt-Glaser, J. K. (2009). Psychoneuroimmunology: Psychology's gateway to the biomedical future. *Perspectives on Psychological Science, 4*, 367–369.

Kiecolt-Glaser, J. K., Loving, T. J., Stowell, J. R., Malarkey, W. B., Lemeshow, S., Dickinson, S. L., & Glaser, R. (2005). Hostile marital interactions, proinflammatory cytokine production, and wound healing. *Archives of General Psychiatry, 62*, 1377–1384.

Kiecolt-Glaser, J. K., Page, G. G., Marucha, P. T., MacCallum, R. C., & Glaser, R. (1998). Psychological influences on surgical recovery: Perspectives from psychoneuroimmunology. *American Psychologist, 53*, 1209–1218.

Kiehl, K. A., & Buckholtz, J. W. (2010). Inside the mind of a psychopath. *Scientific American Mind, 21*, 22–29.

Kihlstrom, J. (2019). The motivational unconscious. *Social and Personality Psychology Compass, 13*, e12466.

Kihlstrom, J. F. (2005). Dissociative disorders. *Annual Review of Clinical Psychology, 1*, 227–253.

Kilgore, A. (2017, November 9). Aaron Hernandez suffered from most severe CTE ever found in a person his age. *The Washington Post.* https://tinyurl.com/ycj8mx64

Kille, D. R., Forest, A. L., & Wood, J. V. (2013). Tall, dark, and stable: Embodiment motivates mate selection preferences. *Psychological Science, 24*, 112–114.

Kilpatrick, L. A., Suyenobu, B. Y., Smith, S. R., Bueller, J. A., Goodman, T., Creswell, J. D., Tillisch, K., Mayer, E. A., & Naliboff, B. D. (2011). Impact of mindfulness-based stress reduction training on intrinsic brain activity. *Neuroimage, 56*, 290–298.

Kilpeläinen, T. O., Qi, L. Brage, S., Sharp, S. J., Sonestedt, E., Demerath, E., Ahmad, T., Mora, S., Kaakinen, M., Sandholt, C. H., Holzapfel, C., Autenrieth, C. S., Hyppönen, E., Cauchi, S., He, M., Kutalik, Z., Kumari, M., Stančáková, A., Meidtner, K., . . . Loos, R. J. F. (2012). Physical activity attenuates the influence of FTO variants on obesity risk: A meta-analysis of 218,166 adults and 19,268 children. *PLOS Medicine, 8*, e1001116.

Kim, B. S. K., Ng, G. F., & Ahn, A. J. (2005). Effects of client expectation for counseling success, client-counselor worldview match, and client adherence to Asian and European American cultural values on counseling process with Asian Americans. *Journal of Counseling Psychology, 52*, 67–76.

Kim, E. S., Hagan, K. A., Grodstein, F., DeMeo, D. L., De Vivo, I., & Kubzansky, L. D. (2017). Optimism and cause-specific mortality: A prospective cohort study. *American Journal of Epidemiology, 185,* 21–29.

Kim, H., & Markus, H. R. (1999). Deviance or uniqueness, harmony or conformity? A cultural analysis. *Journal of Personality and Social Psychology, 77,* 785–800.

Kim, H., Schimmack, U., Oishi, S., & Tsutsui, Y. (2018). Extraversion and life satisfaction: A cross-cultural examination of student and nationally representative samples. *Journal of Personality, 86,* 604–618.

Kim, J., Suh, W., Kim, S., & Gopalan, H. (2012). Coping strategies to manage acculturative stress: Meaningful activity participation, social support, and positive emotion among Korean immigrant adolescents in the USA. *International Journal of Qualitative Studies on Health and Well-Being, 7,* 1–10.

Kim, J., Wang, C., Nunez, N., Kim, S., Smith, T., & Sahgal, N. (2015). Paranormal beliefs: Using survey trends from the USA to suggest a new area of research in Asia. *Asian Journal for Public Opinion Research, 2,* 279–306.

Kim, M., Kim, C.-H., Jung, H. H., Kim, S. J., & Chang, J. W. (2018). Treatment of major depressive disorder via magnetic resonance-guided focused ultrasound surgery. *Biological Psychiatry, 83,* e17–e18.

Kim, S. H., Hwang, J. H., Park, H. S., & Kim, S. E. (2008). Resting brain metabolic correlates of neuroticism and extraversion in young men. *NeuroReport, 19,* 883–886.

Kim, S. H., Vincent, L. C., & Goncalo, J. A. (2013). Outside advantage: Can social rejection fuel creative thought? *Journal of Experimental Psychology: General, 142,* 605–611.

Kim, Y. S., Leventhal, B. L., Koh, Y., Fombonne, E., Laska, E., Lim, E., Cheon, K. A., Kim, S. J., Kim, Y. K., Lee, H., Song, D. H., & Grinker, R. R. (2011). Prevalence of autism spectrum disorders in a total population sample. *The American Journal of Psychiatry, 168,* 904–912.

Kimata, H. (2001). Effect of humor on allergen-induced wheal reactions. *Journal of the American Medical Association, 285,* 737.

Kimble, G. A. (1981). *Biological and cognitive constraints on learning.* In L. T. Benjamin, Jr. (Ed.), *The G. Stanley Hall lecture series, Vol. 1* (pp. 11–60). American Psychological Association.

Kindt, M., Soeter, M., & Vervliet, B. (2009). Beyond extinction: Erasing human fear responses and preventing the return of fear. *Nature Neuroscience, 12,* 256–258.

King, D. W., King, L. A., Park, C. L., Lee, L. O., Pless Kaiser, A., Spiro, A., III, Moore, J. L., Kaloupek, D. G., & Keane, T. M. (2015). Positive adjustment among American repatriated prisoners of the Vietnam War: Modeling the long-term effects of captivity. *Clinical Psychological Science, 3,* 861–876.

King, L. A., Heintzelman, S. J., & Ward, S. J. (2016). Beyond the search for meaning: A contemporary science of the experience of meaning in life. *Current Directions in Psychological Science, 25,* 211–216.

King, S., St.-Hilaire, A., & Heidkamp, D. (2010). Prenatal factors in schizophrenia. *Current Directions in Psychological Science, 19,* 209–213.

Kinnier, R. T., & Metha, A. T. (1989). Regrets and priorities at three stages of life. *Counseling and Values, 33,* 182–193.

Kinsella, E. L., Ritchie, T. D., & Igou, E. R. (2015). Zeroing in on heroes: A prototype analysis of hero features. *Journal of Personality and Social Psychology, 108,* 114–127.

Kinsey, A. C., Pomeroy, W. B., & Martin, C. E. (1948). *Sexual behavior in the human male.* Indiana University Press.

Kinsey, A. C., Pomeroy, W. B., Martin, C. E., & Gebhard, P. H. (1953). *Sexual behavior in the human female.* W. B. Saunders.

Kipnis, J. (2018, August). The seventh sense. *Scientific American,* pp. 28–35.

Kirby, D. (2002). Effective approaches to reducing adolescent unprotected sex, pregnancy, and childbearing. *Journal of Sex Research, 39,* 51–57.

Kirby, T. (2015, September). Ketamine for depression: The highs and lows. *The Lancet Psychiatry, 2,* 783–784.

Kirk, M., Rasmussen, K. W., Overgaard, S. B., & Berntsen, D. (2019). Five weeks of immersive reminiscence therapy improves autobiographical memory in Alzheimer's disease. *Memory, 27,* 441–454.

Kirkpatrick, B., Fenton, W. S., Carpenter, W. T., Jr., & Marder, S. R. (2006). The NIMH-MATRICS consensus statement on negative symptoms. *Schizophrenia Bulletin, 32,* 214–219.

Kirkpatrick, L. (1999). Attachment and religious representations and behavior. In J. Cassidy & P. R. Shaver (Eds.), *Handbook of attachment.* Guilford.

Kirmayer, L. J., & Sartorius, N. (2007). Cultural models and somatic syndromes. *Psychosomatic Medicine, 69,* 832–840.

Kirsch, I. (2010). *The emperor's new drugs: Exploding the antidepressant myth.* Basic Books.

Kirsch, I. (2016). *The emperor's new drugs: Medication and placebo in the treatment of depression.* In Behind and beyond the brain. Symposium conducted by the Bial Foundation, March 30–April 2.

Kirsch, I., Deacon, B. J., Huedo-Medina, T. B., Scoboria, A., Moore, T. J., & Johnson, B. T. (2008). Initial severity and antidepressant benefits: A meta-analysis of data submitted to the Food and Drug Administration. *Public Library of Science Medicine, 5,* e45.

Kirsch, I., Kong, J., Sadler, P., Spaeth, R., Cook, A., Kaptchuk, T. J., & Gollub, R. (2014). Expectancy and conditioning in placebo analgesia: Separate or connected processes? *Psychology of Consciousness; Theory, Research, and Practice, 1,* 51–59.

Kirsch, I., & Sapirstein, G. (1998). Listening to Prozac but hearing placebo: A meta-analysis of antidepressant medication. *Prevention & Treatment, 1,* 2a.

Kisely, S., Li, A., Warren, N., & Siskind, D. (2018). A systematic review and meta-analysis of deep brain stimulation for depression. *Depression and Anxiety, 35,* 468–480.

Kisley, M. A., Wood, S., & Burrows, C. L. (2007). Looking at the sunny side of life: Age-related change in an event-related potential measure of the negativity bias. *Psychological Science, 18,* 838–843.

Kisor, H. (1990). *What's that pig outdoors? A memoir of deafness.* Hill and Wang.

Kitahara, C. M., Flint, A. J., de Gonzalez, A. B., Bernstein, L., Brotzman, M., MacInnis, R. J., Moore, S. C., Robien, K., Rosenberg, P. S., Singh, P. H., Weiderpass, E., Adami, H. O., Anton-Culver, H., Ballard-Barbash, R., Buring, J. E., Freedman, D. M., Fraser, G. E., Beane Freeman, L. E., Gapstur, S. M., . . . Hartge, P. (2014, July 8). Association between class III obesity (BMI of 40–59 kg/m2) and mortality: A pooled analysis of 20 prospective studies. *PLOS Medicine, 11*(7), e1001673.

Kitaoka, A. (2016, September 11). Facebook post. https://www.facebook.com/photo.php?fbid=102078 06660899237&set=a.2215289566523&type=3&theater

Kitayama, S., Conway, L. G., III, Pietromonaci, P. R., Park, H., & Plaut, V. C. (2010). Ethos of independence across regions in the United States: The production-adoption model of cultural change. *American Psychologist, 65,* 559–574.

Kitayama, S., Ishii, K., Imada, T., Takemura, K., & Ramaswamy, J. (2006). Voluntary settlement and the spirit of independence: Evidence from Japan's "northern frontier." *Journal of Personality and Social Psychology, 91,* 369–384.

Kitayama, S., Park, J., Boylan, J. M., Miyamoto, Y., Levine, C. S., Markus, H. R., Karasawa, M., Coe, C. L., Kawakami, N., Love, G. D., & Ryff, C. D. (2015). Expression of anger and ill health in two cultures: An examination of inflammation and cardiovascular risk. *Psychological Science, 26,* 211–220.

Kitayama, S., Park, H., Sevincer, A. T., Karasawa, M., & Uskul, A. K. (2009). A cultural task analysis of implicit independence: Comparing North America, Western Europe, and East Asia. *Journal of Personality and Social Psychology, 97,* 236–255.

Kivimaki, M., Leino-Arjas, P., Luukkonen, R., Rihimaki, H., & Kirjonen, J. (2002). Work stress and risk of cardiovascular mortality: Prospective cohort study of industrial employees. *British Medical Journal, 325,* 857.

Kivipelto, M., & Håkansson, K. (2017, April). A rare success against Alzheimer's. *Scientific American,* pp. 33–37.

Kivisto, A. J., Magee, L. A., Phalen, P. L., & Ray, B. R. (2019). Firearm ownership and domestic versus nondomestic homicide in the U.S. *American Journal of Preventive Medicine, 57,* 311–320.

Kivlighan, D. M., Goldberg, S. B., Abbas, M., Pace, B. T., Yulish, N. E., Thomas, J. G., Cullen, M. M., Flückiger, C., & Wampold, B. E. (2015). The enduring effects of psychodynamic treatments vis-à-vis alternative treatments: A multilevel longitudinal meta-analysis. *Clinical Psychology Review, 40,* 1–14.

Klahr, A. M., & Burt, S. A. (2014). Elucidating the etiology of individual differences in parenting: A meta-analysis of behavioral genetic research. *Psychological Bulletin, 140,* 544–586.

Klayman, J., & Ha, Y.-W. (1987). Confirmation, disconfirmation, and information in hypothesis testing. *Psychological Review, 94,* 211–228.

Klein, D. N. (2010). Chronic depression: Diagnosis and classification. *Current Directions in Psychological Science, 19,* 96–100.

Klein, D. N., & Kotov, R. (2016). Course of depression in a 10-year prospective study: Evidence for qualitatively distinct subgroups. *Journal of Abnormal Psychology, 125,* 337–348.

Klein, R. A., Ratliff, K. A., Vianello, M., Adams, R. B., Jr., Bahník, Š., Bernstein, M. J., Bocian, K., Brandt, M. J., Brooks, B., Brumbaugh, C. C., Cemalcilar, Z., Chandler, J., Cheong, W., Davis, W. E., Devos, T., Eisner, M., Frankowska, N., Furrow, D., Galliani, E. M., . . . Nosek, B. A. (2014). Investigating variation in replicability: A "many labs" replication project. *Social Psychology, 45,* 142–152.

Klein, R. A., Vianello, M., Hasselman, F., Adams, B. G., Adams, R. B., Alper, S., Aveyard, M., Axt, J. R., Babalola, M. T. Bahník, Š., Batra, R., Berkics, M., Bernstein, M. J., Berry, D. R., Bialobrzeska, O., Binan, E. D., Bocian, K., Brandt, M. J., Busching, R., . . . Nosek, B. A. (2018). Many Labs 2: Investigating variation in replicability across samples and settings. *Advances in Methods and Practices in Psychological Science, 1,* 443–490.

Kleinke, C. L. (1986). Gaze and eye contact: A research review. *Psychological Bulletin, 1000,* 78–100.

Kleinman, D., & Gollan, T. H. (2016). Speaking two languages for the price of one: Bypassing language control mechanisms via accessibility-driven switches. *Psychological Science, 27,* 700–714.

Kleinmuntz, B., & Szucko, J. J. (1984). A field study of the fallibility of polygraph lie detection. *Nature, 308,* 449–450.

Kleitman, N. (1960, November). Patterns of dreaming. *Scientific American,* pp. 82–88.

Klemm, W. R. (1990). Historical and introductory perspectives on brainstem-mediated behaviors. In W. R. Klemm & R. P. Vertes (Eds.), *Brainstem mechanisms of behavior* (pp. 3–32). Wiley.

Klimstra, T. A., Hale, W. W., III, Raaijmakers, Q. A. W., Branje, S. J. T., & Meeus, W. H. J. (2009). Maturation of personality in adolescence. *Journal of Personality and Social Psychology, 96,* 898–912.

Klimstra, T. A., Kuppens, P., Luyckx, K., Branje, S., Hale, W. W., Oosterwegel, A., Koot, H. M., & Meeus, W. H. J. (2015). Daily dynamics of adolescent mood and identity. *Journal of Research on Adolescence, 26,* 459–473.

Klimstra, T. A., Noftle, E. E., Luyckx, K., Goossens, L., & Robins, R. W. (2018). Personality development and adjustment in college: A multifaceted, cross-national view. *Journal of Personality and Social Psychology, 115,* 338–361.

Kline, D., & Schieber, F. (1985). Vision and aging. In J. E. Birren & K. W. Schaie (Eds.), *Handbook of the psychology of aging* (2nd ed., pp. 296–331). Van Nostrand Reinhold.

Kline, N. S. (1974). *From sad to glad.* Ballantine Books.

Klinke, R., Kral, A., Heid, S., Tillein, J., & Hartmann, R. (1999). Recruitment of the auditory cortex in congenitally deaf cats by long-term cochlear electrostimulation. *Science, 285,* 1729–1733.

Kluemper, D. H., McLarty, B. D., Bishop, T. R., & Sen, A. (2015). Interviewee selection test and evaluator assessments of general mental ability, emotional intelligence and extraversion: Relationships with structured behavioral and situational interview performance. *Journal of Business and Psychology, 30,* 543–563.

Knapp, S., & VandeCreek, L. (2000). Recovered memories of childhood abuse: Is there an underlying professional consensus? *Professional Psychology: Research and Practice, 31,* 365–371.

Knickmeyer, E. (2001, August 7). In Africa, big is definitely better. *Seattle Times,* p. A7.

Knight, R. T. (2007). Neural networks debunk phrenology. *Science, 316,* 1578–1579.

Knight, W. (2004, August 2). *Animated face helps deaf with phone chat.* NewScientist.com. https://www.newscientist.com/article/dn6228-animated-face-helps-deaf-with-phone-chat/

Knoblich, G., & Oellinger, M. (2006, October/November). The Eureka moment. *Scientific American Mind,* pp. 38–43.

Knolle, F., Goncalves, R. P., Morton, J. A. (2017, November 8). Sheep recognize familiar and unfamiliar human faces from two-dimensional images. *Royal Society Open Science, 4,* 171228.

Knouse, L. E., Teller, J., & Brooks, M. A. (2017). Meta-analysis of cognitive–behavioral treatments for adult ADHD. *Journal of Consulting and Clinical Psychology, 85,* 737–750.

Knowles, E. E. M., Mathias, S. R., McKay, D. R., Sprooten, E., Blangero, H., Almasy, L., & Glahn, D. C. (2014). Genome-wide analyses of working-memory ability: A review. *Current Behavioral Neuroscience Reports, 1,* 224–233.

Knuts, I. J. E., Cosci, F., Esquivel, G., Goossens, L., van Duinen, M., Bareman, M., Overbeek, T., Griez, E. J., & Schruers, K. R. J. (2010). Cigarette smoking and 35% CO_2 induced panic in panic disorder patients. *Journal of Affective Disorders, 124,* 215–218.

Knutsen, J., Mandell, D. S., & Frye, D. (2015). Children with autism are impaired in the understanding of teaching. *Developmental Science, 20,* e12368.

Knutsson, A., & Bøggild, H. (2010). Gastrointestinal disorders among shift workers. *Scandinavian Journal of Work, Environment & Health,* 85–95.

Kobayashi, K., & Hsu, M. (2019). Common neural code for reward and information value. *PNAS, 116,* 13061–13066.

Kocevar, G., Suprano, I., Stamile, C., Hannoun, S., Fourneret, P., Revol, O., Nusbaum, F., & Sappey-Marinier, D. (2019). Brain structural connectivity correlates with fluid intelligence in children: A DTI graph analysis. *Intelligence, 72,* 67–75.

Koch, C. (2015, January/February). The face as entryway to the self. *Scientific American Mind,* pp. 26–29.

Koch, C. (2016, November/December). Sleeping while awake. *Scientific American Mind,* pp. 20–23.

Kocsis, J. H. (2018). Internet-based psychotherapy: How far can we go? *American Journal of Psychiatry, 175,* 202–203.

Koenen, K. C., Moffitt, T. E., Roberts, A. L., Martin, L. T., Kubzansky, L., Harrington, H., Poulton, R., & Caspi, A. (2009). Childhood IQ and adult mental disorders: A test of the cognitive reserve hypothesis. *American Journal of Psychiatry, 166,* 50–57.

Koenig, H. G., & Larson, D. B. (1998). Use of hospital services, religious attendance, and religious affiliation. *Southern Medical Journal, 91,* 925–932.

Koenig, L. B., & Vaillant, G. E. (2009). A prospective study of church attendance and health over the life-span. *Health Psychology, 28,* 117–124.

Koenigs, M., Young, L., Adolphs, R., Tranel, D., Cushman, F., Hauser, M., & Damasio, A. (2007). Damage to the prefrontal cortex increases utilitarian moral judgements. *Nature, 446,* 908–911.

Koerner, B. (2003, March 28). *What does a "thumbs up" mean in Iraq?* Slate. https://slate.com/news-and-politics/2003/03/what-does-a-thumbs-up-mean-in-iraq.html

Kofler, M. J., Raiker, J. S., Sarver, D. E., Wells, E. L., & Soto, E. F. (2016). Is hyperactivity ubiquitous in ADHD or dependent on environmental demands? Evidence from meta-analysis. *Clinical Psychology Review, 46,* 12–24.

Koh, A. W. L., Lee, S. C., & Lim, S. W. H. (2018). The learning benefits of teaching: A retrieval practice hypothesis. *Applied Cognitive Psychology, 32,* 401–410.

Kohlberg, L. (1981). *The philosophy of moral development: Essays on moral development* (Vol. 1). Harper & Row.

Kohlberg, L. (1984). *The psychology of moral development: Essays on moral development* (Vol. 2). Harper & Row.

Kohler, I. (1962, May). Experiments with goggles. *Scientific American,* pp. 62–72.

Köhler, W. (1925; reprinted 1957). *The mentality of apes.* Pelican.

Kolassa, I.-T., & Elbert, T. (2007). Structural and functional neuroplasticity in relation to traumatic stress. *Current Directions in Psychological Science, 16,* 321–325.

Kolb, B. (1989). Brain development, plasticity, and behavior. *American Psychologist, 44,* 1203–1212.

Kolb, B., & Whishaw, I. Q. (1998). Brain plasticity and behavior. *Annual Review of Psychology, 49,* 43–64.

Kolb, B., & Whishaw, I. Q. (2006). *An introduction to brain and behavior* (2nd ed.) Worth.

Koltko-Rivera, M. E. (2006). Rediscovering the later version of Maslow's hierarchy of needs: Self-transcendence and opportunities for theory, research, and unification. *Review of General Psychology, 10,* 302–317.

Komisaruk, B. R., & Whipple, B. (2011). Non-genital orgasms. *Sexual and Relationship Therapy, 26,* 356–372.

Kondoh, K., Lu, Z., Olson, D. P., Lowell, B. B., & Buck, L. B. (2016). A specific area of olfactory cortex involved in stress hormone responses to predator odours. *Nature, 532,* 103–106.

Kong, A., Thorleifsson, G., Frigge, M. L., Vilhjalmsson, B. J., Young, A. I., Thorgeirsson, T. E., Benonisdottir, S., Oddsson, A., Halldorsson, B. V., Masson, G., Gudbjartsson, D. F., Helgason, A., Bjornsdottir, G., Thorsteinsdottir, U., & Stefansson, K. (2018). The nature of nurture: Effects of parental genotypes. *Science, 359,* 424–428.

Konkle, T., Brady, T. F., Alvarez, G. A., & Oliva, A. (2010). Conceptual distinctiveness supports detailed visual long-term memory for real-world objects. *Journal of Experimental Psychology: General, 139,* 558–578.

Kontula, O., & Haavio-Mannila, E. (2009). The impact of aging on human sexual activity and sexual desire. *Journal of Sex Research, 46,* 46–56.

Koole, S. L., Greenberg, J., & Pyszczynski, T. (2006). Introducing science to the psychology of the soul. *Current Directions in Psychological Science, 15,* 212–216.

Koops, S., Blom, J. D., Bouachmir, O., Slot, M. I., Neggers, B., & Sommer, I. E. (2018). Treating auditory hallucinations with transcranial direct current stimulation in a double-blind, randomized trial. *Schizophrenia Research, 201,* 329–336.

Kornell, N., & Bjork, R. A. (2008). Learning concepts and categories: Is spacing the "enemy of induction?" *Psychological Science, 19,* 585–592.

Kosslyn, S. M. (2005). Reflective thinking and mental imagery: A perspective on the development of posttraumatic stress disorder. *Development and Psychopathology, 17,* 851–863.

Kosslyn, S. M., & Koenig, O. (1992). *Wet mind: The new cognitive neuroscience.* Free Press.

Kotchick, B. A., Shaffer, A., & Forehand, R. (2001). Adolescent sexual risk behavior: A multi-system perspective. *Clinical Psychology Review, 21,* 493–519.

Koten, J. W., Jr., Wood, G., Hagoort, P., Goebel, R., Propping, P., Willmes, K., & Boomsma, D. I. (2009). Genetic contribution to variation in cognitive function: An fMRI study in twins. *Science, 323,* 1737–1740.

Kotkin, M., Daviet, C., & Gurin, J. (1996). The *Consumer Reports* mental health survey. *American Psychologist, 51,* 1080–1082.

Kouider, S., Stahlhut, C., Gelskov, S. V., Barbosa, L. S., Dutat, M., de Gardelle, V., Christophe, A., Dehaene, S., & Dehaene-Lambertz, G. (2013). A neural marker of perceptual consciousness in infants. *Science, 340,* 376–380.

Kounios, J., & Beeman, M. (2014). The cognitive neuroscience of insight. *Annual Review of Psychology, 65,* 71–93.

Kovács, Á. M., Téglás, E., & Endress, A. D. (2010). The social sense: Susceptibility to others' beliefs in human infants and adults. *Science, 330,* 1830–1834.

Kovelman, I., Shalinsky, M. H., Berens, M. S., & Petitto, L. (2014). Words in the bilingual brain: An fNIRS brain imaging investigation of lexical processing in sign-speech bimodal bilinguals. *Frontiers in Human Neuroscience, 8,* article 606.

Kowalski, R. M., Limber, S. P., & McCord, A. (2018). A developmental approach to cyberbullying: Prevalence and protective factors. *Aggression and Violent Behavior, 45,* 20–32.

Koyanagi, A., Oh, H., Carvalho, A. F., Smith, L., Haro, J. M., Vancampfort, D., Stubbs, B., & Devylder, J. E. (2019). Bullying victimization and suicide attempt among adolescents aged 12–15 years from 48 countries. *Journal of the American Academy of Child & Adolescent Psychiatry, 58,* 907–918.

Kposowa, A., Hamilton, D., & Wang, K. (2016). Impact of firearm availability and gun regulation on state suicide rates. *Suicide and Life-Threating Behavior, 46,* 678–696.

Kposowa, A. J., & D'Auria, S. (2009). Association of temporal factors and suicides in the United States, 2000–2004. *Social Psychiatry and Psychiatric Epidemiology, 45,* 433–445.

Kraft, C. (1978). A psychophysical approach to air safety: Simulator studies of visual illusions in night approaches. In H. L. Pick, H. W. Leibowitz, J. E. Singer, A. Steinschneider, & H. W. Stevenson (Eds.), *Psychology: From research to practice*. Plenum Press.

Kraft, T., & Pressman, S. (2012). Grin and bear it: The influence of the manipulated facial expression on the stress response. *Psychological Science, 23*, 137–1378.

Krahé, B., & Berger, A. (2017). Longitudinal pathways of sexual victimization, sexual self-esteem, and depression in women and men. *Psychological Trauma: Theory, Research, Practice, and Policy, 9*, 147–155.

Krahé, B., Lutz, J., & Sylla, I. (2018). Lean back and relax: Reclined seating position buffers the effect of frustration on anger and aggression. *European Journal of Social Psychology, 48*, 718–723.

Krakow, B., Germain, A., Warner, T. D., Schrader, R., Koss, M. P., Hollifeld, M., Tandberg, D., Melendrez, D., & Johnston, L. (2001). The relationship of sleep quality and posttraumatic stress to potential sleep disorders in sexual assault survivors with nightmares, insomnia, and PTSD. *Journal of Traumatic Stress, 14*, 647–665.

Krakow, B., Schrader, R., Tandberg, D., Hollifeld, M., Koss, M. P., Yau, C. L., & Cheng, D. T. (2002). Nightmare frequency in sexual assault survivors with PTSD. *Journal of Anxiety Disorders, 16*, 175–190.

Kramer, A. (2010). Personal communication.

Kramer, A. D. I. (2012). The spread of emotion via Facebook. *Proceedings of the SIGCHI Conference on Human Factors in Computing Systems*. ACM (Association for Computing Machinery), New York, 767–770.

Kramer, A. F., & Colcombe, S. (2018). Fitness effects on the cognitive function of older adults: A meta-analytic study—revisited. *Perspectives on Psychological Science, 13*, 213–217.

Kramer, A. F., & Erickson, K. I. (2007). Capitalizing on cortical plasticity: Influence of physical activity on cognition and brain function. *Trends in Cognitive Sciences, 11*, 342–348

Kramer, P. D. (2011, July 9). In defense of antidepressants. *The New York Times*. https://www.nytimes.com/2011/07/10/opinion/sunday/10antidepressants.html?

Kranz, F., & Ishai, A. (2006). Face perception is modulated by sexual preference. *Current Biology, 16*, 63–68.

Kranz, G. S., Hahn, A., Kaufmann, U., Küblböck, M., Hummer, A., Ganger, S., Seiger, R., Winkler, D., Swaab, D. F., Windischberger, C., Kasper, S., & Lanzenberger, R. (2014). White matter microstructure in transsexuals and controls investigated by diffusion tensor imaging. *The Journal of Neuroscience, 34*, 15466–15475.

Kranzler, E. C., Schmälzle, R., O'Donnell, M. B., Pei, R., & Falk, E. B. (2019). Adolescent neural responses to antismoking messages, perceived effectiveness, and sharing intention. *Media Psychology, 22*, 323–349.

Kraul, C. (2010, October 12). Chief engineer knew it would take a miracle. *The Los Angeles Times*. https://www.latimes.com/archives/la-xpm-2010-oct-12-la-fg-chile-miners-rescuer-20101013-story.html

Kremen, W. S., Jacobsen, K. C., Xian, H., Eisen, S. A., Eaves, L. J., Tsuang, M. T., & Lyons, M. J. (2007). Genetics of verbal working memory processes: a twin study of middle-aged men. *Neuropsychology, 21*, 569–580.

Kret, M. E., & De Dreu, C. K. W. (2019). The power of pupil size in establishing trust and reciprocity. *Journal of Experimental Psychology: General, 148*(8), 1299–1311.

Kretch, K. S., Franchak, J. M., & Adolph, K. E. (2014). Crawling and walking infants see the world differently. *Child Development, 85*, 1503–1518.

Kreuder, A. K., Wassermann, L., Wollseifer, M., Ditzen, B., Eckstein, M., Stoffel-Wagner, B., Hennig, J., Hurlemann, R., & Scheele, D. (2018). Oxytocin enhances the pain-relieving effects of social support in romantic couples. *Human Brain Mapping, 40*(1), 242–251.

Kring, A. M., & Caponigro, J. M. (2010). Emotion in schizophrenia: Where feeling meets thinking. *Current Directions in Psychological Science, 19*, 255–259.

Kring, A. M., & Gordon, A. H. (1998). Sex differences in emotion: Expression, experience, and physiology. *Journal of Personality and Social Psychology, 74*, 686–703.

Kringelbach, M. L., & Berridge, K. C. (2012, August). The joyful mind. *Scientific American*, pp. 40–45.

Krishnan, A., Zhang, R., Yao, V., Theesfeld, C. L., Wong, A. K., Tadych, A., Volfovsky, N., Packer, A., Lash, A., & Troyanskaya, O. G. (2016). Genome-wide prediction and functional characterization of the genetic basis of autism spectrum disorder. *Nature Neuroscience, 19*, 1454–1462.

Kristof, N. (2017, February 11). Husbands are deadlier than terrorists. *The New York Times*. https://www.nytimes.com/2017/02/11/opinion/sunday/husbands-are-deadlier-than-terrorists.html?

Kristof, N. (2019, March 16). This 8-year-old chess champion will make you smile. *The New York Times*. https://www.nytimes.com/2019/03/16/opinion/sunday/chess-champion-8-year-old-homeless-refugee-.html

Kristof, N. D. (2004, July 21). Saying no to killers. *The New York Times*. https://www.nytimes.com/2004/07/21/opinion/saying-no-to-killers.html?

Krizan, Z., & Herlache, A. D. (2018). The narcissism spectrum model: A synthetic view of narcissistic personality. *Personality and Social Psychology Review, 22*, 3–31.

Krizan, Z., & Hisler, G. (2019). Sleepy anger: Restricted sleep amplifies angry feelings. *Journal of Experimental Psychology: General, 148*, 1239–1250.

Krosnick, J. A., & Alwin, D. F. (1989). Aging and susceptibility to attitude change. *Journal of Personality and Social Psychology, 57*, 416–425.

Krosnick, J. A., Betz, A. L., Jussim, L. J., & Lynn, A. R. (1992). Subliminal conditioning of attitudes. *Personality and Social Psychology Bulletin, 18*, 152–162.

Kross, E., & Ayduk, O. (2011). Making meaning out of negative experiences by self-distancing. *Current Directions in Psychological Science, 20*, 187–191.

Kross, E., Berman, M., Mischel, W., Smith, E. E., & Wager, T. (2011). Social rejection shares somatosensory representations with physical pain. *PNAS, 108*, 6270–6275.

Kross, E., Bruehlman-Senecal, E., Park, J., Burson, A., Dougherty, A., Shablack, H., Bremner, R., Moser, J., & Ayduk, O. (2014). Self-talk as a regulatory mechanism: How you do it matters. *Journal of Personality and Social Psychology, 106*, 304–324.

Krueze, L. J., Pijnenborg, G. H. M., de Jonge, Y. B., & Nauta, M. H. (2018). Cognitive-behavior therapy for children and adolescents with anxiety disorders: A meta-analysis of secondary outcomes. *Journal of Anxiety Disorders, 60*, 43–57.

Kruger, J., & Dunning, D. (1999). Unskilled and unaware of it: How difficulties in recognizing one's own incompetence lead to inflated self-assessments. *Journal of Personality and Social Psychology, 77*, 1121–1134.

Kruger, J., Epley, N., Parker, J., & Ng, Z.-W. (2005). Egocentrism over e-mail: Can we communicate as well as we think? *Journal of Personality and Social Psychology, 89*, 925–936.

Krumhansl, C. L. (2010). Plink: "Thin slices" of music. *Music Perception, 27*, 337–354.

Krupenye, C., Kano, F., Hirata, S., Call, J., & Tomasello, M. (2016). Great apes anticipate that other individuals will act according to false beliefs. *Science, 354*, 110–113.

Krützen, M., Mann, J., Heithaus, M. R., Connor, R. C., Bejder, L., & Sherwin, W. B. (2005). Cultural transmission of tool use in bottlenose dolphins. *PNAS, 102*, 8939–8943.

Krynen, R. C., & McBeath, M. K. (2019). Baseball's sight-audition farness effect (SAFE) when umpiring baserunners: Judging precedence of competing visual versus auditory events. *Journal of Experimental Psychology: Human Perception and Performance, 45*, 67–81.

Kteily, N. S., & Bruneau, E. (2017). Darker demons of our nature: The need to (re)focus attention on blatant forms of dehumanization. *Current Directions in Psychological Science, 26*, 487–494.

Kubzansky, L. D., Koenen, K. C., Jones, C., & Eaton, W. W. (2009). A prospective study of posttraumatic stress disorder symptoms and coronary heart disease in women. *Health Psychology, 28*, 125–130.

Kubzansky, L. D., Sparrow, D., Vokanas, P., & Kawachi, I. (2001). Is the glass half empty or half full? A prospective study of optimism and coronary heart disease in the normative aging study. *Psychosomatic Medicine, 63*, 910–916.

Kuchynka, S. L., Salomon, K., Bosson, J. K., El-Hout, M., Kiebel, E., Cooperman, C., & Toomey, R. (2018). Hostile and benevolent sexism and college women's STEM outcomes. *Psychology of Women Quarterly, 42*, 72–87.

Kuehn, B. (2019). Vaping and pregnancy. *JAMA, 321*, 1344.

Kuehner, C. (2017). Why is depression more common among women than among men? *The Lancet Psychiatry, 4*, 146–158.

Kuhl, P. K. (2015, November). Baby talk. *Scientific American*, pp. 65–69.

Kuhl, P. K., & Meltzoff, A. N. (1982). The bimodal perception of speech in infancy. *Science, 218*, 1138–1141.

Kuhl, P. K., Ramírez, R. R., Bosseler, A., Lin, J. L., & Imada, T. (2014). Infants' brain responses to speech suggest analysis by synthesis. *PNAS, 111*, 11238–11245.

Kumar, A., & Epley, N. (2018). Undervaluing gratitude: Expressers misunderstand the consequences of showing appreciation. *Psychological Science, 29*, 1423–1435.

Kumar, A., & Gilovich, T. (2013). Talking about what you did and what you have: The differential story utility of experiential and material purchases. *Advances in Consumer Research, 41*.

Kumar, A., & Gilovich, T. (2015). Some "thing" to talk about? Differential story utility from experiential and material purchases. *Personality and Social Psychology Bulletin, 41*, 1320–1331.

Kumar, M. B &., Tjepkema, M. (2019). *Suicide among First Nations people, Métis and Inuit (2011–2016): Findings from the 2011 Canadian census health and environment cohort (CanCHEC)*. https://www150.statcan.gc.ca/n1/pub/99-011-x/99-011-x2019001-eng.htm

Kuncel, N. R., & Hezlett, S. A. (2007). Standardized tests predict graduate students' success. *Science, 315*, 1080–1081.

Kuncel, N. R., & Hezlett, S. A. (2010). Fact and fiction in cognitive ability testing for admissions and hiring decisions. *Current Directions in Psychological Science, 19*, 339–345.

Kunst-Wilson, W. & Zajonc, R. (1980). Affective discrimination of stimuli that cannot be recognized. *Science, 207*, 557–558.

Kupfer, D. J. (2012, June 1). *Dr. Kupfer defends DSM-5*. https://www.medscape.com/viewarticle/764735

Kurdi, B., Seitchik, A. E., Axt, J. R., Carroll, T. J., Karapetyan, A., Kaushik, N., Tomezsko, D., Greenwald, A. G., & Banaji, M. R. (2019). Relationship between the Implicit Association Test and intergroup behavior: A meta-analysis. *American Psychologist, 74,* 569–586.

Kurtycz, L. M. (2015). Choice and control for animals in captivity. *The Psychologist, 28,* 892–893.

Kushlev, K., & Dunn, E. W. (2015). Checking email less frequently reduces stress. *Computers in Human Behavior, 43,* 220–228.

Kushner, M. G., Kim, S. W., Conahue, C., Thuras, P., Adson, D., Kotlyar, M., McCabe, J., Peterson, J., & Foa, E. B. (2007). D-cycloserine augmented exposure therapy for obsessive-compulsive disorder. *Biological Psychiatry, 62,* 835–838.

Kutas, M. (1990). Event-related brain potential (ERP) studies of cognition during sleep: Is it more than a dream? In R. R. Bootzin, J. F. Kihlstrom, & D. Schacter (Eds.), *Sleep and cognition.* American Psychological Association.

Kutcher, E. J., & Bragger, J. D. (2004). Selection interviews of overweight job applicants: Can structure reduce the bias? *Journal of Applied Social Psychology, 34,* 1993–2022.

Kuttler, A. F., La Greca, A. M., & Prinstein, M. J. (1999). Friendship qualities and social-emotional functioning of adolescents with close, cross-sex friendships. *Journal of Research on Adolescence, 9,* 339–366.

Kuypers, K. P. C., Ng, L., Erritzoe, D., Knudsen, G. M., Nichols, C. D., Nichols, D. E., Pani, L., Soula, A., & Nutt, D. (2019). Microdosing psychedelics: More questions than answers? An overview and suggestions for future research. *Journal of Psychopharmacology, 33,* 1039–1056.

Kuzawa, C. W., Chugani, H. T., Grossman, L. I., Lipovich, L., Muzik, O., Hof, P. R., Wildman, D. E., Sherwood, C. C., Leonard, W. R., & Lange, N. (2014). Metabolic costs and evolutionary implications of human brain development. *PNAS, 111,* 13010–13015.

Kwauk, C., Petrova, D., & Robinson, J. P. (2016). *Sesame Street: Combining education and entertainment to bring early childhood education to children around the world.* Center for Universal Education at Brookings (brookings.edu). https://bit.ly/38Pje3x

Kwong, A. S. F., Manley, D., Timpson, N. J., Pearson, R. M., Heron, J., Sallis, H., Stergiakouli, E., Davis, O. S., & Leckie, G. (2019). Identifying critical points of trajectories of depressive symptoms from childhood to young adulthood. *Journal of Youth and Adolescence, 48,* 815–827.

Kyaga, S., Landén, M., Boman, M., Hultman, C. M., Långström, N., Lichtenstein, P. (2013). Mental illness, suicide, and creativity: 40-year prospective total population study. *Journal of Psychiatric Research, 47,* 83–90.

L'Engle, M. (1973). *A wind in the door.* Farrar, Straus and Giroux.

Labella, M. H., Johnson, W. F., Martin, J., Ruiz, S. K., Shankman, J. L., Englund, M. M., Collins, W. A., Roisman, G. I., & Simpson, J. A. (2018). Multiple dimensions of childhood abuse and neglect prospectively predict poorer adult romantic functioning. *Personality and Social Psychology Bulletin, 44,* 238–251.

LaCapria, K. (2015, December 17). *Kindergarten, stop.* Snopes. https://www.snopes.com/fact-check/toddlers-killed-americans-terrorists/

Lacey, M. (2010, December 11). He found bag of cash, but did the unexpected. *The New York Times.* https://www.nytimes.com/2010/12/12/us/12backpack.html

Lachman, M. E. (2004). Development in midlife. *Annual Review of Psychology, 55,* 305–331.

Ladd, G. T. (1887). *Elements of physiological psychology.* Scribner's.

Laeng, B., & Sulutvedt, U. (2014). The eye pupil adjusts to imaginary light. *Psychological Science, 25,* 188–197.

Lafleur, D. L., Pittenger, C., Kelmendi, B., Gardner, T., Wasylink, S., Malison, R. T., Sanacora, G., Krystal, J. H., & Coric, V. (2006). N-acetylcysteine augmentation in serotonin reuptake inhibitor refractory obsessive-compulsive disorder. *Psychopharmacology, 184,* 254–256.

LaFreniere, L. S., & Newman, M. G. (2019). Exposing worry's deceit: Percentage of untrue worries in generalized anxiety disorder treatment. *Behavior Therapy.* Advance online publication. https://doi.org/10.1016/j.beth.2019.07.003

Laird, J. D. (1974). Self-attribution of emotion: The effects of expressive behavior on the quality of emotional experience. *Journal of Personality and Social Psychology, 29,* 475–486.

Laird, J. D. (1984). The real role of facial response in the experience of emotion: A reply to Tourangeau and Ellsworth, and others. *Journal of Personality and Social Psychology, 47,* 909–917.

Laird, J. D., & Lacasse, K. (2014). Bodily influences on emotional feelings: Accumulating evidence and extensions of William James's theory of emotion. *Emotion Review, 6,* 27–34.

Lakin, J. L., Chartrand, T. L., & Arkin, R. M. (2008). I am too just like you: Nonconscious mimicry as an automatic behavioral response to social exclusion. *Psychological Science, 19,* 816–822.

Lally, P., Van Jaarsveld, C. H. M., Potts, H. W. W., & Wardle, J. (2010). How are habits formed: Modelling habit formation in the real world. *European Journal of Social Psychology, 40,* 998–1009.

La Londe, K. B., Mahoney, A., Edwards, T. L., Cox, C., Weetjens, B., Durgin, A., & Poling, A. (2015). Training pouched rats to find people. *Journal of Applied Behavior Analysis, 48,* 1–10.

Lam, C. B., & McBride-Chang, C. A. (2007). Resilience in young adulthood: The moderating influences of gender-related personality traits and coping flexibility. *Sex Roles, 56,* 159–172.

Lam, M., Chen, C. Y., Li, Z., Martin, A. R., Bryois, J., Ma, X., Gaspar, H., Ikeda, M., Benyamin, B., Brown, B. C., Liu, R., Zhou, W., Guan, L., Kamatani, Y., Kim, S.-W., Kubo, M., Kusumawardhani, A. A., Liu, C.-M., Ma, H., . . . Huang, H. (2019). Comparative genetic architectures of schizophrenia in East Asian and European populations. *Nature Genetics, 51,* 1670–1678.

Lambert, J.-C., Ibrahim-Verbaas, C. A., Harold, D., Naj, A. C., Sims, R., Bellenguiez, C., DeStafano, A. L., Bis, J. C., Beecham, G. W., Grenier-Boley, B., Russo, G., Thorton-Wells, T. A., Jones, N., Smith, A. V., Chouraki, V., Thomas, C., Ikram, M. A., Zelenika, D., Vardarajan, B. N., Kamatani, Y., . . . Amouyel, P. (2013). Meta-analysis of 74,046 individuals identifies 11 new susceptibility loci for Alzheimer's disease. *Nature Genetics, 45,* 1452–1458.

Lambert, N. M., DeWall, C. N., Bushman, B. J., Tillman, T. F., Fincham, F. D., Pond, R. S., Jr., & Gwinn, A. M. (2011). *Lashing out in lust: Effect of pornography on nonsexual, physical aggression against relationship partners* [Paper]. Presented at the Society for Personality and Social Psychology convention.

Lambert, W. E. (1992). Challenging established views on social issues: The power and limitations of research. *American Psychologist, 47,* 533–542.

Lambert, W. E., Genesee, F., Holobow, N., & Chartrand, L. (1993). Bilingual education for majority English-speaking children. *European Journal of Psychology of Education, 8,* 3–22.

Lambird, K. H., & Mann, T. (2006). When do ego threats lead to self-regulation failure? Negative consequences of defensive high self-esteem. *Personality and Social Psychology Bulletin, 32,* 1177–1187.

Lammers, J., & Baldwin, M. (2018). Past-focused temporal communication overcomes conservatives' resistance to liberal political ideas. *Journal of Personality and Social Psychology, 114,* 599–619.

Lampert, M. (2017). *Majority of humanity say we are not alone in the universe.* Glocalities. http://www.glocalities.com/reports/majority-of-humanity-say-we-are-not-alone-in-the-universe

Landau, E., Verjee, Z., & Mortensen, A. (2014, February 24). *Uganda president: Homosexuals are 'disgusting.'* CNN. https://www.cnn.com/2014/02/24/world/africa/uganda-homosexuality-interview/index.html

Landberg, J., & Norström, T. (2011). Alcohol and homicide in Russia and the United States: A comparative analysis. *Journal of Studies on Alcohol and Drugs, 72,* 723–730.

Landor, A. M., & Smith, S. M. (2019). Skin-tone trauma: Historical and contemporary influences on the health and interpersonal outcomes of African Americans. *Perspectives on Psychological Science, 14,* 797–815.

Landry, M. J. (2002). MDMA: A review of epidemiologic data. *Journal of Psychoactive Drugs, 34,* 163–169.

Lange, N., & McDougle, C. J. (2013). Help for the child with autism. *Scientific American, 25,* 72–77.

Lange, S., Probst, C., Gmel, G., Rehm, J., Burd, L., & Popova, S. (2017). Global prevalence of fetal alcohol spectrum disorder among children and youth: A systematic review and meta-analysis. *JAMA Pediatrics, 171,* 948–956.

Langer, E. J. (1983). *The psychology of control.* Sage.

Langer, E. J., & Abelson, R. P. (1974). A patient by any other name . . .: Clinician group differences in labeling bias. *Journal of Consulting and Clinical Psychology, 42,* 4–9.

Langer, E. J., & Imber, L. (1980). The role of mindlessness in the perception of deviance. *Journal of Personality and Social Psychology, 39,* 360–367.

Langkaas, T. F., Hoffart, A., Øktedalen, T., Ulvenes, P., Hembree, E. A., & Smucker, M. (2017). Exposure to non-fear emotions: A randomized controlled study of exposure-based and rescripting-based imagery in PTSD treatment. *Behavior Research Therapy, 97,* 33–42.

Langlois, J. H., Kalakanis, L., Rubenstein, A. J., Larson, A., Hallam, M., & Smoot, M. (2000). Maxims or myths of beauty? A meta-analytic and theoretical review. *Psychological Bulletin, 126,* 390–423.

Langmeyer, A., Guglhör-Rudan, A., & Tarnai, C. (2012). What do music preferences reveal about personality? A cross-cultural replication using self-ratings and ratings of music samples. *Journal of Individual Differences, 33,* 119–130.

Långström, N. H., Rahman, Q., Carlström, E., & Lichtenstein, P. (2010). Genetic and environmental effects on same-sex sexual behavior: A population study of twins in Sweden. *Archives of Sexual Behavior, 39,* 75–80.

Lankford, A. (2009). Promoting aggression and violence at Abu Ghraib: The U.S. military's transformation of ordinary people into torturers. *Aggression and Violent Behavior, 14,* 388–395.

Lanman, J. A., & Buhrmester, M. D. (2017). Religious actions speak louder than words: Exposure to credibility-enhancing displays predicts theism. *Religion, Brain & Behavior, 7,* 3–16.

Lansdall-Welfare, T., Lightman, S., & Cristianini, N. (2019). Seasonal variation in antidepressant prescriptions, environmental light and web queries for seasonal affective disorder. *The British Journal of Psychiatry, 215,* 481–484.

Lapidos, R. (2016, August 2). *Five things we learned from Kristen Stewart's struggle with anxiety.* Well + Good. https://www.wellandgood.com/good-advice/kristen-stewart-anxiety/

Lapp, D. (2019, December 17). *Gellert Dornay on the benefits of employee-ownership: 5 questions with family studies.* Institute for Family Studies. https://ifstudies.org/blog/gellert-dornay-on-the-benefits-of-employee-ownership-5-questions-with-family-studies

Larkin, J. E., Brasel, A. M., & Pines, H. A. (2013). Cross-disciplinary applications of I/O psychology concepts: Predicting student retention and employee turnover. *Review of General Psychology, 17,* 82–92.

Larkin, K., Resko, J. A., Stormshak, F., Stellflug, J. N., & Roselli, C. E. (2002). *Neuroanatomical correlates of sex and sexual partner preference in sheep* [Paper]. Presented at Society for Neuroscience convention.

Larrick, R. P., Timmerman, T. A., & Carton, A. M., & Abrevaya, J. (2011). Temper, temperature, and temptation: Heat-related retaliation in baseball. *Psychological Science, 22,* 423–428.

Larsen, R. J., & Diener, E. (1987). Affect intensity as an individual difference characteristic: A review. *Journal of Research in Personality, 21,* 1–39.

Larson, R. W., & Verma, S. (1999). How children and adolescents spend time across the world: Work, play, and developmental opportunities. *Psychological Bulletin, 125,* 701–736.

Larzelere, R. E. (2000). Child outcomes of non-abusive and customary physical punishment by parents: An updated literature review. *Clinical Child and Family Psychology Review, 3,* 199–221.

Larzelere, R. E., Gunnoe, M. L., Ferguson, C. J., & Roberts, M. W. (2019). The insufficiency of the evidence used to categorically oppose spanking and its implications for families and psychological science: Comment on Gershoff et al. (2018). *American Psychologist, 74,* 497–499.

Lashley, K. S. (1950). In search of the engram. In J. F. Danielli & R. Brown (Eds.), *Symposia of the Society for Experimental Biology: Vol. 4. Physiological mechanisms in animal behaviour* (pp. 454–482). Cambridge University Press.

Lassek, W. D., & Gaulin, S. J. C. (2018). Do the low WHRs and BMIs judged most attractive indicate higher fertility? *Evolutionary Psychology, 16(4),* 147470491880063.

Lassek, W. D., & Gaulin, S. J. C. (2019). Evidence supporting nubility and reproductive value as the key to human female physical attractiveness. *Evolution and Human Behavior, 40,* 408–419.

Lassiter, G. D., & Irvine, A. A. (1986). Video-taped confessions: The impact of camera point of view on judgments of coercion. *Journal of Personality and Social Psychology, 16,* 268–276.

Latané, B. (1981). The psychology of social impact. *American Psychologist, 36,* 343–356.

Latané, B., & Dabbs, J. M., Jr. (1975). Sex, group size and helping in three cities. *Sociometry, 38,* 180–194.

Latzman, R. D., Patrick, C. J., Freeman, H. D., Schapiro, S. J., & Hopkins, W. D. (2017). Etiology of triarchic psychopathy dimensions in chimpanzees (Pan troglodytes). *Clinical Psychological Science, 5,* 341–354.

Laudenslager, M. L., & Reite, M. L. (1984). Losses and separations: Immunological consequences and health implications. *Review of Personality and Social Psychology, 5,* 285–312.

Lauer, J. E., Yhang, E., & Lourenco, S. F. (2019). The development of gender differences in spatial reasoning: A meta-analytic review. *Psychological Bulletin, 145,* 537–565.

Laukka, P., Elfenbein, H. A., Thingujam, N. S., Rockstuhl, T., Iraki, F. K., Chui, W., & Althoff, J. (2016). The expression and recognition of emotions in the voice across five nations: A lens model analysis based on acoustic features. *Journal of Personality and Social Psychology, 111,* 686–705.

Launay, J. M., Mouillet-Richard, S., Baudry, A., Pietri, M., & Kellermann, O. (2011). Raphe-mediated signals control the hippocampal response to SRI antidepressants via miR-16. *Translational Psychiatry, 1,* e56.

Lavi, I., Katz, L. F., Ozer, E. J., & Gross, J. J. (2019). Emotion reactivity and regulation in maltreated children: A meta-analysis. *Child Development, 90,* 1503–1524.

Laws, K. R., & Kokkalis, J. (2007). Ecstasy (MDMA) and memory function: A meta-analytic update. *Human Psychopharmacology: Clinical and Experimental, 22,* 381–388.

Layous, K., & Lyubomirsky, S. (2014). The how, who, what, when, and why of happiness: Mechanisms underlying the success of positive activity interventions. In J. Gruber & J. T. Moskowitz (Eds.), *Positive emotions: Integrating the light and dark sides* (pp. 473–495). Oxford University Press.

Lazarov, A., Suarez-Jimenez, B., Tamman, A., Falzon, L., Zhu, X., Edmondson, D. E., & Neria, Y. (2019). Attention to threat in posttraumatic stress disorder as indexed by eye-tracking indices: a systematic review. *Psychological Medicine, 49,* 705–726.

Lazaruk, W. (2007). Linguistic, academic, and cognitive benefits of French immersion. *Canadian Modern Language Review, 63,* 605–628.

Lazarus, R. S. (1990). Theory-based stress measurement. *Psychological Inquiry, 1,* 3–13.

Lazarus, R. S. (1991). Progress on a cognitive-motivational-relational theory of emotion. *American Psychologist, 46,* 352–367.

Lazarus, R. S. (1998). *Fifty years of the research and theory of R. S. Lazarus: An analysis of historical and perennial issues.* Erlbaum.

Lea, S. E. G. (2000). Towards an ethical use of animals. *The Psychologist, 13,* 556–557.

Leaper, C., & Ayres, M. M. (2007). A meta-analytic review of gender variations in adults' language use: Talkativeness, affiliative speech, and assertive speech. *Personality and Social Psychology Review, 11,* 328–363.

Leaper, C., & Starr, C. R. (2019). Helping and hindering undergraduate women's STEM motivation: experiences With STEM encouragement, STEM-related gender bias, and sexual harassment. *Psychology of Women Quarterly, 43,* 165–183.

Leary, M. R. (2018). Self-awareness, hypo-egoicism, and psychological well-being. In J. E. Maddux (Ed.), *Subjective well-being and life satisfaction.* Routledge.

Leary, M. R., Diebels, K. J., Davisson, E. K., Jongman-Sereno, K. P., Isherwood, J. C., Raimi, K. T., Deffler, S. A., & Hoyle, R. H. (2017). Cognitive and interpersonal features of intellectual humility. *Personality and Social Psychology Bulletin, 43,* 793–813.

Leary, M. R., Kowalski, R. M., Smith, L., & Phillips, S. (2003). Teasing, rejection, and violence: Case studies of the school shootings. *Aggressive Behavior, 29,* 202–214.

Lebedev, A. V., Lövdén, M., Rosenthal, G., Feilding, A., Nutt, D. J., & Carhart-Harris, R. L. (2015). Finding the self by losing the self: Neural correlates of ego-dissolution under psilocybin. *Human Brain Mapping, 36,* 3137–3153.

Leckelt, M., Geukes, K., Küfner, A. C., Niemeyer, L. M., Hutteman, R., Osterholz, S., Egloff, B., Nestler, S., & Back, M. D. (2020). A longitudinal field investigation of narcissism and popularity over time: How agentic and antagonistic aspects of narcissism shape the development of peer relationships. *Personality and Social Psychology Bulletin, 46(4),* 463–659.

Leding, J. K. (2019). Adaptive memory: Animacy, threat, and attention in free recall. *Memory & Cognition, 47,* 383–394.

LeDoux, J. (1996). *The emotional brain: The mysterious underpinnings of emotional life.* Simon & Schuster.

LeDoux, J. (2002). *The synaptic self.* Macmillan.

LeDoux, J. (2009, July/August). Quoted by K. McGowan in Out of the past. *Discover,* pp. 28–37.

LeDoux, J. (2015). *Anxious: Using the brain to understand and treat fear and anxiety.* Viking.

LeDoux, J. E., & Armony, J. (1999). Can neurobiology tell us anything about human feelings? In D. Kahneman, E. Diener, & N. Schwartz (Eds.), *Well-being: The foundations of hedonic psychology.* Sage.

LeDoux, J. E., & Brown, R. (2017). A higher-order theory of emotional consciousness. *PNAS, 114,* E2016–E2025.

Lee, B. S., McIntyre, R. S., Gentle, J. E., Park, N. S., Chiriboga, D. A., Lee, Y., Singh, S., & McPherson, M. A. (2018). A computational algorithm for personalized medicine in schizophrenia. *Schizophrenia Research, 192,* 131–136.

Lee, C. A., Derefinko, K. J., Milich, R., Lynam, D. R., & DeWall, C. N. (2017). Longitudinal and reciprocal relations between delay discounting and crime. *Personality and Individual Differences, 111,* 193–198.

Lee, D. C., Sui, X., Artero, E. G., Lee, I. M., Church, T. S., McAuley, P. A., Stanford, F. C., Kohl, H. W., III, & Blair, S. N. (2011). Long-term effects of changes in cardiorespiratory fitness and body mass index on all-cause and cardiovascular disease mortality in men. The Aerobics Center Longitudinal Study. *Circulation, 124,* 2483–2490.

Lee, D. S., Kim, E., & Schwartz, N. (2015). Something smells fishy: Olfactory suspicion cues improve performance on the Moses illusion and Wason rule discovery task. *Journal of Experimental Social Psychology, 59,* 47–50.

Lee, G. Y., & Kisilevsky, B. S. (2014). Fetuses respond to father's voice but prefer mother's voice after birth. *Developmental Psychobiology, 56,* 1–11.

Lee, J. J., Wedow, R., Okbay, A., Kong, E., Maghzian, O., Zacher, M., Nguyen-Viet, A., Bowers, P., Sidorenko, J., Karlsson Linnér, R., Fontana, M. A., Kundu, T., Lee, C., Li, H., Li, R., Royer, R., Timshel, P. N., Walters, R. K., Willoughby, E. A., . . . Cesarini, D. (2018). Gene discovery and polygenic prediction from a 1.1-million-person GWAS of educational attainment. *Nature Genetics, 50,* 1112–1121.

Lee, L., Frederick, S., & Ariely, D. (2006). Try it, you'll like it: The influence of expectation, consumption, and revelation on preferences for beer. *Psychological Science, 17,* 1054–1058.

Lee, L. O., James, P., Zevon, E. S., Kim, E. S., Trudel-Fitzgerald, C., Spiro, A., Grodstein, F., & Kubzansky, L. D. (2019). Optimism is associated with exceptional longevity in 2 epidemiologic cohorts of men and women. *PNAS, 116,* 18357–18362.

Lee, M. R., Boness, C. L., McDowell, Y. E., Vergés, A., Steinley, D. L., & Sher, K. J. (2018). Desistance and severity of alcohol use disorder: A lifespan-developmental investigation. *Clinical Psychological Science, 6,* 90–105.

Lee, S. J., Zhang, J., Neale, M. C., Styner, M., Zhu, H., & Gilmore, J. H. (2019). Quantitative tract-based white matter heritability in 1-and 2-year-old twins. *Human Brain Mapping, 40,* 1164–1173.

Lee, S. W. S., & Schwarz, N. (2012). Bidirectionality, mediation, and moderation of metaphorical effects: The embodiment of social suspicions and fishy smells. *Journal of Personality and Social Psychology, 103,* 737–749.

Lefcourt, H. M. (1982). *Locus of control: Current trends in theory and research.* Erlbaum.

Legault, J., Grant, A., Fang, S. Y., & Li, P. (2019). A longitudinal investigation of structural brain changes during second language learning. *Brain and Language, 197,* 104661.

Legendre, G., Andrillon, T., Koroma, M., & Kouider, S. (2019). Sleepers track informative speech in a multitalker environment. *Nature Human Behaviour*, 3, 274–283.

Leger, K. A., Charles, S. T., & Almeida, D. M. (2018). Let it go: Lingering negative affect in response to daily stressors is associated with physical health years later. *Psychological Science*, 29, 1283–1290.

Lehman, D. R., Wortman, C. B., & Williams, A. F. (1987). Long-term effects of losing a spouse or child in a motor vehicle crash. *Journal of Personality and Social Psychology*, 52, 218–231.

Lehtonen, M., Soveri, A., Laine, A., Järvenpää, J., de Bruin, A., & Antfolk, J. (2018). Is bilingualism associated with enhanced executive functioning in adults? A meta-analytic review. *Psychological Bulletin*, 144, 394–425.

Leichsenring, F., & Leweke, F. (2017). Social anxiety disorder. *The New England Journal of Medicine*, 376, 2255–2264.

Leichsenring, F., & Rabung, S. (2008). Effectiveness of long-term psychodynamic psychotherapy: A meta-analysis. *JAMA*, 300, 1551–1565.

Leitenberg, H., & Henning, K. (1995). Sexual fantasy. *Psychological Bulletin*, 117, 469–496.

Lemonick, M. D. (2002, June 3). Lean and hungrier. *Time*, p. 54.

LeMoult, J., & Gotlib, I. H. (2019). Depression: A cognitive perspective. *Clinical Psychology Review*, 69, 51–66.

Lenneberg, E. H. (1967). *Biological foundations of language*. Wiley.

Lennox, B. R., Bert, S., Park, G., Jones, P. B., & Morris, P. G. (1999). Spatial and temporal mapping of neural activity associated with auditory hallucinations. *The Lancet*, 353, 644.

Lenton, A. P., & Francesconi, M. (2010). How humans cognitively manage an abundance of mate options. *Psychological Science*, 21, 528–533.

Lepp, A., Barkley, J. E., & Karpinski, A. C. (2014). The relationship between cell phone use, academic performance, anxiety, and satisfaction with life in college students. *Computers in Human Behavior*, 31, 343–350.

Lesage, A., Lemasson, M., Medina, K., Tsopmo, J., Sebti, N., Potvin, S., & Patry, S. (2016). The prevalence of electroconvulsive therapy use since 1973: A meta-analysis. *Journal of ECT*, 32, 236–242.

Leschak, C. J., & Eisenberger, N. L. (2019). Two distinct immune pathways linking social relationships with health: Inflammatory and antiviral processes. *Psychosomatic Medicine*, 81, 711–719.

Leshner, A. I. (2019). Stop blaming mental illness. *Science*, 365, 623.

Leucht, S., Barnes, T. R. E., Kissling, W., Engel, R. R., Correll, C., & Kane, J. M. (2003). Relapse prevention in schizophrenia with new-generation antipsychotics: A systematic review and exploratory meta-analysis of randomized, controlled trials. *American Journal of Psychiatry*, 160, 1209–1222.

Leucht, S., Chaimani, A., Leucht, C., Huhn, M., Mavridis, D., Helfer, B., Samara, M., Cipriani, A., Geddes, J. R., Salanti, G., & Davis, J. M. (2018). 60 years of placebo-controlled antipsychotic drug trials in acute schizophrenia: Meta-regression of predictors of placebo response. *Schizophrenia Research*, 201, 315–323.

Leucht, S., Crippa, A., Siafis, S., Patel, M. X., Orsini, N., & Davis, J. M. (2020). Dose-response meta-analysis of antipsychotic drugs for acute schizophrenia. *American Journal of Psychiatry*, 177(4), 342–353.

LeVay, S. (1991). A difference in hypothalamic structure between heterosexual and homosexual men. *Science*, 253, 1034–1037.

LeVay, S. (2011). *Gay, straight, and the reason why: The science of sexual orientation*. Oxford University Press.

Levenson, R. M., Krupinski, E. A., Navarro, V. M., & Wasserman, E. A. (2015, November 18). Pigeons (*Columba livia*) as trainable observers of pathology and radiology breast cancer images. *PLOS ONE*, 10, e0141357.

Levin, M. E., Stocke, K., Pierce, B., & Levin, C. (2018). Do college students use online self-help? A survey of intentions and use of mental health resources. *Journal of College Student Psychotherapy*, 32, 181–198.

Levin, R., & Nielsen, T. A. (2007). Disturbed dreaming, posttraumatic stress disorder, and affect distress: A review and neurocognitive model. *Psychological Bulletin*, 133, 482–528.

Levin, R., & Nielsen, T. A. (2009). Nightmares, bad dreams, and emotion dysregulation. *Current Directions in Psychological Science*, 18, 84–87.

Levine, J. A., Lanningham-Foster, L. M., McCrady, S. K., Krizan, A. C., Olson, L. R., Kane, P. H., Jensen, M. D., & Clark, M. M. (2005). Interindividual variation in posture allocation: Possible role in human obesity. *Science*, 307, 584–586.

Levine, R. (2016). *Stranger in the mirror: The scientific search for self*. Princeton University Press.

Levine, R., Sato, S., Hashimoto, T., & Verma, J. (1995). Love and marriage in eleven cultures. *Journal of Cross-Cultural Psychology*, 26, 554–571.

Levine, R. V., & Norenzayan, A. (1999). The pace of life in 31 countries. *Journal of Cross-Cultural Psychology*, 30, 178–205.

Levy, B., & Langer, E. (1992). Avoidance of the memory loss stereotype: Enhanced memory among the elderly deaf [Paper]. Presented at American Psychological Association convention, Washington, DC.

Levy, D. J., Heissel, J. A., Richeson, J. A., & Adam, E. K. (2016). Psychological and biological responses to race-based social stress as pathways to disparities in educational outcomes. *American Psychologist*, 71, 455–473.

Levy, N., Harmon-Jones, C., & Harmon-Jones, E. (2018). Dissonance and discomfort: Does a simple cognitive inconsistency evoke a negative affective state? *Motivation Science*, 4, 95–108.

Levy, P. E. (2003). *Industrial/organizational psychology: Understanding the workplace*. Houghton Mifflin.

Lewald, J. (2007). More accurate sound localisation induced by short-term light deprivation. *Neuropsychologia*, 45, 1215–1222.

Lewandowski, G. W., Jr., Aron, A., & Gee, J. (2007). Personality goes a long way: The malleability of opposite-sex physical attractiveness. *Personality Relationships*, 14, 571–585.

Lewin, K. (1935). *A dynamic theory of personality*. McGraw-Hill.

Lewinsohn, P. M., Hoberman, H., Teri, L., & Hautziner, M. (1985). An integrative theory of depression. In S. Reiss & R. Bootzin (Eds.), *Theoretical issues in behavior therapy* (pp. 331–359). Academic Press.

Lewinsohn, P. M., Petit, J., Joiner, T. E., Jr., & Seeley, J. R. (2003). The symptomatic expression of major depressive disorder in adolescents and young adults. *Journal of Abnormal Psychology*, 112, 244–252.

Lewinsohn, P. M., Rohde, P., & Seeley, J. R. (1998). Major depressive disorder in older adolescents: Prevalence, risk factors, and clinical implications. *Clinical Psychology Review*, 18, 765–794.

Lewis, C. S. (1960). *Mere Christianity*. Macmillan.

Lewis, C. S. (1967). *Christian reflections*. Eerdmans.

Lewis, D. M. G., Al-Shawaf, L., Conroy-Beam, D., Asao, K., & Buss, D. M. (2017). Evolutionary psychology: A how-to guide. *American Psychologist*, 72, 353–373.

Lewis, D. M. G., Russell, E. M., Al-Shawaf, L., & Buss, D. M. (2015). Lumbar curvature: A previously undiscovered standard of attractiveness. *Evolution and Human Behavior*, 36, 345–350.

Lewis, D. O., Pincus, J. H., Bard, B., Richardson, E., Prichep, L. S., Feldman, M., & Yeager, C. (1988). Neuropsychiatric, psychoeducational, and family characteristics of 14 juveniles condemned to death in the United States. *American Journal of Psychiatry*, 145, 584–589.

Lewis, M. (2016). *The undoing project: A friendship that changed our minds*. W.W. Norton.

Lewis, M. B. (2018). The interactions between botulinum-toxin-based facial treatments and embodied emotions. *Scientific Reports*, 8, 14720.

Lewis, N. A., Jr., & Earl, A. (2018). Seeing more and eating less: Effects of portion size granularity on the perception and regulation of food consumption. *Journal of Personality and Social Psychology*, 114, 786–803.

Lewontin, R. (1982). *Human diversity*. Scientific American Library.

Li, J., Laursen, T. M., Precht, D. H., Olsen, J., & Mortensen, P. B. (2005). Hospitalization for mental illness among parents after the death of a child. *New England Journal of Medicine*, 352, 1190–1196.

Li, J., Zhao, Y., Lin, L., Chen, J., & Wang, S. (2018). The freedom to persist: Belief in free will predicts perseverance for long-term goals among Chinese adolescents. *Personality and Individual Differences*, 121, 7–10.

Li, L., Abutalebi, J., Emmorey, K., Gong, G., Yan, X., Feng, X., Zou, L., & Ding, G. (2017). How bilingualism protects the brain from aging: Insights from bimodal bilinguals. *Human Brain Mapping*, 38, 4109–4124.

Li, L., Wang, Y. Y., Wang, S. B., Zhang, L., Li, L., Xu, D. D., Ng, C. H., Ungvari, G. S., Cui, X., Liu, Z.-M., De Li, S., Jia, F.-J., & Xiang, Y.-T (2018). Prevalence of sleep disturbances in Chinese university students: a comprehensive meta-analysis. *Journal of Sleep Research*, 27, e12648.

Li, N., & DiCarlo, J. J. (2008). Unsupervised natural experience rapidly alters invariant object representation in visual cortex. *Science*, 321, 1502–1506.

Li, N. P., & Kanazawa, S. (2016). Country roads, take me home . . . to my friends: How intelligence, population density, and friendship affect modern happiness. *British Journal of Psychology*, 107, 675–697.

Li, S., Stampfer, M. J., Williams, D. R., & Vander-Weele, T. J. (2016). Association of religious service attendance with mortality among women. *JAMA Internal Medicine*, 176, 777–785.

Li, T., Yan, X., Li, Y., Wang, J., Li, Q., Li, H., & Li, J. (2017). Neuronal correlates of individual differences in the Big Five personality traits: Evidences from cortical morphology and functional homogeneity. *Frontiers in Neuroscience*, 11, 414.

Li, Y., Johnson, E. J., & Zaval, L. (2011). Local warming: Daily temperature change influences belief in global warming. *Psychological Science*, 22, 454–459.

Li, Z. H., Jiang, D., Pepler, D., & Craig, W. (2010). Adolescent romantic relationships in China and Canada: A cross-national comparison. *International Journal of Behavioral Development*, 34, 113–120.

Liberman, M. C. (2015, August). Hidden hearing loss. *Scientific American*, pp. 49–53.

Libertus, M. E., & Brannon, E. M. (2009). Behavioral and neural basis of number sense in infancy. *Current Directions in Psychological Science*, 18, 346–351.

Licata, A., Taylor, S., Berman, M., & Cranston, J. (1993). Effects of cocaine on human aggression. *Pharmacology Biochemistry and Behavior*, 45, 549–552.

Lichtenstein, E., Zhu, S.-H., & Tedeschi, G. J. (2010). Smoking cessation quitlines: An underrecognized intervention success story. *American Psychologist*, 65, 252–261.

Liddle, J. R., Shackelford, T. K., & Weekes-Shackelford, V. W. (2012). Why can't we all just get along?: Evolutionary perspectives on violence, homicide, and war. *Review of General Psychology, 16*, 24–36.

Lieberman, M. D., & Eisenberger, N. I. (2015). The dorsal anterior cingulate is selective for pain: Results from large-scale fMRI reverse inference. *PNAS, 12*, 15250–15255.

Lieberman, M. D., Eisenberger, N. L., Crockett, M. J., Tom, S. M., Pfeifer, J. H., & Way, B. M. (2007). Putting feelings into words: Affect labeling disrupts amygdala activity in response to affective stimuli. *Psychological Science, 18*, 421–428.

Lieberman, M. D., Straccia, M. A., Meyer, M. L., Du, M., & Tan, K. M. (2019). Social, self, (situational), and affective processes in medial prefrontal cortex (MPFC): Causal, multivariate, and reverse inference evidence. *Neuroscience & Biobehavioral Reviews, 99*, 311–328.

Lieberman, P. (2013). Synapses, language, and being human. *Science, 342*, 944–945.

Lievens, F., Dilchert, S., & Ones, D. S. (2009). The importance of exercise and dimension factors in assessment centers: Simultaneous examinations of construct-related and criterion-related validity. *Human Performance, 22*, 375–390.

Lifton, R. J. (1961). *Thought reform and the psychology of totalism: A study of "brainwashing" in China*. Norton.

Lilienfeld, S. O. (2009, Winter). Tips for spotting psychological pseudoscience: A student-friendly guide. *Eye of Psi Chi*, pp. 23–26.

Lilienfeld, S. O. (2017). Clinical psychological science: Then and now. *Clinical Psychological Science, 5*, 3–13.

Lilienfeld, S. O., Lynn, S. J., Kirsch, I., Chaves, J. F., Sarbin, T. R., Ganaway, G. K., & Powell, R. A. (1999). Dissociative identity disorder and the sociocognitive model: Recalling the lessons of the past. *Psychological Bulletin, 125*, 507–523. ok

Lilienfeld, S. O., Marshall, J., Todd, J. T., & Shane, H. C. (2015a). The persistence of fad interventions in the face of negative scientific evidence: Facilitated communication for autism as a case example. *Evidence-Based Communication Assessment and Intervention, 8*, 62–101.

Lilienfeld, S. O., Ritschel, L. A., Lynn, S. J., Cautin, R. L., & Latzman, R. D. (2015b). Science–practice gap. *Encyclopedia of Clinical Psychology* (1–7). Wiley.

Lilienfeld, S. O., Sauvigné, K. C., Reber, J., Watts, A. L., Hamann, S., Smith, S. F., Patrick, C. J., Bowes, S. M., & Tranel, D. (2017). Potential effects of severe bilateral amygdala damage on psychopathic features: A case report. *Personality Disorders: Theory, Research, and Treatment, 9*, 112–121.

Lilienfeld, S. O., Smith, S. F., & Watts, A. L. (2016). Fearless dominance and its implications for psychopathy: Are the right stuff and the wrong stuff flip sides of the same coin? In V. Zeigler-Hill, & D. K. Marcus (Eds.), *The dark side of personality: Science and practice in social, personality, and clinical psychology* (pp. 65–86). American Psychological Association.

Lilienfeld, S. O., Waldman, I. D., Landfield, K., Watts, A. L., Rubenzer, S., & Fashingbauer, T. R. (2012). Fearless dominance and the U.S. presidency: Implications of psychopathic personality traits for successful and unsuccessful political leadership. *Journal of Personality and Social Psychology, 103*, 489–505. ok

Lilienfeld, S. O., Wood, J. M., & Garb, H. N. (2001, May). What's wrong with this picture? *Scientific American*, pp. 81–87.

Lillard, D. (2015). Tweet. https://twitter.com/dame_lillard/status/555485512492785665?lang=en

Lim, D., & DeSteno, D. (2016). Suffering and compassion: The links among adverse life experiences, empathy, compassion, and prosocial behavior. *Emotion, 16*, 175–182.

Lim, J., & Dinges, D. F. (2010). A meta-analysis of the impact of short-term sleep deprivation on cognitive variables. *Psychological Bulletin, 136*, 375–389.

Lin, F. R., Ferrucci, L., Metter, E. J., An, Y., Zonderman, A. B., & Resnick, S. M. (2011a). Hearing loss and cognition in the Baltimore longitudinal study of aging. *Neuropsychology, 25*, 763–770.

Lin, F. R., Metter, E. J., O'Brien, R. J., Resnick, S. M., Zonderman, A. B., & Ferrucci, L. (2011b). Hearing loss and incident dementia. *Archives of Neurology, 68*, 214–220.

Lin, F. R., Yaffe, K., Xia, J., Xue, Q.-L., Harris, T. B., Purchase-Helzner, E., Satterfield, S., Ayonayon, H. N., Ferrucci, L., & Simonsick, E. M. (2013). Hearing loss and cognitive decline in older adults. *JAMA, 173*, 293–299.

Lin, P. (2016). Risky behaviors: Integrating adolescent egocentrism with the theory of planned behavior. *Review of General Psychology, 20*, 392–398.

Lin, X., Chen, W., Wei, F., Ying, M., Wei, W., & Xie, X. (2015). Night-shift work increases morbidity of breast cancer and all-cause mortality: A meta-analysis of 16 prospective cohort studies. *Sleep Medicine, 16*, 1381–1387.

Lin, Z., & Murray, S. O. (2015). More power to the unconscious: Conscious, but not unconscious, exogenous attention requires location variation. *Psychological Science, 26*, 221–230.

Linardon, J., Cuijpers, P., Carlbring, P., Messer, M., & Fuller-Tyszkiewicz, M. (2019). The efficacy of app-supported smartphone interventions for mental health problems: A meta-analysis of randomized controlled trials. *World Psychiatry, 18*, 325–336.

Linardon, J., Wade, T. D., de la Piedad Garcia, X., & Brennan, L. (2017). The efficacy of cognitive-behavioral therapy for eating disorders: A systematic review and meta-analysis. *Journal of Consulting and Clinical Psychology, 85*, 1080–1094.

Lind, A., Hall, L., Breidegard, B., Balkenius, C., & Johansson, P. (2014). Speakers' acceptance of real-time speech exchange indicates that we use auditory feedback to specify the meaning of what we say. *Psychological Science, 25*, 1198–1205.

Lindberg, S. M., Hyde, J. S., Linn, M. C., & Petersen, J. L. (2010). New trends in gender and mathematics performance: A meta-analysis. *Psychological Bulletin, 136*, 1125–1135.

Linder, D. (1982). Social trap analogs: The tragedy of the commons in the laboratory. In V. J. Derlega & J. Grzelak (Eds.), *Cooperative and helping behavior: Theories and research*. Academic Press.

Lindner, I., Echterhoff, G., Davidson, P. S. R., & Brand, M. (2010). Observation inflation: Your actions become mine. *Psychological Science, 21*, 1291–1299.

Lindsay, E. K., Chin, B., Greco, C. M., Young, S., Brown, K. W., Wright, A. G., Smyth, J. M., Burkett, D., & Creswell, J. D. (2018). How mindfulness training promotes positive emotions: Dismantling acceptance skills training in two randomized controlled trials. *Journal of Personality and Social Psychology, 115*, 944–973.

Lindskold, S. (1978). Trust development, the GRIT proposal, and the effects of conciliatory acts on conflict and cooperation. *Psychological Bulletin, 85*, 772–793.

Lindskold, S., & Han, G. (1988). GRIT as a foundation for integrative bargaining. *Personality and Social Psychology Bulletin, 14*, 335–345.

Lindson-Hawley, N., Banting, M., West, R., Michie, S., Shinkins, B., & Aveyard, P. (2016). Gradual versus abrupt smoking cessation: A randomized, controlled noninferiority trial. *Annals of Internal Medicine, 164*, 585–592.

Lindström, B., Golkar, A., Jangard, S., Tobler, P. N., & Olsson, A. (2019). Social threat learning transfers to decision making in humans. *PNAS, 116*, 4732–4737.

Linehan, M. M., Korslund, K. E., Harned, M. S., Gallop, R. J., Lungu, A., Neacsiu, A. D., McDavid, J., Comtois, K. A., & Murray-Gregory, A. M. (2015). Dialectical behavior therapy for high suicide risk in individuals with borderline personality disorder: A randomized clinical trial and component analysis. *JAMA Psychiatry, 72*, 475–482.

Ling, S., Umbach, R., & Raine, A. (2019). Biological explanations of criminal behavior. *Psychology, Crime & Law, 25*, 626–640.

Lionetti, F., Palladino, B. E., Moses Passini, C., Casonato, M., Hamzallari, O., Ranta, M., Dellagiulia, A., & Keijsers, L. (2019). The development of parental monitoring during adolescence: A meta-analysis. *European Journal of Developmental Psychology, 16*, 552–580.

Lippa, R. A. (2007). The relation between sex drive and sexual attraction to men and women: A cross-national study of heterosexual, bisexual, and homosexual men and women. *Archives of Sexual Behavior, 36*, 209–222.

Lippa, R. A. (2009). Sex differences in sex drive, sociosexuality, and height across 53 nations: Testing evolutionary and social structural theories. *Archives of Sexual Behavior, 38*, 631–651.

Lipsitt, L. P. (2003). Crib death: A biobehavioral phenomenon? *Current Directions in Psychological Science, 12*, 164–170.

Littlewood, D. L., Kyle, S. D., Carter, L. A., Peters, S., Pratt, D., & Gooding, P. (2019). Short sleep duration and poor sleep quality predict next-day suicidal ideation: An ecological momentary assessment study. *Psychological Medicine, 49*, 403–411.

Littman, R. (2018). Perpetrating violence increases identification with violent groups: Survey evidence from former combatants. *Personality and Social Psychology Bulletin, 44*, 1077–1089.

Liu, D., & Baumeister, R. F. (2016). Social networking online and personality of self-worth: A meta-analysis. *Journal of Research in Personality, 64*, 79–89.

Liu, J., Zhao, S., Chen, X., Falk, E., & Albarracín, D. (2017). The influence of peer behavior as a function of social and cultural closeness: A meta-analysis of normative influence on adolescent smoking initiation and continuation. *Psychological Bulletin, 143*, 1082–1115.

Liu, P. Z., & Nusslock, R. (2018). Exercise-mediated neurogenesis in the hippocampus via BDNF. *Frontiers in Neuroscience, 12*, 52.

Liu, S., Huang, J. L., & Wang, M. (2014). Effectiveness of job search interventions: A meta-analytic review. *Psychological Bulletin, 140*, 1009–1041.

Liu, X., Hodgson, J. J., & Buchon, N. (2017). Drosophila as a model for homeostatic, antibacterial, and antiviral mechanisms in the gut. *PLOS Pathogens, 13*, e1006.

Liu, Y., Balaraman, Y., Wang, G., Nephew, K. P., & Zhou, F. C. (2009). Alcohol exposure alters DNA methylation profiles in mouse embryos at early neurulation. *Epigenetics, 4*, 500–511.

Livi, A., Lanzilotto, M., Maranesi, M., Fogassi, L., Rizzolatti, G., & Bonini, L. (2019). Agent-based representations of objects and actions in the monkey pre-supplementary motor area. *PNAS, 116*, 2691–2700.

Livingston, G. (2019, February 20). *The way U.S. teens spend their time is changing, but differences between boys and girls persist*. Pew Research Center. https://pewrsr.ch/2ILALhO

Livingston, G., & Parker, K. (2011). *A tale of two fathers: More are active, but more are absent.* Pew Research Center. https://www.pewsocialtrends.org/2011/06/15/a-tale-of-two-fathers/

Lo, J. C., Chong, P. L., Ganesan, S., Leong, R. L., & Chee, M. W. (2016). Sleep deprivation increases formation of false memory. *Journal of Sleep Research, 25*, 673-682.

LoBello, S. G., & Mehta, S. (2019). No evidence of seasonal variation in mild forms of depression. *Journal of Behavior Therapy and Experimental Psychiatry, 62*, 72–79.

Locke, A. E., Kahali, B., Berndt, S. I., Justice, A. E., Pers, T. H., Day, F. R., . . . Speliotes, E. K. (2015). Genetic studies of body mass index yield new insights for obesity biology. *Nature, 518*, 195–206.

Locke, K. D., Church, A. T., Mastor, K. A., Curtis, G. J., Sadler, P., McDonald, K., Vargas-Flores, J. J., Ibáñez-Reyes, J., Morio, H., Reyes, J. A. S., Cabrera, H. F., Mazuera Arias, R., Rincon, B. C., Albornoz Arias, N. C., Muñoz, A., & Ortiz, F. A. (2017). Cross-situational self-consistency in nine cultures: The importance of separating influences of social norms and distinctive dispositions. *Personality and Social Psychology Bulletin, 43*, 1033–1049.

Lodder, P., Ong, H. H., Grasman, R. P., & Wicherts, J. M. (2019). A comprehensive meta-analysis of money priming. *Journal of Experimental Psychology: General, 148*, 688–712.

Loehlin, J. C. (2016). What can an adoption study tell us about the effect of prenatal environment on a trait. *Behavior Genetics, 46*, 329–333.

Loehlin, J. C., Horn, J. M., & Ernst, J. L. (2007). Genetic and environmental influences on adult life outcomes: Evidence from the Texas adoption project. *Behavior Genetics, 37*, 463–476.

Loehlin, J. C. & Martin, N. G. (2018). Personality types: A twin study. *Personality and Individual Differences, 122*, 99–103.

Loehlin, J. C., & Nichols, R. C. (1976). *Heredity, environment, and personality.* University of Texas Press.

Loewenstein, G., Krishnamurti, T., Kopsic, J., & McDonald, D. (2015). Does increased sexual frequency enhance happiness? *Journal of Economic Behavior & Organization, 116*, 206–218.

Loffman, M. (2020). *Asian Americans describe 'gut punch' of racist attacks during coronavirus pandemic.* PBS News Hour. https://www.pbs.org/newshour/nation/asian-americans-describe-gut-punch-of-racist-attacks-during-coronavirus-pandemic

Loftus, E. F. (2001, November). Imagining the past. *The Psychologist, 14*, 584–587.

Loftus, E. F. (2012, July). *Manufacturing memories.* Invited address to the International Congress of Psychology, Cape Town.

Loftus, E. F., & Ketcham, K. (1994). *The myth of repressed memory: False memories and allegations of sexual abuse.* St. Martin's Press.

Loftus, E. F., Levidow, B., & Duensing, S. (1992). Who remembers best? Individual differences in memory for events that occurred in a science museum. *Applied Cognitive Psychology, 6*, 93–107.

Loftus, E. F., & Loftus, G. R. (1980). On the permanence of stored information in the human brain. *American Psychologist, 35*, 409–420

Loftus, E. F., & Palmer, J. C. (October, 1974). Reconstruction of automobile destruction: An example of the interaction between language and memory. *Journal of Verbal Learning & Verbal Behavior, 13*, 585–589.

Logan, G. D. (2018). Automatic control: How experts act without thinking. *Psychological Review, 125*, 453–485.

Logan, J. A., Justice, L. M., Yumus, M., & Chaparro-Moreno, L. J. (2019). When children are not read to at home: The million word gap. *Journal of Developmental & Behavioral Pediatrics, 40*, 383–386.

Logan, T. K., Walker, R., Cole, J., & Leukefeld, C. (2002). Victimization and substance abuse among women: Contributing factors, interventions, and implications. *Review of General Psychology, 6*, 325–397.

Logel, C., Kathmandu, A., & Cohen, G. L. (2019). Affirmation prevents long-term weight gain. *Journal of Experimental Social Psychology, 81*, 70–75.

Logue, A. W. (1998a). Laboratory research on self-control: Applications to administration. *Review of General Psychology, 2*, 221–238.

Logue, A. W. (1998b). Self-control. In W. T. O'Donohue (Ed.), *Learning and behavior therapy.* Allyn & Bacon.

London, P. (1970). The rescuers: Motivational hypotheses about Christians who saved Jews from the Nazis. In J. Macaulay & L. Berkowitz (Eds.), *Altruism and helping behavior.* Academic Press.

Lonsdorf, E. V. (2017). Sex differences in nonhuman primate behavioral development. *Journal of Neuroscience Research, 95*, 213–221.

Loomes, R., Hull, L., & Mandy, W. P. L. (2017). What is the male-to-female ratio in autism spectrum disorder? A systematic review and meta-analysis. *Journal of the American Academy of Child & Adolescent Psychiatry, 56*, 466–474.

Lopez, D. J. (2002, January/February). Snaring the fowler: Mark Twain debunks phrenology. *Skeptical Inquirer.* https://skepticalinquirer.org/2002/01/snaring-the-fowler-mark-twain-debunks-phrenology/

Lopez-Quintero, C., de los Cobos, P., Hasin, D. S., Okuda, M., Wang, S., Grant, B. F., & Blanco, C. (2011). Probability and predictors of transition from first use to dependence on nicotine, alcohol, cannabis, and cocaine: Results of the national epidemiologic survey on alcohol and related conditions (NESARC). *Drug and Alcohol Dependence, 115*, 120–130.

Loprinzi, P. D., Loenneke, J. P., & Blackburn, E. H. (2015). Movement-based behaviors and leukocyte telomere length among US adults. *Medical Science and Sports Exercise, 47*, 2347–2352.

Lord, C. G., Lepper, M. R., & Preston, E. (1984). Considering the opposite: A corrective strategy for social judgment. *Journal of Personality and Social Psychology, 47*, 1231–1247.

Lord, C. G., Ross, L., & Lepper, M. (1979). Biased assimilation and attitude polarization: The effects of prior theories on subsequently considered evidence. *Journal of Personality and Social Psychology, 37*, 2098–2109.

Lorenz, K. (1937). The companion in the bird's world. *Auk, 54*, 245–273.

Loughrey, D. G., Kelly, M. E, Kelley, G. A., Brennan, S., & Lawlor, B. A. (2018). Association of age-related hearing loss with cognitive function, cognitive impairment, and dementia: A systematic review and meta-analysis. *JAMA Otolaryngology Head Neck Surgery, 144*, 115–126.

Louie, K., & Wilson, M. A. (2001). Temporally structured replay of awake hippocampal ensemble activity during rapid eye movement sleep. *Neuron, 29*, 145–156.

Lourenco, O., & Machado, A. (1996). In defense of Piaget's theory: A reply to 10 common criticisms. *Psychological Review, 103*, 143–164.

Lovaas, O. I. (1987). Behavioral treatment and normal educational and intellectual functioning in young autistic children. *Journal of Consulting and Clinical Psychology, 55*, 3–9.

Low, P. (2012). *The Cambridge declaration on consciousness* [PDF file]. Publicly proclaimed in Cambridge, UK, on July 7, 2012, at the Francis Crick Memorial Conference on Consciousness in Human and Non-Human Animals. fcmconference.org/img/CambridgeDeclarationOnConsciousness.pdf

Lowe, H., Haddock, G., Mulligan, L. D., Gregg, L., Carter, L-A., Fuzellier-Hart, A., & Kyle, S. D. (2019). Does exercise improve sleep for adults with insomnia? A systematic review with quality appraisal. *Clinical Psychology Review, 68*, 1–12.

Lozano, A. M., & Mayberg, H. S. (2015, February). Treating depression at the source. *Scientific American*, pp. 68–73.

Lu, J., Zhong, X., Liu, H., Hao, L., Huang, C. T. L., Sherafat, M. A., Jones, J., Ayala, M., Li, L., & Zhang, S. C. (2016). Generation of serotonin neurons from human pluripotent stem cells. *Nature Biotechnology, 34*, 89–94.

Lu, J. G., Martin, A., Usova, A., & Galinsky, A. D. (2018). Creativity and humor across cultures: Where Aha meets Haha. In S. R. Luria, J. Baer, & J. C. Kaufman (Eds.), *Creativity and humor* (pp. 183–203). Academic Press.

Lu, Z.-L., Williamson, S. J., & Kaufman, L. (1992). Behavioral lifetime of human auditory sensory memory predicted by physiological measures. *Science, 258*, 1668–1670.

Luan, Z., Poorthuis, A. M., Hutteman, R., Denissen, J. J., Asendorpf, J. B., & van Aken, M. A. (2019). Unique predictive power of other-rated personality: An 18-year longitudinal study. *Journal of Personality, 87*, 532–545.

Lubinski, D. (2009). Cognitive epidemiology: With emphasis on untangling cognitive ability and socioeconomic status. *Intelligence, 37*, 625–633.

Lubinski, D. (2016). From Terman to today: A century of findings on intellectual precocity. *Review of Educational Research, 86*, 900–944.

Lubinski, D., Benbow, C. P., & Kell, H. J. (2014). Life paths and accomplishments of mathematically precocious males and females four decades later. *Psychological Science, 25*, 2217–2232.

Luby, J. L., Belden, A., Harms, M. P., Tillman, R., & Barch, D. M. (2016). Preschool is a sensitive period for the influence of maternal support on the trajectory of hippocampal development. *PNAS, 113*, 5742–5747.

Lucas, R. E., Clark, A. E., Georgellis, Y., & Diener, E. (2004). Unemployment alters the set point for life satisfaction. *Psychological Science, 15*, 8–13.

Lucas, R. E., & Donnellan, M. B. (2007). How stable is happiness? Using the STARTS model to estimate the stability of life satisfaction. *Journal of Research in Personality, 41*, 1091–1098.

Lucas, R. E., & Donnellan, M. B. (2009). Age differences in personality: Evidence from a nationally representative Australian sample. *Developmental Psychology, 45*, 1353–1363.

Luciano, M., Gow, A. J., Harris, S. E., Hayward, C., Allerhand, M., Starr, J. M., Visscher, P. M., & Deary, I. J. (2009). Cognitive ability at age 11 and 70 years, information processing speed, and APOE variation: The Lothian birth cohort 1936 study. *Psychology and Aging, 24*, 129–138.

Ludwig, A. M. (1995). *The price of greatness: Resolving the creativity and madness controversy.* Guilford Press.

Ludwig, D. S., & Friedman, M. I. (2014). Increasing adiposity: Consequence or cause of overeating? *JAMA, 311*, 2167–2168.

Luhmann, M., & Hawkley, L. C. (2016). Age differences in loneliness from late adolescence to oldest old age. *Developmental Psychology, 52*, 943–959.

Luhmann, M., Hofmann, W., Eid, M., & Lucas, R. E. (2012). Subjective well-being and adaptation to life events: A meta-analysis. *Journal of Personality and Social Psychology, 102*, 592–615.

Luna, V. M., Anacker, C., Burghardt, N. S., Khandaker, H., Andreu, V., Millette, A., Leary, P., Ravenelle, R., Jimenez, J. C. Mastrodonato, A., Denny, C. A., Fenton, A. A., Scharfman, H. E., & Hen, R. (2019). Adult-born hippocampal neurons bidirectionally modulate entorhinal inputs into the dentate gyrus. *Science, 364,* 578–583.

Lund, T. J., & Dearing, E. (2012). Is growing up affluent risky for adolescents or is the problem growing up in an affluent neighborhood? *Journal of Research on Adolescence, 23,* 274–282.

Lundy, A. C. (1985). The reliability of the Thematic Apperception Test. *Journal of Personality Assessment, 49,* 141–145.

Luo, D., Kwok, V. P., Li, P., Liu, Q., Li, W., Yang, Y., Zhou, K., Xu, M., Gao, J. H., & Tan, L. H. (2019). Microstructural plasticity in the bilingual brain. *Brain and Language, 196,* 104654.

Luria, A. M. (1968). In L. Solotaroff (Trans.), *The mind of a mnemonist.* Basic Books.

Lustig, C., & Buckner, R. L. (2004). Preserved neural correlates of priming in old age and dementia. *Neuron, 42,* 865–875.

Lutgendorf, S. K., & Andersen, B. L. (2015). Biobehavioral approaches to cancer progression and survival. *American Psychologist, 70,* 186–197.

Lutgendorf, S. K., Lamkin, D. M., Jennings, N. B., Arevalo, J. M. G., Penedo, F., DeGeest, K., Langley, R. R., Lucci, J. A., III, Cole, S. W., Lubaroff, D. M., & Sood, A. K. (2008). Biobehavioral influences on matrix metalloproteinase expression in ovarian carcinoma. *Clinical Cancer Research, 14,* 6839–6846.

Lutgendorf, S. K., Russell, D., Ullrich, P., Harris, T. B., & Wallace, R. (2004). Religious participation, interleukin-6, and mortality in older adults. *Health Psychology, 23,* 465–475.

Luthar, S. S., Barkin, S. H., & Crossman, E. J. (2013). "I can, therefore I must": Fragility in the upper-middle classes. *Development and Psychopathology, 25,* 1529–1549.

Lutz, P. E., Gross, J. A., Dhir, S. K., Maussion, G., Yang, J., Bramoullé, A., Meaney, M. J., & Turecki, G. (2017). Epigenetic regulation of the kappa opioid receptor by child abuse. *Biological Psychiatry, 84,* 751–761.

Luyckx, K., Tildesley, E. A., Soenens, B., Andrews, J. A., Hampson, S. E., Peterson, M., & Duriez, B. (2011). Parenting and trajectories of children's maladaptive behaviors: A 12-year prospective community study. *Journal of Clinical Child and Adolescent Psychology, 40,* 468–478.

Lyall, S. (2005, November 29). What's the buzz? Rowdy teenagers don't want to hear it. *The New York Times.* https://www.nytimes.com/2005/11/29/world/europe/whats-the-buzz-rowdy-teenagers-dont-want-to-hear-it.html?

Lykes, V. A., & Kemmelmeier, M. (2014). What predicts loneliness? Cultural difference between individualistic and collectivistic societies in Europe. *Journal of Cross-Cultural Psychology, 45,* 468–490.

Lykken, D. T. (1991). *Science, lies, and controversy: An epitaph for the polygraph.* Invited address upon receipt of the Senior Career Award for Distinguished Contribution to Psychology in the Public Interest, American Psychological Association convention.

Lykken, D. T. (1995). *The antisocial personalities.* Erlbaum.

Lykken, D. T. (2006). The mechanism of emergenesis. *Genes, Brain & Behavior, 5,* 306–310.

Lynch, G. (2002). Memory enhancement: The search for mechanism-based drugs. *Nature Neuroscience, 5* (suppl.), 1035–1038.

Lynch, G., Palmer, L. C., & Gall, C. M. (2011). The likelihood of cognitive enhancement. *Pharmacology, Biochemistry and Behavior, 99,* 116–129.

Lynch, G., & Staubli, U. (1991). Possible contributions of long-term potentiation to the encoding and organization of memory. *Brain Research Reviews, 16,* 204–206.

Lynn, M. (1988). The effects of alcohol consumption on restaurant tipping. *Personality and Social Psychology Bulletin, 14,* 87–91.

Lynn, R. (2009). What has caused the Flynn effect? Secular increases in the development quotients of infants. *Intelligence, 37,* 16–24.

Lynn, R., Cheng, H., & Wang, M. (2016). Differences in the intelligence of children across thirty-one provinces and municipalities of China and their economic and social correlates. *Intelligence, 58,* 10–13.

Lynn, R., & Harvey, J. (2008). The decline of the world's intelligence. *Intelligence, 36,* 112–120.

Lynn, R., & Kanazawa, S. (2011). A longitudinal study of sex differences in intelligence at ages 7, 11 and 16 years. *Personality and Individual Differences, 51,* 321–324.

Lynn, R., Sakar, C., & Cheng, H. (2015). Regional differences in intelligence, income and other socio-economic variables in Turkey. *Intelligence, 50,* 144–149.

Lynn, R., & Vanhanen, T. (2012). *Intelligence: A unifying construct for the social sciences.* Ulster Institute for Social Research.

Lynn, S. J., Laurence, J., & Kirsch, I. (2015). Hypnosis, suggestion, and suggestibility: An integrative model. *American Journal of Clinical Hypnosis, 57,* 314–329.

Lynn, S. J., Lilienfeld, S. O., Merckelbach, H., Giesbrecht, T., McNally, R. J., Loftus, E. F., Bruck, M., Garry, M., & Malaktaris, A. (2014). The trauma model of dissociation: Inconvenient truths and stubborn fictions. Comment on Dalenberg et al. (2012). *Psychological Bulletin, 140,* 896–910.

Lynn, S. J., Rhue, J. W., & Weekes, J. R. (1990). Hypnotic involuntariness: A social cognitive analysis. *Psychological Review, 97,* 169–184.

Lyons, A. (2015). Resilience in lesbians and gay men: A review and key findings from a nationwide Australian survey. *International Review of Psychiatry, 27,* 435–443.

Lyons, B. D., Hoffman, B. J., Michel, J. W., & Williams, K. J. (2011). On the predictive efficiency of past performance and physical ability: The case of the National Football League. *Human Performance, 24,* 158–172.

Lyons, D. E., Young, A. G., & Keil, F. C. (2007). The hidden structure of overimitation. *PNAS, 104,* 19751–19756.

Lyons, L. (2004, February 3). *Growing up lonely: Examining teen alienation.* https://news.gallup.com/poll/10465/growing-lonely-examining-teen-alienation.aspx

Lyons, M. J., Panizzon, M. S., Liu, W., McKenzie, R., Bluestone, N. J., Grant, M. D., Franz, C. E., Vuoksimaa, E. P., Toomey, R., Jacobson, K. C., Reynolds, C. A., Kremen, W. S., & Xian, H. (2017). A longitudinal twin study of general cognitive ability over four decades. *Developmental Psychology, 53,* 1170–1177.

Lyubomirsky, S. (2001). Why are some people happier than others? The role of cognitive and motivational processes in well-being. *American Psychologist, 56,* 239–249.

Lyubomirsky, S. (2008). *The how of happiness.* Penguin.

Lyubomirsky, S., Sousa, L., & Dickerhoof, R. (2006). The costs and benefits of writing, talking, and thinking about life's triumphs and defeats. *Journal of Personality and Social Psychology, 90,* 690–708.

Ma, A., Landau, M. J., Narayanan, J., & Kay, A. C. (2017). Thought-control difficulty motivates structure seeking. *Journal of Experimental Psychology: General, 146,* 1067–1072.

Ma, D. S., Correll, J., Wittenbrink, B., Bar-Anan, Y., Sriram, N., & Nosek, B. A. (2013). When fatigue turns deadly: The association between fatigue and racial bias in the decision to shoot. *Basic and Applied Social Psychology, 35,* 515–524.

Ma, L. (1997, September). On the origin of Darwin's ills. *Discover,* p. 27.

Maas, J. B. (1999). *Power sleep. The revolutionary program that prepares your mind and body for peak performance.* HarperCollins.

Maas, J. B., & Robbins, R. S. (2010). *Sleep for success: Everything you must know about sleep but are too tired to ask.* Author House.

Macan, T. H., & Dipboye, R. L. (1994). The effects of the application on processing of information from the employment interview. *Journal of Applied Social Psychology, 24,* 1291–1314.

MacCabe, J. H., Lambe, M. P., Cnattingius, S., Torrång, A., Björk, C., Sham, P. C., David, A. S., Murray, R. M., & Hultman, C. M. (2008). Scholastic achievement at age 16 and risk of schizophrenia and other psychoses: A national cohort study. *Psychological Medicine, 38,* 1133–1140.

Macchia, L., Plagnol, A. C., & Powdthavee, N. (2019). Buying happiness in an unequal world: Rank of income more strongly predicts well-being in more unequal countries. *Personality and Social Psychology Bulletin.* Advance online publication. https://doi.org/10.1177/0146167219877413

Maccoby, E. (1980). *Social development: Psychological growth and the parent-child relationship.* Harcourt Brace Jovanovich.

Maccoby, E. E. (1990). Gender and relationships: A developmental account. *American Psychologist, 45,* 513–520.

Maccoby, E. E. (1998). *The paradox of gender.* Harvard University Press.

Maccoby, E. E. (2002). Gender and group process: A developmental perspective. *Current Directions in Psychological Science, 11,* 54–58.

Maccoby, E. E., & Martin, J. A. (1983). Socialization in the context of the family: Parent-child interaction. In P. H. Mussen, & E. M. Hetherington (Eds.), *Handbook of child psychology: Vol. 4. Socialization, Personality, and Social Development* (pp. 1–101). Wiley.

MacCormack, J. K., & Lindquist, K. A. (2016). Bodily contribution to emotion: Schachter's legacy for a psychological constructionist view on emotion. *Emotion Review, 9,* 36–45.

MacDonald, B., Pennington, B. F., Willcutt, E. G., Dmitrieva, J., Samuelsson, S., Byrne, B., & Olson, R. K. (2019). Cross-country differences in parental reporting of symptoms of ADHD. *Journal of Cross-Cultural Psychology, 50,* 806–824.

MacDonald, G., & Leary, M. R. (2005). Why does social exclusion hurt? The relationship between social and physical pain. *Psychological Bulletin, 131,* 202–223.

Macdonald, K., Germine, L., Anderson, A., Christodoulou, J., & McGrath, L. M. (2017). Dispelling the myth: Training in education or neuroscience decreases but does not eliminate beliefs in neuromyths. *Frontiers in Psychology, 8,* 16.

MacDonald, T. K., & Hynie, M. (2008). Ambivalence and unprotected sex: Failure to predict sexual activity and decreased condom use. *Journal of Applied Social Psychology, 38,* 1092–1107.

MacDonald, T. K., Zanna, M. P., & Fong, G. T. (1995). Decision making in altered states: Effects of alcohol on attitudes toward drinking and driving. *Journal of Personality and Social Psychology, 68,* 973–985.

MacFarlane, A. (1978, February). What a baby knows. *Human Nature,* pp. 74–81.

Macfarlane, J. W. (1964). Perspectives on personality consistency and change from the guidance study. *Vita Humana, 7*, 115–126.

Maciejewski, P. K., Maercker, A., Boelen, P. A., & Prigerson, H. G. (2016). "Prolonged grief disorder" and "persistent complex bereavement disorder", but not "complicated grief," are one and the same diagnostic entity: An analysis of data from the Yale Bereavement Study. *World Psychiatry, 15*, 266–275.

MacInnis, C. C., & Hodson, G. (2015). Do American states with more religious or conservative populations search more for sexual content on Google? *Archives of Sexual Behavior, 44*, 137–147.

Mack, A., & Rock, I. (2000). *Inattentional blindness.* MIT Press.

MacKay, D. M. (1978). Selves and brains. *Neuroscience, 3*, 599–606.

Mackenzie, J. L., Aggen, S. H., Kirkpatrick, R. M., Kendler, K. S., & Amstadter, A. B. (2015). A longitudinal twin study of insomnia symptoms in adults. *Sleep, 38*, 1423–1430.

MacKenzie, M. J., Nicklas, E., Waldfogel, J., & Brooks-Gunn, J. (2013). Spanking and child development across the first decade of life. *Pediatrics, 132*, e1118–1125.

MacKerron, G., & Mourato, S. (2013). Happiness is greater in natural environments. *Global Environmental Change, 23*, 992–1000.

Mackey, S., Allgaier, N., Chaarani, B., Spechler, P., Orr, C., Bunn, J., Allen, N. B., Alia-Klein, N., Batalla, A., Blaine, S., Brooks, S., Caparelli, E., Chye, Y. Y., Cousijn, J., Dagher, A., Desrivieres, S., Feldstein-Ewing, S., Foxe, J. J., Goldstein, R. Z., . . . ENIGMA Addiction Working Group. (2019). Mega-analysis of gray matter volume in substance dependence: General and substance-specific regional effects. *The American Journal of Psychiatry, 176*, 119–128.

MacLeod, C., & Clarke, P. J. F. (2015). The attentional bias modification approach to anxiety intervention. *Clinical Psychological Science, 3*, 58–78.

MacLeod, C. M., & Bodner, G. E. (2017). The production effect in memory. *Current Directions in Psychological Science, 26*, 390–395.

Macmillan, M., & Lena, M. L. (2010). Rehabilitating Phineas Gage. *Neuropsychological Rehabilitation, 17*, 1–18.

Macnamara, B. N., Hambrick, D. Z., & Oswald, F. L. (2014). Deliberate practice and performance in music, games, sports, education, and professions: A meta-analysis. *Psychological Science, 25*, 1608–1618.

Macnamara, B. N., Moreau, D., & Hambrick, D. Z. (2016). The relationship between deliberate practice and performance in sports: A meta-analysis. *Perspectives on Psychological Science, 11*, 333–350.

MacNeilage, P. F., & Davis, B. L. (2000). On the origin of internal structure of word forms. *Science, 288*, 527–531.

MacNeilage, P. F., Rogers, L. J., & Vallortigara, G. (2009, July). Origins of the left and right brain. *Scientific American*, pp. 60–67.

MacPherson, S. E., Turner, M. S., Bozzali, M., Cipolotti, L., & Shallice, T. (2016). The Doors and People Test: The effect of frontal lobe lesions on recall and recognition memory performance. *Neuropsychology, 30*, 332–337.

Maddieson, I. (1984). *Patterns of sounds.* Cambridge University Press.

Madigan, S., Cyr, C., Eirich, R., Fearon, R. P., Ly, A., Rash, C., Poole, J. C., & Alink, L. R. (2019). Testing the cycle of maltreatment hypothesis: Meta-analytic evidence of the intergenerational transmission of child maltreatment. *Development and Psychopathology, 31*, 23–51.

Madison, G., Mosling, M. A., Verweij, K. J. H., Pedersen, N. L., & Ullen, F. (2016). Common genetic influences

on intelligence and auditory simple reaction time in a large Swedish sample. *Intelligence, 59*, 157–162.

Madrid-Valero, J. J., Ordoñana, J. R., Klump, K. L., & Burt, S. A. (2019). Children sleep and antisocial behavior: Differential association of sleep with aggression and rule-breaking. *Journal of Abnormal Child Psychology, 47*, 791–799.

Maes, H. H. M., Neale, M. C., & Eaves, L. J. (1997). Genetic and environmental factors in relative body weight and human adiposity. *Behavior Genetics, 27*, 325–351.

Maes, H. H., Neale, M. C., Ohlsson, H., Zahery, M., Lichtenstein, P., Sundquist, K., Sundquist, J., & Kendler, K. S. (2016). A bivariate genetic analysis of drug abuse ascertained through medical and criminal registries in Swedish twins, siblings and half-siblings. *Behavior Genetics, 46*, 735–741.

Maestripieri, D. (2003). Similarities in affiliation and aggression between cross-fostered rhesus macaque females and their biological mothers. *Developmental Psychobiology, 43*, 321–327.

Maestripieri, D. (2005). Early experience affects the intergenerational transmission of infant abuse in rhesus monkeys. *PNAS, 102*, 9726–9729.

Magill, M., Ray, L., Kiluk, B., Hoadley, A., Bernstein, M., Tonigan, J. S., & Carroll, K. (2019). A meta-analysis of cognitive-behavioral therapy for alcohol or other drug use disorders: Treatment efficacy by contrast condition. *Journal of Consulting and Clinical Psychology, 87*, 1093–1105.

Magnuson, K. A., Ruhm, C., & Waldfogel, J. (2007). Does prekindergarten improve school preparation and performance? *Economics of Education Review, 26*, 33–51.

Magnussen, S., Andersson, J., Cornoldi, C., De Beni, R., Endestad, T., Goodman, G. S., Helstrup, T., Koriat, A., Larsson, M., Melinder, A., Nilsson, L. G., Rönnberg, J., & Zimmer, H. (2006). What people believe about memory. *Memory, 4*, 595–613.

Magnusson, D. (1990). Personality research—challenges for the future. *European Journal of Personality, 4*, 1–17.

Maguire, E. A., Gadian, D. G., Johnsrude, I. S., Good, C. D., Ashburner, J., Frackowiak, R. S. J., & Frith, C. D. (2000). Navigation-related structural change in the hippocampi of taxi drivers. *PNAS, 97*, 4398–4403.

Maguire, E. A., Spiers, H. J., Good, C. D., Hartley, T., Frackowiak, R. S. J., & Burgess, N. (2003a). Navigation expertise and the human hippocampus: A structural brain imaging analysis. *Hippocampus, 13*, 250–259.

Maguire, E. A., Valentine, E. R., Wilding, J. M., & Kapur, N. (2003b). Routes to remembering: The brains behind superior memory. *Nature Neuroscience, 6*, 90–95.

Maguire, E. A., Woollett, & Spiers, H. J. (2006). London taxi drivers and bus drivers: A structural MRI and neuropsychological analysis. *Hippocampus, 16*, 1091–1101.

Mah, C. D., Mah, K. E., Kezirian, E. J., & Dement, W. C. (2011). The effects of sleep extension on the athletic performance of collegiate basketball players. *Sleep, 34*, 943–950.

Mahadevan, N., Gregg, A. P., & Sedikides, C. (2019). Is self-regard a sociometer or a hierometer? Self-esteem tracks status and inclusion, narcissism tracks status. *Journal of Personality and Social Psychology, 116*, 444.

Maharani, A., Dawes, P., Nazroo, J., Tampubolon, G., & Pendleton, N. (2018). Longitudinal relationship between hearing aid use and cognitive function in older Americans. *Journal of the American Geriatrics Society, 66*, 1130–1136.

Maher, S., Ekstrom, T., & Chen, Y. (2014). Greater perceptual sensitivity to happy facial expression. *Perception, 43*, 1353–1364.

Mai, Q. D., Hill, T. D., Vila-Henninger, L., & Grandner, M. A. (2019). Employment insecurity and sleep disturbance: Evidence from 31 European countries. *Journal of Sleep Research, 28*, e12763.

Maia, T. V., & Frank, M. J. (2017). An integrative perspective on the role of dopamine in schizophrenia. *Biological Psychiatry, 81*, 52–66.

Maier, M., & Abdel Rahman, R. (2018). Native language promotes access to visual consciousness. *Psychological Science, 29*, 1757–1772.

Maier, S. F., & Seligman, M. E. P. (2016). Learned helplessness at fifty: Insights from neuroscience. *Psychological Review, 123*, 349–367.

Maier, S. F., Watkins, L. R., & Fleshner, M. (1994). Psychoneuroimmunology: The interface between behavior, brain, and immunity. *American Psychologist, 49*, 1004–1017.

Maiti, S., Kumar, K. H. B. G., Castellini, C. A., O'Reilly, R., & Singh, S. M. (2011). Ontonogenetic de novo copy number variations (CNVs) as a source of genetic individuality: Studies on two families with MZD twins for schizophrenia. *PLOS ONE, 6*, e17125.

Major, B., Carrington, P. I., & Carnevale, P. J. D. (1984). Physical attractiveness and self-esteem: Attribution for praise from an other-sex evaluator. *Personality and Social Psychology Bulletin, 10*, 43–50.

Major, B., Schmidlin, A. M., & Williams, L. (1990). Gender patterns in social touch: The impact of setting and age. *Journal of Personality and Social Psychology, 58*, 634–643.

Makel, M. C., Kell, H. J., Lubinski, D., Putallaz, M., & Benbow, C. P. (2016). When lightning strikes twice: Profoundly gifted, profoundly accomplished. *Psychological Science, 27*, 1004–1018.

Malaktaris, A. L., & Lynn, S. J. (2019). The phenomenology and correlates of flashbacks in individuals with posttraumatic stress symptoms. *Clinical Psychological Science, 7*, 249–264.

Malamuth, N. (2018). "Adding fuel to the fire"? Does exposure to non-consenting adult or to child pornography increase risk of sexual aggression? *Aggression and Violent Behavior, 41*, 74–89.

Malani, P., Singer, D., Clark, S., Kirch, M., & Solway, E. (2018, May). *Let's talk about sex.* National poll on healthy aging. University of Michigan. https://www.healthyagingpoll.org/report/lets-talk-about-sex

Maldonado-Molina, M. M., Reingle, J. M., Jennings, W. G., & Prado, G. (2011). Drinking and driving among immigrant and US-born Hispanic young adults: Results from a longitudinal and nationally representative study. *Addictive Behaviors, 36*, 381–388.

Malkiel, B. G. (2016). *A random walk down Wall Street: The time-tested strategy for successful investing* (11th Ed.). Norton.

Malle, B. F. (2006). The actor–observer asymmetry in attribution: A (surprising) meta-analysis. *Psychological Bulletin, 132*, 895–919.

Malle, B. F., Knobe, J. M., & Nelson, S. E. (2007). Actor–observe asymmetries in explanations of behavior: New answers to an old question. *Journal of Personality and Social Psychology, 93*, 491–514.

Malmquist, C. P. (1986). Children who witness parental murder: Post-traumatic aspects. *Journal of the American Academy of Child Psychiatry, 25*, 320–325.

Malouff, J. M., & Schutte, N. S. (2017). Can psychological interventions increase optimism? A meta-analysis. *The Journal of Positive Psychology, 12*, 594–604.

Maltby, N., Tolin, D. F., Worhunsky, P., O'Keefe, T. M., & Kiehl, K. A. (2005). Dysfunctional action monitoring hyperactivates frontal-striatal circuits in obsessive-compulsive disorder: An event-related fMRI study. *NeuroImage, 24*, 495–503.

Mampe, B., Friederici, A. D., Christophe, A., & Wermke, K. (2009). Newborns' cry melody is shaped by their native language. *Current Biology, 19,* 1–4.

Mandelli, L., Arminio, A., Atti, A. R., & De Ronchi, D. (2019). Suicide attempts in eating disorder subtypes: a meta-analysis of the literature employing DSM-IV, DSM-5, or ICD-10 diagnostic criteria. *Psychological Medicine, 49,* 1237–1249.

Mandsager, K., Harb, S., Cremer, P., Phelan, D., Nissen, S. E., & Jaber, W. (2018). Association of cardiorespiratory fitness with long-term mortality among adults undergoing exercise treadmill testing. *JAMA Network Open, 1,* e183605–e183605.

Maner, J. K., DeWall, C. N, Baumeister, R. F., & Schaller, M. (2007). Does social exclusion motivate interpersonal reconnection? Resolving the "porcupine problem." *Journal of Personality and Social Psychology, 92,* 42–55.

Maner, J. K., Kenrick, D. T., Neuberg, S. L., Becker, D. V., Robertson, T., Hofer, B., Neuberg, S. L., Delton, A. W., Butner, J., & Schaller, M. (2005). Functional projection: How fundamental social motives can bias interpersonal perception. *Journal of Personality and Social Psychology, 88,* 63–78.

Mangelsdorf, J., Eid, M., & Luhmann, M. (2019). Does growth require suffering? A systematic review and meta-analysis on genuine posttraumatic and postecstatic growth. *Psychological Bulletin, 145,* 302–338.

Mani, A., Mullainathan, S., Shafir, E., & Zhao, J. (2013). Poverty impedes cognitive function. *Science, 341,* 976–980.

Mann, T., Tomiyama, A. J., & Ward, A. (2015). Promoting public health in the context of the "obesity epidemic": False starts and promising new directions. *Perspectives on Psychological Science, 10,* 706–710.

Manning, W., & Cohen, J. A. (2012). Premarital cohabitation and marital dissolution: An examination of recent marriages. *Journal of Marriage and Family 74,* 377–387.

Manson, J. E. (2002). Walking compared with vigorous exercise for the prevention of cardiovascular events in women. *New England Journal of Medicine, 347,* 716–725.

Manuck, S. B., & McCaffery, J. M. (2014). Gene-environment interaction. *Annual Review of Psychology, 65,* 41–70.

Maquet, P. (2001). The role of sleep in learning and memory. *Science, 294,* 1048–1052.

Maquet, P., Peters, J.-M., Aerts, J., Delfiore, G., Degueldre, C., Luxen, A., & Franck, G. (1996). Functional neuroanatomy of human rapid-eye-movement sleep and dreaming. *Nature, 383,* 163–166.

Mar, R. A., & Oatley, K. (2008). The function of fiction is the abstraction and simulation of social experience. *Perspectives on Psychological Science, 3,* 173–192.

Mar, R. A., Oatley, K., & Peterson, J. B. (2009). Exploring the link between reading fiction and empathy: Ruling out individual differences and examining outcomes. *Communications: The European Journal of Communication, 34,* 407–428.

Marangolo, P., Fiori, V., Sabatini, U., De Pasquale, G., Razzano, C., Caltagirone, C., & Gili, T. (2016). Bilateral transcranial direct current stimulation language treatment enhances functional connectivity in the left hemisphere: Preliminary data from aphasia. *Journal of Cognitive Neuroscience, 28,* 724–738.

Marceau, K., McMaster, M. T. B., Smith, T. F., Daams, J. G., van Beijsterveldt, C. E. M., Boomsma, D. I., & Knopik, V. S. (2016). The prenatal environment in twin studies: A review on chorionicity. *Behavior Genetics, 46,* 286–303.

Marcinkowska, U. M., Kaminski, G., Little, A. C., & Jasienska, G. (2018). Average ovarian hormone levels, rather than daily values and their fluctuations, are related to facial preferences among women. *Hormones and Behavior, 102,* 114–119.

Mariani, J., Simonini, M. V., Palejev, D., Tomasini, L., Coppola, G., Szekely, A. M., Horvath, T. L., & Vaccarino, F. M. (2012). Modeling human cortical development in vitro using induced pluripotent stem cells. *PNAS, 109,* 12779–12775.

Marinak, B. A., & Gambrell, L. B. (2008). Intrinsic motivation and rewards: What sustains young children's engagement with text? *Literacy Research and Instruction, 47,* 9–26.

Marjonen, H., Sierra, A., Nyman, A., Rogojin, V., Gröhn, O., Linden, A.-M., Hautaniemi, S., & Kaminen-Ahola, N. (2015). Early maternal alcohol consumption alters hippocampal DNA methylation, gene expression and volume in a mouse model. *PLOS ONE, 10,* e0124931.

Markey, P. M., & Ferguson, C. J. (2017). Moral combat: Why the war on violent video games is wrong. BenBella Books.

Marks, A. K., Patton, F., & Coll, C. G. (2011). Being bicultural: A mixed-methods study of adolescents' implicitly and explicitly measured multiethnic identities. *Developmental Psychology, 47,* 270–288.

Marks, E. H., Franklin, A. R., & Zoellner, L. A. (2018). Can't get it out of my mind: A systematic review of predictors of intrusive memories of distressing events. *Psychological Bulletin, 144,* 584–640.

Markus, G. B. (1986). Stability and change in political attitudes: Observe, recall, and "explain." *Political Behavior, 8,* 21–44.

Markus, H. R., & Kitayama, S. (1991). Culture and the self: Implications for cognition, emotion, and motivation. *Psychological Review, 98,* 224–253.

Markus, H. R., & Nurius, P. (1986). Possible selves. *American Psychologist, 41,* 954–969.

Markus, H. R., Uchida, Y., Omoregie, H., Townsend, S. S. M., & Kitayama, S. (2006). Going for the gold: Models of agency in Japanese and American contexts. *Psychological Science, 17,* 103–112.

Marmot, M. G., Bosma, H., Hemingway, H., Brunner, E., & Stansfeld, S. (1997). Contribution to job control and other risk factors to social variations in coronary heart disease incidents. *The Lancet, 350,* 235–239.

Marsh, A. A., Rhoads, S. A., & Ryan, R. M. (2019). A multi-semester classroom demonstration yields evidence in support of the facial feedback effect. *Emotion, 19(8),* 1500–1504.

Marsh, H. W., & Craven, R. G. (2006). Reciprocal effects of self-concept and performance from a multidimensional perspective: Beyond seductive pleasure and unidimensional perspectives. *Perspectives on Psychological Science, 1,* 133–163.

Marsh, H. W., & Parker, J. W. (1984). Determinants of student self-concept: Is it better to be a relatively large fish in a small pond even if you don't learn to swim as well? *Journal of Personality and Social Psychology, 47,* 213–231.

Marshall, M. J. (2002). Why spanking doesn't work. Bonneville Books.

Marshall, P. J., & Meltzoff, A. N. (2014). Neural mirroring mechanisms and imitation in human infants. *Philosophical Transactions of the Royal Society: Series B, 369.*

Martel, M. M., Levinson, C. A., Langer, J. K., & Nigg, J. T. (2016). A network analysis of developmental change in ADHD symptom structure from pre-school to adulthood. *Clinical Psychological Science, 4,* 988–1001.

Martela, F., & Steger, M. F. (2016). The three meanings of meaning in life: Distinguishing coherence, purpose, and significance. *The Journal of Positive Psychology, 11,* 531–545.

Martin, C. K., Anton, S. D., Walden, H., Arnett, C., Greenway, F. L., & Williamson, D. A. (2007). Slower eating rate reduces the food intake of men, but not women: Implications for behavioural weight control. *Behaviour Research and Therapy, 45,* 2349–2359.

Martin, C. L., & Ruble, D. (2004). Children's search for gender cues. *Current Directions in Psychological Science, 13,* 67–70.

Martin, C. L., Ruble, D. N., & Szkrybalo, J. (2002). Cognitive theories of early gender development. *Psychological Bulletin, 128,* 903–933.

Martín, R., Bajo-Grañeras, R., Moratalla, R., Perea, G., & Araque, A. (2015). Circuit-specific signaling in astrocyte-neuron networks in basal ganglia pathways. *Science, 349,* 730–734.

Martin, S. J., Kelly, I. W., & Saklofske, D. H. (1992). Suicide and lunar cycles: A critical review over 28 years. *Psychological Reports, 71,* 787–795.

Martín-María, N., Miret, M., Caballero, F. F., Rico-Uribe, L., Steptoe, A., Chatterji, S., & Ayuso-Mateos, J. (2017). The impact of subjective well-being on mortality: A meta-analysis of longitudinal studies in the general population. *Psychosomatic Medicine, 79,* 565–575.

Martínez-Rivera, F. J., Martínez, N. A., Martínez, M., Ayala-Pagán, R. N., Silva, W. I., & Barreto-Estrada, J. L. (2019). Neuroplasticity transcript profile of the ventral striatum in the extinction of opioid-induced conditioned place preference. *Neurobiology of Learning and Memory, 163,* 107031.

Martini, M., Bufalari, I., Stazi, M. A., & Aglioti, S. M. (2015). Is that me or my twin? Lack of self-face recognition advantage in identical twins. *PLOS ONE, 10,* e0120900.

Martins, N., & Weaver, A. (2019). The role of media exposure on relational aggression: A meta-analysis. *Aggression and Violent Behavior, 47,* 90–99.

Martins, Y., Preti, G., Crabtree, C. R., & Wysocki, C. J. (2005). Preference for human body odors is influenced by gender and sexual orientation. *Psychological Science, 16,* 694–701.

Marty-Dugas, J., Ralph, B. C. W., Oakman, J. M., & Smilek, D. (2018). The relation between smartphone use and everyday inattention. *Psychology of Consciousness: Theory, Research, and Practice, 5,* 46–62.

Marzoli, D., Custodero, M., Pagliara, A., & Tommasi, L. (2013). Sun-induced frowning fosters aggressive feelings. *Cognition and Emotion, 27,* 1513–1521.

Mashour, G. A. (2018). The controversial correlates of consciousness. *Science, 360,* 493–494.

Maslow, A. H. (1970). *Motivation and personality* (2nd ed.). Harper & Row.

Maslow, A. H. (1971). *The farther reaches of human nature.* Viking Press.

Mason, A. E., Sbarra, D. A., & Mehl, M. R. (2010). Thin-slicing divorce: Thirty seconds of information predict changes in psychological adjustment over 90 days. *Psychological Science, 21,* 1420–1422.

Mason, C., & Kandel, E. R. (1991). Central visual pathways. In E. R. Kandel, J. H. Schwartz, & T. M. Jessell (Eds.), *Principles of neural science* (3rd ed.). Elsevier.

Mason, M. F., & Morris, M. W. (2010). Culture, attribution and automaticity: A social cognitive neuroscience view. *Social Cognitive and Affective Neuroscience, 5,* 292–306.

Mason, R. A., & Just, M. A. (2004). How the brain processes causal inferences in text. *Psychological Science, 15,* 1–7.

Mason, R. A., & Just, M. A. (2016). Neural representations of physics concepts. *Psychological Science, 27,* 904–913.

Massimini, M., Ferrarelli, F., Huber, R., Esser, S. K., Singh, H., & Tononi, G. (2005). Breakdown of cortical effective connectivity during sleep. *Science, 309,* 2228–2232.

Masten, A. S. (2001). Ordinary magic: Resilience processes in development. *American Psychologist, 56*, 227–238.

Masters, K. S. (2010). The role of religion in therapy: Time for psychologists to have a little faith? *Cognitive and Behavioral Practice, 17*, 393–400.

Masters, K. S., & Hooker, S. A. (2013). Religiousness/spirituality, cardiovascular disease, and cancer: Cultural integration for health research and intervention. *Journal of Consulting and Clinical Psychology, 81*, 206–216.

Masters, W. H., & Johnson, V. E. (1966). *Human sexual response.* Little, Brown.

Mastroianni, G. R. (2015). Obedience in perspective: Psychology and the Holocaust. *Theory and Psychology, 25*, 657–669.

Mastroianni, G. R., & Reed, G. (2006). Apples, barrels, and Abu Ghraib. *Sociological Focus, 39*, 239–250.

Masuda, T., Ellsworth, P. C., Mesquita, B., Leu, J., Tanida, S., & Van de Veerdonk, E. (2008). Placing the face in context: Cultural differences in the perception of facial emotion. *Journal of Personality and Social Psychology, 94*, 365–381.

Mata, A., Ferreira, M. B., & Sherman, S. J. (2013). The metacognitive advantage of deliberative thinkers: A dual-process perspective on overconfidence. *Journal of Personality and Social Psychology, 105*, 353–373.

Mata, R., Josef, A. K., & Hertwig, R. (2016). Propensity for risk taking across the life span and around the globe. *Psychological Science, 27*, 231–243.

Mataix-Cols, D., Rosario-Campos, M. C., & Leckman, J. F. (2005). A multidimensional model of obsessive-compulsive disorder. *American Journal of Psychiatry, 162*, 228–238.

Mataix-Cols, D., Wooderson, S., Lawrence, N., Brammer, M. J., Speckens, A., & Phillips, M. L. (2004). Distinct neural correlates of washing, checking, and hoarding symptom dimensions in obsessive-compulsive disorder. *Archives of General Psychiatry, 61*, 564–576.

Mather, M. (2016). The affective neuroscience of aging. *Annual Review of Psychology, 67*, 213–238.

Mather, M., & Sutherland, M. (2012, February). *The selective effects of emotional arousal on memory.* APA Science Brief. https://www.apa.org/science/about/psa/2012/02/emotional-arousal

Mather, M., Cacioppo, J. T., & Kanwisher, N. (2013). How fMRI can inform cognitive theories. *Perspectives on Psychological Science, 8*, 108–113.

Mather, M., Canli, T., English, T., Whitfield, S., Wais, P., Ochsner, K., Gabrieli, J. D., & Carstensen, L. L. (2004). Amygdala responses to emotionally valenced stimuli in older and younger adults. *Psychological Science, 15*, 259–263.

Mathur, M. B., & VanderWeele, T. J. (2019). Finding common ground in meta-analysis "wars" on violent video games. *Perspectives on Psychological Science, 14*, 705–708.

Matoba, N., Akiyama, M., Ishigaki, K., Kanai, M., Takahashi, A., Momozawa, Y., Ikegawa, S., Ikeda, M., Iwata, N., Hirata, M., Matsuda, K., Kubo, M., Okada, Y., & Kamatani, Y. (2019). GWAS of smoking behaviour in 165,436 Japanese people reveals seven new loci and shared genetic architecture. *Nature Human Behaviour, 3*, 471–477.

Matson, J. L., & Boisjoli, J. A. (2009). The token economy for children with intellectual disability and/or autism: A review. *Research on Developmental Disabilities, 30*, 240–248.

Matsumoto, D. (1994). *People: Psychology from a cultural perspective.* Brooks/Cole.

Matsumoto, D., & Ekman, P. (1989). American-Japanese cultural differences in intensity ratings of facial expressions of emotion. *Motivation and Emotion, 13*, 143–157.

Matsumoto, D., Frank, M. G., & Hwang, H. C. (2015). The role of intergroup emotions on political violence. *Current Directions in Psychological Science, 24*, 369–373.

Matsumoto, D., & Willingham, B. (2006). The thrill of victory and the agony of defeat: Spontaneous expressions of medal winners of the 2004 Athens Olympic Games. *Journal of Personality and Social Psychology, 91*, 568–581.

Matsumoto, D., & Willingham, B. (2009). Spontaneous facial expressions of emotion of congenitally and noncongenitally blind individuals. *Journal of Personality and Social Psychology, 96*, 1–10.

Matsumoto, D., Willingham, B., & Olide, A. (2009). Sequential dynamics of culturally moderated facial expressions of emotion. *Psychological Science, 20*, 1269–1275.

Mattanah, J. F., Lopez, F. G, & Govern, J. M. (2011). The contributions of parental attachment bonds to college student development and adjustment: A meta-analytic review. *Journal of Counseling Psychology, 58*, 565–596.

Mattheisen, M., Samuels, J. F., Wang, Y., Greenberg, B. D., Fyer, A. J., McCracken, J. T., Geller, D. A., Murphy, D. L., Knowles, J. A., Grados, M. A., Riddle, M. A., Rasmussen, S. A., McLaughlin, N. C., Nurmi, E. L., Askland, K. D., Qin, H.-D., Cullen, B. A., Piacentini, J., Pauls, D. L., . . . Nestadt, G. (2015). Genome-wide association study in obsessive-compulsive disorder: Results from OCGAS. *Molecular Psychiatry, 20*, 337–344.

Matthews, N. L., & Goldberg, W. A. (2018). Theory of mind in children with and without autism spectrum disorder: Associations with the sibling constellation. *Autism, 22*, 311–321.

Matthews, R. N., Domjan, M., Ramsey, M., & Crews, D. (2007). Learning effects on sperm competition and reproductive fitness. *Psychological Science, 18*, 758–762.

Matz, S. C., Kosinski, M., Nave, G., & Stillwell, D. J. (2017). Psychological targeting as an effective approach to digital mass persuasion. *PNAS, 114*, 12714–12719.

Maurer, D., & Maurer, C. (1988). *The world of the newborn.* New York: Basic Books.

Mautz, B., Wong, B., Peters, R., & Jennions, M. (2013). Penis size interacts with body shape and height to influence male attractiveness. *PNAS, 110*, 6925–6693.

May, C., & Hasher, L. (1998). Synchrony effects in inhibitory control over thought and action. *Journal of Experimental Psychology: Human Perception and Performance, 24*, 363–380.

May, P. A., Chambers, C. D., Kalberg, W. O., Zellner, J., Feldman, H., Buckley, D., Kopald, D., Hasken, J. M., Xu, R., Honerkamp-Smith, G., Taras, H., Manning, M. A., Robinson, L. K., Adam, M. P., Abdul-Rahman, M. D., Vaux, K., Jewett, T., Elliott, A. J., Kable, J. A., . . . Hoyme, E. (2018). Prevalence of fetal alcohol spectrum disorders in 4 US communities. *JAMA, 319*, 474–482.

May, R. (1982). The problem of evil: An open letter to Carl Rogers. *Journal of Humanistic Psychology, 22*, 10–21.

Mayer, J. D., Caruso, D. R., & Salovey, P. (2016). The ability model of emotional intelligence: Principles and updates. *Emotion Review, 8*, 290–300.

Mayer, J. D., Salovey, P., & Caruso, D. R. (2002). *The Mayer-Salovey-Caruso emotional intelligence test (MSCEIT).* Multi-Health Systems, Inc.

Mayer, J. D., Salovey, P., & Caruso, D. R. (2012). The validity of the MSCEIT: Additional analyses and evidence. *Emotion Review, 4*, 403–408.

Mazei, J., Hüffmeier, J., Freund, P. A., Stuhlmacher, A. F., Bilke, L., & Hertel, G. (2015). A meta-analysis on gender differences in negotiation outcomes and their moderators. *Psychological Bulletin, 141*, 85–104.

Mazure, C., Keita, G., & Blehar, M. (2002). *Summit on women and depression: Proceedings and recommendations.* American Psychological Association.

Mazza, S., Gerbier, E., Gustin, M. P., Kasikci, Z., Koenig, O., Toppino, T. C., & Magnin, M. (2016). Relearn faster and retain longer: Along with practice, sleep makes perfect. *Psychological Science, 27*, 1321–1330.

Mazzei, P. (2019, March 24). After 2 apparent student suicides, Parkland grieves again. *The New York Times.* https://www.nytimes.com/2019/03/24/us/parkland-suicide-marjory-stoneman-douglas.html?

Mazzoni, G., Clark, A., De Bartolo, A., Guerrini, C., Nahouli, Z., Duzzi, D., De Marco, M., McGeown, W., & Venneri, A. (2019). Brain activation in highly superior autobiographical memory: The role of the precuneus in the autobiographical memory retrieval network. *Cortex, 120*, 588–602.

Mazzoni, G., Scoboria, A., & Harvey, L. (2010). Nonbelieved memories. *Psychological Science, 21*, 1334–1340.

Mazzoni, G., & Vannucci, M. (2007). Hindsight bias, the misinformation effect, and false autobiographical memories. *Social Cognition, 25*, 203–220.

McAdams, D. P., & Guo, J. (2015). Narrating the generative life. *Psychological Science, 26*, 475–483.

McBurney, D. H. (1996). *How to think like a psychologist: Critical thinking in psychology.* Prentice-Hall.

McBurney, D. H., & Collings, V. B. (1984). *Introduction to sensation and perception* (2nd ed.). Prentice-Hall.

McBurney, D. H., & Gent, J. F. (1979). On the nature of taste qualities. *Psychological Bulletin, 86*, 151–167.

McCabe, K. O., & Fleeson, W. (2016). Are traits useful? Explaining trait manifestations as tools in the pursuit of goals. *Journal of Personality and Social Psychology, 110*, 287–301.

McCain, J. (2017, February 18). McCain attacks Trump administration and inability to "separate truth from lies." *The Guardian.* https://www.theguardian.com/us-news/2017/feb/18/john-mccain-savages-donald-trump-administration-inability-separate-truth-from-lies

McCall, W. V., Lisanby, S. H., Rosenquist, P. B., Dooley, M., Husain, M. M., Knapp, R. G., Petrides, G., Rudorfer, M. V., Young, R. C., McClintock, S. M., Mueller, M., Prudic, J., Greenberg, R. M., Weiner, R. D., Bailine, S. H., Riley, M. A., McCloud, L., Kellner, C. H., & CORE/PRIDE Work Group. (2017). Effects of a right unilateral ultrabrief pulse electroconvulsive therapy course on health related quality of life in elderly depressed patients. *Journal of Affective Disorders, 209*, 39–45.

McCann, I. L., & Holmes, D. S. (1984). Influence of aerobic exercise on depression. *Journal of Personality and Social Psychology, 46*, 1142–1147.

McCann, U. D., Eligulashvili, V., & Ricaurte, G. A. (2001). (+–)3,4–Methylenedioxymethamphetamine ('Ecstasy')-induced serotonin neurotoxicity: Clinical studies. *Neuropsychobiology, 42*, 11–16.

McCarthy, J. (2017, June 28). *Americans more positive about effects of immigration.* Gallup. https://news.gallup.com/poll/213146/americans-positive-effects-immigration.aspx

McCarthy, J. (2018, October 22). *Two in three Americans now support legalizing marijuana.* Gallup News. https://news.gallup.com/poll/243908/two-three-americans-support-legalizing-marijuana.aspx

McCarthy, J. (2019, May 22). *U.S. support for same-sex marriage stable, at 63%.* Gallup. https://news.gallup.com/poll/257705/support-gay-marriage-stable.aspx

McCarthy, P. (1986, July). Scent: The tie that binds? *Psychology Today*, pp. 6, 10.

McCauley, C. R. (2002). Psychological issues in understanding terrorism and the response to terrorism. In C. E. Stout (Ed.), *The psychology of terrorism* (Vol. 3, pp. 3–29). Praeger/Greenwood.

McCauley, C. R., & Segal, M. E. (1987). Social psychology of terrorist groups. In C. Hendrick (Ed.), *Group processes and intergroup relations: Review of personality and social psychology* (Vol. 9, pp. 231–256). Sage.

McCauley, E., Berk, M. S., Asarnow, J. R., Adrian, M., Cohen, J., Korslund, K., Avina, C., Hughes, J., Harned, M, Gallop, R., & Linehan, M. M. (2018). Efficacy of dialectical behavior therapy for adolescents at high risk for suicide: A randomized clinical trial. *JAMA Psychiatry, 75,* 777–785.

McClendon, B. T., & Prentice-Dunn, S. (2001). Reducing skin cancer risk: An intervention based on protection motivation theory. *Journal of Health Psychology, 6,* 321–328.

McClintock, M. K., & Herdt, G. (1996, December). Rethinking puberty: The development of sexual attraction. *Current Directions in Psychological Science, 5,* 178–183.

McClung, M., & Collins, D. (2007). "Because I know it will!": Placebo effects of an ergogenic aid on athletic performance. *Journal of Sport & Exercise Psychology, 29,* 382–394.

McClure, E. B. (2000). A meta-analytic review of sex differences in facial expression processing and their development in infants, children, and adolescents. *Psychological Bulletin, 126,* 424–453.

McClure, M. J., & Lydon, J. E. (2014). Anxiety doesn't become you: How attachment compromises relational opportunities. *Journal of Personality and Social Psychology, 106,* 89–111.

McConnell, A. R., Brown, C. M., Shoda, T. M., Stayton, L. E., & Martin, C. E. (2011). Friends with benefits: On the positive consequences of pet ownership. *Journal of Personality and Social Psychology, 101,* 1239–1252.

McCord, J. (1978). A thirty-year follow-up on treatment effects. *American Psychologist, 33,* 284–289.

McCord, J. (1979). Following up on Cambridge-Somerville. *American Psychologist, 34,* 727.

McCrae, R. R., & Costa, P. T., Jr. (1986). Clinical assessment can benefit from recent advances in personality psychology. *American Psychologist, 41,* 1001–1003.

McCrae, R. R., & Costa, P. T., Jr. (1990). *Personality in adulthood.* Guilford.

McCrae, R. R., & Costa, P. T., Jr. (1994). The stability of personality: Observations and evaluations. *Current Directions in Psychological Science, 3,* 173–175.

McCrae, R. R., & Costa, P. T., Jr. (2008). The Five-Factor Theory of personality. In O. P. John, R. W., Robins, & L. A. Pervin (Eds.), *Handbook of personality: Theory and research, 3rd edition.* Guilford.

McCrae, R. R., Terracciano, A., & 78 members of the Personality Profiles and Cultures Project. (2005). Universal features of personality traits from the observer's perspective: Data from 50 cultures. *Journal of Personality and Social Psychology, 88,* 547–561.

McCrink, K., & Wynn, K. (2004). Large-number addition and subtraction by 9-month-old infants. *Psychological Science, 15,* 776–781.

McCrory, E. J., De Brito, S. A., Sebastian, C. L., Mechelli, A., Bird, G., Kelly, P. A., & Viding, E. (2011). Heightened neural reactivity to threat in child victims of family violence. *Current Biology, 21,* R947–948.

McCullough, M. E., Hoyt, W. T., Larson, D. B., Koenig, H. G., & Thoresen, C. (2000). Religious involvement and mortality: A meta-analytic review. *Health Psychology, 19,* 211–222.

McCullough, M. E., & Laurenceau, J.-P. (2005). Religiousness and the trajectory of self-rated health across adulthood. *Personality and Social Psychology Bulletin, 31,* 560–573.

McCullough, M. E., & Willoughby, B. L. B. (2009). Religion, self-regulation, and self-control: Associations, explanations, and implications. *Psychological Bulletin, 135,* 69–93.

McDaniel, M. A., Bugg, J. M., Liu, Y., & Brick, J. (2015). When does the test-study-test sequence optimize learning and retention? *Journal of Experimental Psychology: Applied, 21,* 370–382.

McDaniel, M. A., Howard, D. C., & Einstein, G. O. (2009). The read-recite-review study strategy: Effective and portable. *Psychological Science, 20,* 516–522.

McDermott, R., Tingley, D., Cowden, J., Frazzetto, G., & Johnson, D. D. P. (2009). Monoamine oxidase A gene (MAOA) predicts behavioral aggression following provocation. *PNAS, 106,* 2118–2123.

McDonald, P. (2012). Workplace sexual harassment 30 years on: A review of the literature. *International Journal of Management Reviews, 14,* 1–17.

McDuff, D., Kodra, E., el Kallouby, R., & LaFrance, M. (2017). A large-scale analysis of sex differences in facial expressions. *PLOS ONE, 12,* e0173942.

McElwain, N. L., Ravindran, N., Emery, H. T., & Swartz, R. (2019). Theory of mind as a mechanism linking mother–toddler relationship quality and child–friend interaction during the preschool years. *Social Development, 28,* 998–1015.

McEvoy, S. P., Stevenson, M. R., McCartt, A. T., Woodward, M., Hawroth, C., Palamara, P., & Ceracelli, R. (2005). Role of mobile phones in motor vehicle crashes resulting in hospital attendance: A case-crossover study. *British Medical Journal, 33,* 428.

McEvoy, S. P., Stevenson, M. R., & Woodward, M. (2007). The contribution of passengers versus mobile phone use to motor vehicle crashes resulting in hospital attendance by the driver. *Accident Analysis and Prevention, 39,* 1170–1176.

McFarland, C., & Ross, M. (1987). The relation between current impressions and memories of self and dating partners. *Psychological Bulletin, 13,* 228–238.

McGaugh, J. L. (1994). Quoted by B. Bower, Stress hormones hike emotional memories. *Science News, 146,* 262.

McGaugh, J. L. (2003). *Memory and emotion: The making of lasting memories.* Columbia University Press.

McGaugh, J. L. (2015). Consolidating memories. *Annual Review of Psychology, 66,* 1–24.

McGaugh, J. L., & LePort, A. (2014). Remembrance of all things past. *Scientific American, 310,* 40–45.

McGeehan, P. (February 6, 2018). Failure to screen for sleep apnea led to two recent train crashes. *The New York Times.* https://www.nytimes.com/2018/02/06/nyregion/train-crash-sleep-apnea.html?

McGhee, P. E. (June, 1976). Children's appreciation of humor: A test of the cognitive congruency principle. *Child Development, 47,* 420–426.

McGrath, J. J., & Welham, J. L. (1999). Season of birth and schizophrenia: A systematic review and meta-analysis of data from the Southern hemisphere. *Schizophrenia Research, 35,* 237–242.

McGrath, J. J., Welham, J., & Pemberton, M. (1995). Month of birth, hemisphere of birth and schizophrenia. *British Journal of Psychiatry, 167,* 783–785.

McGrath, R. E. (2015). Character strengths in 75 nations: An update. *The Journal of Positive Psychology, 10,* 41–52.

McGue, M. (2010). The end of behavioral genetics? *Behavioral Genetics, 40,* 284–296.

McGue, M., & Bouchard, T. J., Jr. (1998). Genetic and environmental influences on human behavioral differences. *Annual Review of Neuroscience, 21,* 1–24.

McGue, M., Bouchard, T. J., Jr., Iacono, W. G., & Lykken, D. T. (1993). Behavioral genetics of cognitive ability: A life-span perspective. In R. Plomin &

G. E. McClearn (Eds.), *Nature, nurture and psychology.* American Psychological Association.

McGue, M., & Christensen, K. (2013). Growing old but not growing apart: Twin similarity in the latter half of the lifespan. *Behavior Genetics, 43,* 1–12.

McGurk, H., & MacDonald, J. (1976). Hearing lips and seeing voices. *Nature, 264,* 746–748.

McHugh, P. R. (1995). Resolved: Multiple personality disorder is an individually and socially created artifact. *Journal of the American Academy of Child and Adolescent Psychiatry, 34,* 957–959.

McIntosh, A. M., & Relton, C. (2018). Do depression and stressful events cause premature aging? *American Journal of Psychiatry, 175,* 714–715.

McKay, J. (2000). Building self-esteem in children. In M. McKay & P. Fanning (Eds.), *Self-esteem.* New Harbinger/St. Martins.

McKellar, J., Stewart, E., & Humphreys, K. (2003). Alcoholics Anonymous involvement and positive alcohol-related outcomes: Cause, consequence, or just a correlate? A prospective 2-year study of 2,319 alcohol-dependent men. *Journal of Consulting and Clinical Psychology, 71,* 302–308.

McKenna, K. Y. A., Green, A. S., & Gleason, M. E. J. (2002). What's the big attraction? Relationship formation on the internet. *Journal of Social Issues, 58,* 9–31.

McKinney, B. C. (2017). Epigenetic programming: A putative neurobiological mechanism linking childhood maltreatment and risk for adult psychopathology. *American Journal of Psychiatry, 174,* 1134–1136.

McKinnon, M. C., Palombo, D. J., Nazarov, A., Kumar, N., Khuu, W., & Levine, B. (2015). Threat of death and autobiographical memory: A study of passengers from flight AT236. *Clinical Psychological Science, 3,* 487–502.

McKone, E., Kanwisher, N., & Duchaine, B. C. (2007). Can generic expertise explain special processing for faces? *Trends in Cognitive Sciences, 11,* 8–15.

McLaughlin, K. A., Sheridan, M. A., Tibu, F., Fox, N. A., Zeanah, C. H., & Nelson, C. A. (2015). Causal effects of the early caregiving environment on development of stress response systems in children. *PNAS, 112,* 5637–5642.

McLaughlin, M. (2010, October 2). J. K. Rowling: Depression, the "terrible place that allowed me to come back stronger." *The Scotsman* (scotsman.com).

McLean, C. P., & Anderson, E. R. (2009). Brave men and timid women? A review of the gender differences in fear and anxiety. *Clinical Psychology Review, 29,* 496–505.

McManus, S., Gunnell, D., Cooper, C., Bebbington, P. E., Howard, L. M., Brugha, T., Jenkins, R., Hassiotis, A., Weich, S., & Appleby, L. (2019). Prevalence of non-suicidal self-harm and service contact in England, 2000–14: Repeated cross-sectional surveys of the general population. *The Lancet Psychiatry, 6,* 573–581.

McMurray, B. (2007). Defusing the childhood vocabulary explosion. *Science, 317,* 631.

McNally, R. J. (2003). *Remembering trauma.* Harvard University Press.

McNally, R. J. (2007). Betrayal trauma theory: A critical appraisal. *Memory, 15,* 280–294.

McNally, R. J. (2012). Are we winning the war against posttraumatic stress disorder? *Science, 336,* 872–874.

McNally, R. J., & Geraerts, E. (2009). A new solution to the recovered memory debate. *Perspectives on Psychological Science, 4,* 126–134.

McNeil, J., Ellis, S. J., & Eccles, F. J. R. (2017). Suicide in trans populations: A systematic review of prevalence and correlates. *Psychology of Sexual Orientation and Gender Diversity, 4,* 341–353.

McNulty, J. K., Olson, M. A., Jones, R. E., & Acosta, L. M. (2017). Automatic associations between one's partner and one's affect as the proximal mechanism of change in relationship satisfaction: Evidence from evaluative conditioning. *Psychological Science, 28*, 1031–1040.

Meador, B. D., & Rogers, C. R. (1984). Person-centered therapy. In R. J. Corsini (Ed.), *Current psychotherapies* (3rd ed.). Peacock.

Mednick, S. A., Huttunen, M. O., & Machon, R. A. (1994). Prenatal influenza infections and adult schizophrenia. *Schizophrenia Bulletin, 20*, 263–267.

Meerwijk, E. L., & Sevelius, J. M. (2017). Transgender population size in the United States: A meta-regression of population-based probability samples. *American Journal of Public Health, 107*, e1–e8.

Meeussen, L., Van Laar, C., & Verbruggen, M. (2019). Looking for a family man? Norms for men are toppling in heterosexual relationships. *Sex Roles, 80*, 429–442.

Mehl, M., Gosling, S. D., & Pennebaker, J. W. (2006). Personality in its natural habitat: Manifestations and implicit folk theories of personality in daily life. *Journal of Personality and Social Psychology, 90*, 862–877.

Mehta, D., Klengel, T., Conneely, K. N., Smith, A. K., Altmann, A., Pace, T. W., Rex-Haffner, M., Loeschner, A., Gonik, M., Mercer, K. B., Bradley, B., Müller-Myhsok, B., Ressler, K. J., & Binder, E. B. (2013). Childhood maltreatment is associated with distinct genomic and epigenetic profiles in posttraumatic stress disorder. *PNAS, 110*, 8302–8307.

Meichenbaum, D. (1977). *Cognitive-behavior modification: An integrative approach.* Plenum Press.

Meichenbaum, D. (1985). *Stress inoculation training.* Pergamon.

Meis, L. A., Noorbaloochi, S., Hagel Campbell, E. M., Erbes, C. R., Polusny, M. A., Velasquez, T. L., Bangerter, A., Cutting, A., Eftekhari, A., Rosen, C. S., Tuerk, P. W., Burmeister, L. B., & Spoont, M. R. (2019). Sticking it out in trauma-focused treatment for PTSD: It takes a village. *Journal of Consulting and Clinical Psychology, 87*, 246–256.

Melby-Lervåg, M., Redick, T. S., & Hulme, C. (2016). Working memory training does not improve performance on measures of intelligence or other measures of "far transfer": Evidence from a meta-analytic review. *Perspectives on Psychological Science, 11*, 512–534.

Meleady, R., Crisp, R. J., Hodson, G., & Earle, M. (2019). On the generalization of intergroup contact: A taxonomy of transfer effects. *Current Directions in Psychological Science, 28*, 430–435.

Melioli, T., Bauer, S., Franko, D. L., Moessner, M., Ozer, F., Chabrol, H., & Rodgers, R. F. (2016). Reducing eating disorder symptoms and risk factors using the internet: A meta-analytic review. *International Journal of Eating Disorders, 49*, 19–31.

Mellers, B., Stone, E., Atanasov, P., Rohrbaugh, N., Metz, S. E., Ungar, L., Bishop, M. M., Horowitz, M., Merkle, E., & Tetlock, P. (2015). The psychology of intelligence analysis: Drivers of prediction accuracy in world politics. *Journal of Experimental Psychology: Applied, 21*, 1–14.

Meltzer, A. L., Makhanova, A., Hicks, L. L., French, J. E., McNulty, J. K., & Bradbury, T. N. (2017). Quantifying the sexual afterglow: The lingering benefits of sex and their implications for pair-bonded relationships. *Psychological Science, 28*, 587–598.

Meltzoff, A. N. (1988). Infant imitation after a 1-week delay: Long-term memory for novel acts and multiple stimuli. *Developmental Psychology, 24*, 470–476.

Meltzoff, A. N., Kuhl, P. K., Movellan, J., & Sejnowski, T. J. (2009). Foundations for a new science of learning. *Science, 325*, 284–288.

Meltzoff, A. N., & Moore, M. K. (1989). Imitation in newborn infants: Exploring the range of gestures imitated and the underlying mechanisms. *Developmental Psychology, 25*, 954–962.

Meltzoff, A. N., & Moore, M. K. (1997). Explaining facial imitation: A theoretical model. *Early Development and Parenting, 6*, 179–192.

Melzack, R. (1992, April). Quoted in "Phantom limbs." *Scientific American*, pp. 120–126.

Melzack, R. (1998, February). Quoted in "Phantom limbs." *Discover*, p. 20.

Melzack, R. (2005). Evolution of the neuromatrix theory of pain. *Pain Practice, 5*, 85–94.

Melzack, R., & Katz, J. (2013). Pain. *Wiley Interdisciplinary Reviews: Cognitive Science, 4*, 1–15.

Melzack, R., & Wall, P. D. (1965). Pain mechanisms: A new theory. *Science, 150*, 971–979.

Melzack, R., & Wall, P. D. (1983). *The challenge of pain.* Basic Books.

Mende-Siedlecki, P., Said, C. P., & Todorov, A. (2013). The social evaluation of faces: A meta-analysis of functional neuroimaging studies. *SCAN, 8*, 285–299.

Mendelson, J. L., Gates, J. A., & Lerner, M. D. (2016). Friendship in school-age boys with autism spectrum disorders: A meta-analytic summary and developmental, process-based model. *Psychological Bulletin, 142*, 601–622.

Mendes, E. (2010, June 2). *U.S. exercise levels up, but demographic differences remain.* Gallup. https://news.gallup.com/poll/139340/exercise-levels-demographic-differences-remain.aspx

Mendolia, M., & Kleck, R. E. (1993). Effects of talking about a stressful event on arousal: Does what we talk about make a difference? *Journal of Personality and Social Psychology, 64*, 283–292.

Mennella, J. A., Coren, P., Jagnow, M. S., & Beauchamp, G. K. (2001). Prenatal and postnatal flavor learning by human infants. *Pediatrics, 107*, E88.

Mensa. (2019, accessed October 6). *About us.* Mensa International. http://www.mensa.org/mensa/about-us

Merari, A. (2002). *Explaining suicidal terrorism: Theories versus empirical evidence* [Invited address]. The American Psychological Association.

Mercado, M. C., Holland, K., Leemis, R. W., Stone, D. M., & Wang, J. (2017). Trends in emergency department visits for nonfatal self-inflicted injuries among youth aged 10 to 24 years in the United States, 2001–2015. *JAMA, 318*, 1931–1933.

Mercer, T. (2015). Wakeful rest alleviates interference-based forgetting. *Memory, 23*, 127–137.

Meriac, J. P., Hoffman, B. J., Woehr, D. J., & Fleisher, M. S. (2008). Further evidence for the validity of assessment center dimensions: A meta-analysis of the incremental criterion-related validity of dimension ratings. *Journal of Applied Psychology, 93*, 1042–1052.

Merikangas, K. R., Jin, R., He, J. P., Kessler, R. C., Lee, S., Sampson, N. A., Viana, M. C., Andrade, L. H., Hu, C., Karam, E. G., Ladea, M., Medina-Mora, M. E., Ono, Y., Posada-Villa, J., Sagar, R., Wells, J. E., & Zarkov, Z. (2011). Prevalence and correlates of bipolar spectrum disorder in the World Mental Health Survey initiative. *Archives of General Psychiatry, 68*, 241–251.

Merskey, H. (1992). The manufacture of personalities: The production of multiple personality disorder. *British Journal of Psychiatry, 160*, 327–340.

Merz, J., Schwarzer, G., & Gerger, H. (2019). Comparative efficacy and acceptability of pharmacological, psychotherapeutic, and combination treatments in adults with posttraumatic stress disorder: a network meta-analysis. *JAMA Psychiatry, 76*, 904–913.

Merzenich, M. (2007). Quoted in the Posit Science Brain Fitness Program (positscience.com).

Mesman, J., van Ijzendoorn, M., Behrens, K., Carbonell, O. A., Cárcamo, R., Cohen-Paraira, I., Kondo-Ikemura, K., Mels, C., Mooya, H., Murtisari, S., Nóblega, M., Ortiz, J. A., Sagi-Schwartz, A., Sichimba, F., Soares, I., Steele, H., Steele, M., Pape, M., van Ginkel, J., . . . Zreik, G. (2015). Is the ideal mother a sensitive mother? Beliefs about early childhood parenting in mothers across the globe. *International Journal of Behavioral Development, 40*, 385–397.

Mesoudi, A. (2009). How cultural evolutionary theory can inform social psychology and vice versa. *Psychological Review, 116*, 929–952.

Messias, E., Eaton, W. W., & Grooms, A. N. (2011). Economic grand rounds: Income inequality and depression prevalence across the United States: An ecological study. *Psychiatric Services, 62*, 710–712.

Meston, C. M., & Buss, D. M. (2007). Why humans have sex. *Archives of Sexual Behavior, 36*, 477–507.

Metcalfe, J. (1986). Premonitions of insight predict impending error. *Journal of Experimental Psychology: Learning, Memory, and Cognition, 12*, 623–634.

Metcalfe, J. (1998). Cognitive optimism: Self-deception or memory-based processing heuristics. *Personality and Social Psychology Review, 2*, 100–110.

Metzler, D. (2011, Spring). Vocabulary growth in adult cross-fostered chimpanzees. *Friends of Washoe, 32*, 11–13.

Meyer, A., Carlton, C., Chong, L. J., & Wissemann, K. (2019). The presence of a controlling parent is related to an increase in the error-related negativity in 5-7 year-old children. *Journal of Abnormal Child Psychology, 47*, 935–945.

Meyer-Bahlburg, H. F. L. (1995). Psychoneuroendocrinology and sexual pleasure: The aspect of sexual orientation. In P. R. Abramson & S. D. Pinkerton (Eds.), *Sexual nature/sexual culture* (pp. 135–153). University of Chicago Press.

Meyer, I. H. (2003). Prejudice, social stress, and mental health in lesbian, gay, and bisexual populations: Conceptual issues and research evidence. *Psychological Bulletin, 129*, 674–697.

Meyerhoff, J., & Rohan, K. J. (2016). Treatment expectations for cognitive-behavioral therapy and light therapy for seasonal affective disorder: Change across treatment and relation to outcome. *Journal of Consulting and Clinical Psychology, 84*, 898–906.

Mez, J., Daneshvar, D. H., Kiernan, P. T., Abdolmohammadi, B., Alvarez, V. E., Huber, B. R., Alosco, M. L., Solomon, T. M., Nowinski, C. J., McHale, L., Cormier, K. A., Kubilius, C. A., Martin, B. M., Murphy, L., Baugh, C. M., Montenigro, P. H., Chaisson, C. E., Tripodis, Y., Kowall, N. W., . . . McKee, A. C. (2017). Clinicopathological evaluation of chronic traumatic encephalopathy in players of American football. *JAMA, 318*, 360–370.

Miao, C., Humphrey, R. H., & Qian, S. (2016). Leader emotional intelligence and subordinate job satisfaction: A meta-analysis of main, mediator, and moderator effects. *Personality and Individual Differences, 102*, 13–24.

Michael, R. B., Garry, M., & Kirsch, I. (2012). Suggestion, cognition, and behavior. *Current Directions in Psychological Science, 21*, 151–156.

Michaels, J. W., Bloomel, J. M., Brocato, R. M., Linkous, R. A., & Rowe, J. S. (1982). Social facilitation and inhibition in a natural setting. *Replications in Social Psychology, 2*, 21–24.

Michalka, S. W., Kong, L., Rosen, M. L., Shinn-Cunningham, B., & Somers, D. C. (2015). Short-term memory for space and time flexibly recruit complementary sensory-biased frontal lobe attention networks. *Neuron, 87*, 882–892.

Michel, M., Beck, D., Block, N., Blumenfeld, H., Brown, R., Carmel, D., Dehaene, S., Fleming, S. M., Frith, C., Haggard, P., He, B. J., Heyes, C., Goodale, M. A., Irvine, L., Kawato, M., Kentridge, R., King, J.

R., Knight, R. T., Kouider, S., . . . Yoshida, M. (2019). Opportunities and challenges for a maturing science of consciousness. *Nature Human Behaviour, 3,* 104–107.

Michener, J. A. (1978, February 3). *External forces and inner voices.* Speech at the Chapel of the Four Chaplains, Philadelphia, PA.

Middlebrooks, J. C., & Green, D. M. (1991). Sound localization by human listeners. *Annual Review of Psychology, 42,* 135–159.

Miech, R., Patrick, M. E., O'Malley, P. M., & Johnston, L. D. (2017). E-cigarette use as a predictor of cigarette smoking: Results from a 1-year follow-up of a national sample of 12th grade students. *Tobacco Control, 26,* e2.

Miech, R. A., Johnston, L. D., O'Malley, P. M., Bachman, J. G., & Schulenberg, J. E. (2016). *Monitoring the Future national survey results on drug use, 1975–2015: Volume I, Secondary school students.* Institute for Social Research (The University of Michigan). https://eric.ed.gov/?id=ED578604

Miech, R. A., Schulenberg, J. E., Johnston, L. D., Bachman, J. G., O'Malley, P. M., & Patrick, M. E. (2019, December 19). *National adolescent drug trends in 2019: Findings released. Monitoring the Future.* Institute for Social Research. https://www.ncbi.nlm.nih.gov/pmc/articles/PMC6411424/

Miers, R. (2009, Spring). Calum's road. *Scottish Life,* pp. 36–39, 75.

Mihura, J. L., Meyer, G. J., Bombel, G., & Dumitrascu, N. (2015). Standards, accuracy, and questions of bias in Rorschach meta-analyses: Reply to Wood, Garb, Nezworski, Lilienfeld, and Duke (2015). *Psychological Bulletin, 141,* 250–260.

Mihura, J. L., Meyer, G. J., Dumitrascu, N., & Bombel, G. (2013). The validity of individual Rorschach variables: Systematic reviews and meta-analyses of the comprehensive system. *Psychological Bulletin, 139,* 548–605.

Mikalson, P., Pardo, S., & Green, J. (2012). *First, do no harm: Reducing disparities for lesbian, gay, bisexual, transgender, queer and questioning populations in California.* National Council on Crime & Delinquency. https://www.nccdglobal.org/newsroom/news-of-interest/first-do-no-harm-reducing-disparities-lesbian-gay-bisexual-transgender

Mikhail, J. (2007). Universal moral grammar: Theory, evidence and the future. *Trends in Cognitive Sciences, 11,* 143–152.

Mikkelsen, T. S., & The Chimpanzee Sequencing and Analysis Consortium. (2005). Initial sequence of the chimpanzee genome and comparison with the human genome. *Nature, 437,* 69–87.

Mikulincer, M., Florian, V., & Hirschberger, G. (2003). The existential function of close relationships: Introducing death into the science of love. *Personality and Social Psychology Review, 7,* 20–40.

Mikulincer, M., & Shaver, P. R. (2001). Attachment theory and intergroup bias: Evidence that priming the secure base schema attenuates negative reactions to out-groups. *Journal of Personality and Social Psychology, 81,* 97–115.

Milan, R. J., Jr., & Kilmann, P. R. (1987). Interpersonal factors in premarital contraception. *Journal of Sex Research, 23,* 289–321.

Milas, G., Wright, P., & Štulhofer, A. (2019). Longitudinal assessment of the association between pornography use and sexual satisfaction in adolescence. *The Journal of Sex Research, 57*(1), 16–28.

Milek, A., Butler, E. A., Tackman, A. M., Kaplan, D. M., Raison, C. L., Sbarra, D. A., Vazire, S., & Mehl, M. R. (2018). "Eavesdropping on happiness" revisited: A pooled, multisample replication of the association between life satisfaction and observed daily conversation quantity and quality. *Psychological Science, 29,* 1451–1462.

Miles, D. R., & Carey, G. (1997). Genetic and environmental architecture of human aggression. *Journal of Personality and Social Psychology, 72,* 207–217.

Miles-Novelo, A., & Anderson, C. A. (2019). Climate change and psychology: Effects of rapid global warming on violence and aggression. *Current Climate Change Reports, 5,* 36–46.

Milgram, S. (1963). Behavioral study of obedience. *Journal of Abnormal and Social Psychology, 67,* 371–378.

Milgram, S. (1974). *Obedience to authority.* Harper & Row.

Miller, A. B., Eisenlohr-Moul, T., Glenn, C. R., Turner, B. J., Chapman, A. L., Nock, M. K., & Prinstein, M. J. (2019). Does higher-than-usual stress predict nonsuicidal self-injury? Evidence from two prospective studies in adolescent and emerging adult females. *Journal of Child Psychology and Psychiatry, 60,* 1076–1084.

Miller, D. I., Nolla, K. M., Eagly, A. H., & Uttal, D. H. (2018). The development of children's gender-science stereotypes: A meta-analysis of 5 decades of U.S. Draw-A-Scientist studies. *Child Development, 89,* 1943–1955.

Miller, D. J., McBain, K. A., Li, W. W., & Raggatt, P. T. (2019). Pornography, preference for porn like sex, masturbation, and men's sexual and relationship satisfaction. *Personal Relationships, 26,* 93–113.

Miller, G. (2004). Axel, Buck share award for deciphering how the nose knows. *Science, 306,* 207.

Miller, G. (2012). Drone wars: Are remotely piloted aircraft changing the nature of war? *Science, 336,* 842–843.

Miller, G. A. (1956). The magical number seven, plus or minus two: Some limits on our capacity for processing information. *Psychological Review, 63,* 81–97.

Miller, G. E., & Blackwell, E. (2006). Turning up the heat: Inflammation as a mechanism linking chronic stress, depression, and heart disease. *Current Directions in Psychological Science, 15,* 269–272.

Miller, G. E., & Chen, E. (2010). Harsh family climate in early life presages the emergence of a proinflammatory phenotype in adolescence. *Psychological Science, 21,* 848–856.

Miller, J. F., Neufang, M., Solway, A., Brandt, A., Trippel, M., Mader, I., Hefft, S., Merkow, M., Polyn, S. M., Jacobs, J., Kahana, M. J., & Schulze-Bonhage, A. (2013). Neural activity in human hippocampal formation reveals the spatial context of retrieved memories. *Science, 342,* 1111–1114.

Miller, J. G., Goyal, N., & Wice, M. (2017). A cultural psychology of agency: Morality, motivation, and reciprocity. *Perspectives on Psychological Science, 12,* 867–875.

Miller, L. K. (1999). The savant syndrome: Intellectual impairment and exceptional skill. *Psychological Bulletin, 125,* 31–46.

Miller, M., Azrael, D., & Hemenway, D. (2002). Household firearm ownership levels and suicide across U.S. regions and states, 1988–1997. *Epidemiology, 13,* 517–524.

Miller, M., Swanson, S. A., & Azrael, D. (2016). Are we missing something pertinent? A bias analysis of unmeasured confounding in the firearm-suicide literature. *Epidemiologic Reviews, 38,* 62–69.

Miller, M. A., Kruisbrink, M., Wallace, J., Ji, C., & Cappuccio, F. P. (2018). Sleep duration and incidence of obesity in infants, children, and adolescents: a systematic review and meta-analysis of prospective studies. *Sleep, 41,* zsy018.

Miller, N. E. (1985, February). Rx: Biofeedback. *Psychology Today,* pp. 54–59.

Miller, P. (2012, January). A thing or two about twins. *National Geographic,* pp. 38–65.

Miller, P. J. O., Aoki, K., Rendell, L. E., & Amano, M. (2008). Stereotypical resting behavior of the sperm whale. *Current Biology, 18,* R21–R23.

Miller, S. L., & Maner, J. K. (2010). Scent of a woman: Men's testosterone responses to olfactory ovulation cues. *Psychological Science, 21,* 276–283.

Miller, S. L., & Maner, J. K. (2011). Ovulation as a male mating prime: Subtle signs of women's fertility influence men's mating cognition and behavior. *Journal of Personality and Social Psychology, 100,* 295–308.

Milling, L. S., Gover, M. C., & Moriarty, C. L. (2018). The effectiveness of hypnosis as an intervention for obesity: A meta-analytic review. *Psychology of Consciousness: Theory, Research, and Practice, 5,* 29–45.

Milling, L. S., Kirsch, I., Meunier, S. A., & Levine, M. R. (2002). Hypnotic analgesia and stress inoculation training: Individual and combined effects in analog treatment of experimental pain. *Cognitive Therapy and Research, 26,* 355–371.

Milner, A. D., & Goodale, M. A. (2008). Two visual systems reviewed. *Neuropsychologia, 46,* 774–785.

Mineka, S. (1985). The frightful complexity of the origins of fears. In F. R. Brush & J. B. Overmier (Eds.), *Affect, conditioning and cognition: Essays on the determinants of behavior.* Erlbaum.

Mineka, S. (2002). Animal models of clinical psychology. In N. Smelser & P. Baltes (Eds.), *International encyclopedia of the social and behavioral sciences.* Elsevier Science.

Mineka, S., & Oehlberg, K. (2008). The relevance of recent developments in classical conditioning to understanding the etiology and maintenance of anxiety disorders. *Acta Psychologica, 127,* 567–580.

Mineka, S., & Zinbarg, R. (1996). Conditioning and ethological models of anxiety disorders: Stress-in-dynamic-context anxiety models. In D. Hope (Ed.), *Perspectives on anxiety, panic, and fear* (Nebraska Symposium on Motivation). University of Nebraska Press.

Minică, C. C., Verweij, K. J., van der Most, P. J., Mbarek, H., Bernard, M., van Eijk, K. R., Lind, P. A., Liu, M. Z., Maciejewski, D. F., Palviainen, T., Sánchez-Mora, C., Sherva, R., Taylor, M., Walters, R. K., Abdellaoui, A., Bigdeli, T. V., Branje, S. J. T., Brown, S. A., Casas, M., . . . Derks, E. M. (2018). Genome-wide association meta-analysis of age at first cannabis use. *Addiction, 113,* 2073–2086.

Minns, S., Levihn-Coon, A., Carl, E., Smits, J. A., Miller, W., Howard, D., Papini, S., Quiroz, S., Lee-Furman, E., Telch, M., Carlbring, P., Xanthopoulos, D., & Powers, M. B. (2019). Immersive 3D exposure-based treatment for spider fear: A randomized controlled trial. *Journal of Anxiety Disorders, 61,* 37–44.

Minsky, M. (1986). *The society of mind.* Simon & Schuster.

Mischel, W. (1968). *Personality and assessment.* Wiley.

Mischel, W. (1981). Current issues and challenges in personality. In L. T. Benjamin, Jr. (Ed.), *The G. Stanley Hall Lecture Series* (Vol. 1). American Psychological Association.

Mischel, W. (2014). *The marshmallow test: Mastering self-control.* Little, Brown.

Mischkowski, D., Kross, E., & Bushman, B. (2012). Flies on the wall are less aggressive: Self-distancing "in the heat of the moment" reduces aggressive thoughts, angry feelings and aggressive behavior. *Journal of Experimental Social Psychology, 48,* 1187–1191.

Miserandino, M. (1991). Memory and the seven dwarfs. *Teaching of Psychology, 18,* 169–171.

Mishkin, M. (1982). A memory system in the monkey. *Philosophical Transactions of the Royal Society of London: Biological Sciences, 298,* 83–95.

Mishkin, M., Suzuki, W. A., Gadian, D. G., & Vargha-Khadem, F. (1997). Hierarchical organization of cognitive memory. *Philosophical Transactions of the Royal Society of London: Biological Sciences, 352,* 1461–1467.

Mishra, A., & Mishra, H. (2010). Border bias: The belief that state borders can protect against disasters. *Psychological Science, 21*, 1582–1586.

Mita, T. H., Dermer, M., & Knight, J. (1977). Reversed facial images and the mere-exposure hypothesis. *Journal of Personality and Social Psychology, 35*, 597–601.

Mitani, J. C., Watts, D. P., & Amsler, S. J. (2010). Lethal intergroup aggression leads to territorial expansion in wild chimpanzees. *Current Biology, 20*, R507–R509.

Mitchell, G. (2012). Revisiting truth or triviality: The external validity of research in the psychological laboratory. *Perspectives on Psychological Science, 7*, 109–117.

Mitchell, J. P. (2009). Social psychology as a natural kind. *Cell, 13*, 246–251.

Mitricheva, E., Kimura, R., Logothetis, N. K., & Noori, H. R. (2019). Neural substrates of sexual arousal are not sex dependent. *PNAS, 116*, 15671–15676.

Mitte, K. (2008). Memory bias for threatening information in anxiety and anxiety disorders: A meta-analytic review. *Psychological Bulletin, 134*, 886–911.

Miu, A. S., & Yeager, D. S. (2015). Preventing symptoms of depression by teaching adolescents that people can change: Effects of a brief incremental theory of personality intervention at 9-month follow-up. *Clinical Psychological Science, 3*, 726–743.

Miyamoto, Y., & Kitayama, S. (2018). Cultural differences in correspondence bias are systematic and multifaceted. *Advances in Methods and Practices in Psychological Science, 1*, 497–498.

Miyatsu, T., Nguyen, K., & McDaniel, M. A. (2018). Five popular study strategies: Their pitfalls and optimal implementations. *Perspectives on Psychological Science, 13*, 390–407.

Mobbs, D., Yu, R., Meyer, M., Passamonti, L., Seymour, B., Calder, A. J., Schweizer, S., Frith, C. D., & Dalgeish, T. (2009). A key role for similarity in vicarious reward. *Science, 324*, 900.

Moffitt, T. E. (2005). The new look of behavioral genetics in developmental psychopathology: Gene-environment interplay in antisocial behaviors. *Psychological Bulletin, 131*, 533–554.

Moffitt, T. E. (2018). Male antisocial behavior in adolescence and beyond. *Nature Human Behavior, 2*, 177–186.

Moffitt, T. E., Arsenault, L., Belsky, D., Dickson, N., Hancox, R. J., Harrington, H., Houts, R., Poulton, R., Roberts, B. W., Ross, S., Sears, M. R., Thompson, W. M., & Caspi, A. (2011). A gradient of childhood self-control predicts health, wealth, and public safety. *PNAS, 108*, 2693–2698.

Moffitt, T. E., Caspi, A., Harrington, H., & Milne, B. J. (2002). Males on the life-course—persistent and adolescence-limited antisocial pathways: Follow-up at age 26 years. *Development and Psychopathology, 14*, 179–207.

Moffitt, T. E., Caspi, A., & Rutter, M. (2006). Measured gene-environment interactions in psychopathology: Concepts, research strategies, and implications for research, intervention, and public understanding of genetics. *Perspectives on Psychological Science, 1*, 5–27.

Moffitt, T. E., Poulton, R., & Caspi, A. (2013). Lifelong impact of early self-control. *American Scientist, 101*, 352–359.

Moghaddam, F. M. (2005). The staircase to terrorism: A psychological exploration. *American Psychologist, 60*, 161–169.

Mogilner, C., & Norton, M. I. (2016). Time, money, and happiness. *Current Opinion in Psychology, 10*, 12–16.

Moholdt, T., Lavie, C., & Nauman, J. (2018). Sustained physical activity, not weight loss, associated with improved survival in coronary heart disease. *Journal of the American College of Cardiology. 71*, 1094–1101.

Molenberghs, P., Ogilvie, C., Louis, W. R., Decety, J., Bagnall, J., & Bain, P. G. (2015). The neural correlates of justified and unjustified killing: An fMRI study. *Social Cognitive and Affective Neuroscience, 10*, 1397–1404.

Möller-Levet, C. S., Archer, S. N., Bucca, G., Laing, E. E., Slak, A., Kabiljo, R., Lo, J. C. Y., Santhi, N., von Schantz, M., Smith, C. P., & Dijk, D.-J. (2013). Effects of insufficient sleep on circadian rhythmicity and expression amplitude of the human blood transcriptome. *PNAS, 110*, E1132–E1141.

Mommersteeg, P. M. C., Schoemaker, R. G., Naudé, P. J., Eisel, U. L., Garrelds, I. M., Schalkwijk, C. G., Westerhuis, B. W. J. J. M., Kop, W. J., & Denollet, J. (2016). Depression and markers of inflammation as predictors of all-cause mortality in heart failure. *Brain, Behavior, and Immunity, 57*, 144–150.

Mondloch, C. J., Lewis, T. L., Budreau, D. R., Maurer, D., Dannemiller, J. L., Stephens, B. R., & Kleiner-Gathercoal, K. A. (1999). Face perception during early infancy. *Psychological Science, 10*, 419–422.

Money, J. (1987). Sin, sickness, or status? Homosexual gender identity and psychoneuroendocrinology. *American Psychologist, 42*, 384–399.

Money, J., Berlin, F. S., Falck, A., & Stein, M. (1983). *Antiandrogenic and counseling treatment of sex offenders.* Johns Hopkins University School of Medicine, Department of Psychiatry and Behavioral Sciences.

Monroe, S. M., & Reid, M. W. (2009). Life stress and major depression. *Current Directions in Psychological Science, 18*, 68–72.

Monroe, S. M., & Simons, A. D. (1991). Diathesis-stress theories in the context of life stress research: Implications for the depressive disorders. *Psychological Bulletin, 110*, 406–425.

Montagne, A., Barnes, S. R., Sweeney, M. D., Halliday, M. R., Sagare, A. P., Zhao, Z., Toga, A. W., Jacobs, R. E., Liu, C. Y., Amezcua, L., Harrington, M. G., Chui, H. C., Law, M., & Zlokovic, B. V. (2015). Blood-brain barrier breakdown in the aging human hippocampus. *Neuron, 85*, 296–302.

Monteiro, B. M., Moreira, F. A., Massensini, A. R., Moraes, M. F., & Pereira, G. S. (2014). Enriched environment increases neurogenesis and improves social memory persistence in socially isolated adult mice. *Hippocampus, 24*, 239–248.

Montgomery, G. H., DuHamel, K. N., & Redd, W. H. (2000). A meta-analysis of hypnotically induced analgesia: How effective is hypnosis? *International Journal of Clinical and Experimental Hypnosis, 48*, 138–153.

Montoya, R. M., & Horton, R. S. (2013). A meta-analytic investigation of the processes underlying the similarity-attraction effect. *Journal of Social and Personal Relationships, 30*, 64–94.

Montoya, R. M., & Horton, R. S. (2014). A two-dimensional model for the study of interpersonal attraction. *Personality and Social Psychology Review, 18*, 59–86.

Montoya, R. M., Horton, R. S., Vevea, J. L., Citkowicz, M., & Lauber, E. A. (2017). A re-examination of the mere exposure effect: The influence of repeated exposure on recognition, familiarity, and liking. *Psychological Bulletin, 143*, 459–498.

Mook, D. G. (1983). In defense of external invalidity. *American Psychologist, 38*, 379–387.

Moon, C., Lagercrantz, H., & Kuhl, P. K. (2013). Language experienced in utero affects vowel perception after birth: A two-country study. *Acta Paediatrica, 102*, 156–160.

Moorcroft, W. H. (2003). *Understanding sleep and dreaming.* Kluwer Academic/Plenum Press.

Moore, D. M., D'Mello, A. M., McGrath, L. M., & Stoodley, C. J. (2017). The developmental relationship between specific cognitive domains and grey matter in the cerebellum. *Developmental Cognitive Neuroscience, 24*, 1–11.

Moore, D. W. (2004, December 17). *Sweet dreams go with a good night's sleep.* Gallup News Service. https://news.gallup.com/poll/14380/sweet-dreams-good-nights-sleep.aspx

Moore, S. C., Lee, I., Weiderpass, E., Campbell, P. T., Sampson, J. N., Kitahara, C. M., Keadle, S. K., Arem, H., Berrington de Gonzalez, A., Hartge, P., Adami, H. O., Blair, C. K., Borch, K. B., Boyd, E., Check, D. P., Fournier, A., Freedman, N. D., Gunter, M., Johannson, M., . . . Patel, A. V. (2016). Association of leisure-time physical activity with risk of 26 types of cancer in 1.44 million adults. *JAMA Internal Medicine, 176*, 816–825.

Moos, R. H., & Moos, B. S. (2005). Sixteen-year changes and stable remission among treated and untreated individuals with alcohol use disorders. *Drug and Alcohol Dependence, 80*, 337–347.

Moos, R. H., & Moos, B. S. (2006). Participation in treatment and Alcoholics Anonymous: A 16-year follow-up of initially untreated individuals. *Journal of Clinical Psychology, 62*, 735–750.

Mor, N., & Winquist, J. (2002). Self-focused attention and negative affect: A meta-analysis. *Psychological Bulletin, 128*, 638–662.

More, H. L., Hutchinson, J. R., Collins, D. F., Weber, D. J., Aung, S. K. H., & Donelan, J. M. (2010). Scaling of sensorimotor control in terrestrial mammals. *Proceedings of the Royal Society: Series B, 277*, 3563–3568.

Moreira, M. T., Smith, L. A., & Foxcroft, D. (2009). Social norms interventions to reduce alcohol misuse in university or college students. *Cochrane Database of Systematic Reviews*, Issue 3, Art. No. CD006748.

Moreland, R. L., & Zajonc, R. B. (1982). Exposure effects in person perception: Familiarity, similarity, and attraction. *Journal of Experimental Social Psychology, 18*, 395–415.

Morelli, G. A., Rogoff, B., Oppenheim, D., & Goldsmith, D. (1992). Cultural variation in infants' sleeping arrangements: Questions of independence. *Developmental Psychology, 26*, 604–613.

Moreno, C., Laje, G., Blanco, C., Jiang, H., Schmidt, A. B., & Olfson, M. (2007). National trends in the outpatient diagnosis and treatment of bipolar disorder in youth. *Archives of General Psychiatry, 64*, 1032–1039.

Morewedge, C. K., & Norton, M. I. (2009). When dreaming is believing: The (motivated) interpretation of dreams. *Journal of Personality and Social Psychology, 96*, 249–264.

Morey, R. A., Inan, S., Mitchell, T. V., Perkins, D. O., Lieberman, J. A., & Belger, A. (2005). Imaging frontostriatal function in ultra-high-risk, early, and chronic schizophrenia during executive processing. *Archives of General Psychiatry, 62*, 254–262.

Morgan, A. B., & Lilienfeld, S. O. (2000). A meta-analytic review of the relation between antisocial behavior and neuropsychological measures of executive function. *Clinical Psychology Review, 20*, 113–136.

Morgan, C., Webb, R. T., Carr, M. J., Kontopantelis, E., Green, J., Chew-Graham, C. A., Kapur, N., & Ashcroft, D. M. (2017). Incidence, clinical management, and mortality risk following self-harm among children and adolescents: Cohort study in primary care. *BMJ, 359*, j4351.

Morgenthaler, T. I., Hashmi, S., Croft, J. B., Dort, L., Heald, J. L., & Mullington, J. (2016). High school start times and the impact on high school students: What we know and what we hope to learn. *Journal of Clinical Sleep Medicine, 12*, 1681–1689.

Mori, K., & Mori, H. (2009). Another test of the passive facial feedback hypothesis: When your face smiles, you feel happy. *Perceptual and Motor Skills, 109,* 1–3.

Morris, G., Baker-Ward, L., & Bauer, P. J. (2010). What remains of that day: The survival of children's autobiographical memories across time. *Applied Cognitive Psychology, 24,* 527–544.

Morris, M. (2015, September 18). Opinion: Damaging labels do transgender people a disservice. *Edmonton Journal.* https://www.usatoday.com/story/news/politics/2019/05/28/transgender-rights-supreme-court-wont-hear-school-bathroom-challenge/1258665001/

Morris, M. C., Wang, Y., Barnes, L. L., Bennett, D. A., Dawson-Hughes, B., & Booth, S. L. (2018). Nutrients and bioactives in green leafy vegetables and cognitive decline: Prospective study. *Neurology, 90*(3), e214–e222.

Morrison, A. R. (2003). The brain on night shift. *Cerebrum, 5,* 23–36.

Morrison, M., Tay, L., & Diener, E. (2014). *Subjective well-being across the lifespan worldwide* [Paper]. Presented at the Society for Personality and Social Psychology convention, Austin, Texas.

Morrison, R., & Reiss, D. (2018). Precocious development of self-awareness in dolphins. *PLOS ONE, 13,* e0189813.

Mortensen, P. B. (1999). Effects of family history and place and season of birth on the risk of schizophrenia. *New England Journal of Medicine, 340,* 603–608.

Moscovici, S. (1985). Social influence and conformity. In G. Lindzey & E. Aronson (Eds.), *The handbook of social psychology* (3rd ed., pp. 347–412). Erlbaum.

Moses, E. B., & Barlow, D. H. (2006). A new unified treatment approach for emotional disorders based on emotion science. *Current Directions in Psychological Science, 15,* 146–150.

Mosher, C. E., & Danoff-Burg, S. (2008). Agentic and communal personality traits: Relations to disordered eating behavior, body shape concern, and depressive symptoms. *Eating Behaviors, 9,* 497–500.

Mosher, W. D., Chandra, A., & Jones, J. (2005, September 15). *Sexual behavior and selected health measures: Men and women 15–44 years of age, United States, 2002.* Advance Data from Vital and Health Statistics, No. 362, National Center for Health Statistics, Centers for Disease Control and Prevention, U.S. Department of Health and Human Services.

Mosing, M. A., Butkovic, A., & Ullen, F. (2018). Can flow experiences be protective of work-related depressive symptoms and burnout? A genetically informative approach. *Journal of Affective Disorders, 226,* 6–11.

Mosing, M. A., Zietsch, B. P., Shekar, S. N., Wright, M. J., & Martin, N. G. (2009). Genetic and environmental influences on optimism and its relationship to mental and self-rated health: A study of aging twins. *Behavior Genetics, 39,* 597–604.

Moskowitz, T. J., & Wertheim, L. J. (2011). *Scorecasting: The hidden influences behind how sports are played and games are won.* Crown Archetype.

Mosnier, I., Bebear, J.-P., Marx, M., Fraysse, B., Truy, E., Lina-Granade, G., Mondain, M., Sterkers-Artières, F., Bordure, P., Robier, A., Godey, B., Meyer, B., Frachet, B., Poncet-Wallet, C., Bouccara, D., & Sterkers, O. (2015). Improvement of cognitive function after cochlear implantation in elderly patients. *JAMA Otolaryngology—Head & Neck Surgery, 141,* 442–450.

Moss, A. C., & Albery, I. P. (2009). A dual-process model of the alcohol-behavior link for social drinking. *Psychological Bulletin, 135,* 516–530.

Moss, A. J., Allen, K. F., Giovino, G. A., & Mills, S. L. (1992, December 2). *Recent trends in adolescent smoking, smoking-update correlates, and expectations about the future.* CDC. Advance Data No. 221.

Moss-Racusin, C. A., Pietri, E. S., Hennes, E. P., Dovidio, J. F., Brescoll, V. L., Roussos, G., & Handelsman, J. (2018). Reducing STEM gender bias with VIDS (video interventions for diversity in STEM). *Journal of Experimental Psychology: Applied, 24,* 236–260.

Motivala, S. J., & Irwin, M. R. (2007). Sleep and immunity: Cytokine pathways linking sleep and health outcomes. *Current Directions in Psychological Science, 16,* 21–25.

Mõttus, R., Briley, D. A., Zheng, A., Mann, F. D., Engelhardt, L. E., Tackett, J. L., Harden, K. P., & Tucker-Drob, E. M. (2019). Kids becoming less alike: A behavioral genetic analysis of developmental increases in personality variance from childhood to adolescence. *Journal of Personality and Social Psychology, 117,* 635–658.

Motyl, M., Demos, A. P., Carsel, T. S., Hanson, B. E., Melton, Z. J., Mueller, A. B., Prims, J. P., Sun, J., Washburn, A. N., Wong, K. M., Yantis, C., & Skitka, L. J. (2017). The state of social and personality science: Rotten to the core, not so bad, getting better, or getting worse? *Journal of Personality and Social Psychology, 113,* 34–58.

Moulin, S., Waldfogel, J., & Washbrook, E. (2014). Baby bonds: Parenting, attachment, and a secure base for children. *Sutton Trust,* 1–42.

Moxley, J. H., Ericsson, K. A., Charness, N., & Krampe, R. T. (2012). The role of intuition and deliberative thinking in experts' superior tactical decision-making. *Cognition, 124,* 72–78.

Mroczek, D. K., & Kolarz, D. M. (1998). The effect of age on positive and negative affect: A developmental perspective on happiness. *Journal of Personality and Social Psychology, 75,* 1333–1349.

Muchnik, L., Aral, S., Taylor, S. J. (2013). Social influence bias: A randomized experiment. *Science, 341,* 647–651.

Mueller, P. A., & Oppenheimer, D. M. (2014). The pen is mightier than the keyboard: Advantages of longhand over laptop note-taking. *Psychological Science, 25,* 1159–1168.

Mueller, S., Wagner, J., Smith, J., Voelkle, M. C., & Gerstorf, D. (2018). The interplay of personality and functional health in old and very old age: Dynamic within-person interrelations across up to 13 years. *Journal of Personality and Social Psychology, 115,* 1127.

Mueller, S. C., De Cuypere, G., & T'Sjoen, G. (2017). Transgender research in the 21st century: A selective critical review from a neurocognitive perspective. *The American Journal of Psychiatry, 174,* 1155–1162.

Muenks, K., Yang, J. S., & Wigfield, A. (2018). Associations between grit, motivation, and achievement in high school students. *Motivation Science, 4,* 158–176.

Muggleton, N. K., Tarran, S. R., & Fincher, C. L. (2019). Who punishes promiscuous women? Both women and men are prejudiced towards sexually-accessible women, but only women inflict costly punishment. *Evolution and Human Behavior, 40,* 259–268.

Muhlnickel, W. (1998). Reorganization of auditory cortex in tinnitus. *PNAS, 95,* 10340–10343.

Muise, A., Schimmack, U., & Impett, E. A. (2016). Sexual frequency predicts greater well-being, but more is not always better. *Social Psychological and Personality Science, 7,* 295–302.

Mulcahy, N. J., & Call, J. (2006). Apes save tools for future use. *Science, 312,* 1038–1040.

Muldoon, S., Taylor, S. C., & Norma, C. (2016). The survivor master narrative in sexual assault. *Violence Against Women, 22,* 565–587.

Mulick, A., Walker, J., Puntis, S., Burke, K., Symeonides, S., Gourley, C., Wanat, M., Frost, C., & Sharpe, M. (2018). Does depression treatment improve the survival of depressed patients with cancer? A long-term follow-up of participants in the SMaRT oncology-2 and 3 trials. *The Lancet Psychiatry, 5,* 321–326.

Mull, A. (2019, May 31). What 10,000 steps will really get you. *The Atlantic.* https://www.theatlantic.com/health/archive/2019/05/10000-steps-rule/590785/

Muller, J. E., Mittleman, M. A., Maclure, M., Sherwood, J. B., & Tofler, G. H. (1996). Triggering myocardial infarction by sexual activity. *Journal of the American Medical Association, 275,* 1405–1409.

Müller, M. J., Bosy-Westphal, A., & Heymsfield, S. B. (2010). Is there evidence for a set point that regulates human body weight? *F1000 Medicine Reports, 2,* 59.

Mullin, C. R., & Linz, D. (1995). Desensitization and resensitization to violence against women: Effects of exposure to sexually violent films on judgments of domestic violence victims. *Journal of Personality and Social Psychology, 69,* 449–459.

Mulrow, C. D. (1999, March). Treatment of depression—newer pharmacotherapies: Summary. *Evidence Report/Technology Assessment, 7.* Agency for Health Care Policy and Research. https://www.ncbi.nlm.nih.gov/books/NBK11912/

Murayama, K., Pekrun, R., Lichtenfeld, S., & vom Hofe, R. (2013). Predicting long-term growth in students' mathematics achievement: The unique contributions of motivation and cognitive strategies. *Child Development, 84,* 1475–1490.

Mure, L. S., Le, H. D., Benegiamo, G., Chang, M. W., Rios, L., Jillani, N., Ngotho, M., Kariuki, T., Dkhissi-Benyahya, O., Cooper, H. M., & Panda, S. (2018). Diurnal transcriptome atlas of a primate across major neural and peripheral tissues. *Science, 359*(6381), eaao0318.

Murphy, G., Loftus, E. F., Grady, R. F., Levine, L. J., & Greene, C. M. (2019). False memories for fake news during Ireland's abortion referendum. *Psychological Science, 30,* 1449–1459.

Murphy, K. R., & Cleveland, J. N. (1995). *Understanding performance appraisal: Social, organizational, and goal-based perspectives.* Sage.

Murphy, S., & Dalton, P. (2016). Out of touch? Visual load induces inattentional numbness. *Journal of Experimental Psychology: Human Perception and Performance, 42,* 761–765.

Murphy, S., & Dalton, P. (2018). Inattentional numbness and the influence of task difficulty. *Cognition, 178,* 1–6.

Murphy, S. T., Monahan, J. L., & Zajonc, R. B. (1995). Additivity of nonconscious affect: Combined effects of priming and exposure. *Journal of Personality and Social Psychology, 69,* 589–602.

Murray, H. (1938). *Explorations in personality.* Oxford University Press.

Murray, H. A. (1933). The effect of fear upon estimates of the maliciousness of other personalities. *Journal of Social Psychology, 4,* 310–329.

Murray, H. A., & Wheeler, D. R. (1937). A note on the possible clairvoyance of dreams. *Journal of Psychology, 3,* 309–313.

Murray, R., Jones, P., O'Callaghan, E., Takei, N., & Sham, P. (1992). Genes, viruses, and neurodevelopmental schizophrenia. *Journal of Psychiatric Research, 26,* 225–235.

Murray, S. L., Bellavia, G. M., Rose, P., & Griffin, D. W. (2003). Once hurt, twice hurtful: How perceived regard regulates daily marital interactions. *Journal of Personality and Social Psychology, 84,* 126–147.

Murthy, V. (2017, September). Work and the loneliness epidemic. *Harvard Business Review.* https://hbr.org/cover-story/2017/09/work-and-the-loneliness-epidemic

Murty, V. P., Calabro, F., & Luna, B. (2016). The role of experience in adolescent cognitive development: integration of executive, memory, and mesolimbic systems. *Neuroscience & Biobehavioral Reviews, 70,* 46–58.

Musick, M. A., Herzog, A. R., & House, J. S. (1999). Volunteering and mortality among older adults: Findings from a national sample. *Journals of Gerontology, 54B,* 173–180.

Mutz, J., Vipulananthan, V., Carter, B., Hurlemann, R., Fu, C. H. Y., & Young, A. H. (2019). Comparative efficacy and acceptability of non-surgical brain stimulation for the acute treatment of major depressive episodes in adults: Systematic review and network meta-analysis. *BMJ: British Medical Journal, 364,* 13.

Muusses, L. D., Kerkhof, P., & Finkenauer, C. (2015). Internet pornography and relationship quality: A longitudinal study of within and between partner effects of adjustment, sexual satisfaction and sexually explicit internet material among newlyweds. *Computers in Human Behavior, 45,* 77–84.

Mydans, S. (2002, May 17). In Pakistan, rape victims are the 'criminals.' *The New York Times.* https://www.nytimes.com/2002/05/17/world/in-pakistan-rape-victims-are-the-criminals.html

Myers, D. G. (1993). *The pursuit of happiness.* Harper.

Myers, D. G. (2000). *The American paradox: Spiritual hunger in an age of plenty.* Yale University Press.

Myers, D. G. (2010). *Social psychology,* 10th edition. McGraw-Hill.

Myers, D. G. (2018, August 23). *Do more immigrants equal greater acceptance or greater fear of immigrants?* TalkPsych. https://bit.ly/2UEvGNT

Myers, D. G. (2018, December 6). *Does exercise benefit as much as smoking harms?* https://community.macmillan.com/community/the-psychology-community/blog/2018/12/06/does-exercise-benefit-as-much-as-smoking-harms

Myers, D. G. (2019, May). The likely aftermath of adversity: harm, resilience, or growth? *APS Observer.* https://www.psychologicalscience.org/observer/teaching-current-directions-in-psychological-science-57#adversity

Myers, D. G., & Bishop, G. D. (1970). Discussion effects on racial attitudes. *Science, 169,* 778–779.

Myers, D. G., & Diener, E. (1995). Who is happy? *Psychological Science, 6,* 10–19.

Myers, D. G., & Diener, E. (1996, May). The pursuit of happiness (PDF). *Scientific American.* http://www.davidmyers.org/davidmyers/assets/Pursuit.Happ.scientific.american.pdf

Myers, D. G., & Scanzoni, L. D. (2005). *What God has joined together?* Harper.

Myers, D. G., & Twenge, J. M. (2019). *Social psychology,* 13th edition. McGraw-Hill.

Myers, I. B. (1987). *Introduction to type: A description of the theory and applications of the Myers-Briggs Type Indicator.* Consulting Psychologists Press.

Myre, G. (2000, April 27). McCain still can't forgive guards at "Hanoi Hilton." *The Washington Post.* https://www.washingtonpost.com/archive/politics/2000/04/27/mccain-still-cant-forgive-guards-at-hanoi-hilton/3dc0cd5c-5596-4bd7-852b-e6e44a15750f/

Nagourney, A. (2002, September 25). For remarks on Iraq, Gore gets praise and scorn. *The New York Times.* https://www.nytimes.com/2002/09/25/us/threats-responses-former-vice-president-for-remarks-iraq-gore-gets-praise-scorn.html

Nagourney, A., Sanger, D. E., & Barr, J. (2018, January 13). Hawaii panics after alert about incoming missile is sent in error. *The New York Times.* https://www.nytimes.com/2018/01/13/us/hawaii-missile.html?

Nairne, J. S., Coverdale, M. E., & Pandeirada, J. N. (2019). Adaptive memory: The mnemonic power of survival-based generation. *Journal of Experimental Psychology: Learning. Memory, and Cognition, 45,* 1970–1982.

Nakamura, K., Arai, S., & Kawabata, H. (2017). Prioritized identification of attractive and romantic partner faces in rapid serial visual presentation. *Archives of Sexual Behavior, 46,* 2327–2338.

Nakamura, Y., Gaetano, L., Matsushita, T., Anna, A., Sprenger, T., Radue, E. W., Wuerfel, J., Bauer, L., Amann, M., Shinoda, K., Isobe, N., Yamasaki, R., Saida, T., Kappos, L., & Isobe, N. (2018). A comparison of brain magnetic resonance imaging lesions in multiple sclerosis by race with reference to disability progression. *Journal of Neuroinflammation, 15,* 255.

Nam, B., Wilcox, H. C., Hilimire, M., & DeVylder, J. E. (2018). Perceived need for care and mental health service utilization among college students with suicidal ideation. *Journal of American College Health, 66*(8), 713–719.

Nancekivell, S. E., Shah, P., & Gelman, S. A. (2019). Maybe they're born with it, or maybe it's experience: Toward a deeper understanding of the learning style myth. *Journal of Educational Psychology, 112*(2), 221–235.

Napolitan, D. A., & Goethals, G. R. (1979). The attribution of friendliness. *Journal of Experimental Social Psychology, 15,* 105–113.

NAS. (2011, accessed May 11). *Statistics: How many people have autistic spectrum disorders?* National Autistic Society. Retrieved from autism.org.uk

NAS. (2019). *Fostering healthy mental, emotional, and behavioral development in children and youth: A national agenda.* National Academies Press.

Nasie, M., Diamond, A. H., & Bar-Tal, D. (2016). Young children in intractable conflicts: The Israeli case. *Personality and Social Psychology Review, 20,* 365–392.

Nathan, D. (2011). *Sybil exposed: The extraordinary story behind the famous multiple personality case.* Simon and Schuster.

Nathanson, L., Rivers, S. E., Flynn, L. M., & Brackett, M. A. (2016). Creating emotionally intelligent schools with RULER. *Emotion Review, 8,* 1–6.

National Academies of Sciences, Engineering, and Medicine. (2017). *The health effects of cannabis and cannabinoids: The current state of evidence and recommendations for research.* National Academies Press.

National Center for Health Statistics. (1990). *Health, United States, 1989.* U.S. Department of Health and Human Services.

National Council on Aging. (1999). *The consequences of untreated hearing loss in older persons.* Washington, DC: Author (ncoa.org).

National Institute on Aging (NIA). (2019). *Parkinson's disease.* National Institutes of Health. https://www.nia.nih.gov//health/parkinsons-disease

National Safety Council. (2019). *Deaths by transportation mode: Passenger death rates, United States, 2007–2017.* https://injuryfacts.nsc.org/home-and-community/safety-topics/deaths-by-transportation-mode/

National Science Foundation. (2019). *Number of women with U.S. doctorates in science, engineering, or health employed in the United States more than doubles since 1997* [PDF file]. Info brief. National Centers for Science and Engineering Statistics. nsf.gov/statistics/2019/nsf19307/nsf19307.pdf

Natsuaki, M. N., Neiderhiser, J. M., Harold, G. T., Shaw, D. S., Reiss, D., & Leve, L. D. (2019). Siblings reared apart: a sibling comparison study on rearing environment differences. *Developmental Psychology, 55,* 1182–1190.

Nature. (2016). Character traits: Scientific virtue. *Nature, 532,* 139.

Naumann, L. P., Vazire, S., Rentfrow, P. J., & Gosling, S. D. (2009). Personality judgments based on physical appearance. *Personality and Social Psychology Bulletin, 35,* 1661–1671.

Nausheen, B., Carr, N. J., Peveler, R. C., Moss-Morris, R., Verrill, C., Robbins, E., Nugent, K. P., Baker, A. M., Judd, M., & Gidron, Y. (2010). Relationship between loneliness and proangiogenic cytokines in newly diagnosed tumors of colon and rectum. *Psychosomatic Medicine, 72,* 912–916.

Nave, G., Minxha, J., Greenberg, D. M., Kosinski, M., Stillwell, D., & Rentfrow, J. (2018). Musical preferences predict personality: Evidence from active listening and Facebook likes. *Psychological Science, 29,* 1145–1158.

NCASA. (2007). *Wasting the best and the brightest: Substance abuse at America's colleges and universities.* https://www.centeronaddiction.org/newsroom/op-eds/wasting-best-and-brightest-alcohol-and-drug-abuse-college-campuses

NCD Risk Factor Collaboration. (2016). Trends in adult body-mass index in 200 countries from 1975 to 2014: A pooled analysis of 1698 population-based measurement studies with 19.2 million participants. *The Lancet, 387,* 1377–1396.

NCEE. (2018, February 22). *Statistic of the month: How much time do students spend in school?* National Center on Education and the Economy. http://ncee.org/2018/02/statistic-of-the-month-how-much-time-do-students-spend-in-school/

Neal, D. T., Wood, W., & Drolet, A. (2013). How do people adhere to goals when willpower is low? The profits (and pitfalls) of strong habits. *Journal of Personality and Social Psychology, 104,* 959–975.

Neatby, L. H. & Mercer, K. (2018). Sir John Franklin. *The Canadian Encyclopedia.* https://www.thecanadianencyclopedia.ca/en/article/sir-john-franklin

Nedeltcheva, A. V., Kilkus, J. M., Imperial, J., Schoeller, D. A., & Penev, P. D. (2010). Insufficient sleep undermines dietary efforts to reduce adiposity. *Annals of Internal Medicine, 153,* 435–441.

NEEF. (2015). *Fact sheet: Children's health and nature.* National Environmental Education Foundation. https://www.jeffersfoundation.org/real-research.php

Neese, R. M. (1991, November/December). What good is feeling bad? The evolutionary benefits of psychic pain. *The Sciences,* pp. 30–37.

Neimeyer, R. A., & Currier, J. M. (2009). Grief therapy: Evidence of efficacy and emerging directions. *Current Directions in Psychological Science, 18,* 352–356.

Neisser, U. (1979). The control of information pickup in selective looking. In A. D. Pick (Ed.), *Perception and its development: A tribute to Eleanor J. Gibson.* Erlbaum.

Neisser, U., Boodoo, G., Bouchard, T. J., Jr., Boykin, A. W., Brody, N., Ceci, S. J., Halpern, D. F., Loehlin, J. C., Perloff, R., Sternberg, R. J., & Urbina, S. (1996). Intelligence: Knowns and unknowns. *American Psychologist, 51,* 77–101.

Neitz, J., Carroll, J., & Neitz, M. (2001). Color vision: Almost reason enough for having eyes. *Optics & Photonics News, 12,* 26–33.

Neitz, J., Geist, T., & Jacobs, G. H. (1989). Color vision in the dog. *Visual Neuroscience, 3,* 119–125.

Nelson, B. W., & Allen, N. B. (2018). Extending the passive-sensing toolbox: Using smart-home technology in psychological science. *Perspectives on Psychological Science, 13,* 718–733.

Nelson, C. A., III, Fox, N. A., & Zeanah, C. H., Jr. (2013, April). Anguish of the abandoned child. *Scientific American,* pp. 62–67.

Nelson, C. A., III, Fox, N. A., & Zeanah, C. H., Jr. (2014). *Romania's abandoned children.* Harvard University Press.

Nelson, C. A., III, Furtado, E. Z., Fox, N. A., & Zeanah, C. H., Jr. (2009). The deprived human brain. *American Scientist, 97,* 222–229.

Nelson, J., Klumparendt, A., Doebler, P., & Ehring, T. (2017). Childhood maltreatment and characteristics of adult depression: A meta-analysis. *The British Journal of Psychiatry, 210,* 96–104.

Nelson, L. D., Simmons, J., & Simonsohn, U. (2018). Psychology's renaissance. *Annual Review of Psychology, 69,* 511–534.

Nelson, M. D., Saykin, A. J., Flashman, L. A., & Riordan, H. J. (1998). Hippocampal volume reduction in schizophrenia as assessed by magnetic resonance imaging. *Archives of General Psychiatry, 55,* 433–440.

Nelson-Coffey, S. K., Killingsworth, M., Layous, K., Cole, S. W., & Lyubomirsky, S. (2019). Parenthood is associated with greater well-being for fathers than mothers. *Personality and Social Psychology Bulletin, 45,* 1378–1390.

Nemeroff, C. B. (2018). Ketamine: Quo vadis? *American Journal of Psychiatry, 175,* 297-299.

Nemeth, C. J., & Ormiston, M. (2007). Creative idea generation: Harmony versus stimulation. *European Journal of Social Psychology, 37,* 524–535.

Nemmi, F., Nymberg, C., Helander, E., & Klingberg, T. (2016). Grit is associated with structure of nucleus accumbens and gains in cognitive training. *Journal of Cognitive Neuroscience, 28,* 1688–1699.

Nes, R. B. (2010). Happiness in behaviour genetics: Findings and implications. *Journal of Happiness Studies, 11,* 369–381.

Ness, E. (2016, January/February). FDA OKs sex drug for women. *Discover.* https://www.discovermagazine.com/health/fda-oks-sex-drug-for-women

Nestler, E. J. (2011). Hidden switches in the mind. *Scientific American, 305,* 76–83.

Nestoriuc, Y., Rief, W., & Martin, A. (2008). Meta-analysis of biofeedback for tension-type headache: Efficacy, specificity, and treatment moderators. *Journal of Consulting and Clinical Psychology, 76,* 379–396.

Nettle, D., Andrews, C., & Bateson, M. (2017). Food insecurity as a driver of obesity in humans: The insurance hypothesis. *Behavioral and Brain Sciences, 40,* e105.

Neubauer, D. N. (1999). Sleep problems in the elderly. *American Family Physician, 59,* 2551–2558.

Neumann, R., & Strack, F. (2000). "Mood contagion": The automatic transfer of mood between persons. *Journal of Personality and Social Psychology, 79,* 211–223.

Newcomb, M. D., & Harlow, L. L. (1986). Life events and substance use among adolescents: Mediating effects of perceived loss of control and meaninglessness in life. *Journal of Personality and Social Psychology, 51,* 564–577.

Newell, B. R. (2015). "Wait! Just let me not think about that for a minute": What role do implicit processes play in higher-level cognition? *Current Directions in Psychological Science, 24,* 65–70.

Newell, F. N., & Mitchell, K. J. (2016). Multisensory integration and cross-modal learning in synaesthesia: A unifying model. *Neuropsychologia, 88,* 140–150.

Newman, L. S., & Ruble, D. N. (1988). Stability and change in self-understanding: The early elementary school years. *Early Child Development and Care, 40,* 77–99.

Newport, C., Wallis, G., Reshitnyk, Y., & Siebeck, U. E. (2016). Discrimination of human faces by archerfish (*Toxotes chatareus*). *Scientific Reports, 6,* 27523.

Newport, E. L. (1990). Maturational constraints on language learning. *Cognitive Science, 14,* 11–28.

Newport, F. (1999, accessed April 28, 2016). Americans today much more accepting of a woman, Black, Catholic, or Jew as president. Gallup. Retrieved from https://news.gallup.com/poll/3979/americans-today-much-more-accepting-woman-black-catholic.aspx

Newport, F. (2001, February). Americans see women as emotional and affectionate, men as more aggressive. *The Gallup Poll Monthly,* pp. 34–38.

Newport, F. (2012, December 19). To stop shootings, Americans focus on police, mental health. Gallup. https://news.gallup.com/poll/159422/stop-shootings-americans-focus-police-mental-health.aspx

Newport, F. (2013b, July 31). Most U. S. smokers want to quit, have tried multiple times. Gallup. https://news.gallup.com/poll/163763/smokers-quit-tried-multiple-times.aspx

Newport, F. (2015, July 9). Most U.S. smartphone owners check phone at least hourly. Gallup. https://news.gallup.com/poll/184046/smartphone-owners-check-phone-least-hourly.aspx

Newport, F. (2018, May 22). In U.S. estimate of LGBT population rises to 4.5%. Gallup. https://news.gallup.com/poll/234863/estimate-lgbt-population-rises.aspx

Newport, F., Argrawal, S., & Witters, D. (2010, December 23). Very religious Americans lead healthier lives. Gallup. https://news.gallup.com/poll/145379/religious-americans-lead-healthier-lives.aspx

Newport, F., & Pelham, B. (2009, December 14). Don't worry, be 80: Worry and stress decline with age. Gallup. https://news.gallup.com/poll/124655/dont-worry-be-80-worry-stress-decline-age.aspx

Newport, F., & Wilke, J. (2013, August 2). Most in U.S. want marriage, but its importance has dropped. Gallup Poll. https://news.gallup.com/poll/163802/marriage-importance-dropped.aspx

Newton, E. L. (1991). The rocky road from actions to intentions. *Dissertation Abstracts International, 51,* 4105.

Newton, I. (1704). *Opticks: Or, a treatise of the reflexions, refractions, inflexions and colours of light.* Royal Society.

Newton, P. M., & Miah, M. (2017). Evidence-based higher education–Is the learning styles 'myth' important? *Frontiers in Psychology, 8,* 444.

Ng, J. Y. Y., Ntoumanis, N., Thøgersen-Ntoumani, C., Deci, E. L., Ryan, R. M., Duda, J. L., & Williams, G. C. (2012). Self-determination theory applied to health contexts: A meta-analysis. *Perspectives on Psychological Science, 7,* 325–340.

Ng, S. H. (1990). Androcentric coding of man and his in memory by language users. *Journal of Experimental Social Psychology, 26,* 455–464.

Ng, T. W. H., & Feldman, D. C. (2009). How broadly does education contribute to job performance. *Personnel Psychology, 62,* 89–134.

Ng, T. W. H., Sorensen, K. L., & Eby, L. T. (2006). Locus of control at work: A meta-analysis. *Journal of Organizational Behavior, 27,* 1057–1087.

Ng, T. W. H., Sorensen, K. L., & Yim, F. H. K. (2009). Does the job satisfaction—job performance relationship vary across cultures? *Journal of Cross-Cultural Psychology, 40,* 761–796.

Nguyen, H.-H. D., & Ryan, A. M. (2008). Does stereotype threat affect test performance of minorities and women? A meta-analysis of experimental evidence. *Journal of Applied Psychology, 93,* 1314–1334.

Nguyen, T. T., Ryan, R. M., & Deci, E. L. (2018). Solitude as an approach to affective self-regulation. *Personality and Social Psychology Bulletin, 44,* 92–106.

Nguyen, T. V., Werner, K. M., & Soenens, B. (2019). Embracing me-time: Motivation for solitude during transition to college. *Motivation and Emotion, 43,* 571–591.

NHS. (2020, accessed January 6). *Mental health.* National Health Service England. Retrieved from https://www.england.nhs.uk/five-year-forward-view/next-steps-on-the-nhs-five-year-forward-view/mental-health/

NHTSA. (2000). *Traffic safety facts 1999: Older population.* National Highway Traffic Safety Administration (ntl.bts.gov).

Nichols, R. M., & Loftus, E. F. (2019). Who is susceptible in three false memory tasks? *Memory, 27,* 962–984.

Nicholson, I. (2011). "Torture at Yale": Experimental subjects, laboratory torment and the "rehabilitation" of Milgram's "Obedience to Authority." *Theory and Psychology, 21,* 737–761.

Nickel, L. B., Roberts, B. W., & Chernyshenko, O. S. (2019). No evidence of a curvilinear relation between conscientiousness and relationship, work, and health outcomes. *Journal of Personality and Social Psychology, 116,* 296–312.

Nickell, J. (2005, July/August). The case of the psychic detectives. *Skeptical Inquirer.* https://skepticalinquirer.org/2005/07/the-case-of-the-psychic-detectives/

Nickerson, R. S. (1999). How we know—and sometimes misjudge—what others know: Imputing one's own knowledge to others. *Psychological Bulletin, 125,* 737–759.

Nickerson, R. S. (2002). The production and perception of randomness. *Psychological Review, 109,* 330–357.

Nickerson, R. S. (2005). Bertrand's chord, Buffon's needles, and the concept of randomness. *Thinking & Reasoning, 11,* 67–96.

Nickerson, R. S., & Adams, M. J. (1979). Long-term memory for a common object. *Cognitive Psychology, 11,* 287–307.

Nicol, S. E., & Gottesman, I. I. (1983). Clues to the genetics and neurobiology of schizophrenia. *American Scientist, 71,* 398–404.

Nicolas, S., & Levine, Z. (2012). Beyond intelligence testing: Remembering Alfred Binet after a century. *European Psychologist, 17,* 320–325.

Nicolaus, L. K., Cassel, J. F., Carlson, R. B., & Gustavson, C. R. (1983). Taste-aversion conditioning of crows to control predation on eggs. *Science, 220,* 212–214.

Nicolelis, M. A. L. (2011). *Beyond boundaries: The new neuroscience of connecting brains with machines—and how it will change our lives.* Times Books.

NIDA (National Institute on Drug Abuse). (2017). *The science of drug use: Discussion points.* https://www.drugabuse.gov/related-topics/criminal-justice/science-drug-use-discussion-points

NIDA. (2002). *Methamphetamine abuse and addiction.* Research Report Series. NIH Publication Number 02–4210.

NIDA. (2005, May). *Methamphetamine.* NIDA Info Facts.

NIDA. (2018). *Overdose death rates.* https://www.drugabuse.gov/related-topics/trends-statistics/overdose-death-rates

Niederkrotenthaler, T., Stack, S., Till, B., Sinyor, M., Pirkis, J., Garcia, D., Rockett, I. R., & Tran, U. S. (2019). Association of increased youth suicides in the United States with the release of *13 Reasons Why.* *JAMA Psychiatry, 76*(9), 933–940.

NIEHS. (2019). Institutional review board. National Institute of Environmental Health Sciences, National Institutes of Health. Retrieved on May 8, 2019, from https://www.niehs.nih.gov/about/boards/irb/index.cfm

Nielsen, K. M., Faergeman, O., Larsen, M. L., & Foldspang, A. (2006). Danish singles have a twofold risk of acute coronary syndrome: Data from a cohort of 138,290 persons. *Journal of Epidemiology and Community Health, 60,* 721–728.

Nielsen, M., & Tomaselli, K. (2010). Overimitation in Kalahari Bushman children and the origins of human cultural cognition. *Psychological Science, 21,* 729–736.

Nielssen, O., Karin, E., Staples, L., Titov, N., Gandy, M., Fogliati, V. J., & Dear, B. F. (2019). Opioid use before and after completion of an online pain management program. *Journal of Consulting and Clinical Psychology, 87,* 904–917.

Niemiec, C. P., Ryan, R. M., & Deci, E. L. (2009). The path taken: Consequences of attaining intrinsic and extrinsic aspirations in post-college life. *Journal of Research in Personality, 43,* 291–306.

Niessen, A. S., & Meijer, R. R. (2017). On the use of broadened admission criteria in higher education. *Perspectives on Psychological Science, 12,* 436–448.

Nietzsche, F. (1889/1990). *Twilight of the idols and the Anti-Christ: Or how to philosophize with a hammer* (R. J. Hollindale, translator). Penguin Classics.

Nieuwenstein, M. R., Wierenga, T., Morey, R. D., Wicherts, J. M., Blom, T. N., Wagenmakers, E., & van Rijn, H. (2015). On making the right choice: A meta-analysis and large-scale replication attempt of the unconscious thought advantage. *Judgment and Decision Making, 10,* 1–17.

NIH. (2001, July 20). *Workshop summary: Scientific evidence on condom effectiveness for sexually transmitted disease (STD) prevention.* National Institute of Allergy and Infectious Diseases, National Institutes of Health.

NIH. (2010). *Teacher's guide: Information about sleep.* http://sleep.boomja.com/index.php?ITEM=61174

NIH. (2013, January 24). *Prenatal inflammation linked to autism risk.* https://www.nih.gov/news-events/news-releases/prenatal-inflammation-linked-autism-risk

NIH. (2019). *All of us health surveys.* https://allofus.nih.gov/

Nikitin, E. S., Roshchin, M. V., Ierusalimsky, V. N., Egorov, A. V., & Balaban, P. M. (2019). Optogenetic stimulation of the axons of visual cortex and hippocampus pyramidal neurons in living brain slices. *Neuroscience and Behavioral Physiology, 49,* 227–232.

Nikles, M., Stiefel, F., & Bourquin, C. (2017). What medical students dream of: A standardized and data-driven approach. *Dreaming, 27,* 177–192.

Nikolas, M. A., & Burt, A. (2010). Genetic and environmental influences on ADHD symptom dimensions of inattention and hyperactivity: A meta-analysis. *Journal of Abnormal Psychology, 119,* 1–17.

Nikolova, H., & Lamberton, C. (2016). Men and the middle: Gender differences in dyadic compromise effects. *Journal of Consumer Research, 43,* 355–371.

Niles, A. N., Craske, M. G., Lieberman, M. D., & Hur, C. (2015). Affect labeling enhances exposure effectiveness for public speaking anxiety. *Behavior Research and Therapy, 68,* 27–36.

NIMH. (2017, accessed February 27). *Research Domain Criteria (RDoC).* National Institute of Mental Health. https://www.nimh.nih.gov/research/research-funded-by-nimh/rdoc/index.shtml

NIMH. (2019, accessed June 16). *Adolescent Brain Cognitive Development (ABCD) Study.* https://www.nimh.nih.gov/research/research-funded-by-nimh/research-initiatives/adolescent-brain-cognitive-development-abcd-study.shtml

Ninio, J., & Stevens, K. A. (2000) Variations on the Hermann grid: an extinction illusion. *Perception, 29,* 1209–1217.

Niparko, J. K., Tobey, E. A., Thal, D. J., Eisenberg, L. S., Wang, N., Quittner, A. L., & Fink, N. E. (2010). Spoken language development in children following cochlear implantation. *JAMA, 303,* 1498–1506.

Nir, Y., & Tononi, G. (2010). Dreaming and the brain: From phenomenology to neurophysiology. *Trends in Cognitive Sciences, 14,* 88–100.

Nisbett, R. (2015). *Mindware: Tools for smart thinking.* Farrar, Straus and Giroux.

Nisbett, R. E. (1987). Lay personality theory: Its nature, origin, and utility. In N. E. Grunberg, R. E. Nisbett et al. (Eds.), *A distinctive approach to psychological research: The influence of Stanley Schachter.* Erlbaum.

Nisbett, R. E. (2003). *The geography of thought: How Asians and Westerners think differently . . . and why.* Free Press.

Nisbett, R. E. (2009). *Intelligence and how to get it: Why schools and culture count.* Norton.

Nisbett, R. E., Aronson, J., Blair, C., Dickens, W., Flynn, J., Halpern, D. F., & Turkheimer, E. (2012). Intelligence: New findings and theoretical developments. *American Psychologist, 67,* 130–159.

Nisbett, R. E., & Cohen, D. (1996). *Culture of honor: The psychology of violence in the South.* Westview Press.

Nisbett, R. E., & Ross, L. (1980). *Human inference: Strategies and shortcomings of social judgment.* Prentice-Hall.

Nitschke, J. P., Krol, S. A., & Bartz, J. A. (2019). Oxytocin and human sociality: An interactionist perspective on the hormone of love. *Biological Psychiatry: Cognitive Neuroscience and Neuroimaging.* In press.

Noah, T., Schul, Y., & Mayo, R. (2018). When both the original study and its failed replication are correct: Feeling observed eliminates the facial-feedback effect. *Journal of Personality and Social Psychology, 114,* 657–664.

Noble, W., & Spires-Jones, T. L. (2019). Sleep well to slow Alzheimer's progression? *Science, 363,* 813–814.

Nock, M. (2016, May 6). Five myths about suicide. *The Washington Post* (washingtonpost.com).

Nock, M. K., Borges, G., Bromet, E. J., Alonso, J., Angermeyer, M., Beautrais, A., Bruffaerts, R., Chiu, W. T., de Girolamo, G., Gluzman, S., de Graaf, R., Gureje, O., Haro, J. M., Huang, Y., Karam, E., Kessler, R. C., Lepine, J. P., Levinson, D., Medina-Mora, M. E., . . . Williams, D. (2008). Cross-national prevalence and risk factors for suicidal ideation, plans, and attempts. *British Journal of Psychiatry, 192,* 98–105.

Nock, M. K., & Kessler, R. C. (2006). Prevalence of and risk factors for suicide attempts versus suicide gestures: Analysis of the National Comorbidity Survey. *Journal of Abnormal Psychology, 115,* 616–623.

Noel, J. G., Forsyth, D. R., & Kelley, K. N. (1987). Improving the performance of failing students by overcoming their self-serving attributional biases. *Basic and Applied Social Psychology, 8,* 151–162.

Noice, H., & Noice, T. (2006). What studies of actors and acting can tell us about memory and cognitive functioning. *Current Directions in Psychological Science, 15,* 14–18.

Nolen-Hoeksema, S. (2001). Gender differences in depression. *Current Directions in Psychological Science, 10,* 173–176.

Nolen-Hoeksema, S. (2003). *Women who think too much: How to break free of overthinking and reclaim your life.* Holt.

Nolen-Hoeksema, S., & Larson, J. (1999). *Coping with loss.* Erlbaum.

Nollet, M., Hicks, H., McCarthy, A. P., Wu, H., Moller-Levet, C. S., Laing, E. E., Malki, K., Lawless, N., Wafford, K. A., Dijk, D.-J., & Winsky-Sommerer, R. (2019). REM sleep: Unique associations with corticosterone regulation, apoptotic pathways and behavior in chronic stress in mice. *PNAS, 116,* 2733–2742.

Nook, E. C., Ong, D. C., Morelli, S. A., Mitchell, J. P., & Zaki, J. (2016). Prosocial conformity: Prosocial norms generalize across behavior and empathy. *Personality and Social Psychology Bulletin, 42,* 1045–1062.

Norberg, M. M., Krystal, J. H., & Tolin, D. F. (2008). A meta-analysis of d-cycloserine and the facilitation of fear extinction and exposure therapy. *Biological Psychiatry, 63,* 1118–1126.

Nørby, S. (2015). Why forget? On the adaptive value of memory loss. *Perspectives on Psychological Science, 10,* 551–578.

NORC. (2016a). General Social Survey data, 1972 through 2014. Accessed via sda.berkeley.edu.

NORC. (2016b). *New insights into Americans' perceptions and misperceptions of obesity treatments, and the struggles many face.* National Opinion Research Center and the American Society for Metabolic and Bariatric Surgery (norc.org).

NORC. (2019). *General social survey.* NORC (formerly National Opinion Research Center), University of Chicago.

Nordgren, L. F., McDonnell, M.-H. M., & Loewenstein, G. (2011). What constitutes torture? Psychological impediments to an objective evaluation of enhanced interrogation tactics. *Psychological Science, 22,* 689–694.

Nordgren, L. F., van der Pligt, J., & van Harreveld, F. (2006). Visceral drives in retrospect: Explanations about the inaccessible past. *Psychological Science, 17,* 635–640.

Nordgren, L. F., van der Pligt, J., & van Harreveld, F. (2007). Evaluating Eve: Visceral states influence the evaluation of impulsive behavior. *Journal of Personality and Social Psychology, 93,* 75–84.

Nordgren, L. F., van Harreveld, F., & van der Pligt, J. (2009). The restraint bias: How the illusion of self-restraint promoted impulsive behavior. *Psychological Science, 20,* 1523–1528.

Norem, J. K. (2001). *The positive power of negative thinking: Using defensive pessimism to harness anxiety and perform at your peak.* Basic Books.

Norenzayan, A., & Hansen, I. G. (2006). Belief in supernatural agents in the face of death. *Personality and Social Psychology Bulletin, 32,* 174–187.

Norko, M. A., Freeman, D., Phillips, J., Hunter, W., Lewis, R., & Viswanathan, R. (2017). Can religion protect against suicide? *Journal of Nervous and Mental Disease, 205,* 9–14.

Norman, D. A. (2001). *The perils of home theater.* https://jnd.org/the_perils_of_home_theater/

Norman, E. (2010). "The unconscious" in current psychology. *European Psychologist, 15,* 193–201.

Norman, Y., Yeagle, E. M., Khuvis, S., Harel, M., Mehta, A. D., & Malach, R. (2019). Hippocampal sharp-wave ripples linked to visual episodic recollection in humans. *Science, 365*(6454), eaax1030.

Norris, A. L., Marcus, D. K., & Green, B. A. (2015). Homosexuality as a discrete class. *Psychological Science, 26,* 1843–1853.

Northey, J. M., Cherbuin, N., Pumpa, K. L., Smee, D. J., & Rattray, B. (2018). Exercise interventions for cognitive function in adults older than 50: A systematic review with meta-analysis. *British Journal of Sports Medicine, 52,* 154.

Norton, K. L., Olds, T. S., Olive, S., & Dank, S. (1996). Ken and Barbie at life size. *Sex Roles, 34,* 287–294.

Nosek, B. A., Ebersole, C. R., DeHaven, A. C., & Mellor, D. T. (2018). The preregistration revolution. *PNAS, 115,* 2600–2606.

Novén, M., Schremm, A., Nilsson, M., Horne, M., & Roll, M. (2019). Cortical thickness of Broca's area and right homologue is related to grammar learning aptitude and pitch discrimination proficiency. *Brain and Language, 188,* 42–47.

NPR. (2009, July 11). *Afraid to fly? Try living on a plane.* https://www.npr.org/templates/story/story.php?storyId=106498235

NPR. (2018, October 1). *They always remember a face: What it takes to be a Scotland Yard 'super recognizer.'* NPR Here & Now. https://www.wbur.org/hereand now/2018/10/01/skripal-poisoning-super-recognizer

NSC. (2019). *Odds of dying.* https://injuryfacts.nsc .org/all-injuries/preventable-death-overview /odds-of-dying/data-details/

NSF. (2001, October 24). *Public bounces back after Sept. 11 attacks, national study shows.* National Science Foundation. https://www.nsf.gov/od/lpa/news /press/01/pr0185.htm

NSF. (2006). *The ABC's of back-to-school sleep schedules: The consequences of insufficient sleep.* National Sleep Foundation press release (sleepfoundation.org).

NSF. (2008). *2008 sleep in America poll: Summary of findings* [PDF file]. https://www.sleepfoundation .org/sites/default/files/2018-11/2008_POLL_SOF.pdf

NSF. (2013). *2013 International bedroom poll: Summary of findings* [PDF file]. https://www.sleepfoundation .org/sites/default/files/inline-files/RPT495a.pdf

Nugent, N. R., Goldberg, A., & Uddin, M. (2016). Topical review: The emerging field of epigenetics: Informing models of pediatric trauma and physical health. *Journal of Pediatric Psychology, 41,* 55–64.

Nunziata, L. (2015). Immigration and crime: Evidence from victimization data. *Journal of Population Economics, 28,* 697–736.

Nurmikko, A. V., Donoghue, J. P., Hochberg, L. R., Patterson, W. R., Song, Y.-K., Bull, C. W., Borton, D. A., Laiwalla, F., Park, S., Ming, Y., & Aceros, J. (2010). Listening to brain microcircuits for interfacing with external world—Progress in wireless implantable microelectronic neuroengineering devices. *Proceedings of the IEEE, 98,* 375–388.

Nussinovitch, U., & Shoenfeld, Y. (2012). The role of gender and organ specific autoimmunity. *Autoimmunity Reviews, 11,* A377–A385.

Nuttin, J. M., Jr. (1987). Affective consequences of mere ownership: The name letter effect in twelve European languages. *European Journal of Social Psychology, 17,* 381–402.

Nye, C. D., Su, R., Rounds, J., & Drasgow, F. (2012). Vocational interests and performance: A quantitative summary of over 60 years of research. *Perspectives on Psychological Science, 7,* 384–403.

O'Brien, E., & Ellsworth, P. C. (2012). Saving the last for best: A positivity bias for end experiences. *Psychological Science, 23,* 163–165.

O'Brien, E., & Smith, R. W. (2019). Unconventional consumption methods and enjoying things consumed: Recapturing the "first-time" experience. *Personality and Social Psychology Bulletin, 45,* 67–80.

O'Brien, F., Bible, J., Liu, D., & Simons-Morton, B. (2017). Do young drivers become safer after being involved in a collision? *Psychological Science, 28,* 407–413.

O'Brien, L., Albert, D., Chein, J., & Steinberg, L. (2011). Adolescents prefer more immediate rewards when in the presence of their peers. *Journal of Research on Adolescence, 21,* 747–753.

O'Callaghan, C., Shine, J. M., Hodges, J. R., Andrews-Hanna, J. R., & Irish, M. (2019). Hippocampal atrophy and intrinsic brain network dysfunction relate to alterations in mind wandering in neurodegeneration. *PNAS, 116,* 3316–3321.

O'Connor, P., & Brown, G. W. (1984). Supportive relationships: Fact or fancy? *Journal of Social and Personal Relationships, 1,* 159–175.

O'Connor, R. J., Fix, B. V., McNeill, A., Goniewicz, M. L., Bansal-Travers, M., Heckman, B. W., Cummings, M. K., Hitchman, S., Borland, R., Hammond, D., Levy, D. T., Gravely, S., & Fong, G. (2019). Characteristics of nicotine vaping products used by participants in the 2016 ITC Four Country Smoking and Vaping Survey. *Addiction, 114,* Suppl 1, 15–23.

O'Donnell, L., Stueve, A., O'Donnell, C., Duran, R., San Doval, A., Wilson, R. F., Haber, E. P., & Pleck, J. H. (2002). Long-term reduction in sexual initiation and sexual activity among urban middle schoolers in the Reach for Health service learning program. *Journal of Adolescent Health, 31,* 93–100.

O'Donovan, A., Neylan, T. C., Metzler, T., & Cohen, B. E. (2012). Lifetime exposure to traumatic psychological stress is associated with elevated inflammation in the Heart and Soul Study. *Brain, Behavior, and Immunity, 26,* 642–649.

O'Hara, R. E., Gibbons, F. X., Gerrard, M., Li, Z., & Sargent, J. D. (2012). Greater exposure to sexual content in popular movies predicts earlier sexual debut and increased sexual risk taking. *Psychological Science, 23,* 984–993.

O'Leary, K. D., O'Leary, S., & Becker, W. C. (1967). Modification of a deviant sibling interaction pattern in the home. *Behaviour Research and Therapy, 5,* 113–120.

O'Leary, T., Williams, A. H., Franci, A., & Marder, E. (2014). Cell types, network homeostasis, and pathological compensation from a biologically plausible ion channel expression model. *Neuron, 82,* 809–821.

O'Neill, M. J. (1993). *The relationship between privacy, control, and stress responses in office workers* [Paper]. Presented to the Human Factors and Ergonomics Society convention.

O'Sullivan, M., Frank, M. G., Hurley, C. M., & Tiwana, J. (2009). Police lie detection accuracy: The effect of lie scenario. *Law and Human Behavior, 33,* 530–538.

Oakley, D. A., & Halligan, P. W. (2013). Hypnotic suggestion: Opportunities for cognitive neuroscience. *Nature Reviews Neuroscience, 14,* 565–576.

Obama, B. (2017, January 10). President Obama's farewell address. *The New York Times.* https://www .nytimes.com/video/us/politics/100000004864201 /watch-live-president-obamas-farewell-speech .html?

Oberauer, K., Lewandowsky, S., Awh, E., Brown, G. D. A., Conway, A., Cowan, N., Donkin, C., Farrell, S., Hitch, G. J., Hurlstone, M. J., Ma, W. J., Morey, C. C., Nee, D. E., Schweppe, J., Vergauwe, E., & Ward, G. (2018). Benchmarks for models of short-term and working memory. *Psychological Bulletin, 144,* 885–958.

Oberman, L. M., & Ramachandran, V. S. (2007). The simulating social mind: The role of the mirror neuron system and simulation in the social and communicative deficits of autism spectrum disorders. *Psychological Bulletin, 133,* 310–327.

Obermeyer, Z., Powers, B., Vogeli, C., & Mullainathan, S. (2019). Dissecting racial bias in an algorithm used to manage the health of populations. *Science, 366,* 447–453.

Obschonka, M., Zhou, M., Zhou, Y., Zhang, J., & Silbereisen, R. K. (2018). "Confucian" traits, entrepreneurial personality, and entrepreneurship in China: a regional analysis. *Small Business Economics,* 1–19.

Ochsner, K. N., Ray, R. R., Hughes, B., McRae, K., Cooper, J. C., Weber, J., Gabrieli, J. D., & Gross, J. J. (2009). Bottom-up and top-down processes in emotion generation: Common and distinct neural mechanisms. *Psychological Science, 20,* 1322–1331.

Odgers, C. L., Caspi, A., Nagin, D. S., Piquero, A. R., Slutske, W. S., Milne, B. J., Dickson, N., Poulton, R., & Moffitt, T. E. (2008). Is it important to prevent early exposure to drugs and alcohol among adolescents? *Psychological Science, 19,* 1037–1044.

Odic, D., & Wojcik, E. H. (2020). The publication gender gap in psychology. *American Psychologist, 75,* 92–103.

OECD. (2018). *Employment: Time spent in paid and unpaid work, by sex.* Organisation for Economic Co-operation and Development. https://stats.oecd.org /index.aspx?queryid=54757

Offer, D., Ostrov, E., Howard, K. I., & Atkinson, R. (1988). *The teenage world: Adolescents' self-image in ten countries.* Plenum Press.

Offner, M., Coles, A., Decou, M. L., Minh, T. D. Bienek, A., Snider, J., & Ugnat, A.-M. (2018). *Autism Spectrum Disorder among children and youth in Canada 2018: A report of the National Autism Spectrum Disorder Surveillance System.* Public Health Agency of Canada. https://www.nimh.nih.gov/research/research -funded-by-nimh/rdoc/index.shtml

Ofosu, E. K., Chambers, M. K., Chen, J. M., & Hehman, E. (2019). Same-sex marriage legalization associated with reduced implicit and explicit anti-gay bias. *PNAS, 116,* 8846–8851.

Ogden, J. (2012, January 16). HM, the man with no memory. *Psychology Today.* https://www.psycho logytoday.com/us/blog/trouble-in-mind/201201 /hm-the-man-no-memory

Ogihara, Y., Fujita, H., Tominaga, H., Ishigaki, S., Kashimoto, T., Takahashi, A., Toyohara, K., & Uchida, Y. (2015). Are common names becoming less common? The rise in uniqueness and individualism in Japan. *Frontiers in Psychology, 6,* article 1490.

Ogunnaike, O., Dunham, Y., & Banaji, M. R. (2010). The language of implicit preferences. *Journal of Experimental Social Psychology, 46,* 999–1003.

Ohgami, H., Terao, T., Shiotsuki, I., Ishii, N., & Iwata, N. (2009). Lithium levels in drinking water and risk of suicide. *British Journal of Psychiatry, 194,* 464–465.

Ohi, K., Shimada, T., Nitta, Y., Kihara, H., Okubo, H., Uehara, T., & Kawasaki, Y. (2016). The five-factor model personality traits in schizophrenia: A meta-analysis. *Psychiatry Research, 240,* 34–41.

Öhman, A. (2009). Of snakes and fears: An evolutionary perspective on the psychology of fear. *Scandinavian Journal of Psychology, 50,* 543–552.

Öhman, A., Lundqvist, D., & Esteves, F. (2001). The face in the crowd revisited: A threat advantage with schematic stimuli. *Journal of Personality and Social Psychology, 80,* 381–396.

Oishi, S., & Diener, E. (2014). Can and should happiness be a policy goal? *Policy Insights from Behavioral and Brain Sciences, 1,* 195–203.

Oishi, S., Diener, E. F., Lucas, R. E., & Suh, E. M. (1999). Cross-cultural variations in predictors of life satisfaction: Perspectives from needs and values. *Personality and Social Psychology Bulletin, 25,* 980–990.

Oishi, S., Kesebir, S., & Diener, E. (2011). Income inequality and happiness. *Psychological Science, 22,* 1095–1100.

Oishi, S., Kesebir, S., Miao, F., Talhelm, T., Endo, U., Uchida, Y., Shibanai, Y., & Norasakkunkit, V. (2013a). Residential mobility increases motivation to expand social network. But why? *Journal of Experimental Social Psychology, 49,* 217–223.

Oishi, S., & Schimmack, U. (2010). Culture and well-being: A new inquiry into the psychological wealth of nations. *Perspectives in Psychological Science, 5,* 463–471.

Okada, K., & Samreth, S. (2013). A study on the socio-economic determinants of suicide: Evidence from 13 European OECD countries. *Journal of Behavioral Economics, 45,* 78–85.

Okimoto, T. G., & Brescoll, V. L. (2010). The price of power: Power seeking and backlash against female politicians. *Personality and Social Psychology Bulletin, 36,* 923–936.

Okuyama, T., Kitamura, T., Roy, D. S., Itohara, S., & Tonegawa, S. (2016). Ventral CA1 neurons store social memory. *Science, 353,* 1536–1541.

Olatunji, B. O., & Wolitzky-Taylor, K. B. (2009). Anxiety sensitivity and the anxiety disorders: A meta-analytic review and synthesis. *Psychological Bulletin, 135,* 974–999.

Olds, J. (1958). Self-stimulation of the brain. *Science, 127*, 315–324.

Olds, J. (1975). Mapping the mind onto the brain. In F. G. Worden, J. P. Swazey, & G. Adelman (Eds.), *The neurosciences: Paths of discovery* (pp. 375–400). MIT Press.

Olds, J., & Milner, P. (1954). Positive reinforcement produced by electrical stimulation of the septal area and other regions of rat brain. *Journal of Comparative and Physiological Psychology, 47*, 419–427.

Olff, M., Langeland, W., Draijer, N., & Gersons, B. P. R. (2007). Gender differences in posttraumatic stress disorder. *Psychological Bulletin, 135*, 183–204.

Olfson, M., Gerhard, T., Huang, C., Crystal, S., & Stroup, T. S. (2015). Premature mortality among adults with schizophrenia in the United States. *JAMA Psychiatry, 72*, 1172–1181.

Olfson, M., & Marcus, S. C. (2009). National patterns in antidepressant medication treatment. *Archives of General Psychiatry, 66*, 848–856.

Olfson, M., Wall, M., Liu, S-M., Morin, C. MN., & Blanco, C. (2018). Insomnia and impaired quality of life in the United States. *Journal of Clinical Psychiatry, 79*(5), 17m12020.

Olfson, M., Wang, S., Wall, M., Marcus, S. C., & Blanco, C. (2019). Trends in serious psychological distress and outpatient mental health care of U.S. adults. *JAMA Psychiatry, 76*, 152–161.

Oliner, S. P., & Oliner, P. M. (1988). *The altruistic personality: Rescuers of Jews in Nazi Europe*. Free Press.

Oliveira, D. F., Ma, Y., Woodruff, T. K., & Uzzi, B. (2019). Comparison of National Institutes of Health grant amounts to first-time male and female principal investigators. *JAMA, 321*, 898–900.

Olivola, C. Y., & Todorov, A. (2010). Elected in 100 milliseconds: Appearance-based trait inferences and voting. *Journal of Nonverbal Behavior, 54*, 83–110.

Olshansky, S. J. (2011). Aging of U.S. Presidents. *Journal of the American Medical Association, 306*, 2328–2329.

Olson, K. R., & Gülgöz, S. (2018). Early findings from the TransYouth Project: Gender development in transgender children. *Child Development Perspectives, 12*, 93–97.

Olson, K. R., Key, A. C., & Eaton, N. R. (2015). Gender cognition in transgender children. *Psychological Science, 26*, 467–474.

Olson, R. L., Hanowski, R. J., Hickman, J. S., & Bocanegra, J. (2009, September). *Driver distraction in commercial vehicle operations* [PDF file]. U.S. Department of Transportation, Federal Motor Carrier Safety Administration. https://www.fmcsa.dot.gov/sites/fmcsa.dot.gov/files/docs/DriverDistraction Study.pdf

Olsson, A., Nearing, K. I., & Phelps, E. A. (2007). Learning fears by observing others: The neural systems of social fear transmission. *Social Cognitive and Affective Neuroscience, 2*, 3–11.

Oltmanns, J. R., Smith, G. T., Oltmanns, T. F., & Widiger, T. A. (2018). General factors of psychopathology, personality, and personality disorder: Across domain comparisons. *Clinical Psychological Science, 6*, 581–589.

Oman, D., Kurata, J. H., Strawbridge, W. J., & Cohen, R. D. (2002). Religious attendance and cause of death over 31 years. *International Journal of Psychiatry in Medicine, 32*, 69–89.

Oman, D., & Syme, S. L. (2018). Weighing the evidence: What is revealed by 100+ meta-analyses and systematic reviews of religion/spirituality and health? In D. Oman (Ed.) *Why religion and spirituality matter for public health: Evidence, implications, and resources* (pp. 261–281). Springer.

ONS. (2018). *Measuring national well-being: Quality of life in the UK, 2018*. Office of National Statistics. https://www.ons.gov.uk/releases/measuringnational wellbeinglifeintheukapril2018

ONS. (2019, September 3). *Suicides in the UK: 2018 registrations*. Office for National Statistics. https://bit.ly/34Y9a7c

Onyeador, I. N., Wittlin, N. M., Burke, S. E., Dovidio, J. F., Perry, S. P., Hardeman, R. R., Dyrbye, L. N., Herrin, J., Phelan, S. M., & van Ryn, M. (2020). The value of interracial contact for reducing anti-Black bias among non-Black physicians: A cognitive habits and growth evaluation (CHANGE) study report. *Psychological Science, 31*(1), 18–30. Open Science Collaboration. (2015). Estimating the reproducibility of psychological science. *Science, 349*, 943.

Opp, M. R., & Krueger, J. M. (2015). Sleep and immunity: A growing field with clinical impact. *Brain, Behavior, and Immunity, 47*, 1–3.

Oquendo, M. A., Galfalvy, H. C., Currier, D., Grunebaum, M. F., Sher, L., Sullivan, G. M., Burke, A. K., Harkavy-Friedman, J., Sublette, M. E., Parsey, R. V., & Mann, J. J. (2011). Treatment of suicide attempters with bipolar disorder: A randomized clinical trial comparing lithium and valproate in the prevention of suicidal behavior. *The American Journal of Psychiatry, 168*, 1050–1056.

Orehek, E., & Human, L. J. (2017). Self-expression on social media: Do tweets present accurate and positive portraits of impulsivity, self-esteem, and attachment style? *Personality and Social Psychology Bulletin, 43*, 60–70.

Oren, D. A., & Terman, M. (1998). Tweaking the human circadian clock with light. *Science, 279*, 333–334.

Orth, U., Erol, R. Y., & Luciano, E. C. (2018). Development of self-esteem from age 4 to 94 years: A meta-analysis of longitudinal studies. *Psychological Bulletin, 144*, 1045–1080.

Orth, U., & Robins, R. W. (2014). The development of self-esteem. *Current Directions in Psychological Science, 23*, 381–387.

Orth, U., Robins, R. W., Meier, L. L., & Conger, R. D. (2016). Refining the vulnerability model of low self-esteem and depression: Disentangling the effects of genuine self-esteem and narcissism. *Journal of Personality and Social Psychology, 110*, 133–149.

Orth, U., Robins, R. W., Trzesniewski, K. H., Maes, J., & Schmitt, M. (2009). Low self-esteem is a risk factor for depressive symptoms from young adulthood to old age. *Journal of Abnormal Psychology, 118*, 472–478.

Ortiz-Ospina, E. (2019, July 17). *Are we happier when we spend more time with others?* Our World in Data. https://ourworldindata.org/happiness-and-friends

Osborne, L. (1999, October 27). A linguistic big bang. *The New York Times Magazine*. https://archive.nytimes.com/www.nytimes.com/library/magazine/home/19991024mag-sign-language.html

Osgood, C. E. (1962). *An alternative to war or surrender*. University of Illinois Press.

Osgood, C. E. (1980). GRIT: A strategy for survival in mankind's nuclear age? [Paper]. Presented at the Pugwash Conference on New Directions in Disarmament.

Oskarsson, A. T., Van Voven, L., McClelland, G. H., & Hastie, R. (2009). What's next? Judging sequences of binary events. *Psychological Bulletin, 135*, 262–285.

Osler, M., Rozing, M. P., Christensen, G. T., Andersen, P. K., & Jørgensen, M. B. (2018). Electroconvulsive therapy and risk of dementia in patients with affective disorders: A cohort study. *The Lancet Psychiatry, 5*, 348–356.

Osoegawa, C., Gomes, J. S., Grigolon, R. B., Brietzke, E., Gadelha, A., Lacerda, A. L., Dias, A. M., Cordeiro, Q., Laranjeira, R., de Jesus, D., Daskalakis, Z. J., Brunelin, J., Cordes, J., & Paulino Trevizol, A. (2018). Non-invasive brain stimulation for negative symptoms in schizophrenia: An updated systematic review and meta-analysis. *Schizophrenia Research, 197*, 34–44.

OSS Assessment Staff. (1948). *The assessment of men*. Rinehart.

Ossher, L., Flegal, K. E., & Lustig, C. (2012). Everyday memory errors in older adults. *Aging, Neuropsychology, and Cognition, 20*, 220–242.

Ossola, A. (2014). This woman sees 100 times more colors than the average person. *Popular Science*. https://www.popsci.com/article/science/woman-sees-100-times-more-colors-average-person/

Öst, L. G., Havnen, A., Hansen, B., & Kvale, G. (2015). Cognitive behavioral treatments of obsessive-compulsive disorder. A systematic review and meta-analysis of studies published 1993–2014. *Clinical Psychology Review, 40*, 156–169.

Öst, L. G., & Hugdahl, K. (1981). Acquisition of phobias and anxiety response patterns in clinical patients. *Behaviour Research and Therapy, 16*, 439–447.

Österman, K., Björkqvist, K., & Wahlbeck, K. (2014). Twenty-eight years after the complete ban on the physical punishment of children in Finland: Trends and psychosocial concomitants. *Aggressive Behavior, 40*, 568–581.

Ostfeld, A. M., Kasl, S. V., D'Atri, D. A., & Fitzgerald, E. F. (1987). *Stress, crowding, and blood pressure in prison*. Erlbaum.

Osvath, M., & Karvonen, E. (2012). Spontaneous innovation for future deception in a male chimpanzee. *PLOS ONE, 7*, e36782.

Oswald, F. L., Mitchell, G., Blanton, H., Jaccard, J., & Tetlock, P. E. (2013). Predicting ethnic and racial discrimination: A meta-analysis of IAT criterion studies. *Journal of Personality and Social Psychology, 105*, 171–192.

Oswald, F. L., Mitchell, G., Blanton, H., Jaccard, J., & Tetlock, P. E. (2015). Using the IAT to predict ethnic and racial discrimination: Small effect sizes of unknown societal significance. *Journal of Personality and Social Psychology, 108*, 562–571.

Otgaar, H., & Baker, A. (2018). When lying changes memory for the truth. *Memory, 1*, 2–14.

Otgaar, H., Howe, M. L., Patihis, L., Merckelbach, H., Lynn, S. J., Lilienfeld, S. O., & Loftus, E. F. (2019). The return of the repressed: The persistent and problematic claims of long-forgotten trauma. *Perspectives on Psychological Science, 14*, 1072–1095.

Ott, B. (2007, June 14). Investors, take note: Engagement boosts earnings. *Gallup Business Journal*. https://news.gallup.com/businessjournal/27799/investors-take-note-engagement-boosts-earnings.aspx

Ott, C. H., Lueger, R. J., Kelber, S. T., & Prigerson, H. G. (2007). Spousal bereavement in older adults: Common, resilient, and chronic grief with defining characteristics. *Journal of Nervous and Mental Disease, 195*, 332–341.

Ouellette, J. A., & Wood, W. (1998). Habit and intention in everyday life: The multiple processes by which past behavior predicts future behavior. *Psychological Bulletin, 124*, 54–74.

Our World in Data. (2019). *Human height*. https://ourworldindata.org/human-height

Owczarski, W. (2018). Adaptive nightmares of Holocaust survivors: The Auschwitz camp in the former inmates' dreams. *Dreaming, 28*, 287–302.

Owen, A. (2017a). Into the gray zone: A neuroscientist explores the border between life and death. Scribner.

Owen, A. (2017b, August). Adrian Owen: At the flimsy border between life and death [Interview]. *The Psychologist*. https://thepsychologist.bps.org.uk/volume-30/august-2017/flimsy-border-between-life-and-death

Owen, A. M., Coleman, M. R., Boly, M., Davis, M. H., Laureys, S., & Pickard, J. D. (2006). Detecting awareness in the vegetative state. *Science, 313,* 1402.

Owen, R. (1814). First essay in *New view of society or the formation of character.* Quoted in *The story of New Lamark.* New Lamark Conservation Trust, 1993.

OWN. (2018, April 20). *Oprah and Amy Schumer on being secret introverts* [Video file]. http://www.oprah.com/own-supersoulsessions/oprah-and-amy-schumer-on-being-secret-introverts-video_2

Oxfam. (2005, March 26). *Three months on: New figures show tsunami may have killed up to four times as many women as men.* https://reliefweb.int/report/india/south-asia-three-months-new-figures-show-tsunami-may-have-killed-four-times-many-women

Özçaliskan, S., Lucero, C., & Goldin-Meadow, S. (2016). Is *seeing gesture* necessary to *gesture* like a native speaker? Psychological Science, 27, 737–747.

Ozer, E. J., Best, S. R., Lipsey, T. L., & Weiss, D. S. (2003). Predictors of posttraumatic stress disorder and symptoms in adults: A meta-analysis. *Psychological Bulletin, 1,* 52–73.

Ozer, E. J., & Weiss, D. S. (2004). Who develops posttraumatic stress disorder? *Current Directions in Psychological Science, 13,* 169–172.

Özgen, E. (2004). Language, learning, and color perception. *Current Directions in Psychological Science, 13,* 95–98.

Pace-Schott, E. P., & Spencer, R. M. C. (2011). Age-related changes in the cognitive function of sleep. *Progress in Brain Research, 191,* 75–89.

Pachankis, J. E., & Bränström, R. (2018). Hidden from happiness: Structural stigma, sexual orientation concealment, and life satisfaction across 28 countries. *Journal of Consulting and Clinical Psychology, 86,* 403–415.

Pachankis, J. E., Hatzenbuehler, M. L., Wang, K., Burton, C. L., Crawford, F. W., Phelan, J. C., & Link, B. G. (2018). The burden of stigma on health and well-being: A taxonomy of concealment, course, disruptiveness, aesthetics, origin, and peril across 93 stigmas. *Personality and Social Psychology Bulletin, 44,* 451–474.

Padgett, V. R. (1989). *Predicting organizational violence: An application of 11 powerful principles of obedience* [Paper]. Presented to the American Psychological Association convention.

Painter, D. R., Dwyer, M. F., Kamke, M. R., & Mattingley, J. B. (2018). Stimulus-driven cortical hyperexcitability in individuals with Charles Bonnet hallucinations. *Current Biology, 28,* 3475–3480.

Palagini, L., Bastien, C. H., Marazziti, D., Ellis, J. G., & Riemann, D. (2019). The key role of insomnia and sleep loss in the dysregulation of multiple systems involved in mood disorders: A proposed model. *Journal of Sleep Research, 28,* e12841.

Palladino, J. J., & Carducci, B. J. (1983). *"Things that go bump in the night": Students' knowledge of sleep and dreams* [Paper]. Presented at the meeting of the Southeastern Psychological Association.

Paller, K. A., & Oudiette, D. (2018, November). Sleep learning gets real. *Scientific American,* pp. 27–31.

Palmer, B. (2013, May 9). *Investigative intuition: Do psychics ever solve crimes? Why do police consult them?* Slate. https://slate.com/news-and-politics/2013/05/psychic-sylvia-browne-said-amanda-berry-was-dead-why-do-police-consult-psychics.html

Palmer, D. C. (1989). A behavioral interpretation of memory. In L. J. Hayes (Ed.), *Dialogues on verbal behavior: The first international institute on verbal relations* (pp. 261–279). Context Press.

Palmese, L. B., DeGeorge, P. C., Ratliff, J. C., Srihari, V. H., Wexler, B. E., Krystal, A. D., & Tek, C. (2011). Insomnia is frequent in schizophrenia and associated with night eating and obesity. *Schizophrenia Research, 133,* 238–243.

Palomar-García, M. Á., Bueicheků, E., Ávila, C., Sanjuán, A., Strijkers, K., Ventura-Campos, N., & Costa, A. (2015). Do bilinguals show neural differences with monolinguals when processing their native language? *Brain and Language, 142,* 36–44.

Palombo, D. J., McKinnon, M. C., McIntosh, A. R., Anderson, A. K., Todd, R. M., & Levine, B. (2015). The neural correlates of memory for a life-threatening event: An fMRI study of passengers from Flight AT236. *Clinical Psychological Science, 4,* 312–319.

Paluck, E. L., Green, S. A., & Green, D. P. (2018). The contact hypothesis re-evaluated. *Behavioural Public Policy,* 1–30.

Pan, S. C., & Rickard, T. C. (2018). Transfer of test-enhanced learning: Meta-analytic review and synthesis. *Psychological Bulletin, 144,* 710–756.

Pandey, J., Sinha, Y., Prakash, A., & Tripathi, R. C. (1982). Right-left political ideologies and attribution of the causes of poverty. *European Journal of Social Psychology, 12,* 327–331.

Pänkäläinen, M., Kerola, T., Kampman, O., Kauppi, M., & Hintikka, J. (2016). Pessimism and risk of death from coronary heart disease among middle-aged and older Finns: An eleven-year follow-up study. *BMC Public Health, 16,* 1124.

Panksepp, J. (2007). Neurologizing the psychology of affects: How appraisal-based constructivism and basic emotion theory can coexist. *Perspectives on Psychological Science, 2,* 281–295.

Pantev, C., Oostenveld, R., Engelien, A., Ross, B., Roberts, L. R., & Hoke, M. (1998). Increased auditory cortical representation in musicians. *Nature, 392,* 811–814.

Papadatou-Pastou, M., Gritzali, M., & Barrable, A. (2018, November). The learning styles educational neuromyth: Lack of agreement between teachers' judgments, self-assessment, and students' intelligence. In *Frontiers in Education* (Vol. 3, pp. 1–5).

Pappas, A. (2016, August 26). Alexi Pappas shares secrets from the Olympic Village. *The New York Times.* https://well.blogs.nytimes.com/2016/08/26/alexi-pappas-shares-secrets-from-the-olympic-village/

Pardiñas, A. F., Holmans, P., Pocklington, A. J., Escott-Price, V., Ripke, S., Carrera, N., Legge, S. E., Bishop, S., Cameron, D., Hamshere, M. L., Han, J., Hubbard, L., Lynham, A., Mantripragada, K., Rees, E., MacCabe, J. H., McCarroll, S. A., Baune, B. T., Breen, G., . . . Walters, J. T. R. (2018). Common schizophrenia alleles are enriched in mutation-intolerant genes and in regions under strong background selection. *Nature Genetics, 50,* 381–389.

Pardini, D. A., Raine, A., Erickson, K., & Loeber, R. (2014). Lower amygdala volume in men is associated with childhood aggression, early psychopathic traits, and future violence. *Biological Psychiatry, 75,* 73–80.

Park, C. L. (2007). Religiousness/spirituality and health: A meaning systems perspective. *Journal of Behavioral Medicine, 30,* 319–328.

Park, D. C., & McDonough, I. M. (2013). The dynamic aging mind: Revelations from functional neuroimaging research. *Perspectives on Psychological Science, 8,* 62–67.f

Park, G., Schwartz, H. A., Eichstaedt, J. C., Kern, M. L., Kosinski, M., Stillwell, D. J., Ungar, L. H., & Seligman, M. E. P. (2015). Automatic personality assessment through social media language. *Journal of Personality and Social Psychology, 108,* 934–952.

Park, G., Yaden, D. R., Schwartz, H. A., Kern, M. L., Eichstaedt, J. C., Kosinski, M., Stillwell, D., Ungar, L. H., & Seligman, M. E. P. (2016). Women are warmer but no less assertive than men: Gender and language on Facebook. *PLOS ONE, 11,* e0155885.

Park, K., Lee, S., Yang, J., Song, T., & Hong, G. R. S. (2019). A systematic review and meta-analysis on the effect of reminiscence therapy for people with dementia. *International Psychogeriatrics, 31,* 1581–1597.

Park, Y. C., & Pyszczynski, T. (2019). Reducing defensive responses to thoughts of death: Meditation, mindfulness, and Buddhism. *Journal of Personality and Social Psychology, 116,* 101–118.

Parker, E. S., Cahill, L., & McGaugh, J. L. (2006). A case of unusual autobiographical remembering. *Neurocase, 12,* 35–49.

Parker, K., & Wang, W. (2013). *Modern parenthood. roles of moms and dads converge as they balance work and family* [PDF file]. Pew Research Center, Social & Demographic Trends. https://www.pewsocialtrends.org/wp-content/uploads/sites/3/2013/03/FINAL_modern_parenthood_03-2013.pdf

Parkes, A., Wight, D., Hunt, K., Henderson, M., & Sargent, J. (2013). Are sexual media exposure, parental restrictions on media use and co-viewing TV and DVDs with parents and friends associated with teenagers' early sexual behavior? *Journal of Adolescence, 36,* 1121–1133.

Parkinson's Foundation. (2018). *Statistics.* https://www.parkinson.org/Understanding-Parkinsons/Statistics

Parnia, S., Spearpoint, K., de Vos, G., Fenwick, P., Goldberg, D., Yang, J., Zhu, J., Baker, K., Killingback, H., McLean, P., Wood, M., Zafari, A. M., Dickert, N., Beisteiner, R., Sterz, F., Berger, M., Warlow, C., Bullock, S., Lovett, S., . . . Schoenfeld, E. R. (2014). AWARE—AWAreness during REsuscitation—A prospective study. *Resuscitation, 85,* 1799–1805.

Parsaik, A. K., Mascarenhas, S. S., Hashmi, A., Prokop, L. J., John, V., Okusaga, O., & Singh, B. (2016). Role of botulinum toxin in depression. *Journal of Psychiatric Practice, 22,* 99–110.

Partanen, E., Kujala, T., Näätänen, R., Liitola, A., Sambeth, A., & Huotilainen, M. (2013). Learning-induced neural plasticity of speech processing before birth. *PNAS, 110,* 15145–15150.

Parthasarathy, S., Vasquez, M. M., Halonen, M., Bootzin, R., Quan, S. F., Martinez, F. D., & Guerra, S. (2015). Persistent insomnia is associated with mortality risk. *American Journal of Medicine, 128,* 268–275.

Paşca, A. M., Sloan, S. A., Clarke, L. E., Tian, Y., Makinson, C. D., Huber, N., Kim, C. H., Park, J. Y. O'Rourke, N. A., Nguyen, K. D. Smith, S. J., Huguenard, J. R., Geschwind, D. H., Barres, B. A., & Paşca, S. P. (2015). Functional cortical neurons and astrocytes from human pluripotent stem cells in 3D culture. *Nature Methods, 12,* 671–678.

Pascoe, E. A., & Richman, L. S. (2009). Perceived discrimination and health: A meta-analytic review. *Psychological Bulletin, 135,* 531–554.

Passell, P. (1993, March 9). Like a new drug, social programs are put to the test. *The New York Times.* https://www.nytimes.com/1993/03/09/science/like-a-new-drug-social-programs-are-put-to-the-test.html?

Patihis, L. (2016). Individual differences and correlates of highly superior autobiographical memory. *Memory, 24,* 961–978.

Patihis, L., Frenda, S. J., & Loftus, E. F. (2018). False memory tasks do not reliably predict other false memories. *Psychology of Consciousness: Theory, Research, and Practice, 5,* 140.

Patihis, L., Ho, L. Y., Tingen, I. W., Lilienfeld, S. O., & Loftus, E. F. (2014a). Are the "memory wars" over? A scientist-practitioner gap in beliefs about repressed memory. *Psychological Science, 25,* 519–530.

Patihis, L., Lilienfeld, S. O., Ho, L. Y., & Loftus, E. F. (2014b). Unconscious repressed memory is scientifically questionable. *Psychological Science, 25,* 1967–1968.

Patterson, D. R., & Jensen, M. P. (2003). Hypnosis and clinical pain. *Psychological Bulletin, 129,* 495–521.

Patterson, F. (1978, October). Conversations with a gorilla. *National Geographic,* pp. 438–465.

Patterson, G. R., Chamberlain, P., & Reid, J. B. (1982). A comparative evaluation of parent training procedures. *Behavior Therapy, 13,* 638–650.

Patterson, G. R., Ray, R. S., & Shaw, D. A. (1968). Direct intervention in families of deviant children. *Oregon Research Institute Research Bulletin,* 8(No. 9). Oregon Research Institute and University of Oregon.

Patterson, M., Warr, P., & West, M. (2004). Organizational climate and company productivity: The role of employee affect and employee level. *Journal of Occupational and Organizational Psychology, 77,* 193–216.

Patterson, R. (1951). *The riddle of Emily Dickinson.* Houghton Mifflin.

Patton, C. L., Smith, S. F., & Lilienfeld, S. O. (2018). Psychopathy and heroism in first responders: Traits cut from the same cloth? *Personality Disorders: Theory, Research, and Treatment, 9,* 354–368.

Pauker, K., Weisbuch, M., Ambady, N., Sommers, S. R., Adams, R. B., Jr., & Ivcevic, Z. (2009). Not so Black and White: Memory for ambiguous group members. *Journal of Personality and Social Psychology, 96,* 795–810.

Paulesu, E., Démonet, J.-F., Fazio, F., McCrory, E., Chanoine, V., Brunswick, N., Cappa, S. F., Cossu, G., Habib, M., Frith, C. D., & Frith, U. (2001). Dyslexia: Cultural diversity and biological unity. *Science, 291,* 2165–2167.

Pauletti, R. E., Menon, M., Cooper, P. J., Aults, C. D., & Perry, D. G. (2017). Psychological androgyny and children's mental health: A new look with new measures. *Sex Roles, 76,* 705–718.

Pauly, K., Finkelmeyer, A., Schneider, F., & Habel, U. (2013). The neural correlates of positive self-evaluation and self-related memory. *Social Cognitive and Affective Neuroscience, 8,* 878–886.

Paus, T., Zijdenbos, A., Worsley, K., Collins, D. L., Blumenthal, J., Giedd, J. N., Rapoport, J. L., & Evans, A. C. (1999). Structural maturation of neural pathways in children and adolescents: In vivo study. *Science, 283,* 1908–1911.

Pavlenko, A. (2014). *The bilingual mind and what it tells us about language and thought.* Cambridge University Press.

Pavlov, I. (1927). *Conditioned reflexes: An investigation of the physiological activity of the cerebral cortex.* Oxford University Press.

Payne, B. K. (2006). Weapon bias: Split-second decisions and unintended stereotyping. *Current Directions in Psychological Science, 15,* 287–291.

Payne, B. K., Krosnick, J. A., Pasek, J., Lelkes, Y., Akhtar, O., & Tompson, T. (2010). Implicit and explicit prejudice in the 2008 American presidential election. *Journal of Experimental Social Psychology, 46,* 367–374.

Payne, K. (2017). *The broken ladder: How inequality affects the way we think, live, and die.* Viking.

PBS. (2019). Alfred Kinsey's life, and sex research and social policies in America. *PBS American Experience.* https://www.pbs.org/wgbh/americanexperience/features/kinsey-timeline/

Pearce, M. J., Koenig, H. G., Robins, C. J., Nelson, B., Shaw, S. F., Cohen, H. J., & King, M. B. (2015). Religiously integrated cognitive behavioral therapy: A new method of treatment for major depression in patients with chronic medical illness. *Psychotherapy, 52,* 56–66.

Pedersen, A., Zachariae, R., & Bovbjerg, D. H. (2010). Influence of psychological stress on upper respiratory infection—A meta-analysis of prospective studies. *Psychosomatic Medicine, 72,* 823–832.

Peigneux, P., Laureys, S., Fuchs, S., Collette, F., Perrin, F., Reggers, J., Phillips, C., Degueldre, C., Del Fiore, G., Aerts, J., Luxen, A., & Maquet, P. (2004). Are spatial memories strengthened in the human hippocampus during slow wave sleep? *Neuron, 44,* 535–545.

Pelham, B., & Crabtree, S. (2008, October 8). Worldwide, highly religious more likely to help others. Gallup. https://news.gallup.com/poll/111013/worldwide-highly-religious-more-likely-help-others.aspx

Pelham, B. W. (1993). On the highly positive thoughts of the highly depressed. In R. F. Baumeister (Ed.), *Self-esteem: The puzzle of low self-regard.* Plenum.

Pelham, W. E., Jr., Fabiano, G. A., Waxmonsky, J. G., Greiner, A. R., Gnagy, E. M., Pelham, W. E., III, Coxe, S., Verley, J., Bhatia, I., Hart, K., Karch, K., Konijnendijk, E., Tresco, K., Nahum-Shani, I., & Murphy, S. A. (2016). Treatment sequencing for childhood ADHD: A multiple-randomization study of adaptive medication and behavioral interventions. *Journal of Clinical Child and Adolescent Psychology, 45,* 396–415.

Peng, Y., & Tullis, J. G. (2019). Theories of intelligence influence self-regulated study choices and learning. *Journal of Experimental Psychology: Learning, Memory, and Cognition,* in press.

Pennebaker, J. (1990). *Opening up: The healing power of confiding in others.* William Morrow.

Pennebaker, J. W. (1985). Traumatic experience and psychosomatic disease: Exploring the roles of behavioral inhibition, obsession, and confiding. *Canadian Psychology, 26,* 82–95.

Pennebaker, J. W. (2011). *The secret life of pronouns: What our words say about us.* Bloomsbury Press.

Pennebaker, J. W., Barger, S. D., & Tiebout, J. (1989). Disclosure of traumas and health among Holocaust survivors. *Psychosomatic Medicine, 51,* 577–589.

Pennebaker, J. W., Gosling, S. D., & Ferrell, J. D. (2013). Daily online testing in large classes: Boosting college performance while reducing achievement gaps. *PLOS ONE, 8,* e79774.

Pennebaker, J. W., & O'Heeron, R. C. (1984). Confiding in others and illness rate among spouses of suicide and accidental death victims. *Journal of Abnormal Psychology, 93,* 473–476.

Pennycook, G., De Neys, W., Evans, J. S. B., Stanovich, K. E., & Thompson, V. A. (2018). The mythical dual-process typology. *Trends in Cognitive Sciences, 22,* 667–668.

Pennycook, G., & Rand, D. G. (2019). Fighting misinformation on social media using crowdsourced judgments of news source quality. *PNAS, 116,* 2521–2526.

Pennycook, G., & Rand, D. G. (2019). Lazy, not biased: Susceptibility to partisan fake news is better explained by lack of reasoning than by motivated reasoning. *Cognition, 188,* 39–50.

Peplau, L. A., & Fingerhut, A. W. (2007). The close relationships of lesbians and gay men. *Annual Review of Psychology, 58,* 405–424.

Pepler, D., & Craig, W. (2012, November 15). *Health development depends on healthy relationships* [Paper]. Prepared for the Division of Childhood and Adolescence, Centre for Health Promotion, Public Health Agency of Canada. PREVNet and York University.

Pepperberg, I. M. (2009). *Alex & me: How a scientist and a parrot discovered a hidden world of animal intelligence—and formed a deep bond in the process.* Harper.

Pepperberg, I. M. (2012). Further evidence for addition and numerical competence by a grey parrot (Psittacus erithacus). *Animal Cognition, 15,* 711–717.

Pepperberg, I. M. (2013). Abstract concepts: Data from a grey parrot. *Behavioural Processes, 93,* 82–90.

Perdue, K. L., Jensen, S. K., Kumar, S., Richards, J. E., Kakon, S. H., Haque, R., Petri, W. A., Jr., Lloyd-Fox, S., Elwell, C., & Nelson, C. A. (2019). Using functional near-infrared spectroscopy to assess social information processing in poor urban Bangladeshi infants and toddlers. *Developmental Science, 22,* e12839.

Pereg, D., Gow, R., Mosseri, M., Lishner, M., Rieder, M., Van Uum, S., & Koren, G. (2011). Hair cortisol and the risk for acute myocardial infarction in adult men. *Stress, 14,* 73–81.

Pereira, A. C., Huddleston, D. E., Brickman, A. M., Sosunov, A. A., Hen, R., McKhann, G. M., Sloan, R., Gage, F. H., Brown, T. R., & Small, S. A. (2007). An *in vivo* correlate of exercise-induced neurogenesis in the adult dentate gyrus. *PNAS, 104,* 5638–5643.

Pereira, G. M., & Osburn, H. G. (2007). Effects of participation in decision making on performance and employee attitudes: A quality circles meta-analysis. *Journal of Business Psychology, 22,* 145–153.

Pérez-Vigil, A., Fernández de, l. C., Brander, G., Isomura, K., Jangmo, A., Feldman, I., Hesselmark, E., Serlachius, E., Lázaro, L., Rück, C., Kuja-Halkola, R., D'Onofrio, B. M., Larsson, H., & Mataix-Cols, D. (2018). Association of obsessive-compulsive disorder with objective indicators of educational attainment: A nationwide register-based sibling control study. *JAMA Psychiatry, 75,* 47–55.

Pergamin-Hight, L., Bakermans-Kranenburg, M. J., van IJzendoorn, M. H., & Bar-Haim, Y. (2012). Variations in the promoter region of the serotonin transporter gene and biased attention for emotional information: A meta-analysis. *Biological Psychiatry, 71,* 373–379.

Perilloux, C., Easton, J. A., & Buss, D. M. (2012). The misperception of sexual interest. *Psychological Science, 23,* 146–151.

Perilloux, H. K., Webster, G. D., & Gaulin, S. J. (2010). Signals of genetic quality and maternal investment capacity: The dynamic effects of fluctuating asymmetry and waist-to-hip ratio on men's ratings of women's attractiveness. *Social Psychological and Personality Science, 1,* 34–42.

Perkins, A., & Fitzgerald, J. A. (1997). Sexual orientation in domestic rams: Some biological and social correlates. In L. Ellis & L. Ebertz (Eds.), *Sexual orientation: Toward biological understanding.* Praeger Publishers.

Perkins, A. M., Inchley-Mort, S. L., Pickering, A. D., Corr, P. J., & Burgess, A. P. (2012). A facial expression for anxiety. *Journal of Personality and Social Psychology, 102,* 910–924.

Perrachione, T. K., Del Tufo, S. N., & Gabrieli, J. D. E. (2011). Human voice recognition depends on language ability. *Science, 333,* 595.

Perrett, D. I., Harries, M., Mistlin, A. J., & Chitty, A. J. (1990). Three stages in the classification of body movements by visual neurons. In H. Barlow, C. Blakemore, & M. Weston-Smith (Eds.), *Images and understanding* (pp. 94–108). Cambridge University Press.

Perrett, D. I., Hietanen, J. K., Oram, M. W., & Benson, P. J. (1992). Organization and functions of cells responsive to faces in the temporal cortex. *Philosophical Transactions of the Royal Society of London: Series B, 335,* 23–30.

Perrett, D. I., May, K. A., & Yoshikawa, S. (1994). Facial shape and judgments of female attractiveness. *Nature, 368,* 239–242.

Perry, G. (2013). *Behind the shock machine: The untold story of the notorious Milgram psychology experiments.* New Press.

Perry, G. (2018). *The lost boys: Inside Muzafer Sherif's Robbers Cave experiment.* Scribe.

Person, C., Tracy, M., & Galea, S. (2006). Risk factors for depression after a disaster. *Journal of Nervous and Mental Disease, 194,* 659–666.

Pert, C. B. (1986). Quoted in J. Hooper & D. Teresi, *The three-pound universe.* Macmillan.

Pert, C. B., & Snyder, S. H. (1973). Opiate receptor: Demonstration in nervous tissue. *Science, 179,* 1011–1014.

Perugini, E. M., Kirsch, I., Allen, S. T., Coldwell, E., Meredith, J., Montgomery, G. H., & Sheehan, J. (1998). Surreptitious observation of responses to hypnotically suggested hallucinations: A test of the compliance hypothesis. *International Journal of Clinical and Experimental Hypnosis, 46,* 191–203.

Peschel, E. R., & Peschel, R. E. (1987). Medical insights into the castrati in opera. *American Scientist, 75,* 578–583.

Pescosolido, B. A., Martin, J. K., Long, J. S., Medina, T. R., Phelan, J. C., & Link, B. G. (2010). "A disease like any other?" A decade of change in public reactions to schizophrenia, depression, and alcohol dependence. *American Journal of Psychiatry, 167,* 1321–1330.

Pesko, M. F. (2014). Stress and smoking: Associations with terrorism and causal impact. *Contemporary Economic Policy, 32,* 351–371.

Peter, C. J., Fischer, L. K., Kundakovic, M., Garg, P., Jakovcevski, M, Dincer, A., Amaral, S. C., Ginns, E., Galdzicka, M., Bryce, C. P., Ratner, C., Waber, D. P., Mokler, D., Medford, G., Champagne, F. A., Rosene, D. L., McGaughy, J. A., Sharp, A. J., Galler, J. R. & Akbarian, S. (2016). DNA methylation signatures of early childhood malnutrition associated with impairments in attention and cognition. *Biological Psychiatry, 80,* 765–774.

Peter, J., & Valkenburg, P. M. (2016). Adolescents and pornography: A review of 20 years of research. *Journal of Sex Research, 53,* 509–531.

Peters, K., & Kashima, Y. (2015). A multimodal theory of affect diffusion. *Psychological Bulletin, 141,* 966–992.

Peters, M., Rhodes, G., & Simmons, L. W. (2007). Contributions of the face and body to overall attractiveness. *Animal Behaviour, 73,* 937–942.

Petersen, J. L., & Hyde, J. S. (2010). A meta-analytic review of research on gender differences in sexuality, 1993–2007. *Psychological Bulletin, 136,* 21–38.

Petersen, J. L., & Hyde, J. S. (2011). Gender differences in sexual attitudes and behaviors: A review of meta-analytic results and large datasets. *Journal of Sex Research, 48,* 149–165.

Peterson, C., & Barrett, L. C. (1987). Explanatory style and academic performance among university freshmen. *Journal of Personality and Social Psychology, 53,* 603–607.

Peterson, C., Peterson, J., & Skevington, S. (1986). Heated argument and adolescent development. *Journal of Social and Personal Relationships, 3,* 229–240.

Peterson, C. C., & Siegal, M. (1999). Representing inner worlds: Theory of mind in autistic, deaf, and normal hearing children. *Psychological Science, 10,* 126–129.

Peterson, C. K., & Harmon-Jones, E. (2012). Anger and testosterone: Evidence that situationally-induced anger relates to situationally-induced testosterone. *Emotion, 12,* 899–902.

Peterson, G. B. (2004). A day of great illumination: B. F. Skinner's discovery of shaping. *Journal of the Experimental Analysis of Behavior, 82,* 317–328.

Peterson, L. R., & Peterson, M. J. (1959). Short-term retention of individual verbal items. *Journal of Experimental Psychology, 58,* 193–198.

Peterson, R. S., Dvorak, R. D., Stevenson, B. L., Kramer, M. P., Pinto, D. A., Mora, E. T., & Leary, A. V. (2019). Protective behavioral strategies and alcohol-related regretted sex among college students. *Experimental and Clinical Psychopharmacology, 28*(1), 6–12.

Petitto, L. A., & Marentette, P. F. (1991). Babbling in the manual mode: Evidence for the ontogeny of language. *Science, 251,* 1493–1496.

Petsko, C. D., & Bodenhausen, G. V. (2019). Race–crime congruency effects revisited: Do we take defendants' sexual orientation into account? *Social Psychological and Personality Science, 10,* 73–81.

Pettegrew, J. W., Keshavan, M. S., & Minshew, N. J. (1993). 31P nuclear magnetic resonance spectroscopy: Neurodevelopment and schizophrenia. *Schizophrenia Bulletin, 19,* 35–53.

Pettersson, E., Lichtenstein, P., Larsson, H., Song, J., Attention Deficit/Hyperactivity Disorder Working Group of the iPSYCH-Broad-PGC Consortium, Autism Spectrum Disorder Working Group of the iPSYCH-Broad-PGC Consortium, Bipolar Disorder Working Group of the PGC, Eating Disorder Working Group of the PGC, Major Depressive Disorder Working Group of the PGC, Obsessive Compulsive Disorders and Tourette Syndrome Working Group of the PGC, Schizophrenia CLOZUK, Substance Use Disorder Working Group of the PGC, Agrawal, A., Børglum, A. D., Bulik, C. M., Daly, M. J., Davis, L. K., Demontis, D., Edenberg, H. J., . . . Polderman, T. J. C. (2019). Genetic influences on eight psychiatric disorders based on family data of 4,408,646 full and half-siblings, and genetic data of 333,748 cases and controls. *Psychological Medicine, 49,* 1166–1173.

Petticrew, C., Bell, R., & Hunter, D. (2002). Influence of psychological coping on survival and recurrence in people with cancer: Systematic review. *British Medical Journal, 325,* 1066.

Petticrew, M., Fraser, J. M., & Regan, M. F. (1999). Adverse life events and risk of breast cancer: A meta-analysis. *British Journal of Health Psychology, 4,* 1–17.

Pettigrew, T. F., & Tropp, L. R. (2011). *When groups meet: The dynamics of intergroup contact.* Psychology Press.

Pew. (2007, July 18). *Modern marriage: "I like hugs. I like kisses. But what I really love is help with the dishes."* https://www.pewsocialtrends.org/2007/07/18/modern-marriage/

Pew. (2013a, June 4). *The global divide on homosexuality.* Global Attitudes Project. https://www.pewresearch.org/global/2013/06/04/the-global-divide-on-homosexuality/

Pew. (2013b, June 13). *A survey of LGBT Americans.* https://www.pewsocialtrends.org/2013/06/13/a-survey-of-lgbt-americans/

Pew. (2014). *Global views of morality.* Global Attitudes Project. https://www.pewresearch.org/global/interactives/global-morality/

Pew. (2015). *Teen girls more likely to text, call and use social media to get in touch; boys more likely to use gaming.* https://www.pewresearch.org/internet/2015/08/06/teens-technology-and-friendships/2015-08-06_teens-and-friendships_2-06/

Pew. (2015, November 4). *Raising kids and running a household: How working parents share the load.* https://www.pewsocialtrends.org/2015/11/04/raising-kids-and-running-a-household-how-working-parents-share-the-load/

Pew. (2016, September 28). *Where the public stands on religious liberty vs. nondiscrimination.* https://www.pewforum.org/2016/09/28/where-the-public-stands-on-religious-liberty-vs-nondiscrimination/

Pew. (2017). *Internet/Broadband technology fact sheet.* pewinternet.org/fact-sheet/internet-broadband/

Pew. (2019, January 31). *Religion's relationship to happiness, civic engagement and health around the world.* https://www.pewforum.org/2019/01/31/religions-relationship-to-happiness-civic-engagement-and-health-around-the-world/

Pfaff, L. A., Boatwright, K. J., Potthoff, A. L., Finan, C., Ulrey, L. A., & Huber, D. M. (2013). Perceptions of women and men leaders following 360-degree feedback evaluations. *Performance Improvement Quarterly, 26,* 35–56.

Phelps, E. A., & Hofmann, S. G. (2019). Memory editing from science fiction to clinical practice. *Nature, 572,* 43–50.

Phelps, J. A., Davis J. O., & Schartz, K. M. (1997). Nature, nurture, and twin research strategies. *Current Directions in Psychological Science, 6,* 117–120.

Philbeck, J. W., & Witt, J. K. (2015). Action-specific influences on perception and postperceptual processes: Present controversies and future directions. *Psychological Bulletin, 141,* 1120–1144.

Philip Morris. (2003). Philip Morris USA youth smoking prevention. Teenage attitudes and behavior study, 2002. In *Raising kids who don't smoke.* Series, Vol. 1(2).

Phillips, A. C., Batty, G. D., Gale, C. R., Deary, I. J., Osborn, D., MacIntyre, K., & Carroll, D. (2009). Generalized anxiety disorder, major depressive disorder, and their comorbidity as predictors of all-cause and cardiovascular mortality: The Vietnam Experience Study. *Psychosomatic Medicine, 71,* 395–403.

Phillips, A. L. (2011). A walk in the woods. *American Scientist, 69,* 301–302.

Phillips, D. P. (1985). Natural experiments on the effects of mass media violence on fatal aggression: Strengths and weaknesses of a new approach. In L. Berkowitz (Ed.), *Advances in experimental social psychology* (Vol. 19, pp. 207–250). Academic Press.

Phillips, D. P., Carstensen, L. L., & Paight, D. J. (1989). Effects of mass media news stories on suicide, with new evidence on the role of story content. In C. R. Pfeffer (Ed.), *Suicide among youth: Perspectives on risk and prevention* (pp. 101–116). American Psychiatric Press.

Phillips, J. L. (1969). *Origins of intellect: Piaget's theory.* Freeman.

Phillips, J. L., Norris, S., Talbot, J., Birmingham, M., Hatchard, T., Ortiz, A., Owoeye, O., Batten, L. A., & Blier, P. (2019). Single, repeated, and maintenance ketamine infusions for treatment-resistant depression: a randomized controlled trial. *American Journal of Psychiatry, 176,* 401–409.

Phillips, W. J., Fletcher, J. M., Marks, A. D. G., & Hine, D. W. (2016). Thinking styles and decision making: A meta-analysis. *Psychological Bulletin, 142,* 260–290.

Philpot, R., Liebst, L. S., Levine, M., Bernasco, W., & Lindegaard, M. R. (2019). Would I be helped? Cross-national CCTV footage shows that intervention is the norm in public conflicts. *American Psychologist, 75*(1), 66–75.

Piaget, J. (1930). *The child's conception of physical causality.* Routledge & Kegan Paul.

Piaget, J. (1932). *The moral judgment of the child* (M. Gabain, Trans.). Harcourt, Brace & World.

Piazza, J. R., Charles, S. T., Silwinski, M. J., Mogle, J., & Almeida, D. M. (2013). Affective reactivity to daily stressors and long-term risk of reporting a chronic health condition. *Annals of Behavioral Medicine, 45,* 110–120.

Picardi, A., Fagnani, C., Nisticò, L., & Stazi, M. A. (2011). A twin study of attachment style in young adults. *Journal of Personality, 79,* 965–992.

Picchioni, M. M., & Murray, R. M. (2007). Schizophrenia. *British Medical Journal, 335,* 91–95.

Picci, G., Gotts, S. J., & Scherf, K. S. (2016). A theoretical rut: Revisiting and critically evaluating the generalized under/over-connectivity hypothesis of autism. *Developmental Science, 19,* 524–549.

Picci, G., & Scherf, K. S. (2016). From caregivers to peers: Puberty shapes human face perception. *Psychological Science, 27,* 1461–1473.

Piekarski, D. J., Routman, D. M., Schoomer, E. E., Driscoll, J. R., Park, J. H., Butler, M. P., & Zucker, I. (2009). Infrequent low dose testosterone treatment maintains male sexual behavior in Syrian hamsters. *Hormones and Behavior, 55,* 182–189.

Pierce, L. J., Klein, D., Chen, J., Delcenserie, A., & Genesee, F. (2014). Mapping the unconscious maintenance of a lost first language. *PNAS, 111,* 17314–17319.

Pietschnig, J., & Voracek, M. (2015). One century of global IQ gains: A formal meta-analysis of the Flynn effect (1909–2013). *Perspectives on Psychological Science, 10,* 282–306.

Piliavin, J. A. (2003). Doing well by doing good: Benefits for the benefactor. In C.L.M. Keyes & J. Haidt (Eds.), *Flourishing: Positive psychology and the life well-lived* (pp. 227–247). American Psychological Association.

Pillemer, D. (1998). *Momentous events, vivid memories.* Harvard University Press.

Pillemer, D. B., Ivcevic, Z., Gooze, R. A., & Collins, K. A. (2007). Self-esteem memories: Feeling good about achievement success, feeling bad about relationship distress. *Personality and Social Psychology Bulletin, 33,* 1292–1305.

Pilley, J. W. (2013). Chaser: Unlocking the genius of the dog who knows a thousand words. Houghton Mifflin.

Pinker, S. (1995). The language instinct. *The General Psychologist, 31,* 63–65.

Pinker, S. (1998). Words and rules. *Lingua, 106,* 219–242.

Pinker, S. (2005, April 22). *The science of gender and science: A conversation with Elizabeth Spelke.* Harvard University. The Edge. https://www.edge.org/event/the-science-of-gender-and-science-pinker-vs-spelke-a-debate

Pinker, S. (2007). *The stuff of thought.* Viking.

Pinker, S. (2008). *The sexual paradox: Men, women, and the real gender gap.* Scribner.

Pinker, S. (2010). 2010: How is the internet changing the way you think? Not at all. Edge. https://www.edge.org/inthenews/how-is-the-internet-changing-the-way-you-think

Pinker, S. (2011, September 27). A history of violence. Edge. https://www.edge.org/3rd_culture/pinker07/pinker07_index.html

Pinker, S. (2015, June 8). The trauma of residential schools is passed down through the generations. *The Globe and Mail.* https://www.theglobeandmail.com/opinion/the-trauma-of-residential-schools-is-passed-down-through-the-generations/article24828005/

Pinker, S. A. [@sapinker]. (2019, March 10). [Tweet.] https://twitter.com/sapinker/status/1104610776420139008?lang=en

Pinquart, M. (2016). Associations of parenting styles and dimensions with academic achievement in children and adolescents: A meta-analysis. *Educational Psychology Review, 28,* 475–493.

Pinto, Y., de Haan, E. H. F., Lamme, V. A. F. (2017). The split-brain phenomenon revisited: A single conscious agent with split perception. *Trends in Cognitive Sciences, 21,* 835–851.

Pipe, M.-E., Lamb, M. E., Orbach, Y., & Esplin, P. W. (2004). Recent research on children's testimony about experienced and witnessed events. *Developmental Review, 24,* 440–468.

Pipher, M. (2002). *The middle of everywhere: The world's refugees come to our town.* Harcourt Brace.

Pitcher, D., Walsh, V., Yovel, G., & Duchaine, B. (2007). TMS evidence for the involvement of the right occipital face area in early face processing. *Current Biology, 17,* 1568–1573.

Pitman, R. K., Sanders, K. M., Zusman, R. M., Healy, A. R., Cheema, F., Lasko, N. B., Cahill, L., & Orr, S. P. (2002). Pilot study of secondary prevention of posttraumatic stress disorder with propranolol. *Biological Psychiatry, 51,* 189–192.

Pittenger, D. J. (1993). The utility of the Myers-Briggs Type Indicator. *Review of Educational Research, 63,* 467–488.

Pittinsky, T. L., & Diamante, N. (2015). Global bystander nonintervention. *Peace and Conflict: Journal of Peace Psychology, 21,* 226–247.

Pizzagalli, D. A., Berretta, S., Wooten, D., Goer, F., Pilobello, K. T., Kumar, P., Murray, L., Beltzer, M., Boyer-Boiteau, A., Alpert, N., El Fakhri, G., Mechawar, N., Vitaliano, G., Turecki, G., & Normandin, M. (2019). Assessment of striatal dopamine transporter binding in individuals with major depressive disorder: In vivo positron emission tomography and postmortem evidence. *JAMA Psychiatry, 76,* 854–861.

Place, S. S., Todd, P. M., Penke, L., & Asendorph, J. B. (2009). The ability to judge the romantic interest of others. *Psychological Science, 20,* 22–26.

PLAN USA. (2018). *The state of gender equality for U.S. adolescents* [PDF file]. https://www.planusa.org/docs/state-of-gender-equality-summary-2018.pdf

Plana-Ripoll, O., Pedersen, C. B., Holtz, Y., Benros, M. E., Dalsgaard, S., de Jonge, P., Fan, C. C., Degenhardt, L., Ganna, A., Greve, A. N., Gunn, J., Moesgaard Iburg, K., Vedel Kessing, L., Lee, B. K., Lim, C. C. W., Mors, O., Nordentoft, M., Prior, A., Roest, A. M., . . . McGrath, J. J. (2019). Exploring comorbidity within mental disorders among a Danish national population. *JAMA Psychiatry, 76,* 259–270.

Plant, E. A., & Peruche, B. M. (2005). The consequences of race for police officers' responses to criminal suspects. *Psychological Science, 16,* 180–183.

Plassmann, H., O'Doherty, J., Shiv, B., & Rangel, A. (2008). Marketing actions can modulate neural representations of experienced pleasantness. *PNAS, 105,* 1050–1054.

Platek, S. M., & Singh, D. (2010) Optimal waist-to-hip ratios in women activate neural reward centers in men. *PLOS ONE, 5,* e9042.

Pliner, P. (1982). The effects of mere exposure on liking for edible substances. *Appetite: Journal for Intake Research, 3,* 283–290.

Pliner, P., Pelchat, M., & Grabski, M. (1993). Reduction of neophobia in humans by exposure to novel foods. *Appetite, 20,* 111–123.

Plomin, R. (1999). Genetics and general cognitive ability. *Nature, 402,* C25–C29.

Plomin, R. (2011). Why are children in the same family so different? Nonshared environment three decades later. *International Journal of Epidemiology, 40,* 582–592.

Plomin, R. (2018). *Blueprint: How DNA makes us who we are.* MIT Press.

Plomin, R. (2018b, December 14). In the nature–nurture war, nature wins [Blog]. *Scientific American.* https://blogs.scientificamerican.com/observations/in-the-nature-nurture-war-nature-wins/

Plomin, R., & Bergeman, C. S. (1991). The nature of nurture: Genetic influence on "environmental" measures. *Behavioral and Brain Sciences, 14,* 373–427.

Plomin, R., & DeFries, J. C. (1998). The genetics of cognitive abilities and disabilities. *Scientific American, 278,* 62–69.

Plomin, R., DeFries, J. C., Knopik, V. S., & Neiderhiser, J. M. (2016). Top 10 replicated findings from behavioral genetics. *Perspectives on Psychological Science, 11,* 3–23.

Plomin, R., DeFries, J. C., McClearn, G. E., & Rutter, M. (1997). *Behavioral genetics.* Freeman.

Plomin, R., McClearn, G. E., Pedersen, N. L., Nesselroade, J. R., & Bergeman, C. S. (1988). Genetic influence on childhood family environment perceived retrospectively from the last half of the life span. *Developmental Psychology, 24,* 37–45.

Plomin, R., & McGuffin, P. (2003). Psychopathology in the postgenomic era. *Annual Review of Psychology, 54,* 205–228.

Plomin, R., Reiss, D., Hetherington, E. M., & Howe, G. W. (1994, January). Nature and nurture: Genetic contributions to measures of the family environment. *Developmental Psychology, 30,* 32–43.

Plomin, R., & von Stumm, S. (2018). The new genetics of intelligence. *Nature Reviews Neuroscience, 19,* 148–159.

Plotkin, H. (1994). *Darwin machines and the nature of knowledge.* Harvard University Press.

Plotnik, J. M., Brubaker, D. L., Dale, R., Tiller, L. N., Mumby, H. S., & Clayton, N. S. (2019). Elephants have a nose for quantity. *PNAS, 116,* 12566–12571.

Plous, S., & Herzog, H. A. (2000). Poll shows researchers favor lab animal protection. *Science, 290,* 711.

Pluess, M., & Belsky, J. (2013). Vantage sensitivity: Individual differences in response to positive experiences. *Psychological Bulletin, 139,* 901–916.

Poelmans, G., Pauls, D. L., Buitelaar, J. K., & Franke, B. (2011). Integrated genomewide association study findings: Identification of a neurodevelopmental network for attention deficit hyperactivity disorder. *American Journal of Psychiatry, 168,* 365–377.

Polák, J., Rádlová, S., Janovcová, M., Flegr, J., Landová, E., & Frynta, D. (2019). Scary and nasty beasts: Self-reported fear and disgust of common phobic animals. *British Journal of Psychology.* https://doi.org/10.1111/bjop.12409

Polanin, J. R., Espelage, D. L., & Pigott, T. D. (2012). A meta-analysis of school-based bully prevention programs' effects on bystander intervention behavior. *School Psychology Review, 41,* 47–65.

Polderman, T. J. C., Benyamin, B., de Leeuw, C. A., Sullivan, P. F., van Bochoven, A., Visscher, P. M., & Posthuma, D. (2015). Meta-analysis of the heritability of human traits based on fifty years of twin studies. *Nature Genetics, 47,* 702–709.

Poldrack, R. A. (2018). *The new mind readers: What neuroimaging can and cannot reveal about our thoughts.* Princeton University Press.

Polivy, J., Herman, C. P., & Coelho, J. S. (2008). Caloric restriction in the presence of attractive food cues: External cues, eating, and weight. *Physiology and Behavior, 94,* 729–733.

Pollak, S. D., & Kistler, D. J. (2002). Early experience is associated with the development of categorical representations for facial expressions of emotion. *PNAS, 99,* 9072–9076.

Pollak, S. D., & Tolley-Schell, S. A. (2003). Selective attention to facial emotion in physically abused children. *Journal of Abnormal Psychology, 112,* 323–328.

Pollard, R. (1992). *100 years in psychology and deafness: A centennial retrospective.* Invited address to the American Psychological Association convention, Washington, DC.

Pollatsek, A., Romoser, M. R. E., & Fisher, D. L. (2012). Identifying and remediating failures of selective attention in older drivers. *Current Directions in Psychological Science, 21,* 3–7.

Pollick, A. S., & de Waal, F. B. M. (2007). Ape gestures and language evolution. *PNAS, 104,* 8184–8189.

Poole, D. A., & Lindsay, D. S. (1995). Interviewing preschoolers: Effects of nonsuggestive techniques, parental coaching and leading questions on reports of nonexperienced events. *Journal of Experimental Child Psychology, 60,* 129–154.

Poole, D. A., & Lindsay, D. S. (2001). Children's eyewitness reports after exposure to misinformation from parents. *Journal of Experimental Psychology: Applied, 7,* 27–50.

Poorthuis, A. M., Slagt, M., van Aken, M. A., Denissen, J. J., & Thomaes, S. (2019). Narcissism and popularity among peers: A cross-transition longitudinal study. *Self and Identity, 1–15.*

Pope, D., & Simonsohn, U. (2011). Round numbers as goals: Evidence from baseball, SAT takers, and the lab. *Psychological Science, 22,* 71–79.

Pope Francis. (2015). *Encyclical letter* Laudato Si' *of the Holy Father Francis on care for our common home* (official English-language text of encyclical). https://bit.ly/2ycGx9Z

Popova, S., Lange, S., Shield, K., Burd, L., & Rehm, J. (2019). Prevalence of fetal alcohol spectrum disorder among special subpopulations: A systematic review and meta-analysis. *Addiction, 114,* 1150–1172.

Popova, V., Daly, E. J., Trivedi, M., Cooper, K., Lane, R., Lim, P., Mazzucco, C., Hough, D., Thase, M. E., Shelton, R. C., Molero, P., Vieta, E., Bajbouj, M., Manji, H., Drevets, W. C., & Singh, J. B. (2019). Efficacy and safety of flexibly dosed esketamine nasal spray combined with a newly initiated oral antidepressant in treatment-resistant depression: A randomized double-blind active-controlled study. *The American Journal of Psychiatry, 176,* 428–438

Porfiri, M., Sattanapalle, R. R., Nakayama, S., Macinko, J., & Sipahi, R. (2019). Media coverage and firearm acquisition in the aftermath of a mass shooting. *Nature Human Behaviour, 3,* 913–921.

Poropat, A. E. (2014). Other-rated personality and academic performance: Evidence and implications. *Learning and Individual Differences, 34,* 24–32.

Porter, D., & Neuringer, A. (1984). Music discriminations by pigeons. *Journal of Experimental Psychology: Animal Behavior Processes, 10,* 138–148.

Porter, S., Birt, A. R., Yuille, J. C., & Lehman, D. R. (2000, November). Negotiating false memories: Interviewer and rememberer characteristics relate to memory distortion. *Psychological Science, 11,* 507–510.

Porter, S., & Peace, K. A. (2007). The scars of memory: A prospective, longitudinal investigation of the consistency of traumatic and positive emotional memories in adulthood. *Psychological Science, 18,* 435–441.

Potter, G. D. M., Cade, J. E., & Hardie, L. J. (2017). Longer sleep is associated with lower BMI and favorable metabolic profiles in UK adults: Findings from the National Diet and Nutrition Survey. *PLOS ONE 12(7),* e0182195.

Poulton, R., Moffitt, T. E., & Silva, P. A. (2015). The Dunedin multidisciplinary health and development study: Overview of the first 40 years, with an eye to the future. *Social Psychiatry and Psychiatric Epidemiology, 50,* 679–693.

Poundstone, W. (2014). *How to predict the unpredictable. The art of outsmarting almost everyone.* OneWorld.

Powell, R., Digdon, N. A., Harris, B., & Smithson, C. (2014). Correcting the record on Watson, Rayner and Little Albert: Albert Barger as "Psychology's Lost Boy." *American Psychologist, 69,* 600–611.

Powell, R. A., & Boer, D. P. (1994). Did Freud mislead patients to confabulate memories of abuse? *Psychological Reports, 74,* 1283–1298.

Powell, R. A., & Schmaltz, R. M. (2017, July). *Did Little Albert actually acquire a conditioned fear of animals? What the film evidence tells us* [Paper]. Presented at the Vancouver International Conference on the Teaching of Psychology.

PPP (Public Policy Polling). (2016, December 9). *Trump remains unpopular; voters prefer Obama on SCOTUS pick* [PDF file]. https://www.publicpolicypolling.com/wp-content/uploads/2017/09/PPP_Release_National_120916.pdf

Prather, A. A., Janicki-Deverts, D., Hall, M. H., & Cohen, S. (2015). Behaviorally assessed sleep and susceptibility to the common cold. *Sleep, 38,* 1353–1359.

Pratt, L. A., Brody, D. J., & Gu, Q. (2017, August). Antidepressant use among persons aged 12 and over: United States, 2011–2014. *NCHS Data Brief, 283,* 1–8.

Preckel, F., Lipnevich, A., Boehme, K., Branderner, L., Georgi, K., Könen, T., Mursin, K., & Roberts, R. (2013). Morningness–eveningness and educational outcomes: The lark has an advantage over the owl at high school. *British Journal of Educational Psychology, 83,* 114–134.

Preller, K. H., Razi, A., Zeidman, P., Stämpfli, P., Friston, K. J., & Vollenweider, F. X. (2019). Effective connectivity changes in LSD-induced altered states of consciousness in humans. *PNAS, 116,* 2743–2748.

Premack, D. G. (2007). Human and animal cognition: Continuity and discontinuity. *PNAS, 104,* 13861–13867.

Premack, D. G., & Woodruff, G. (1978). Does the chimpanzee have a theory of mind? *Behavioral and Brain Sciences, 1,* 515–526.

Prentice, D. A., & Miller, D. T. (1993). Pluralistic ignorance and alcohol use on campus: Some consequences of misperceiving the social norm. *Journal of Personality and Social Psychology, 64,* 243–256.

Prescott, A. T., Sargent, J. D., & Hull, J. G. (2018). Metaanalysis of the relationship between violent video game play and physical aggression over time. *PNAS, 115,* 9882–9888.

Presley, C. A., Meilman, P. W., & Lyerla, R. (1997). *Alcohol and drugs on American college campuses: Issues of violence and harassment.* Core Institute, Southern Illinois University.

Primack, B. A., Shensa, A., Escobar-Viera, C. G., Barrett, E. L., Sidani, J. E., Colditz, J. B., & James, A. E. (2016). Use of multiple social media platforms and symptoms of depression and anxiety: A nationally-representative study among U.S. young adults. *Computers in Human Behavior, 69,* 1–9.

Prochaska, J. J. (2019). The public health consequences of e-cigarettes: A review by the National Academies of Sciences. A call for more research, a need for regulatory action. *Addiction, 114,* 587–589.

Prochazkova, E., Prochazkova, L., Giffin, M. R., Scholte, H. S., De Dreu, C. K., & Kret, M. E. (2018). Pupil mimicry promotes trust through the theory-of-mind network. *PNAS, 115,* E7265–E7274.

Profet, M. (1992). Pregnancy sickness as adaptation: A deterrent to maternal ingestion of teratogens. In J. H. Barkow, L. Cosmides, and J. Tooby (Eds). *The adapted mind: Evolutionary psychology and the generation of culture* (pp. 327–366). Oxford University Press.

Proffitt, D. R. (2006a). Distance perception. *Current Directions in Psychological Research, 15,* 131–135.

Proffitt, D. R. (2006b). Embodied perception and the economy of action. *Perspectives on Psychological Science, 1,* 110–122.

Project Match Research Group. (1997). Matching alcoholism treatments to client heterogeneity: Project MATCH posttreatment drinking outcomes. *Journal of Studies on Alcohol, 58,* 7–29.

Pronin, E. (2007). Perception and misperception of bias in human judgment. *Trends in Cognitive Sciences, 11,* 37–43.

Pronin, E. (2013). When the mind races: Effects of thought speed on feeling and action. *Current Directions in Psychological Science, 22,* 283–288.

Pronin, E., & Ross, L. (2006). Temporal differences in trait self-ascription: When the self is seen as another. *Journal of Personality and Social Psychology, 90,* 197–209.

Propper, R. E., Stickgold, R., Keeley, R., & Christman, S. D. (2007). Is television traumatic? Dreams, stress, and media exposure in the aftermath of September 11, 2001. *Psychological Science, 18,* 334–340.

Prot, S., Gentile, D. A., Anderson, C. A., Suzuki, K., Swing, E., Lim, K. M., Horiuchi, Y., Jelic, M., Krahé, B., Liuqing, W., Liau, A. K., Khoo, A., Petrescu. P. D., Sakamoto, A., Tajima, S., Toma, R. A., Warburton, W., Zhang, X., & Lam, B. C. P. (2014). Long-term relations among prosocial-media use, empathy, and prosocial behavior. *Psychological Science, 25,* 358–368.

Protzko, J., Aronson, J., & Blair, C. (2013). How to make a young child smarter: Evidence from the database of raising intelligence. *Perspectives on Psychological Science, 8,* 25–40.

Provine, R. R. (2001). *Laughter: A scientific investigation.* Penguin.

Provine, R. R. (2012). *Curious behavior: Yawning, laughing, hiccupping, and beyond.* Harvard University Press.

Pryor, J. H., Hurtado, S., Saenz, V. B., Korn, J. S., Santos, J. L., & Korn, W. S. (2006). *The American freshman: National norms for fall 2006.* UCLA Higher Education Research Institute.

Pryor, L. (2019, March 15). Mental illness isn't all in your head. *The New York Times* https://www.nytimes.com/2019/03/15/opinion/preventing-mental-illness.html

Przybylski, A. K., Weinstein, N., & Murayama, K. (2017). Internet gaming disorder: Investigating the clinical relevance of a new phenomenon. *American Journal of Psychiatry, 174,* 230–236.

Psaltopoulou, T., Sergentanis, T. N., Panagiotakos, D. B., Sergentanis, I. N., Kosti, R., & Scarmeas, N. (2013). Mediterranean diet, stroke, cognitive impairment, and depression: A meta-analysis. *Annals of Neurology, 74,* 580–591.

Psychologist. (2003). Who's the greatest? *The Psychologist, 16,* 170–175.

PTC. (2007, January 10). *Dying to entertain: Violence on prime time broadcast TV, 1998 to 2006.* Parents Television Council.

Puhl, R. M., Latner, J. D., O'Brien, K., Luedicke, J., Forhan, M., & Danielsdottir, S. (2015). Cross-national perspectives about weight-based bullying in youth: Nature, extent and remedies. *Pediatric Obesity, 11,* 241–250.

Punamäki, R. L., & Joustie, M. (1998). The role of culture, violence, and personal factors affecting dream content. *Journal of Cross-Cultural Psychology, 29,* 320–342.

Puterman, E., Gemmill, A., Karasek, D., Weir, D., Adler, N. E., Prather, A. A., & Epel, E. S. (2016). Lifespan adversity and later adulthood telomere length in the nationally representative U.S. Health and Retirement Study. *PNAS, 113,* E6335–E6342.

Putnam, A. L., Ross, M. Q., Soter, L. K., & Roediger, H. L. (2018). Collective narcissism: Americans exaggerate the role of their home state in appraising U.S. history. *Psychological Science, 29,* 1414–1422.

Putnam, F. W. (1991). Recent research on multiple personality disorder. *Psychiatric Clinics of North America, 14,* 489–502.

Puttonen, S., Kivimäki, M., Elovainio, M., Pulkki-Råback, L., Hintsanen, M., Vahtera, J., Telama, R., Juonala, M., Viikari, J. S., Raitakari, O. T., & Keltikangas-Järvinen, L. (2009). Shift work in young adults and carotid artery intima-media thickness: The Cardiovascular Risk in Young Finns study. *Atherosclerosis, 205,* 608–613.

Pyszczynski, T. A., Motyl, M., Vail, K. E., III, Hirschberger, G., Arndt, J., & Kesebir, P. (2012). Drawing attention to global climate change decreases support for war. *Peace and Conflict: Journal of Peace Psychology, 18,* 354–368.

Pyszczynski, T. A., Rothschild, Z., & Abdollahi, A. (2008). Terrorism, violence, and hope for peace: A terror management perspective. *Current Directions in Psychological Science, 17,* 318–322.

Pyszczynski, T. A., Solomon, S., & Greenberg, J. (2002). *In the wake of 9/11: The psychology of terror.* American Psychological Association.

Qaseem, A., Kansagara, D., Forciea, M. A., Cooke, M., & Denberg, T. D., for the Clinical Guidelines Committee of the American College of Physicians. (2016). Management of chronic insomnia disorder in adults: A clinical practice guideline from the American College of Physicians. *Annals of Internal Medicine, 165,* 125–133.

Qin, H.-F., & Piao, T.-J. (2011). Dispositional optimism and life satisfaction of Chinese and Japanese college students: Examining the mediating effects of affects and coping efficacy. *Chinese Journal of Clinical Psychology, 19,* 259–261.

Qiu, L., Lin, H., Ramsay, J., & Yang, F. (2012). You are what you tweet: Personality expression and perception on Twitter. *Journal of Research in Personality, 46,* 710–718.

Quaedflieg, C. W. E. M., & Schwabe, L. (2017). Memory dynamics under stress. *Memory, 26,* 364–376.

Quasha, S. (1980). *Albert Einstein: An intimate portrait.* Forest.

Quinn, P. C., Bhatt, R. S., Brush, D., Grimes, A., & Sharpnack, H. (2002). Development of form similarity as a Gestalt grouping principle in infancy. *Psychological Science, 13,* 320–328.

Quiroga, R. Q., Fried, I., & Koch, C. (2013, February). Brain cells for grandmother. *Scientific American,* pp. 30–35.

Quoidbach, J., Dunn, E. W., Hansenne, M., & Bustin, G. (2015). The price of abundance: How a wealth of experiences impoverishes savoring. *Personality and Social Psychology Bulletin, 41,* 393–404.

Quoidbach, J., Dunn, E. W., Petrides, K. V., & Mikolajczak, M. (2010). Money giveth, money taketh away: The dual effect of wealth on happiness. *Psychological Science, 21,* 759–763.

Quoidbach, J., Gilbert, D. T., & Wilson, T. D. (2013). The end of history illusion. *Science, 339,* 96–98.

Quoidbach, J., Taquet, M., Desseilles, M., de Montjoye, Y., & Gross, J. J. (2019). Happiness and social behavior. *Psychological Science, 30,* 1111–1122.

Rabbitt, P. (2006). Tales of the unexpected: 25 years of cognitive gerontology. *The Psychologist, 19,* 674–676.

Rabinowicz, T., Dean, D. E., Petetot, J. M., & de Courten-Myers, G. M. (1999). Gender differences in the human cerebral cortex: More neurons in males; more processes in females. *Journal of Child Neurology, 14,* 98–107.

Rabinowicz, T., deCourten-Myers, G. M., Petetot, J. M., Xi, G., & de los Reyes, E. (1996). Human cortex development: Estimates of neuronal numbers indicate major loss late during gestation. *Journal of Neuropathology and Experimental Neurology, 55,* 320–328.

Raby, K. L., Cicchetti, D., Carlson, E. A., Cutuli, J. J., Englund, M. M., & Egeland, B. (2012). Genetic and care-giving-based contributions to infant attachment: Unique associations with distress reactivity and attachment security. *Psychological Science, 23,* 1016–1023.

Raby, K. L., Roisman, G. I., Fraley, R. C., & Simpson, J. A. (2014). The enduring predictive significance of early maternal sensitivity: Social and academic competence through age 32 years. *Child Development, 86,* 695–708.

Racsmány, M., Conway, M. A., & Demeter, G. (2010). Consolidation of episodic memories during sleep: Long-term effects of retrieval practice. *Psychological Science, 21,* 80–85.

Radford, B. (2010, March 5). *Missing persons and abductions reveal psychics' failures.* DiscoveryNews. https://culteducation.com/group/1104-psychics/22804-missing-persons-and-abductions-reveal-psychics-failures.html

Rae, J. R., Gülgöz, S., Durwood, L., DeMeules, M., Lowe, R., Lindquist, G., & Olson, K. R. (2019). Predicting early-childhood gender transitions. *Psychological Science, 30,* 669–681.

Rahl, H. A., Lindsay, E. K., Pacilio, L. E., Brown, K. W., & Creswell, J. D. (2017). Brief mindfulness meditation training reduces mind wandering: The critical role of acceptance. *Emotion, 17,* 224–230.

Rahman, A., Khan, M. N., Hamdani, S. U., Chiumento, A., Akhtar, P., Nazir, H., Nisar, A., Masood, A., Din, I. U., Khan, N. A., Bryant, R. A., Dawson, K. S., Sijbrandij, M., Wang, D., & van Ommeren, M. (2019). Effectiveness of a brief group psychological intervention for women in a post-conflict setting in Pakistan: A single-blind, cluster, randomised controlled trial. *The Lancet, 393*(10182), 1733–1744.

Rahman, Q. (2015, July 24). "Gay genes": Science is on the right track, we're born this way. Let's deal with it. *The Guardian.* https://www.theguardian.com/science/blog/2015/jul/24/gay-genes-science-is-on-the-right-track-were-born-this-way-lets-deal-with-it

Rahman, Q., & Koerting, J. (2008). Sexual orientation-related differences in allocentric spatial memory tasks. *Hippocampus, 18,* 55–63.

Rahman, Q., & Wilson, G. D. (2003). Born gay? The psychobiology of human sexual orientation. *Personality and Individual Differences, 34,* 1337–1382.

Rahman, Q., Wilson, G. D., & Abrahams, S. (2004). Biosocial factors, sexual orientation and neuro-cognitive functioning. *Psychoneuroendocrinology, 29,* 867–881.

Raichle, M. (2010, March). The brain's dark energy. *Scientific American,* pp. 44–49.

Raichlen, D. A., & Polk, J. D. (2013). Linking brains and brawn: Exercise and the evolution of human neurobiology. *Proceedings of the Royal Society of Biology, 280,* 20122250.

Raila, H., Scholl, B. J., & Gruber, J. (2015). Seeing the world through rose-colored glasses: People who are happy and satisfied with life preferentially attend to positive stimuli. *Emotion, 15,* 449–462.

Raine, A. (1999). Murderous minds: Can we see the mark of Cain? *Cerebrum: The Dana Forum on Brain Science 1,* 15–29.

Raine, A. (2005). The interaction of biological and social measures in the explanation of antisocial and violent behavior. In D. M. Stoff & E. J. Susman (Eds.), *Developmental psychobiology of aggression.* Cambridge University Press.

Raine, A. (2013). *The anatomy of violence: The biological roots of crime.* Pantheon.

Raine, A., Ang, R. P., Choy, O., Hibbeln, J. R., Ho, R., Lim, C. G., Lim-Ashworth, N. S. J., Ling, S., Liu, J. C. J., Ooi, Y. P., Tan, Y. R., & Fung, D. S. S. (2018). Omega-3 (ω-3) and social skills interventions for reactive aggression and childhood externalizing behavior problems: A randomized, stratified, double-blind, placebo-controlled, factorial trial. *Psychological Medicine.* Advance online publication. doi: 10.1017/S0033291718000983.

Raine, A., Brennan, P., Mednick, B., & Mednick, S. A. (1996). High rates of violence, crime, academic problems, and behavioral problems in males with both early neuromotor deficits and unstable family environments. *Archives of General Psychiatry, 53,* 544–549.

Raine, A., Lencz, T., Bihrle, S., LaCasse, L., & Colletti, P. (2000). Reduced prefrontal gray matter volume and reduced autonomic activity in antisocial personality disorder. *Archives of General Psychiatry, 57,* 119–127.

Rainville, P., Duncan, G. H., Price, D. D., Carrier, B., & Bushnell, M. C. (1997). Pain affect encoded in human anterior cingulate but not somatosensory cortex. *Science, 277,* 968–971.

Raison, C. L., Klein, H. M., & Steckler, M. (1999). The moon and madness reconsidered. *Journal of Affective Disorders, 53,* 99–106.

Rajangam, S., Tseng, P. H., Yin, A., Lehew, G., Schwarz, D., Lebedev, M. A., & Nicolelis, M. A. (2016). Wireless cortical brain-machine interface for whole-body navigation in primates. *Scientific Reports, 6,* 22170.

Raji, C. A., Merrill, D. A., Eyre, H., Mallam, S., Torosyan, N., Erickson, K.I., Lopez, O. L., Becker, J. T., Carmichael, O. T., Gach, H. M., Thompson, P. M., Longstreth, W. T., & Kuller, L. H. (2016). Longitudinal relationships between caloric expenditure and gray matter in the cardiovascular health study. *Journal of Alzheimer's Disease, 52,* 719–729.

Ramachandran, V. S., & Blakeslee, S. (1998). *Phantoms in the brain: Probing the mysteries of the human mind.* Morrow.

Ramírez-Esparza, N., Gosling, S. D., Benet-Martínez, V., Potter, J. P., & Pennebaker, J. W. (2006). Do bilinguals have two personalities? A special case of cultural frame switching. *Journal of Research in Personality, 40,* 99–120.

Ramos, M. R., Cassidy, C., Reicher, S., & Haslam, S. A. (2012). A longitudinal investigation of the rejection-identification hypothesis. *British Journal of Social Psychology, 51,* 642–660.

Ramot, M., Walsh, C., & Martin, A. (2019). Multifaceted integration: Memory for faces is subserved by widespread connections between visual, memory, auditory, and social networks. *Journal of Neuroscience, 39,* 4976–4985.

Rand, D. G., Tomlin, D., Bear, A., Ludvig, E. A., & Cohen, J. D. (2017). Cyclical population dynamics of automatic versus controlled processing: An evolutionary pendulum. *Psychological Review, 124,* 626–642.

Randall, D. K. (2012, September 22). Rethinking sleep. *The New York Times.* https://www.nytimes.com/2012/09/23/opinion/sunday/rethinking-sleep.html?

Randi, J. (1999, February 4). 2000 club mailing list e-mail letter.

Randler, C. (2008). Morningness–eveningness and satisfaction with life. *Social Indicators Research, 86,* 297–302.

Randler, C. (2009). Proactive people are morning people. *Journal of Applied Social Psychology, 39,* 2787–2797.

Ranzini, M., & Girelli, L. (2019). Colours + Numbers differs from colours of numbers: cognitive and visual illusions in grapheme-colour synaesthesia. *Attention, Perception, & Psychophysics, 81,* 1500–1511.

Rapoport, J. L. (1989). The biology of obsessions and compulsions. *Scientific American, 260,* 83–89.

Räsänen, S., Pakaslahti, A., Syvalahti, E., Jones, P. B., & Isohanni, M. (2000). Sex differences in schizophrenia: A review. *Nordic Journal of Psychiatry, 54,* 37–45.

Rashbaum, W. K. (2019, April 23). For first time, pharmaceutical distributor faces federal criminal charges over opioid crisis. *The New York Times.* https://www.nytimes.com/2019/04/23/nyregion/opioid-crisis-drug-trafficking-rochester.html?

Rasmussen, K. (2016). Entitled vengeance: A meta-analysis relating narcissism to provoked aggression. *Aggressive Behavior, 42,* 362–379.

Rath, T., & Harter, J. K. (2010, August 19). Your friends and your social well-being: Close friendships are vital to health, happiness, and even workplace productivity. *Gallup Business Journal.* https://news.gallup.com/businessjournal/127043/friends-social-wellbeing.aspx

Rathbone, C. J., Salgado, S., Akan, M., Havelka, J., & Berntsen, D. (2016). Imagining the future: A cross-cultural perspective on possible selves. *Consciousness and Cognition, 42,* 113–124.

Rattan, A., Savani, K., Naidu, N. V. R., & Dweck, C. S. (2012). Can everyone become highly intelligent? Cultural differences in and societal consequences of beliefs about the universal potential for intelligence. *Journal of Personality and Social Psychology, 103,* 787–803.

Ravizza, S. M., Uitvlught, M. G., & Fenn, K. M. (2017). Logged in and zoned out. *Psychological Science, 28,* 171–180.

Ray, J., & Kafka, S. (2014, May 6). *Life in college matters for life after college.* Gallup. https://news.gallup.com/poll/168848/life-college-matters-life-college.aspx

Ray, O., & Ksir, C. (1990). *Drugs, society, and human behavior* (5th ed.). Times Mirror/Mosby.

Ray, R., Sanes, M., & Schmitt, J. (2013). No-vacation nation revisited. *Center for Economic and Policy Research,* 1–22.

Raynor, H. A., & Epstein, L. H. (2001). Dietary variety, energy regulation, and obesity. *Psychological Bulletin, 127,* 325–341.

Raz, A., Fan, J., & Posner, M. I. (2005). Hypnotic suggestion reduces conflict in the human brain. *PNAS, 102,* 9978–9983.

Reason, J. (1987). The Chernobyl errors. *Bulletin of the British Psychological Society, 40,* 201–206.

Reason, J., & Mycielska, K. (1982). *Absent-minded? The psychology of mental lapses and everyday errors.* Prentice-Hall.

Rebar, A. L., Stanton, R., Geard, D., Short, C., Duncan, M. J., & Vandelanotte, C. (2015). A meta-meta-analysis of the effect of physical activity on depression and anxiety in non-clinical adult populations. *Health Psychology Review, 9,* 366–378.

Rechenberg, K. (2016). Nutritional interventions in clinical depression. *Clinical Psychological Science, 4,* 144–162.

Redden, J. P., Mann, T., Vickers, Z., Mykerezi, E., Reicks, M., & Elsbernd, E. (2015). Serving first in isolation increases vegetable intake among elementary schoolchildren. *PLOS ONE, 10,* e0121283.

Redick, T. (2019). The hype cycle of working memory training. *Current Directions in Psychological Science, 28,* 423–429.

Redick, T. S., Unsworth, N., Kane, M. J., & Hambrick, D. Z. (2017). Don't shoot the messenger: Still no evidence that video-game experience is related to cognitive abilities—A reply to Green et al. (2017). *Psychological Science, 28,* 683–686.

Reed, D. (2012, January). Quoted by Miller, P. in A thing or two about twins. *National Geographic.* https://www.nationalgeographic.com/magazine/2012/01/identical-twins-science-dna-portraits/.

Rees, M. (1999). *Just six numbers: The deep forces that shape the universe.* Basic Books.

Reger, M. A., Stanley, M. S., & Joiner, T. E. (2020). Suicide mortality and coronavirus disease 2019—a perfect storm? *JAMA Psychiatry.* Advance online publication. doi:10.1001/jamapsychiatry.2020.1060

Régner, I., Thinus-Blanc, C., Netter, A., Schmader, T., & Huguet, P. (2019). Committees with implicit biases promote fewer women when they do not believe gender bias exists. *Nature Human Behaviour, 3,* 1171–1179.

Rehm, J., & Shield, K. D. (2019). Global burden of disease and the impact of mental and addictive disorders. *Current Psychiatry Reports, 21*(2), 10.

Reichenberg, A., Cederlöf, M., McMillan, A., Trzaskowski, M., Kapara, O., Fruchter, E., Ginat, K., Davidson, M., Weiser, M., Larsson, H., Plomin, R., & Lichtenstein, P. (2016). Discontinuity in the genetic and environmental causes of the intellectual disability spectrum. *PNAS, 113,* 1098–1103.

Reichenberg, A., & Harvey, P. D. (2007). Neuropsychological impairments in schizophrenia: Integration of performance-based and brain imaging findings. *Psychological Bulletin, 133,* 833–858.

Reichert, R. A., Robb, M. B., Fender, J. G., & Wartella, E. (2010). Word learning from baby videos. *Archives of Pediatrics & Adolescent Medicine, 164,* 432–437.

Reichow, B. (2012). Overview of meta-analyses on early intensive behavioral intervention for young children with autism spectrum disorders. *Journal of Autism and Developmental Disorders, 42,* 512–520.

Reid, V. M., Dunn, K., Young, R. J., Amu, J., Donovan, T., & Reissland, N. (2017). The human fetus preferentially engages with face-like visual stimuli. *Current Biology, 27,* 1825–1828.

Reifman, A. S., Larrick, R. P., & Fein, S. (1991). Temper and temperature on the diamond: The heat-aggression relationship in major league baseball. *Personality and Social Psychology Bulletin, 17,* 580–585.

Reilly, D., Neumann, D. L., & Andrews, G. (2019). Gender differences in reading and writing achievement: Evidence from the National Assessment of Educational Progress (NAEP). *American Psychologist, 74,* 445–458.

Reimann, F., Cox, J. J., Belfer, I., Diatchenko, L., Zaykin, D. V., McHale, D. P., Drenth, J. P., Dai, F., Wheeler, J., Sanders, F., Wood, L., Wu, T. X., Karppinen, J., Nikolaisen, L., Männikkö, M., Max, M. B., Kiselycznyk, C., Poddar, M., Te Morsche, R. H., . . . Woods, C. G. (2010). Pain perception is altered by a nucleotide polymorphism in SCN9A. *PNAS, 107,* 5148–5153.

Reimão, R. N., & Lefévre, A. B. (1980). Prevalence of sleep-talking in childhood. *Brain and Development, 2,* 353–357.

Reiner, W. G., & Gearhart, J. P. (2004). Discordant sexual identity in some genetic males with cloacal exstrophy assigned to female sex at birth. *New England Journal of Medicine, 350,* 333–341.

Reis, H. (2018). *Relationships, well-being and behaviour: Selected works of Harry T. Reis.* Routledge.

Reis, H. T., & Aron, A. (2008). Love: What is it, why does it matter, and how does it operate? *Perspectives on Psychological Science, 3,* 80–86.

Reis, M., Ramiro, L., Camacho, I., Tomé, G., Brito, C., & Gaspar de Matos, G. (2017). Does having a pet make a difference? Highlights from the HBSC Portuguese study. *European Journal of Developmental Psychology, 15,* 548–564.

Reis, S. M. (2001). Toward a theory of creativity in diverse creative women. In M. Bloom & T. Gullotta (Eds.), *Promoting creativity across the life span* (pp. 231–275). CWLA Press.

Reisenzein, R. (1983). The Schachter theory of emotion: Two decades later. *Psychological Bulletin, 94,* 239–264.

Reitz, A. K., Motti-Stefanidi, F., & Asendorpf, J. B. (2016). Me, us, and them: Testing sociometer theory in a socially diverse real-life context. *Journal of Personality and Social Psychology, 110,* 908–920.

Reitzle, M. (2006). The connections between adulthood transitions and the self-perception of being adult in the changing contexts of East and West Germany. *European Psychologist, 11,* 25–38.

Reivich, K., Gillham, J. E., Chaplin, T. M., & Seligman, M. E. P. (2013). *From helplessness to optimism: The role of resilience in treating and preventing depression in youth.* Springer Science + Business Media.

Rekker, R., Keijsers, L., Branje, S., & Meeus, W. (2015). Political attitudes in adolescence and emerging adulthood: Developmental changes in mean level, polarization, rank-order stability, and correlates. *Journal of Adolescence, 41,* 136–147.

Remick, A. K., Polivy, J., & Pliner, P. (2009). Internal and external moderators of the effect of variety on food intake. *Psychological Bulletin, 135,* 434–451.

Remington, A., Swettenham, J., Campbell, R., & Coleman, M. (2009). Selective attention and perceptual load in autism spectrum disorder. *Psychological Science, 20,* 1388–1393.

Remley, A. (1988, October). From obedience to independence. *Psychology Today,* pp. 56–59.

Ren, D., Wesselmann, E., & Williams, K. D. (2016). Evidence for another response to ostracism: Solitude seeking. *Social Psychological and Personality Science, 7*(3), 204–212.

Ren, X., & Canavero, S. (2017). HEAVEN in the making: Between the rock (the academe) and a hard case (a head transplant). *AJOB Neuroscience, 8,* 200–205.

Ren, X., Kim, C. Y., & Canavero, S. (2019). Bridging the gap: Spinal cord fusion as a treatment of chronic spinal cord injury. *Surgical Neurology International, 10,* 51.

Renner, M. J., & Renner, C. H. (1993). Expert and novice intuitive judgments about animal behavior. *Bulletin of the Psychonomic Society, 31,* 551–552.

Renner, M. J., & Rosenzweig, M. R. (1987). *Enriched and impoverished environments: Effects on brain and behavior.* Springer-Verlag.

Renninger, K. A., & Granott, N. (2005). The process of scaffolding in learning and development. *New Ideas in Psychology, 23,* 111–114.

Rentfrow, P. J., & Gosling, S. D. (2003). The do re mi's of everyday life: The structure and personality correlates of music preferences. *Journal of Personality and Social Psychology, 84,* 1236–1256.

Rentfrow, P. J., & Gosling, S. D. (2006). Message in a ballad: The role of music preferences in interpersonal perception. *Psychological Science, 17,* 236–242.

Repacholi, B. M., Meltzoff, A. N., Toub, T. S., & Ruba, A. L. (2016). Infants' generalizations about other people's emotions: Foundations for trait-like attributions. *Developmental Psychology, 52,* 364.

Rescorla, R. A., & Wagner, A. R. (1972). A theory of Pavlovian conditioning: Variations in the effectiveness of reinforcement and nonreinforcement. In A. H. Black & W. F. Perokasy (Eds.), *Classical conditioning II: Current theory.* Appleton-Century-Crofts.

Resnick, M. D., Bearman, P. S., Blum, R. W., Bauman, K. E., Harris, K. M., Jones, J., Tabor, J., Beuhring, T., Sieving, R. E., Shew M., Ireland, M., Bearinger, L. H., & Udry, J. R. (1997). Protecting adolescents from harm. Findings from the National Longitudinal Study on Adolescent Health. *Journal of the American Medical Association, 278,* 823–832.

Resnick, S. M. (1992). Positron emission tomography in psychiatric illness. *Current Directions in Psychological Science, 1,* 92–98.

Retraction Watch. (2015, December 8). *Diederik Stapel now has 58 retractions.* https://www.retractionwatch.com/category/diederik-stapel

Reuters. (2000, July 5). *Many teens regret decision to have sex.* National Campaign to Prevent Teen Pregnancy survey.

Reuters. (2019). *Factbox: South African athlete Semenya loses appeal against testosterone rule.* https://www.reuters.com/article/us-athletics-semenya-factbox/factbox-south-african-athlete-semenya-loses-appeal-against-testosterone-rule-idUSKCN1S73XX

Reyna, V. F., Chick, C. F., Corbin, J. C., & Hsia, A. N. (2014). Developmental reversals in risky decision making: Intelligence agents show larger decision biases than college students. *Psychological Science, 25,* 76–84.

Reynolds, G. (2009, November 18). Phys ed: Why exercise makes you less anxious. *The New York Times* blog. https://well.blogs.nytimes.com/2009/11/18/phys-ed-why-exercise-makes-you-less-anxious/?

Reynolds, G. (2019, January 16). How exercise may help keep our memory sharp. *The New York Times*. https://www.nytimes.com/2019/01/16/well/move/exercise-brain-memory-irisin-alzheimer-dementia.html?

Reynolds, J., Stewart, M., MacDonald, R., & Sischo, L. (2006). Have adolescents become too ambitious? High school seniors' educational and occupational plans, 1976 to 2000. *Social Problems, 53*, 186–206.

Reynolds, J. P., Archer, S., Pilling, M., Kenny, M., Hollands, G. J., & Marteau, T. M. (2019). Public acceptability of nudging and taxing to reduce consumption of alcohol, tobacco, and food: A population-based survey experiment. *Social Science & Medicine, 236*, 112395.

Rhodes, E. (2017, August). Back to academia . . . and elephants. *The Psychologist*, pp. 12–13.

Rhodes, M. G., & Anastasi, J. S. (2012). The own-age bias in face recognition: A meta-analytic and theoretical review. *Psychological Bulletin, 138*, 146–174.

Ribeiro, J. D., Huang, X., Fox, K. R., Walsh, C. G., & Linthicum, K. P. (2019). Predicting imminent suicidal thoughts and nonfatal attempts: The role of complexity. *Clinical Psychological Science, 7*, 941–957.

Riccelli, R., Toschi, N., Nigro, S., Terracciano, A., & Passamonti, L. (2017). Surface-based morphometry reveals the neuroanatomical basis of the five-factor model of personality. *Social Cognitive and Affective Neuroscience, 12*, 671–684.

Ricciardelli, L. A., & McCabe, M. P. (2004). A biopsychosocial model of disordered eating and the pursuit of muscularity in adolescent boys. *Psychological Bulletin, 130*, 179–205.

Rice, M. E., & Grusec, J. E. (1975). Saying and doing: Effects on observer performance. *Journal of Personality and Social Psychology, 32*, 584–593.

Richardson, G. B., La Guardia, A. C., & Klay, P. M. (2018). Determining the roles of father absence and age at menarche in female psychosocial acceleration. *Evolution and Human Behavior, 39*, 437–446.

Richardson, J. (1993). The curious case of coins: Remembering the appearance of familiar objects. *The Psychologist: Bulletin of the British Psychological Society, 6*, 360–366.

Richardson, J. T. E., & Zucco, G. M. (1989). Cognition and olfaction: A review. *Psychological Bulletin, 105*, 352–360.

Richardson, M., Abraham, C., & Bond, R. (2012). Psychological correlates of university students' academic performance: A systematic review and meta-analysis. *Psychological Bulletin, 138*, 353–387.

Richeson, J. A., & Shelton, J. N. (2007). Negotiating interracial interactions. *Current Directions in Psychological Science, 16*, 316–320.

Richtel, M., & Kaplan, S. (2018, August 27). Did Juul lure teenagers and get 'customers for life'? *The New York Times*. https://www.nytimes.com/2018/08/27/science/juul-vaping-teen-marketing.html?

Rieff, P. (1979). *Freud: The mind of a moralist* (3rd ed.). University of Chicago Press.

Rieger, G., Savin-Williams, R., Chivers, M. L., & Bailey, J. M. (2016). Sexual arousal and masculinity-femininity of women. *Journal of Personality and Social Psychology, 111*, 265–283.

Rigoni, J. B., & Asplund, J. (2016a, July 7). *Strengths-based development: The business results*. Gallup. https://www.gallup.com/workplace/236297/strengths-based-employee-development-business-results.aspx

Rigoni, J. B., & Asplund, J. (2016b, July 12). *Global study: ROI for strengths-based development*. Gallup.

https://www.gallup.com/workplace/236288/global-study-roi-strengths-based-development.aspx

Rihm, J. S., Menz, M. M., Schultz, H., Bruder, L., Schilbach, L., Schmid, S. M., & Peters, J. (2019). Sleep deprivation selectively up-regulates an amygdala-hypothalamic circuit involved in food reward. *Journal of Neuroscience, 39*, 888–899.

Riley, L. D., & Bowen, C. (2005). The sandwich generation: Challenges and coping strategies of multigenerational families. *The Family Journal, 13*, 52–58.

Rimfeld, K., Kovas, Y., Dale, P. S., & Plomin, R. (2016). True grit and genetics: Predicting academic achievement from personality. *Journal of Personality and Social Psychology, 111*, 780–789

Rindermann, H., & Becker, D. (2018). FLynn-effect and economic growth: Do national increases in intelligence lead to increases in GDP? *Intelligence, 69*, 87–93.

Rindermann, H., Becker, D., & Coyle, T. R. (2016). Survey of expert opinion on intelligence: The Flynn effect and the future of intelligence. *Personality and Individual Differences, 106*, 242–247.

Rindermann, H., & Ceci, S. J. (2009). Educational policy and country outcomes in international cognitive competence studies. *Perspectives on Psychological Science, 4*, 551–577.

Riordan, M. (2013, March 19). *Tobacco warning labels: Evidence of effectiveness*. Washington, DC: The Campaign for Tobacco-Free Kids (tobaccofreekids.org).

Ritchie, H., Roser, M., & Ortiz-Espina, E. (2019a). Suicide (by age). Our World in Data. ourworldindata.org/suicide#suicide-by-age

Ritchie, H., Roser, M., & Ortiz-Ospina, E. (2019b). Suicide (by gender). Our World in Data. ourworldindata.org/suicide#suicide-by-gender

Ritchie, H., Roser, M., & Ortiz-Ospina, E. (2020). Suicide. Our World in Data. https://ourworldindata.org/suicide

Ritchie, S. J., Cox, S. R., Shen, X., Lombardo, M. V., Reus, L. M., Alloza, C., Harris, M. A., Alderson, H. L., Hunter, S., Neilson, E., Liewald, D. C. M., Auyeung, B., Whalley, H. C., Lawrie, S. M., Gale, C. R., Bastin, M. E., McIntosh, A. M., & Deary, I. J. (2018). Sex differences in the adult human brain: Evidence from 5216 UK Biobank participants. *Cerebral Cortex, 28*, 2959–2975.

Ritchie, S. J., Dickie, D. A., Cox, S. R., Valdes Hernandez Mdel, C., Corley, J., Royle, N. A., Pattie, A., Aribisala, B. S., Redmond, P., Muñoz Maniega, S., Taylor, A. M., Sibbett, R., Gow, A. J., Starr, J. M., Bastin, M. E., Wardlaw, J. M., & Deary, I. J. (2015). Brain volumetric changes and cognitive ageing during the eighth decade of life. *Human Brain Mapping, 36*, 4910–4925.

Ritchie, S. J., & Tucker-Drob, E. M. (2018). How much does education improve intelligence? A meta-analysis. *Psychological Science, 29*, 1358–1369.

Ritchie, S. J., Wiseman, R., & French, C. C. (2012). Failing the future: Three unsuccessful attempts to replicate Bem's "retroactive facilitation of recall" effect. *PLOS ONE, 7*, e33r23.

Ritter, S. M., Damian, R. I., Simonton, D. K., van Baaren, R. B., Strick, M., Derks, J., & Dijksterhuis, A. (2012). Diversifying experiences enhance cognitive flexibility. *Journal of Experimental Social Psychology, 48*, 961–964.

Rivera, M., Locke, A. E., Corre, T., Czamara, D., Wolf, C., Ching-Lopez, A., Milaneschi, Y., Kloiber, S., Cohen-Woods, S., Rucker, J., Aitchison, K. J., Bergmann, S., Boomsma, D. I., Craddock, N., Gill, M., Holsboer, F., Hottenga, J. J., Korszun, A., Kutalik, Z., . . . McGuffin, P. (2017). Interaction between the FTO gene, body mass index and depression: Metaanalysis of 13701 individuals. *The British Journal of Psychiatry, 211*, 70–76.

Rizzolatti, G., Fadiga, L., Fogassi, L., & Gallese, V. (2002). From mirror neurons to imitation: Facts and speculations. In A. N. Meltzoff & W. Prinz (Eds.), *The imitative mind: Development, evolution, and brain bases*. Cambridge University Press.

Rizzolatti, G., Fogassi, L., & Gallese, V. (2006, November). Mirrors in the mind. *Scientific American, 295*, 54–61.

Roberson, D., Davidoff, J., Davies, I. R. L., & Shapiro, L. R. (2004). The development of color categories in two languages: A longitudinal study. *Journal of Experimental Psychology: General, 133*, 554–571.

Roberson, D., Davies, I. R. L., Corbett, G. G., & Vandervyver, M. (2005). Free-sorting of colors across cultures: Are there universal grounds for grouping? *Journal of Cognition and Culture, 5*, 349–386.

Roberti, J. W., Storch, E. A., & Bravata, E. A. (2004). Sensation seeking, exposure to psychosocial stressors, and body modifications in a college population. *Personality and Individual Differences, 37*, 1167–1177.

Roberts, B. W., & DelVecchio, W. F. (2000). The rank-order consistency of personality traits from childhood to old age: A quantitative review of longitudinal studies. *Psychological Bulletin, 126*, 3–25.

Roberts, B. W., Donnellan, M. B., & Hill, P. L. (2013). Personality trait development in adulthood. In H. Tennen, J. Suls, & I. B. Weiner (Eds.), *Handbook of psychology, Vol. 5: Personality and social psychology* (2nd ed.). Wiley.

Roberts, B. W., Kuncel, N. R., Shiner, R., Caspi, A., & Goldberg, L. R. (2007). The power of personality: The comparative validity of personality traits, socioeconomic status, and cognitive ability for predicting important life outcomes. *Perspectives on Psychological Science, 2*, 313–345.

Roberts, B. W., Luo, J., Briley, D. A., Chow, P. I., Su, R., & Hill, P. L. (2017). A systematic review of personality trait change through intervention. *Psychological Bulletin, 143*, 117–141.

Roberts, J. A., & David, M. E. (2016). My life has become a major distraction from my cell phone: Partner phubbing and relationship satisfaction among romantic partners. *Computers in Human Behavior, 54*, 134–141.

Roberts, L. (1988). Beyond Noah's ark: What do we need to know? *Science, 242*, 1247.

Roberts, P., & Stewart, B. A. (2018). Defining the 'generalist specialist' niche for Pleistocene Homo sapiens. *Nature Human Behaviour, 2*, 542–550.

Roberts, T.-A. (1991). Determinants of gender differences in responsiveness to others' evaluations. *Dissertation Abstracts International, 51*(8–B).

Robine, J.-M., & Allard, M. (1999). Jeanne Calment: Validation of the duration of her life. In B. Jeune & J. W. Vaupel (Eds.), *Validation of exceptional longevity*. Odense University Press. https://www.demogr.mpg.de/books/odense/6/09.htm

Robins, L., & Regier, D. (Eds.). (1991). *Psychiatric disorders in America*. Free Press.

Robins, L. N., Davis, D. H., & Goodwin, D. W. (1974). Drug use by U.S. Army enlisted men in Vietnam: A follow-up on their return home. *American Journal of Epidemiology, 99*, 235–249.

Robinson, F. P. (1970). *Effective study*. Harper & Row.

Robinson, J. P., & Martin, S. (2008). What do happy people do? *Social Indicators Research, 89*, 565–571.

Robinson, J. P., & Martin, S. (2009). Changes in American daily life: 1965–2005. *Social Indicators Research, 93*, 47–56.

Robinson, O. J., Cools, R., Carlisi, C. O., & Drevets, W. C. (2012). Ventral striatum response during reward and punishment reversal learning in unmedicated major depressive disorder. *American Journal of Psychiatry, 169*, 152–159.

Robinson, T. E., & Berridge, K. C. (2003). Addiction. *Annual Review of Psychology, 54*, 25–53.

Robinson, T. N., Borzekowski, D. L. G., Matheson, D. M., & Kraemer, H. C. (2007). Effects of fast food branding on young children's taste preferences. *Archives of Pediatric and Adolescent Medicine, 161,* 792–797.

Robinson, V. M. (1983). Humor and health. In P. E. McGhee & J. H. Goldstein (Eds.), *Handbook of humor research: Vol. II. Applied studies.* Springer-Verlag.

Robles, T. F. (2015). Marital quality and health: Implications for marriage in the 21st century. *Current Directions in Psychological Science, 23,* 427–432.

Rochat, F. (1993). *How did they resist authority? Protecting refugees in Le Chambon during World War II* [Paper]. Presented at the American Psychological Association convention.

Rock, I., & Palmer, S. (1990, December). The legacy of Gestalt psychology. *Scientific American,* pp. 84–90.

Rodin, J. (1986). Aging and health: Effects of the sense of control. *Science, 233,* 1271–1276.

Rodriguez, D. N., & Strange, D. (2015). False memories for dissonance inducing events. *Memory, 23,* 203-212.

Rodríguez, G., & Hall, G. (2019). Explaining learned predictiveness: Roles of attention and integration of associative structures. *Journal of Experimental Psychology: Animal Learning and Cognition, 45,* 163–173.

Roediger, H. L. (1980). Memory metaphors in cognitive psychology. *Memory & Cognition, 8,* 231–246.

Roediger, H. L., III. (2013). Applying cognitive psychology to education: Translational educational science. *Psychological Science in the Public Interest, 14,* 1–3.

Roediger, H. L., III, & DeSoto, K. A. (2016). Was Alexander Hamilton president? *Psychological Science, 27,* 644–650.

Roediger, H. L., III, & Finn, B. (2010, March/April). The pluses of getting it wrong. *Scientific American Mind,* pp. 39–41.

Roediger, H. L., III, & Karpicke, J. D. (2006). Test-enhanced learning: Taking memory tests improves long-term retention. *Psychological Science, 17,* 249–255.

Roediger, H. L., III, & Karpicke, J. D. (2018). Reflections on the resurgence of interest in the testing effect. *Perspectives on Psychological Science, 13,* 236–241.

Roediger, H. L., III, & McDaniel, M. A. (2007). Illusory recollection in older adults: Testing Mark Twain's conjecture. In M. Garry H. Hayne (Ed.), *Do justice and let the sky fall: Elizabeth F. Loftus and her contributions to science, law, and academic freedom.* Erlbaum.

Roediger, H. L., III, & McDermott, K. B. (1995). Creating false memories: Remembering words not presented in lists. *Journal of Experimental Psychology: Learning, Memory, and Cognition, 21,* 803–814.

Roediger, H. L., III, Meade, M. L., & Bergman, E. T. (2001). Social contagion of memory. *Psychonomic Bulletin & Review, 8,* 365–371.

Roediger, H. L., III, Wheeler, M. A., & Rajaram, S. (1993). Remembering, knowing, and reconstructing the past. In D. L. Medin (Ed.), *The psychology of learning and motivation: Advances in research and theory* (Vol. 30). Academic Press.

Roehling, P. V., Roehling, M. V., & Moen, P. (2001). The relationship between work-life policies and practices and employee loyalty: A life course perspective. *Journal of Family and Economic Issues, 22,* 141–170.

Roelofs, T. (2010, September 22). Somali refugee takes oath of U.S. citizenship year after his brother. *The Grand Rapids Press* (mlive.com).

Roenneberg, T., Kuehnle, T., Pramstaller, P. P., Ricken, J., Havel, M., Guth, A., & Merrow, M. (2004). A marker for the end of adolescence. *Current Biology, 14,* R1038–R1039.

Roepke, A. M. (2015). Psychosocial interventions and posttraumatic growth: A meta-analysis. *Journal of Consulting and Clinical Psychology, 83,* 129.

Roese, N. J., & Summerville, A. (2005). What we regret most . . . and why. *Personality and Social Psychology Bulletin, 31,* 1273–1285.

Roese, N. J., & Vohs, K. D. (2012). Hindsight bias. *Perspectives on Psychological Science, 7,* 411–426.

Roesser, R. (1998). *What you should know about hearing conservation.* betterhearing.org/

Rogers, C. R. (1961). *On becoming a person: A therapist's view of psychotherapy.* Houghton Mifflin.

Rogers, C. R. (1980). *A way of being.* Houghton Mifflin.

Rogers, C. R. (1985, February). Quoted by M. L. Wallach & L. Wallach, How psychology sanctions the cult of the self. *Washington Monthly,* pp. 46–56.

Rogers, T., & Feller, A. (2016). Discouraged by peer excellence: Exposure to exemplary peer performance causes quitting. *Psychological Science, 27,* 365–374.

Rogers, T., & Milkman, K. L. (2016). Reminders through association. *Psychological Science, 27,* 973–986.

Rogers, T., Moore, D. A., & Norton, M. I. (2017). The belief in a favorable future. *Psychological Science, 28,* 1290–1301.

Rohner, R. P., & Veneziano, R. A. (2001). The importance of father love: History and contemporary evidence. *Review of General Psychology, 5,* 382–405.

Rohrer, J. M., Egloff, B., Kosinski, M., Stillwell, D., & Schmukle, S. C. (2018). In your eyes only? Discrepancies and agreement between self- and other-reports of personality from age 14 to 29. *Journal of Personality and Social Psychology, 115,* 304–320.

Rohrer, J. M., Egloff, B., & Schmukle, S. C. (2015). Examining the effects of birth order on personality. *PNAS, 112,* 14224–14229.

Roiser, J. P., Cook, L. J., Cooper, J. D., Rubinsztein, D. C., & Sahakian, B. J. (2005). Association of a functional polymorphism in the serotonin transporter gene with abnormal emotional processing in Ecstasy users. *American Journal of Psychiatry, 162,* 609–612.

Rokach, A., Orzeck, T., Moya, M., & Exposito, F. (2002). Causes of loneliness in North America and Spain. *European Psychologist, 7,* 70–79.

Romano, A., Balliet, D., Yamagishi, T., & Liu, J. H. (2017). Parochial trust and cooperation across 17 societies. *PNAS, 114,* 12702–12707.

Romelsjö, A., Danielsson, A., Wennberg, P., & Hibell, B. (2014). Cannabis use and drug related problems among adolescents in 27 European countries: The utility of the prevention paradox. *Nordic Studies on Alcohol and Drugs, 31,* 359–369.

Ronay, R., & von Hippel, W. (2010). The presence of an attractive woman elevates testosterone and physical risk taking in young men. *Social Psychology and Personality Science, 1,* 57–64.

Roper, K. R. (2016, July 19). Public Facebook post. https://www.facebook.com/kate.riffleroper/posts/1746348308987959

Roper, S. D., & Chaudhari, N. (2017). Taste buds: Cells, signals, and synapses. *Nature Reviews Neuroscience, 18,* 485–497.

Roque, L., Verissimo, M., Oliveira, T. F., & Oliveira, R. F. (2012). Attachment security and HPA axis reactivity to positive and challenging emotional situations in child-mother dyads in naturalistic settings. *Developmental Psychobiology, 54,* 401–411.

Rosch, E. (1978). Principles of categorization. In E. Rosch & B. L. Lloyd (Eds.), *Cognition and categorization.* Erlbaum.

Rose, A. J., & Rudolph, K. D. (2006). A review of sex differences in peer relationship processes: Potential trade-offs for the emotional and behavioral development of girls and boys. *Psychological Bulletin, 132,* 98–131.

Rose, H., & Rose, S. (2016). *Can neuroscience change our minds?* Polity.

Rose, J. S., Chassin, L., Presson, C. C., & Sherman, S. J. (1999). Peer influences on adolescent cigarette smoking: A prospective sibling analysis. *Merrill-Palmer Quarterly, 45,* 62–84.

Rose, R. J., Kaprio, J., Winter, T., Dick, D. M., Viken, R. J., Pulkkinen, L., & Koskenvuo, M. (2002). Femininity and fertility in sisters with twin brothers: Prenatal androgenization? Cross-sex socialization? *Psychological Science, 13,* 263–266.

Roselli, C. E., Larkin, K., Schrunk, J. M., & Stormshak, F. (2004). Sexual partner preference, hypothalamic morphology and aromatase in rams. *Physiology and Behavior, 83,* 233–245.

Roselli, C. E., Resko, J. A., & Stormshak, F. (2002). Hormonal influences on sexual partner preference in rams. *Archives of Sexual Behavior, 31,* 43–49.

Rosenbaum, M. (1986). The repulsion hypothesis: On the nondevelopment of relationships. *Journal of Personality and Social Psychology, 51,* 1156–1166.

Rosenberg, B. D., & Siegel, J. T. (2018). A 50-year review of psychological reactance theory: Do not read this article. *Motivation Science, 4,* 281–300.

Rosenberg, E. L., Zanesco, A. P., King, B. G., Aichele, S. R., Jacobs, R. L., Bridwell, D. A., MacLean, K. A., Shaver, P. R., Ferrer, E., Sahdra, B. K., Lavy, S., Wallace, B. A., & Saron, C. D. (2015). Intensive meditation training influences emotional responses to suffering. *Emotion, 15,* 775–790.

Rosenberg, N. A., Pritchard, J. K., Weber, J. L., Cann, H. M., Kidd, K. K., Zhivotosky, L. A., & Feldman, M. W. (2002). Genetic structure of human populations. *Science, 298,* 2381–2385.

Rosenberg, T. (2010, November 1). The opt-out solution. *The New York Times* (nytimes.com).

Rosenberg, T. (2019, Dec. 17). Five who spread hope in 2019. *The New York Times.* https://www.nytimes.com/2019/12/17/opinion/spread-hope-2019.html?

Rosenblum, L. D. (2013, January). A confederacy of senses. *Scientific American,* pp. 73–78.

Rosenfeld, M. J. (2014). Couple longevity in the era of same-sex marriage in the United States. *Journal of Marriage and Family, 76,* 905–911.

Rosenfeld, M. J., Reuben, T. J., & Falcon, M. (2011). *How couples meet and stay together, Waves 1, 2, and 3: Public version 3.04. Machine Readable Data File.* Stanford University Libraries. https://data.stanford.edu/hcmst

Rosenfeld, M. J., Thomas, R. J., & Hausen, S. (2018). *How couples meet and stay together 2017 fresh sample.* Stanford University Libraries. https://data.stanford.edu/hcmst2017

Rosenfeld, M. J., Thomas, R. J., & Hausen. S. (2019). Disintermediating your friends: How online dating in the United States displaces other ways of meeting. *PNAS, 116,* 17753–17758.

Rosenquist, P. B., McCall, W. V., & Youssef, N. (2016). Charting the course of electroconvulsive therapy: Where have we been and where are we headed? *Psychiatric Annals, 46,* 647–651.

Rosenthal, E. (2009, November 1). When texting kills, Britain offers path of prison. *The New York Times.* https://www.nytimes.com/2009/11/02/technology/02texting.html?

Rosenthal, R., Hall, J. A., Archer, D., DiMatteo, M. R., & Rogers, P. L. (1979). The PONS test: Measuring sensitivity to nonverbal cues. In S. Weitz (Ed.), *Nonverbal communication* (2nd ed.). Oxford University Press.

Rosenzweig, M. R. (1984). Experience, memory, and the brain. *American Psychologist, 39,* 365–376.

Rosenzweig, M. R., Krech, D., Bennett, E. L., & Diamond, M. C. (1962). Effects of environmental complexity and training on brain chemistry and anatomy: A replication and extension. *Journal of Comparative and Physiological Psychology, 55*, 429–437.

Roser, M. (2019). *Life expectancy*. Our World in Data. https://ourworldindata.org/life-expectancy

Roseth, C. J., Johnson, D. W., & Johnson, R. T. (2008). Promoting early adolescents' achievement and peer relationships: The effects of cooperative, competitive, and individualistic goal structures. *Psychological Bulletin, 134*, 223–246.

Rosling, H., Rosling Rönnlund, A., & Rosling, O. (2018). *Factfulness: Ten reasons we're wrong about the world—and why things are better than you think.* Flatiron Books.

Ross, E. L., Zivin, K., & Maixner, D. F. (2018). Cost-effectiveness of electroconvulsive therapy vs pharmacotherapy/psychotherapy for treatment-resistant depression in the United States. *JAMA Psychiatry, 75*, 713–722.

Ross, J. (2006, December). Sleep on a problem . . . it works like a dream. *The Psychologist, 19*, 738–740.

Ross, L. (1977). The intuitive psychologist and his shortcomings: Distortions in the attribution process. In L. Berkowitz (Ed.) *Advances in experimental social psychology* (Vol. 10). Academic Press.

Ross, L. (2018). From the fundamental attribution error to the truly fundamental attribution error and beyond: My research journey. *Perspectives on Psychological Science, 13*, 750–769.

Ross, L. E., Salway, T., Tarasoff, L. A., MacKay, J. M., Hawkins, B. W., & Fehr, C. P. (2018). Prevalence of depression and anxiety among bisexual people compared to gay, lesbian, and heterosexual individuals: A systematic review and meta-analysis. *Journal of Sex Research, 55*(4–5), 435–456.

Ross, M., McFarland, C., & Fletcher, G. J. O. (1981). The effect of attitude on the recall of personal histories. *Journal of Personality and Social Psychology, 40*, 627–634.

Ross, M., Xun, W. Q. E., & Wilson, A. E. (2002). Language and the bicultural self. *Personality and Social Psychology Bulletin, 28*, 1040–1050.

Rossi, A. S., & Rossi, P. H. (1993). *Of human bonding: Parent-child relations across the life course.* Aldine de Gruyter.

Rossi, P. J. (1968). Adaptation and negative after-effect to lateral optical displacement in newly hatched chicks. *Science, 160*, 430–432.

Rotge, J.-Y., Lemogne, C., Hinfray, S., Huguet, P., Grynszpan, O., Tartour, E., George, N., & Fossati, P. (2015). A meta-analysis of the anterior cingulate contribution to social pain. *Social Cognitive and Affective Neuroscience, 10*, 19–27.

Roth, B., Becker, N., Romeyke, S., Schäfer, S., Domnick, F., & Spinath, F. M. (2015). Intelligence and school grades: A meta-analysis. *Intelligence, 53*, 118–137.

Roth, T., Roehrs, T., Zwyghuizen-Doorenbos, A., Stpeanski, E., & Witting, R. (1988). Sleep and memory. In I. Hindmarch & H. Ott (Eds.), *Benzodiazepine receptor ligans, memory and information processing.* Springer-Verlag.

Rothbart, M., Fulero, S., Jensen, C., Howard, J., & Birrell, P. (1978). From individual to group impressions: Availability heuristics in stereotype formation. *Journal of Experimental Social Psychology, 14*, 237–255.

Rothbaum, F., & Tsang, B. Y.-P. (1998). Lovesongs in the United States and China: On the nature of romantic love. *Journal of Cross-Cultural Psychology, 29*, 306–319.

Rotheneichner, P., Lange, S., O'Sullivan, A., Marschallinger, J., Zaunmair, P., Geretsegger, C., Aigner, L., & Couillard-Despres, S. (2014). Hippocampal neurogenesis and antidepressive therapy: Shocking relations. *Neural Plasticity, 2014*, 723915.

Rottenberg, J., Devendorf, A. R., Panaite, V., Disabato, D. J., & Kashdan, T. B. (2019). Optimal well-being after major depression. *Clinical Psychological Science, 7*, 621–627.

Rottensteiner, M., Leskinen, T., Niskanen, E., Aaltonen, S., Mutikainen, S., Wikgren, J., Heikkilä, K., Kovanen, V., Kainulainen, H., Kaprio, J., Tarkka, I. M., & Kujala, U. M. (2015). Physical activity, fitness, glucose homeostasis, and brain morphology in twins. *Medicine and Science in Sports and Exercise, 47*, 509–518.

Rotton, J., & Kelly, I. W. (1985). Much ado about the full moon: A meta-analysis of lunar-lunacy research. *Psychological Bulletin, 97*, 286–306.

Rounds, J., & Su, R. (2014). The nature and power of interests. *Current Directions in Psychological Science, 23*, 98–103.

Rovee-Collier, C. (1989). The joy of kicking: Memories, motives, and mobiles. In P. R. Solomon, G. R. Goethals, C. M. Kelley, & B. R. Stephens (Eds.), *Memory: Interdisciplinary approaches.* Springer-Verlag.

Rovee-Collier, C. (1993). The capacity for long-term memory in infancy. *Current Directions in Psychological Science, 2*, 130–135.

Rovee-Collier, C. (1999). The development of infant memory. *Current Directions in Psychological Science, 8*, 80–85.

Rowe, D. C. (1990). As the twig is bent? The myth of child-rearing influences on personality development. *Journal of Counseling and Development, 68*, 606–611.

Rowe, D. C., Almeida, D. M., & Jacobson, K. C. (1999). School context and genetic influences on aggression in adolescence. *Psychological Science, 10*, 277–280.

Rowe, D. C., Vazsonyi, A. T., & Flannery, D. J. (1994). No more than skin deep: Ethnic and racial similarity in developmental process. *Psychological Review, 101*, 396.

Rowe, D. C., Vazsonyi, A. T., & Flannery, D. J. (1995). Ethnic and racial similarity in developmental process: A study of academic achievement. *Psychological Science, 6*, 33–38.

Roy, J., & Forest, G. (2018). Greater circadian disadvantage during evening games for the National Basketball Association (NBA), National Hockey League (NHL) and National Football League (NFL) teams travelling westward. *Journal of Sleep Research, 27*, 86–89.

Royal, K. (2019, September 14). *What engaged employees do differently*. Gallup. https://www.gallup.com/workplace/266822/engaged-employees-differently.aspx

Røysamb, E., & Nes, R. B. (2019). The role of genetics in subjective well-being. *Nature Human Behavior, 3*(1), 3.

Rozin, P., Dow, S., Mosovitch, M., & Rajaram, S. (1998). What causes humans to begin and end a meal? A role for memory for what has been eaten, as evidenced by a study of multiple meal eating in amnesic patients. *Psychological Science, 9*, 392–396.

Rozin, P., Haddad, B., Nemeroff, C., & Slovic, P. (2015). Psychological aspects of the rejection of recycled water: Contamination, purification and disgust. *Judgment and Decision Making, 10*, 50–63.

Rozin, P., Millman, L., & Nemeroff, C. (1986). Operation of the laws of sympathetic magic in disgust and other domains. *Journal of Personality and Social Psychology, 50*, 703–712.

Ruau, D., Liu, L. Y., Clark, J. D., Angst, M. S., & Butte, A. J. (2012). Sex differences in reported pain across 11,000 patients captured in electronic medical records. *Journal of Pain, 13*, 228–234.

Ruback, R. B., Carr, T. S., & Hopper, C. H. (1986). Perceived control in prison: Its relation to reported crowding, stress, and symptoms. *Journal of Applied Social Psychology, 16*, 375–386.

Rubel, J. A., Hilpert, P., Wolfer, C., Held, J., Vîslă, A., & Flückiger, C. (2019). The working alliance in manualized CBT for generalized anxiety disorder: Does it lead to change and does the effect vary depending on manual implementation flexibility? *Journal of Consulting and Clinical Psychology, 87*, 989–1002.

Rubenstein, J. S., Meyer, D. E., & Evans, J. E. (2001). Executive control of cognitive processes in task switching. *Journal of Experimental Psychology: Human Perception and Performance, 27*, 763–797.

Rubenstein, L. M., Freed, R. D., Shapero, B. G., Fauber, R. L., & Alloy, L. B. (2016, June). Cognitive attributions in depression: Bridging the gap between research and clinical practice. *Journal of Psychotherapy Integration, 26*, 103–115.

Ruberton, P. M., Gladstone, J., & Lyubomirsky, S. (2016). How your bank balance buys happiness. *Emotion, 16*, 575–580.

Rubin, D. C., Rahhal, T. A., & Poon, L. W. (1998). Things learned in early adulthood are remembered best. *Memory and Cognition, 26*, 3–19.

Rubin, J. Z., Pruitt, D. G., & Kim, S. H. (1994). *Social conflict: Escalation, stalemate, and settlement.* McGraw-Hill.

Rubin, L. B. (1985). *Just friends: The role of friendship in our lives.* Harper & Row.

Rubin, Z. (1970). Measurement of romantic love. *Journal of Personality and Social Psychology, 16*, 265–273.

Rubinstein, G. (2016). Modesty doesn't become me: Narcissism and the Big Five among male and female candidates for the *Big Brother* TV show. *Journal of Individual Differences, 37*, 223–230.

Rubio, G., & López-Ibor, J. J. (2007). Generalized anxiety disorder: A 40-year follow-up study. *Acta Psychiatrica Scandinavica, 115*, 372–379.

Rubio-Fernández, P., & Geurts, B. (2013). How to pass the false-belief task before your fourth birthday. *Psychological Science, 24*, 27–33.

Ruchlis, H. (1990). *Clear thinking: A practical introduction.* Prometheus Books.

Ruddock, H. K., Brunstrom, J. M., Vartanian, L. R., & Higgs, S. (2019). A systematic review and meta-analysis of the social facilitation of eating. *American Journal of Clinical Nutrition, 110*, 842–861.

Rudert, S. C., Keller, M. D., Hales, A. H., Walker, M., & Greifeneder, R. (2019). Who gets ostracized? A personality perspective on risk and protective factors of ostracism. *Journal of Personality and Social Psychology*, in press.

Rueckert, L., Doan, T., & Branch, B. (2010). Emotion and relationship effects on gender differences in empathy. Presented at the annual meeting of the Association for Psychological Science, Boston, MA.

Rueger, S. Y., Malecki, C. K., Pyun, Y., Aycock, C., & Coyle, S. (2016). A meta-analytic review of the association between perceived social support and depression in childhood and adolescence. *Psychological Bulletin, 142*, 1017–1067.

Ruffin, C. L. (1993). Stress and health—little hassles vs. major life events. *Australian Psychologist, 28*, 201–208.

Rule, B. G., & Ferguson, T. J. (1986). The effects of media violence on attitudes, emotions, and cognitions. *Journal of Social Issues, 42*, 29–50.

Rumbaugh, D. M. (1977). *Language learning by a chimpanzee: The Lana project.* Academic Press.

Rumbaugh, D. M., & Washburn, D. A. (2003). *Intelligence of apes and other rational beings.* Yale University Press.

Ruotsalainen, H., Kyngäs, H., Tammelin, T., & Kääriäinen, M. (2015). Systematic review of physical activity and exercise interventions on body mass indices, subsequent physical activity and psychological symptoms in overweight and obese adolescents. *Journal of Advanced Nursing, 71*, 2461–2477.

Rusanen, M., Kivipelto, M., Quesenberry, C. P., Jr., Zhou, J., & Whitmer, R. A. (2011). Heavy smoking in midlife and long-term risk of Alzheimer disease and vascular dementia. *Archives of Internal Medicine, 171*, 333–339.

Rusch, H. L., Rosario, M., Levison, L. M., Olivera, A., Livingston, W. S., Wu, T., & Gill, J. M. (2019). The effect of mindfulness meditation on sleep quality: a systematic review and meta-analysis of randomized controlled trials. *Annals of the New York Academy of Sciences, 1445*, 5–16.

Rushton, J. P. (1975). Generosity in children: Immediate and long-term effects of modeling, preaching, and moral judgment. *Journal of Personality and Social Psychology, 31*, 459–466.

Russell, B. (1930/1985). *The conquest of happiness.* Unwin Paperbacks.

Ruthsatz, J., & Urbach, J. B. (2012). Child prodigy: A novel cognitive profile places elevated general intelligence, exceptional working memory and attention to detail at the root of prodigiousness. *Intelligence, 40*, 419–426.

Rutledge, R. B., Skandali, N., Dayan, P., & Dolan, R. J. (2014). A computational and neural model of momentary subjective well-being. *PNAS, 111*, 12252–12257.

Rutz, C., Klump, B. C., Komarczyk, L., Leighton, R., Kramer, R., Wischnewski, S., Sugasawa, S., Morrissey, M. B., James, R., St. Clair, J. J., Switzer, R. A., & Masuda, B. M. (2016). Discovery of species-wide tool use in the Hawaiian crow. *Nature, 537*, 403–407.

Ruzich, E., Allison, C., Chakrabarti, B., Smith, P., Musto, H., Ring, H., & Baron-Cohen, S. (2015). Sex and STEM occupation predict autism-spectrum quotient (AQ) scores in half a million people. *PLOS ONE 10*(10), e0141229.

Ruzich, E., Crespo-García, M., Dalal, S. S., & Schneiderman, J. F. (2019). Characterizing hippocampal dynamics with MEG: A systematic review and evidence-based guidelines. *Human Brain Mapping, 40*, 1353–1375.

Ryan, B. (2016, March 8). *Women's life ratings get better with full-time jobs.* Gallup. https://news.gallup.com/opinion/gallup/189854/women-life-ratings-better-full-time-jobs.aspx

Ryan, P. (2015, December 15). Quoted by Editorial Board of *The New York Times* in Don't blame mental illness for gun violence. *The New York Times.* https://www.nytimes.com/2015/12/16/opinion/dont-blame-mental-illness-for-gun-violence.html?

Ryan, R. M., & Deci, E. L. (2000). Self-determination theory and the facilitation of intrinsic motivation, social development, and well-being. *American Psychologist, 55*, 68–78.

Ryan, R. M., & Deci, E. L. (2004). Avoiding death or engaging life as accounts of meaning and culture: Comment on Pyszczynski et al. (2004). *Psychological Bulletin, 130*, 473–477.

Rydell, M., Lundström, S., Gillberg, C., Lichtenstein, P., & Larsson, H. (2018). Has the attention deficit hyperactivity disorder phenotype become more common in children between 2004 and 2014? Trends over 10 years from a Swedish general population sample. *Journal of Child Psychology and Psychiatry, 59*, 863–871.

Rydell, R. J., Rydell, M. T., & Boucher, K. L. (2010). The effect of negative performance stereotypes on learning. *Journal of Personality and Social Psychology, 99*, 883–896.

Ryder, A. G., Yang, J., Zhu, X., Yao, S., Yi, J., Heine, S. J., & Bagby, R. M. (2008). The cultural shaping of depression: somatic symptoms in China, psychological symptoms in North America? *Journal of Abnormal Psychology, 117*, 300–313.

Ryder, J. G., & Holtzheimer, P. E. (2016). Deep brain stimulation for depression: An update. *Current Behavioral Neuroscience Reports, 3*, 102–108.

Saad, L. (2002, November 21). *Most smokers wish they could quit.* Gallup News Service. https://news.gallup.com/poll/7270/most-smokers-wish-they-could-quit.aspx

Saad, L. (2015, July 13). *Nearly half of smartphone users can't imagine life without it.* Gallup. https://news.gallup.com/poll/184085/nearly-half-smartphone-users-imagine-life-without.aspx

Saad, L. (2019, August 16). *10 major social changes in the 50 years since Woodstock.* Gallup. https://news.gallup.com/opinion/gallup/265490/major-social-changes-years-woodstock.aspx

Sabbagh, M. A., Xu, F., Carlson, S. M., Moses, L. J., & Lee, K. (2006). The development of executive functioning and theory of mind: A comparison of Chinese and U.S. preschoolers. *Psychological Science, 17*, 74–81.

Sabesan, R., Schmidt, B. P., Tuten, W. S., & Roorda, A. (2016). The elementary representation of spatial and color vision in the human retina. *Science Advances, 2*, e1600797.

Sabini, J. (1986). Stanley Milgram (1933–1984). *American Psychologist, 41*, 1378–1379.

Sachdev, P., & Sachdev, J. (1997). Sixty years of psychosurgery: Its present status and its future. *Australian and New Zealand Journal of Psychiatry, 31*, 457–464.

Sackett, P. R., Kuncel, N. R., Beatty, A. S., Rigdon, J. L., Shen, W., & Kiger, T. B. (2012). The role of socioeconomic status in SAT-grade relationships and in college admissions decisions. *Psychological Science, 23*, 1000–1007.

Sacks, O. (1985). *The man who mistook his wife for a hat.* Summit Books.

Sadato, N., Pascual-Leone, A., Grafman, J., Ibanez, V., Deiber, M.-P., Dold, G., & Hallett, M. (1996). Activation of the primary visual cortex by Braille reading in blind subjects. *Nature, 380*, 526–528.

Sadler, M. S., Correll, J., Park, B., & Judd, C. M. (2012a). The world is not Black and White: Racial bias in the decision to shoot in a multiethnic context. *Journal of Social Issues, 68*, 286–313.

Sadler, M. S., Meagor, E. L., & Kaye, M. E. (2012b). Stereotypes of mental disorders differ in competence and warmth. *Social Science and Medicine, 74*, 915–922.

Saffran, J. A. (2009). What can statistical learning tell us about infant learning? In A. Woodward & A. Needham (Eds.), *Learning and the infant mind.* Oxford University Press.

Saffran, J. R., Aslin, R. N., & Newport, E. L. (1996). Statistical learning by 8-month-old infants. *Science, 274*, 1926–1928.

Sagan, C. (1977). *The dragons of Eden: Speculations on the evolution of human intelligence.* Ballantine.

Sagan, C. (1987, February 1). *The fine art of baloney detection* [PDF file]. www.inf.fu-berlin.de/lehre/pmo/eng/Sagan-Baloney.pdf

Saint Louis, C. (2017, February 2). Pregnant women turn to marijuana, perhaps harming infants. *The New York Times.* https://www.nytimes.com/2017/02/02/health/marijuana-and-pregnancy.html

Saito, A., Shinozuka, K., Ito, Y., & Hasegawa, T. (2019). Domestic cats (Felis catus) discriminate their names from other words. *Scientific Reports, 9*, 5394.

Sajous-Turner, A., Anderson, N. E., Widdows, M., Nyalakanti, P., Harenski, K., Harenski, C., Koenigs, M., Decety, J., & Kiehl, K. A. (2019). Aberrant brain gray matter in murderers. *Brain Imaging and Behavior.* Advance online publication. https://doi.org/10.1007/s11682-019-00155-y

Sakaluk, J. K., Williams, A. J., Kilshaw, R. E., & Rhyner, K. T. (2019). Evaluating the evidential value of empirically supported psychological treatments (ESTs): A meta-scientific review. *Journal of Abnormal Psychology, 128*, 500–509.

Saks, E. (2007, August 27). A memoir of schizophrenia. *Time* (time.com).

Sala, G., Tatlidil, K. S., & Gobet, F. (2018). Video game training does not enhance cognitive ability: A comprehensive meta-analytic investigation. *Psychological Bulletin, 144*, 111–139.

Salas-Wright, C., Vaughn, M. G., Goings, T. C., Miller, D. P., & Schwartz, S. J. (2018). Immigrants and mental disorders in the United States: New evidence on the healthy migrant hypothesis. *Psychiatry Research, 267*, 438–445.

Salas-Wright, C. P., Vaughn, M. G., Hodge, D. R., & Perron, B. E. (2012). Religiosity profiles of American youth in relation to substance use, violence, and delinquency. *Journal of Youth and Adolescence, 41*, 1560–1575.

Salazar Kämpf, M., Liebermann, H., Kerschreiter, R., Krause, S., Nestler, S., & Schmukle, S. C. (2018). Disentangling the sources of mimicry: Social relations analyses of the link between mimicry and liking. *Psychological Science, 29*, 131–138.

Salchegger, S. (2016). Selective school systems and academic self-concept: How explicit and implicit school-level tracking relate to the big-fish–little-pond effect across cultures. *Journal of Educational Psychology, 108*, 405–423.

Salehi, I., Hosseini, S. M., Haghighi, M., Jahangard, L., Bajoghli, H., Gerber, M., Pühse, U., Holsboer-Trachsler, E., & Brand, S. (2016). Electroconvulsive therapy (ECT) and aerobic exercise training (AET) increased plasma BDNF and ameliorated depressive symptoms in patients suffering from major depressive disorder. *Journal of Psychiatric Research, 76*, 1–8.

Salgado, J. F., & Moscoso, S. (2002). Comprehensive meta-analysis of the construct validity of the employment interview. *European Journal of Work and Organizational Psychology, 11*, 299–326.

Salk, R. H., Hyde, J. S., & Abramson, L. Y. (2017). Gender differences in depression in representative national samples: Meta-analyses of diagnoses and symptoms. *Psychological Bulletin, 143*, 783–822.

Salles, A., Bjaalie, J. G., Evers, K., Farisco, M., Fothergill, B. T., Guerrero, M., Maslen, H., Muller, J., Prescott, T., Stahl, B. C., Walter, H., Zilles, K., & Amunts, K. (2019). The Human Brain Project: Responsible brain research for the benefit of society. *Neuron, 101*, 380–384.

Salmela-Aro, K., Tolvanen, A., & Nurmi, J. (2009). Achievement strategies during university studies predict early career burnout and engagement. *Journal of Vocational Behavior, 75*, 162–172.

Salmon, P. (2001). Effects of physical exercise on anxiety, depression, and sensitivity to stress: A unifying theory. *Clinical Psychology Review, 21*, 33–61.

Salovey, P. (1990, January/February). Interview. *American Scientist*, pp. 25–29.

Salthouse, T. A. (2010). Selective review of cognitive aging. *Journal of the International Neuropsychological Society, 16*, 754–760.

Salthouse, T. A. (2013). Within-cohort age-related differences in cognitive functioning. *Psychological Science, 24*, 123–130.

Salthouse, T. A. (2014). Why are there different age relations in cross-sectional and longitudinal comparisons of cognitive functioning? *Current Directions in Psychological Science, 23*, 252–256.

Salthouse, T. A., & Mandell, A. R. (2013). Do age-related increases in tip-of-the-tongue experiences signify episodic memory impairments? *Psychological Science, 24*, 2489–2497.

SAMHSA. (2018). *Key substance use and mental health indicators in the United States: Results from the 2017 National Survey on Drug Use and Health* (HHS Publication No. SMA 18-5068, NSDUH Series H-53). Center for Behavioral Health Statistics and Quality, Substance Abuse and Mental Health Services Administration.

SAMHSA. (2019). *Results from the 2018 National Survey on Drug Use and Health: Graphics from the key findings report*. Center for Behavioral Health Statistics and Quality, Substance Abuse and Mental Health Services Administration, U.S. Department of Health and Human Services.

Samson, D. R., Crittenden, A. N., Mabulla, I. A., Mabulla, A. Z. P., & Nunn, C. L. (2017). Chronotype variation drives night-time sentinel-like behaviour in hunter-gatherers. *Proceedings of the Royal Society B, 284*(1858), 20170967.

Samuels, J., & Nestadt, G. (1997). Epidemiology and genetics of obsessive-compulsive disorder. *International Review of Psychiatry, 9*, 61–71.

Sánchez-Álvarez, N., Extremera, N., & Fernández-Berrocal, P. (2016). The relation between emotional intelligence and subjective well-being: A meta-analytic investigation. *Journal of Positive Psychology, 11*, 276–285.

Sánchez-Villegas, A., Henríquez-Sánchez, P., Ruiz-Canela, M., Lahortiga, F., Molero, P., Toledo, E., & Martínez-González, M. A. (2015). A longitudinal analysis of diet quality scores and the risk of incident depression in the SUN Project. *BMC Medicine, 13*, 1.

Sanders, A. R., Beecham, G. W., Guo, S., Dawood, K., Rieger, G., Badner, J. A., Gershon, E. S., Krishnappa, R. S., Kolundzija, A. B., Duan, J., MGS Collaboration, Gejman, P. V., Bailey, J. M., & Martin, E. R. (2017). Genome-wide association study of male sexual orientation. *Nature: Scientific Reports, 7*(1), 16950.

Sanders, A. R., Martin, E. R., Beecham, G. W., Guo, S., Dawood, K. Rieger, G., Badner, J. A., Gershon, E. S., Krishnappa, R. S., Kolundzija, A. B., Duan, J., Gejman, P. V., & Bailey, J. M. (2015). Genome-wide scan demonstrates significant linkage for male sexual orientation. *Psychological Medicine, 45*, 1379–1388.

Sandler, W., Meir, I., Padden, C., & Aronoff, M. (2005). The emergence of grammar: Systematic structure in a new language. *PNAS, 102*, 2261–2265.

Sandoval, M., Leclerc, J. A., & Gómez, R. L. (2017). Words to sleep on: Naps facilitate verb generalization in habitually and nonhabitually napping preschoolers. *Child Development, 88*(5), 1615–1626.

Sandstrom, A. (2015, December 2). *Religious groups' policies on transgender members vary widely*. Pew Research Center. https://www.pewresearch.org/fact-tank/2015/12/02/religious-groups-policies-on-transgender-members-vary-widely/

Sanson, M., Strange, D., & Garry, M. (2019). Trigger warnings are trivially helpful at reducing negative affect, intrusive thoughts, and avoidance. *Clinical Psychological Science, 7*, 778–793.

Santangelo, V., Cavallina, C., Colucci, P., Santori, A., Macri, S., McGaugh, J. L., & Campolongo, P. (2018). Enhanced brain activity associated with memory access in highly superior autobiographical memory. *PNAS, 115*, 7795–7800.

Santavirta, T., Santavirta, N., & Gilman, S. E. (2018). Association of the World War II Finnish evacuation of children with psychiatric hospitalization in the next generation. *JAMA Psychiatry, 75*, 21–27.

Santomauro, J., & French, C. C. (2009). Terror in the night. *The Psychologist, 22*, 672–675.

Santos, H. C., Varnum, M. E. W., & Grossmann, I. (2017). Global increases in individualism. *Psychological Science, 28*, 1228–1239.

Sanz, C., Blicher, A., Dalke, K., Gratton-Fabbri, L., McClure-Richards, T., & Fouts, R. (1998, Winter-Spring). Enrichment object use: Five chimpanzees' use of temporary and semi-permanent enrichment objects. *Friends of Washoe, 19*, 9–14.

Sanz, C., Morgan, D., & Gulick, S. (2004). New insights into chimpanzees, tools, and termites from the Congo Basin. *American Naturalist, 164*, 567–581.

Sapadin, L. A. (1988). Friendship and gender: Perspectives of professional men and women. *Journal of Social and Personal Relationships, 5*, 387–403.

Sapolsky, R. (2003). Taming stress. *Scientific American, 289*, 86–95.

Sapolsky, R. (2005). The influence of social hierarchy on primate health. *Science, 308*, 648–652.

Sapolsky, R. (2010, November 14). This is your brain on metaphors. *The New York Times*. https://opinionator.blogs.nytimes.com/2010/11/14/this-is-your-brain-on-metaphors/?

Sapolsky, R. (2015, September 3). *Caitlyn Jenner and our cognitive dissonance*. Nautilus. http://nautil.us/issue/28/2050/caitlyn-jenner-and-our-cognitive-dissonance

Sapolsky, R. M. (2018, November). The science of inequality. *Scientific American*, pp. 54–67.

Saposnik, G., Redelmeier, D., Ruff, C. C., & Tobler, P. N. (2016). Cognitive biases associated with medical decisions: A systematic review. *BMC Medical Informatics and Decision Making, 16*, 138.

Sarrasin, J. B., Nenciovici, L., Foisy, L.-M. B., Allaire-Duquette, G., Riopel, M., Masson, S. (2018). Effects of teaching the concept of neuroplasticity to induce a growth mindset on motivation, achievement, and brain activity: A meta-analysis. *Trends in Neuroscience and Education, 12*, 22–31.

Sarro, E. C., Wilson, D. A., & Sullivan, R. M. (2014). Maternal regulation of infant brain state. *Current Biology, 24*, 1664–1669.

Sassenberg, K., & Ditrich, L. (2019). Research in social psychology changed between 2011 and 2016: Larger sample sizes, more self-report measures, and more online studies. *Advances in Methods and Practices in Psychological Science, 2*(2), 107–114.

Sasser, T. R., Bierman, K. L., Heinrichs, B., & Nix, R. L. (2017). Preschool intervention can promote sustained growth in the executive-function skills of children exhibiting early deficits. *Psychological Science, 28*, 1719–1730.

Satel, S., & Lilienfeld, S. G. (2013). *Brainwashed: The seductive appeal of mindless neuroscience*. Basic Books.

Sato, K. (1987). Distribution of the cost of maintaining common resources. *Journal of Experimental Social Psychology, 23*, 19–31.

Sauce, B., & Matzel, L. D. (2018). The paradox of intelligence: Heritability and malleability coexist in hidden gene-environment interplay. *Psychological Bulletin, 144*, 26–47.

Saulny, S. (2006, June 21). A legacy of the storm: Depression and suicide. *The New York Times*. https://www.nytimes.com/2006/06/21/us/a-legacy-of-the-storm-depression-and-suicide.html?

Saunders, G. R. B., Elkins, I. J., Christensen, K., & McGue, M. (2018). The relationship between subjective well-being and mortality within discordant twin pairs from two independent samples. *Psychology and Aging, 33*, 439–447.

Saunders-Scott, D., Braley, M. B., & Stennes-Spidahl, N. (2018). Traditional and psychological factors associated with academic success: investigating best predictors of college retention. *Motivation and Emotion, 42*, 459–465.

Saurat, M., Agbakou, M., Attigui, P., Golmard, J., & Arnulf, I. (2011). Walking dreams in congenital and acquired paraplegia. *Consciousness and Cognition, 20*, 1425–1432.

Savage, J. E., Jansen, P. R., Stringer, S., Watanabe, K., Bryois, J., de Leeuw, C. A., Nagel, M., Awasthi, S., Barr, P. B., Coleman, J., Grasby, K. L., Hammerschlag, A. R., Kaminski, J. A., Karlsson, R., Krapohl, E., Lam, M., Nygaard, M., Reynolds, C. A., Trampush, J. W., . . . Grasby, K. L. (2018). Genome-wide association meta-analysis in 269,867 individuals identifies new genetic and functional links to intelligence. *Nature Genetics, 50*, 912–919.

Savage-Rumbaugh, E. S., Murphy, J., Sevcik, R. A., Brakke, K. E., Williams, S. L., & Rumbaugh, D. M., with commentary by Bates, E. (1993). Language comprehension in ape and child. *Monographs of the Society for Research in Child Development, 58*, 1–254.

Savage-Rumbaugh, E. S., Rumbaugh, D., & Fields, W. M. (2009). Empirical Kanzi: The ape language controversy revisited. *Skeptic, 15*, 25–33.

Savani, K., & Job, V. (2017). Reverse ego-depletion: Acts of self-control can improve subsequent performance in Indian cultural contexts. *Journal of Personality and Social Psychology, 113*, 589–607.

Savani, K., & Rattan, A. (2012). A choice mind-set increases the acceptance and maintenance of wealth inequality. *Psychological Science, 23*, 796–804.

Savelieva, K., Pulkki-Råback, L., Jokela, M., Kubzansky, L. D., Elovainio, M., Mikkilä, V., Tammelin, T., Juonala, M., Raitakari, O. T., & Keltikangas-Järvinen, L. (2016). Intergenerational transmission of socioeconomic position and ideal cardiovascular health: 32-year follow-up study. *Health Psychology, 36*, 270–279.

Savic, I., Berglund, H., & Lindstrom, P. (2005). Brain response to putative pheromones in homosexual men. *PNAS, 102*, 7356–7361.

Savic, I., & Lindström, P. (2008). PET and MRI show differences in cerebral asymmetry and functional connectivity between homo- and heterosexual subjects. *PNAS, 105*, 9403–9408.

Savin-Williams, R., Joyner, K., & Rieger, G. (2012). Prevalence and stability of self-reported sexual orientation identity during young adulthood. *Archives of Sexual Behavior, 41*, 103–110.

Savitsky, K., Epley, N., & Gilovich, T. D. (2001). Do others judge us as harshly as we think? Overestimating the impact of our failures, shortcomings, and mishaps. *Journal of Personality and Social Psychology, 81*, 44–56.

Savitsky, K., & Gilovich, T. D. (2003). The illusion of transparency and the alleviation of speech anxiety. *Journal of Experimental Social Psychology, 39*, 618–625.

Savoy, C., & Beitel, P. (1996). Mental imagery for basketball. *International Journal of Sport Psychology, 27*, 454–462.

Sawyer, A. C. P., Miller-Lewis, L. R., Searle, A. K., & Sawyer, M. G. (2015). Is greater improvement in early self-regulation associated with fewer behavioral problems later in childhood? *Developmental Psychology, 51*, 1740–1755.

Sawyer, S. M., Azzopardi, P. S., Wickremarathne, D., & Patton, G. C. (2018). The age of adolescence. *Lancet Child and Adolescent Health, 2*, 223–228.

Sayal, K., Chudal, R., Hinkka-Yli-Salomäki, S., Joelsson, P., & Sourander, A. (2017). Relative age within the school year and diagnosis of attention-deficit hyperactivity disorder: A nationwide population-based study. *The Lancet Psychiatry, 4*(11), 868–875.

Sayer, L. C. (2016). Trends in women's and men's time use, 1965–2012: Back to the future? In S. M. McHale, V. King, J. Van Hook, and A. Booth (Eds.), *Gender and couple relationships*. Springer International.

Sayette, M. A., Loewenstein, G., Griffin, K. M., & Black, J. J. (2008). Exploring the cold-to-hot empathy gap in smokers. *Psychological Science, 19,* 926–932.

Sayette, M. A., Reichle, E. D., & Schooler, J. W. (2009). Lost in the sauce: The effects of alcohol on mind wandering. *Psychological Science, 20,* 747–752.

Sayette, M. A., Schooler, J. W., & Reichle, E. D. (2010). Out for a smoke: The impact of cigarette craving on zoning out during reading. *Psychological Science, 21,* 26–30.

Sayre, R. F. (1979). The parents' last lessons. In D. D. Van Tassel (Ed.), *Aging, death, and the completion of being.* University of Pennsylvania Press.

Sbarra, D. A., Hasselmo, K., & Bourassa, K. J. (2015). Divorce and health: Beyond individual differences. *Current Directions in Psychological Science, 24,* 109–113.

Scaini, S., Belotti, R., Ogliari, A., & Battaglia, M. (2016). A comprehensive meta-analysis of cognitive-behavioral interventions for social anxiety disorder in children and adolescents. *Journal of Anxiety Disorders, 42,* 105–112.

Scarborough, E., & Furumoto, L. (1987). *Untold lives: The first generation of American women psychologists.* Columbia University Press.

Scarf, D., Boy, K., Reinert, A. U., Devine, J., Güntürkün, O., & Colombo, M. (2016). Orthographic processing in pigeons (*Columba livia*). PNAS, 113, 11272–11276.

Scarr, S. (1984, May). What's a parent to do? A conversation with E. Hall. *Psychology Today,* pp. 58–63.

Scarr, S. (1989). Protecting general intelligence: Constructs and consequences for interventions. In R. J. Linn (Ed.), *Intelligence: Measurement, theory, and public policy.* University of Illinois Press.

Scarr, S. (1990). Back cover comments on J. Dunn & R. Plomin (1990), *Separate lives: Why siblings are so different.* Basic Books.

Scarr, S. (1993, May/June). So long, superparents. *Psychology Today.* https://www.psychologytoday.com/us/articles/199305/so-long-superparents

Schab, F. R. (1991). Odor memory: Taking stock. *Psychological Bulletin, 109,* 242–251.

Schachter, S., & Singer, J. E. (1962). Cognitive, social and physiological determinants of emotional state. *Psychological Review, 69,* 379–399.

Schacter, D. L. (1992). Understanding implicit memory: A cognitive neuroscience approach. *American Psychologist, 47,* 559–569.

Schacter, D. L. (1996). *Searching for memory: The brain, the mind, and the past.* Basic Books.

Schaefer, J. D., Moffitt, T. E., Arseneault, L., Danese, A., Fisher, H. L., Houts, R., Sheridan, M. A., Wertz, J., & Caspi, A. (2018). Adolescent victimization and early-adult psychopathology: Approaching causal inference using a longitudinal twin study to rule out noncausal explanations. *Clinical Psychological Science, 6,* 352–371.

Schaefer, M., Cherkasskiy, L., Denke, C., Spies, C., Song, H., Malahy, S., Heinz, A., Ströhle, A., & Bargh, J. A. (2018). Incidental haptic sensations influence judgment of crimes. *Scientific Reports, 8,* 6039.

Schafer, G. (2005). Infants can learn decontextualized words before their first birthday. *Child Development, 76,* 87–96.

Schaffer, A., Isometsä, E. T., Tondo, L., Moreno, D., Turecki, G., Reis, C., Cassidy, F., Sinyor, M., Azorin, J. M., Kessing, L. V., Ha, K., Goldstein, T., Weizman, A., Beautrais, A., Chou, Y.-H., Diazgranados, N., Levitt, A. J., Zarate, C. A., Jr., Rihmer, Z., & Yatham, L. N. (2015). International society for bipolar disorders task force on suicide: Meta-analyses and meta-regression of correlates of suicide attempts and suicide deaths in bipolar disorder. *Bipolar Disorders, 17,* 1–16.

Schaie, K. W. (1994). The life course of adult intellectual abilities. *American Psychologist, 49,* 304–313.

Schaie, K. W., & Geiwitz, J. (1982). *Adult development and aging.* Little, Brown.

Schalock, R. L., Borthwick-Duffy, S., Bradley, V. J., Buntinx, W. H. E., Coulter, D. L., Craig, E. M. (2010). *Intellectual disability: Definition, classification, and systems of supports* (11th edition). American Association on Intellectual and Developmental Disabilities.

Schatzberg, A. F. (2019). A word to the wise about intranasal esketamine. *The American Journal of Psychiatry, 176,* 422–424.

Schein, E. H. (1956). The Chinese indoctrination program for prisoners of war: A study of attempted brainwashing. *Psychiatry, 19,* 149–172.

Scheufele, D. A., Xenos, M. A., Howell, E. L., Rose, K. M., Brossard, D., & Hardy, B. W. (2017). U.S. attitudes on human genome editing. *Science, 357,* 553–554.

Schick, V., Herbenick, D., Reece, M., Sanders, S. A., Dodge, B., Middlestadt, S. E., & Fortenberry, J. D. (2010). Sexual behaviors, condom use, and sexual health of Americans over 50: Implications for sexual health promotion for older adults. *Journal of Sexual Medicine, 7*(Suppl. 5), 315–329.

Schiffenbauer, A., & Schiavo, R. S. (1976). Physical distance and attraction: An intensification effect. *Journal of Experimental Social Psychology, 12,* 274–282.

Schiffer, L. P., & Roberts, T. A. (2018). The paradox of happiness: Why are we not doing what we know makes us happy?. *The Journal of Positive Psychology, 13,* 252–259.

Schiffman, J., Abrahamson, A., Cannon, T., LaBrie, J., Parnas, J., Schulsinger, F., & Mednick, S. (2001). Early rearing factors in schizophrenia. *International Journal of Mental Health, 30,* 3-16.

Schilt, T., de Win, M. M. L, Koeter, M., Jager, G., Korf, D. J., van den Brink, W., & Schmand, B. (2007). Cognition in novice Ecstasy users with minimal exposure to other drugs. *Archives of General Psychiatry, 64,* 728–736.

Schimel, J., Arndt, J., Pyszczynski, T., & Greenberg, J. (2001). Being accepted for who we are: Evidence that social validation of the intrinsic self reduces general defensiveness. *Journal of Personality and Social Psychology, 80,* 35–52.

Schlaug, G., Jancke, L., Huang, Y., & Steinmetz, H. (1995). In vivo evidence of structural brain asymmetry in musicians. *Science, 267,* 699–701.

Schlomer, G. L., Del Giudice, M., & Ellis, B. J. (2011). Parent–offspring conflict theory: An evolutionary framework for understanding conflict within human families. *Psychological Review, 118,* 496–521.

Schloss, J. (2009). Does evolution explain human nature? Totally, for a Martian. In *Celebrating the bicentenary of the birth of Charles Darwin.* John Templeton Foundation (templeton.org).

Schmid, S. M., Hallschmid, M., & Schultes, B. (2015). The metabolic burden of sleep loss. *The Lancet Diabetes & Endocrinology, 3,* 52–62.

Schmidt, A., Dirk, J., & Schmiedek, F. (2019). The importance of peer relatedness at school for affective well-being in children: Between-and within-person associations. *Social Development, 28,* 873–892.

Schmidt, C., Collette, F., Leclercq, Y., Sterpenich, V., Vandewalle, G., Berthomier, P., Phillips, C., Tinguely, G., Darsaud, A., Gais, S., Schabus, M., Desseilles, M., Dang-Vu, T. T., Salmon, E., Balteau, E., Degueldre, C., Luxen, A., Maquet, P., Cajochen, C., & Peigneux, P. (2009). Homeostatic sleep pressure and responses to sustained attention in the suprachiasmatic area. *Science, 324,* 516–519.

Schmidt, F. L., & Hunter, J. E. (1998). The validity and utility of selection methods in personnel psychology: Practical and theoretical implications of 85 years of research findings. *Psychological Bulletin, 124,* 262–274.

Schmidt, F. L., & Hunter, J. E. (2004). General mental ability in the world of work: Occupational attainment and job performance. *Journal of Personality and Social Psychology, 86,* 162–173.

Schmidt, F. T. C., Nagy, G., Fleckenstein, J., Möller, J., & Retelsdorf, J. (2018). Same same, but different? Relations between facets of conscientiousness and grit. *European Journal of Personality, 32,* 705–720.

Schmidt, I. D., Pfeifer, B. J., & Strunk, D. R. (2019). Putting the "cognitive" back in cognitive therapy: Sustained cognitive change as a mediator of in-session insights and depressive symptom improvement. *Journal of Consulting and Clinical Psychology, 87,* 446–456.

Schmidt, S. (2018, April 4). Twin sisters known for battle with debilitating OCD die in possible 'suicide pact.' *The Washington Post* (washingtonpost.com).

Schmitt, D. P. (2003). Universal sex differences in the desire for sexual variety; tests from 52 nations, 6 continents, and 13 islands. *Journal of Personality and Social Psychology, 85,* 85–104.

Schmitt, D. P. (2007). Sexual strategies across sexual orientations: How personality traits and culture relate to sociosexuality among gays, lesbians, bisexuals, and heterosexuals. *Journal of Psychology and Human Sexuality, 18,* 183–214.

Schmitt, D. P., & Allik, J. (2005). Simultaneous administration of the Rosenberg Self-esteem Scale in 53 nations: Exploring the universal and culture-specific features of global self-esteem. *Journal of Personality and Social Psychology, 89,* 623–642.

Schmitt, D. P., Allik, J., McCrae, R. R., & Benet-Martínez, V., Reips, U.-D. (2007). The geographic distribution of Big Five personality traits: Patterns and profiles of human self-description across 56 nations. *Journal of Cross-Cultural Psychology, 38,* 173–212.

Schmitt, D. P., & Fuller, R. C. (2015). On the varieties of sexual experience: Cross-cultural links between religiosity and human mating strategies. *Psychology of Religion and Spirituality, 7,* 314–326.

Schmitt, D. P., Jonason, P. K., Byerley, G. J., Flores, S. D., Illbeck, B. E., O'Leary, K. N., & Qudrat, A. (2012). A reexamination of sex differences in sexuality: New studies reveal old truths. *Current Directions in Psychological Science, 21,* 135–139.

Schmitt, D. P., & Pilcher, J. J. (2004). Evaluating evidence of psychological adaptation: How do we know one when we see one? *Psychological Science, 15,* 643–649.

Schnall, E., Wassertheil-Smoller, S., Swencionis, C., Zemon, V., Tinker, L., O'Sullivan, M. J., Van Horn, L., & Goodwin, M. (2010). The relationship between religion and cardiovascular outcomes and all-cause mortality in the women's health initiative observational study. *Psychology and Health, 25,* 249–263.

Schnall, S., Haidt, J., Clore, G. L., & Jordan, A. (2008). Disgust as embodied moral judgment. *Personality and Social Psychology Bulletin, 34,* 1096–1109.

Schneider, M. (2019, October 10). *A year after Michael, Florida community still in crisis.* Associated Press. https://apnews.com/0d260a9ec44545458ab1f25b6f969a5a

Schneider, S. L. (2001). In search of realistic optimism: Meaning, knowledge, and warm fuzziness. *American Psychologist, 56,* 250–263.

Schneider, W. J., & McGrew, K. S. (2012). The Cattell-Horn-Carroll model of intelligence In Flanagan D. P., Harrison P. L. (Eds.), *Contemporary intellectual assessment: Theories, tests, and issues* (3rd ed.). Guilford Press.

Schneier, B. (2007, May 17). *Virginia Tech lesson: Rare risks breed irrational responses.* Schneir on Security. https://www.schneier.com/essays/archives/2007/05/virginia_tech_lesson.html

Schnur, J. B., Kafer, I., Marcus, C., & Montgomery, G. H. (2008). Hypnosis to manage distress related to medical procedures: a meta-analysis. *Contemporary Hypnosis*, 25, 114–128.

Schoeneman, T. J. (1994). Individualism. In V. S. Ramachandran (Ed.), *Encyclopedia of human behavior* (Vol. 2, pp. 631–643). Academic Press.

Schofield, J. W. (1986). Black-White contact in desegregated schools. In M. Hewstone & R. Brown (Eds.), *Contact and conflict in intergroup encounters* (pp. 79–92). Basil Blackwell.

Scholaske, L., Buss, C., Wadhwa, P. D., & Entringer, S. (2018). Acculturation and interleukin (IL)-6 concentrations across pregnancy among Mexican-American women. *Brain, Behavior, and Immunity*, 73, 731–735.

Scholtz, S., Miras, A. D., Chhina, N., Prechtl, C. G., Sleeth, M. L., Daud, N. M., Ismail, N. A. Durighel, G., Ahmed, A. R., Olbers, T., Vincent, R. P., Alaghband-Zadeh, J., Ghatei, M. A., Waldman, A. D., Frost, G. S., Bell, J. D., le Roux, C. W., & Goldstone, A. P. (2013). Obese patients after gastric bypass surgery have lower brain-hedonic responses to food than after gastric banding. *Gut*, 63, 891–902.

Schonfield, D., & Robertson, B. A. (1966). Memory storage and aging. *Canadian Journal of Psychology*, 20, 228–236.

Schooler, J. W., Gerhard, D., & Loftus, E. F. (1986). Qualities of the unreal. *Journal of Experimental Psychology: Learning, Memory, and Cognition*, 12, 171–181.

Schorr, E. A., Fox, N. A., van Wassenhove, V., & Knudsen, E. I. (2005). Auditory–visual fusion in speech perception in children with cochlear implants. *PNAS*, 102, 18748–18750.

Schrauzer, G. N., & Shrestha, K. P. (1990). Lithium in drinking water and the incidences of crimes, suicides, and arrests related to drug addictions. *Biological Trace Element Research*, 25, 105–113.

Schrauzer, G. N., & Shrestha, K. P. (2010). Lithium in drinking water. *British Journal of Psychiatry*, 196, 159.

Schreiber, F. R. (1973). *Sybil*. Regnery.

Schroeder, J., Caruso, E. M., & Epley, N. (2016). Many hands make overlooked work: Over-claiming of responsibility increases with group size. *Journal of Experimental Psychology: Applied*, 22, 238–246.

Schroeder, J., & Epley, N. (2015). The sound of intellect: Speech reveals a thoughtful mind, increasing a job candidate's appeal. *Psychological Science*, 26, 877–891.

Schroeder, J., & Epley, N. (2016). Mistaking minds and machines: How speech affects dehumanization and anthropomorphism. *Journal of Experimental Psychology: General*, 145, 1427–1437.

Schuch, F., Vancampfort, D., Firth, J., Rosenbaum, S., Ward, P., Silva, E. S., Hallgren, M., Ponce De Leon, A., Dunn, A. L., Deslandes, A. C., Fleck, M. P., Carvalho, A. F., & Stubbs, B. (2018). Physical activity and incident depression: A meta-analysis of prospective cohort studies. *American Journal of Psychiatry*, 175, 631–648.

Schuch, F. B., Vancampfort, D., Rosenbaum, S., Richards, J., Ward, P. B., & Stubbs, B. (2016). Exercise improves physical and psychological quality of life in people with depression: A meta-analysis including the evaluation of control group response. *Psychiatry Research*, 241, 47–54.

Schulte-Rüther, M., Otte, E., Adigüzel, K., Firk, C., Herpertz-Dahlmann, B., Koch, I., & Konrad, K. (2016). Intact mirror mechanisms for automatic facial emotions in children and adolescents with autism spectrum disorder. *Autism Research*, 10, 298–310.

Schultheiss, O. C., & Pang, J. S. (2007). Measuring implicit motives. In R. W. Robins, R. C. Fraley, & R. F.

Krueger (Eds.), *Handbook of research methods in personality psychology* (pp. 322–345). Guilford Press.

Schultheiss, O., Wiemers, U. & Wolf, O. (2014). Implicit need for achievement predicts attenuated cortisol responses to difficult tasks. *Journal of Research in Personality*, 48, 84–92.

Schuman, H., & Scott, J. (June, 1989). Generations and collective memories. *American Sociological Review*, 54, 359–381.

Schumann, K., & Ross, M. (2010). Why women apologize more than men: Gender differences in thresholds for perceiving offensive behavior. *Psychological Science*, 21, 1649–1655.

Schutte, N. S., Malouff, J. M., Thorsteinsson, E. B., Bhullar, N., & Rooke, S. E. (2007). A meta-analytic investigation of the relationship between emotional intelligence and health. *Personality and Individual Differences*, 42, 921–933.

Schutte, N. S., Palanisamy, S. K. A., & McFarlane, J. R. (2016). The relationship between positive characteristics and longer telomeres. *Psychology & Health*, 31, 1466–1480.

Schuyler, A. C., Kintzle, S., Lucas, C. L., Moore, H., & Castro, C. A. (2017). Military sexual assault (MSA) among veterans in Southern California: Associations with physical health, psychological health, and risk behaviors. *Traumatology*, 23, 223–234.

Schwaba, T., & Bleidorn, W. (2019). Personality trait development across the transition to retirement. *Journal of Personality and Social Psychology*, 116, 651–665.

Schwartz, B. (1984). *Psychology of learning and behavior* (2nd ed.). Norton.

Schwartz, B. (2000). Self-determination: The tyranny of freedom. *American Psychologist*, 55, 79–88.

Schwartz, B. (2004). *The paradox of choice: Why more is less*. Ecco/HarperCollins.

Schwartz, H. A., Eichstaedt, J. C., Kern, M. L., Dziurzynski, L., Ramones, S. M., Agrawal, M., Shah, A., Kosinski, M., Stillwell, D., Seligman, M. E., & Ungar, L. H. (2013). Personality, gender, and age in the language of social media: The open-vocabulary approach. *PLOS ONE*, 8, e73791.

Schwartz, J. M., Stoessel, P. W., Baxter, L. R., Jr., Martin, K. M., & Phelps, M. E. (1996). Systematic changes in cerebral glucose metabolic rate after successful behavior modification treatment of obsessive-compulsive disorder. *Archives of General Psychiatry*, 53, 109–113.

Schwartz, P. J. (2011). Season of birth in schizophrenia: A maternal-fetal chronobiological hypothesis. *Medical Hypotheses*, 76, 785–793.

Schwartz, S. (2012). Dreams, emotions and brain plasticity. In *Aquém e além do cérebro* [Behind and beyond the brain]. Fundação Bial Institution of Public Utility.

Schwartz, S. H., & Rubel-Lifschitz, T. (2009). Cross-national variation in the size of sex differences in values: Effects of gender equality. *Journal of Personality and Social Psychology*, 97, 171–185.

Schwartz, S. J., Lilienfeld, S. O., Meca, A., & Sauvigné, K. C. (2016). The role of neuroscience within psychology: A call for inclusiveness over exclusiveness. *American Psychologist*, 71, 52–70.

Schwartzman-Morris, J., & Putterman, C. (2012). Gender differences in the pathogenesis and outcome of lupus and of lupus nephritis. *Clinical and Developmental Immunology*, 2012, 604892.

Schwarz, A. (2012, June 9). Risky rise of the good-grade pill. *The New York Times*. https://www.nytimes.com/2012/06/10/education/seeking-academic-edge-teenagers-abuse-stimulants.html?

Schwarz, N., Strack, F., Kommer, D., & Wagner, D. (1987). Soccer, rooms, and the quality of your life:

Mood effects on judgments of satisfaction with life in general and with specific domains. *European Journal of Social Psychology*, 17, 69–79.

Schwemmer, M. A., Skomrock, N. D., Sederberg, P. B., Ting, J. E., Sharma, G., Bockbrader, M. A., & Friedenberg, D. A. (2018). Meeting brain–computer interface user performance expectations using a deep neural network decoding framework. *Nature Medicine*, 24, 1669–1676.

Scinicariello, F., Przybyla, J., Carroll, Y., Eichwald, J., Decker, J., & Breysse, P. N. (2019). Age and sex differences in hearing loss association with depressive symptoms: Analyses of NHANES 2011–2012. *Psychological Medicine*, 49, 962–968.

Sclafani, A. (1995). How food preferences are learned: Laboratory animal models. *PNAS*, 54, 419–427.

Scoboria, A., Wade, K. A., Lindsay, D. S., Azad, T., Strange, D., Ost, J., & Hyman, I. E. (2017). A mega-analysis of memory reports from eight peer-reviewed false memory implantation studies. *Memory*, 25, 146–163.

Scopelliti, I., Loewenstein, G., & Vosgerau, J. (2015). You call it "self-exuberance"; I call it "bragging": Miscalibrated predictions of emotional responses to self-promotion. *Psychological Science*, 26, 903–914.

Scott, D. J., Stohler, C. S., Egnatuk, C. M., Wang, H., Koeppe, R. A., & Zubieta, J.-K. (2007). Individual differences in reward responding explain placebo-induced expectations and effects. *Neuron*, 55, 325–336.

Scott, K. M., Wells, J. E., Angermeyer, M., Brugha, T. S., Bromet, E., Demyttenaere, K., de Girolamo, G., Gureje, O., Haro, J. M., Jin, R., Karam, A. N., Kovess, V., Lara, C., Levinson, D., Ormel, J., Posada-Villa, J., Sampson, N., Takeshima, T., Zhang, M., & Kessler, R. C. (2010). Gender and the relationship between marital status and first onset of mood, anxiety and substance use disorders. *Psychological Medicine*, 40, 1495–1505.

Scott-Sheldon, L., Carey, K. B., Elliott, J. C., Garey, L., & Carey, M. P. (2014). Efficacy of alcohol interventions for first-year college students: A meta-analytic review of randomized controlled trials. *Journal of Consulting and Clinical Psychology*, 82, 177–188.

Scullin, M. K. (2019). The eight hour sleep challenge during final exams week. *Teaching of Psychology*, 46, 55–63.

Scullin, M. K., & Bliwise, D. L. (2015). Sleep, cognition, and normal aging: Integrating a half century of multidisciplinary research. *Perspectives on Psychological Science*, 10, 97–137.

Scullin, M. K., & McDaniel, M. A. (2010). Remembering to execute a goal: Sleep on it! *Psychological Science*, 21, 1028–1035.

Scully, I. D., Napper, L. E., & Hupbach, A. (2017). Does reactivation trigger episodic memory change? A meta-analysis. *Neurobiology of Learning and Memory*, 142, 99–107.

Sdorow, L. M. (2005). The people behind psychology. In B. Perlman, L. McCann, & W. Buskist (Eds.), *Voices of experience: Memorable talks from the National Institute on the Teaching of Psychology*. American Psychological Society.

Seal, K. H., Bertenthal, D., Miner, C. R., Sen, S., & Marmar, C. (2007). Bringing the war back home: Mental health disorders among 103,788 U.S. veterans returning from Iraq and Afghanistan seen at Department of Veterans Affairs facilities. *Archives of Internal Medicine*, 167, 467–482.

Seamon, J., Punjabi, P., & Busch, E. (2010). Memorizing Milton's *Paradise Lost*: A study of a septuagenarian exceptional memoriser. *Memory*, 18, 498–503.

Sedley, W., Gander, P. E., Kumar, S., Oya, H., Kovach, C. K., Nourski, K. V., Kawasaki, H., Howard, M. A., & Griffiths, T. D. (2015). Intracranial mapping of a cortical tinnitus system using residual inhibition. *Current Biology, 25*, 1208–1214.

Sedlmeier, P., Eberth, J., Schwarz, M., Zimmermann, D., Haarig, F., Jaeger, S., & Kunze, S. (2012). The psychological effects of meditation: A meta-analysis. *Psychological Bulletin, 138*, 1139–1171.

Seehagen, S., Konrad, C., Herbert, J. S., & Schneider, S. (2015). Timely sleep facilitates declarative memory consolidation in infants. *PNAS, 112*, 1625–1629.

Seeman, P., Guan, H.-C., & Van Tol, H. H. M. (1993). Dopamine D4 receptors elevated in schizophrenia. *Nature, 365*, 441–445.

Seery, M. D. (2011). Resilience: A silver lining to experiencing adverse life events. *Current Directions in Psychological Science, 20*, 390–394.

Segal, N. L. (2005). *Indivisible by two: Lives of extraordinary twins*. Harvard University Press.

Segal, N. L. (2013). Personality similarity in unrelated look-alike pairs: Addressing a twin study challenge. *Personality and Individual Differences, 54*, 23–28.

Segal, N. L., Graham, J. L., & Ettinger, U. (2013). Unrelated look-alikes: Replicated study of personality similarity and qualitative findings on social relatedness. *Personality and Individual Differences, 55*, 169–174.

Segal, N. L., McGuire, S. A., & Stohs, J. H. (2012). What virtual twins reveal about general intelligence and other behaviors. *Personality and Individual Differences, 53*, 405–410.

Segal, N. L., & Montoya, Y. S. (2018). *Accidental brothers: The story of twins exchanged at birth and the power of nature and nurture*. Macmillan.

Segall, M. H., Dasen, P. R., Berry, J. W., & Poortinga, Y. H. (1990). *Human behavior in global perspective: An introduction to cross-cultural psychology*. Pergamon.

Segerstrom, S. C. (2007). Stress, energy, and immunity. *Current Directions in Psychological Science, 16*, 326–330.

Segerstrom, S. C., Taylor, S. E., Kemeny, M. E., & Fahey, J. L. (1998). Optimism is associated with mood, coping, and immune change in response to stress. *Journal of Personality and Social Psychology, 74*, 1646–1655.

Seibert, S. E., Wang, G., & Courtright, S. H. (2011). Antecedents and consequences of psychological and team empowerment in organizations: A meta-analytic review. *Journal of Applied Psychology, 96*, 981–1003.

Sejnowski, T. (2016, January 20). Quoted in *Memory capacity of brain is 10 times more than previously thought*. Salk News. https://www.salk.edu/news-release/memory-capacity-of-brain-is-10-times-more-than-previously-thought/

Selby, E. A., Kranzler, A., Lindqvist, J., Fehling, K. B., Brillante, J., Yuan, F., Gao, X., & Miller, A. L. (2019). The dynamics of pain during nonsuicidal self-injury. *Clinical Psychological Science, 7*, 302–320.

Self, C. E. (1994). *Moral culture and victimization in residence halls* [Unpublished master's thesis]. Bowling Green University.

Seli, P., Risko, E. F., Smilek, D., & Schacter, D. L. (2016). Mind-wandering with and without intention. *Trends in Cognitive Sciences, 20*, 605–617.

Seligman, M. (2016). How positive psychology happened and where it is going. In R. J. Sternberg, S. T. Fiske & D. J. Foss (Eds.), *Scientists making a difference: One hundred eminent behavioral and brain scientists talk about their most important contributions* (pp. 478–480). Cambridge University Press.

Seligman, M. E. P. (1975). *Helplessness: On depression, development and death*. Freeman.

Seligman, M. E. P. (1991). *Learned optimism: How to change your mind and your life*. Knopf.

Seligman, M. E. P. (1995). The effectiveness of psychotherapy: The *Consumer Reports* study. *American Psychologist, 50*, 965–974.

Seligman, M. E. P. (2002). *Authentic happiness: Using the new positive psychology to realize your potential for lasting fulfillment*. Free Press.

Seligman, M. E. P. (2012, May 8). Quoted in A. C. Brooks, America and the value of 'earned success.' *The Wall Street Journal*. https://www.wsj.com/articles/SB10001424052702304749904577385650652966894

Seligman, M. E. P., Allen, A. R., Vie, L. L., Ho, T. E., Scheier, L. M., Cornum, R., & Lester, P. B. (2019). PTSD: Catastrophizing in combat as risk and protection. *Clinical Psychological Science, 7*, 516–529.

Seligman, M. E. P., Ernst, R. M., Gillham, J., Reivich, K., & Linkins, M. (2009). Positive education: Positive psychology and classroom interventions. *Oxford Review of Education, 35*, 293–311.

Seligman, M. E. P., & Maier, S. F. (1967). Failure to escape traumatic shock. *Journal of Experimental Psychology, 74*, 1–9.

Seligman, M. E. P., Peterson, C., Barsky, A. J., Boehm, J. K., Kubzansky, L. D., Park, N., & Labarthe, D. (2011). *Positive health and health assets: Re-analysis of longitudinal datasets* [Unpublished manuscript]. University of Pennsylvania.

Seligman, M. E. P., Steen, T. A., Park, N., & Peterson, C. (2005). Positive psychology progress: Empirical validation of interventions. *American Psychologist, 60*, 410–421.

Seligman, M. E. P., & Yellen, A. (1987). What is a dream? *Behavior Research and Therapy, 25*, 1–24.

Selimbeyoglu, A., & Parvizi, J. (2010). Electrical stimulation of the human brain: Perceptual and behavioral phenomena reported in the old and new literature. *Frontiers in Human Neuroscience, 4*, 1–11.

Selye, H. (1936). A syndrome produced by diverse nocuous agents. *Nature, 138*, 32.

Selye, H. (1976). *The stress of life*. McGraw-Hill.

Senghas, A., & Coppola, M. (2001). Children creating language: How Nicaraguan Sign Language acquired a spatial grammar. *Psychological Science, 12*, 323–328.

Sergeant, S., & Mongrain, M. (2014). An online optimism intervention reduces depression in pessimistic individuals. *Journal of Consulting and Clinical Psychology, 82*, 263–274.

Serruya, M. D., Hatsopoulos, N. G., Paninski, L., Fellow, M. R., & Donoghue, J. P. (2002). Instant neural control of a movement signal. *Nature, 416*, 141–142.

Servant, M., Cassey, P., Woodman, G. F., & Logan, G. D. (2018). Neural bases of automaticity. *Journal of Experimental Psychology: Learning, Memory, and Cognition, 44*, 440–464.

Service, R. F. (1994). Will a new type of drug make memory-making easier? *Science, 266*, 218–219.

Servick, K. (2019). Warning signs. *Science, 365*, 742–744.

Sest, N., & March, E. (2017). Constructing the cybertroll: Psychopathy, sadism, and empathy. *Personality and Individual Differences, 119*, 69–72.

Sezer, O., Gino, F., & Norton, M. I. (2018). Humblebragging: A distinct—and ineffective—self-presentation strategy. *Journal of Personality and Social Psychology, 114*, 52–74.

Sforzini, L., Pariante, C. M., Palacios, J. E., Tylee, A., Carvalho, L. A., Viganò, C. A., & Nikkheslat, N. (2019). Inflammation associated with coronary heart disease predicts onset of depression in a three-year prospective follow-up: A preliminary study. *Brain, Behavior, and Immunity, 81*, 659–664.

Shackman, A. J., Tromp, D. P., Stockbridge, M. D., Kaplan, C. M., Tillman, R. M., & Fox, A. S. (2016). Dispositional negativity: An integrative psychological and neurobiological perspective. *Psychological Bulletin, 142*, 1275–1314.

Shadish, W. R., & Baldwin, S. A. (2005). Effects of behavioral marital therapy: A meta-analysis of randomized controlled trials. *Journal of Consulting and Clinical Psychology, 73*, 6–14.

Shadish, W. R., Montgomery, L. M., Wilson, P., Wilson, M. R., Bright, I., & Okwumabua, T. (1993). Effects of family and marital psychotherapies: A meta-analysis. *Journal of Consulting and Clinical Psychology, 61*, 992–1002.

Shafir, E. (Ed.) (2013). *The behavioral foundations of public policy*. Princeton University Press.

Shafir, E., & LeBoeuf, R. A. (2002). Rationality. *Annual Review of Psychology, 53*, 491–517.

Shakeshaft, N. G., Trzaskowski, M., McMillan, A., Rimfeld, K., Krapohl, E., Haworth, C. M. A., Dale, P. S., & Plomin, R. (2013). Strong genetic influence on a UK nationwide test of educational achievement at the end of compulsory education at age 16. *PLOS ONE 8*, e80341.

Shaki, S. (2013). What's in a kiss? Spatial experience shapes directional bias during kissing. *Journal of Nonverbal Behavior, 37*, 43–50.

Shalev, I., Moffitt, T. E., Sugden, K., Williams, B., Houts, R. M., Danese, A., Mill, J., Arseneault, L., & Caspi, A. (2013). Exposure to violence during childhood is associated with telomere erosion from 5 to 10 years of age: A longitudinal study. *Molecular Psychiatry, 18*, 576–581.

Shallcross, A. J., Ford, B. Q., Floerke, V. A., & Mauss, I. B. (2013). Getting better with age: The relationship between age, acceptance, and negative affect. *Journal of Personality and Social Psychology, 104*, 734–749.

Shanahan, L., McHale, S. M., Osgood, D. W., & Crouter, A. C. (2007). Conflict frequency with mothers and fathers from middle childhood to late adolescence: Within- and between-families comparisons. *Developmental Psychology, 43*, 539–550.

Shannon, B. J., Raichle, M. E., Snyder, A. Z., Fair, D. A., Mills, K. L., Zhang, D., Bache, K., Calhoun, V. D., Nigg, J. T., Nagel, B. J., Stevens, A. A., & Kiehl, K. A. (2011). Premotor functional connectivity predicts impulsivity in juvenile offenders. *PNAS, 108*, 11241–11245.

Shapin, S. (2013, October 15). The man who forgot everything. *The New Yorker* (newyorker.com).

Shapiro, D. (1999). *Psychotherapy of neurotic character*. Basic Books.

Shapiro, K. A., Moo, L. R., & Caramazza, A. (2006). Cortical signatures of noun and verb production. *PNAS, 103*, 1644–1649.

Shappell, S., Detweiler, C., Holcomb, K., Hackworth, C., Boquet, A., & Wiegmann, D. A. (2007). Human error and commercial aviation accidents: An analysis using the human factors analysis and classification system. *Human Factors, 49*, 227–242.

Shargorodsky, J., Curhan, S. G., Curhan, G. C., & Eavey, R. (2010). Changes of prevalence of hearing loss in US adolescents. *JAMA, 304*, 772–778.

Shariff, A. F., Greene, J. D., Karremans, J. C., Luguri, J. B., Clark, C. J., Schooler, J. W., Baumeister, R. F., & Vohs, K. D. (2014). Free will and punishment: A mechanistic view of human nature reduces retribution. *Psychological Science, 25*, 1563–1570.

Sharma, A. R., McGue, M. K., & Benson, P. L. (1998). The psychological adjustment of United States adopted adolescents and their nonadopted siblings. *Child Development, 69*, 791–802.

Shattuck, P. T. (2006). The contribution of diagnostic substitution to the growing administrative prevalence of autism in US special education. *Pediatrics, 117*, 1028–1037.

Shave, R. E., Lieberman, D. E., Drane, A. L., Brown, M. G., Batterham, A. M., Worthington, S., Atencia, R., Feltrer, Y., Neary, J., Weiner, R. B., & Wasfy, M. M. (2019). Selection of endurance capabilities and the trade-off between pressure and volume in the evolution of the human heart. PNAS, 116, 19905–19910.

Shaver, P. R., Morgan, H. J., & Wu, S. (1996). Is love a basic emotion? Personal Relationships, 3, 81–96.

Shaw, B. A., Liang, J., & Krause, N. (2010). Age and race differences in the trajectories of self-esteem. Psychology and Aging, 25, 84–94.

Shaw, J. (2018). How can researchers tell whether someone has a false memory? Coding strategies in autobiographical false memory research. A reply to Wade, Garry, and Pezdek. Psychological Science, 29, 477–480.

Shedler, J. (2009, March 23). That was then, this is now: Psychoanalytic psychotherapy for the rest of us [Unpublished manuscript]. Department of Psychiatry, University of Colorado Health Sciences Center.

Shedler, J. (2010). The efficacy of psychodynamic psychotherapy. American Psychologist, 65, 98–109.

Sheeber, L. B., Feil, E. G., Seeley, J. R., Leve, C., Gau, J. M., Davis, B., Sorensen, E., & Allan, S. (2017). Momnet: Evaluation of an internet-facilitated cognitive behavioral intervention for low-income depressed mothers. Journal of Consulting and Clinical Psychology, 85, 355–366.

Sheehan, S. (1982). Is there no place on earth for me? Houghton Mifflin.

Sheikh, S., & Janoff-Bulman, R. (2013). Paradoxical consequences of prohibitions. Journal of Personality and Social Psychology, 105, 301–315.

Sheldon, K. M., Elliot, A. J., Kim, Y., & Kasser, T. (2001). What is satisfying about satisfying events? Testing 10 candidate psychological needs. Journal of Personality and Social Psychology, 80, 325–339.

Sheldon, K. M., & Lyubomirsky, S. (2012). The challenge of staying happier: Testing the hedonic adaptation prevention model. Personality and Social Psychology Bulletin, 38, 670–680.

Shelton, L. T., Elliott, E. M., Matthews, R. A., Hill, B. H., & Gouvier, W. D. (2010). The relationships of working memory, secondary memory, and general fluid intelligence: working memory is special. Journal of Experimental Psychology, 36, 813–820.

Shen, L., Fishbach, A., & Hsee, C. K. (2015, February). The motivating-uncertainty effect: Uncertainty increases resource investment in the process of reward pursuit. Journal of Consumer Research, 41, 1301–1315.

Shen, W., Yuan, Y., Liu, C., & Luo, J. (2017). The roles of the temporal lobe in creative insight: An integrated review. Thinking & Reasoning, 23, 321–375.

Shen, Y. A., Shoda, Y., & Fine, I. (2018). Too few women authors on research papers in leading journals. Nature, 555, 7695.

Shenton, M. E. (1992). Abnormalities of the left temporal lobe and thought disorder in schizophrenia: A quantitative magnetic resonance imaging study. New England Journal of Medicine, 327, 604–612.

Shepard, R. N. (1990). Mind sights. Freeman.

Shepherd, C., Kohut, J. J., & Sweet, R. (1990). More news of the weird. Penguin/Plume Books.

Shepperd, J. A., Waters, E., Weinstein, N. D., & Klein, W. M. P. (2015). A primer on unrealistic optimism. Current Directions in Psychological Science, 24, 232–237.

Shergill, S. S., Bays, P. M., Frith, C. D., & Wolpert, D. M. (2003). Two eyes for an eye: The neuroscience of force escalation. Science, 301, 187.

Sherif, M. (1966). In common predicament: Social psychology of intergroup conflict and cooperation. Houghton Mifflin.

Sherif, M., Radhakrishnan, R., D'Souza, D. C., & Ranganathan, M. (2016). Human laboratory studies on cannabinoids and psychosis. Biological Psychiatry, 79, 526–538.

Sherman, G. D., Lee, J. J., Cuddy, A. J. C., Renshon, J., Oveis, C., Gross, J. J., & Lerner, J. S. (2012). Leadership is associated with lower levels of stress. PNAS, 109, 17903–17907.

Sherman, L. E., Payton, A. A., Hernandez, L. M., Greenfield, P. M., & Dapretto, M. (2016). The power of the like in adolescence: Effects of peer influence on neural and behavioral responses to social media. Psychological Science, 27, 1027–1035.

Sherman, P. W., & Flaxman, S. M. (2001). Protecting ourselves from food. American Scientist, 89, 142–151.

Sherman, R. A., Rauthmann, J. F., Brown, N. A., Serfass, D. S., & Jones, A. B. (2015). The independent effects of personality and situations on real-time expressions of behavior and emotion. Journal of Personality and Social Psychology, 109, 872–888.

Sherry, D., & Vaccarino, A. L. (1989). Hippocampus and memory for food caches in black-capped chickadees. Behavioral Neuroscience, 103, 308–318.

Shettleworth, S. J. (1973). Food reinforcement and the organization of behavior in golden hamsters. In R. A. Hinde & J. Stevenson-Hinde (Eds.), Constraints on learning. Academic Press.

Shettleworth, S. J. (1993). Where is the comparison in comparative cognition? Alternative research programs. Psychological Science, 4, 179–184.

Shiell, M. M., Champoux, F., & Zatorre, R. (2014). Enhancement of visual motion detection thresholds in early deaf people. PLOS ONE, 9, e90498.

Shilsky, J. D., Hartman, T. J., Kris-Etherton, P. M., Rogers, C. J., Sharkey, N. A., & Nickols-Richardson, S. M. (2012). Partial sleep deprivation and energy balance in adults: An emerging issue for consideration by dietetics practitioners. Journal of the Academy of Nutrition and Dietetics, 112, 1785–1797.

Shimamura, A. P. (2010). Bridging psychological and biological science: The good, bad, and ugly. Perspectives on Psychological Science, 5, 772–775.

Shimizu, M., & Pelham, B. W. (2008). Postponing a date with the grim reaper. Basic and Applied Social Psychology, 30, 36–45.

Shin, J. E., Suh, E. M., Li, N. P., Eo, K., Chong, S. C., & Tsai, M. H. (2019). Darling, get closer to me: Spatial proximity amplifies interpersonal liking. Personality and Social Psychology Bulletin, 45, 300–309.

Shinkareva, S. V., Mason, R. A., Malave, V. L., Wang, W., Mitchell, T. M., & Just, M. A. (2008, January 2). Using fMRI brain activation to identify cognitive states associated with perceptions of tools and dwellings. PLOS ONE, 3, 31394.

Shirazi, T. N., Self, H., Dawood, K., Rosenfield, K. A., Penke, L., Carré, J. M., Ortiz, T., & Puts, D. A. (2019). Hormonal predictors of women's sexual motivation. Evolution and Human Behavior, 40, 336–344.

Shockley, K. M., Ispas, D., Rossi, M. E., & Levine, E. L. (2012). A meta-analytic investigation of the relationship between state affect, discrete emotions, and job performance. Human Performance, 25, 377–411.

Shor, E., Roelfs, D. J., Bugyi, P., & Schwartz, J. E. (2012). Meta-analysis of marital dissolution and mortality: Reevaluating the intersection of gender and age. Social Science & Medicine, 75, 46–59.

Shors, T. J. (2014). The adult brain makes new neurons, and effortful learning keeps them alive. Current Directions in Psychological Science, 23, 311–318.

Short, M., Gradisar, M., Wright, H., Dewald, J., Wolfson, A., & Carskadon, M. (2013). A cross-cultural comparison of sleep duration between U.S. and Australian adolescents: The effect of school start time, parent-set bedtimes, and extra-curricular load. Health Education Behavior, 40, 323–330.

Short, S. J., Lubach, G. R., Karasin, A. I., Olsen, C. W., Styner, M., Knickmeyer, R. C., Gilmore, J. H., & Coe, C. L. (2010). Maternal influenza infection during pregnancy impacts postnatal brain development in the rhesus monkey. Biological Psychiatry, 67, 965–973.

Shotland, R. L. (1984, March 12). Quoted in Maureen Dowd, 20 years after the murder of Kitty Genovese, the question remains: Why? The New York Times, p. B1.

Showers, C. (1992). The motivational and emotional consequences of considering positive or negative possibilities for an upcoming event. Journal of Personality and Social Psychology, 63, 474–484.

Shrestha, A., Nohr, E. A., Bech, B. H., Ramlau-Hansen, C. H., & Olsen, J. (2011). Smoking and alcohol during pregnancy and age of menarche in daughters. Human Reproduction, 26, 259–265.

Shrira, I. (2020). Population diversity and ancestral diversity as distinct contributors to outgroup prejudice. Personality and Social Psychology Bulletin. Advance online publication. doi: 10.1177/0146167219880190

Shuffler, M. L., Burke, C. S., Kramer, W. S., & Salas, E. (2013). Leading teams: Past, present, and future perspectives. In M. G. Rumsey (Ed.), The Oxford handbook of leadership. Oxford University Press.

Shuffler, M. L., DiazGranados, D., & Salas, E. (2011). There's a science for that: Team development interventions in organizations. Current Directions in Psychological Science, 20, 365–372.

Shuwairi, S. M., & Johnson, S. P. (2013). Oculomotor exploration of impossible figures in early infancy. Infancy, 18, 221–232.

Siclari, F., Baird, B., Perogamvros, L., Bernardi, G., LaRocque, J. J., Riedner, B., Boly, M., Postle, B. R., & Tononi, G. (2017). The neural correlates of dreaming. Nature Neuroscience, 20, 872–878.

Sieber, V., Flückiger, L., Mata, J., Bernecker, K., & Job, V. (2019). Autonomous goal striving promotes a nonlimited theory about willpower. Personality and Social Psychology Bulletin, 45, 1295–1307.

Siegel, E. H., Sands, M. K., Van den Noortgate, W., Condon, P., Chang, Y., Dy, J., Quigley, K. S., & Barrett, L. F. (2018). Emotion fingerprints or emotion populations? A meta-analytic investigation of autonomic features of emotion categories. Psychological Bulletin, 144, 343–393.

Siegel, J. M. (1990). Stressful life events and use of physician services among the elderly: The moderating role of pet ownership. Journal of Personality and Social Psychology, 58, 1081–1086.

Siegel, J. M. (2009). Sleep viewed as a state of adaptive inactivity. Nature Reviews Neuroscience, 10, 747–753.

Siegel, J. M. (2012). Suppression of sleep for mating. Science, 337, 1610–1611.

Siegel, R. K. (1977, October). Hallucinations. Scientific American, pp. 132–140.

Siegel, R. K. (1980). The psychology of life after death. American Psychologist, 35, 911–931.

Siegel, R. K. (1982, October). Quoted by J. Hooper, Mind tripping. Omni, pp. 72–82, 159–160.

Siegel, R. K. (1984, March 15). Personal communication.

Siegel, R. K. (1990). Intoxication: Life in pursuit of artificial paradise. Pocket Books.

Siegel, S. (2005). Drug tolerance, drug addiction, and drug anticipation. Current Directions in Psychological Science, 14, 296–300.

Silber, M. H., Ancoli-Israel, S., Bonnet, M. H., Chokroverty, S., Grigg-Damberger, M. M., Hirshkowitz, M.,

Kapen, S., Keenan, S. A., Kryger, M. H., Penzel, T., Pressman, M. R., & Iber, C. (2007). The visual scoring of sleep in adults. *Journal of Clinical Sleep Medicine, 3,* 121–131.

Silbersweig, D. A., Stern, E., Frith, C., Cahill, C., Holmes, A., Grootoonk, S., Seaward, J., McKenna, P., Chua, S. E., Schnorr, L., Jones, T., & Frackowiak, R. S. J. (1995). A functional neuroanatomy of hallucinations in schizophrenia. *Nature, 378,* 176–179.

Silston, B., Bassett, D. S., & Mobbs, D. (2018). How dynamic brain networks tune social behavior in real time. *Current Directions in Psychological Science, 27,* 413–421.

Silva, C. E., & Kirsch, I. (1992). Interpretive sets, expectancy, fantasy proneness, and dissociation as predictors of hypnotic response. *Journal of Personality and Social Psychology, 63,* 847–856.

Silver, M., & Geller, D. (1978). On the irrelevance of evil: The organization and individual action. *Journal of Social Issues, 34,* 125–136.

Silver, N. (2012). *The signal and the noise: Why so many predictions fail—but some don't.* Penguin.

Silver, R. C., Holman, E. A., Anderson, J. P., Poulin, M., McIntosh, D. N., & Gil-Rivas, V. (2013). Mental- and physical-health effects of acute exposure to media images of the September 11, 2001 attacks and Iraq War. *Psychological Science, 24,* 1623–1634.

Silver, R. C., Holman, E. A., McIntosh, D. N., Poulin, M., & Gil-Rivas, V. (2002). Nationwide longitudinal study of psychological responses to September 11. *Journal of the American Medical Association, 288,* 1235–1244.

Silverman, K., Evans, S. M., Strain, E. C., & Griffiths, R. R. (1992). Withdrawal syndrome after the double-blind cessation of caffeine consumption. *New England Journal of Medicine, 327,* 1109–1114.

Silverstein, B. H., Snodgrass, M., Shevrin, H., & Kushwaha, R. (2015). P3b, consciousness, and complex unconscious processing. *Cortex, 73,* 216–227.

Silwa, J., & Frehwald, W. A. (2017). A dedicated network for social interaction processing in the primate brain. *Science, 356,* 745–749.

Simek, T. C., & O'Brien, R. M. (1981). *Total golf: A behavioral approach to lowering your score and getting more out of your game.* B-MOD Associates.

Simek, T. C., & O'Brien, R. M. (1988). A chaining-mastery, discrimination training program to teach Little Leaguers to hit a baseball. *Human Performance, 1,* 73–84.

Simon, G. E., Johnson, E., Lawrence, J. M., Rossom, R. C., Ahmedani, B., Lynch, F. L., Beck, A., Waitzfelder, B., Ziebell, R., Penfold, R. B., & Shortreed, S. M. (2018). Predicting suicide attempts and suicide deaths following outpatient visits using electronic health records. *The American Journal of Psychiatry, 175,* 951–960.

Simon, V., Czobor, P., Bálint, S., Mésáros, A., & Bitter, I. (2009). Prevalence and correlates of adult attention-deficit hyperactivity disorder: Meta-analysis. *British Journal of Psychiatry, 194,* 204–211.

Simon-Kutscher, K., Wanke, N., Hiller, C., & Schwabe, L. (2019). Fear without context: Acute stress modulates the balance of cue-dependent and contextual fear learning. *Psychological Science, 30(8),* 1123–1135.

Simons, D. J., Boot, W. R., Charness, N., Gathercole, S. E., Chabris, C. F., Hambrick, D. Z., & Stine-Morrow, E. A. L. (2016). Do "brain-training" programs work? *Psychological Science in the Public Interest, 17,* 103–186.

Simons, D. J., & Chabris, C. F. (1999). Gorillas in our midst: Sustained inattentional blindness for dynamic events. *Perception, 28,* 1059–1074.

Simons, D. J., & Chabris, C. F. (2011). What people believe about how memory works: A representative survey of the U.S. population. *PLOS ONE, 6,* e22757.

Simons, D. J., & Levin, D. T. (1998). Failure to detect changes to people during a real-world interaction. *Psychonomic Bulletin & Review, 5,* 644–649.

Simonsohn, U., & Gino, F. (2013). Daily horizons: Evidence of narrow bracketing in judgment from 10 years of M.B.A. admissions interviews. *Psychological Science, 24,* 219–224.

Simonton, D. K. (1988). Age and outstanding achievement: What do we know after a century of research? *Psychological Bulletin, 104,* 251–267.

Simonton, D. K. (1990). Creativity in the later years: Optimistic prospects for achievement. *The Gerontologist, 30,* 626–631.

Simonton, D. K. (1992). The social context of career success and course for 2,026 scientists and inventors. *Personality and Social Psychology Bulletin, 18,* 452–463.

Simonton, D. K. (2000). Methodological and theoretical orientation and the long-term disciplinary impact of 54 eminent psychologists. *Review of General Psychology, 4,* 13–24.

Simonton, D. K. (2012a). Teaching creativity: Current findings, trends, and controversies in the psychology of creativity. *Teaching of Psychology, 39,* 217–222.

Simonton, D. K. (2012b, November–December). The science of genius. *Scientific American Mind,* pp. 35–41.

Sims, C. R. (2018). Efficient coding explains the universal law of generalization in human perception. *Science, 360,* 652–656.

Sin, N. L., Graham-Engeland, J. E., Ong, A. D., & Almeida, D. M. (2015). Affective reactivity to daily stressors is associated with elevated inflammation. *Health Psychology, 34,* 154–1165.

Sinclair, R. C., Hoffman, C., Mark, M. M., Martin, L. L., & Pickering, T. L. (1994). Construct accessibility and the misattribution of arousal: Schachter and Singer revisited. *Psychological Science, 5,* 15–18.

Singer, J. L. (1981). Clinical intervention: New developments in methods and evaluation. In L. T. Benjamin, Jr. (Ed.), *The G. Stanley Hall Lecture Series* (Vol. 1). American Psychological Association.

Singer, T., Seymour, B., O'Doherty, J., Kaube, H., Dolan, R. J., & Frith, C. (2004). Empathy for pain involves the affective but not sensory components of pain. *Science, 303,* 1157–1162.

Singh, D. (1993). Adaptive significance of female physical attractiveness: Role of waist-to-hip ratio. *Journal of Personality and Social Psychology, 65,* 293–307.

Singh, D., & Randall, P. K. (2007). Beauty is in the eye of the plastic surgeon: Waist-hip ration (WHR) and women's attractiveness. *Personality and Individual Differences, 43,* 329–340.

Singh, S. (1997). *Fermat's enigma: The epic quest to solve the world's greatest mathematical problem.* Bantam Books.

Singh, S., & Riber, K. A. (1997, November). Fermat's last stand. *Scientific American,* pp. 68–73.

Sio, U. N., Monahan, P., & Ormerod, T. (2013). Sleep on it, but only if it is difficult: Effects of sleep on problem solving. *Memory and Cognition, 41,* 159–166.

SIOP. (2018, August 28). *Materials for incorporating I-O into an introductory psychology textbook.* https://www.siop.org/Events-Education/Educators/Incorporating-I-O

Sipski, M. L., Alexander, C. J., & Rosen, R. C. (1999). Sexual response in women with spinal cord injuries: Implications for our understanding of the able bodied. *Journal of Sexual & Marital Therapy, 25,* 11–22.

Sireteanu, R. (1999). Switching on the infant brain. *Science, 286,* 59–61.

Sisk, V. F., Burgoyne, A. P., Sun, J., Butler, J. L., & Macnamara, B. N. (2018). To what extent and under which circumstances are growth mind-sets important to academic achievement? Two meta-analyses. *Psychological Science, 29,* 549–571.

Skeem, J. L., & Cooke, D. J. (2010). Is criminal behavior a central component of psychopathy? Conceptual directions for resolving the debate. *Psychological Assessment, 22,* 433–445.

Skinner, B. F. (1953). *Science and human behavior.* Macmillan.

Skinner, B. F. (1956). A case history in scientific method. *American Psychologist, 11,* 221–233.

Skinner, B. F. (1960). Pigeons in a pelican. *American Psychologist, 15,* 28–37.

Skinner, B. F. (1961, November). Teaching machines. *Scientific American, 205,* 90–112.

Skinner, B. F. (1966). *The behavior of organisms: An experimental analysis.* Appleton-Century-Crofs. (Original work published 1938.)

Skinner, B. F. (1983, September). Origins of a behaviorist. *Psychology Today,* pp. 22–33.

Skinner, B. F. (1989). Teaching machines. *Science, 243,* 1535.

Skitka, L. J., Bauman, C. W., & Mullen, E. (2004). Political tolerance and coming to psychological closure following the September 11, 2001, terrorist attacks: An integrative approach. *Personality and Social Psychology Bulletin, 30,* 743–756.

Sklar, L. S., & Anisman, H. (1981). Stress and cancer. *Psychological Bulletin, 89,* 369–406.

Skoog, G., & Skoog, I. (1999). A 40-year follow-up of patients with obsessive-compulsive disorder. *Archives of General Psychiatry, 56,* 121–127.

Skov, R. B., & Sherman, S. J. (1986). Information-gathering processes: Diagnosticity, hypothesis-confirmatory strategies, and perceived hypothesis confirmation. *Journal of Experimental Social Psychology, 22,* 93–121.

Slagt, M., Dubas, J. S., Deković, M., & van Aken, M. A. (2016). Differences in sensitivity to parenting depending on child temperament: A meta-analysis. *Psychological Bulletin, 142,* 1068–1110.

Slater, E., & Meyer, A. (1959). *Confinia psychiatra.* S. Karger AG.

Slaughter, V., Imuta, K., Peterson, C. C., & Henry, J. D. (2015). Meta-analysis of theory of mind and peer popularity in the preschool and early school years. *Child Development, 86,* 1159–1174.

Slee, A., Nazareth, I., Bondaronek, P., Liu, Y., Cheng, Z., & Freemantle, N. (2019). Pharmacological treatments for generalised anxiety disorder: a systematic review and network meta-analysis. *The Lancet, 393,* 768–777.

Slemp, G. R., Kern, M. L., Patrick, K. J., & Ryan, R. M. (2018). Leader autonomy support in the workplace: A meta-analytic review. *Motivation and Emotion, 42,* 706–724.

Sloan, R. P. (2005). *Field analysis of the literature on religion, spirituality, and health* [PDF file]. Columbia University. https://metanexus.net/archive/templetonadvancedresearchprogram/pdf/TARP-Sloan.pdf

Sloan, R. P., & Bagiella, E. (2002). Claims about religious involvement and health outcomes. *Annals of Behavioral Medicine, 24,* 14–21.

Sloan, R. P., Bagiella, E., & Powell, T. (1999). Religion, spirituality, and medicine. *The Lancet, 353,* 664–667.

Sloan, R. P., Bagiella, E., VandeCreek, L., & Poulos, P. (2000). Should physicians prescribe religious activities? *New England Journal of Medicine, 342,* 1913–1917.

Slopen, N., Glynn, R. J., Buring, J., & Albert, M. A. (2010, November 23). Job strain, job insecurity, and incident cardiovascular disease in the Women's

Health Study. *Circulation, 122*(21, Suppl.), Abstract A18520.

Slovic, P. (2007). "If I look at the mass I will never act": Psychic numbing and genocide. *Judgment and Decision Making, 2,* 79–95.

Slovic, P., Västfjälla, D., Erlandsson, A., & Gregory, R. (2017). Iconic photographs and the ebb and flow of empathic response to humanitarian disasters. *PNAS, 114,* 640–644.

Slutske, W. S., Moffitt, T. E., Poulton, R., & Caspi A. (2012). Under-controlled temperament at age 3 predicts disordered gambling at age 32: A longitudinal study of a complete birth cohort. *Psychological Science, 23,* 510–516.

Smalarz, L., & Wells, G. L. (2015). Contamination of eyewitness self-reports and the mistaken identification problem. *Current Directions in Psychological Science, 24,* 120–124.

Smaldino, P. E., & McElreath, R. (2016). The natural selection of bad science. *Royal Society Open Science, 3,* 160384.

Small, M. F. (1997). Making connections. *American Scientist, 85,* 502–504.

Smedley, A., & Smedley, B. D. (2005). Race as biology is fiction, racism as a social problem is real: Anthropological and historical perspectives on the social construction of race. *American Psychologist, 60,* 16–26.

Smith, A. (1776). *An inquiry into the nature and causes of the wealth of nations.* W. Strahan and T. Cadell.

Smith, A. (1983). Personal correspondence.

Smith, A. (2016, February 11). *15% of American adults have used online dating sites or mobile dating apps.* Pew Research Center. https://www.pewresearch.org/internet/2016/02/11/15-percent-of-american-adults-have-used-online-dating-sites-or-mobile-dating-apps/

Smith, B. C. (2011, January 16). *The senses and the multi-sensory.* Edge. https://www.edge.org/response-detail/11677

Smith, C. (2006, January 7). Nearly 100, LSD's father ponders his "problem child." *The New York Times.* https://www.nytimes.com/2006/01/07/pageoneplus/world/the-saturday-profile-nearly-100-lsds-father-ponders-his.html?

Smith, G. E. (2016). Healthy cognitive aging and dementia prevention. *American Psychologist, 71,* 268–275.

Smith, J. A., & Rhodes, J. E. (2014). Being depleted and being shaken: An interpretative phenomenological analysis of the experiential features of a first episode of depression. *Psychology and Psychotherapy: Theory, Research and Practice, 88,* 197–209.

Smith, J. C., Nielson, K. A., Woodard, J. L., Seidenberg, M., Durgerian, S., Hazlett, K. E., Figueroa, C. M., Kandah, C. C., Kay, C. D., Matthews, M. A., & Rao, S. M. (2014, April 23). Physical activity reduces hippocampal atrophy in elders at genetic risk for Alzheimer's disease. *Frontiers in Aging Neuroscience, 6,* 61.

Smith, K. (2018). Sex and drugs and self-control: How the teen brain navigates risk. *Nature, 554,* 426-428.

Smith, L. K., & Wissel, E. F. (2019). Microbes and the mind: How bacteria shape affect, neurological processes, cognition, social relationships, development, and pathology. *Perspectives on Psychological Science, 14,* 397–418.

Smith, M. (2017). Hyperactive around the world? The history of ADHD in global perspective. *Social History of Medicine, 30,* 767–787.

Smith, M. B. (1978). Psychology and values. *Journal of Social Issues, 34,* 181–199.

Smith, M. L., & Glass, G. V. (1977). Meta-analysis of psychotherapy outcome studies. *American Psychologist, 32,* 752–760.

Smith, M. L., Glass, G. V., & Miller, R. L. (1980). *The benefits of psychotherapy.* Johns Hopkins Press.

Smith, M. M., Sherry, S. B., Chen, S., Saklofske, D. H., Mushquash, C., Flett, G. L., & Hewitt, P. L. (2018). The perniciousness of perfectionism: A meta-analytic review of the perfectionism–suicide relationship. *Journal of Personality, 86,* 522–542.

Smith, P. B., & Tayeb, M. (1989). Organizational structure and processes. In M. Bond (Ed.), *The cross-cultural challenge to social psychology.* Sage.

Smith, S. G., Jackson, S. E., Kobayashi, L. C., & Steptoe, A. (2018). Social isolation, health literacy, and mortality risk: Findings from the English Longitudinal Study of Ageing. *Health Psychology, 37,* 160–169.

Smith, S. L., Pieper, K., & Choueiti, M. (2017, February). *Inclusion in the director's chair? Gender, race, & age of film directors across 1,000 films from 2007–2016* [PDF file]. University of Southern California Annenberg School for Communications and Journalism. https://bit.ly/2QRRkNw

Smith, T. W., & Baucom, B. R. W. (2017). Intimate relationships, individual adjustment, and coronary heart disease: Implications of overlapping associations in psychosocial risk. *American Psychologist, 72,* 578–589.

Smith-Woolley, E., Selzam, S., & Plomin, R. (2019). Polygenic score for educational attainment captures DNA variants shared between personality traits and educational achievement. *Journal of Personality and Social Psychology, 117,* 1145–1163.

Smits, I. A. M., Dolan, C. V., Vorst, H. C. M., Wicherts, J. M., & Timmerman, M. E. (2011). Cohort differences in Big Five personality traits over a period of 25 years. *Journal of Personality and Social Psychology, 100,* 1124–1138.

Smolak, L., & Murnen, S. K. (2002). A meta-analytic examination of the relationship between child sexual abuse and eating disorders. *International Journal of Eating Disorders, 31,* 136–150.

Smoller, J. W. (2019). Psychiatric genetics begins to find its footing. *American Journal of Psychiatry, 176,* 609–614.

Snedeker, J., Geren, J., & Shafto, C. L. (2007). Starting over: International adoption as a natural experiment in language development. *Psychological Science, 18,* 79–86.

Snell, J., & Grainger, J. (2019). Readers are parallel processors. *Trends in Cognitive Sciences, 23,* 537–546.

Sniekers, S., Stringer, S., Watanabe, K., Jansen, P. R., Coleman, J. R. I., Krapohl, E., Taskesen, E., Hammerschlag, A. R., Okbay, A., Zabaneh, D., Amin, N., Breen, G., Desarini, D., Chabris, C. F., Iacono, W. G., Ikram, M. A., Johannesson, M., Koellinger, P., Lee, J. J., . . . Posthuma, D. (2017). Genome-wide association meta-analysis of 78,308 individuals identifies new loci and genes influencing human intelligence. *Nature Genetics, 49,* 1107–1112.

Snipes, D. J., Calton, J. M., Green, B. A., Perrin, P. B., & Benotsch, E. G. (2017). Rape and posttraumatic stress disorder (PTSD): Examining the mediating role of explicit sex-power beliefs for men versus women. *Journal of Interpersonal Violence, 32,* 2453–2470.

Snodgrass, S. E., Higgins, J. G., & Todisco, L. (1986). *The effects of walking behavior on mood* [Paper]. Presented at the American Psychological Association convention.

Snyder, F., & Scott, J. (1972). The psychophysiology of sleep. In N. S. Greenfield & R. A. Sterbach (Eds.), *Handbook of psychophysiology.* Holt, Rinehart & Winston.

Snyder, S. H. (1984). Neurosciences: An integrative discipline. *Science, 225,* 1255–1257.

Snyder-Mackler, N., Sanz, J., Kohn, J. N., Brinkworth, J. F., Morrow, S., Shaver, A. O., Grenier, J. C.,

Pique-Regi, R., Johnson, Z. P., Wilson, M. E., Barreiro, L. B. & Tung, J. (2016). Social status alters immune regulation and response to infection in macaques. *Science, 354,* 1041–1045.

Society for Personality Assessment. (2005). The status of the Rorschach in clinical and forensic practice: An official statement by the Board of Trustees of the Society for Personality Assessment. *Journal of Personality Assessment, 85,* 219–237.

Soderstrom, N. C., Kerr, T. K., & Bjork, R. A. (2016). The critical importance of retrieval—and spacing—for learning. *Psychological Science, 27,* 223–230.

Sofer, C., Dotsch, R., Wigboldus, D. H. J., & Todorov, A. (2015). What is typical is good: The influence of face typicality on perceived trustworthiness. *Psychological Science, 26,* 39–47.

Solano, I., Eaton, N. R., & O'Leary, K. D. (2018). Pornography consumption, modality and function in a large internet sample. *The Journal of Sex Research, 57*(1), 92–103.

Solomon, D. A., Keitner, G. I., Miller, I. W., Shea, M. T., & Keller, M. B. (1995). Course of illness and maintenance treatments for patients with bipolar disorder. *Journal of Clinical Psychiatry, 56,* 5–13.

Solomon, Z., Greene, T., Ein-Dor, T., Zerach, G., Benyamini, Y., & Ohry, A. (2014). The long-term implications of war captivity for mortality and health. *Journal of Behavioral Medicine, 37,* 849–859.

Solomon, Z., Tsur, N., Levin, Y., Uziel, O., Lahav, M., & Ohry, A. (2017). The implications of war captivity and long-term psychopathology trajectories for telomere length. *Psychoneuroendocrinology, 81,* 122–128.

Somerville, L. H., Jones, R. M., Ruberry, E. J., Dyke, J. P., Glover, G., & Casey, B. J. (2013). The medial prefrontal cortex and the emergence of self-conscious emotion in adolescence. *Psychological Science, 24,* 1554–1562.

Sommet, N., Morselli, D., & Spini, D. (2018). Income inequality affects the psychological health of only the people facing scarcity. *Psychological Science, 29,* 1911–1921.

Song, S. (2006, March 27). Mind over medicine. *Time,* p. 47.

Sontag, S. (1978). *Illness as metaphor.* Farrar, Straus, & Giroux.

Sood, A. K., Armaiz-Pena, G. N., Halder, J., Nick, A. M., Stone, R. L., Hu, W., Carroll, A. R., Spannuth, W. A., Deavers, M. T., Allen, J. K., Han, L. Y., Kamat, A. A., Shahzad, M. M., McIntyre, B. W., Diaz-Montero, C. M., Jennings, N. B., Lin, Y. G., Merritt, W. M., DeGeest, K., . . . Lutgendorf, S. K. (2010). Adrenergic modulation of focal adhesion kinase protects human ovarian cancer cells from anoikis. *Journal of Clinical Investigation, 120,* 1515–1523.

Soral, W., Bilewicz, M., & Winiewski, M. (2018). Exposure to hate speech increases prejudice through desensitization. *Aggressive Behavior, 44,* 136–146.

Sorrells, S., Alvarez-Buylla, A. A., & Paredes, M. (2018). No evidence for new adult neurons. *American Scientist, 106,* 152–155.

Soto, C. J. (2019). How replicable are links between personality traits and consequential life outcomes? The Life Outcomes of Personality Replication Project. *Psychological Science, 30,* 711–727.

Soto, C. J., & John, O. P. (2017). The next Big Five inventory (BFI-2): Developing and assessing a hierarchical model with 15 facets to enhance bandwidth, fidelity, and predictive power. *Journal of Personality and Social Psychology, 113,* 117–143.

Soussignan, R. (2001). Duchenne smile, emotional experience, and autonomic reactivity: A test of the facial feedback hypothesis. *Emotion, 2,* 52–74.

South, S. C., Krueger, R. F., Johnson, W., & Iacono, W. G. (2008). Adolescent personality moderates genetic and environmental influences on relationships with parents. *Journal of Personality and Social Psychology, 94*, 899–912.

Sowell, T. (1991, May/June). Cultural diversity: A world view. *American Enterprise*, pp. 44–55.

Spanos, N. P. (1986). Hypnosis, nonvolitional responding, and multiple personality: A social psychological perspective. *Progress in Experimental Personality Research, 14*, 1–62.

Spanos, N. P. (1994). Multiple identity enactments and multiple personality disorder: A sociocognitive perspective. *Psychological Bulletin, 116*, 143–165.

Spanos, N. P. (1996). *Multiple identities and false memories: A sociocognitive perspective.* American Psychological Association Books.

Spanos, N. P., & Coe, W. C. (1992). A social-psychological approach to hypnosis. In E. Fromm & M. R. Nash (Eds.), *Contemporary hypnosis research* (pp. 102–130). Guilford Press.

Spark, A., Stansmore, T., & O'Connor, P. (2018). The failure of introverts to emerge as leaders: The role of forecasted affect. *Personality and Individual Differences, 121*, 84–88.

Sparkman, G., & Walton, G. M. (2017). Dynamic norms promote sustainable behavior, even if it is counternormative. *Psychological Science, 28*, 1663–1674.

Sparkman, G., & Walton, G. M. (2019). Witnessing change: Dynamic norms help resolve diverse barriers to personal change. *Journal of Experimental Social Psychology, 82*, 238–252.

Sparks, S., Cunningham, S. J., & Kritikos, A. (2016). Culture modulates implicit ownership-induced self-bias in memory. *Cognition, 153*, 89–98.

Spearman, C. (1904). "General intelligence," objectively determined and measured. *American Journal of Psychology, 15*, 201–292.

Spector, T. (2012). *Identically different: Why you can change your genes.* Weidenfeld & Nicolson.

Speer, N. K., Reynolds, J. R., Swallow, K. M., & Zacks, J. M. (2009). Reading stories activates neural representations of visual and motor experiences. *Psychological Science, 20*, 989–999.

Spelke, E. S., Bernier, E. P., & Skerry, A. E. (2013). Core social cognition. In M. R. Banaji & S. A. Gelman (Eds.), *Navigating the social world: What infants, children, and other species can teach us.* Oxford University Press.

Spencer, K. M., Nestor, P. G., Perlmutter, R., Niznikiewicz, M. A., Klump, M. C., Frumin, M., Shenton, M. E., & McCarley, R. W. (2004). Neural synchrony indexes disordered perception and cognition in schizophrenia. PNAS, 101, 17288–17293.

Spencer, S. J., Logel, C., & Davies, P. G. (2016). Stereotype threat. *Annual Review of Psychology, 67*, 415–437.

Spencer, S. J., Steele, C. M., & Quinn, D. M. (1997). *Stereotype threat and women's math performance.* Unpublished manuscript. Hope College, Michigan.

Sperry, R. W. (1964). *Problems outstanding in the evolution of brain function* [Lecture]. The James Arthur Lecture, delivered at the American Museum of Natural History, New York, NY. Cited by R. Ornstein (1977) in *The psychology of consciousness* (2nd ed.). Harcourt Brace Jovanovich.

Sperry, R. W. (1985). Changed concepts of brain and consciousness: Some value implications. *Zygon, 20*, 41–57.

Sperry, R. W. (1992, Summer). Turnabout on consciousness: A mentalist view. *Journal of Mind & Behavior, 13*, 259–280.

Spiegel, A. (2015, January 8). *Dark thoughts.* From "Invisibilia," National Public Radio. https://www.npr.org/2015/01/09/375928124/dark-thoughts

Spiegel, D. (2007). The mind prepared: Hypnosis in surgery. *Journal of the National Cancer Institute, 99*, 1280–1281.

Spiegel, D. (2008, January 31). *Coming apart: Trauma and the fragmentation of the self.* Dana Foundation. https://www.dana.org/article/coming-apart-trauma-and-the-fragmentation-of-the-self/

Spielberger, C., & London, P. (1982). Rage boomerangs. *American Health, 1*, 52–56.

Sprecher, S., Treger, S., & Sakaluk, J. K. (2013). Premarital sexual standards and sociosexuality: Gender, ethnicity, and cohort differences. *Archives of Sexual Behavior, 42*, 1395–1405.

Spring, B., Pingitore, R., Bourgeois, M., Kessler, K. H., & Bruckner, E. (1992). *The effects and non-effects of skipping breakfast: Results of three studies.* Paper presented at the American Psychological Association convention.

Sproesser, G., Schupp, H. T., & Renner, B. (2014). The bright side of stress-induced eating: Eating more when stressed but less when pleased. *Psychological Science, 25*, 58–65.

Sprong, S., Jetten, J., Wang, Z., Peters, K., Verkuyten, M., Bastian, B., Ariyanto, A., Autin, F., Ayub, N., Badea, C., Besta, T., Butera, F., Costa-Lopes, R., Cui, L., Fantini, C., Finchilescu, G., Gaertner, L., Gollwitzer, M., Gómez, Á., . . . Wohl, J. A. (2019). "Our country needs a strong leader right now": Economic inequality enhances the wish for a strong leader. *Psychological Science, 30*(11), 1625–1637.

Squire, L. R., & Zola-Morgan, S. (1991, September 20). The medial temporal lobe memory system. *Science, 253*, 1380–1386.

Srivastava, A., Locke, E. A., & Bartol, K. M. (2001). Money and subject well-being: It's not the money, it's the motives. *Journal of Personality and Social Psychology, 80*, 959–971.

Srivastava, S., McGonigal, K. M., Richards, J. M., Butler, E. A., & Gross, J. J. (2006). Optimism in close relationships: How seeing things in a positive light makes them so. *Journal of Personality and Social Psychology, 91*, 143–153.

St-Onge, M.-P., McReynolds, A., Trivedi, Z. B., Roberts, A. L., Sy, M., & Hirsch, J. (2012). Sleep restriction leads to increased activation of brain regions sensitive to food stimuli. *American Journal of Clinical Nutrition, 95*, 818–824.

St. Clair, D., Xu, M., Wang, P., Yu, Y., Fang, Y., Zhang, F., Zheng, X., Gu, N., Feng, G., Sham, P., & He, L. (2005). Rates of adult schizophrenia following prenatal exposure to the Chinese famine of 1959–1961. *Journal of the American Medical Association, 294*, 557–562.

Stacey, D., Bilbao, A., Maroteaux, M., Jia, T., Easton, A. C., Longueville, S., Nymberg, C., Banaschewski, T., Barker, G. J., Büchel, C., Carvalho, F., Conrod, P. J., Desriviéres, S., Fauth-Bühler, M., Fernandez-Medarde, A., Flor, H., Gallinat, J., Garavan, H., Bokde, A. L., . . . IMAGEN Consortium. (2012). RASGRF2 regulates alcohol-induced reinforcement by influencing mesolimbic dopamine neuron activity and dopamine release. PNAS, 109, 21128–21133.

Stafford, T., & Dewar, M. (2014). Tracing the trajectory of skill learning with a very large sample of online game players. *Psychological Science, 25*, 511–518.

Stager, C. L., & Werker, J. F. (1997). Infants listen for more phonetic detail in speech perception than in word-learning tasks. *Nature, 388*, 381–382.

Stahl, A. E., & Feigenson, L. (2015). Observing the unexpected enhances infants' learning and exploration. *Science, 348*, 91–94.

Stahl, E. A., Breen, G., Forstner, A. J., McQuillin, A., Ripke, S., Trubetskoy, V., Mattheisen, M., Wang, Y., Coleman, J. R., Gaspar, H. A., de Leeuw, C. A. Steinberg, S., Whitehead Pavlides, J. M., Trzaskowski, M., Byrne, E. M., Pers, T. H., Holmans, P. A., Richards, A. L., Abbott, L., . . . Bipolar Disorder Working Group

of the Psychiatric Genomics Consortium. (2019). Genome-wide association study identifies 30 loci associated with bipolar disorder. *Nature Genetics, 51*, 793–803.

Stamkou, E., van Kleef, G. A., Homan, A. C., Gelfand, M. J., van de Vijver, F. J., van Egmond, M. C., Boer, D., Phiri, N., Ayub, N., Kinias, Z., Cantarero, K., Efrat Treister, D., Figueiredo, A., Hashimoto, H., Hofmann, E. B., Lima, R. P., & Lee, I. C. (2019). Cultural collectivism and tightness moderate responses to norm violators: Effects on power perception, moral emotions, and leader support. *Personality and Social Psychology Bulletin, 45*, 947–964.

Stanley, D., Phelps, E., & Banaji, M. (2008). The neural basis of implicit attitudes. *Current Directions in Psychological Science, 17*, 164–170.

Stanley, S. M., Rhoades, G. K., Amato, P. R., Markman, H. J., & Johnson, C. A. (2010). The timing of cohabitation and engagement: Impact on first and second marriages. *Journal of Marriage and Family, 72*, 906–918.

Stanley, S., & Rhoades, G. (2016a, July 19). *Testing a relationship is probably the worst reason to cohabit.* Institute for Family Studies. https://ifstudies.org/blog/testing-a-relationship-is-probably-the-worst-reason-to-cohabit

Stanley, S., & Rhoades, G. (2016b, July/August). The perils of sowing your wild oats. *Psychology Today*, pp. 40–42.

Stanley, T. D., Carter, E. C., & Doucouliagos, H. (2018). What meta-analyses reveal about the replicability of psychological research. *Psychological Bulletin, 144*, 1325–1346.

Stanovich, K. (1996). *How to think straight about psychology.* HarperCollins.

Stanovich, K. E., West, R. F., & Toplak, M. E. (2013). My side bias, rational thinking, and intelligence. *Current Directions in Psychological Science, 22*, 259–264.

Stanovich, K. E., West, R. F., & Toplak, M. E. (2016). *The rationality quotient: Toward a test of rational thinking.* MIT Press.

Stanton, K., Khoo, S., Watson, D., Gruber, J., Zimmerman, M., & Weinstock, L. M. (2019). Unique and transdiagnostic symptoms of hypomania/mania and unipolar depression. *Clinical Psychological Science, 7*, 471–487.

Starcke, K., & Brand, M. (2016). Effects of stress on decisions under uncertainty: A meta-analysis. *Psychological Bulletin, 142*, 909–933.

Stark, R. (2003a). *For the glory of God: How monotheism led to reformations, science, witch-hunts, and the end of slavery.* Princeton University Press.

Stark, R. (2003b, October–November). False conflict: Christianity is not only compatible with science—it created it. *American Enterprise*, pp. 27–33.

Starzynski, L. L., Ullman, S. E., & Vasquez, A. L. (2017). Sexual assault survivors' experiences with mental health professionals: A qualitative study. *Women & Therapy, 40*, 228–246.

Statista. (2017). *Reported violent crime in the United States from 1990 to 2015.* https://www.statista.com/statistics/191219/reported-violent-crime-rate-in-the-usa-since-1990/

Statista. (2018). *Matchmaking—United States.* https://www.statista.com/outlook/371/109/matchmaking/united-states

Statista. (2019, October 10). *Anti-Semitic violence on the rise in Germany.* https://www.statista.com/chart/19608/anti-semitic-crimes-in-germany/

Statistics Canada. (2011). *Marital status: Overview, 2011.* Table 2: Divorces and crude divorce rates, Canada, provinces and territories, 1981 to 2008. https://www150.statcan.gc.ca/n1/pub/91-209-x/2013001/article/11788/tbl/tbl2-eng.htm

Statistics Canada. (2013). Table A.5.1. *Second language immersion program enrolments in public elementary and secondary schools, Canada, provinces and territories, 2005/2006 to 2009/2010.* https://www150.statcan.gc.ca/n1/pub/81-595-m/2011095/tbl/tbla.5.1-eng.htm

Statistics Canada. (2016). "Chart 10: Prevalence of fair/poor mental health and mood disorders, female population aged 12 to 19, Canada, 2003 to 2014." https://www150.statcan.gc.ca/n1/pub/89-503-x/2015001/article/14324/c-g/c-g10-eng.htm

Statistics Canada. (2019, February 7). *National Cannabis Survey, fourth quarter 2018.* https://www150.statcan.gc.ca/n1/daily-quotidien/190207/dq190207b-eng.htm

Statistics Canada. (2019). *Mental health characteristics: Ability to handle stress and sources of stress.* https://www150.statcan.gc.ca/t1/tbl1/en/tv.action?pid=1310080201

Staub, E. (1989). *The roots of evil: The psychological and cultural sources of genocide.* Cambridge University Press.

Stavrinos, D., Pope, C. N., Shen, J., & Schwebel, D. C. (2017). Distracted walking, bicycling, and driving: Systematic review and meta-analysis of mobile technology and youth crash risk. *Child Development, 89,* 118–128.

Stavrova, O., & Ehlebracht, D. (2018). The cynical genius illusion: Exploring and debunking lay beliefs about cynicism and competence. *Personality and Social Psychology Bulletin, 45*(2), 254–269.

Steel, P., Schmidt, J., & Schultz, J. (2008). Refining the relationship between personality and subject well-being. *Psychological Bulletin, 134,* 138–161.

Steele, C. M. (1990, May). A conversation with Claude Steele. *APS Observer,* pp. 11–17.

Steele, C. M. (1995, August 31). Black students live down to expectations. *The New York Times.* https://www.nytimes.com/1995/08/31/opinion/black-students-live-down-to-expectations.html

Steele, C. M. (2010). *Whistling Vivaldi: And other clues to how stereotypes affect us.* Norton.

Steele, C. M., & Josephs, R. A. (1990). Alcohol myopia: Its prized and dangerous effects. *American Psychologist, 45,* 921–933.

Steele, C. M., Spencer, S. J., & Aronson, J. (2002). Contending with group image: The psychology of stereotype and social identity threat. *Advances in Experimental Social Psychology, 34,* 379–440.

Stein, J. Y., Levin, Y., Lahav, Y., Uziel, O., Abumock, H., & Solomon, Z. (2018). Perceived social support, loneliness, and later life telomere length following wartime captivity. *Health Psychology, 37,* 1067–1076.

Stein, M. B., & Rothbaum, B. O. (2018). 175 years of progress in PTSD therapeutics: Learning from the past. *The American Journal of Psychiatry, 175,* 508–516.

Stein, R. (2018, December 18). *Surgeon General warns youth vaping is now an 'epidemic.'* National Public Radio. https://www.npr.org/sections/health-shots/2018/12/18/677755266/surgeon-general-warns-youth-vaping-is-now-an-epidemic

Steinberg, L. (1987, September). Bound to bicker. *Psychology Today,* pp. 36–39.

Steinberg, L. (2012, Spring). Should the science of adolescent brain development inform public policy? *Issues in Science and Technology, 28,* pp. 67–78.

Steinberg, L. (2013). The influence of neuroscience on U.S. Supreme Court decisions involving adolescents' criminal culpability. *Nature Reviews Neuroscience, 14,* 513–518.

Steinberg, L. (2015). How to improve the health of American adolescents. *Perspectives on Psychological Science, 10,* 711–715.

Steinberg, L., Cauffman, E., Woolard, J., Graham, S., & Banich, M. (2009). Are adolescents less mature than adults? Minors' access to abortion, the juvenile death penalty, and the alleged APA "flip-flop." *American Psychologist, 64,* 583–594.

Steinberg, L., Icenogle, G., Shulman, E. P., Breiner, K., Chein, J., Bacchini, D., Chang, L., Chaudhary, N., Giunta, L. D., Dodge, K. A., Fanti, K. A., Lansford, J. E., Malone, P. S., Oburu, P., Pastorelli, C., Skinner, A. T., Sorbring, E., Tapanya, S., Tirado, L. M. U., . . . Takash, H. M. S. (2018). Around the world, adolescence is a time of heightened sensation seeking and immature self-regulation. *Developmental Science, 21,* e12532.

Steinberg, L., Lamborn, S. D., Darling, N., Mounts, N. S., & Dornbusch, S. M. (1994). Over-time changes in adjustment and competence among adolescents from authoritative, authoritarian, indulgent, and neglectful families. *Child Development, 65,* 754–770.

Steinberg, L., & Morris, A. S. (2001). Adolescent development. *Annual Review of Psychology, 52,* 83–110.

Steinberg, L., & Scott, E. S. (2003). Less guilty by reason of adolescence: Developmental immaturity, diminished responsibility, and the juvenile death penalty. *American Psychologist, 58,* 1009–1018.

Steinberg, N. (1993, February). Astonishing love stories (from an earlier United Press International report). *Games,* p. 47.

Steiner, J. L., Murphy, E. A., McClellan, J. L., Carmichael, M. D., & Davis, J. M. (2011). Exercise training increases mitochondrial biogenesis in the brain. *Journal of Applied Physiology, 111,* 1066–1071.

Steinert, C., Munder, T., Rabung, S., Hoyer, J., & Leichsenring, F. (2017). Psychodynamic therapy: As efficacious as other empirically supported treatments? A meta-analysis testing equivalence of outcomes. *American Journal of Psychiatry, 174,* 943–953.

Steinglass, J. E, Glasofer, D. R., Walsh, E., Guzman, G., Peterson, C. B., Walsh, B. T., Attia, E., & Wonderlich, S. A. (2018). Targeting habits in anorexia nervosa: A proof-of-concept randomized trial. *Psychological Medicine, 48,* 2584–2591.

Steinhausen, H.-C., Mohr Jensen, C., & Lauritsen, M. B. (2016). A systematic review and meta-analysis of the long-term overall outcome of autism spectrum disorders in adolescence and adulthood. *Acta Psychiatrica Scandinavica, 133,* 445–452.

Stellar, J. E., John-Henderson, N., Anderson, C. L., Gordon, A. M., McNeil, G. D., & Keltner, D. (2015). Positive affect and markers of inflammation: Discrete positive emotions predict lower levels of inflammatory cytokines. *Emotion, 15,* 129–133.

Stender, J., Gosseries, O., Bruno, M.-A., Charland-Verville, V., Vanhaudenhuyse, A., Demertzi, A., Chatelle, C., Thonnard, M., Thibaut, A., Heine, L., Soddu, A., Boly, M., Schnakers, C., Gjedde, A., & Laureys, S. (2014). Diagnostic precision of PET imaging and functional MRI in disorders of consciousness: A clinical validation study. *The Lancet, 384,* 514–522.

Stephan, Y., Sutin, A. R., Kornadt, A., Caudroit, J., & Terracciano, A. (2018). Higher IQ in adolescence is related to a younger subjective age in later life: Findings from the Wisconsin Longitudinal Study. *Intelligence, 69,* 195–199.

Stephens-Davidowitz, S. (2013, December 7). How many American men are gay? *The New York Times.* https://www.nytimes.com/2013/12/08/opinion/sunday/how-many-american-men-are-gay.html?

Stephens-Davidowitz, S. (2014). The effects of racial animus on a black candidate: Evidence using Google search data. *Journal of Public Economics, 118,* 26–40.

Stephens-Davidowitz, S. (2017). *Everybody lies: Big data, new data, and what the internet can tell us about who we really are.* Dey St. (Morrow).

Steptoe, A., Chida, Y., Hamer, M., & Wardle, J. (2010). Author reply: Meta-analysis of stress-related factors in cancer. *Nature Reviews: Clinical Oncology, 7,* 1.

Steptoe, A., & Wardle, J. (2011). Positive affect measured using ecological momentary assessment and survival in older men and women. *PNAS, 108,* 18244–18248.

Steptoe, A., & Wardle, J. (2017). Life skills, wealth, health, and wellbeing later in life. *PNAS, 114,* 4354–4359.

Sterling, R. (2003). *The traveling curmudgeon: Irreverent notes, quotes, and anecdotes on dismal destinations, excess baggage, the full upright position, and other reasons not to go there* (p. 102). Sasquatch Books.

Stern, M., & Karraker, K. H. (1989). Sex stereotyping of infants: A review of gender labeling studies. *Sex Roles, 20,* 501–522.

Sternberg, E. M. (2009). *Healing spaces: The science of place and well-being.* Harvard University Press.

Sternberg, R. (2017). ACCEL: A new model for identifying the gifted. *Roeper Review, 39,* 152–169.

Sternberg, R. J. (1985). *Beyond IQ: A triarchic theory of human intelligence.* Cambridge University Press.

Sternberg, R. J. (1988). Applying cognitive theory to the testing and teaching of intelligence. *Applied Cognitive Psychology, 2,* 231–255.

Sternberg, R. J. (2003). Our research program validating the triarchic theory of successful intelligence: Reply to Gottfredson. *Intelligence, 31,* 399–413.

Sternberg, R. J. (2006). The Rainbow Project: Enhance the SAT through assessments of analytical, practical, and creative skills. *Intelligence, 34,* 321–350.

Sternberg, R. J. (2015). Successful intelligence: A model for testing intelligence beyond IQ tests. *European Journal of Education and Psychology, 8,* 76–84.

Sternberg, R. J., & Grajek, S. (1984). The nature of love. *Journal of Personality and Social Psychology, 47,* 312–329.

Sternberg, R. J., & Kaufman, J. C. (1998). Human abilities. *Annual Review of Psychology, 49,* 479–502.

Sternberg, R. J., & Lubart, T. I. (1991). An investment theory of creativity and its development. *Human Development, 34,* 1–31.

Sternberg, R. J., & Lubart, T. I. (1992). Buy low and sell high: An investment approach to creativity. *Psychological Science, 1,* 1–5.

Sterzing, P. R., Shattuck, P. T., Narendorf, S. C., Wagner, M., & Cooper, B. P. (2012). Bullying involvement and autism spectrum disorders: prevalence and correlates of bullying involvement among adolescents with an autism spectrum disorder. *Archives of Pediatric and Adolescent Medicine, 166,* 1058–1064.

Stetter, F., & Kupper, S. (2002). Autogenic training: A meta-analysis of clinical outcome studies. *Applied Psychophysiology and Biofeedback, 27,* 45–98.

Stevenson, R. J. (2014). Flavor binding: Its nature and cause. *Psychological Bulletin, 140,* 487–510.

Stevenson, R. J., & Francis, H. M. (2017). The hippocampus and the regulation of human food intake. *Psychological Bulletin, 143,* 1011–1032.

Steyvers, M., Hawkins, G. E., Karayanidis, F., & Brown, S. D. (2019). A large-scale analysis of task switching practice effects across the lifespan. *PNAS, 116,* 17735–17740.

Stice, E. (2002). Risk and maintenance factors for eating pathology: A meta-analytic review. *Psychological Bulletin, 128,* 825–848.

Stice, E., Ng, J., & Shaw, H. (2010). Risk factors and prodromal eating pathology. *Journal of Child Psychology and Psychiatry, 51,* 518–525.

Stice, E., Spangler, D., & Agras, W. S. (2001). Exposure to media-portrayed thin-ideal images adversely affects vulnerable girls: A longitudinal experiment. *Journal of Social and Clinical Psychology, 20*, 270–288.

Stickgold, R. (2000, March 7). Quoted by S. Blakeslee, For better learning, researchers endorse "sleep on it" adage. *The New York Times*, p. F2.

Stickgold, R. (2012). Sleep, memory and dreams: Putting it all together. In *Aquém e além do Cérebro* [Behind and beyond the brain]. Fundação Bial Institution of Public Utility.

Stillman, T. F., Baumeister, R. F., Vohs, K. D., Lambert, N. M., Fincham, F. D., & Brewer, L. E. (2010). Personal philosophy and personnel achievement: Belief in free will predicts better job performance. *Social Psychological and Personality Science, 1*, 43–50.

Stillman, T. F., Lambet, N. M., Fincham, F. D., & Baumeister, R. F. (2011). Meaning as magnetic force: Evidence that meaning in life promotes interpersonal appeal. *Social Psychological and Personality Science, 2*, 13–20.

Stinson, D. A., Logel, C., Zanna, M. P., Holmes, J. G., Cameron, J. J., Wood, J. V., & Spencer, S. J. (2008). The cost of lower self-esteem: Testing a self- and social-bonds model of health. *Journal of Personality and Social Psychology, 94*, 412–428.

Stipek, D. (1992). The child at school. In M. H. Bornstein & M. E. Lamb (Eds.), *Developmental psychology: An advanced textbook*. Erlbaum.

Stith, S. M., Rosen, K. H., Middleton, K. A., Busch, A. L., Lunderberg, K., & Carlton, R. P. (2000). The intergenerational transmission of spouse abuse: A meta-analysis. *Journal of Marriage and the Family, 62*, 640–654.

Stjepanovic, D. & LaBar, K. S. (2018). Fear learning. In Wixted, J.T.(Ed.), *Stevens' Handbook of Experimental Psychology*, 4th Ed., Vol. 1. Wiley.

Stockton, M. C., & Murnen, S. K. (1992, June). *Gender and sexual arousal in response to sexual stimuli: A meta-analytic review* [Paper]. Presented at the Fourth Annual Convention of the American Psychological Society, San Diego.

Stoet, G., & Geary, D. C. (2018). The gender-equality paradox in science, technology, engineering, and mathematics education. *Psychological Science, 29*, 581–593.

Stokoe, W. C. (1960). Sign language structure: An outline of the visual communication systems of the American Deaf. *Studies in Linguistics: Occasional papers (No. 8)*. Dept. of Anthropology and Linguistics, University of Buffalo.

Stoll, G., Rieger, S., Lüdtke, O., Nagengast, B., Trautwein, U., & Roberts, B. W. (2017). Vocational interests assessed at the end of high school predict life outcomes assessed 10 years later over and above IQ and Big Five personality traits. *Journal of Personality and Social Psychology, 113*, 167–184.

Stolzenberg, E. B., Eagan, M. K., Aragon, M. C., Cesar-Davis, N. M., Jacobo, S., Couch, V., & Rios-Aguilar, C. (2019). *The American freshman: National norms fall 2017*. Higher Education Research Institute, UCLA.

Stone, A. A., & Neale, J. M. (1984). Effects of severe daily events on mood. *Journal of Personality and Social Psychology, 46*, 137–144.

Stone, A. A., Schwartz, J. E., Broderick, J. E., & Deaton, A. (2010). A snapshot of the age distribution of psychological well-being in the United States. *PNAS, 107*, 9985–9990.

Stone, A. A., Schwartz, J. E., Broderick, J. E., & Shiffman, S. S. (2005). Variability of momentary pain predicts recall of weekly pain: A consequence of the peak (or salience) memory heuristic. *Personality and Social Psychology Bulletin, 31*, 1340–1346.

Stone, G. (2006, February 17). *Homeless man discovered to be lawyer with amnesia*. ABC News. https://abcnews.go.com/US/story?id=1629645&page=1

Stone, M. & Vogelstein, R. (2019, March 7). *Celebrating #MeToo's global impact*. Foreign Policy. https://foreignpolicy.com/2019/03/07/metooglobalimpactinternationalwomens-day/

Stop Street Harassment. (2018). *The facts behind the #MeToo movement: A national study on sexual harassment and assault* [PDF file]. http://www.stopstreetharassment.org/wp-content/uploads/2018/01/Executive-Summary-2018-National-Study-on-Sexual-Harassment-and-Assault.pdf

Storbeck, J., Robinson, M. D., & McCourt, M. E. (2006). Semantic processing precedes affect retrieval: The neurological case for cognitive primary in visual processing. *Review of General Psychology, 10*, 41–55.

Storm, B. C., & Jobe, T. A. (2012). Retrieval-induced forgetting predicts failure to recall negative autobiographical memories. *Psychological Science, 23*, 1356–1363.

Storm, L., Tressoldi, P. E., & Di Risio, L. (2010a). A meta-analysis with nothing to hide: Reply to Hyman (2010). *Psychological Bulletin, 136*, 491–494.

Storm, L., Tressoldi, P. E., & Di Risio, L. (2010b). Meta-analysis of free-response studies, 1992–2008: Assessing the noise reduction model in parapsychology. *Psychological Bulletin, 136*, 471–485.

Storms, M. D. (1973). Videotape and the attribution process: Reversing actors' and observers' points of view. *Journal of Personality and Social Psychology, 27*, 165–175.

Storms, M. D. (1981). A theory of erotic orientation development. *Psychological Review, 88*, 340–353.

Storms, M. D., & Thomas, G. C. (1977). Reactions to physical closeness. *Journal of Personality and Social Psychology, 35*, 412–418.

Stothart, C., Mitchum, A., & Yehnert, C. (2015). The attentional cost of receiving a cell phone notification. *Journal of Experimental Psychology: Human Perception and Performance, 41*, 893–897.

Stout, D. M., Glenn, D. E., Acheson, D. T., Spadoni, A. D., Risbrough, V. B., & Simmons, A. N. (2018). Neural measures associated with configural threat acquisition. *Neurobiology of Learning and Memory, 150*, 99–106.

Stowell, J. R., Oldham, T., & Bennett, D. (2010). Using student response systems ("clickers") to combat conformity and shyness. *Teaching of Psychology, 37*, 135–140.

Strack, F. (2016). Reflection on the smiling preregistered replication report. *Perspectives on Psychological Science, 11*, 929–930.

Strain, J. F., Womack, K. B., Didenbani, N., Spence, J. S., Conover, H., Hart, J., Jr., Kraut, M. A., & Cullum, C. M. (2015). Imaging correlates of memory and concussion history in retired National Football League athletes. *JAMA Neurology, 72*, 773–780.

Strand, L. B., Mukamal, K. J., Halasz, J., Vatten, L. J., & Janszky, I. (2016). Short-term public health impact of the July 22, 2011, terrorist attacks in Norway: A nationwide register-based study. *Psychosomatic Medicine, 78*, 525–531.

Strang, S., Utikal, V., Fischbacher, U., Weber, B., & Falk, A. (2014). Neural correlates of receiving an apology and active forgiveness: An fMRI study. *PLOS ONE, 9*, e87654.

Strange, D., Hayne, H., & Garry, M. (2008). A photo, a suggestion, a false memory. *Applied Cognitive Psychology, 22*, 587–603.

Strasburger, V. C., Jordan, A. B., & Donnerstein, E. (2010). Health effects of media on children and adolescents. *Pediatrics, 125*, 756–767.

Stratton, G. M. (1896). Some preliminary experiments on vision without inversion of the retinal image. *Psychological Review, 3*, 611–617.

Straus, M. A., & Gelles, R. J. (1980). *Behind closed doors: Violence in the American family*. Anchor/Doubleday.

Straus, M. A., Sugarman, D. B., & Giles-Sims, J. (1997). Spanking by parents and subsequent antisocial behavior of children. *Archives of Pediatric Adolescent Medicine, 151*, 761–767.

Strauss, M. (2018, August 16). *Americans are divided over the use of animals in scientific research*. Pew Research Center. https://www.pewresearch.org/fact-tank/2018/08/16/americans-are-divided-over-the-use-of-animals-in-scientific-research/

Strawbridge, W. J. (1999). *Mortality and religious involvement: A review and critique of the results, the methods, and the measures* [Paper]. Presented at a Harvard University conference on religion and health, sponsored by the National Institute for Health Research and the John Templeton Foundation.

Strawbridge, W. J., Cohen, R. D., & Shema, S. J. (1997). Frequent attendance at religious services and mortality over 28 years. *American Journal of Public Health, 87*, 957–961.

Strayhorn, J., Jr. (2019). Editorial: Cognitive-behavior therapy versus serotonin reuptake inhibitors for pediatric obsessive-compulsive disorder. *Journal of the American Academy of Child & Adolescent Psychiatry, 59*, 219–221.

Strick, M., Dijksterhuis, A., Bos, M. W., Sjoerdsma, A., & van Baaren, R. B. (2011). A meta-analysis on unconscious thought effects. *Social Cognition, 29*, 738–762.

Strick, M., Dijksterhuis, A., & van Baaren, R. B. (2010). Unconscious-thought effects take place off-line, not on-line. *Psychological Science, 21*, 484–488.

Strickland, B. (1992, February 20). *Gender differences in health and illness* [Lecture]. Sigma Xi national lecture delivered at Hope College, Michigan.

Striem-Amit, E., Vannuscorps, G., & Caramazza, A. (2018). Plasticity based on compensatory effector use in the association but not primary sensorimotor cortex of people born without hands. *PNAS, 115*, 7801–7806.

Stroebe, M., Finenauer, C., Wijngaards-de Meij, L., Schut, H., van den Bout, J., & Stroebe, W. (2013). Partner-oriented self-regulation among bereaved parents: The costs of holding in grief for the partner's sake. *Psychological Science, 24*, 395–402.

Stroebe, W. (2012). The truth about Triplett (1898), but nobody seems to care. *Perspectives on Psychological Science, 7*, 54–57.

Stroebe, W. (2013). Firearm possession and violent death: A critical review. *Aggression and Violent Behavior, 18*, 709–721.

Stroebe, W., Gadenne, V., & Nijstad, B. A. (2018). Do our psychological laws apply only to college students? External validity revisited. *Basic and Applied Social Psychology, 40*, 384–395.

Stroebe, W., Leander, N. P., & Kruglanski, A. W. (2017). Is it a dangerous world out there? The motivational bases of American gun ownership. *Personality and Social Psychology Bulletin, 43*, 1071–1085.

Stroebe, W., Schut, H., & Stroebe, M. S. (2005). Grief work, disclosure and counseling: Do they help the bereaved? *Clinical Psychology Review, 25*, 395–414.

Stroud, L. R., Panadonatos, G. D., Rodriguez, D., McCallum, M., Salisbury, A. L., Phipps, M. G., Lester, B., Huestis, M. A., Niaura, R., Padbury, J. F., & Marsit, C. J. (2014). Maternal smoking during pregnancy and infant stress response: Test of a prenatal programming hypothesis. *Psychoneuroendocrinology, 48*, 29–40.

Strully, K. W. (2009). Job loss and health in the U.S. labor market. *Demography, 46*, 221–246.

Stuart, G. J., & Spruston, N. (2015). Dendritic integration: 60 years of progress. *Nature Neuroscience, 18*, 1713–1721.

Stubbs, B., Vancampfort, D., Rosenbaum, S., Firth, J., Cosco, T., Veronese, N., Salum, G. A., & Schuch, F. B.

(2017). An examination of the anxiolytic effects of exercise for people with anxiety and stress-related disorders: A meta-analysis. *Psychiatry Research, 249,* 102–108.

Studte, S., Bridger, E., & Mecklinger, A. (2017). Sleep spindles during a nap correlate with post sleep memory performance for highly rewarded word-pairs. *Brain and Language, 167,* 28–35.

Štulhofer, A., Šoh, D., Jelaska, N., Baćak, V., & Landripet, I. (2011). Religiosity and sexual risk behavior among Croatian college students, 1998–2008. *Journal of Sex Research, 48,* 360–371.

Stutzer, A., & Frey, B. S. (2006). Does marriage make people happy, or do happy people get married? *Journal of Socio-Economics, 35,* 326–347.

Subotnik, R. F., Olszewski-Kubilius, P., & Worrell, F. C. (2011). Rethinking giftedness and gifted education: A proposed direction forward based on psychological science. *Psychological Science in the Public Interest, 12,* 3–54.

Suchotzki, K., Verschuere, B., Van Bockstaele, B., Ben-Shakhar, G., & Crombez, G. (2017). Lying takes time: A meta-analysis on reaction time measures of deception. *Psychological Bulletin, 143,* 428–453.

Suddath, R. L., Christison, G. W., Torrey, E. F., Casanova, M. F., & Weinberger, D. R. (1990). Anatomical abnormalities in the brains of monozygotic twins discordant for schizophrenia. *New England Journal of Medicine, 322,* 789–794.

Suddendorf, T. (2018, September). Two key features created the human mind. *Scientific American,* pp. 43–47.

Sue, S., Zane, N., Hall, G. C. N., & Berger, L. K. (2009). The case for cultural competency in psychotherapeutic interventions. *Annual Review of Psychology, 60,* 525–548.

Suedfeld, P., & Mocellin, J. S. P. (1987). The "sensed presence" in unusual environments. *Environment and Behavior, 19,* 33–52.

Sugaya, L., Hasin, D. S., Olfson, M., Lin, K.-H., Grant, B. F., & Blanco, C. (2012). Child physical abuse and adult mental health: A national study. *Journal of Traumatic Stress, 25,* 384–392.

Sulik, M. J., Blair, C., Mills-Koonce, R., Berry, D., Greenberg, M., & Family Life Project Investigators. (2015). Early parenting and the development of externalizing behavior problems: Longitudinal mediation through children's executive function. *Child Development, 86,* 1588–1603.

Sullivan, K. T., Pasch, L. A., Johnson, M. D., & Bradbury, T. N. (2010). Social support, problem solving, and the longitudinal course of newlywed marriage. *Journal of Personality and Social Psychology, 98,* 631–644.

Sullivan, P. F., Neale, M. C., & Kendler, K. S. (2000). Genetic epidemiology of major depression: Review and meta-analysis. *American Journal of Psychiatry, 157,* 1552–1562.

Suls, J. M., & Tesch, F. (1978). Students' preferences for information about their test performance: A social comparison study. *Journal of Experimental Social Psychology, 8,* 189–197.

Summers, M. (1996, December 9). Mister Clean. *People Weekly,* pp. 139–142.

Sumner, R., Burrow, A. L., & Hill, P. L. (2018). The development of purpose in life among adolescents who experience marginalization: Potential opportunities and obstacles. *American Psychologist, 73,* 740–752.

Sun, G. J., Zhou, Y., Ito, S., Bonaguidi, M. A., Stein-O'Brien, G., Kawasaki, N. K., Modak, N., Zhu, Y., Ming, G. L., & Song, H. (2015). Latent tri-lineage potential of adult hippocampal neural stem cells revealed by Nf1 inactivation. *Nature Neuroscience, 18,* 1722–1724.

Sun, X., Zheng, B., Lv, J., Guo, Y., Bian, Z., Yang, L., Chen, Y., Fu, Z., Guo, H., Liang, P., Chen, Z., Chen, J., Li, L., Yu, C., & China Kadoorie Biobank (CKB) Collaborative Group. (2018). Sleep behavior and depression: Findings from the China Kadoorie Biobank of 0.5 million Chinese adults. *Journal of Affective Disorders, 229,* 120–124.

Sunahara, C. S., Zelkowitz, P., Bolger, N., Sadikaj, G., Samuel, S., Gold, I., Hayton, B., Feeley, N., Carter, C. S., & Bartz, J. A. (2019). Maternal oxytocin predicts relationship survival during the perinatal transition period: Preliminary evidence. *International Journal of Psychophysiology, 136,* 33–38.

Sundstrom, E., De Meuse, K. P., & Futrell, D. (1990). Work teams: Applications and effectiveness. *American Psychologist, 45,* 120–133.

Sung, S., Simpson, J. A., Griskevicius, V., Sally, I., Kuo, C., Schlomer, G. L., & Belsky, J. (2016). Secure infant-mother attachment buffers the effect of early-life stress on age of menarche. *Psychological Science, 27,* 667–674.

Sunstein, C. R., Bobadilla-Suarez, S., Lazzaro, S. C., & Sharot, T. (2016). How people update beliefs about climate change: Good news and bad news [PDF file]. *Cornell Law Review, 102*(6). https://scholarship.law.cornell.edu/cgi/viewcontent.cgi?article=4736&context=clr

Sunstein, C. R., Reisch, L. A., & Kaiser, M. (2019). Trusting nudges? Lessons from an international survey. *Journal of European Public Policy, 26,* 1417–1443.

Sunstein, C. R. & Thaler, R. (2016, December 7). The two friends who changed how we think about how we think. *The New Yorker.* https://www.newyorker.com/books/page-turner/the-two-friends-who-changed-how-we-think-about-how-we-think

Suomi, S. J. (1986). Anxiety-like disorders in young nonhuman primates. In R. Gettleman (Ed.), *Anxiety disorders of childhood.* Guilford Press.

Suomi, S. J., Collins, M. L., Harlow, H. F., & Ruppenthal, G. C. (1976). Effects of maternal and peer separations on young monkeys. *Journal of Child Psychology and Psychiatry, 17,* 101–112.

Suppes, P. (1982). Quoted in R. H. Ennis, Children's ability to handle Piaget's propositional logic: A conceptual critique. In S. Modgil & C. Modgil (Eds.), *Jean Piaget: Consensus and controversy* (pp. 101–130). Praeger.

Surgeon General. (1986). *The Surgeon General's workshop on pornography and public health,* June 22–24. Report prepared by E. P. Mulvey & J. L. Haugaard and released by Office of the Surgeon General on August 4, 1986.

Surgeon General. (1999). *Mental health: A report of the Surgeon General.* U.S. Department of Health and Human Services.

Surgeon General. (2012). *Preventing tobacco use among youth and young adults: A report of the Surgeon General.* Department of Health and Human Services, Office of the Surgeon General.

Susser, E., & Martínez-Alés, G. (2018). Putting psychosis into sociocultural context: An international study in 17 locations. *JAMA Psychiatry, 75,* 9–10."

Susser, E. S. (1999). Life course cohort studies of schizophrenia. *Psychiatric Annals, 29,* 161–165.

Susser, E. S., Neugenbauer, R., Hoek, H. W., Brown, A. S., Lin, S., Labovitz, D., & Gorman, J. M. (1996). Schizophrenia after prenatal famine. *Archives of General Psychiatry, 53,* 25–31.

Svaldi, J., Schmitz, F., Baur, J., Hartmann, A. S., Legenbauer, T., Thaler, C., von Wietersheim, J., de Zwaan, M., & Tuschen-Caffier, B. (2019). Efficacy of psychotherapies and pharmacotherapies for bulimia nervosa. *Psychological Medicine, 49,* 898–910.

Swami, V. (2015). Cultural influences on body size ideals: Unpacking the impact of Westernization and modernization. *European Psychologist, 20,* 44–51.

Swami, V., Frederick, D. A., Aavik, T., Alcalay, L., Allik, J., Anderson, D., Andrianto, S., Arora, A., Brännström, A., Cunningham, J., Danel, D., Dorosqewicz, K., Forbes, G. B., Furnham, A., Greven, C. U., Halberstadt, J., Hao, S., Haubner, T., Hwang, C. S., . . . Zivcic-Becirevic, I. (2010). The attractive female body weight and female body dissatisfaction in 26 countries across 10 world regions: Results of the International Body Project I. *Personality and Social Psychology Bulletin, 36,* 309–325.

Swann, W. B., Jr., Chang-Schneider, C., & McClarty, K. L. (2007). Do people's self-views matter? Self-concept and self-esteem in everyday life. *American Psychologist, 62,* 84–94.

Swartz, J. R., Hariri, A. R. & Williamson, D. E. (2016). An epigenetic mechanism links socioeconomic status to changes in depression-related brain function in high-risk adolescents. *Molecular Psychiatry, 22,* 209–214.

Sweeny, K., & Falkenstein, A. (2017). Even optimists get the blues: Interindividual consistency in the tendency to brace for the worst. *Journal of Personality, 85,* 807–816.

Swift, A. (2013, October 28). *Personal safety top reason Americans own guns today.* Gallup. https://news.gallup.com/poll/165605/personal-safety-top-reason-americans-own-guns-today.aspx

Swift, A. (2016, November 9). *Americans' perceptions of U.S. crime problem are steady.* Gallup. https://news.gallup.com/poll/197318/americans-perceptions-crime-problem-steady.aspx

Swift, A. (2017). *In U.S., belief in creationist view of humans at new low.* Gallup. https://news.gallup.com/poll/210956/belief-creationist-view-humans-new-low.aspx

Symbaluk, D. G., Heth, C. D., Cameron, J., & Pierce, W. D. (1997). Social modeling, monetary incentives, and pain endurance: The role of self-efficacy and pain perception. *Personality and Social Psychology Bulletin, 23,* 258–269.

Symond, M. B., Harris, A. W. F., Gordon, E., & Williams, L. M. (2005). "Gamma synchrony" in first-episode schizophrenia: A disorder of temporal connectivity? *American Journal of Psychiatry, 162,* 459–465.

Symons, C. S., & Johnson, B. T. (1997). The self-reference effect in memory: A meta-analysis. *Psychological Bulletin, 121,* 371–394.

Szkodny, L. E., Newman, M. G., & Goldfried, M. R. (2014). Clinical experiences in conducting empirically supported treatments for generalized anxiety disorder. *Behavior Therapy, 45,* 7–20.

Szutorisz, H., & Hurd, J. L. (2016). Epigenetic effects of cannabis exposure. *Biological Psychiatry, 79,* 586–594.

Tackett, J. L., Herzhoff, K., Kushner, S. C., & Rule, N. (2016). Thin slices of child personality: Perceptual, situational, and behavioral contributions. *Journal of Personality and Social Psychology, 110,* 150–166.

Taha, F. A. (1972). A comparative study of how sighted and blind perceive the manifest content of dreams. *National Review of Social Sciences, 9,* 28.

Taheri, S. (2004, December 20). Does the lack of sleep make you fat? *University of Bristol Research News.* https://www.bristol.ac.uk/news/2004/1113989409.html

Taheri, S., Lin, L., Austin, D., Young, T., & Mignot, E. (2004). Short sleep duration is associated with reduced leptin, elevated ghrelin, and increased body mass index. *PLOS Medicine, 1,* e62.

Tajfel, H. (Ed.). (1982). *Social identity and intergroup relations.* Cambridge University Press.

Takizawa, R., Maughan, B., & Arseneault, L. (2014). Adult health outcomes of childhood bullying victimization: Evidence from a five-decade longitudinal British birth cohort. *American Journal of Psychiatry, 171,* 777–784.

Talarico, J. M., Bohn, A., & Wessel, I. (2019). The role of event relevance and congruence to social groups in flashbulb memory formation. *Memory, 27,* 985–997.

Talarico, J. M., & Moore, K. M. (2012). Memories of "the rivalry": Differences in how fans of the winning and losing teams remember the same game. *Applied Cognitive Psychology, 26,* 746–756.

Talbot, M. (1999, October). The Rorschach chronicles. *The New York Times.* https://www.nytimes.com/1999/10/17/magazine/the-rorschach-chronicles.html?

Talhelm, T., Oishi, S., & Zhang, X. (2019). Who smiles while alone? Rates of smiling lower in China than U.S. *Emotion, 19,* 741–745.

Talhelm, T., Zhang, X., & Oishi, S. (2018). Moving chairs in Starbucks: Observational studies find rice-wheat cultural differences in daily life in China. *Science Advances, 4,* eaap8469.

Talhelm, T., Zhang, X., Oishi, S., Shimin, C., Duan, D., Lan, X., & Kitayama, S. (2014). Large-scale psychological differences within China explained by rice versus wheat agriculture. *Science, 344,* 603–608.

Talvitie, E., Hintsanen, M., Pulkki-Råback, L., Lipsanen, J., Merjonen, P., Hakulinen, C., Elovainio, M., Rosenström, T., Lehtimäki, T., Raitakari, O., & Keltikangas-Järvinen, L. (2019). Adverse childhood environment and self-reported sleep in adulthood: The Young Finns Study. *Health Psychology, 38,* 705–715.

Talwar, S. K., Xu, S., Hawley, E. S., Weiss, S. A., Moxon, K. A., & Chapin, J. K. (2002). Rat navigation guided by remote control. *Nature, 417,* 37–38.

Tam, T. (2018). *The Chief Public Health Officer's report on the state of public health in Canada 2018: Preventing problematic substance use in youth.* Public Health Agency of Canada. https://www.canada.ca/en/public-health/corporate/publications/chief-public-health-officer-reports-state-public-health-canada/2018-preventing-problematic-substance-use-youth.html

Tamminen, J., & Mebude, M. (2019). Reinstatement of odour context cues veridical memories but not false memories. *Memory, 27,* 575–579.

Tamres, L. K., Janicki, D., & Helgeson, V. S. (2002). Sex differences in coping behavior: A meta-analytic review and an examination of relative coping. *Personality and Social Psychology Review, 6,* 2–30.

Tan, Y., Singhal, S. M., Harden, S. W., Cahill, K. M., Nguyen, D. T. M., Colon-Perez, L. M., Sahagian, T. J., Thinschmidt, J. S., de Kloet, A. D., Febo, M., Frazier, C. J., & Krause, E. G. (2019). Oxytocin receptors are expressed by glutamatergic prefrontal cortical neurons that selectively modulate social recognition. *Journal of Neuroscience, 39,* 3249–3263.

Tang, S.-H., & Hall, V. C. (1995). The overjustification effect: A meta-analysis. *Applied Cognitive Psychology, 9,* 365–404.

Tangney, J. P., Baumeister, R. F., & Boone, A. L. (2004). High self-control predicts good adjustment, less pathology, better grades, and interpersonal success. *Journal of Personality, 72*(2), 271–324.

Tannen, D. (1990). *You just don't understand: Women and men in conversation.* Morrow.

Tannen, D. (2001). *You just don't understand: Women and men in conversation.* Harper.

Tanner, J. M. (1978). *Fetus into man: Physical growth from conception to maturity.* Harvard University Press.

Tardif, T., Fletcher, P., Liang, W., Zhang, Z., Kaciroti, N., & Marchman, V. A. (2008). Baby's first 10 words. *Developmental Psychology, 44,* 929–938.

Tarrant, M., Branscombe, N. R., Warner, R. H., & Weston, D. (2012). Social identity and perceptions of torture: It's moral when we do it. *Journal of Experimental Social Psychology, 48,* 513–518.

Tasbihsazan, R., Nettelbeck, T., & Kirby, N. (2003). Predictive validity of the Fagan test of infant intelligence. *British Journal of Developmental Psychology, 21,* 585–597.

Taub, E. (2004). Harnessing brain plasticity through behavioral techniques to produce new treatments in neurorehabilitation. *American Psychologist, 59,* 692–698.

Taubes, G. (2001). The soft science of dietary fat. *Science, 291,* 2536–2545.

Taubes, G. (2002, July 7). What if it's all been a big fat lie? *The New York Times.* https://www.nytimes.com/2002/07/07/magazine/what-if-it-s-all-been-a-big-fat-lie.html?

Tavernise, S. (2013, February 13). To reduce suicide rates, new focus turns to guns. *The New York Times.* https://www.nytimes.com/2013/02/14/us/to-lower-suicide-rates-new-focus-turns-to-guns.html

Tavernise, S. (2016, February 29). "Female Viagra" only modestly increases sexual satisfaction, study finds. *The New York Times.* https://www.nytimes.com/2016/03/01/health/female-viagra-addyi-flibanserin-sex-drive-women.html?

Tavris, C. (1982, November). Anger defused. *Psychology Today,* pp. 25–35.

Tavris, C., & Aronson, E. (2007). *Mistakes were made (but not by me).* Harcourt.

Tay, L., & Diener, E. (2011). Needs and subjective well-being around the world. *Journal of Personality and Social Psychology, 101,* 354–365.

Tay, R. Y. L., & Ng, B. C. (2019). Effects of affective priming through music on the use of emotion words. *PLOS ONE, 14,* e0214482.

Taylor, C. (2017). Creativity and mood disorder: A systematic review and meta-analysis. *Perspectives on Psychological Science, 12,* 1040–1076.

Taylor, K., & Rohrer, D. (2010). The effects of interleaved practice. *Applied Cognitive Psychology, 24,* 837–848.

Taylor, L. E., Swerdfeger, A. L., & Eslick, G. D. (2014). Vaccines are not associated with autism: An evidence-based meta-analysis of case-control and cohort studies. *Vaccine, 32,* 3623–3629.

Taylor, P. (2014). *The next America: Boomers, millennials, and the looming generational showdown.* Public Affairs.

Taylor, P. J., Gooding, P., Wood, A. M., & Tarrier, N. (2011). The role of defeat and entrapment in depression, anxiety, and suicide. *Psychological Bulletin, 137,* 391–420.

Taylor, P. J., Russ-Eft, D. F., & Chan, D. W. L. (2005). A meta-analytic review of behavior modeling training. *Journal of Applied Psychology, 90,* 692–709.

Taylor, R. J., & Garry, M. (2019). People infuse their passwords with autobiographical information. *Memory, 27,* 581–591.

Taylor, S. (2013). Molecular genetics of obsessive-compulsive disorder: A comprehensive meta-analysis of genetic association studies. *Molecular Psychiatry, 18,* 799–805. ok

Taylor, S. E. (2002). *The tending instinct: How nurturing is essential to who we are and how we live.* Times Books.

Taylor, S. E. (2006). Tend and befriend: Biobehavioral bases of affiliation under stress. *Current Directions in Psychological Science, 15,* 273–277.

Taylor, S. E., Pham, L. B., Rivkin, I. D., & Armor, D. A. (1998). Harnessing the imagination: Mental simulation, self-regulation, and coping. *American Psychologist, 53,* 429–439.

Taylor, S. P., & Chermack, S. T. (1993). Alcohol, drugs and human physical aggression. *Journal of Studies on Alcohol, Supplement 11,* 78–88.

Taylor-Covill, G. A., & Eves, F. F. (2016). Carrying a biological "backpack": Quasi-experimental effects of weight status and body fat change on perceived steepness. *Journal of Experimental Psychology: Human Perception and Performance, 42,* 331–338.

Teachman, B. A., McKay, D., Barch, D. M., Prinstein, M. J., Hollon, S. D., & Chambless, D. L. (2019). How psychosocial research can help the National Institute of Mental Health achieve its grand challenge to reduce the burden of mental illnesses and psychological disorders. *American Psychologist, 74,* 415–431.

Teasdale, T. W., & Owen, D. R. (2008). Secular declines in cognitive test scores: A reversal of the Flynn effect. *Intelligence, 36,* 121–126.

Tebbett-Mock, A. A., Saito, E., McGee, M., Woloszyn, P., & Venuti, M. (2019). Efficacy of dialectical behavior therapy versus treatment as usual for acute-care inpatient adolescents. *Journal of the American Academy of Child & Adolescent Psychiatry, 59,* 149–156.

Tedeschi, R. G., & Calhoun, L. G. (2004). Posttraumatic growth: Conceptual foundations and empirical evidence. *Psychological Inquiry, 15,* 1–18.

Teghtsoonian, R. (1971). On the exponents in Steven's law and the constant in Ekman's law. *Psychological Review, 78,* 71–80.

Teicher, M. H., & Samson, J. A. (2016). Annual research review: Enduring neurobiological effects of childhood abuse and neglect. *Journal of Child Psychology and Psychiatry, 57,* 241–266.

Teller. (2009, April 20). Quoted by J. Lehrer in *Magic and the brain: Teller reveals the neuroscience of illusion.* Wired Magazine. https://www.wired.com/2009/04/ff-neuroscienceofmagic/

Telzer, E. H., Flannery, J., Shapiro, M., Humphreys, K. L., Goff, B., Gabard-Durman, L., Gee, D. D., & Tottenham, N. (2013). Early experience shapes amygdala sensitivity to race: An international adoption design. *Journal of Neuroscience, 33,* 13484–13488.

ten Brinke, L., Vohs, K. D., & Carney, D. (2016). Can ordinary people detect deception after all? *Trends in Cognitive Sciences, 20,* 579–588.

Tenenbaum, H. R., & Leaper, C. (2002). Are parents' gender schemas related to their children's gender-related cognitions? A meta-analysis. *Developmental Psychology, 38,* 615–630.

Teng, Z., Nie, Q., Guo, C., Zhang, Q., Liu, Y., & Bushman, B. J. (2019). A longitudinal study of link between exposure to violent video games and aggression in Chinese adolescents: The mediating role of moral disengagement. *Developmental Psychology, 55,* 184–195.

Tenney, E. R., Logg, J. M., & Moore, D. A. (2015). (Too) optimistic about optimism: The belief that optimism improves performance. *Journal of Personality and Social Psychology, 108,* 377–399.

Tenopyr, M. L. (1997). Improving the workplace: Industrial/organizational psychology as a career. In R. J. Sternberg (Ed.), *Career paths in psychology: Where your degree can take you.* American Psychological Association.

Tepper, S. J. (2000). Fiction reading in America: Explaining the gender gap. *Poetics, 27,* 255–275.

Terada, S., Sakurai, Y., Nakahara, H., & Fujisawa, S. (2017). Temporal and rate coding for discrete event sequences in the hippocampus. *Neuron, 94,* 1248–1262.

Terao, T., Ohgami, H., Shlotsuki, I., Ishii, N., & Iwata, N. (2010). Author's reply. *British Journal of Psychiatry, 196,* 160.

Terman, L. (1930). *Autobiography of Lewis Terman.* In C. A. Murchison & E. G. Boring (Eds.) *A history of psychology in autobiography.* Clark University Press.

Terracciano, A., Costa, P. T., Jr., & McCrae, R. R. (2006). Personality plasticity after age 30. *Personality and Social Psychology Bulletin, 32,* 999–1009.

Terrace, H. S. (1979, November). How Nim Chimpsky changed my mind. *Psychology Today,* pp. 65–76.

Terre, L., & Stoddart, R. (2000). Cutting edge specialties for graduate study in psychology. *Eye on Psi Chi*, 23–26.

Terrell, J., Kofink, A., Middleton, J., Rainear, C., Murphy-Hill, E., Parnin, C., & Stallings, J. (2017). Gender differences and bias in open source: Pull request acceptance of women versus men. *PeerJ Computer Science, 3*, e111.

Tesser, A., Forehand, R., Brody, G., & Long, N. (1989). Conflict: The role of calm and angry parent-child discussion in adolescent development. *Journal of Social and Clinical Psychology, 8*, 317–330.

Testa, R. J., Michaels, M. S., Bliss, W., Rogers, M. L., Balsam, K. F., & Joiner, T. (2017). Suicidal ideation in transgender people: Gender minority stress and interpersonal factors. *Journal of Abnormal Psychology, 126*, 125–136.

Teter, C. J., DiRaimo, C. G., West, B. T., Schepis, T. S., & McCabe, S. E. (2018). Nonmedical use of prescription stimulants among U.S. high school students to help study: Results from a national survey. *Journal of Pharmacy Practice, 33*(1), 38–47.

Tetlock, P. E. (1988). Monitoring the integrative complexity of American and Soviet policy rhetoric: What can be learned? *Journal of Social Issues, 44*, 101–131.

Tetlock, P. E. (1998). Close-call counterfactuals and belief-system defenses: I was not almost wrong but I was almost right. *Journal of Personality and Social Psychology, 75*, 639–652.

Tetlock, P. E. (2005). *Expert political judgment: How good is it? How can we know?* Princeton University Press.

Tetlock, P. E., & Gardner, D. (2016). *Superforecasting: The art and science of prediction.* Broadway Books.

Thaler, L., Arnott, S. R., & Goodale, M. A. (2011). Neural correlates of natural human echolocation in early and late blind echolocation experts. *PLOS ONE, 6*, e20162.

Thaler, L., Milne, J. L., Arnott, S. R., Kish, D., & Goodale, M. A. (2014). Neural correlates of motion processing through echolocation, source hearing, and vision in blind echolocation experts and sighted echolocation novices. *Journal of Neurophysiology, 111*, 112–127.

Thaler, R. H. (2015, May 8). Unless you are Spock, irrelevant things matter in economic behavior. *The New York Times.* https://www.nytimes.com/2015/05/10/upshot/unless-you-are-spock-irrelevant-things-matter-in-economic-behavior.html?

Thaler, R. H., & Sunstein, C. R. (2008). *Nudge: Improving decisions about health, wealth, and happiness.* Yale University Press.

Thalmann, M., Souza, A. S., & Oberauer, K. (2019). How does chunking help working memory? *Journal of Experimental Psychology: Learning, Memory, and Cognition, 45*, 37–55.

Thalmayer, A. G., Saucier, G., Ole-Kotikash, L., & Payne, D. (2019). Personality structure in east and west Africa: Lexical studies of personality in Maa and Supyire-Senufo. *Journal of Personality and Social Psychology.* Advance online publication. doi: 10.1037/pspp0000264

Tharmaratnam, T., Iskandar, M. A., Tabobondung, T. C., Tobbia, I., Gopee-Ramanan, P., & Tabobondung, T. A. (2018). Chronic traumatic encephalopathy in professional American football players: Where are we now? *Frontiers in Neurology, 9*, 445.

Thatcher, R. W., Walker, R. A., & Giudice, S. (1987). Human cerebral hemispheres develop at different rates and ages. *Science, 236*, 1110–1113.

Thayer, R. E. (1987). Energy, tiredness, and tension effects of a sugar snack versus moderate exercise. *Journal of Personality and Social Psychology, 52*, 119–125.

Thayer, R. E. (1993). Mood and behavior (smoking and sugar snacking) following moderate exercise: A partial test of self-regulation theory. *Personality and Individual Differences, 14*, 97–104.

Théoret, H., Halligan, H., Kobayashi, M., Fregni, F., Tager-Flusberg, H., & Pascual-Leone, A. (2005). Impaired motor facilitation during action observation in individuals with autism spectrum disorder. *Current Biology, 15*, R84–R85.

Thibodeau, R., Jorgensen, R. S., & Kim, S. (2006). Depression, anxiety, and resting frontal EEG asymmetry: A meta-analytic review. *Journal of Abnormal Psychology, 115*, 715–729.

Thiebaut de Schotten, M., Dell'Acqua, F., Ratiu, P., Leslie, A., Howells, H., Cabanis, E., Iba-Zizen, M. T., Plaisant, O., Simmons, A., Dronkers, N. F., Corkin, S., & Catani, M. (2015). From Phineas Gage and Monsieur Leborgne to HM: Revisiting disconnection syndromes. *Cerebral Cortex, 25*, 4812–4827.

Thiel, A., Hadedank, B., Herholz, K., Kessler, J., Winhuisen, L., Haupt, W. F., & Heiss, W.-D. (2006). From the left to the right: How the brain compensates progressive loss of language function. *Brain and Language, 98*, 57–65.

Thomas, A., & Chess, S. (1986). The New York Longitudinal Study: From infancy to early adult life. In R. Plomin & J. Dunn (Eds.), *The study of temperament: Changes, continuities, and challenges.* Erlbaum.

Thomas, E. F., Zubielevitch, E., Sibley, C. G., & Osborne, D. (2019). Testing the social identity model of collective action longitudinally and across structurally disadvantaged and advantaged groups. *Personality and Social Psychology Bulletin.* Advance online publication. doi: 10.1177/0146167219879111

Thomas, L. (1974). *The lives of a cell.* Viking Press.

Thomas, L. (1992). *The fragile species.* Scribner's.

Thompson, G. (2010). The $1 million dollar challenge. *Skeptic Magazine, 15*, 8–9.

Thompson, J. K., Jarvie, G. J., Lahey, B. B., & Cureton, K. J. (1982). Exercise and obesity: Etiology, physiology, and intervention. *Psychological Bulletin, 91*, 55–79.

Thompson, P. M., Cannon, T. D., Narr, K. L., van Erp, T., Poutanen, V.-P., Huttunen, M., Lönnqvist, J., Standertskjöld-Nordenstam, C. G., Kaprio, J., Khaledy, M., Dail, R., Zoumalan, C. I., & Toga, A. W. (2001). Genetic influences on brain structure. *Nature Neuroscience, 4*, 1253–1258.

Thompson, P. M., Giedd, J. N., Woods, R. P., MacDonald, D., Evans, A. C., & Toga, A. W. (2000). Growth patterns in the developing brain detected by using continuum mechanical tensor maps. *Nature, 404*, 190–193.

Thompson, R., Emmorey, K., & Gollan, T. H. (2005). "Tip of the fingers" experiences by Deaf signers. *Psychological Science, 16*, 856–860.

Thompson-Hollands, J., Marx, B. P., Lee, D. J., Resick, P. A., & Sloan, D. M. (2018). Long-term treatment gains of a brief exposure-based treatment for PTSD. *Depression and Anxiety, 35*, 985–991.

Thompson-Schill, S. L., Ramscar, M., & Chrysikou, E. G. (2009). Cognition without control: When a little frontal lobe goes a long way. *Current Directions in Psychological Science, 18*, 259–263.

Thomson, K. S., & Oppenheimer, D. M. (2016). Investigating an alternate form of the cognitive reflection test. *Judgment and Decision Making, 11*, 99–113.

Thorarinsdottir, E. H., Bjornsdottir, E., Benediktsdottir, B., Janson, C., Gislason, T., Aspelund, T., Kuna, S. T., Pack, A. I., & Arnardottir, E. S. (2019). Definition of excessive daytime sleepiness in the general population: Feeling sleepy relates better to sleep-related symptoms and quality of life than the Epworth Sleepiness Scale score. Results from an epidemiological study. *Journal of Sleep Research, 28*, e12852.

Thorndike, E. L. (1898). Animal intelligence: An experimental study of the associative processes in animals. *Psychological Review Monograph Supplement, 2*, 4–160.

Thorne, J., with Larry Rothstein. (1993). *You are not alone: Words of experience and hope for the journey through depression.* Harper Perennial.

Thornicroft, G., Chatterji, S., Evans-Lacko, S., Gruber, M., Sampson, N., Aguilar-Gaxiola, S., Al-Hamzawi, A., Alonso, J., Andrade, L., Borges, G., Bruffaerts, R., Buntin, B., Caldas de Almeida, J. M., Florescu, S., de Girolamo, G., Gureje, O., Hara, J. M., He, Y., Hinkov, H., . . . Kessler, R. C. (2017). Undertreatment of people with major depressive disorder in 21 countries. *British Journal of Psychiatry, 210*, 119–124.

Thornton, A. (2019, February 8). *This is how many animals we eat each year.* World Economic Forum. https://www.weforum.org/agenda/2019/02/chart-of-the-day-this-is-how-many-animals-we-eat-each-year/

Thornton, B., & Moore, S. (1993). Physical attractiveness contrast effect: Implications for self-esteem and evaluations of the social self. *Personality and Social Psychology Bulletin, 19*, 474–480.

Thorpe, W. H. (1974). *Animal nature and human nature.* Metheun.

Tick, B., Bolton, P., Happé, F., Rutter, M., & Rijsdijk, F. (2016). Heritability of autism spectrum disorders: A meta-analysis of twin studies. *Journal of Child Psychology and Psychiatry, 57*, 585–595.

Tickle, J. J., Hull, J. G., Sargent, J. D., Dalton, M. A., & Heatherton, T. F. (2006). A structural equation model of social influences and exposure to media smoking on adolescent smoking. *Basic and Applied Social Psychology, 28*, 117–129.

Tiedens, L. Z. (2001). Anger and advancement versus sadness and subjugation: The effect of negative emotion expressions on social status conferral. *Journal of Personality and Social Psychology, 80*, 86–94.

Tielbeek, J. J., Johansson, A., Polderman, T. J., Rautiainen, M. R., Jansen, P., Taylor, M., Tong, X., Lu, Q., Burt, A. S., Tiemeier, H., Viding, E., Plomin, R., Martin, N. G., Heath, A. C., Madden, P. A. F., Montgomery, G., Beaver, K. M., Waldman, I., Gelernter, J., . . . Broad Antisocial Behavior Consortium collaborators. (2017). Genome-wide association studies of a broad spectrum of antisocial behavior. *JAMA Psychiatry, 74*, 1242–1250.

Tierney, J., & Baumeister, R. F. (2019). *The power of bad: How the negativity effect rules us and how we can rule it.* Penguin.

Tigbe, W. W., Granat, M. H., Sattar, N., & Lean, M. E. J. (2017). Time spent in sedentary posture is associated with waist circumference and cardiovascular risk. *International Journal of Obesity, 41*, 689–696.

Tiggemann, M., & Miller, J. (2010). The Internet and adolescent girls' weight satisfaction and drive for thinness. *Sex Roles, 63*, 79–90.

Tiihonen, J., Lönnqvist, J., Wahlbeck, K., Klaukka, T., Niskanen, L., Tanskanen, A., & Haukka, J. (2009). 11-year follow-up of mortality in patients with schizophrenia: A population-based cohort study (FIN11 study). *The Lancet, 374*, 260–267.

Tiihonen, J., Rautiainen, M. R., Ollila, H. M., Repo-Tiihonen, E., Virkkunen, M., Palotie, A., Pietiläinen, O., Kristiansson, K., Joukamaa, M., Lauerma, H., Saarela, J., Tyni, S., Vartiainen, H., Paananen, J., Goldman, D., & Paunio, T. (2015). Genetic background of extreme violent behavior. *Molecular Psychiatry, 20*, 786–792.

Timerman, J. (1980). *Prisoner without a name, cell without a number.* University of Wisconsin Press.

Timmerman, T. A. (2007). "It was a thought pitch": Personal, situational, and target influences on hit-by-pitch events across time. *Journal of Applied Psychology, 92*, 876–884.

Timmermann, C., Spriggs, M. J., Kaelen, M., Leech, R., Nutt, D. J., Moran, R. J., Carhart-Harris, R. L., & Muthukumaraswamy, S. D. (2018). LSD modulates effective connectivity and neural adaptation mechanisms in an auditory oddball paradigm. *Neuropharmacology, 142*, 251–262.

Tinbergen, N. (1951). *The study of instinct.* Clarendon.

Tirrell, M. E. (1990). Personal communication.

Tobin, D. D., Menon, M., Menon, M., Spatta, B. C., Hodges, E. V. E., & Perry, D. G. (2010). The intrapsychics of gender: A model of self-socialization. *Psychological Review, 117*, 601–622

Todd, R. M., MacDonald, M. J., Sedge, P., Robertson, A., Jetly, R., Taylor, M. J., & Pang, E. W. (2015). Soldiers with posttraumatic stress disorder see a world full of threat: Magnetoencephalography reveals enhanced tuning to combat-related cues. *Biological Psychiatry, 78*, 821–829.

Todes, D. P. (2014). *Ivan Pavlov: A Russian life in science.* Oxford University Press.

Toews, P. (2004, December 30). *Dirk Willems: A heart undivided.* Mennonite Brethren Historical Commission. https://mbhistory.org/profiles/dirk/

Tolin, D. F. (2010). Is cognitive-behavioral therapy more effective than other therapies? A meta-analytic review. *Clinical Psychology Review, 30*, 710–720.

Tolin, D. F., Wootton, B. M., Levy, H. C., Hallion, L. S., Worden, B. L., Diefenbach, G. J., Jaccard, J., & Stevens, M. C. (2019). Efficacy and mediators of a group cognitive–behavioral therapy for hoarding disorder: A randomized trial. *Journal of Consulting and Clinical Psychology, 87*, 590–602.

Tolman, E. C., & Honzik, C. H. (1930). Introduction and removal of reward, and maze performance in rats. *University of California Publications in Psychology, 4*, 257–275.

Tolstoy, L. (1904). *My confessions.* Dana Estes.

Toma, C., & Hancock, J. (2013). Self-affirmation underlies Facebook use. *Personality and Social Psychology Bulletin, 369*, 321–331.

Tomaka, J., Blascovich, J., & Kelsey, R. M. (1992). Effects of self-deception, social desirability, and repressive coping on psychophysiological reactivity to stress. *Personality and Social Psychology Bulletin, 18*, 616–624.

Tomasello, M. (2019). *Becoming human.* Belknap Press.

Tomasello, M. (2019). The moral psychology of obligation. *Behavioral and Brain Sciences*, 1–33.

Tomita, K. K., Testa, R. J., & Balsam, K. F. (2018). Gender-affirming medical interventions and mental health in transgender adults. *Psychology of Sexual Orientation and Gender Diversity, 6*, 182–193.

Tompkins, D. A., Hobelmann, J. G., & Compton, P. (2017). Providing chronic pain management in the "Fifth Vital Sign" Era: Historical and treatment perspectives on a modern-day medical dilemma. *Drug and Alcohol Dependence, 173*, S11–S21.

Toni, N., Buchs, P.-A., Nikonenko, I., Bron, C. R., & Muller, D. (1999). LTP promotes formation of multiple spine synapses between a single axon terminal and a dendrite. *Nature, 402*, 421–442.

Topolinski, S., & Reber, R. (2010). Gaining insight into the "aha" experience. *Current Directions in Psychological Science, 19*, 401–405.

Torrey, E. F. (1986). *Witchdoctors and psychiatrists.* Harper & Row.

Torrey, E. F., & Miller, J. (2002). *The invisible plague: The rise of mental illness from 1750 to the present.* Rutgers University Press.

Torrey, E. F., Miller, J., Rawlings, R., & Yolken, R. H. (1997). Seasonality of births in schizophrenia and bipolar disorder: A review of the literature. *Schizophrenia Research, 28*, 1–38.

Toschi, N., Riccelli, R., Indovina, I., Terracciano, A., & Passamonti, L. (2018). Functional connectome of the five-factor model of personality. *Personality Neuroscience, 1*, e2.

Totterdell, P., Kellett, S., Briner, R. B., & Teuchmann, K. (1998). Evidence of mood linkage in work groups. *Journal of Personality and Social Psychology, 74*, 1504–1515.

Towers, S., Gomez-Lievano, A., Khan, M., Mubayi, A., & Castillo-Chavez, C. (2015) Contagion in mass killings and school shootings. *PLOS ONE, 10*, e0117259.

Townsend, S. S. M., Stephens, N. M., Smallets, S., & Hamedani, M. G. (2019). Empowerment through difference: An online difference-education intervention closes the social class achievement gap. *Personality and Social Psychology Bulletin, 45*(7), 1068–1083.

Tracy, J. L., Cheng, J. T., Robins, R. W., & Trzesniewski, K. H. (2009). Authentic and hubristic pride: The affective core of self-esteem and narcissism. *Self and Identity, 8*, 196–213.

Tracy, J. L., & Robins, R. W. (2004). Show your pride: Evidence for a discrete emotion expression. *Psychological Science, 15*, 194–197.

Tracy, J. L., Shariff, A. F., Zhao, W., & Henrich, J. (2013). Cross-cultural evidence that the nonverbal expression of pride is an automatic status signal. *Journal of Experimental Psychology: General, 142*, 163–180.

Traffanstedt, M. K., Mehta, S., & LoBello, S. G. (2016). Major depression with seasonal variation: Is it a valid construct? *Clinical Psychological Science, 4*, 825–834.

Trahan, L. H., Stuebing, K. K., Fletcher, J. M., & Hiscock, M. (2014). The Flynn effect: A meta-analysis. *Psychological Bulletin, 140*, 1332–1360.

Tran, U. S., Hofer, A. A., & Voracek, M. (2014). Sex differences in general knowledge: Meta-analysis and new data on the contribution of school-related moderators among high-school students. *PLOS ONE, 9*, e110391.

Trautwein, U., Lüdtke, O., Köller, O., & Baumert, J. (2006). Self-esteem, academic self-concept, and achievement: How the learning environment moderates the dynamics of self-concept. *Journal of Personality and Social Psychology, 90*, 334–349.

Treanor, M., Brown, L. A., Rissman, J., & Craske, M. G. (2017). Can memories of traumatic experiences or addiction be erased or modified? A critical review of research on the disruption of memory reconsolidation and its applications. *Perspectives on Psychological Science, 12*, 290–305.

Treffert, D. A. (2010). *Islands of genius: The beautiful mind of the autistic, acquired, and sudden savant.* Jessica Kinsley.

Treffert, D. A., & Christensen, D. D. (2005, December). Inside the mind of a savant. *Scientific American*, pp. 108–113.

Treisman, A. (1987). Properties, parts, and objects. In K. R. Boff, L. Kaufman, & J. P. Thomas (Eds.), *Handbook of perception and human performance* (pp. 159–198). Wiley.

Tremblay, P., & Dick, A. S. (2016). Broca and Wernicke are dead, or moving past the classic model of language neurobiology. *Brain and Language, 162*, 60–71.

Tremblay, R. E., Pihl, R. O., Vitaro, F., & Dobkin, P. L. (1994). Predicting early onset of male antisocial behavior from preschool behavior. *Archives of General Psychiatry, 51*, 732–739.

Tremblay, R. E., Vitaro, F., & Côté, S. M. (2018). Developmental origins of chronic physical aggression: A bio-psycho-social model for the next generation of preventive interventions. *Annual Review of Psychology, 69*, 383–407.

Triandis, H. C. (1981). *Some dimensions of intercultural variation and their implications for interpersonal behavior.* Paper presented at the American Psychological Association convention.

Triandis, H. C. (1994). *Culture and social behavior.* McGraw-Hill.

Trickett, E. (2009). Community psychology: Individuals and interventions in community context. *Annual Review of Psychology, 60*, 395–419.

Trillin, C. (2006, March 27). Alice off the page. *The New Yorker*, p. 44.

Trimmer, C., Keller, A., Murphy, N. R., Snyder, L. L., Willer, J. R., Nagai, M. H., Katsanis, N., Vosshall, L. B., Matsunami, H., & Mainland, J. D. (2019). Genetic variation across the human olfactory receptor repertoire alters odor perception. *PNAS, 116*, 9475–9480.

Triplett, N. (1898). The dynamogenic factors in pacemaking and competition. *American Journal of Psychology, 9*, 507–533.

Troeger, C., Khalil, I., Rao, P. C., Cao, S., Blacker, B. F., Ahmed, T., Armah, G., Bines, J. E., Brewer, T. G., Colombara, D. V., Kang, G., Kirkpatrick, B. D., Kirkwood, C. D., Mwenda, J. M., Parashar, U. D., Petri, W. A., Jr., Riddle, M. S., Steele, A. D., Thompson, R. L., . . . Reiner, R. C., Jr. (2018, October). Rotavirus vaccination and the global burden of rotavirus diarrhea among children younger than 5 years. *JAMA Pediatrics, 172*, 958–965.

Tropp, L. R., & Barlow, F. K. (2018). Making advantaged racial groups care about inequality: Intergroup contact as a route to psychological investment. *Current Directions in Psychological Science, 27*, 194–199.

Trotter, J. (2014). The power of positive coaching. *Sports Illustrated.* https://www.si.com/nfl/2014/01/23/power-positive-coaching

Troy, A. S., Shallcross, A. J., Brunner, A., Friedman, R., & Jones, M. C. (2018). Cognitive reappraisal and acceptance: Effects on emotion, physiology, and perceived cognitive costs. *Emotion, 18*, 58–74.

Trumbo, M. C., Leiting, K. A., McDaniel, M. A., & Hodge, G. K. (2016). Effects of reinforcement on test-enhanced learning in a large, diverse introductory college psychology course. *Journal of Experimental Psychology: Applied, 22*, 148–160.

Trut, L. N. (1999). Early canid domestication: The farm-fox experiment. *American Scientist, 87*, 160–169.

Tsai, J. L., Ang, J. Y. Z., Blevins, E., Goernandt, J., Fung, H. H., Jiang, D., Elliott, J., Kölzer, A., Uchida, Y., Lee, Y. C., Lin, Y., Zhang, X., Govindama, Y., & Haddouk, L. (2016). Leaders' smiles reflect cultural differences in ideal affect. *Emotion, 16*, 183–195.

Tsai, J. L., & Chentsova-Dutton, Y. (2003). Variation among European Americans in emotional facial expression. *Journal of Cross-Cultural Psychology, 34*, 650–657.

Tsai, J. L., Knutson, B., & Fung, H. H. (2006). Cultural variation in affect valuation. *Journal of Personality and Social Psychology, 90*, 288–307.

Tsang, Y. C. (1938). Hunger motivation in gastrectomized rats. *Journal of Comparative Psychology, 26*, 1–17.

Tsao, D. Y. (2019, February). Face values. *Scientific American*, pp. 23–29.

Tskhay, K. O., Zhu, R., Zou, C., & Rule, N. O. (2018). Charisma in everyday life: Conceptualization and validation of the General Charisma Inventory. *Journal of Personality and Social Psychology, 114*, 131–152.

Tsui, A. S. M., Byers-Heinlein, K., & Fennell, C. T. (2019). Associative word learning in infancy: A meta-analysis of the switch task. *Developmental Psychology, 55*, 934–950.

Tsvetkova, M., & Macy, M. W. (2014). The social contagion of generosity. *PLOS ONE, 9*(2), e87275.

Tuber, D. S., Miller, D. D., Caris, K. A., Halter, R., Linden, F., & Hennessy, M. B. (1999). Dogs in animal shelters: Problems, suggestions, and needed expertise. *Psychological Science, 10*, 379–386.

Tucker, R. P. (2019). Suicide in transgender veterans: Prevalence, prevention, and implications of current policy. *Perspectives on Psychological Science, 14*, 452–468.

Tucker-Drob, E. (2012). Preschools reduce early academic-achievement gaps: A longitudinal twin approach. *Psychological Science, 23*, 310–319.

Tucker-Drob, E., & Briley, D. A. (2014). Continuity of genetic and environmental influences on cognition across the life span: A meta-analysis of longitudinal twin and adoption studies. *Psychological Bulletin, 140*, 949–979.

Tucker-Drob, E., Brandmaier, A. M., & Lindenberger, U. (2019). Coupled cognitive changes in adulthood: A meta-analysis. *Psychological Bulletin, 145*, 273–301.

Tucker-Drob, E. M., & Bates, T. C. (2016). Large cross-national differences in gene x socioeconomic status interaction on intelligence. *Psychological Science, 27*, 138–149.

Tuerk, P. W. (2005). Research in the high-stakes era: Achievement, resources, and No Child Left Behind. *Psychological Science, 16*, 419–425.

Tuk, M. A., Zhang, K., & Sweldens, S. (2015). The propagation of self-control: Self-control in one domain simultaneously improves self-control in other domains. *Journal of Experimental Psychology: General, 144*, 639–654.

Tullett, A. M., Kay, A. C., & Inzlicht, M. (2015). Randomness increases self-reported anxiety and neurophysiological correlates of performance monitoring. *Social Cognitive and Affective Neuroscience, 10*, 628–635.

Tully, T. (2003). Reply: The myth of a myth. *Current Biology, 13*, R426.

Turban, J. L., Beckwith, N., Reisner, S. L., & Keuroghlian, A. S. (2020). Association between recalled exposure to gender identity conversion efforts and psychological distress and suicide attempts among transgender adults. *JAMA Psychiatry, 77*, 68–76.

Turkheimer, E., Pettersson, E., & Horn, E. E. (2014). A phenotypic null hypothesis for the genetics of personality. *Annual Review of Psychology, 65*, 515–540.

Turner, B. L., Caruso, E. M., Dilich, M. A., & Roese, N. J. (2019). Body camera footage leads to lower judgments of intent than dash camera footage. *PNAS, 116*, 1201–1206.

Turner, N., Barling, J., & Zacharatos, A. (2002). Positive psychology at work. In C. R. Snyder & S. J. Lopez (Eds.), *The handbook of positive psychology*. Oxford University Press.

Turpin, A. (2005, April 3). The science of psi. *FT Weekend*, pp. W1, W2.

Tversky, A. (1985, June). Quoted in K. McKean, Decisions, decisions. *Discover*, pp. 22–31.

Tversky, A., & Kahneman, D. (1974). Judgment under uncertainty: Heuristics and biases. *Science, 185*, 1124–1131.

Twenge, J. M. (2006). *Generation me*. Free Press.

Twenge, J. M. (2017). *iGen: Why today's superconnected kids are growing up less rebellious, more tolerant, less happy — and completely unprepared for adulthood—and what that means for the rest of us*. Atria Books.

Twenge, J. M., Abebe, E. M., & Campbell, W. K. (2010a). Fitting in or standing out: Trends in American parents' choices for children's names, 1880–2007. *Social Psychology and Personality Science, 1*, 19–25.

Twenge, J. M., Baumeister, R. F., Tice, D. M., & Stucke, T. S. (2001). If you can't join them, beat them: Effects of social exclusion on aggressive behavior. *Journal of Personality and Social Psychology, 81*, 1058–1069.

Twenge, J. M., & Campbell, W. K. (2008). Increases in positive self-views among high school students: Birth-cohort changes in anticipated performance, self-satisfaction, self-liking, and self-competence. *Psychological Science, 19*, 1082–1086.

Twenge, J. M., & Campbell, W. K. (2019). Media use is linked to lower psychological well-being: Evidence from three datasets. *Psychiatric Quarterly, 90*, 311–331.

Twenge, J. M., Dawson, L., & Campbell, W. K. (2016a). Still standing out: Children's names in the United States during the Great Recession and correlations with economic indicators. *Journal of Applied Social Psychology, 46*, 663–670.

Twenge, J. M., & Foster, J. D. (2010). Birth cohort increases in narcissistic personality traits among American college students, 1982–2009. *Social Psychological and Personality Science, 1*, 99–106.

Twenge, J. M., Gentile, B., DeWall, C. N., Ma, D., Lacefield, K., & Schurtz, D. R. (2010b). Birth cohort increases in psychopathology among young Americans, 1938–2007: A cross-temporal meta-analysis of the MMPI. *Clinical Psychology Review, 30*, 145–154.

Twenge, J. M., Martin, G. N., & Spitzberg, B. H. (2019). Trends in U.S. adolescents' media use, 1976–2016: The rise of digital media, the decline of TV, and the (near) demise of print. *Psychology of Popular Media Culture, 8*, 329–345.

Twenge, J. M., & Park, H. (2019). The decline in adult activities among U.S. adolescents, 1976–2016. *Child Development, 90*, 638–654.

Twenge, J. M., Sherman, R. A., & Wells, B. E. (2017). Declines in sexual frequency among American adults, 1989–2014. *Archives of Sexual Behavior, 46*, 2389–2401.

Twenge, J. M., Zhang, L., & Im, C. (2004). It's beyond my control: A cross-temporal meta-analysis of increasing externality in locus of control, 1960–2002. *Personality and Social Psychology Review, 8*, 308–319.

Twiss, C., Tabb, S., & Crosby, F. (1989). Affirmative action and aggregate data: The importance of patterns in the perception of discrimination. In F. Blanchard & F. Crosby (Eds.), *Affirmative action: Social psychological perspectives*. Springer-Verlag.

Úbeda, Y., Ortín, S., St. Leger, J., Llorente, M., & Almunia, J. (2018). Personality in captive killer whales (Orcinus orca): A rating approach based on the five-factor model. *Journal of Comparative Psychology, 133*, 252–261.

Uchida, Y., & Kitayama, S. (2009). Happiness and unhappiness in East and West: Themes and variations. *Emotion, 9*, 441–456.

Uchida, Y., Kitayama, S., Akutsu, S., Park, J., & Cole, S. W. (2018). Optimism and the conserved transcriptional response to adversity. *Health Psychology, 37*, 1077–1080.

Uchino, B. N., & Way, B. M. (2017). Integrative pathways linking close family ties to health: A neurochemical perspective. *American Psychologist, 72*, 590–600.

Udo, T., & Grilo, C. M. (2019). Psychiatric and medical correlates of DSM-5 eating disorders in a nationally representative sample of adults in the United States. *International Journal of Eating Disorders, 52*, 42–50.

Udry, J. R. (2000). Biological limits of gender construction. *American Sociological Review, 65*, 443–457.

Uga, V., Lemut, M. C., Zampi, C., Zilli, I., & Salzarulo, P. (2006). Music in dreams. *Consciousness and Cognition, 15*, 351–357.

Uhlhaas, P. J., Grent-Jong, T., & Gross, J. (2018). Magnetoencephalography and translational neuroscience in psychiatry. *JAMA Psychiatry, 75*, 969–971.

Ullén, F., Hambrick, D. Z., & Mosing, M. A. (2016). Rethinking expertise: A multifactorial gene-environment interaction model of expert performance. *Psychological Bulletin, 142*, 427–446.

Ullsperger, J. M., & Nikolas, M. A. (2017). A meta-analytic review of the association between pubertal timing and psychopathology in adolescence: Are there sex differences in risk? *Psychological Bulletin, 143*, 903–938.

Ulrich, R. E. (1991). Animal rights, animal wrongs and the question of balance. *Psychological Science, 2*, 197–201.

UN. (2015). *The world's women: Trends and statistics* [PDF file]. United Nations Department of Economic and Social Affairs. https://unstats.un.org/unsd/gender/downloads/worldswomen2015_report.pdf

UNAIDS. (2013, accessed May 17). *Data and analysis*. Joint United Nations Programme on HIV/AIDS. https://www.unaids.org/en/data-analysis

Underwood, E. (2016). Cadaver study challenges brain stimulation methods. *Science, 352*, 397.

UNESCO. (2017). *Women in science* [PDF file]. http://uis.unesco.org/sites/default/files/documents/fs43-women-in-science-2017-en.pdf

UNFPA. (2016). *Changing attitudes towards gender equality: Update from the World Values Survey*. United Nations Population Fund (unstats.un.org).

Ungar, L. (2014). Quiz: How long will you live? *Time Magazine*. https://bit.ly/2tnbjdQ

Ungerleider, S. (2005). *Mental training for peak performance, revised & updated edition*. Rodale.

UNICEF. (2014). *Hidden in plain sight: A statistical analysis of violence against children*. UNICEF.

United Nations. (2017). *World population prospects: The 2017 revision* [PDF file]. United Nations Division of Economic and Social Affairs. https://population.un.org/wpp/Publications/Files/WPP2017_Data Booklet.pdf

Unsworth, N., & Engle, R. W. (2007). The nature of individual differences in working memory capacity: Active maintenance in primary memory and controlled search from secondary memory. *Psychological Review, 114*, 104–132.

Urbain, C., De Tiège, X., De Beeck, M. O., Bourguignon, M., Wens, V., Verheulpen, D., Van Bogaert, P., & Peigneux, P. (2016). Sleep in children triggers rapid reorganization of memory-related brain processes. *NeuroImage, 134*, 213–222.

Urcelay, G. P., & Jonkman, S. (2019). Delayed rewards facilitate habit formation. *Journal of Experimental Psychology: Animal Learning and Cognition, 45*(4), 413–421.

Urquhart, J. A., Sivakumaran, M. H., Macfarlane, J. A., & O'Connor, A. R. (2018). fMRI evidence supporting the role of memory conflict in the déjà vu experience. *Memory, 20*, 1–12.

Urry, H. L., & Gross, J. J. (2010). Emotion regulation in older age. *Current Directions in Psychological Science, 19*, 352–357.

Urry, H. L., Nitschke, J. B., Dolski, I., Jackson, D. C., Dalton, K. M., Mueller, C. J., Rosenkranz, M. A., Ryff, C. D., Singer, B. H., & Davidson, R. J. (2004). Making a life worth living: Neural correlates of well-being. *Psychological Science, 15*, 367–372.

U.S. Senate Intelligence Committee. (2004, July 9). *Report of the Select Committee on Intelligence on the U.S. intelligence community's prewar intelligence assessments on Iraq*. Washington, DC: Author.

U.S.D.O.J. (United States Department of Justice). (2018). *Sexual assault*. Office on Violence Against Women. https://www.justice.gov/ovw/sexual-assault

U.S.E.E.O.C. (Equal Employment Opportunity Commission). (2018). *Sexual harassment*. https://www.eeoc.gov/laws/types/sexual_harassment.cfm

Uskul, A. K., & Over, H. (2017). Culture, social interdependence, and ostracism. *Current Directions in Psychological Science, 26*, 371–376.

Uttal, W. R. (2001). *The new phrenology: The limits of localizing cognitive processes in the brain*. MIT Press.

Uy, J. P., Goldenberg, D., Tashjian, S. M., Do, K. T., & Galván, A. (2019). Physical home environment is associated with prefrontal cortical thickness in adolescents. *Developmental Science*, e12834.

Vaci, N., Edelsbrunner, P., Stern, E., Neubauer, A., Bilalić, M., & Grabner, R. H. (2019). The joint influence of intelligence and practice on skill development throughout the life span. *PNAS, 116*, 18363–18369.

Vaillant, G. (2013, May). What makes us happy, revisited. *The Atlantic*. https://www.theatlantic.com/magazine/archive/2013/05/thanks-mom/309287/

Vaillant, G. E. (1977). *Adaptation to life*. Little, Brown.

Vaillant, G. E. (2002). *Aging well: Surprising guideposts to a happier life from the landmark Harvard study of adult development*. Little, Brown.

Valenstein, E. S. (1986). *Great and desperate cures: The rise and decline of psychosurgery*. Basic Books.

Valentine, S. E., & Shipherd, J. C. (2018). A systematic review of social stress and mental health among transgender and gender non-conforming people in the United States. *Clinical Psychology Review, 66*, 24–38.

Valenza, E. Simion, F., Cassia, V. M., & Umiltà, C. (1996). Face preference at birth. *Journal of Experimental Psychology: Human Perception and Performance, 22*, 892–903.

Valkenburg, P. M., & Peter, J. (2009). Social consequences of the Internet for adolescents: A decade of research. *Current Directions in Psychological Science, 18*, 1–5.

van Anders, S. M. (2012). Testosterone and sexual desire in healthy women and men. *Archives of Sexual Behavior, 41*, 1471–1484.

Van Bavel, J. J., Baicker, K., Boggio, P., Capraro, V., Chichocka, A., Crockett, M., Cikara, M., Crum, A., Douglas, K., Druckman, J., Drury, J., Dube, O., Ellemers, N., Finkel, E. J., Fowler, J. H., Gelfand, M., Han, S., Haslam, S., Jetten, J., . . . Willer, R. (2020). Using social and behavioural science to support COVID-19 pandemic response. In press. https://doi.org/10.31234/osf.io/y38m9

van Beijsterveldt, C. E. M., Overbeek, L. I. H., Rozendaal, L., McMaster, M. T. B., Glasner, T. J., Bartels, M., Vink, M. J., Martin, N. G., Dolan, C. V., & Boomsma, D. I. (2016). Chorionicity and heritability estimates from twin studies: The prenatal environment of twins and their resemblance across a large number of traits. *Behavior Genetics, 46*, 304–314.

Van Blerkom, D. L. (2012). *Orientation to learning* (7th ed.). Wadsworth.

Van Bockstaele, B., Verschuere, B., Tibboel, H., De Houwer, J., Crombez, G., & Koster, E. H. W. (2014). A review of current evidence for the causal impact of attentional bias on fear and anxiety. *Psychological Bulletin, 140*, 682–721.

Van Boven, L., Ramos, J., Montal-Rosenberg, R., Kogut, T., Sherman, D. K., & Slovic, P. (2019). It depends: Partisan evaluation of conditional probability importance. *Cognition, 188*, 51–63.

Van Dam, N. T., van Vugt, M. K., Vago, D. R., Schmalzl, L., Saron, C. D., Olendzki, A., Meissner, T., Lazar, S.

W., Kerr, C. E., Gorchov, J., Fox, K. C. R., Field, B. A., Britton, W. B., Brefczynski-Lewis, J. A., & Meyer, D. E. (2018). Mind the hype: A critical evaluation and prescriptive agenda for research on mindfulness and meditation. *Perspectives on Psychological Science, 13*, 36–61.

van de Bongardt, D., Reitz, E., Sandfort, T., & Deković, M. (2015). A meta-analysis of the relations between three types of peer norms and adolescent sexual behavior. *Personality and Social Psychology Review, 19*, 203–234.

van de Waal, E., Borgeaud, C., & Whiten, A. (2013). Potent social learning and conformity shape a wild primate's foraging decisions. *Science, 340*, 483–485.

Van den Akker, A. L., Asscher, J., & Prinzie, P. (2014). Mean-level personality development across childhood and adolescence: A temporary defiance of the maturity principle and bidirectional associations with parenting. *Journal of Personality and Social Psychology, 107*, 736–750.

van den Berg, S. M., de Moor, M. H., Verweij, K. J., Krueger, R. F., Luciano, M., Vasquez, A. A., Matteson, L. K., Derringer, J., Esko, T., Amin, N., Gordon, S. D., Hansell, N. K., Hart, A. B., Seppälä, I., Huffman, J. E., Konte, B., Lahti, J., Lee, M., Miller, M., . . . Boomsma, D. I. (2016). Meta-analysis of genome-wide association studies for extraversion: Findings from the Genetics of Personality Consortium. *Behavior Genetics, 46*, 170–182.

van den Boom, D. C. (1994). The influence of temperament and mothering on attachment and exploration: An experimental manipulation of sensitive responsiveness among lower-class mothers with irritable infants. *Child Development, 65*, 1457–1477.

van den Bos, K., & Spruijt, N. (2002). Appropriateness of decisions as a moderator of the psychology of voice. *European Journal of Social Psychology, 32*, 57–72.

Van den Broeck, A., Ferris, D. L., Chang, C. H., & Rosen, C. C. (2016). A review of self-determination theory's basic psychological needs at work. *Journal of Management, 42*, 1195–1229.

Van den Bulck, J., Çetin, Y., Terzi, Ö., & Bushman, B. J. (2016). Violence, sex, and dreams: Violent and sexual media content infiltrate our dreams at night. *Dreaming, 26*, 271–279.

van der Linden, S. L., Leiserowitz, A. A., Feinberg, G. D., & Maibach, E. W. (2015). The scientific consensus on climate change as a gateway belief: Experimental evidence. *PLOS ONE, 10*, e0118489.

Van Dessel, P., Mertens, G., Smith, C. T., & De Houwer, J. (2019). Mere exposure effects on implicit stimulus evaluation: The moderating role of evaluation task, number of stimulus presentations, and memory for presentation frequency. *Personality and Social Psychology Bulletin, 45*, 447–460.

van Dijk, W. W., Van Koningsbruggen, G. M., Ouwerkerk, J. W., & Wesseling, Y. M. (2011). Self-esteem, self-affirmation, and schadenfreude. *Emotion, 11*, 1445–1449.

Van Dyke, C., & Byck, R. (1982, March). Cocaine. *Scientific American*, pp. 128–141.

van Egmond, L., Ekman, M., & Benedict, C. (2019). Bed and rise times during the Age of Enlightenment: A case report. *Journal of Sleep Research, 28*, e12862.

van Emmerik, A. A. P., Reijntjes, A., & Kamphuis, J. H. (2013). Writing therapy for posttraumatic stress: A meta-analysis. *Psychotherapy and Psychosomatics, 82*, 82–88.

van Engen, M. L., & Willemsen, T. M. (2004). Sex and leadership styles: A meta-analysis of research published in the 1990s. *Psychological Reports, 94*, 3–18.

van Geel, M., Goemans, A., & Vedder, P. (2015). A meta-analysis on the relation between peer victimization and adolescent non-suicidal self-injury. *Psychiatry Research, 230*, 364–368.

van Gelderen, M., Kautonen, T., Wincent, J., & Biniari, M. (2018). Implementation intentions in the entrepreneurial process: Concept, empirical findings, and research agenda. *Small Business Economics, 51*, 923–941.

van Haren, N. E., Rijsdijk, F., Schnack, H. G., Picchioni, M. M., Toulopoulou, T., Weisbrod, M., Sauer, H., van Erp, T. G., Cannon, T. D., Huttunen, M. O., Boomsma, D. I., Hulshoff Pol, H. E., Murray, R. M., & Kahn, R. S. (2012). The genetic and environmental determinants of the association between brain abnormalities and schizophrenia: The schizophrenia twins and relatives consortium. *Biological Psychiatry, 71*, 915–921.

van Haren, N. E., Schnack, H. G., Koevoets, M. G., Cahn, W., Pol, H. E. H., & Kahn, R. S. (2016). Trajectories of subcortical volume change in schizophrenia: A 5-year follow-up. *Schizophrenia Research, 173*, 140–145.

van Hemert, D. A., Poortinga, Y. H., & van de Vijver, F. J. R. (2007). Emotion and culture: A meta-analysis. *Cognition and Emotion, 21*, 913–943.

van Honk, J., Schutter, D. J., Bos, P. A., Kruijt, A.-W., Lentje, E. G., & Baron-Cohen, S. (2011). Testosterone administration impairs cognitive empathy in women depending on second-to-fourth digit ratio. *PNAS, 108*, 3448–3452.

Van Horn, J., Irimia, A., Torgerson, C., Chambers, M., Kikinis, R., & Toga, A. (2012). Mapping connectivity damage in the case of Phineas Gage. *PLOS ONE, 7*, e37454.

van IJzendoorn, M., Fearon, P., & Bakermans-Kranenburg, M. (2017). Attachment—public and scientific. *The Psychologist, 30*, 6–9.

van IJzendoorn, M. H., & Juffer, F. (2006). The Emanuel Miller Memorial Lecture 2006: Adoption as intervention. Meta-analytic evidence for massive catch-up and plasticity in physical, socioemotional, and cognitive development. *Journal of Child Psychology and Psychiatry, 47*, 1228–1245.

van IJzendoorn, M. H., Juffer, F., & Poelhuis, C. W. K. (2005). Adoption and cognitive development: A meta-analytic comparison of adopted and nonadopted children's IQ and school performance. *Psychological Bulletin, 131*, 301–316.

van IJzendoorn, M. H., & Kroonenberg, P. M. (1988). Cross-cultural patterns of attachment: A meta-analysis of the strange situation. *Child Development, 59*, 147–156.

van IJzendoorn, M. H., Luijk, M. P. C. M., & Juffer, F. (2008). IQ of children growing up in children's homes: A meta-analysis on IQ delays in orphanages. *Merrill-Palmer Quarterly, 54*, 341–366.

Van Kesteren, P. J. M., Asscheman, H., Megens, J. A. J., & Gooren, J. G. (1997). Mortality and morbidity in transsexual subjects treated with cross-sex hormones. *Clinical Endocrinology, 47*, 337–342.

Van Leeuwen, M. S. (1978). A cross-cultural examination of psychological differentiation in males and females. *International Journal of Psychology, 13*, 87–122.

Van Munster, C. E., Jonkman, L. E., Weinstein, H. C., Uitdehaag, B. M., & Geurts, J. J. (2015). Gray matter damage in multiple sclerosis: Impact on clinical symptoms. *Neuroscience, 303*, 446–461.

van Praag, H. (2009). Exercise and the brain: Something to chew on. *Trends in Neuroscience, 32*, 283–290.

Van Tongeren, D. R., DeWall, C. N., Chen, Z., Sibley, C. G., & Bulbulia, J. (2020). Religious residue: Cross-cultural evidence that religious psychology and behavior persist following deidentification. *Journal of Personality and Social Psychology*. Advance online publication. doi: 10.1037/pspp0000288

Van Tongeren, D. R., DeWall, C. N., Green, J. D., Cairo, A. H., Davis, D. E., & Hook, J. N. (2018). Self-regulation facilitates meaning in life. *Review of General Psychology, 22*, 95–106.

Van Yperen, N. W., & Buunk, B. P. (1990). A longitudinal study of equity and satisfaction in intimate relationships. *European Journal of Social Psychology, 20*, 287–309.

Van Zeijl, J., Mesman, J., Van IJzendoorn, M. H., Bakermans-Kranenburg, M. J., Juffer, F., Stolk, M. N., Koot, H. M., & Alink, L. R. A. (2006). Attachment-based intervention for enhancing sensitive discipline in mothers of 1- to 3-year-old children at risk for externalizing behavior problems: A randomized controlled trial. *Journal of Consulting and Clinical Psychology, 74*, 994–1005.

van Zuiden, M., Geuze, E., Willemen, H. L., Vermetten, E., Maas, M., Amarouchi, K., Kevelaars, A. & Heijnen, C. J. (2012). Glucocorticoid receptor pathway components predict posttraumatic stress disorder symptom development: A prospective study. *Biological Psychiatry, 71*, 309–316.

Vancampfort, D., Stubbs, B., Smith, L., Hallgren, M., Firth, J., Herring, M. P., Probst, M., & Koyanagi, A. (2018). Physical activity and sleep problems in 38 low-and middle-income countries. *Sleep Medicine, 48*, 140–147.

Vance, E. (2018, June). Can you super-charge your baby? *Scientific American*, pp. 35–39.

Vance, E. B., & Wagner, N. N. (1976). Written descriptions of orgasm: A study of sex differences. *Archives of Sexual Behavior, 5*, 87–98.

vanDellen, M. R., Campbell, W. K., Hoyle, R. H., & Bradfield, E. K. (2011). Compensating, resisting, and breaking: A meta-analytic examination of reactions to self-esteem threat. *Personality and Social Psychological Review, 15*, 51–74.

VanderLaan, D. P., Forrester, D. L., Petterson, L. J., & Vasey, P. L. (2012). Offspring production among the extended relatives of Samoan men and Fa'afafi ne. *PLOS ONE, 7*, e36088.

VanderLaan, D. P., & Vasey, P. L. (2011). Male sexual orientation in Independent Samoa: Evidence for fraternal birth order and maternal fecundity effects. *Archives of Sexual Behavior, 40*, 495–503.

VanderWeele, T. J. (2017, May 30). *What the New York Times gets wrong about marriage, health, and well-being*. Institute for Family Studies. https://ifstudies.org/blog/what-the-new-york-times-gets-wrong-about-marriage-health-and-well-being

VanderWeele, T. J. (2018, September 18). *Religious upbringing and adolescence*. Institute for Family Studies. https://ifstudies.org/blog/religious-upbringing-and-adolescence

VanderWeele, T. J., Li, S., & Kawachi, I. (2017). Religious service attendance and suicide rates—reply. *JAMA Psychiatry, 74*, 197–198.

VanderWeele, T. J., Li, S., Tsai, A. C., & Kawachi, I. (2016). Association between religious service attendance and lower suicide rates among US women. *JAMA Psychiatry, 73*, 845–851.

Vanhalst, J., Soenens, B., Luyckx, K., Van Petegem, S., Weeks, M. S., & Asher, S. R. (2015). Why do the lonely stay lonely? Chronically lonely adolescents' attributions and emotions in situations of social inclusion and exclusion. *Journal of Personality and Social Psychology, 109*, 932–948.

Varnum, M. E. W., Grossmann, I., Kitayama, S., & Nisbett, R. E. (2010). The origin of cultural differences in cognition: The social orientation hypothesis. *Current Directions in Psychological Science, 19*, 9–13.

Vasilev, M. R., Kirkby, J. A., & Angele, B. (2018). Auditory distraction during reading: A Bayesian meta-analysis of a continuing controversy. *Perspectives on Psychological Science, 13*, 567–597.

Vaughn, K. B., & Lanzetta, J. T. (1981). The effect of modification of expressive displays on vicarious emotional arousal. *Journal of Experimental Social Psychology, 17*, 16–30.

Vaz, A. P., Inati, S. K., Brunel, N., & Zaghloul, K. A. (2019). Coupled ripple oscillations between the medial temporal lobe and neocortex retrieve human memory. *Science, 363*, 975–978.

Vazsonyi, A. T., Ksinan, A. J., Jiskrova, G. K., Mikuška, J., Javakhishvili, M., & Cui, G. (2019). To grit or not to grit, that is the question! *Journal of Research in Personality, 78*, 215–226.

Vecera, S. P., Vogel, E. K., & Woodman, G. F. (2002). Lower region: A new cue for figure-ground assignment. *Journal of Experimental Psychology: General, 13*, 194–205.

Veenhoven, R. (2014, accessed March 17). *World database of happiness*. https://worlddatabaseofhappiness.eur.nl/

Veenhoven, R. (2015). Informed pursuit of happiness: What we should know, do know and can get to know. *Journal of Happiness Studies, 16*, 1035–1071.

Vekassy, L. (1977). Dreams of the blind. *Magyar Pszichologiai Szemle, 34*, 478–491.

Velikonja, T., Fett, A. K., & Velthorst, E. (2019). Patterns of nonsocial and social cognitive functioning in adults with autism spectrum disorder: a systematic review and meta-analysis. *JAMA Psychiatry, 76*, 135–151.

Velliste, M., Perel, S., Spalding, M. C., Whitford, A. S., & Schwartz, A. B. (2008). Cortical control of a prosthetic arm for self-feeding. *Nature, 453*, 1098–1101.

Verdolini, N., Pacchiarotti, I., Köhler, C. A., Reinares, M., Samalin, L., Colom, F., Totorella, A., Stubbs, B., Carvalho, A. F., Vieta, E., & Murru, A. (2018). Violent criminal behavior in the context of bipolar disorder: Systematic review and meta-analysis. *Journal of Affective Disorders, 239*, 161–170.

Verduyn, P., Ybarra, O., Résibois, M., Jonides, J., & Kross, E. (2017). Do social network sites enhance or undermine subjective well-being? A critical review. *Social Issues and Policy Review, 11*, 274–302.

Vergauwe, J., Wille, B., Hofmans, J., Kaiser, R. B., & De Fruyt, F. (2018). The double-edged sword of leader charisma: Understanding the curvilinear relationship between charismatic personality and leader effectiveness. *Journal of Personality and Social Psychology, 114*, 110–130.

Vergunst, F., Tremblay, R. E., Nagin, D., Algan, Y., Beasley, E., Park, J., Galera, C., Vitaro, F., & Côté, S. M. (2019). Association between childhood behaviors and adult employment earnings in Canada. *JAMA Psychiatry, 76*, 1044–1051.

Verhaeghen, P., & Salthouse, T. A. (1997). Meta-analyses of age–cognition relations in adulthood: Estimates of linear and nonlinear age effects and structural models. *Psychological Bulletin, 122*, 231–249.

Vermetten, E., Schmahl, C., Lindner, S., Loewenstein, R. J., & Bremner, J. D. (2006). Hippocampal and amygdalar volumes in dissociative identity disorder. *American Journal of Psychiatry, 163*, 630–636.

Verona, E., & Sullivan, E. A. (2008). Emotional catharsis and aggression revisited: Heart rate reduction following aggressive responding. *Emotion, 8*, 331–340.

Verschuere, B., & Meijer, E. H. (2014). What's on your mind? Recent advances in memory detection using the concealed information test. *European Psychologist, 19*, 162–171.

Vezzali, L., Stathi, S., Giovannini, D., Capozza, D., & Trifiletti, E. (2015). The greatest magic of Harry Potter: Reducing prejudice. *Journal of Applied Social Psychology, 45*, 105–121.

Vigliocco, G., & Hartsuiker, R. J. (2002). The interplay of meaning, sound, and syntax in sentence production. *Psychological Bulletin, 128*, 442–472.

Villalba, D. K., Lindsay, E. K., Marsland, A. L., Greco, C. M., Young, S., Brown, K. W., Smyth, J. M., Walsh, C. P., Gray, K., Chin, B., & Creswell, J. D. (2019). Mindfulness training and systemic low-grade inflammation in stressed community adults: Evidence from two randomized controlled trials. *PLOS ONE, 14*, e0219120.

Vining, E. P. G., Freeman, J. M., Pillas, D. J., Uematsu, S., Carson, B. S., Brandt, J., Boatman, D., Pulsifer, M. B., & Zukerberg, A. (1997). Why would you remove half a brain? The outcome of 58 children after hemispherectomy—The Johns Hopkins Experience: 1968 to 1996. *Pediatrics, 100*, 163–171.

Vinkhuyzen, A. A. E., van der Sluis, S., Posthuma, D., & Boomsma, D. I. (2009). The heritability of aptitude and exceptional talent across different domains in adolescents and young adults. *Behavior Genetics, 39*, 380–392.

Visich, P. S., & Fletcher, E. (2009). Myocardial infarction. In J. K. Ehrman, P. M. Gordon, P. S. Visich, & S. J. Keleyian (Eds.). *Clinical exercise physiology* (2nd ed.). Human Kinetics.

Visser, B. A., Ashton, M. C., & Vernon, P. A. (2006). Beyond *g*: Putting multiple intelligences theory to the test. *Intelligence, 34*, 487–502.

Vita, A. J., Terry, R. B., Hubert, H. B., & Fries, J. F. (1998). Aging, health risks, and cumulative disability. *New England Journal of Medicine, 338*, 1035–1041.

Vitello, P. (2012, August 1). George A. Miller. A pioneer in cognitive psychology, is dead at 92. *The New York Times*. https://www.nytimes.com/2012/08/02/us/george-a-miller-cognitive-psychology-pioneer-dies-at-92.html?

Vitiello, M. V. (2009). Recent advances in understanding sleep and sleep disturbances in older adults: Growing older does not mean sleeping poorly. *Current Directions in Psychological Science, 18*, 316–320.

Vitória, P. D., Salgueiro, M. F., Silva, S. A., & De Vries, H. (2009). The impact of social influence on adolescent intention to smoke: Combining types and referents of influence. *British Journal of Health Psychology, 14*, 681–699.

Vlasic, B. (2015, Feb. 4). Despite recalls, G.M. pays workers a big bonus. *The New York Times*. https://www.nytimes.com/2015/02/05/business/gm-reports-2-8-billion-profit-in-2014.html?

Vliegenthart, J., Noppe, G., van Rossum, E. F. C., Koper, J. W., Raat, H., & van den Akker, E. L. T. (2016). Socioeconomic status in children is associated with hair cortisol levels as a biological measure of chronic stress. *Psychoneuroendocrinology, 65*, 9–14.

Vocks, S., Tuschen-Caffier, B., Pietrowsky, R., Rustenbach, S. J., Kersting, A., & Herpertz, S. (2010). Meta-analysis of the effectiveness of psychological and pharmacological treatments for binge eating disorder. *International Journal of Eating Disorders, 43*, 205–217.

Vogel, G. (2010). Long-fought compromise reached on European animal rules. *Science, 329*, 1588–1589.

Vogel, N., Schilling, O. K., Wahl, H.-W., Beekman, A. T. F., & Penninx, B. W. J. H. (2013). Time-to-death-related change in positive and negative affect among older adults approaching the end of life. *Psychology and Aging, 28*, 128–141.

Volkow, N. D., & Boyle, M. (2018). Neuroscience of addiction: Relevance to prevention and treatment. *The American Journal of Psychiatry, 175,* 729–740.

Volkow, N. D., Wang, G. J., Kollins, S. H., Wigal, T. L., Newcorn, J. H., Telang, F., Fowler, J. S., Zhu, W., Logan, J., Ma, Y., Pradhan, K., Wong, C., & Swanson, J. M. (2009). Evaluating dopamine reward pathway in ADHD: Clinical implications. *Journal of the American Medical Association, 302,* 1084–1091

von Békésy, G. (1957, August). The ear. *Scientific American,* pp. 66–78.

von Dawans, B., Ditzen, B., Trueg, A., Fischbacher, U., & Heinrichs, M. (2019). Effects of acute stress on social behavior in women. *Psychoneuroendocrinology, 99,* 137–144.

von Hippel, W. (2007). Aging, executive functioning, and social control. *Current Directions in Psychological Science, 16,* 240–244.

von Hippel, W. (2015, July 17). *Do people become more prejudiced as they grow older?* BBC News Magazine. https://www.bbc.com/news/magazine-33523313

von Hippel, W. & Trivers, R. (2011). The evolution and psychology of self-deception. *Behavioral and Brain Sciences, 34,* 1–56.

von Senden, M. (1932). *The perception of space and shape in the congenitally blind before and after operation.* Free Press.

von Soest, T., Wagner, J., Hansen, T., & Gerstorf, D. (2018). Self-esteem across the second half of life: The role of socioeconomic status, physical health, social relationships, and personality factors. *Journal of Personality and Social Psychology, 114,* 945–958.

von Stumm, S., Hell, B., & Chamorro-Premuzic, T. (2011). The hungry mind: Intellectual curiosity is the third pillar of academic performance. *Perspectives on Psychological Science, 6,* 574–588.

Vonk, J., Jett, S. E., & Mosteller, K. W. (2012). Concept formation in American black bears, *Ursus americanus. Animal Behaviour, 84,* 953–964.

Vosoughi, S., Roy, D., & Aral, S. (2018). The spread of true and false news online. *Science, 359,* 1146–1151.

Voss, U., Tuin, I., Schermelleh-Engel, K., & Hobson, A. (2011). Waking and dreaming: Related but structurally independent. Dream reports of congenitally paraplegic and deaf-mute persons. *Consciousness and Cognition, 20,* 673–687.

Voyer, D., & Voyer, S. D. (2014). Gender differences in scholastic achievement: A meta-analysis. *Psychological Bulletin, 140,* 1174–1204.

VPC. (2015, June). *Firearm justifiable homicides and non-fatal self-defense gun use: An analysis of Federal Bureau of Investigation and National Crime Victimization Survey Data.* Violence Policy Center.

VPC. (2016, January 4). *States with weak gun laws and higher gun ownership lead nation in gun deaths, new data for 2014 confirms.* Violence Policy Center. http://vpc.org/press/states-with-weak-gun-laws-and-higher-gun-ownership-lead-nation-in-gun-suicides/

Vrij, A., & Fisher, R. P. (2016). Which lie detection tools are ready for use in the criminal justice system? *Journal of Applied Research in Memory and Cognition, 5,* 302–307.

Vukasović, T., & Bratko, D. (2015). Heritability of personality: A meta-analysis of behavior genetic studies. *Psychological Bulletin, 141,* 769–785.

Vyse, S. (2016, March/April). Guns: Feeling safe ≠ being safe. *Skeptical Inquirer,* pp. 27–30.

Waber, R. L., Shiv, B., Carmon, & Ariely, D. (2008). Commercial features of placebo and therapeutic efficacy. *Journal of the American Medical Association, 299,* 1016–1017.

Wacker, J., Chavanon, M.-L., & Stemmler, G. (2006). Investigating the dopaminergic basis of extraversion in humans: A multilevel approach. *Journal of Personality and Social Psychology, 91,* 177–187.

Wade, K. A., Garry, M., & Pezdek, K. (2018). Deconstructing rich false memories of committing crime: Commentary on Shaw and Porter (2015). *Psychological Science, 29,* 471–476.

Wade, K. A., Garry, M., Read, J. D., & Lindsay, D. S. (2002). A picture is worth a thousand lies: Using false photographs to create false childhood memories. *Psychonomic Bulletin & Review, 9,* 597–603.

Wadley, J., & Lee, J. (2016, September 23). *Compared with Europe, American teens have high rates of illicit drug use.* Michigan News (University of Michigan). https://news.umich.edu/compared-with-europe-american-teens-have-high-rates-of-illicit-drug-use/

Wadman, M. (2018). 'Rapid onset' of transgender identity ignites storm. *Science, 361,* 958–959.

Wadman, M. (2018). Watching the teen brain grow. *Science, 359,* 13.

Wagemans, J., Elder, J. H., Kubovy, M., Palmer, S. E., Peterson, M. A., Singh, M., & von der Heydt, R. (2012a). A century of Gestalt psychology in visual perception: I. Perceptual grouping and figure–ground organization. *Psychological Bulletin, 138,* 1172–1217.

Wagemans, J., Feldman, J., Gepshtein, S., Kimchi, R., Pomerantz, J. R, van der Helm, P., & van Leeuwen, C. (2012b). A century of Gestalt psychology in visual perception: II. Conceptual and theoretical foundations. *Psychological Bulletin, 138,* 1218–1252.

Wagenmakers, E.-J. (2014, June 25). *Bem is back: A skeptic's review of a meta-analysis on psi.* Open Science Collaboration. http://osc.centerforopenscience.org/2014/06/25/a-skeptics-review/

Wagenmakers, E.-J., Wetzels, R., Borsboom, D., & van der Maas, H. (2011). Why psychologists must change the way they analyze their data: The case of psi. *Journal of Personality and Social Psychology, 100,* 1–12.

Wager, R. D., & Atlas, L. Y. (2013). How is pain influenced by cognition? Neuroimaging weighs in. *Perspectives on Psychological Science, 8,* 91–97.

Wagner, D., Becker, B., Koester, P., Gouzoulis-Mayfrank, E., & Daumann, J. (2012b). A prospective study of learning, memory, and executive function in new MDMA users. *Addiction, 108,* 136–145.

Wagner, D. D., Altman, M., Boswell, R. G., Kelley, W. M., & Heatherton, T. F. (2013). Self-regulatory depletion enhances neural responses to rewards and impairs top-down control. *Psychological Science, 24,* 2262–2271.

Wagner, J., Lüdtke, O., & Robitzsch, A. (2019). Does personality become more stable with age? Disentangling state and trait effects for the Big Five across the life span using local structural equation modeling. *Journal of Personality and Social Psychology, 116,* 666–680.

Wagner, J., Ram, N., Smith, J., & Gerstorf, D. (2016). Personality trait development at the end of life: Antecedents and correlates of mean-level trajectories. *Journal of Personality and Social Psychology, 111,* 411–429.

Wagner, K., & Dobkins, K. R. (2011). Synaesthetic associations decrease during infancy. *Psychological Science, 22,* 1067–1072.

Wagstaff, G. (1982). Attitudes to rape: The "just world" strikes again? *Bulletin of the British Psychological Society, 13,* 275–283.

Wai, J., Brown, M., & Chabris, C. (2018). Using standardized test scores to include general cognitive ability in education research and policy. *Journal of Intelligence, 6,* 37.

Wakefield, J. C., Schmitz, M. F., First, M. B., & Horwitz, A. V. (2007). Extending the bereavement exclusion for major depression to other losses: Evidence from the National Comorbidity Survey. *Archives of General Psychiatry, 64,* 433–440.

Wakefield, J. C., & Spitzer, R. L. (2002). Lowered estimates—but of what? *Archives of General Psychiatry, 59,* 129–130.

Walasek, L., Juanchich, M., & Sirota, M. (2019). Adaptive cooperation in the face of social exclusion. *Journal of Experimental Social Psychology, 82,* 35–46.

Walker, D. M., Cates, H. M., Loh, Y. H. E., Purushothaman, I., Ramakrishnan, A., Cahill, K. M., Lardner, C. K., Godino, A., Kronman, H. G., Rabkin, J., Lorsch, Z. S., Mews, P., Doyle, M. A., Feng, J., Labonté, B., Koo, J. W., Bagot, R. C., Logan, R. W., Seney, M. L., . . . Nestler, E. J. (2018). Cocaine self-administration alters transcriptome-wide responses in the brain's reward circuitry. *Biological Psychiatry, 84,* 867–880.

Walker, E., Shapiro, D., Esterberg, M., & Trotman, H. (2010). Neurodevelopment and schizophrenia: Broadening the focus. *Current Directions in Psychological Science, 19,* 204–208.

Walker, M., & Keller, M. (2019). Beyond attractiveness: A multi-method approach to study enhancement in self-recognition on the Big Two personality dimensions. *Journal of Personality and Social Psychology, 117(3),* 483–499.

Walker, M. P., & van der Helm, E. (2009). Overnight therapy? The role of sleep in emotional brain processing. *Psychological Bulletin, 135,* 731–748.

Wall, P. D. (2000). *Pain: The science of suffering.* Columbia University Press.

Wallace, D. S., Paulson, R. M., Lord, C. G., & Bond, C. F., Jr. (2005). Which behaviors do attitudes predict? Meta-analyzing the effects of social pressure and perceived difficulty. *Review of General Psychology, 9,* 214–227.

Wallace, L. E., Anthony, R., End, C. M., & Way, B. M. (2018). Does religion stave off the grave? Religious affiliation in one's obituary and longevity. *Social Psychological and Personality Science, 10,* 662–670.

Wallach, M. A., & Wallach, L. (1983). *Psychology's sanction for selfishness: The error of egoism in theory and therapy.* Freeman.

Walsh, C. G., Ribeiro, J. D., & Franklin, J. C. (2017). Predicting risk of suicide attempts over time through machine learning. *Clinical Psychological Science, 5,* 457–469.

Walsh, J. L., Fielder, R. L., Carey, K. B., & Carey, M. P. (2013). Female college students' media use and academic outcomes: Results from a longitudinal cohort study. *Emerging Adulthood, 1,* 219–232.

Walsh, L. C., Boehm, J. K., & Lyubomirsky, S. (2018). Does happiness promote career success? Revisiting the evidence. *Journal of Career Assessment, 26,* 199–219.

Walsh, R. (2011). Lifestyle and mental health. *American Psychologist, 66,* 579–592.

Walster (Hatfield), E., Aronson, V., Abrahams, D., & Rottman, L. (1966). Importance of physical attractiveness in dating behavior. *Journal of Personality and Social Psychology, 4,* 508–516.

Walters, G. D. (2018). Predicting short-and long-term desistance from crime with the NEO personality inventory-short form: Domain scores and interactions in high risk delinquent youth. *Journal of Research in Personality, 75,* 37–45.

Walton, G. M., & Spencer, S. J. (2009). Latent ability: Grades and test scores systematically underestimate the intellectual ability of negatively stereotyped students. *Psychological Science, 20,* 1132–1139.

Walton, G. M., & Wilson, T. D. (2018). Wise interventions: Psychological remedies for social and personal problems. *Psychological Review, 125,* 617–655.

Wampold, B. E. (2007). Psychotherapy: The humanistic (and effective) treatment. *American Psychologist, 62,* 857–873.

Wampold, B. E., Flückiger, C., Del Re, A. C., Yulish, N. E., Frost, N. D., Pace, B. T., Goldberg, S. B., Miller, S. D., Baardseth, T. P., Laska, K. M., & Hilsenroth, M. J. (2017). In pursuit of truth: A critical examination of meta-analyses of cognitive behavior therapy. *Psychotherapy Research, 27,* 14–32.

Wang, F., DesMeules, M., Luo, W., Dai, S., Lagace, C., & Morrison, H. (2011). Leisure-time physical activity and marital status in relation to depression between men and women: A prospective study. *Health Psychology, 30,* 204–211.

Wang, G., Cao, M., Sauciuvenaite, J., Bissland, R., Hacker, M., Hambly, C., Vaanholt, L. M., Niu, C., Faries, M. D., & Speakman, J. R. (2018). Different impacts of resources on opposite sex ratings of physical attractiveness by males and females. *Evolution and Human Behavior, 39,* 220–225.

Wang, G., Holmes, Jr., R. M., Devine, R. A., & Bishoff, J. (2018). CEO gender differences in careers and the moderating role of country culture: A meta-analytic investigation. *Organizational Behavior and Human Decision Processes, 148,* 30–53.

Wang, J., Cheng, G. H., Chen, T., & Leung, K. (2019). Team creativity/innovation in culturally diverse teams: A meta-analysis. *Journal of Organizational Behavior, 40,* 693–708.

Wang, J., He, L., Liping, J., Tian, J., & Benson, V. (2015a). The "positive effect" is present in older Chinese adults: Evidence from an eye tracking study. *PLOS ONE, 10,* e0121372.

Wang, J., Rao, Y., & Houser, D. E. (2017a). An experimental analysis of acquired impulse control among adult humans intolerant to alcohol. *PNAS, 114,* 1299–1304.

Wang, J., Wei, Q., Bai, T., Zhou, X., Sun, H., Becker, B., Tian, Y., Wang, K, & Kendrick, K. (2017b). Electroconvulsive therapy selectively enhanced feedforward connectivity from fusiform face area to amygdala in major depressive disorder. *Social Cognitive and Affective Neuroscience, 2,* 1983–1992.

Wang, Q., Hoi, S. P., Wang, Y., Song, C., Li, T., Lam, C. M., Fang, F., & Yi, L. (2020). Out of mind, out of sight? Investigating abnormal face scanning in autism spectrum disorder using gaze-contingent paradigm. *Developmental Science, 23*(1), e12856.

Wang, S. (2014, March 29). How to think about the risk of autism. *The New York Times.* https://www.nytimes.com/2014/03/30/opinion/sunday/how-to-think-about-the-risk-of-autism.html?

Wang, S., Dai, J., Li, J., Wang, X., Chen, T., Yang, X., He, M., & Gong, Q. (2018). Neuroanatomical correlates of grit: Growth mindset mediates the association between gray matter structure and trait grit in late adolescence. *Human Brain Mapping, 39,* 1688–1699.

Wang, S. B., Haynos, A. F., Wall, M. M., Chen, C., Eisenberg, M. E., & Neumark-Sztainer, D. (2019). Fifteen-year prevalence, trajectories, and predictors of body dissatisfaction from adolescence to middle adulthood. *Clinical Psychological Science, 7,* 1403–1415.

Wang, S.-H., Baillargeon, R., & Brueckner, L. (2004). Young infants' reasoning about hidden objects: Evidence from violation-of-expectation tasks with test trials only. *Cognition, 93,* 167–198.

Wang, W., & Wilcox, W. B. (2019). *Less stable, less important: Cohabiting families' comparative disadvantage across the globe.* Institute for Family Studies.

https://ifstudies.org/blog/less-stable-less-important-cohabiting-families-comparative-disadvantage-across-the-globe

Wang, X., Gallegos, D. A., Pogorelov, V. M., O'Hare, J. K., Calakos, N., Wetsel, W. C., & West, A. E. (2018). Parvalbumin interneurons of the mouse nucleus accumbens are required for amphetamine-induced locomotor sensitization and conditioned place preference. *Neuropsychopharmacology, 43,* 953–963.

Wang, Y., Highhouse, S., Lake, C. J., Petersen, N. L., & Rada, T. B. (2017). Meta-analytic investigations of the relation between intuition and analysis. *Journal of Behavioral Decision Making, 30,* 15–25.

Wang, Y., & Olson, I. R. (2018). The original social network: White matter and social cognition. *Trends in Cognitive Sciences, 22,* 504–516.

Wang, Z., Lukowski, S. L., Hart, S. A., Lyons, I. M., Thompson, L. A., Kovas, Y., Mazzocco, M. M., Plomin, R., & Petrill, S. A. (2015). Is math anxiety always bad for math learning? The role of math motivation. *Psychological Science, 26,* 1863–1876.

Wann, J. P., Poulter, D. R., & Purcell, C. (2011). Reduced sensitivity to visual looming inflates the risk posed by speeding vehicles when children try to cross the road. *Psychological Science, 22,* 429–434.

Ward-Griffin, E., Klaiber, P., Collins, H. K., Owens, R. L., Coren, S., & Chen, F. S. (2018). Petting away pre-exam stress: The effect of therapy dog sessions on student well-being. *Stress and Health, 34,* 468–473.

Ward, A., & Mann, T. (2000). Don't mind if I do: Disinhibited eating under cognitive load. *Journal of Personality and Social Psychology, 78,* 753–763.

Ward, C. (1994). Culture and altered states of consciousness. In W. J. Lonner & R. Malpass (Eds.), *Psychology and culture.* Allyn & Bacon.

Ward, K. D., Klesges, R. C., & Halpern, M. T. (1997). Predictors of smoking cessation and state-of-the-art smoking interventions. *Journal of Social Issues, 53,* 129–145.

Ward, L. M., Seabrook, R. C., Grower, P., Giaccardi, S., & Lippman, J. R. (2018). Sexual object or sexual subject? Media use, self-sexualization, and sexual agency among undergraduate women. *Psychology of Women Quarterly, 42,* 29–43.

Wardle, J., Cooke, L. J., Gibson, L., Sapochnik, M., Sheiham, A., & Lawson, M. (2003). Increasing children's acceptance of vegetables: A randomized trial of parent-led exposure. *Appetite, 40,* 155–162.

Wargo, E. (2007, December). Understanding the have-knots. *APS Observer,* pp. 18–21.

Warne, R. T., & Burningham, C. (2019). Spearman's *g* found in 31 non-Western nations: Strong evidence that *g* is universal. *Psychological Bulletin, 145,* 237–272.

Wason, P. C. (1960). On the failure to eliminate hypotheses in a conceptual task. *Quarterly Journal of Experimental Psychology, 12,* 129–140.

Wason, P. C. (1981). The importance of cognitive illusions. *The Behavioral and Brain Sciences, 4,* 356.

Wasserman, E. A. (1993). Comparative cognition: Toward a general understanding of cognition in behavior. *Psychological Science, 4,* 156–161.

Wasserman, E. A. (1995). The conceptual abilities of pigeons. *American Scientist, 83,* 246–255.

Wastell, C. A. (2002). Exposure to trauma: The long-term effects of suppressing emotional reactions. *Journal of Nervous and Mental Disorders, 190,* 839–845.

Waterhouse, L. (2006). Inadequate evidence for multiple intelligences, Mozart effect, and emotional intelligence theories. *Educational Psychologist, 41,* 247–255.

Waterman, A. S. (1988). Identity status theory and Erikson's theory: Commonalities and differences. *Developmental Review, 8,* 185–208.

Waters, E. A., Klein, W. M. P., Moser, R. P., Yu, M., Waldron, W. R., McNeel, T. S., & Freedman, A. N. (2011). Correlates of unrealistic risk beliefs in a nationally representative sample. *Journal of Behavioral Medicine, 34,* 225–235.

Waters, T. E., Köber, C., Raby, K. L., Habermas, T., & Fivush, R. (2019). Consistency and stability of narrative coherence: An examination of personal narrative as a domain of adult personality. *Journal of Personality, 87,* 151–162.

Watkins, E. R. (2008). Constructive and unconstructive repetitive thought. *Psychological Bulletin, 134,* 163–206.

Watson, D. (2000). *Mood and temperament.* Guilford Press.

Watson, H. J., Yilmaz, Z., Thornton, L. M., Hübel, C., Coleman, J. R., Gaspar, H. A., Bryois, J., Hinney, A., Leppä, V.M., Mattheisen, M., Medland, S. E., Ripke, S., Yao, S., Giusti-Rodríguez, P., Anorexia Nervosa Genetics Initiative, Hanscombe, K. B., Purves, K. L., Eating Disorders Working Group of the Psychiatric Genomics Consortium, Adan, R. A. H., Alfredsson, L., . . . Bulik, C. M. (2019). Genome-wide association study identifies eight risk loci and implicates metabo-psychiatric origins for anorexia nervosa. *Nature Genetics, 51,* 1207–1214.

Watson, J. B. (1913). Psychology as the behaviorist views it. *Psychological Review, 20,* 158–177.

Watson, J. B. (1924). The unverbalized in human behavior. *Psychological Review, 31,* 339–347.

Watson, J. B., & Rayner, R. (1920). Conditioned emotional reactions. *Journal of Experimental Psychology, 3,* 1–14.

Watson, R. I., Jr. (1973). Investigation into deindividuation using a cross-cultural survey technique. *Journal of Personality and Social Psychology, 25,* 342–345.

Watts, T. W., Duncan, G. J., & Quan, H. (2018). Revisiting the marshmallow task: A conceptual replication investigating links between early delay of gratification and later outcomes. *Psychological Science, 29,* 1159–1177.

Way, B. M., Creswell, J. D., Eisenberger, N. I., & Lieberman, M. D. (2010). Dispositional mindfulness and depressive symptomatology: Correlations with limbic and self-referential neural activity during rest. *Emotion, 10,* 12–24.

Wayment, H. A., & Peplau, L. A. (1995). Social support and well-being among lesbian and heterosexual women: A structural modeling approach. *Personality and Social Psychology Bulletin, 21,* 1189–1199.

Waytz, A., & Gray, K. (2018). Does online technology make us more or less sociable? A preliminary review and call for research. *Perspectives on Psychological Science, 13,* 473–491.

Waytz, A., Young, L. L., & Ginges, J. (2014). Motive attribution asymmetry for love vs. hate drives intractable conflict. *PNAS, 111,* 15687–15692.

Webb, C. A., Cohen, Z. D., Beard, C., Forgeard, M., Peckham, A. D., & Björgvinsson, T. (2020). Personalized prognostic prediction of treatment outcome for depressed patients in a naturalistic psychiatric hospital setting: A comparison of machine learning approaches. *Journal of Consulting and Clinical Psychology, 88,* 25–38.

Webb, C. E., Rossignac-Milon, M., & Higgins, E. T. (2017). Stepping forward together: Could walking facilitate interpersonal conflict resolution? *American Psychologist, 72,* 374–385.

Webb, M. E., Cropper, S. J., & Little, D. R. (2019). "Aha!" is stronger when preceded by a "huh?":

Presentation of a solution affects ratings of aha experience conditional on accuracy. *Thinking & Reasoning, 25,* 324–364.

Weber, A., Fernald, A., & Diop, Y. (2017). When cultural norms discourage talking to babies: Effectiveness of a parenting program in rural Senegal. *Child Development, 88,* 1513–1526.

Weber, B., Koschutnig, K., Schwerdtfeger, A., Rominger, C., Papousek, I., Weiss, E. M., Tilp, M., & Fink, A. (2019). Learning unicycling evokes manifold changes in gray and white matter networks related to motor and cognitive functions. *Scientific Reports, 9,* 4324.

Webster, G. D., DeWall, C. N., Pond, R. S., Jr., Deckman, T., Jonason, P. K., Le, B. M., Nichols, A. L., Schember, T. O., Crysel, L. C., Crosier, B. S., Smith, C. V., Paddock, E. L., Nezlek, J. B., Kirkpatrick, L. A., Bryan, A. D., & Bator, R. J. (2014). The Brief Aggression Questionnaire: Psychometric and behavioral evidence for an efficient measure of trait aggression. *Aggressive Behavior, 40,* 120–139.

Wechsler, D. (1972). "Hold" and "Don't Hold" tests. In S. M. Chown (Ed.), *Human aging.* Penguin.

Wegner, D. M. (2002). *The illusion of conscious will.* MIT Press.

Wegner, D. M., & Ward, A. F. (2013). How Google is changing your brain. *Scientific American, 309,* 58–61.

Wei, Q., Fentress, H. M., Hoversten, M. T., Zhang, L., Hebda-Bauer, E. K., Watson, S. J., Seasholtz, A. F., & Akil, H. (2012). Early-life forebrain glucocorticoid receptor overexpression increases anxiety behavior and cocaine sensitization. *Biological Psychiatry, 71,* 224–231.

Weichbold, V., Holzer, A., Newesely, G., & Stephan, K. (2012). Results from high-frequency hearing screening in 14- to 15-year old adolescents and their relation to self-reported exposure to loud music. *International Journal of Audiology, 51,* 650–654.

Weidman, A. C., Tracy, J. L., & Elliot, A. J. (2016). The benefits of following your pride: Authentic pride promotes achievement. *Journal of Personality, 84,* 607–622.

Weinberg, A., & Doyle, N. (2017). *Psychology at work: Improving wellbeing and productivity in the workplace.* British Psychological Society. https://www.bps.org.uk/news-and-policy/psychology-work-improving-wellbeing-and-productivity-workplace

Weinberger, D. R. (2019). Thinking about schizophrenia in an era of genomic medicine. *American Journal of Psychiatry, 176,* 12–20.

Weiner, B., Perry, R. P., & Magnusson, J. (1988). An attributional analysis of reactions to stigmas. *Journal of Personality and Social Psychology, 55,* 738–748.

Weiner, J. (2017, October 6). The flagrant sexual hypocrisy of conservative men. *The New York Times.* https://www.nytimes.com/2017/10/06/opinion/sunday/conservative-men-abortion-hypocrisy.html?

Weingarden, H., & Renshaw, K. D. (2012). Early and late perceived pubertal timing as risk factors for anxiety disorders in adult women. *Journal of Psychiatric Research, 46,* 1524–1529.

Weingarten, E., Chen, Q., McAdams, M., Yi, J., Hepler, J., & Albarracín, D. (2016). From primed concepts to action: A meta-analysis of the behavioral effects of incidentally presented words. *Psychological Bulletin, 142,* 472.

Weingarten, G. (2002, March 10). Below the beltway. *The Washington Post,* p. WO3.

Weinstein, J. J., van de Giessen, E., Rosengard, R. J., Xu, X., Ojeil, N., Brucato, G., Gil, R. B., Kegeles, L. S., Laruelle, M., Slifstein, M., & Abi-Dargham, A. (2018).

PET imaging of dopamine-D2 receptor internalization in schizophrenia. *Molecular Psychiatry, 23,* 1506–1511.

Weinstein, N. D. (1980). Unrealistic optimism about future life events. *Journal of Personality and Social Psychology, 39,* 806–820.

Weinstein, N. D., Ryan, W. S., DeHaan, C. R., Przybylski, A. K., Legate, N., & Ryan, R. M. (2012). Parental autonomy support and discrepancies between implicit and explicit sexual identities: Dynamics of self-acceptance and defense. *Journal of Personality and Social Psychology, 102,* 815–832.

Weinstein, Y., Levav, I., Gelkopf, M., Roe, D., Yoffe, R., Pugachova, I., & Levine, S. Z. (2018b). Association of maternal exposure to terror attacks during pregnancy and the risk of schizophrenia in the offspring: A population-based study. *Schizophrenia Research, 199,* 163–167.

Weir, K. (2013, May). Captive audience. *Monitor on Psychology,* pp. 44–49.

Weir, W. (2010, May 17). Middletown man, age 76, has memorized epic poem "Paradise Lost." *Hartford Courant* (courant.com).

Weisbuch, M., Ivcevic, Z., & Ambady, N. (2009). On being liked on the web and in the "real world": Consistency in first impressions across personal webpages and spontaneous behavior. *Journal of Experimental Social Psychology, 45,* 573–576.

Weiser, E. B. (2015). #Me: Narcissism and its facets as predictors of selfie-posting frequency. *Personality and Individual Differences, 86,* 477–481.

Weiskrantz, L. (2009). *Blindsight.* Oxford University Press.

Weiskrantz, L. (2010). Blindsight in hindsight. *The Psychologist, 23,* 356–358.

Weisman, K., Dweck, C. S., & Markman, E. M. (2017). Rethinking people's conceptions of mental life. *PNAS, 114,* 11374–11379.

Weiss, A., Wilson, M. L., Collins, D. A., Mhungu, D., Kamenya, S., Foerster, S., & Pusey, A. E. (2017). Personality in the chimpanzees of Gombe National Park. *Nature: Scientific Data, 4,* #170146.

Weiss, B., Lavner, J. A., & Miller, J. D. (2017). Self- and partner-reported psychopathic traits' relations with couples' communication, marital satisfaction trajectories, and divorce in a longitudinal sample. *Personality Disorders: Theory, Research, and Treatment, 9,* 239–249.

Weissman, M. M., Wickramaratne, P., Gameroff, M. J., Warner, V., Pilowsky, D., Kohad, R. G., Verdeli, H., Skipper, J., & Talati, A. (2016). Offspring of depressed parents: 30 years later. *American Journal of Psychiatry, 173,* 1024–1032.

Weisz, J. R., Kuppens, S., Ng, M. Y., Eckshtain, D., Ugueto, A. M., Vaughn-Coaxum, R., Jensen-Doss, A., Hawley, K. M., Krumholz Marchette, L. S., Chu, B. C., Weersing, V. R., & Fordwood, S. R. (2017). What five decades of research tells us about the effects of youth psychological therapy: A multilevel meta-analysis and implications for science and practice. *American Psychologist, 72,* 79–117.

Welborn, B. L., Gunter, B. C., Vesich, I. S., & Lieberman, M. D. (2017). Neural correlates of the false consensus effect: Evidence for motivated projection and regulatory restraint. *Journal of Cognitive Neuroscience, 29,* 708–717.

Welch, J. M., Lu, J., Rodriquiz, R. M., Trotta, N. C., Peca, J., Ding, J.-D., Feliciano, C., Chen, M., Adams, J. P., Luo, J., Dudek, S. M., Weinberg, R. J., Calakos, N., Wetsel, W. C., & Feng, G. (2007). Cortico-striatal synaptic defects and OCD-like behaviours in *Sapap3*-mutant mice. *Nature, 448,* 894–900.

Welch, W. W. (2005, February 28). Trauma of Iraq war haunting thousands returning home. *USA*

Today. https://archive.commondreams.org/script files/headlines05/0228-01.htm

Welham, J., Isohanni, M., Jones, P., & McGrath, J. (2009). The antecedents of schizophrenia: A review of birth cohort studies. *Schizophrenia Bulletin, 35,* 603–623.

Welker, K. M., Baker, L., Padilla, A., Holmes, H., Aron, A., & Slatcher, R. B. (2014). Effects of self-disclosure and responsiveness between couples on passionate love within couples. *Personal Relationships, 21,* 692–708.

Weller, S. C., & Davis-Beaty, K. (2002). Condom effectiveness in reducing heterosexual HIV transmission. *Cochrane Database of Systematic Reviews,* Issue 1, Article CD003255.

Wells, D. L. (2009). The effects of animals on human health and well-being. *Journal of Social Issues, 65,* 523–543.

Wells, G. L. (1981). Lay analyses of causal forces on behavior. In J. Harvey (Ed.), *Cognition, social behavior and the environment.* Erlbaum.

Wenze, S. J., Gunthert, K. C., & German, R. E. (2012). Biases in affective forecasting and recall in individuals with depression and anxiety symptoms. *Personality and Social Psychology Bulletin, 38,* 895–906.

Werker, J. F., Yeung, H. H., & Yoshida, K. A. (2012). How do infants become experts at native-speech perception? *Current Directions in Psychological Science, 21,* 221–226.

Werner, L., Geisler, J., & Randler, C. (2015). Morningness as a personality predictor of punctuality. *Current Psychology, 34,* 130–139.

Wertz, J., Caspi, A., Belsky, D. W., Beckley, A. L., Arseneault, L., Barnes, J. C., Corcoran, D. L., Hogan, S., Houts, R. M., Morgan, N., Odgers, C. L., Prinz, J. A., Sugden, K., Williams, B. S., Poulton, R., & Moffitt, T. E. (2018). Genetics and crime: Integrating new genomic discoveries into psychological research about antisocial behavior. *Psychological Science, 29,* 791–803.

Westen, D. (1996). *Is Freud really dead? Teaching psychodynamic theory to introductory psychology* [Presentation]. Annual Institute on the Teaching of Psychology, St. Petersburg Beach, FL.

Westen, D. (1998). The scientific legacy of Sigmund Freud: Toward a psychodynamically informed psychological science. *Psychological Bulletin, 124,* 333–371.

Westen, D. (2007). *The political brain: The role of emotion in deciding the fate of the nation.* PublicAffairs.

Westen, D., & Morrison, K. (2001). A multidimensional meta-analysis of treatments for depression, panic, and generalized anxiety disorder: An empirical examination of the status of empirically supported therapies. *Journal of Consulting and Clinical Psychology, 69,* 875–899.

Westermeyer, J. (2018). Assessing and treating posttraumatic stress disorder: An update. *Journal of Nervous and Mental Disease, 206*(1), 1–2.

Whalen, P. J., Shin, L. M., McInerney, S. C., Fisher, H., Wright, C. I., & Rauch, S. L. (2001). A functional MRI study of human amygdala responses to facial expressions of fear versus anger. *Emotion, 1,* 70–83.

Wheelock, M. D., Hect, J. L., Hernandez-Andrade, E., Hassan, S. S., Romero, R., Eggebrecht, A. T., & Thomason, M. E. (2019). Sex differences in functional connectivity during fetal brain development. *Developmental Cognitive Neuroscience, 36,* 100632.

Whelan, R., Conrod, P. J., Poline, J.-B., Lourdusamy, A., Banaschewski, T., Barker, G. J., Bellgrove, M. A., Büchel, C., Byrne, M., Cummins, T. D. R.,

Fauth-Bühler, Flor, H., Gallinat, J., Heinz, A., Ittermann, B., Mann, K., Martinot, J.-L., Lalor, E. C., Lathrop, M., . . . IMAGEN Consortium. (2012). Adolescent impulsivity phenotypes characterized by distinct brain networks. *Nature Neuroscience, 15*, 920–925.

Whillans, A. (2019). Time poor and unhappy. *Harvard Business Review*. https://bit.ly/3agABLB

Whillans, A. V., Christie, C. D., Cheung, S., Jordan, A. H., & Chen, F. S. (2017). From misperception to social connection: Correlates and consequences of overestimating others' social connectedness. *Personality and Social Psychology Bulletin, 43*, 1696–1711.

Whillans, A. V., Weidman, A. C., & Dunn, E. W. (2016). Valuing time over money is associated with greater happiness. *Social Psychological and Personality Science, 7*, 213–222.

Whisman, M. A., Gilmour, A. L., & Salinger, J. M. (2018). Marital satisfaction and mortality in the United States adult population. *Health Psychology, 37*, 1041–1044.

Whisman, M. A., Johnson, D. P., & Rhee, S. H. (2014). A behavior genetic analysis of pleasant events, depressive symptoms, and their covariation. *Clinical Psychological Science, 2*, 535–544.

Whitaker, K. J., Vértes, P. E., Romero-Garcia, R., Váša, F., Moutoussis, M., Prabhu, G., Weiskopf, N., Callaghan, M. F., Wagstyl, K., Rittman, T., Tait, R., Ooi, C., Suckling, J., Inkster, B., Fonagy, P., Dolan, R. J., Jones, P. B., Goodyer, I. M., NSPN Consortium, & Bullmore, E. T. (2016). Adolescence is associated with genomically patterned consolidation of the hubs of the human brain connectome. *PNAS, 113*, 9105–9110.

White, H. R., Brick, J., & Hansell, S. (1993). A longitudinal investigation of alcohol use and aggression in adolescence. *Journal of Studies on Alcohol, Supplement 11*, 62–77.

White, L., & Edwards, J. (1990). Emptying the nest and parental well-being: An analysis of national panel data. *American Sociological Review, 55*, 235–242.

White, R. A. (1998). Intuition, heart knowledge, and parapsychology. *Journal of the American Society for Psychical Research, 92*, 158–171.

White, R. E., Kross, E., & Duckworth, A. L. (2015). Spontaneous self-distancing and adaptive self-reflection across adolescence. *Child Development, 86*, 1272–1281.

Whitehouse, H. (2018). Dying for the group: Towards a general theory of extreme self-sacrifice. *Behavioral and Brain Sciences, 7*, 1–64.

Whitehurst, L. N., Cellini, N., McDevitt, E. A., Duggan, K. A., & Mednick, S. C. (2016). Autonomic activity during sleep predicts memory consolidation in humans. *PNAS, 113*, 7272–7277.

Whiten, A., & Boesch, C. (2001, January). Cultures of chimpanzees. *Scientific American*, pp. 60–67.

Whiten, A., & Byrne, R. W. (1988). Tactical deception in primates. *Behavioral and Brain Sciences, 11*, 233–244, 267–273.

Whiten, A., Goodall, J., McGrew, W. C., Nishidas, T., Reynolds, V., Sugiyama, Y., Tutin, C. E. G., Wrangham, R. W., & Boesch, C. (1999). Cultures in chimpanzees. *Nature, 399*, 682–685.

Whiten, A., Spiteri, A., Horner, V., Bonnie, K. E., Lambeth, S. P., Schapiro, S. J., & de Waal, F. B. M. (2007). Transmission of multiple traditions within and between chimpanzee groups. *Current Biology, 17*, 1038–1043.

Whiting, B. B., & Edwards, C. P. (1988). *Children of different worlds: The formation of social behavior*. Harvard University Press.

Whitley, B. E., Jr. (1999). Right-wing authoritarianism, social dominance orientation, and prejudice. *Journal of Personality and Social Psychology, 77*, 126–134.

Whitlock, J. R., Heynen, A. L., Shuler, M. G., & Bear, M. F. (2006). Learning induces long-term potentiation in the hippocampus. *Science, 313*, 1093–1097.

Whitmore, L. M., & Smith, T. C. (2018). Isolating the association of sleep, depressive state, and other independent indicators for suicide ideation in United States teenagers. *Archives of Suicide Research, 23*, 471–490.

WHO. (2000). *Effectiveness of male latex condoms in protecting against pregnancy and sexually transmitted infections*. https://bit.ly/2vjBcN7

WHO. (2003). *The male latex condom: Specification and guidelines for condom procurement*. Department of Reproductive Health and Research, Family and Community Health, World Health Organization.

WHO. (2004a). *Prevention of mental disorders: Effective interventions and policy options. Summary report* [PDF file]. https://www.who.int/mental_health/evidence/en/prevention_of_mental _disorders_sr.pdf

WHO. (2004b). *Promoting mental health: Concepts, emerging evidence, practice. Summary report* [PDF file]. https://www.who.int/mental_health /evidence/en/promoting_mhh.pdf

WHO. (2012, May). *Tobacco: Fact sheet N339*. https://www.ncbi.nlm.nih.gov/pmc/articles/PMC3850892/

WHO. (2012b, November 23). *WHO recommends seasonal influenza vaccination to pregnant women as the highest priority*. https://www.who.int/immunization/newsroom/newsstory_seasonal_influenza _vaccination_pregnancy/en/

WHO. (2014). *Global status report on alcohol and health 2014* [PDF file]. https://www.who.int/substance_abuse/publications/global_alcohol_report /msb_gsr_2014_1.pdf

WHO. (2014b, accessed September 20). *Chain-free initiative*. emro.who.int/mental-health/chain-free -initiative

WHO. (2016). *Global status on road safety 2015* [PDF file]. https://www.who.int/violence_injury _prevention/road_safety_status/2018/English -Summary-GSRRS2018.pdf.

WHO. (2016). *Growing recognition of transgender health*. https://www.who.int/bulletin/volumes/94 /11/16-021116/en/

WHO. (2016b). *World Health Statistics 2016* [PDF file]. https://www.who.int/gho/publications/world _health_statistics/2016/en/

WHO. (2016a, November). *Violence against women. Intimate partner and sexual violence against women. Fact Sheet.*

WHO. (2017a). *Depression*. https://www. who.int /mediacentre/factsheets/fs369/en

WHO. (2017b). *Mental disorders*. https://www.who .int/mediacentre/factsheets/fs396/en

WHO. (2018). *Gaming disorder*. https://www.who.int /features/qa/gaming-disorder/en/

WHO. (2018). *Report on global sexually transmitted infection surveillance 2018*. https://www.who.int /reproductivehealth/publications/stis-surveillance -2018/en/

WHO. (2018a). (V. Poznyak & D. Rekve, Eds.). *Global status report on alcohol and health 2018* https: //www.who.int/substance_abuse/publications /global_alcohol_report/en/

WHO. (2018b). *Adolescent alcohol-related behaviours: Trends and inequalities in the WHO European Region, 2002–2014*. http://www.euro.who.int/en /publications/abstracts/adolescent-alcohol-related -behaviours-trends-and-inequalities-in-the-who -european-region,-20022014-2018

WHO. (2018e, July 17). *Suicide rate estimates, age-standardized: Estimates by country*. https://apps .who.int/gho/data/node.main.MHSUICIDEASDR? lang=en

WHO. (2019). *Burn-out an "occupational phenomenon": International classification of diseases*. https://www.who.int/mental_health/evidence /burn-out/en/

WHO. (2019, March 20). *Deafness and hearing loss*. https://www.who.int/news-room/fact-sheets/detail /deafness-and-hearing-loss

Whooley, M. A., de Jonge, P., Vittinghoff, E., Otte, C., Noos, R., Carney, R. M., Ali, S., Dowray, S., Na, B., Feldman, M. D., Schiller, N. B., & Browner, W. S. (2008). Depressive symptoms, health behaviors, and risk of cardiovascular events in patients with coronary heart disease. *JAMA, 300*, 2379–2388.

Whorf, B. L. (1956). Science and linguistics. In J. B. Carroll (Ed.), *Language, thought, and reality: Selected writings of Benjamin Lee Whorf*. MIT Press.

Wicherts, J. M., Dolan, C. V., Carlson, J. S., & van der Maas, H. L. J. (2010). Raven's test performance of sub-Saharan Africans: Mean level, psychometric properties, and the Flynn effect. *Learning and Individual Differences, 20*, 135–151.

Wickelgren, I. (2009, September/October). I do not feel your pain. *Scientific American Mind*, pp. 51–57.

Wickelgren, W. A. (1977). *Learning and memory*. Prentice-Hall.

Widén, S. E., Båsjö, S., Möller, C., & Kähäri, K. (2017). Headphone listening habits and hearing thresholds in Swedish adolescents. *Noise & Health, 19*, 125–132.

Widiger, T. A., Sellbom, M., Chmielewski, M., Clark, L. A., DeYoung, C. G., Kotov, R., Krueger, R. F., Lynam, D. R., Miller, J. D., Mullins-Sweatt, S., Samuel., D. B., South, S. C., Tackett, J. L., Thomas, K. M., Watson, D., & Wright, A. G. C. (2019). Personality in a hierarchical model of psychopathology. *Clinical Psychological Science, 7*, 77–92.

Wielgosz, J., Goldberg, S. B., Kral, T. R., Dunne, J. D., & Davidson, R. J. (2019). Mindfulness meditation and psychopathology. *Annual Review of Clinical Psychology, 15*, 285–316.

Wiens, A. N., & Menustik, C. E. (1983). Treatment outcome and patient characteristics in an aversion therapy program for alcoholism. *American Psychologist, 38*, 1089–1096.

Wierenga, L. M., Bos, M. G., van Rossenberg, F., & Crone, E. A. (2019). Sex effects on development of brain structure and executive functions: Greater variance than mean effects. *Journal of Cognitive Neuroscience, 31*, 730–753.

Wierson, M., & Forehand, R. (1994). Parent behavioral training for child noncompliance: Rationale, concepts, and effectiveness. *Current Directions in Psychological Science, 3*, 146–149.

Wierzbicki, M. (1993). Psychological adjustment of adoptees: A meta-analysis. *Journal of Clinical Child Psychology, 22*, 447–454.

Wiese, C. W., Kuykendall, L., & Tay, L. (2018). Get active? A meta-analysis of leisure-time physical activity and subjective well-being. *The Journal of Positive Psychology, 13*, 57–66.

Wiese, H., Tüttenberg, S. C., Ingram, B. T., Chan, C. Y., Gurbuz, Z., Burton, A. M., & Young, A. W. (2019). A robust neural index of high face familiarity. *Psychological Science, 30*, 261–272.

Wiesel, T. N. (1982). Postnatal development of the visual cortex and the influence of environment. *Nature, 299*, 583–591.

Wiesner, W. H., & Cronshaw, S. P. (1988). A meta-analytic investigation of the impact of interview format and degree of structure on the validity of the employment interview. *Journal of Occupational Psychology, 61,* 275–290.

Wigdor, A. K., & Garner, W. R. (1982). *Ability testing: Uses, consequences, and controversies.* National Academy Press.

Wilar, G., Shinoda, Y., Sasaoka, T., & Fukunaga, K. (2019). Crucial role of dopamine D2 receptor signaling in nicotine-induced conditioned place preference. *Molecular Neurobiology,* 1–18.

Wilcox, W. B., & DeRose, L. (2017, March 27). *In Europe, cohabitation is stable . . . right?* Brookings Institution. https://www.brookings.edu/blog/social-mobility-memos/2017/03/27/in-europe-cohabitation-is-stable-right/

Wilcox, W. B., & Marquardt, E. (2011, December). *When baby makes three: How parenthood makes life meaningful and how marriage makes parenthood bearable.* National Marriage Project, University of Virginia.

Wilcox, W. B., Van Leeuwen, J., & Price, J. (2018, October 17). *The family geography of the American dream: New neighborhood data on single parenthood, prisons, and poverty.* Institute for Family Studies. https://ifstudies.org/blog/the-family-geography-of-the-american-dream-new-neighborhood-data-on-single-parenthood-prisons-and-poverty

Wilcox, W. B., & Wolfinger, N. H. (2017, February). *Men & marriage: Debunking the ball and chain myth* [PDF file]. Institute for Family Studies. https://ifstudies.org/wp-content/uploads/2017/02/IFS MenandMarriageResearchBrief2.pdf

Wilder, D. A. (1981). Perceiving persons as a group: Categorization and intergroup relations. In D. L. Hamilton (Ed.), *Cognitive processes in stereotyping and intergroup behavior* (pp. 213–257). Erlbaum.

Wildman, D. E., Uddin, M., Liu, G., Grossman, L. I., & Goodman, M. (2003). Implications of natural selection in shaping 99.4% nonsynonymous DNA identity between humans and chimpanzees: Enlarging genus Homo. *PNAS, 100,* 7181–7188.

Wiley, J., & Jarosz, A. F. (2012). Working memory capacity, attentional focus, and problem solving. *Current Directions in Psychological Science, 21,* 258–262.

Wilford, J. N. (1999, February 9). New findings help balance the cosmological books. *The New York Times.* https://www.nytimes.com/1999/02/09/science/new-findings-help-balance-the-cosmological-books.html?

Wilkey, E. D., Cutting, L. E., & Price, G. R. (2018). Neuroanatomical correlates of performance in a state-wide test of math achievement. *Developmental Science, 21,* e12545.

Wilkinson, M. J., Manoogian, E. N., Zadourian, A., Lo, H., Fakhouri, S., Shoghi, A., Wang, X., Fleischer, J. G., Navlakha, S., Panda, S., & Taub, P. R. (2020). Ten-hour time-restricted eating reduces weight, blood pressure, and atherogenic lipids in patients with metabolic syndrome. *Cell Metabolism, 31*(1), 92–104.

Wilkinson, R. G., & Pickett, K. (2009). *The spirit level: Why greater equality makes societies stronger.* Bloomsbury Press.

Wilkinson, R. G., & Pickett, K. (2017a). Inequality and mental illness. *The Lancet Psychiatry, 4,* 512–513.

Wilkinson, R. G., & Pickett, K. E. (2017b). The enemy between us: The psychological and social costs of inequality. *European Journal of Social Psychology, 47,* 11–24.

Willett, L. L., Halvorsen, A. J., McDonald, F. S., Chaudhry, S. I., & Arora, V. M. (2015). Gender differences in salary of internal medicine residency directors: A national survey. *The American Journal of Medicine, 128,* 659–665.

Williams, C. L., & Berry, J. W. (1991). Primary prevention of acculturative stress among refugees. *American Psychologist, 46,* 632–641.

Williams, J. E., & Best, D. L. (1990). *Measuring sex stereotypes: A multination study.* Sage.

Williams, K. D. (2007). Ostracism. *Annual Review of Psychology, 58,* 425–452.

Williams, K. D. (2009). Ostracism: A temporal need-threat model. *Advances in Experimental Social Psychology, 41,* 275–313.

Williams, L. A., & DeSteno, D. (2009). Adaptive social emotion or seventh sin? *Psychological Science, 20,* 284–288.

Williams, N. M., Zaharieva, I., Martin, A., Langley, K., Mantripragada, K., Fossdal, R., Steffanson, H., Steffanson, K., Magnusson, P., Gudmundsson, O. O., Gustafsson, O., Holmans, P., Owen, M. J., O'Donovan, M., & Thapar, A. (2010). Rare chromosomal deletions and duplications in attention-deficit hyperactivity disorder: A genome-wide analysis. *The Lancet, 376,* 1401–1408.

Williams, S. (2018, March 1). Are the brains of transgender people different from those of cisgender people? *The Scientist.* https://www.the-scientist.com/features/are-the-brains-of-transgender-people-different-from-those-of-cisgender-people-30027

Williams, S. L. (1987). *Self-efficacy and mastery-oriented treatment for severe phobias* [Paper]. Presented to the American Psychological Association convention.

Williams, T. (2015, March 17). Missouri executes killer who had brain injury. *The New York Times.* https://www.nytimes.com/2015/03/18/us/missouri-executes-killer-who-had-brain-injury.html?

Williams, W. W., & Ceci, S. (2015). National hiring experiments reveal 2:1 faculty preference for women on tenure track. *PNAS, 112,* 5360–5365.

Willingham, D. T. (2010, Summer). Have technology and multitasking rewired how students learn? *American Educator, 34,* 23–28, 42.

Willingham, W. W., Lewis, C., Morgan, R., & Ramist, L. (1990). *Predicting college grades: An analysis of institutional trends over two decades.* Educational Testing Service.

Willis, B. L., Leonard, D., Barlow, C. E., Martin, S. B., DeFina, L. F., & Trivedi, M. H. (2018). Association of midlife cardiorespiratory fitness with incident depression and cardiovascular death after depression in later life. *JAMA Psychiatry, 75,* 911–917.

Willis, J., & Todorov, A. (2006). First impressions: Making up your mind after a 100-ms. exposure to a face. *Psychological Science, 17,* 592–598.

Willmuth, M. E. (1987). Sexuality after spinal cord injury: A critical review. *Clinical Psychology Review, 7,* 389–412.

Willoughby, B. J., Carroll, J. S., & Busby, D. M. (2014). Differing relationship outcomes when sex happens before, on, or after first dates. *Journal of Sex Research, 51,* 52–61.

Willoughby, E. A., Love, A. C., McGue, M., Iacono, W. G., Quigley, J., & Lee, J. J. (2019). Free will, determinism, and intuitive judgments about the heritability of behavior. *Behavior Genetics, 49,* 136–153.

Wilmot, M. P., & Ones, D. S. (2019). A century of research on conscientiousness at work. *PNAS, 116,* 23004–23010.

Wilmot, M. P., Wanberg, C. R., Kammeyer-Mueller, J. D., & Ones, D. S. (2019). Extraversion advantages at work: A quantitative review and synthesis of the meta-analytic evidence. *Journal of Applied Psychology, 104*(12), 1447–1470.

Wilson, A. E., & Ross, M. (2001). From chump to champ: People's appraisals of their earlier and present selves. *Journal of Personality and Social Psychology, 80,* 572–584.

Wilson, B., Smith, K., & Petkov, C. I. (2015). Mixed-complexity artificial grammar learning in humans and macaque monkeys: Evaluating learning strategies. *European Journal of Neuroscience, 41,* 568–578.

Wilson, B. S., Tucci, D. L., Merson, M. H., & O'Donoghue, G. M. (2017). Global hearing health care: New findings and perspectives. *The Lancet, 390,* 2503–2515.

Wilson, J. P., Hugenberg, K., & Rule, N. O. (2017). Racial bias in judgments of physical size and formidability: From size to threat. *Journal of Personality and Social Psychology, 113,* 59–80.

Wilson, R. S. (1979). Analysis of longitudinal twin data: Basic model and applications to physical growth measures. *Acta Geneticae Medicae et Gemellologiae, 28,* 93–105.

Wilson, R. S., Arnold, S. E., Schneider, J. A., Tang, Y., & Bennett, D. A. (2007a). The relationship between cerebral Alzheimer's disease pathology and odour identification in old age. *Journal of Neurology, Neurosurgery, and Psychiatry, 78,* 30–35.

Wilson, R. S., Beck, T. L., Bienias, J. L., & Bennett, D. A. (2007b). Terminal cognitive decline: Accelerated loss of cognition in the last years of life. *Psychosomatic Medicine, 69,* 131–137.

Wilson, R. S., & Matheny, A. P., Jr. (1986). Behavior-genetics research in infant temperament: The Louisville twin study. In R. Plomin & J. Dunn (Eds.), *The study of temperament: Changes, continuities, and challenges.* Erlbaum.

Wilson, T. D. (2002). *Strangers to ourselves: Discovering the adaptive unconscious.* Harvard University Press.

Wilson, T. D., Reinhard, D. A., Westgate, E. C., Gilbert, D. T., Ellerbeck, N., Hahn, C., Brown, C. L., & Shaked, A. (2014). Just think: The challenges of the disengaged mind. *Science, 345,* 75–77.

Wimber, M., Alink, A., Charest, I., Kriegeskorte, N., & Anderson, M. C. (2015). Retrieval induces adaptive forgetting of competing memories via cortical pattern suppression. *Nature Neuroscience, 18,* 582–589.

Wimmer, R. D., Schmitt, L. I., Davidson, T. J., Nakajima, M., Deisseroth, K., & Halassa, M. M. (2015). Thalamic control of sensory selection in divided attention. *Nature, 526,* 705–709.

Windholz, G. (1989, April–June). The discovery of the principles of reinforcement, extinction, generalization, and differentiation of conditional reflexes in Pavlov's laboratories. *Pavlovian Journal of Biological Science, 26,* 64–74.

Windholz, G. (1997). Ivan P. Pavlov: An overview of his life and psychological work. *American Psychologist, 52,* 941–946.

Wingfield, A., McCoy, S. L., Peelle, J. E., Tun, P. A., & Cox, L. C. (2005). Effects of adult aging and hearing loss on comprehension of rapid speech varying in syntactic complexity. *Journal of the American Academy of Audiology, 17,* 487–497.

Winkler, A., Dörsing, B., Rief, W., Shen, Y., & Glombiewski, J. A. (2013). Treatment of internet addiction: A meta-analysis. *Clinical Psychology Review, 33,* 317–329.

Winter, W. C., Hammond, W. R., Green, N. H., Zhang, Z., & Bilwise, D. L. (2009). Measuring circadian advantage in major league baseball: A 10-year retrospective study. *International Journal of Sports Physiology and Performance, 4,* 394–401.

Wirth, J. H., Sacco, D. F., Hugenberg, K., & Williams, K. D. (2010). Eye gaze as relational evaluation: Averted eye gaze leads to feelings of ostracism and relational devaluation. *Personality and Social Psychology Bulletin, 36*, 869–882.

Wiseman, R., & Greening, E. (2002). The Mind Machine: A mass participation experiment into the possible existence of extra-sensory perception. *British Journal of Psychology, 93*, 487–499.

Witelson, S. (2011). Sandra Witelson. http://www .science.ca/scientists/scientistprofile.php?pID=273

Witt, J. K., Linkenauger, S. A., & Proffitt, D. R. (2012). Get me out of this slump! Visual illusions improve sports performance. *Psychological Science, 23*, 397–399.

Witteman, H. O., Hendricks, M., Straus, S., & Tannenbaum, C. (2019). Are gender gaps due to evaluations of the applicant or the science? A natural experiment at a national funding agency. *Lancet, 393*, 531–540.

Witters, D. (2014, October 20). *U.S. adults with children at home have greater joy, stress.* Gallup. https://news.gallup.com/poll/178631/adults-children home-greaterjoy-stress.aspx

Witters, D., & Wood, J. (2015, January 14). *Heart attacks and depression closely linked.* Gallup. https://news.gallup.com/poll/180470/heart-attacks -depression-closely-linked.aspx

Wittgenstein, L. (1922). *Tractatus logico-philosophicus* (C. K. Ogden, Trans.). Harcourt, Brace.

Witvliet, C. V. O., & Vrana, S. R. (1995). Psychophysiological responses as indices of affective dimensions. *Psychophysiology, 32*, 436–443.

Wixted, J. T., & Ebbesen, E. B. (1991). On the form of forgetting. *Psychological Science, 2*, 409–415.

Wixted, J. T., Mickes, L., & Fisher, R. P. (2018). Rethinking the reliability of eyewitness memory. *Perspectives on Psychological Science, 13*, 324–335.

WKYT. (2017). *Kentucky fans set crowd roar world record.* https://www.wkyt.com/content/news /Kentucky-fans-set-crowd-roar-world-record-4120 59133.html

Wolf, R. (2019). *Supreme Court lets stand Pennsylvania school district's bathroom accommodations for transgender students.* USA Today. https://www .usatoday.com/story/news/politics/2019/05/28 /transgender-rights-supreme-court-wont-hear -school-bathroom-challenge/1258665001/

Wolfe, M. B., & Williams, T. J. (2018). Poor metacognitive awareness of belief change. *The Quarterly Journal of Experimental Psychology, 71*, 1898–1910.

Wolfinger, N. H. (2015). *Want to avoid divorce? Wait to get married, but not too long.* Institute for Family Studies. https://ifstudies.org/blog/want-to-avoid -divorce-wait-to-get-married-but-not-too-long/

Wolfson, A. R., & Carskadon, M. A. (1998). Sleep schedules and daytime functioning in adolescents. *Child Development, 69*, 875–887.

Wolpe, J. (1958). *Psychotherapy by reciprocal inhibition.* Stanford University Press.

Wolpe, J., & Plaud, J. J. (1997). Pavlov's contributions to behavior therapy: The obvious and the not so obvious. *American Psychologist, 52*, 966–972.

Wolpe, P. (2018, June 12). *A human head transplant would be reckless and ghastly. It's time to talk about it.* Vox. https://www.vox.com/the-big-idea/2018 /4/2/17173470/human-head-transplant-canavero -ethics-bioethics

Won, J., Alfini, A. J., Weiss, L. R., & Michelson, C. S. (2019). Semantic memory activation after acute exercise in healthy older adults. *Journal of the International Neuropsychological Society, 25*, 557–568.

Wonderlich, S. A., Joiner, T. E., Jr., Keel, P. K., Williamson, D. A., & Crosby, R. D. (2007). Eating disorder diagnoses: Empirical approaches to classification. *American Psychologist, 62*, 167–180.

Wondra, J. D., & Ellsworth, P. C. (2015). An appraisal theory of empathy and other vicarious emotional experiences. *Psychological Review, 122*, 411–428.

Wong, D. F., Wagner, H. N., Tune, L. E., Dannals, R. F., Pearlson, G. D., Links, J. M., Tamminga, C. A., Broussolle, E. P., Ravert, H. T., Wilson, A. A., Toung, J. K., Malat, J., Williams, J. A., O'Tuama, L. A., Snyder, S. H., Kuhar, M. J., & Gjedde, A. (1986). Positron emission tomography reveals elevated D$_2$ dopamine receptors in drug-naive schizophrenics. *Science, 234*, 1588–1593.

Wong, J. (2019). *Why Arthur creator Marc Brown enjoyed 'blowing up Twitter' with gay wedding.* CBC News. https://www.cbc.ca/news/entertainment /arthur-gay-wedding-reaction-1.5135547

Wong, M. M., Craun, E. A., Bravo, A. J., & Pearson, M. R. (2019). Insomnia symptoms, cannabis protective behavioral strategies, and hazardous cannabis use among U.S. college students. *Experimental and Clinical Psychopharmacology, 27*, 309–317.

Wong, M. M., & Csikszentmihalyi, M. (1991). Affiliation motivation and daily experience: Some issues on gender differences. *Journal of Personality and Social Psychology, 60*, 154–164.

Wongupparaj, P., Kumari, V., & Morris, R. G. (2015). A cross-temporal meta-analysis of Raven's Progressive Matrices: Age groups and developing versus developed countries. *Intelligence, 49*, 1–9.

Wood, C. (2018, October 1). *Thought-reading AI helps a person with quadriplegia play Guitar Hero.* Popular Science. https://www.popsci.com/machine-learn ing-quadriplegia-brain-interface/

Wood, D., Bruner, J., & Ross, G. (1976). The role of tutoring in problem solving. *Journal of Child Psychology and Child Psychiatry, 17*, 89–100.

Wood, J. M. (2003, May 19). Quoted in R. Mestel, Rorschach tested? Blot out the famous method? Some experts say it has no place in psychiatry. *The Los Angeles Times.*

Wood, J. M., Bootzin, R. R., Kihlstrom, J. F., & Schacter, D. L. (1992). Implicit and explicit memory for verbal information presented during sleep. *Psychological Science, 3*, 236–239.

Wood, J. M., Garb, H. N., Nezworski, M. T., Lilienfeld, S. O., & Duke, M. C. (2015). A second look at the validity of widely used Rorschach indices: Comment on Mihura, Meyer, Dumitrascu, and Bombel (2013). *Psychological Bulletin, 141*, 236–249.

Wood, J. M., Nezworski, M. T., Garb, H. N., & Lilienfeld, S. O. (2006). The controversy over Exner's Comprehensive System for the Rorschach: The critics speak. *Independent Practitioner, 26*, 73–82.

Wood, W. (1987). Meta-analytic review of sex differences in group performance. *Psychological Bulletin, 102*, 53–71.

Wood, W. (2017). Habit in personality and social psychology. *Personality and Social Psychology Review, 21*, 389–403.

Wood, W., & Eagly, A. H. (2002). A cross-cultural analysis of the behavior of women and men: Implications for the origins of sex differences. *Psychological Bulletin, 128*, 699–727.

Wood, W., & Eagly, A. H. (2007). Social structural origins of sex differences in human mating. In S. W. Gagestad & J. A. Simpson (Eds.), *The evolution of mind: Fundamental questions and controversies.* Guilford Press.

Wood, W., Lundgren, S., Ouellette, J. A., Busceme, S., & Blackstone, T. (1994). Minority influence: A meta-analytic review of social influence processes. *Psychological Bulletin, 115*, 323–345.

Wooden, J. (1977). Wooden preaches preparation. Reported by Cromwell, C. *Lubbock Avalanche-Journal,* p. D3.

Woolcock, N. (2004, September 3). Driver thought everyone else was on wrong side. *The Times,* p. 22.

Woolett, K., & Maguire, E. A. (2011). Acquiring "the knowledge" of London's layout drives structural brain changes. *Current Biology, 21*, 2109–2114.

Woollett, K., & Maguire, E. A. (2012). Exploring anterograde associative memory in London taxi drivers. *Neuroreport, 23*, 885–888.

Woolley, A. W., Chabris, C. F., Pentland, A., Hasmi, N., & Malone, T. W. (2010). Evidence for a collective intelligence factor in the performance of human groups. *Science, 330*, 686–688.

Woolley, K., & Fishbach, A. (2017). Immediate rewards predict adherence to long-term goals. *Personality and Social Psychology Bulletin, 43*, 151–162.

Woolley, K., & Fishbach, A. (2018). It's about time: Earlier rewards increase intrinsic motivation. *Journal of Personality and Social Psychology, 114*, 877–890.

Woolley, K., & Risen, J. L. (2018). Closing your eyes to follow your heart: Avoiding information to protect a strong intuitive preference. *Journal of Personality and Social Psychology, 114*, 230–245.

World Bank. (2019, accessed June 10). *Life expectancy at birth, total (years).* https://data.worldbank .org/indicator/sp.dyn.le00.in

World Federation for Mental Health. (2005). *ADHD: The hope behind the hype.* www.wfmh.org

Worobey, J., & Blajda, V. M. (1989). Temperament ratings at 2 weeks, 2 months, and 1 year: Differential stability of activity and emotionality. *Developmental Psychology, 25*, 257–263.

Worthman, C. M., & Trang, K. (2018). Dynamics of body time, social time and life history at adolescence. *Nature, 554*, 451–457.

Wortman, C. B., & Silver, R. C. (1989). The myths of coping with loss. *Journal of Consulting and Clinical Psychology, 57*, 349–357.

Wren, C. S. (1999, April 8). Drug survey of children finds middle school a pivotal time. *The New York Times* (nytimes.com).

Wright, J. (2006, March 16). *Boomers in the bedroom: Sexual attitudes and behaviours in the boomer generation.* https://www.ipsos.com/en-ca/boomers -bedroom-sexual-attitudes-and-behaviours -boomer-generation

Wright, P., Takei, N., Rifkin, L., & Murray, R. M. (1995). Maternal influenza, obstetric complications, and schizophrenia. *American Journal of Psychiatry, 152*, 1714–1720.

Wright, P. J., Bridges, A. J., Sun, C., Ezzell, M. B., Johnson, J. A. (2018). Personal pornography viewing and sexual satisfaction: A quadratic analysis. *Journal of Sex and Marital Therapy, 44*, 308–315.

Wright, P. J., & Vangeel, L. (2019). Pornography, permissiveness, and sex differences: An evaluation of social learning and evolutionary explanations. *Personality and Individual Differences, 143*, 128–138.

Wrzesniewski, A., & Dutton, J. E. (2001). Crafting a job: Revisioning employees as active crafters of their work. *Academy of Management Review, 26*, 179–201.

Wrzesniewski, A., Schwartz, B., Cong, X., Kane, M., Omar, A., & Kolditz, T. (2014). Multiple types of motives don't multiply the motivation of West Point cadets. *PNAS, 111*, 10990–10995.

Wu, L., Wang, D., & Evans, J. A. (2019). Large teams develop and small teams disrupt science and technology. *Nature, 566*, 378–382.

Wu, S., Wu, F., Ding, Y., Hou, J., Bi, J., & Zhang, Z. (2017). Advanced parental age and autism risk in children: A systematic review and meta-analysis. *Acta Psychiatrica Scandinavica, 135*, 29–41.

Wu, W., & Small, S. A. (2006). Imaging the earliest stages of Alzheimer's disease. *Current Alzheimer Research, 3*, 529–539.

Wu, X., Kaminga, A. C., Dai, W., Deng, J., Wang, Z., Pan, X., & Liu, A. (2019). The prevalence of moderate-to-high posttraumatic growth: A systematic review and meta-analysis. *Journal of Affective Disorders, 243,* 408–415.

Wu, X., Zhang, Z., Zhao, F., Wang, W., Li, Y., Bi, L., Qian, Z. Z., Lu, S. S., Feng, F., Hu, C. Y., Gong, F. F., & Sun, Y. (2016). Prevalence of internet addiction and its association with social support and other related factors among adolescents in China. *Journal of Adolescence, 52,* 103–111.

Wucherpfennig, F., Rubel, J. A., Hofmann, S. G., & Lutz, W. (2017). Processes of change after a sudden gain and relation to treatment outcome—Evidence for an upward spiral. *Journal of Consulting and Clinical Psychology, 85,* 1199–1210.

Wyatt, J. K., & Bootzin, R. R. (1994). Cognitive processing and sleep: Implications for enhancing job performance. *Human Performance, 7,* 119–139.

Wynn, K. (1992). Addition and subtraction by human infants. *Nature, 358,* 749–759.

Wynn, K. (2000). Findings of addition and subtraction in infants are robust and consistent: Reply to Wakeley, Rivera, and Langer. *Child Development, 71,* 1535–1536.

Wynn, K. (2008). Some innate foundations of social and moral cognition. In K. Wynn (Ed.) *The innate mind. Volume 3: Foundations and the future* (pp. 330–347). Oxford University Press.

Wynn, K., Bloom, P., Jordan, A., Marshall, J., & Sheskin, M. (2018). Not noble savages after all: Limits to early altruism. *Current Directions in Psychological Science, 27,* 3–8.

Wynne, C. D. L. (2004). *Do animals think?* Princeton University Press.

Wynne, C. D. L. (2008). Aping language: A skeptical analysis of the evidence for nonhuman primate language. *Skeptic, 13,* 10–13.

Wysocki, C. J., & Gilbert, A. N. (1989). National Geographic Smell Survey: Effects of age are heterogeneous. *Annals of the New York Academy of Sciences, 561,* 12–28.

Xie, L., Kang, H., Xu, Q., Chen, M. J., Liao, Y., Thiyagarajan, M., O'Donnell, J., Christensen, D. J., Nicholson, C., Iliff, J. J., Takano, T., Deane, R., & Nedergaard, M. (2013). Sleep drives metabolite clearance from the adult brain. *Science, 342,* 373–377.

Xu, J., Murphy, S. L., Kochanek, K. D., & Bastian B. A. (2016, February 16). Deaths: Final data for 2013. *National Vital Statistics Report, 64*(2), 1–119. Centers for Disease Control and Prevention.

Xu, J., & Potenza, M. N. (2012). White matter integrity and five-factor personality measures in healthy adults. *NeuroImage, 59,* 800–807.

Xu, Y., & Corkin, S. (2001). H.M. revisits the Tower of Hanoi puzzle. *Neuropsychology, 15,* 69–79.

Yamaguchi, M., Masuchi, A., Nakanishi, D., Suga, S., Konishi, N., Yu, Y. Y., & Ohtsubo, Y. (2015). Experiential purchases and prosocial spending promote happiness by enhancing social relationships. *The Journal of Positive Psychology,* 1–9.

Yang, J., & Hofmann, J. (2015). Action observation and imitation in autism spectrum disorders: An ALE meta-analysis of fMRI studies. *Brain Imaging and Behavior, 10,* 960–969.

Yang, S. Y., Lin, C. Y., Huang, Y. C., & Chang, J. H. (2018). Gender differences in the association of smartphone use with the vitality and mental health of adolescent students. *Journal of American College Health, 66,* 693–701.

Yang, Y., Cao, S., Shields, G. S., Teng, Z., & Liu, Y. (2017). The relationships between rumination and core executive functions: A meta-analysis. *Depression and Anxiety, 34,* 37–50.

Yang, Y., & Raine, A. (2009). Prefrontal structural and functional brain imaging findings in antisocial, violent, and psychopathic individuals: A meta-analysis. *Psychiatry Research: Neuroimaging, 174,* 81–88.

Yang, Y. C., Boen, C., Gerken, K., Li, T., Schorpp, K., & Harris, K. M. (2016). Social relationships and physiological determinants of longevity across the human life span. *PNAS, 113,* 578–583.

Yankelovich Partners. (1995, May/June). Growing old. *American Enterprise,* p. 108.

Yarnell, P. R., & Lynch, S. (1970, April 25). Retrograde memory immediately after concussion. *The Lancet,* pp. 863–865.

Yasmin, S. (2017). Experts debunk study that found Holocaust trauma is inherited. *Chicago Tribune.* https://www.chicagotribune.com/lifestyles/health /ct-holocaust-trauma-not-inherited-20170609-story .html

Yates, A. (1989). Current perspectives on the eating disorders: I. History, psychological and biological aspects. *Journal of the American Academy of Child and Adolescent Psychiatry, 28,* 813–828.

Yates, A. (1990). Current perspectives on the eating disorders: II. Treatment, outcome, and research directions. *Journal of the American Academy of Child and Adolescent Psychiatry, 29,* 1–9.

Yau, J. O. Y., & McNally, G. P. (2018). Brain mechanisms controlling Pavlovian fear conditioning. *Journal of Experimental Psychology: Animal Learning and Cognition, 44,* 341–357.

Ybarra, O. (1999). Misanthropic person memory when the need to self-enhance is absent. *Personality and Social Psychology Bulletin, 25,* 261–269.

Yeager, D. S., Dahl, R. E., & Dweck, C. S. (2018). Why interventions to influence adolescent behavior often fail but could succeed. *Perspectives on Psychological Science, 13,* 101–122.

Yeager, D. S., Hanselman, P., Walton, G. M., Murray, J. S., Crosnoe, R., Muller, C., Tipton, E., Schneider, B., Hulleman, C. S., Hinojosa, C. P., Paunesku, D., Romero, C., Flint, K., Robert, A., Trott, J., Iachan, R., Buontempo, J., Yang, S. M., Carvalho, C. M., . . . Dweck, C. S. (2019). A national experiment reveals where a growth mindset improves achievement. *Nature, 573,* 364–369.

Yehuda, R., Daskalakis, N. P., Bierer, L. M., Bader, H. N., Klengel, T., Holsboer, F., & Binder E. B. (2016). Holocaust exposure induced intergenerational effects on FKBP5 methylation. *Biological Psychiatry, 80,* 372–380.

Yengo, L., Robinson, M. R., Keller, M. C., Kemper, K. E., Yang, Y., Trzaskowski, M., Gratten, J., Turley, P., Cesarini, D., Banjamin, D. J., Wray, N. R., Goddard, M. E., Yang, J., & Visscher, P. M. (2018). Imprint of assortative mating on the human genome. *Nature Human Behaviour, 2,* 948–954.

Yerkes, R. M., & Dodson, J. D. (1908). The relation of strength of stimulus to rapidity of habit-formation. *Journal of Comparative Neurology and Psychology, 18,* 459–482.

Yesavage, J. A., Fairchild, J. K., Mi, Z., Biswas, K., Davis-Karim, A., Phibbs, C. S., Forman, S. D., Thase, M., Williams, L. M., Etkin, A., O'Hara, R., Georgette, G., Beale, T., Huang, G. D., Noda, A., George, M. S., & VA Cooperative Studies Program Study Team. (2018). Effect of repetitive transcranial magnetic stimulation on treatment-resistant major depression in US veterans: A randomized clinical trial. *JAMA Psychiatry, 75,* 884–893.

Yilmaz, Z., Hardaway, J. A. & Bulik, C. M. (2015). Genetics and epigenetics of eating disorders. *Advances in Genomics and Genetics, 5,* 131–150.

Yin, L., & Weber, B. (2019). I lie, why don't you: Neural mechanisms of individual differences in self-serving lying. *Human Brain Mapping, 40,* 1101–1113.

Yokum, D., Ravishankar, A., & Coppock, A. (2019). A randomized control trial evaluating the effects of police body-worn cameras. *PNAS, 116,* 10329–10332.

Yong, H. H., Borland, R., Cummings, K. M., Gravely, S., Thrasher, J. F., McNeill, A., Hitchman, S., Greenhalgh, E., Thompson, M. E., & Fong, G. T. (2019). Reasons for regular vaping and for its discontinuation among smokers and recent ex-smokers: Findings from the 2016 ITC Four Country Smoking and Vaping Survey. *Addiction, 114, Suppl 1,* 35–48.

Yoshimoto, C., & Frauenheim, E. (2018, February 27). *The best companies to work for are beating the marketplace.* Fortune. https://fortune.com/2018/02/27 /the-best-companies-to-work-for-are-beating-the -market/

Young, C., & Lim, C. (2014). Time as a network good: Evidence from unemployment and the standard workweek. *Sociological Science, 1,* 10–27.

Young, S. G., Hugenberg, K., Bernstein, M. J., & Sacco, D. F. (2012). Perception and motivation in face recognition: A critical review of theories of the cross-race effect. *Personality and Social Psychology Review, 16,* 116–142.

Young, S. M., & Pinsky, D. (2006). Narcissism and celebrity. *Journal of Personality, 40,* 463–471.

Youngentob, S. L., & Glendinning, J. I. (2009). Fetal ethanol exposure increases ethanol intake by making it smell and taste better. *PNAS, 106,* 5359.

Youngentob, S. L., Kent, P. F., Scheehe, P. R., Molina, J. C., Spear, N. E., & Youngentob, L. M. (2007). Experience-induced fetal plasticity: The effect of gestational ethanol exposure on the behavioral and neurophysiologic olfactory response to ethanol odor in early postnatal and adult rats. *Behavioral Neuroscience, 121,* 1293–1305.

Younger, J., Aron, A., Parke, S., Chatterjee, N., & Mackey, S. (2010) Viewing pictures of a romantic partner reduces experimental pain: Involvement of neural reward systems. *PLOS ONE, 5,* e13309.

Yount, K. M., James-Hawkins, L., Cheong, Y. F., & Naved, R. T. (2017). Men's perpetration of partner violence in Bangladesh: Community gender norms and violence in childhood. *Psychology of Men & Masculinity, 19,* 117–130.

Youyou, W., Kosinski, M., & Stillwell, D. (2015). Computer-based personality judgments are more accurate than those made by humans. *PNAS, 112,* 1036–1040.

Yu, H., McCoach, D. V., Gottfried, A. W., & Gottfried, A. E. (2018). Stability of intelligence from infancy through adolescence: An autoregressive latent variable model. *Intelligence, 69,* 8–15.

Yu, H., Yan, H., Wang, L., Li, J., Tan, L., Deng, W., Chen, Q., Yang, G., Zhang, F., Lu, T., Yang, J., Li, K., Lv, L., Tan, Q., Zhang, H., Xiao, X., Li, M., Ma, X., Yang, F., . . . Chinese Antipsychotics Pharmacogenomics Consortium. (2018b). Five novel loci associated with antipsychotic treatment response in patients with schizophrenia: A genome-wide association study. *The Lancet Psychiatry, 5,* 327–338.

Yudkin, D., Hawkins, S., Dixon, T. (2019b, June). *The perception gap: How false impressions are pulling Americans apart* [PDF file]. More in Common. https://perceptiongap.us/media/zaslaroc/percep tion-gap-report-1-0-3.pdf

Yudkin, D. A., Van Bavel, J. J., & Rhodes, M. (2019). Young children police group members at personal cost. *Journal of Experimental Psychology: General, 149,* 182–191.

Yuen, R. K., Merico, D., Cao, H., Pellecchia, G., Alipanahi, B., Thiruvahindrapuram, B., Tong, X., Sun, Y., Cao, D., Zhang, T., Wu, X., Jin, X., Zhou, Z., Liu, X., Nalpathamkalam, T., Walker, S., Howe, J. L., Wang, Z., MacDonald, . . . Schere, S. W. (2016).

Genome-wide characteristics of de novo mutations in autism. *NPJ Genomic Medicine, 1*, 1–10.

Yuki, M., Maddux, W. W., & Masuda. T. (2007). Are the windows to the soul the same in the East and West? Cultural differences in using the eyes and mouth as cues to recognize emotions in Japan and the United States. *Journal of Experimental Social Psychology, 43*, 303–311.

Zagorsky, J. L. (2007). Do you have to be smart to be rich? The impact of IQ on wealth, income and financial distress. *Intelligence, 35*, 489–501.

Zahrt, O. H., & Crum, A. J. (2017). Perceived physical activity and mortality: Evidence from three nationally representative U.S. samples. *Health Psychology, 36*, 1017–1025.

Zainulbhai, H. (2016, March 8). *Strong global support for gender equality, especially among women.* Pew Research Center. https://www.pewresearch.org/fact-tank/2016/03/08/strong-global-support-for-gender-equality-especially-among-women/

Zajonc, R. B. (1965). Social facilitation. *Science, 149*, 269–274.

Zajonc, R. B. (1980). Feeling and thinking: Preferences need no inferences. *American Psychologist, 35*, 151–175.

Zajonc, R. B. (1984). On the primacy of affect. *American Psychologist, 39*, 117–123.

Zajonc, R. B. (1998). Emotions. In D. Gilbert, S. T. Fiske, & G. Lindzey (Eds.), *Handbook of social psychology* (4th ed.). McGraw-Hill.

Zajonc, R. B. (2001). Mere exposure: A gateway to the subliminal. *Current Directions in Psychological Science, 10*, 224–228.

Zajonc, R. B., & Markus, G. B. (1975). Birth order and intellectual development. *Psychological Review, 82*, 74–88.

Zanarini, M. C., Williams, A. A., Lewis, R. E., Reich, R. B., Vera, S. C., Marino, M. F., Levin, A., Yong, L., & Frankenburg, R. F. (1997). Reported pathological childhood experiences associated with the development of borderline personality disorder. *American Journal of Psychiatry, 154*, 1101–1106.

Zannas, A. S., Provençal, N., & Binder, E. B. (2015). Epigenetics of posttraumatic stress disorder: current evidence, challenges, and future directions. *Biological Psychiatry, 78*, 327–335.

Zaslavsky, O., Palgi, Y., Rillamas-Sun, E., LaCroix, A. Z., Schnall, E., Woods, N. F., Cochrane, B. B., Garcia, L., Hingle, M., Post, S., Seguin, R., Tindle, H., & Shrira, A. (2015). Dispositional optimism and terminal decline in global quality of life. *Developmental Psychology, 51*, 856–863.

Zauberman, G., & Lynch, J. G., Jr. (2005). Resource slack and propensity to discount delayed investments of time versus money. *Journal of Experimental Psychology: General, 134*, 23–37.

Zaval, L., Keenan, E. A., Johnson, E. J., & Weber, E. U. (2014). How warm days increase belief in global warming. *Nature Climate Change, 4*, 143–147.

Zeelenberg, R., Wagenmakers, E.-J., & Rotteveel, M. (2006). The impact of emotion on perception. *Psychological Science, 17*, 287–291.

Zeidner, M. (1990). Perceptions of ethnic group modal intelligence: Reflections of cultural stereotypes or intelligence test scores? *Journal of Cross-Cultural Psychology, 21*, 214–231.

Zeineh, M. M., Engel, S. A., Thompson, P. M., & Bookheimer, S. Y. (2003). Dynamics of the hippocampus during encoding and retrieval of face-name pairs. *Science, 299*, 577–580.

Zelenski, J. M., & Nisbet, E. K. (2014). Happiness and feeling connected: The distinct role of nature relatedness. *Environmental Behavior, 46*, 3–23.

Zell, E., & Alicke, M. D. (2010). The local dominance effect in self-evaluation: Evidence and

explanations. *Personality and Social Psychology Review, 14*, 368–384.

Zell, E., Krizan, Z., & Teeter, S. R. (2015). Evaluating gender similarities and differences using meta-synthesis. *American Psychologist, 70*, 10–20.

Zell, E., Strickhouser, J. E., & Krizan, Z. (2018). Subjective social status and health: A meta-analysis of community and society ladders. *Health Psychology, 37*, 979–987.

Zentner, M., & Eagly, A. H. (2015). A sociocultural framework for understanding partner preferences of women and men: Integration of concepts and evidence. *European Journal of Social Psychology, 26*, 328–373.

Zerr, C. L., Berg, J. J., Nelson, S. M., Fishell, A. K., Savalia, N. K., & McDermott, K. B. (2018). Learning efficiency: Identifying individual differences in learning rate and retention in healthy adults. *Psychological Science, 29*, 1436–1450.

Zerubavel, N., Hoffman, M. A., Reich, A., Ochsner, K. N., & Bearman, P. (2018). Neural precursors of future liking and affective reciprocity. *PNAS, 115*, 4375–4380.

Zetsche, U., Bürkner, P.-C., & Renneberg, B. (2019). Future expectations in clinical depression: Biased or realistic? *Journal of Abnormal Psychology, 128*, 678–688.

Zhang, H., Gross, J., De Dreu, C., & Ma, Y. (2019). Oxytocin promotes coordinated out-group attack during intergroup conflict in humans. *eLife, 8*, e40698.

Zhang, J. (2016, July 2). Personal correspondence from Dept. of Psychology and Behavioral Science, Zhejiang University, Hangzhou, China, based on "2015–2016 Nationwide Psychology Specialty Ranking."

Zhang, J., Fang, L., Yow-Wu, B. W., & Wieczorek, W. F. (2013). Depression, anxiety, and suicidal ideation among Chinese Americans: A study of immigration-related factors. *The Journal of Nervous and Mental Disease, 201*, 17–22.

Zhang, W., Jiao, B., Zhou, M., Zhou, T., & Shen, L. (2016). Modeling Alzheimer's disease with induced pluripotent stem cells: Current challenges and future concerns. *Stem Cells International, 2016*, 7828049.

Zhong, C.-B., Dijksterhuis, A., & Galinsky, A. D. (2008). The merits of unconscious thought in creativity. *Psychological Science, 19*, 912–918.

Zhou, J., Park, C. Y., Theesfeld, C. L., Wong, A. K., Yuan, Y., Scheckel, C., Fak, J. J., Funk, J., Yao, K., Tajima, Y., Packer, A., Darnell, R. B., & Troyanskaya, O. G. (2019). Whole-genome deep-learning analysis identifies contribution of noncoding mutations to autism risk. *Nature Genetics, 51*, 973–980.

Zhou, S., DeFranco, J. P., Blaha, N. T., Dwivedy, P., Culver, A., Nallamala, H., Chelluri, S., & Dumas, T. C. (2019). Aversive conditioning in the tardigrade, *Dactylobiotus dispar. Journal of Experimental Psychology: Animal Learning and Cognition, 45*(4), 405–412.

Zhou, S., Page-Gould, E., Aron, A., Moyer, A., & Hewstone, M. (2019). The extended contact hypothesis: A meta-analysis on 20 years of research. *Personality and Social Psychology Review, 23*, 132–160.

Zhou, Y., Zou, M., Woods, S. A., & Wu, C.-H. (2019). The restorative effect of work after unemployment: An intraindividual analysis of subjective well-being recovery through reemployment. *Journal of Applied Psychology, 104*, 1195–1206.

Zilbergeld, B. (1983). *The shrinking of America: Myths of psychological change.* Little, Brown.

Zilcha-Mano, S., Errázuriz, P., Yaffe-Herbst, L., German, R. E., & DeRubeis, R. J. (2019). Are there any robust predictors of "sudden gainers," and how is sustained improvement in treatment outcome

achieved following a gain? *Journal of Consulting and Clinical Psychology, 87*, 491–500.

Zill, N., & Wilcox, W. B. (2017, June 8). *What happens at home doesn't stay there: It goes to school.* Institute for Family Studies. https://ifstudies.org/blog/what-happens-at-home-doesnt-stay-there-it-goes-to-school

Zillmann, D. (1989). Effects of prolonged consumption of pornography. In D. Zillmann & J. Bryant (Eds.), *Pornography: Research advances and policy considerations* (pp. 127–157). Erlbaum.

Zillmann, D., & Bryant, J. (1984). Effects of massive exposure to pornography. In N. Malamuth & E. Donnerstein (Eds.), *Pornography and sexual aggression.* Academic Press.

Zimbardo, P., Wilson, G., & Coulombe, N. (2016). How porn is messing with your manhood. *Skeptic.* https://www.skeptic.com/reading_room/how-porn-is-messing-with-your-manhood

Zimbardo, P. G. (1970). The human choice: Individuation, reason, and order versus deindividuation, impulse, and chaos. In W. J. Arnold & D. Levine (Eds.), *Nebraska Symposium on Motivation, 1969.* University of Nebraska Press.

Zimbardo, P. G. (2007, September). Person x situation x system dynamics. *The Observer* (Association for Psychological Science), p. 43.

Zimmermann, T. D., & Meier, B. (2006). The rise and decline of prospective memory performance across the lifespan. *Quarterly Journal of Experimental Psychology, 59*, 2040–2046.

Zinzow, H. M., Amstadter, A. B., McCauley, J. L., Ruggiero, K. J., Resnick, H. S., & Kilpatrick, D. G. (2011). Self-rated health in relation to rape and mental health disorders in a national sample of college women. *Journal of American College Health, 59*, 588–594.

Zogby, J. (2006, March). *Survey of teens and adults about the use of personal electronic devices and head phones.* Zogby International.

Zoma, M., & Gielen, U. P. (2015). How many psychologists are there in the world? *International Psychology Bulletin, 19*, 47–50.

Zou, L. Q., van Hartevelt, T. J., Kringelbach, M. L., Cheung, E. F., & Chan, R. C. (2016). The neural mechanism of hedonic processing and judgment of pleasant odors: An activation likelihood estimation meta-analysis. *Neuropsychology, 30*, 970–979.

Zubieta, J.-K., Bueller, J. A., Jackson, L. R., Scott, D. J., Xu, Y., Koeppe, R. A., Nichols, T. E., & Stohler, C. S. (2005). Placebo effects mediated by endogenous opioid activity on μ-opioid receptors. *Journal of Neuroscience, 25*, 7754–7762.

Zubieta, J.-K., Heitzeg, M. M., Smith, Y. R., Bueller, J. A., Xu, K., Xu, Y., Koeppe, R. A., Stohler, C. S., & Goldman, D. (2003). COMT val158met genotype affects μ-opioid neurotransmitter responses to a pain stressor. *Science, 299*, 1240–1243.

Zucco, G. M. (2003). Anomalies in cognition: Olfactory memory. *European Psychologist, 8*, 77–86.

Zucker, G. S., & Weiner, B. (1993). Conservatism and perceptions of poverty: An attributional analysis. *Journal of Applied Social Psychology, 23*, 925–943.

Zuckerman, M. (1979). *Sensation seeking: Beyond the optimal level of arousal.* Erlbaum.

Zuckerman, M. (1999). *Vulnerability to psychopathology: A biosocial model.* American Psychological Association.

Zuckerman, M. (2009). Sensation seeking. In M. Zuckerman (Ed.), *Handbook of individual differences in social behavior.* Guilford Press.

Zuckerman, M., Li, C., & Hall, J. A. (2016). When men and women differ in self-esteem and when they don't: A meta-analysis. *Journal of Research in Personality, 64*, 34–51.

Zunick, P. V., Fazio, R. H., & Vasey, M. W. (2015). Directed abstraction: Encouraging broad, personal generalizations following a success experience. *Journal of Personality and Social Psychology, 109,* 1–19.

Zuromski, K. L., Dempsey, C. L., Ng, T. H. H., Riggs-Donovan, C. A., Brent, D. A., Heeringa, S. G., Kessler, R. C., Stein, M. B., Ursano, R. J., Benedek, D., & Nock, M. K. (2019). Utilization of and barriers to treatment among suicide decedents: Results from the Army Study to Assess Risk and Resilience Among Servicemembers (Army STARRS). *Journal of Consulting and Clinical Psychology, 87,* 671–683.

Zuzanek, J. (2013). Does being well-off make us happier? Problems of measurement. *Journal of Happiness Studies, 14,* 795–815.

Zvolensky, M. J., Bakhshaie, J., Sheffer, C., Perez, A., & Goodwin, R. D. (2015). Major depressive disorder and smoking relapse among adults in the United States: A 10-year, prospective investigation. *Psychiatry Research, 226,* 73–77.

Zvolensky, M. J., & Bernstein, A. (2005). Cigarette smoking and panic psychopathology. *Current Directions in Psychological Science, 14,* 301–305.

Zwaan, R. A., Etz, A., Lucas, R. E., & Donnellan, M. B. (2018). Making replication mainstream. *Behavioral and Brain Sciences, 41,* 13.

Zych, I., Farrington, D. P., & Ttofi, M. M. (2018). Protective factors against bullying and cyberbullying: A systematic review of meta-analyses. *Aggression and Violent Behavior, 45,* 4–19.

Name Index

Subject Index